L

Defender 90 110 130 Parts Catalogue

Covering Vehicles 1987-2006 MY

Part No. STC9021CC

October 2001

LAND ROVER PARTS LTD

DEFENDER

Engine	B
Gearbox	C
Transfer Box	D
Axles & Suspension	E
Steering	F
Vehicle & Engine Controls	G
Braking Systems	H
Fuel & Emission Systems	J
Exhaust Systems	K
Cooling & Heating	L
Body Electrics	M
Body & Chassis	N
Interior Trim	P
Seats	R

CONTENTS

TYPE LD VIN CODE BREAKDOWN - NON NAS

VIN POSITION	SUBJECT	CHARACTER	MEANING
1-3	World Manufacturer Identifier	SAL	Land Rover (UK)
4-5	Vehicle Type	LD	Defender
6	Class	H	110" Standard
		K	130" Standard
		V	90" Standard
		A	90" Extra Heavy/Duty
		B	110" Extra Heavy/Duty
		C	130" Extra Heavy/Duty
7	Body Style	A	Regular
		B	3 Door Station Wagon
		F	4 Door Crew Cab Non H/Cap
		H	H/Cap with or without 4 Door Crew Cab
		M	4 Door Station Wagon
8	Engine	B	2.5 Diesel Turbo (Falcon)
		C	2.5 Diesel Nat Asp
		D	2.5 Petrol Carb
		F	2.5 Tdi Non EEGR/Cat (Gem)
		V	3.5 V8 Petrol Carb Non Cat
		6	2.5 Tdi EEGR &/or Cat (Gem)
		Y	2.0 Lti Petrol Cat
		8	2.5 (Td5)
	M : 4 V8 EFI	9	2.8 Petrol M52 (BMW)
9	Transmission & Hand of Steering	RHD / LHD	
		7 / 8	5 Speed Manual
		3 / 4	4 Speed Automatic
10	Model Year	V	1997
		W	1998
		X	1999
		Y	2000
11	Assembly Plant	A	Solihull

AH3

VEHICLE IDENTIFICATION NUMBER

REGULAR

VIN CODE	ENGINE	GEARBOX	STEERING
SALLDVAH7AA	2.25 PETROL	5 SPEED	RH STG
SALLDVAH8AA	2.25 PETROL	5 SPEED	LH STG
SALLDVAD7AA	2.5 PETROL	5 SPEED	RH STG
SALLDVAD8AA	2.5 PETROL	5 SPEED	LH STG
SALLDVAC7AA	2.5 DIESEL	5 SPEED	RH STG
SALLDVAC8AA	2.5 DIESEL	5 SPEED	LH STG
SALLDVAB7AA	2.5 DIESEL	TURBO 5 SPEED	RH STG
SALLDVAB8AA	2.5 DIESEL	TURBO 5 SPEED	LH STG
SALLDVAV7AA	3.5 PETROL	5 SPEED	RH STG
SALLDVAV8AA	3.5 PETROL	5 SPEED	LH STG
SALLDVAD7 ••	2.5 PETROL	5 SPEED	RH STG
SALLDVAD8 ••	2.5 PETROL	5 SPEED	LH STG
SALLDVAC7 ••	2.5 DIESEL	5 SPEED	RH STG
SALLDVAC8 ••	2.5 DIESEL	5 SPEED	LH STG
SALLDVAB7 ••	2.5 DIESEL	TURBO 5 SPEED	RH STG
SALLDVAB8 ••	2.5 DIESEL	TURBO 5 SPEED	LH STG
SALLDVAV7 ••	3.5 PETROL	5 SPEED	RH STG
SALLDVAV8 ••	3.5 PETROL	5 SPEED	LH STG
SALLDVAD7 ••	2.5 PETROL	5 SPEED	RH STG
SALLDVAD8 ••	2.5 PETROL	5 SPEED	LH STG
SALLDVAC7 ••	2.5 DIESEL	5 SPEED	RH STG
SALLDVAC8 ••	2.5 DIESEL	5 SPEED	LH STG
SALLDVAF7 ••	2.5 DIESEL TDI	5 SPEED	RH STG
SALLDVAF8 ••	2.5 DIESEL TDI	5 SPEED	LH STG
SALLDVAV7 ••	3.5 PETROL	5 SPEED	RH STG
SALLDVAV8 ••	3.5 PETROL	5 SPEED	LH STG
SALLDHAD7 ••	2.5 PETROL	5 SPEED	RH STG
SALLDHAD8 ••	2.5 PETROL	5 SPEED	LH STG
SALLDHAB7 ••	2.5 DIESEL	TURBO 5 SPEED	RH STG
SALLDHAB8 ••	2.5 DIESEL	TURBO 5 SPEED	LH STG
SALLDHAC7 ••	2.5 DIESEL	5 SPEED	RH STG
SALLDHAC8 ••	2.5 DIESEL	5 SPEED	LH STG
SALLDHAF7 ••	300 TDI NO CAT	5 SPEED	RH STG
SALLDHAF8 ••	300 TDI NO CAT	5 SPEED	LH STG
SALLDHAV7 ••	3.5 PETROL	5 SPEED	RH STG
SALLDHAV8 ••	3.5 PETROL	5 SPEED	LH STG
SALLDHA67 ••	300 TDI NO CAT	5 SPEED	RH STG
SALLDHA68 ••	300 TDI NO CAT	5 SPEED	LH STG
SALLDKAF7 ••	300 TDI NO CAT	5 SPEED	RH STG
SALLDKAF8 ••	300 TDI NO CAT	5 SPEED	LH STG
SALLDKAV7 ••	3.5 PETROL	5 SPEED	RH STG
SALLDKAV8 ••	3.5 PETROL	5 SPEED	LH STG
SALLDKA67 ••	300 TDI NO CAT	5 SPEED	RH STG
SALLDKA68 ••	300 TDI NO CAT	5 SPEED	LH STG

AH6

VEHICLE IDENTIFICATION NUMBER

STATION WAGON

VIN CODE	ENGINE	GEARBOX	STEERING
SALLDVBH7AA	2.25 PETROL	5 SPEED	RH STG
SALLDVBH8AA	2.25 PETROL	5 SPEED	LH STG
SALLDVBD7AA	2.5 PETROL	5 SPEED	RH STG
SALLDVBD8AA	2.5 PETROL	5 SPEED	LH STG
SALLDVBC7AA	2.5 DIESEL	5 SPEED	RH STG
SALLDVBC8AA	2.5 DIESEL	5 SPEED	LH STG
SALLDVBB7AA	2.5 DIESEL	TURBO 5 SPEED	RH STG
SALLDVBB8AA	2.5 DIESEL	TURBO 5 SPEED	LH STG
SALLDVBV7AA	3.5 PETROL	5 SPEED	RH STG
SALLDVBV8AA	3.5 PETROL	5 SPEED	LH STG
SALLDVBD7 ••	2.5 PETROL	5 SPEED	RH STG
SALLDVBD8 ••	2.5 PETROL	5 SPEED	LH STG
SALLDVBC7 ••	2.5 DIESEL	5 SPEED	RH STG
SALLDVBC8 ••	2.5 DIESEL	5 SPEED	LH STG
SALLDVBB7 ••	2.5 DIESEL	TURBO 5 SPEED	RH STG
SALLDVBB8 ••	2.5 DIESEL	TURBO 5 SPEED	LH STG
SALLDVBV7 ••	3.5 PETROL	5 SPEED	RH STG
SALLDVBV8 ••	3.5 PETROL	5 SPEED	LH STG
SALLDVBD7 ••	2.5 PETROL	5 SPEED	RH STG
SALLDVBD8 ••	2.5 PETROL	5 SPEED	LH STG
SALLDVBC7 ••	2.5 DIESEL	5 SPEED	RH STG
SALLDVBC8 ••	2.5 DIESEL	5 SPEED	LH STG
SALLDVBF7 ••	2.5 DIESEL TDI	5 SPEED	RH STG
SALLDVBF8 ••	2.5 DIESEL TDI	5 SPEED	LH STG
SALLDVBM8VA ••	4.0 V8I - JAPAN		
SALLDVBV7 ••	3.5 PETROL	5 SPEED	RH STG
SALLDVBV8 ••	3.5 PETROL	5 SPEED	LH STG
SALLDHMD7 ••	2.5 PETROL	5 SPEED	RH STG
SALLDHMD8 ••	2.5 PETROL	5 SPEED	LH STG
SALLDHMB7 ••	2.5 DIESEL	TURBO 5 SPEED	RH STG
SALLDHMB8 ••	2.5 DEISEL	TURBO 5 SPEED	LH STG
SALLDHMC7 ••	2.5 DIESEL	5 SPEED	RH STG
SALLDHMC8 ••	2.5 DIESEL	5 SPEED	LH STG
SALLDHMF7 ••	300 TDI NO CAT	5 SPEED	RH STG
SALLDHMF8 ••	300 TDI NO CAT	5 SPEED	LH STG
SALLDHMV7 ••	3.5 PETROL	5 SPEED	RH STG
SALLDHMV8 ••	3.5 PETROL	5 SPEED	LH STG
SALLDHM67 ••	300 TDI NO CAT	5 SPEED	RH STG
SALLDHM68 ••	300 TDI NO CAT	5 SPEED	LH STG

AH7

VEHICLE IDENTIFICATION NUMBER

HIGH CAPACITY PICK-UP

VIN CODE		ENGINE		GEARBOX	STEERING	
SALLDHHD7	••	2.5	PETROL	5 SPEED	RH	STG
SALLDHHD8	••	2.5	PETROL	5 SPEED	LH	STG
SALLDHHB7	••	2.5	DIESEL	TURBO 5 SPEED	RH	STG
SALLDHHB8	••	2.5	DIESEL	TURBO 5 SPEED	LH	STG
SALLDHHC7	••	2.5	DIESEL	5 SPEED	RH	STG
SALLDHHC8	••	2.5	DIESEL	5 SPEED	LH	STG
SALLDHHF7	••	300	TDI NO CAT	5 SPEED	RH	STG
SALLDHHF8	••	300	TDI NO CAT	5 SPEED	LH	STG
SALLDHHV7	••	3.5	PETROL	5 SPEED	RH	STG
SALLDHHV8	••	3.5	PETROL	5 SPEED	LH	STG
SALLDHH67	••	300	TDI NO CAT	5 SPEED	RH	STG
SALLDHH68	••	300	TDI NO CAT	5 SPEED	LH	STG
SALLDKHF7	••	300	TDI NO CAT	5 SPEED	RH	STG
SALLDKAF8	••	300	TDI NO CAT	5 SPEED	LH	STG
SALLDKAV7	••	3.5	PETROL	5 SPEED	RH	STG
SALLDKAV8	••	3.5	PETROL	5 SPEED	LH	STG
SALLDKA67	••	300	TDI NO CAT	5 SPEED	RH	STG
SALLDKA68	••	300	TDI NO CAT	5 SPEED	LH	STG

••	BA - 1987	MODEL YEAR
••	EA - 1988	MODEL YEAR
••	FA - 1989	MODEL YEAR
••	GA - 1990	MODEL YEAR
••	HA - 1991	MODEL YEAR
••	JA - 1992	MODEL YEAR
••	KA - 1993	MODEL YEAR
••	LA - 1994	MODEL YEAR
••	MA - 1995	MODEL YEAR
••	TA - 1996	MODEL YEAR
••	VA - 1997	MODEL YEAR
••	WA - 1998	MODEL YEAR

AH8

SERIAL NUMBER IDENTIFICATION

ENGINES - DIESEL

11L00001	200 TDI 1991 MY
12J00001C	2.5 NA
16L0001A	300 TDI 1995 MY
19J0001C	2.5 Turbo
23L00001	300 TDI - (ELECTRONIC EGR) 1995 MY
10P00001	Td5 - NOT JAPAN
11P00001	Td5 - JAPAN ONLY

(SERVICE ENGINES Td5)
-12P STRIPPED ENGINE
-13P STRIPPED ENGINE - LESS CYLINDER HEAD
-14P - SHORT ENGINE

ENGINES - PETROL

10H00001A	2.25 PETROL	8 : 1	CR NON DETOXED
11H00001A	2.25 PETROL	8 : 1	CR DETOXED
14G00001	3.5 LITRE V8	8.13 : 1	CR NON DETOXED
15G00001	3.5 LITRE V8	8.13 :1	CR DETOXED
17H00001A	2.5 PETROL	8 : 1	CR
17H00001C	2.5		
19G00001	3.5 LITRE V8	SAUDI ARABIAN SPEC.	
20G00001	3.5 LITRE V8	8.13 : 1 CR NON DETOXED	
21G00001	3.5 LITRE V8	8.13 : 1 CR DETOXED	
22G00001	3.5 LITRE V8	AUSTRALIAN SPEC.	
24G00001	3.5 LITRE V8	8.13 : 1 CR DETOXED	
24G00001C	3.5 LITRE V8	8.13 : 1 CR DETOXED	
30G00001	4.0 LITRE V8i	9.13 : 1 JAPAN	
31G00001	4.0 LITRE V8	EFI 50LE	

TRANSFER GEARBOX - LT230T TYPE

13D00001	4 CYLINDER PETROL / DIESEL	
20D00001	4 CYLINDER PETROL / DIESEL	1.6 : 1
22D00001	4 CYLINDER	1.4 : 1
25D00001	V8 PETROL	
29D00001	V8 PETROL	1.2 : 1
32D00001	V8	1.2 : 1

LT230Q TYPE

38D00001	V8	1.2 : 1
40D00001	JAPAN / SOUTH AFRICA	
43D00001	Td5	

AH3.1C

SERIAL NUMBER IDENTIFICATION

GEARBOX - R380 MANUAL TYPE

43A00001	V8
44A00001	TDI
56A00001J	300 TDI
50A00001J	4 CYLINDER PETROL (NOT TDI)
60A00001J	V8
61A00001J	V8 COOLED
70A00001J	SOUTH AFRICA
68A00001L	Td5 NON COOLED
74A00001L	Td5 COOLED

GEARBOX - LT85 MANUAL TYPE

20C00001	5 SPEED V8 CARB.
22C00001	5 SPEED V8 CARB.

GEARBOX - LT77 MANUAL TYPE

50A00001	5 SPEED 4 CYLINDER

GEARBOX - LT77S MANUAL TYPE

56A00001	5 SPEED 200 TDI 1991 MY
60A00001	5 SPEED V8
61A00001	5 SPEED V8 WITH OIL COOLER

GEARBOX - AUTOMATIC TYPE

2F	4 SPEED	JAPAN

AH3.2A

SERIAL NUMBER IDENTIFICATION

AXLE SERIAL NUMBERS
FRONT

20L00001A	RHS		
21L00001A	LHS		
22L00001A	RHS	90	
23L00001A	LHS	90	
61L00001	RHS	90	4 CYLINDER
62L00001	LHS	90	4 CYLINDER
63L00001	RHS	90	V8 AND 4 CYLINDER HEAVY DUTY (VENTED)
63L00001A	RHS	110	
64L00001	LHS	90	V8 AND 4 CYLINDER HEAVY DUTY (VENTED)
64L00001A			SOUTH AFRICA
64L00001J	LHS	110	
91L00001A			MISFIRE DETECTION - JAPAN
10M00001		90	BASE
11M00001		90	BASE WIDEWHEEL LOCKSTOPS
12M00001		90	BASE ABS
13M00001		90	BASE ABS WIDEWHEEL LOCKSTOPS
14M00001		90	H/D 110/130 BASE (VENTED)
15M00001		90	H/D 110/130 BASE (VENTED) WIDEWHEEL LOCKSTOPS
16M00001		90	H/D 110/130 BASE (VENTED) ABS
17M00001		90	H/D 110/130 BASE (VENTED) ABS WIDEWHEEL LOCKSTOPS
18M00001		110	H/D ROLLING CHASSIS
98L00001A			V8/TDI HEAVY DUTY AX STOPS

REAR

21S0001A		
22S00001A	90	
23L00001A	90	HEAVY
38S00001A	110	HEAVY DUTY
39S00001A	90/110	STANDARD
42S00001	90	2 PIN 4 CYLINDER AND V8
44S00001	90	4 PIN V8 AND HEAVY DUTY
53S00001A		MISFIRE DETECTION - JAPAN
58S00001	90	
59S00001	90	ABS
60S00001	110	
61S00001	110	ABS
62S00001	110	H/D/130

AH3.3

EXTERIOR PAINT CODES

PAINT COLOUR CODES ARE RECORDED ON THE VEHICLE IDENTIFICATION PLATE

BODY COLOUR	CODE	LRC NUMBER
AA YELLOW	FUN	584
ALPINE WHITE	NUC	456
ALVESTON RED	CDX	696
ANTIGUA BLUE	JFN	645
ARIZONA TAN	ABA	341
ARRAN BEIGE	SUB	433
ARROW RED	CUF	390
ATLANTIS BLUE	JYW	632
ATLANTIC GREEN	SPECIAL	LRR726HZA
BLENHEIM SILVER	MAL	642
BONATTI GREY	LAL	659
BRITISH RACING GREEN	HNA	617
BRONZE GREEN	HCC	1
CALEDONIAN BLUE	JUT	507
CARMEN PEARL	COG	843
CHAWTON WHITE	NAL	603
COBAR BLUE	JAV	624
CONISTON GREEN	HYJ	637
EASTNOR GREEN	HUJ	419
EPSOM GREEN	HAF	961
HIGHLAND GREEN	HPG	639
ICELANDIC BLUE	JEL	621
IVORY/DAVOS WHITE	NCM	354
JAVA BLACK	PNF	697
KAROO BLUE	JFB	698
KENT GREEN	HEX	647
LIMESTONE	NCJ	7
MARINE BLUE	JCC	6
MASAI RED	CCC	234
MONTE CARLO BLUE	JZD	608
MONZA RED	CCZ	590
NIAGARA GREY	LVD	574
OSLO BLUE	JFM	644
OXFORD BLUE	JSJ	602
PACIFIC BLUE	JUH	424
PENNINE/PEMBROKE GREY	LUS	476
ROAN BROWN	ACV	324
RUTLAND RED	CPQ	607
SHIRE BLUE	JUG	392
SLATE GREY	LCN	348
STRATOS BLUE	JCP	327
TINTERN GREEN	HEW	656
TRIDENT GREEN	HCM	325
VENETIAN MAUVE	KMH	622
VENETIAN RED	CCL	301
WILLOW GREEN	HOR	970

FITTING INSTRUCTION FOR INTERMEDIATE SEAT BELT MOUNTINGS LOWER - LR 110

1.0 Jack up rear of vehicle, support on stands, remove road wheels.

2.0 Fold intermediate seats forward (or remove) and remove rear load space mat or carpet.

3.0 Outer Lower Mounting:
Remove existing bolt (A), floor to bodyframe and ensure a full 5/16" clearance.

3.1 Fit bracket (347844) under wheelarch and temporarily secure at lower end using bolt (SH605081L) and nut (SH605041L). Ensure that the slots in the bracket are located over the outer pair of pop rivets.

3.2 Drill upper fixing hole 5/16" from under wheelarch and fit bolt (255227) to locate bracket.

3.3 Mark position of lower seat belt fixing point on the underside of the wheelarch. Remove bracket and drill seat belt fixing with 1/4" pilot hole and then open up to 5/8".

3.4 Refit bracket using bolt (SH605081L) 1 off at lower fixing and bolt (255227) 1 off at the upper fixing. Secure using plain washer (3830L), spring washer (WM600051L) and nut (NH605041L).

4.0 Floor Mounting.
Locate step in wheelbox and draw a vertical line down to floor. Find mid point between rivets in floor and draw a line across the floor.

4.1 Measure 6 1/2" and 10 1/4" from either side of wheelarch and mark position. Drill 1/4" pilot holes through floor and crossmember.

4.2 On outer holes open up to 5/8" through floor skin only, open pilot holes to 5/16" in crossmember. On inner holes open up to 5/8" through floor and crossmember.

4.3 In outer holes fit spacers, screws, washers and nuts and tighten. Place anchor point tube in inner holes, drill holes 3/16" for rivets and rivet to floor.

4.4 From under vehicle fit screws, washer and tabwashers. Tighten screw and bend tabwasher over screws and crossmember.

5.0 Replace rear mat or carpet and replace seats.

6.0 Replace road wheels and remove vehicle from stands.

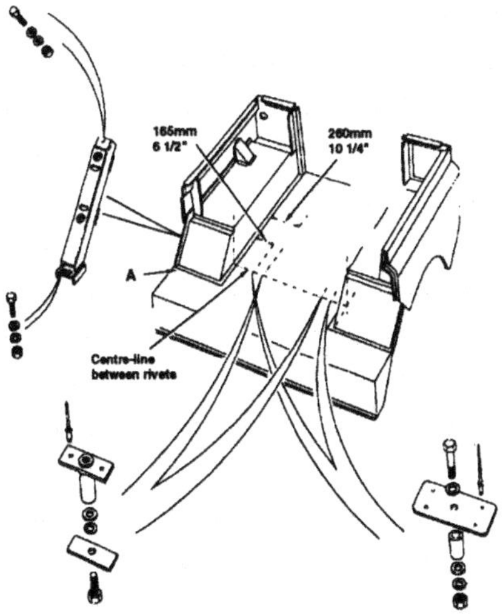

AH10

FITTING INSTRUCTIONS FOR REAR INWARD FACING SEAT BELT MOULDINGS - LR 110

1.0 Remove inward facing seats.

2.0 Jack up vehicles, support on stands and remove rear road wheels.

3.0 Remove rear light covers and the rear tool retaining strap from wheelarch.

4.0 Check stiffeners and open holes for monobolts *ref* A on illustration to 17/64".

5.0 Mark position for stiffeners as follows:
Front Stiffener (B)
From step in wheelarch box measure 7 1/4", draw a line from wheelarch inner edge to bodyside. Measure 1 5/8" from bodyside and drill 1/4" pilot hole.

5.1 Centre Stiffener (C)
From step in wheelarch box measure 23 1/8" and 24 5/16", draw a line from wheelarch inner edge to bodyside. Measure 1 5/8" from bodyside and drill 1/4" pilot holes.

5.2 Rear Stiffener (D)
From step in wheelarch box measure 43 1/8", draw a line from wheelarch inner edge to bodyside. Measure 4 5/8" from bodyside and drill 1/4" pilot hole.

5.3 Open up pilot holes to 5/8" and deburr.

6.0 Front and Centre Stiffener.
From under vehicle position stiffeners to wheelarch box, locate angle bracket and use 7/16" UNF bolt and washer to position stiffeners, tighten bolt, drill 3/16" holes for rivets *ref* E, deburr and rivet, dril holes 17/64" for monobolts *ref* A, deburr and rivet up.

6.1 Rear Stiffener.
From under wheelarch at rear of vehicle remove rubber protector for rear lamp wiring, trim 1/4" to 1/2" from top of protector to allow stiffener to fit body. Remove excess sealer as required and refit rubber protector. Position stiffener to wheelarch box, use 7/16" UNF bolt and washer to position stiffener, drill 3/16" holes for rivets, deburr and rivet, drill holes 17/64" for monobolts deburr and rivet up.

7.0 Remove 7/16" bolts and repeat operations for opposite wheelarch.

8.0 Refit light covers and re-position tool retaining strap to forward edge of centre angle bracket.
Fit seatbelts with long end of belt in centre fixings and tighten.

9.0 Refit seats - road wheels and remove from stands.

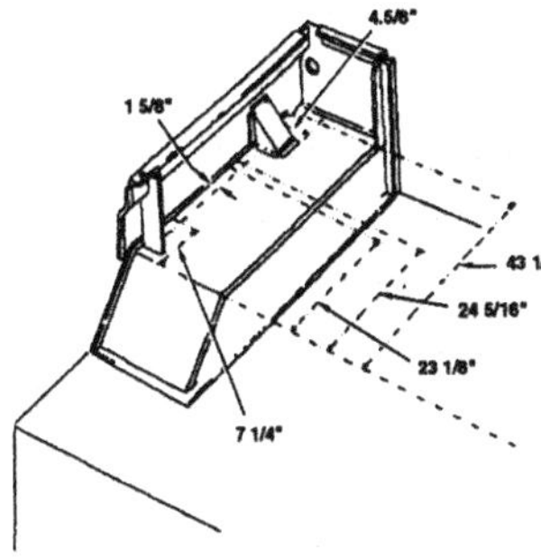

AH11

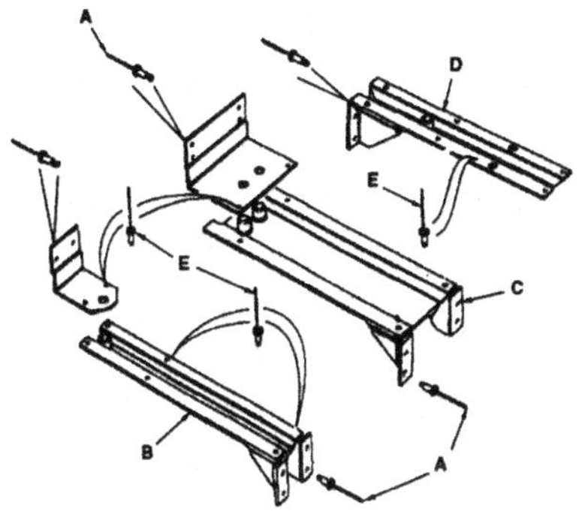

AH12

TECHNICAL INFORMATION

CIRCULATE TO:			
SERVICE MGR.	X		
RECEPTION	X		
WORKSHOP	X	SUBJECT	03/12/93
PARTS	X	**Axle Swivel and Hub Seals - New Part Information**	170/93/EN
MODEL **Range Rover Discovery Defender**		AFFECTED VEHICLES **All derivatives from LH 632889 - LJ 045306 - LD925688**	

DETAIL

To improve axle swivel and hub sealing a new range of seals have been introduced at the above VIN numbers. These seals are directly interchangeable with the previous parts.

The information provided on seal FTC 3401 supersedes that provided on Technical Bulletin 083/93.

ACTION REQUIRED

If the new type swivel/hub seals leak in service, please submit a Product Report accompanied by a copy of the illustration overleaf identifying the area of the leak. Should customers complain of leaks in this area fit the new seals.

PARTS INFORMATION

Swivel seal FTC 3401 replaces FRC 2889

Hub seal FTC 2783 replaces FRC 8221

Stub axle seal FTC 3145 replaces FRC 0951

ILLUSTRATION

PROCEDURE

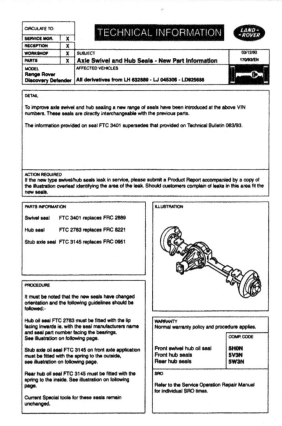

It must be noted that the new seals have changed orientation and the following guidelines should be followed:-

Hub oil seal FTC 2783 must be fitted with the lip facing inwards ie. with the seal manufacturers name and seal part number facing the bearings.
See illustration on following page.

Stub axle oil seal FTC 3145 on front axle application must be fitted with the spring to the outside,
see illustration on following page.

Rear hub oil seal FTC 3145 must be fitted with the spring to the inside. See illustration on following page.

Current Special tools for these seals remain unchanged.

WARRANTY

Normal warranty policy and procedure applies.

	COMP. CODE
Front swivel hub oil seal	**5H0N**
Front hub seals	**5V3N**
Rear hub seals	**5W3N**

SRO

Refer to the Service Operation Repair Manual for individual SRO times.

TECHNICAL INFORMATION

Page 2 of 3	SUBJECT **Axle Swivel and Hub Seals - New Part Information**	03/12/93 170/93/EN
MODEL **Range Rover Discovery Defender**	AFFECTED VEHICLES **All derivatives from LH 632889 - LJ 045306 - LD925688**	

REAR AXLE HUB ASSEMBLY

A - Rear axle hub assembly - oil seal FTC 3145 fitted with spring inwards.
B - Rear axle hub assembly - oil seal FTC 2783 (Springless type)

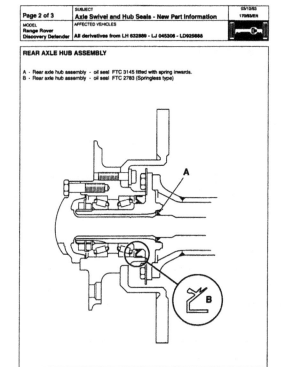

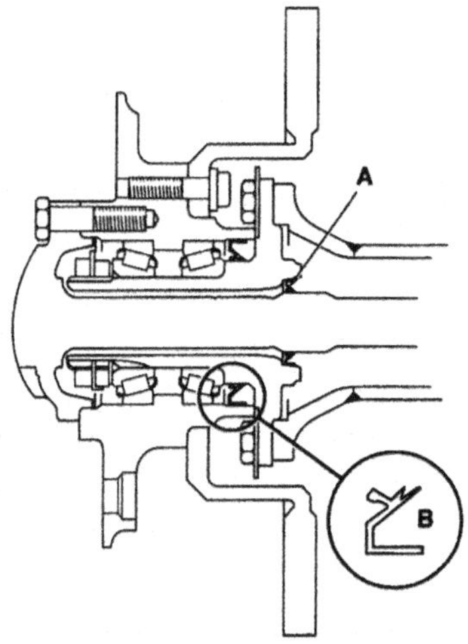

TECHNICAL INFORMATION

Page 3 of 3	SUBJECT **Axle Swivel and Hub Seals - New Part Information**	03/12/93 170/93/EN
MODEL **Range Rover Discovery Defender**	AFFECTED VEHICLES **All derivatives from LH 632889 - LJ 045306 - LD925688**	

FRONT AXLE HUB ASSEMBLY

C - Front axle oil seal - FTC3145 fitted with spring outwards.
D - Swivel housing oil seal - FTC 3401
E - Front axle hub oil seal - FTC 2783 (Springless type)

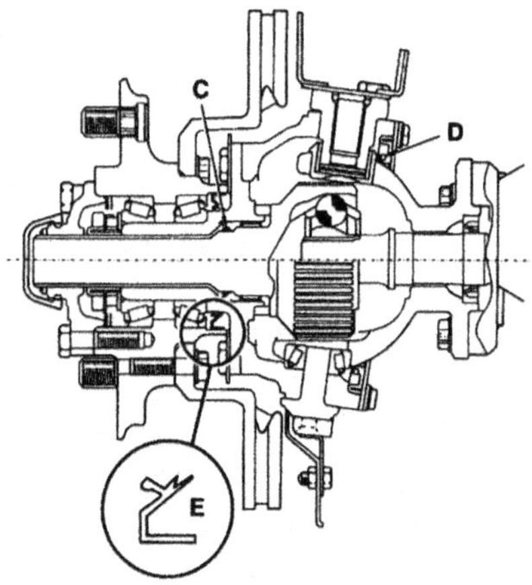

Absorber-crankshaft vibration	B374
Absorber-transfer box vibration	D 9
Actuator-central door locking-passenger's	N194
Actuator-central door locking-passenger's	N197
Actuator-waste gate turbocharger	B177
Actuator-waste gate turbocharger	B218
Actuator-waste gate turbocharger	B255
Adapter-crankcase breather	B338
Adapter-crankcase breather	B339
Adapter-crankcase breather	J 60
Adaptor	E 6
Adaptor	E 27
Adaptor	E 51
Adaptor	E 29
Adaptor	L 71
Adaptor	M 13
Adaptor	N161
Adaptor	N184
Adaptor assembly-oil filter	B 18
Adaptor assembly-oil filter	B 66
Adaptor assembly-oil filter	B117
Adaptor assembly-oil filter	B165
Adaptor assembly-oil filter	B206
Adaptor assembly-oil filter	B314
Adaptor fuel lines	J 5
Adaptor fuel lines	J 6
Adaptor fuel lines	J 59
Adaptor-air cleaner	J 60
Adaptor-air cleaner	J 61
Adaptor-air cleaner	J 73
Adaptor-air cleaner-with raised air intake	J 37
Adaptor-air conditioning compressor hose	L 50
Adaptor-air conditioning compressor hose	L 58
Adaptor-air conditioning compressor hose	L 80
Adaptor-carburettor-only with stromberg	B334
Adaptor-clutch housing	C 53
Adaptor-clutch housing	C 40
Adaptor-handle window regulator	N159
Adaptor-inlet manifold bypass	B385
Adaptor-inlet manifold heater feed	B385
Adaptor-oil cooler	L 30
Adaptor-oil drain pipe turbocharger	B178
Adaptor-oil drain pipe turbocharger	B218
Adaptor-oil drain pipe turbocharger	B255
Adaptor-oil filter	B 17
Adaptor-oil filter	B 18
Adaptor-oil filter	B 65
Adaptor-oil filter	B 66
Adaptor-oil filter	B116
Adaptor-oil filter	B117
Adaptor-oil filter	B165
Adaptor-oil filter	B206
Adaptor-oil filter	B243
Adaptor-oil filter	L 30
Adaptor-oil filter-diesel	B291
Adaptor-oil pressure switch	B116
Adaptor-oil pressure switch	B117
Adaptor-oil pressure switch	B165
Adaptor-oil pressure switch	B243
Adaptor-outlet engine exhaust	B324
Adaptor-pipe coolant	B 24
Adaptor-pipe coolant	B 72
Adaptor-pipe coolant	B125
Adaptor-pipe coolant	B172
Adaptor-pipe coolant	B207
Adaptor-pipe coolant	B244
Adaptor-pipe coolant	L 27
Adaptor-pipe coolant	L 30
Adaptor-pipe coolant	L 2
Adaptor-pipe-dual male	B216
Adaptor-pipe-dual male	C 86
Adaptor-pipe-dual male	H 21
Adaptor-servo to dash	H 6
Adaptor-spare wheel	S 14
Adaptor-transmitter	B 19
Adaptor-transmitter-water temperature	B 67
Adaptor-tube-drain evaporator tube	L 49
Adaptor-vacuum pipe injection pump	H 1
Adaptor-vacuum pipe injection pump	H 5
Adhesive	N221
Adhesive-sealing-300ml	U 1
Adjuster assembly-transfer box brake shoe	D 41
Adjuster unit-headlamp	M 5
Adjuster-door latch	N188
Adjuster-door latch	N193
Aerial front fender-metal	M121
Aerial front fender-metal	M122
Aerial front fender-metal	M124
Aerial front fender-metal	M127
Aerial front fender-rubberised	T 12
Air cleaner assembly	J 33
Air cleaner assembly	J 34
Air cleaner assembly	J 35
Air cleaner assembly	J 36
Air cleaner assembly	J 37
Air cleaner assembly	J 38
Air cleaner assembly	J 39
Air cleaner assembly	J 41
Air cleaner assembly	J 43
Air cleaner assembly-raised	J 45
Air cleaner assembly-raised	J 46
Airbox assembly blower-heater-rhd	L 35
Alternator assembly-115/45-exchange	B359
Alternator assembly-115/45-lra356-exchange	B 91
Alternator assembly-115/45-lra356-exchange	B138
Alternator assembly-120 amp-new	B296
Alternator assembly-a127-100 amp-	B261
Alternator assembly-a127-100 amp-new	B396
Alternator assembly-a133-65 amp	B361
Alternator assembly-exchange-115/45	B358
Alternator assembly-lra406-exchange-a133-	B 43
Alternator assembly-lra406-exchange-a133-	B 93
Alternator assembly-lra406-exchange-a133-	B140
Alternator assembly-machine sensed-115/45-	B 43
Alternator assembly-new-a127-45 amp	B 92
Alternator assembly-new-a127-45 amp	B139
Alternator assembly-new-a127-45 amp	B186
Alternator assembly-new-a127-45 amp	B226
Alternator assembly-new-a127-45 amp-lucas	B355
Alternator assembly-new-a127-45 amp-lucas	B360
Alternator assembly-new-a127-65 amp	B261
Alternator assembly-new-a127-65 amp-rh	B 94
Alternator assembly-new-a127-65 amp-rh	B141
Alternator assembly-new-a127-65 amp-rh	B187
Alternator assembly-new-a127-65 amp-rh	B226
Alternator assembly-new-a127-65 amp-rh	B356
Alternator assembly-new-a127-65 amp-rh	B362
Ammeter-12v	M115
Amplifier	B354
Angle mounting	N114
Angle mounting-rear	N 68
Angle mounting-rear	N 75
Angle mounting-rear	N 79
Angle mounting-rear	N 87
Angle mounting-rear	N 69
Angle mounting-rear	N 73
Angle mounting-rear	N 76
Angle mounting-rear	N 80
Angle mounting-rear	N 88
Angle mounting-rear	N101
Angle mounting-rear	N 70
Angle mounting-rear	N 74
Angle mounting-rear	N 77
Angle mounting-rear	N 81
Angle mounting-rear	N 71
Angle mounting-rear	N 78
Angle mounting-rear	N 82
Angle mounting-rear	N 83
Angle mounting-rear	N 84
Angle mounting-rear	N 85
Angle mounting-rear	N 86
Angle mounting-rh	N 41
Angle protection-corner-rh	N 41
Angle reinforcing	N 90
Angle reinforcing-rh	N 41
Antifreeze-1ltr	U 2
Arm & bush assembly-exhaust valve rocker	B120
Arm & bush assembly-exhaust valve rocker	B168
Arm & bush assembly-exhaust valve rocker-	B208
Arm & bush assembly-inlet valve rocker-lh	B208
Arm assembly-backlight wiper	M143
Arm assembly-backlight wiper	M144
Arm assembly-radius front suspension	E 56
Arm assembly-tensioner	B260
Arm assembly-windscreen wiper	M129
Arm-clutch release clutch	C 2
Arm-clutch release clutch	C 3
Arm-clutch release clutch	C 28
Arm-clutch release clutch	C 41
Arm-clutch release clutch	C 42
Arm-clutch release clutch	C 43
Arm-clutch release clutch	C 44
Arm-clutch release clutch	C 45
Arm-exhaust valve rocker-rh	B 20
Arm-exhaust valve rocker-rh	B 68
Arm-exhaust valve rocker-rh	B120
Arm-exhaust valve rocker-rh	B168
Arm-inlet valve rocker-rh	B 20
Arm-inlet valve rocker-rh	B 68
Arm-inlet valve rocker-rh	B120
Arm-inlet valve rocker-rh	B168
Arm-mirror	N221
Arm-radius front suspension-rhd	E 57
Arm-rotor distributor	B350
Arm-rotor distributor	B351
Arm-rotor distributor	B352
Arm-rotor distributor-lucas	B 42
Arm-rotor distributor-lucas	B 90
Arm-transfer box differential lock	D 36
Arm-transfer box differential lock connecting	D 36
Arm-transfer box differential lock connecting	D 37
Arm-transfer box differential lock connecting	D 38
Arm-transfer box gearchange	D 29
Arm-transfer box gearchange	D 30
Arm-transfer box gearchange	D 33
Arm-transfer box gearchange	D 35
Arm-transfer box gearchange	D 31
Ashtray assembly-facia	P 6
Axle assembly-stub front suspension	E 23
Axle-rear suspension hub stub	E 46
Axle-rear suspension hub stub	E 48
Axle-stub-hub front suspension	E 23
Axle-stub-hub front suspension	E 25
Axle-stub-hub front suspension	E 22
Axle/drive unit assembly 4x4-front	E 4
Axle/drive unit assembly 4x4-front-steel	E 5
Axle/drive unit-4x4 rear	E 27
Axle/drive unit-4x4 rear	E 28
Axle/drive unit-4x4 rear	E 29
Axle/drive unit-4x4 rear	E 30
Backlight assembly-convertible hood plastic-	N227
Backlight assembly-convertible hood plastic-	N230
Backlight assembly-convertible hood plastic-	N231
Backlight assembly-convertible hood plastic-	N223
Backlight assembly-convertible hood plastic-	N228
Backplate-brake pad inner-rh	H 28
Backplate-front & rear door handle	N187
Backplate-transmission brake assembly	D 41
Backplate-transmission brake assembly	D 42
Badge	N124

Badge	P 2
Badge-camel trophy-large	V 8
Badge-front-silver on black background	N205
Badge-front-silver on black background	N207
Badge-front-wing-light grey	N217
Badge-grille-land rover-silver.	N205
Badge-grille-land rover-silver.	N206
Badge-grille-land rover-silver.	N207
Badge-grille-land rover-silver.	N208
Badge-grille-land rover-silver.	N209
Badge-land rover	N209
Badge-land rover-gold on green background	L 74
Badge-land rover-rear-gold on green	N206
Badge-land rover-rear-gold on green	N208
Badge-land rover-rear-gold on green	N222
Badge-rear panel	N209
Badge-td5 -moulded-plastic-dark grey	N209
Badge-td5 -no pattern-silver.	N206
Badge-td5 -no pattern-silver.	N208
Badge-tdi-front-wing-light grey	N215
Badge-tdi-front-wing-silver on black	N214
Badge-tdi-front-wing-silver on black	N216
Baffle-engine oil	B319
Baffle-oil separator	B211
Baffle-oil separator	B248
Baffle-oil separator-side cover	B123
Bag-accessory-umbrella	T 54
Bag-jack assembly stowage	S 6
Bag-locking wheel nut key/extractor	E 55
Ball-detent manual transmission	C 21
Ball-detent manual transmission	C 24
Ball-detent manual transmission	C 32
Ball-detent manual transmission	C 33
Ball-detent manual transmission	C 36
Ball-detent manual transmission	C 46
Ball-detent manual transmission	C 68
Ball-detent manual transmission	C 34
Ball-detent manual transmission	D 29
Ball-detent manual transmission	D 24
Ball-detent manual transmission	D 22
Ball-detent manual transmission	D 28
Ball-detent manual transmission	F 13
Ball-detent manual transmission	T 5
Ball-towing attachment-50mm	T 37
Ball-towing attachment-50mm	T 38
Ball-towing attachment-50mm	T 42
Ball-towing attachment-bracket to rear	T 30
Ball-towing attachment-tie-bar to chassis-	T 31
Banjo-clutch special	G 5
Bar assembly-anti-roll rear suspension	E 68
Bar assembly-nudge-front-black-a frame	N 21
Bar assembly-nudge-front-compatable with	T 15
Bar assembly-nudge-front-wrap round with	N 22
Bar-actuating	L 76
Bar-anti-roll front suspension	E 60
Bar-roll over	N219
Bar-roof sports	T 18
Bar-tie straight	S 15
Bar-tie straight	S 16
Bar-tie straight-bracket to extension assy-lh	T 31
Bar-tie straight-rh	T 30
Bar-tie straight-spare wheel clamp	S 14
Bar-tie-bent forging	R 67
Bar-tie-bent forging-rh	R 61
Bar-tie-bent forging-rhd	F 7
Bar-tie-bent forging-rhd	F 8
Bar-tie-bent forging-rhd	F 9
Bar-tie-bent forging-rhd	F 10
Bar-tie-bent forging-rhd	F 11
Bar-tie-bent machining-rh	R 59
Bar-transverse-roll cage-lh	N250
Bar-transverse-roll cage-lh	N252
Bar-underside protection	N 20
Base assembly-cab	N 41
Base assembly-front seat mounting-with tool	N 35
Base assembly-front seat mounting-with tool	N 36
Base assembly-front seat mounting-with tool	N 37
Base assembly-seat-rear forward facing	N 38
Base-map lamp roof trim cantrail	M 17
Battery-091-bbms-standard-wet	M 27
Battery-091-bbms-standard-wet	M 28
Battery-transmitter burglar alarm	M104
Bearing bush-connecting rod small end	B199
Bearing bush-connecting rod small end	B236
Bearing clutch	C 42
Bearing intermediate shaft assembly	D 15
Bearing steering gear-power assisted steering	B340
Bearing steering gear-power assisted steering	F 16
Bearing-alternator front	B 43
Bearing-alternator front	B 91
Bearing-alternator front	B 92
Bearing-alternator front	B 93
Bearing-alternator front	B138
Bearing-alternator front	B139
Bearing-alternator front	B140
Bearing-alternator front	B141
Bearing-alternator front	B186
Bearing-alternator front	B187
Bearing-alternator front	B226
Bearing-alternator front	B355
Bearing-alternator front	B358
Bearing-alternator front	B359
Bearing-alternator front	B360
Bearing-alternator front	B361
Bearing-alternator front	B362
Bearing-alternator front	B 44
Bearing-alternator front-new alternator-rh	B356
Bearing-alternator front-slip ring end	B 94
Bearing-ball	B 11
Bearing-ball	B 15
Bearing-ball	B 40
Bearing-ball	B 87
Bearing-ball	B205
Bearing-ball	B225
Bearing-ball	B349
Bearing-ball	C 32
Bearing-ball	C 33
Bearing-ball	D 18
Bearing-ball	D 19
Bearing-ball	F 15
Bearing-ball	T 5
Bearing-ball-rear	C 35
Bearing-camshaft front	B 3
Bearing-camshaft front	B 51
Bearing-camshaft front	B 52
Bearing-camshaft front	B102
Bearing-camshaft front	B104
Bearing-camshaft front	B152
Bearing-camshaft front	B153
Bearing-camshaft front	B195
Bearing-camshaft front	B233
Bearing-camshaft rear	B 3
Bearing-camshaft rear	B 51
Bearing-camshaft rear	B 52
Bearing-camshaft rear	B102
Bearing-camshaft rear	B104
Bearing-camshaft rear	B152
Bearing-camshaft rear	B153
Bearing-camshaft rear	B195
Bearing-camshaft rear	B233
Bearing-clutch release	B 47
Bearing-clutch release	B 98
Bearing-clutch release	B191
Bearing-clutch release	B230
Bearing-clutch release	B370
Bearing-clutch release	B147
Bearing-clutch release	C 2
Bearing-clutch release	C 3
Bearing-clutch release	C 28
Bearing-clutch release	C 41
Bearing-clutch release	C 43
Bearing-clutch release	C 45
Bearing-front/rear axle hub	E 23
Bearing-front/rear axle hub	E 25
Bearing-front/rear axle hub	E 46
Bearing-front/rear axle hub	E 48
Bearing-front/rear axle hub-swivel pin	E 22
Bearing-half big end connecting rod	B268
Bearing-main-crankshaft	B268
Bearing-needle roller	B340
Bearing-needle roller	C 11
Bearing-needle roller	C 12
Bearing-needle roller	C 32
Bearing-needle roller	C 33
Bearing-needle roller	C 35
Bearing-needle roller	C 67
Bearing-needle roller	D 17
Bearing-needle roller	D 24
Bearing-needle roller	F 12
Bearing-needle roller	F 15
Bearing-needle roller manual transmission	C 59
Bearing-needle roller manual transmission	C 63
Bearing-needle roller manual transmission	C 64
Bearing-needle roller manual transmission	C 13
Bearing-needle roller manual transmission	C 65
Bearing-needle roller manual transmission	C 14
Bearing-roller	C 35
Bearing-roller-viscous fan to cover	B273
Bearing-taper roller	C 64
Bearing-taper roller	C 15
Bearing-taper roller	D 29
Bearing-taper roller	D 21
Bearing-taper roller	D 24
Bearing-taper roller	D 28
Bearing-taper roller	E 8
Bearing-taper roller	E 11
Bearing-taper roller	E 14
Bearing-taper roller differential	E 40
Bearing-taper roller differential	E 42
Bearing-taper roller differential	E 14
Bearing-taper roller differential-crownwheel	E 43
Bearing-taper roller differential-crownwheel	E 45
Bearing-taper roller-differential final drive	E 40
Bearing-taper roller-differential final drive	E 42
Bearing-taper roller-differential final drive	E 43
Bearing-taper roller-differential final drive	E 45
Bearing-taper roller-differential final drive	E 32
Bearing-taper roller-differential final drive	E 35
Bearing-taper roller-differential final drive	E 39
Bearing-taper roller-lower	E 20
Bearing-taper roller-lower	E 22
Bearing-taper roller-man trans	C 16
Bearing-taper roller-man trans	C 18
Bearing-taper roller-man trans	C 66
Bearing-taper roller-man trans	C 46
Bearing-taper roller-man trans	C 57
Bearing-taper roller-man trans	C 10
Bearing-taper roller-man trans primary shaft-	C 58
Bearing-thrust crankshaft	B268
Bellcrank-door	N194
Belt-engine timing	B112
Belt-engine timing	B161
Belt-engine timing	B203
Belt-engine timing	B240
Belt-front camshaft drive	B 39
Belt-front camshaft drive	B 86
Belt-polyvee air conditioning compressor	B 86
Belt-polyvee air conditioning compressor	B135
Belt-polyvee air conditioning compressor	B183
Belt-polyvee air conditioning compressor	B223

Belt-polyvee air conditioning compressor B259
Belt-polyvee alternator .... B 91
Belt-polyvee alternator .... B 92
Belt-polyvee alternator .... B 93
Belt-polyvee alternator .... B 94
Belt-polyvee alternator B114
Belt-polyvee alternator B138
Belt-polyvee alternator B139
Belt-polyvee alternator B140
Belt-polyvee alternator B141
Belt-polyvee alternator B162
Belt-polyvee alternator B163
Belt-polyvee alternator B186
Belt-polyvee alternator B187
Belt-polyvee alternator B204
Belt-polyvee alternator B226
Belt-polyvee alternator B277
Belt-polyvee alternator B278
Belt-polyvee alternator B312
Belt-polyvee alternator B313
Belt-polyvee alternator B355
Belt-polyvee alternator B356
Belt-polyvee alternator B359
Belt-polyvee alternator B360
Belt-polyvee alternator B362
Belt-polyvee alternator B380
Belt-polyvee alternator B394
Belt-polyvee coolant pump .... B 61
Belt-polyvee coolant pump .... B 62
Belt-polyvee coolant pump B113
Belt-polyvee coolant pump B242
Belt-polyvee coolant pump B313
Belt-polyvee coolant pump .... B 14
Belt-polyvee power assisted steering .... B 36
Belt-polyvee power assisted steering .... B 37
Belt-polyvee power assisted steering .... B 83
Belt-polyvee power assisted steering .... B 84
Belt-polyvee power assisted steering B132
Belt-polyvee power assisted steering B133
Belt-polyvee power assisted steering B181
Belt-polyvee power assisted steering B221
Belt-vee air conditioning compressor B313
Belt-vee air conditioning compressor B347
Belt-vee power assisted steering B312
Belt-vee power assisted steering B313
Belt-vee power assisted steering B341
Bezel-clock M120
Bezel-door handle-black-rh .... P 21
Bezel-door handle-black-rh .... P 22
Bezel-door handle-black-rh .... P 20
Bezel-facia heater control .... P 12
Bezel-headlamp-black .... M 5
Bezel-headlamp-quartz halogen-black .... M 3
Bezel-headlamp-sealed beam-black .... M 2
Bezel-headlamp-sealed beam-chrome .... M 1
Bezel-radio .... P 4
Bezel-speaker-radio-speaker M122
Bezel-speaker-radio-speaker M124
Bezel-sunroof handle N134
Bimetal assembly-carburettor choke B333
Bin-facia console stowage .... P 4
Blade connector-wiper earth M128
Blade-windscreen and backlight wiper M143
Blade-windscreen and backlight wiper- M144
Blade-windscreen and backlight wiper- M129
Blank assembly-facia switch-electric window .... M 89
Blank-evaporator speaker .... P 7
Blank-facia switch .... M 89
Block-fixing-catch slide window N111
Blower air conditioning .... L 51
Blower assembly heater-rhd .... L 35
Blower assembly-air conditioning .... L 52
Body assembly-lower rear .... N 72
Body assembly-lower rear .... N 75
Body assembly-lower rear .... N 87
Body assembly-lower rear .... N 89
Body assembly-lower rear .... N 73
Body assembly-lower rear .... N 76
Body assembly-lower rear .... N 88
Body assembly-lower rear .... N 77
Body assembly-lower rear .... N 78
Body assembly-lower rear .... N 82
Body assembly-lower rear .... N 83
Body assembly-lower rear-front and rear fuel .... N 84
Body assembly-lower rear-front fuel filler .... N 85
Body assembly-lower rear-less fuel filler .... N 86
Body assembly-lower rear-less rope cleats .... N 68
Body assembly-lower rear-less rope cleats .... N 69
Body assembly-lower rear-less rope cleats .... N 70
Body assembly-lower rear-less rope cleats .... N 74
Body assembly-lower rear-less rope cleats .... N 71
Body assembly-lower rear-rear fuel filler .... N 80
Body assembly-lower rear-rear fuel filler .... N 81
Body assembly-lower rear-rear fuel filler .... N 79
Body assembly-rear .... N 89
Body side assembly-rear-front and rear fuel .... N 84
Body side assembly-rear-rh .... N 68
Body side assembly-rear-rh .... N 72
Body side assembly-rear-rh .... N 69
Body side assembly-rear-rh .... N 73
Body side assembly-rear-rh .... N 70
Body side assembly-rear-rh .... N 74
Body side assembly-rear-rh .... N 71
Body side assembly-rear-rh .... N 82
Body side assembly-rear-rh .... N 83
Body side assembly-rear-rh-front fuel filler .... N 85
Body side assembly-rear-rh-less fuel filler .... N 86
Body side assembly-rear-rh-less rope cleats .... N 80
Body side assembly-rear-rh-rear fuel filler .... N 81
Body side assembly-rear-rh-rear fuel filler .... N 79
Body side assembly-rh .... N 92
Body side-lh-less rope cleats .... N 80
Body side-lh-less rope cleats .... N 81
Body side-lh-less rope cleats .... N 82
Body side-lh-less rope cleats .... N 83
Body side-lh-less rope cleats .... N 86
Body side-lh-with rope cleats .... N 79
Body side-lh-with rope cleats .... N 84
Body side-lh-with rope cleats .... N 85
Body side-rh-front and rear fuel filler .... N 84
Body side-rh-front fuel filler aperture-with .... N 85
Body side-rh-less fuel filler aperture-less .... N 86
Body side-rh-rear fuel filler aperture-less .... N 80
Body side-rh-rear fuel filler aperture-less .... N 81
Body side-rh-rear fuel filler aperture-less .... N 82
Body side-rh-rear fuel filler aperture-less .... N 83
Body side-rh-rear fuel filler aperture-with .... N 79
Body side-upper-lh-with fixed side window N104
Body side-upper-rh-with fixed side window N104
Body side/wheelarch assembly .... N 75
Body side/wheelarch assembly-rh .... N 87
Body side/wheelarch assembly-rh .... N 76
Body side/wheelarch assembly-rh .... N 88
Body side/wheelarch assembly-rh .... N 77
Body side/wheelarch assembly-rh .... N 78
Body-carburettor float needle .... B 28
Body-carburettor float needle .... B 31
Body-carburettor float needle .... B 76
Body-carburettor-lh B333
Body-headlamp .... M 5
Body-headlamp-quartz halogen .... M 3
Body-headlamp-sealed beam .... M 1
Body-headlamp-sealed beam .... M 2
Body-transmission oil pump .... C 7
Body-transmission oil pump .... C 8
Body-upper fuel system .... B 28
Bolt .... B 11
Bolt .... B 21
Bolt .... B 52
Bolt .... B 69
Bolt B102
Bolt B104
Bolt B121
Bolt B131
Bolt B153
Bolt B169
Bolt B173
Bolt B180
Bolt B195
Bolt B209
Bolt B220
Bolt B233
Bolt B246
Bolt B267
Bolt B274
Bolt B279
Bolt B287
Bolt B327
Bolt B334
Bolt B337
Bolt B365
Bolt B375
Bolt B280
Bolt .... C 36
Bolt .... C 54
Bolt .... C 72
Bolt .... C 83
Bolt .... D 41
Bolt .... D 42
Bolt .... E 32
Bolt .... E 40
Bolt .... E 43
Bolt .... E 45
Bolt .... E 62
Bolt .... E 69
Bolt .... E 13
Bolt .... F 10
Bolt .... H 29
Bolt .... J 1
Bolt .... J 8
Bolt .... J 10
Bolt .... J 52
Bolt .... J 58
Bolt .... J 67
Bolt .... K 31
Bolt .... K 33
Bolt .... L 26
Bolt .... M 10
Bolt M132
Bolt M133
Bolt M136
Bolt M138
Bolt M139
Bolt M140
Bolt M141
Bolt M142
Bolt .... N 90
Bolt .... N 92
Bolt N139
Bolt N175
Bolt N201
Bolt N203
Bolt .... N 99
Bolt N179
Bolt .... R 15
Bolt .... R 63
Bolt .... R 68
Bolt .... R 30
Bolt .... S 8
Bolt .... S 9

Bolt .... S 10
Bolt .... T 39
Bolt .... V 5
Bolt & washer assembly-sump B376
Bolt & washer assembly-sump-5/16unc B306
Bolt differential .... E 43
Bolt differential .... E 45
Bolt-1/2unf x 4 9/16 .... B 19
Bolt-1/2unf x 4 9/16 .... B 67
Bolt-1/2unf x 4 9/16 .... B119
Bolt-1/4unc x 1 1/2-hexagonal head B341
Bolt-1/4unc x 1 1/2-hexagonal head B342
Bolt-1/4unc x 1 1/2-hexagonal head B343
Bolt-1/4unc x 1 1/4 .... B314
Bolt-1/4unf x 7/8 .... F 17
Bolt-3/8-unf .... E 1
Bolt-3/8-unf .... E 3
Bolt-3/8-unf .... T 6
Bolt-3/8unc x 1 1/4 .... D 18
Bolt-3/8unc x 2.79 .... B319
Bolt-3/8unc x 2.79 .... B382
Bolt-3/8unf .... E 42
Bolt-3/8unf x 1 3/4 .... D 19
Bolt-5/16unc B325
Bolt-5/16unc B385
Bolt-5/16unc x 3 .... B307
Bolt-5/16unf x 0.58 .... B399
Bolt-5/16unf x 1 1/2 .... B304
Bolt-5/16unf x 1 1/2 .... B363
Bolt-5/16unf-counter sunk N168
Bolt-5/8unf x 3 1/2 .... E 56
Bolt-7/16unc x 2.71 .... B381
Bolt-7/16unc x 2.71 .... B317
Bolt-7/16unf-hexagonal head .... F 7
Bolt-adhesive-patch-m10 x 40 .... B294
Bolt-banjo .... B 19
Bolt-banjo .... B 36
Bolt-banjo .... B 67
Bolt-banjo .... B 83
Bolt-banjo B116
Bolt-banjo B117
Bolt-banjo B119
Bolt-banjo B132
Bolt-banjo B165
Bolt-banjo B167
Bolt-banjo B175
Bolt-banjo B177
Bolt-banjo B216
Bolt-banjo B253
Bolt-banjo B255
Bolt-banjo B293
Bolt-banjo B323
Bolt-banjo .... C 37
Bolt-banjo .... C 83
Bolt-banjo .... C 56
Bolt-banjo .... D 5
Bolt-banjo .... E 50
Bolt-banjo .... E 51
Bolt-banjo .... J 52
Bolt-banjo .... J 55
Bolt-banjo .... J 56
Bolt-banjo fuel lines B253
Bolt-banjo-6mm B217
Bolt-banjo-6mm B254
Bolt-banjo-boost capsule B251
Bolt-banjo-fixing feed pipe B178
Bolt-banjo-no1-no2-no3 .... B129
Bolt-banjo-no1-no2-no3 .... B176
Bolt-banjo-oil feed B218
Bolt-bar to body N219
Bolt-bracket to block B296
Bolt-bracket to block-hexagonal head-m8 x .... B 95
Bolt-bracket to block-hexagonal head-m8 x B188
Bolt-bracket to block-hexagonal head-m8 x B227
Bolt-bracket to block-hexagonal head-m8 x .... B 83
Bolt-bracket to body-hexagonal head-m8 x .... K 2
Bolt-bracket to catalyst-hexagonal head- .... K 17
Bolt-bump stop to body-flanged head-m8 x .... N 91
Bolt-caliper -m12 x 35 .... H 31
Bolt-caliper -m12 x 35 .... H 33
Bolt-caliper assy to set pad .... H 27
Bolt-chain retained-m6 x 55 .... N121
Bolt-clutch special banjo .... G 5
Bolt-compressor to block-flanged head B295
Bolt-compressor to plate-hexagonal head- .... B 40
Bolt-compressor to plate-hexagonal head- .... B 87
Bolt-compressor to plate-hexagonal head- B184
Bolt-compressor to plate-hexagonal head- B224
Bolt-connecting rod .... B 6
Bolt-connecting rod .... B 55
Bolt-connecting rod B107
Bolt-connecting rod B156
Bolt-connecting rod B199
Bolt-connecting rod B236
Bolt-connecting rod-11/32uns-3a B305
Bolt-connecting rod-to cap B269
Bolt-counter sunk-torx drive N176
Bolt-counter sunk-torx drive N177
Bolt-cover to block-flanged head-m10 x 40 .... B273
Bolt-cover to block-m8 x 55 .... B291
Bolt-crankshaft pulley .... B 5
Bolt-crankshaft pulley .... B 54
Bolt-crankshaft pulley B106
Bolt-crankshaft pulley B155
Bolt-crankshaft pulley B198
Bolt-crankshaft pulley B235
Bolt-crankshaft pulley B304
Bolt-crankshaft pulley B374
Bolt-cylinder head fixing B280
Bolt-cylinder head fixing-7/16unc x 2 1/4 .... B381
Bolt-cylinder head fixing-7/16unc x 2 1/4 .... B317
Bolt-cylinder head fixing-short-m12 x 100 .... B207
Bolt-cylinder head fixing-short-m12 x 100 .... B244
Bolt-dmf to crankshaft B268
Bolt-dog point B304
Bolt-drain plug fuel tank .... J 1
Bolt-drain plug fuel tank .... J 3
Bolt-drain plug fuel tank .... J 8
Bolt-drain plug fuel tank .... J 10
Bolt-duo taptite-m6 x 12 .... H 24
Bolt-exhaust manifold heat shield pillar .... B 97
Bolt-exhaust manifold heat shield pillar- .... B 46
Bolt-exhaust manifold heat shield pillar-shield .... B 75
Bolt-extention to rear crossmembers- .... T 31
Bolt-fixing box-m12 x 100-hexagonal head .... F 8
Bolt-fixing flywheel crankshaft-long .... B 47
Bolt-fixing flywheel crankshaft-long .... B 98
Bolt-fixing flywheel crankshaft-long B191
Bolt-fixing flywheel crankshaft-long B230
Bolt-fixing flywheel crankshaft-long B147
Bolt-fixing flywheel crankshaft-short B148
Bolt-fixing flywheel crankshaft-short B263
Bolt-fixing hinge N124
Bolt-flanged head .... B 3
Bolt-flanged head .... B 51
Bolt-flanged head B152
Bolt-flanged head B240
Bolt-flanged head .... C 55
Bolt-flanged head .... K 10
Bolt-flanged head .... K 23
Bolt-flanged head-1/4unc x 1 3/8 .... B388
Bolt-flanged head-3/8unc x 1 3/8 .... B385
Bolt-flanged head-3/8unc x 3 1/4 .... B394
Bolt-flanged head-3/8unc x 5/8 .... B393
Bolt-flanged head-3/8unc x 5/8 .... B393
Bolt-flanged head-5/16unc x 2 1/4 .... B390
Bolt-flanged head-5/16unc x 2 1/8 .... B378
Bolt-flanged head-acoustic pad to engine B284
Bolt-flanged head-cover to block-m6 x 65 .... B202
Bolt-flanged head-m10 x 100 .... L 53
Bolt-flanged head-m10 x 35 .... B263
Bolt-flanged head-m10 x 40 .... B297
Bolt-flanged head-m10 x 45 .... C 53
Bolt-flanged head-m10 x 50 .... C 52
Bolt-flanged head-m10 x 50 .... E 23
Bolt-flanged head-m10 x 50 .... E 47
Bolt-flanged head-m10 x 65 .... B373
Bolt-flanged head-m10 x 70 .... B203
Bolt-flanged head-m10 x 75 .... B379
Bolt-flanged head-m12 x 40 .... T 40
Bolt-flanged head-m6 .... L 80
Bolt-flanged head-m6 x 25 .... L 80
Bolt-flanged head-m6 x 30-self tapping .... H 24
Bolt-flanged head-m6 x 40 .... B213
Bolt-flanged head-m6 x 40 .... L 9
Bolt-flanged head-m6 x 40 .... S 14
Bolt-flanged head-m6 x 40 .... S 15
Bolt-flanged head-m6 x 55 .... B248
Bolt-flanged head-m8 x 110 .... B396
Bolt-flanged head-m8 x 110 .... J 57
Bolt-flanged head-m8 x 120 .... B241
Bolt-flanged head-m8 x 125 .... B261
Bolt-flanged head-m8 x 125 .... F 2
Bolt-flanged head-m8 x 130 .... B241
Bolt-flanged head-m8 x 16 .... B354
Bolt-flanged head-m8 x 16 .... H 7
Bolt-flanged head-m8 x 16 .... L 13
Bolt-flanged head-m8 x 16 .... L 23
Bolt-flanged head-m8 x 30 .... G 8
Bolt-flanged head-m8 x 35 .... B204
Bolt-flanged head-m8 x 40 .... B211
Bolt-flanged head-m8 x 40 .... B364
Bolt-flanged head-m8 x 40 .... C 69
Bolt-flanged head-m8 x 40 .... K 1
Bolt-flanged head-m8 x 40 .... K 7
Bolt-flanged head-m8 x 40 .... K 8
Bolt-flanged head-m8 x 40 .... K 11
Bolt-flanged head-m8 x 40 .... K 19
Bolt-flanged head-m8 x 40 .... K 20
Bolt-flanged head-m8 x 40 .... K 22
Bolt-flanged head-m8 x 40 .... L 47
Bolt-flanged head-m8 x 45 .... C 43
Bolt-flanged head-m8 x 50 .... B245
Bolt-flanged head-m8 x 50 .... B253
Bolt-flanged head-m8 x 50 .... C 41
Bolt-flanged head-m8 x 50 .... C 45
Bolt-flanged head-m8 x 50 .... R 40
Bolt-flanged head-m8 x 50 .... R 21
Bolt-flanged head-m8 x 50 .... R 28
Bolt-flanged head-m8 x 55 .... B 13
Bolt-flanged head-m8 x 55 .... B110
Bolt-flanged head-m8 x 55 .... B113
Bolt-flanged head-m8 x 55 .... B120
Bolt-flanged head-m8 x 55 .... B159
Bolt-flanged head-m8 x 55 .... B168
Bolt-flanged head-m8 x 55 .... D 35
Bolt-flanged head-m8 x 55 .... D 5
Bolt-flanged head-m8 x 55 .... D 34
Bolt-flanged head-m8 x 55 .... D 32
Bolt-flanged head-m8 x 55 .... H 14
Bolt-flanged head-m8 x 70 .... B202
Bolt-flanged head-m8 x 80 .... B214
Bolt-flanged head-m8 x 80 .... B238
Bolt-flanged head-m8 x 80 .... D 9
Bolt-flanged head-m8 x 85 .... B251
Bolt-flanged head-m8 x 95 .... B394
Bolt-fuse box cover .... P 12
Bolt-gearbox to engine-hexagonal head-m10 .... C 51
Bolt-head to block-1/2unf x 4 9/16 .... B167
Bolt-hexagonal head .... S 16

Bolt-hexagonal head-3/8unc x 2 .... C 73
Bolt-hexagonal head-3/8unc x 2 .... G 5
Bolt-hexagonal head-5/16unc x 3 1/4 .... B 45
Bolt-hexagonal head-5/16unc x 5 .... B308
Bolt-hexagonal head-5/16unc x 5 .... B309
Bolt-hexagonal head-5/16unc x 5 1/2 .... B349
Bolt-hexagonal head-5/16unf x 1 1/4 .... B225
Bolt-hexagonal head-5/16unf x 1 1/4 .... R 62
Bolt-hexagonal head-m10 x 100 .... B137
Bolt-hexagonal head-m10 x 100 .... K 18
Bolt-hexagonal head-m10 x 110 .... E 63
Bolt-hexagonal head-m10 x 110 .... E 66
Bolt-hexagonal head-m10 x 110 .... N204
Bolt-hexagonal head-m10 x 120 .... B348
Bolt-hexagonal head-m10 x 120 .... N 24
Bolt-hexagonal head-m10 x 120 .... N 20
Bolt-hexagonal head-m10 x 35 .... B 23
Bolt-hexagonal head-m10 x 35 .... B 47
Bolt-hexagonal head-m10 x 35 .... B 98
Bolt-hexagonal head-m10 x 35 .... B124
Bolt-hexagonal head-m10 x 35 .... B171
Bolt-hexagonal head-m10 x 35 .... B212
Bolt-hexagonal head-m10 x 35 .... E 20
Bolt-hexagonal head-m10 x 35 .... E 21
Bolt-hexagonal head-m10 x 40 .... D 6
Bolt-hexagonal head-m10 x 50 .... R 71
Bolt-hexagonal head-m6 x 25 .... B303
Bolt-hexagonal head-m6 x 25 .... D 33
Bolt-hexagonal head-m6 x 25 .... D 31
Bolt-hexagonal head-m6 x 30 .... C 7
Bolt-hexagonal head-m6 x 30 .... C 8
Bolt-hexagonal head-m6 x 30 .... H 10
Bolt-hexagonal head-m8 .... E 22
Bolt-hexagonal head-m8 x 100 .... N 7
Bolt-hexagonal head-m8 x 65 .... K 13
Bolt-hexagonal head-m8 x 70 .... B 20
Bolt-hexagonal head-m8 x 70 .... B 68
Bolt-hexagonal head-m8 x 70 .... B114
Bolt-hexagonal head-m8 x 70 .... B162
Bolt-hexagonal head-m8 x 70 .... B163
Bolt-hexagonal head-m8 x 70 .... K 15
Bolt-hexagonal head-m8 x 70 .... N100
Bolt-hexagonal head-m8 x 80 .... B142
Bolt-hexagonal head-m8 x 90 .... B 36
Bolt-hexagonal head-m8 x 90 .... B 37
Bolt-hexagonal head-m8 x 90 .... B 84
Bolt-hexagonal head-m8 x 90 .... B132
Bolt-hexagonal head-m8 x 90 .... B133
Bolt-hexagonal head-m8 x 90 .... B181
Bolt-hexagonal head-m8 x 90 .... B221
Bolt-hexagonal head-m8 x 90 .... D 4
Bolt-hexagonal socket .... E 61
Bolt-hexagonal socket-m12 x 70 .... C 29
Bolt-hexagonal socket-pintle to .... T 35
Bolt-housing to block-m10 x 45 .... B191
Bolt-housing to block-m10 x 45 .... B230
Bolt-housing to extension-hexagonal head- .... C 24
Bolt-housing to g/box-m12 x 45 .... C 6
Bolt-ladder frame to block-flanged head-m8 .... B200
Bolt-m10 x 45 .... B143
Bolt-m10 x 45 .... B144
Bolt-m10 x 45 .... B146
Bolt-m10 x 45 .... B148
Bolt-m10 x 45 .... B189
Bolt-m10 x 45 .... C 30
Bolt-m10 x 45 .... D 10
Bolt-m10 x 45 .... D 8
Bolt-m10 x 45 .... E 26
Bolt-m10 x 45 .... E 49
Bolt-m10 x 45 .... J 3
Bolt-m10 x 60-long .... D 11
Bolt-m10 x 60-long .... F 18
Bolt-m10-hexagonal .... E 18
Bolt-m12 .... E 19
Bolt-m12 x 100-hexagonal head .... F 9
Bolt-m12 x 100-hexagonal head .... F 11
Bolt-m12 x 30 .... B322
Bolt-m12 x 45 .... B249
Bolt-m12 x 50 .... E 7
Bolt-m12 x 50 .... E 9
Bolt-m12 x 50 .... E 33
Bolt-m12 x 50 .... E 36
Bolt-m12 x 50 .... E 34
Bolt-m12 x 50 .... E 37
Bolt-m12 x 50 .... E 35
Bolt-m14 x 80 .... E 57
Bolt-m16 x 60-dacromat .... T 37
Bolt-m16 x 60-dacromat .... T 38
Bolt-m5 .... D 36
Bolt-m6 x 20 .... N240
Bolt-m6 x 20 .... N243
Bolt-m6 x 20 .... N245
Bolt-m6 x 45 .... H 11
Bolt-m6 x 50 .... M 32
Bolt-m6 x 75 .... B 24
Bolt-m6 x 75 .... B 72
Bolt-m6 x 75 .... B172
Bolt-m8 x 18 .... C 42
Bolt-m8 x 20 .... B147
Bolt-m8 x 20-flanged head .... J 5
Bolt-m8 x 20-flanged head .... J 6
Bolt-m8 x 35 .... N138
Bolt-m8 x 35 .... R 59
Bolt-m8 x 45 .... F 6
Bolt-m8 x 45 .... H 19
Bolt-m8 x 45 .... H 36
Bolt-m8 x 45 .... K 3
Bolt-m8 x 45 .... K 14
Bolt-m8 x 45 .... K 24
Bolt-m8 x 45 .... K 25
Bolt-m8 x 90 .... L 54
Bolt-m8 x 95 .... B 9
Bolt-m8 x 95 .... B 58
Bolt-m8-domed N174
Bolt-manifold to head-flanged head-m8 x 50 .... B 25
Bolt-manifold to head-flanged head-m8 x 50 .... B 73
Bolt-manifold to head-hexagonal head-m8 x .... B 26
Bolt-manifold to head-hexagonal head-m8 x .... B 74
Bolt-pintle to crossmember .... T 35
Bolt-pintle to crossmember-hexagonal .... T 34
Bolt-powerlok-special B316
Bolt-pulley to hub-hexagonal head-m6 x 25 .... B 62
Bolt-pulley to pump-flanged head-m8 x 55 .... B 61
Bolt-pump to block-m6 x 25 .... B271
Bolt-retaining-hexagonal head-m10 x 35 .... B 71
Bolt-rh outlet-m6-70mm B125
Bolt-rocker shaft B208
Bolt-shaft to head B282
Bolt-shear head B253
Bolt-shear-mounting steering column .... M 86
Bolt-shield disc to disc solid-m10 .... H 30
Bolt-shield disc to disc solid-m10 .... H 32
Bolt-shouldered .... R 2
Bolt-shouldered .... R 29
Bolt-shouldered .... R 31
Bolt-shouldered .... R 24
Bolt-shouldered .... R 27
Bolt-shouldered-pin clevis to checker N181
Bolt-side cover-flanged head-m8 x 40 .... B123
Bolt-silencer to silencer-flanged head-m8 x .... K 9
Bolt-special egr pipe to exhaust manifold .... J 76
Bolt-special-cowl mounting-m8 x 60 .... B 10
Bolt-starter to flywheel-m10 x 45 .... B229
Bolt-strap to bracket-flanged head-m8 x 50 .... N185
Bolt-sump to block-m8 x 80 .... B270
Bolt-t piece to pipe brake-hexagonal head- .... H 22
Bolt-tensioner to block B277
Bolt-tensioner to block B278
Bolt-terminal cable-battery .... M 30
Bolt-terminal cable-battery .... M 31
Bolt-tie bar to chassis-hexagonal head-m10 .... T 30
Bolt-to bracket mounting-hexagonal head- .... N 15
Bolt-to bracket mounting-hexagonal head- .... N 16
Bolt-to bumperette-flanged head-m10 x 70 .... N 23
Bolt-to crossmember-hexagonal head-m10 x .... N 8
Bolt-to dash assembly-m12 x 180 .... N 28
Bolt-to disc solid-m10 .... H 25
Bolt-to floor plate .... N 44
Bolt-to hinge assembly-counter sunk N157
Bolt-to panel outer .... N 57
Bolt-torx-flange .... N 30
Bolt-torx-pan-m10 x 30 .... N138
Bolt-torx-pan-m10 x 30 .... N250
Bolt-torx-pan-m10 x 30 .... N251
Bolt-torx-pan-m10 x 30 .... N252
Bolt-torx-pan-m10 x 30 .... V 4
Bolt-towing hook to crossmember-m12 x .... T 33
Bolt-towing jaw to rear crossmember .... T 32
Bolt-turbo to bracket-flanged head-m8 x 40 .... B293
Bolt-u .... K 1
Bolt-u .... K 3
Bolt-u .... K 8
Bolt-u .... K 9
Bolt-u .... K 10
Bolt-u .... K 11
Bolt-u .... K 12
Bolt-u .... K 20
Bolt-u .... K 22
Bolt-u .... K 23
Bolt-u .... K 25
Bolt-u .... K 15
Bolt-u .... K 21
Bolt-u .... L 24
Bolt-u .... L 32
Bolt-u .... S 12
Bolt-u-downpipe support .... K 2
Bolt-upper-counter sunk N169
Bolt-use if sx110251 is too short-hexagonal .... E 48
Bolt-washer-m6 x 12-m6 x 12 .... L 16
Bolt-washer-m8 x 50 .... S 13
Bolt-zinc-m10 x 120 .... N 19
Bonnet assembly N139
Bonnet assembly N140
Bonnet assembly-less spare wheel carrier N140
Bonnet assembly-spare wheel carrier N140
Boot-cable .... M 7
Boot-clutch release lever .... C 44
Box assembly-brush alternator B358
Box assembly-brush alternator B359
Box assembly-brush starter motor B369
Box assembly-brush starter motor B397
Box assembly-brush starter motor-bosch B144
Box assembly-brush starter motor-bosch B145
Box assembly-brush starter motor-bosch B190
Box assembly-brush starter motor-bosch B228
Box assembly-brush starter motor-bosch B262
Box assembly-brush starter motor-valeo B189
Box assembly-brush starter motor-valeo B229
Box assembly-pulsair-lh B339
Box assembly-steering .... F 7
Box assembly-steering-adwest-lightweight- .... F 11
Box assembly-steering-adwest-new- .... F 10
Box assembly-steering-adwest-new-rhd .... F 8
Box assembly-steering-gemmer-new-rhd .... F 9
Box-gun .... T 28
Box-immobiliser housing .... N 38
Box-key pad radio M124
Box-skis .... T 18
Box-tool stowage .... N 35
Box-tool stowage .... N 36

Bracket .... B 20
Bracket .... B 53
Bracket B105
Bracket B110
Bracket B120
Bracket B122
Bracket B143
Bracket B154
Bracket B159
Bracket B170
Bracket B205
Bracket B210
Bracket B296
Bracket B321
Bracket B342
Bracket B343
Bracket B363
Bracket B364
Bracket .... B 59
Bracket .... C 42
Bracket .... D 38
Bracket .... E 20
Bracket .... E 22
Bracket .... G 10
Bracket .... J 10
Bracket .... J 40
Bracket .... J 51
Bracket .... J 69
Bracket .... J 73
Bracket .... K 14
Bracket .... K 16
Bracket .... L 7
Bracket .... L 61
Bracket .... L 64
Bracket .... L 46
Bracket .... M 66
Bracket .... M 82
Bracket .... M 83
Bracket M143
Bracket .... M 75
Bracket .... N 49
Bracket .... N 52
Bracket .... N 53
Bracket N180
Bracket N201
Bracket .... N 46
Bracket N146
Bracket .... N 48
Bracket .... P 34
Bracket .... P 56
Bracket .... P 63
Bracket .... P 65
Bracket .... P 67
Bracket .... P 60
Bracket .... P 61
Bracket .... R 60
Bracket .... S 5
Bracket .... S 10
Bracket .... V 5
Bracket .... V 6
Bracket & modulator assembly antilock .... H 7
Bracket air conditioning .... L 56
Bracket anchor .... R 71
Bracket anti roll bar-rh-rear .... N 7
Bracket assembly power assisted steering .... F 20
Bracket assembly-air cleaner .... J 38
Bracket assembly-air cleaner .... J 40
Bracket assembly-air cleaner-lh .... J 34
Bracket assembly-blower mounting .... L 57
Bracket assembly-body mounting-rear-rh N100
Bracket assembly-canister support .... J 65
Bracket assembly-canister support .... J 72
Bracket assembly-charcoal canister .... J 66
Bracket assembly-check arm pivot N180
Bracket assembly-check arm pivot N181
Bracket assembly-check arm pivot-rh-rh N153
Bracket assembly-coolant & power assisted B294
Bracket assembly-exhaust mounting .... K 24
Bracket assembly-footrest .... P 32
Bracket assembly-footrest-rh .... N 7
Bracket assembly-front radius arm mounting- .... N 10
Bracket assembly-front seat belt lower .... R 48
Bracket assembly-front seat belt lower .... R 50
Bracket assembly-fuel filter .... J 56
Bracket assembly-fuel tank fuel tank .... J 10
Bracket assembly-harness .... R 59
Bracket assembly-harness .... R 60
Bracket assembly-harness .... R 65
Bracket assembly-harness .... R 67
Bracket assembly-harness engine M106
Bracket assembly-horn mounting M103
Bracket assembly-horn mounting-horn- M102
Bracket assembly-intermediate exhaust .... K 24
Bracket assembly-intermediate exhaust .... K 31
Bracket assembly-intermediate exhaust .... K 32
Bracket assembly-intermediate exhaust .... K 6
Bracket assembly-mounting air cleaner .... J 35
Bracket assembly-mounting air cleaner .... J 42
Bracket assembly-mounting multi point B216
Bracket assembly-pedal box mountng .... H 10
Bracket assembly-radiator mounting-lh .... L 2
Bracket assembly-radiator upper mounting-lh .... L 2
Bracket assembly-radio housing-(use 95my M121
Bracket assembly-rear damper-upper .... E 63
Bracket assembly-rear damper-upper .... E 66
Bracket assembly-rear door checker-rh N170
Bracket assembly-safety harness mounting- .... R 58
Bracket assembly-sensor mounting .... K 5
Bracket assembly-spare wheel retention .... S 16
Bracket assembly-support air conditioning .... L 45
Bracket assembly-support power assisted .... F 23
Bracket assembly-throttle wire mounting B388
Bracket assembly-throttle wire mounting B391
Bracket assembly-trailing link mounting-rh .... N 10
Bracket assembly-transmission mounting- .... N 16
Bracket condenser-lh-top .... L 48
Bracket exhaust system-front .... K 26
Bracket exhaust system-front .... K 27
Bracket exhaust system-front .... K 28
Bracket exhaust system-front .... K 29
Bracket exhaust system-front .... K 30
Bracket exhaust system-rear .... K 5
Bracket exhaust system-rear .... K 17
Bracket exhaust system-rear .... K 18
Bracket fixing .... F 5
Bracket fixing .... P 17
Bracket fusebox .... J 68
Bracket fusebox .... M 91
Bracket fusebox .... M 94
Bracket fusebox .... M 48
Bracket harness .... B 47
Bracket harness B146
Bracket harness B148
Bracket harness B153
Bracket harness B159
Bracket harness B244
Bracket harness B253
Bracket harness B257
Bracket harness B263
Bracket harness .... B 59
Bracket harness .... M 65
Bracket harness .... M 66
Bracket harness M146
Bracket harness .... M 58
Bracket harness-clip to housing .... B 98
Bracket harness-harness clip B191
Bracket harness-harness clip B230
Bracket mounting .... H 31
Bracket mounting .... N 67
Bracket mounting .... N 97
Bracket mounting body-outer .... N 11
Bracket mounting-body N101
Bracket mounting-lh-c post N138
Bracket pedal .... G 7
Bracket power assisted steering reservoir .... F 19
Bracket rear axle .... E 32
Bracket receiver dryer .... L 45
Bracket receiver dryer .... L 54
Bracket speedometer cable M118
Bracket support .... F 25
Bracket support .... F 27
Bracket support .... F 23
Bracket support .... J 70
Bracket support .... N 11
Bracket support N114
Bracket support N153
Bracket support-rh N191
Bracket support-rh N192
Bracket support-rh .... N 8
Bracket support-upper .... N 87
Bracket support-upper .... N 88
Bracket windscreen-rh N185
Bracket-5th gear selector fork support- .... C 23
Bracket-abutment clutch hose to pipe assy .... G 5
Bracket-abutment-throttle cable multi point B336
Bracket-abutment-throttle cable multi point .... G 13
Bracket-air cleaner .... J 36
Bracket-air cleaner .... J 37
Bracket-air cleaner .... J 40
Bracket-air cleaner .... J 67
Bracket-air compressor .... B 40
Bracket-air compressor .... B 87
Bracket-air compressor B137
Bracket-air compressor B184
Bracket-air compressor B224
Bracket-air compressor B259
Bracket-air compressor B348
Bracket-ancillary mounting B394
Bracket-ancillary mounting .... N 12
Bracket-antilock brake harness .... H 7
Bracket-bell housing clutch hose .... G 5
Bracket-blower mounting .... L 57
Bracket-body B341
Bracket-body/chassis mounting .... N 8
Bracket-bonnet stay .... L 3
Bracket-bonnet stay .... L 2
Bracket-bonnet stay N140
Bracket-bonnet stay-pivot bush end N147
Bracket-brake pipe .... E 32
Bracket-brake pipe tee connector .... H 16
Bracket-brake pipe tee connector .... H 17
Bracket-brake pipe tee connector .... H 18
Bracket-brake pipe tee connector .... H 19
Bracket-brake pipe tee connector .... H 15
Bracket-brake pipe tee connector .... H 24
Bracket-brake pipe tee connector-t piece to .... H 21
Bracket-brake pipe-rh .... E 21
Bracket-brake pipe-rh .... H 25
Bracket-cable N124
Bracket-cable N126
Bracket-cable abutment handbrake .... G 12
Bracket-cable choke .... G 6
Bracket-canister support .... J 65
Bracket-canister support .... J 68
Bracket-canister support .... J 72
Bracket-chain N125
Bracket-chassis frame body mounting .... N 11
Bracket-chassis frame body mounting-front N100
Bracket-chassis frame body mounting-front N101
Bracket-clamp roll bar mounting .... E 60

Bracket-clipping-steel B244
Bracket-clipping-steel D 8
Bracket-clipping-steel K 5
Bracket-clipping-steel M146
Bracket-clipping-steel M118
Bracket-clutch housing lifting C 53
Bracket-coil ignition-where module is with B354
Bracket-column support steering F 3
Bracket-column support steering F 2
Bracket-compressor air conditioning B137
Bracket-compressor air conditioning B184
Bracket-compressor air conditioning B224
Bracket-compressor/idler assembly air B 40
Bracket-compressor/idler assembly air B 87
Bracket-connector engine B320
Bracket-connector engine B378
Bracket-console trim P 17
Bracket-coolant bottom hose L 12
Bracket-coolant bottom hose L 18
Bracket-coolant hose support B241
Bracket-coolant hose support L 20
Bracket-coolant pump support B241
Bracket-cowl mounting B 10
Bracket-diesel G 10
Bracket-door lock security R 44
Bracket-drive end c/w bearing alternator e-lh B355
Bracket-drive end c/w bearing alternator e-lh B360
Bracket-drive end c/w bearing alternator e- B141
Bracket-drive end c/w bearing alternator e- B356
Bracket-drive end c/w bearing alternator e-rh B 92
Bracket-drive end c/w bearing alternator e-rh B 94
Bracket-drive end c/w bearing alternator e-rh B139
Bracket-drive end c/w bearing alternator e-rh B186
Bracket-drive end c/w bearing alternator e-rh B187
Bracket-drive end c/w bearing alternator e-rh B226
Bracket-drive end c/w bearing alternator e-rh B362
Bracket-electronic control unit mounting M100
Bracket-engine mounting B128
Bracket-engine mounting B175
Bracket-engine mounting-lh C 38
Bracket-engine mounting-lh N 13
Bracket-engine mounting-rear-rh N 16
Bracket-engine mounting-rh B 8
Bracket-engine mounting-rh B 57
Bracket-engine mounting-rh B109
Bracket-engine mounting-rh B158
Bracket-engine mounting-rh B201
Bracket-engine mounting-rh B377
Bracket-engine mounting-rh N 12
Bracket-engine mounting-rh N 14
Bracket-engine mounting-rh N 9
Bracket-exhaust gas recirculation pipe J 76
Bracket-exhaust gas recirculation valve J 77
Bracket-exhaust mounting K 1
Bracket-exhaust mounting K 2
Bracket-exhaust mounting K 11
Bracket-exhaust mounting K 12
Bracket-exhaust mounting K 14
Bracket-exhaust mounting K 26
Bracket-exhaust mounting K 28
Bracket-exhaust mounting K 31
Bracket-exhaust mounting K 32
Bracket-exhaust mounting/lashing hanger K 8
Bracket-exhaust mounting/lashing hanger K 9
Bracket-exhaust mounting/lashing hanger K 22
Bracket-exhaust mounting/lashing hanger K 21
Bracket-expansion tank support L 9
Bracket-expansion tank-for 200tdi L 8
Bracket-facia M 49
Bracket-facia console mounting-rh P 4
Bracket-fan mounting-lower-rhd L 55
Bracket-fan mounting-upper L 45
Bracket-female catch S 11
Bracket-fender support-rh N 61
Bracket-for reel R 64
Bracket-front J 67
Bracket-front fender-lh V 4
Bracket-front fender-rh N 58
Bracket-front mounting B348
Bracket-front mudflap retention-rh T 51
Bracket-front mudflap retention-rh T 53
Bracket-front seat slide frame R 14
Bracket-front seat support R 3
Bracket-front seat support R 28
Bracket-front seat support-rh R 43
Bracket-front spring mounting-driver-side E 59
Bracket-front subframe-front R 69
Bracket-fuel filter J 57
Bracket-fuel filter support J 51
Bracket-fuel filter support J 58
Bracket-fuel pipe J 6
Bracket-fuel pipe-breather J 5
Bracket-fuel tank rear mounting J 1
Bracket-fuel tank rear mounting J 7
Bracket-fuel tank rear mounting J 8
Bracket-gear change cable assembly C 84
Bracket-gearbox to engine C 51
Bracket-handbrake H 36
Bracket-harness C 40
Bracket-harness clip B 4
Bracket-harness clip B197
Bracket-harness clip to side cover M 65
Bracket-harness engine M 69
Bracket-heater feed pipe L 42
Bracket-heater feed pipe L 43
Bracket-heater feed pipe L 60
Bracket-heater pipe assembly L 63
Bracket-heatshield B 26
Bracket-heatshield B 74
Bracket-heatshield exhaust system B386
Bracket-horn mounting M101
Bracket-hose air conditioning L 62
Bracket-hose brake H 22
Bracket-hose brake H 24
Bracket-idler mounting ancillary drive B277
Bracket-idler mounting ancillary drive B278
Bracket-idler mounting ancillary drive B295
Bracket-inertia reel seat belts P 57
Bracket-injection pump diesel B253
Bracket-inlet manifold support B323
Bracket-jack stowage mounting S 1
Bracket-jack stowage mounting S 2
Bracket-jack stowage mounting S 5
Bracket-jack stowage-lh S 1
Bracket-lashing N 93
Bracket-lashing N124
Bracket-lh N252
Bracket-lh R 67
Bracket-lh-front N251
Bracket-lifting body-front B 19
Bracket-lifting body-front B 67
Bracket-lifting body-front B119
Bracket-lifting body-front B167
Bracket-lifting engine front B207
Bracket-lifting engine front B244
Bracket-lifting engine front B381
Bracket-lifting engine front B393
Bracket-lifting engine front B280
Bracket-lifting engine front-front-lh B317
Bracket-lifting engine rear B207
Bracket-lifting engine rear B244
Bracket-lifting engine rear B320
Bracket-lifting engine rear B381
Bracket-lifting engine rear B280
Bracket-load/tail door spare wheel mounting S 15
Bracket-lock stop E 19
Bracket-lower L 45
Bracket-mounting B202
Bracket-mounting B111
Bracket-mounting B160
Bracket-mounting M 88
Bracket-mounting P 13
Bracket-mounting air cleaner J 44
Bracket-mounting cage-lh N251
Bracket-mounting cage-rh V 4
Bracket-mounting engine-electric control M 99
Bracket-mounting oil cooler L 24
Bracket-mounting oil cooler L 32
Bracket-mounting oil pipe B178
Bracket-mounting oil pipe B218
Bracket-mounting oil pipe L 22
Bracket-mounting pedal G 1
Bracket-mounting power assisted steering B133
Bracket-mounting power assisted steering B221
Bracket-mounting power assisted steering B258
Bracket-mounting power assisted steering B294
Bracket-mounting power assisted steering B393
Bracket-mounting power assisted steering B342
Bracket-mounting power assisted steering B343
Bracket-mounting power assisted steering B 37
Bracket-mounting power assisted steering B 84
Bracket-mounting power assisted steering B181
Bracket-mounting-alternator B 45
Bracket-mounting-alternator B 95
Bracket-mounting-alternator B142
Bracket-mounting-alternator B188
Bracket-mounting-alternator B227
Bracket-mounting-alternator B363
Bracket-mounting-alternator B384
Bracket-mounting-alternator-65 amp B357
Bracket-mounting-alternator-65 amp B366
Bracket-mounting-alternator-lh B365
Bracket-mounting-exhaust-rear K 5
Bracket-mounting-exhaust-rear K 26
Bracket-mounting-exhaust-rear K 27
Bracket-mounting-exhaust-rear K 28
Bracket-mounting-exhaust-rear K 29
Bracket-mounting-exhaust-rear K 30
Bracket-mounting-exhaust-rear K 31
Bracket-mounting-exhaust-rear K 33
Bracket-mounting-interior-rear-lh M138
Bracket-mounting-lamp-interior M 19
Bracket-mounting-lh V 4
Bracket-mounting-outer-rh R 27
Bracket-mounting-rear N 72
Bracket-mounting-rear-rh T 53
Bracket-mounting-rh N 18
Bracket-mounting-rh N251
Bracket-mounting-steel M146
Bracket-mounting-with central door locking N197
Bracket-oil cooler C 70
Bracket-oil dipstick tube B303
Bracket-pedestal B 68
Bracket-pipe clip-rear J 30
Bracket-pipe mounting B323
Bracket-pipe to pipe transmission cooling L 23
Bracket-pivot D 37
Bracket-pivot D 39
Bracket-pivot 5th fork C 36
Bracket-pivot check arm N181
Bracket-pivot check arm N169
Bracket-pivot check arm N158
Bracket-power assisted steering B 36
Bracket-power assisted steering B 37
Bracket-power assisted steering B 83
Bracket-power assisted steering B132
Bracket-power assisted steering B133
Bracket-power assisted steering B181
Bracket-power assisted steering B221
Bracket-power assisted steering-mounting B 84

Bracket-pulley support belt tensioner B349
Bracket-pulsair box-lh B339
Bracket-pump/actuator B 15
Bracket-pump/actuator B115
Bracket-pump/actuator B164
Bracket-pump/actuator B 64
Bracket-pump/actuator-support B 63
Bracket-purge valve mounting J 66
Bracket-radiator closing panel-rh N 55
Bracket-radiator grille support N147
Bracket-radiator mounting-rh L 4
Bracket-radiator pipe to cowl B 24
Bracket-radiator pipe to cowl B172
Bracket-radiator pipe to cowl-cowl mounting B 72
Bracket-radiator pipe to cowl-rh outlet B125
Bracket-radiator upper mounting-lh L 3
Bracket-radiator upper mounting-rh L 2
Bracket-radio housing M124
Bracket-radio housing-philips M121
Bracket-radio housing-philips M122
Bracket-rear J 24
Bracket-rear J 25
Bracket-rear J 28
Bracket-rear J 27
Bracket-rear axle fulcrum E 62
Bracket-rear axle fulcrum E 69
Bracket-rear body mounting-front-rh N100
Bracket-rear door checker N181
Bracket-rear door glass guide N184
Bracket-rear mudflap retention-rear-rh T 53
Bracket-rear mudflap retention-rh T 52
Bracket-rear seat belt anchorage-upper-rh R 66
Bracket-rear seat belt anchorage-upper-rh R 68
Bracket-rear seat mounting R 28
Bracket-rear seat mounting-inner R 29
Bracket-rear seat retention R 40
Bracket-rear sub frame angle-outer N100
Bracket-rear subframe-centre R 69
Bracket-rear vehicle recovery N 24
Bracket-relay mounting M 83
Bracket-relay mounting M 84
Bracket-relay mounting M 93
Bracket-relay mounting M 95
Bracket-relay mounting-overspeed monitor M109
Bracket-return spring-attachment accelerator B335
Bracket-rh E 62
Bracket-rh M130
Bracket-rh N 43
Bracket-rh N 49
Bracket-rh N121
Bracket-rh N222
Bracket-rh R 63
Bracket-rh R 40
Bracket-rh-corner-rear end door N118
Bracket-rh-corner-rear end door N123
Bracket-rh-corner-tailboard N115
Bracket-rh-corner-tailboard N117
Bracket-rh-front N138
Bracket-rh-front N250
Bracket-rhd J 37
Bracket-rhd J 38
Bracket-rocker shaft B168
Bracket-roll cage hoop intermediate mounting N252
Bracket-roll cage hoop intermediate V 3
Bracket-roof grab handle rear N196
Bracket-shield rear brake H 31
Bracket-shield rear brake H 33
Bracket-side T 48
Bracket-sill extension fixing-lh N 48
Bracket-spacer block-rh R 71
Bracket-spare wheel retention mounting S 15
Bracket-spare wheel retention mounting S 17
Bracket-spare wheel retention mounting V 5
Bracket-starter heatshield B229
Bracket-steering column cover inner support F 5
Bracket-stiffener mounting-rh N 43
Bracket-support air cleaner/pipe J 35
Bracket-support air conditioning L 46
Bracket-support alternator B365
Bracket-support downpipe K 2
Bracket-support downpipe K 13
Bracket-support engine cable control M 63
Bracket-support king lead B318
Bracket-support starter motor B103
Bracket-support-lh V 4
Bracket-top mounting condenser L 47
Bracket-towing T 30
Bracket-towing T 31
Bracket-towing-front & rear-less spoiler N 24
Bracket-track rod protection E 8
Bracket-track rod protection E 11
Bracket-transmission mounting-lh N 15
Bracket-transmission mounting-rear-lh C 38
Bracket-transmission mounting-rear-lh N 16
Bracket-transmission mounting-rh N 17
Bracket-tube support fresh air intake J 63
Bracket-tube support fresh air intake-lhd J 37
Bracket-tube support fresh air intake-lhd J 38
Bracket-upper-rh P 55
Bracket-valve brake H 19
Bracket-warning flare N 64
Bracket-washer bottle-rh M131
Bracket-washer bottle-rh M135
Bracket-wiper motor M128
Bracket-wiper mounting M143
Brake fluid U 2
Breather assembly-crankcase B105
Breather assembly-crankcase B153
Breather assembly-crankcase B154
Breather assembly-crankcase B197
Breather assembly-crankcase B211
Breather assembly-crankcase-side cover B123
Breather assembly-manual transmission C 37
Breather fuel filler J 17
Breather manual transmission C 37
Breather-assembly J 17
Brush alternator B 91
Brush alternator B 93
Brush alternator B138
Brush alternator B140
Brush alternator B358
Brush alternator B359
Brush alternator B361
Brush alternator-machine sensed B 43
Brush-timing belt cover torsional vibration B 11
Brush-timing belt cover torsional vibration B 12
Brush-timing belt cover torsional vibration B 60
Brush-wiper motor M128
Buckle N223
Buckle N224
Buckle N227
Buckle N228
Buckle N230
Buckle N231
Buckle N233
Buckle N234
Buffer rubber N114
Buffer rubber R 43
Buffer rubber-seat front R 37
Buffer rubber-seat front S 10
Buffer rubber-seat front V 5
Buffer rubber-seat front-centre squab R 3
Buffer rubber-seat rear R 35
Buffer-bonnet N139
Buffer-bonnet N 28
Buffer-bonnet N141
Buffer-front door N181
Buffer-front door N158
Buffer-spare wheel S 8
Buffer-spare wheel S 9
Buffer-spare wheel S 10
Buffer-stop N114
Buffer-stop N124
Buffer-stop-clear glass N107
Buffer-stop-rh clear N109
Buffer-stop-rubber-short N180
Buffer-stop-rubber-short-1"-3/8 N169
Buffer-stop-rubber-short-1"-3/8 N179
Buffer-stop-tinted glass N108
Buffer-stop-tinted glass N110
Buffer-tailgate N127
Bulb M 7
Bulb M 24
Bulb & holder assembly M114
Bulb & holder assembly M119
Bulb illumination assembly L 72
Bulb-12v-2w M 70
Bulb-12v-2w M 71
Bulb-12v-2w M119
Bulb-233-t8/4-4 watt-12v M 10
Bulb-233-t8/4-4 watt-12v M 11
Bulb-245-r19/10-10 watt M 18
Bulb-245-r19/10-10 watt M 26
Bulb-272-10 watt-festoon-36x10.5mm M 19
Bulb-281-ba7s-2 watt M 70
Bulb-281-ba7s-2 watt M 71
Bulb-281-ba7s-2 watt-clock illumination M120
Bulb-281-ba7s-2 watt-clock illumination M115
Bulb-380-p25/2-21/5 watt-12v M 10
Bulb-380-p25/2-21/5 watt-12v M 11
Bulb-382-p25/1-21 watt-12v M 6
Bulb-382-p25/1-21 watt-12v M 11
Bulb-382-p25/1-21 watt-12v M 13
Bulb-382-p25/1-21 watt-12v M 14
Bulb-382-p25/1-21 watt-12v M 15
Bulb-382-p25/1-21 watt-12v M 16
Bulb-382-p25/1-21 watt-12v M 17
Bulb-382-p25/1-21 watt-12v M 18
Bulb-382-p25/1-21 watt-12v M 24
Bulb-382-p25/1-21 watt-indicator-12v M 10
Bulb-501-w10/5-5 watt-12v M 7
Bulb-501-w10/5-5 watt-side repeater-12v M 8
Bulb-504-w10/3-3 watt L 71
Bulb-504-w10/3-3 watt-air con controls M 70
Bulb-headlamp-h3-55 watt-type h3 T 9
Bulb-headlamp-h3-55 watt-type h3 T 10
Bulb-headlamp-h4-60/65 watt-main & M 1
Bulb-headlamp-h4-60/65 watt-main & M 5
Bulb-headlamp-h4-60/65 watt-main & M 4
Bulb-headlamp-quartz halogen-cewe-type M 9
Bulb-headlamp-quartz halogen-cewe-type T 10
Bulb-illumination M 90
Bulb-instruments-12v-2w M114
Bulb-lucas lamps M 6
Bulb-wedge illumination P 13
Bulb-wedge illumination-12v-1.2 watt M 89
Bulb-wedge illumination-12v-1.2 watt M111
Bulb-wedge illumination-12v-1.2 watt M119
Bulb-wedge illumination-12v-1.2 watt M115
Bulb-wedge illumination-12v-1.2 watt M116
Bulbholder-5/21w M 11
Bulkhead assembly-body front N 87
Bulkhead assembly-body front N 88
Bulkhead front assembly N 90
Bumper cleaner-black-500ml W 5
Bumper mounting-front T 7
Bumper-front-galvanised N 19
Bumperette-front-galvanised N 19
Bumperette-rear-rh N 23
Bung-rubber radio fixing M122

Circlip .... B 6
Circlip .... B 34
Circlip .... B 36
Circlip .... B 38
Circlip .... B 39
Circlip .... B 40
Circlip .... B 55
Circlip .... B 81
Circlip .... B 83
Circlip .... B 85
Circlip .... B 86
Circlip .... B 87
Circlip B132
Circlip B134
Circlip B135
Circlip B182
Circlip B183
Circlip B222
Circlip B223
Circlip B273
Circlip B335
Circlip B346
Circlip B347
Circlip .... B 16
Circlip .... C 32
Circlip .... C 35
Circlip .... C 68
Circlip .... C 74
Circlip .... C 17
Circlip .... C 20
Circlip .... C 23
Circlip .... D 18
Circlip .... D 29
Circlip .... D 30
Circlip .... D 33
Circlip .... D 35
Circlip .... D 16
Circlip .... D 32
Circlip .... E 1
Circlip .... E 2
Circlip .... E 12
Circlip .... E 40
Circlip .... E 42
Circlip .... E 3
Circlip .... F 13
Circlip .... F 14
Circlip .... F 15
Circlip .... F 16
Circlip .... G 11
Circlip .... G 12
Circlip .... L 26
Circlip .... R 5
Circlip .... R 12
Circlip-1st & 2nd hub .... C 13
Circlip-axle shaft to hub driving member .... E 24
Circlip-axle shaft to hub driving member .... E 26
Circlip-axle shaft to hub driving member .... E 47
Circlip-axle shaft to hub driving member .... E 49
Circlip-countershaft B336
Circlip-front axle shaft to cv joint .... E 16
Circlip-front axle shaft to cv joint .... E 17
Circlip-gear/layshaft .... C 16
Circlip-large .... D 19
Circlip-man trans 5th gear synchroniser hub .... C 33
Circlip-man trans 5th gear synchroniser hub .... C 15
Circlip-man trans mainshaft/centre plate .... C 64
Circlip-piston B107
Circlip-piston B156
Circlip-piston B199
Circlip-piston B236
Circlip-piston B269
Circlip-pivot pin .... C 36
Circlip-selector shaft .... C 22
Clamp B173
Clamp B337
Clamp .... C 83
Clamp .... C 86
Clamp .... J 45
Clamp .... J 65
Clamp .... J 68
Clamp .... J 72
Clamp .... K 12
Clamp .... K 25
Clamp .... L 16
Clamp .... L 22
Clamp .... L 23
Clamp .... L 26
Clamp .... L 27
Clamp .... L 28
Clamp .... L 29
Clamp .... L 30
Clamp .... L 31
Clamp .... L 42
Clamp .... L 43
Clamp .... L 49
Clamp .... L 50
Clamp .... L 57
Clamp .... L 60
Clamp .... L 61
Clamp .... L 63
Clamp .... L 64
Clamp .... L 65
Clamp N148
Clamp N185
Clamp N239
Clamp N240
Clamp N241
Clamp N242
Clamp N243
Clamp N245
Clamp N246
Clamp .... S 14
Clamp .... S 15
Clamp .... S 16
Clamp fuel injector B217
Clamp fuel injector B254
Clamp fuel injector B279
Clamp fuel injector B287
Clamp-'y' piece exhaust .... K 3
Clamp-2 pipes B217
Clamp-bar B303
Clamp-bar N137
Clamp-bar .... R 33
Clamp-blower motor .... L 66
Clamp-cable .... C 84
Clamp-distributor .... B 90
Clamp-distributor B350
Clamp-distributor B351
Clamp-distributor B352
Clamp-exhaust downpipe to manifold .... K 14
Clamp-exhaust downpipe to manifold .... K 16
Clamp-exhaust downpipe to manifold .... K 13
Clamp-exhaust intermediate pipe assembly .... K 1
Clamp-exhaust intermediate pipe assembly .... K 2
Clamp-exhaust intermediate pipe assembly .... K 11
Clamp-exhaust intermediate pipe assembly .... K 4
Clamp-fixing battery .... M 27
Clamp-fixing battery .... M 28
Clamp-heater hose B339
Clamp-hose B178
Clamp-hose fuel lines .... J 23
Clamp-hose fuel lines .... J 66
Clamp-inlet manifold gasket seal B325
Clamp-inlet manifold gasket seal B385
Clamp-lock steering column .... M 86
Clamp-lower .... F 4
Clamp-manifold to head B126
Clamp-manifold to head .... B 26
Clamp-manifold to head .... B 74
Clamp-rear exhaust .... K 10
Clamp-rear exhaust .... K 23
Clamp-rocker shaft B208
Clamp-rocker shaft B245
Clamp-tail pipe .... K 21
Clamp-tail pipe to rear exhaust .... K 8
Clamp-tail pipe to rear exhaust .... K 9
Clamp-tail pipe to rear exhaust .... K 20
Clamp-tail pipe to rear exhaust .... K 22
Clamp-top .... F 5
Clamp-tube .... F 17
Cleaner dashboard .... W 5
Cleaner fabric-300ml .... W 5
Cleaner leather-300ml .... W 5
Cleaner-alloy wheel-500ml .... W 5
Cleaner-glazing-500ml .... W 5
Cleaner-liquid-200ml .... U 1
Cleaner-liquid-hand-orange-400ml .... U 3
Cleat .... N 97
Cleat N122
Cleat N123
Cleat N239
Cleat N240
Cleat N242
Cleat N245
Cleat N246
Cleat .... N 96
Cleat .... N 58
Clip .... B 19
Clip .... B 67
Clip .... B 78
Clip .... B 80
Clip B129
Clip B173
Clip B176
Clip B178
Clip B255
Clip B303
Clip B320
Clip B323
Clip B330
Clip B333
Clip B335
Clip B377
Clip B387
Clip .... C 28
Clip .... C 41
Clip .... C 42
Clip .... C 43
Clip .... C 45
Clip .... D 36
Clip .... D 21
Clip .... D 24
Clip .... D 22
Clip .... F 15
Clip .... G 6
Clip .... H 10
Clip .... H 11
Clip .... H 36
Clip .... H 20
Clip .... H 22
Clip .... H 24
Clip .... J 5
Clip .... J 7
Clip .... J 24
Clip .... J 31
Clip .... J 32
Clip .... J 34
Clip .... J 35
Clip .... J 45
Clip .... J 46

Clip .... J 48
Clip .... J 61
Clip .... J 67
Clip .... J 73
Clip .... L 5
Clip .... L 7
Clip .... L 11
Clip .... L 14
Clip .... L 15
Clip .... L 38
Clip .... L 54
Clip .... L 34
Clip .... L 37
Clip M138
Clip M139
Clip M140
Clip M141
Clip M142
Clip .... M 57
Clip .... M 58
Clip N135
Clip N187
Clip N184
Clip N155
Clip .... P 4
Clip .... P 18
Clip .... P 23
Clip .... P 24
Clip .... R 2
Clip .... R 46
Clip .... R 47
Clip .... R 51
Clip .... R 54
Clip .... S 1
Clip .... S 2
Clip .... V 9
Clip brake pipe .... H 10
Clip brake pipe .... H 12
Clip brake pipe .... H 13
Clip brake pipe .... H 16
Clip brake pipe .... H 17
Clip brake pipe .... H 18
Clip brake pipe .... H 15
Clip brake pipe .... H 20
Clip brake pipe .... H 22
Clip brake pipe N193
Clip brake pipe N189
Clip glass holder N159
Clip glass holder N160
Clip-2 holes .... H 17
Clip-5mm-6.5mm hole M150
Clip-8mm .... J 22
Clip-8mm .... J 49
Clip-8mm .... J 50
Clip-8mm .... J 65
Clip-8mm .... J 72
Clip-8mm .... J 71
Clip-black-mesh type .... T 25
Clip-bonnet prop-single N144
Clip-brake pipe double .... H 10
Clip-brake pipe double .... H 12
Clip-brake pipe double .... H 13
Clip-brake pipe double .... H 16
Clip-brake pipe double .... H 17
Clip-brake pipe double .... H 15
Clip-brake pipe double .... H 20
Clip-brake pipe double .... H 22
Clip-brake pipe double .... H 24
Clip-brake pipe treble .... H 12
Clip-brake pipe treble .... H 16
Clip-brake pipe treble .... H 17
Clip-brake pipe treble .... H 18
Clip-brake pipe treble .... H 15
Clip-brake pipe treble-4.75mm .... H 20
Clip-bulb-quartz halogen .... M 3
Clip-cable B178
Clip-cable B210
Clip-cable B218
Clip-cable B254
Clip-cable B320
Clip-cable .... C 52
Clip-cable .... C 84
Clip-cable .... E 22
Clip-cable .... G 6
Clip-cable .... G 12
Clip-cable .... G 13
Clip-cable .... K 5
Clip-cable .... L 39
Clip-cable .... L 40
Clip-cable .... M 61
Clip-cable M128
Clip-cable N142
Clip-cable-8mm hole .... B 4
Clip-cable-8mm hole .... B 53
Clip-cable-8mm hole .... B 98
Clip-cable-8mm hole .... B 59
Clip-cable-8mm hole .... E 50
Clip-cable-8mm hole .... M 59
Clip-cable-8mm hole .... M 60
Clip-cable-8mm hole .... M 65
Clip-cable-8mm hole .... M 66
Clip-cable-8mm hole M127
Clip-cable-8mm hole M150
Clip-cable-8mm hole .... M 57
Clip-cable-8mm hole .... M 46
Clip-cable-gearbox to engine .... C 51
Clip-cable-lh B334
Clip-cable-lh .... L 17
Clip-cable-rear .... H 2
Clip-carburettor breather .... B 30
Clip-clutch release-pivot post .... C 2
Clip-clutch release-pivot post .... C 28
Clip-clutch release-pivot post .... C 43
Clip-clutch release-pivot post .... C 45
Clip-coolant hose .... L 17
Clip-cradle-panel fixing-13mm-8mm hole M149
Clip-cup retainer .... P 25
Clip-double .... L 17
Clip-double fuel lines .... J 24
Clip-double fuel lines .... J 31
Clip-double fuel lines .... J 32
Clip-double-6 - 8mm .... J 23
Clip-double-6 - 8mm .... J 40
Clip-e .... C 84
Clip-edge harness .... C 53
Clip-edge harness .... K 5
Clip-edge harness .... P 55
Clip-edge harness-12mm-clear. M150
Clip-fuel feed pipe-single-9mm .... J 27
Clip-fuel injector multi point injection B387
Clip-fuel pipe edge .... J 65
Clip-handle assembly link N159
Clip-handle assembly link N161
Clip-harness B395
Clip-harness M106
Clip-harness .... R 12
Clip-harness engine .... M 60
Clip-harness engine .... M 65
Clip-harness engine .... M 69
Clip-harness engine .... M 63
Clip-harness engine .... M 68
Clip-harness-14.5mm-6.5mm hole .... F 25
Clip-harness-14.5mm-6.5mm hole .... F 27
Clip-harness-14.5mm-6.5mm hole .... F 23
Clip-harness-14mm-6mm hole M151
Clip-hose .... B 33
Clip-hose .... B 61
Clip-hose .... B 62
Clip-hose .... B 79
Clip-hose .... B 80
Clip-hose B113
Clip-hose B114
Clip-hose B122
Clip-hose B162
Clip-hose B163
Clip-hose B170
Clip-hose B177
Clip-hose B204
Clip-hose B213
Clip-hose B218
Clip-hose B251
Clip-hose B255
Clip-hose B284
Clip-hose B324
Clip-hose B329
Clip-hose B334
Clip-hose B338
Clip-hose B389
Clip-hose .... B 14
Clip-hose B239
Clip-hose .... B 30
Clip-hose .... E 52
Clip-hose .... F 20
Clip-hose .... H 6
Clip-hose .... H 8
Clip-hose .... H 9
Clip-hose .... H 2
Clip-hose .... H 5
Clip-hose .... J 6
Clip-hose .... J 14
Clip-hose .... J 17
Clip-hose .... J 20
Clip-hose .... J 22
Clip-hose .... J 23
Clip-hose .... J 33
Clip-hose .... J 36
Clip-hose .... J 37
Clip-hose .... J 38
Clip-hose .... J 39
Clip-hose .... J 41
Clip-hose .... J 43
Clip-hose .... J 45
Clip-hose .... J 46
Clip-hose .... J 49
Clip-hose .... J 50
Clip-hose .... J 53
Clip-hose .... J 60
Clip-hose .... J 61
Clip-hose .... J 68
Clip-hose .... J 69
Clip-hose .... J 70
Clip-hose .... J 73
Clip-hose .... J 74
Clip-hose .... J 75
Clip-hose .... J 42
Clip-hose .... L 3
Clip-hose .... L 8
Clip-hose .... L 11
Clip-hose .... L 13
Clip-hose .... L 10
Clip-hose M127
Clip-hose M138
Clip-hose M139
Clip-hose M140
Clip-hose M141
Clip-hose M142
Clip-hose .... T 4
Clip-hose-14.5mm-steel-25/64" hole .... G 3
Clip-hose-14.5mm-steel-25/64" hole M146
Clip-hose-20mm .... B 22

Clip-hose-20mm ... B 70
Clip-hose-20mm ... F 25
Clip-hose-20mm ... F 27
Clip-hose-22mm ... L 20
Clip-hose-25mm ... B 24
Clip-hose-25mm ... B 72
Clip-hose-25mm ... B125
Clip-hose-25mm ... B172
Clip-hose-25mm ... B178
Clip-hose-25mm ... B211
Clip-hose-25mm ... B248
Clip-hose-25mm ... F 24
Clip-hose-25mm ... F 26
Clip-hose-25mm ... F 23
Clip-hose-25mm ... L 39
Clip-hose-25mm ... L 42
Clip-hose-25mm ... L 61
Clip-hose-25mm ... L 62
Clip-hose-26mm ... B385
Clip-hose-27mm-green ... L 40
Clip-hose-30mm ... B241
Clip-hose-30mm ... B339
Clip-hose-30mm ... J 18
Clip-hose-30mm ... L 43
Clip-hose-30mm ... L 44
Clip-hose-30mm ... L 60
Clip-hose-30mm ... L 63
Clip-hose-30mm ... L 64
Clip-hose-4mm/id ... B293
Clip-hose-50mm-less spring assist ... E 1
Clip-hose-50mm-less spring assist ... L 14
Clip-hose-50mm-less spring assist ... L 15
Clip-hose-50mm-less spring assist ... L 17
Clip-hose-50mm-less spring assist ... L 19
Clip-hose-60mm ... L 12
Clip-hose-antenna ... M124
Clip-hose-antenna ... M123
Clip-hose-double wire ... J 74
Clip-hose-heater end-25mm ... L 41
Clip-hose-main tank ... J 16
Clip-hose-side cover-25mm ... B123
Clip-hose-spring-band ... B387
Clip-hose-spring-band-60mm ... L 13
Clip-hose-top hose ... L 18
Clip-hose-worm drive ... J 5
Clip-hose-worm drive ... J 6
Clip-hose-worm drive ... J 17
Clip-linkage ... N188
Clip-linkage ... N193
Clip-linkage ... N189
Clip-linkage ... N194
Clip-linkage ... N197
Clip-linkage ... N190
Clip-linkage ... R 43
Clip-manifold to head ... B126
Clip-omega-grey-10.5 x 8mm-6.5mm hole ... M137
Clip-omega-grey-10.5 x 8mm-6.5mm hole ... M145
Clip-on seat base ... R 50
Clip-only with stromberg carburettors ... B321
Clip-overspeed monitor-5mm-6.5mm hole ... M109
Clip-p ... B244
Clip-p ... H 2
Clip-p ... H 20
Clip-p ... H 22
Clip-p ... H 24
Clip-p ... H 5
Clip-p ... J 18
Clip-p ... J 67
Clip-p ... J 74
Clip-p ... J 77
Clip-p ... M118
Clip-p-3/4" ... H 36
Clip-p-3/8" ... J 75
Clip-p-5/16" ... D 5
Clip-p-5mm ... M 63
Clip-p-8mm ... J 65
Clip-p-8mm ... J 72
Clip-p-black-13.6mm-plastic ... M145
Clip-p-front breather-5/16" ... E 50
Clip-p-m12 ... H 8
Clip-p-m12 ... M100
Clip-p-only with su carburettors ... B334
Clip-p-plastic-adjustable-black-11.0/20.0mm ... M127
Clip-p-plastic-adjustable-black-11.0/20.0mm ... M 58
Clip-p-plastic-adjustable-white.-4.0/12.0mm ... M 57
Clip-p-plastic-adjustable-white.-4.0/12.0mm ... M 46
Clip-p-rear breather ... E 51
Clip-p-single-5/16" ... C 37
Clip-panel fixing-5mm-4.8mm hole ... B 30
Clip-panel fixing-5mm-4.8mm hole ... M 59
Clip-panel fixing-5mm-4.8mm hole ... M 60
Clip-panel fixing-5mm-4.8mm hole ... M150
Clip-pipe ... B 32
Clip-pipe ... B254
Clip-pipe ... C 6
Clip-pipe ... C 83
Clip-pipe ... C 56
Clip-pipe ... D 36
Clip-pipe ... F 25
Clip-pipe ... F 27
Clip-pipe ... F 23
Clip-pipe ... H 10
Clip-pipe ... H 12
Clip-pipe-10mm ... L 11
Clip-pipe-double ... C 37
Clip-pipe-double ... J 19
Clip-pipe-double ... J 20
Clip-pipe-double ... J 21
Clip-pipe-double ... J 22
Clip-pipe-double ... J 23
Clip-pipe-double ... J 25
Clip-pipe-double ... J 28
Clip-pipe-double ... J 49
Clip-pipe-double ... J 50
Clip-pipe-double ... J 65
Clip-pipe-double ... J 72
Clip-pipe-double ... J 27
Clip-pipe-double ... J 30
Clip-pipe-double ... M 82
Clip-pipe-front breather ... E 50
Clip-pipe-front breather ... E 51
Clip-pipe-gearbox to engine ... C 51
Clip-pipe-only with stromberg carburettors ... B334
Clip-pipe-single ... D 8
Clip-pipe-single ... G 5
Clip-pipe-single ... J 74
Clip-pipe-single ... M 82
Clip-pipe-single ... M 31
Clip-pipe-single ... M118
Clip-pivot-snap-13-17mm-7mm hole-grey ... M151
Clip-plastic-hose to engine ... L 41
Clip-plastic-large ... L 20
Clip-push rod ... C 2
Clip-push rod to lever ... C 3
Clip-rear seat belt stowage-black ... R 54
Clip-retainer pin ... T 35
Clip-retaining ... J 42
Clip-retaining ... M131
Clip-retaining ... M133
Clip-retaining ... M134
Clip-retaining ... M135
Clip-retaining ... M136
Clip-retaining ... M137
Clip-retaining ... N159
Clip-retaining ... N162
Clip-retaining ... P 25
Clip-retaining-ball ... B 11
Clip-retaining-buzzer mounting ... M109
Clip-retaining-flasher unit ... M 93
Clip-retaining-short ... J 41
Clip-scissor prop ... N143
Clip-self adhesive-6mm ... M145
Clip-single-9mm ... G 3
Clip-single-9mm ... G 10
Clip-single-9mm ... J 19
Clip-single-9mm ... J 21
Clip-single-9mm ... J 25
Clip-single-9mm ... J 28
Clip-single-9mm ... J 30
Clip-snap-sack ... H 35
Clip-snap-sack ... P 17
Clip-snap-sack ... P 18
Clip-snap-sack ... P 21
Clip-snap-sack ... P 22
Clip-snap-sack ... P 44
Clip-snap-sack ... P 20
Clip-snap-sack ... P 45
Clip-snap-sack ... P 37
Clip-spacer ... F 27
Clip-spacer-high tension lead ignition ... B324
Clip-spacer-high tension lead ignition ... B350
Clip-spacer-high tension lead ignition ... B395
Clip-spacer-high tension lead ignition ... B353
Clip-spring band ... L 20
Clip-spring band ... L 43
Clip-spring band-14mm ... L 11
Clip-spring band-23mm ... L 41
Clip-spring band-heater end ... L 42
Clip-spring connector ... L 38
Clip-spring connector ... L 76
Clip-spring steel ... B391
Clip-spring steel ... C 24
Clip-spring steel ... D 30
Clip-spring steel ... D 35
Clip-support boss ... F 23
Clip-support boss-pipe ... F 25
Clip-support boss-pipe ... F 27
Clip-support-exhaust gas recirculation pipe ... J 76
Clip-swivel ... F 25
Clip-swivel ... F 27
Clip-swivel ... F 23
Clip-swivel ... G 3
Clip-swivel ... J 19
Clip-swivel ... J 65
Clip-swivel ... J 66
Clip-swivel ... J 72
Clip-swivel ... J 71
Clip-swivel-10 x 10mm ... J 25
Clip-swivel-10 x 10mm ... J 28
Clip-swivel-10 x 10mm ... J 27
Clip-swivel-10 x 10mm ... J 30
Clip-swivel-10 x 10mm ... M149
Clip-tailgate lock retaining ... B177
Clip-trim retention ... R 28
Clock analogue-in centre dash panel-round ... M120
Clock analogue-round ... M115
Clutch set-magnetic air conditioning ... B 38
Clutch set-magnetic air conditioning ... B 39
Clutch set-magnetic air conditioning ... B 85
Clutch set-magnetic air conditioning ... B 86
Clutch set-magnetic air conditioning ... B134
Clutch set-magnetic air conditioning ... B135
Clutch set-magnetic air conditioning ... B182
Clutch set-magnetic air conditioning ... B183
Clutch set-magnetic air conditioning ... B222
Clutch set-magnetic air conditioning ... B223
Clutch set-magnetic air conditioning ... B346
Clutch set-magnetic air conditioning ... B347
Clutch-drive-assy ... B 38
Clutch-drive-assy ... B 39

Clutch-drive-assy ... B 85
Clutch-drive-assy ... B 86
Clutch-drive-assy ... B134
Clutch-drive-assy ... B135
Clutch-drive-assy ... B182
Clutch-drive-assy ... B183
Clutch-drive-assy ... B222
Clutch-drive-assy ... B223
Clutch-drive-assy ... B346
Clutch-drive-assy ... B347
Coil and bracket assembly-ignition-where ... B354
Coil ignition ... B 42
Coil ignition ... B 89
Coil ignition ... B395
Coil ignition-lucas ... B354
Coil-engine immobilizer ... M105
Collar ... N 90
Collar ... N 92
Collar ... N 93
Collar ... N 95
Collar ... N 97
Collar ... N 98
Collar ... N124
Collar-distance manual transmission ... C 55
Collar-distance manual transmission ... C 14
Collar-layshaft ... C 66
Collar-layshaft ... C 67
Collar-oil seal ... C 7
Collar-oil seal ... C 8
Collar-oil seal-3.00mm ... C 34
Collet-cylinder head valve ... B279
Collet-cylinder head valve ... B283
Column-upper-steering ... F 1
Column-upper-steering ... F 3
Compressor assembly air conditioning ... B 38
Compressor assembly air conditioning ... B 39
Compressor assembly air conditioning ... B 85
Compressor assembly air conditioning ... B 86
Compressor assembly air conditioning ... B134
Compressor assembly air conditioning ... B135
Compressor assembly air conditioning ... B182
Compressor assembly air conditioning ... B183
Compressor assembly air conditioning ... B222
Compressor assembly air conditioning ... B223
Compressor assembly air conditioning ... B295
Compressor assembly air conditioning ... B346
Compressor assembly air conditioning ... B347
Compressor assembly air conditioning ... B394
Compressor assembly-r134a air conditioning ... B 85
Compressor assembly-r134a air conditioning ... B 86
Compressor assembly-r134a air conditioning ... B135
Compressor assembly-r134a air conditioning ... B222
Compressor assembly-r134a air conditioning ... B223
Compressor assembly-r134a air conditioning ... B259
Compressor assembly-r134a air conditioning ... B346
Compressor assembly-r134a air conditioning ... B347
Compressor assembly-r134a air conditioning- ... B134
Condenser air conditioning ... L 47
Condenser assembly air conditioning ... L 45
Condenser assembly air conditioning ... L 48
Condenser ignition ... B350
Condenser/fan & frame assembly ... L 47
Cone-synchronizer inner ... C 13
Cone-synchronizer inner ... C 14
Connecting rod assembly brake-for old type ... D 41
Connector assembly-fuel block ... B279
Connector assembly-fuel block ... B287
Connector brake ... H 19
Connector brake ... H 21
Connector brake ... H 23
Connector fit ... B 79
Connector fit ... B 30
Connector fit ... C 81
Connector fit ... J 67
Connector fit ... J 70
Connector fit ... J 74
Connector fit ... M138
Connector fit ... M139
Connector fit ... M140
Connector fit ... M141
Connector fit ... M142
Connector fit-0.5-1.0mm cable ... M 46
Connector fit-detoxed ... B 25
Connector fuel lines ... B 79
Connector fuel lines ... J 20
Connector fuel lines ... J 22
Connector fuel lines ... J 49
Connector fuel lines ... J 50
Connector harness ... J 1
Connector harness ... J 9
Connector harness-to convert prc5602 where ... M 77
Connector harness-to convert prc5602 where ... M 57
Connector-inlet manifold adaptor ... B 42
Connector-inlet manifold adaptor ... B 52
Connector-inlet manifold adaptor ... B 73
Connector-inlet manifold adaptor ... B 90
Connector-inlet manifold adaptor ... B104
Connector-inlet manifold adaptor ... B119
Connector-inlet manifold adaptor ... B153
Connector-inlet manifold adaptor ... B167
Connector-inlet manifold adaptor ... B323
Connector-inlet manifold adaptor ... B390
Connector-inlet manifold adaptor ... G 4
Connector-inlet manifold adaptor ... J 12
Connector-inlet manifold adaptor ... J 36
Connector-inlet manifold adaptor ... J 37
Connector-inlet manifold adaptor ... J 73
Connector-inlet manifold adaptor ... L 29
Connector-inlet manifold adaptor ... L 49
Connector-inlet manifold adaptor ... L 70
Connector-inlet manifold adaptor-servo ... B 25
Connector-inlet manifold adaptor-transmitter ... B314
Connector-straight ... J 49
Console assembly-tunnel ... P 17
Container & pump assembly-windscreen ... M143
Container assembly-windscreen wash ... M130
Container-windscreen wash ... M131
Container-windscreen wash ... M132
Container-windscreen wash ... M133
Container-windscreen wash ... M134
Container-windscreen wash ... M135
Container-windscreen wash ... M136
Container-windscreen wash ... M137
Container-windscreen wash ... M138
Container-windscreen wash ... M139
Container-windscreen wash ... M140
Container-windscreen wash ... M141
Container-windscreen wash ... M142
Control assembly heater ... L 71
Control assembly heater-lhd ... L 68
Control assembly heater-rhd ... L 36
Control assembly-air conditioning ... L 73
Control rod-long ... J 51
Control rod-short ... J 51
Control unit burglar alarm-433 mhz ... M104
Control unit daytime running lamps ... M 76
Control unit daytime running lamps ... M 77
Control unit dim dip-quartz halogen ... M 95
Control unit-self levelling ... E 69
Converter assembly automatic transmission ... C 73
Coolant-1ltr ... U 2
Cooler assembly-exhaust gas recirculation ... L 13
Cotter-antiluce ... N115
Cotter-antiluce ... N117
Cotter-valve ... B 21
Cotter-valve ... B121
Cotter-valve ... B169
Cotter-valve ... B209
Cotter-valve ... B246
Cotter-valve ... B319
Cotter-valve ... B381
Cotter-valve-split halves ... B 69
Counter shaft-carb ... G 12
Counter shaft-carb ... G 13
Coupling ... B 42
Coupling ... B 66
Coupling ... B115
Coupling ... B117
Coupling ... B164
Coupling ... B165
Coupling ... B206
Coupling ... L 26
Coupling ... L 27
Coupling ... L 50
Coupling ... L 58
Coupling-drive ... B 90
Coupling-engine fan viscous ... B 62
Coupling-engine fan viscous ... B114
Coupling-engine fan viscous ... B162
Coupling-engine fan viscous ... B163
Coupling-engine fan viscous ... B204
Coupling-engine fan viscous ... B242
Coupling-engine fan viscous ... B311
Coupling-engine fan viscous ... B380
Coupling-engine fan viscous ... B 14
Coupling-small ... L 45
Cover alternator ... B 93
Cover alternator ... B140
Cover alternator ... B361
Cover alternator-24079b90 ... B358
Cover alternator-lra356 ... B 43
Cover alternator-lra356 ... B 91
Cover alternator-lra356 ... B138
Cover alternator-lra356 ... B359
Cover assembly-camshaft carrier ... B284
Cover assembly-convertible hood tonneau ... T 24
Cover assembly-coverter automatic ... C 73
Cover assembly-engine acoustic ... B284
Cover assembly-facia console ... M120
Cover assembly-facia console ... P 8
Cover assembly-front ... B 38
Cover assembly-front ... B 39
Cover assembly-front ... B 85
Cover assembly-front ... B 86
Cover assembly-front ... B134
Cover assembly-front ... B135
Cover assembly-front ... B182
Cover assembly-front ... B183
Cover assembly-front ... B202
Cover assembly-front ... B222
Cover assembly-front ... B223
Cover assembly-front ... B346
Cover assembly-front ... B347
Cover assembly-front ... C 31
Cover assembly-front seat cushion-centre- ... R 18
Cover assembly-front seat cushion-centre- ... R 17
Cover assembly-front seat cushion-centre- ... R 19
Cover assembly-front seat cushion-cloth ... R 4
Cover assembly-front seat cushion-cloth ... R 5
Cover assembly-front seat cushion-cloth- ... R 13
Cover assembly-front seat cushion-cloth- ... R 20
Cover assembly-front seat squab-centre- ... R 20
Cover assembly-front seat squab-centre- ... R 18
Cover assembly-front seat squab-centre- ... R 17
Cover assembly-front seat squab-centre- ... R 19
Cover assembly-front seat squab-cloth ... R 16
Cover assembly-front seat squab-cloth-blue ... R 11
Cover assembly-front seat squab-cloth- ... R 5
Cover assembly-fuel filter-rear ... J 58
Cover assembly-fuel filter-rear ... J 59

Downpipe assembly exhaust system K 2
Downpipe assembly exhaust system K 5
Downpipe assembly exhaust system K 11
Downpipe assembly exhaust system K 12
Downpipe assembly exhaust system K 14
Downpipe assembly exhaust system K 16
Downpipe assembly exhaust system K 18
Downpipe assembly exhaust system-less K 17
Downpipe assembly exhaust system-lh K 3
Downpipe assembly-exhaust manifold-with K 18
Drain channel N241
Drain channel N242
Drain channel N243
Drain channel N245
Drain channel-top-rh N238
Drive assembly starter motor B143
Drive assembly starter motor B367
Drive assembly starter motor B368
Drive assembly starter motor B369
Drive assembly starter motor B397
Drive assembly starter motor-bosch B144
Drive assembly starter motor-bosch B145
Drive assembly starter motor-bosch B190
Drive assembly starter motor-bosch B228
Drive assembly starter motor-bosch B262
Drive assembly starter motor-new starter B 96
Drive assembly starter motor-new-with B 46
Drive assembly starter motor-valeo B189
Drive assembly starter motor-valeo B229
Drive assembly-freewheel-automatic C 80
Drive assembly-oil pump B 63
Drive assembly-oil pump B115
Drive assembly-oil pump B164
Drive assembly-oil pump B205
Drive assembly-oil pump B 16
Driveshaft-front-rh-23 spline shaft E 16
Driveshaft-front-rh-24 spline shaft E 17
Drum brake H 29
Drum-splined M129
Drum-transmission brake-black D 41
Drum-transmission brake-black D 42
Duct air cleaner to elbow J 61
Duct air-upper-rh J 41
Duct air-upper-rh J 63
Duct assembly air cleaner to elbow J 73
Duct assembly air cleaner to elbow-s.u. B338
Duct assembly air cleaner to elbow-s.u. J 60
Duct assembly-air cleaner/turbocharger J 42
Duct assembly-air floor L 73
Duct assembly-air floor-rh L 38
Duct assembly-air floor-rh L 76
Duct assembly-cold air intake induction L 34
Duct assembly-fresh air B339
Duct assembly-fresh air J 45
Duct assembly-fresh air L 65
Duct assembly-fresh air-upper J 62
Duct-air cleaner to hose turbocharger B218
Duct-air cleaner to hose turbocharger J 38
Duct-air cleaner to hose turbocharger J 39
Duct-air inlet heater L 5
Duct-air intake-air cleaner J 64
Duct-demist windscreen-rh L 38
Duct-demist windscreen-rh L 75
Duct-elbow induction system J 61
Duct-elbow induction system-duct to valve J 73
Duct-engine intake L 66
Duct-face level vent-lh L 70
Duct-heater-rhd-without speaker-less P 9
Duct-water separator to air cleaner air intake J 41
Duct-water separator to air cleaner air intake J 64
Dump valve & bracket assy J 39
Dump valve & bracket assy J 41
Earth lead J 13
Ecu-egr-located under front centre seat M 97
Ecu-one touch f/lamp M 98
Edging strip J 46
Edging strip N132
Edging strip N 66
Edging strip N 99
Edging strip N103
Edging strip N116
Edging strip N129
Edging strip N131
Edging strip R 40
Edging strip R 38
Edging strip T 53
Edging strip T 52
Elbow B177
Elbow B289
Elbow J 38
Elbow assembly-engine coolant to outlet B324
Elbow fuel tank J 49
Elbow fuel tank J 50
Elbow-carburettor air inlet B 80
Elbow-carburettor air inlet B338
Elbow-carburettor air inlet B339
Elbow-carburettor air inlet J 60
Elbow-carburettor air inlet J 61
Elbow-carburettor air inlet-non detoxed B 29
Elbow-engine coolant outlet B 24
Elbow-engine coolant outlet B 72
Elbow-engine coolant outlet B172
Elbow-engine coolant outlet B213
Elbow-engine coolant outlet B250
Elbow-engine coolant outlet B385
Elbow-engine coolant outlet-rh outlet B125
Elbow-exhaust outlet B218
Elbow-only with stromberg carburettors B334
Elbow-rh J 73
Elbow-rubber J 65
Elbow-rubber J 67
Elbow-rubber J 68
Elbow-rubber J 70
Elbow-rubber J 72
Elbow-rubber J 74
Electric control unit & traction control- M 96
Electric control unit-fuel control M 99
Electric control unit-fuel control M100
Element air cleaner J 33
Element air cleaner J 34
Element air cleaner J 35
Element air cleaner J 36
Element air cleaner J 37
Element air cleaner J 38
Element air cleaner J 39
Element air cleaner J 41
Element-filter B 28
Element-filter J 43
Element-filter J 52
Element-filter-flyscreen N 30
Element-fuel filter diesel J 52
Element-fuel filter diesel J 59
Element-inline fuel filter B 31
Element-inline fuel filter B 76
Element-inline fuel filter J 12
Element-inline fuel filter J 20
Element-inline fuel filter J 22
End assembly-track rod F 17
End cap-front bumper N 20
End cap-hood N223
End cap-hood N224
End cap-hood N227
End cap-hood N228
End cap-hood N230
End cap-hood N231
End cap-hood N233
End cap-hood N234
End cap-rear bumper-lh N 24
End-yoke B255
Engine assembly - short B232
Engine assembly - short B372
Engine assembly-power unit B 50
Engine assembly-power unit B149
Engine assembly-power unit B300
Engine assembly-power unit-complete B 99
Engine assembly-power unit-short B151
Engine assembly-power unit-short. B101
Engine base unit-part B 2
Engine base unit-part B266
Engine base unit-part-8.13:1 B302
Engine base unit-part-short B194
Engine unit-stripped B264
Engine unit-stripped B371
Engine unit-stripped-exchange B100
Engine unit-stripped-exchange B301
Engine unit-stripped-new B 1
Engine unit-stripped-new B100
Engine unit-stripped-new B150
Engine unit-stripped-new B193
Engine unit-stripped-new B231
Engine unit-stripped-new B301
Engine unit-stripped-reconditioned B 49
Engine-power unit B 48
Engine-power unit B192
Engine-power unit B265
Escutcheon-door-lock-black P 21
Escutcheon-door-lock-black P 22
Escutcheon-door-lock-black P 20
Escutcheon-front door release assembly N187
Escutcheon-rear door release assembly P 25
Escutcheon-sunroof handle N135
Escutcheon-window regulator-black N159
Escutcheon-window regulator-black N161
Escutcheon-window regulator-black N184
Evaporator air conditioning L 50
Evaporator assembly-air conditioning L 52
Evaporator assembly-air conditioning-lhd L 50
Evaporator assembly-air conditioning-rhd L 49
Evaporator assembly-r134a air conditioning L 73
Evaporator assembly-r134a air conditioning- L 49
Excluder mud B 58
Excluder mud-not needed when err1632 is B307
Excluder mud-single lip seal B 9
Exhaust silencer-intermediate K 14
Expander assembly-transfer box brake shoe D 41
Extension assembly-plenum closing L 69
Extension-rear tailpipe aperture K 27
Extinguisher-fire T 27
Extractor blade fuse M 92
Extractor blade fuse M 49
Eyebrow-front wheelarch-lh-stratos blue N 63
Eyebrow-front wheelarch-rh-black-plastic- N 62
Eyebrow-rear wheelarch-black-plastic- N198
Eyelet connector N223
Eyelet connector N224
Eyelet connector N227
Eyelet connector N228
Eyelet connector N230
Eyelet connector N231
Eyelet connector N233
Eyelet connector N234
Facia assembly L 74
Facia assembly-front end L 72
Fan alternator B 91
Fan alternator B 92
Fan alternator B 93
Fan alternator B 94
Fan alternator B138
Fan alternator B139
Fan alternator B140

Fan alternator B141
Fan alternator B186
Fan alternator B187
Fan alternator B226
Fan alternator B355
Fan alternator B356
Fan alternator B358
Fan alternator B359
Fan alternator B360
Fan alternator B361
Fan alternator B362
Fan alternator B 44
Fan assembly-condenser L 47
Fan assembly-cooling B276
Fan assembly-cooling-5 blade B310
Fan assembly-cooling-7 blade B311
Fan blower-heater L 57
Fan-condenser L 45
Fan-condenser L 48
Fan-cooling B 13
Fan-cooling B 61
Fan-cooling B 62
Fan-cooling B113
Fan-cooling B114
Fan-cooling B162
Fan-cooling B163
Fan-cooling B242
Fan-cooling-11 blade-17"-black B380
Fan-cooling-7 blade B204
Fastener-drive P 38
Fastener-drive P 45
Fastener-drive P 11
Fastener-drive-black L 11
Fastener-drive-black P 43
Fastener-drive-brushwood-plastic P 44
Fastener-drive-grey M 90
Fastener-drive-grey M125
Fastener-drive-grey P 3
Fastener-drive-radio housing-grey M123
Fastener-drive-slate grey H 35
Fastener-drive-slate grey P 17
Fastener-drive-slate grey P 41
Fastener-drive-slate grey P 37
Fastener-dzus-female L 4
Fastener-fir tree M100
Fastener-fir tree N 25
Fastener-fir tree N 20
Fastener-fir tree P 21
Fastener-fir tree P 22
Fastener-fir tree P 20
Fastener-fir tree-2 1/4" M130
Fastener-fir tree-2 1/4" M131
Fastener-fir tree-2 1/4" M132
Fastener-fir tree-2 1/4" M133
Fastener-fir tree-2 1/4" M135
Fastener-fir tree-2 1/4" M136
Fastener-fir tree-black N 63
Fastener-fir tree-inertia reel seat belts-white P 57
Fastener-fir tree-light grey P 66
Fastener-fir tree-light grey P 60
Fastener-fir tree-mid grey P 55
Fastener-fir tree-white. P 53
Fastener-fir tree-white. P 56
Fastener-fir tree-white. P 64
Fastener-fir tree-white. P 63
Fastener-fir tree-white. P 65
Felt-nvh N 65
Felt-nvh N113
Felt-nvh N108
Felt-nvh-clear glass N107
Felt-nvh-intermediate P 44
Felt-nvh-intermediate P 46
Felt-nvh-rh clear N109
Felt-nvh-tinted glass N110
Felt-sliding glass-cab-rear panel-top N107
Felt-sliding glass-cab-rear panel-top N108
Felt-tunnel P 35
Fender assembly-front-rh N 54
Fender assembly-front-rh N 55
Ferrule M128
Filler assembly-fuel J 14
Filler assembly-fuel J 18
Filler assembly-fuel J 70
Filler assembly-fuel J 74
Filler sloping-rh N155
Filler strip N 65
Filler strip N112
Filler strip N105
Filler strip N129
Filler strip N131
Filler strip N111
Filler strip-clear glass N107
Filler strip-rh clear N109
Filler strip-tinted glass N108
Filler strip-tinted glass N110
Filler-body-rh N165
Filler-oil B320
Filler-oil B383
Filler-rear-corner N165
Filler-rear-corner N155
Filter assembly-fuel.-unheated J 54
Filter assembly-fuel.-unheated J 56
Filter assembly-in line fuel lines J 34
Filter assembly-in line fuel lines J 57
Filter assembly-in line fuel lines J 69
Filter-air fuel C 30
Filter-air fuel H 1
Filter-exhaust gas recirculation solenoid J 77
Filter-fuel pump tank J 1
Filter-fuel pump tank J 12
Filter-in line fuel lines J 20
Filter-in line fuel lines J 22
Filter-in line fuel lines J 59
Filter-reservoir F 19
Filter/sedimentor assembly-diesel J 58
Finger assembly-transfer box high/low D 28
Finisher N200
Finisher assembly comp-facia assembly L 72
Finisher assembly-d post N103
Finisher assembly-d post N105
Finisher assembly-facia assembly L 71
Finisher assembly-front door waist-rh N155
Finisher assembly-quarterlight-rh P 53
Finisher facia vent N 32
Finisher-assembly-cantrail-rh P 53
Finisher-b post-rh P 64
Finisher-b post-rh P 63
Finisher-b post-rh-ripple grey P 66
Finisher-bc post P 56
Finisher-bc post-mid grey P 54
Finisher-cab back-rh P 65
Finisher-cantrail-intermediate-rh P 56
Finisher-corner capping N117
Finisher-corner capping N116
Finisher-corner capping N119
Finisher-d post-static-rh P 57
Finisher-dash strip L 71
Finisher-dash strip L 72
Finisher-demist vent windscreen P 1
Finisher-edge strip M 58
Finisher-facia air conditioning control L 71
Finisher-facia air conditioning control L 72
Finisher-facia assembly-lh P 31
Finisher-facia assembly-rhd P 12
Finisher-footwell upper-rh P 28
Finisher-footwell upper-rh P 29
Finisher-front console automatic selector-ash P 17
Finisher-front-rear N111
Finisher-grab handle L 72
Finisher-headlamp-steel grey-rh-stainless N 57
Finisher-headlining-rear-ripple grey P 59
Finisher-outer N113
Finisher-outer N 66
Finisher-pillar-cab-rear-rh P 65
Finisher-pillar-cab-rear-rh-ripple grey P 66
Finisher-quarter trim strip-rh P 57
Finisher-rh N102
Finisher-rh N104
Finisher-rh N106
Finisher-roof cantrail-rh-mid grey P 60
Finisher-roof trim sunroof aperture N134
Finisher-seat plinth R 15
Finisher-seat plinth-front R 30
Finisher-seat plinth-front R 35
Finisher-sixthlight lower P 53
Finisher-sixthlight lower P 57
Finisher-sixthlight upper P 53
Finisher-sixthlight upper P 57
Finisher-sunroof N136
Finisher-trim exhaust tailpipe K 7
Finisher-trim exhaust tailpipe K 10
Finisher-trim exhaust tailpipe K 19
Finisher-trim exhaust tailpipe K 23
Finisher-trim exhaust tailpipe-rear K 27
Finisher-trim exhaust tailpipe-rear K 30
Finisher-trim retention R 4
Finisher-trim retention R 5
Finisher-trim retention R 15
Finisher-trim retention R 16
Finisher-trim retention R 17
Finisher-trim retention R 18
Finisher-trim retention R 19
Finisher-trim retention R 14
Finisher-trim retention-rh-mid grey P 55
Finisher-trim retention-rh-side R 30
Finisher-trim retention-rh-side R 35
Finisher-windscreen a post-rh P 53
Finisher-windscreen a post-rh P 54
Finisher-windscreen a post-rh P 56
Finisher-windscreen a post-rh P 64
Finisher-windscreen a post-rh P 66
Finisher-windscreen a post-rh P 63
Flame trap-crankcase breather B338
Flame trap-crankcase breather B339
Flame trap-crankcase breather J 60
Flame trap-crankcase breather-rocker cover B321
Flange & mudshield-front & rear axle E 11
Flange & mudshield-front & rear axle E 39
Flange assembly rear hub E 32
Flange assembly-front output D 18
Flange assembly-rear output D 19
Flange-adaptor-bearing to viscous fan B273
Flange-coupling T 6
Flange-driveshaft coupling differential E 11
Flange-driveshaft coupling differential-4 bolt E 8
Flange-driveshaft coupling differential-4 bolt E 39
Flange-driveshaft coupling differential-4 E 35
Flange-driving shaft joint E 23
Flange-driving shaft joint E 26
Flange-driving shaft joint E 47
Flange-driving shaft joint E 49
Flap & seals assembly blower-heater L 38
Flap & seals assembly blower-heater L 76
Flap-oil filler B284
Flasher unit electronic-2 pin-without trailer M 93
Flasher unit electronic-3 pin-without trailer M 94
Flinger-crankshaft pulley B106
Flinger-crankshaft pulley B155
Flinger-crankshaft pulley B198
Flinger-crankshaft pulley B235

Float assembly-carburettor ..... B 28
Float assembly-carburettor ..... B 31
Float assembly-carburettor ..... B 76
Float assembly-carburettor B332
Float-carburettor-lh B333

Floor assembly ..... N 75
Floor assembly ..... N 87
Floor assembly ..... N 90
Floor assembly ..... N 76
Floor assembly ..... N 88

Floor assembly ..... N 77
Floor assembly ..... N 78
Fluid-automatic transmission-dextron 2 ..... U 2
Fluid-de-lacquering-205ltr ..... U 2
Flywheel engine ..... B 47

Flywheel engine ..... B 98
Flywheel engine B146
Flywheel engine B148
Flywheel engine B191
Flywheel engine B230

Flywheel engine B263
Flywheel engine B299
Flywheel engine B370
Foam N163
Foam N167

Foam ..... P 17
Foam cushion ..... R 30
Foam cushion ..... R 37
Foam cushion ..... R 34
Foam cushion-driver & passenger side seats ..... R 2

Foam-pad-self adhesive ..... N 40
Foam-squab ..... R 29
Foam-squab-3 seat ..... R 39
Foam-squab-driver & passenger side seats ..... R 2
Follower assembly-valve camshaft finger B283

Follower assembly-valve camshaft finger B280
Footrest assembly-front floor ..... P 32
Footrest assembly-front floor-rh ..... R 58
Fork assembly-3rd & 4th manual transmission ..... C 68
Fork assembly-3rd & 4th manual transmission ..... C 23

Fork assembly-5th manual transmission ..... C 36
Fork assembly-5th manual transmission ..... C 68
Fork assembly-selector-1st/2nd manual ..... C 21
Fork assembly-selector-1st/2nd manual ..... C 36
Fork assembly-selector-1st/2nd manual ..... C 68

Fork-high/low selector ..... D 29
Fork-high/low selector ..... D 28
Fork-selector ..... T 5
Fork-selector-3rd/4th manual transmission ..... C 36
Fork-selector-5th gear ..... C 23

Fork-selector-cross shaft ..... D 29
Fork-transfer box differential lock selector ..... D 21
Fork-transfer box differential lock selector ..... D 24
Frame assembly-battery box-split charge ..... M 29
Frame assembly-bench seat-rh ..... R 39

Frame assembly-body side-rh N166
Frame assembly-chassis ..... N 1
Frame assembly-chassis ..... N 2
Frame assembly-chassis ..... N 3
Frame assembly-chassis ..... N 4

Frame assembly-chassis ..... N 5
Frame assembly-chassis ..... N 6
Frame assembly-manual convertible hood N241
Frame assembly-manual convertible hood N243
Frame assembly-manual front seat ..... R 1

Frame assembly-rear-inward facing-bench- ..... R 36
Frame assembly-windscreen N185
Frame spare wheel carrier ..... S 10
Frame spare wheel carrier ..... V 5
Frame-radiator grille-hand operated bonnet N145

Frame-radiator-lh ..... L 3
Frame-seat assembly outer ..... R 29
Frame-seat assembly-centre ..... R 29
Frame-sunroof N134
Frame-sunroof centre N135

Frame-sunroof front-upper N136
Front screen hoop assy N137
Fuel cooler assembly B292
Fuel tap assembly-heelboard ..... J 51
Fuel-filler ..... J 15

Fuse-15 amp M111
Fuse-30 amp-auto-standard ..... M 80
Fuse-5 amp ..... M 47
Fuse-5 amp-auto-standard ..... M 92
Fuse-7.5 amp-auto-standard. M106

Fuse-condenser fan-35 amp ..... M 79
Fuse-heated rear window-20 amp-maxi- ..... M 91
Fuseblock ..... M 46
Fusebox ..... M 92
Fusebox assembly engine compartment ..... M 91

Fusebox assembly passenger compartment M111
Fusebox assembly passenger compartment ..... M 79
Gaiter-gear lever assembly-transfer box ..... C 69
Gaiter-gear lever assembly-transfer box ..... N 34
Gaiter-gear lever assembly-transfer box ..... P 17

Gaiter-propshaft sliding joint ..... E 1
Gaiter-propshaft sliding joint ..... E 2
Gaiter-propshaft sliding joint ..... E 3
Gaiter-self levelling unit ball joint-upper ..... E 69
Gasket B103

Gasket B153
Gasket B196
Gasket B202
Gasket B327
Gasket ..... G 5

Gasket ..... J 45
Gasket ..... L 66
Gasket ..... N 97
Gasket ..... N 42
Gasket ..... N 96

Gasket ..... N 38
Gasket ..... T 5
Gasket door lockface-rh N190
Gasket exhaust system-intermediate to rear ..... K 31
Gasket exhaust system-intermediate to rear ..... K 32

Gasket exhaust system-intermediate to rear ..... K 6
Gasket exhaust system-manifold to downpipe ..... K 2
Gasket exhaust system-manifold to downpipe ..... K 3
Gasket exhaust system-manifold to downpipe ..... K 5
Gasket exhaust system-manifold to downpipe ..... K 12

Gasket exhaust system-manifold to downpipe ..... K 17
Gasket exhaust system-turbo outlet to ..... K 18
Gasket selector mechanism-top cover ..... C 37
Gasket-adaptor. ..... L 29
Gasket-adaptor. ..... L 30

Gasket-axle shaft drive member ..... E 23
Gasket-axle shaft drive member ..... E 26
Gasket-axle shaft drive member ..... E 47
Gasket-axle shaft drive member ..... E 49
Gasket-axle shaft drive member-salisbury ..... E 32

Gasket-camshaft cover B284
Gasket-carburettor ..... B 31
Gasket-carburettor air elbow-asbestos ..... B 80
Gasket-carburettor air elbow-asbestos ..... B 29
Gasket-carburettor to induction manifold- B330

Gasket-carburettor to induction manifold- B331
Gasket-carburettor-12,000 mile service B344
Gasket-carburettor-needle valve ..... B 76
Gasket-carburettor-only with stromberg B334
Gasket-centre plate to extension case ..... C 26

Gasket-centre plate to extension case- ..... C 4
Gasket-centre plate to extension case- ..... C 5
Gasket-centre plate to main case ..... C 26
Gasket-centrifuge oil-drain pipe-diesel B291
Gasket-clutch pedal box to bulkhead ..... G 7

Gasket-clutch pedal box top cover ..... G 7
Gasket-clutch pedal box top cover ..... G 8
Gasket-converter housing lower access ..... C 73
Gasket-coolant outlet elbow B289
Gasket-coolant outlet elbow B323

Gasket-coolant outlet elbow B324
Gasket-coolant outlet elbow B385
Gasket-coolant pump body ..... B 13
Gasket-coolant pump body ..... B 61
Gasket-coolant pump body ..... B 62

Gasket-coolant pump body B113
Gasket-coolant pump body B114
Gasket-coolant pump body B162
Gasket-coolant pump body B163
Gasket-coolant pump body B204

Gasket-coolant pump body B241
Gasket-coolant pump body B379
Gasket-coolant pump body-asbestos ..... B 9
Gasket-coolant pump body-asbestos B110
Gasket-coolant pump body-asbestos B159

Gasket-coolant pump body-asbestos B202
Gasket-coolant pump body-to front cover- ..... B 58
Gasket-coolant pump distance piece to B241
Gasket-cover front B202
Gasket-cover front B307

Gasket-cover front B378
Gasket-cover front-asbestos B110
Gasket-cover front-asbestos B160
Gasket-crankcase oil sump B306
Gasket-crankcase oil sump B376

Gasket-crankcase rear oil seal housing B233
Gasket-cylinder block coolant pump B308
Gasket-cylinder block coolant pump B309
Gasket-cylinder block oil pump B271
Gasket-cylinder block oil pump B314

Gasket-cylinder block oil pump-asbestos ..... B 15
Gasket-cylinder block oil pump-asbestos B115
Gasket-cylinder block oil pump-asbestos B164
Gasket-cylinder block oil pump-asbestos free ..... B 63
Gasket-cylinder block oil pump-asbestos free B205

Gasket-cylinder block side cover ..... B 4
Gasket-cylinder block side cover ..... B 53
Gasket-cylinder block side cover B105
Gasket-cylinder block side cover B123
Gasket-cylinder block side cover B154

Gasket-cylinder block side cover B197
Gasket-cylinder block side cover B211
Gasket-cylinder block side cover-asbestos B248
Gasket-cylinder block to oil filter adaptor B243
Gasket-cylinder block to oil filter adaptor- B165

Gasket-cylinder block to oil filter adaptor- B206
Gasket-cylinder block water gallery plate ..... B 10
Gasket-cylinder block water gallery plate ..... B 59
Gasket-cylinder head ..... B 19
Gasket-cylinder head ..... B 67

Gasket-cylinder head B381
Gasket-cylinder head B316
Gasket-cylinder head-1.27mm-1 hole B280
Gasket-cylinder head-1.30mm-1 hole B207
Gasket-cylinder head-1.30mm-1 hole B244

Gasket-cylinder head-asbestos B119
Gasket-cylinder head-asbestos free B167
Gasket-differential cover plate ..... E 32
Gasket-differential housing to axle case ..... E 41
Gasket-differential housing to axle case ..... E 15

Gasket-end cover automatic transmission ..... C 74
Gasket-engine inlet/exhaust manifold B214
Gasket-engine rocker cover B122
Gasket-engine rocker cover B170
Gasket-engine rocker cover B210

Gasket-engine rocker cover B247
Gasket-engine rocker cover B320
Gasket-engine rocker cover B383
Gasket-engine rocker cover-asbestos ..... B 22
Gasket-engine rocker cover-asbestos ..... B 70

Gasket-exhaust gas recirculation pipe to ..... J 75
Gasket-exhaust gas recirculation valve to ..... J 76
Gasket-exhaust gas recirculation valve to B255
Gasket-exhaust gas recirculation valve to ..... J 75
Gasket-exhaust gas recirculation valve to ..... J 76

Gasket-exhaust manifold B286
Gasket-exhaust manifold to turbocharger B177
Gasket-exhaust manifold to turbocharger B218
Gasket-exhaust manifold to turbocharger B286
Gasket-exhaust manifold-asbestos ..... B 25

Gasket-exhaust manifold-asbestos ..... B 73
Gasket-exhaust manifold-no1 ..... B386
Gasket-external drain pipe B234
Gasket-external drain pipe B237
Gasket-flywheel/drive plate B230

Gasket-front cover manual transmission ..... C 9
Gasket-front cover manual transmission ..... C 26
Gasket-front housing to main case ..... D 4
Gasket-front housing to main case ..... D 40
Gasket-front plate to timing chain cover B239

Gasket-fuel connector block B279
Gasket-fuel connector block B287
Gasket-fuel gauge sender unit ..... J 1
Gasket-fuel gauge sender unit ..... J 9
Gasket-fuel lift pump B127

Gasket-fuel lift pump B174
Gasket-fuel lift pump B215
Gasket-fuel lift pump-side cover B252
Gasket-fuel tank pump unit-external ..... J 12
Gasket-fuel tank spill return pipe ..... J 1

Gasket-fuel tank spill return pipe ..... J 9
Gasket-fuel tank spill return pipe ..... J 11
Gasket-headlamp lens ..... M 5
Gasket-headlamp lens-quartz halogen ..... M 3
Gasket-headlamp lens-sealed beam ..... M 1

Gasket-headlamp lens-sealed beam ..... M 2
Gasket-injection pump-diesel engine B216
Gasket-injection pump-diesel engine B253
Gasket-injection pump-diesel engine- B128
Gasket-injection pump-diesel engine- B175

Gasket-inlet manifold ..... B 25
Gasket-inlet manifold ..... B 73
Gasket-inlet manifold B126
Gasket-inlet manifold B173
Gasket-inlet manifold B251

Gasket-inlet manifold B285
Gasket-inlet manifold B325
Gasket-inlet manifold B385
Gasket-lower swivel pin-asbestos free ..... E 20
Gasket-lower swivel pin-asbestos free ..... E 22

Gasket-master cylinder to pedal box ..... G 4
Gasket-motor blower-heater ..... L 34
Gasket-oil cooler-adaptor B291
Gasket-oil drain turbocharger B255
Gasket-oil filter housing B291

Gasket-oil filter housing ..... J 12
Gasket-oil filter housing-asbestos ..... B 17
Gasket-oil filter housing-asbestos ..... B 18
Gasket-oil filter housing-asbestos ..... B 65
Gasket-oil filter housing-asbestos ..... B 66

Gasket-oil filter housing-asbestos B116
Gasket-oil filter housing-asbestos B117
Gasket-oil separator B284
Gasket-pedal box-brake ..... G 9
Gasket-potentiometer-throttle multi point B388

Gasket-quarterlight glass hinge-lower N185
Gasket-rear extension housing ..... C 83
Gasket-sealing-12mm-inside diameter- B243
Gasket-sealing-50ml B237
Gasket-sealing-50ml ..... U 1

Gasket-sealing-asbestos B110
Gasket-sealing-asbestos B159
Gasket-sealing-asbestos B160
Gasket-seating lamp ..... M 7
Gasket-seating lamp ..... M 17

Gasket-seating lamp ..... M 18
Gasket-seating lens ..... M 7
Gasket-stepping motor B388
Gasket-stepping motor B398
Gasket-stub axle-front axle-asbestos free ..... E 23

Gasket-stub axle-front axle-asbestos free ..... E 22
Gasket-stub axle-rear axle ..... E 46
Gasket-stub axle-rear axle-asbestos free ..... E 48
Gasket-sump ..... B 7
Gasket-sump ..... B 56

Gasket-sump B108
Gasket-sump B270
Gasket-sump oil strainer B306
Gasket-sump oil strainer B376
Gasket-sump/transmission case automatic ..... C 74

Gasket-swivel pin bearing housing to axle ..... E 18
Gasket-thermostat housing B250
Gasket-thermostat housing-asbestos-top ..... B 24
Gasket-thermostat housing-asbestos-top B172
Gasket-thermostat housing-top-asbestos ..... B 72

Gasket-thermostat housing-top-asbestos B125
Gasket-thermostat housing-top-asbestos B213
Gasket-timing gear cover plate B239
Gasket-timing gear housing drain plate ..... B 9
Gasket-timing gear housing drain plate ..... B 58

Gasket-timing gear housing drain plate B110
Gasket-timing gear housing drain plate B159
Gasket-timing gear housing drain plate B202
Gasket-timing gear housing drain plate B238
Gasket-transfer box bottom cover ..... D 10

Gasket-transfer box bottom cover ..... D 40
Gasket-transfer box bottom cover ..... D 9
Gasket-transfer box cover to case ..... D 40
Gasket-transfer box cover to case ..... D 5
Gasket-transfer box gear change housing ..... C 37

Gasket-transfer box gear change housing ..... D 33
Gasket-transfer box gear change housing ..... D 35
Gasket-transfer box gear change housing ..... D 40
Gasket-transfer box gear change housing ..... D 32
Gasket-transfer box gear change housing ..... D 30

Gasket-transfer box gear change housing ..... D 33
Gasket-transfer box gear change housing ..... D 35
Gasket-transfer box gear change housing ..... D 40
Gasket-transfer box gear change housing ..... D 31
Gasket-transfer box power take off cover ..... D 10

Gasket-transfer box power take off cover ..... D 40
Gasket-transfer box power take off cover ..... D 8
Gasket-transfer box side cover ..... D 4
Gasket-transfer box side cover ..... D 40
Gasket-transfer box side cover-joint ..... C 30

Gasket-transfer box speedometer housing ..... D 7
Gasket-transfer box speedometer housing ..... D 10
Gasket-transfer box speedometer housing ..... D 40
Gasket-turbocharger elbow to inlet manifold B177
Gasket-turbocharger elbow to inlet manifold B218

Gasket-turbocharger outlet B293
Gasket-vacuum pump B131
Gasket-vacuum pump B180
Gasket-vacuum pump B220
Gasket-vacuum pump B257

Gasket-water jacket to plenum chamber B388
Gauge-fuel M119
Gauge-fuel-12v M115
Gauge-oil temperature-12v M120
Gauge-oil-12v M120

Gauge-temperature M119
Gauge-temperature-12v M115
Gauge-tyre pressure ..... S 18
Gauge-tyre pressure ..... S 7
Gear & coupling assembly B350

Gear & coupling assembly B351
Gear & coupling assembly B352
Gear 5th speed assembly ..... C 35
Gear 5th speed assembly ..... C 34
Gear assembly-planetary automatic ..... C 82

Gear differential ..... E 43
Gear differential ..... E 45
Gear-1st & 2nd synchroniser mainshaft ..... C 12
Gear-1st driven manual transmission ..... C 33
Gear-1st driven manual transmission ..... C 13

Gear-1st driven manual transmission ..... C 60
Gear-1st driven manual transmission ..... C 61
Gear-2nd driven manual transmission ..... C 12
Gear-2nd driven manual transmission ..... C 33
Gear-2nd driven manual transmission ..... C 59

Gear-3rd driven manual transmission ..... C 11
Gear-3rd driven manual transmission ..... C 32
Gear-3rd driven manual transmission-27 teeth ..... C 63
Gear-5th driven manual transmission ..... C 64
Gear-5th driven manual transmission ..... C 34

Gear-5th speed countershaft manual ..... C 66
Gear-5th speed countershaft manual ..... C 20
Gear-5th speed countershaft manual ..... C 67
Gear-5th speed main shaft manual ..... C 14
Gear-5th speed-layshaft ..... C 16

Gear-automatic transmission sun ..... C 82
Gear-crankshaft timing drive ..... B 23
Gear-crankshaft timing drive ..... B 71
Gear-crankshaft timing drive B198
Gear-drive-distributor B322

Gear-high output ..... D 29
Gear-high output-1.6 : 1 ..... D 27
Gear-intermediate shaft ..... D 17
Gear-intermediate shaft-1.4 : 1 ..... D 15
Gear-low output ..... D 25

Gear-low output ..... D 29
Gear-mainshaft-26 teeth ..... D 12
Gear-mainshaft-26 teeth ..... D 13
Gear-mainshaft-26 teeth-1.4 : 1 ..... D 14
Gear-oil pump B314

Gear-oil pump ..... C 7
Gear-oil pump ..... C 8
Gear-oil pump ..... C 30
Gear-oil pump idler-10 teeth ..... B 15
Gear-oil pump idler-10 teeth ..... B 63

Gear-oil pump idler-10 teeth B115
Gear-oil pump idler-10 teeth B164
Gear-oil pump idler-10 teeth B205
Gear-oil pump idler-10 teeth ..... B 64
Gear-oil pump-10 teeth ..... B 15

Gear-oil pump-10 teeth B115
Gear-oil pump-10 teeth B164
Gear-oil pump-10 teeth B205
Gear-oil pump-10 teeth ..... B 64
Gear-oil pump-wheel driver-10 teeth ..... B 63

Gear-parking automatic transmission ..... C 83
Gear-reverse idler assembly manual ..... C 35
Gear-reverse idler assembly manual ..... C 67
Gear-reverse manual transmission ..... C 64
Gear-reverse manual transmission ..... C 17

Gear-reverse manual transmission ..... C 65
Gear-reverse manual transmission ..... C 67
Gear-reverse manual transmission ..... C 20
Gear-ring automatic transmission-front ..... C 82
Gear-ring-flywheel engine B146

Gear-ring-flywheel engine B148
Gear-ring-flywheel engine B191
Gear-ring-flywheel engine B230
Gear-ring-flywheel engine B263
Gear-ring-flywheel engine B299

Gear-ring-flywheel engine B370
Gear-ring-flywheel engine B399
Gear-speedometer drive ..... D 19
Gearbox & transfer box-casing ..... C 30
Glass assembly- load/tail door-clear N174

Lamp-auxiliary lighting side marker M 6
Lamp-auxiliary lighting side repeater M 7
Lamp-auxiliary lighting side repeater M 8
Lamp-front direction indicator M 6
Lamp-front lighting fog-rally 1000 T 10
Lamp-front lighting side M 6
Lamp-front long range driving-rally 1000 M 9
Lamp-front long range driving-rally 1000 T 10
Lamp-front long range driving-safari 5000 M 25
Lamp-front long range driving-safari 5000 T 9
Lamp-hand-cewe T 54
Lamp-interior courtesy M 17
Lamp-interior courtesy M 18
Lamp-interior courtesy M 19
Lamp-interior courtesy-with on/off switch M 26
Lamp-rear fog-12v M 16
Lamp-rear fog-red M 14
Lamp-rear fog-red M 15
Lamp-rear high mounted stop M 13
Lamp-rear licence plate M 10
Lamp-rear licence plate M 11
Lamp-rear reverse M 14
Lamp-rear reverse-12v M 16
Lamp-rear reverse-clear. M 15
Lash-adjuster B283
Latch assembly-front door-rh N187
Latch assembly-rear seat cushion-rh R 43
Latch assembly-tailgate N124
Latch assembly-tunnel console lid P 15
Latch assembly-tunnel console lid P 16
Latch assembly-tunnel console lid P 17
Latch-front door-rh N188
Latch-rear door-rh N193
Lead link-terminal post to diode M 82
Lead link-windscreen wiper motor-lhd M129
Lead-brake pad wear warning indicator M 70
Lead-earth bonding M 58
Lead-high tension ignition-no1 B353
Lead-high tension ignition-to number one B395
Lead-king ignition B353
Lead-link radio M121
Lead-link radio M123
Lead-link radio M125
Lead-link radio T 12
Lead-link-chassis harness to rear light M 20
Lead-link-diode to terminal box M 82
Lead-link-solenoid fuel shut off B 30
Lead-link-solenoid fuel shut off M 59
Lead-link-solenoid fuel shut off M 60
Lead-link-solenoid fuel shut off M 70
Lead-link-washer pump-service M135
Lens & body assy-front indicator M 6
Lens & body-rear indicator M 11
Lens & body-stop/tail M 11
Lens assembly-rear lamp M 10
Lens assembly-rear lamp-with number plate M 24
Lens-auxiliary lighting side repeater M 7
Lens-fog T 9
Lens-fog-rear-red M 14
Lens-fog-rear-red M 15
Lens-front direction indicator M 6
Lens-interior lamp M 17
Lens-lamp-side M 6
Lens-rear licence plate lamp M 10
Lens-replacement T 9
Lens-replacement-rally 1000 T 10
Lens-reverse-clear. M 14
Lens-reverse-clear. M 15
Level-carburettor throttle B 31
Level-carburettor throttle B128
Level-carburettor throttle B175
Level-carburettor throttle B333
Level-carburettor throttle B335
Level-carburettor throttle B336
Level-carburettor throttle B 77
Level-carburettor throttle G 12
Level-carburettor throttle G 13
Lever & grip assembly handbrake-rhd H 34
Lever assembly bell crank D 30
Lever assembly bell crank D 33
Lever assembly bell crank D 35
Lever assembly bell crank D 32
Lever assembly-carburettor accelerator pump J 51
Lever assembly-carburettor-rh B336
Lever assembly-gear selector manual C 37
Lever assembly-gear selector manual C 69
Lever assembly-gear selector manual C 25
Lever assembly-hand throttle B 34
Lever assembly-hand throttle B 81
Lever assembly-hand throttle G 10
Lever assembly-operating automatic C 84
Lever assembly-operating/selector automatic C 84
Lever assembly-rear protection-loadspace T 5
Lever assembly-selector selector mechanism C 73
Lever assembly-tailgate release N180
Lever assembly-throttle G 11
Lever assembly-throttle tbi B391
Lever handbrake H 36
Lever-bonnet release assembly N142
Lever-carburettor accelerator pump G 12
Lever-carburettor accelerator pump G 13
Lever-carburettor camshaft-lh B333
Lever-carburettor vacuum switch operating B 28
Lever-detent automatic transmission C 73
Lever-drop arm steering-rhd F 7
Lever-drop arm steering-rhd F 8
Lever-drop arm steering-rhd F 9
Lever-drop arm steering-rhd F 10
Lever-drop arm steering-rhd F 11
Lever-hand throttle G 11
Lever-handbrake cable relay G 11
Lever-lower manual transmission C 24
Lever-lower manual transmission C 69
Lever-operating automatic transmission- C 84
Lever-selector selector mechanism C 36
Lever-selector selector mechanism C 68
Lever-selector selector mechanism C 22
Lever-selector selector mechanism C 20
Lever-selector selector mechanism D 38
Lever-selector selector mechanism-reverse C 17
Lever-starting control B 28
Lever-starting control B 31
Lever-starting control B 77
Lever-throttle cam B335
Lever-throttle multi point injection B388
Lever-throttle multi point injection B391
Lever-tool kit nut cover removal E 55
Lever-transfer box D 30
Lever-transfer box D 34
Lever-transfer box-differential lock D 37
Lever-transfer box-differential lock D 39
Lever-transfer box-rubber mounted D 35
Lever-transmission brake D 42
Lever. J 51
Lid assembly-facia fuse box P 17
Lid assembly-locker N 39
Lid assembly-locker-centre N 39
Lid assembly-ventilator-dashboard-rh N 30
Lid immobiliser box N 38
Lid-air cleaner J 41
Lid-tool locker-rear forward facing seat N 38
Lid-tunnel console P 17
Lifting ring N 23
Light unit-headlamp-sealed beam-rhd M 1
Light unit-lhd-wipac-quartz halogen M 5
Light unit-rhd-wipac-quartz halogen M 3
Light unit-wagner-rhd-sealed beam M 2
Liner-carpet protection-loadspace T 22
Liner-front wheelarch-rh N 63
Link - locks-inner handle-rh N193
Link assembly-drag N180
Link assembly-lower-rear suspension E 61
Link assembly-rear suspension upper-rh E 62
Link door latch N194
Link intermediate N194
Link rod-bellcrank to actuator-with central N194
Link threaded-rh N188
Link threaded-rh N193
Link-adjuster alternator B357
Link-adjuster alternator B363
Link-adjuster alternator B364
Link-adjuster alternator B365
Link-adjuster alternator B366
Link-adjuster alternator-a127 alternator B188
Link-adjuster alternator-a127 alternator B227
Link-adjuster alternator-a133 alternator B 45
Link-adjuster alternator-a133 alternator B 95
Link-adjuster alternator-a133 alternator B142
Link-adjusting compressor B 40
Link-adjusting compressor B 87
Link-adjusting compressor B137
Link-adjusting compressor B184
Link-adjusting compressor B224
Link-carburettor/throttle connecting B 28
Link-carburettor/throttle connecting B 31
Link-carburettor/throttle connecting B128
Link-carburettor/throttle connecting B175
Link-carburettor/throttle connecting B335
Link-carburettor/throttle connecting B336
Link-carburettor/throttle connecting B 77
Link-front door lock/latch-external lock-rh N189
Link-front door sill button/latch N194
Link-front door sill button/latch N190
Link-front door sill button/latch-rh N187
Link-fusible-100 amp-blue. M 92
Link-fusible-air conditioning-in line M 80
Link-fusible-in line M 79
Link-load/tail door exterior release N196
Link-power assisted steering pump adjusting B341
Link-power assisted steering pump adjusting B342
Link-power assisted steering pump adjusting B343
Link-rear door crank/latch-with central door N194
Link-squab hinge-rh R 43
Link-transfer box differential lock connecting D 24
Link-transfer box differential lock connecting- D 21
Load stop adjustable-set of 4 T 18
Load/tail door assembly-spare wheel carrier N171
Load/tail door assembly-spare wheel carrier- N174
Location rear-seat cushion-front seat R 4
Location rear-seat cushion-front seat R 15
Location rear-seat cushion-front seat R 16
Location rear-seat cushion-front seat R 17
Location rear-seat cushion-front seat R 6
Location rear-seat cushion-front seat R 18
Location rear-seat cushion-front seat R 19
Location rear-seat cushion-front seat R 14
Lock & keys M 87
Lock & keys P 17
Lock & keys-1 barrel/2 keys J 15
Lock & keys-front door N186
Lock & keys-front door N187
Lock assembly-door N196
Lock assembly-steering column M 86
Lock set P 14
Lock set P 15
Lock set P 16
Lock strip N222
Lock-tailgate-basic-rh N122
Lock-tilt & remove sunroof frame N134
Locknut B178

Locknut B298
Locknut C 24
Locknut D 16
Locknut D 24
Locknut E 25
Locknut E 32
Locknut E 62
Locknut E 47
Locknut E 49
Locknut F 15
Locknut G 4
Locknut G 9
Locknut L 49
Locknut-10x32unf B335
Locknut-m10 B214
Locknut-m10 D 22
Locknut-m10 L 39
Locknut-m10 L 62
Locknut-m10 T 5
Locknut-reverse light switch-m10 M 14
Locknut-stub axle E 23
Loop-hood R 62
Loop-luggage tie down S 19
Lubricant U 2
Lubricant-aerosol U 2
Lubricant-silicone-aerosol-200ml U 1
Lug assembly-5th & reverse manual C 36
Lug-1st & 2nd manual transmission C 36
Lug-fixing-front seat R 61
Lug-reverse-manual transmission C 36
Luggage top box T 18
Magazine-automatic changer compact disc M126
Main floor centre assembly N 99
Mainshaft bearing D 14
Manifold assembly-engine exhaust B 25
Manifold assembly-engine exhaust-conical B 73
Manifold assembly-engine inlet B126
Manifold assembly-engine inlet B285
Manifold assembly-engine inlet B323
Manifold assembly-engine inlet B385
Manifold-engine exhaust B173
Manifold-engine exhaust B214
Manifold-engine exhaust B286
Manifold-engine exhaust-lh B251
Manifold-engine exhaust-lh B326
Manifold-engine exhaust-lh B327
Manifold-engine exhaust-olive end B126
Manifold-engine exhaust-rh B386
Manifold-engine inlet B 25
Manifold-engine inlet B 73
Manifold-engine inlet B173
Manifold-engine inlet B214
Manifold-engine inlet B251
Manifold-engine inlet B329
Manifold-engine inlet B385
Master cylinder assembly brake H 1
Master cylinder assembly brake H 3
Master cylinder assembly brake-anti-lock H 6
Master cylinder clutch G 4
Mat-centre console P 17
Mat-floor cover heel T 19
Mat-footwell set-intermediate-footwell T 19
Mat-front floor drop in-rh-rhd P 39
Mat-front floor drop in-rh-rhd P 69
Mat-front floor-front footwell.-pair T 19
Mat-intermediate floor-rubber P 46
Mat-loadspace P 48
Mat-loadspace T 23
Mat-loadspace-full-nylon T 22
Mat-rear bumper step N203
Mat-rear bumper step N204
Mat-rear floor drop in-cab floor P 49
Mat-rear floor drop in-rear-pair T 19
Matrix-evaporator-r134a automatic air L 51
Matrix-heater L 49
Matrix-heater L 50
Matrix-heater-with horizontal inlet/outlet L 35
Mechanism assembly-air vent operation N 30
Mechanism assembly-transfer box gear D 30
Mechanism assembly-transfer box gear D 33
Mechanism assembly-transfer box gear D 31
Member-rh-inner R 71
Micro switch n.c contacts C 84
Micro switch n.o contacts C 84
Mirror assembly-interior-non dipping N221
Mirror assembly-external head-convex N221
Modulator antilock brakes H 7
Module-distributor-3 pin B352
Module-warning light M119
Monitor unit- overspeed-black M109
Monobolt N 90
Monobolt N 92
Monobolt N124
Monobolt N 38
Monobolt R 66
Monobolt-1/4" N122
Monobolt-1/4" N147
Monobolt-1/4" R 69
Monobolt-3/16 dia T 14
Monobolt-stiffener to tailgate-1/4" N 41
Motor & bracket assembly-backlight wiper M144
Motor & bracket assembly-backlight wiper- M143
Motor and rotor assembly L 49
Motor blower-heater L 49
Motor blower-heater L 57
Motor-cooling fan condenser L 45
Motor-multi point injection stepping B388
Motor-multi point injection stepping B398
Motor-starter engine-bosch-new B369
Motor-starter engine-bosch-new B397
Motor-starter engine-exchange-bosch B145
Motor-starter engine-exchange-lucas B367
Motor-starter engine-new B297
Motor-starter engine-new-bosch B144
Motor-starter engine-new-bosch B190
Motor-starter engine-new-bosch B228
Motor-starter engine-new-bosch B262
Motor-starter engine-new-lucas B143
Motor-starter engine-new-lucas B368
Motor-starter engine-new-valeo B189
Motor-starter engine-new-valeo B229
Motor-starter engine-with m78r starter B 46
Motor-starter engine-with m78r starter B 96
Motor-vacuum-air con L 65
Motor-vacuum-air con L 66
Motor-vacuum-air con L 69
Motor-vacuum-air con L 70
Motor-vacuum-air con L 71
Motor-windscreen wiper M128
Moulding assembly-facia switch panel M 90
Moulding-centre console switch pack P 4
Moulding-facia stowage shelf-rhd P 4
Moulding-fuel tank J 5
Moulding-fuel tank J 6
Moulding-headlining-rear end P 56
Mount-radiator rubber L 3
Mount-radiator rubber L 4
Mount-radiator rubber L 2
Mounting assembly-bonnet lock N140
Mounting assembly-rear suspension E 69
Mounting-bonnet lock N140
Mounting-engine rubber B 8
Mounting-engine rubber B 57
Mounting-engine rubber B109
Mounting-engine rubber B158
Mounting-engine rubber B201
Mounting-engine rubber B377
Mounting-engine rubber N 13
Mounting-engine rubber N 14
Mounting-engine rubber N 15
Mounting-engine rubber N 16
Mounting-engine rubber-imperial C 38
Mounting-flexible-fan cowl L 5
Mounting-gearbox-rh N 18
Mounting-lower link flexible rubber E 61
Mounting-rear lamp-fog or reverse lamps N 94
Mounting-rubber J 1
Mounting-rubber J 3
Mounting-rubber J 7
Mounting-rubber J 8
Mounting-rubber J 10
Mounting-rubber J 13
Mounting-rubber J 40
Mounting-rubber J 41
Mounting-rubber J 44
Mounting-rubber J 75
Mounting-rubber J 42
Mounting-rubber J 77
Mounting-rubber L 4
Mounting-rubber exhaust system K 24
Mounting-rubber exhaust system-front & K 17
Mounting-rubber exhaust system-front & K 18
Mounting-rubber exhaust system-front & K 28
Mounting-rubber exhaust system-front & K 29
Mounting-rubber exhaust system-front & K 30
Mounting-rubber exhaust system-front & K 31
Mounting-rubber exhaust system-front & K 32
Mounting-rubber exhaust system-front & K 6
Mounting-rubber exhaust system-rear K 26
Mounting-rubber exhaust system-rear K 27
Mounting-rubber flexible support J 35
Mounting-rubber flexible support L 12
Mounting-rubber-rh N 17
Mounting-tailgate hinge N 7
Mudflap-rear T 53
Mudflap-rear-rh T 51
Mudflaps-front-pair T 51
Mudflaps-front-pair T 53
Mudguard-power take off T 5
Mudguard-power take off T 6
Mudshield-front & rear differential E 8
Mudshield-front & rear differential E 11
Mudshield-front & rear differential E 35
Mudshield-front & rear differential E 39
Mudshield-rear lamp N199
Mudshield-transfer box oil seal D 18
Mudshield-transfer box oil seal D 19
Needle & seat assembly-carburettor float B333
Needle assembly-carburettor jet B333
Needle-carburettor jet B332
Nipple-cable automatic transmission C 84
Nipple-grease S 10
Nipple-grease V 5
Nipple-grease-for propshaft universal joint- E 1
Nipple-grease-unf E 2
Nipple-grease-unf E 3
Nozzle-injection diesel B129
Nozzle-injection diesel B176
Nut B 36
Nut B 38
Nut B 39
Nut B 85
Nut B 86
Nut B132
Nut B134
Nut B135
Nut B140
Nut B173
Nut B182
Nut B183

Nut-hexagonal head-nyloc-m6 .... N170
Nut-hexagonal head-nyloc-m6 .... R 31
Nut-hexagonal head-nyloc-m6 .... R 45
Nut-hexagonal head-nyloc-m6 .... S 14
Nut-hexagonal head-nyloc-m6 .... S 15
Nut-hexagonal head-nyloc-m6 .... S 11
Nut-hexagonal head-nyloc-m6 .... T 14
Nut-hexagonal head-nyloc-m6 .... V 6
Nut-hexagonal-backrest to frame .... R 36
Nut-hexagonal-centre squab-m5 .... R 3
Nut-hexagonal-elbow to carb-m5 .... B 80
Nut-hexagonal-fixing facia plate-m5 .... M113
Nut-hexagonal-fog lamp-m5 .... M 14
Nut-hexagonal-gearbox to engine-m5 .... C 51
Nut-hexagonal-instrument cover-m5 .... M123
Nut-hexagonal-instrument cover-m5 .... M125
Nut-hexagonal-m12 .... N 28
Nut-hexagonal-m4 .... B 19
Nut-hexagonal-m4 .... B 67
Nut-hexagonal-m4 .... B244
Nut-hexagonal-m4 .... F 23
Nut-hexagonal-m4 .... J 50
Nut-hexagonal-m4 .... M 83
Nut-hexagonal-m4 .... M 84
Nut-hexagonal-m4 .... M119
Nut-hexagonal-m4 .... M116
Nut-hexagonal-m4 .... N 32
Nut-hexagonal-m4 .... N187
Nut-hexagonal-m4 .... N188
Nut-hexagonal-m4 .... N193
Nut-hexagonal-m4 .... N184
Nut-hexagonal-m4 .... N127
Nut-hexagonal-m4 .... P 1
Nut-hexagonal-m5 .... B128
Nut-hexagonal-m5 .... B175
Nut-hexagonal-m5 .... B178
Nut-hexagonal-m5 .... B218
Nut-hexagonal-m5 .... B 29
Nut-hexagonal-m5 .... F 4
Nut-hexagonal-m5 .... G 13
Nut-hexagonal-m5 .... H 36
Nut-hexagonal-m5 .... J 51
Nut-hexagonal-m5 .... L 3
Nut-hexagonal-m5 .... M 15
Nut-hexagonal-m5 .... M 16
Nut-hexagonal-m5 .... M109
Nut-hexagonal-m5 .... M120
Nut-hexagonal-m5 .... M 12
Nut-hexagonal-m5 .... M 63
Nut-hexagonal-m5 .... M 57
Nut-hexagonal-m5 .... M 58
Nut-hexagonal-m5 .... N132
Nut-hexagonal-m5 .... N163
Nut-hexagonal-m5 .... N182
Nut-hexagonal-m5 .... P 8
Nut-hexagonal-m5 .... P 2
Nut-hexagonal-m5 .... R 2
Nut-hexagonal-m5 .... R 37
Nut-hexagonal-m5 .... S 8
Nut-hexagonal-m5 .... S 9
Nut-hexagonal-m5 .... T 45
Nut-hexagonal-m5 .... T 46
Nut-hexagonal-nyloc .... E 61
Nut-hexagonal-nyloc .... F 8
Nut-hexagonal-nyloc .... F 10
Nut-hexagonal-nyloc-1/2unf .... F 8
Nut-hexagonal-nyloc-1/2unf .... F 10
Nut-hexagonal-nyloc-5/8unf .... E 56
Nut-hexagonal-nyloc-m20 .... D 18
Nut-hexagonal-nyloc-m20 .... D 19
Nut-hexagonal-nyloc-m5 .... D 33
Nut-hexagonal-nyloc-m5 .... D 36
Nut-hexagonal-nyloc-m5 .... D 31
Nut-hexagonal-nyloc-m5 .... L 39
Nut-hexagonal-nyloc-m5 .... L 62
Nut-hexagonal-nyloc-m5 .... M 13
Nut-hexagonal-nyloc-m5 .... N139
Nut-hexagonal-nyloc-m5 .... N239
Nut-hexagonal-nyloc-m5 .... N240
Nut-hexagonal-nyloc-m5 .... N242
Nut-hexagonal-nyloc-m5 .... N245
Nut-hexagonal-nyloc-m5 .... S 10
Nut-hexagonal-nyloc-m5 .... T 37
Nut-hexagonal-nyloc-m5 .... T 38
Nut-hexagonal-nyloc-m5 .... T 43
Nut-hexagonal-nyloc-m5 .... V 5
Nut-hexagonal-nyloc-m6 .... B354
Nut-hexagonal-nyloc-m6 .... B147
Nut-hexagonal-nyloc-m6 .... C 24
Nut-hexagonal-nyloc-m6 .... C 29
Nut-hexagonal-nyloc-m6 .... C 69
Nut-hexagonal-nyloc-m6 .... F 23
Nut-hexagonal-nyloc-m6 .... H 10
Nut-hexagonal-nyloc-m6 .... H 25
Nut-hexagonal-nyloc-m6 .... J 13
Nut-hexagonal-nyloc-m6 .... J 20
Nut-hexagonal-nyloc-m6 .... J 22
Nut-hexagonal-nyloc-m6 .... J 33
Nut-hexagonal-nyloc-m6 .... J 36
Nut-hexagonal-nyloc-m6 .... J 37
Nut-hexagonal-nyloc-m6 .... J 38
Nut-hexagonal-nyloc-m6 .... J 46
Nut-hexagonal-nyloc-m6 .... K 14
Nut-hexagonal-nyloc-m6 .... K 16
Nut-hexagonal-nyloc-m6 .... L 8
Nut-hexagonal-nyloc-m6 .... L 17
Nut-hexagonal-nyloc-m6 .... L 24
Nut-hexagonal-nyloc-m6 .... L 32
Nut-hexagonal-nyloc-m6 .... L 42
Nut-hexagonal-nyloc-m6 .... L 43
Nut-hexagonal-nyloc-m6 .... L 60
Nut-hexagonal-nyloc-m6 .... L 61
Nut-hexagonal-nyloc-m6 .... L 63
Nut-hexagonal-nyloc-m6 .... L 64
Nut-hexagonal-nyloc-m6 .... M 27
Nut-hexagonal-nyloc-m6 .... M 28
Nut-hexagonal-nyloc-m6 .... M 32
Nut-hexagonal-nyloc-m6 .... M130
Nut-hexagonal-nyloc-m6 .... M131
Nut-hexagonal-nyloc-m6 .... M135
Nut-hexagonal-nyloc-m6 .... M 46
Nut-hexagonal-nyloc-m6 .... N 39
Nut-hexagonal-nyloc-m6 .... N 41
Nut-hexagonal-nyloc-m6 .... N 44
Nut-hexagonal-nyloc-m6 .... N 49
Nut-hexagonal-nyloc-m6 .... N 53
Nut-hexagonal-nyloc-m6 .... N 67
Nut-hexagonal-nyloc-m6 .... N 93
Nut-hexagonal-nyloc-m6 .... N 95
Nut-hexagonal-nyloc-m6 .... N 97
Nut-hexagonal-nyloc-m6 .... N114
Nut-hexagonal-nyloc-m6 .... N115
Nut-hexagonal-nyloc-m6 .... N117
Nut-hexagonal-nyloc-m6 .... N118
Nut-hexagonal-nyloc-m6 .... N125
Nut-hexagonal-nyloc-m6 .... N133
Nut-hexagonal-nyloc-m6 .... N139
Nut-hexagonal-nyloc-m6 .... N142
Nut-hexagonal-nyloc-m6 .... N149
Nut-hexagonal-nyloc-m6 .... N181
Nut-hexagonal-nyloc-m6 .... N187
Nut-hexagonal-nyloc-m6 .... N191
Nut-hexagonal-nyloc-m6 .... N192
Nut-hexagonal-nyloc-m6 .... N196
Nut-hexagonal-nyloc-m6 .... N198
Nut-hexagonal-nyloc-m6 .... N239
Nut-hexagonal-nyloc-m6 .... N243
Nut-hexagonal-nyloc-m6 .... N246
Nut-hexagonal-nyloc-m6 .... N 34
Nut-hexagonal-nyloc-m6 .... N 96
Nut-hexagonal-nyloc-m6 .... N 99
Nut-hexagonal-nyloc-m6 .... N126
Nut-hexagonal-nyloc-m6 .... N129
Nut-hexagonal-nyloc-m6 .... N131
Nut-hexagonal-nyloc-m6 .... N161
Nut-hexagonal-nyloc-m6 .... N169
Nut-hexagonal-nyloc-m6 .... N197
Nut-hexagonal-nyloc-m6 .... N 37
Nut-hexagonal-nyloc-m6 .... N 38
Nut-hexagonal-nyloc-m6 .... N 58
Nut-hexagonal-nyloc-m6 .... N179
Nut-hexagonal-nyloc-m6 .... R 15
Nut-hexagonal-nyloc-m6 .... R 29
Nut-hexagonal-nyloc-m6 .... R 44
Nut-hexagonal-nyloc-m6 .... R 51
Nut-hexagonal-nyloc-m6 .... R 63
Nut-hexagonal-nyloc-m6 .... R 66
Nut-hexagonal-nyloc-m6 .... R 68
Nut-hexagonal-nyloc-m6 .... R 37
Nut-hexagonal-nyloc-m6 .... R 40
Nut-hexagonal-nyloc-m6 .... S 4
Nut-hexagonal-nyloc-m6 .... S 12
Nut-hexagonal-nyloc-m6 .... T 45
Nut-hexagonal-nyloc-m6 .... T 46
Nut-hexagonal-nyloc-m6 .... T 48
Nut-hexagonal-nyloc-m6 .... T 53
Nut-hexagonal-solid prop-m4 .... N143
Nut-hexagonal-thin .... E 20
Nut-hexagonal-thin-5/16unf B308
Nut-hexagonal-thin-5/16unf B309
Nut-hexagonal-thin-5/16unf B363
Nut-hexagonal-thin-5/16unf B364
Nut-hexagonal-thin-5/16unf .... G 4
Nut-hexagonal-thin-7/16unf .... G 5
Nut-hexagonal-thin-m12 .... E 22
Nut-hexagonal-thin-m12 .... E 19
Nut-hexagonal-thin-m12 .... G 3
Nut-hexagonal-thin-m12 .... H 25
Nut-hexagonal-thin-m12 .... S 10
Nut-hexagonal-thin-m12 .... V 5
Nut-hinge to tailgate N122
Nut-locking B208
Nut-locking B245
Nut-locking-alloy road wheels-code a .... E 55
Nut-locking-m8 .... B293
Nut-locking-m8 .... K 28
Nut-locking-m8 .... K 29
Nut-locking-m8 .... K 31
Nut-locking-m8 .... K 33
Nut-locking-m8 .... N174
Nut-locking-manifold to block-m8 .... B286
Nut-lokut .... F 1
Nut-lokut .... L 72
Nut-lokut .... L 34
Nut-lokut .... M 6
Nut-lokut .... M 11
Nut-lokut .... M 18
Nut-lokut M120
Nut-lokut M127
Nut-lokut .... N 30
Nut-lokut .... N 44
Nut-lokut N145
Nut-lokut N159
Nut-lokut N187
Nut-lokut N193
Nut-lokut .... N 31
Nut-lokut .... N 34
Nut-lokut N146
Nut-lokut N184
Nut-lokut N189

Nut-lokut N194
Nut-lokut .... N 37
Nut-lokut .... N 61
Nut-lokut N162
Nut-lokut .... N 48
Nut-lokut .... N 57
Nut-lokut .... P 1
Nut-lokut .... P 4
Nut-lokut .... P 7
Nut-lokut .... P 8
Nut-lokut .... P 25
Nut-lokut .... P 2
Nut-lokut .... P 10
Nut-lokut .... P 30
Nut-lokut .... T 47
Nut-lokut .... T 48
Nut-lokut-antenna M124
Nut-lokut-antenna M123
Nut-lokut-front plate to dash .... N 32
Nut-lokut-grey .... P 21
Nut-lokut-grey .... P 20
Nut-lokut-headlamp to body .... M 1
Nut-lokut-headlamp to body .... M 5
Nut-lokut-headlamp to body .... M 4
Nut-lokut-instrument cover M125
Nut-lokut-rh nozzle .... L 75
Nut-lower-hexagonal-nyloc-1/2unf .... E 58
Nut-m10 .... K 1
Nut-m10 .... K 2
Nut-m10 .... K 11
Nut-m10 .... K 26
Nut-m10 .... K 27
Nut-m10-flanged head B240
Nut-m10-flanged head .... J 3
Nut-m12-hexagonal .... E 65
Nut-m12-hexagonal .... E 66
Nut-m16 .... S 10
Nut-m16 .... T 3
Nut-m16 .... V 5
Nut-m16-hexagonal head .... N 24
Nut-m16-hexagonal head .... T 37
Nut-m16-hexagonal head .... T 38
Nut-m6 .... P 3
Nut-m6-hexagonal .... F 19
Nut-m8 .... B177
Nut-m8 .... B218
Nut-m8 .... C 84
Nut-m8 .... K 5
Nut-m8 .... K 28
Nut-m8 .... K 29
Nut-m8 .... K 30
Nut-m8 .... K 6
Nut-m8 .... N 25
Nut-m8 .... N138
Nut-manifold to head-hexagonal head-m8 .... B 25
Nut-manifold to head-hexagonal head-m8 .... B 73
Nut-mudflap attachment-hexagonal-nyloc- .... T 51
Nut-mudflap attachment-hexagonal-nyloc- .... T 52
Nut-narrow .... F 18
Nut-no10-unf B336
Nut-nyloc-m8 .... B 95
Nut-nyloc-m8 .... B112
Nut-nyloc-m8 .... B128
Nut-nyloc-m8 .... B142
Nut-nyloc-m8 .... B161
Nut-nyloc-m8 .... B175
Nut-nyloc-m8 .... B188
Nut-nyloc-m8 .... B227
Nut-nyloc-m8 .... B309
Nut-nyloc-m8 .... D 36
Nut-nyloc-m8 .... D 37
Nut-nyloc-m8 .... D 38
Nut-nyloc-m8 .... D 39
Nut-nyloc-m8 .... D 21
Nut-nyloc-m8 .... F 6
Nut-nyloc-m8 .... G 2
Nut-nyloc-m8 .... G 4
Nut-nyloc-m8 .... H 3
Nut-nyloc-m8 .... H 19
Nut-nyloc-m8 .... J 1
Nut-nyloc-m8 .... J 8
Nut-nyloc-m8 .... J 17
Nut-nyloc-m8 .... L 12
Nut-nyloc-m8 .... N 11
Nut-nyloc-m8 .... N 16
Nut-nyloc-m8 .... N 43
Nut-nyloc-m8 .... N124
Nut-nyloc-m8 .... N151
Nut-nyloc-m8 .... N201
Nut-nyloc-m8 .... R 5
Nut-nyloc-m8 .... R 28
Nut-nyloc-m8 .... S 8
Nut-nyloc-m8 .... S 9
Nut-nyloc-m8 .... S 13
Nut-pintle to crossmember-hexagonal head- .... T 34
Nut-pintle to crossmember-hexagonal-m12 .... T 35
Nut-plastic N204
Nut-plate M128
Nut-plate N192
Nut-plate N195
Nut-plate .... R 16
Nut-plate .... R 31
Nut-plate .... R 70
Nut-plate .... R 6
Nut-plate .... R 21
Nut-plate .... R 14
Nut-retaining N145
Nut-rivet-steel N140
Nut-rivet-steel-m10-hexagonal .... J 5
Nut-rivet-steel-m10-hexagonal .... J 6
Nut-rivet-steel-m10-hexagonal N203
Nut-rubber to foot-hexagonal head-coarse .... B 8
Nut-rubber to foot-hexagonal head-coarse .... B 57
Nut-rubber to foot-hexagonal head-coarse B201
Nut-seat frame to wheelarch-hexagonal- .... R 36
Nut-shield to manifold-hexagonal head-m8 .... B 27
Nut-sill panel to outer wing-hexagonal- .... N 46
Nut-spacer fixings-hexagonal-nyloc-m6 .... M 29
Nut-special .... B 93
Nut-special spigot .... B 83
Nut-spiralok .... J 67
Nut-spiralok .... N 39
Nut-spiralok .... N 44
Nut-spiralok N132
Nut-spiralok .... N 99
Nut-spiralok N129
Nut-spiralok N131
Nut-spiralok .... N 57
Nut-spiralok .... P 33
Nut-spiralok-drivers & passenger squab .... R 3
Nut-spire .... P 4
Nut-spring-flat .... N 57
Nut-spring-flat-cover grommet fixing-with .... P 24
Nut-spring-flat-with rear wash/wipe .... M 75
Nut-spring-flat-with rear wash/wipe .... P 23
Nut-spring-flat-with rear wash/wipe .... P 11
Nut-spring-u type .... L 38
Nut-spring-u type .... M 6
Nut-spring-u type M143
Nut-spring-u type .... N 57
Nut-spring-u type-no 6 .... M 32
Nut-spring-u type-no 6 .... P 2
Nut-spring-u type-no 6 .... P 12
Nut-spring-u type-no 8 .... P 7
Nut-spring-u type-rh nozzle .... L 75
Nut-spring-u type-wiper motor fixing .... P 23
Nut-spring-u type-wiper motor fixing .... P 24
Nut-square N240
Nut-square N242
Nut-square N245
Nut-stake .... C 20
Nut-stake-man trans countershaft .... C 16
Nut-stake-man trans countershaft .... C 66
Nut-starter to flywheel-hexagonal head- B189
Nut-steering wheel-1/2"-unf-imperial .... F 1
Nut-support to capping-hexagonal-nyloc- .... R 33
Nut-throttle spindle multi point injection B388
Nut-throttle spindle multi point injection B391
Nut-towing hook to crossmember- .... T 33
Nut-towing jaw to rear crossmember- .... T 32
Nut-tube-female .... L 29
Nut-tube-female-m12 .... J 19
Nut-tube-female-m12 .... J 20
Nut-tube-female-m12 .... J 21
Nut-tube-female-m12 .... J 25
Nut-tube-female-m12 .... J 28
Nut-tube-female-m12 .... J 50
Nut-tube-female-m12 .... J 4
Nut-tube-female-m12 .... J 27
Nut-tube-female-m12 .... J 30
Nut-unf B303
Nut-unf B320
Nut-unf .... M 10
Nut-windscreen wiper special M129
Nut-wing .... J 33
Nut-wing .... J 36
Nut-wing .... J 38
Nut-wing .... J 39
Nut-wing .... S 14
Nut-wing .... S 15
Nut-wing .... S 16
Nut-wing-m6 .... M 27
Nutsert-blind .... E 69
Nutsert-blind .... F 23
Nutsert-blind .... J 36
Nutsert-blind .... J 37
Nutsert-blind .... L 22
Nutsert-blind .... L 26
Nutsert-blind .... L 27
Nutsert-blind .... L 29
Nutsert-blind .... N 52
Nutsert-blind-8mm .... N 28
Nutsert-blind-for seat runner to seat base .... R 14
Nutsert-blind-hexagonal-m8 .... N 9
Nutsert-blind-m5-black .... M 12
Nutsert-blind-m5-black .... N 30
Nutsert-blind-m6 .... C 86
Nutsert-blind-m6 .... F 25
Nutsert-blind-m6 .... F 27
Nutsert-blind-m6 .... J 51
Nutsert-blind-m6 .... M131
Nutsert-blind-m6 .... M135
Nutsert-blind-m6 .... N 93
Nutsert-blind-m6 .... N141
Nutsert-blind-m6 .... N 58
Nutsert-blind-m6 .... P 14
Nutsert-blind-m6 .... P 15
Nutsert-blind-m6 .... P 16
Nutsert-blind-m6 .... P 17
Nutsert-blind-m6 .... P 33
Nutsert-blind-m6 .... R 35
Nutsert-blind-m6 .... R 28
Nutsert-blind-m6 .... T 51
Nutsert-blind-m6 .... T 53
Nutsert-blind-m6 .... T 52
Nutsert-m5 .... P 10
Nutsert-m6 .... T 27
O ring .... B 7
O ring .... B 15
O ring .... B 17

O ring ... B 18
O ring ... B 31
O ring ... B 38
O ring ... B 39
O ring ... B 47
O ring ... B 52
O ring ... B 56
O ring ... B 63
O ring ... B 65
O ring ... B 66
O ring ... B 76
O ring ... B 85
O ring ... B 86
O ring ... B104
O ring ... B108
O ring ... B115
O ring ... B116
O ring ... B117
O ring ... B122
O ring ... B123
O ring ... B124
O ring ... B131
O ring ... B134
O ring ... B135
O ring ... B146
O ring ... B153
O ring ... B157
O ring ... B164
O ring ... B165
O ring ... B170
O ring ... B171
O ring ... B177
O ring ... B180
O ring ... B182
O ring ... B183
O ring ... B200
O ring ... B205
O ring ... B206
O ring ... B211
O ring ... B212
O ring ... B220
O ring ... B222
O ring ... B223
O ring ... B243
O ring ... B248
O ring ... B250
O ring ... B279
O ring ... B287
O ring ... B288
O ring ... B291
O ring ... B303
O ring ... B320
O ring ... B334
O ring ... B346
O ring ... B347
O ring ... B350
O ring ... B352
O ring ... B377
O ring ... B378
O ring ... B383
O ring ... B385
O ring ... B398
O ring ... B 64
O ring ... C 26
O ring ... C 30
O ring ... C 68
O ring ... C 73
O ring ... C 75
O ring ... C 82
O ring ... C 83
O ring ... C 84
O ring ... C 86
O ring ... C 22
O ring ... C 34
O ring ... C 56
O ring ... D 7
O ring ... D 10
O ring ... D 15
O ring ... D 17
O ring ... D 19
O ring ... D 20
O ring ... D 29
O ring ... D 30
O ring ... D 33
O ring ... D 35
O ring ... D 5
O ring ... D 16
O ring ... D 21
O ring ... D 24
O ring ... D 34
O ring ... D 9
O ring ... D 32
O ring ... D 28
O ring ... E 21
O ring ... F 24
O ring ... F 26
O ring ... J 33
O ring ... J 35
O ring ... J 36
O ring ... J 37
O ring ... J 52
O ring ... J 58
O ring ... L 3
O ring ... L 16
O ring ... L 23
O ring ... L 25
O ring ... L 26
O ring ... L 28
O ring ... L 29
O ring ... L 31
O ring ... L 50
O ring ... L 2
O ring ... M 8
O ring ... M108
O ring ... T 5
O ring air conditioning ... B 38
O ring air conditioning ... B 39
O ring air conditioning ... B 85
O ring air conditioning ... B 86
O ring air conditioning ... B134
O ring air conditioning ... B135
O ring air conditioning ... B182
O ring air conditioning ... B183
O ring air conditioning ... B222
O ring air conditioning ... B223
O ring air conditioning ... B346
O ring air conditioning ... B347
O ring air conditioning ... L 51
O ring air conditioning ... L 78
O ring air conditioning ... L 79
O ring-11.2mm od-7.6mm id-1.8mm thick- ... L 54
O ring-15.7mm od-10.9mm id-2.4mm thick ... L 77
O ring-8mm od-4.5mm id-1.8mm thick ... L 52
O ring-auto trans strainer to control unit ... C 74
O ring-breather ... B 70
O ring-breather combined ... B 22
O ring-collar ... C 7
O ring-collar ... C 8
O ring-crankshaft to toothed pulley ... B235
O ring-dipstick tube ... B272
O ring-dipstick tube assembly to engine ... B237
O ring-interlock retainer ... C 23
O ring-large ... B340
O ring-less cfc free refrigerant ... L 45
O ring-less cfc free refrigerant-no 10- ... L 58
O ring-man trans thermostat housing ... C 55
O ring-oil pump seal ... C 55
O ring-oil suction pipe seal ... B237
O ring-oil suction pipe seal ... B271
O ring-pas box to return hose-6mm ... F 25
O ring-pas box to return hose-6mm ... F 27
O ring-pump to steering box ... F 22
O ring-radiator filler plug ... L 1
O ring-small ... B387
O ring-suction ... B295
O ring-transfer box intermediate shaft ... D 40
O ring-transmission oil cooler hose ... C 70
Oil cooler assembly transmission ... C 70
Oil cooler assembly transmission ... C 86
Oil cooler assembly transmission ... L 24
Oil cooler assembly transmission ... L 25
Oil cooler assembly-engine-diesel ... B291
Oil cooler-engine ... L 32
Oil-525 visc ... B 39
Oil-525 visc ... B 86
Oil-525 visc ... B135
Oil-525 visc ... B183
Oil-525 visc ... B223
Oil-525 visc ... B347
Oil-shpd-1ltr ... U 2
Olive ... B200
Olive ... B330
Olive ... B331
Olive ... B333
Olive ... F 13
Olive ... J 19
Olive ... J 20
Olive ... J 25
Olive ... J 28
Olive ... J 4
Olive ... K 25
Olive-exhaust downpipe ... K 3
Olive-exhaust pipe joint flange ... K 5
Olive-exhaust pipe joint flange ... K 12
Olive-exhaust pipe joint flange ... K 14
Olive-exhaust pipe joint flange ... K 24
Olive-exhaust pipe joint flange-rear ... K 9
Olive-exhaust pipe joint flange-rear ... K 10
Olive-exhaust pipe joint flange-rear ... K 22
Olive-exhaust pipe joint flange-rear ... K 23
Olive-fuel tank pipe ... J 21
Olive-fuel tank pipe ... J 50
Olive-fuel tank pipe ... J 27
Olive-fuel tank pipe ... J 30
Olive-intermediate pipe to rear pipe ... K 2
Outrigger assembly-rh-no1-front ... N 10
Overlay-front seat squab centre-cloth ... R 15
Overlay-front seat squab-cloth ... R 4
Overlay-seat-front-cushion-centre-cloth ... R 15
Overlay-seat-front-cushion-centre-cloth ... R 16
Packing piece ... N100
Packing piece ... N123
Packing rubber-drivers & passenger squab ... R 3
Packing strip ... B195
Packing strip ... B233
Packing strip ... F 3
Packing strip ... F 2
Packing strip ... N 7
Pad mounting-rear floor ... N 90
Pad mounting-rear floor-5.0mm ... N 95
Pad mounting-rear floor-5.0mm ... N 97
Pad mounting-rear floor-5.0mm ... N 98
Pad steering wheel-plastic ... F 1
Pad-5th gear selector fork ... C 23
Pad-acoustic ... N 25
Pad-adhesive-to cab stiffeners ... N 43
Pad-anti rattle ... N164
Pad-anti rattle ... S 2
Pad-anti rattle ... V 9
Pad-buffer ... C 36

Pad-buffer ... F 13
Pad-buffer ... F 14
Pad-buffer-reverse gear ... C 17
Pad-clutch release lever slipper ... C 3
Pad-clutch release lever slipper ... C 41
Pad-clutch release lever slipper ... C 42
Pad-dash insulation ... P 26
Pad-dash insulation-dash vent ... P 50
Pad-detachable-key radio ... M124
Pad-detachable-key radio ... M126
Pad-engine acoustic ... N 25
Pad-facia crash assembly-black ... P 1
Pad-front door casing insulation ... N153
Pad-front floor insulation-lh ... P 50
Pad-front footwell insulation-lhd ... P 39
Pad-front seat pan insulation-rh ... P 42
Pad-front seat pan insulation-rh ... R 12
Pad-front seat pan insulation-rhd ... P 43
Pad-heelboard insulation-centre-rhd ... P 50
Pad-insulation ... B 8
Pad-insulation ... B 57
Pad-insulation ... B103
Pad-insulation ... B153
Pad-insulation ... B279
Pad-insulation ... B287
Pad-insulation ... L 70
Pad-insulation ... M 17
Pad-insulation ... N 34
Pad-insulation ... N129
Pad-insulation ... N131
Pad-insulation ... P 17
Pad-insulation bonnet ... P 34
Pad-insulation-air duct-top ... L 67
Pad-insulation-fuel tank ... J 5
Pad-insulation-fuel tank ... J 6
Pad-insulation-rh-black ... P 42
Pad-insulation-seatbase covers ... N 40
Pad-insulation-swivel ... C 36
Pad-insulation-toebox-lh-rhd ... P 50
Pad-lever-pedal ... G 1
Pad-lever-pedal ... G 2
Pad-lever-pedal ... G 7
Pad-lever-pedal ... G 8
Pad-lever-pedal ... G 9
Pad-mid floor insulation-lh ... P 50
Pad-reverse gear selector lever ... C 20
Pad-roof rack rail assembly ... N137
Pad-rubber ... M128
Pad-rubber ... N137
Pad-rubber ... R 28
Pad-tunnel insulation-rh ... P 50
Padding-rear squab face panel-2 seat ... R 36
Padding-rh ... N252
Paint-aerosol spray-alpine white-solid- ... W 3
Paint-aerosol spray-davas white-ivory- ... W 4
Paint-pencil-alpine white-solid-(lrc456) ... W 1
Paint-pencil-county red-trocadero red- ... W 2
Pan assembly-oil transmission case- ... C 74
Panel assembly-bodyside trim-front ... N 68
Panel assembly-bodyside trim-front ... N 72
Panel assembly-bodyside trim-front ... N 69
Panel assembly-bodyside trim-front ... N 73
Panel assembly-bodyside trim-front ... N 70
Panel assembly-bodyside trim-front ... N 74
Panel assembly-bodyside trim-front ... N 71
Panel assembly-bodyside trim-front-front ... N 84
Panel assembly-bodyside trim-front-front ... N 85
Panel assembly-bodyside trim-front-rear ... N 79
Panel assembly-bodyside trim-front-rear ... N 80
Panel assembly-bodyside trim-front-rear ... N 81
Panel assembly-bodyside trim-front-rear ... N 82
Panel assembly-bodyside trim-front-rear ... N 83
Panel assembly-bodyside trim-front-rear ... N 86
Panel assembly-electrical equipment ... N 37
Panel assembly-fender side-rh ... N 56
Panel assembly-switch mounting-rhd ... P 11
Panel battery tray-split charge ... M 29
Panel closing-rhd ... P 12
Panel cover-rear lamps-rh ... N 51
Panel extension-rh ... N 98
Panel extension-rh ... N101
Panel header roof ... N237
Panel header roof ... V 3
Panel outer-rear ... N 65
Panel rear quarter-glazed-rh ... N222
Panel rear quarter-lh ... N 48
Panel side -hard top-glazed-rh ... N222
Panel trim-windscreen-rh-ash grey ... P 68
Panel waterdam-rh ... N170
Panel-air flow divider ... N 31
Panel-back-seat-front-squab-brushwood ... R 15
Panel-blanking-headlining-ripple grey ... P 63
Panel-bodyside trim-rh-mid grey ... P 54
Panel-bodyside-end and side window ... N102
Panel-bodyside-end and side window ... N106
Panel-bodyside-rh ... N 75
Panel-bodyside-rh ... N 87
Panel-bodyside-rh ... N 76
Panel-bodyside-rh ... N 88
Panel-bodyside-rh ... N 77
Panel-bodyside-rh ... N 78
Panel-extension-rh ... N 40
Panel-facia ... L 71
Panel-facia-rhd-less air conditioning-black ... P 1
Panel-facia-rhd-less air conditioning-dark ... P 3
Panel-facia-rhd-less air conditioning-vince ... P 3
Panel-fender front-rh ... N 54
Panel-fender front-rh ... N 55
Panel-front door facing-rh ... N153
Panel-front end trim plenum closing ... L 69
Panel-front seat squab face-brushwood ... R 4
Panel-headlamp mounting-rh ... N 54
Panel-headlamp mounting-rh ... N 55
Panel-inner-rh ... N 93
Panel-inner-rh ... N154
Panel-inner-side-rh ... N164
Panel-instrument mounting ... M119
Panel-instrument mounting-rhd ... P 7
Panel-lower rear trim ... P 65
Panel-lower rear trim-ripple grey ... P 66
Panel-main floor-front-rh ... N 44
Panel-rear end-rh ... N 68
Panel-rear end-rh ... N 72
Panel-rear end-rh ... N 75
Panel-rear end-rh ... N 79
Panel-rear end-rh ... N 87
Panel-rear end-rh ... N 69
Panel-rear end-rh ... N 73
Panel-rear end-rh ... N 76
Panel-rear end-rh ... N 80
Panel-rear end-rh ... N 88
Panel-rear end-rh ... N 70
Panel-rear end-rh ... N 74
Panel-rear end-rh ... N 77
Panel-rear end-rh ... N 81
Panel-rear end-rh ... N 71
Panel-rear end-rh ... N 78
Panel-rear end-rh ... N 82
Panel-rear end-rh ... N 83
Panel-rear end-rh ... N 84
Panel-rear end-rh ... N 85
Panel-rear end-rh ... N 86
Panel-rear seat squab main face ... R 36
Panel-rear seat squab main face ... R 39
Panel-rubber ... P 30
Panel-seat base ... R 30
Panel-seat base ... R 35
Panel-splash-vent-grille-lh ventilator ... N 30
Panel-sunroof glass lid ... N134
Panel-sunroof glass lid ... N135
Panel-sunroof glass lid ... N136
Panel-switch-housing ... M 32
Panel-switches mounting ... L 74
Panel-toe box ... P 30
Panel-valance-front-rh ... N 93
Parcel shelf-front-rhd ... P 11
Pawl-parklock automatic transmission ... C 83
Pedal assembly accelerator ... G 1
Pedal assembly clutch ... G 8
Pedal assembly clutch-rhd ... G 7
Pedal assembly-brake ... G 9
Pedal box ... G 9
Peg locating ... B118
Peg locating ... B166
Peg-air cleaner mtg-engine ... B323
Penthouse vent-radiator-cooling ... L 2
Pillar-cylinder head rocker support ... B319
Pillar-cylinder head rocker support ... B382
Pillar-rear body-lower ... N 92
Pin ... C 24
Pin ... C 36
Pin ... C 69
Pin ... D 36
Pin ... D 37
Pin ... D 38
Pin ... D 39
Pin ... E 21
Pin ... E 60
Pin ... E 68
Pin ... G 7
Pin ... G 8
Pin ... G 9
Pin ... G 11
Pin ... H 1
Pin ... H 36
Pin ... J 34
Pin ... J 51
Pin ... L 37
Pin ... N 30
Pin ... T 5
Pin ... T 39
Pin assembly-clevis ... G 3
Pin assembly-clevis ... H 36
Pin assembly-clevis ... N125
Pin assembly-clevis ... N218
Pin-38mm ... N 98
Pin-42mm ... N 95
Pin-42mm ... N 97
Pin-anti rotation-3.00mm ... C 34
Pin-centre squab ... R 2
Pin-clevis ... C 36
Pin-clevis ... D 37
Pin-clevis ... D 38
Pin-clevis ... D 39
Pin-clevis ... G 9
Pin-clevis/pivot ... D 30
Pin-clevis/pivot ... D 33
Pin-clevis/pivot ... D 35
Pin-clevis/pivot ... D 36
Pin-clevis/pivot ... D 37
Pin-clevis/pivot ... D 38
Pin-clevis/pivot ... D 39
Pin-clevis/pivot ... D 32
Pin-clevis/pivot ... G 3
Pin-clevis/pivot ... G 10
Pin-clevis/pivot ... N180
Pin-clevis/pivot ... N181
Pin-clevis/pivot ... N158
Pin-clevis/pivot ... T 5
Pin-clevis/pivot-5th fork ... C 36

Pin-clevis/pivot-5th gear fork ..... C 23
Pin-clevis/pivot-8 x 22mm ..... H 34
Pin-clevis/pivot-8 x 22mm ..... H 36
Pin-clevis/pivot-new starter motor-with ..... B 96
Pin-clevis/pivot-scissor prop N143
Pin-clevis/pivot-with 2m100 starter motor ..... B 46
Pin-locating ..... C 37
Pin-locking ..... T 35
Pin-locking-anti rotation-5.0mm ..... C 34
Pin-lower ..... E 20
Pin-piston gudgeon ..... B 6
Pin-piston gudgeon ..... B 55
Pin-piston gudgeon B199
Pin-piston gudgeon B236
Pin-reverse gear selector lever pivot ..... C 4
Pin-reverse gear selector lever pivot ..... C 5
Pin-reverse gear selector lever pivot ..... C 17
Pin-reverse gear selector lever pivot ..... C 20
Pin-roll B350
Pin-roll B351
Pin-roll B352
Pin-roll ..... C 24
Pin-roll ..... C 17
Pin-roll ..... C 20
Pin-roll ..... E 12
Pin-roll ..... E 42
Pin-roll-roll ..... C 69
Pin-roll-spring tension B205
Pin-roll-spring tension B254
Pin-roll-spring tension B373
Pin-roll-spring tension ..... C 73
Pin-roll-spring tension ..... E 7
Pin-roll-spring tension ..... E 9
Pin-roll-spring tension ..... E 33
Pin-roll-spring tension ..... E 36
Pin-roll-spring tension ..... E 34
Pin-roll-spring tension ..... E 37
Pin-selector lever/shaft manual transmission ..... C 21
Pin-selector lever/shaft manual transmission ..... C 68
Pin-selector manual transmission ..... C 68
Pin-spirol ..... C 44
Pin-split B319
Pin-split B382
Pin-split ..... C 36
Pin-split ..... C 84
Pin-split ..... D 36
Pin-split ..... D 37
Pin-split ..... D 38
Pin-split ..... D 39
Pin-split ..... D 34
Pin-split ..... D 22
Pin-split ..... E 62
Pin-split ..... E 8
Pin-split ..... E 11
Pin-split ..... E 35
Pin-split ..... E 39
Pin-split ..... G 3
Pin-split ..... G 9
Pin-split ..... G 10
Pin-split ..... H 34
Pin-split ..... H 36
Pin-split N121
Pin-split N125
Pin-split N180
Pin-split N181
Pin-split N188
Pin-split N193
Pin-split N218
Pin-split ..... N 50
Pin-split N158
Pin-split ..... T 5
Pin-split-3.2 x 25 ..... E 60
Pin-split-3.2 x 32 ..... E 68
Pin-split-3.2 x 32 ..... F 17
Pin-split-scissor prop N143
Pin-spring B304
Pin-spring B310
Pin-spring ..... C 55
Pin-spring ..... C 64
Pin-spring ..... C 68
Pin-spring ..... C 69
Pin-spring ..... C 84
Pin-spring ..... C 25
Pin-spring ..... G 1
Pin-spring ..... L 29
Pin-spring N238
Pin-spring-quadrant to shaft ..... C 22
Pin-spring-top cover ..... C 37
Pin-tensioner pivot B202
Pin-timing chain guide B274
Pin-towing pintle ..... T 29
Pin-towing pintle ..... T 35
Pin-upper swivel ..... E 20
Pinion primary ..... C 10
Pipe B323
Pipe ..... J 67
Pipe - fuel injection-no1 ..... B129
Pipe - fuel injection-no1 ..... B176
Pipe assembly brake ..... H 19
Pipe assembly brake ..... J 46
Pipe assembly brake-g valve ..... H 10
Pipe assembly brake-master cylinder to jump ..... H 16
Pipe assembly brake-master cylinder to pcrv ..... H 12
Pipe assembly brake-master cylinder to pcrv ..... H 13
Pipe assembly brake-master cylinder to valve ..... H 14
Pipe assembly brake-primary-rhd ..... H 11
Pipe assembly brake-rear-rh ..... H 22
Pipe assembly brake-rear-rh ..... H 24
Pipe assembly brake-rh ..... H 17
Pipe assembly brake-rh ..... H 18
Pipe assembly brake-rh ..... H 23
Pipe assembly brake-valve to rear ..... H 21
Pipe assembly clutch ..... C 44
Pipe assembly clutch ..... G 5
Pipe assembly clutch-rhd ..... G 4
Pipe assembly power assisted steering-rhd ..... F 14
Pipe assembly power assisted steering- ..... F 13
Pipe assembly turbocharger oil feed B177
Pipe assembly-canister to separator ..... J 66
Pipe assembly-coolant B290
Pipe assembly-coolant to heater ..... L 61
Pipe assembly-coolant to heater ..... L 64
Pipe assembly-coolant to heater-rhd ..... L 42
Pipe assembly-coolant to heater-rhd ..... L 43
Pipe assembly-coolant to heater-rhd ..... L 60
Pipe assembly-coolant to heater-rhd ..... L 63
Pipe assembly-coolant-feed ..... L 29
Pipe assembly-cooler to filter oil-rh-front ..... L 22
Pipe assembly-crankcase breather oil B303
Pipe assembly-engine coolant-diesel B241
Pipe assembly-engine coolant-diesel B250
Pipe assembly-engine oil feed ..... B 19
Pipe assembly-engine oil feed ..... B 67
Pipe assembly-engine oil feed B119
Pipe assembly-engine oil feed B167
Pipe assembly-engine oil feed B178
Pipe assembly-engine oil feed B218
Pipe assembly-engine oil feed ..... L 26
Pipe assembly-evap/vs to canister ..... L 51
Pipe assembly-exhaust gas recirculation ..... J 76
Pipe assembly-heater ..... L 16
Pipe assembly-heater feed B385
Pipe assembly-intercooler turbocharger ..... L 12
Pipe assembly-intercooler-metal ..... L 13
Pipe assembly-oil cooler to transmission ..... C 70
Pipe assembly-oil cooler to transmission ..... C 86
Pipe assembly-oil cooler to transmission ..... L 25
Pipe assembly-pump to steering box ..... F 24
Pipe assembly-pump to steering box ..... F 26
Pipe assembly-pump to steering box-lhd ..... F 22
Pipe assembly-pump to steering box-rhd ..... F 21
Pipe assembly-purge B388
Pipe assembly-steering box to reservoir ..... F 24
Pipe assembly-steering box to reservoir ..... F 26
Pipe assembly-steering box to reservoir ..... F 22
Pipe assembly-steering box to reservoir ..... F 27
Pipe assembly-transmission to oil cooler ..... C 70
Pipe assembly-transmission to oil cooler ..... C 86
Pipe boost control B251
Pipe catch-pipe ..... J 67
Pipe fuel ..... B 33
Pipe fuel ..... B 79
Pipe fuel B330
Pipe fuel B331
Pipe fuel ..... B 30
Pipe fuel ..... J 1
Pipe fuel ..... J 13
Pipe fuel ..... J 49
Pipe fuel ..... J 50
Pipe fuel ..... J 56
Pipe fuel ..... J 73
Pipe fuel ..... J 74
Pipe fuel ..... J 9
Pipe fuel ..... J 11
Pipe fuel-canister to catch tank ..... J 72
Pipe fuel-engine to connector ..... J 24
Pipe fuel-lift pump to filter ..... J 53
Pipe fuel-lift pump to filter ..... J 55
Pipe fuel-pump to filter ..... J 32
Pipe fuel-rear sedimentor to tap ..... J 30
Pipe fuel-rear tank to lift pump ..... J 26
Pipe fuel-rear tank to tap-feed ..... J 27
Pipe fuel-sedimentor to engine to tank ..... J 31
Pipe fuel-tank to filter ..... J 23
Pipe fuel-tank to pump ..... J 19
Pipe fuel-tank to pump ..... J 25
Pipe fuel-tank to pump feed ..... J 21
Pipe fuel-tank to sedimentor ..... J 28
Pipe fuel-tank to sedimentor ..... J 29
Pipe fuel-to carburetter ..... J 22
Pipe fuel-to vapour separator-metal ..... J 20
Pipe induction system B390
Pipe induction system-turbo to injection B218
Pipe turbocharger oil feed B255
Pipe-adaptor turbocharger B153
Pipe-adaptor turbocharger B178
Pipe-adaptor turbocharger B218
Pipe-adaptor turbocharger B255
Pipe-air cleaner case ..... J 38
Pipe-air cleaner case ..... J 61
Pipe-air cleaner case ..... J 73
Pipe-altn/vac pump oil feed B296
Pipe-brake-rh ..... H 11
Pipe-brake-tee piece ..... H 10
Pipe-brake-to g valve ..... H 20
Pipe-breather fuel tank ..... J 7
Pipe-breather fuel tank ..... J 18
Pipe-breather fuel tank-fuel filler to catch ..... J 70
Pipe-canister to catch tank ..... J 65
Pipe-carburettor breather vent ..... B 80
Pipe-carburettor breather vent ..... B 30
Pipe-carburettor vacuum ..... B 78
Pipe-carburettor vacuum-31" B330
Pipe-carburettor vacuum-31" B331
Pipe-carburettor vacuum-31" B337
Pipe-carburettor vacuum-advance ..... B 32
Pipe-carburettor vacuum-sensor to valve- ..... J 73
Pipe-carburettor vent B330
Pipe-carburettor vent B331
Pipe-carburettor vent-only with stromberg B334

Pipe-carburettor vent-only with su B334
Pipe-centrifuge oil-drain B291
Pipe-condenser/receiver dryer ..... L 78
Pipe-coolant ..... L 18
Pipe-cylinder 1-high pressure fuel injection B217
Pipe-cylinder 1-high pressure fuel injection B254
Pipe-cylinder 2-high pressure fuel injection B217
Pipe-cylinder 2-high pressure fuel injection B254
Pipe-cylinder 3-high pressure fuel injection B217
Pipe-cylinder 3-high pressure fuel injection B254
Pipe-cylinder 4-high pressure fuel injection B217
Pipe-cylinder 4-high pressure fuel injection B254
Pipe-dipstick automatic transmission ..... C 74
Pipe-engine oil suction B271
Pipe-engine to oil cooler ..... L 28
Pipe-engine to oil cooler ..... L 31
Pipe-evaporator air conditioning ..... L 50
Pipe-evaporator/compressor air conditioning ..... L 79
Pipe-exhaust gas recirculation ..... J 75
Pipe-exhaust gas recirculation ..... L 13
Pipe-exhaust gas recirculation-green ..... J 77
Pipe-exhaust-extension ..... K 10
Pipe-exhaust-extension ..... K 23
Pipe-exhaust-extension ..... K 25
Pipe-exhaust-extension ..... K 30
Pipe-feed-fuel lines B333
Pipe-front axle breather ..... E 50
Pipe-front axle breather ..... E 51
Pipe-fuel feed-fuel tank ..... J 4
Pipe-fuel lines feed-filter to pump ..... J 32
Pipe-fuel return fuel tank ..... J 1
Pipe-fuel return fuel tank ..... J 9
Pipe-fuel return fuel tank ..... J 11
Pipe-heater feed B290
Pipe-heater to hose coolant ..... L 39
Pipe-heater to hose coolant ..... L 40
Pipe-heater to hose coolant ..... L 62
Pipe-hose to carburettor ..... B 33
Pipe-lh B329
Pipe-oil cooler to engine ..... L 26
Pipe-oil cooler to engine ..... L 27
Pipe-oil cooler to engine ..... L 28
Pipe-oil cooler to engine ..... L 31
Pipe-oil cooler to engine-except to rhd ..... L 30
Pipe-oil cooler to gearbox ..... L 23
Pipe-oil cooler/transmission ..... L 23
Pipe-oil drain turbocharger B234
Pipe-oil drain turbocharger B255
Pipe-oil drain turbocharger B293
Pipe-oil feed-turbocharger B293
Pipe-outlet stub B385
Pipe-outlet to heater coolant B385
Pipe-outlet to inlet manifold coolant B324
Pipe-plenum chamber breather B368
Pipe-plenum chamber breather ..... L 69
Pipe-ram B390
Pipe-rear axle breather ..... E 50
Pipe-rear axle breather ..... E 51
Pipe-rear elbow ..... J 65
Pipe-receiver dry/evaporator air conditioning ..... L 79
Pipe-solenoid valve/exhaust gas recirculation ..... J 75
Pipe-spill return fuel injection B129
Pipe-spill return fuel injection B176
Pipe-spill return fuel injection B217
Pipe-spill return fuel injection B254
Pipe-spill return fuel injection B387
Pipe-suction automatic transmission ..... C 74
Pipe-sump assembly oil drain B178
Pipe-sump assembly oil drain B218
Pipe-sump assembly oil drain B237
Pipe-transmission oil inlet ..... C 7
Pipe-transmission oil inlet ..... C 8
Pipe-transmission oil inlet ..... C 55
Pipe-transmission/oil cooler ..... L 25
Pipe-vacuum exhaust gas recirculation valve ..... J 77
Pipe-vacuum exhaust gas recirculation valve ..... J 75
Pipe-vacuum heater/air conditioning ..... L 59
Pipe-vent fuel lines-front elbow to rear-lhd ..... J 65
Pipe-vent fuel tank ..... J 7
Piston front caliper ..... H 26
Piston power assisted steering ..... F 15
Piston power assisted steering ..... F 16
Piston-clutch-automatic ..... C 77
Piston-clutch-automatic ..... C 78
Piston-clutch-automatic ..... C 79
Piston-clutch-automatic ..... C 80
Piston-clutch-automatic ..... C 81
Piston-engine B269
Piston-engine-hepworth/grandidge pistons- B107
Piston-engine-standard ..... B 6
Piston-engine-standard ..... B 55
Piston-engine-standard B156
Piston-engine-standard B236
Piston-engine-standard.-'x' B199
Piston-engine-standard.-8.13:1 ..... B305
Piston-engine-standard.-high compression B375
Piston-rear caliper brake ..... H 30
Piston-rear caliper brake ..... H 32
Pivot bracket-rh ..... R 33
Pivot-clutch release lever ..... C 2
Pivot-clutch release lever ..... C 28
Pivot-clutch release lever ..... C 42
Pivot-clutch release lever ..... C 45
Pivot-spare wheel harness ..... V 5
Pivot-transfer box differential lock shaft/arm ..... D 24
Pivot-transfer box differential lock shaft/arm ..... D 22
Plate ..... B 38
Plate ..... B 39
Plate ..... B 41
Plate ..... B 85
Plate ..... B 86
Plate B134
Plate B135
Plate B136
Plate B159
Plate B182
Plate B183
Plate B222
Plate B223
Plate B304
Plate B323
Plate B346
Plate B347
Plate ..... B 10
Plate ..... B 59
Plate ..... C 12
Plate ..... C 41
Plate ..... C 42
Plate ..... C 45
Plate ..... C 74
Plate ..... C 83
Plate ..... D 41
Plate ..... F 12
Plate ..... F 27
Plate ..... F 23
Plate ..... G 7
Plate ..... G 8
Plate ..... H 35
Plate ..... J 11
Plate ..... L 29
Plate ..... L 51
Plate ..... L 72
Plate ..... M 18
Plate M138
Plate M139
Plate M140
Plate M141
Plate M142
Plate ..... N 11
Plate ..... N 23
Plate ..... N 97
Plate N100
Plate N123
Plate N124
Plate N149
Plate N150
Plate N199
Plate N221
Plate ..... N 42
Plate ..... N 96
Plate N170
Plate ..... R 31
Plate ..... R 43
Plate ..... R 45
Plate ..... R 62
Plate ..... S 4
Plate ..... S 8
Plate ..... S 17
Plate ..... T 5
Plate & weld nut assembly-seat belt rear ..... R 70
Plate & weldnut assembly N191
Plate & weldnut assembly ..... N 8
Plate & weldnut assembly ..... S 15
Plate & weldnut assembly-to support bracket ..... N 7
Plate air cleaner mounting bracket ..... J 44
Plate assembly ..... B 22
Plate assembly ..... B 36
Plate assembly B132
Plate assembly B221
Plate assembly B147
Plate assembly ..... C 3
Plate assembly ..... D 17
Plate assembly ..... H 29
Plate assembly ..... J 13
Plate assembly ..... N 58
Plate assembly-drive torque converter B399
Plate assembly-front B202
Plate assembly-front-rhd ..... N 32
Plate assembly-front-rhd ..... N 31
Plate assembly-pump ..... B 83
Plate assembly-rear-floor ..... N 68
Plate assembly-rear-floor ..... N 72
Plate assembly-rear-floor ..... N 69
Plate assembly-rear-floor ..... N 73
Plate assembly-rear-floor ..... N 70
Plate assembly-rear-floor ..... N 74
Plate assembly-rear-floor ..... N 71
Plate assembly-retaining ..... C 35
Plate assembly-rh ..... R 43
Plate assembly-tow bar mounting ..... T 33
Plate assembly-tow bar mounting ..... T 34
Plate assembly-tow bar mounting ..... T 35
Plate assembly-tow bar mounting ..... T 40
Plate cover N123
Plate cover ..... S 9
Plate mounting-rh ..... N 15
Plate mounting-rh ..... N 16
Plate- guide ..... C 83
Plate-2 seats ..... R 37
Plate-5th gear synchroniser support ..... C 14
Plate-adjusting-hook N142
Plate-automatic transmission clutch end ..... C 79
Plate-backing ..... C 2
Plate-backing ..... C 28
Plate-baffle ..... B 20
Plate-baffle ..... B 68
Plate-baffle ..... C 46
Plate-baffle ..... J 34
Plate-baffle-rh N149
Plate-blanking ..... C 30

Plunger-oil pump relief valve B314
Plunger-oil pump relief valve ..... B 64
Plunger-oil pump relief valve-ten tooth idler ..... B 15
Plunger-reverse switch ..... C 24
Pointer-engine timing ..... B 9
Pointer-engine timing ..... B 58
Pointer-engine timing B307
Pop out unit cigar lighter M111
Post-terminal ..... M 82
Post-terminal ..... M 83
Post-terminal ..... M 84
Potentiometer & pedal-assembly ..... G 2
Potentiometer-throttle diesel B253
Potentiometer-throttle multi point injection B388
Potentiometer-throttle multi point injection B398
Printed circuit board instrument pack M119
Printed circuit board instrument pack M116
Propellor shaft-front ..... E 1
Propellor shaft-rear ..... E 2
Propellor shaft-rear ..... E 3
Protector-driving lamp-pair ..... T 9
Protector-edge M138
Protector-edge M139
Protector-edge M140
Protector-edge M141
Protector-edge M142
Protector-edge ..... M 79
Protector-headlamp-perspex-pair ..... T 16
Protector-pipe fuel ..... J 23
Protector-tail door N182
Pulley & torsional vibration damper- B106
Pulley & torsional vibration damper- B155
Pulley & torsional vibration damper- B198
Pulley alternator ..... B 43
Pulley alternator ..... B 91
Pulley alternator ..... B 92
Pulley alternator ..... B 93
Pulley alternator ..... B 94
Pulley alternator B138
Pulley alternator B139
Pulley alternator B140
Pulley alternator B141
Pulley alternator B186
Pulley alternator B187
Pulley alternator B226
Pulley alternator B355
Pulley alternator B356
Pulley alternator B360
Pulley alternator B361
Pulley alternator B362
Pulley assembly-crankshaft ..... B 5
Pulley assembly-crankshaft ..... B 54
Pulley assembly-pump fuel injection pump B216
Pulley coolant pump B162
Pulley coolant pump B163
Pulley coolant pump B204
Pulley coolant pump B241
Pulley coolant pump B242
Pulley coolant pump B310
Pulley coolant pump B380
Pulley coolant pump-single groove ..... B 13
Pulley coolant pump-single groove ..... B 61
Pulley coolant pump-single groove B113
Pulley coolant pump-single groove B311
Pulley coolant pump-twin groove ..... B 62
Pulley fuel inj pump B128
Pulley fuel inj pump B175
Pulley power assisted steering pump ..... B 37
Pulley power assisted steering pump ..... B 84
Pulley power assisted steering pump B133
Pulley power assisted steering pump B181
Pulley power assisted steering pump B221
Pulley power assisted steering pump B258
Pulley power assisted steering pump B294
Pulley power assisted steering pump B342
Pulley power assisted steering pump-single B341
Pulley power assisted steering pump-twin B343
Pulley-alternator B358
Pulley-alternator B359
Pulley-assembly B276
Pulley-assembly B393
Pulley-camshaft B124
Pulley-camshaft B171
Pulley-camshaft B212
Pulley-camshaft B253
Pulley-camshaft-timing belt B249
Pulley-crankshaft B106
Pulley-crankshaft B155
Pulley-crankshaft B235
Pulley-crankshaft B304
Pulley-drive air conditioning ..... B 41
Pulley-drive air conditioning ..... B 88
Pulley-drive air conditioning B136
Pulley-drive air conditioning B185
Pulley-drive power assisted steering ..... B 36
Pulley-drive power assisted steering ..... B 83
Pulley-drive power assisted steering B132
Pulley-driven air conditioning ..... B 38
Pulley-driven air conditioning ..... B 39
Pulley-driven air conditioning ..... B 85
Pulley-driven air conditioning ..... B 86
Pulley-driven air conditioning B134
Pulley-driven air conditioning B135
Pulley-driven air conditioning B182
Pulley-driven air conditioning B183
Pulley-driven air conditioning B222
Pulley-driven air conditioning B223
Pulley-driven air conditioning B346
Pulley-driven air conditioning B347
Pulley-idler ancillary drive ..... B 36
Pulley-idler ancillary drive ..... B 41
Pulley-idler ancillary drive ..... B 83
Pulley-idler ancillary drive ..... B 88
Pulley-idler ancillary drive B132
Pulley-idler ancillary drive B136
Pulley-idler ancillary drive B185
Pulley-idler ancillary drive B260
Pulley-idler ancillary drive B277
Pulley-idler ancillary drive B278
Pulley-idler ancillary drive B295
Pulley-polyvee alternator-61mm B261
Pulley-tensioner ancillary drive B225
Pulley-tensioner ancillary drive B260
Pulley-tensioner ancillary drive B349
Pulley-tensioner ancillary drive B379
Pulley-tensioner ancillary drive B394
Pump assembly power assisted steering ..... B 36
Pump assembly power assisted steering ..... B 37
Pump assembly power assisted steering ..... B 83
Pump assembly power assisted steering ..... B 84
Pump assembly power assisted steering B132
Pump assembly power assisted steering B133
Pump assembly power assisted steering B181
Pump assembly power assisted steering B221
Pump assembly power assisted steering B258
Pump assembly power assisted steering B294
Pump assembly power assisted steering B393
Pump assembly power assisted steering-v B341
Pump assembly-backlight wash M135
Pump assembly-backlight wash M136
Pump assembly-backlight wash M141
Pump assembly-backlight wash-black wire M137
Pump assembly-engine coolant ..... B 13
Pump assembly-engine coolant ..... B 61
Pump assembly-engine coolant B113
Pump assembly-engine coolant B204
Pump assembly-engine coolant B241
Pump assembly-engine coolant B308
Pump assembly-engine coolant B309
Pump assembly-engine coolant B379
Pump assembly-engine coolant-a127 ..... B114
Pump assembly-engine coolant-a127 ..... B162
Pump assembly-engine coolant-a127 ..... B163
Pump assembly-engine coolant-a133 ..... B 62
Pump assembly-engine oil B205
Pump assembly-engine oil B271
Pump assembly-fuel injection diesel-new B128
Pump assembly-headlamp wash M138
Pump assembly-headlamp wash M139
Pump assembly-headlamp wash M140
Pump assembly-headlamp wash M141
Pump assembly-headlamp wash M142
Pump assembly-windscreen wash M130
Pump assembly-windscreen wash M131
Pump assembly-windscreen wash M132
Pump assembly-windscreen wash M133
Pump assembly-windscreen wash M134
Pump assembly-windscreen wash M135
Pump assembly-windscreen wash M136
Pump assembly-windscreen wash M137
Pump assembly-windscreen wash M139
Pump assembly-windscreen wash M140
Pump assembly-windscreen wash M141
Pump assembly-windscreen wash M142
Pump assembly-windscreen wash M143
Pump body assembly-engine oil ..... B 15
Pump body assembly-engine oil ..... B 63
Pump body assembly-engine oil B115
Pump body assembly-engine oil B164
Pump body casting-engine oil ..... B 64
Pump brake vacuum B131
Pump brake vacuum B180
Pump brake vacuum B220
Pump brake vacuum B257
Pump sub assembly power assisted steering B340
Pump-expansion tank ejector ..... L 8
Pump-expansion tank ejector ..... L 18
Pump-foot ..... S 18
Pump-foot ..... T 54
Pump-fuel injection-new B175
Pump-fuel injection-new B216
Pump-fuel injection-new B253
Pump-fuel mechanical B127
Pump-fuel mechanical B174
Pump-fuel mechanical B215
Pump-fuel mechanical B252
Pump-fuel tank ..... J 1
Pump-fuel tank ..... J 5
Pump-fuel tank ..... J 6
Pump-fuel tank ..... J 7
Pump-fuel tank-external-12v ..... J 12
Pump-fuel tank-extra 10 gallon ..... J 11
Pump-fuel tank-extra 15 gallon ..... J 9
Pump-fuel tank-low pressure. ..... J 4
Pump-transmission oil ..... C 55
Pump-transmission oil ..... C 75
Pump-water. B275
Quadrant-selector rail ..... C 22
Quarter-rear lower-rh ..... N 92
Rack assembly-roof N137
Rack assembly-roof-1600mm ..... T 17
Rack-ladder N218
Rack-ladder ..... T 17
Radiator & intercooler assembly-cooling ..... L 3
Radiator assembly ..... L 1
Radiator assembly ..... L 3
Radiator assembly ..... L 2
Radiator-cooling system-diesel-diesel ..... L 4
Radio cassette assembly- electronic M121
Radio cassette assembly- electronic M122

Radio cassette assembly- electronic ..... T 12
Radio cassette assembly- electronic-philips- M124
Radio cassette electronic-auto/reversal M126
Rail assembly-multi point injection fuel B387
Rail diagonal side rear-rh N137
Rail guide-draught-clear glass N107
Rail guide-draught-rh clear N109
Rail guide-draught-tinted glass N108
Rail guide-draught-tinted glass N110
Rail lower front screen hoop N137
Rail-anchorage-s/harness ..... R 61
Ratchet assembly handbrake ..... B 11
Rear assembly exhaust system ..... K 5
Rear assembly exhaust system ..... K 7
Rear assembly exhaust system ..... K 8
Rear assembly exhaust system ..... K 10
Rear assembly exhaust system ..... K 19
Rear assembly exhaust system ..... K 20
Rear assembly exhaust system ..... K 23
Rear assembly exhaust system ..... K 24
Rear assembly exhaust system ..... K 25
Rear assembly exhaust system ..... K 26
Rear assembly exhaust system ..... K 28
Rear assembly exhaust system ..... K 30
Rear assembly exhaust system ..... K 31
Rear assembly exhaust system ..... K 32
Rear assembly exhaust system-rear ..... K 9
Rear assembly exhaust system-rear ..... K 22
Rear floor assembly ..... N 44
Rear rail roof rack support frame N137
Receiver dryer assembly air conditioning ..... L 45
Receiver dryer assembly air conditioning ..... L 54
Reciever dryer assembly-air con ..... L 53
Rectifier-alternator ..... B 91
Rectifier-alternator ..... B 92
Rectifier-alternator ..... B 93
Rectifier-alternator ..... B 94
Rectifier-alternator B138
Rectifier-alternator B139
Rectifier-alternator B140
Rectifier-alternator B141
Rectifier-alternator B186
Rectifier-alternator B187
Rectifier-alternator B226
Rectifier-alternator B355
Rectifier-alternator B358
Rectifier-alternator B359
Rectifier-alternator B360
Rectifier-alternator B361
Rectifier-alternator B362
Rectifier-alternator-machine sensed ..... B 43
Rectifier-alternator-new alternator-rh B356
Reflector-rear-rectangular ..... M 15
Reflector-rear-rectangular ..... M 16
Reflector-rear-round ..... M 14
Regulator & brush box assembly alternator ..... B 92
Regulator & brush box assembly alternator ..... B 94
Regulator & brush box assembly alternator B139
Regulator & brush box assembly alternator B141
Regulator & brush box assembly alternator B186
Regulator & brush box assembly alternator B187
Regulator & brush box assembly alternator B226
Regulator & brush box assembly alternator B355
Regulator & brush box assembly alternator B360
Regulator & brush box assembly alternator B362
Regulator & brush box assembly alternator- B356
Regulator assembly alternator-24079b90 ..... B358
Regulator assembly alternator-lra356 ..... B 43
Regulator assembly alternator-lra356 ..... B 91
Regulator assembly alternator-lra356 ..... B 93
Regulator assembly alternator-lra356 ..... B138
Regulator assembly alternator-lra356 ..... B140
Regulator assembly alternator-lra356 ..... B359
Regulator assembly alternator-lra356 ..... B361
Regulator-front door glass-rh N159
Regulator-front door glass-rh N161
Regulator-fuel pressure B387
Regulator-rear door glass-rh N184
Reinforcement ..... R 67
Reinforcement ..... V 5
Reinforcement assembly-cable retained N122
Reinforcement assembly-chain retained N121
Reinforcement assembly-headlamp closing-rh ..... N 54
Reinforcement assembly-headlamp closing-rh ..... N 55
Reinforcement assembly-load door spare ..... S 8
Reinforcement-bc post N220
Reinforcement-bracket ..... S 10
Reinforcement-nut plate N191
Reinforcement-rh N192
Reinforcement-rh ..... S 9
Reinforcement-spare wheel retention-upper ..... S 10
Reinforcement-spare wheel retention-upper ..... V 5
Relay ..... L 50
Relay ..... L 73
Relay ..... M 83
Relay ..... T 46
Relay assembly multi function ..... M 94
Relay normally open-black ..... M 94
Relay-33ra w/proof assy ..... M 84
Relay-a/c blower fan ..... M 80
Relay-air conditioning ..... M 81
Relay-blower fan-changeover-green ..... M 79
Relay-brake system check-changeover- ..... M 93
Relay-changeover-green ..... M 70
Relay-changeover-green ..... M 76
Relay-changeover-green ..... M 77
Relay-emissions maintenance M110
Relay-hrw-changeover-green M112
Relay-ignition heater plug-12v ..... M 95
Relay-normally open-black ..... L 56
Relay-twin make-brown M105
Relay-wiper-delay unit-12v-red ..... M 94
Release assembly-bonnet-rh N150
Reservoir assembly power assisted steering ..... F 19
Reservoir assembly power assisted steering ..... F 20
Resistor ..... L 50
Resistor ..... L 58
Resistor ..... M 33
Resistor ..... M 95
Resistor ..... M 34
Resistor ..... M 35
Resistor ..... M 37
Resistor ..... M 38
Resistor ..... M 40
Resistor pack-speed control-blower-heater ..... L 51
Resistor-air conditioning ..... M 81
Resonator induction system ..... J 36
Restrictor-air flow B331
Restrictor-fuel hose fuel lines ..... B 79
Restrictor-fuel hose fuel lines ..... J 20
Restrictor-inlet manifold-engine B323
Retainer ..... B 38
Retainer ..... B 39
Retainer ..... B 85
Retainer ..... B 86
Retainer B134
Retainer B135
Retainer B182
Retainer B183
Retainer B222
Retainer B223
Retainer B342
Retainer B343
Retainer B346
Retainer B347
Retainer ..... D 36
Retainer ..... E 64
Retainer ..... E 67
Retainer N180
Retainer N242
Retainer N245
Retainer N246
Retainer ..... P 6
Retainer ..... P 13
Retainer ..... P 26
Retainer ..... P 41
Retainer ..... P 31
Retainer ..... S 5
Retainer ..... S 8
Retainer-10ml ..... U 1
Retainer-bearing automatic transmission ..... C 76
Retainer-except 3 stud fixing-spare wheel ..... S 9
Retainer-gear lever assembly gaiter-upper ..... P 17
Retainer-headlining ..... P 65
Retainer-ht cables B320
Retainer-inner ..... E 63
Retainer-inner ..... E 65
Retainer-inner ..... E 66
Retainer-inner ..... S 11
Retainer-interlock ..... C 68
Retainer-interlock ..... C 56
Retainer-interlock-attachment plate ..... C 23
Retainer-mat N182
Retainer-mat-floor. ..... P 52
Retainer-outer ..... P 44
Retainer-outer ..... P 46
Retainer-rear door-top N173
Retainer-rh N132
Retainer-rh N163
Retainer-rh N203
Retainer-rh N173
Retainer-rh ..... P 49
Retainer-rh ..... P 30
Retainer-seal N182
Retaining-strip N242
Retaining-strip N245
Retaining-strip N246
Retention-bearing clutch release ..... C 2
Retention-bearing clutch release ..... C 3
Retention-bearing clutch release ..... C 28
Retention-bearing clutch release ..... C 41
Retention-bearing clutch release ..... C 42
Retention-bearing clutch release ..... C 43
Retention-bearing clutch release ..... C 45
Ring power assisted steering ..... F 15
Ring power assisted steering ..... F 16
Ring pull-seat lock-rear seats ..... R 43
Ring set assembly-piston ..... C 79
Ring set assembly-piston-standard. ..... B 6
Ring set assembly-piston-standard. B199
Ring set assembly-piston-standard. B305
Ring set assembly-piston-standard. B375
Ring starter-flywheel-engine ..... B 47
Ring starter-flywheel-engine. ..... B 98
Ring-backing automatic transmission ..... C 79
Ring-backing automatic transmission ..... C 80
Ring-backing automatic transmission ..... C 82
Ring-baulk ..... C 11
Ring-baulk ..... C 12
Ring-baulk ..... C 32
Ring-baulk ..... C 33
Ring-baulk ..... C 63
Ring-baulk ..... C 34
Ring-baulk ..... C 62
Ring-baulk-1st/2nd gear ..... C 59
Ring-baulk-5th gear ..... C 64
Ring-baulk-5th gear ..... C 14
Ring-differential locking ..... D 20
Ring-differential locking ..... D 23
Ring-differential locking ..... E 7

Ring-differential locking .... E 9
Ring-differential locking .... E 33
Ring-differential locking .... E 36
Ring-differential locking .... E 34
Ring-differential locking .... E 37
Ring-locking fuel tank .... J 1
Ring-locking fuel tank .... J 5
Ring-locking fuel tank .... J 6
Ring-locking fuel tank .... J 4
Ring-locking fuel tank-extra 15 gallon .... J 9
Ring-locking fuel tank-red .... J 7
Ring-mainshaft oil feed .... C 31
Ring-mainshaft oil feed .... C 55
Ring-mainshaft oil feed .... C 64
Ring-mainshaft oil feed-asbestos .... C 7
Ring-mainshaft oil feed-asbestos .... C 8
Ring-piston-forward shaft automatic .... C 79
Ring-pulsar antilock brakes .... H 33
Ring-retention .... C 64
Ring-retention .... E 59
Ring-retention .... L 59
Ring-retention .... L 66
Ring-retention-gauge M115
Ring-retention-rubber .... S 1
Ring-retention-rubber .... S 2
Ring-retention-rubber .... S 5
Ring-retention-speedometer M114
Ring-sealing fuel tank .... J 4
Ring-slip alternator .... B 91
Ring-slip alternator B138
Ring-slip alternator-machine sensed .... B 43
Ring-snap B115
Ring-snap B164
Ring-snap .... E 62
Ring-snap .... F 1
Ring-snap .... F 3
Ring-snap automatic transmission .... C 77
Ring-snap automatic transmission .... C 78
Ring-snap automatic transmission .... C 79
Ring-snap automatic transmission .... C 81
Ring-snap automatic transmission .... C 82
Ring-snap automatic transmission-large .... C 80
Ring-snap-later type locking ring .... B 16
Ring-snap-locking .... B 63
Ring-snap-manual .... C 68
Ring-snap-outer B205
Ring-support .... C 77
Ring-synchroniser friction .... C 14
Ring-synchroniser inner .... C 59
Ring-synchroniser inner .... C 63
Ring-synchroniser inner .... C 62
Ring-synchroniser intermediate .... C 59
Ring-synchroniser intermediate .... C 63
Ring-synchroniser intermediate .... C 62
Ring-towing-front .... N 20
Ring-transfer box differential retaining .... D 11
Rivet .... B 9
Rivet .... B 58
Rivet .... H 19
Rivet .... J 8
Rivet .... J 34
Rivet M143
Rivet .... M 46
Rivet .... N 64
Rivet .... N 92
Rivet .... N 93
Rivet N112
Rivet N113
Rivet N124
Rivet N180
Rivet N201
Rivet N209
Rivet N223
Rivet N224
Rivet N227
Rivet N228
Rivet N230
Rivet N231
Rivet N233
Rivet N239
Rivet N240
Rivet N241
Rivet N242
Rivet N243
Rivet N245
Rivet .... N 31
Rivet .... N 66
Rivet N167
Rivet N234
Rivet N170
Rivet N173
Rivet N111
Rivet .... P 17
Rivet .... P 65
Rivet .... P 67
Rivet .... R 2
Rivet .... R 31
Rivet .... R 64
Rivet .... R 69
Rivet .... R 40
Rivet .... S 2
Rivet .... S 14
Rivet .... S 16
Rivet .... T 3
Rivet .... T 16
Rivet .... T 39
Rivet-3/16" x 0.45"lng N140
Rivet-3/16" x 0.45"lng .... P 45
Rivet-3/16" x 0.575"lng .... N 90
Rivet-3/16" x 0.575"lng .... N 95
Rivet-3/16" x 0.575"lng .... N 97
Rivet-3/16" x 0.575"lng .... N 98
Rivet-3/16" x 0.575"lng N182
Rivet-3/16" x 0.575"lng N203
Rivet-3/16" x 0.575"lng N246
Rivet-3/16" x 0.575"lng .... N 42
Rivet-3/16" x 0.575"lng .... N 57
Rivet-3/16" x 0.575"lng .... P 34
Rivet-3/16" x 0.575"lng .... P 63
Rivet-3/16" x 0.575"lng .... P 61
Rivet-3/16" x 0.575"lng .... R 60
Rivet-3/16" x 0.575"lng .... R 62
Rivet-3/16" x 0.575"lng .... R 65
Rivet-3/16" x 0.575"lng .... R 3
Rivet-3/16" x 0.575"lng .... R 37
Rivet-3/16" x 0.7lng .... J 15
Rivet-5/32" x 0.335"lng N147
Rivet-5mm B279
Rivet-aluminium-1/8" x 0.482"lng N103
Rivet-aluminium-1/8" x 0.482"lng N105
Rivet-aluminium-1/8" x 0.482"lng N129
Rivet-aluminium-1/8" x 0.482"lng N131
Rivet-aluminium-1/8" x 0.482"lng .... R 6
Rivet-aluminium-1/8" x 0.482"lng .... R 38
Rivet-aluminium-1/8" x 0.482"lng .... R 21
Rivet-aluminium-1/8" x 0.482"lng .... R 14
Rivet-angle to cab base-pop-3/16" x 0.45"lng .... N 41
Rivet-bifurcated .... N 40
Rivet-bracket to tailgate-pop-3/16" x 0.45"lng N123
Rivet-chain retained-pop-3/16" x 0.45"lng N121
Rivet-long N204
Rivet-plastic-drive .... L 72
Rivet-plastic-drive N198
Rivet-plastic-drive .... N 63
Rivet-plastic-drive-black .... P 21
Rivet-plastic-drive-redundant holes N122
Rivet-plastic-snap in .... J 5
Rivet-plastic-snap in .... J 6
Rivet-pop-3/16" x 0.45"lng .... H 36
Rivet-pop-3/16" x 0.45"lng .... L 80
Rivet-pop-3/16" x 0.45"lng .... N 35
Rivet-pop-3/16" x 0.45"lng .... N 51
Rivet-pop-3/16" x 0.45"lng .... N 54
Rivet-pop-3/16" x 0.45"lng .... N 68
Rivet-pop-3/16" x 0.45"lng .... N 72
Rivet-pop-3/16" x 0.45"lng .... N 75
Rivet-pop-3/16" x 0.45"lng .... N 79
Rivet-pop-3/16" x 0.45"lng .... N 87
Rivet-pop-3/16" x 0.45"lng N115
Rivet-pop-3/16" x 0.45"lng N117
Rivet-pop-3/16" x 0.45"lng N118
Rivet-pop-3/16" x 0.45"lng N122
Rivet-pop-3/16" x 0.45"lng N132
Rivet-pop-3/16" x 0.45"lng N148
Rivet-pop-3/16" x 0.45"lng N163
Rivet-pop-3/16" x 0.45"lng N181
Rivet-pop-3/16" x 0.45"lng N238
Rivet-pop-3/16" x 0.45"lng .... N 20
Rivet-pop-3/16" x 0.45"lng .... N 28
Rivet-pop-3/16" x 0.45"lng .... N 36
Rivet-pop-3/16" x 0.45"lng .... N 40
Rivet-pop-3/16" x 0.45"lng .... N 55
Rivet-pop-3/16" x 0.45"lng .... N 69
Rivet-pop-3/16" x 0.45"lng .... N 73
Rivet-pop-3/16" x 0.45"lng .... N 76
Rivet-pop-3/16" x 0.45"lng .... N 80
Rivet-pop-3/16" x 0.45"lng .... N 88
Rivet-pop-3/16" x 0.45"lng .... N 96
Rivet-pop-3/16" x 0.45"lng N116
Rivet-pop-3/16" x 0.45"lng N119
Rivet-pop-3/16" x 0.45"lng N244
Rivet-pop-3/16" x 0.45"lng .... N 37
Rivet-pop-3/16" x 0.45"lng .... N 70
Rivet-pop-3/16" x 0.45"lng .... N 74
Rivet-pop-3/16" x 0.45"lng .... N 77
Rivet-pop-3/16" x 0.45"lng .... N 81
Rivet-pop-3/16" x 0.45"lng .... N 71
Rivet-pop-3/16" x 0.45"lng .... N 78
Rivet-pop-3/16" x 0.45"lng .... N 82
Rivet-pop-3/16" x 0.45"lng .... N 63
Rivet-pop-3/16" x 0.45"lng .... N 83
Rivet-pop-3/16" x 0.45"lng .... N 84
Rivet-pop-3/16" x 0.45"lng .... N 85
Rivet-pop-3/16" x 0.45"lng .... N 86
Rivet-pop-3/16" x 0.45"lng .... P 46
Rivet-pop-3/16" x 0.45"lng .... P 49
Rivet-pop-3/16" x 0.45"lng .... R 44
Rivet-pop-3/16" x 0.45"lng .... S 1
Rivet-pop-3/16" x 0.45"lng .... S 3
Rivet-pop-3/16" x 0.45"lng .... S 5
Rivet-pop-3/16" x 0.45"lng .... S 12
Rivet-pop-3/16" x 0.45"lng .... S 15
Rivet-pop-3/16" x 0.45"lng .... S 17
Rivet-pop-3/16" x 0.45"lng .... T 47
Rivet-pop-3/16" x 0.45"lng .... T 48
Rivet-pop-aluminium B391
Rivet-pop-aluminium .... L 48
Rivet-pop-aluminium .... M 83
Rivet-pop-aluminium .... M 84
Rivet-pop-aluminium .... N 30
Rivet-pop-aluminium .... N 90
Rivet-pop-aluminium .... N 92
Rivet-pop-aluminium .... N 93
Rivet-pop-aluminium N149
Rivet-pop-aluminium N241
Rivet-pop-aluminium N243
Rivet-pop-aluminium N246
Rivet-pop-aluminium .... R 1
Rivet-pop-aluminium .... R 4
Rivet-pop-aluminium .... S 8

Rivet-pop-aluminium .... S 9
Rivet-pop-aluminium .... S 17
Rivet-pop-aluminium-0.125" .... N 39
Rivet-pop-aluminium-0.125" .... P 56
Rivet-pop-aluminium-0.125" .... P 60
Rivet-required when bonnet lock fitted-pop- N139
Rivet-short N249
Rivnut .... N 52
Road atlas .... T 54
Rocker & arm assembly B280
Rocker & arm assembly-fuel injectors B282
Rocker assembly-cylinder head-rh B245
Rocker assembly-cylinder head-rh B319
Rocker assembly-cylinder head-rh B382
Rocker cover assembly .... B 70
Rocker cover assembly-breather separate .... B 22
Rod assembly-connecting .... B 6
Rod assembly-connecting .... B 55
Rod assembly-connecting B107
Rod assembly-connecting B156
Rod assembly-connecting B269
Rod assembly-connecting .... D 38
Rod assembly-connecting .... T 5
Rod assembly-connecting .... T 6
Rod assembly-kickdown automatic .... C 73
Rod assembly-linkage connecting .... D 36
Rod assembly-linkage connecting .... D 37
Rod assembly-linkage connecting .... D 39
Rod assembly-push slave cylinder .... C 2
Rod assembly-push slave cylinder .... C 28
Rod assembly-push slave cylinder .... C 45
Rod assembly-tie .... F 1
Rod assembly-tie .... F 3
Rod assembly-tie N179
Rod-crankshaft connecting B199
Rod-crankshaft connecting B236
Rod-crankshaft connecting B305
Rod-crankshaft connecting B375
Rod-engine push .... B 21
Rod-engine push .... B 69
Rod-engine push B121
Rod-engine push B169
Rod-engine push B209
Rod-engine push B246
Rod-engine push B319
Rod-engine push B382
Rod-front suspension panhard .... E 57
Rod-push slave cylinder .... C 3
Rod-push slave cylinder .... C 41
Rod-push slave cylinder .... C 42
Rod-push slave cylinder .... C 43
Rod-push slave cylinder .... C 44
Rod-rear seats-inward facing .... R 36
Rod-rear seats-inward facing .... R 39
Rod-transmission support .... C 83
Roll-tool stowage .... S 6
Roll-tool stowage .... S 7
Roller B335
Roller .... C 68
Roller .... G 12
Roller-countershaft B336
Roller-quadrant shaft .... C 22
Roller-tappet guide .... B 21
Roller-tappet guide .... B 69
Roller-tappet guide B121
Roller-tappet guide B169
Roller-tappet guide B209
Roller-tappet guide B246
Roof assembly-alpine white N132
Roof assembly-alpine white N133
Roof assembly-alpine white-less sunroof N130
Roof assembly-with sunroof-external N130
Roof assembly-without alpine lights-less N128
Roof assembly-without alpine lights-less N128
Rope-hood side curtain N225
Rope-hood side curtain N226
Rope-hood side curtain N229
Rope-hood side curtain N232
Rope-hood side curtain N235
Rope-hood side curtain N236
Rope-hood-elastic N225
Rope-hood-elastic N226
Rope-hood-elastic N229
Rope-hood-elastic N232
Rope-hood-elastic N235
Rope-hood-elastic N236
Rope-hood-rear curtain N223
Rope-hood-rear curtain N224
Rope-hood-rear curtain N227
Rope-hood-rear curtain N228
Rope-hood-rear curtain N230
Rope-hood-rear curtain N231
Rope-hood-side N233
Rope-hood-side N234
Rope-top and sides-hood N233
Rope-top and sides-hood N234
Rope-towing .... T 41
Rotor blade-vacuum pump B131
Rotor blade-vacuum pump B180
Rotor blade-vacuum pump B220
Rotor, ... B291
Rotor-oil pump inner B238
Rotor-oil pump outer B238
Rubbing strip-spare wheel retention .... S 14
Rubbing strip-spare wheel retention .... S 15
Rubbing strip-spare wheel retention .... S 17
Rubbing strip-tailgate N124
Scraper-ice .... T 54
Screen wash-250ml .... W 5
Screw .... B 13
Screw .... B 22
Screw .... B 38
Screw .... B 39
Screw .... B 42
Screw .... B 61
Screw .... B 62
Screw .... B 85
Screw .... B 86
Screw B113
Screw B114
Screw B134
Screw B135
Screw B162
Screw B163
Screw B173
Screw B182
Screw B183
Screw B204
Screw B222
Screw B223
Screw B274
Screw B282
Screw B299
Screw B323
Screw B332
Screw B333
Screw B346
Screw B347
Screw B280
Screw .... C 73
Screw .... C 79
Screw .... C 83
Screw .... D 6
Screw .... D 41
Screw .... E 46
Screw .... F 12
Screw .... F 15
Screw .... F 16
Screw .... H 20
Screw .... H 22
Screw .... H 24
Screw .... H 29
Screw .... H 35
Screw .... J 1
Screw .... J 14
Screw .... J 15
Screw .... J 11
Screw .... K 16
Screw .... K 31
Screw .... K 32
Screw .... L 5
Screw .... L 6
Screw .... L 7
Screw .... L 23
Screw .... L 52
Screw .... L 72
Screw .... L 74
Screw .... L 37
Screw .... L 76
Screw .... M 10
Screw M142
Screw M116
Screw N134
Screw N192
Screw N111
Screw .... P 4
Screw .... P 41
Screw .... P 45
Screw .... P 57
Screw .... P 12
Screw .... R 43
Screw .... R 44
Screw .... R 45
Screw .... R 30
Screw .... R 40
Screw .... V 6
Screw adjust-tension adjustment power B340
Screw-1/4unc x 7/8 .... B383
Screw-10 x 3/8-self tapping B321
Screw-10 x 3/8-self tapping M100
Screw-10unc x 9/16 .... B320
Screw-10unf x 3/4 .... B336
Screw-10unf x 3/4 .... T 16
Screw-3.5 x 16 .... M 13
Screw-3/8unc x 1 1/2 .... B367
Screw-3/8unc x 1 1/2 .... B368
Screw-3/8unc x 3/4 .... B341
Screw-6 x 7/8 .... M121
Screw-83mm-long .... C 74
Screw-adjusting .... B 28
Screw-adjusting .... B 31
Screw-antenna-self tapping M123
Screw-backrest to frame-hexagonal head- .... R 36
Screw-black .... M 5
Screw-bleed .... F 13
Screw-bleed .... F 14
Screw-bleed .... L 20
Screw-bleed brake .... H 28
Screw-bleed brake .... H 26
Screw-bleed brake .... H 31
Screw-bleed brake .... H 33
Screw-bleed clutch slave cylinder .... C 41
Screw-bleed clutch slave cylinder .... C 42
Screw-bleed clutch slave cylinder .... C 43
Screw-bleed-unheated .... J 54
Screw-bleed-unheated .... J 56
Screw-block-flanged head-m8 x 30 .... B 95
Screw-body to chassis-hexagonal socket- .... N 98
Screw-bracket fixing-flanged head-m8 x 25 .... M103
Screw-bracket fixing-hexagonal head-m6 x M102

Screw-hexagonal head-1/4unf x 5/8 ... B330
Screw-hexagonal head-1/4unf x 5/8 ... G 12
Screw-hexagonal head-10unf x 5/16 ... B335
Screw-hexagonal head-3/8bsf x 5/8 ... E 8
Screw-hexagonal head-3/8bsf x 5/8 ... E 11
Screw-hexagonal head-3/8unc x 1 1/2 ... B350
Screw-hexagonal head-3/8unc x 1 1/2 ... B352
Screw-hexagonal head-3/8unc x 1 1/4 ... B326
Screw-hexagonal head-3/8unc x 1 1/8 ... B386
Screw-hexagonal head-3/8unc x 3/4 ... H 36
Screw-hexagonal head-3/8unc x 7/8 ... B318
Screw-hexagonal head-5/16unc x 1 1/8 ... B307
Screw-hexagonal head-5/16unc x 1 1/8 ... B381
Screw-hexagonal head-5/16unc x 3/4 ... B384
Screw-hexagonal head-5/16unc x 7/8 ... B377
Screw-hexagonal head-5/16unf x 1 ... E 62
Screw-hexagonal head-5/16unf x 1 1/2 ... B351
Screw-hexagonal head-5/16unf x 3/4 ... B342
Screw-hexagonal head-5/16unf x 3/4 ... B343
Screw-hexagonal head-5/16unf x 5/8 ... B328
Screw-hexagonal head-7/16unc x 1 ... B370
Screw-hexagonal head-m10 x 16 ... F 1
Screw-hexagonal head-m10 x 16 ... F 3
Screw-hexagonal head-m10 x 16 ... K 14
Screw-hexagonal head-m10 x 25 ... E 59
Screw-hexagonal head-m10 x 25 ... E 64
Screw-hexagonal head-m10 x 25 ... E 67
Screw-hexagonal head-m10 x 25 ... N 19
Screw-hexagonal head-m10 x 25 ... N251
Screw-hexagonal head-m10 x 25 ... R 58
Screw-hexagonal head-m10 x 25 ... V 4
Screw-hexagonal head-m10 x 30 ... B144
Screw-hexagonal head-m10 x 35 ... E 60
Screw-hexagonal head-m10 x 35 ... E 68
Screw-hexagonal head-m12 x 20 ... T 5
Screw-hexagonal head-m12 x 25 ... B 8
Screw-hexagonal head-m12 x 25 ... B 57
Screw-hexagonal head-m12 x 25 ... B109
Screw-hexagonal head-m12 x 25 ... B158
Screw-hexagonal head-m12 x 25 ... C 38
Screw-hexagonal head-m12 x 25 ... N 16
Screw-hexagonal head-m12 x 30 ... C 6
Screw-hexagonal head-m5 ... M 12
Screw-hexagonal head-m5 x 12 ... J 67
Screw-hexagonal head-m5 x 12 ... L 39
Screw-hexagonal head-m5 x 12 ... L 62
Screw-hexagonal head-m5 x 16 ... C 52
Screw-hexagonal head-m5 x 16 ... M 63
Screw-hexagonal head-m5 x 16 ... S 8
Screw-hexagonal head-m5 x 20 ... G 13
Screw-hexagonal head-m5 x 20 ... M105
Screw-hexagonal head-m5 x 25 ... B178
Screw-hexagonal head-m5 x 25 ... B218
Screw-hexagonal head-m5-6mm ... G 8
Screw-hexagonal head-m6 x 12 ... F 23
Screw-hexagonal head-m6 x 12 ... J 33
Screw-hexagonal head-m6 x 12 ... J 36
Screw-hexagonal head-m6 x 12 ... J 37
Screw-hexagonal head-m6 x 12 ... L 24
Screw-hexagonal head-m6 x 12 ... L 32
Screw-hexagonal head-m6 x 12 ... M131
Screw-hexagonal head-m6 x 12 ... M135
Screw-hexagonal head-m6 x 12 ... R 39
Screw-hexagonal head-m6 x 14 ... B 17
Screw-hexagonal head-m6 x 14 ... B 18
Screw-hexagonal head-m6 x 14 ... B 65
Screw-hexagonal head-m6 x 14 ... B 66
Screw-hexagonal head-m6 x 14 ... B116
Screw-hexagonal head-m6 x 14 ... B117
Screw-hexagonal head-m6 x 14 ... B165
Screw-hexagonal head-m6 x 14 ... B206
Screw-hexagonal head-m6 x 14 ... J 65
Screw-hexagonal head-m6 x 14 ... J 72
Screw-hexagonal head-m6 x 14 ... M101
Screw-hexagonal head-m6 x 16 ... B354
Screw-hexagonal head-m6 x 16 ... C 46
Screw-hexagonal head-m6 x 16 ... C 68
Screw-hexagonal head-m6 x 16 ... F 19
Screw-hexagonal head-m6 x 16 ... N 58
Screw-hexagonal head-m6 x 20 ... J 38
Screw-hexagonal head-m6 x 20 ... J 45
Screw-hexagonal head-m6 x 20 ... L 9
Screw-hexagonal head-m6 x 25 ... T 45
Screw-hexagonal head-m6 x 30 ... C 29
Screw-hexagonal head-m6 x 30 ... L 47
Screw-hexagonal head-m6 x 30 ... L 63
Screw-hexagonal head-m6 x 30 ... L 64
Screw-hexagonal head-m6 x 30-long ... E 69
Screw-hexagonal head-m6 x 35 ... C 54
Screw-hexagonal head-m6 x 35 ... L 25
Screw-hexagonal head-m6 x 35 ... N197
Screw-hexagonal head-m6 x 45 ... G 1
Screw-hexagonal head-m8 x 12 ... B159
Screw-hexagonal head-m8 x 12 ... J 73
Screw-hexagonal head-m8 x 125 ... G 9
Screw-hexagonal head-m8 x 14 ... B380
Screw-hexagonal head-m8 x 14 ... B 27
Screw-hexagonal head-m8 x 15 ... R 5
Screw-hexagonal head-m8 x 16 ... L 12
Screw-hexagonal head-m8 x 16 ... N 24
Screw-hexagonal head-m8 x 25 ... B108
Screw-hexagonal head-m8 x 25 ... K 29
Screw-hexagonal head-m8 x 30 ... J 70
Screw-hexagonal head-m8 x 40 ... C 8
Screw-hexagonal head-m8 x 40 ... C 31
Screw-hexagonal head-m8 x 45 ... B357
Screw-hexagonal head-m8 x 45 ... B366
Screw-hexagonal head-m8 x 70 ... K 25
Screw-hexagonal head-shouldered-m12 x ... E 22
Screw-hexagonal socket-high tensile-m8 x ... N 28
Screw-hinge to bonnet assembly-m6 x 20- ... N140
Screw-hinge to tailgate-m8 x 60 ... N122
Screw-hoodsticks-flanged head-m8 x 25 ... N241
Screw-housing ... M125
Screw-housing to block-flanged head-m10 x ... B191
Screw-housing to block-hexagonal head- ... B306
Screw-idle mixture ... B 76
Screw-ladder frame to block-flanged head- ... B200
Screw-later type locking ring ... B 16
Screw-link to plate-flanged head-m8 x 25 ... B184
Screw-long ... R 54
Screw-m10 x 25-hexagonal head ... E 23
Screw-m10 x 25-hexagonal head ... E 48
Screw-m10 x 30 ... J 5
Screw-m10 x 30 ... J 6
Screw-m12 ... D 29
Screw-m4 x 12 ... H 34
Screw-m5 ... M 93
Screw-m6 x 14 ... B 14
Screw-m6 x 16 ... M 91
Screw-m6 x 16 ... M128
Screw-m6 x 16 ... N 90
Screw-m6 x 16 ... N139
Screw-m6 x 16 ... N249
Screw-m6 x 16 ... R 31
Screw-m6 x 16 ... T 14
Screw-m6 x 16 ... T 27
Screw-m6 x 20 ... P 32
Screw-m6 x 20-counter sunk-recessed ... D 32
Screw-m6 x 20-counter sunk-recessed ... R 4
Screw-m6 x 20-counter sunk-recessed ... R 15
Screw-m6 x 28 ... C 75
Screw-m8 ... L 3
Screw-m8 x 16 ... M 83
Screw-m8 x 16 ... M 84
Screw-m8 x 16 ... P 13
Screw-m8 x 20-counter sunk ... D 42
Screw-m8 x 70-hexagonal head ... K 1
Screw-m8 x 70-hexagonal head ... K 2
Screw-m8 x 70-hexagonal head ... K 3
Screw-m8 x 70-hexagonal head ... K 7
Screw-m8 x 70-hexagonal head ... K 8
Screw-m8 x 70-hexagonal head ... K 11
Screw-m8 x 70-hexagonal head ... K 12
Screw-m8 x 70-hexagonal head ... K 19
Screw-m8 x 70-hexagonal head ... K 20
Screw-m8 x 70-hexagonal head ... K 22
Screw-machine-3/8unc x 1-counter sunk ... B365
Screw-machine-3/8unc x 1-counter sunk ... B318
Screw-manifold to downpipe-flanged head- ... B285
Screw-manifold to head-flanged head-m8 x ... B 25
Screw-manifold to head-hexagonal head-m8 ... B 73
Screw-mounting to engine-hexagonal head- ... N 14
Screw-mudflap attachment-flanged head-m6 ... T 51
Screw-mudflap attachment-flanged head-m6 ... T 52
Screw-no 10 x 1" ... P 7
Screw-no 8 ... P 24
Screw-nut lokut to wheelarch-self tapping- ... N 61
Screw-on seat base-self tapping-no 10 x 5 x ... R 51
Screw-paint clearing-m6 x 20 ... H 32
Screw-paint clearing-m6 x 25 ... F 5
Screw-paint clearing-m6 x 25 ... M144
Screw-pan ... C 84
Screw-pan ... L 34
Screw-pan ... N241
Screw-pan ... N244
Screw-pan ... P 34
Screw-pan ... P 41
Screw-pan ... P 67
Screw-pan ... P 61
Screw-pan ... R 2
Screw-pan ... T 45
Screw-pan ... T 46
Screw-pan head-m5 x 12 ... J 2
Screw-pan head-m5 x 12 ... J 4
Screw-pan head-m5 x 12 ... J 9
Screw-pan head-m5 x 12 ... M109
Screw-pan head-m5 x 12 ... M 79
Screw-pan head-m5 x 12 ... M 57
Screw-pan head-m5 x 12 ... M 58
Screw-pan head-m5 x 12 ... P 2
Screw-pan head-m5 x 40 ... F 4
Screw-pan head-m5 x 40 ... T 37
Screw-pan head-m5 x 40 ... T 38
Screw-pan head-m5 x 40 ... T 43
Screw-pan head-m6 x 20 ... M 94
Screw-pan head-m6 x 20 ... N 95
Screw-pan head-m8 x 25 ... N200
Screw-pan head-m8 x 50 ... N178
Screw-pan-10 seats-m6 x 40 ... P 55
Screw-pan-centre squab ... R 3
Screw-pan-instrument cover-8 x 1/2 ... M123
Screw-pan-instrument cover-8 x 1/2 ... M125
Screw-pan-m5 x 16 ... F 4
Screw-pan-m5 x 16 ... H 36
Screw-pan-m6 x 25 ... N238
Screw-pan-m6 x 25 ... P 13
Screw-pan-m6 x 35 ... P 14
Screw-pan-m6 x 35 ... P 15
Screw-pan-pan head-m6 x 12 ... B110
Screw-pan-pan head-m6 x 12 ... B160
Screw-pan-pan head-m6 x 12 ... F 1
Screw-pan-pan head-m6 x 12 ... M 93
Screw-pan-pan head-m6 x 12 ... M130
Screw-pan-pan head-m6 x 12 ... M 48
Screw-pan-squab to frame ... R 37
Screw-pan-to bonnet assembly-m8 x 40 ... N141
Screw-panel diaphragm to seal-self tapping- ... N 33
Screw-panel to body-pan head-m5 x 12 ... N 51
Screw-plastic ... N204

Screw-plate to bar ... N219
Screw-plate to bonnet-hexagonal head-m5 x ... S 9
Screw-pulley to hub-hexagonal head-1/4unf ... B310
Screw-pump to bracket-flanged head-m6 x ... B 84
Screw-quartz halogen-black ... M 3
Screw-rack guide power assisted steering ... F 13
Screw-rack guide power assisted steering ... F 14
Screw-rear breather ... E 50
Screw-rear breather ... E 51
Screw-recessed-pan head-m5 x 16 ... L 36
Screw-recessed-pan head-m5 x 16 ... N163
Screw-reflector-self tapping-no 8 x 1/2 ... M 14
Screw-relay base-self tapping-no 8 x 1/2 ... M 77
Screw-retainer to door rear-self tapping-no ... N173
Screw-retainer to seal rear door-recessed- ... N182
Screw-retainer-hexagonal head-m10 x 20 ... N203
Screw-sealed beam-black ... M 2
Screw-seat base to box immobiliser housing- ... N 38
Screw-seat frame to wheelarch-pan head-m6 ... R 38
Screw-seat slide to floor-m6 x 20-counter ... R 1
Screw-seat to bracket-hexagonal head-m8 x ... R 28
Screw-secondary adjust ... B 77
Screw-self tapping ... B391
Screw-self tapping ... J 41
Screw-self tapping ... J 63
Screw-self tapping ... J 64
Screw-self tapping ... J 42
Screw-self tapping ... L 4
Screw-self tapping ... L 48
Screw-self tapping ... L 72
Screw-self tapping ... L 34
Screw-self tapping ... M 16
Screw-self tapping ... M127
Screw-self tapping ... N135
Screw-self tapping ... N199
Screw-self tapping ... N 94
Screw-self tapping ... P 4
Screw-self tapping ... P 11
Screw-self tapping ab ... L 69
Screw-self tapping ab-m8 x 12 ... B298
Screw-self tapping ab-m8 x 12 ... B377
Screw-self tapping ab-m8 x 12 ... B395
Screw-self tapping ab-m8 x 12 ... G 10
Screw-self tapping ab-m8 x 12 ... M 75
Screw-self tapping ab-m8 x 12 ... N134
Screw-self tapping ab-no 6 x 1/4 ... B 22
Screw-self tapping ab-no 6 x 1/4 ... L 70
Screw-self tapping ab-no 6 x 3/4 ... P 1
Screw-self tapping b-no 8 x 1 1/4 ... T 16
Screw-self tapping-counter sunk ... N111
Screw-self tapping-counter sunk-no 6 x 1 ... P 2
Screw-self tapping-m8 x 13-self tapping ... P 17
Screw-self tapping-m8 x 13-self tapping ... P 21
Screw-self tapping-m8 x 13-self tapping ... P 22
Screw-self tapping-m8 x 13-self tapping ... P 20
Screw-self tapping-no 10 x 5 x 8 ... M 46
Screw-self tapping-no 10 x 5 x 8 ... R 46
Screw-self tapping-no 10 x 5 x 8 ... R 47
Screw-self tapping-no 12 x 5/8 ... M 95
Screw-self tapping-no 14 x 3/4 ... B 89
Screw-self tapping-no 14 x 3/4 ... J 19
Screw-self tapping-no 14 x 3/4 ... J 20
Screw-self tapping-no 14 x 3/4 ... J 48
Screw-self tapping-no 14 x 3/4 ... P 1
Screw-self tapping-no 6 ... B307
Screw-self tapping-no 6 x 1" ... P 53
Screw-self tapping-no 6 x 1" ... P 54
Screw-self tapping-no 6 x 1" ... P 64
Screw-self tapping-no 6 x 1" ... P 63
Screw-self tapping-no 6 x 1/2 ... C 84
Screw-self tapping-no 6 x 1/2 ... M 6
Screw-self tapping-no 6 x 1/2 ... M 17
Screw-self tapping-no 6 x 1/2 ... M 18
Screw-self tapping-no 6 x 1/2 ... P 3
Screw-self tapping-no 6 x 1/2 ... P 23
Screw-self tapping-no 6 x 1/2 ... P 44
Screw-self tapping-no 6 x 1/2 ... P 46
Screw-self tapping-no 6 x 1/2 ... P 30
Screw-self tapping-no 6 x 1/2 ... P 31
Screw-self tapping-no 6 x 3/4 ... B 9
Screw-self tapping-no 6 x 3/4 ... B 58
Screw-self tapping-no 6 x 3/4 ... P 14
Screw-self tapping-no 6 x 5/8 ... M132
Screw-self tapping-no 6 x 5/8 ... M138
Screw-self tapping-no 6 x 5/8 ... M139
Screw-self tapping-no 6 x 5/8 ... M140
Screw-self tapping-no 6 x 5/8 ... M141
Screw-self tapping-no 6 x 5/8 ... P 66
Screw-self tapping-no 8 x 1 ... P 18
Screw-self tapping-no 8 x 1/2 ... J 62
Screw-self tapping-no 8 x 1/2 ... L 38
Screw-self tapping-no 8 x 1/2 ... L 75
Screw-self tapping-no 8 x 1/2 ... M 15
Screw-self tapping-no 8 x 1/2 ... M 16
Screw-self tapping-no 8 x 1/2 ... T 47
Screw-self tapping-no 8 x 1/2 ... T 48
Screw-self tapping-no 8 x 3/4 ... N187
Screw-self tapping-no 8 x 3/4 ... P 21
Screw-self tapping-no 8 x 3/4 ... P 56
Screw-self tapping-no 8 x 3/4 ... P 20
Screw-self tapping-no 8 x 3/4 ... P 67
Screw-self tapping-no 8 x 3/4 ... P 61
Screw-self tapping-no 8 x 3/8 ... G 10
Screw-self tapping-no 8 x 3/8 ... M 70
Screw-self tapping-no 8 x 3/8 ... M 76
Screw-self tapping-no 8 x 3/8 ... M 95
Screw-self tapping-no 8 x 3/8 ... M120
Screw-self tapping-no 8 x 3/8 ... P 8
Screw-self tapping-no 8 x 3/8 ... T 46
Screw-self tapping-no 8 x 3/8-long ... M 82
Screw-self tapping-no8 x 5/8 ... P 10
Screw-self tapping-no8 x 5/8 ... P 65
Screw-self tapping-sealed beam-pan head- ... M 1
Screw-self tapping-to wheelarch-8 x 1/4 ... N 61
Screw-self tapping-wiper motor fixing-m8 x ... M143
Screw-self tapping-wiper motor fixing-m8 x ... P 23
Screw-self tapping-wiper motor fixing-m8 x ... P 24
Screw-shield disc to disc solid-flanged ... H 30
Screw-shield disc to disc solid-hexagonal ... H 25
Screw-silencer to chassis-m8 x 70- ... K 9
Screw-solid prop-m4 x 10 ... N143
Screw-speaker-6 x 7/8 ... M122
Screw-speaker-self tapping-no 6 x 40 ... M124
Screw-starter heatshield-flanged head-m5 x ... B229
Screw-starter to flywheel-hexagonal head- ... B189
Screw-stay to body-flanged head-m6 x 20 ... N 96
Screw-stay to body-pan head-m6 x 20 ... N 97
Screw-step to sill-flanged head-m8 x 25 ... N201
Screw-striker to spacer ... N195
Screw-striker to tailgate-hexagonal head-m6 ... N123
Screw-sunroof ... N135
Screw-sunroof to body ... N136
Screw-tappet adjusting ... B 20
Screw-tappet adjusting ... B 68
Screw-tappet adjusting ... B120
Screw-tappet adjusting ... B168
Screw-taptite ... N102
Screw-taptite ... N104
Screw-taptite ... N106
Screw-taptite-plate to chassis-m6 x 12-long ... N 11
Screw-tie bar to bracket-flanged head-m10 x ... T 30
Screw-tie bar to bracket-flanged head-m10 x ... T 31
Screw-to base assembly - front seat-flanged ... N 37
Screw-to bonnet assembly-m6 x 16 ... N141
Screw-to bracket mounting-flanged head-m8 ... N 48
Screw-to bracket mounting-hexagonal head- ... N 12
Screw-to bracket support-m6 x 16 ... N153
Screw-to bracket transmission mounting- ... N 17
Screw-to bracket-flanged head-m8 x 16 ... J 40
Screw-to bracket-hexagonal socket-high ... N 50
Screw-to bumperette-flanged head ... N 23
Screw-to button sill-self tapping-no 6 x 1/2 ... N194
Screw-to channel top-self tapping-6 x 3/8 ... N159
Screw-to channel top-self tapping-6 x 3/8 ... N161
Screw-to channel top-self tapping-6 x 3/8 ... N184
Screw-to cover plate centre-self tapping-no ... N 39
Screw-to crossmember-hexagonal head- ... N 8
Screw-to dash assembly-m8 x 25 ... N 29
Screw-to dash ventilator-hexagonal head- ... N 30
Screw-to finisher ... R 35
Screw-to floor assembly-self tapping-no 14 ... N 44
Screw-to floor-flanged head-m8 x 25 ... R 21
Screw-to frame grille-recessed-pan head- ... N147
Screw-to front plate-self tapping-no 8 x 1/2 ... N 31
Screw-to grille assembly-flanged head-m8 x ... N151
Screw-to grille assembly-self tapping-no 6 x ... N145
Screw-to handle assy-m5 ... N193
Screw-to hexsert-flanged head-m8 x 20 ... N 25
Screw-to nut plate-m6 x 16 ... N196
Screw-to nut spring-self tapping ... N146
Screw-to panel-centre tunnel console-self ... N 34
Screw-to plate catch-flanged head-m6 x 20 ... N142
Screw-to pull door-self tapping-pan head- ... N162
Screw-to vacuum tank-self tapping-no 6 x ... H 9
Screw-to wheelarch-hexagonal head-1/4unf ... R 33
Screw-torx drive-black-m10 x 25 ... N137
Screw-torx drive-black-m10 x 25 ... N220
Screw-torx drive-black-m10 x 25 ... N252
Screw-torx-flange-m5 x 30 ... C 55
Screw-torx-pan ... P 25
Screw-upper ... R 68
Screw-upper bracket-self tapping-no 8 x 1/2 ... P 55
Screw-washer ... M 6
Screw-washer ... M 10
Screw-washer to mounting plate-hexagonal ... N 15
Screw-washer-handle window regulator to ... N162
Screw-washer-m5 x 10 ... N159
Screw-washer-no 8 x 19 ... P 18
Screw-washer-to handle assembly door-no ... N189
Screw-washer-to handle assy-no 8 x 19 ... N193
Screw-washer-to handle window regulator- ... N184
Screw-washer-to panel waterdam-no 8 x 19 ... N170
Screw-wiper motor fixing ... M143
Screw-with rear wash/wipe ... M 75
Screw-with trim ... N221
Screwdriver-tool kit ... S 6
Screwdriver-tool kit ... S 18
Screwdriver-tool kit ... S 7
Seal ... B 31
Seal ... B110
Seal ... B159
Seal ... B202
Seal ... B210
Seal ... B291
Seal ... B 77
Seal ... C 9
Seal ... C 26
Seal ... C 75
Seal ... C 86
Seal ... D 40
Seal ... E 69
Seal ... F 5
Seal ... F 15
Seal ... F 16
Seal ... F 19
Seal ... G 9
Seal ... H 1
Seal ... H 26
Seal ... J 1
Seal ... J 12

Shaft-sun gear ... C 82
Shaft-transfer box differential lock selector ... D 21
Shaft-transfer box differential lock selector ... D 24
Shaft-transfer box-intermediate ... D 15
Shaft-universal joint steering ... F 6
Shampoo-500ml ... W 5
Shedder-front door water-rh ... N153
Shedder-rear door water ... N164
Shield-bonnet latch ... N142
Shield-disc front brake-rh ... H 25
Shield-disc rear brake-rh ... H 30
Shield-disc rear brake-rh ... H 32
Shield-rear flange oil deflector-not needed ... B304
Shim ... F 12
Shim ... F 16
Shim ... N 95
Shim ... N 98
Shim ... N159
Shim ... N183
Shim ... N196
Shim ... N197
Shim ... N 61
Shim ... N170
Shim-0.003" ... E 20
Shim-0.003" ... E 21
Shim-0.038"-imperial ... E 44
Shim-0.060"-imperial ... E 35
Shim-0.70mm ... N191
Shim-1.15mm ... C 33
Shim-1.20/1.25mm ... B399
Shim-2.8mm ... C 75
Shim-2mm ... D 20
Shim-2mm ... D 23
Shim-3.07mm ... C 32
Shim-3.15mm ... D 8
Shim-3.15mm ... D 14
Shim-bearing differential-0.060" ... E 8
Shim-bearing differential-0.060" ... E 35
Shim-bearing differential-2.155mm ... E 10
Shim-bearing differential-2.155mm ... E 38
Shim-channel ... N161
Shim-differential final drive pinion-0.038"- ... E 41
Shim-differential final drive pinion-0.038"- ... E 14
Shim-differential final drive pinion-1.548mm- ... E 42
Shim-differential final drive pinion-1.548mm- ... E 15
Shim-door hinge ... N157
Shim-door hinge ... N169
Shim-front axle half shaft-0.45mm ... E 24
Shim-front axle half shaft-0.45mm ... E 26
Shim-man trans 5th gear synchroniser hub- ... C 15
Shim-man trans countershaft bearing/centre ... C 49
Shim-man trans countershaft bearing/centre ... C 50
Shim-man trans countershaft bearing/front ... C 19
Shim-man trans countershaft bearing/front ... C 16
Shim-man trans differential bearing-0.003" ... E 45
Shim-man trans mainshaft bearing/centre ... C 47
Shim-man trans mainshaft bearing/centre ... C 48
Shim-man trans primary shaft bearing/front ... C 9
Shim-man trans primary shaft bearing/front ... C 10
Shim-man trans reverse gear bush- ... C 65
Shoe assembly rear brake system ... H 28
Shroud ... B118
Shroud ... B166
Shroud ... N123
Shroud ... N197
Shroud air conditioning ... B259
Shroud air conditioning ... L 45
Shroud-central door locking latch-rh ... N191
Side angle roof trim-ripple grey ... P 66
Side rail roof rack support frame-rh ... N137
Silencer assembly exhaust system ... K 7
Silencer assembly exhaust system ... K 8
Silencer assembly exhaust system ... K 10
Silencer assembly exhaust system ... K 19
Silencer assembly exhaust system ... K 20
Silencer assembly exhaust system ... K 23
Silencer assembly exhaust system ... K 24
Silencer assembly exhaust system ... K 25
Silencer assembly exhaust system ... K 26
Silencer assembly exhaust system ... K 27
Silencer assembly exhaust system ... K 30
Silencer assembly exhaust system ... K 31
Silencer assembly exhaust system ... K 32
Silencer assembly exhaust system-centre ... K 28
Silencer assembly exhaust system-centre ... K 29
Silencer assembly exhaust system-rear ... K 9
Silencer assembly exhaust system-rear ... K 22
Sill-front-rh ... N 45
Sill-front-rh ... N 49
Sixthlight assembly-front-rh ... P 53
Slave cylinder clutch ... C 2
Slave cylinder clutch ... C 3
Slave cylinder clutch ... C 28
Slave cylinder clutch ... C 41
Slave cylinder clutch ... C 42
Slave cylinder clutch ... C 43
Slave cylinder clutch ... C 44
Slave cylinder clutch ... C 45
Sleeve ... B175
Sleeve ... D 29
Sleeve ... G 7
Sleeve ... G 9
Sleeve ... N125
Sleeve-guide clutch ... B 47
Sleeve-guide clutch ... B 98
Sleeve-guide clutch ... B191
Sleeve-guide clutch ... B230
Sleeve-guide clutch ... B370
Sleeve-guide clutch ... B147
Sleeve-guide clutch ... C 2
Sleeve-guide clutch ... C 3
Sleeve-guide clutch ... C 28
Sleeve-insulation heat protection-asbestos ... B 25
Sleeve-insulation heat protection-asbestos ... B 73
Sleeve-locking speed stop ... B128
Sleeve-short ... C 74
Slide selector mechanism ... C 84
Slide-front seat left hand side-rh-basic ... R 1
Slide-front seat right hand side-rh-control ... R 1
Slide-tappet guide ... B 21
Slide-tappet guide ... B 69
Slide-tappet guide ... B121
Slide-tappet guide ... B169
Slide-tappet guide ... B209
Slide-tappet guide ... B246
Slug-windscreen mirror fixing ... N221
Socket-electrical towing-7 pin ... T 45
Socket-electrical towing-7 pin ... T 46
Socket-power take off accessory ... T 5
Solenoid shut off-fuel injection pump ... B253
Solenoid starter motor ... B 28
Solenoid starter motor ... B 31
Solenoid starter motor ... B143
Solenoid starter motor ... B369
Solenoid starter motor ... B397
Solenoid starter motor-0 331 303 165-bosch ... B144
Solenoid starter motor-0 331 303 165-bosch ... B145
Solenoid starter motor-0 331 303 165-bosch ... B190
Solenoid starter motor-0 331 303 165-bosch ... B228
Solenoid starter motor-0 331 303 165-bosch ... B262
Solenoid starter motor-cut off ... B 76
Solenoid starter motor-new starter motor- ... B 96
Solenoid starter motor-valeo ... B189
Solenoid starter motor-valeo ... B229
Solenoid starter motor-with 2m100 starter ... B 46
Solenoid starter motor-with m78r starter ... B367
Solenoid starter motor-with m78r starter ... B368
Solenoid-carburettor vent valve ... B 31
Solenoid-carburettor vent valve ... B 29
Solenoid-carburettor vent valve ... B 77
Solenoid-gear change lock ... C 84
Solenoid-vacuum blower-heater ... M 81
Sounder unit burglar alarm-with battery back ... M105
Spacer ... B 9
Spacer ... B 58
Spacer ... B 61
Spacer ... B 92
Spacer ... B 93
Spacer ... B113
Spacer ... B138
Spacer ... B139
Spacer ... B140
Spacer ... B141
Spacer ... B142
Spacer ... B162
Spacer ... B173
Spacer ... B186
Spacer ... B187
Spacer ... B188
Spacer ... B207
Spacer ... B211
Spacer ... B226
Spacer ... B227
Spacer ... B245
Spacer ... B320
Spacer ... B322
Spacer ... B341
Spacer ... B342
Spacer ... B343
Spacer ... B355
Spacer ... B356
Spacer ... B358
Spacer ... B359
Spacer ... B361
Spacer ... B398
Spacer ... B 44
Spacer ... C 32
Spacer ... C 35
Spacer ... C 70
Spacer ... C 86
Spacer ... C 10
Spacer ... C 17
Spacer ... C 67
Spacer ... C 20
Spacer ... D 17
Spacer ... D 18
Spacer ... D 19
Spacer ... D 16
Spacer ... E 9
Spacer ... E 16
Spacer ... E 36
Spacer ... E 46
Spacer ... E 61
Spacer ... E 17
Spacer ... E 47
Spacer ... E 57
Spacer ... G 8
Spacer ... H 21
Spacer ... H 36
Spacer ... J 3
Spacer ... J 8
Spacer ... J 70
Spacer ... K 1
Spacer ... K 2
Spacer ... K 3
Spacer ... K 7
Spacer ... K 8
Spacer ... K 9
Spacer ... K 10
Spacer ... K 11

Spacer ... K 12
Spacer ... K 19
Spacer ... K 20
Spacer ... K 22
Spacer ... K 23
Spacer ... K 25
Spacer ... K 15
Spacer ... L 49
Spacer ... L 69
Spacer ... L 10
Spacer ... L 37
Spacer ... M 27
Spacer ... M 29
Spacer ... M 32
Spacer ... M138
Spacer ... M139
Spacer ... M140
Spacer ... M141
Spacer ... M142
Spacer ... N 24
Spacer ... N185
Spacer ... N192
Spacer ... N195
Spacer ... N203
Spacer ... N222
Spacer ... N 20
Spacer ... N197
Spacer ... N111
Spacer ... P 34
Spacer ... P 53
Spacer ... P 67
Spacer ... P 60
Spacer ... P 61
Spacer ... R 45
Spacer ... R 40
Spacer ... R 28
Spacer ... S 14
Spacer ... S 15
Spacer ... S 16
Spacer ... T 5
Spacer ... T 16
Spacer ... T 39
Spacer ... T 40
Spacer ... T 53
Spacer ... T 52
Spacer spare wheel retention ... S 12
Spacer-15.5mm-purple ... E 26
Spacer-15.5mm-purple ... E 49
Spacer-a133 alternator ... B363
Spacer-bias spring ... C 37
Spacer-collapsible ... E 45
Spacer-crank/drive plate automatic ... B399
Spacer-distance piece ... G 7
Spacer-evaporator expansion valve ... L 49
Spacer-extention to rear crossmembers ... T 31
Spacer-fan to water pump ... B 13
Spacer-foam ... P 18
Spacer-foam ... P 21
Spacer-foam ... P 22
Spacer-foam ... P 56
Spacer-foam ... P 20
Spacer-idler ... B278
Spacer-inertia reel seat belts ... P 57
Spacer-inner ... C 83
Spacer-kit ... B 91
Spacer-mainshaft ... C 58
Spacer-pinion bearing ... E 8
Spacer-pinion bearing ... E 11
Spacer-pinion bearing ... E 35
Spacer-pinion bearing ... E 39
Spacer-plunger housing ... C 24
Spacer-pulley ... B 94
Spacer-pulley ... B360
Spacer-pulley ... B362
Spacer-rocker shaft ... B208
Spacer-side cover ... B123
Spacer-sliding ... C 33
Spacer-sliding ... C 34
Spacer-synchro-hub/pilot ... C 13
Spacer-towing jaw to rear crossmember ... T 32
Spacer-tube-flanged condenser ... L 33
Spacer-twin tube ... R 71
Spacer-twintube ... N204
Spanner-tool kit ... S 6
Spanner-tool kit plug ... S 6
Spanner-tool kit plug ... S 18
Spanner-tool kit plug ... S 7
Spanner-tool kit-10mm x 13mm ... S 7
Spanner-tool kit-3/16" x 1/4" ... S 18
Speaker assembly rear ... M126
Speaker assembly rear-bokhara-philips ... T 12
Speaker assembly-front active ... M126
Speaker assembly-front active ... T 12
Speaker assembly-front single cone ... M121
Speaker assembly-front single cone ... M122
Speaker assembly-front single cone ... M124
Speaker-cover ... M127
Speaker-front & rear single cone ... M127
Speedometer-mph ... M114
Speedometer-mph ... M119
Spigot ... B 36
Spigot ... B132
Spigot-flywheel alignment ... B399
Spigot-idler arm mounting ... B 83
Spindle-hood ret ... N238
Spindle-oil pump ... B 15
Spindle-oil pump ... B115
Spindle-oil pump ... B164
Spindle-oil pump ... B205
Spindle-oil pump ... B 64
Spindle-oil pump-idler wheel ... B 63
Spindle-throttle multi point injection ... B388
Splashguard-engine compartment ... M100
Split charge-towing electrics ... T 43
Spool-interlock-1/2/3/4 ... C 23
Spring ... B 28
Spring ... B332
Spring ... B340
Spring ... B391
Spring ... C 32
Spring ... C 33
Spring ... C 77
Spring ... C 78
Spring ... C 80
Spring ... C 81
Spring ... C 34
Spring ... H 27
Spring ... L 26
Spring ... L 38
Spring ... N175
Spring ... N180
Spring ... N201
Spring ... N203
Spring ... N238
Spring ... N176
Spring ... N177
Spring ... R 31
Spring ... R 45
Spring ... T 5
Spring 1st & 2nd synchroniser ... C 11
Spring 1st & 2nd synchroniser ... C 12
Spring 1st & 2nd synchroniser ... C 14
Spring clip ... N142
Spring ring ... B323
Spring ring ... C 59
Spring ring ... C 63
Spring ring ... C 64
Spring ring ... C 62
Spring ring ... E 69
Spring ring-collar ... C 7
Spring ring-collar ... C 8
Spring ring-collar ... C 34
Spring-carburettor jet needle ... B333
Spring-carburettor throttle return ... B 31
Spring-carburettor throttle return ... B 34
Spring-carburettor throttle return ... B 81
Spring-carburettor throttle return ... B128
Spring-carburettor throttle return ... B175
Spring-carburettor throttle return ... B335
Spring-carburettor throttle return ... B336
Spring-carburettor throttle return ... B 77
Spring-carburettor yellow piston ... B333
Spring-coil ... B144
Spring-coil ... B145
Spring-coil ... B189
Spring-coil ... B190
Spring-coil ... B228
Spring-coil ... B229
Spring-coil ... B262
Spring-coil ... C 24
Spring-cylinder head valve ... B 21
Spring-cylinder head valve ... B 69
Spring-cylinder head valve ... B121
Spring-cylinder head valve ... B169
Spring-cylinder head valve ... B209
Spring-cylinder head valve ... B246
Spring-cylinder head valve ... B279
Spring-cylinder head valve ... B283
Spring-cylinder head valve ... B319
Spring-cylinder head valve ... B381
Spring-detent manual transmission ... C 21
Spring-detent manual transmission ... C 24
Spring-detent manual transmission ... C 46
Spring-detent manual transmission ... C 68
Spring-detent manual transmission ... D 33
Spring-housing ... C 37
Spring-idle spring screw ... B 76
Spring-lever detent selector mechanism ... C 73
Spring-oil pump relief valve ... B 15
Spring-oil pump relief valve ... B 63
Spring-oil pump relief valve ... B115
Spring-oil pump relief valve ... B164
Spring-oil pump relief valve ... B205
Spring-oil pump relief valve ... B238
Spring-oil pump relief valve ... B314
Spring-oil pump relief valve ... B 64
Spring-parking pawl automatic transmission ... C 83
Spring-pin ... C 35
Spring-plunger manual transmission ... C 24
Spring-plunger manual transmission ... C 69
Spring-primary butterfly ... B 31
Spring-pump-carburettor ... B 28
Spring-pump-carburettor ... B 31
Spring-pump-carburettor ... B 76
Spring-rear suspension coil helper ... E 67
Spring-release button selector mechanism ... C 84
Spring-return ... B 28
Spring-return ... B 31
Spring-return ... B 77
Spring-return ... N142
Spring-return brake ... G 9
Spring-return-clutch ... G 7
Spring-return-clutch ... G 8
Spring-return-green ... D 41
Spring-return-tension accelerator ... B391
Spring-return-tension accelerator ... G 1
Spring-reverse hinge ... C 36
Spring-road-coil-front-blue.-green ... E 59
Spring-road-coil-rear-blue.-blue ... E 67
Spring-road-coil-rear-red-blue. ... E 64

Spring-rocker shaft B 20
Spring-rocker shaft B 68
Spring-rocker shaft B120
Spring-rocker shaft B168
Spring-rocker shaft B208

Spring-rocker shaft B245
Spring-rocker shaft B319
Spring-rocker shaft B382
Spring-shoe return-brake abutment end H 29
Spring-shoe return-brake cylinder end H 29

Spring-short C 74
Spring-tensioner B 11
Spring-torsion C 24
Spring-torsion C 69
Spring-torsion C 56

Spring-torsion G 8
Spring-transfer box detent D 29
Spring-transfer box detent D 24
Spring-transfer box detent D 22
Spring-transfer box detent D 28

Spring-transfer box differential lock D 21
Spring-transfer box differential lock D 24
Spring-valve B 77
Sprocket-camshaft B322
Sprocket-camshaft B384

Sprocket-crankshaft B 5
Sprocket-crankshaft B 54
Sprocket-crankshaft B274
Sprocket-crankshaft B304
Sprocket-crankshaft B374

Squab assembly-front-centre-seat-cloth R 15
Squab assembly-front-centre-seat-cloth R 16
Squab assembly-front-centre-seat-cloth- R 20
Squab assembly-front-centre-seat-cloth- R 18
Squab assembly-front-centre-seat-vinyl- R 17

Squab assembly-front-centre-seat-vinyl- R 19
Squab assembly-side-rh-cloth-blue grey- R 9
Squab assembly-side-rh-cloth-morland R 10
Squab cover-rh-centre R 45
Squab-assembly-cloth-brushwood R 4

Squab-assembly-cloth-brushwood R 5
Squab-assembly-front seat-vinyl-black R 2
Squab-large split rear seat-cloth- R 25
Squab-rear seat fixed bench-2 seat-cloth- R 36
Squab-rear seat fixed bench-blue grey- R 39

Squab-rear seat individual- R 29
Squab-rear seat individual-cloth-morland R 32
Squab-small split rear seat-cloth- R 22
Staple N239
Staple N240

Staple N241
Staple N242
Staple N243
Staple N245
Staple N246

Staple T 3
Staple-required when bonnet lock fitted N139
Stay N 95
Stay T 47
Stay T 48

Stay-back-rh N220
Stay-bonnet N144
Stay-bonnet-scissor prop N143
Stay-front N 49
Stay-front N 47

Stay-rh N 97
Stay-rh N 99
Stay-roll cage hoop-inner N250
Stay-roll cage hoop-lower N251
Stay-roll cage hoop-lower V 4

Step & bumper-rear T 49
Step assembly-rear end T 49
Step assembly-rear end-fixed contact N204
Step assembly-rear end-folding N203
Step assembly-side-black T 49

Step assembly-side-folding N201
Step assembly-side-stirrup type N200
Step rear retractable N203
Step-side runner-black-pair N202
Step-side runner-black-pair T 50

Stiffener-cab base assembly-rh N 43
Stiffener-chassis frame-lh N 8
Stiffener-door pillar-rh N 41
Stiffener-front main floor H 35
Stiffener-front mudflap T 51

Stiffener-front mudflap T 53
Stiffener-inst cowl-rh-rhd P 7
Stiffener-lower N 99
Stiffener-rear N105
Stiffener-rh S 12

Stiffener-seat frame R 40
Stiffener-tow equipment angle iron T 40
Stiffener-wheel arch rear floor-front R 69
Stop ladder-bracket N218
Stop-bump-galvanised-rh N 91

Stop-front suspension rebound E 56
Stop-rear seat locating N 39
Stop-rebound rear suspension-2 holes E 61
Stop-release rod selector lever C 24
Strainer and pipe assembly-oil B205

Strainer and pipe assembly-oil B237
Strainer and pipe assembly-oil B306
Strainer and pipe assembly-oil B376
Strainer-fuel filter B279
Strainer-fuel filter B287

Strainer-oil B 15
Strainer-oil B 63
Strainer-oil B115
Strainer-oil B159
Strainer-oil B164

Strainer-oil B314
Strainer-oil B 64
Strainer-oil-automatic transmission fluid C 74
Strainer-oil-drainage hole B110
Strainer-transmission oil C 7

Strainer-transmission oil C 8
Strainer-transmission oil C 55
Strap assembly-retaining T 3
Strap assembly-retaining-black R 33
Strap assembly-retaining-front J 34

Strap assembly-retaining-green R 33
Strap assembly-retaining-rh P 18
Strap assembly-retaining-rh P 21
Strap assembly-retaining-rh P 20
Strap fuel tank J 5

Strap fuel tank J 6
Strap-air cleaner J 40
Strap-bolt-protector rear suspension E 68
Strap-centre cushion-front seats R 2
Strap-convertible hood tonneau retaining N241

Strap-convertible hood tonneau retaining N243
Strap-convertible hood tonneau retaining V 9
Strap-hood-khaki green N238
Strap-oil filler flap retaining B284
Strap-retaining N224

Strap-retaining N230
Strap-retaining-centre squab R 3
Strap-retaining-levelling-3 holes E 69
Strap-roof rack lashing-pair-2 metres T 18
Strap-spare wheel jack retention S 1

Strap-spare wheel jack retention S 2
Strap-spare wheel jack retention S 5
Strap-tool kit retention S 18
Strap-windscreen N185
Straps-load R 37

Striker assembly-door lock P 16
Striker courtesy light N173
Striker-bonnet N139
Striker-bonnet N141
Striker-centre console stowage box lid P 15

Striker-centre console stowage box lid P 16
Striker-door lock N123
Striker-door lock N191
Striker-door lock N192
Striker-door lock N195

Striker-door lock N196
Striker-rear seat squab-rh R 31
Striker-seat lock R 44
Striker-seat lock-except centre squab R 45
Strip rubbing-spare wheel stowage S 16

Strip-anti rattle F 5
Strip-edge protection-89mm M151
Strip-flexible adhesive D 37
Strip-flexible adhesive D 38
Strip-flexible adhesive D 39

Strip-glazing N174
Strip-glazing N108
Strip-glazing N172
Strip-glazing-5 mm glass N111
Strip-glazing-5mm glass N105

Strip-glazing-clear glass N107
Strip-glazing-rh clear N109
Strip-glazing-tinted glass N110
Strip-protection mounting bracket S 14
Strip-protection mounting bracket S 16

Strip-retainer-washer bag-lh N173
Strip-rubbing-black R 14
Strip-sealing G 9
Strip-self adhesive packing P 63
Strip-self adhesive packing P 67

Strip-self adhesive packing P 61
Strip-self adhesive packing-front N 33
Stripper-gasket-200ml U 1
Strut-alternator-65 amp B357
Strut-alternator-65 amp B366

Strut-tailgate gas N222
Stud B 13
Stud B 58
Stud B119
Stud B166

Stud B173
Stud B255
Stud B259
Stud B323
Stud B334

Stud B342
Stud B343
Stud B 10
Stud B111
Stud B160

Stud C 7
Stud C 8
Stud C 83
Stud D 7
Stud D 8

Stud D 9
Stud E 25
Stud E 46
Stud E 49
Stud F 13

Stud H 33
Stud J 41
Stud J 63
Stud J 64
Stud M 13

Stud N114
Stud N191
Stud N192
Stud N241
Stud N242

Stud N245
Stud N246
Stud N 40
Stud N126
Stud N244

Stud N 38
Stud P 38
Stud P 45
Stud R 2
Stud R 3

Stud R 35
Stud plate N 49
Stud plate N102
Stud plate N104
Stud plate N106

Stud plate N196
Stud plate N 47
Stud-1/4unc x 1 B328
Stud-3/8unf x 1 1/4 E 6
Stud-3/8unf x 1 1/4 E 31

Stud-3/8unf x 1 1/8 B341
Stud-5/16unc x 1 3/8 B303
Stud-5/16unc/unf x 2 x 1/8 lng B308
Stud-5/16unc/unf x 2 x 1/8 lng B309
Stud-5/16unf x 1 1/2 B326

Stud-5/16unf x 1 1/2 B327
Stud-bell housing-m10 x 30 B191
Stud-black P 20
Stud-bolt D 7
Stud-bolt D 10

Stud-bolt D 9
Stud-bolt N 30
Stud-bolt N181
Stud-bolt N169
Stud-carb to inlet/manifold-m8 x 40 B 73

Stud-carburetter to inlet manifold-m8 x 35 B 25
Stud-head to block B167
Stud-m10 B126
Stud-m10 x 25 B207
Stud-m10 x 25 B240

Stud-m10 x 25 B297
Stud-m10 x 30 B 47
Stud-m10 x 30 B 98
Stud-m10 x 30 B146
Stud-m10 x 30 B148

Stud-m10 x 30 B230
Stud-m10 x 30 B263
Stud-m10 x 35 B294
Stud-m10 x 75 B241
Stud-m6 x 22 B385

Stud-m8 B120
Stud-m8 x 15 B 7
Stud-m8 x 15 B 52
Stud-m8 x 15 B 56
Stud-m8 x 15 B102

Stud-m8 x 15 B104
Stud-m8 x 15 B108
Stud-m8 x 15 B152
Stud-m8 x 15 B153
Stud-m8 x 15 B195

Stud-m8 x 20 B 4
Stud-m8 x 20 B 53
Stud-m8 x 20 B105
Stud-m8 x 20 B154
Stud-m8 x 20 B197

Stud-m8 x 25 B 11
Stud-m8 x 25 B 12
Stud-m8 x 25 B 19
Stud-m8 x 25 B 60
Stud-m8 x 25 B 67

Stud-m8 x 25 B118
Stud-m8 x 25 B214
Stud-m8 x 25 B244
Stud-m8 x 25 B251
Stud-m8 x 25 B293

Stud-m8 x 25 B386
Stud-m8 x 30 B112
Stud-m8 x 30 B161
Stud-m8 x 30 B202
Stud-m8 x 30 B285

Stud-m8 x 30 B239
Stud-m8 x 32 B177
Stud-m8 x 32 B218
Stud-m8 x 40 B 20
Stud-m8 x 40 B 68

Stud-m8 x 70 B273
Stud-m8 x 70 B280
Stud-m8 x 90 B204
Stud-manifold to block-m8 x 25 B286
Stud-mounting for cab-5/16unf N 67

Stud-rocker cover fixing-m8 B168
Stud-rocker shaft B245
Stud-shoulder L 13
Stud-stub axle E 23
Subframe & slide assembly-front seat-rh R 4

Subframe & slide assembly-front seat-rh R 5
Subframe & slide assembly-front seat-rh R 12
Sump assembly-engine oil B200
Sump assembly-engine oil B270
Sump assembly-engine oil-use with cyclone B108

Sump-engine oil B 7
Sump-engine oil B 56
Sump-engine oil B108
Sump-engine oil B157
Sump-engine oil B237

Sump-engine oil B306
Sump-engine oil B376
Sunvisor assembly-front header-rh P 33
Support assembly-centre facia-radio P 4
Support assembly-hood N242

Support assembly-hood N243
Support assembly-hood N245
Support assembly-hood-front N239
Support assembly-hood-front N240
Support assembly-hood-front N241

Support assembly-hood-intermediate N246
Support assembly-side step N201
Support bracket B296
Support wing N 58
Support-adjuster link alternator B357

Support-adjuster link alternator B366
Support-bulkhead-rh N138
Support-rear body N 44
Support-roll cage-lh N250
Support-seat-10 seats R 43

Support-seat-rh R 32
Support-seat-rh-centre R 1
Suppressor M 68
Switch & bracket assembly-bonnet burglar M105
Switch assembly clutch L 71

Switch assembly-air conditioning rotary- L 73
Switch assembly-pressure antilock brakes H 11
Switch assembly-pressure condenser fan L 68
Switch assembly-push push heated rear M 90
Switch assembly-push push seat-heat M 89

Switch assembly-rotary headlamp leveling M 89
Switch assembly-stop lamp G 9
Switch assembly-transfer box low ratio D 4
Switch assembly-vacuum control-heater L 49
Switch assembly-vacuum control-heater L 68

Switch auxiliary-lamp M 94
Switch auxiliary-lamp M 88
Switch choke G 6
Switch handbrake unit H 34
Switch master lighting M 87

Switch parking-screen wipers M128
Switch trinary L 54
Switch-accessory push push-non-illuminated M 88
Switch-contact courtesy light M 18
Switch-contact courtesy light M 88

Switch-contact courtesy light-front door M 23
Switch-contact wash/wipe-rear M112
Switch-contact-bonnet burglar alarm M105
Switch-electronic diesel control B216
Switch-electronic diesel control B253

Switch-electronic diesel control G 5
Switch-engine thermostat-green B172
Switch-engine thermostat-green B213
Switch-engine thermostat-yellow B324
Switch-engine thermostat-yellow B385

Switch-fuel changeover B128
Switch-fuel changeover B175
Switch-fuel changeover J 51
Switch-fuel changeover M 88
Switch-high/low D 24

Switch-high/low D 22
Switch-indicator/horn/ headlamp dip M 87
Switch-inertia remote fuel pump B298
Switch-inertia remote fuel pump B398
Switch-inhibitor change selector C 73

Switch-master M 32
Switch-oil pressure engine B 17
Switch-oil pressure engine B 18
Switch-oil pressure engine B 65
Switch-oil pressure engine B 66

Switch-oil pressure engine B116
Switch-oil pressure engine B117
Switch-oil pressure engine B165
Switch-oil pressure engine B206
Switch-oil pressure engine B243

Switch-oil pressure engine B291
Switch-oil pressure engine B314
Switch-oil pressure engine B378
Switch-pressure air conditioning control-high L 45
Switch-push push fog-front M 89

Switch-push push fog-rear-one touch M 88
Switch-push push hazard-12v M 89
Switch-push push heated rear window M 89
Switch-push push heated windscreen M 89
Switch-rear fog lamp rocker M 88

Switch-rear fog lamps M 89
Switch-rear fog lamps M 88
Switch-rear fog momentary M 88
Switch-rear wash-momentary M 89
Switch-rear wash-momentary M 90

Switch-rear wipe push push M 89
Switch-rear wipe push push M 90
Switch-reverse lamp C 30
Switch-reverse lamp M 14
Switch-reverse light manual transmission C 55

Switch-rocker T 10
Switch-rocker electric window lift M 89
Switch-rocker hazard-24v M 88
Switch-rocker heated rear window M112
Switch-rotary heatr/fan control L 74

Switch-starter M 86
Switch-starter-without steering column lock M 87
Switch-temp control and capillary temp probe L 74
Switch-thumbwheel illumination control L 72
Switch-transmission oil cooler temperature C 86

Switch-tri pressure-r134a air conditioning L 51
Switch-vacuum-evaporator-air conditioning L 50
Switch-volt sensitive M 84
Switch-volt sensitive-45 amp M 83
Switch-volt sensitive-heated rear window-45 M112

Switch-wash/wipe windscreen M 87
Synchroniser assembly-1st & 2nd mainshaft C 12
Synchroniser assembly-1st & 2nd mainshaft C 33
Synchroniser assembly-1st & 2nd mainshaft C 59
Synchroniser assembly-1st & 2nd mainshaft C 62

Synchroniser assembly-3rd & 4th mainshaft .... C 11
Synchroniser assembly-3rd & 4th mainshaft .... C 32
Synchroniser assembly-3rd & 4th mainshaft .... C 63
Synchroniser assembly-5th gear mainshaft .... C 64
Synchroniser assembly-5th gear mainshaft .... C 34
Synchroniser assembly-5th gear mainshaft .... C 14
T piece .... B 22
T piece .... B 70
T piece .... B 30
T piece .... H 8
T piece .... H 9
T piece .... J 50
T piece .... J 67
T piece .... J 70
T piece .... J 74
T piece .... L 15
T piece .... L 59
T piece .... L 66
T piece M130
T piece M138
T piece M139
T piece M140
T piece M141
T piece M142
T piece-rear .... H 10
T piece-rear .... H 11
T piece-rear .... H 19
T piece-rear .... H 22
T piece-rear .... H 24
Tab-differential locking ring .... E 7
Tab-differential locking ring .... E 9
Tab-differential locking ring .... E 33
Tab-differential locking ring .... E 36
Tab-differential locking ring .... E 34
Tab-differential locking ring .... E 37
Tachometer M119
Tachometer M115
Tailgate assembly N124
Tailgate assembly-chain retained N121
Tailgate assembly-glazed N222
Tailgate assembly-spare wheel carrier N122
Tailpipe assembly-exhaust system .... K 29
Tailpipe exhaust system .... K 8
Tailpipe exhaust system .... K 9
Tailpipe exhaust system .... K 20
Tailpipe exhaust system .... K 22
Tailpipe exhaust system .... K 27
Tank assembly fuel .... J 7
Tank assembly fuel-12 gallons .... J 1
Tank assembly fuel-extra 10 gallon .... J 10
Tank assembly fuel-extra 15 gallon .... J 8
Tank assembly fuel-less evaporator loss-18 .... J 3
Tank-cooling system expansion .... L 9
Tank-cooling system expansion-diesel .... L 11
Tank-radiator expansion .... L 8
Tape sidestripe-strobe blue-rh N216
Tape-'turbo'-rear N211
Tape-'turbo'-rear-grey N212
Tape-'turbo'-rear-grey N213
Tape-black-25mm diameter .... N 37
Tape-door/wing-beige-rh N210
Tape-front door-light grey-dark grey-rh N215
Tape-front door-multi green-rh N214
Tape-front door-multi green-rh N216
Tape-grille-defender-silver on black N206
Tape-grille-defender-silver on black N208
Tape-light grey-dark grey-rh N217
Tape-self adhesive-foam .... L 9
Tappet-engine valve hydraulic B209
Tappet-engine valve hydraulic B246
Tappet-engine valve hydraulic B319
Tappet-engine valve hydraulic B382
Tappet-engine valve mechanical .... B 21
Tappet-engine valve mechanical .... B 69
Tappet-engine valve mechanical B121
Tappet-engine valve mechanical B169
Tappet-engine valve mechanical B209
Tappet-engine valve mechanical B246
Tensioner assembly .... B 11
Tensioner-automatic ancillary drive B241
Tensioner-timing belt B112
Tensioner-timing belt B161
Tensioner-timing belt B203
Tensioner-timing belt B240
Tensioner-timing belt B277
Tensioner-timing belt B278
Tensioner-timing chain .... B 12
Tensioner-timing chain .... B 60
Tensioner-timing chain B274
Terminal connector-plus .... M 82
Thermostat assembly-oil .... B 18
Thermostat assembly-oil .... B 66
Thermostat assembly-oil B117
Thermostat assembly-oil B165
Thermostat assembly-oil B206
Thermostat assembly-oil B243
Thermostat assembly-oil .... L 26
Thermostat assembly-oil .... L 29
Thermostat evaporator-air conditioning .... L 49
Thermostat evaporator-air conditioning .... L 50
Thermostat-engine B250
Thermostat-engine-82 degrees c .... B 24
Thermostat-engine-82 degrees c .... B 72
Thermostat-engine-82 degrees c B125
Thermostat-engine-82 degrees c B172
Thermostat-engine-82 degrees c B324
Thermostat-engine-88 degrees c B213
Thermostat-engine-88 degrees c B385
Thread-locking-sealing-10ml .... U 1
Throttle body-engine .... B 28
Throttle body-engine .... B 31
Throttle body-engine .... B 77
Throttle-traction control secondary .... G 11
Tie bar N239
Tie bar N242
Tie bar N246
Tie bar-front N243
Tie bar-front N245
Tie bar-front and rear N241
Tie bar-rear N240
Tie bar-roll cage .... V 3
Tie bracket-lh .... N 10
Tie-cable .... J 68
Tie-cable .... L 37
Tie-cable .... M 70
Tie-cable .... M 85
Tie-cable M130
Tie-cable-3.5 x 300mm-inside serated .... L 74
Tie-cable-4.8 x 270mm-inside serated .... H 9
Tie-cable-4.8 x 270mm-inside serated .... H 2
Tie-cable-4.8 x 270mm-inside serated .... H 5
Tie-cable-4.8 x 270mm-inside serated .... J 17
Tie-cable-4.8 x 270mm-inside serated .... J 23
Tie-cable-4.8 x 270mm-inside serated .... M 65
Tie-cable-4.8 x 270mm-inside serated .... M 76
Tie-cable-4.8 x 270mm-inside serated .... M 77
Tie-cable-6.5mm hole-8.0 x 155mm .... G 3
Tie-cable-6.5mm hole-8.0 x 155mm .... J 44
Tie-cable-6.5mm hole-8.0 x 155mm M118
Tie-cable-6.5mm hole-8.0 x 155mm .... M 57
Tie-cable-6.5mm hole-8.0 x 155mm .... M 46
Tie-cable-black-13.0 x 540mm-inside .... L 60
Tie-cable-black-13.0 x 540mm-inside .... L 61
Tie-cable-black-13.0 x 540mm-inside .... L 62
Tie-cable-black-13.0 x 540mm-inside .... L 63
Tie-cable-black-13.0 x 540mm-inside .... L 64
Tie-cable-black-2.5 x 100mm-inside serated B318
Tie-cable-black-2.5 x 100mm-outside M101
Tie-cable-black-2.5 x 100mm-outside M109
Tie-cable-black-2.5 x 100mm-outside M147
Tie-cable-black-3.5 x 150mm-inside serated .... G 10
Tie-cable-black-3.5 x 150mm-inside serated .... L 10
Tie-cable-black-3.5 x 150mm-inside serated M100
Tie-cable-black-3.5 x 150mm-inside serated M134
Tie-cable-black-3.5 x 150mm-inside serated M137
Tie-cable-black-3.5 x 150mm-inside serated .... T 45
Tie-cable-black-4.8 x 115mm-inside serated .... M 14
Tie-cable-black-4.8 x 115mm-inside serated M102
Tie-cable-black-4.8 x 115mm-inside serated M103
Tie-cable-black-4.8 x 115mm-inside serated M127
Tie-cable-black-4.8 x 135mm-inside serated B110
Tie-cable-black-4.8 x 135mm-inside serated .... B 59
Tie-cable-black-4.8 x 135mm-inside serated .... M 59
Tie-cable-black-4.8 x 135mm-inside serated .... M 60
Tie-cable-black-4.8 x 135mm-inside serated .... M 66
Tie-cable-black-4.8 x 135mm-inside serated .... M 63
Tie-cable-black-8.8 x 770mm-releasable .... C 24
Tie-cable-black-8.8 x 770mm-releasable .... C 69
Tie-cable-black-8.8 x 770mm-releasable .... N 34
Tie-cable-front breather-white.-4.6 x .... E 50
Tie-cable-front breather-white.-4.6 x .... E 51
Tie-cable-only with su carburettors-white.- B339
Tie-cable-panel fixing-plastic-adjustable- M148
Tie-cable-pipe to tie bar .... J 71
Tie-cable-retaining vent pipe B334
Tie-cable-white.-4.6 x 385mm-inside serated B338
Tie-cable-white.-4.6 x 385mm-inside serated .... G 6
Tie-cable-white.-4.6 x 385mm-inside serated .... J 37
Tie-cable-white.-4.6 x 385mm-inside serated .... J 60
Tie-cable-white.-4.6 x 385mm-inside serated .... J 63
Tie-cable-white.-4.6 x 385mm-inside serated .... L 19
Timer headlamp wash M138
Timer headlamp wash M139
Timer headlamp wash M140
Timer headlamp wash M141
Timer headlamp wash M142
Tongue assembly-seat belt-double-rear- .... R 57
Tool curtain .... S 4
Tool curtain-black .... S 3
Torsion bar & collar-rear end door N181
Torsion bar-rh N169
Torsion bar-rh N158
Torsional vibration damper-engine crankshaft B235
Tow jaw-3500kg .... T 32
Tow jaw-5000kg .... T 34
Towing attachment assembly .... T 31
Towing attachment assembly .... T 35
Towing attachment assembly .... T 37
Towing attachment assembly .... T 38
Towing attachment assembly-adjustable .... T 29
Towing socket-s type .... T 43
Transducer coolant temperature .... B 17
Transducer coolant temperature .... B 18
Transducer coolant temperature .... B 19
Transducer coolant temperature .... B 65
Transducer coolant temperature .... B 66
Transducer coolant temperature .... B 67
Transducer coolant temperature B119
Transducer coolant temperature B167
Transducer coolant temperature B324
Transducer coolant temperature .... L 26
Transducer oil pressure B116
Transducer oil pressure B117
Transducer oil pressure B165
Transducer oil pressure B314
Transducer oil temperature B314
Transducer oil temperature-24v B116
Transducer oil temperature-24v B117
Transducer oil temperature-24v B165
Transducer oil temperature-24v M120

Transducer oil temperature-basic .... C 8
Transducer oil temperature-basic .... C 56
Transducer speed .... D 8
Transducer speed M108
Transfer gearbox assembly-exchange-1.4 : 1 .... D 3
Transfer gearbox assembly-new-1.6 : 1 .... D 1
Transfer gearbox assembly-new-1.6 : 1 .... D 2
Transmission assembly automatic -new .... C 71
Transmission assembly manual-new .... C 27
Transmission assembly-exchange .... C 1
Transmission assembly-new .... C 39
Transmission assembly-new .... C 40
Transmitter plip burglar alarm-433 mhz M104
Trap-fuel-intake engine-electric control unit B337
Tray assembly-electrical equipment .... N 37
Tray battery .... N 35
Tray battery .... N 36
Tray battery .... N 37
Tray-console picnic .... P 14
Tread plate .... N 51
Tread plate N201
Tread plate-front fender-counter sunk- N248
Tread plate-front fender-counter sunk-matt- .... T 14
Tread plate-tailboard N249
Triangle-warning .... T 54
Trim panel .... R 4
Trim panel-aluminium .... P 16
Trim panel-front-mid grey .... P 54
Trunnion-clutch pedal .... G 7
Trunnion-clutch pedal .... G 8
Tube B118
Tube B166
Tube B329
Tube B339
Tube B342
Tube B343
Tube .... B 77
Tube .... J 15
Tube .... L 33
Tube .... L 38
Tube .... L 49
Tube .... L 75
Tube M128
Tube M138
Tube M139
Tube .... S 10
Tube .... V 5
Tube assembly-hood stick tie N247
Tube assembly-oil dipstick .... B 7
Tube assembly-oil dipstick .... B 56
Tube assembly-oil dipstick B108
Tube assembly-oil dipstick B157
Tube assembly-oil dipstick B200
Tube assembly-oil dipstick B272
Tube assembly-rh-front .... R 70
Tube assy-child s/belt mtg .... R 58
Tube bearing .... R 35
Tube-breather transmission case .... C 6
Tube-breather transmission case .... C 37
Tube-breather transmission case .... C 83
Tube-breather transmission case .... C 56
Tube-breather transmission case .... D 5
Tube-centre squab .... R 3
Tube-crossmember N138
Tube-drain evaporator tube .... L 52
Tube-inward facing rear seats support .... R 35
Tube-motor to wheel box-rhd M129
Tube-oil dipstick B237
Tube-oil dipstick B303
Tube-oil dipstick B377
Tube-primary .... B 28
Tube-primary .... B 31
Tube-primary .... B 76
Tube-spacer B327
Tube-tie bar .... F 17
Tube-upper inlet manifold inner B126
Tunnel assembly-main floor .... N 33
Turbocharger assembly-new B177
Turbocharger assembly-new B218
Turbocharger assembly-new B255
Turbocharger assembly-new B293
Tyre .... E 54
Tyron safety band-6.5"-steel wheel-tubed- .... T 1
Underlay-front floor insulation-rh .... P 37
Undertray assembly-rear .... N 25
Union-delivery .... B 37
Union-delivery .... B 83
Union-delivery .... B 84
Union-delivery B133
Union-delivery B181
Unit assembly-immobilization-spider M105
Unit-protection-phase tap-820 ohm .... M 68
Vacuum tank .... H 9
Vacuum tank .... L 59
Valve assembly air intake .... J 33
Valve assembly air intake .... J 34
Valve assembly air intake .... J 35
Valve assembly air intake .... J 36
Valve assembly air intake .... J 37
Valve assembly air intake .... J 38
Valve assembly air intake .... J 39
Valve assembly air intake .... J 43
Valve assembly air intake .... J 62
Valve assembly air intake .... J 73
Valve assembly air intake .... L 34
Valve assembly brake .... H 8
Valve assembly brake-pdwa switch .... H 11
Valve assembly-depression control B284
Valve assembly-depression control .... J 42
Valve assembly-exhaust gas recirculation .... J 77
Valve assembly-oil cooler .... L 26
Valve assembly-power assisted steering B340
Valve assembly-power assisted steering .... F 9
Valve assembly-solenoid .... J 50
Valve brake .... H 19
Valve brake-40 prf 24 .... H 14
Valve-air cleaner dump .... J 42
Valve-air conditioning pressure relief .... B 38
Valve-air conditioning pressure relief .... B 39
Valve-air conditioning pressure relief .... B 85
Valve-air conditioning pressure relief .... B 86
Valve-air conditioning pressure relief B134
Valve-air conditioning pressure relief B135
Valve-air conditioning pressure relief B182
Valve-air conditioning pressure relief B183
Valve-air conditioning pressure relief B222
Valve-air conditioning pressure relief B223
Valve-air conditioning pressure relief B346
Valve-air conditioning pressure relief B347
Valve-air control B329
Valve-air control B338
Valve-air control B339
Valve-air control .... J 60
Valve-air control .... J 73
Valve-bearing housing jet B103
Valve-bearing housing jet B104
Valve-bearing housing jet B153
Valve-bearing housing jet B196
Valve-bearing housing jet B234
Valve-block .... C 74
Valve-block oil flow flap B280
Valve-carburettor throttle overrun B332
Valve-charging air conditioning .... L 45
Valve-control-exhaust gas recirculation .... B 29
Valve-cylinder head exhaust .... B 21
Valve-cylinder head exhaust .... B 69
Valve-cylinder head exhaust B121
Valve-cylinder head exhaust B169
Valve-cylinder head exhaust B209
Valve-cylinder head exhaust B246
Valve-cylinder head exhaust B279
Valve-cylinder head exhaust B283
Valve-cylinder head exhaust B381
Valve-cylinder head exhaust B316
Valve-cylinder head inlet .... B 21
Valve-cylinder head inlet .... B 69
Valve-cylinder head inlet B121
Valve-cylinder head inlet B169
Valve-cylinder head inlet B209
Valve-cylinder head inlet B246
Valve-cylinder head inlet B279
Valve-cylinder head inlet B283
Valve-cylinder head inlet B381
Valve-cylinder head inlet B316
Valve-exhaust gas recirculation engine .... J 75
Valve-exhaust gas recirculation engine .... J 76
Valve-expansion evaporator-air conditioning .... L 50
Valve-expansion evaporator-air conditioning .... L 51
Valve-expansion evaporator-air conditioning .... L 52
Valve-fuel cut fuel tank B253
Valve-fuel cut fuel tank .... J 7
Valve-inlet manifold non return B323
Valve-non return brake vacuum .... H 1
Valve-non return brake vacuum .... H 3
Valve-one way fuel lines .... J 53
Valve-pressure vacuum .... J 69
Valve-solenoid-exhaust gas recirculation .... J 75
Valve-suction air conditioning compressor .... L 50
Valve-suction air conditioning compressor .... L 58
Valve-vacuum delay-blue. .... B 32
Valve-vacuum delay-blue. .... B 78
Valve-vacuum delay-orange B331
Valve-wash system non return-4mm M131
Valve-wash system non return-4mm M133
Valve-wash system non return-4mm M134
Valve-wash system non return-4mm M137
Valve-wash system non return-4mm M140
Valve-wash system non return-4mm M141
Valve-wash system non return-4mm M142
Valve-wash system non return-windscreen M135
Valve-wash system non return-windscreen M136
Valve-waste gate-control turbocharger B293
Vent assembly-face level driver facia .... L 71
Vent-air extractor N129
Vent-air extractor N131
Vent-elbow .... B 77
Venturi auxilary-centre device-carburettor- .... B 28
Venturi auxilary-centre device-carburettor- .... B 31
Venturi auxilary-centre device-carburettor- .... B 76
Warning light assembly-12v M119
Warning light assembly-12v M116
Wash 'n' wax-300ml .... W 5
Washer .... B 3
Washer .... B 8
Washer .... B 22
Washer .... B 23
Washer .... B 31
Washer .... B 38
Washer .... B 39
Washer .... B 41
Washer .... B 42
Washer .... B 51
Washer .... B 57
Washer .... B 85
Washer .... B 86
Washer .... B 88
Washer B102
Washer B109
Washer B119
Washer B134

Washer-m6 .... R 63
Washer-m6 .... R 68
Washer-m6 .... T 48
Washer-m6-oversize .... H 10
Washer-m6-oversize .... J 48

Washer-m6-oversize .... M 28
Washer-m6-oversize .... M 91
Washer-m6-oversize M130
Washer-m6-oversize M131
Washer-m6-oversize M135

Washer-m6-oversize .... N 39
Washer-m6-oversize .... N 53
Washer-m6-oversize .... S 14
Washer-m6-rectangular .... F 19
Washer-m6-rectangular .... N 61

Washer-m8 .... B103
Washer-m8 .... N200
Washer-m8 .... N 50
Washer-m8 .... N 29
Washer-m8 .... N178

Washer-m8 .... N 7
Washer-m8 .... R 16
Washer-m8 .... R 42
Washer-m8 .... R 59
Washer-m8 .... R 64

Washer-m8 .... R 67
Washer-m8 .... R 24
Washer-m8 .... R 21
Washer-m8 .... R 27
Washer-m8 .... S 15

Washer-m8-large .... R 48
Washer-m8-large .... R 50
Washer-m8-large .... S 19
Washer-m8-standard B174
Washer-m8-standard B175

Washer-m8-standard B366
Washer-m8-standard .... C 36
Washer-m8-standard .... D 24
Washer-nylon .... L 62
Washer-nylon N168

Washer-nylon N221
Washer-nylon N157
Washer-nylon N178
Washer-nylon .... N 8
Washer-oil pressure switch engine B314

Washer-oversize .... J 3
Washer-panel fixing-sprung-m6 .... M 29
Washer-plain .... B 19
Washer-plain .... B 20
Washer-plain .... B 62

Washer-plain .... B 67
Washer-plain .... B 68
Washer-plain B112
Washer-plain B114
Washer-plain B119

Washer-plain B120
Washer-plain B124
Washer-plain B161
Washer-plain B162
Washer-plain B163

Washer-plain B167
Washer-plain B168
Washer-plain B171
Washer-plain B204
Washer-plain B212

Washer-plain B260
Washer-plain B304
Washer-plain B308
Washer-plain B309
Washer-plain B319

Washer-plain B322
Washer-plain B323
Washer-plain B326
Washer-plain B327
Washer-plain B328

Washer-plain B341
Washer-plain B342
Washer-plain B343
Washer-plain B357
Washer-plain B363

Washer-plain B364
Washer-plain B365
Washer-plain B366
Washer-plain B381
Washer-plain B382

Washer-plain B386
Washer-plain .... B 14
Washer-plain .... B 74
Washer-plain B317
Washer-plain .... E 40

Washer-plain .... E 42
Washer-plain .... E 43
Washer-plain .... E 56
Washer-plain .... E 69
Washer-plain .... E 8

Washer-plain .... E 11
Washer-plain .... E 14
Washer-plain .... E 35
Washer-plain .... E 19
Washer-plain .... E 39

Washer-plain .... G 7
Washer-plain .... H 30
Washer-plain .... H 32
Washer-plain .... H 20
Washer-plain .... H 22

Washer-plain .... H 24
Washer-plain .... J 1
Washer-plain .... J 8
Washer-plain .... J 10
Washer-plain .... J 14

Washer-plain .... J 15
Washer-plain .... K 1
Washer-plain .... K 2
Washer-plain .... K 3
Washer-plain .... K 7

Washer-plain .... K 8
Washer-plain .... K 9
Washer-plain .... K 10
Washer-plain .... K 11
Washer-plain .... K 12

Washer-plain .... K 18
Washer-plain .... K 19
Washer-plain .... K 20
Washer-plain .... K 22
Washer-plain .... K 23

Washer-plain .... K 25
Washer-plain .... K 29
Washer-plain .... K 31
Washer-plain .... K 32
Washer-plain .... K 15

Washer-plain .... L 3
Washer-plain .... L 12
Washer-plain .... L 33
Washer-plain .... L 39
Washer-plain .... L 62

Washer-plain .... L 37
Washer-plain .... M 32
Washer-plain M101
Washer-plain M134
Washer-plain M137

Washer-plain .... N 30
Washer-plain N102
Washer-plain N104
Washer-plain N106
Washer-plain N121

Washer-plain N124
Washer-plain N125
Washer-plain N139
Washer-plain N163
Washer-plain N181

Washer-plain N182
Washer-plain N191
Washer-plain N199
Washer-plain N201
Washer-plain N203

Washer-plain N238
Washer-plain N251
Washer-plain N252
Washer-plain .... N 50
Washer-plain N197

Washer-plain .... N 47
Washer-plain .... N 61
Washer-plain N127
Washer-plain N170
Washer-plain .... N 48

Washer-plain N179
Washer-plain .... P 7
Washer-plain .... P 13
Washer-plain .... P 30
Washer-plain .... R 5

Washer-plain .... R 31
Washer-plain .... R 62
Washer-plain .... R 66
Washer-plain .... R 68
Washer-plain .... R 37

Washer-plain .... R 71
Washer-plain .... R 38
Washer-plain .... S 1
Washer-plain .... S 2
Washer-plain .... S 5

Washer-plain .... S 14
Washer-plain .... T 16
Washer-plain .... T 47
Washer-plain .... T 48
Washer-plain .... V 4

Washer-plain-1/4 dia .... R 45
Washer-plain-10mm id .... S 13
Washer-plain-8mm .... D 36
Washer-plain-8mm .... H 34
Washer-plain-8mm .... T 53

Washer-plain-bracket fixing M103
Washer-plain-centre flange/head .... B 26
Washer-plain-centre squab .... R 3
Washer-plain-coil bracket-m6 .... B 42
Washer-plain-fan to viscous B311

Washer-plain-fixing bracket-8mm .... M 82
Washer-plain-fixing facia plate-large-black M113
Washer-plain-large-black M120
Washer-plain-large-black .... M 12
Washer-plain-large-black N145

Washer-plain-large-black .... P 8
Washer-plain-large-m5 .... G 10
Washer-plain-large-m5 .... N 30
Washer-plain-large-m5 .... N 51
Washer-plain-large-m5 .... N147

Washer-plain-m10 .... D 9
Washer-plain-m10-oversize B377
Washer-plain-m10-oversize .... E 62
Washer-plain-m10-oversize N204
Washer-plain-m10-oversize .... N 8

Washer-plain-m12 .... N 20
Washer-plain-m12 x 22 .... E 22
Washer-plain-m12 x 28 .... E 60
Washer-plain-m12 x 28 .... E 68
Washer-plain-m12 x 28 .... F 17

Washer-plain-m12 x 28 .... K 13
Washer-plain-m4 .... B244
Washer-plain-m4 .... F 23
Washer-plain-m4 .... J 50
Washer-plain-m4 .... M 32

Washer-plain-m4 .... M121
Washer-plain-m4 .... M139
Washer-plain-m4 .... M140
Washer-plain-m4 .... M141
Washer-plain-m4 .... M142

Washer-plain-m4 .... N 32
Washer-plain-m4 .... N 90
Washer-plain-m4 .... N187
Washer-plain-m4 .... N184
Washer-plain-m4 .... N189

Washer-plain-m4 .... N194
Washer-plain-m4 .... P 1
Washer-plain-m4 .... P 3
Washer-plain-m4 .... P 13
Washer-plain-m4 .... P 11

Washer-plain-m5 .... L 72
Washer-plain-m5 .... M109
Washer-plain-m5-oversize .... M 57
Washer-plain-m6 .... B 89
Washer-plain-m6 .... J 19

Washer-plain-m6 .... J 20
Washer-plain-m6 .... K 14
Washer-plain-m6 .... K 16
Washer-plain-m6 .... L 31
Washer-plain-m6 .... M127

Washer-plain-m6 .... M143
Washer-plain-m6 .... N 33
Washer-plain-m6 .... N 44
Washer-plain-m6 .... N 34
Washer-plain-m6 .... N 99

Washer-plain-m6 .... N249
Washer-plain-m6 .... P 1
Washer-plain-m6 .... T 14
Washer-plain-m6-standard B354
Washer-plain-m6-standard .... F 19

Washer-plain-m6-standard .... J 37
Washer-plain-m6-standard .... J 38
Washer-plain-m6-standard .... J 45
Washer-plain-m8 .... B 41
Washer-plain-m8 .... B 88

Washer-plain-m8 .... B136
Washer-plain-m8 .... B185
Washer-plain-m8 .... J 73
Washer-plain-m8 .... M 86
Washer-plain-m8 .... M 58

Washer-plain-m8 .... R 6
Washer-plain-m8 .... R 14
Washer-plain-m8 .... S 8
Washer-plain-m8 .... S 9
Washer-plain-manifold to head .... B 25

Washer-plain-manifold to head .... B 73
Washer-plain-no 10 .... R 71
Washer-plain-normal o.d. .... N 67
Washer-plain-p-clip to bulkhead .... M 46
Washer-plain-radius arm-m12 x 28 .... E 57

Washer-plain-scissor prop N143
Washer-plain-sill panel to outer wing- .... N 46
Washer-plain-speaker-m4 .... M122
Washer-plain-speaker-m4 .... M124
Washer-plain-standard .... B 32

Washer-plain-standard .... B 78
Washer-plain-standard B307
Washer-plain-standard .... J 8
Washer-plain-standard .... K 26
Washer-plain-standard .... K 27

Washer-plain-standard .... K 28
Washer-plain-standard .... K 30
Washer-plain-standard .... N 15
Washer-plain-standard .... N 16
Washer-plain-standard .... N 49

Washer-plain-standard .... N 53
Washer-plain-standard N114
Washer-plain-standard N188
Washer-plain-standard N193
Washer-plain-standard N198

Washer-plain-standard .... N 37
Washer-plain-standard .... N 38
Washer-plain-standard .... N 58
Washer-plain-standard .... R 1
Washer-plain-standard .... R 15

Washer-plain-standard .... R 44
Washer-plain-standard .... R 28
Washer-plain-standard-m12 .... F 8
Washer-plain-standard-m12 .... G 3
Washer-plain-standard-m12 .... N 28

Washer-plain-standard-m5 .... B178
Washer-plain-standard-m5 .... B 29
Washer-plain-standard-m5 .... C 52
Washer-plain-standard-m5 .... F 4
Washer-plain-standard-m5 .... J 45

Washer-plain-standard-m5 .... J 67
Washer-plain-standard-m5 .... L 36
Washer-plain-standard-m5 .... L 38
Washer-plain-standard-m5 .... L 39
Washer-plain-standard-m5 .... L 62

Washer-plain-standard-m5 .... L 75
Washer-plain-standard-m5 .... M 15
Washer-plain-standard-m5 .... M 16
Washer-plain-standard-m5 .... M 70
Washer-plain-standard-m5 .... M 76

Washer-plain-standard-m5 .... M121
Washer-plain-standard-m5 .... M 75
Washer-plain-standard-m5 .... M 79
Washer-plain-standard-m5 .... M 58
Washer-plain-standard-m5 .... N 90

Washer-plain-standard-m5 .... N148
Washer-plain-standard-m5 .... N188
Washer-plain-standard-m5 .... N193
Washer-plain-standard-m5 .... N201
Washer-plain-standard-m5 .... N 31

Washer-plain-standard-m5 .... N 94
Washer-plain-standard-m5 .... N244
Washer-plain-standard-m5 .... R 37
Washer-plain-standard-m5 .... S 8
Washer-plain-standard-m5 .... S 9

Washer-plain-standard. N146
Washer-plain-steering drop arm to crossrod- .... F 18
Washer-plain-striker to bonnet-m12- N141
Washer-plain-thick N203
Washer-plain-thin .... B 34

Washer-plain-thin .... B 81
Washer-plain-thin .... N 8
Washer-plain-thin .... R 35
Washer-plastic M144
Washer-plastic .... N 25

Washer-plastic N180
Washer-plastic N204
Washer-plastic .... P 10
Washer-plastic .... P 30
Washer-plastic .... R 2

Washer-plastic .... R 29
Washer-plastic .... T 3
Washer-plastic-retaining .... L 4
Washer-plate to block-sprung-m6 .... B212
Washer-pump to bracket-8mm .... B 84

Washer-pump to bracket-8mm B133
Washer-pump to bracket-m8-standard B181
Washer-relay base-plain-standard-m5 .... M 77
Washer-retaining .... B 71
Washer-retaining .... N 98

Washer-retaining-m5 .... G 13
Washer-retaining-m5 .... J 51
Washer-retaining-m5 .... J 2
Washer-retaining-m5 .... J 4
Washer-retaining-m5 .... J 9

Washer-retaining-m5 .... M 10
Washer-retaining-m5 .... M 63
Washer-retaining-m5 .... N163
Washer-retaining-m5 .... N182
Washer-retaining-m5 .... P 7

Washer-retaining-m5 .... T 45
Washer-retaining-m5 .... T 46
Washer-rubber .... B 22
Washer-rubber .... F 18
Washer-rubber .... R 29

Washer-rubber-drivers & passenger squab .... R 2
Washer-scissor prop N143
Washer-sealing .... B 3
Washer-sealing .... B 15
Washer-sealing .... B 17

Washer-sealing .... B 18
Washer-sealing .... B 19
Washer-sealing .... B 21
Washer-sealing .... B 22
Washer-sealing .... B 24

Washer-sealing .... B 25
Washer-sealing .... B 31
Washer-sealing .... B 37
Washer-sealing .... B 51
Washer-sealing .... B 52

Washer-sealing .... B 65
Washer-sealing .... B 66
Washer-sealing .... B 67
Washer-sealing .... B 69
Washer-sealing .... B 70

Washer-sealing .... B 72
Washer-sealing .... B 73
Washer-sealing .... B 76
Washer-sealing .... B 83
Washer-sealing .... B 84

Washer-sealing B102
Washer-sealing B103
Washer-sealing B104
Washer-sealing B115
Washer-sealing B116

Washer-sealing B117
Washer-sealing B119
Washer-sealing B121
Washer-sealing B122
Washer-sealing B125

Washer-sealing B133
Washer-sealing B152
Washer-sealing B164
Washer-sealing B165
Washer-sealing B167

Washer-sealing B169
Washer-sealing B170
Washer-sealing B172
Washer-sealing B177
Washer-sealing B178

Washer-sealing B181
Washer-sealing B196
Washer-sealing B205
Washer-sealing B206
Washer-sealing B207

Washer-sealing B209
Washer-sealing B213
Washer-sealing B216
Washer-sealing B217
Washer-sealing B243

Washer-sealing B244
Washer-sealing B246
Washer-sealing B247
Washer-sealing B251
Washer-sealing B253

Washer-sealing B254
Washer-sealing B274
Washer-sealing B279
Washer-sealing B287
Washer-sealing B289

Washer-sealing B293
Washer-sealing B314
Washer-sealing B323
Washer-sealing B324
Washer-sealing B378
Washer-sealing B385
Washer-sealing B390
Washer-sealing B 64
Washer-sealing B239
Washer-sealing C 26
Washer-sealing C 37
Washer-sealing C 55
Washer-sealing C 75
Washer-sealing C 83
Washer-sealing C 86
Washer-sealing C 56
Washer-sealing D 4
Washer-sealing D 7
Washer-sealing D 40
Washer-sealing D 5
Washer-sealing E 51
Washer-sealing E 19
Washer-sealing J 52
Washer-sealing J 59
Washer-sealing L 26
Washer-sealing L 27
Washer-sealing L 30
Washer-sealing N 32
Washer-sealing-alternatives B 7
Washer-sealing-asbestos B202
Washer-sealing-asbestos B111
Washer-sealing-asbestos B160
Washer-sealing-axle breather hose banjo E 50
Washer-sealing-diesel injector to cylinder B129
Washer-sealing-diesel injector to cylinder B176
Washer-sealing-drain plug-automatic C 74
Washer-sealing-fuel tank drain plug J 1
Washer-sealing-fuel tank drain plug J 3
Washer-sealing-fuel tank drain plug J 8
Washer-sealing-fuel tank drain plug J 10
Washer-sealing-jet assembly-top B153
Washer-sealing-joint oil relief B 63
Washer-sealing-man trans drain plug C 4
Washer-sealing-man trans drain plug C 46
Washer-sealing-man trans drain plug C 5
Washer-sealing-man trans extension case C 7
Washer-sealing-man trans extension case C 8
Washer-sealing-man trans extension case C 30
Washer-sealing-steering swivel pin housing E 21
Washer-sealing-sump drain plug B 56
Washer-sealing-sump drain plug B108
Washer-sealing-sump drain plug B157
Washer-sealing-sump drain plug B200
Washer-sealing-sump drain plug B237
Washer-sealing-sump drain plug B270
Washer-sealing-sump drain plug B306
Washer-sealing-sump drain plug B376
Washer-sealing-transfer box drain plug D 10
Washer-sealing-transfer box drain plug D 9
Washer-sealing-turbocharger oil drain pipe B218
Washer-sealing-turbocharger oil feed pipe B255
Washer-sealing-unheated J 54
Washer-sealing-unheated J 56
Washer-seat to bracket-m8 R 28
Washer-shield to manifold-8mm B 27
Washer-sill panel to outer wing-sprung-m6 N 46
Washer-special idler pulley B249
Washer-spring B 4
Washer-spring B354
Washer-spring J 1
Washer-spring J 50
Washer-spring J 9
Washer-spring J 11
Washer-spring M 7
Washer-spring M 82
Washer-spring M100
Washer-spring M 12
Washer-spring N121
Washer-spring N149
Washer-spring N 58
Washer-spring P 18
Washer-spring R 36
Washer-spring R 39
Washer-spring R 45
Washer-spring R 62
Washer-spring S 15
Washer-spring-1/4 dia-square B 32
Washer-spring-1/4 dia-square B 42
Washer-spring-1/4 dia-square B 78
Washer-spring-1/4 dia-square B306
Washer-spring-1/4 dia-square B307
Washer-spring-1/4 dia-square B310
Washer-spring-1/4 dia-square B320
Washer-spring-1/4 dia-square B324
Washer-spring-1/4 dia-square B337
Washer-spring-1/4 dia-square B370
Washer-spring-1/4 dia-square B376
Washer-spring-1/4 dia-square B385
Washer-spring-1/4 dia-square J 13
Washer-spring-1/4 dia-square L 3
Washer-spring-1/4 dia-square R 30
Washer-spring-1/4 dia-square R 33
Washer-spring-3/16 dia-square B303
Washer-spring-3/16 dia-square B323
Washer-spring-3/16 dia-square B335
Washer-spring-3/16 dia-square B336
Washer-spring-3/16 dia-square M 14
Washer-spring-3/16 dia-square M 58
Washer-spring-3/16 dia-square N102
Washer-spring-3/16 dia-square P 2
Washer-spring-3/16 dia-square R 44
Washer-spring-3/16 dia-square R 35
Washer-spring-3/8 C 38
Washer-spring-3/8 C 73
Washer-spring-5/16" B 45
Washer-spring-5/16" B131
Washer-spring-5/16" B180
Washer-spring-5/16" B220
Washer-spring-5/16" B225
Washer-spring-5/16" B308
Washer-spring-5/16" B309
Washer-spring-5/16" B330
Washer-spring-5/16" B331
Washer-spring-5/16" B334
Washer-spring-5/16" B341
Washer-spring-5/16" B342
Washer-spring-5/16" B343
Washer-spring-5/16" B349
Washer-spring-5/16" B363
Washer-spring-5/16" B364
Washer-spring-5/16" B365
Washer-spring-5/16" B377
Washer-spring-5/16" B381
Washer-spring-5/16" E 62
Washer-spring-5/16" E 63
Washer-spring-5/16" E 59
Washer-spring-5/16" E 64
Washer-spring-5/16" E 66
Washer-spring-5/16" E 67
Washer-spring-5/16" G 7
Washer-spring-5/16" H 29
Washer-spring-5/16" J 34
Washer-spring-5/16" K 3
Washer-spring-5/16" L 43
Washer-spring-5/16" M 63
Washer-spring-5/16" N 14
Washer-spring-5/16" N 53
Washer-spring-5/16" N 67
Washer-spring-5/16" N 50
Washer-spring-5/16" N 47
Washer-spring-5/16" R 68
Washer-spring-6mm N 11
Washer-spring-double coil-1/4"-imperial L 7
Washer-spring-fixing radiator cowl-double L 5
Washer-spring-front to rear sill panel-m6- N 46
Washer-spring-m4 P 1
Washer-spring-m6 P 23
Washer-spring-m6 P 24
Washer-spring-m6-square C 2
Washer-spring-m6-square C 28
Washer-spring-m6-square L 17
Washer-spring-m6-square N 49
Washer-spring-m6-square N 99
Washer-spring-no 10-single coil-rectangular J 14
Washer-spring-no 10-single coil-rectangular J 15
Washer-spring-no 10-single coil-rectangular T 16
Washer-spring-rectangular N146
Washer-spring-solid prop N143
Washer-sprung-7/16" N 14
Washer-sprung-m5 M120
Washer-sprung-m5 P 8
Washer-sprung-m6 B 13
Washer-sprung-m6 B 24
Washer-sprung-m6 B 61
Washer-sprung-m6 B 62
Washer-sprung-m6 B 72
Washer-sprung-m6 B113
Washer-sprung-m6 B114
Washer-sprung-m6 B124
Washer-sprung-m6 B125
Washer-sprung-m6 B131
Washer-sprung-m6 B162
Washer-sprung-m6 B163
Washer-sprung-m6 B171
Washer-sprung-m6 B172
Washer-sprung-m6 B180
Washer-sprung-m6 B204
Washer-sprung-m6 B220
Washer-sprung-m6 B 59
Washer-sprung-m6 C 86
Washer-sprung-m6 C 23
Washer-sprung-m6 E 19
Washer-sprung-m6 G 1
Washer-sprung-m6 J 33
Washer-sprung-m6 J 36
Washer-sprung-m6 J 37
Washer-sprung-m6 J 46
Washer-sprung-m6 J 65
Washer-sprung-m6 L 25
Washer-sprung-m6 L 27
Washer-sprung-m6 L 32
Washer-sprung-m6 L 42
Washer-sprung-m6 L 43
Washer-sprung-m6 L 60
Washer-sprung-m6 L 61
Washer-sprung-m6 L 63
Washer-sprung-m6 L 64
Washer-sprung-m6 M101
Washer-sprung-m6 M 46
Washer-sprung-m6 N 41
Washer-sprung-m6 N 67
Washer-sprung-m6 N 93
Washer-sprung-m6 N115
Washer-sprung-m6 N123
Washer-sprung-m6 N124
Washer-sprung-m6 N139
Washer-sprung-m6 N142
Washer-sprung-m6 N159
Washer-sprung-m6 N180
Washer-sprung-m6 N187

Washer-sprung-m6 N196
Washer-sprung-m6 N198
Washer-sprung-m6 N246
Washer-sprung-m6 N126
Washer-sprung-m6 N161
Washer-sprung-m6 N 37
Washer-sprung-m6 N 38
Washer-sprung-m6 N179
Washer-sprung-m6 P 24
Washer-sprung-m6 P 33
Washer-sprung-m6 R 15
Washer-sprung-m6 R 44
Washer-sprung-m6 R 51
Washer-sprung-m6 R 66
Washer-sprung-m6 R 33
Washer-sprung-m6 S 4
Washer-sprung-m6 S 12
Washer-sprung-m6 T 5
Washer-sprung-m6 T 52
Washer-sprung-m6 B 7
Washer-sprung-m8 B 9
Washer-sprung-m8 B 11
Washer-sprung-m8 B 15
Washer-sprung-m8 B 19
Washer-sprung-m8 B 20
Washer-sprung-m8 B 36
Washer-sprung-m8 B 45
Washer-sprung-m8 B 53
Washer-sprung-m8 B 56
Washer-sprung-m8 B 58
Washer-sprung-m8 B 67
Washer-sprung-m8 B 68
Washer-sprung-m8 B 83
Washer-sprung-m8 B 95
Washer-sprung-m8 B105
Washer-sprung-m8 B106
Washer-sprung-m8 B108
Washer-sprung-m8 B115
Washer-sprung-m8 B120
Washer-sprung-m8 B129
Washer-sprung-m8 B132
Washer-sprung-m8 B142
Washer-sprung-m8 B154
Washer-sprung-m8 B155
Washer-sprung-m8 B157
Washer-sprung-m8 B164
Washer-sprung-m8 B168
Washer-sprung-m8 B176
Washer-sprung-m8 B188
Washer-sprung-m8 B197
Washer-sprung-m8 B198
Washer-sprung-m8 B205
Washer-sprung-m8 B227
Washer-sprung-m8 B 10
Washer-sprung-m8 B 14
Washer-sprung-m8 B 74
Washer-sprung-m8 C 2
Washer-sprung-m8 C 3
Washer-sprung-m8 C 28
Washer-sprung-m8 C 31
Washer-sprung-m8 C 35
Washer-sprung-m8 C 42
Washer-sprung-m8 C 54
Washer-sprung-m8 D 33
Washer-sprung-m8 D 31
Washer-sprung-m8 G 9
Washer-sprung-m8 H 1
Washer-sprung-m8 H 36
Washer-sprung-m8 H 35
Washer-sprung-m8 J 10
Washer-sprung-m8 J 73
Washer-sprung-m8 K 1
Washer-sprung-m8 K 2
Washer-sprung-m8 K 3
Washer-sprung-m8 K 7
Washer-sprung-m8 K 8
Washer-sprung-m8 K 9
Washer-sprung-m8 K 10
Washer-sprung-m8 K 11
Washer-sprung-m8 K 12
Washer-sprung-m8 K 19
Washer-sprung-m8 K 20
Washer-sprung-m8 K 22
Washer-sprung-m8 K 23
Washer-sprung-m8 K 24
Washer-sprung-m8 K 25
Washer-sprung-m8 K 4
Washer-sprung-m8 K 15
Washer-sprung-m8 L 3
Washer-sprung-m8 L 33
Washer-sprung-m8 M 82
Washer-sprung-m8 N 43
Washer-sprung-m8 N114
Washer-sprung-m8 N145
Washer-sprung-m8 N150
Washer-sprung-m8 N151
Washer-sprung-m8 N 48
Washer-sprung-m8 T 6
Washer-standard N 57
Washer-standard R 30
Washer-standard.-black-10mm N137
Washer-starlock G 3
Washer-starlock G 5
Washer-starlock H 36
Washer-starlock M 95
Washer-starlock R 35
Washer-starlock-1/2"-imperial F 1
Washer-starlock-14mm F 3
Washer-starlock-centre squab R 3
Washer-starlock-m5 P 2
Washer-starlock-m6 N141
Washer-starlock-no 8-3mm P 7
Washer-starter to flywheel-m10 B229
Washer-steering box drop arm nut tab- F 8
Washer-steering box drop arm nut tab- F 10
Washer-steering box drop arm nut tab- F 11
Washer-steering box drop arm nut tab- F 7
Washer-steering box drop arm nut tab- F 9
Washer-steering box drop arm nut tab- F 12
Washer-sump assembly drain plug B 8
Washer-sump assembly drain plug B 57
Washer-sump assembly drain plug B103
Washer-sump assembly drain plug B153
Washer-sump assembly drain plug B196
Washer-sump assembly drain plug B234
Washer-thrust B115
Washer-thrust B164
Washer-thrust D 11
Washer-thrust E 20
Washer-thrust manual transmission C 64
Washer-thrust manual transmission-1st/2nd C 13
Washer-thrust-5th gear C 33
Washer-thrust-gear differential E 43
Washer-thrust-gear differential E 45
Washer-thrust-later type locking ring B 16
Washer-thrust-pinion differential-rear E 43
Washer-thrust-pinion differential-rear E 45
Washer-thrust-thrust B 63
Washer-tie bar to chassis-m10 T 30
Washer-towing hook to crossmember-plain- T 33
Washer-waved B319
Washer-waved B382
Washer-waved N 32
Washer-wing to bracket N 58
Water control valve L 60
Water control valve L 61
Water control valve L 62
Water control valve L 63
Water control valve L 64
Wax polish-500ml W 5
Waxstat adaptor B206
Waxstat adaptor B243
Weatherstrip-alpine light-5mm glass N105
Weatherstrip-alpine light-5mm glass N129
Weatherstrip-alpine light-5mm glass N131
Weatherstrip-rear quarter-5 mm glass N 65
Weight-crankshaft balance-.17oz B304
Weight-crankshaft balance-0.75 oz B399
Weight-crankshaft balance-0.75 oz C 72
Weight-crankshaft balance-5gm B374
Weight-governor C 83
Well-spare wheel S 15
Wheel assembly-steering-plastic-black F 1
Wheel assembly-steering-plastic-deep F 3
Wheel blower L 49
Wheel-alloy road-7.0 x 16-tornado-silver E 53
Wheel-steel road-5.5f x 16-riveted-primed- E 53
Wheelarch assembly-front-rh N 59
Wheelarch assembly-front-rh N 60
Wheelbrace S 6
Wheelbrace S 18
Wheelguard-rh T 47
Wheelguard-rh T 48
Winch-electric-m6000-c/w fittings T 7
Wiper rack M128
Wire rope-winch T 7
Wire-trim retention P 4
Worm & valve assembly-power assisted F 16
Worm & valve assembly-power assisted F 12
Worm & valve assembly-power assisted F 15
Y-piece B339
Y-piece J 69
Yoke assembly starter motor B144
Yoke assembly starter motor B189
Yoke assembly starter motor B229
Yoke assembly-selector rod D 29
Yoke-shift rod manual transmission C 68
Yoke-shift rod manual transmission C 22
Yoke-shift rod manual transmission C 23

This page is intentionally left blank

Illus	Part Number	Description	Quantity	Change Point	Remarks
1	RTC2918N	Engine unit-stripped-new	1		
1	STC8276E	Engine unit-stripped-exchange	1		

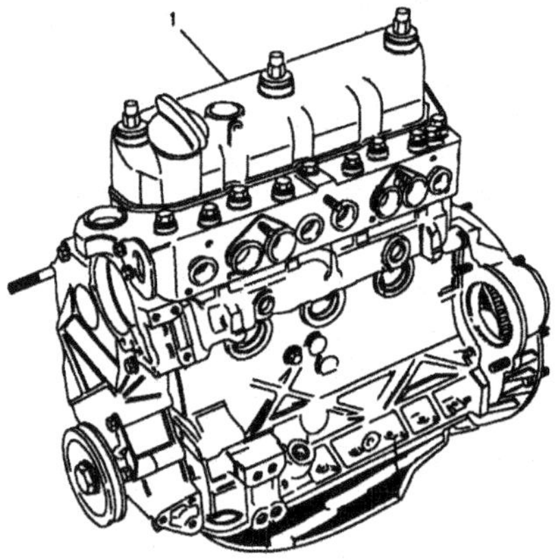

Illus	Part Number	Description	Quantity	Change Point	Remarks
1	RTC2978	Engine base unit-part	1		2250 cc 4 Cylinder Petrol

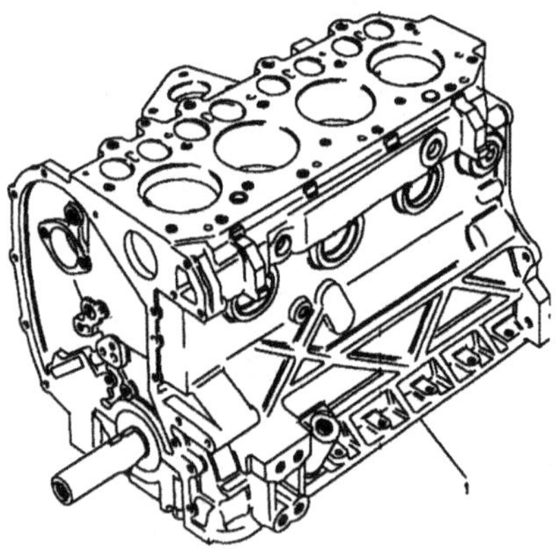

DEFENDER	GROUP B	Engine 2250 - Petrol Cylinder Block

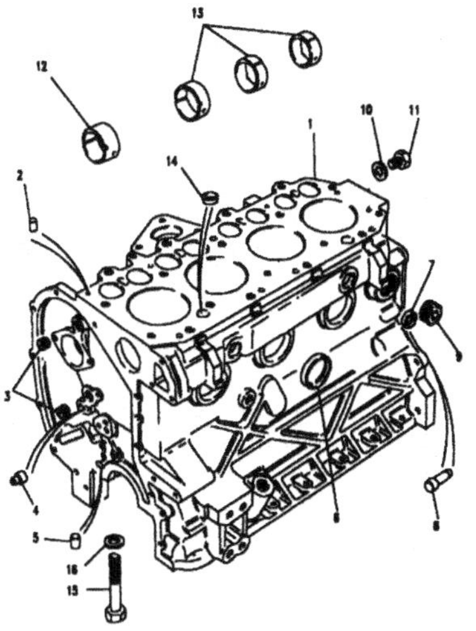

Illus	Part Number	Description	Quantity	Change Point	Remarks
1	ERC9348	CYLINDER BLOCK-ENGINE	1		
2	247965	• Plug	1		
3	247127	• Plug-cylinder block oil way	2		
4	213700	• Dowel	2		
5	501593	• Dowel	10		
6	ERC4996	• Plug-core	6		
7	597586	• Plug-core	3		
8	ERC4644	• Dowel	2		
9	527269	• Plug	1		
10	243959	• Washer-sealing	2		
11	536577	• Plug-drain	2		
12	90519054	• Bearing-camshaft front	1		
13	90519055	• Bearing-camshaft rear	3		
14	ERC4995	• Plug-core	2		
15	ETC7596	• Bolt-flanged head	10		
16	504006	• Washer	10		

DEFENDER	GROUP B	Engine 2250 - Petrol Cover Side

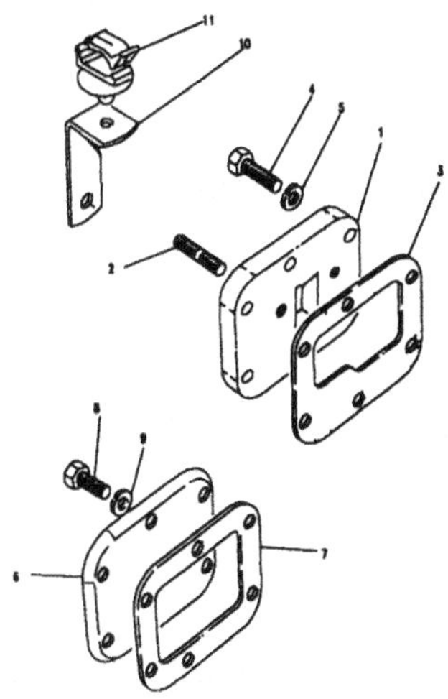

Illus	Part Number	Description	Quantity	Change Point	Remarks
1	ETC4799	COVER-CYLINDER BLOCK SIDE	1		
2	TE108041L	• Stud-M8 x 20	2		
3	ERR1475	Gasket-cylinder block side cover	1		
4	FS108251L	Screw-flanged head-M8 x 25	NLA		Use FS108257L.
5	WL1O8001L	Washer-spring	6		
6	ERC2869	Cover-engine	1		
7	247555	Gasket-cylinder block side cover	NLA		Use ERR3605.
7	ERR3605	Gasket-cylinder block side cover-asbestos	NLA		Use ERR2026.
7	ERR2026	Gasket-cylinder block side cover-asbestos free	1		
8	FS108207L	Screw-flanged head-M8 x 20	6		
9	WL1O8001L	Washer-spring	6		
10	ERC9480	Bracket-harness clip	1		
11	AFU1090L	Clip-cable-8mm hole	1		

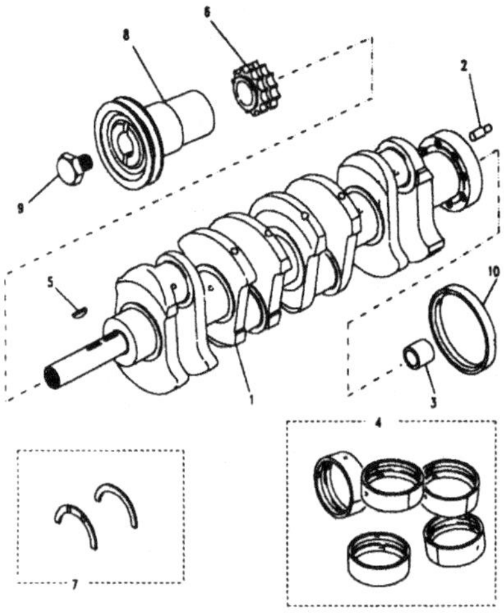

Illus	Part Number	Description	Quantity	Change Point	Remarks
1	ERC5014	CRANKSHAFT ASSEMBLY-ENGINE	1		
2	ERR1630	• Dowel-flywheel to crankshaft	1		
3	8566L	• Bush-crankshaft	1		
		SET-CRANKSHAFT BEARINGS			
4	RTC2626	standard	A/R		
4	RTC262610	0.010" undersize	A/R		
4	RTC262620	0.020 undersize	A/R		
5	235770	Key-crankshaft	1		
6	568333	Sprocket-crankshaft	1		
		WASHER-CRANKSHAFT THRUST			
7	RTC2825	standard.-pair	A/R		
7	538131	oversize.-0.0025"-pair	A/R		
7	538132	oversize.-0.005"-pair	A/R		
7	538133	oversize.-0.0075"-pair	A/R		
7	538134	oversize.-0.01"-pair	A/R		
8	ERC5349	Pulley assembly-crankshaft	1		Note (1)
8	ERC5128	Pulley assembly-crankshaft	1		Note (2)
8	ERC5127	Pulley assembly-crankshaft	1		Note (3)
8	ERC7089	Pulley assembly-crankshaft	1		Note (4)
9	ETC7934	Bolt-crankshaft pulley	1		
10	ERR1535	Seal-crankshaft rear	NLA		Use ERR2532.
10	ERR2532	Seal-crankshaft rear	1		

Remarks:
(1) Except power steering And air conditioning
(2) power steering Except air conditioning
(3) air conditioning Except power steering
(4) power steering air conditioning

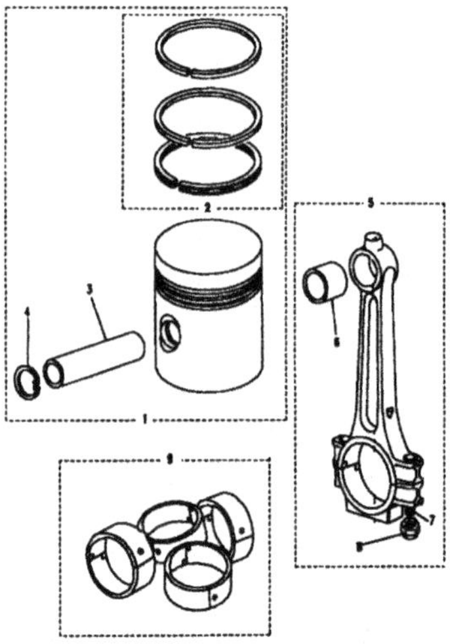

Illus	Part Number	Description	Quantity	Change Point	Remarks
		PISTON-ENGINE			
1	RTC4188S	STANDARD	4		
1	RTC418820	0.020" OVERSIZE	4		
1	RTC418840	0.040" OVERSIZE	4		
2	RTC4190S	• Ring set assembly-piston-standard.	1		Part of RTC4188S.
3	265169	• Pin-piston gudgeon	1		
4	265175	• Circlip	2		
2	RTC419020	• Ring set assembly-piston-0.020" oversize	1		Part of RTC418820.
2	RTC419040	• Ring set assembly-piston-0.040" oversize	1		Part of RTC418840.
5	ETC5157	ROD ASSEMBLY-CONNECTING	4		
6	528004	• Bush	1		
7	ERC8751	• Bolt-connecting rod	2		
8	ETC5155	• Nut-connecting rod	2		
		SET-CONNECTING ROD BEARING			
9	RTC1730	standard	1		
9	RTC173010	0.010" undersize	1		
9	RTC173020	0.020 undersize	1		

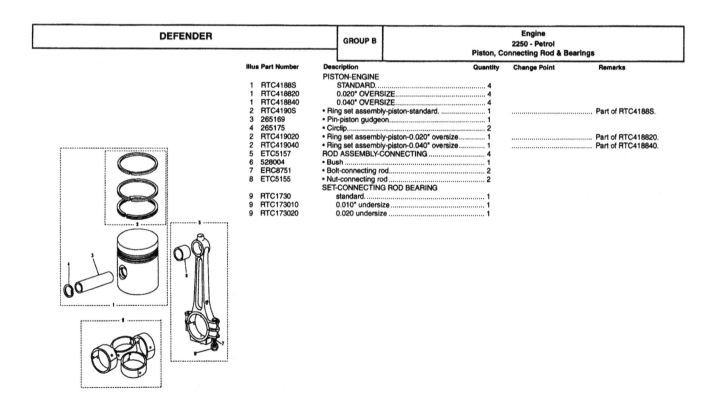

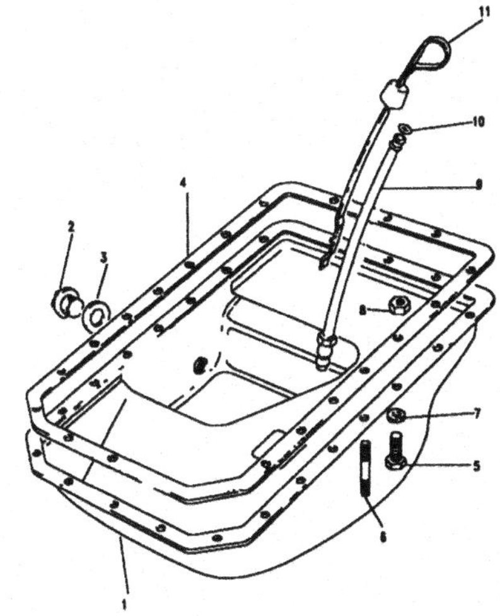

Illus	Part Number	Description	Quantity	Change Point	Remarks
1	RTC4841	KIT-SUMP	1	Note (1)	
	ERR4716	• SUMP-ENGINE OIL	1		
2	599552	• • Plug-drain	1		
3	FRC4808	• • Washer-sealing-alternatives	1		
4	546841	• Gasket-sump	1		
5	FS108161L	• Screw-flanged head-M8 x 16	21		
6	TE108031L	• Stud-M8 x 15	1		
7	WL108001L	• Washer-sprung-M8	22		
8	NH108041L	• Nut-hexagonal head-M8	1		
5	FS108161L	Screw-flanged head-M8 x 16			
2	536577	Plug-drain-non magnetic	1	Note (2)	
3	243959	Washer-sealing-sump drain plug	1		
2	ETC5577	Plug-drain-magnetic	1		
3	FRC4808	Washer-sealing-alternatives	1		
4	546841	Gasket-sump	1		
5	FS108251L	Screw-flanged head-M8 x 25	NLA		Use FS108257L.
5	FS108257L	Screw-flanged head-M8 x 25	1		
6	TE108041L	Stud-M8 x 20	1		
5	FS108161L	Screw-flanged head-M8 x 16	21		
6	TE108031L	Stud-M8 x 15	1		
7	WL108001L	Washer-sprung-M8	22		
8	NH108041L	Nut-hexagonal head-M8	1		
9	ERC8980	Tube assembly-oil dipstick	1		
10	532387	O ring	1		
11	ETC7867	Dipstick-oil	1		

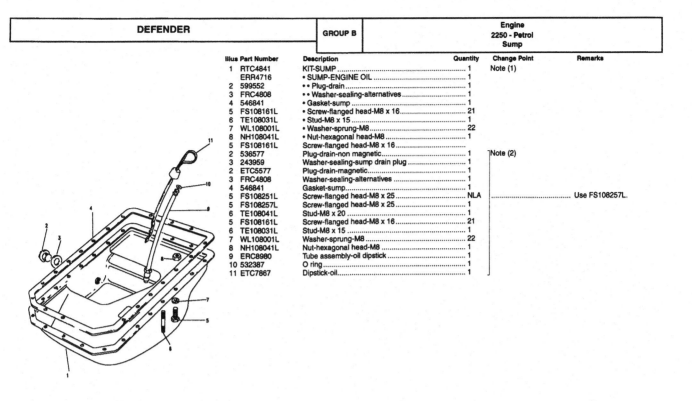

CHANGE POINTS:
(1) From (V) LA 935269
(2) To (V) LA 935268

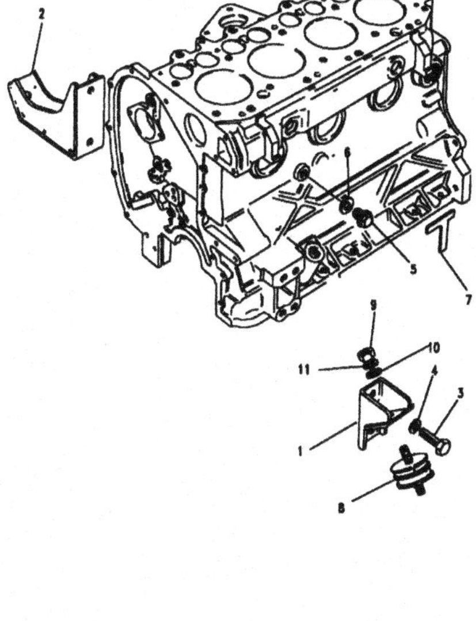

Illus	Part Number	Description	Quantity	Change Point	Remarks
1	NRC5434	Bracket-engine mounting-RH	1		
2	NRC9557	Bracket-engine mounting-LH	1		
3	SH112251L	Screw-hexagonal head-M12 x 25	4		
4	WL112001L	Washer	4		
5	ERC9410	Plug-drain	1		
6	AFU1882L	Washer-sump assembly drain plug	1		
7	ERC5086	Pad-insulation	2		
8	NRC9560	Mounting-engine rubber	NLA	Note (1)	Use ANR1808.
8	ANR1808	Mounting-engine rubber	2	Note (2)	
9	NH110041L	Nut-rubber to foot-hexagonal head-coarse thread-M10	4		
10	WC110061L	Washer-rubber to foot-plain-M10-oversize	2		
11	WL110001L	Washer-M10	4		

CHANGE POINTS:
(1) To (V) JA 920702
(2) From (V) JA 920703

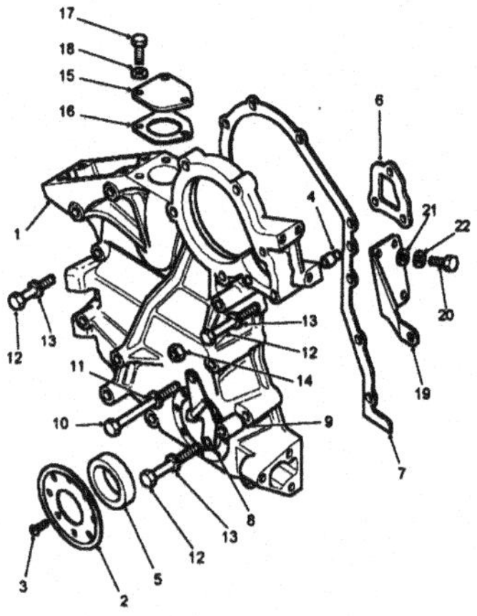

AHBFEA1A

Illus	Part Number	Description	Quantity	Change Point	Remarks
1	ERC9519	COVER-ENGINE-FRONT-WITH SINGLE LIP SEAL	1		Except air conditioning
2	247766	• Excluder mud-single lip seal	1		
	RJ608603	• Rivet	8		
4	6395L	• Dowel-single lip seal	4		
5	ERC7987	• Seal-crankshaft front oil-with single lip seal	1		
1	ERC9528	COVER-ENGINE-FRONT-WITH SINGLE LIP SEAL	1		Air conditioning
2	247766	• Excluder mud-single lip seal	1		
	RJ608603	• Rivet	8		
4	6395L	• Dowel-single lip seal	4		
5	516028	• Seal-crankshaft front oil-with single lip seal	1		
1	ETC6081	COVER-ENGINE-FRONT-WITH TWIN LIP SEAL	1		Except air conditioning
2	247766	• Excluder mud-twin lip seal	1		
3	AB606061L	• Screw-self tapping-No 6 x 3/4	8		
4	6395L	• Dowel-twin lip seal	2		
5	ETC5187	• Seal-crankshaft front oil-twin lip seal-with twin lip seal	1		
1	ETC6082	COVER-ENGINE-FRONT-WITH TWIN LIP SEAL	1		Air conditioning
2	247766	• Excluder mud-twin lip seal	1		
4	6395L	• Dowel-twin lip seal	2		
5	ETC5187	• Seal-crankshaft front oil-with twin lip seal	1		
6	538038	Gasket-coolant pump body-asbestos	NLA		Use ERR1607.
6	ERR1607	Gasket-coolant pump body-to front cover-asbestos free	1		
7	538039	Gasket-timing gear housing drain plate	1		
8	ERC5361	Pointer-engine timing	1		
9	ERC6869	Spacer	1		
10	ERC8964	Bolt-M8 x 95	1		
11	WL108001L	Washer-sprung-M8	1		
		NON AIR CONDITIONING			
10	ETC4994	Bolt-special-cowl mounting-M8 x 80	1		
12	BH108151L	Bolt-hexagonal head-M8 x 70	1		
12	FB108101L	Bolt-flanged head-M8 x 50	6		
13	WL108001L	Washer-sprung-M8	8		
14	NH108041L	Nut-hexagonal head-M8	1		

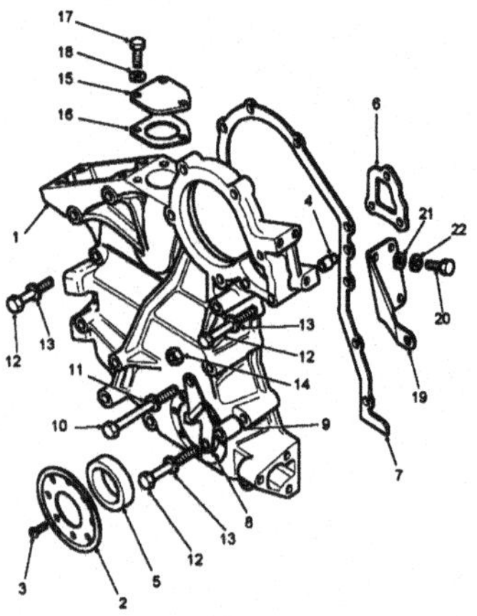

AHBFEA1A

Illus	Part Number	Description	Quantity	Change Point	Remarks
10	ETC4995	Bolt-special-cowl mounting-M8 x 60	1		Air conditioning
10	ERC8964	Bolt-special-M8 x 95	2		
	ERC9468	Stud	1		
12	BH108131L	Bolt-hexagonal head-M8 x 65	1		
12	BH108151L	Bolt-hexagonal head-M8 x 70	2		
12	FB108101L	Bolt-flanged head-M8 x 50	2		
12	BH108201L	Bolt-hexagonal head-M8 x 100	1		
13	WL108001L	Washer-sprung-M8	9		
14	NH108041L	Nut-hexagonal head-M8	1		
15	574469	Plate	1		
16	542636	Gasket-cylinder block water gallery plate	1		
17	FS106201L	Screw-flanged head-M6 x 20	3		
18	WL106001L	Washer-sprung-M6	3		
19	ERC6479	Bracket-cowl mounting	1		
20	FS108207L	Screw-flanged head-M8 x 20	3		
21	WL108001L	Washer-sprung-M8	3		
22	WA108051L	Washer-8mm	1		
10	ETC4994	Bolt-M8 x 80	1		Split charge
12	FB108101L	Bolt-flanged head-M8 x 50	5		
	ERC9468	Stud	1		
14	NH108041L	Nut-hexagonal head-M8	1		

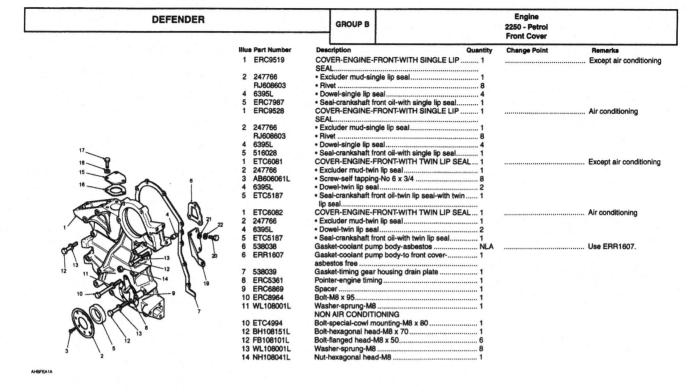

Illus	Part Number	Description	Quantity	Change Point	Remarks
1	ETC4499	Chain-engine timing	1		
2	3739	Bearing-ball	1		
3	233328	Clip-retaining-ball	1		
4	233326	Spring-tensioner	1		
5	267451	Spring-ratchet	1		
6	ERC8975	Bolt	1		
7	247912	Tensioner assembly	1		
8	546026	Ratchet assembly handbrake	1		
9	236067	Idler assembly-timing belt	1		
10	234124	Bush	1		
11	277388	Cylinder-tensioner	1		
12	TE108051L	Stud-M8 x 25	1		
13	FS108307L	Screw-flanged head-M8 x 30	1		
14	WL108001L	Washer-sprung-M8	1		
15	NH108041L	Nut-hexagonal head-M8	1		
16	275234	Brush-timing belt cover torsional vibration damper	1		
17	SH106121L	Screw-hexagonal head-M6 x 12	2		
18	557523	Washer-lock	2		

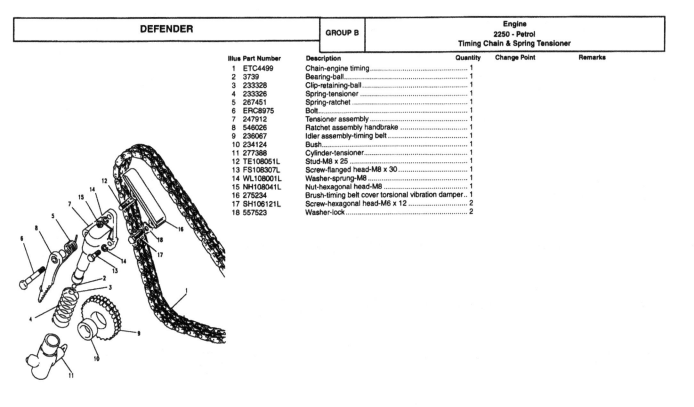

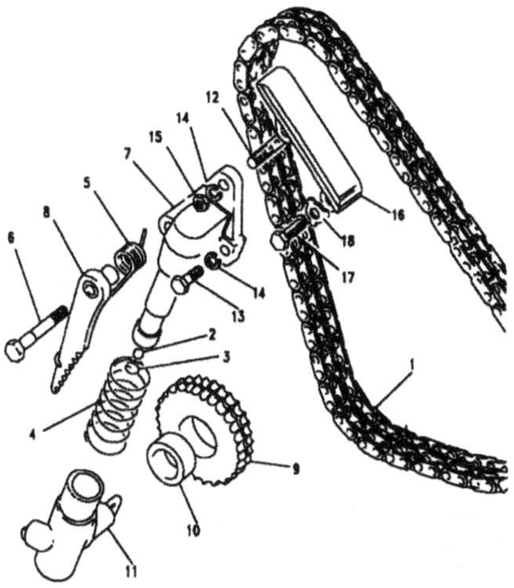

Illus	Part Number	Description	Quantity	Change Point	Remarks
1	ETC5191	Chain-engine timing	1		
2	ETC5190	Tensioner-timing chain	1		
3	FS108207L	Screw-flanged head-M8 x 20	2		
4	TE108051L	Stud-M8 x 25	1		
5	WA108051L	Washer-8mm	3		
6	NH108041L	Nut-hexagonal head-M8	1		
7	275234	Brush-timing belt cover torsional vibration damper	1		
8	SH106121L	Screw-hexagonal head-M6 x 12	2		
9	557523	Washer-lock	2		

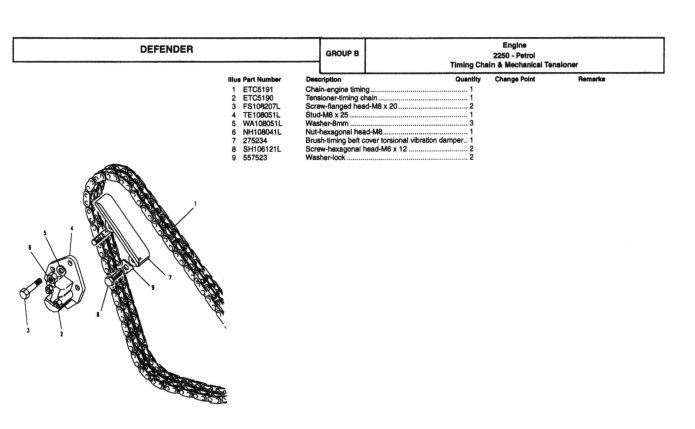

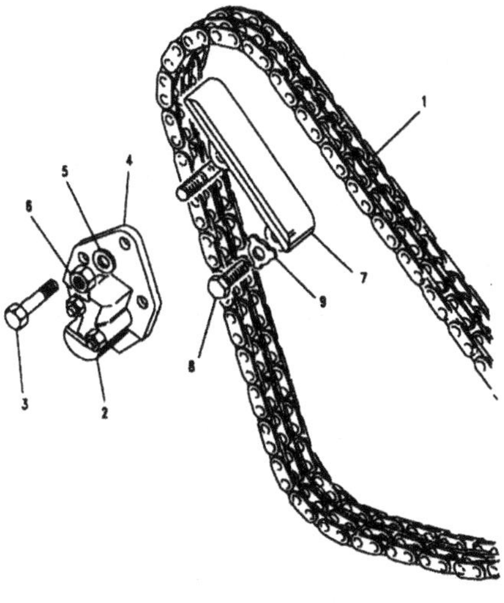

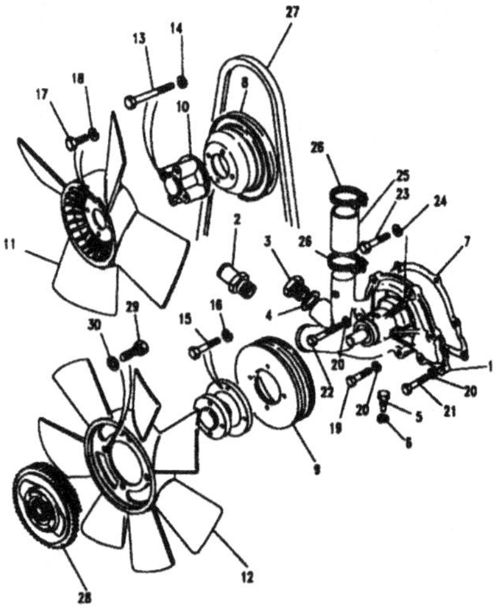

Illus	Part Number	Description	Quantity	Change Point	Remarks
1	RTC3644	Pump assembly-engine coolant	1		Except air conditioning
2	ERC7313	Stud	1		Except air conditioning
7	ERC5655	Gasket-coolant pump body	1		Except air conditioning
1	RTC6333	PUMP ASSEMBLY-ENGINE COOLANT-A133 ALTERNATOR	NLA		Use STC640. Air conditioning
1	STC640	PUMP ASSEMBLY-ENGINE COOLANT-A133 ALTERNATOR	1		Air conditioning
3	ERC7312	• Plug	1		
4	232046	• Washer-copper	1		
	ERC5600	• Screw	1		
16	WL106001L	• Washer-sprung-M6	1		
7	ERC5655	• Gasket-coolant pump body	1		
		PULLEY COOLANT PUMP			
8	ERC5578	single groove	1		Except air conditioning
9	ERC8890	twin groove	1		Air conditioning
9	ERC7871	twin groove	1		Split charge except air conditioning
10	ERC7489	Spacer-fan to water pump	1		Except air conditioning
11	ERC5545	Fan-cooling	1		Except air conditioning
12	ERR3380	Fan-cooling	1		Air conditioning
13	FB108111L	Bolt-flanged head-M8 x 55	4		Except air conditioning
14	WL108001L	Washer-sprung-M8	4		Except air conditioning
15	BH106051L	Bolt-pulley to hub-hexagonal head-M6 x 25	4		Air conditioning
16	WL106001L	Washer-sprung-M6	4		Air conditioning
17	FS108161L	Screw-flanged head-M8 x 16	4		Air conditioning
18	WL108001L	Washer-sprung-M8	4		Air conditioning
19	BH108161L	Bolt-pump to block-hexagonal head-M8 x 80	2		
20	WL108001L	Washer-sprung-M8	4		
21	BH108171L	Bolt-pump to block-hexagonal head-M8 x 85	1		
22	BH108151L	Bolt-pump to block-hexagonal head-M8 x 70	1		
23	BH108161L	Bolt-pump to cover-hexagonal head-M8 x 80	3		

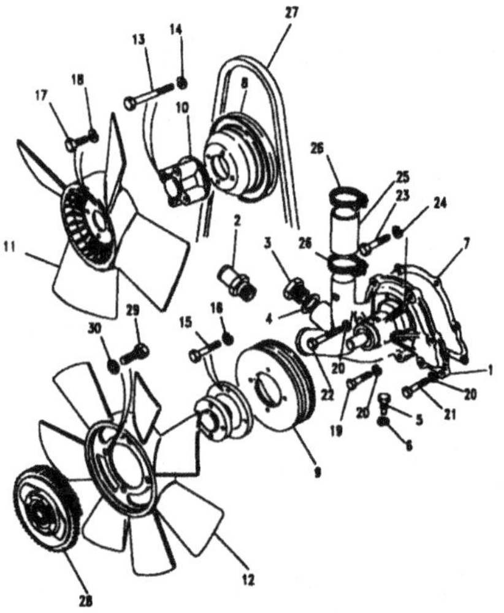

Illus	Part Number	Description	Quantity	Change Point	Remarks
24	WL108001L	Washer-sprung-M8	5		
25	ERC5654	Hose assembly water-outlet	1		
26	CN100408L	Clip-hose	2		
27	563132	Belt-polyvee coolant pump	1		
27	ERC8938	Belt-polyvee coolant pump	1		Split charge
28	ERC5708	Coupling-engine fan viscous	1		Air conditioning
29	ERC5709	Screw-M6 x 14	4		Air conditioning
30	4589L	Washer-plain	4		Air conditioning

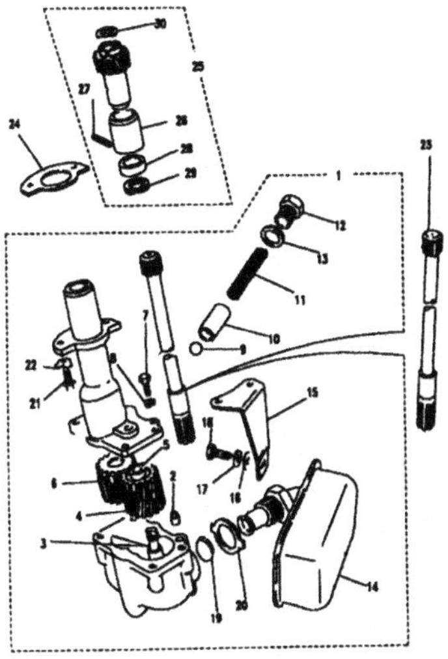

Illus	Part Number	Description	Quantity	Change Point	Remarks
1	ERR1117	PUMP BODY ASSEMBLY-ENGINE OIL	1		Oil cooler (air cooled)
2	236257	• Dowel	2		
3	ERR1063	• Spindle-oil pump	1		
4	ERR1088	• Gear-oil pump idler-10 teeth	1		
6	ERC9706	• Gear-oil pump-10 teeth	1		
7	FS108207L	• Screw-flanged head-M8 x 20	4		
8	WL108001L	• Washer-sprung-M8	4		
10	ETC4880	• Plunger-oil pump relief valve-ten tooth idler	1		
11	564456	• Spring-oil pump relief valve	1		
12	564455	• Plug	1		
13	232044	• Washer-sealing	1		
14	ERC7530	• Strainer-oil	1		
15	ERC7940	• Bracket-pump/actuator	1		
16	WA108051L	• Washer-8mm	1		
17	WL108001L	• Washer-sprung-M8	1		
7	FS108207L	• Screw-flanged head-M8 x 20	1		
19	244488	• O ring	1		
20	244487	• Washer-lock	1		
22	247665	• Washer-lock	2		
21	FS108251L	Screw-flanged head-M8 x 25	NLA		Use FS108257L.
4	278109	Gear-oil pump idler-9 teeth	1		
5	214995	Bush	1		
6	240555	Gear-oil pump-9 teeth	1		
9	3748	Bearing-ball	1		
10	273711	Plunger-oil pump relief valve-nine tooth idler	1		
12	549909	Plug-end oil relief	1		Except oil cooler (air cooled)
17	WL108001L	Washer-sprung-M8	1		
23	ERR850	Shaft-oil pump	1		
24	ERC8408	Gasket-cylinder block oil pump-asbestos	NLA		Use ERR3606.
24	ERR3606	Gasket-cylinder block oil pump-asbestos free	1		

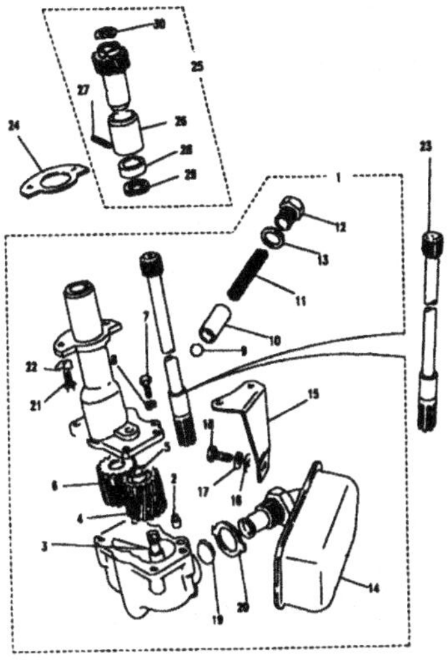

Illus	Part Number	Description	Quantity	Change Point	Remarks
25	ETC6139	DRIVE ASSEMBLY-OIL PUMP	1		
26	522745	• Bush-later type locking ring	1		
28	ETC6137	• Washer-thrust-later type locking ring	1		
29	ETC6138	• Ring-snap-later type locking ring	1		
27	ETC6142	• Screw-later type locking ring	1		
27	ERC8976	Screw-earlier type spring ring	1		
28	530178	Washer-thrust-earlier type spring ring	1		
29	530179	Ring-snap-earlier type spring ring	1		
30	247742	Circlip	1		

Illus	Part Number	Description	Quantity	Change Point	Remarks
1	ETC5347	ADAPTOR-OIL FILTER	1		Except oil cooler (air cooled)
2	RTC6851	• Plug	1		
3	213961	• Washer-sealing	1		
4	ERC5913	• O ring	1		
5	ERC9884	• Cover-oil filter	1		
6	ETC4021	• Plug	1		
7	SH106141L	• Screw-hexagonal head-M6 x 14	2		
8	WA106041L	• Washer-6mm	2		
9	ERR3340	Cartridge-engine oil filter	1		
10	FS110301L	Screw-filter to block-flanged head-M10 x 30-top	2		
11	WL110001L	Washer-filter to block-M10	2		
12	ETC7582	Gasket-oil filter housing-asbestos	NLA		Use ERR4934.
12	ERR4934	Gasket-oil filter housing-asbestos free	1		
13	PRC6387	Switch-oil pressure engine	1		
14	PRC2505	Transducer coolant temperature	1		

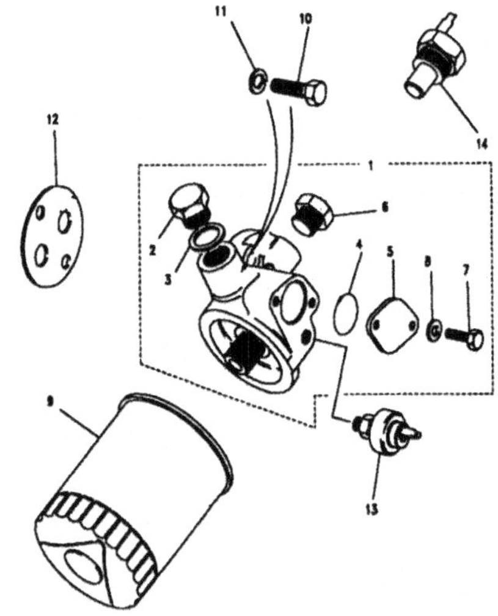

Illus	Part Number	Description	Quantity	Change Point	Remarks
1	ERR1347	ADAPTOR ASSEMBLY-OIL FILTER	1		Oil cooler (air cooled)
2	ERC5923	• Thermostat assembly-oil	1		
3	ETC4022	• Adaptor-oil filter	1		
4	ERC5913	• O ring	1		
5	ETC4021	• Plug	1		
6	SH106141L	• Screw-hexagonal head-M6 x 14	2		
7	WA106041L	• Washer-6mm	2		
8	ERR3340	Cartridge-engine oil filter	1		
9	FS110301L	Screw-filter to block-flanged head-M10 x 30-top	2		
11	ETC7582	Gasket-oil filter housing-asbestos	NLA		Use ERR4934.
11	ERR4934	Gasket-oil filter housing-asbestos free	1		
12	PRC6387	Switch-oil pressure engine	1		
13	232039	Washer-sealing	1		
14	PRC2505	Transducer coolant temperature	1		

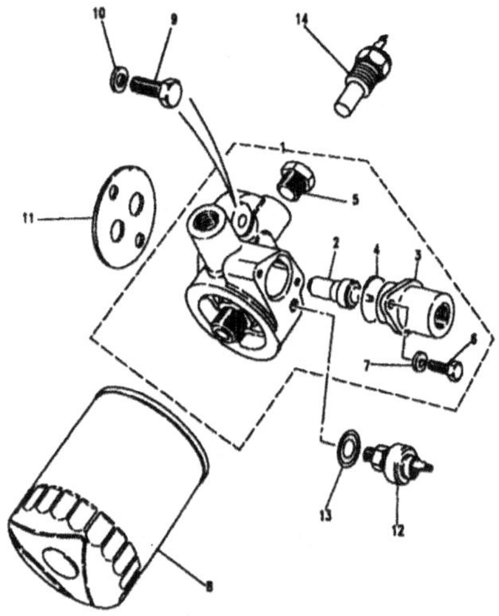

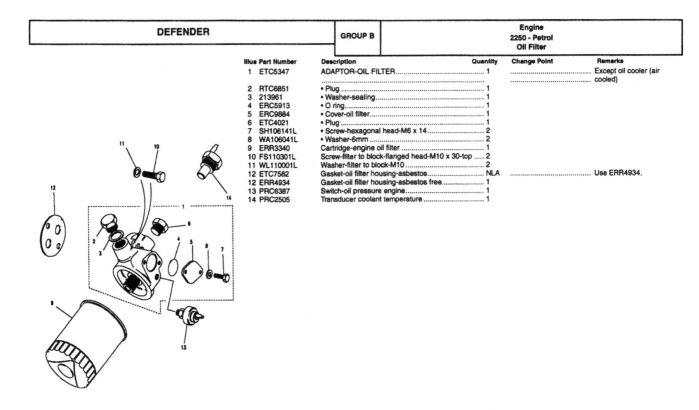

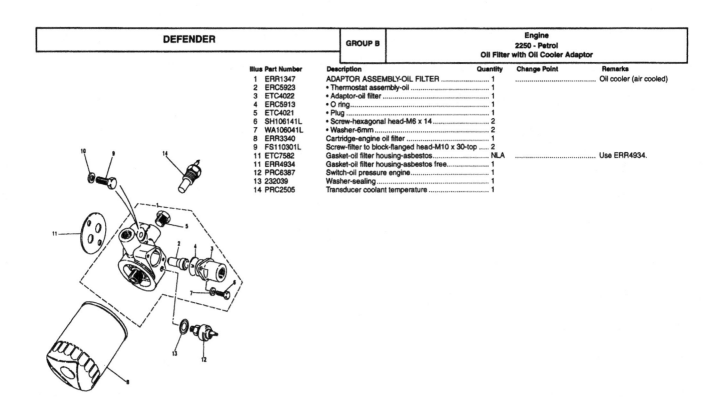

Engine
2250 - Petrol
Cylinder Head

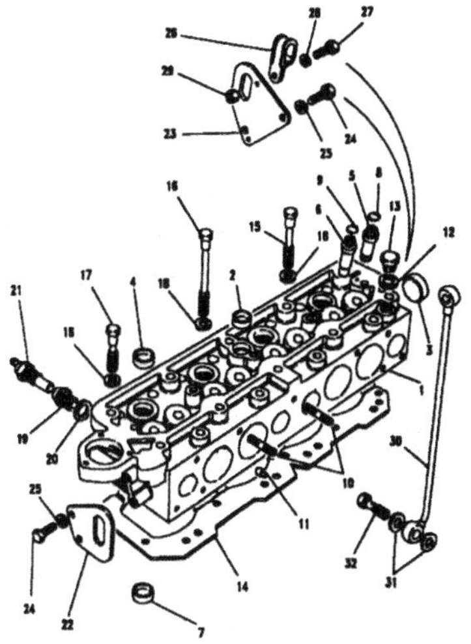

Illus	Part Number	Description	Quantity	Change Point	Remarks
1	ETC5412	CYLINDER HEAD ASSEMBLY-ENGINE	1		
2	525497	• Plug-core	1		
3	524765	• Plug-core	1		
4	549702	• Plug	4		
5	568686	• Guide-valve-cylinder head inlet	4		
6	568687	• Guide-valve-cylinder head exhaust	4		
7	ETC6278	• Insert-cylinder head exhaust valve seat	4		
8	ETC4709	Seal-inlet valve	4		
9	ETC4751	Seal-exhaust	4		
10	TE108051L	Stud-M8 x 25	3		
11	213700	Dowel	2		
12	AFU1890L	Washer-sealing	1		
13	ERC9448	Plug	1		
14	ERC6380	Gasket-cylinder head	1		
15	247051	Bolt-1/2UNF x 4 9/16	9		
16	279648	Bolt-1/2UNF x 2 5/16	4		
17	554621	Bolt-1/2UNF x 4 1/8	5		
18	ERC6821	Washer-plain	18		
19	ERC8973	Adaptor-transmitter	1		
20	AFU1890L	Washer-sealing	1		
21	PRC2505	Transducer coolant temperature	1		
22	ERC2254	Bracket-lifting body-front	1		
23	ETC7135	Bracket-lifting body-rear	1		
24	FS108207L	Screw-bracket to head-flanged head-M8 x 20	4		
25	WL108001L	Washer-sprung-M8	4		
26	543589	Clip	1		
27	SH104121L	Screw-hexagonal head-M4 x 12	1		
28	WA104001L	Washer-plain-M4	1		
29	NH104041L	Nut-hexagonal-M4	1		
30	275679	Pipe assembly-engine oil feed	1		
31	ETC6510	Washer-sealing	4		
32	ETC4498	Bolt-banjo	2		

Engine
2250 - Petrol
Rocker Shaft

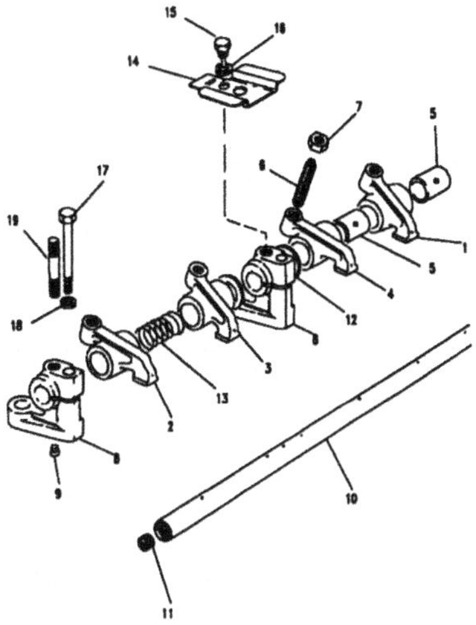

Illus	Part Number	Description	Quantity	Change Point	Remarks
1	ERC9103	ARM-EXHAUST VALVE ROCKER-RH	2		
2	ERC9102	ARM-EXHAUST VALVE ROCKER-LH	2		
3	ERC9107	ARM-INLET VALVE ROCKER-RH	2		
4	ERC9106	ARM-INLET VALVE ROCKER-LH	2		
5	247614	• Bush	8		
6	ERC9054	Screw-tappet adjusting	8		
7	NT108041L	Nut-hexagonal head	8		
8	ERC9138	Bracket	5		
9	277956	Dowel-ring	3		
10	ERC6341	SHAFT-ROCKER	1		
11	ERC6337	• Plug	2		
12	525389	Washer-plain	6		
13	247040	Spring-rocker shaft	4		
14	ERC9278	Plate-baffle	1		
15	ETC4460	Screw	1		
16	WL108001L	Washer-sprung-M8	1		
17	BH108151L	Bolt-hexagonal head-M8 x 70	5		
18	WL108001L	Washer-sprung-M8	5		
19	TE108081L	Stud-M8 x 40	3		

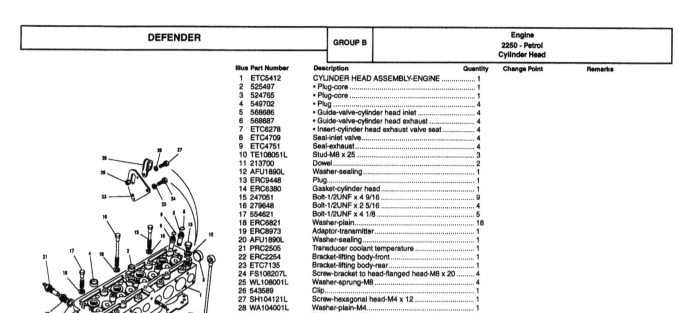

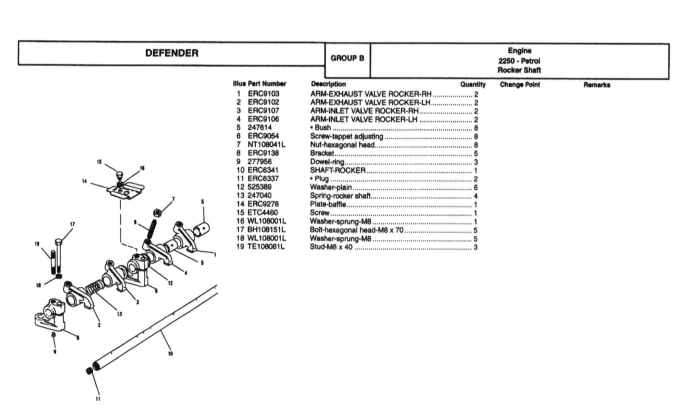

DEFENDER	GROUP B	Engine 2250 - Petrol Valves

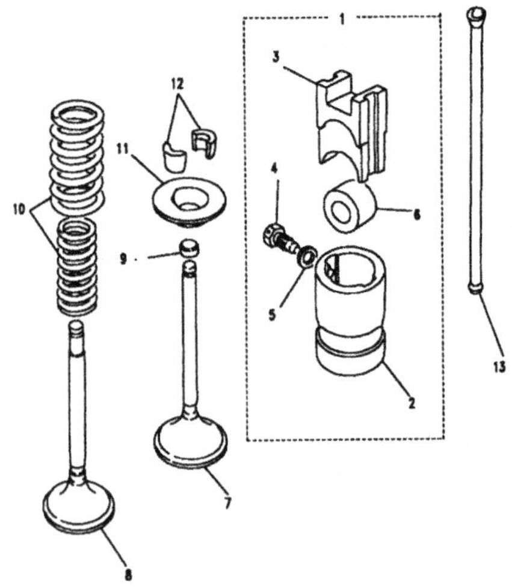

Illus	Part Number	Description	Quantity	Change Point	Remarks
1	507829	TAPPET-ENGINE VALVE MECHANICAL	8		
2	502473	• Slide-tappet guide	8		
3	ERR607	• Tappet-engine valve mechanical	8		
4	ETC4246	• Bolt	8		
5	273069	• Washer-sealing	8		
6	ERR561	• Roller-tappet guide	8		
7	ETC4067	Valve-cylinder head inlet	4		
8	ETC5866	Valve-cylinder head exhaust	4		
9	ETC7203	Cap-valve stem	8		Optional
10	ERR4640	Spring-cylinder head valve	8		
11	ETC4068	Cap-cylinder head valve spring	8		
12	ETC4069	Cotter-valve	16		
13	546798	Rod-engine push	8		

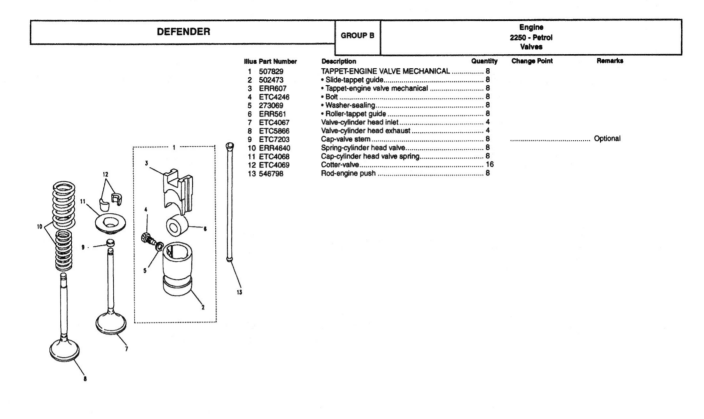

DEFENDER	GROUP B	Engine 2250 - Petrol Rocker Cover & Breather

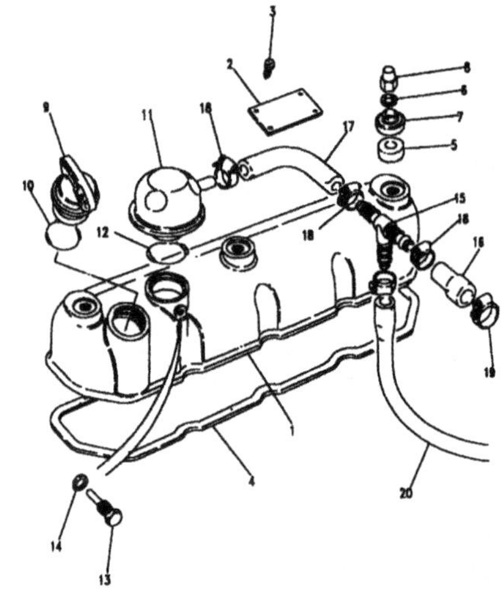

Illus	Part Number	Description	Quantity	Change Point	Remarks
1	ERC2866	ROCKER COVER ASSEMBLY-BREATHER SEPARATE	1		
2	247634	• Plate assembly	1		
3	AB606021L	• Screw-self tapping AB-No 6 x 1/4	4		
1	ETC5955	Rocker cover assembly-breather combined	1		
11	ERR1454	CAP ASSEMBLY-OIL FILLER-BREATHER COMBINED	1		
12	ERR736	• O ring-breather combined	1		
4	ETC6439	Gasket-engine rocker cover-asbestos	1		
4	ERR4933	Gasket-engine rocker cover-asbestos free	1		
5	506069	Washer	3		
6	273069	Washer-sealing	3		
7	247624	Washer-rubber	3		
8	ERC9220	Nut-domed-M8	3		
9	625038	Cap-oil filler	1		
10	564258	O ring-filler cap	1		
11	574658	Cap assembly-oil filler-breather separate	1		
12	268887	O ring-breather separate	1		
13	515291	Screw	1		
14	232037	Washer	1		
15	ERC6200	T piece	1		
16	ERC9032	Hose assembly-breather	1		
17	ERC9031	Hose assembly-breather	1		
18	CN100208L	Clip-hose-20mm	4		
19	CN100148L	Clip-hose	1		
20	ERC9033	Hose-T piece to carb	1		

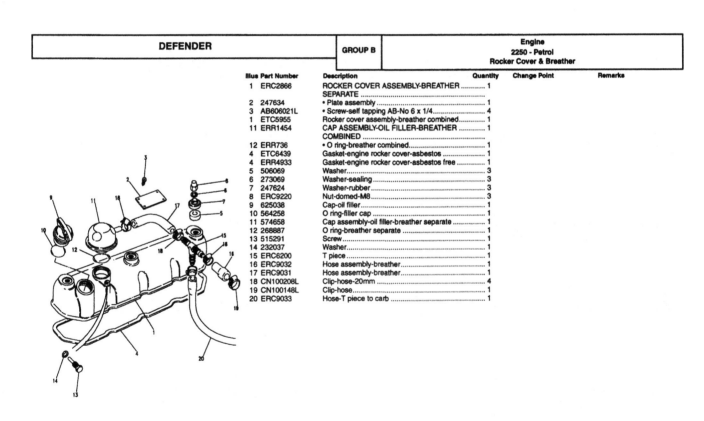

Engine
2250 - Petrol
Camshaft

Illus	Part Number	Description	Quantity	Change Point	Remarks
1	ETC7128	Camshaft assembly-engine	1		
2	ERC1561	Plate-camshaft retaining	1		
3	FS106167L	Screw-flanged head-flanged head-M6 x 16	2		
4	230313	Key	1		
5	ETC5172	Gear-crankshaft timing drive	1		
6	ETC4140	Washer	1		
7	BX110071M	Bolt-hexagonal head-M10 x 35	1		
8	2995	Washer-lock	2		

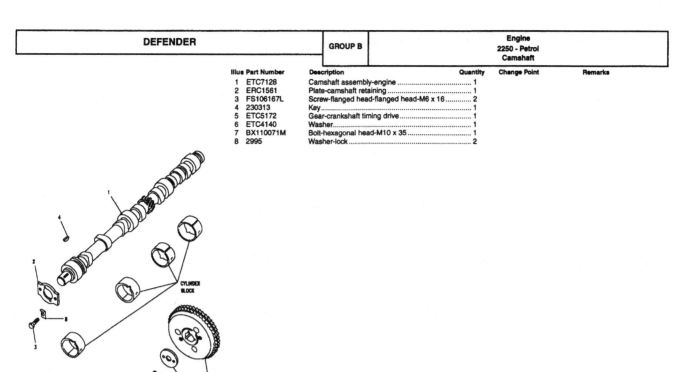

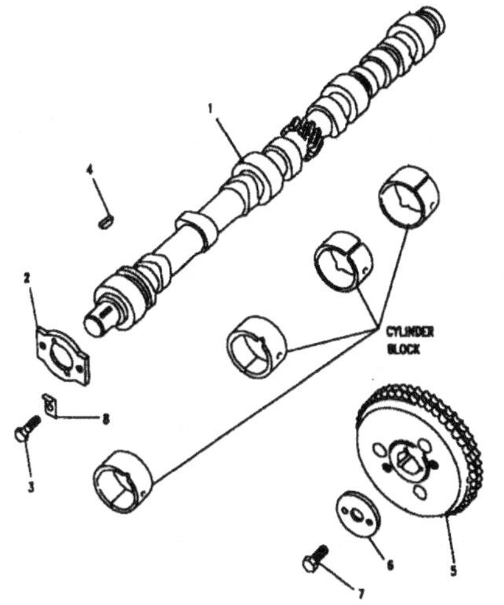

Engine
2250 - Petrol
Thermostat Housing

Illus	Part Number	Description	Quantity	Change Point	Remarks
1	ERC8758	Housing-thermostat	1		
		THERMOSTAT-ENGINE			
2	ETC4763	82 degrees C	NLA		Use 602687.
2	602687	82 degrees C	1		
2	ETC4761	74 degrees C	1		Optional
3	ERR977	Gasket-thermostat housing-asbestos-top	1		
3	ERR3682	Gasket-thermostat housing-top-asbestos free	1		
4	247874	Gasket-thermostat housing-bottom	1		
5	ERC7510	Hose to pipe-coolant	1	Note (1)	
5	BTR6141	Hose to pipe-coolant	1	Note (2)	
6	CN100258L	Clip-hose-25mm	2		
7	ETC5967	Elbow-engine coolant outlet	1		Except air conditioning
7	ETC5958	Elbow-engine coolant outlet	1		Air conditioning
8	ETC5965	Bracket-radiator pipe to cowl	1		
9	BH106151L	Bolt-M6 x 75	3		
10	WL106001L	Washer-sprung-M6	3		
11	624091	Adaptor-pipe coolant	2		
12	243959	Washer-sealing	2		
13	PRC3366	Sensor-temperature-Blue	1		Air conditioning
13	PRC3541	Sensor-temperature-Red	1		
14	C457593	Washer-sealing	2		

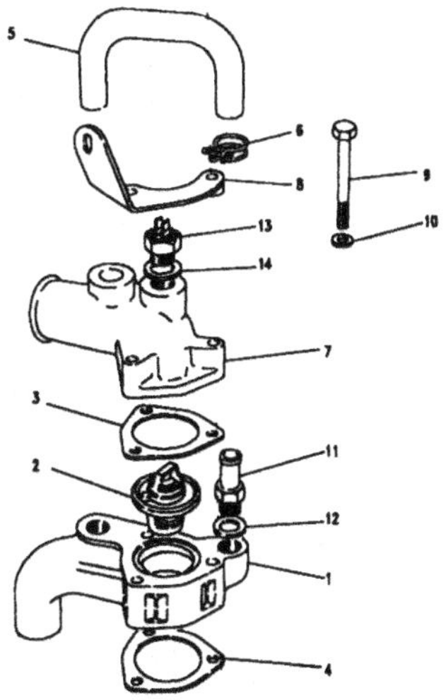

CHANGE POINTS:
(1) To (V) JA 920214
(2) From (V) JA 920215

Illus	Part Number	Description	Quantity	Change Point	Remarks
1	ERC9069	Manifold-engine inlet	1		
2	90513171	Connector-inlet manifold adaptor-servo	1		
2	587517	Connector-inlet manifold adaptor-servo-detoxed	1		
3	243958	Washer-sealing	1		
3	243958	Washer-sealing-detoxed	2		
4	ERC6691	Connector fit-detoxed	1		
5	TE108071L	Stud-carburetter to inlet manifold-M8 x 35	4		Alternatives
5	TE108071L	Stud-carburetter to inlet manifold (hand throttle)-M8 x 35	2		Alternatives
5	TE108081L	Stud-carburetter to inlet manifold (hand throttle)-M8 x 40	2		Alternatives
6	ERC8645	Washer-asbestos	2		
6	ERR4385	Washer-asbestos free	2		
7	564307	Gasket-inlet manifold	2		
8	ERC8460	Sleeve-insulation heat protection-asbestos	1		
8	ERR4386	Sleeve-insulation heat protection-asbestos free	1		
9	NH108041L	Nut-manifold to head-hexagonal head-M8	2		
10	FB108101L	Bolt-manifold to head-flanged head-M8 x 50	2		
11	587405	Washer-plain-manifold to head	4		
12	WA108051L	Washer-8mm	4		
13	NH108041L	Nut-manifold to manifold-hexagonal head-M8	4		
14	WL108001L	Washer-sprung-M8	4		
15	ERC8124	Gasket-exhaust manifold-asbestos	1		
15	ERR4387	Gasket-exhaust manifold-asbestos free	1		
16	ERC9071	Manifold assembly-engine exhaust	1		
17	TE108131L	Stud-manifold to manifold-M8 x 65	4		
18	AFU1848L	Stud-fixing exhaust pipe-M10	3		
19	BH108141L	Bolt-manifold to head-hexagonal head-M8 x 70	2		
20	FS108307L	Screw-manifold to head-flanged head-M8 x 30	2		
21	596490	Washer-exhaust manifold to cylinder head tab	2		
22	587405	Washer-plain-manifold to head	4		

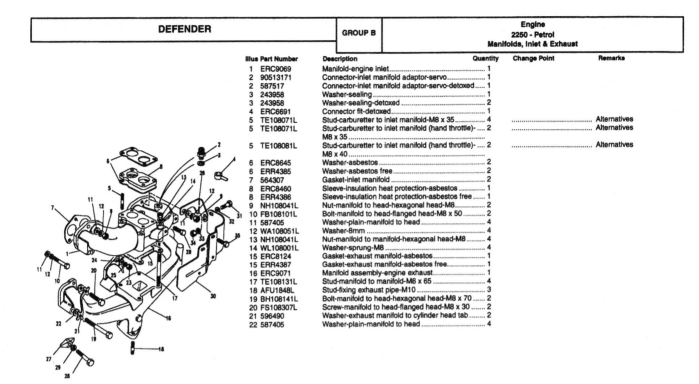

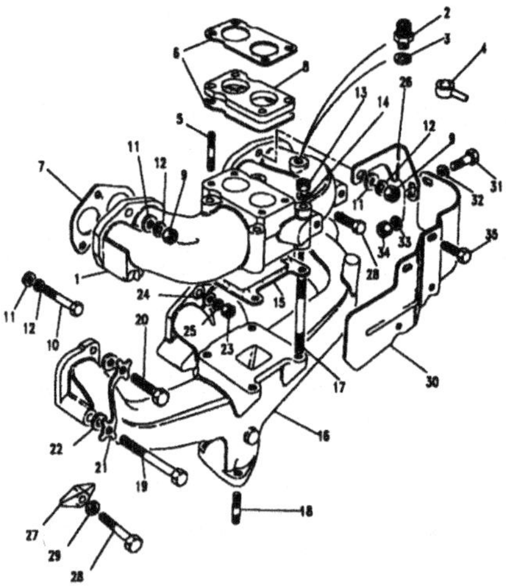

Illus	Part Number	Description	Quantity	Change Point	Remarks
23	NH108041L	Nut-centre flange to head-hexagonal head-M8	1		
24	587405	Washer-plain-centre flange/head	1		
25	WL108001L	Washer-flange/head-sprung-M8	1		
26	ETC5040	Bracket-heatshield	1		
27	564308	Clamp-manifold to head	2		
28	BH108141L	Bolt-manifold to head-hexagonal head-M8 x 70	2		
29	WL108001L	Washer-sprung-M8	3		
30	ERC8712	Heatshield-exhaust manifold	1		
31	BH108201L	Bolt-shield to manifold-hexagonal head-M8 x 100	1		

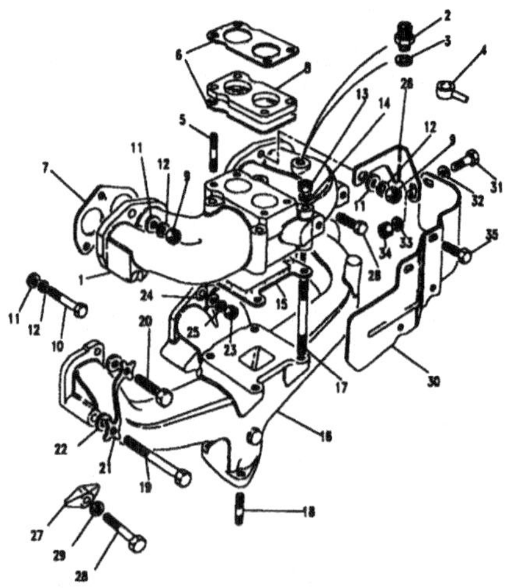

Illus	Part Number	Description	Quantity	Change Point	Remarks
32	WA108051L	Washer-shield to manifold-8mm	4		
33	WL108001L	Washer-sprung-M8	4		
34	NH108041L	Nut-shield to manifold-hexagonal head-M8	1		
35	SH108141L	Screw-hexagonal head-M8 x 14	2		

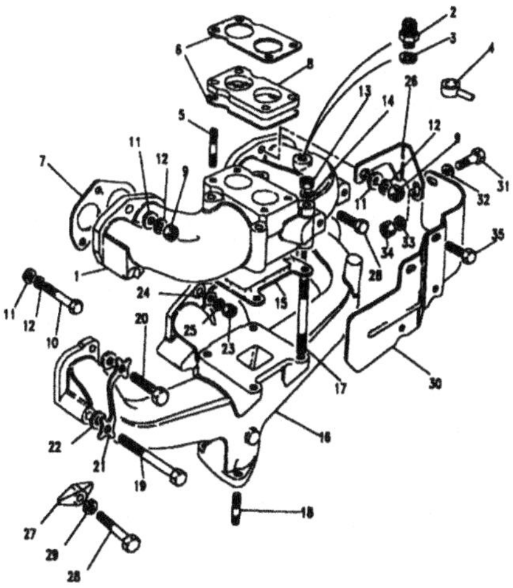

Illus	Part Number	Description	Quantity	Change Point	Remarks
	ETC5305	Carburettor-engine	NLA		Fit carburetter STC3374 and new air intake elbow ERR539..
	STC3374	Carburettor-engine	1		
	RTC3948	Kit-conversion-carburettor	1		
	ETC5306	Carburettor-engine-detoxed	1		
	RTC3948	Kit-conversion-carburettor-detoxed	1		
1	AEU2587	Element-filter	1		
2	AEU2586	Body-upper fuel system	1		
3	AEU2585	Venturi auxilary-centre device-carburettor-primary	2		
4	AEU2584	Body-carburettor float needle	1		
5	AEU2583	Float assembly-carburettor	1		
6	AEU2582	Holder-jet	2		
7	AEU2581	Jet-carburettor-primary idler-primary	1		
7	AEU2580	Jet-carburettor-secondary idling-secondary	1		
8	AEU2579	Screw-adjusting	2		
9	AEU2578	Jet-carburettor	1		
10	AEU2577	Spring	1		
11	RTC4850	Solenoid starter motor	1		
12	AEU2575	Spring-pump-carburettor	1		
13	AEU2572	Plate-throttle body setting-full power valve	1		
14	AEU2569	Spring-return	1		
15	AEU2568	Jet-carburettor-primary main	1		
15	AEU2567	Jet-carburettor-secondary main	1		
16	AEU2566	Tube-primary	2		
17	AEU2565	Jet-carburettor-primary	2		
18	AEU2564	Spring-return	1		
19	AEU2563	Lever-starting control	1		
20	AEU2562	Link-carburettor/throttle connecting	1		
21	AEU2561	Lever-carburettor vacuum switch operating	1		
22	AEU2560	Throttle body-engine	1		

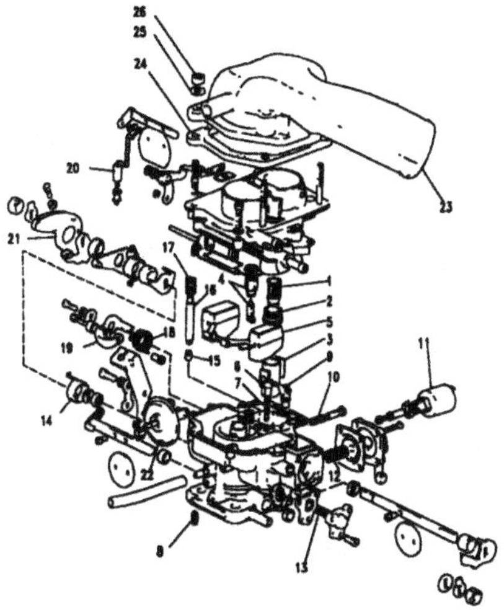

Illus	Part Number	Description	Quantity	Change Point	Remarks
23	ERC8631	Elbow-carburettor air inlet-non detoxed	NLA		Use ERR539.
23	ERR539	Elbow-carburettor air inlet-non detoxed	1		
23	ERC9896	Elbow-carburettor air inlet-detoxed	1		
24	ERC7922	Gasket-carburettor air elbow-asbestos	1		
24	ERR4384	Gasket-carburettor air elbow-asbestos free	1		
25	WA105001L	Washer-plain-standard-M5	4		
26	NH105041L	Nut-hexagonal-M5	4		
	RTC3663	Solenoid-carburettor vent valve	1		
	RTC3664	Washer-solenoid	1		
	RTC3665	Seal-rubber	1		
	ERC7343	Valve-control-exhaust gas recirculation engine exhaust	1		

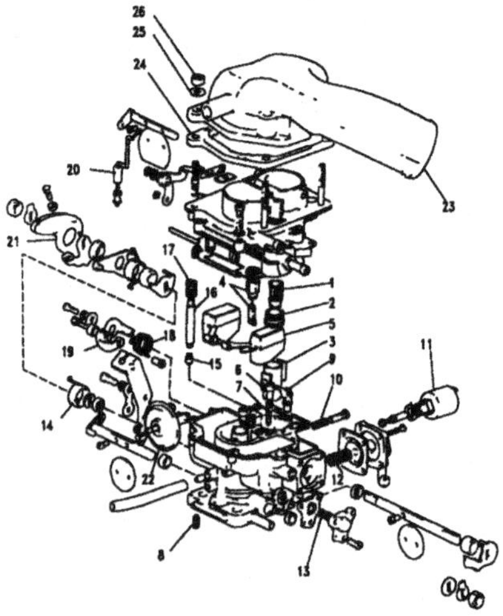

Illus	Part Number	Description	Quantity	Change Point	Remarks
	AEU2557	Kit-gasket-carburetter overhaul-single solenoid	1		
	RTC5863	Kit-gasket-carburetter overhaul-twin solenoid	1		
	RTC3948	Kit-conversion-carburettor	1		
	ETC5603	Pipe fuel	1		
	ETC5605	Connector fit	3		
	C435996L	Clip-hose	6		
	RTC3949	T piece	1		
	ERC298	Pipe-carburettor breather vent	1		
	ETC4959	Clip-carburettor breather	1		
	PRC3702	Clip-panel fixing-5mm-4.8mm hole	1		
	PRC3494	Plate-clips ignition	1		
	PRC4376	Lead-link-solenoid fuel shut off	1		

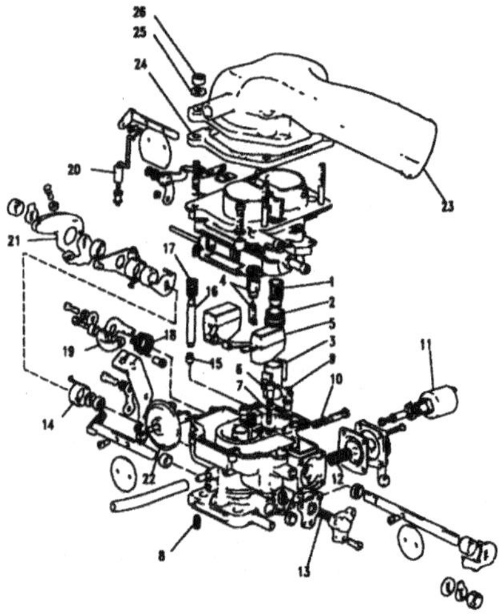

Carburetter Electric Pump

Illus	Part Number	Description	Quantity	Change Point	Remarks
1	ETC5305	Carburettor-engine	NLA		Fit carburetter STC3374 and new air intake elbow ERR539..
1	ETC5306	Carburettor-engine-detoxed	1		
2	RTC4421	Element-inline fuel filter	1		
3	RTC4420	Washer-sealing	1		
4	RTC4419	Hose-carburettor fuel pipe	1		
5	AEU2583	Float assembly-carburettor	1		
6	RTC4896	Gasket-carburettor	1		
7	AEU2584	Body-carburettor float needle	1		
8	AEU2565	Jet-carburettor-primary	2		
9	AEU2566	Tube-primary	2		
10	AEU2582	Holder-jet	2		
11	AEU2581	Jet-carburettor-primary	1		
11	AEU2580	Jet-carburettor-secondary	1		
12	AEU2578	Jet-carburettor-pump	1		
13	AEU2585	Venturi auxilary-centre device-carburettor-primary	2		
14	AEU2577	Spring-primary butterfly	1		
15	RTC4898	Screw-carburettor fast idle adjusting	1		
16	RTC4900	O ring	1		
17	RTC4850	Solenoid starter motor	1		
18	RTC3664	Washer	2		
19	AEU2575	Spring-pump-carburettor	1		
20	RTC4901	Diaphragm.	1		
21	RTC4903	Seal	1		
22	AEU2573	Shaft primary manual transmission	1		
24	AEU2574	Plate-throttle body setting	1		
25	RTC4860	Diaphragm.	1		
26	RTC4851	Spring	1		
27	AEU2579	Screw-adjusting	2		
29	AEU2572	Plate-throttle body setting	1		
30	AEU2569	Spring-return	1		
31	AEU2564	Spring-return	1		
32	RTC4853	Level-carburettor throttle	1		
33	AEU2560	Throttle body-engine	1		
34	AEU2564	Spring-return	1		
35	AEU2563	Lever-starting control	1		
36	AEU2562	Link-carburettor/throttle connecting	1		
38	RTC3665	Seal-rubber	1		
39	RTC4908	Spring-carburettor throttle return	1		
40	RTC3663	Solenoid-carburettor vent valve	1		
	RTC5863	Kit-gasket-carburetter overhaul	1		

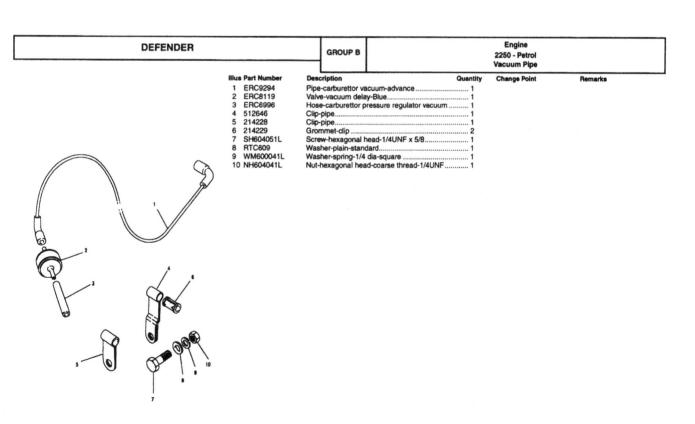

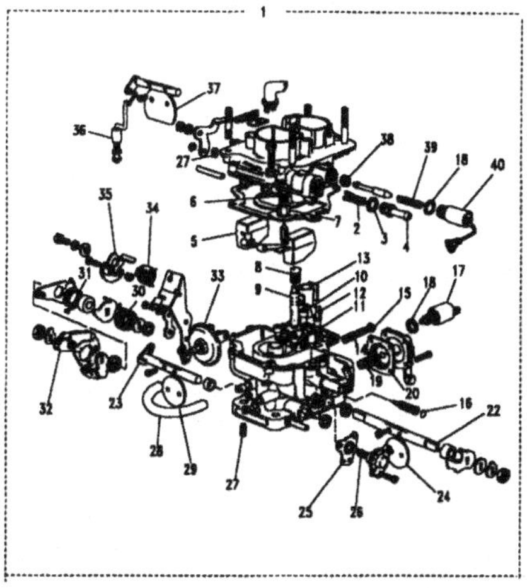

Vacuum Pipe

Illus	Part Number	Description	Quantity	Change Point	Remarks
1	ERC9294	Pipe-carburettor vacuum-advance	1		
2	ERC8119	Valve-vacuum delay-Blue	1		
3	ERC6996	Hose-carburettor pressure regulator vacuum	1		
4	512646	Clip-pipe	1		
5	214228	Clip-pipe	1		
6	214229	Grommet-clip	2		
7	SH604051L	Screw-hexagonal head-1/4UNF x 5/8	1		
8	RTC609	Washer-plain-standard	1		
9	WM600041L	Washer-spring-1/4 dia-square	1		
10	NH604041L	Nut-hexagonal head-coarse thread-1/4UNF	1		

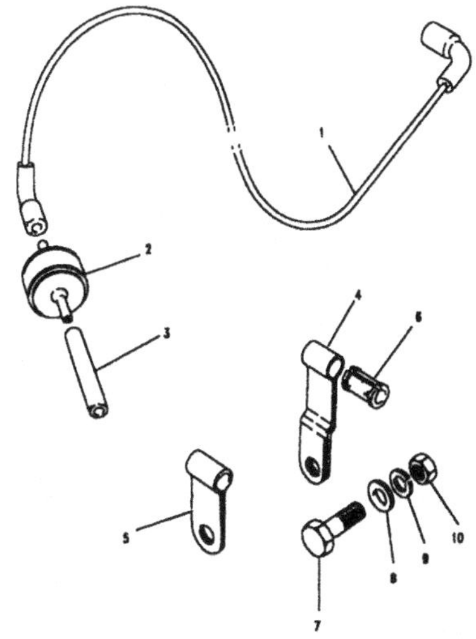

Illus	Part Number	Description	Quantity	Change Point	Remarks
1	ETC4925	Pipe fuel	1		
2	587684	Pipe-hose to carburettor	2		
3	572839	Clip-hose	4		

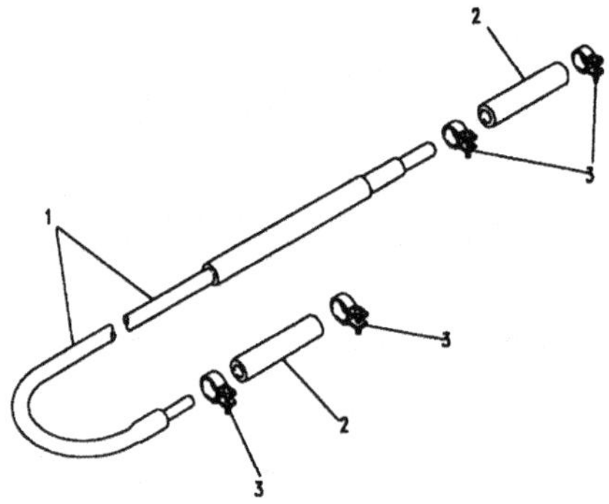

Illus	Part Number	Description	Quantity	Change Point	Remarks
1	ERC9708	LEVER ASSEMBLY-HAND THROTTLE	1		
2	ERC9693	• Lever assembly-hand throttle	1		
3	ERC9704	• Spring-carburettor throttle return	1		
4	WB600071L	• Washer-plain-thin	1		
5	CR120115L	• Circlip	1		

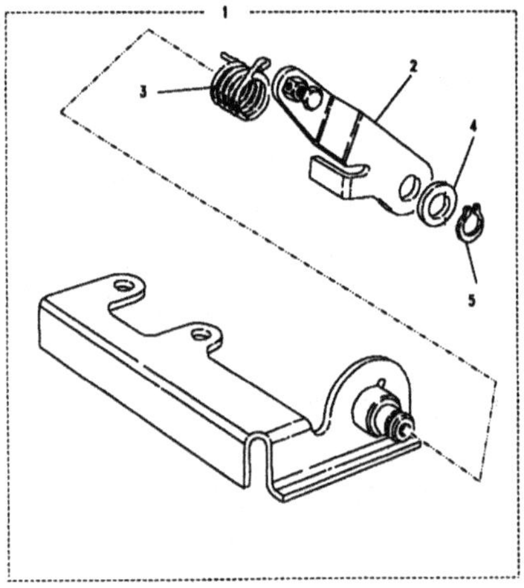

DEFENDER | GROUP B | Engine 2250 - Petrol Gaskets

Illus	Part Number	Description	Quantity	Change Point	Remarks
		SET-ENGINE GASKET			
1	RTC2889	decarbonising-asbestos	1		
1	STC1640	decarbonising-asbestos free	1		
2	RTC2890	overhaul-asbestos	1		
2	STC1467	overhaul-asbestos free	1		

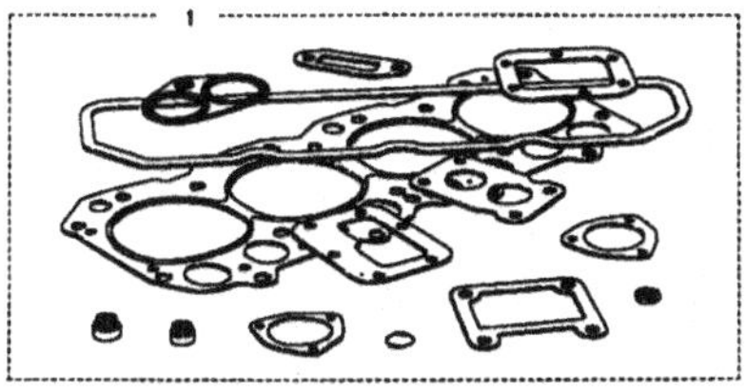

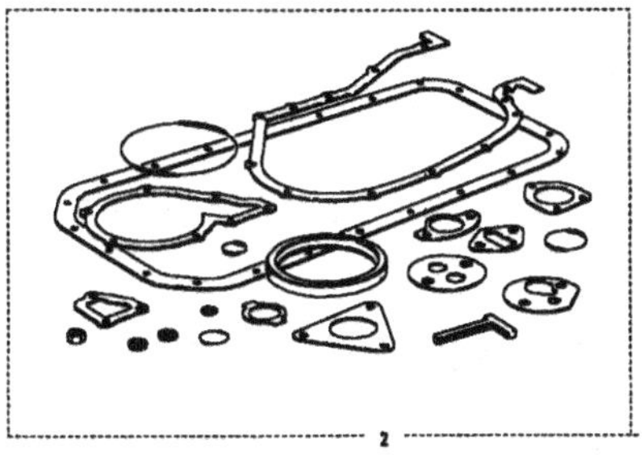

DEFENDER | GROUP B | Engine 2250 - Petrol Power Steering Pump-Adwest

Illus	Part Number	Description	Quantity	Change Point	Remarks
1	ERC8447	PUMP ASSEMBLY POWER ASSISTED STEERING	NLA		Use ETC9077 Hobourn Eaton Pump.
	AEU4119	• Washer power assisted steering	1		
	RTC4485	• Bolt-banjo	1		
2	ERC6974	Bracket-power assisted steering	1		
3	FS108251L	Screw-flanged head-M8 x 25	NLA		Use FS108257L.
4	WL108001L	Washer-sprung-M8	3		
5	FS108307L	Screw-flanged head-M8 x 30	1		
6	WL108001L	Washer-sprung-M8	1		
7	BH108181L	Bolt-hexagonal head-M8 x 90	NLA		
8	WL108001L	Washer-sprung-M8	1		
9	ERC6976	Spigot	1		
10	ERC6977	Nut	1		
11	ERC5145	Pulley-drive power assisted steering	1		
12	ERC6975	Plate assembly	1		
13	SH108141L	Screw-hexagonal head-M8 x 14	3		
14	WL108001L	Washer-sprung-M8	3		
15	FS106201L	Screw-flanged head-M6 x 20	4		
16	WL106001L	Washer-sprung-M6	4		
17	FS108251L	Screw-flanged head-M8 x 25	NLA		Use FS108257L.
18	WL108001L	Washer-sprung-M8	3		
19	ETC4153	PULLEY-IDLER ANCILLARY DRIVE	1		
20	SH108401L	• Screw-hexagonal head-M8 x 40	1		
21	WL108001L	• Washer-sprung-M8	1		
22	CR120195	Circlip	2		
23	ERC5146	Belt-polyvee power assisted steering	1		Except air conditioning
23	ETC4272	Belt-polyvee power assisted steering	1		Air conditioning
	AEU4119	Washer power assisted steering-on power steering pump	2		

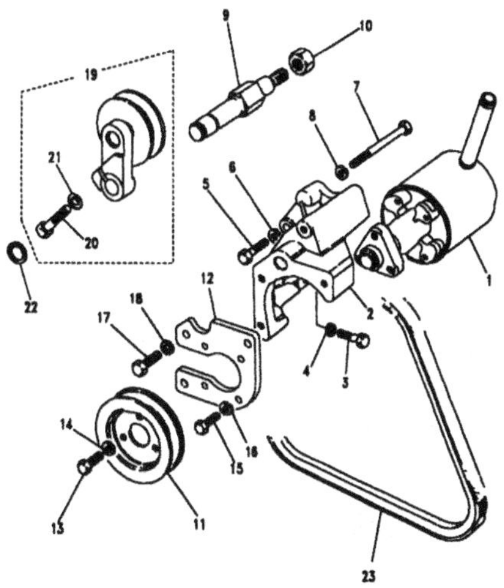

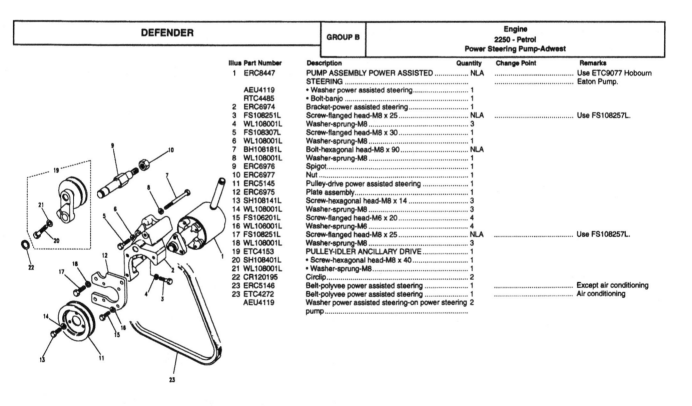

Illus	Part Number	Description	Quantity	Change Point	Remarks
1	ETC9077	PUMP ASSEMBLY POWER ASSISTED STEERING	1		
	RTC5674	• Union-delivery	1		
	RTC5675	• Washer-sealing	2		
2	ERC6974	Bracket-power assisted steering	1		
3	FS106201L	Screw-flanged head-M6 x 20	4		
4	FS108251L	Screw-flanged head-M8 x 25	NLA		Use FS108257L.
5	WA108051L	Washer-8mm	2		
6	WL106001L	Washer-sprung-M6	4		
7	WL108001L	Washer-sprung-M8	3		
8	ETC5783	Pulley power assisted steering pump	1		
9	SH108141L	Screw-hexagonal head-M8 x 14	3		
10	WL108001L	Washer-sprung-M8	3		
11	ETC5944	Bracket-mounting power assisted steering pump-mounting	NLA		Use ERR1976.
12	ETC5815	Belt-polyvee power assisted steering	1		
13	BH108181L	Bolt-hexagonal head-M8 x 90	NLA		
14	FS108251L	Screw-flanged head-M8 x 25	NLA		Use FS108257L.
14	FS108307L	Screw-flanged head-M8 x 30	1		
15	WL108001L	Washer-sprung-M8	5		
16	RTC5935	Kit-power assisted steering pump seal	NLA	Note (1)	Use STC1633.
16	STC1633	Kit-power assisted steering pump seal	1	Note (2)	

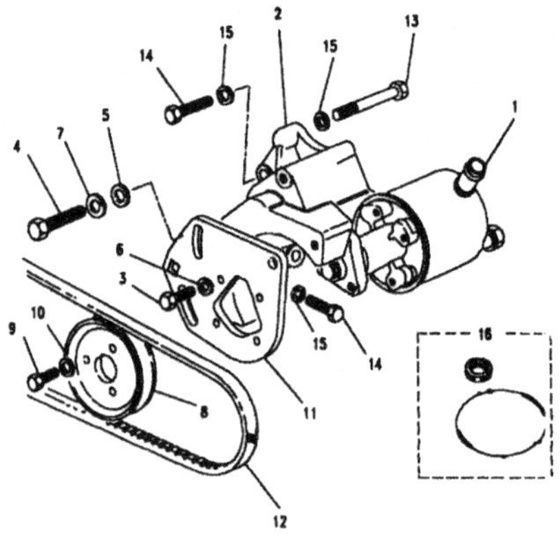

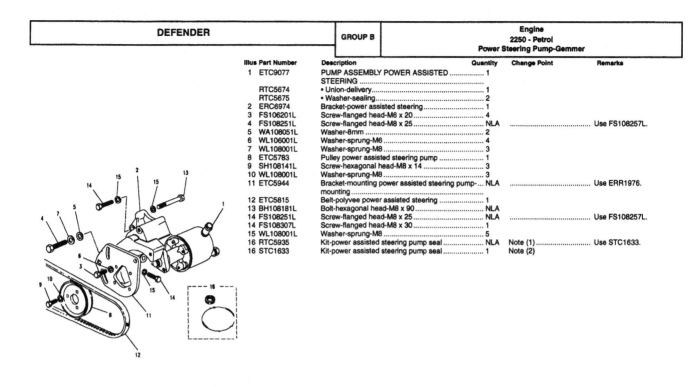

CHANGE POINTS:
(1) To (E)11L 22454A
(2) From (E)11L 22455A

Illus	Part Number	Description	Quantity	Change Point	Remarks
	ERC6480	COMPRESSOR ASSEMBLY AIR CONDITIONING	1		
1	AEU1782	• Pulley-driven air conditioning	1		
2	AEU1694	• Key	1		
3	AEU1780	• Screw	6		
4	AEU1779	• Washer	6		
5	AEU1784	• Screw	4		
6	AEU1775	• Nut	1		
7	AEU1778	• Clutch set-magnetic air conditioning compressor	1		
8	AEU1777	• Retainer	1		
9	AEU1785	• Cover assembly-front	1		
10	AEU1776	• Clutch-drive-assy	1		
	AEU1792	• CYLINDER	1		
	AEU1791	• • Kit-thrust washer-air conditioning	1		
	AEU1790	• • Kit-steering box sector shaft seal	1		
	AEU1192	• • O RING AIR CONDITIONING	1		
	AEU1690	• • • O ring	2		
	AEU1788	• Plate	4		
	AEU1787	• Circlip	4		
	AEU1786	• Housing assembly compressor	1		
	AEU1689	• Valve-air conditioning pressure relief	1		
	AEU1688	• Kit-superheat switch	1		

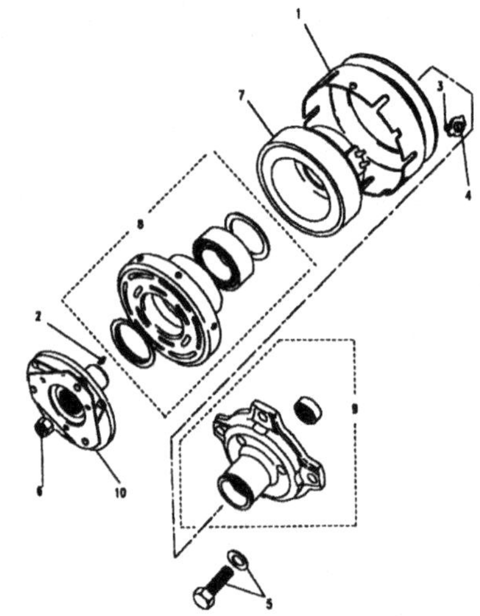

DEFENDER | GROUP B | Engine 2250 - Petrol Air Conditioning Pump Kits

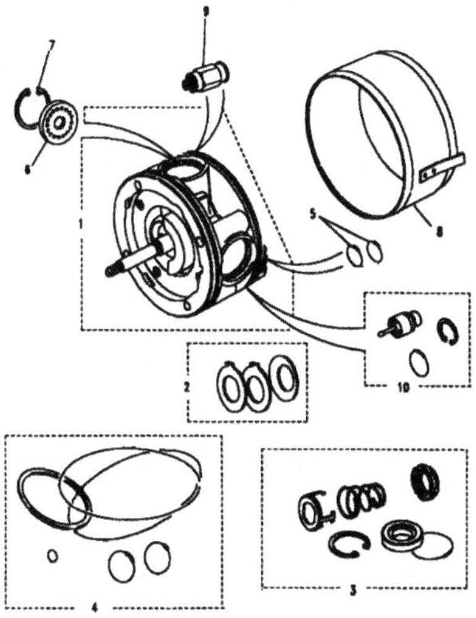

Illus	Part Number	Description	Quantity	Change Point	Remarks
	ERC6480	COMPRESSOR ASSEMBLY AIR CONDITIONING	1		
	AEU1782	• Pulley-driven air conditioning	1		
	AEU1694	• Key	1		
	AEU1780	• Screw	6		
	AEU1779	• Washer	6		
	AEU1784	• Screw	4		
	AEU1775	• Nut	1		
	AEU1778	• Clutch set-magnetic air conditioning compressor	1		
	AEU1777	• Retainer	1		
	AEU1785	• Cover assembly-front	1		
	AEU1776	• Clutch-drive-assy	1		
1	AEU1792	• CYLINDER	1		
2	AEU1791	• • Kit-thrust washer-air conditioning	1		
3	AEU1790	• • Kit-steering box sector shaft seal	1		
4	AEU1192	• • O RING AIR CONDITIONING	1		
5	AEU1690	• • • O ring	2		
6	AEU1788	• Plate	4		
7	AEU1787	• Circlip	4		
8	AEU1786	• Housing assembly compressor	1		
9	AEU1689	• Valve-air conditioning pressure relief	1		
10	AEU1688	• Kit-superheat switch	1		
11	ERC6072	Belt-front camshaft drive	2		
	AEU1691	Oil-525 visc	A/R		

DEFENDER | GROUP B | Engine 2250 - Petrol Air Conditioning Pump Fixings

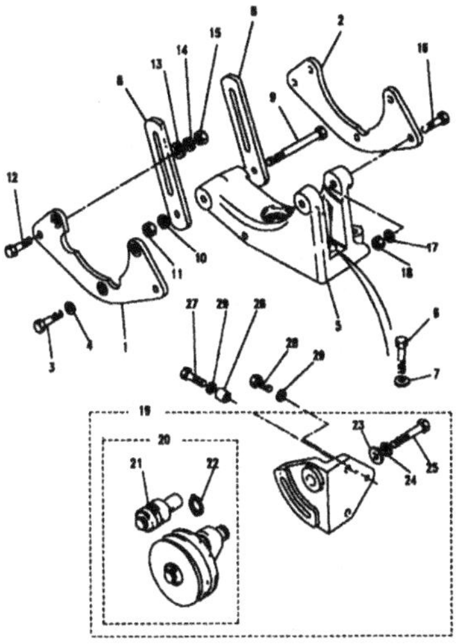

Illus	Part Number	Description	Quantity	Change Point	Remarks
1	ERC7082	Plate-front	1		
2	ERC5152	Plate-rear	1		
3	BH110201L	Bolt-compressor to plate-hexagonal head-M10 x 100	3		
4	WL110001L	Washer-M10	3		
5	ETC4882	Bracket-air compressor	NLA		Use ERR3091.
6	BH110101L	Bolt-bracket to cover-hexagonal head-M10 x 50-long	4		
7	WA110061L	Washer-M10	4		
8	ERC5155	Link-adjusting compressor	2		
9	BH108181L	Bolt-link to bracket-hexagonal head-M8 x 90	NLA		
10	WL108001L	Washer-sprung-M8	1		
11	NH108041L	Nut-hexagonal head-M8	1		
12	FS108251L	Screw-flanged head-M8 x 25	NLA		Use FS108257L.
13	WA108051L	Washer-8mm	2		
14	WL108001L	Washer-sprung-M8	2		
15	NH108041L	Nut-hexagonal head-M8	2		
16	FB108081L	Bolt-bracket to plate-flanged head-M8 x 40	2		
17	WL108001L	Washer-sprung-M8	2		
18	NH108041L	Nut-hexagonal head-M8	2		
19	ERC5386	BRACKET-COMPRESSOR/IDLER ASSEMBLY AIR CONDITIONING	1		
20	ERC5387	• IDLER-ARM	1		
21	90613049	• • Bearing-ball	1		
22	CR120171L	• • Circlip	1		
23	WC108051L	• Washer-idler arm clamp-M8	1		
24	WL108001L	• Washer-sprung-M8	1		
25	FB108081L	• Bolt-flanged head-M8 x 40	1		
26	ERC6071	Dowel	2		
27	FS108307L	Screw-flanged head-M8 x 30	2		
28	FS108251L	Screw-link to plate-flanged head-M8 x 25	NLA		Use FS108257L.
29	WL108001L	Washer-sprung-M8	3		

Illus	Part Number	Description	Quantity	Change Point	Remarks
1	ETC7756	PULLEY-DRIVE AIR CONDITIONING	1		
2	554971	• PULLEY-IDLER ANCILLARY DRIVE	1		
3	RTC6077	• • Nut-5/16UNF	1		
4	4095	• Washer	1		
5	WB108051L	• Washer-plain-M8	1		
6	ETC4212	• Plate	1		

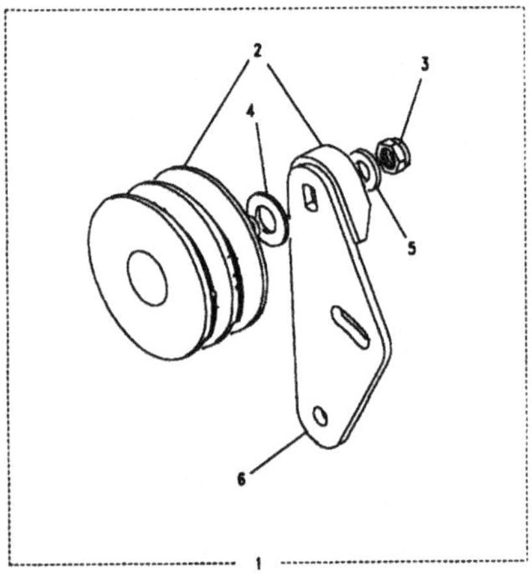

Illus	Part Number	Description	Quantity	Change Point	Remarks
1	ERC8520	DISTRIBUTOR ASSEMBLY IGNITION	1		
2	RTC3278	• Cap-distributor ignition-Lucas	1		
3	RTC3614	• Arm-rotor distributor-Lucas	1		
4	RTC3282	• Set-distributor contact-Lucas	1		
5	RTC3474	• Capacitor ignition coil-Lucas	1		
6	RTC315	• Set-distributor contact-Lucas	1		
7	AEU1034	• Capsule-vacuum distributor-Lucas	1		
2	RTC4932	• Cap-distributor ignition-Ducellier	1		
3	RTC4933	• Arm-rotor distributor-Ducellier	1		
4	RTC4934	• Set-distributor contact-Ducellier	1		
5	RTC4935	• Capacitor ignition coil-Ducellier	1		
7	AEU1684	• Capsule-vacuum distributor-Ducellier	1		
	RTC4936	• Plate-Ducellier	1		
8	549610	Connector-inlet manifold adaptor	1		
9	52278	Washer	1		
10	WB106041L	Washer-M6	1		
11	WM600041L	Washer-spring-1/4 dia-square	1		
12	253205	Screw	1		
13	FS108257L	Screw-flanged head-M8 x 25	3		
14	WA108051L	Washer-8mm	3		
15	WL108001L	Washer-sprung-M8	1		
16	549611	Coupling	1		
17	247212	Washer	1		
18	ERC3256	Set-high tension lead ignition	1		
19	RTC3570	Plug-sparking-8:1-com/ratio-N12Y	4		
19	RTC3571	Plug-sparking-7:1-com/ratio	4		
20	PRC9858	Coil ignition	1		
21	AB614061L	Screw-coil bracket-self tapping-No 14 x 3/4	2		
22	WJ106001L	Washer-plain-coil bracket-M6	2		

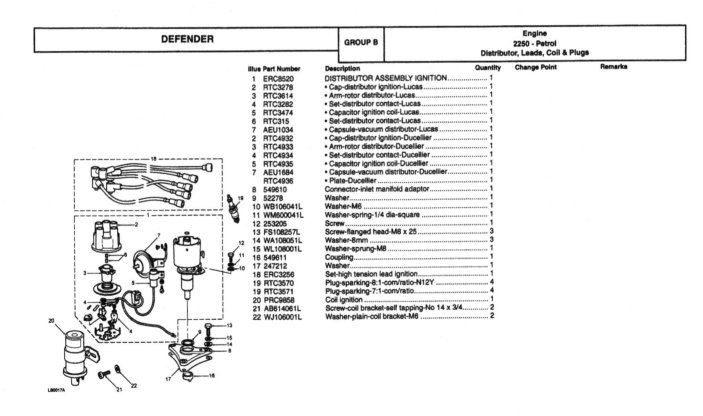

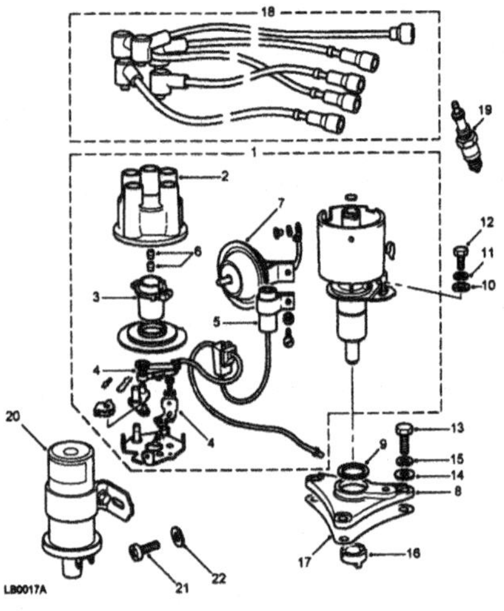

Illus	Part Number	Description	Quantity	Change Point	Remarks
1	RTC5083E	ALTERNATOR ASSEMBLY-MACHINE SENSED-115/45-LRA356-EXCHANGE	1		Except air conditioning
2	AEU2507	• Cover alternator-LRA356	1		
3	AEU3076	• Regulator assembly alternator-LRA356	1		
4	BAU1825	• Rectifier-alternator-machine sensed	1		
5	BAU2193	• Ring-slip alternator-machine sensed	1		
6	BAU2195	• Brush alternator-machine sensed	1		
7	RTC3215	• Brush alternator-machine sensed	1		
1	RTC5088E	ALTERNATOR ASSEMBLY-BATTERY SENSED-115/45-24079B90-EXCHANGE	1		Except air conditioning
2	AEU1814	• Cover alternator-24079B90	1		
3	AEU2464L	• Regulator assembly alternator-24079B90	1		
4	BAU1825	• Rectifier-alternator-battery sensed	1		
5	BAU2193	• Ring-slip alternator-battery sensed	1		
6	BAU2195	• Brush alternator-battery sensed	1		
7	RTC3215	• Brush alternator-battery sensed	1		
8	STC130	• Diode pack alternator	1		
1	RTC5218E	ALTERNATOR ASSEMBLY-LRA406-EXCHANGE-A133-65 AMP	1		Air conditioning
2	AEU1725	• Cover alternator	1		
3	AEU3076	• Regulator assembly alternator-LRA356	1		
4	AEU1527	• Rectifier-alternator	1		
7	RTC3292	• Brush alternator	1		
8	STC130	• Diode pack alternator	1		
10	AEU1726	• Kit-bearing-drive end alternator	1		
11	AEU1532	• Bearing-alternator front	1		
9	568788	Pulley alternator	1		Except air conditioning
9	ERC8986	Pulley alternator	1		Split charge

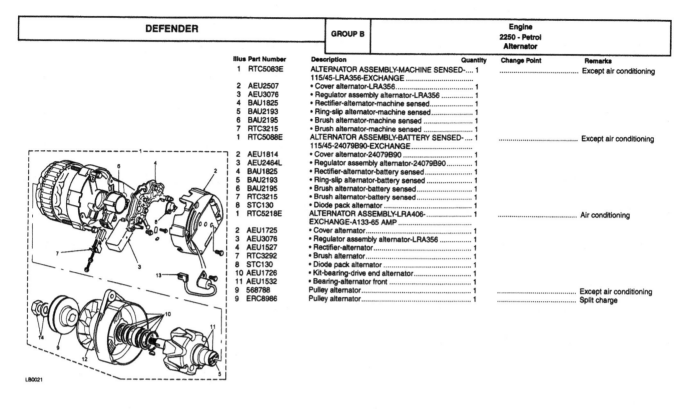

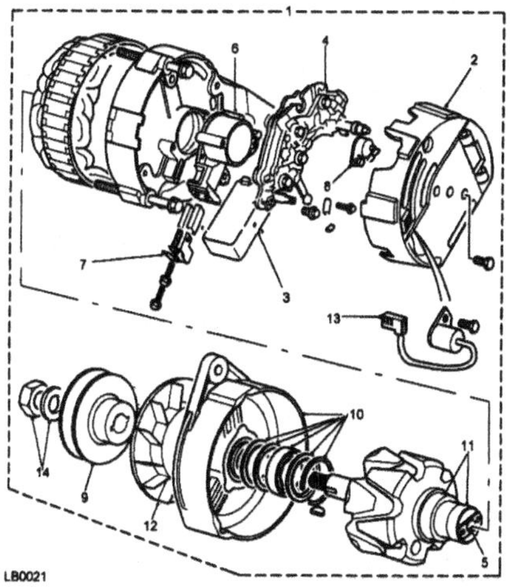

LB0021

Illus	Part Number	Description	Quantity	Change Point	Remarks
	ERC8987	Nut	1		Air conditioning
10	18G8619L	Kit-bearing-drive end alternator	1		Except air conditioning
10	AEU1726	Kit-bearing-drive end alternator	1		Air conditioning
11	AEU1532	Bearing-alternator front	1		
12	C37222L	Fan alternator	1		Except air conditioning
12	ADU4928L	Fan alternator	1		Air conditioning
13	AEU1616	Capacitor alternator	1		Air conditioning
	AEU1706	Kit-screw	1		
14	AEU1710	Kit-fixings alternator/vacuum pump-sundry parts	1		
	AEU1709	Kit-alternator-terminal	1		Air conditioning
	AEU1942	Spacer	1		Except air conditioning
	AEU1708	Spacer	1		Air conditioning

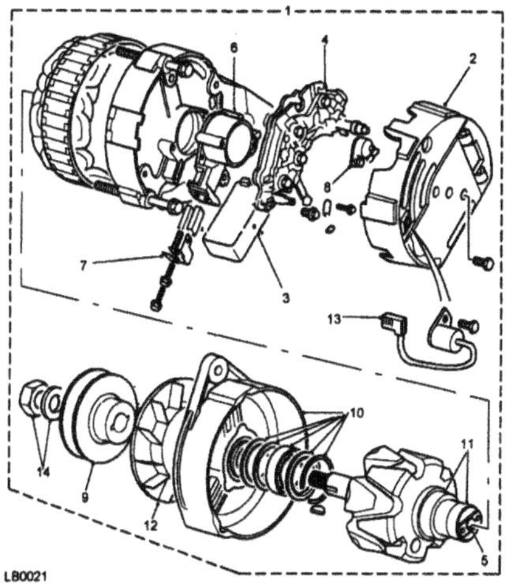

LB0021

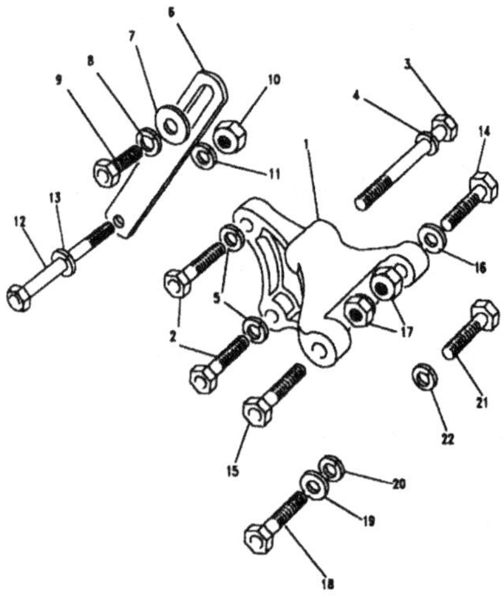

Illus	Part Number	Description	Quantity	Change Point	Remarks
1	ETC4357	Bracket-mounting-alternator	1		Except air conditioning
2	FS108307L	Screw-flanged head-M8 x 30	2		Except air conditioning
3	BH605261L	Bolt-hexagonal head-5/16UNC x 3 1/4	1		Alternatives except air conditioning
11	WM600051L	Washer-spring-5/16"	1		
3	BH108161L	Bolt-hexagonal head-M8 x 80	1		
4	WL108001L	Washer-sprung-M8	1		
5	WL108001L	Washer-sprung-M8	2		Except air conditioning
		LINK-ADJUSTER ALTERNATOR			
6	ERC5139	A133 alternator	1		
6	ERC6683	A127 alternator	1		Air conditioning
6	ERC6683	A127 alternator	1		Split charge
7	2266L	Washer-link to alternator	1		
8	WL108001L	Washer-sprung-M8	1		
9	FS108251L	Screw-flanged head-M8 x 25	NLA		Use FS108257L.
10	NH605041L	Nut-hexagonal head-5/16UNF	1		Air conditioning
11	WM600051L	Washer-spring-5/16"	1		
12	BH108201L	Bolt-hexagonal head-M8 x 100	1		Except air conditioning
13	WL108001L	Washer-sprung-M8	1		
14	FB108081L	Bolt-flanged head-M8 x 40	1		Manual steering
15	BH108091L	Bolt-M8 x 45	1		
16	WC108051L	Washer-M8	1		
17	NY108041L	Nut-nyloc-M8	2		
18	FS108357	Screw-flanged head-M8 x 35	1		Power steering
19	WC108051L	Washer-M8	1		
20	WL108001L	Washer-sprung-M8	1		
21	SH108401L	Screw-hexagonal head-M8 x 40	1		
22	WL108001L	Washer-sprung-M8	1		

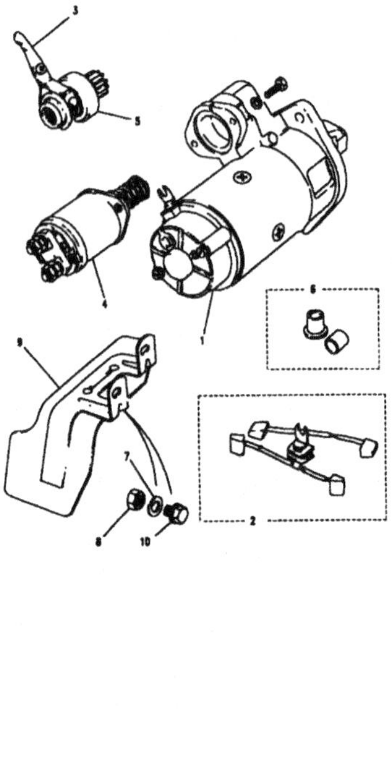

Illus	Part Number	Description	Quantity	Change Point	Remarks
1	PRC6613N	MOTOR-STARTER ENGINE-WITH M78R STARTER MOTOR-LUCAS-NEW	1		
1	PRC6613E	MOTOR-STARTER ENGINE-EXCHANGE	1		
2	RTC5967	• Kit-brush starter motor-with 2m100 starter motor-Lucas	1		
3	520455	• Pin-clevis/pivot-with 2m100 starter motor	1		
4	STC1519	• Solenoid starter motor-with 2m100 starter motor-Lucas	1		
5	AEU2502	• Drive assembly starter motor-new-with 2m100 starter motor-Lucas	1		
2	RTC5048	• Kit-brush starter motor-with M78R starter motor-Lucas	1		
4	RTC5049	• Solenoid starter motor-with M78R starter motor-Lucas	1		
5	STC742	• Drive assembly starter motor-new-with M78R starter motor-Lucas	1		
6	608352	Kit-brush starter motor-with 2m100 starter motor	1		
6	RTC5563	Kit-brush starter motor-with M78R starter motor	1		
7	WL110001L	Washer-M10	2		
8	NH110041L	Nut-hexagonal head-coarse thread-M10	2		
9	ETC4133	Heatshield starter motor	1		
10	ERC8722	Bolt-exhaust manifold heat shield pillar-heatshield	2		
	608395	Kit-starter motor sundry parts-standard	1		
	90608178	Kit-starter motor sundry parts-with 2m100 starter motor	1		
	RTC5577	Kit-starter motor-with M78R starter motor	1		

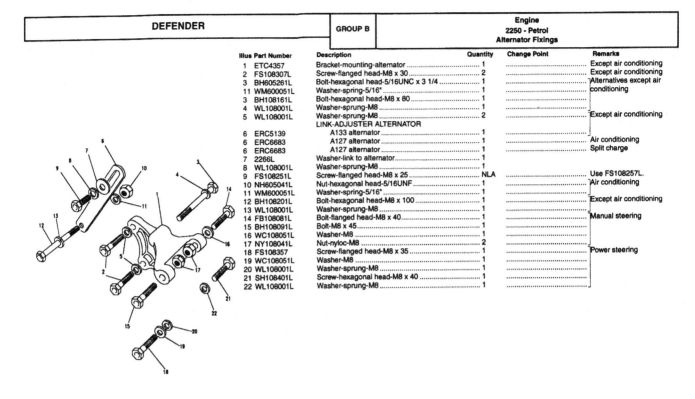

DEFENDER	GROUP B	Engine 2250 - Petrol Clutch & Flywheel

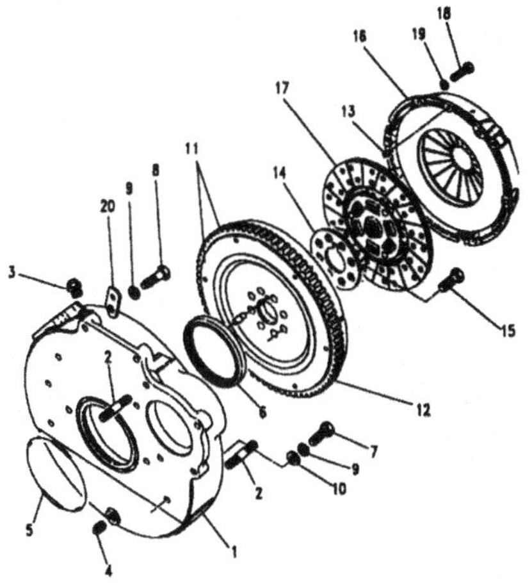

Illus	Part Number	Description	Quantity	Change Point	Remarks
1	ETC6394	HOUSING-FLYWHEEL ASSEMBLY	1		
2	TE110061L	• Stud-M10 x 30	13		
3	ERC7295	• Plug-rubber	1		
	NH110041L	Nut-hexagonal head-coarse thread-M10	11		
4	3290	Plug-coolant drain	1		
5	ERC6432	O ring	1		
6	ERR1535	Seal-crankshaft rear	NLA		Use ERR2532.
6	ERR2532	Seal-crankshaft rear	1		
7	FS110301L	Screw-flanged head-M10 x 30-top	6		
8	BX110071M	Bolt-hexagonal head-M10 x 35	2		
9	WL110001L	Washer-M10	2		
10	WA110061L	Washer-M10	6		
11	ERC6408	FLYWHEEL ENGINE	1		
12	ERC5293	• Ring starter-flywheel-engine	1		
13	502116	• Dowel-flywheel to crankshaft	3		
14	ERC4658	Plate-reinforcement	NLA		Engineering have found that the reinforcing plate is not required. When refitting flywheel omit plate , and fit new bolts ERR4574..
15	ERC6551	Bolt-fixing flywheel crankshaft-long	8		
15	ERR4574	Bolt-fixing flywheel crankshaft-short	8		
16	576557	Cover-clutch assembly	1		
17	FRC2671	Plate-clutch-driven-asbestos	1		
17	FTC159	Plate-clutch-driven-asbestos free	1		
	STC8359	KIT-CLUTCH	1		
17	FTC159	• Plate-clutch-driven-asbestos free	1		
16	576557	• Cover-clutch assembly	1		
	FRC9568	• BEARING-CLUTCH RELEASE	NLA		Use FTC5200.
	FRC4078	• • Sleeve-guide clutch	1		
	FTC5200	Bearing-clutch release			
18	SX108201L	Bolt-M8 x 20	6		
19	WL108001L	Washer-sprung-M8	6		
20	ERC9404	Bracket harness	2		

DEFENDER	GROUP B	Engine 2500 - Petrol Complete Engine

Illus	Part Number	Description	Quantity	Change Point	Remarks
1	ETC5900N	Engine-power unit	1		17H

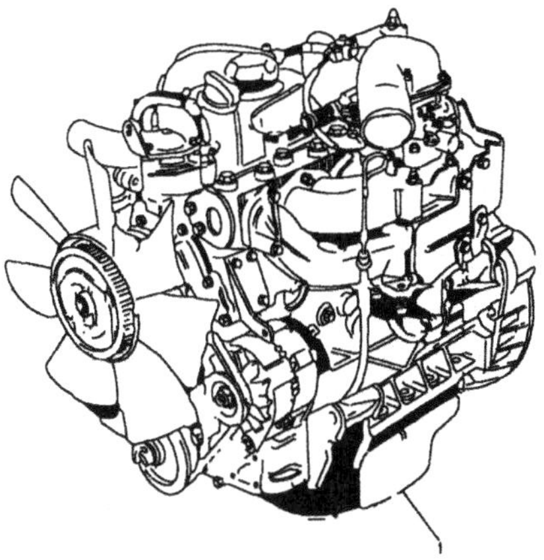

Illus	Part Number	Description	Quantity	Change Point	Remarks
		ENGINE UNIT-STRIPPED			
1	RTC4595R	reconditioned	1	To (E)17H 25700C	
1	RTC6800R	reconditioned	1	From (E)17H 25701C	
1	RTC6800N	new	1		

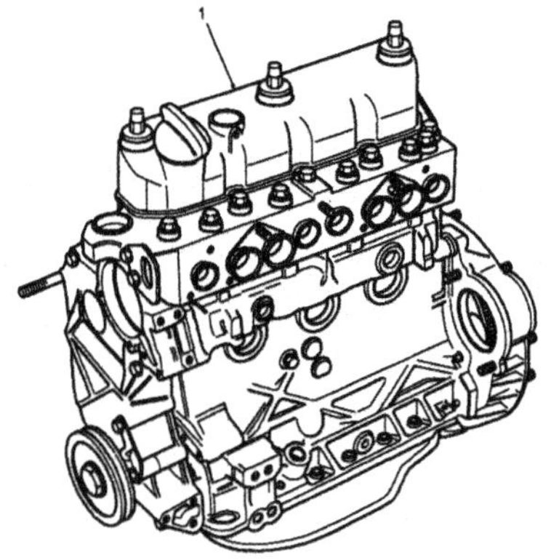

AHBFAC1A

Illus	Part Number	Description	Quantity	Change Point	Remarks
1	RTC6793	Engine assembly-power unit	1		

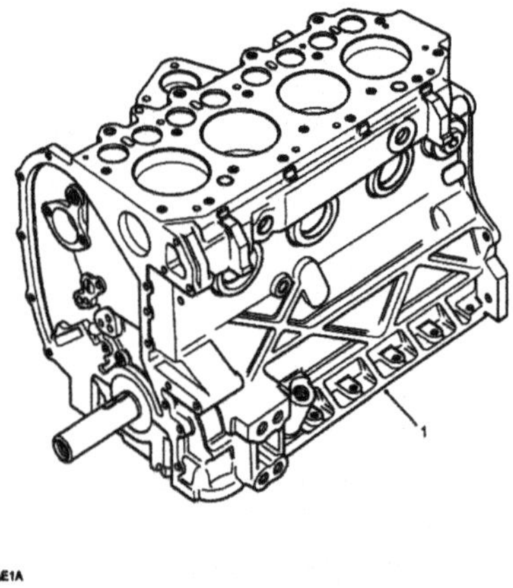

AHBFAE1A

Illus	Part Number	Description	Quantity	Change Point	Remarks
1	RTC3985	CYLINDER BLOCK-ENGINE	1		
2	247965	• Plug-tappet hole feed	1		
3	247127	• Plug-cylinder block oil way	2		
4	501593	• Dowel	10		
5	ERC4996	• Plug-core	6		
6	597586	• Plug-core	3		
7	ERC4644	• Dowel	2		
8	527269	• Plug-immersion heater	1		
9	243959	• Washer-sealing	2		
10	ETC4922	• Plug-gallery pipe	2		
11	90519054	• Bearing-camshaft front	1		
12	90519055	• Bearing-camshaft rear	3		
13	ERC4995	• Plug-core	2		
14	ETC7596	• Bolt-flanged head	10		
15	504006	• Washer	10		
	ERR5034	Plug-camshaft blanking-camshaft oil feed-rubber	3		

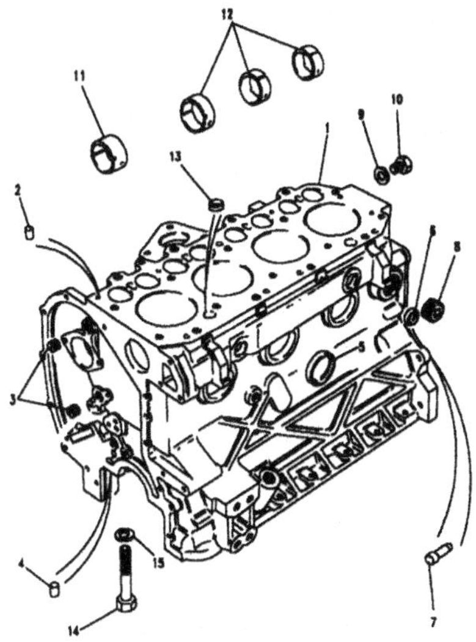

Illus	Part Number	Description	Quantity	Change Point	Remarks
1	ERR477	CYLINDER BLOCK-ENGINE	1		
2	247127	• Plug-cylinder block oil way	2		
3	501593	• Dowel-bearing cap	10		
4	ERC4996	• Plug-core	6		
5	597586	• Plug-core	3		
6	ETC8442	• Bearing-camshaft front	1		
7	90519055	• Bearing-camshaft rear	3		
8	ETC4529	• Plug-core	1		
9	ERC4995	• Plug-core	2		
10	ETC8074	• Bolt	10		
11	TE108031L	• Stud-M8 x 15	1		
12	ETC5577	• Plug-drain	1		
13	213961	• Washer-sealing	1		
14	ETC8362	• Plug-blanking-metal	1		
15	ERR586	• Connector-inlet manifold adaptor	1		
16	ERR531	• O ring	1		
	ERC9188	• Set-engine cylinder liner & piston	4		
	ERR5034	• Plug-camshaft blanking-camshaft-rubber	3		

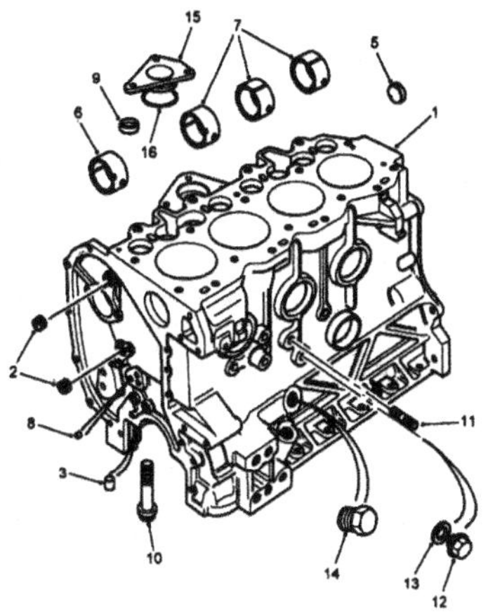

AHBFBA2A

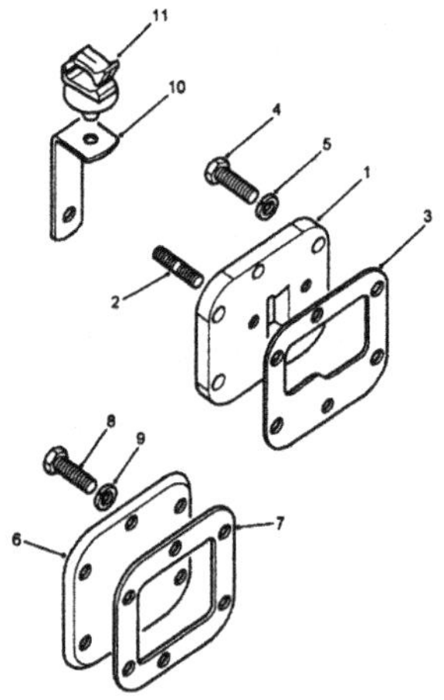

AHBFBC1A

Illus	Part Number	Description	Quantity	Change Point	Remarks
1	ETC4799	COVER-CYLINDER BLOCK SIDE	1		
2	TE108041L	• Stud-M8 x 20	2		
3	247554	Gasket-cylinder block side cover	NLA		Use ERR1475.
3	ERR1475	Gasket-cylinder block side cover	1		
4	FS108207L	Screw-flanged head-M8 x 20	6		
5	WL108001L	Washer-sprung-M8	6		
6	ERC2869	Cover-engine	1		
7	247555	Gasket-cylinder block side cover	NLA		Use ERR3605.
7	ERR3605	Gasket-cylinder block side cover-asbestos	NLA		Use ERR2026.
7	ERR2026	Gasket-cylinder block side cover-asbestos free	1		
8	FS108207L	Screw-flanged head-M8 x 20	6		
9	WL108001L	Washer-sprung-M8	6		
10	ERC9480	Bracket	1		
11	AFU1090L	Clip-cable-8mm hole	1		

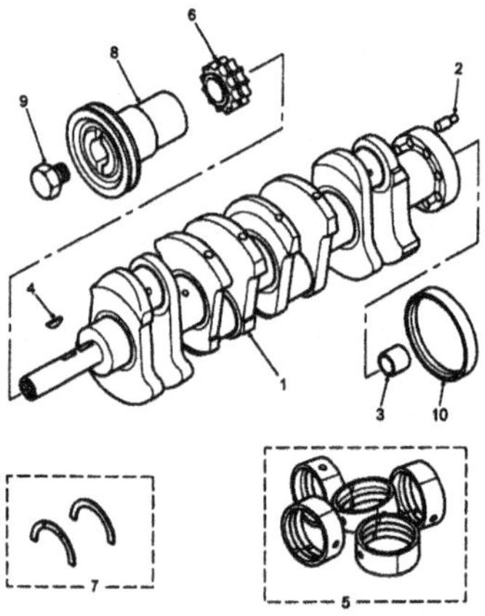

AHBFCA1A

Illus	Part Number	Description	Quantity	Change Point	Remarks
1	ETC8829	Crankshaft-engine	1	To (V) August 1989	
1	ERR1181	CRANKSHAFT-ENGINE	1	From (V) August 1989	
2	ERR1630	• Dowel-flywheel to crankshaft	1		
3	8566L	• Bush-crankshaft	1		
4	235770	• Key-crankshaft	2		
2	ERR1630	Dowel-flywheel to crankshaft	1		
3	8566L	Bush-crankshaft	1		
4	235770	Key-crankshaft	1		
		SET-CRANKSHAFT BEARINGS			
5	RTC2992	standard	A/R	To (E)17H 25700C	
5	RTC299210	0.010" undersize	A/R		
5	RTC4783	standard	NLA	From (E)17H 25701C	Use STC3395.
5	STC3395	standard	1		
5	RTC478310	0.010" undersize	1		
6	568333	Sprocket-crankshaft	1		
		WASHER-CRANKSHAFT THRUST			
7	RTC2825	standard.-pair	A/R	Note (1)	
7	538131	oversize.-0.0025"-pair	A/R		
7	538132	oversize.-0.005"-pair	A/R		
7	538134	oversize.-0.01"-pair	A/R		
8	ERC5349	Pulley assembly-crankshaft	1		Note (1)
8	ERC5128	Pulley assembly-crankshaft	1		Note (2)
8	ERC5127	Pulley assembly-crankshaft	1		Note (3)
8	ERC7089	Pulley assembly-crankshaft	1		Note (4)
9	ETC7934	Bolt-crankshaft pulley	1	To (V) August 1989	
9	ERR605	Bolt-crankshaft pulley	1	From (V) August 1989	
7	ERR705	Washer-crankshaft thrust	1		
10	ERR1535	Seal-crankshaft rear	NLA		Use ERR2532.
10	ERR2532	Seal-crankshaft rear	1		

CHANGE POINTS:
(1) To (V) August 1989

Remarks:
(1) manual steering Except air conditioning
(2) power steering Except air conditioning
(3) manual steering air conditioning
(4) power steering air conditioning

DEFENDER	GROUP B	Engine 2500 - Petrol Piston, Connecting Rod & Bearings

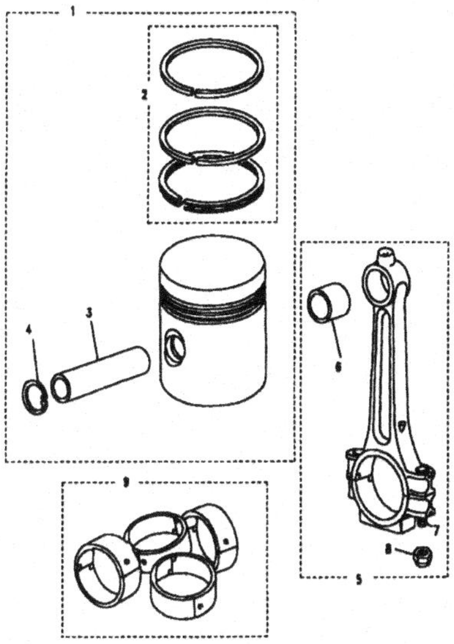

Illus	Part Number	Description	Quantity	Change Point	Remarks
1	RTC4734S	PISTON-ENGINE-STANDARD.	4		
2	RTC4374S	• Kit-piston ring-standard.	NLA		Use STC199.
3	ETC5994	• Pin-piston gudgeon	4		
4	265175	• Circlip	8		
1	RTC473420	PISTON-ENGINE-OVERSIZE.	4		
2	RTC437420	• Kit-piston ring-oversize.	NLA		Use STC19920.
3	ETC5994	• Pin-piston gudgeon	4		
4	265175	• Circlip	8		
2	STC199	Kit-piston ring-standard			
2	STC19920	Kit-piston ring-0.020" oversize			
5	ERR595	ROD ASSEMBLY-CONNECTING	4		
6	528004	• Bush	4		
7	ETC7357	• Bolt-connecting rod	8	From (E)17H 18677E	
8	ETC8191	• Nut-connecting rod	8		
7	ERC8751	Bolt-connecting rod	8	To (E)17H 18676E	
8	ETC5155	Nut-connecting rod	8		
9	RTC2993	Set-connecting rod big end half bearing-standard.	1		
9	RTC299310	Set-connecting rod big end half bearing-0.010" undersize	1		

DEFENDER	GROUP B	Engine 2500 - Petrol Sump

Illus	Part Number	Description	Quantity	Change Point	Remarks
	RTC4841	KIT-SUMP	1		
1	ERR4716	• SUMP-ENGINE OIL	1		
2	599552	• • Plug-drain	1		
3	FRC4808	• • Washer-sealing-sump drain plug	1		
4	546841	• Gasket-sump	1		
5	FS108161L	• Screw-flanged head-M8 x 16	21		
6	TE108031L	• Stud-M8 x 15	1		
7	WL108001L	• Washer-sprung-M8	22		
8	NH108041L	• Nut-hexagonal head-M8	1		
9	ERC8980	Tube assembly-oil dipstick	1		
10	532387	O ring	1		
11	ETC7867	Dipstick-oil	1		
5	FS108257L	Screw-flanged head-M8 x 25	1		
6	TE108041L	Stud-M8 x 20	1		

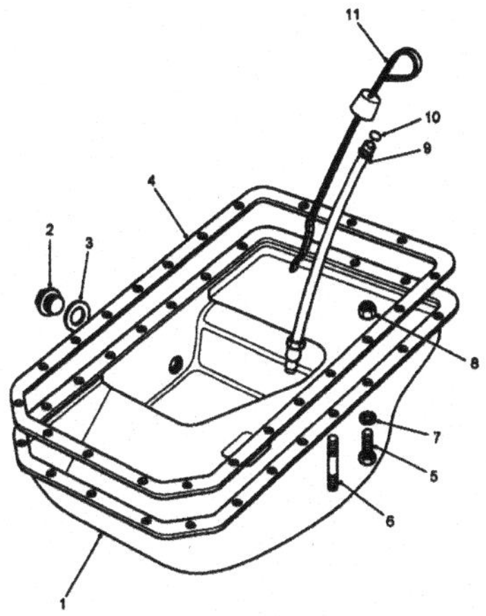

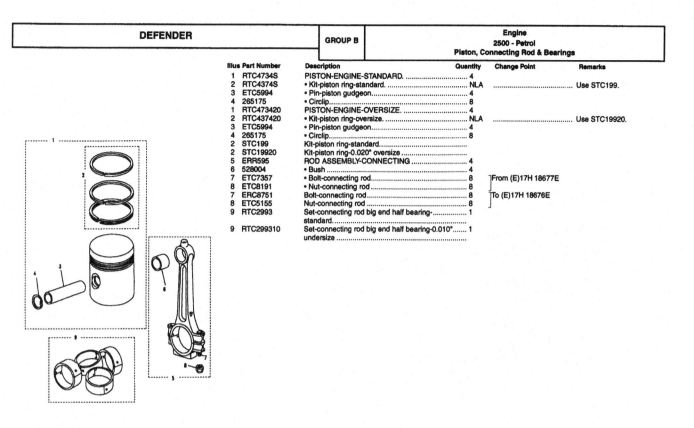

Illus	Part Number	Description	Quantity	Change Point	Remarks
1	NRC5434	Bracket-engine mounting-RH	1		
2	NRC9557	Bracket-engine mounting-LH	1		
3	SH112251L	Screw-hexagonal head-M12 x 25	4		
4	WL112001L	Washer	4		
5	ERC9410	Plug-drain	1		
6	AFU1882L	Washer-sump assembly drain plug	1		
7	ERC5086	Pad-insulation	2		
8	ANR1808	Mounting-engine rubber	2		
9	NH110041L	Nut-rubber to foot-hexagonal head-coarse thread-M10	4		
10	WC110061L	Washer-rubber to foot-plain-M10-oversize	2		
11	WL110001L	Washer-M10	4		

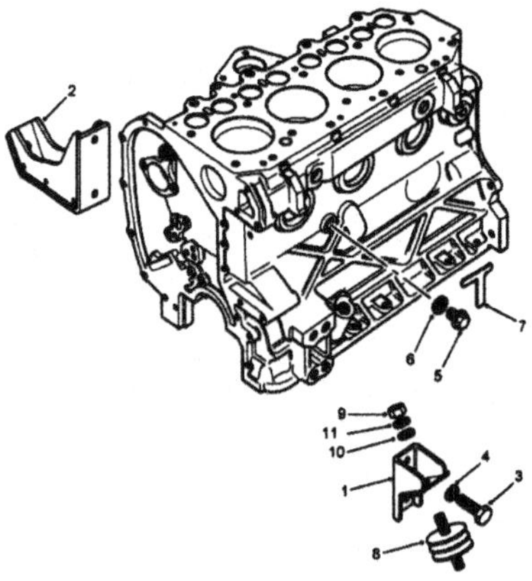

AHBFDC1A

Illus	Part Number	Description	Quantity	Change Point	Remarks
1	ERC9519	COVER-ENGINE-FRONT-WITH SINGLE LIP SEAL	1		Except air conditioning
1	ERC9528	COVER-ENGINE-FRONT-WITH SINGLE LIP SEAL	1		Air conditioning
2	247766	• Excluder mud	1		
	RJ608603	• Rivet	8		
4	6395L	• Dowel	4		
5	ERC7987	• Seal-crankshaft front oil-with single lip seal	1		Part of ERC9519.
5	516028	• Seal-crankshaft front oil-with single lip seal	1		Part of ERC9528.
1	ETC6081	COVER-ENGINE-FRONT-WITH TWIN LIP SEAL	1		Except air conditioning
1	ETC7947	COVER-ENGINE-FRONT-WITH TWIN LIP SEAL	1		Air conditioning
2	247766	• Excluder mud	1		
3	AB606061L	• Screw-self tapping-No 6 x 3/4	8		
4	6395L	• Dowel	2		
5	ETC5187	• Seal-crankshaft front oil-with twin lip seal	1		
6	ERR1607	Gasket-coolant pump body-to front cover-asbestos free	1		
7	538039	Gasket-timing gear housing drain plate	1		
8	ERC5361	Pointer-engine timing	1		
9	ERC6869	Spacer	1		
10	ERC8964	Bolt-M8 x 95	1		
11	WL108001L	Washer-sprung-M8	1		
12	ETC4994	Bolt-Special-cowl mounting-M8 x 80	1		Except air conditioning
12	FB108101L	Bolt-flanged head-M8 x 50	6		
12	BH108151L	Bolt-hexagonal head-M8 x 70	1		
12	FB108101L	Bolt-flanged head-M8 x 50	6		
13	WL108001L	Washer-sprung-M8	8		
22	WA108051L	Washer-8mm	1		
12	ETC4995	Bolt-M8 x 60	1		Air conditioning
	ERC9468	Stud	1		
12	BH108131L	Bolt-hexagonal head-M8 x 65	1		
12	BH108151L	Bolt-hexagonal head-M8 x 70	1		
12	FB108101L	Bolt-flanged head-M8 x 50	2		
12	BH108201L	Bolt-hexagonal head-M8 x 100	1		
12	FB108101L	Bolt-flanged head-M8 x 50	2		
10	ERC8964	Bolt-M8 x 95	2		
12	BH108201L	Bolt-hexagonal head-M8 x 100	1		
13	WL108001L	Washer-sprung-M8	9		

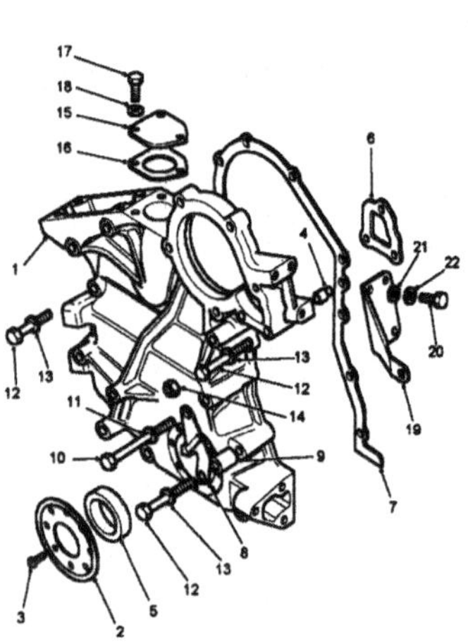

AHBFEA1A

Front Cover

Illus	Part Number	Description	Quantity	Change Point	Remarks
14	NH108041L	Nut-hexagonal head-M8	1		Air conditioning
15	574469	Plate	1		
16	542636	Gasket-cylinder block water gallery plate	1		
17	FS106201L	Screw-flanged head-M6 x 20	3		
18	WL106001L	Washer-sprung-M6	3		
19	ERC6479	Bracket	1		
20	FS108207L	Screw-flanged head-M8 x 20	3		
21	WL108001L	Washer-sprung-M8	3		
	ERC9404	Bracket harness	2		
	AFU1090L	Clip-cable-8mm hole	2		
20	FS108161L	Screw-flanged head-M8 x 16	2		
	RTC3772	Tie-cable-Black-4.8 x 135mm-inside serated	2		

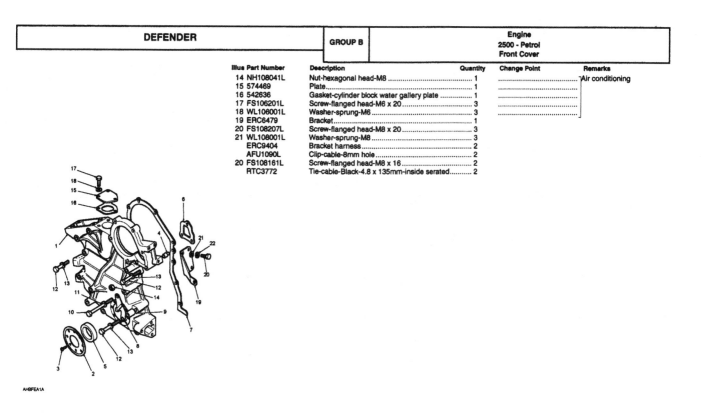

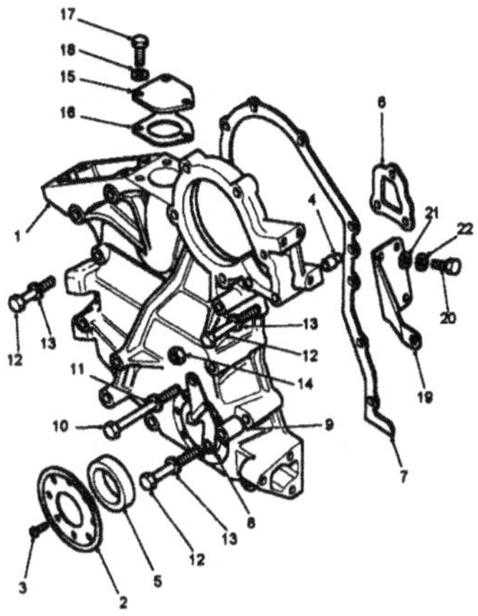

AHBFEA1A

Timing Chain & Tensioner

Illus	Part Number	Description	Quantity	Change Point	Remarks
1	ETC5191	Chain-engine timing	1		
2	ETC5190	Tensioner-timing chain	1		
3	FS108207L	Screw-flanged head-M8 x 20	2		
4	TE108051L	Stud-M8 x 25	1		
5	WA108051L	Washer-8mm	3		
6	NH108041L	Nut-hexagonal head-M8	1		
6	FN108041L	Nut-flange-M8	NLA		Use FN108047L.
7	275234	Brush-timing belt cover torsional vibration damper	1		
8	SH106121L	Screw-hexagonal head-M6 x 12	2		
9	557523	Washer-lock	2		

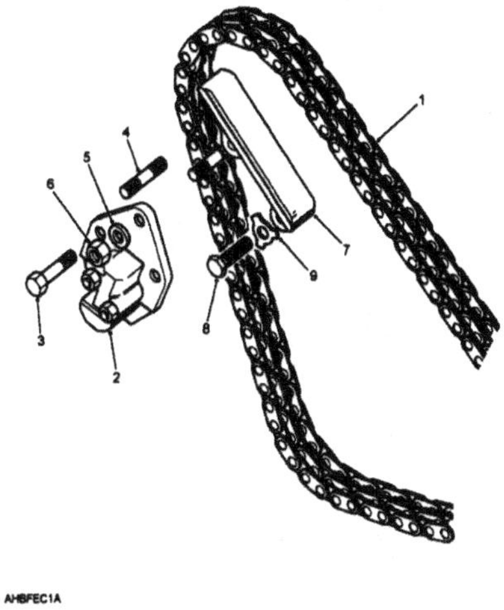

AHBFEC1A

DEFENDER	GROUP B	Engine 2500 - Petrol Water Pump-Basic

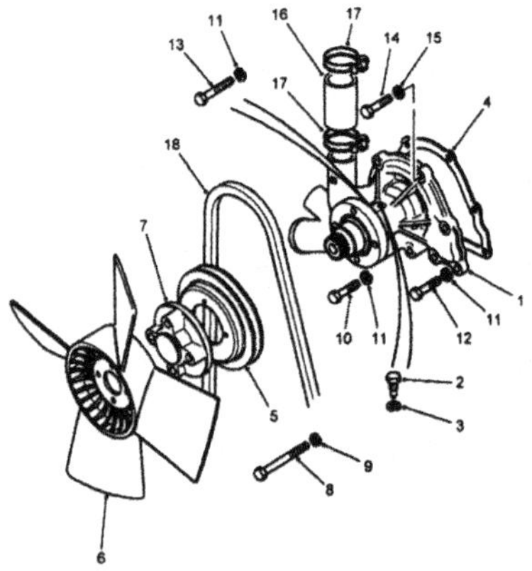

AHBFEE1A

Illus	Part Number	Description	Quantity	Change Point	Remarks
1	STC637	PUMP ASSEMBLY-ENGINE COOLANT	1		
	ERC7312	• Plug	1		
	232046	• Washer-copper	1		
2	ERC5600	• Screw	1		
3	WL106001L	• Washer-sprung-M6	1		
4	ERC5655	• Gasket-coolant pump body	1		
5	ERC5578	Pulley coolant pump-single groove	1		
6	ERC5545	Fan-cooling	1		
7	ERC7489	Spacer	1		
8	FB108111L	Bolt-pulley to pump-flanged head-M8 x 55	4		
9	WL108001L	Washer-sprung-M8	4		
10	BH108161L	Bolt-pump to block-hexagonal head-M8 x 80	2		
11	WL108001L	Washer-sprung-M8	4		
12	BH108171L	Bolt-pump to block-hexagonal head-M8 x 85	1		
13	BH108151L	Bolt-pump to block-hexagonal head-M8 x 70	1		
15	WL108001L	Washer-sprung-M8	3		
16	ERC5654	Hose assembly water-outlet	1		
17	CN100408L	Clip-hose	2		
18	563132	Belt-polyvee coolant pump	1		

DEFENDER	GROUP B	Engine 2500 - Petrol Water Pump-Air Conditioning

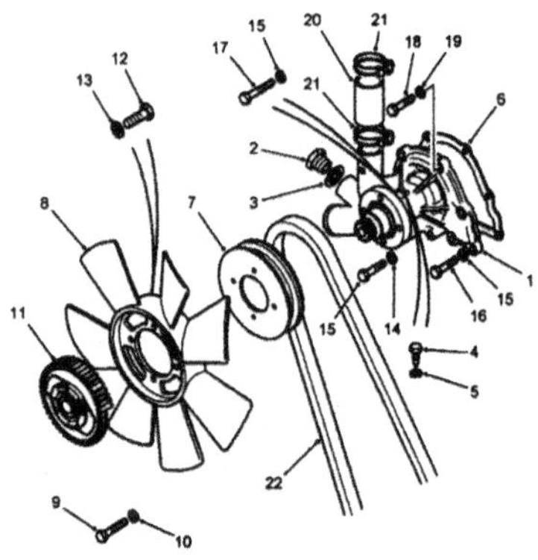

AHBFEE2A

Illus	Part Number	Description	Quantity	Change Point	Remarks
1	STC640	PUMP ASSEMBLY-ENGINE COOLANT-A133 ALTERNATOR	1		
1	STC635	PUMP ASSEMBLY-ENGINE COOLANT-A127 ALTERNATOR	1		
2	ERC7312	• Plug	1		
3	232046	• Washer-copper	1		
4	ERC5600	• Screw	1		
5	WL106001L	• Washer-sprung-M6	1		
6	ERC5655	• Gasket-coolant pump body	1		
7	ERC8890	Pulley coolant pump-twin groove	1		
8	ERR3380	Fan-cooling	1		
9	BH106051L	Bolt-pulley to hub-hexagonal head-M6 x 25	4		
10	WL106001L	Washer-sprung-M6	4		
11	ERC5708	Coupling-engine fan viscous	1		
12	ERC5709	Screw-M6 x 14	4		
13	4589L	Washer-plain	4		
14	BH108161L	Bolt-pump to block-hexagonal head-M8 x 80	2		
15	WL108001L	Washer-sprung-M8	4		
16	BH108171L	Bolt-pump to block-hexagonal head-M8 x 85	1		
17	BH108151L	Bolt-pump to block-hexagonal head-M8 x 70	1		
18	BH108161L	Bolt-pump to cover-hexagonal head-M8 x 80	3		
19	WL108001L	Washer-sprung-M8	3		
20	ERC5654	Hose assembly water-outlet	1		
21	CN100408L	Clip-hose	2		
22	ERC8938	Belt-polyvee coolant pump	1		

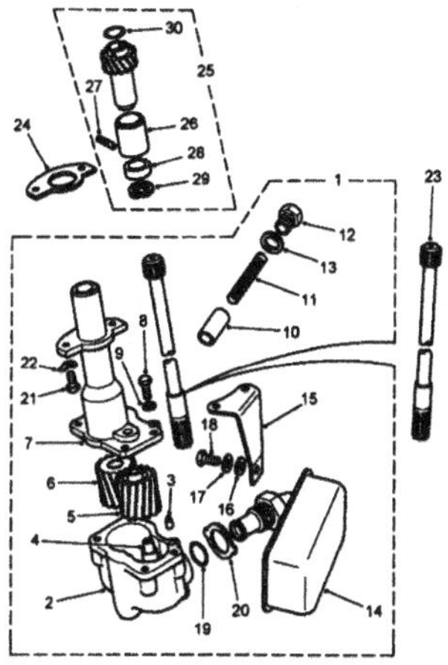

AHBFFA1A

Illus	Part Number	Description	Quantity	Change Point	Remarks
1	ERR1117	PUMP BODY ASSEMBLY-ENGINE OIL	1		
3	236257	• Dowel	2		
4	ERR1063	• Spindle-oil pump-idler wheel	1		
5	ERR1088	• Gear-oil pump idler-10 teeth	1		
6	ERC9706	• Gear-oil pump-wheel driver-10 teeth	1		
8	FS108207L	• Screw-flanged head-M8 x 20	4		
9	WL108001L	• Washer-fixing pump head with strainer to pump body-sprung-M8	4		
10	ETC4880	• Plunger-oil pump relief valve	1		
11	564456	• Spring-oil pump relief valve	1		
12	564455	• Plug-end oil relief	1		
13	232044	• Washer-sealing-joint oil relief	1		
14	ERC7530	• Strainer-oil	1		
15	ERC7940	• Bracket-pump/actuator-support	1		
16	WA108051L	• Washer-8mm	1		
9	WL108001L	• Washer-fixing bracket-sprung-M8	1		
8	FS108207L	• Screw-filter-flanged head-M8 x 20	1		
19	244488	• O ring	1		
20	244487	• Washer-lock	1		
21	FS108257L	• Screw-flanged head-M8 x 25	2		
22	247665	• Washer-lock-fixing pump head with strainer	2		
23	ERR850	Shaft-oil pump	1		
24	ERR3606	Gasket-cylinder block oil pump-asbestos free	1		
25	ETC6139	DRIVE ASSEMBLY-OIL PUMP	1		
26	522745	• Bush	1		
28	ETC6137	• Washer-thrust-thrust	1		
29	ETC6138	• Ring-snap-locking	1		
27	ETC6142	• Screw	1		

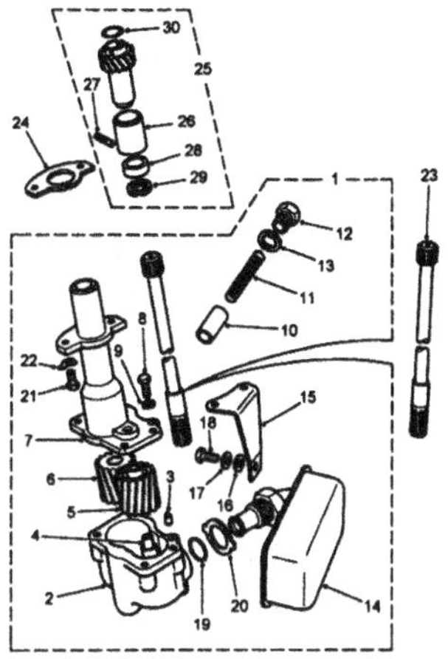

AHBFFA1A

Illus	Part Number	Description	Quantity	Change Point	Remarks
2	ETC5609	PUMP BODY CASTING-ENGINE OIL	1		
3	236257	• Dowel	2		
4	ERR1063	• Spindle-oil pump	1		
5	ERR1088	• Gear-oil pump idler-10 teeth	1		
6	ERC9706	• Gear-oil pump-10 teeth	1		
8	FS108207L	• Screw-flanged head-M8 x 20	4		
9	WL108001L	• Washer-fixing pump head without strainer to body-sprung-M8	4		
10	ETC4880	• Plunger-oil pump relief valve	1		
11	564456	• Spring-oil pump relief valve	1		
12	564455	• Plug	1		
13	232044	• Washer-sealing	1		
14	ERC7530	• Strainer-oil	1		
15	ERC7940	• Bracket-pump/actuator	1		
16	WA108051L	• Washer-8mm	1		
19	244488	• O ring	1		
20	244487	• Washer-lock	1		
21	FS108257L	• Screw-flanged head-M8 x 25	2		
22	247665	• Washer-lock-fixing pump head without strainer	2		

Illus	Part Number	Description	Quantity	Change Point	Remarks
1	ETC5347	ADAPTOR-OIL FILTER	1		
2	RTC6851	• Plug	1		
3	213961	• Washer-sealing	1		
4	ERC5913	• O ring	1		
5	ERC9884	• Cover-oil filter	1		
6	ETC4021	• Plug	1		
7	SH106141L	• Screw-hexagonal head-M6 x 14	2		
8	WA106041L	• Washer-6mm	2		
9	ERR3340	Cartridge-engine oil filter	1		
10	FS110301L	Screw-filter to block-flanged head-M10 x 30-top	2		
11	WL110001L	Washer-filter to block-M10	2		
12	ETC7582	Gasket-oil filter housing-asbestos	NLA	Note (1)	Use ERR4934.
12	ERR4934	Gasket-oil filter housing-asbestos free	1	Note (2)	
13	PRC6387	Switch-oil pressure engine	1		
14	PRC2505	Transducer coolant temperature	1		

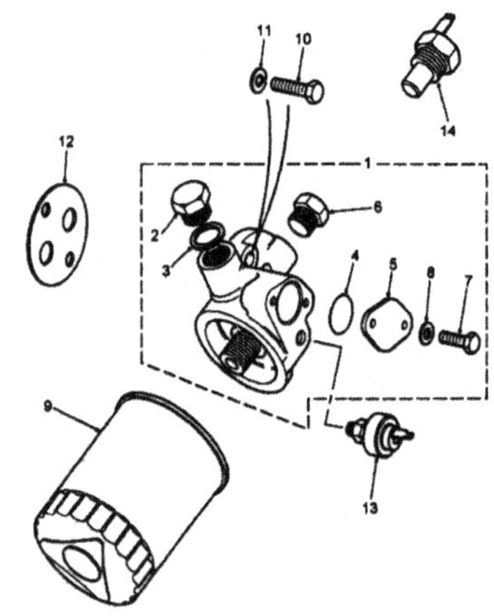

AHBFFA2A

CHANGE POINTS:
(1) To (E)17H 27415C
(2) From (E)17H 27416C

Illus	Part Number	Description	Quantity	Change Point	Remarks
1	ERR1347	ADAPTOR ASSEMBLY-OIL FILTER	1		
2	ERC5923	• Thermostat assembly-oil	1		
3	ETC4022	• Adaptor-oil filter	1		
4	ERC5913	• O ring	1		
5	ETC4021	• Plug	1		
6	SH106141L	• Screw-hexagonal head-M6 x 14	2		
7	WA106041L	• Washer-6mm	2		
8	ERR3340	Cartridge-engine oil filter	1		
9	FS110301L	Screw-filter to block-flanged head-M10 x 30-top	2		
10	WL110301L	Washer-filter to block	2		
11	ETC7582	Gasket-oil filter housing-asbestos	NLA	Note (1)	Use ERR4934.
11	ERR4934	Gasket-oil filter housing-asbestos free	1	Note (2)	
12	PRC6387	Switch-oil pressure engine	1		
13	232039	Washer-sealing	1		
14	NRC8618	Coupling	1		
	PRC2505	Transducer coolant temperature	1		

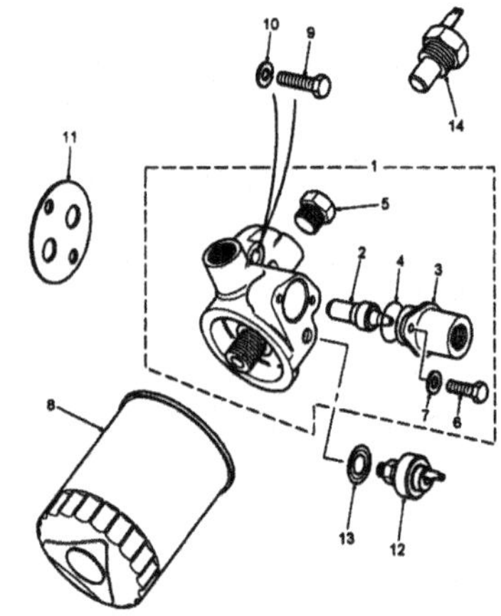

AHBFFA3A

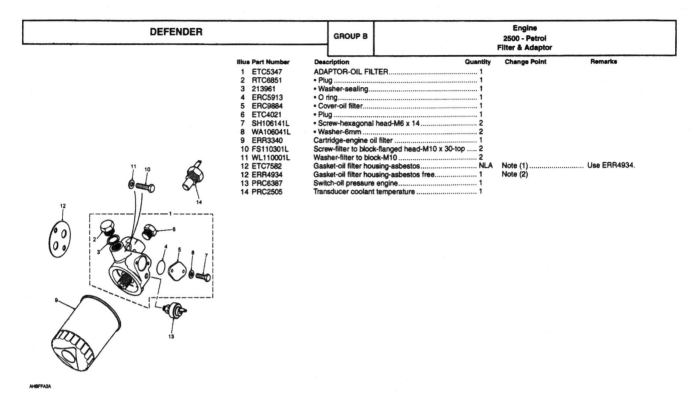

CHANGE POINTS:
(1) To (E)17H 27415C
(2) From (E)17H 27416C

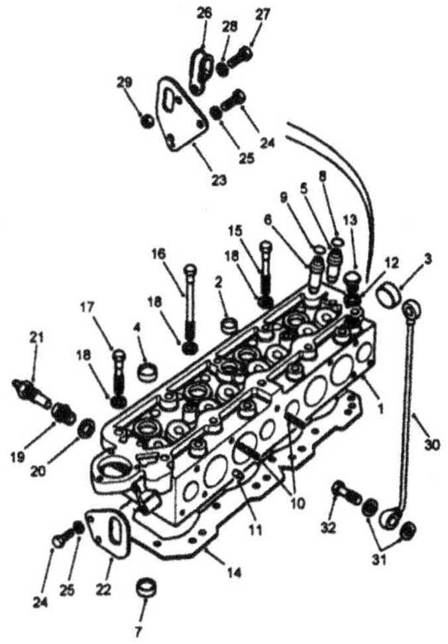

AHBFGA1A

Illus	Part Number	Description	Quantity	Change Point	Remarks
1	ETC5412	CYLINDER HEAD ASSEMBLY-ENGINE	1		
2	525497	• Plug-core	1		
3	524765	• Plug-core	1		
4	549702	• Plug	4		
5	568686	• Guide-valve-cylinder head inlet	4		
6	568687	• Guide-valve-cylinder head exhaust	4		
7	ETC6278	• Insert-cylinder head exhaust valve seat	4		
8	ERR1510	Seal-cylinder head valve stem oil-inlet	4		
9	ETC4751	Seal-exhaust	4		
10	TE108051L	Stud-M8 x 25	3		
11	213700	Dowel	2		
12	AFU1890L	Washer-sealing	1		
13	ERC9448	Plug	1		
14	ERC6380	Gasket-cylinder head	1		
15	247051	Bolt-1/2UNF x 4 9/16	9		
16	279648	Bolt-1/2UNF x 2 5/16	4		
17	554621	Bolt-1/2UNF x 4 1/8	5		
18	ERC6821	Washer-plain	18		
19	ERC8973	Adaptor-transmitter-water temperature	1	To (V) April 1989	
20	AFU1890L	Washer-sealing	1		
21	PRC2505	Transducer coolant temperature	1	To (V) April 1989	
21	PRC6663	Transducer coolant temperature	1	Note (1)	
21	YCB100390	Transducer coolant temperature	1	Note (2)	
22	ERC2254	Bracket-lifting body-front	1		
23	ETC7135	Bracket-lifting body-rear	1		
24	FS108207L	Screw-flanged head-M8 x 20	4		
25	WL108001L	Washer-sprung-M8	4		
26	543589	Clip	1		
27	SH104121L	Screw-hexagonal head-M4 x 12	1		
28	WA104001L	Washer-plain-M4	1		
29	NH104041L	Nut-hexagonal-M4	1		
30	275679	Pipe assembly-engine oil feed	1		
31	ETC6510	Washer-sealing	4		
32	ETC4498	Bolt-banjo	2		

CHANGE POINTS:
(1) From (V) April 1989 To (V) WA 159806
(2) From (V) XA 159807

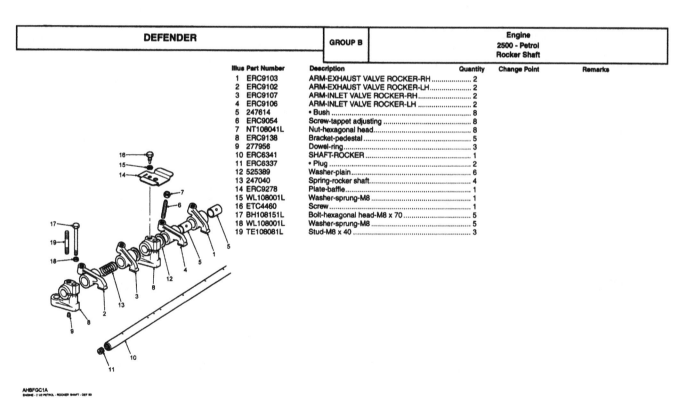

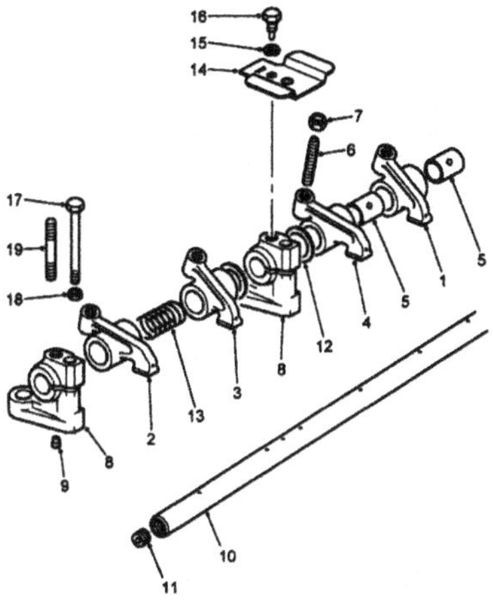

AHBFGC1A
ENGINE - 2 1/2 PETROL - ROCKER SHAFT - DEF 90

Illus	Part Number	Description	Quantity	Change Point	Remarks
1	ERC9103	ARM-EXHAUST VALVE ROCKER-RH	2		
2	ERC9102	ARM-EXHAUST VALVE ROCKER-LH	2		
3	ERC9107	ARM-INLET VALVE ROCKER-RH	2		
4	ERC9106	ARM-INLET VALVE ROCKER-LH	2		
5	247614	• Bush	8		
6	ERC9054	Screw-tappet adjusting	8		
7	NT108041L	Nut-hexagonal head	8		
8	ERC9138	Bracket-pedestal	5		
9	277956	Dowel-ring	3		
10	ERC6341	SHAFT-ROCKER	1		
11	ERC6337	• Plug	2		
12	525389	Washer-plain	6		
13	247040	Spring-rocker shaft	4		
14	ERC9278	Plate-baffle	1		
15	WL108001L	Washer-sprung-M8	1		
16	ETC4460	Screw	1		
17	BH108151L	Bolt-hexagonal head-M8 x 70	5		
18	WL108001L	Washer-sprung-M8	5		
19	TE108081L	Stud-M8 x 40	3		

Illus	Part Number	Description	Quantity	Change Point	Remarks
1	507829	TAPPET-ENGINE VALVE MECHANICAL	8		
2	502473	• Slide-tappet guide	8		
3	ERR607	• Tappet-engine valve mechanical	8		
4	ETC4246	• Bolt	8		
5	273069	• Washer-sealing	8		
6	ERR561	• Roller-tappet guide	8		
7	ETC4067	Valve-cylinder head inlet	4		
8	ETC5866	Valve-cylinder head exhaust	4		
9	ERR4175	Cap-valve stem	NLA	To (V) VA 128878	Use LJC100270.
9	LJC100270	Cap-valve stem	8	From (V) VA 128879	
10	ERR4640	Spring-cylinder head valve	8		
11	ETC4068	Cap-cylinder head valve spring	8		
12	ETC4069	Cotter-valve-split halves	16		
13	546798	Rod-engine push	8		

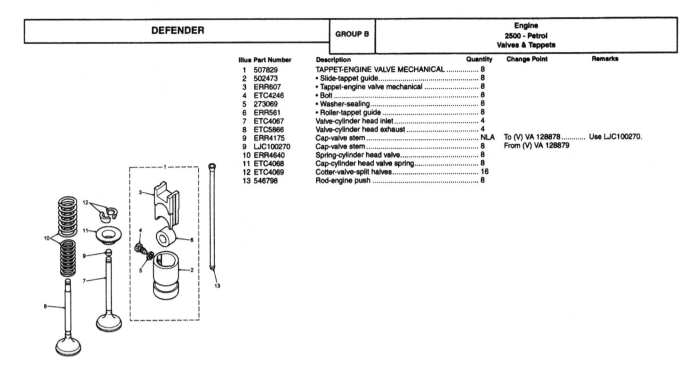

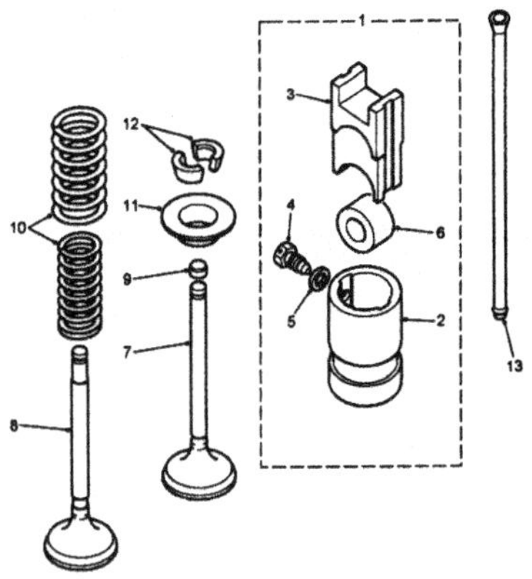

AHBFGE1A

Illus	Part Number	Description	Quantity	Change Point	Remarks
1	ETC5955	Rocker cover assembly	1		
2	ETC6439	Gasket-engine rocker cover-asbestos	1		
2	ERR4933	Gasket-engine rocker cover-asbestos free	1		2500 cc 4 Cylinder Petrol
3	ERC9220	Nut-domed-M8	3		
4	273069	Washer-sealing	3		
5	ERR1454	CAP ASSEMBLY-OIL FILLER	1		
6	ERR736	• O ring-breather	1		
7	ERC6200	T piece	1		
8	ERC9032	Hose assembly-breather-tee piece to elbow	1		
9	ERC9031	Hose assembly-breather-rocker to T piece	1		
10	CN100208L	Clip-hose-20mm	4		
11	CN100148L	Clip-hose	1		
12	ERC9033	Hose-T piece to carb	1		

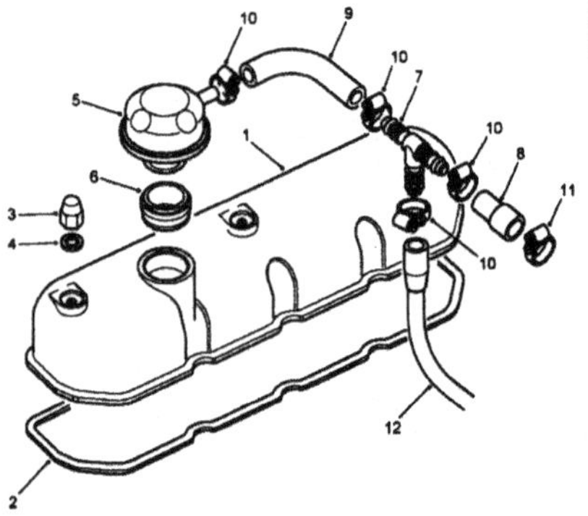

AHBFGG1A
ENGINE - 2 1/2 PETROL - ROCKER COVER AND BREATHER - DEF 90

DEFENDER

GROUP B — **Engine** / **2500 - Petrol** / **Camshaft**

Illus	Part Number	Description	Quantity	Change Point	Remarks
1	ETC7128	Camshaft assembly-engine	1		
2	ERC1561	Plate-camshaft retaining-thrust	1		
3	FS106167L	Screw-flanged head-flanged head-M6 x 16	2		
4	230313	Key-woodruff	1		
5	ETC5172	Gear-crankshaft timing drive	1		
6	ETC4140	Washer-retaining	1		
7	BX110071M	Bolt-retaining-hexagonal head-M10 x 35	1		
8	2995	Washer-lock	2		

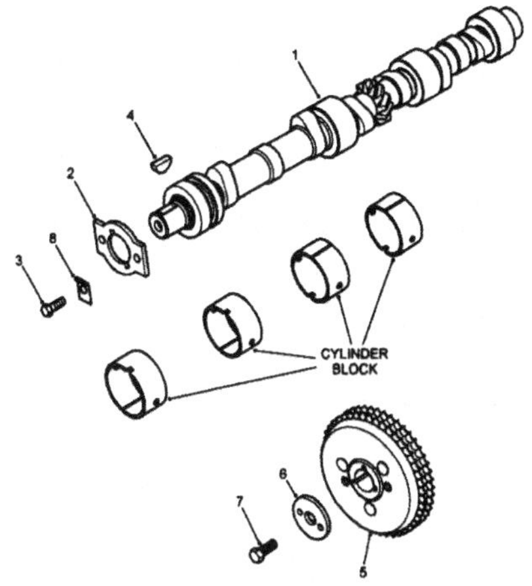

AHBFGI1A

DEFENDER

GROUP B — **Engine** / **2500 - Petrol** / **Thermostat Housing**

Illus	Part Number	Description	Quantity	Change Point	Remarks
1	ERC8758	Housing-thermostat	1		
		THERMOSTAT-ENGINE			
2	ETC4763	82 degrees C	NLA		Use 602687.
2	602687	82 degrees C	1		
2	ETC4761	74 degrees C	1		Optional
3	ERR3682	Gasket-thermostat housing-top-asbestos free	1		
4	247874	Gasket-thermostat housing-bottom	1		
5	ERC7510	Hose to pipe-coolant	1		
6	CN100258L	Clip-hose-25mm	2		
7	ETC5967	Elbow-engine coolant outlet	1		Except air conditioning
7	ETC5958	Elbow-engine coolant outlet	1		Air conditioning
8	ETC5965	Bracket-radiator pipe to cowl-cowl mounting	1		
9	BH106151L	Bolt-M6 x 75	3		
10	WL106001L	Washer-sprung-M6	3		
11	624091	Adaptor-pipe coolant	2		
12	243959	Washer-sealing	2		
13	PRC3366	Sensor-temperature-Blue	1		Air conditioning
13	PRC3541	Sensor-temperature-Red	1		Air conditioning
14	C457593	Washer-sealing	2		Air conditioning

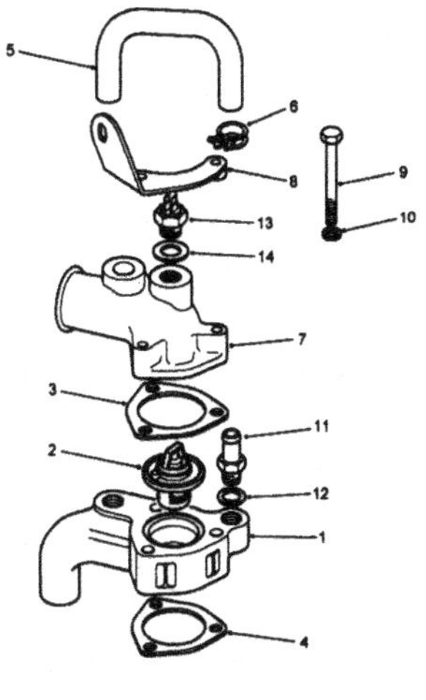

AHBFGK1A

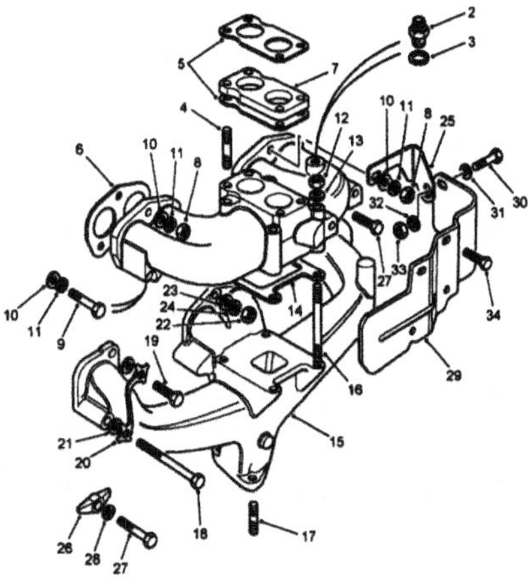

AHBFHA1A

Illus	Part Number	Description	Quantity	Change Point	Remarks
1	ERC9069	Manifold-engine inlet	1		
2	90513171	Connector-inlet manifold adaptor	1		
	ETC6929	Hose assembly-banjo fuel lines	1		
3	243958	Washer-sealing	1		
4	TE108081L	Stud-carb to inlet/manifold-M8 x 40	4		
5	ERC8645	Washer-asbestos	1		
5	ERR4385	Washer-asbestos free	2		
6	564307	Gasket-inlet manifold	2		
7	ERC8460	Sleeve-insulation heat protection-asbestos	1		
7	ERR4386	Sleeve-insulation heat protection-asbestos free	1		
8	NH108041L	Nut-manifold to head-hexagonal head-M8	2		
9	FB108101L	Bolt-manifold to head-flanged head-M8 x 50	2		2500 cc Petrol
10	587405	Washer-plain-manifold to head	4		
11	WL108001L	Washer-manifold to head-sprung-M8	4		
12	NH108041L	Nut-manifold to manifold-hexagonal head-M8	4		
13	WA108051L	Washer-8mm	4		
14	ERC8124	Gasket-exhaust manifold-asbestos	1		
14	ERR4387	Gasket-exhaust manifold-asbestos free	1		
15	ERC9071	Manifold assembly-engine exhaust-conical bore	1		
15	ETC5330	Manifold assembly-engine exhaust-parallel sided bore	1		
16	TE108131L	Stud-manifold to manifold-M8 x 65	4		
17	AFU1848L	Stud-exhaust pipe-M10	3		
18	BH108141L	Bolt-manifold to head-hexagonal head-M8 x 70	2		
34	SH108301L	Screw-manifold to head-hexagonal head-M8 x 30	NLA		Use FS108307L.
19	FS108307L	Screw-manifold to head-flanged head-M8 x 30	2		
20	596490	Washer-exhaust manifold to cylinder head tab	2		
21	587405	Washer-plain-manifold to head	4		
8	NH108041L	Nut-centre flange to head-hexagonal head-M8	1		
22	FN108041L	Nut-centre flange to head-flange-M8	NLA		Use FN108047L.

Illus	Part Number	Description	Quantity	Change Point	Remarks
23	587405	Washer-plain	1		
24	WL108001L	Washer-sprung-M8	1		
25	ETC5040	Bracket-heatshield	1		
26	564308	Clamp-manifold to head	2		
27	BH108141L	Bolt-manifold to head-hexagonal head-M8 x 70	2		
28	WL108001L	Washer-sprung-M8	2		
29	ERC8712	Heatshield-exhaust manifold	1		
30	FS108207L	Screw-heatshield to bracket-flanged head-M8 x 20	1		

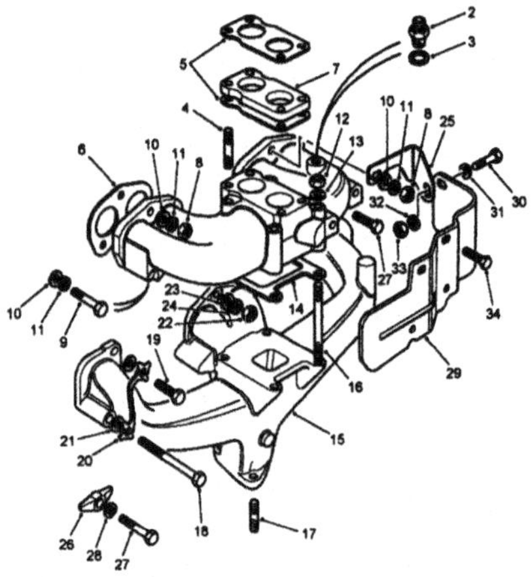

AHBFHA1A

Illus	Part Number	Description	Quantity	Change Point	Remarks
31	WA108051L	Washer-heatshield to bracket-8mm	4		
32	WL108001L	Washer-heatshield to bracket-sprung-M8	3		
33	NH108041L	Nut-heatshield to bracket-hexagonal head-M8	1		
34	SH108141L	Screw-heatshield to bracket-hexagonal head-M8 x 14	2		
	ERC8722	Bolt-exhaust manifold heat shield pillar-shield to manifold	2		

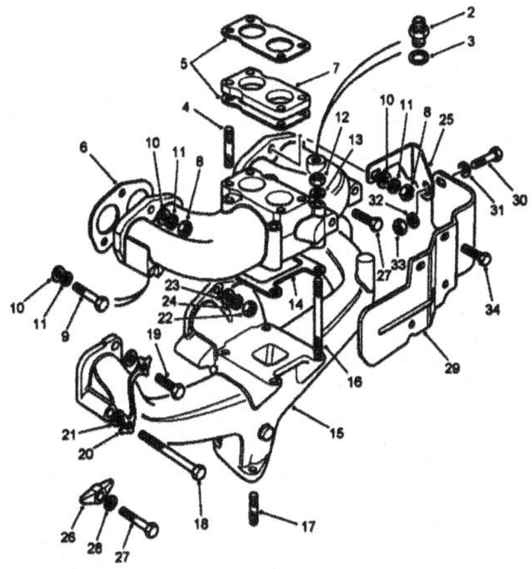

AHBFHA1A

Illus	Part Number	Description	Quantity	Change Point	Remarks
1	ETC6350	CARBURETTOR-ENGINE	1	To (E)17H 08822C	
1	ETC7144	CARBURETTOR-ENGINE	1	From (E)17H 08823C	
2	RTC4421	• Element-inline fuel filter	1		
3	RTC4420	• Washer-sealing	1		
4	RTC4419	• Hose-carburettor fuel pipe	1		
5	AEU2583	• Float assembly-carburettor	1		
6	RTC4896	• Gasket-carburettor-needle valve	1		
	AEU2584	• Body-carburettor float needle	1		
8	AEU2565	• Jet-carburettor-primary	1		
8	RTC4858	• Jet-carburettor-secondary	1		
9	AEU2566	• Tube-primary	1		
9	RTC4857	• Tube-secondary	1		
10	RTC4852	• Jet-carburettor	2		
11	AEU2582	• Holder-jet	1		
12	RTC4849	• Jet-carburettor-primary	1		
12	AEU2580	• Jet-carburettor-secondary	1		
13	RTC4897	• O ring	1		
14	AEU2578	• Jet-carburettor-pump	1		
15	AEU2585	• Venturi auxilary-centre device-carburettor-primary	1		
15	RTC4859	• Venturi auxilary-centre device-carburettor-secondary	1		
16	AEU2577	• Spring-idle spring screw	1		
17	RTC4898	• Screw-carburettor fast idle adjusting	1		
18	RTC4899	• Screw-idle mixture	1		
19	RTC4900	• O ring-mixture screw	1		
20	RTC4850	• Solenoid starter motor-cut off	1		
21	AEU2575	• Spring-pump-carburettor	1		
22	RTC4901	• Diaphragm.	1		

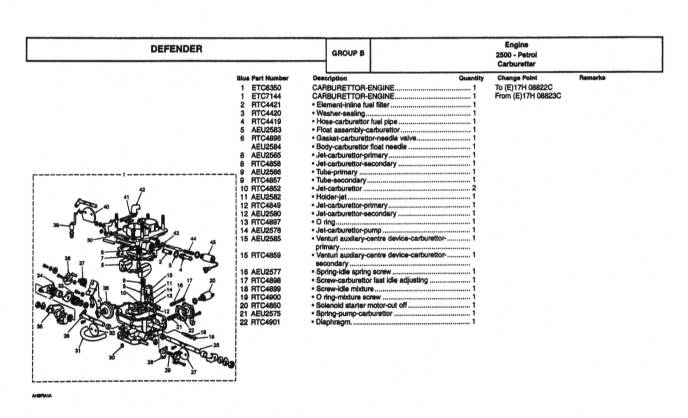

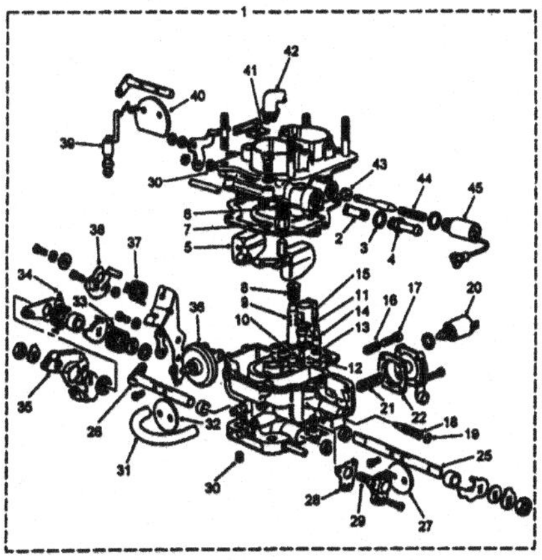

AHBFIA1A

Illus	Part Number	Description	Quantity	Change Point	Remarks
24	RTC4903	• Seal	3		
25	AEU2573	• Shaft primary manual transmission	1		
27	AEU2574	• Plate-throttle body setting	1		
28	RTC4860	• Diaphragm.	1		
29	RTC4851	• Spring-valve	1		
30	AEU2579	• Screw-secondary adjust	1		
31	RTC4904	• Tube	1		
33	AEU2569	• Spring-return	1		
34	AEU2564	• Spring-return	1		Part of ETC6350, ETC7144, ETC7144.
35	RTC4853	• Level-carburettor throttle	1		
36	AEU2560	• Throttle body-engine	1		
38	AEU2563	• Lever-starting control	1		
39	AEU2562	• Link-carburettor/throttle connecting	1		
41	RTC4906	• Seal	1		
42	RTC4861	• Vent-elbow	1		
43	RTC3665	• Seal-rubber	1		
44	RTC4908	• Spring-carburettor throttle return	1		
45	RTC3663	• Solenoid-carburettor vent valve	1		
	RTC5970	• Kit-carburettor seal	1		
	RTC5863	Kit-gasket-carburetter overhaul	1		
	RTC5608	Kit-gaskèt-overhaul	1		

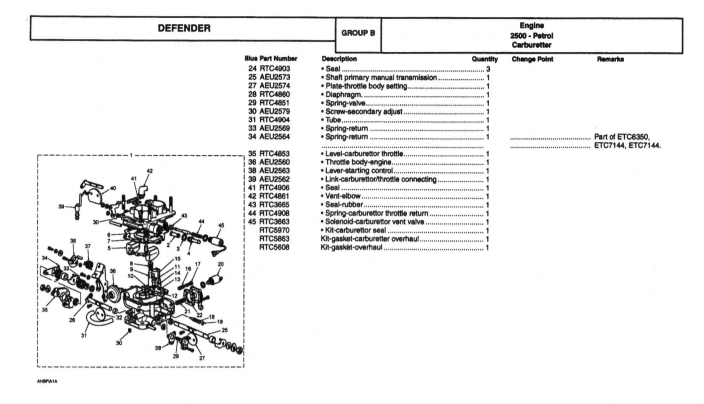

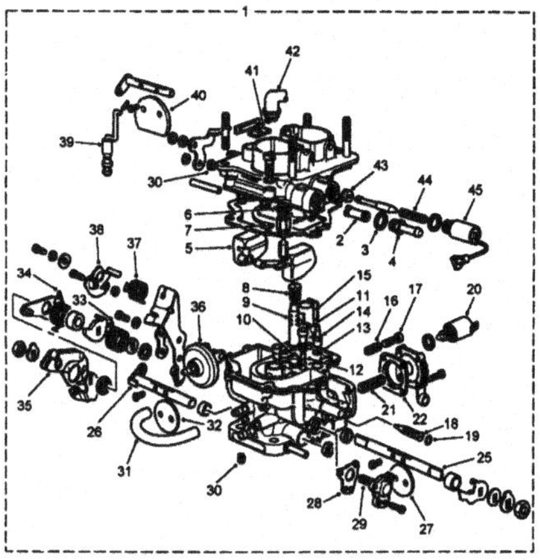

AHBFIA1A

Illus	Part Number	Description	Quantity	Change Point	Remarks
1	ERC9294	Pipe-carburettor vacuum	1		
2	ERC8119	Valve-vacuum delay-Blue	1		
3	ERC6996	Hose-carburettor pressure regulator vacuum	1		
4	512646	Clip	1		
5	214228	Clip	1		
6	214229	Grommet	2		
7	SH604051L	Screw-hexagonal head-1/4UNF x 5/8	1		
8	RTC609	Washer-plain-standard	1		
9	WM600041L	Washer-spring-1/4 dia-square	1		
10	NH604041L	Nut-hexagonal head-coarse thread-1/4UNF	1		

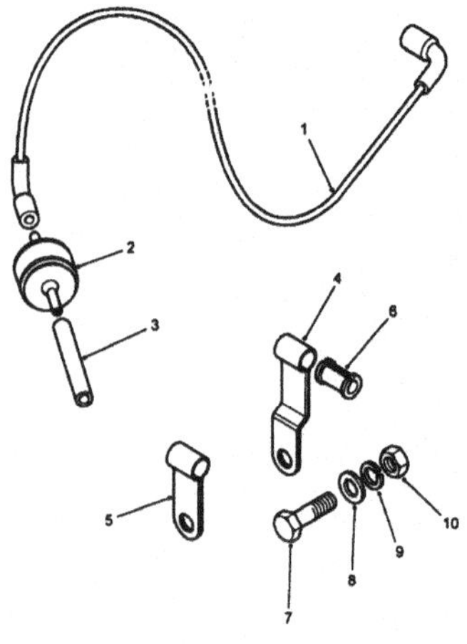

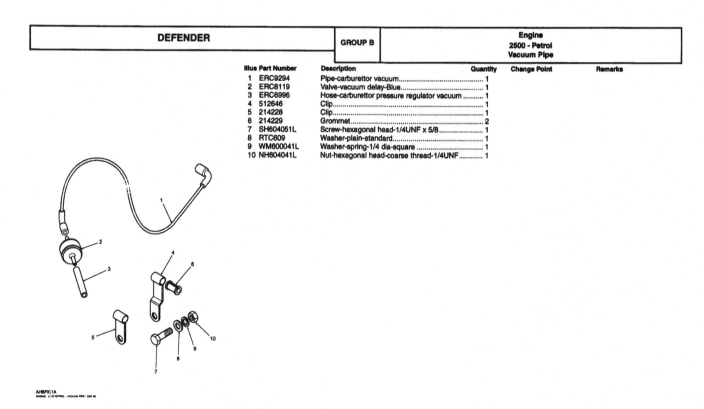

AHBFIC1A
ENGINE - 2 1/2 PETROL - VACUUM PIPE - DEF 90

DEFENDER | GROUP B | Engine 2500 - Petrol Fuel Rail

Illus	Part Number	Description	Quantity	Change Point	Remarks
1	ETC5027	Pipe fuel	1		
2	ETC6155	Connector fuel lines	1		
3	EAC32151	Clip-hose	2		
4	ETC6156	Connector fit	1		
5	EAU32151	Clip-hose	2		
6	ETC6243	Restrictor-fuel hose fuel lines	1		

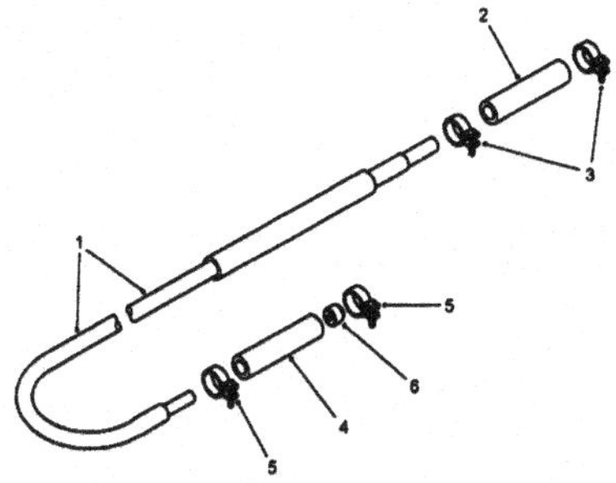

AHBFIE1A

DEFENDER | GROUP B | Engine 2500 - Petrol Air Inlet System

Illus	Part Number	Description	Quantity	Change Point	Remarks
1	ERR539	Elbow-carburettor air inlet	1		
2	ERC7922	Gasket-carburettor air elbow-asbestos	1	To (V) LA 939341	
2	ERR4384	Gasket-carburettor air elbow-asbestos free	1	From (V) LA 939342	
3	ERC298	Pipe-carburettor breather vent	1		
4	AAU1979	Clip-hose	NLA		Use PYC101150.
4	PYC101150	Clip-hose	1		
5	ETC4959	Clip	1		
6	NH105041L	Nut-hexagonal-elbow to carb-M5	4		
7	WL105001L	Washer-elbow to carb-retaining-M5	4		

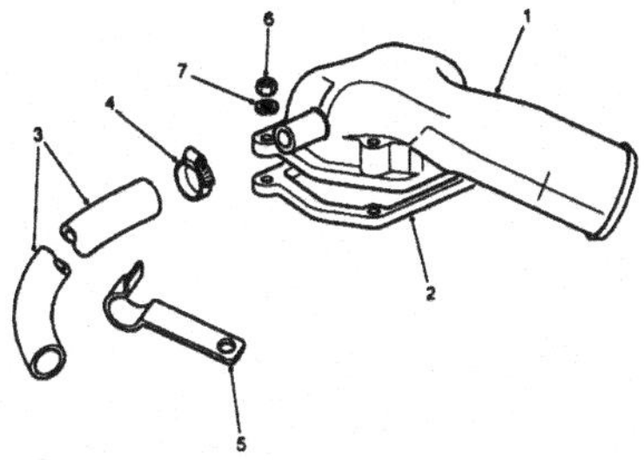

AHBFIG1A

Illus	Part Number	Description	Quantity	Change Point	Remarks
1	ERC9708	LEVER ASSEMBLY-HAND THROTTLE	1		
2	ERC9693	• Lever assembly-hand throttle	1		
3	ERC9704	• Spring-carburettor throttle return	1		
4	WB600071L	• Washer-plain-thin	1		
5	CR120115L	• Circlip	1		

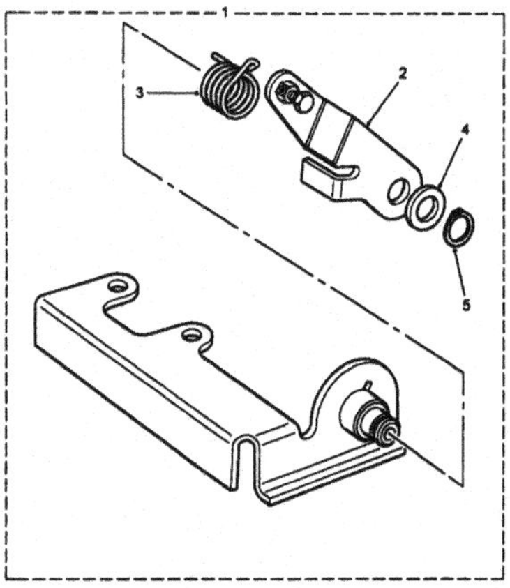

AHBFIA2A

Illus	Part Number	Description	Quantity	Change Point	Remarks
		SET-ENGINE GASKET			
1	RTC2889	decarbonising-asbestos	1	To (V) LA 939341	
1	STC1640	decarbonising-asbestos free	1	From (V) LA 939342	
2	RTC2890	overhaul-asbestos	1	To (V) LA 939341	
2	STC1467	overhaul-asbestos free	1	From (V) LA 939342	

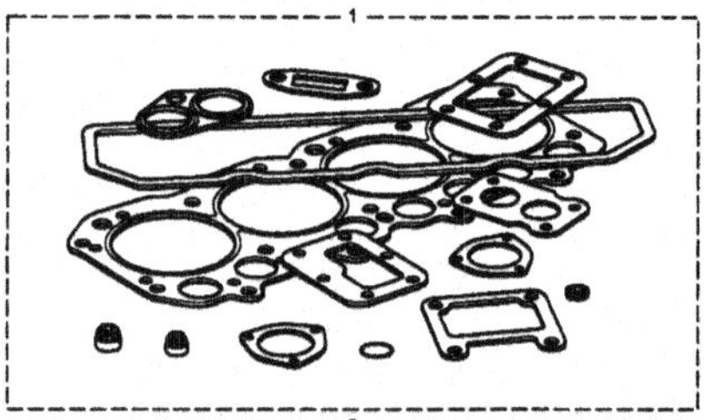

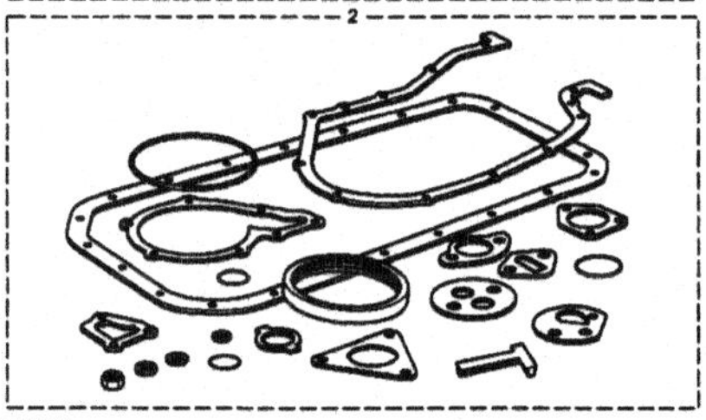

AHBFMA1A

DEFENDER

GROUP B

Engine
2500 - Petrol
Power Steering Pump-Adwest

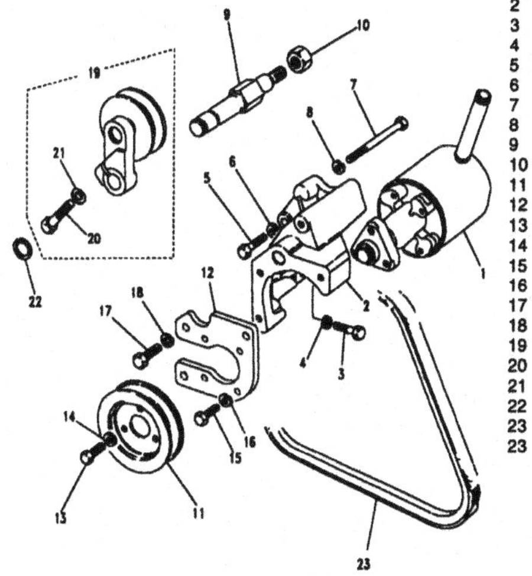

Illus	Part Number	Description	Quantity	Change Point	Remarks
1	ERC8447	PUMP ASSEMBLY POWER ASSISTED STEERING	NLA		Use ETC9077 Hobourn Eaton Pump.
	AEU4119	• Washer power assisted steering	1		
	RTC4485	• Bolt-banjo	1		
1	ETC9077	PUMP ASSEMBLY POWER ASSISTED STEERING	1	Note (1)	
	RTC5674	• Union-delivery	1		
	RTC5675	• Washer-sealing	2		
2	ERC6974	Bracket-power assisted steering	1		
3	FS108251L	Screw-bracket to cover-flanged head-M8 x 25	NLA		Use FS108257L.
4	WL108001L	Washer-sprung-M8	3		
5	FS108307L	Screw-flanged head-M8 x 30	1		
6	WL108001L	Washer-sprung-M8	1		
7	BH108181L	Bolt-bracket to block-hexagonal head-M8 x 90	NLA		
8	WL108001L	Washer-sprung-M8	1		
9	ERC6976	Spigot-idler arm mounting	1		
10	ERC6977	Nut-special spigot	1		
11	ERC5145	Pulley-drive power assisted steering	1		
12	ERC6975	Plate assembly-pump	1		
13	SH108141L	Screw-pulley to pump-hexagonal head-M8 x 14	3		
14	WL108001L	Washer-sprung-M8	3		
15	FS106201L	Screw-pump to plate-flanged head-M6 x 20	4		
16	WL106001L	Washer-pump to plate-sprung-M6	4		
17	FS108251L	Screw-plate to bracket-flanged head-M8 x 25	NLA		Use FS108257L.
18	WL108001L	Washer-sprung-M8	3		
19	ETC4153	PULLEY-IDLER ANCILLARY DRIVE	1		
20	SH108401L	• Screw-idler arm clamp-hexagonal head-M8 x 40	1		
21	WL108001L	• Washer-idler arm-sprung-M8	1		
22	CR120195	Circlip	2		
23	ERC5146	Belt-polyvee power assisted steering	1		Except air conditioning
23	ETC4272	Belt-polyvee power assisted steering	1		Air conditioning

CHANGE POINTS:
(1) To (V) June 1989

DEFENDER

GROUP B

Engine
2500 - Petrol
Power Steering Pump-Gemmer

Illus	Part Number	Description	Quantity	Change Point	Remarks
1	ETC9077	PUMP ASSEMBLY POWER ASSISTED STEERING	1	To (V) June 1989	
	RTC5674	• Union-delivery	1		
	RTC5675	• Washer-sealing	2		
1	NTC8287	Pump assembly power assisted steering	1	From (V) June 1989 To (V) June 1992	
1	NTC9070	Pump assembly power assisted steering	1	From (V) June 1992	
2	ERC6974	Bracket-power assisted steering-mounting	1	To (V) June 1989	
2	ETC8854	Bracket-power assisted steering-mounting	1	From (V) June 1989	
3	FS106201L	Screw-pump to bracket-flanged head-M6 x 20	4	To (V) LA 939975	
3	FS106207L	Screw-pump to bracket-flanged head-M6 x 20	4	From (V) MA 939976	
4	FS108251L	Screw-pump to bracket-flanged head-M8 x 25	NLA		Use FS108257L.
5	WA108051L	Washer-pump to bracket-8mm	2		
6	WL106001L	Washer-sprung-M6	4		
7	WL108001L	Washer-sprung-M8	3		
8	ETC5783	Pulley power assisted steering pump	1		
9	SH108141L	Screw-pulley to pump-hexagonal head-M8 x 14	3		
10	WL108001L	Washer-sprung-M8	3		
11	ETC5944	Bracket-mounting power assisted steering pump-mounting	NLA	To (V) June 1989	Use ERR1976.
11	ERR1976	Bracket-mounting power assisted steering pump-mounting	1	From (V) June 1989 To (V) June 1992	
11	ERR2605	Bracket-mounting power assisted steering pump-mounting	1	From (V) June 1992	
12	ETC5815	Belt-polyvee power assisted steering	1		
13	BH108181L	Bolt-hexagonal head-M8 x 90	NLA		
14	FS108251L	Screw-flanged head-M8 x 25	NLA		Use FS108257L.
14	FS108307L	Screw-flanged head-M8 x 30	1		
15	WL108001L	Washer-sprung-M8	5		
16	RTC5935	Kit-power assisted steering pump seal	NLA	To (V) JA 918809	Use STC1633.
16	STC1633	Kit-power assisted steering pump seal	1	From (V) JA 918810	

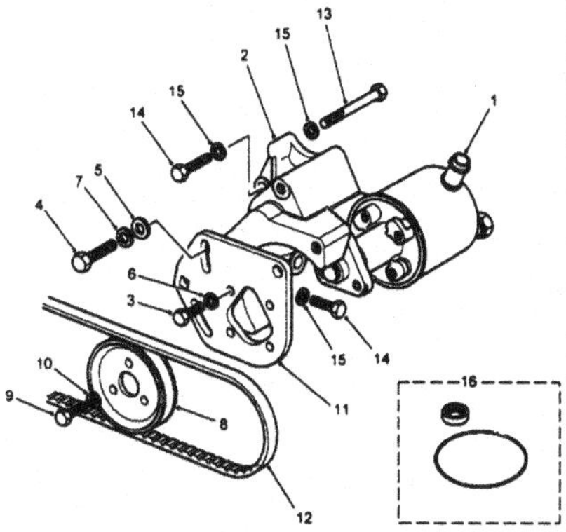

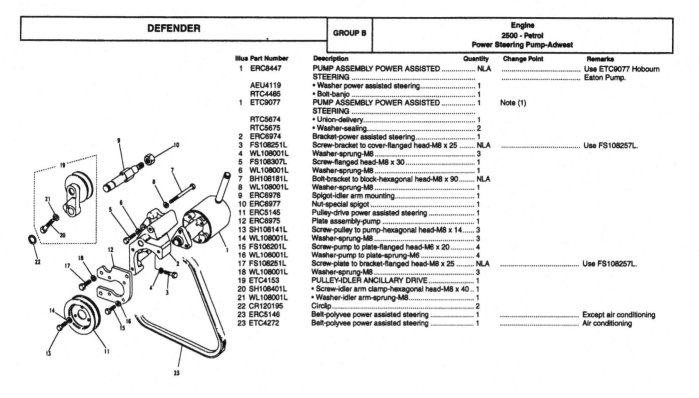

AHBFNC2A

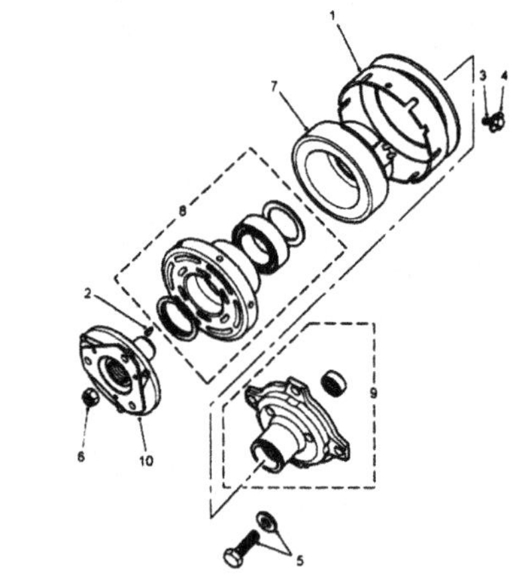

AHBFNE1A

Illus	Part Number	Description	Quantity	Change Point	Remarks
	BTR9419	Compressor assembly-R134a air conditioning	1	From (V) MA 949375	
	ERC6480	COMPRESSOR ASSEMBLY AIR CONDITIONING	1	To (V) MA 949374	
1	AEU1782	• Pulley-driven air conditioning	1		
	AEU1694	• Key	1		
3	AEU1780	• Screw	6		
4	AEU1779	• Washer	6		
5	AEU1784	• Screw	4		
6	AEU1775	• Nut	1		
7	AEU1778	• Clutch set-magnetic air conditioning compressor	1		
8	AEU1777	• Retainer	1		
9	AEU1785	• Cover assembly-front	1		
10	AEU1776	• Clutch-drive-assy	1		
	AEU1792	• CYLINDER	1		
	AEU1791	• • Kit-thrust washer-air conditioning	1		
	AEU1790	• • Kit-steering box sector shaft seal	1		
	AEU1192	• • O RING AIR CONDITIONING	1		
	AEU1690	• • • O ring	2		
	AEU1788	• Plate	4		
	AEU1787	• Circlip	4		
	AEU1786	• Housing assembly compressor	1		
	AEU1689	• Valve-air conditioning pressure relief	1		
	AEU1688	• Kit-superheat switch	1		

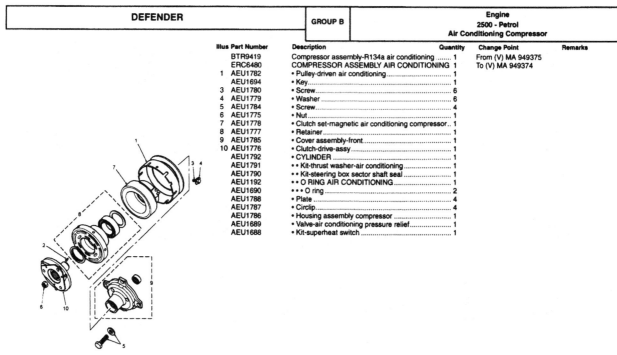

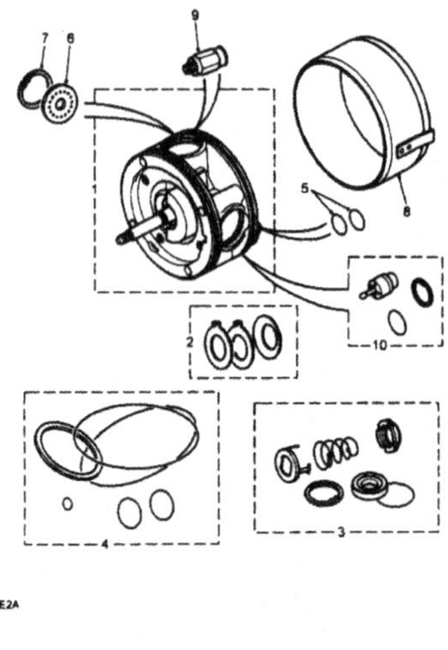

AHBFNE2A

Illus	Part Number	Description	Quantity	Change Point	Remarks
	BTR9419	Compressor assembly-R134a air conditioning	1	Note (1)	
	ERC6480	COMPRESSOR ASSEMBLY AIR CONDITIONING	1	Note (2)	
	AEU1782	• Pulley-driven air conditioning	1		
	AEU1694	• Key	1		
	AEU1780	• Screw	6		
	AEU1779	• Washer	6		
	AEU1784	• Screw	4		
	AEU1775	• Nut	1		
	AEU1778	• Clutch set-magnetic air conditioning compressor	1		
	AEU1777	• Retainer	1		
	AEU1785	• Cover assembly-front	1		
	AEU1776	• Clutch-drive-assy	1		
1	AEU1792	• CYLINDER	1		
2	AEU1791	• • Kit-thrust washer-air conditioning	1		
3	AEU1790	• • Kit-steering box sector shaft seal	1		
4	AEU1192	• • O RING AIR CONDITIONING	1		
5	AEU1690	• • • O ring	2		
6	AEU1788	• Plate	4		
7	AEU1787	• Circlip	4		
8	AEU1786	• Housing assembly compressor	1		
9	AEU1689	• Valve-air conditioning pressure relief	1		
10	AEU1688	• Kit-superheat switch	1		
	ERC6072	Belt-front camshaft drive	2		
	ETC4371	Belt-polyvee air conditioning compressor	1		
	AEU1691	Oil-525 visc	A/R		

CHANGE POINTS:
(1) From (V) MA 949375
(2) To (V) MA 949374

Illus	Part Number	Description	Quantity	Change Point	Remarks
1	ERC7082	Plate-mounting-front	1		
2	ERC5152	Plate-mounting-rear	1		
3	BH110201L	Bolt-compressor to plate-hexagonal head-M10 x 100	3		
4	WL110001L	Washer-M10	3		
5	ETC4882	Bracket-air compressor	NLA	Note (1)	Use ERR3091.
5	ERR3091	Bracket-air compressor	1	Note (2)	
6	BH110101L	Bolt-bracket to cover-hexagonal head-M10 x 50-long	4		
7	WA110061L	Washer-M10	4		
8	ERC5155	Link-adjusting compressor	2		
9	BH108181L	Bolt-link to bracket-hexagonal head-M8 x 90	NLA		
10	WL108001L	Washer-sprung-M8	1		
11	NH108041L	Nut-hexagonal head-M8	1	Note (1)	
11	FN108041L	Nut-flange-M8	NLA	Note (2)	Use FN108047L.
12	FS108251L	Screw-flanged head-M8 x 25	NLA		Use FS108257L.
13	WA108051L	Washer-8mm	2		
14	WL108001L	Washer-sprung-M8	2		
15	NH108041L	Nut-hexagonal head-M8	2	Note (1)	
15	FN108041L	Nut-flange-M8	NLA	Note (2)	Use FN108047L.
16	FB108081L	Bolt-bracket to plate-flanged head-M8 x 40	2		
17	WL108001L	Washer-sprung-M8	2		
18	NH108041L	Nut-hexagonal head-M8	2	Note (1)	
18	FN108041L	Nut-flange-M8	NLA	Note (2)	Use FN108047L.
19	ERC5386	BRACKET-COMPRESSOR/IDLER ASSEMBLY AIR CONDITIONING	1		
20	ERC5387	• IDLER-ARM	1		
21	90613049	• • Bearing-ball	1		
22	CR120171L	• • Circlip	1		
23	WC108051L	• Washer-idler arm clamp-M8	1		
24	WL108001L	• Washer-sprung-M8	1		
25	FB108081L	• Bolt-idler arm clamp-flanged head-M8 x 40	1		
26	ERC6071	Dowel	2		
27	FS108301L	Screw-flanged head-M8 x 30	NLA		Use FS108307L.
28	FS108251L	Screw-link to plate-flanged head-M8 x 25	NLA		Use FS108257L.
29	WL108001L	Washer-sprung-M8	3		

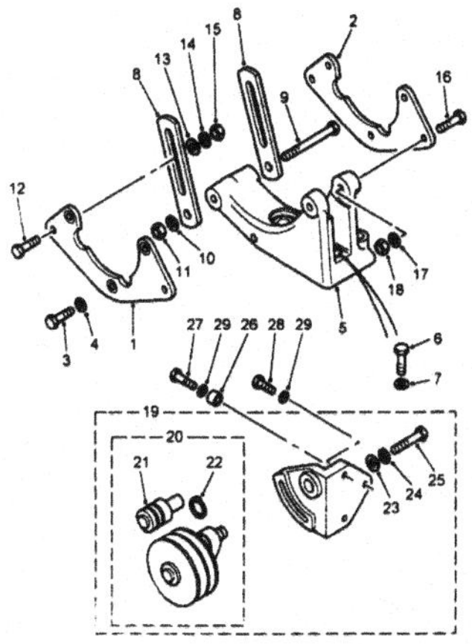

AHBFNE3A

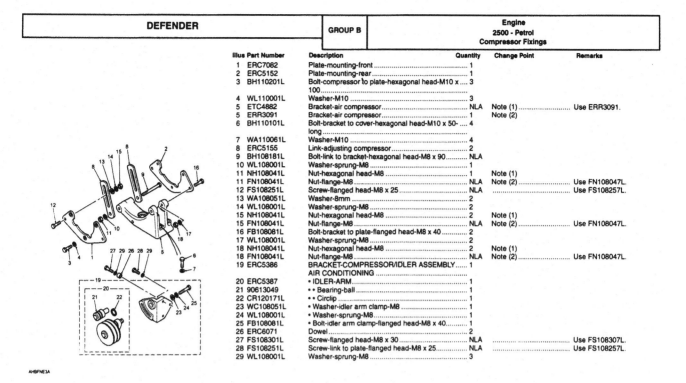

CHANGE POINTS:
(1) To (V) LA 939975
(2) From (V) MA 939976

Illus	Part Number	Description	Quantity	Change Point	Remarks
1	ETC7756	PULLEY-DRIVE AIR CONDITIONING	1		
2	554971	• PULLEY-IDLER ANCILLARY DRIVE	1		
3	RTC6077	• • Nut-5/16UNF	1		
4	4095	• Washer	1		
5	WB108051L	• Washer-plain-M8	1		
6	ETC4212	• Plate-mounting	1		

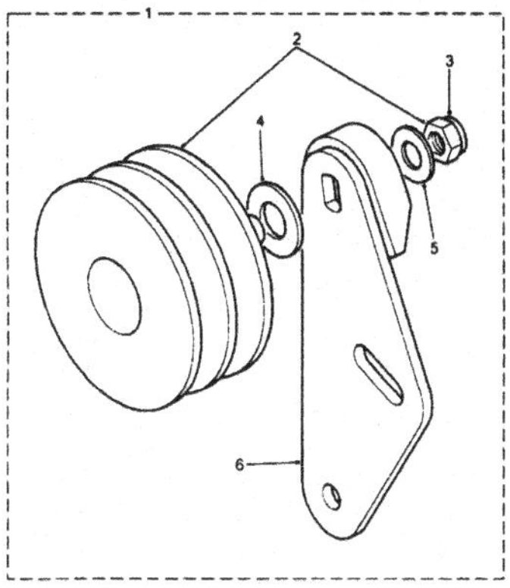

AHBFNE4A

Illus	Part Number	Description	Quantity	Change Point	Remarks
1	RTC5629	Coil ignition	NLA		Use PRC9858.
1	PRC9858	Coil ignition	1		
2	AB614061L	Screw-self tapping-No 14 x 3/4	2		
3	WJ106001L	Washer-plain-M6	2		

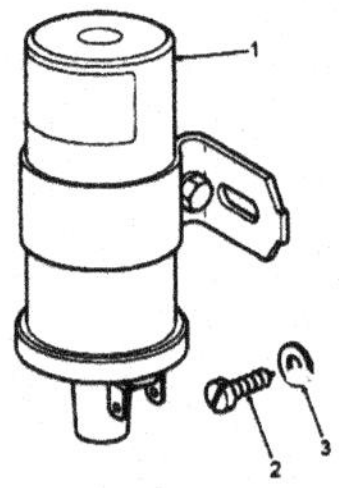

AHBFPA2A

Illus	Part Number	Description	Quantity	Change Point	Remarks
1	ETC5835	DISTRIBUTOR IGNITION	1		2500 cc 4 Cylinder Petrol
2	RTC3278	• Cap-distributor ignition-Lucas	1		
3	RTC3614	• Arm-rotor distributor-Lucas	1		
4	RTC6627	• Set-distributor contact-sliding contact	1		
4	RTC5947	• Set-distributor contact-fixed contact	1		
5	RTC3474	• Capacitor ignition coil-Lucas	1		
6	AEU1034	• Capsule-vacuum distributor-Lucas	1		
7	245003	• Clamp-distributor	1		
		PLUG-SPARKING			
8	RTC3812	N9YC	4		Alternatives
8	ERR743	RN9YC	4		
8	ERR3799	RN11YC	4		
9	ERC3256	Set-high tension lead ignition	1		
10	549611	Coupling-drive	1		
11	52278	Washer-cork	1		
12	ETC4466	Connector-inlet manifold adaptor	1		
13	247212	Washer-joint	1		
14	FS108201L	Screw-flanged head-M8 x 20	NLA	Note (1)	Use FS108207L.
14	FS108207L	Screw-flanged head-M8 x 20	3	Note (2)	
15	WL108001L	Washer-sprung-M8	3		
16	WA108051L	Washer-8mm	3		
17	FS106167L	Screw-flanged head-flanged head-M6 x 16	1		
18	WL106001L	Washer-sprung-M6	1		
19	WB106041L	Washer-M6	1		

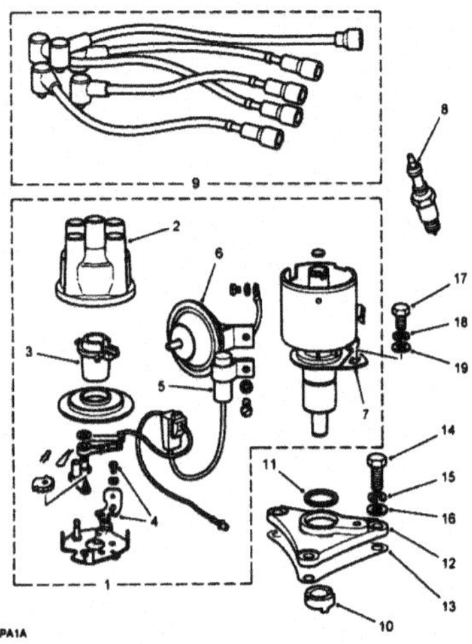

AHBFPA1A

CHANGE POINTS:
(1) To (V) LA 939975
(2) From (V) MA 939976

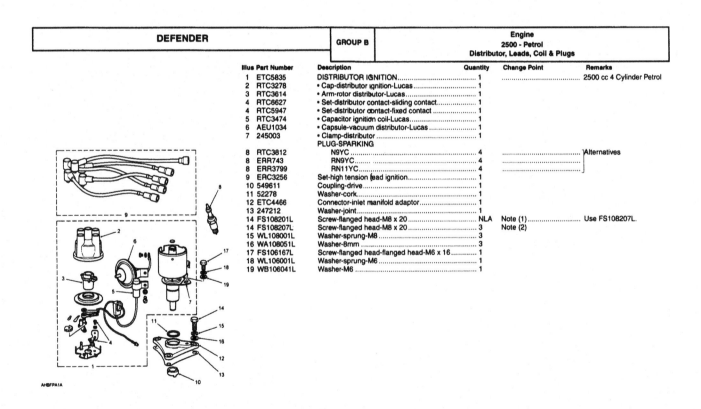

Illus	Part Number	Description	Quantity	Change Point	Remarks
1	RTC5083E	ALTERNATOR ASSEMBLY-115/45-LRA356-EXCHANGE	1		
2	AEU2507	• Cover alternator-LRA356	1		
3	AEU3076	• Regulator assembly alternator-LRA356	1		
4	BAU1825	• Rectifier-alternator	1		
5	BAU2193	• Ring-slip alternator	1		
6	BAU2195	• Brush alternator	1		
7	RTC3215	• Brush alternator	1		
8	568788	Pulley alternator	1		
9	18G8619L	Kit-bearing-drive end alternator	1		
10	AEU1532	Bearing-alternator front	1		
11	C37222L	Fan alternator	1		
12	ETC7939	Belt-polyvee alternator	1		
	AEU1706	Kit-screw	1		
	AEU1710	Kit-fixings alternator/vacuum pump	1		
	AEU1942	Spacer-kit	1		

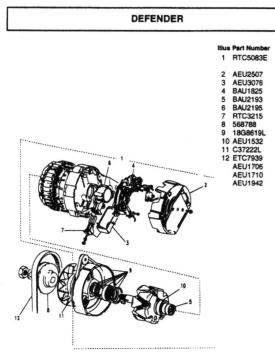

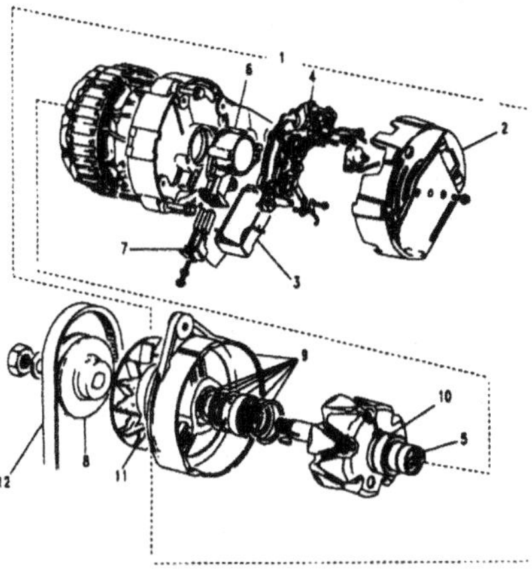

Illus	Part Number	Description	Quantity	Change Point	Remarks
1	RTC5682N	ALTERNATOR ASSEMBLY-NEW-A127-45 AMP	1		
1	RTC5682E	ALTERNATOR ASSEMBLY-EXCHANGE-A127-45 AMP	1		
2	RTC5670	• Regulator & brush box assembly alternator	1		
3	RTC5684	• Rectifier-alternator	1		
4	RTC5926	• Bearing-alternator front	1		
5	RTC5687	• Bracket-drive end c/w bearing alternator e-RH	1		
6	RTC5925	• Kit-fixings alternator/vacuum pump-LH	1		
7	RTC5685	Fan alternator	1		
8	RTC5686	Pulley alternator	1		
9	ETC7939	Belt-polyvee alternator	1		
	RTC5689	Spacer	1		

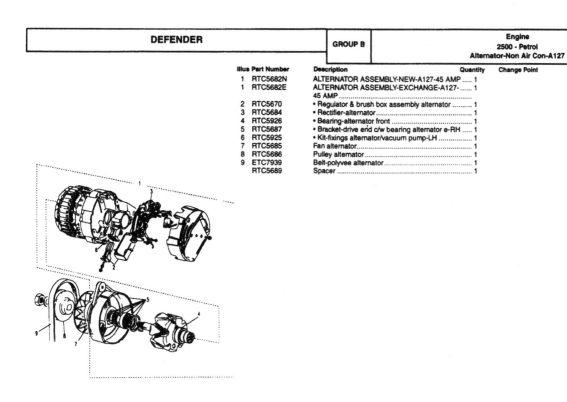

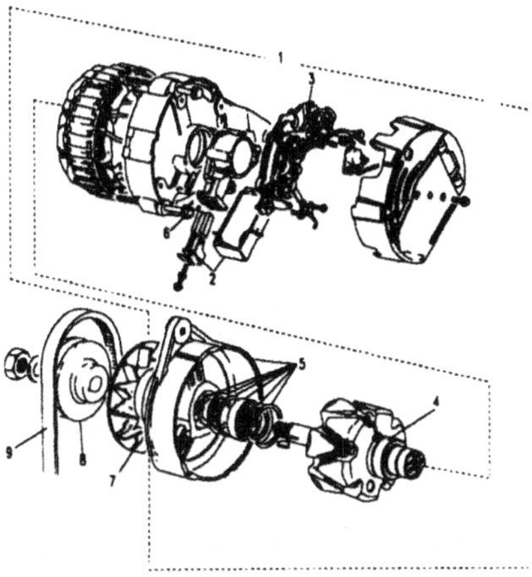

Illus	Part Number	Description	Quantity	Change Point	Remarks
1	RTC5218E	ALTERNATOR ASSEMBLY-LRA406-EXCHANGE-A133-65 AMP	1		
2	AEU1725	• Cover alternator	1		
3	AEU3076	• Regulator assembly alternator-LRA356	1		
4	AEU1527	• Rectifier-alternator	1		
5	RTC3292	• Brush alternator	1		
6	STC130	• Diode pack alternator	1		
7	AEU1726	• Kit-bearing-drive end alternator	1		
8	AEU1532	• Bearing-alternator front	1		
9	AEU1710	Kit-fixings alternator/vacuum pump	1		
	ERC8987	Nut-special	1		
10	ADU4928L	Fan alternator	1		
11	ERC8986	Pulley alternator	1		
12	AEU1616	Capacitor alternator	1		
13	ETC7939	Belt-polyvee alternator	1		
	AEU1706	Kit-screw	1		
	AEU1708	Spacer	1		
	AEU1709	Kit-alternator	1		

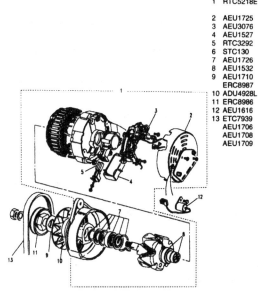

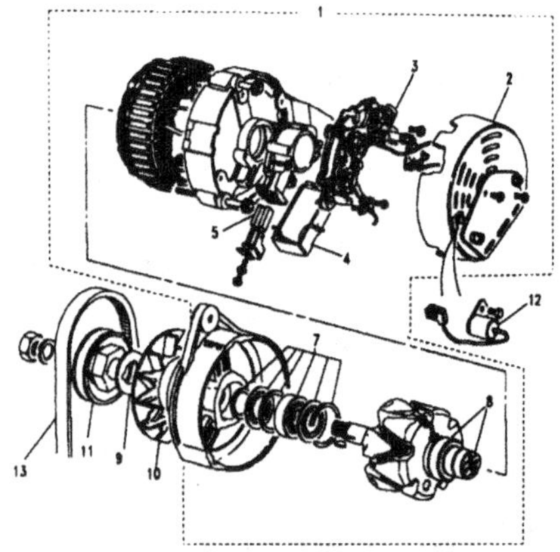

Illus	Part Number	Description	Quantity	Change Point	Remarks
		ALTERNATOR ASSEMBLY			
1	RTC5680N	NEW-A127-65 AMP-RH	NLA		Use STC234.
1	STC234	NEW-A127-65 AMP-RH	1		
1	RTC5680E	EXCHANGE-A127-65 AMP-RH	1		
2	RTC5670	• Regulator & brush box assembly alternator	1		
3	RTC5671	• Rectifier-alternator	1		
4	RTC5926	• Bearing-alternator front-slip ring end	1		Part of RTC5680N, RTC5680E.
5	RTC5687	• Bracket-drive end c/w bearing alternator e-RH	1		
6	RTC5046	• Kit-fixings alternator/vacuum pump-RH	1		
	RTC6114	• Capacitor alternator	1		Part of STC234.
7	AAU2249L	Fan alternator	1		
8	RTC5686	Pulley alternator	1		
9	ETC7939	Belt-polyvee alternator	1		
	RTC5689	Spacer-pulley	1		

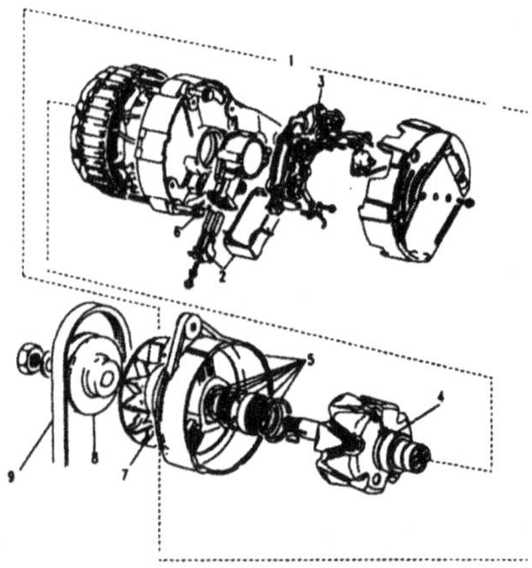

DEFENDER	GROUP B	Engine 2500 - Petrol Alternator Fixings

Illus	Part Number	Description	Quantity	Change Point	Remarks
1	ETC4357	Bracket-mounting-alternator	1		
2	FS108307L	Screw-block-flanged head-M8 x 30	2		
3	WL108001L	Washer-sprung-M8	2		
4	BH108161L	Bolt-bracket to block-hexagonal head-M8 x 80	1		
5	WL108001L	Washer-sprung-M8	1		
6	ERC5139	Link-adjuster alternator-A133 alternator	1		
6	ERC6266	Link-adjuster alternator-A127 alternator	1		
7	2266L	Washer-link to alternator	1		
8	WL108001L	Washer-sprung-M8	1		
9	FS108251L	Screw-link to alternator-flanged head-M8 x 25	NLA		Use FS108257L.
10	BH108201L	Bolt-link to block-hexagonal head-M8 x 100	1		
11	WL108001L	Washer-sprung-M8	1		
12	FB108081L	Bolt-flanged head-M8 x 40	1		
13	BH108091L	Bolt-M8 x 45	1		
14	WC108051L	Washer-M8	1		
15	NY108041L	Nut-nyloc-M8	2		

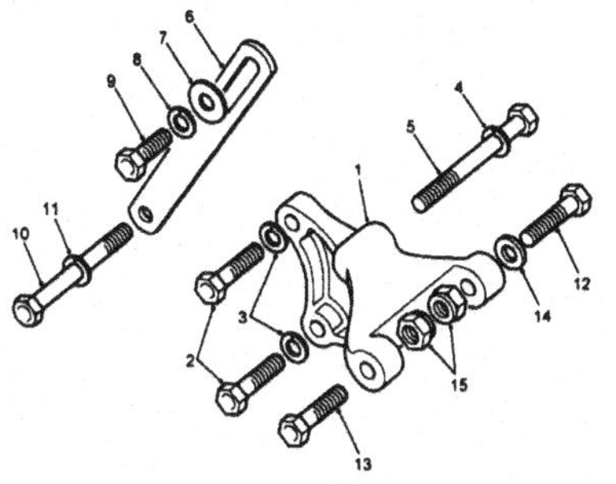

AHBFPC5A

DEFENDER	GROUP B	Engine 2500 - Petrol Starter Motor

Illus	Part Number	Description	Quantity	Change Point	Remarks
1	PRC6613N	MOTOR-STARTER ENGINE-WITH M78R STARTER MOTOR-LUCAS-NEW	1	To (E)17H 26367c	
1	PRC6613E	MOTOR-STARTER ENGINE-EXCHANGE	1		
2	RTC5967	• Kit-brush starter motor-new starter motor-with 2m100 starter motor-Lucas	1		
3	520455	• Pin-clevis/pivot-new starter motor-with 2m100 starter motor	1		
4	STC1519	• Solenoid starter motor-new starter motor-with 2m100 starter motor-Lucas	1		
5	AEU2502	• Drive assembly starter motor-new starter motor-with 2m100 starter motor-Lucas	1		
2	RTC5048	• Kit-brush starter motor-new starter motor-with M78R starter motor-Lucas	1	From (E)17H 26368c	Part of PRC6613N.
4	RTC5049	• Solenoid starter motor-new starter motor-with M78R starter motor-Lucas	1		Part of PRC6613N.
5	STC742	• Drive assembly starter motor-new starter motor-with M78R starter motor-Lucas	1		
2	RTC5048	• Kit-brush starter motor-with M78R starter motor-Lucas	1		Part of PRC6613E.
4	RTC5049	• Solenoid starter motor-with M78R starter motor-Lucas	1		Part of PRC6613E.
1	NAD10040	MOTOR-STARTER ENGINE-BOSCH-NEW	1	From (E)17H 26368c	
2	NAK100050	• Kit-brush starter motor-Bosch	1		
4	NAF100170	• Solenoid starter motor-Bosch	1		
5	NAJ100100	• Drive assembly starter motor-Bosch	1		
1	NAD10040E	MOTOR-STARTER ENGINE-BOSCH-EXCHANGE	1	From (E)17H 26368c	
2	NAK100050	• Kit-brush starter motor-Bosch	1		
4	NAF100170	• Solenoid starter motor-Bosch	1		
5	NAJ100100	• Drive assembly starter motor-Bosch	1		
6	RTC5563	Kit-brush starter motor-with M78R starter motor	1	From (E)17H 26368c	
7	WL110001L	Washer-M10	2		

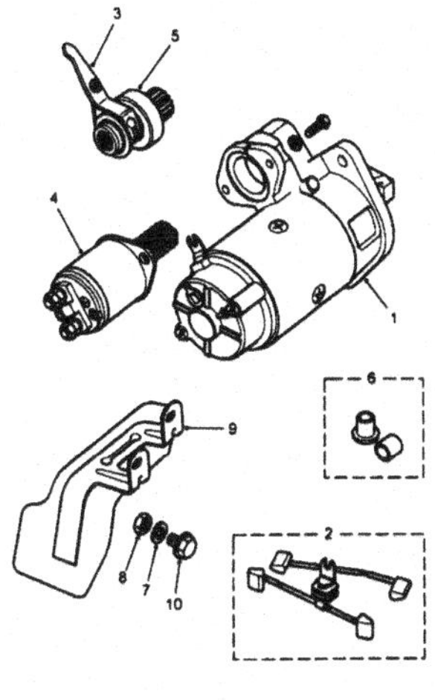

AHBFPE1A

Illus	Part Number	Description	Quantity	Change Point	Remarks
8	NH110041L	Nut-hexagonal head-coarse thread-M10	2		
9	ETC4133	Heatshield starter motor	1		
10	ERC8722	Bolt-exhaust manifold heat shield pillar	2		
	608395	Kit-starter motor sundry parts-standard	1		
	90608178	Kit-starter motor sundry parts-with 2m100 starter motor	1		
	RTC5577	Kit-starter motor-with M78R starter motor	1		

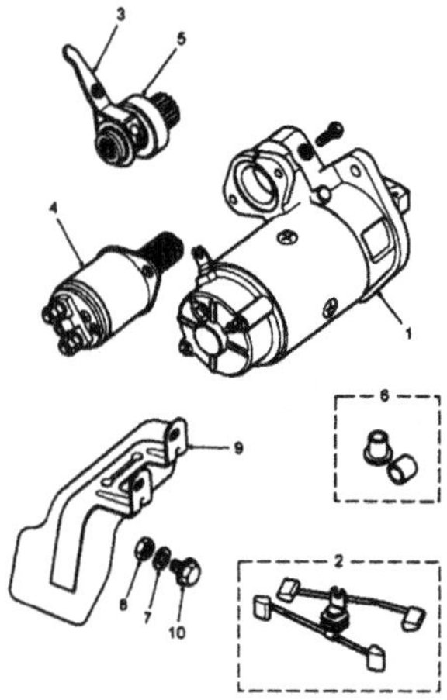

AHBFPE1A

Illus	Part Number	Description	Quantity	Change Point	Remarks
1	ETC6394	HOUSING-FLYWHEEL ASSEMBLY	1		
2	TE110061L	• Stud-M10 x 30	13		
3	ERC7295	• Plug-rubber	1		
	NH110041L	Nut-hexagonal head-coarse thread-M10	11		
4	ERC7295	Plug-rubber	1		
5	ERR1535	Seal-crankshaft rear	NLA	To (E)17H 22797C	Use ERR2532.
5	ERR2532	Seal-crankshaft rear	1	From (E)17H 22798C	
6	FS110301L	Screw-flanged head-M10 x 30-top	6		
7	BX110071M	Bolt-hexagonal head-M10 x 35	2		
8	WL110001L	Washer-M10	2		
9	WA110061L	Washer-M10	6		
10	ERC6408	FLYWHEEL ENGINE	1		
11	ERC5293	• Ring starter-flywheel-engine	1		
12	502116	• Dowel-flywheel to crankshaft	3		
13	ERC4658	Plate-reinforcement	NLA	To (V) December 1993	Engineering have found that the reinforcing plate is not required. When refitting flywheel omit plate , and fit new bolts ERR4574..
14	ERC6551	Bolt-fixing flywheel crankshaft-long	8		
14	ERR4574	Bolt-fixing flywheel crankshaft-short	8		
16	FRC2671	Plate-clutch-driven-asbestos	1		
16	FTC3196	Plate-clutch-driven-asbestos free	1	Note (1)	
16	FTC4661	Plate-clutch-driven-asbestos free	1	From (E)17H 32577C	
	STC8359	KIT-CLUTCH	1	To (V) January 1993	
16	FTC159	• Plate-clutch-driven-asbestos free	1		
15	576557	• Cover-clutch assembly	1		
	FRC9568	• BEARING-CLUTCH RELEASE	NLA		Use FTC5200.
	FRC4078	• • Sleeve-guide clutch	1		
	FTC5200	Bearing-clutch release			
17	SX108201L	Bolt-set-M8 x 20	6		
18	WL108001L	Washer-sprung-M8	6		
19	ERC9404	Bracket harness-clip to housing	2		
	AFU1090L	Clip-cable-8mm hole	2		

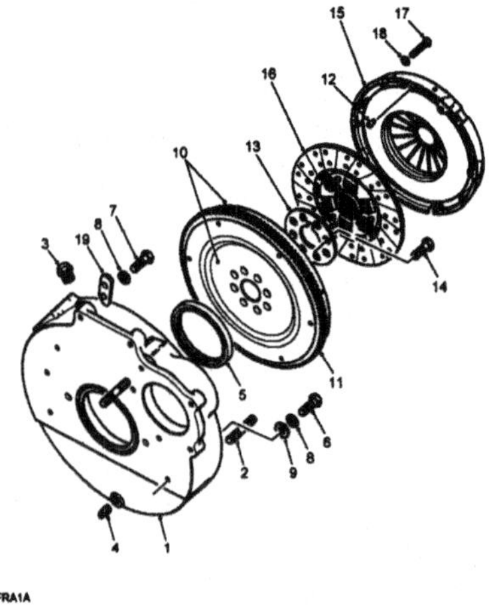

AHBFRA1A

CHANGE POINTS:
(1) From (V) January 1993 To (E)17H 32576C

Illus	Part Number	Description	Quantity	Change Point	Remarks
1	STC3164	Engine assembly-power unit-complete	NLA	Note (1)	Use STC1257.
1	STC1257	Engine assembly-power unit-complete	NLA	Note (1)	Complete Engine no longer available. Short Engine only available Part number STC3867..

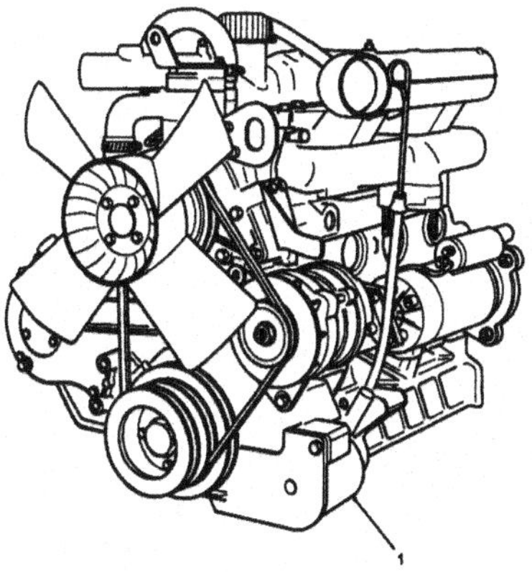

AHBGAA1A

CHANGE POINTS:
(1) From (E)12J 000001C

Illus	Part Number	Description	Quantity	Change Point	Remarks
		ENGINE UNIT-STRIPPED			
1	RTC6801N	new	1		
1	RTC4059E	exchange	1	To (E)12J 43824C	
1	RTC6801E	exchange	1	From (E)12J 43825C	

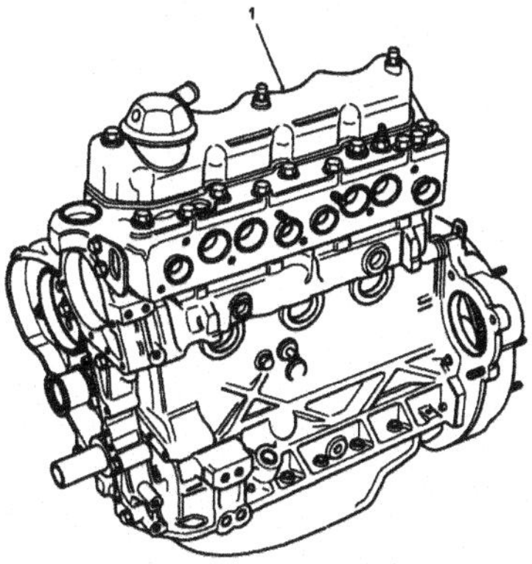

AHBGAC1A

Illus	Part Number	Description	Quantity	Change Point	Remarks
1	STC1481	Engine assembly-power unit-short.	1	Note (1)	
1	STC3867	Engine assembly-power unit-short.	1	Note (2)	

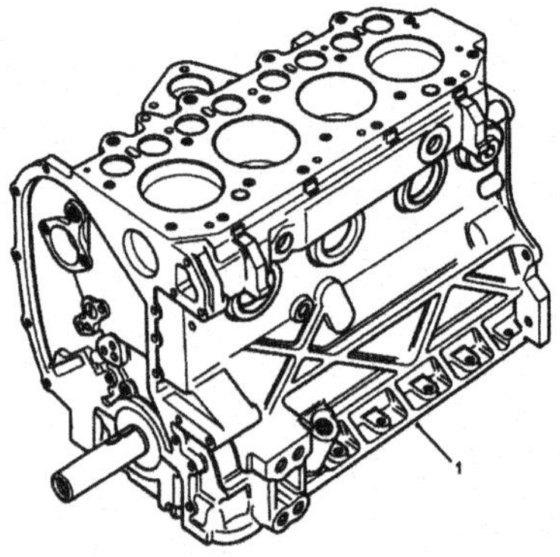

AHBGAE1A

CHANGE POINTS:
(1) To (V) LA 939975
(2) From (V) MA 939976

Illus	Part Number	Description	Quantity	Change Point	Remarks
1	RTC2991	CYLINDER BLOCK-ENGINE	NLA	To (E)12J 43824C	Use ERR478 qty 01 Superseded to later block and bearings with RTC4783 qty 01.
2	247965	• Plug-tappet hole feed	1		
3	247127	• Plug-cylinder block oil way	2		
4	ETC4529	• Plug-core	1		
5	501593	• Dowel	10		
6	ERC4996	• Plug-core	6		
7	597586	• Plug-core	3		
8	ERC4644	• Dowel	2		
9	243959	• Washer-sealing	1		
10	536577	• Plug-drain	2		
11	90519054	• Bearing-camshaft front	1		
12	90519055	• Bearing-camshaft rear	3		
13	ERC4995	• Plug-core	2		
14	247755	• Bolt	10		
	ETC7596	• Bolt-flanged head	10		
15	504006	• Washer	10		
	ERR5034	• Plug-camshaft blanking-camshaft oil feed-rubber	3		
16	TE108031L	Stud-M8 x 15	1		

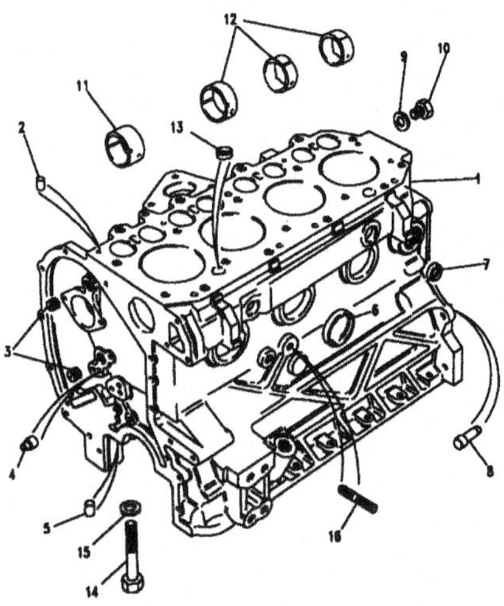

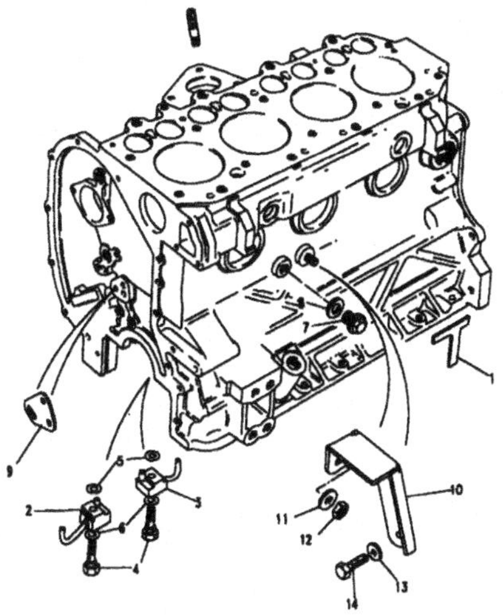

Illus	Part Number	Description	Quantity	Change Point	Remarks
1	ERC5086	Pad-insulation	2		
2	ETC6531	Jet assembly-piston cooling-No1-No3	2		
3	ETC6532	Jet assembly-piston cooling-No2-No4	2		
4	ETC5592	Valve-bearing housing jet	4		
5	AFU1879L	Washer-sealing	4		
6	AFU1887L	Washer-sealing	4		
7	ERC9410	Plug-drain	1		
8	AFU1882L	Washer-sump assembly drain plug	1		
9	ERC8864	Gasket	1		
10	ETC4697	Bracket-support starter motor	1		
11	WC108051L	Washer-M8	1		
12	NH108041L	Nut-hexagonal head-M8	1		
13	WA106041L	Washer-6mm	2		
14	FS106167L	Screw-flanged head-flanged head-M6 x 16	2		

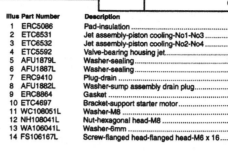

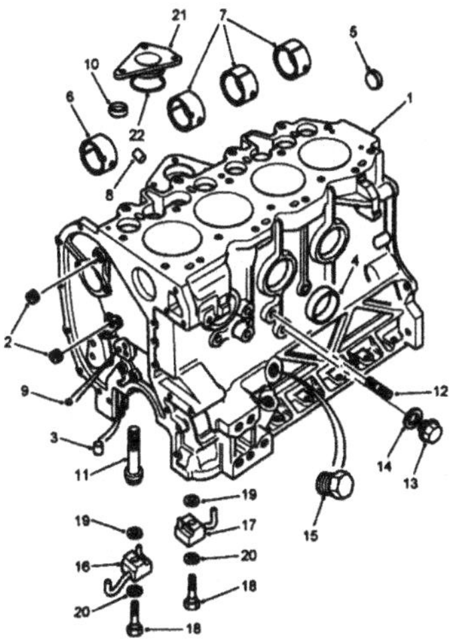

AHBGBA3A

Illus	Part Number	Description	Quantity	Change Point	Remarks
1	ERR478	CYLINDER BLOCK-ENGINE	NLA	To (E)12J 43824C	Use ERR2639.
1	ERR2639	CYLINDER BLOCK-ENGINE	1	From (E)12J 43825C	
2	247127	• Plug-cylinder block oil way	2		
3	501593	• Dowel	10		
4	ERC4996	• Plug-core	6		
5	597586	• Plug-core	3		
6	ETC8442	• Bearing-camshaft front	1		
7	90519055	• Bearing-camshaft rear	3		
8	ERR5034	• Plug-camshaft blanking-rubber	3		
9	ETC4529	• Plug-core	1		
10	ERC4995	• Plug-core	2		
11	ETC8074	• Bolt	10		
12	TE108031L	• Stud-M8 x 15	1		
13	ETC5577	• Plug-drain	1		
14	213961	• Washer-sealing	1		
15	ETC8362	• Plug-blanking-metal	1		
16	ETC6531	• Jet assembly-piston cooling-No1-No3	2		
17	ETC6532	• Jet assembly-piston cooling-No2-No4	2		
18	ETC5592	• Valve-bearing housing jet	4		
19	AFU1879L	• Washer-sealing	4		
20	AFU1887L	• Washer-sealing	4		
21	ERR586	• Connector-inlet manifold adaptor	1		
22	ERR531	• O ring	1		
	ERC9188	• Set-engine cylinder liner & piston	4		

DEFENDER	GROUP B	Engine 2500 - Diesel - Naturally Aspirated Cover Side

Illus	Part Number	Description	Quantity	Change Point	Remarks
1	ERC9073	COVER PLATE-SIDE	1	To (E)12J 39054C	
2	ETC7929	COVER PLATE-SIDE	1	From (E)12J 39055C	
3	TE108041L	• Stud-M8 x 20	2		
4	ERR1475	Gasket-cylinder block side cover	1		
5	FS108251L	Screw-flanged head-M8 x 25	NLA		Use FS108257L.
5	FS108257L	Screw-flanged head-M8 x 25	1		
6	WL108001L	Washer-sprung-M8	6		
7	541010	Breather assembly-crankcase	1		
8	ERC9480	Bracket	1		
9	FS108207L	Screw-flanged head-M8 x 20	3		
9	FS108251L	Screw-flanged head-M8 x 25	NLA		Use FS108257L.
9	FS108257L	Screw-flanged head-M8 x 25	1		
10	WA108051L	Washer-8mm	3		
11	WL108001L	Washer-sprung-M8	6		
12	247555	Gasket-cylinder block side cover	NLA		Use ERR3605.
12	ERR3605	Gasket-cylinder block side cover-asbestos	NLA		Use ERR2026.
12	ERR2026	Gasket-cylinder block side cover-asbestos free	1		

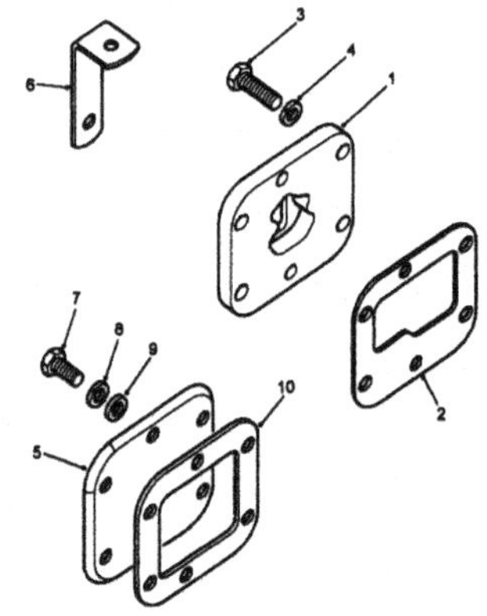

AHBGBC1A

DEFENDER	GROUP B	Engine 2500 - Diesel - Naturally Aspirated Crankshaft & Bearings

Illus	Part Number	Description	Quantity	Change Point	Remarks
1	ETC8829	Crankshaft-engine	1	To (V) 399927	
1	ERR1181	CRANKSHAFT-ENGINE	1	From (V) 399928	
2	ERR1630	• Dowel-flywheel to crankshaft	1		
3	8566L	• Bush-crankshaft	1		
4	235770	• Key-crankshaft	2		
2	ERR1630	Dowel-flywheel to crankshaft	1		
3	8566L	Bush-crankshaft	1		
4	235770	Key-crankshaft	2		
		SET-CRANKSHAFT BEARINGS			
5	RTC2992	standard.	1	To (E)12J 43824C	
5	RTC299210	0.010" undersize	1		
5	RTC4783	standard.	NLA	From (E)12J 43825C	Use STC3395.
5	STC3395	standard.	1		
5	RTC478310	0.010" undersize	1		
		WASHER-CRANKSHAFT THRUST			
6	RTC2825	standard.-pair	A/R	Note (1)	
6	538131	oversize.-0.0025"-pair	A/R	Note (1)	
6	538132	oversize.-0.005"-pair	A/R	Note (1)	
6	538134	oversize.-0.01"-pair	A/R	Note (1)	
7	ETC4077	Pulley & torsional vibration damper-crankshaft	1		Note (1)
7	ETC4105	Pulley & torsional vibration damper-crankshaft	1		Note (2)
7	ERC6860	Pulley & torsional vibration damper-crankshaft	1		Note (3)
7	ERC6859	Pulley & torsional vibration damper-crankshaft	1		Note (4)
7	ERC6861	PULLEY & TORSIONAL VIBRATION DAMPER-CRANKSHAFT	1		Note (5)
	WL108001L	• Washer-sprung-M8	4		
	FS108251L	Screw-flanged head-M8 x 25	NLA		Use FS108257L.
8	ETC4390	Flinger-crankshaft pulley	1		
9	ERC9765	Pulley-crankshaft	1		
10	ETC7934	Bolt-crankshaft pulley	1	To (V) 399927	
10	ERR605	Bolt-crankshaft pulley	1	From (V) 399928	
6	ERR705	Washer-crankshaft thrust	1		
11	ERR1535	Seal-crankshaft rear	NLA		Use ERR2532.
11	ERR2532	Seal-crankshaft rear	1		

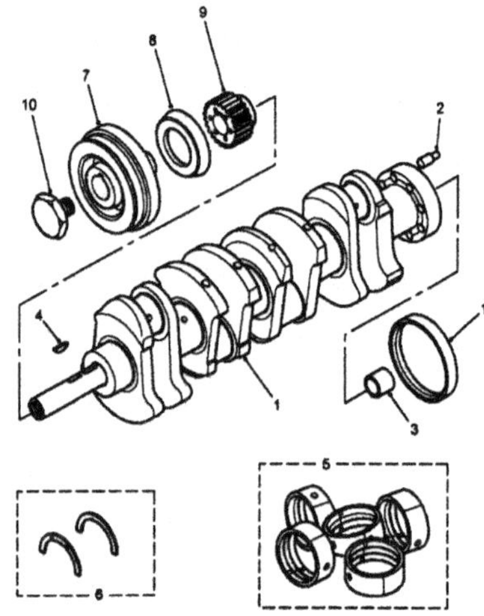

AHBGCA1A

CHANGE POINTS:
(1) To (V) 399927

Remarks:
(1) manual steering Except air conditioning
(2) power steering air conditioning
(3) manual steering air conditioning
(4) power steering air conditioning Standard on
(5) power steering Except air conditioning

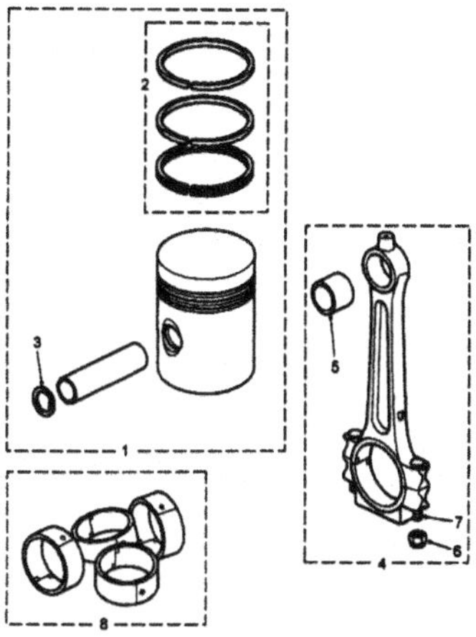

AHBGCC1A
ENGINE - 2 1/2 DIESEL - PISTON, CONNECTING ROD AND BEARINGS - DEF 90

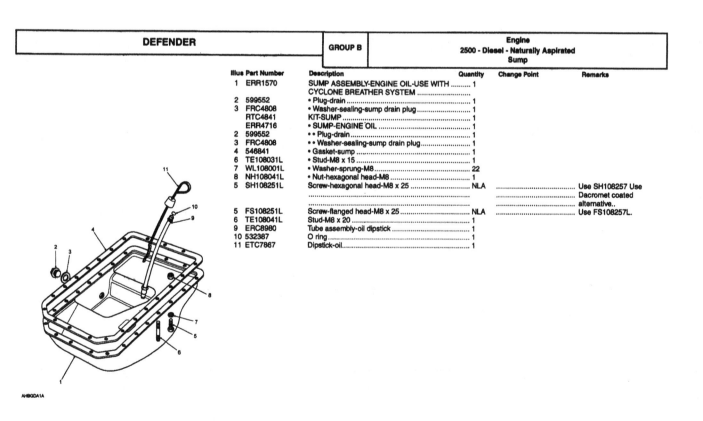

Illus	Part Number	Description	Quantity	Change Point	Remarks
1	RTC6442S	PISTON-ENGINE-HEPWORTH/GRANDIDGE PISTONS-STANDARD.	4		
1	RTC644220	PISTON-ENGINE-HEPWORTH/GRANDIDGE PISTONS-0.020" OVERSIZE	4		
2	RTC4778S	• Kit-piston ring-Hepworth/Grandidge pistons-standard.	4		Part of RTC6442S.
3	266945	• Circlip-piston	8		
2	RTC477820	• Kit-piston ring-0.020" oversize	4		Part of RTC644220.
		KIT-PISTON RING			
2	STC772S	GKN pistons only-standard.	4		
2	STC77220	GKN pistons only-oversize.-0.02"	4		
2	STC77240	GKN pistons only-0.040" oversize	4		
4	ERR593	ROD ASSEMBLY-CONNECTING	4		
5	247583	• Bush	4		
7	ERC8751	• Bolt-connecting rod	8	To (E)12J 45357	
7	ETC7357	• Bolt-connecting rod	8	From (E)12J 45358E	
6	ETC5155	• Nut-connecting rod	8	To (E)12J 45357	
6	ETC8191	• Nut-connecting rod	8	From (E)12J 45358E	
8	RTC2993	Set-connecting rod big end half bearing-standard.	1		
8	RTC299310	Set-connecting rod big end half bearing-0.010" undersize	1		
	ERC9188	Set-engine cylinder liner & piston	4		

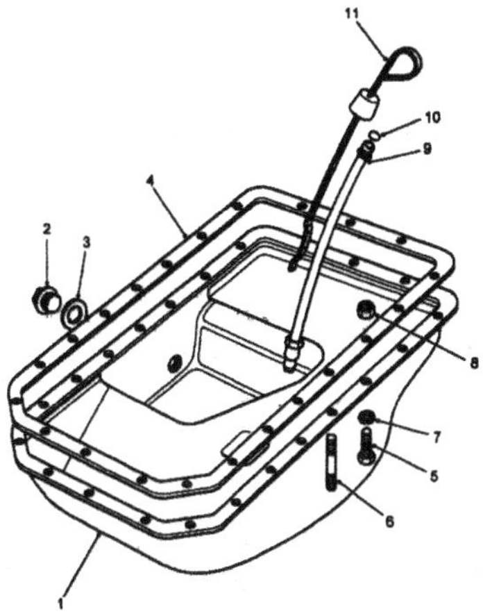

AHBGDA1A

Illus	Part Number	Description	Quantity	Change Point	Remarks
1	ERR1570	SUMP ASSEMBLY-ENGINE OIL-USE WITH CYCLONE BREATHER SYSTEM	1		
2	599552	• Plug-drain	1		
3	FRC4808	• Washer-sealing-sump drain plug	1		
	RTC4841	KIT-SUMP	1		
	ERR4716	• SUMP-ENGINE OIL	1		
2	599552	• • Plug-drain	1		
3	FRC4808	• • Washer-sealing-sump drain plug	1		
4	546841	• Gasket-sump	1		
6	TE108031L	• Stud-M8 x 15	1		
7	WL108001L	• Washer-sprung-M8	22		
8	NH108041L	• Nut-hexagonal head-M8	1		
5	SH108251L	Screw-hexagonal head-M8 x 25	NLA		Use SH108257 Use Dacromet coated alternative..
5	FS108251L	Screw-flanged head-M8 x 25	NLA		Use FS108257L.
6	TE108041L	Stud-M8 x 20	1		
9	ERC8980	Tube assembly-oil dipstick	1		
10	532387	O ring	1		
11	ETC7867	Dipstick-oil	1		

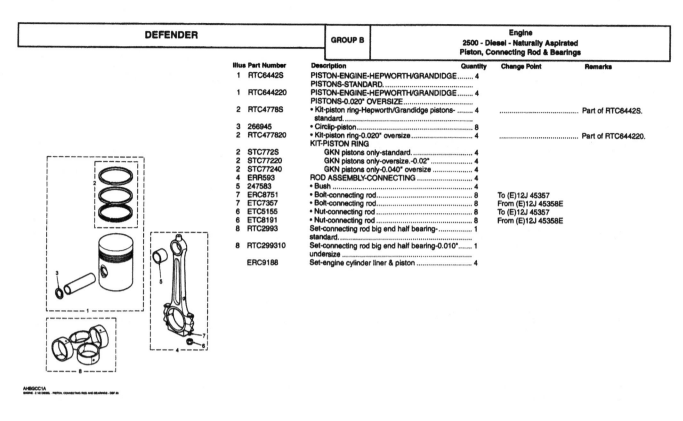

DEFENDER	GROUP B	Engine 2500 - Diesel - Naturally Aspirated Engine Mountings

Illus	Part Number	Description	Quantity	Change Point	Remarks
1	NRC5434	Bracket-engine mounting-RH	1		
2	NRC9557	Bracket-engine mounting-LH	1		
3	SH112251L	Screw-hexagonal head-M12 x 25	4		
4	WL112001L	Washer	4		
5	NRC9560	Mounting-engine rubber	NLA	To (V) JA 920702	Use ANR1808.
5	ANR1808	Mounting-engine rubber	1	To (C) JA 920703	
6	NH110041L	Nut-hexagonal head-coarse thread-M10	4		
7	WC110061L	Washer-plain-M10-oversize	2		
8	WL110001L	Washer-M10	4		

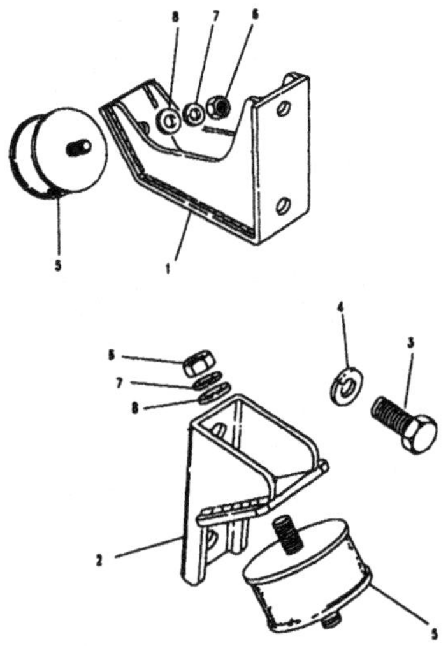

DEFENDER	GROUP B	Engine 2500 - Diesel - Naturally Aspirated Front Cover

Illus	Part Number	Description	Quantity	Change Point	Remarks
1	ETC4421	Cover-engine-front	1		Except air conditioning
1	ETC5672	Cover-engine-front	1		Air conditioning
2	6395L	Dowel	4		
3	ETC5064	Seal-camshaft oil	1		
4	ETC5065	Seal-crankshaft front oil	NLA		Use ERR1632.
4	ERR1632	Seal-crankshaft front oil	NLA		Use ERR6490.
4	ERR6490	Seal-crankshaft front oil	1		
5	538038	Gasket-coolant pump body-asbestos	NLA		Use ERR1607.
5	ERR1607	Gasket-coolant pump body-to front cover-asbestos free	1		
6	538039	Gasket-timing gear housing drain plate	1		
7	FB108111L	Bolt-flanged head-M8 x 55	1		
8	FB108121L	Bolt-flanged head-M8 x 60	4		
9	BH108201L	Bolt-hexagonal head-M8 x 100	1		
10	FB108251	Bolt-flanged head-M8 x 125	2		
11	WA108051L	Washer-8mm	8		
12	ETC4422	Cover-plate.	1		
12	ETC5675	Cover-plate.	1		
13	ETC4154	Seal	1		
14	BH108131L	Bolt-hexagonal head-M8 x 65	1		
15	WA108051L	Washer-8mm	1		
16	FS108251L	Screw-flanged head-M8 x 25	NLA		Use FS108257L.
17	WA108051L	Washer-8mm	7		
18	ERC6479	Bracket	1		
19	ETC4996	Bolt	1		
20	FS108207L	Screw-flanged head-M8 x 20	3		
21	WL108001L	Washer-sprung-M8	3		
22	ERC7295	Plug-rubber	1		
23	RTC3772	Tie-cable-Black-4.8 x 135mm-inside serated	1		
24	ETC4058	Plate-drainage hole	1		
25	ETC4122	Gasket-sealing-asbestos	NLA		Use ERR3615.
25	ERR3615	Gasket-sealing-asbestos free	1		
26	FS106207L	Screw-flanged head-M6 x 20	4		
27	WA106041L	Washer-6mm	4		
28	ETC4063	Strainer-oil-drainage hole	1		
29	ERC9199	Nut-bulkhead plate	1		
30	ERC9201	Gasket-sealing-asbestos	NLA		Use ERR3614.
30	ERR3614	Gasket-sealing-asbestos free	1		
31	ETC4420	Gasket-cover front-asbestos	NLA		Use ERR3616.
31	ERR3616	Gasket-cover front-asbestos free	1		
32	SE106121L	Screw-pan-pan head-M6 x 12	3		

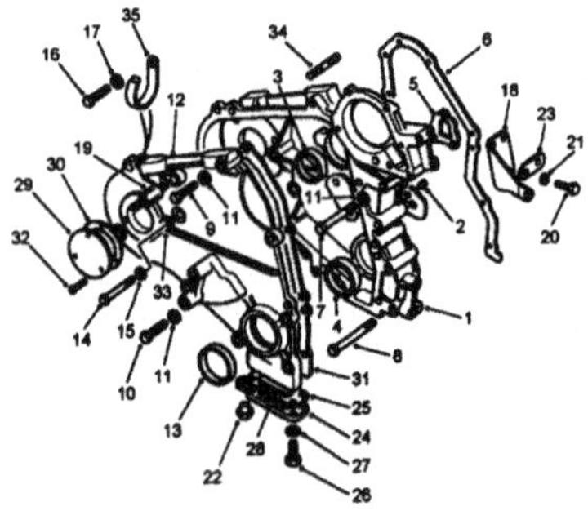

AHBGEA1A

DEFENDER	GROUP B	Engine 2500 - Diesel - Naturally Aspirated Front Cover

Illus	Part Number	Description	Quantity	Change Point	Remarks
33	ETC4124	Washer-sealing-asbestos	NLA		Use ERR3604.
33	ERR3604	Washer-sealing-asbestos free	1		
34	ETC4873	Stud	3		
35	ETC4630	Bracket-mounting	1		

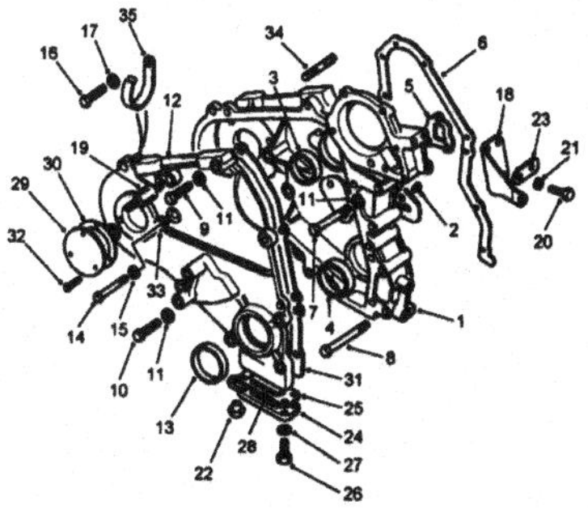

AHBGEA1A

DEFENDER	GROUP B	Engine 2500 - Diesel - Naturally Aspirated Timing Belt & Tensioner

Illus	Part Number	Description	Quantity	Change Point	Remarks
1	ETC7333	Belt-engine timing	1		
2	ERC8861	Tensioner-timing belt	1		
3	4594L	Washer-plain	2		
4	TE108061L	Stud-M8 x 30	2		
5	NY108041L	Nut-nyloc-M8	2		

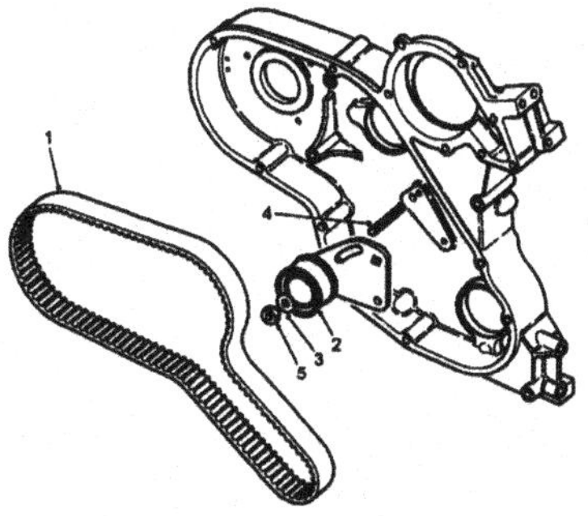

AHBGEC1A

Illus	Part Number	Description	Quantity	Change Point	Remarks
1	STC637	PUMP ASSEMBLY-ENGINE COOLANT	1		Non viscous coupling
2	ERC7312	• Plug	1		
3	232046	• Washer-copper	1		
4	ERC5600	• Screw	1		
5	WL106001L	• Washer-sprung-M6	1		
6	ERC5655	• Gasket-coolant pump body	1		
7	ERC5578	Pulley coolant pump-single groove	1		
7	ETC4650	Pulley coolant pump-double groove	1		
8	ERC7489	Spacer	1		
9	ERC5545	Fan-cooling	1		
10	FB108111L	Bolt-flanged head-M8 x 55	4		
11	WL108001L	Washer-sprung-M8	4		
12	FS108307L	Screw-flanged head-M8 x 30	3		
13	WL108001L	Washer-sprung-M8	3		
14	BH108151L	Bolt-hexagonal head-M8 x 70	1		
15	BH108161L	Bolt-hexagonal head-M8 x 80	2		
16	BH108171L	Bolt-hexagonal head-M8 x 85	1		
17	WL108001L	Washer-sprung-M8	4		
18	ERC5654	Hose assembly water-outlet	1		
19	CN100408L	Clip-hose	2		
20	563132	Belt-polyvee coolant pump	1		

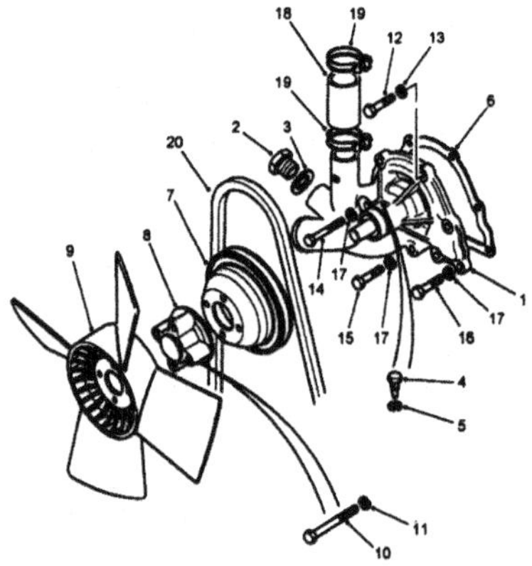

AHBGEE1A

Illus	Part Number	Description	Quantity	Change Point	Remarks
1	STC635	PUMP ASSEMBLY-ENGINE COOLANT-A127 ALTERNATOR	1		
2	ERC7312	• Plug	1		
3	232046	• Washer-copper	1		
4	ERC5600	• Screw	1		
5	WL106001L	• Washer-sprung-M6	1		
8	ERC5655	• Gasket-coolant pump body	1		
9	ERC5708	Coupling-engine fan viscous	1		
10	ERC5709	Screw-M6 x 14	4		
11	4589L	Washer-plain	4		
12	ERR3380	Fan-cooling	1		
13	FS108307L	Screw-flanged head-M8 x 30	3		
14	WL108001L	Washer-sprung-M8	3		
15	BH108151L	Bolt-hexagonal head-M8 x 70	1		
16	BH108161L	Bolt-hexagonal head-M8 x 80	2		
17	BH108171L	Bolt-hexagonal head-M8 x 85	1		
18	WL108001L	Washer-sprung-M8	8		
19	ERC5654	Hose assembly water-outlet	1		
20	CN100408L	Clip-hose	2		
21	ETC7939	Belt-polyvee alternator	1		

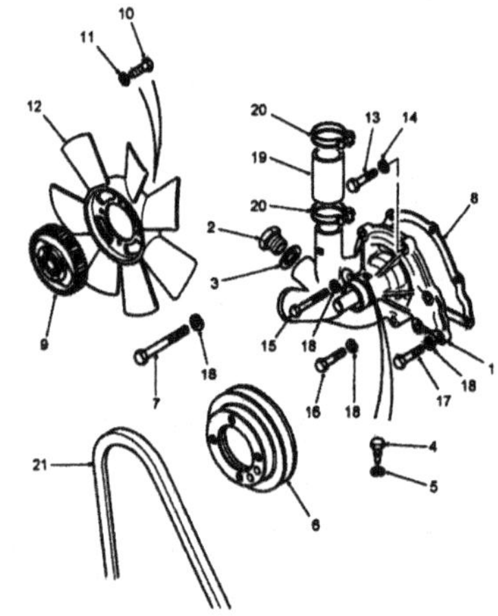

AHBGEE2A

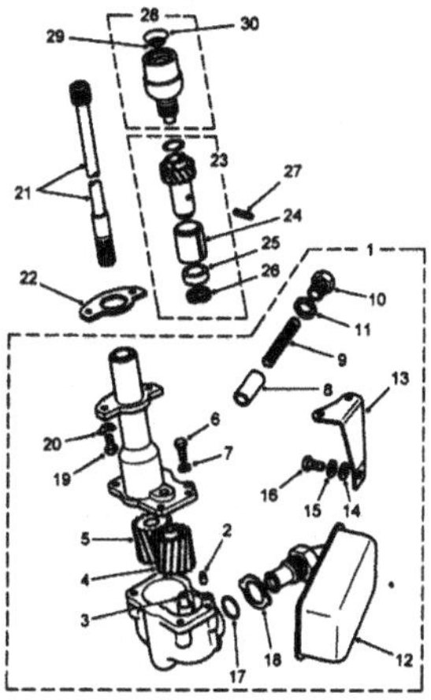

AHBGFA1A

Illus	Part Number	Description	Quantity	Change Point	Remarks
1	ERR1117	PUMP BODY ASSEMBLY-ENGINE OIL	1		
2	236257	• Dowel	2		
3	ERR1063	• Spindle-oil pump	1		
4	ERR1088	• Gear-oil pump idler-10 teeth	1		
5	ERC9706	• Gear-oil pump-10 teeth	1		
6	FS108207L	• Screw-flanged head-M8 x 20	4		
7	WL108001L	• Washer-sprung-M8	4		
8	ETC4880	• Plunger-oil pump relief valve	1		
9	564456	• Spring-oil pump relief valve	1		
10	564455	• Plug	1		
11	232044	• Washer-sealing	1		
12	ERC7530	• Strainer-oil	1		
13	ERC7940	• Bracket-pump/actuator	1		
14	WA108051L	• Washer-8mm	1		
15	WL108001L	• Washer-sprung-M8	1		
16	FS108207L	• Screw-flanged head-M8 x 20	1		
17	244488	• O ring	1		
18	244487	• Washer-lock	1		
20	247665	• Washer-lock	2		
19	FS108251L	Screw-flanged head-M8 x 25	NLA		Use FS108257L.
21	ERR850	Shaft-oil pump	1		
22	ERC8408	Gasket-cylinder block oil pump-asbestos	NLA		Use ERR3606.
22	ERR3606	Gasket-cylinder block oil pump-asbestos free	1		
23	ETC6139	DRIVE ASSEMBLY-OIL PUMP	1		
24	522745	• Bush	1		
25	ETC6137	• Washer-thrust	1		
26	ETC6138	• Ring-snap	1		
27	ETC6142	• Screw	1		
28	ETC4706	COUPLING	1		
29	RTC6167	• O ring-inner	1		
30	RTC6168	• O ring-outer	1		

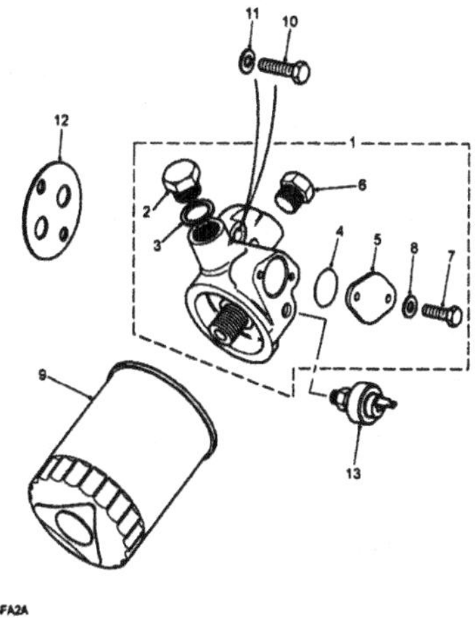

AHBGFA2A

Illus	Part Number	Description	Quantity	Change Point	Remarks
1	ETC5347	ADAPTOR-OIL FILTER	1		
2	RTC6851	• Plug	1		
3	213961	• Washer-sealing	1		
4	ERC5913	• O ring	1		
5	ERC9884	• Cover-oil filter	1		
6	ETC4021	• Plug	1		
7	SH106141L	• Screw-hexagonal head-M6 x 14	2		
8	WA106041L	• Washer-6mm	2		
9	ERR3340	Cartridge-engine oil filter	1		
10	FS110301L	Screw-flanged head-M10 x 30-top	2		
11	WL110001L	Washer-M10	2		
12	ETC7582	Gasket-oil filter housing-asbestos	NLA		Use ERR4934.
12	ERR4934	Gasket-oil filter housing-asbestos free	1		
13	PRC6387	Switch-oil pressure engine	1		
	PRC4043	Transducer oil pressure	1		
	ETC4033	Adaptor-oil pressure switch	1		
	ETC4034	Bolt-banjo	1		
	PRC4372	Transducer oil temperature-24V	1		

DEFENDER	GROUP B	Engine 2500 - Diesel - Naturally Aspirated Oil Filter with Oil Cooler

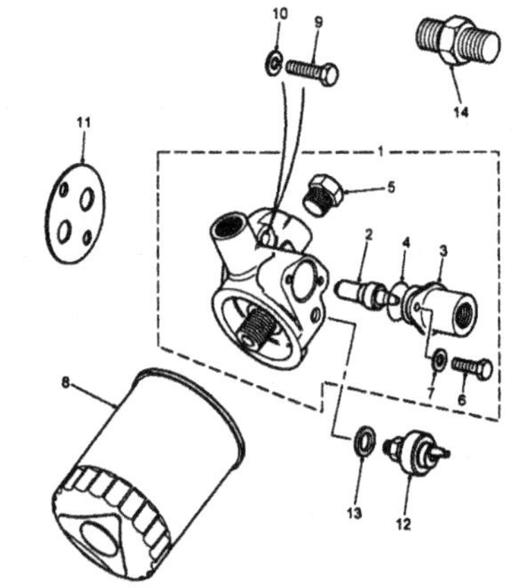

AHBGFA3A

Illus	Part Number	Description	Quantity	Change Point	Remarks
1	ERR1347	ADAPTOR ASSEMBLY-OIL FILTER	1		
2	ERC5923	• Thermostat assembly-oil	1		
3	ETC4022	• Adaptor-oil filter	1		
4	ERC5913	• O ring	1		
5	ETC4021	• Plug	1		
6	SH106141L	• Screw-hexagonal head-M6 x 14	2		
7	WA106041L	• Washer-6mm	2		
8	ERR3340	Cartridge-engine oil filter	1		
9	FS110301L	Screw-flanged head-M10 x 30-top	2		
10	WL110001L	Washer-M10	2		
11	ETC7582	Gasket-oil filter housing-asbestos	NLA		Use ERR4934.
11	ERR4934	Gasket-oil filter housing-asbestos free	1		
12	PRC6387	Switch-oil pressure engine	1		
13	232039	Washer-sealing	1		
14	NRC8618	Coupling	1		
	PRC4043	Transducer oil pressure	1		
	ETC4033	Adaptor-oil pressure switch	1		
	ETC4034	Bolt-banjo	1		
	PRC4372	Transducer oil temperature-24V	1		

DEFENDER	GROUP B	Engine 2500 - Diesel - Naturally Aspirated Cylinder Head Assembly

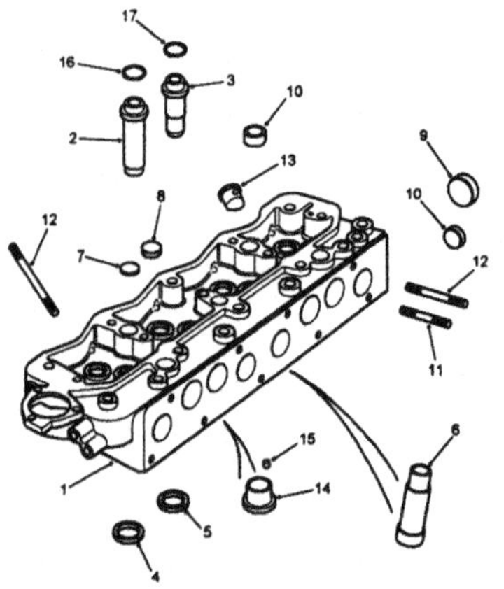

AHBGGA1A

Illus	Part Number	Description	Quantity	Change Point	Remarks
1	ETC4649	CYLINDER HEAD ASSEMBLY-ENGINE-NEW	1	To (V) April 1989	
2	568688	• Guide-valve-cylinder head inlet	4	To (E)17H 26286A	
3	568689	• Guide-valve-cylinder head exhaust	NLA		Use SFR47.
3	SFR47	• Guide-valve-cylinder head exhaust	4		
4	ERC9631	• Insert-cylinder head exhaust valve seat	4		
5	ETC4643	• Insert-inlet valve seat-cylinder head	4		
6	ERC8663	• Tube	8		
7	250830	• Plug-core	2		
8	525497	• Plug-core	9		
9	524765	• Plug-core	1		
10	602289	• Plug-cup	1		
1	STC803	CYLINDER HEAD ASSEMBLY-ENGINE-NEW	1	From (V) April 1989	
2	ERR2861	• Guide-valve-cylinder head inlet	4	From (E)17H 26287A	
3	ERR2860	• Guide-valve-cylinder head exhaust	4		
4	ERR3081	• Insert-cylinder head exhaust valve seat	4		
5	ERR3082	• Insert-inlet valve seat-cylinder head	4		
6	ERC8663	• Tube	8		
7	250830	• Plug-core	2		
8	525497	• Plug-core	9		
9	524765	• Plug-core	1		
10	602289	• Plug-cup	2		
11	TE108051L	Stud-M8 x 25	5		
12	TE108071L	Stud-M8 x 35	12		
13	ERC9501	Shroud	4		
14	ETC8620	Hot Plug	NLA		Use ERR1223.
14	ERR1223	Hot Plug	4		
15	PA105101L	Peg locating	4		
16	ERR1510	Seal-cylinder head valve stem oil-inlet	4		
17	ETC4751	Seal-exhaust	4		

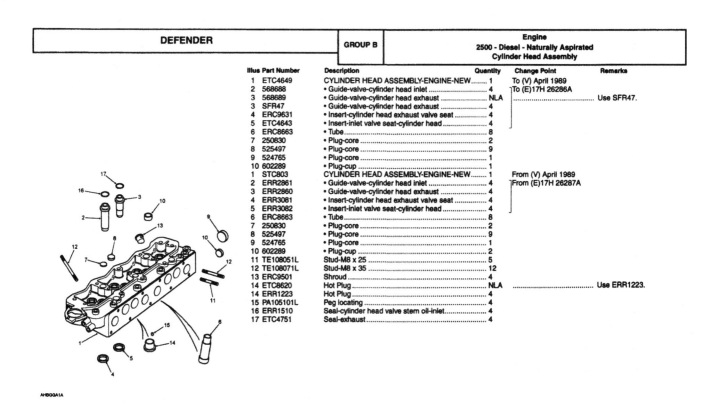

DEFENDER	GROUP B	Engine 2500 - Diesel - Naturally Aspirated Cylinder Head Components

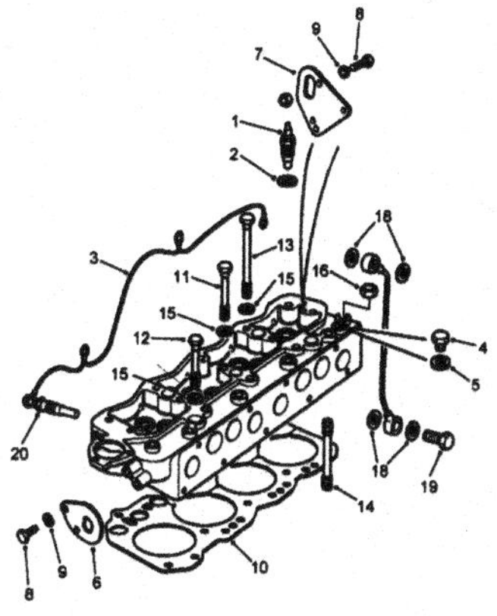

AHBGGA2A

Illus	Part Number	Description	Quantity	Change Point	Remarks
1	PRC2505	Transducer coolant temperature	1	Note (1)	
1	PRC6663	Transducer coolant temperature	1	Note (2)	
1	YCB100390	Transducer coolant temperature	1	Note (3)	
	ERC9432	Connector-inlet manifold adaptor	1	To (V) April 1989	
2	10802070	Washer	1		
3	PRC6295	Cable-heater plug ignition	1		
4	ERC9448	Plug	1	To (V) April 1989	
4	RTC6851	Plug	1	From (V) April 1989	
5	AFU1890L	Washer-sealing	2	To (V) April 1989	
5	243960	Washer-sealing	1	From (V) April 1989	
6	ERC2254	Bracket-lifting body-front	1		
7	ETC7135	Bracket-lifting body-rear	1		
8	FS108207L	Screw-flanged head-M8 x 20	4		
9	WL108001L	Washer-sprung-M8	4		
10	ETC5301	Gasket-cylinder head-asbestos	1		
10	ERR3618	Gasket-cylinder head-asbestos free	1		
11	247051	Bolt-1/2UNF x 4 9/16	9		
12	247683	Bolt-1/2UNF x 2 1/2	2		
13	247723	Bolt-1/2UNF x 6	5		
14	90518466	Stud	2		
15	ERC6821	Washer-plain	18		
16	NH608061L	Nut-hexagonal	2		
17	275679	Pipe assembly-engine oil feed	1		
18	ETC6510	Washer-sealing	4		
19	ETC4498	Bolt-banjo	2		
20	ERC8450	Plug-heater ignition	4		

CHANGE POINTS:
(1) To (V) April 1989
(2) From (V) April 1989 To (V) WA 159806
(3) From (V) XA 159807

DEFENDER	GROUP B	Engine 2500 - Diesel - Naturally Aspirated Rockershaft

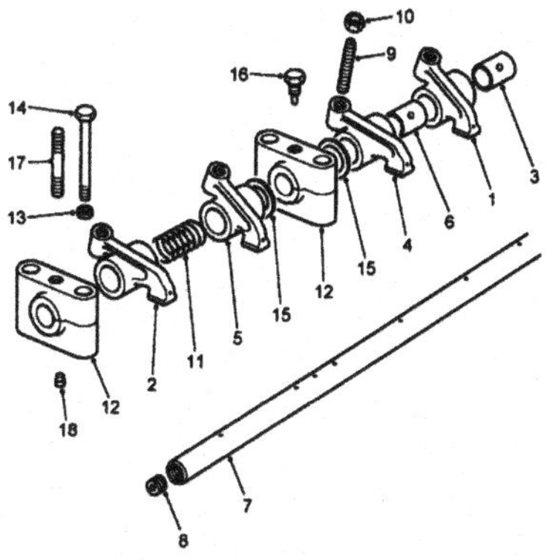

AHBGGC1A

Illus	Part Number	Description	Quantity	Change Point	Remarks
1	ERC9060	ARM-EXHAUST VALVE ROCKER-RH	2		
3	247738	• Arm & bush assembly-exhaust valve rocker	4		
2	ERC9059	ARM-EXHAUST VALVE ROCKER-LH	2		
3	247738	• Arm & bush assembly-exhaust valve rocker	4		
5	ERC9056	ARM-INLET VALVE ROCKER-RH	2		
4	ERC9055	ARM-INLET VALVE ROCKER-LH	2		
6	247737	• Bush	4		
7	ERC6341	SHAFT-ROCKER	1		
8	ERC6337	• Plug	2		
9	ERC9054	Screw-tappet adjusting	8		
10	NT108041L	Nut-hexagonal head	8		
11	247040	Spring-rocker shaft	4		
12	ERC9137	Bracket	5		
13	WL108001L	Washer-sprung-M8	5		
14	FB108111L	Bolt-flanged head-M8 x 55	5		
15	247153	Washer-plain	8		
16	ETC4460	Screw	1		
17	TD108091L	Stud-M8	3		
18	277956	Dowel-ring	3		

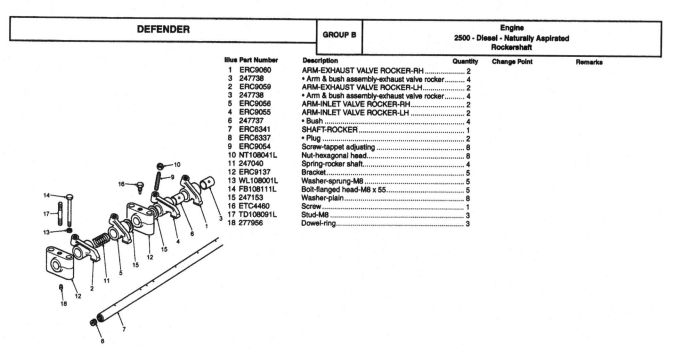

Illus	Part Number	Description	Quantity	Change Point	Remarks
1	507829	TAPPET-ENGINE VALVE MECHANICAL	8		
2	502473	• Slide-tappet guide	8		
3	ERR607	• Tappet-engine valve mechanical	8		
4	ETC4246	• Bolt	8		
5	273069	• Washer-sealing	8		
6	ERR561	• Roller-tappet guide	8		
7	ETC5739	Valve-cylinder head inlet	4		
8	ERR1230	Valve-cylinder head exhaust	4		
9	ERR4175	Cap-valve stem	NLA	Note (1)	Use LJC100270.
9	LJC100270	Cap-valve stem	8	Note (2)	
10	ETC4068	Cap-cylinder head valve spring	8		
11	ETC4069	Cotter-valve	16		
12	ERR4640	Spring-cylinder head valve	8		
13	546799	Rod-engine push	8		

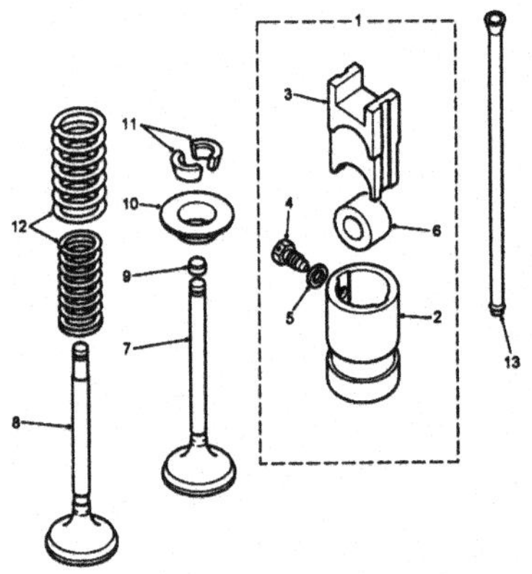

AHBGGE1A

CHANGE POINTS:
(1) To (V) VA 128878
(2) From (V) VA 128879

Illus	Part Number	Description	Quantity	Change Point	Remarks
1	ETC6924	Cover-valve rocker	1		
2	ETC6438	Gasket-engine rocker cover	1		
3	273069	Washer-sealing	3		
4	ERC9220	Nut-domed-M8	3		
5	ERR1454	CAP ASSEMBLY-OIL FILLER	1	To (E)12J 42593C	
5	ERR737	CAP ASSEMBLY-OIL FILLER	1	From (E)12J 42594C	
6	ERR736	• O ring	1		
7	ERC9728	Hose-camshaft cover to inlet manifold breather	1	To (E)12J 42593C	
7	ETC7969	Hose-camshaft cover to inlet manifold breather	1	From (E)12J 42594C	
8	RTC3499	Clip-hose	2		
9	ETC5588	Bracket	1		Air conditioning

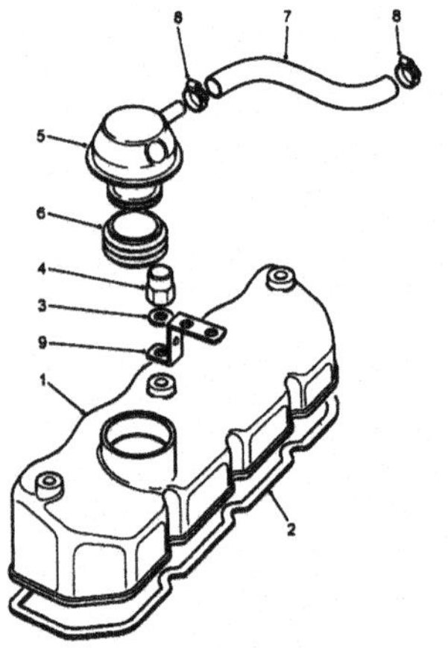

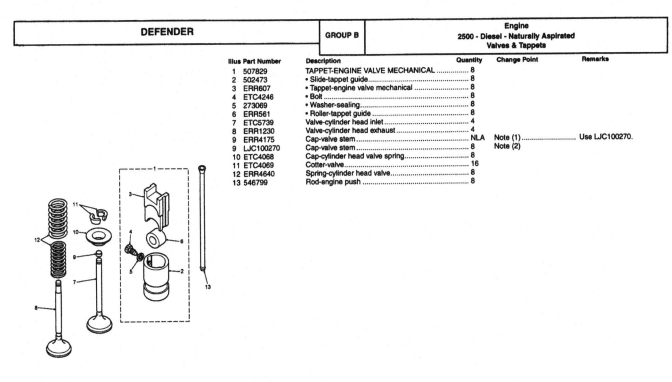

AHBGGG1A

Illus	Part Number	Description	Quantity	Change Point	Remarks
1	ERR506	Breather assembly-crankcase-side cover	1		
2	FB108081L	Bolt-side cover-flanged head-M8 x 40	1		
3	FS108257L	Screw-flanged head-M8 x 25	5		
4	247555	Gasket-cylinder block side cover	NLA		Use ERR3605.
4	ERR3605	Gasket-cylinder block side cover-asbestos	NLA		Use ERR2026.
4	ERR2026	Gasket-cylinder block side cover-asbestos free	1		
5	ERR874	Baffle-oil separator-side cover	1		
6	79026	Screw-side cover-No 6 x 5/16	1		
7	ERR877	Hose-crankcase breather flexible-side cover	1		
8	CN100258L	Clip-hose-side cover-25mm	2		
9	ERR1471	SEPARATOR ASSEMBLY-CRANKCASE BREATHER OIL-SIDE COVER	1		
	LLO100000	• O ring	1		
10	FB106121L	Bolt-side cover-flanged head-M6 x 60	2		
11	ERR1605	Hose-oil separator drain-side cover	1		
12	CN100208L	Clip-hose-side cover-20mm	2		
13	ERR1729	Hose-cyclone-air cleaner-side cover	1		
14	CN100258L	Clip-hose-side cover-25mm	2		
15	ERR878	Clip-hose-side cover	1		
16	ERR879	Spacer-side cover	1		
17	SH110201L	Screw-side cover-hexagonal head-M10 x 20	1		

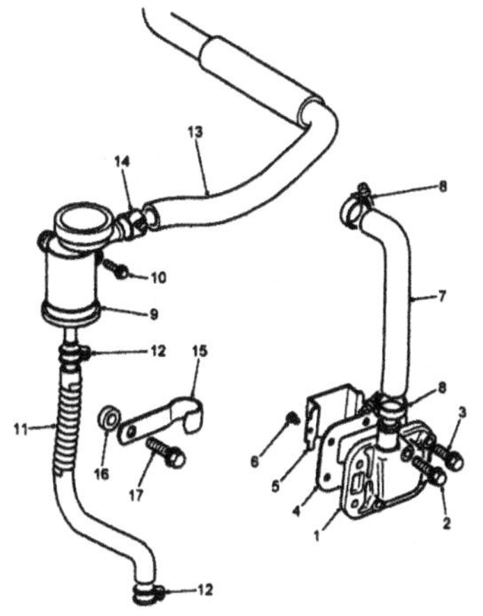

Illus	Part Number	Description	Quantity	Change Point	Remarks
1	ETC7128	Camshaft assembly-engine	1		
2	ERC1561	Plate-camshaft retaining	1		
3	FS106167L	Screw-flanged head-flanged head-M6 x 16	2		
4	WL106001L	Washer-sprung-M6	2		
5	ETC4014	Pulley-camshaft	1		
6	230313	Key	1		
7	BX110071M	Bolt-hexagonal head-M10 x 35	1		
8	ETC4670	Washer-plain	1		
9	ERC8847	Plate-camshaft pulley retaining	1		
10	ERC8849	O ring	1		
11	ETC4076	O ring	1		
12	2995	Washer-lock	2		

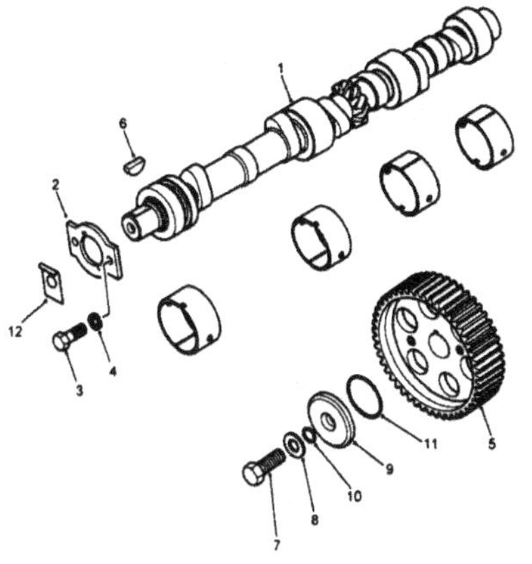

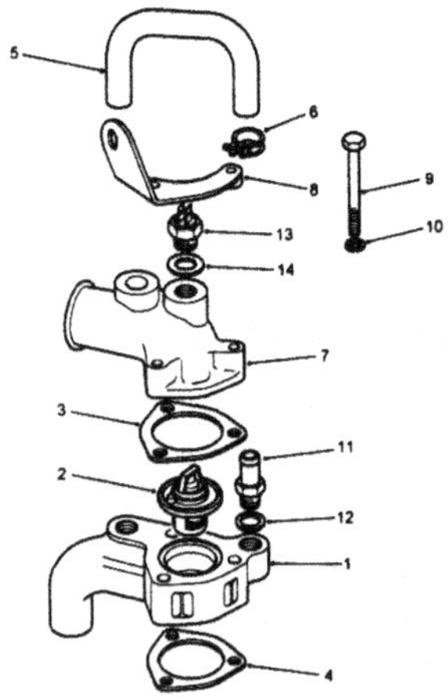

AHBGGK1A

Illus	Part Number	Description	Quantity	Change Point	Remarks
1	ERC8758	Housing-thermostat	1		
2	602687	Thermostat-engine-82 degrees C	1		
2	ETC4761	Thermostat-engine-74 degrees C	1		Optional
3	ERR3682	Gasket-thermostat housing-top-asbestos free	1		
4	247874	Gasket-thermostat housing-bottom	1		
5	ERC7510	Hose to pipe-coolant	1		
6	CN100258L	Clip-hose-25mm	2		
		ELBOW-ENGINE COOLANT OUTLET			
7	ERC8757	RH outlet	1		Except air conditioning
7	ETC5967	LH outlet	1		
7	ETC4217	RH outlet	1		Air conditioning
7	ETC5958	LH outlet	1		
8	ERC6478	Bracket-radiator pipe to cowl-RH outlet	1		
8	ETC5965	Bracket-radiator pipe to cowl-LH outlet	1		
9	BH106141L	Bolt-RH outlet-M6-70mm	1		
9	BH106151L	Bolt-RH outlet-M6 x 75	2		
9	BH106151L	Bolt-LH outlet-M6 x 75	3		
10	WL106001L	Washer-sprung-M6	3		
11	624091	Adaptor-pipe coolant	2		
12	243959	Washer-sealing	2		
13	PRC3366	Sensor-temperature-Blue	1		
13	PRC3541	Sensor-temperature-Red	1		
14	C457593L	Washer	2		

Illus	Part Number	Description	Quantity	Change Point	Remarks
1	ERC6939	Manifold assembly-engine inlet	1	To (E)12J 42593C	
1	ERR362	Manifold assembly-engine inlet	1	From (E)12J 42594C	
2	525428	Plug-cup	1		
3	ERC6047	Tube-upper inlet manifold inner	1		
4	ETC5312	Gasket-inlet manifold	1	To (E)12J 48876C	
4	ETC7750	Gasket-inlet manifold	1	From (E)12J 48877C	
5	564308	Clamp-manifold to head	4		
6	574654	Clip-manifold to head	1		
7	NH108041L	Nut-hexagonal head-M8	9		
8	WA108051L	Washer-8mm	9		
9	WL108001L	Washer-sprung-M8	9		
10	ERC9688	Manifold-engine exhaust-Olive end	1	Note (1)	
10	ETC5331	Manifold-engine exhaust	1	Note (2)	
11	AFU1848L	Stud-M10	3		

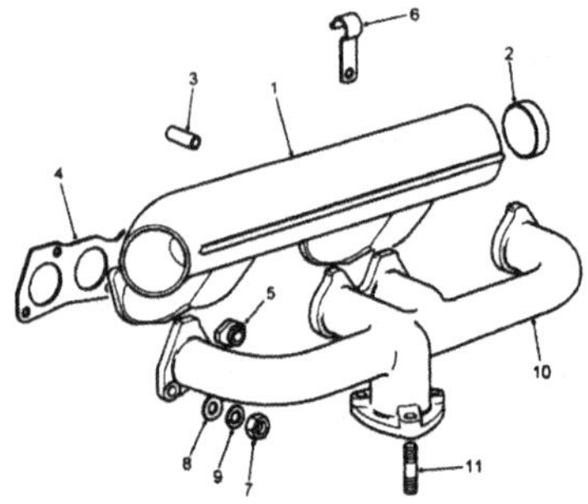

AHBGHA1A

CHANGE POINTS:
(1) To (V) FA 375546
(2) From (V) FA 375547

Illus	Part Number	Description	Quantity	Change Point	Remarks
1	ETC7869	Pump-fuel mechanical	NLA		Use STC1190.
	RTC6180	Kit-fuel pump repair	NLA		
	STC1190	Kit-fuel pump repair	1		
2	ETC7970	Gasket-fuel lift pump	NLA		Use ERR2028.
2	ERR2028	Gasket-fuel lift pump	2		
3	SS108301L	Screw-flanged head-M8 x 30	2		
4	WA108051L	Washer-8mm	2		

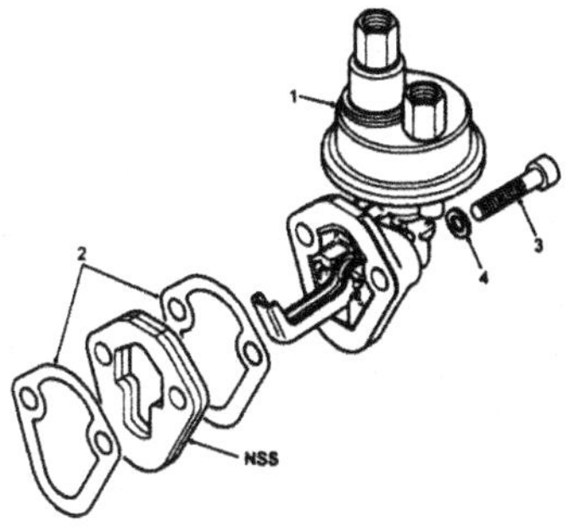

AHBGKA1A

Illus	Part Number	Description	Quantity	Change Point	Remarks
1	ERC6761	Pump assembly-fuel injection diesel-new	1		
1	ERC6761E	Pump assembly-fuel injection diesel-exchange	1		
2	ETC4070	Bracket-engine mounting	1		
3	WA108051L	Washer-8mm	2		
4	FS108251L	Screw-flanged head-M8 x 25	NLA		Use FS108257L.
5	NY108041L	Nut-nyloc-M8	1		
6	NY108041L	Nut-nyloc-M8	3		
7	WA108051L	Washer-8mm	3		
8	ETC5717	Pulley fuel inj pump	1		
9	RTC5077	Key-oil pump drive	1		
10	NH112041L	Nut-hexagonal-M12	1		
11	ETC6675	Level-carburettor throttle	1		
12	ETC4417	Link-carburettor/throttle connecting	1		
13	NH105041L	Nut-hexagonal-M5	2		
14	WA105001L	Washer-plain-standard-M5	2		
15	ETC4440	Gasket-injection pump-diesel engine-asbestos	1		
15	ERR3617	Gasket-injection pump-diesel engine-asbestos free	1		
16	BAU4611L	Switch-fuel changeover	1		
17	ETC4752	Sleeve-locking speed stop	1		
18	RTC5891	Spring-carburettor throttle return	1		

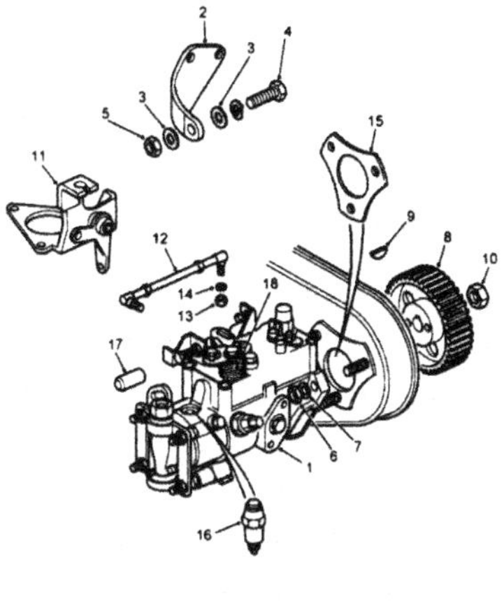

AHBGKC1A

Illus	Part Number	Description	Quantity	Change Point	Remarks
1	ERC4480	Pipe-spill return fuel injection	1		
2	ETC4291	Pipe - fuel injection-No1	1		
3	ETC4292	Pipe - fuel injection-No2	1		
4	ETC4293	Pipe - fuel injection-No3	1		
5	ETC4294	Pipe - fuel injection-No4	1		
6	ERR1266	INJECTOR ASSEMBLY-DIESEL HOLDER & NOZZLE-NEW	4		
	247726	• Nozzle-injection diesel	4		
6	564332E	INJECTOR ASSEMBLY-DIESEL HOLDER & NOZZLE-EXCHANGE	4		
	247726	• Nozzle-injection diesel	4		
7	NH108041L	Nut-hexagonal head-M8	8		
8	WL108001L	Washer-sprung-M8	8		
9	247179	Washer-injector sealing	4		
10	12H220L	Washer-sealing-diesel injector to cylinder head	4		
11	ETC4156	Clip	2		
12	ETC4308	Clip	1		
13	273069	Washer-sealing-diesel injector spill return pipe banjo	8		
14	273521	Bolt-banjo-No1-No2-No3	3		
14	563195	Bolt-banjo-No4	1		

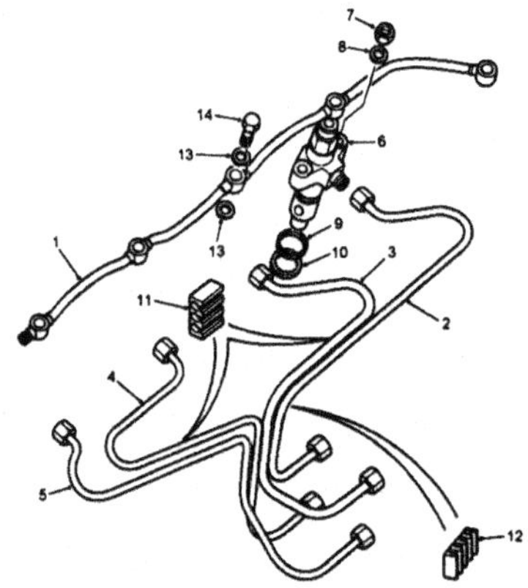

AHBGKE1A

Illus	Part Number	Description	Quantity	Change Point	Remarks
1	STC1562	Set-cylinder head gasket-decarbonising	1		
2	RTC6084	Kit-gasket-overhaul-asbestos	NLA		Use STC1559.
2	STC1559	Kit-gasket-overhaul-asbestos free	1		

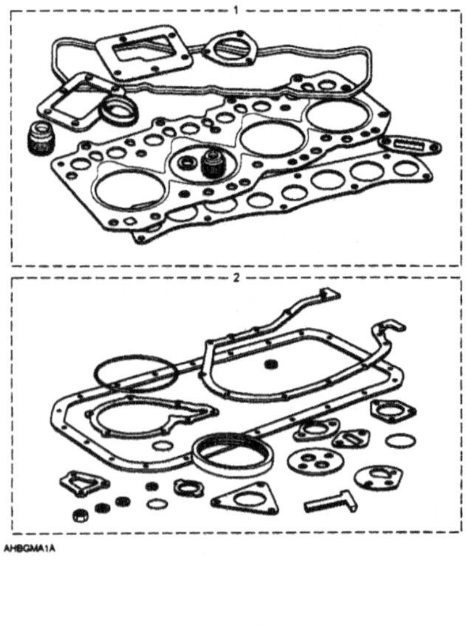

AHBGMA1A

Illus	Part Number	Description	Quantity	Change Point	Remarks
1	ERR535	PUMP BRAKE VACUUM	1		
2	AEU2720	• Bolt	4		
3	WL106001L	• Washer-sprung-M6	4		
4	AEU2718	• Rotor blade-vacuum pump	4		
5	AEU2719	• O ring	1		
6	ETC4616	Gasket-vacuum pump	2		
7	SS108301L	Screw-flanged head-M8 x 30	3		
8	WM600051L	Washer-spring-5/16"	3		

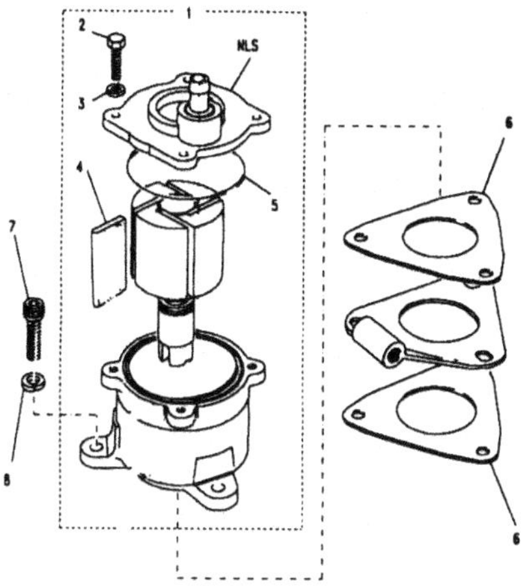

Illus	Part Number	Description	Quantity	Change Point	Remarks
1	ERC8447	PUMP ASSEMBLY POWER ASSISTED STEERING	NLA		Use ETC9077 Hobourn Eaton Pump.
	AEU4119	• Washer power assisted steering	1		
	RTC4485	• Bolt-banjo	1		
2	ERC6974	Bracket-power assisted steering	1		
3	FS108251L	Screw-flanged head-M8 x 25	NLA		Use FS108257L.
4	WL108001L	Washer-sprung-M8	3		
5	FS108307L	Screw-flanged head-M8 x 30	1		
6	WL108001L	Washer-sprung-M8	1		
7	BH108181L	Bolt-hexagonal head-M8 x 90	NLA		
8	WL108001L	Washer-sprung-M8	3		
9	ERC6976	Spigot	1		
10	ERC6977	Nut	1		
11	ERC5145	Pulley-drive power assisted steering	1		
12	ERC6975	Plate assembly	1		
13	SH108141L	Screw-hexagonal head-M8 x 14	3		
14	WL108001L	Washer-sprung-M8	1		
15	FS106201L	Screw-flanged head-M6 x 20	4		
16	WL108001L	Washer-sprung-M8	3		
17	FS108251L	Screw-flanged head-M8 x 25	NLA		Use FS108257L.
19	ETC4153	PULLEY-IDLER ANCILLARY DRIVE	1		
20	SH108401L	• Screw-hexagonal head-M8 x 40	1		
21	WL108001L	• Washer-sprung-M8	1		
22	CR120195	Circlip	2		
23	ERC5146	Belt-polyvee power assisted steering	1		Except air conditioning
23	ETC4272	Belt-polyvee power assisted steering	1		Air conditioning
	AEU4119	Washer power assisted steering-on power steering pump	2		

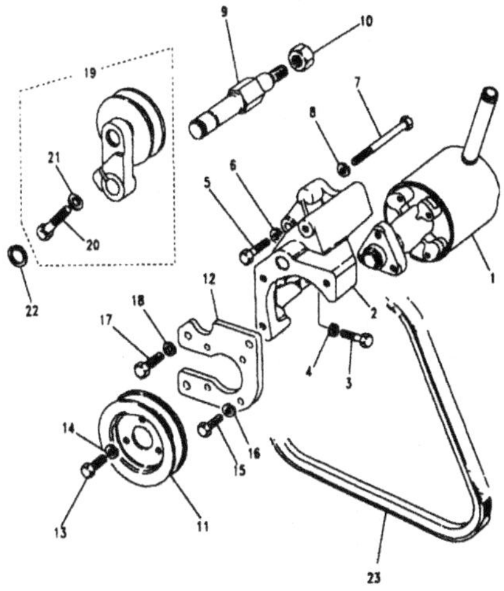

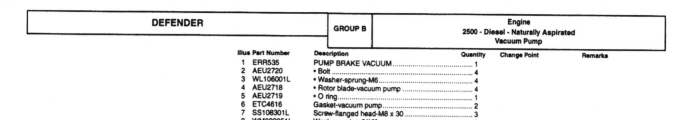

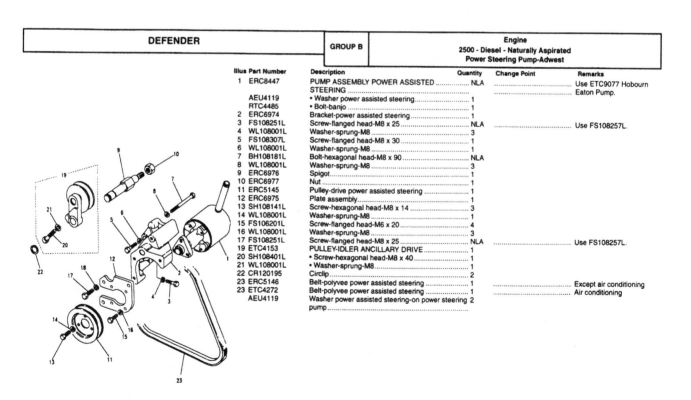

DEFENDER

GROUP B

Engine
2500 - Diesel - Naturally Aspirated
Power Steering Pump-Hobourn Eaton

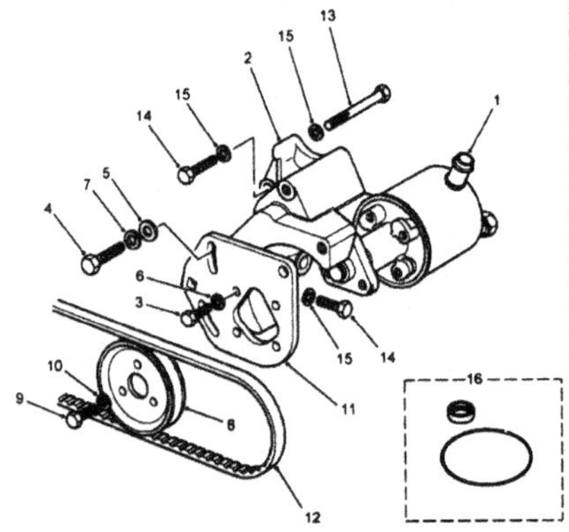

AHBGNC2A

Illus	Part Number	Description	Quantity	Change Point	Remarks
1	ETC9077	PUMP ASSEMBLY POWER ASSISTED STEERING	1	Note (1)	
	RTC5674	• Union-delivery	1		
	RTC5675	• Washer-sealing	2		
1	NTC8287	Pump assembly power assisted steering	1	Note (2)	
1	NTC9070	Pump assembly power assisted steering	1	Note (3)	
2	ERC6974	Bracket-power assisted steering	1	To (V) June 1989	
2	ETC8854	Bracket-power assisted steering	1	From (V) June 1989	
3	FS106201L	Screw-flanged head-M6 x 20	4	To (V) LA 939975	
4	FS108251L	Screw-flanged head-M8 x 25	NLA		Use FS108257L.
5	WA108051L	Washer-pump to bracket-8mm	2	To (V) LA 939975	
6	WL106001L	Washer-sprung-M6	4		
7	WL108001L	Washer-sprung-M8	3		
8	ETC5783	Pulley power assisted steering pump	1		
9	SH108141L	Screw-hexagonal head-M8 x 14	3		
10	WL108001L	Washer-sprung-M8	3		
11	ETC5944	Bracket-mounting power assisted steering pump	NLA	To (E)11L 10733A	Use ERR1976.
11	ERR1976	Bracket-mounting power assisted steering pump	1	Note (4)	
11	ERR2605	Bracket-mounting power assisted steering pump	1	From (V) JA 918810	
12	ETC5815	Belt-polyvee power assisted steering	1	To (V) LA 939975	
13	BH108181L	Bolt-hexagonal head-M8 x 90	NLA	To (V) LA 939975	
14	FS108251L	Screw-flanged head-M8 x 25	NLA		Use FS108257L.
14	FS108307L	Screw-flanged head-M8 x 30	1		
15	WL108001L	Washer-sprung-M8	4	To (V) LA 939975	
16	RTC5935	Kit-power assisted steering pump seal	NLA		Use STC1633.
16	STC1633	Kit-power assisted steering pump seal	1	To (V) LA 939975	

CHANGE POINTS:
(1) To (V) June 1989
(2) From (V) June 1989 To (V) July 1992
(3) From (V) July 1992
(4) From (E)11L 10734A To (V) JA 918809

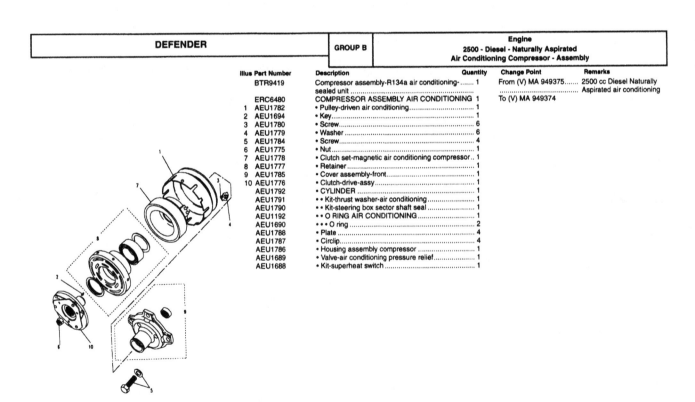

DEFENDER

GROUP B

Engine
2500 - Diesel - Naturally Aspirated
Air Conditioning Compressor - Assembly

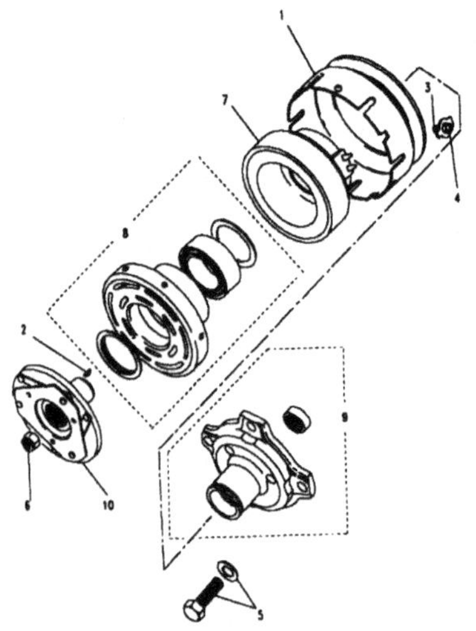

Illus	Part Number	Description	Quantity	Change Point	Remarks
	BTR9419	Compressor assembly-R134a air conditioning-sealed unit	1	From (V) MA 949375	2500 cc Diesel Naturally Aspirated air conditioning
	ERC6480	COMPRESSOR ASSEMBLY AIR CONDITIONING	1	To (V) MA 949374	
1	AEU1782	• Pulley-driven air conditioning	1		
2	AEU1694	• Key	1		
3	AEU1780	• Screw	6		
4	AEU1779	• Washer	6		
5	AEU1784	• Screw	4		
6	AEU1775	• Nut	1		
7	AEU1778	• Clutch set-magnetic air conditioning compressor	1		
8	AEU1777	• Retainer	1		
9	AEU1785	• Cover assembly-front	1		
10	AEU1776	• Clutch-drive-assy	1		
	AEU1792	• CYLINDER	1		
	AEU1791	• • Kit-thrust washer-air conditioning	1		
	AEU1790	• • Kit-steering box sector shaft seal	1		
	AEU1192	• • O RING AIR CONDITIONING	1		
	AEU1690	• • • O ring	2		
	AEU1788	• Plate	4		
	AEU1787	• Circlip	4		
	AEU1786	• Housing assembly compressor	1		
	AEU1689	• Valve-air conditioning pressure relief	1		
	AEU1688	• Kit-superheat switch	1		

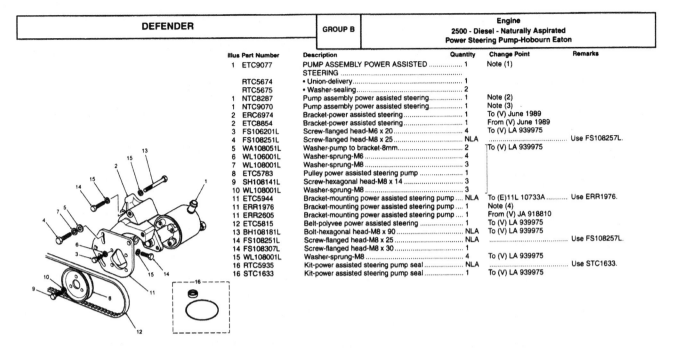

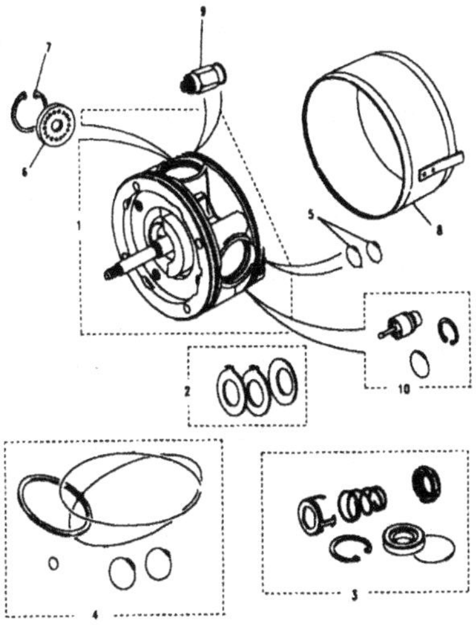

Illus	Part Number	Description	Quantity	Change Point	Remarks
	ERC6480	COMPRESSOR ASSEMBLY AIR CONDITIONING	1	To (V) MA 949374	
	AEU1782	• Pulley-driven air conditioning	1		
	AEU1694	• Key	1		
	AEU1780	• Screw	6		
	AEU1779	• Washer	6		
	AEU1784	• Screw	4		
	AEU1775	• Nut	1		
	AEU1778	• Clutch set-magnetic air conditioning compressor	1		
	AEU1777	• Retainer	1		
	AEU1785	• Cover assembly-front	1		
	AEU1776	• Clutch-drive-assy	1		
1	AEU1792	• CYLINDER	1		
2	AEU1791	• • Kit-thrust washer-air conditioning	1		
3	AEU1790	• • Kit-steering box sector shaft seal	1		
4	AEU1192	• • O RING AIR CONDITIONING	1		
5	AEU1690	• • • O ring	2		
6	AEU1788	• Plate	4		
7	AEU1787	• Circlip	4		
8	AEU1786	• Housing assembly compressor	1		
9	AEU1689	• Valve-air conditioning pressure relief	1		
10	AEU1688	• Kit-superheat switch	1		
	BTR9419	Compressor assembly-R134a air conditioning	1	From (V) MA 949375	
11	ETC4371	Belt-polyvee air conditioning compressor	1		
	AEU1691	Oil-525 visc	A/R		

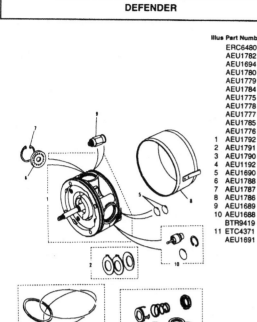

Illus	Part Number	Description	Quantity	Change Point	Remarks
1	ETC7756	PULLEY-DRIVE AIR CONDITIONING	1		
2	554971	• PULLEY-IDLER ANCILLARY DRIVE	1		
3	RTC6077	• • Nut-5/16UNF	1		
4	4095	• Washer	1		
5	WB108051L	• Washer-plain-M8	1		
6	ETC4212	• Plate	1		

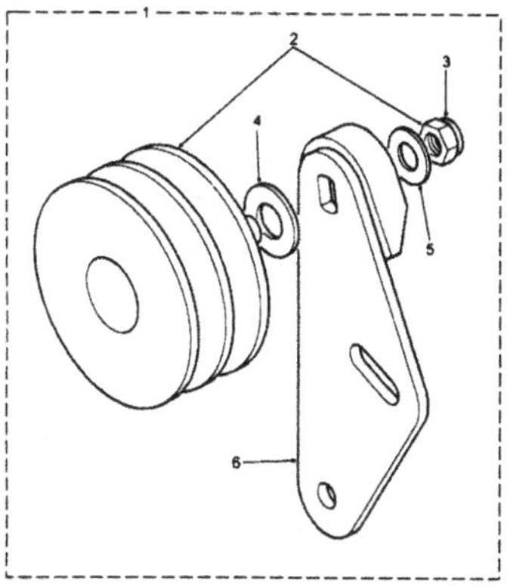

AHBGNE4A

Compressor Fixings

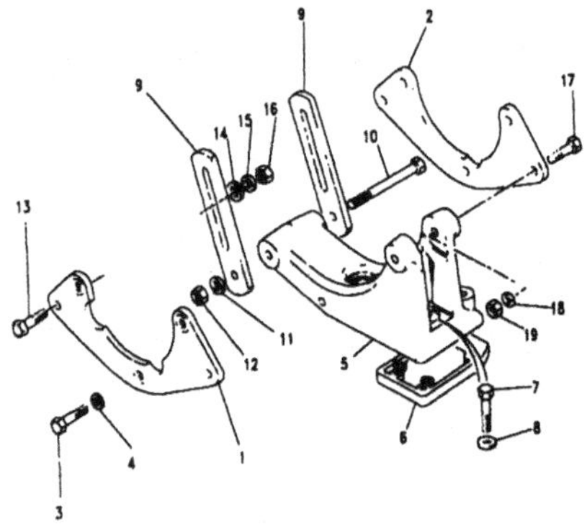

Illus	Part Number	Description	Quantity	Change Point	Remarks
1	ERC7082	Plate-front	1		
2	ERC5152	Plate-rear	1		
3	BH110201L	Bolt-hexagonal head-M10 x 100	3		
4	WL110001L	Washer-M10	3		
5	ETC4882	Bracket-air compressor	NLA		Use ERR3091.
5	ERR3091	Bracket-air compressor	1		
6	ETC4197	Bracket-compressor air conditioning	1		
7	BH110101L	Bolt-hexagonal head-M10 x 50-long	4		
8	WA110061L	Washer-M10	4		
9	ERC5155	Link-adjusting compressor	2		
10	BH108181L	Bolt-hexagonal head-M8 x 90	NLA		
11	WL108001L	Washer-sprung-M8	1		
12	NH108041L	Nut-hexagonal head-M8	1		
13	FS108251L	Screw-flanged head-M8 x 25	NLA		Use FS108257L.
14	WA108051L	Washer-8mm	2		
15	WL108001L	Washer-sprung-M8	2		
16	NH108041L	Nut-hexagonal head-M8	2		
17	FB108081L	Bolt-flanged head-M8 x 40	2		
18	WL108001L	Washer-sprung-M8	2		
19	NH108041L	Nut-hexagonal head-M8	2		

Alternator-Non Air Con-A115

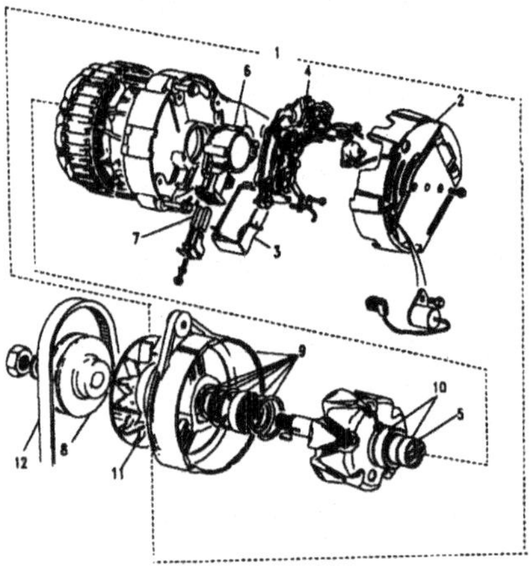

Illus	Part Number	Description	Quantity	Change Point	Remarks
1	RTC5083E	ALTERNATOR ASSEMBLY-115/45-LRA356-EXCHANGE	1		
2	AEU2507	• Cover alternator-LRA356	1		
3	AEU3076	• Regulator assembly alternator-LRA356	1		
4	BAU1825	• Rectifier-alternator	1		
5	BAU2193	• Ring-slip alternator	1		
6	BAU2195	• Brush alternator	1		
7	RTC3215	• Brush alternator	1		
8	568788	Pulley alternator	1		
9	18G8619L	Kit-bearing-drive end alternator	1		
10	AEU1532	Bearing-alternator front	1		
11	C37222L	Fan alternator	1		
12	ERC6886	Belt-polyvee alternator	NLA		Use ETC7939.
12	ETC7939	Belt-polyvee alternator	1		
	AEU1706	Kit-screw	1		
	AEU1710	Kit-fixings alternator/vacuum pump	1		
	AEU1942	Spacer	1		

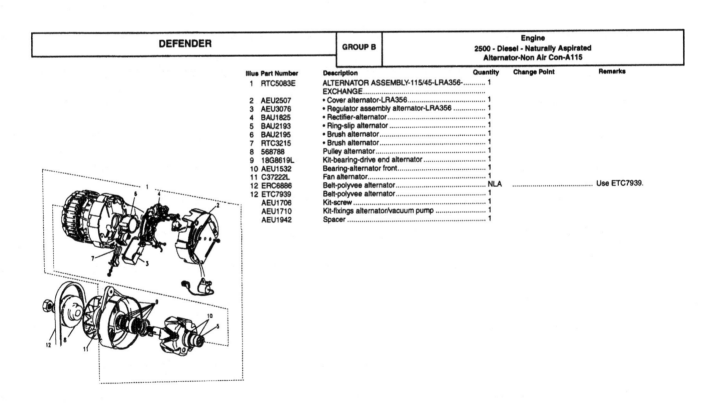

Illus	Part Number	Description	Quantity	Change Point	Remarks
1	RTC5682N	ALTERNATOR ASSEMBLY-NEW-A127-45 AMP	1		
1	RTC5682E	ALTERNATOR ASSEMBLY-EXCHANGE-A127-45 AMP	1		
2	RTC5670	• Regulator & brush box assembly alternator	1		
3	RTC5684	• Rectifier-alternator	1		
	RTC5926	• Bearing-alternator front	1		
4	RTC5687	• Bracket-drive end c/w bearing alternator e-RH	1		
	RTC5925	• Kit-fixings alternator/vacuum pump-LH	1		
7	RTC5685	Fan alternator	1		
8	RTC5686	Pulley alternator	1		
9	ETC7939	Belt-polyvee alternator	1		
	RTC5689	Spacer	1		

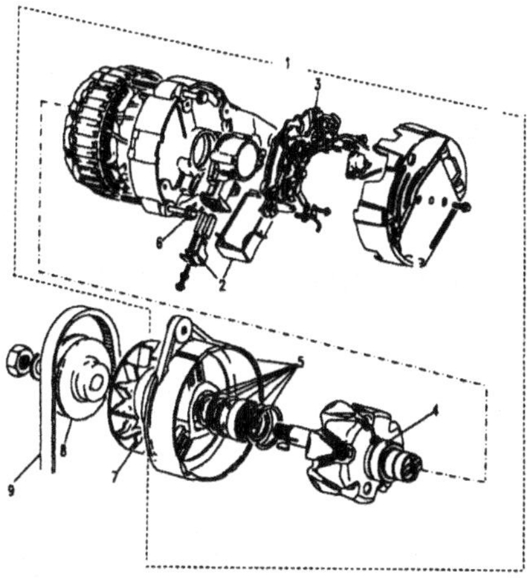

Illus	Part Number	Description	Quantity	Change Point	Remarks
1	RTC5218E	ALTERNATOR ASSEMBLY-LRA406-EXCHANGE-A133-65 AMP	1		
2	AEU1725	• Cover alternator	1		
3	AEU3076	• Regulator assembly alternator-LRA356	1		
4	AEU1527	• Rectifier-alternator	1		
5	RTC3292	• Brush alternator	1		
6	STC130	• Diode pack alternator	1		
7	AEU1726	• Kit-bearing-drive end alternator	1		
8	AEU1532	• Bearing-alternator front	1		
9	AEU1710	Kit-fixings alternator/vacuum pump-sundry parts	1		
	ERC8987	Nut	1		
10	ADU4928L	Fan alternator	1		
11	ERC8986	Pulley alternator	1		
12	AEU1616	Capacitor alternator	1		
13	ETC7939	Belt-polyvee alternator	1		
	AEU1706	Kit-screw	1		
	AEU1708	Spacer	1		
	AEU1709	Kit-alternator-terminal	1		

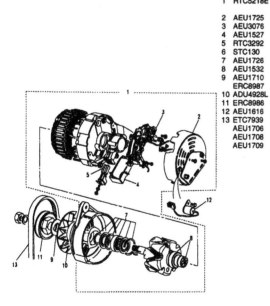

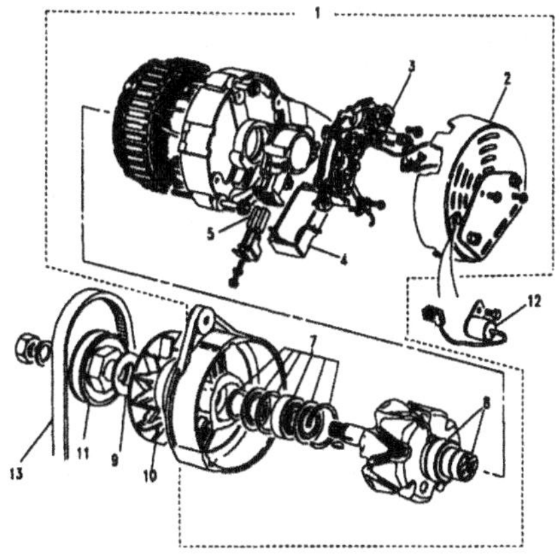

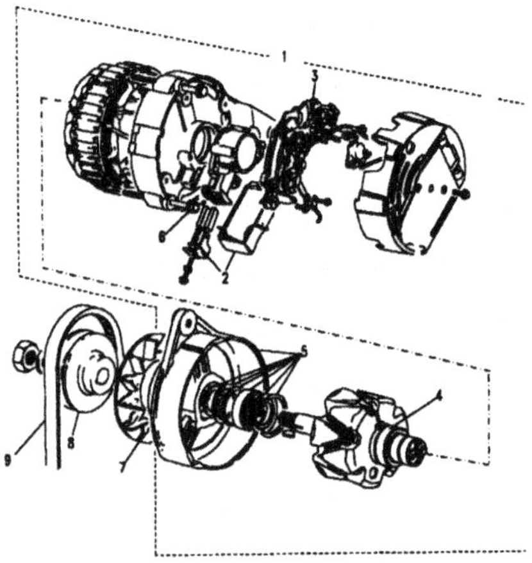

Illus	Part Number	Description	Quantity	Change Point	Remarks
		ALTERNATOR ASSEMBLY			
1	RTC5680N	NEW-A127-65 AMP-RH	NLA		Use STC234.
1	STC234	NEW-A127-65 AMP-RH	1		
1	RTC5680E	EXCHANGE-A127-65 AMP-RH	1		
2	RTC5670	• Regulator & brush box assembly alternator	1		
3	RTC5671	• Rectifier-alternator	1		
4	RTC5926	• Bearing-alternator front	1		Part of RTC5680N, RTC5680E.
5	RTC5687	• Bracket-drive end c/w bearing alternator e-new alternator-RH-RH	1		
6	RTC5046	• Kit-fixings alternator/vacuum pump-new alternator-RH-RH	1		
	RTC6114	• Capacitor alternator	1		Part of STC234.
7	AAU2249L	Fan alternator	1		
8	RTC5686	Pulley alternator	1		
9	ETC7939	Belt-polyvee alternator	1		
	RTC5689	Spacer	1		

Illus	Part Number	Description	Quantity	Change Point	Remarks
1	ETC4357	Bracket-mounting-alternator	1		
2	BH108161L	Bolt-hexagonal head-M8 x 80	1		
3	FS110301L	Screw-flanged head-M10 x 30-top	2		
4	WL108001L	Washer-sprung-M8	1		
5	WL108001L	Washer-sprung-M8	2		
6	ERC5139	Link-adjuster alternator-A133 alternator	1		
6	ERC6266	Link-adjuster alternator-A127 alternator	1		
7	FS108207L	Screw-flanged head-M8 x 20	1		
8	WL108001L	Washer-sprung-M8	1		
9	2266L	Washer	1		
10	ERC8964	Bolt-M8 x 95	1		
11	WL108001L	Washer-sprung-M8	1		
12	BH108081L	Bolt-hexagonal head-M8 x 40	1		
13	BH108091L	Bolt-M8 x 45	1		
14	WC108051L	Washer-M8	1		
15	NY108041L	Nut-nyloc-M8	2		
16	ERC7974	Spacer	1		

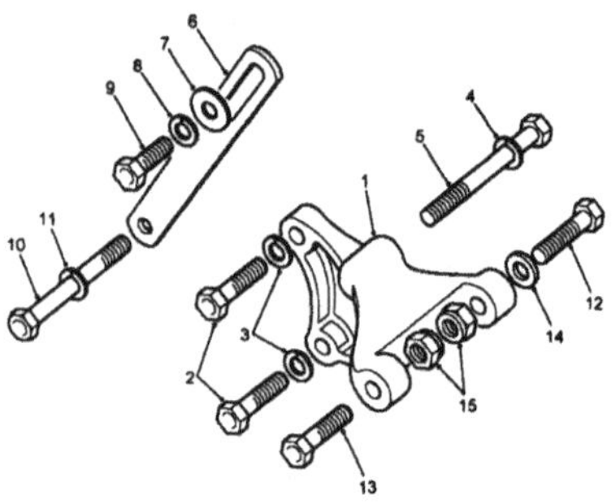

AHBGPC8A

Engine
2500 - Diesel - Naturally Aspirated
Starter Motor-Lucas-Type M113

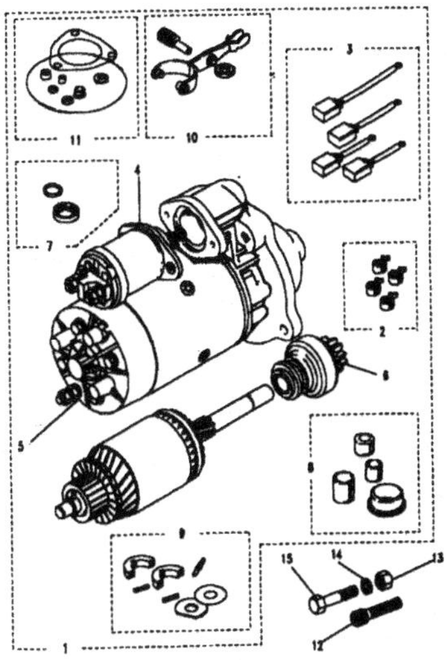

Illus	Part Number	Description	Quantity	Change Point	Remarks
1	RTC5249N	MOTOR-STARTER ENGINE-NEW-LUCAS	1		
1	RTC5249E	MOTOR-STARTER ENGINE-EXCHANGE-LUCAS	1		
2	27H5932L	• Kit-brush starter motor	1		
3	AEU4151	• Kit-brush starter motor	1		
4	STC1518	• Solenoid starter motor	1		
5	AEU4147	• Bracket	1		
6	AEU2792	• Drive assembly starter motor	1		
7	AEU4148	• Kit-starter motor retention	1		
8	AEU4149	• Kit-starter motor	1		
9	37H6171L	• Kit-starter motor	1		
10	AEU1613	• Kit-starter motor	1		
11	37H7618L	• Kit-starter motor	1		
12	FS110301L	Screw-flanged head-M10 x 30-top	1		
13	NH110041L	Nut-hexagonal head-coarse thread-M10	2		
14	WL110001L	Washer-M10	3		
15	BH110091L	Bolt-M10 x 45	4		
	AEU4150	Kit-starter motor sundry parts	1		

Engine
2500 - Diesel - Naturally Aspirated
Starter Motor-Lucas-Type M47

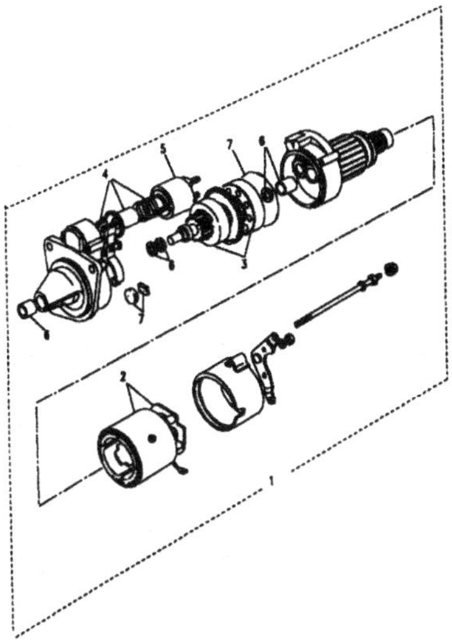

Illus	Part Number	Description	Quantity	Change Point	Remarks
1	ERR5009	MOTOR-STARTER ENGINE-NEW-BOSCH	1	Note (1)	
2	STC1246	• Box assembly-brush starter motor-Bosch	1		
	STC1254	• Spring-coil	4		
	STC1247	• Guide-starter motor brush	4		
3	STC1244	• Drive assembly starter motor-Bosch	1		
5	STC1245	• Solenoid starter motor-0 331 303 165-Bosch	1		
5	STC3715	• Solenoid starter motor-9 330 331 006-Bosch	1		
	STC1250	• Bush-starter motor-centre	2		
	STC1251	• Bush-starter motor-rear	1		
	STC1255	• Bush-starter motor-front	1		
1	PRC5109N	MOTOR-STARTER ENGINE-NEW-VALEO	NLA	Note (1)	Use NAD10039.
1	PRC5109E	MOTOR-STARTER ENGINE-EXCHANGE-VALEO	1	Note (1)	
2	RTC4981	• Box assembly-brush starter motor-Valeo	1		
3	RTC4982	• Drive assembly starter motor-Valeo	1		
4	RTC4979	• Yoke assembly starter motor	1		
5	RTC4978	• Solenoid starter motor-Valeo	1		
6	RTC4980	• Kit-starter motor	1		
7	RTC4983	• Kit-starter motor sundry parts	1		
1	NAD10039	MOTOR-STARTER ENGINE-LUCAS	NLA		Use ERR5009.
2	STC1246	• Box assembly-brush starter motor-Bosch	1		
	STC1254	• Spring-coil	4		
	STC1247	• Guide-starter motor brush	4		
3	STC1244	• Drive assembly starter motor-Bosch	1		
5	STC1245	• Solenoid starter motor-0 331 303 165-Bosch	1		
5	STC3715	• Solenoid starter motor-9 330 331 006-Bosch	1		
	STC1250	• Bush-starter motor-centre	2		
	STC1251	• Bush-starter motor-rear	1		
	STC1255	• Bush-starter motor-front	1		
	PRC5538	Harness earth bond	1		
	SH110301L	Screw-hexagonal head-M10 x 30	NLA		Use FS110301L.
	FS110301L	Screw-flanged head-M10 x 30-top	1		
	NH110041L	Nut-hexagonal head-coarse thread-M10	2		
	WL110001L	Washer-M10	3		
	BH110091L	Bolt-M10 x 45	4		

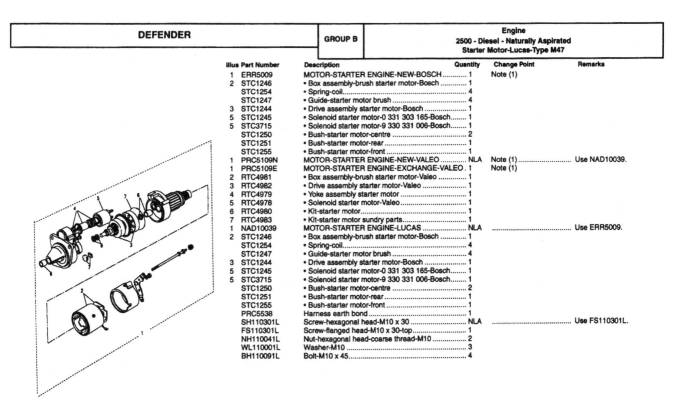

CHANGE POINTS:
(1) To (E)12J 52162C

Illus	Part Number	Description	Quantity	Change Point	Remarks
1	ERR5009E	MOTOR-STARTER ENGINE-EXCHANGE-BOSCH	1	From (E)12J 52163C	
1	ERR5009	MOTOR-STARTER ENGINE-NEW-BOSCH	1	From (E)12J 52163C	
2	STC1246	• Box assembly-brush starter motor-Bosch	1		
3	STC1254	• Spring-coil	4		
4	STC1247	• Guide-starter motor brush	4		
5	STC1244	• Drive assembly starter motor-Bosch	1		
6	STC1245	• Solenoid starter motor-0 331 303 165-Bosch	1		
6	STC3715	• Solenoid starter motor-9 330 331 006-Bosch	1		
7	STC1250	• Bush-starter motor-centre	2		
8	STC1251	• Bush-starter motor-rear	1		
9	STC1255	• Bush-starter motor-front	1		

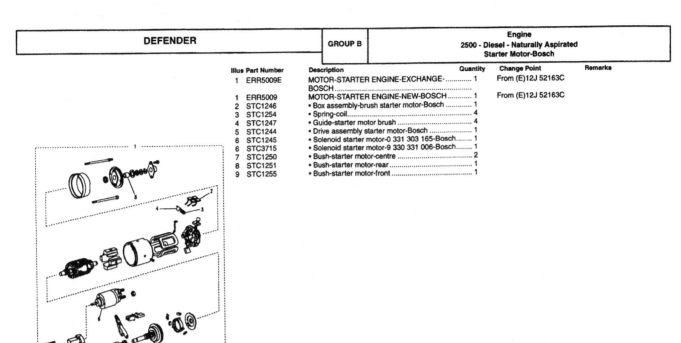

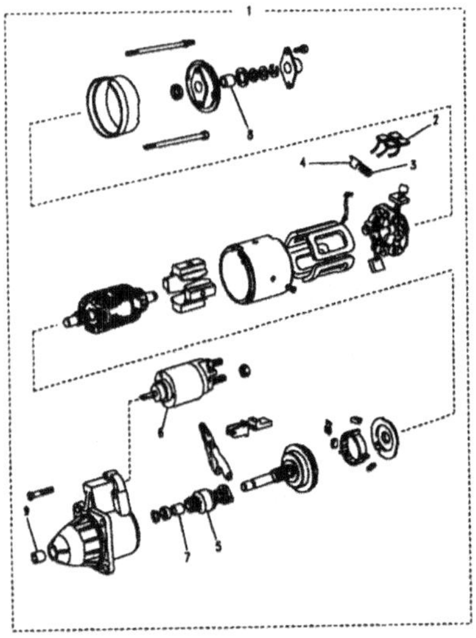

Illus	Part Number	Description	Quantity	Change Point	Remarks
1	ETC7336	Housing assembly-clutch	1	To (V) January 1993	
1	ERR3920	Housing assembly-clutch	1	From (V) January 1993	
2	TE110061L	Stud-M10 x 30	11		
3	ERC9240	Stud-M10	1		
4	TE106041L	Stud	2	To (E)12J 10960C	
5	ERC7295	Plug-rubber	2		
6	ERC6432	O ring	1	To (E)12J 10960C	
20	NH110041L	Nut-hexagonal head-coarse thread-M10	11		
7	FS110301L	Screw-flanged head-M10 x 30-top	6		
8	BH110091L	Bolt-M10 x 45	2		
9	WA110061L	Washer-M10	8		
10	ERC9404	Bracket harness	2		
11	ETC5780	FLYWHEEL ENGINE	1		
12	568431	• Gear-ring-flywheel engine	1		
13	502116	• Dowel-flywheel to crankshaft	3		

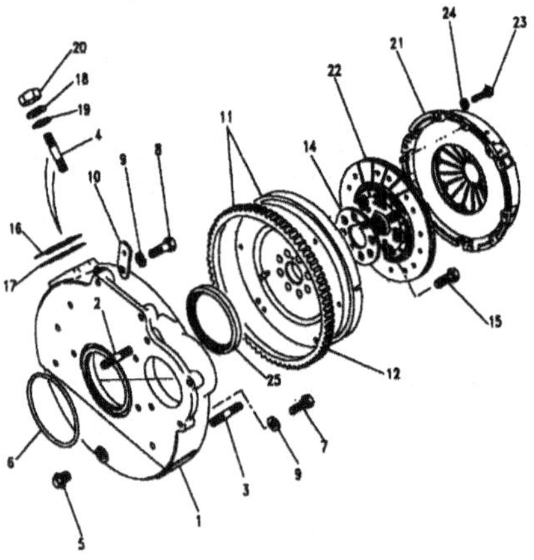

Illus	Part Number	Description	Quantity	Change Point	Remarks
14	ERC4658	Plate-reinforcement	NLA	To (V) December 1993	Engineering have found that the reinforcing plate is not required. When refitting flywheel omit plate , and fit new bolts ERR4574..
15	ERC6551	Bolt-fixing flywheel crankshaft-long	8	To (V) December 1993	
15	ERR4574	Bolt-fixing flywheel crankshaft-short	8	From (V) December 1993	
	ETC5155	Nut-connecting rod	8	To (E)12J 45357	
16	56140	Plate assembly	1	To (E)12J 10960C	
17	50216	Washer	1		
18	WL106001L	Washer-sprung-M6	1		
19	WA106041L	Washer-6mm	2		
20	NH106041L	Nut-hexagonal-nyloc-M6	2		
	STC8358	KIT-CLUTCH	1	Note (1)	Except 130"
21	FTC575	• Cover-clutch assembly	NLA		Use URB100760.
22	FTC2149	• Plate-clutch-driven	NLA		Use FTC4204.
	FRC9568	• BEARING-CLUTCH RELEASE	NLA		Use FTC5200.
	FRC4078	• • Sleeve-guide clutch	1		
	FTC5200	Bearing-clutch release			
21	FTC575	Cover-clutch assembly	NLA		Use URB100760.
21	URB100760	Cover-clutch assembly	1		
22	FTC2149	Plate-clutch-driven	NLA		Use FTC4204.
23	SX108201L	Bolt-M8 x 20	6		
24	WL108001L	Washer-sprung-M8	6		
25	ERR2532	Seal-crankshaft rear	1		

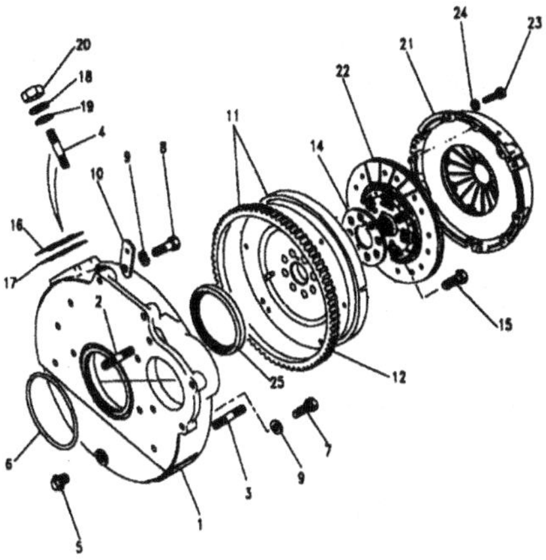

CHANGE POINTS:
(1) To (V) MA 962814

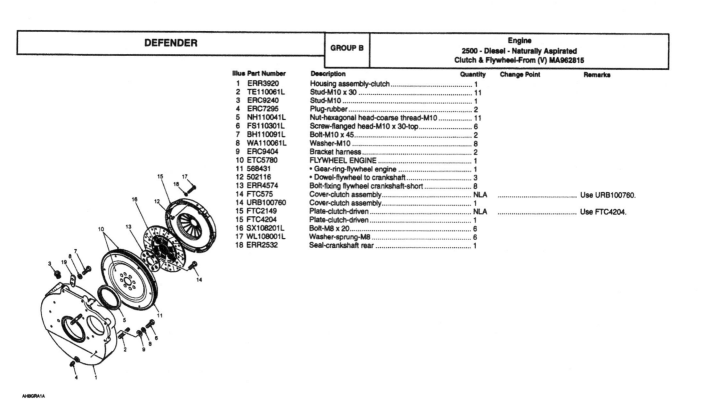

Illus	Part Number	Description	Quantity	Change Point	Remarks
1	ERR3920	Housing assembly-clutch	1		
2	TE110061L	Stud-M10 x 30	11		
3	ERC9240	Stud-M10	1		
4	ERC7295	Plug-rubber	2		
5	NH110041L	Nut-hexagonal head-coarse thread-M10	11		
6	FS110301L	Screw-flanged head-M10 x 30-top	6		
7	BH110091L	Bolt-M10 x 45	2		
8	WA110061L	Washer-M10	8		
9	ERC9404	Bracket harness	2		
10	ETC5780	FLYWHEEL ENGINE	1		
11	568431	• Gear-ring-flywheel engine	1		
12	502116	• Dowel-flywheel to crankshaft	3		
13	ERR4574	Bolt-fixing flywheel crankshaft-short	8		
14	FTC575	Cover-clutch assembly	NLA		Use URB100760.
14	URB100760	Cover-clutch assembly	1		
15	FTC2149	Plate-clutch-driven	NLA		Use FTC4204.
15	FTC4204	Plate-clutch-driven	1		
16	SX108201L	Bolt-M8 x 20	6		
17	WL108001L	Washer-sprung-M8	6		
18	ERR2532	Seal-crankshaft rear	1		

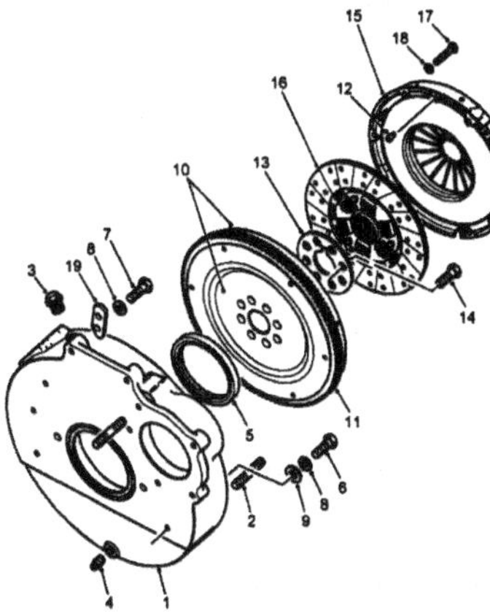

AHBGRA1A

Illus	Part Number	Description	Quantity	Change Point	Remarks
1	ETC5700	Engine assembly-power unit	1	From (E)19J 00001C	Note (1)
1	ETC6881	Engine assembly-power unit	1		Note (2)
1	ETC6882	Engine assembly-power unit	1		Note (3)
1	ETC6883	Engine assembly-power unit	1		Note (4)
1	ETC6884	Engine assembly-power unit			Note (5)
1	ETC6885	Engine assembly-power unit	1		Note (6)
1	ETC6886	Engine assembly-power unit	1		Note (7)
1	ETC6887	Engine assembly-power unit	1		Note (8)

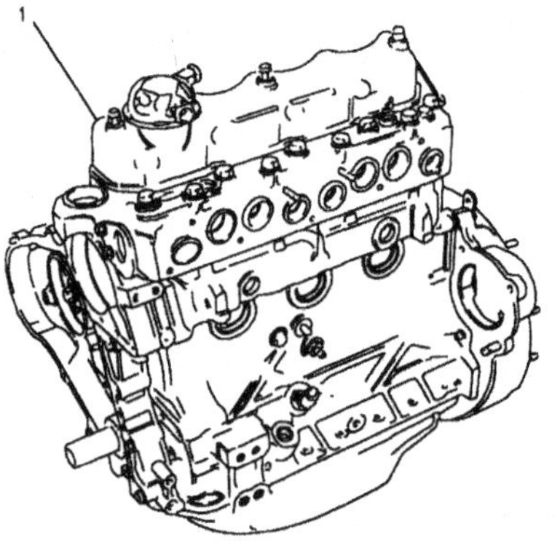

Remarks:
(1) manual steering Europe UK Except air conditioning
(2) power steering UK Europe Except air conditioning
(3) manual steering air conditioning Europe UK
(4) power steering air conditioning Europe UK
(5) manual steering Rest of World Except air conditioning
(6) power steering Rest of World Except air conditioning
(7) manual steering air conditioning Rest of World
(8) power steering air conditioning Rest of World

Illus	Part Number	Description	Quantity	Change Point	Remarks
		ENGINE UNIT-STRIPPED			
1	RTC6802N	new	1		
1	RTC5265E	exchange	1	Note (1)	
1	RTC6802E	exchange	1	Note (2)	

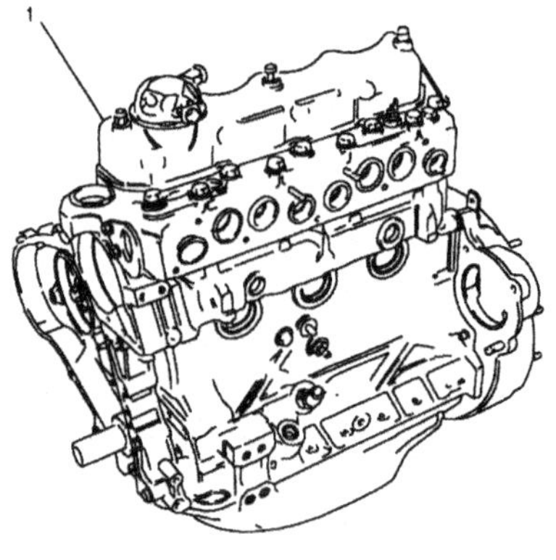

CHANGE POINTS:
(1) To (E)19J 15451C
(2) From (E)19J 15452C

Illus	Part Number	Description	Quantity	Change Point	Remarks
1	RTC6795	Engine assembly-power unit-short	1		

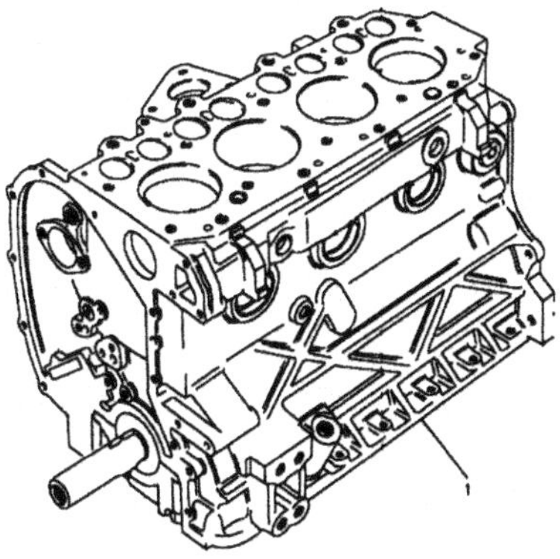

Illus	Part Number	Description	Quantity	Change Point	Remarks
1	ETC8767	CYLINDER BLOCK-ENGINE	1		
2	247965	• Plug-tappet feed hole	1		
3	247127	• Plug-cylinder block oil way	2		
4	ETC4529	• Plug-core	1		
5	501593	• Dowel	10		
6	ERC4996	• Plug-core-side/ends	5		
7	597586	• Plug-core-water rail-ends	3		
8	ERC4644	• Dowel-flywheel housing	2		
9	243959	• Washer-sealing	2		
10	536577	• Plug-drain-gallery pipe	2		
11	90519054	• Bearing-camshaft front	1		
12	90519055	• Bearing-camshaft rear	3		
13	ERC4995	• Plug-core-top fitting	2		
14	ETC7596	Bolt-flanged head	1		
15	504006	Washer	10		
	ERR5034	Plug-camshaft blanking-blanking camshaft-rubber	3		
16	TE108031L	Stud-M8 x 15	1		

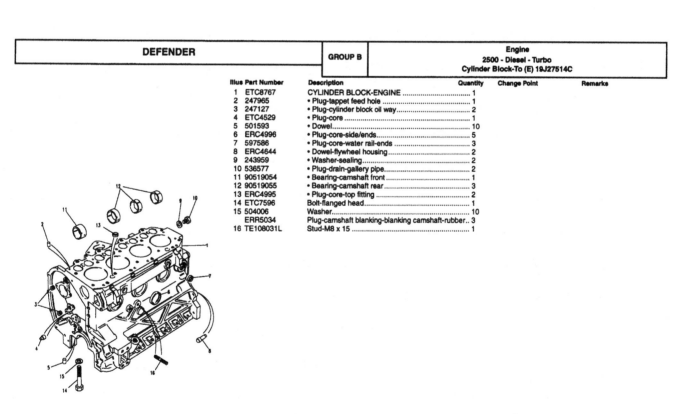

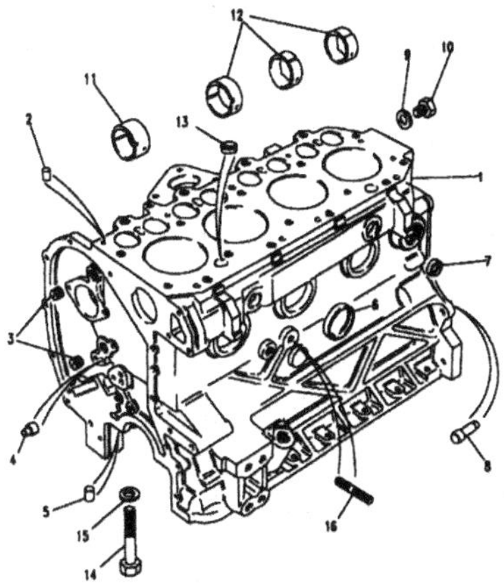

Engine
2500 - Diesel - Turbo
Cylinder Block-From (E) 19J27515C

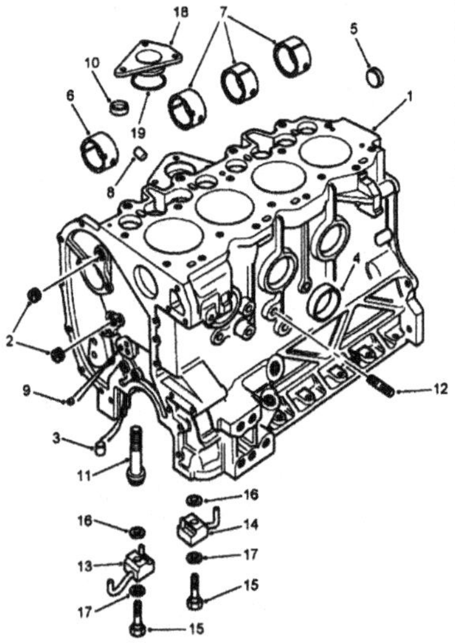

LB0018

Illus	Part Number	Description	Quantity	Change Point	Remarks
1	ERR479	CYLINDER BLOCK-ENGINE	1		
2	247127	• Plug-cylinder block oil way	1		
3	501593	• Dowel	10		
4	ERC4996	• Plug-core	6		
5	597586	• Plug-core	3		
6	ETC8442	• Bearing-camshaft front	1		
7	90519055	• Bearing-camshaft rear	3		
8	ERR5034	• Plug-camshaft blanking-rubber	3		
9	ETC4529	• Plug-core	1		
10	ERC4995	• Plug-core	2		
11	ETC8074	• Bolt	10		
12	TE108031L	• Stud-M8 x 15	1		
13	ETC6531	• Jet assembly-piston cooling-No1-No3	2		
14	ETC6532	• Jet assembly-piston cooling-No2-No4	2		
15	ETC5592	• Valve-bearing housing jet	4		
16	AFU1879L	• Washer-sealing-jet assembly-top	4		
17	AFU1887L	• Washer-sealing-jet assembly-bottom	4		
18	ERR586	• Connector-inlet manifold adaptor	1		
19	ERR531	• O ring	1		
	ERC5086	Pad-insulation	2		
	ERC9410	Plug-drain	1		
	AFU1882L	Washer-sump assembly drain plug	1		
	ERC8864	Gasket	1		
	ERC9404	Bracket harness	1		
	WA108051L	Washer-8mm	1		
	FS108161L	Screw-flanged head-M8 x 16	1		
	ETC8530	Breather assembly-crankcase	1		
	ETC5755	Pipe-adaptor turbocharger	1		

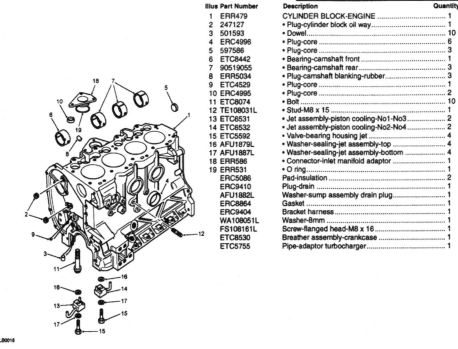

Engine
2500 - Diesel - Turbo
Cover Side

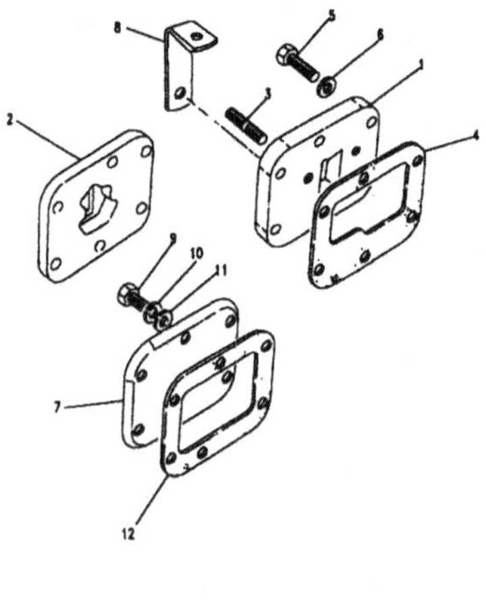

Illus	Part Number	Description	Quantity	Change Point	Remarks
1	ERC9073	COVER PLATE-SIDE	1	To (E)19J 14097C	
2	ETC7929	COVER PLATE-SIDE	1	From (E)19J 14098C	
3	TE108041L	• Stud-M8 x 20	2		
4	ERR1475	Gasket-cylinder block side cover	1		
5	FS108251L	Screw-flanged head-M8 x 25	NLA		Use FS108257L.
6	WL108001L	Washer-sprung-M8	6		
7	541010	Breather assembly-crankcase	1		
8	ERC9480	Bracket	1		
9	FS108207L	Screw-flanged head-M8 x 20	1		
10	WA108051L	Washer-8mm	3		
11	WL108001L	Washer-sprung-M8	6		
12	ERR3605	Gasket-cylinder block side cover-asbestos	NLA		Use ERR2026.
12	ERR2026	Gasket-cylinder block side cover-asbestos free	1		

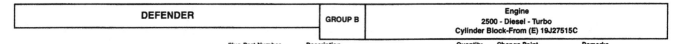

DEFENDER

GROUP B

Engine
2500 - Diesel - Turbo
Crankshaft & Bearings

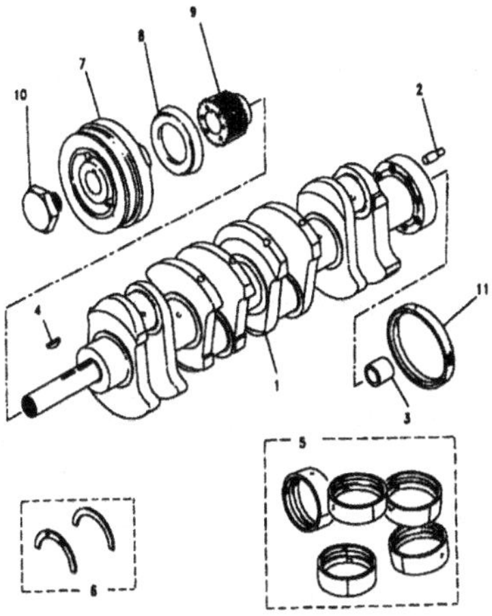

Illus	Part Number	Description	Quantity	Change Point	Remarks
1	ETC8829	Crankshaft-engine	1	To (V) August 1989	
1	ERR1181	CRANKSHAFT-ENGINE	1	From (V) August 1989	
2	ERR1630	• Dowel-flywheel to crankshaft	1		
3	8566L	• Bush-crankshaft	1		
4	235770	• Key-crankshaft	2		
		SET-CRANKSHAFT BEARINGS			
5	RTC4783	standard.	NLA		Use STC3395.
5	STC3395	standard.	1		
5	RTC478310	0.010" undersize	1		
		WASHER-CRANKSHAFT THRUST			
6	RTC2825	standard.-pair	A/R	Note (1)	
6	538131	oversize.-0.0025"-pair	A/R		
6	538132	oversize.-0.005"-pair	A/R		
6	538134	oversize.-0.01"-pair	A/R		
7	ETC4077	Pulley & torsional vibration damper-crankshaft	1		Note (1)
7	ETC4105	Pulley & torsional vibration damper-crankshaft	1		Note (2)
7	ERC6859	Pulley & torsional vibration damper-crankshaft	1		Note (3)
7	ERC6860	Pulley & torsional vibration damper-crankshaft	1		Note (4)
7	ERC6861	PULLEY & TORSIONAL VIBRATION DAMPER-CRANKSHAFT	1		Note (5)
	WL108001L	• Washer-sprung-M8	4		
	FS108251L	Screw-flanged head-M8 x 25	NLA		Use FS108257L.
	SH108251L	Screw-hexagonal head-M8 x 25	NLA		Use SH108257 Use Dacromet coated alternative..
	FS108251L	Screw-flanged head-M8 x 25	NLA		Use FS108257L.
	WL108001	Washer-sprung-M8	NLA		Use WL108001L.
	WL108001L	Washer-sprung-M8	1		
8	ETC4390	Flinger-crankshaft pulley	1		
9	ERC9765	Pulley-crankshaft	1		
10	ETC7934	Bolt-crankshaft pulley	1	To (V) August 1989	
10	ERR605	Bolt-crankshaft pulley	1	From (V) August 1989	
6	ERR705	Washer-crankshaft thrust	1		
11	ERR1535	Seal-crankshaft rear	NLA		Use ERR2532.
11	ERR2532	Seal-crankshaft rear	1		

CHANGE POINTS:
(1) To (V) August 1989

Remarks:
(1) manual steering Except air conditioning
(2) power steering air conditioning Optional on
(3) power steering air conditioning Standard on
(4) manual steering air conditioning
(5) power steering Except air conditioning

DEFENDER

GROUP B

Engine
2500 - Diesel - Turbo
Piston & Rings

Illus	Part Number	Description	Quantity	Change Point	Remarks
1	ETC8676	Piston-engine-standard	NLA		Use ETC8670S.
1	ETC8670S	PISTON-ENGINE-STANDARD.	4		
2	RTC6174S	• Kit-piston ring-standard.	4		
3	266945	• Circlip-piston	8		
1	RTC599320	PISTON-ENGINE-0.020" OVERSIZE	4		
2	RTC617420	• Kit-piston ring-oversize.	4		
3	266945	• Circlip-piston	8		
4	ERR593	ROD ASSEMBLY-CONNECTING	4		
5	247583	• Bush	4		
6	ERC8751	• Bolt-connecting rod	8	To (E)19J 23245	
6	ETC7357	• Bolt-connecting rod	8	From (E)19J 23246E	
7	ETC5155	• Nut-connecting rod	8	To (E)19J 23245	
7	ETC8191	• Nut-connecting rod	8	From (E)19J 23246E	
8	RTC2993	Set-connecting rod big end half bearing-standard.	1		
8	RTC299310	Set-connecting rod big end half bearing-0.010" undersize	1		

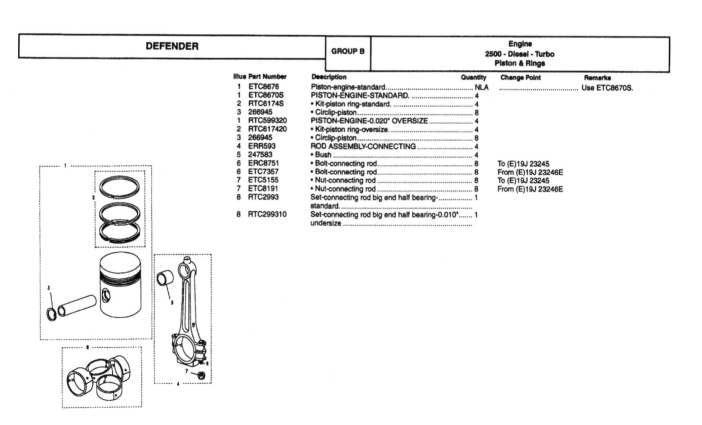

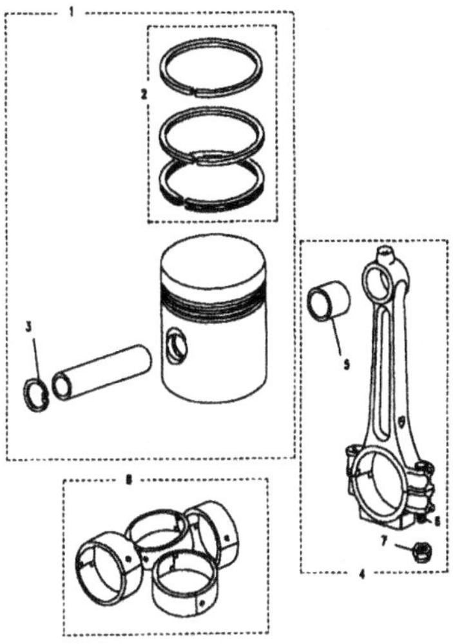

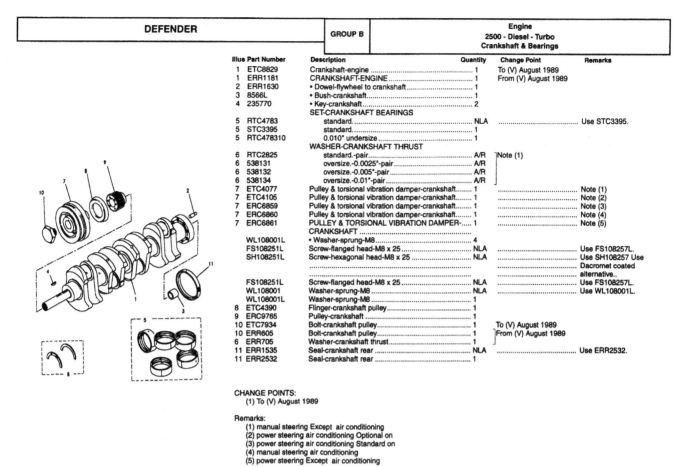

Illus	Part Number	Description	Quantity	Change Point	Remarks
1	ERR4716	SUMP-ENGINE OIL	1		
2	599552	• Plug-drain	1		
3	FRC4808	• Washer-sealing-sump drain plug	1		
4	FS108161L	Screw-flanged head-M8 x 16	22		
5	WL108001L	Washer-sprung-M8	22		
6	ERC8980	Tube assembly-oil dipstick	1		
7	532387	O ring	1		
8	ETC7867	Dipstick-oil	1		

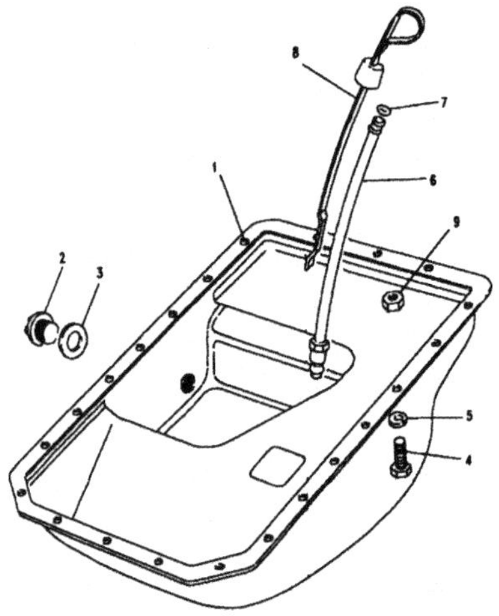

Illus	Part Number	Description	Quantity	Change Point	Remarks
1	NRC5434	Bracket-engine mounting-RH	1		
2	NRC9557	Bracket-engine mounting-LH	1		
3	SH112251L	Screw-hexagonal head-M12 x 25	4		
4	WL112001L	Washer	4		
5	NRC9560	Mounting-engine rubber	NLA	To (C) JA 920702	Use ANR1808.
5	ANR1808	Mounting-engine rubber	1	From (C) JA 920703	
6	NH110041L	Nut-hexagonal head-coarse thread-M10	4		
7	WC110061L	Washer-plain-M10-oversize	2		
8	WL110001L	Washer-M10	4		

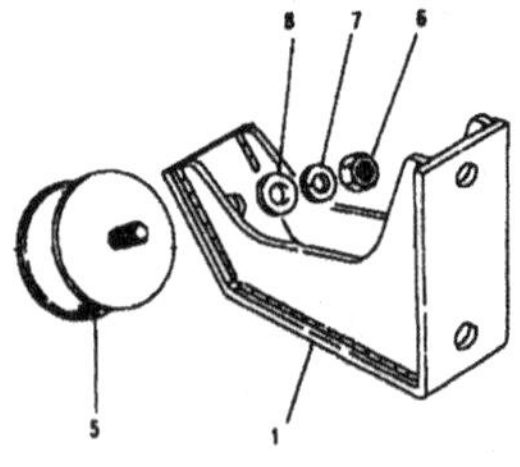

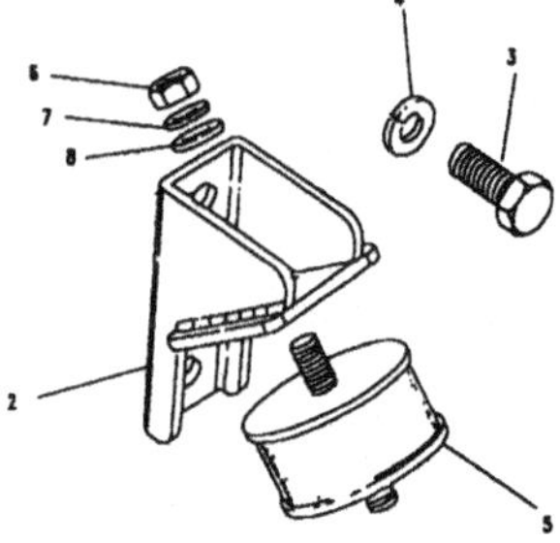

DEFENDER	GROUP B	Engine 2500 - Diesel - Turbo Front Cover

Illus	Part Number	Description	Quantity	Change Point	Remarks
1	ETC4421	Cover-engine-front	1		
1	ETC5672	Cover-engine-front	1		
2	6395L	Dowel	1		
3	ETC5064	Seal-camshaft oil	1		
4	ETC5065	Seal-crankshaft front oil	NLA		Use ERR1632.
4	ERR1632	Seal-crankshaft front oil	NLA		Use ERR6490.
4	ERR6490	Seal-crankshaft front oil	1		
5	538038	Gasket-coolant pump body-asbestos	NLA		Use ERR1607.
5	ERR1607	Gasket-coolant pump body-to front cover-asbestos free	1		
6	538039	Gasket-timing gear housing drain plate	1		
7	FB108111L	Bolt-flanged head-M8 x 55	1		
8	FB108121L	Bolt-flanged head-M8 x 60	4		
9	BH108201L	Bolt-hexagonal head-M8 x 100	1		
10	FB108251	Bolt-flanged head-M8 x 125	2		
11	WA108051L	Washer-8mm	8		
12	ETC4422	Cover-plate.	1		
12	ETC5675	Cover-plate.	1		
13	ETC4154	Seal	1		
14	BH108131L	Bolt-hexagonal head-M8 x 65	1		
15	WA108051L	Washer-8mm	1		
16	SH108121L	Screw-hexagonal head-M8 x 12	1		
16	FS108251L	Screw-flanged head-M8 x 25	NLA		Use FS108257L.
17	WA108051L	Washer-8mm	8		
18	ERC6479	Bracket	1		
19	ETC4996	Bolt	1		
20	FS108207L	Screw-flanged head-M8 x 20	3		
21	WL108001L	Washer-sprung-M8	3		
22	ERC7295	Plug-rubber	1		
23	ERC9404	Bracket harness	1		
24	ETC4058	Plate	1		
25	ETC4122	Gasket-sealing-asbestos	NLA		Use ERR3615.
25	ERR3615	Gasket-sealing-asbestos free	1		
26	FS106201L	Screw-flanged head-M6 x 20	4		
26	FS106207L	Screw-flanged head-M6 x 20	4		
27	WA106041L	Washer-6mm	1		
28	ETC4063	Strainer-oil	1		
29	ERC9199	Nut-bulkhead plate	1		

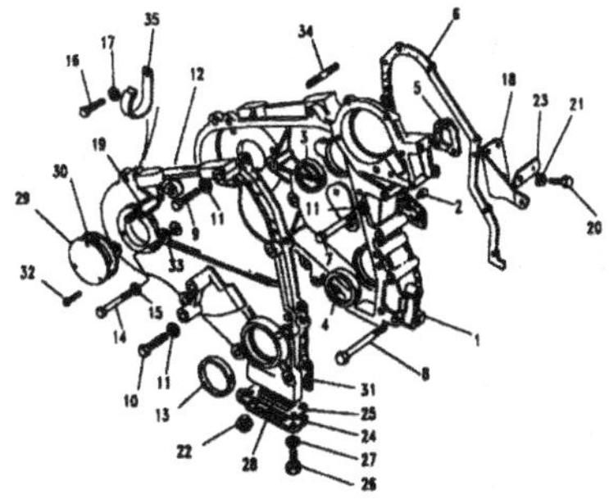

DEFENDER	GROUP B	Engine 2500 - Diesel - Turbo Front Cover

Illus	Part Number	Description	Quantity	Change Point	Remarks
		GASKET-COVER FRONT			
30	ERC9201	asbestos	NLA		Use ERR3614.
30	ERR3614	asbestos free	1		
31	ETC4420	asbestos	NLA		Use ERR3616.
31	ERR3616	asbestos free	1		
32	SE106121L	Screw-pan-pan head-M6 x 12	3		
33	ETC4124	Washer-sealing-asbestos	NLA		Use ERR3604.
33	ERR3604	Washer-sealing-asbestos free	1		
34	ETC4873	Stud	3		
35	ETC4630	Bracket-mounting	1		

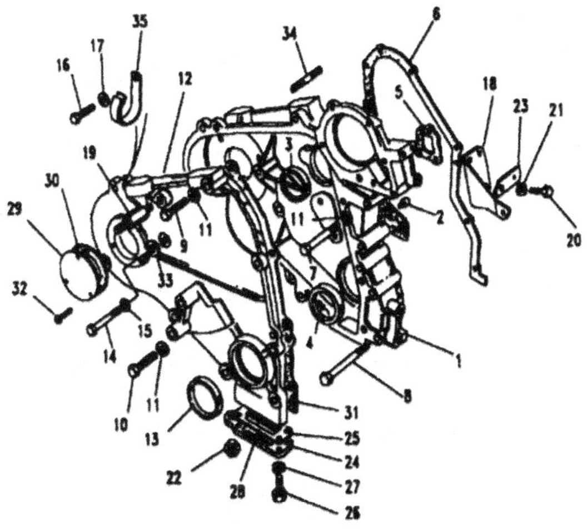

Illus	Part Number	Description	Quantity	Change Point	Remarks
1	ETC7333	Belt-engine timing	1		
2	ERC8861	Tensioner-timing belt	1		
3	4594L	Washer-plain	2		
4	TE108061L	Stud-M8 x 30	2		
5	NY108041L	Nut-nyloc-M8	2		

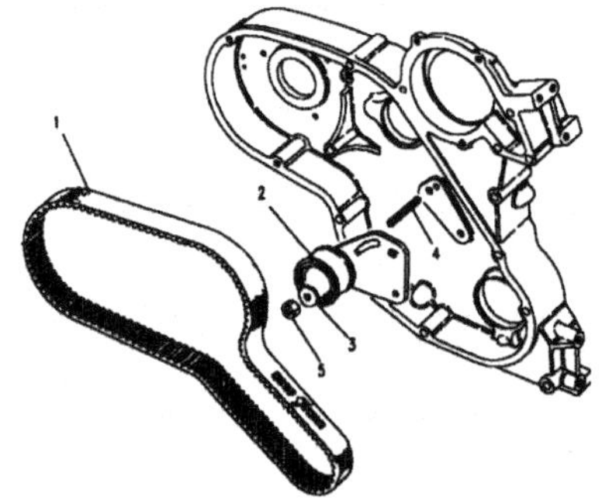

Illus	Part Number	Description	Quantity	Change Point	Remarks
1	STC635	PUMP ASSEMBLY-ENGINE COOLANT-A127 ALTERNATOR	1		
	ERC7312	• Plug	1		
	232046	• Washer-copper	1		
2	ERC5600	• Screw	1		
3	WL106001L	• Washer-sprung-M6	1		
4	ERC5655	• Gasket-coolant pump body	1		
5	ETC4785	Pulley coolant pump	1		
6	FS108161L	Screw-flanged head-M8 x 16	4		
7	WL108001L	Washer-sprung-M8	4		
8	ERC7489	Spacer	1		
9	ERR3380	Fan-cooling	1		Europe UK
10	ETC7238	Coupling-engine fan viscous	1		
11	4589L	Washer-plain	4		
12	ERC5709	Screw-M6 x 14	4		
9	ETC6852	Fan-cooling	1		Rest of World
10	ETC6841	Coupling-engine fan viscous	1		
11	587405	Washer-plain	4		
12	SH505051L	Screw-hexagonal head-5/16UNC x 5/8	4		
13	FS108307L	Screw-flanged head-M8 x 30	3		
13	FS108301L	Screw-flanged head-M8 x 30	NLA		Use FS108307L.
14	WL108001	Washer-sprung-M8	NLA		Use WL108001L.
15	BH108151L	Bolt-hexagonal head-M8 x 70	1		
16	BH108161L	Bolt-hexagonal head-M8 x 80	2		
17	BH108171L	Bolt-hexagonal head-M8 x 85	1		
18	WL108001	Washer-sprung-M8	NLA		Use WL108001L.
19	ERC5654	Hose assembly water-outlet	1		
20	CN100408L	Clip-hose	2		
21	ETC7939	Belt-polyvee alternator	1		

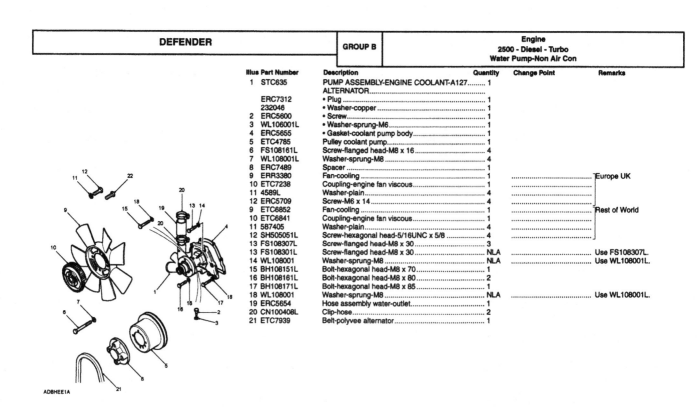

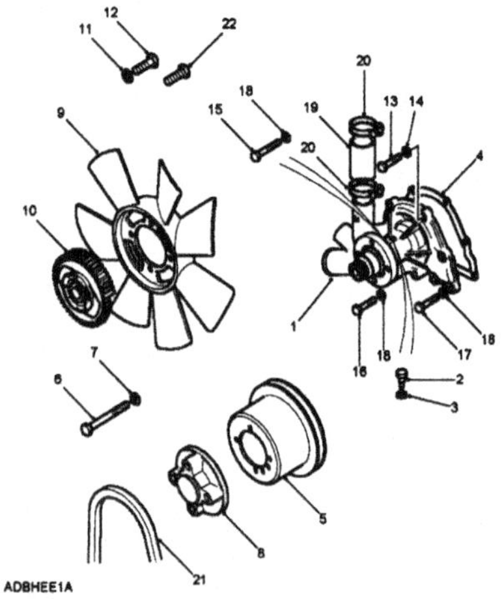

ADBHEE1A

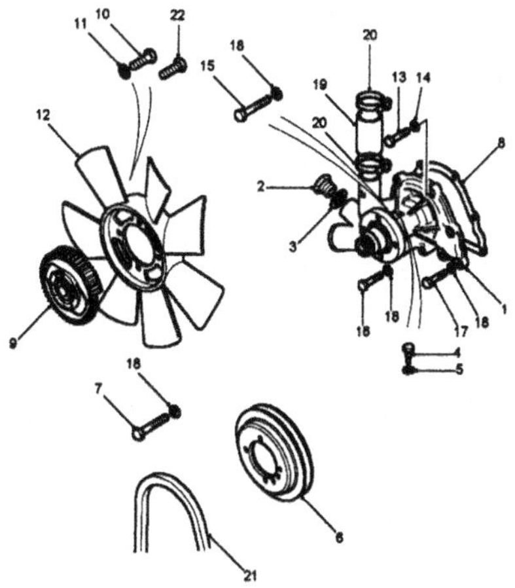

ADBHEE2A

Illus	Part Number	Description	Quantity	Change Point	Remarks
1	STC635	PUMP ASSEMBLY-ENGINE COOLANT-A127 ALTERNATOR	1		
2	ERC7312	• Plug	1		
3	232046	• Washer-copper	1		
4	ERC5600	• Screw	1		
5	WL106001L	• Washer-sprung-M6	1		
8	ERC5655	• Gasket-coolant pump body	1		
6	ETC4785	Pulley coolant pump			
9	ETC7238	Coupling-engine fan viscous	1		UK Europe
10	ERC5709	Screw-M6 x 14	4		
11	4589L	Washer-plain	4		
12	ERC7834	Fan-cooling	NLA		Use ETC7554. Europe UK
12	ETC7554	Fan-cooling-7 blade	NLA		Use ERR3380. Europe UK
12	ERR3380	Fan-cooling	1		Europe UK
9	ETC6841	Coupling-engine fan viscous	1		Rest of World
22	SH505051L	Screw-hexagonal head-5/16UNC x 5/8	4		
11	587405	Washer-plain	4		
12	ETC6852	Fan-cooling	1		
13	FS108301L	Screw-flanged head-M8 x 30	NLA		Use FS108307L.
13	FS108307L	Screw-flanged head-M8 x 30	3		
14	WL108001	Washer-sprung-M8	NLA		Use WL108001L.
14	WL108001L	Washer-sprung-M8	3		
15	BH108151L	Bolt-hexagonal head-M8 x 70	1		
16	BH108161L	Bolt-hexagonal head-M8 x 80	2		
17	BH108171L	Bolt-hexagonal head-M8 x 85	1		
18	WL108001L	Washer-sprung-M8	4		
19	ERC5654	Hose assembly water-outlet	1		
20	CN100408L	Clip-hose	2		
21	ERC6504	Belt-polyvee alternator	NLA		Use ETC7939.
21	ETC7939	Belt-polyvee alternator	1		

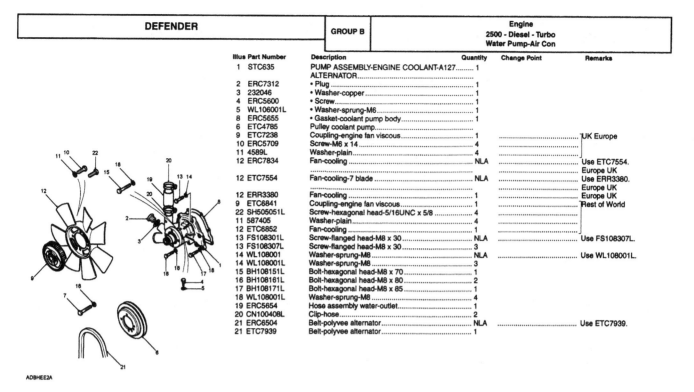

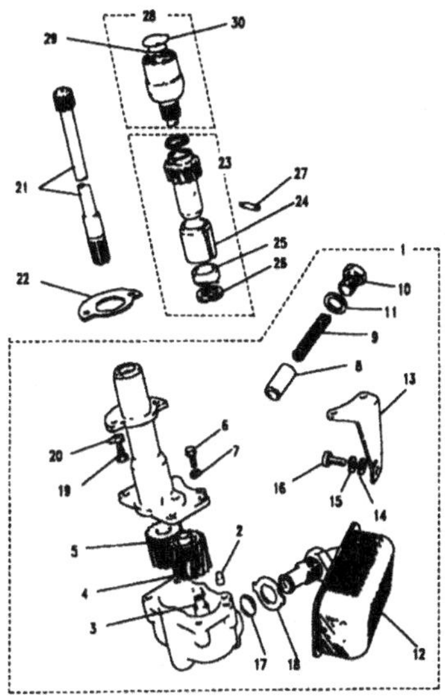

Illus	Part Number	Description	Quantity	Change Point	Remarks
1	ERR1117	PUMP BODY ASSEMBLY-ENGINE OIL	1		
2	236257	• Dowel	2		
3	ERR1063	• Spindle-oil pump	1		
4	ERR1088	• Gear-oil pump idler-10 teeth	1		
5	ERC9706	• Gear-oil pump-10 teeth	1		
6	FS108207L	• Screw-flanged head-M8 x 20	4		
7	WL108001L	• Washer-sprung-M8	4		
8	ETC4880	• Plunger-oil pump relief valve	1		
9	564456	• Spring-oil pump relief valve	1		
10	564455	• Plug	1		
11	232044	• Washer-sealing	1		
12	ERC7530	• Strainer-oil	1		
13	ERC7940	• Bracket-pump/actuator	1		
14	WA108051L	• Washer-8mm	1		
15	WL108001L	• Washer-sprung-M8	1		
16	FS108207L	• Screw-flanged head-M8 x 20	1		
17	244488	• O ring	1		
18	244487	• Washer-lock	1		
20	247665	• Washer-lock	2		
19	FS108251L	Screw-flanged head-M8 x 25	NLA		Use FS108257L.
21	ERR850	Shaft-oil pump	1		
22	ERC8408	Gasket-cylinder block oil pump-asbestos	NLA		Use ERR3606.
22	ERR3606	Gasket-cylinder block oil pump-asbestos free	1		
23	ETC6139	DRIVE ASSEMBLY-OIL PUMP	1		
24	522745	• Bush	1		
25	ETC6137	• Washer-thrust	1		
26	ETC6138	• Ring-snap	1		
27	ETC6142	• Screw	1		
28	ETC4706	COUPLING	1		
29	RTC6167	• O ring-inner	1		
30	RTC6168	• O ring-outer	1		

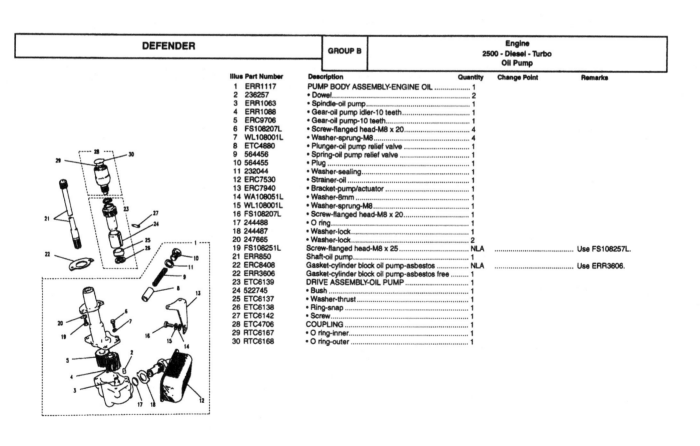

DEFENDER

GROUP B

Engine
2500 - Diesel - Turbo
Oil Pump & Filter

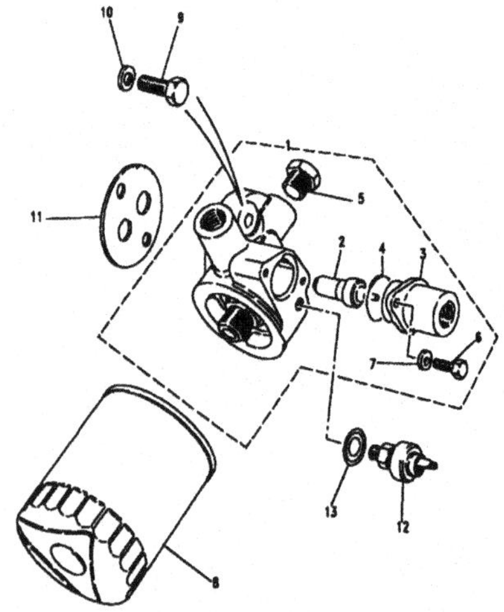

Illus	Part Number	Description	Quantity	Change Point	Remarks
1	ERR1347	ADAPTOR ASSEMBLY-OIL FILTER	1		2500 cc Diesel Turbo
2	ERC5923	• Thermostat assembly-oil	1		
3	ETC4022	• Adaptor-oil filter	1		
4	ERC5913	• O ring	1		
5	ETC4021	• Plug	1		
6	SH106141L	• Screw-hexagonal head-M6 x 14	2		
7	WA106041L	• Washer-6mm	2		
8	ERR3340	Cartridge-engine oil filter	1		
	PRC4372	Transducer oil temperature-24V	1		Optional
9	FS110301L	Screw-flanged head-M10 x 30-top	2		
10	WL110001L	Washer-M10	2		
11	ETC5276	Gasket-cylinder block to oil filter adaptor-asbestos	1		
11	ERR3607	Gasket-cylinder block to oil filter adaptor-asbestos free	1		
12	PRC6387	Switch-oil pressure engine	1		
13	232039	Washer-sealing	1		
	NRC8618	Coupling	1		Optional
	PRC4043	Transducer oil pressure	1		
	ETC4033	Adaptor-oil pressure switch	1		
	ETC4034	Bolt-banjo	1		

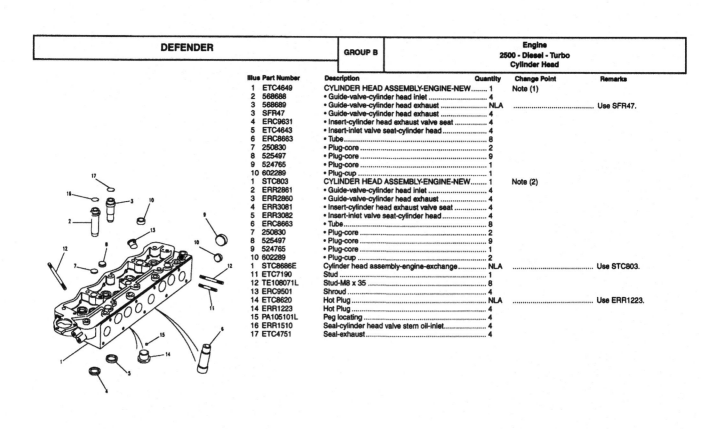

DEFENDER

GROUP B

Engine
2500 - Diesel - Turbo
Cylinder Head

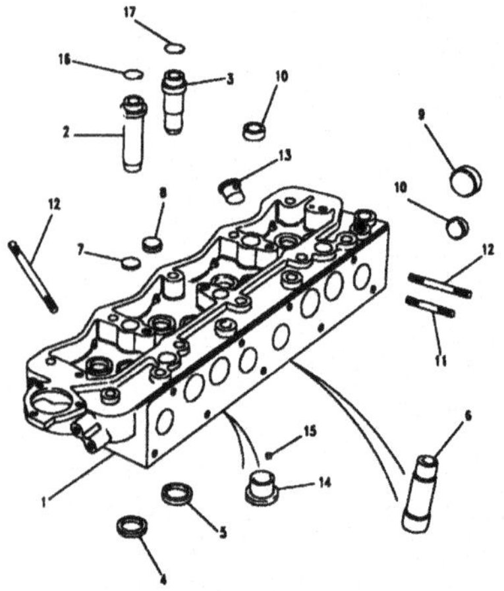

Illus	Part Number	Description	Quantity	Change Point	Remarks
1	ETC4649	CYLINDER HEAD ASSEMBLY-ENGINE-NEW	1	Note (1)	
2	568688	• Guide-valve-cylinder head inlet	4		
3	568689	• Guide-valve-cylinder head exhaust	NLA		Use SFR47.
3	SFR47	• Guide-valve-cylinder head exhaust	4		
4	ERC9631	• Insert-cylinder head exhaust valve seat	4		
5	ETC4643	• Insert-inlet valve seat-cylinder head	4		
6	ERC8663	• Tube	8		
7	250830	• Plug-core	2		
8	525497	• Plug-core	9		
9	524765	• Plug-core	1		
10	602289	• Plug-cup	1		
1	STC803	CYLINDER HEAD ASSEMBLY-ENGINE-NEW	1	Note (2)	
2	ERR2861	• Guide-valve-cylinder head inlet	4		
3	ERR2860	• Guide-valve-cylinder head exhaust	4		
4	ERR3081	• Insert-cylinder head exhaust valve seat	4		
5	ERR3082	• Insert-inlet valve seat-cylinder head	4		
6	ERC8663	• Tube	8		
7	250830	• Plug-core	2		
8	525497	• Plug-core	9		
9	524765	• Plug-core	1		
10	602289	• Plug-cup	2		
1	STC8686E	Cylinder head assembly-engine-exchange	NLA		Use STC803.
11	ETC7190	Stud	1		
12	TE108071L	Stud-M8 x 35	8		
13	ERC9501	Shroud	4		
14	ETC8620	Hot Plug	NLA		Use ERR1223.
14	ERR1223	Hot Plug	4		
15	PA105101L	Peg locating	4		
16	ERR1510	Seal-cylinder head valve stem oil-inlet	4		
17	ETC4751	Seal-exhaust	4		

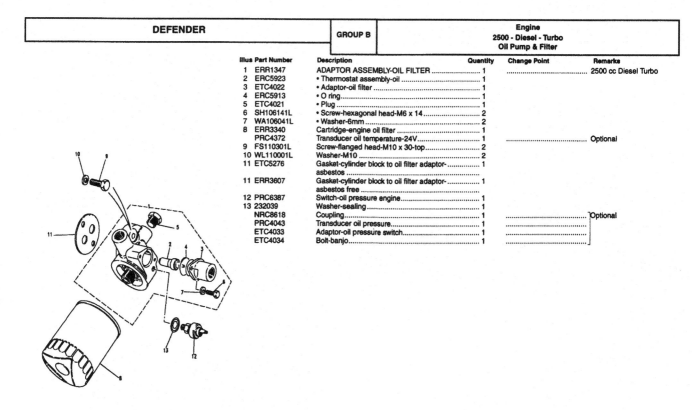

CHANGE POINTS:
(1) To (E)19J 25183C
(2) From (E)19J 25184C

DEFENDER | GROUP B | Engine 2500 - Diesel - Turbo Cylinder Head Components

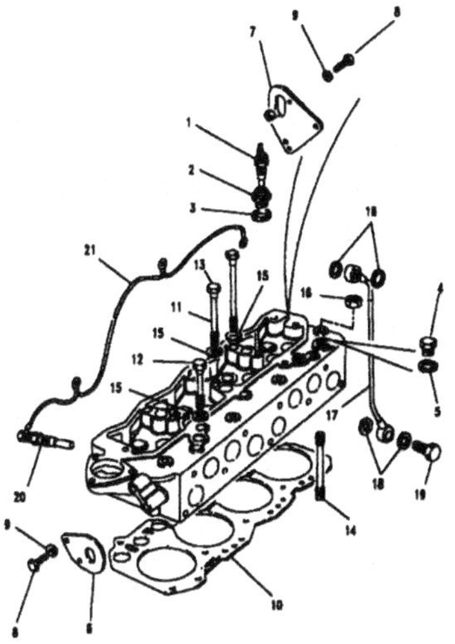

Illus	Part Number	Description	Quantity	Change Point	Remarks
1	PRC2505	Transducer coolant temperature	1	To (E)19J 25183C	
1	PRC6663	Transducer coolant temperature	1	From (E)19J 25184C	
2	ERC9432	Connector-inlet manifold adaptor	1	To (E)19J 25183C	
3	10802070	Washer	1		
4	ERC9448	Plug	1	To (E)19J 25183C	
4	RTC6851	Plug	1	From (E)19J 25184C	
5	AFU1890L	Washer-sealing	1	To (E)19J 25183C	
5	243960	Washer-sealing	1	From (E)19J 25184C	
6	ERC2254	Bracket-lifting body-front	1		
7	ETC5816	Bracket-lifting body-rear	1		
8	FS108207	Screw-bracket to head-flanged head	NLA		Use FS108207L.
8	FS108207L	Screw-bracket to head-flanged head-M8 x 20	4		
9	WL108001L	Washer-sprung-M8	4		
10	ERR3618	Gasket-cylinder head-asbestos free	1		
11	247051	Bolt-head to block-1/2UNF x 4 9/16	9		
12	247683	Bolt-head to block-1/2UNF x 2 1/2	2		
13	247723	Bolt-head to block-1/2UNF x 6	5		
14	90518466	Stud-head to block	2		
15	ERC6821	Washer-plain	18		
16	NH608061L	Nut-hexagonal	2		
17	275679	Pipe assembly-engine oil feed	1		
18	ETC6510	Washer-sealing	4		
19	ETC4498	Bolt-banjo	2		
20	ERC8450	Plug-heater ignition	4		
21	PRC6295	Cable-heater plug ignition	1		

DEFENDER | GROUP B | Engine 2500 - Diesel - Turbo Rockershaft

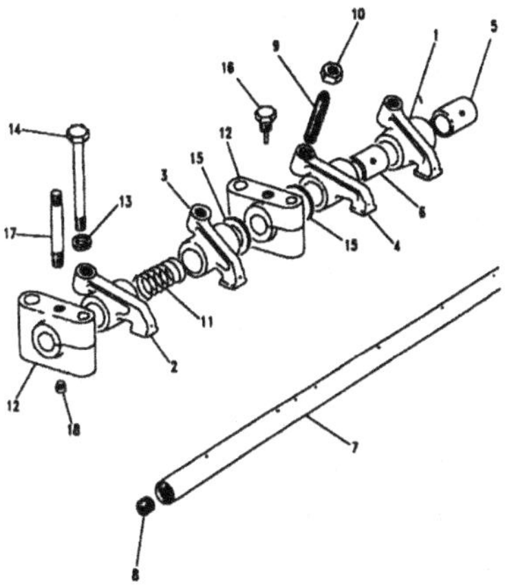

Illus	Part Number	Description	Quantity	Change Point	Remarks
1	ERC9060	ARM-EXHAUST VALVE ROCKER-RH	2		
2	ERC9059	ARM-EXHAUST VALVE ROCKER-LH	2		
3	247738	• Arm & bush assembly-exhaust valve rocker	4		
4	ERC9056	ARM-INLET VALVE ROCKER-RH	2		
5	ERC9055	ARM-INLET VALVE ROCKER-LH	2		
6	247737	• Bush-inlet rockers	4		
7	ERC6341	SHAFT-ROCKER	8		
8	ERC6337	• Plug	2		
9	ERC9054	Screw-tappet adjusting	8		
10	NT108041L	Nut-hexagonal head	8		
11	247040	Spring-rocker shaft	4		
12	ERC9137	Bracket-rocker shaft	5		
13	WL108001L	Washer-sprung-M8	5		
14	FB108111L	Bolt-flanged head-M8 x 55	5		
15	247153	Washer-plain	8		
16	ETC4460	Screw	1		
17	TD108091L	Stud-rocker cover fixing-M8	3		
18	277956	Dowel-ring	3		

DEFENDER | **GROUP B** | **Engine**

2500 - Diesel - Turbo
Valves & Tappets

Illus	Part Number	Description	Quantity	Change Point	Remarks
1	507829	TAPPET-ENGINE VALVE MECHANICAL	8		
2	502473	• Slide-tappet guide	8		
3	ERR607	• Tappet-engine valve mechanical	8		
4	ETC4246	• Bolt	8		
5	273069	• Washer-sealing	8		
6	ERR561	• Roller-tappet guide	8		
7	ETC5739	Valve-cylinder head inlet	4		
8	ETC5740	Valve-cylinder head exhaust	4		
9	ERR4175	Cap-valve stem	NLA		Use LJC100270.
10	ERR4640	Spring-cylinder head valve	8		
11	ETC4068	Cap-cylinder head valve spring	8		
12	ETC4069	Cotter-valve	16		
13	546799	Rod-engine push	8		

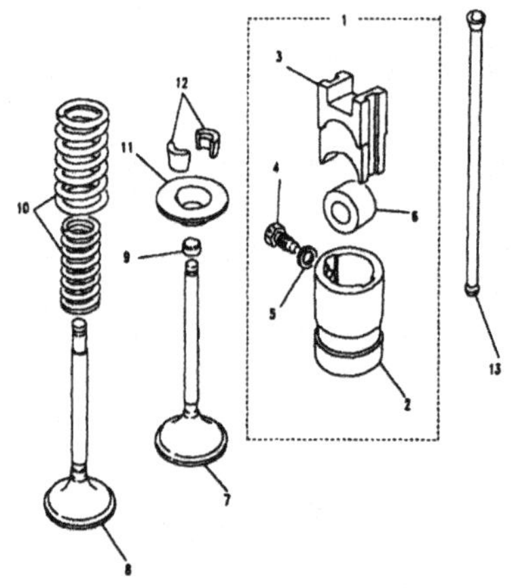

DEFENDER | **GROUP B** | **Engine**

2500 - Diesel - Turbo
Rocker Cover & Breather

Illus	Part Number	Description	Quantity	Change Point	Remarks
1	ETC6924	Cover-valve rocker	1	To (E)19J 15451C	
2	ETC8600	Cover-valve rocker	1	From (E)19J 15452C	
3	ETC6438	Gasket-engine rocker cover	1		
4	273069	Washer-sealing	3		
5	ERC9220	Nut-domed-M8	3		
6	ETC7774	Cap assembly-oil filler	1	To (E)19J 15451C	
7	ETC7909	Cap assembly-oil filler	1	From (E)19J 15452C	
7	ERR737	CAP ASSEMBLY-OIL FILLER	1	From (E)12J 42594C	
8	ERR736	• O ring	1		
8	ERC8049	O ring	1	To (E)19J 15451C	
8	ERR736	O ring	1	From (E)19J 15452C	
9	ETC7187	Hose assembly-breather	1	To (E)19J 15451C	
10	ETC8636	Hose assembly-breather	1	From (E)19J 15452C	
11	ETC7059	Hose assembly-breather-standard air intake	1		
11	RRC5728	Hose assembly-breather-raised air intake	1		
12	CJ600224	Clip-hose	2		
13	ETC5588	Bracket	1		

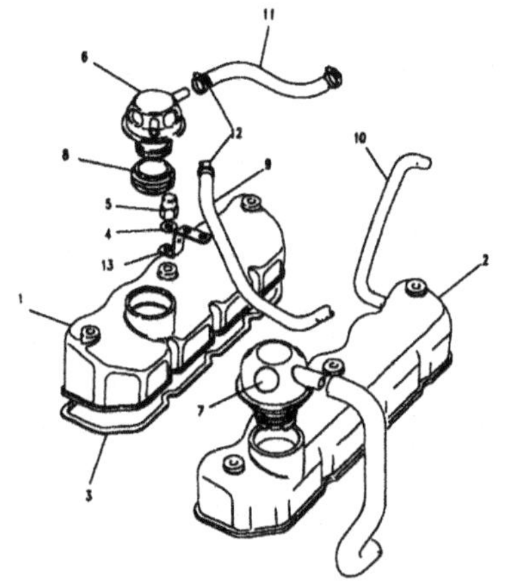

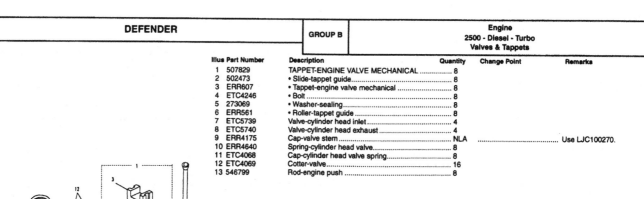

DEFENDER

GROUP B

Engine
2500 - Diesel - Turbo
Camshaft

Illus	Part Number	Description	Quantity	Change Point	Remarks
1	ETC7128	Camshaft assembly-engine	1		
2	ERC1561	Plate-camshaft retaining	1		
3	FS106167P	Screw-flanged head-M6	2		
4	WL106001L	Washer-sprung-M6	2		
5	ETC4014	Pulley-camshaft	1		
6	230313	Key	1		
7	BX110071M	Bolt-hexagonal head-M10 x 35	1		
8	ETC4670	Washer-plain	1		
9	ERC8847	Plate-camshaft pulley retaining	1		
10	ERC8849	O ring	1		
11	ETC4076	O ring	1		
12	2995	Washer-lock	2		

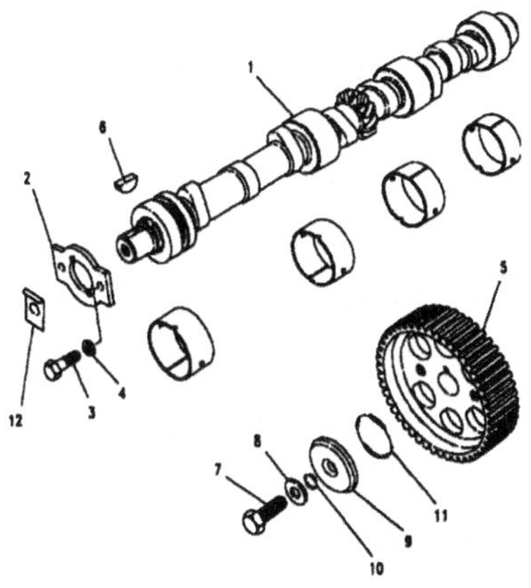

DEFENDER

GROUP B

Engine
2500 - Diesel - Turbo
Thermostat Housing

Illus	Part Number	Description	Quantity	Change Point	Remarks
1	ERC8758	Housing-thermostat	1		
2	602687	Thermostat-engine-82 degrees C	1	....	Standard on
2	ETC4761	Thermostat-engine-74 degrees C	1	....	Optional
3	ERR977	Gasket-thermostat housing-asbestos-top	1		
3	ERR3682	Gasket-thermostat housing-top-asbestos free	1		
4	247874	Gasket-thermostat housing-bottom	1		
5	ERC7510	Hose to pipe-coolant	1		
6	CN100258L	Clip-hose-25mm	2		
7	ETC5967	Elbow-engine coolant outlet	1	....	Except air conditioning
7	ETC5958	Elbow-engine coolant outlet	1	....	Air conditioning
8	ETC5965	Bracket-radiator pipe to cowl	1		
9	BH106151L	Bolt-M6 x 75	3		
10	WL106001L	Washer-sprung-M6	3		
11	624091	Adaptor-pipe coolant	2		
12	243959	Washer-sealing	2		
13	PRC3359	Switch-engine thermostat-Green	1		
13	PRC3505	Switch-engine thermostat-Yellow..	1		
14	C457593	Washer-sealing	1		

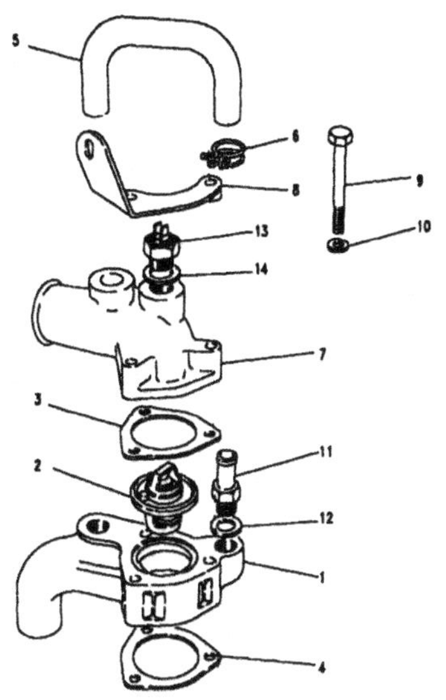

Illus	Part Number	Description	Quantity	Change Point	Remarks
1	ETC6492	Manifold-engine inlet	1		
2	525428	Plug	2		
3	ETC7750	Gasket-inlet manifold	1		
4	564308	Clamp	4		
5	574654	Clip	1		
6	NH108065L	Nut	1		
7	WA108051L	Washer-8mm	1		
8	ETC6910	Bolt	2		
9	ETC7917	Screw	3		
	ETC7503	Spacer	3	To (E)19J 15397C	
10	ETC7917	Screw	2		
11	ETC7395	Bolt	1		
12	WJ108001	Washer-M8-large	2		
13	ETC7633	Manifold-engine exhaust	1		
	ETC6970	Stud	2		
6	NH108065L	Nut	2		

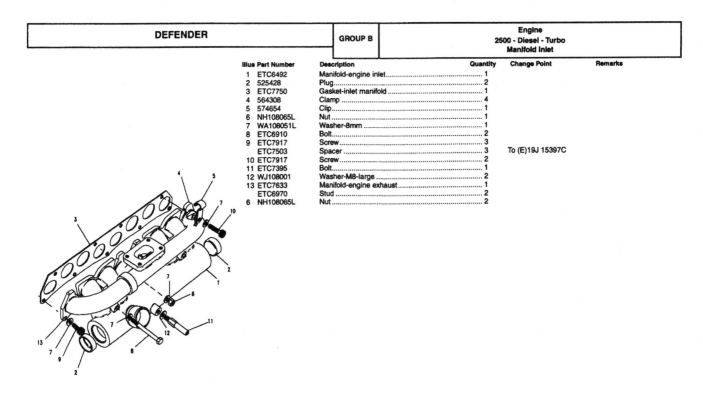

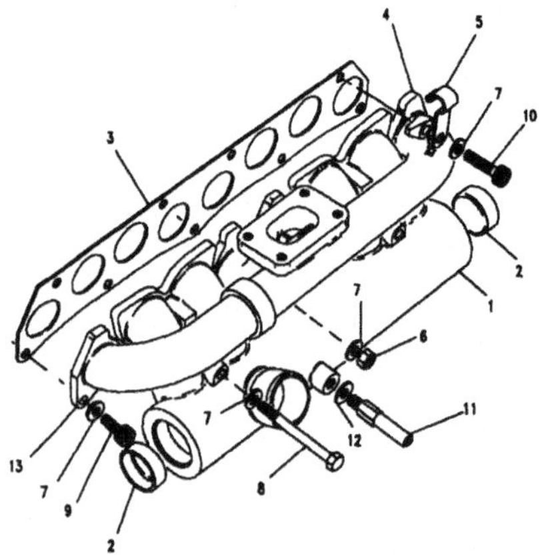

Illus	Part Number	Description	Quantity	Change Point	Remarks
1	ETC7869	Pump-fuel mechanical	NLA		Use STC1190.
	STC1190	Kit-fuel pump repair	1		
2	ETC7970	Gasket-fuel lift pump	NLA		Use ERR2028.
2	ERR2028	Gasket-fuel lift pump	1		
3	SS108301L	Screw-flanged head-M8 x 30	2		
4	WA108051	Washer-M8-standard	NLA		Use WA108051L.

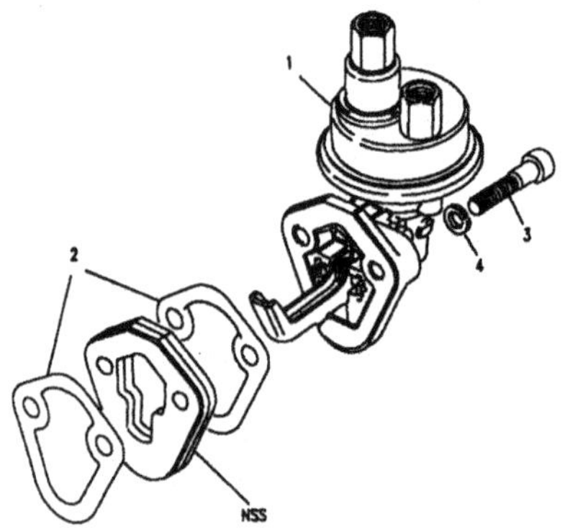

DEFENDER

GROUP B

Engine
2500 - Diesel - Turbo
Injection Pump

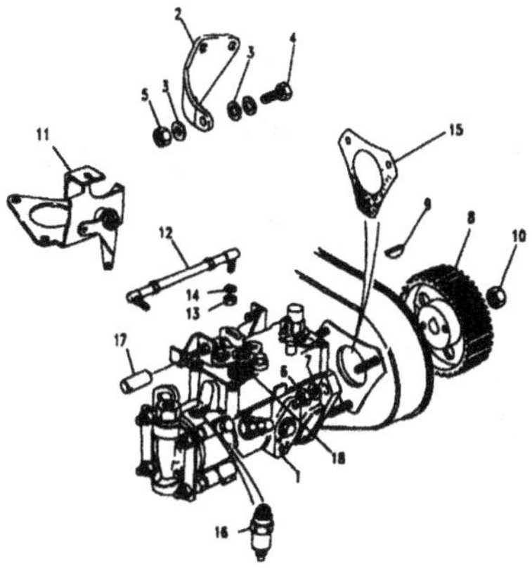

Illus	Part Number	Description	Quantity	Change Point	Remarks
1	ETC7136	Pump-fuel injection-new	1		
1	ETC7136E	Pump-fuel injection-exchange	1		
2	ETC4070	Bracket-engine mounting	1		
3	WA108051	Washer-M8-standard	NLA		Use WA108051L.
4	FS108251L	Screw-flanged head-M8 x 25	NLA		Use FS108257L.
5	NY108041L	Nut-nyloc-M8	1		
6	NH108041L	Nut-hexagonal head-M8	3		
7	WA108051L	Washer-8mm	1		
8	ETC5717	Pulley fuel inj pump	1		
9	RTC5077	Key-oil pump drive	1		
10	NH112041L	Nut-hexagonal-M12	1		
11	ETC6675	Level-carburettor throttle	1		
12	ETC4417	Link-carburettor/throttle connecting	1		
13	NH105041L	Nut-hexagonal-M5	2		
14	WA105001L	Washer-plain-standard-M5	3		
15	ERR3617	Gasket-injection pump-diesel engine-asbestos free	1		
16	BAU4611L	Switch-fuel changeover	1		
17	ETC4752	Sleeve	1		
	ETC7091	Bolt-banjo	2		
	517976	Washer-copper	2		
18	RTC5891	Spring-carburettor throttle return	1		

DEFENDER

GROUP B

Engine
2500 - Diesel - Turbo
Injectors & Pipes

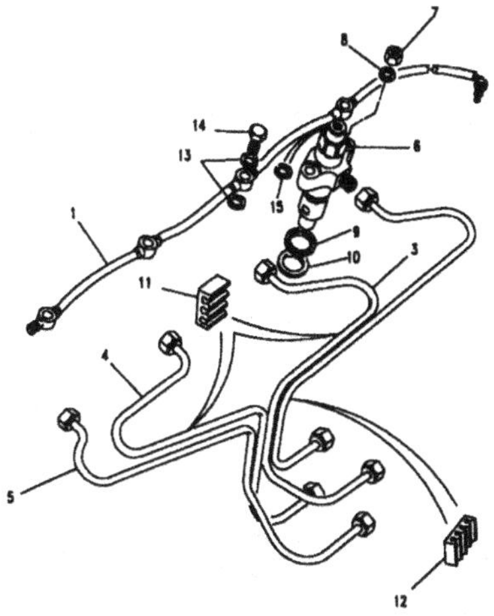

Illus	Part Number	Description	Quantity	Change Point	Remarks
1	ERR1259	Pipe-spill return fuel injection	1		
2	ETC4291	Pipe - fuel injection-No1	1		
3	ETC4292	Pipe - fuel injection-No2	1		
4	ETC4293	Pipe - fuel injection-No3	1		
5	ETC4294	Pipe - fuel injection-No4	1		
6	564332	Injector assembly-diesel holder & nozzle-new	4	Note (1)	
6	564332E	INJECTOR ASSEMBLY-DIESEL HOLDER & NOZZLE-EXCHANGE	4		
6	ERR1266	INJECTOR ASSEMBLY-DIESEL HOLDER & NOZZLE-NEW	4	Note (2)	
	247726	• Nozzle-injection diesel	4		
7	NH108041L	Nut-hexagonal head-M8	8		
8	WL108001L	Washer-sprung-M8	8		
9	12H220L	Washer-sealing-diesel injector to cylinder head	4		
10	247179	Washer-injector sealing	4		
11	ETC4156	Clip	2		
12	ETC4308	Clip	1		
13	273069	Washer-sealing-diesel injector spill return pipe banjo	8		
14	273521	Bolt-banjo-No1-No2-No3	4		
15	517976	Washer-copper	4		

CHANGE POINTS:
(1) To (V) GA 432367
(2) From (V) GA 432368

DEFENDER	GROUP B	Engine 2500 - Diesel - Turbo Turbocharger

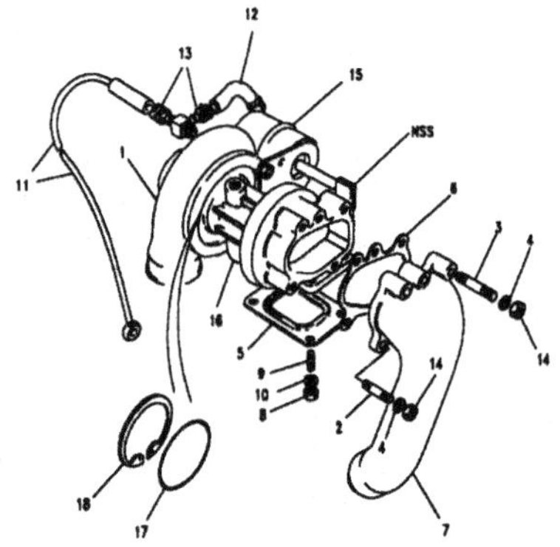

Illus	Part Number	Description	Quantity	Change Point	Remarks
1	STC99N	Turbocharger assembly-new	1		
1	STC99E	Turbocharger assembly-exchange	1		
2	RTC6094	Stud-M8 x 32	1		
3	RTC6093	Stud-M8 x 48	4		
	ERR1125	Bolt-banjo	1		
	FRC4808	Washer-sealing	2		
4	WA108051L	Washer-8mm	5		
5	ETC5710	Gasket-exhaust manifold to turbocharger	1		
6	ETC5898	Gasket-turbocharger elbow to inlet manifold	1		
7	ETC7058	Elbow	1		
8	ETC7184	Nut-M8	8		
9	ETC7667	Stud	4		
10	WA108051L	Washer-8mm	4		
	ETC7186	Plate-turbocharger blanking	1		
11	ETC7331	Pipe assembly turbocharger oil feed	1	To (E)19J 35152	
11	ERR1260	Pipe assembly turbocharger oil feed	1	From (E)19J 35153	
12	RTC5099	Hose-intercooler turbocharger-66mm-long	1		
13	UKC3803L	Clip-hose	3		
14	NH108041L	Nut-hexagonal head-M8	4		
15	RTC6543	Actuator-waste gate turbocharger	1		
16	RTC6540	Housing assembly turbine	1		
17	RTC6541	O ring	1		
18	RTC6542	Clip-tailgate lock retaining	1		

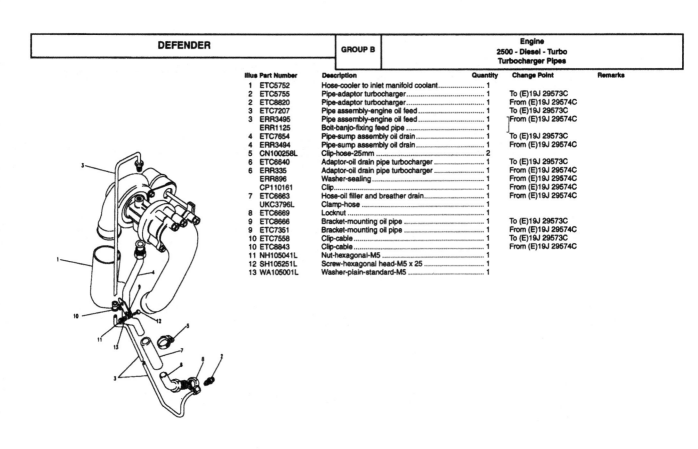

DEFENDER	GROUP B	Engine 2500 - Diesel - Turbo Turbocharger Pipes

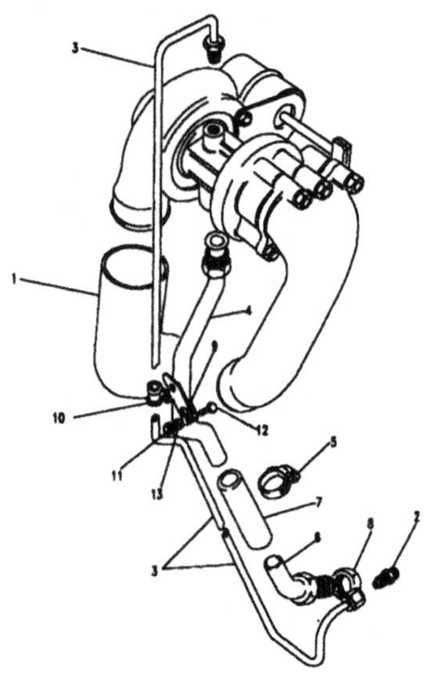

Illus	Part Number	Description	Quantity	Change Point	Remarks
1	ETC5752	Hose-cooler to inlet manifold coolant	1		
2	ETC5755	Pipe-adaptor turbocharger	1	To (E)19J 29573C	
2	ETC8820	Pipe-adaptor turbocharger	1	From (E)19J 29574C	
3	ETC7207	Pipe assembly-engine oil feed	1	To (E)19J 29573C	
3	ERR3495	Pipe assembly-engine oil feed	1	From (E)19J 29574C	
	ERR1125	Bolt-banjo-fixing feed pipe	1		
4	ETC7654	Pipe-sump assembly oil drain	1	To (E)19J 29573C	
4	ERR3494	Pipe-sump assembly oil drain	1	From (E)19J 29574C	
5	CN100258L	Clip-hose-25mm	2		
6	ETC6640	Adaptor-oil drain pipe turbocharger	1	To (E)19J 29573C	
6	ERR335	Adaptor-oil drain pipe turbocharger	1	From (E)19J 29574C	
	ERR896	Washer-sealing	1	From (E)19J 29574C	
	CP110161	Clip	1	From (E)19J 29574C	
7	ETC6663	Hose-oil filler and breather drain	1	From (E)19J 29574C	
	UKC3796L	Clamp-hose	1		
8	ETC6669	Locknut	1		
9	ETC8666	Bracket-mounting oil pipe	1	To (E)19J 29573C	
9	ETC7351	Bracket-mounting oil pipe	1	From (E)19J 29574C	
10	ETC7558	Clip-cable	1	To (E)19J 29573C	
10	ETC8843	Clip-cable	1	From (E)19J 29574C	
11	NH105041L	Nut-hexagonal-M5	1		
12	SH105251L	Screw-hexagonal head-M5 x 25	1		
13	WA105001L	Washer-plain-standard-M5	1		

DEFENDER	GROUP B	Engine 2500 - Diesel - Turbo Gaskets

Illus	Part Number	Description	Quantity	Change Point	Remarks
1	RTC5774	Set-cylinder head gasket	1		
2	RTC5775	Set-engine gasket-asbestos	1		
2	STC1558	Set-engine gasket-asbestos free	1		

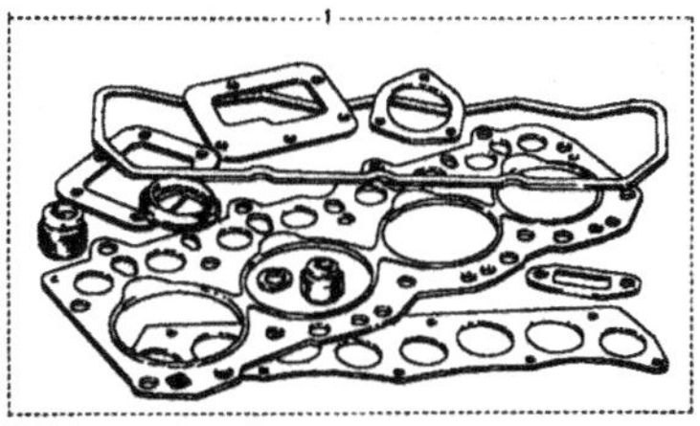

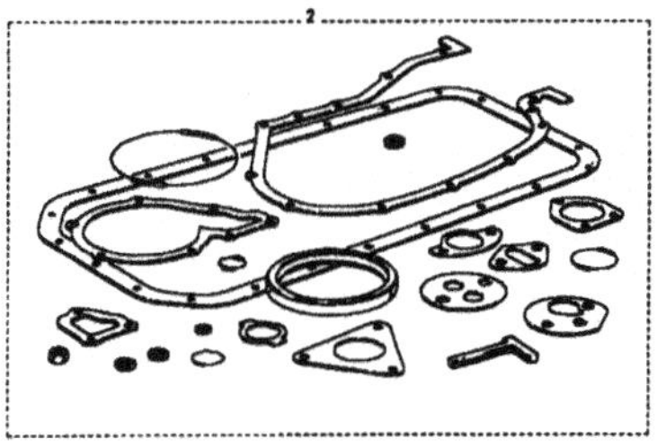

DEFENDER	GROUP B	Engine 2500 - Diesel - Turbo Vacuum Pump

Illus	Part Number	Description	Quantity	Change Point	Remarks
1	ERR535	PUMP BRAKE VACUUM	1		
2	AEU2720	• Bolt	4		
3	WL106001L	• Washer-sprung-M6	4		
4	AEU2718	• Rotor blade-vacuum pump	4		
5	AEU2719	• O ring	1		
6	ETC4616	Gasket-vacuum pump	2		
7	SS108301L	Screw-flanged head-M8 x 30	3		
8	WM600051L	Washer-spring-5/16"	3		

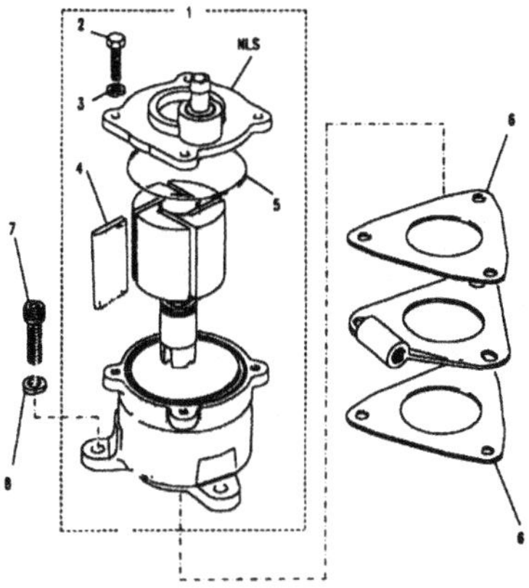

Power Steering Pump

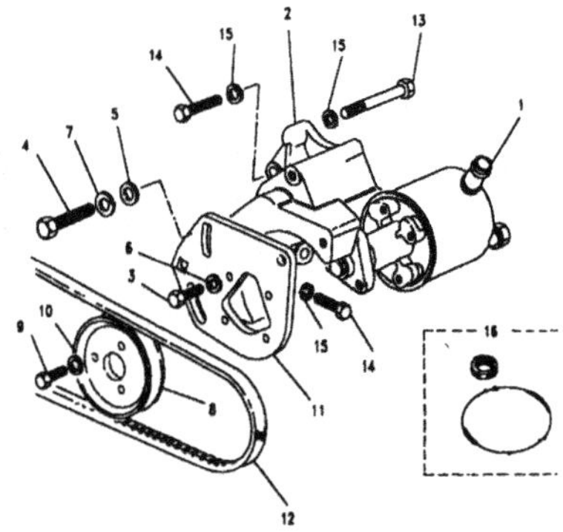

Illus	Part Number	Description	Quantity	Change Point	Remarks
1	ETC9077	PUMP ASSEMBLY POWER ASSISTED STEERING	1	Note (1)	
	RTC5674	• Union-delivery	1		
	RTC5675	• Washer-sealing	2		
1	NTC8287	Pump assembly power assisted steering	1	Note (2)	
1	NTC9070	Pump assembly power assisted steering	1	Note (3)	
2	ERC6974	Bracket-power assisted steering	1	Note (1)	
2	ETC8854	Bracket-power assisted steering	1	Note (4)	
3	FS106201L	Screw-flanged head-M6 x 20	4		
4	FS108251L	Screw-pump to bracket-flanged head-M8 x 25	NLA		Use FS108257L.
4	FS108251L	Screw-pump to bracket-flanged head-M8 x 25	NLA		Use FS108257L.
5	WA108051	Washer-pump to bracket-M8-standard	NLA		Use WA108051L.
6	WL106001L	Washer-sprung-M6	4		
7	WL108001L	Washer-sprung-M8	3		
8	ETC5783	Pulley power assisted steering pump	1		
9	SH108141L	Screw-pulley to pump-hexagonal head-M8 x 14	3		
10	WL108001L	Washer-sprung-M8	3		
11	ERR1976	Bracket-mounting power assisted steering pump-mounting	1	Note (5)	
11	ERR2605	Bracket-mounting power assisted steering pump-mounting	1	Note (3)	
12	ETC5815	Belt-polyvee power assisted steering	1		
13	BH108181L	Bolt-hexagonal head-M8 x 90	NLA		
14	FS108251L	Screw-flanged head-M8 x 25	NLA		Use FS108257L.
14	FS108307L	Screw-flanged head-M8 x 30	1		
15	WL108001L	Washer-sprung-M8	4		
16	RTC5935	Kit-power assisted steering pump seal	NLA		Use STC1633.
16	STC1633	Kit-power assisted steering pump seal	1		

CHANGE POINTS:
(1) To (E)19J 27245C
(2) From (E)19J 27246c To (V) July 1992
(3) From (V) July 1992
(4) From (E)19J 27246c
(5) To (V) July 1992

DEFENDER | **GROUP B** | **Engine**
2500 - Diesel - Turbo

Air Conditioning Compressor

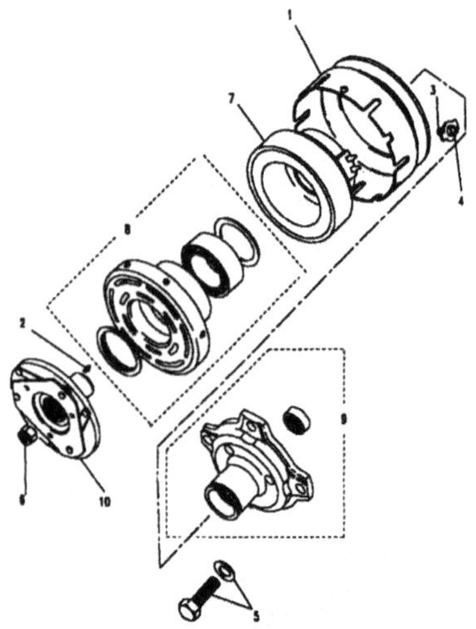

Illus	Part Number	Description	Quantity	Change Point	Remarks
	ERC6480	COMPRESSOR ASSEMBLY AIR CONDITIONING	1		
1	AEU1782	• Pulley-driven air conditioning	1		
2	AEU1694	• Key	1		
3	AEU1780	• Screw	6		
4	AEU1779	• Washer	6		
5	AEU1784	• Screw	4		
6	AEU1775	• Nut	1		
7	AEU1778	• Clutch set-magnetic air conditioning compressor	1		
8	AEU1777	• Retainer	1		
9	AEU1785	• Cover assembly-front	1		
10	AEU1776	• Clutch-drive-assy	1		
	AEU1792	• CYLINDER	1		
	AEU1791	• • Kit-thrust washer-air conditioning	1		
	AEU1790	• • Kit-steering box sector shaft seal	1		
	AEU1192	• • O RING AIR CONDITIONING	1		
	AEU1690	• • • O ring	2		
	AEU1788	• Plate	4		
	AEU1787	• Circlip	4		
	AEU1786	• Housing assembly compressor	1		
	AEU1689	• Valve-air conditioning pressure relief	1		
	AEU1688	• Kit-superheat switch	1		

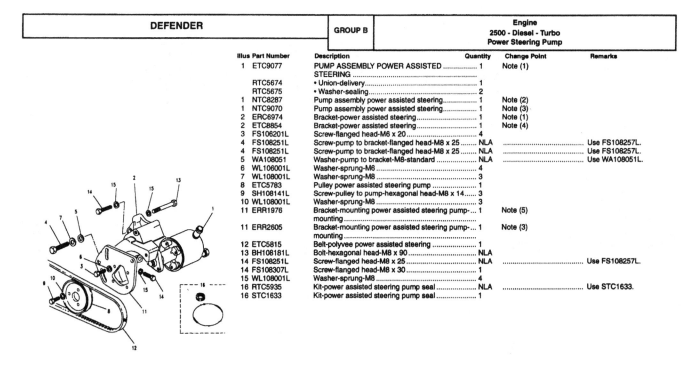

Engine
2500 - Diesel - Turbo
Air Conditioning Compressor-Kits

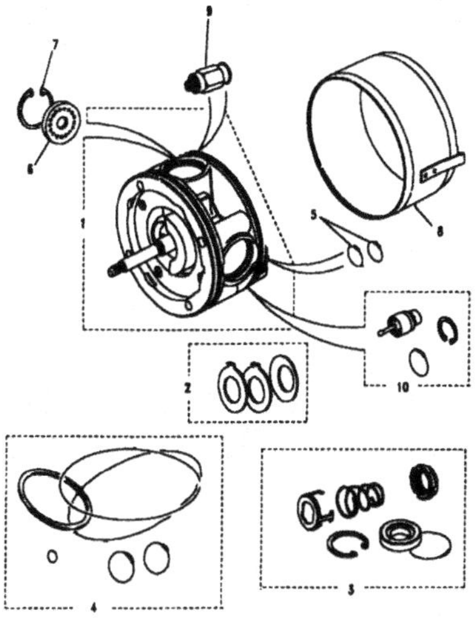

Illus	Part Number	Description	Quantity	Change Point	Remarks
	ERC6480	COMPRESSOR ASSEMBLY AIR CONDITIONING	1		
	AEU1782	• Pulley-driven air conditioning	1		
	AEU1694	• Key	1		
	AEU1780	• Screw	6		
	AEU1779	• Washer	6		
	AEU1784	• Screw	4		
	AEU1775	• Nut	1		
	AEU1778	• Clutch set-magnetic air conditioning compressor	1		
	AEU1777	• Retainer	1		
	AEU1785	• Cover assembly-front	1		
	AEU1776	• Clutch-drive-assy	1		
1	AEU1792	• CYLINDER	1		
2	AEU1791	• • Kit-thrust washer-air conditioning	1		
3	AEU1790	• • Kit-steering box sector shaft seal	1		
4	AEU1192	• • O RING AIR CONDITIONING	1		
5	AEU1690	• • • O ring	2		
6	AEU1788	• Plate	4		
7	AEU1787	• Circlip	4		
8	AEU1786	• Housing assembly compressor	1		
9	AEU1689	• Valve-air conditioning pressure relief	1		
10	AEU1688	• Kit-superheat switch	1		
11	ETC4371	Belt-polyvee air conditioning compressor	1		
	AEU1691	Oil-525 visc	A/R		

Engine
2500 - Diesel - Turbo
Air Conditioning Compressor Fixings

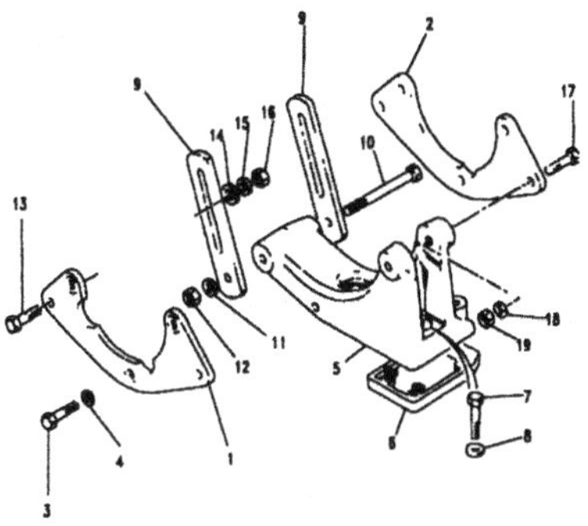

Illus	Part Number	Description	Quantity	Change Point	Remarks
1	ERC7082	Plate-mounting-front	1		
2	ERC5152	Plate-mounting-rear	1		
3	BH110201L	Bolt-compressor to plate-hexagonal head-M10 x 100	3		
4	WL110001L	Washer-M10	3		
5	ETC4882	Bracket-air compressor	NLA		Use ERR3091.
5	ERR3091	Bracket-air compressor	1		
6	ETC4197	Bracket-compressor air conditioning	1		
7	BH110101L	Bolt-bracket to cover-hexagonal head-M10 x 50-long	4		
8	WA110061L	Washer-M10	4		
9	ERC5155	Link-adjusting compressor	2		
10	BH108181L	Bolt-link to bracket-hexagonal head-M8 x 90	NLA		
11	WL108001L	Washer-sprung-M8	1		
12	NH108041L	Nut-hexagonal head-M8	1		
13	FS108251L	Screw-link to plate-flanged head-M8 x 25	NLA		Use FS108257L.
13	FS108251L	Screw-link to plate-flanged head-M8 x 25	NLA		Use FS108257L.
14	WA108051	Washer-M8-standard	NLA		Use WA108051L.
15	WL108001L	Washer-sprung-M8	2		
16	NH108041L	Nut-hexagonal head-M8	2		
17	FB108081L	Bolt-bracket to plate-flanged head-M8 x 40	2		
18	WL108001L	Washer-sprung-M8	2		
19	NH108041L	Nut-hexagonal head-M8	2		

Illus	Part Number	Description	Quantity	Change Point	Remarks
1	ETC7756	PULLEY-DRIVE AIR CONDITIONING	1		
2	554971	• PULLEY-IDLER ANCILLARY DRIVE	1		
3	RTC6077	• • Nut-5/16UNF	1		
4	4095	• Washer	1		
5	WB108051L	• Washer-plain-M8	1		
6	ETC4212	• Plate-mounting	1		

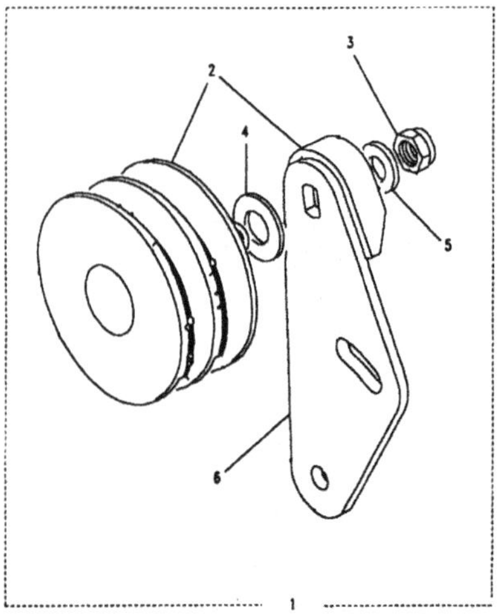

Illus	Part Number	Description	Quantity	Change Point	Remarks
1	RTC5682N	ALTERNATOR ASSEMBLY-NEW-A127-45 AMP	1		
1	RTC5682E	ALTERNATOR ASSEMBLY-EXCHANGE-A127-45 AMP	1		
2	RTC5670	• Regulator & brush box assembly alternator	1		
3	RTC5684	• Rectifier-alternator	1		
4	RTC5926	• Bearing-alternator front	1		
5	RTC5687	• Bracket-drive end c/w bearing alternator e-RH	1		
6	RTC5925	• Kit-fixings alternator/vacuum pump-LH	1		
7	RTC5685	Fan alternator	1		
8	RTC5686	Pulley alternator	1		
9	ETC7939	Belt-polyvee alternator	1		
	RTC5689	Spacer	1		

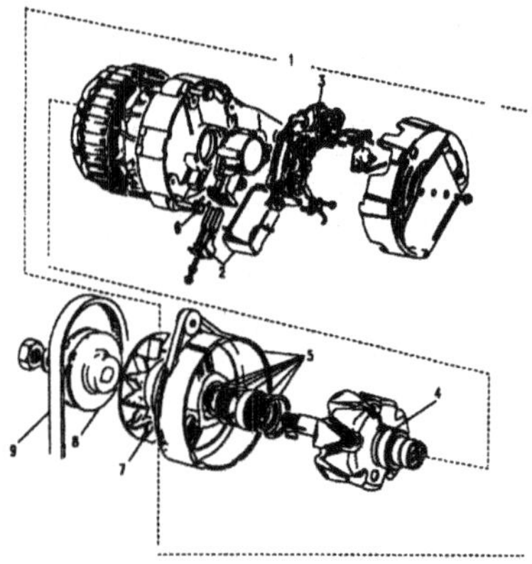

Illus	Part Number	Description	Quantity	Change Point	Remarks
		ALTERNATOR ASSEMBLY			
1	RTC5680N	NEW-A127-65 AMP-RH	NLA		Use STC234.
1	STC234	NEW-A127-65 AMP-RH	1		
1	RTC5680E	EXCHANGE-A127-65 AMP-RH	1		
2	RTC5670	• Regulator & brush box assembly alternator	1		
3	RTC5671	• Rectifier-alternator	1		
4	RTC5926	• Bearing-alternator front	1		Part of RTC5680N, RTC5680E.
5	RTC5687	• Bracket-drive end c/w bearing alternator e-RH	1		
6	RTC5046	• Kit-fixings alternator/vacuum pump-RH	1		
	RTC6114	• Capacitor alternator	1		Part of STC234.
7	AAU2249L	Fan alternator	1		
8	RTC5686	Pulley alternator	1		
9	ETC7939	Belt-polyvee alternator	1		
	RTC5689	Spacer	1		

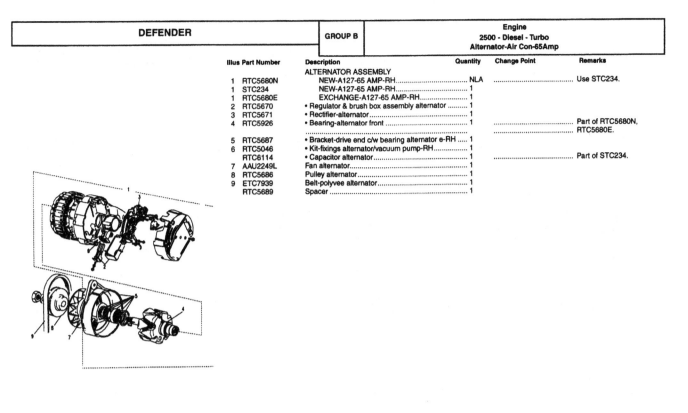

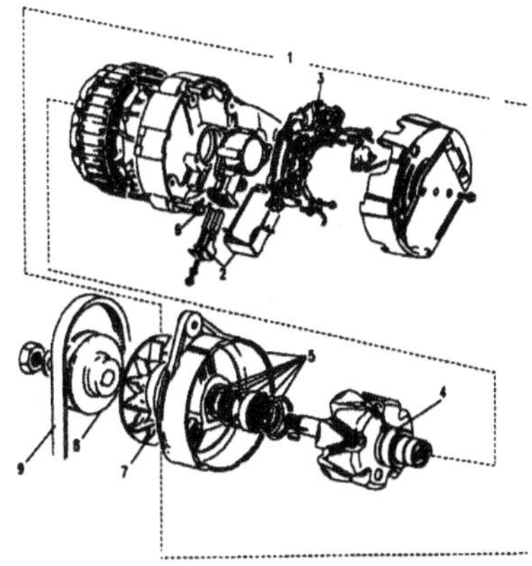

Illus	Part Number	Description	Quantity	Change Point	Remarks
1	ETC4357	Bracket-mounting-alternator	1		
2	BH108161L	Bolt-bracket to block-hexagonal head-M8 x 80	1		
3	FS110301L	Screw-bracket to block-flanged head-M10 x 30-top	2		
4	WL108001L	Washer-sprung-M8	1		
5	WL108001L	Washer-sprung-M8	1		
6	ERC6266	Link-adjuster alternator-A127 alternator	1		
6	ERC5139	Link-adjuster alternator-A133 alternator	1		
7	FS108207L	Screw-flanged head-M8 x 20	1		
8	WL108001L	Washer-sprung-M8	2		
9	2266L	Washer	1		
10	ERC8964	Bolt-link to block-M8 x 95	1		
11	WL108001L	Washer-sprung-M8	1		
12	FB108081L	Bolt-bracket to block-flanged head-M8 x 40	1		
13	BH108091L	Bolt-bracket to block-M8 x 45	1		
	ERC7974	Spacer	1		
14	WC108051L	Washer-M8	1		
15	NY108041L	Nut-nyloc-M8	2		

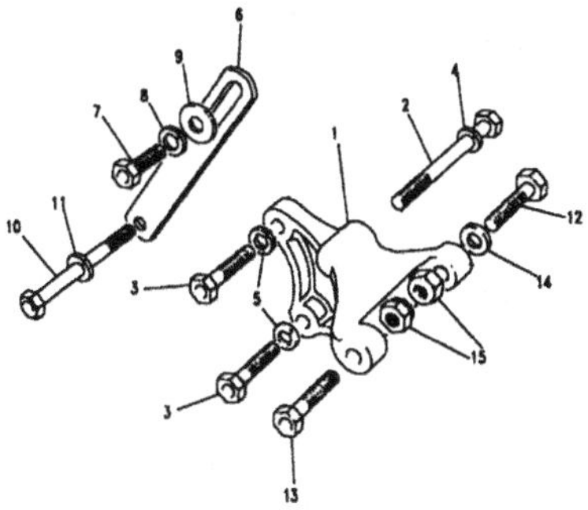

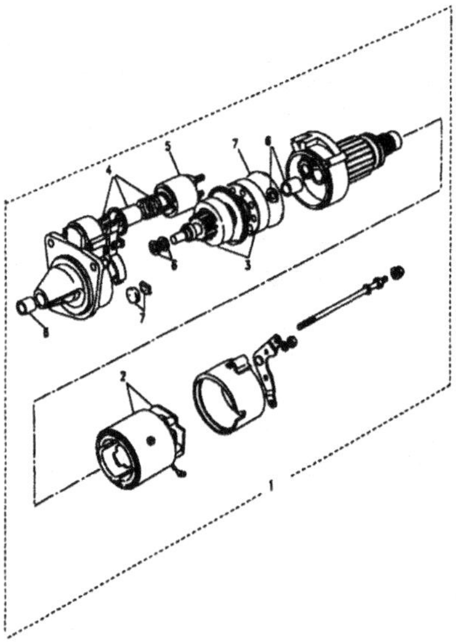

Illus	Part Number	Description	Quantity	Change Point	Remarks
1	PRC5109N	MOTOR-STARTER ENGINE-NEW-VALEO	NLA		Use NAD10039.
1	PRC5109E	MOTOR-STARTER ENGINE-EXCHANGE-VALEO	1		
2	RTC4981	• Box assembly-brush starter motor-Valeo	1		
3	RTC4982	• Drive assembly starter motor-Valeo	1		
4	RTC4979	• Yoke assembly starter motor	1		
5	RTC4978	• Solenoid starter motor-Valeo	1		
6	RTC4980	• Kit-starter motor	1		
7	RTC4983	• Kit-starter motor sundry parts	1		
1	NAD10039	MOTOR-STARTER ENGINE-LUCAS	NLA		Use ERR5009.
1	ERR5009	MOTOR-STARTER ENGINE-NEW-BOSCH	1		
2	STC1246	• Box assembly-brush starter motor-Bosch	1		
	STC1254	• Spring-coil	4		
	STC1247	• Guide-starter motor brush	4		
3	STC1244	• Drive assembly starter motor-Bosch	1		
5	STC1245	• Solenoid starter motor-0 331 303 165-Bosch	1		
5	STC3715	• Solenoid starter motor-9 330 331 006-Bosch	1		
	STC1250	• Bush-starter motor-centre	2		
	STC1251	• Bush-starter motor-rear	1		
	STC1255	• Bush-starter motor-front	1		
	PRC5538	Harness earth bond	1		
	WL110001L	Washer-M10	3		
	SH110301L	Screw-starter to flywheel-hexagonal head-M10 x 30	NLA		Use FS110301L.
	NH110041L	Nut-starter to flywheel-hexagonal head-coarse thread-M10	2		
	BH110091L	Bolt-M10 x 45	4		

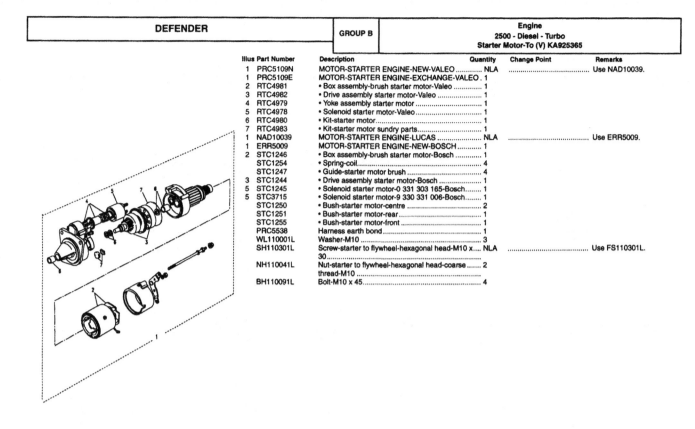

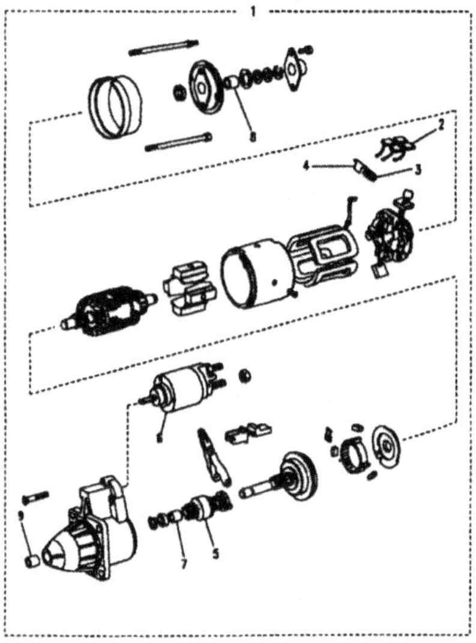

Illus	Part Number	Description	Quantity	Change Point	Remarks
1	ERR5009	MOTOR-STARTER ENGINE-NEW-BOSCH	1		
1	ERR5009E	MOTOR-STARTER ENGINE-EXCHANGE-BOSCH	1		
2	STC1246	• Box assembly-brush starter motor-Bosch	1		
3	STC1254	• Spring-coil	4		
4	STC1247	• Guide-starter motor brush	4		
5	STC1244	• Drive assembly starter motor-Bosch	1		
6	STC1245	• Solenoid starter motor-0 331 303 165-Bosch	1		
6	STC3715	• Solenoid starter motor-9 330 331 006-Bosch	1		
7	STC1250	• Bush-starter motor-centre	2		
8	STC1251	• Bush-starter motor-rear	1		
9	STC1255	• Bush-starter motor-front	1		

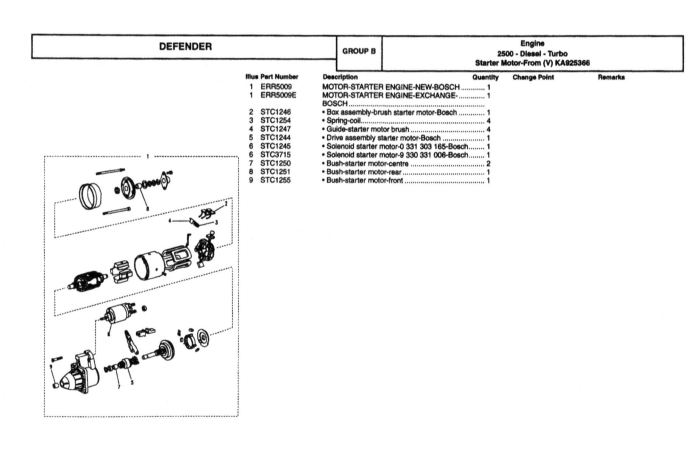

DEFENDER	GROUP B	Engine 2500 - Diesel - Turbo Clutch & Flywheel

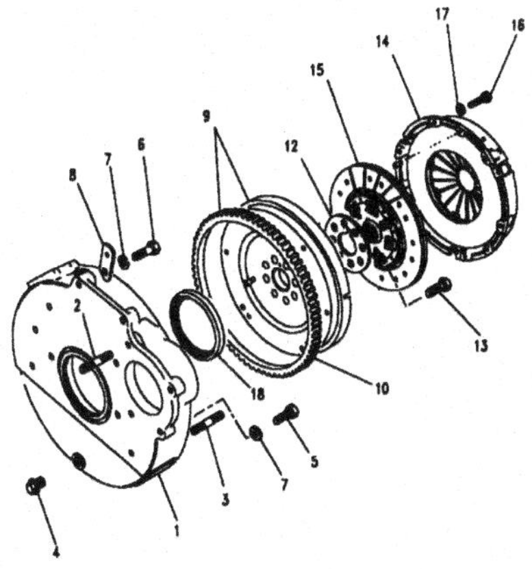

Illus	Part Number	Description	Quantity	Change Point	Remarks
1	ETC7336	Housing assembly-clutch	1		
2	TE110061L	Stud-bell housing-M10 x 30	11		
3	ERC9240	Stud-starter motor-M10	1		
4	ERC7295	Plug-rubber	1		
5	FS110301L	Screw-housing to block-flanged head-M10 x 30-top	6		
6	BH110091L	Bolt-housing to block-M10 x 45	2		
7	WA110061L	Washer-housing to block-M10	8		
8	ERC9404	Bracket harness-harness clip	2		
9	ETC5780	FLYWHEEL ENGINE	1		
10	568431	• Gear-ring-flywheel engine	1		
11	502116	• Dowel-flywheel to crankshaft	3		
12	ERC4658	Plate-reinforcement	NLA		Engineering have found that the reinforcing plate is not required. When refitting flywheel omit plate , and fit new bolts ERR4574..
13	ERC6551	Bolt-fixing flywheel crankshaft-long	8		
13	ERR4574	Bolt-fixing flywheel crankshaft-short	8		
	STC8358	KIT-CLUTCH	1		Except 130"
14	FTC575	• Cover-clutch assembly	NLA		Use URB100760.
15	FTC2149	• Plate-clutch-driven	NLA		Use FTC4204.
	FRC9568	• BEARING-CLUTCH RELEASE	NLA		Use FTC5200.
	FRC4078	• • Sleeve-guide clutch	1		
14	URB100760	Cover-clutch assembly			
16	SX108201L	Bolt-M8 x 20	6		
17	WL108001L	Washer-sprung-M8	6		
18	ERR1535	Seal-crankshaft rear	NLA		Use ERR2532.
18	ERR2532	Seal-crankshaft rear	1		

DEFENDER	GROUP B	Engine 2500 - Diesel - Turbo - 200 Tdi Engine Complete

Illus	Part Number	Description	Quantity	Change Point	Remarks
1	STC308	Engine-power unit	1	From (E)11L 00001	

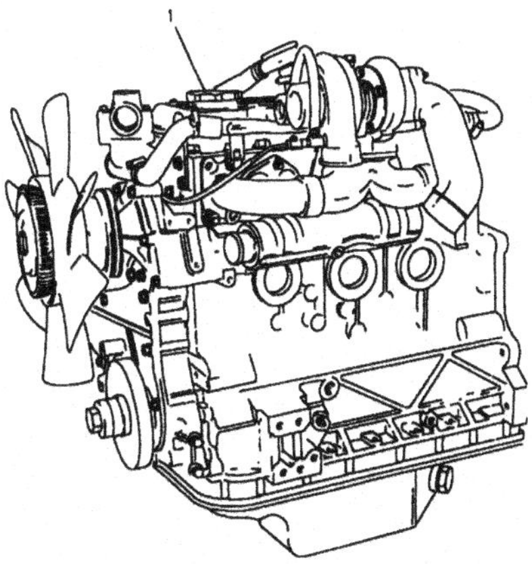

Illus	Part Number	Description	Quantity	Change Point	Remarks
1	STC309N	Engine unit-stripped-new	1	From (E)11L 00001	
1	STC309E	Engine unit-stripped-exchange	1		

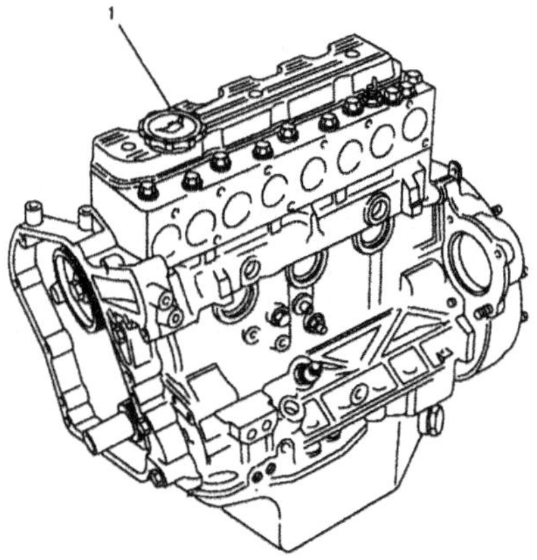

Illus	Part Number	Description	Quantity	Change Point	Remarks
1	RTC6635	Engine base unit-part-short	1	From (E)11L 00001	

CYL BLOCK/CRANK/MAIN BEARINGS/CON ROD/PISTONS

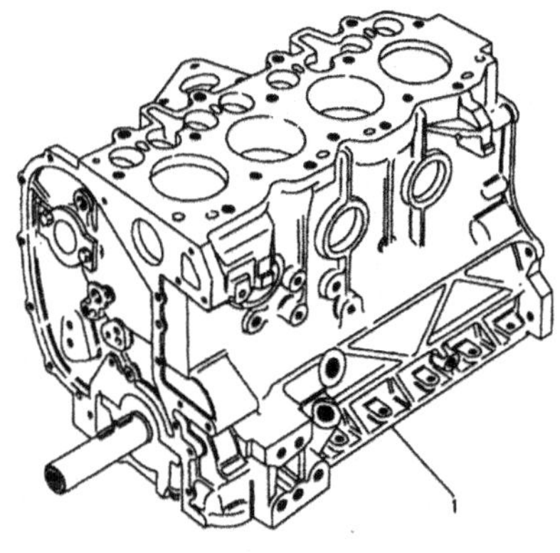

Illus	Part Number	Description	Quantity	Change Point	Remarks
1	ERR3	CYLINDER BLOCK-ENGINE	1		
2	501593	• Dowel	10		
3	ERC4996	• Plug-core	7		
4	597586	• Plug-core	1		
5	ETC8442	• Bearing-camshaft front	1		
6	90519055	• Bearing-camshaft rear	3		
7	ETC4529	• Plug-core	1		
8	ETC8074	• Bolt	10		
	FS108161L	• Screw-flanged head-M8 x 16	1		
9	TE108031L	Stud-M8 x 15	1		
10	247127	Plug-cylinder block oil way	1		
11	ERC4644	Dowel-flywheel housing	2		
12	ETC4922	Plug-gallery pipe	1		
13	ERR5034	Plug-camshaft blanking-camshaft oil feed-rubber	3		
14	ETC8352	Dowel-ring-head to block	2		
15	ERR913	Packing strip	2		

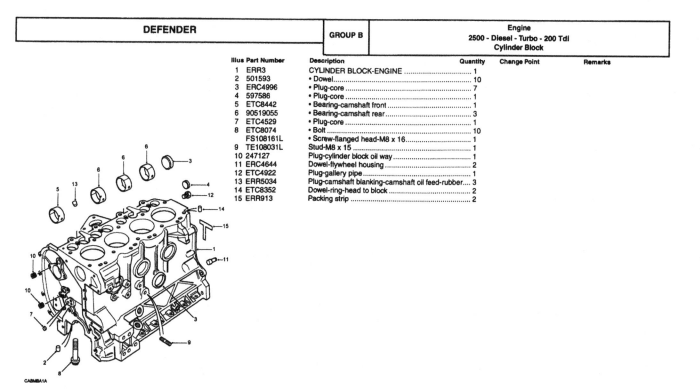

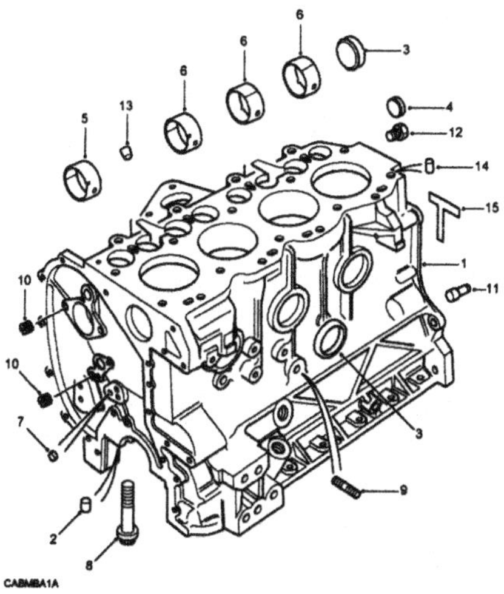

Illus	Part Number	Description	Quantity	Change Point	Remarks
1	ETC6531	Jet assembly-piston cooling-No1-No3	2		
2	ETC6532	Jet assembly-piston cooling-No2-No4	2		
3	ETC5592	Valve-bearing housing jet	4		
4	AFU1879L	Washer-sealing	4		
5	AFU1887L	Washer-sealing	4		
6	ERC9410	Plug-drain	1		
7	AFU1882L	Washer-sump assembly drain plug	1		
8	ERC8864	Gasket	1		

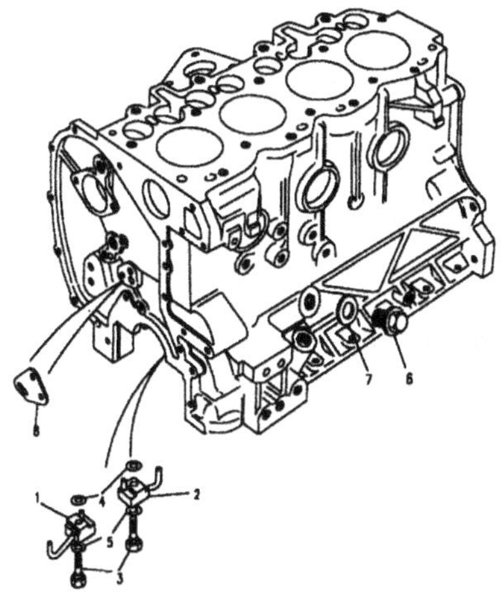

DEFENDER	GROUP B	Engine 2500 - Diesel - Turbo - 200 Tdl Cover Side

Illus	Part Number	Description	Quantity	Change Point	Remarks
1	ETC7929	COVER PLATE-SIDE	1		
2	TE108041L	• Stud-M8 x 20	2		
3	ERR1475	Gasket-cylinder block side cover	1		
4	FS108251L	Screw-flanged head-M8 x 25	NLA		Use FS108257L.
5	WL108001L	Washer-sprung-M8	12		
6	ERR506	Breather assembly-crankcase	1		
7	247555	Gasket-cylinder block side cover	NLA		Use ERR3605.
7	ERR3605	Gasket-cylinder block side cover-asbestos	NLA		Use ERR2026.
7	ERR2026	Gasket-cylinder block side cover-asbestos free	1		
8	ERC9480	Bracket-harness clip	1		
9	WA108051L	Washer-8mm	3		

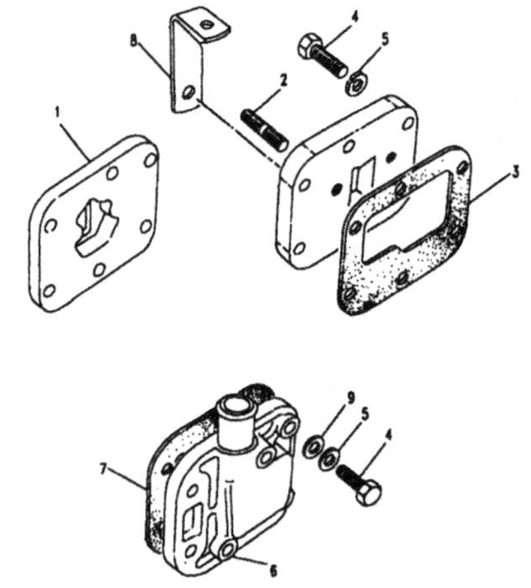

DEFENDER	GROUP B	Engine 2500 - Diesel - Turbo - 200 Tdl Crankshaft & Bearings

Illus	Part Number	Description	Quantity	Change Point	Remarks
1	ERR1181	CRANKSHAFT-ENGINE	1		
2	ERR1630	• Dowel-flywheel to crankshaft	1		
3	8566L	• Bush-crankshaft	1		
4	235770	• Key-crankshaft	2		
5	RTC4783	Set-crankshaft bearings-standard	NLA		Use STC3395.
5	STC3395	Set-crankshaft bearings-standard	1		
5	RTC478310	Set-crankshaft bearings-0.010" undersize	1		
		WASHER-CRANKSHAFT THRUST			
6	RTC2825	standard.-pair	A/R		
6	538131	oversize.-0.0025"-pair	A/R		
6	538132	oversize.-0.005"-pair	A/R		
6	538133	oversize.-0.0075"-pair	A/R		
6	538134	oversize.-0.01"-pair	A/R		
7	ETC4077	Pulley & torsional vibration damper-crankshaft	1		Note (1)
7	ERR751	PULLEY & TORSIONAL VIBRATION DAMPER-CRANKSHAFT	1		Note (2)
	ETC4390	• Flinger-crankshaft pulley	1		
8	ERR1642	Gear-crankshaft timing drive	1		
9	ERC6859	Pulley & torsional vibration damper-crankshaft	1		Note (2)
9	ERC6861	PULLEY & TORSIONAL VIBRATION DAMPER-CRANKSHAFT	1		Note (3)
12	FS108257L	• Screw-flanged head-M8 x 25	4		
	WL108001L	• Washer-sprung-M8	4		
9	ERC6859	Pulley & torsional vibration damper-crankshaft	1		Note (2)
10	ERR605	Bolt-crankshaft pulley	1		
11	ERR705	Washer-crankshaft thrust	1		
12	FS108207L	Screw-flanged head-M8 x 20	4		

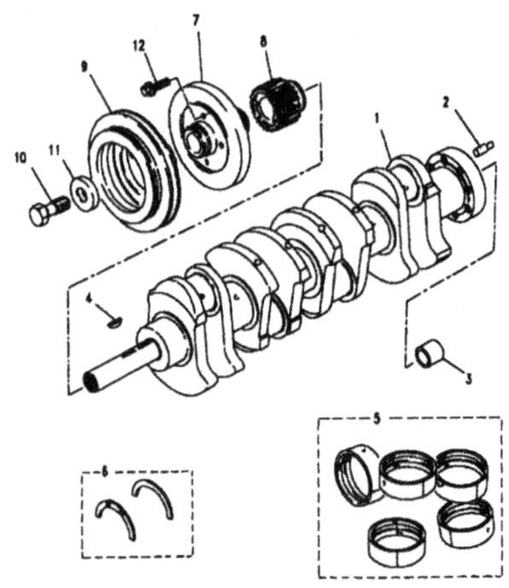

Remarks:
(1) manual steering Except air conditioning
(2) power steering air conditioning
(3) power steering Except air conditioning

DEFENDER

GROUP B

Engine
2500 - Diesel - Turbo - 200 Tdi
Piston, Connecting Rod & Bearings

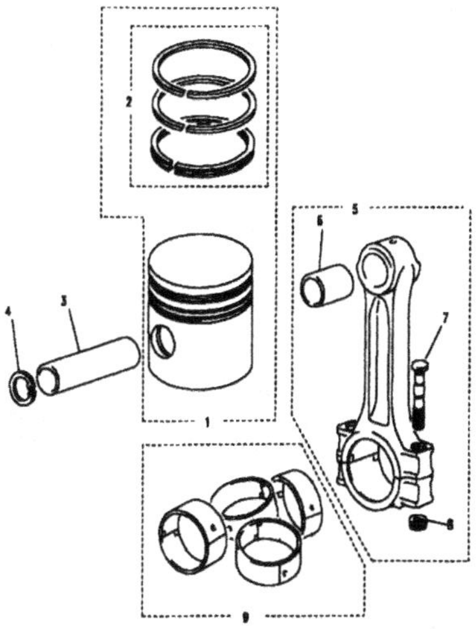

Illus	Part Number	Description	Quantity	Change Point	Remarks
1	ERR1390	PISTON-ENGINE-STANDARD.-'X'	4		
1	ERR1391	PISTON-ENGINE-STANDARD.-'Y'	4		
2	RTC6457	• Ring set assembly-piston-standard.	4		
1	STC1052020	PISTON-ENGINE-0.020" OVERSIZE	4		
2	RTC645720	• Ring set assembly-piston-0.020" oversize	4		
1	STC1052040	PISTON-ENGINE-0.040" OVERSIZE	4		
2	RTC645740	• Ring set assembly-piston-0.040" oversize	4		
3	ERR703	Pin-piston gudgeon	4		
4	266945	Circlip-piston	2		
5	ETC8086	ROD-CRANKSHAFT CONNECTING	4		
6	ETC7286	• Bearing bush-connecting rod small end	4		
7	ETC7357	• Bolt-connecting rod	2		
8	ETC8191	• Nut-connecting rod	2		
9	RTC2993	Set-connecting rod big end half bearing-standard.	1		
9	RTC299310	Set-connecting rod big end half bearing-0.010" undersize	1		

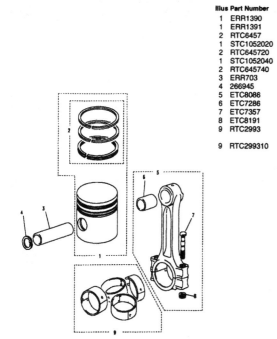

DEFENDER

GROUP B

Engine
2500 - Diesel - Turbo - 200 Tdi
Sump/Ladder Frame

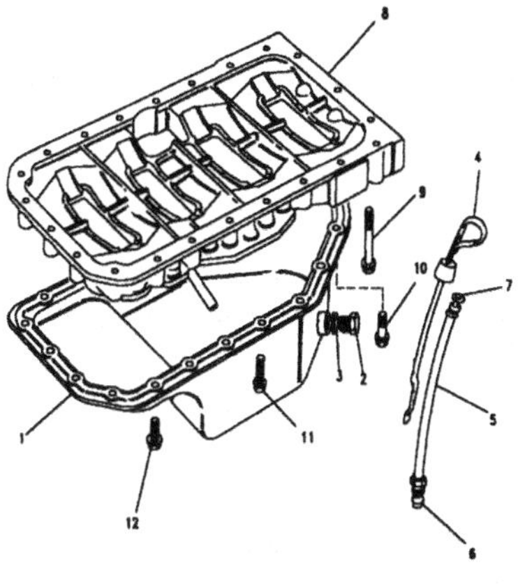

Illus	Part Number	Description	Quantity	Change Point	Remarks
1	ERR1790	Sump assembly-engine oil	1		
2	603659	Plug-sump assembly oil drain	1		
3	213961	Washer-sealing-sump drain plug	1	To (E)11L 38389A	
3	ETC7398	Washer-sealing	1	From (E)11L 38390A	
4	ETC7867	Dipstick-oil	1		
5	ERC8980	Tube assembly-oil dipstick	1		
6	236408	Olive	1		
7	532387	O ring	1		
8	ERR1291	Cylinder block/ladder assembly	1		
9	FB108251	Bolt-ladder frame to block-flanged head-M8 x 125	2		
10	FB108121L	Bolt-ladder frame to block-flanged head-M8 x 60	4		
11	FS108307L	Screw-ladder frame to block-flanged head-M8 x 30	3		
10	FB108121L	Bolt-sump to ladder frame/block-flanged head-M8 x 60	12		
12	FS108251L	Screw-sump to ladder frame/block-flanged head-M8 x 25	NLA		Use FS108257L.
	STC611	Sealant-sump to ladder frame/block-Hylomar 2000.	1		

Illus	Part Number	Description	Quantity	Change Point	Remarks
1	NRC5434	Bracket-engine mounting-RH	1		
2	NRC9557	Bracket-engine mounting-LH	1		
3	SH112251L	Screw-foot to block-hexagonal head-M12 x 25	4		
4	WL112001L	Washer-foot to block	4		
5	NRC9560	Mounting-engine rubber	NLA	To (V) JA 920702	Use ANR1808.
5	ANR1808	Mounting-engine rubber	2	From (V) JA 920703	
6	NH110041L	Nut-rubber to foot-hexagonal head-coarse thread-M10	4		
7	WC110061L	Washer-rubber to foot-plain-M10-oversize	2		
8	WL110001L	Washer-rubber to foot-M10	4		

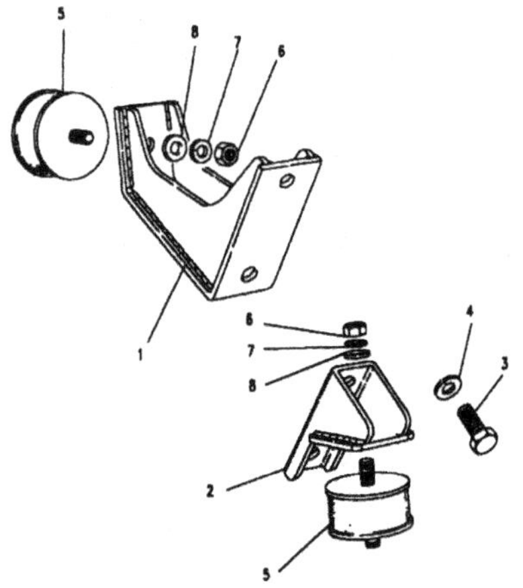

Illus	Part Number	Description	Quantity	Change Point	Remarks
1	ERR1273	Cover assembly-front	NLA		Use ERR1274.
1	ERR1274	Cover assembly-front	1		
2	6395L	Dowel	4		
3	ETC5064	Seal-camshaft oil	1		
4	ETC5065	Seal-crankshaft front oil	NLA		Use ERR1632.
5	538038	Gasket-coolant pump body-asbestos	NLA		Use ERR1607.
5	ERR1607	Gasket-coolant pump body-to front cover-asbestos free	1		
6	538039	Gasket-timing gear housing drain plate	1		
7	FC108137	Bolt-flanged head-cover to block-M6 x 65	1		
8	FS108207L	Screw-cover to block-flanged head-M8 x 20	2		
9	ERR2375	Pin-tensioner pivot	1		
10	ERR1253	Plate assembly-front	NLA		Use ERR1256.
10	ERR1256	Plate assembly-front	1		
11	ETC4154	Seal	1		
12	FB108141L	Bolt-flanged head-M8 x 70	2		
13	FB108151L	Bolt-flanged head-M8 x 75	4		
14	FB108201L	Bolt-flanged head-M8 x 100	1		
15	FB108101L	Bolt-flanged head-M8 x 50	1		
16	FS108251L	Screw-flanged head-M8 x 25	NLA		Use FS108257L.
17	ERR25	Plate-timing belt cover	1		Except air conditioning
17	ETC8853	Plate-timing belt cover	1		Air conditioning
18	ERR635	Gasket	1		
19	ERR1553	Gasket-cover front	1		
20	FS106101L	Screw-flanged head-M6 x 10	3		
21	ETC4124	Washer-sealing-asbestos	NLA		Use ERR3604.
21	ERR3604	Washer-sealing-asbestos free	1		
22	TE108061L	Stud-M8 x 30	3		
23	ETC4630	Bracket-mounting	1		
24	WA108051L	Washer-8mm	1		
25	SH108121L	Screw-hexagonal head-M8 x 12	1		
26	ERR394	Gasket-front cover	1		

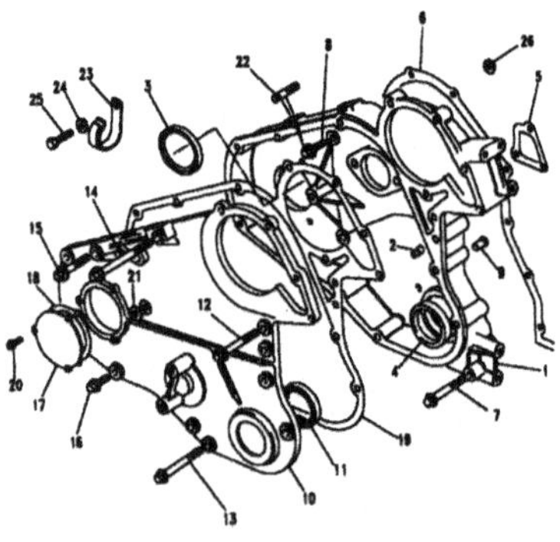

Illus	Part Number	Description	Quantity	Change Point	Remarks
1	ETC8550	Belt-engine timing	1		
2	ERR118	Tensioner-timing belt	NLA		Use ERR2530.
2	ERR2530	Tensioner-timing belt	1		
3	ERR900	Washer	1		
4	FB110141L	Bolt-flanged head-M10 x 70	1		

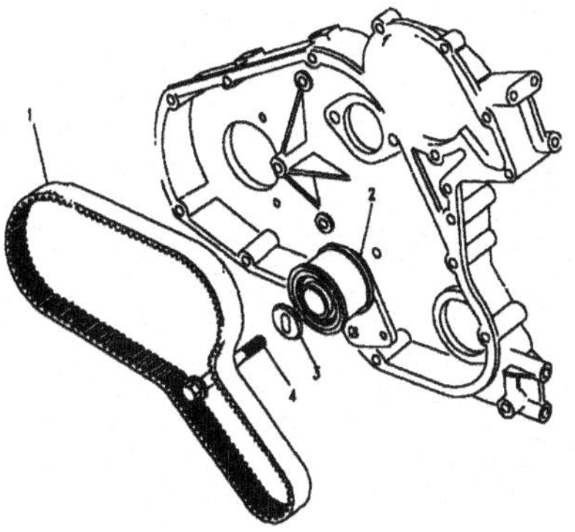

Illus	Part Number	Description	Quantity	Change Point	Remarks
1	STC639	Pump assembly-engine coolant	1		
2	ERC5600	Screw	1		
3	WL106001L	Washer-sprung-M6	1		
4	ERC5655	Gasket-coolant pump body	1		
5	ETC4785	Pulley coolant pump	1		
6	FS108161L	Screw-flanged head-M8 x 16	4		
7	WL108001L	Washer-sprung-M8	4		
8	ETC7554	Fan-cooling-7 blade	NLA	To (V) December 1992	Use ERR3380.
8	ERR3380	Fan-cooling	1	From (V) December 1992	
9	ETC7238	Coupling-engine fan viscous	1		
10	4589L	Washer-plain	4		
11	ERC5709	Screw-M6 x 14	4		
12	FB108071L	Bolt-flanged head-M8 x 35	3		
13	FB108151L	Bolt-flanged head-M8 x 75	1		
14	FB108171L	Bolt-flanged head-M8 x 85-long	2		
15	FN108041L	Nut-flange-M8	NLA		Use FN108047L.
16	TD108181	Stud-M8 x 90	1		
17	ERR1424	Hose-bypass to pump coolant	1		
18	CN100408L	Clip-hose	2		
19	ETC7939	Belt-polyvee alternator	1		

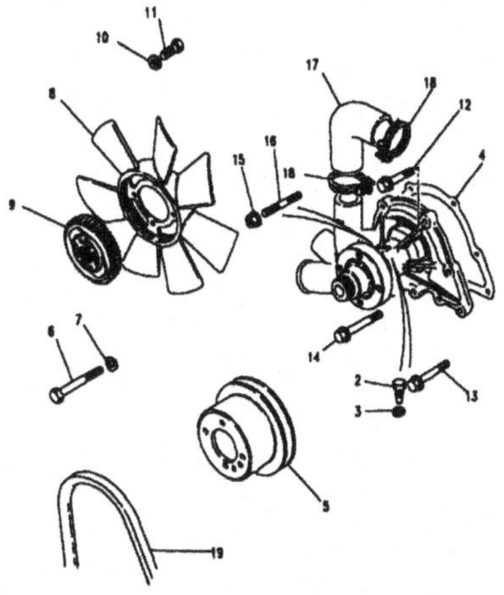

DEFENDER

GROUP B

Engine
2500 - Diesel - Turbo - 200 Tdi
Oil Pump

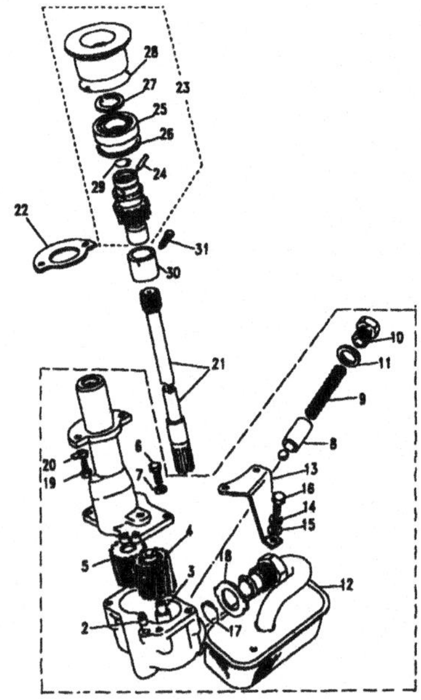

Illus	Part Number	Description	Quantity	Change Point	Remarks
1	ERR1178	PUMP ASSEMBLY-ENGINE OIL	1		
2	236257	• Dowel	2		
3	ERR1063	• Spindle-oil pump	1		
4	ERR1088	• Gear-oil pump idler-10 teeth	1		
5	ERC9706	• Gear-oil pump-10 teeth	1		
6	FS108201L	• Screw-flanged head-M8 x 20	NLA		Use FS108207L.
7	WL108001L	• Washer-sprung-M8	4		
8	ETC4880	• Plunger-oil pump relief valve	1		
9	564456	• Spring-oil pump relief valve	1		
10	564455	• Plug	1		
11	232044	• Washer-sealing	1		
12	ERR1521	• Strainer and pipe assembly-oil	1		
13	ERR541	• Bracket	1		
14	WA108051L	• Washer-8mm	1		
15	WL108001L	• Washer-sprung-M8	1		
16	FS108201L	• Screw-flanged head-M8 x 20	NLA		Use FS108207L.
17	244488	• O ring	1		
18	244487	• Washer-lock	1		
19	FS108251L	• Screw-flanged head-M8 x 25	NLA		Use FS108257L.
20	247665	• Washer-lock	2		
21	ERR850	Shaft-oil pump	1		
22	ERR3606	Gasket-cylinder block oil pump-asbestos free	1		
23	ERR928	DRIVE ASSEMBLY-OIL PUMP	1		
24	ERR309	• Pin-roll-spring tension	1		
25	ERR528	• Bearing-ball	1		
26	CR120305	• Ring-snap-outer	1		
27	ERR530	• Ring-snap-inner	1		
28	ERR531	• O ring	1		
29	ERR532	• O ring	1		
30	ERR500	Bush	1		
31	ERR848	Screw	1		

DEFENDER

GROUP B

Engine
2500 - Diesel - Turbo - 200 Tdi
Filter & Adaptor

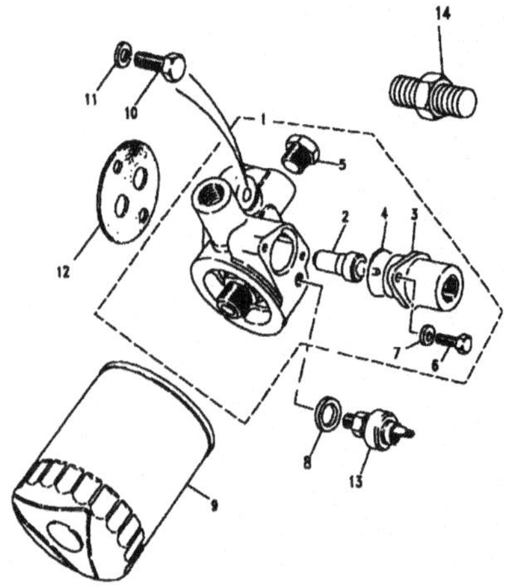

Illus	Part Number	Description	Quantity	Change Point	Remarks
1	ERR1299	ADAPTOR ASSEMBLY-OIL FILTER	1	To (E)11L 25129A	
1	ERR2711	ADAPTOR ASSEMBLY-OIL FILTER	1	From (E)11L 25130A	
2	ERC5923	• Thermostat assembly-oil	1		
3	ETC4022	• Adaptor-oil filter	1		Part of ERR1299.
4	ERC5913	• O ring	1		
5	ETC4021	• Plug	1		
6	SH106141L	• Screw-hexagonal head-M6 x 14	2		
7	WA106041L	• Washer-6mm	2		
3	ERR2623	• Adaptor-oil filter	1		Part of ERR2711.
	ERR2241	• Waxstat adaptor	1		Part of ERR2711.
8	ETC7398	Washer-sealing	2		
9	ERR3340	Cartridge-engine oil filter	1		
10	FS110301L	Screw-flanged head-M10 x 30-top	2		
11	WL110001L	Washer-M10	2		
12	ETC5276	Gasket-cylinder block to oil filter adaptor-asbestos	1		
12	ERR3607	Gasket-cylinder block to oil filter adaptor-asbestos free	1		
13	PRC6387	Switch-oil pressure engine	1		
14	NRC8618	Coupling	2		

DEFENDER	GROUP B	Engine 2500 - Diesel - Turbo - 200 Tdi Cylinder Head

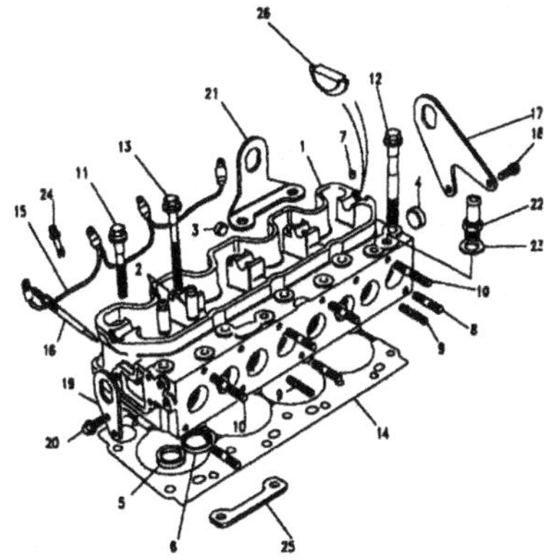

Illus	Part Number	Description	Quantity	Change Point	Remarks
1	RTC6896	CYLINDER HEAD ASSEMBLY-ENGINE	1		
2	ETC8003	• Guide-cylinder head valve	NLA		Use LGJ100880.
3	525497	• Plug-core	1		
4	524765	• Plug-core	1		
5	ETC8002	• Insert-cylinder head exhaust valve seat	4		
6	ETC8001	• Insert-inlet valve seat-cylinder head	4		
7	ETC8194	• Dowel-ring	1		
8	TE110051L	Stud-M10 x 25	5		
9	TE108051L	Stud-M8 x 25	2		
10	TE110071L	Stud-M10 x 35	2		
11	ETC8808	Bolt-cylinder head fixing-short-M12 x 100	4		
12	ETC8809	Bolt-cylinder head fixing-long	10		
13	ETC8810	Bolt-cylinder head fixing-M10 x 117	4		
		GASKET-CYLINDER HEAD			
14	ERR5261	1.30mm-1 hole	1		
14	ERR5262	1.40mm-2 holes	1		
14	ERR5263	1.50mm-3 holes	1		
15	PRC6947	Cable-heater plug ignition	1	To (E)11L 33656A	
15	AMR2425	Cable-heater plug ignition	1	From (E)11L 33657A	
16	ETC8847	Plug-heater ignition	4		
17	ETC8036	Bracket-lifting engine rear	1		
18	FS108251L	Screw-flanged head-M8 x 25	NLA		Use FS108257L.
19	ETC8031	Bracket-lifting engine front	1		
20	FS108251L	Screw-flanged head-M8 x 25	NLA		Use FS108257L.
21	ERR978	Bracket-lifting engine rear	1		
22	624091	Adaptor-pipe coolant	1		
23	243959	Washer-sealing	1		
24	ERR1019	Stud-injector clamp	1		
25	ERR1536	Spacer	1		
26	ERR765	Plug-cylinder block oil way-rubber	2		

DEFENDER	GROUP B	Engine 2500 - Diesel - Turbo - 200 Tdi Rockershaft

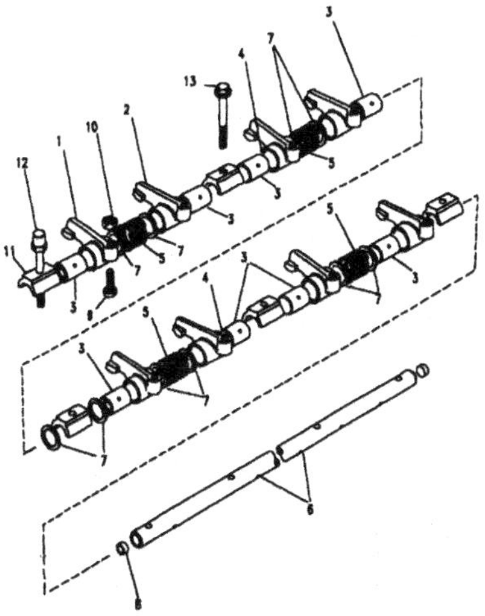

Illus	Part Number	Description	Quantity	Change Point	Remarks
1	ERR1202	ARM & BUSH ASSEMBLY-EXHAUST VALVE ROCKER-RH	4		
3	ERR1203	• Bush-cylinder head rocker arm	4		
2	ERR1201	ARM & BUSH ASSEMBLY-INLET VALVE ROCKER-LH	4		
3	ERR1203	• Bush-cylinder head rocker arm	4		
4	ERR1209	Spacer-rocker shaft	6		
5	ETC8095	Spring-rocker shaft	1		
6	ERR1197	Shaft-rocker	NLA	To (V) LA 939817	Use ERR4682.
6	ERR4682	Shaft-rocker	1	From (V) LA 939818	
7	ERR1210	SPACER-ROCKER SHAFT	10		
8	ETC8103	• Plug	2		
9	ERR559	Screw-engine tappet adjustment	8		
10	ERR560	Nut-locking	8		
11	ERR1107	Clamp-rocker shaft	5		
12	ETC7530	Bolt-rocker shaft	3		
13	FB108101L	Bolt-flanged head-M8 x 50	2		

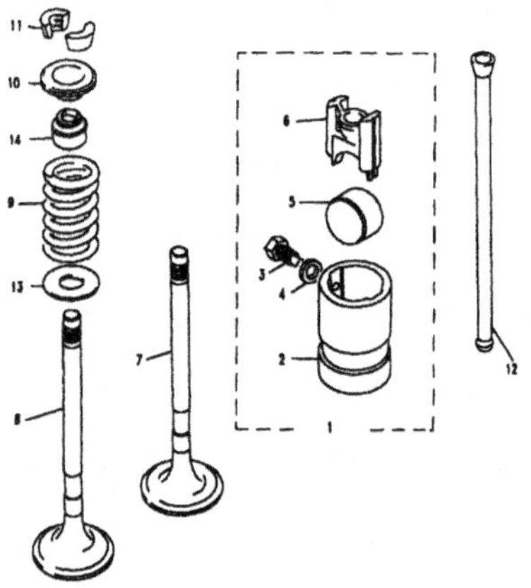

Illus	Part Number	Description	Quantity	Change Point	Remarks
1	RTC6564	TAPPET-ENGINE VALVE HYDRAULIC	8		
2	502473	• Slide-tappet guide	8		
3	ETC4246	• Bolt	8		
4	273069	• Washer-sealing	8		
5	ERR561	• Roller-tappet guide	8		
6	ERR607	• Tappet-engine valve mechanical	8		
7	ERR1157	Valve-cylinder head inlet	4		
8	ERR1156	Valve-cylinder head exhaust	4		
9	ERR314	Spring-cylinder head valve	8	To (E)11L 37880A	
9	ERR4640	Spring-cylinder head valve	8	From (E)11L 37881A	
10	ETC4068	Cap-cylinder head valve spring	8		
11	ETC4069	Cotter-valve	16		
12	546799	Rod-engine push	8		
13	ETC8193	Seat-cylinder head valve spring	8		
14	ETC8663	Seal-cylinder head valve stem	8		
	ERR4175	Cap-valve stem	NLA		Use LJC100270.

Illus	Part Number	Description	Quantity	Change Point	Remarks
1	ERR1530	Cover assembly-valve rocker	1	To (V) JA 916016	
1	ERR3368	Cover assembly-valve rocker	1	From (V) JA 916017	
2	ERR2393	Gasket-engine rocker cover	1		
3	ERR455	Cap-oil filler	1	To (V) April 1992	
3	ERR2529	Cap-oil filler	NLA	From (V) April 1992	Use ERR5041.
3	ERR5041	Cap-oil filler	1		
4	FS106255L	Screw-flanged head-M6 x 25	3		
5	ERR663	Seal	3		
6	ERR1621	Bracket	1		
7	NRC8332	Clip-cable	1		

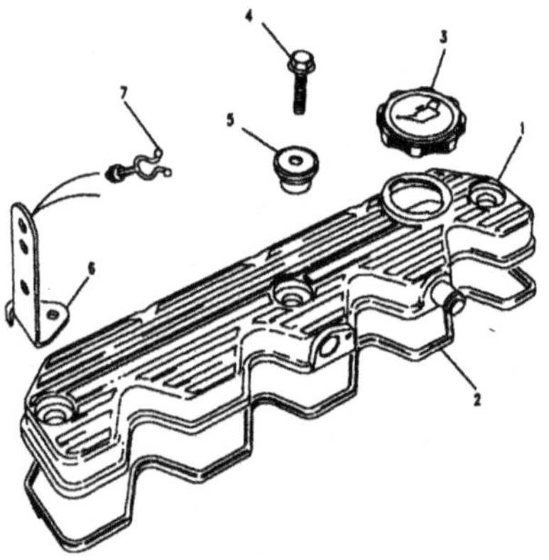

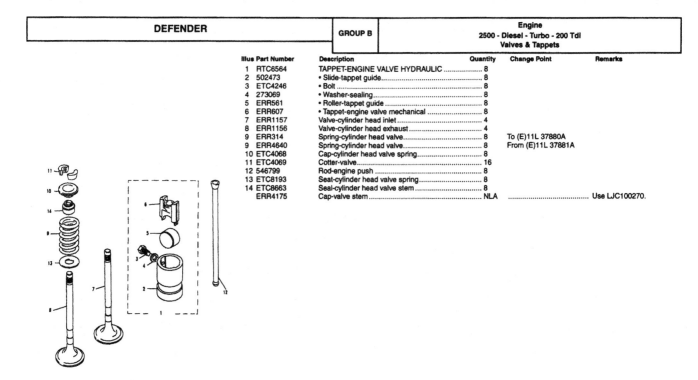

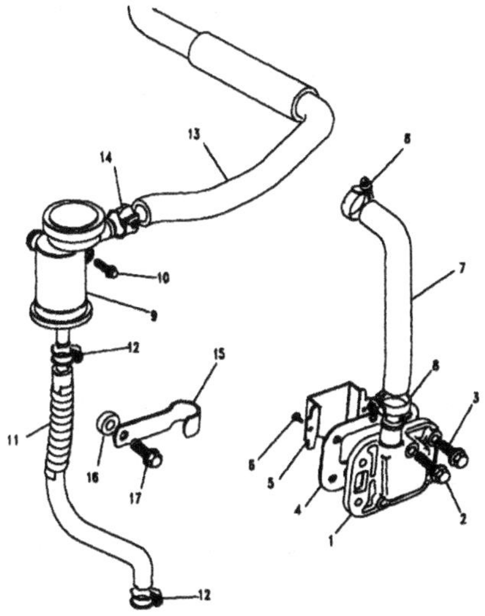

Illus	Part Number	Description	Quantity	Change Point	Remarks
1	ERR506	Breather assembly-crankcase	1	To (V) JA 916016	
1	541010	Breather assembly-crankcase	1	From (V) JA 916017	
2	FB108081L	Bolt-flanged head-M8 x 40	1		
3	FS108251L	Screw-flanged head-M8 x 25	NLA		Use FS108257L.
4	247555	Gasket-cylinder block side cover	NLA		Use ERR3605.
4	ERR3605	Gasket-cylinder block side cover-asbestos	NLA		Use ERR2026.
4	ERR2026	Gasket-cylinder block side cover-asbestos free	1		
5	ERR874	Baffle-oil separator	1		
6	79026	Screw-No 6 x 5/16	1		
7	ERR877	Hose-crankcase breather flexible	1		
8	CN100258L	Clip-hose-25mm	2		
9	ERR1471	SEPARATOR ASSEMBLY-CRANKCASE BREATHER OIL	1		
	LLO100000	• O ring	1		
10	FB106121L	Bolt-flanged head-M6 x 60	2		
11	ERR1605	Hose-oil separator drain	1		
12	CN100208L	Clip-hose-20mm	2		
13	ERR1729	Hose-cyclone-air cleaner	1		
14	CN100258L	Clip-hose-25mm	2		
15	ERR878	Clip-hose	1		
16	ERR879	Spacer	1		
17	SH110201L	Screw-hexagonal head-M10 x 20	1		

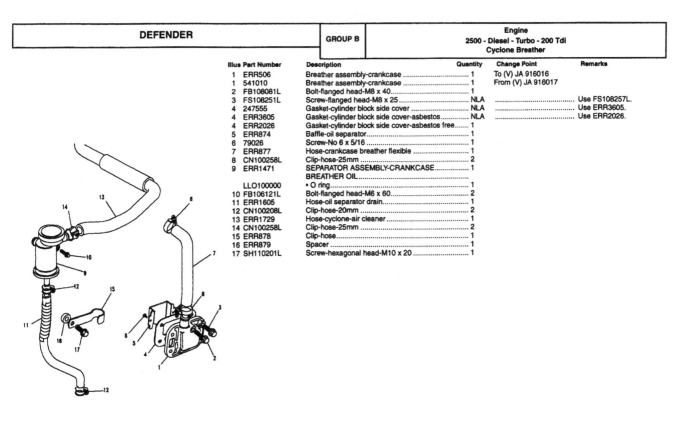

Illus	Part Number	Description	Quantity	Change Point	Remarks
1	ETC7128	Camshaft assembly-engine	1		
2	ERC1561	Plate-camshaft retaining	1		
3	FS106167L	Screw-flanged head-flanged head-M6 x 16	2		
4	WL106001L	Washer-plate to block-sprung-M6	2		
5	ERR666	Pulley-camshaft	1		
6	230313	Key	1		
7	BX110071M	Bolt-hexagonal head-M10 x 35	1		
8	ETC4670	Washer-plain	1		
9	ERC8847	Plate-camshaft pulley retaining	1		
10	ERC8849	O ring	1		
11	ETC4076	O ring	1		

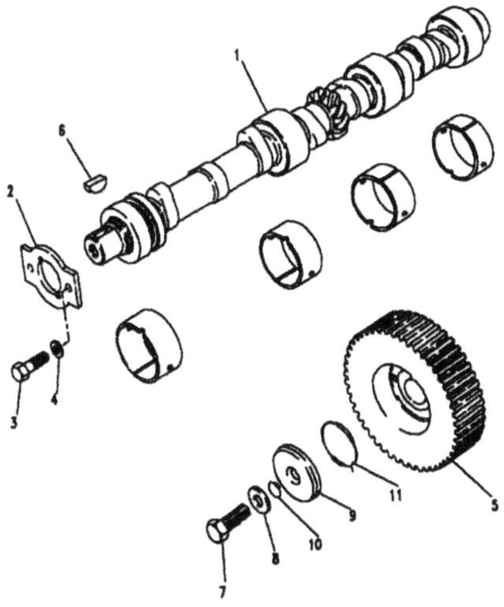

Engine
2500 - Diesel - Turbo - 200 Tdi
Thermostat Housing

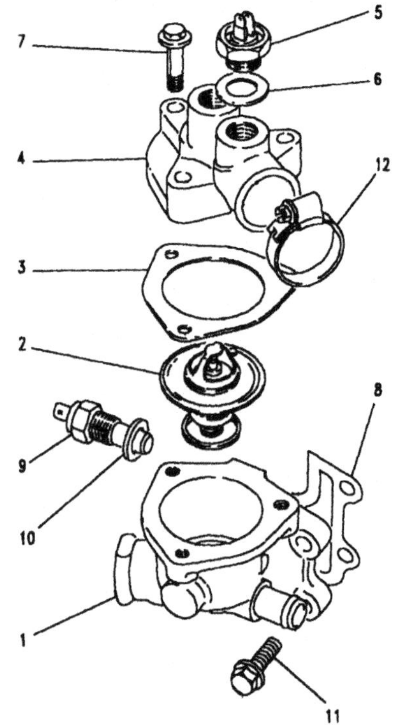

Illus	Part Number	Description	Quantity	Change Point	Remarks
1	ERR1499	Housing-thermostat	1		
2	ERR2803	Thermostat-engine-88 degrees C	1		
3	ERR3682	Gasket-thermostat housing-top-asbestos free	1		
4	ETC5967	Elbow-engine coolant outlet	1		Except air conditioning
4	ETC5958	Elbow-engine coolant outlet	1		Air conditioning
	BTR6141	Hose to pipe-coolant	1		
5	PRC3359	Switch-engine thermostat-Green	1		
6	ERR696	Washer-copper-M14	1		
7	FB106081L	Bolt-flanged head-M6 x 40	3		
8	ETC8007	Gasket-thermostat housing-bottom	1		
9	PRC8593	Sensor-temperature	1		
10	90568054	Washer-sealing	1		
11	FS108251L	Screw-flanged head-M8 x 25	NLA		Use FS108257L.
12	CJ600304L	Clip-hose	1		

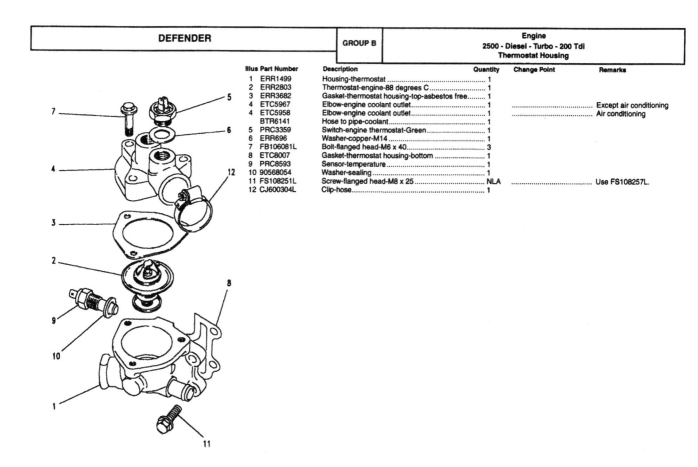

Engine
2500 - Diesel - Turbo - 200 Tdi
Manifolds

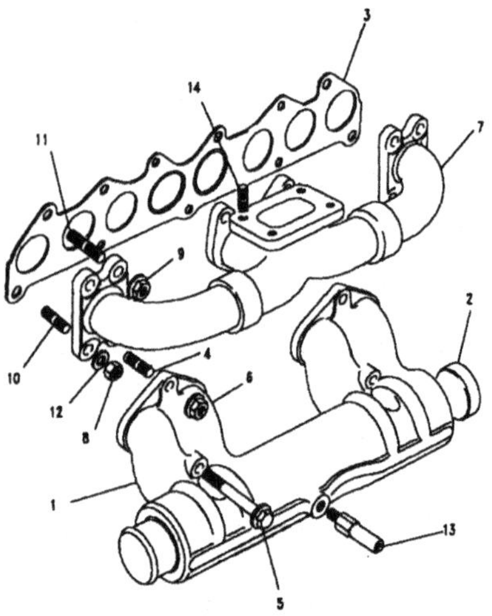

Illus	Part Number	Description	Quantity	Change Point	Remarks
1	ERR1435	Manifold-engine inlet	1		
2	525428	Plug	1		
3	ERR1208	Gasket-engine inlet/exhaust manifold	1		
4	TE108051L	Stud-M8 x 25	2		
5	FB108161L	Bolt-flanged head-M8 x 80	2		
6	FN108041L	Nut-flange-M8	NLA		Use FN108047L.
7	ERR678	Manifold-engine exhaust	1		
8	ERR597	Nut-flange-nyloc-M10	2		
	FX110041L	Nut-flange-M10	NLA		Use FX110047L.
9	NT110041L	Locknut-M10	2		
10	TE110051L	Stud-M10 x 25	5		
11	TE110071L	Stud-M10 x 35	2		
12	WA110061L	Washer-M10	7		
13	ETC7395	Bolt-support heatshield	1		
14	ERR551L	Stud-M8 x 25	4		

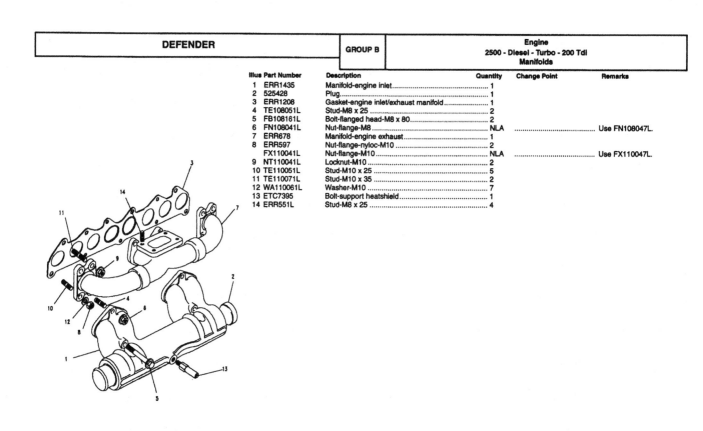

Fuel Pump

Illus	Part Number	Description	Quantity	Change Point	Remarks
1	ETC7869	Pump-fuel mechanical	NLA		Use STC1190.
	STC1190	Kit-fuel pump repair	1		
2	ETC7970	Gasket-fuel lift pump	NLA	To (V) LA 939817	Use ERR2028.
2	ERR2028	Gasket-fuel lift pump	2	From (V) LA 939818	
3	SS108301L	Screw-flanged head-M8 x 30	2		
4	WA108051L	Washer-8mm	2		

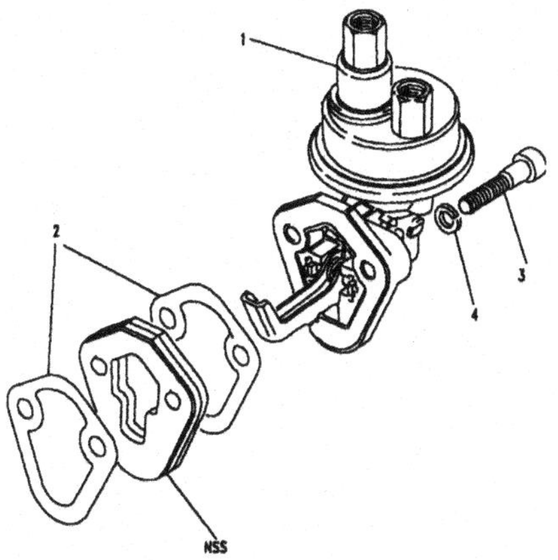

Injection Pump

Illus	Part Number	Description	Quantity	Change Point	Remarks
1	ERR1333	Pump-fuel injection-new	1		
1	ERR1333E	Pump-fuel injection-exchange	1		
3	ERR631	Gasket-injection pump-diesel engine	1		
4	FN108041L	Nut-flange-M8	NLA		Use FN108047L.
5	ERR1662	Bracket assembly-mounting multi point injection	1		
6	FN108041L	Nut-flange-M8	NLA		Use FN108047L.
7	FS108207L	Screw-flanged head-M8 x 20	2		
8	ERR667	Pulley assembly-pump fuel injection pump drive	1		
9	ERR359	Plate-retaining-pulley	1		
10	FN108041L	Nut-flange-M8	NLA		Use FN108047L.
11	WA108051L	Washer-8mm	6		
12	ERR886	Bolt-banjo	1		
13	ERR894	Washer-sealing	2		
14	ERR1125	Bolt-banjo-fuel inlet	1		
15	RTC6702	Switch-electronic diesel control	1		
16	STC262	Adaptor-pipe-dual male	4		

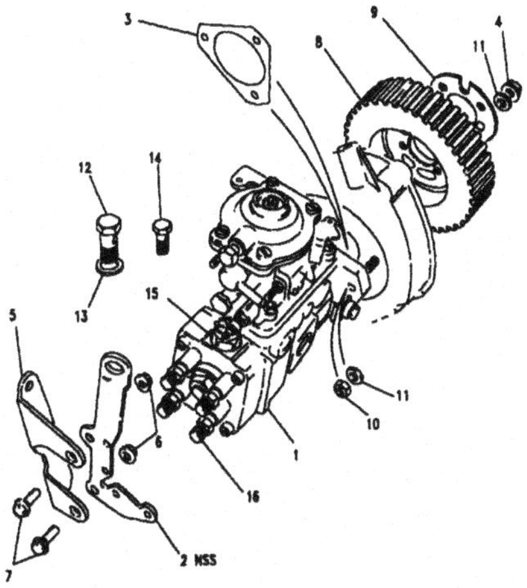

DEFENDER	GROUP B	Engine 2500 - Diesel - Turbo - 200 Tdi Injectors & Pipes

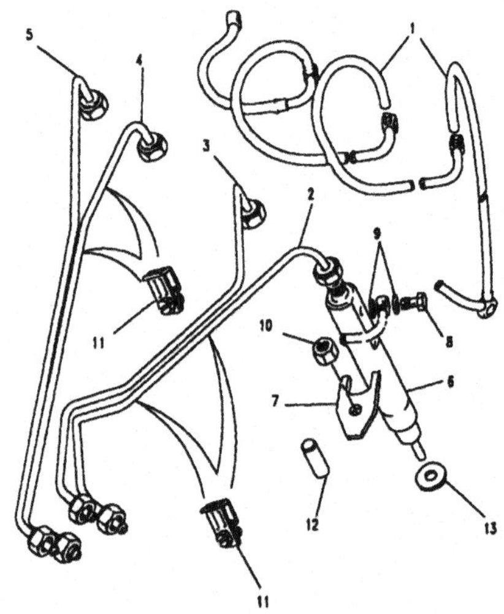

Illus	Part Number	Description	Quantity	Change Point	Remarks
1	ERR3652	Pipe-spill return fuel injection	1		
2	STC793	Pipe-cylinder 1-high pressure fuel injection	1		
3	STC794	Pipe-cylinder 2-high pressure fuel injection	1		
4	STC795	Pipe-cylinder 3-high pressure fuel injection	1		
5	STC796	Pipe-cylinder 4-high pressure fuel injection	1		
6	ETC8412	Injector assembly-diesel holder & nozzle-new	4		
6	ETC8412E	Injector assembly-diesel holder & nozzle-exchange	4		
7	ERR1509	Clamp fuel injector	4		
8	ERR1200	Bolt-banjo-6mm	NLA		Use STC3297.
8	STC3297	BOLT-BANJO	1		
9	ERR1304	• Washer-sealing	8		
10	FN108041L	Nut-flange-M8	NLA		Use FN108047L.
11	AEU2129L	Clamp-2 pipes	4		
12	ETC8470	Dowel-ring	4		
13	ETC8042	Washer-sealing-diesel injector to cylinder head	1	To (E)11L 38460A	
13	ERR4621	Washer-sealing-diesel injector to cylinder head	1	From (E)11L 38461A	

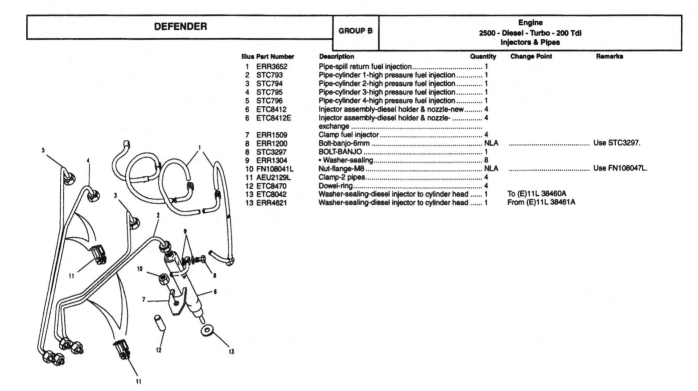

DEFENDER	GROUP B	Engine 2500 - Diesel - Turbo - 200 Tdi Turbocharger

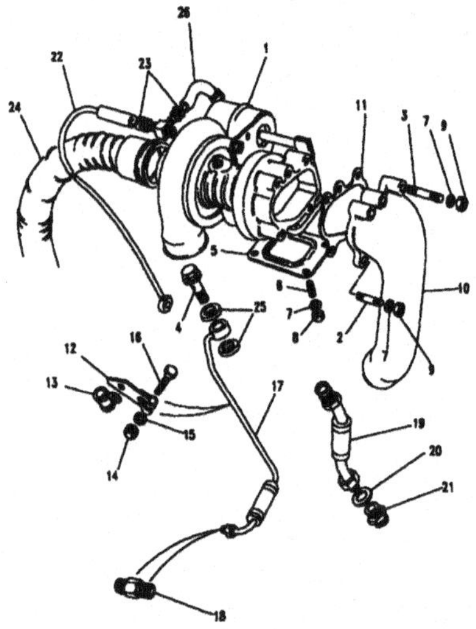

Illus	Part Number	Description	Quantity	Change Point	Remarks
1	ETC8751	Turbocharger assembly-new	1		
1	ETC8751E	Turbocharger assembly-exchange	1		
	STC960	Actuator-waste gate turbocharger	1		
2	RTC6094	Stud-M8 x 32	1		
3	RTC6093	Stud-M8 x 48	4		
4	ERR1125	Bolt-banjo-oil feed	1		
5	ETC5710	Gasket-exhaust manifold to turbocharger	1		
6	ERR551L	Stud-M8 x 25	4		
7	WA108051L	Washer-8mm	9		
8	ETC7184	Nut-M8	4		
9	NH108065L	Nut	5		
10	ETC7058	Elbow-exhaust outlet	1		
11	ETC5898	Gasket-turbocharger elbow to inlet manifold	1		
12	ETC7351	Bracket-mounting oil pipe	1		
13	ETC8843	Clip-cable	1		
14	NH105041L	Nut-hexagonal-M5	1		
15	WA105001L	Washer-plain-standard-M5	1		
16	SH105251L	Screw-hexagonal head-M5 x 25	1		
17	ERR333	Pipe assembly-engine oil feed	1	To (V) 922728	
17	ERR3495	Pipe assembly-engine oil feed	1	From (V) 922729	
18	ETC8820	Pipe-adaptor turbocharger	1		
19	ERR334	Pipe-sump assembly oil drain	1	To (V) 922728	
19	ERR3494	Pipe-sump assembly oil drain	1	From (V) 922729	
20	ERR896	Washer-sealing-turbocharger oil drain pipe adaptor	1		
21	ERR335	Adaptor-oil drain pipe turbocharger	1		
22	ERR1458	Pipe induction system-turbo to injection pump	1		
23	UKC3803L	Clip-hose	2		
24	ESR415	Duct-air cleaner to hose turbocharger	1		
25	FRC4808	Washer-sealing-oil feed pipe banjo	2		
26	RTC5099	Hose-intercooler turbocharger-66mm-long	1		Alternatives
	STC1896	Hose-turbocharger to pipe-230mm-long	1		Alternatives

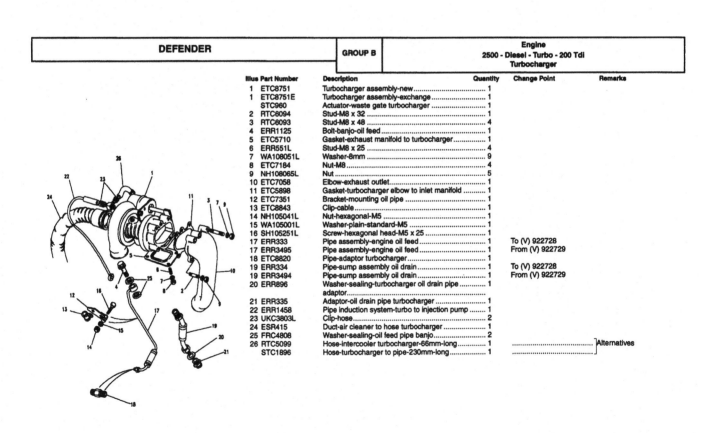

Illus	Part Number	Description	Quantity	Change Point	Remarks
1	STC363	Set-engine gasket-asbestos	NLA		Use STC1557.
1	STC1557	Set-engine gasket-asbestos free	1		
2	STC1172	Set-cylinder head gasket	1		

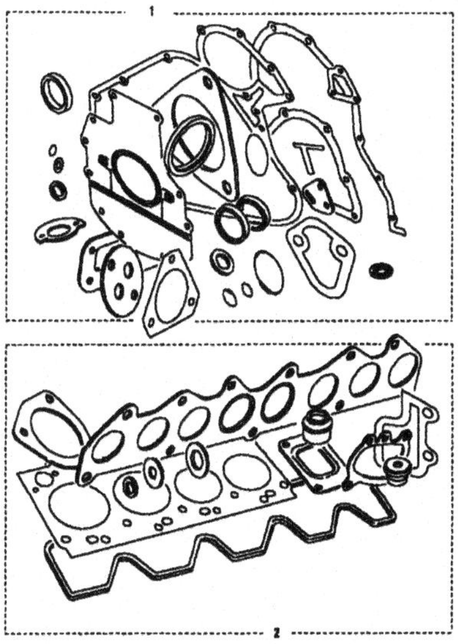

Illus	Part Number	Description	Quantity	Change Point	Remarks
1	ERR535	PUMP BRAKE VACUUM	1		
2	AEU2720	• Bolt	4		
3	WL106001L	• Washer-sprung-M6	4		
4	AEU2718	• Rotor blade-vacuum pump	4		
5	AEU2719	• O ring	1		
6	ETC4616	Gasket-vacuum pump	1		
7	SS108251L	Bolt-hexagonal socket-M8 x 25	3		
8	WM600051L	Washer-spring-5/16"	3		

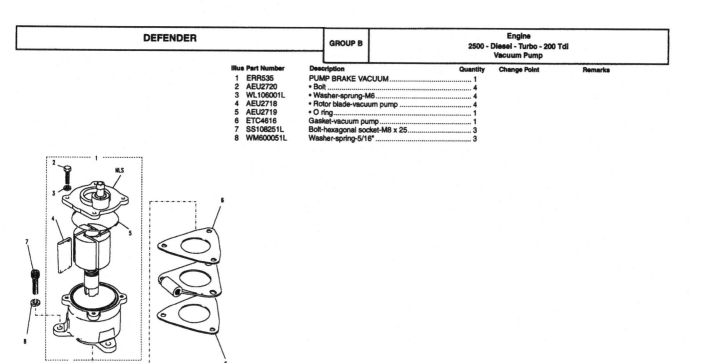

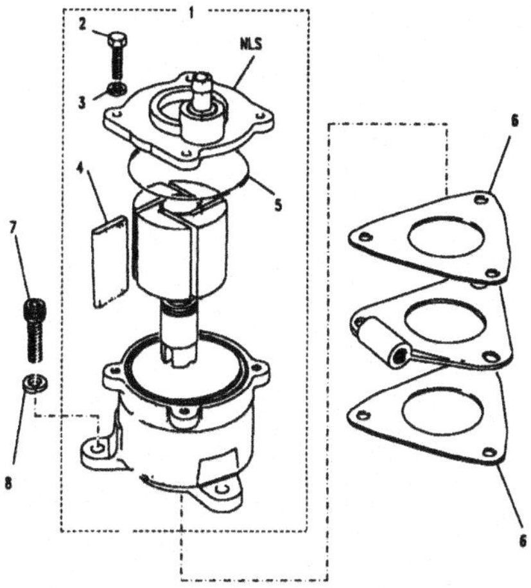

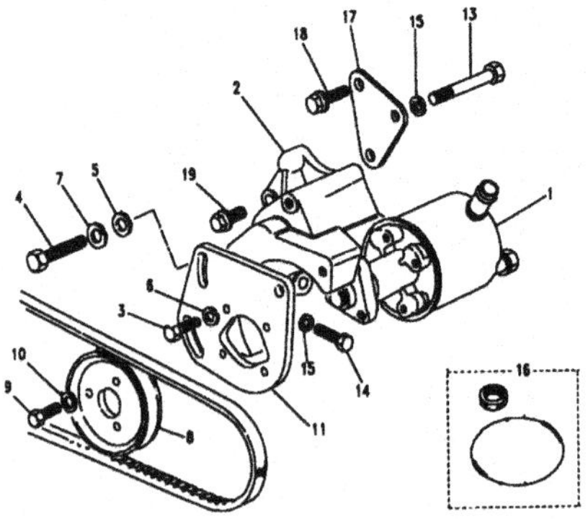

Illus	Part Number	Description	Quantity	Change Point	Remarks
1	NTC8287	Pump assembly power assisted steering	1	To (E)11L 22454A	
1	NTC9070	Pump assembly power assisted steering	1	From (E)11L 22455A	
2	ETC8854	Bracket-power assisted steering	1		
3	FS106201L	Screw-flanged head-M6 x 20	4		
4	FS108251L	Screw-flanged head-M8 x 25	NLA		Use FS108257L.
5	WA108051L	Washer-8mm	2		
6	WL106001L	Washer-sprung-M6	4		
7	WL108001L	Washer-sprung-M8	3		
8	ETC5783	Pulley power assisted steering pump	1		
9	SH108141L	Screw-hexagonal head-M8 x 14	3		
10	WL108001L	Washer-sprung-M8	3		
11	ERR1976	Bracket-mounting power assisted steering pump	1	To (E)11L 22454A	
11	ERR2605	Bracket-mounting power assisted steering pump	1	From (E)11L 22455A	
12	ETC5815	Belt-polyvee power assisted steering	1		
13	BH108181L	Bolt-hexagonal head-M8 x 90	NLA		
14	FS108251L	Screw-flanged head-M8 x 25	NLA		Use FS108257L.
14	FS108307L	Screw-flanged head-M8 x 30	1		
15	WL108001L	Washer-sprung-M8	4		
16	RTC5935	Kit-power assisted steering pump seal	NLA	To (E)11L 22454A	Use STC1633.
16	STC1633	Kit-power assisted steering pump seal	1	From (E)11L 22455A	
17	ERR1264	Plate assembly	1		
18	FS108161L	Screw-flanged head-M8 x 16	1		
19	FS108307L	Screw-flanged head-M8 x 30	1		

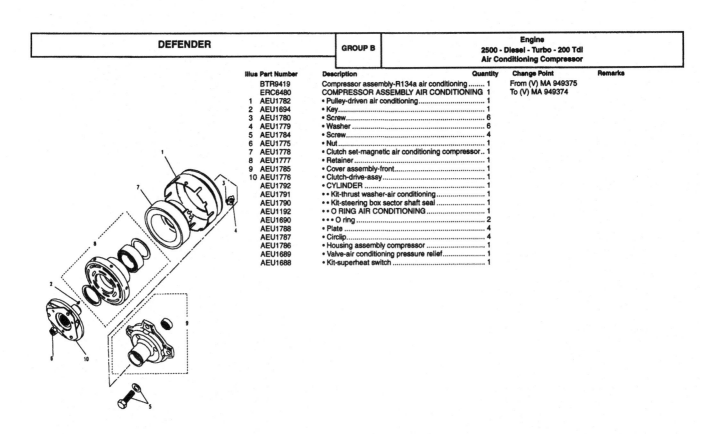

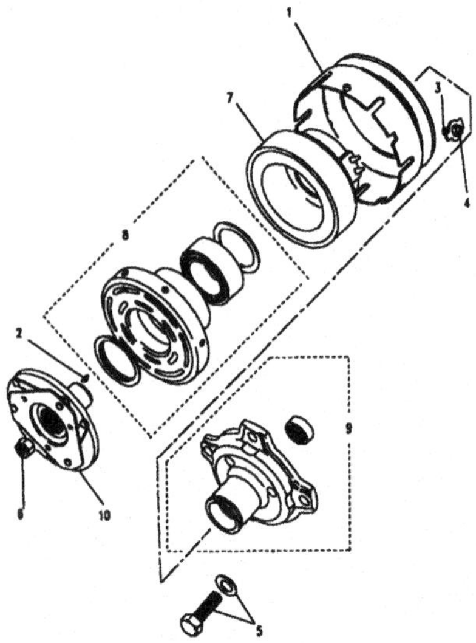

Illus	Part Number	Description	Quantity	Change Point	Remarks
	BTR9419	Compressor assembly-R134a air conditioning	1	From (V) MA 949375	
	ERC6480	COMPRESSOR ASSEMBLY AIR CONDITIONING	1	To (V) MA 949374	
1	AEU1782	• Pulley-driven air conditioning	1		
2	AEU1694	• Key	1		
3	AEU1780	• Screw	6		
4	AEU1779	• Washer	6		
5	AEU1784	• Screw	4		
6	AEU1775	• Nut	1		
7	AEU1778	• Clutch set-magnetic air conditioning compressor	1		
8	AEU1777	• Retainer	1		
9	AEU1785	• Cover assembly-front	1		
10	AEU1776	• Clutch-drive-assy	1		
	AEU1792	• CYLINDER	1		
	AEU1791	• • Kit-thrust washer-air conditioning	1		
	AEU1790	• • Kit-steering box sector shaft seal	1		
	AEU1192	• • O RING AIR CONDITIONING	1		
	AEU1690	• • • O ring	2		
	AEU1788	• Plate	4		
	AEU1787	• Circlip	4		
	AEU1786	• Housing assembly compressor	1		
	AEU1689	• Valve-air conditioning pressure relief	1		
	AEU1688	• Kit-superheat switch	1		

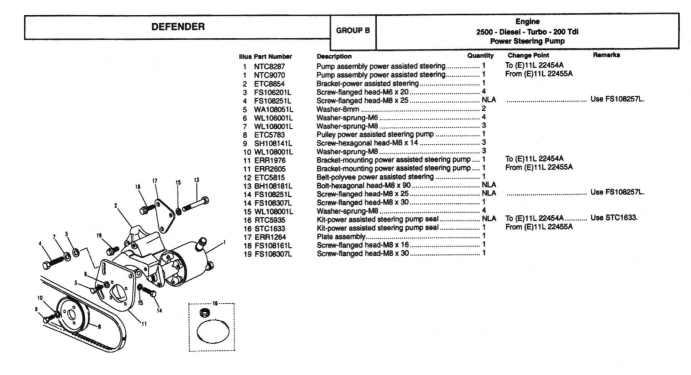

DEFENDER

GROUP B

Engine
2500 - Diesel - Turbo - 200 Tdi
Air Conditioning Compressor-Kits

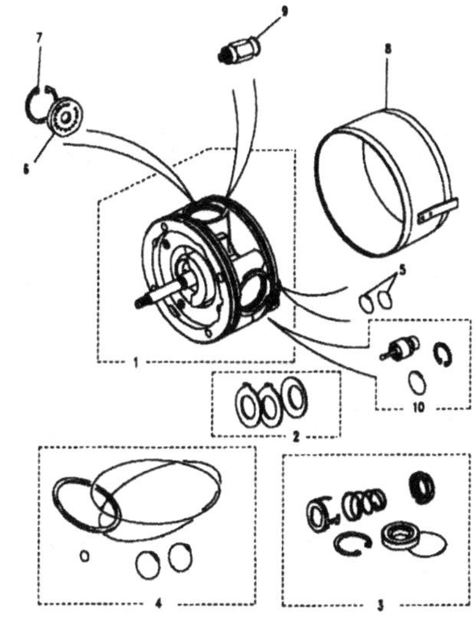

Illus	Part Number	Description	Quantity	Change Point	Remarks
	BTR9419	Compressor assembly-R134a air conditioning	1	From (V) MA 949375	
	ERC6480	COMPRESSOR ASSEMBLY AIR CONDITIONING	1	To (V) MA 949374	
	AEU1782	• Pulley-driven air conditioning	1		
	AEU1694	• Key	1		
	AEU1780	• Screw	6		
	AEU1779	• Washer	6		
	AEU1784	• Screw	4		
	AEU1775	• Nut	1		
	AEU1778	• Clutch set-magnetic air conditioning compressor	1		
	AEU1777	• Retainer	1		
	AEU1785	• Cover assembly-front	1		
	AEU1776	• Clutch-drive-assy	1		
1	AEU1792	• CYLINDER	1		
2	AEU1791	• • Kit-thrust washer-air conditioning	1		
3	AEU1790	• • Kit-steering box sector shaft seal	1		
4	AEU1192	• • O RING AIR CONDITIONING	1		
5	AEU1690	• • • O ring	2		
6	AEU1788	• Plate	4		
7	AEU1787	• Circlip	4		
8	AEU1786	• Housing assembly compressor	1		
9	AEU1689	• Valve-air conditioning pressure relief	1		
10	AEU1688	• Kit-superheat switch	1		
11	ETC4371	Belt-polyvee air conditioning compressor	1		
	AEU1691	Oil-525 visc	A/R		

DEFENDER

GROUP B

Engine
2500 - Diesel - Turbo - 200 Tdi
Air Conditioning Compressor-Fixings

Illus	Part Number	Description	Quantity	Change Point	Remarks
1	ERC7082	Plate-front	1		
2	ERC5152	Plate-rear	1		
3	BH110201L	Bolt-compressor to plate-hexagonal head-M10 x 100	3		
4	WL110001L	Washer-M10	3		
5	ETC4882	Bracket-air compressor	NLA		Use ERR3091.
5	ERR3091	Bracket-air compressor	1		
6	ETC4197	Bracket-compressor air conditioning	1		
7	BH110101L	Bolt-bracket to cover-hexagonal head-M10 x 50-long	4		
8	WA110061L	Washer-M10	4		
9	ERC5155	Link-adjusting compressor	2		
10	BH108181L	Bolt-link to bracket-hexagonal head-M8 x 90	NLA		
11	WL108001L	Washer-sprung-M8	1		
12	NH108041L	Nut-hexagonal head-M8	1		
13	FS108251L	Screw-flanged head-M8 x 25	NLA		Use FS108257L.
14	WA108051L	Washer-8mm	2		
15	WL108001L	Washer-sprung-M8	2		
16	NH106041L	Nut-hexagonal-nyloc-M6	2		
17	FB108081L	Bolt-flanged head-M8 x 40	2		
18	WL108001L	Washer-sprung-M8	2		
19	NH108041L	Nut-hexagonal head-M8	2		

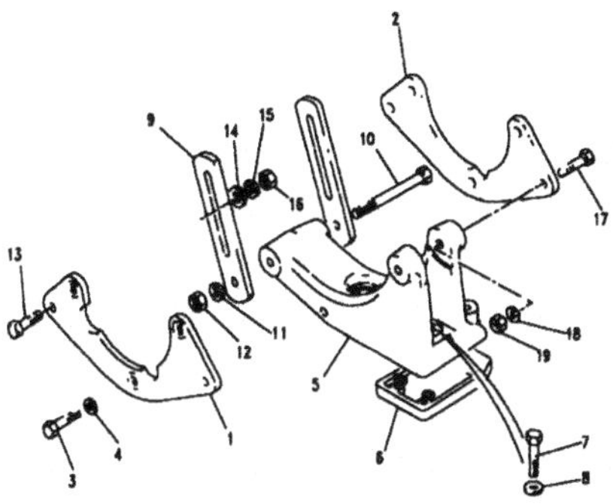

DEFENDER	GROUP B	Engine 2500 - Diesel - Turbo - 200 Tdi Air Conditioning Idler Pulley

Illus	Part Number	Description	Quantity	Change Point	Remarks
1	614718	PULLEY-TENSIONER ANCILLARY DRIVE	1		
	614154	• Bearing-ball	1		
2	BH605101L	Bolt-hexagonal head-5/16UNF x 1 1/4	1		
3	WM600051L	Washer-spring-5/16"	1		

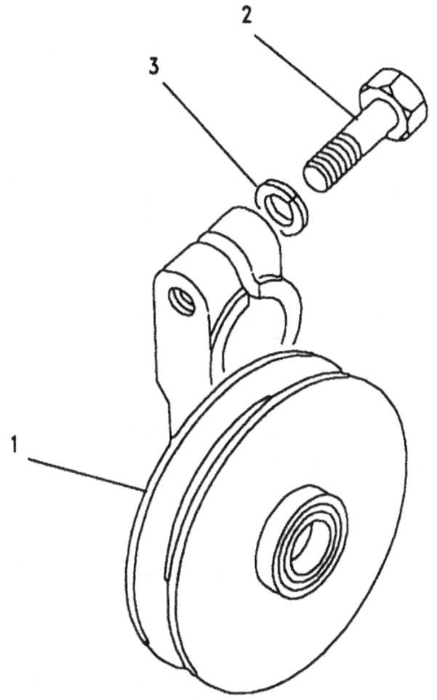

DEFENDER	GROUP B	Engine 2500 - Diesel - Turbo - 200 Tdi Alternator

Illus	Part Number	Description	Quantity	Change Point	Remarks
1	RTC5682N	ALTERNATOR ASSEMBLY-NEW-A127-45 AMP	1		Standard on
1	RTC5682E	ALTERNATOR ASSEMBLY-EXCHANGE-A127-45 AMP	1		
2	RTC5670	• Regulator & brush box assembly alternator	1		
3	RTC5684	• Rectifier-alternator	1		
4	RTC5926	• Bearing-alternator front	1		
5	RTC5687	• Bracket-drive end c/w bearing alternator e-RH	1		
6	RTC5925	• Kit-fixings alternator/vacuum pump-LH	1		
		ALTERNATOR ASSEMBLY			
1	RTC5680N	NEW-A127-65 AMP-RH	NLA		Use STC234.
					Optional
1	STC234	NEW-A127-65 AMP-RH	1		Optional
1	RTC5680E	EXCHANGE-A127-65 AMP-RH	1		Optional
2	RTC5670	• Regulator & brush box assembly alternator	1		
3	RTC5671	• Rectifier-alternator	1		
4	RTC5926	• Bearing-alternator front	1		Part of RTC5680N, RTC5680E.
5	RTC5687	• Bracket-drive end c/w bearing alternator e-RH	1		
6	RTC5046	• Kit-fixings alternator/vacuum pump-RH	1		
	RTC6114	• Capacitor alternator	1		Part of STC234.
7	AAU2249L	Fan alternator	1		
8	RTC5686	Pulley alternator	1		
9	ETC7939	Belt-polyvee alternator	1		
	RTC5689	Spacer	1		

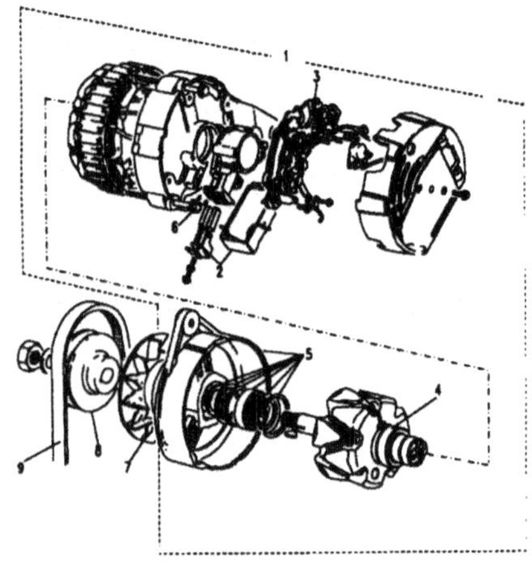

Illus	Part Number	Description	Quantity	Change Point	Remarks
1	ETC4357	Bracket-mounting-alternator	1		
2	BH108161L	Bolt-bracket to block-hexagonal head-M8 x 80	1		
3	FS110301L	Screw-bracket to block-flanged head-M10 x 30-top	2		
4	WL108001L	Washer-sprung-M8	1		
5	WL108001L	Washer-sprung-M8	1		
6	ERC6266	Link-adjuster alternator-A127 alternator	1		
7	FS108207L	Screw-link to alternator-flanged head-M8 x 20	1		
8	WL108001L	Washer-sprung-M8	2		
9	2266L	Washer	1		
10	ERC8964	Bolt-link to block-M8 x 95	1		
11	WL108001L	Washer-sprung-M8	1		
12	FB108081L	Bolt-bracket to block-flanged head-M8 x 40	1		
13	BH108091L	Bolt-bracket to block-M8 x 45	1		
	ERC7974	Spacer	1		
14	WC108051L	Washer-M8	1		
15	NY108041L	Nut-nyloc-M8	2		

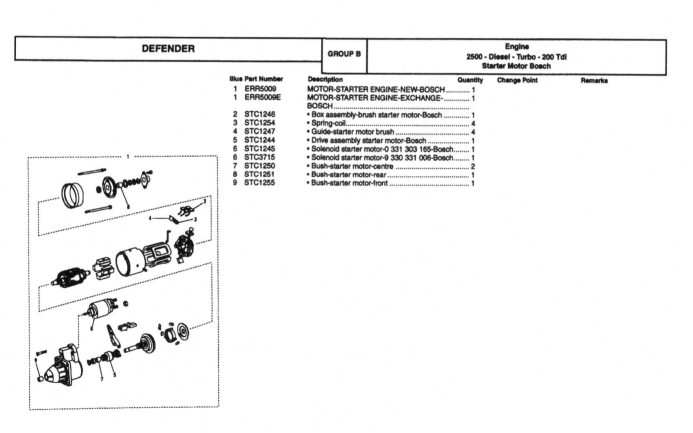

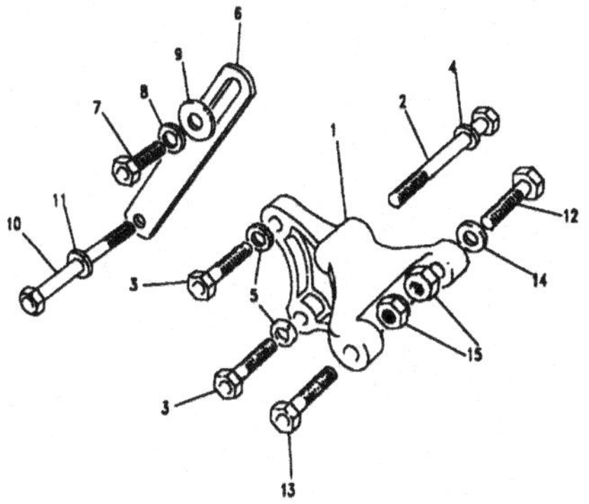

Illus	Part Number	Description	Quantity	Change Point	Remarks
1	ERR5009	MOTOR-STARTER ENGINE-NEW-BOSCH	1		
1	ERR5009E	MOTOR-STARTER ENGINE-EXCHANGE-BOSCH	1		
2	STC1246	• Box assembly-brush starter motor-Bosch	1		
3	STC1254	• Spring-coil	4		
4	STC1247	• Guide-starter motor brush	4		
5	STC1244	• Drive assembly starter motor-Bosch	1		
6	STC1245	• Solenoid starter motor-0 331 303 165-Bosch	1		
6	STC3715	• Solenoid starter motor-9 330 331 006-Bosch	1		
7	STC1250	• Bush-starter motor-centre	2		
8	STC1251	• Bush-starter motor-rear	1		
9	STC1255	• Bush-starter motor-front	1		

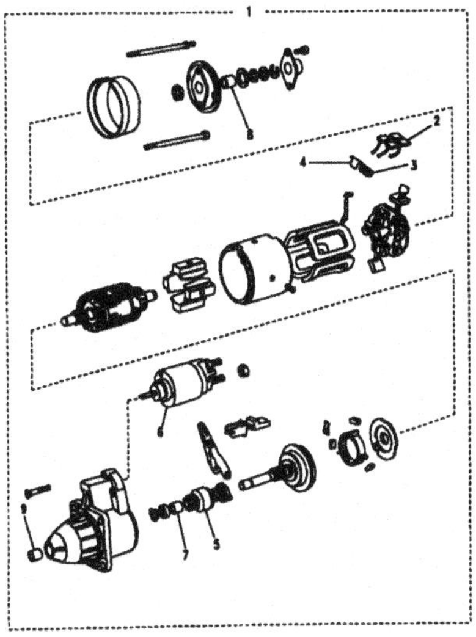

DEFENDER | GROUP B | Engine 2500 - Diesel - Turbo - 200 Tdi Starter Motor Valeo

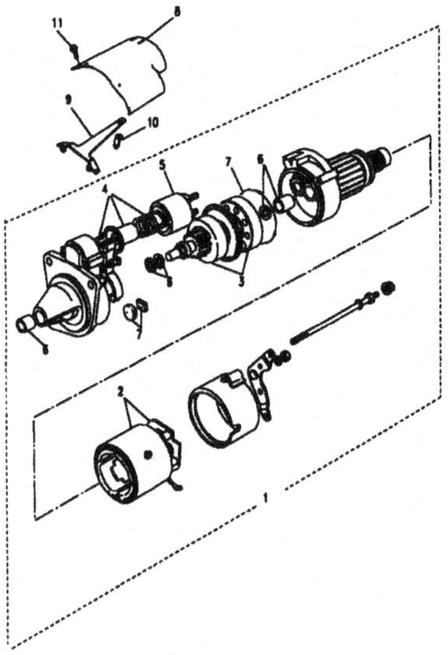

Illus	Part Number	Description	Quantity	Change Point	Remarks
1	PRC5109N	MOTOR-STARTER ENGINE-NEW-VALEO	NLA		Use NAD10039.
1	PRC5109N	MOTOR-STARTER ENGINE-NEW-VALEO	NLA	To (E)11L 24823A	Use NAD10039.
1	PRC5109E	MOTOR-STARTER ENGINE-EXCHANGE-VALEO	1	To (E)11L 24823A	
2	RTC4981	• Box assembly-brush starter motor-Valeo	1		
3	RTC4982	• Drive assembly starter motor-Valeo	1		
4	RTC4979	• Yoke assembly starter motor	1		
5	RTC4978	• Solenoid starter motor-Valeo	1		
6	RTC4980	• Kit-starter motor	1		
7	RTC4983	• Kit-starter motor sundry parts	1		
1	NAD10039	MOTOR-STARTER ENGINE-LUCAS	NLA		Use ERR5009.
1	ERR5009	MOTOR-STARTER ENGINE-NEW-BOSCH	1		
2	STC1246	• Box assembly-brush starter motor-Bosch	1		
	STC1254	• Spring-coil	4		
	STC1247	• Guide-starter motor brush	4		
3	STC1244	• Drive assembly starter motor-Bosch	1		
5	STC1245	• Solenoid starter motor-0 331 303 165-Bosch	1		
5	STC3715	• Solenoid starter motor-9 330 331 006-Bosch	1		
	STC1250	• Bush-starter motor-centre	2		
	STC1251	• Bush-starter motor-rear	1		
	STC1255	• Bush-starter motor-front	1		
	PRC5538	Harness earth bond	1	To (E)11L 24823A	
8	ERR806	Heatshield-starter motor	1		
9	ERR807	Bracket-starter heatshield	1		
10	ERR808	Bracket-starter heatshield	1		
11	FS105107L	Screw-starter heatshield-flanged head-M5 x 10	4		
	FS110301L	Screw-starter to flywheel-flanged head-M10 x 30-top	1		
	FN110047	Nut-flange-starter to flywheel-flange-M10	2		
	WL110001L	Washer-starter to flywheel-M10	3		
	BH110091L	Bolt-starter to flywheel-M10 x 45	1		

DEFENDER | GROUP B | Engine 2500 - Diesel - Turbo - 200 Tdi Flywheel & Clutch

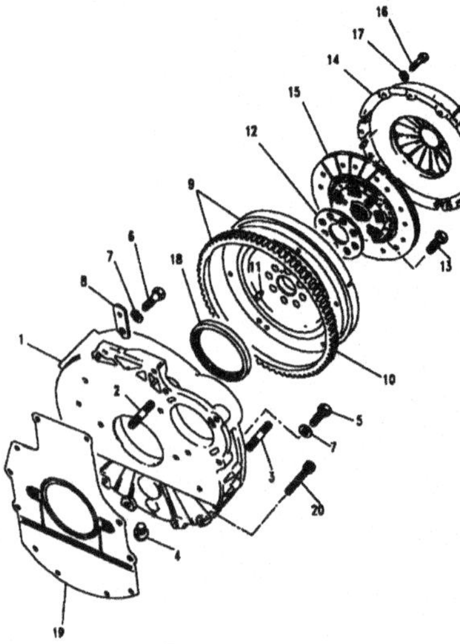

Illus	Part Number	Description	Quantity	Change Point	Remarks
1	ERR1330	Housing assembly differential/final drive wheel	1	To (E) 60160A	
1	ERR3924	Housing assembly differential/final drive wheel	1	From (E) 60161A	
2	TE110061L	Stud-M10 x 30	13		
3	ERC9240	Stud-M10	1		
4	ERC7295	Plug-rubber	1		
5	FS110301L	Screw-flanged head-M10 x 30-top	6		
6	BH110091L	Bolt-housing to block-M10 x 45	2		
7	WA110061L	Washer-housing to block-M10	6		
8	ERC9404	Bracket harness-harness clip	2		
9	ERR4908	Flywheel engine	NLA		Use ERR719.
9	ERR719	FLYWHEEL ENGINE	1		
11	568431	• Gear-ring-flywheel engine	1		
10	502116	• Dowel-flywheel to crankshaft	3		
12	ERC4658	Plate-reinforcement	NLA		Engineering have found that the reinforcing plate is not required. When refitting flywheel omit plate , and fit new bolts ERR4574..
13	ERC6551	Bolt-fixing flywheel crankshaft-long	8		
13	ERR4574	Bolt-fixing flywheel crankshaft-short	8		
15	FTC576	Plate-clutch-driven-standard duty	NLA		Use FTC2149.
15	FTC1994	Plate-clutch-driven-Valeo	1		
	STC8358	KIT-CLUTCH	1		Except 130"
14	FTC575	• Cover-clutch assembly	NLA		Use URB100760.
15	FTC2149	• Plate-clutch-driven	NLA		Use FTC4204.
	FRC9568	• BEARING-CLUTCH RELEASE	NLA		Use FTC5200.
	FRC4078	• • Sleeve-guide clutch	1		
	FTC5200	Bearing-clutch release	1		
16	SX108201L	Bolt-M8 x 20	6		
17	WL108001L	Washer-sprung-M8	6		
18	ERR1535	Seal-crankshaft rear	NLA		Use ERR2532.
18	ERR2532	Seal-crankshaft rear	1		
19	ERR1440	Gasket-flywheel/drive plate housing/crankcase	1		
20	SS110801	Screw-M10 x 80	4		

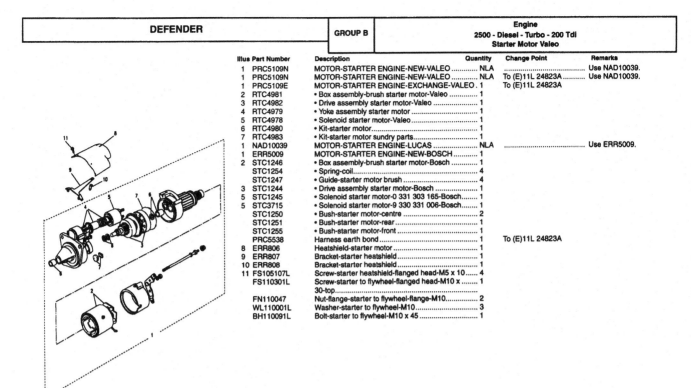

Illus	Part Number	Description	Quantity	Change Point	Remarks
1	STC1736N	Engine unit-stripped-new	1		
1	STC1736E	Engine unit-stripped-exchange	1		

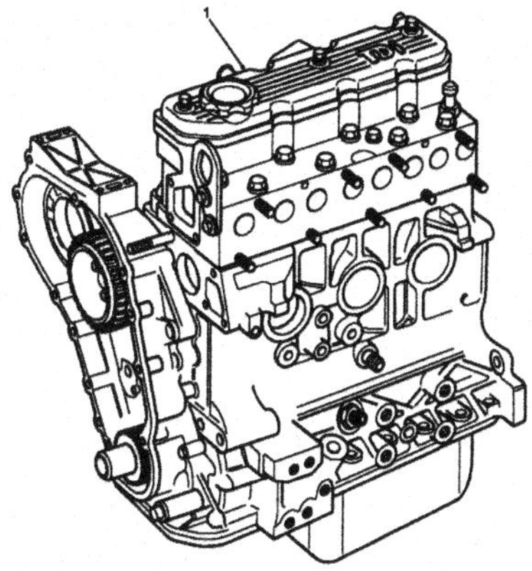

AHBNAC1A

Illus	Part Number	Description	Quantity	Change Point	Remarks
1	STC1675	Engine assembly - Short	1		

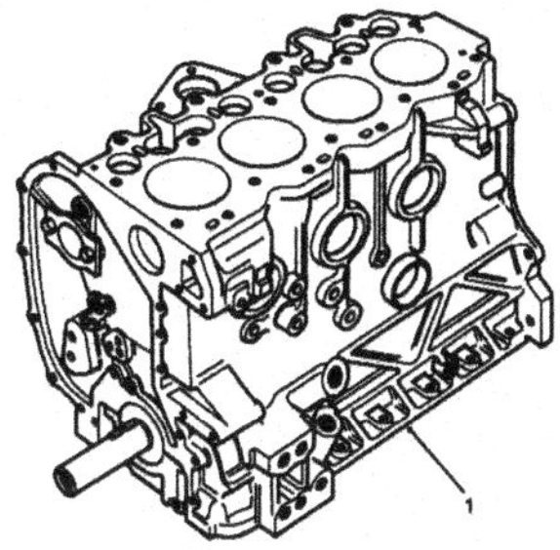

AHBNAE1A

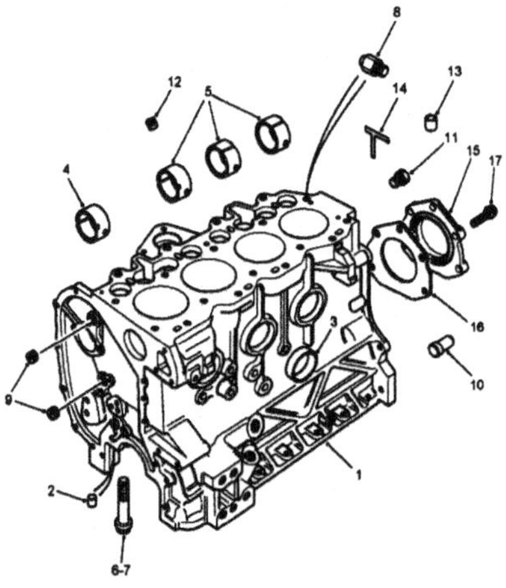

AHBNBA1A

Illus	Part Number	Description	Quantity	Change Point	Remarks
1	ERR1919	CYLINDER BLOCK-ENGINE	1		
2	501593	• Dowel	10		
3	ERC4996	• Plug-core	6		
4	ETC8442	• Bearing-camshaft front	1		
5	90519055	• Bearing-camshaft rear	3		
6	ETC8074	• Bolt	8		
7	ERR3419	• Setscrew-cylinder block main bearing cap	2		
8	ERR2767	Jet-camshaft oil	1		
9	247127	Plug-cylinder block oil way	2		
10	FRC2482	Dowel-ring-15.0mm	2		
11	ETC4922	Plug-gallery pipe	2		
12	ERR5034	Plug-camshaft blanking-rubber	3		
13	ETC8352	Dowel-ring	2		
14	ERR913	Packing strip	2		
15	ERR4179	Seal-crankshaft rear oil	NLA	Note (1)	Use ERR6818 qty 1 with ERR6811 qty 1.
15	ERR6818	Seal-crankshaft rear oil	NLA	Note (2)	Use LUF100430.
15	LUF100430	Seal-crankshaft rear oil	1	Note (3)	
16	ERR4861	Gasket-crankcase rear oil seal housing	NLA	To (E)16L 39342A	Use ERR6811.
16	ERR6811	Gasket-crankcase rear oil seal housing	1	From (E)16L 39343A	
17	FS108257L	Screw-flanged head-M8 x 25	5		

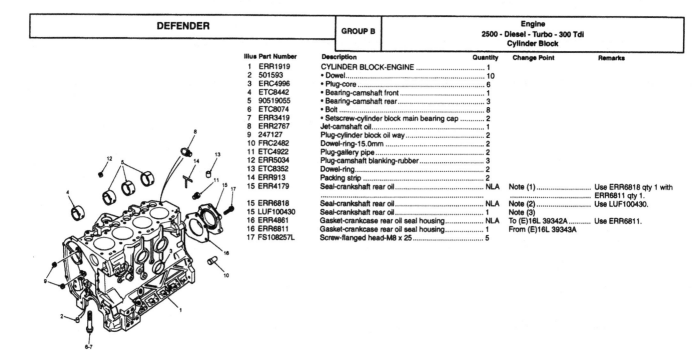

CHANGE POINTS:
(1) To (E)16L 39342A
(2) From (E)16L 39343A To (V) WA 138479
(3) From (V) WA 138480

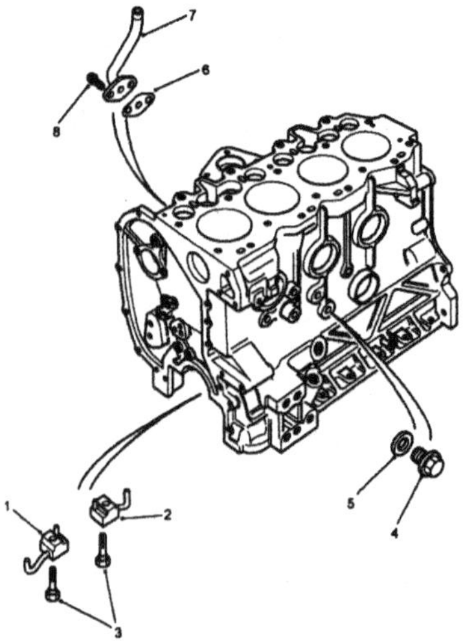

AHBNBA2A

Illus	Part Number	Description	Quantity	Change Point	Remarks
1	ETC6531	Jet assembly-piston cooling-No1-No3	2		
2	ETC6532	Jet assembly-piston cooling-No2-No4	2		
3	ETC5592	Valve-bearing housing jet	4		
4	ERC9410	Plug-drain	1		
5	AFU1882L	Washer-sump assembly drain plug	1		
6	ERR1653	Gasket-external drain pipe	1		
7	ERR1094	Pipe-oil drain turbocharger	1		
8	FS108207L	Screw-flanged head-M8 x 20	2		

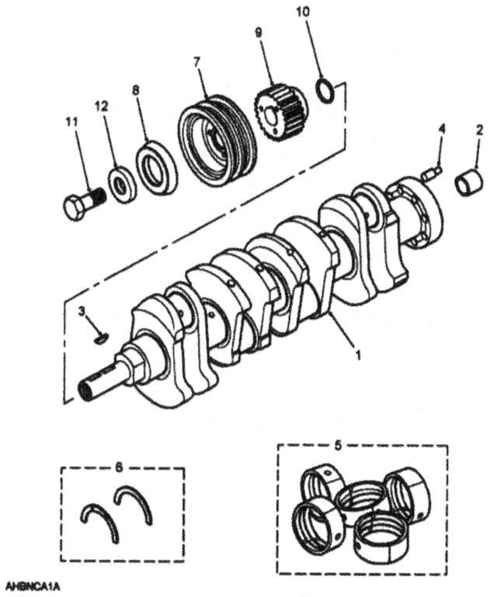

AHBNCA1A

Illus	Part Number	Description	Quantity	Change Point	Remarks
1	ERR2112	CRANKSHAFT-ENGINE	1		
2	8566L	• Bush-crankshaft	1		
3	ERR3987	• Key-crankshaft	NLA		Use ERR5215.
3	ERR5215	• Key-crankshaft	2		
4	ERR1630	Dowel-flywheel to crankshaft	1		
		SET-CRANKSHAFT BEARINGS			
5	RTC4783	standard.	NLA		Use STC3395.
5	STC3395	standard.	1		
5	RTC478310	0.010" undersize	1		
		WASHER-CRANKSHAFT THRUST			
6	RTC2825	standard.-pair	A/R		
6	538131	oversize.-0.0025"-pair	A/R		
6	538132	oversize.-0.005"-pair	A/R		
7	ERR2220	Torsional vibration damper-engine crankshaft	1		
8	ERR2100	Flinger-crankshaft pulley	1		
9	ERR4707	Pulley-crankshaft	1	To (V) VA 117353	
9	LHH100660	Pulley-crankshaft	1	From (V) VA 117354	
10	ERR4710	O ring-crankshaft to toothed pulley	1		
11	ERR5087	Bolt-crankshaft pulley	1		
12	ERR1564	Washer-crankshaft thrust	1		

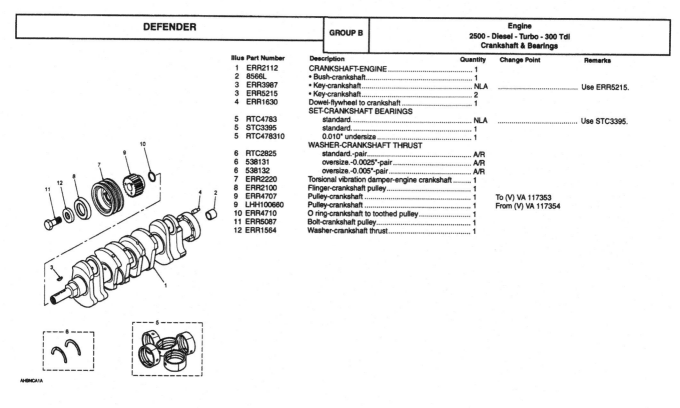

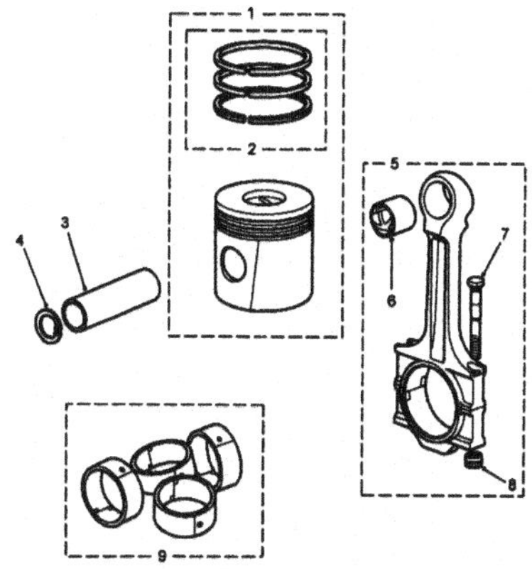

AHBNCC1A

Illus	Part Number	Description	Quantity	Change Point	Remarks
		PISTON-ENGINE			
1	ERR2410	STANDARD.	4		
1	STC298210	0.010" OVERSIZE	4		
1	STC298220	0.020" OVERSIZE	4		
2	STC958	• Kit-piston ring	4		
3	ERR703	Pin-piston gudgeon	4		
4	266945	Circlip-piston	8		
5	ERR2418	ROD-CRANKSHAFT CONNECTING	4		
6	ERR2419	• Bearing bush-connecting rod small end	4		
7	ETC7357	• Bolt-connecting rod	8		
8	ETC8191	• Nut-connecting rod	8		
9	RTC2993	Set-connecting rod big end half bearing-standard.	A/R		
9	RTC299310	Set-connecting rod big end half bearing-0.010" undersize	A/R		

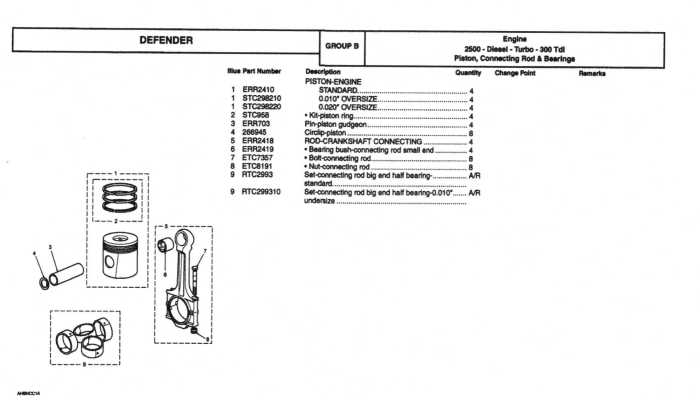

DEFENDER	GROUP B	Engine 2500 - Diesel - Turbo - 300 Tdi Sump

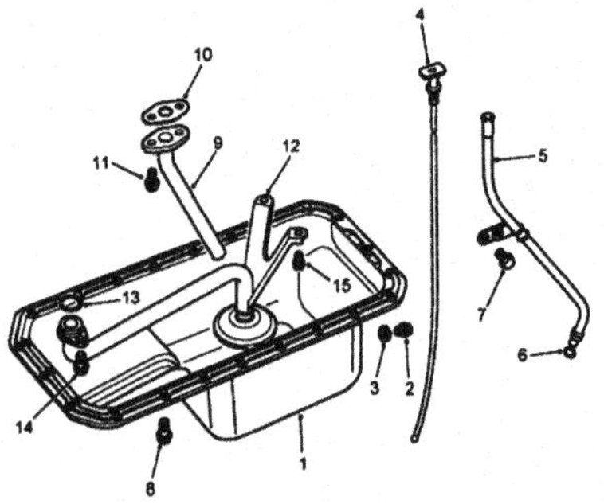

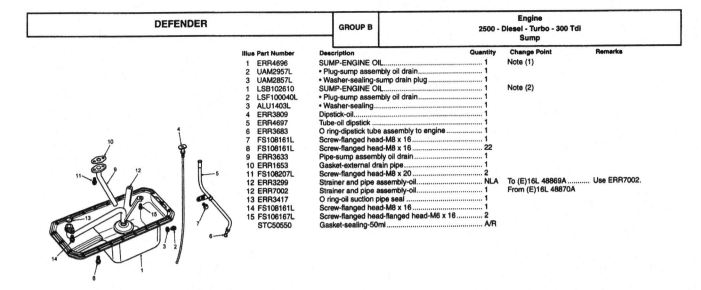

AHBNDA1A
ENGINE - 2 1/2 TURBO DIESEL 300 TDI - SUMP - DEF 110

Illus	Part Number	Description	Quantity	Change Point	Remarks
1	ERR4696	SUMP-ENGINE OIL	1	Note (1)	
2	UAM2957L	• Plug-sump assembly oil drain	1		
3	UAM2857L	• Washer-sealing-sump drain plug	1		
1	LSB102610	SUMP-ENGINE OIL	1	Note (2)	
2	LSF100040L	• Plug-sump assembly oil drain	1		
3	ALU1403L	• Washer-sealing	1		
4	ERR3809	Dipstick-oil	1		
5	ERR4697	Tube-oil dipstick	1		
6	ERR3683	O ring-dipstick tube assembly to engine	1		
7	FS108161L	Screw-flanged head-M8 x 16	1		
8	FS108161L	Screw-flanged head-M8 x 16	22		
9	ERR3633	Pipe-sump assembly oil drain	1		
10	ERR1653	Gasket-external drain pipe	1		
11	FS108207L	Screw-flanged head-M8 x 20	2		
12	ERR3299	Strainer and pipe assembly-oil	NLA	To (E)16L 48869A	Use ERR7002.
12	ERR7002	Strainer and pipe assembly-oil	1	From (E)16L 48870A	
13	ERR3417	O ring-oil suction pipe seal	1		
14	FS108161L	Screw-flanged head-M8 x 16	1		
15	FS106167L	Screw-flanged head-flanged head-M6 x 16	2		
	STC50550	Gasket-sealing-50ml	A/R		

AJBNDA1A

CHANGE POINTS:
(1) To (E)16L 88228A; To (E)23L 88228A
(2) From (E)16L 88229A; From (E)23L 88229A

DEFENDER	GROUP B	Engine 2500 - Diesel - Turbo - 300 Tdi Front Cover

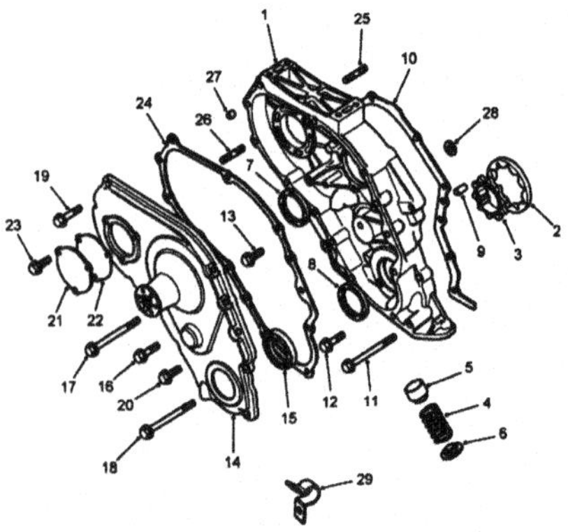

AHBNEA1A

Illus	Part Number	Description	Quantity	Change Point	Remarks
1	ERR4664	COVER-TIMING BELT-INNER	1		
2	ERR1040	• Rotor-oil pump outer	NLA		Use STC3407 matched pair of inner and outer rotor.
2	STC3407	• Rotor-oil pump outer	1		
3	ERR1041	• Rotor-oil pump inner	NLA		Use STC3407 matched pair of inner and outer rotor.
4	ERR1084	• Spring-oil pump relief valve	1		
5	ERR1085	• Plunger-oil pump relief valve	1		
6	ERR1086	• Plug	1		
7	ERR3356	• Seal-camshaft oil	1		
8	ERR4575	• Seal-crankshaft front oil-inner	1		
9	6395L	Dowel	4		
10	ERR4860	Gasket-timing gear housing drain plate	1		
11	FB108161L	Bolt-flanged head-M8 x 80	2		
12	FB108071L	Bolt-flanged head-M8 x 35	3		
13	FS108257L	Screw-flanged head-M8 x 25	5		
14	ERR4578	Cover-engine-front	NLA		Use ERR7147 qty 1 on Wolf vehicles with vented front cover.Note fit new boost pipe MSP100980 and plug old pipe connection in ERR4664 cover assembly or ERR7146 qty 1 on all other applications.
15	ERR4576	Seal-crankshaft front oil-outer	1	Note (1)	
15	ERR7143	Seal-crankshaft front oil	1	Note (2)	
16	FB108071L	Bolt-flanged head-M8 x 35	5		
16	FB108081L	Bolt-flanged head-M8 x 40	2		
17	FB108201L	Bolt-flanged head-M8 x 100	2		
18	FB108221	Bolt-flanged head-M8 x 110	2		
19	FB108101L	Bolt-flanged head-M8 x 50	2		
20	FS108257L	Screw-flanged head-M8 x 25	1		

CHANGE POINTS:
(1) To (E)15L 01620A
(2) From (E)15L 01621A

Illus	Part Number	Description	Quantity	Change Point	Remarks
21	ERR1560	Cover plate	NLA		Use ERR7249.
21	ERR7249	Cover plate	1		
22	ERR1561	Gasket-front plate to timing chain cover	1		
23	FS108127L	Screw-flanged head-flanged head-M8 x 12	3		
23	FS108127L	Screw-flanged head-flanged head-M8 x 12	3		
24	ERR4120	Gasket-timing gear cover plate	NLA		Use ERR7293.
24	ERR7293	Gasket-timing gear cover plate	1		
25	TE108061L	Stud-M8 x 30	3		
26	TE110051L	Stud-M10 x 25	1		
27	ERR3286	Dowel-front cover securing	2		
28	ERR2344	Washer-sealing	1		
29	ERR4824	Clip-hose	2		

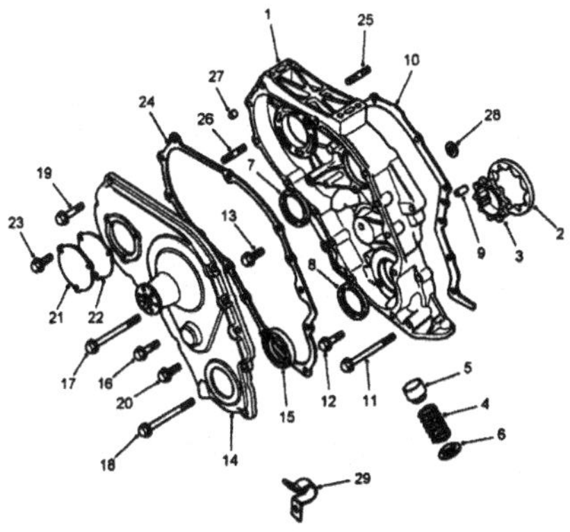

AHBNEA1A

Illus	Part Number	Description	Quantity	Change Point	Remarks
1	ERR1092	Belt-engine timing	1		
2	ERR1972	Tensioner-timing belt	1	To (V) VA 117353	
2	LHP100860	Tensioner-timing belt	1	From (V) VA 117354	
3	ERR900	Washer	1		
4	FN110041	Nut-M10-flanged head	NLA		Use FN110047.
4	FN110047	Nut-flange-flange-M10	1		
5	FB110131	Bolt-flanged head	1		
6	ETC8560	Idler-timing belt	1	To (V) VA 117353	
6	LHV100150	Idler-timing belt	1	From (V) VA 117354	
7	ERR1973	Washer	1		
8	TE110051L	Stud-M10 x 25	1	To (E)16L 67364B To (E)23L 38372B	
8	TE110061L	Stud-M10 x 30	1	From (E)16L 67365B From (E)23L 38373B	
9	FX110041L	Nut-flange-M10	NLA	To (E)16L 67364B To (E)23L 38372B	Use FX110047L.
9	LYH100500	Nut-flange-M10	1	From (E)16L 67365B From (E)23L 38373B	

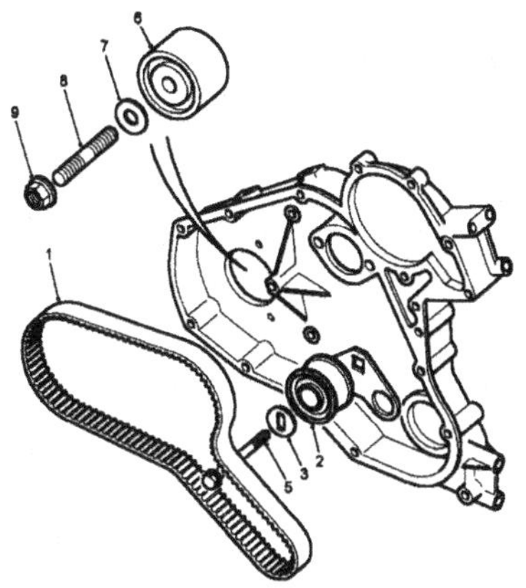

LB0027

DEFENDER

GROUP B

Engine
2500 - Diesel - Turbo - 300 Tdi
Coolant Pump

Illus	Part Number	Description	Quantity	Change Point	Remarks
1	STC1086	PUMP ASSEMBLY-ENGINE COOLANT	1		
2	ERR3284	• Gasket-coolant pump body	1		
3	FS108307L	Screw-flanged head-M8 x 30	5		
4	PEP102840	Pipe assembly-engine coolant-diesel	1		
5	ERR3736	Bracket-coolant pump support	1		
6	FC108247	Bolt-flanged head-M8 x 120	3		
7	ERR5259	Bracket-coolant hose support	1		
8	TE110151	Stud-M10 x 75	1		
9	ERR4708	Tensioner-automatic ancillary drive	1		
10	FN110047	Nut-flange-flange-M10	1		
11	PET100790	Gasket-coolant pump distance piece to block-water in to block	1		
12	ERR5691	Stud-M8 x 52	1		
13	FC108137	Bolt-flanged head-M6 x 65	1		
14	FB108261	Bolt-flanged head-M8 x 130	1		
15	FX108041	Nut-flange-M8	2		
16	ERR3734	Pulley coolant pump	1		
17	FS108127L	Screw-flanged head-flanged head-M8 x 12	3		
18	ERR5099	Hose-bypass to pump coolant	1		
19	CN100308L	Clip-hose-30mm	2		

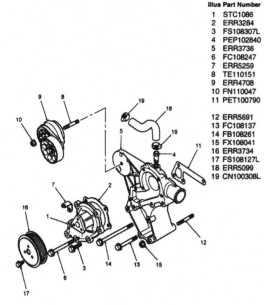

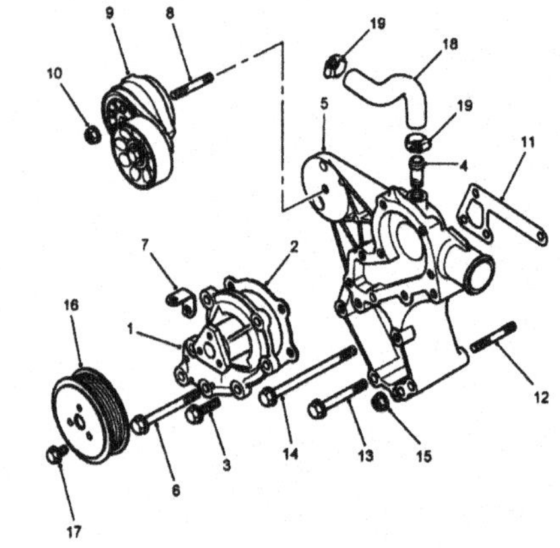

LB0033

DEFENDER

GROUP B

Engine
2500 - Diesel - Turbo - 300 Tdi
Cooling Fan & Belt

Illus	Part Number	Description	Quantity	Change Point	Remarks
1	ERR2789	Fan-cooling	1		
2	ERR2266	Coupling-engine fan viscous	1		
3	ERR3735	Pulley coolant pump	1		
4	FS108127L	Screw-flanged head-flanged head-M8 x 12	4		
5	ERR3287	Belt-polyvee coolant pump	1	To (E)16L 25164	
5	ERR5911	Belt-polyvee coolant pump	1	From (E)16L 25165	
6	SS108161L	Screw-hexagon socket-M8 x 16	4		

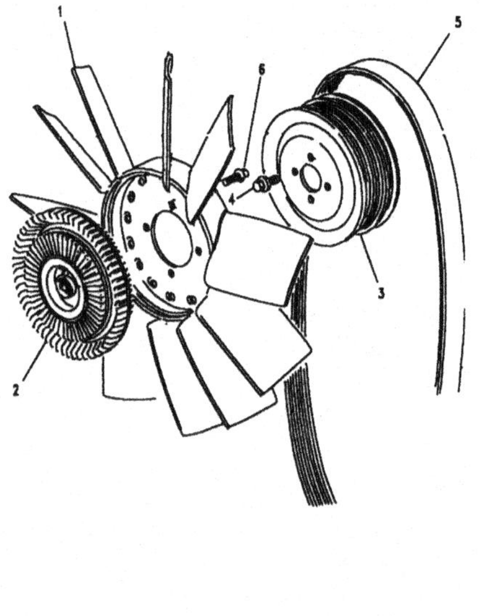

Illus	Part Number	Description	Quantity	Change Point	Remarks
1	ERR2317	ADAPTOR-OIL FILTER	1		
2	ERC5923	• Thermostat assembly-oil	1		
3	ERR2241	• Waxstat adaptor	1		
4	ERC5913	• O ring	1		
5	PRC6387	• Switch-oil pressure engine	1		
6	FS106167L	• Screw-flanged head-flanged head-M6 x 16	2		
7	AFU1887L	• Washer-sealing	1		
8	ERR3340	Cartridge-engine oil filter	1		
9	FS110301L	Screw-flanged head-M10 x 30-top	4		
10	ERR3283	Gasket-cylinder block to oil filter adaptor	1		
5	NUC100280L	Switch-oil pressure engine	1		
7	MDY100080L	Gasket-sealing-12mm-inside diameter-18mm-outside diameter	1		
	LQS105070	Adaptor-oil pressure switch	1		
7	ADU6847L	Washer-sealing	1		

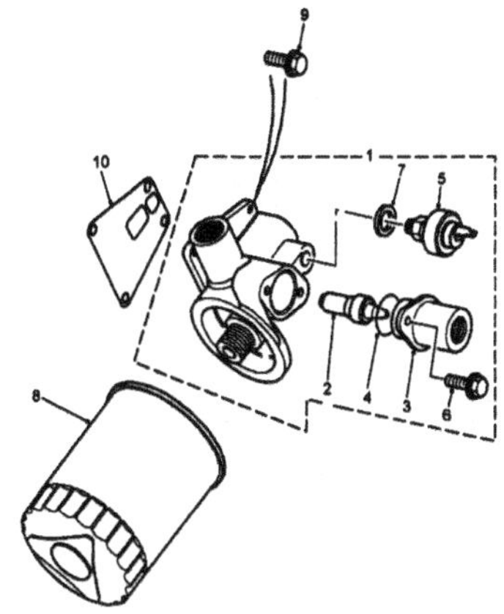

AHBNFC1A

Illus	Part Number	Description	Quantity	Change Point	Remarks
1	ERR5027	CYLINDER HEAD-ENGINE-LESS CORE PLUGS	1		
2	LGJ100880	• Guide-cylinder head valve	8		
4	ERR3753	• Insert-cylinder head exhaust valve seat	4		
3	ERR2396	• Insert-inlet valve seat-cylinder head	4	Note (1)	
5	525497	Plug-core	1		
6	524765	Plug-core	1		
7	TE108051L	Stud-M8 x 25	2		
8	TE110071	Stud-M10 x 35	10		
		BOLT-CYLINDER HEAD FIXING			
9	ETC8808	short-M12 x 100	4		
10	ERR1939	long-M12 x 140	10		
11	ETC8810	M10 x 117	4		
		GASKET-CYLINDER HEAD			
12	ERR5261	1.30mm-1 hole	A/R		
12	ERR5262	1.40mm-2 holes	A/R		
12	ERR5263	1.50mm-3 holes	A/R		
12	ERR7154	1.60mm.	A/R		
13	AMR2425	Cable-heater plug ignition	1		
14	NH104041L	Nut-hexagonal-M4	4		
15	WA104001L	Washer-plain-M4	4		
16	WE104001L	Washer- shakeproof-M4	4		
17	ETC8847	Plug-heater ignition	4		
18	ETC8036	Bracket-lifting engine rear	1		
19	FS108257L	Screw-flanged head-M8 x 25	2		
20	CP108251L	Clip-p	1		
21	PRC2979	Bracket-clipping-steel	1		
22	390939	Bush	1		
23	ETC8031	Bracket-lifting engine front	1		
24	FS108207L	Screw-flanged head-M8 x 20	2		
25	624091	Adaptor-pipe coolant	1		
26	ERR1019	Stud-injector clamp	4		
27	ERC9404	Bracket harness	1		
28	FS108161L	Screw-flanged head-M8 x 16	1		
29	ETC5577	Plug-drain	1		
30	FRC4808	Washer-sealing	1		
31	ERR2081	Sensor-temperature	1		
32	ERR894	Washer-sealing	1		

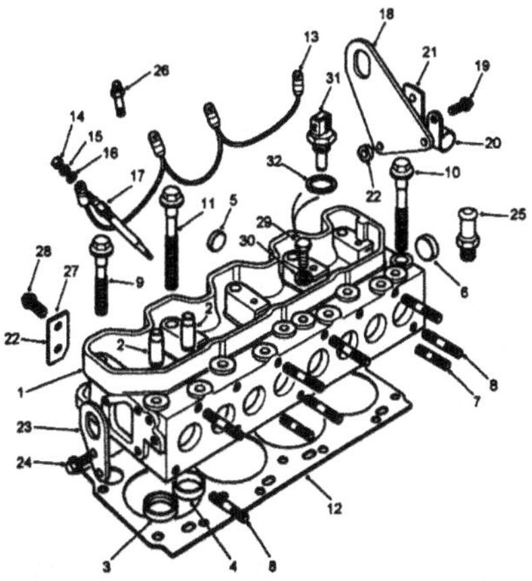

LB0012

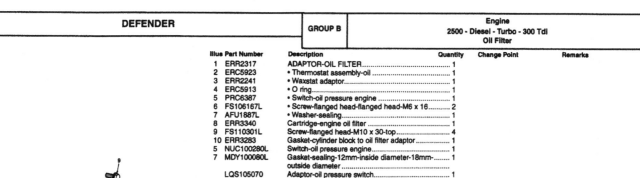

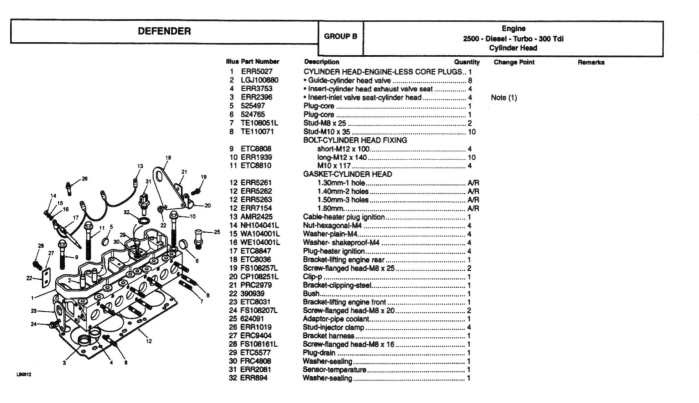

CHANGE POINTS:
(1) From (E)16L 00088L

DEFENDER	GROUP B	Engine 2500 - Diesel - Turbo - 300 Tdi Rockershaft

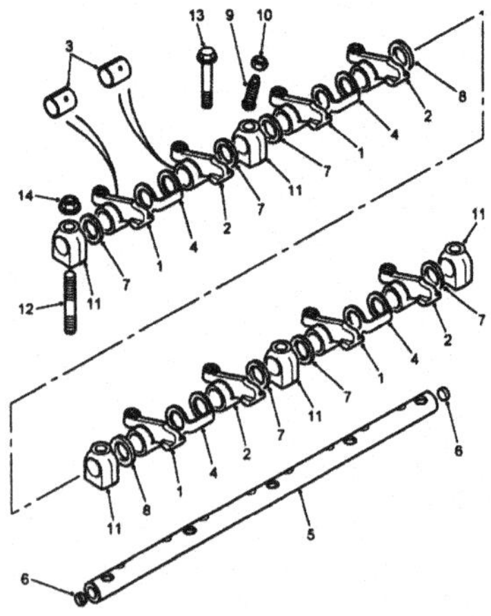

Illus	Part Number	Description	Quantity	Change Point	Remarks
1	ERR3343	ROCKER ASSEMBLY-CYLINDER HEAD-RH	4		
2	ERR3342	ROCKER ASSEMBLY-CYLINDER HEAD-LH	4		
3	ERR1203	• Bush-cylinder head rocker arm	8		
4	ERR2405	Spring-rocker shaft	4		
5	ERR4848	SHAFT-ROCKER	1		
6	ERR3457	• Plug	2		
7	ERR1209	Spacer	6		
8	ERR2732	Spacer	2		
9	ERR4883	Screw-engine tappet adjustment	8		
10	ERR560	Nut-locking	8		
11	ERR3779	Clamp-rocker shaft	5		
12	ERR4687	Stud-rocker shaft	3		
13	FB108101L	Bolt-flanged head-M8 x 50	2		
14	FN108047L	Nut-flange-flanged head-M8	3		

DEFENDER	GROUP B	Engine 2500 - Diesel - Turbo - 300 Tdi Valves & Tappets

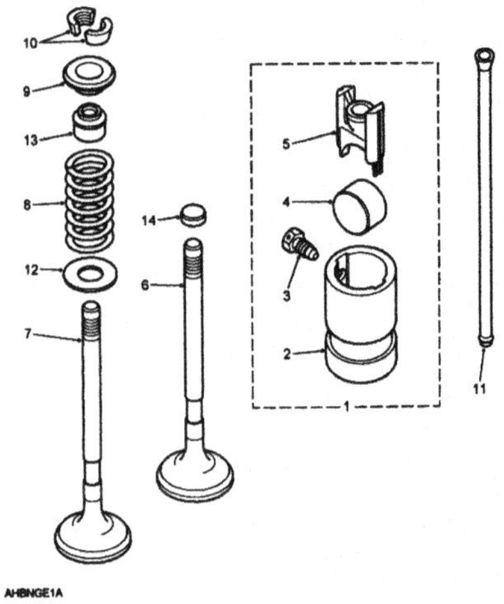

Illus	Part Number	Description	Quantity	Change Point	Remarks
1	RTC6564	TAPPET-ENGINE VALVE HYDRAULIC	8		
2	502473	• Slide-tappet guide	8		
3	ETC4246	• Bolt	8		
	273069	• Washer-sealing	8		
4	ERR561	• Roller-tappet guide	8		
5	ERR607	• Tappet-engine valve mechanical	8		
6	ERR3777	Valve-cylinder head inlet	4		
7	ERR1156	Valve-cylinder head exhaust	4		
8	ERR4640	Spring-cylinder head valve	8		
9	ETC4068	Cap-cylinder head valve spring	8		
10	ETC4069	Cotter-valve	16		
11	546799	Rod-engine push	8		
12	ETC8193	Seat-cylinder head valve spring	8		
13	ETC8663	Seal-cylinder head valve stem	8		
14	ERR4175	Cap-valve stem	NLA	To (V) VA 128878	Use LJC100270.
14	LJC100270	Cap-valve stem	8	From (V) VA 128879	

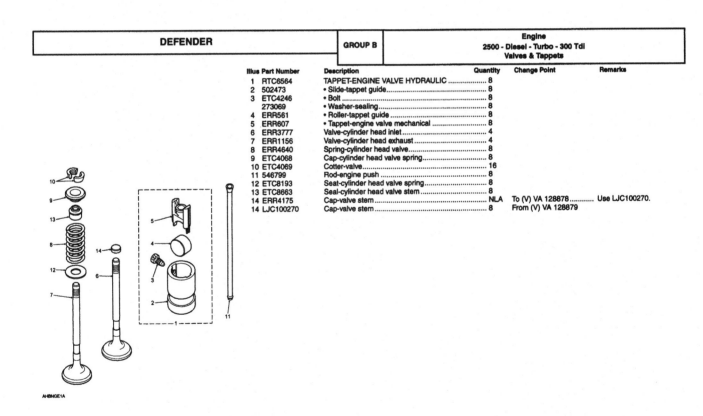

DEFENDER

GROUP B

Engine
2500 - Diesel - Turbo - 300 Tdi
Rocker Cover

Illus	Part Number	Description	Quantity	Change Point	Remarks
1	ERR4691	Cover assembly-valve rocker	1		
2	ERR2409	Gasket-engine rocker cover	1		
3	ERR5041	Cap-oil filler	1		
4	ERR4834	Screw-cover	3		
5	ERR3424	Washer-sealing	3		
6	ERR4632	Cover-engine-top	1		

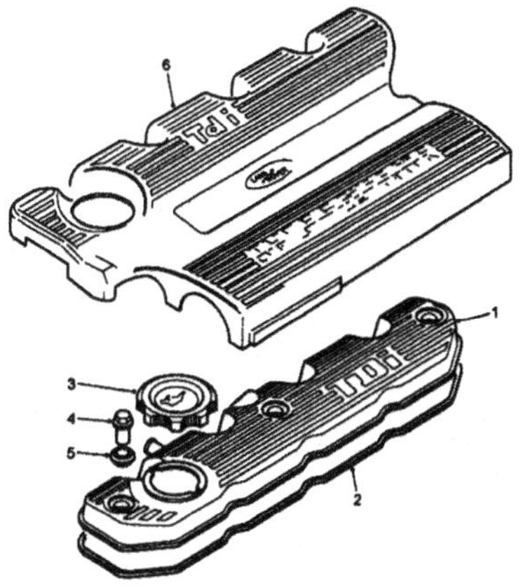

AHBNGG1A

DEFENDER

GROUP B

Engine
2500 - Diesel - Turbo - 300 Tdi
Engine Breather

Illus	Part Number	Description	Quantity	Change Point	Remarks
1	ERR4706	Cover-breather	1		
2	FS108257L	Screw-flanged head-M8 x 25	3		
3	ERR2026	Gasket-cylinder block side cover-asbestos free	1		
4	ERR874	Baffle-oil separator	1		
5	79027	Screw-6 x 3/8	1		
6	ERR7340	Hose-crankcase breather	NLA		Use ERR3084.
6	ERR3084	Hose-crankcase breather	1		
7	CN100258L	Clip-hose-25mm	2		
8	ERR1471	SEPARATOR ASSEMBLY-CRANKCASE BREATHER OIL	1		
14	LLO100000	• O ring	1		
9	FB106111L	Bolt-flanged head-M6 x 55	1		
10	ERR1351	Hose-oil separator drain	1		
11	CN100208L	Clip-hose-20mm	2		
12	ERR4926	Hose-cyclone-air cleaner	1		
13	CN100258L	Clip-hose-25mm	2		

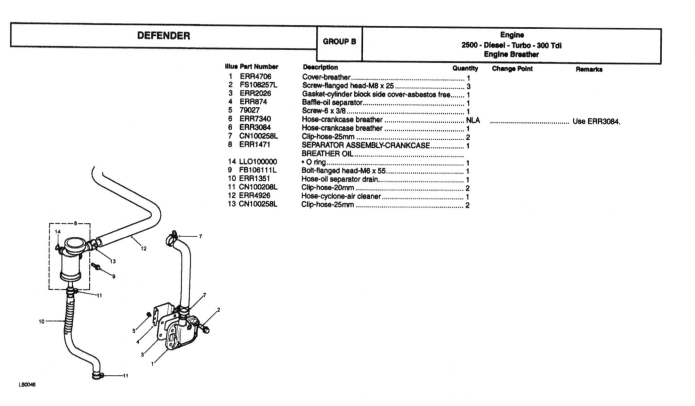

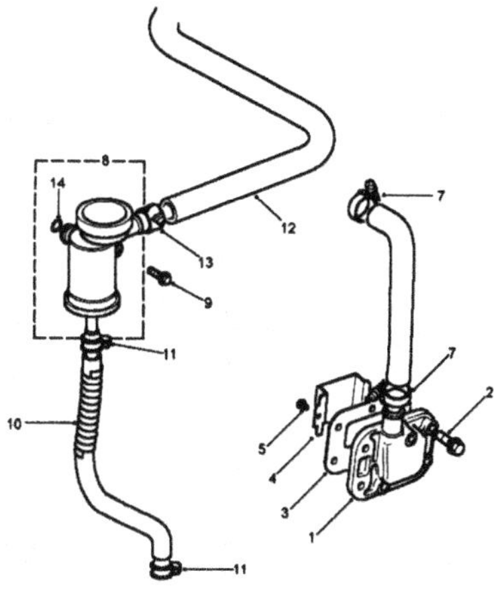

LB0048

Camshaft

Illus	Part Number	Description	Quantity	Change Point	Remarks
1	ERR3547	Camshaft-engine	1		
2	ERR3754	Plate-camshaft retaining	1		
3	FS106167	Screw-flanged head-M6 x 16	NLA		Use FS106167L.
3	FS106167L	Screw-flanged head-flanged head-M6 x 16	2		
4	ERR3545	Pulley-camshaft-timing belt	1		
5	BX112091	Bolt-M12 x 45	1	Note (1)	
11	FS112401L	Screw-flanged head-M12 x 40	1	Note (2)	
6	BDU1496L	Washer-special idler pulley	1	Note (1)	
7	ERR2216	Plate-camshaft pulley retaining	1		
8	ERR4709	Dowel-pin-camshaft	1		
9	FS108161L	Screw-flanged head-M8 x 16	3		
10	ERR3756	Hub-camshaft pulley	1		

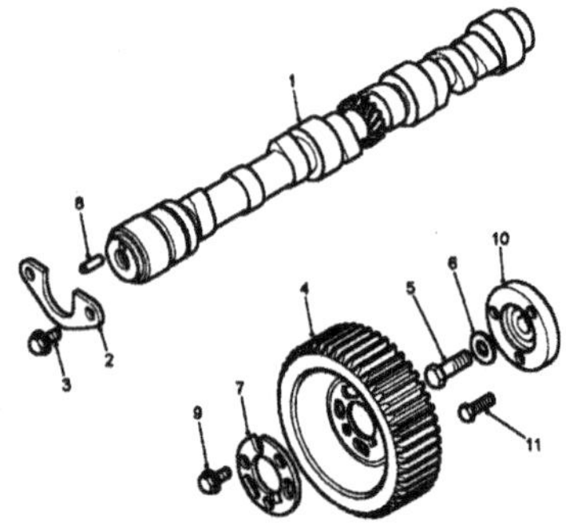

AHBNGI1A

CHANGE POINTS:
(1) To (V) TA 999222
(2) From (V) VA 999223

Thermostat Housing

Illus	Part Number	Description	Quantity	Change Point	Remarks
1	ERR3479	HOUSING-THERMOSTAT	1		Except air conditioning
1	ERR5098	HOUSING-THERMOSTAT	1		Air conditioning
2	ERR3291	• Thermostat-engine	1		
3	ERR4685	• O ring	1		
4	ERR4686	• Plug	1		
5	ERR3622	• Pipe assembly-engine coolant-diesel	1	Note (1)	
5	PEP102840	• Pipe assembly-engine coolant-diesel	1	Note (2)	
6	ERR3737	• Elbow-engine coolant outlet	1		Part of ERR3479.
7	FS108257L	• Screw-flanged head-M8 x 25	2		
	ERR4821	• Housing-thermostat	1		Part of ERR5098.
6	ERR3738	• Elbow-engine coolant outlet	1		Part of ERR5098.
8	ERR3490	Gasket-thermostat housing	1		
9	FS108257L	Screw-flanged head-M8 x 25	4		
10	AMR3321	Sensor-temperature	1		

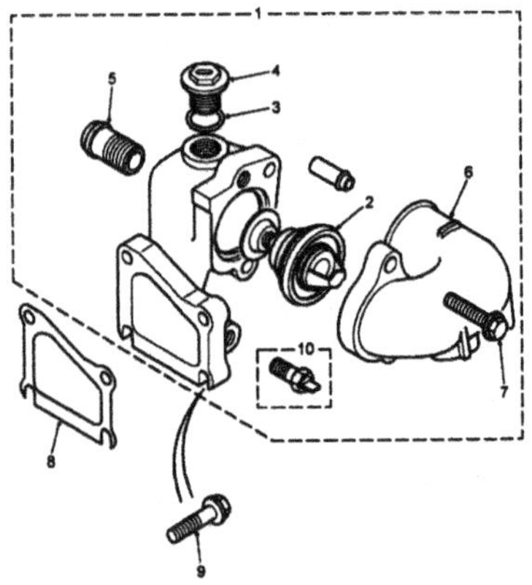

AHBNGK1A

CHANGE POINTS:
(1) To (V) WA 138479
(2) From (V) WA 138480

DEFENDER	GROUP B	Engine 2500 - Diesel - Turbo - 300 Tdi Manifolds

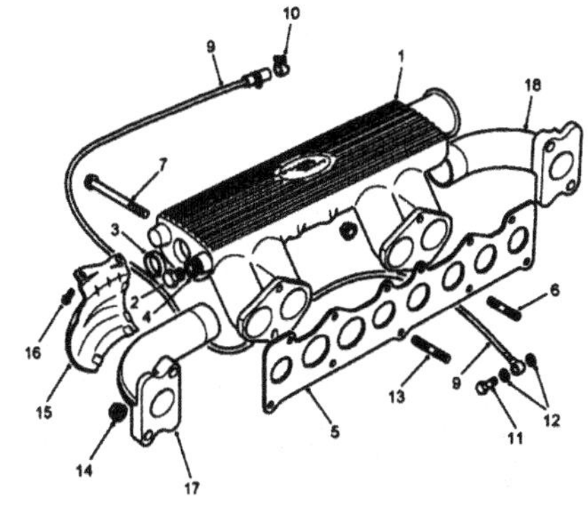

AHBNHA1A

Illus	Part Number	Description	Quantity	Change Point	Remarks
1	ERR3481	Manifold-engine inlet	1		
2	ETC5577	Plug-drain	1		
3	524765	Plug-core	1		
4	ERR894	Washer-sealing	1		
5	ERR3785	Gasket-inlet manifold	1		
6	TE108051L	Stud-M8 x 25	2		
7	FB108171	Bolt-flanged head-M8 x 85	2		
8	FN108041L	Nut-flange-M8	NLA		Use FN108047L.
9	ERR4699	Pipe boost control	1		
10	UKC3803L	Clip-hose	1		
11	ERR886	Bolt-banjo-boost capsule	1		
12	273069	Washer-sealing	2		
13	TE110071	Stud-M10 x 35	7		
14	FX110041L	Nut-flange-M10	NLA		Use FX110047L.
15	ESR2422	Heatshield-exhaust manifold	1		
16	FS105101	Screw-flanged head-M5 x 10	2		Except 90"
17	ERR4000	Manifold-engine exhaust-LH	NLA		Use ERR4802 Supplied part of the turbocharger assembly.
18	ERR4001	Manifold-engine exhaust-RH	NLA		Use ERR4802 Supplied part of the turbocharger assembly.

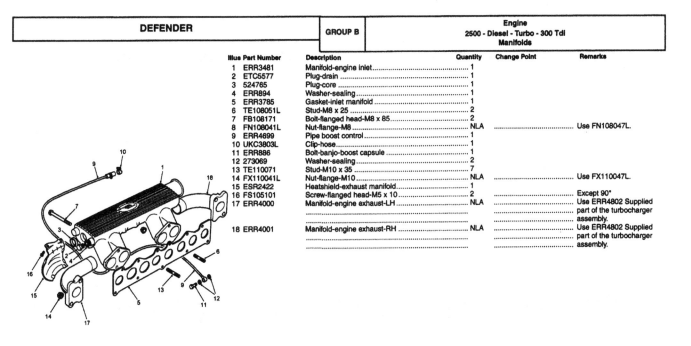

DEFENDER	GROUP B	Engine 2500 - Diesel - Turbo - 300 Tdi Fuel Pump

Illus	Part Number	Description	Quantity	Change Point	Remarks
1	ERR5057	Pump-fuel mechanical	1		
2	ERR2028	Gasket-fuel lift pump-side cover	1		
3	FS108301L	Screw-flanged head-M8 x 30	NLA		Use FS108307L.

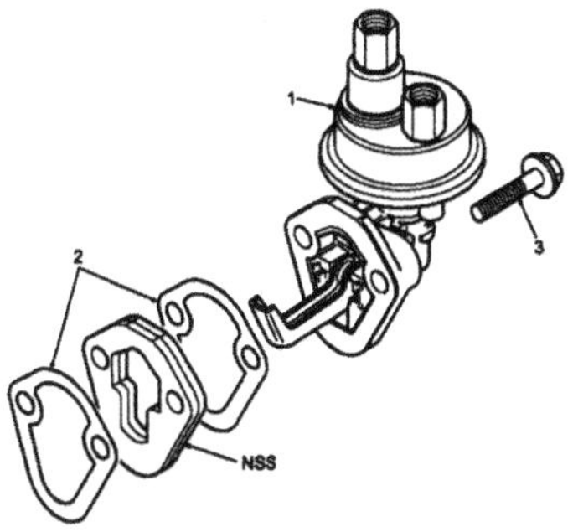

AHBNKA1A

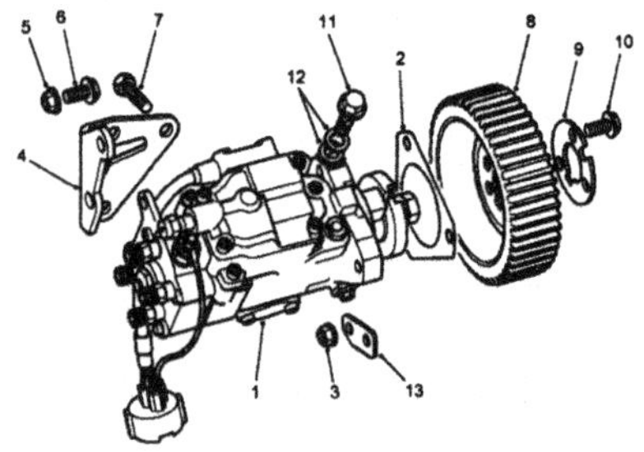

AHBNKC1A

CTP LOGISTICS LTD

Illus	Part Number	Description	Quantity	Change Point	Remarks
		PUMP-FUEL INJECTION			
1	ERR4419	NEW	1		Non EGR
1	ERR4046	NEW	1		EGR except immobilisation
1	ERR4419E	EXCHANGE	1		Non EGR
2	RTC6702	• Switch-electronic diesel control	1		
3	STC3597	• Bolt-banjo fuel lines	1		
4	STC3624	• Potentiometer-throttle diesel	1		
5	ERR6700	PUMP-FUEL INJECTION-NEW	1		EGR immobilisation
8	STC3254	• Solenoid shut off-fuel injection pump	1		
7	STC3253	• Bolt-shear head	2		
6	STC3252	• Valve-fuel cut fuel tank	1		
9	STC4389	• Potentiometer-throttle diesel	1		
10	ERR2023	Gasket-injection pump-diesel engine	1		
11	FN108041L	Nut-flange-M8	NLA		Use FN108047L.
12	ERR4725	Bracket-injection pump diesel	NLA		Use ERR6835.
12	ERR6835	Bracket-injection pump diesel	1		
13	FN108041L	Nut-flange-M8	NLA		Use FN108047L.
14	FS108207L	Screw-flanged head-M8 x 20	2		
15	FB108101L	Bolt-flanged head-M8 x 50	3		
16	ERR3545	Pulley-camshaft	1		
17	ERR2216	Plate-camshaft pulley retaining	1		
18	FS108161L	Screw-flanged head-M8 x 16	3		
23	ERR886	Bolt-banjo	1		
22	ERR894	Washer-sealing	2		
21	ERC9404	Bracket harness	1		
15	FB108051	Bolt-flanged head-M8 x 25	3		
20	ERR894	Washer-sealing	2		
23	ERR1125	Bolt-banjo	1		

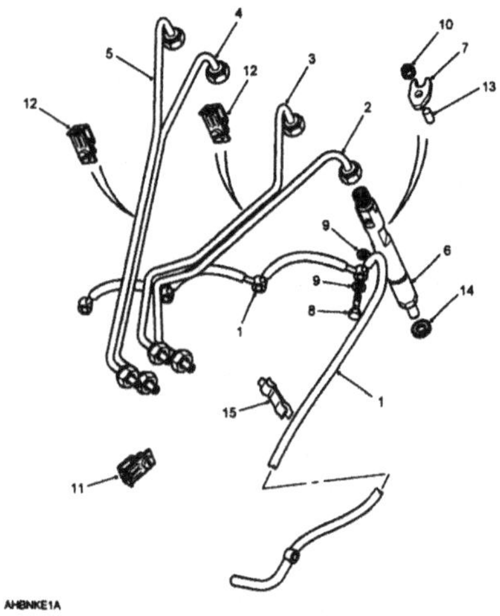

AHBNKE1A

Illus	Part Number	Description	Quantity	Change Point	Remarks
1	MJN100910	Pipe-spill return fuel injection	1		
2	STC1694	Pipe-cylinder 1-high pressure fuel injection	1		
3	STC1695	Pipe-cylinder 2-high pressure fuel injection	1		
4	STC1696	Pipe-cylinder 3-high pressure fuel injection	1		
5	STC1697	Pipe-cylinder 4-high pressure fuel injection	1		
6	ERR3339	Injector assembly-diesel holder & nozzle-new	4		
6	ERR3339E	Injector assembly-diesel holder & nozzle-exchange	4		
7	ERR3780	Clamp fuel injector	4		
8	ERR1200	Bolt-banjo-6mm	NLA		Use STC3297.
8	STC3297	BOLT-BANJO	1		
	ERR1304	• Washer-sealing	8		
10	FN108047L	Nut-flange-flanged head-M8	4		
11	STC1738	Clip-pipe	2		
12	STC1739	Clip-pipe	2		
13	ERR3468	Pin-roll-spring tension	4		
14	ERR4621	Washer-sealing-diesel injector to cylinder head	4		
15	DCP7384L	Clip-cable	1		

Illus	Part Number	Description	Quantity	Change Point	Remarks
1	ERR4802	TURBOCHARGER ASSEMBLY-NEW	1		
1	ERR4802E	TURBOCHARGER ASSEMBLY-EXCHANGE	1		
2	STC3159	• Stud	3		
3	STC3084	• Actuator-waste gate turbocharger	1		
4	STC3592	• Clip	1		
5	STC4614	• Nut	3		
6	STC4615	• End-yoke	1		
7	PYC101800L	• Clip-hose	2		
8	STC4617	• Hose wastegate control	1		
9	ERR1125	Bolt-banjo	1		
10	FRC4808	Washer-sealing-turbocharger oil feed pipe banjo	2		
11	ERR4894	Pipe turbocharger oil feed	1		
12	ERR4895	Pipe-oil drain turbocharger	1		
13	ERR2109	Gasket-oil drain turbocharger	1		
14	ERR335	Adaptor-oil drain pipe turbocharger	1		
15	FS108207L	Screw-flanged head-M8 x 20	2		
16	ETC8820	Pipe-adaptor turbocharger	1		
17	ERR4698	Plate-turbocharger blanking	1		
18	ERR4852	Gasket-exhaust gas recirculation valve to pipe	1		
19	SS108201	Screw-hexagon socket-M8 x 20	2		

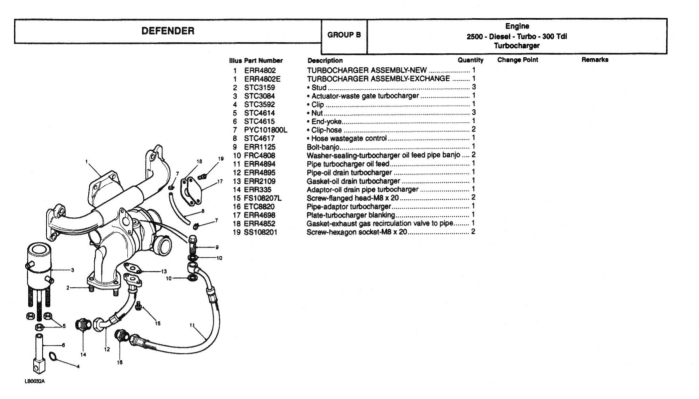

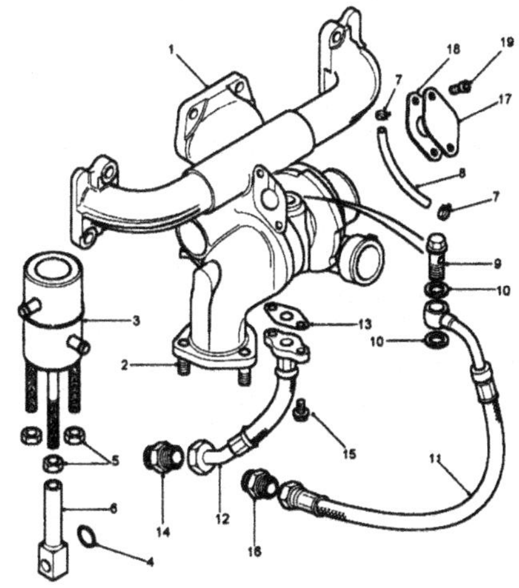

LB0032A

Illus	Part Number	Description	Quantity	Change Point	Remarks
1	STC2802	Kit-gasket-decarbonising	1		
2	STC2801	Kit-gasket-overhaul	1		

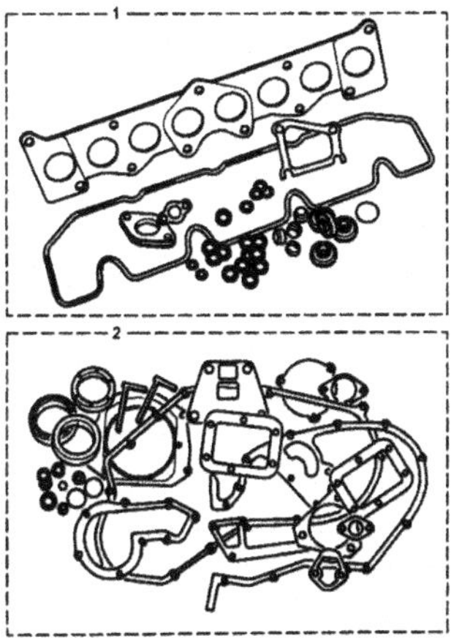

AHBNMA1A

Illus	Part Number	Description	Quantity	Change Point	Remarks
1	ERR3539	Pump brake vacuum	1		
2	FS108207L	Screw-flanged head-M8 x 20	2		
3	ERR2027	Gasket-vacuum pump	1		
4	ERC9404	Bracket harness	1		

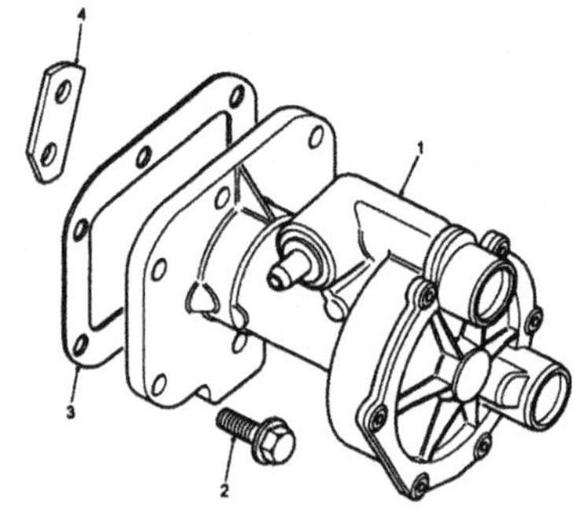

AHBNNA1A

Illus	Part Number	Description	Quantity	Change Point	Remarks
1	ANR2157	Pump assembly power assisted steering	1		
2	ERR2228	Bracket-mounting power assisted steering pump	1		
3	FS108161L	Screw-flanged head-M8 x 16	3		
4	FS108207L	Screw-flanged head-M8 x 20	4		
5	ERR3733	Pulley power assisted steering pump	1		
6	FS108127L	Screw-flanged head-flanged head-M8 x 12	3		

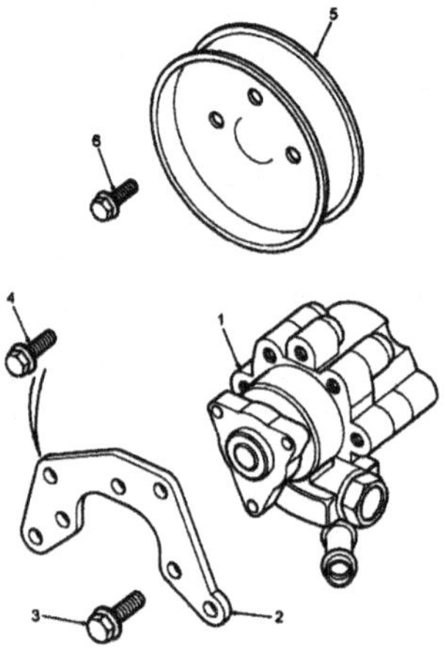

AHBNNC1A

Illus	Part Number	Description	Quantity	Change Point	Remarks
1	BTR8505	Compressor assembly-R134a air conditioning	1	Note (1)	
1	JPB101200	Compressor assembly-R134a air conditioning	1	Note (2)	
2	ERR2215	Belt-polyvee air conditioning compressor	1		Except South Africa
3	TE108221	Stud	3		
4	FN108047L	Nut-flange-flanged head-M8	3		
5	ERR4638	Bracket-air compressor	1		
6	FS110301L	Screw-flanged head-M10 x 30-top	4		
7	ERR4639	Shroud air conditioning	1		300 TDI

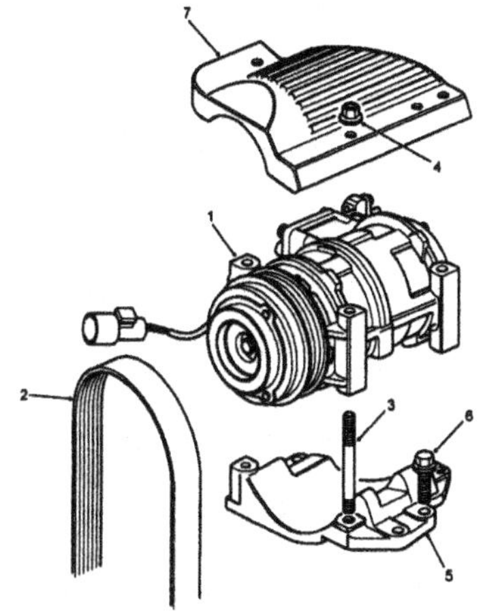

AHBNNE1A

CHANGE POINTS:
(1) To (V) WA 159806
(2) From (V) XA 159807

Illus	Part Number	Description	Quantity	Change Point	Remarks
1	ERR4543	PULLEY-TENSIONER ANCILLARY DRIVE	NLA	Note (1)	Use ERR7386 qty 1 with ERR7387 qty 1.
4	ERR3807	• Cover-air conditioning belt tensioner	1		
6	FS110301L	• Screw-flanged head-M10 x 30-top	1		
2	ERR7387	PULLEY-TENSIONER ANCILLARY DRIVE	1	Note (2)	
3	ERR7296	• Pulley-tensioner ancillary drive	1		
4	ERR7297	• Cover-air conditioning belt tensioner	2		
6	FS110301L	• Screw-flanged head-M10 x 30-top	1		
5	WJ110001	• Washer-plain	1		
7	ERR7386	Arm assembly-tensioner	1		
6	FS108257L	Screw-flanged head-M8 x 25	1		
3	ERR2798	Pulley-idler ancillary drive	1		
6	FS110301L	Screw-flanged head-M10 x 30-top	1		

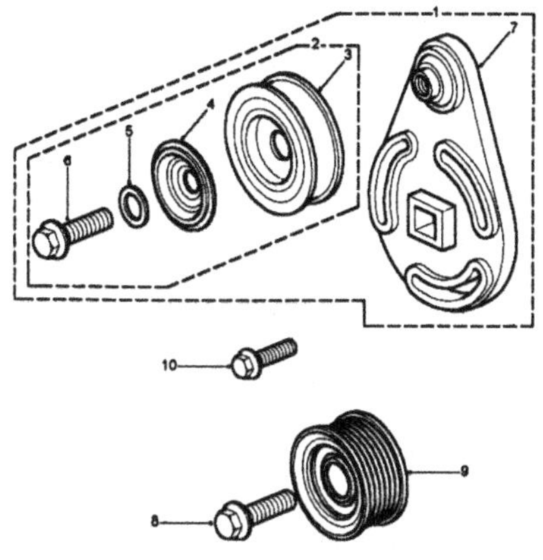

LB0142

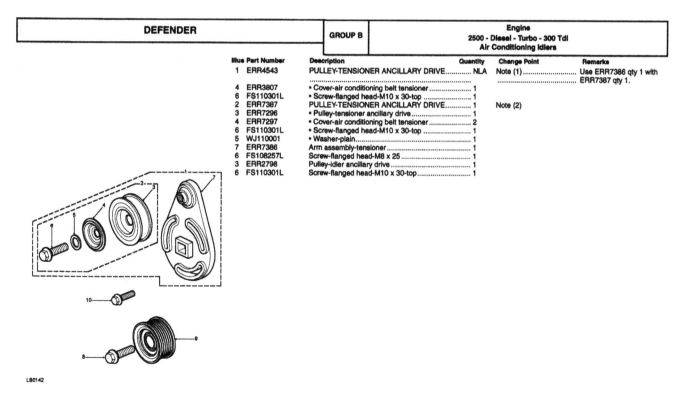

CHANGE POINTS:
(1) To (V) MA 962814
(2) From (V) MA 962815

Illus	Part Number	Description	Quantity	Change Point	Remarks
1	AMR3412	ALTERNATOR ASSEMBLY-NEW-A127-65 AMP	1	To (V) MA 969102	
1	AMR3412E	ALTERNATOR ASSEMBLY-EXCHANGE-A127-65 AMP	NLA	To (V) MA 969102	Use AMR4249E Use pulley from old unit AMR3412E.
	STC1796	• Pulley-polyvee alternator-61mm	1		
1	AMR4249E	Alternator assembly-exchange-A127-65 amp	1		
1	AMR4249	ALTERNATOR ASSEMBLY-NEW-A127-65 AMP	1	From (V) TA 969103	
	STC3202	• Pulley-polyvee alternator-49mm	1	From (V) TA 969103	
1	AMR4249E	Alternator assembly-exchange-A127-65 amp	1	From (V) TA 969103	
1	AMR4247E	Alternator assembly-A127-100 amp-exchange	1		
2	FB108251	Bolt-flanged head-M8 x 125	1		
3	FS108307L	Screw-flanged head-M8 x 30	1		
4	FX108047L	Nut-flange-flange-M8	1		
5	ERR4859	Heatshield alternator	1		
6	AMR2217	Nut & washer set-flanged head-5.0m	3		
7	FN105041L	Nut-flange-M5-D Terminal	1		Alternatives
7	FN105047L	Nut-flanged head-M5	1		Alternatives

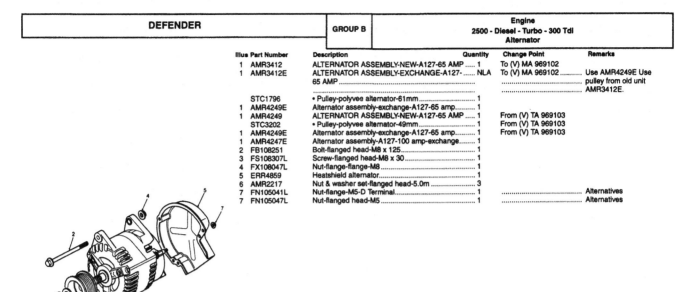

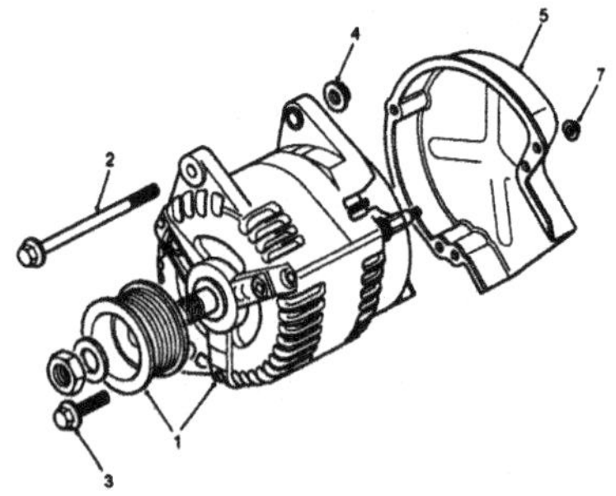

AHBNPC1A

Illus	Part Number	Description	Quantity	Change Point	Remarks
1	ERR5009	MOTOR-STARTER ENGINE-NEW-BOSCH	1		
1	ERR5009E	MOTOR-STARTER ENGINE-EXCHANGE-BOSCH	1		
2	STC1246	• Box assembly-brush starter motor-Bosch	1		
3	STC1254	• Spring-coil	4		
4	STC1247	• Guide-starter motor brush	4		
5	STC1244	• Drive assembly starter motor-Bosch	1		
6	STC1245	• Solenoid starter motor-0 331 303 165-Bosch	1		
6	STC3715	• Solenoid starter motor-9 330 331 006-Bosch	1		
7	STC1250	• Bush-starter motor-centre	2		
8	STC1251	• Bush-starter motor-rear	1		
9	STC1255	• Bush-starter motor-front	1		
10	FN110047	Nut-flange-flange-M10	1		
11	FS110301L	Screw-flanged head-M10 x 30-top	2		
12	FN108047L	Nut-flange-flanged head-M8	1		

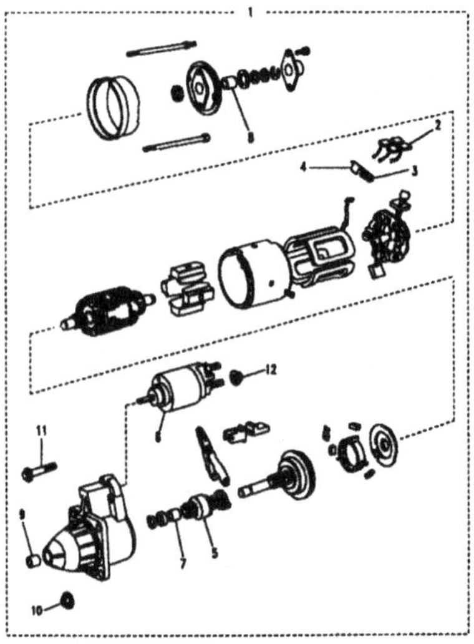

Illus	Part Number	Description	Quantity	Change Point	Remarks
1	ERR4723	HOUSING ASSEMBLY-CLUTCH	1		
2	TE110061L	• Stud-M10 x 30	13		
3	TE110051L	• Stud-M10 x 25	1		
4	ERC7295	Plug-rubber	1		
5	FS110301L	Screw-flanged head-M10 x 30-top	6		
6	FB110071L	Bolt-flanged head-M10 x 35	2		
7	WA110061L	Washer-housing to block-M10	2		
8	ERC9404	Bracket harness	2		
9	ERR4908	Flywheel engine	NLA		Use ERR719.
9	ERR719	FLYWHEEL ENGINE	1		
10	568431	• Gear-ring-flywheel engine	1		
11	502116	• Dowel-flywheel to crankshaft	3		
12	ERR4574	Bolt-fixing flywheel crankshaft-short	8		
13	FTC575	Cover-clutch assembly	NLA	To (V) WA 138479	Use URB100760.
13	URB100760	Cover-clutch assembly	1	From (V) WA 138480	
14	FTC2149	Plate-clutch-driven	NLA		Use FTC4204.
14	FTC4204	Plate-clutch-driven	1		
14	FTC1994	Plate-clutch-driven-Valeo	1		
	STC8358	Kit-clutch	1		LT 77 16L except 130"
	STC50501	Kit-clutch	1		R 380
15	SX108201L	Bolt-M8 x 20	6		
16	WL108001L	Washer-sprung-M8	6		

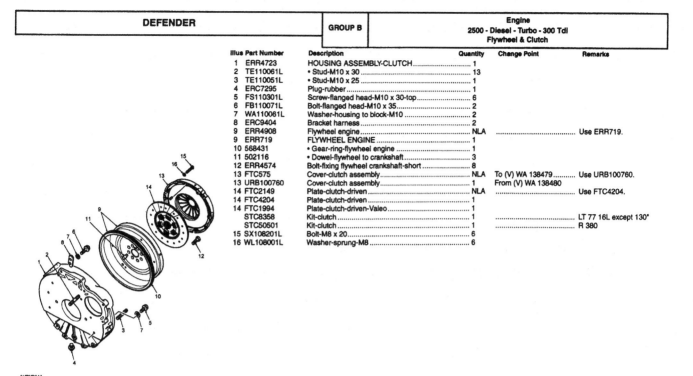

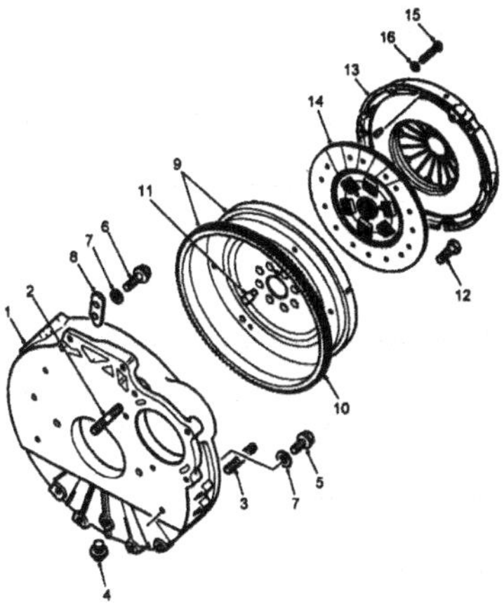

AHBNRA1A

Illus	Part Number	Description	Quantity	Change Point	Remarks
1	LBB111670	Engine unit-stripped	1	To (V) ECD3	
1	LBB001190	Engine unit-stripped	1	From (V) ECD3	

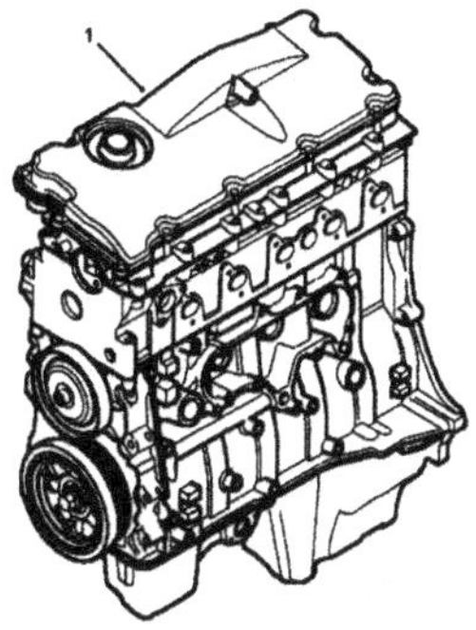

CFBNAC1A

Illus	Part Number	Description	Quantity	Change Point	Remarks
	LBB111680	Engine-power unit	1		

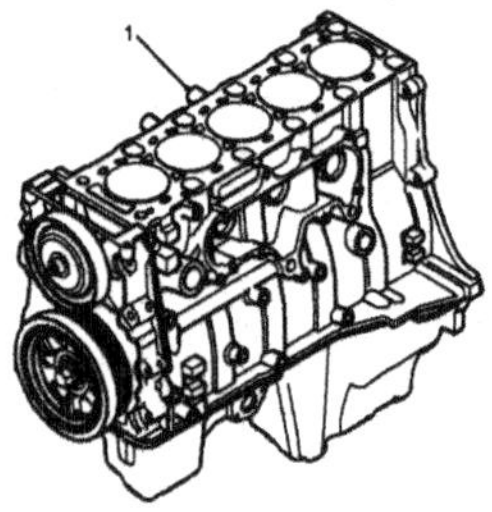

LB0095

Illus	Part Number	Description	Quantity	Change Point	Remarks
1	LBB111690	Engine base unit-part	1	To (V) ECD3	
1	LBB001200	Engine base unit-part	1	From (V) ECD3	

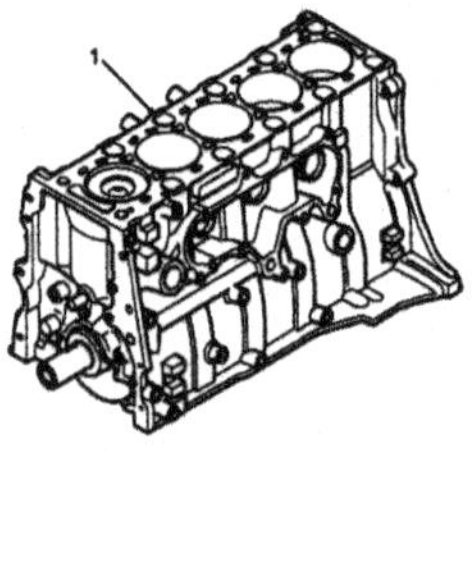

LB0096

Illus	Part Number	Description	Quantity	Change Point	Remarks
1	ERR6977	CYLINDER BLOCK-ENGINE	1		
2	ERR5278	• Bolt	12		
3	LCM100160	• Plug-cylinder block oil way	1		
4	LYQ100080	• Plug	NLA		Use LYQ100080L.
4	LYQ100080L	• Plug	2		
5	12H4636L	Dowel-ring	2		
6	37D2260L	Plug-core	3		
7	LCL100020L	Dowel	2		
8	FRC2482	Dowel-ring-15.0mm	2		
9	LYQ100120L	Plug	2		
10	LCM100150	Plug-blanking	1		
11	BDU1649L	Dowel	2		
12	LUF100420	Seal-crankshaft rear oil	1		
13	FS106167L	Screw-flanged head-flanged head-M6 x 16	5		
14	LFQ100310	Jet assembly-piston cooling	5		
15	SB106121	Screw-cap head-M6	5		

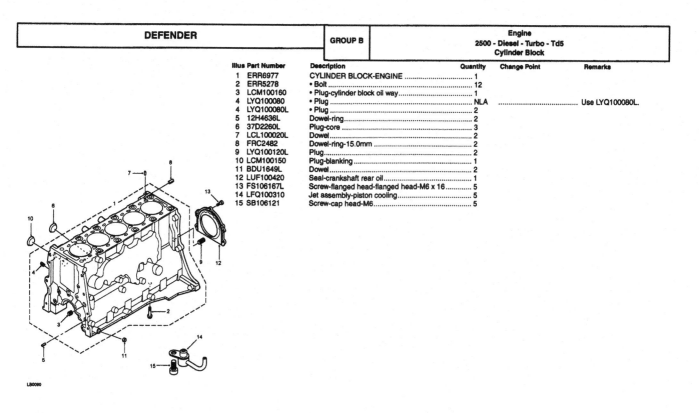

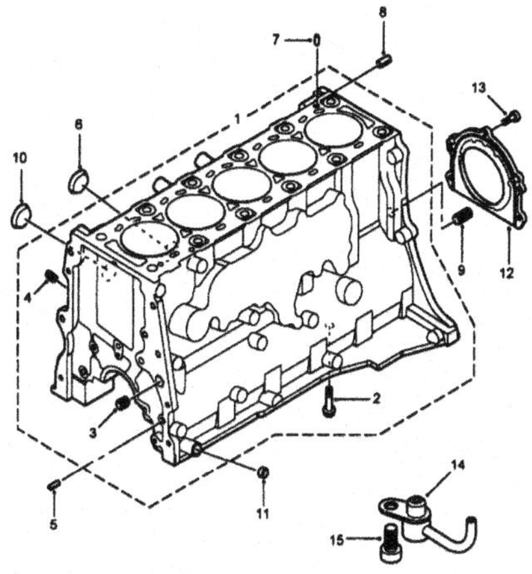

LB0090

Illus	Part Number	Description	Quantity	Change Point	Remarks
1	ERR5291	CRANKSHAFT ASSEMBLY-ENGINE	1		
2	8566L	• Bush-crankshaft	1		
3	6395L	• Dowel	1		
4	ERR5215	• Key-crankshaft	1		
5	ERR6581	Bolt-DMF to crankshaft	8		
5	FTC4738	Bolt-drive plate to crankshaft	8		
6	LHG100580	Damper-crankshaft	1		
7	LYG101190	Bolt-damper to crank	1		
8	STC3299	Bearing-main-crankshaft	1		
9	ERR5345	Bearing-thrust crankshaft	2		
10	STC3300	Kit-bearing-big end	1		
11	LFB101630	Bearing-half big end connecting rod	5		

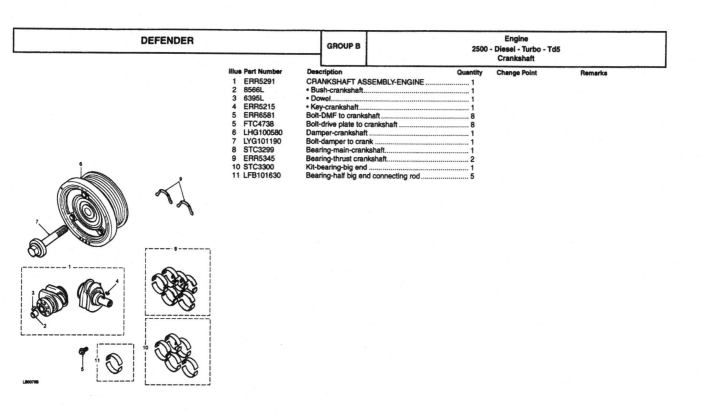

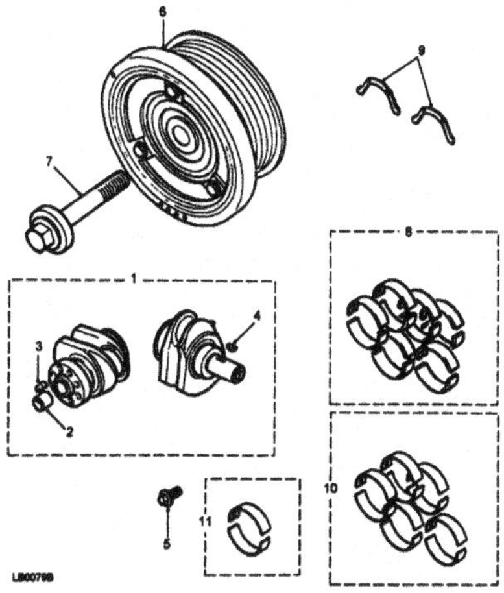

LB0079B

DEFENDER	GROUP B	Engine 2500 - Diesel - Turbo - Td5 Piston & Rings

Illus	Part Number	Description	Quantity	Change Point	Remarks
1	ERR7177	PISTON-ENGINE	5	To (E)10P 13888B	
2	LFT100300	• Kit-piston ring	1		
3	LFN10006L	• Circlip-piston	2		
1	LFL000460	PISTON-ENGINE	5	From (E)10P 13889B	
2	STC4668	• Kit-piston ring	1		
3	LFN10006L	• Circlip-piston	2		
1	LFL105300	PISTON-ENGINE	5		
2	STC4745	• Kit-piston ring	1		
3	LFN10006L	• Circlip-piston	2		
4	ERR6953	ROD ASSEMBLY-CONNECTING	5		
5	ERR6954L	• Bolt-connecting rod-to cap	2		
6	ERR6978	• Bush-small end	1		

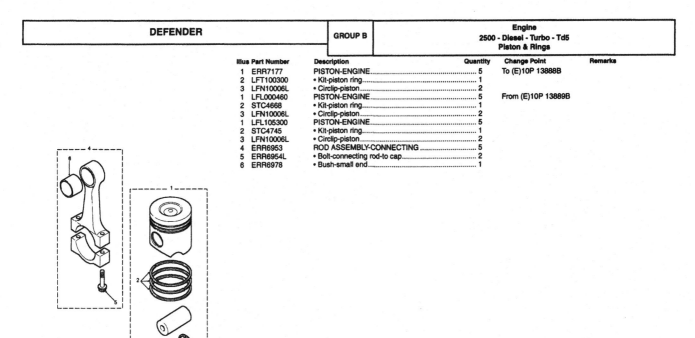

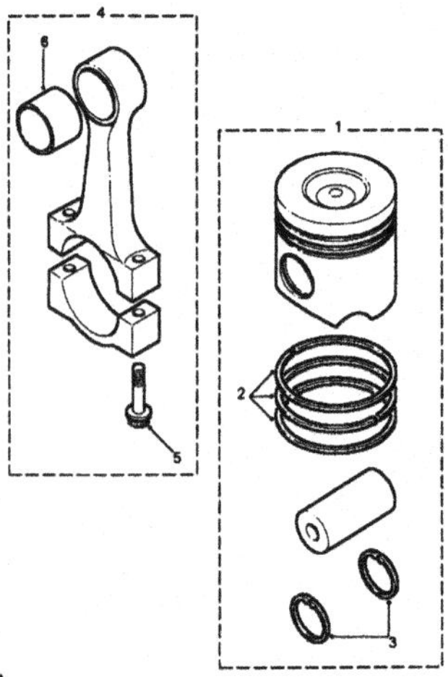

CFBSCC1A

DEFENDER	GROUP B	Engine 2500 - Diesel - Turbo - Td5 Sump

Illus	Part Number	Description	Quantity	Change Point	Remarks
1	LSB102550	SUMP ASSEMBLY-ENGINE OIL	1		
2	TRL100040	• Plug-sump assembly oil drain	1		
3	CDU1001L	• Washer-sealing-sump drain plug	1		
4	LVF100380	Gasket-sump	1		
5	FS108257L	Screw-flanged head-M8 x 25	16		
6	FB108167	Bolt-sump to block-M8 x 80	1		
7	FB108087	Bolt-sump to block-flanged head-M8 x 40	1		
8	FB108267	Bolt-sump to block-M8 x 130	2		

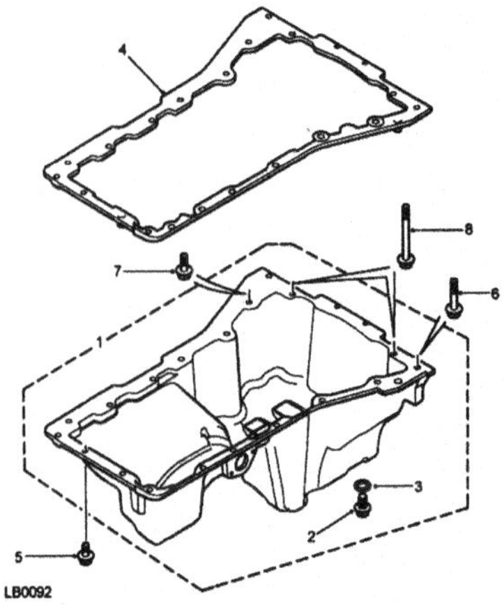

LB0092

DEFENDER	GROUP B	Engine 2500 - Diesel - Turbo - Td5 Oil Pump

Illus	Part Number	Description	Quantity	Change Point	Remarks
1	LPF101250	Pump assembly-engine oil	1		
2	LVG100340	Gasket-cylinder block oil pump	1		
3	FT106257M	Bolt-pump to block-M6 x 25	10		
4	FC106087M	Bolt-pump to block-M6 x 40	12		
5	LSP100640	PIPE-ENGINE OIL SUCTION	1		
8	ERR6401	• O ring-oil suction pipe seal	1		
6	LYP101160	Screw-flanged head-M6 x 20	3		
7	12H4636L	Dowel-ring	2		

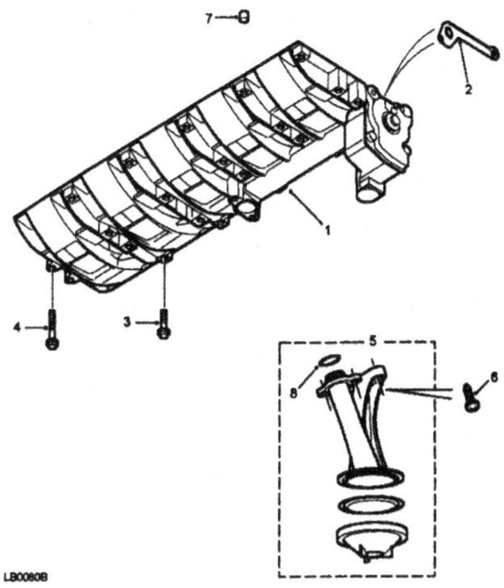

LB0080B

DEFENDER	GROUP B	Engine 2500 - Diesel - Turbo - Td5 Dipstick

Illus	Part Number	Description	Quantity	Change Point	Remarks
1	LQM100880	Dipstick-oil	1		
2	LQN101070	TUBE ASSEMBLY-OIL DIPSTICK	1		
3	ERR3683	• O ring-dipstick tube	1		
4	FS106107L	Screw-flanged head-M6 x 10	1		

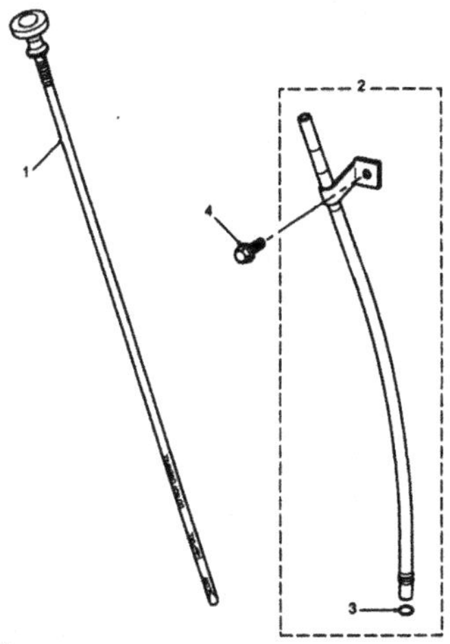

CFBSDA2A

Illus	Part Number	Description	Quantity	Change Point	Remarks
1	LJR103670	COVER-ENGINE-FRONT	1		
2	CR110625	• Circlip	1		
3	ERR7042	• Shaft assembly-bearing to viscous fan	1		
4	ERR7043	• Flange-adaptor-bearing to viscous fan	1		
5	ERR5285	• Bearing-roller-viscous fan to cover	1		
6	TE108147	Stud-M8 x 70	1		
7	FS108357	Screw-cover to block-flanged head-M8 x 35	4		
8	FB110087	Bolt-cover to block-flanged head-M10 x 40	3		
9	FS110207L	Screw-flanged head-cover to block-M10 x 20	1		
10	ERR5992	Seal-crankshaft front oil	1		
11	FN108047L	Nut-flange-flanged head-M8	1		

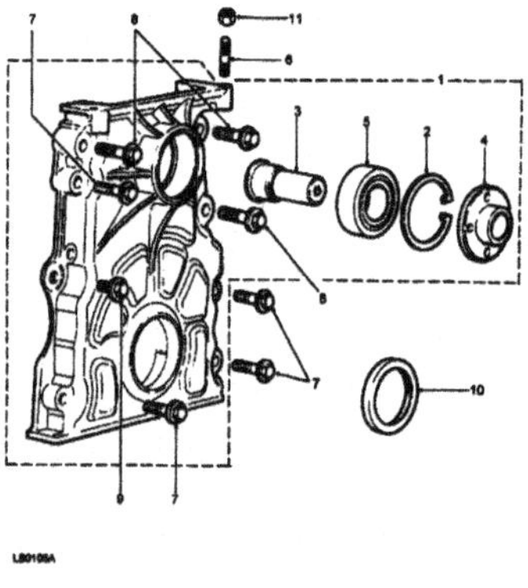

Illus	Part Number	Description	Quantity	Change Point	Remarks
1	LXB100090	Kit-ancillary belt tensioner repair	1	To (V) ECD3	
17	LHA000030	Kit-chain drive	1	From (V) ECD3	
2	ERR7070	Screw	3		
3	LGJ100690	Guide-timing chain	1		
4	FS106307L	Screw-flanged head	1		
5	LGQ100500	TENSIONER-TIMING CHAIN	1	To (V) ECD3	
6	LJR104820	• Cover-tensioner arm	1		
18	LGQ000020	Tensioner-timing chain	1	From (V) ECD3	
7	LHP100700	TENSIONER-TIMING CHAIN	1	To (V) ECD3	
7	LHP000020	TENSIONER-TIMING CHAIN-BLACK DOT- BLACK DOT	1	From (V) ECD3	
8	LXI100000	• Washer-sealing	1		
9	FS108357	Screw-flanged head-M8 x 35	1		
10	ERR6378	Pin-timing chain guide	1	To (E)10A 43740A	
10	LXU100050	Pin-timing chain guide	1	From (E)10P 43741A	
11	FS110307	Screw-M10 x 30	1		
12	LQX100130	Set-oil pump chain/ sprocket	1		
13	LYG101210	Bolt	1		
14	ERR6885	Sprocket-crankshaft	1		
15	LNL100000	Jet-chain lubrication	1		
16	FS106125L	Screw-flanged head-M6 x 12	1		

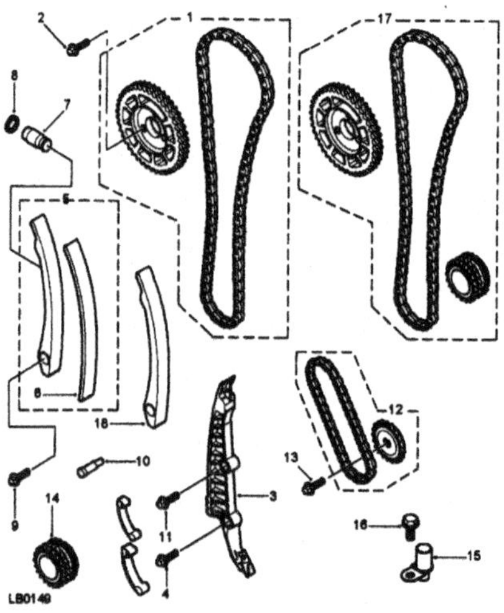

Illus	Part Number	Description	Quantity	Change Point	Remarks
1	ERR6505	Pump-water	1		
2	ERR7047	Cover-coolant pump	1		
3	FS106257L	Screw-flanged head-M6 x 25	5		
4	ERR6711	Seal-coolant pump	1		
5	PFQ10001L	Set-coolant pump D ring	1		

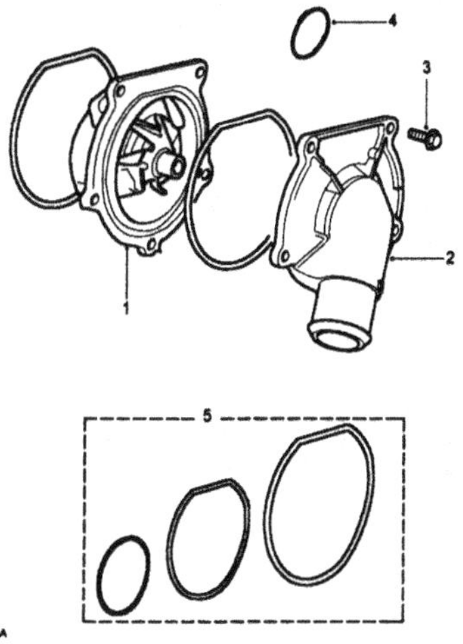

LB0043A

Illus	Part Number	Description	Quantity	Change Point	Remarks
1	PGG101050	Fan assembly-cooling	1		
2	ERR6948	Pulley-assembly	1		
3	FS108127L	Screw-flanged head-flanged head-M8 x 12	3		

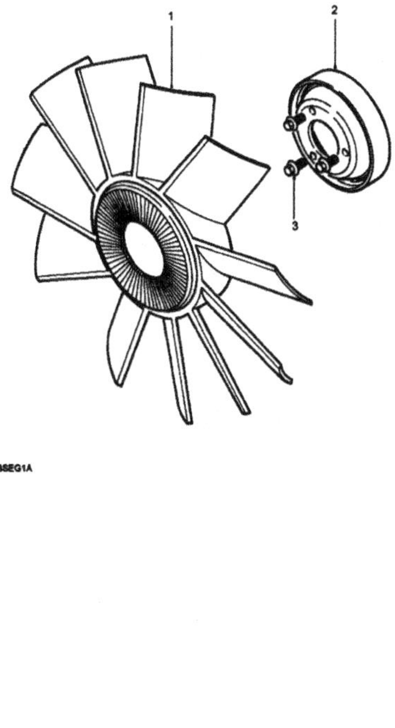

CFBSEG1A

Illus	Part Number	Description	Quantity	Change Point	Remarks
1	ERR6951	Tensioner-timing belt	1		
2	PYG10006L	Bolt-tensioner to block	1		
3	PQS101500	Belt-polyvee alternator	1		
4	ERR6949	BRACKET-IDLER MOUNTING ANCILLARY DRIVE	1		
5	ERR6658	• PULLEY-IDLER ANCILLARY DRIVE	1		
	ERR6659	• • Bolt	1		
6	FRC2481	Dowel	2		

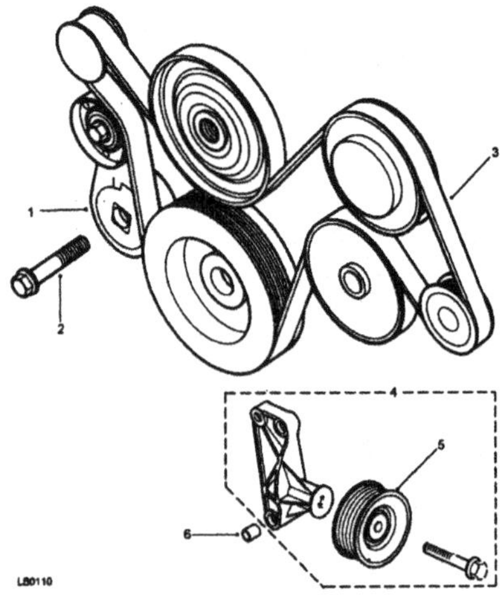

LB0110

Illus	Part Number	Description	Quantity	Change Point	Remarks
1	ERR6951	Tensioner-timing belt	1		
2	PYG10006L	Bolt-tensioner to block	1		
3	ERR6493	IDLER ASSEMBLY-TIMING BELT	1		
4	ERR5958	• Bolt-idler to head	1		
5	ERR6220	• Spacer-idler	1		
6	PQS101490	Belt-polyvee alternator	1		
7	ERR6949	BRACKET-IDLER MOUNTING ANCILLARY DRIVE	1		
8	ERR6658	• PULLEY-IDLER ANCILLARY DRIVE	1		
	ERR6659	• • Bolt	1		
9	FRC2481	Dowel	2		

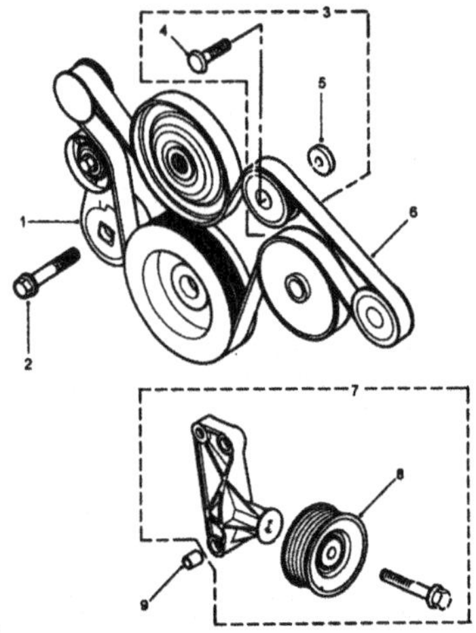

LB0111

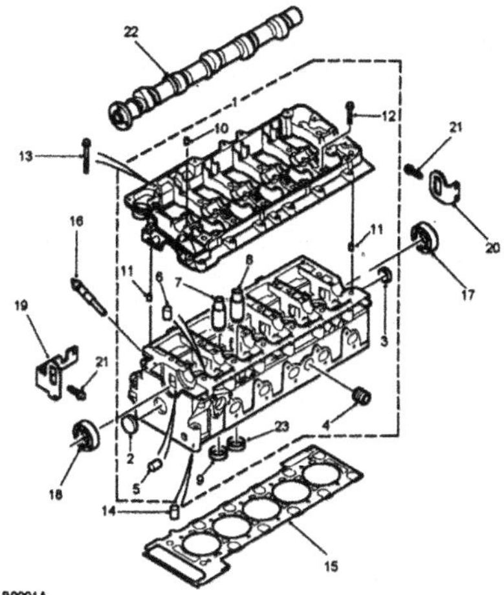

LB0091A

Illus	Part Number	Description	Quantity	Change Point	Remarks
	LDF107860	CYLINDER HEAD ASSEMBLY-ENGINE	1		
1	ERR6862	• CYLINDER HEAD-ENGINE	1		
3	37D2260L	• • Plug-core	1		
6	LYQ100040	• • Rivet-5mm	1		
9	ERR7049	• • Insert-cylinder head inlet valve seat	5		
23	ERR7050	• • Insert-cylinder head exhaust valve seat	5		
7	ERR7225	• • Guide-cylinder head valve	10		
10	ETC8194	• • Dowel-ring	1		
11	ERR5617	• • Dowel	2		
12	FS108357	• • Screw-flanged head-M8 x 35	13		
4	ERR7060	• • Plug	1	Note (1)	
4	LCM100170	• • Plug	1	Note (2)	
2	ERR6674	• Plug-core	1		
5	LYQ100170	• Rivet-12mm	4		
	ERR6064	• Clamp fuel injector	1		
	ERR6616	• Pad-insulation	1		
	ERR6761	• O ring	1		
	MAE100010	• Strainer-fuel filter	1		
	MBD100050	• Bolt	5		
	MSC100670	• INJECTOR & SENSOR ASSEMBLY-DIESEL-NEW	5		
	ERR7004	• • O ring	1		
	ERR6417	• • Washer-injector sealing	1		
	MSO100010	• CONNECTOR ASSEMBLY-FUEL BLOCK	1		
	ERR2081	• • Sensor-temperature	1		
	ERR6192	• • Washer-sealing	1		
	STC4509	• • O ring	2		
	MSX100080	• Gasket-fuel connector block	1		
16	ERR6066	• Plug-heater ignition	5		
	ERR3907	• Collet-cylinder head valve	20		
	ERR6013	• Cap-valve	10		
	ERR6354	• Spring-cylinder head valve	10		
	ERR6611	• Valve-cylinder head inlet	5		
	ERR6612	• Valve-cylinder head exhaust	5		
22	ERR6676	• Camshaft-engine	1		

CHANGE POINTS:
(1) To (E)10P 57369A
(2) From (E)10P 57370A

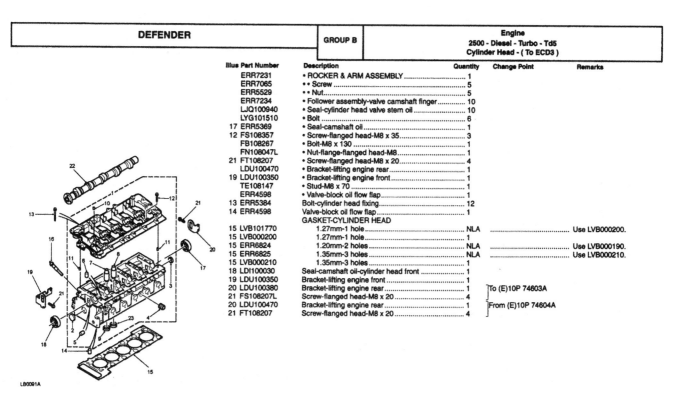

DEFENDER | GROUP B | Engine
2500 - Diesel - Turbo - Td5
Cylinder Head - (To ECD3)

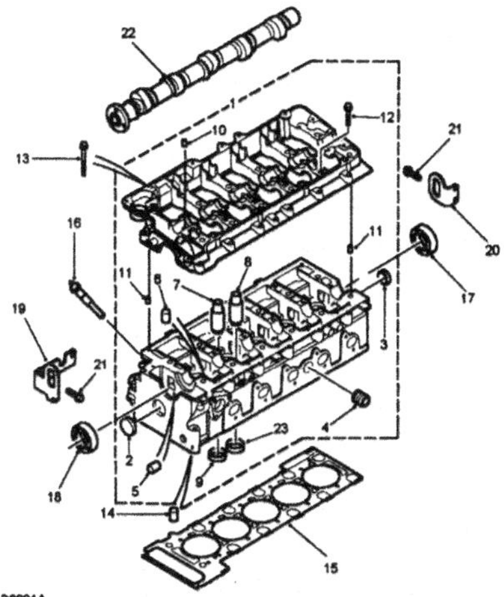

LB0091A

Illus	Part Number	Description	Quantity	Change Point	Remarks
	ERR7231	• ROCKER & ARM ASSEMBLY	1		
	ERR7065	• • Screw	5		
	ERR5529	• • Nut	5		
	ERR7234	• Follower assembly-valve camshaft finger	10		
	LJQ100940	• Seal-cylinder head valve stem oil	10		
	LYG101510	• Bolt	6		
17	ERR5369	• Seal-camshaft oil	1		
12	FS108357	• Screw-flanged head-M8 x 35	3		
	FB108267	• Bolt-M8 x 130	1		
	FN108047L	• Nut-flange-flanged head-M8	1		
21	FT108207	• Screw-flanged head-M8 x 20	4		
	LDU100470	• Bracket-lifting engine rear	1		
19	LDU100350	• Bracket-lifting engine front	1		
	TE108147	• Stud-M8 x 70	1		
	ERR4598	• Valve-block oil flow flap	1		
13	ERR5384	Bolt-cylinder head fixing	12		
14	ERR4598	Valve-block oil flow flap	1		
		GASKET-CYLINDER HEAD			
15	LVB101770	1.27mm-1 hole	NLA		Use LVB000200.
15	LVB000200	1.27mm-1 hole	1		
15	ERR6824	1.20mm-2 holes	NLA		Use LVB000190.
15	ERR6825	1.35mm-3 holes	NLA		Use LVB000210.
15	LVB000210	1.35mm-3 holes	1		
18	LDI100030	Seal-camshaft oil-cylinder head front	1		
19	LDU100350	Bracket-lifting engine front	1		
20	LDU100380	Bracket-lifting engine rear	1	To (E)10P 74603A	
21	FS108207L	Screw-flanged head-M8 x 20	4		
20	LDU100470	Bracket-lifting engine rear	1	From (E)10P 74604A	
21	FT108207	Screw-flanged head-M8 x 20	4		

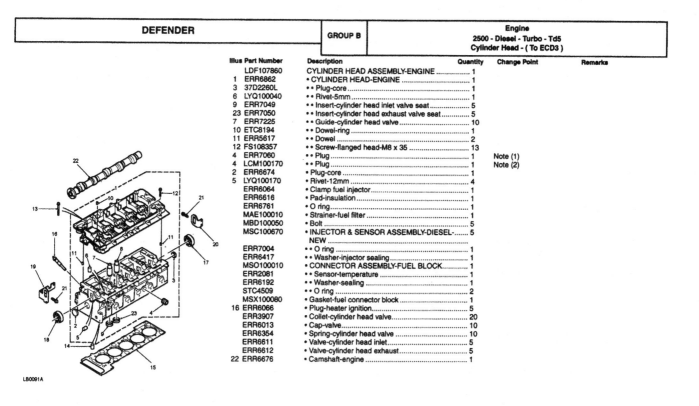

Illus	Part Number	Description	Quantity	Change Point	Remarks
1	LDF000890	Cylinder head assembly-engine	1		
	LGC107280	Camshaft-engine	1		

NOT ILLUSTRATED
PAS ILLUSTREE
NICHT ILLUSTRIERT
SENZA IL DISEGNO
SIN EL DISENO
SEM ILLUSTRACAO
NIET AFGEBEELD

TF 0097

Illus	Part Number	Description	Quantity	Change Point	Remarks
1	ERR7231	ROCKER & ARM ASSEMBLY-FUEL INJECTORS	1	To (V) ECD3	
2	ERR7065	• Screw	5		
3	ERR5529	• Nut	5		
		CHECK INJECTOR COLOUR CODE TO ENSURE CORRECT SCREW FITMENT			
4	MUI000040	Rocker & arm assembly-without adjusting screws and nuts	1	From (V) ECD3	
2	ERR7065	Screw	5	To (V) ECD3	
2	LGV000020	Screw	5	From (V) ECD3	
3	ERR5529	Nut	5		
4	FC108175	Bolt-shaft to head	6	To (E)10P 09891A	
4	LYG101510	Bolt-shaft to head	6	From (E)10P 09892A	

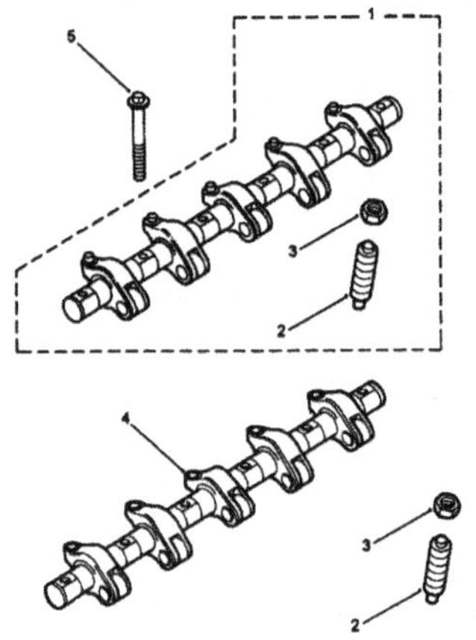

LB0067A

Illus	Part Number	Description	Quantity	Change Point	Remarks
1	ERR7236	Valve-cylinder head inlet	NLA		Use ERR6611.
1	ERR6611	Valve-cylinder head inlet	5		
2	ERR7237	Valve-cylinder head exhaust	NLA		Use ERR6612.
2	ERR6612	Valve-cylinder head exhaust	5		
3	ERR6354	Spring-cylinder head valve	10		
4	ERR6013	Cap-valve	10		
5	ERR3907	Collet-cylinder head valve	20		
6	LJQ100940	Seal-cylinder head valve stem oil	10		
7	ERR7233	Lash-adjuster	10		
8	ERR7234	Follower assembly-valve camshaft finger	10		

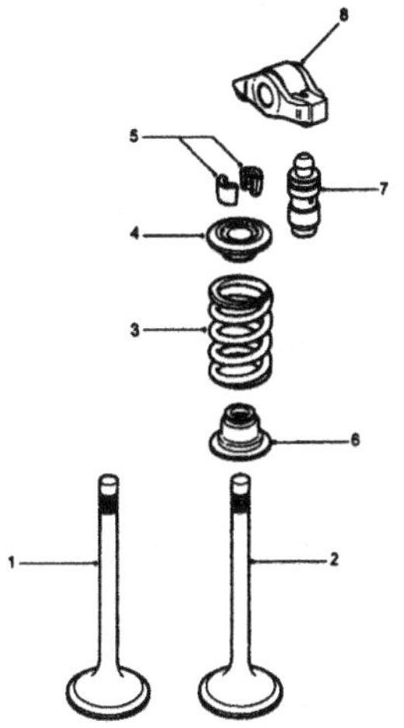

LB0093

Illus	Part Number	Description	Quantity	Change Point	Remarks
1	ERR6859	COVER ASSEMBLY-CAMSHAFT CARRIER	1	To (V) ECD3	
2	ERR7155	• Gasket-oil separator	1		
3	ERR7266	• Grommet-sealing	13		
4	ERR7094	• Gasket-camshaft cover	1		
5	FS106307L	Screw-flanged head-cover to block	13		
1	LDR000020	COVER ASSEMBLY-CAMSHAFT CARRIER	1	From (V) ECD3	
3	ERR7266	• Grommet-sealing	13		
4	LVP000020	• Gasket-camshaft cover-with identification tag	1		
6	LQC100270L	CAP ASSEMBLY-OIL FILLER-YELLOW.	1		
7	LUD100040L	• Seal-engine oil filler cap	1		
8	LBH100370	COVER ASSEMBLY-ENGINE ACOUSTIC	1		
9	ERR6709	• Flap-oil filler	1		
	LBL100000	• Strap-oil filler flap retaining	1		
10	PYA10011L	• Grommet	3		
8	LBH000090	COVER ASSEMBLY-ENGINE ACOUSTIC	1	From (V) ECD3	
9	ERR6709	• Flap-oil filler	1		
10	PYA10011L	• Grommet	3		
11	LYG101200	Bolt-flanged head-acoustic pad to engine	3		
11	LYG000230	Bolt-flanged head-acoustic pad to engine	3	From (V) 2A 622424	
12	WA110068L	Washer-acoustic pad to engine-Black	1		
13	LBH100360	COVER ASSEMBLY-ENGINE ACOUSTIC	1		
14	PYA10011L	• Grommet	2		
15	FS106167L	Screw-flanged head-cover to cylinder head-flanged head-M6 x 16	2		
16	ERR7134	Dowel-M6	2		
17	ERR7135	Dowel-M8	2		
18	LLN100140L	Valve assembly-depression control	1		
19	LLH102680	Hose-camshaft cover/breather valve breather	NLA		Use LLH000070.
19	LLH000070	Hose-camshaft cover/breather valve breather	1		
20	PYC101410L	Clip-hose	1		

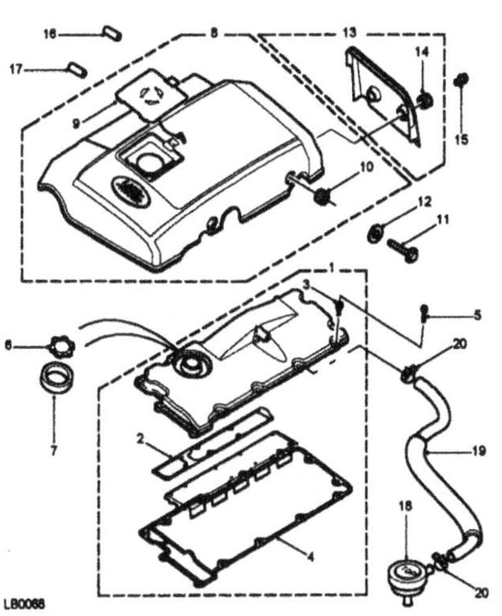

LB0088

Illus	Part Number	Description	Quantity	Change Point	Remarks
1	LKB108110	MANIFOLD ASSEMBLY-ENGINE INLET	1		
2	37D2260L	• Plug-core	1		
3	ERR7072	Gasket-inlet manifold	NLA		Use LKJ000010.
4	MHK100640	Sensor-temperature	1		
5	FS106167L	Screw-flanged head-sensor to inlet manifold-flanged head-M6 x 16	2		
6	TE108061L	Stud-M8 x 30	3		
7	FN108047L	Nut-flange-manifold to downpipe-flanged head-M8	3		
8	FS108307L	Screw-manifold to downpipe-flanged head-M8 x 30	7		

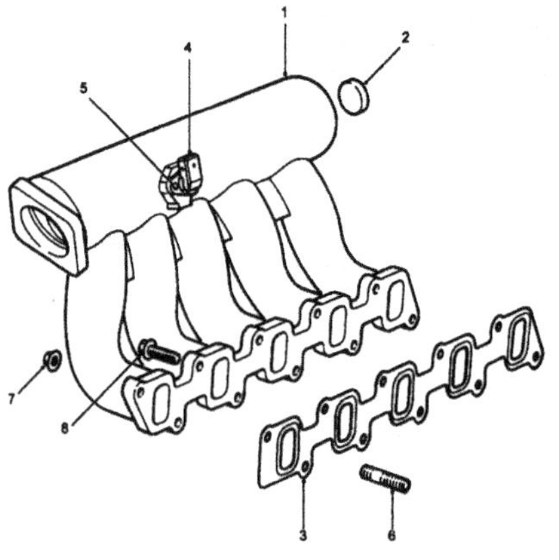

CFBSHA1A

Illus	Part Number	Description	Quantity	Change Point	Remarks
1	LKC102020	Manifold-engine exhaust	1		
2	LKG100470	Gasket-exhaust manifold	1		
3	TE108051L	Stud-manifold to block-M8 x 25	10		
4	ESR2033	Nut-locking-manifold to block-M8	10		
5	ERR6768	Gasket-exhaust manifold to turbocharger	1		
6	LWQ100270	Heatshield-exhaust manifold	1		
7	FS108127L	Screw-flanged head-heatshield fixing-flanged head-M8 x 12	3		

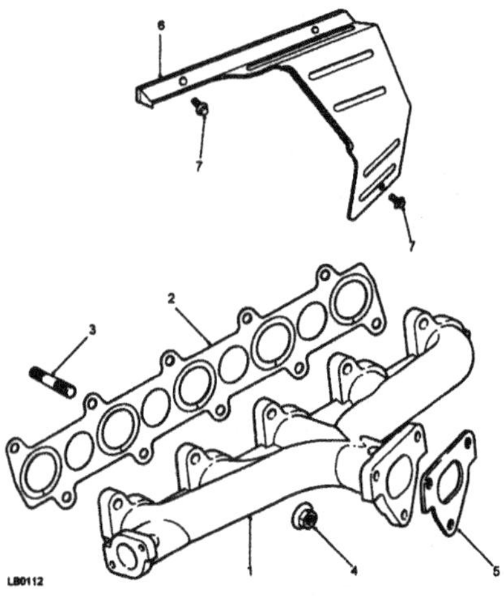

LB0112

DEFENDER	GROUP B	Engine 2500 - Diesel - Turbo - Td5 Injector, Pipes & Filter

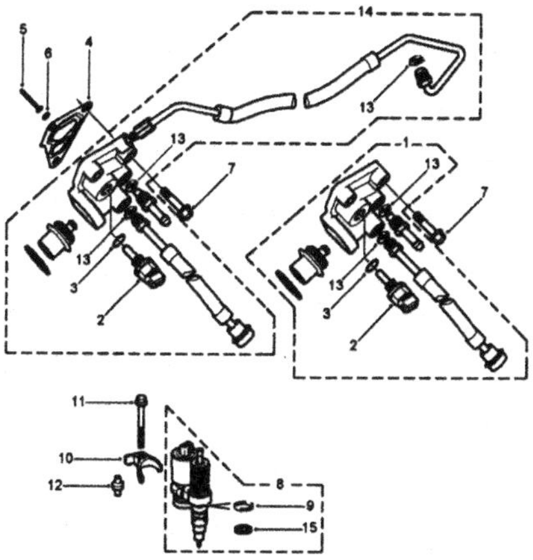

LB0150

Illus	Part Number	Description	Quantity	Change Point	Remarks
1	MSO100010	CONNECTOR ASSEMBLY-FUEL BLOCK	1	To (E)10P 15967B	
1	MSO000080	CONNECTOR ASSEMBLY-FUEL BLOCK	1	From (E)10P 15968B	
14	MSO000060	CONNECTOR ASSEMBLY-FUEL BLOCK	1	From (V) ECD3	
2	ERR2081	• Sensor-temperature	1		
3	ERR6192	• Washer-sealing	1		
13	STC4509	• O ring	2		
4	MSX100080	Gasket-fuel connector block	1	To (E)10P 15967B	
4	MSX000010	Gasket-fuel connector block	1	From (E)10P 15968B	
5	MAE100010	Strainer-fuel filter	1		
6	ERR6761	O ring	1		
7	FS108357	Screw-con block to head-flanged head-M8 x 35 TO ECD3	3		
8	MSC100670	INJECTOR & SENSOR ASSEMBLY-DIESEL-NEW	5	To (V) ECD3	
9	ERR7004	• O ring	1		
15	ERR6417	• Washer-injector sealing	1		
8	MSC100670E	Injector & sensor assembly-diesel-exchange	NLA		
8	MSC000040	INJECTOR & SENSOR ASSEMBLY-DIESEL-BLUE.	5	To (V) ECD3	
6	ERR7004	• O ring	1		
15	ERR6417	• Washer-injector sealing FROM ECD3	1		
8	STC4786	Kit-injector-fuel multi point injection	NLA	From (V) ECD3	Use MSC000030 qty 1 with LGV000020 qty 1.
8	MSC000030	INJECTOR & SENSOR ASSEMBLY-DIESEL-GREEN	5	From (V) ECD3	
9	ERR7004	• O ring	1		
15	ERR6417	• Washer-injector sealing	1		
10	ERR6064	Clamp fuel injector	5		
11	MBD100050	Bolt	5		
12	ERR6616	Pad-insulation	5		

DEFENDER	GROUP B	Engine 2500 - Diesel - Turbo - Td5 Harness Fuel Injector

Illus	Part Number	Description	Quantity	Change Point	Remarks
1	AMR6103	HARNESS-FUEL INJECTOR ENGINE	1		
2	NYX100080	• O ring	2		

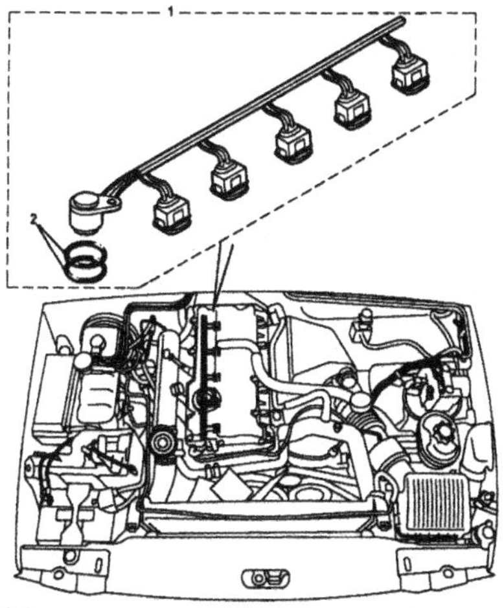

LB0081

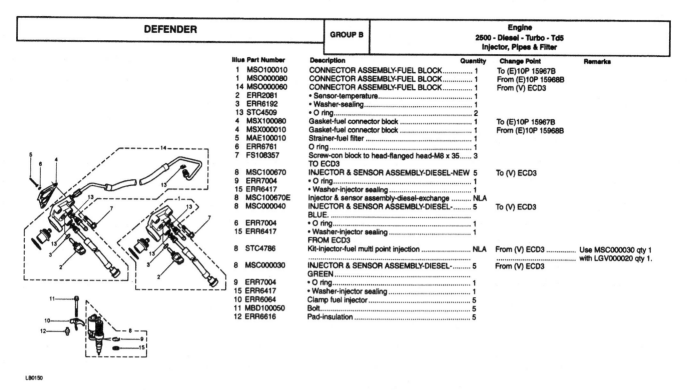

Illus	Part Number	Description	Quantity	Change Point	Remarks
1	ERR7097	Elbow	1		
2	ERR7032	Gasket-coolant outlet elbow	1	To (E)10P 86382A	
2	LVJ000010	Gasket-coolant outlet elbow	1	From (E)10P 86383A	
3	FS108207L	Screw-elbow to head-flanged head-M8 x 20	3		
4	ERR2081	Sensor-temperature	1		
5	ERR6192	Washer-sealing	1		

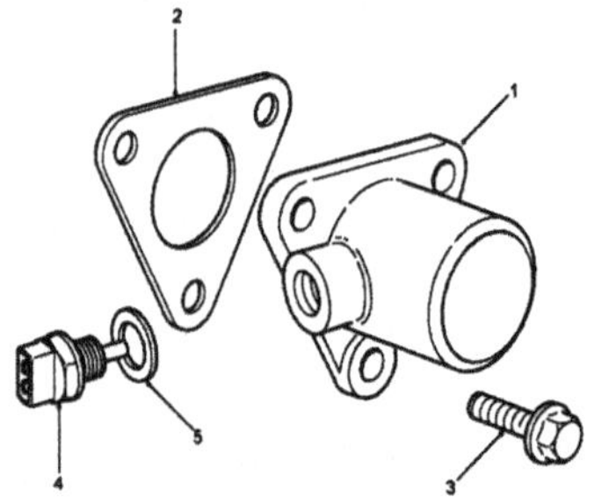

LB0094

Illus	Part Number	Description	Quantity	Change Point	Remarks
1	PEP102670	Pipe-heater feed	1		
2	PIP100030	Pipe assembly-coolant	1		
3	ERR6689	Hose-heater to oil cooler	1		

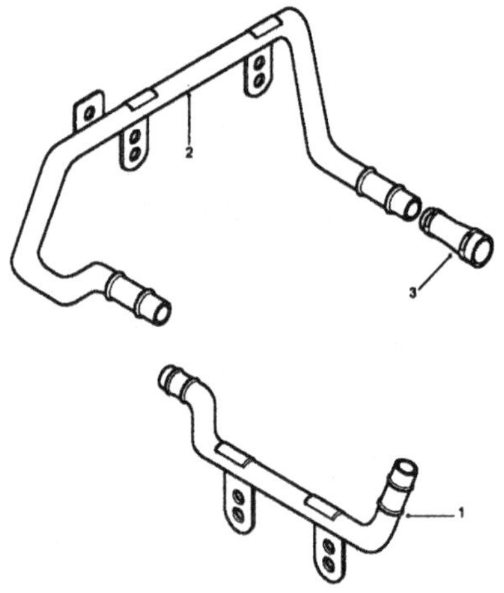

LB0046

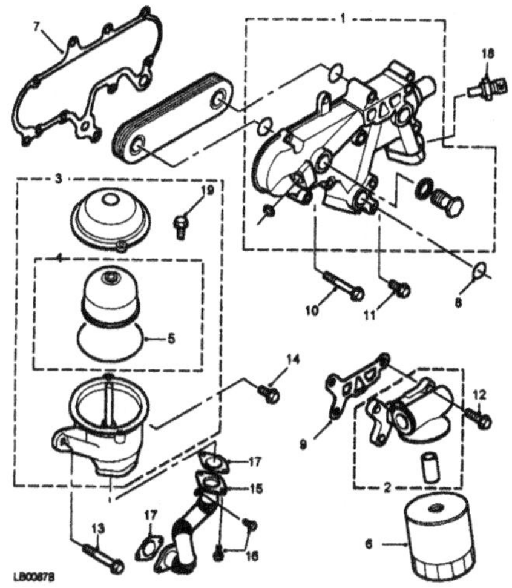

LB0087B

Illus	Part Number	Description	Quantity	Change Point	Remarks
1	PBC101270	Oil cooler assembly-engine-diesel	1		
2	LPY100160	Adaptor-oil filter-diesel	1		
3	LPD100010	CENTRIFUGE - OIL COOLER	1		
4	ERR6299	• ROTOR,	1		
5	ERR7247	• • Seal	1		
19	FS106207L	• Screw-flanged head-M6 x 20	2		
6	LPX100590	Cartridge-engine oil filter	1		
7	ERR7220	Gasket-oil cooler-adaptor	1		
8	ERR7098	O ring	1		
9	LVH100230	Gasket-oil filter housing	1		
10	FB108117	Bolt-cover to block-M8 x 55	2		
11	FS108207L	Screw-cover to block-flanged head-M8 x 20	3		
12	FS108307	Screw-flanged head-housing to cover-M8 x 30	3		
13	FB108167	Bolt-centrifuge to cover-M8 x 80	2		
14	FS108257L	Screw-centrifuge to cover-flanged head-M8 x 25	1		
15	LQP100680	Pipe-centrifuge oil-drain	1		
16	FS106167L	Screw-flanged head-pipe to cover-flanged head-M6 x 16	2		
16	FS106167L	Screw-flanged head-pipe to sump-flanged head-M6 x 16	2		
17	LRJ100000	Gasket-centrifuge oil-drain pipe-diesel	1		
18	NUC10003	Switch-oil pressure engine	1		

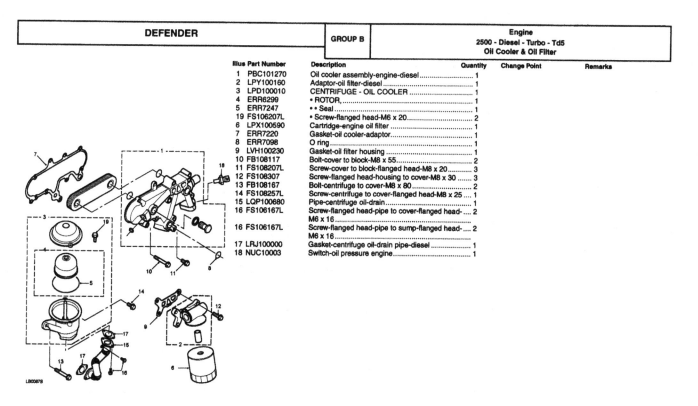

Illus	Part Number	Description	Quantity	Change Point	Remarks
1	PIB100050	FUEL COOLER ASSEMBLY	1	To (V) ECD3	
2	PYH100400	• Nut-caged-M8	1		
1	PIB000070	FUEL COOLER ASSEMBLY	1	From (V) ECD3	
2	PYH100400	• Nut-caged-M8	1		
5	PIB000060	Fuel cooler assembly	1	To (V) ECD3	
3	FS108127ML	Screw-flanged head-M8 x 12-patch lock	2		
4	FS108207L	Screw-flanged head-M8 x 20	2		

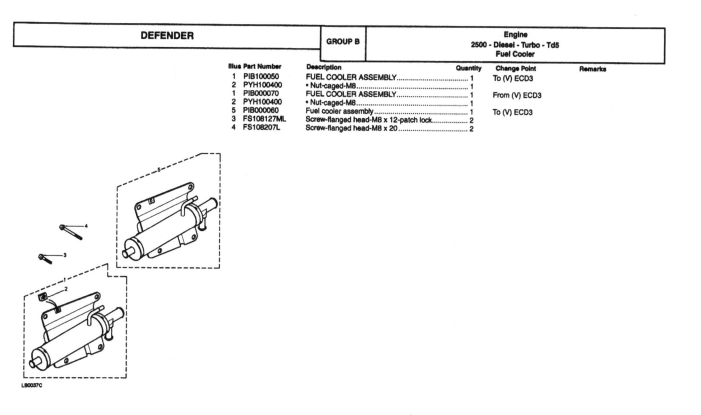

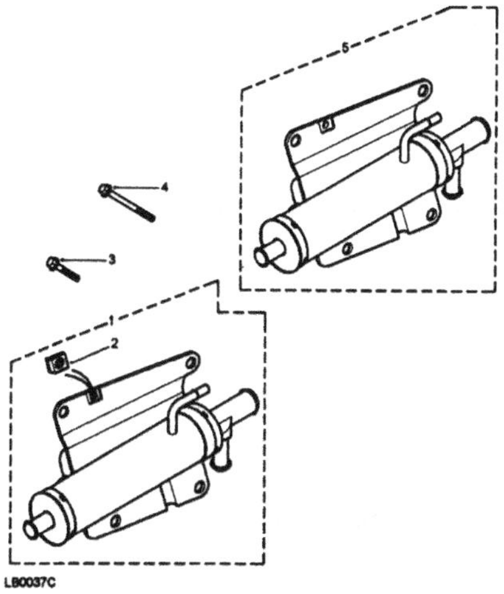

LB0037C

DEFENDER	GROUP B	Engine 2500 - Diesel - Turbo - Td5 Turbo Charger

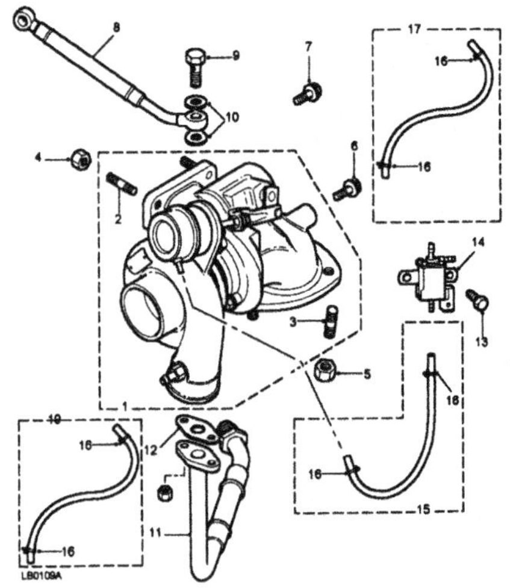

LB0109A

Illus	Part Number	Description	Quantity	Change Point	Remarks
1	PMF100460	TURBOCHARGER ASSEMBLY-NEW	1	To (V) ECD3	
2	ERR551L	• Stud-M8 x 25	3		
3	UAM2368L	• Stud	3		
1	PMF100460E	TURBOCHARGER ASSEMBLY-EXCHANGE	1	To (V) ECD3	
2	ERR551L	• Stud-M8 x 25	3		
3	UAM2368L	• Stud	3		
1	PMF000040	TURBOCHARGER ASSEMBLY-NEW	1	From (V) ECD3	
2	ERR551L	• Stud-M8 x 25	3		
3	UAM2368L	• Stud	3		
4	ESR2033	Nut-locking-M8	3		
5	ESR2034	Nut-flange-nyloc-M10	3		
6	FB108087	Bolt-turbo to bracket-flanged head-M8 x 40	1		
7	FB108117	Bolt-bracket to head-M8 x 55	2		
8	PNP101280	Pipe-oil feed-turbocharger	1		
9	SYG100510L	Bolt-banjo	2		
10	ADU6847L	Washer-sealing	4		
11	PNH101840	Pipe-oil drain turbocharger	1		
12	PNT100030	Gasket-turbocharger outlet	1		
13	FS106127L	Screw-flanged head-M6 x 12	2		
14	PMK100130	Valve-waste gate-control turbocharger	1		
15	PNH101570	HOSE ASSEMBLY-VACUUM WASTEGATE CONTROL	1		
16	MYC100230L	• Clip-hose-4mm/ID	2		
17	PNH101680	HOSE WASTEGATE CONTROL	1		
19	PNH101670	HOSE-MODULATOR VALVE TO AIR CLEANER-200MM	1		
16	MYC100230L	• Clip-hose-4mm/ID	2		

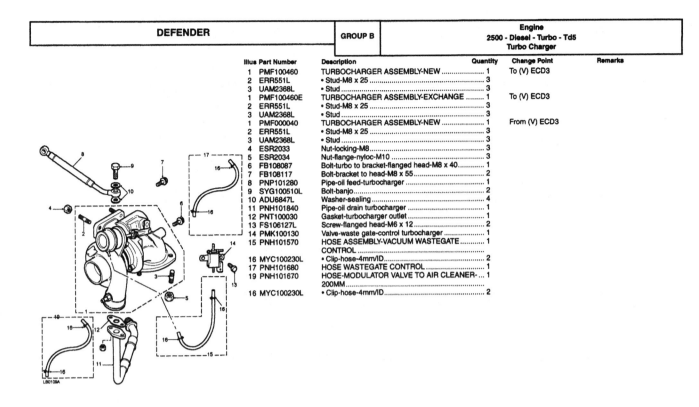

DEFENDER	GROUP B	Engine 2500 - Diesel - Turbo - Td5 Power Steering Pump

Illus	Part Number	Description	Quantity	Change Point	Remarks
1	QVB101350	Pump assembly power assisted steering	1		
2	ERR6711	Seal-coolant pump	1		
3	ERR7033	Pulley power assisted steering pump	1		
4	FS108127L	Screw-flanged head-flanged head-M8 x 12	3		
5	QVU10037	Bracket-mounting power assisted steering pump	1		
6	FS108207L	Screw-flanged head-M8 x 20	2		
7	FS108807	Screw-M8 x 80	2		
8	PEU102770	Bracket assembly-coolant & power assisted steering pump-diesel	1		
9	FN110047	Nut-flange-flange-M10	1		
10	TE110071L	Stud-M10 x 35	1		
11	FB110081S	Bolt-adhesive-patch-M10 x 40	5		

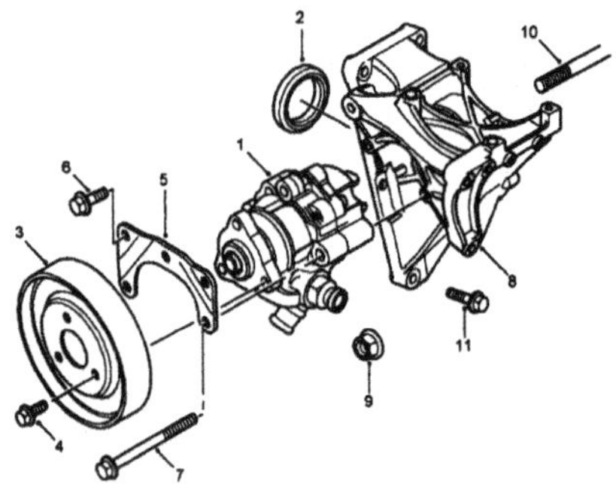

CFBSNC1A

Air Conditioning Compressor

Illus	Part Number	Description	Quantity	Change Point	Remarks
1	JPB101330	COMPRESSOR ASSEMBLY AIR CONDITIONING	1		
	STC3176	• O ring-suction	1		
	STC3177	• O ring-discharge	1		
2	FB108177	Bolt-compressor to block-flanged head	4		
	FRC2481	Dowel	2		
3	ERR6949	BRACKET-IDLER MOUNTING ANCILLARY DRIVE	1		
4	ERR6658	• PULLEY-IDLER ANCILLARY DRIVE	1		
	ERR6659	• • Bolt	1		
	FRC2481	Dowel	2		
	FS108357	Screw-flanged head-M8 x 35	3		
4	PQR101070	Pulley-idler ancillary drive-80mm	NLA		Use PQR101150.
4	PQR101150	Pulley-idler ancillary drive-80mm	1		

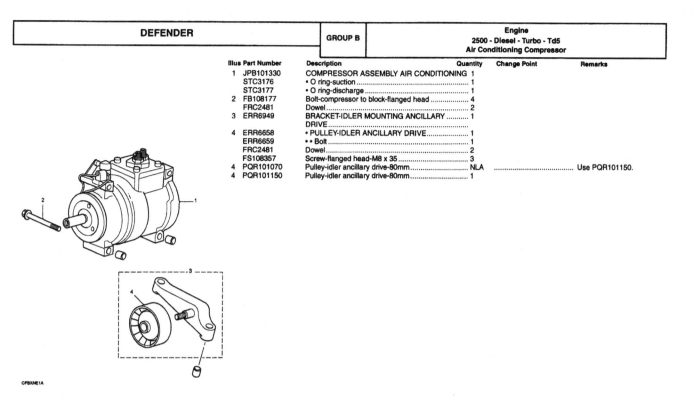

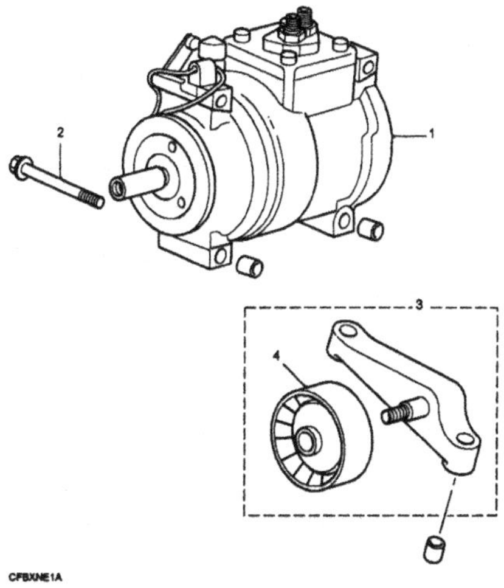

CFBXNE1A

DEFENDER | GROUP B | Engine
2500 - Diesel - Turbo - Td5

Alternator

Illus	Part Number	Description	Quantity	Change Point	Remarks
1	ERR6999	Alternator assembly-120 amp-new	1		
1	ERR6999E	Alternator assembly-120 amp-exchange	1		
2	ERR6997	Bracket	1		
3	FB110127	Bolt-bracket to block	3		
4	ERR7000	Support bracket	1		
5	FS108207L	Screw-flanged head-M8 x 20	2		
6	FB110227	Bolt-alternator to bracket-flanged head-M10	1		
7	FN110047	Nut-flange-alternator to bracket-flange-M10	1		
8	YKL100120	Pipe-altn/vac pump oil feed	1		
9	517976	Washer-copper	2		
10	ERR6996	Pipe-vacuum pump oil drain	1		

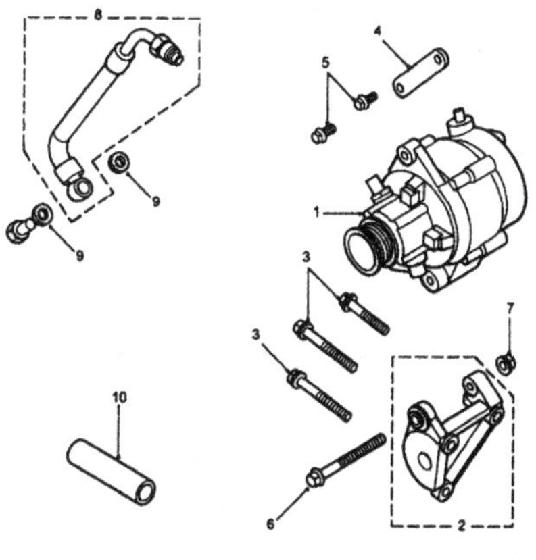

LB0108

DEFENDER	GROUP B	Engine 2500 - Diesel - Turbo - Td5 Starter Motor

Illus	Part Number	Description	Quantity	Change Point	Remarks
1	NAD101240	MOTOR-STARTER ENGINE-NEW	1		
2	NYH100090	• Nut	1		
1	NAD101240E	Motor-starter engine-exchange	1		
3	FB110087	Bolt-flanged head-M10 x 40	2		
4	TE110051L	Stud-M10 x 25	1		
5	FN110047	Nut-flange-flange-M10	1		

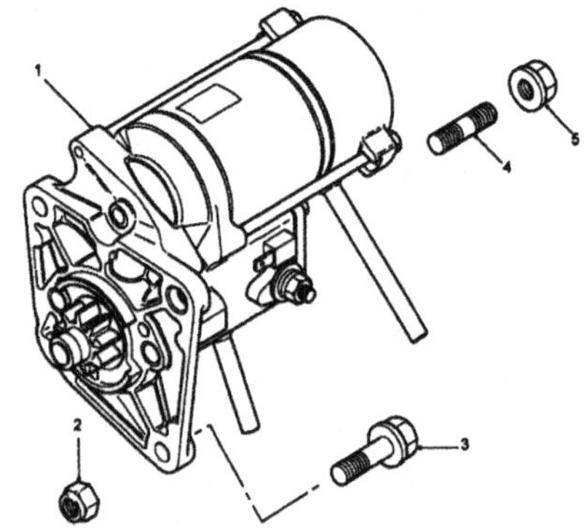

CFBSPE1A

DEFENDER	GROUP B	Engine 2500 - Diesel - Turbo - Td5 Sensors

Illus	Part Number	Description	Quantity	Change Point	Remarks
1	NSC100790	Sensor-crank engine	1		
2	FS106127L	Screw-flanged head-sensor to crankcase-M6 x 12	1		
3	WQT100030L	Switch-inertia remote fuel pump	1		
4	AB610041L	Screw-self tapping AB-M8 x 12	2		
5	CZG1946	Locknut	2		

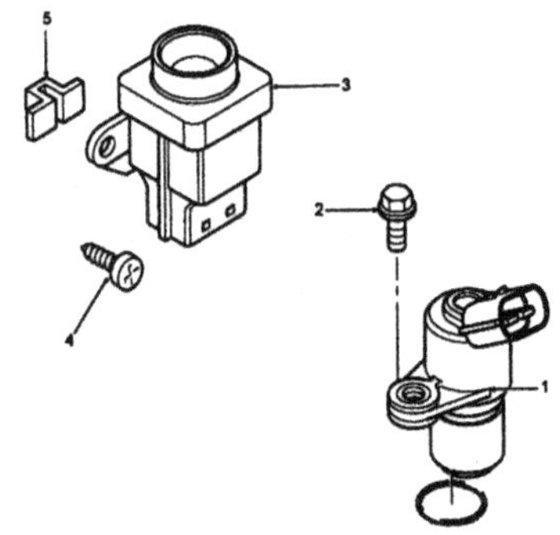

LB0075

DEFENDER	GROUP B	Engine 2500 - Diesel - Turbo - Td5 Flywheel - Manual

Illus	Part Number	Description	Quantity	Change Point	Remarks
1	PSD103040	Flywheel engine	NLA		Use PSD103470.
1	PSD103470	FLYWHEEL ENGINE	1		
2	PSF100140	• Gear-ring-flywheel engine	1		
3	FTC4631	Plate-clutch-driven	1		
4	FTC4630	Cover-clutch assembly	1		
5	NH108041L	Nut-hexagonal head-M8	6		
6	KSP101410	Plate-engine/gearbox shim	1		
7	FS110167	Screw	2		

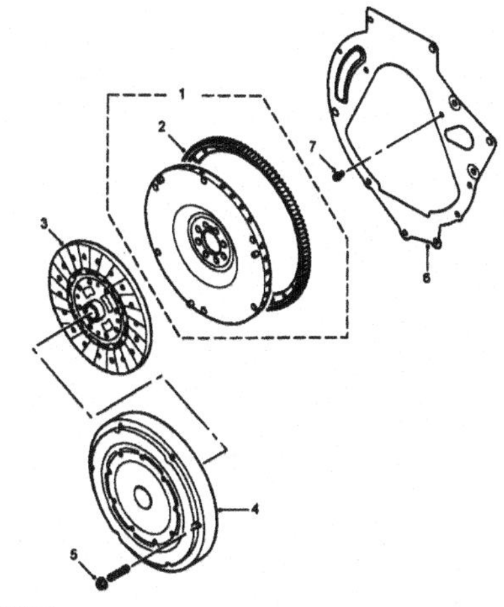

DEFENDER	GROUP B	Engine V8 Petrol - Carburetter Engine Complete

Illus	Part Number	Description	Quantity	Change Point	Remarks
1	ETC8445	Engine assembly-power unit	NLA		Use ETC7714 Short Engine.

NOTE-ENGINE IS WITHOUT AIR RAILS &
DETOXED
THROUGH THE CARBURETTTERS

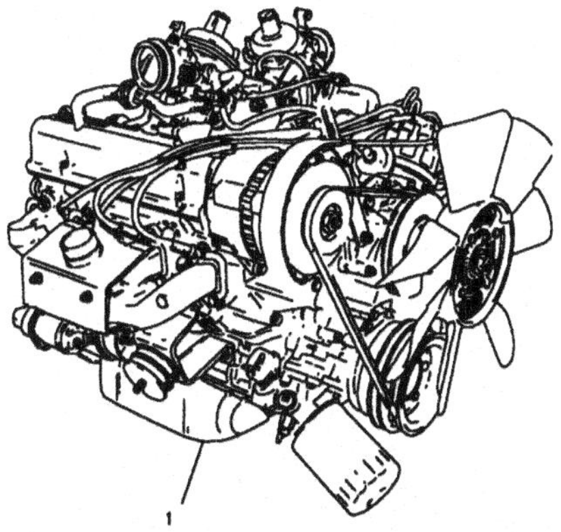

Illus	Part Number	Description	Quantity	Change Point	Remarks
1	RTC2972N	Engine unit-stripped-new	1		14G 20G 24G
1	RTC2972E	Engine unit-stripped-exchange	1		
1	RTC2973N	Engine unit-stripped-new	NLA		Use ETC7714 Short Engine and re-use ancillary components. 15G 21G
1	RTC5856N	Engine unit-stripped-5/8" bore air rails-new	1		24G
1	RTC5856E	Engine unit-stripped-exchange	1		

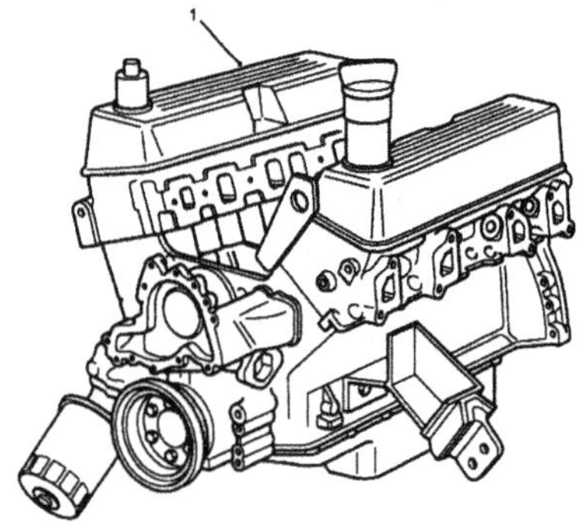

AHBQAC1A

CTP LOGISTICS LTD

Illus	Part Number	Description	Quantity	Change Point	Remarks
1	ETC7714	Engine base unit-part-8.13:1	1		

NOTE:COMPRISES BLOCK, PISTON & CRANKSHAFT

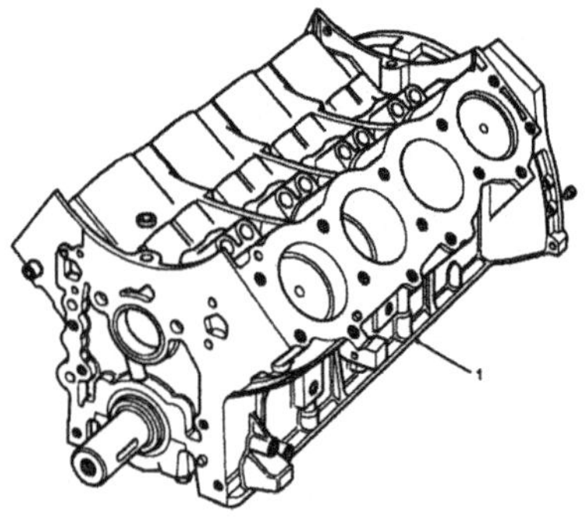

AHBQAE1A

Cylinder Block

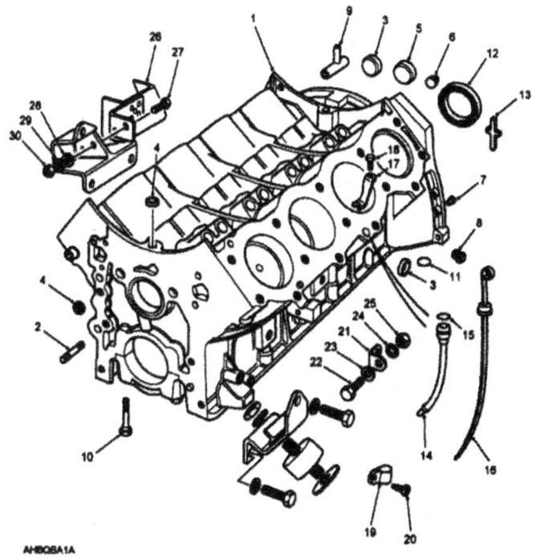

Illus	Part Number	Description	Quantity	Change Point	Remarks
1	ERC6934	CYLINDER BLOCK-ENGINE	1		
2	252513	• Stud-5/16UNC x 1 3/8	1		
3	602152	• Plug-cup	8		
4	602147	• Plug-cylinder block oil way	4		
5	602146	• Plug-cam bore	1		
6	602212	• Plug-blanking.-tappet line rear	2		
7	602141	• Dowel-flywheel housing	2		
8	3290	• Plug-coolant drain	2		
9	ERC5761	• Pipe assembly-crankcase breather oil	1		
10	602130	• Setscrew-cylinder block main bearing cap	10		
11	612898	Plug-rear block	2		
12	ERR2640	Seal-crankshaft rear oil	1		
13	611089	Seal-main bearing rear cap half joint	2		
14	ERR4556	Tube-oil dipstick	1		
15	602545	O ring	1		
16	ERR1922L	Dipstick-oil	1		
17	614585	Clamp-bar	1		
18	SH604031L	Screw-bracket/head-hexagonal head	1		
19	610489	Clip	1		
20	78862	Screw-10UNC x 9/16	1		21G 24G
21	ERC2973	Bracket-oil dipstick tube	1		
22	257017	Screw-M5 x 16	1		
23	WA702101L	Washer	1		
24	WM702001L	Washer-spring-3/16 dia-square	1		
25	HN2005L	Nut-UNF	1		
26	NRC3301	Heatshield engine exhaust-LH	1		
26	577846	Heatshield engine exhaust-RH	1		
27	BH106051L	Bolt-hexagonal head-M6 x 25	4		
28	WA106041L	Washer-6mm	4		
29	WL106001L	Washer-sprung-M6	4		
30	NH106041L	Nut-hexagonal-nyloc-M6	4		

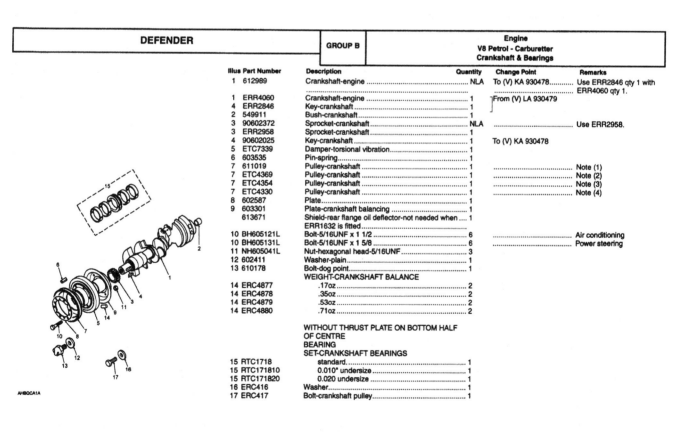

Crankshaft & Bearings

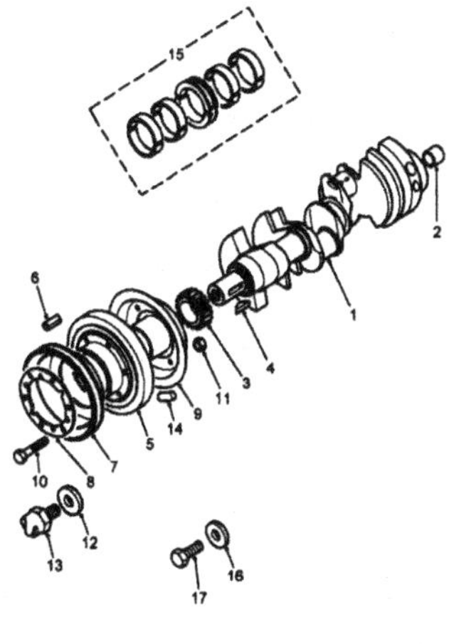

Illus	Part Number	Description	Quantity	Change Point	Remarks
1	612989	Crankshaft-engine	NLA	To (V) KA 930478	Use ERR2846 qty 1 with ERR4060 qty 1.
1	ERR4060	Crankshaft-engine	1	From (V) LA 930479	
4	ERR2846	Key-crankshaft	1		
2	549911	Bush-crankshaft	1		
3	90602372	Sprocket-crankshaft	NLA		Use ERR2958.
3	ERR2958	Sprocket-crankshaft	1		
4	90602025	Key-crankshaft	1	To (V) KA 930478	
5	ETC7339	Damper-torsional vibration	1		
6	603535	Pin-spring	1		
7	611019	Pulley-crankshaft	1		Note (1)
7	ETC4369	Pulley-crankshaft	1		Note (2)
7	ETC4354	Pulley-crankshaft	1		Note (3)
7	ETC4330	Pulley-crankshaft	1		Note (4)
8	602587	Plate	1		
9	603301	Plate-crankshaft balancing	1		
	613671	Shield-rear flange oil deflector-not needed when ERR1632 is fitted	1		
10	BH605121L	Bolt-5/16UNF x 1 1/2	6		Air conditioning
10	BH605131L	Bolt-5/16UNF x 1 5/8	6		Power steering
11	NH605041L	Nut-hexagonal head-5/16UNF	3		
12	602411	Washer-plain	1		
13	610178	Bolt-dog point	1		
		WEIGHT-CRANKSHAFT BALANCE			
14	ERC4877	.17oz	2		
14	ERC4878	.35oz	2		
14	ERC4879	.53oz	2		
14	ERC4880	.71oz	2		
		WITHOUT THRUST PLATE ON BOTTOM HALF OF CENTRE BEARING			
		SET-CRANKSHAFT BEARINGS			
15	RTC1718	standard	1		
15	RTC171810	0.010" undersize	1		
15	RTC171820	0.020 undersize	1		
16	ERC416	Washer	1		
17	ERC417	Bolt-crankshaft pulley	1		

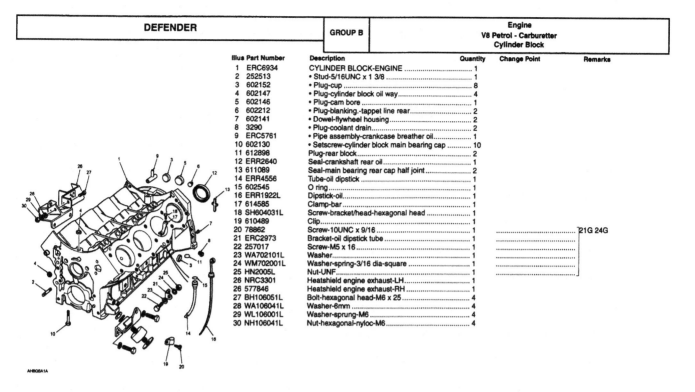

Remarks:
(1) Except power steering And air conditioning
(2) power steering Except air conditioning
(3) air conditioning Except power steering
(4) power steering air conditioning

Illus	Part Number	Description	Quantity	Change Point	Remarks
1	RTC2186S	PISTON-ENGINE-STANDARD.-8.13:1	8		
2	RTC2408	• Ring set assembly-piston-standard.	8		
1	RTC218620	PISTON-ENGINE-0.020" OVERSIZE-8.13:1	8		
2	RTC240820	• Ring set assembly-piston-0.020" oversize	8		
3	602082	ROD-CRANKSHAFT CONNECTING	8		
4	602609	• Bolt-connecting rod-11/32UNS-3A	16		
5	602061	• Nut-connecting rod-11/32UNS-3B	16		
		SET-CONNECTING ROD BIG END HALF BEARING			
6	RTC2117	standard.	1		
6	RTC211710	0.010" undersize	1		
6	RTC211720	0.020 undersize	1		

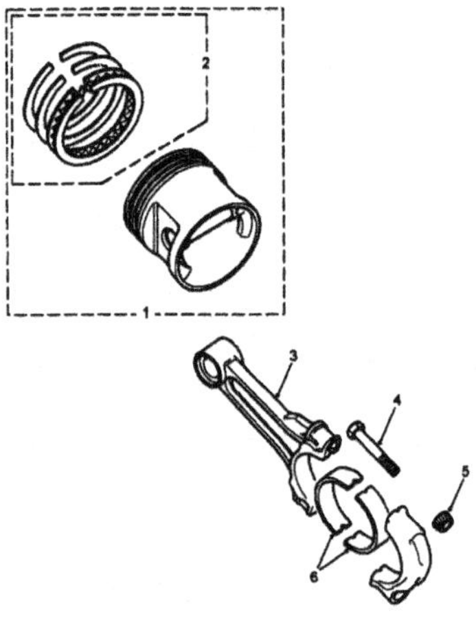

AHBQCC1A

Illus	Part Number	Description	Quantity	Change Point	Remarks
1	612710	Strainer and pipe assembly-oil	NLA		Use ERR3677.
1	ERR3677	Strainer and pipe assembly-oil	1		
2	90602068	Gasket-sump oil strainer	1		
2	ERR3788	Gasket-sump oil strainer	1		
3	SH506081L	Screw-housing to block-hexagonal head-3/8" x 1"	2		
4	WM600041L	Washer-spring-1/4 dia-square	2		
5	602070	Cover-oil strainer	1		
6	ERR4633	Sump-engine oil	1		
7	603659	Plug-sump assembly oil drain	1		
8	213961	Washer-sealing-sump drain plug	1		
9	602199	Bolt & washer assembly-sump-5/16UNC	NLA		Use LSO100000.
9	LSO100000	Bolt & washer assembly-sump	16		
	602087	Gasket-crankcase oil sump	1		Optional

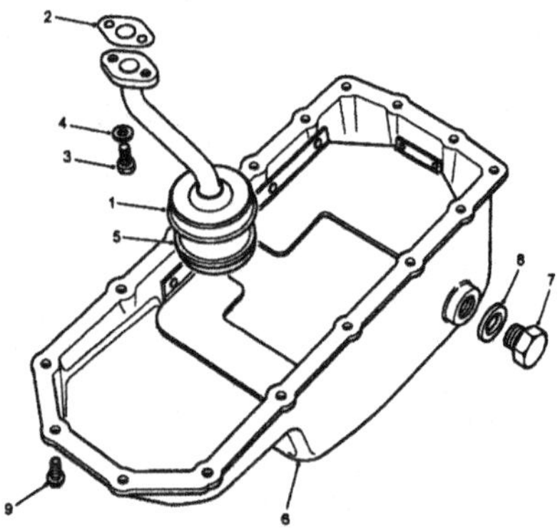

AHBQDA1A

Illus	Part Number	Description	Quantity	Change Point	Remarks
1	ETC7385	COVER-ENGINE-FRONT	1		
2	602201	• Dowel	2		
3	ETC5065	• Seal-crankshaft front oil	NLA		Use ERR1632.
3	ERR1632	• Seal-crankshaft front oil	NLA		Use ERR6490.
3	ERR6490	• Seal-crankshaft front oil	1		
4	154545	• Plug-core	1		
6	90602202	• Dowel	2		
	247766	Excluder mud-not needed when ERR1632 is fitted	1		
	78782	Screw-self tapping-No 6	8		
5	ERR4936	Gasket-cover front	1		
7	BH505241L	Bolt-5/16UNC x 3	1		
8	SH505091L	Screw-hexagonal head-5/16UNC x 1 1/8	2		
9	602388	Bolt-5/16UNC x 3.8	1		
10	WA108051L	Washer-8mm	4		
11	4075L	Washer-plain-M8	1		
12	NH605041L	Nut-hexagonal head-5/16UNF	1		
13	ETC7345	Pointer-engine timing	1		
14	SH504051L	Screw-hexagonal head-1/4UNF x 5/8	2		
15	WM600041L	Washer-spring-1/4 dia-square	2		
16	RTC609	Washer-plain-standard	1		

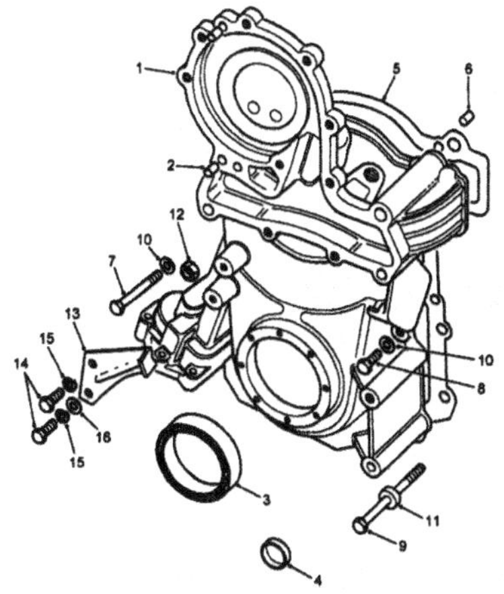

AHBQEA1A

Illus	Part Number	Description	Quantity	Change Point	Remarks
1	STC1611	PUMP ASSEMBLY-ENGINE COOLANT	1		Non viscous coupling
2	612326	• Gasket-cylinder block coolant pump	NLA		Use ERR2428.
2	ERR2428	Gasket-cylinder block coolant pump			
3	BH505401L	Bolt-hexagonal head-5/16UNC x 5	3		
4	BH505401L	Bolt-hexagonal head-5/16UNC x 5	1		
5	WA108051L	Washer-8mm	4		
6	BH504101L	Bolt-1/4UNC x 1 1/4	6		
7	BH504151L	Bolt-hexagonal head-1/4UNC x 1 7/8	2		
8	BH504161L	Bolt-1/4UNC x 2	1		
9	WC106041L	Washer-M6-oversize	9		
10	252516	Stud-5/16UNC/UNF x 2 x 1/8 lng	1		
11	4421	Washer-plain	1		
12	WM600051L	Washer-spring-5/16"	1		
13	NT605041L	Nut-hexagonal-thin-5/16UNF	1		
14	BH505121L	Bolt-flanged head-5/16UNC x 1 1/2	1		
15	WM600051L	Washer-spring-5/16"	1		

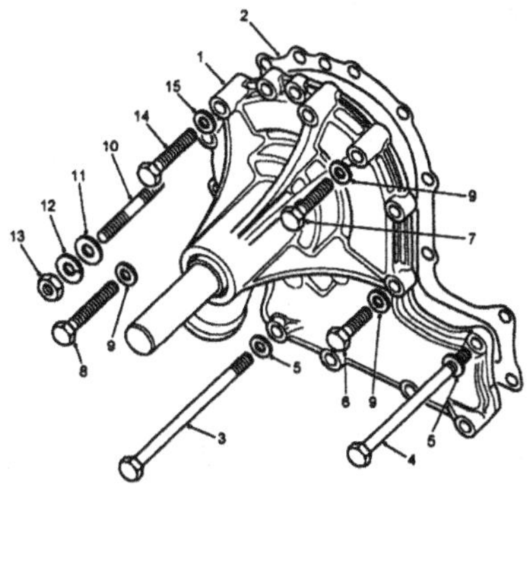

AHBQEE1A

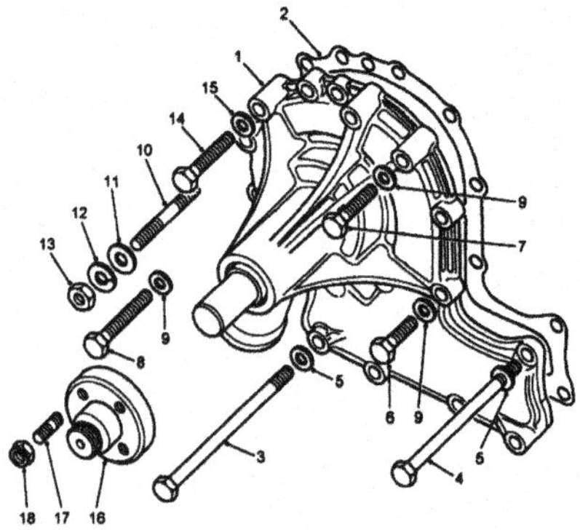

AHBQEE2A

Illus	Part Number	Description	Quantity	Change Point	Remarks
1	RTC6337	PUMP ASSEMBLY-ENGINE COOLANT	NLA		Use STC487.
1	STC487	PUMP ASSEMBLY-ENGINE COOLANT	1		Except air conditioning
1	RTC6338	PUMP ASSEMBLY-ENGINE COOLANT	NLA		Use STC488.
1	STC488	PUMP ASSEMBLY-ENGINE COOLANT	1		Air conditioning
2	612326	• Gasket-cylinder block coolant pump	NLA		Use ERR2428.
2	ERR2428	Gasket-cylinder block coolant pump			Air conditioning
3	BH505401L	Bolt-hexagonal head-5/16UNC x 5	3		Except air conditioning
3	BH505401L	Bolt-hexagonal head-5/16UNC x 5	1		Air conditioning
4	BH505401L	Bolt-hexagonal head-5/16UNC x 5	1		
5	WA108051L	Washer-8mm	4		
6	BH504101L	Bolt-1/4UNC x 1 1/4	6		
7	BH504151L	Bolt-hexagonal head-1/4UNC x 1 7/8	2		
8	BH504161L	Bolt-1/4UNC x 2	1		90°
8	BH505121L	Bolt-flanged head-5/16UNC x 1 1/2	2		
8	BH505161L	Bolt	1		
9	WC106041L	Washer-M6-oversize	9		
6	BH504101L	Bolt-1/4UNC x 1 1/4	2		Air conditioning except power steering
7	BH505121L	Bolt-flanged head-5/16UNC x 1 1/2	2		
15	WM600051L	Washer-spring-5/16"	2		
9	WC106041L	Washer-M6-oversize	3		
6	BH504101L	Bolt-1/4UNC x 1 1/4	4		Power steering except air conditioning
7	BH504151L	Bolt-hexagonal head-1/4UNC x 1 7/8	2		
8	BH504161L	Bolt-1/4UNC x 2	1		
9	WC106041L	Washer-M6-oversize	7		
10	252516	Stud-5/16UNC/UNF x 2 x 1/8 lng	1		
12	WM600051L	Washer-spring-5/16"	1		
11	4421	Washer-plain	1		Except air conditioning
12	WM600051L	Washer-spring-5/16"	1		
13	NT605041L	Nut-hexagonal-thin-5/16UNF	1		
14	BH505121L	Bolt-flanged head-5/16UNC x 1 1/2	1		
15	WM600051L	Washer-spring-5/16"	1		
16	ERC5705	Hub assembly-front & rear	1		
17	TE108041L	Stud-M8 x 20	1		
18	NY108041L	Nut-nyloc-M8	4		

Illus	Part Number	Description	Quantity	Change Point	Remarks
1	613087	Fan assembly-cooling-5 blade	1		
2	602582	Pulley coolant pump	1		
3	SH504051L	Screw-pulley to hub-hexagonal head-1/4UNF x 5/8	3		
4	WM600041L	Washer-spring-1/4 dia-square	3		
5	SH505061L	Screw-fan to pump-hexagonal head-5/16UNC x 3/4	4		
6	WM600051L	Washer-spring-5/16"	4		
7	610578	HUB-DOWEL ASSEMBLY-WATER PUMP	1		
8	603428	• Pin-spring	1		

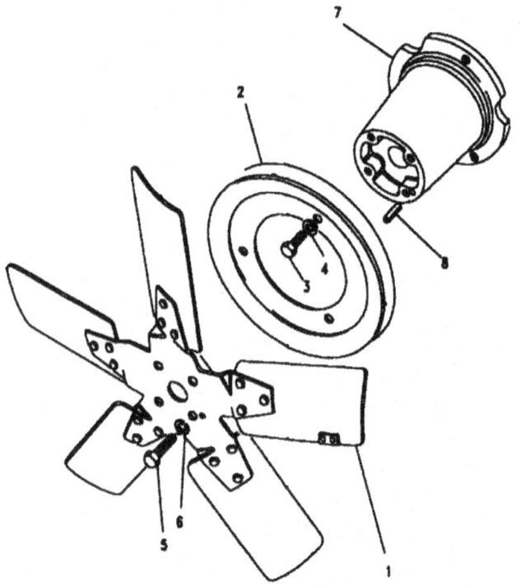

Illus	Part Number	Description	Quantity	Change Point	Remarks
1	ETC7553L	Fan assembly-cooling-7 blade	1		
1	ERC8164	Fan assembly-cooling-11 blade	1		Optional
2	ERC5707	Pulley coolant pump-single groove	1		Note (1)
3	ERC6540	Pulley coolant pump-twin groove	1		Note (2)
4	ERC5708	Coupling-engine fan viscous	1		
5	ERC5709	Screw-fan to viscous drive-M6 x 14	4		
6	4589L	Washer-plain-fan to viscous	4		

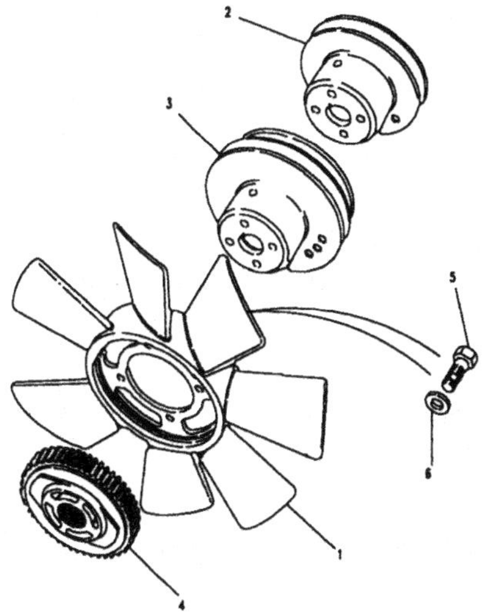

Remarks:
(1) manual steering Except air conditioning
(2) power steering air conditioning

Illus	Part Number	Description	Quantity	Change Point	Remarks
1	ETC7394	Belt-polyvee alternator	1		
2	ETC7394	Belt-polyvee alternator	1		
3	614106	Belt-vee power assisted steering	NLA		Use ERC675.
3	ERC675	Belt-vee power assisted steering	1		

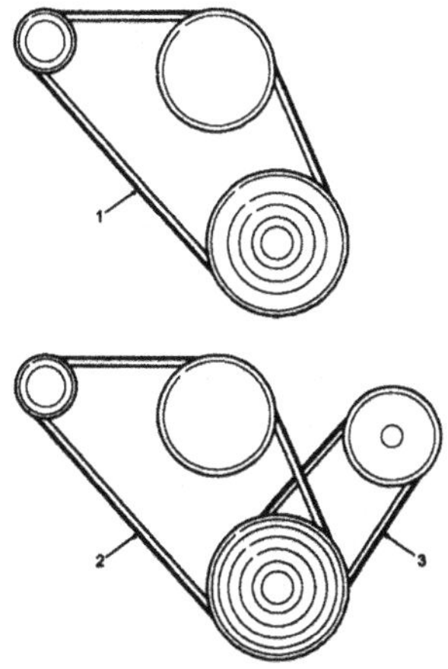

AHBQEG3A

Illus	Part Number	Description	Quantity	Change Point	Remarks
1	614670	Belt-polyvee coolant pump	1		
2	603713	Belt-vee air conditioning compressor	1		
3	614106	Belt-vee power assisted steering	NLA		Use ERC675.
3	ERC675	Belt-vee power assisted steering	1		
4	ERR2073	Belt-polyvee alternator	1		
5	614670	Belt-polyvee coolant pump	1		Power steering
6	603713	Belt-vee air conditioning compressor	1		Power steering
7	614106	Belt-vee power assisted steering	NLA		Use ERC675.
7	ERC675	Belt-vee power assisted steering	1		Power steering
8	ERR2073	Belt-polyvee alternator	1		

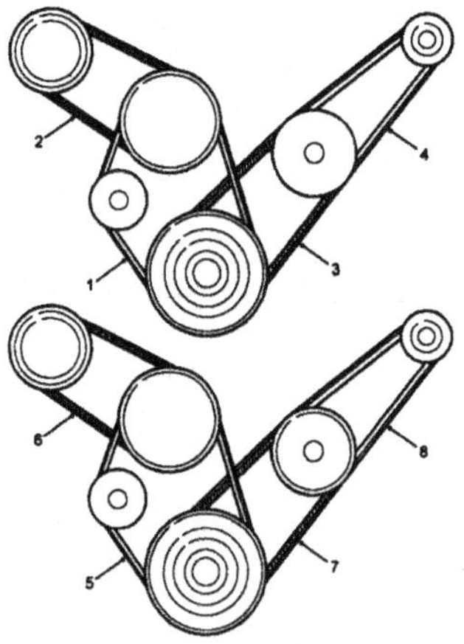

AHBQEG4A

Illus	Part Number	Description	Quantity	Change Point	Remarks
1	ERC1351	Shaft-oil pump	1		
2	614037	Gear-oil pump	1		
3	ETC4276	ADAPTOR ASSEMBLY-OIL FILTER	1		
4	614202	• Strainer-oil	1		
5	90602064	• Plunger-oil pump relief valve	1		
6	602067	• Spring-oil pump relief valve	1		
7	602071	• Plug-oil pump relief valve	1		
8	ETC8833	• Washer-oil pressure switch engine	1		
10	243968	• Washer-sealing	1		
	273166	• Plug	1		
9	PRC7204	Switch-oil pressure engine	NLA	To (V) KA 925365	Use AMR2092.
9	AMR2092	Switch-oil pressure engine	NLA	From (V) KA 925366	Use STC4104.
9	STC4104	Switch-oil pressure engine	1		
10	243968	Washer-sealing	1		
11	DRC2479	Transducer oil pressure	1		
12	243967	Washer-sealing	1		
13	PRC2507	Transducer oil temperature	1		
14	611514	Connector-inlet manifold adaptor-transmitter	1		
15	243968	Washer-sealing	1		
16	90602072	Gasket-cylinder block oil pump	1	To (V) JA 915290	
16	ERR1990	Gasket-cylinder block oil pump	1	From (V) JA 915291	
17	602912	Bolt-1/4UNC x 1 1/4	2		
17	602910	Bolt-1/4UNC x 7/8	3		
17	602913	Bolt-1/4UNC x 9/16	1		
18	ERR3340	Cartridge-engine oil filter	1		
	RTC4477	Kit-oil pump repair	1		

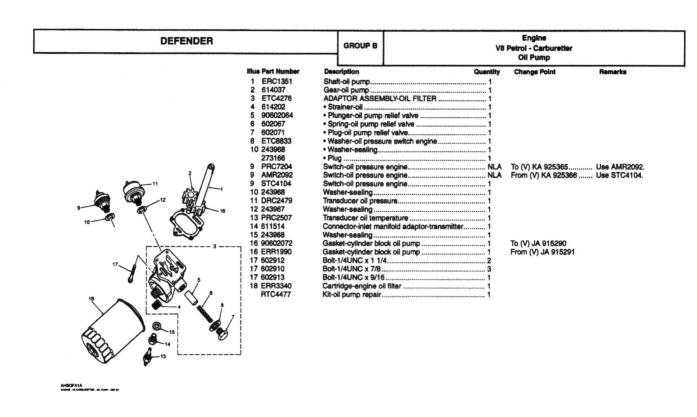

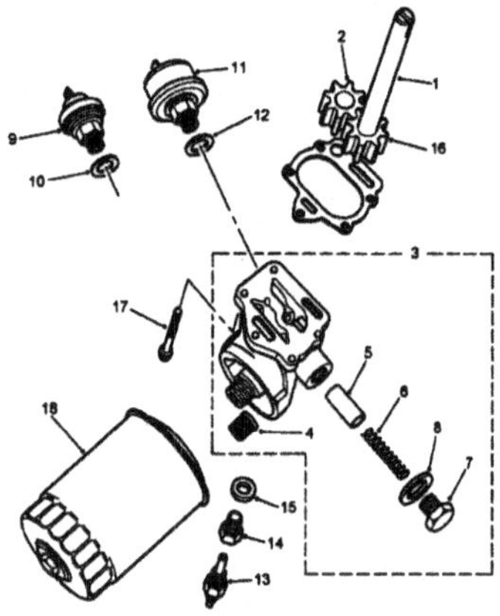

AHBQFA1A

DEFENDER	GROUP B	Engine V8 Petrol - Carburetter Cylinder Head

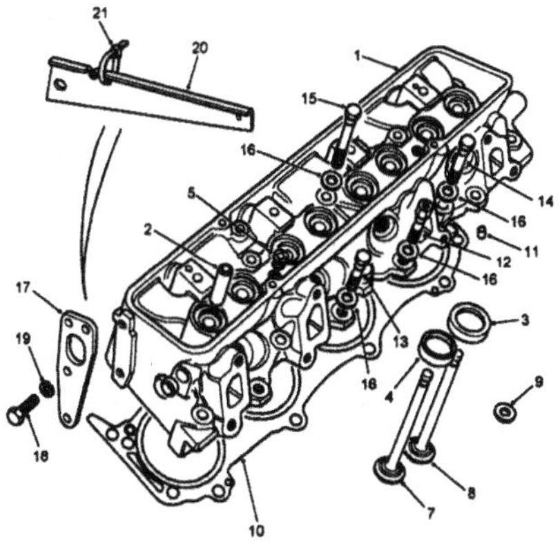

AHBQGA1A

Illus	Part Number	Description	Quantity	Change Point	Remarks
1	ERC215	CYLINDER HEAD ASSEMBLY-ENGINE-NON DETOXED	NLA		Use ERR2943 qty 7 with ERR2944 qty 3 with ERR4735 qty 1 with ERR5448 qty 1.
1	ERC676	CYLINDER HEAD ASSEMBLY-ENGINE-DETOXED	2		15G 21G
4	ERC210	• Seat-cylinder head exhaust valve-standard	4		
3	ERC224	• Seat-cylinder head inlet valve-standard	4		
5	602123	• Plug-core	2		
6	602289	• Plug-cup	2		
2	ERR3648	• Guide-cylinder head valve	NLA		Use LGJ100900. Part of ERC676.
1	ETC6471	CYLINDER HEAD ASSEMBLY-ENGINE-DETOXED-WITH AIR RAIL	2	Note (1)	24G
1	ERC3346	CYLINDER HEAD ASSEMBLY-ENGINE-DETOXED-WITHOUT AIR RAIL	NLA	To (E) November 1991	Use ERC3346L. 24G
2	603554	• Guide-cylinder head valve	16		
4	ERC210	• Seat-cylinder head exhaust valve-standard	4		
3	ERC224	• Seat-cylinder head inlet valve-standard	4		
5	602123	• Plug-core	2		
6	602289	• Plug-cup	2		
1	ERC3346L	CYLINDER HEAD ASSEMBLY-ENGINE-DETOXED	NLA	Note (2)	Fit ERR3650 new Cyl head, ERR1780 Inlet valve, ERR1782 stem seals. Use either exh valve ERR1781 for the Pi or ERR2551 for carb engine.
2	603554	• Guide-cylinder head valve	16		
3	ERC224	• Seat-cylinder head inlet valve-standard	8		
3	ERC225	• Seat-cylinder head inlet valve-0.010" oversize	8		
4	ERC210	• Seat-cylinder head exhaust valve-standard	8		
4	ERC211	• Seat-cylinder head exhaust valve-0.010" oversize	8		
5	602123	• Plug-core	4		
6	602289	• Plug-cup	4		

CHANGE POINTS:
(1) To (E) November 1991
(2) To (V) LA 921745

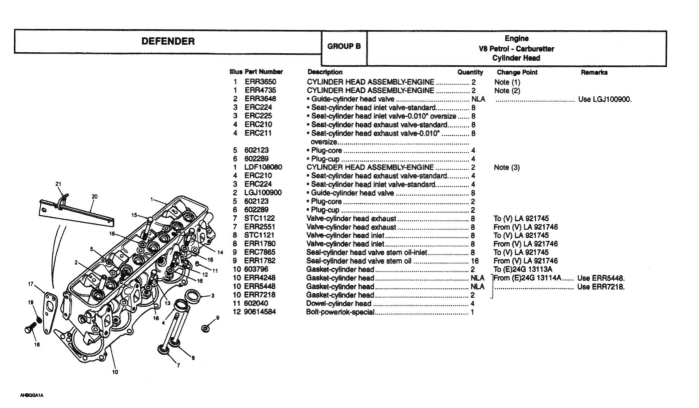

DEFENDER	GROUP B	Engine V8 Petrol - Carburetter Cylinder Head

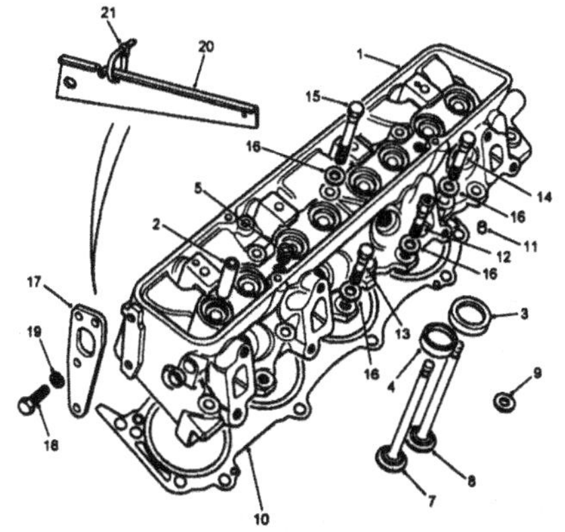

AHBQGA1A

Illus	Part Number	Description	Quantity	Change Point	Remarks
1	ERR3650	CYLINDER HEAD ASSEMBLY-ENGINE	2	Note (1)	
1	ERR4735	CYLINDER HEAD ASSEMBLY-ENGINE	2	Note (2)	
2	ERR3648	• Guide-cylinder head valve	NLA		Use LGJ100900.
3	ERC224	• Seat-cylinder head inlet valve-standard	8		
3	ERC225	• Seat-cylinder head inlet valve-0.010" oversize	8		
4	ERC210	• Seat-cylinder head exhaust valve-standard	8		
4	ERC211	• Seat-cylinder head exhaust valve-0.010" oversize	8		
5	602123	• Plug-core	4		
6	602289	• Plug-cup	4		
1	LDF108080	CYLINDER HEAD ASSEMBLY-ENGINE	2	Note (3)	
4	ERC210	• Seat-cylinder head exhaust valve-standard	4		
3	ERC224	• Seat-cylinder head inlet valve-standard	4		
2	LGJ100900	• Guide-cylinder head valve	8		
5	602123	• Plug-core	2		
6	602289	• Plug-cup	2		
7	STC1122	Valve-cylinder head exhaust	8	To (V) LA 921745	
7	ERR2551	Valve-cylinder head exhaust	8	From (V) LA 921746	
8	STC1121	Valve-cylinder head inlet	8	To (V) LA 921745	
8	ERR1780	Valve-cylinder head inlet	8	From (V) LA 921746	
9	ERC7865	Seal-cylinder head valve stem oil-inlet	8	To (V) LA 921745	
9	ERR1782	Seal-cylinder head valve stem oil	16	From (V) LA 921746	
10	603796	Gasket-cylinder head	2	To (E)24G 13113A	
10	ERR4248	Gasket-cylinder head	NLA	From (E)24G 13114A	Use ERR5448.
10	ERR5448	Gasket-cylinder head	NLA		Use ERR7218.
10	ERR7218	Gasket-cylinder head	2		
11	602040	Dowel-cylinder head	4		
12	90614584	Bolt-powerlok-special	1		

CHANGE POINTS:
(1) From (E)23D 18155A To (E)24G 13113A
(2) From (E)24G 13114A To (V) WA 152500
(3) To (V) WA 152501

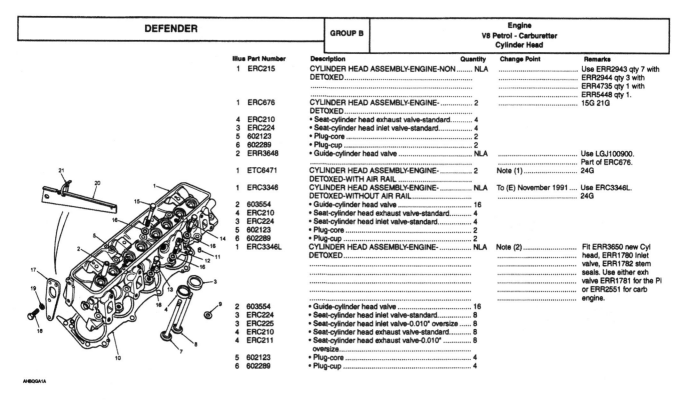

Illus	Part Number	Description	Quantity	Change Point	Remarks
13	602191	Bolt-cylinder head fixing-7/16UNC x 2 1/4	7		
14	602192	Bolt-cylinder head fixing-7/16UNC x 2.71	14		Except air conditioning
14	602192	Bolt-cylinder head fixing-7/16UNC x 2.71	13		Air conditioning
14	ERR2943	Bolt-cylinder head fixing-7/16UNC x 2.6	13	From (E)24G 13114A	
15	602193	Bolt-cylinder head fixing-7/16UNC x 3.91	6		
15	ERR2944	Bolt-cylinder head fixing-7/16UNC x 3.78	6	From (E)24G 13114A	
16	602098	Washer-plain	1		
	602200	Bolt-7/16UNC x 2.71	1		
17	603031	Bracket-lifting engine front-front-LH	1		Manual steering
17	90611812	Bracket-lifting engine front-front-LH	1		Power steering

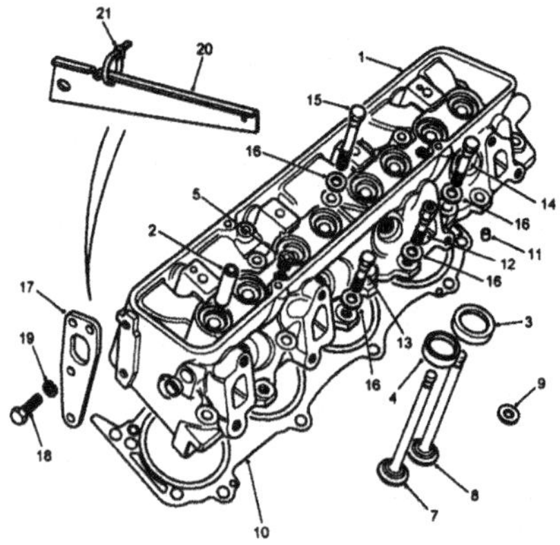

AHBQGA1A

Illus	Part Number	Description	Quantity	Change Point	Remarks
18	SH506071L	Screw-hexagonal head-3/8UNC x 7/8	2		Except power steering
19	WM600061L	Washer-3/8"-square	2		
18	SH506071L	Screw-hexagonal head-3/8UNC x 7/8	3		Power steering air conditioning
19	WM600061L	Washer-3/8"-square	3		
	SA506081L	Screw-machine-3/8UNC x 1-counter sunk	1		
20	ERC2920	Bracket-support king lead	1		Except air conditioning
21	DRC1538	Tie-cable-Black-2.5 x 100mm-inside serated	NLA		Use C43640.
					Except air conditioning
21	C43640	Tie-cable-Black-2.5 x 100mm-outside serated	2		Except air conditioning
	ETC6474	Plug	2		

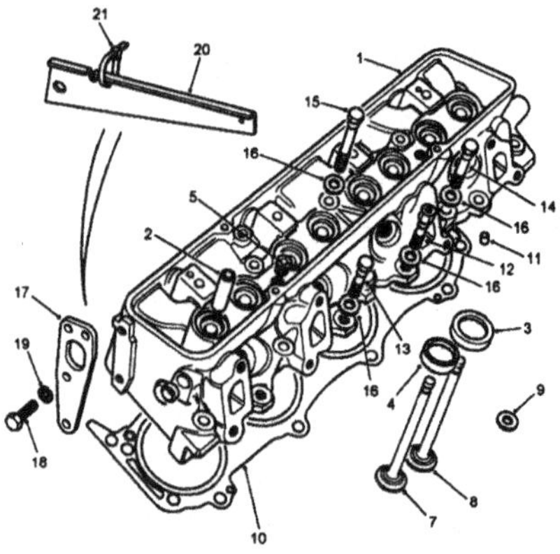

AHBQGA1A

DEFENDER | **GROUP B** | **Engine — V8 Petrol - Carburetter — Rocker Shaft**

Illus	Part Number	Description	Quantity	Change Point	Remarks
1	611659L	SHAFT-ROCKER	2		
2	154545	• Plug-core	4		
3	603734	Pillar-cylinder head rocker support	8		
4	602142	Spring-rocker shaft	6		
5	602148	Washer-waved	4		
6	602186	Washer-plain	4		
7	PS606101L	Pin-split	4		
8	602153	Rocker assembly-cylinder head-RH	8		
9	602154	Rocker assembly-cylinder head-LH	8		
10	602097	Bolt-3/8UNC x 2.79	8		
11	602172	Baffle-engine oil	2		
12	ERR4628	Spring-cylinder head valve	16		
13	ERR1921	Cap-cylinder head valve spring	16		
14	ERC1637	Cotter-valve	32		
15	603378	Rod-engine push	16		
16	ERC4949	Tappet-engine valve hydraulic	16		

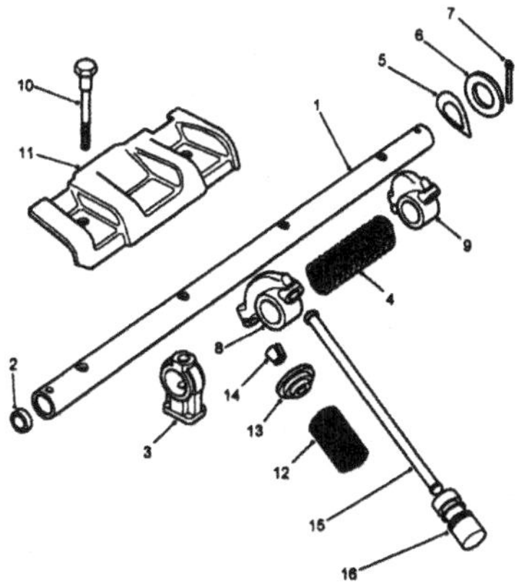

AHBQGC1A

DEFENDER | **GROUP B** | **Engine — V8 Petrol - Carburetter — Rocker Cover**

Illus	Part Number	Description	Quantity	Change Point	Remarks
		COVER-VALVE ROCKER			
1	RTC2348	RH	1		
2	RTC2349	LH	NLA		Use ETC8604.
2	ETC8604	LH	1		
3	ERC2989	Filler-oil	1		
4	ERC5512	Retainer-HT cables	1		
5	78862	Screw-10UNC x 9/16	1		
6	603675	Retainer-HT cables	1		
7	78861	Screw-10UNC x 5/8	1		
8	602512	Gasket-engine rocker cover	NLA	Note (1)	Use ERR7288.
8	ERR7288	Gasket-engine rocker cover	2	Note (2)	
8	LVC100260	Gasket-engine rocker cover	2	Note (3)	
9	603127	Screw-1/4UNC x 1 5/16	4		
9	SY504072L	Screw-1/4UNC x 7/8	4		
10	WM600041L	Washer-spring-1/4 dia-square	8		
11	WB106041L	Washer-M6	8		
12	625038	Cap-oil filler	1		
13	564258	O ring	1		
14	ERC614	Bracket-lifting engine rear	1		
15	WM600061L	Washer-3/8"-square	2		
16	SH506071L	Screw-hexagonal head-3/8UNC x 7/8	2		
17	586440	Clip-cable	1		
18	WM600041L	Washer-spring-1/4 dia-square	1		
19	WB106041L	Washer-M6	1		
20	SH604041L	Screw-hexagonal head-1/4UNF x 1/2	1		
21	ERC2144	Spacer	1		
22	603184	Clip	1		
23	78593	Screw-10UNF x 1/2	2		
24	WA702101L	Washer	2		
25	HN2005L	Nut-UNF	2		
	ETC5594	Bracket-connector engine	2		

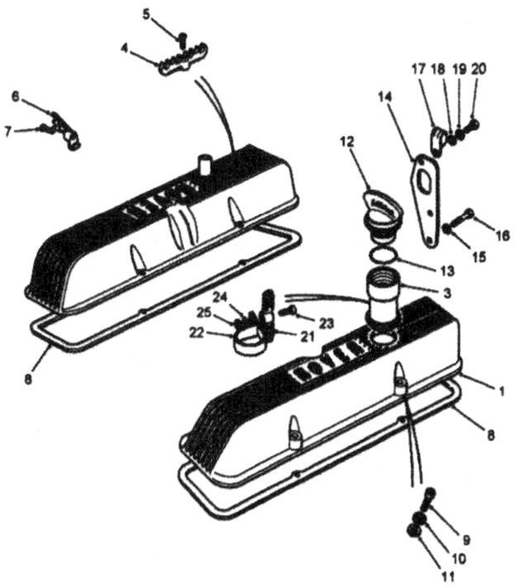

AHBQGG1A

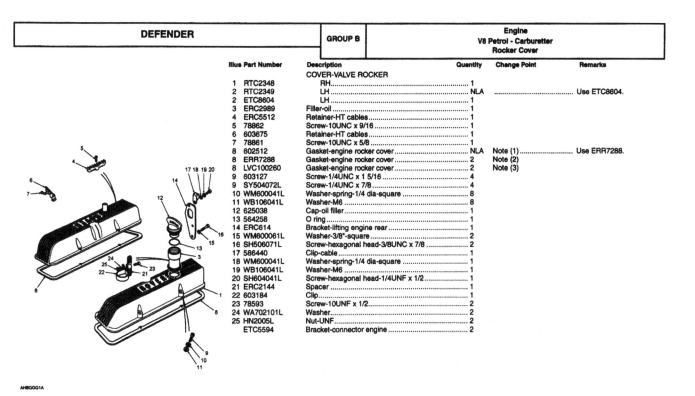

CHANGE POINTS:
(1) To (V) VA 121694
(2) From (V) VA 121695 To (V) WA 138479
(3) From (V) WA 138480

Illus	Part Number	Description	Quantity	Change Point	Remarks
1	603330	Flame trap-crankcase breather-rocker cover	2		
2	603376	Clip-only with Stromberg carburettors	2		
2	90513220	Clip-only with SU carburettors	1		
3	611351	Bracket	1		
4	AB610031L	Screw-10 x 3/8-self tapping	2		
5	611114	Hose assembly-breather-only with Stromberg carburettors-LH	1		
6	90611112	Hose-carburettor fuel pipe-only with Stromberg carburettors-LH	1		
5	613718L	Hose assembly-breather-only with SU carburettors-LH	1		
6	613402	Hose-carburettor fuel pipe-only with SU carburettors-LH	1		
7	ERC3930	Hose assembly fuel-RH	1		
8	ERC3931	Hose assembly fuel-RH	1		
9	ERC4670	Bracket	1		

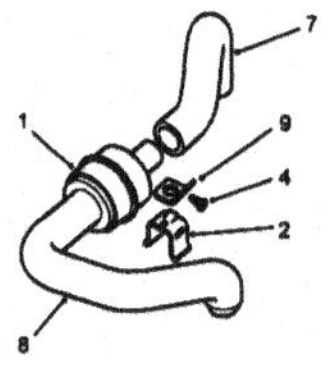

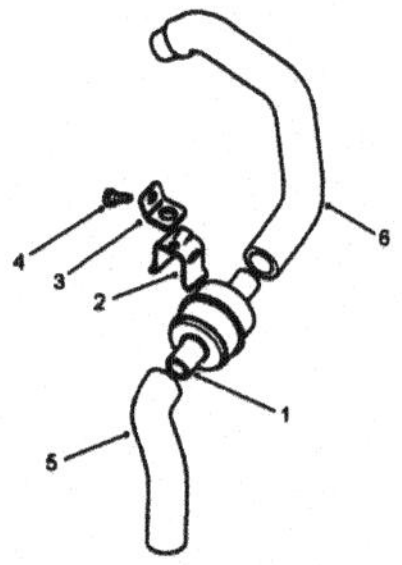

AHBQIG4A

Illus	Part Number	Description	Quantity	Change Point	Remarks
1	ETC6849	Camshaft-engine	1		14G 20G
1	ETC6850L	Camshaft-engine	1		15G 21G 24G
2	ERC2838	Key-camshaft location-camshaft	1		
3	610289	Sprocket-camshaft	1		
4	ERC2839	Spacer	1		
5	614188	Gear-drive-distributor	1		
6	ERC6552	Washer-plain	1		
7	ERC5749	Bolt-M12 x 30	1		14G 20G
7	602227	Bolt-7/16UNC x 1 1/8	1		15G 21G 24G
8	ERC7929	Chain-engine timing	1		
	RTC5918	Set-camshaft bearings	1		

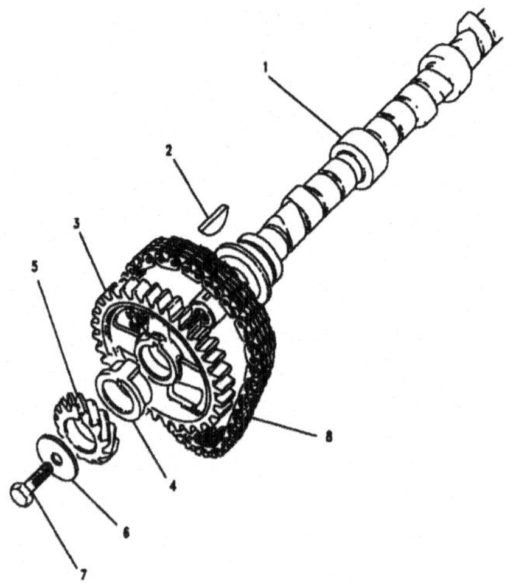

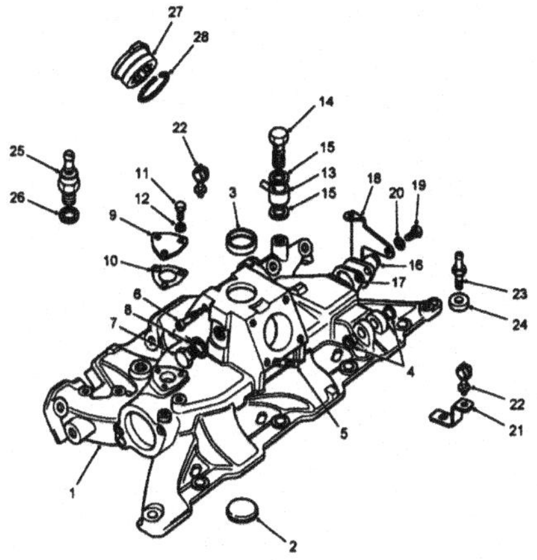

AHBQHA1A

Illus	Part Number	Description	Quantity	Change Point	Remarks
1	ERC2135	MANIFOLD ASSEMBLY-ENGINE INLET	1	To (E)24G 02088A	
1	ETC7915	MANIFOLD ASSEMBLY-ENGINE INLET	1	From (E)24G 02089A	
2	602152	• Plug-cup	1		
3	ERC256	• Plug-core	2		
4	522932	• Bush	2		
5	252514	• Stud	8		
7	603224	• Plug-blanking	1		Part of ERC2135.
8	232043	• Washer-sealing	1		
6	ERC4820	• Connector-inlet manifold adaptor	1		
7	603224	• Plug-blanking	1		Part of ETC7915.
					20G
9	598006	Plate	1		
10	236022	Washer-sealing	1		
11	257064	Screw	3		
12	WM702001L	Washer-spring-3/16 dia-square	3		
13	603277	Bolt-banjo	1		20G
13	610246	Bolt-banjo	1		21G 24G
14	534897	Bolt-banjo	1		
15	267604	Washer-sealing	2		
16	ERC3561	Pipe	1		
17	603441	Gasket-coolant outlet elbow	1	To (V) January 1994	
17	ERR4935	Gasket-coolant outlet elbow	1	From (V) January 1994	
18	603561	Bracket-inlet manifold support	1		
19	SH504061L	Setscrew-1/4UNC x 3/4	2		
20	WM600041L	Washer-spring-1/4 dia-square	2		
21	NRC2864	Bracket-pipe mounting	2		
22	CRC1226	Clip	A/R		
23	ERC2297	Peg-air cleaner mtg-engine	2		
24	4594L	Washer-plain	2		
25	578620	Valve-inlet manifold non return	1		
26	232043	Washer-sealing	1		
27	ERC3493	Restrictor-inlet manifold-engine	2		
28	ERC3729	Spring ring	2		

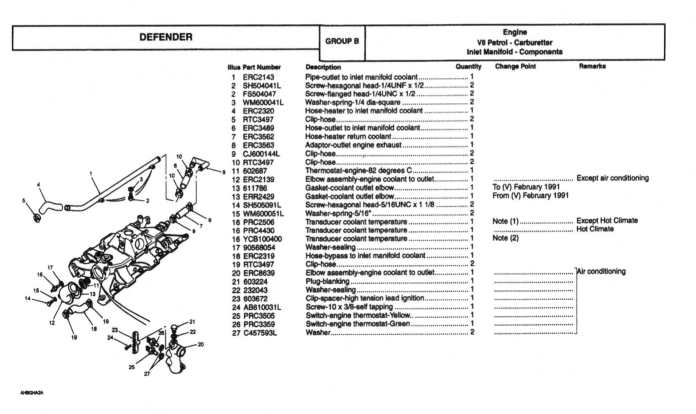

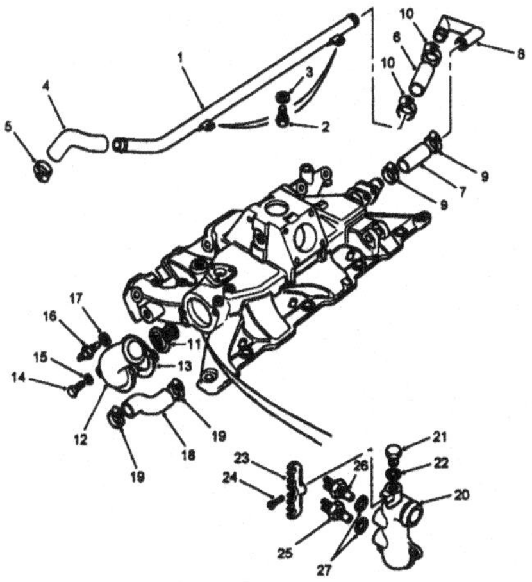

AHBQHA2A

Illus	Part Number	Description	Quantity	Change Point	Remarks
1	ERC2143	Pipe-outlet to inlet manifold coolant	1		
2	SH504041L	Screw-hexagonal head-1/4UNF x 1/2	2		
2	FS504047	Screw-flanged head-1/4UNC x 1/2	2		
3	WM600041L	Washer-spring-1/4 dia-square	2		
4	ERC2320	Hose-heater to inlet manifold coolant	1		
5	RTC3497	Clip-hose	2		
6	ERC3489	Hose-outlet to inlet manifold coolant	1		
7	ERC3562	Hose-heater return coolant	1		
8	ERC3563	Adaptor-outlet engine exhaust	1		
9	CJ600144L	Clip-hose	2		
10	RTC3497	Clip-hose	2		
11	602687	Thermostat-engine-82 degrees C	1		
12	ERC2139	Elbow assembly-engine coolant to outlet	1		Except air conditioning
13	611786	Gasket-coolant outlet elbow	1	To (V) February 1991	
13	ERR2429	Gasket-coolant outlet elbow	1	From (V) February 1991	
14	SH505091L	Screw-hexagonal head-5/16UNC x 1 1/8	2		
15	WM600051L	Washer-spring-5/16"	2		
16	PRC2506	Transducer coolant temperature	1	Note (1)	Except Hot Climate
16	PRC4430	Transducer coolant temperature	1		Hot Climate
16	YCB100400	Transducer coolant temperature	1	Note (2)	
17	90568054	Washer-sealing	1		
18	ERC2319	Hose-bypass to inlet manifold coolant	1		
19	RTC3497	Clip-hose	2		
20	ERC8639	Elbow assembly-engine coolant to outlet	1		Air conditioning
21	603224	Plug-blanking	1		Air conditioning
22	232043	Washer-sealing	1		Air conditioning
23	603672	Clip-spacer-high tension lead ignition	1		Air conditioning
24	AB610031L	Screw-10 x 3/8-self tapping	1		Air conditioning
25	PRC3505	Switch-engine thermostat-Yellow	1		Air conditioning
26	PRC3359	Switch-engine thermostat-Green	1		Air conditioning
27	C457593L	Washer	2		Air conditioning

CHANGE POINTS:
(1) To (V) WA 159806
(2) From (V) XA 159807

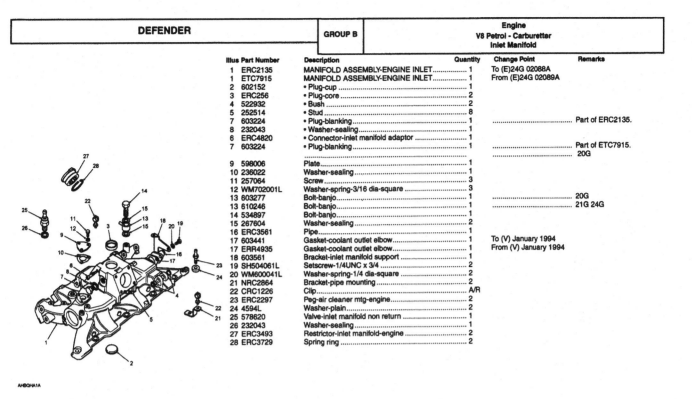

DEFENDER	GROUP B	Engine V8 Petrol - Carburetter Inlet Manifold-Gasket

Illus	Part Number	Description	Quantity	Change Point	Remarks
1	ERR4923	Gasket-inlet manifold	NLA		Use ERR7306.
1	ERR7306	Gasket-inlet manifold	1		
2	602099	Seal-inlet manifold gasket	NLA		Use ERR7282 qty 1 with ERR7283 qty 1.
2	ERR7283	Seal-inlet manifold gasket	2		
3	602076	Clamp-inlet manifold gasket seal	2		
4	602236	Bolt-5/16UNC	2		
5	BH506161L	Bolt-hexagonal head-3/8UNC x 2	2		
6	BH506121L	Bolt-hexagonal head-3/8UNC x 1 1/2	6		
7	90611504	Bolt-3/8UNC x 1 5/16	4		
8	2204L	Washer	12		

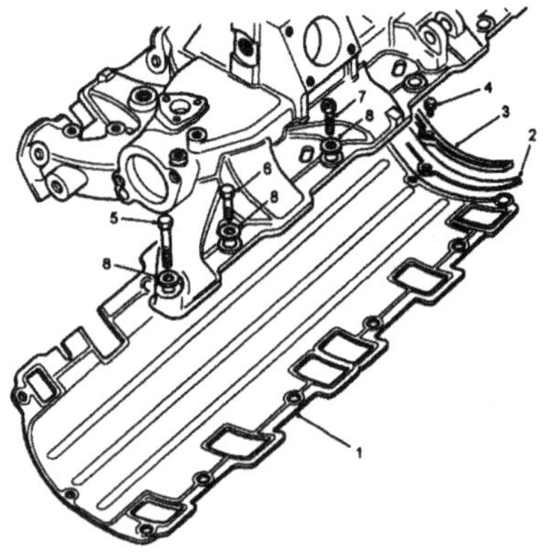

AHBQHA3A

DEFENDER	GROUP B	Engine V8 Petrol - Carburetter Exhaust Manifold-Without Heat Transfer Cover

Illus	Part Number	Description	Quantity	Change Point	Remarks
1	ETC5329	Manifold-engine exhaust-LH	1	To (E)24G 06490B	
1	ERC5068	Manifold-engine exhaust-LH	NLA	From (E)24G 06491B	Use ERR2535 Exhaust manifold and 3 off TE108051L Metrc studs in order to fit existing exhaust pipe.
1	ERR2535	Manifold-engine exhaust-LH	1	From (E)24G 06736G	
2	252623	Stud-5/16UNF x 1 1/2	6		
2	TE108051L	Stud-M8 x 25	6		
3	SH506101L	Screw-hexagonal head-3/8UNC x 1 1/4	8		
4	3036L	Washer-plain	8		
5	ERC7321	Washer-exhaust manifold to cylinder head tab	4		
6	ETC6535	Manifold-engine exhaust-less heat transfer cover-RH	1	To (E)24G 06490B	
6	ERC3102	Manifold-engine exhaust-less heat transfer cover-RH	NLA	From (E)24G 06491B	Use ERR2533 Exhaust manifold and 3 off TE108051L Metric studs in order to fit the existing exhaust pipe.
6	ERR2533	Manifold-engine exhaust-less heat transfer cover-RH	1	From (E)24G 06736G	
7	252623	Stud-5/16UNF x 1 1/2	3		
7	TE108051L	Stud-M8 x 25	3		
8	SH506101L	Screw-hexagonal head-3/8UNC x 1 1/4	7		
9	614443	Screw-3/8UNC x 1 1/8	1		
10	3036L	Washer-plain	8		
11	ERC7321	Washer-exhaust manifold to cylinder head tab	4		

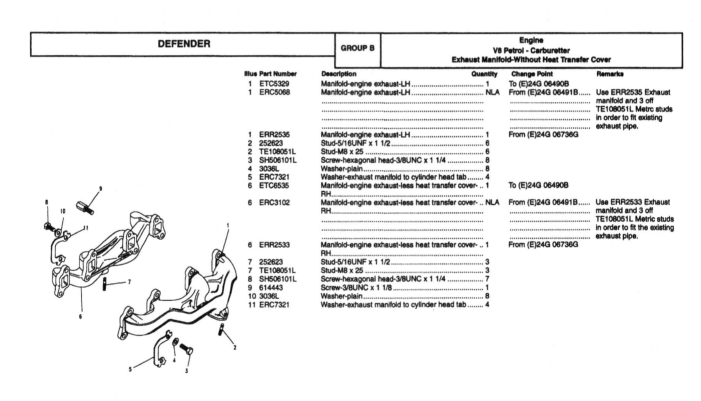

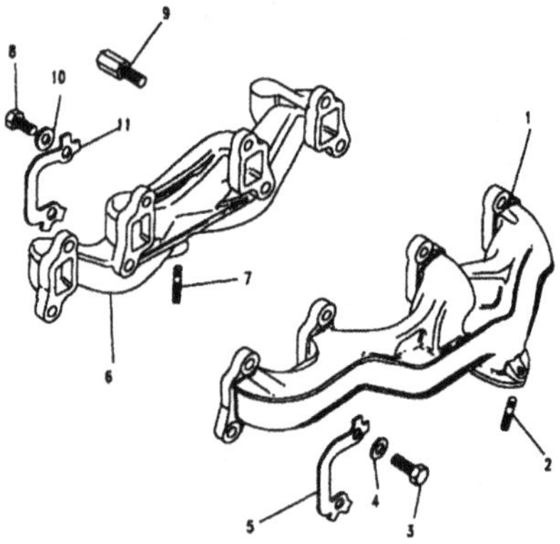

Engine
V8 Petrol - Carburetter
Exhaust Manifold-With Heat Transfer Cover

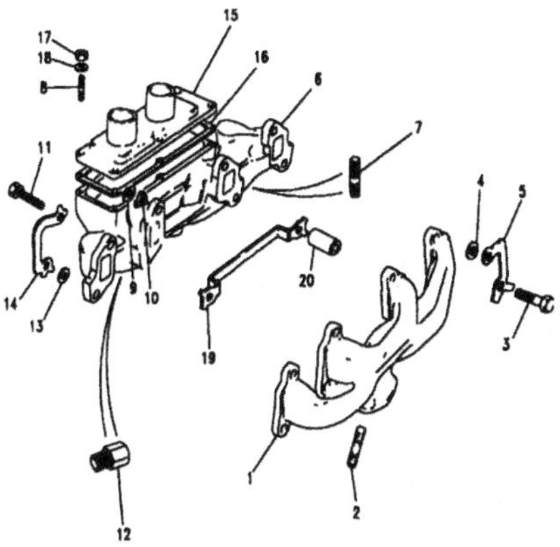

Illus	Part Number	Description	Quantity	Change Point	Remarks
1	ERC5068	Manifold-engine exhaust-LH	NLA		Use ERR2535 Exhaust manifold and 3 off TE108051L Metrc studs in order to fit existing exhaust pipe.
2	252623	Stud-5/16UNF x 1 1/2	3		
3	SH506091L	Screw-hexagonal head	8		
4	3036L	Washer-plain	8		
5	ERC7321	Washer-exhaust manifold to cylinder head tab	4		
6	ERC5925	Manifold-engine exhaust-with heat transfer cover-RH	1		
7	252623	Stud-5/16UNF x 1 1/2	3		
8	ERC3690	Stud-1/4UNC x 1	6		
9	ERC3699	Washer	2		
10	612689	Washer	2		
11	SH506091L	Screw-hexagonal head	5		
	BH506441L	Bolt	2		
12	614443	Screw-3/8UNC x 1 1/8	1		
13	3036L	Washer-plain	4		
14	ERC7321	Washer-exhaust manifold to cylinder head tab	6		
15	ERC7611	Cover heat exchanger	1		
16	ERC4989	Gasket	1		
17	RTC609	Washer-plain-standard	6		
18	NR604090L	Nut-hexagonal	6		
19	ERC7896	Washer	1		
20	ERC7897	Tube-spacer	2		

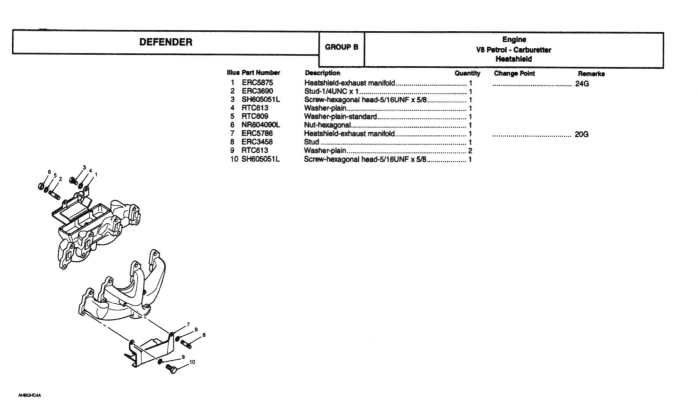

Engine
V8 Petrol - Carburetter
Heatshield

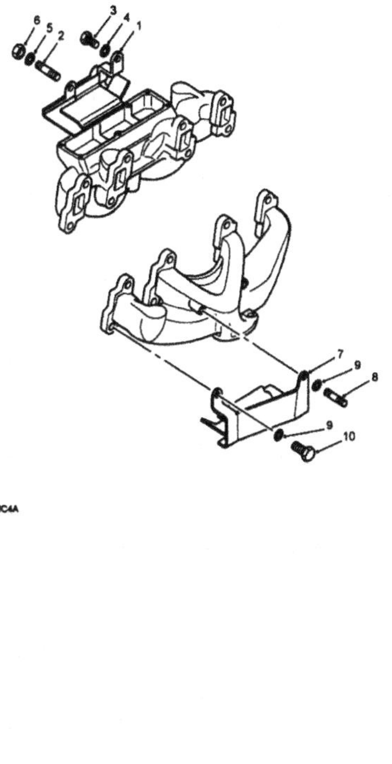

AHBQHC4A

Illus	Part Number	Description	Quantity	Change Point	Remarks
1	ERC5875	Heatshield-exhaust manifold	1		24G
2	ERC3690	Stud-1/4UNC x 1	1		
3	SH605051L	Screw-hexagonal head-5/16UNF x 5/8	1		
4	RTC613	Washer-plain	1		
5	RTC609	Washer-plain-standard	1		
6	NR604090L	Nut-hexagonal	1		
7	ERC5786	Heatshield-exhaust manifold	1		20G
8	ERC3458	Stud	1		
9	RTC613	Washer-plain	2		
10	SH605051L	Screw-hexagonal head-5/16UNF x 5/8	1		

Illus	Part Number	Description	Quantity	Change Point	Remarks
1	ERC9035	Manifold-engine inlet	2		
2	ERC3588	Tube	4		
3	ERC4204	Tube-LH	2		
4	ERC4203	Tube-RH	2		
5	ERC6878	Valve-air control	2		
6	ERC7629	Pipe-LH	1		
7	ERC7630	Pipe-RH	1		
8	ERC9039	Hose-valve to elbow	2		
9	ERC7631	Hose intake	2		
10	RTC3499	Clip-hose	4		
11	CN100308L	Clip-hose-30mm	4		
11	ESR3607	Clip-hose-26mm	4		

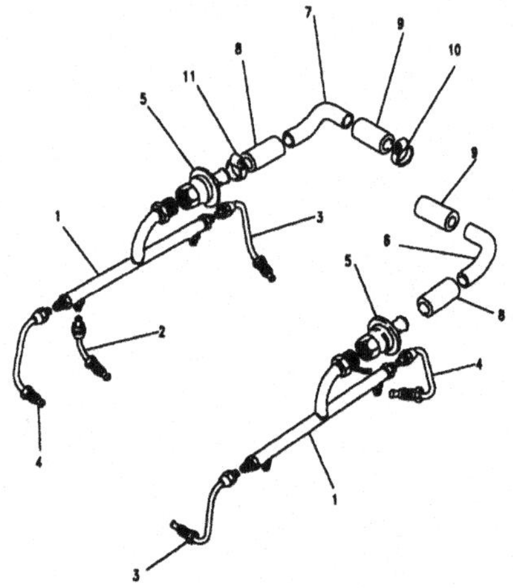

Illus	Part Number	Description	Quantity	Change Point	Remarks
1	ERC6364	Carburettor-engine-Stromberg-LH	1		
2	ERC6365	Carburettor-engine-Stromberg-RH	1		
3	610849	Insulator assembly-carburettor inlet manifold	2		
4	611026	Guide-carburettor jet needle	1		
5	ERC2154	Gasket-carburettor to induction manifold-asbestos	4	To (V) January 1994	
5	ERR4381	Gasket-carburettor to induction manifold-asbestos free	4	From (V) January 1994	20G
6	WM600051L	Washer-spring-5/16"	8		
7	NH605041L	Nut-hexagonal head-5/16UNF	8		
8	612505	PIPE FUEL	1		
9	614555	• Olive	2		
10	534790	• Nut-7/16UNF	2		
11	613514	PIPE-CARBURETTOR VENT	1		
12	611015	• Olive	2		
13	90611014	• Nut-3/8UNF	2		
14	614891	Pipe-carburettor vacuum-31"	A/R		
15	AEU1449	Clip	1		
16	541215	Grommet	1		
17	SH504051L	Screw-hexagonal head-1/4UNF x 5/8	1		
18	WM600041L	Washer-spring-1/4 dia-square	1		

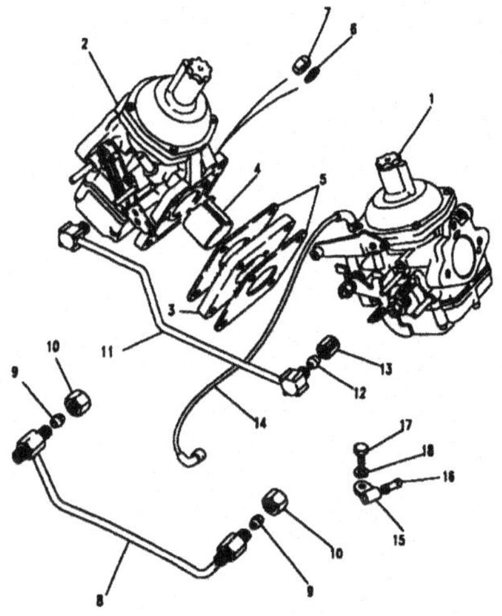

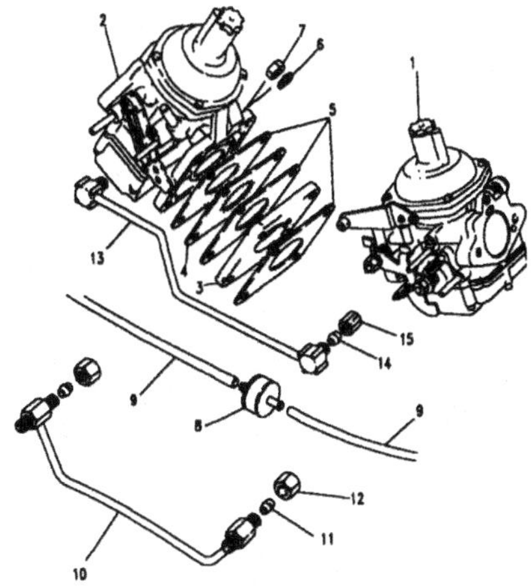

Illus	Part Number	Description	Quantity	Change Point	Remarks
1	ERC6362	Carburettor-engine-Stromberg-LH	1		
2	ERC6363	Carburettor-engine-Stromberg-RH	1		
3	610833	Insulator assembly-carburettor inlet manifold-asbestos	2	To (V) January 1994	
3	ERR4383	Insulator assembly-carburettor inlet manifold-asbestos free	2	From (V) January 1994	
4	566737	Restrictor-air flow	2		
5	ERC2154	Gasket-carburettor to induction manifold-asbestos	6	To (V) January 1994	
5	ERR4381	Gasket-carburettor to induction manifold-asbestos-free	6	From (V) January 1994	
6	WM600051L	Washer-spring-5/16"	8		
7	NH605041L	Nut-hexagonal head-5/16UNF	8		
8	ERC6997	Valve-vacuum delay-Orange	1		
9	614891	Pipe-carburettor vacuum-31"	A/R		
10	612505	PIPE FUEL	1		
11	614555	• Olive	2		
12	534790	• Nut-7/16UNF	2		
13	613514	PIPE-CARBURETTOR VENT	1		
14	611015	• Olive	2		
15	90611014	• Nut-3/8UNF	2		

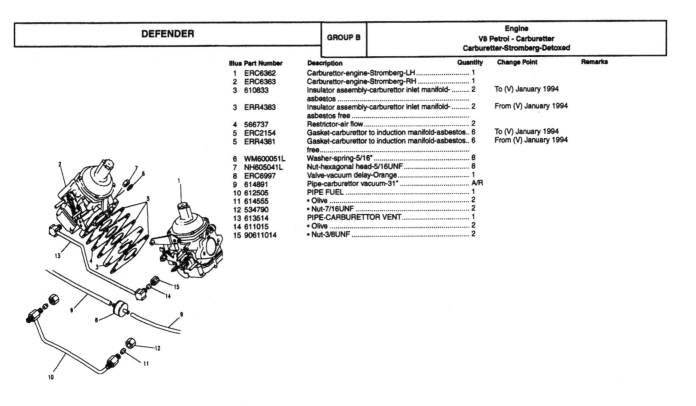

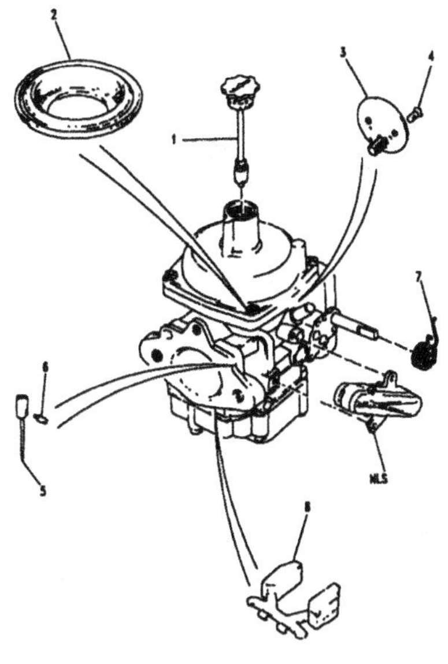

Illus	Part Number	Description	Quantity	Change Point	Remarks
1	605848	Damper assembly-carburettor	2		
2	JS499L	Diaphragm assembly-carburettor	2		
3	605800	Valve-carburettor throttle overrun	2		20G
3	AAU7604	Valve-carburettor throttle overrun	2		21G
4	601845	Screw	2		
5	AEU3077	Needle-carburettor jet	2		21G
5	AEU2462	Needle-carburettor jet	2		20G
6	518653	Screw-grub	2		
7	516951	Spring	2		
8	605833	Float assembly-carburettor	2		

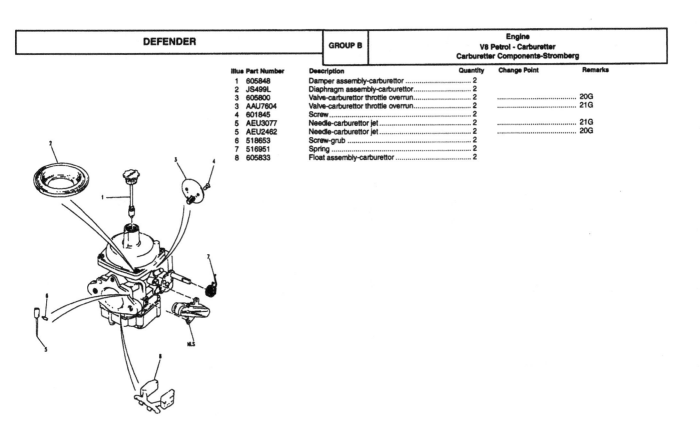

DEFENDER	GROUP B	Engine V8 Petrol - Carburetter Carburetter & Components-SU

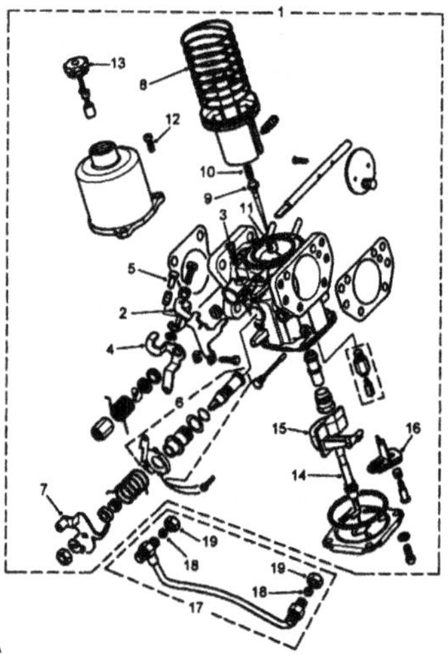

AHBQIA4A

Illus	Part Number	Description	Quantity	Change Point	Remarks
1	ETC7122	CARBURETTOR-ENGINE-S.U.-LH	1		
1	ETC7123	CARBURETTOR-ENGINE-S.U.-RH	1		
2	LZX2107L	• Level-carburettor throttle	1		
3	JZX1303L	• Screw-carburettor fast idle adjusting	2		
4	AUD4771L	• Clip	2		
5	JZX1181L	• Screw-carburettor slow run adjusting	2		
6	STC509	• Body-carburettor-LH	1		Part of ETC7122.
7	LZX1988L	• Lever-carburettor camshaft-LH	1		Part of ETC7122.
8	AUD4398L	• Spring-carburettor yellow piston	2		
9	NZX8076L	• Needle assembly-carburettor jet	2		
10	AUD3306L	• Spring-carburettor jet needle	2		
11	JZX1039L	• Guide-carburettor jet needle	2		
12	JZX1394L	• Screw	6		
13	LZX1505	• Damper assembly-carburettor	2		
14	CUD2788L	• Jet-carburettor-LH	1		Part of ETC7122.
15	RTC3566	• Float-carburettor-LH	1		Part of ETC7122.
16	CUD2399L	• Bimetal assembly-carburettor choke	2		
6	STC510	• Body-carburettor-RH	1		Part of ETC7123.
7	LZX1989L	• Lever-carburettor camshaft-RH	1		Part of ETC7123.
14	CUD2785L	• Jet-carburettor-RH	1		Part of ETC7123.
15	LZX1600L	• Float-carburettor-RH	1		Part of ETC7123.
17	ETC7127	PIPE-FEED-FUEL LINES	1		
18	612064	• Olive	2		
19	534790	• Nut-7/16UNF	2		
20	STC205	Needle & seat assembly-carburettor float	2		
	RTC6072	Kit-carburettor seal	1		
	WZX1505	Kit-gasket	1		

DEFENDER	GROUP B	Engine V8 Petrol - Carburetter Carburetter Adaptors

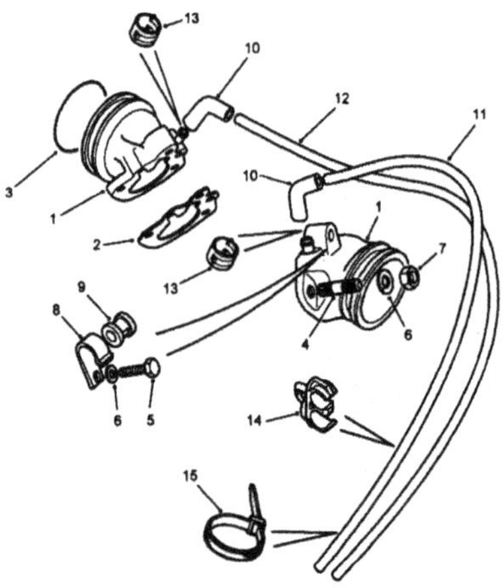

AHBQIC1A

Illus	Part Number	Description	Quantity	Change Point	Remarks
1	ERC9213	Adaptor-carburettor-only with Stromberg carburettors	2		
2	610327	Gasket-carburettor-only with Stromberg carburettors	2		
1	ETC7126	Adaptor-carburettor-only with SU carburettors	2		
2	612435	Gasket-carburettor-only with SU carburettors-asbestos	2	Note (1)	
2	PKX100030	Gasket-carburettor-only with SU carburettors-asbestos free	2	Note (2)	
3	602634	O ring	2		
4	TE505105L	Stud	4		
5	BH505111L	Bolt	2		
6	WM600051L	Washer-spring-5/16"	6		
7	NH605041L	Nut-hexagonal head-5/16UNF	4		
8	239600	Clip-cable-LH	1		
8	523203	Clip-cable-RH	1		
9	273370	Grommet-only with Stromberg carburettors-LH	1		
10	NRC223	Elbow-only with Stromberg carburettors	1		
11	ERC8906	Pipe-carburettor vent-only with Stromberg carburettors-LH	1		
12	ERC8907	Pipe-carburettor vent-only with Stromberg carburettors-RH	1		
10	577458	Elbow-only with SU carburettors-rubber	2		
11	NTC3793	Pipe-carburettor vent-only with SU carburettors-LH	1		
12	NTC3794	Pipe-carburettor vent-only with SU carburettors-RH	1		
13	UKC3803L	Clip-hose	2		
14	AFU1342L	Clip-pipe-only with Stromberg carburettors	1		
15	573256	Tie-cable-retaining vent pipe	1		
15	C43640	Tie-cable-only with Stromberg carburettors-Black-2.5 x 100mm-outside serated	1		
15	568680	Tie-cable-only with Stromberg carburettors-4.8 x 270mm-inside serated	1		
	50641	Clip-p-only with SU carburettors	1		
9	589254	Grommet-only with SU carburettors-17/32" hole	1		
14	NTC2292	Clip-pipe-only with SU carburettors	1		
15	594594	Tie-cable-only with SU carburettors-White.-4.8 x 385mm-inside serated	1		

CHANGE POINTS:
(1) To (V) LA 939224
(2) From (V) LA 939225

DEFENDER

GROUP B

Engine
V8 Petrol - Carburetter
Throttle Linkage-SU

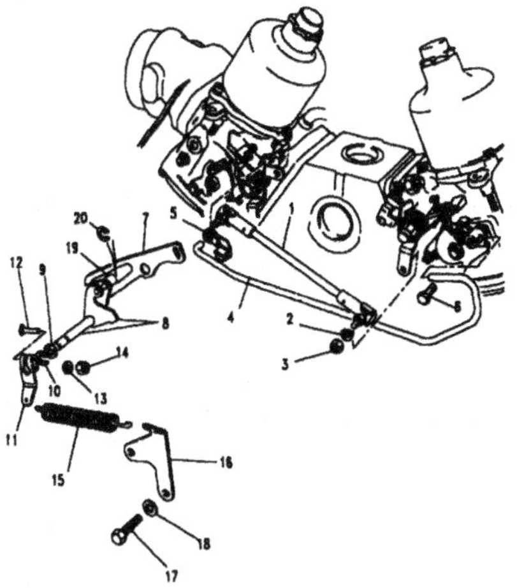

Illus	Part Number	Description	Quantity	Change Point	Remarks
1	ETC4728L	Link-carburettor/throttle connecting	1		
2	WM702001L	Washer-spring-3/16 dia-square	2		
3	NH910011L	Locknut-10x32UNF	2		
4	NSP	Rod assembly-carburettor choke	1		
5	614538L	Clip	1		
6	SH910101	Screw-hexagonal head-10UNF x 5/16	1		
7	ETC7061	Lever-throttle cam	1		
8	ETC8513	Link-carburettor/throttle connecting	1		
9	WA108051L	Washer-8mm	1		
10	521453	Circlip	1		
11	AUD2437L	Level-carburettor throttle	1		
12	SH910241L	Screw-hexagonal head-10UNF x 3/4	1		
13	WA702101L	Washer	1		
14	NH910241L	Nut-hexagonal	1		
15	603622	Spring-carburettor throttle return	1		
16	ERC8626	Bracket-return spring-attachment accelerator	1		
17	FS504047	Screw-flanged head-1/4UNC x 1/2	3		
18	WA106041L	Washer-6mm	3		
2	WM600041L	Washer-spring-1/4 dia-square	1		
19	ETC8511	Roller	1		
20	521452	Circlip	1		

DEFENDER

GROUP B

Engine
V8 Petrol - Carburetter
Throttle Linkage-Stromberg

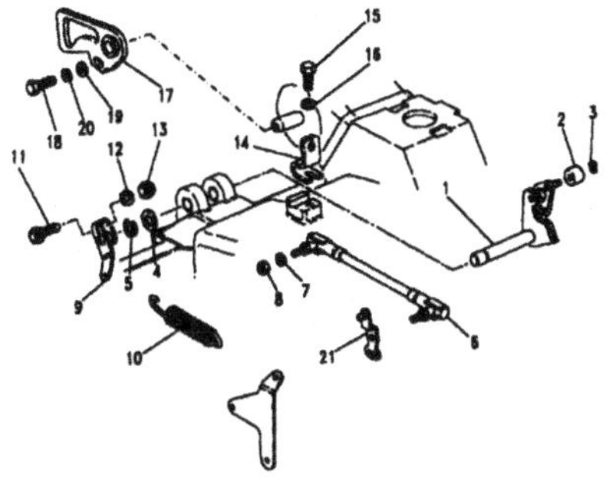

Illus	Part Number	Description	Quantity	Change Point	Remarks
1	ERC2446	Link-carburettor/throttle connecting	1	Note (1)	
2	603237	Roller-countershaft	1		
1	ETC8513	Link-carburettor/throttle connecting	1	Note (2)	
2	ETC8511	Roller-countershaft	1		
3	521452	Circlip-countershaft	1		
4	WA108051L	Washer-8mm	1		
5	521453	Circlip	1		
6	ERC7744	Link-carburettor/throttle connecting	1		
7	WM702001L	Washer-spring-3/16 dia-square	2		
8	257011	Nut-No10-UNF	2		
9	AUD2437L	Level-carburettor throttle	1		
10	603622	Spring-carburettor throttle return	1		
11	257020	Screw-10UNF x 3/4	1		
12	WA702101L	Washer	1		
13	HN2005L	Nut-UNF	1		
14	ERC3163	Bracket-abutment-throttle cable multi point injection/tbi	1		
15	SH504051L	Screw-hexagonal head-1/4UNF x 5/8	1		
16	WA106041L	Washer-6mm	1		
17	610333	Level-carburettor throttle-LH	1		
18	257123	Setscrew	1		
19	WA702101L	Washer	1		
20	WM702001L	Washer-spring-3/16 dia-square	1		
21	612320	Lever assembly-carburettor-RH	1		

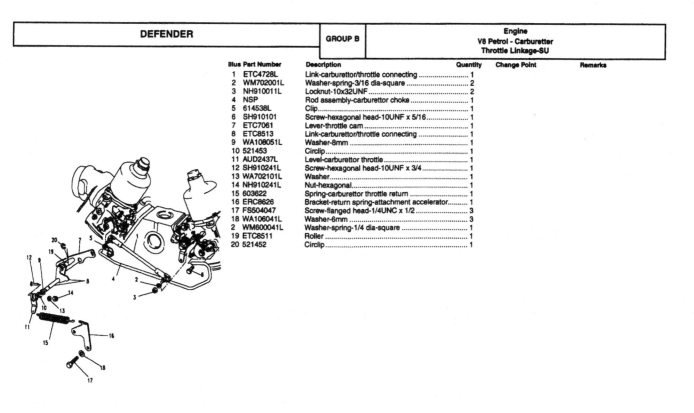

CHANGE POINTS:
(1) To (C)24G 02663B
(2) From (V)24G 02264B

Illus	Part Number	Description	Quantity	Change Point	Remarks
1	ERC2042L	Trap-fuel-intake engine-electric control unit	1		
2	ERC4193	Clamp	1		
3	253942	Bolt	1		
4	WA702101L	Washer	2		
5	257071	Nut	1		
6	614891	Pipe-carburettor vacuum-31"	A/R		
7	FS504047	Screw-flanged head-1/4UNC x 1/2	2		90"
7	SH504041L	Screw-hexagonal head-1/4UNF x 1/2	2		Except 90"
8	WM600041L	Washer-spring-1/4 dia-square	2		

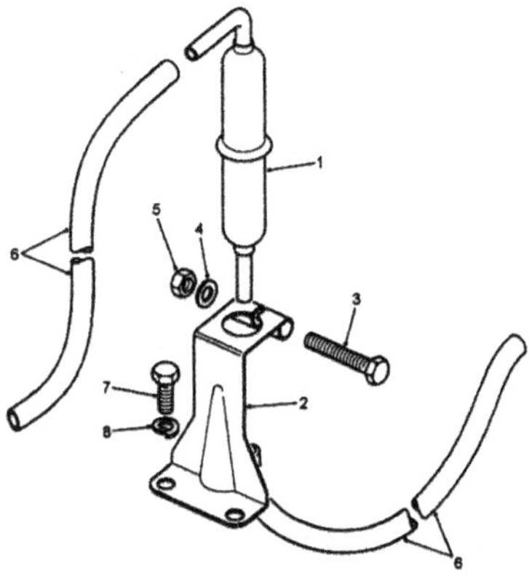

AHBQIC2A

Illus	Part Number	Description	Quantity	Change Point	Remarks
1	ETC7193	Duct assembly air cleaner to elbow-S.U.	1		
2	ERC3956	Hose-air cleaner	1		
3	ERC5247	Elbow-carburettor air inlet	2		
4	ERC3915	Hose-air duct/aircleaner	2		
5	RTC3518	Clip-hose	4		
6	ETC7199	Hose assembly-breather	1		
7	UKC3799L	Clip-hose-18.3mm	2		
8	ETC7201	Adapter-crankcase breather	1		
9	ERC6878	Valve-air control	1		
10	ETC7189	Hose assembly-breather	1		
11	ETC7188	Flame trap-crankcase breather	1		
12	611092	Hose breather-RH	1		
13	611097	Hose breather-RH	1		
14	594594	Tie-cable-White.-4.6 x 385mm-inside serated	1		

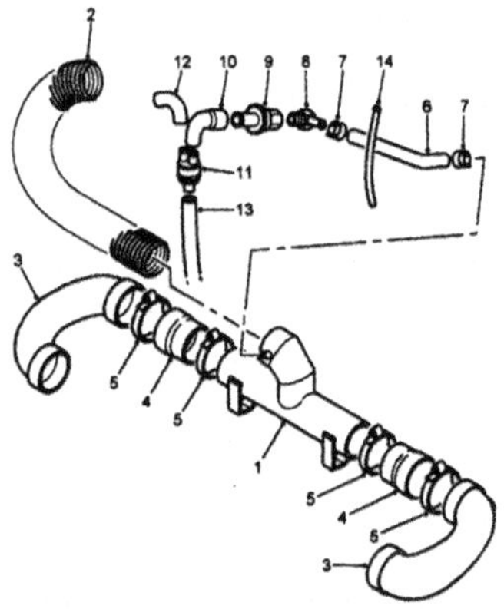

AHBQIG1A

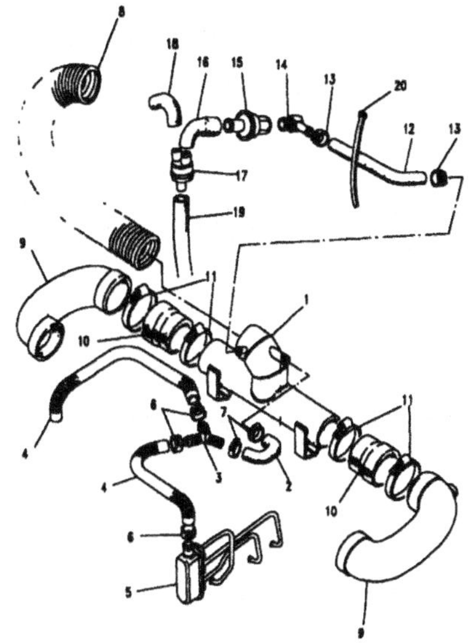

Illus	Part Number	Description	Quantity	Change Point	Remarks
1	ETC7195	Duct assembly-fresh air	1	Note (1)	
2	ERC9398	Hose-valve to air cleaner pulse air system	1	Note (1)	
3	ETC6579	Y-piece	1	Note (1)	
4	ETC6581	Hose-Y piece to carburettor	2	Note (1)	
		BOX ASSEMBLY-PULSAIR			
5	ETC5989	LH	NLA	Note (1)	Use ETC6331.
5	ETC6331	LH	1	Note (1)	
5	ETC5990	RH	1	Note (1)	Except air conditioning
5	ETC6912	RH	1	Note (1)	Air conditioning
	ETC6550	Bracket-pulsair box-LH	1	Note (1)	
	ETC6549	Bracket-RH	1	Note (1)	Except air conditioning
	ETC6249	Bracket-RH	1	Note (1)	Air conditioning
	ETC7012	Bracket-RH	1	Note (1)	
6	UKC3802L	Clamp-heater hose	4		
7	CN100308L	Clip-hose-30mm	2		
7	ESR3607	Clip-hose-26mm	2		
8	ERC3956	Hose-air cleaner	1		
9	ERC5247	Elbow-carburettor air inlet	2		
10	ERC3915	Hose-air duct/aircleaner	2		
11	RTC3518	Clip-hose	4		
12	ETC7199	Hose assembly-breather	1		
13	UKC3799L	Clip-hose-18.3mm	2		
14	ETC7201	Adapter-crankcase breather	1		
15	ERC6878	Valve-air control	1		
16	ETC7189	Hose assembly-breather	1		
17	ETC7188	Flame trap-crankcase breather	1		
18	611092	Hose breather-RH	1		
19	611097	Hose breather-RH	1		
20	594594	Tie-cable-only with SU carburettors-White.-4.6 x 385mm-inside serated	1		
	ETC5918	Tube	2		

CHANGE POINTS:
(1) To (V) 328516

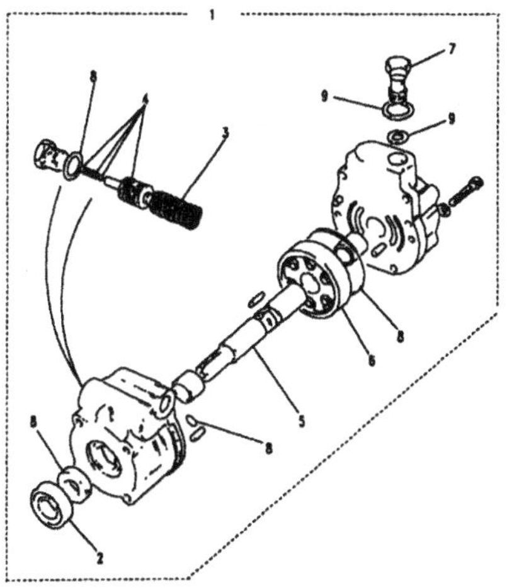

Illus	Part Number	Description	Quantity	Change Point	Remarks
1	610020	PUMP SUB ASSEMBLY POWER ASSISTED STEERING	1	Note (1)	
2	605181	• Bearing-needle roller	1		
3	536373	• Spring	1		
4	RTC327	• Valve assembly-power assisted steering pump	1		
5	605180	• Shaft & flinger assembly	1		
6	605174	• Bearing steering gear-power assisted steering	1		
7	536382	Screw adjust-tension adjustment power assisted steering pump belt	1		
8	ABU7142	Kit-power assisted steering pump seal	1	Note (1)	
9	ABU7145	Kit-gasket	1		
1	ETC5689	Pump sub assembly power assisted steering	1	Note (2)	
1	ETC6496	PUMP SUB ASSEMBLY POWER ASSISTED STEERING	NLA	Note (3)	Use NTC8286.
	RTC6074	• O ring-large	1		
	RTC6075	• O ring-small	1		
8	RTC5935	• Kit-power assisted steering pump seal	NLA		Use STC1633.
8	STC1633	Kit-power assisted steering pump seal		Note (3)	

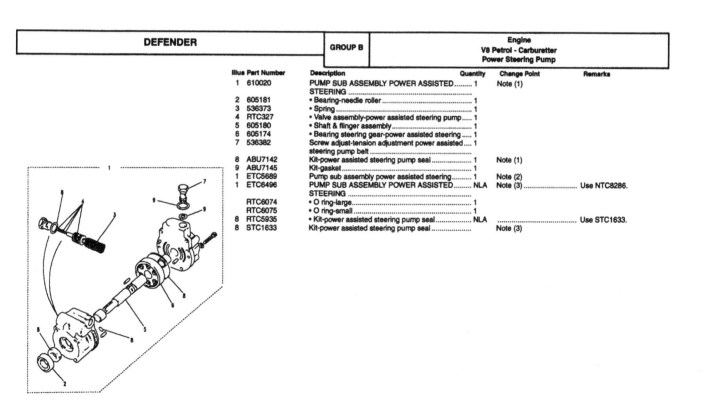

CHANGE POINTS:
(1) To (V) AA 243977 RHD; To (V) 244542 LHD
(2) From (E)19G 00008 To (E)19G 00042; From (E)20G 00504 To (E)20G 01144; From (E)21G 01043 To (E)21G 02209; From (E)22G To (E)22G 00355
(3) From (E)19G 00043; From (E)20G 01145; From (E)21G 02210; From (E)22G 00356

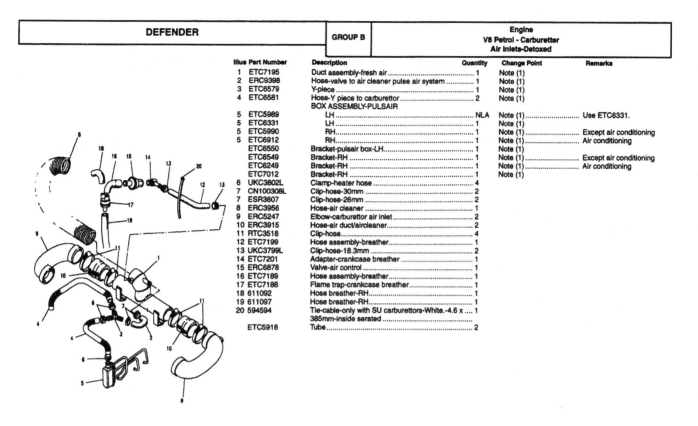

Power Steering Pump & Mountings-200 Series

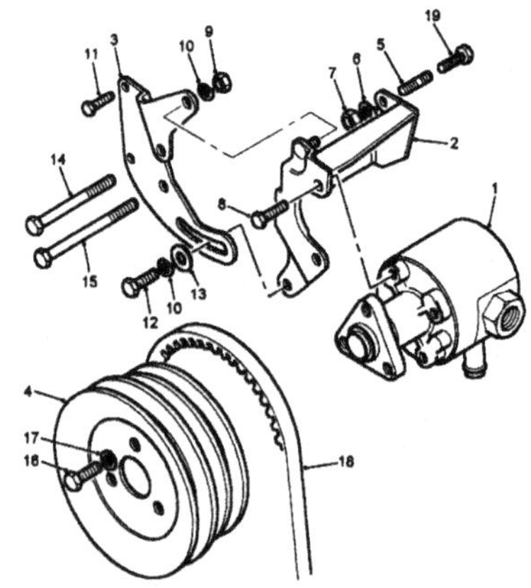

ADBGNC4A

Illus	Part Number	Description	Quantity	Change Point	Remarks
1	ANR2003	Pump assembly power assisted steering-V belt drive	1	Note (1)	
	RTC6760	Spacer	1		
1	NTC9198	Pump assembly power assisted steering	1	Note (2)	
2	ETC6486	Bracket-body	1		
3	ETC6607	Link-power assisted steering pump adjusting	1		
		PULLEY POWER ASSISTED STEERING PUMP			
4	ETC6647	single groove	1		Except air conditioning
4	ETC5665	twin groove-A133 alternator	1		Air conditioning
4	ETC6408	twin groove-A127 alternator	1		Air conditioning
5	TE506101L	Stud-3/8UNF x 1 1/8	1	Note (3)	
6	WM600061L	Washer-3/8"-square	1	Note (3)	
7	NH606041L	Nut-hexagonal head-3/8UNF	1	Note (3)	
19	SS506060	Screw-3/8UNC x 3/4	1	Note (4)	
8	FS106167L	Screw-flanged head-flanged head-M6 x 16	3		
9	NH108041L	Nut-hexagonal head-M8	1		
10	WM600051L	Washer-spring-5/16"	3		
11	BH504121L	Bolt-1/4UNC x 1 1/2-hexagonal head	3		
12	FS108251L	Screw-adjusting bracket-flanged head-M8 x 25	NLA		Use FS108257L.
13	4594L	Washer-plain	1		
14	BH505401L	Bolt-hexagonal head-5/16UNC x 5	1		
15	BH505401L	Bolt-hexagonal head-5/16UNC x 5	1		
16	FS108207L	Screw-flanged head-M8 x 20	3		
17	WA108051L	Washer-8mm	3		
18	614106	Belt-vee power assisted steering	NLA		Use ERC675.
18	ERC675	Belt-vee power assisted steering	1		
	554880	Key	1		
	2217L	Spacer	1		
12	SH505071L	Screw-centre hole pulley fixing-hexagonal head-5/16UNC x 7/8	1		
	RTC5935	Kit-power assisted steering pump seal	NLA	Note (5)	Use STC1633.
	STC1633	Kit-power assisted steering pump seal	1	Note (6)	

CHANGE POINTS:
(1) To (V)24G 10889A
(2) From (E)24G 10890A
(3) To (V) KA 929427
(4) From (V) KA 929428
(5) To (V) January 1994
(6) From (V) January 1994

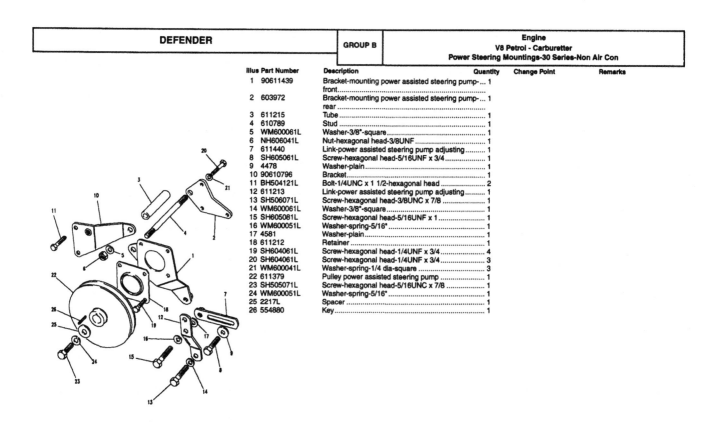

Power Steering Mountings-30 Series-Non Air Con

Illus	Part Number	Description	Quantity	Change Point	Remarks
1	90611439	Bracket-mounting power assisted steering pump-front	1		
2	603972	Bracket-mounting power assisted steering pump-rear	1		
3	611215	Tube	1		
4	610789	Stud	1		
5	WM600061L	Washer-3/8"-square	1		
6	NH606041L	Nut-hexagonal head-3/8UNF	1		
7	611440	Link-power assisted steering pump adjusting	1		
8	SH605061L	Screw-hexagonal head-5/16UNF x 3/4	1		
9	4478	Washer-plain	1		
10	90610796	Bracket	1		
11	BH504121L	Bolt-1/4UNC x 1 1/2-hexagonal head	2		
12	611213	Link-power assisted steering pump adjusting	1		
13	SH506071L	Screw-hexagonal head-3/8UNC x 7/8	1		
14	WM600061L	Washer-3/8"-square	1		
15	SH605081L	Screw-hexagonal head-5/16UNF x 1	1		
16	WM600051L	Washer-spring-5/16"	1		
17	4581	Washer-plain	1		
18	611212	Retainer	1		
19	SH604061L	Screw-hexagonal head-1/4UNF x 3/4	4		
20	SH604061L	Screw-hexagonal head-1/4UNF x 3/4	3		
21	WM600041L	Washer-spring-1/4 dia-square	3		
22	611379	Pulley power assisted steering pump	1		
23	SH505071L	Screw-hexagonal head-5/16UNC x 7/8	1		
24	WM600051L	Washer-spring-5/16"	1		
25	2217L	Spacer	1		
26	554880	Key	1		

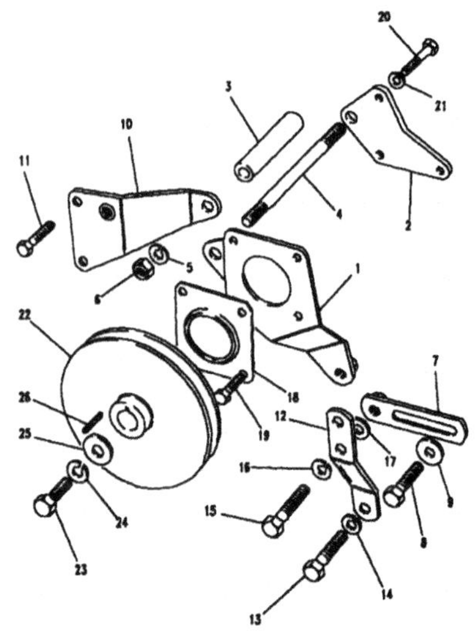

DEFENDER | GROUP B | Engine — V8 Petrol - Carburetter — Power Steering Mountings-30 Series-Air Con

Illus	Part Number	Description	Quantity	Change Point	Remarks
1	614743	Bracket-mounting power assisted steering pump-front	1		
2	603972	Bracket-mounting power assisted steering pump-rear	1		
3	611215	Tube	1		
4	610789	Stud	1		
5	WM600061L	Washer-3/8"-square	1		
6	NH606041L	Nut-hexagonal head-3/8UNF	1		
7	611440	Link-power assisted steering pump adjusting	1		
8	SH605061L	Screw-hexagonal head-5/16UNF x 3/4	1		
9	4478	Washer-plain	1		
10	90610796	Bracket	1		
11	BH504121L	Bolt-1/4UNC x 1 1/2-hexagonal head	2		
12	611213	Link-power assisted steering pump adjusting	1		
13	SH506071L	Screw-hexagonal head-3/8UNC x 7/8	1		
14	WM600061L	Washer-3/8"-square	1		
15	SH605081L	Screw-hexagonal head-5/16UNF x 1	1		
16	WM600051L	Washer-spring-5/16"	1		
17	4581	Washer-plain	1		
18	611212	Retainer	1		
19	SH604061L	Screw-hexagonal head-1/4UNF x 3/4	4		
20	SH604061L	Screw-hexagonal head-1/4UNF x 3/4	3		
21	WM600041L	Washer-spring-1/4 dia-square	3		
22	610792	Pulley power assisted steering pump-twin groove	1		
23	SH505071L	Screw-hexagonal head-5/16UNC x 7/8	1		
24	WM600051L	Washer-spring-5/16"	1		
25	2217L	Spacer	1		

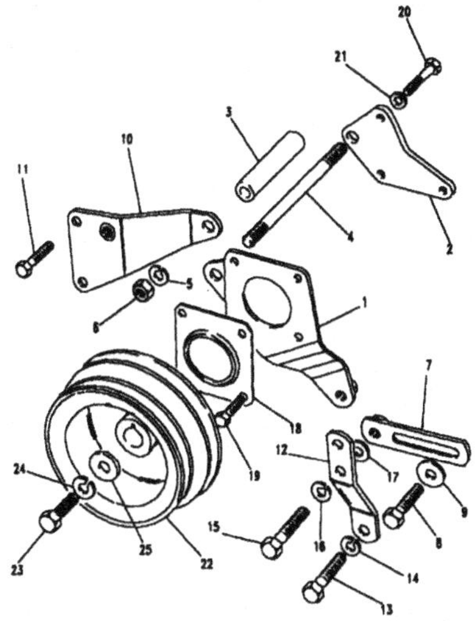

DEFENDER | GROUP B | Engine — V8 Petrol - Carburetter — Gasket Kits-Carburetter

Illus	Part Number	Description	Quantity	Change Point	Remarks
1	RTC1481	Kit-carburettor seal	1		
2	AAU7219L	Gasket-carburettor-12,000 mile service	1		
3	BHM1079L	Kit-carburettor needle & seat	1		
4	AAU2967	Kit-gasket-24,000 mile service	1		

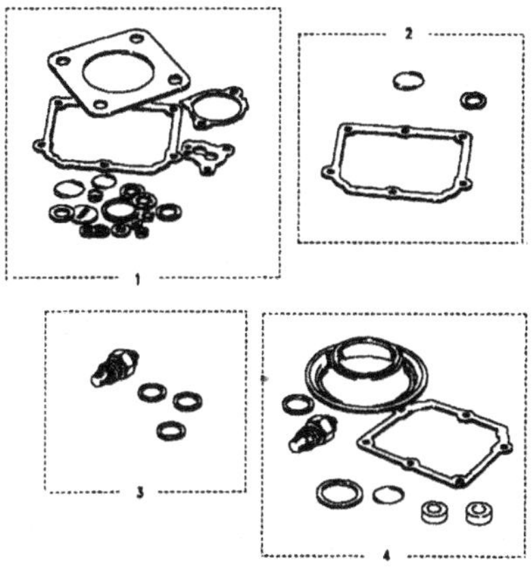

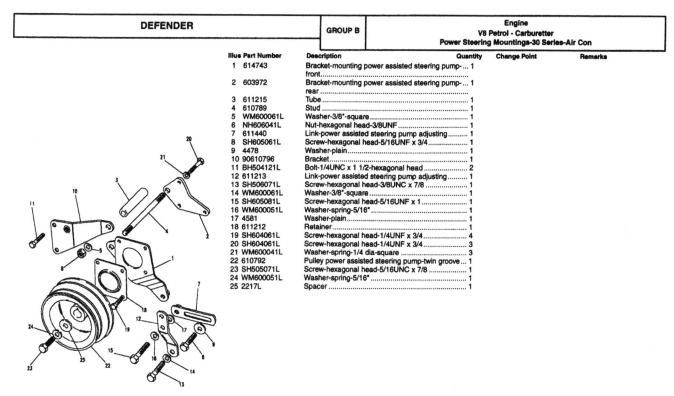

Illus	Part Number	Description	Quantity	Change Point	Remarks
		SET-ENGINE GASKET			
1	RTC2104	asbestos-overhaul	NLA		Use STC1639.
1	STC1639	asbestos free-overhaul	1		
2	RTC2913	asbestos-decarbonising	NLA		Use STC1566.
2	STC1566	asbestos free-decarbonising	1		

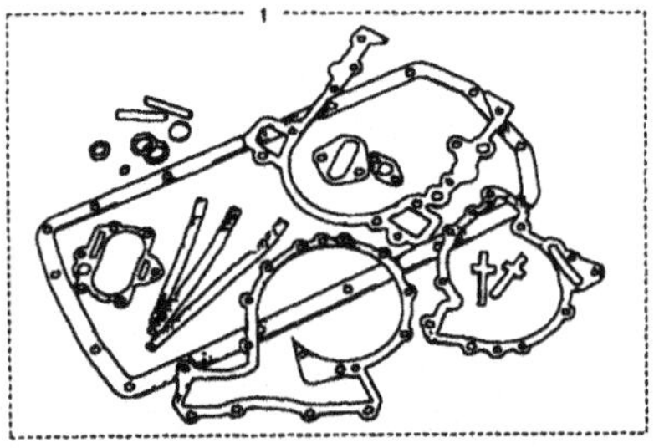

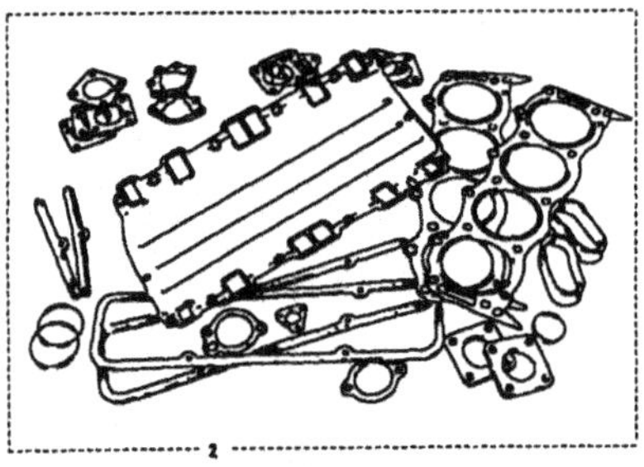

Illus	Part Number	Description	Quantity	Change Point	Remarks
	BTR9419	Compressor assembly-R134a air conditioning	1	Note (1)	
	ERC6480	COMPRESSOR ASSEMBLY AIR CONDITIONING	1	Note (2)	
1	AEU1782	• Pulley-driven air conditioning	1		
2	AEU1694	• Key	1		
3	AEU1780	• Screw	6		
4	AEU1779	• Washer	6		
5	AEU1784	• Screw	4		
6	AEU1775	• Nut	1		
7	AEU1778	• Clutch set-magnetic air conditioning compressor	1		
8	AEU1777	• Retainer	1		
9	AEU1785	• Cover assembly-front	1		
10	AEU1776	• Clutch-drive-assy	1		
	AEU1792	• CYLINDER	1		
	AEU1791	• • Kit-thrust washer-air conditioning	1		
	AEU1790	• • Kit-steering box sector shaft seal	1		
	AEU1192	• • O RING AIR CONDITIONING	1		
	AEU1690	• • • O ring	2		
	AEU1788	• Plate	4		
	AEU1787	• Circlip	4		
	AEU1786	• Housing assembly compressor	1		
	AEU1689	• Valve-air conditioning pressure relief	1		
	AEU1688	• Kit-superheat switch	1		

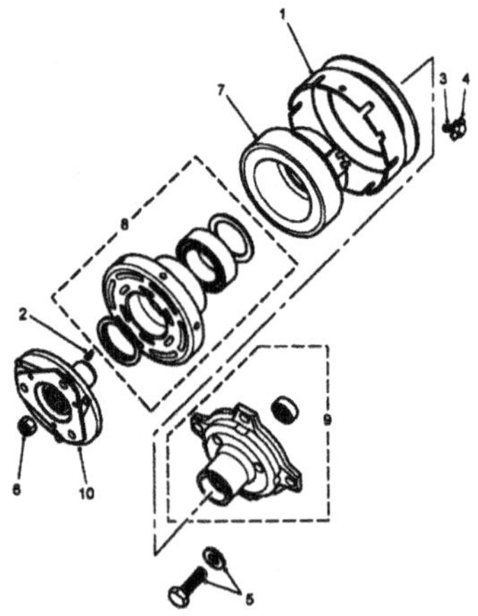

AHBQNE1A

CHANGE POINTS:
(1) From (V) MA 949375
(2) To (V) MA 949374

Illus	Part Number	Description	Quantity	Change Point	Remarks
	BTR9419	Compressor assembly-R134a air conditioning	1	Note (1)	
	ERC6480	COMPRESSOR ASSEMBLY AIR CONDITIONING	1	Note (2)	
	AEU1782	• Pulley-driven air conditioning	1		
	AEU1694	• Key	1		
	AEU1780	• Screw	6		
	AEU1779	• Washer	6		
	AEU1784	• Screw	4		
	AEU1775	• Nut	1		
	AEU1778	• Clutch set-magnetic air conditioning compressor	1		
	AEU1777	• Retainer	1		
	AEU1785	• Cover assembly-front	1		
	AEU1776	• Clutch-drive-assy	1		
1	AEU1792	• CYLINDER	1		
2	AEU1791	• • Kit-thrust washer-air conditioning	1		
3	AEU1790	• • Kit-steering box sector shaft seal	1		
4	AEU1192	• • O RING AIR CONDITIONING	1		
5	AEU1690	• • • O ring	2		
6	AEU1788	• Plate	4		
7	AEU1787	• Circlip	4		
8	AEU1786	• Housing assembly compressor	1		
9	AEU1689	• Valve-air conditioning pressure relief	1		
10	AEU1688	• Kit-superheat switch	1		
11	603713	Belt-vee air conditioning compressor	1		
	AEU1691	Oil-525 visc	A/R		

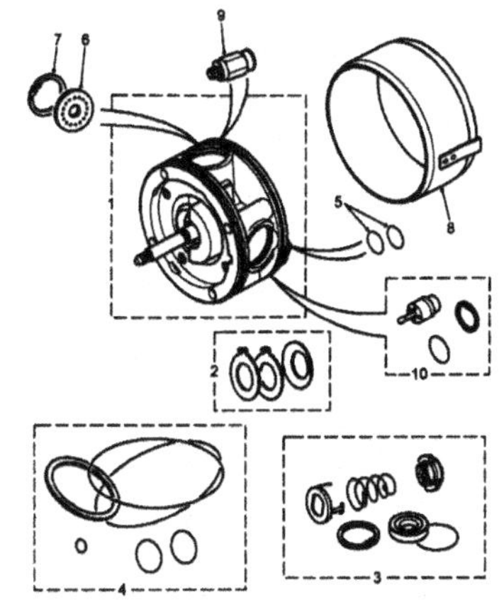

AHBQNE2A

CHANGE POINTS:
(1) From (V) MA 949375
(2) To (V) MA 949374

Illus	Part Number	Description	Quantity	Change Point	Remarks
1	ERC7494	Bracket-air compressor	1	Note (1)	
1	ERR4524	Bracket-air compressor	1	Note (2)	
2	ERC6545	Bracket-front mounting	1		
3	FS110301L	Screw-flanged head-M10 x 30-top	2		
4	WA110061L	Washer-M10	2		
5	BH110241L	Bolt-hexagonal head-M10 x 120	2		
6	BH110221L	Bolt-hexagonal head-M10 x 110	2		
7	WA110061L	Washer-M10	3		
8	4067	Washer	2		
9	BH506111L	Bolt-hexagonal head-3/8UNC x 1 3/8	2		
10	4866L	Washer	1		
11	BH505201L	Bolt-hexagonal head-5/16UNC x 2 1/2	1		

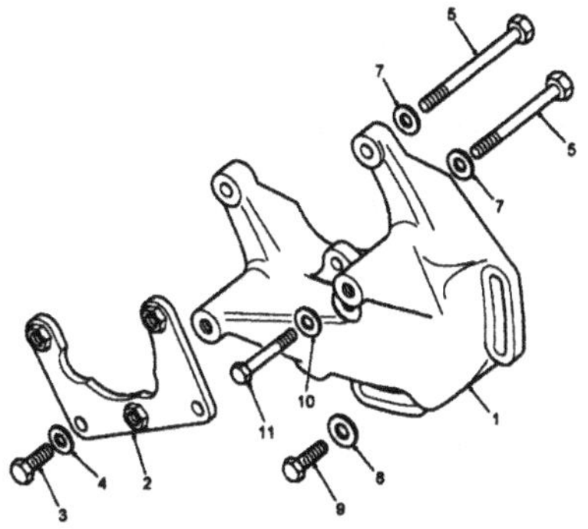

AHBQNE3A

CHANGE POINTS:
(1) To (V)24G 12353B
(2) From (V)24G 12354B

DEFENDER

GROUP B

Engine
V8 Petrol - Carburetter
Air Conditioning-Pulley

Illus	Part Number	Description	Quantity	Change Point	Remarks
1	613540	Bracket-pulley support belt tensioner	1		
2	BH505441L	Bolt-hexagonal head-5/16UNC x 5 1/2	2		
3	BH504151L	Bolt-hexagonal head-1/4UNC x 1 7/8	1		
4	614718	PULLEY-TENSIONER ANCILLARY DRIVE	1		
	614154	• Bearing-ball	1		
5	BH605101L	Bolt-hexagonal head-5/16UNF x 1 1/4	1		
6	WM600051L	Washer-spring-5/16"	1		

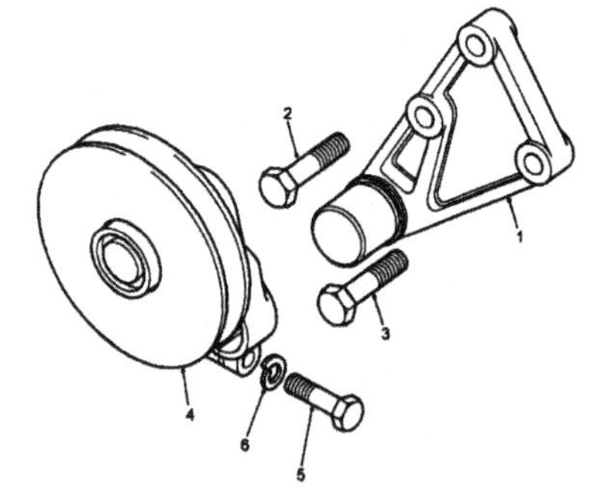

AHBQNE4A

DEFENDER

GROUP B

Engine
V8 Petrol - Carburetter
Distributor-Stromberg-14G/15G/17G

Illus	Part Number	Description	Quantity	Change Point	Remarks
1	ERC4536	DISTRIBUTOR IGNITION-STROMBERG	1		15G
1	ERC5745	DISTRIBUTOR IGNITION-STROMBERG	1		14G
1	ERC7131	DISTRIBUTOR IGNITION-STROMBERG	1		17G
2	RTC3197	• Cap-distributor ignition	1		
3	RTC3618	• Arm-rotor distributor	1		
4	RTC3286	• Set-distributor contact	1		
5	RTC3472	• Condenser ignition	1		
6	608197	• Harness-link-low tension ignition coil	1		
	RTC5014	• Bush	1		
7	AAU8452	• Capsule-vacuum distributor	1		Part of ERC4536.
7	AEU1422	• Capsule-vacuum distributor	1		Part of ERC5745.
7	608266	• Capsule-vacuum distributor	1		Part of ERC7131.
8	603446	O ring	1		
9	ERC1353	GEAR & COUPLING ASSEMBLY	1		
10	602953	• Pin-roll	1		
11	613857	Clamp-distributor	1		
12	SH506121L	Screw-hexagonal head-3/8UNC x 1 1/2	1		
13	ETC5617	Set-high tension lead ignition	1		
14	RTC3570	Plug-sparking-N12Y	8		Alternatives
14	ERR3799	Plug-sparking-RN11YC	8		Alternatives
15	603672	Clip-spacer-high tension lead ignition	1	Note (1)	
16	603673	Clip-spacer-high tension lead ignition	4		

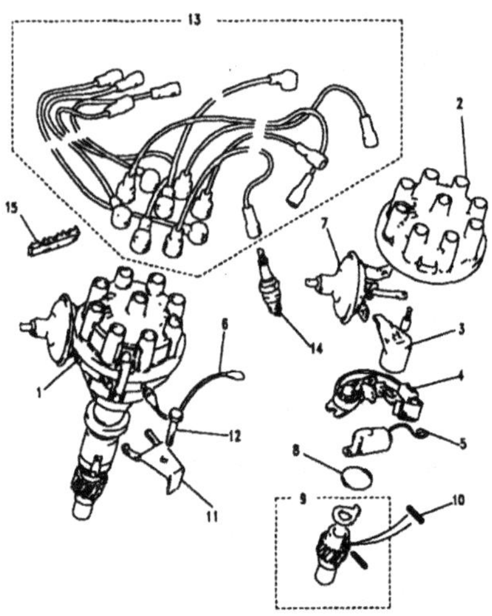

CHANGE POINTS:
(1) To (E)24G 03883B

Distributor-Stromberg-19G/20G/21G/22G

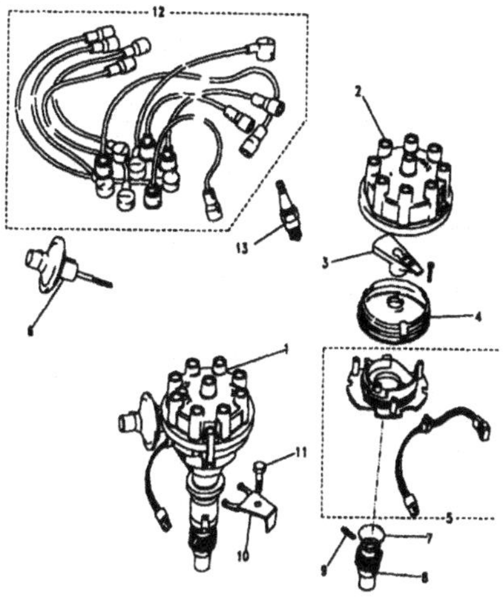

Illus	Part Number	Description	Quantity	Change Point	Remarks
1	ETC4715	DISTRIBUTOR IGNITION	1		22G
1	ETC4717	DISTRIBUTOR IGNITION	1		20G
1	ETC5090	DISTRIBUTOR IGNITION	1		19G
1	ETC5354	DISTRIBUTOR IGNITION	1		21G
2	RTC3197	• Cap-distributor ignition	1		
3	STC1857	• Arm-rotor distributor	1		
4	RTC5971	• Kit-distributor	1		
5	RTC3198	• Plate-mounting distributor	1		
6	608266	• Capsule-vacuum distributor	1		Part of ETC4715.
6	RTC3201	• Capsule-vacuum distributor-2 pin	1		Part of ETC4717.
6	AAU8452	• Capsule-vacuum distributor	1		Part of ETC5090, ETC5354.
8	ERC1353	GEAR & COUPLING ASSEMBLY	1		
9	602953	• Pin-roll	1		
10	613857	Clamp-distributor	1		
11	SH605121L	Screw-hexagonal head-5/16UNF x 1 1/2	1		
12	ETC5617	Set-high tension lead ignition	1		
13	RTC3570	Plug-sparking-N12Y	8		Alternatives
13	ERR3799	Plug-sparking-RN11YC	8		Alternatives

Distributor-SU

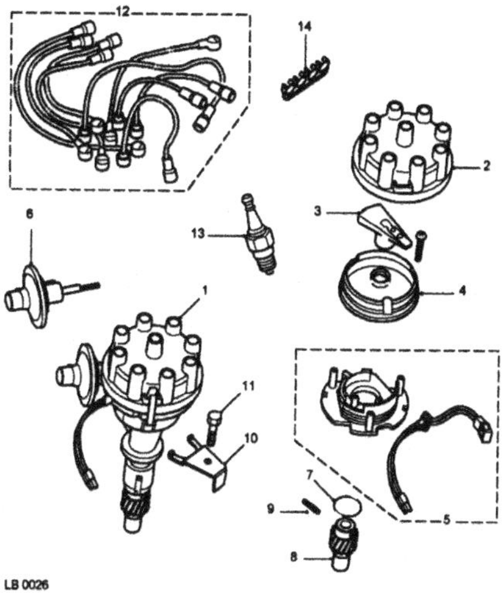

LB 0026

Illus	Part Number	Description	Quantity	Change Point	Remarks
1	ETC6586	DISTRIBUTOR IGNITION	1	Note (1)	90"
2	RTC3197	• Cap-distributor ignition	1		
3	STC1857	• Arm-rotor distributor	1		
4	RTC5971	• Kit-distributor	1		
5	RTC3198	• Plate-mounting distributor	1		
6	RTC3201	• Capsule-vacuum distributor-2 pin	1		
7	603446	• O ring	1		
1	ETC6976	DISTRIBUTOR IGNITION	1	Note (2)	90"
	STC1184	• Module-distributor-3 pin	1		
	STC1212	• Harness-link-3 pin	1		
6	RTC5092	• Capsule-vacuum distributor	1		
2	RTC3197	• Cap-distributor ignition	1		
3	STC1857	• Arm-rotor distributor	1		
5	RTC5090	• Plate-mounting distributor	1		
7	603446	• O ring	1		
4	RTC5971	• Kit-distributor	1		
1	ERR4285	DISTRIBUTOR IGNITION	1		Except 90"
	STC1184	• Module-distributor-3 pin	1		
2	RTC3197	• Cap-distributor ignition	1		
3	STC1857	• Arm-rotor distributor	1		
4	RTC5971	• Kit-distributor	1		
5	RTC5090	• Plate-mounting distributor	1		
6	RTC5092	• Capsule-vacuum distributor	1		
7	603446	• O ring	1		
8	ERC1353	GEAR & COUPLING ASSEMBLY	1		
9	602953	• Pin-roll	1		
10	613857	Clamp-distributor	1		
11	SH506121L	Screw-hexagonal head-3/8UNC x 1 1/2	1		

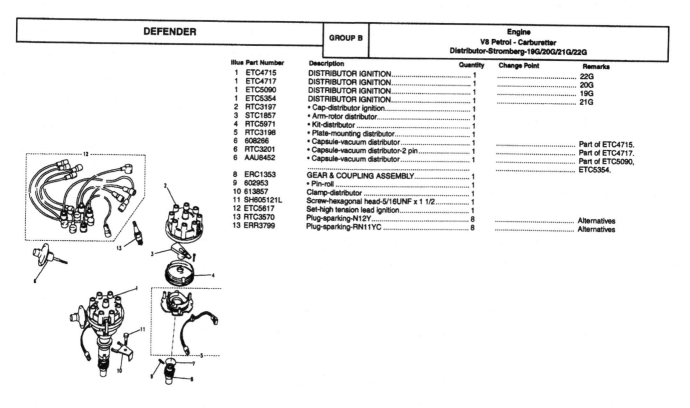

CHANGE POINTS:
(1) To (E)20G 01607A; To (E)24G 00235A
(2) From (E)20G 01608A; From (E)24G 00236A

DEFENDER

GROUP B

Engine
V8 Petrol - Carburetter
Distributor-SU

Illus	Part Number	Description	Quantity	Change Point	Remarks
12	ETC6484	KIT-HIGH TENSION LEADS IGNITION-CARBON	1		
	ETC8610	• Lead-high tension ignition-No1	NLA		Use STC3843 qty 1 for NAS markets only or STC8658 qty 1 for ROW markets only.
	ETC8611	• Lead-high tension ignition-No3	NLA		Use STC3845 qty 1 for NAS markets only or STC8661 qty 1 for ROW markets only.
	ETC8612	• Lead-high tension ignition-No5	1		
	ETC8613	• Lead-high tension ignition-No2	NLA		Use STC3844 qty 1 for NAS markets only or STC8660 qty 1 for ROW markets only.
	ETC8614	• Lead-high tension ignition-No4	1		
	ETC8615	• Lead-high tension ignition-No6	NLA		Use STC3843.
	ETC8616	• Lead-high tension ignition-No8	NLA		Use STC3850 qty 1 for NAS markets only or STC8660 qty 1 for ROW markets only.
	ETC8617	• Lead-high tension ignition-No7	NLA		Use STC3849.
	ETC8618	• Lead-king ignition	1		
13	RTC3570	Plug-sparking-N12Y	8		
14	603672	Clip-spacer-high tension lead ignition	1	To (E)24G 03883B	
14	ETC8720	Clip-spacer-high tension lead ignition	1	From (E)24G 03884B	
15	603673	Clip-spacer-high tension lead ignition	4		

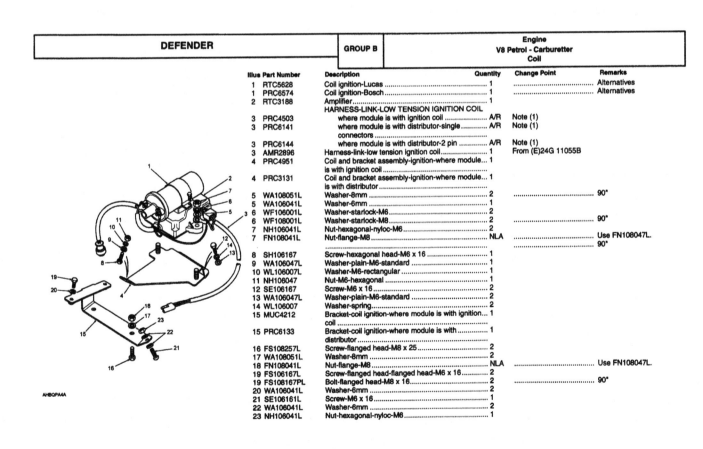

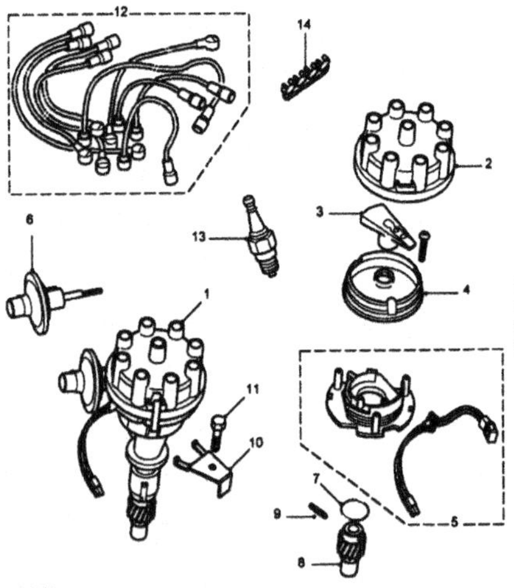

LB 0026

DEFENDER

GROUP B

Engine
V8 Petrol - Carburetter
Coil

Illus	Part Number	Description	Quantity	Change Point	Remarks
1	RTC5628	Coil ignition-Lucas	1		Alternatives
1	PRC6574	Coil ignition-Bosch	1		Alternatives
2	RTC3188	Amplifier	1		
		HARNESS-LINK-LOW TENSION IGNITION COIL			
3	PRC4503	where module is with ignition coil	A/R	Note (1)	
3	PRC6141	where module is with distributor-single connectors	A/R	Note (1)	
3	PRC6144	where module is with distributor-2 pin	A/R	Note (1)	
3	AMR2896	Harness-link-low tension ignition coil	1	From (E)24G 11055B	
4	PRC4951	Coil and bracket assembly-ignition-where module is with ignition coil	1		
4	PRC3131	Coil and bracket assembly-ignition-where module is with distributor	1		
5	WA108051L	Washer-8mm	2		90"
5	WA106041L	Washer-6mm	1		
6	WF106001L	Washer-starlock-M6	2		
6	WF108001L	Washer-starlock-M8	2		90"
7	NH106041L	Nut-hexagonal-nyloc-M6	2		
7	FN108041L	Nut-flange-M8	NLA		Use FN108047L. 90"
8	SH106167	Screw-hexagonal head-M6 x 16	1		
9	WA106047L	Washer-plain-M6-standard	1		
10	WL106007L	Washer-M6-rectangular	1		
11	NH106047	Nut-M6-hexagonal	1		
12	SE106167	Screw-M6 x 16	2		
13	WA106047L	Washer-plain-M6-standard	2		
14	WL106007	Washer-spring	2		
15	MUC4212	Bracket-coil ignition-where module is with ignition coil	1		
15	PRC6133	Bracket-coil ignition-where module is with distributor	1		
16	FS108257L	Screw-flanged head-M8 x 25	2		
17	WA108051L	Washer-8mm	2		
18	FN108041L	Nut-flange-M8	NLA		Use FN108047L.
19	FS106167L	Screw-flanged head-flanged head-M6 x 16	2		
19	FS108167PL	Bolt-flanged head-M8 x 16	2		90"
20	WA106041L	Washer-6mm	2		
21	SE106161L	Screw-M6 x 16	1		
22	WA106041L	Washer-6mm	2		
23	NH106041L	Nut-hexagonal-nyloc-M6	1		

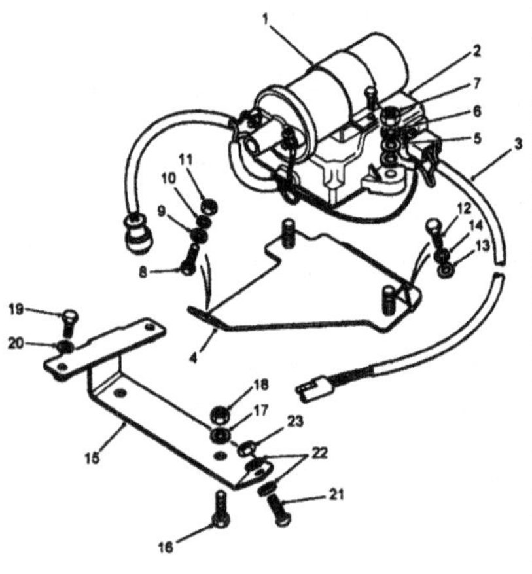

AHBQPA4A

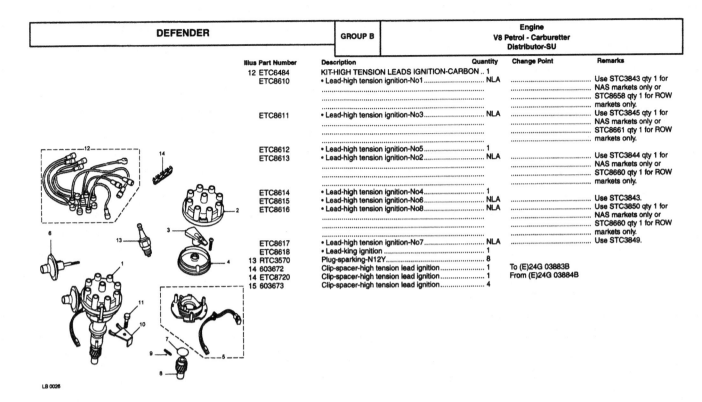

CHANGE POINTS:
(1) To (E)24G 11054B

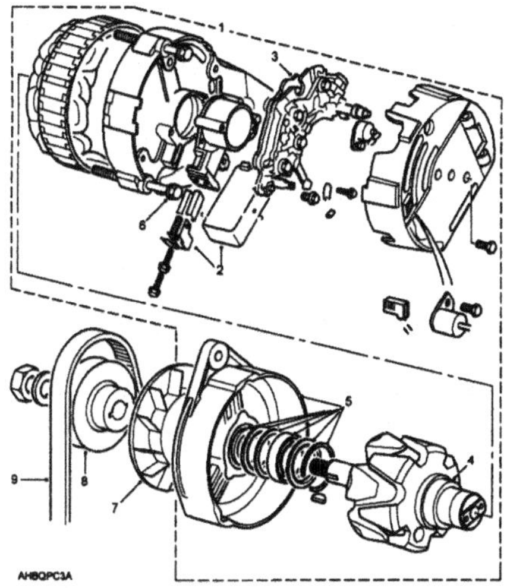

AHBQPC3A

Illus	Part Number	Description	Quantity	Change Point	Remarks
1	RTC5683N	ALTERNATOR ASSEMBLY-NEW-A127-45 AMP-LUCAS	1		
1	RTC5683E	ALTERNATOR ASSEMBLY-EXCHANGE-A127-45 AMP	1		
2	RTC5044	• Regulator & brush box assembly alternator	1		
3	RTC5045	• Rectifier-alternator	1		
4	RTC5047	• Bearing-alternator front	NLA		Use RTC5926.
5	RTC5688	• BRACKET-DRIVE END C/W BEARING ALTERNATOR E-LH	1		
6	RTC5925	• • Kit-fixings alternator/vacuum pump-LH	1		
	RTC6114	• • Capacitor alternator	1		
4	RTC5926	Bearing-alternator front			
7	RTC5685	Fan alternator	1		
8	RTC5686	Pulley alternator	1		
9	ETC7394	Belt-polyvee alternator	1		
	RTC5689	Spacer	1		

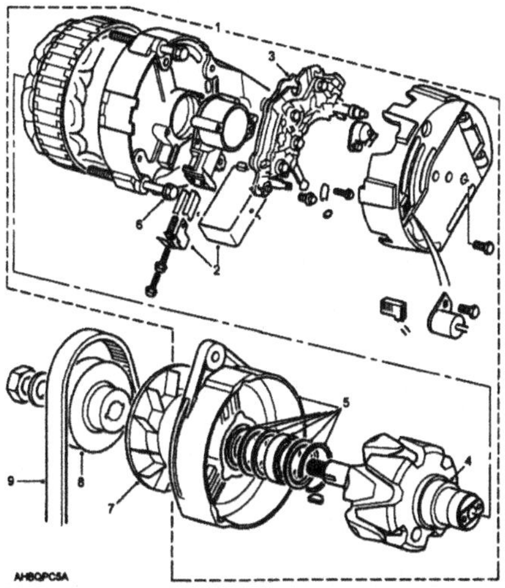

AHBQPC5A

Illus	Part Number	Description	Quantity	Change Point	Remarks
		ALTERNATOR ASSEMBLY			
1	RTC5680N	NEW-A127-65 AMP-RH	NLA		Use STC234.
1	STC234	NEW-A127-65 AMP-RH	1		
1	RTC5680E	EXCHANGE-A127-65 AMP-RH	1		
2	RTC5670	• Regulator & brush box assembly alternator-new alternator-RH	1		
3	RTC5671	• Rectifier-alternator-new alternator-RH	1		
4	RTC5926	• Bearing-alternator front-new alternator-RH	1		Part of RTC5680N, RTC5680E.
5	RTC5687	• Bracket-drive end c/w bearing alternator e-new alternator-RH-RH	1		
6	RTC5046	• Kit-fixings alternator/vacuum pump-new alternator-RH-RH	1		
	RTC6114	• Capacitor alternator	1		Part of STC234.
1	RTC5681N	ALTERNATOR ASSEMBLY-NEW-A127-65 AMP-LH	1		
1	RTC5681E	ALTERNATOR ASSEMBLY-EXCHANGE-A127-65 AMP-LH	1		
2	RTC5670	• Regulator & brush box assembly alternator-new alternator-LH	1		
3	RTC5671	• Rectifier-alternator-new alternator-LH	1		
4	RTC5926	• Bearing-alternator front-new alternator-LH	1		
5	RTC5688	• BRACKET-DRIVE END C/W BEARING ALTERNATOR E-NEW ALTERNATOR-LH-LH	1		
6	RTC5925	• • Kit-fixings alternator/vacuum pump-new alternator-LH-LH	1		
	RTC6114	• • Capacitor alternator-new alternator-LH	1		
7	AAU2249L	Fan alternator	1		
8	RTC5686	Pulley alternator	1		
9	ERR2073	Belt-polyvee alternator	1		
	RTC5689	Spacer	1		

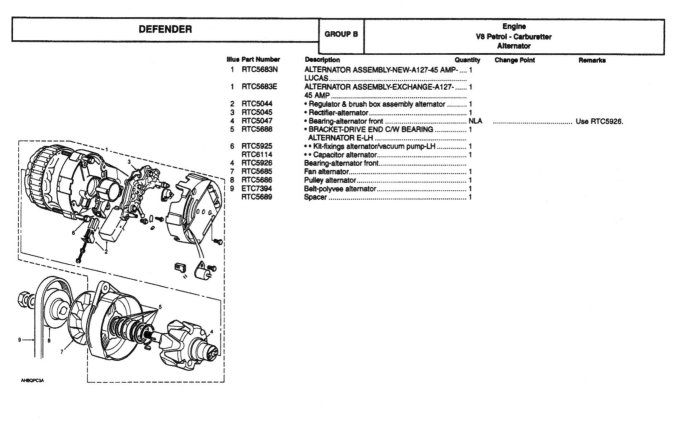

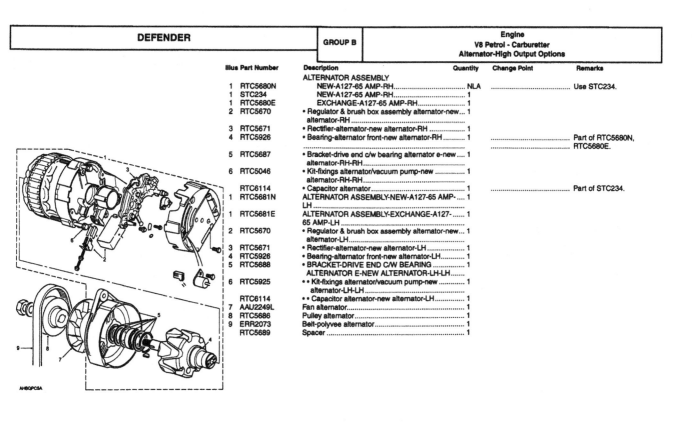

Alternator Mountings

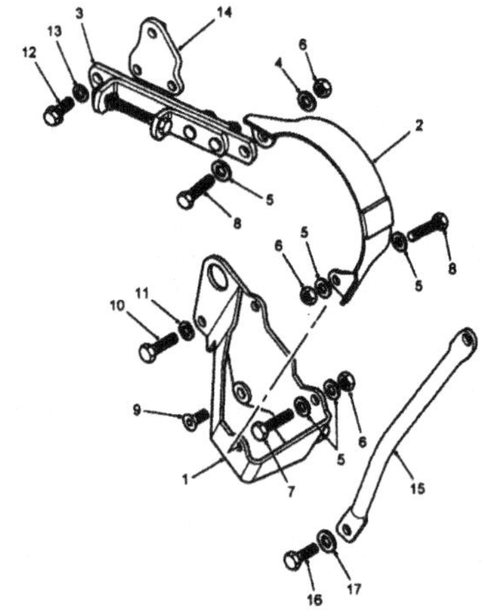

AHBQPCSA

Illus	Part Number	Description	Quantity	Change Point	Remarks
1	ETC5576	Bracket-mounting-alternator-65 amp	1		
2	ETC8441	Guard-fan alternator-65 amp	1		
	ERC5830	Grommet	2		
	ETC8559	Bush	2		
3	ERR1574	Link-adjuster alternator	1		
4	4594L	Washer-plain	1		
5	WA108051L	Washer-8mm	8		
6	NH108041L	Nut-hexagonal head-M8	3		
7	SH108451L	Screw-hexagonal head-M8 x 45	1		
8	SH108401L	Screw-hexagonal head-M8 x 40	2		
9	ETC8765	Screw-3/8UNC x 1	1		
10	SH506071L	Screw-hexagonal head-3/8UNC x 7/8	1		
11	WM600061L	Washer-3/8"-square	1		
12	FS108207L	Screw-flanged head-M8 x 20	1		
13	WL108001L	Washer-sprung-M8	1		
14	ERR1885	Support-adjuster link alternator	1		
15	ETC8579	Strut-alternator-65 amp	1		
16	SH506101L	Screw-hexagonal head-3/8UNC x 1 1/4	1		
17	WA110061L	Washer-M10	1		

Alternator-Battery Sensed

Illus	Part Number	Description	Quantity	Change Point	Remarks
1	RTC5086E	ALTERNATOR ASSEMBLY-EXCHANGE-115/45	1	Note (1)	
2	AEU1814	• Cover alternator-24079B90	1		
3	AEU2464L	• Regulator assembly alternator-24079B90	1		
4	BAU1825	• Rectifier-alternator	1		
5	18G8619L	• Kit-bearing-drive end alternator	1		
6	AEU1532	• Bearing-alternator front	1		
	BAU2195L	• Box assembly-brush alternator	1		
7	RTC3215	• Brush alternator	1		
8	AEU1710	• Kit-fixings alternator/vacuum pump	1		
	AEU1706	• Kit-screw	1		
	AEU1942	• Spacer	1		
9	STC130	• Diode pack alternator	1		
10	C37222L	Fan alternator	1	Note (1)	
11	602505	Pulley-alternator	1	Note (1)	
12	AEU1616	Capacitor alternator	1	Note (1)	

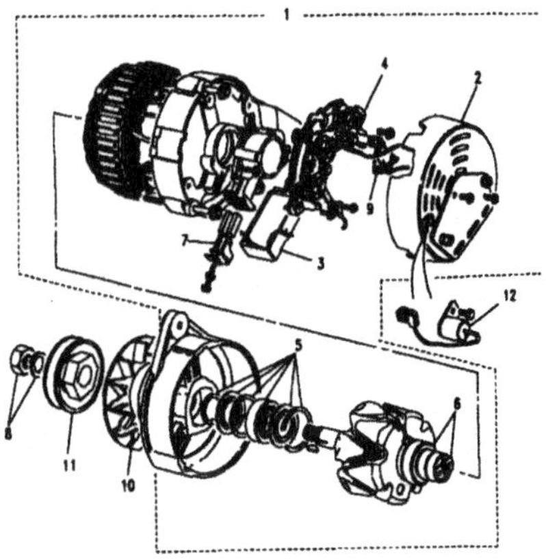

CHANGE POINTS:
(1) To (E)14G 01446; To (E)15G 02240; To (E)17G 00182

Illus	Part Number	Description	Quantity	Change Point	Remarks
1	RTC5085E	ALTERNATOR ASSEMBLY-115/45-EXCHANGE	1	Note (1)	
2	AEU2507	• Cover alternator-LRA356	1		
3	AEU3076	• Regulator assembly alternator-LRA356	1		
4	BAU1825	• Rectifier-alternator	1		
5	18G8619L	• Kit-bearing-drive end alternator	1		
6	AEU1532	• Bearing-alternator front	1		
	BAU2195L	• Box assembly-brush alternator	1		
7	RTC3215	• Brush alternator	1		
8	AEU1710	• Kit-fixings alternator/vacuum pump	1		
	AEU1706	• Kit-screw	1		
	AEU1942	• Spacer	1		
9	C37222L	Fan alternator	1	Note (1)	
10	602505	Pulley-alternator	1		
11	AEU1616	Capacitor alternator	1		
12	ETC7394	Belt-polyvee alternator	1		

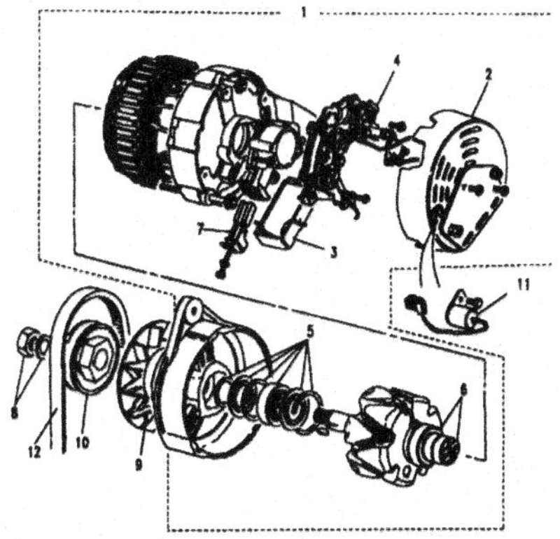

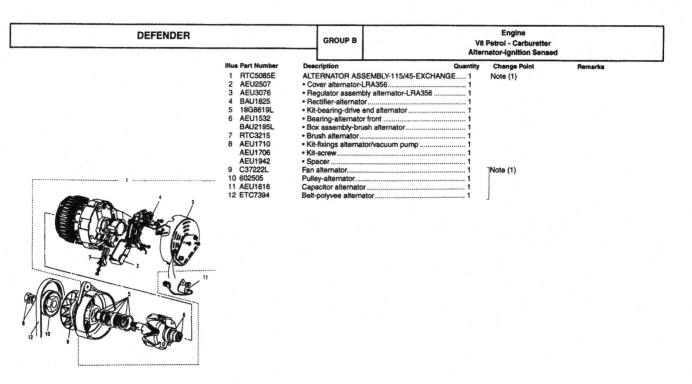

CHANGE POINTS:
(1) From (E)14G 01447; From (E)15G 02241; From (E)17G 00183; From (E)20G; From (E)21G

Illus	Part Number	Description	Quantity	Change Point	Remarks
1	RTC5683N	ALTERNATOR ASSEMBLY-NEW-A127-45 AMP-LUCAS	1		
1	RTC5683E	ALTERNATOR ASSEMBLY-EXCHANGE-A127-45 AMP	1		
2	RTC5044	• Regulator & brush box assembly alternator	1		
3	RTC5045	• Rectifier-alternator	1		
4	RTC5047	• Bearing-alternator front	NLA		Use RTC5926.
5	RTC5688	• BRACKET-DRIVE END C/W BEARING ALTERNATOR E-LH	1		
6	RTC5925	• • Kit-fixings alternator/vacuum pump-LH	1		
	RTC6114	• • Capacitor alternator	1		
4	RTC5926	Bearing-alternator front			
7	RTC5685	Fan alternator	1		
8	RTC5686	Pulley alternator	1		
9	ETC7394	Belt-polyvee alternator	1		
	RTC5689	Spacer-pulley	1		

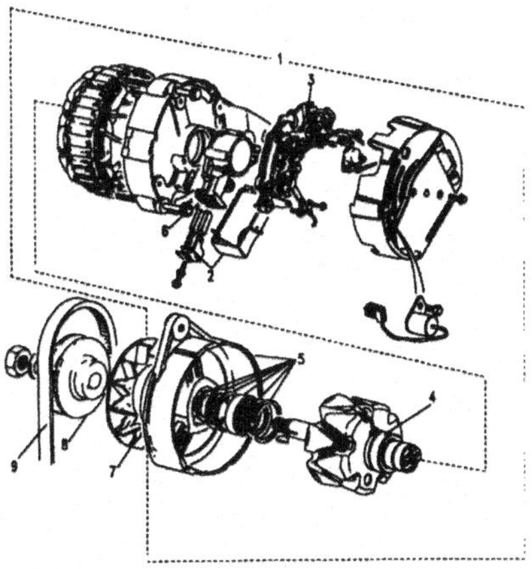

Alternator-A133/65Amp

Illus	Part Number	Description	Quantity	Change Point	Remarks
1	RTC5087E	ALTERNATOR ASSEMBLY-A133-65 AMP	1		Split charge
1	RTC5218E	ALTERNATOR ASSEMBLY-LRA406-EXCHANGE-A133-65 AMP	1		Power steering air conditioning
2	AEU1725	• Cover alternator	1		
3	AEU3076	• Regulator assembly alternator-LRA356	1		
4	AEU1527	• Rectifier-alternator	1		
5	AEU1726	• Kit-bearing-drive end alternator	1		
6	AEU1532	• Bearing-alternator front	1		
7	RTC3292	• Brush alternator	1		
8	AEU1710	• Kit-fixings alternator/vacuum pump	1		Part of RTC5087E.
	AEU1706	• Kit-screw	1		Part of RTC5087E.
	AEU1708	• Spacer	1		Part of RTC5087E.
	AEU1709	• Kit-alternator	1		Part of RTC5087E.
9	STC130	• Diode pack alternator	1		
10	ADU4928L	Fan alternator	1		
11	ERC3345	Pulley alternator	1		Split charge
11	ERC8851	Pulley alternator	1		Power steering air conditioning
	AEU1616	Capacitor alternator	1		

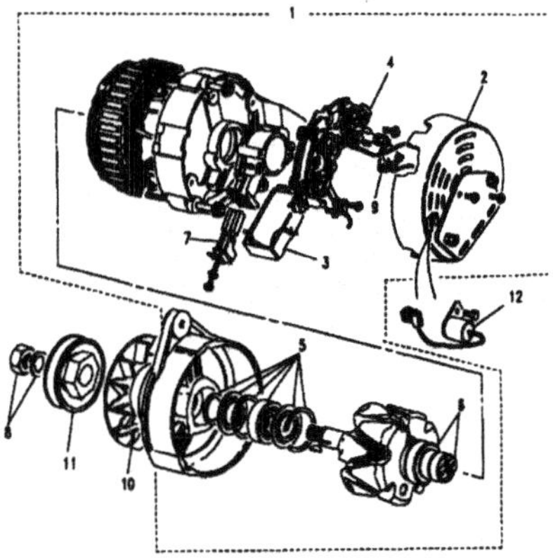

Alternator-A127/65Amp

Illus	Part Number	Description	Quantity	Change Point	Remarks
		ALTERNATOR ASSEMBLY			
1	RTC5680N	NEW-A127-65 AMP-RH	NLA		Use STC234.
1	STC234	NEW-A127-65 AMP-RH	1		
1	RTC5680E	EXCHANGE-A127-65 AMP-RH	1		
1	RTC5681N	NEW-A127-65 AMP-LH	1		
1	RTC5681E	EXCHANGE-A127-65 AMP-LH	1		
2	RTC5670	• Regulator & brush box assembly alternator	1		
3	RTC5671	• Rectifier-alternator	1		
4	RTC5926	• Bearing-alternator front	1		Part of RTC5680N, RTC5680E, RTC5681N, RTC5681E.
5	RTC5687	• Bracket-drive end c/w bearing alternator e-RH	1		Part of RTC5680N, STC234, RTC5680E.
6	RTC5046	• Kit-fixings alternator/vacuum pump-RH	1		Part of RTC5680N, STC234, RTC5680E.
	RTC6114	• Capacitor alternator	1		Part of STC234.
5	RTC5688	• BRACKET-DRIVE END C/W BEARING ALTERNATOR E-LH	1		Part of RTC5681N, RTC5681E.
6	RTC5925	• • Kit-fixings alternator/vacuum pump-LH	1		
	RTC6114	• • Capacitor alternator	1		
7	AAU2249L	Fan alternator	1		
8	RTC5686	Pulley alternator	1		
9	ERR2073	Belt-polyvee alternator	1		
10	RTC5689	Spacer-pulley	1		

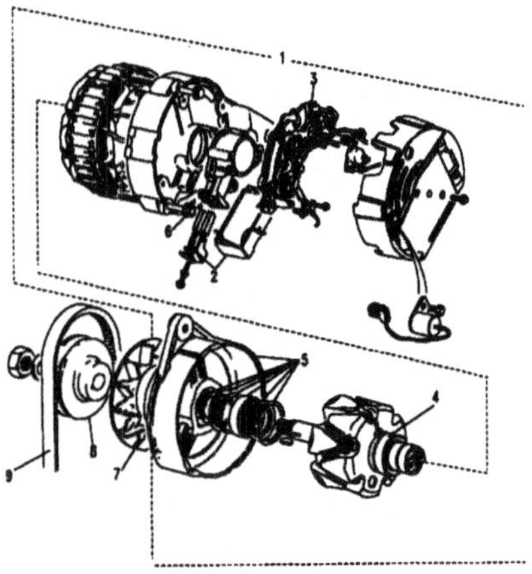

DEFENDER	GROUP B	Engine V8 Petrol - Carburetter Alternator Fixings-A115 & A133-type

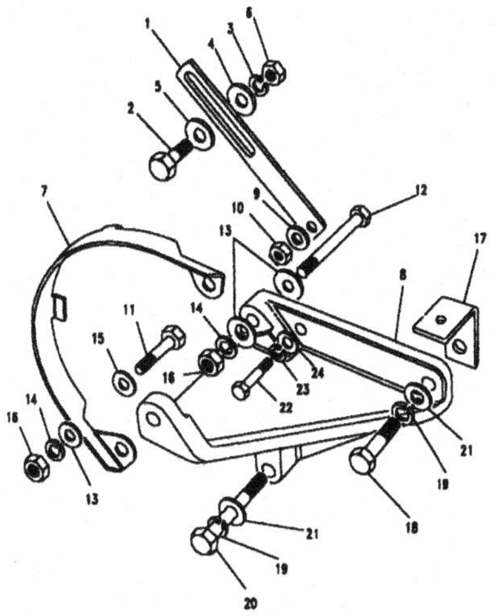

Illus	Part Number	Description	Quantity	Change Point	Remarks
1	614939	Link-adjuster alternator	1		
2	FS108357	Screw-flanged head-M8 x 35	1		
3	WM600051L	Washer-spring-5/16"	1		
4	2217L	Spacer-A133 Alternator	1		
5	2266L	Washer	1		
6	NH108041L	Nut-hexagonal head-M8	1		
7	613244	Guard-fan alternator	1		
8	611022	Bracket-mounting-alternator	1	Note (1)	
8	ERR4519L	Bracket-mounting-alternator	1	Note (2)	
9	WM600051L	Washer-spring-5/16"	1		
10	NT605041L	Nut-hexagonal-thin-5/16UNF	1		
11	BH605121L	Bolt-5/16UNF x 1 1/2	1		
12	BH605201L	Bolt	1		
13	WA108051L	Washer-8mm	3		
14	WM600051L	Washer-spring-5/16"	2		
15	2266L	Washer	1		
16	NH605041L	Nut-hexagonal head-5/16UNF	2		
17	613620	Bracket	1		
18	BH506111L	Bolt-hexagonal head-3/8UNC x 1 3/8	2		
19	WM600061L	Washer-3/8"-square	2		
20	BH506201L	Bolt	1		
21	3036L	Washer-plain	3		
22	BH505111L	Bolt	1		
23	WM600051L	Washer-spring-5/16"	1		
24	WA108051L	Washer-8mm	1		

CHANGE POINTS:
(1) To (E)24G 12353B
(2) From (E)24G 12354B

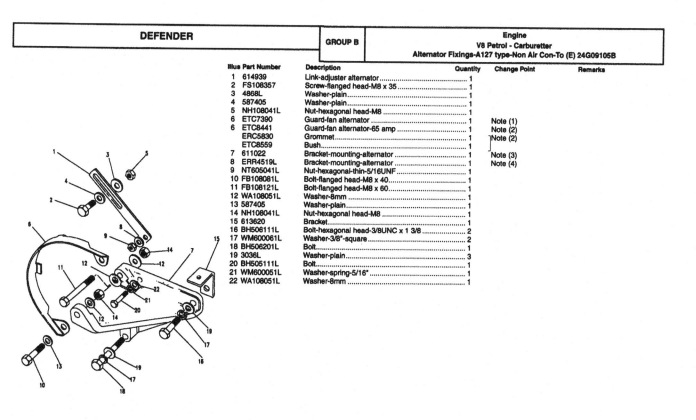

DEFENDER	GROUP B	Engine V8 Petrol - Carburetter Alternator Fixings-A127 type-Non Air Con-To (E) 24G09105B

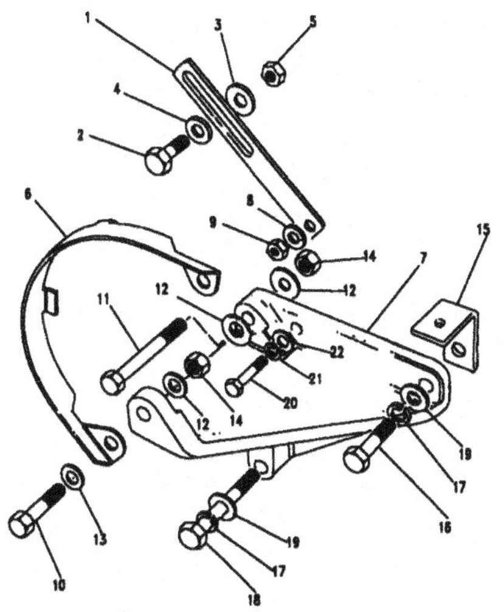

Illus	Part Number	Description	Quantity	Change Point	Remarks
1	614939	Link-adjuster alternator	1		
2	FS108357	Screw-flanged head-M8 x 35	1		
3	4868L	Washer-plain	1		
4	587405	Washer-plain	1		
5	NH108041L	Nut-hexagonal head-M8	1		
6	ETC7390	Guard-fan alternator	1	Note (1)	
6	ETC8441	Guard-fan alternator-65 amp	1	Note (2)	
	ERC5830	Grommet	1	Note (2)	
	ETC8559	Bush	1		
7	611022	Bracket-mounting-alternator	1	Note (3)	
8	ERR4519L	Bracket-mounting-alternator	1	Note (4)	
9	NT605041L	Nut-hexagonal-thin-5/16UNF	1		
10	FB108081L	Bolt-flanged head-M8 x 40	1		
11	FB108121L	Bolt-flanged head-M8 x 60	1		
12	WA108051L	Washer-8mm	1		
13	587405	Washer-plain	1		
14	NH108041L	Nut-hexagonal head-M8	1		
15	613620	Bracket	1		
16	BH506111L	Bolt-hexagonal head-3/8UNC x 1 3/8	2		
17	WM600061L	Washer-3/8"-square	2		
18	BH506201L	Bolt	1		
19	3036L	Washer-plain	3		
20	BH505111L	Bolt	1		
21	WM600051L	Washer-spring-5/16"	1		
22	WA108051L	Washer-8mm	1		

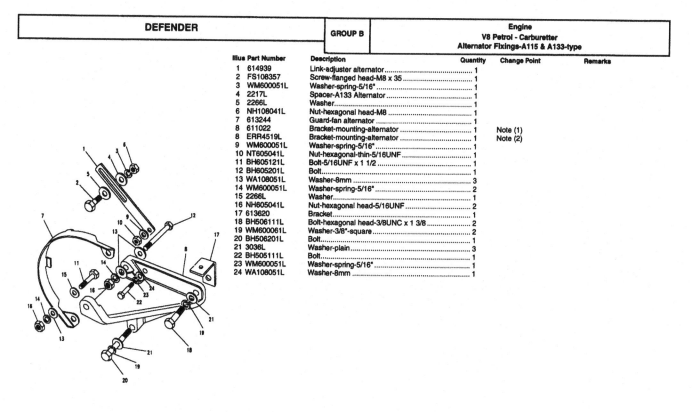

CHANGE POINTS:
(1) To (E)24G 02919B
(2) From (E)24G 02920B
(3) To (E)24G 12353B
(4) From (E)24G 12354B

DEFENDER	GROUP B	Engine V8 Petrol - Carburetter Alternator Fixings-Air Con-To (E) 24G09105B

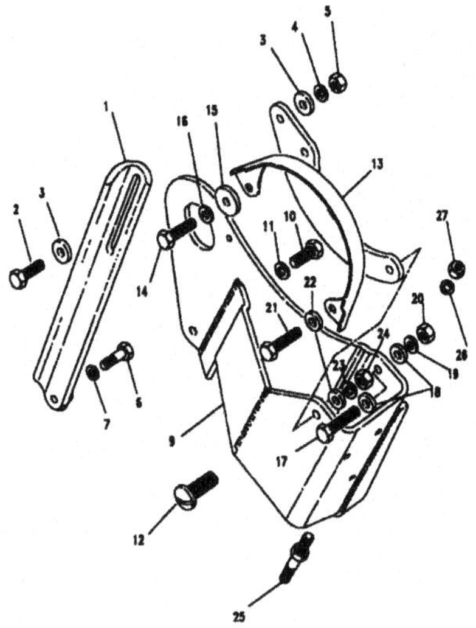

Illus	Part Number	Description	Quantity	Change Point	Remarks
1	ERC7548	Link-adjuster alternator	1		
2	FS108357	Screw-flanged head-M8 x 35	1		
3	4866L	Washer	1		
4	WM600051L	Washer-spring-5/16"	1		
5	NH108041L	Nut-hexagonal head-M8	1		
6	BH605111L	Bolt	1		
7	WL108001L	Washer-sprung-M8	1		
8	ERC6547	Bracket-support alternator	1		
9	ERC6538	Bracket-mounting-alternator-LH	1		
10	SH506071L	Screw-hexagonal head-3/8UNC x 7/8	1		
11	WM600061	Washer-lock	NLA		Use WM600061L.
12	SA506081L	Screw-machine-3/8UNC x 1-counter sunk	1		
13	90613442	Guard-fan alternator	1	Note (1)	
13	ETC8440	Guard-fan alternator-80 amp	1	Note (2)	
	ERC5830	Grommet	2		
	ETC8559	Bush	2		
14	FS108251L	Screw-flanged head-M8 x 25	NLA		Use FS108257L.
15	4594L	Washer-plain	1		
16	WM600051L	Washer-spring-5/16"	1		L/R V8 Petrol Twin Carburettor
17	FB108081L	Bolt-flanged head-M8 x 40	1		
18	WA108051L	Washer-8mm	2		
19	WM600051L	Washer-spring-5/16"	1		
20	NH108041L	Nut-hexagonal head-M8	1		
22	WA108051L	Washer-8mm	1		
23	WM600051L	Washer-spring-5/16"	1		
24	NH108041L	Nut-hexagonal head-M8	1		
25	602200	Bolt-7/16UNC x 2.71	1		
26	WM600061L	Washer-3/8"-square	2		
27	NH604041L	Nut-hexagonal head-coarse thread-1/4UNF	1		

CHANGE POINTS:
(1) To (E)24G 02919B
(2) From (E)24G 02920B

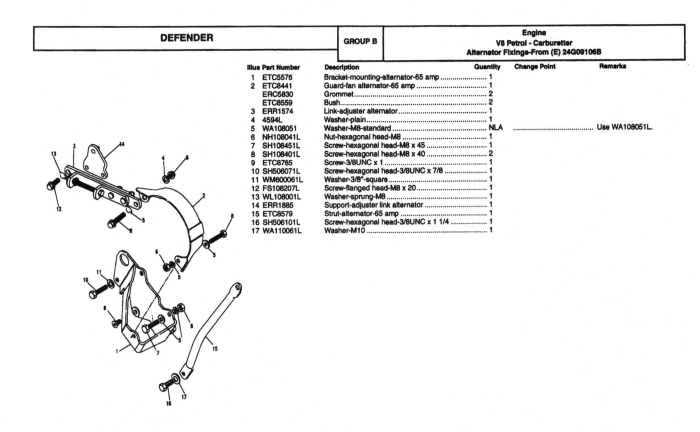

DEFENDER	GROUP B	Engine V8 Petrol - Carburetter Alternator Fixings-From (E) 24G09106B

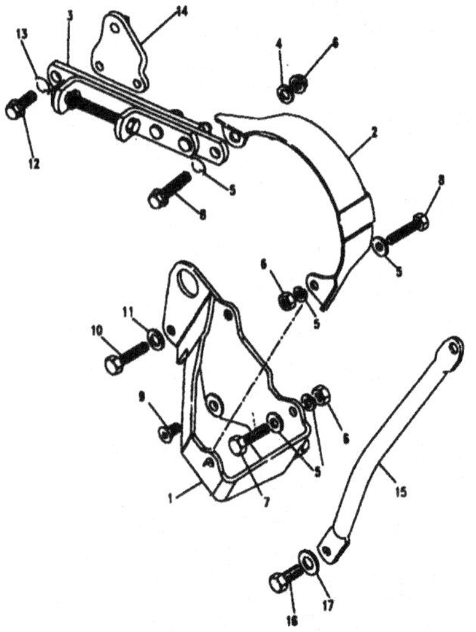

Illus	Part Number	Description	Quantity	Change Point	Remarks
1	ETC5576	Bracket-mounting-alternator-65 amp	1		
2	ETC8441	Guard-fan alternator-65 amp	1		
	ERC5830	Grommet	2		
	ETC8559	Bush	2		
3	ERR1574	Link-adjuster alternator	1		
4	4594L	Washer-plain	1		
5	WA108051	Washer-M8-standard	NLA		Use WA108051L.
6	NH108041L	Nut-hexagonal head-M8	1		
7	SH108451L	Screw-hexagonal head-M8 x 45	1		
8	SH108401L	Screw-hexagonal head-M8 x 40	2		
9	ETC8765	Screw-3/8UNC x 1	1		
10	SH506071L	Screw-hexagonal head-3/8UNC x 7/8	1		
11	WM600061L	Washer-3/8"-square	1		
12	FS108207L	Screw-flanged head-M8 x 20	1		
13	WL108001L	Washer-sprung-M8	1		
14	ERR1885	Support-adjuster link alternator	1		
15	ETC8579	Strut-alternator-65 amp	1		
16	SH506101L	Screw-hexagonal head-3/8UNC x 1 1/4	1		
17	WA110061L	Washer-M10	1		

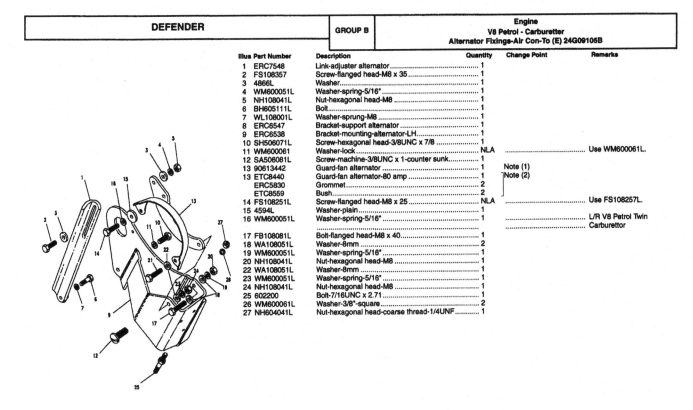

Illus	Part Number	Description	Quantity	Change Point	Remarks
1	RTC5228E	MOTOR-STARTER ENGINE-EXCHANGE-LUCAS	1		
	RTC5048	• Kit-brush starter motor-with M78R starter motor-Lucas	1		
	RTC5049	• Solenoid starter motor-with M78R starter motor-Lucas	1		
	RTC5050	• Drive assembly starter motor	1		
11	SS506121L	Screw-3/8UNC x 1 1/2	2		
12	WM600061	Washer-lock	NLA		Use WM600061L.
13	WA110061L	Washer-M10	1		
8	90608178	Kit-starter motor sundry parts-with 2m100 starter motor	1		

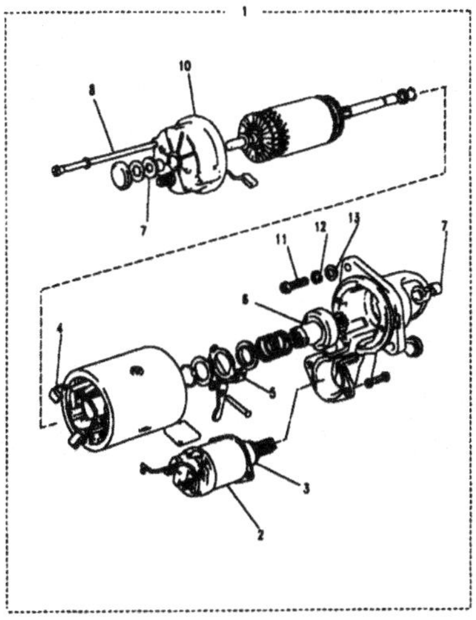

Illus	Part Number	Description	Quantity	Change Point	Remarks
1	RTC6061N	MOTOR-STARTER ENGINE-NEW-LUCAS	1		
	RTC5049	• Solenoid starter motor-with M78R starter motor-Lucas	1		
	RTC5048	• Kit-brush starter motor-with M78R starter motor-Lucas	1		
	RTC5050	• Drive assembly starter motor	1		
	RTC5577	Kit-starter motor-with M78R starter motor	1		
	SS506121L	Screw-3/8UNC x 1 1/2	2		
	WM600061L	Washer-3/8"-square	2		
	WA110061L	Washer-M10	2		

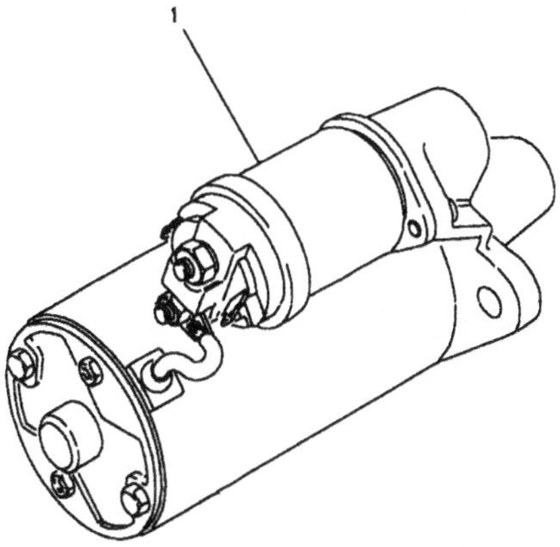

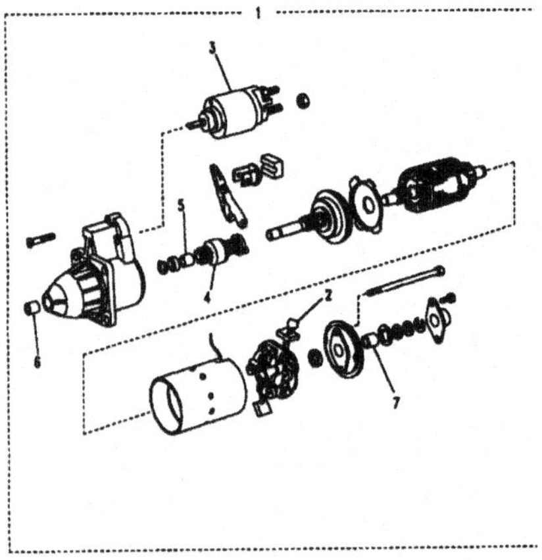

Illus	Part Number	Description	Quantity	Change Point	Remarks
		MOTOR-STARTER ENGINE			
1	NAD10038	BOSCH-NEW	NLA	Note (1)	Use ESR2191.
1	ESR2191	BOSCH-NEW	NLA	Note (2)	Use ERR6087.
1	ERR6087	BOSCH-NEW	NLA	Note (3)	Use NAD101190.
1	NAD10038E	BOSCH-EXCHANGE	NLA	Note (1)	Use ERR6087E.
1	ERR6087E	BOSCH-EXCHANGE	1	Note (4)	
2	STC1243	• Box assembly-brush starter motor	1		
3	STC1242	• Solenoid starter motor	1		
4	STC1241	• Drive assembly starter motor	1		
5	STC1250	• Bush-starter motor-centre	2		
6	STC1252	• Bush-starter motor-front	1		
7	STC1253	• Bush-starter motor-rear	1		
		MOTOR-STARTER ENGINE			
1	NAD101190	BOSCH-NEW	NLA	Note (5)	Use NAD101490.
1	NAD101490	BOSCH-NEW	1	Note (6)	
1	NAD101190E	BOSCH-EXCHANGE	NLA	Note (6)	Use NAD101490E.
1	NAD101490E	BOSCH-EXCHANGE	1	Note (6)	
2	STC4465	• Box assembly-brush starter motor	1		
3	STC4462	• Solenoid starter motor	1		
4	STC4464	• Drive assembly starter motor	1		
5	STC1250	• Bush-starter motor-centre	2		
7	STC1253	• Bush-starter motor-rear	1		
6	STC1255	• Bush-starter motor-front	1		

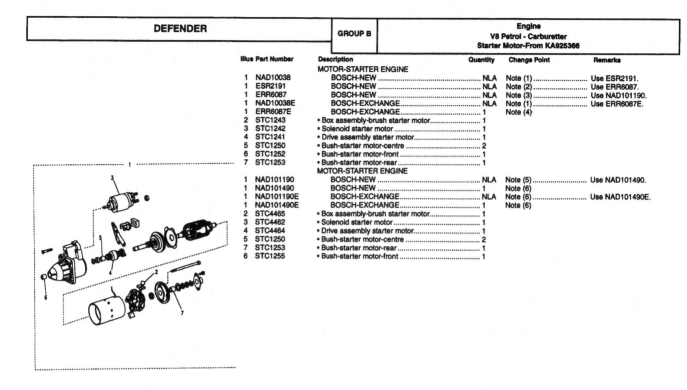

CHANGE POINTS:
(1) To (V) LA 939975
(2) From (V) MA 939976 To (V) MA 966723
(3) From (V) MA 966724 To (V) VA 124530
(4) From (V) MA 939976 To (V) XA 175501
(5) From (V) VA 124531 To (V) XA 175501
(6) From (V) XA 175502

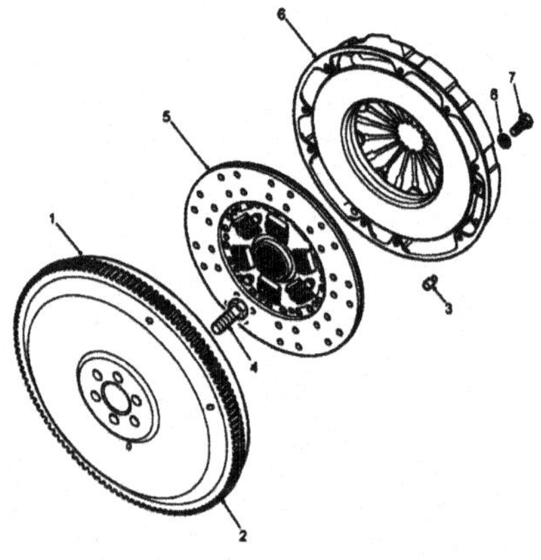

AHBQRA1A

Illus	Part Number	Description	Quantity	Change Point	Remarks
	STC8361	KIT-CLUTCH-ASBESTOS FREE	1		
	STC50503	KIT-CLUTCH	1	Note (1)	
5	FTC160	• Plate-clutch-driven-asbestos free	NLA		Use FTC3197.
					Part of STC8361.
6	576476	• Cover-clutch assembly	1		
	FRC9568	• BEARING-CLUTCH RELEASE	NLA		Use FTC5200.
	FRC4078	• • Sleeve-guide clutch	1		
5	FTC4662	• Plate-clutch-driven-asbestos free	1		Part of STC50503.
	FTC5200	Bearing-clutch release			
1	ERR2264	FLYWHEEL ENGINE	NLA		Use ERR5575.
1	ERR5575	FLYWHEEL ENGINE	1	Note (2)	
2	611323	• Gear-ring-flywheel engine	1		
3	6395L	• Dowel	3		
4	SH607081L	Screw-hexagonal head-7/16UNC x 1	6		
7	SH606061L	Screw-hexagonal head-3/8UNC x 3/4	6		
8	WM600041L	Washer-spring-1/4 dia-square	6		

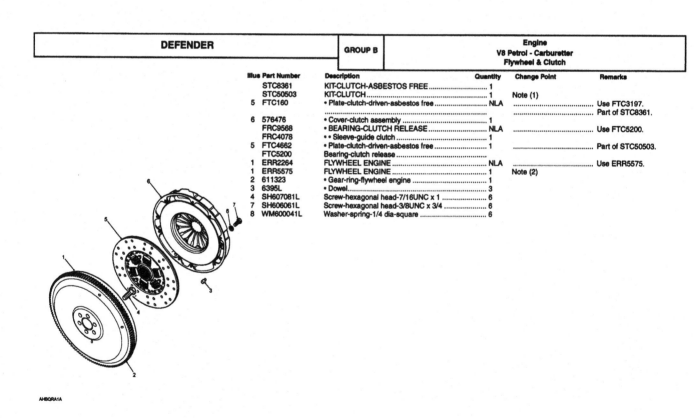

CHANGE POINTS:
(1) From (E)24G 14148B
(2) From (V)24G 13679B

Illus	Part Number	Description	Quantity	Change Point	Remarks
1	STC3319	Engine unit-stripped	1		

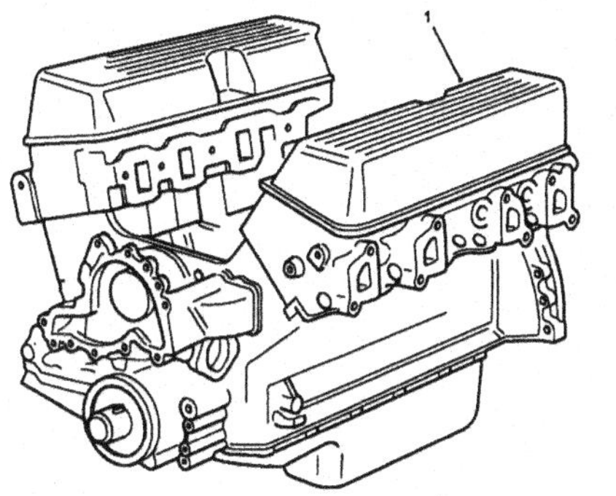

AMBRAC2A

Illus	Part Number	Description	Quantity	Change Point	Remarks
1	STC1891	Engine assembly - Short	1		

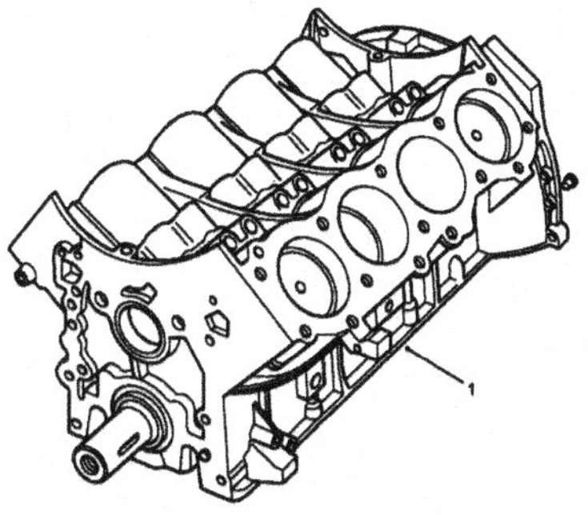

AMBRAE1A

DEFENDER	GROUP B	Engine V8 Petrol - EFi Cylinder Block

Illus	Part Number	Description	Quantity	Change Point	Remarks
1	ERR4199	CYLINDER BLOCK-ENGINE	NLA		Use LCF104860.
1	LCF104860	CYLINDER BLOCK-ENGINE	NLA		
1	LCF104560	CYLINDER BLOCK-ENGINE	1		
2	602152	• Plug-cup	8		
3	602130	• Setscrew-cylinder block main bearing cap	10		
4	612898	• Plug	2		
5	ERR3330	• Seal-19mm OD	8		
6	ERR3331	• Seal-16mm OD	2		
7	ERR3693	• Housing-crankshaft sensor	1	Note (1)	Part of ERR4199, LCF104860.
8	ERR4157	• Pin-roll-spring tension	1		
9	FB110137	• Bolt-flanged head-M10 x 65	8		
10	SS110555	• Screw-hexagon socket-M10 x 55	2		
11	STC1961	• Set-camshaft bearings-unfinished	1		
7	EIQ100020	• Housing-crankshaft sensor	1	Note (2)	Part of LCF104560.
12	602147	Plug-cylinder block oil way	4		
13	602146	Plug	1		
14	602141	Dowel	2		
15	ERR4314	Plug	2		
16	ERR4315	Plug-drain	2		
17	90602202	Dowel	2		
18	ERR2640	Seal-crankshaft rear oil	1		
19	611089	Seal-main bearing rear cap half joint	2		

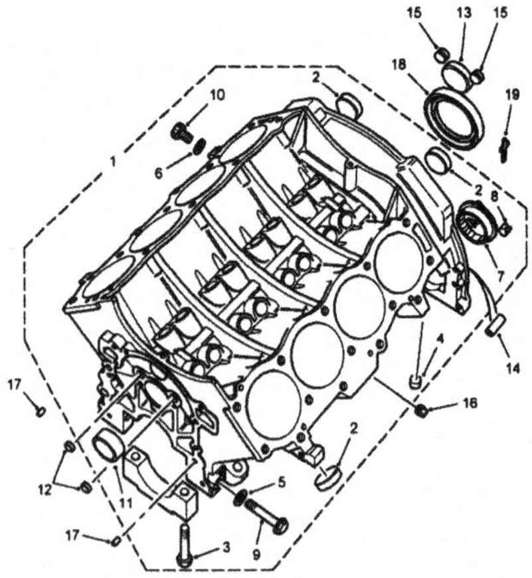

AMBRBA2B

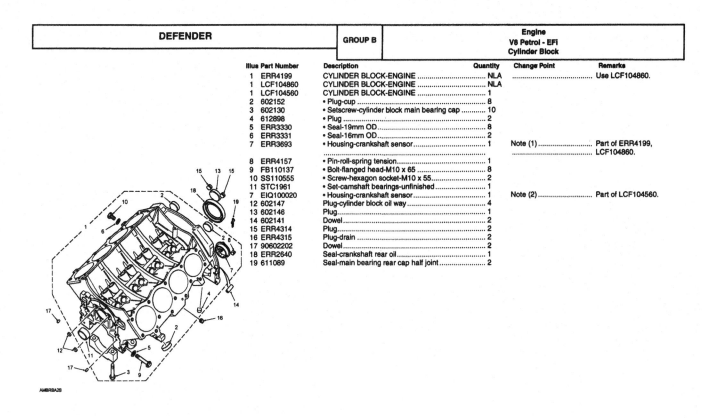

CHANGE POINTS:
(1) To (V) VA 138868
(2) From (V) WA 138869

DEFENDER	GROUP B	Engine V8 Petrol - EFi Crankshaft & Bearings

Illus	Part Number	Description	Quantity	Change Point	Remarks
1	ERR5090	CRANKSHAFT-ENGINE	1		
2	ERR1101	• Dowel-flywheel to crankshaft	1		
5	ERR2846	• Key-crankshaft	1		
3	549911	Bush-crankshaft	1		
4	ERR2958	Sprocket-crankshaft	1		
5	ERR2846	Key-crankshaft	1		
6	STC4299	Set-crankshaft bearings-standard	1		
7	ERR4922	Absorber-crankshaft vibration	1		
		WEIGHT-CRANKSHAFT BALANCE			
8	ERR3758	5gm	A/R		
8	ERR3592	10gm	A/R		
8	ERR3759	15gm	A/R		
8	ERR3760	20gm	A/R		
8	ERR5391	30gm	A/R		
9	ERC417	Bolt-crankshaft pulley	1		
10	ERC416	Washer	1		
	ERR6117	Heatshield-crankshaft sensor	1		

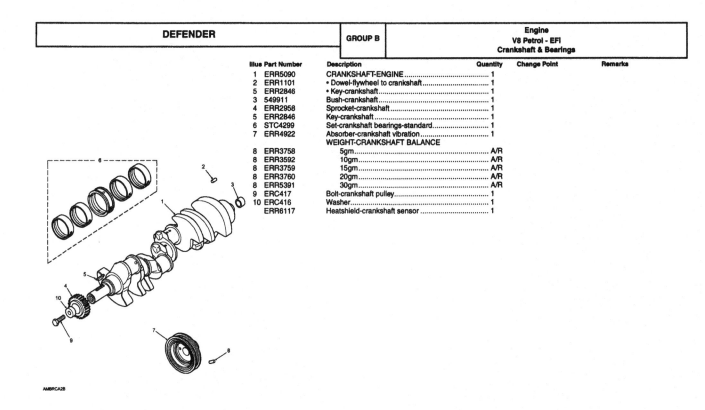

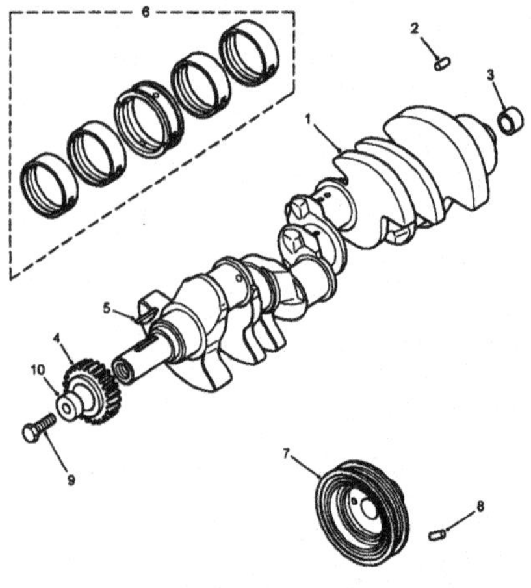

AMBRCA2B

Illus	Part Number	Description	Quantity	Change Point	Remarks
1	ERR5553	PISTON-ENGINE-STANDARD.-HIGH COMPRESSION	8		
2	STC1427	• Ring set assembly-piston-standard.	8		
3	ERR4837	ROD-CRANKSHAFT CONNECTING	8		
4	ERR1772	• Bolt	16		
5	ERR1773	Set-connecting rod bearing-standard.	1		

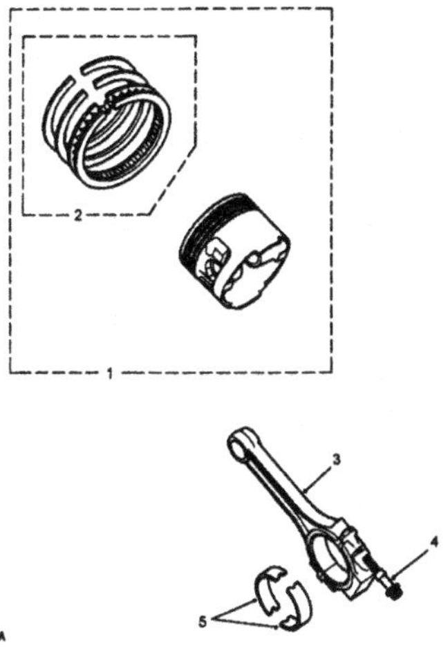

AMBRCC2A

Illus	Part Number	Description	Quantity	Change Point	Remarks
1	ERR4633	Sump-engine oil	1		
2	213961	Washer-sealing-sump drain plug	1		
3	603659	Plug-sump assembly oil drain	1		
4	602087	Gasket-crankcase oil sump	1		
5	LSO100000	Bolt & washer assembly-sump	16		
6	ERR3788	Gasket-sump oil strainer	1		
7	SH504061L	Setscrew-1/4UNC x 3/4	2		
8	WM600041L	Washer-spring-1/4 dia-square	2		
9	ERR3677	Strainer and pipe assembly-oil	1		
10	602070	Cover-oil strainer	1		

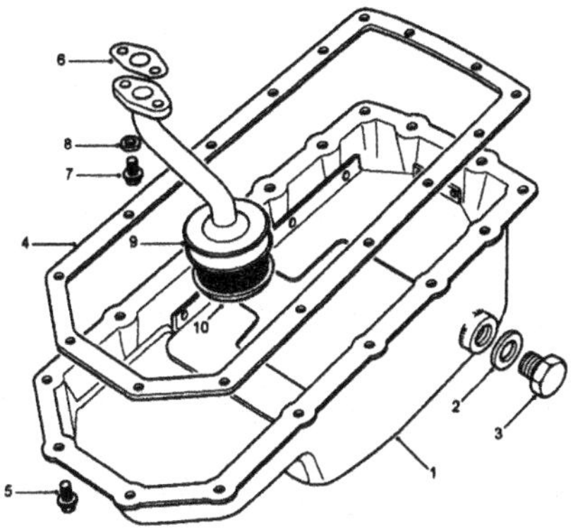

AMBRDA1A

Illus	Part Number	Description	Quantity	Change Point	Remarks
1	ANR4697	Bracket-engine mounting-RH	1		
2	ANR4696	Bracket-engine mounting-LH	1		
3	NTC4205	Heatshield-front engine mounting-LH	1		
4	KKB103120	Mounting-engine rubber	2		
5	WC110061L	Washer-plain-M10-oversize	2		
6	WL110001L	Washer-M10	4		
7	FX112041	Nut-flange-prevailing torque	4		
8	SH505071L	Screw-hexagonal head-5/16UNC x 7/8	2		
9	WM600051L	Washer-spring-5/16"	2		
10	SH507091L	Screw-hexagonal head-7/16UNC x 1 1/8	4		
11	WM600071L	Washer-sprung-7/16"	4		
12	ERR4905	Dipstick-oil	1		
13	ERR4450	Tube-oil dipstick	1		
14	602545	O ring	1		
15	610489	Clip	1		
16	AB610041L	Screw-self tapping AB-M8 x 12	1		
18	SH604071L	Screw-hexagonal head-1/4UNF x 7/8	2		
19	WA106041L	Washer-6mm	2		
20	WM600041L	Washer-spring-1/4 dia-square	2		
21	NH604041L	Nut-hexagonal head-coarse thread-1/4UNF	2		

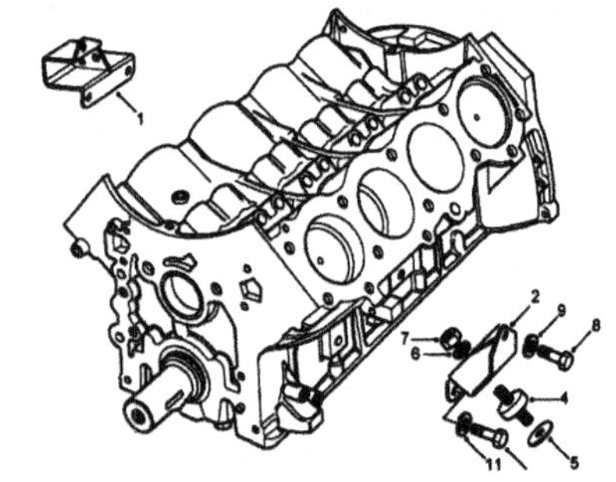

AM8QDC1A

Illus	Part Number	Description	Quantity	Change Point	Remarks
1	ERR6126	COVER-ENGINE-FRONT	1		
2	ERR6490	• Seal-crankshaft front oil	1		
3	ERR7280	Gasket-cover front	1		
4	FB505171S	Bolt-flanged head-5/16UNC x 2 1/8	5		
5	FB505241S	Bolt-flanged head-5/16UNC x 3	4		
6	STC4104	Switch-oil pressure engine	1		
7	243967	Washer-sealing	1		
8	STC3372	O ring	1		
9	ERR3340	Cartridge-engine oil filter	1		
10	ERR6107	Bracket-connector engine	1		

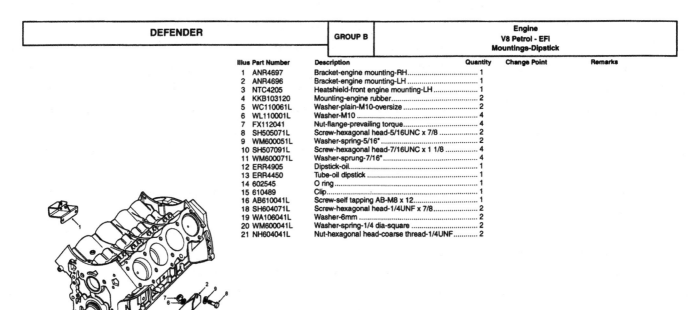

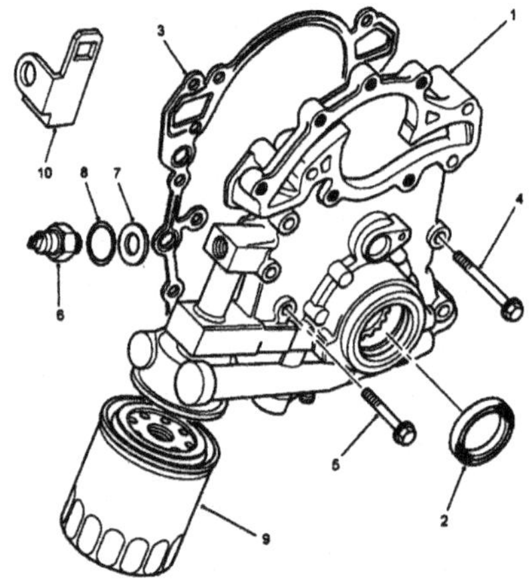

AM8REA2B

Illus	Part Number	Description	Quantity	Change Point	Remarks
1	STC1693	PUMP ASSEMBLY-ENGINE COOLANT	NLA		Use STC4378.
2	ERR4077	• Gasket-coolant pump body	1		
1	STC4378	PUMP ASSEMBLY-ENGINE COOLANT	1		
2	ERR4077	• Gasket-coolant pump body	1		
3	FS106255L	Screw-flanged head-M6 x 25	6		
4	ERR3440	Pulley-tensioner ancillary drive	1		
5	FB110151L	Bolt-flanged head-M10 x 75	6		

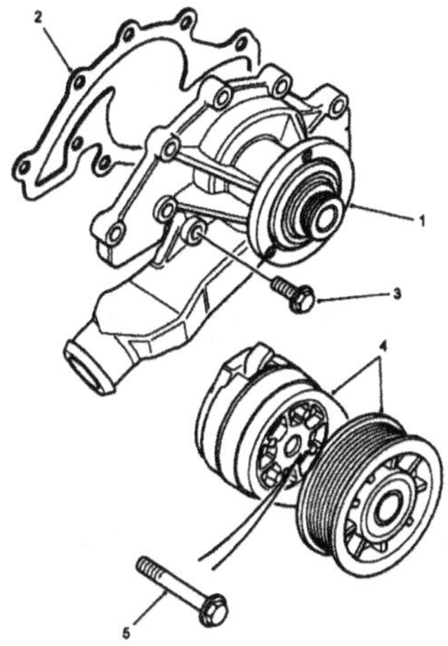

AMBREE18

Illus	Part Number	Description	Quantity	Change Point	Remarks
1	PQR101050	Pulley coolant pump	1		
2	FS108127L	Screw-flanged head-flanged head-M8 x 12	3		
3	ERR3443	Coupling-engine fan viscous	1		
4	ERR3439	Fan-cooling-11 blade-17"-Black	1		
5	ERR4194	Screw-hexagonal head-M8 x 14	4		
6	ERR5579	Belt-polyvee alternator	1		

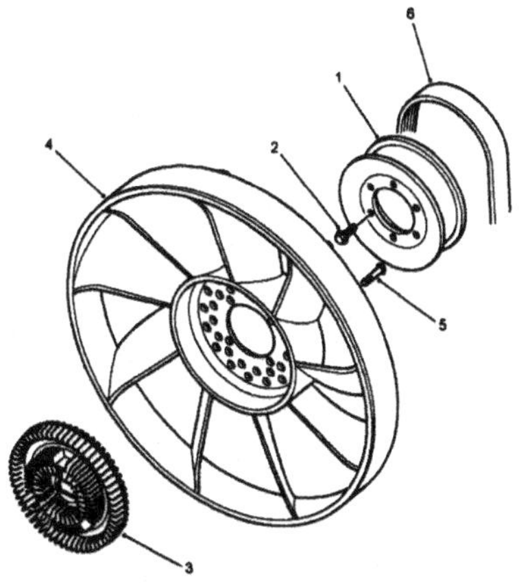

AMBREG2A

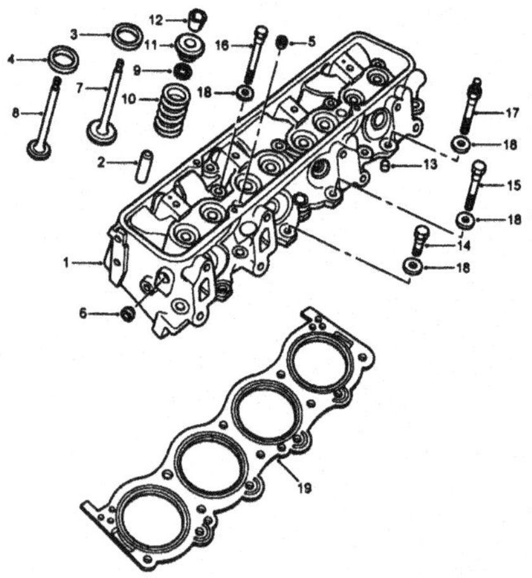

Illus	Part Number	Description	Quantity	Change Point	Remarks
1	LDF108090	CYLINDER HEAD ASSEMBLY-ENGINE	2		
2	ERR3648	• Guide-cylinder head valve	NLA		Use LGJ100900.
2	LGJ100900	• Guide-cylinder head valve	8		
3	ERC224	• Seat-cylinder head inlet valve-standard	4		
4	ETC8596	• Seat-cylinder head exhaust valve-standard	4		
5	602123	• Plug-core	2		
6	602289	• Plug-cup	2		
7	ERR1780	Valve-cylinder head inlet	8		
8	ERR7338	Valve-cylinder head exhaust	8		
9	ERR1782	Seal-cylinder head valve stem oil	16		
10	ERR4628	Spring-cylinder head valve	16		
11	ERC573	Cap-cylinder head valve spring	16		
12	ERC1637	Cotter-valve	32		
13	602040	Dowel	4		
14	602191	Bolt-cylinder head fixing-7/16UNC x 2 1/4	8		
15	ERR2943	Bolt-cylinder head fixing-7/16UNC x 2.6	13		
16	ERR2944	Bolt-cylinder head fixing-7/16UNC x 3.78	6		
17	602200	Bolt-7/16UNC x 2.71	1		
18	602098	Washer-plain	28		
19	ERR7217	Gasket-cylinder head	2		
	ETC5964	Bracket-lifting engine front	1		
	SH505091L	Screw-hexagonal head-5/16UNC x 1 1/8	1		
	WM600051L	Washer-spring-5/16"	1		
	SH506071L	Screw-hexagonal head-3/8UNC x 7/8	2		
	WM600061L	Washer-3/8"-square	2		
	ERC614	Bracket-lifting engine rear	1		
	SH506071L	Screw-hexagonal head-3/8UNC x 7/8	2		
	WM600061L	Washer-3/8"-square	2		

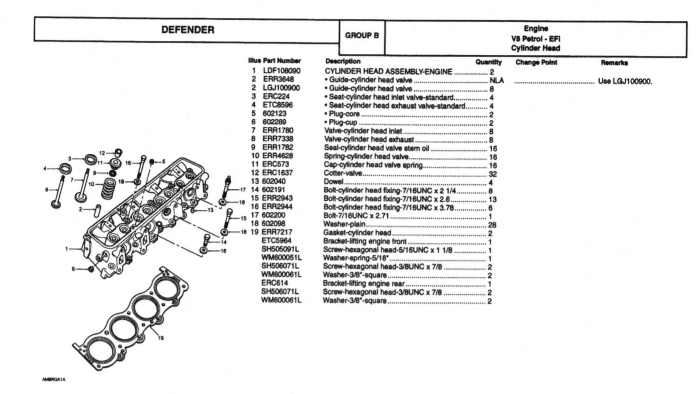

Illus	Part Number	Description	Quantity	Change Point	Remarks
1	611660	SHAFT ASSEMBLY-ROCKER	2		
2	611659L	• SHAFT-ROCKER	2		
10	154545	• • Plug-core	4		
3	602153	• Rocker assembly-cylinder head-RH	8		
4	602154	• Rocker assembly-cylinder head-LH	8		
5	603734	• Pillar-cylinder head rocker support	8		
6	602142	• Spring-rocker shaft	6		
7	602148	• Washer-waved	4		
8	602186	• Washer-plain	4		
9	PS606101L	• Pin-split	4		
11	602097	Bolt-3/8UNC x 2.79	8		
12	603378	Rod-engine push	16		
13	ERC4949	Tappet-engine valve hydraulic	16		

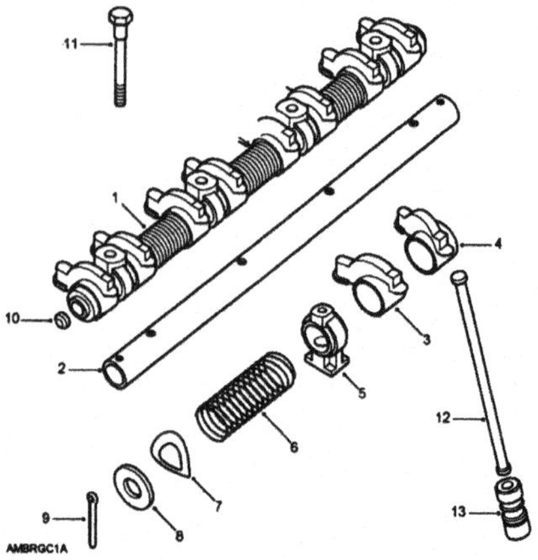

DEFENDER | GROUP B | Engine V8 Petrol - EFi Rocker Cover

Illus	Part Number	Description	Quantity	Change Point	Remarks
1	ERR5439	COVER ASSEMBLY-VALVE ROCKER-LH	NLA		Use ERR7365.
2	ERR5217	• Filler-oil	1		
3	602512	• Gasket-engine rocker cover	NLA		Use ERR7288.
3	ERR7288	• Gasket-engine rocker cover	1		
4	ERR5218	CAP ASSEMBLY-OIL FILLER	1		
5	ERR5219	• Seal-dust	1		
6	564258	O ring	1		
7	ERR5000	COVER ASSEMBLY-VALVE ROCKER-RH	NLA		Use ERR7367.
8	602512	• Gasket-engine rocker cover	NLA		Use ERR7288.
8	ERR7288	• Gasket-engine rocker cover	1		
	ERR4563	• Separator-crankcase breather oil	1		
9	ERR4818	Screw-1/4UNC x 7/8	4		
10	ERR4819	Screw-1/4UNC x 1 1/4	4		
11	ERR4258	Hose assembly-breather-rocker to ram housing	1		
12	ERR4237	Hose assembly-breather-rocker to plenum	1		

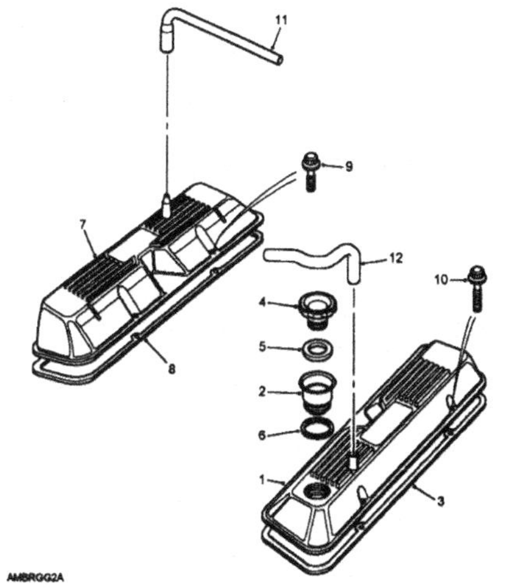

AMBRGG2A

DEFENDER | GROUP B | Engine V8 Petrol - EFi Camshaft

Illus	Part Number	Description	Quantity	Change Point	Remarks
1	ERR3720	Camshaft-engine	1		
2	ERR5086	Sprocket-camshaft	1		
3	ERC7929	Chain-engine timing	1		
4	ERR2609	Key-camshaft location	1		
5	SH505061L	Screw-hexagonal head-5/16UNC x 3/4	2		
6	FS110301L	Screw-flanged head-M10 x 30-top	1		

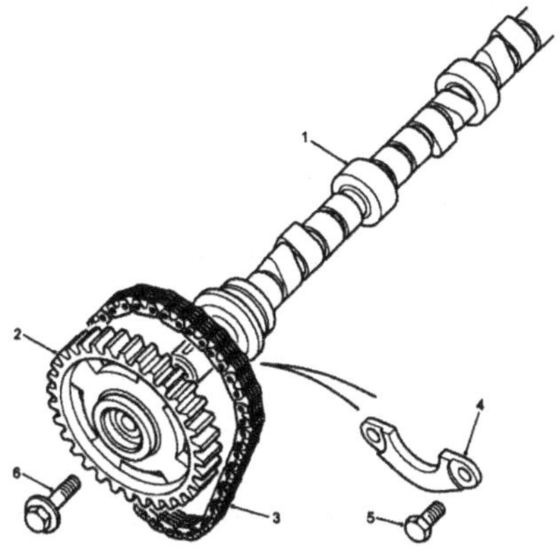

AMBRGI2A

DEFENDER	GROUP B	Engine V8 Petrol - EFI Inlet Manifold

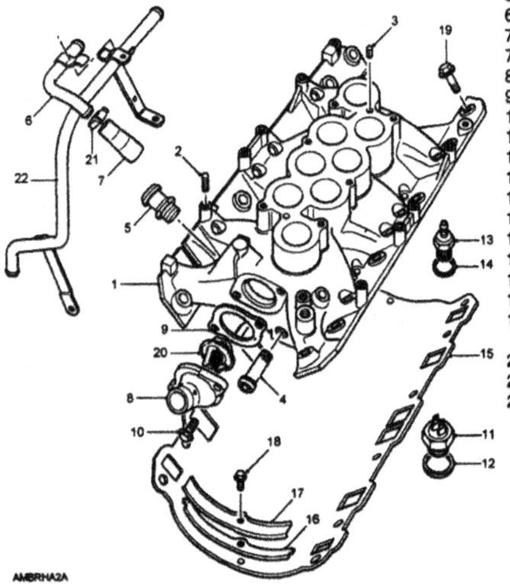

AMBRHA2A

Illus	Part Number	Description	Quantity	Change Point	Remarks
1	ERR5045	MANIFOLD ASSEMBLY-ENGINE INLET	1		
2	ERR4309	• Stud-M6 x 22	4		
	ERR4389	• Pipe-outlet stub	NLA		Use PEP103530.
	ERR4886	• Manifold-engine inlet	1		
	ETC7388	• Plug-blanking	1		
3	602040	• Dowel-cylinder block to cylinder head	2		
3	602201	• Dowel-locating	2		
4	ETC6547	Adaptor-inlet manifold bypass	1		
5	ERR4820	Adaptor-inlet manifold heater feed	1		
6	ERR5473	Pipe assembly-heater feed	1		
7	ERR5238	Hose-heater to pump coolant	NLA		Use PEH101170.
7	PEH101170	Hose-heater to pump coolant	1		
8	ETC4596	Elbow-engine coolant outlet	1		
9	ERR2429	Gasket-coolant outlet elbow	1		
10	FS505077	Screw-flanged head-5/16UNC x 7/8	2		
11	PRC3505	Switch-engine thermostat-Yellow..	1		
12	C457593	Washer-sealing	1		
13	AMR1425	Sensor-temperature	1		
14	243967	Washer-sealing	1		
15	ERR7306	Gasket-inlet manifold	1		
16	ERR7283	Seal-inlet manifold gasket	2		
17	602076	Clamp-inlet manifold gasket seal	2		
18	602236	Bolt-5/16UNC	2		
19	FB506115	Bolt-flanged head-3/8UNC x 1 3/8	10		
19	FB506155	Bolt-flanged head-3/8UNC x 1 7/8	NLA		Use LYG101450 Use bolt with retained washer..
20	ETC4765	Thermostat-engine-88 degrees C	1		
21	ESR3607	Clip-hose-26mm	2		
22	ERR5474	PIPE-OUTLET TO HEATER COOLANT	1		
	NTC4609	• Plug-drain/filler level	1		
	NTC5171	• O ring	1		
	SH504061L	• Setscrew-1/4UNC x 3/4	2		
	WM600041L	• Washer-spring-1/4 dia-square	2		

DEFENDER	GROUP B	Engine V8 Petrol - EFI Exhaust Manifold

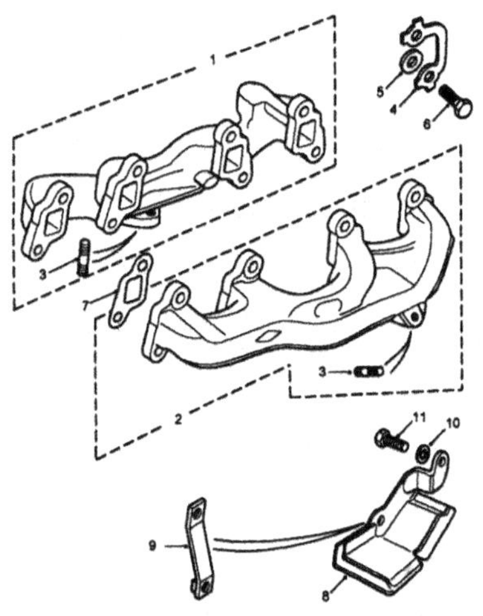

AMBRHC1A

Illus	Part Number	Description	Quantity	Change Point	Remarks
1	ERR5023	MANIFOLD-ENGINE EXHAUST-RH	1		
2	ERR5024	MANIFOLD-ENGINE EXHAUST-LH	1		
3	ERR551L	• Stud-M8 x 25	6		
4	ERC7321	Washer-exhaust manifold to cylinder head tab	4		
5	3036L	Washer-plain	16		
6	SH506095L	Screw-hexagonal head-3/8UNC x 1 1/8	14		
6	614443	Screw-3/8UNC x 1 1/8	2		
7	ERR5008	Gasket-exhaust manifold-No1	2		
7	ERR5010	Gasket-exhaust manifold-No2	2		
8	ERC5875	Heatshield-exhaust manifold	1		
9	ERR117	Bracket-heatshield exhaust system	1		
10	RTC613	Washer-plain	3		
11	SH605051L	Screw-hexagonal head-5/16UNF x 5/8	3		
12	ERR5795	Heatshield-exhaust manifold	NLA		Use KKJ100110.
12	KKJ100110	Heatshield-exhaust manifold	1		
13	SH505091L	Screw-hexagonal head-5/16UNC x 1 1/8	1		
14	WA108051L	Washer-8mm	1		

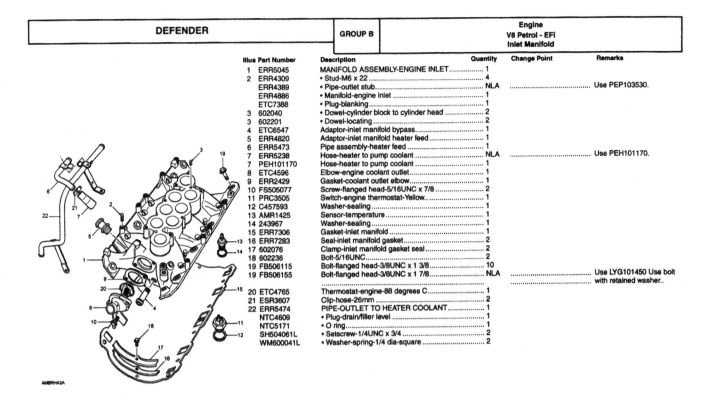

Illus	Part Number	Description	Quantity	Change Point	Remarks
1	ERR4937	Rail assembly-multi point injection fuel distribution	1		
2	FN106047L	Nut-flange-M6	4		
3	ETC6661	Sensor-fuel temperature multi point injection/tbi	1		
4	ERR722	INJECTOR-FUEL MULTI POINT INJECTION	8		
5	BAU5325L	• O ring-small	NLA		Use RTC5679.
5	RTC5679	• O ring-small	16		
6	EAC2414L	O ring-centre-large	8		
7	ETC6375	Clip-fuel injector multi point injection	8		
8	ETC8494	Regulator-fuel pressure	1		
9	FS106127L	Screw-flanged head-M6 x 12	2		
10	ETC7305	Hose-vacuum induction system	1		
11	ERR4541	Pipe-spill return fuel injection	1		
12	MXC1848	Clip	1		
13	ERR2966	Hose-return fuel	1		
14	WJM10006	Clip-hose-spring-band	2		

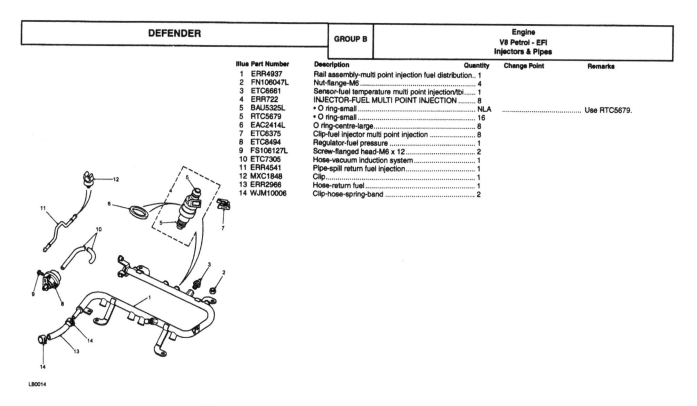

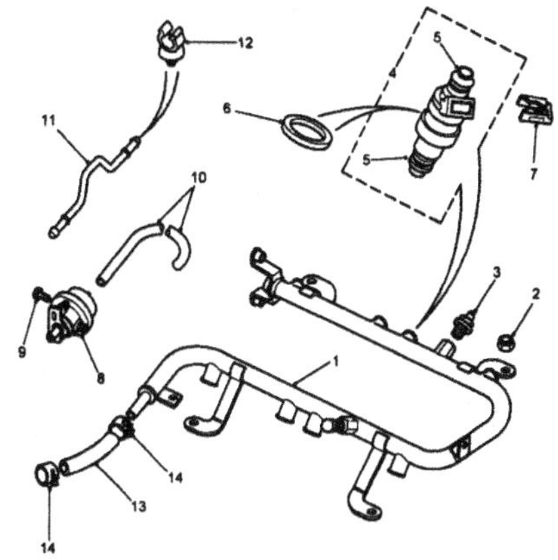

LB0014

Illus	Part Number	Description	Quantity	Change Point	Remarks
1	ERR6794	PLENUM ASSEMBLY	1		
2	ERC255	• Plug-cup	A/R		
3	ERR1756	• Bush-throttle spindle tbi	2		
4	AUD3577L	• Seal-throttle spindle multi point injection	1		
5	ERR4318	• Seal-throttle spindle multi point injection	1		
6	ERR4225	• Spindle-throttle multi point injection	1		
7	ETC6222	• Disc-carburettor throttle	1		
8	ERC3579	Nut-throttle spindle multi point injection	1		
9	ST606080	Setscrew	1		
10	ERR5007	Pipe-plenum chamber breather	1		
11	ERR6704	Bracket assembly-throttle wire mounting	1		
12	ERR5103	Lever-throttle multi point injection	1		
13	SS108801	Screw-hexagon socket-M8 x 80	1		
14	SS108555	Screw-hexagon socket-M8 x 55	5		
15	WA108051L	Washer-8mm	6		
16	ERR4352	Motor-multi point injection stepping	1		
17	ERR3359	Gasket-stepping motor	1		
18	FS104147M	Screw-flanged head-M4 x 14	2		
19	FS104207M	Screw-flanged head-M4 x 20	2		
20	ERR1262	COVER ASSEMBLY-WATER JACKET	1		
21	ERR1261	• Pipe-plenum chamber breather	2		
22	ETC7353	Gasket-water jacket to plenum chamber	1		
23	FB504117S	Bolt-flanged head-1/4UNC x 1 3/8	1		
24	FS504087S	Screw-flanged head-1/4UNC x 1	3		
25	ETC6874	Cap-tamperproof	1		
26	ERR6189	Pipe assembly-purge	1		
27	ERR4278	Potentiometer-throttle multi point injection	1		
28	ERR4944	Gasket-potentiometer-throttle multi point injection	1		
29	RTC5965	Screw-carburettor throttle disc	2		

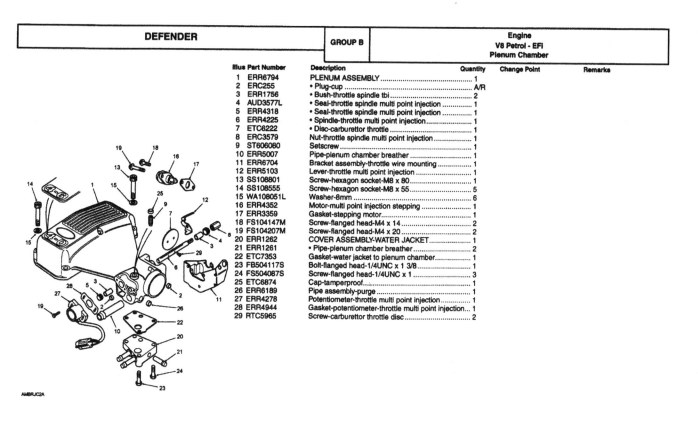

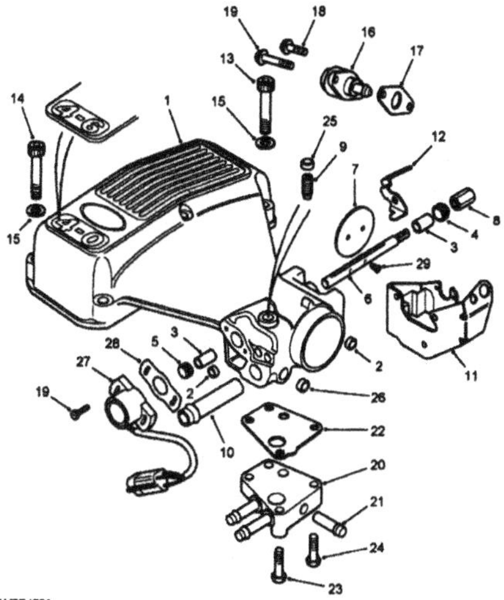
AMBRJC2A

Illus	Part Number	Description	Quantity	Change Point	Remarks
1	ERR4388	Hose-manifold to plenum de icer	1		
2	EAC32151	Clip-hose	2		
3	ERR4258	Hose assembly-breather-rocker to ram housing	1		
4	ERR5039	Hose-rocker to plenum	1		

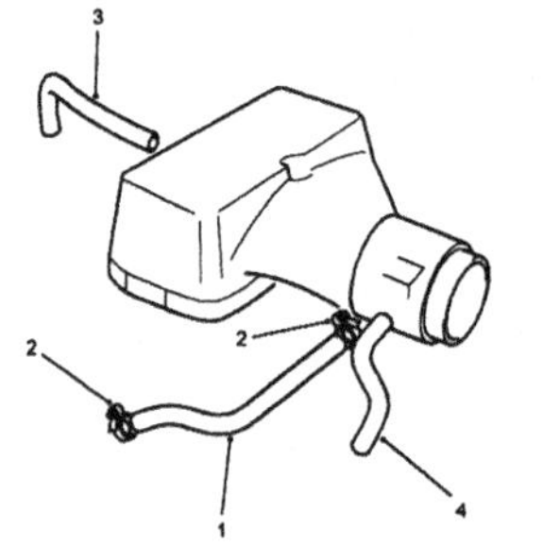

AMBRJE1A

Illus	Part Number	Description	Quantity	Change Point	Remarks
1	ERR4021	HOUSING-RAM PIPES	1		
	ERR4566	• Pipe induction system	1		
2	ERC9110	• Pipe-ram	8		
3	ERR4235	• Connector-inlet manifold adaptor	1		
4	232043	• Washer-sealing	1		
5	FB505181	Bolt-flanged head-5/16UNC x 2 1/4	6		

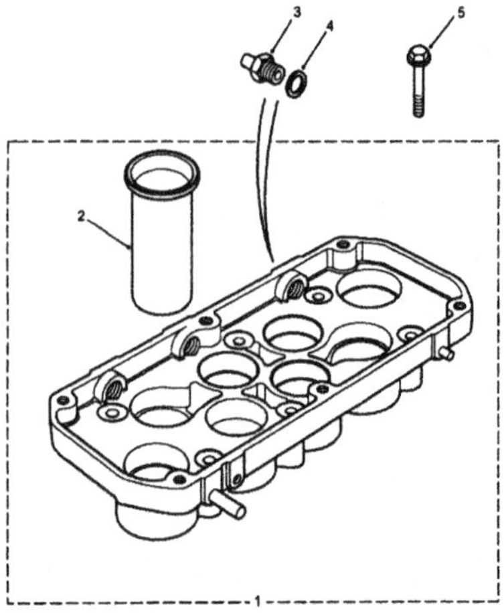

AMBRJG2B

Illus	Part Number	Description	Quantity	Change Point	Remarks
1	ERR6704	Bracket assembly-throttle wire mounting	1		
2	ETC7887	LEVER ASSEMBLY-THROTTLE TBI	1		
3	ETC7884	• Clip-spring steel	2		
10	ERC3792L	• Spring-return-tension accelerator	1		
5	ERC4215	• Bush-spherical	1		
4	ERR3712	Housing bearing	2		
6	RA612183	Rivet-pop-aluminium	2		
7	C43231L	Washer-lock	1		
8	ERC3579	Nut-throttle spindle multi point injection	1		
9	ETC5524	Spring	1		
11	ETC7769	Lever-throttle multi point injection	1		
12	ETC7668M	Screw-self tapping	1		
13	FS504047	Screw-flanged head-1/4UNC x 1/2	3		

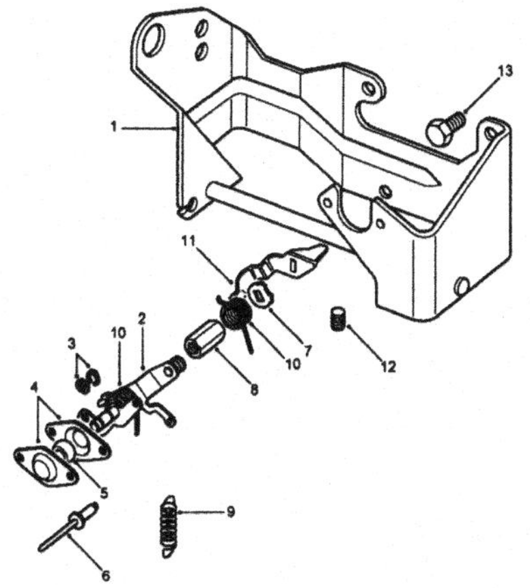

AMBRJI1A

Illus	Part Number	Description	Quantity	Change Point	Remarks
1	STC1639	Set-engine gasket-asbestos free-overhaul	1		
2	STC1641	Set-cylinder head gasket	1		

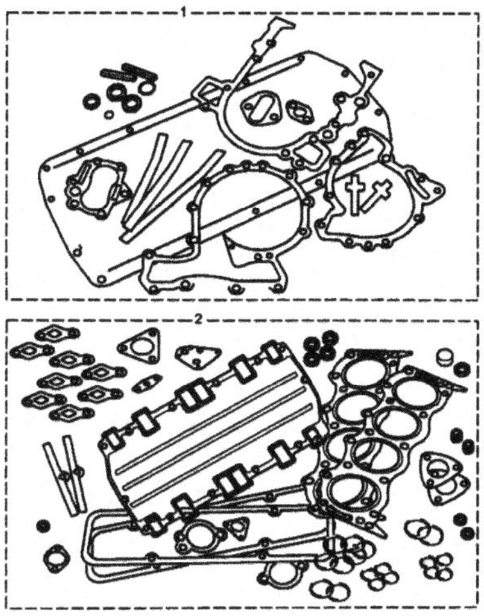

AMBRMA1A

Illus	Part Number	Description	Quantity	Change Point	Remarks
1	ERR4066	PUMP ASSEMBLY POWER ASSISTED STEERING	NLA		Use QVB101110.
2	ERR4054	• Bracket-mounting power assisted steering pump-centre	1		
3	FS108201L	• Screw-flanged head-M8 x 20	NLA		Use FS108207L.
4	FS108207L	Screw-flanged head-M8 x 20	2		
5	ERR4053	Bracket-mounting power assisted steering pump-rear	1		
6	FB506211	Bolt-flanged head-3/8UNC x 5/8	1		
7	FB506267	Bolt-flanged head-3/8UNC x 3 1/4	NLA		Use FC506267S.
7	FC506267S	Bolt-flanged head-3/8UNC x 3 1/4	1		
8	ERR4427	Bracket-mounting power assisted steering pump-front	1		
9	ERR3062	Bolt-flanged head-3/8UNC x 5 1/4	1		
10	FS108207L	Screw-flanged head-M8 x 20	5		
11	ERR4868	Pulley-assembly	1		
12	FS108127ML	Screw-flanged head-M8 x 12-patch lock	3		
13	ERR4679	Bracket-lifting engine front	1		

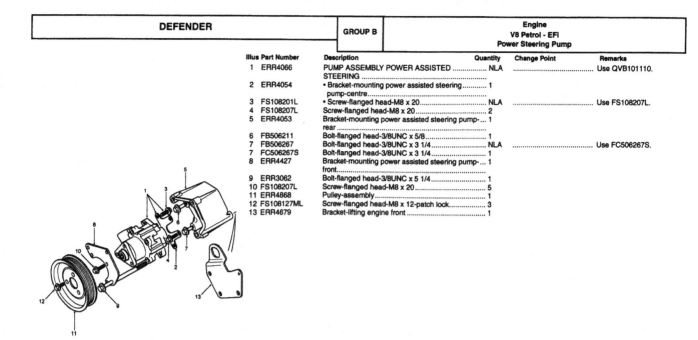

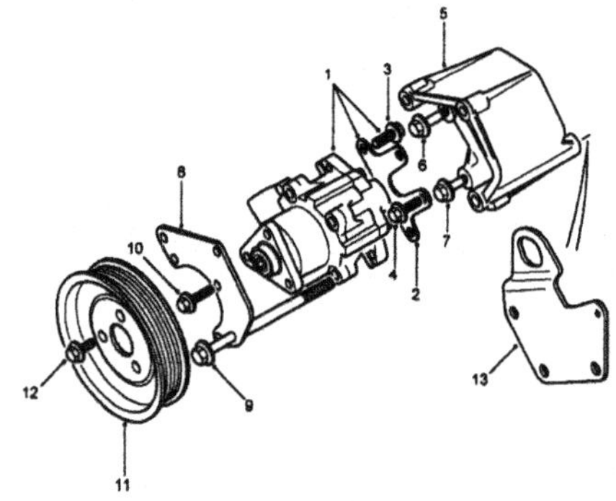

AMBRNC1A

Illus	Part Number	Description	Quantity	Change Point	Remarks
1	BTR5750	Compressor assembly air conditioning	1		
2	ERR3671	Heatshield assembly air conditioning compressor	1		
3	ERR4052	Dowel	2		
4	FB108197	Bolt-flanged head-M8 x 95	4		
5	ERR3440	Pulley-tensioner ancillary drive	1		
6	FB110151L	Bolt-flanged head-M10 x 75	1		
7	ERR4513	Bracket-ancillary mounting	1		
8	ERR3062	Bolt-flanged head-3/8UNC x 5 1/4	2		
9	FB506267	Bolt-flanged head-3/8UNC x 3 1/4	NLA		Use FC506267S.
9	FC506267S	Bolt-flanged head-3/8UNC x 3 1/4	2		
10	ERR5579	Belt-polyvee alternator	1		

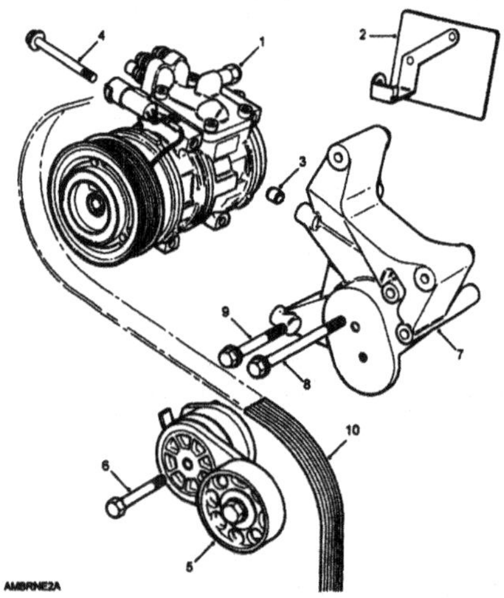

AMBRNE2A

Illus	Part Number	Description	Quantity	Change Point	Remarks
1	ERR6269	COIL IGNITION	1		
2	ERR2970	• Harness-link-low tension ignition coil	1		
3	YYC10017	Clip-harness	1		
		LEAD-HIGH TENSION IGNITION			
4	STC8663	to number one cylinder	1		
4	ERR4410	to number two cylinder-No2	1		
4	STC8665	to number three cylinder	1		
4	STC8668	to number four cylinder	1		
4	STC8663	to number five cylinder	1		
4	STC8668	to number six cylinder	1		
4	ERR4415	to number seven cylinder-No7	1		
4	STC8667	to number eight cylinder	1		
5	ERR3799	Plug-sparking-RN11YC	8		
6	603672	Clip-spacer-high tension lead ignition	6		
7	587477	Clip-spacer-high tension lead ignition	2		
8	ADU7828L	Clip-spacer-high tension lead ignition-outer	5		
9	AB610041L	Screw-self tapping AB-M8 x 12	4		

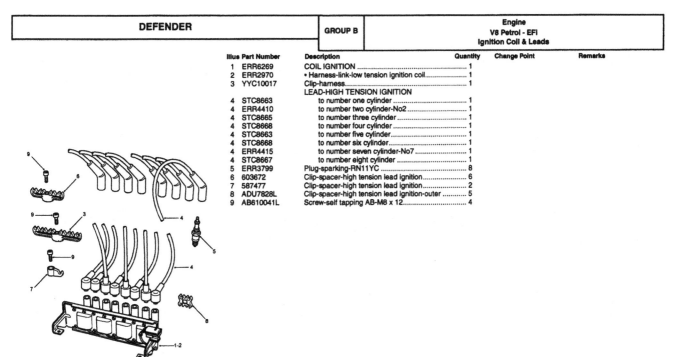

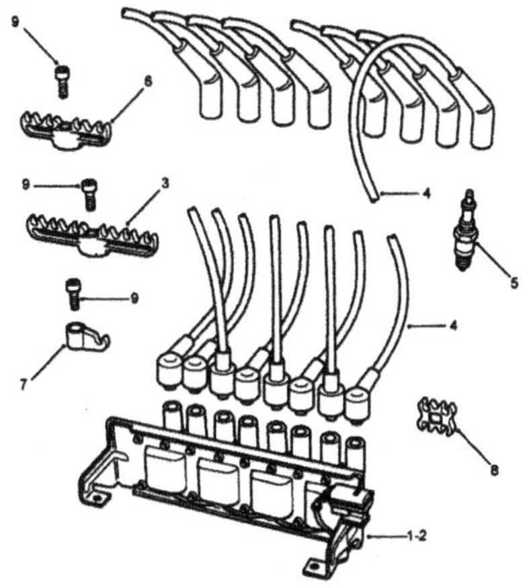

AMBRPA4A

Illus	Part Number	Description	Quantity	Change Point	Remarks
1	AMR4247	Alternator assembly-A127-100 amp-new	1		
2	AMR2218	Nut & washer set-6mm	1		
3	AMR4939	Cover-terminal alternator	1		
4	FB108227	Bolt-flanged head-M8 x 110	2		
5	FN108047L	Nut-flange-flanged head-M8	2		

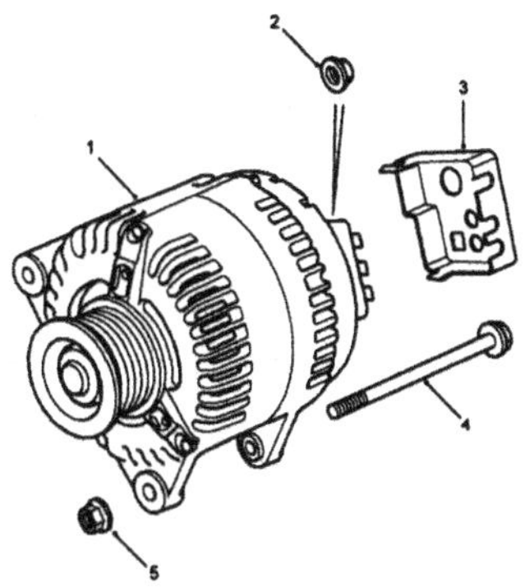

AMBRPC1A

Illus	Part Number	Description	Quantity	Change Point	Remarks
		MOTOR-STARTER ENGINE			
1	NAD101490	BOSCH-NEW	1		
1	NAD101190E	BOSCH-EXCHANGE	NLA		Use NAD101490E.
1	NAD101490E	BOSCH-EXCHANGE	1		
2	STC4465	• Box assembly-brush starter motor	1		
3	STC4462	• Solenoid starter motor	1		
4	STC4464	• Drive assembly starter motor	1		
5	STC1250	• Bush-starter motor-centre	2		
6	STC1255	• Bush-starter motor-front	1		
7	STC1253	• Bush-starter motor-rear	1		

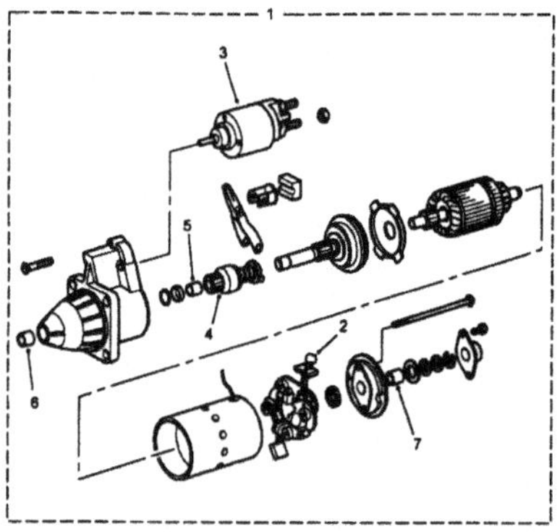

AMBQPE2A

Illus	Part Number	Description	Quantity	Change Point	Remarks
3	WQT100030L	Switch-inertia remote fuel pump	1		
4	ERR6170	Sensor-camshaft engine	1		
5	ERR4815	O ring	1		
6	ERR6119	SENSOR-CRANK ENGINE	1		
8	ADU7346	• Spacer	1		
9	ERR5594	Sensor-knock ignition	2		
10	ERR4278	Potentiometer-throttle multi point injection	1		
11	ERR5032	Plate-throttle potentiometer	1		
12	ERR4352	Motor-multi point injection stepping	1		
13	ERR3359	Gasket-stepping motor	1		
14	ETC8496	Sensor-temperature	1		

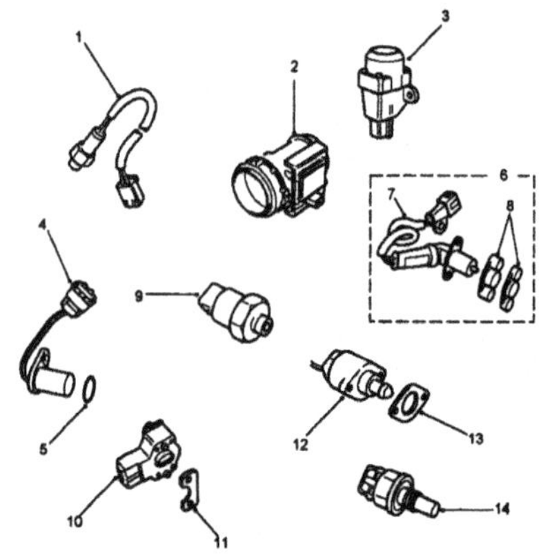

AMBRPG1A

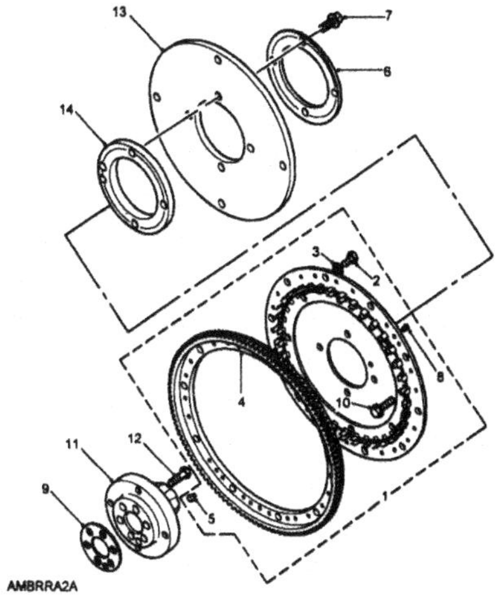

AMBRRA2A

Illus	Part Number	Description	Quantity	Change Point	Remarks
1	ERR5658	PLATE ASSEMBLY-DRIVE TORQUE CONVERTER	1		
2	FTC4388	• Bolt-5/16UNF x 0.58	10		
3	610736	• Washer	10		
4	603340	• GEAR-RING-FLYWHEEL ENGINE	1		
5	529364	• • Dowel-flywheel spigot alignment	2		
6	FTC1117	Plate-support-drive plate automatic transmission	1		
7	FS110251M	Screw-flanged head-M10 x 25	4		
8	571134	Dowel	1		
		SHIM			
9	FTC1680	1.20/1.25mm	A/R		
9	FTC1681	1.30/1.35mm	A/R		
9	FTC1682	1.40/1.45mm	A/R		
9	FTC1683	1.50/1.55mm	A/R		
9	FTC1684	1.60/1.65mm	A/R		
9	FTC1685	1.70/1.75mm	A/R		
9	FTC1686	1.80/1.85mm	A/R		
9	FTC1687	1.90/1.95mm	A/R		
9	FTC1688	2.00/2.05mm	A/R		
9	FTC1689	2.10/2.15mm	A/R		
10	FS110141M	Screw-flanged head-M10 x 14	A/R		
11	FTC1977	Spigot-flywheel alignment	NLA		Use FTC4606.
11	FTC4606	Spigot-flywheel alignment	1		
12	SS607160	Screw-hexagon socket-7/16UNF x 2	6		
13	FTC4607	Plate-drive automatic transmission	1		
14	FTC4608	Spacer-crank/drive plate automatic transmission	1		
	STC3272	KIT-ENGINE BALANCE WEIGHTS	1		
	546198	• Weight-crankshaft balance-0.75 oz	5		
	535781	• Weight-crankshaft balance-1.00 oz	5		
	535782	• Weight-crankshaft balance-1.75 oz	5		
	546194	• Weight-crankshaft balance-2.00 oz	5		

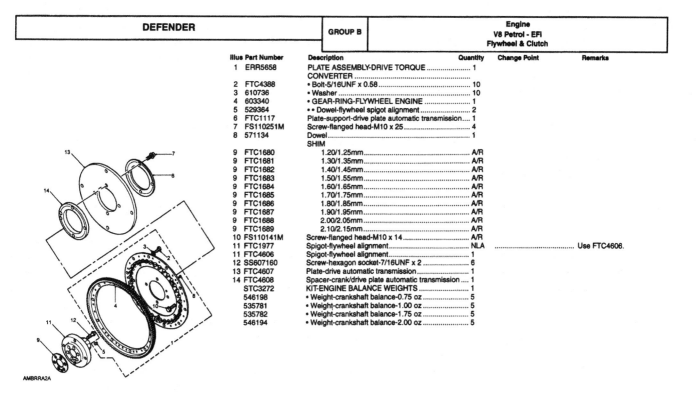

DEFENDER	GROUP C	Gearbox 77mm-5 Speed-Manual Gearbox Assembly

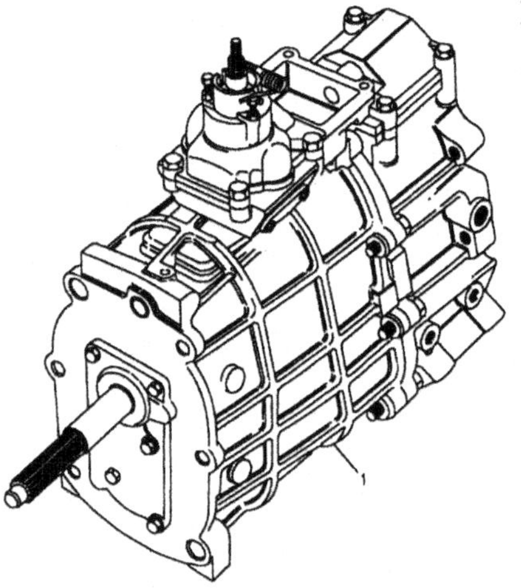

Illus	Part Number	Description	Quantity	Change Point	Remarks
1	FRC5928E	Transmission assembly-exchange	1		50A Suffix A Suffix B Suffix C Suffix D Suffix E
1	RTC6999E	Transmission assembly-exchange	1		50A Suffix F
1	RTC6868E	Transmission assembly-exchange	1		50A Suffix G
1	STC1004E	Transmission assembly-exchange	1		V8 60A
1	STC1005E	Transmission assembly-exchange	1		V8 61A Use with Oil Cooler
1	STC1006E	Transmission assembly-exchange	1		50A Suffix H
1	STC1007E	Transmission assembly-exchange	1		56A Suffix H
1	STC8583E	Transmission assembly-exchange	1		TDi 56A Suffix G
1	STC1549N	Transmission assembly-new	1	Note (1)	50A kit to be used when fitting a new gearbox Suffix E Suffix F Suffix G Suffix H Suffix J
1	TRC102920	Transmission assembly-new	1	Note (2)	50A Suffix K kit to be used when fitting a new gearbox
1	TRC103150	Transmission assembly-new	1		50A kit to be used when fitting a new gearbox Suffix L
	STC2770	Kit-fitting-gearbox R380	1		Kit to be used when fitting a new gearbox
1	FTC4502	Transmission assembly-new	1		44A kit to be used when fitting a new gearbox Suffix J
	STC2770	Kit-fitting-gearbox R380	1		Kit to be used when fitting a new gearbox
1	FTC4506	Transmission assembly	1		43A kit to be used when fitting a new gearbox Suffix J
	STC2770	Kit-fitting-gearbox R380	1		Kit to be used when fitting a new gearbox

CHANGE POINTS:
(1) To (G) 0623639J
(2) From (G) 0623640K

DEFENDER	GROUP C	Gearbox 77mm-5 Speed-Manual Clutch Release-V8

Illus	Part Number	Description	Quantity	Change Point	Remarks
1	UKC8677L	Slave cylinder clutch	NLA		Use FTC5071 which has thicker flange that eliminates the need for backing plate FRC2402.
1	FTC5071	Slave cylinder clutch	1		
	BHM7063L	Kit-repair clutch slave cylinder	1		
2	FRC2402	Plate-backing	1		
3	FS108251L	Screw-flanged head-M8 x 25	NLA		Use FS108257L.
4	WL108001L	Washer-sprung-M8	2		
5	571160	Rod assembly-push slave cylinder	1		
6	576723	Clip-push rod	1		
7	FRC9568	BEARING-CLUTCH RELEASE	NLA		Use FTC5200.
	FRC4078	• Sleeve-guide clutch	1		
7	FTC5200	Bearing-clutch release	1		
8	576137	Arm-clutch release clutch	1		
9	FRC2975	Cap-clutch release lever pivot	1		
10	FRC2528	Pivot-clutch release lever	1		
11	571161	Insert-clutch lever	1		
12	FS106101L	Screw-flanged head-M6 x 10	1		
13	WM106001L	Washer-spring-M6-square	1		
14	571163	Clip-clutch release-pivot post	1		
15	576203	Retention-bearing clutch release	1		
16	FRC4803	Guide-clutch release bearing	1		
17	FRC2481	Dowel	2		
18	SH108401L	Screw-hexagonal head-M8 x 40	1		
19	WL108001L	Washer-sprung-M8	2		

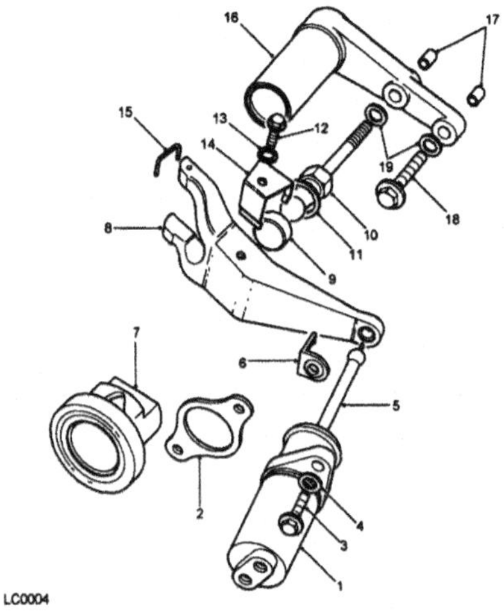

LC0004

Illus	Part Number	Description	Quantity	Change Point	Remarks
1	FRC9568	BEARING-CLUTCH RELEASE	NLA		Use FTC5200.
	FRC4078	• Sleeve-guide clutch	1		
1	FTC5200	Bearing-clutch release	1		
2	FTC2957	Arm-clutch release clutch	1		
3	FRC5255	Pad-clutch release lever slipper	2		
4	FRC5180	Plate assembly	1		
5	FS108307L	Screw-flanged head-M8 x 30	2		
6	WL108001L	Washer-sprung-M8	2		
7	FRC3416	Retention-bearing clutch release	1		
8	591231	Slave cylinder clutch	1		
9	FS108251L	Screw-flanged head-M8 x 25	NLA		Use FS108257L.
10	WL108001L	Washer-sprung-M8	2		
11	591988	Plate-packing	1		
12	FRC3417	Rod-push slave cylinder	1		
13	FRC3327	Clip-push rod to lever	1		

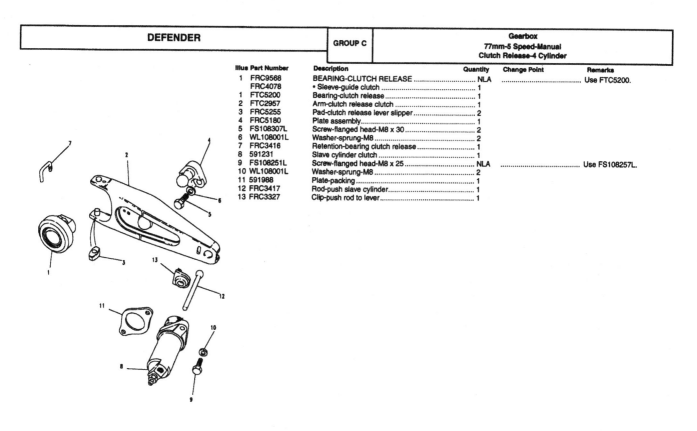

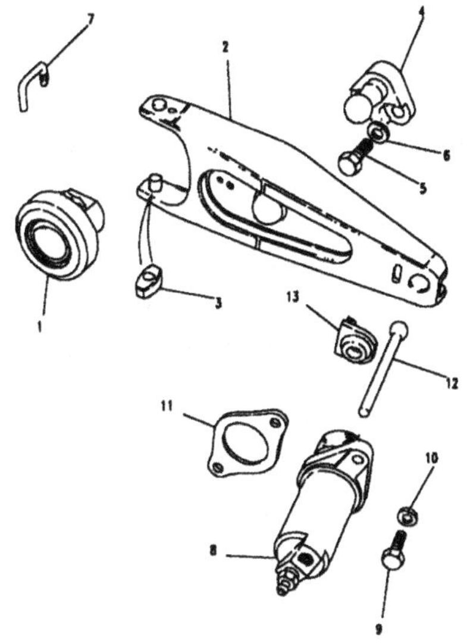

Illus	Part Number	Description	Quantity	Change Point	Remarks
		UP TO SUFFIX E INCLUSIVE			
1	STC471	CASE-MANUAL TRANSMISSION	1		
2	FRC8383	• Pin-reverse gear selector lever pivot	1		
3	WA110061L	• Washer-M10	1		
4	WL110001L	• Washer-M10	1		
5	NH110041L	• Nut-hexagonal head-coarse thread-M10	1		
6	UKC170L	• Dowel	2		
7	FRC6145	Plug and magnet assembly-transmission case	1		
8	FTC4112	Washer-sealing-man trans drain plug	1		
9	TKC1229L	Gasket-centre plate to extension case-gearcase to. plate	1		
10	TKC1235L	Gasket-centre plate to extension case	1		
11	3292	Plug-level	1		
12	UKC24L	Plug-core-6mm	1		
12	UKC30L	Plug-core-9mm	1		
14	TKC5779L	Catcher-manual transmission oil	1		
13	FRC9803	Plug-core-9mm	1		
6	UKC25L	Dowel	1		
2	FRC8383	Pin-reverse gear selector lever pivot	1		
3	WA110061L	Washer-M10	1		
4	WL110001L	Washer-M10	1		
5	NH110041L	Nut-hexagonal head-coarse thread-M10	1		

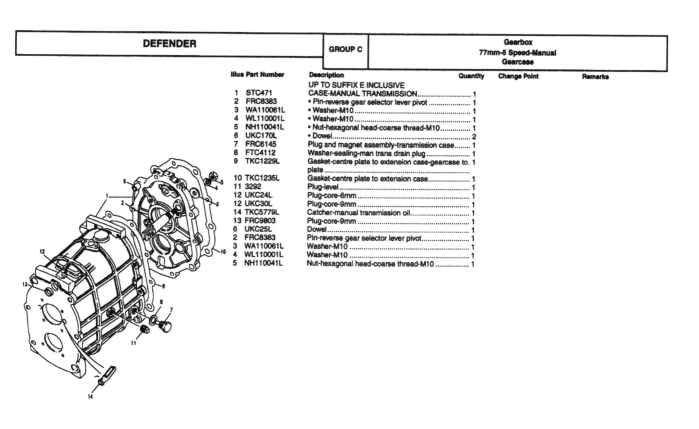

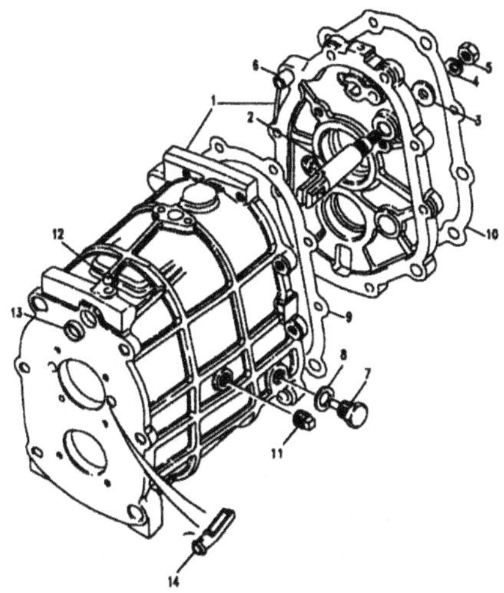

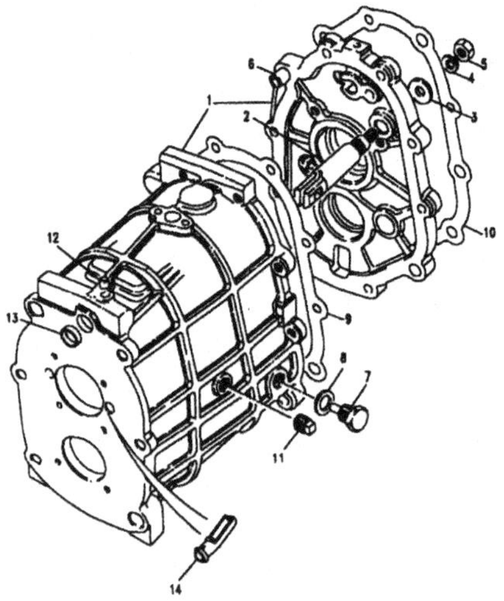

Illus	Part Number	Description	Quantity	Change Point	Remarks
		FROM SUFFIX F			
1	STC1036	CASE-MANUAL TRANSMISSION	1		50A Suffix F
6	UKC170L	• Dowel	2		
1	FTC918	CASE-MANUAL TRANSMISSION	NLA		Use FTC2192 qty 1 with FTC2193 qty 2 with FTC2195 qty 2 with BLS112L qty 2. 50A 56A Suffix G
6	UKC170L	• Dowel	2		
1	FTC2192	Case-manual transmission	1		50A 56A 60A 61A Suffix H
2	FRC8383	Pin-reverse gear selector lever pivot	1		
3	WA110061L	Washer-M10	1		
4	WL110001L	Washer-M10	1		
5	NH110041L	Nut-hexagonal head-coarse thread-M10	1		
6	UKC170L	Dowel	2		
7	FRC6145	Plug and magnet assembly-transmission case	1		
8	FTC4112	Washer-sealing-man trans drain plug	1		
9	TKC1229L	Gasket-centre plate to extension case-gearcase to. plate	1		
10	TKC1235L	Gasket-centre plate to extension case	1		
11	3292	Plug-level	1		
12	UKC24L	Plug-core-6mm	1		
12	UKC30L	Plug-core-9mm	1		
14	TKC5779L	Catcher-manual transmission oil	1		

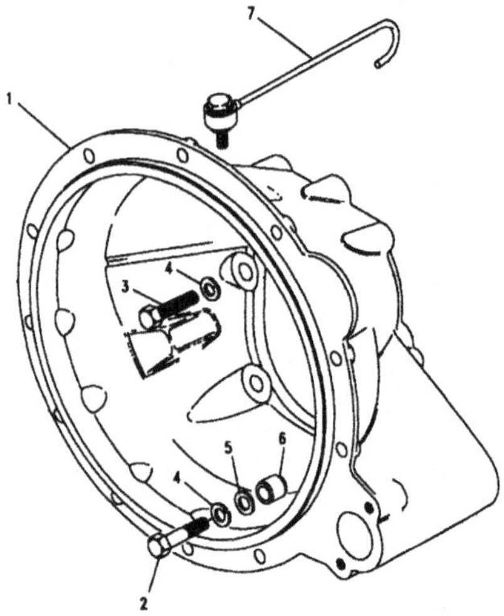

Illus	Part Number	Description	Quantity	Change Point	Remarks
1	FRC9865	Housing-clutch manual transmission	1		50A 56A
1	FRC6154	Housing-clutch manual transmission	1		60A 61A
2	BH112091L	Bolt-housing to g/box-M12 x 45	2		
3	SH112301L	Screw-hexagonal head-M12 x 30	4		
4	WL112001L	Washer	6		
5	WA112081L	Washer-housing to g/box-plain-standard-M12	2		
6	UKC25L	Dowel-hollow	2		
6	FRC8758	Dowel-plug	2		
7	FRC6375	Tube-breather transmission case	1	Note (1)	
7	FRC9428	Tube-breather transmission case	1	Note (2)	
8	FN110047	Nut-flange-gearbox to engine-flange-M10	11		
9	WA110061L	Washer-gearbox to engine-M10	11		
	FTC5409	Clip-pipe	A/R		Td5

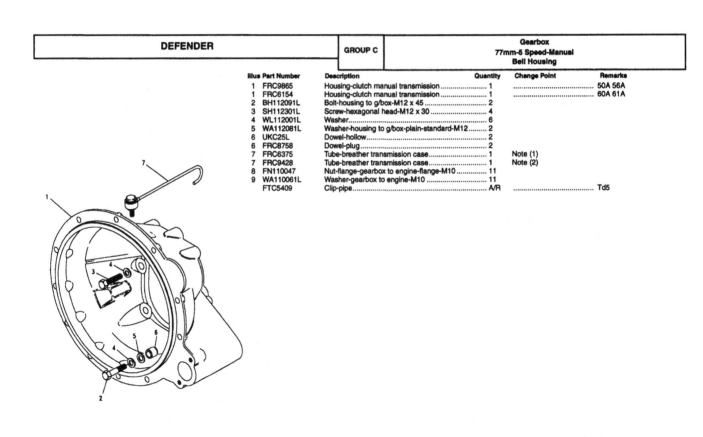

CHANGE POINTS:
(1) To (V) September 1987
(2) From (V) September 1987 To (V) LA 939975

DEFENDER

GROUP C

Gearbox
77mm-5 Speed-Manual
Extension case & Oil Pump To suffix F Inclusive

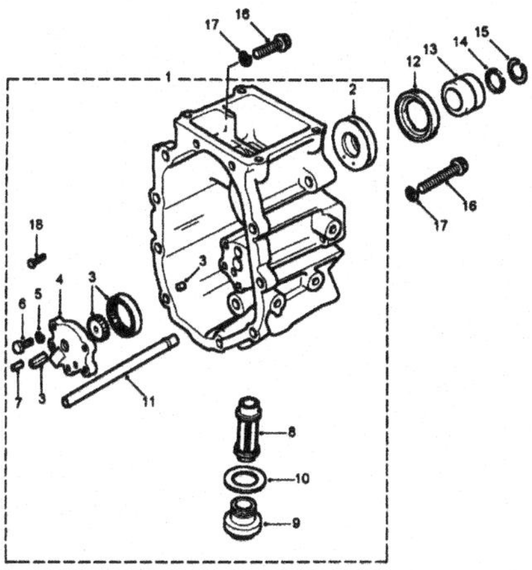

LC0011

Illus	Part Number	Description	Quantity	Change Point	Remarks
1	STC536	CASE-EXTENSION-GEARBOX-EARLY TYPE-TWO HOLES	1		
1	FTC1518	CASE-EXTENSION-GEARBOX-LATER TYPE-ONE HOLE	1		
2	FRC4449	• Ring-mainshaft oil feed-asbestos	1		
7	UKC2738L	• Dowel	2		
8	FRC6244	• Strainer-transmission oil	1		
9	90571104	• Plug	1		
10	FRC4810	• Washer-sealing-man trans extension case drain plug	1		
11	FRC8104	• Pipe-transmission oil inlet	1		
	FTC890	• Stud	1		Part of FTC1518.
	FTC1533	• Screw-grub	1		Part of FTC1518.
2	FTC2210	• Ring-mainshaft oil feed-asbestos free	1		Part of FTC1518.
3	STC822	• Gear-oil pump	1		Part of FTC1518.
4	FTC1403	• Body-transmission oil pump	1	To (G) 0207405H	Part of FTC1518.
4	FTC3623	• Body-transmission oil pump	1	From (G) 0207406H	Part of FTC1518.
5	WA106001L	• Washer-M6	3		Part of FTC1518.
6	BH106061L	• Bolt-hexagonal head-M6 x 30	3		Part of FTC1518.
	RTC2057	Kit-oil pump repair	NLA		Use STC820.
	STC820	Kit-oil pump repair	1		
4	FRC6246	Body-transmission oil pump	1		
17	WL106001L	Washer-sprung-M6	3		
18	FS106201L	Screw-flanged head-M6 x 20	3		
12	FRC2365	Seal-oil	1		
13	FRC4493	Collar-oil seal	1		
14	FRC4501	O ring-collar	1		
15	FRC4494	Spring ring-collar	1		
16	FB108101L	Bolt-extension to gearbox-flanged head-M8 x 50	2		
16	FRC4282	Bolt-extension to gearbox-flanged head-M8 x 60	8		
17	WL108001L	Washer-sprung-M8	10		

DEFENDER

GROUP C

Gearbox
77mm-5 Speed-Manual
Extension case & Oil Pump From Suffix G

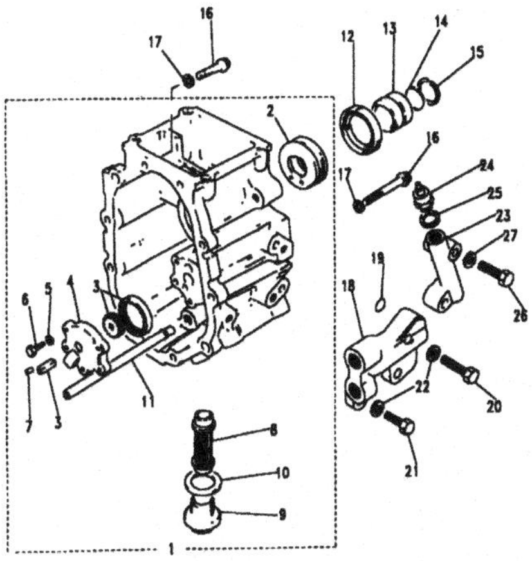

Illus	Part Number	Description	Quantity	Change Point	Remarks
1	FTC1518	CASE-EXTENSION-GEARBOX	1		50A Suffix G Suffix H
1	FTC1518	CASE-EXTENSION-GEARBOX	1		56A Suffix G Suffix H
1	FTC2102	CASE-EXTENSION-GEARBOX	1		60A Suffix G
1	FTC2190	CASE-EXTENSION-GEARBOX	1		61A Suffix G
	FTC890	• Stud	1		
	FTC1533	• Screw-grub	1		
2	FRC4449	• Ring-mainshaft oil feed-asbestos	1		
2	FTC2210	• Ring-mainshaft oil feed-asbestos free	1		
3	STC822	• Gear-oil pump	1		
4	FTC1403	• Body-transmission oil pump	1	Note (1)	
4	FTC3623	• Body-transmission oil pump	1	Note (2)	
5	WA106001L	• Washer-M6	3		
6	BH106061L	• Bolt-hexagonal head-M6 x 30	3		
7	UKC2738L	• Dowel	2		
8	FRC6244	• Strainer-transmission oil	1		
9	90571104	• Plug	1		
10	FRC4810	• Washer-sealing-man trans extension case drain plug	1		
11	FRC8104	• Pipe-transmission oil inlet	1		
12	FRC2365	Seal-oil	1		
13	FRC4493	Collar-oil seal	1		
14	FRC4501	O ring-collar	1		
15	FRC4494	Spring ring-collar	1		
16	FB108101L	Bolt-flanged head-M8 x 50	2		
16	FRC4282	Bolt-flanged head-M8 x 60	8		
17	WL108001L	Washer-sprung-M8	10		
18	FTC1404	Housing-transmission thermostat	1		61A
19	FTC1441	O ring-man trans thermostat housing	2		
20	SH108401L	Screw-hexagonal head-M8 x 40	1		
21	FS108307L	Screw-flanged head-M8 x 30	2		61A
22	WA108051L	Washer-8mm	3		
23	FTC2104	Housing-transmission thermostat	1		60A
24	PRC8873	Transducer oil temperature-basic	1		
25	232042	Washer-sealing	1		
26	SH108401L	Screw-hexagonal head-M8 x 40	2		
27	WA108051L	Washer-8mm	2		

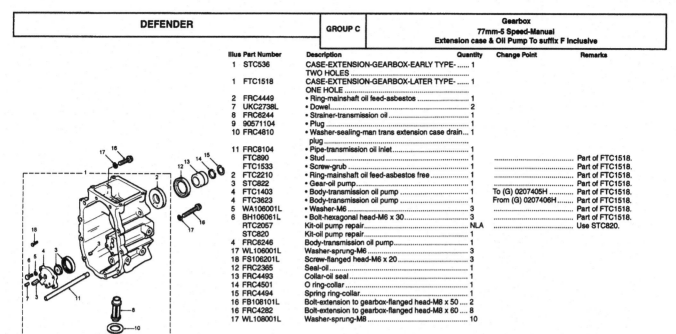

CHANGE POINTS:
(1) To (G) 0207405H
(2) From (G) 0207406H

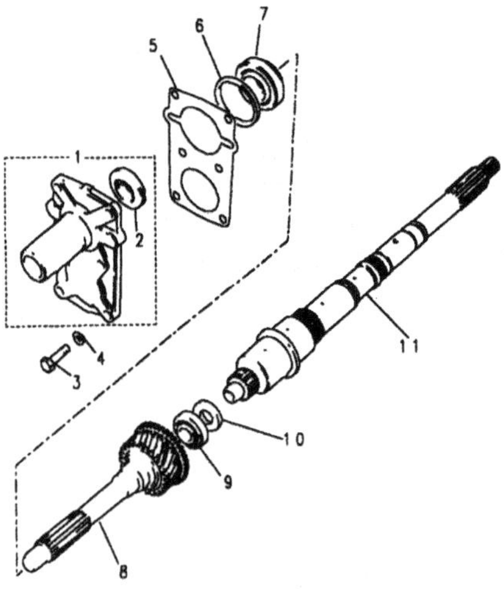

Illus	Part Number	Description	Quantity	Change Point	Remarks
1	FRC4856	COVER-END MANUAL TRANSMISSION	1		Suffix A Suffix B Suffix C Suffix D Suffix E
1	FTC311	COVER-END MANUAL TRANSMISSION-FRONT-LONG	1		Suffix F
1	FTC1438	COVER-END MANUAL TRANSMISSION	1		Suffix G
1	FTC1438	COVER-END MANUAL TRANSMISSION	1	To (G) 0242819H	50A 56A 60A 61A Suffix H
1	FTC2822	COVER-END MANUAL TRANSMISSION-FRONT-SHORT	1	From (G) 0242820H	50A 56A 60A 61A Suffix H
2	UKC1060L	• Seal	NLA		Use FTC5303.
2	FTC5303	• Seal	1		
3	FS108251L	Screw-flanged head-M8 x 25	NLA		Use FS108257L.
4	WA108051L	Washer-8mm	6		
5	FRC4873	Gasket-front cover manual transmission	1		Suffix A Suffix B Suffix C Suffix D Suffix E
5	FTC316	Gasket-front cover manual transmission	1		Suffix F
6	FRC4327	Shim-man trans primary shaft bearing/front cover-1.51mm	A/R		
6	FRC4329	Shim-man trans primary shaft bearing/front cover-1.57mm	A/R		
6	FRC4331	Shim-man trans primary shaft bearing/front cover-1.63mm	A/R		
6	FRC4333	Shim-man trans primary shaft bearing/front cover-1.69mm	A/R		
6	FRC4335	Shim-man trans primary shaft bearing/front cover-1.75mm	A/R		
6	FRC4337	Shim-man trans primary shaft bearing/front cover-1.81mm	A/R		
6	FRC4339	Shim-man trans primary shaft bearing/front cover-1.87mm	A/R		
6	FRC4341	Shim-man trans primary shaft bearing/front cover-1.93mm	A/R		
6	FRC4343	Shim-man trans primary shaft bearing/front cover-1.99mm	A/R		
6	FRC4345	Shim-man trans primary shaft bearing/front cover-2.05mm	A/R		
6	FRC4347	Shim-man trans primary shaft bearing/front cover-2.11mm	A/R		

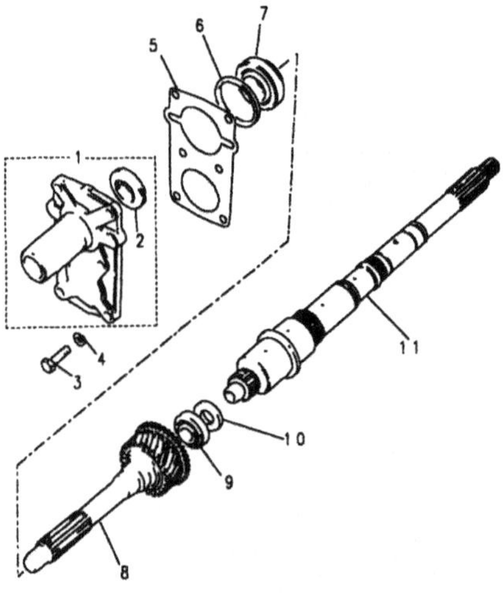

Illus	Part Number	Description	Quantity	Change Point	Remarks
6	FRC4349	Shim-man trans primary shaft bearing/front cover-2.17mm	A/R		
6	FRC4351	Shim-man trans primary shaft bearing/front cover-2.23mm	A/R		
6	FRC4353	Shim-man trans primary shaft bearing/front cover-2.29mm	A/R		
6	FRC4355	Shim-man trans primary shaft bearing/front cover-2.35mm	A/R		
6	FRC4357	Shim-man trans primary shaft bearing/front cover-2.41mm	A/R		
6	FRC4359	Shim-man trans primary shaft bearing/front cover-2.47mm	A/R		
6	FRC4361	Shim-man trans primary shaft bearing/front cover-2.53mm	A/R		
6	FRC4363	Shim-man trans primary shaft bearing/front cover-2.59mm	A/R		
6	FRC4365	Shim-man trans primary shaft bearing/front cover-2.65mm	A/R		
6	FRC4367	Shim-man trans primary shaft bearing/front cover-2.71mm	A/R		
6	FRC4369	Shim-man trans primary shaft bearing/front cover-2.77mm	A/R		
7	RTC6751	Bearing-taper roller-man trans mainshaft/primary shaft-35.0 x 68.5	1		
8	FRC4845	SHAFT-PINION DIFFERENTIAL	1		50A Suffix E Suffix F
8	FTC347	SHAFT-PINION DIFFERENTIAL	1		60A 61A Suffix H
	FTC1293	• Disc synchro stop-mainshaft	1		
8	FTC1406	SHAFT-PINION DIFFERENTIAL	1		50A Suffix G Suffix H
8	FTC1428	SHAFT-PINION DIFFERENTIAL	1		56A Suffix G Suffix H
	FTC1112	• Disc synchro stop-mainshaft	1		
9	UKC8L	Bearing-taper roller-man trans mainshaft/centre plate-17.5 x 40.0	1		
	FTC4504	Pinion primary	1		
10	UKC37L	Spacer	1		
11	FRC5305	Shaft-main manual transmission	1		50A Suffix E Suffix F
11	FTC1446	Shaft-main manual transmission	1		50A 56A Suffix G
11	FTC1282	Shaft-main manual transmission	NLA		Use STC1889.
11	STC1889	Shaft-main manual transmission	1	Note (1)	50A 56A 60A 61A Suffix H
11	STC1889	Shaft-main manual transmission	1	Note (2)	50A 56A 60A 61A Suffix H

CHANGE POINTS:
(1) To (G) 0242819H
(2) From (G) 0242820H

DEFENDER	GROUP C	Gearbox 77mm-5 Speed-Manual Mainshaft Gears 3/4th

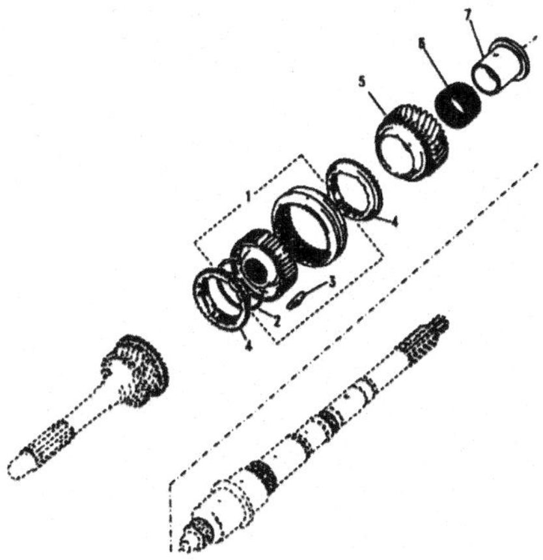

Illus	Part Number	Description	Quantity	Change Point	Remarks
1	FRC9792L	SYNCHRONISER ASSEMBLY-3RD & 4TH MAINSHAFT ASSEMBLY	1	Note (1)	50A 56A 60A 61A
2	UKC31L	• Spring 1st & 2nd synchroniser	2		
3	UKC3530L	• Plate-synchroniser	3		
4	FRC8232	• Ring-baulk	2		
5	TKC6962L	Gear-3rd driven manual transmission	1		50A Suffix A Suffix B Suffix C Suffix D Suffix E Suffix F
5	FTC358	Gear-3rd driven manual transmission	1		50A 56A Suffix G
5	FTC2504	Gear-3rd driven manual transmission	1		60A 61A
5	FTC2505	Gear-3rd driven manual transmission	1		50A 56A Suffix H
6	FTC1313	Bearing-needle roller	1		50A 56A 60A 61A Suffix H
7	FTC1310	Bush-3rd gear	1		

CHANGE POINTS:
(1) To (V) LA 939975

DEFENDER	GROUP C	Gearbox 77mm-5 Speed-Manual Mainshaft Gears 1st/2nd/5th

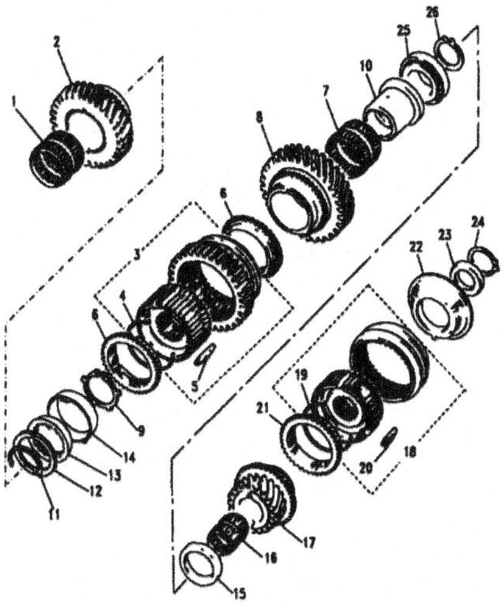

Illus	Part Number	Description	Quantity	Change Point	Remarks
		1ST AND 2ND GEARS			
1	FRC5678	Bearing-needle roller	2		50A 56A Suffix A Suffix B Suffix C Suffix D Suffix E Suffix F Suffix G
1	FTC1312	Bearing-needle roller	NLA		Use TUK10011L.
1	TUK10011L	Bearing-needle roller	1		50A 56A 60A 61A Suffix H
2	FRC5279	Gear-2nd driven manual transmission	1		50A Suffix A Suffix B Suffix C Suffix D Suffix E Suffix F
2	FTC357	Gear-2nd driven manual transmission	1		50A 56A Suffix G
2	FTC2462	Gear-2nd driven manual transmission	1		50A 56A 60A 61A Suffix H
3	FRC6670	Synchroniser assembly-1st & 2nd mainshaft assembly	1	To (G) 0173664	50A Suffix A Suffix B Suffix C Suffix D Suffix E Suffix F
3	FRC9386	SYNCHRONISER ASSEMBLY-1ST & 2ND MAINSHAFT ASSEMBLY	1	From (G) 0173665	50A Suffix A Suffix B Suffix C Suffix D Suffix E Suffix F
4	UKC31L	• Spring 1st & 2nd synchroniser	2		
5	UKC3531L	• Plate-synchroniser	3		
6	FRC8232	• Ring-baulk	2		
3	FTC1327	SYNCHRONISER ASSEMBLY-1ST & 2ND MAINSHAFT ASSEMBLY	1		50A 56A Suffix G
4	UKC31L	• Spring 1st & 2nd synchroniser	1		
5	UKC3531L	• Plate-synchroniser	3		
6	FTC2282	Ring-baulk-1st/2nd gear	NLA		Land Rover recommend replacement of 1st & 2nd syncro assy to STC8577 if this baulk ring fails..
3	STC8577	SYNCHRONISER ASSEMBLY-1ST & 2ND MAINSHAFT ASSEMBLY	1		50A 56A 60A 61A Suffix H
4	FTC2285	• Spring 1st & 2nd synchroniser	2		
5	FTC4011	• Plate-synchroniser-manual	3		
6	FTC4007	• Ring-baulk	1		
	FTC1361	Gear-1st & 2nd synchroniser mainshaft reversal	1		
	FTC3373	Plate	3		61A Suffix H

DEFENDER	GROUP C	Gearbox 77mm-5 Speed-Manual Mainshaft Gears 1st/2nd/5th

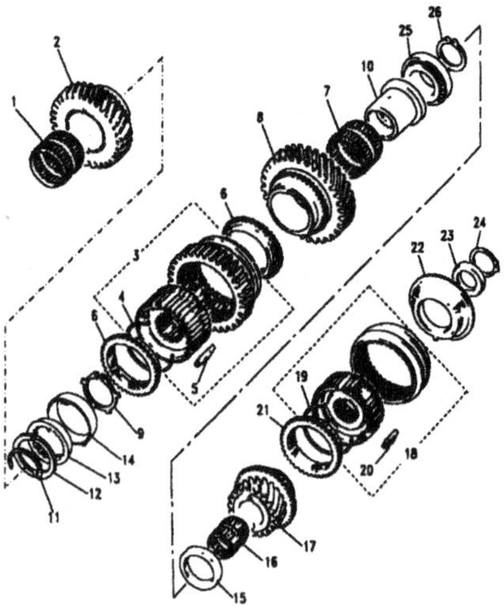

Illus	Part Number	Description	Quantity	Change Point	Remarks
7	FRC5679	Bearing-needle roller manual transmission	1		Suffix A Suffix B Suffix C
					Suffix D Suffix E Suffix F
					Suffix G
7	FTC1311	Bearing-needle roller manual transmission	NLA		Use TUK100340.
					Suffix H
7	TUK100340	Bearing-needle roller manual transmission	1		Suffix H
8	FRC5253	Gear-1st driven manual transmission	1		50A Suffix A Suffix B
					Suffix C Suffix D Suffix E
					Suffix F
8	FTC2089	Gear-1st driven manual transmission	1		50A Suffix G
8	FTC2090	Gear-1st driven manual transmission	1		TDi 56A Suffix G
8	FTC1760	Gear-1st driven manual transmission	1		50A Suffix H
8	FTC1989	Gear-1st driven manual transmission	1		56A 60A 61A Suffix H
	UKC37L	Spacer-synchro-hub/pilot	1		
9	FTC2084	Circlip-1st & 2nd Hub	2	Note (1)	
9	FTC4009	Circlip-1st & 2nd Hub	2	Note (2)	
		BUSH-1ST GEAR SELECTIVE			
10	FRC5243	40.16 to 40.21mm	A/R		50A 56A Suffix A Suffix B
10	FRC5244	40.21 to 40.26mm	A/R		Suffix C Suffix D Suffix E
10	FRC5245	40.26 to 40.31mm	A/R		Suffix F Suffix G
10	FRC5246	40.31 to 40.36mm	A/R		
10	FRC5247	40.36 to 40.41mm	A/R		
		BUSH-1ST GEAR SELECTIVE			
10	FTC2005	30.905 to 30.955mm	NLA		Use TUJ100050.
					50A 56A 60A 61A Suffix H
10	FTC2006	30.955 to 31.005mm	1		50A 56A 60A 61A Suffix H
10	FTC2007	31.005 to 31.055mm	1		50A 56A 60A 61A Suffix H
10	FTC2008	31.055 to 31.105mm	1		50A 56A 60A 61A Suffix H
10	FTC2009	31.105 to 31.155mm	1		50A 56A 60A 61A Suffix H
10	TUJ100050	30.905 to 30.955mm	1		50A 56A 60A 61A Suffix H
11	FTC1752	Circlip-man trans 2nd gear thrust washer	1		50A 56A 60A 61A Suffix H
12	FTC1301	Washer-thrust manual transmission-1st/2nd gear	1		50A 56A 60A 61A Suffix H
13	FTC2283	Cone-synchronizer inner	NLA		Land Rover recommends
					that if this cone needs
					replacement it should be
					replaced with new
					1st/2nd synchro cone
					STC8577.
					50A 56A 60A 61A Suffix
					H

CHANGE POINTS:
(1) To (G) 0242819H
(2) From (G) 0242820H

DEFENDER	GROUP C	Gearbox 77mm-5 Speed-Manual Mainshaft Gears 1st/2nd/5th

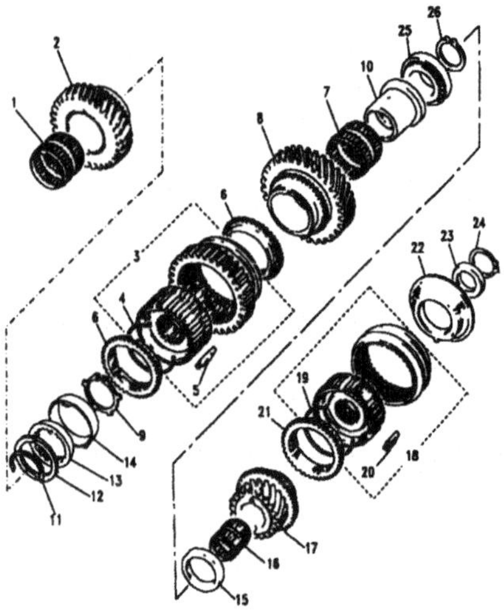

Illus	Part Number	Description	Quantity	Change Point	Remarks
14	FTC2284	Ring-synchroniser friction	1		50A 56A 60A 61A Suffix H
13	FTC4008	Cone-synchronizer inner	1	Note (1)	
14	FTC4010	Ring-synchroniser friction	1		
		5TH GEAR			
15	FRC4321	Collar-distance manual transmission	1		Suffix A Suffix B Suffix C
					Suffix D Suffix E Suffix F
15	FTC916	Collar-distance manual transmission	1		Suffix G
16	FRC5280	Bearing-needle roller manual transmission	1		
17	RKC5098L	Gear-5th speed main shaft manual transmission	1		50A Suffix A Suffix B
					Suffix C Suffix D Suffix E
					Suffix F
17	FTC1791	Gear-5th speed main shaft manual transmission	1		50A 56A 60A 61A Suffix G
					Suffix H
18	FRC9389	Synchroniser assembly-5th gear mainshaft assembly	1		50A Suffix A Suffix B
					Suffix C Suffix D Suffix E
					Suffix F
18	FTC1455	SYNCHRONISER ASSEMBLY-5TH GEAR MAINSHAFT ASSEMBLY	1		50A 56A 60A 61A Suffix G
					Suffix H
19	UKC31L	• Spring 1st & 2nd synchroniser	2		
20	UKC3530L	• Plate-synchroniser	3		
21	FRC8232	Ring-baulk-5th gear	1		
22	FRC5235	Plate-5th gear synchroniser support	1		

CHANGE POINTS:
(1) From (G) 0242820H

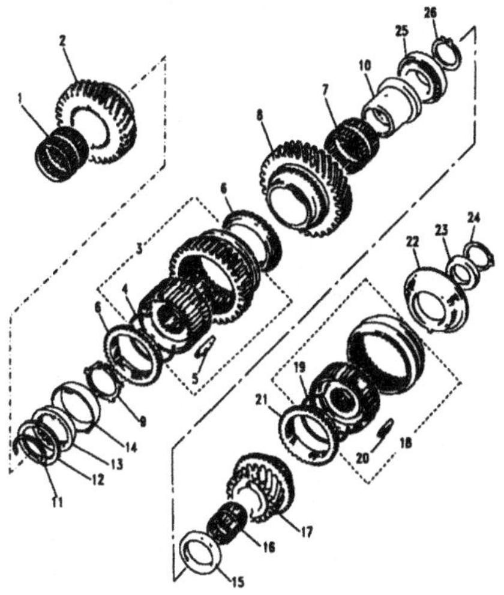

Illus	Part Number	Description	Quantity	Change Point	Remarks
		SHIM			
23	FRC5284	man trans 5th gear synchroniser hub-5.10mm			
23	FRC5286	man trans 5th gear synchroniser hub-5.16mm	A/R		
23	FRC5288	man trans 5th gear synchroniser hub-5.22mm	A/R		
23	FRC5290	man trans 5th gear synchroniser hub-5.28mm	A/R		
23	FRC5292	man trans 5th gear synchroniser hub-5.34mm	A/R		
23	FRC5294	man trans 5th gear synchroniser hub-5.40mm	A/R		
23	FRC5296	man trans 5th gear synchroniser hub-5.46mm	A/R		
23	FRC5298	man trans 5th gear synchroniser hub-5.52mm	A/R		
23	FRC5300	man trans 5th gear synchroniser hub-5.58mm	A/R		
23	FRC5302	man trans 5th gear synchroniser hub-5.64mm	A/R		
24	FRC9526	Circlip-man trans 5th gear synchroniser hub	1		
25	RTC2914	Bearing-taper roller	1		
26	FRC9812	Circlip	1		

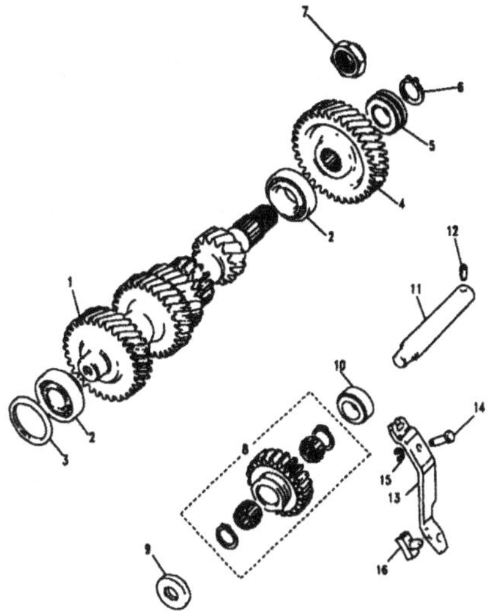

Illus	Part Number	Description	Quantity	Change Point	Remarks
1	FRC7575	Shaft-lay	1	To (G) 0173664	
1	FRC8141	Shaft-lay	1	From (G) 0173665	
2	ULC1796L	Bearing-taper roller-man trans countershaft/centre plate	1		
2	ULC1796L	Bearing-taper roller-man trans countershaft/main case	1		
3	TKC4633	Shim-man trans countershaft bearing/front cover-1.69mm	A/R		
3	TKC4635L	Shim-man trans countershaft bearing/front cover-1.75mm	A/R		
3	TKC4637	Shim-man trans countershaft bearing/front cover-1.81mm	A/R		
3	TKC4639	Shim-man trans countershaft bearing/front cover-1.87mm	A/R		
3	TKC4641	Shim-man trans countershaft bearing/front cover-1.93mm	A/R		
3	TKC4643L	Shim-man trans countershaft bearing/front cover-1.99mm	A/R		
3	TKC4645	Shim-man trans countershaft bearing/front cover-2.05mm	A/R		
3	TKC4647L	Shim-man trans countershaft bearing/front cover-2.11mm	A/R		
3	TKC4649	Shim-man trans countershaft bearing/front cover-2.17mm	A/R		
3	TKC4651L	Shim-man trans countershaft bearing/front cover-2.23mm	A/R		
3	TKC4653L	Shim-man trans countershaft bearing/front cover-2.29mm	A/R		
3	TKC4655L	Shim-man trans countershaft bearing/front cover-2.35mm	A/R		
3	TKC4657L	Shim-man trans countershaft bearing/front cover-2.41mm	A/R		
3	TKC4659L	Shim-man trans countershaft bearing/front cover-2.47mm	A/R		
3	TKC4661L	Shim-man trans countershaft bearing/front cover-2.53mm	A/R		
3	TKC4663L	Shim-man trans countershaft bearing/front cover-2.59mm	A/R		
4	FRC5162	Gear-5th speed-layshaft	1		
5	UKC1689L	Washer-5th speed layshaft	1		
6	UKC1690L	Circlip-gear/layshaft	1		
7	FRC7214	Nut-stake-man trans countershaft	1		

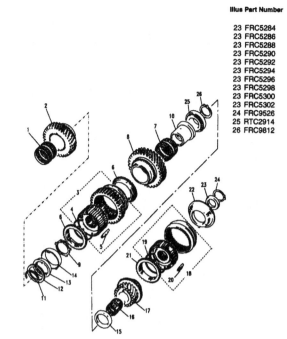

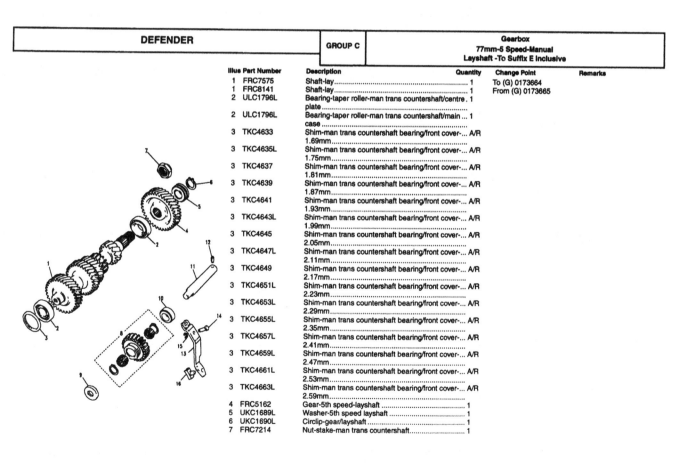

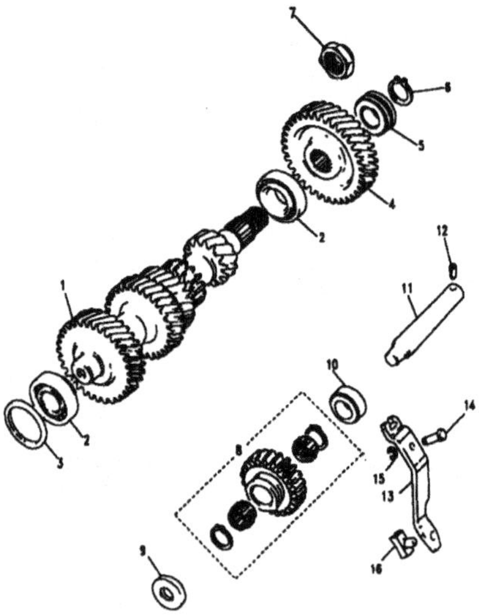

Illus	Part Number	Description	Quantity	Change Point	Remarks
8	FRC7602	Gear-reverse manual transmission	1	To (G) 0173664	
8	FRC8285	Gear-reverse manual transmission	1	From (G) 0173665	
9	FRC4947	Spacer	1		
10	FRC5186	Spacer-rear	1		
11	FRC5095	Shaft-reverse idler assembly-manual transmission	1		
12	UKC18L	Pin-roll	1		
13	TKC1428L	Lever-selector selector mechanism-reverse	1	To (G) 0173664	
13	FRC8246	Lever-selector selector mechanism-reverse	1	From (G) 0173665	
14	UKC2662L	Pin-reverse gear selector lever pivot	1	To (G) 0173664	
14	FRC8382	Pin-reverse gear selector lever pivot	1	From (G) 0173665	
15	13H2023L	Circlip	1		
16	FRC4946	Pad-buffer-reverse gear	1	To (G) 0173664	
16	FRC8384	Pad-buffer-reverse gear	1	From (G) 0173665	

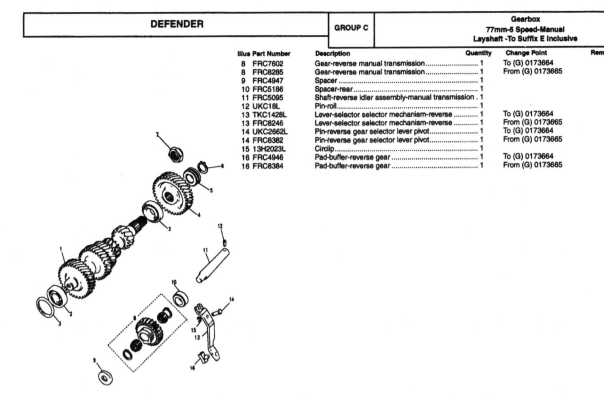

Illus	Part Number	Description	Quantity	Change Point	Remarks
1	FRC9761	Shaft-lay	1		50A Suffix A Suffix B Suffix C Suffix D Suffix E Suffix F
1	FTC1416	Shaft-lay	1		50A Suffix G Suffix H
1	FTC1074	Shaft-lay	1		56A 60A 61A
2	FTC317	Bearing-taper roller-man trans countershaft/centre plate-31.75 x 59.0	1		
3	FTC248	Bearing-taper roller-man trans countershaft/main case-31.75 x 62.0	1		

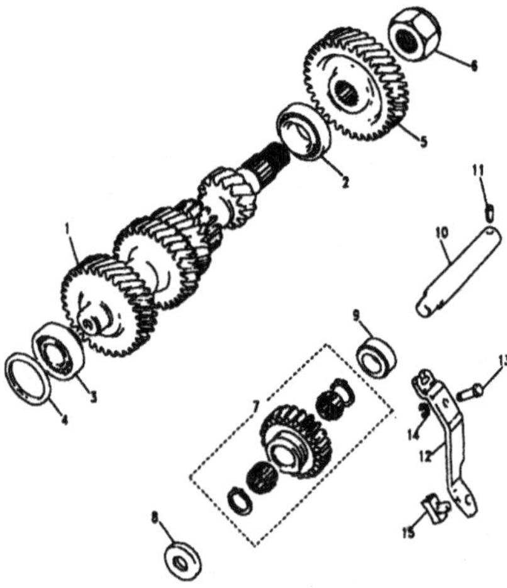

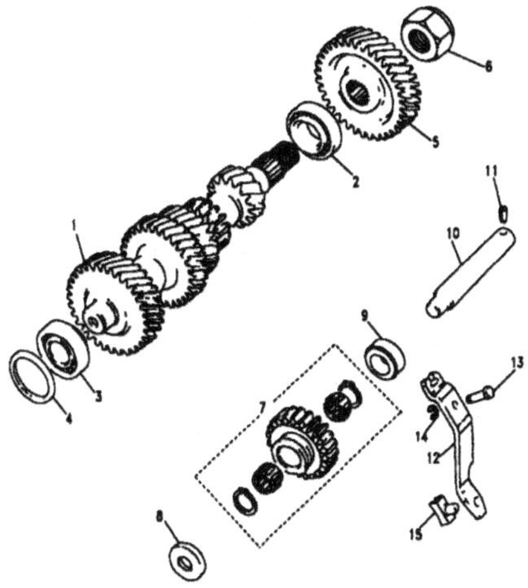

Illus	Part Number	Description	Quantity	Change Point	Remarks
4	FTC263	Shim-man trans countershaft bearing/front cover-1.39mm	1		
4	FTC265	Shim-man trans countershaft bearing/front cover-1.45mm	1		
4	FTC267	Shim-man trans countershaft bearing/front cover-1.51mm	1		
4	FTC269	Shim-man trans countershaft bearing/front cover-1.57mm	1		
4	FTC271	Shim-man trans countershaft bearing/front cover-1.63mm	1		
4	FTC273	Shim-man trans countershaft bearing/front cover-1.69mm	1		
4	FTC275	Shim-man trans countershaft bearing/front cover-1.75mm	1		
4	FTC277	Shim-man trans countershaft bearing/front cover-1.81mm	1		
4	FTC279	Shim-man trans countershaft bearing/front cover-1.87mm	1		
4	FTC281	Shim-man trans countershaft bearing/front cover-1.93mm	1		
4	FTC283	Shim-man trans countershaft bearing/front cover-1.99mm	1		
4	FTC285	Shim-man trans countershaft bearing/front cover-2.05mm	1		
4	FTC287	Shim-man trans countershaft bearing/front cover-2.11mm	1		
4	FTC289	Shim-man trans countershaft bearing/front cover-2.17mm	1		
4	FTC291	Shim-man trans countershaft bearing/front cover-2.23mm	1		
4	FTC293	Shim-man trans countershaft bearing/front cover-2.29mm	1		
4	FTC295	Shim-man trans countershaft bearing/front cover-2.35mm	1		

Illus	Part Number	Description	Quantity	Change Point	Remarks
5	FRC9758	Gear-5th speed countershaft manual transmission	1		50A Suffix A Suffix B Suffix C Suffix D Suffix E Suffix F
5	FTC419	Gear-5th speed countershaft manual transmission	1		50A Suffix G Suffix H
5	FTC419	Gear-5th speed countershaft manual transmission	1		56A 60A 61A
6	FRC7214	Nut-stake	1		
7	FRC8285	Gear-reverse manual transmission	1		
8	FRC4947	Spacer	1		
9	FRC5186	Spacer-rear	1		
10	FRC5095	Shaft-reverse idler assembly-manual transmission	1		
11	UKC18L	Pin-roll	1		
12	FRC8246	Lever-selector selector mechanism	1		
13	FRC8382	Pin-reverse gear selector lever pivot	1		
14	13H2023L	Circlip	1		
15	FTC1435	Pad-reverse gear selector lever	1		

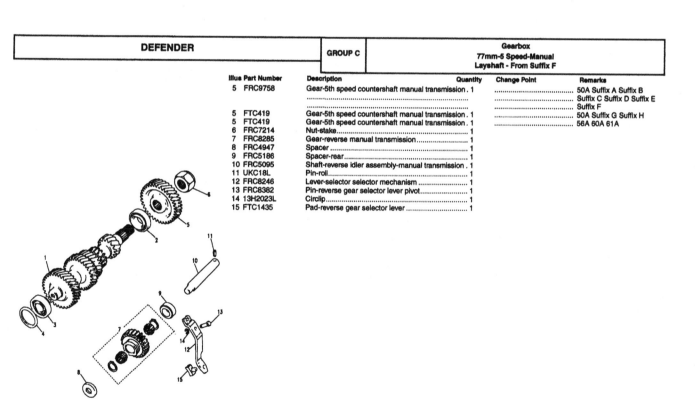

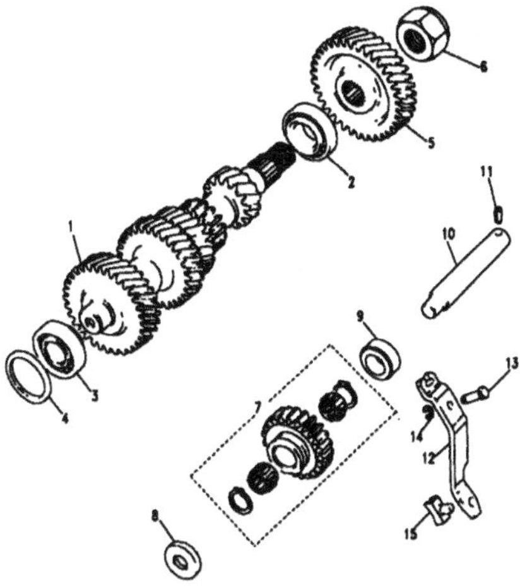

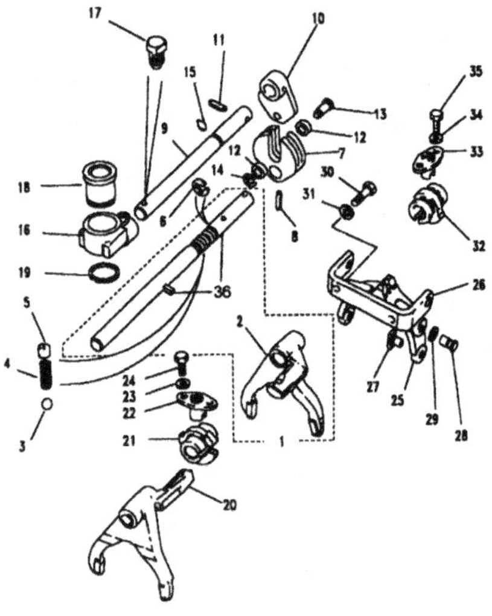

Illus	Part Number	Description	Quantity	Change Point	Remarks
1	FTC1814	SHAFT & LEVER ASSEMBLY-SELECTOR MANUAL TRANSMISSION	1	To (V) LA 939975	50A Suffix A Suffix B Suffix C Suffix D Suffix E Suffix F Suffix G
2	FTC1490	• Fork assembly-selector-1st/2nd manual transmission	1		
36	FRC8127	• Pin-selector lever/shaft manual transmission	2		
1	FTC1765	SHAFT & LEVER ASSEMBLY-SELECTOR MANUAL TRANSMISSION	NLA	To (V) LA 939975	Use FTC1764. 50A Suffix H
1	FTC1764	• SHAFT & LEVER ASSEMBLY-SELECTOR MANUAL TRANSMISSION	1		
2	FTC2450	• • Fork assembly-selector-1st/2nd manual transmission	1		
36	FRC8127	• • Pin-selector lever/shaft manual transmission	2		
1	FTC1765	SHAFT & LEVER ASSEMBLY-SELECTOR MANUAL TRANSMISSION	NLA	To (V) LA 939975	Use FTC1764. 56A 60A 61A
1	FTC1764	• SHAFT & LEVER ASSEMBLY-SELECTOR MANUAL TRANSMISSION	1		
2	FTC2450	• • Fork assembly-selector-1st/2nd manual transmission	1		
36	FRC8127	• • Pin-selector lever/shaft manual transmission	2		
3	BLS112L	Ball-detent manual transmission	1	To (V) LA 939975	50A Suffix A Suffix B
4	FRC7195	Spring-detent manual transmission	1		Suffix C Suffix D Suffix E
5	UKC75L	Plug-spring retaining	1		Suffix F Suffix G
3	BLS112L	Ball-detent manual transmission	1		50A Suffix H
3	BLS112L	Ball-detent manual transmission	1		56A 60A 61A
4	FTC3382	Spring-detent manual transmission	1		50A Suffix H
4	FTC3382	Spring-detent manual transmission	1		56A 60A 61A

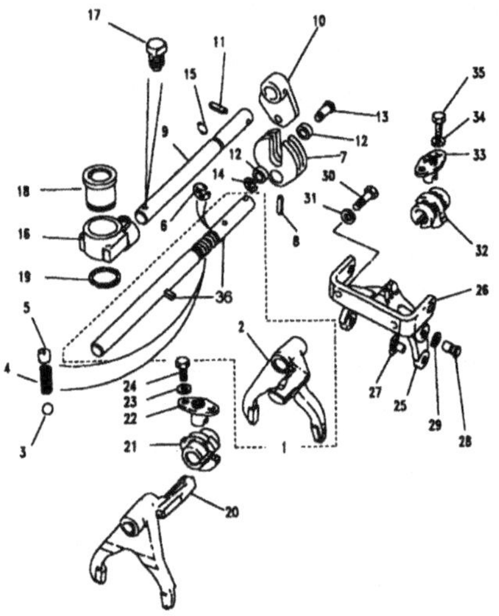

Illus	Part Number	Description	Quantity	Change Point	Remarks
5	FTC2193	Plug	1		50A Suffix H
5	FTC2193	Plug	1		56A 60A 61A
6	UKC73L	Circlip-selector shaft	1		
7	FRC7330	Quadrant-selector rail	1		
8	FRC7332	Pin-spring-quadrant to shaft	1		
9	FRC7334	Shaft-selector manual transmission	1		
10	FRC7333	Lever-selector selector mechanism	1		
11	FRC7335	Pin-spring	1		
12	FRC4435	Roller-quadrant shaft	1		
13	FRC4434	Shaft-gear change change piece roller	1		
14	CR120105L	Circlip-quadrant shaft	1		
15	FRC4509	O ring	NLA	To (V) LA 939975	Use FRC4951.
15	FRC4951	O ring-selector shaft remote	1		
16	FRC5864	Yoke-shift rod manual transmission	1		

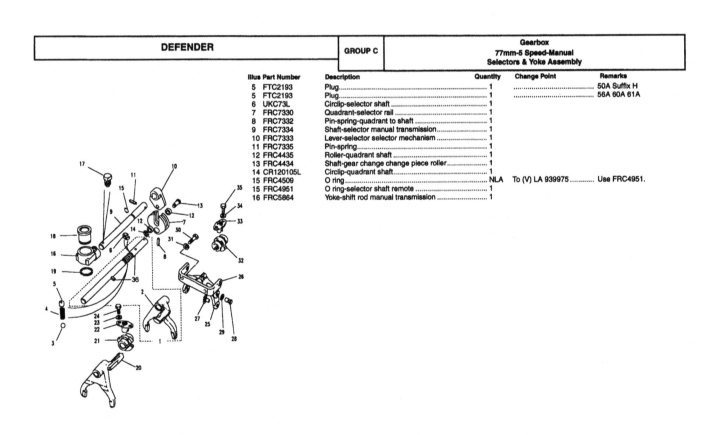

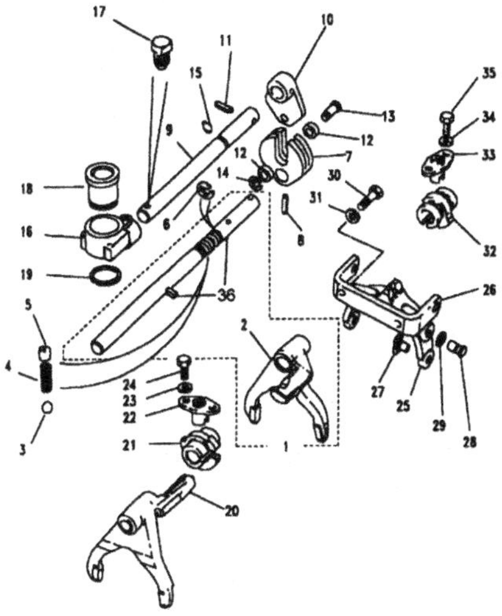

Illus	Part Number	Description	Quantity	Change Point	Remarks
17	FTC4536	Screw-grub	1		
18	FRC5859	Yoke-shift rod manual transmission	1		
19	CR120335L	Circlip	1		
20	FTC1489	Fork assembly-3rd & 4th manual transmission	1		
21	TKC290L	Spool-interlock-1/2/3/4	1	To (C)DA 300721 approx	
22	UKC3660L	Retainer-interlock-attachment plate	1		
22	FRC8239	Retainer-interlock-attachment plate	1	From (C)DA 300722	
15	FRC8170	O ring-interlock retainer	1	approx	
23	WL106001L	Washer-sprung-M6	2		
24	FS106167L	Screw-flanged head-flanged head-M6 x 16	1		
25	TKC2596	Fork-selector-5th gear	1		
26	UKC3115	Bracket-5th gear selector fork support-support	1		
27	532943	Pad-5th gear selector fork	2		
28	UKC2089L	Pin-clevis/pivot-5th gear fork	2		
29	UKC2105L	Circlip	2		
30	FS108251L	Screw-flanged head-M8 x 25	NLA		Use FS108257L.
31	WL108001L	Washer-sprung-M8	2		Suffix A Suffix B Suffix C
					Suffix D Suffix E Suffix F
	WA108051L	Washer-8mm	2		Suffix G
32	FRC7192	Spool-interlock-5th gear	1		
33	FRC4905	Retainer-interlock	1	To (C)DA 300721 approx	
33	FRC8240	Retainer-interlock	1	From (C)DA 300722 approx	
34	WA106001L	Washer-M6	2	To (V) LA 939975	Suffix G
35	FS106167L	Screw-flanged head-flanged head-M6 x 16	2		Suffix F

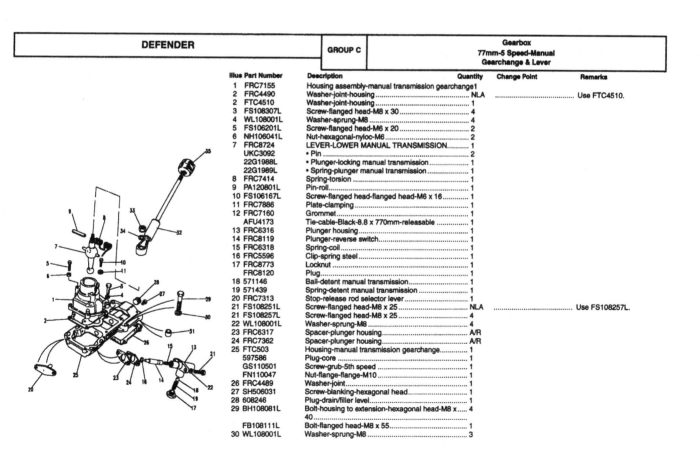

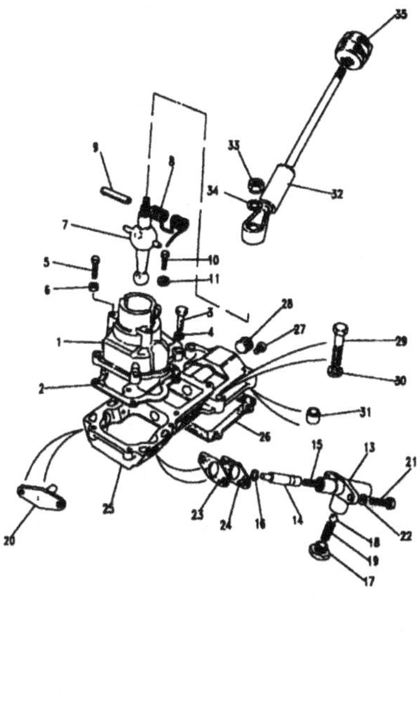

Illus	Part Number	Description	Quantity	Change Point	Remarks
1	FRC7155	Housing assembly-manual transmission gearchange	1		
2	FRC4490	Washer-joint-housing	NLA		Use FTC4510.
2	FTC4510	Washer-joint-housing	1		
3	FS108307L	Screw-flanged head-M8 x 30	4		
4	WL108001L	Washer-sprung-M8	4		
5	FS106201L	Screw-flanged head-M6 x 20	2		
6	NH106041L	Nut-hexagonal-nyloc-M6	2		
7	FRC8724	LEVER-LOWER MANUAL TRANSMISSION	1		
	UKC3092	• Pin	2		
	22G1988L	• Plunger-locking manual transmission	1		
	22G1989L	• Spring-plunger manual transmission	1		
8	FRC7414	Spring-torsion	1		
9	PA120801L	Pin-roll	1		
10	FS106167L	Screw-flanged head-flanged head-M6 x 16	1		
11	FRC7886	Plate-clamping	1		
12	FRC7160	Grommet	1		
	AFU4173	Tie-cable-Black-8.8 x 770mm-releasable	1		
13	FRC6316	Plunger housing	1		
14	FRC8119	Plunger-reverse switch	1		
15	FRC6318	Spring-coil	1		
16	FRC5596	Clip-spring steel	1		
17	FRC8773	Locknut	1		
	FRC8120	Plug	1		
18	571146	Ball-detent manual transmission	1		
19	571439	Spring-detent manual transmission	1		
20	FRC7313	Stop-release rod selector lever	1		
21	FS108251L	Screw-flanged head-M8 x 25	NLA		Use FS108257L.
21	FS108257L	Screw-flanged head-M8 x 25	4		
22	WL108001L	Washer-sprung-M8	4		
23	FRC6317	Spacer-plunger housing	A/R		
24	FRC7362	Spacer-plunger housing	A/R		
25	FTC503	Housing-manual transmission gearchange	1		
	597586	Plug-core	1		
	GS110501	Screw-grub-5th speed	1		
	FN110047	Nut-flange-flange-M10	1		
26	FRC4489	Washer-joint	1		
27	SH506031	Screw-blanking-hexagonal head	1		
28	608246	Plug-drain/filler level	1		
29	BH108081L	Bolt-housing to extension-hexagonal head-M8 x 40	4		
	FB108111L	Bolt-flanged head-M8 x 55	1		
30	WL108001L	Washer-sprung-M8	3		

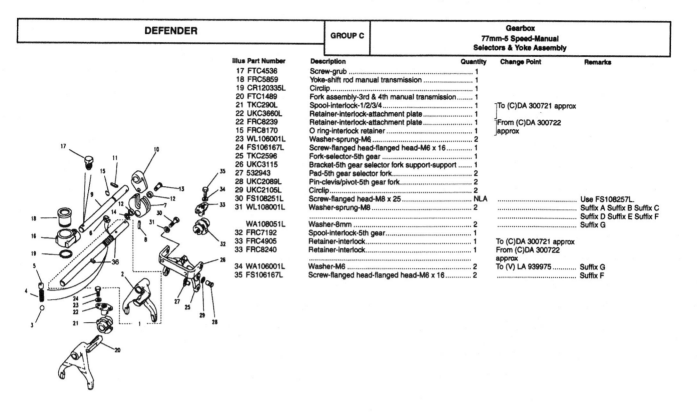

Illus	Part Number	Description	Quantity	Change Point	Remarks
31	FRC2626	Pin-spring	2		
32	FRC7860	Lever assembly-gear selector manual transmission	1		
32	FRC7493	Lever assembly-gear selector manual transmission	1		
33	NY110047L	Nut-gear lever assembly-flange-nyloc-M10	1		
34	WA110061L	Washer-M10	1		
35	FRC8722	Knob assembly-change manual transmission	1		

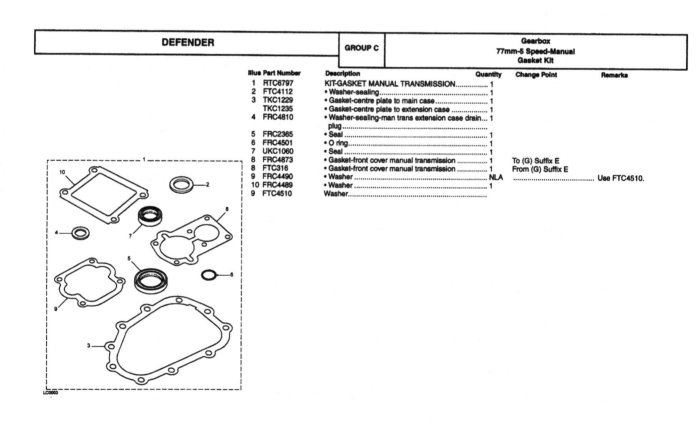

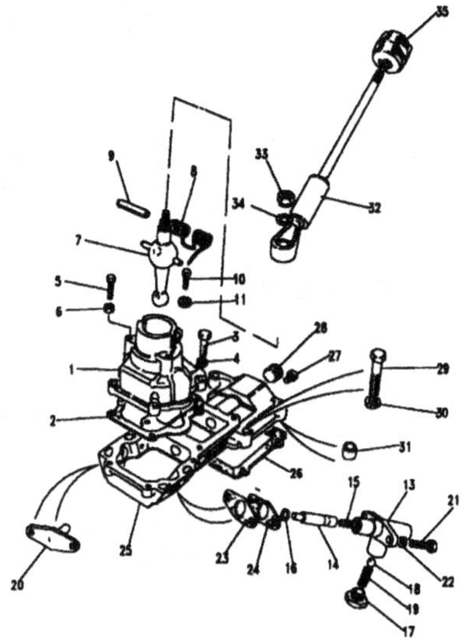

Illus	Part Number	Description	Quantity	Change Point	Remarks
1	RTC6797	KIT-GASKET MANUAL TRANSMISSION	1		
2	FTC4112	• Washer-sealing	1		
3	TKC1229	• Gasket-centre plate to main case	1		
	TKC1235	• Gasket-centre plate to extension case	1		
4	FRC4810	• Washer-sealing-man trans extension case drain plug	1		
5	FRC2365	• Seal	1		
6	FRC4501	• O ring	1		
7	UKC1060	• Seal	1		
8	FRC4873	• Gasket-front cover manual transmission	1	To (G) Suffix E	
8	FTC316	• Gasket-front cover manual transmission	1	From (G) Suffix E	
9	FRC4490	• Washer	NLA		Use FTC4510.
10	FRC4489	• Washer	1		
9	FTC4510	Washer			

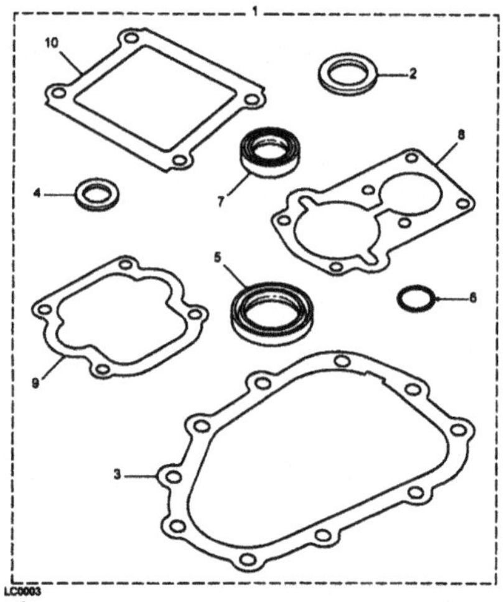

LC0003

Illus	Part Number	Description	Quantity	Change Point	Remarks
1	FTC322N	Transmission assembly manual-new	1		20C 22C
1	FTC322E	Transmission assembly manual-exchange	1		22C
1	FRC7904E	Transmission assembly manual-exchange	1		20C

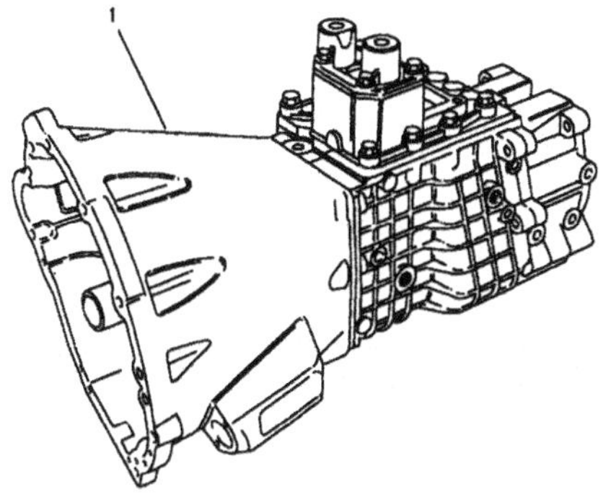

Illus	Part Number	Description	Quantity	Change Point	Remarks
19	FRC7757	Gear-5th driven manual transmission	1		20C
	FRC8211	Gear 5th speed assembly	NLA		Use STC3314.
	STC3314	Kit-gears-5th/reverse	1		
20	FRC8176	Synchroniser assembly-5th gear mainshaft assembly	1		
21	FRC8777	Ring-baulk	1		
22	BLS108L	Ball-detent manual transmission	3		
23	503805	Spring	3		
24	FRC7752	Spacer-sliding	3		
25	FRC7753	Plate-stop manual transmission-5th speed hub-3.00mm	1	To (G)22C 00845	
25	STC700	Plate-stop manual transmission-5th speed hub-5.0mm	1	From (G)22C 00846	
26	FRC8409	Pin-anti rotation-3.00mm	1	To (G)22C 00845	
	STC581	Pin-locking-anti rotation-5.0mm	1	From (G)22C 00846	
27	FRC2457	O ring	1		
28	FRC5317	Collar-oil seal-3.00mm	NLA	To (G)22C 00845	Use STC581 qty 1 with STC582 qty 1 with STC700 qty 1.
28	STC582	Collar-oil seal-5.0mm	1	From (G)22C 00846	
		WASHER			
29	FRC5602	4.25mm	A/R		
29	FRC5603	4.30mm	A/R		
29	FRC5604	4.35mm	A/R		
29	FRC5605	4.40mm	A/R		
29	FRC5606	4.45mm	A/R		
29	FRC5607	4.50mm	A/R		
29	FRC5608	4.55mm	A/R		
29	FRC5609	4.60mm	A/R		
29	FRC5610	4.65mm	A/R		
29	FRC5611	4.70mm	A/R		
		WASHER			
29	FRC5612	4.75mm	A/R		
29	FRC5613	4.80mm	A/R		
29	FRC5614	4.85mm	A/R		
29	FRC5615	4.90mm	A/R		
29	FRC5616	4.95mm	A/R		
30	FRC4494	Spring ring-collar	1		

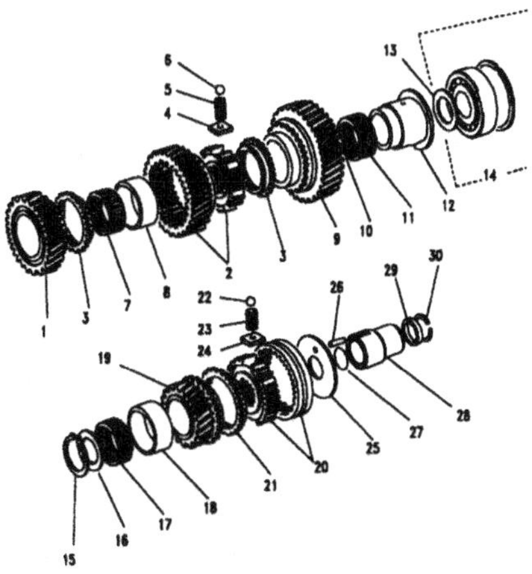

Illus	Part Number	Description	Quantity	Change Point	Remarks
1	FRC8529	Case clutch housing	1		
2	BH112141L	Bolt-hexagonal socket-M12 x 70	6		
3	WL112001L	Washer	6		
4	SH106301L	Screw-hexagonal head-M6 x 30	1		
5	NH106041L	Nut-hexagonal-nyloc-M6	1		
	3290	Plug-coolant drain	1		

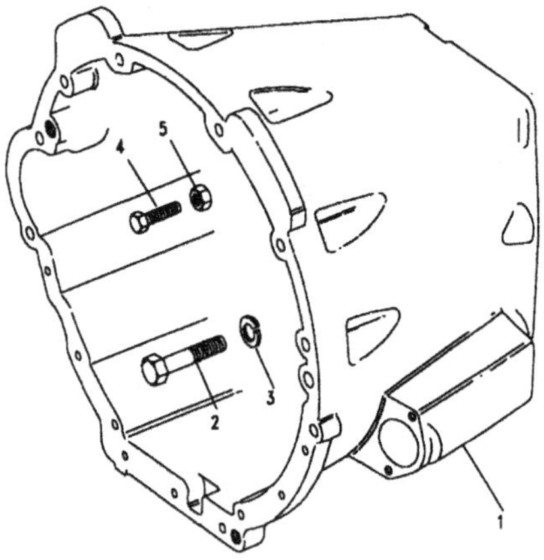

Illus	Part Number	Description	Quantity	Change Point	Remarks
1	FRC3731	Gearbox & transfer box-casing	1		20C
1	FRC8397	Gearbox & transfer box-casing	1		22C
1	FRC9524	Gearbox & transfer box-split gearcase	1		22C
2	FRC2309	Dowel	2		
3	FRC5306	Case assembly-extension	1		
4	FRC2365	Seal-oil-extension case	1		
5	FRC2465	Gasket-transfer box side cover-joint	1		
6	FRC2482	Dowel-ring-15.0mm	2		
7	BH110091L	Bolt-M10 x 45	3		
8	BH110101L	Bolt-hexagonal head-M10 x 50-long	3		
9	BH110121L	Bolt-M10 x 60-long	2		
10	WL110001L	Washer-M10	8		
11	NH110041L	Nut-hexagonal head-coarse thread-M10	1		
12	FRC3073	Gasket-transfer box side cover-joint	2		
13	FRC2542	Plate-blanking	1		
14	FRC3166	Screw-grub	1		
15	90571086	Gear-oil pump	NLA		Use STC3860 qty 1 Use kit on 85mm gearboxes only. or STC3861 qty 1 Use kit on 95mm gearboxes only.. 20C
15	STC3860	Gear-oil pump	1		
16	591227	Gear-oil pump	NLA		Use STC3860.
16	STC3860	Gear-oil pump	1		
17	576220	Filter-air fuel	1		20C
18	FRC2468	O ring	1		20C
19	90571104	Plug-main gear casing	1		20C
20	FRC4810	Washer-sealing-man trans extension case drain plug	1		20C
	STC820	Kit-oil pump repair	1		
	608246	Plug-drain/filler level	1		
19	571944	Plug-reverse switch hole	1		
	PRC1039	Switch-reverse lamp	1		
23	FRC5674	Washer-reverse switch	1		
21	FRC2370	Bolt-reverse lever	1		
22	3292	Plug-level-oil	1		

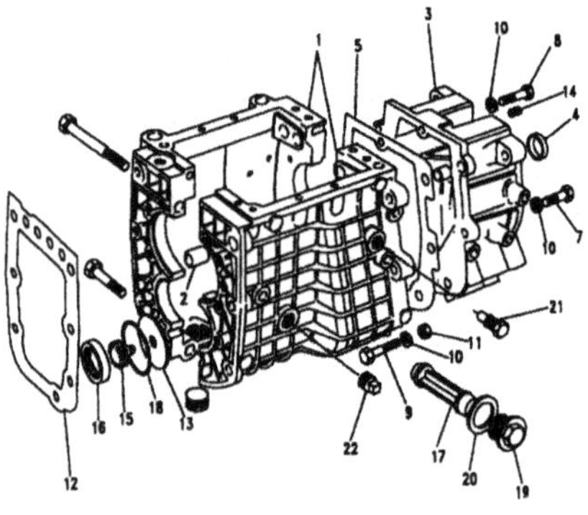

Illus	Part Number	Description	Quantity	Change Point	Remarks
1	FRC4875	Cover assembly-front	1	....	20C
1	FRC9620	Cover assembly-front	1	....	22C
	GS108081L	Screw-grub	1	....	20C
2	FRC2361	Seal-oil	1		
3	591394	Ring-mainshaft oil feed	1		
4	SH108401L	Screw-hexagonal head-M8 x 40	8		
5	WL108001L	Washer-sprung-M8	8	....	V8
6	571134	Dowel-front cover	1		
7	FRC3072	Washer-joint	1	....	20C
7	FRC8215	Washer-joint	1	....	22C

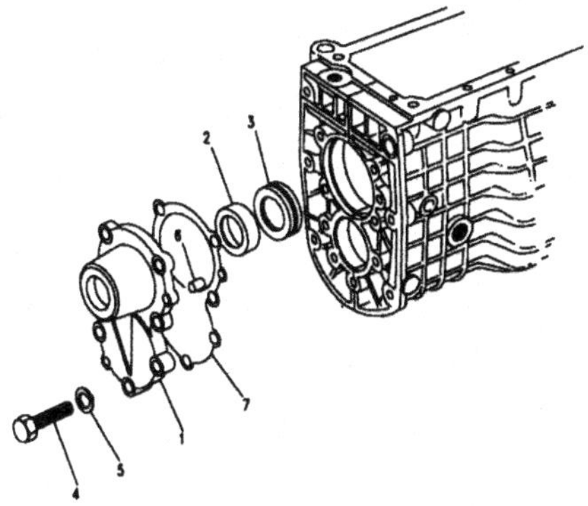

Illus	Part Number	Description	Quantity	Change Point	Remarks
1	FRC4714	Shaft-main manual transmission	1	....	20C
2	FRC7852	Joint-constant velocity	1	....	
1	FRC8214	Shaft-main manual transmission	1	....	22C
2	FRC9621	Joint-constant velocity	1	....	
3	FRC2301	Bearing-ball	1		
4	FRC2445	Shim-3.07mm	A/R		
4	FRC2446	Shim-3.02mm	A/R		
4	FRC2447	Shim-2.97mm	A/R		
4	FRC2448	Shim-2.92mm	A/R		
4	FRC2449	Shim-2.87mm	A/R		
5	FRC2488	Circlip	2		
6	571142	Seal-oil	1		
7	6397	Bearing-needle roller	1		
8	FRC2554	Shim-man trans primary shaft bearing/front cover-3.48mm	A/R		
8	FRC2555	Shim-man trans primary shaft bearing/front cover-3.43mm	A/R		
8	FRC2556	Shim-man trans primary shaft bearing/front cover-3.38mm	A/R		
9	FRC8139	Synchroniser assembly-3rd & 4th mainshaft assembly	1		
10	FRC8777	Ring-baulk	2		
11	FRC7752	Spacer	3		
12	503805	Spring	3		
13	BLS108L	Ball-detent manual transmission	1		
14	FRC3898	Spacer	1		
15	FRC7764	Gear-3rd driven manual transmission	1	....	20C
15	FRC8210	Gear-3rd driven manual transmission	1	....	22C
16	FRC2334	Bearing-needle roller	1		

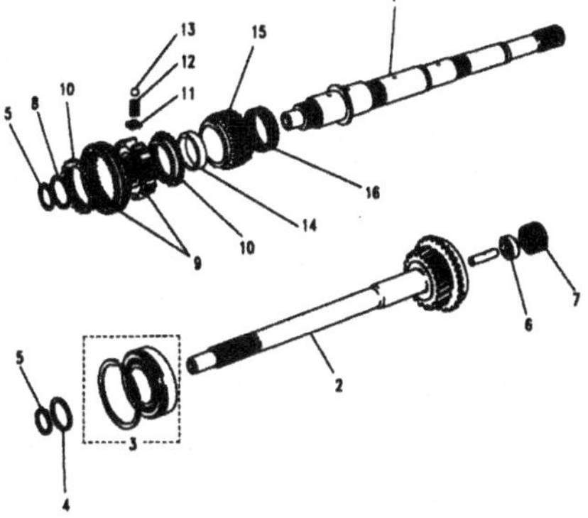

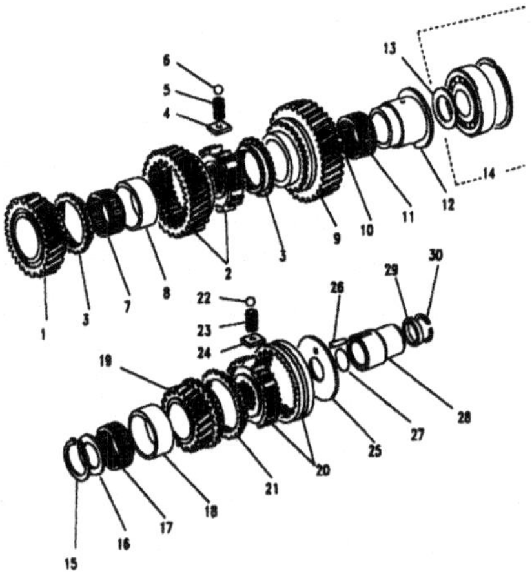

Illus	Part Number	Description	Quantity	Change Point	Remarks
1	FRC7763	Gear-2nd driven manual transmission	1		20C
1	FRC8209	Gear-2nd driven manual transmission	1		22C
2	FRC8129	Synchroniser assembly-1st & 2nd mainshaft assembly	1		20C
2	FRC8129	Synchroniser assembly-1st & 2nd mainshaft assembly	1	To (G)22C 00193	22C
2	FRC9556	Synchroniser assembly-1st & 2nd mainshaft assembly	1	From (G)22C 00194	22C
3	FRC8777	Ring-baulk	2		
4	FRC7752	Spacer-sliding	3		
5	503805	Spring	3		
6	BLS108L	Ball-detent manual transmission	3		
7	FRC2334	Bearing-needle roller	1		
8	FRC3898	Spacer	1		
9	FRC7761	Gear-1st driven manual transmission	1		20C
9	FRC8208	Gear-1st driven manual transmission	1		22C
10	FRC3897	Spacer-1st speed	1		
11	FRC2334	Bearing-needle roller	1		
12	FRC8422	Bush-1st speed	1		
		SHIM			
13	FRC8400	1.15mm	A/R		
13	FRC8401	1.20mm	A/R		
13	FRC8402	1.25mm	A/R		
13	FRC8403	1.30mm	A/R		
13	FRC8404	1.35mm	A/R		
13	FRC8405	1.40mm	A/R		
13	FRC8406	1.45mm	A/R		
14	FRC2301	Bearing-ball	1		
15	FRC2488	Circlip-man trans 5th gear synchroniser hub	1		
16	FRC5978	Washer-thrust-5th gear	1		
17	FRC2479	Bearing-needle roller	1		
18	FRC3896	Spacer-5th gear	1		

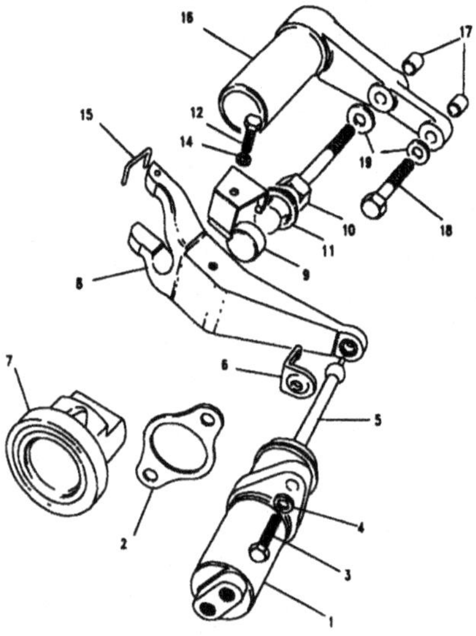

Illus	Part Number	Description	Quantity	Change Point	Remarks
1	UKC8677L	Slave cylinder clutch	NLA		Use FTC5071 which has thicker flange that eliminates the need for backing plate FRC2402.
1	FTC5071	Slave cylinder clutch	1		
	BHM7063L	Kit-repair clutch slave cylinder	1		
2	FRC2402	Plate-backing	1		
3	FS108251L	Screw-flanged head-M8 x 25	NLA		Use FS108257L.
4	WL108001L	Washer-sprung-M8	2		
5	571160	Rod assembly-push slave cylinder	1		
6	576723	Clip	1		
7	FRC9568	BEARING-CLUTCH RELEASE	NLA		Use FTC5200.
	FRC4078	• Sleeve-guide clutch	1		
7	FTC5200	Bearing-clutch release	1		
8	576137	Arm-clutch release clutch	1		
9	FRC2975	Cap-clutch release lever pivot	1		
10	FRC2528	Pivot-clutch release lever	1		
11	571161	Insert-clutch lever	1		
12	FS106101L	Screw-flanged head-M6 x 10	1		
13	WM106001L	Washer-spring-M6-square	1		
14	571163	Clip-clutch release-pivot post	1		
15	576203	Retention-bearing clutch release	1		
16	FRC4803	Guide-clutch release bearing	1		
17	FRC2481	Dowel	2		
18	SH108401L	Screw-hexagonal head-M8 x 40	1		
19	WL108001L	Washer-sprung-M8	2		

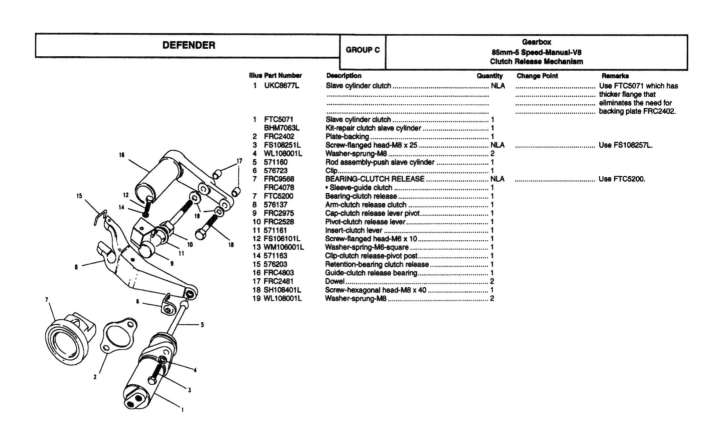

DEFENDER	GROUP C	Gearbox 85mm-5 Speed-Manual-V8 Layshaft

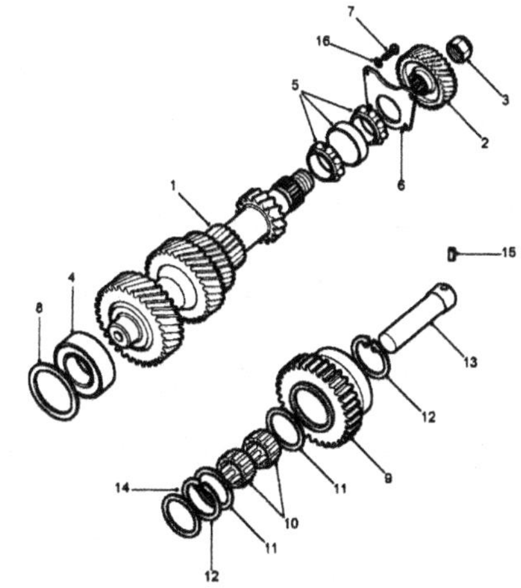

AFCGIE1A

Illus	Part Number	Description	Quantity	Change Point	Remarks
1	FRC3732	Shaft-lay	1		V8 20C
1	FRC8213	Shaft-lay	1		V8 22C
2	FRC8211	Gear 5th speed assembly	NLA		Use STC3314.
	STC3314	Kit-gears-5th/reverse	1		
3	FRC3806	Nut	1		
4	FRC2578	Bearing-roller	1		
5	FRC2470	Bearing-ball-rear	1		
6	FRC8380	Plate assembly-retaining	1		
7	SB108201L	Screw-hexagon socket-front	2		
	FS108307L	Screw-flanged head-M8 x 30	2		
16	WL108001L	Washer-sprung-M8	2		V8
8	FRC3987	Spacer	1		
9	FRC3319	Gear-reverse idler assembly manual transmission	1		
10	FRC1032	Bearing-needle roller	2		
11	FRC1034	Washer	2		
12	FRC1035	Circlip	2		
13	FRC3112	Shaft-reverse idler assembly-manual transmission	1		
14	FRC8421	Washer-thrust	1		
15	591519	Spring-pin	1		

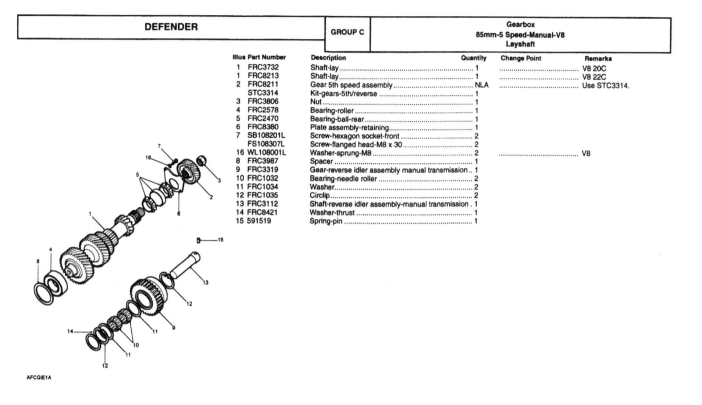

DEFENDER	GROUP C	Gearbox 85mm-5 Speed-Manual-V8 Selectors & Shafts

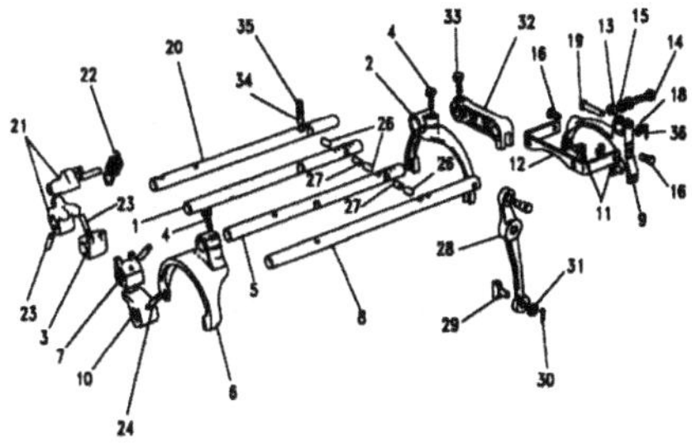

Illus	Part Number	Description	Quantity	Change Point	Remarks
1	FRC2381	Shaft-selector manual transmission-1st/2nd	1		
2	FRC7769	Fork assembly-selector-1st/2nd manual transmission	1		
3	FRC8452	Lug-1st & 2nd manual transmission	1		
4	SX108351	Bolt	1		
5	FRC3118	Shaft-selector manual transmission-3rd & 4th	1		
6	FRC7754	Fork-selector-3rd/4th manual transmission	1		
7	FRC8452	Lug-1st & 2nd manual transmission	1		
8	FRC3282	Shaft-selector manual transmission	1		
9	FRC7767	Fork assembly-5th manual transmission	1		
10	FRC8454	Lug assembly-5th & reverse manual transmission	1		
11	622388	Pad-insulation-swivel	2		
12	FRC7766	Bracket-pivot 5th fork	1		
13	FRC2481	Dowel	2		
14	FS108307L	Screw-flanged head-M8 x 30	2		
15	WA108051	Washer-M8-standard	NLA		Use WA108051L.
16	UKC2089L	Pin-clevis/pivot-5th fork	2		
17	UKC2105L	Circlip-pivot pin	2		
18	WA106041L	Washer-6mm	1		
19	PC106561L	Pin-clevis	1		
20	FRC8270	Shaft-selector manual transmission	1		
21	FRC8455	Lug-reverse-manual transmission	1		
22	FRC3481	Spring-reverse hinge	1		
23	571158	Spring	4		
24	PS103121L	Pin-split	1		
25	FS108307L	Screw-flanged head-M8 x 30	2		
26	FRC2577	Plunger-locking manual transmission	3		
27	FRC3117	Pin	2		
28	FRC2390	Lever-selector selector mechanism	1		
29	571043	Pad-buffer	1		
30	PS103121L	Pin-split	1		
31	WA108051	Washer-M8-standard	NLA		Use WA108051L.
32	FRC2368	Shaft-selector lever	1		
33	FRC2370	Bolt-reverse lever	1		
34	571146	Ball-detent manual transmission	4		
35	593802	Spring	4		
36	PS103121L	Pin-split	1		

DEFENDER	GROUP C	Gearbox 85mm-5 Speed-Manual-V8 Gearchange & Lever

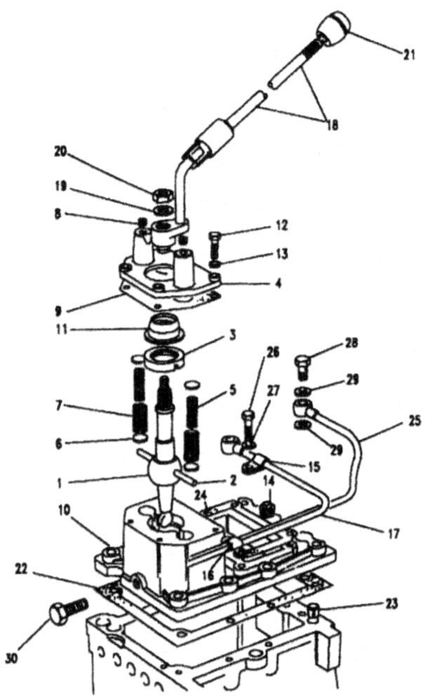

Illus	Part Number	Description	Quantity	Change Point	Remarks
1	FRC8250	GUIDE-GEAR LEVER-LOWER	1		
2	FRC2622	• Pin-locating	2		
3	FRC2612	Seat-change ball lever manual transmission	1		
4	FRC2583	Spring-housing	1		
5	FRC2587	Spring-bias inner	2		
6	FRC2623	Spacer-bias spring	4		
7	FRC3146	Spring-bias outer	2		
8	GS112141L	Screw-grub	2		
9	FRC2648	Washer-joint	1		
10	FRC5698	Housing-gear selector	1		
11	FRC8271	Grommet-gear lever lower	1		
12	FS106257L	Screw-flanged head-M6 x 25	4		
13	WL106001L	Washer-sprung-M6	4		
14	3292	Plug-level-filler	1		
15	BAU1689	Clip-p-single-5/16"	1		
16	622324	Clip-pipe-double	1		
	FRC9430	TUBE-BREATHER TRANSMISSION CASE	1		
29	232039	• Washer-sealing	1		
28	595478	• Bolt-banjo	1		
17	FRC4062	Breather assembly-manual transmission	1		
18	FRC8863	Lever assembly-gear selector manual transmission	1		
19	WA110061L	Washer-M10	1		
20	NY110041L	Nut-hexagonal head-nyloc-M10	NLA		Use NY110047L.
21	FRC8722	Knob assembly-change manual transmission	1		
22	FRC2487	Gasket selector mechanism-top cover	1		
23	FRC2626	Pin-spring-top cover	1		
24	FRC6306	Gasket-transfer box gear change housing	NLA	Note (1)	Use FTC4036.
24	FTC4036	Gasket-transfer box gear change housing	1	Note (2)	
25	FRC9429	Breather manual transmission	1		
26	SH108401L	Screw-hexagonal head-M8 x 40	8		
27	WL108001L	Washer-sprung-M8	8		
28	595478	Bolt-banjo	2		
29	232039	Washer-sealing	4		
	FTC5409	Clip-pipe	A/R		Td5

CHANGE POINTS:
(1) To (E) 299332E
(2) From (E) 299333E

DEFENDER	GROUP C	Gearbox 85mm-5 Speed-Manual-V8 Transmission Mountings

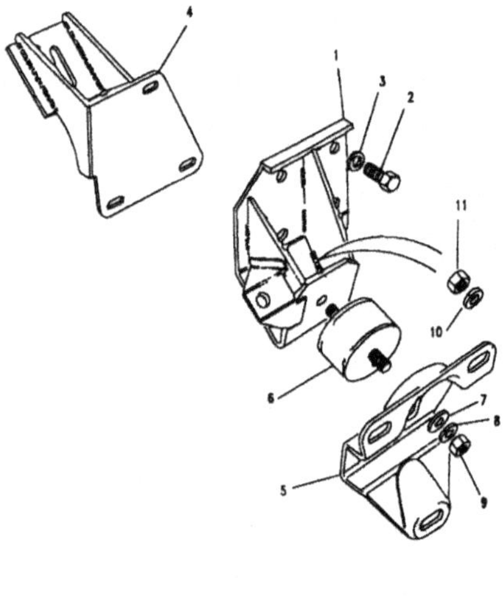

Illus	Part Number	Description	Quantity	Change Point	Remarks
1	NRC9501	Bracket-engine mounting-LH	1		
2	SH112251L	Screw-hexagonal head-M12 x 25	4		
3	WL112001L	Washer	4		
4	NTC1201	Bracket-engine mounting-rear-RH	NLA	Note (1)	Use ANR4657.
4	ANR4657	Bracket-engine mounting-rear-RH	1	Note (2)	
5	90575585	Bracket-transmission mounting-rear-LH	1	Note (3)	
5	ANR2820	Bracket-transmission mounting-rear-LH	2	Note (4)	
6	NTC5900	Mounting-engine rubber-imperial	NLA		Use RTC6115.
6	RTC6115	MOUNTING-ENGINE RUBBER	NLA		Use STC434.
6	STC434	MOUNTING-ENGINE RUBBER	2		
7	WC110061L	• Washer-plain-M10-oversize	2		
8	WL110001L	• Washer-metric fixing-M10	4		
9	NH110041L	• Nut-hexagonal head-coarse thread-M10	4		
9	NH606041L	Nut-hexagonal head-3/8UNF	2		
10	WL600061L	Washer-spring-3/8	2		
11	NH606041L	Nut-hexagonal head-3/8UNF	2		

CHANGE POINTS:
(1) To (V) TA 970049
(2) From (V) TA 970050
(3) To (V) LA 939975
(4) From (V) MA 939976

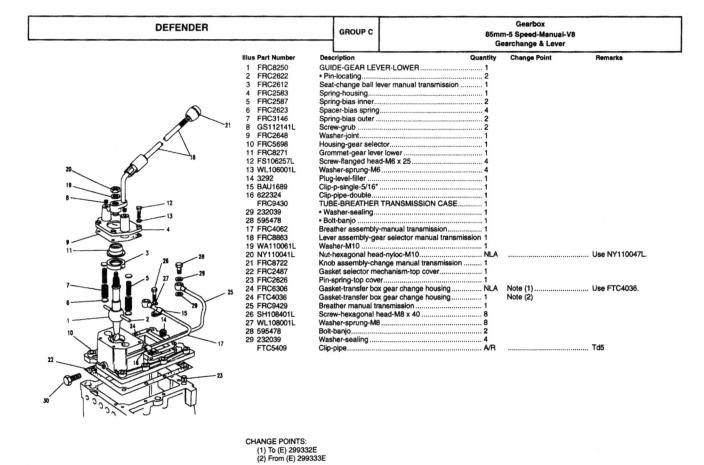

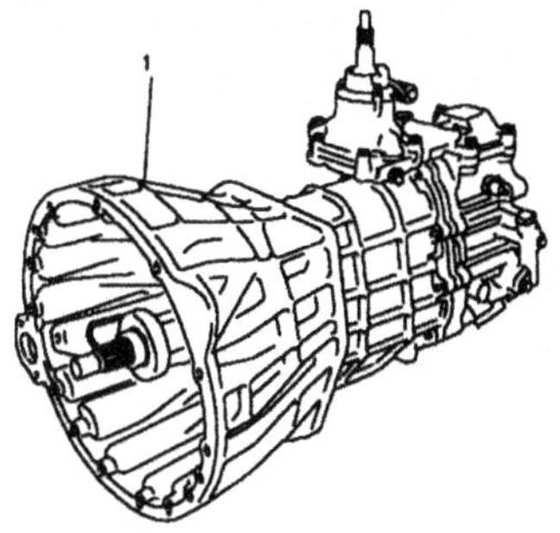

Illus	Part Number	Description	Quantity	Change Point	Remarks
		TRANSMISSION ASSEMBLY			
1	STC1546N	new	1	Note (1)	TDi 56A Suffix J
1	STC1546E	exchange	1		TDi 56A
1	TRC102980	new	NLA	Note (2)	Use TRC103160. TDi 56A Suffix K
1	TRC103160E	exchange	1		56A Suffix L except oil cooler (air cooled)
		TRANSMISSION ASSEMBLY			
1	STC1547N	new	1	Note (1)	V8 Twin Carburettor 60A Suffix J
1	STC1547E	exchange	1		V8 Twin Carburettor 60A
1	TRC103010	new	1	Note (2)	V8 Twin Carburettor 60A Suffix K
		TRANSMISSION ASSEMBLY			
1	STC1548N	cooled-new	1	Note (1)	V8 EFi 61A Suffix J
1	STC1548E	cooled-exchange	1		V8 EFi 61A
1	TRC103030	new	1	Note (2)	V8 EFi 61A Suffix K
1	TRC103030E	exchange	1		V8 EFi 61A Suffix K
1	TRC103210E	exchange	1		V8 EFi 61A Suffix L
		TRANSMISSION ASSEMBLY			
1	STC1549N	new	1	Note (1)	4 Cylinder 50A Suffix J except TDi
1	STC1549E	exchange	1		4 Cylinder 50A
1	TRC102920	new	1	Note (2)	4 Cylinder 50A Suffix K except TDi

CHANGE POINTS:
(1) To (G) 0623639J
(2) From (G) 0623640K

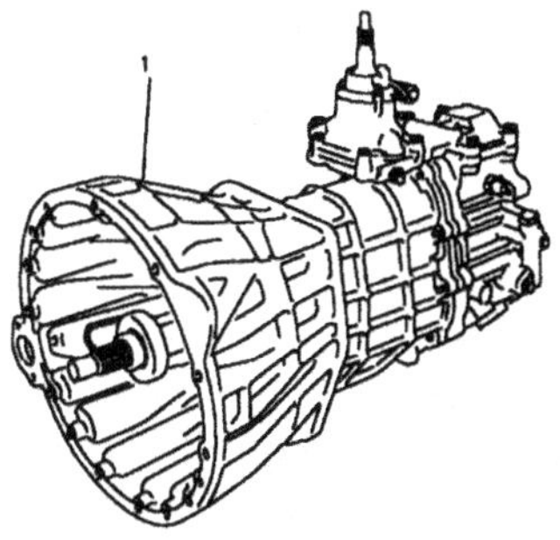

Illus	Part Number	Description	Quantity	Change Point	Remarks
		SHOT PEENED GEARS-FROM SUFFIX 'L'			
1	TRC103260	Transmission assembly-new	1		Diesel 68A Td5 except oil cooler (air cooled)
1	TRC103330	Transmission assembly	1		Diesel 74A Td5 oil cooler (air cooled)
1	TRC103260E	Transmission assembly-exchange	1		68A Td5 Suffix L
1	TRC103240	Transmission assembly-new	1		BMW M52 Suffix L
1	TRC103210	Transmission assembly-new	1		V8 EFi 61A Suffix L oil cooler (air cooled)
1	TRC103190	Transmission assembly-new	1		V8 Twin Carburettor 60A Suffix L except oil cooler (air cooled)
1	TRC103180	Transmission assembly-new	1		TDi 58A Suffix L oil cooler (air cooled)
1	TRC103140	Transmission assembly-new	1		44A Suffix L
1	TRC103160	Transmission assembly-new	1		4 Cylinder TDi 56A Suffix L except oil cooler (air cooled)
1	TRC103150	Transmission assembly-new	1		4 Cylinder Petrol Single Carburettor 50A Suffix L
1	TRC103150	Transmission assembly-new	1		4 Cylinder Diesel Natural-Aspirated 50A Suffix L
1	TRC103010E	Transmission assembly-exchange	1	Note (1)	3500 cc Petrol 60A
1	TRC102980E	Transmission assembly-exchange	1	Note (1)	Diesel 56A Tdi Suffix K
1	TRC103160E	Transmission assembly-exchange	1		Diesel 56A Tdi Suffix L
2	1247357	Bracket-harness	2		6 Cylinder
3	FTC4461	Housing-clutch manual transmission	1		
4	2943111	Adaptor-clutch housing	1		

CHANGE POINTS:
(1) From (G) 0623640K

DEFENDER

GROUP C

Gearbox
R380-5 Speed-Manual
Clutch Release Mechanism-TDI

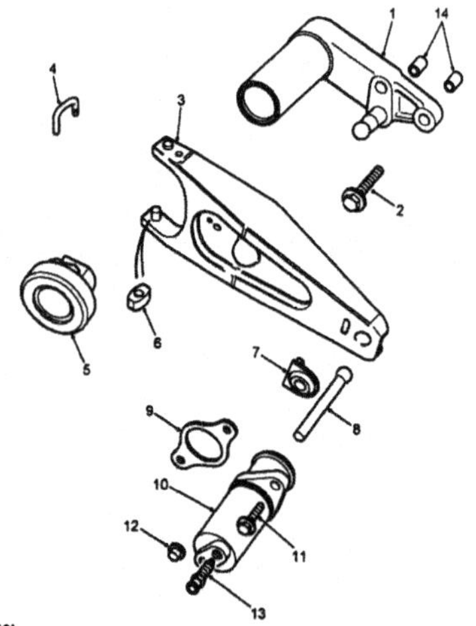

AHCFCA2A

Illus	Part Number	Description	Quantity	Change Point	Remarks
1	FTC1271	Guide-clutch release bearing-aluminium	NLA		Use FTC5218.
1	FTC5218	Guide-clutch release bearing-cast iron	1		
2	FB108101L	Bolt-flanged head-M8 x 50	2		
3	FTC2957	Arm-clutch release clutch	1		
4	FRC3416	Retention-bearing clutch release	1		
5	FRC9568	Bearing-clutch release	NLA	Note (1)	Use FTC5200.
5	FTC5200	Bearing-clutch release	1	Note (2)	
6	FRC5255	Pad-clutch release lever slipper	2		
7	FRC3327	Clip	1		
8	FTC3912	Rod-push slave cylinder	1	Note (1)	
8	FTC5199	Rod-push slave cylinder	1	Note (2)	
9	FRC2402	Plate	1		
10	FTC3911	Slave cylinder clutch	NLA	Note (3)	Use FTC5072, which has a thicker flange eliminating the need for backing plate FRC2402.
10	FTC5072	Slave cylinder clutch	1	Note (1)	
10	FTC5202	Slave cylinder clutch	1	Note (2)	
	STC2818	Kit-repair clutch slave cylinder	1		
11	FB108161L	Bolt-flanged head-M8 x 80	2		
12	594091	Cap-protective	1		
13	606733	Screw-bleed clutch slave cylinder	1		
14	FRC2481	Dowel	2		

CHANGE POINTS:
(1) To (G)56A 0669086K
(2) From (G)56A 0669087K
(3) To (V) TA 9975718

DEFENDER

GROUP C

Gearbox
R380-5 Speed-Manual
Clutch Release Mechanism-4cyl Naturally Aspirated 2.5P/D

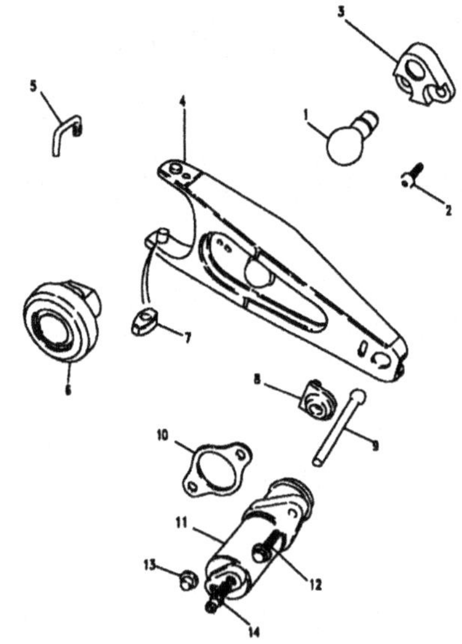

Illus	Part Number	Description	Quantity	Change Point	Remarks
1	FTC4173	Pivot-clutch release lever	1		
2	FTC4209	Bolt-M8 x 18	2		
3	FTC4174	Plate	1		
4	FTC2957	Arm-clutch release clutch	1		
5	FRC3416	Retention-bearing clutch release	1		
6	FTC4177	Bearing clutch	1		4 Cylinder Naturally Aspirated
6	UTJ100210	Bearing clutch	1		4 Cylinder Naturally Aspirated
7	FRC5255	Pad-clutch release lever slipper	2		
8	FRC3327	Clip	1		
9	FTC4229	Rod-push slave cylinder	1		
10	FRC2402	Plate	1		
11	FRC8531	Slave cylinder clutch	1		
12	FS108257L	Screw-flanged head-M8 x 25	2	To (V) LA 939975	
13	594091	Cap-protective	1		
14	606733	Screw-bleed clutch slave cylinder	1		
	NRC7441	Bracket	1		
	WL108001L	Washer-sprung-M8	2	To (V) LA 939975	

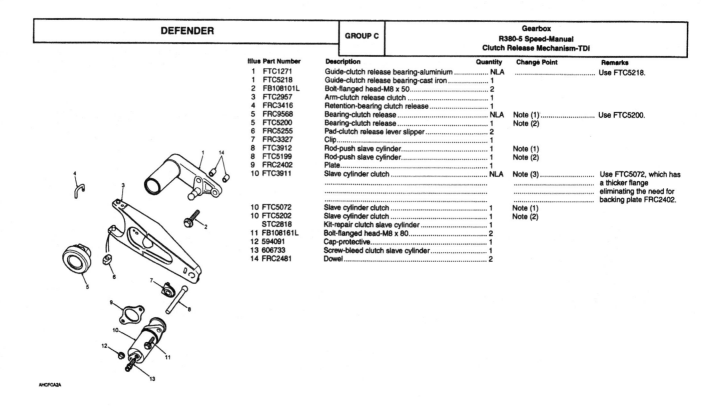

DEFENDER	GROUP C	Gearbox R380-5 Speed-Manual Clutch Release Mechanism-5cyl Diesel

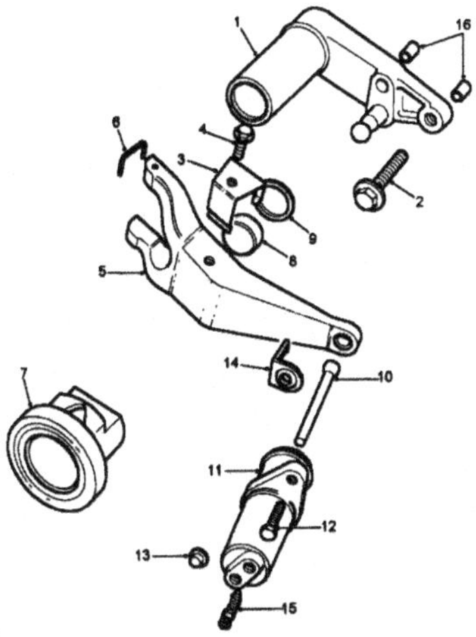

LC0033

Illus	Part Number	Description	Quantity	Change Point	Remarks
1	FTC4720	Guide-clutch release bearing	1		
2	FB108091L	Bolt-flanged head-M8 x 45	2		
3	571163	Clip-clutch release-pivot post	1		
4	FS106101	Screw-flanged head	1		
5	576137	Arm-clutch release clutch	1		
6	576203	Retention-bearing clutch release	1		
7	FTC5200	Bearing-clutch release	1		
8	571161	Insert-clutch lever	1		
9	FRC2975	Cap-clutch release lever pivot	1		
10	FTC5199	Rod-push slave cylinder	1		
11	FTC5202	Slave cylinder clutch	1		
12	FS108251ML	Screw-flanged head-M8 x 25	2		
13	594091	Cap-protective	1		
14	576723	Clip	1		
15	606733	Screw-bleed clutch slave cylinder	1		
16	FRC2481	Dowel	2		

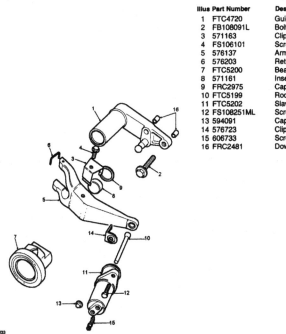

DEFENDER	GROUP C	Gearbox R380-5 Speed-Manual Clutch Release Mechanism-6cyl

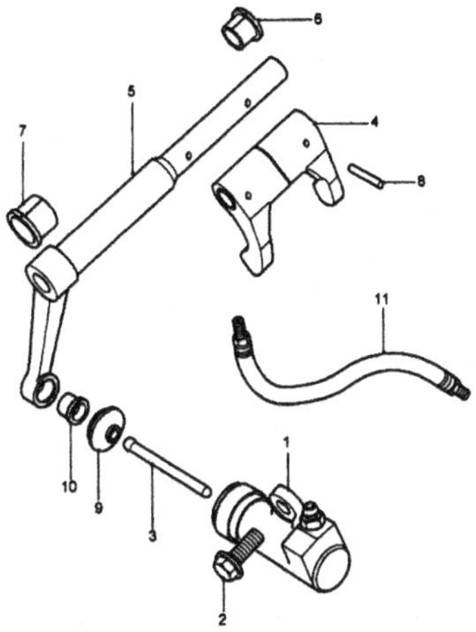

AKCFCA1A

Illus	Part Number	Description	Quantity	Change Point	Remarks
1	ANR2967	Slave cylinder clutch	1		
	STC2818	Kit-repair clutch slave cylinder	1		
	2943344	Heatshield-clutch slave cylinder	1		
2	FS110301L	Screw-flanged head-M10 x 30-top	2		
3	FTC2170	Rod-push slave cylinder	1		
4	FTC1667	Arm-clutch release clutch	1		
5	FTC4085	Shaft & lever assembly clutch	1		
6	FTC1010	Bush-lever release assembly clutch-small	1		
7	FTC2169	Bush-lever release assembly clutch-large	1		
8	FTC1692	Pin-spirol	2		
9	FTC2174	Boot-clutch release lever	1		
10	FTC2189	Insert-release lever	1		
11	2943144	Pipe assembly clutch	1		

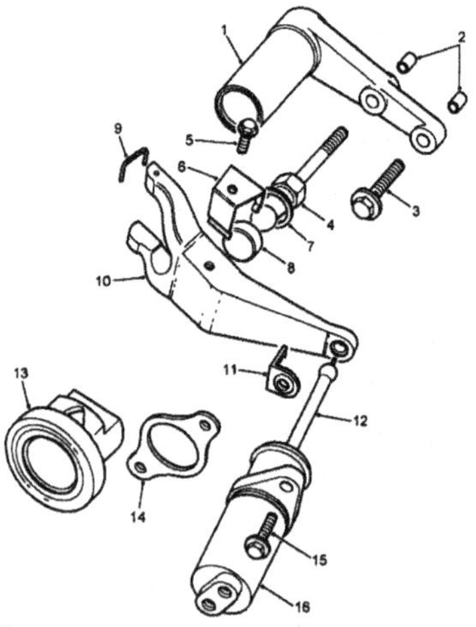

AHCFCA3A

Illus	Part Number	Description	Quantity	Change Point	Remarks
		CLUTCH RELEASE MECHANISM-V8			
1	FRC4803	Guide-clutch release bearing	1		
2	FRC2481	Dowel	2		
3	FB108101L	Bolt-flanged head-M8 x 50	1		
4	FRC2528	Pivot-clutch release lever	1		
5	FS106101L	Screw-flanged head-M6 x 10	1		
6	571163	Clip-clutch release-pivot post	1		
7	FRC2975	Cap-clutch release lever pivot	1		
8	571161	Insert-clutch lever	1		
9	576203	Retention-bearing clutch release	1		
10	576137	Arm-clutch release clutch	1		
11	576723	Clip	1		
12	571160	Rod assembly-push slave cylinder	1		
13	FRC9568	Bearing-clutch release	NLA		Use FTC5200.
13	FTC5200	Bearing-clutch release	1		
14	FRC2402	Plate	1		
15	FS108251L	Screw-flanged head-M8 x 25	NLA		Use FS108257L.
16	UKC8677L	Slave cylinder clutch	NLA		Use FTC5071 which has thicker flange that eliminates the need for backing plate FRC2402.
16	FTC5071	Slave cylinder clutch	1		
	BHM7063L	Kit-repair clutch slave cylinder	1		

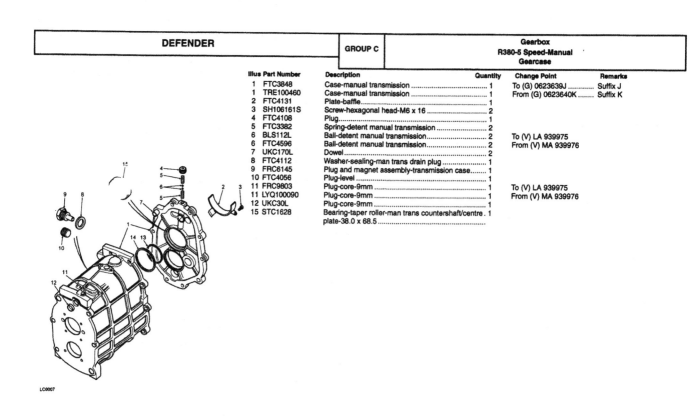

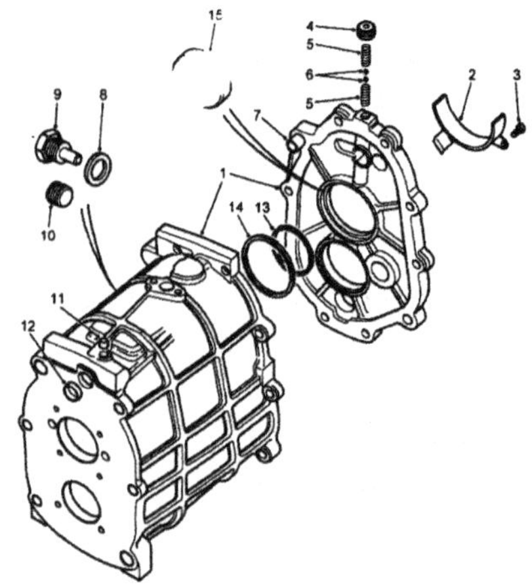

LC0007

Illus	Part Number	Description	Quantity	Change Point	Remarks
1	FTC3848	Case-manual transmission	1	To (G) 0623639J	Suffix J
1	TRE100460	Case-manual transmission	1	From (G) 0623640K	Suffix K
2	FTC4131	Plate-baffle	1		
3	SH106161S	Screw-hexagonal head-M6 x 16	2		
4	FTC4108	Plug	1		
5	FTC3382	Spring-detent manual transmission	2		
6	BLS112L	Ball-detent manual transmission	2	To (V) LA 939975	
6	FTC4596	Ball-detent manual transmission	2	From (V) MA 939976	
7	UKC170L	Dowel	2		
8	FTC4112	Washer-sealing-man trans drain plug	1		
9	FRC6145	Plug and magnet assembly-transmission case	1		
10	FTC4056	Plug-level	1		
11	FRC9803	Plug-core-9mm	1	To (V) LA 939975	
11	LYQ100090	Plug-core-9mm	1	From (V) MA 939976	
12	UKC30L	Plug-core-9mm	1		
15	STC1628	Bearing-taper roller-man trans countershaft/centre plate-38.0 x 68.5	1		

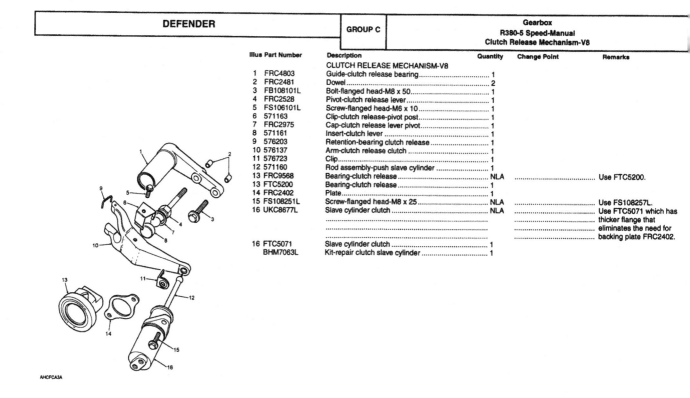

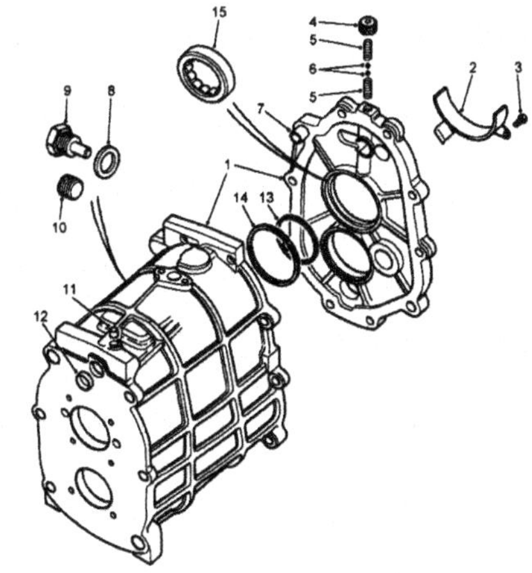

LC0007

Illus	Part Number	Description	Quantity	Change Point	Remarks
		SHIM			
13	FTC3739	man trans mainshaft bearing/centre plate- 1.740/1.715mm	A/R		
13	FTC3741	man trans mainshaft bearing/centre plate- 1.790/1.765mm	A/R		
13	FTC3743	man trans mainshaft bearing/centre plate- 1.840/1.815mm	A/R		
13	FTC3745	man trans mainshaft bearing/centre plate- 1.890/1.865mm	A/R		
13	FTC3747	man trans mainshaft bearing/centre plate- 1.940/1.915mm	A/R		
13	FTC3749	man trans mainshaft bearing/centre plate- 1.990/1.965mm	A/R		
13	FTC3751	man trans mainshaft bearing/centre plate- 2.040/2.015mm	A/R		
13	FTC3753	man trans mainshaft bearing/centre plate- 2.090/2.065mm	A/R		
13	FTC3755	man trans mainshaft bearing/centre plate- 2.140/2.115mm	A/R		
13	FTC3757	man trans mainshaft bearing/centre plate- 2.190/2.165mm	A/R		

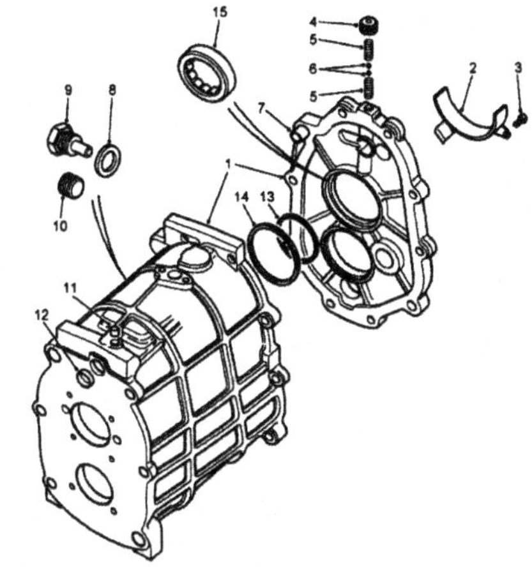

LC0007

Illus	Part Number	Description	Quantity	Change Point	Remarks
13	FTC3759	Shim-man trans mainshaft bearing/centre plate- 2.240/2.215mm	A/R		
13	FTC3761	Shim-man trans mainshaft bearing/centre plate- 2.290/2.265mm	A/R		
13	FTC3763	Shim-man trans mainshaft bearing/centre plate- 2.340/2.315mm	A/R		
13	FTC3765	Shim-man trans mainshaft bearing/centre plate- 2.390/2.365mm	A/R		
13	FTC3767	Shim-man trans mainshaft bearing/centre plate- 2.440/2.415mm	A/R		
13	FTC3769	Shim-man trans mainshaft bearing/centre plate- 2.490/2.465mm	A/R		
13	FTC3771	Shim-man trans mainshaft bearing/centre plate- 2.540/2.515mm	A/R		
13	FTC3773	Shim-man trans mainshaft bearing/centre plate- 2.590/2.565mm	A/R		
13	FTC3775	Shim-man trans mainshaft bearing/centre plate- 2.640/2.615mm	A/R		
13	FTC3777	Shim-man trans mainshaft bearing/centre plate- 2.690/2.665mm	A/R		
13	FTC3779	Shim-man trans mainshaft bearing/centre plate- 2.740/2.715mm	A/R		
13	FTC3781	Shim-man trans mainshaft bearing/centre plate- 2.790/2.765mm	A/R		
13	FTC3783	Shim-man trans mainshaft bearing/centre plate- 2.840/2.815mm	A/R		
13	FTC3785	Shim-man trans mainshaft bearing/centre plate- 2.890/2.865mm	A/R		
13	FTC3787	Shim-man trans mainshaft bearing/centre plate- 2.940/2.915mm	A/R		

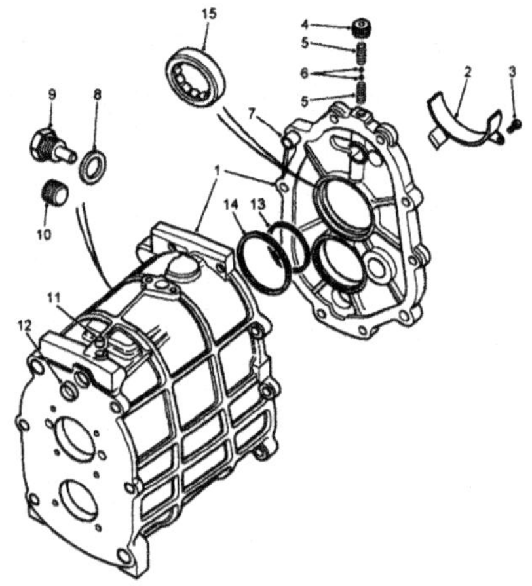

LC0007

Illus	Part Number	Description	Quantity	Change Point	Remarks
14	FTC4296	Shim-man trans countershaft bearing/centre plate-. 1.477/1.452mm	A/R	To (G) 0623639J	Suffix J
14	FTC4298	Shim-man trans countershaft bearing/centre plate-. 1.527/1.502mm	A/R		
14	FTC4300	Shim-man trans countershaft bearing/centre plate-. 1.577/1.552mm	A/R		
14	FTC4302	Shim-man trans countershaft bearing/centre plate-. 1.627/1.602mm	A/R		
14	FTC4304	Shim-man trans countershaft bearing/centre plate-. 1.677/1.652mm	A/R		
14	FTC4306	Shim-man trans countershaft bearing/centre plate-. 1.727/1.702mm	A/R		
14	FTC4308	Shim-man trans countershaft bearing/centre plate-. 1.777/1.752mm	A/R		
14	FTC4310	Shim-man trans countershaft bearing/centre plate-. 1.827/1.802mm	A/R		
14	FTC4312	Shim-man trans countershaft bearing/centre plate-. 1.877/1.852mm	A/R		
14	FTC4314	Shim-man trans countershaft bearing/centre plate-. 1.927/1.902mm	A/R		
14	FTC4316	Shim-man trans countershaft bearing/centre plate-. 1.977/1.952mm	A/R		
14	FTC4318	Shim-man trans countershaft bearing/centre plate-. 2.027/2.002mm	A/R		
14	FTC4320	Shim-man trans countershaft bearing/centre plate-. 2.077/2.052mm	A/R		
14	FTC4322	Shim-man trans countershaft bearing/centre plate-. 2.127/2.102mm	A/R		
14	FTC4324	Shim-man trans countershaft bearing/centre plate-. 2.177/2.152mm	A/R		
14	FTC4326	Shim-man trans countershaft bearing/centre plate-. 2.227/2.202mm	A/R		

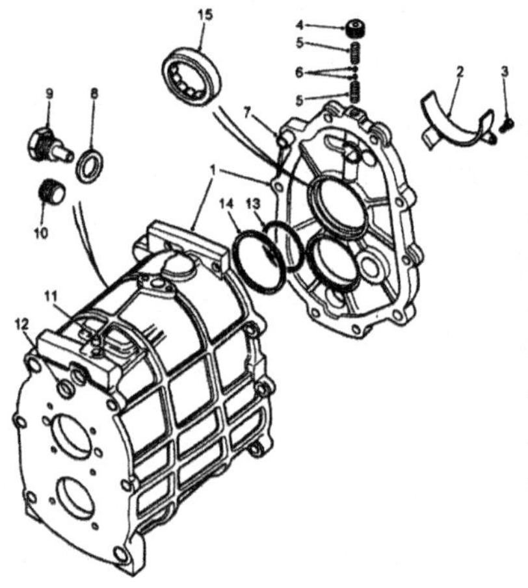

LC0007

Illus	Part Number	Description	Quantity	Change Point	Remarks
		SHIM			
14	TUZ100020	man trans countershaft bearing/centre plate-... 1.477/1.452mm	A/R	From (G) 0623640K	Suffix K
14	TUZ100040	man trans countershaft bearing/centre plate-... 1.502/1.477mm	A/R		
14	TUZ100060	man trans countershaft bearing/centre plate-... 1.577/1.552mm	A/R		
14	TUZ100080	man trans countershaft bearing/centre plate-... 1.627/1.602mm	A/R		
14	TUZ100100	man trans countershaft bearing/centre plate-... 1.677/1.652mm	A/R		
14	TUZ100120	man trans countershaft bearing/centre plate-... 1.727/1.702mm	A/R		
14	TUZ100140	man trans countershaft bearing/centre plate-... 1.777/1.752mm	A/R		
14	TUZ100160	man trans countershaft bearing/centre plate-... 1.827/1.802mm	A/R		
14	TUZ100180	man trans countershaft bearing/centre plate-... 1.877/1.852mm	A/R		
14	TUZ100200	man trans countershaft bearing/centre plate-... 1.927/1.902mm	A/R		
14	TUZ100220	man trans countershaft bearing/centre plate-... 1.977/1.952mm	A/R		
14	TUZ100240	man trans countershaft bearing/centre plate-... 2.027/2.002mm	A/R		
14	TUZ100270	man trans countershaft bearing/centre plate-... 2.077/2.052mm	A/R		
14	TUZ100290	man trans countershaft bearing/centre plate-... 2.127/2.102mm	A/R		
14	TUZ100310	man trans countershaft bearing/centre plate-... 2.177/2.152mm	A/R		
14	TUZ100330	man trans countershaft bearing/centre plate-... 2.227/2.202mm	A/R		

Illus	Part Number	Description	Quantity	Change Point	Remarks
1	FTC3921	Housing-clutch manual transmission	1		TDi
1	FTC3922	Housing-clutch manual transmission	NLA		Use UNB100190 qty 1 with FTC4720 qty 1. V8
1	FTC4018	HOUSING-CLUTCH MANUAL TRANSMISSION	1		4 Cylinder
	FRC6110	• Plug	1		
	FS112401	Screw-flanged head-flanged head-M12 x 40	6		
	FS112401	Screw-flanged head-flanged head-M12 x 40	5		4 Cylinder Naturally Aspirated
2	FTC4616	Screw-counter sunk-M12 x 40	1		4 Cylinder Naturally Aspirated
3	UKC25L	Dowel-housing to gearcase	2		
	3290	Plug-coolant drain	1		
	BH110221L	Bolt-gearbox to engine-hexagonal head-M10 x 110	4		TDi
	FN110047	Nut-flange-gearbox to engine-flange-M10	9		Manual TDi
2	SH108141L	Screw-gearbox to engine-hexagonal head-M8 x 14	1		TDi
	WA110061L	Washer-gearbox to engine-M10	4		
3	571134	Dowel-gearbox to engine	2		TDi
	622324	Clip-pipe-gearbox to engine	1		TDi
	BH506161L	Bolt-gearbox to engine-hexagonal head-3/8UNC x 2	8		V8
	PRC2978	Bracket-gearbox to engine	1		
	586440	Clip-cable-gearbox to engine	1		
	NH105041L	Nut-hexagonal-gearbox to engine-M5	1		
2	SH105161L	Screw-gearbox to engine-hexagonal head-M5 x 16	1		
	WA105001L	Washer-gearbox to engine-plain-standard-M5	2		
	WL105001L	Washer-gearbox to engine-retaining-M5	1		
	FN110047	Nut-flange-gearbox to engine-flange-M10	11		

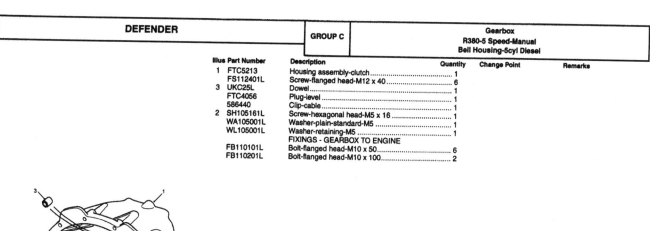

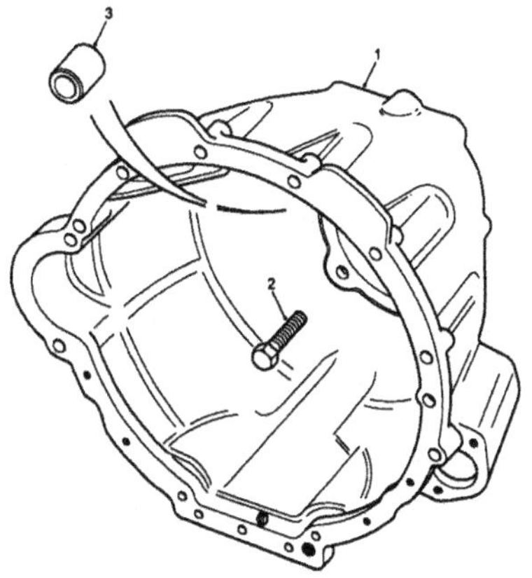

AHCFEA2A

Illus	Part Number	Description	Quantity	Change Point	Remarks
1	FTC5213	Housing assembly-clutch	1		
	FS112401L	Screw-flanged head-M12 x 40	6		
3	UKC25L	Dowel	1		
	FTC4056	Plug-level	1		
	586440	Clip-cable	1		
2	SH105161L	Screw-hexagonal head-M5 x 16	1		
	WA105001L	Washer-plain-standard-M5	1		
	WL105001L	Washer-retaining-M5	1		
		FIXINGS - GEARBOX TO ENGINE			
	FB110101L	Bolt-flanged head-M10 x 50	6		
	FB110201L	Bolt-flanged head-M10 x 100	2		

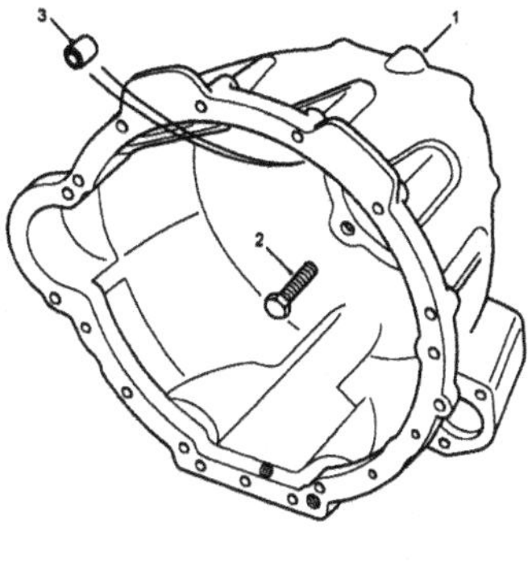

CFCFEA2A

Illus	Part Number	Description	Quantity	Change Point	Remarks
1	FTC4461	Housing-clutch manual transmission	1		
2	UKC25L	Dowel	2		
3	FS112401L	Screw-flanged head-M12 x 40	6		
4	2943111	Adaptor-clutch housing	1		
5	FTC2167	Seal-oil clutch housing	1		
6	FTC2168	Plug-core	1		
	FTC4833	Jacket-g/box-insul-lower	1		
	FTC4832	Jacket-g/box-insul-upper	1		
7	FTC2694	Guide-clutch release bearing	1		
8	FB110091L	Bolt-flanged head-M10 x 45	6		
8	FB110101	Bolt-flanged head-M10 x 50	2		
9	FRC2481	Dowel	A/R		
8	FB108161L	Bolt-flanged head-M8 x 80	4		
8	FB110221L	Bolt-flanged head-M10 x 110	2		
8	FB112101L	Bolt-flanged head-M12 x 50	2		
8	FB112201L	Bolt-flanged head-M12 x 100	2		
	FTC2162	Dowel-starter location starter motor	1		
	FTC4392	Bracket-clutch housing lifting	1		
3	FS106101L	Screw-flanged head-M6 x 10	1		
	ERR5194	Clip-edge harness	1		

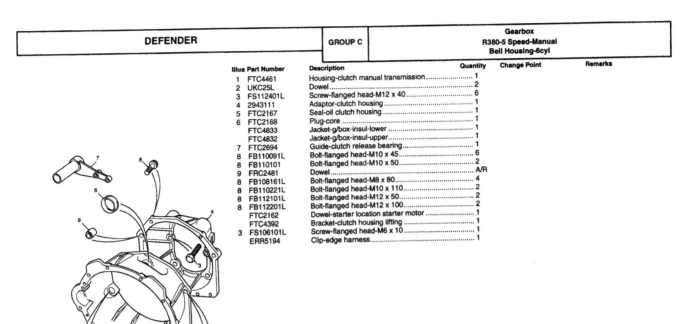

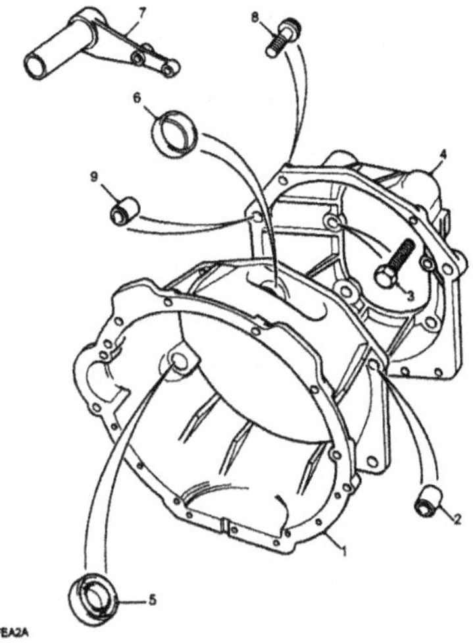

AKCFEA2A

Illus	Part Number	Description	Quantity	Change Point	Remarks
1	FRC2859	Cover-bell housing-bottom	1		
2	594087	Seal-bottom	1		
	SH106351L	Screw-hexagonal head-M6 x 35	5		
3	FS106255L	Screw-flanged head-M6 x 25	2		
4	FN106047L	Nut-flange-M6	5		
5	594134	Bolt	2		
6	WL108001L	Washer-sprung-M8	2		

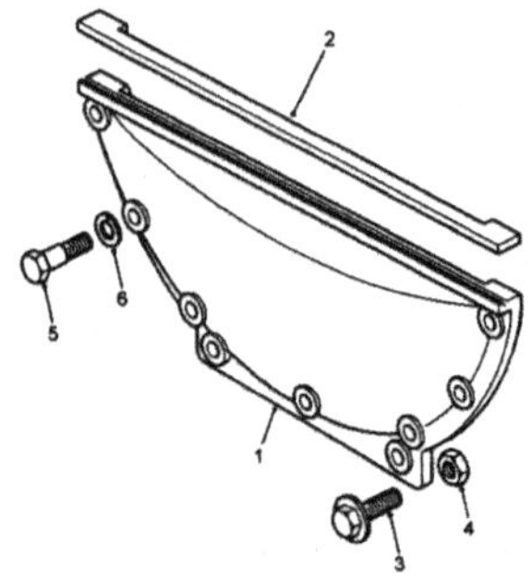

AHCFEA3A

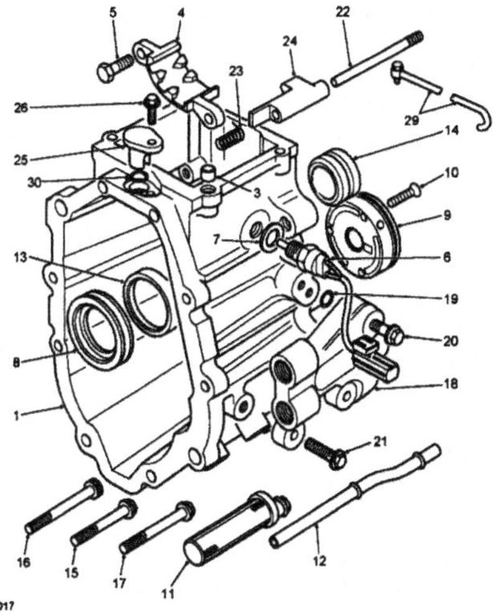

LC0017

Illus	Part Number	Description	Quantity	Change Point	Remarks
1	FTC4241	CASE ASSEMBLY-EXTENSION	1	To (V) MA 949874	
1	FTC4522	CASE ASSEMBLY-EXTENSION	1	From (V) MA 949875	
	FTC3730	• Case-extension-gearbox	1		
2	LYQ100050	• Plug-blanking	1		
3	FRC2626	• Pin-spring	2		
4	FTC2392	• Guide-gear lever	1		
5	FS108257L	• Screw-flanged head-M8 x 25	2		
6	CDU51	• Switch-reverse light manual transmission	1		Part of FTC4241.
7	ALU1403L	• Washer-sealing	1		
6	AMR3918	• Switch-reverse light manual transmission	1		Part of FTC4522.
	AMR3859	Harness-link	1		
8	FTC3701	Ring-mainshaft oil feed	1	To (G) 410128J	
8	FTC4991	Ring-mainshaft oil feed	1	From (G) 410129J	
9	FTC4206	PUMP-TRANSMISSION OIL	1		
	BZV1051	• O ring-oil pump seal	1		
10	FTC4449	Screw-torx-flange-M5 x 30	3		
11	FRC7855	Strainer-transmission oil	1		
12	FTC3387	Pipe-transmission oil inlet	1		
13	FTC2383	Seal-man trans output shaft	1		
14	FTC4021	Collar-distance manual transmission	1		
15	FB108111	Bolt-flanged head	6		
16	FB108171	Bolt-flanged head-M8 x 85	2		
17	SS108701S	Screw-M8 x 70	2	Note (3)	
17	FB108141S	Screw-M8 x 70	2	Note (2)	
17	TYG100650	Bolt	2	Note (4)	
	FTC4053	Pipe-transmission oil inlet	1		4 Cylinder
	FTC4053	Pipe-transmission oil inlet	1		5 Cylinder Diesel
18	FTC2104	Housing-transmission thermostat	1		V8 except oil cooler (air cooled)
18	FTC2687	Housing-transmission thermostat	1		V8 oil cooler (air cooled)
18	FTC2687	Housing-transmission thermostat	1	Note (1)	BMW M52 6 Cylinder
19	FTC1441	O ring-man trans thermostat housing	2		
20	FB108081	Bolt-M8 x 40-basic	2		
21	FS108307L	Screw-flanged head-M8 x 30	2		

CHANGE POINTS:
- (1) From (V) XA 159807
- (2) To (G) Suffix J
- (3) To (V) VA 106672
- (4) From (G) Suffix k

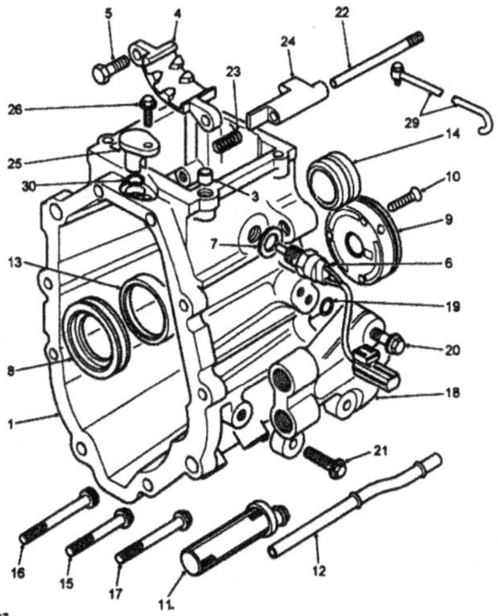

LC0017

Illus	Part Number	Description	Quantity	Change Point	Remarks
22	FTC3711	Shaft-camshaft reverse lock	1		
23	FTC4483	Spring-torsion	1		
24	FTC3713	Camshaft-reverse lock manual transmission	1		
25	FTC3587	Retainer-interlock	1		
26	FS106161M	Screw-flanged head-M6 x 16	1		
27	PRC8873	Transducer oil temperature-basic	1		V8
28	232042	Washer-sealing	1		V8
29	FRC9428	Tube-breather transmission case	1		4 Cylinder Petrol
29	FRC9430	TUBE-BREATHER TRANSMISSION CASE	1		TDi
	232039	• Washer-sealing	1		
	595478	• Bolt-banjo	1		
29	FRC9430	TUBE-BREATHER TRANSMISSION CASE	1		V8 Petrol
	232039	• Washer-sealing	1		
	595478	• Bolt-banjo	1		
30	FTC3975	O ring	1		
	FTC5409	Clip-pipe	A/R		Td5

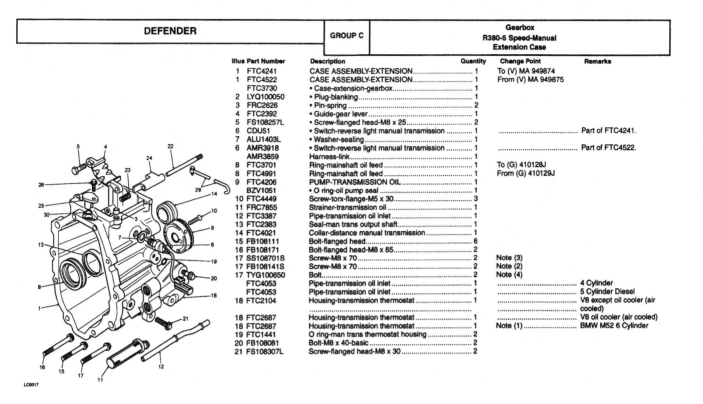

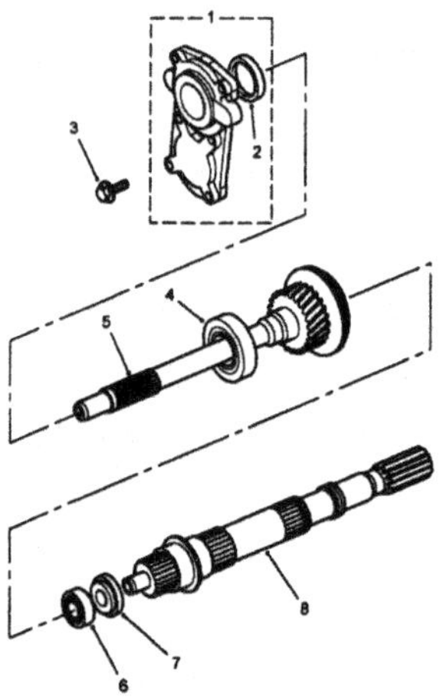

AHCFIA1A

Illus	Part Number	Description	Quantity	Change Point	Remarks
1	FTC4238	COVER-END MANUAL TRANSMISSION-FRONT	1	Note (1)	4 Cylinder Suffix J
1	FTC3696	COVER-END MANUAL TRANSMISSION-FRONT	NLA		Use FTC5371. V8
1	FTC3696	COVER-END MANUAL TRANSMISSION-FRONT	NLA		Use FTC5371. TDi
2	UKC1060L	• Seal-man trans primary shaft	NLA		Use FTC5303.
1	FTC5372	COVER-END MANUAL TRANSMISSION	1	Note (2)	4 Cylinder Suffix J
2	FTC5303	• Seal-man trans primary shaft	1		
1	FTC5371	COVER-END MANUAL TRANSMISSION	1	Note (2)	V8 Suffix J
2	FTC5303	• Seal-man trans primary shaft	1		
1	FTC5371	COVER-END MANUAL TRANSMISSION	1	Note (2)	TDi Suffix J
2	FTC5303	• Seal-man trans primary shaft	1		
1	FTC5371	COVER-END MANUAL TRANSMISSION	1	Note (2)	6 Cylinder Suffix J
2	FTC5303	• Seal-man trans primary shaft	1		
1	TVQ100200	COVER-END MANUAL TRANSMISSION	1	Note (3)	4 Cylinder Suffix K
2	FTC5303	• Seal-man trans primary shaft	1		
1	TVQ100130	COVER-END MANUAL TRANSMISSION	1	Note (3)	V8 Suffix K
2	FTC5303	• Seal-man trans primary shaft	1		
1	TVQ100130	COVER-END MANUAL TRANSMISSION	1	Note (3)	TDi Suffix K
2	FTC5303	• Seal-man trans primary shaft	1		
1	TVQ100130	COVER-END MANUAL TRANSMISSION	1	Note (3)	6 Cylinder Suffix K
2	FTC5303	• Seal	1		
3	FS108251S	Screw-flanged head-M8 x 25	6	To (G) 0623639J	
3	FS108301S	Screw-flanged head-M8 x 30	6	From (G) 0623640K	
4	RTC6751	Bearing-taper roller-man trans mainshaft/primary shaft-35.0 x 68.5	1	To (G) 0623639J	
4	TZZ100190	Bearing-taper roller-man trans mainshaft/primary shaft-35.0 x 72.0	1	From (G) 0623640K	

CHANGE POINTS:
(1) To (V) VA 103081
(2) From (V) VA 103082 To (G) 0623639J
(3) From (G) 0623640K

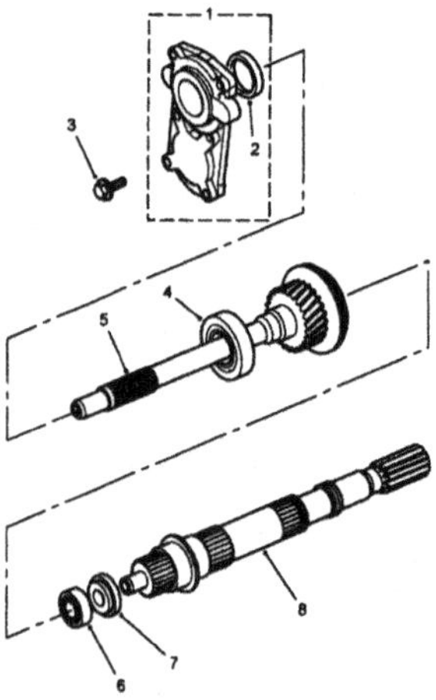

AHCFIA1A

Illus	Part Number	Description	Quantity	Change Point	Remarks
5	FTC3366	Shaft primary manual transmission	1	Note (1)	4 Cylinder
5	FTC3927	Shaft primary manual transmission	NLA		Fit new primary pinion FTC5046 and 3/4 synchro & 3rd gear kit STC3376.. TDi
5	FTC3928	Shaft primary manual transmission	NLA		Fit new primary pinion FTC5044, new 3/4 synchro and 3rd speed gear kit STC3376.. V8
5	FTC5056	Shaft primary manual transmission	1	Note (2)	4 Cylinder
5	FTC5046	Shaft primary manual transmission	1		TDi
5	FTC5044	Shaft primary manual transmission	1		V8
5	TUD101910	Shaft primary manual transmission	1	Note (3)	4 Cylinder
5	TUD101970	Shaft primary manual transmission	1		TDi
5	TUD102340	Shaft primary manual transmission	1	Note (4)	V8
5	TUD102820	Shaft primary manual transmission	1	Note (5)	4 Cylinder
5	TUD102580	Shaft primary manual transmission	1		TDi
5	TUD101830	Shaft primary manual transmission	1		5 Cylinder Diesel
5	TUD102580	Shaft primary manual transmission	1		BMW M52 6 Cylinder
6	UKC8L	Bearing-taper roller-man trans primary shaft-17.5 x 40.0	1		
7	FTC2737	Spacer-mainshaft	1		
8	FTC3703	Shaft-main manual transmission	NLA	Note (6)	Use FTC5287 qty 1 Mainshaft strengthened, need to change mainshaft and fit new pair of thrust washer segments and with FTC5288 qty 1 with FTC4990 qty 2.
8	FTC5287	Shaft-main manual transmission	1	Note (7)	Suffix J
8	TUD101720	Shaft-main manual transmission	1	Note (4)	Suffix K

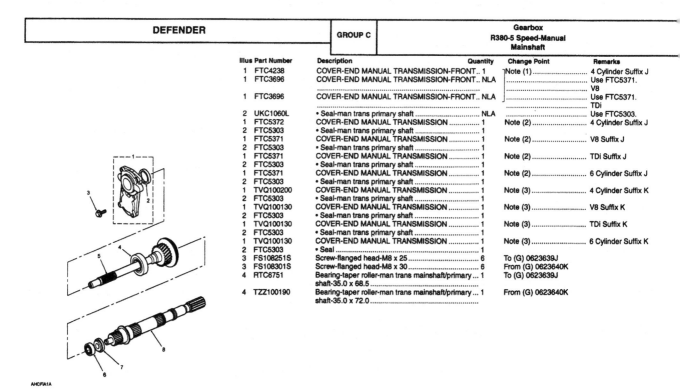

CHANGE POINTS:
(1) To (G) 417152J
(2) From (G) 417153J To (G) 0623639J
(3) From (G) 0623640K To (G) Suffix L
(4) From (G) 0623640K
(5) From (G) Suffix L
(6) To (G) 506331J
(7) From (G) 506332J To (G) 0623639J

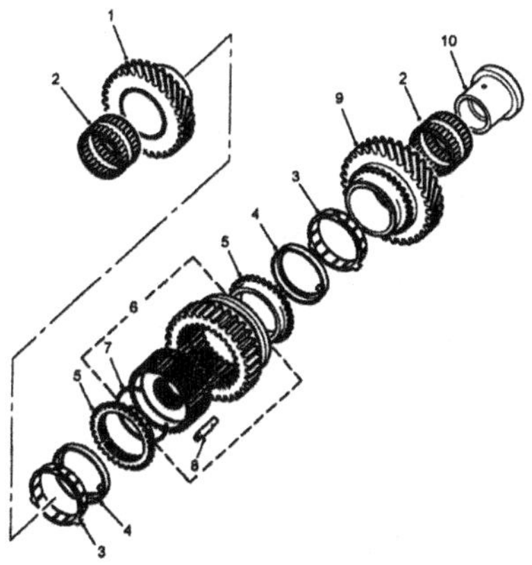

AHCFIC1A

Illus	Part Number	Description	Quantity	Change Point	Remarks
1	FTC2714	Gear-2nd driven manual transmission	1	Note (1)	
1	FTC5038	Gear-2nd driven manual transmission	1	Note (2)	
1	TUB101620	Gear-2nd driven manual transmission-27 teeth	1	Note (3)	
2	FTC1311	Bearing-needle roller manual transmission	NLA	Note (4)	Use TUK100340.
2	TUK100340	Bearing-needle roller manual transmission	2		
2	TUK100340	Bearing-needle roller manual transmission	2	Note (5)	
3	FTC2397	Ring-synchroniser inner	NLA	Note (1)	Use FTC5019.
3	FTC5019	Ring-synchroniser inner	2	Note (6)	
4	FTC2396	Ring-synchroniser intermediate	2		
5	FTC3584	Ring-baulk-1st/2nd gear	2		
6	FTC2733	SYNCHRONISER ASSEMBLY-1ST & 2ND MAINSHAFT ASSEMBLY	1	Note (1)	
7	FTC4172	• Spring ring	NLA		Use FTC4992.
8	FTC4171	• Plate-synchroniser	3		
7	FTC4992	Spring ring			
6	FTC5100	SYNCHRONISER ASSEMBLY-1ST & 2ND MAINSHAFT ASSEMBLY	1	Note (6)	
7	FTC4992	• Spring ring	2		
8	FTC4171	• Plate-synchroniser	3		

CHANGE POINTS:
(1) To (G) 417152J
(2) From (G) 417153J To (G) Suffix L
(3) From (G) Suffix L
(4) To (G) 0623639J
(5) From (G) 0623640K
(6) From (G) 417153J

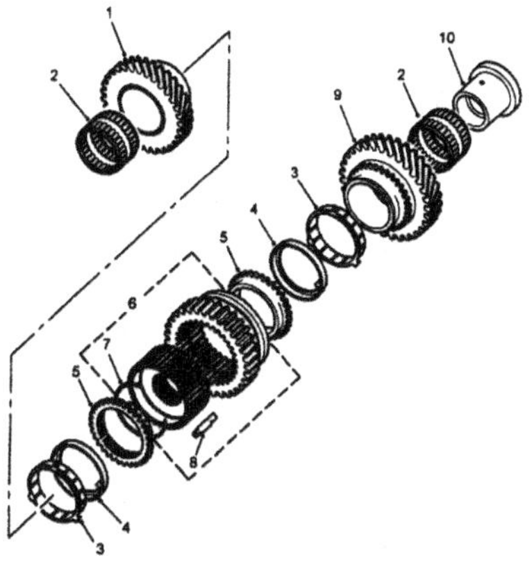

AHCFIC1A

Illus	Part Number	Description	Quantity	Change Point	Remarks
9	FTC2948	Gear-1st driven manual transmission	NLA	To (G) 417152J	Use FTC5037 qty 1 FTC5038 and synchro kit STC3375 for diesel or FTC5040 qty 1 For Defender 4 cyl diesel MOD, BMC SANAYI Turkey and DAF 0 series & XUD9A fit FTC5037, FTC5040 and synchro kit STC3375. V8 Petrol
9	FTC2948	Gear-1st driven manual transmission	NLA	To (G) 417152J	Use FTC5037 qty 1 FTC5038 and synchro kit STC3375 for diesel or FTC5040 qty 1 For Defender 4 cyl diesel MOD, BMC SANAYI Turkey and DAF 0 series & XUD9A fit FTC5037, FTC5040 and synchro kit STC3375. TDi
9	FTC5037	Gear-1st driven manual transmission-32 teeth	1	From (G) 417153J To (G) 0623639J	V8 TDi
9	TUB101800	Gear-1st driven manual transmission-32 teeth	1	From (G) 0623640K	TDi
9	TUB101800	Gear-1st driven manual transmission-32 teeth	1	To (G) Suffix L	V8
9	TUB101610	Gear-1st driven manual transmission-32 teeth	1	From (G) Suffix L	TDi
9	TUB101610	Gear-1st driven manual transmission-32 teeth	1		5 Cylinder Diesel
9	TUB101610	Gear-1st driven manual transmission-32 teeth	1		BMW M52 6 Cylinder
9	TUB101610	Gear-1st driven manual transmission-32 teeth	1		V8

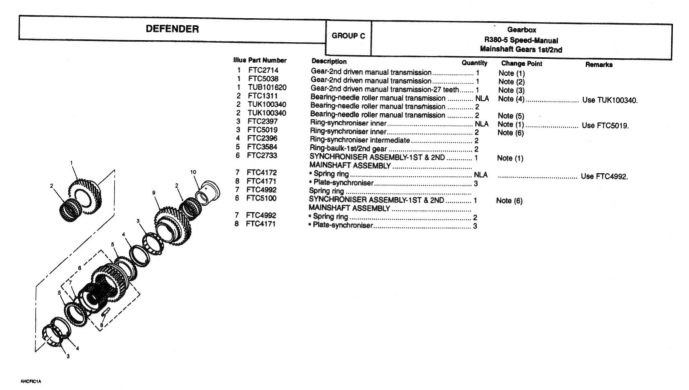

Illus	Part Number	Description	Quantity	Change Point	Remarks
9	FTC2716	Gear-1st driven manual transmission	NLA	To (G) 417152J	Fit new 1st/2nd synchro kit STC3375 with 1st gear FTC5036 and 2nd gear FTC5038. 4 Cylinder except TDi
9	FTC5036	Gear-1st driven manual transmission-31 teeth	1	From (G) 417153J To (G) 0623639J	4 Cylinder except TDi
9	TUB101830	Gear-1st driven manual transmission-31 teeth	1	From (G) 0623640K To (G) Suffix L	4 Cylinder except TDi
9	TUB101680	Gear-1st driven manual transmission-31 teeth	1	From (G) Suffix L	4 Cylinder except TDi

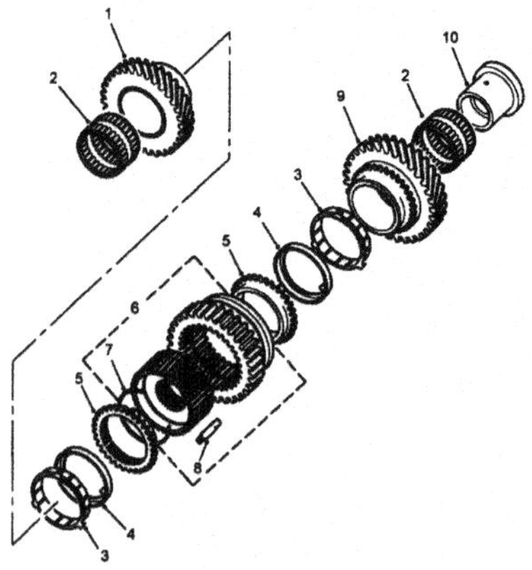

AHCFIC1A

Illus	Part Number	Description	Quantity	Change Point	Remarks
10	FTC2005	Bush-1st gear selective-30.905 to 30.955mm	NLA	To (G) 0623639J	Use TUJ100050.
10	TUJ100050	Bush-1st gear selective-30.905 to 30.955mm	1	From (G) 0623640K	
	STC3375	KIT-GEARS-1ST/2ND	1		
3	FTC5019	• Ring-synchroniser inner	2		
4	FTC2396	• Ring-synchroniser intermediate	2		
5	FTC3584	• Ring-baulk	2		
6	FTC5100	• SYNCHRONISER ASSEMBLY-1ST & 2ND MAINSHAFT ASSEMBLY	1		
7	FTC4992	• • Spring ring	2		
8	FTC4171	• • Plate-synchroniser	3		

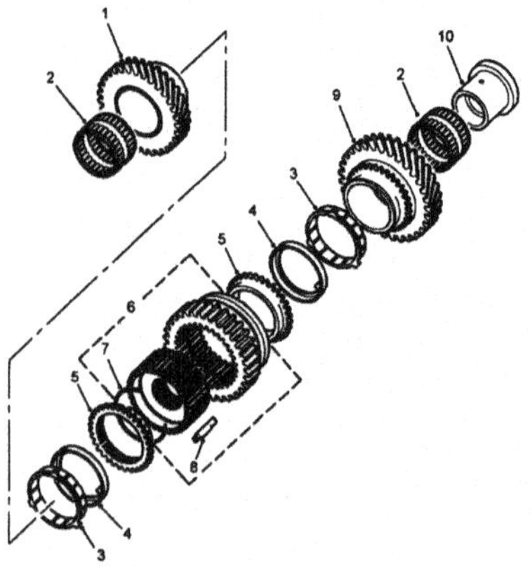

AHCFIC1A

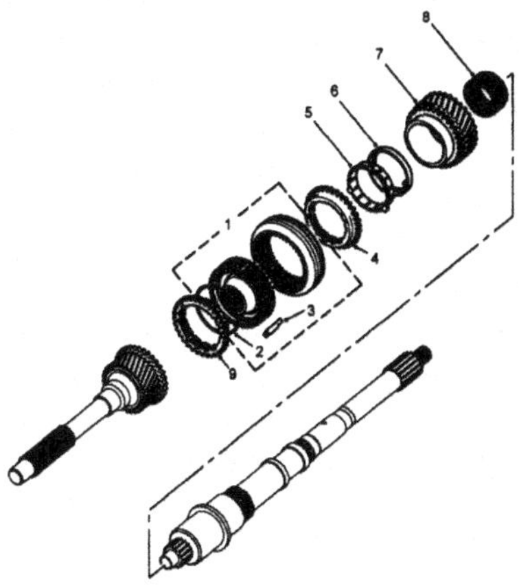

AHCFIC2A

Illus	Part Number	Description	Quantity	Change Point	Remarks
1	FTC2887	SYNCHRONISER ASSEMBLY-3RD & 4TH MAINSHAFT ASSEMBLY	1	Note (1)	
2	FTC4172	• Spring ring	NLA		Use FTC4992.
2	FTC4992	• Spring ring	1		
3	FTC4171	• Plate-synchroniser	3		
1	FTC5101	SYNCHRONISER ASSEMBLY-3RD & 4TH MAINSHAFT ASSEMBLY	1	Note (2)	
2	FTC4992	• Spring ring	2		
	FTC4171	• Plate-synchroniser	3		
4	FTC3584	Ring-baulk	1		
5	FTC2396	Ring-synchroniser intermediate	1		
6	FTC2397	Ring-synchroniser inner	NLA	Note (1)	Use FTC5019.
6	FTC5019	Ring-synchroniser inner	1	Note (2)	
		MAINSHAFT - 3RD & 4TH GEARS - MANUAL			
7	FTC2712	Gear-3rd driven manual transmission-27 teeth	1	Note (1)	
7	FTC5041	Gear-3rd driven manual transmission-27 teeth	1	Note (3)	
7	TUB101630	Gear-3rd driven manual transmission-27 teeth		Note (4)	
8	FTC1311	Bearing-needle roller manual transmission	NLA	Note (5)	Use TUK100340.
8	TUK100340	Bearing-needle roller manual transmission	1	Note (4)	
9	FTC2731	Ring-baulk-3rd/4th/5th gear	NLA	Note (1)	
9	FTC5018	Ring-baulk-3rd/4th/5th gear	1	Note (2)	
	STC3376	KIT-GEARS-3RD/4TH	1	Note (5)	
	STC4348	KIT-GEARS-3RD/4TH	1	Note (4)	
1	FTC5101	• SYNCHRONISER ASSEMBLY-3RD & 4TH MAINSHAFT ASSEMBLY	1		
2	FTC4992	• • Spring ring	2		
3	FTC4171	• • Plate-synchroniser	3		
4	FTC3584	• Ring-baulk	1		
6	FTC5019	• Ring-synchroniser inner	1		
5	FTC2396	• Ring-synchroniser intermediate	1		
7	FTC5041	• Gear-3rd driven manual transmission-27 teeth	1		Part of STC3376.
7	TUB101630	• Gear-3rd driven manual transmission-27 teeth	1		Part of STC4348.
9	FTC5018	• Ring-baulk	1		Part of STC4348.

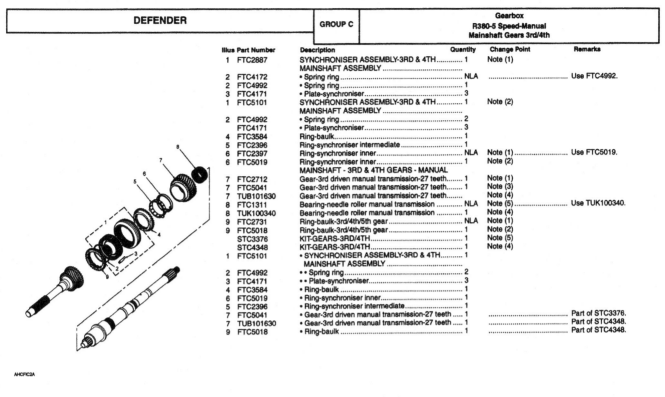

CHANGE POINTS:
(1) To (G) 417152J
(2) From (G) 417153J
(3) From (G) 417153J To (G) Suffix L
(4) From (G) Suffix L
(5) To (G) Suffix L

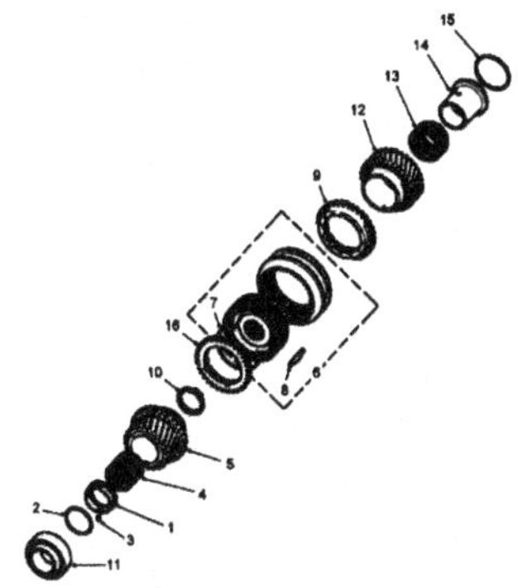

LC0027

Illus	Part Number	Description	Quantity	Change Point	Remarks
1	FTC3699	Washer-thrust manual transmission	NLA	Note (1)	Use FTC4989 qty 2 with FTC4990 qty 1 with FTC4991 qty 1.
1	FTC4989	Washer-thrust manual transmission	NLA	Note (2)	Use FTC5288.
1	FTC5288	Washer-thrust manual transmission	1	Note (3)	
2	FTC3700	Ring-retention	NLA		Use FTC4524.
2	FTC4524	Ring-retention	1	To (G) 410128J	
	FTC4991	Ring-mainshaft oil feed	1	From (G) 410129J	
3	PA108101L	Pin-spring	1	To (G) 410128J	
4	FRC5280	Bearing-needle roller manual transmission	1		
5	FTC4539	Gear-5th driven manual transmission	NLA	To (G) 417152J	Fit new 5th/reverse synchro & reverse gear kit STC3377 and 5th gear FTC5043..
5	FTC5043	Gear-5th driven manual transmission-19 teeth	1	From (G) 417153J	
6	FTC2727	SYNCHRONISER ASSEMBLY-5TH GEAR MAINSHAFT ASSEMBLY	1	To (G) 417152J	
7	FTC4245	• Spring ring	2		
8	FTC4171	• Plate-synchroniser	3		
		MAINSHAFT - 5TH GEAR & REVERSE - MANUAL			
9	FTC2731	Ring-baulk-5th gear	NLA	To (G) 417152J	
9	FTC5018	Ring-baulk-5th gear	1	From (G) 417153J	
10	FTC3697	Circlip-man trans mainshaft/centre plate bearing	1		
11	FTC3371	Bearing-taper roller	1		
	STC3377	KIT-SYNCHRONISER ASSEMBLY-MAIN SHAFT-5TH & REVERSE GEAR	1	From (G) 417153J	
6	FTC5102	• SYNCHRONISER ASSEMBLY-5TH GEAR MAINSHAFT ASSEMBLY	1		
7	FTC4992	• • Spring ring	2		
8	FTC4171	• • Plate-synchroniser	3		
12	FTC5070	• Gear-reverse manual transmission	1		
9	FTC5018	• Ring-baulk	1		
16	FTC3584	• Ring-baulk	1		
1	FTC4989	• Washer-thrust manual transmission	NLA		Use FTC5288.
1	FTC5288	• Washer-thrust manual transmission	2		
2	FTC4990	• Ring-retention	1		
	FTC4991	• Ring-mainshaft oil feed	1		

CHANGE POINTS:
(1) To (G) 410129J
(2) From (G) 410129J To (G) 506331J
(3) From (G) 506332J

DEFENDER	GROUP C	Gearbox R380-5 Speed-Manual Mainshaft Gears 5th/Reverse

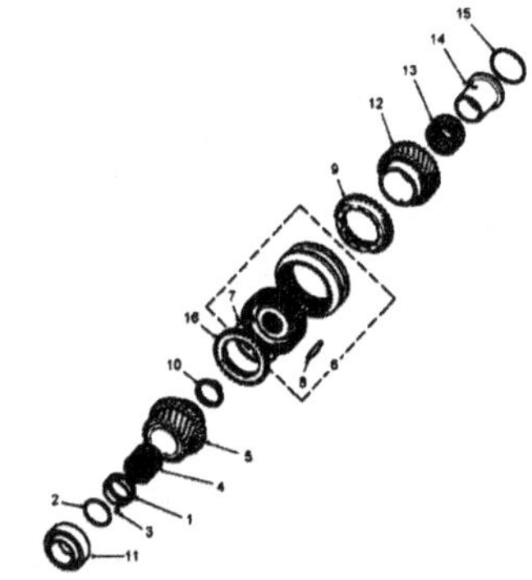

LC0027

Illus	Part Number	Description	Quantity	Change Point	Remarks
14	FTC2005	Bush-1st gear selective-30.905 to 30.955mm	NLA	To (G) 417152J	Use TUJ100050.
14	TUJ100050	Bush-1st gear selective-30.905 to 30.955mm	1	From (G) 417153J	
12	FTC4242	Gear-reverse manual transmission...........................	1	To (G) 417152J	
12	FTC5070	Gear-reverse manual transmission...........................	1	From (G) 417153J	
13	FTC1311	Bearing-needle roller manual transmission	NLA	To (G) Suffix L.................	Use TUK100340.
13	TUK100340	Bearing-needle roller manual transmission	1	From (G) Suffix L	
15	FTC3951	Shim-man trans reverse gear bush-2.475/2.450mm	A/R		
15	FTC3953	Shim-man trans reverse gear bush-2.425/2.400mm	A/R		
15	FTC3955	Shim-man trans reverse gear bush-2.375/2.350mm	A/R		
15	FTC3957	Shim-man trans reverse gear bush-2.325/2.300mm	A/R		
15	FTC3959	Shim-man trans reverse gear bush-2.275/2.250mm	A/R		
15	FTC3961	Shim-man trans reverse gear bush-2.225/2.200mm	A/R		
15	FTC3963	Shim-man trans reverse gear bush-2.175/2.150mm	A/R		
15	FTC3965	Shim-man trans reverse gear bush-2.125/2.100mm	A/R		
15	FTC3967	Shim-man trans reverse gear bush-2.075/2.050mm	A/R		
15	FTC3969	Shim-man trans reverse gear bush-2.025/2.000mm	A/R		

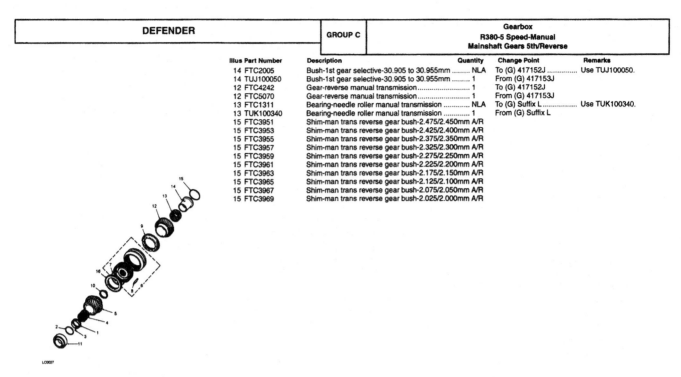

DEFENDER	GROUP C	Gearbox R380-5 Speed-Manual Layshaft

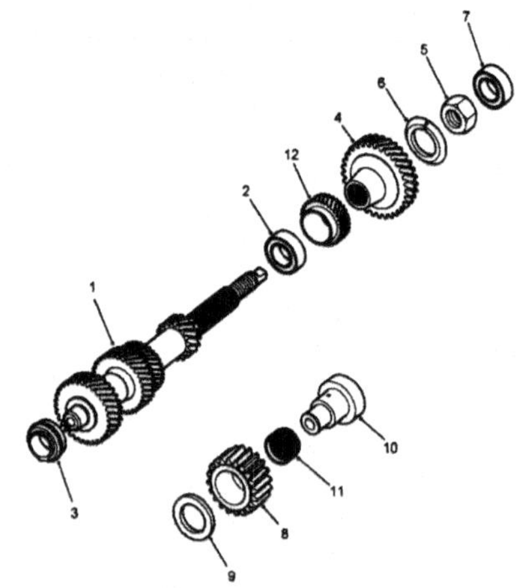

AJCFIE1A

Illus	Part Number	Description	Quantity	Change Point	Remarks
1	FTC2941	Shaft-lay..	NLA	Note (1)............................	Fit layshaft FTC4982 and 5th gear kit STC3378.. TDi
1	FTC2941	Shaft-lay..	NLA	....	Fit layshaft FTC4982 and 5th gear kit STC3378.. V8
1	FTC4982	Shaft-lay..	1	Note (2)............................	V8 Petrol Suffix J
1	FTC4982	Shaft-lay..	1	....	TDi Suffix J
1	FTC4982	Shaft-lay..	1	....	6 Cylinder
1	TUO100240	Shaft-lay..	1	Note (3)............................	V8 Suffix K
1	TUO100240	Shaft-lay..	1	....	TDi
1	TUO100240	Shaft-lay..	1	....	BMW M52 6 Cylinder
1	TUO100100	Shaft-lay..	1	Note (4)............................	V8
1	TUO100100	Shaft-lay..	1	....	TDi
1	TUO100100	Shaft-lay..	1	....	BMW M52 6 Cylinder
1	TUO100100	Shaft-lay..	1	....	5 Cylinder
1	FTC2974	Shaft-lay..	1	Note (1)............................	4 Cylinder except TDi
1	FTC4984	Shaft-lay..	1	Note (2)............................	4 Cylinder except TDi
1	TUO100160	Shaft-lay..	1	Note (5)............................	4 Cylinder except TDi
1	TUO100370	Shaft-lay..	1	Note (4)	
		BEARING-TAPER ROLLER			
2	FTC317	man trans countershaft/centre plate-31.75 x 59.0....................	1	To (G) 0623639J	
2	TZZ100200	man trans countershaft/centre plate-31.75 x 62.0....................	1	From (G) 0623640K	
3	FTC248	man trans countershaft/main case-31.75 x 62.01			
4	FTC2945	Gear-5th speed countershaft manual transmission .	1	To (G) 416033J	
4	FTC4978	Gear-5th speed countershaft manual transmission-37 teeth....................	1	From (G) 416034J	
5	EJP7738L	Nut-stake-man trans countershaft............................	1		
6	FAM9270	Collar-layshaft..	1	From (G) 416034J	
7	FTC2385	Bearing-taper roller-man trans countershaft/extension case	1		

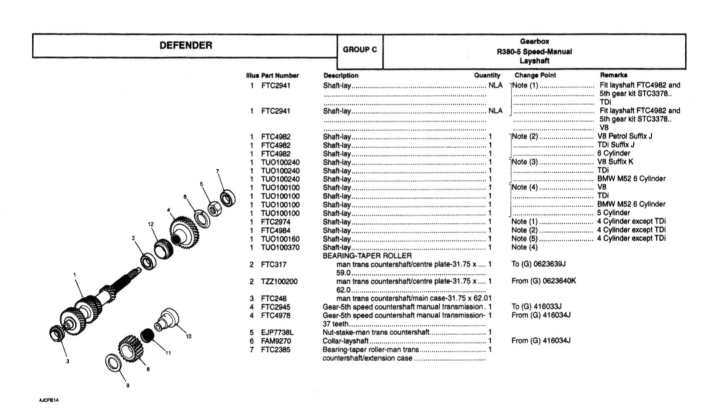

CHANGE POINTS:
(1) To (G) 416033J
(2) From (G) 416034J To (G) 0623639J
(3) From (G) 0623640K To (G) Suffix L
(4) From (G) Suffix L
(5) From (G) 0623640K

Illus	Part Number	Description	Quantity	Change Point	Remarks
8	FTC2725	Gear-reverse idler assembly manual transmission	1	To (G) Suffix L	
8	TUB102000	Gear-reverse idler assembly manual transmission	1	From (G) Suffix L	
9	FTC3847	Spacer	1	To (G) 0623639J	
9	TUZ100000	Spacer	1	From (G) 0623640K	
10	FTC3850	Shaft-reverse idler assembly-manual transmission	1		
11	FTC2582	Bearing-needle roller	1		
12	FTC3391	Gear-reverse manual transmission	1	To (G) 0623639J	Suffix J
12	TUB101500	Gear-reverse manual transmission	NLA	From (G) 0623640K	Use TUB101990. Suffix K
12	TUB101990	Gear-reverse manual transmission	1		Suffix L
	STC3378	KIT-GEAR 5TH SPEED	1	Note (1)	
4	FTC4978	• Gear-5th speed countershaft manual transmission-37 teeth	1		
6	FAM9270	• Collar-layshaft	1		

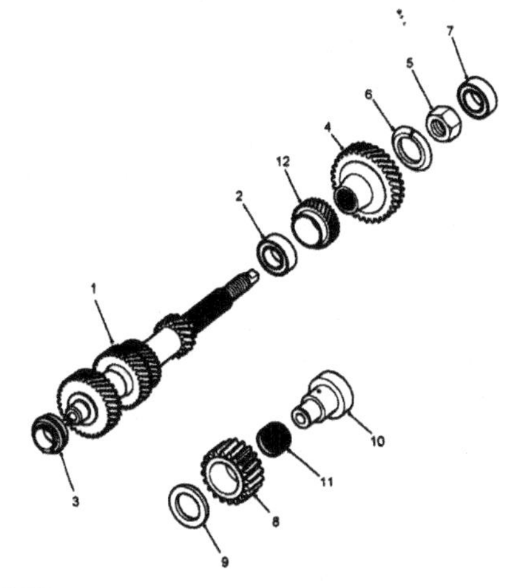

AJCFIE1A

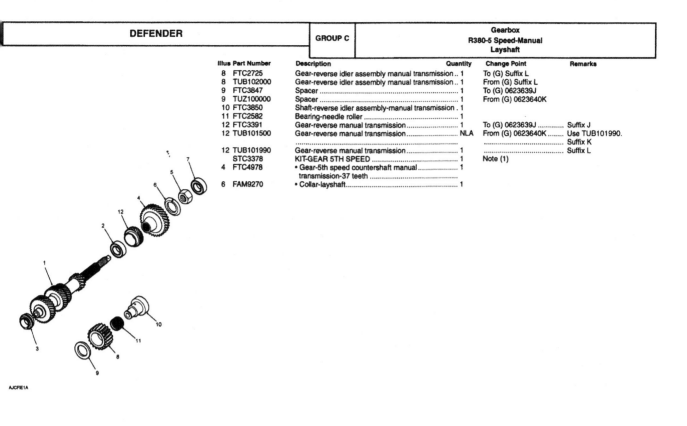

CHANGE POINTS:
(1) From (G) 416034J

Illus	Part Number	Description	Quantity	Change Point	Remarks
1	FTC4588	Shaft-selector manual transmission	1		
2	FTC3581	Fork assembly-selector-1st/2nd manual transmission	1		
3	FTC4596	Ball-detent manual transmission	2		
4	FTC4585	Lever-selector selector mechanism	NLA		Use FTC5120.
4	FTC5120	Lever-selector selector mechanism	1		
	FTC4458	Ring-snap-manual	1		
5	FTC1488	Pin-selector manual transmission	1	To (V) LA 939975	
5	FTC4617	Pin-selector manual transmission	1	From (V) MA 939976	
6	FRC7334	Shaft-selector manual transmission	1		
7	FRC7333	Lever-selector selector mechanism	1		
8	FRC7335	Pin-spring	1		
9	FRC4435	Roller	1		
10	FRC4434	Shaft-gear change change piece roller	1		
11	CR120105L	Circlip	1		
12	FRC4951	O ring	1		
13	FRC5864	Yoke-shift rod manual transmission	1		
14	FTC4536	Screw-grub	1		
15	FRC5859	Yoke-shift rod manual transmission	1		
16	CR120335L	Circlip	1		
17	FTC3582	Fork assembly-3rd & 4th manual transmission	1		
18	FTC3370	Interlock manual transmission	1		
19	FRC8239	Retainer-interlock	1		
20	FRC8170	O ring	1		
21	FTC4597	Fork assembly-5th manual transmission	1		
22	FTC2885	Interlock-5th/reverse	1		
23	FTC3382	Spring-detent manual transmission	2		
24	FTC4108	Plug	1		
25	SH106161M	Screw-hexagonal head-M6 x 16	2		
26	FRC8127	Pin-selector lever/shaft manual transmission	2		

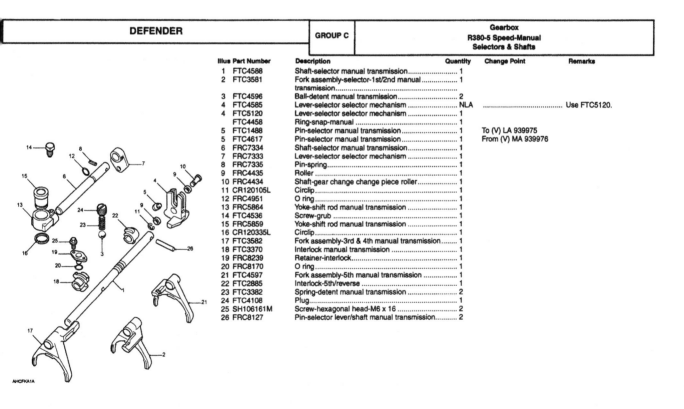

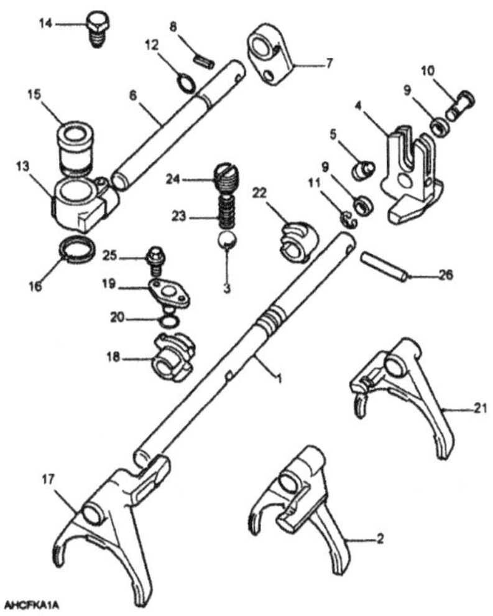

AHCFKA1A

Illus	Part Number	Description	Quantity	Change Point	Remarks
1	FRC7155	Housing assembly-manual transmission gearchange	1		
2	FTC4510	Washer-joint	1		
3	FS108257L	Screw-flanged head-M8 x 25	4		
4	FS106201L	Screw-flanged head-M6 x 20	2		
5	NH106041L	Nut-hexagonal-nyloc-M6	2		
6	FRC8724	LEVER-LOWER MANUAL TRANSMISSION	1		
	UKC3092	• Pin	2		
7	22G1988L	• Plunger-locking manual transmission	1		
8	22G1989L	• Spring-plunger manual transmission	1		
9	FRC7414	Spring-torsion	1		
10	PA120801L	Pin-roll-roll	1		
11	FS106167L	Screw-flanged head-flanged head-M6 x 16	1		
12	FRC7886	Plate-retaining	1		
13	FRC7160	Grommet	1		
14	AFU4173	Tie-cable-Black-8.8 x 770mm-releasable	1		
15	BTR1698	Gaiter-gear lever assembly-transfer box	1		
16	FTC3915	Housing assembly-transfer box gear change	1		
17	GS110501	Screw-grub-5th speed stop	1		
18	FN110047	Nut-flange-flange-M10	1		
19	597586	Plug-core	1		
20	FB108081L	Bolt-flanged head-M8 x 40	3		
21	FB108111L	Bolt-flanged head-M8 x 55	1		
22	FRC2626	Pin-spring	2		
23	FRC7860	Lever assembly-gear selector manual transmission	1		RHD
23	FRC7493	Lever assembly-gear selector manual transmission	1		LHD
24	NY110047L	Nut-sheradized-flange-nyloc-M10	1		
25	WC110061L	Washer-plain-M10-oversize	1		
26	BTR9270	Knob assembly-change manual transmission-plastic	1		Standard / County
26	STC60508	Knob assembly-change manual transmission-aluminium	1		Tdi Hardtop 50th Tomb Raider
26	UKJ000010	Knob assembly-change manual transmission	1		X-Tech LE

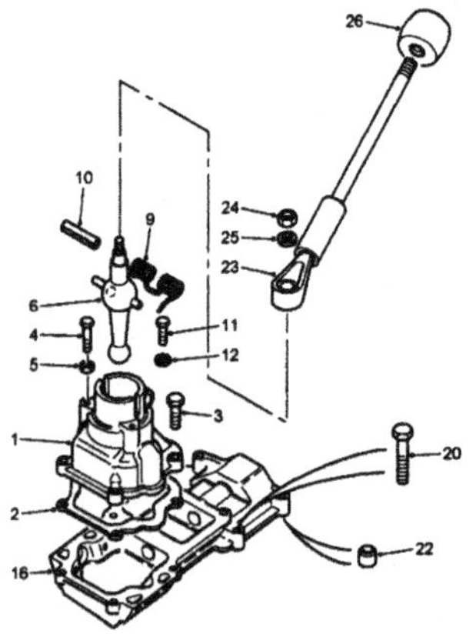

AJCFKC1A

Illus	Part Number	Description	Quantity	Change Point	Remarks
1	FTC5360	Oil cooler assembly transmission	1		
	2943346	Bracket-oil cooler	1		
	FTC5361	Spacer	2		
2	FS108351L	Screw-flanged head-M8 x 40-long	NLA		Use FS108357.
3	2943348	Pipe assembly-transmission to oil cooler	1		
4	2943349	Pipe assembly-oil cooler to transmission	1		
5	1742636	O ring-transmission oil cooler hose	4		

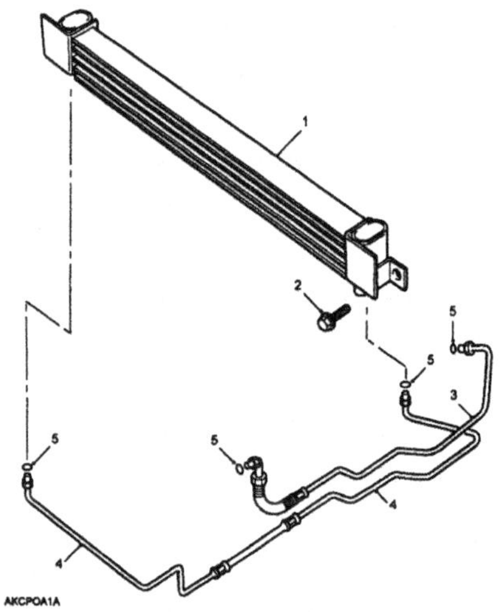

AKCPOA1A

Illus	Part Number	Description	Quantity	Change Point	Remarks
1	FTC4969	Transmission assembly automatic -new	1		

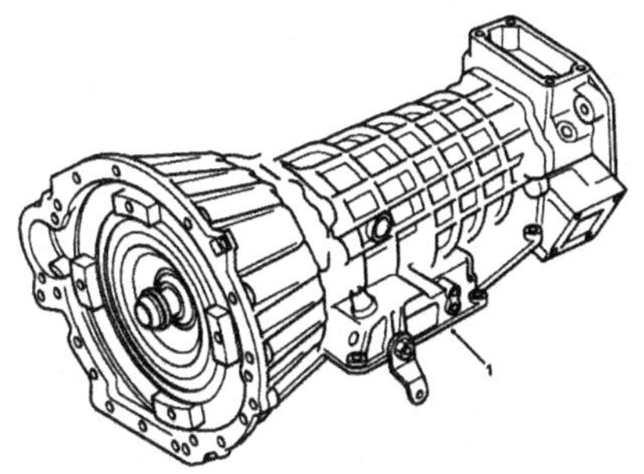

AMCPAA1A

Illus	Part Number	Description	Quantity	Change Point	Remarks
1	594087	Seal-bottom	1		
	546198	Weight-crankshaft balance-0.75 oz	1		
2	FRC2859	Cover-bell housing-bottom	1		
3	FS106255L	Screw-flanged head-M6 x 25	7		
4	594134	Bolt	2		

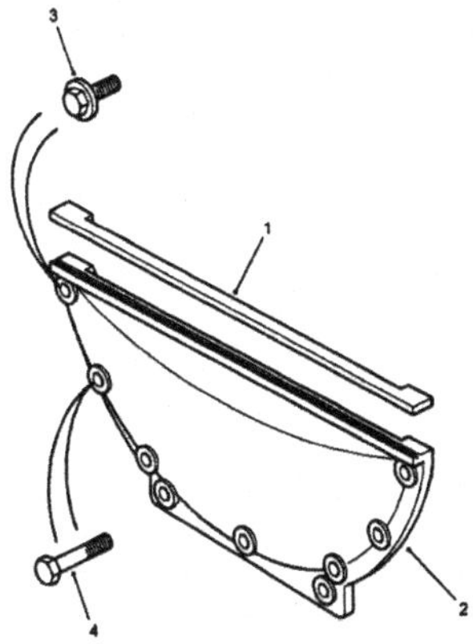

AMCPEA1A

DEFENDER

GROUP C

Gearbox
ZF-4 Speed-Automatic
Torque Convertor & Housing

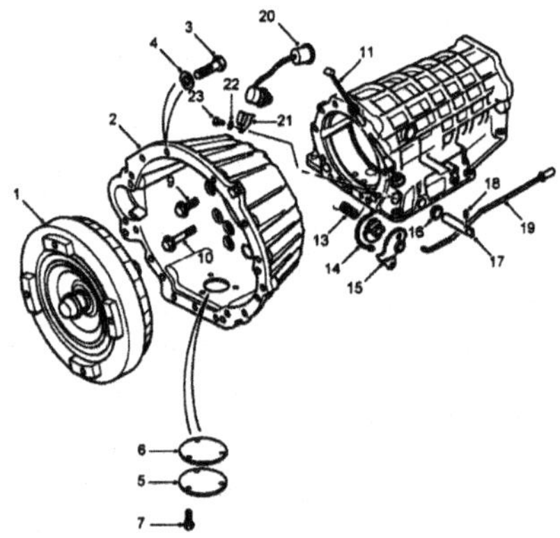

AMCPEA2A

Illus	Part Number	Description	Quantity	Change Point	Remarks
1	FRC5981	Converter assembly automatic transmission	1	Note (1)	
1	STC3600	Converter assembly automatic transmission	1	Note (2)	
2	RTC6594	Housing assembly-torque converter automatic transmission	1		
3	BH506161L	Bolt-hexagonal head-3/8UNC x 2	8		
4	WL600061L	Washer-spring-3/8	8		
5	FRC7706	Cover assembly-coverter automatic transmission	1		
6	FRC7707	Gasket-converter housing lower access cover	1		
7	FS106167L	Screw-flanged head-flanged head-M6 x 16	3		
8	WM600041L	Washer-spring-1/4 dia-square	6		
9	FB110301L	Bolt-hexagonal head-M10 x 30	6		
10	FB110141L	Bolt-flanged head-M10 x 70	12		
11	RTC4854	Cable assembly-kickdown automatic transmission	1		
12	RTC4648	O ring	1		
13	RTC4288	Spring-lever detent selector mechanism	1		
14	RTC4658	Lever assembly-selector selector mechanism	1		
15	RTC4286	Lever-detent automatic transmission	1		
16	RTC4289	Seal selector mechanism	1		
17	RTC4285	Shaft automatic transmission	1		
18	RTC4290	Pin-roll-spring tension	1		
19	RTC4291	Rod assembly-kickdown automatic transmission	1		
20	RTC4937	Switch-inhibitor change selector	1		
	RTC5203	Plate-transfer box detent spring retaining	1		
21	RTC4644	Plate-inhibitor switch detent	1		
22	RTC4643	Washer-spring	1		
23	RTC4645	Screw	1		

CHANGE POINTS:
(1) To (E)36D 52139C
(2) From (E)36D 52140C

DEFENDER

GROUP C

Gearbox
ZF-4 Speed-Automatic
Casing & Sump

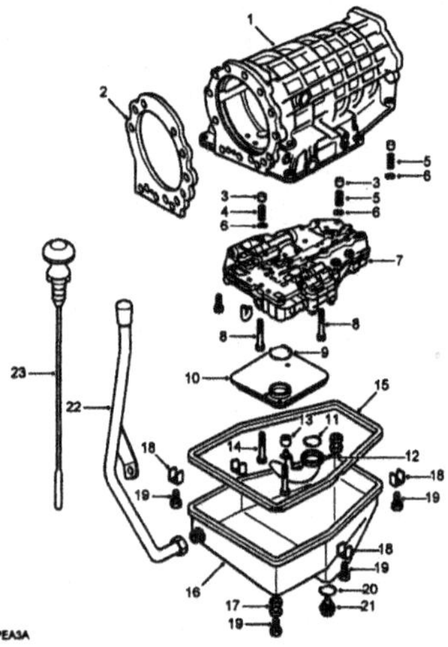

AMCPEA3A

Illus	Part Number	Description	Quantity	Change Point	Remarks
2	RTC4320	Gasket-end cover automatic transmission	1		
3	RTC4280	Sleeve-short	8		
3	RTC5209	Sleeve-long	1		
4	RTC4281	Spring-short	4		
5	RTC4282	Spring-long	5		
6	RTC4657	Circlip	9		
7	STC930	Valve-block	1		
8	RTC4649	Screw-83mm-long	1		
8	RTC4278	Screw-65mm-long	4		
8	RTC4277	Screw-60mm-long	3		
8	RTC4279	Screw-30mm-long	8		
9	RTC4276	O ring-auto trans strainer to control unit	1		
10	RTC4653	Strainer-oil-automatic transmission fluid automatic transmission	1		
11	RTC5818	O ring-auto trans fluid suction pipe	1		
12	RTC4655	Pipe-suction automatic transmission	NLA		Use TQW100030 Suction pipe now includes sleeve.
12	TQW100030	Pipe-suction automatic transmission	1		
13	RTC4656	Sleeve	1		
14	RTC4278	Screw-65mm-long	2		
14	RTC4649	Screw-83mm-long	1		
15	RTC4268	Gasket-sump/transmission case automatic transmission	1		
16	RTC4652	Pan assembly-oil transmission case-automatic	NLA		Use STC4097 qty 01 Changed size of sump plug. Supply latest sump with new plug washer and magnet. with STC4098 qty 01 with STC4099 qty 01 with STC4100 qty 01.
17	RTC5733	Plate	4		
18	RTC5734	Plate	2		
19	RTC5735	Screw	6		
20	STC1060	Washer-sealing-drain plug-automatic transmission	1		
21	RTC4647	Plug and magnet assembly-transmission case	1		
22	FTC1356	Pipe-dipstick automatic transmission	1		
23	FTC4474	Dipstick automatic transmission-693mm	1		

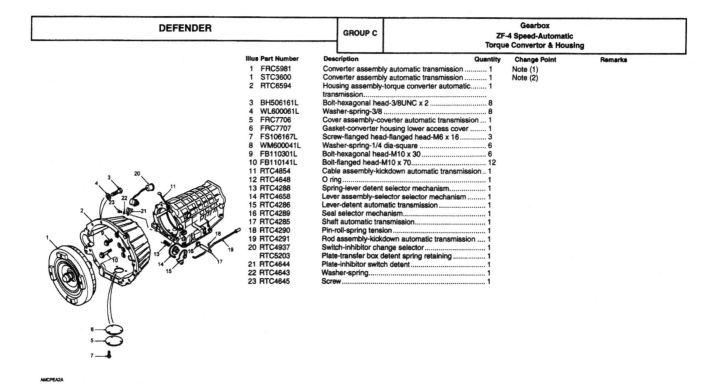

Illus	Part Number	Description	Quantity	Change Point	Remarks
1	RTC5102	Seal	1		
2	STC1836	Pump-transmission oil	1		
3	RTC5105	Screw-M6 x 28	8		
4	RTC5106	Dowel-pin	1		
5	RTC5103	O ring	1		
6	RTC5107	Plate-intermediate	1		
7	RTC4339	Washer-sealing	1		
8	RTC4335	Plug-blanking	1		
9	RTC4338	Washer-sealing	1		
10	RTC4336	Plug-blanking	1		
		SHIM			
11	RTC5108	2.8mm	A/R		
11	RTC5109	2.6mm	A/R		
11	RTC5111	2.20mm	A/R		
11	RTC5112	2.00mm	A/R		
11	RTC5113	1.80mm	A/R		
11	RTC5114	1.6mm	A/R		
11	RTC5115	1.40mm	A/R		
11	RTC5116	1.20mm	A/R		
11	RTC5117	1.0mm	A/R		

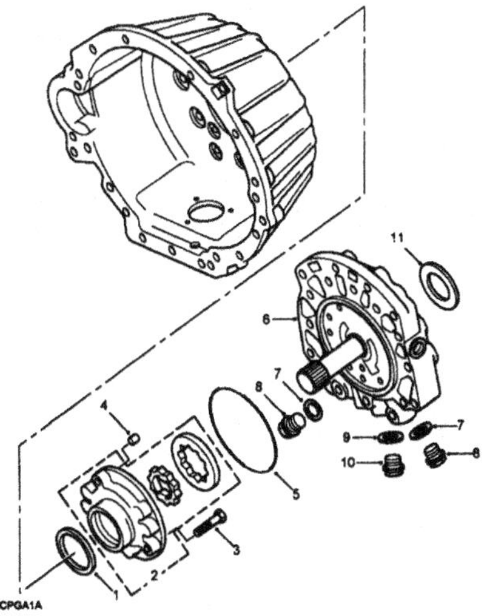

AMCPGA1A

Illus	Part Number	Description	Quantity	Change Point	Remarks
5	RTC5101	Kit-automatic transmission bearing overhaul	1		
1	RTC5143	Retainer-bearing automatic transmission	1		
2	RTC5141	Shaft-counter automatic transmission	1		
3	RTC5142	Kit-clutch-automatic	1		
4	RTC5144	Carrier-gear automatic transmission	1		

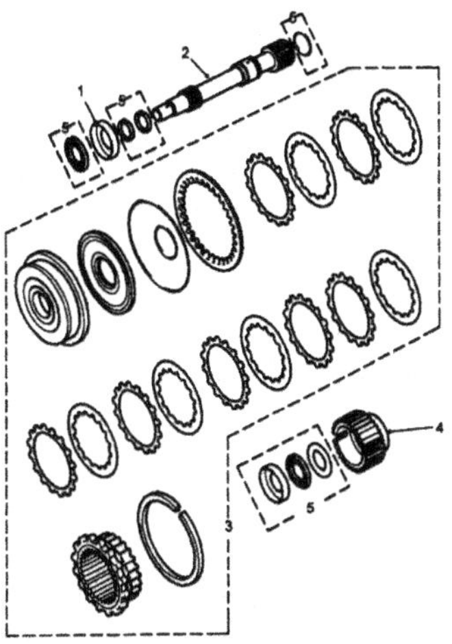

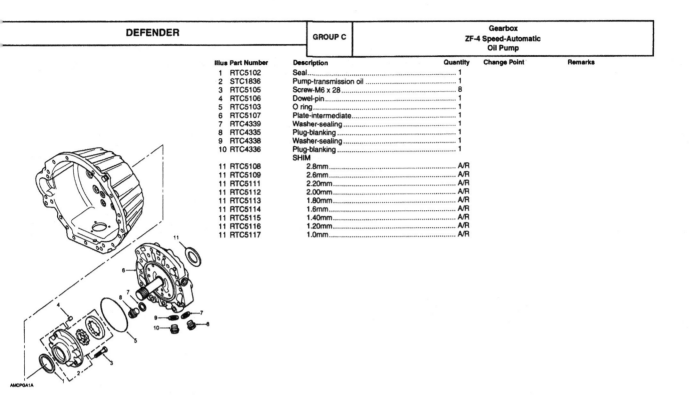

AMCPGE1A

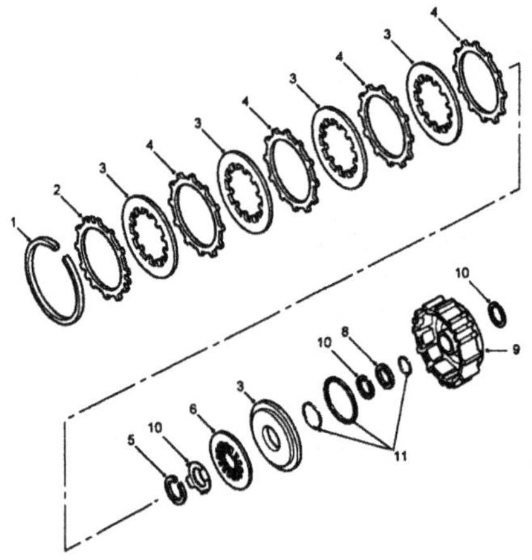

AMCPGE2A

Illus	Part Number	Description	Quantity	Change Point	Remarks
1	RTC5124	Ring-snap automatic transmission	1		
2	RTC5123	Disc-clutch automatic transmission-end	1		
3	RTC5122	Disc-clutch automatic transmission-lined	4		
4	RTC5121	Disc-clutch automatic transmission-outer-steel	4		
5	RTC5148	Ring-snap automatic transmission	1		
6	RTC5147	Spring	1		
7	RTC5146	Piston-clutch-automatic	1		
8	RTC5149	Ring-support	1		
9	RTC5145	Guide automatic transmission	1		
10	RTC5100	Kit-gasket automatic transmission	NLA		Use STC4448 qty 1 For transmission type 4HP22 hydraulic - fitted to all Defender, Discovery 1, and ZF-equipped Range Rover Classic Models or STC4449 qty 1 For transmission types 4HP22 EH & 4HP24 EH - fitted to all Discovery 2 and New Range Rover models.
11	RTC5101	Kit-automatic transmission bearing overhaul	1		

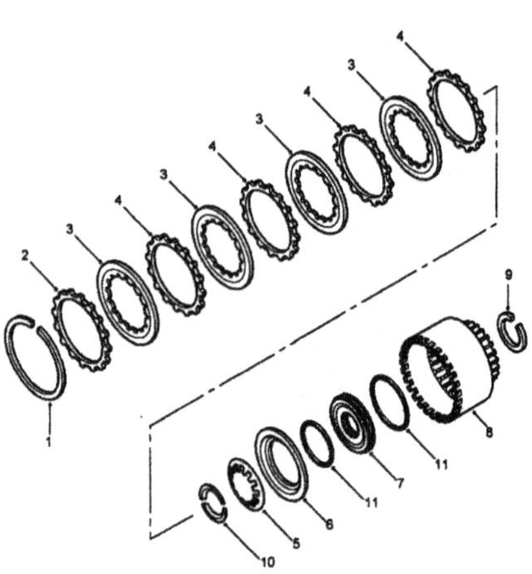

AMCPGE3B

Illus	Part Number	Description	Quantity	Change Point	Remarks
1	RTC5137	Ring-snap automatic transmission	1		
2	RTC5139	Disc-clutch automatic transmission-end	1		
3	RTC5135	Disc-clutch automatic transmission-lined	4		
4	RTC5138	Disc-clutch automatic transmission-outer	4		
5	RTC5164	Spring	1		
6	RTC5163	Plate-forward clutch pressure	1		
7	RTC5162	Piston-clutch-automatic	1		
8	RTC5161	Cylinder	1		
9	RTC5171	Ring-snap automatic transmission-small	1		
10	RTC5101	Kit-automatic transmission bearing overhaul	1		
11	RTC5100	Kit-gasket automatic transmission	NLA		Use STC4448 qty 1 For transmission type 4HP22 hydraulic - fitted to all Defender, Discovery 1, and ZF-equipped Range Rover Classic Models or STC4449 qty 1 For transmission types 4HP22 EH & 4HP24 EH - fitted to all Discovery 2 and New Range Rover models.

Illus	Part Number	Description	Quantity	Change Point	Remarks
1	RTC5137	Ring-snap automatic transmission	1		
2	RTC5136	Plate-automatic transmission clutch end	1		
3	RTC5135	Disc-clutch automatic transmission-lined	4		
4	RTC5134	Disc-clutch automatic transmission	4		
5	RTC5160	Ring-backing automatic transmission	1		
6	RTC5159	Disc-brake spring	1		
7	RTC5158	Piston-clutch-automatic	1		
8	RTC5157	Ring-piston-forward shaft automatic transmission	2		
9	RTC5155	Cylinder	1		
10	RTC5156	Screw	10		
11	RTC4660	Ring set assembly-piston	3		
12	RTC5101	Kit-automatic transmission bearing overhaul	1		

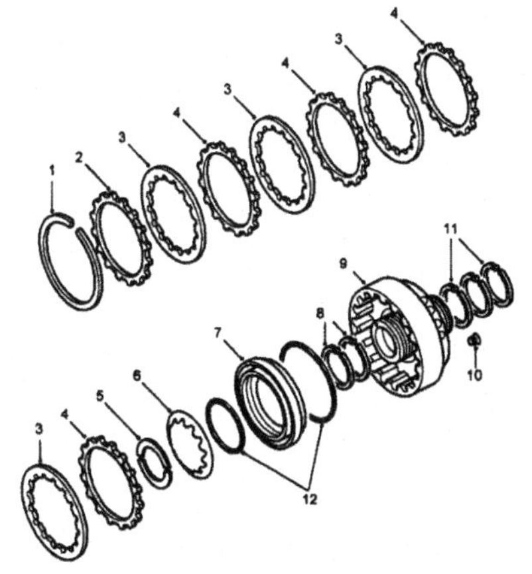

AMCPGG1A

Illus	Part Number	Description	Quantity	Change Point	Remarks
1	RTC5173	Ring-snap automatic transmission-large	1		
2	RTC5174	Plate-centre	1		
3	RTC5175	Piston-clutch-automatic	1		
4	RTC5176	Spring	1		
5	RTC5177	Ring-backing automatic transmission	1		
6	RTC5122	Disc-clutch automatic transmission-lined	4		
7	RTC5126	Disc-clutch automatic transmission-outer	4		
8	RTC5123	Disc-clutch automatic transmission-end	1		
9	RTC5178	Drive assembly-freewheel-automatic	1		
10	RTC5177	Ring-backing automatic transmission	1		
11	RTC5176	Spring	1		
12	RTC5179	Piston-clutch-automatic	1		
13	RTC5100	Kit-gasket automatic transmission	NLA		Use STC4448 qty 1 For transmission type 4HP22 hydraulic - fitted to all Defender, Discovery 1, and ZF-equipped Range Rover Classic Models or STC4449 qty 1 For transmission types 4HP22 EH & 4HP24 EH - fitted to all Discovery 2 and New Range Rover models.

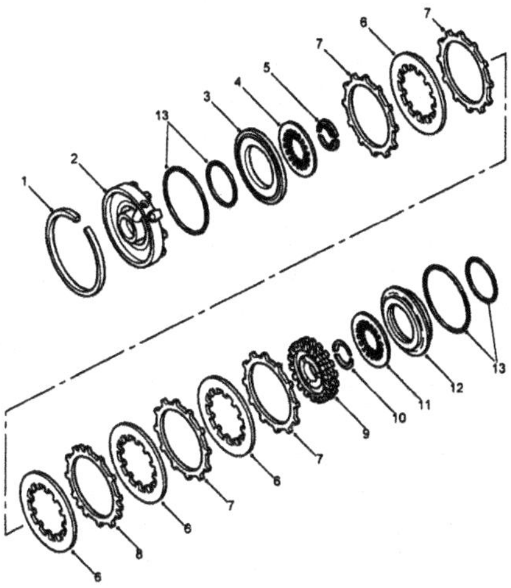

DEFENDER	GROUP C	Gearbox ZF-4 Speed-Automatic Brake 'D'

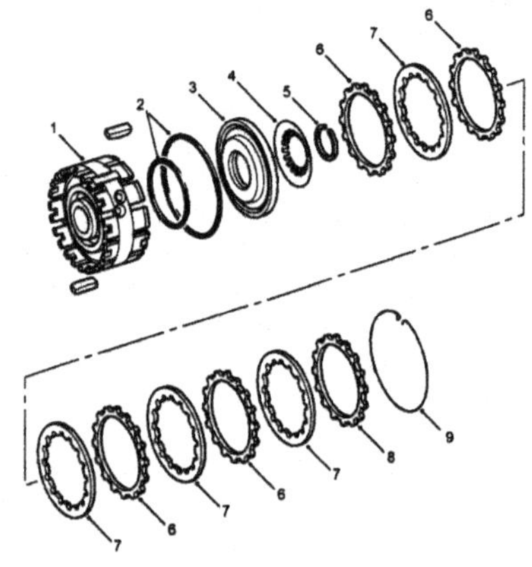

AMCPGG3B

Illus	Part Number	Description	Quantity	Change Point	Remarks
1	RTC5151	Cylinder	1		
2	RTC5100	Kit-gasket automatic transmission	NLA		Use STC4448 qty 1 For transmission type 4HP22 hydraulic - fitted to all Defender, Discovery 1, and ZF-equipped Range Rover Classic Models or STC4449 qty 1 For transmission types 4HP22 EH & 4HP24 EH - fitted to all Discovery 2 and New Range Rover models.
3	RTC5152	Piston-clutch-automatic	1		
4	RTC5153	Spring	1		
5	RTC5154	Connector fit	1		
6	RTC5126	Disc-clutch automatic transmission-outer	4		
7	RTC5127	Disc-clutch automatic transmission-lined	4		
8	RTC5125	Disc-clutch automatic transmission-outer	1		
9	RTC5128	Ring-snap automatic transmission	1		

DEFENDER	GROUP C	Gearbox ZF-4 Speed-Automatic Web Shaft & Fourth Gear

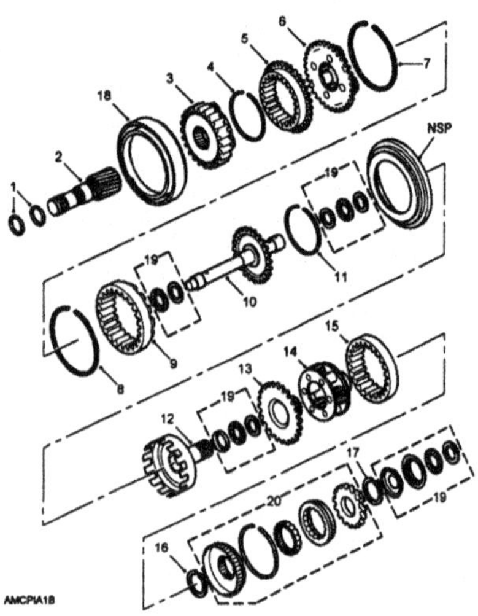

AMCPIA1B

Illus	Part Number	Description	Quantity	Change Point	Remarks
1	RTC5183	Set-ring automatic transmission	2		
2	RTC5182	Shaft-sun gear	1		
	STC334	O ring	3		
3	RTC5185	Gear assembly-planetary automatic transmission-front	1		
4	RTC5181	Ring-snap automatic transmission	1		
5	RTC5180	Gear-ring automatic transmission-front	1		
6	RTC5188	Gear assembly-planetary automatic transmission-front	1		
7	RTC5190	Ring-snap automatic transmission-large-rear	1		
8	RTC5181	Ring-snap automatic transmission	1		
9	RTC5184	Gear-ring automatic transmission-centre	1		
10	RTC5186	Shaft-intermediate transmission	1		
11	RTC5187	Ring-snap automatic transmission-rear	1		
12	STC996	Shaft-spider	1		
13	RTC5191	Gear-automatic transmission sun	1		
14	RTC5192	Gear assembly-planetary automatic transmission-rear	NLA		Use STC997.
14	STC997	Gear assembly-planetary automatic transmission	1		
15	RTC5193	Gear-ring automatic transmission-rear	1		
16	RTC5171	Ring-snap automatic transmission-small	1		
17	RTC5172	Ring-snap automatic transmission-small	1		
18	RTC5129	Ring-backing automatic transmission	1		
19	RTC5101	Kit-automatic transmission bearing overhaul	1		
20	STC330	Housing-freewheel assembly automatic transmission	1		

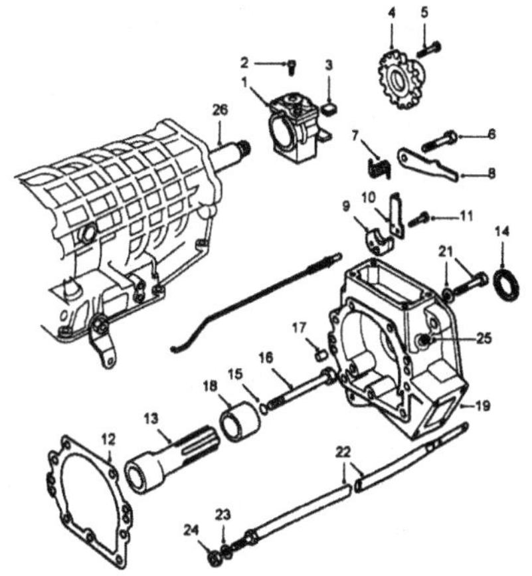

AMCPII1A

Illus	Part Number	Description	Quantity	Change Point	Remarks
1	RTC4314	Hub-governor	1		
	RTC5792	Weight-governor	1		
2	RTC4313	Screw	2		
3	RTC4315	Clamp	1		
4	RTC4662	Gear-parking automatic transmission	1		
5	RTC4313	Screw	4		
6	RTC4661	Bolt	1		
7	RTC4308	Spring-parking pawl automatic transmission	1		
8	RTC4307	Pawl-parklock automatic transmission	1		
9	RTC5212	Plate- guide	1		
10	RTC4663	Plate	1		
11	RTC5211	Screw	1		
12	RTC4295	Gasket-rear extension housing	1		
13	FTC5090	Shaft automatic transmission	1		
14	RTC4650	Seal-auto trans output shaft	1		
15	FRC5575	O ring	1		
16	BH110261	Bolt-M10 x 130-long	1		
17	RTC4301	Dowel	2		
18	RTC4300	Spacer-inner	1		
19	RTC4659	Housing-governor extension	1		
20	SH106121L	Screw-hexagonal head-M6 x 12	9		
21	WA106041L	Washer-6mm	9		
22	FRC7500	ROD-TRANSMISSION SUPPORT	1		
	FS108207L	• Screw-flanged head-M8 x 20	2		
23	WA108051L	• Washer-8mm	2		
23	WA110061L	Washer-M10	1		
24	NY110047L	Nut-flange-nyloc-M10	1		
25	FRC9427	TUBE-BREATHER TRANSMISSION CASE	1		
	232039	• Washer-sealing	1		
	595478	• Bolt-banjo	1		
	RTC5150	Shaft assembly-main automatic transmission	1		
	FTC890	Stud	1		
	FTC5409	Clip-pipe	A/R		Td5

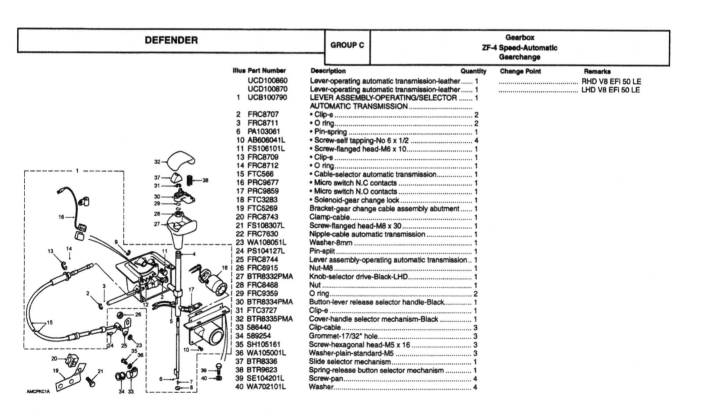

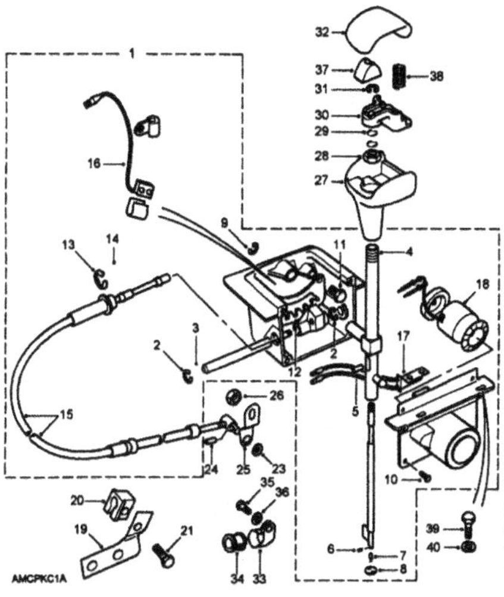

AMCPKC1A

Illus	Part Number	Description	Quantity	Change Point	Remarks
	UCD100860	Lever-operating automatic transmission-leather	1		RHD V8 EFi 50 LE
	UCD100870	Lever-operating automatic transmission-leather	1		LHD V8 EFi 50 LE
1	UCB100790	LEVER ASSEMBLY-OPERATING/SELECTOR AUTOMATIC TRANSMISSION	1		
2	FRC8707	• Clip-e	2		
3	FRC8711	• O ring	2		
6	PA103061	• Pin-spring	1		
10	AB606041L	• Screw-self tapping-No 6 x 1/2	4		
11	FS106101L	• Screw-flanged head-M6 x 10	1		
13	FRC8709	• Clip-e	1		
14	FRC8712	• O ring	1		
15	FTC566	• Cable-selector automatic transmission	1		
16	PRC9677	• Micro switch N.C contacts	1		
17	PRC9859	• Micro switch N.O contacts	1		
18	FTC3283	• Solenoid-gear change lock	1		
19	FTC5269	Bracket-gear change cable assembly abutment	1		
20	FRC8743	Clamp-cable	1		
21	FS108307L	Screw-flanged head-M8 x 30	1		
22	FRC7630	Nipple-cable automatic transmission	1		
23	WA108051L	Washer-8mm	1		
24	PS104127L	Pin-split	1		
25	FRC8744	Lever assembly-operating automatic transmission	1		
26	FRC6915	Nut-M8	1		
27	BTR8332PMA	Knob-selector drive-Black-LHD	1		
28	FRC8468	Nut	1		
29	FRC9359	O ring	2		
30	BTR8334PMA	Button-lever release selector handle-Black	1		
31	FTC3727	Clip-e	1		
32	BTR8335PMA	Cover-handle selector mechanism-Black	1		
33	586440	Clip-cable	3		
34	589254	Grommet-17/32" hole	3		
35	SH105161	Screw-hexagonal head-M5 x 16	3		
36	WA105001L	Washer-plain-standard-M5	3		
37	BTR8336	Slide selector mechanism	1		
38	BTR9623	Spring-release button selector mechanism	1		
39	SE104201L	Screw-pan	4		
40	WA702101L	Washer	4		

Illus	Part Number	Description	Quantity	Change Point	Remarks
1	RTC5100	Kit-gasket automatic transmission	NLA		Use STC4448 qty 1 For transmission type 4HP22 hydraulic - fitted to all Defender, Discovery 1, and ZF-equipped Range Rover Classic Models or STC4449 qty 1 For transmission types 4HP22 EH & 4HP24 EH - fitted to all Discovery 2 and New Range Rover models.
	RTC5101	Kit-automatic transmission bearing overhaul	1		

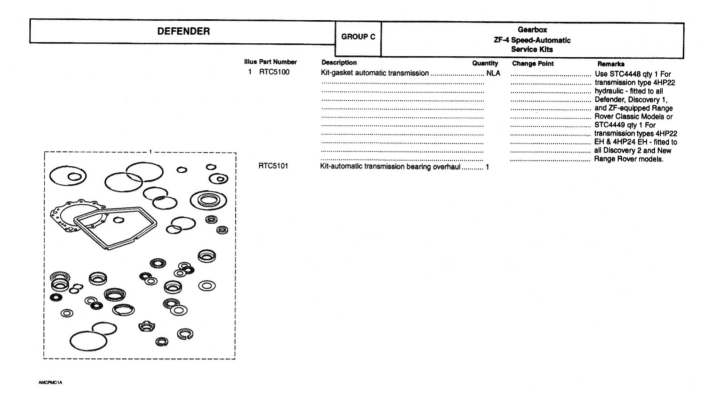

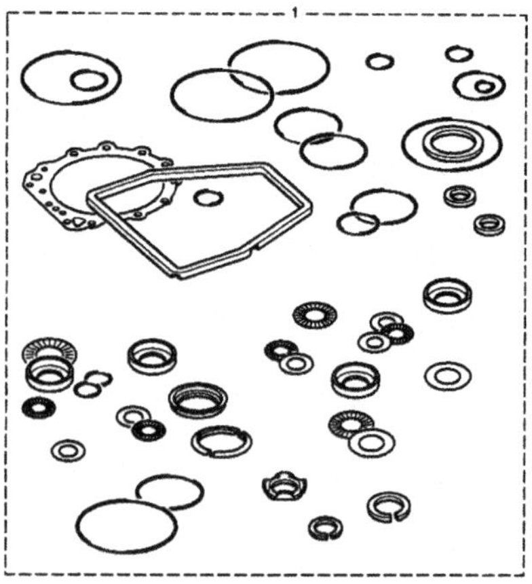

AMCPMC1A

Illus	Part Number	Description	Quantity	Change Point	Remarks
1	FTC5360	Oil cooler assembly transmission	1		
	FTC5361	Spacer	2		
2	FS108357	Screw-flanged head-M8 x 35	2		
3	ESR4219	Pipe assembly-transmission to oil cooler	1		
4	ESR3695	Hose-pipe to oil cooler-intermediate	1		
5	ESR4218	Pipe assembly-oil cooler to transmission	1		
6	ESR1594L	O ring	6		
7	ESR2806	Clamp	2		
8	SH106351L	Screw-hexagonal head-M6 x 35	1		
9	WL106001L	Washer-sprung-M6	1		
10	NN106021	Nutsert-blind-M6	1		
11	NTC6847	Clamp	1		
12	FS106167L	Screw-flanged head-flanged head-M6 x 16	1		
13	NY106041	Nut-flange-nyloc-M6	1		
14	AMR4948	Switch-transmission oil cooler temperature	1		
15	232039	Washer-sealing	1		
16	ESR1253	Adaptor-pipe-dual male	2		
17	FTC1525	Seal	2		

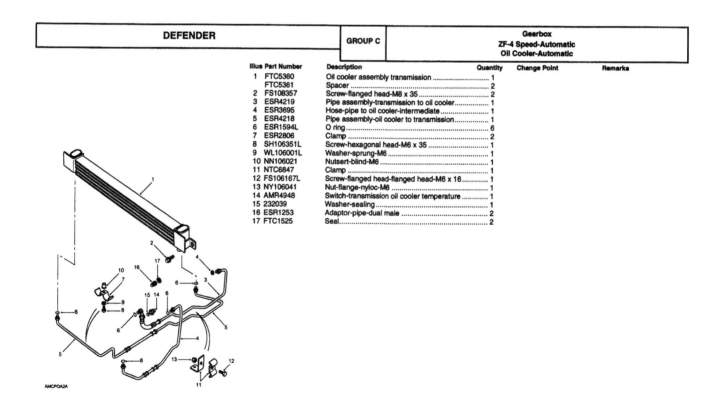

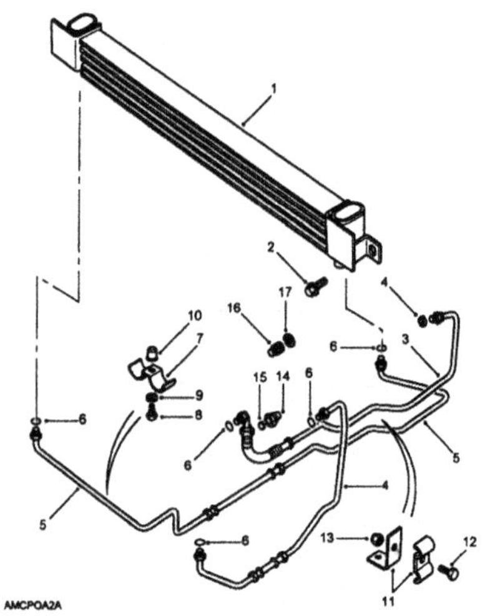

AMCPOA2A

LT230
Transfer Assembly

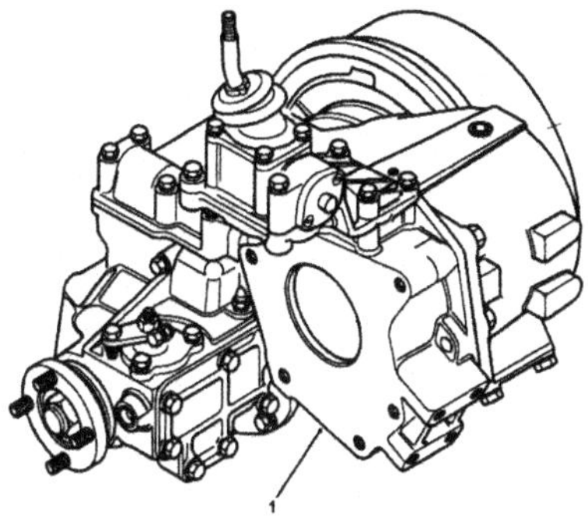

AHDBAA1A

Illus	Part Number	Description	Quantity	Change Point	Remarks
1	FRC9469N	Transfer gearbox assembly-new-1.6 : 1	1	Note (1)	20D 4 Cylinder Petrol except 90"
1	FRC9469N	Transfer gearbox assembly-new-1.6 : 1	1	Note (1)	20D 4 Cylinder Diesel Naturally Aspirated except 90"
1	FRC9468N	Transfer gearbox assembly-new-1.4 : 1	1	Note (1)	25D V8 Petrol Twin Carburettor except 90"
1	FRC9470N	Transfer gearbox assembly-new-1.4 : 1	1	Note (1)	22D 4 Cylinder Diesel Turbo except 90"
1	FRC9470N	Transfer gearbox assembly-new-1.4 : 1	1	Note (1)	22D 4 Cylinder 90"
1	FRC9471N	Transfer gearbox assembly-new-1.2 : 1	1	Note (1)	29D V8 Petrol Twin Carburettor 90"
1	STC1017	Transfer gearbox assembly-new-1.2 : 1	1	Note (1)	32D V8 Petrol Twin Carburettor 90"
1	STC8683E	Transfer gearbox assembly-exchange-1.6 : 1	1	Note (1)	20D 4 Cylinder Petrol Note (1) except 90"
1	STC8683E	Transfer gearbox assembly-exchange-1.6 : 1	1	Note (1)	20D 4 Cylinder Diesel Naturally Aspirated Note (1) except 90"
1	STC8682E	Transfer gearbox assembly-exchange-1.4 : 1	1	Note (1)	25D V8 Petrol Twin Carburettor Note (1) except 90"
1	STC8682E	Transfer gearbox assembly-exchange-1.4 : 1	1	Note (1)	22D 4 Cylinder Diesel Turbo Note (1) except 90"
1	STC8682E	Transfer gearbox assembly-exchange-1.4 : 1	1	Note (1)	22D 4 Cylinder Note (1) 90"
1	STC8959E	Transfer gearbox assembly-exchange-1.2 : 1	1	Note (1)	29D V8 Petrol Twin Carburettor Note (1) 90"
1	STC8959E	Transfer gearbox assembly-exchange-1.2 : 1	1	Note (1)	32D V8 Petrol Twin Carburettor Note (1) 90"

CHANGE POINTS:
(1) To (T) 551441F

Remarks:
(1) Transfer boxes do not come with transmission brake assembly, any sensors, gear change linkage or speedo pinion

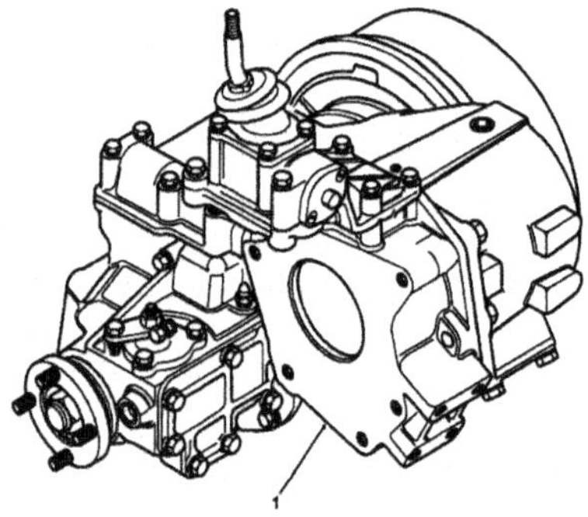

AHDBAA1A

Illus	Part Number	Description	Quantity	Change Point	Remarks
1	STC3610	Transfer gearbox assembly-new-1.6 : 1	1	Note (1)	20D 4 Cylinder Petrol Note (1) except 90"
1	STC3610	Transfer gearbox assembly-new-1.6 : 1	1	Note (1)	20D 4 Cylinder Diesel Naturally Aspirated Note (1) except 90"
1	STC3609	Transfer gearbox assembly-new-1.4 : 1	1	Note (1)	25D V8 Petrol Twin Carburettor Note (1) except 90"
1	STC3609	Transfer gearbox assembly-new-1.4 : 1	1	Note (1)	22D 4 Cylinder Diesel Turbo Note (1) except 90"
1	STC3609	Transfer gearbox assembly-new-1.4 : 1	1	Note (1)	22D 4 Cylinder Note (1) 90"
1	STC3608	Transfer gearbox assembly-new-1.2 : 1	1	Note (1)	29D V8 Petrol Twin Carburettor Note (1) 90"
1	STC3608	Transfer gearbox assembly-new-1.2 : 1	1	Note (1)	32D V8 Petrol Twin Carburettor Note (1) 90"
1	STC3608	Transfer gearbox assembly-new-1.2 : 1	1	Note (1)	38D V8 Petrol EFi Note (1) 90" except shift interlock
1	STC3611	Transfer gearbox assembly-new-1.2 : 1	1	Note (1)	40D V8 Petrol EFi Note (1) shift interlock 90"
1	STC3610E	Transfer gearbox assembly-exchange-1.6 : 1	1	Note (1)	20D 4 Cylinder Petrol Note (1) except 90"
1	STC3610E	Transfer gearbox assembly-exchange-1.6 : 1	1	Note (1)	20D 4 Cylinder Diesel Naturally Aspirated Note (1) except 90"

CHANGE POINTS:
(1) From (T) 551442G

Remarks:
(1) Transfer boxes do not come with transmission brake assembly, any sensors, gear change linkage or speedo pinion

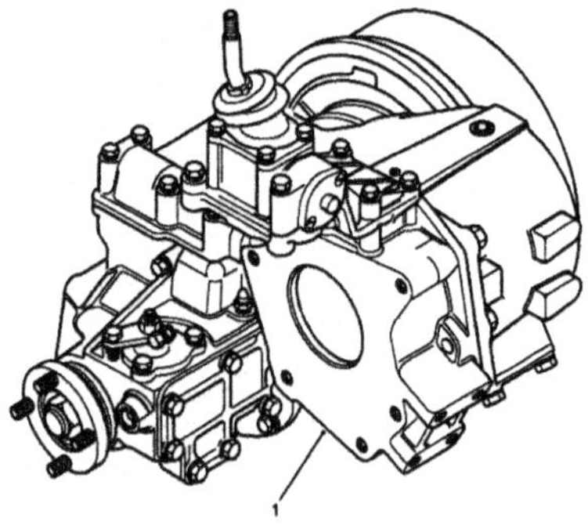

AHDBAA1A

Illus	Part Number	Description	Quantity	Change Point	Remarks
1	STC3609E	Transfer gearbox assembly-exchange-1.4 : 1	1	Note (1)	25D V8 Petrol Twin Carburettor Note (1) except 90"
1	STC3609E	Transfer gearbox assembly-exchange-1.4 : 1	1	Note (1)	22D 4 Cylinder Diesel Turbo Note (1) except 90"
1	STC3609E	Transfer gearbox assembly-exchange-1.4 : 1	1	Note (1)	22D 4 Cylinder Note (1) 90"
1	STC3608E	Transfer gearbox assembly-exchange-1.2 : 1	1	Note (1)	29D V8 Petrol Twin Carburettor Note (1) 90"
1	STC3608E	Transfer gearbox assembly-exchange-1.2 : 1	1	Note (1)	32D V8 Petrol Twin Carburettor Note (1) 90"
1	STC3608E	Transfer gearbox assembly-exchange-1.2 : 1	1	Note (1)	38D V8 Petrol EFi Note (1) 90" except shift interlock
1	IAB100040	Transfer gearbox assembly-new-1.6 : 1	1		47D 4 Cylinder Petrol Note (1)
1	IAB100030	Transfer gearbox assembly-manual-new-1.4 : 1	1		43D Td5 Note (1)
1	IAB100030	Transfer gearbox assembly-manual-new-1.4 : 1	1		43D Note (1) 300 TDI
1	IAB100030	Transfer gearbox assembly-manual-new-1.4 : 1	1		43D V8 Petrol Note (1) except 90"
1	IAB100020	Transfer gearbox assembly-new-1.2 : 1	1		45D V8 Petrol Note (1) 90" except shift interlock
1	IAB100050	Transfer gearbox assembly-new-1.2 : 1	1		45D V8 Petrol Note (1) shift interlock 90"
		4 CYL VEHICLES WITH 7.50X16 TYRES MAY REQUIRE A DIFFERENT SPEEDO PINION, USE OLD ONE OR SEE REAR FLANGE/SPEEDO PINION SECTION			

CHANGE POINTS:
(1) From (T) 551442G

Remarks:
(1) Transfer boxes do not come with transmission brake assembly, any sensors, gear change linkage or speedo pinion

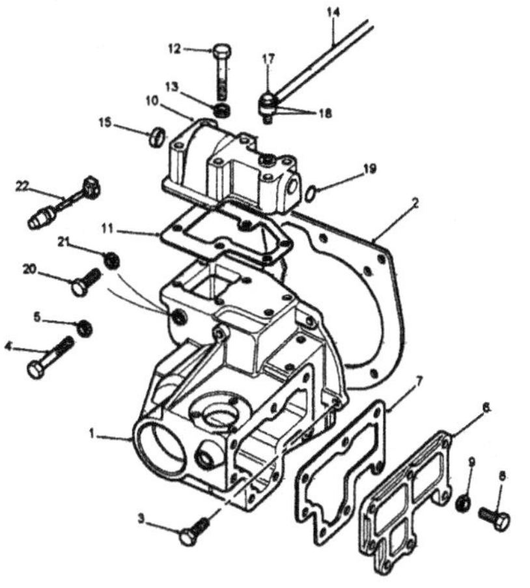

LD0021

Illus	Part Number	Description	Quantity	Change Point	Remarks
1	FRC8299	Housing-output shaft front	NLA	Note (1)	Use FTC4178. Use liquid gasket instead of paper to obtain the correct bearing preload if insufficient shim range available.
1	FTC4178	Housing-output shaft front	1	Note (2)	
2	FRC6103	Gasket-front housing to main case	1	Note (1)	
2	RTC3254	Sealant-silicone	1	Note (2)	
1	ICB100070	Housing-output shaft front	1	Note (3)	
22	IGM100000	Switch assembly-transfer box low ratio detect	1	Note (3)	Td5
20	SH214141	Plug	1	Note (3)	Except Td5
21	ALU1403L	Washer-sealing	1	Note (3)	
3	FS108251L	Screw-flanged head-M8 x 25	NLA	Note (1)	Use FS108257L. 13D
3	FS108301L	Screw-flanged head-M8 x 30	NLA		Use FS108307L. LT 77S 22D 32D
3	FS108307L	Screw-flanged head-M8 x 30	7		LT 77S 22D 32D
3	FS108251ML	Screw-flanged head-M8 x 25	7	Note (2)	
4	BH108181L	Bolt-hexagonal head-M8 x 90	NLA	Note (1)	13D
4	BH108181L	Bolt-hexagonal head-M8 x 90	NLA		LT 85 except 13D
4	FB108181M	Bolt-flanged head-M8 x 90	NLA		LT 77S 22D 32D
4	FB108181ML	Bolt-flanged head-M8 x 90	1	Note (2)	
5	WA108051L	Washer-8mm	8	Note (1)	
6	FRC6104	Cover-transfer box front housing	1		
7	FRC6105	Gasket-transfer box side cover	1	Note (1)	
7	RTC3254	Sealant-silicone	1	Note (2)	

CHANGE POINTS:
(1) To (V) LA 939975
(2) From (V) MA 939976
(3) From (T)43D Suffix G

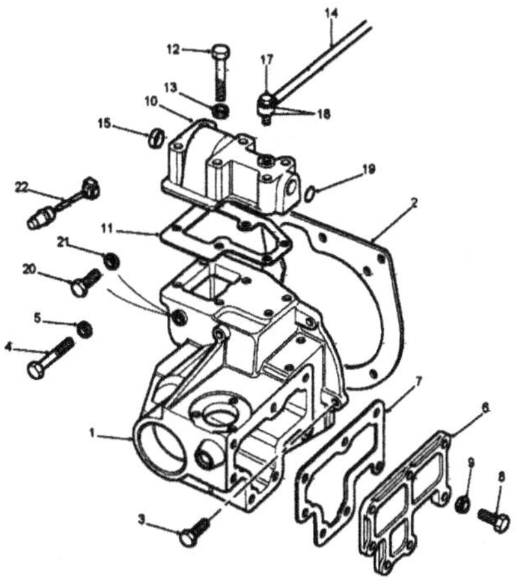

LD0021

Illus	Part Number	Description	Quantity	Change Point	Remarks
8	FS108257L	Screw-flanged head-M8 x 25	7	Note (1)	
8	FS108251ML	Screw-flanged head-M8 x 25	7	Note (2)	
9	WA108051L	Washer-8mm	7	Note (1)	
10	FRC6106	Housing-cross shaft	1	Note (3)	
10	FTC5421	Housing-cross shaft	1	Note (4)	
11	FRC7998	Gasket-transfer box cover to case	1	Note (1)	
11	RTC3254	Sealant-silicone	1	Note (2)	
12	FB108111L	Bolt-flanged head-M8 x 55	6		
13	WA108051L	Washer-8mm	6	Note (1)	
14	FRC167	Tube-breather transmission case	1		LT 85 except 90"
14	FRC9427	TUBE-BREATHER TRANSMISSION CASE	1		LT 77S except 90"
18	232039	• Washer-sealing	1		
17	595478	• Bolt-banjo	1		
14	FRC168	Tube-breather transmission case	1	Note (1)	LT 77S 13D 90"
14	FRC167	Tube-breather transmission case	1	Note (1)	LT 77S 22D 32D 90"
14	FRC167	Tube-breather transmission case	1	Note (1)	LT 85 90"
14	FRC9430	TUBE-BREATHER TRANSMISSION CASE	1	Note (2)	90"
	232039	• Washer-sealing	1		
	595478	• Bolt-banjo	1		
15	FTC5427	Plug	1	Note (3)	
15	FTC5422	Plug	1	Note (4)	
16	BAU1689	Clip-p-5/16"	1	Note (1)	
17	595478	Bolt-banjo	1		
18	232039	Washer-sealing-transfer box breather pipe banjo	2		
19	FRC5575	O ring	2	Note (1)	13D
19	FRC5575	O ring	1		LT 77S 22D 32D
19	FRC5575	O ring	1		LT 85 except 13D
19	FRC5575	O ring	1	Note (2)	

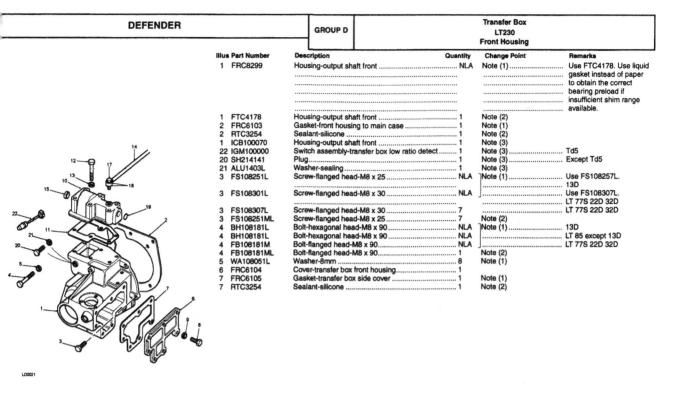

CHANGE POINTS:
(1) To (V) LA 939975
(2) From (V) MA 939976
(3) To (T)43D
(4) From (T)43D Suffix G

DEFENDER	GROUP D	Transfer Box LT230 Adaptor Housing-LT85

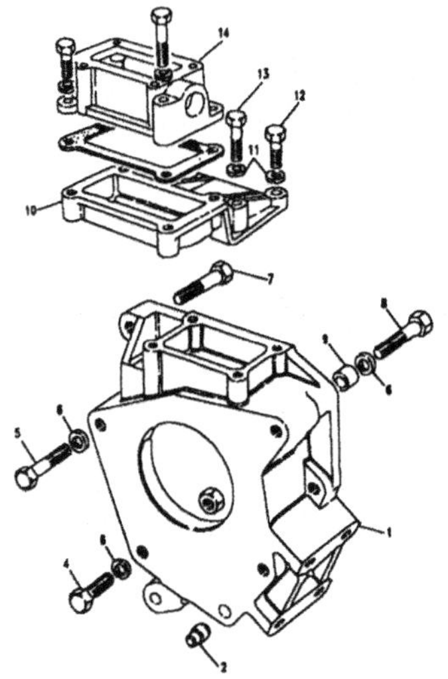

Illus	Part Number	Description	Quantity	Change Point	Remarks
1	FRC5622	Housing-transfer box power take off bearing	1		
2	571134	Dowel	1		
3	NH110041L	Nut-hexagonal head-coarse thread-M10	2		
4	FRC5053	Screw	1		
5	SH110401L	Screw-hexagonal head-M10 x 40	3		
6	WL110001L	Washer-M10	12		
7	BH110081L	Bolt-hexagonal head-M10 x 40	3		
8	BH110091L	Bolt-M10 x 45	1		
9	FRC2482	Dowel-ring-15.0mm	1		
10	FRC8558	Housing-manual transmission gearchange	1		
11	WL108001L	Washer-sprung-M8	4		
12	SH108251L	Screw-hexagonal head-M8 x 25	NLA		Use SH108257 Use Dacromet coated alternative..
13	FB108111L	Bolt-flanged head-M8 x 55	13		
14	FRC8751	Housing assembly- gear change cross shaft	1		

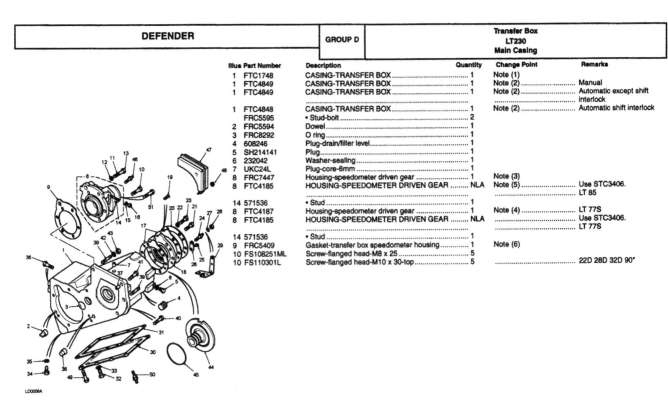

DEFENDER	GROUP D	Transfer Box LT230 Main Casing

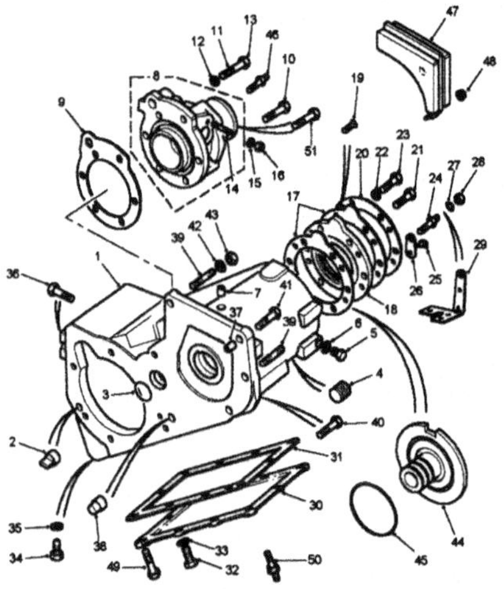

LD0006A

Illus	Part Number	Description	Quantity	Change Point	Remarks
1	FTC1748	CASING-TRANSFER BOX	1	Note (1)	
1	FTC4849	CASING-TRANSFER BOX	1	Note (2)	Manual
1	FTC4849	CASING-TRANSFER BOX	1	Note (2)	Automatic except shift interlock
1	FTC4848	CASING-TRANSFER BOX	1	Note (2)	Automatic shift interlock
	FRC5595	• Stud-bolt	2		
2	FRC5594	Dowel	1		
3	FRC8292	O ring	1		
4	608246	Plug-drain/filler level	1		
5	SH214141	Plug	1		
6	232042	Washer-sealing	1		
7	UKC24L	Plug-core-6mm	1		
8	FRC7447	Housing-speedometer driven gear	1	Note (3)	
8	FTC4185	HOUSING-SPEEDOMETER DRIVEN GEAR	NLA	Note (5)	Use STC3406. LT 85
14	571536	• Stud	1		
8	FTC4187	Housing-speedometer driven gear	1	Note (4)	LT 77S
8	FTC4185	HOUSING-SPEEDOMETER DRIVEN GEAR	NLA		Use STC3406. LT 77S
14	571536	• Stud	1		
9	FRC5409	Gasket-transfer box speedometer housing	1	Note (6)	
10	FS108251ML	Screw-flanged head-M8 x 25	5		
10	FS110301L	Screw-flanged head-M10 x 30-top	5		22D 28D 32D 90"

CHANGE POINTS:
(1) To (T) 551442F
(2) From (T) 551443G
(3) To (T)22D 309416E
(4) From (T)22D 309417E
(5) From (T)25D 309417E
(6) To (V) LA 939975

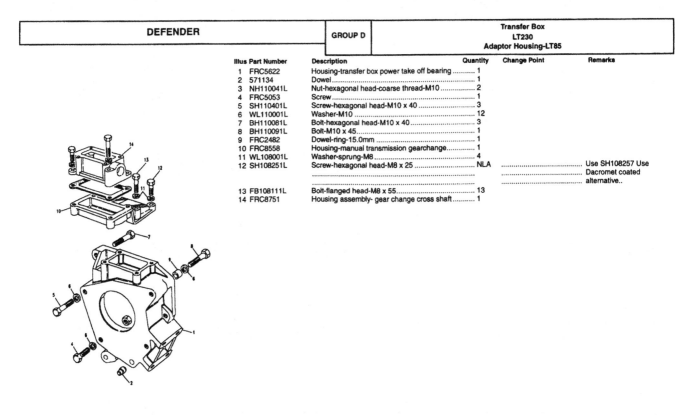

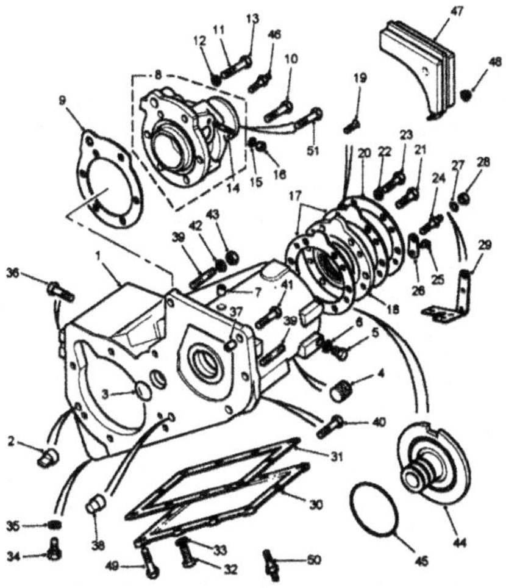

LD0006A

Illus	Part Number	Description	Quantity	Change Point	Remarks
10	FS110301L	Screw-flanged head-M10 x 30-top	5	Note (1)	
10	FS110301L	Screw-flanged head-M10 x 30-top	2	Note (2)	
11	BH110091L	Bolt-M10 x 45	1		
12	WA110061L	Washer-M10	6		
13	FB110091ML	Bolt-flanged head-M10 x 45	1		
14	571536	Stud	1	Note (3)	
15	WA106041L	Washer-6mm	1	Note (3)	
16	NY106041	Nut-flange-nyloc-M6	1	To (T)43D	
51	FS106201M	Screw-flanged head-M6 x 20-flanged head-patch lock	1	Note (4)	
	YBE100530	Transducer speed	1	Note (2)	Td5
17	FRC5413	Gasket-transfer box power take off cover	2		
	RTC3254	Sealant-silicone	1	Note (5)	
18	FRC6943	Housing-bearing shaft	1	Note (6)	
18	FTC4866	Housing-bearing shaft	1	Note (7)	
19	SF108251L	Screw-M8 x 25	1		
20	FTC2061	Cover-transfer box power take off	1	Note (8)	
20	FTC3178	Cover-transfer box power take off	1	Note (5)	
	FRC9926	Shim-3.15mm	1		
	FRC9963	Shim	1		
21	BX110071M	Bolt-hexagonal head-M10 x 35	6		
22	WA110061L	Washer-M10	6		
23	FB110081ML	Bolt-flanged head-M10 x 40	5	Note (9)	
	PRC2979	Bracket-clipping-steel	1	Note (9)	
24	FTC1919	Stud	1		
25	PRC3180	Clip-pipe-single	1	Note (10)	
26	ANR3227	Heatshield-bracket	1		

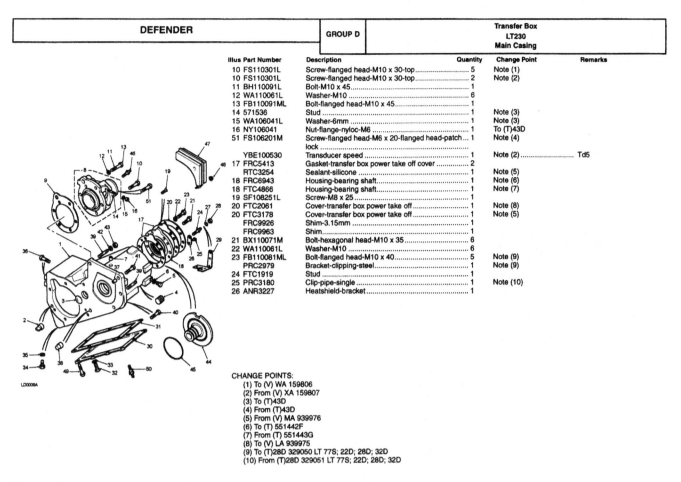

CHANGE POINTS:
(1) To (V) WA 159806
(2) From (V) XA 159807
(3) To (T)43D
(4) From (T)43D
(5) From (V) MA 939976
(6) To (T) 551442F
(7) From (T) 551443G
(8) To (V) LA 939975
(9) To (T)28D 329050 LT 77S; 22D; 28D; 32D
(10) From (T)28D 329051 LT 77S; 22D; 28D; 32D

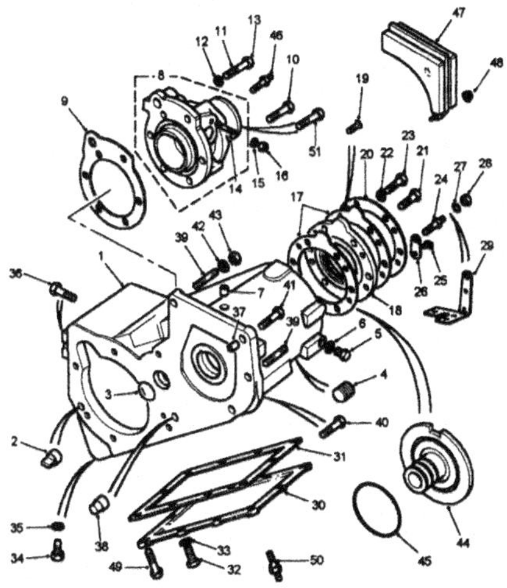

LD0006A

Illus	Part Number	Description	Quantity	Change Point	Remarks
27	WA110001L	Washer-plain-M10	1		
28	FN110047	Nut-flange-flange-M10	1		
29	ANR3227	Heatshield-bracket	1		LHD
30	FRC5415	Cover-transfer box	1		
31	FRC5416	Gasket-transfer box bottom cover	1		
	RTC3254	Sealant-silicone	1		
49	FB108161L	Bolt-flanged head-M8 x 80	10		25D 29D
32	FS108307L	Screw-flanged head-M8 x 30	10		22D 28D 32D
32	FS108251ML	Screw-flanged head-M8 x 25	8		43D
50	IYR100000	Stud-bolt	2		43D
33	WA108051L	Washer-8mm	10		
34	599552	Plug-drain	1		
35	FRC4808	Washer-sealing-transfer box drain plug	1		
36	FS108307L	Screw-earth wire fixing-flanged head-M8 x 30	1		
37	FRC2482	Dowel-ring-15.0mm	1		
38	571134	Dowel	1		
39	FTC890	Stud	2		
40	BH110081L	Bolt-hexagonal head-M10 x 40	3		
40	BH110091L	Bolt-M10 x 45	1		
41	FB110091ML	Bolt-flanged head-M10 x 45	1		
41	FB110071ML	Bolt-flanged head-M10 x 35	3		
42	WL110001L	Washer-M10	2		
43	FN110047	Nut-flange-flange-M10	2		
44	STC3615K	Kit-plate & seal-oil guide	1		
45	FTC4994	O ring	1	From (T)22D 445132E	
46	IYR100010	Stud	3	Note (1)	
47	IAI100030	Absorber-transfer box vibration	1	Note (1)	Td5
48	FX110047L	Nut-flange-M10	3	Note (1)	Td5

CHANGE POINTS:
(1) From (T)43D

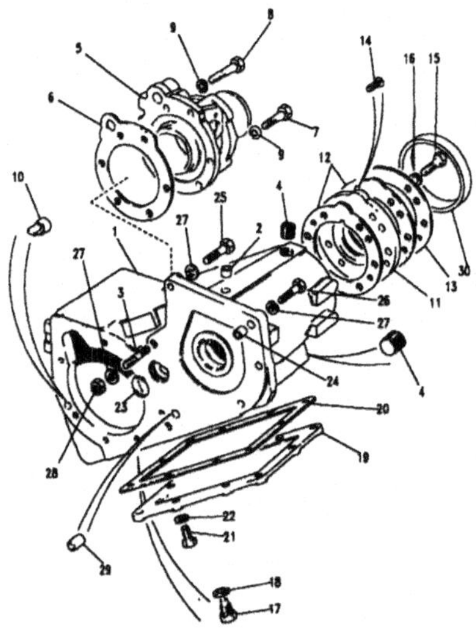

Illus	Part Number	Description	Quantity	Change Point	Remarks
1	FRC7026	CASING-TRANSFER BOX	NLA		Use FRC9467N qty 1 or FRC9473N qty 1.
2	UKC24L	• Plug-core-6mm	1		
3	FRC5595	• Stud-bolt	2		
4	608246	Plug-drain/filler level	2		
5	FRC6578	Housing assembly-speedometer driven gear	1		
6	FRC5409	Gasket-transfer box speedometer housing	1		
7	FS110301L	Screw-flanged head-M10 x 30-top	5		
8	BH110091L	Bolt-M10 x 45	1		
9	WA110061L	Washer-M10	6		
10	FRC5594	Dowel	1		
11	FRC6943	Housing-bearing shaft	1		
12	FRC5413	Gasket-transfer box power take off cover	2		
13	FTC2061	Cover-transfer box power take off	1		
14	SF108251L	Screw-M8 x 25	2		
15	BX110071M	Bolt-hexagonal head-M10 x 35	6		
16	WA110061L	Washer-M10	6		
17	599552	Plug-drain	1		
18	FRC4808	Washer-sealing-transfer box drain plug	1		
19	FRC5415	Cover-transfer box	1		
20	FRC5416	Gasket-transfer box bottom cover	1		
21	FS108301L	Screw-flanged head-M8 x 30	NLA		Use FS108307L.
22	WA108051	Washer-M8-standard	NLA		Use WA108051L.
23	FRC5419	O ring	1		
24	FRC2482	Dowel-ring-15.0mm	1		
25	BH110081L	Bolt-hexagonal head-M10 x 40	3		
26	BH110091L	Bolt-M10 x 45	1		
27	WL110001L	Washer-M10	6		
28	FN110041L	Nut-flange-M10	NLA		Use FN110047.
29	571134	Dowel	1	Note (1)	
30	602146	Plug	1		

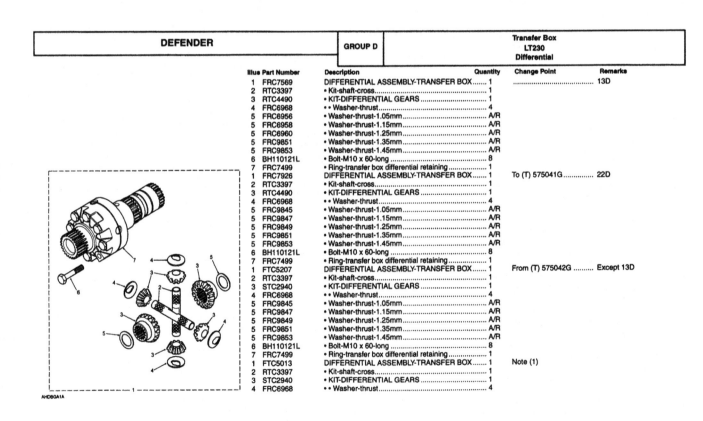

CHANGE POINTS:
(1) To (V) LA 939975

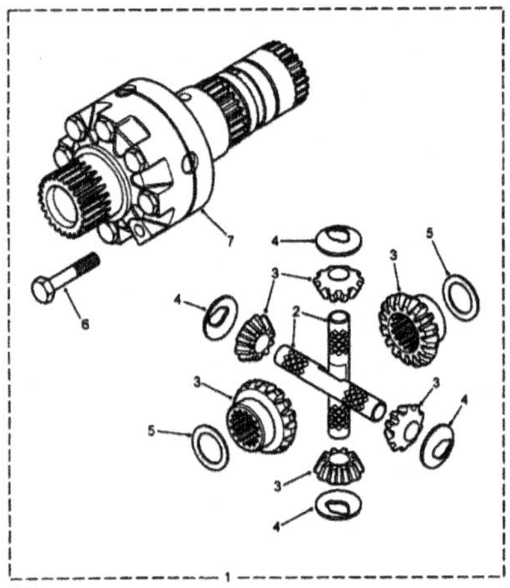

AHDBGA1A

Illus	Part Number	Description	Quantity	Change Point	Remarks
1	FRC7569	DIFFERENTIAL ASSEMBLY-TRANSFER BOX	1		13D
2	RTC3397	• Kit-shaft-cross	1		
3	RTC4490	• KIT-DIFFERENTIAL GEARS	1		
4	FRC6968	• • Washer-thrust	4		
5	FRC6956	• Washer-thrust-1.05mm	A/R		
5	FRC6958	• Washer-thrust-1.15mm	A/R		
5	FRC6960	• Washer-thrust-1.25mm	A/R		
5	FRC9851	• Washer-thrust-1.35mm	A/R		
5	FRC9853	• Washer-thrust-1.45mm	A/R		
6	BH110121L	• Bolt-M10 x 60-long	8		
7	FRC7499	• Ring-transfer box differential retaining	1		
1	FRC7926	DIFFERENTIAL ASSEMBLY-TRANSFER BOX	1	To (T) 575041G	22D
2	RTC3397	• Kit-shaft-cross	1		
3	RTC4490	• KIT-DIFFERENTIAL GEARS	1		
4	FRC6968	• • Washer-thrust	4		
5	FRC9845	• Washer-thrust-1.05mm	A/R		
5	FRC9847	• Washer-thrust-1.15mm	A/R		
5	FRC9849	• Washer-thrust-1.25mm	A/R		
5	FRC9851	• Washer-thrust-1.35mm	A/R		
5	FRC9853	• Washer-thrust-1.45mm	A/R		
6	BH110121L	• Bolt-M10 x 60-long	8		
7	FRC7499	• Ring-transfer box differential retaining	1		
1	FTC5207	DIFFERENTIAL ASSEMBLY-TRANSFER BOX	1	From (T) 575042G	Except 13D
2	RTC3397	• Kit-shaft-cross	1		
3	STC2940	• KIT-DIFFERENTIAL GEARS	1		
4	FRC6968	• • Washer-thrust	4		
5	FRC9845	• Washer-thrust-1.05mm	A/R		
5	FRC9847	• Washer-thrust-1.15mm	A/R		
5	FRC9849	• Washer-thrust-1.25mm	A/R		
5	FRC9851	• Washer-thrust-1.35mm	A/R		
5	FRC9853	• Washer-thrust-1.45mm	A/R		
6	BH110121L	• Bolt-M10 x 60-long	8		
7	FRC7499	• Ring-transfer box differential retaining	1		
1	FTC5013	DIFFERENTIAL ASSEMBLY-TRANSFER BOX	1	Note (1)	
2	RTC3397	• Kit-shaft-cross	1		
3	STC2940	• KIT-DIFFERENTIAL GEARS	1		
4	FRC6968	• • Washer-thrust	4		

CHANGE POINTS:
(1) From (T)43D

Illus	Part Number	Description	Quantity	Change Point	Remarks
1	FRC5428	Gear-mainshaft-26 teeth	1	Note (1)	22D 4 Cylinder 90°
1	FRC5428	Gear-mainshaft-26 teeth	1	Note (2)	29D V8 Petrol Twin Carburettor 90°
1	FRC8917	Gear-mainshaft-26 teeth	NLA	Note (3); Note (4)	For manual variants use FTC5089 gear. For automatic variants use FTC5089 gear and FTC5090 shaft.. 29D V8 Petrol Twin Carburettor 90°
1	FRC8917	Gear-mainshaft-26 teeth	NLA	Note (5); Note (6)	For manual variants use FTC5089 gear. For automatic variants use FTC5089 gear and FTC5090 shaft.. 22D 4 Cylinder 90°
1	FRC8917	Gear-mainshaft-26 teeth	NLA	Note (7)	For manual variants use FTC5089 gear. For automatic variants use FTC5089 gear and FTC5090 shaft.. 20D 4 Cylinder Petrol except 90°
1	FRC8917	Gear-mainshaft-26 teeth	NLA	Note (7)	For manual variants use FTC5089 gear. For automatic variants use FTC5089 gear and FTC5090 shaft.. 20D 4 Cylinder Diesel Naturally Aspirated except 90°

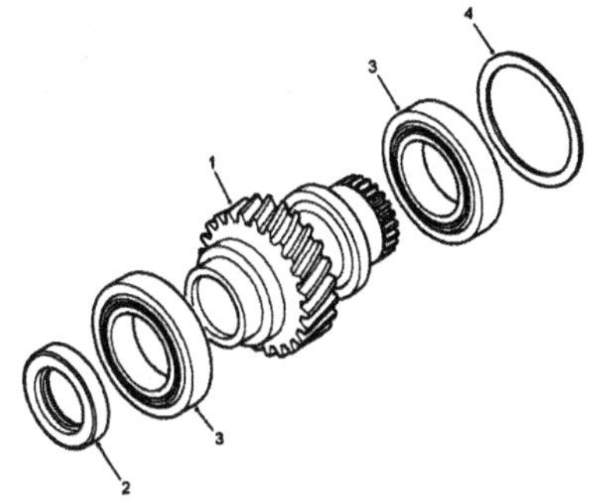

AHDBIA1A

CHANGE POINTS:
(1) To (T)22D Suffix B
(2) To (T)29D Suffix B
(3) From (T)29D Suffix C
(4) To (T)29D Suffix F
(5) From (T)22D Suffix C
(6) To (T)22D Suffix F
(7) To (T) 551441F

Illus	Part Number	Description	Quantity	Change Point	Remarks
1	FRC8917	Gear-mainshaft-26 teeth	NLA	Note (1)	For manual variants use FTC5089 gear. For automatic variants use FTC5089 gear and FTC5090 shaft.. 25D V8 Petrol Twin Carburettor except 90°
1	FRC8917	Gear-mainshaft-26 teeth	NLA	Note (1)	For manual variants use FTC5089 gear. For automatic variants use FTC5089 gear and FTC5090 shaft.. 22D 4 Cylinder Diesel Turbo except 90°
1	FRC8917	Gear-mainshaft-26 teeth	NLA	Note (2)	For manual variants use FTC5089 gear. For automatic variants use FTC5089 gear and FTC5090 shaft.. 32D V8 Petrol Twin Carburettor 90°
1	FTC4188	Gear-mainshaft-28 teeth	NLA	Note (3)	Manual use FTC5087; auto use FTC5087 & FTC5090; later gear has longer internal spline, lubricating holes & dog teeth which old may not have. 32D V8 Petrol Twin Carburettor 90°
1	FTC4962	Gear-mainshaft-26 teeth-1.4 : 1	1	Note (4)	20D 4 Cylinder Petrol except 90°
1	FTC4962	Gear-mainshaft-26 teeth-1.4 : 1	1	Note (4)	20D 4 Cylinder Diesel Naturally Aspirated except 90°

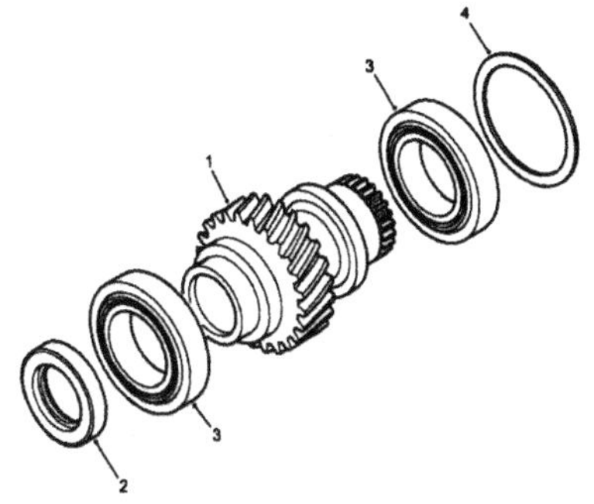

AHDBIA1A

CHANGE POINTS:
(1) To (T) 551441F
(2) To (T)32D 309416D
(3) From (T)32D 309417E To (T) 551441F
(4) From (T) 551442G

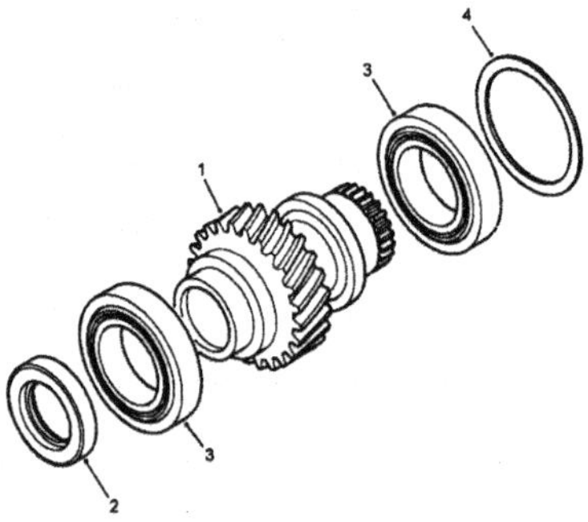

AHDBIA1A

Illus	Part Number	Description	Quantity	Change Point	Remarks
1	FTC4962	Gear-mainshaft-26 teeth-1.4 : 1	1	Note (1)	25D V8 Petrol Twin Carburettor except 90"
1	FTC4962	Gear-mainshaft-26 teeth-1.4 : 1	1	Note (1)	22D 4 Cylinder Diesel Turbo except 90"
1	FTC4845	Gear-mainshaft-1.2 : 1	1	Note (1)	29D V8 Petrol Twin Carburettor 90"
1	FTC4845	Gear-mainshaft-1.2 : 1	1	Note (1)	32D V8 Petrol Twin Carburettor 90"
1	FTC4845	Gear-mainshaft-1.2 : 1	1	Note (1)	38D V8 Petrol EFi 90" except shift interlock
1	FTC4845	Gear-mainshaft-1.2 : 1	1	Note (1)	40D V8 Petrol EFi shift interlock 90"
1	FTC4962	Gear-mainshaft-26 teeth-1.4 : 1	1		47D 4 Cylinder Petrol
1	FTC4962	Gear-mainshaft-26 teeth-1.4 : 1	1		43D Td5
1	FTC4962	Gear-mainshaft-26 teeth-1.4 : 1	1		43D 300 TDI
1	FTC4962	Gear-mainshaft-26 teeth-1.4 : 1	1		43D V8 Petrol except 90"
1	FTC4850	Gear-mainshaft-38 teeth-1.2 : 1	1		45D V8 Petrol 90"
2	FRC2365	Seal-transfer box input	1	Note (2)	
2	ICV100000	Seal-transfer box input	1	Note (3)	
3	FRC5564	Mainshaft bearing	2		
4	FRC9926	Shim-3.15mm	A/R		
4	FRC9928	Shim-3.20mm	A/R		
4	FRC9930	Shim-3.25mm	A/R		
4	FRC9932	Shim-3.30mm	A/R		
4	FRC9934	Shim-3.35mm	A/R		
4	FRC9936	Shim-3.40mm	A/R		
4	FRC9938	Shim-3.45mm	A/R		
4	FRC9940	Shim-3.50mm	A/R		
4	FRC9942	Shim-3.55mm	A/R		
4	FRC9944	Shim-3.6mm	A/R		
4	FRC9946	Shim-3.65mm	A/R		
4	FRC9948	Shim-3.70mm	A/R		
4	FRC9950	Shim-3.75mm	A/R		
4	FRC9952	Shim-3.80mm	A/R		
4	FRC9954	Shim-3.85mm	A/R		
4	FRC9956	Shim-3.90mm	A/R		
4	FRC9958	Shim-3.95mm	A/R		
4	FRC9960	Shim-4.00mm	A/R		

CHANGE POINTS:
(1) From (T) 551442G
(2) To (T) 677403
(3) From (T) 677404G

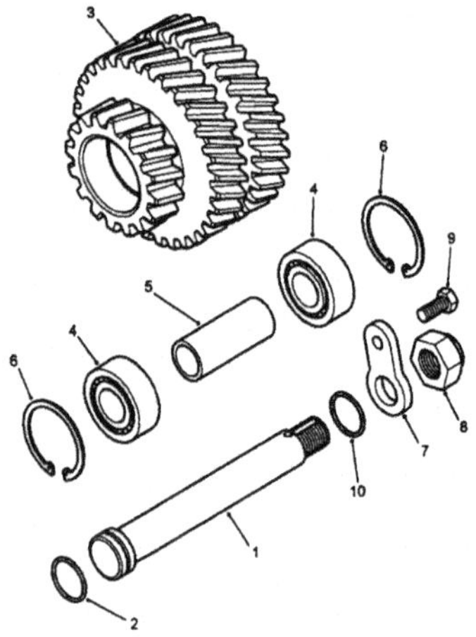

AHDBIA2A

Illus	Part Number	Description	Quantity	Change Point	Remarks
1	FRC8291	Shaft-transfer box-intermediate	1		
2	FRC7439	O ring	1		Except 32D
2	FRC8292	O ring	1		32D
3	FRC7884	Gear-intermediate shaft-1.4 : 1	1	Note (1)	22D
3	FRC9460	Gear-intermediate shaft-1.4 : 1	1	Note (2)	22D
3	FRC9552	Gear-intermediate shaft-1.2 : 1	1	Note (3)	32D V8 Petrol 90"
3	FTC4190	Gear-intermediate shaft-1.2 : 1	1	Note (4)	32D V8 Petrol 90"
3	FRC7428	Gear-intermediate shaft-1.2 : 1	1	Note (5)	29D V8 Petrol 90"
3	FRC9552	Gear-intermediate shaft-1.2 : 1	1	Note (6)	29D V8 Petrol 90"
3	FTC4846	Gear-intermediate shaft-1.2 : 1	1	Note (7)	29D V8 Petrol 90"
3	FRC9462	Gear-intermediate shaft-1.6 : 1	1		20D
3	FRC9460	Gear-intermediate shaft-1.4 : 1	1		25D V8 Petrol Twin Carburettor except 90"
3	FTC4846	Gear-intermediate shaft-1.2 : 1	1		45D
3	FRC9460	Gear-intermediate shaft-1.4 : 1	1		43D
3	FRC9462	Gear-intermediate shaft-1.6 : 1	1		47D
4	FRC7810	Bearing intermediate shaft assembly	NLA	Note (8)	Use STC3185.
4	STC3185	Bearing intermediate shaft assembly	2	Note (7)	

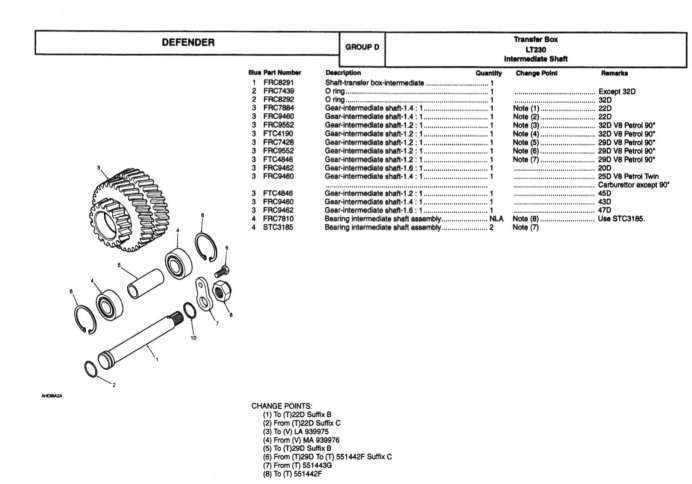

CHANGE POINTS:
(1) To (T)22D Suffix B
(2) From (T)22D Suffix C
(3) To (V) LA 939975
(4) From (V) MA 939976
(5) To (T)29D Suffix B
(6) From (T)29D To (T) 551442F Suffix C
(7) From (T) 551443G
(8) To (T) 551442F

Illus	Part Number	Description	Quantity	Change Point	Remarks
5	FRC7437	Spacer	1	Note (1)	
5	IEJ100010	Spacer-58.350	1	Note (2)	
5	IEJ100030	Spacer-58.400	1		
5	IEJ100050	Spacer-58.450	1		
5	IEJ100070	Spacer-58.500	1		
5	IEJ100090	Spacer-58.550	1		
5	IEJ100110	Spacer-58.600	1		
5	IEJ100130	Spacer-58.650	1		
5	IEJ100150	Spacer-58.700	1		
5	IEJ100170	Spacer-58.750	1		
5	IEJ100190	Spacer-58.800	1		
5	IEJ100210	Spacer-58.850	1		
5	IEJ100230	Spacer-58.900	1		
5	IEJ100250	Spacer-58.950	1		
5	IEJ100270	Spacer-59.000	1		
5	IEJ100290	Spacer-59.050	1		
5	IEJ100310	Spacer-59.100	1		
5	IEJ100330	Spacer-59.150	1		
5	IEJ100350	Spacer-59.200	1		
5	IEJ100370	Spacer-59.250	1		
5	IEJ100390	Spacer-59.300	1		
6	FRC7454	Circlip	2		
7	FRC7452	Plate-transfer box anti rotation	1		
8	FRC7453	Locknut	1		
9	FS108207L	Screw-flanged head-M8 x 20	1	Note (3)	
9	FS108251ML	Screw-flanged head-M8 x 25	1	Note (4)	
	WA108051L	Washer-8mm	1	Note (3)	
10	FRC7439	O ring	1	Note (4)	

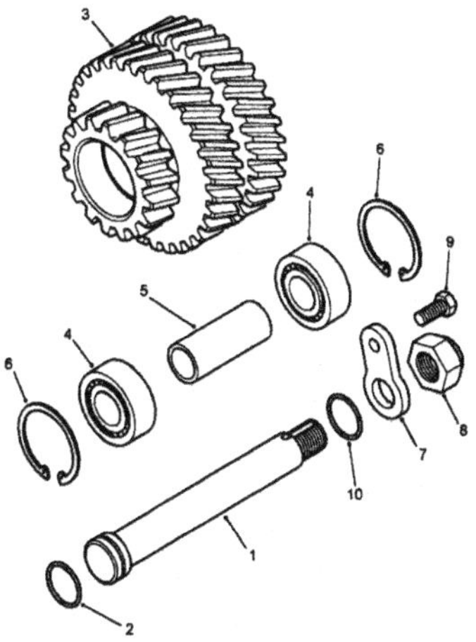

AHDBIA2A

CHANGE POINTS:
(1) To (T)43D
(2) From (T)43D
(3) To (V) LA 939975
(4) From (V) MA 939976

Illus	Part Number	Description	Quantity	Change Point	Remarks
1	FRC5454	Shaft-intermediate transmission	1		
	FRC3196	Plug	2		
2	532323	O ring	1		
3	FRC5424	Gear-intermediate shaft	1		
4	594290	Bearing-needle roller	2		
5	FRC2317	Spacer	1		
6	FRC6861	Washer	2		
7	FRC5494	Plate assembly	1		
8	WA108051L	Washer-8mm	1		
9	FS108207L	Screw-flanged head-M8 x 20	1		

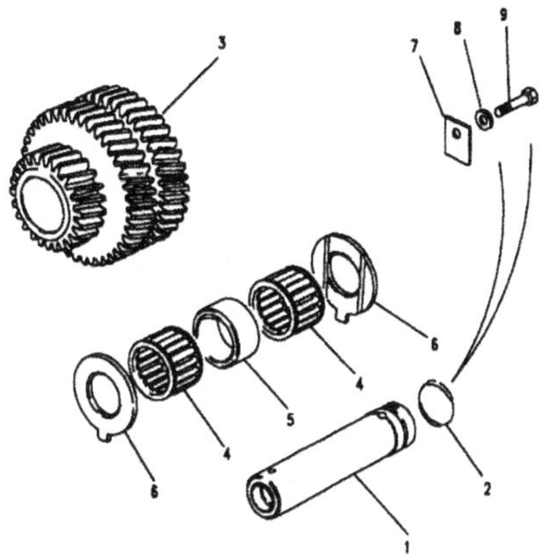

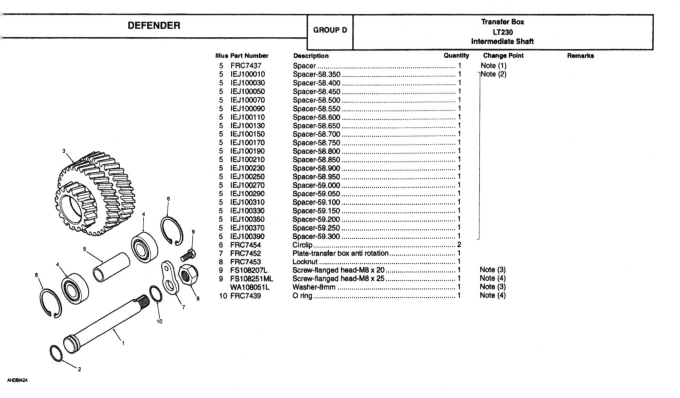

DEFENDER	GROUP D	Transfer Box LT230 Front Flange

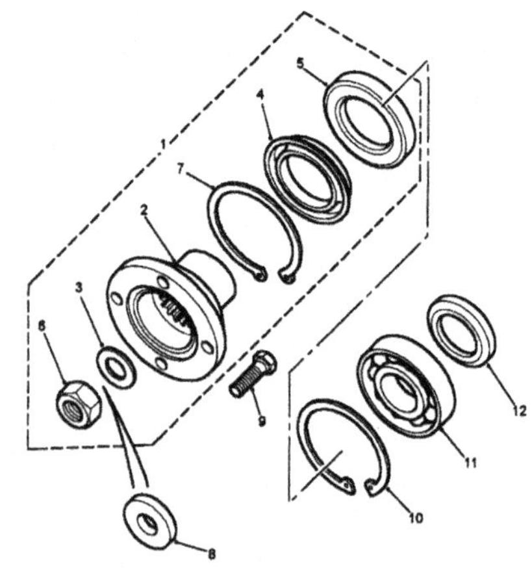

LD0011

Illus	Part Number	Description	Quantity	Change Point	Remarks
1	STC3432	FLANGE ASSEMBLY-FRONT OUTPUT	1	Note (1); Note (2)	
2	FRC5442	• Flange assembly-front output	1		
3	FRC2464	• Washer	1		
4	FTC4940	• Mudshield-transfer box oil seal	1		
5	FTC4939	• Seal-transfer box output	1		
6	NY120041L	• Nut-hexagonal-nyloc-M20	1		
1	STC4370	FLANGE ASSEMBLY-FRONT OUTPUT	1	Note (3)	
2	IEC100020	• Flange assembly-front output	1		
3	FRC2464	• Washer	1		
4	ICN100000	• Mudshield-transfer box oil seal	1		
5	FTC4939	• Seal-transfer box output	1		
6	NY120041L	• Nut-hexagonal-nyloc-M20	1		
7	571682	• Circlip	1		
4	FRC6121	Mudshield-transfer box oil seal	1	Note (4); Note (5); Note (6)	
5	FRC7043	Seal-transfer box output	1	Note (4); Note (5)	
8	571468	Washer	1		
9	BT606101L	Bolt-3/8UNC x 1 1/4	4		
10	216962	Circlip-large	1		
11	STC1130	Bearing-ball	1		
12	FRC5439	Spacer	1		

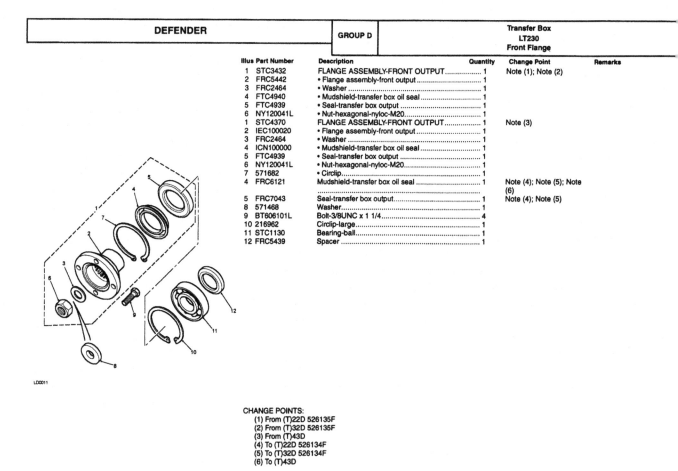

CHANGE POINTS:
(1) From (T)22D 526135F
(2) From (T)32D 526135F
(3) From (T)43D
(4) To (T)22D 526134F
(5) To (T)32D 526134F
(6) To (T)43D

DEFENDER	GROUP D	Transfer Box LT230 Rear Flange

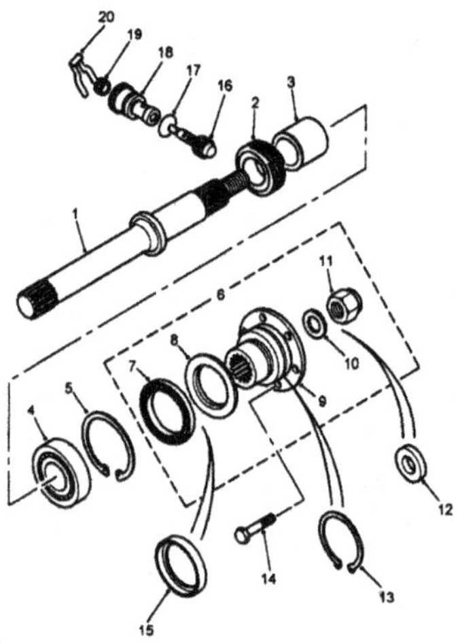

AHD8IA4A

Illus	Part Number	Description	Quantity	Change Point	Remarks
1	FRC5450	Shaft assembly-rear output	1		
2	FRC3162	Gear-speedometer drive	1		
3	FRC5446	Spacer	1		
4	STC1130	Bearing-ball	1		
5	216962	Circlip-large	1		
6	STC3433	KIT-FLANGE-REAR	1		
7	FTC4939	• Seal-transfer box output	1	Note (1)	
8	FTC4941	• Mudshield-transfer box oil seal	1		
9	FTC4942	• Flange assembly-rear output	1		
10	FRC2464	• Washer	1		
11	NY120041L	• Nut-hexagonal-nyloc-M20	1		
7	FRC7043	Seal-transfer box output	1	Note (2)	
9	FRC5438	Flange assembly-rear output	1		
12	571468	Washer	1		
13	571682	Circlip	1		
14	FRC3602	Bolt-3/8UNF x 1 3/4	1		
15	571970	Mudshield-transfer box oil seal-rear	1		
		GEAR-SPEEDOMETER DRIVE			
16	FRC3310	20 teeth-Blue.	1	Note (3)	750 x 16 tyre 90"
16	FRC3310	20 teeth-Blue.	1	Note (4)	90" except 205 x 16 tyre
16	FRC3310	20 teeth-Blue.	1		Except 90"
16	FRC3311	21 teeth-Green	1		90" except 50 LE
16	FRC3312	22 teeth-Yellow.	1		205 x 16 tyre 90"
16	FRC3313	24 teeth-Red	1		29D V8 Petrol Twin Carburettor 90"
17	571665	O ring	1		
18	FRC3286	Housing-spindle	1		
19	AAU2304	Seal-oil speedometer pinion	1		
20	533765	Plate-oil seal retainer	1	Note (3)	

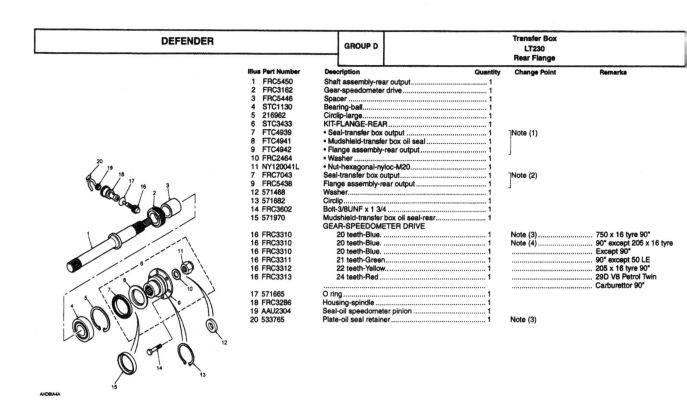

CHANGE POINTS:
(1) From (T)22D 526135F; From (T)32D 526135F
(2) To (V) LA 939975
(3) To (V) WA 159806
(4) From (V) XA 159807

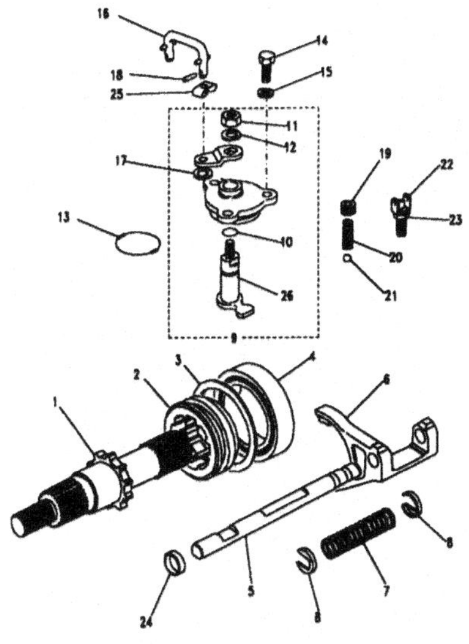

Illus	Part Number	Description	Quantity	Change Point	Remarks
1	FRC5449	Shaft assembly-front output	1		
2	FRC5440	Ring-differential locking	1		
	FRC5575	O ring	1		
		SHIM			
3	FTC726	2mm	1		
3	FTC728	2.05mm	1		
3	FTC730	2.10mm	1		
3	FTC732	2.15mm	1		
3	FTC734	2.20mm	1		
3	FTC736	2.25mm	1		
3	FTC738	2.30mm	1		
3	FTC740	2.35mm	1		
3	FTC742	2.40mm	1		
3	FTC744	2.45mm	1		
3	FTC746	2.50mm	1		
3	FTC748	2.55mm	1		
3	FTC750	2.60mm	1		
3	FTC752	2.65mm	1		
3	FTC754	2.70mm	1		
3	FTC756	2.75mm	1		
3	FTC758	2.8mm	1		
3	FTC760	2.85mm	1		
3	FTC762	2.90mm	1		
3	FTC764	2.95mm	1		
3	FTC766	3.0mm	1		
3	FTC768	3.05mm	1		
3	FTC770	3.10mm	1		
3	FTC772	3.15mm	1		
3	FTC774	3.20mm	1		
3	FTC776	3.25mm	1		

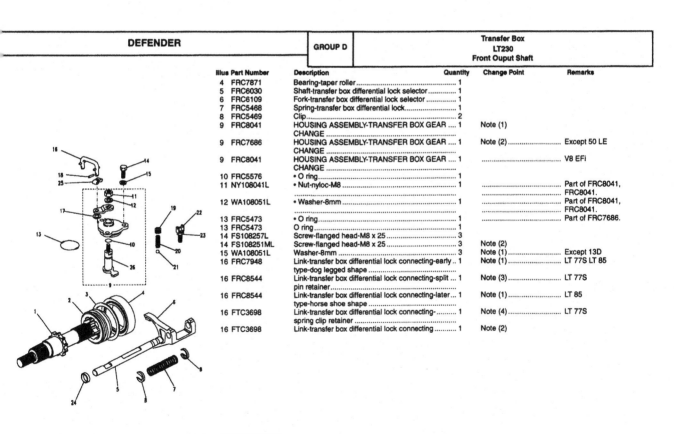

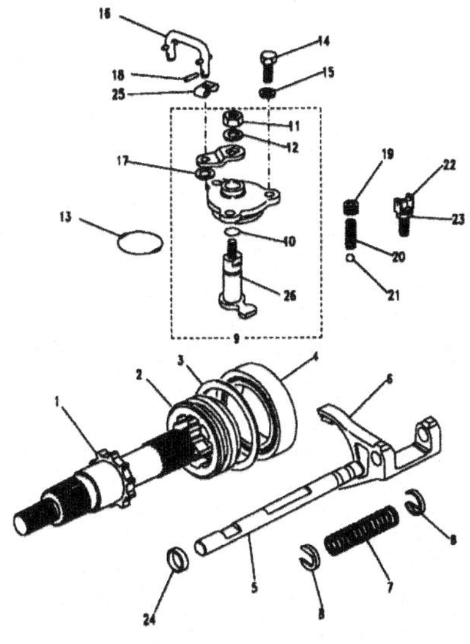

Illus	Part Number	Description	Quantity	Change Point	Remarks
4	FRC7871	Bearing-taper roller	1		
5	FRC6030	Shaft-transfer box differential lock selector	1		
6	FRC6109	Fork-transfer box differential lock selector	1		
7	FRC5468	Spring-transfer box differential lock	1		
8	FRC5469	Clip	2		
9	FRC8041	HOUSING ASSEMBLY-TRANSFER BOX GEAR CHANGE	1	Note (1)	
9	FRC7686	HOUSING ASSEMBLY-TRANSFER BOX GEAR CHANGE	1	Note (2)	Except 50 LE
9	FRC8041	HOUSING ASSEMBLY-TRANSFER BOX GEAR CHANGE	1		V8 EFi
10	FRC5576	• O ring	1		
11	NY108041L	• Nut-nyloc-M8	1		Part of FRC8041, FRC8041.
12	WA108051L	• Washer-8mm	1		Part of FRC8041, FRC8041.
13	FRC5473	• O ring	1		Part of FRC7686.
13	FRC5473	O ring	1		
14	FS108257L	Screw-flanged head-M8 x 25	3		
14	FS108251ML	Screw-flanged head-M8 x 25	3	Note (2)	
15	WA108051L	Washer-8mm	3	Note (1)	Except 13D
16	FRC7948	Link-transfer box differential lock connecting-early type-dog legged shape	1	Note (1)	LT 77S LT 85
16	FRC8544	Link-transfer box differential lock connecting-split pin retainer	1	Note (3)	LT 77S
16	FRC8544	Link-transfer box differential lock connecting-later type-horse shoe shape	1	Note (1)	LT 85
16	FTC3698	Link-transfer box differential lock connecting-spring clip retainer	1	Note (4)	LT 77S
16	FTC3698	Link-transfer box differential lock connecting	1	Note (2)	

CHANGE POINTS:
(1) To (V) LA 939975
(2) From (V) MA 939976
(3) To (T)28D 274897E
(4) From (T)28D 274898E To (V) LA 939975

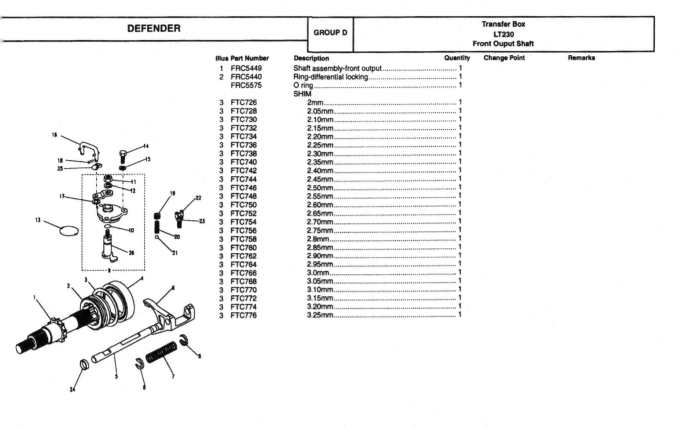

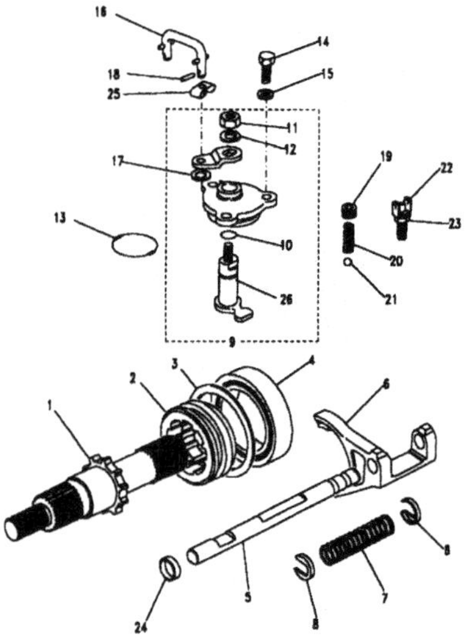

Illus	Part Number	Description	Quantity	Change Point	Remarks
17	WA106041L	Washer-6mm	2		
25	FTC3674	Clip	2	Note (1)	LT 77S 22D 32D
25	FTC3674	Clip	2	Note (2)	
18	PS103121L	Pin-split	2	Note (3)	LT 77S 22D 32D
18	PS103121L	Pin-split	2	Note (4)	LT 85
19	SU112101S	Plug-M12 x 10-patch lock	1		
20	FRC5562	Spring-transfer box detent	1		
21	571146	Ball-detent manual transmission	1		
22	PRC2911	Switch-high/low	1		
23	NT110041L	Locknut-M10	1		
27	UYF100160	Locknut	1		
24	FRC6110	Plug	1		
26	FRC7098	Pivot-transfer box differential lock shaft/arm	1	Note (4)	LT 77S 22D 32D
26	FRC7098	Pivot-transfer box differential lock shaft/arm	1	Note (2)	

CHANGE POINTS:
(1) From (T)28D 274898E To (V) LA 939975
(2) From (V) MA 939976
(3) To (T)28D 274897E
(4) To (V) LA 939975

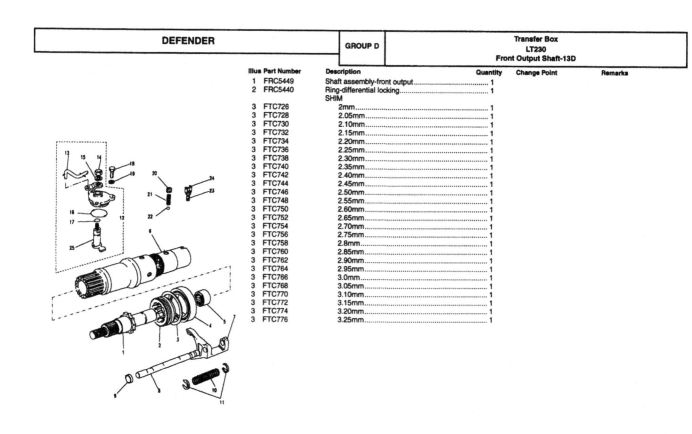

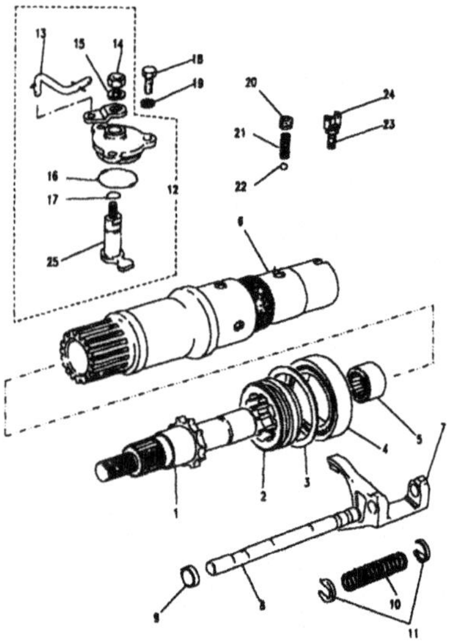

Illus	Part Number	Description	Quantity	Change Point	Remarks
1	FRC5449	Shaft assembly-front output	1		
2	FRC5440	Ring-differential locking	1		
		SHIM			
3	FTC726	2mm	1		
3	FTC728	2.05mm	1		
3	FTC730	2.10mm	1		
3	FTC732	2.15mm	1		
3	FTC734	2.20mm	1		
3	FTC736	2.25mm	1		
3	FTC738	2.30mm	1		
3	FTC740	2.35mm	1		
3	FTC742	2.40mm	1		
3	FTC744	2.45mm	1		
3	FTC746	2.50mm	1		
3	FTC748	2.55mm	1		
3	FTC750	2.60mm	1		
3	FTC752	2.65mm	1		
3	FTC754	2.70mm	1		
3	FTC756	2.75mm	1		
3	FTC758	2.8mm	1		
3	FTC760	2.85mm	1		
3	FTC762	2.90mm	1		
3	FTC764	2.95mm	1		
3	FTC766	3.0mm	1		
3	FTC768	3.05mm	1		
3	FTC770	3.10mm	1		
3	FTC772	3.15mm	1		
3	FTC774	3.20mm	1		
3	FTC776	3.25mm	1		

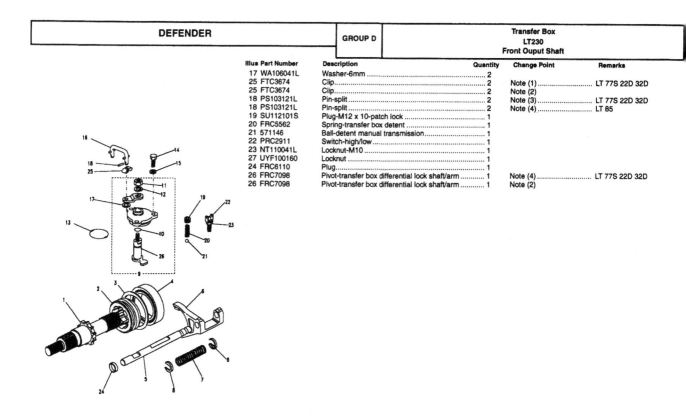

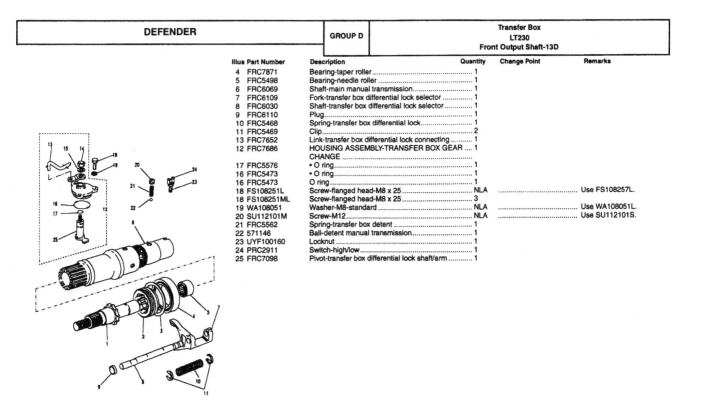

DEFENDER	GROUP D	Transfer Box LT230 Front Output Shaft-13D

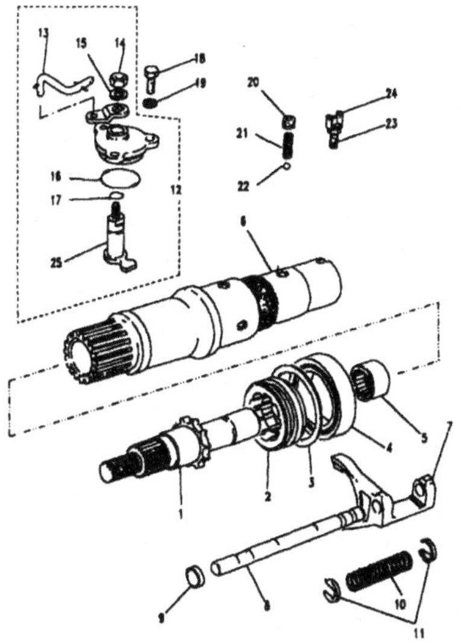

Illus	Part Number	Description	Quantity	Change Point	Remarks
4	FRC7871	Bearing-taper roller	1		
5	FRC5498	Bearing-needle roller	1		
6	FRC6069	Shaft-main manual transmission	1		
7	FRC6109	Fork-transfer box differential lock selector	1		
8	FRC6030	Shaft-transfer box differential lock selector	1		
9	FRC6110	Plug	1		
10	FRC5468	Spring-transfer box differential lock	1		
11	FRC5469	Clip	2		
13	FRC7652	Link-transfer box differential lock connecting	1		
12	FRC7686	HOUSING ASSEMBLY-TRANSFER BOX GEAR CHANGE	1		
17	FRC5576	• O ring	1		
16	FRC5473	• O ring	1		
16	FRC5473	O ring	1		
18	FS108251L	Screw-flanged head-M8 x 25	NLA		Use FS108257L.
18	FS108251ML	Screw-flanged head-M8 x 25	3		
19	WA108051	Washer-M8-standard	NLA		Use WA108051L.
20	SU112101M	Screw-M12	NLA		Use SU112101S.
21	FRC5562	Spring-transfer box detent	1		
22	571146	Ball-detent manual transmission	1		
23	UYF100160	Locknut	1		
24	PRC2911	Switch-high/low	1		
25	FRC7098	Pivot-transfer box differential lock shaft/arm	1		

DEFENDER	GROUP D	Transfer Box LT230 High/Low Gear

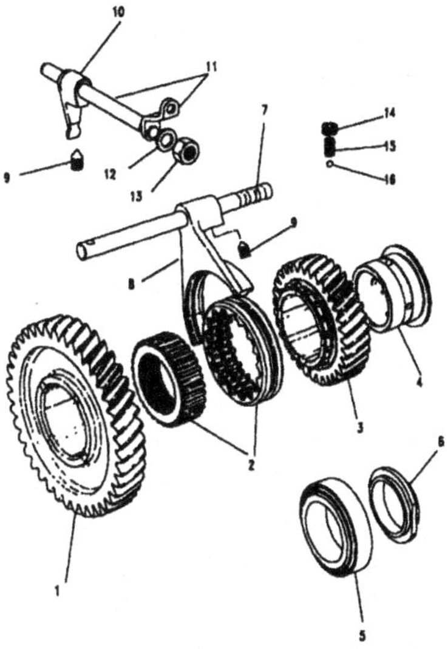

Illus	Part Number	Description	Quantity	Change Point	Remarks
1	FRC7434	Gear-low output	1	Note (1)	22D 4 Cylinder 90"
1	FRC7434	Gear-low output	1	Note (1)	22D 4 Cylinder Diesel Turbo except 90"
1	FTC1084	Gear-low output	1	Note (2)	22D 4 Cylinder 90"
1	FTC1084	Gear-low output	1	Note (2)	22D Diesel Turbo 4 Cylinder except 90"
1	FTC1084	Gear-low output	1		32D V8 Petrol Twin Carburettor 90"
1	FTC1084	Gear-low output	1		43D 300 TDI
1	FTC1084	Gear-low output	1		43D Td5
1	FRC7434	Gear-low output	1		29D V8 Petrol Twin Carburettor 90"
1	FRC7434	Gear-low output	1		25D V8 Petrol Twin Carburettor except 90"

CHANGE POINTS:
(1) To (T)22D Suffix D
(2) From (T)22D Suffix E

DEFENDER	GROUP D	Transfer Box LT230 High/Low Gear

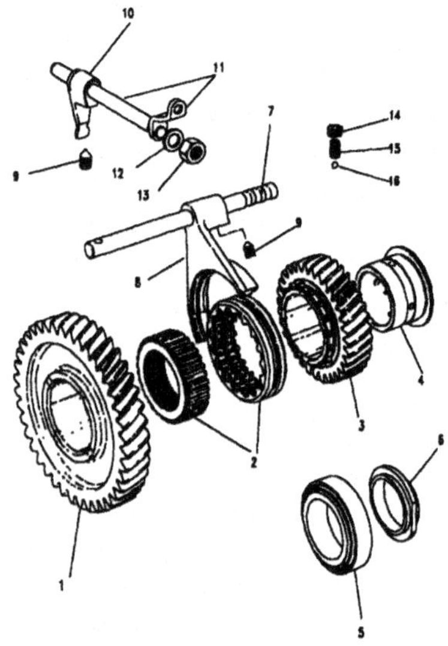

Illus	Part Number	Description	Quantity	Change Point	Remarks
2	RTC4373	Hub & sleeve assembly- transfer box	1	Note (1)	22D 4 Cylinder 90"
2	RTC4373	Hub & sleeve assembly- transfer box	1	Note (1)	22D 4 Cylinder Diesel Turbo except 90"
2	FTC382	Hub & sleeve assembly- transfer box	1	Note (2)	22D 4 Cylinder 90"
2	FTC382	Hub & sleeve assembly- transfer box	1	Note (2)	22D Diesel Turbo 4 Cylinder except 90"
2	FTC382	Hub & sleeve assembly- transfer box	1		32D V8 Petrol Twin Carburettor 90"
2	RTC5064	Hub & sleeve assembly- transfer box	1		29D V8 Petrol Twin Carburettor 90"
2	RTC4373	Hub & sleeve assembly- transfer box	1		25D V8 Petrol Twin Carburettor except 90"
2	IEQ100000	Hub & sleeve assembly- transfer box	1	Note (3)	22D 4 Cylinder Suffix G 90"
2	IEQ100000	Hub & sleeve assembly- transfer box	1	Note (3)	22D 4 Cylinder Diesel Turbo Suffix G except 90"
2	FTC5099	Hub & sleeve assembly- transfer box	1		43D Td5
2	FTC5099	Hub & sleeve assembly- transfer box	1		43D 300 TDI
2	FTC5099	Hub & sleeve assembly- transfer box	1		43D 3500 cc V8 Petrol Twin Carburettor except 90"
2	RTC4373	Hub & sleeve assembly- transfer box	1		38D 50 LE

CHANGE POINTS:
(1) To (T)22D Suffix D
(2) From (T)22D Suffix E
(3) From (T)22D 681983 Suffix G

DEFENDER	GROUP D	Transfer Box LT230 High/Low Gear

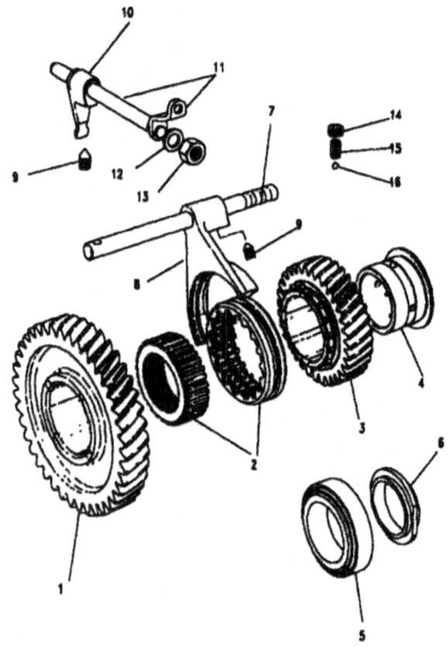

Illus	Part Number	Description	Quantity	Change Point	Remarks
		GEAR-HIGH OUTPUT			
3	FRC7427	1.6 : 1	1	Note (1)	20D Petrol 4 Cylinder except 90"
3	FRC7427	1.6 : 1	1		20D 4 Cylinder Diesel Naturally Aspirated except 90"
3	FTC1823	1.6 : 1	1	Note (2)	20D 4 Cylinder Petrol except 90"
3	FTC1823	1.6 : 1	1		20D Diesel Naturally Aspirated except 90"
3	FRC7885	1.4 : 1	1	Note (3)	22D 4 Cylinder 90"
3	FRC7885	1.4 : 1	1		22D 4 Cylinder Diesel Turbo except 90"
3	FTC1741	1.4 : 1	1	Note (4)	22D 4 Cylinder 90"
3	FTC1741	1.4 : 1	1		22D 4 Cylinder Diesel Turbo except 90"
3	FTC1741	1.4 : 1	1		43D 300 TDI
3	FTC1741	1.4 : 1	1		43D Td5
3	FRC7885	1.4 : 1	1		25D except 90"
		GEAR-HIGH OUTPUT			
3	FTC1085	1.2 : 1	1	Note (5)	32D V8 Petrol Twin Carburettor 90"
3	FTC4189	1.2 : 1	1	Note (6)	32D V8 Petrol Twin Carburettor 90"
3	FTC4847	1.2 : 1	1	Note (7)	32D V8 Petrol Twin Carburettor 90"
3	FRC7429	1.2 : 1	1		29D V8 Petrol Twin Carburettor Suffix B 90"
3	FRC9551	1.2 : 1	1		29D V8 Petrol Twin Carburettor Suffix C 90"

CHANGE POINTS:
(1) To (T)20D 226368E
(2) From (T)20D 226369E
(3) To (T)22D Suffix D
(4) From (T)22D Suffix E
(5) To (V) LA 939975
(6) From (V) MA 939976 To (T) 551442F
(7) From (T) 551443G

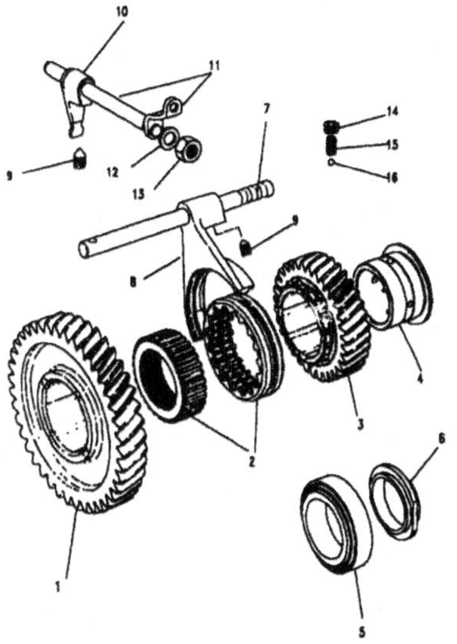

Illus	Part Number	Description	Quantity	Change Point	Remarks
4	FRC7441	Bush	NLA	Note (1)	Use IEE100050.
4	IEE100050	Bush	1	Note (2)	
5	606474	Bearing-taper roller	1		
6	FRC7970	Nut	1		
7	FRC9513	Shaft-selector lever	NLA		Use FTC3627.
7	FTC3627	Shaft-selector lever	1		
8	FRC5458	FORK-HIGH/LOW SELECTOR	NLA	Note (3)	Use FTC2859. 29D 90"
8	FTC2859	FORK-HIGH/LOW SELECTOR	NLA	Note (4)	Use FTC2827 qty 1 with FTC4536 qty 1. LT 85 90"
9	FRC7018	• Screw-grub	NLA		Use FTC4536.
8	FTC2827	FORK-HIGH/LOW SELECTOR	1	Note (4)	
9	FTC4536	• Screw-grub	1		
10	FRC7929	Finger assembly-transfer box high/low selector	1		
11	FRC8900	Shaft assembly-high/low selector	1		LT 77S
11	FRC8899	Shaft assembly-high/low selector	1		LT 85
12	WA108051L	Washer-8mm	1	Note (3)	LT 77S 22D 32D
13	NY108041L	Nut-nyloc-M8	1		
14	SU112101S	Plug-M12 x 10-patch lock	1	Note (3)	Suffix B
14	FRC9549	Plug	1		LT 77S Suffix C
14	FRC9549	Plug	1		LT 85 Suffix C
14	FRC9549	Plug	1	Note (4)	
15	FRC5562	Spring-transfer box detent	1	Note (5)	LT 77S Suffix B
15	FRC9546	Spring-transfer box detent	1	Note (3)	LT 77S Suffix C
15	FRC5562	Spring-transfer box detent	1		LT 85 Suffix B
15	FRC9546	Spring-transfer box detent	1		LT 85 Suffix C
15	FRC9546	Spring-transfer box detent	1	Note (4)	
16	571146	Ball-detent manual transmission	1		
	FRC5575	O ring	1	Note (4)	

CHANGE POINTS:
(1) To (T) 551442F
(2) From (T) 551443G
(3) To (V) LA 939975
(4) From (V) MA 939976
(5) From (T)28D 274402E To (V) LA 939975

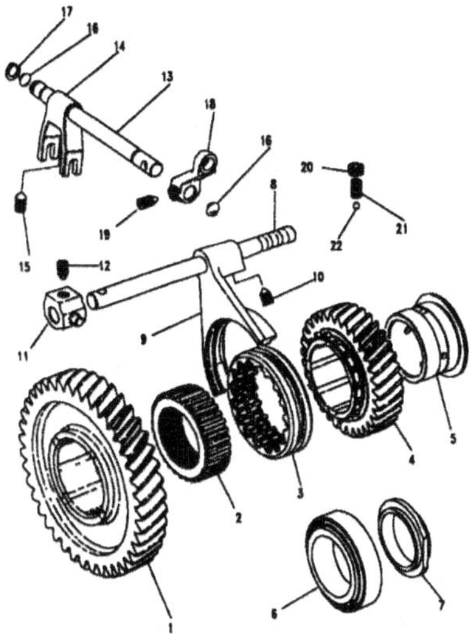

Illus	Part Number	Description	Quantity	Change Point	Remarks
1	FRC5435	Gear-low output	1		
2	FRC5681	Hub-forward clutch	1		
3	FRC7326	Sleeve	1		
4	FRC5425	Gear-high output	1		
5	FRC5436	Screw-grub	1		
6	606474	Bearing-taper roller	1		
7	FRC6098	Nut	1		
8	FRC5459	Shaft-selector manual transmission	1		
9	FTC2859	FORK-HIGH/LOW SELECTOR	NLA		Use FTC2827 qty 1 with FTC4536 qty 1.
10	FRC7018	• Screw-grub	NLA		Use FTC4536.
9	FTC2827	FORK-HIGH/LOW SELECTOR	1		
10	FTC4536	• Screw-grub	1		
11	FRC5460	Yoke assembly-selector rod	1		
12	FTC4536	Screw-grub	1		
13	FRC7021	Shaft & flinger assembly	1		
14	FRC5461	Fork-selector-cross shaft	1		
15	FTC4536	Screw-grub	1		
16	FRC5575	O ring	2		
17	CR120125L	Circlip	1		
18	FRC5465	Arm-transfer box gearchange	1		
19	FTC4536	Screw-grub	1		
20	SU112101M	Screw-M12	NLA		Use SU112101S.
21	FRC5562	Spring-transfer box detent	1		
22	571146	Ball-detent manual transmission	1		

Illus	Part Number	Description	Quantity	Change Point	Remarks
1	FRC9555	MECHANISM ASSEMBLY-TRANSFER BOX GEAR CHANGE	1	Note (1)	LT 77S 22D 32D
2	FRC6873	• Plate-transfer box gearchange grommet retaining	1		
3	FRC6872	• Grommet	1		
4	FS106201L	• Screw-flanged head-M6 x 20	4		
6	FRC8561	• Plate-gear lever retention	1		
7	FTC4037	• Gasket-transfer box gear change housing plate	1		
8	FRC5478	• Arm-transfer box gearchange	1		
9	FS106251M	• Screw-flanged head-patch lock-M6 x 25	NLA		Use FS106251ML.
	FRC8751	• Housing assembly- gear change cross shaft	1		
18	FRC5574	• Plate-transfer box selector cross shaft end	1		
19	SF106201L	• Screw-M6 x 20-counter sunk-recessed	2		
20	FRC8292	• O ring	1		
21	FRC4951	• O ring	2		
22	FRC5480	• Lever assembly bell crank	1		
23	FRC5479	• O ring	1		
24	FRC8203	• Shaft-gear change cross	1		
25	FRC8766	• Pin-clevis/pivot	1		
26	FRC4499	• Bush	4		
	ETC7884	• Clip-spring steel	2		
29	FRC7487	• Lever-transfer box	1		
30	FRC5076	• Bush-joint selector rod/yoke manual transmission	1		
31	CR120215	• Circlip	1		
5	WA106001L	• Washer-M6	4		
9	FS106251ML	Screw-flanged head-patch lock-M6 x 25			LT 77S 22D 32D

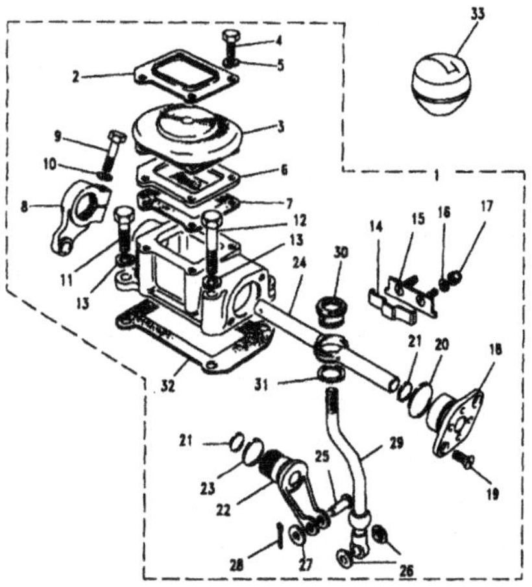

CHANGE POINTS:
(1) From (V) MA 939976

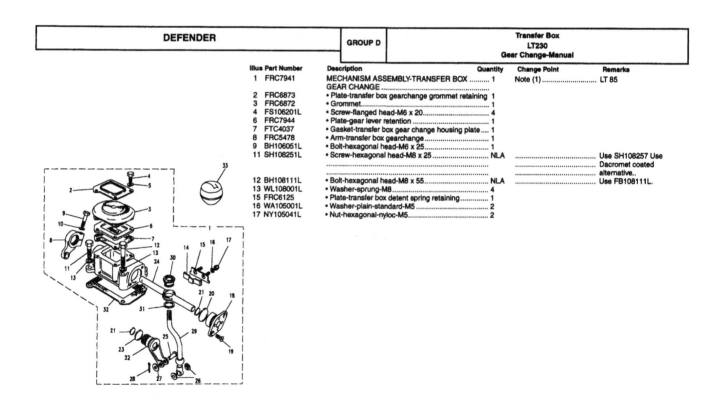

Illus	Part Number	Description	Quantity	Change Point	Remarks
1	FRC7941	MECHANISM ASSEMBLY-TRANSFER BOX GEAR CHANGE	1	Note (1)	LT 85
2	FRC6873	• Plate-transfer box gearchange grommet retaining	1		
3	FRC6872	• Grommet	1		
4	FS106201L	• Screw-flanged head-M6 x 20	4		
6	FRC7944	• Plate-gear lever retention	1		
7	FTC4037	• Gasket-transfer box gear change housing plate	1		
8	FRC5478	• Arm-transfer box gearchange	1		
9	BH106051L	• Bolt-hexagonal head-M6 x 25	1		
11	SH108251L	• Screw-hexagonal head-M8 x 25	NLA		Use SH108257 Use Dacromet coated alternative..
12	BH108111L	• Bolt-hexagonal head-M8 x 55	NLA		Use FB108111L.
13	WL108001L	• Washer-sprung-M8	4		
15	FRC6125	• Plate-transfer box detent spring retaining	1		
16	WA105001L	• Washer-plain-standard-M5	2		
17	NY105041L	• Nut-hexagonal-nyloc-M5	2		

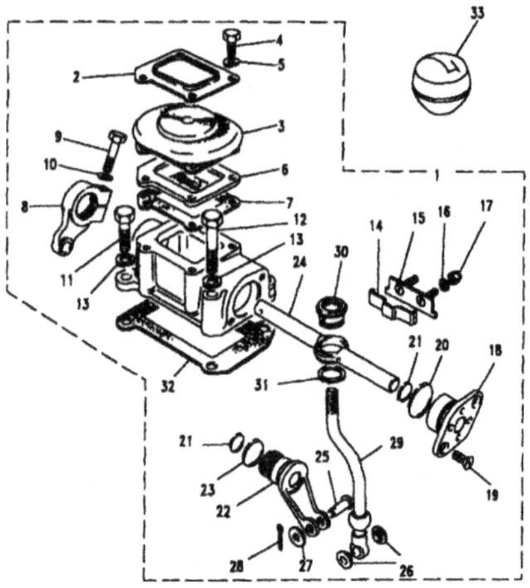

CHANGE POINTS:
(1) To (V) LA 939975

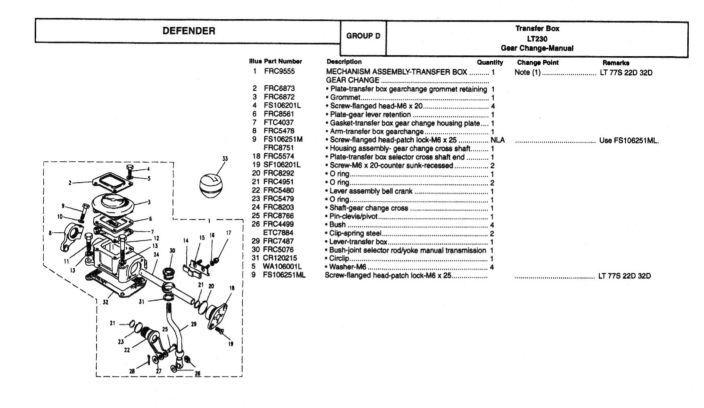

Illus	Part Number	Description	Quantity	Change Point	Remarks
18	FRC5574	• Plate-transfer box selector cross shaft end	1		
19	SF106201L	• Screw-M6 x 20-counter sunk-recessed	2		
20	FRC4565	• O ring	1		
21	FRC4509	• O ring	NLA		Use FRC4951.
22	FRC5480	• Lever assembly bell crank	1		
23	FRC5479	• O ring	3		
24	FRC6117	• Shaft-gear change cross	1		
25	PC108321L	• Pin-clevis/pivot	1		
26	FRC4499	• Bush	2		
27	WA108051L	• Washer-8mm	1		
30	FRC5076	• Bush-joint selector rod/yoke manual transmission	1		
31	CR120215L	• Circlip	1		
32	FRC6306	• Gasket-transfer box gear change housing	NLA		Use FTC4036.
32	FTC4036	• Gasket-transfer box gear change housing	1		
12	FB108111L	• Bolt-flanged head-M8 x 55	1		
33	FRC6595	Knob assembly-transfer box change-plastic	1	Note (1)	Standard / County
33	FTC3852	Knob assembly-transfer box change-plastic	1	Note (2)	Standard / County
33	STC60509	Knob assembly-transfer box change-aluminium	1		Tdi Hardtop 50th Tomb Raider

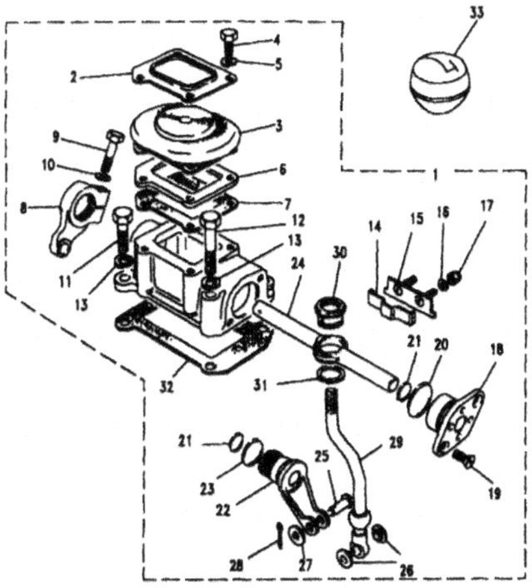

CHANGE POINTS:
(1) To (V) LA 935624
(2) From (V) LA 935625

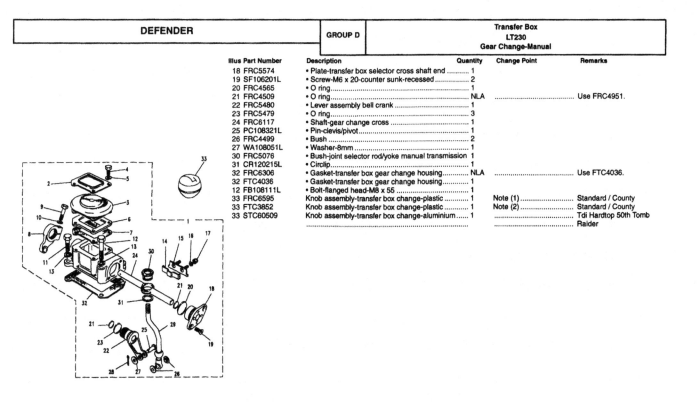

Illus	Part Number	Description	Quantity	Change Point	Remarks
1	FRC7941	MECHANISM ASSEMBLY-TRANSFER BOX GEAR CHANGE	1	Note (1)	
2	FRC6873	• Plate-transfer box gearchange grommet retaining	1		
3	FRC6872	• Grommet	1		
4	FS106201L	• Screw-flanged head-M6 x 20	4		
6	FRC7944	• Plate-gear lever retention	1		
7	FTC4037	• Gasket-transfer box gear change housing plate	1		
8	FRC5478	• Arm-transfer box gearchange	1		
9	BH106051L	• Bolt-hexagonal head-M6 x 25	1		
11	SH108251L	• Screw-hexagonal head-M8 x 25	NLA		Use SH108257 Use Dacromet coated alternative..
12	BH108111L	• Bolt-hexagonal head-M8 x 55	NLA		Use FB108111L.
13	WL108001L	• Washer-sprung-M8	4		
14	RTC1956	• Spring-detent manual transmission	1		
15	FRC6125	• Plate-transfer box detent spring retaining	1		
16	WA105001L	• Washer-plain-standard-M5	2		
17	NY105041L	• Nut-hexagonal-nyloc-M5	2		
18	FRC5574	• Plate-transfer box selector cross shaft end	1		
19	SF106201L	• Screw-M6 x 20-counter sunk-recessed	2		
20	FRC4565	• O ring	1		
21	FRC4509	• O ring	NLA		Use FRC4951.
22	FRC5480	• Lever assembly bell crank	1		
23	FRC5479	• O ring	3		
24	FRC6117	• Shaft-gear change cross	1		
25	PC108321L	• Pin-clevis/pivot	1		
26	FRC4499	• Bush	2		
27	WA108051L	• Washer-8mm	1		
30	FRC5076	• Bush-joint selector rod/yoke manual transmission	1		
31	CR120215L	• Circlip	1		
32	FRC6306	• Gasket-transfer box gear change housing	NLA	Note (2)	Use FTC4036.
32	FTC4036	• Gasket-transfer box gear change housing	1	Note (3)	
	FB108111L	• Bolt-flanged head-M8 x 55	1		

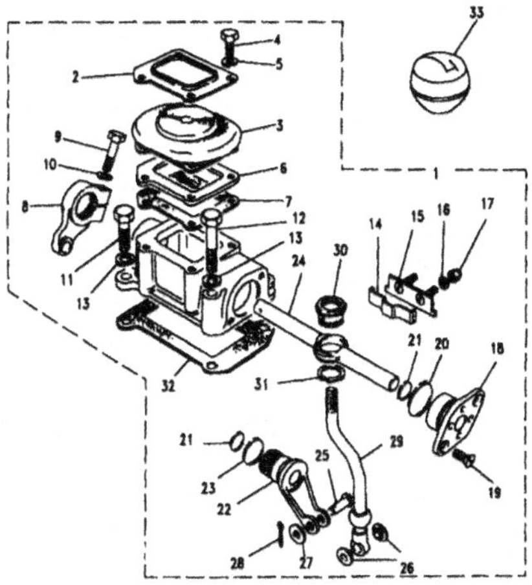

CHANGE POINTS:
(1) To (V) LA 939975
(2) To (T)20D 299332E
(3) From (T)20D 299333E To (V) LA 939975

Illus	Part Number	Description	Quantity	Change Point	Remarks
11	FS108251L	Screw-flanged head-M8 x 25	NLA		Use FS108257L.
12	FB108111L	Bolt-flanged head-M8 x 55			
21	FRC4951	O ring			
5	WA108051L	Washer-8mm	4	Note (1)	
10	WL106001L	Washer-sprung-M6	1	Note (1)	
28	PS104127L	Pin-split	1	Note (1)	
29	FRC7487	Lever-transfer box	1	Note (1)	
33	FRC6595	Knob assembly-transfer box change-plastic	1	Note (2)	
33	FTC3852	Knob assembly-transfer box change-plastic	1	Note (3)	

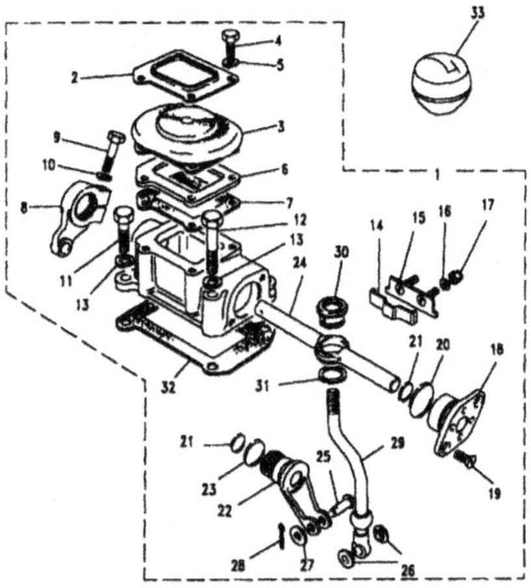

CHANGE POINTS:
(1) To (V) LA 939975
(2) To (V) LA 935624
(3) From (V) LA 935625 To (V) LA 939975

Illus	Part Number	Description	Quantity	Change Point	Remarks
1	FRC8561	Plate-gear lever retention	1		
2	FTC4037	Gasket-transfer box gear change housing plate	1		
3	FRC5574	Plate-transfer box selector cross shaft end	1		
4	FRC5478	Arm-transfer box gearchange	1		
5	FS108251ML	Screw-flanged head-M8 x 25	1		
6	SF106201L	Screw-M6 x 20-counter sunk-recessed	2		
7	FRC8292	O ring	1		
8	FRC4951	O ring	2		
9	FRC5480	Lever assembly bell crank	1		
10	FRC5479	O ring	3		
11	FRC8203	Shaft-gear change cross	1		
12	FRC8766	Pin-clevis/pivot	1		
13	FRC4499	Bush	2		
14	FTC4735	Lever-transfer box-rubber mounted	1		
15	ETC7884	Clip-spring steel	1		
16	CR120215L	Circlip	1		
17	FRC5076	Bush-joint selector rod/yoke manual transmission	1		
18	FRC8751	Housing assembly- gear change cross shaft	1		
19	FRC6873	Plate-transfer box gearchange grommet retaining	1		
20	FRC6872	Grommet	1		
21	FS106207L	Screw-flanged head-M6 x 20	4		
22	FTC4036	Gasket-transfer box gear change housing	1		
23	FS108257L	Screw-flanged head-M8 x 25	2		
24	FB108111L	Bolt-flanged head-M8 x 55	1		
25	IGC100020	Knob assembly-transfer box change-alloy.	1		
25	IGC100010	Knob assembly-transfer box change-leather covered	1		
25	STC60169	Knob assembly-transfer box change-aluminium	1		
26	FRC5575	O ring	1		

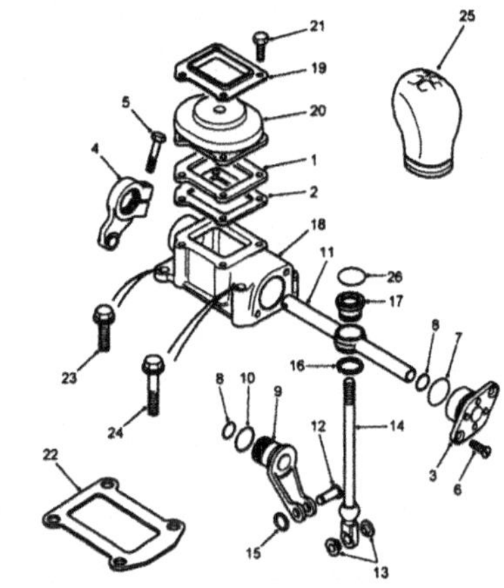

AMD8MA1A

Rod Assembly-LT77S-Without Pivot

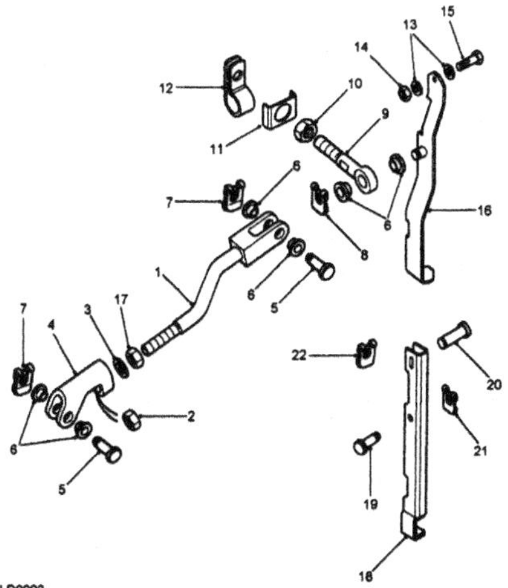

LD0003

Illus	Part Number	Description	Quantity	Change Point	Remarks
1	FRC6000	Rod assembly-linkage connecting	1	Note (1)	
1	FTC3675	Rod assembly-linkage connecting	1	Note (2)	
2	NY108041L	Nut-nyloc-M8	1		
3	WA108001	Washer-plain-8mm	1		
4	FRC8075	Arm-transfer box differential lock connecting rod adjusting	1		
5	FRC8767	Pin-clevis/pivot	2		
6	FRC4499	Bush	6		
7	FRC8548	Pin-split	2		
8	FRC8548	Pin-split	1		
9	FRC8202	Pin	1		
10	NH108041L	Nut-hexagonal head-M8	1		
10	FN108041L	Nut-flange-M8	NLA		Use FN108047L.
11	FRC9310	Retainer	1		
12	622324	Clip-pipe	1		
13	WA106041L	Washer-6mm	2	Note (2)	
14	NY105041L	Nut-hexagonal-nyloc-M5	1		
15	FB105051L	Bolt-M5	1	Note (2)	
16	FTC4095	Arm-transfer box differential lock	1	Note (2)	
17	NT108041L	Nut-hexagonal head	1		
18	FRC8204	Arm-transfer box differential lock	1	Note (1)	
19	FRC8547	Pin-clevis/pivot	1	Note (1)	
20	FRC8768	Pin-clevis/pivot	1		
21	FRC8548	Pin-split	2		
22	FRC8769	Clip	1		

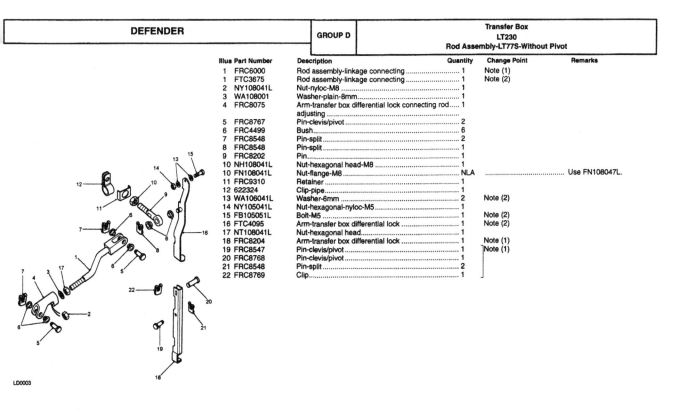

CHANGE POINTS:
(1) To (V) LA 939975
(2) From (V) MA 939976

Rod Assembly-LT77S-With Pivot

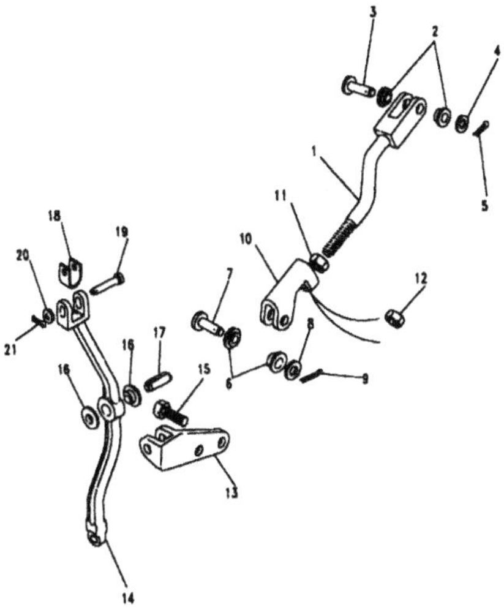

Illus	Part Number	Description	Quantity	Change Point	Remarks
1	FRC6000	Rod assembly-linkage connecting	1	Note (1)	
1	FTC3675	Rod assembly-linkage connecting	1	Note (2)	
2	FRC4499	Bush	2		
3	PC108321L	Pin-clevis/pivot	1		
4	WA108051L	Washer-8mm	1		
5	PS104127L	Pin-split	1		
6	FRC4499	Bush	2		
7	PC108321L	Pin-clevis/pivot	1		
8	WA108051L	Washer-8mm	1		
9	PS104127L	Pin-split	1		
10	FRC8075	Arm-transfer box differential lock connecting rod adjusting	1		
11	NY108041L	Nut-nyloc-M8	1		
12	NT108041L	Nut-hexagonal head	1		
13	FRC6066	Bracket-pivot	1		
14	FRC7315	Lever-transfer box-differential lock	1		
15	FS108251L	Screw-flanged head-M8 x 25	NLA		Use FS108257L.
16	FRC4499	Bush	2		
17	FRC7325	Pin	1		
18	FRC4505	Strip-flexible adhesive	1		
19	PC105401L	Pin-clevis	1		
20	WA105001L	Washer-plain-standard-M5	1		
21	PS103101L	Pin-split	1		

CHANGE POINTS:
(1) To (T)28D 274488E
(2) From (T)28D 274489E To (V) LA 939975

Illus	Part Number	Description	Quantity	Change Point	Remarks
1	FRC7946	Rod assembly-connecting	1	To (V) LA 939975	
2	FRC4499	Bush	2	To (V) LA 939975	
3	PC108321L	Pin-clevis/pivot	1		
4	WA108051L	Washer-8mm	1		
5	PS104121L	Pin-split	1		
6	FRC4499	Bush	2		
7	PC108321L	Pin-clevis/pivot	1		
8	WA108051L	Washer-8mm	1		
9	PS104121L	Pin-split	1		
10	FRC8075	Arm-transfer box differential lock connecting rod adjusting	1		
11	NY108041L	Nut-nyloc-M8	1		
12	NT108041L	Nut-hexagonal head	1		
13	FRC8033	Bracket	1		
14	FRC8859	Lever-selector selector mechanism	1		
15	FS108251L	Screw-flanged head-M8 x 25	NLA		Use FS108257L.
16	FRC4499	Bush	2		
17	FRC7325	Pin	1		
18	FRC4505	Strip-flexible adhesive	1		
19	PC105401L	Pin-clevis	1		
20	WA105001L	Washer-plain-standard-M5	1		
21	PS103101L	Pin-split	1		

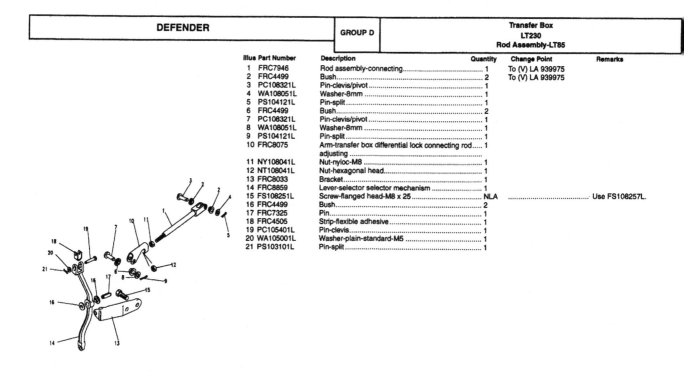

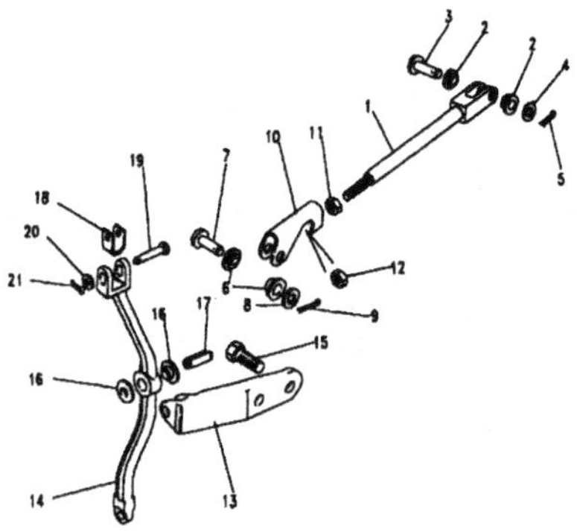

Illus	Part Number	Description	Quantity	Change Point	Remarks
1	FRC6000	Rod assembly-linkage connecting	1	Note (1)	
1	FTC3675	Rod assembly-linkage connecting	1	Note (2)	
2	FRC5998	Pin-clevis	1		
3	NY108041L	Nut-nyloc-M8	1		
4	FRC4499	Bush	4		
5	PC108321L	Pin-clevis/pivot	1		
6	WA108051L	Washer-8mm	1		
7	PS104127L	Pin-split	2		
8	FRC7315	Lever-transfer box-differential lock	1		
9	FRC6066	Bracket-pivot	1		
10	FS108251L	Screw-flanged head-M8 x 25	NLA		Use FS108257L.
11	FRC7325	Pin	1		
12	FRC4499	Bush	2		
13	PC105401L	Pin-clevis	1		
14	FRC4505	Strip-flexible adhesive	1		
15	WA105001L	Washer-plain-standard-M5	1		
16	PS103101L	Pin-split	1		

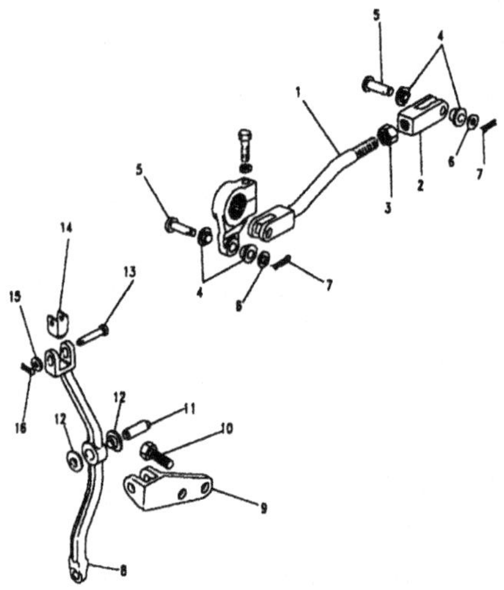

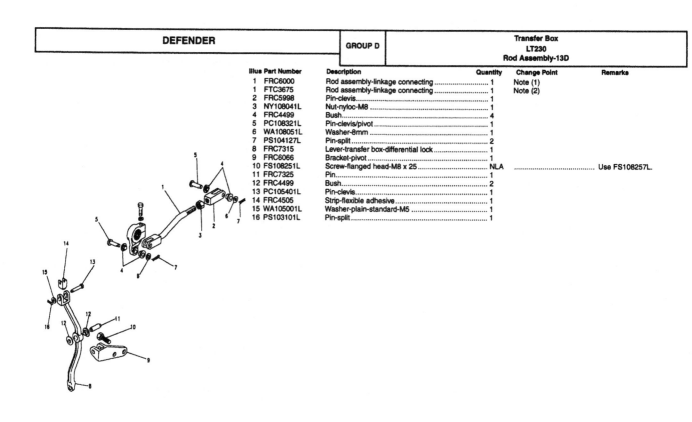

CHANGE POINTS:
(1) To (T)28D 274488E
(2) From (T)28D 274489E

Transfer Box
LT230
Gasket Kit

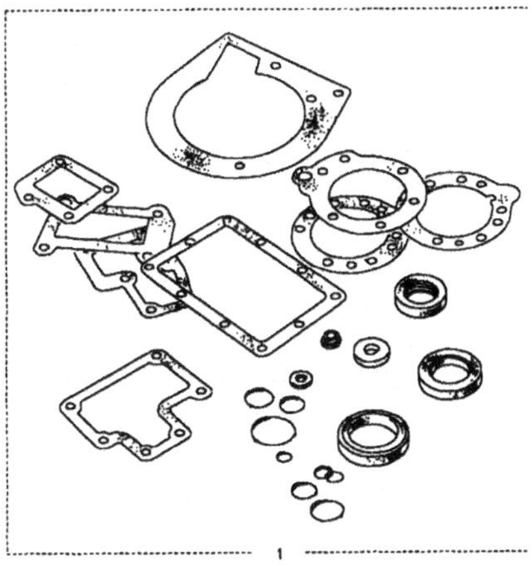

Illus	Part Number	Description	Quantity	Change Point	Remarks
1	RTC3890	KIT-GASKET AND SEAL	1	Note (1)	LT 77S
1	RTC3890	KIT-GASKET AND SEAL	1	Note (1)	LT 85
	FRC5409	• Gasket-transfer box speedometer housing	1		
	FRC5413	• Gasket-transfer box power take off cover	2		
	FRC5416	• Gasket-transfer box bottom cover	1		
	FRC5486	• Gasket-transfer box gear change housing plate	NLA		Use FTC4037.
	FRC6103	• Gasket-front housing to main case	1		
	FRC6105	• Gasket-transfer box side cover	1		
	FRC6306	• Gasket-transfer box gear change housing	NLA		Use FTC4036.
	FTC4037	• Gasket-transfer box gear change housing plate	1		
	FTC4036	• Gasket-transfer box gear change housing	1		
	FRC7998	• Gasket-transfer box cover to case	1		
	FRC2464	• Washer	2		
	AAU2304	• Seal-oil speedometer pinion	1		
	FRC2365	• Seal	1		
	FRC7043	• Seal-transfer box output	2		
	FRC8292	• O ring-transfer box intermediate shaft	2		
	532323	• O ring-transfer box intermediate shaft	1		
	571665	• O ring-speedometer spindle housing	1		
	FRC4509	• O ring-cross shaft	NLA		Use FRC4951.
	FRC5419	• O ring-transfer box intermediate shaft	1		
	FRC5473	• O ring-selector mechanism	1		
	FRC5479	• O ring-crank arm	1		
	FRC5575	• O ring	2		
	FRC5576	• O ring-pivot shaft	1		
	FRC7439	• O ring-transfer box intermediate shaft	1		
	FRC4808	• Washer-sealing	1		
	FRC4951	O ring			LT 77S

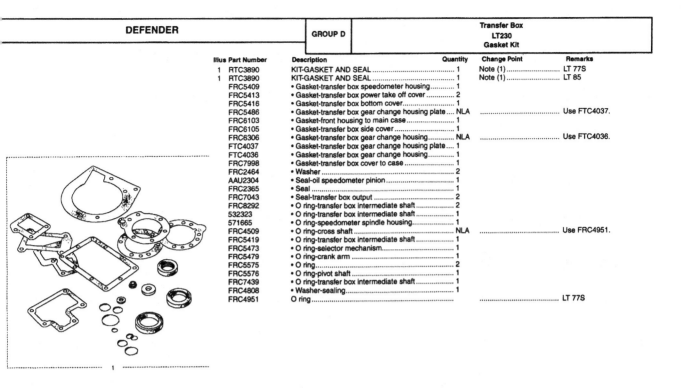

CHANGE POINTS:
(1) To (V) LA 939975

Transfer Box
LT230
Transmission Brake-Rod Operated

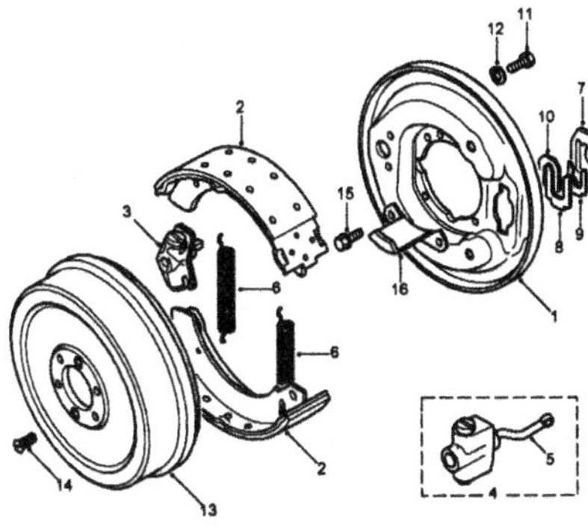

LD0004

Illus	Part Number	Description	Quantity	Change Point	Remarks
1	AEU2733	Backplate-transmission brake assembly	1	Note (1)	LT 77S LT 85
2	RTC3403	Kit-transmission brake shoe-asbestos	1		
3	37H4558L	ADJUSTER ASSEMBLY-TRANSFER BOX BRAKE SHOE	1		
	8G7019L	• Kit-transmission brake adjuster	1		
1	STC963	Backplate-transmission brake assembly	1	Note (2)	LT 77S LT 85
2	RTC6179	Kit-transmission brake shoe-asbestos free	1		
3	STC244	Adjuster assembly-transfer box brake shoe	1		
	STC245	KIT-TRANSMISSION BRAKE ADJUSTER	1		
3	STC244	• Adjuster assembly-transfer box brake shoe	1		
4	AEU2734	EXPANDER ASSEMBLY-TRANSFER BOX BRAKE SHOE	1	Note (3)	LT 77S LT 85
5	STC964	• Connecting rod assembly brake-for old type expander assembly	1		
5	AEU2736	Connecting rod assembly brake-for old type expander assembly	NLA		Use STC964.
	AEU2735	Kit-transmission brake adjuster-for old type expander assembly	1	Note (3)	LT 77S LT 85
6	FRC8549	Spring-return-Green	1	Note (1)	
6	STC246	Spring-return-Green	1	Note (2)	
7	515466	Cover-dust wheel cylinder	1	Note (3)	
8	515467	Plate-locking	1		
9	515470	Plate-packing	1		
10	515468	Plate	1		
11	AEU2737	Screw	2		
12	AEU2738	Washer	2		
13	FRC3502	Drum-transmission brake-Black	1		
14	SA108201L	Screw-M8 x 20-counter sunk	2		
15	AFU1400	Bolt	4		
16	FRC8093	Catcher-transfer box transmission brake oil	1		

CHANGE POINTS:
(1) To (V) July 1989
(2) From (V) July 1989
(3) To (V) LA 935629

Illus	Part Number	Description	Quantity	Change Point	Remarks
1	STC1533	Backplate-transmission brake assembly	1	Note (1)	
1	ICL100010	Backplate-transmission brake assembly	1	Note (2)	
2	STC1526	Kit-transmission brake shoe retention	1	Note (1)	
2	ICW100050	Kit-transmission brake shoe retention	1	Note (2)	
3	STC1527	Kit-transmission brake adjuster	1	Note (3)	
4	STC1532	Kit-transmission brake shoe retention	1	Note (4)	
12	ICW100000	Kit-transmission brake shoe retention	1		
5	STC1525	Kit-transmission brake shoe	1	Note (3)	
5	ICW100030	Kit-transmission brake shoe	1	Note (2)	
6	STC1536	Shaft-cross-transmission brake	1	Note (3)	
7	STC1538	Lever-transmission brake	1	Note (4)	
11	ICW100010	Kit-lever rear brake	1	Note (5)	
8	AFU1400	Bolt	4	Note (3)	
9	FRC3502	Drum-transmission brake-Black	1	Note (4)	
9	NTC9859	Drum-transmission brake-Silver	1	Note (5)	
10	SA108201L	Screw-M8 x 20-counter sunk	1	Note (3)	

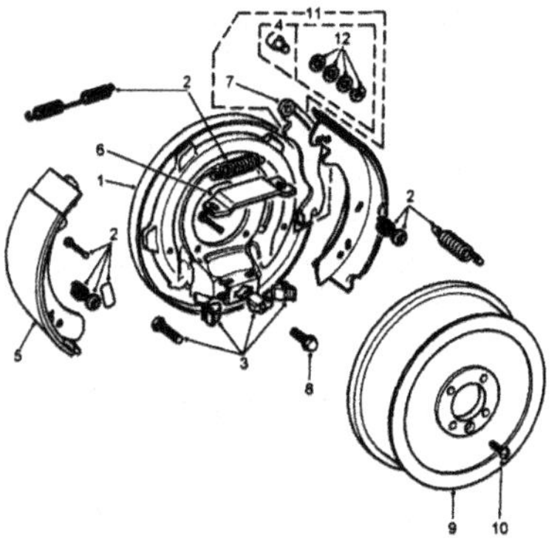

LD0007A

CHANGE POINTS:
(1) From (V) LA 935630 To (V) XA 175163
(2) From (V) XA 175164
(3) From (V) LA 935630
(4) From (V) LA 935630 To (V) WA 159806
(5) From (V) XA 159807

DEFENDER	GROUP E	Axles & Suspension Propshafts Propshaft Front

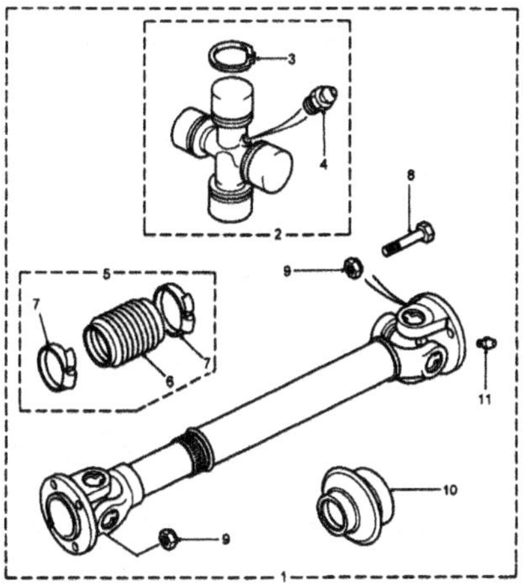

LE0005

Illus	Part Number	Description	Quantity	Change Point	Remarks
1	FRC5566	PROPELLOR SHAFT-FRONT	1	Note (1)	4 Cylinder
1	FRC6243	PROPELLOR SHAFT-FRONT	1	Note (2)	V8
2	RTC3346	• JOINT-PROPSHAFT UNIVERSAL	2		
3	242522	• • Circlip	8		
4	549229	• Nipple-grease-for propshaft universal joint-UNF	NLA		Use TYL100030.
11	234532	• Nipple-grease-propshaft coupling-ANF	1		
4	TYL100030	Nipple-grease-for propshaft universal joint-UNF		Note (3)	
1	FRC8390	PROPELLOR SHAFT-FRONT	1	Note (4)	
1	FRC8390	PROPELLOR SHAFT-FRONT	1	Note (5)	4 Cylinder Petrol
1	FRC8386	PROPELLOR SHAFT-FRONT	1	Note (6)	
1	FRC8386	PROPELLOR SHAFT-FRONT	1	Note (7)	Diesel
2	RTC3458	• JOINT-PROPSHAFT UNIVERSAL	2		
3	242522	• • Circlip	8		
4	549229	• Nipple-grease-UNF	NLA		Use TYL100030.
11	234532	• Nipple-grease-ANF	1		
1	TVB000130	Propellor shaft-front	1	Note (8)	
1	TVB100610	PROPELLOR SHAFT-FRONT	1	Note (9)	
10	TVE100000	• Gaiter-propshaft sliding joint	1		
2	STC4807	• JOINT-PROPSHAFT UNIVERSAL	2		
3	242522	• • Circlip	4		
4	STC4808	• • Nipple-grease	1		
5	276484	GAITER-PROPSHAFT SLIDING JOINT	1		
6	276483	• Gaiter-propshaft sliding joint	1		
7	CN100508L	• Clip-hose-50mm-less spring assist	1		
7	ESR3353	• Clip-hose-50mm-with spring assist	1		
8	509045P	Bolt-3/8-UNF	4		
9	NZ606041L	Nut-3/8-UNF	8		
10	STC2955	Gaiter-propshaft sliding joint	NLA		Use TVE100000.
10	TVE100000	Gaiter-propshaft sliding joint	1		
11	234532	Nipple-grease-ANF	1		

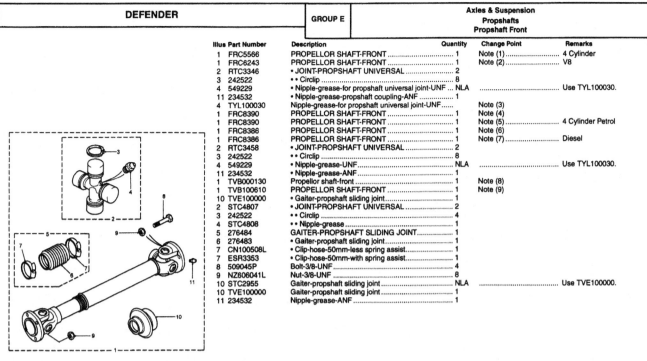

CHANGE POINTS:
(1) To (V) CA 252578
(2) To (V) CA 254406
(3) To (V) ZA 612404
(4) From (V) CA 252579 To (V) LA 939975 4 Cylinder
(5) From (V) MA 939976
(6) From (V) CA 254407 V8
(7) From (V) MA 939976 To (V) ZA 612404
(8) From (V) 1A 608154
(9) From (V) 1A 612405

DEFENDER	GROUP E	Axles & Suspension Propshafts Propshaft Rear

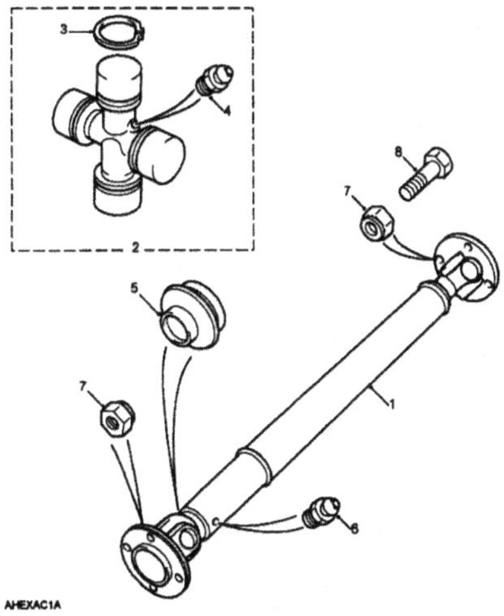

AHEXAC1A

Illus	Part Number	Description	Quantity	Change Point	Remarks
		DEFENDER 90			
		REAR DRUM BRAKES			
1	FRC7732	PROPELLOR SHAFT-REAR	1	Note (1)	4 Cylinder
1	FRC8385	PROPELLOR SHAFT-REAR	1	Note (2)	V8
2	RTC3346	• JOINT-PROPSHAFT UNIVERSAL	2		
3	242522	• • Circlip	8		
4	549229	• Nipple-grease-UNF	NLA		Use TYL100030.
6	234532	• Nipple-grease-ANF	1		
6	TYL100030	Nipple-grease-UNF			
1	FRC8392	PROPELLOR SHAFT-REAR	1	Note (3)	4 Cylinder
1	FRC8393	PROPELLOR SHAFT-REAR	1	Note (4)	V8
2	RTC3458	• JOINT-PROPSHAFT UNIVERSAL	2		
3	242522	• • Circlip	8		
5	STC2955	• Gaiter-propshaft sliding joint	NLA		Use TVE100000.
6	234532	• Nipple-grease-ANF	1		
		REAR DISC BRAKES			
1	FRC8392	PROPELLOR SHAFT-REAR	1		4 Cylinder Petrol
1	FRC8392	PROPELLOR SHAFT-REAR	1	Note (5)	4 Cylinder Diesel
1	FRC8393	PROPELLOR SHAFT-REAR	1		V8
1	FRC8393	PROPELLOR SHAFT-REAR	1	Note (6)	Diesel
2	RTC3458	• JOINT-PROPSHAFT UNIVERSAL	2		
3	242522	• • Circlip	8		
5	STC2955	• Gaiter-propshaft sliding joint	NLA		Use TVE100000.
6	234532	• Nipple-grease-ANF	1		

CHANGE POINTS:
(1) To (V) CA 252578
(2) To (V) CA 254406
(3) From (V) CA 252579
(4) From (V) CA 254407
(5) To (V) LA 939975
(6) From (V) MA 939976

Axles & Suspension
Propshafts
Propshaft Rear

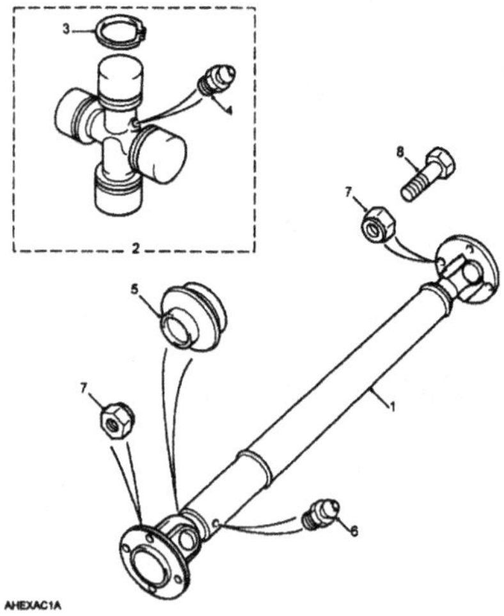

AHEXAC1A

Illus	Part Number	Description	Quantity	Change Point	Remarks
		DEFENDER 110/130			
		REAR DRUM BRAKES			
1	FRC8391	PROPELLOR SHAFT-REAR	1	Note (1)	4 Cylinder 110"
1	FTC3245	PROPELLOR SHAFT-REAR	1	Note (2)	4 Cylinder 110"
1	FRC8389	PROPELLOR SHAFT-REAR	1		V8 110"
1	FTC1250	PROPELLOR SHAFT-REAR	1	Note (3)	4 Cylinder 130"
1	RRC2303	PROPELLOR SHAFT-REAR	1	Note (3)	V8 130"
1	FTC1249	PROPELLOR SHAFT-REAR	1	Note (4)	130"
2	RTC3458	• JOINT-PROPSHAFT UNIVERSAL	2		
3	242522	• • Circlip	8		
4	549229	• Nipple-grease-UNF	NLA		Use TYL100030.
6	234532	• Nipple-grease-ANF	1		
6	TYL100030	Nipple-grease-UNF			
		REAR DISC BRAKES			
1	FTC3245	PROPELLOR SHAFT-REAR	1		4 Cylinder Petrol 110"
1	FRC8389	PROPELLOR SHAFT-REAR	1	Note (5)	V8 110"
1	FTC3905	PROPELLOR SHAFT-REAR	1	Note (6)	V8 110"
1	FTC3905	PROPELLOR SHAFT-REAR	1		Diesel 110"
1	FTC1250	PROPELLOR SHAFT-REAR	1	Note (3)	130"
1	FTC1249	PROPELLOR SHAFT-REAR	1	Note (4)	130"
2	RTC3458	• JOINT-PROPSHAFT UNIVERSAL	2		
3	242522	• • Circlip	8		
4	549229	• Nipple-grease-UNF	NLA		Use TYL100030.
6	234532	• Nipple-grease-ANF	1		
6	TYL100030	Nipple-grease-UNF			4 Cylinder Petrol non-
					ventilated disc brakes-
					rear 110"
5	TVE100000	Gaiter-propshaft sliding joint			90"
5	TVE100000	Gaiter-propshaft sliding joint	1		110"
7	NZ606041L	Nut-3/8-UNF	8		
8	509045P	Bolt-3/8-UNF	4		

CHANGE POINTS:
(1) To (V) KA 925786
(2) From (V) KA 925787
(3) To (V) June 1989
(4) From (V) June 1989
(5) To (V) LA 937639
(6) From (V) LA 937640

Axles & Suspension
Front Axle
Front Axle Assembly

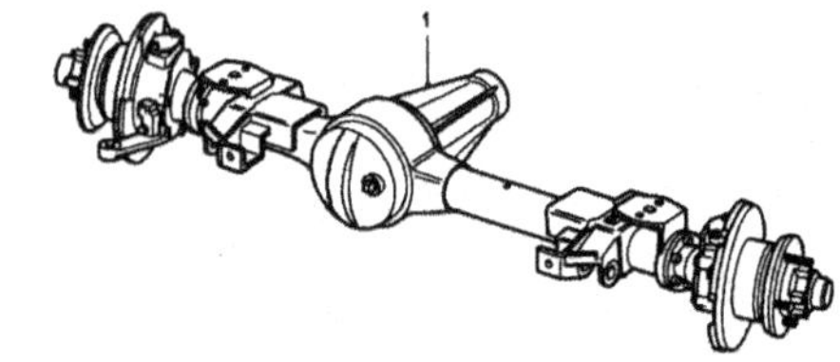

AHEXCA1A

Illus	Part Number	Description	Quantity	Change Point	Remarks
		90			
		REAR DRUM BRAKES			
1	FRC9454	Axle/drive unit assembly 4x4-front	NLA		Use FRC8782.
					RHD 22L
1	FRC8782	Axle/drive unit assembly 4x4-front	1	Note (1)	RHD 22L
1	FTC3280	Axle/drive unit assembly 4x4-front	1	Note (2)	RHD 22L
1	FRC9455	Axle/drive unit assembly 4x4-front	NLA		Use FRC8783 Axle-front
					but retain Calipers &
					Pads from old axle.
					LHD 23L
1	FRC8783	Axle/drive unit assembly 4x4-front	1	Note (3)	LHD
1	FTC3281	Axle/drive unit assembly 4x4-front	1	Note (4)	LHD
		REAR DISC BRAKES-SOLID FRONT DISCS			
1	FTC3302	Axle/drive unit assembly 4x4-front	1		RHD 61L
1	FTC3303	Axle/drive unit assembly 4x4-front	1		LHD 62L
1	TAG100090	Axle/drive unit assembly 4x4-front-steel wheel	1		10M except Antilock
					Brakes
1	TAG100120	Axle/drive unit assembly 4x4-front-alloy wheel	1		11M except Antilock
					Brakes
1	TAG100130	Axle/drive unit assembly 4x4-front-steel wheel	1		12M Antilock Brakes
1	TAG100140	Axle/drive unit assembly 4x4-front-alloy wheel	1		13M Antilock Brakes
		REAR DISC BRAKE-VENTED FRONT DISCS			
1	FTC3300	Axle/drive unit assembly 4x4-front	1		RHD 63L
1	FTC3301	Axle/drive unit assembly 4x4-front	1		LHD 64L
1	TAG100200	Axle/drive unit assembly 4x4-front	1		98L 50 LE
1	FTC5210	Axle/drive unit assembly 4x4-front	1		V8 EFi Japan NAS 49
					States

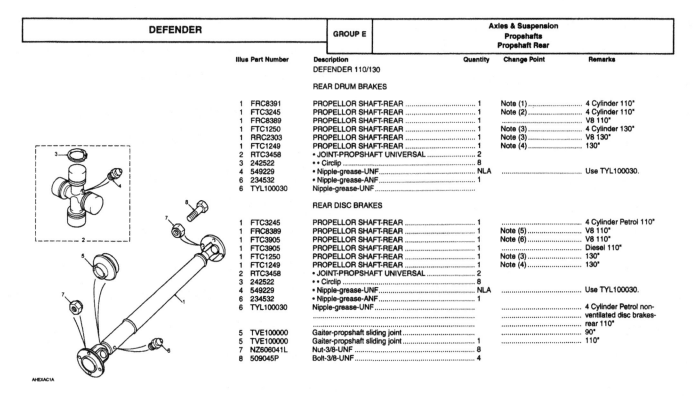

CHANGE POINTS:
(1) To (A)22L 12545C
(2) From (A)22L 12546C
(3) To (A)23L 16310C
(4) From (A)23L 16311C

Illus	Part Number	Description	Quantity	Change Point	Remarks
		90 CONTINUED			
1	TAG100150	Axle/drive unit assembly 4x4-front-steel wheel	1		14M Heavy duty except Antilock Brakes
1	TAG100160	Axle/drive unit assembly 4x4-front-alloy wheel	1		15M Heavy duty except Antilock Brakes
1	TAG100170	Axle/drive unit assembly 4x4-front-steel wheel	1		16M Heavy duty Antilock Brakes
1	TAG100180	Axle/drive unit assembly 4x4-front-alloy wheel	1		17M Heavy duty Antilock Brakes
		110/130			
		REAR DRUM BRAKES			
1	FRC8782	Axle/drive unit assembly 4x4-front	1	Note (1)	RHD
1	FTC3280	Axle/drive unit assembly 4x4-front	1	Note (2)	RHD
1	FRC8783	Axle/drive unit assembly 4x4-front	1	Note (3)	LHD
1	FTC3281	Axle/drive unit assembly 4x4-front	1	Note (4)	LHD
		REAR DISC BRAKES-VENTED FRONT DISCS			
1	FTC3300	Axle/drive unit assembly 4x4-front	1		63L RHD
1	FTC3301	Axle/drive unit assembly 4x4-front	1		64L LHD
1	TAG100150	Axle/drive unit assembly 4x4-front-steel wheel	1		14M except Antilock Brakes
1	TAG100160	Axle/drive unit assembly 4x4-front-alloy wheel	1		15M except Antilock Brakes
1	TAG100170	Axle/drive unit assembly 4x4-front-steel wheel	1		16M Antilock Brakes
1	TAG100180	Axle/drive unit assembly 4x4-front-alloy wheel	1		17M Antilock Brakes

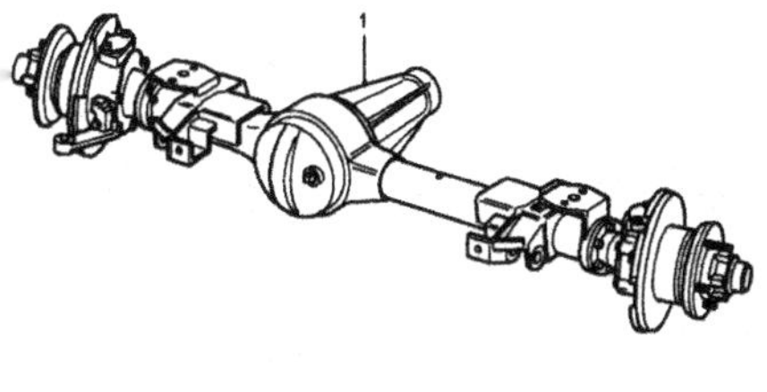

AHEXCA1A

CHANGE POINTS:
(1) To (A)20L 77036C
(2) From (A)20L 77037C
(3) To (A)21L 56452C
(4) From (A)21L 56453C

Illus	Part Number	Description	Quantity	Change Point	Remarks
1	FRC4307	CASE-FRONT AXLE	1		20L 21L 22L 23L drum brakes-rear
2	561195	• Stud-3/8UNF x 1 1/4	4		
3	561196	• Stud-3/8UNF x 1 3/4	6		
4	608246	• Plug-drain/filler level	2		
1	FTC2223	CASE-FRONT AXLE	NLA	Note (1); Note (2)	Use FTC4413. 61L 62L non-ventilated disc brakes-front
2	561195	• Stud-3/8UNF x 1 1/4	4		
3	561196	• Stud-3/8UNF x 1 3/4	6		
4	608246	• Plug-drain/filler level	2		
1	FTC4413	CASE-FRONT AXLE	1	Note (3); Note (4)	61L 62L non-ventilated disc brakes-front
3	561196	• Stud-3/8UNF x 1 3/4	10		
4	608246	• Plug-drain/filler level	2		
1	FTC4413	CASE-FRONT AXLE	1		63L 64L ventilated disc brakes-front
3	561196	• Stud-3/8UNF x 1 3/4	10		
4	608246	• Plug-drain/filler level	2		
1	TAJ100020	CASE-FRONT AXLE	1		10M 11M 12M 13M non-ventilated disc brakes-front
3	561196	• Stud-3/8UNF x 1 3/4	10		
4	608246	• Plug-drain/filler level	1		
5	FTC5085	• Adaptor	1		
1	TAJ100020	CASE-FRONT AXLE	1		14M 15M 16M 17M ventilated disc brakes-front
3	561196	• Stud-3/8UNF x 1 3/4	10		
4	608246	• Plug-drain/filler level	1		
5	FTC5085	• Adaptor	1		

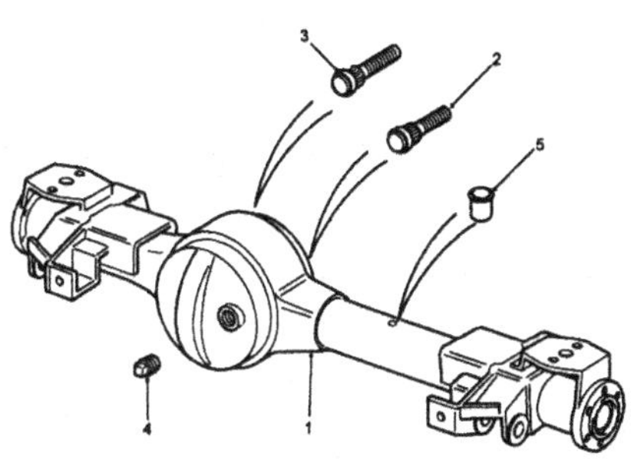

LE0045

CHANGE POINTS:
(1) To (A)61L 04174A
(2) To (A)62L 01997A
(3) From (A)61L 04175A
(4) From (A)62L 01998A

DEFENDER

GROUP E

Axles & Suspension
Front Axle
Differential Front-To (V) KA930434

Illus	Part Number	Description	Quantity	Change Point	Remarks
1	FTC782N	DIFFERENTIAL ASSEMBLY DIFFERENTIAL-NEW	NLA	Note (1)	20L 21L drum brakes-rear except 90"
1	FTC782E	DIFFERENTIAL ASSEMBLY DIFFERENTIAL-10 SPLINE SHAFT-EXCHANGE	1	Note (1)	Drum brakes-rear 2 pin differential 20L 21L
1	FTC2750	DIFFERENTIAL ASSEMBLY DIFFERENTIAL-NEW-10 SPLINE SHAFT-4 BOLT FLANGE	1	Note (2)	20L 21L drum brakes-rear except 90"
1	FTC2750	DIFFERENTIAL ASSEMBLY DIFFERENTIAL-NEW-10 SPLINE SHAFT-4 BOLT FLANGE	1		Drum brakes-rear 22L 90"
1	FTC2750E	DIFFERENTIAL ASSEMBLY DIFFERENTIAL-EXCHANGE-10 SPLINE SHAFT	1	Note (2)	Drum brakes-rear
2	FRC5690	• HOUSING ASSEMBLY DIFFERENTIAL/FINAL DRIVE WHEEL-WITH FILLER/LEVEL PLUG	1		Part of FTC782N, FTC2750, FTC2750, FTC2750E.
3	BH112101L	• • Bolt-M12 x 50	4		
2	FRC4112	• HOUSING ASSEMBLY DIFFERENTIAL/FINAL DRIVE WHEEL-LESS FILLER/LEVEL PLUG	1		
3	BH112101L	• • Bolt-M12 x 50	4		
4	FRC5204	• Ring-differential locking	NLA		Use FTC4210.
4	FTC4210	• Ring-differential locking	2		
5	FRC5661	• Tab-differential locking ring	2		
6	576159	• Pin-roll-spring tension	2		
7	NY606041L	• Nut-hexagonal head-nyloc-3/8-UNF	10		

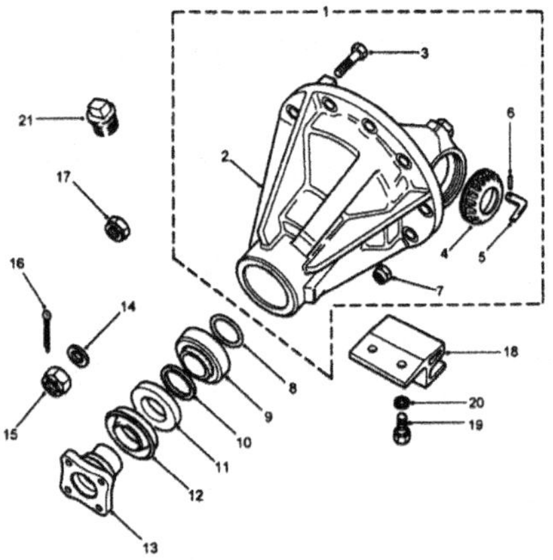

LE0039

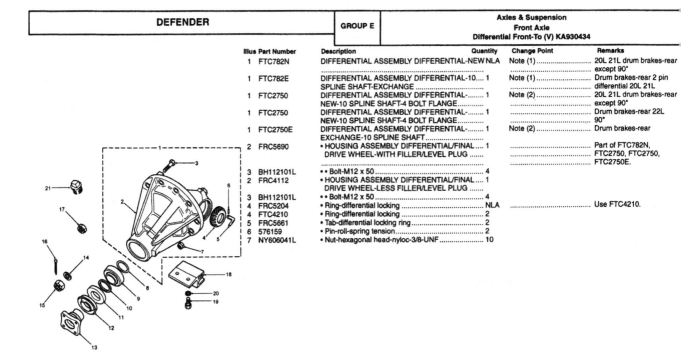

CHANGE POINTS:
(1) To (V) JA 917433
(2) From (V) JA 917434

DEFENDER

GROUP E

Axles & Suspension
Front Axle
Differential Front-To (V) KA930434

Illus	Part Number	Description	Quantity	Change Point	Remarks
		SHIM-BEARING DIFFERENTIAL			
8	FRC1193	0.060"	NLA		Use 549252.
8	FRC1195	0.062"	A/R		
8	FRC1197	0.064"	A/R		
8	FRC1199	0.066"	A/R		
8	FRC1201	0.068"	A/R		
8	FRC1203	0.070"	A/R		
8	539718	0.072"	A/R		
8	539720	0.074"	A/R		
8	539722	0.076"	A/R		
8	539724	0.080"	A/R		
9	539707	Bearing-taper roller	1		
10	539745	Spacer-pinion bearing	1		
11	FRC8220	Seal-differential final drive pinion-front & rear	1		
12	FRC8154	Mudshield-front & rear differential	1		
13	FRC3002	Flange-driveshaft coupling differential-4 bolt flange	1		
14	90513454	Washer-plain	1		
15	3259	Nut-castle	1	Note (1)	
16	PS608101L	Pin-split	1		
17	NY116041L	Nut-hexagonal head-nyloc-M16	1	Note (2)	
18	NRC9713	Bracket-track rod protection	1		
19	SH406061L	Screw-hexagonal head-3/8BSF x 5/8	2		
20	WM600061L	Washer-3/8"-square	2		
21	608246	Plug-drain/filler level	1		

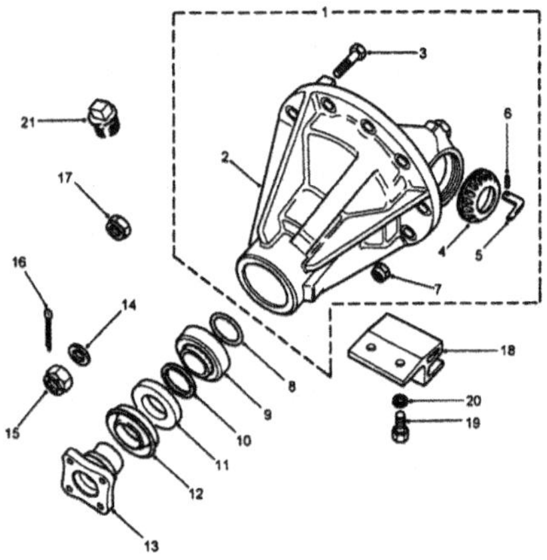

LE0039

CHANGE POINTS:
(1) To (V) KA 929665
(2) From (V) KA 929666

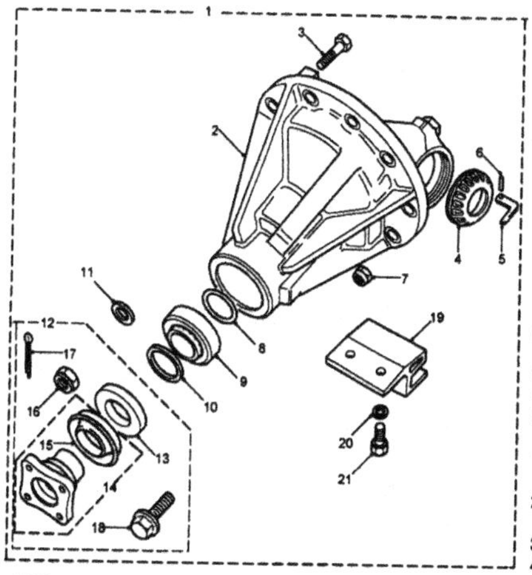

LE0040

Illus	Part Number	Description	Quantity	Change Point	Remarks
1	FTC3272	DIFFERENTIAL ASSEMBLY DIFFERENTIAL-NEW-24 SPLINE SHAFT-4 BOLT FLANGE	1	Note (1)	61L 62L 63L 64L 98L
1	FTC3272E	DIFFERENTIAL ASSEMBLY DIFFERENTIAL-EXCHANGE-24 SPLINE SHAFT-4 BOLT FLANGE.	1	Note (1)	
2	FRC5690	• HOUSING ASSEMBLY DIFFERENTIAL/FINAL DRIVE WHEEL-WITH FILLER/LEVEL PLUG	1		
3	BH112101L	• • Bolt-M12 x 50	4		
2	FRC4112	• HOUSING ASSEMBLY DIFFERENTIAL/FINAL DRIVE WHEEL-LESS FILLER/LEVEL PLUG	1		
3	BH112101L	• • Bolt-M12 x 50	4		
4	FRC5204	• Ring-differential locking	NLA		Use FTC4210.
4	FTC4210	• Ring-differential locking	2		
5	FRC5661	• Tab-differential locking ring	2		
6	576159	• Pin-roll-spring tension	2		
7	NY606041L	• Nut-hexagonal head-nyloc-3/8-UNF	10		
1	TBV100020	DIFFERENTIAL ASSEMBLY DIFFERENTIAL-24 SPLINE SHAFT-4 BOLT FLANGE-NEW	NLA	Note (2)	Use FTC5142 qty 1 Rover unable to supply differential together with spacers. with TYF101160 qty 2. 10M 11M 12M 13M 14M 15M 16M 17M
1	FTC5142	• DIFFERENTIAL ASSEMBLY DIFFERENTIAL-24 SPLINE SHAFT-4 BOLT FLANGE-NEW	1		
2	FRC4112	• • HOUSING ASSEMBLY DIFFERENTIAL/FINAL DRIVE WHEEL-LESS FILLER/LEVEL PLUG	1		
3	BH112101L	• • • Bolt-M12 x 50	4		
4	FTC4210	• • Ring-differential locking	2		
6	576159	• • Pin-roll-spring tension	2		
	TYF101160	• Spacer	2		
1	FTC5142	DIFFERENTIAL ASSEMBLY DIFFERENTIAL-24 SPLINE SHAFT-4 BOLT FLANGE-NEW	1		10M 11M 12M 13M 14M 15M 16M 17M
2	FRC4112	• HOUSING ASSEMBLY DIFFERENTIAL/FINAL DRIVE WHEEL-LESS FILLER/LEVEL PLUG	1		
3	BH112101L	• • Bolt-M12 x 50	4		
4	FTC4210	• Ring-differential locking	2		
6	576159	• Pin-roll-spring tension	2		

CHANGE POINTS:
(1) To (V) WA 159806
(2) From (V) XA 159807

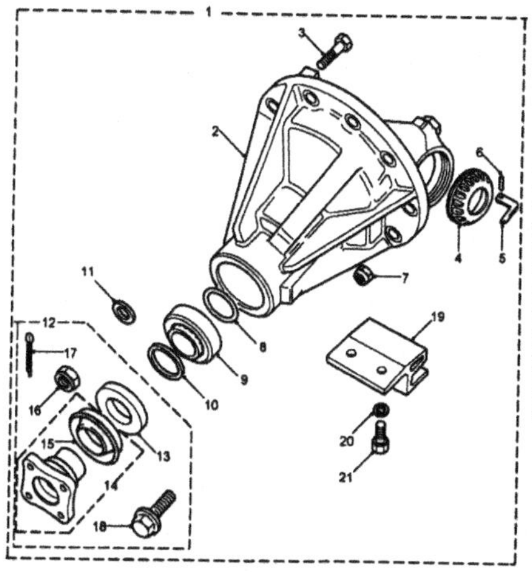

LE0040

Illus	Part Number	Description	Quantity	Change Point	Remarks
		SHIM-BEARING DIFFERENTIAL			
8	FTC3869	2.155mm	A/R	Note (1); Note (2)	61L 62L 63L 64L 98L
8	FTC3871	2.105mm	A/R		
8	FTC3873	2.055mm	A/R		
8	FTC3875	2.005mm	A/R		
8	FTC3877	1.955mm	A/R		
8	FTC3879	1.905mm	A/R		
8	FTC3881	1.855mm	A/R		
8	FTC3883	1.805mm	A/R		
8	FTC3885	1.755mm	A/R		
8	FTC3887	1.705mm	A/R		
8	FTC3889	1.655mm	A/R		
8	FTC3891	1.605mm	A/R		
8	FTC3893	1.555mm	A/R		
8	FTC3895	1.505mm	A/R		
8	TYS101040	2.155mm	A/R	Note (3)	
8	TYS101060	2.105mm	A/R		
8	TYS101080	2.055mm	A/R		
8	TYS101100	2.005mm	A/R		
8	TYS101120	1.955mm	A/R		
8	TYS101140	1.905mm	A/R		
8	TYS101160	1.855mm	A/R		
8	TYS101180	1.805mm	A/R		
8	TYS101200	1.755mm	A/R		
8	TYS101220	1.705mm	A/R		
8	TYS101240	1.655mm	A/R		
8	TYS101260	1.605mm	A/R		
8	TYS101280	1.555mm	A/R		
8	TYS101300	1.505mm	A/R		

CHANGE POINTS:
(1) From (A)22L 12546C RHD
(2) From (A)23L 16311C LHD
(3) From (V) WA 140851

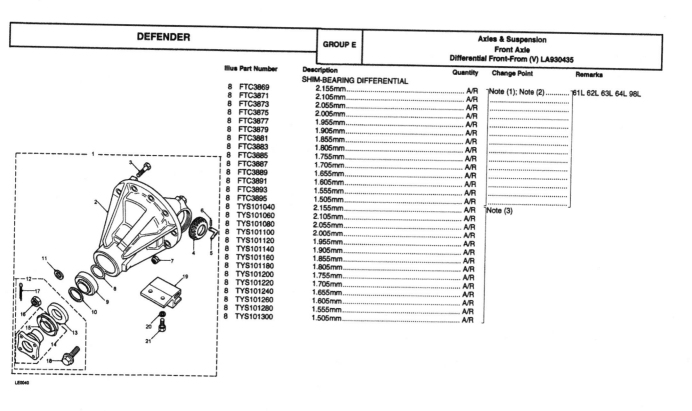

Illus	Part Number	Description	Quantity	Change Point	Remarks
9	539707	Bearing-taper roller	1		
10	539745	Spacer-pinion bearing	1		
11	90513454	Washer-plain	1	Note (1); Note (2)	
12	STC3722	FLANGE & MUDSHIELD-FRONT & REAR AXLE	1	Note (3); Note (4)	
13	FTC5258	• Seal-front & rear	1		
14	FTC5322	• FLANGE-DRIVESHAFT COUPLING DIFFERENTIAL	1		
15	FTC5317	• • Mudshield-front & rear differential	1		
16	NY116041L	• Nut-hexagonal head-nyloc-M16	1		
17	PS608101L	• Pin-split	1		
18	FS112301P	• Screw-flanged head-M12 x 30	1		
11	FTC5413	• Washer-plain	1		
13	FRC8220	Seal-front & rear	1	Note (1); Note (2)	
14	FRC3002	Flange-driveshaft coupling differential-4 bolt flange	1	Note (1); Note (2)	
15	FRC8154	Mudshield-front & rear differential	1	Note (1); Note (2)	
16	NY116041L	Nut-hexagonal head-nyloc-M16	1	Note (1); Note (2)	
17	PS608101L	Pin-split	1	Note (1); Note (2)	
19	NRC9713	Bracket-track rod protection	1	Note (5)	
19	QEU101060	Bracket-track rod protection	1	Note (6)	
20	WM600061L	Washer-differential-3/8"-square	2		
21	SH406061L	Screw-hexagonal head-3/8BSF x 5/8	2		

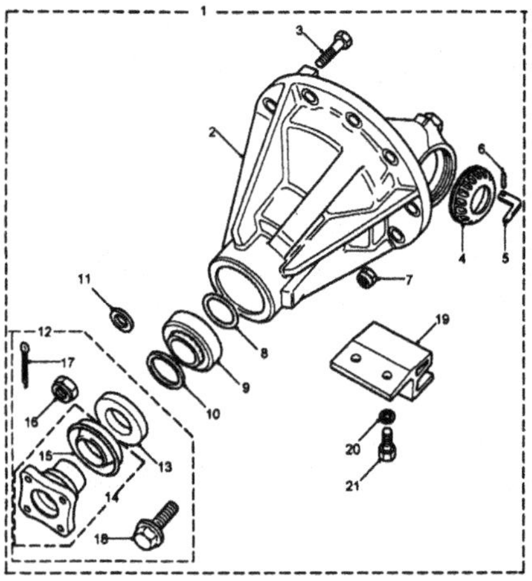

LE0040

CHANGE POINTS:
(1) To (A)61L 18557A
(2) To (A)62L 12289A
(3) From (A)61L 18558A
(4) From (A)62L 12290A
(5) To (V) VA 127829
(6) From (V) VA 127830

Illus	Part Number	Description	Quantity	Change Point	Remarks
1	FRC2933	Case differential-10 spline shaft	1		Drum brakes-rear 20L 22L 23L
1	FRC2933	Case differential-10 spline shaft	1	Note (1); Note (2); Note (3); Note (4)	
1	FTC3269	Case differential-24 spline shaft	1	Note (5); Note (6); Note (7); Note (8)	
1	FTC5399	Case differential	1		10M 11M 12M 13M 14M 15M 16M 17M
2	STC851	KIT-DIFFERENTIAL GEARS-10 SPLINE SHAFT	NLA		Use STC1768. 20L 21L 22L 23L
2	STC1768	KIT-DIFFERENTIAL GEARS-10 SPLINE SHAFT	1		20L 21L 22L 23L
2	STC1846	KIT-DIFFERENTIAL GEARS-24 SPLINE SHAFT	1		61L 62L 63L 64L
3	599945	• Cross shaft differential	1		
4	CCN110L	• Circlip	2		
2	TCI100060	KIT-DIFFERENTIAL GEARS-24 SPLINE SHAFT	1		10M 11M 12M 13M 14M 15M 16M 17M
3	FTC5401	• Cross shaft differential	1		
12	FTC5402	• Pin-roll	1		

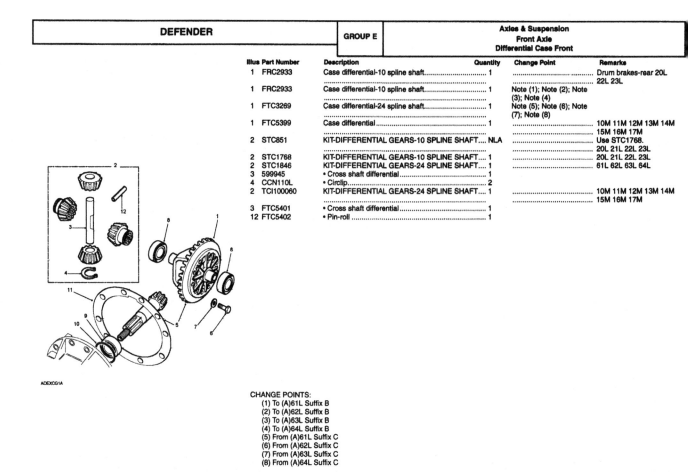

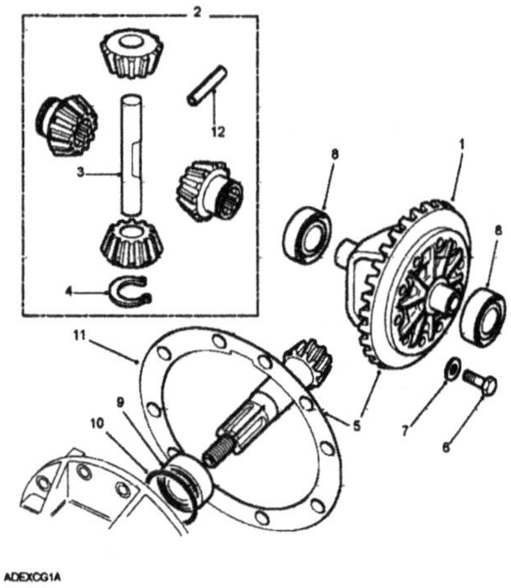

ADEXCG1A

CHANGE POINTS:
(1) To (A)61L Suffix B
(2) To (A)62L Suffix B
(3) To (A)63L Suffix B
(4) To (A)64L Suffix B
(5) From (A)61L Suffix C
(6) From (A)62L Suffix C
(7) From (A)63L Suffix C
(8) From (A)64L Suffix C

Illus	Part Number	Description	Quantity	Change Point	Remarks
5	594493	Crownwheel and pinion assembly-4 spline	1		Use with FRC8521
5	FTC781	Crownwheel and pinion assembly	NLA		Use FTC3620 qty 1 with NY116041L qty 1. Use with FTC782N
5	FTC3620	Crownwheel and pinion assembly	1	Note (1); Note (2); Note (3); Note (4)	
5	TBH100040	Crownwheel and pinion assembly	1	Note (5); Note (6); Note (7); Note (8)	Use with 24 spline halfshaft 10M 11M 12M 13M 14M 15M 16M 17M
6	593692	Bolt	NLA	Note (9); Note (10); Note (11); Note (12)	Use FTC3586. Use with 10 spline halfshaft
6	FTC3586	Bolt-3/8UNF	10	Note (13); Note (14); Note (15); Note (16)	
6	FTC5150	Bolt-3/8UNF	10		10M 11M 12M 13M 14M 15M 16M 17M

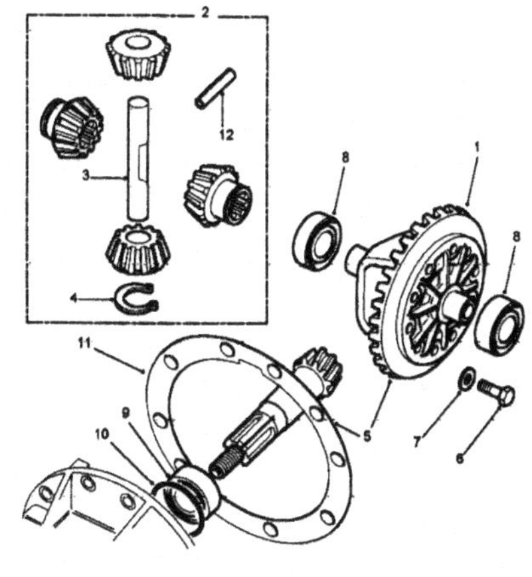

ADEXCG1A

CHANGE POINTS:
(1) To (A)61L 21114A
(2) To (A)62L 15728A
(3) To (A)63L 31579A
(4) To (A)64L 30972A
(5) From (A)61L 21115A
(6) From (A)62L 15729A
(7) From (A)63L 31580A
(8) From (A)64L 30973A
(9) To (A)61L Suffix B
(10) To (A)62L Suffix B
(11) To (A)63L Suffix B
(12) To (A)64L Suffix B
(13) From (A)61L Suffix C
(14) From (A)62L Suffix C
(15) From (A)63L Suffix C
(16) From (A)64L Suffix C

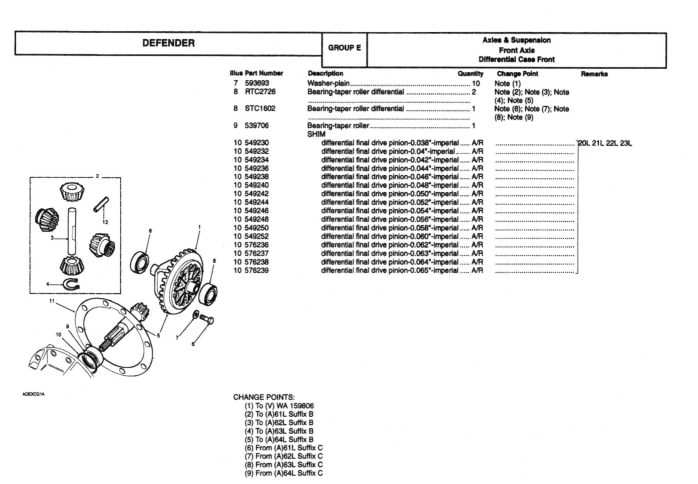

Illus	Part Number	Description	Quantity	Change Point	Remarks
7	593693	Washer-plain	10	Note (1)	
8	RTC2726	Bearing-taper roller differential	2	Note (2); Note (3); Note (4); Note (5)	
8	STC1602	Bearing-taper roller differential	1	Note (6); Note (7); Note (8); Note (9)	
9	539706	Bearing-taper roller	1		
		SHIM			
10	549230	differential final drive pinion-0.038"-imperial	A/R		20L 21L 22L 23L
10	549232	differential final drive pinion-0.04"-imperial	A/R		
10	549234	differential final drive pinion-0.042"-imperial	A/R		
10	549236	differential final drive pinion-0.044"-imperial	A/R		
10	549238	differential final drive pinion-0.046"-imperial	A/R		
10	549240	differential final drive pinion-0.048"-imperial	A/R		
10	549242	differential final drive pinion-0.050"-imperial	A/R		
10	549244	differential final drive pinion-0.052"-imperial	A/R		
10	549246	differential final drive pinion-0.054"-imperial	A/R		
10	549248	differential final drive pinion-0.056"-imperial	A/R		
10	549250	differential final drive pinion-0.058"-imperial	A/R		
10	549252	differential final drive pinion-0.060"-imperial	A/R		
10	576236	differential final drive pinion-0.062"-imperial	A/R		
10	576237	differential final drive pinion-0.063"-imperial	A/R		
10	576238	differential final drive pinion-0.064"-imperial	A/R		
10	576239	differential final drive pinion-0.065"-imperial	A/R		

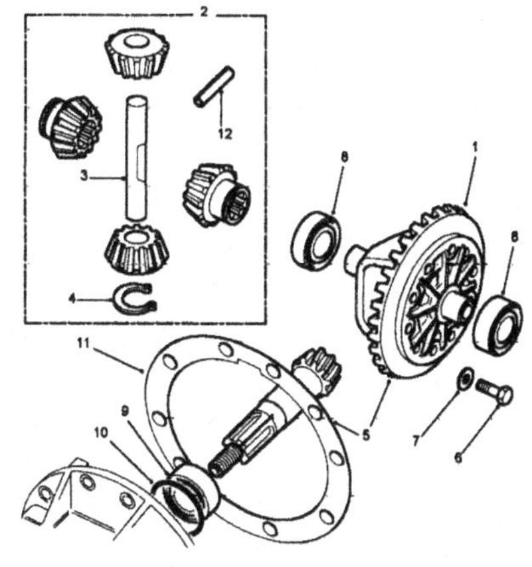

ADEXCG1A

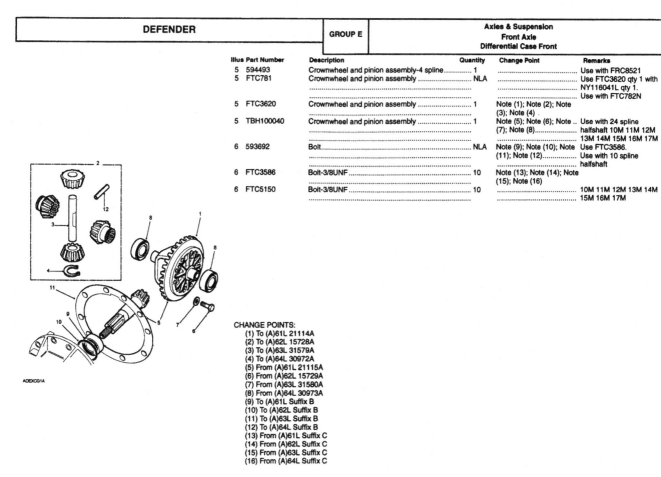

CHANGE POINTS:
(1) To (V) WA 159806
(2) To (A)61L Suffix B
(3) To (A)62L Suffix B
(4) To (A)63L Suffix B
(5) To (A)64L Suffix B
(6) From (A)61L Suffix C
(7) From (A)62L Suffix C
(8) From (A)63L Suffix C
(9) From (A)64L Suffix C

Illus	Part Number	Description	Quantity	Change Point	Remarks
		SHIM			
10	FTC3853	differential final drive pinion-1.548mm-metric	A/R		61L 62L 63L 64L
10	FTC3855	differential final drive pinion-1.498mm-metric	A/R		
10	FTC3857	differential final drive pinion-1.448mm-metric	A/R		
10	FTC3859	differential final drive pinion-1.398mm-metric	A/R		
10	FTC3861	differential final drive pinion-1.348mm-metric	A/R		
10	FTC3863	differential final drive pinion-1.298mm-metric	A/R		
10	FTC3865	differential final drive pinion-1.248mm-metric	A/R		
10	FTC3867	differential final drive pinion-1.198mm-metric	A/R		
10	TYS100870	differential final drive pinion-2.255mm-metric	A/R	Note (1)	
10	TYS100900	differential final drive pinion-2.210mm-metric	A/R	Note (1)	
10	TYS100940	differential final drive pinion-2.150mm-metric	A/R	Note (1)	
10	TYS100970	differential final drive pinion-2.105mm-metric	A/R	Note (1)	
10	TYS101000	differential final drive pinion-2.060mm-metric	A/R	Note (1)	
11	7316	Gasket-differential housing to axle case	1		
	RTC3254	Sealant-silicone	1	Note (2)	

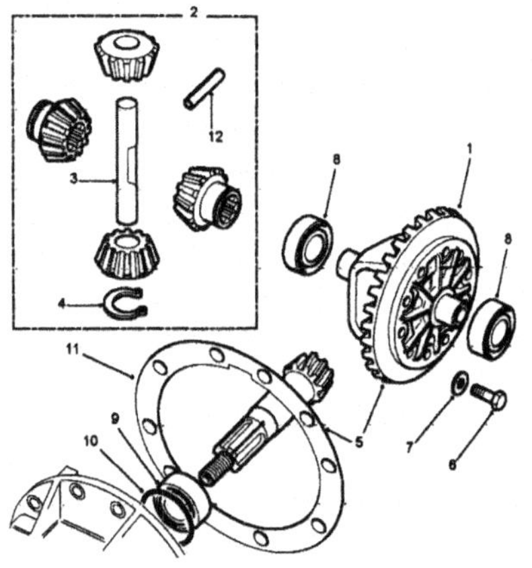
ADEXCG1A

CHANGE POINTS:
(1) From (A) Dec 1997
(2) From (V) MA 939976

Illus	Part Number	Description	Quantity	Change Point	Remarks
1	FRC3890	DRIVESHAFT-FRONT-RH-23 SPLINE SHAFT	1	Note (1); Note (2)	90"
1	FRC3890	DRIVESHAFT-FRONT-RH-23 SPLINE SHAFT	1	Note (3); Note (4)	110"
1	FRC3890	DRIVESHAFT-FRONT-RH-23 SPLINE SHAFT	1	Note (3); Note (4)	130"
2	AEU2522	• Joint-constant velocity	1		
3	AEU2520	• Shaft-front axle half-RH	1		
4	FTC254	• Spacer	1		
5	RTC4820	• Circlip-front axle shaft to CV joint	1		
1	FRC3891	DRIVESHAFT-FRONT-LH-23 SPLINE SHAFT	1	Note (1); Note (2)	90"
1	FRC3891	DRIVESHAFT-FRONT-LH-23 SPLINE SHAFT	1	Note (3); Note (4)	110"
1	FRC3891	DRIVESHAFT-FRONT-LH-23 SPLINE SHAFT	1	Note (3); Note (4)	130"
2	AEU2522	• Joint-constant velocity	1		
3	AEU2521	• Shaft-front axle half-LH	1		
4	FTC254	• Spacer	1		
5	RTC4820	• Circlip-front axle shaft to CV joint	1		
1	FTC1332	DRIVESHAFT-FRONT-RH-33 SPLINE SHAFT	1	Note (5); Note (6)	90"
1	FTC1332	DRIVESHAFT-FRONT-RH-33 SPLINE SHAFT	1	Note (7); Note (8)	110"
1	FTC1332	DRIVESHAFT-FRONT-RH-33 SPLINE SHAFT	1	Note (7); Note (8)	130"
2	RTC6862	• Joint-constant velocity	1		
3	RTC6754	• Shaft-front axle half-RH	1		
4	RTC5841	• Spacer	1		
5	STC579	• Circlip-front axle shaft to CV joint	1		
1	FTC1333	DRIVESHAFT-FRONT-LH-33 SPLINE SHAFT	1	Note (5); Note (6)	90"
1	FTC1333	DRIVESHAFT-FRONT-LH-33 SPLINE SHAFT	1	Note (7); Note (8)	110"
1	FTC1333	DRIVESHAFT-FRONT-LH-33 SPLINE SHAFT	1	Note (7); Note (8)	130"
2	RTC6862	• Joint-constant velocity	1		
3	RTC6755	• Shaft-front axle half-LH	1		
4	RTC5841	• Spacer	1		
5	STC579	• Circlip-front axle shaft to CV joint	1		

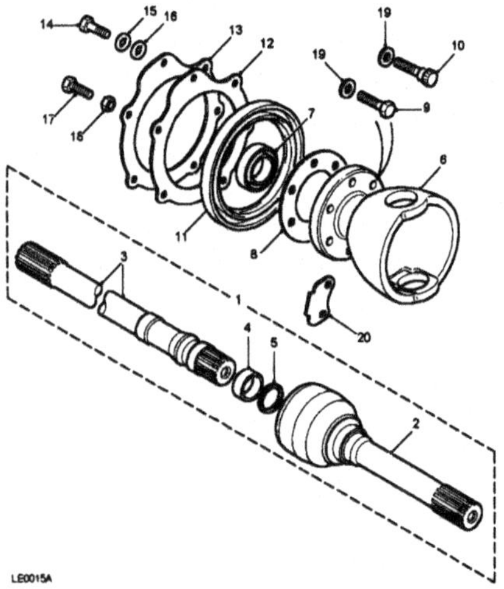
LE0015A

CHANGE POINTS:
(1) To (A)22L 27847 RHD
(2) To (A)23L 12092 LHD
(3) To (A)20L 48865 RHD
(4) To (A)21L 33355 LHD
(5) From (A)22L 27848 RHD
(6) From (A)23L 12093 LHD
(7) From (A)20L 48866 RHD
(8) From (A)21L 33356 LHD

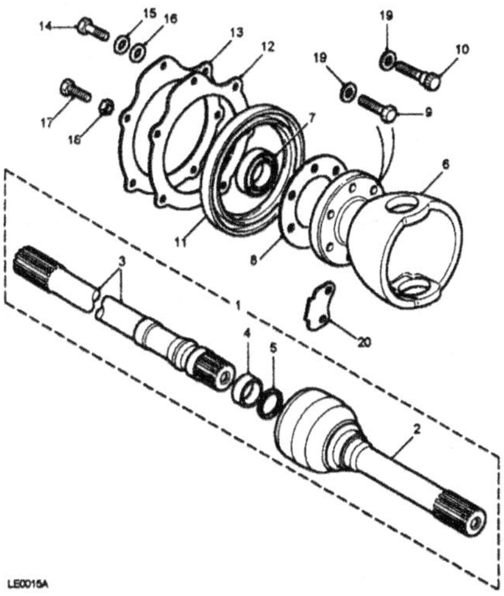

LE0015A

Illus	Part Number	Description	Quantity	Change Point	Remarks
1	FTC3148	DRIVESHAFT-FRONT-RH-24 SPLINE SHAFT	NLA		Use FTC3146. 61L 62L 63L 64L except Antilock Brakes
2	STC3051	• Joint-constant velocity	1		
3	STC3049	• Shaft-front axle half-RH-RH	1		
4	RTC5841	• Spacer	1		
5	STC579	• Circlip-front axle shaft to CV joint	1		
1	FTC3149	DRIVESHAFT-FRONT-LH-24 SPLINE SHAFT	NLA		Use FTC3147. 61L 62L 63L 64L except Antilock Brakes
2	STC3051	• Joint-constant velocity	1		
3	STC3050	• Shaft-front axle half-LH	1		
4	RTC5841	• Spacer	1		
5	STC579	• Circlip-front axle shaft to CV joint	1		
1	FTC3146	DRIVESHAFT-FRONT-RH-24 SPLINE SHAFT	1	Note (1)	61L 62L 63L 64L
2	STC3051	• Joint-constant velocity	1		
3	STC3049	• Shaft-front axle half-RH-RH	1		
4	RTC5841	• Spacer	1		
5	STC579	• Circlip-front axle shaft to CV joint	1		
1	FTC3147	DRIVESHAFT-FRONT-LH-24 SPLINE SHAFT	1	Note (1)	61L 62L 63L 64L
2	STC3051	• Joint-constant velocity	1		
3	STC3050	• Shaft-front axle half-LH	1		
4	RTC5841	• Spacer	1		
5	STC579	• Circlip-front axle shaft to CV joint	1		
1	TDB000180	DRIVESHAFT-FRONT-RH-24 SPLINE SHAFT	1	Note (2)	10M 11M 12M 13M 14M 15M 16M 17M
2	TDJ000010	• Joint-constant velocity	1		
3	TDC000020	• Shaft-front axle half-RH	1		
4	TYF000010	• Spacer	1		
5	TDL000010	• Circlip-front axle shaft to CV joint	1		
1	TDB000190	DRIVESHAFT-FRONT-LH-24 SPLINE SHAFT	1	Note (2)	10M 11M 12M 13M 14M 15M 16M 17M
2	TDJ000010	• Joint-constant velocity	1		
3	TDC000030	• Shaft-front axle half-LH	1		
4	TYF000010	• Spacer	1		
5	TDL000010	• Circlip-front axle shaft to CV joint	1		

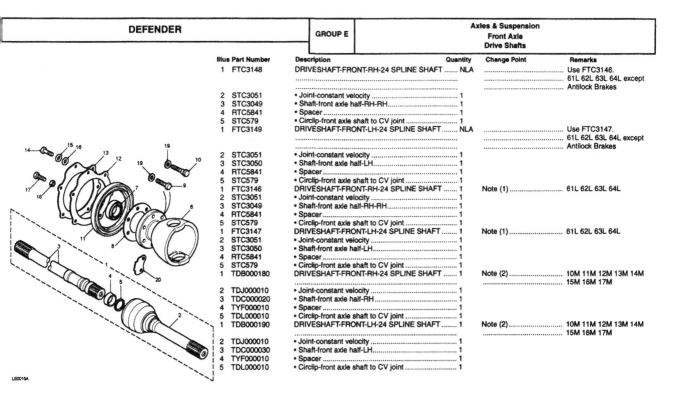

CHANGE POINTS:
(1) From (V) LA 930456 To (V) WA 159806
(2) From (V) XA 159807

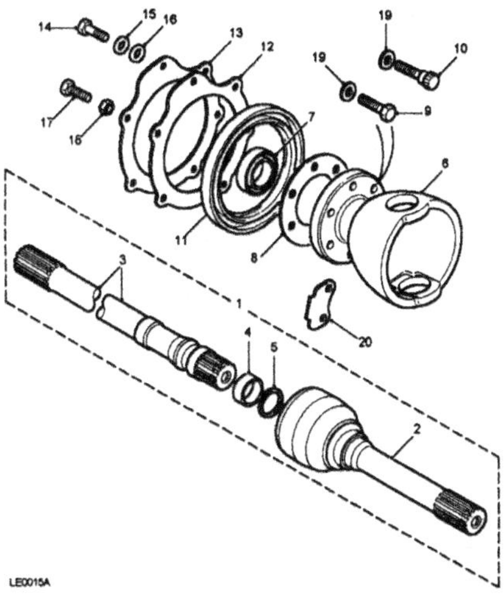

LE0015A

Illus	Part Number	Description	Quantity	Change Point	Remarks
6	FRC2644	Housing-swivel pin bearing	NLA		Use FTC5105. 20L 21L 22L 23L
6	FTC5105	Housing-swivel pin bearing	1		20L 21L 22L 23L
6	FRC7065	Housing-swivel pin bearing	2		61L 62L 63L 64L
6	TIR100000	Housing-swivel pin bearing	2		10M 11M 12M 13M 14M 15M 16M 17M
7	571718	Seal-front driveshaft	2		Drum brakes-rear 20L 22L 23L
7	FTC3276	Seal-front driveshaft	2		Non-ventilated disc brakes-rear 61L 62L 63L 64L
8	FTC3646	Gasket-swivel pin bearing housing to axle case	2		
9	FTC3456	Bolt-M10-hexagonal	12	Note (1)	
9	TYG100590	Bolt-M10-double hex	12	Note (2)	
10	FTC3454	Bolt-dowel-hexagonal-M10	2	Note (1)	
10	TYG100580	Bolt-dowel-M10-double hex	2	Note (2)	
11	FRC2889	Seal-swivel pin housing-9mm	2	Note (3); Note (4)	
11	FTC3401	Seal-swivel pin housing-9mm	2	Note (5); Note (6)	

CHANGE POINTS:
(1) To (V) VA 118090
(2) From (V) VA 118091
(3) To (A)20L 74081C RHD
(4) To (A)21L 55147C LHD
(5) From (A)20L 740082C RHD
(6) From (A)21L 55148C LHD

Illus	Part Number	Description	Quantity	Change Point	Remarks
12	FRC4206	Washer-sealing	2		Drum brakes-rear 20L 22L 23L
13	FRC4142	Plate-oil seal retainer	2		20L 21L 22L 23L
13	571755	Plate-oil seal retainer	4		61L 62L 63L 64L
14	FS106125L	Screw-flanged head-M6 x 12	12		
14	SH106121L	Screw-hexagonal head-M6 x 12	14		Drum brakes-rear 20L 22L 23L
15	WL106001L	Washer-sprung-M6	14		
16	WA106001L	Washer-M6	14		
17	AFU1234	Bolt-M12	2		Drum brakes-rear 20L 22L 23L except 90"
18	NT112041L	Nut-hexagonal-thin-M12	2		
19	FRC8530	Washer-plain	14		61L 62L 63L 64L
20	TAU100170	Bracket-lock stop	1		10M 11M 12M 13M 14M 15M 16M 17M

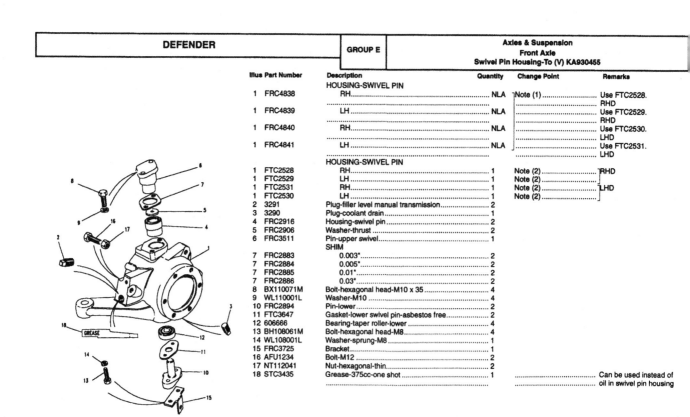

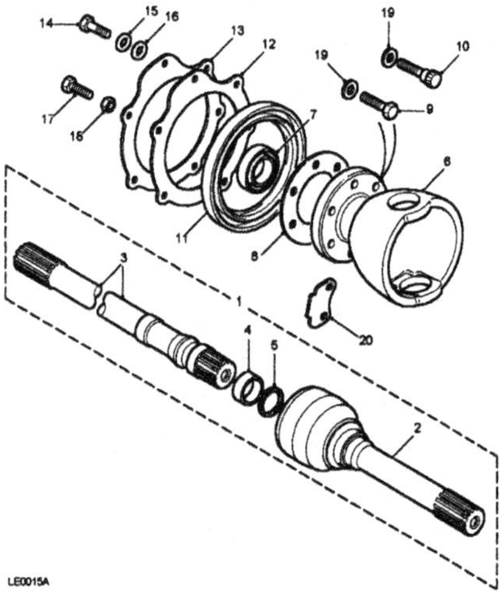

LE0015A

Illus	Part Number	Description	Quantity	Change Point	Remarks
		HOUSING-SWIVEL PIN			
1	FRC4838	RH	NLA	Note (1)	Use FTC2528. RHD
1	FRC4839	LH	NLA		Use FTC2529. RHD
1	FRC4840	RH	NLA		Use FTC2530. LHD
1	FRC4841	LH	NLA		Use FTC2531. LHD
		HOUSING-SWIVEL PIN			
1	FTC2528	RH	1	Note (2)	RHD
1	FTC2529	LH	1	Note (2)	
1	FTC2531	RH	1	Note (2)	LHD
1	FTC2530	LH	1	Note (2)	
2	3291	Plug-filler level manual transmission	2		
3	3290	Plug-coolant drain	1		
4	FRC2916	Housing-swivel pin	2		
5	FRC2906	Washer-thrust	2		
6	FRC3511	Pin-upper swivel	1		
		SHIM			
7	FRC2883	0.003"	2		
7	FRC2884	0.005"	2		
7	FRC2885	0.01"	2		
7	FRC2886	0.03"	2		
8	BX110071M	Bolt-hexagonal head-M10 x 35	4		
9	WL110001L	Washer-M10	4		
10	FRC2894	Pin-lower	2		
11	FTC3647	Gasket-lower swivel pin-asbestos free	2		
12	606666	Bearing-taper roller-lower	4		
13	BH108061M	Bolt-hexagonal head-M8	4		
14	WL108001L	Washer-sprung-M8	1		
15	FRC3725	Bracket	1		
16	AFU1234	Bolt-M12	2		
17	NT112041	Nut-hexagonal-thin	2		
18	STC3435	Grease-375cc-one shot	1		Can be used instead of oil in swivel pin housing

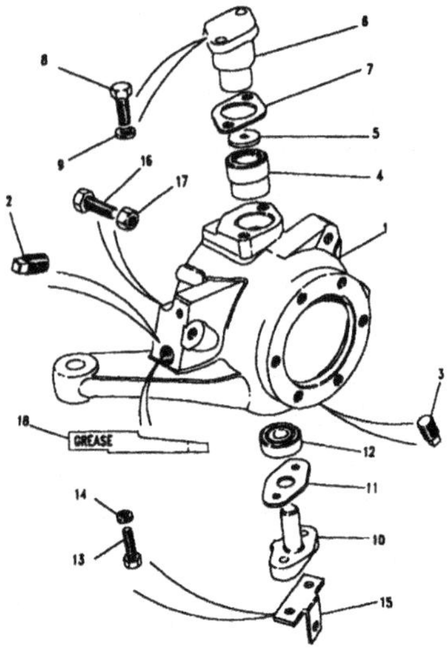

CHANGE POINTS:
(1) To (V) JA 909205
(2) From (V) JA 909206

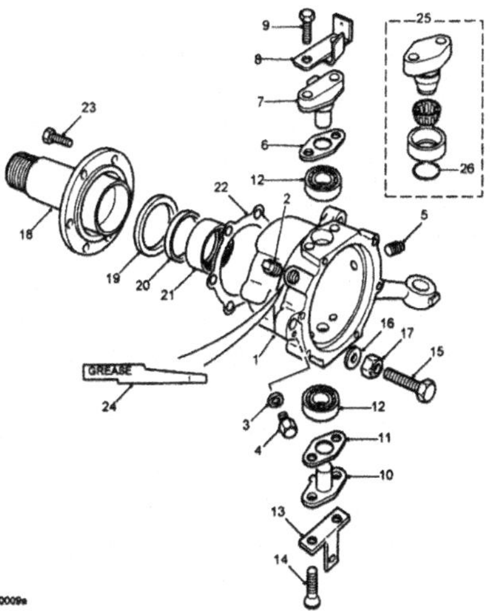

LE0009a

Illus	Part Number	Description	Quantity	Change Point	Remarks
		HOUSING-SWIVEL PIN			
1	FTC3308	RH	1	Note (1)	RHD
1	FTC3309	LH	1		
1	FTC3310	RH	1		LHD
1	FTC3311	LH	1		
1	FTC5296	RH	1	Note (2)	RHD
1	FTC5297	LH	1		
1	FTC5298	RH	1		LHD
1	FTC5299	LH	1		
2	3292	Plug-level	1		
3	230511	Washer-sealing-steering swivel pin housing drain plug	1		
4	236070	Plug-drain	1		
5	FTC3670	Plug-hexagonal	1		
		SHIM			
6	FRC2883	0.003"	2		
6	FRC2884	0.005"	2		
6	FRC2885	0.01"	2		
6	FRC2886	0.03"	2		
7	FTC2882	Pin	2		
25	TAR100050	KIT-SWIVEL PIN-UPPER	1		12M 13M 16M 17M Antilock Brakes
26	TYX100570	• O ring	1		
25	TAR100040	KIT-SWIVEL PIN-UPPER	1		10M 11M 14M 15M except Antilock Brakes
26	TYX100570	• O ring	1		
8	FRC7202	Bracket-brake pipe-RH	1	Note (3)	
8	ANR5784	Bracket-brake pipe-RH	1	Note (4)	
8	FRC7201	Bracket-brake pipe-LH	1	Note (3)	
8	ANR5783	Bracket-brake pipe-LH	1	Note (4)	
9	BX110071M	Bolt-hexagonal head-M10 x 35	4		
10	FRC2894	Pin-lower	2		

CHANGE POINTS:
(1) To (V) VA 104814
(2) From (V) VA 104815
(3) To (V) WA 159806
(4) From (V) XA 159807

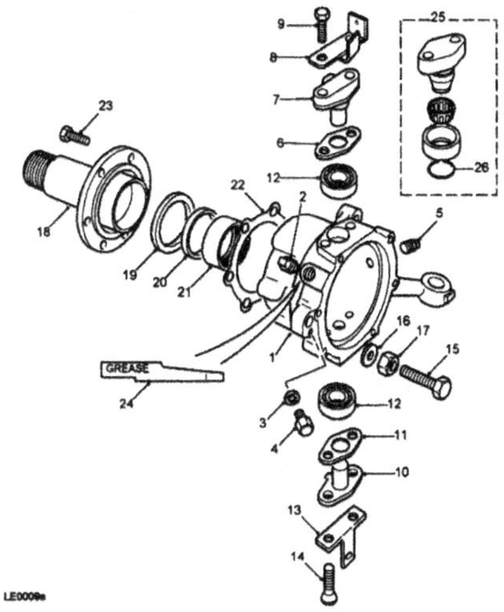

LE0009a

Illus	Part Number	Description	Quantity	Change Point	Remarks
11	FTC3647	Gasket-lower swivel pin-asbestos free	2		
12	606666	Bearing-taper roller-lower	4		
13	FRC3725	Bracket	2		
14	BH108061M	Bolt-hexagonal head-M8	4		
15	FTC4111	Bolt-steering lock stop-M12	2		50 LE
15	SH112505	Screw-hexagonal head-shouldered-M12 x 50	2		Except 50 LE
16	WB112081L	Washer-plain-M12 x 22	2		
17	NT112041L	Nut-hexagonal-thin-M12	2		
	NTC6994	Clip-cable	2		
18	FTC3154	Axle-stub-hub front suspension	2		
19	FTC56	Washer-front hub thrust	2		
20	FTC840	Seal-stub axle-outer	2	Note (1); Note (2)	
20	FTC3145	Seal-stub axle	NLA	Note (3); Note (4)	Use FTC5268.
20	FTC5268	Seal-stub axle-inner	1	Note (5)	
21	FTC861	Bearing-front/rear axle hub-swivel pin housing	2		
22	FTC3648	Gasket-stub axle-front axle-asbestos free	2		
23	SX110251M	Screw-M10 x 25-hexagonal head	12	Note (6)	
23	SX110257M	Screw-M10 x 25-hexagonal head	12	Note (7)	
24	STC3435	Grease-375cc-one shot	1		Can be used instead of oil in swivel pin housing
	FTC1616	Damper-swivel pin-RH	1		50 LE
	FTC1617	Damper-swivel pin-LH	1		50 LE

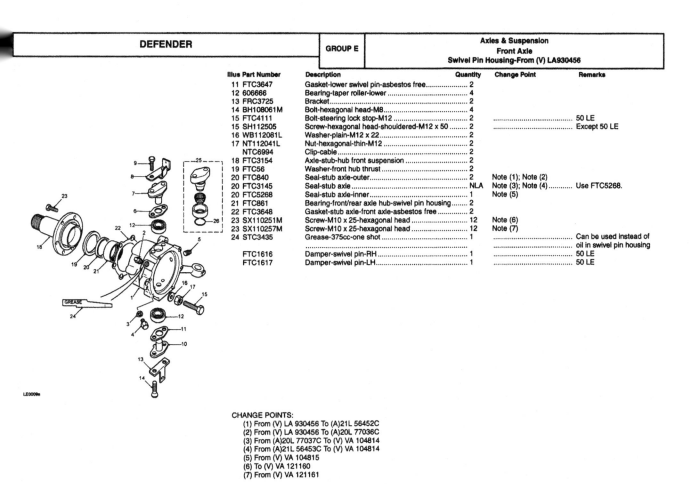

CHANGE POINTS:
(1) From (V) LA 930456 To (A)21L 56452C
(2) From (V) LA 930456 To (A)20L 77036C
(3) From (A)20L 77037C To (V) VA 104814
(4) From (A)21L 56453C To (V) VA 104814
(5) From (V) VA 104815
(6) To (V) VA 121160
(7) From (V) VA 121161

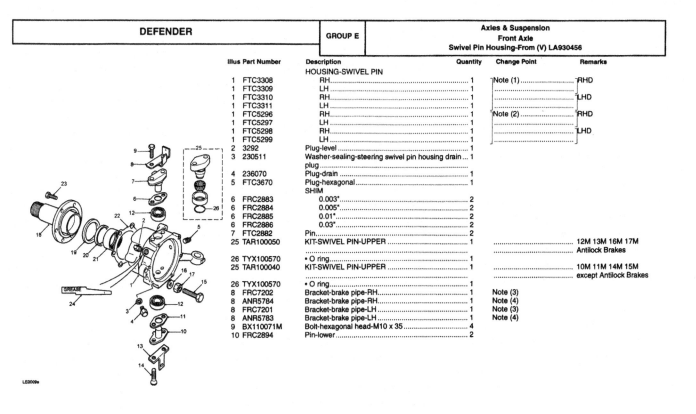

Illus	Part Number	Description	Quantity	Change Point	Remarks
1	FRC4320	AXLE-STUB-HUB FRONT SUSPENSION	2		
2	FRC3099	• Seal-stub axle	2		
3	FRC4319	• Axle assembly-stub front suspension	2		
4	FTC3648	Gasket-stub axle-front axle-asbestos free	2		
5	FRC2310	Plate-front & rear stub axle locking	2		
6	SX110251M	Screw-M10 x 25-hexagonal head	12		
7	WL110001L	Washer-M10	12		
8	RTC3511	Seal assembly-front/rear hub	2	Note (1); Note (2)	90"
8	FRC8221	Seal assembly-front/rear hub-inner	2	Note (3); Note (4)	Except 90"
8	FTC2783	Seal assembly-front/rear hub-inner	NLA	Note (5); Note (6); Note (7); Note (8)	Use FTC4785.
9	RTC3429	Bearing-front/rear axle hub	NLA		Use STC4382.
9	STC4382	Bearing-front/rear axle hub	2		
10	FRC6139	HUB ASSEMBLY FRONT	2		
11	FRC6137	• Stud-stub axle	10		
12	217352	Washer-front & rear hub nut tab	2		
13	FRC8700	Locknut-stub axle	4		
14	217353	Washer-lock-stub axle	2		
15	FRC3988	Gasket-axle shaft drive member	2		
16	FRC5806	Flange-driving shaft joint	2		
17	RYG101010L	Bolt-flanged head-M10 x 50	10		
18	WL110001L	Washer-M10	10		

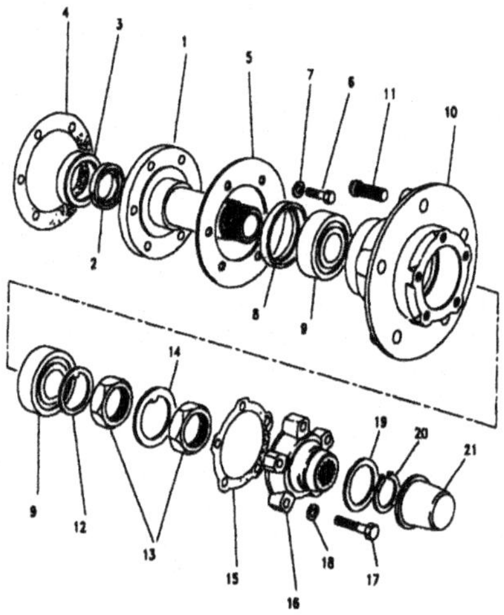

CHANGE POINTS:
(1) To (A)22L 06071B RHD
(2) To (A)23L 03666B LHD
(3) To (A)20L 70575C
(4) To (A)21L 52060C
(5) From (A)22L 06072B RHD
(6) From (A)23L 03667B LHD
(7) From (A)20L 70576C
(8) From (A)21L 52061C

DEFENDER | GROUP E | Axles & Suspension
Front Axle
Front Hubs-To (V) KA930455

Illus	Part Number	Description	Quantity	Change Point	Remarks
		SHIM-FRONT AXLE HALF SHAFT			
19	FRC6782	0.45mm	2		
19	FRC6783	0.60mm	4		
19	FRC6784	0.75mm	4		
19	FRC6785	0.90mm	4		
19	FRC6786	1.05mm	4		
19	FRC6787	1.20mm	4		
19	FRC6788	1.35mm	4		
19	FRC6789	1.50mm	4		
19	FRC6790	1.65mm	4		
20	549473	Circlip-axle shaft to hub driving member	2		
21	FRC4377	Cap-driveshaft coupling bolt locking-polyurethane	2		

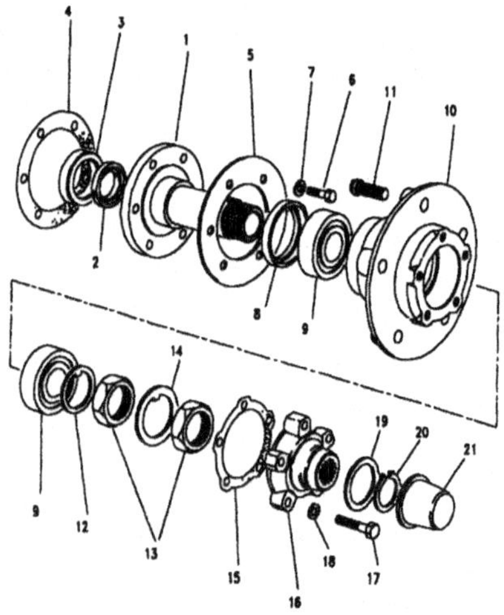

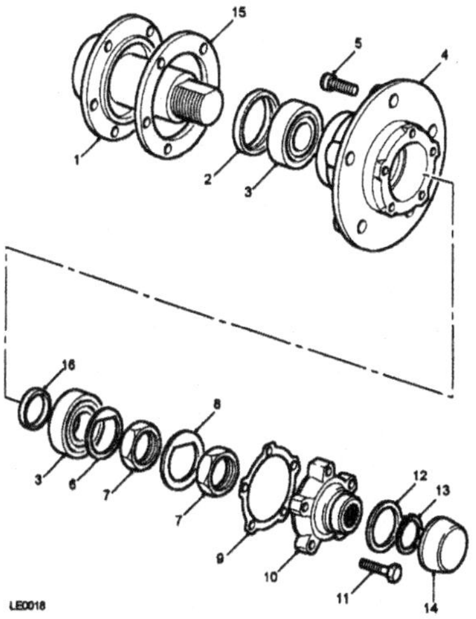

LE0018

Illus	Part Number	Description	Quantity	Change Point	Remarks
1	FTC3154	Axle-stub-hub front suspension	2		
2	FTC2783	Seal assembly-front/rear hub-inner	NLA	Note (1)	Use FTC4785.
2	FTC4785	Seal assembly-front/rear hub-inner	2	Note (2)	
3	RTC3429	Bearing-front/rear axle hub	NLA		Use STC4382. 61L 62L 63L 64L
3	STC4382	Bearing-front/rear axle hub	4		10M 11M 12M 13M 14M 15M 16M 17M
4	FTC942	HUB ASSEMBLY-FRONT & REAR	2		61L 62L 63L 64L
5	FRC5926	• Stud	10		
4	RUB101740	HUB ASSEMBLY-FRONT & REAR	2		10M 11M 12M 13M 14M 15M 16M 17M
5	FRC5926	• Stud	5		
6	FTC3185	Washer-front & rear hub nut tab	2	Note (3)	
6	FTC5241	Washer-front & rear hub nut tab	2	Note (4)	
7	FRC8700	Locknut	4		61L 62L 63L 64L
7	RFD100000	Locknut	2		10M 11M 12M 13M 14M 15M 16M 17M

CHANGE POINTS:
(1) To (V) TA 987746
(2) From (V) TA 987747
(3) From (V) TA 996892
(4) From (V) TA 996893

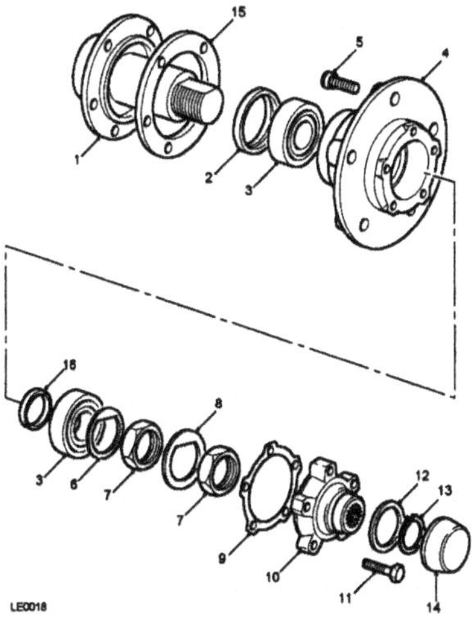

LE0018

Illus	Part Number	Description	Quantity	Change Point	Remarks
8	FTC3179	Washer-lock-outer	2		61L 62L 63L 64L
9	571752	Gasket-axle shaft drive member	2	Note (1)	
10	FTC859	Flange-driving shaft joint	2		
11	BX110095M	Bolt-M10 x 45	10		
		SHIM-FRONT AXLE HALF SHAFT			
12	FRC6782	0.45mm	2		61L 62L 63L 64L
12	FRC6783	0.60mm	2		
12	FRC6784	0.75mm	2		
12	FRC6785	0.90mm	2		
12	FRC6786	1.05mm	2		
12	FRC6787	1.20mm	2		
12	FRC6788	1.35mm	2		
12	FRC6789	1.50mm	2		
12	FRC6790	1.65mm	2		
13	549473	Circlip-axle shaft to hub driving member	2		
14	FTC943	Cap-driveshaft coupling bolt locking-without logo	2	Note (2)	
14	FTC5414	Cap-driveshaft coupling bolt locking-with Land Rover logo	2	Note (3)	
15	FRC2310	Plate-front & rear stub axle locking	2		
16	TOF100000	Spacer-15.5mm-Purple	A/R		10M 11M 12M 13M 14M 15M 16M 17M
16	TOF100010	Spacer-15.4mm-Yellow.	A/R		
16	TOF100020	Spacer-15.3mm-Red	A/R		
16	TOF100030	Spacer-15.2mm-Blue	A/R		
16	TOF100040	Spacer-15.1mm-Green	A/R		
16	TOF100050	Spacer-15.0mm-Black	A/R		
16	TOF100060	Spacer-14.9mm-White	A/R		

CHANGE POINTS:
(1) From (V) LA 930456
(2) To (V) VA 110615
(3) From (V) VA 110616

Illus	Part Number	Description	Quantity	Change Point	Remarks
		REAR DRUM BRAKES			
1	FRC8786	Axle/drive unit-4x4 rear	1	Note (1)	4 Cylinder except Heavy duty
1	FTC1633	Axle/drive unit-4x4 rear	1	Note (2)	
1	FRC8787	Axle/drive unit-4x4 rear	1	Note (3)	4 Cylinder Heavy duty
1	FTC1636	Axle/drive unit-4x4 rear	1	Note (4)	
1	FRC8787	Axle/drive unit-4x4 rear	1	Note (3)	V8
1	FTC1636	Axle/drive unit-4x4 rear	1	Note (4)	
		REAR DISC BRAKES			
1	FTC3688	Axle/drive unit-4x4 rear	1		42S 4 Cylinder except Heavy duty
1	FTC3974	Axle/drive unit-4x4 rear	1		44S 4 Cylinder Heavy duty
1	FTC3974	Axle/drive unit-4x4 rear	1		44S V8
1	FTC5300	Axle/drive unit-4x4 rear	1		42S 50 LE
1	TVK100440	Axle/drive unit-4x4 rear	1		58S except Antilock Brakes
1	TVK100450	Axle/drive unit-4x4 rear	1		59S Antilock Brakes
2	FTC5085	Adaptor	1		58S 59S 60S 61S 62S 63S

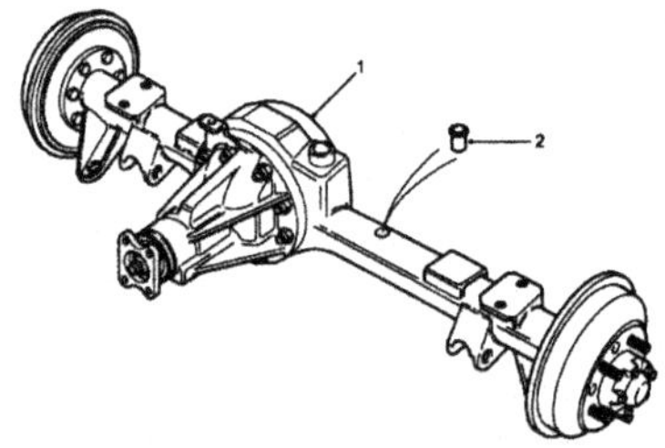

LE0041

CHANGE POINTS:
(1) To (A)22S 07618C
(2) From (A)22S 07619C
(3) To (A)23S 07618C
(4) From (A)23S 07619C

Illus	Part Number	Description	Quantity	Change Point	Remarks
		REAR DRUM BRAKES			
1	FTC2352	AXLE/DRIVE UNIT-4X4 REAR	1		21S 110" except Heavy duty
2	FTC3721	• Case-rear axle	1		
1	FTC2353	AXLE/DRIVE UNIT-4X4 REAR	1		24S 110" Heavy duty
1	FTC2353	AXLE/DRIVE UNIT-4X4 REAR	1		24S 130"
2	FTC2212	• Case-rear axle	1		

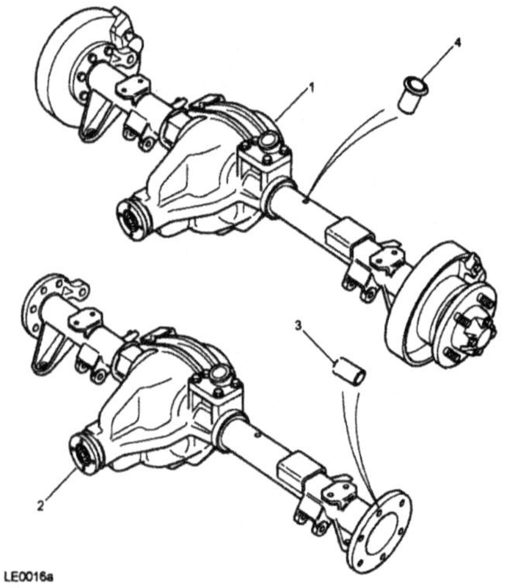

LE0016a

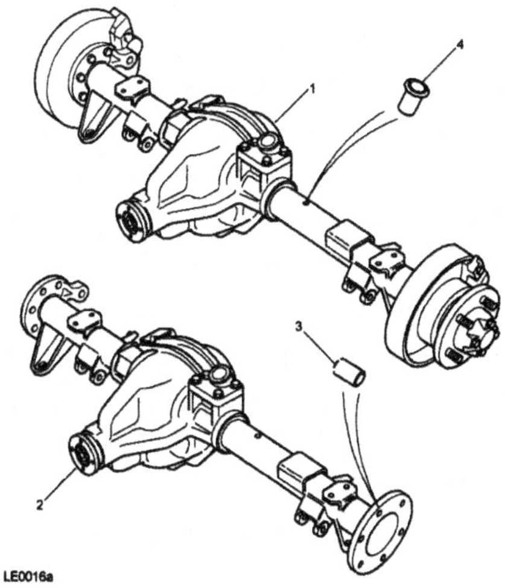

LE0016a

Illus	Part Number	Description	Quantity	Change Point	Remarks
		REAR DISC BRAKES			
1	FTC3304	AXLE/DRIVE UNIT-4X4 REAR	1		39S 110" except Heavy duty
2	FTC3721	• Case-rear axle	1		
1	FTC3232	AXLE/DRIVE UNIT-4X4 REAR	1		38S 110" Heavy duty
1	FTC3232	AXLE/DRIVE UNIT-4X4 REAR	1		38S 130"
		110" - EXCEPT ABS			
1	TVK100460	AXLE/DRIVE UNIT-4X4 REAR	1		60S except Heavy duty
2	TVK100420	• Case-rear axle	1		
1	TVK100480	AXLE/DRIVE UNIT-4X4 REAR	1		62S Heavy duty
2	TVK100430	• Case-rear axle	1		
		110" - WITH ABS			
1	TVK100470	AXLE/DRIVE UNIT-4X4 REAR	1		61S except Heavy duty
2	TVK100420	• Case-rear axle	1		
3	FTC1384	• Bush	2		
1	TVK100490	AXLE/DRIVE UNIT-4X4 REAR	1		63S Heavy duty
2	TVK100430	• Case-rear axle	1		
3	FTC1384	• Bush	2		
		130"			
1	TVK100480	AXLE/DRIVE UNIT-4X4 REAR	1		62S except Antilock Brakes
1	TVK100490	AXLE/DRIVE UNIT-4X4 REAR	1		63S Antilock Brakes
2	TVK100430	• Case-rear axle	1		
3	FTC1384	• Bush	2		Part of TVK100490.
4	FTC5085	Adaptor	1		60S 61S 62S 63S

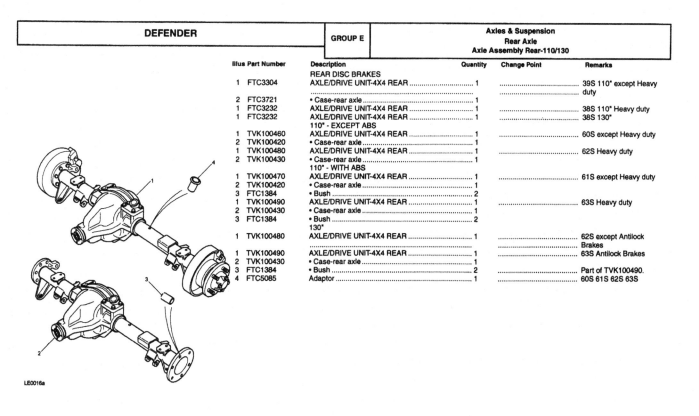

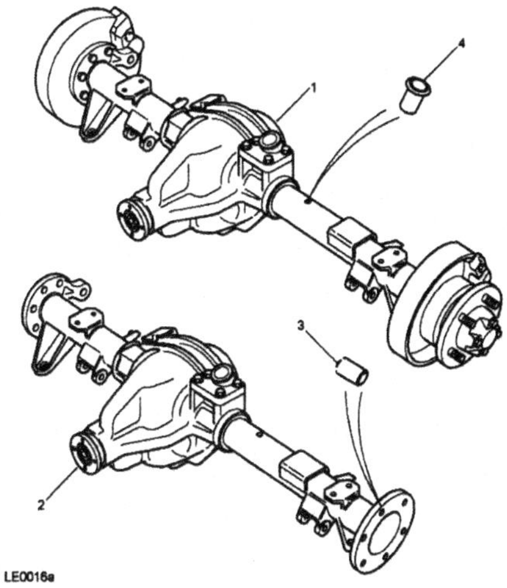

LE0016a

Illus	Part Number	Description	Quantity	Change Point	Remarks
1	TVK000120	AXLE/DRIVE UNIT-4X4 REAR	1	Note (1)	10S 110" except Antilock Brakes
2	TVK100420	• Case-rear axle	1		
1	TVK000130	AXLE/DRIVE UNIT-4X4 REAR	1	Note (1)	Antilock Brakes 12S 110" except 130"
2	TVK100420	• Case-rear axle	1		
1	TVK000140	AXLE/DRIVE UNIT-4X4 REAR	1	Note (1)	12S 110" except Antilock Brakes
2	TVK100430	• Case-rear axle	1		
1	TVK000140	AXLE/DRIVE UNIT-4X4 REAR	1	Note (1)	HICAP 12S 130" except Antilock Brakes
2	TVK100430	• Case-rear axle	1		
1	TVK000170	AXLE/DRIVE UNIT-4X4 REAR	1	Note (1)	Antilock Brakes 12S 130"
2	TVK100430	• Case-rear axle	1		
1	TVK000170	AXLE/DRIVE UNIT-4X4 REAR	1	Note (1)	HICAP 13S 130"
2	TVK100430	• Case-rear axle	1		
1	TVK000170	AXLE/DRIVE UNIT-4X4 REAR	1	Note (1)	Antilock Brakes 14S 130"
2	TVK100430	• Case-rear axle	1		

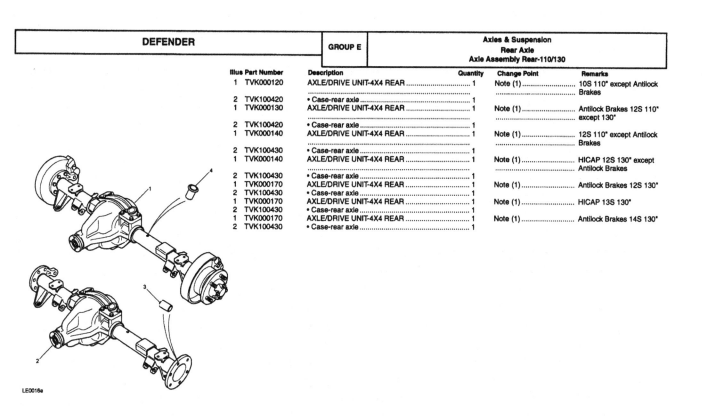

CHANGE POINTS:
(1) From (V) 2A 622424

Case Assembly Rear

Illus	Part Number	Description	Quantity	Change Point	Remarks
1	FRC7231	CASE-REAR AXLE	1		22S 23S 90" drum brakes-rear
2	561195	• Stud-3/8UNF x 1 1/4	4		
3	561196	• Stud-3/8UNF x 1 3/4	6		
4	608246	• Plug-drain/filler level	2		
1	FTC3434	CASE-REAR AXLE	1		42S 44S 90" non-ventilated disc brakes-rear except 50 LE
2	561196	• Stud-3/8UNF x 1 3/4	6	Note (1)	
3	561195	• Stud-3/8UNF x 1 1/4	4	Note (1)	
2	561196	• Stud-3/8UNF x 1 3/4	10	Note (2)	
4	608246	• Plug-drain/filler level	2		
1	FTC3437	CASE-REAR AXLE	1		42S 90" 50 LE
1	TVI100130	CASE-REAR AXLE	1		58S 59S 90"
2	561196	• Stud-3/8UNF x 1 3/4	10		
4	608246	• Plug-drain/filler level	2		
5	FTC1384	Bush	2		Antilock Brakes 59S

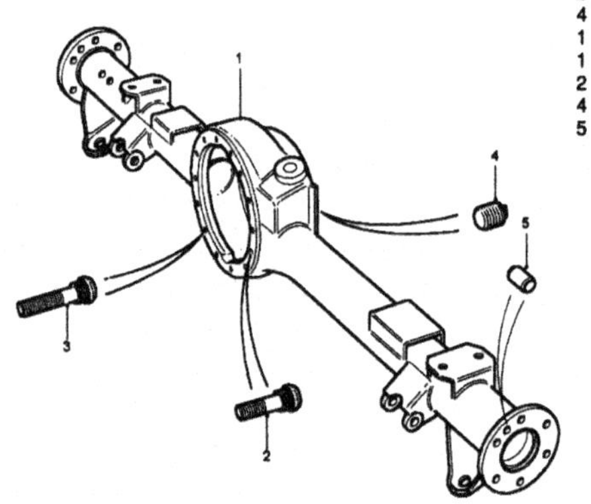

LE0017

CHANGE POINTS:
(1) To (A)42S 04615A
(2) From (A)42S 04616A

Case Assembly Rear-Salisbury Type

Illus	Part Number	Description	Quantity	Change Point	Remarks
1	607163	Bolt	4		
2	RTC1139	Gasket-differential cover plate	1		
3	RTC844	Cover-rear axle differential	1		
4	607173	Bolt	10		
5	AAU2825	Washer	10		
6	608246	Plug-drain/filler level	2		
7	RTC845	Plate-gear lever assembly face	1		
8	NRC8024	Bracket-brake pipe	1		
9	NRC5346	Bracket-brake pipe	1		
10	NRC9607	Bracket rear axle	1		
11	AEU2508	Bolt	4		
12	607181	Bearing-taper roller-differential final drive pinion outer	1		
13	607182	Washer	1		
14	607183	Gasket-axle shaft drive member-salisbury type	1		
15	AEU2515	Seal differential-differential final drive pinion-rear	1	Note (1)	
15	STC4401	Seal differential-rear	1	Note (2)	
16	607185	Flange assembly rear hub	1	Note (1)	
	STC4403	Kit-flange	1	Note (2)	
17	607357	Washer-differential gear thrust	1		
18	90608545	Locknut	1		

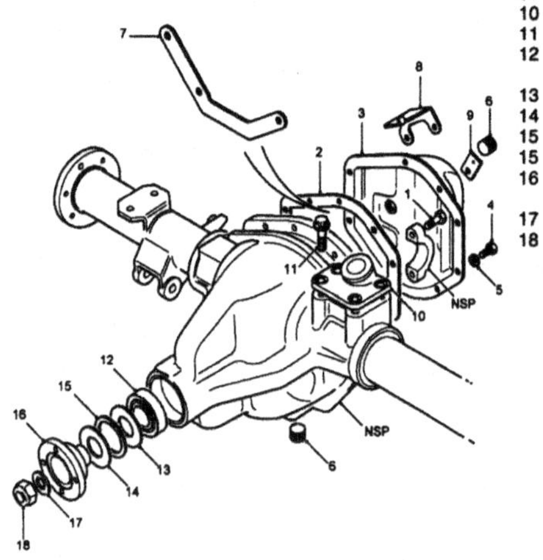

AJEXEC1A

CHANGE POINTS:
(1) To (V) WA 159806
(2) From (V) XA 159807

Illus	Part Number	Description	Quantity	Change Point	Remarks
	FTC782N	DIFFERENTIAL ASSEMBLY DIFFERENTIAL-NEW	NLA	Note (1)	2 pin differential drum brakes-rear
	FTC782E	DIFFERENTIAL ASSEMBLY DIFFERENTIAL-10 SPLINE SHAFT-EXCHANGE	1	Note (1)	Drum brakes-rear 2 pin differential 20L 21L
	FTC2750	DIFFERENTIAL ASSEMBLY DIFFERENTIAL-NEW-10 SPLINE SHAFT-4 BOLT FLANGE	1	Note (2)	2 pin differential drum brakes-rear
	FTC2750E	DIFFERENTIAL ASSEMBLY DIFFERENTIAL-EXCHANGE-10 SPLINE SHAFT	1	Note (2)	2 pin differential drum brakes-rear
1	FRC5690	• HOUSING ASSEMBLY DIFFERENTIAL/FINAL DRIVE WHEEL-WITH FILLER/LEVEL PLUG	1		Part of FTC782N, FTC2750, FTC2750E.
2	BH112101L	• • Bolt-M12 x 50	4		
1	FRC4112	• HOUSING ASSEMBLY DIFFERENTIAL/FINAL DRIVE WHEEL-LESS FILLER/LEVEL PLUG	1		
2	BH112101L	• • Bolt-M12 x 50	4		
4	FRC5204	• Ring-differential locking	NLA		Use FTC4210.
4	FTC4210	• Ring-differential locking	2		
5	FRC5661	• Tab-differential locking ring	2		
6	576159	• Pin-roll-spring tension	2		
7	NY606041L	• Nut-hexagonal head-nyloc-3/8-UNF	10		

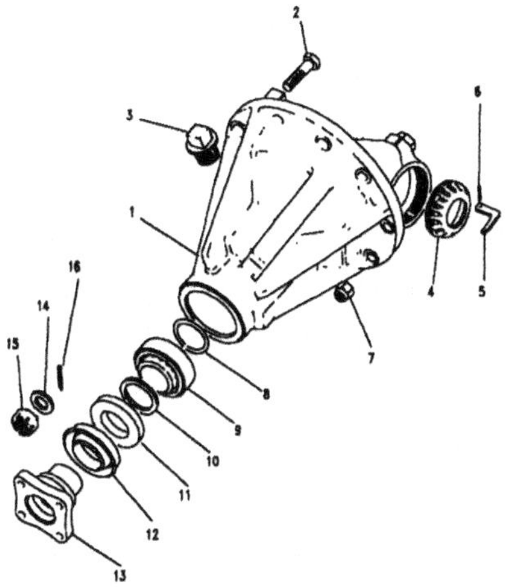

CHANGE POINTS:
(1) To (V) JA 917433
(2) From (V) JA 917434

Illus	Part Number	Description	Quantity	Change Point	Remarks
	FRC8611	Differential assembly differential	NLA		23S 4 pin differential drum brakes-rear
	FTC785	DIFFERENTIAL ASSEMBLY DIFFERENTIAL-NEW	NLA		Use FTC4663. 4 pin differential
	FTC785R	DIFFERENTIAL ASSEMBLY DIFFERENTIAL-RECONDITIONED	NLA		Use FTC4663E. 4 pin differential
1	FRC5690	• HOUSING ASSEMBLY DIFFERENTIAL/FINAL DRIVE WHEEL-WITH FILLER/LEVEL PLUG	1		
1	FRC4112	• HOUSING ASSEMBLY DIFFERENTIAL/FINAL DRIVE WHEEL-LESS FILLER/LEVEL PLUG	1		
2	BH112101L	• • Bolt-M12 x 50	4		
4	FRC5204	• Ring-differential locking	NLA		Use FTC4210.
4	FTC4210	• Ring-differential locking	2		
5	FRC5661	• Tab-differential locking ring	2		
6	576159	• Pin-roll-spring tension	2		
7	NY606041L	• Nut-hexagonal head-nyloc-3/8-UNF	10		

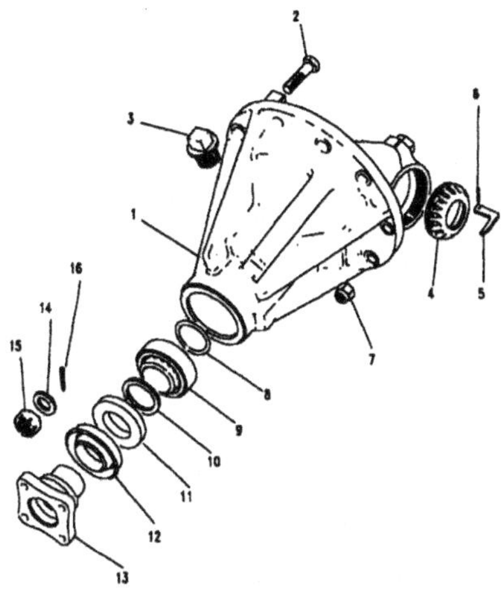

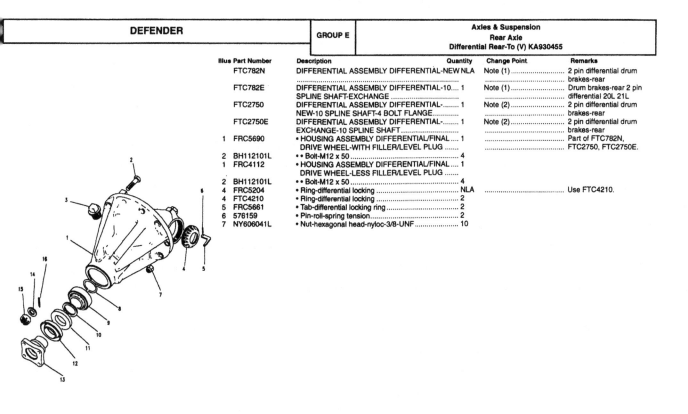

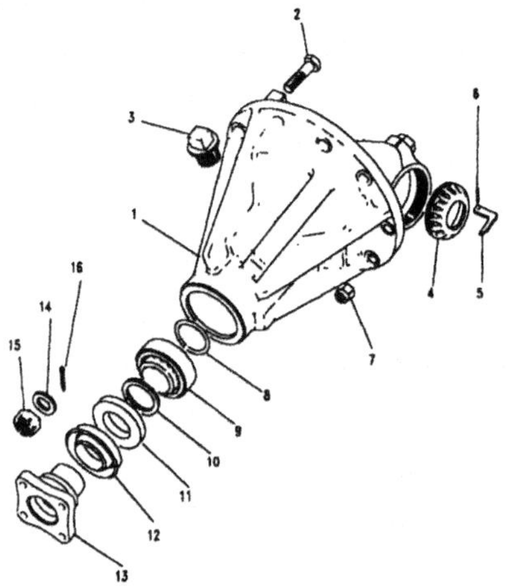

Illus	Part Number	Description	Quantity	Change Point	Remarks
1	FRC5690	HOUSING ASSEMBLY DIFFERENTIAL/FINAL DRIVE WHEEL-WITH FILLER/LEVEL PLUG	1	Note (1)	
1	FRC4112	HOUSING ASSEMBLY DIFFERENTIAL/FINAL DRIVE WHEEL-LESS FILLER/LEVEL PLUG	1	Note (2)	
2	BH112101L	• Bolt-M12 x 50	4		
3	608246	Plug-drain/filler level	1		
8	FRC1193	Shim-bearing differential-0.060"	NLA		Use 549252.
8	549252	Shim-0.060"-imperial	A/R		
8	FRC1195	Shim-bearing differential-0.062"	A/R		
8	FRC1197	Shim-bearing differential-0.064"	A/R		
8	FRC1199	Shim-bearing differential-0.066"	A/R		
8	FRC1201	Shim-bearing differential-0.068"	A/R		
8	FRC1203	Shim-bearing differential-0.070"	A/R		
8	539718	Shim-bearing differential-0.072"	A/R		
8	539720	Shim-bearing differential-0.074"	A/R		
8	539722	Shim-bearing differential-0.076"	A/R		
8	539724	Shim-bearing differential-0.080"	A/R		
9	539707	Bearing-taper roller-differential final drive pinion outer	1		
10	539745	Spacer-pinion bearing	1		
11	FRC4586	Seal-differential final drive pinion	1	Note (3)	
11	FRC8220	Seal-differential final drive pinion-front & rear	1	Note (4)	
12	236072	Mudshield-front & rear differential	1	Note (3)	
12	FRC8154	Mudshield-front & rear differential	1	Note (4)	
13	236632	Flange-driveshaft coupling differential-4 spline	1		Use on FRC5688, FRC8521 and FRC8611
13	FRC3002	Flange-driveshaft coupling differential-4 bolt flange	1		Use with FTC785 Use with FTC782N
14	90513454	Washer-plain	1		
15	3259	Nut-castle	1		
16	PS608101L	Pin-split	1		

CHANGE POINTS:
(1) To (A)42S 11257A
(2) From (A)42S 11258A
(3) To (A)22S 08283B
(4) From (A)22S 08284B

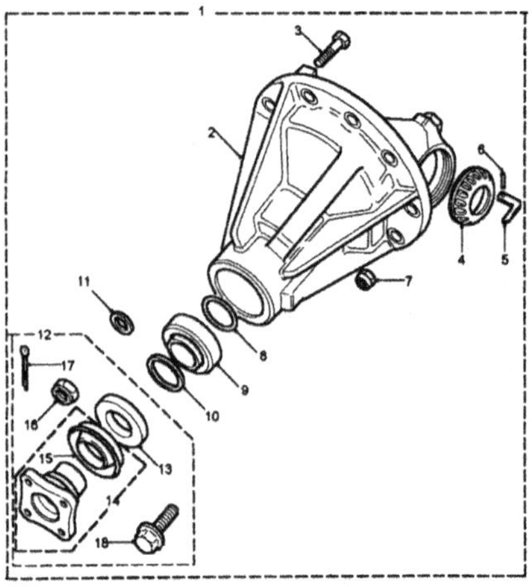

LE0044

Illus	Part Number	Description	Quantity	Change Point	Remarks
		2 PINION DIFFERENTIALS			
1	FTC3272	DIFFERENTIAL ASSEMBLY DIFFERENTIAL-NEW-24 SPLINE SHAFT-4 BOLT FLANGE	1	To (V) WA 159806	42S 2 pin differential
1	FTC3272E	DIFFERENTIAL ASSEMBLY DIFFERENTIAL-EXCHANGE-24 SPLINE SHAFT-4 BOLT FLANGE.	1	To (V) WA 159806	42S 2 pin differential
2	FRC5690	• HOUSING ASSEMBLY DIFFERENTIAL/FINAL DRIVE WHEEL-WITH FILLER/LEVEL PLUG	1		
3	BH112101L	• • Bolt-M12 x 50	4		
2	FRC4112	• HOUSING ASSEMBLY DIFFERENTIAL/FINAL DRIVE WHEEL-LESS FILLER/LEVEL PLUG	1		
3	BH112101L	• • Bolt-M12 x 50	4		
4	FRC5204	• Ring-differential locking	NLA		Use FTC4210.
4	FTC4210	• Ring-differential locking	2		
5	FRC5661	• Tab-differential locking ring	2		
6	576159	• Pin-roll-spring tension	2		
7	NY606041L	• Nut-hexagonal head-nyloc-3/8-UNF	10		
1	TBV100020	DIFFERENTIAL ASSEMBLY DIFFERENTIAL-24 SPLINE SHAFT-4 BOLT FLANGE-NEW	NLA	From (V) XA 159807	Use FTC5142 qty 1 Rover unable to supply differential together with spacers. with TYF101160 qty 2. 58S 59S 2 pin differential
1	FTC5142	• DIFFERENTIAL ASSEMBLY DIFFERENTIAL-24 SPLINE SHAFT-4 BOLT FLANGE-NEW	1		
2	FRC4112	• • HOUSING ASSEMBLY DIFFERENTIAL/FINAL DRIVE WHEEL-LESS FILLER/LEVEL PLUG	1		
3	BH112101L	• • • Bolt-M12 x 50	4		
4	FTC4210	• • Ring-differential locking	2		
6	576159	• • Pin-roll-spring tension	2		
	TYF101160	• Spacer	2		

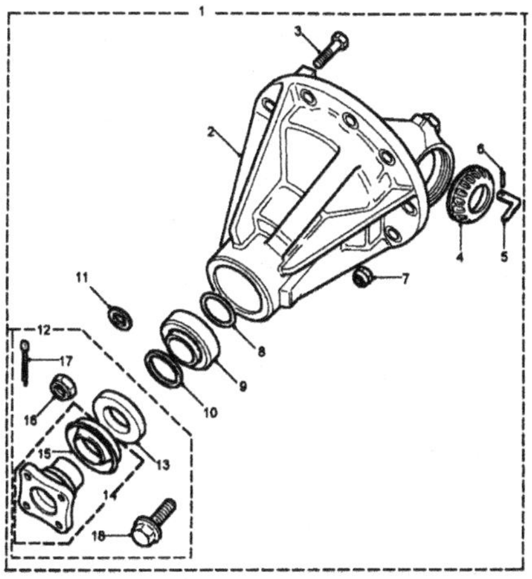

LE0044

Illus	Part Number	Description	Quantity	Change Point	Remarks
		4 PINION DIFFERENTIALS			
1	FTC785	DIFFERENTIAL ASSEMBLY DIFFERENTIAL-NEW	NLA		Use FTC4663. 44S 4 pin differential
1	FTC785R	DIFFERENTIAL ASSEMBLY DIFFERENTIAL-RECONDITIONED	NLA		Use FTC4663E. 4 pin differential
1	FTC4663	DIFFERENTIAL ASSEMBLY DIFFERENTIAL-NEW	NLA	To (V) WA 159806	Use TBB100980. 44S 4 pin differential From (v) XA159807 use FTC5142 strengthened 2 pin diff
1	FTC4663E	DIFFERENTIAL ASSEMBLY DIFFERENTIAL-EXCHANGE	1		44S 4 pin differential
1	TBB100980	DIFFERENTIAL ASSEMBLY DIFFERENTIAL-NEW-4 PIN	1		44S 4 pin differential
2	FRC5690	• HOUSING ASSEMBLY DIFFERENTIAL/FINAL DRIVE WHEEL-WITH FILLER/LEVEL PLUG	1		Part of FTC785, FTC785R, FTC4663, FTC4663E.
3	BH112101L	• • Bolt-M12 x 50	4		
2	FRC4112	• HOUSING ASSEMBLY DIFFERENTIAL/FINAL DRIVE WHEEL-LESS FILLER/LEVEL PLUG	1	From (A)42S 11258A	Part of FTC785, FTC785R.
3	BH112101L	• • Bolt-M12 x 50	4		
4	FRC5204	• Ring-differential locking	NLA	To (A)42S 11257A	Use FTC4210. Part of FTC785, FTC785R.
4	FTC4210	• Ring-differential locking	2	From (A)42S 11258A	Part of FTC785,
5	FRC5661	• Tab-differential locking ring	2	To (A)42S 11257A	FTC785R.
6	576159	• Pin-roll-spring tension	2		
7	NY606041L	• Nut-hexagonal head-nyloc-3/8-UNF	10		
2	FRC4112	• HOUSING ASSEMBLY DIFFERENTIAL/FINAL DRIVE WHEEL-LESS FILLER/LEVEL PLUG	1		Part of FTC4663, FTC4663E, TBB100980.
3	BH112101L	• • Bolt-M12 x 50	4		
4	FRC5204	• Ring-differential locking	NLA		Use FTC4210. Part of FTC4663, FTC4663E.
4	FTC4210	• Ring-differential locking	2		Part of FTC4663, FTC4663E, TBB100980.
5	FRC5661	• Tab-differential locking ring	2		Part of FTC4663, FTC4663E.
	TYU100110	• Dowel	4		Part of TBB100980.

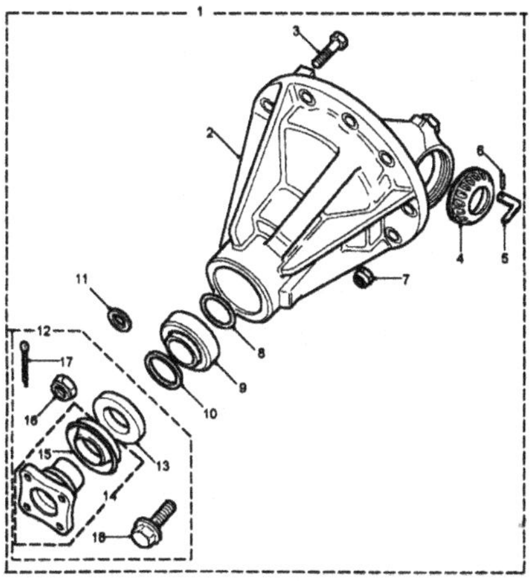

LE0044

Illus	Part Number	Description	Quantity	Change Point	Remarks
8	FTC3869	Shim-bearing differential-2.155mm	A/R	Note (1)	
8	FTC3871	Shim-bearing differential-2.105mm	A/R		
8	FTC3873	Shim-bearing differential-2.055mm	A/R		
8	FTC3875	Shim-bearing differential-2.005mm	A/R		
8	FTC3877	Shim-bearing differential-1.955mm	A/R		
8	FTC3879	Shim-bearing differential-1.905mm	A/R		
8	FTC3881	Shim-bearing differential-1.855mm	A/R		
8	FTC3883	Shim-bearing differential-1.805mm	A/R		
8	FTC3885	Shim-bearing differential-1.755mm	A/R		
8	FTC3887	Shim-bearing differential-1.705mm	A/R		
8	FTC3889	Shim-bearing differential-1.655mm	A/R		
8	FTC3891	Shim-bearing differential-1.605mm	A/R		
8	FTC3893	Shim-bearing differential-1.555mm	A/R		
8	FTC3895	Shim-bearing differential-1.505mm	A/R		
8	TYS101040	Shim-bearing differential-2.155mm	A/R	Note (2)	
8	TYS101060	Shim-bearing differential-2.105mm	A/R		
8	TYS101080	Shim-bearing differential-2.055mm	A/R		
8	TYS101100	Shim-bearing differential-2.005mm	A/R		
8	TYS101120	Shim-bearing differential-1.955mm	A/R		
8	TYS101140	Shim-bearing differential-1.905mm	A/R		
8	TYS101160	Shim-bearing differential-1.855mm	A/R		
8	TYS101180	Shim-bearing differential-1.805mm	A/R		
8	TYS101200	Shim-bearing differential-1.755mm	A/R		
8	TYS101220	Shim-bearing differential-1.705mm	A/R		
8	TYS101240	Shim-bearing differential-1.655mm	A/R		
8	TYS101260	Shim-bearing differential-1.605mm	A/R		
8	TYS101280	Shim-bearing differential-1.555mm	A/R		
8	TYS101300	Shim-bearing differential-1.505mm	A/R		

CHANGE POINTS:
(1) To (V) WA 140850
(2) From (V) WA 140851

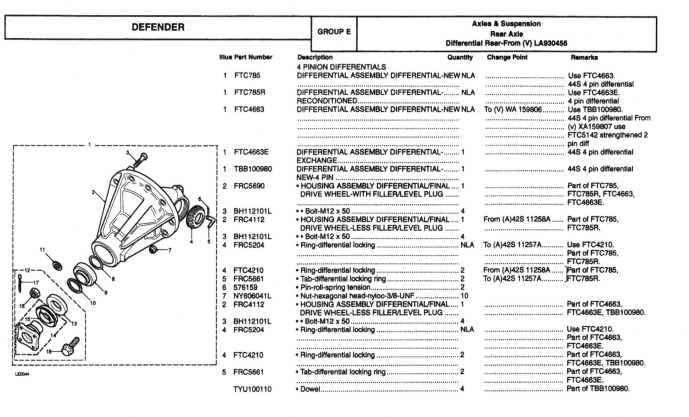

Differential Rear-From (V) LA930456

Illus	Part Number	Description	Quantity	Change Point	Remarks
9	539707	Bearing-taper roller-differential final drive pinion outer	A/R		
10	539745	Spacer-pinion bearing	1		
13	FRC8220	Seal-differential final drive pinion-front & rear	1	Note (1)	
15	FRC8154	Mudshield-front & rear differential	1	Note (1)	
14	FRC3002	Flange-driveshaft coupling differential-4 bolt flange	1	Note (1)	
12	STC3722	FLANGE & MUDSHIELD-FRONT & REAR AXLE	1	Note (2)	
13	FTC5258	• Seal-front & rear	1	Note (2)	
14	FTC5322	• FLANGE-DRIVESHAFT COUPLING DIFFERENTIAL	1	Note (2)	
15	FTC5317	• • Mudshield-front & rear differential	1		
16	NY116041L	• Nut-hexagonal head-nyloc-M16	1	Note (3)	
17	PS608101L	• Pin-split	1		
18	FS112301P	• Screw-flanged head-M12 x 30	1	Note (4)	
11	FTC5413	• Washer-plain	1		

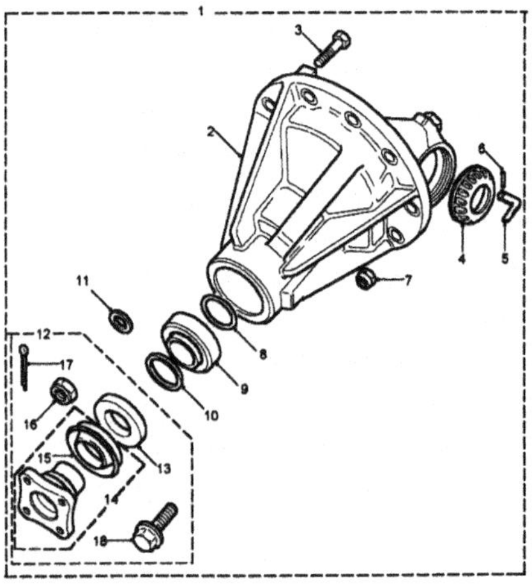

LE0044

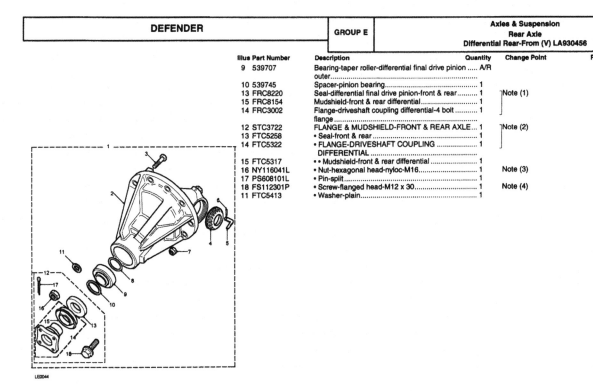

CHANGE POINTS:
(1) To (V) VA 102732
(2) From (V) VA 102733
(3) To (A)42S 41562
(4) From (A)42S 41563

Crownwheel & Pinion-2 Pinion-To (V) KA930455

Illus	Part Number	Description	Quantity	Change Point	Remarks
1	FRC2933	Case differential-10 spline shaft	1		4 Cylinder drum brakes-rear
2	STC851	KIT-DIFFERENTIAL GEARS-10 SPLINE SHAFT	NLA		Use STC1768. 4 Cylinder drum brakes-rear
2	STC1768	KIT-DIFFERENTIAL GEARS-10 SPLINE SHAFT	1		4 Cylinder drum brakes-rear
3	599945	• Cross shaft differential	1		
4	CCN110L	• Circlip	2		
5	FTC3620	Crownwheel and pinion assembly	1		4 Cylinder drum brakes-rear
6	593692	Bolt	NLA		Use FTC3586.
6	FTC3586	Bolt-3/8UNF	10		
7	593693	Washer-plain	10		
8	RTC2726	Bearing-taper roller differential	2		4 Cylinder drum brakes-rear
9	539706	Bearing-taper roller-differential final drive pinion inner	1		

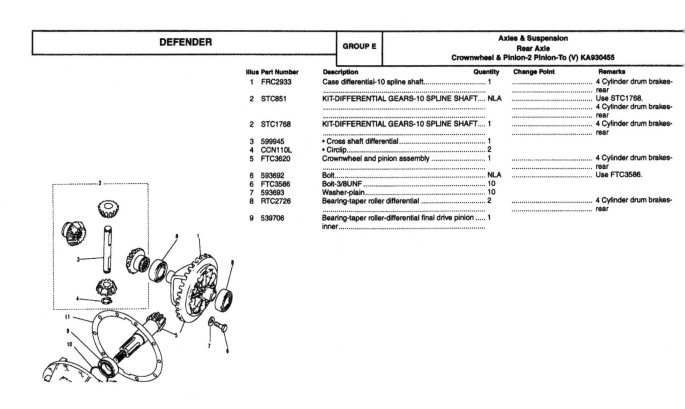

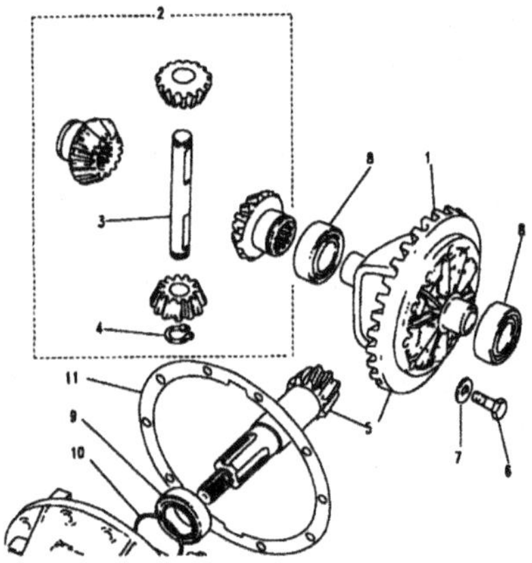

DEFENDER	GROUP E	Axles & Suspension Rear Axle Crownwheel & Pinion-2 Pinion-To (V) KA930455

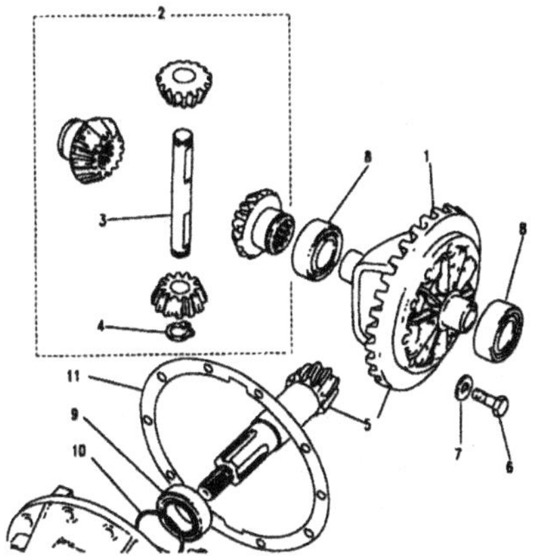

Illus	Part Number	Description	Quantity	Change Point	Remarks
		SHIM			
10	549230	differential final drive pinion-0.038"-imperial	A/R		22S
10	549232	differential final drive pinion-0.04"-imperial	A/R		
10	549234	differential final drive pinion-0.042"-imperial	A/R		
10	549236	differential final drive pinion-0.044"-imperial	A/R		
10	549238	differential final drive pinion-0.046"-imperial	A/R		
10	549240	differential final drive pinion-0.048"-imperial	A/R		
10	549242	differential final drive pinion-0.050"-imperial	A/R		
10	549244	differential final drive pinion-0.052"-imperial	A/R		
10	549246	differential final drive pinion-0.054"-imperial	A/R		
10	549248	differential final drive pinion-0.056"-imperial	A/R		
10	549250	differential final drive pinion-0.058"-imperial	A/R		
10	549252	differential final drive pinion-0.060"-imperial	A/R		
10	576236	differential final drive pinion-0.062"-imperial	A/R		
10	576237	differential final drive pinion-0.063"-imperial	A/R		
10	576238	differential final drive pinion-0.064"-imperial	A/R		
10	576239	differential final drive pinion-0.065"-imperial	A/R		
11	7316	Gasket-differential housing to axle case	1		

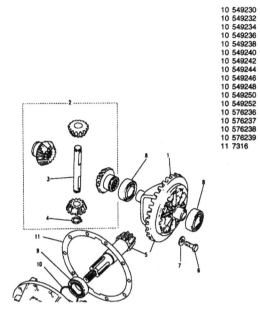

DEFENDER	GROUP E	Axles & Suspension Rear Axle Crownwheel & Pinion-2 Pinion-From (V) LA930456

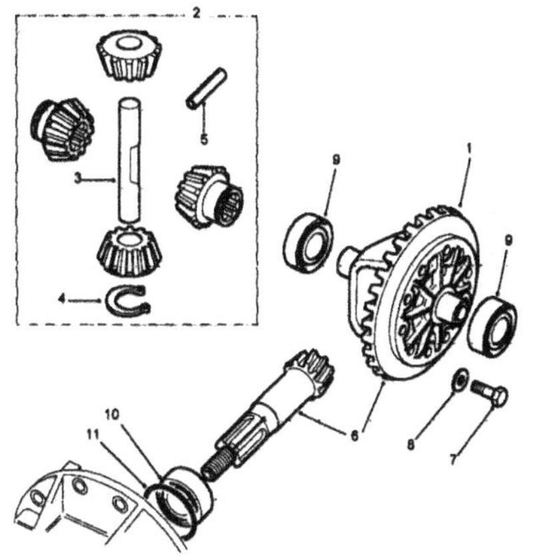

LE0043

Illus	Part Number	Description	Quantity	Change Point	Remarks
1	FTC3269	Case differential-24 spline shaft	1		42S
1	FTC5399	Case differential	1		58S 59S
2	STC1846	KIT-DIFFERENTIAL GEARS-24 SPLINE SHAFT	1		42S
3	599945	• Cross shaft differential	1		
4	CCN110L	• Circlip	2		
2	TCI100060	KIT-DIFFERENTIAL GEARS-24 SPLINE SHAFT	1		58S 59S
3	FTC5401	• Cross shaft differential	1		
5	FTC5402	• Pin-roll	1		
6	FTC3620	Crownwheel and pinion assembly	1	Note (1)	
6	TBH100040	Crownwheel and pinion assembly	1	Note (2)	
7	FTC3586	Bolt-3/8UNF	10		42S
7	FTC5150	Bolt-3/8UNF	10		58S 59S
8	593693	Washer-plain	10		42S
9	RTC3095	Bearing-taper roller differential	2	Note (3)	42S
10	539706	Bearing-taper roller-differential final drive pinion inner	1		42S
		SHIM			
11	FTC3853	differential final drive pinion-1.548mm-metric	A/R	Note (4)	
11	FTC3855	differential final drive pinion-1.498mm-metric	A/R	Note (4)	
11	FTC3857	differential final drive pinion-1.448mm-metric	A/R	Note (4)	
11	FTC3859	differential final drive pinion-1.398mm-metric	A/R	Note (4)	
11	FTC3861	differential final drive pinion-1.348mm-metric	A/R	Note (4)	
11	FTC3863	differential final drive pinion-1.298mm-metric	A/R	Note (4)	
11	FTC3865	differential final drive pinion-1.248mm-metric	A/R	Note (4)	
11	FTC3867	differential final drive pinion-1.198mm-metric	A/R	Note (4)	
11	TYS100870	differential final drive pinion-2.255mm-metric	A/R	Note (5)	
11	TYS100900	differential final drive pinion-2.210mm-metric	A/R	Note (5)	
11	TYS100940	differential final drive pinion-2.150mm-metric	A/R	Note (5)	
11	TYS100970	differential final drive pinion-2.105mm-metric	A/R	Note (5)	
11	TYS101000	differential final drive pinion-2.060mm-metric	A/R	Note (5)	

CHANGE POINTS:
(1) To (A)42S 41562
(2) From (A)42S 41563
(3) From (V) LA 930456
(4) From (A)42S 04616A
(5) From (A) Dec 1997

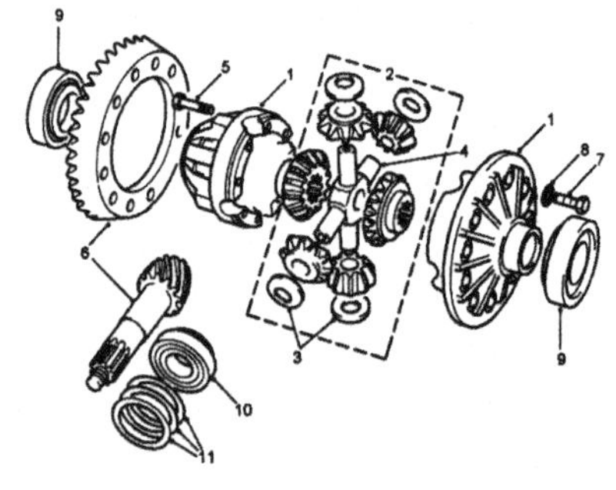

LE0042

Illus	Part Number	Description	Quantity	Change Point	Remarks
1	FRC8187	Case-differential-rear	1		23S 44S Use with
2	RTC4487	KIT-DIFFERENTIAL GEARS	1		FTC785
	FRC8190	• Gear differential	2		
	599944	• Gear differential	4		
3	FRC9979	• Washer-thrust-pinion differential-rear	4		
	FRC8667	• Washer-thrust-gear differential	2		
4	FRC8189	• Shaft-pinion differential	2		
5	FRC8188	Bolt differential	8		23S 44S Use with
6	FTC3620	Crownwheel and pinion assembly	1		FTC785
1	FTC4540	Case-differential-rear	1		44S Use with FTC4663
2	STC1845	KIT-DIFFERENTIAL GEARS	1	Note (1)	Use with FTC4663
4	FTC3429	• Shaft-pinion differential-rear	2		
3	FRC9979	• Washer-thrust-pinion differential-rear	4		
5	BX108130	Bolt differential-M8 x 65	8		44S Use with FTC4663
6	FTC4234	Crownwheel and pinion assembly	1	Note (1)	Use with FTC4663
6	TBH100050	Crownwheel and pinion assembly	1	Note (2)	
7	593692	Bolt	NLA		Use FTC3586.
					23S 44S
8	593693	Washer-plain	10		23S 44S
9	RTC3095	Bearing-taper roller differential-crownwheel	2		
10	539706	Bearing-taper roller-differential final drive pinion inner	1		

CHANGE POINTS:
(1) From (A)44S 00001 To (A)44S 00421A nut securing flange
(2) From (A)44S 00442A bolt securing flange

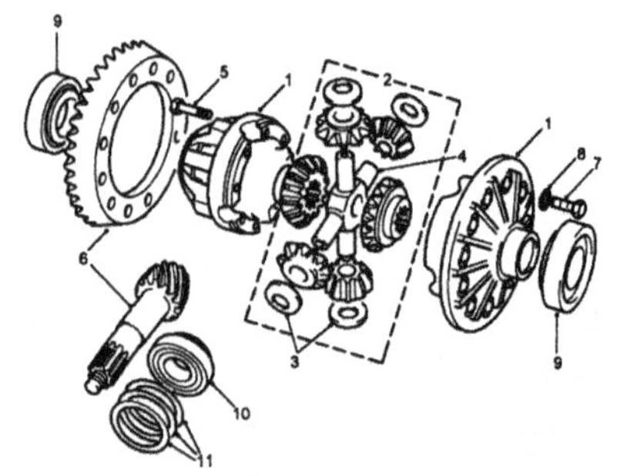

LE0042

Illus	Part Number	Description	Quantity	Change Point	Remarks
11	549230	Shim-0.038"-imperial	A/R	Note (1)	
11	549232	Shim-0.04"-imperial	A/R		
11	549234	Shim-0.042"-imperial	A/R		
11	549236	Shim-0.044"-imperial	A/R		
11	549238	Shim-0.046"-imperial	A/R		
11	549240	Shim-0.048"-imperial	A/R		
11	549242	Shim-0.050"-imperial	A/R		
11	549244	Shim-0.052"-imperial	A/R		
11	549246	Shim-0.054"-imperial	A/R		
11	549248	Shim-0.056"-imperial	A/R		
11	549250	Shim-0.058"-imperial	A/R		
11	549252	Shim-0.060"-imperial	A/R		
11	576236	Shim-0.062"-imperial	A/R		
11	576237	Shim-0.063"-imperial	A/R		
11	576238	Shim-0.064"-imperial	A/R		
11	576239	Shim-0.065"-imperial	A/R	Note (1)	
11	FTC3853	Shim-differential final drive pinion-1.548mm-metric.	A/R	Note (2)	
11	FTC3855	Shim-differential final drive pinion-1.498mm-metric.	A/R		
11	FTC3857	Shim-differential final drive pinion-1.448mm-metric.	A/R		
11	FTC3859	Shim-differential final drive pinion-1.398mm-metric.	A/R		
11	FTC3861	Shim-differential final drive pinion-1.348mm-metric.	A/R		
11	FTC3863	Shim-differential final drive pinion-1.298mm-metric.	A/R		
11	FTC3865	Shim-differential final drive pinion-1.248mm-metric.	A/R		
11	FTC3867	Shim-differential final drive pinion-1.198mm-metric.	A/R		
11	TYS100870	Shim-differential final drive pinion-2.255mm-metric.	A/R	Note (3)	
11	TYS100900	Shim-differential final drive pinion-2.210mm-metric.	A/R		
11	TYS100940	Shim-differential final drive pinion-2.150mm-metric.	A/R		
11	TYS100970	Shim-differential final drive pinion-2.105mm-metric.	A/R		
11	TYS101000	Shim-differential final drive pinion-2.060mm-metric.	A/R		

CHANGE POINTS:
(1) To (A)44S 00029A
(2) From (A)44S 00030A
(3) From (A) Dec 1997

Crownwheel & Pinion-4 Pinion-110/130

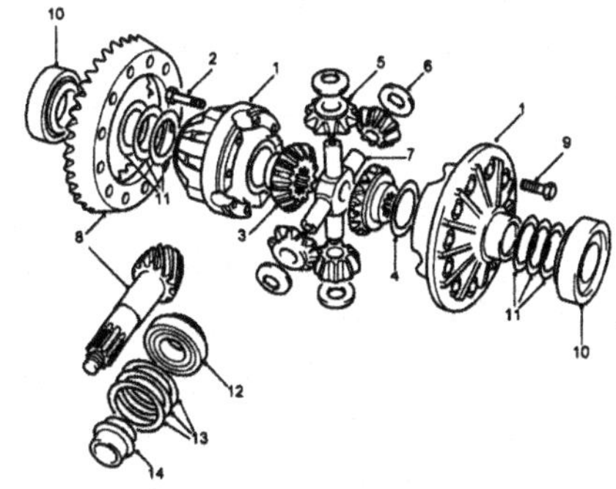

AHEXEG4A

Illus	Part Number	Description	Quantity	Change Point	Remarks
1	AEU1489	Case-differential-rear	1		
2	607165	Bolt differential	8		
	RTC4488	KIT-DIFFERENTIAL GEARS	1		
3	607166	• Gear differential	NLA		Now only available as part of kit RTC4488.
4	607169	• Washer-thrust-gear differential	2		
5	607167	• Gear differential	NLA		Now only available as part of kit RTC4488.
6	607168	• Washer-thrust-pinion differential-rear	4		
7	90607170	Shaft-pinion differential	1		
8	AEU1488	Crownwheel and pinion assembly	1		
9	RTC773	Bolt	12		
10	607187	Bearing-taper roller differential-crownwheel	2		
11	607188	Shim-man trans differential bearing-0.003"	2		
11	607189	Shim-man trans differential bearing-0.005"	2		
11	607190	Shim-man trans differential bearing-0.010"	2		
11	607191	Shim-man trans differential bearing-0.030"	2		
12	607180	Bearing-taper roller-differential final drive pinion inner	1		
13	607177	Shim-differential final drive pinion-0.003"-imperial	2		
13	607178	Shim-differential final drive pinion-0.005"-imperial	2		
13	607179	Shim-differential final drive pinion-0.010"-imperial	2		
14	607197	Spacer-collapsible	1		

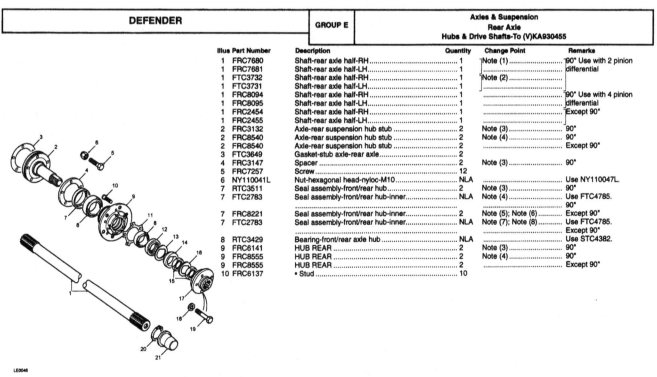

Hubs & Drive Shafts-To (V)KA930455

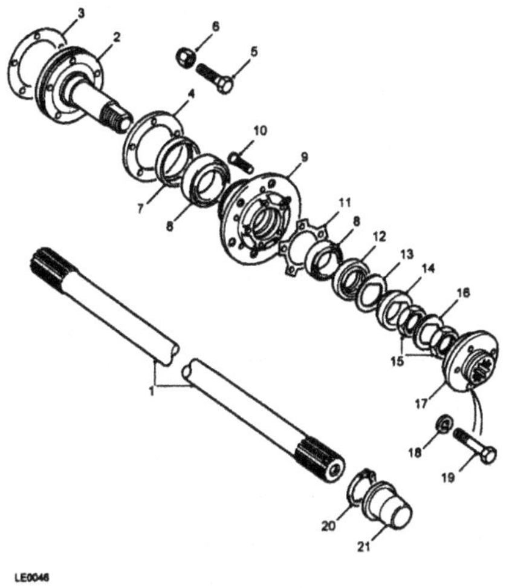

LE0046

Illus	Part Number	Description	Quantity	Change Point	Remarks
1	FRC7680	Shaft-rear axle half-RH	1	Note (1)	90° Use with 2 pinion differential
1	FRC7681	Shaft-rear axle half-LH	1		
1	FTC3732	Shaft-rear axle half-RH	1	Note (2)	
1	FTC3731	Shaft-rear axle half-LH	1		
1	FRC8094	Shaft-rear axle half-RH	1		90° Use with 4 pinion differential
1	FRC8095	Shaft-rear axle half-LH	1		
1	FRC2454	Shaft-rear axle half-RH	1		Except 90°
1	FRC2455	Shaft-rear axle half-LH	1		
2	FRC3132	Axle-rear suspension hub stub	2	Note (3)	90°
2	FRC8540	Axle-rear suspension hub stub	2	Note (4)	90°
2	FRC8540	Axle-rear suspension hub stub	2		Except 90°
3	FTC3649	Gasket-stub axle-rear axle	2		
4	FRC3147	Spacer	2	Note (3)	90°
5	FRC7257	Screw	12		
6	NY110041L	Nut-hexagonal head-nyloc-M10	NLA		Use NY110047L.
7	RTC3511	Seal assembly-front/rear hub	2	Note (3)	90°
7	FTC2783	Seal assembly-front/rear hub-inner	NLA	Note (4)	Use FTC4785. 90°
7	FRC8221	Seal assembly-front/rear hub-inner	2	Note (5); Note (6)	Except 90°
7	FTC2783	Seal assembly-front/rear hub-inner	NLA	Note (7); Note (8)	Use FTC4785. Except 90°
8	RTC3429	Bearing-front/rear axle hub	NLA		Use STC4382.
9	FRC6141	HUB REAR	2	Note (3)	90°
9	FRC8555	HUB REAR	2	Note (4)	90°
9	FRC8555	HUB REAR	2		Except 90°
10	FRC6137	• Stud	10		

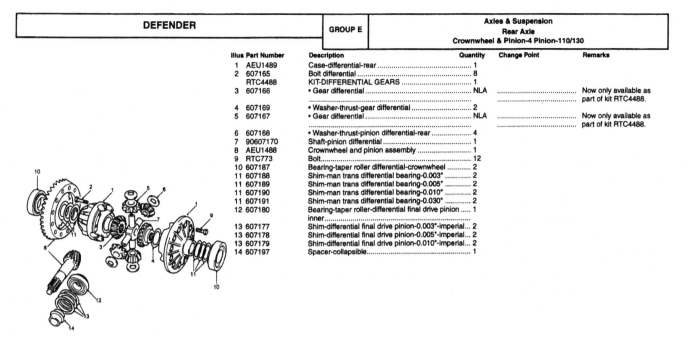

CHANGE POINTS:
- (1) To (A)22S 64620E
- (2) From (A)22S 64621E
- (3) To (A)22S 08283B
- (4) From (A)22S 08284B
- (5) To (A)21S 10027C
- (6) To (A)24S 00521A
- (7) From (A)21S 10028C
- (8) From (A)24S 00522A

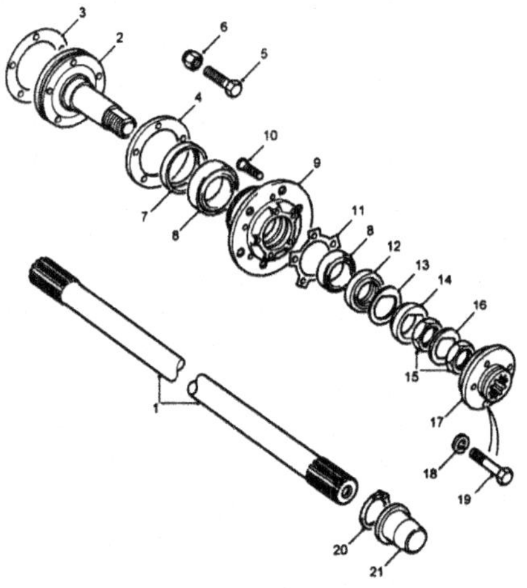

LE0046

Illus	Part Number	Description	Quantity	Change Point	Remarks
11	FRC3988	Gasket-axle shaft drive member	2		
12	FRC8222	Seal assembly-front/rear hub-outer	2		Except 90"
13	217352	Washer-front & rear hub nut tab	2	Note (1)	90"
14	FRC8227	Spacer	2	Note (2)	90"
14	FRC8227	Spacer	2		Except 90"
15	FRC8700	Locknut	4		
16	217353	Washer-lock	2	Note (1)	90"
16	FRC8002	Washer-lock	2	Note (2)	90"
16	FRC8002	Washer-lock	2		Except 90"
17	FRC5806	Flange-driving shaft joint	2		
18	WL110001L	Washer-M10	10		
19	FC110107L	Bolt-flanged head-M10 x 50	NLA		Use RYG101010L.
20	549473	Circlip-axle shaft to hub driving member	2		
21	FRC4377	Cap-driveshaft coupling bolt locking-polyurethane	2	Note (1)	90"
21	FTC943	Cap-driveshaft coupling bolt locking-without logo	2	Note (2)	90"
21	FRC4377	Cap-driveshaft coupling bolt locking-polyurethane	2		Except 90"

CHANGE POINTS:
(1) To (A)22S 08283B
(2) From (A)22S 08284B

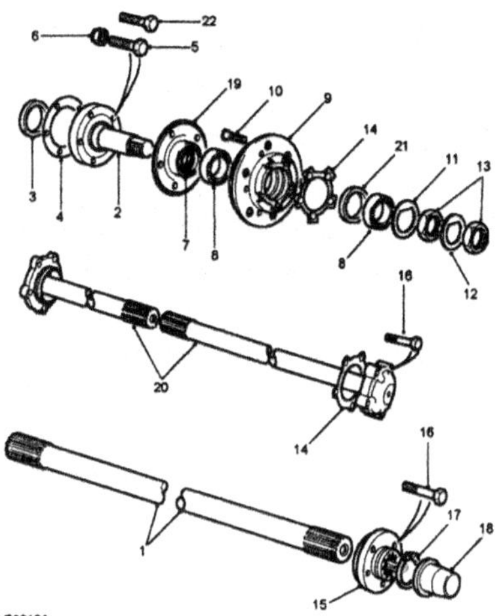

LE0019A

Illus	Part Number	Description	Quantity	Change Point	Remarks
20	FTC3270	Shaft-rear axle half-RH-24 spline shaft	1		90"
20	FTC3271	Shaft-rear axle half-LH-24 spline shaft	1		90"
1	FTC1724	Shaft-rear axle half-RH	1		Except 90"
1	FTC1725	Shaft-rear axle half-LH	1		Except 90"
2	FTC3188	AXLE-REAR SUSPENSION HUB STUB	2		42S 44S 58S 59S 90"
2	FTC1740	AXLE-REAR SUSPENSION HUB STUB	2		38S 39S except 90"
2	FTC3188	AXLE-REAR SUSPENSION HUB STUB	2		60S 61S 62S 63S except 90"
3	FTC5268	• Seal-stub axle-inner	1		
4	FTC3648	Gasket-stub axle-rear axle-asbestos free	2		90"
4	FTC3649	Gasket-stub axle-rear axle	2		Except 90"
4	FTC3650	Gasket-stub axle-asbestos free	2	Note (1)	Antilock Brakes
5	SX110251M	Screw-M10 x 25-hexagonal head	12		90" Alternatives
22	BX110071M	Bolt-use if SX110251 is too short-hexagonal head-M10 x 35	4		90" Alternatives
22	BX110111L	Bolt-M10 x 55-hexagonal head	8		110"
5	SX110301	Screw-M10 x 30-hexagonal head	4		110"
22	BX110071M	Bolt-use if SX110301 is too short-hexagonal head-M10 x 35	4		Alternatives 110"
6	NY110047L	Nut-flange-nyloc-M10	4		Except 90"
7	FTC4785	Seal assembly-front/rear hub-inner	2		
8	STC4382	Bearing-front/rear axle hub	4		

CHANGE POINTS:
(1) From (V) XA 159807

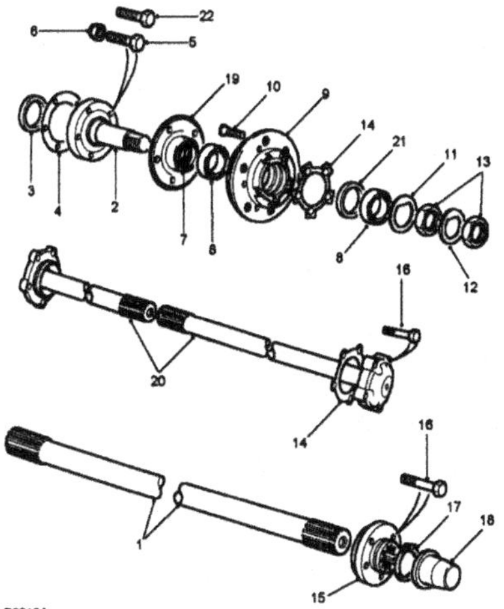

LE0019A

Illus	Part Number	Description	Quantity	Change Point	Remarks
9	FTC942	HUB ASSEMBLY-FRONT & REAR	2	To (V) WA 159806	
10	FRC5926	• Stud	10		
9	RUB101740	HUB ASSEMBLY-FRONT & REAR	2	From (V) XA 159807	
10	FRC5926	• Stud	5		
11	FTC3185	Washer-front & rear hub nut tab	2	To (V) TA 996892	
11	FTC5241	Washer-front & rear hub nut tab	2	From (V) TA 996893	
12	FTC3179	Washer-lock-outer	2	To (V) WA 159806	
13	FRC8700	Locknut	4	To (V) WA 159806	
13	RFD100000	Locknut	2	From (V) XA 159807	
14	571752	Gasket-axle shaft drive member	2		
15	FTC859	Flange-driving shaft joint	2		Except 90"
16	BX110095M	Bolt-M10 x 45	10		
17	549473	Circlip-axle shaft to hub driving member	2		Except 90"
18	FTC943	Cap-driveshaft coupling bolt locking-without logo	2	To (V) VA 110615	Except 90"
18	FTC5414	Cap-driveshaft coupling bolt locking-with Land Rover logo	2	From (V) VA 110616	Except 90"
19	FRC2310	Plate-front & rear stub axle locking	2		
21	TOF100000	Spacer-15.5mm-Purple	A/R	From (V) XA 159807	
21	TOF100010	Spacer-15.4mm-Yellow.	A/R		
21	TOF100020	Spacer-15.3mm-Red	A/R		
21	TOF100030	Spacer-15.2mm-Blue.	A/R		
21	TOF100040	Spacer-15.1mm-Green	A/R		
21	TOF100050	Spacer-15.0mm-Black	A/R		
21	TOF100060	Spacer-14.9mm-White.	A/R		

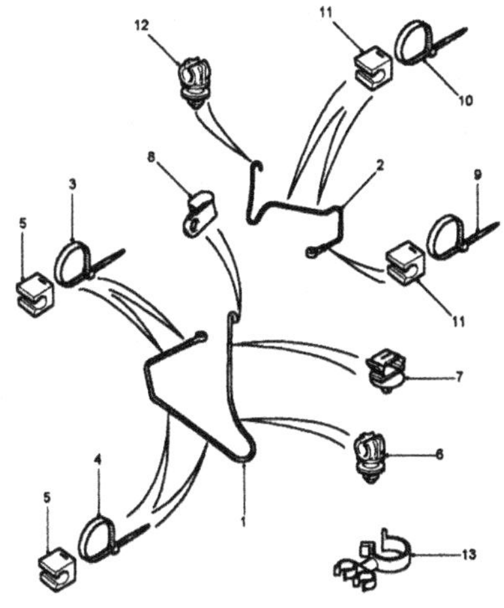

LE0064

Illus	Part Number	Description	Quantity	Change Point	Remarks
1	FTC2175	PIPE-FRONT AXLE BREATHER	1		
2	FTC2176	PIPE-REAR AXLE BREATHER	1		
1	FRC4718	PIPE-FRONT AXLE BREATHER	1	Note (1)	Drum brakes-rear
1	FTC2177	PIPE-FRONT AXLE BREATHER	1	Note (2)	Drum brakes-rear
2	FTC2178	PIPE-REAR AXLE BREATHER	1	Note (2)	Drum brakes-rear
	595478	• Bolt-banjo	1		
	232039	• Washer-sealing-axle breather hose banjo	2		Part of FTC2175, FTC2176, FTC2177.
	232039	• Washer-sealing	1		Part of FRC4718, FTC2178.
2	FRC4719	Pipe-rear axle breather	1	Note (1)	Drum brakes-rear
3	594594	Tie-cable-front breather-White.-4.6 x 385mm-inside serated	2		
4	568680	Tie-cable-front breather-4.8 x 270mm-inside serated	2		
5	NRC9246	Clip-pipe-front breather	4		
6	79123	Clip-pipe-front breather-single	1		
7	AFU1090L	Clip-cable-8mm hole	1		4 Cylinder
8	BAU1689	Clip-p-front breather-5/16"	1		V8
8	ATU1017L	Clip-p-rear breather	1	Note (3)	
9	79004	Screw-rear breather	1		
10	568680	Tie-cable-rear breather-4.8 x 270mm-inside serated	2		
11	NRC9246	Clip-pipe-rear breather	2		
12	79123	Clip-pipe-rear breather-single	1		
13	FTC5409	Clip-pipe	2		Td5

CHANGE POINTS:
(1) To (V) HA 473072
(2) From (V) HA 473073
(3) To (V) KA 930455

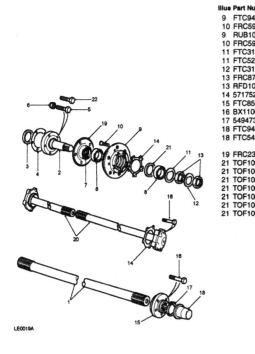

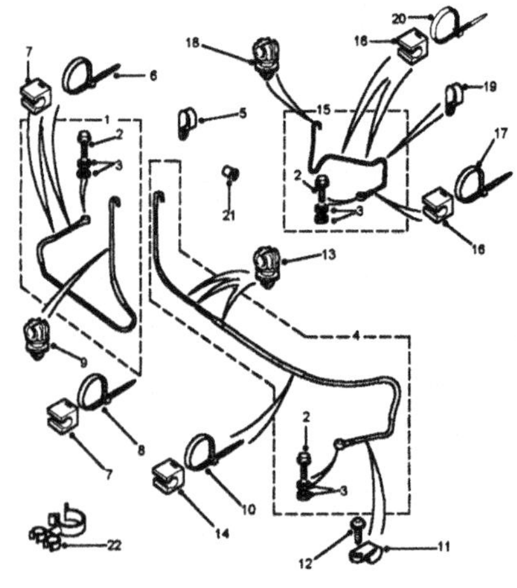

LE0011B

Illus	Part Number	Description	Quantity	Change Point	Remarks
1	FTC2177	PIPE-FRONT AXLE BREATHER	1	Note (1)	
2	595478	• Bolt-banjo	1		
3	232039	• Washer-sealing	2		
1	TAP100010	Pipe-front axle breather	1	Note (2)	Normal duty suspension
1	TAP100020	Pipe-front axle breather	1	Note (2)	Heavy duty suspension
15	FTC2178	PIPE-REAR AXLE BREATHER	1	Note (3)	Except 90"
15	FTC3904	PIPE-REAR AXLE BREATHER	1	Note (4)	Except 90"
4	FTC2179	PIPE-REAR AXLE BREATHER	1	Note (5)	90"
2	595478	• Bolt-banjo	1		
3	232039	• Washer-sealing	2		
4	TVP100010	Pipe-rear axle breather	1	Note (2)	Normal duty suspension
4	TVP100030	Pipe-rear axle breather	1		Heavy duty suspension
		FIXINGS - FRONT BREATHER			
5	622324	Clip-pipe-front breather	1		
6	594594	Tie-cable-front breather-White.-4.6 x 385mm-inside serated	2		
7	NRC9246	Clip-pipe-front breather	4		
8	568680	Tie-cable-front breather-4.8 x 270mm-inside serated	2		
9	79123	Clip-pipe-front breather-single	1		
		FIXINGS - REAR BREATHER			
10	568680	Tie-cable-rear breather-4.8 x 270mm-inside serated	2		Except 90"
11	ATU1017L	Clip-p-rear breather	1		
12	79004	Screw-rear breather	1		
13	79123	Clip-pipe-rear breather-single	3		
14	NRC9246	Clip-pipe-rear breather	2		
16	NRC9246	Clip-pipe	3		90"
17	568680	Tie-cable-4.8 x 270mm-inside serated	2		
18	79123	Clip-pipe-single	2		
19	622324	Clip-pipe	1		
20	594594	Tie-cable-White.-4.6 x 385mm-inside serated	1		
21	FTC5085	Adaptor	1	Note (2)	
22	FTC5409	Clip-pipe	2		Td5

CHANGE POINTS:
(1) From (V) LA 930456 To (V) WA 159806
(2) From (V) XA 159807
(3) To (V) LA 937639
(4) From (V) LA 937640
(5) From (V) LA 930456

Illus	Part Number	Description	Quantity	Change Point	Remarks
1	RTC3826	KIT-GAITER-OUTER JOINT DRIVESHAFT	1		
2	RTC3519	• Clip-hose	2		

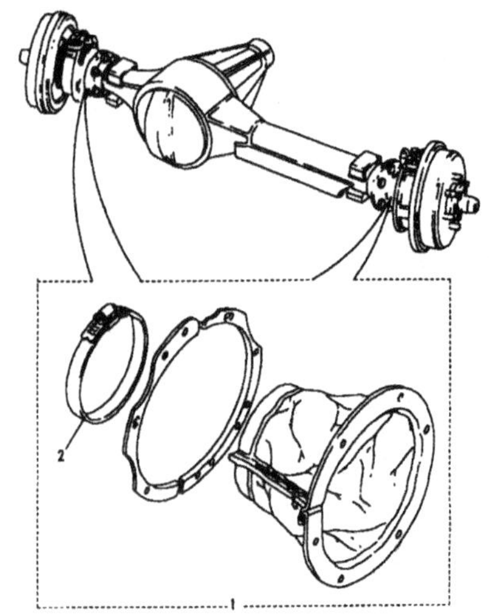

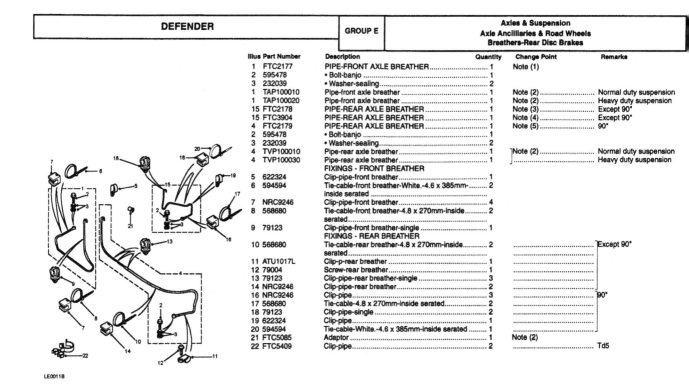

Illus	Part Number	Description	Quantity	Change Point	Remarks
		WHEEL-STEEL ROAD			
1	NRC7578PM	5.5F x 16-riveted-primed-tubed	5	To (V) TA 792779	
1	ANR4636PM	5.5F x 16-welded-primed-tubed	5	From (V) TA 792780	
1	ANR1534PM	6.5L x 16-riveted-primed-tubed	5	To (V) TA 999222	Heavy duty suspension
2	ANR5593PM	6.5J x 16-welded-primed-tubed	5	From (V) VA 999223	Heavy duty suspension
2	ANR4583PM	6.5J x 16-welded-primed-tubeless	5	From (V) VA 999223	Heavy duty suspension
3	NTC4135PM	6.0J x 16-riveted-primed	NLA	To (V) TA 792779	Use ANR4635PM.
3	ANR4635PM	6.0J x 16-welded-primed	5	From (V) TA 792780	
4	NTC5193MUE	7.0 X 16-5 spoke-Quicksilver	5		
		WHEEL-ALLOY ROAD			
5	ANR1689MNH	7.0 X 16-Tornado-Silver Sparkle	5	To (V) TA 998909	90" Note (1)
5	ANR5307MNH	7.0 X 16-Tornado-Silver Sparkle	5	From (V) TA 998910	90" Note (1)
5	STC60715	7.0 X 16-Tornado-Atlantic Green.	5		90" Heritage
5	STC60717	7.0 X 16-Tornado-Bronze Green	5		90" Heritage
5	ANR5307RJQ	7.0 X 16-Tornado-Arken Grey Nave/Silver Sparkle Rim	5		90" 50 LE UK
6	RTC9526	7.0 X 16-Styled-Quicksilver	5		90" Note (1)
6	RTC9526POL	7.0 X 16-Styled-Bright-polished	5		90" Note (1)
7	NTC9976MUE	7.0 X 16-Castor-Quicksilver	5		90" Note (1)
7	NTC9976MNH	7.0 X 16-Castor-Silver Sparkle	5		90" Note (1)
8	RRC110870MNH	7.0 X 16-5 spoke-Silver Sparkle	5		90" Note (1)
8	RRC110870MNH	7.0 X 16-5 spoke-Silver Sparkle	5		90" 50 LE Europe Japan
8	RRC110870MNH	7.0 X 16-5 spoke-Silver Sparkle	5		90" X-Tech LE
9	STC8126	7.0 X 16-Sports-Quicksilver-unpolished	5		90" Note (1)
10	2943433	7.0 X 16-Deep dish-Silver Sparkle	5		90" South Africa
10	STC60718	7.0 X 16-Deep dish-Atlantic Green.	5		110" Heritage
10	STC60716	7.0 X 16-Deep dish-Bronze Green	5		110" Heritage
10	ANR3631MNH	7.0 X 16-Deep dish-Silver Sparkle	5		Except 130"
11	RRC110870RHO	7.0 X 16-5 spoke-Pewter/Bright-tubeless	5	Note (1)	Tomb Raider

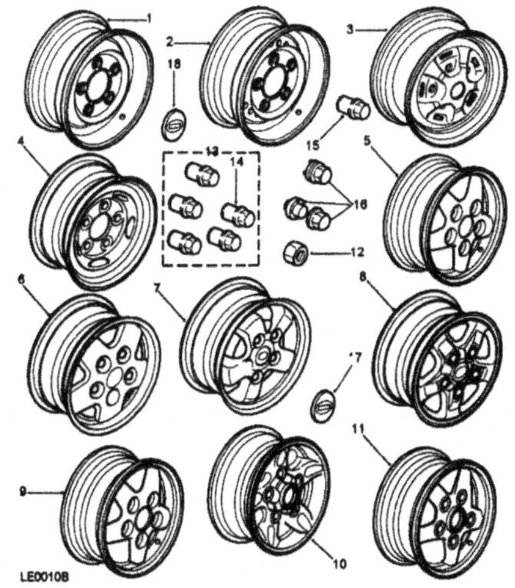

LE0010B

CHANGE POINTS:
(1) From (V) 1A 612404

Remarks:
(1) non-ventilated disc brakes-rear to fit these wheels to vehicles as an accessory anti roll bars must be fitted front and rear

Illus	Part Number	Description	Quantity	Change Point	Remarks
12	90577473	Nut wheel retention-16mm-steel wheel	20	To (V) VA 126656	
12	NTC7396	Nut wheel retention-M16-steel wheel	20	From (V) VA 126657	
13	RTC9563	NUT WHEEL RETENTION-ALLOY-SET OF 20	1		
14	NRC7415	• Nut-alloy road wheels	20		
15	ANR2763MMM	Nut-alloy road wheels-capped	20		
15	ANR2763MMM	Nut-alloy road wheels	20	Note (1)	Tomb Raider
		KIT-LOCKING NUT ROAD WHEELS			
16	RTC9535	set of 5-steel	1		
16	STC7623	set of 5-alloy-use with Deep dish wheel	1		
16	STC8843AA	set of 5-alloy-except Deep dish wheel	1		
17	ANR3861	Cap assembly-centre-road wheel-steel wheel-White	5		
18	ANR2391MUE	Cap assembly-centre alloy wheel-Quicksilver-with logo	5		
18	ANR2391MNH	Cap assembly-centre alloy wheel-Silver Sparkle-with logo	5		
18	ANR2391LAL	Cap assembly-centre alloy wheel-Pewter-with logo	5	Note (1)	Tomb Raider
18	STC60745	Cap assembly-centre alloy wheel-Green-with logo	5		
	2943289	Tyre	5		90" South Africa

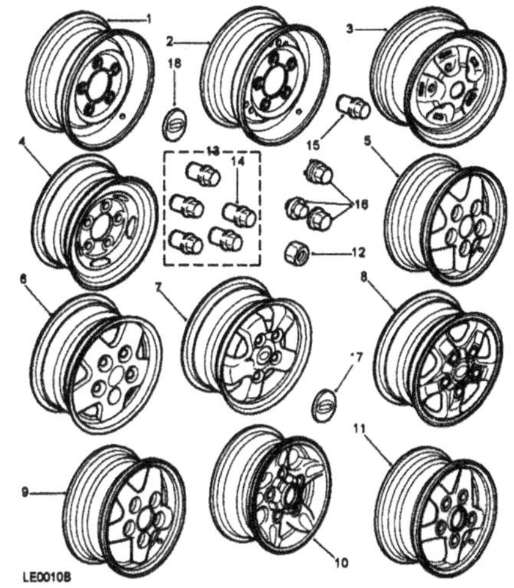

LE0010B

CHANGE POINTS:
(1) From (V) 1A 612404

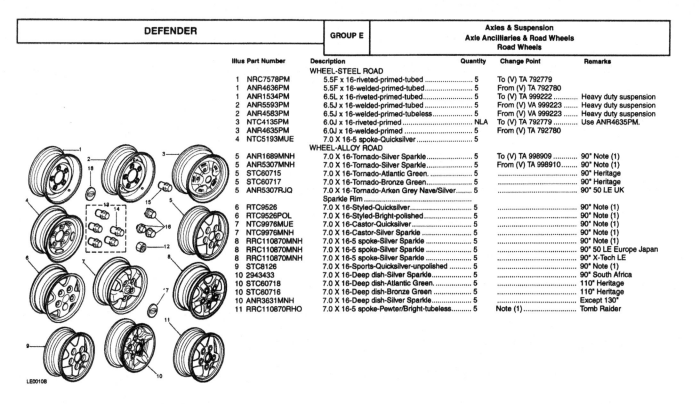

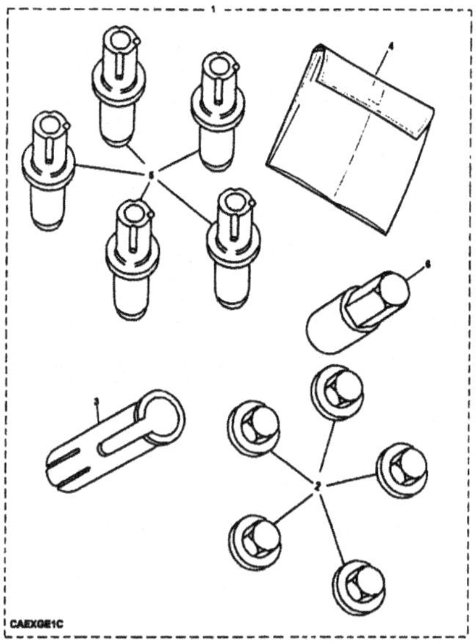

Illus	Part Number	Description	Quantity	Change Point	Remarks
1	STC3601	KIT-LOCKING NUT ROAD WHEELS	1		
2	ANR5435	• Cover-wheel nut	NLA		Use RRJ100120.
2	RRJ100120	• Cover-wheel nut	5		
3	ANR5436	• Lever-tool kit nut cover removal	1		
4	RRW100010	• Bag-locking wheel nut key/extractor	1		
		NUT-LOCKING-ALLOY ROAD WHEELS			
5	STC3410	Code A	5		
5	STC3411	Code B	5		
5	STC3412	Code C	5		
5	STC3413	Code D	5		
5	STC3414	Code E	5		
5	STC3415	Code F	5		
5	STC3416	Code G	5		
5	STC3417	Code H	5		
5	STC3418	Code I	5		
5	STC3419	Code J	5		
		KEY-TOOL KIT LOCKING WHEEL NUT			
6	STC3420	Code A	1		
6	STC3421	Code B	1		
6	STC3422	Code C	1		
6	STC3423	Code D	1		
6	STC3424	Code E	1		
6	STC3425	Code F	1		
6	STC3426	Code G	1		
6	STC3427	Code H	1		
6	STC3428	Code I	1		
6	STC3429	Code J	1		

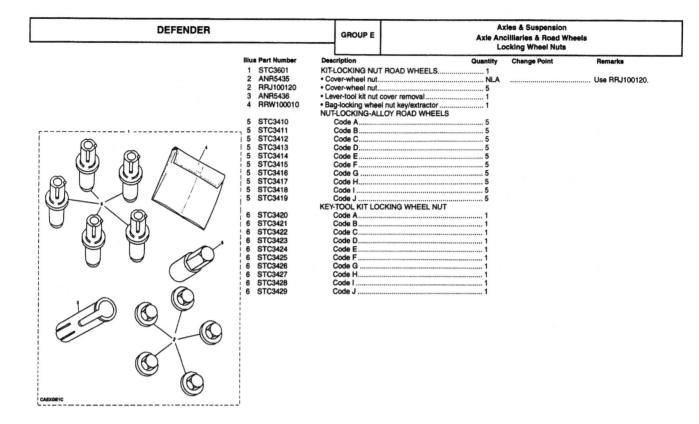

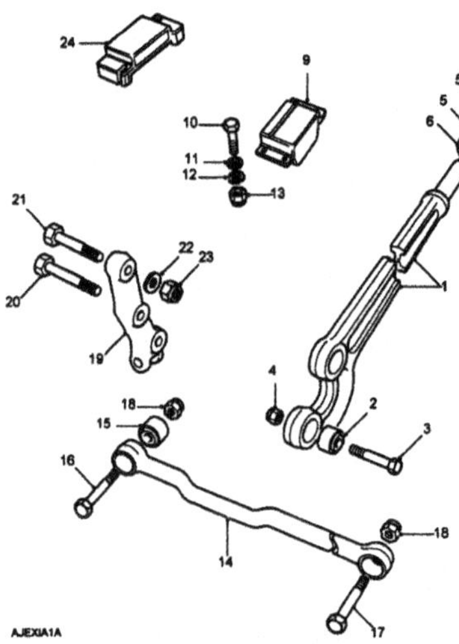

Illus	Part Number	Description	Quantity	Change Point	Remarks
1	NTC2705	ARM ASSEMBLY-RADIUS FRONT SUSPENSION.	2	Note (1)	
2	NTC7307	• Bush-front suspension radius arm	4		
1	NTC7331	ARM ASSEMBLY-RADIUS FRONT SUSPENSION.	2	Note (2)	
2	NTC6781	• Bush-front suspension radius arm	4		
3	BH610281L	Bolt-5/8UNF x 3 1/2	4	Note (1)	
3	BH116207	Bolt-M16-Dacromet	4	Note (3)	
3	BH116187	Bolt-M16 x 90-dacromat	4	Note (4)	
4	NY610041	Nut-hexagonal-nyloc-5/8UNF	4	Note (1)	
4	NV116047	Nut-hexagonal-nyloc-M16	4	Note (2)	
5	NRC4514	Bush	4	Note (5)	
5	ANR6971	Bush	4	Note (6)	
6	NRC4515	Washer-cup	2		
7	NRC4516	Washer-plain	2	Note (5)	
7	RDB100070	Washer-plain	2	Note (6)	
8	NY120041L	Nut-hexagonal-nyloc-M20	2		
9	575707	Stop-front suspension rebound	NLA	Note (7)	Use ANR4188.
9	ANR4188	Stop-front suspension rebound	2	Note (8)	
10	FS108207L	Screw-flanged head-M8 x 20	4		
10	FB108101L	Bolt-front suspension rebound stop-flanged head-M8 x 50	4		130"
11	WA108051L	Washer-front suspension rebound stop-8mm	4		
12	WL108001L	Washer-front suspension rebound stop-sprung-M8	4		
13	NY108041L	Nut-front suspension rebound stop-nyloc-M8	4		
13	FN108047L	Nut-flange-flanged head-M8	4		130"

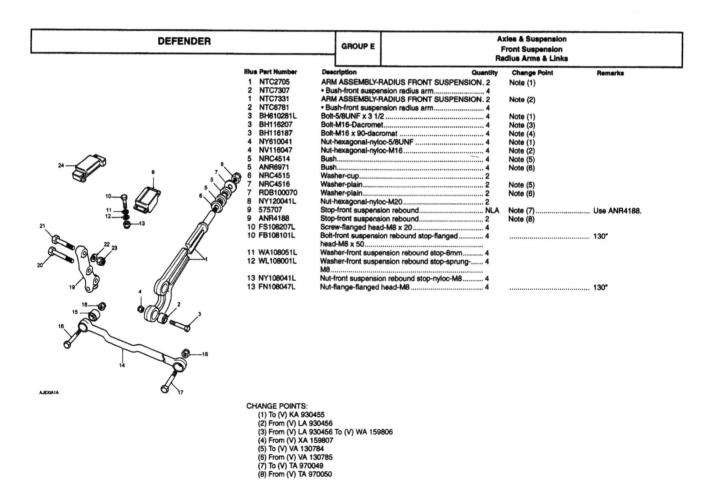

CHANGE POINTS:
(1) To (V) KA 930455
(2) From (V) LA 930456
(3) From (V) LA 930456 To (V) WA 159806
(4) From (V) XA 159807
(5) To (V) VA 130784
(6) From (V) VA 130785
(7) To (V) TA 970049
(8) From (V) TA 970050

DEFENDER	GROUP E	Axles & Suspension Front Suspension Radius Arms & Links

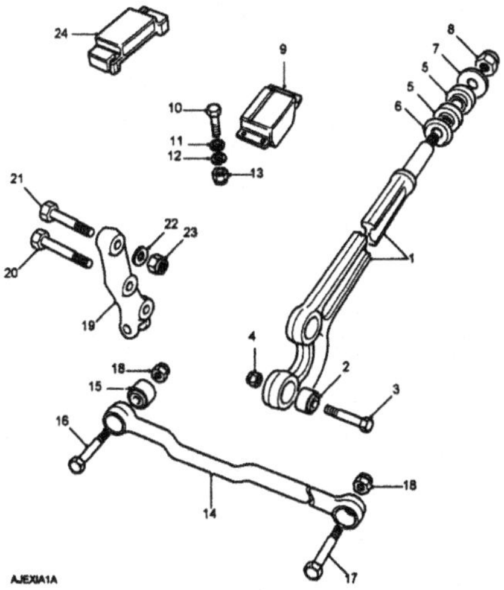

Illus	Part Number	Description	Quantity	Change Point	Remarks
14	NRC9729	ROD-FRONT SUSPENSION PANHARD	1	Note (1)	90"
15	ANR3410	• Bush-panhard rod	2		
14	NRC9729	ROD-FRONT SUSPENSION PANHARD	1	Note (1)	Except 90"
15	ANR3410	• Bush-panhard rod	2		
14	RBI100000	ROD-FRONT SUSPENSION PANHARD	1	Note (2)	
15	ANR3410	• Bush-panhard rod	2		
16	BH114167	Bolt-M14 x 80	1		
17	BH114167	Bolt-M14 x 80	1		
18	NV114047	Nut	2		
23	NY114041	Nut-radius arm-M14-hexagonal-nyloc	2		110"
19	NTC9462	Arm-radius front suspension-RHD	1		
19	NTC9461	Arm-radius front suspension-LHD	1		
20	253952	Bolt-1/2UNF x 6 1/2	1	Note (4)	
20	253948	Bolt-1/2UNF x 6 1/4	1	Note (5)	L/R
21	BH608461	Bolt-radius arm-1/2UNF x 5 3/4	1	Note (4)	
21	BH608381	Bolt-1/2UNF x 4 3/4	1	Note (5)	
22	WC112081L	Washer-plain-radius arm-M12 x 28	2		
23	NY608041L	Nut-radius arm-hexagonal-nyloc-1/2UNF	2		
24	RRC2281	Spacer	2		Extra heavy duty 130"
3	BX116201L	Bolt-radius arm to axle-short-high tensile	4	Note (6)	Except 90"
23	NY116051L	Nut-radius arm-M16-hexagonal-nyloc	4		
10	FB108101L	Bolt-front suspension rebound stop-flanged head-M8 x 50	2		Extra heavy duty 130"
11	WA108051L	Washer-front suspension rebound stop-8mm	2		Extra heavy duty 130"
12	WL108001L	Washer-sprung-M8	2		Extra heavy duty 130"
13	FN108047L	Nut-flange-flanged head-M8	2		Extra heavy duty 130"

CHANGE POINTS:
(1) To (V) VA 117813
(2) From (V) VA 117814
(4) To (V) WA 159806
(5) From (V) XA 159807
(6) From (V) LA 930435 To (V) LA 939975

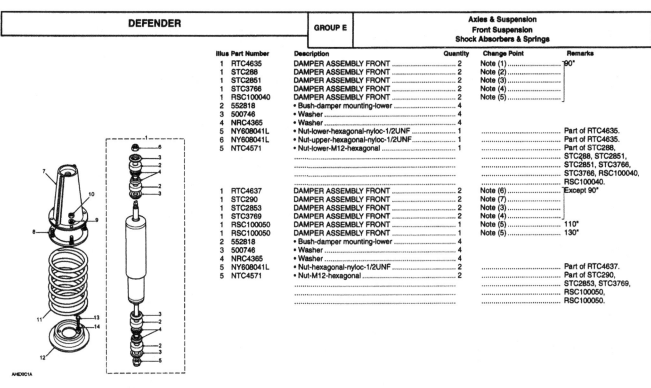

DEFENDER	GROUP E	Axles & Suspension Front Suspension Shock Absorbers & Springs

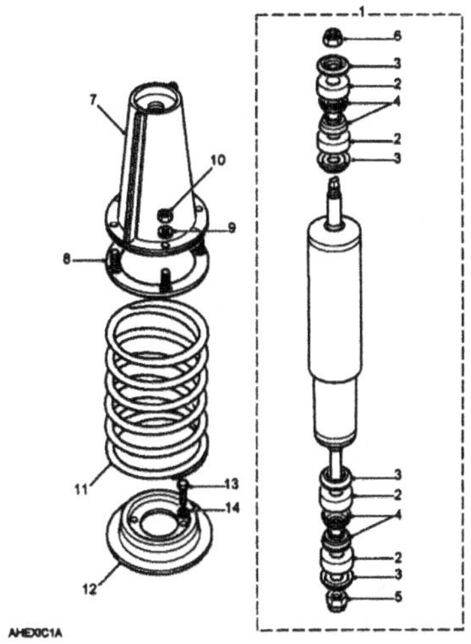

Illus	Part Number	Description	Quantity	Change Point	Remarks
1	RTC4635	DAMPER ASSEMBLY FRONT	2	Note (1)	90"
1	STC288	DAMPER ASSEMBLY FRONT	2	Note (2)	
1	STC2851	DAMPER ASSEMBLY FRONT	2	Note (3)	
1	STC3766	DAMPER ASSEMBLY FRONT	2	Note (4)	
1	RSC100040	DAMPER ASSEMBLY FRONT	2	Note (5)	
2	552818	• Bush-damper mounting-lower	4		
3	500746	• Washer	4		
4	NRC4365	• Washer	4		
5	NY608041L	• Nut-lower-hexagonal-nyloc-1/2UNF	1		Part of RTC4635.
6	NY608041L	• Nut-upper-hexagonal-nyloc-1/2UNF	1		Part of RTC4635.
5	NTC4571	• Nut-lower-M12-hexagonal	1		Part of STC288, STC288, STC2851, STC2851, STC3766, STC3766, RSC100040, RSC100040.
1	RTC4637	DAMPER ASSEMBLY FRONT	2	Note (6)	Except 90"
1	STC290	DAMPER ASSEMBLY FRONT	2	Note (7)	
1	STC2853	DAMPER ASSEMBLY FRONT	2	Note (3)	
1	STC3769	DAMPER ASSEMBLY FRONT	2	Note (4)	
1	RSC100050	DAMPER ASSEMBLY FRONT	1	Note (5)	110"
1	RSC100050	DAMPER ASSEMBLY FRONT	1	Note (5)	130"
2	552818	• Bush-damper mounting-lower	4		
3	500746	• Washer	4		
4	NRC4365	• Washer	4		
5	NY608041L	• Nut-hexagonal-nyloc-1/2UNF	2		Part of RTC4637.
5	NTC4571	• Nut-M12-hexagonal	2		Part of STC290, STC2853, STC3769, RSC100050, RSC100050.

CHANGE POINTS:
(1) To (V) HA 476189
(2) From (V) HA 476190 To (V) MA 967602
(3) From (V) MA 967603 To (V) VA 998899
(4) From (V) VA 998900 To (V) WA 159806
(5) From (V) XA 159807
(6) To (V) HA 475249
(7) From (V) HA 475250 To (V) MA 967602

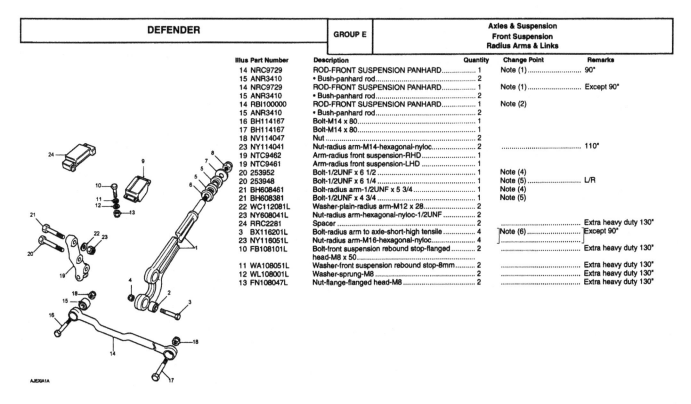

Shock Absorbers & Springs

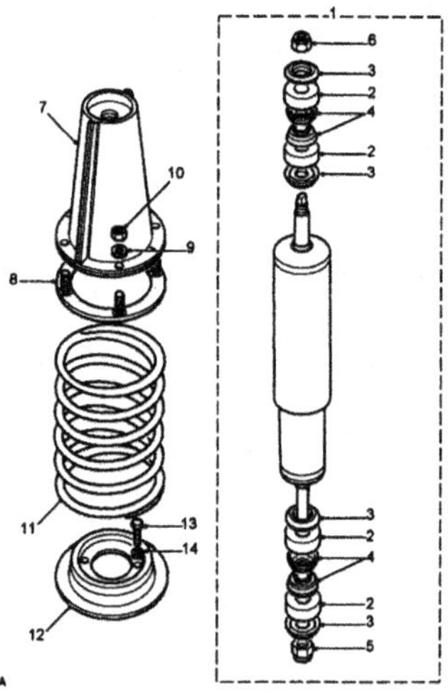

AHEXIC1A

Illus	Part Number	Description	Quantity	Change Point	Remarks
7	NRC6372	Bracket-front spring mounting-driver-side suspension-upper	2		
8	572087	Ring-retention	2		
9	WM600051L	Washer-spring-5/16"	8		
10	NH605041L	Nut-hexagonal head-5/16UNF	8		
11	NRC9446	Spring-road-coil-front-Blue.-Green	1		90" Driver
11	NRC9447	Spring-road-coil-front-Blue/Yellow.	1		90" Passenger
11	NRC8044	Spring-road-coil-front-White.-White.	1		110" Driver normal duty suspension
11	NRC8045	Spring-road-coil-front-Yellow.-Yellow.	1		110" Passenger normal duty suspension
11	NRC9448	Spring-road-coil-front-Red-Blue.	1		110" Driver heavy duty suspension
11	NRC9449	Spring-road-coil-front-Yellow.-White	1		110" Passenger heavy duty suspension
11	NRC9448	Spring-road-coil-front-Red-Blue.	1		130" Driver
11	NRC9449	Spring-road-coil-front-Yellow.-White	1		130" Passenger
12	NRC9700	Seat-suspension spring lower	2		
13	SH110251L	Screw-hexagonal head-M10 x 25	4		
14	WM110001L	Washer-spring-5/16"	4		

Anti Roll Bar

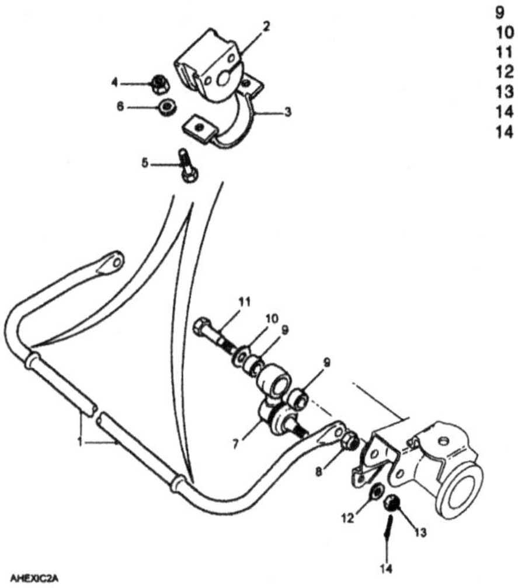

AHEXIC2A

Illus	Part Number	Description	Quantity	Change Point	Remarks
1	NTC6837	Bar-anti-roll front suspension	1		Heavy duty suspension
2	NTC6828	Bush-anti-roll bar-front	2		Heavy duty suspension
3	NTC6776	Bracket-clamp roll bar mounting	2		Heavy duty suspension
4	NY110047L	Nut-flange-nyloc-M10	4		Heavy duty suspension
5	SH110351L	Screw-hexagonal head-M10 x 35	4		Heavy duty suspension
6	WA110061L	Washer-M10	4		Heavy duty suspension
7	NTC1888	Joint-ball-lower arm front/rear suspension	2		Heavy duty suspension
8	NV116041L	Nut-M16	2		Heavy duty suspension
9	552819	Bush-lower arm front/rear suspension	4		Heavy duty suspension
10	264024	Washer	2		Heavy duty suspension
11	NTC8202	Pin	2		Heavy duty suspension
12	WC112081L	Washer-plain-M12 x 28	2		Heavy duty suspension
13	NC112041	Nut-castle-M12	2		Heavy duty suspension
14	PS106251L	Pin-split-3.2 x 25	2		110"
14	PS106321L	Pin-split-3.2 x 32	2		

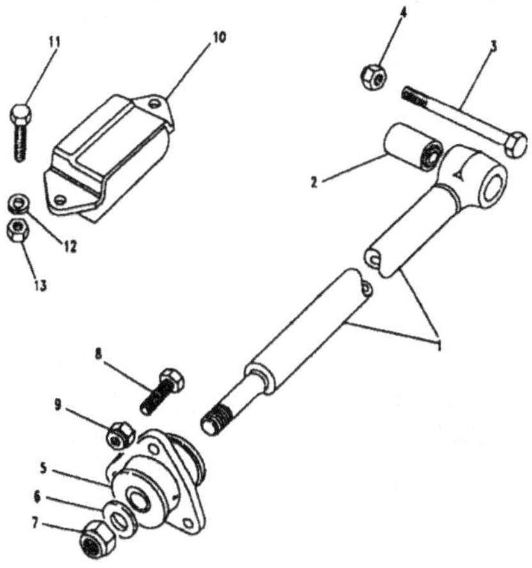

Illus	Part Number	Description	Quantity	Change Point	Remarks
1	NTC4720	LINK ASSEMBLY-LOWER-REAR SUSPENSION	NLA	Note (1)	When replacing NTC4720 use NTC8328 Link assembly which must be fitted as a pair.
1	NTC8328	LINK ASSEMBLY-LOWER-REAR SUSPENSION	2	Note (2)	
2	NTC1772	• Bush-rear-lower arm rear suspension	2		
3	BH610321L	Bolt-hexagonal socket	2		
4	NY610041L	Nut-hexagonal-nyloc	2		
5	STC618	Mounting-lower link flexible rubber	1	Note (3)	
5	NTC9027	Mounting-lower link flexible rubber	2	Note (4)	
6	WA120001	Washer	2		
7	NY120041L	Nut-hexagonal-nyloc-M20	2		
8	SH110301	Screw-flanged head-M10 x 30	6	Note (5)	
8	SX110301	Screw-M10 x 30-hexagonal head	6	Note (6)	
9	NY110041	Nut-hexagonal head-nyloc	6	Note (5)	
9	NY110051L	Nut-hexagonal head-nyloc	6	Note (6)	
10	90575789	Stop-rebound rear suspension-2 holes	NLA	Note (7)	Use ANR4189.
10	ANR4189	Stop-rebound rear suspension	2	Note (8)	
11	FS108207L	Screw-flanged head-M8 x 20	2		
12	WL108001L	Washer-sprung-M8	4		
13	NY108041L	Nut-nyloc-M8	4		
		SPACERS - LINK TO CHASSIS			
	IPV000010	KIT SERVICE FIXINGS	1		Petrol heavy duty suspension
	KVX000010	• Spacer	2		
	SX110401	• Screw-M10 x 40	6		
	NY110051L	• Nut-hexagonal head-nyloc	6		

CHANGE POINTS:
(1) To (V) HA 470427
(2) From (V) HA 470428
(3) To (V) JA 910736
(4) From (V) JA 910737
(5) To (V) YA 185790
(6) From (V) YA 185791
(7) To (V) TA 970049
(8) From (V) TA 970050

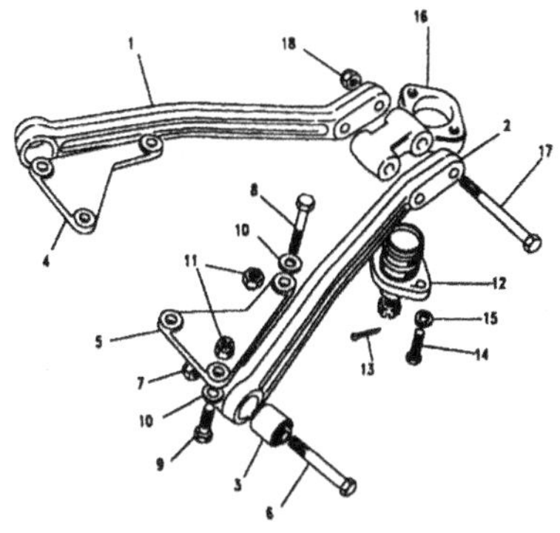

Illus	Part Number	Description	Quantity	Change Point	Remarks
1	NTC2706	LINK ASSEMBLY-REAR SUSPENSION UPPER-RH	1		
2	NTC2707	LINK ASSEMBLY-REAR SUSPENSION UPPER-LH	1		
3	NTC1773	• Bush-rear suspension upper link	2		
4	575615	Bracket-RH	1		
5	575616	Bracket-LH	1		
6	BH612321	Bolt	2		
7	NY612041	Locknut	2		
8	BX110111L	Bolt-M10 x 55-hexagonal head	2		
9	BX110091L	Bolt	4		
10	WC110061L	Washer-plain-M10-oversize	6		
11	NY110051L	Nut-hexagonal head-nyloc	6		
12	572337	Joint-rear suspension upper link ball	1	Note (1)	90°
12	NTC4260	JOINT-REAR SUSPENSION UPPER LINK BALL	1	Note (2)	
12	NTC9932	JOINT-REAR SUSPENSION UPPER LINK BALL	1	Note (3)	
12	ANR1799	JOINT-REAR SUSPENSION UPPER LINK BALL	1	Note (4)	
	NTC4618	• Nut-20mm	1		
	WB120001	• Washer-20mm	1		
13	PS608101L	Pin-split	1	Note (5)	
13	PS106321L	Pin-split-3.2 x 32	1	Note (6)	
	592445	Ring-snap	1	Note (1)	90°
	572338	Cover-dust ball joint-outer	1	Note (1)	90°
14	SH605081L	Screw-hexagonal head-5/16UNF x 1	2	Note (7)	
14	FS108207L	Screw-flanged head-M8 x 20	2	Note (4)	
15	WM600051L	Washer-spring-5/16"	2	Note (7)	
16	NRC3923	Bracket-rear axle fulcrum	1	Note (7)	
16	ANR3037	Bracket-rear axle fulcrum	1	Note (4)	
17	253952	Bolt-1/2UNF x 6 1/2	2		
18	NY608041L	Nut-rear suspension upper link to chassis bracket-hexagonal-nyloc-1/2UNF	2		

CHANGE POINTS:
(1) To (V) EA 329986
(2) From (V) EA 329987 To (V) JA 914425
(3) From (V) JA 914426 To (V) KA 930263
(4) From (V) KA 930264
(5) To (V) JA 914425
(6) From (V) JA 914426
(7) To (V) KA 930263

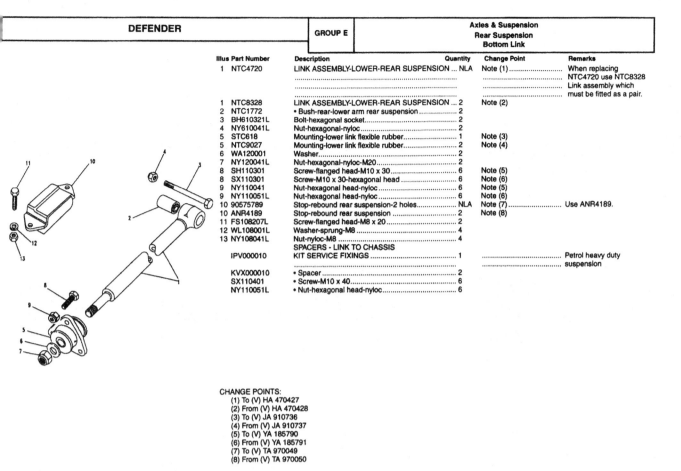

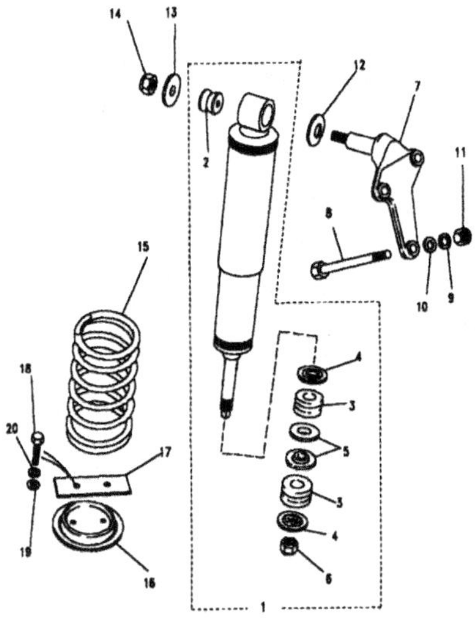

Illus	Part Number	Description	Quantity	Change Point	Remarks
1	RTC4636	DAMPER ASSEMBLY REAR	2	Note (1)	
1	STC289	DAMPER ASSEMBLY REAR	2	Note (2)	
1	STC2852	DAMPER ASSEMBLY REAR	2	Note (3)	
1	STC3767	DAMPER ASSEMBLY REAR	2	Note (4)	
2	NRC5593	• Bush-damper mounting-rear-upper	2		
3	552818	• Bush-damper mounting-lower	4		
4	500746	• Washer-damper lower fixing	4		
5	NRC6235	• Washer-damper lower fixing	4		
6	NY608041L	• Nut-damper mounting-hexagonal-nyloc-1/2UNF	2		Part of RTC4636.
6	NV608041L	• Nut-alternative-hexagonal head	2		Part of RTC4636.
6	NTC4571	• Nut-M12-hexagonal	2		Part of STC289, STC2852, STC3767.
1	RPM100070	DAMPER ASSEMBLY REAR	2	Note (5)	
3	RNF100090	• Bush-damper mounting-lower-lower	1		
4	ANR1895	• Washer-damper lower fixing	1		
6	NTC4571	• Nut-damper upper fixing-M12-hexagonal	1		
11	NY112041	• Nut-hexagonal head-nyloc-M12	1		
12	NRC5602	• Retainer-inner	1		
13	NRC5603	• Retainer-outer	1		
7	NRC7981	Bracket assembly-rear damper-upper	2		
8	BH110221L	Bolt-hexagonal head-M10 x 110	6		
9	WM110001L	Washer-spring-5/16"	6		
10	WC110061L	Washer-plain-M10-oversize	6		
11	NH110041L	Nut-hexagonal head-coarse thread-M10	6		
12	NRC5602	Retainer-inner	2	Note (6)	
13	NRC5603	Retainer-outer	2	Note (6)	
14	NY112041L	Nut-damper upper fixing-M12-hexagonal head-nyloc	2		

CHANGE POINTS:
(1) To (V) HA 475839
(2) From (V) HA 475840 To (V) MA 967602
(3) From (V) MA 967603 To (V) VA 998899
(4) From (V) VA 998900
(5) From (V) XA 159807
(6) To (V) WA 159806

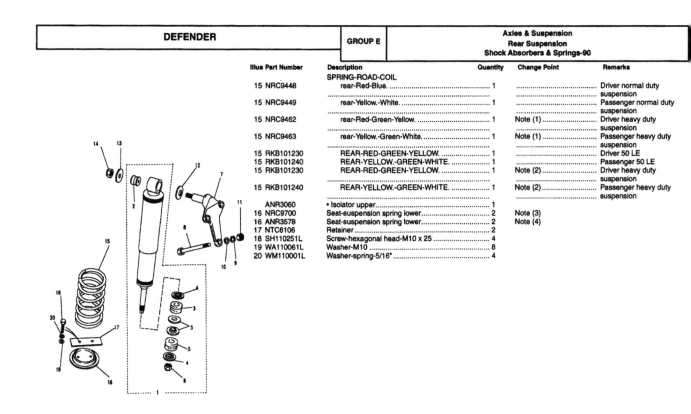

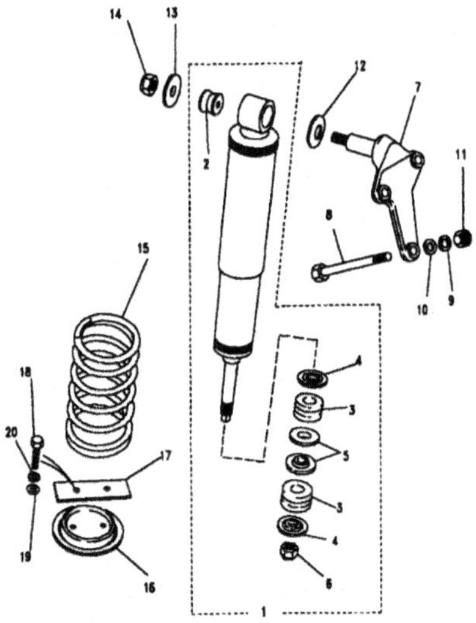

Illus	Part Number	Description	Quantity	Change Point	Remarks
		SPRING-ROAD-COIL			
15	NRC9448	rear-Red-Blue.	1		Driver normal duty suspension
15	NRC9449	rear-Yellow.-White.	1		Passenger normal duty suspension
15	NRC9462	rear-Red-Green-Yellow.	1	Note (1)	Driver heavy duty suspension
15	NRC9463	rear-Yellow.-Green-White.	1	Note (1)	Passenger heavy duty suspension
15	RKB101230	REAR-RED-GREEN-YELLOW.	1		Driver 50 LE
15	RKB101240	REAR-YELLOW.-GREEN-WHITE.	1		Passenger 50 LE
15	RKB101230	REAR-RED-GREEN-YELLOW.	1	Note (2)	Driver heavy duty suspension
15	RKB101240	REAR-YELLOW.-GREEN-WHITE.	1	Note (2)	Passenger heavy duty suspension
	ANR3060	• Isolator upper	1		
16	NRC9700	Seat-suspension spring lower	2	Note (3)	
16	ANR3578	Seat-suspension spring lower	2	Note (4)	
17	NTC6106	Retainer	2		
18	SH110251L	Screw-hexagonal head-M10 x 25	4		
19	WA110061L	Washer-M10	8		
20	WM110001L	Washer-spring-5/16"	4		

CHANGE POINTS:
(1) To (V) WA 159806
(2) From (V) XA 159807
(3) To (V) LA 939975
(4) From (V) MA 939976

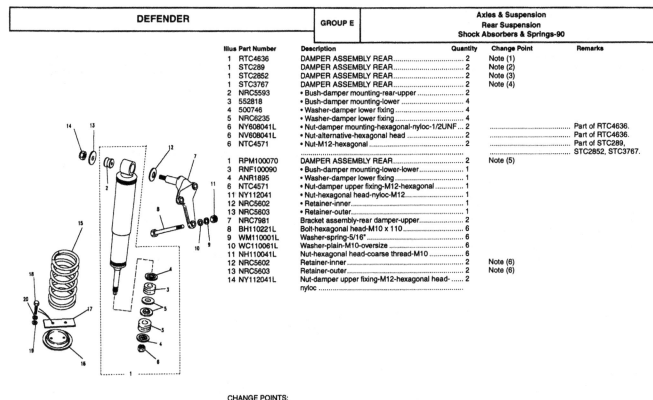

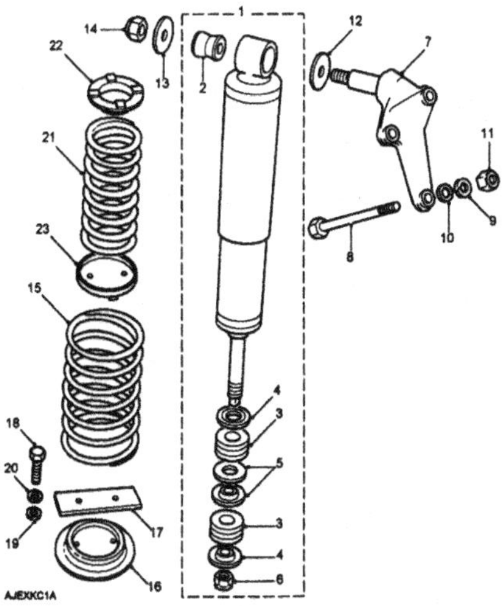

Illus	Part Number	Description	Quantity	Change Point	Remarks
		110" WHEELBASE			
1	RTC4638	Damper assembly rear	1	Note (1)	Self levelling suspension
1	STC291	DAMPER ASSEMBLY REAR	2	Note (2)	
1	STC2854	DAMPER ASSEMBLY REAR	2	Note (3)	
1	STC3770	DAMPER ASSEMBLY REAR	2	Note (4)	
1	RTC4639	DAMPER ASSEMBLY REAR	2	Note (5)	Normal duty suspension
1	STC292	DAMPER ASSEMBLY REAR	2	Note (6)	
1	STC2855	DAMPER ASSEMBLY REAR	2	Note (3)	
1	STC3771	DAMPER ASSEMBLY REAR	2	Note (4)	
1	STC293	DAMPER ASSEMBLY REAR	2	Note (8)	Heavy duty suspension
1	STC2856	DAMPER ASSEMBLY REAR	2	Note (3)	
1	STC3772	DAMPER ASSEMBLY REAR	2	Note (4)	
2	NRC5593	• Bush-damper mounting-rear-upper	2		
3	552818	• Bush-damper mounting-lower	4		
4	500746	• Washer	4		
5	NRC6235	• Washer	4		
6	NTC4571	• Nut-M12-hexagonal	2		
1	RPM100080	DAMPER ASSEMBLY REAR	2	Note (7)	
2	RNF100090	• Bush-damper mounting-lower-lower	1		
4	ANR1895	• Washer	1		
6	NTC4571	• Nut-M12-hexagonal	1		
12	NRC5602	• Retainer-inner	1		
13	NRC5603	• Retainer-outer	1		
14	NY112041	• Nut-hexagonal head-nyloc-M12	1		

CHANGE POINTS:
(1) To (V) HA 473822
(2) From (V) HA 473823 To (V) MA 967602
(3) From (V) MA 967603 To (V) VA 998899
(4) From (V) VA 998900 To (V) WA 159806
(5) To (V) HA 478284
(6) From (V) HA 478285 To (V) MA 967602
(7) From (V) XA 159807
(8) To (V) MA 967602

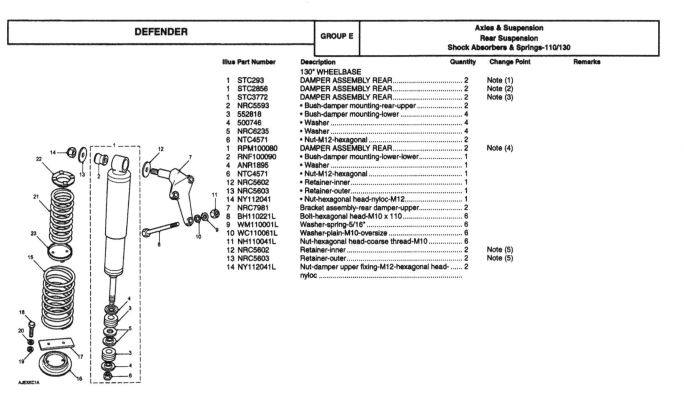

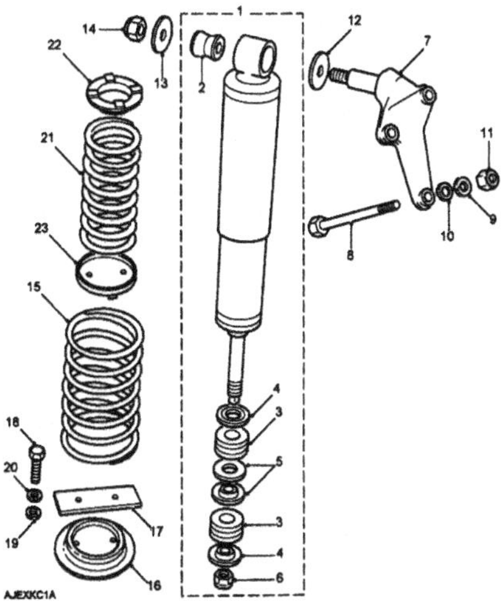

Illus	Part Number	Description	Quantity	Change Point	Remarks
		130" WHEELBASE			
1	STC293	DAMPER ASSEMBLY REAR	2	Note (1)	
1	STC2856	DAMPER ASSEMBLY REAR	2	Note (2)	
1	STC3772	DAMPER ASSEMBLY REAR	2	Note (3)	
2	NRC5593	• Bush-damper mounting-rear-upper	2		
3	552818	• Bush-damper mounting-lower	4		
4	500746	• Washer	4		
5	NRC6235	• Washer	4		
6	NTC4571	• Nut-M12-hexagonal	2		
1	RPM100080	DAMPER ASSEMBLY REAR	2	Note (4)	
2	RNF100090	• Bush-damper mounting-lower-lower	1		
4	ANR1895	• Washer	1		
6	NTC4571	• Nut-M12-hexagonal	1		
12	NRC5602	• Retainer-inner	1		
13	NRC5603	• Retainer-outer	1		
14	NY112041	• Nut-hexagonal head-nyloc-M12	1		
7	NRC7981	Bracket assembly-rear damper-upper	2		
8	BH110221L	Bolt-hexagonal head-M10 x 110	6		
9	WM110001L	Washer-spring-5/16"	6		
10	WC110061L	Washer-plain-M10-oversize	6		
11	NH110041L	Nut-hexagonal head-coarse thread-M10	6		
12	NRC5602	Retainer-inner	2	Note (5)	
13	NRC5603	Retainer-outer	2	Note (5)	
14	NY112041L	Nut-damper upper fixing-M12-hexagonal head-nyloc	2		

CHANGE POINTS:
(1) To (V) MA 967602
(2) From (V) MA 967603 To (V) VA 998899
(3) From (V) VA 998900 To (V) WA 159806
(4) From (V) XA 159807
(5) To (V) WA 159806

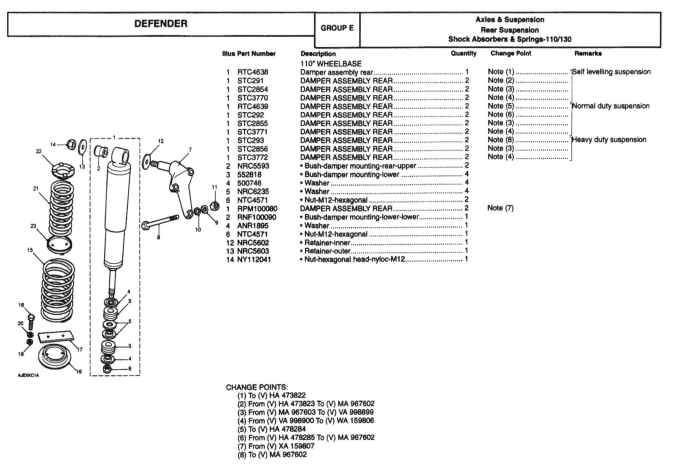

Rear Suspension
Shock Absorbers & Springs-110/130

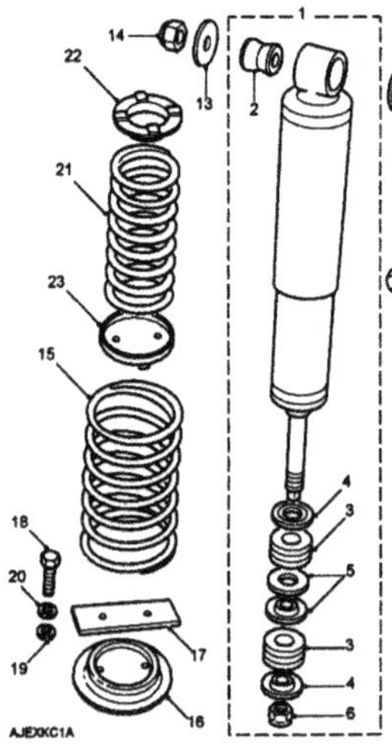

AJEXXC1A

Illus	Part Number	Description	Quantity	Change Point	Remarks
15	NRC6388	Spring-road-coil-rear-Blue.-Blue.	1	Note (1)	110" Driver self levelling suspension
15	NRC7000	Spring-road-coil-rear-Green-White.	1		110" Passenger self levelling suspension
15	NRC6389	Spring-road-coil-rear-Red-Red	1		110" Driver except self levelling suspension
15	NRC6904	Spring-road-coil-rear-Red-Green	1		110" Passenger except self levelling suspension
15	RKB101111	SPRING-ROAD-COIL-REAR-BROWN-PURPLE	2	Note (2)	
	ANR3060	• Isolator upper	1		
15	NRC6389	Spring-road-coil-rear-Red-Red	1	Note (1)	130" Driver
15	NRC6904	Spring-road-coil-rear-Red-Green	1		130" Passenger
15	RKB101111	SPRING-ROAD-COIL-REAR-BROWN-PURPLE	2	Note (2)	130"
	ANR3060	• Isolator upper	1		
16	NRC4317	Seat-suspension spring lower	2		
17	NRC4318	Retainer	2		
18	SH110251L	Screw-hexagonal head-M10 x 25	4		110" normal duty suspension
18	FS110301L	Screw-flanged head-M10 x 30-top	4		Heavy duty suspension
19	WA110061L	Washer-M10	8		110" normal duty suspension
19	WA110001L	Washer-plain-M10	4		Heavy duty suspension
20	WM110001L	Washer-spring-5/16"	4		
21	RRC3266	Spring-rear suspension coil helper	2	Note (3)	110" heavy duty suspension
21	RRC3266	Spring-rear suspension coil helper	2		130" extra heavy duty
22	RRC3352	Retainer	2		Heavy duty suspension
23	RRC3355	Retainer	2		Heavy duty suspension

CHANGE POINTS:
(1) To (V) WA 159806
(2) From (V) XA 159807
(3) From (V) WA 138480 Except Station Wagon

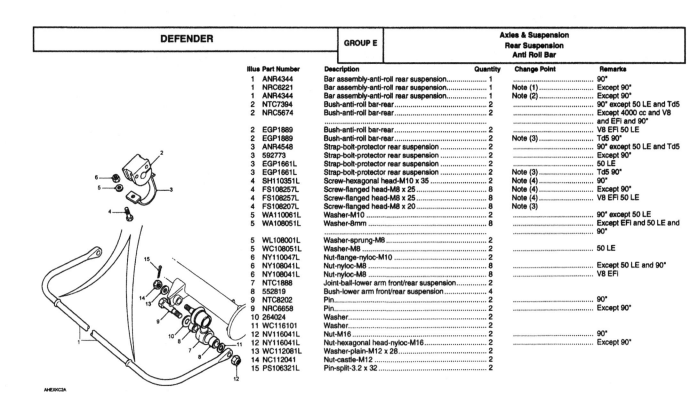

Rear Suspension
Anti Roll Bar

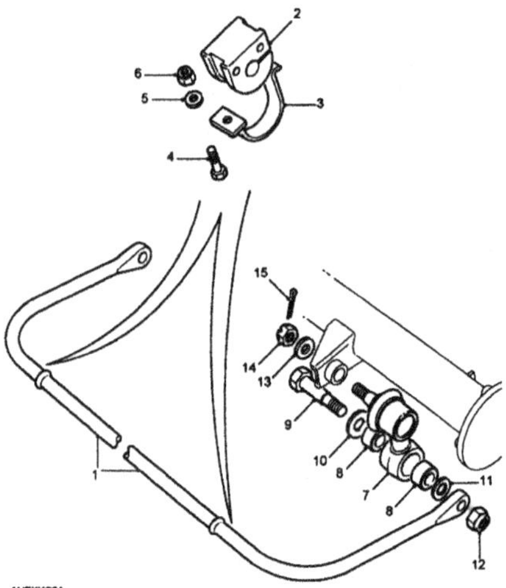

AHEXXC2A

Illus	Part Number	Description	Quantity	Change Point	Remarks
1	ANR4344	Bar assembly-anti-roll rear suspension	1		90"
1	NRC6221	Bar assembly-anti-roll rear suspension	1	Note (1)	Except 90"
1	ANR4344	Bar assembly-anti-roll rear suspension	1	Note (2)	Except 90"
2	NTC7394	Bush-anti-roll bar-rear	2		90" except 50 LE and Td5
2	NRC5674	Bush-anti-roll bar-rear	2		Except 4000 cc and V8 and EFi and 90"
2	EGP1889	Bush-anti-roll bar-rear	2		V8 EFi 50 LE
2	EGP1889	Bush-anti-roll bar-rear	2	Note (3)	Td5 90"
3	ANR4548	Strap-bolt-protector rear suspension	2		90" except 50 LE and Td5
3	592773	Strap-bolt-protector rear suspension	2		Except 90"
3	EGP1661L	Strap-bolt-protector rear suspension	2		50 LE
3	EGP1661L	Strap-bolt-protector rear suspension	2	Note (3)	Td5 90"
4	SH110351L	Screw-hexagonal head-M10 x 35	2	Note (4)	90"
4	FS108257L	Screw-flanged head-M8 x 25	8	Note (4)	Except 90"
4	FS108257L	Screw-flanged head-M8 x 25	8	Note (4)	V8 EFi 50 LE
4	FS108207L	Screw-flanged head-M8 x 20	8	Note (3)	
5	WA110061L	Washer-M10	2		90" except 50 LE
5	WA108051L	Washer-8mm	8		Except EFi and 50 LE and 90"
5	WL108001L	Washer-sprung-M8	2		
5	WC108051L	Washer-M8	2		50 LE
6	NY110047L	Nut-flange-nyloc-M10	2		
6	NY108041L	Nut-nyloc-M8	8		Except 50 LE and 90"
6	NY108041L	Nut-nyloc-M8	8		V8 EFi
7	NTC1888	Joint-ball-lower arm front/rear suspension	2		
8	552819	Bush-lower arm front/rear suspension	4		
9	NTC8202	Pin	2		90"
9	NRC6658	Pin	2		Except 90"
10	264024	Washer	2		
11	WC116101	Washer	2		
12	NV116041L	Nut-M16	2		90"
12	NY116041L	Nut-hexagonal head-nyloc-M16	2		Except 90"
13	WC112081L	Washer-plain-M12 x 28	2		
14	NC112041	Nut-castle-M12	2		
15	PS106321L	Pin-split-3.2 x 32	2		

CHANGE POINTS:
(1) To (V) MA 960429
(2) From (V) MA 960430
(3) From (V) XA 159807
(4) To (V) WA 159806

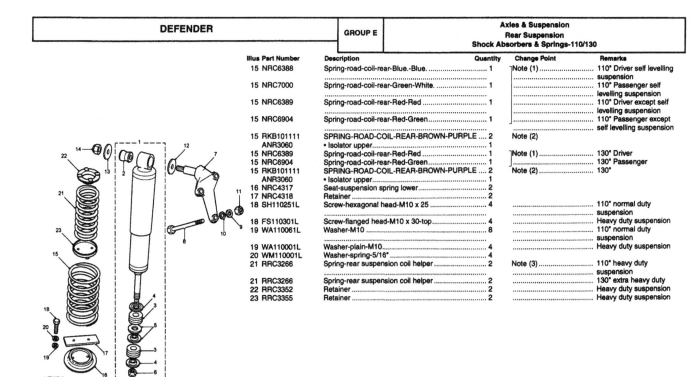

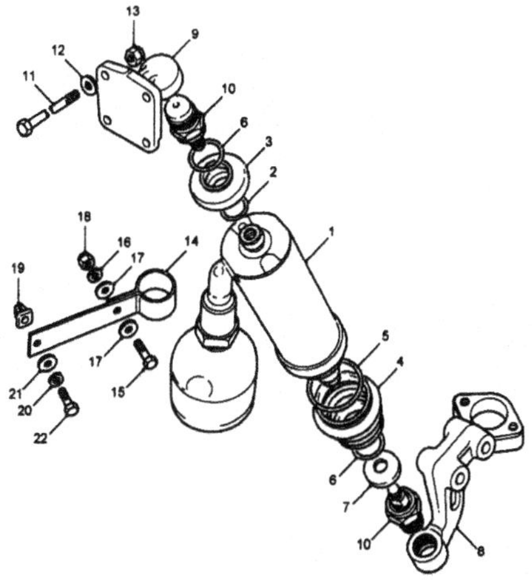

AJEXKG1A

Illus	Part Number	Description	Quantity	Change Point	Remarks
1	NRC7050	Control unit-self levelling	1		110"
2	NRC7066	Spring ring	1		
3	NRC5707	Gaiter-self levelling unit ball joint-upper	1		
4	NRC6561	Gaiter-self levelling unit ball joint-lower	1		
5	577703	Spring ring	1		
6	90577704	Spring ring	1		
7	NRC8007	Seal	1		
8	90575878	Bracket-rear axle fulcrum	1	Note (4)	
8	ANR3036	Bracket-rear axle fulcrum-metric fixing	1	Note (1)	
9	NRC8375	Mounting assembly-rear suspension	1		
10	575882	Joint-self levelling unit ball	2		
11	BH110351	Bolt	4		
12	NRC5758	Washer	4		
13	NY110041L	Nut-hexagonal head-nyloc-M10	NLA		
14	NRC6320	Strap-retaining-levelling-3 holes	1		
14	NRC8518	Strap-retaining-levelling-2 holes	1		
15	SH106301	Screw-hexagonal head-M6 x 30-long	1		
16	WL106001L	Washer-sprung-M6	1		
17	2215L	Washer-plain	1		
18	NH106041L	Nut-hexagonal-nyloc-M6	1		
19	NN106011	Nutsert-blind	1	Note (2)	
19	AWR6715	Nutsert-blind-M6	1	Note (3)	
20	WL106001L	Washer-sprung-M6	1		
21	2215L	Washer-plain	1		
22	FS106201L	Screw-flanged head-M6 x 20	1		

CHANGE POINTS:
(1) To (V) KA 930264
(2) To (V) VA 999222
(3) From (V) VA 999223
(4) To (V) KA 930263

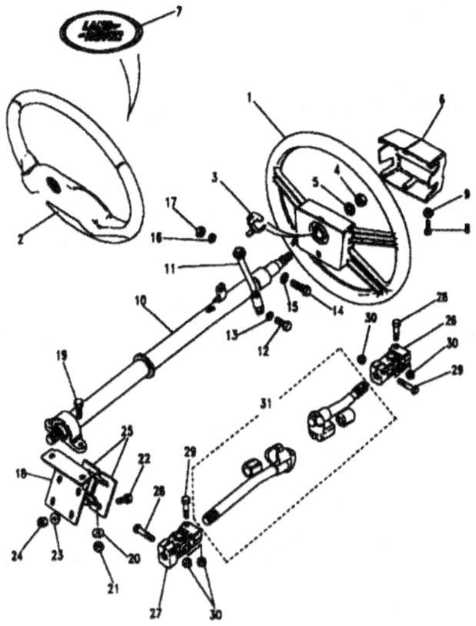

Illus	Part Number	Description	Quantity	Change Point	Remarks
		WHEEL ASSEMBLY-STEERING			
1	NRC5281	plastic-Black	1	Note (1)	
1	NTC4844	leather covered	1		
2	NTC8847	plastic-deep grained	1	Note (2)	
2	ANR3231	plastic-deep grained	1	Note (3)	
3	NRC7636	Ring-snap	1		
4	CRC2015	Nut-steering wheel-1/2"-UNF-imperial	1		
4	CRC209	Nut-steering wheel-14mm-metric	1		
5	WE600081L	Washer-starlock-1/2"-imperial	1		
5	WE114001L	Washer-starlock-14mm-metric	1		
6	NRC6747	Pad steering wheel-plastic	1	To (V) HA 906579	
6	NTC7731	Pad steering wheel-leather covered	1		
7	NTC8848	Cover steering wheel nut	1	From (V) JA 906580	
8	SE106121L	Screw-pan-pan head-M6 x 12	1		
9	NK106081	Nut-lokut	1		
10	NRC7635	Column-upper-steering	1	To (V) HA 906579	
10	NTC9068	Column-upper-steering	1	From (V) JA 906580	
11	NRC9711	Rod assembly-tie	1		
12	SH110161L	Screw-hexagonal head-M10 x 16	1		
13	WL110001L	Washer-M10	1		
14	FS110301L	Screw-flanged head-M10 x 30-top	1		
15	WA110061L	Washer-M10	1		

CHANGE POINTS:
(1) To (V) JA 906579
(2) From (V) JA 906581 To (V) LA 936926
(3) From (V) LA 936927

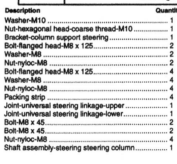

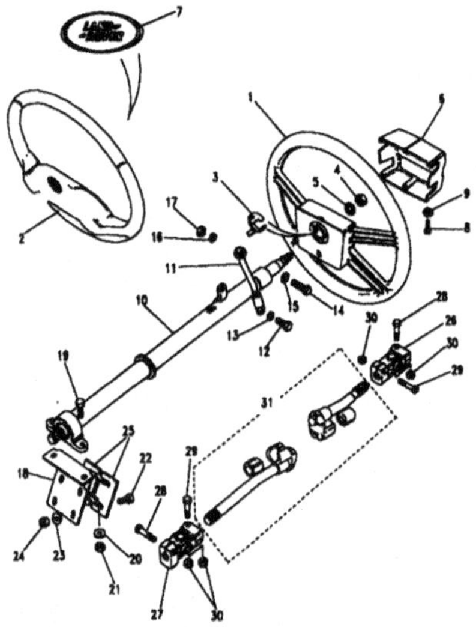

Illus	Part Number	Description	Quantity	Change Point	Remarks
16	WL110001L	Washer-M10	1		
17	NH110041L	Nut-hexagonal head-coarse thread-M10	1		
18	NRC7127	Bracket-column support steering	1		
19	FB108251	Bolt-flanged head-M8 x 125	2		
20	WC108051L	Washer-M8	2		
21	NY108041L	Nut-nyloc-M8	2		
22	FB108251	Bolt-flanged head-M8 x 125	4		
23	WC108051L	Washer-M8	4		
24	NY108041L	Nut-nyloc-M8	4		
25	569522	Packing strip	4		
26	NRC7387	Joint-universal steering linkage-upper	1		
27	NRC7704	Joint-universal steering linkage-lower	1		
28	BH108091L	Bolt-M8 x 45	2		
29	BH108091L	Bolt-M8 x 45	2		
30	NY108041L	Nut-nyloc-M8	4		
31	RTC4738	Shaft assembly-steering steering column	1		

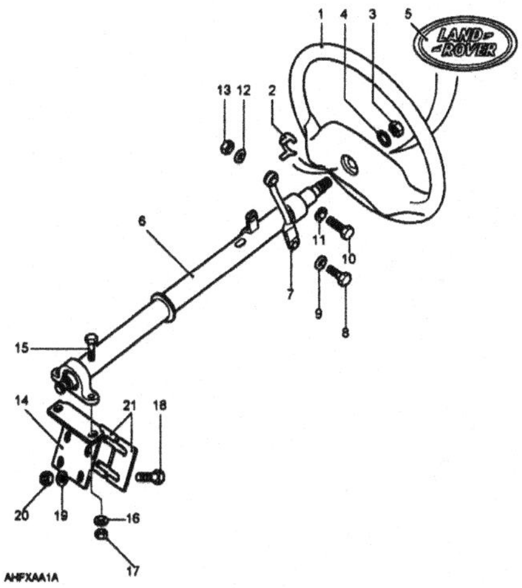

AHFXAA1A

Illus	Part Number	Description	Quantity	Change Point	Remarks
		WHEEL ASSEMBLY-STEERING			
1	ANR3231	plastic-deep grained	1	Note (1); Note (2)	Standard / County
1	ANR1972	plastic-deep grained	1	Note (3)	Standard / County
1	QTB102760	leather covered-Dark Granite	1		V8 EFi 50 LE
1	STC60751	leather covered-Green	1		Heritage
1	STC60510	leather covered-Black	1		Tdi Hardtop 50th
1	QTB102760PMA	leather covered-Black	1		Tomb Raider
2	NRC7636	Ring-snap	1		
3	CRC209	Nut-14mm-metric	1		
4	WE114001	Washer-starlock-14mm	1		
5	NTC8848	Cover steering wheel nut	1	Note (2); Note (1)	
5	QTF100220	Cover steering wheel nut	1	Note (3)	
6	NTC9068	Column-upper-steering	1	Note (2); Note (1)	
6	QMB101620	Column-upper-steering	1	Note (3)	
6	QMB101620	Column-upper-steering	1	Note (4)	Tomb Raider
7	NRC9711	Rod assembly-tie	1		
8	SH110161L	Screw-hexagonal head-M10 x 16	1		
9	WL110001L	Washer-M10	1		
10	FS110301L	Screw-flanged head-M10 x 30-top	1		
11	WA110061L	Washer-M10	1	Note (5)	
11	WF110001L	Washer-lock-10mm ID	1	Note (6)	
12	WL110001L	Washer-M10	1	Note (5)	
12	WF110001L	Washer-lock-10mm ID	1	Note (6)	
13	NH110041L	Nut-hexagonal head-coarse thread-M10	1		
14	NRC7127	Bracket-column support steering	1		
15	FS108257L	Screw-flanged head-M8 x 25	2		
16	WC108051L	Washer-M8	2		
17	NY108041L	Nut-nyloc-M8	2		
18	FS108207L	Screw-flanged head-M8 x 20	4		
19	WC108051L	Washer-M8	4		
20	NY108041L	Nut-nyloc-M8	4		
21	569522	Packing strip	4		

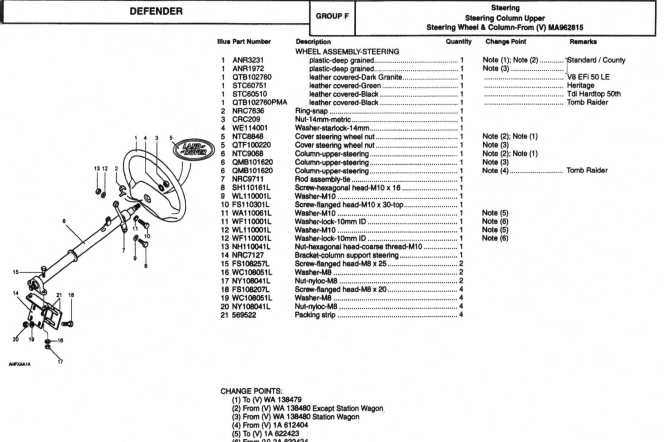

CHANGE POINTS:
(1) To (V) WA 138479
(2) From (V) WA 138480 Except Station Wagon
(3) From (V) WA 138480 Station Wagon
(4) From (V) 1A 612404
(5) To (V) 1A 622423
(6) From (V) 2A 622424

Illus	Part Number	Description	Quantity	Change Point	Remarks
1	MTC3499	Cover assembly-steering column-upper	1		
2	MTC3801	Cover assembly-steering column-lower	1		
3	SE105401	Screw-pan head-M5 x 40	2		
4	AB608031L	Screw-self tapping-No 8 x 3/8	2		
5	SE105161	Screw-pan-M5 x 16	1		
6	NRC7836	Clamp-lower	1		
7	NRC7835	Clamp-upper	1		
8	SH105121	Screw-hexagonal head-M5 x 12	2		
9	WA105001L	Washer-plain-standard-M5	2		
10	NH105041	Nut-hexagonal-M5	2		
11	331083	Plug-blanking	1		

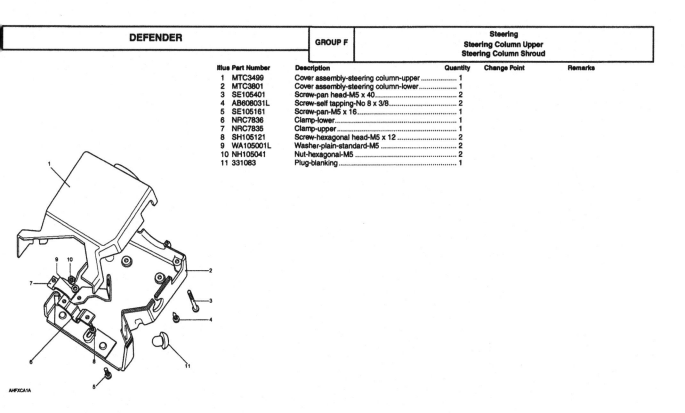

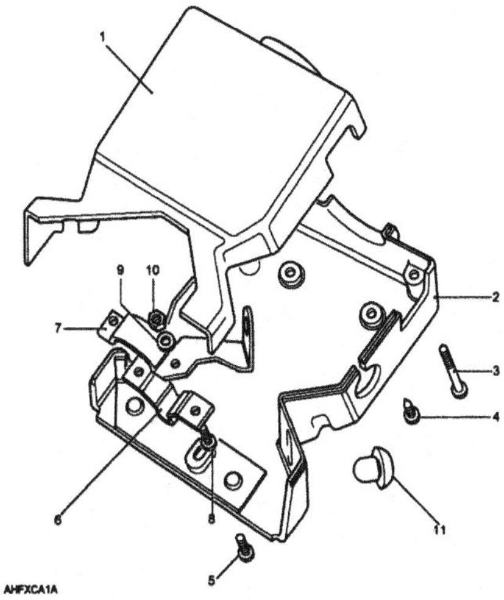

AHFXCA1A

DEFENDER	GROUP F	Steering Steering Column Upper Steering Column Top Support

Illus	Part Number	Description	Quantity	Change Point	Remarks
1	MTC1382	Bracket-steering column cover inner support	1		
2	MUC7000	Seal	1		
3	346722	Clamp-top	1		
4	MTC1078	Clamp-lower	1		
5	348747	Strip-anti rattle	1		
6	FS108257L	Screw-flanged head-M8 x 25	2		
7	WA108051L	Washer-8mm	1		
8	MTC4771	Bracket fixing	1		
9	WL108001L	Washer-sprung-M8	2		
	NN108021	Nut-blind-M8	2		
10	GG108251L	Screw-fixing bracket-hexagonal head-M8 x 125	2		
11	WL108001L	Washer-sprung-M8	2		
12	WA108051L	Washer-8mm	2		
13	GG106251L	Screw-paint clearing-M6 x 25	2		
14	WL106001L	Washer-sprung-M6	2		
15	WA106041L	Washer-6mm	2		

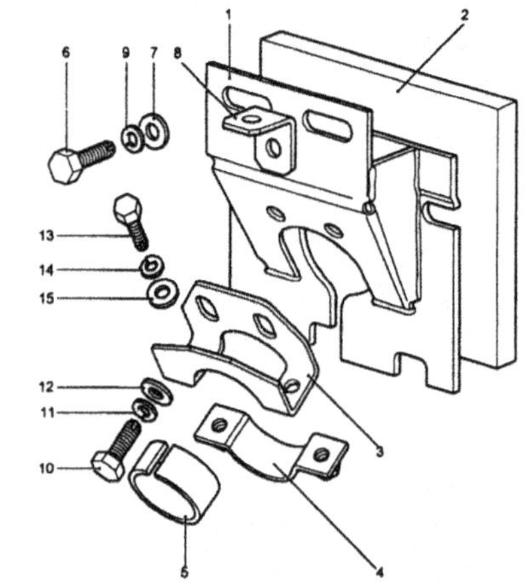

AHFXEA1A

DEFENDER	GROUP F	Steering Steering Column Lower Lower Steering Shaft

Illus	Part Number	Description	Quantity	Change Point	Remarks
1	RTC4738	Shaft assembly-steering steering column	1	Note (1)	
2	NRC7387	Joint-universal steering linkage-upper	1		
3	NRC7704	Joint-universal steering linkage-lower	1		
4	BH108091L	Bolt-M8 x 45	4		
5	NY108041L	Nut-nyloc-M8	4		
6	QLG100000	Shaft-universal joint steering	1	Note (2)	
7	QLC100080	Joint-universal steering linkage	1		
8	BH108077	Bolt-M8 x 35	3		

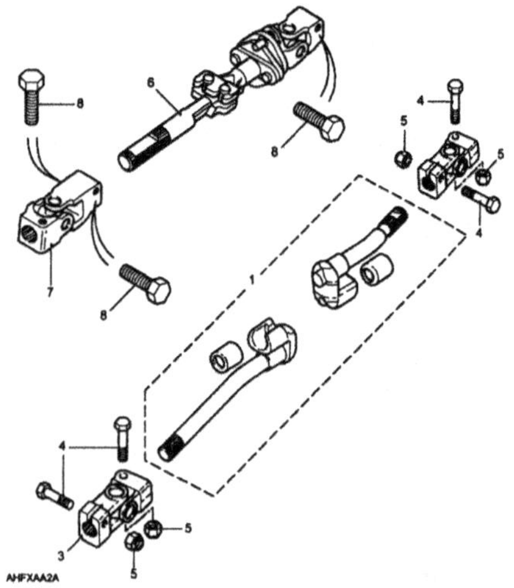

AHFXAA2A

CHANGE POINTS:
(1) To (V) VA 133508
(2) From (V) VA 133509

DEFENDER

GROUP F

Steering
Steering Column Lower
Steering Box-Manual-Gemmer

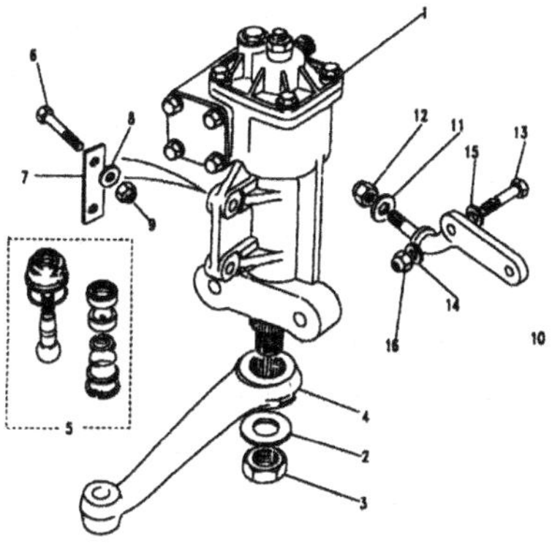

Illus	Part Number	Description	Quantity	Change Point	Remarks
1	NRC8588	Box assembly-steering	NLA	To (V) 311627 RHD	Use NTC2590.
1	NRC8589	Box assembly-steering	NLA	To (V) 322575 LHD	Use NTC2591.
		BOX ASSEMBLY-STEERING			
1	NTC2590	GEMMER-NEW-RHD	NLA		Use NTC8224.
1	NTC2591	GEMMER-NEW-LHD	NLA		Use NTC8223.
1	NTC2590E	GEMMER-EXCHANGE-RHD	1		
1	NTC2591E	GEMMER-EXCHANGE-LHD	1		
2	AEU4025	• Washer-steering box drop arm nut tab-Gemmer	1		
3	AEU4026	• Nut	1		
4	RTC6398	Lever-drop arm steering-RHD	1		
4	RTC6399	Lever-drop arm steering-LHD	1		
5	AEU2761	Joint-ball-outer steering gear-steering lever arm	1	Note (1); Note (2)	
6	BH607381	Bolt-7/16UNF-hexagonal head	4		
5	RTC4198	Joint-ball-outer steering gear-RH	NLA	Note (3); Note (4)	Use STC3295.
6	BX112201	Bolt-M12 x 100-hexagonal head	4		
7	572077	Washer	2		
8	WA600071L	Washer	8	Note (1); Note (2)	
9	NY607041L	Nut-nyloc-7/16UNF	2		
8	WA112081L	Washer-plain-standard-M12	4	Note (3); Note (4)	
10	594947	Bar-tie-bent forging-RHD	NLA	To (V) LA 939975	Use ANR2994 qty 1 with BH607201L qty 2.
10	594946	Bar-tie-bent forging-LHD	NLA		Use ANR2994 qty 1 with BH607201L qty 2.
10	ANR2994	Bar-tie-bent forging	2	From (V) MA 939976	
11	4905	Washer-1/2"	1	To (V) MA 940009	
12	NY608041L	Nut-hexagonal-nyloc-1/2UNF	1		
13	253963	Bolt	2	To (V) MA 940009	
14	217245	Washer-plain-No 10	2		
15	3261	Washer-plain	2		
16	NY607041L	Nut-nyloc-7/16UNF	2		
13	BH112121L	Bolt-M12 x 60	2	From (V) MA 940010	
14	WA112081L	Washer-plain-standard-M12	2		
15	WA112081L	Washer-plain-standard-M12	2		
16	NY112041L	Nut-M12-hexagonal head-nyloc	2		

CHANGE POINTS:
(1) To (V) 311627 RHD
(2) To (V) 322575 LHD
(3) From (V) 311628 RHD
(4) From (V) 322576 LHD

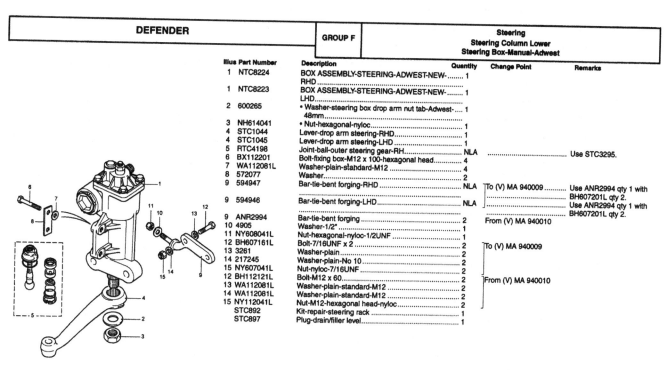

DEFENDER

GROUP F

Steering
Steering Column Lower
Steering Box-Manual-Adwest

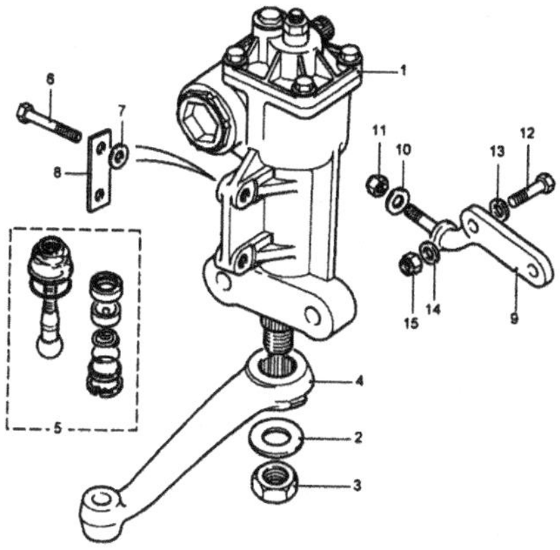

AHFXGA3A

Illus	Part Number	Description	Quantity	Change Point	Remarks
1	NTC8224	BOX ASSEMBLY-STEERING-ADWEST-NEW-RHD	1		
1	NTC8223	BOX ASSEMBLY-STEERING-ADWEST-NEW-LHD	1		
2	600265	• Washer-steering box drop arm nut tab-Adwest-48mm	1		
3	NH614041	• Nut-hexagonal-nyloc	1		
4	STC1044	Lever-drop arm steering-RHD	1		
4	STC1045	Lever-drop arm steering-LHD	1		
5	RTC4198	Joint-ball-outer steering gear-RH	NLA		Use STC3295.
6	BX112201	Bolt-fixing box-M12 x 100-hexagonal head	4		
7	WA112081L	Washer-plain-standard-M12	4		
8	572077	Washer	2		
9	594947	Bar-tie-bent forging-RHD	NLA	To (V) MA 940009	Use ANR2994 qty 1 with BH607201L qty 2.
9	594946	Bar-tie-bent forging-LHD	NLA		Use ANR2994 qty 1 with BH607201L qty 2.
9	ANR2994	Bar-tie-bent forging	2	From (V) MA 940010	
10	4905	Washer-1/2"	1		
11	NY608041L	Nut-hexagonal-nyloc-1/2UNF	1		
12	BH607161L	Bolt-7/16UNF x 2	2	To (V) MA 940009	
13	3261	Washer-plain	2		
14	217245	Washer-plain-No 10	2		
15	NY607041L	Nut-nyloc-7/16UNF	2		
12	BH112121L	Bolt-M12 x 60	2	From (V) MA 940010	
13	WA112081L	Washer-plain-standard-M12	2		
14	WA112081L	Washer-plain-standard-M12	2		
15	NY112041L	Nut-M12-hexagonal head-nyloc	2		
	STC892	Kit-repair-steering rack	1		
	STC897	Plug-drain/filler level	1		

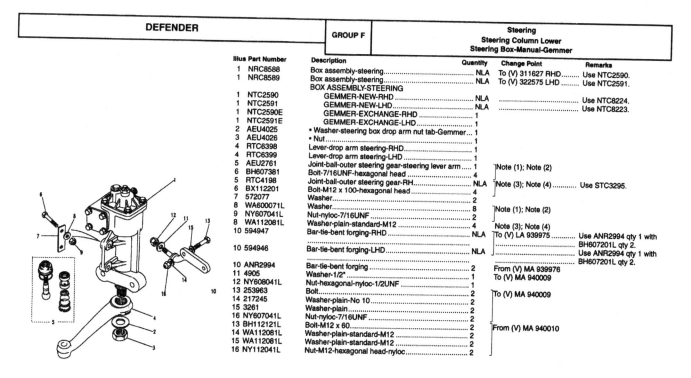

DEFENDER	GROUP F	Steering Steering Column Lower Steering Box-Power-Gemmer

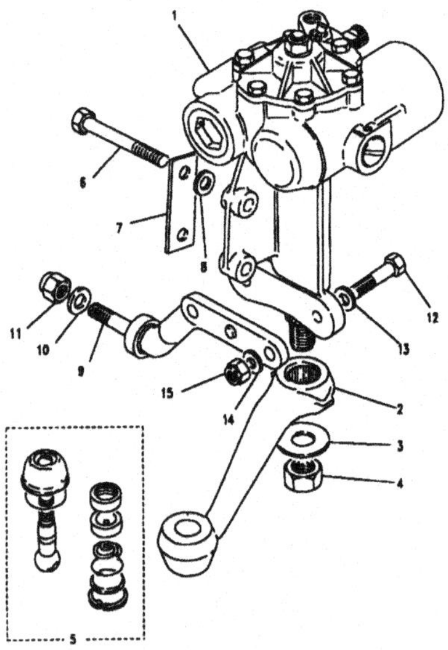

Illus	Part Number	Description	Quantity	Change Point	Remarks
		BOX ASSEMBLY-STEERING			
1	NTC1582	Gemmer-new-RHD	1		
1	NTC1583	Gemmer-new-LHD	1		
1	NTC1582E	Gemmer-exchange-RHD	1		
1	NTC1583E	Gemmer-exchange-LHD	1		
2	RTC6398	Lever-drop arm steering-RHD	1		
2	RTC6399	Lever-drop arm steering-LHD	1		
3	AEU4025	Washer-steering box drop arm nut tab-Gemmer	1		
4	AEU4026	Nut	1		
5	RTC4198	Joint-ball-outer steering gear-RH	NLA		Use STC3295.
6	BX112201	Bolt-M12 x 100-hexagonal head	4		
7	572077	Washer	2		
8	WA112081L	Washer-plain-standard-M12	4		
9	594947	Bar-tie-bent forging-RHD	NLA		Use ANR2994 qty 1 with BH607201L qty 2.
9	594946	Bar-tie-bent forging-LHD	NLA		Use ANR2994 qty 1 with BH607201L qty 2.
10	4905	Washer-1/2"	1		
11	NY608041L	Nut-hexagonal-nyloc-1/2UNF	1		
12	BH607161L	Bolt-7/16UNF x 2	2		
13	3261	Washer-plain	2		
14	217245	Washer-plain-No 10	2		
15	NY607041L	Nut-nyloc-7/16UNF	2		
	RTC5068	Valve assembly-power assisted steering pump	1		
	RTC5069	Shaft-front output-LHD	1		
	RTC5070	Shaft-front output-RHD	1		
	RTC5071	Kit-power assisted steering box seal	1		
	RTC5072	Kit-repair-steering rack	1		
	RTC5073	Cover assembly-trochoid power assisted steering	1		
	RTC5074	Kit-bearing	1		

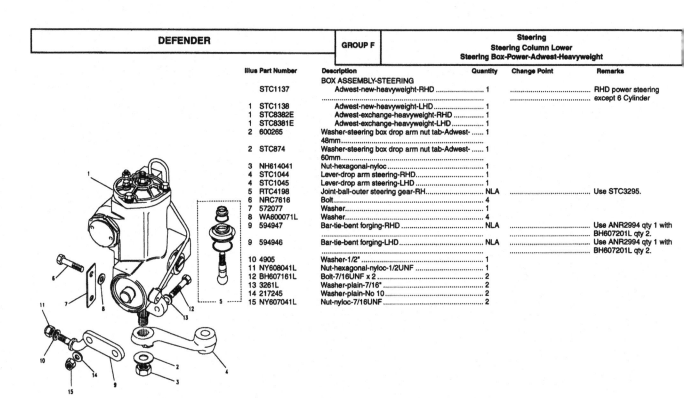

DEFENDER	GROUP F	Steering Steering Column Lower Steering Box-Power-Adwest-Heavyweight

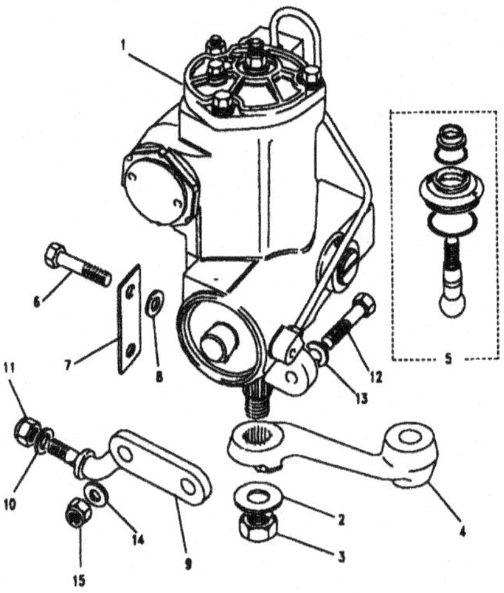

Illus	Part Number	Description	Quantity	Change Point	Remarks
		BOX ASSEMBLY-STEERING			
	STC1137	Adwest-new-heavyweight-RHD	1		RHD power steering except 6 Cylinder
1	STC1138	Adwest-new-heavyweight-LHD	1		
1	STC8382E	Adwest-exchange-heavyweight-RHD	1		
1	STC8381E	Adwest-exchange-heavyweight-LHD	1		
2	600265	Washer-steering box drop arm nut tab-Adwest-48mm	1		
2	STC874	Washer-steering box drop arm nut tab-Adwest-60mm	1		
3	NH614041	Nut-hexagonal-nyloc	1		
4	STC1044	Lever-drop arm steering-RHD	1		
4	STC1045	Lever-drop arm steering-LHD	1		
5	RTC4198	Joint-ball-outer steering gear-RH	NLA		Use STC3295.
6	NRC7616	Bolt	4		
7	572077	Washer	1		
8	WA600071L	Washer	4		
9	594947	Bar-tie-bent forging-RHD	NLA		Use ANR2994 qty 1 with BH607201L qty 2.
9	594946	Bar-tie-bent forging-LHD	NLA		Use ANR2994 qty 1 with BH607201L qty 2.
10	4905	Washer-1/2"	1		
11	NY608041L	Nut-hexagonal-nyloc-1/2UNF	1		
12	BH607161L	Bolt-7/16UNF x 2	2		
13	3261L	Washer-plain-7/16"	2		
14	217245	Washer-plain-No 10	2		
15	NY607041L	Nut-nyloc-7/16UNF	2		

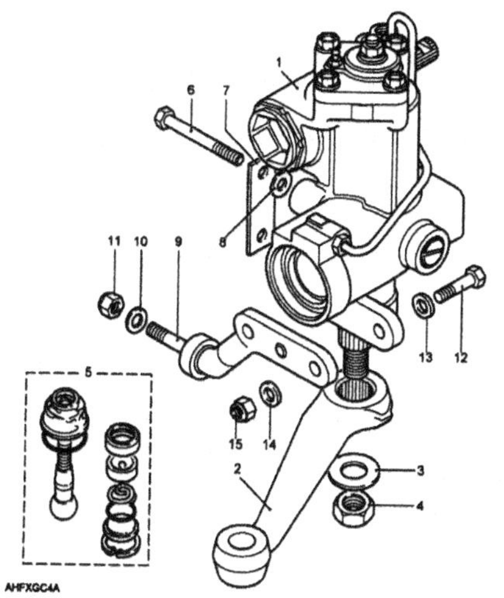

AHFXGC4A

Illus	Part Number	Description	Quantity	Change Point	Remarks
		BOX ASSEMBLY-STEERING			
1	STC398	Adwest-lightweight-RHD-new	1	To (V) JA 919038	
1	STC837	Adwest-lightweight-RHD-new	NLA	From (V) JA 919039	Use STC887.
1	STC887	Adwest-lightweight-RHD-new	1	To (V) MA 955519	
1	STC888	Adwest-lightweight-LHD-new	1		
1	STC2846	Adwest-lightweight-RHD-new	1	Note (1)	
1	STC2845	Adwest-lightweight-LHD-new	1		
1	QAF000140	Adwest-lightweight-RHD-new	1	Note (2)	Except 6 Cylinder and 50 LE
1	QAF000150	Adwest-lightweight-LHD-new	1	Note (2)	
1	STC3947	Adwest-lightweight-new	1		6 Cylinder
1	STC8384E	Adwest-lightweight-RHD-exchange	1		
1	STC8383E	Adwest-lightweight-LHD-exchange	1		
2	STC1044	Lever-drop arm steering-RHD	1		
2	STC1045	Lever-drop arm steering-LHD	1		
3	600265	Washer-steering box drop arm nut tab-Adwest-48mm	1		Power steering
3	STC874	Washer-steering box drop arm nut tab-Adwest-60mm	1		Power steering
4	NT614041L	Nut-drop arm to steering box	1		
5	RTC4198	Joint-ball-outer steering gear-RH	NLA		Use STC3295.
5	STC3295	Joint-ball-outer steering gear-RH	1		
6	BX112201	Bolt-M12 x 100-hexagonal head	4		
7	572077	Washer	2		
8	WA112081L	Washer-plain-standard-M12	4		
9	594947	Bar-tie-bent forging-RHD	NLA	To (V) MA 940009	Use ANR2994 qty 1 with BH607201L qty 2.
9	594946	Bar-tie-bent forging-LHD	NLA		
9	ANR2994	Bar-tie-bent forging	1	From (V) MA 940010	
10	4905	Washer-1/2"	1		
11	NY608041L	Nut-hexagonal-nyloc-1/2UNF	1		
12	BH607161L	Bolt-7/16UNF x 2	2	To (V) MA 940009	
13	3261L	Washer-plain-7/16"	2		
14	217245	Washer-plain-No 10	2		
15	NY607041L	Nut-nyloc-7/16UNF	2		
12	BH112121L	Bolt-M12 x 60	2	From (V) MA 940010	
13	WA112081L	Washer-plain-standard-M12	2		
14	WA112081L	Washer-plain-standard-M12	2		
15	NY112041L	Nut-M12-hexagonal head-nyloc	2		

CHANGE POINTS:
(1) From (V) MA 955520 To (V) ZA 999999
(2) From (V) 2A 622424

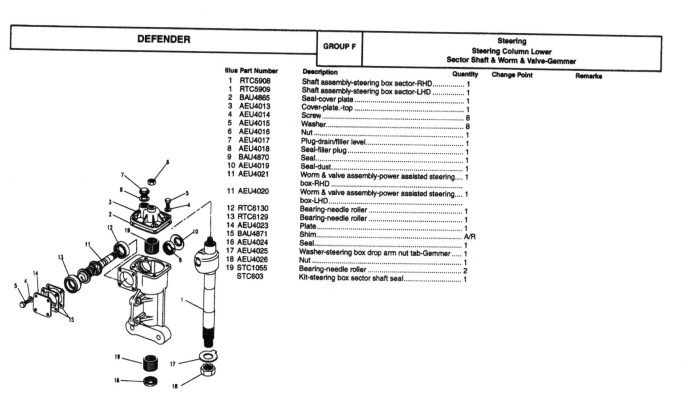

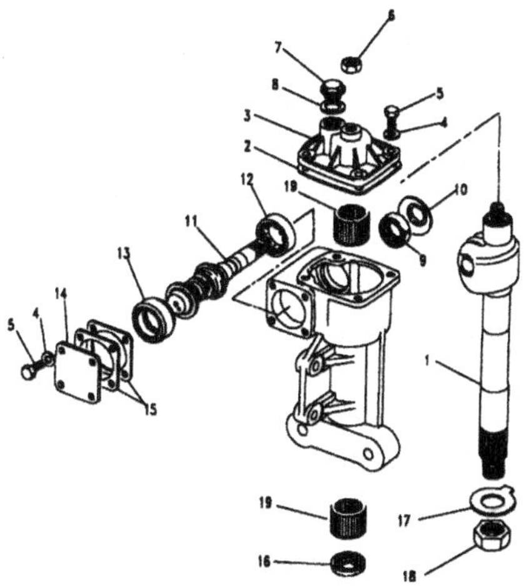

Illus	Part Number	Description	Quantity	Change Point	Remarks
1	RTC5908	Shaft assembly-steering box sector-RHD	1		
1	RTC5909	Shaft assembly-steering box sector-LHD	1		
2	BAU4865	Seal-cover plate	1		
3	AEU4013	Cover-plate.-top	1		
4	AEU4014	Screw	8		
5	AEU4015	Washer	8		
6	AEU4016	Nut	1		
7	AEU4017	Plug-drain/filler level	1		
8	AEU4018	Seal-filler plug	1		
9	BAU4870	Seal	1		
10	AEU4019	Seal-dust	1		
11	AEU4021	Worm & valve assembly-power assisted steering box-RHD	1		
11	AEU4020	Worm & valve assembly-power assisted steering box-LHD	1		
12	RTC6130	Bearing-needle roller	1		
13	RTC6129	Bearing-needle roller	1		
14	AEU4023	Plate	1		
15	BAU4871	Shim	A/R		
16	AEU4024	Seal	1		
17	AEU4025	Washer-steering box drop arm nut tab-Gemmer	1		
18	AEU4026	Nut	1		
19	STC1055	Bearing-needle roller	2		
	STC603	Kit-steering box sector shaft seal	1		

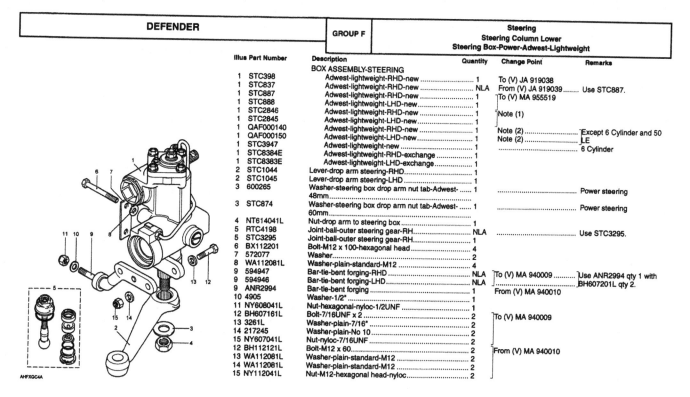

DEFENDER

GROUP F

Steering
Steering Column Lower
Sector Shaft-Adwest Heavyweight

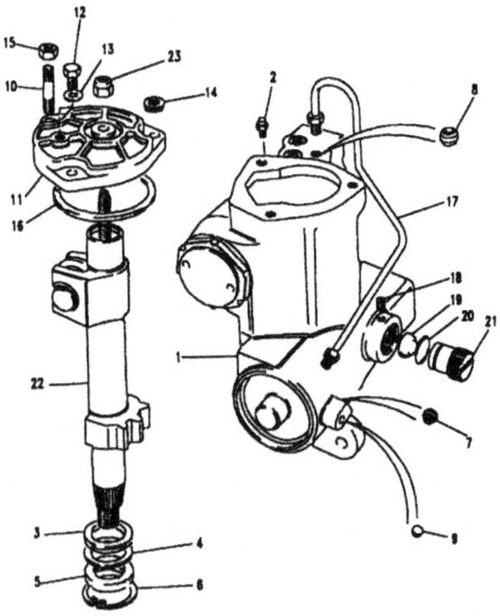

Illus	Part Number	Description	Quantity	Change Point	Remarks
1	AEU1358	Housing assembly-RHD	1		
1	AEU1359	Housing assembly-LHD	1		
2	606564	Plug	1		
3	STC1042	KIT-STEERING BOX SECTOR SHAFT SEAL	NLA		Use STC2848.
4	608068	• Washer	NLA		Use STC1042.
6	606551	• Circlip	NLA		Use STC1042.
11	RTC6110	• Seal-dust & dirt	NLA		Use STC1042.
3	STC2848	Kit-steering box sector shaft seal	1		
7	11987L	Olive	1		
8	11988L	Olive	1		
9	BLS108L	Ball-detent manual transmission	1		
10	RTC297	Stud	3		
11	RTC6110	Seal-dust & dirt	NLA		Use STC1042.
	RTC294	Cover-power assisted steering box piston retaining	1		
12	11015L	Screw-bleed	1		
13	608069	Seal	1		
14	RTC298	Washer	3		
15	RTC299	Nut	3		
16	RTC295	Seal	1		
		PIPE ASSEMBLY POWER ASSISTED STEERING			
17	AEU1029	straight end-RHD	1		
17	RTC307	straight end-LHD	1		
17	RTC6782	right angled end-RHD	1		
17	RTC6783	right angled end-LHD	1		
18	11011L	Screw-grub	1		
19	606544	Pad-buffer	1		
20	608065	Seal-steering rack pinion-rack adjustment screw	1		
21	606545	Screw-rack guide power assisted steering	1		
22	RTC300	Shaft assembly-steering box sector-RHD	1		
22	RTC301	Shaft assembly-steering box sector-LHD	1		
23	90606566	Nut	1		

DEFENDER

GROUP F

Steering
Steering Column Lower
Sector Shaft-Adwest Lightweight

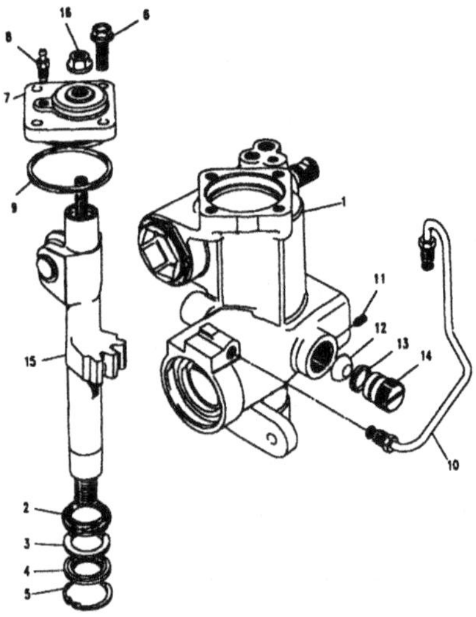

Illus	Part Number	Description	Quantity	Change Point	Remarks
1	RTC4391	Housing assembly	NLA		RHD
1	RTC4392	Housing assembly	NLA		LHD
1	STC416	Housing assembly-Adwest-lightweight-RHD-new	1		
2	608066	Seal-inner output shaft	NLA		Use STC1042.
4	RTC6110	Seal-dust & dirt	NLA		Use STC1042.
6	RTC4393	Screw-cover power steering box	4		
7	STC418	Cover-power assisted steering box piston retaining	NLA		Part no longer available steering box must now be replaced choose either new or exchange box from catalogue.
8	RTC4395	Screw-bleed	1		
10	RTC4400	Pipe assembly power assisted steering-RHD	1		
10	RTC4401	Pipe assembly power assisted steering-LHD	1		
11	11011L	Screw-grub	1		
12	606544	Pad-buffer	1		
13	608065	Seal-steering rack pinion	1		
14	606545	Screw-rack guide power assisted steering	1		
15	RTC4398	SHAFT ASSEMBLY-STEERING BOX SECTOR-RHD	1		
15	RTC4399	SHAFT ASSEMBLY-STEERING BOX SECTOR-LHD	1		
16	RTC4394	• Nut	1		
	STC890	Kit-power assisted steering box seal	NLA	Note (1)	Use STC2847.
	STC2847	Kit-power assisted steering box seal	1	Note (2)	
	STC1042	KIT-STEERING BOX SECTOR SHAFT SEAL	NLA	Note (1)	Use STC2848.
	608068	• Washer	NLA		Use STC1042.
	606551	• Circlip	NLA		Use STC1042.
4	RTC6110	• Seal-dust & dirt	NLA		Use STC1042.
	STC2848	Kit-steering box sector shaft seal	1	Note (2)	
	STC1040	KIT-POWER ASSISTED STEERING BOX SEAL-PAD ADJUSTER	NLA		Use STC4385.
11	11011L	• Screw-grub	1		
14	606545	• Screw-rack guide power assisted steering	1		
	STC4385	Kit-power assisted steering box seal-pad adjuster	1		

CHANGE POINTS:
(1) To (V) MA 955519
(2) From (V) MA 955520

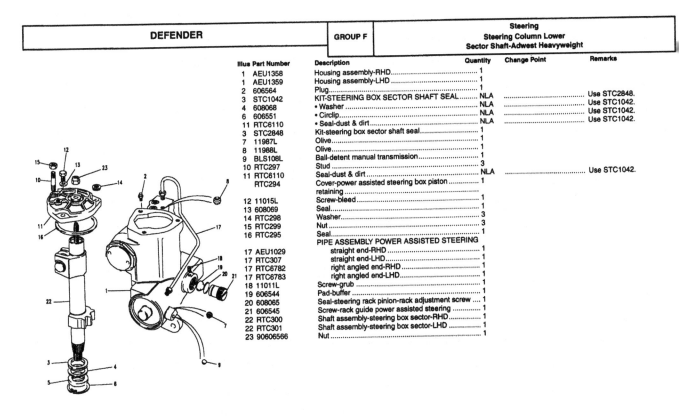

DEFENDER

GROUP F | **Steering — Steering Column Lower — Worm & Valve-Adwest Heavyweight**

Illus	Part Number	Description	Quantity	Change Point	Remarks
1	606542	Piston power assisted steering	1	Note (1)	
2	RTC308	Kit-power assisted steering pump seal	1	Note (1)	
3	606543	Cover-power assisted steering box piston retaining	1	Note (1)	
4	11009L	Clip	NLA	Note (1)	
5	STC1041	Kit-steering box sector shaft seal	NLA	Note (1)	Use STC875.
5	STC875	Kit-steering box sector shaft seal	NLA	Note (1)	Use STC889.
5	STC889	Kit-steering box sector shaft seal	1		
6	AEU1248	Seal	NLA	Note (1)	Use STC1041.
7	605061	Bearing-needle roller	1	Note (1)	
8	RTC2762	Set-shim	1	Note (1)	
9	606538	Bearing-ball	2	Note (1)	
10	608000	Ring power assisted steering	4	Note (1)	
11	606567	Circlip	1	Note (1)	
12	AEU1356	Worm & valve assembly-power assisted steering box-RHD	1	Note (1)	
12	AEU1357	Worm & valve assembly-power assisted steering box-LHD	1	Note (1)	
13	608073	Seal	1	Note (1)	
14	RTC306	Screw	1	Note (1)	
15	606553	Locknut	1	Note (1)	

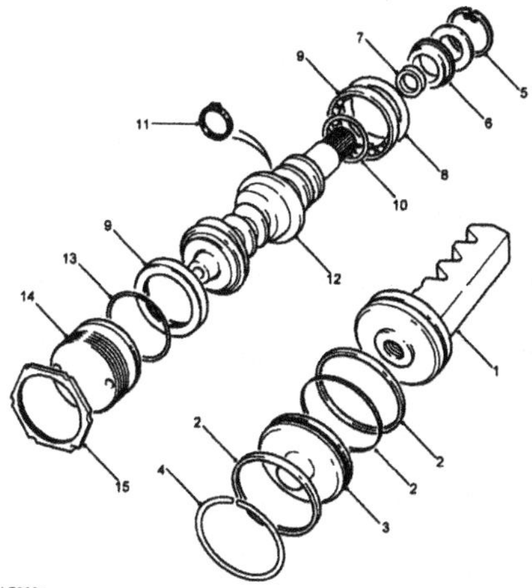

LF0004

CHANGE POINTS:
(1) To (V) AA 244022

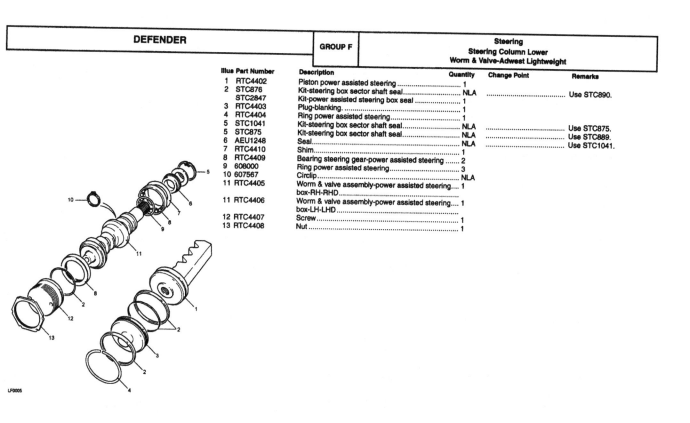

DEFENDER

GROUP F | **Steering — Steering Column Lower — Worm & Valve-Adwest Lightweight**

Illus	Part Number	Description	Quantity	Change Point	Remarks
1	RTC4402	Piston power assisted steering	1		
2	STC876	Kit-steering box sector shaft seal	NLA		Use STC890.
	STC2847	Kit-power assisted steering box seal	1		
3	RTC4403	Plug-blanking.	1		
4	RTC4404	Ring power assisted steering	1		
5	STC1041	Kit-steering box sector shaft seal	NLA		Use STC875.
5	STC875	Kit-steering box sector shaft seal	NLA		Use STC889.
6	AEU1248	Seal	NLA		Use STC1041.
7	RTC4410	Shim	1		
8	RTC4409	Bearing steering gear-power assisted steering	2		
9	608000	Ring power assisted steering	3		
10	607567	Circlip	NLA		
11	RTC4405	Worm & valve assembly-power assisted steering box-RH-RHD	1		
11	RTC4406	Worm & valve assembly-power assisted steering box-LH-LHD	1		
12	RTC4407	Screw	1		
13	RTC4408	Nut	1		

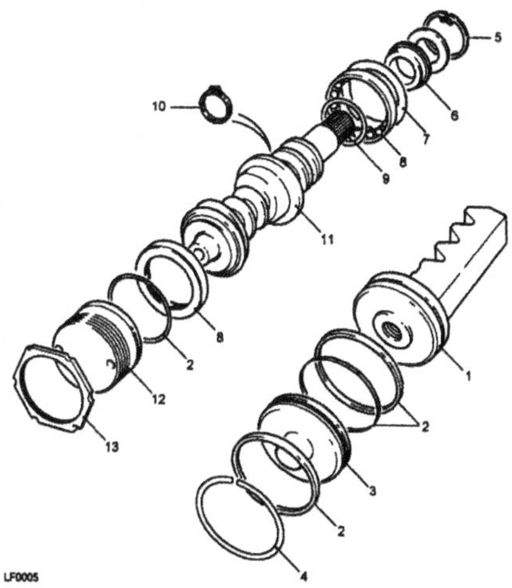

LF0005

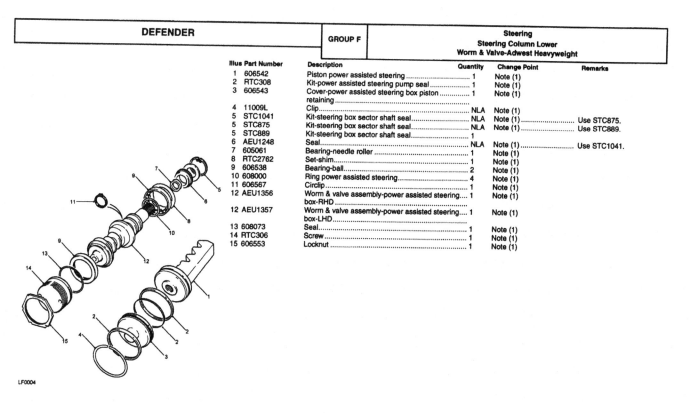

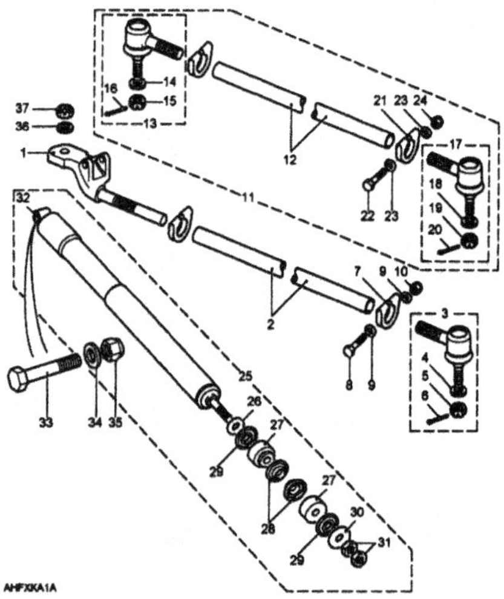

AHFXKA1A

Illus	Part Number	Description	Quantity	Change Point	Remarks
		CROSS ROD-EYE END			
1	NRC8231	RHD	1	Note (1)	
1	NRC8232	LHD	1	Note (1)	
1	ANR2858	RHD	1	Note (2)	
1	ANR2859	LHD	1	Note (2)	
2	NRC5582	Tube-tie bar	1	Note (3)	
2	NRC9741	Tube-tie bar	1	Note (4)	
2	ANR2860	Tube-tie bar	1	Note (2)	
3	RTC5869	KIT-BALL JOINT-RH-R/H THREAD	1		
4	WC112081L	• Washer-plain-M12 x 28	2		
5	NC112041	• Nut-castle-M12	2		
6	PS106321L	• Pin-split-3.2 x 32	1		
7	577898	Clamp-tube	2		
8	BH604151L	Bolt-1/4UNF x 7/8	2		
9	WA106041L	Washer-6mm	4		
10	NY604041L	Nut-1/4"-hexagonal-nyloc	2		
11	NRC9743	END ASSEMBLY-TRACK ROD	1		
12	NRC9742	• Tube-track rod	1		
13	RTC5869	• KIT-BALL JOINT-RH-R/H THREAD	1		
14	WC112081L	• • Washer-plain-M12 x 28	2		
15	NC112041	• • Nut-castle-M12	2		
16	PS106321L	• • Pin-split-3.2 x 32	1		
17	RTC5870	• KIT-BALL JOINT-LH-L/H THREAD	1		
18	WC112081L	• • Washer-plain-M12 x 28	1		
19	NC112041	• • Nut-castle-M12	1		
20	PS106321L	• • Pin-split-3.2 x 32	1		
21	577898	• Clamp-tube	2		
22	BH604151L	• Bolt-1/4UNF x 7/8	2		
23	WA106041L	• Washer-6mm	4		
24	NY604041L	• Nut-1/4"-hexagonal-nyloc	2		

CHANGE POINTS:
(1) To (V) LA 939975
(2) From (V) MA 939976
(3) To (V) JA 917433
(4) From (V) JA 917434 To (V) LA 939975

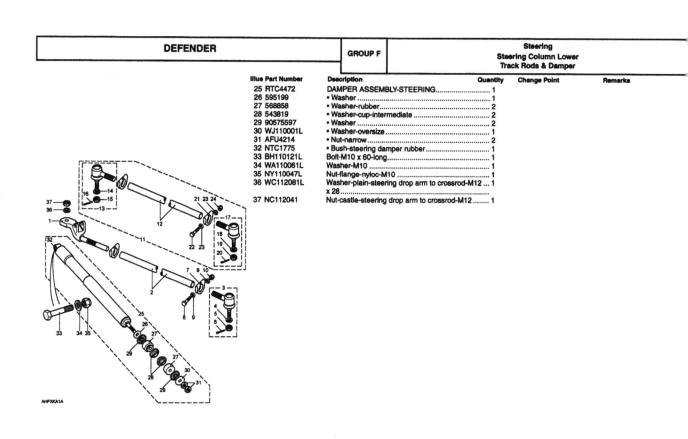

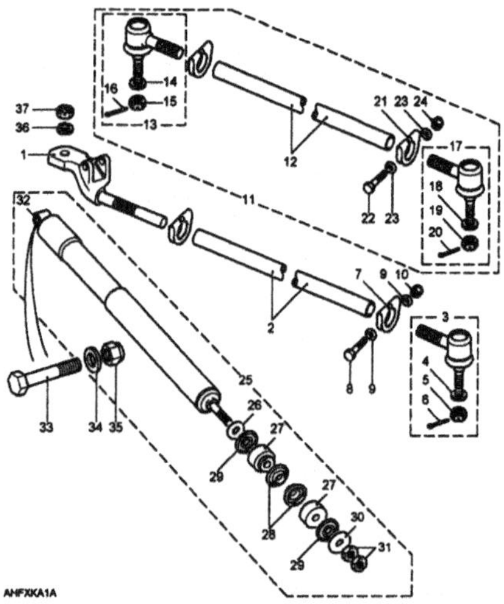

AHFXKA1A

Illus	Part Number	Description	Quantity	Change Point	Remarks
25	RTC4472	DAMPER ASSEMBLY-STEERING	1		
26	595199	• Washer	1		
27	568858	• Washer-rubber	2		
28	543819	• Washer-cup-intermediate	2		
29	90575597	• Washer	2		
30	WJ110001L	• Washer-oversize	1		
31	AFU4214	• Nut-narrow	2		
32	NTC1775	• Bush-steering damper rubber	1		
33	BH110121L	Bolt-M10 x 60-long	1		
34	WA110061L	Washer-M10	1		
35	NY110047L	Nut-flange-nyloc-M10	1		
36	WC112081L	Washer-plain-steering drop arm to crossrod-M12 x 28	1		
37	NC112041	Nut-castle-steering drop arm to crossrod-M12	1		

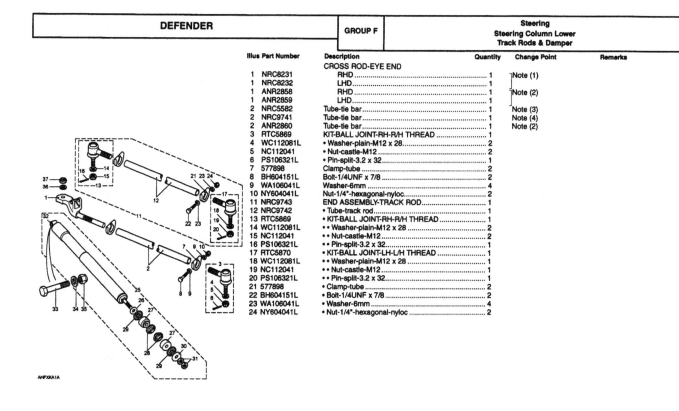

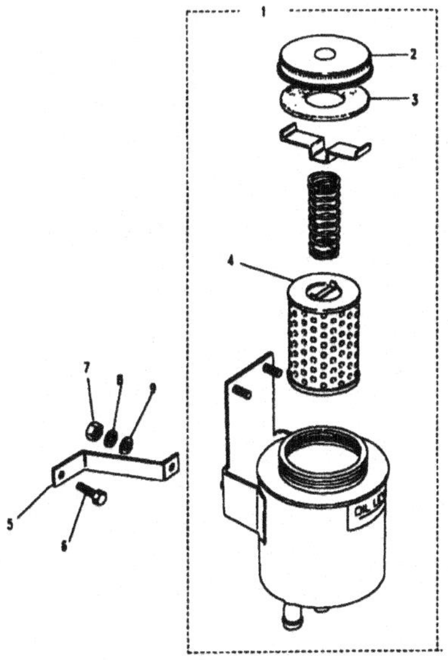

Illus	Part Number	Description	Quantity	Change Point	Remarks
1	NRC9551	RESERVOIR ASSEMBLY POWER ASSISTED STEERING FLUID	1	Note (1)	Except air conditioning
1	NRC9552	RESERVOIR ASSEMBLY POWER ASSISTED STEERING FLUID	1	Note (2)	
2	RTC3056	• Cap power assisted steering reservoir	1		
3	RTC3962	• Seal	1		
4	RTC3058	• Filter-reservoir	1		
5	NRC5982	Bracket power assisted steering reservoir	1		
6	SH106167	Screw-hexagonal head-M6 x 16	1		
7	NH106047	Nut-M6-hexagonal	4		
8	WA106047L	Washer-plain-M6-standard	4		
9	WL106007L	Washer-M6-rectangular	1		

CHANGE POINTS:
(1) To (V) AA 244022
(2) From (V) AA 244023 To (V) AA 270226

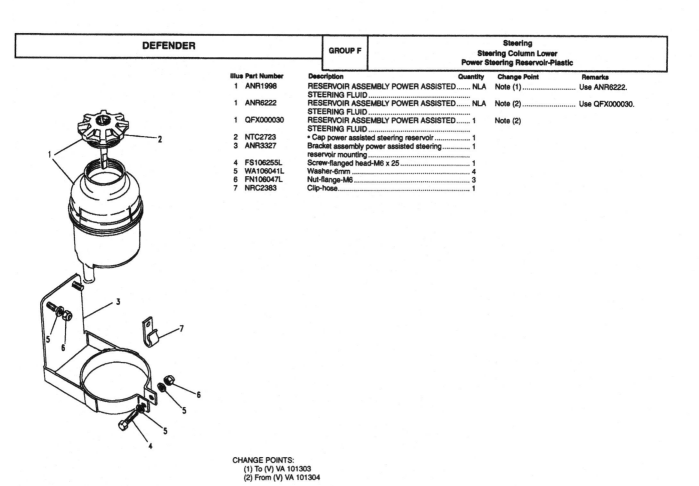

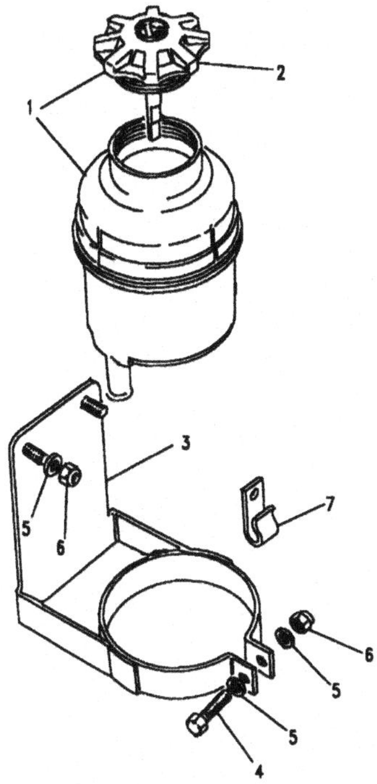

Illus	Part Number	Description	Quantity	Change Point	Remarks
1	ANR1998	RESERVOIR ASSEMBLY POWER ASSISTED STEERING FLUID	NLA	Note (1)	Use ANR6222.
1	ANR6222	RESERVOIR ASSEMBLY POWER ASSISTED STEERING FLUID	NLA	Note (2)	Use QFX000030.
1	QFX000030	RESERVOIR ASSEMBLY POWER ASSISTED STEERING FLUID	1	Note (2)	
2	NTC2723	• Cap power assisted steering reservoir	1		
3	ANR3327	Bracket assembly power assisted steering reservoir mounting	1		
4	FS106255L	Screw-flanged head-M6 x 25	1		
5	WA106041L	Washer-6mm	4		
6	FN106047L	Nut-flange-M6	3		
7	NRC2383	Clip-hose	1		

CHANGE POINTS:
(1) To (V) VA 101303
(2) From (V) VA 101304

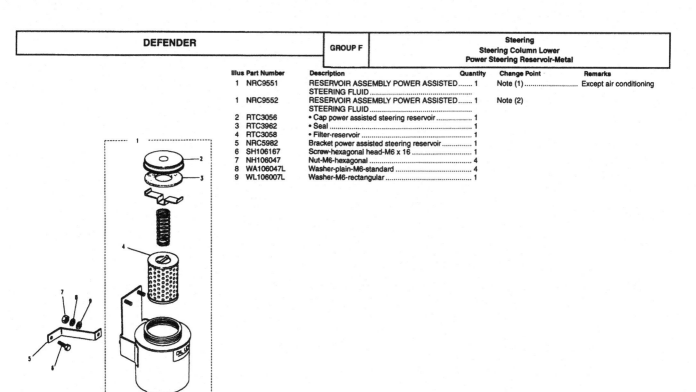

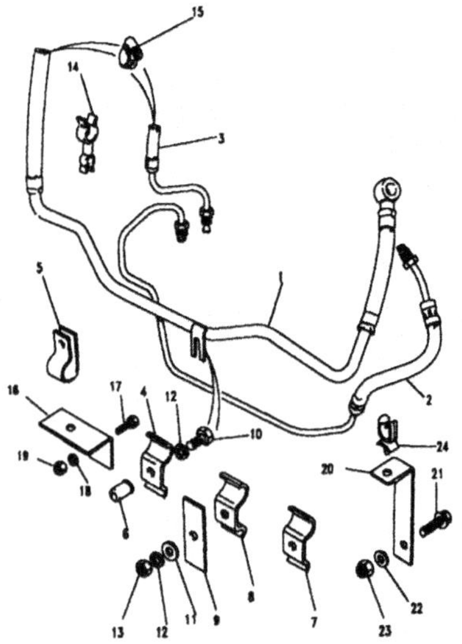

Illus	Part Number	Description	Quantity	Change Point	Remarks
1	NRC8286	Hose-power assisted steering reservoir to pump	1	Note (1)	Petrol
1	NRC8286	Hose-power assisted steering reservoir to pump	1		Diesel Naturally Aspirated
1	NTC1691	Hose-power assisted steering reservoir to pump	1	Note (2)	Petrol
1	NTC1691	Hose-power assisted steering reservoir to pump	1		Diesel Naturally Aspirated
1	NTC6863	Hose-power assisted steering reservoir to pump	1	Note (3)	Petrol
1	NTC6863	Hose-power assisted steering reservoir to pump	1		Diesel Naturally Aspirated
1	NTC3066	Hose-power assisted steering reservoir to pump	1	Note (4)	Diesel Turbo
1	NTC6863	Hose-power assisted steering reservoir to pump	1	Note (5)	Diesel Turbo
1	NTC8192	Hose-power assisted steering reservoir to pump	1	Note (6)	Diesel TDi Turbo
1	NRC5975	Hose-power assisted steering reservoir to pump	1	Note (1)	V8 Petrol
1	NTC1685	Hose-power assisted steering reservoir to pump	1	Note (7)	
1	NTC2595	Hose-power assisted steering reservoir to pump	1	Note (9)	
		PIPE ASSEMBLY-PUMP TO STEERING BOX			
2	NRC8290	RHD	1	To (V) AA 244022	Petrol
2	NRC8290	RHD	1		Diesel Naturally Aspirated
2	NTC5001	RHD	1	Note (8)	Petrol
2	NTC5001	RHD	1		Diesel Naturally Aspirated
2	NTC6731	RHD	1	From (V) FA 389465	Petrol
2	NTC6731	RHD	1		Diesel Naturally Aspirated
2	NTC5001	RHD	1	To (V) FA 389464	RHD Diesel Turbo
2	NTC6731	RHD	1	From (V) FA 389465	
2	NTC8193	RHD	1	To (V) JA 918809	Diesel Turbo TDi
2	NRC7988	RHD	1	To (V) AA 244022	V8 Petrol
2	NTC1687	RHD	1	Note (7)	
2	NTC2597	Pipe assembly-pump to steering box	1	From (V) 262025	RHD V8 Petrol

CHANGE POINTS:
(1) To (V) AA 244022
(2) From (V) AA 244023 To (V) FA 388915
(3) From (V) FA 388916
(4) To (V) FA 388915
(5) From (V) FA 388916 To (V) HA 455645
(6) From (V) HA 455945
(7) From (V) AA 244023 To (V) 262024
(8) From (V) AA 244023 To (V) FA 389464
(9) From (V) 262025

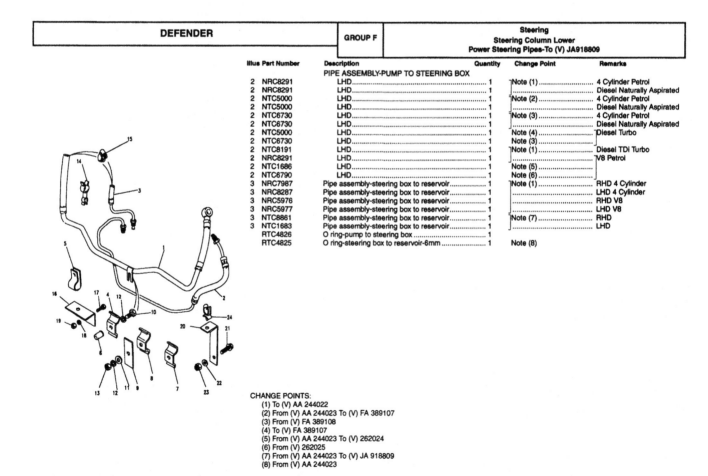

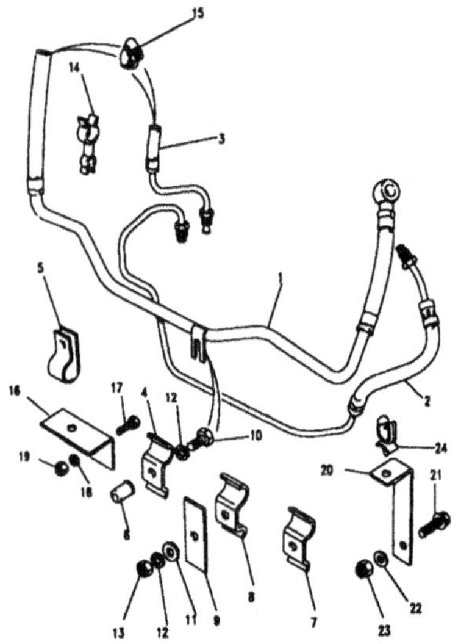

Illus	Part Number	Description	Quantity	Change Point	Remarks
		PIPE ASSEMBLY-PUMP TO STEERING BOX			
2	NRC8291	LHD	1	Note (1)	4 Cylinder Petrol
2	NRC8291	LHD	1		Diesel Naturally Aspirated
2	NTC5000	LHD	1	Note (2)	4 Cylinder Petrol
2	NTC5000	LHD	1		Diesel Naturally Aspirated
2	NTC6730	LHD	1	Note (3)	4 Cylinder Petrol
2	NTC6730	LHD	1		Diesel Naturally Aspirated
2	NTC5000	LHD	1	Note (4)	Diesel Turbo
2	NTC6730	LHD	1	Note (3)	
2	NTC8191	LHD	1	Note (1)	Diesel TDi Turbo
2	NRC8291	LHD	1		V8 Petrol
2	NTC1686	LHD	1	Note (5)	
2	NTC6790	LHD	1	Note (6)	
3	NRC7987	Pipe assembly-steering box to reservoir	1	Note (1)	RHD 4 Cylinder
3	NRC8287	Pipe assembly-steering box to reservoir	1		LHD 4 Cylinder
3	NRC5976	Pipe assembly-steering box to reservoir	1		RHD V8
3	NRC5977	Pipe assembly-steering box to reservoir	1		LHD V8
3	NTC8861	Pipe assembly-steering box to reservoir	1	Note (7)	RHD
3	NTC1683	Pipe assembly-steering box to reservoir	1		LHD
	RTC4826	O ring-pump to steering box	1		
	RTC4825	O ring-steering box to reservoir-6mm	1	Note (8)	

CHANGE POINTS:
(1) To (V) AA 244022
(2) From (V) AA 244023 To (V) FA 389107
(3) From (V) FA 389108
(4) To (V) FA 389107
(5) From (V) AA 244023 To (V) 262024
(6) From (V) 262025
(7) From (V) AA 244023 To (V) JA 918809
(8) From (V) AA 244023

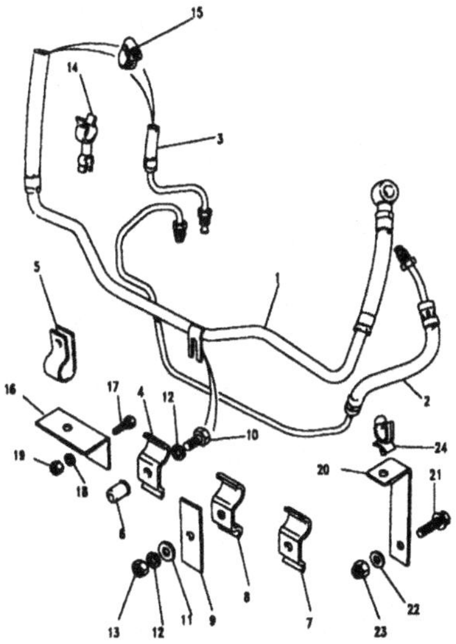

Illus	Part Number	Description	Quantity	Change Point	Remarks
4	NRC6302	Clip-pipe	1		RHD 4 Cylinder Petrol
5	NRC8408	Clip-pipe	1		LHD 4 Cylinder Petrol
	NRC9492	Clip-support boss	1		Diesel
	NTC3791	Clip-support boss	1		Diesel Turbo
6	NN106011	Nutsert-blind	2		
7	NRC6302	Clip-pipe	2		RHD
8	NRC8404	Clip-pipe	2	To (V) HA 465395	
8	NRC6302	Clip-pipe	1	From (V) HA 465396	RHD
9	NRC8405	Plate	1		
10	SH106121L	Screw-hexagonal head-M6 x 12	3		RHD 4 Cylinder
10	SH106121L	Screw-hexagonal head-M6 x 12	4		LHD 4 Cylinder
10	FS106167L	Screw-flanged head-flanged head-M6 x 16	2		RHD V8
10	FS106167L	Screw-flanged head-flanged head-M6 x 16	3		LHD V8
11	WA106041L	Washer-6mm	A/R		
12	WL106001L	Washer-sprung-M6	4		
13	NH106041L	Nut-hexagonal-nyloc-M6	A/R		
14	ADU9081L	Clip-swivel	1		
15	CN100258L	Clip-hose-25mm	2		
15	CN100208L	Clip-hose-20mm	1		
16	NTC7224	Bracket assembly-support power assisted steering. pipes	1	From (V) FA 389460	
17	SH104081L	Screw-hexagonal head-M4 x 8	2		
18	WA104001L	Washer-plain-M4	2		
19	NH104041L	Nut-hexagonal-M4	2		
20	NTC8263	Bracket support	1	From (V) HA 455646	LHD TDi
21	FS106201L	Screw-flanged head-M6 x 20	1		
22	WA106041L	Washer-6mm	1		
23	NY106041L	Nut-hexagonal head-nyloc-M6	NLA		Use NY106047L.
24	ADU8363L	Clip-harness-14.5mm-6.5mm hole	1		LHD TDi

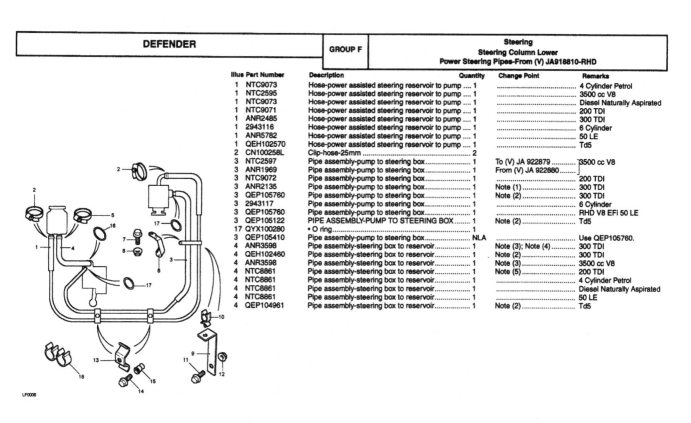

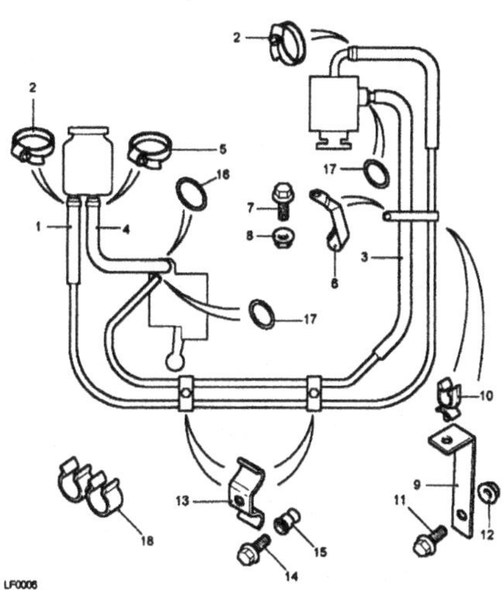

LF0006

Illus	Part Number	Description	Quantity	Change Point	Remarks
1	NTC9073	Hose-power assisted steering reservoir to pump	1		4 Cylinder Petrol
1	NTC2595	Hose-power assisted steering reservoir to pump	1		3500 cc V8
1	NTC9073	Hose-power assisted steering reservoir to pump	1		Diesel Naturally Aspirated
1	NTC9071	Hose-power assisted steering reservoir to pump	1		200 TDI
1	ANR2485	Hose-power assisted steering reservoir to pump	1		300 TDI
1	2943116	Hose-power assisted steering reservoir to pump	1		6 Cylinder
1	ANR5782	Hose-power assisted steering reservoir to pump	1		50 LE
1	QEH102570	Hose-power assisted steering reservoir to pump	1		Td5
2	CN100258L	Clip-hose-25mm	2		
3	NTC2597	Pipe assembly-pump to steering box	1	To (V) JA 922879	3500 cc V8
3	ANR1969	Pipe assembly-pump to steering box	1	From (V) JA 922880	
3	NTC9072	Pipe assembly-pump to steering box	1		200 TDI
3	ANR2135	Pipe assembly-pump to steering box	1	Note (1)	300 TDI
3	QEP105760	Pipe assembly-pump to steering box	1	Note (2)	300 TDI
3	2943117	Pipe assembly-pump to steering box	1		6 Cylinder
3	QEP105760	Pipe assembly-pump to steering box	1		RHD V8 EFi 50 LE
3	QEP105122	PIPE ASSEMBLY-PUMP TO STEERING BOX	1	Note (2)	Td5
17	QYX100280	• O ring	1		
3	QEP105410	Pipe assembly-pump to steering box	NLA		Use QEP105760.
4	ANR3598	Pipe assembly-steering box to reservoir	1	Note (3); Note (4)	300 TDI
4	QEH102460	Pipe assembly-steering box to reservoir	1	Note (2)	300 TDI
4	ANR3598	Pipe assembly-steering box to reservoir	1	Note (3)	3500 cc V8
4	NTC8861	Pipe assembly-steering box to reservoir	1	Note (5)	200 TDI
4	NTC8861	Pipe assembly-steering box to reservoir	1		4 Cylinder Petrol
4	NTC8861	Pipe assembly-steering box to reservoir	1		Diesel Naturally Aspirated
4	NTC8861	Pipe assembly-steering box to reservoir	1		50 LE
4	QEP104961	Pipe assembly-steering box to reservoir	1	Note (2)	Td5

CHANGE POINTS:

(1) From (V) MA 939976 To (V) WA 159806
(2) From (V) XA 159807
(3) From (V) MA 939976
(4) To (V) WA 159806
(5) To (V) LA 939975

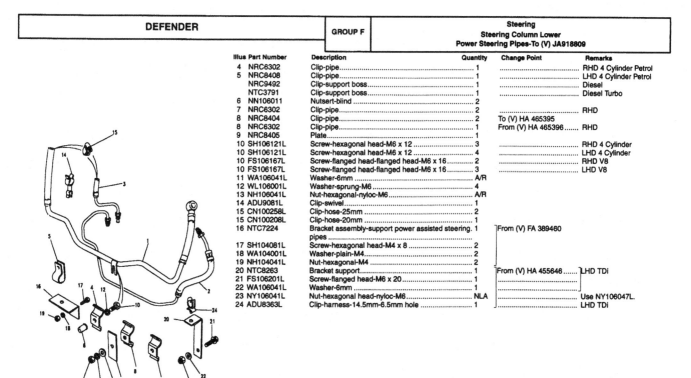

DEFENDER	GROUP F	Steering Steering Column Lower Power Steering Pipes-From (V) JA918810-RHD

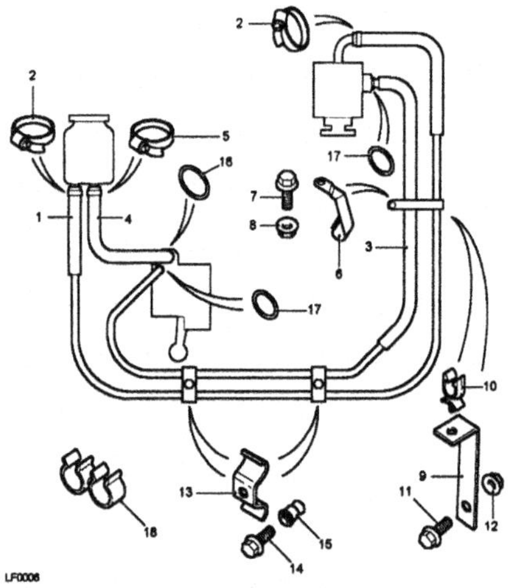

LF0006

Illus	Part Number	Description	Quantity	Change Point	Remarks
5	CN100208L	Clip-hose-20mm	2	....	4 Cylinder Petrol
6	NTC3791	Clip-support boss-pipe	1	....	
7	FS106167L	Screw-flanged head-flanged head-M6 x 16	1	....	
8	FN106047L	Nut-flange-M6	1	....	
6	NTC3791	Clip-support boss-pipe	1	....	Diesel Naturally Aspirated
7	FS106167L	Screw-flanged head-flanged head-M6 x 16	1	....	
8	FN106047L	Nut-flange-M6	1	....	
9	NTC8263	Bracket support	1	....	TDi
10	ADU8363L	Clip-harness-14.5mm-6.5mm hole	1	....	
11	FS106167L	Screw-flanged head-to reinforcement assy-flanged head-M6 x 16	1	....	
12	FN106047L	Nut-flange-M6	1	....	
13	NRC6302	Clip-pipe	2		
14	FS106167L	Screw-flanged head-to clip-flanged head-M6 x 16	2		
15	NN106021	Nutsert-blind-M6	2		
16	RTC4825	O ring-PAS box to return hose-6mm	1		
18	QYC100290	Clip-swivel	1	Note (1)	Td5

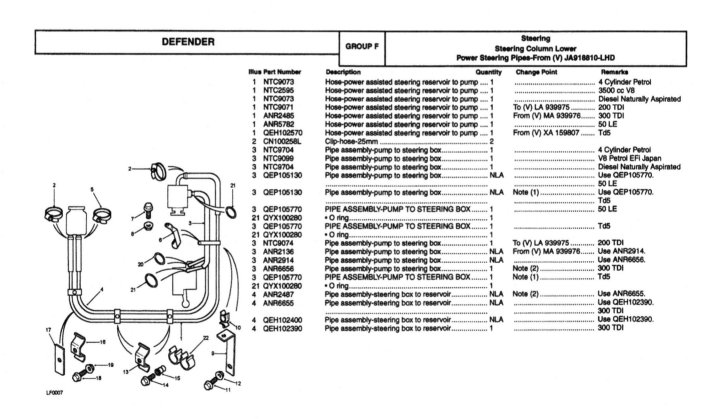

CHANGE POINTS:
(1) From (V) XA 159807

DEFENDER	GROUP F	Steering Steering Column Lower Power Steering Pipes-From (V) JA918810-LHD

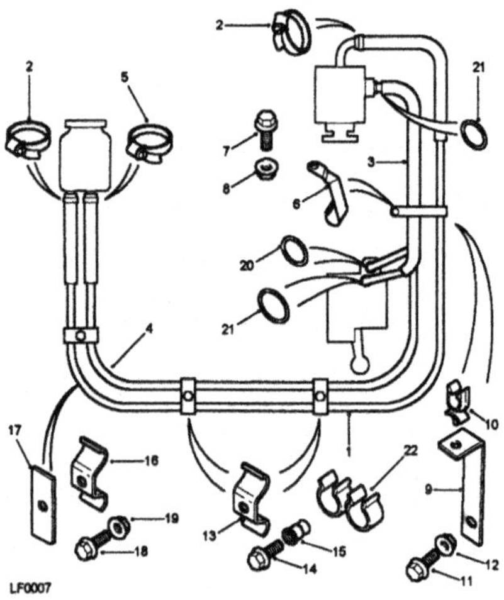

LF0007

Illus	Part Number	Description	Quantity	Change Point	Remarks
1	NTC9073	Hose-power assisted steering reservoir to pump	1	....	4 Cylinder Petrol
1	NTC2595	Hose-power assisted steering reservoir to pump	1	....	3500 cc V8
1	NTC9073	Hose-power assisted steering reservoir to pump	1	....	Diesel Naturally Aspirated
1	NTC9071	Hose-power assisted steering reservoir to pump	1	To (V) LA 939975	200 TDI
1	ANR2485	Hose-power assisted steering reservoir to pump	1	From (V) MA 939976	300 TDI
1	ANR5782	Hose-power assisted steering reservoir to pump	1	....	50 LE
1	QEH102570	Hose-power assisted steering reservoir to pump	1	From (V) XA 159807	Td5
2	CN100258L	Clip-hose-25mm	2		
3	NTC9704	Pipe assembly-pump to steering box	1	....	4 Cylinder Petrol
3	NTC9099	Pipe assembly-pump to steering box	1	....	V8 Petrol EFi Japan
3	NTC9704	Pipe assembly-pump to steering box	1	....	Diesel Naturally Aspirated
3	QEP105130	Pipe assembly-pump to steering box	NLA	....	Use QEP105770. 50 LE
3	QEP105130	Pipe assembly-pump to steering box	NLA	Note (1)	Use QEP105770. Td5
3	QEP105770	PIPE ASSEMBLY-PUMP TO STEERING BOX	1	....	50 LE
21	QYX100280	• O ring	1		
3	QEP105770	PIPE ASSEMBLY-PUMP TO STEERING BOX	1	....	Td5
21	QYX100280	• O ring	1		
3	NTC9074	Pipe assembly-pump to steering box	1	To (V) LA 939975	200 TDI
3	ANR2136	Pipe assembly-pump to steering box	NLA	From (V) MA 939976	Use ANR2914.
3	ANR2914	Pipe assembly-pump to steering box	NLA	....	Use ANR6656.
3	ANR6656	Pipe assembly-pump to steering box	1	Note (2)	300 TDI
3	QEP105770	PIPE ASSEMBLY-PUMP TO STEERING BOX	1	Note (1)	Td5
21	QYX100280	• O ring	1		
4	ANR2487	Pipe assembly-steering box to reservoir	NLA	Note (2)	Use ANR6655.
4	ANR6655	Pipe assembly-steering box to reservoir	NLA	....	Use QEH102390. 300 TDI
4	QEH102400	Pipe assembly-steering box to reservoir	NLA	....	Use QEH102390.
4	QEH102390	Pipe assembly-steering box to reservoir	1	....	300 TDI

CHANGE POINTS:
(1) From (V) XA 159807
(2) From (V) MA 939976

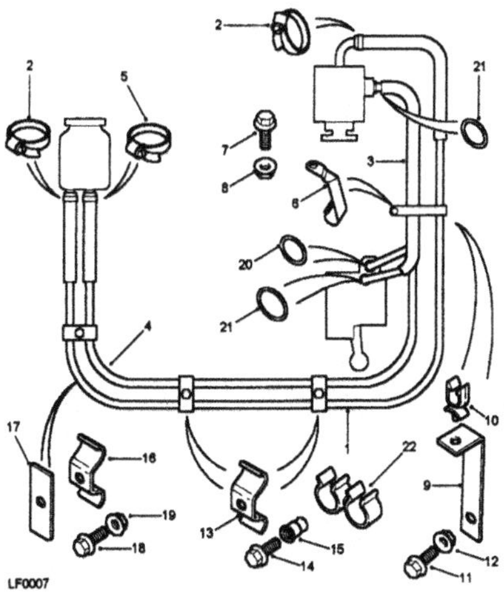

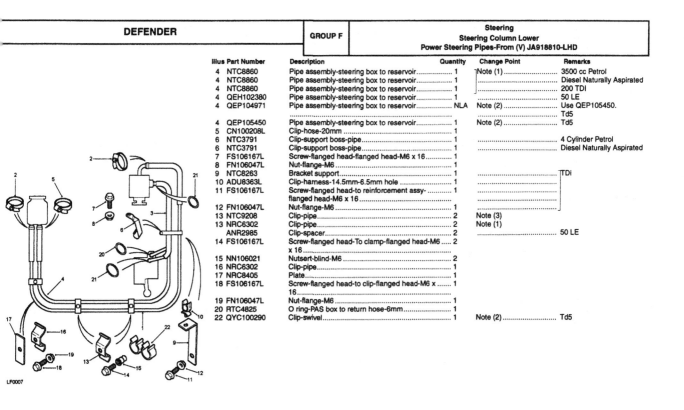

Illus	Part Number	Description	Quantity	Change Point	Remarks
4	NTC8860	Pipe assembly-steering box to reservoir	1	Note (1)	3500 cc Petrol
4	NTC8860	Pipe assembly-steering box to reservoir	1		Diesel Naturally Aspirated
4	NTC8860	Pipe assembly-steering box to reservoir	1		200 TDI
4	QEH102380	Pipe assembly-steering box to reservoir	1		50 LE
4	QEP104971	Pipe assembly-steering box to reservoir	NLA	Note (2)	Use QEP105450. Td5
4	QEP105450	Pipe assembly-steering box to reservoir	1	Note (2)	Td5
5	CN100208L	Clip-hose-20mm	1		
6	NTC3791	Clip-support boss-pipe	1		4 Cylinder Petrol
6	NTC3791	Clip-support boss-pipe	1		Diesel Naturally Aspirated
7	FS106167L	Screw-flanged head-flanged head-M6 x 16	1		
8	FN106047L	Nut-flange-M6	1		
9	NTC8263	Bracket support	1		TDi
10	ADU8363L	Clip-harness-14.5mm-6.5mm hole	1		
11	FS106167L	Screw-flanged head-to reinforcement assy-flanged head-M6 x 16	1		
12	FN106047L	Nut-flange-M6	1		
13	NTC9208	Clip-pipe	2	Note (3)	
13	NRC6302	Clip-pipe	2	Note (1)	
	ANR2985	Clip-spacer	2		50 LE
14	FS106167L	Screw-flanged head-To clamp-flanged head-M6 x 16	2		
15	NN106021	Nutsert-blind-M6	2		
16	NRC6302	Clip-pipe	1		
17	NRC8405	Plate	1		
18	FS106167L	Screw-flanged head-to clip-flanged head-M6 x 16	1		
19	FN106047L	Nut-flange-M6	1		
20	RTC4825	O ring-PAS box to return hose-6mm	1		
22	QYC100290	Clip-swivel	1	Note (2)	Td5

CHANGE POINTS:
(1) To (V) LA 939975
(2) From (V) XA 159807
(3) From (V) MA 939976

Illus	Part Number	Description	Quantity	Change Point	Remarks
1	NRC7827	Pedal assembly accelerator	1		
2	NRC4475	Shaft-pedal-accelerator	1		
3	NRC5220	Bracket-mounting pedal	1		
4	PA105161L	Pin-spring	1		
5	NRC9121	Spring-return-tension accelerator	1		
6	SH106451	Screw-hexagonal head-M6 x 45	1		
7	NH605041L	Nut-hexagonal head-5/16UNF	1		
8	11H1781L	Pad-lever-pedal	1		
9	FS106167L	Screw-flanged head-bracket to body-flanged head-M6 x 16	6		
10	WL106001L	Washer-sprung-M6	6		
11	WA106041L	Washer-6mm	6		
12	NH106041L	Nut-hexagonal-nyloc-M6	6		

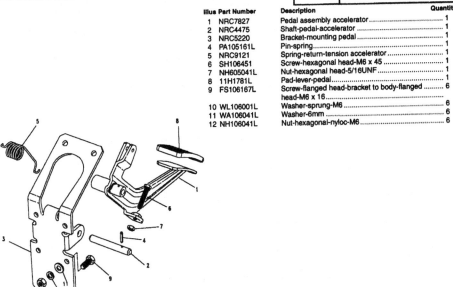

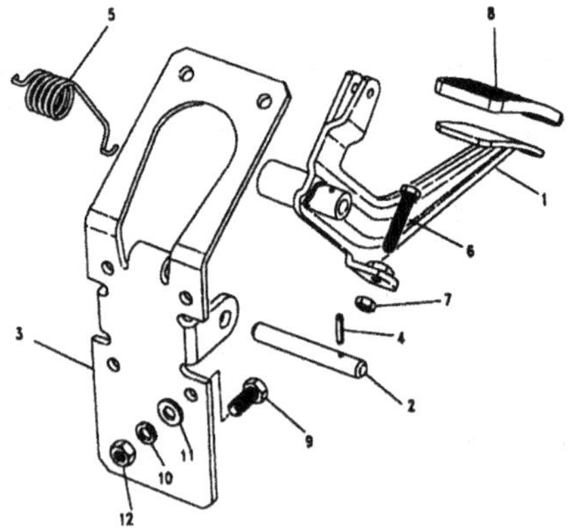

Illus	Part Number	Description	Quantity	Change Point	Remarks
1	SLC100210	POTENTIOMETER & PEDAL-ASSEMBLY	1	Note (1); Note (2)	
2	SAD000010PMA	• Pad-lever-pedal	1		
1	SLC000010PMA	POTENTIOMETER & PEDAL-ASSEMBLY	1	Note (3)	
2	SAD000010PMA	• Pad-lever-pedal	1		
3	SZU100050	Cover-throttle pedal potentiometer	1		
4	FS108307L	Screw-flanged head-M8 x 30	3		
5	WA108051L	Washer-8mm	3		
6	NY108041L	Nut-nyloc-M8	3		

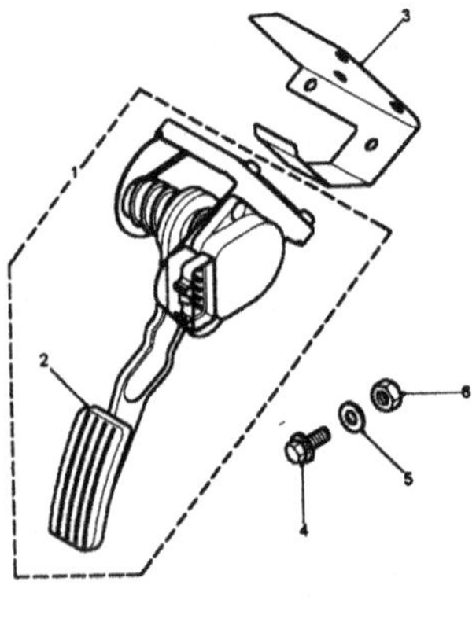

LG0013A

CHANGE POINTS:
(1) From (V) XA 159807
(2) To (V) 1A 607224
(3) From (V) 1A 607225

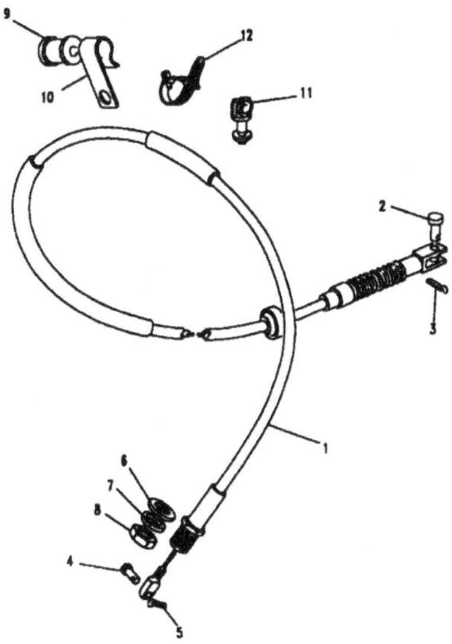

Illus	Part Number	Description	Quantity	Change Point	Remarks
1	NRC8116	Cable assembly accelerator-RHD	1		2250 cc Petrol
1	NRC8117	Cable assembly accelerator-LHD	1		
1	NTC2086	Cable assembly accelerator-RHD	1	To (V) 295722	2500 cc Petrol
1	NTC2087	Cable assembly accelerator-LHD	1	To (V) 295733	
1	NTC3460	Cable assembly accelerator-RHD	1	From (V) 295723	
1	NTC3459	Cable assembly accelerator-LHD	1	From (V) 295734	
1	NRC5494	Cable assembly accelerator	1		V8 Twin Carburettor
1	2943224	Cable assembly accelerator	1		BMW M52
1	SBB104100	Cable assembly accelerator	1		V8 EFi 50 LE
1	NRC7605	Cable assembly accelerator-RHD	1	To (V) 267061	Diesel Naturally Aspirated
1	NRC7606	Cable assembly accelerator-LHD	1		
1	NTC2743	Cable assembly accelerator-RHD	1	From (V) 267062	
1	NTC3396	Cable assembly accelerator-LHD	1		
1	NTC2743	Cable assembly accelerator-RHD	1		Diesel Turbo
1	NTC3396	Cable assembly accelerator-LHD	1		
1	NTC4944	Cable assembly accelerator-RHD	1	Note (1)	200 TDI
1	ANR1419	Cable assembly accelerator-RHD	1	Note (2)	
1	NTC4945	Cable assembly accelerator-LHD	1	Note (3)	
1	NTC9360	Cable assembly accelerator-RHD	1	Note (4)	300 TDI
1	NTC9359	Cable assembly accelerator-LHD	1		
2	562481	Pin-clevis/pivot	1		
3	PS103081L	Pin-split	1	To (V) HA 455945	
3	PS603041L	Pin-split	1	From (V) HA 455946	
4	NRC5502	Pin assembly-clevis	1		
5	PS102081L	Pin-split	1		
6	WA112081L	Washer-plain-standard-M12	1		
7	WF112001L	Washer-starlock	1		
8	NT112041L	Nut-hexagonal-thin-M12	1		
9	6860L	Grommet-rubber-17/64" hole	1	To (V) HA 701009	
10	240407	Clip-hose-14.5mm-steel-25/64" hole	1	Note (5)	RHD
	AFU1077L	Clip-swivel	1	From (V) HA 701010	4 Cylinder Petrol
11	79121	Clip-single-9mm	1		RHD TDi
11	79121	Clip-single-9mm	1	From (V) HA 455946	LHD
12	AAU3686	Tie-cable-6.5mm hole-8.0 x 155mm	1	From (V) HA 455646	
	ESR301	Clip-swivel-10 x 10mm	1	From (V) JA 915380	RHD TDi
	ADU8460	Clip	3		V8 EFi

CHANGE POINTS:
(1) To (V) JA 915380
(2) From (V) JA 915381 To (V) LA 939975
(3) From (V) HA 455646 To (V) LA 939975
(4) From (V) MA 939976
(5) From (V) HA 455946 To (V) HA 701009

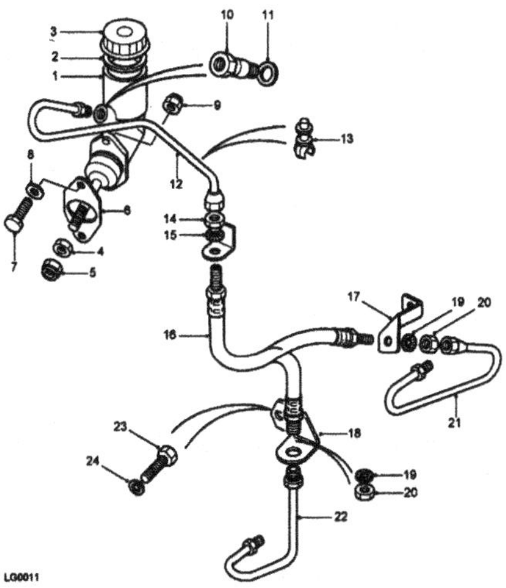

Illus	Part Number	Description	Quantity	Change Point	Remarks
1	550732	MASTER CYLINDER CLUTCH	1	Note (1)	
2	264767	• Seal-tank cap clutch	1		
3	STC976	• Cap assembly-tank clutch	-		
1	STC100410	MASTER CYLINDER CLUTCH	1	Note (2)	
3	STC100440	• Cap assembly-tank clutch	1		
	8G8837L	Kit-repair brake master cylinder	1		
4	NT605041L	Nut-hexagonal-thin-5/16UNF	2		
5	NY605041L	Locknut	1		
6	592358	Gasket-Master cylinder to pedal box	1	To (V) TA 989477	
6	ANR5308	Gasket-Master cylinder to pedal box	1	From (V) TA 989478	
7	FS108307L	Screw-flanged head-M8 x 30	2		
8	WA108051L	Washer-8mm	4		
9	NY108041L	Nut-nyloc-M8	2		
10	139082	Connector-inlet manifold adaptor	1		
11	233220	Gasket	1		
		PIPE ASSEMBLY CLUTCH			
12	NRC8330	RHD	1	Note (3)	
12	ANR2162	RHD	1	Note (4)	
12	NRC8329	LHD	1	Note (3)	
12	ANR2945	LHD	1	Note (4)	
12	2943124	RHD	1		BMW M52 6 Cylinder
12	STG101080	RHD	1	Note (5)	Petrol
12	STG101150	RHD	1		300 TDI
12	STG101100	RHD	1		Td5
12	STG101090	LHD	1		Td5

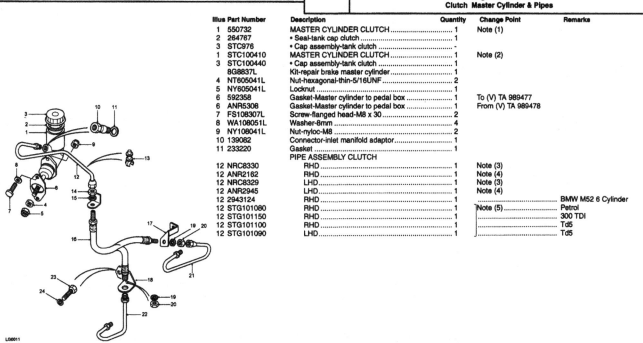

CHANGE POINTS:
(1) To (V) XA 178602
(2) From (V) XA 178603
(3) To (V) LA 939975
(4) From (V) MA 939976
(5) From (V) XA 159807

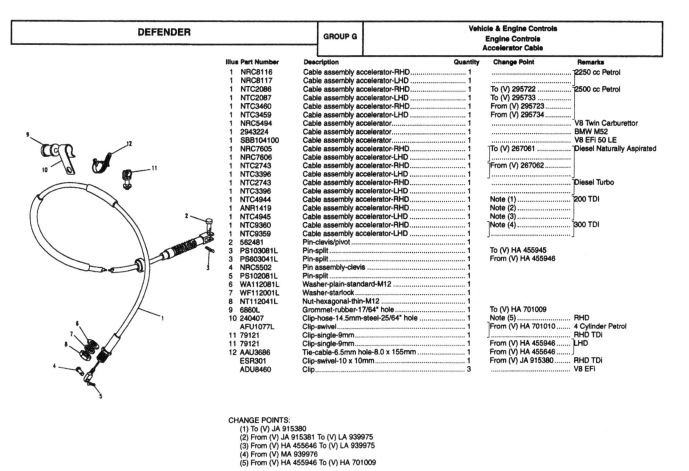

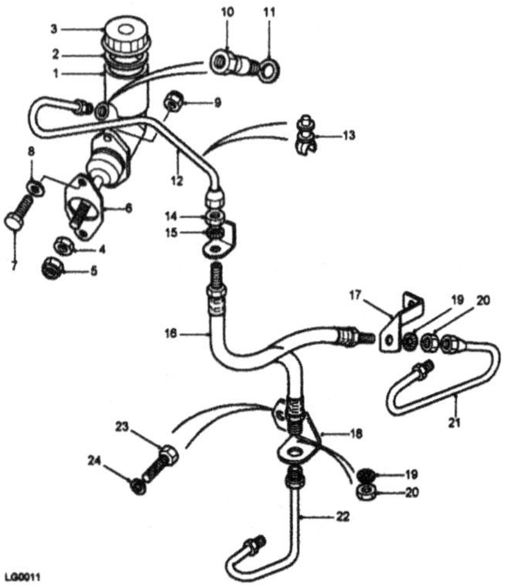

Illus	Part Number	Description	Quantity	Change Point	Remarks
13	79123	Clip-pipe-single	2		Except 90"
13	NTC1175	Clip-pipe	2		RHD 90"
13	NTC1175	Clip-pipe	1		LHD 90"
14	NT607041L	Nut-hexagonal-thin-7/16UNF	2		4 Cylinder
15	WF600071L	Washer-starlock	2		
16	RTC4425	Hose clutch	1		
14	NT604041L	Nut-hexagonal-thin-1/4UNF	1		V8
15	WE600071L	Washer-starlock	1		
16	NRC2211	Hose clutch	1		
16	NRC2211	Hose clutch	1		Td5
16	NRC7139	Hose clutch	1	To (V) LA 939975	200 TDI
16	NTC9055	Hose clutch	1	From (V) MA 939976	300 TDI
16	2943288	Hose clutch	1		6 Cylinder
17	NRC7441	Bracket-abutment clutch hose to pipe assy clutch	1		4 Cylinder
18	90577642	Bracket-bell housing clutch hose	1		V8
19	WE600101L	Washer-starlock	1		
20	2K8686L	Nut	1		
18	STU100250	Bracket-bell housing clutch hose	1	Note (1)	Td5
21	NRC9595	Pipe assembly clutch	1		4 Cylinder
21	2943144	Pipe assembly clutch	1		BMW M52 6 Cylinder
22	577643	Pipe assembly clutch	1		V8
22	ANR2183	Pipe assembly clutch	1	Note (1)	Td5
23	BH506161L	Bolt-hexagonal head-3/8UNC x 2	2		
24	WM600061L	Washer-3/8"-square	2		
25	SVE100010	Banjo-clutch special	1	Note (1)	Td5
26	SVF100010	Bolt-clutch special banjo	1		
27	MSK100050	Switch-electronic diesel control	1		
28	233220	Gasket	2		

CHANGE POINTS:
(1) From (V) XA 159807

Illus	Part Number	Description	Quantity	Change Point	Remarks
		CABLE ASSEMBLY CHOKE			
1	NRC8626	RHD	1	Note (1)	4 Cylinder Petrol
1	NRC8627	LHD	1		
1	NTC1384	RHD	1	Note (2)	
1	NTC1385	LHD	1		
		CABLE ASSEMBLY CHOKE			
1	NRC7792	RHD	1	Note (3)	V8
1	NRC7791	LHD	1		
1	NTC3686	RHD	1	Note (4)	
1	NTC3687	LHD	1		
1	NTC3932	RHD	1	Note (5)	
1	NTC3933	LHD	1		
2	RTC5816	Switch choke	1	From (V) AA 270227	
3	NRC8333	Bracket-cable choke	1		
4	NRC8332	Clip-cable	1		
5	538890L	Clip	1	From (V) AA 268052	
6	594594	Tie-cable-White.-4.6 x 385mm-inside serated	1		

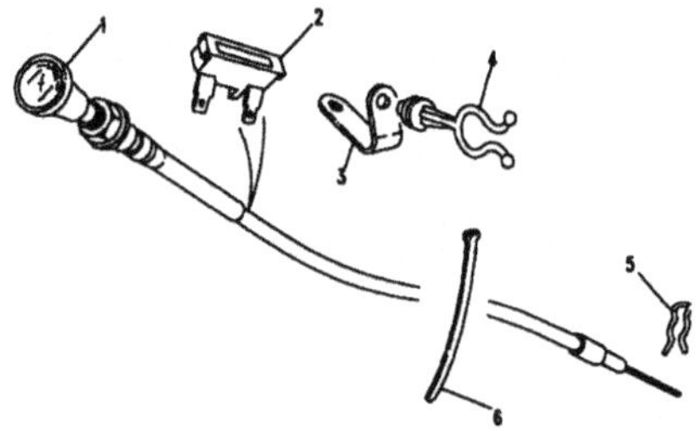

CHANGE POINTS:
(1) To (V) AA 270139
(2) From (V) AA 270140
(3) To (V) AA 268051
(4) From (V) AA 268052 To (V) AA 271213
(5) From (V) AA 271214

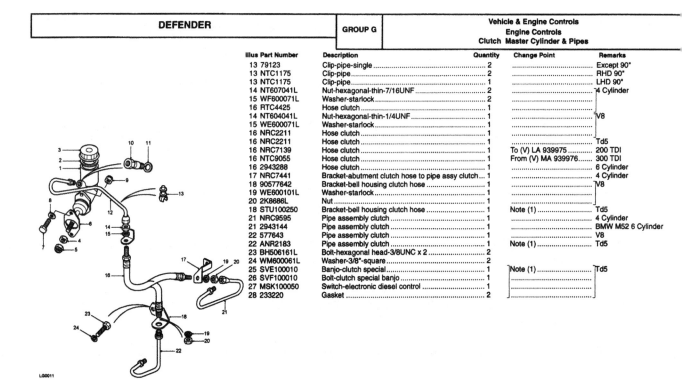

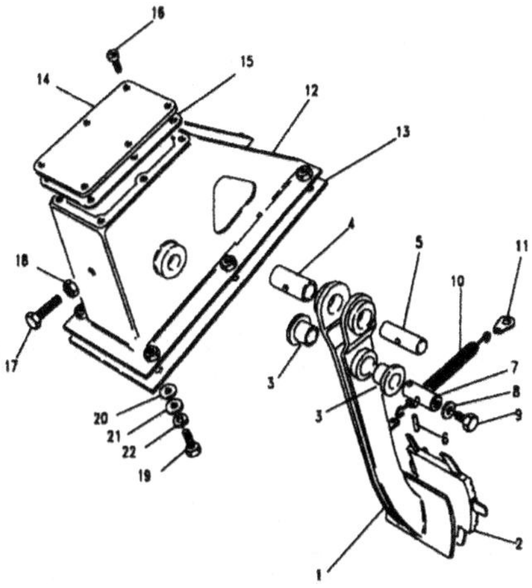

Illus	Part Number	Description	Quantity	Change Point	Remarks
1	568895	Pedal assembly clutch-RHD	1	Note (1)	
1	NRC9217	Pedal assembly clutch-LHD	1		
1	NTC1112	Pedal assembly clutch	1	Note (2)	
2	278166	Pad-lever-pedal	1	Note (1)	Optional
2	61K738	Pad-lever-pedal	1	Note (2)	
3	272714	Bush	1		
4	269783	Spacer-Distance piece	1		
5	568883	Trunnion-clutch pedal	1		
6	50446	Pin	1		
7	272712	Pin-pivot	1		
8	3052	Washer	1		
9	SH604031L	Screw-hexagonal head	1		
10	569701	Spring-return-clutch	1		
	NRC7869	Sleeve	1		
11	240708	Plate	1		
12	272632	Bracket pedal	1		
13	MUC7505	Gasket-clutch pedal box to bulkhead	1		90°
14	272713	Plate-mounting pedal	1		
15	272819	Gasket-clutch pedal box top cover	1		
16	78227	Screw	6		
17	SH604081L	Screw-pedal stop-hexagonal head-M5-6mm	1		
18	NH604041L	Nut-hexagonal head-coarse thread-1/4UNF	1		
19	GG605081	Screw	6		
20	RTC610	Washer-plain	5		
21	4594L	Washer-plain	1		
22	WM600051L	Washer-spring-5/16"	6		

CHANGE POINTS:
(1) To (V) AA 234187
(2) From (V) AA 234188 To (V) LA 939891

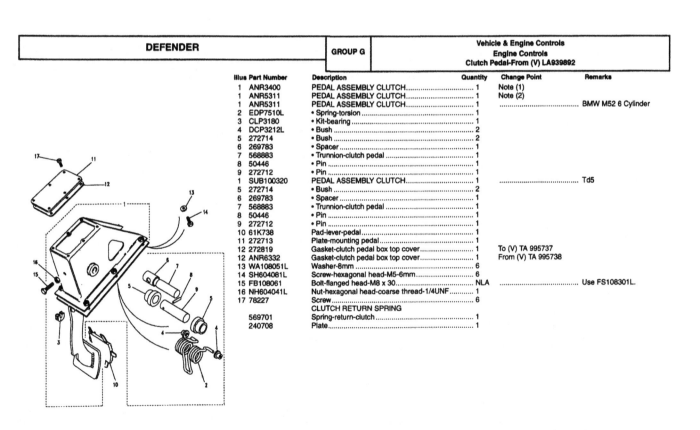

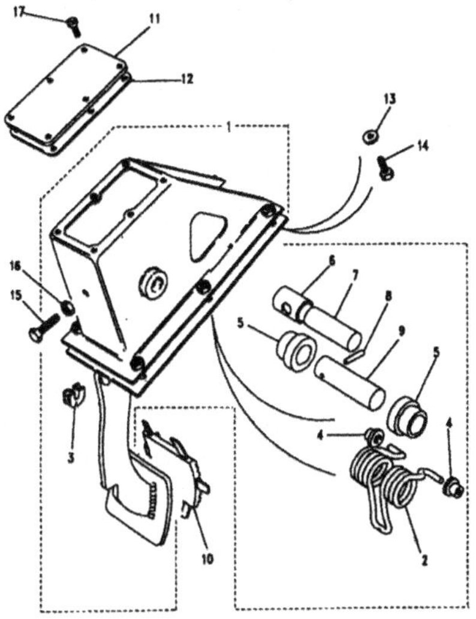

Illus	Part Number	Description	Quantity	Change Point	Remarks
1	ANR3400	PEDAL ASSEMBLY CLUTCH	1	Note (1)	
1	ANR5311	PEDAL ASSEMBLY CLUTCH	1	Note (2)	
1	ANR5311	PEDAL ASSEMBLY CLUTCH	1		BMW M52 6 Cylinder
2	EDP7510L	• Spring-torsion	1		
3	CLP3180	• Kit-bearing	1		
4	DCP3212L	• Bush	2		
5	272714	• Bush	2		
6	269783	• Spacer	1		
7	568883	• Trunnion-clutch pedal	1		
8	50446	• Pin	1		
9	272712	• Pin	1		
1	SUB100320	PEDAL ASSEMBLY CLUTCH	1		Td5
5	272714	• Bush	2		
6	269783	• Spacer	1		
7	568883	• Trunnion-clutch pedal	1		
8	50446	• Pin	1		
9	272712	• Pin	1		
10	61K738	Pad-lever-pedal	1		
11	272713	Plate-mounting pedal	1		
12	272819	Gasket-clutch pedal box top cover	1	To (V) TA 995737	
12	ANR6332	Gasket-clutch pedal box top cover	1	From (V) TA 995738	
13	WA108051L	Washer-8mm	6		
14	SH604081L	Screw-hexagonal head-M5-6mm	6		
15	FB108061	Bolt-flanged head-M8 x 30	NLA		Use FS108301L.
16	NH604041L	Nut-hexagonal head-coarse thread-1/4UNF	1		
17	78227	Screw	6		
		CLUTCH RETURN SPRING			
	569701	Spring-return-clutch	1		
	240708	Plate	1		

CHANGE POINTS:
(1) From (V) LA 939892 To (V) TA 989477
(2) From (V) TA 989478

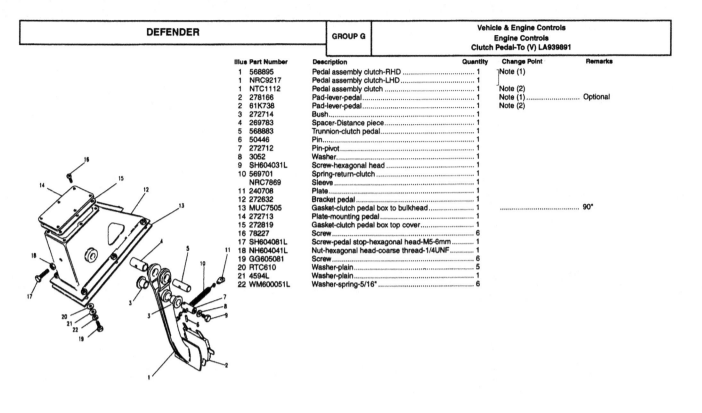

DEFENDER

GROUP G

Vehicle & Engine Controls
Engine Controls
Brake Pedal

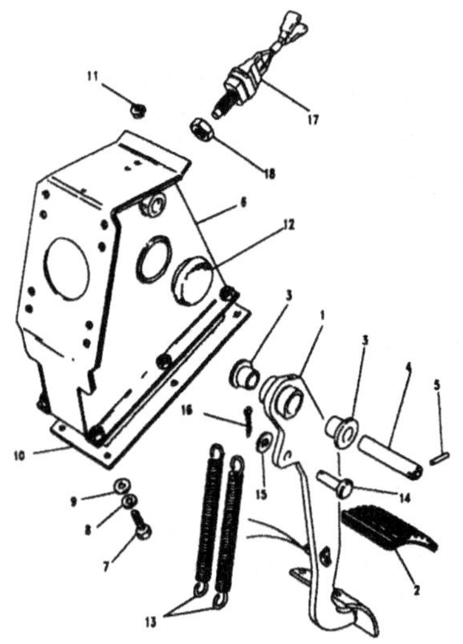

Illus	Part Number	Description	Quantity	Change Point	Remarks
1	NRC9183	Pedal assembly-brake	1	To (V) AA 234187	
1	NTC1210	Pedal assembly-brake	1	From (V) AA 234188	
1	ANR6472	Pedal assembly-brake	1		V8 EFi
2	NRC9224	Pad-lever-pedal	1	To (V) AA 234187	Optional
2	61K738	Pad-lever-pedal	1	From (V) AA 234188	
2	ANR6476	Pad-lever-pedal	1		V8 EFi
3	564816	Bush-pedal pivot-brake	2		
4	564813	Shaft-pedal-accelerator	1		
5	50446	Pin	1		
6	NRC6058	Pedal box	1	To (V) HA 701009	
6	NTC7933	Pedal box	1	From (V) HA 701010	
7	GG108251L	Screw-hexagonal head-M8 x 125	6		
8	WL108001L	Washer-sprung-M8	6		
9	WA108051L	Washer-8mm	6		
10	MUC7506	Gasket-pedal box-brake	1	To (V) TA 995737	
10	ANR6333	Gasket-pedal box-brake	1	From (V) TA 995738	
11	338013	Plug-blanking-plastic-9.5mm	1		
12	AFU2627	Plug-blanking-plastic-41.5mm	2		
13	569291	Spring-return brake	2		
	NRC7869	Sleeve	1		
14	NRC4665	Pin-clevis	1	To (V) HA 701009	
14	PC112291	Pin-clevis	1	From (V) HA 701010	
15	WA112081L	Washer-plain-standard-M12	1		
16	PS106201	Pin-split	1		
17	PRC4297	Switch assembly-stop lamp	1		
18	BMK1903	Locknut	1		
	NRC9169	Strip-sealing	1		
	NRC9233	Seal	1	To (V) HA 701009	
	NTC5017	Seal	1	From (V) HA 701010	

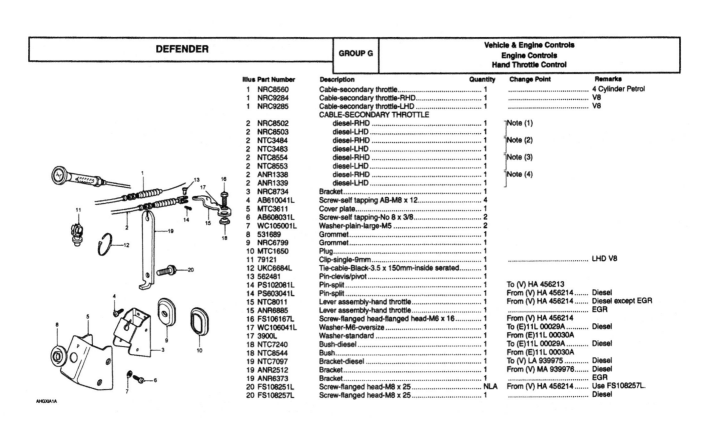

DEFENDER

GROUP G

Vehicle & Engine Controls
Engine Controls
Hand Throttle Control

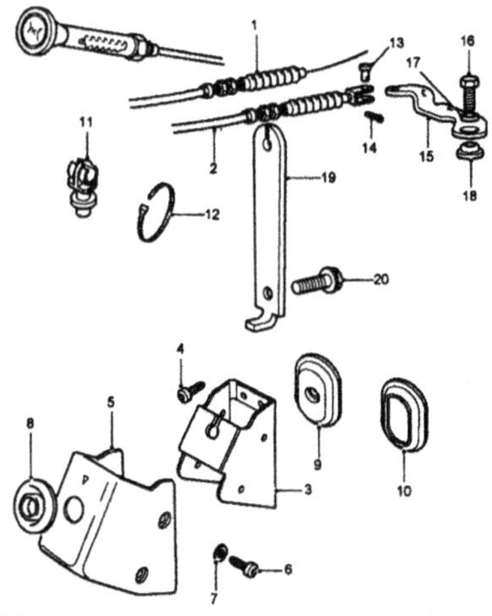

AHGXIA1A

Illus	Part Number	Description	Quantity	Change Point	Remarks
1	NRC8560	Cable-secondary throttle	1		4 Cylinder Petrol
1	NRC9284	Cable-secondary throttle-RHD	1		V8
1	NRC9285	Cable-secondary throttle-LHD	1		V8
		CABLE-SECONDARY THROTTLE			
2	NRC8502	diesel-RHD	1	Note (1)	
2	NRC8503	diesel-LHD	1		
2	NTC3484	diesel-RHD	1	Note (2)	
2	NTC3483	diesel-LHD	1		
2	NTC8554	diesel-RHD	1	Note (3)	
2	NTC8553	diesel-LHD	1		
2	ANR1338	diesel-RHD	1	Note (4)	
2	ANR1339	diesel-LHD	1		
3	NRC8734	Bracket	1		
4	AB610041L	Screw-self tapping AB-M8 x 12	4		
5	MTC3611	Cover plate	1		
6	AB608031L	Screw-self tapping-No 8 x 3/8	2		
7	WC105001L	Washer-plain-large-M5	2		
8	531689	Grommet	1		
9	NRC6799	Grommet	1		
10	MTC1650	Plug	1		
11	79121	Clip-single-9mm	1		LHD V8
12	UKC6684L	Tie-cable-Black-3.5 x 150mm-inside serated	1		
13	562481	Pin-clevis/pivot	1		
14	PS102081L	Pin-split	1	To (V) HA 456213	
14	PS603041L	Pin-split	1	From (V) HA 456214	Diesel
15	NTC8011	Lever assembly-hand throttle	1	From (V) HA 456214	Diesel except EGR
15	ANR6885	Lever assembly-hand throttle	1		EGR
16	FS106167L	Screw-flanged head-flanged head-M6 x 16	1	From (V) HA 456214	
17	WC106041L	Washer-M6-oversize	1	To (E)11L 00029A	Diesel
17	3900L	Washer-standard	1	From (E)11L 00030A	
18	NTC7240	Bush-diesel	1	To (E)11L 00029A	Diesel
18	NTC8544	Bush	1	From (E)11L 00030A	
19	NTC7097	Bracket-diesel	1	To (V) LA 939975	Diesel
19	ANR2512	Bracket	1	From (V) MA 939976	Diesel
19	ANR6373	Bracket	1		EGR
20	FS108251L	Screw-flanged head-M8 x 25	NLA	From (V) HA 456214	Use FS108257L.
20	FS108257L	Screw-flanged head-M8 x 25	1		Diesel

CHANGE POINTS:
(1) To (V) 267061
(2) From (V) 267062 To (V) HA 456213
(3) From (V) HA 456214 To (V) LA 939975
(4) From (V) MA 939976

DEFENDER	GROUP G	Vehicle & Engine Controls Engine Controls Hand Throttle-Additional Parts-4 Cyl-Diesel-Not Tdi

Illus	Part Number	Description	Quantity	Change Point	Remarks
1	ETC6630	THROTTLE-TRACTION CONTROL SECONDARY	1		
2	ETC4678	• Lever-handbrake cable relay	-		
3	613915	• Bush	-		
4	ETC4686	• Pin	-		
5	CR120081L	• Circlip	1		
6	WA108051L	• Washer-8mm	1		
7	ETC5182	LEVER ASSEMBLY-THROTTLE	1		
8	522932	• Bush	1		
9	ETC5183	LEVER-HAND THROTTLE	1		
10	522932	• Bush	1		

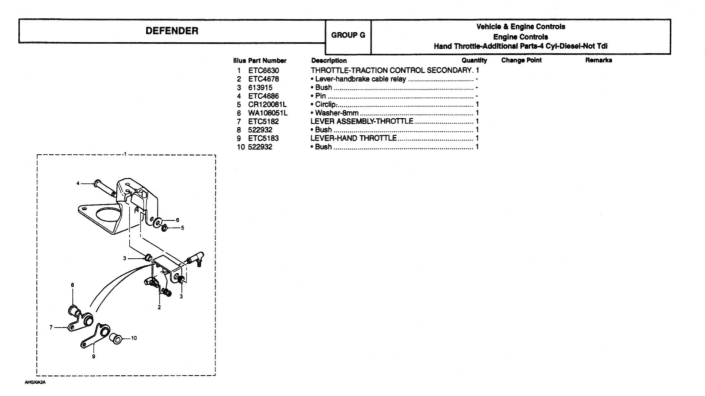

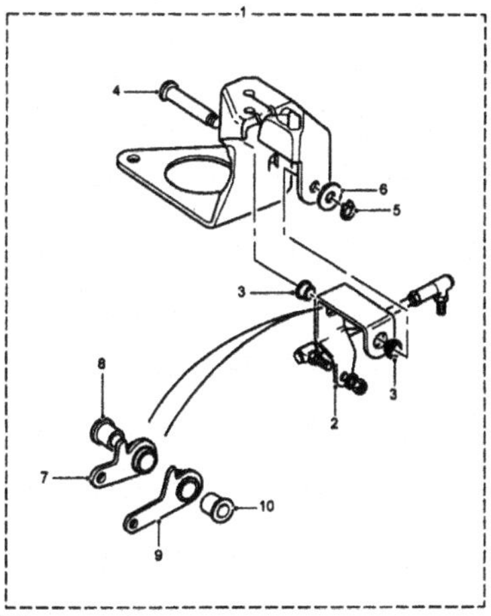

AHGXIA2A

DEFENDER	GROUP G	Vehicle & Engine Controls Engine Controls Hand Throttle-Additional Parts-V8-Su Carburetter

Illus	Part Number	Description	Quantity	Change Point	Remarks
1	613910	Counter shaft-carb	1		
2	613916	LEVEL-CARBURETTOR THROTTLE	1		
3	613915	• Bush	1		
4	90613913	LEVER-CARBURETTOR ACCELERATOR PUMP	1		
5	613915	• Bush	1		
6	239673	Clip-cable	1		
7	ETC7393	Bracket-cable abutment handbrake	1		
8	SH504051L	Screw-hexagonal head-1/4UNF x 5/8	1		
9	WA106041L	Washer-6mm	1		
10	603237	Roller	1		
11	521452	Circlip	1		

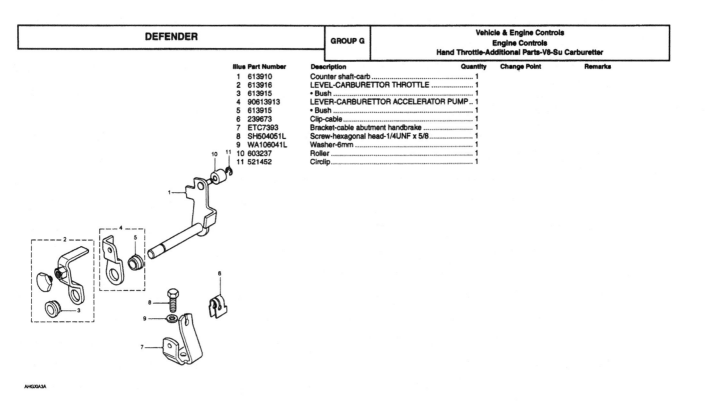

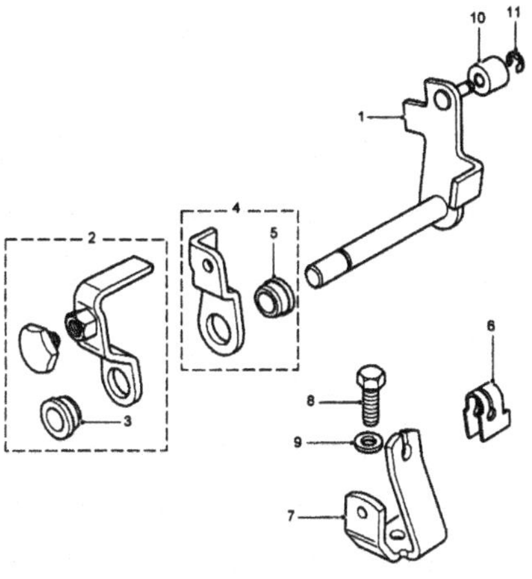

AHGXIA3A

Illus	Part Number	Description	Quantity	Change Point	Remarks
1	613910	Counter shaft-carb	1		
2	613916	LEVEL-CARBURETTOR THROTTLE	1		
3	613915	• Bush	1		
4	SH105201L	Screw-hexagonal head-M5 x 20	1		
5	WL105001L	Washer-retaining-M5	1		
6	NH105041L	Nut-hexagonal-M5	1		
7	90613913	LEVER-CARBURETTOR ACCELERATOR PUMP	1		
8	613915	• Bush	1		
9	239673	Clip-cable	1		
10	ETC4006	Bracket-abutment-throttle cable multi point injection/tbi	1		
11	SH504051L	Screw-hexagonal head-1/4UNF x 5/8	1		
12	WA106041L	Washer-6mm	1		

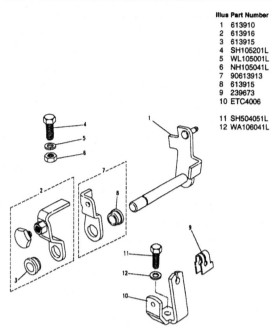

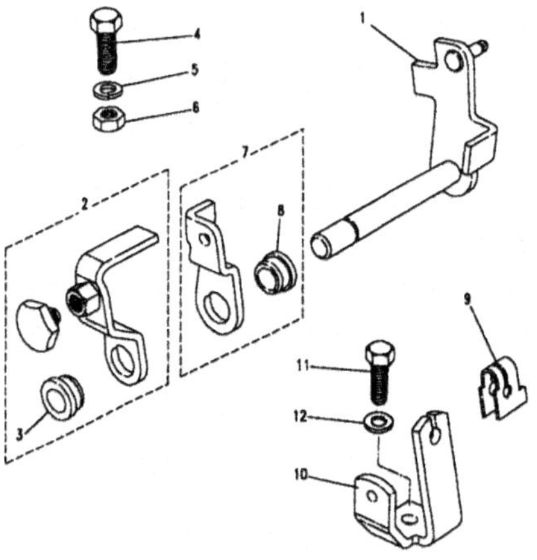

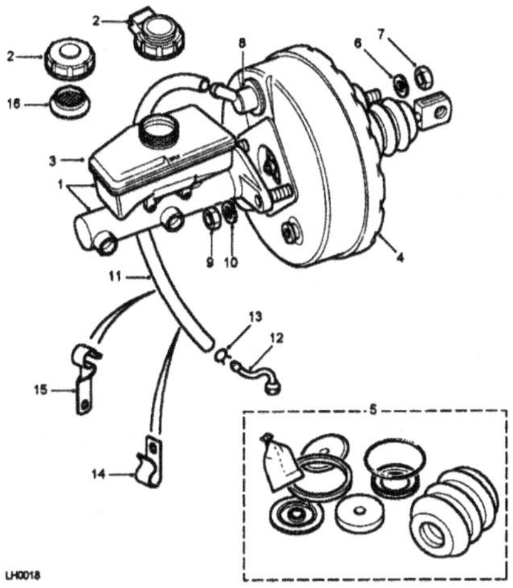

LH0018

Illus	Part Number	Description	Quantity	Change Point	Remarks
1	NRC8690	MASTER CYLINDER ASSEMBLY BRAKE	1		Except 90"
2	RTC4428	• Cap-fluid level warning reservoir indicator	1		
	AEU1045	• Set-cap brake master cylinder	1		
	AEU1044	• Pin	2		
	AEU3015	Kit-repair clutch master cylinder	1		
16	592324	Filter-air fuel	1		
	AEU1891	Seal	1		
1	NRC9529	MASTER CYLINDER ASSEMBLY BRAKE	1		90"
2	NTC4414	• Cap-fluid level warning reservoir indicator	1		
3	RTC3388	• Kit-master cylinder/reservoir & seal brake	1		
	AEU1044	• Pin	2		
	RTC3387	Kit-repair brake master cylinder	1		
	NRC9233	Seal-servo to pedal box	1		
		SERVO ASSEMBLY BRAKE			
4	STC2878	1 port	1		
4	STC2879	2 port	1		
4	NRC4775	Type 50	1		Note (2)
4	NRC4772	Type 80	1		Note (1)
5	18G8951L	Kit-repair brake servo-Type 50	1		
5	AEU2741	Kit-repair brake servo-Type 80	1		
6	WL108001L	Washer-sprung-M8	4		
7	FN108041L	Nut-flange-M8	NLA		Use FN108047L.
8	18G8953L	Valve-non return brake vacuum	1		
9	NH110041L	Nut-hexagonal head-coarse thread-M10	2		
10	WL110001L	Washer-M10	2		
11	CRC2131	Hose brake vacuum-930mm	1		
		HOSE BRAKE VACUUM			
11	NTC3372	LHD-1560mm	1		Diesel Turbo
11	NTC3372	LHD-1560mm	1		TDi
11	CRC2135	RHD-RHD-1092mm	1		V8 Petrol
12	569714	Adaptor-vacuum pipe injection pump	1		4 Cylinder Petrol

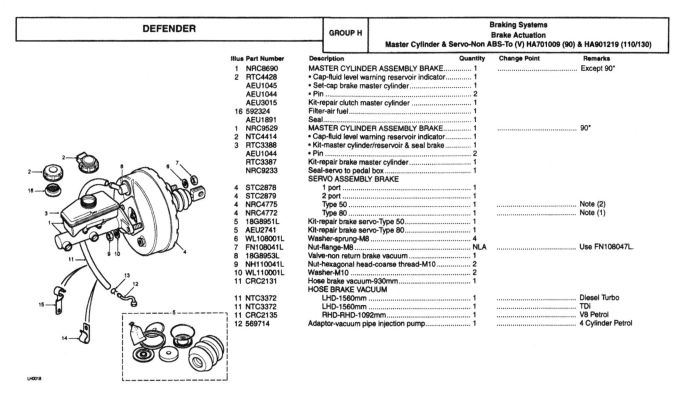

Remarks:
(1) Type 80:- 276 diameter non return valve aperture at top left
(2) Type 50:- 227 mm diameter non return valve aperture at bottom right

Illus	Part Number	Description	Quantity	Change Point	Remarks
13	572548	Clip-hose	NLA		Use CN100168L.
13	CS600244L	Clip-hose	2		LHD Diesel Turbo
	568680	Tie-cable-4.8 x 270mm-inside serated	3		
	568680	Tie-cable-4.8 x 270mm-inside serated	3		LHD TDi
13	CS600244L	Clip-hose	2		
14	240407	Clip-hose-14.5mm-steel-25/64" hole	1		4 Cylinder Petrol
15	614617	Clip-hose	1		V8 Petrol
	NRC9338	Clip-p	1		LHD Diesel Turbo
	NRC9338	Clip-p	1		LHD TDi
	345662	Clip-cable-rear	1		

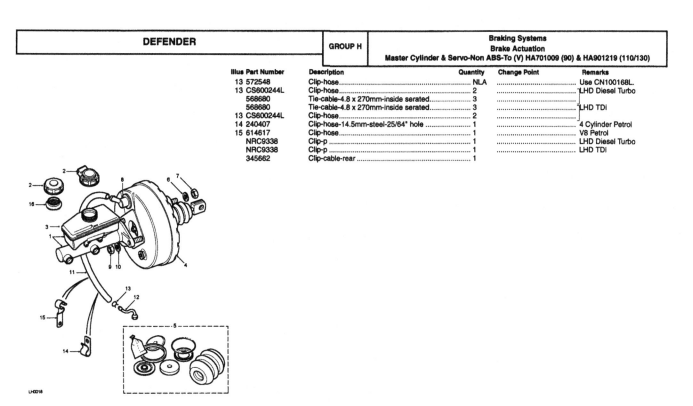

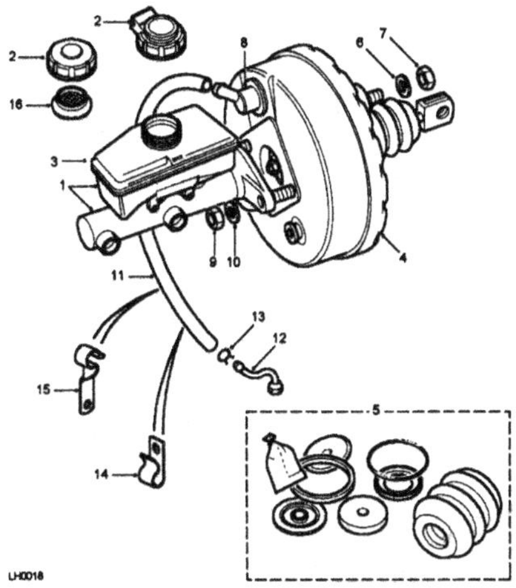

LH0018

Illus	Part Number	Description	Quantity	Change Point	Remarks
1	STC441	MASTER CYLINDER ASSEMBLY BRAKE	1	Note (1)	Except Antilock Brakes
2	NTC4414	• Cap-fluid level warning reservoir indicator	1		
3	STC492	• Kit-brake reservoir	1		
	STC491	Kit-repair brake master cylinder	1		
1	SJC100460	Master cylinder assembly brake	1	Note (2)	
2	SJL100200	Cap-fluid level warning reservoir indicator			
3	SJJ100351	Kit-brake reservoir	1		
4	STC4322	Servo assembly brake	1	Note (3)	
5	WA108051L	Washer-8mm	4		
6	NY108041L	Nut-nyloc-M8	4		
4	STC442	SERVO ASSEMBLY BRAKE	1	Note (4)	
7	STC493	• VALVE-NON RETURN BRAKE VACUUM	1		
	SQQ100000	• • Grommet	1		

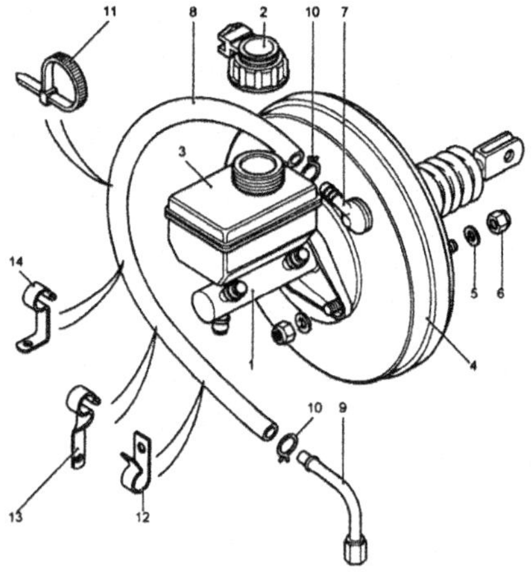

AHHXAA2A

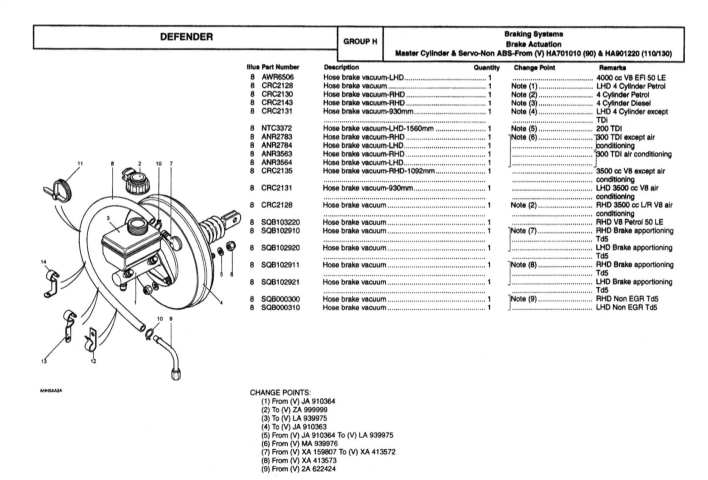

CHANGE POINTS:
(1) To (V) XA 178473
(2) From (V) XA 178474
(3) From (V) XA 159807
(4) From (V) HA 701010 To (V) WA 159806

Illus	Part Number	Description	Quantity	Change Point	Remarks
8	AWR6506	Hose brake vacuum-LHD	1		4000 cc V8 EFi 50 LE
8	CRC2128	Hose brake vacuum	1	Note (1)	LHD 4 Cylinder Petrol
8	CRC2130	Hose brake vacuum-RHD	1	Note (2)	4 Cylinder Petrol
8	CRC2143	Hose brake vacuum-RHD	1	Note (3)	4 Cylinder Diesel
8	CRC2131	Hose brake vacuum-930mm	1	Note (4)	LHD 4 Cylinder except TDi
8	NTC3372	Hose brake vacuum-LHD-1560mm	1	Note (5)	200 TDI
8	ANR2783	Hose brake vacuum-RHD	1	Note (6)	300 TDI except air conditioning
8	ANR2784	Hose brake vacuum-LHD	1		
8	ANR3563	Hose brake vacuum-RHD	1		300 TDI air conditioning
8	ANR3564	Hose brake vacuum-LHD	1		
8	CRC2135	Hose brake vacuum-RHD-1092mm	1		3500 cc V8 except air conditioning
8	CRC2131	Hose brake vacuum-930mm	1		LHD 3500 cc V8 air conditioning
8	CRC2128	Hose brake vacuum	1	Note (2)	RHD 3500 cc L/R V8 air conditioning
8	SQB103220	Hose brake vacuum	1		RHD V8 Petrol 50 LE
8	SQB102910	Hose brake vacuum	1	Note (7)	RHD Brake apportioning Td5
8	SQB102920	Hose brake vacuum	1		LHD Brake apportioning Td5
8	SQB102911	Hose brake vacuum	1	Note (8)	RHD Brake apportioning Td5
8	SQB102921	Hose brake vacuum	1		LHD Brake apportioning Td5
8	SQB000300	Hose brake vacuum	1	Note (9)	RHD Non EGR Td5
8	SQB000310	Hose brake vacuum	1		LHD Non EGR Td5

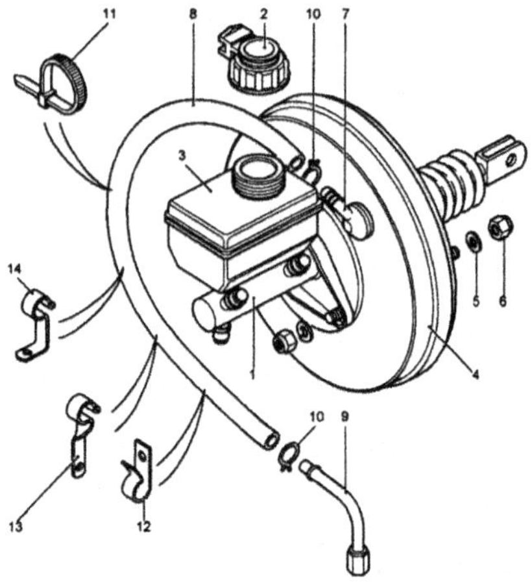

AHHXAA2A

CHANGE POINTS:
(1) From (V) JA 910364
(2) To (V) ZA 999999
(3) To (V) LA 939975
(4) To (V) JA 910363
(5) From (V) JA 910364 To (V) LA 939975
(6) From (V) MA 939976
(7) From (V) XA 159807 To (V) XA 413572
(8) From (V) XA 413573
(9) From (V) 2A 622424

Illus	Part Number	Description	Quantity	Change Point	Remarks
9	569714	Adaptor-vacuum pipe injection pump	1		4 Cylinder Petrol
10	572548	Clip-hose	NLA		Use CN100168L.
10	CN100168L	Clip-hose	2		Except TDi
10	CS600244L	Clip-hose	2		TDi
11	568680	Tie-cable-4.8 x 270mm-inside serated	3		
12	240407	Clip-hose-14.5mm-steel-25/64" hole	1		4 Cylinder Petrol
13	614617	Clip-hose	1		V8
14	NRC9338	Clip-p	1		TDi

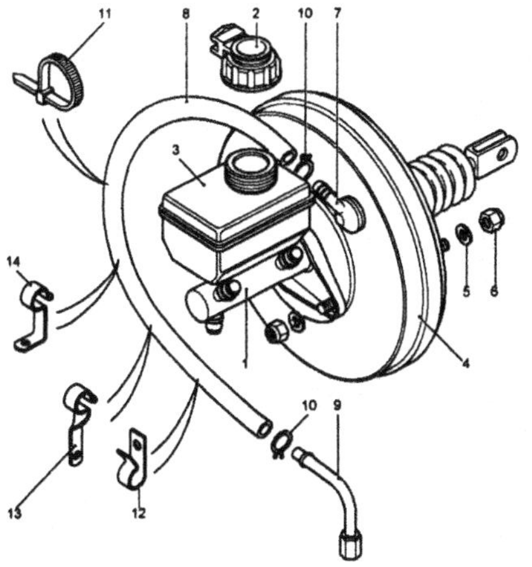

AHHXAA2A

Illus	Part Number	Description	Quantity	Change Point	Remarks
1	SJC100420	MASTER CYLINDER ASSEMBLY BRAKE-ANTI-LOCK BRAKE	1	Note (1)	
2	SJJ100350	• KIT-BRAKE RESERVOIR	1		
3	NTC4414	• • Cap-fluid level warning reservoir indicator	1		
	SJO100080	• • Seal-brake servo	1		
1	SJC100421	Master cylinder assembly brake-anti-lock brake	1	Note (2)	
2	SJJ100351	Kit-brake reservoir			
3	SJL100200	Cap-fluid level warning reservoir indicator			
4	SJG100240	SERVO ASSEMBLY BRAKE	1	Note (3)	
	SJO100080	• Seal-brake servo	1		
	SIH100010	ADAPTOR-SERVO TO DASH	1	Note (3)	
5	FY108047	• Nut-flange-nyloc-M8	4		
6	SQQ100000	Grommet	1	Note (3)	
7	SQB102910	Hose brake vacuum- with non return valve	1	Note (4)	RHD
7	SQB102920	Hose brake vacuum- with non return valve	1		LHD
7	SQB102911	Hose brake vacuum	1	Note (5)	RHD Td5
7	SQB102921	Hose brake vacuum	1		LHD Td5
7	SQB000300	Hose brake vacuum	1	Note (6)	RHD Non EGR Td5
7	SQB000310	Hose brake vacuum	1		LHD Non EGR Td5
8	DYC101410L	Clip-hose	1	Note (3)	

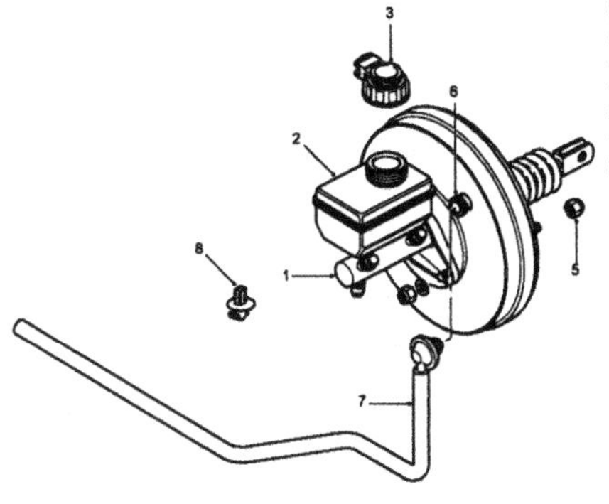

LH0020A

CHANGE POINTS:
(1) To (V) XA 178473
(2) From (V) XA 178474
(3) From (V) XA 159807
(4) From (V) XA 159807 To (V) XA 413572
(5) From (V) XA 413573
(6) From (V) 2A 622424

Illus	Part Number	Description	Quantity	Change Point	Remarks
1	SRB101550	Modulator antilock brakes	1		
2	SRU101970	Bracket & modulator assembly antilock brakes-LHD	1		
2	SRU101920	Bracket & modulator assembly antilock brakes-RHD	1		
3	ANR5265	Bush-antilock brake system modulator to mounting bracket	3		
4	ANR3107	Washer-cup	3		
5	FN106047L	Nut-flange-M6	3		
6	FN108047L	Nut-flange-flanged head-M8	3		RHD
6	FN108047L	Nut-flange-flanged head-M8	2		LHD
7	FS108167PL	Bolt-flanged head-M8 x 16	1		LHD
8	SRU102200	Bracket-antilock brake harness	1		

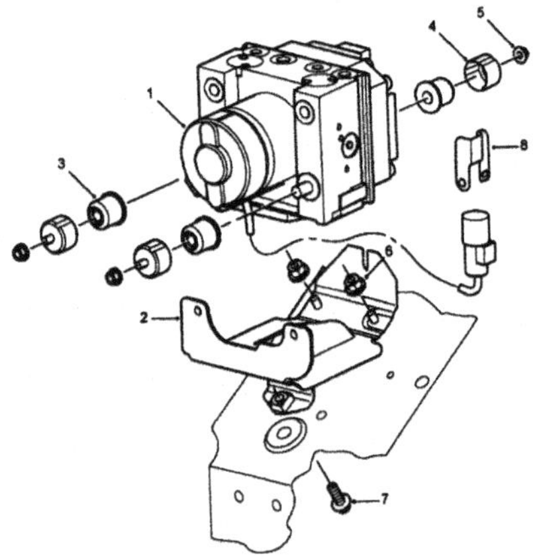

LH0015

Illus	Part Number	Description	Quantity	Change Point	Remarks
1	NRC8349	Hose brake vacuum	1		Petrol
1	CRC2131	Hose brake vacuum-930mm	1		Diesel
1	CRC2135	Hose brake vacuum-RHD-1092mm	1		Diesel Turbo
2	592443	T piece	1		
3	NRC8629	Hose brake vacuum	1		Petrol
3	CRC2134	Hose brake vacuum	1		Diesel
3	CRC2131	Hose brake vacuum-930mm	1		Diesel Turbo
4	NRC8593	Valve assembly brake	1		
		HOSE BRAKE VACUUM			
5	NRC8352	heater/cooler	1		Petrol
5	CRC2131	heater/cooler-930mm	1		Diesel
5	CRC2131	heater/cooler-930mm	1		Diesel Turbo
6	CRC2133	engine	1		4 Cylinder Petrol
6	NRC8352	engine	1		V8
6	CRC2144	pump	1		Diesel
6	CRC2131	pump-930mm	1		Diesel Turbo
7	CS600244L	Clip-hose	8		
8	CP105121L	Clip-p-M12	1		Petrol
9	56667	Clip-p-5/8"	1		Diesel

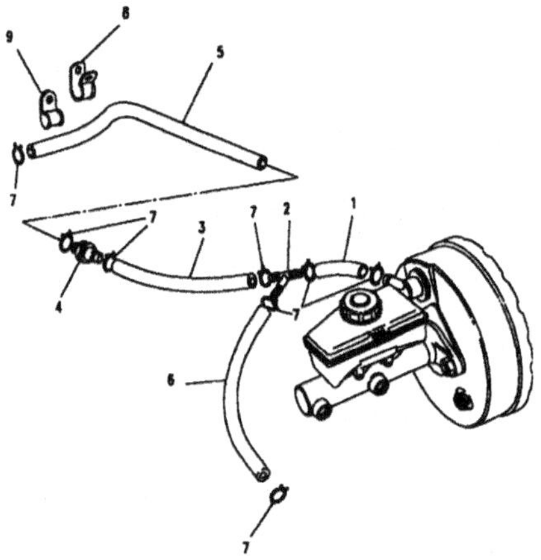

Vacuum Hoses-From (V) AA273532

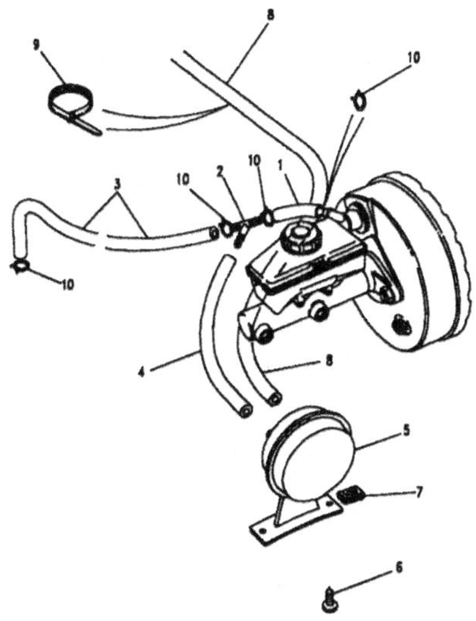

Illus	Part Number	Description	Quantity	Change Point	Remarks
1	NRC8349	Hose brake vacuum	1		LHD
1	CRC2131	Hose brake vacuum-930mm	1		RHD
2	MUC4865	T piece	1		
		HOSE BRAKE VACUUM			
3	CRC2131	Engine-930mm	1		4 Cylinder Petrol
3	NRC8352	Engine	1		LHD V8
3	CRC2131	Engine-930mm	1		RHD V8
3	CRC2131	Pump-930mm	1		Diesel
3	NTC3372	Pump-LHD-1560mm	1		LHD Diesel Turbo
3	NTC3372	LHD-1560mm	1	Note (1)	LHD TDi
3	NTC8592	Hose brake vacuum	1	Note (2)	LHD TDi
4	MUC4866	Hose vacuum	1		
5	MUC1679	Vacuum tank	1		
6	AB606041L	Screw-to vacuum tank-self tapping-No 6 x 1/2	2		
7	AK612011L	Nut	2		
8	MWC4854	Hose brake vacuum	1		
9	568680	Tie-cable-4.8 x 270mm-inside serated	3		
10	CS600244L	Clip-hose	4		

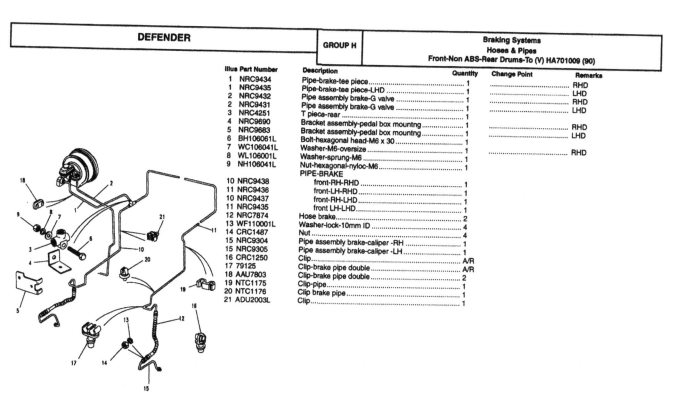

CHANGE POINTS:
(1) From (V) AA 273532 To (V) HA 701009
(2) From (V) HA 701010

Front-Non ABS-Rear Drums-To (V) HA701009 (90)

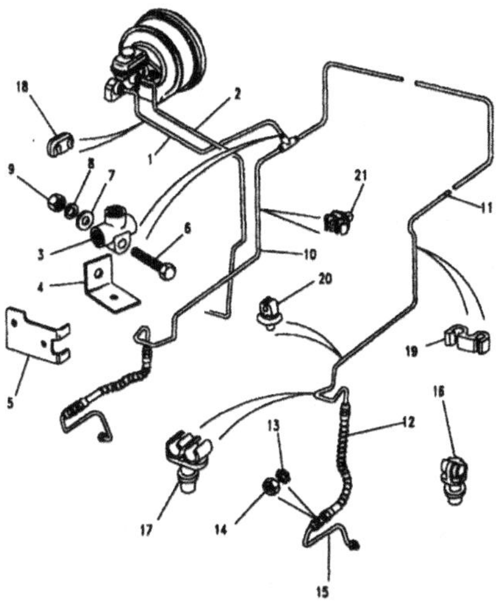

Illus	Part Number	Description	Quantity	Change Point	Remarks
1	NRC9434	Pipe-brake-tee piece	1		RHD
1	NRC9435	Pipe-brake-tee piece-LHD	1		LHD
2	NRC9432	Pipe assembly brake-G valve	1		RHD
2	NRC9431	Pipe assembly brake-G valve	1		LHD
3	NRC4251	T piece-rear	1		
4	NRC9690	Bracket assembly-pedal box mountng	1		RHD
5	NRC9683	Bracket assembly-pedal box mountng	1		LHD
6	BH106061L	Bolt-hexagonal head-M6 x 30	1		
7	WC106041L	Washer-M6-oversize	1		RHD
8	WL106001L	Washer-sprung-M6	1		
9	NH106041L	Nut-hexagonal-nyloc-M6	1		
		PIPE-BRAKE			
10	NRC9438	front-RH-RHD	1		
11	NRC9436	front-LH-RHD	1		
10	NRC9437	front-RH-LHD	1		
11	NRC9435	front LH-LHD	1		
12	NRC7874	Hose brake	2		
13	WF110001L	Washer-lock-10mm ID	4		
14	CRC1487	Nut	4		
15	NRC9304	Pipe assembly brake-caliper -RH	1		
15	NRC9305	Pipe assembly brake-caliper -LH	1		
16	CRC1250	Clip	A/R		
17	79125	Clip-brake pipe double	A/R		
18	AAU7803	Clip-brake pipe double	2		
19	NTC1175	Clip-pipe	1		
20	NTC1176	Clip brake pipe	1		
21	ADU2003L	Clip	1		

Front-Non ABS-Rear Drums-To (V) HA901219 (110/130)

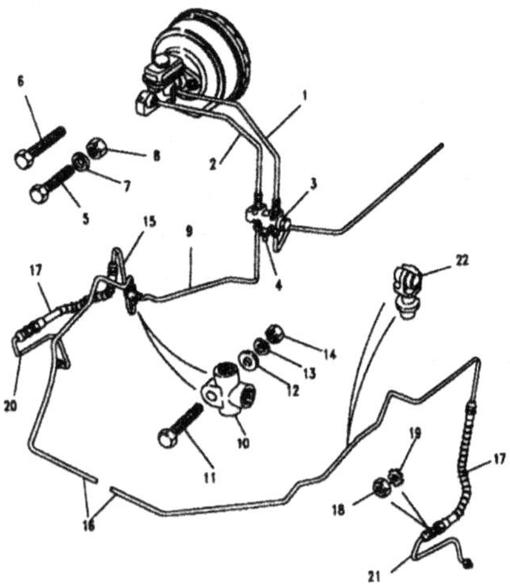

Illus	Part Number	Description	Quantity	Change Point	Remarks
		PIPE ASSEMBLY BRAKE			
1	NRC7901	primary-RHD	1	Note (1)	
1	NRC7902	primary-LHD	1		
2	NRC7903	secondary-RHD	1		
2	NRC7904	secondary-LHD	1		
3	NRC7871	Valve assembly brake-PDWA switch	1		
3	NRC6515	Valve assembly brake-PDWA/PCR	1		
4	AAU1700	Switch assembly-pressure antilock brakes	1		
5	BH106091L	Bolt-M6 x 45	1		
6	BH106111L	Bolt-M6 x 55	1		
7	WL106001	Washer-M6	NLA		Use WL106001L.
8	NH106041	Nut-hexagonal head-M6	NLA		Use NH106041L.
9	NRC9731	Pipe assembly brake	1		
10	NRC4251	T piece-rear	1		
11	BH106061L	Bolt-hexagonal head-M6 x 30	1		
12	WC106041L	Washer-M6-oversize	1		
13	WL106001	Washer-M6	NLA		Use WL106001L.
14	NH106041	Nut-hexagonal head-M6	NLA		Use NH106041L.
15	NRC8721	Pipe-brake-RH	1		
16	NRC7801	Pipe-brake-LH	1		
17	NRC7874	Hose brake	2		
18	CRC1487	Nut	4		
19	WF110001L	Washer-lock-10mm ID	4		
20	NRC9575	Pipe assembly brake-RH	1		
21	NRC7799	Pipe assembly brake-LH	1		
22	CRC1250	Clip	8		

CHANGE POINTS:
(1) To (V) HA 901219

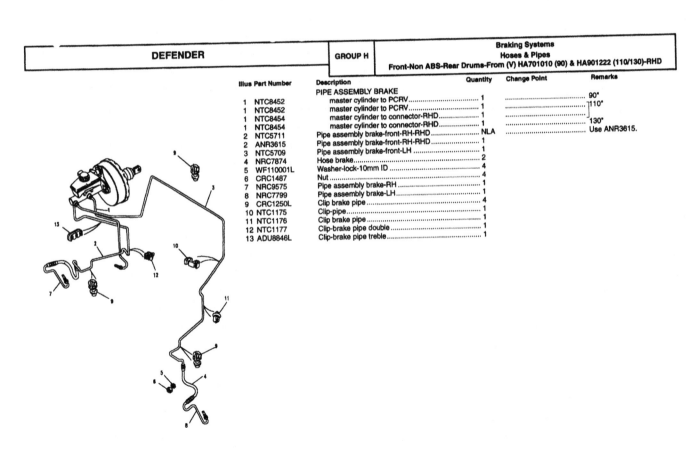

Front-Non ABS-Rear Drums-From (V) HA701010 (90) & HA901222 (110/130)-RHD

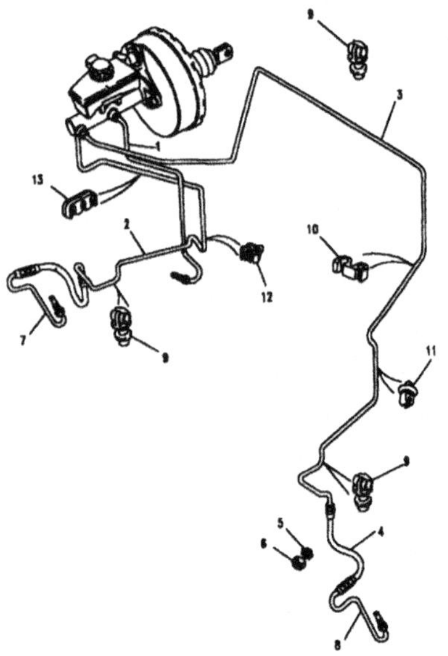

Illus	Part Number	Description	Quantity	Change Point	Remarks
		PIPE ASSEMBLY BRAKE			
1	NTC8452	master cylinder to PCRV	1		90"
1	NTC8452	master cylinder to PCRV	1		110"
1	NTC8454	master cylinder to connector-RHD	1		110"
1	NTC8454	master cylinder to connector-RHD	1		130"
2	NTC5711	Pipe assembly brake-front-RH-RHD	NLA		Use ANR3615.
2	ANR3615	Pipe assembly brake-front-RH-RHD	1		
3	NTC5709	Pipe assembly brake-front-LH	1		
4	NRC7874	Hose brake	2		
5	WF110001L	Washer-lock-10mm ID	4		
6	CRC1487	Nut	4		
7	NRC9575	Pipe assembly brake-RH	1		
8	NRC7799	Pipe assembly brake-LH	1		
9	CRC1250L	Clip brake pipe	4		
10	NTC1175	Clip-pipe	1		
11	NTC1176	Clip brake pipe	1		
12	NTC1177	Clip-brake pipe double	1		
13	ADU8846L	Clip-brake pipe treble	1		

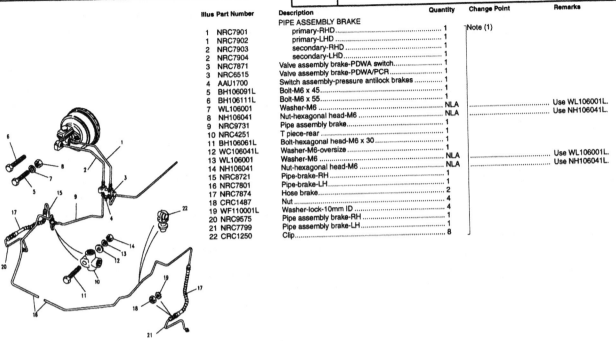

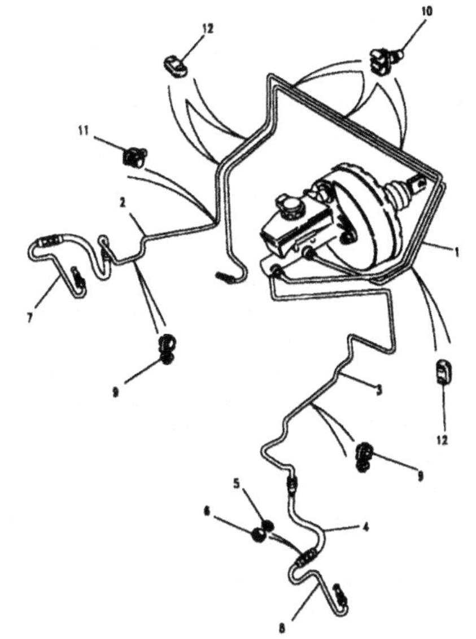

Illus	Part Number	Description	Quantity	Change Point	Remarks
		PIPE ASSEMBLY BRAKE			
1	NTC8451	master cylinder to PCRV	1		90"
1	NTC8451	master cylinder to PCRV	1		110"
1	NTC8453	master cylinder to connector-LHD	1		
1	NTC8453	master cylinder to connector-LHD	1		130"
2	NTC8450	Pipe assembly brake-RH	1		
3	NTC5708	Pipe assembly brake-LH-LHD	1		
4	NRC7874	Hose brake	2		
5	WF110001L	Washer-lock-10mm ID	4		
6	CRC1487	Nut	4		
7	NRC9575	Pipe assembly brake-RH	1		
8	NRC7799	Pipe assembly brake-LH	1		
9	CRC1250L	Clip brake pipe	2		
10	79127	Clip-brake pipe double	3		
11	NTC1177	Clip-brake pipe double	1		
12	AAU7803	Clip-brake pipe double	3		

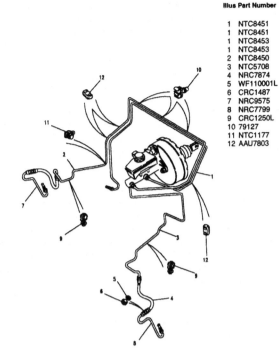

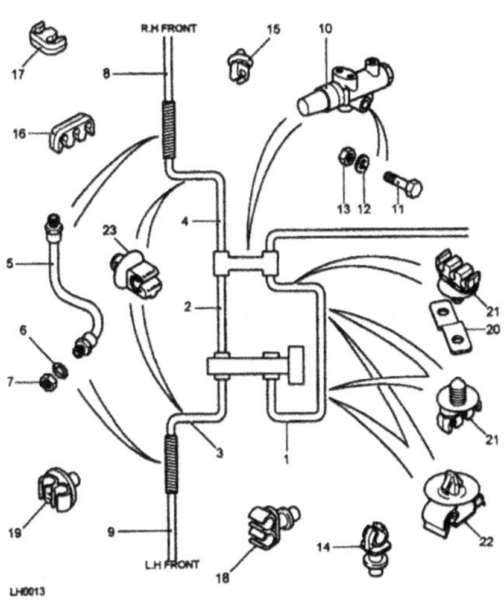

Illus	Part Number	Description	Quantity	Change Point	Remarks
		PIPE ASSEMBLY BRAKE			
1	NTC7961	master cylinder to valve rear-RHD	1		
1	NTC7962	master cylinder to valve rear-LHD	1	Note (1)	
1	ANR3770	master cylinder to valve rear-LHD	1	Note (2)	
1	SGB112440	master cylinder to valve rear-LHD	1	Note (3)	
2	NTC7968	master cylinder to valve front-RHD	1		
2	NTC7970	master cylinder to valve front-LHD	1	Note (1)	
2	ANR3069	master cylinder to valve front-LHD	1	Note (2)	
2	SGB112450	master cylinder to valve front-LHD	1	Note (3)	
3	SGB112430	master cylinder to jump hose-LH-RHD	1		
3	ANR2503	master cylinder to front-RH	1		
4	NTC9726	master cylinder to front-LH-RHD	1		
4	NTC5708	master cylinder to front-LH-LHD	1		
5	NRC7874	Hose brake	2		
6	WF110001L	Washer-lock-10mm ID	4		
7	CRC1487	Nut	4		
8	ANR2946	Pipe assembly brake-RH	1		
9	ANR2947	Pipe assembly brake-LH	1		
10	NTC8836	Valve brake-40 PRF 24	1		90"
10	NRC8215	Valve brake	1	Note (4)	Except 90"
10	ANR1415	Valve brake-29 PRF 43	1	Note (5)	Except 90"
11	FB108111L	Bolt-flanged head-M8 x 55	1		
11	BH106091L	Bolt-M6 x 45	1		
12	WA108051L	Washer-8mm	1		
12	WL106001L	Washer-sprung-M6	1		
13	NY108041L	Nut-nyloc-M8	1		
13	NH106041L	Nut-hexagonal-nyloc-M6	1		

CHANGE POINTS:
(1) From (V) LA 930456 To (V) MA 948860
(2) From (V) MA 948861 To (V) WA 159806
(3) From (V) XA 159807
(4) To (V) LA 939975
(5) From (V) MA 939976

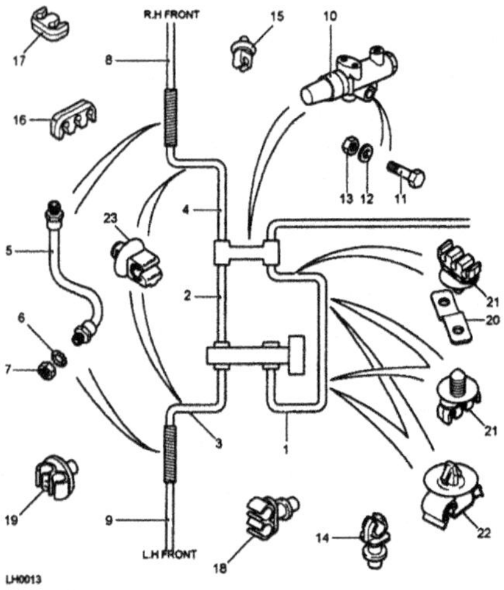

LH0013

Illus	Part Number	Description	Quantity	Change Point	Remarks
14	CRC1250L	Clip brake pipe	A/R		RHD
23	NTC9543L	Clip brake pipe	3	Note (1)	RHD
15	NTC1176	Clip brake pipe	1		RHD
16	ADU8846L	Clip-brake pipe treble	1		RHD
17	AAU7803	Clip-brake pipe double	3		RHD
20	SGI100020	Bracket-brake pipe tee connector	1	Note (1)	RHD
21	SGK100870	Clip-brake pipe treble	1	Note (1)	RHD
22	SGK100860	Clip-brake pipe double	2	Note (1)	RHD
14	CRC1250L	Clip brake pipe	A/R		LHD
23	NTC9543L	Clip brake pipe	3	Note (1)	LHD
15	NTC1176	Clip brake pipe	1		LHD
17	AAU7803	Clip-brake pipe double	3		LHD
18	79127	Clip-brake pipe double	3		LHD
19	NTC1177	Clip-brake pipe double	1		LHD
20	SGI100020	Bracket-brake pipe tee connector	1	Note (1)	LHD

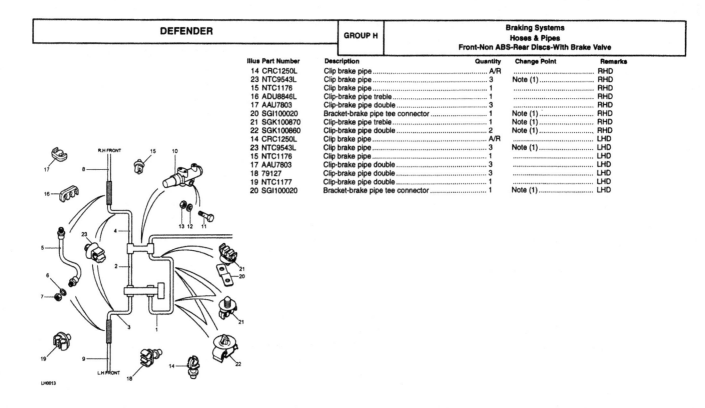

CHANGE POINTS:
(1) From (V) XA 159807

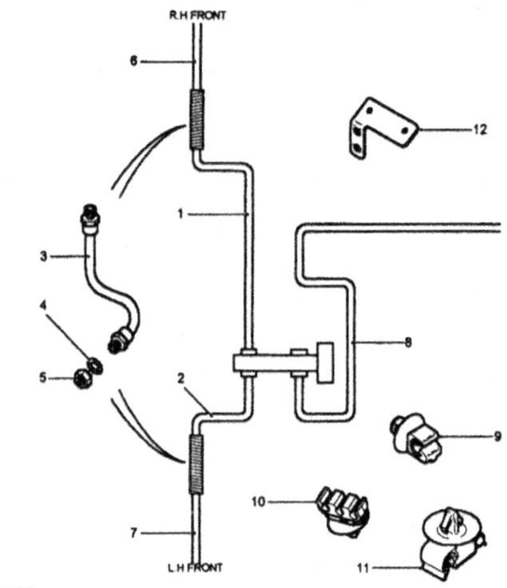

LH0016

Illus	Part Number	Description	Quantity	Change Point	Remarks
		PIPE ASSEMBLY BRAKE			
1	NTC5711	master cylinder to jump hose-front-RH-RHD	NLA		Use ANR3615.
1	ANR3615	master cylinder to jump hose-front-RH-RHD	1	Note (1)	
1	SGB113780	master cylinder to jump hose-RH-RHD	1	Note (2)	
1	ANR2780	master cylinder to jump hose-RH-LHD	1	Note (1)	
1	SGB112370	master cylinder to jump hose-RH-LHD	1	Note (2)	
2	NTC9726	master cylinder to jump hose-LH-RHD	1	Note (1)	
2	SGB112430	master cylinder to jump hose-LH-RHD	1	Note (2)	
2	NTC5708	master cylinder to jump hose-LH-LHD	1		
3	NRC7874	Hose brake	2		
4	WF110001L	Washer-lock-10mm ID	4		
5	CRC1487	Nut	4		
		PIPE ASSEMBLY BRAKE			
6	NRC9575	RH	1		
7	NRC7799	LH	1		
8	NTC8454	master cylinder to connector-RHD	1	Note (1)	
8	NTC8453	master cylinder to connector-LHD	1	Note (1)	
8	SGB114450	master cylinder to connector-LHD	1	Note (3)	TDi
8	SGB112451	LHD	1	Note (4)	Tdi
8	SGB112460	master cylinder to connector-RHD	1	Note (3)	
8	SGB112461	RHD	1	Note (4)	
8	SGB112420	master cylinder to connector-LHD	1	Note (3)	Td5
8	SGB112421	LHD	1	Note (4)	Td5
9	NTC9543L	Clip brake pipe	4	Note (2)	
10	SGK100870	Clip-brake pipe treble	3	Note (2)	LHD
10	SGK100870	Clip-brake pipe treble	1	Note (2)	RHD
11	SGK100860	Clip-brake pipe double	2	Note (2)	RHD
12	SGI100020	Bracket-brake pipe tee connector	1	Note (2)	
13	DCP3969L	Clip-brake pipe double-4.7 x 4.7mm	1	Note (2)	LHD Tdi
14	AAU7803	Clip-brake pipe double	3		LHD
15	SGK100890	Clip-brake pipe treble	1		130"

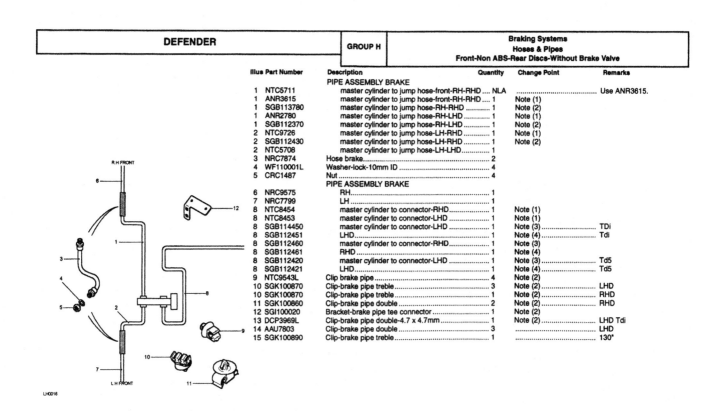

CHANGE POINTS:
(1) To (V) WA 159806
(2) From (V) XA 159807
(3) From (V) XA 159807 To (V) XA 176106
(4) From (V) XA 176107

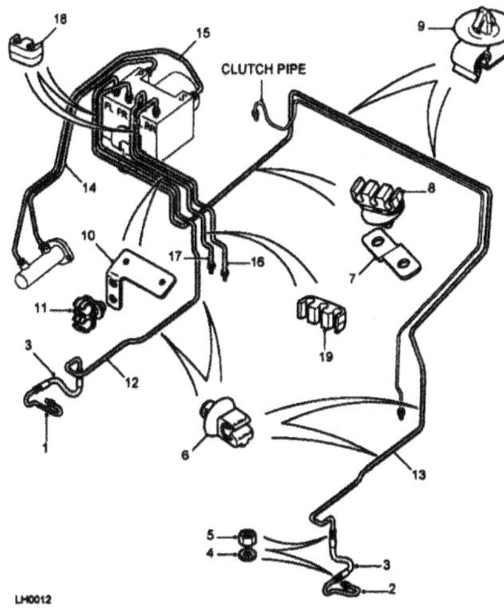

Illus	Part Number	Description	Quantity	Change Point	Remarks
1	ANR2946	Pipe assembly brake-RH	1	Note (1)	
2	ANR2947	Pipe assembly brake-LH	1	Note (1)	
3	NRC7874	Hose brake	2	Note (1)	
4	WF110001L	Washer-lock-10mm ID	4	Note (1)	
5	CRC1487	Nut	4	Note (1)	Antilock Brakes
6	NTC9543	Clip brake pipe	NLA	Note (1)	Use NTC9543L.
7	SGI100020	Bracket-brake pipe tee connector	1	Note (1)	
8	SGK100870	Clip-brake pipe treble	1	Note (1)	
9	SGK100860	Clip-brake pipe double	2	Note (1)	
10	SGI100010	Bracket-brake pipe tee connector	1	Note (1)	
11	NTC9531	Clip-2 holes	2	Note (1)	
12	SGB111910	Pipe assembly brake	1	Note (1)	
13	SGB111920	Pipe assembly brake	1	Note (1)	
14	SGB111890	Pipe assembly brake	1	Note (1)	
15	SGB111900	Pipe assembly brake	1	Note (1)	
16	SGB111930	Pipe assembly brake	1	Note (1)	
16	SGB111930	Pipe assembly brake	1	Note (3)	Td5
16	SGB111931	Pipe assembly brake	1	Note (4)	Td5
17	SGB111940	Pipe assembly brake	1	Note (1)	
17	SGB111940	Pipe assembly brake	1	Note (3)	Td5
17	SGB111941	Pipe assembly brake	1	Note (4)	Td5
18	AAU7803	Clip-brake pipe double	3	Note (1)	
19	ADU8846L	Clip-brake pipe treble	1	Note (1)	

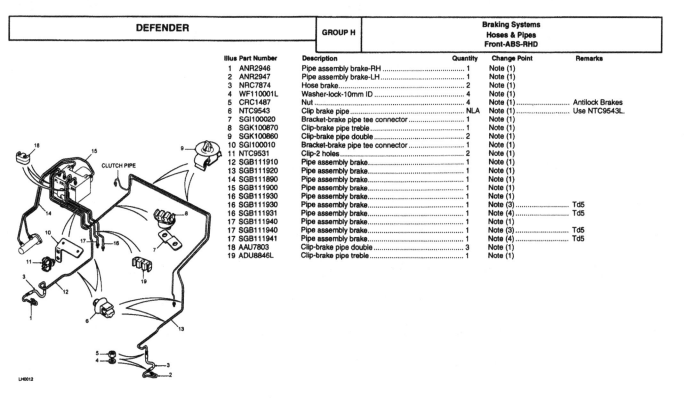

CHANGE POINTS:
(1) From (V) XA 159807
(3) From (V) XA 159807 To (V) XA 176106
(4) From (V) XA 176107

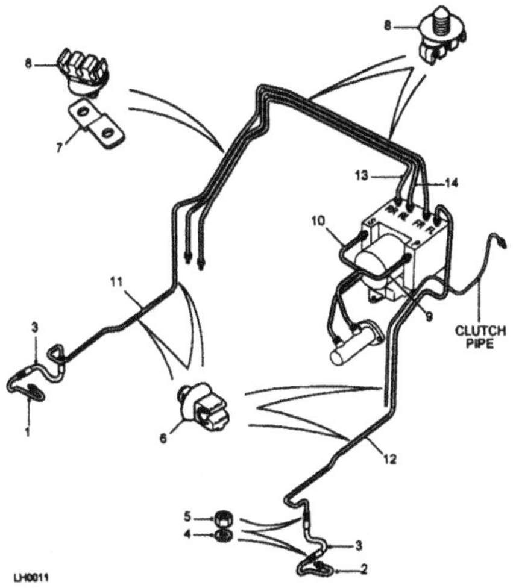

Illus	Part Number	Description	Quantity	Change Point	Remarks
1	ANR2946	Pipe assembly brake-RH	1	Note (1)	
2	ANR2947	Pipe assembly brake-LH	1	Note (1)	
3	NRC7874	Hose brake	2	Note (1)	
4	WF110001L	Washer-lock-10mm ID	4	Note (1)	
5	CRC1487	Nut	4	Note (1)	
6	NTC9543	Clip brake pipe	NLA	Note (1)	Use NTC9543L.
7	SGI100020	Bracket-brake pipe tee connector	1	Note (1)	
8	SGK100870	Clip-brake pipe treble	3	Note (1)	
9	SGB111950	Pipe assembly brake	1	Note (1)	
10	SGB111960	Pipe assembly brake	1	Note (1)	
11	SGB111970	Pipe assembly brake	1	Note (1)	
12	SGB111980	Pipe assembly brake	1	Note (1)	
13	SGB111990	Pipe assembly brake	1	Note (1)	
13	SGB111990	Pipe assembly brake	1	Note (3)	Td5
13	SGB111991	Pipe assembly brake	1	Note (4)	Td5
14	SGB112000	Pipe assembly brake	1	Note (1)	
14	SGB112000	Pipe assembly brake	1	Note (3)	Td5
14	SGB112001	Pipe assembly brake	1	Note (4)	Td5

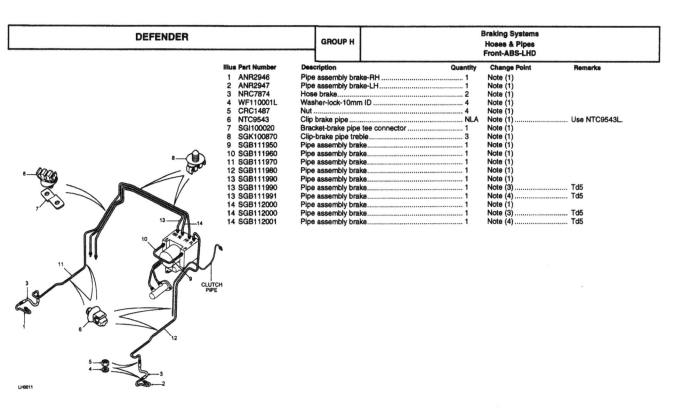

CHANGE POINTS:
(1) From (V) XA 159807
(3) From (V) XA 159807 To (V) XA 176106
(4) From (V) XA 176107

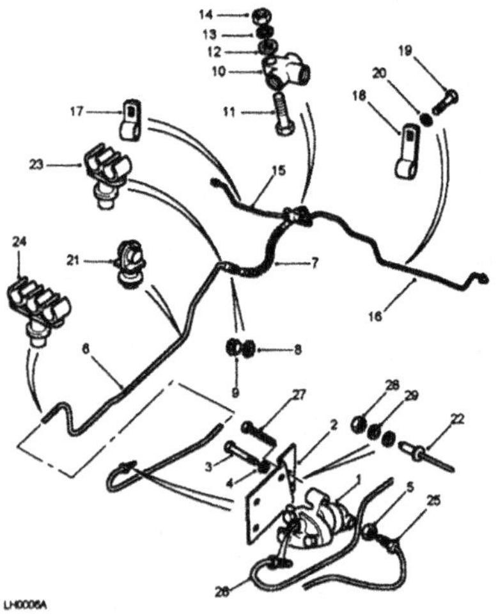

LH0006A

Illus	Part Number	Description	Quantity	Change Point	Remarks
1	NRC8215	Valve brake	1		
2	NRC9035	Bracket-valve brake	1	Note (1)	110"
2	NRC8897	Bracket-valve brake	1		
3	BH108091L	Bolt-M8 x 45	1		
4	WA108051L	Washer-8mm	1	Note (2)	
4	2266L	Washer	2	Note (3)	
5	NY108041L	Nut-nyloc-M8	1		
22	RA612207L	Rivet	2	Note (3)	
6	NTC8543	Pipe assembly brake	1	Note (4)	130"
6	NTC8455	Pipe assembly brake-with G valve	1	Note (5)	110"
6	NTC8456	Pipe assembly brake-with connector	1	Note (6)	110"
6	NTC1792	Pipe assembly brake	1	Note (1)	110"
6	RRC2479	Pipe assembly brake	1	Note (1)	130"
6	NTC1636	Pipe assembly brake	1		90"
	BMK2466	Connector brake	1	Note (5)	110"
7	NRC9455	Hose brake	1	Note (7)	90"
7	NRC9456	Hose brake	1	Note (8)	Except 90"
8	WF110001L	Washer-lock-10mm ID	1		
9	CRC1487	Nut	1		
10	NRC4251	T piece-rear	1		
	FRC8775	Bracket-brake pipe tee connector	NLA		Use FTC4889.
	FTC4889	Bracket-brake pipe tee connector	1		
11	BH106061L	Bolt-hexagonal head-M6 x 30	1		
12	WC106041L	Washer-M6-oversize	1	Note (2)	
13	WL106001L	Washer-sprung-M6	1	Note (2)	
14	NH106041L	Nut-hexagonal-nyloc-M6	1		
		PIPE ASSEMBLY BRAKE			
15	NRC8902	RH	1		
15	NRC7905	RH	1	Note (1)	110"
16	NTC4578	LH	1	Note (5)	110"
16	NRC9757	LH	1		90"
16	NRC7906	LH	1	Note (1)	110"

CHANGE POINTS:
(1) To (V) HA 901219
(2) To (V) HA 701009
(3) From (V) HA 701010 To (V) KA 930455
(4) From (V) HA 901220 To (V) LA 930545 130"
(5) From (V) HA 901220 To (V) KA 930434
(6) From (V) HA 901220 To (V) KA 930455
(7) To (V) LA 930455
(8) To (V) LA 930434

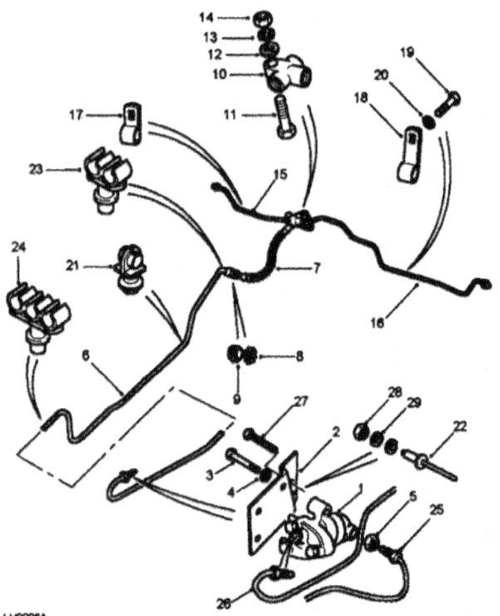

LH0006A

Illus	Part Number	Description	Quantity	Change Point	Remarks
17	577873	Clip-p	2		
18	11820L	Clip	1		
19	79004	Screw	3	Note (1)	
19	SL510031	Screw	3	Note (2)	
19	SL510031	Screw	2	Note (3)	
20	WC702101L	Washer-plain	3	Note (4)	
20	WC702101L	Washer-plain	2	Note (3)	
21	CRC1250L	Clip brake pipe	A/R	Note (3)	
23	79127	Clip-brake pipe double	3	Note (5)	Except 90"
24	AFU1217	Clip-brake pipe treble-4.75mm	3	Note (6)	110"
25	NRC8213	Pipe-brake-to G valve	1		Hard Top 110"
26	NRC8214	Pipe-brake-from G valve	1		Hard Top 110"
27	FS106255L	Screw-flanged head-M6 x 25	1	Note (6)	Hard Top 110"
28	WA106041	Washer	NLA	Note (6)	Use WA106041L.
					Hard Top 110"
29	NY106041L	Nut-hexagonal head-nyloc-M6	NLA	Note (6)	Use NY106047L.
					Hard Top 110"

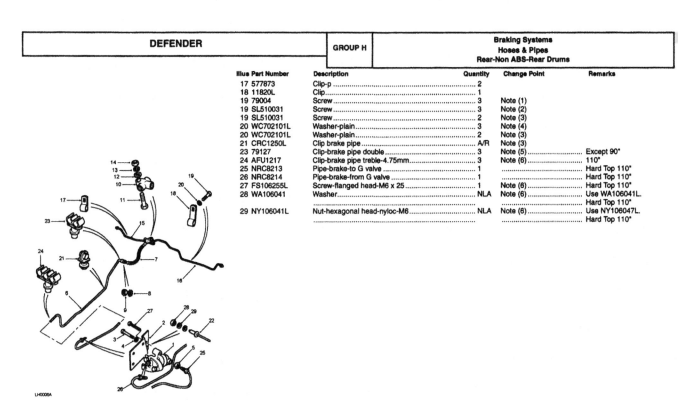

CHANGE POINTS:
(1) To (V) 341764
(2) From (V) 341765 To (V) HA 701009
(3) From (V) HA 701010 To (V) KA 930455
(4) To (V) HA 701009
(5) To (V) LA 930434
(6) To (V) HA 901219

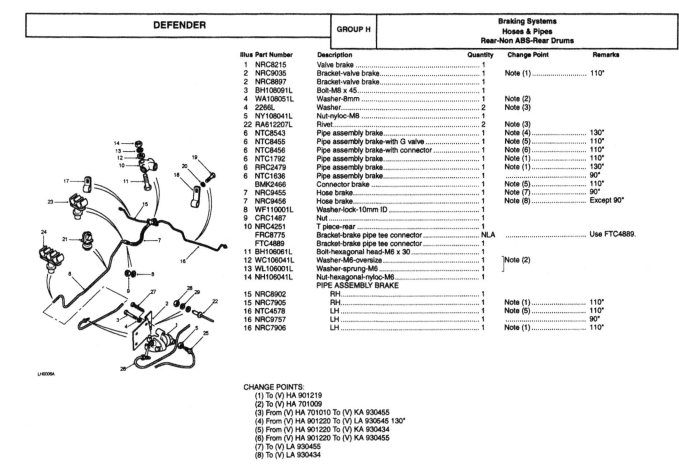

Illus	Part Number	Description	Quantity	Change Point	Remarks
1	FTC4889	Bracket-brake pipe tee connector-T piece to axle	1	Note (1)	
22	TYF101160	Spacer	2		90"
1	SGI100040	Bracket-brake pipe tee connector-T piece to axle	1	Note (2)	Except 90"
2	BMK2466	Connector brake	1		110"
2	BMK2466	Connector brake	1		130"
19	SGL100020	Adaptor-pipe-dual male	1	Note (2)	Brake apportioning except 130"
		PIPE ASSEMBLY BRAKE			
3	ANR2775	valve to rear	1	Note (3)	90"
3	ANR2776	valve to rear	1	Note (4)	Brake apportioning 110"
3	ANR2777	valve to rear	1		110" except Brake apportioning
3	ANR2778	Pipe assembly brake	1		130"
3	SGB112020	Pipe assembly brake	1	Note (2)	90" except Brake apportioning
3	SGB112350	Pipe assembly brake	1		110" except Brake apportioning
3	SGB114490	Pipe assembly brake-front to rear	1		Brake apportioning 90"
3	SGB114500	Pipe assembly brake-front to rear	1		Brake apportioning 110"
3	SGB113700	Pipe assembly brake-front to rear	1	Note (2)	130"
3	SGB113700	Pipe assembly brake-front to rear	1	Note (5)	Td5 130"
3	SGB113701	Pipe assembly brake-front to rear	1	Note (6)	Td5 130"
4	NRC9455	Hose brake	1	Note (3)	90"
4	NRC9456	Hose brake	1	Note (4)	110"
4	SHB101370	Hose brake-rear	1	From (V) XA 159807	

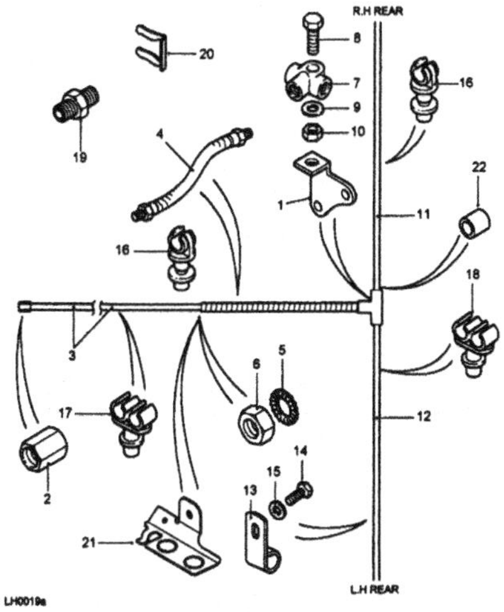

LH0019a

CHANGE POINTS:
(1) From (V) LA 930456
(2) From (V) XA 159807
(3) From (V) LA 930456 To (V) WA 159806
(4) To (V) WA 159806
(5) From (V) XA 159807 To (V) XA 176106
(6) From (V) XA 176107

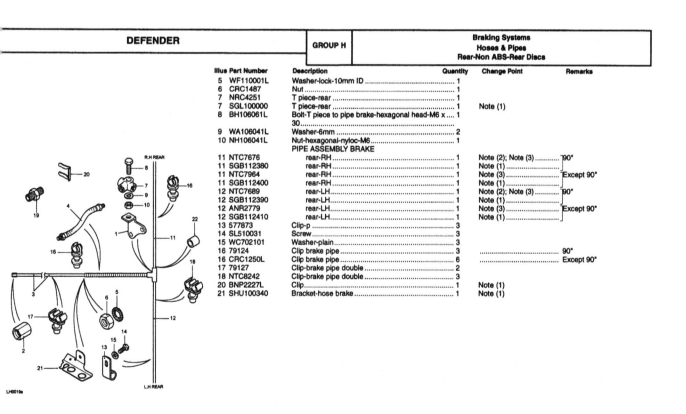

Illus	Part Number	Description	Quantity	Change Point	Remarks
5	WF110001L	Washer-lock-10mm ID	1		
6	CRC1487	Nut	1		
7	NRC4251	T piece-rear	1		
7	SGL100000	T piece-rear	1	Note (1)	
8	BH106061L	Bolt-T piece to pipe brake-hexagonal head-M6 x 30	1		
9	WA106041L	Washer-6mm	2		
10	NH106041L	Nut-hexagonal-nyloc-M6	1		
		PIPE ASSEMBLY BRAKE			
11	NTC7676	rear-RH	1	Note (2); Note (3)	90"
11	SGB112380	rear-RH	1	Note (1)	
11	NTC7964	rear-RH	1	Note (3)	Except 90"
11	SGB112400	rear-RH	1	Note (1)	
12	NTC7689	rear-LH	1	Note (2); Note (3)	90"
12	SGB112390	rear-LH	1	Note (1)	
12	ANR2779	rear-LH	1	Note (3)	Except 90"
12	SGB112410	rear-LH	1	Note (1)	
13	577873	Clip-p	3		
14	SL510031	Screw	3		
15	WC702101	Washer-plain	3		
16	79124	Clip brake pipe	3		90"
16	CRC1250L	Clip brake pipe	6		Except 90"
17	79127	Clip-brake pipe double	2		
18	NTC8242	Clip-brake pipe double	3		
20	BNP2227L	Clip	1	Note (1)	
21	SHU100340	Bracket-hose brake	1	Note (1)	

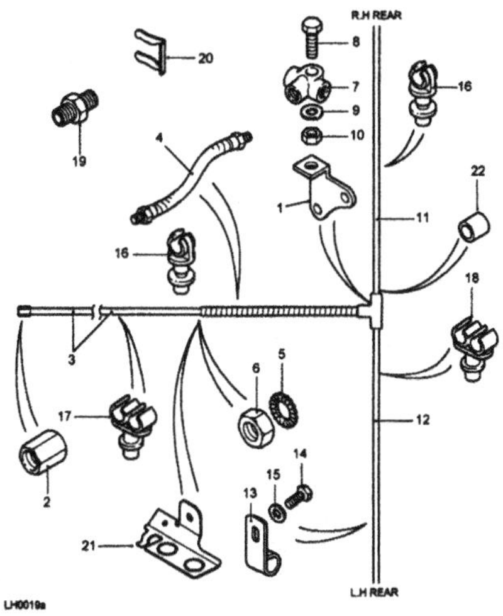

LH0019a

CHANGE POINTS:
(1) From (V) XA 159807
(2) From (V) LA 930456
(3) To (V) WA 159806

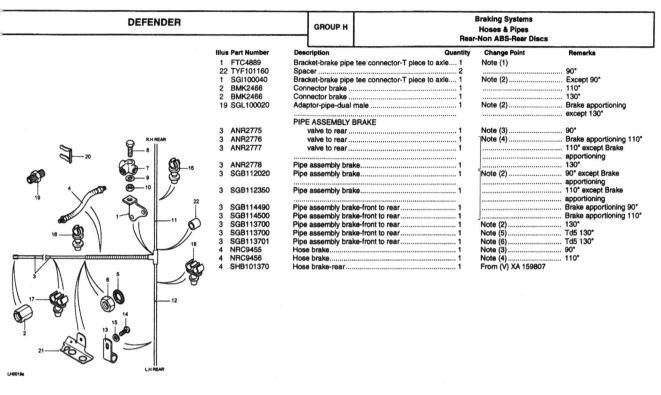

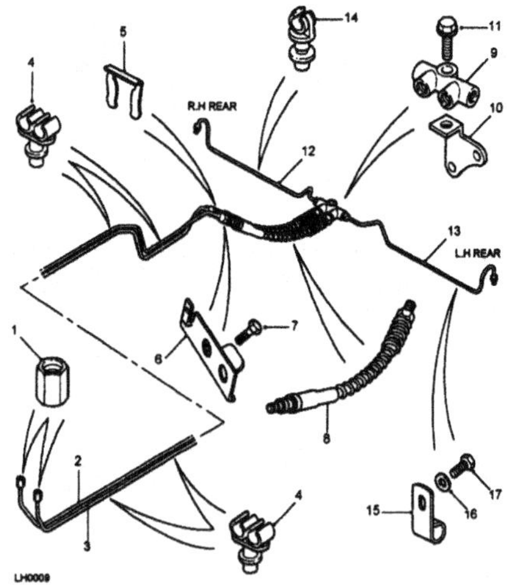

Illus	Part Number	Description	Quantity	Change Point	Remarks
1	BMK2466	Connector brake	2	Note (1)	
2	SGB112020	Pipe assembly brake-RH	1	Note (1)	90"
2	SGB112020	Pipe assembly brake-RH	1	Note (2)	Td5 90"
2	SGB112021	Pipe assembly brake-RH	1	Note (3)	Td5 90"
2	SGB112350	Pipe assembly brake-RH	1	Note (1)	110"
2	SGB112350	Pipe assembly brake-RH	1	Note (2)	Td5 110"
2	SGB112351	Pipe assembly brake-RH	1	Note (4)	110" except Brake apportioning
2	SGB000650	PIPE ASSEMBLY BRAKE-RH	1	Note (5)	110" except Brake apportioning
1	BMK2466	• Connector brake	1		
2	SGB000660	Pipe assembly brake-rear-RH	1	Note (6)	Except 90"
3	SGB114380	Pipe assembly brake-LH	1	Note (1)	90"
3	SGB114380	Pipe assembly brake-LH	1	Note (2)	Td5 90"
3	SGB114381	Pipe assembly brake-LH	1	Note (3)	Td5 90"
3	SGB114390	Pipe assembly brake-LH	1	Note (1)	110"
3	SGB114390	Pipe assembly brake-LH	1	Note (2)	Td5 110"
3	SGB114391	Pipe assembly brake-LH	1	Note (4)	110" except Brake apportioning
3	SGB000640	Pipe assembly brake-LH	1	Note (5)	Antilock Brakes 110" except Brake apportioning
3	SGB000670	Pipe assembly brake-rear-LH	1	Note (6)	Except 90"

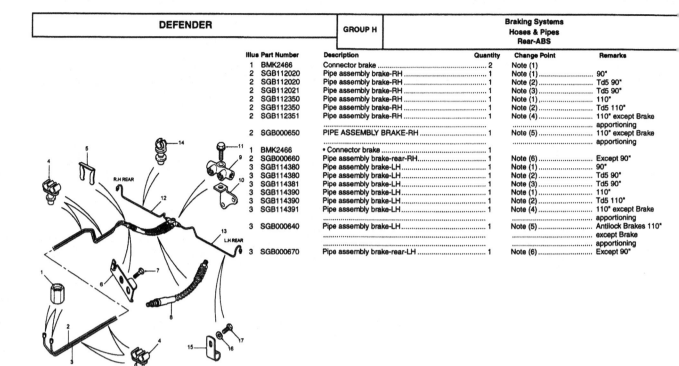

CHANGE POINTS:
(1) From (V) XA 159807
(2) From (V) XA 159807 To (V) XA 176106
(3) From (V) XA 176107
(4) From (V) XA 176107 To (V) ZA 608372
(5) From (V) 1A 608373
(6) From (V) 2A 622424

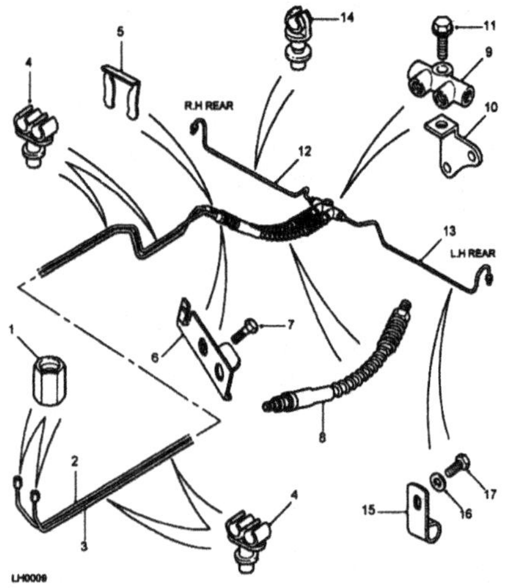

Illus	Part Number	Description	Quantity	Change Point	Remarks
4	79127	Clip-brake pipe double	A/R	Note (1)	
5	BNP2227L	Clip	2	Note (1)	
6	SHU100340	Bracket-hose brake	1	Note (1)	
7	SN106307	Bolt-flanged head-M6 x 30-self tapping	1	Note (1)	
8	SHB101370	Hose brake-RH side-rear	1	Note (1)	
8	SHB101430	Hose brake-LH side-rear	1	Note (1)	
9	SGL100010	T piece-rear	1	Note (1)	
10	SGI100040	Bracket-brake pipe tee connector	1	Note (1)	Except 90"
11	SN106127L	Bolt-duo taptite-M6 x 12	1	Note (1)	
		PIPE ASSEMBLY BRAKE			
12	SGB112380	rear-RH	1	Note (1)	90"
13	SGB112390	rear-LH	1	Note (1)	
12	SGB112400	rear-RH	1	Note (1)	Except 90"
13	SGB112410	rear-LH	1	Note (1)	
14	NTC8242	Clip-brake pipe double	3	Note (1)	90"
15	577873	Clip-p	3	Note (1)	Except 90"
16	WC702101L	Washer-plain	3	Note (1)	
17	SL510031	Screw	3	Note (1)	

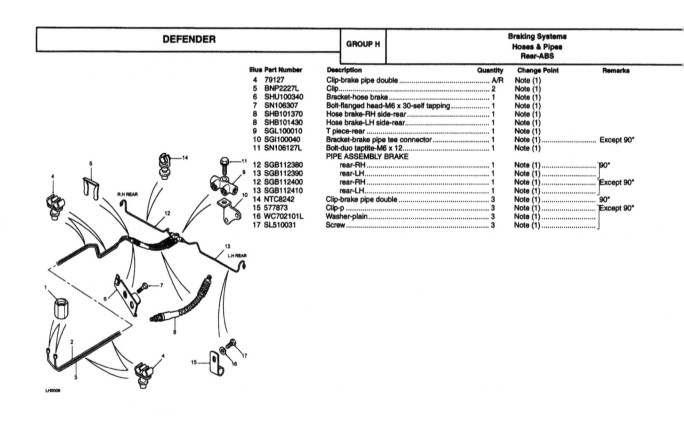

CHANGE POINTS:
(1) From (V) XA 159807

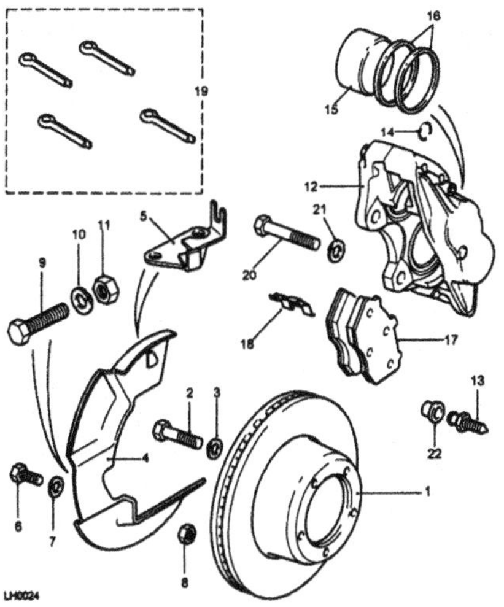

Illus	Part Number	Description	Quantity	Change Point	Remarks
1	FRC7329	Disc-brake.-front	2	Note (1)	
1	FRC7329	Disc-brake.-front	2	Note (2)	Non-ventilated disc brakes-front
1	FTC902	Disc-brake.-front	2	Note (2)	Ventilated disc brakes-front
2	AFU1180	Bolt-to disc solid-M10	NLA		Use FTC1368.
2	FTC1368	Bolt-to disc solid-M10	10		
3	WL110001L	Washer-M10	10	Note (1)	
		SHIELD-DISC FRONT BRAKE			
4	FRC6402	RH	1	Note (1)	
4	FRC6403	LH	1		
4	FTC3278	RH	NLA	Note (3)	Use FTC4838.
4	FTC3279	LH	NLA	Note (3)	Use FTC4839.
4	FTC4838	RH	1	Note (4)	
4	FTC4839	LH	1		
5	FRC7202	Bracket-brake pipe-RH	1	Note (5)	
5	ANR5784	Bracket-brake pipe-RH	1	Note (6)	
5	FRC7201	Bracket-brake pipe-LH	1	Note (5)	
5	ANR5783	Bracket-brake pipe-LH	1	Note (6)	
6	SH106121L	Screw-shield disc to disc solid-hexagonal head-M6 x 12	2		
7	WL106001L	Washer-sprung-M6	2	Note (1)	
8	NH106041L	Nut-hexagonal-nyloc-M6	2		
9	SH106121L	Screw-To shield disc-hexagonal head-M6 x 12	2		
10	WL106001L	Washer-sprung-M6	2		
8	NH106045	Nut-hexagonal head-nyloc-M6	2	Note (2)	
9	SH112505	Screw-To shield disc-hexagonal head-shouldered-M12 x 50	2		
11	NT112041L	Nut-hexagonal-thin-M12	2		

CHANGE POINTS:
(1) To (V) KA 930455
(2) From (V) LA 930456
(3) From (V) LA 930456 To (V) TA 989186
(4) From (V) TA 989187
(5) To (V) WA 159806
(6) From (V) XA 159807

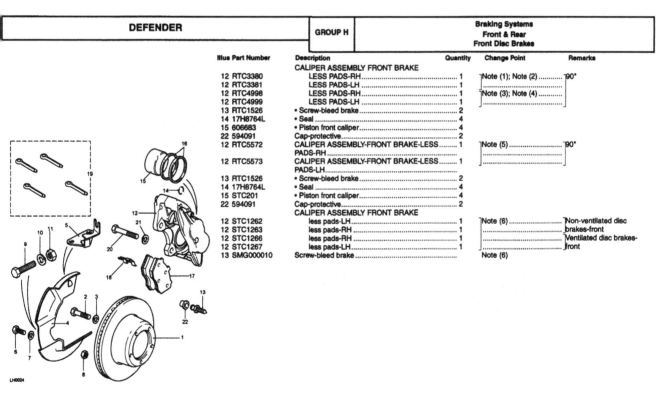

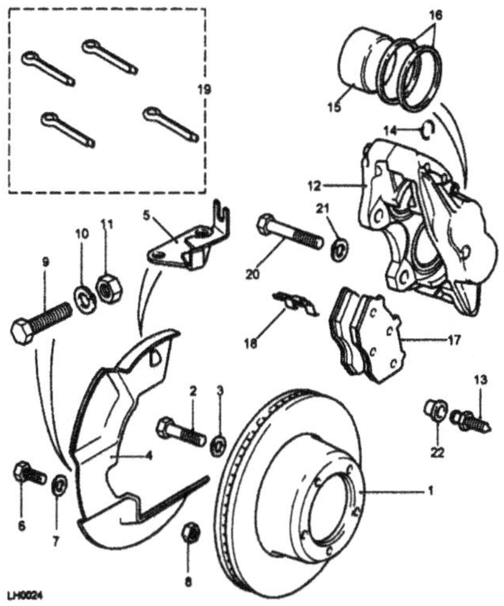

Illus	Part Number	Description	Quantity	Change Point	Remarks
		CALIPER ASSEMBLY FRONT BRAKE			
12	RTC3380	LESS PADS-RH	1	Note (1); Note (2)	90"
12	RTC3381	LESS PADS-LH	1		
12	RTC4998	LESS PADS-RH	1	Note (3); Note (4)	
12	RTC4999	LESS PADS-LH	1		
13	RTC1526	• Screw-bleed brake	2		
14	17H8764L	• Seal	4		
15	606683	• Piston front caliper	4		
22	594091	Cap-protective	2		
12	RTC5572	CALIPER ASSEMBLY-FRONT BRAKE-LESS PADS-RH	1	Note (5)	90"
12	RTC5573	CALIPER ASSEMBLY-FRONT BRAKE-LESS PADS-LH	1		
13	RTC1526	• Screw-bleed brake	2		
14	17H8764L	• Seal	4		
15	STC201	• Piston front caliper	4		
22	594091	Cap-protective	2		
		CALIPER ASSEMBLY FRONT BRAKE			
12	STC1262	less pads-LH	1	Note (6)	Non-ventilated disc brakes-front
12	STC1263	less pads-RH	1		
12	STC1266	less pads-RH	1		Ventilated disc brakes-front
12	STC1267	less pads-LH	1		
13	SMG000010	Screw-bleed brake		Note (6)	

CHANGE POINTS:
(1) To (A)22L 09654 RHD; To (A)23L 05987 LHD
(2) From (A)22L 10192 To (A)22L 10271 RHD; From (A)23L 06060 To (A)23L 06078 LHD
(3) From (A)22L 09655 To (A)22L 10191 RHD; From (A)23L 05988 To (A)23L 06059 LHD
(4) From (A)22L 10272 To (V) HA 701009 RHD; From (A)23L 06079 To (V) HA 701009 LHD
(5) From (V) HA 701010 To (V) KA 930455
(6) From (V) LA 930456

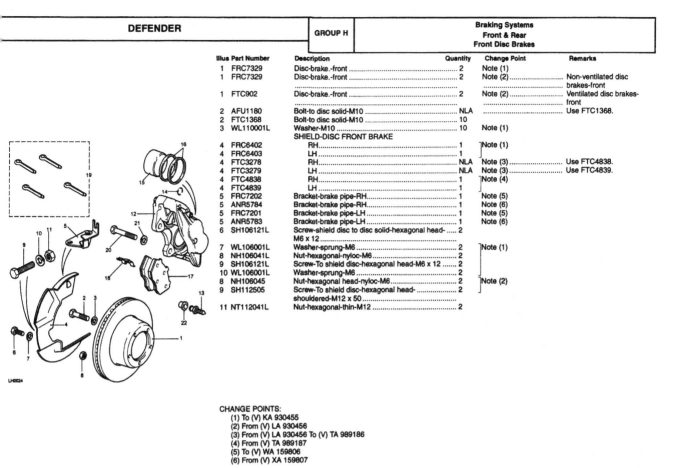

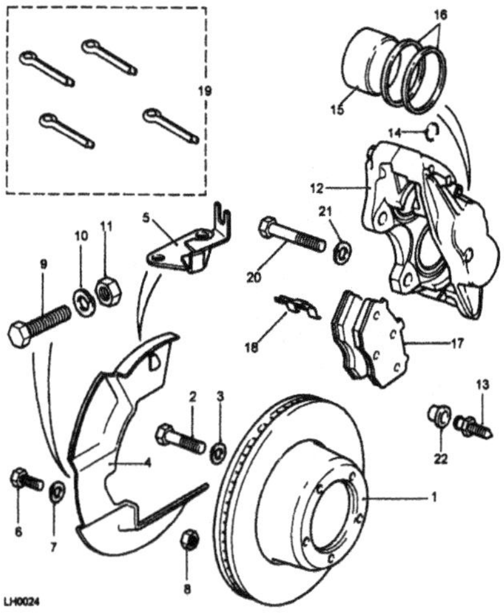

LH0024

Illus	Part Number	Description	Quantity	Change Point	Remarks
17	RTC3163	SET-PAD FRONT BRAKE SYSTEM	1	Note (1); Note (2)	90"
18	606688	• Spring	4		
17	RTC5756	Set-pad front brake system	1	Note (3); Note (4)	90"
17	RTC5574	Set-pad front brake system	1	Note (5)	90"
17	RTC5574	Set-pad front brake system	1	Note (6)	Except 90"
17	STC1275	Set-pad front brake system	1	Note (7)	90"
17	STC1275	Set-pad front brake system	1	Note (8)	Except 90"
17	SFP000140	Set-pad front brake system	1	Note (9)	Except 90"
20	AFU1031	Bolt-Caliper assy to set pad	4	Note (10)	
20	FTC3375	Bolt-Caliper assy to set pad-M12 x 35	4	Note (7)	
21	WL112001L	Washer	4		
	STC1280	Kit caliper piston	1		
16	AEU1547	Kit-brake caliper piston seal	2	Note (11)	
16	AEU2539	Kit-brake caliper piston seal	1	Note (12)	
19	RTC5001	Kit-brake pad retaining-asbestos-front-solid	1		Non-ventilated disc brakes-front
19	RTC6799	Kit-brake pad retaining-front	NLA		Use STC8575.
19	STC8575	Kit-brake pad retaining-asbestos free-front	1		Ventilated disc brakes-front

NOTE: PARTS FRC7329, STC1262 , STC1263 & RTC5001 ARE 4 CYLINDER (NON VENTED)
NOTE: PARTS FTC902, STC1266, STC1267 & RTC6799 ARE 4 CYLINDER HEAVY DUTY AND V8 (VENTED DISCS)

CHANGE POINTS:
(1) To (A)22L 09654 RHD; To (A)23L 05987 LHD
(2) From (A)22L 10192 To (A)22L 10271 RHD; From (A)23L 06060 To (A)23L 06078 LHD
(3) From (A)22L 09655 To (A)22L 10191 RHD; From (A)23L 05988 To (A)23L 06059 LHD
(4) From (A)22L 10272 To (V) HA 701009 RHD; From (A)23L 06079 To (V) HA 701009 LHD
(5) From (V) HA 701010 To (V) KA 930455
(6) To (V) KA 930434
(7) From (V) LA 930456
(8) From (V) LA 930435 To (V) ZA 999999
(9) From (V) 2A 622424
(10) To (V) KA 930455
(11) To (V) HA 701009
(12) From (V) HA 701010

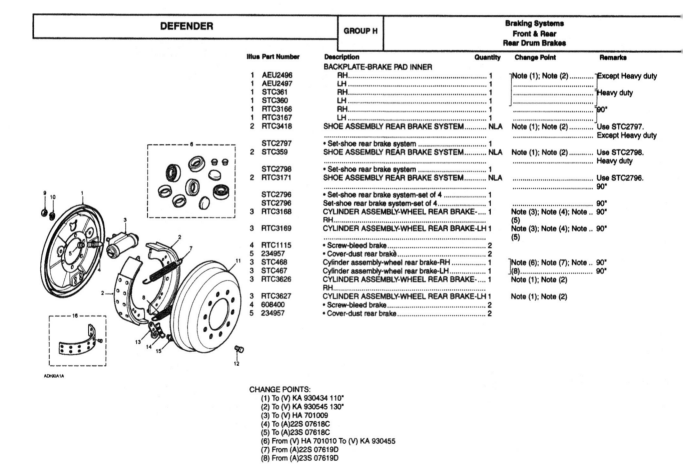

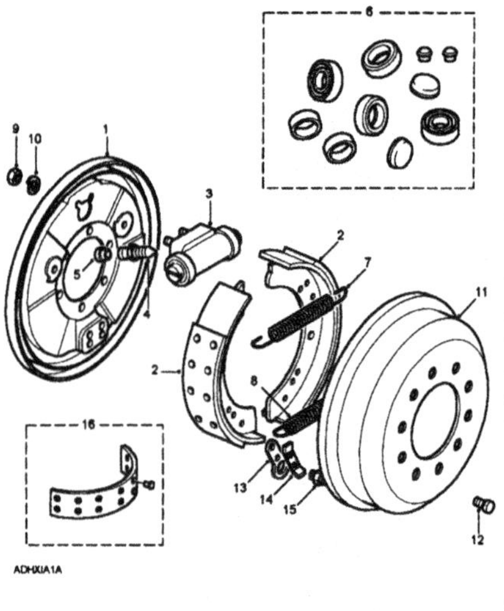

ADHXUA1A

Illus	Part Number	Description	Quantity	Change Point	Remarks
		BACKPLATE-BRAKE PAD INNER			
1	AEU2496	RH	1	Note (1); Note (2)	Except Heavy duty
1	AEU2497	LH	1		
1	STC361	RH	1		Heavy duty
1	STC360	LH	1		
1	RTC3166	RH	1		90"
1	RTC3167	LH	1		
2	RTC3418	SHOE ASSEMBLY REAR BRAKE SYSTEM	NLA	Note (1); Note (2)	Use STC2797. Except Heavy duty
	STC2797	• Set-shoe rear brake system	1		
2	STC359	SHOE ASSEMBLY REAR BRAKE SYSTEM	NLA	Note (1); Note (2)	Use STC2798. Heavy duty
	STC2798	• Set-shoe rear brake system	1		
2	RTC3171	SHOE ASSEMBLY REAR BRAKE SYSTEM	NLA		Use STC2796. 90"
	STC2796	• Set-shoe rear brake system-set of 4	1		
	STC2796	Set-shoe rear brake system-set of 4	1		90"
3	RTC3168	CYLINDER ASSEMBLY-WHEEL REAR BRAKE-RH	1	Note (3); Note (4); Note (5)	90"
3	RTC3169	CYLINDER ASSEMBLY-WHEEL REAR BRAKE-LH	1	Note (3); Note (4); Note (5)	90"
4	RTC1115	• Screw-bleed brake	2		
5	234957	• Cover-dust rear brake	2		
3	STC468	Cylinder assembly-wheel rear brake-RH	1	Note (6); Note (7); Note (8)	90"
3	STC467	Cylinder assembly-wheel rear brake-LH	1		90"
3	RTC3626	CYLINDER ASSEMBLY-WHEEL REAR BRAKE-RH	1	Note (1); Note (2)	
3	RTC3627	CYLINDER ASSEMBLY-WHEEL REAR BRAKE-LH	1	Note (1); Note (2)	
4	608400	• Screw-bleed brake	2		
5	234957	• Cover-dust rear brake	2		

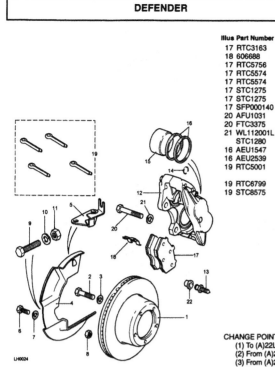

CHANGE POINTS:
(1) To (V) KA 930434 110"
(2) To (V) KA 930545 130"
(3) To (V) HA 701009
(4) To (A)22S 07618C
(5) To (A)23S 07618C
(6) From (V) HA 701010 To (V) KA 930455
(7) From (A)22S 07619D
(8) From (A)23S 07619D

Illus	Part Number	Description	Quantity	Change Point	Remarks
6	RTC3170	Kit-wheel cylinder repair rear brake	2	Note (1); Note (2); Note (3)	90"
6	STC469	Kit-wheel cylinder repair rear brake	2	Note (4); Note (5); Note (6)	90"
6	AEU2498	Kit-wheel cylinder repair rear brake	2	Note (7); Note (8)	
7	503981	Spring-shoe return-brake cylinder end	2		90"
8	218983	Spring-shoe return-brake abutment end	2		
7	548169	Spring-shoe return-brake cylinder end	2	Note (7); Note (8)	
8	531893	Spring-shoe return-brake abutment end	2		
9	NH605041L	Nut-hexagonal head-5/16UNF	4		
10	WM600051L	Washer-spring-5/16"	4		
11	591039	Drum brake	2		90"
11	576973	Drum brake	2	Note (7); Note (8)	
12	SA108161	Screw	2		
13	236993	Disc-brake spring	2		
14	236995	Plate assembly	2		
15	238542	Bolt	4	Note (1); Note (2); Note (3)	
15	RTC207	Bolt	4	Note (4); Note (5); Note (6)	
	RTC3176	Kit-transmission brake adjuster	1	Note (7); Note (8)	

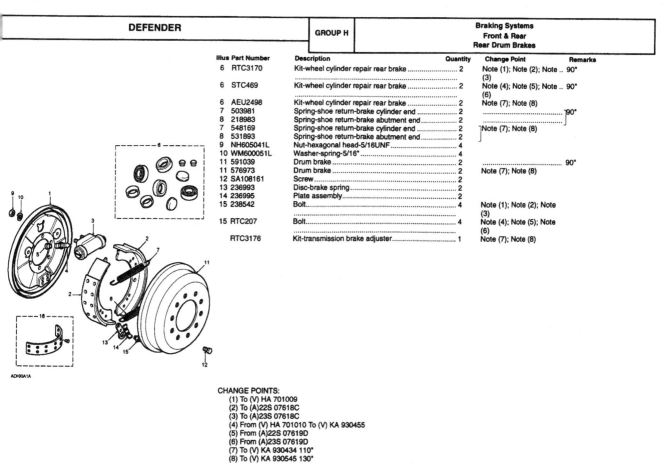

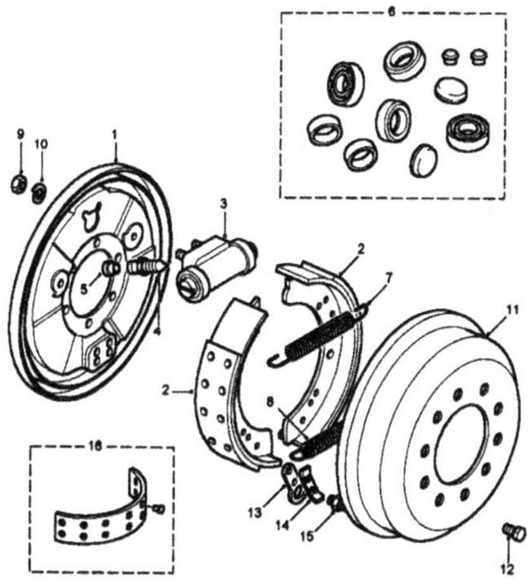

ADHXIA1A

CHANGE POINTS:
(1) To (V) HA 701009
(2) To (A)22S 07618C
(3) To (A)23S 07618C
(4) From (V) HA 701010 To (V) KA 930455
(5) From (A)22S 07619D
(6) From (A)23S 07619D
(7) To (V) KA 930434 110"
(8) To (V) KA 930545 130"

Illus	Part Number	Description	Quantity	Change Point	Remarks
1	FTC1381	Disc-solid brake-rear	2		90"
1	FTC3846	Disc-solid brake	2	Note (1)	Except 90"
1	SDB100980	Disc-solid brake-rear	2	Note (2)	
1	SDB000330	Disc-solid brake-rear	2	Note (3)	Except 90"
2	SMD100260	Shield-disc rear brake-RH	1		
2	SMD100270	Shield-disc rear brake-LH	1		
3	FTC1368	Bolt-shield disc to disc solid-M10	10		
4	FS106207L	Screw-shield disc to disc solid-flanged head-M6 x 20	6		
5	2215L	Washer-plain	6		
6	STC1264	CALIPER ASSEMBLY-REAR BRAKE-RH	1		90"
6	STC1265	CALIPER ASSEMBLY-REAR BRAKE-LH	1		
7	STC1279	• Piston-rear caliper brake	1		
8	8G8587L	Kit-brake caliper piston seal	1		90"
6	STC1268	CALIPER ASSEMBLY-REAR BRAKE-RH	1	Note (4)	Except 90"
6	STC1269	CALIPER ASSEMBLY-REAR BRAKE-LH	1		
7	STC1281	• Piston-rear caliper brake	1		
8	STC1270	• Kit-brake caliper piston seal	1		
6	SMC000180	CALIPER ASSEMBLY-REAR BRAKE-RH	1	Note (3)	Except 90"
6	SMC000190	CALIPER ASSEMBLY-REAR BRAKE-LH	1		
7	SEE000010	• Piston-rear caliper brake	1		
8	SMN000060	• Kit-brake caliper piston seal	1		

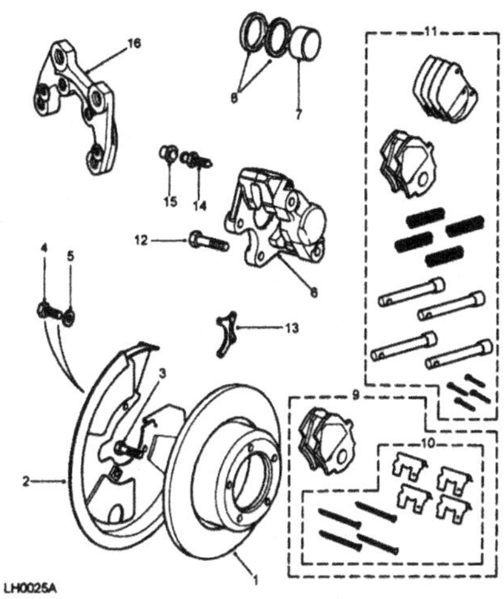

LH0025A

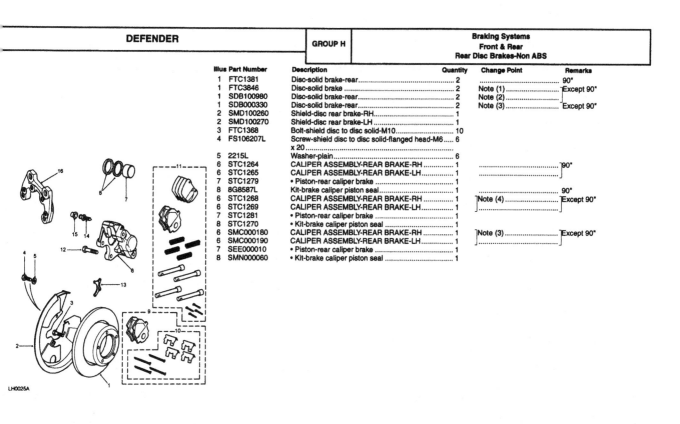

CHANGE POINTS:
(1) To (V) WA 159806
(2) From (V) XA 159807 To (V) ZA 614447
(3) From (V) 1A 614448
(4) To (V) 1A 614447

Rear Disc Brakes-Non ABS

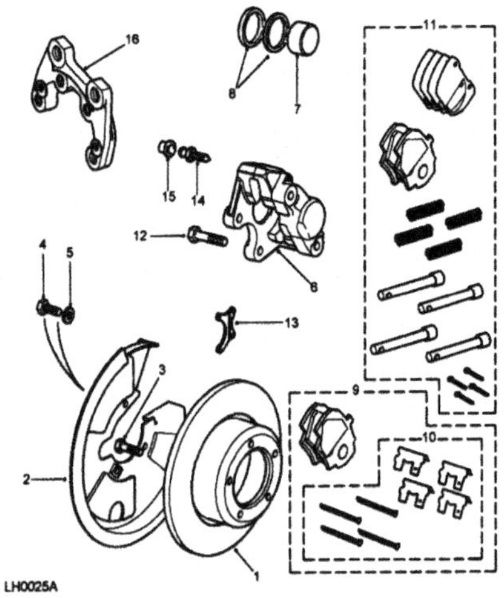

LH0025A

Illus	Part Number	Description	Quantity	Change Point	Remarks
9	STC1276	Set-pad rear brake system	1		90"
10	STC8574	Kit-brake pad retaining-rear	1		
11	SFP000150	Set-pad rear brake system	1	Note (1)	
11	STC1601	Set-pad rear brake system	1	Note (3)	Except 90"
11	SFP000160	Set-pad rear brake system	1	Note (4)	
11	SFP000130	Set-pad rear brake system	1	Note (5)	
12	FTC3375	Bolt-caliper -M12 x 35	4		
13	FTC3299	Bracket-shield rear brake	2		90"
13	FTC4465	Bracket-shield rear brake	2	Note (6)	Except 90"
14	RTC1526	Screw-bleed brake	2	Note (7)	
14	SMG000010	Screw-bleed brake	2	Note (1)	
15	594091	Cap-protective	2		
16	FTC3306	Bracket mounting	2		38S 39S except 90"

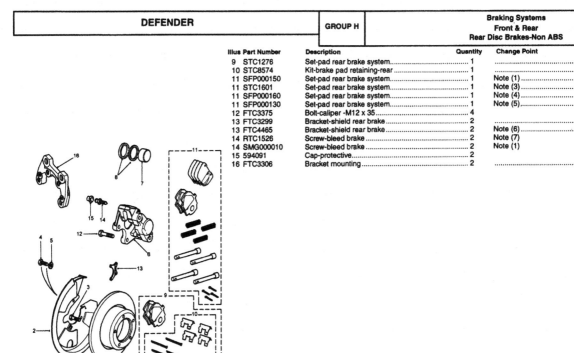

CHANGE POINTS:
(1) From (V) 2A 622424
(3) To (V) WA 159806
(4) From (V) XA 159807 To (V) ZA 614447
(5) From (V) 1A 614448
(6) From (V) XA 159807
(7) To (V) ZA 999999

Rear Disc Brakes-ABS

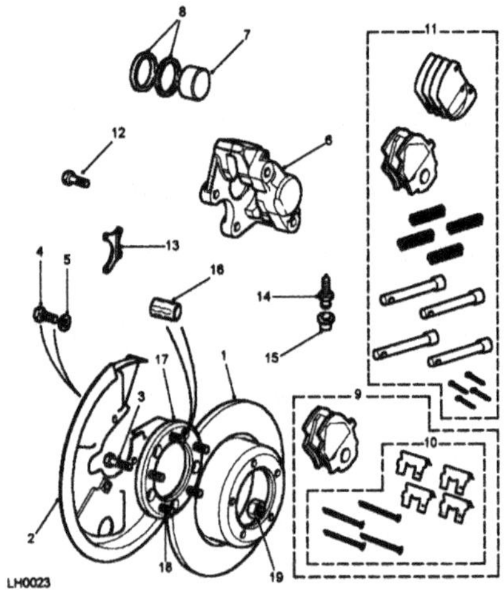

LH0023

Illus	Part Number	Description	Quantity	Change Point	Remarks
1	FTC1381	Disc-solid brake-rear	2		90"
1	SDB100980	Disc-solid brake-rear	2	Note (1)	Except 90"
1	SDB000330	Disc-solid brake-rear	2	Note (2)	
2	SMD100260	Shield-disc rear brake-RH	1		
2	SMD100270	Shield-disc rear brake-LH	1		
3	FTC1368	Bolt-shield disc to disc solid-M10	10		
4	GG106201	Screw-paint clearing-M6 x 20	6		
5	2215L	Washer-plain	6		
6	STC1264	CALIPER ASSEMBLY-REAR BRAKE-RH	1		90"
6	STC1265	CALIPER ASSEMBLY-REAR BRAKE-LH	1		
7	STC1279	• Piston-rear caliper brake	1		
8	8G8587L	Kit-brake caliper piston seal	1		90"
6	STC1268	CALIPER ASSEMBLY-REAR BRAKE-RH	1	Note (3)	Except 90"
6	STC1269	CALIPER ASSEMBLY-REAR BRAKE-LH	1		
7	STC1281	• Piston-rear caliper brake	1		
8	STC1270	• Kit-brake caliper piston seal	1		
6	SMC000190	CALIPER ASSEMBLY-REAR BRAKE-LH	1	Note (2)	Except 90"
6	SMC000180	CALIPER ASSEMBLY-REAR BRAKE-RH	1		
7	SEE000010	• Piston-rear caliper brake	1		
8	SMN000060	• Kit-brake caliper piston seal	1		

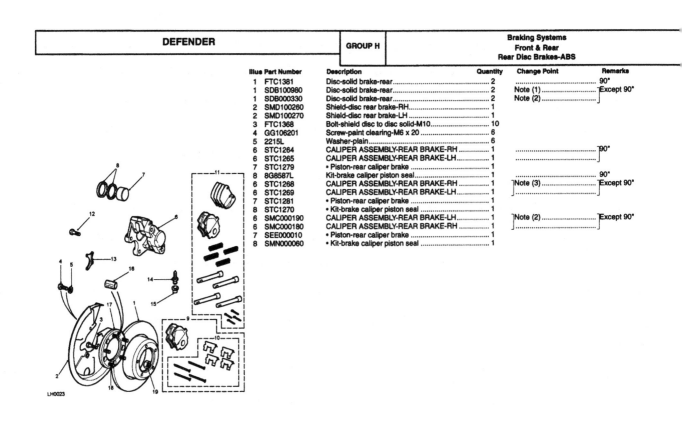

CHANGE POINTS:
(1) To (V) 1A 614447
(2) From (V) 1A 614448
(3) To (V) ZA 614447

Illus	Part Number	Description	Quantity	Change Point	Remarks
9	STC1276	Set-pad rear brake system	1	Note (1)	90°
9	SFP000150	Set-pad rear brake system	1	Note (2)	
10	STC8574	Kit-brake pad retaining-rear	1		
11	STC1601	Set-pad rear brake system	1	Note (4)	Except 90°
11	SFP000160	Set-pad rear brake system	1	Note (5)	
11	SFP000130	Set-pad rear brake system	1	Note (2)	
12	FTC3375	Bolt-caliper -M12 x 35	4		
13	FTC3299	Bracket-shield rear brake	2		90°
13	FTC4465	Bracket-shield rear brake	2		Except 90°
14	RTC1526	Screw-bleed brake	2	Note (1)	
14	SMG000010	Screw-bleed brake	2	Note (2)	
15	594091	Cap-protective	2		
16	FTC1374	Bush-antilock brake system sensor	2		
17	FTC1379	RING-PULSAR ANTILOCK BRAKES	2		
18	TD106041	• Stud	10		
19	NY106041	Nut-flange-nyloc-M6	10		

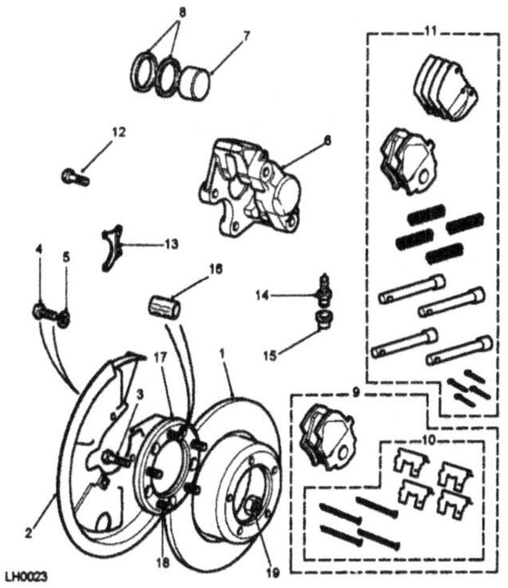
LH0023

CHANGE POINTS:
(1) To (V) ZA 614447
(2) From (V) 1A 614448
(4) To (V) WA 159806
(5) From (V) XA 159807 To (V) ZA 614447

Illus	Part Number	Description	Quantity	Change Point	Remarks
1	NRC9123	LEVER & GRIP ASSEMBLY HANDBRAKE-RHD	1	Note (1)	
1	NTC1557	LEVER & GRIP ASSEMBLY HANDBRAKE-RHD	NLA	Note (2)	Use STC4391.
1	NRC9115	LEVER & GRIP ASSEMBLY HANDBRAKE-LHD	1	Note (3)	
5	NRC2744	• Grip handbrake	1		
1	ANR3692	LEVER & GRIP ASSEMBLY HANDBRAKE-RHD	1	Note (4)	
1	ANR3693	LEVER & GRIP ASSEMBLY HANDBRAKE-LHD	1	Note (4)	
2	EEP191L	• Switch handbrake unit	1		
3	WF104001L	• Washer-4mm	2		
4	SE104124L	• Screw-M4 x 12	2		
5	NRC2744	• Grip handbrake	1		
1	STC4391	Lever & grip assembly handbrake-RHD	1	Note (2)	
6	PS104127L	Pin-split	1	Note (5)	
6	PS104161	Pin-split	1	Note (6)	
7	WA108051L	Washer-8mm	1		
8	FS108257L	Screw-To grip handbrake-flanged head-M8 x 25	2		
9	PC108291L	Pin-clevis/pivot-8 x 22mm	1		
10	WA108251L	Washer-plain-8mm	2	Note (6)	
11	WL108001L	Washer-sprung-M8	2		
12	NH108041L	Nut-hexagonal head-M8	2	Note (7)	
	ADP710040	Nut plate-8mm	1	Note (8)	
16	AMR3095	Harness-link	1	Note (6)	
17	MRC9570	Cover handbrake-RHD	1		
17	MRC9571	Cover handbrake-LHD	1		
13	SE105201L	Screw	1	Note (3)	
14	WA105001L	Washer-plain-standard-M5	3	Note (3)	

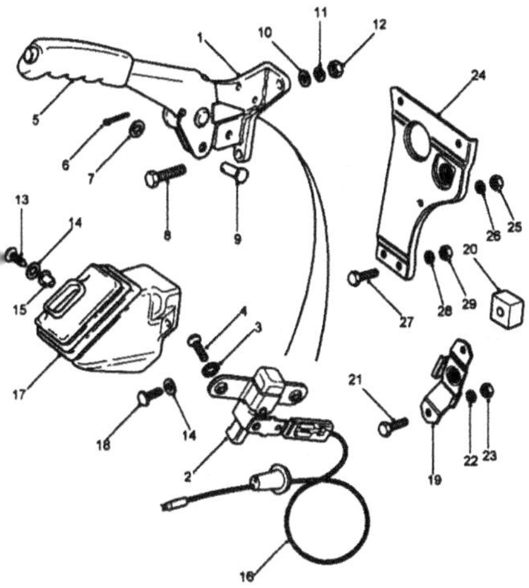
LH0005

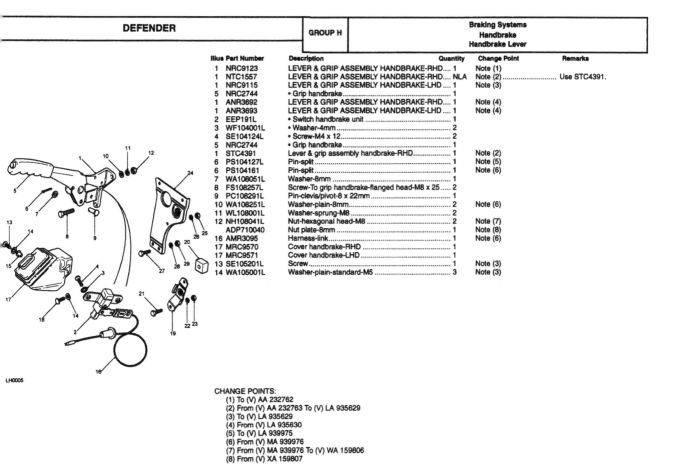

CHANGE POINTS:
(1) To (V) AA 232762
(2) From (V) AA 232763 To (V) LA 935629
(3) To (V) LA 935629
(4) From (V) LA 935630
(5) To (V) LA 939975
(6) From (V) MA 939976
(7) From (V) MA 939976 To (V) WA 159806
(8) From (V) XA 159807

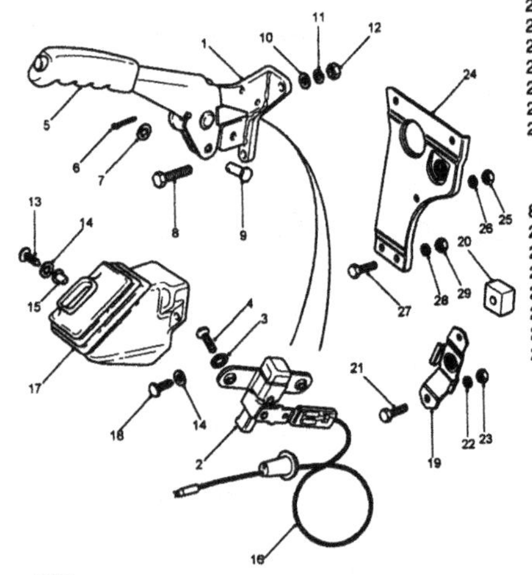

LH0005

Illus	Part Number	Description	Quantity	Change Point	Remarks
18	AR608041	Screw	2	Note (1)	
15	MWC3136	Clip-snap-sack	1	Note (2)	
	AFU1897LDE	Fastener-drive-Slate Grey	3		
		4 CYL AND V8 FROM HA456187-935629			
19	NRC7984	Plate	1		4 Cylinder
19	NRC7984	Plate	1	Note (3)	V8
20	NRC6795	Seal-handbrake lever/body	1		4 Cylinder
20	NRC6795	Seal-handbrake lever/body	1	Note (3)	V8
21	FS108257L	Screw-flanged head-M8 x 25	2		4 Cylinder
21	FS108257L	Screw-flanged head-M8 x 25	2	Note (3)	V8
22	WL108001L	Washer-sprung-M8	2		4 Cylinder
22	WL108001L	Washer-sprung-M8	2	Note (3)	V8
23	FN108047L	Nut-flange-flanged head-M8	2	Note (3)	4 Cylinder
23	FN108047L	Nut-flange-flanged head-M8	2	Note (3)	V8
		V8 UP TO VIN 456186			
8	FS108257L	Screw-flanged head-M8 x 25	2	Note (4)	
24	NTC1224	Stiffener-front main floor	1	Note (4)	RHD
24	NRC6653	Stiffener-front main floor	1	Note (4)	LHD
25	FN108047L	Nut-flange-flanged head-M8	2	Note (4)	
26	WL108001L	Washer-sprung-M8	2	Note (4)	
27	FS108257L	Screw-flanged head-M8 x 25	3	Note (4)	
28	WL108001L	Washer-sprung-M8	3	Note (4)	
29	FN108047L	Nut-flange-flanged head-M8	2	Note (4)	

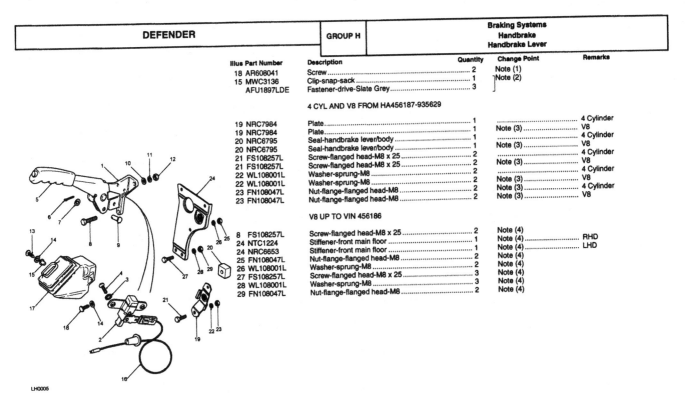

CHANGE POINTS:
(1) To (V) LA 935629
(2) From (V) LA 935630
(3) From (V) HA 456187 To (V) LA 935629
(4) To (V) HA 456186

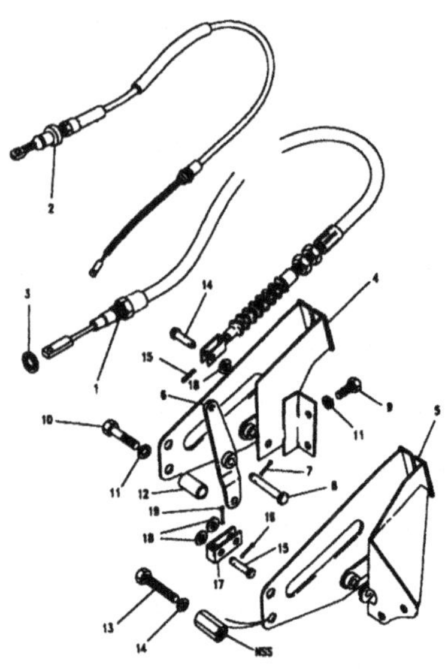

Illus	Part Number	Description	Quantity	Change Point	Remarks
1	NTC3480	Cable assembly handbrake	1	Note (1)	
1	NRC5088	Cable assembly handbrake-RHD	1	To (V) LA 935629	
1	NRC5089	Cable assembly handbrake-LHD	1		
2	STC1530	Cable assembly handbrake	1	From (V) LA 935630	
		NOTE: FOR PART STC1530 BRACKET CABLE TO TRANS BOX ON LHS ONLY SEE FRAME 2C4 - 2C5			
3	WF116001L	Washer-starlock	1		
4	NRC8059	Bracket-handbrake	1	To (V) HA 701009	4 Cylinder
4	NTC1643	Bracket-handbrake	1	From (V) HA 701010	
5	NRC5110	Bracket-handbrake	1		V8
4	NTC1643	Bracket-handbrake	1		
6	NRC7044	Lever handbrake	1		
7	PS104161	Pin-split	1		
8	NRC5104	Pin	1		
10	BH108091L	Bolt-M8 x 45	2	To (V) HA 701009	4 Cylinder
11	WL108001L	Washer-sprung-M8	4		4 Cylinder
12	NRC7124	Spacer	2	To (V) HA 701009	4 Cylinder
13	SH606061L	Screw-hexagonal head-3/8UNC x 3/4	2	From (V) HA 701010	4 Cylinder
13	SH606061L	Screw-hexagonal head-3/8UNC x 3/4	2		V8
14	WM600061L	Washer-3/8"-square	2	From (V) HA 701010	4 Cylinder
14	WM600061L	Washer-3/8"-square	2	From (V) HA 701010	V8
15	PC108291L	Pin-clevis/pivot-8 x 22mm	1		
16	PS104127L	Pin-split	1		
17	NRC7648	Pin assembly-clevis	1		
18	WA108051L	Washer-8mm	2		
19	PS104127L	Pin-split	2		
	NRC9461	Clip	1	Note (2)	RHD
	AEU1446	Clip-p-3/4"	1	Note (3)	LHD
	SE105161	Screw-pan-M5 x 16	1	Note (3)	
14	WL105001L	Washer-retaining-M5	1	To (V) HA 701009	
	NH105041	Nut-hexagonal-M5	1	Note (3)	
	AEU1446	Clip-p-3/4"	1	Note (4)	
	78248	Rivet-pop-3/16" x 0.45"lng	1		

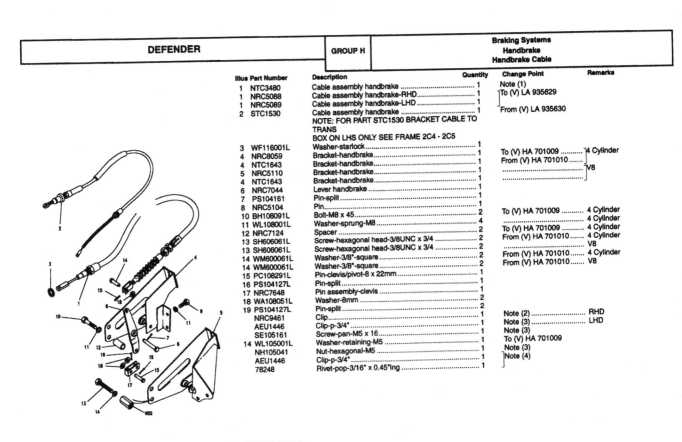

CHANGE POINTS:
(1) To (T)20D 290863E
(2) To (V) HA 455961
(3) To (V) 1991 MY
(4) From (V) 1991 MY

Fuel-Air Cleaner-Evaporative Loss

Fuel Tank Pump & Mountings-To (V) WA159806-90

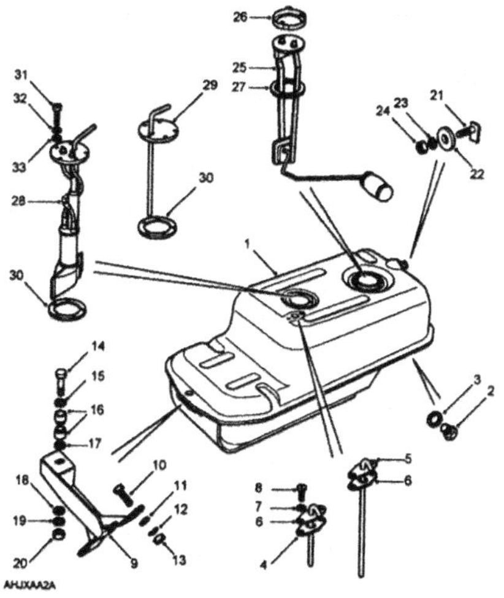

Illus	Part Number	Description	Quantity	Change Point	Remarks
1	NRC9225	TANK ASSEMBLY FUEL-12 GALLONS	1	Note (1)	
1	NTC2088	TANK ASSEMBLY FUEL-12 GALLONS	1	Note (2)	
2	NRC62	• Bolt-drain plug fuel tank	1		
3	243958	• Washer-sealing-fuel tank drain plug	1		
4	NRC9543	Pipe-fuel return fuel tank	1		Petrol
5	NRC9678	Pipe-fuel return fuel tank	1		Diesel
6	267837	Gasket-fuel tank spill return pipe	NLA		Use ESR3277.
6	ESR3277	Gasket-fuel tank spill return pipe	1		
7	3101	Washer-spring	2		
8	3972	Screw	2		
9	NRC9474	Bracket-fuel tank rear mounting	1		
10	SH108401L	Screw-hexagonal head-M8 x 40	3		
11	WA108051L	Washer-8mm	3		
12	WL108001L	Washer-sprung-M8	3		
13	NY108041L	Nut-nyloc-M8	3		
14	NRC4765	Bolt	1		
15	2265L	Washer-plain	1		
16	90508545	Mounting-rubber	2		
17	WP185L	Washer-plain-standard	1		
18	WA108051L	Washer-8mm	1		
19	WL108001L	Washer-sprung-M8	1		
20	FN108041L	Nut-flange-M8	NLA		Use FN108047L.
21	NRC9682	Bolt	2		
22	WC108051L	Washer-M8	4		
23	WL108001L	Washer-sprung-M8	2		
24	FN108041L	Nut-flange-M8	NLA		Use FN108047L.
25	PRC4262	Sensor unit fuel tank	1	Note (1)	
	PRC2476	Filter-fuel pump tank	1		
25	STC1139	Sensor unit fuel tank	1	Note (2)	
26	ARA1501L	Ring-locking fuel tank	1	Note (3)	
27	ARA1502L	Gasket-fuel gauge sender unit	1		
28	PRC7019	Pump-fuel tank	1	Note (3)	Petrol 90"
	RTC6545	Connector harness	1	Note (4)	Petrol
29	NTC2159	Pipe fuel	1		Diesel
	PRC5852	Seal	1	Note (5)	

CHANGE POINTS:
(1) To (V) AA 243342
(2) From (V) AA 243343
(3) To (V) WA 159806
(4) From (V) AA 243343 To (V) 345761
(5) To (V) MA 946570

Illus	Part Number	Description	Quantity	Change Point	Remarks
30	ESR3278	Seal	1	Note (1)	
31	SE105121L	Screw-pan head-M5 x 12	5		
32	WL105001L	Washer-retaining-M5	5		
33	WA105001L	Washer-plain-standard-M5	5		

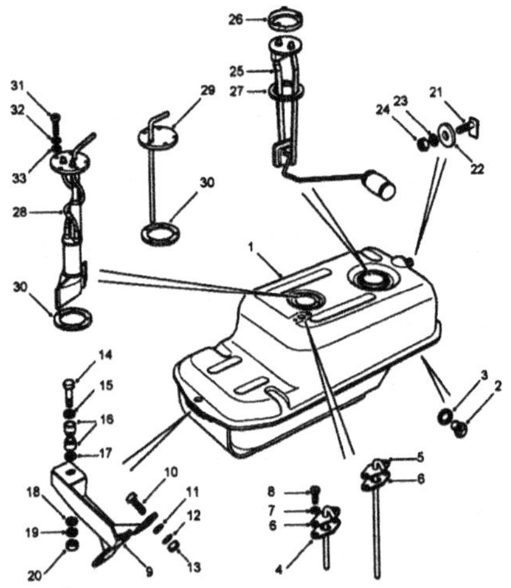

AHJXAA2A

CHANGE POINTS:
(1) From (V) MA 946571

Illus	Part Number	Description	Quantity	Change Point	Remarks
1	NTC2017	TANK ASSEMBLY FUEL-LESS EVAPORATOR LOSS-18 GALLONS	1		
2	NRC62	• Bolt-drain plug fuel tank	1		
3	243958	• Washer-sealing-fuel tank drain plug	1		
4	BH110091L	Bolt-M10 x 45	2		
5	NRC6097	Washer assembly	1		
6	500447	Mounting-rubber	2		
7	NRC4757	Spacer	2		
8	500447	Mounting-rubber	2		
9	WJ110001L	Washer-oversize	2		
9	850641	Washer-standard	2		
10	WL110001L	Washer-M10	2		
11	FN110041	Nut-M10-flanged head	NLA		Use FN110047.
12	NTC2681	Bolt	2		
13	NTC2837	Spacer	2		
14	WA108051	Washer-M8-standard	NLA		Use WA108051L.
15	NY108041L	Nut-nyloc-M8	2		

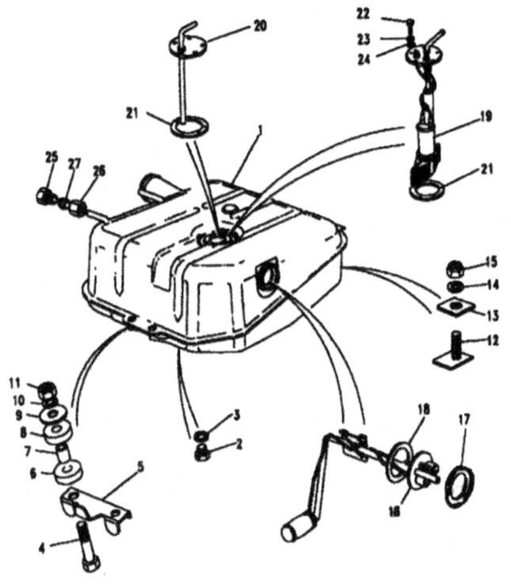

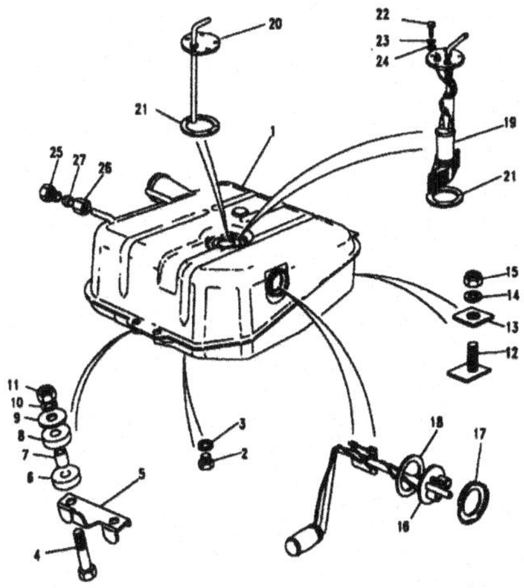

Illus	Part Number	Description	Quantity	Change Point	Remarks
16	PRC8707	Sensor unit fuel tank-without low fuel warning light	1	Note (1)	Petrol
16	STC1482	Sensor unit fuel tank-with low fuel warning light	1	Note (1)	Petrol
16	AMR1496	Sensor unit fuel tank	1	Note (2)	Petrol
16	PRC8463	Sensor unit fuel tank	1	Note (3)	Diesel
16	AMR1495	Sensor unit fuel tank	1	Note (4)	Diesel
17	ARA1501L	Ring-locking fuel tank	1		
18	519965	Ring-sealing fuel tank	1		
19	PRC7020	Pump-fuel tank-low pressure.	1		Petrol
20	NTC2156	Pipe-fuel feed-fuel tank	1		Diesel
21	PRC5852	Seal	1	Note (5)	
21	ESR3278	Seal	1	Note (6)	
22	SE105121L	Screw-pan head-M5 x 12	5		
23	WL105001L	Washer-retaining-M5	5		
24	WA105001L	Washer-plain-standard-M5	5		
25	NTC1612	Plug-M12	1		Diesel
26	NRC9770	Nut-tube-female-M12	1		Diesel
27	NRC9771	Olive	1		Diesel
28	ESR2204	Cradle-fuel tank	1		

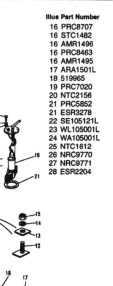

CHANGE POINTS:
(1) To (V) JA 915411
(2) From (V) JA 915412
(3) To (V) JA 915357
(4) From (V) JA 915358
(5) To (V) LA 939975
(6) From (V) MA 939976

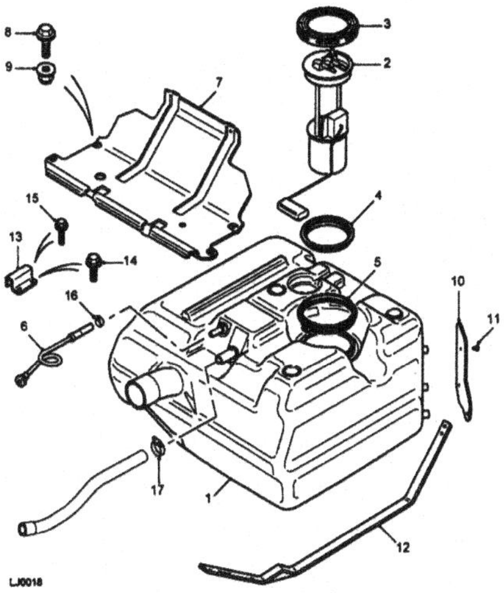

Illus	Part Number	Description	Quantity	Change Point	Remarks
1	WHK100070	Moulding-fuel tank	1	Note (1)	Except 90"
1	WHK100060	Moulding-fuel tank	1	Note (1)	6 Cylinder 90"
2	WQB100450	Pump-fuel tank	1	Note (1)	6 Cylinder 90"
2	WQB100460	Pump-fuel tank	1	Note (1)	6 Cylinder 110"
2	WQB100470	Pump-fuel tank	1	Note (1)	V8 except 90"
2	WQB100470	Pump-fuel tank	1	Note (1)	4 Cylinder Petrol 110"
3	ESR3808	Ring-locking fuel tank	1	Note (1)	
4	ESR3806	Seal-fuel pump unit tank	1	Note (1)	
5	ESR3807	Adaptor fuel lines	1	Note (1)	
6	WFH101750	Hose-vent fuel tank	1	Note (1)	
7	WFI100070	Cradle-fuel tank support	1	Note (1)	90"
7	WFI100080	Cradle-fuel tank support	1	Note (2)	Except 90"
7	WFI100100	Cradle-fuel tank support	1	Note (3)	Except 90"
8	FS110307	Screw-M10 x 30	4	Note (1)	90"
8	FS110307	Screw-M10 x 30	2	Note (1)	Except 90"
9	FY110057	Nut-flange-nyloc	2	Note (1)	
18	WYH100470	Nut-rivet-steel-M10-hexagonal	2	Note (1)	Except 90"
10	WGE100110	Pad-insulation-fuel tank	1	Note (1)	Except 90"
10	WGE100120	Pad-insulation-fuel tank	1	Note (1)	90"
19	MXC5714	Pad-insulation-fuel tank	4	Note (1)	Except 90"
19	MXC5714	Pad-insulation-fuel tank	2	Note (1)	90"
11	WYQ100040	Rivet-plastic-snap in	3	Note (1)	
12	WFS100520	Strap fuel tank	1	Note (2)	Except 90"
12	WFS100530	Strap fuel tank	1	Note (3)	Except 90"
13	WFU100820	Bracket-fuel pipe-breather	1	Note (1)	
14	FA108207	Bolt-M8 x 20-flanged head	2	Note (1)	90"
14	FA108207	Bolt-M8 x 20-flanged head	4	Note (1)	Except 90"
15	FA105201	Screw-M5 x 20	1	Note (1)	
16	ESR3710	Clip	1	Note (1)	
17	PYC102060	Clip-hose-worm drive	1	Note (1)	

CHANGE POINTS:
(1) From (V) XA 159807
(2) From (V) XA 159807 To (V) XA 177325
(3) From (V) YA 177326

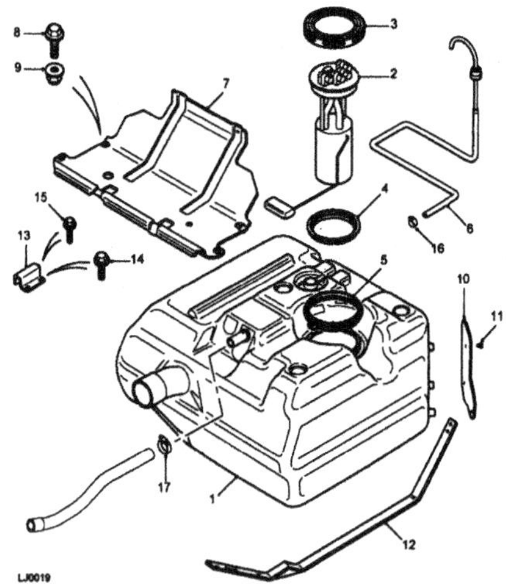
LJ0019

Illus	Part Number	Description	Quantity	Change Point	Remarks
1	WHK100040	Moulding-fuel tank	1	Note (1)	90"
1	WHK100050	Moulding-fuel tank	1	Note (1)	Except 90"
2	WQB100410	Pump-fuel tank	1	Note (1)	Td5 90"
2	WQB100420	Pump-fuel tank	1	Note (1)	Td5 except 90"
2	WQB100430	Pump-fuel tank	1	Note (1)	TDi 90"
2	WQB100440	Pump-fuel tank	1	Note (1)	TDi except 90"
3	ESR3808	Ring-locking fuel tank	1	Note (1)	
4	ESR3806	Seal-fuel pump unit tank	1	Note (1)	
5	ESR3807	Adaptor fuel lines	1	Note (1)	
6	WFH101730	Hose-vent fuel tank-diesel	1	Note (1)	Except 90"
6	WFH101790	Hose-vent fuel tank-diesel	1	Note (1)	90"
7	WFI100070	Cradle-fuel tank support	1	Note (1)	90"
7	WFI100080	Cradle-fuel tank support	1	Note (3)	Except 90"
7	WFI100100	Cradle-fuel tank support	1	Note (4)	Except 90"
8	FS110307	Screw-M10 x 30	4	Note (1)	90"
8	FS110307	Screw-M10 x 30	2	Note (1)	Except 90"
9	FY110057	Nut-flange-nyloc	2	Note (1)	
18	WYH100470	Nut-rivet-steel-M10-hexagonal	2	Note (1)	Except 90"
10	WGE100110	Pad-insulation-fuel tank	1	Note (1)	Except 90"
10	WGE100120	Pad-insulation-fuel tank	1	Note (1)	90"
11	WYQ100040	Rivet-plastic-snap in	3	Note (1)	
12	WFS100520	Strap fuel tank	1	Note (3)	Except 90"
12	WFS100530	Strap fuel tank	1	Note (4)	Except 90"
13	WFU100820	Bracket-fuel pipe	1	Note (1)	
14	FA108207	Bolt-M8 x 20-flanged head	2	Note (1)	90"
14	FA108207	Bolt-M8 x 20-flanged head	4	Note (1)	Except 90"
15	FA105201	Screw-M5 x 20	1	Note (1)	
16	WYC100570	Clip-hose	1	Note (1)	
17	PYC102060	Clip-hose-worm drive	1	Note (1)	
19	MXC5714	Pad-insulation-fuel tank	4	Note (1)	Except 90"
19	MXC5714	Pad-insulation-fuel tank	2	Note (1)	90"

CHANGE POINTS:
(1) From (V) XA 159807
(3) From (V) XA 159807 To (V) XA 177325
(4) From (V) YA 177326

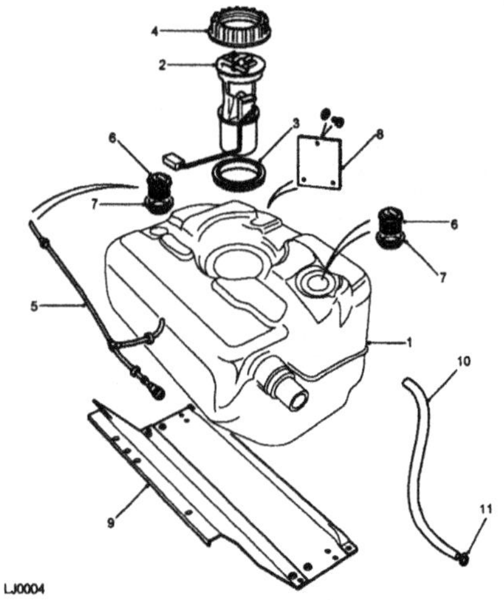
LJ0004

Illus	Part Number	Description	Quantity	Change Point	Remarks
1	ESR2657	Tank assembly fuel	1	Note (1)	4000 cc L/R V8 Petrol
2	ESR3928	Pump-fuel tank	1	Note (1)	EFi 90"
3	NTC5859	Seal-fuel pump unit tank	1	Note (1)	
4	NTC5858	Ring-locking fuel tank-Red	1	Note (1)	
5	ESR2693	PIPE-VENT FUEL TANK	1	Note (1)	
6	NTC4517	• Valve-fuel cut fuel tank	2		
7	NTC5879	Grommet	2	Note (1)	4000 cc L/R V8 Petrol
8	ESR2756	Heatshield-exhaust system fuel tank	1	Note (1)	EFi 90"
9	ESR2692	Bracket-fuel tank rear mounting	1	Note (1)	
	ESR2821	Mounting-rubber	2	Note (1)	
	FS110301L	Screw-flanged head-M10 x 30-top	6	Note (1)	
	WL110001L	Washer-M10	6	Note (1)	
1	ESR2657	Tank assembly fuel	1	Note (1)	2800 cc BMW M52 6
2	ESR3928	Pump-fuel tank	1		Cylinder Petrol
3	NTC5859	Seal-fuel pump unit tank	1		
4	NTC5858	Ring-locking fuel tank-Red	1		
5	ESR2693	PIPE-VENT FUEL TANK	1		
6	NTC4517	• Valve-fuel cut fuel tank	2		
7	NTC5879	Grommet	1	Note (1)	2800 cc BMW M52 6
8	ESR2756	Heatshield-exhaust system fuel tank	1		Cylinder Petrol
9	ESR2692	Bracket-fuel tank rear mounting	1		
10	2943486	Pipe-breather fuel tank	1		
11	1943711	Clip	1		
	ESR2821	Mounting-rubber	1		
	FS110301L	Screw-flanged head-M10 x 30-top	6		
	WL110001L	Washer-M10	6		

CHANGE POINTS:
(1) To (V) WA 159806

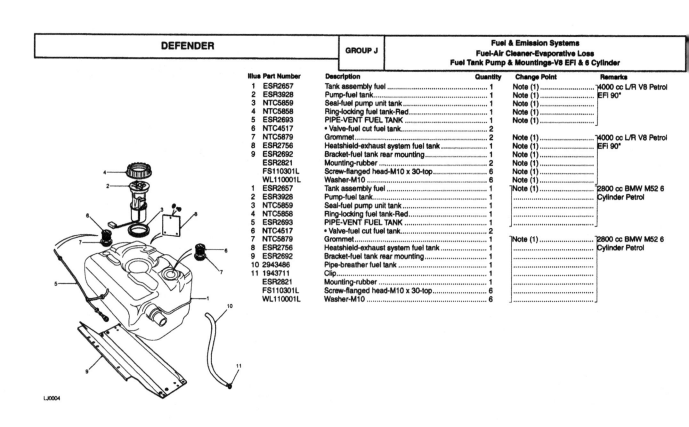

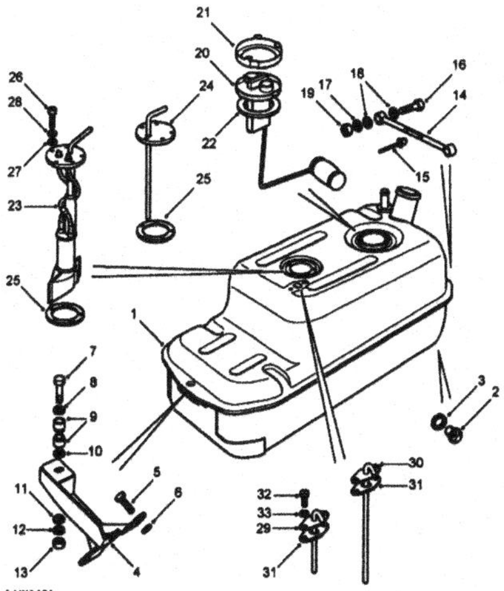

AJJXAA2A

Illus	Part Number	Description	Quantity	Change Point	Remarks
1	NTC2089	TANK ASSEMBLY FUEL-EXTRA 15 GALLON	1		Regular
2	NRC62	• Bolt-drain plug fuel tank	1		
3	243958	• Washer-sealing-fuel tank drain plug	1		
4	NRC9474	Bracket-fuel tank rear mounting	1		
5	FS108207L	Screw-flanged head-M8 x 20	3		
5	FS108251L	Screw-flanged head-M8 x 25	NLA		Use FS108257L.
6	NY108041L	Nut-nyloc-M8	3		
7	NRC4765	Bolt	1		
8	2265L	Washer-plain	1		
9	90508545	Mounting-rubber	2		
10	WP185L	Washer-plain-standard	1		
11	WA108051	Washer-M8-standard	NLA		Use WA108051L.
12	WL108001L	Washer-sprung-M8	1		
13	NH108041L	Nut-hexagonal head-M8	1		
14	NRC6526	Spacer	1		
15	RA608177L	Rivet	2		
16	FS108357	Screw-flanged head-M8 x 35	2		
17	WL108001	Washer-sprung-M8	NLA		Use WL108001L.
18	WC108051	Washer	4		
19	FN108041	Nut-flange-M8	NLA		Use FN108041L.
19	NH108041L	Nut-hexagonal head-M8	1		
20	PRC8708	Sensor unit fuel tank-extra 15 gallon	1		

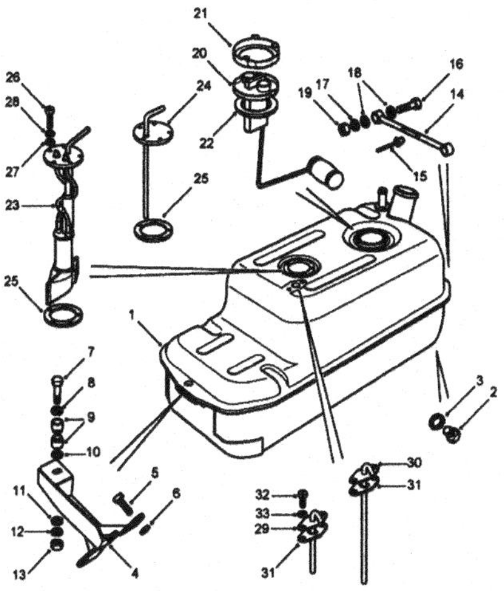

AJJXAA2A

Illus	Part Number	Description	Quantity	Change Point	Remarks
21	ARA1501L	Ring-locking fuel tank-extra 15 gallon	1		Diesel
22	ARA1502L	Gasket-fuel gauge sender unit	1		
23	PRC7018	Pump-fuel tank-extra 15 gallon	1		Petrol
	RTC6545	Connector harness	1	Note (1)	Petrol
24	NTC2180	Pipe fuel	1		Diesel
	PRC5852	Seal	1		
25	ESR3278	Seal	1		90°
26	SE105121L	Screw-pan head-M5 x 12	5		
27	WL105001L	Washer-retaining-M5	1		
28	WA105001L	Washer-plain-standard-M5	5		
29	NRC9543	Pipe-fuel return fuel tank	1		Petrol
30	NRC9562	Pipe-fuel return fuel tank	1		Diesel
31	267837	Gasket-fuel tank spill return pipe	NLA		Use ESR3277.
					90°
31	ESR3277	Gasket-fuel tank spill return pipe	1		
32	3890	Screw	2		
33	3101	Washer-spring	2		

CHANGE POINTS:
(1) From (V) 347499

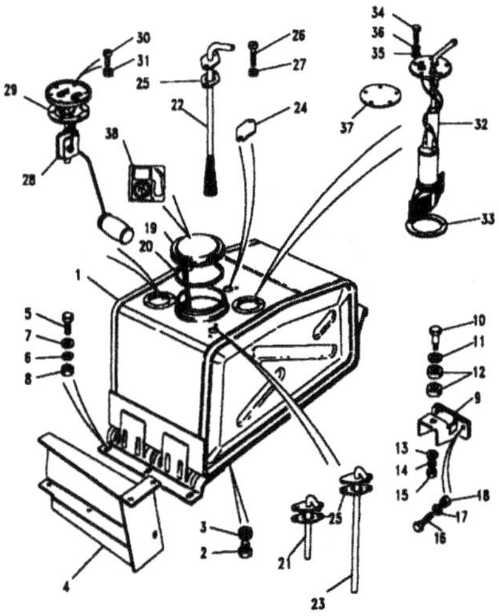

Illus	Part Number	Description	Quantity	Change Point	Remarks
1	NTC2110	TANK ASSEMBLY FUEL-EXTRA 10 GALLON	1		
2	NRC62	• Bolt-drain plug fuel tank	1		
3	243958	• Washer-sealing-fuel tank drain plug	1		
4	NRC9138	Bracket assembly-fuel tank fuel tank	1	Note (1)	
4	NTC5351	Bracket assembly-fuel tank fuel tank	1	Note (2)	
5	FS108251	Screw-flanged head-M8 x 25	NLA		Use FS108251L.
5	FS108251L	Screw-flanged head-M8 x 25	NLA		Use FS108257L.
5	SH108201L	Screw-hexagonal head-M8 x 20	NLA		Use FS108201L.
6	WL108001	Washer-sprung-M8	NLA		Use WL108001L.
7	WA108051	Washer-M8-standard	NLA		Use WA108051L.
8	FN108041L	Nut-flange-M8	NLA		Use FN108047L.
8	NH108041L	Nut-hexagonal head-M8	1		
9	NRC6558	Bracket	1		
10	NRC4765	Bolt	1		
11	2265L	Washer-plain	1		
12	90508545	Mounting-rubber	2		
13	WC108051L	Washer-M8	1		
14	WL108001	Washer-sprung-M8	NLA		Use WL108001L.
15	FN108041L	Nut-flange-M8	NLA		Use FN108047L.
15	NH108041L	Nut-hexagonal head-M8	1		
16	SH108201L	Screw-hexagonal head-M8 x 20	NLA		Use FS108201L.
16	FS108251	Screw-flanged head-M8 x 25	NLA		Use FS108251L.
16	FS108251L	Screw-flanged head-M8 x 25	NLA		Use FS108257L.
17	WL108001	Washer-sprung-M8	NLA		Use WL108001L.
18	FN108041L	Nut-flange-M8	NLA		Use FN108047L.
19	569006	Cap-filler fuel filler-extra 10 gallon-vented	1		
19	NTC3391	Cap-filler fuel filler-extra 10 gallon-non-vented	1		
20	NRC6836	Seal-cap fuel filler	1		

CHANGE POINTS:
(1) To (V) 346179
(2) From (V) 346180

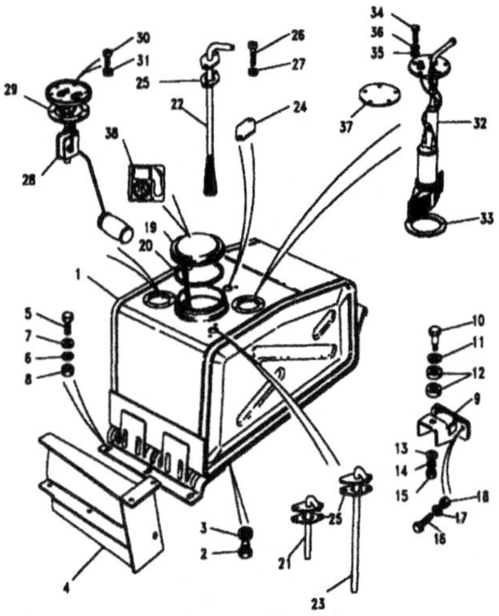

Illus	Part Number	Description	Quantity	Change Point	Remarks
21	NRC9543	Pipe-fuel return fuel tank	1		Petrol
22	NRC5414	Pipe fuel	1		Diesel
23	NRC9678	Pipe-fuel return fuel tank	1		
24	NTC2334	Plate	1		Petrol
25	267837	Gasket-fuel tank spill return pipe	NLA		Use ESR3277.
25	ESR3277	Gasket-fuel tank spill return pipe	2		
26	3972	Screw	4		
27	3101	Washer-spring	4		
28	PRC3098	Sensor unit fuel tank-extra 10 gallon	1		
29	RTC1148	Washer	1		
30	3890	Screw	6		
31	3101	Washer-spring	6		
32	PRC7019	Pump-fuel tank-extra 10 gallon	1		Petrol
33	PRC5852	Seal	1		
34	SE105121L	Screw-pan head-M5 x 12	5		Petrol
35	WL105001L	Washer-retaining-M5	5		
36	WA105001L	Washer-plain-standard-M5	5		
37	NTC2333	Plate	1		
38	NTC7503	Label-caution fuel filler-petrol	1		

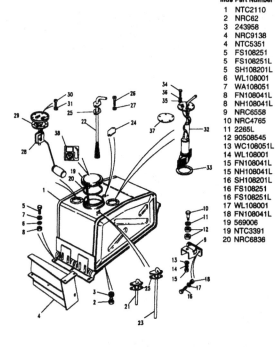

Illus	Part Number	Description	Quantity	Change Point	Remarks
1	PRC3901	Pump-fuel tank-external-12V	1	To (V) MA 962814	Petrol
2	90606262	Filter-fuel pump tank	1		
3	90606261	Gasket-fuel tank pump unit-external	1		
4	572535	Connector-inlet manifold adaptor	2		
5	90577064	Filter-fuel pump tank	1		
6	JS657L	Gasket-oil filter housing	1		
7	JS660L	Element-inline fuel filter	1		
8	AEU1147	Seal	1		
9	606207	Seal	1		

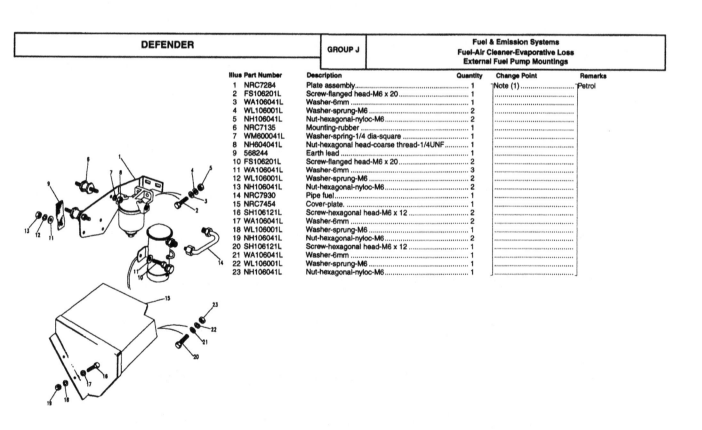

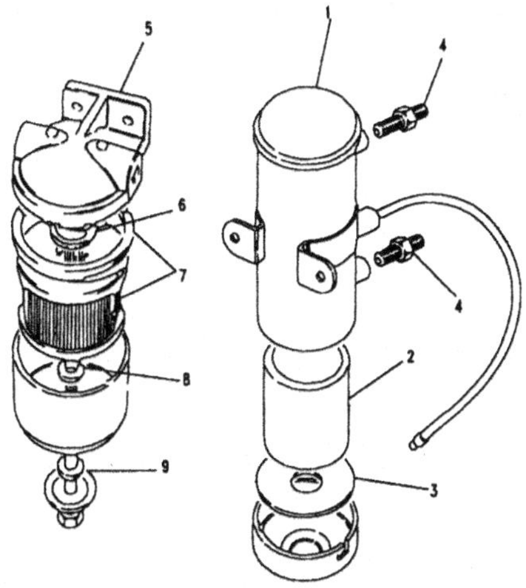

Illus	Part Number	Description	Quantity	Change Point	Remarks
1	NRC7284	Plate assembly	1	Note (1)	Petrol
2	FS106201L	Screw-flanged head-M6 x 20	1		
3	WA106041L	Washer-6mm	1		
4	WL106001L	Washer-sprung-M6	2		
5	NH106041L	Nut-hexagonal-nyloc-M6	2		
6	NRC7135	Mounting-rubber	1		
7	WM600041L	Washer-spring-1/4 dia-square	1		
8	NH604041L	Nut-hexagonal head-coarse thread-1/4UNF	1		
9	568244	Earth lead	1		
10	FS106201L	Screw-flanged head-M6 x 20	2		
11	WA106041L	Washer-6mm	3		
12	WL106001L	Washer-sprung-M6	2		
13	NH106041L	Nut-hexagonal-nyloc-M6	2		
14	NRC7930	Pipe fuel	1		
15	NRC7454	Cover-plate.	1		
16	SH106121L	Screw-hexagonal head-M6 x 12	2		
17	WA106041L	Washer-6mm	2		
18	WL106001L	Washer-sprung-M6	1		
19	NH106041L	Nut-hexagonal-nyloc-M6	2		
20	SH106121L	Screw-hexagonal head-M6 x 12	1		
21	WA106041L	Washer-6mm	1		
22	WL106001L	Washer-sprung-M6	1		
23	NH106041L	Nut-hexagonal-nyloc-M6	1		

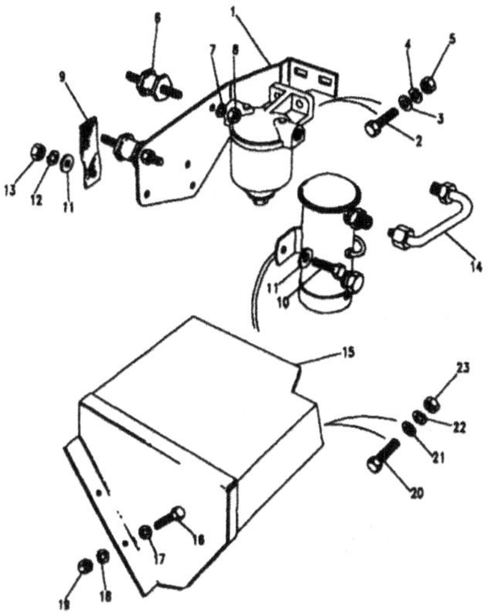

CHANGE POINTS:
(1) To (V) MA 962814

DEFENDER	GROUP J	Fuel & Emission Systems Fuel-Air Cleaner-Evaporative Loss Fuel Filler-To (V) AA259678

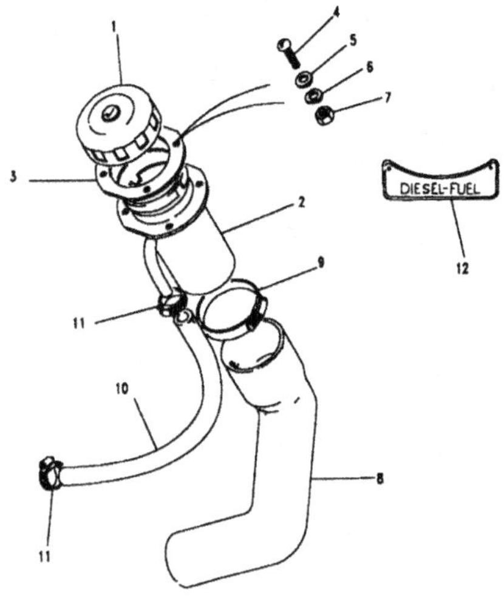

Illus	Part Number	Description	Quantity	Change Point	Remarks
1	NRC9572	Cap-filler fuel filler-vented-2 lug-non-locking	1		
1	NRC9429	Cap-filler fuel filler-non-locking-3 lug-non-vented	1		
2	NRC9424	Filler assembly-fuel	NLA		Use STC3943.
2	STC3943	Filler assembly-fuel-complete with cap and valve-vented	1		
2	NRC9423	Filler assembly-fuel	NLA		Use STC4236.
2	STC4236	FILLER ASSEMBLY-FUEL-NON-VENTED	1		
1	STC4237	• Cap-filler fuel filler-non-vented-3 lug	1		
3	500710	Seal	1		
4	77941	Screw	4		
5	WC702101L	Washer-plain	4		
6	WL700101L	Washer-spring-No 10-single coil-rectangular	4		
7	RTC608	Nut	4		
8	NRC9291	Hose-filler fuel filler	1		
9	594753	Clip-hose	2		
10	NTC1049	Hose-fuel filler pipe breather	NLA		Use ESR1287.
10	ESR1287	Hose-fuel filler pipe breather	1		
11	572548	Clip-hose	NLA		Use CN100168L.
12	502951	Label-fuel caution	1		

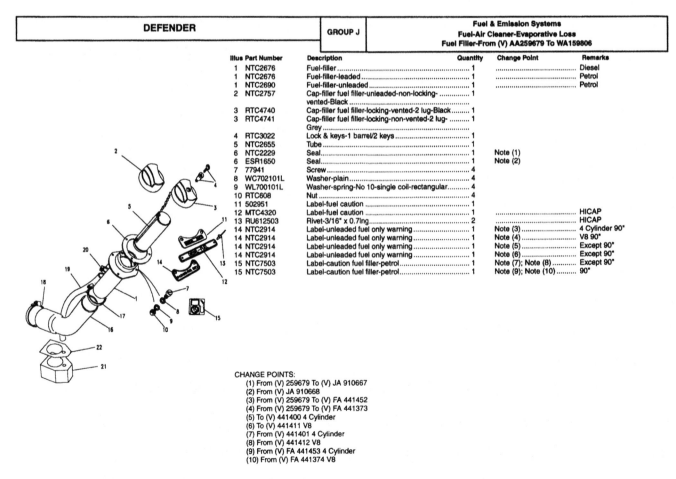

DEFENDER	GROUP J	Fuel & Emission Systems Fuel-Air Cleaner-Evaporative Loss Fuel Filler-From (V) AA259679 To WA159806

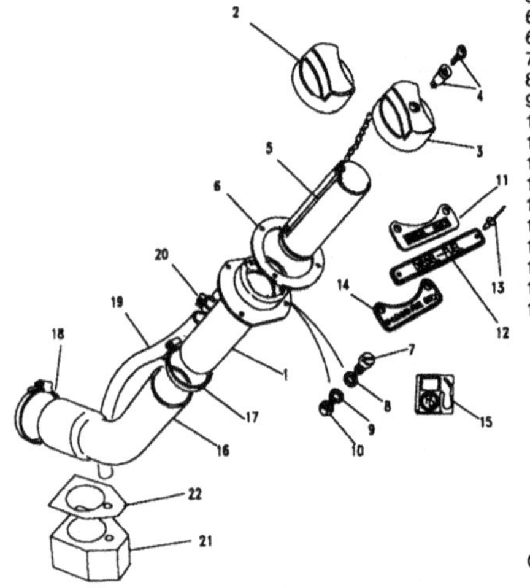

Illus	Part Number	Description	Quantity	Change Point	Remarks
1	NTC2676	Fuel-filler	1		Diesel
1	NTC2676	Fuel-filler-leaded	1		Petrol
1	NTC2690	Fuel-filler-unleaded	1		Petrol
2	NTC2757	Cap-filler fuel filler-unleaded-non-locking-vented-Black	1		
3	RTC4740	Cap-filler fuel filler-locking-vented-2 lug-Black	1		
3	RTC4741	Cap-filler fuel filler-locking-non-vented-2 lug-Grey	1		
4	RTC3022	Lock & keys-1 barrel/2 keys	1		
5	NTC2655	Tube	1		
6	NTC2229	Seal	1	Note (1)	
6	ESR1650	Seal	1	Note (2)	
7	77941	Screw	4		
8	WC702101L	Washer-plain	4		
9	WL700101L	Washer-spring-No 10-single coil-rectangular	4		
10	RTC608	Nut	4		
11	502951	Label-fuel caution	1		
12	MTC4320	Label-fuel caution	1		HICAP
13	RU612503	Rivet-3/16" x 0.7lng	2		HICAP
14	NTC2914	Label-unleaded fuel only warning	1	Note (3)	4 Cylinder 90"
14	NTC2914	Label-unleaded fuel only warning	1	Note (4)	V8 90"
14	NTC2914	Label-unleaded fuel only warning	1	Note (5)	Except 90"
14	NTC2914	Label-unleaded fuel only warning	1	Note (6)	Except 90"
15	NTC7503	Label-caution fuel filler-petrol	1	Note (7); Note (8)	Except 90"
15	NTC7503	Label-caution fuel filler-petrol	1	Note (9); Note (10)	90"

CHANGE POINTS:

(1) From (V) 259679 To (V) JA 910667
(2) From (V) JA 910668
(3) From (V) 259679 To (V) FA 441452
(4) From (V) 259679 To (V) FA 441373
(5) To (V) 441400 4 Cylinder
(6) To (V) 441411 V8
(7) From (V) 441401 4 Cylinder
(8) From (V) 441412 V8
(9) From (V) FA 441453 4 Cylinder
(10) From (V) FA 441374 V8

Fuel Filler-From (V) AA259679 To WA159806

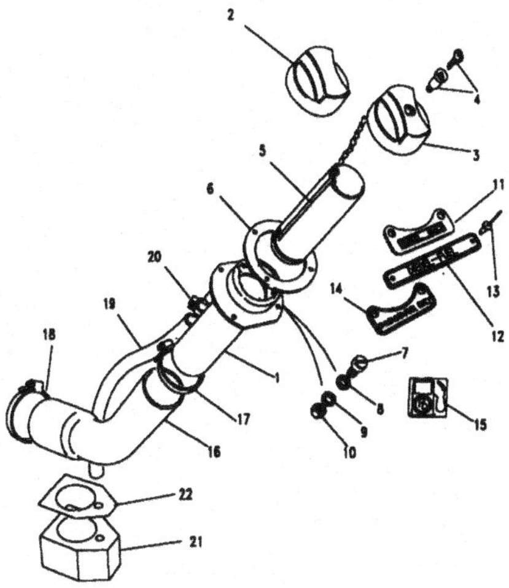

Illus	Part Number	Description	Quantity	Change Point	Remarks
16	NTC2338	Hose-filler fuel filler	1		90"
16	NTC2337	Hose-filler fuel filler-main tank	1		110"
16	NTC2699	Hose-filler fuel filler-side tank	1		110"
16	RRC2593	Hose-filler fuel filler-main tank	1	Note (1)	130"
16	RRC4418	Hose-filler fuel filler-main tank	1	Note (2)	130"
17	594753	Clip-hose-main tank	2		Except 130"
17	CN100908L	Clip-hose-main tank	2		130"
17	594753	Clip-hose-side tank	1		
18	STC128	Clip-hose-side tank	1	Note (3)	130"
18	PYC102350	Clip-hose-side tank	1	Note (4)	130"
19	ESR1287	Hose-fuel filler pipe breather-main tank	1		Except HICAP and 90"
19	543767	Hose-fuel filler pipe breather-main tank	1		HICAP
19	543765	Hose-fuel filler pipe breather-side tank	NLA		Use ESR1287.
19	ESR1287	Hose-fuel filler pipe breather-side tank	1		
20	572839	Clip-hose	2		Except 90"
19	NTC1049	Hose-fuel filler pipe breather	NLA		Use ESR1287.
					90"
19	ESR1287	Hose-fuel filler pipe breather	1		90"
20	572548	Clip-hose	NLA		Use CN100168L.
					90"
21	504233	Grommet-container assembly filler neck	1		Except 90"
22	504673	Washer	2		Except 90"

CHANGE POINTS:
(1) To (V) 25/9/88
(2) From (V) 26/9/88
(3) To (V) 17/6/98
(4) From (V) 18/8/98

Fuel Filler-From (V) XA159807

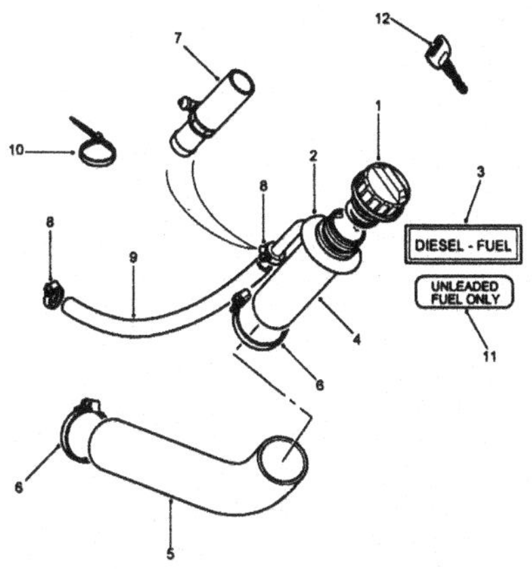

LJ0013A

Illus	Part Number	Description	Quantity	Change Point	Remarks
1	ESR3281	Cap-filler fuel filler-locking	1		UK NAS 49 States
1	WLD100730	Cap-filler fuel filler-locking	1	Note (1)	Rest of World
12	STC4373	Key-blank owner	1		
2	NTC5916	Grommet	1		
11	NTC7503	Label-caution fuel filler-petrol	1		
3	NTC7349	Label-caution fuel filler-diesel	1		
4	WLH100570	Hose-filler fuel filler-diesel	1		
4	WLH100600	Hose-filler fuel filler-petrol	1		
5	WFH101820	Hose-moulded fuel tank	1		90"
5	ESR4414	Hose-moulded fuel tank	1		110" except HICAP
5	WFH101710	Hose-moulded fuel tank	1		130"
5	WFH101710	Hose-moulded fuel tank	1		HICAP 110"
6	PYC102350	Clip-hose	2		
7	WLK100110	Breather fuel filler	1		Diesel 130"
8	PYC102060	Clip-hose-worm drive	2		
9	ESR4290	Breather-assembly	1		Cut to the required length
10	568680	Tie-cable-4.8 x 270mm-inside serated	1		Petrol
	NY108047	Nut-nyloc-M8	1		
	YYG10015	Screw-flanged head-M8 x 22-paint clearing	1		Petrol
	PYC102070	Clip-hose-worm drive	1		

CHANGE POINTS:
(1) From (V) XA 172265

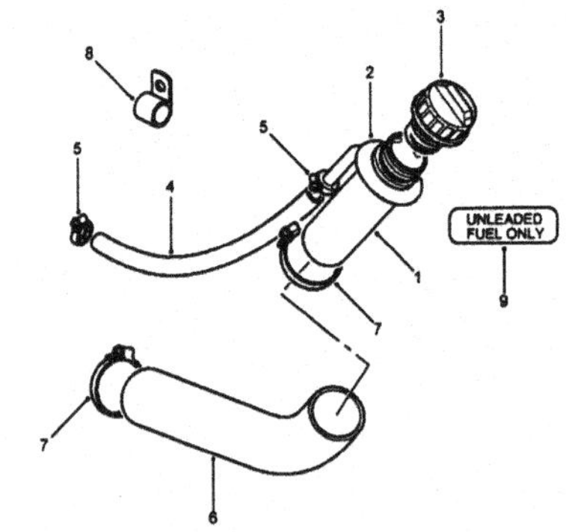

AMJXEA2A

Illus	Part Number	Description	Quantity	Change Point	Remarks
1	ESR2732	Filler assembly-fuel	1		V8
1	2943337	Filler assembly-fuel	1		6 Cylinder
2	NTC5916	Grommet	1		
3	NTC5418	Cap-filler fuel filler-non-locking-English-language warning label	1		
3	WLD100820	Cap-filler fuel filler-non-locking-International symbol warning label	1		
3	ESR3281	Cap-filler fuel filler-locking	1		
4	ESR2694	Pipe-breather fuel tank	1		
5	CN100308L	Clip-hose-30mm	2		
6	ESR2681	Hose-filler fuel filler	1		Japan
6	NTC2337	Hose-filler fuel filler	1		6 Cylinder 110"
6	WLH100600	Hose-filler fuel filler-petrol	1		
7	PYC102350	Clip-hose	2		
8	CP105081	Clip-p	1		
9	ESR387	Label-unleaded fuel only warning	1		Except Japan
9	ESR3482	Label-unleaded fuel only warning	1		Japan

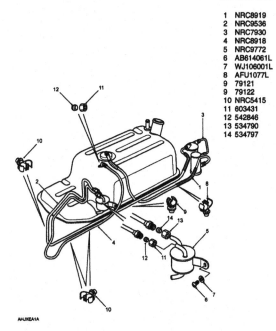

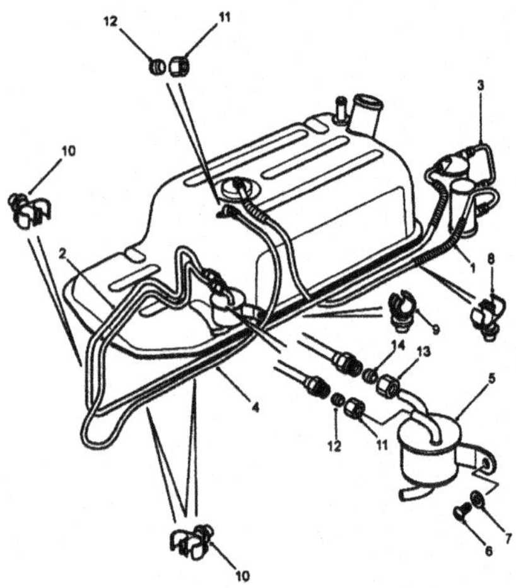

AHJXEA1A

Illus	Part Number	Description	Quantity	Change Point	Remarks
		PIPE FUEL			
1	NRC8919	tank to pump	1		
2	NRC9536	filter to separator	1		
3	NRC7930	pump to filter	1		
4	NRC8918	spill return to tank	1		
5	NRC9772	Separator-vapour fuel lines	1		
6	AB614061L	Screw-self tapping-No 14 x 3/4	2		
7	WJ106001L	Washer-plain-M6	2		
8	AFU1077L	Clip-swivel	1		
9	79121	Clip-single-9mm	7		
9	79122	Clip-8mm	2		
10	NRC5415	Clip-pipe-double	10		
11	603431	Nut-tube-female-M12	A/R		
12	542846	Olive	A/R		
13	534790	Nut-7/16UNF	1		
14	534797	Olive-fuel tank pipe	1		

Illus	Part Number	Description	Quantity	Change Point	Remarks
1	NRC9772	Separator-vapour fuel lines	1		
2	AB614061L	Screw-self tapping-No 14 x 3/4	2		
3	WJ106001L	Washer-plain-M6	2		
4	NRC9771	Olive	2		
5	NRC9770	Nut-tube-female-M12	2		
6	NTC2224	Pipe fuel-to vapour separator-metal	1	Note (1)	
6	NTC3866	Pipe fuel-to vapour separator-plastic	1	Note (2)	
7	RRC2486	Pipe fuel	1		130"
7	NTC2073	Pipe fuel-from vapour separator-metal	1	Note (1)	4 Cylinder 110"
7	NTC3867	Pipe fuel-from vapour separator-plastic	1	Note (2)	4 Cylinder 110"
8	NTC2876	Connector fuel lines	1		
9	CN100168L	Clip-hose	2		
10	79158	Clip-pipe-double	2	Note (1)	
10	NRC5415	Clip-pipe-double	4	Note (2)	
11	NRC9786	FILTER-IN LINE FUEL LINES	1		
	JS660L	• Element-inline fuel filter	1		
12	FS106201L	Screw-flanged head-M6 x 20	2		
13	WA106001L	Washer-M6	2		
14	WL106001L	Washer-sprung-M6	2		
15	NH106041L	Nut-hexagonal-nyloc-M6	2		
16	NTC2077	Pipe fuel-from tank	1		4 Cylinder 90"
17	NTC2078	Pipe fuel-to tank	1		90"
17	NTC2072	Pipe fuel-spill return	1		Except 90"
18	NTC2876	Connector fuel lines	2		
19	CN100168L	Clip-hose	4		
20	NTC2069	Pipe fuel-filter to hose	1	Note (3)	
21	NTC2876	Connector fuel lines	2		4 Cylinder
22	CN100168L	Clip-hose	4		4 Cylinder
23	NTC2223	Restrictor-fuel hose fuel lines	1	Note (1)	4 Cylinder

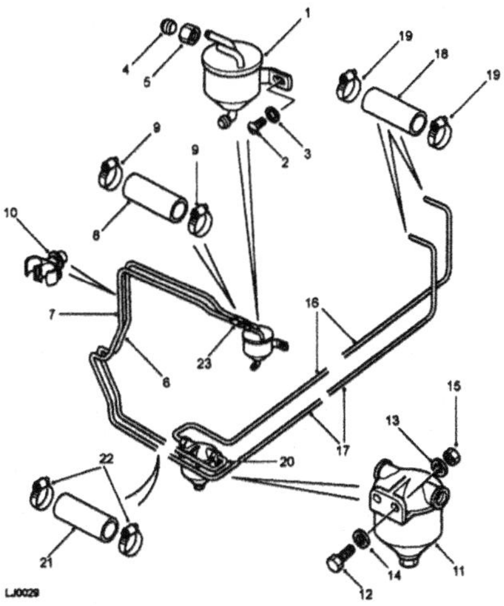

LJ0029

CHANGE POINTS:
(1) To (V) 295565
(2) From (V) 295566
(3) To (V) 296311

Illus	Part Number	Description	Quantity	Change Point	Remarks
1	NRC8919	Pipe fuel-tank to pump feed	1		
2	NRC7930	Pipe fuel-pump to filter	1		
3	NRC8921	Pipe fuel-filter to carburetter	1		
4	NRC8917	Pipe fuel-spill return to tank	1		
5	NRC5415	Clip-pipe-double	3		
6	79121	Clip-single-9mm	4		
7	79122	Clip-8mm	1		
8	AFU1107	Clip-pipe-double	1		
9	603431	Nut-tube-female-M12	A/R		
10	542846	Olive-fuel tank pipe	A/R		

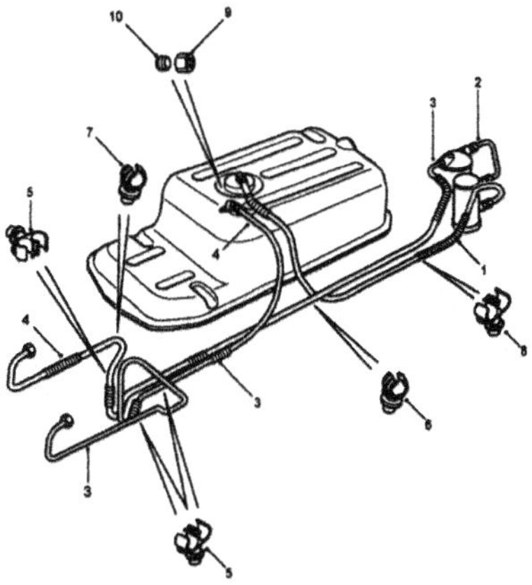

AHJXEA3A

DEFENDER	GROUP J	Fuel & Emission Systems Fuel-Air Cleaner-Evaporative Loss Fuel Pipes Petrol-To (V) WA159806-V8-Internal Pump

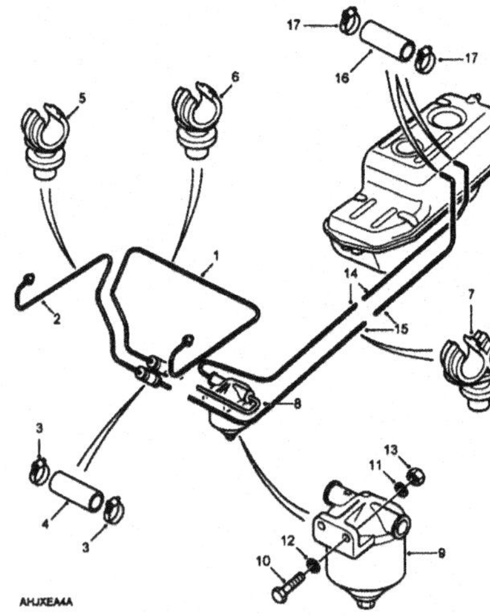

AHJXEA4A

Illus	Part Number	Description	Quantity	Change Point	Remarks
1	NTC2120	Pipe fuel-to carburetter	1		
1	NTC3692	Pipe fuel-filter to carburetter	1		
2	NTC2122	Pipe fuel-carburetter to hose	1		Except 130"
2	RRC6149	Pipe fuel-S.U.	1	Note (1)	130"
3	CN100168L	Clip-hose	2		
4	NTC2876	Connector fuel lines	2		
5	79122	Clip-8mm	1		
6	79121	Clip-single-9mm	3		
7	79158	Clip-pipe-double	5		
8	NTC2069	Pipe fuel	1		
9	NRC9786	FILTER-IN LINE FUEL LINES	1		
	JS660L	• Element-inline fuel filter	1		
10	FS106201L	Screw-flanged head-M6 x 20	2		
11	WA106001L	Washer-M6	2		
12	WL106001L	Washer-sprung-M6	2		
13	NH106041L	Nut-hexagonal-nyloc-M6	2		
14	NTC2077	Pipe fuel-tank to filter	1		90"
14	NTC2225	Pipe fuel-tank to filter	1		Except 90"
15	NTC2078	Pipe fuel-hose to tank	1		90"
15	NTC2072	Pipe fuel-hose to tank	1		Except 90"
16	NTC2876	Connector fuel lines	2		
17	CN100168L	Clip-hose	4		

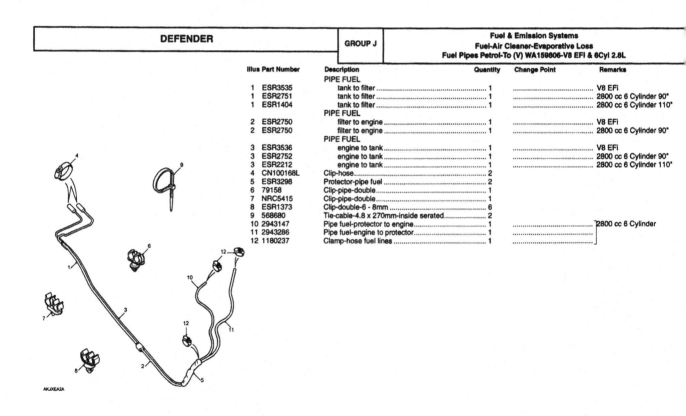

CHANGE POINTS:
(1) From (V) 26/9/88

DEFENDER	GROUP J	Fuel & Emission Systems Fuel-Air Cleaner-Evaporative Loss Fuel Pipes Petrol-To (V) WA159806-V8 EFI & 6Cyl 2.8L

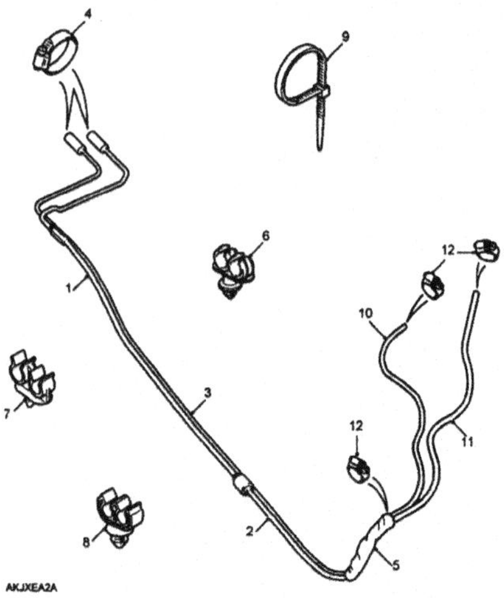

AKJXEA2A

Illus	Part Number	Description	Quantity	Change Point	Remarks
		PIPE FUEL			
1	ESR3535	tank to filter	1		V8 EFi
1	ESR2751	tank to filter	1		2800 cc 6 Cylinder 90"
1	ESR1404	tank to filter	1		2800 cc 6 Cylinder 110"
		PIPE FUEL			
2	ESR2750	filter to engine	1		V8 EFi
2	ESR2750	filter to engine	1		2800 cc 6 Cylinder 90"
		PIPE FUEL			
3	ESR3536	engine to tank	1		V8 EFi
3	ESR2752	engine to tank	1		2800 cc 6 Cylinder 90"
3	ESR2212	engine to tank	1		2800 cc 6 Cylinder 110"
4	CN100168L	Clip-hose	2		
5	ESR3298	Protector-pipe fuel	2		
6	79158	Clip-pipe-double	1		
7	NRC5415	Clip-pipe-double	1		
8	ESR1373	Clip-double-6 - 8mm	6		
9	568680	Tie-cable-4.8 x 270mm-inside serated	2		
10	2943147	Pipe fuel-protector to engine	1		2800 cc 6 Cylinder
11	2943286	Pipe fuel-engine to protector	1		2800 cc 6 Cylinder
12	1180237	Clamp-hose fuel lines	1		2800 cc 6 Cylinder

DEFENDER	GROUP J	Fuel & Emission Systems Fuel-Air Cleaner-Evaporative Loss Fuel Pipes-Petrol-From (V) XA159807

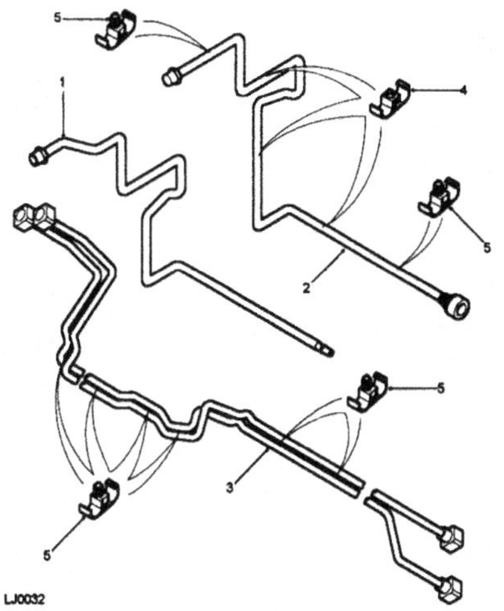

LJ0032

Illus	Part Number	Description	Quantity	Change Point	Remarks
		PIPE FUEL			
1	WJP108030	engine to connector	1		4 Cylinder Petrol
1	WJP108050	engine to connector	1		V8 Petrol 110"
1	WJP108010	engine to connector	1		BMW M52 6 Cylinder
		PIPE FUEL			
2	WJP108020	filter to engine	1		4 Cylinder Petrol
2	WJP108040	filter to engine	1		V8 Petrol
2	WJP108000	filter to engine	1		BMW M52 6 Cylinder
3	WJP108060	Pipe fuel-connector to tank	1		Petrol 90"
3	WJP108070	Pipe fuel-connector to tank-front	1		Petrol except 90"
4	WJC100680	Clip	1		
5	ESR4687	Clip-double fuel lines	1	Note (1)	Petrol
	ESR3135	Bracket-rear	2	Note (1)	BMW M52 Petrol

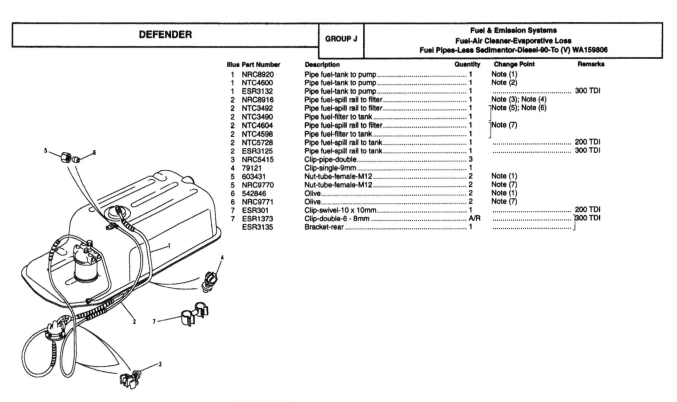

CHANGE POINTS:
(1) From (V) XA 159807

DEFENDER	GROUP J	Fuel & Emission Systems Fuel-Air Cleaner-Evaporative Loss Fuel Pipes-Less Sedimentor-Diesel-90-To (V) WA159806

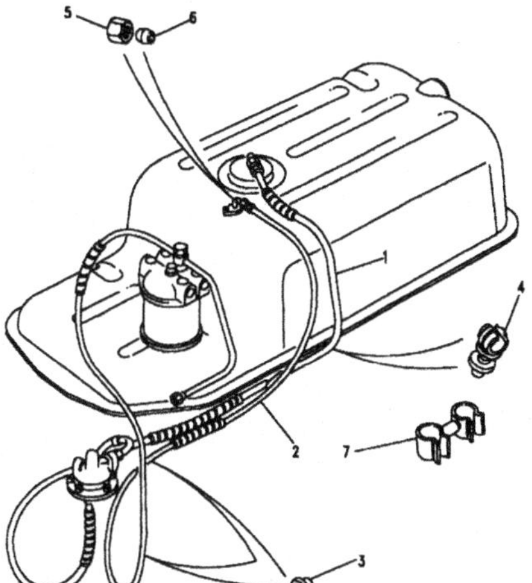

Illus	Part Number	Description	Quantity	Change Point	Remarks
1	NRC8920	Pipe fuel-tank to pump	1	Note (1)	
1	NTC4600	Pipe fuel-tank to pump	1	Note (2)	
1	ESR3132	Pipe fuel-tank to pump	1		300 TDI
2	NRC8916	Pipe fuel-spill rail to filter	1	Note (3); Note (4)	
2	NTC3492	Pipe fuel-spill rail to filter	1	Note (5); Note (6)	
2	NTC3490	Pipe fuel-filter to tank	1		
2	NTC4604	Pipe fuel-spill rail to filter	1	Note (7)	
2	NTC4598	Pipe fuel-filter to tank	1		
2	NTC5728	Pipe fuel-spill rail to tank	1		200 TDI
2	ESR3125	Pipe fuel-spill rail to tank	1		300 TDI
3	NRC5415	Clip-pipe-double	3		
4	79121	Clip-single-9mm	1		
5	603431	Nut-tube-female-M12	2	Note (1)	
5	NRC9770	Nut-tube-female-M12	2	Note (7)	
6	542846	Olive	2	Note (1)	
6	NRC9771	Olive	2	Note (7)	
7	ESR301	Clip-swivel-10 x 10mm	1		200 TDI
7	ESR1373	Clip-double-6 - 8mm	A/R		300 TDI
	ESR3135	Bracket-rear	1		

CHANGE POINTS:
(1) To (V) 327014
(2) From (V) 327015 To (V) LA 939975
(3) To (E)12J 35306C
(4) To (E)19J 07163C
(5) From (E)12J 35307C To (V) 327014
(6) From (E)19J 07164C To (V) 327014
(7) From (V) 327015

Illus	Part Number	Description	Quantity	Change Point	Remarks
1	NRC7979	Pipe fuel-rear tank to lift pump	1	Note (1)	110"
1	ESR246	Pipe fuel-rear tank to lift pump	1	Note (2)	
1	ESR3133	Pipe fuel-rear tank to lift pump	1		110" 300 TDI
1	RRC2644	Pipe fuel-rear tank to lift pump	1	Note (3)	130"
1	ESR3134	Pipe fuel-rear tank to lift pump	1		130" 300 TDI
2	NTC2157	Pipe fuel-rail to filter to rear tank	1	Note (4)	
2	NTC4604	Pipe fuel-spill rail to filter	1	Note (5)	
2	NTC3491	Pipe fuel-filter to rear tank	1	Note (5)	110"
2	RRC2645	Pipe fuel-filter to rear tank	1		130"
2	NTC5729	Pipe fuel-spill rail to rear tank	1		110" 200 TDI
2	ESR3127	Pipe fuel-spill rail to rear tank	1		110" 300 TDI
2	ESR352	Pipe fuel-spill rail to rear tank	1		130" 200 TDI
2	ESR3124	Pipe fuel-spill rail to rear tank	1		130" 300 TDI

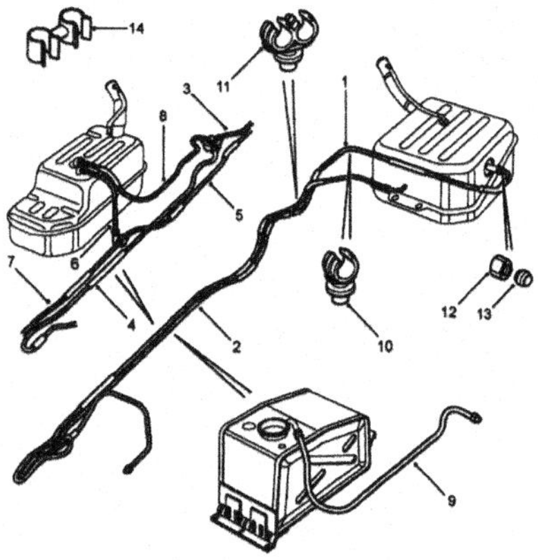

AJJXEC3A

CHANGE POINTS:
(1) To (V) FA 450724
(2) From (V) FA 450725 To (V) LA 939975
(3) To (V) LA 939975
(4) To (V) EA 328280
(5) From (V) EA 328281

Illus	Part Number	Description	Quantity	Change Point	Remarks
		ADDITIONAL FUEL TANK - OPTIONAL			
3	NRC7893	Pipe fuel-Rear tank to tap-feed	1	Note (1)	110"
3	ESR247	Pipe fuel-Rear tank to tap-feed	1	Note (2)	
3	RRC6745	Pipe fuel-Rear tank to tap-feed	1	Note (3)	130"
4	NRC8104	Pipe fuel-Tap to lift pump-feed	1	Note (4)	
4	ESR3299	Pipe fuel-Tap to lift pump-feed	1		300 TDI
5	NTC2179	Pipe fuel-Tap to rear tank-spill	1		110"
5	RRC6746	Pipe fuel-Tap to rear tank-spill	1	Note (3)	130"
6	NRC7310	Pipe fuel-Side tank to tap-spill	1	Note (5)	
6	NTC4596	Pipe fuel-Side tank to tap-spill	1	Note (6)	
7	NRC7351	Pipe fuel-Spill rail to tap	1	Note (5)	
7	NTC3489	Pipe fuel-Filter to tap	1	Note (6)	
7	NTC5750	Pipe fuel-Spill rail to tap	1		200 TDI
7	ESR3300	Pipe fuel-Spill rail to tap	1		300 TDI
8	NRC7303	Pipe fuel-Side tank to tap-feed	1	Note (5)	HICAP
8	NTC4595	Pipe fuel-Side tank to tap-feed	1	Note (6)	
9	NRC8087	Pipe fuel-Side tank to tap-feed	1	Note (5)	Station Wagon
9	NTC4599	Pipe fuel-Side tank to tap-feed	1	Note (6)	
10	79121	Clip-fuel feed pipe-single-9mm	4		
10	79122	Clip-fuel spill pipe-8mm	1		
11	NRC5415	Clip-pipe-double	3		
12	603431	Nut-tube-female-M12	A/R	Note (5)	
12	NRC9770	Nut-tube-female-M12	A/R	Note (6)	
13	542846	Olive-fuel tank pipe	A/R	Note (5)	
13	NRC9771	Olive-fuel tank pipe	A/R	Note (6)	
14	ESR301	Clip-swivel-10 x 10mm	1		200 TDI
14	ESR1373	Clip-double-6 - 8mm	A/R		300 TDI
	ESR3135	Bracket-rear	1		

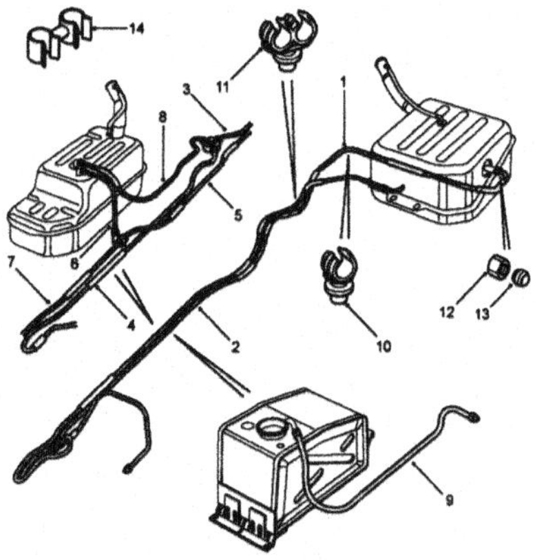

AJJXEC3A

CHANGE POINTS:
(1) To (V) FA 450722
(2) From (V) FA 450723
(3) From (V) October1989
(4) To (V) LA 939975
(5) To (V) EA 328280
(6) From (V) EA 328281

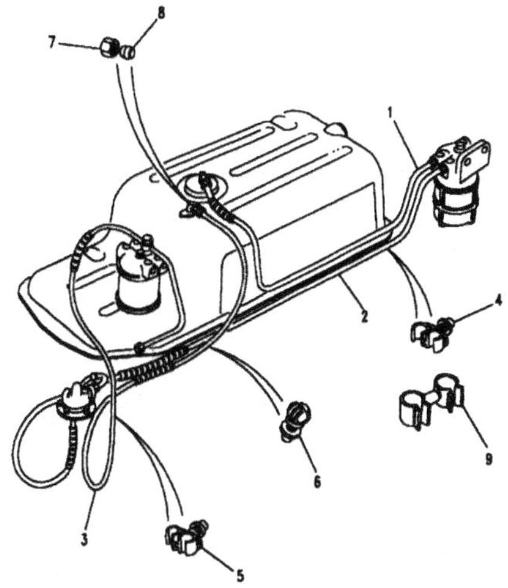

Illus	Part Number	Description	Quantity	Change Point	Remarks
1	NRC8922	Pipe fuel-tank to sedimentor	1	Note (1)	
1	NTC4601	Pipe fuel-tank to sedimentor	1	Note (2)	
2	NRC8923	Pipe fuel-sedimentor to lift pump	1	Note (3)	
2	ESR3129	Pipe fuel-sedimentor to lift pump	1		300 TDI
3	NRC8916	Pipe fuel-spill rail/filter/tank	1	Note (4); Note (5)	
3	NTC3492	Pipe fuel-spill rail to filter	1	Note (6); Note (7)	
3	NTC3490	Pipe fuel-filter to tank	1		
3	NTC4604	Pipe fuel-spill rail to filter	1	Note (2)	
3	NTC4598	Pipe fuel-filter to tank	1		
3	NTC5728	Pipe fuel-spill rail to tank	1		200 TDI
3	ESR3125	Pipe fuel-spill rail to tank	1		300 TDI
4	AFU1107	Clip-pipe-double	1		
5	NRC5415	Clip-pipe-double	3		
6	79121	Clip-single-9mm	1		
7	603431	Nut-tube-female-M12	1	Note (1)	
7	NRC9770	Nut-tube-female-M12	1	Note (2)	
8	542846	Olive	1	Note (1)	
8	NRC9771	Olive	1	Note (2)	
9	ESR301	Clip-swivel-10 x 10mm	1		200 TDI
9	ESR1373	Clip-double-6 - 8mm	A/R		300 TDI
	ESR3135	Bracket-rear	1		

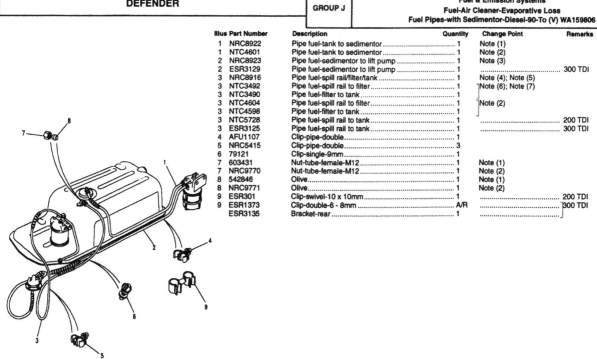

CHANGE POINTS:
(1) To (V) 327014
(2) From (V) 327015
(3) To (V) LA 939975
(4) To (E)12J 35306C
(5) To (E)19J 07163C
(6) From (E)12J 35307C To (V) 327014
(7) From (E)19J 07164C To (V) 327014

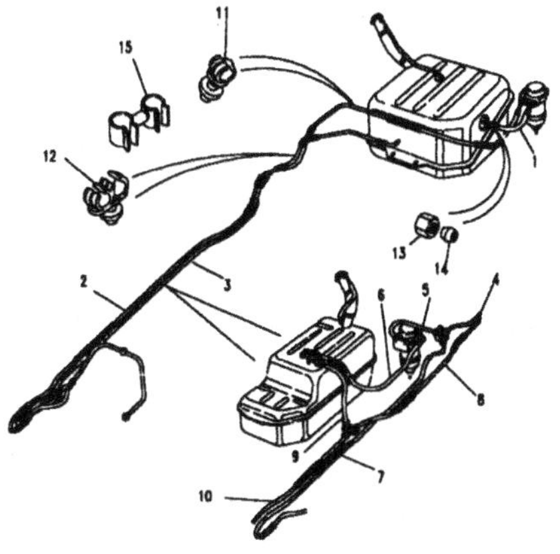

Illus	Part Number	Description	Quantity	Change Point	Remarks
		PIPE FUEL			
1	NRC8462	tank to sedimentor	1	Note (1)	
1	ESR245	tank to sedimentor	1	Note (2)	
2	NRC8103	sedimentor to lift pump	1	Note (3)	110"
2	ESR3130	sedimentor to lift pump	1		110" 300 TDI
2	RRC2475	sedimentor to lift pump	1	Note (4)	130"
2	RRC6744	sedimentor to lift pump	1	Note (5)	
2	ESR3128	sedimentor to lift pump	1		130" 300 TDI
2	NTC2157	rail to filter to rear tank	1	Note (6)	
2	NTC4604	spill rail to filter	1	Note (7)	
2	NTC3491	filter to rear tank	1		
2	NTC5729	spill rail to rear tank	1		110" 200 TDI
2	ESR3127	spill rail to rear tank	1		110" 300 TDI
2	ESR352	spill rail to rear tank	1		130" 200 TDI
2	ESR3124	spill rail to rear tank	1		130" 300 TDI

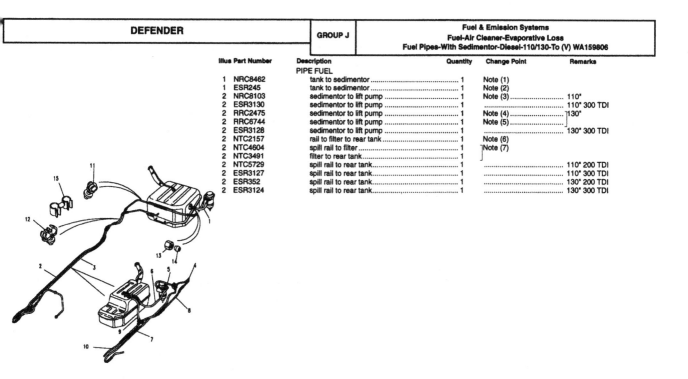

CHANGE POINTS:
(1) To (V) FA 450724
(2) From (V) FA 450725
(3) To (V) LA 939975
(4) To (V) October1989
(5) From (V) October1989 To (V) LA 939975
(6) To (V) EA 328280
(7) From (V) EA 328281

DEFENDER

GROUP J

Fuel & Emission Systems
Fuel-Air Cleaner-Evaporative Loss
Fuel Pipes-With Sedimentor-Diesel-110/130-To (V) WA159806

Illus	Part Number	Description	Quantity	Change Point	Remarks
		ADDITIONAL FUEL TANK - OPTIONAL			
4	NRC7318	Pipe fuel-Rear sedimentor to tap	1		110"
4	RRC6747	Pipe fuel-Rear sedimentor to tap	1	Note (1)	130"
5	NRC7319	Pipe fuel-Front sedimentor to tap	1		
6	NRC8108	Pipe fuel-Side tank to front sedimentor	1	Note (2)	
6	NTC4597	Pipe fuel-Side tank to front sedimentor	1	Note (3)	
7	NRC8104	Pipe fuel-Tap to lift pump-feed	1	Note (4)	
7	ESR3299	Pipe fuel-Tap to lift pump-feed	1		300 TDI
8	NTC2179	Pipe fuel-Tap to rear tank-spill	1		
9	NRC7310	Pipe fuel-Side tank to tap-spill	1	Note (2)	
9	NTC4596	Pipe fuel-Side tank to tap-spill	1	Note (3)	
10	NRC7351	Pipe fuel-Spill rail to tap	1	Note (2)	
10	NTC5750	Pipe fuel-Spill rail to tap	1		200 TDI
10	ESR3300	Pipe fuel-Spill rail to tap	1		300 TDI
		FILTER TO TAP			
10	NTC3489	Pipe fuel-Filter to tap	1		
11	79121	Clip-single-9mm	4		
11	79122	Clip-8mm	1		
12	NRC5415	Clip-pipe-double	7		
13	603431	Nut-tube-female-M12	A/R	Note (2)	
13	NRC9770	Nut-tube-female-M12	A/R	Note (3)	
14	542846	Olive-fuel tank pipe	A/R	Note (2)	
14	NRC9771	Olive-fuel tank pipe	A/R	Note (3)	
15	ESR301	Clip-swivel-10 x 10mm	1		200 TDI
15	ESR1373	Clip-double-6 - 8mm	A/R		300 TDI
	ESR3135	Bracket-pipe clip-rear	1		

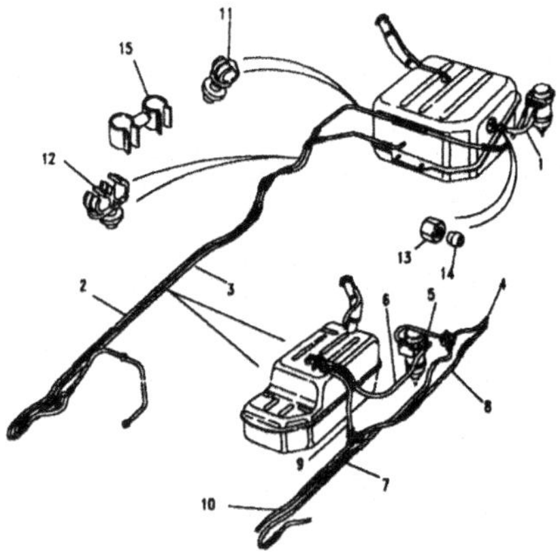

CHANGE POINTS:
(1) From (V) October1989
(2) To (V) EA 328280
(3) From (V) EA 328281
(4) To (V) LA 939975

DEFENDER

GROUP J

Fuel & Emission Systems
Fuel-Air Cleaner-Evaporative Loss
Fuel Pipes-Diesel-300TDi From (V) XA159807

Illus	Part Number	Description	Quantity	Change Point	Remarks
1	WJP107960	Pipe fuel-sedimentor to engine to tank	1		90"
1	WJP107980	Pipe fuel-sedimentor to engine to tank	1		110"
1	WJP107990	Pipe fuel-sedimentor to engine to tank	1		130"
2	WJP107950	Pipe fuel-tank to sedimentor	1		90"
2	WJP107970	Pipe fuel-tank to sedimentor	1		110"
2	WJP107970	Pipe fuel-tank to sedimentor	1		130"
3	WJC100680	Clip	1		
4	ESR4687	Clip-double fuel lines	1	Note (1)	

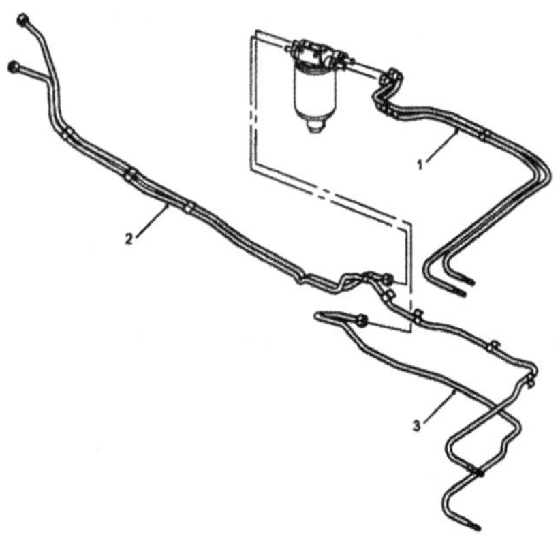

LJ0016

CHANGE POINTS:
(1) From (V) XA 159807

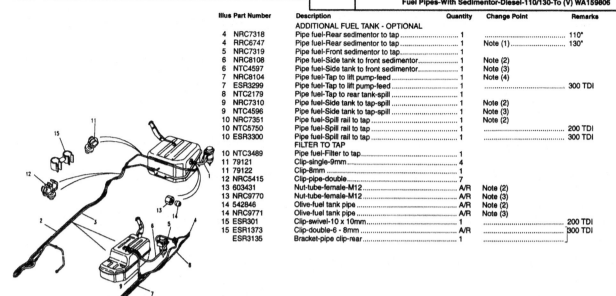

DEFENDER

GROUP J

Fuel & Emission Systems
Fuel-Air Cleaner-Evaporative Loss
Fuel Pipes-Diesel-Td5

Illus	Part Number	Description	Quantity	Change Point	Remarks
		PIPE FUEL			
1	WJP107880	pump to filter	1		90"
1	WJP107940	pump to filter	1		110"
1	WJP107940	pump to filter	1		130"
		PIPE FUEL			
2	WJP107890	pump to engine	1		90"
2	WJP107910	pump to engine	1		110"
2	WJP107920	pump to engine	1		130"
		PIPE-FUEL LINES FEED			
3	WJP107900	filter to pump	1		90"
3	WJP107930	filter to pump	1		110"
3	WJP107930	filter to pump	1		130"
4	WJC100680	Clip	1		
5	ESR4687	Clip-double fuel lines	1		

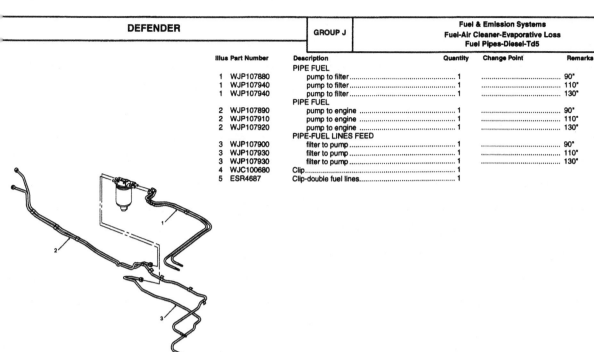

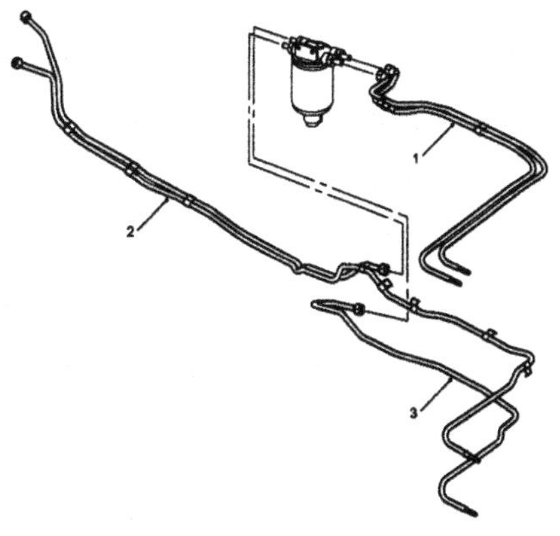

LJ0016

DEFENDER

GROUP J

Fuel & Emission Systems
Fuel-Air Cleaner-Evaporative Loss
Air Cleaner-4 Cyl Petrol

Illus	Part Number	Description	Quantity	Change Point	Remarks
1	RRC4002	AIR CLEANER ASSEMBLY	1	Note (1)	
2	NRC9238	• Element air cleaner	1		
	NRC9239	• Nut-wing	1		
3	RRC3746	• O ring	1		
4	NRC8955	• Valve assembly air intake	1		
1	NTC4183	AIR CLEANER ASSEMBLY	1	Note (2)	
2	NRC9238	• Element air cleaner	1		
3	RRC3746	• O ring	1		
4	NTC3751	• Valve assembly air intake	1		
5	SH106121L	Screw-hexagonal head-M6 x 12	3		
6	WL106001L	Washer-sprung-M6	3		
7	NH106041L	Nut-hexagonal-nyloc-M6	3		
8	NTC1650	Hose-carburettor vent	1		
9	CJ600504L	Clip-hose	2		

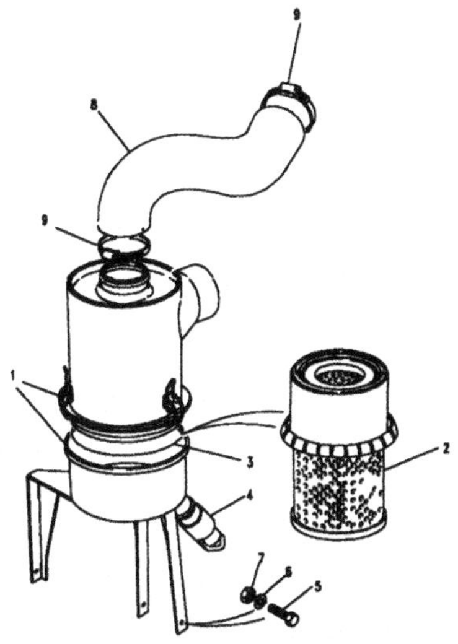

CHANGE POINTS:
(1) To (V) FA 375497
(2) From (V) FA 375498

Air Cleaner-V8 Twin Carb

Illus	Part Number	Description	Quantity	Change Point	Remarks
1	ERC8505	AIR CLEANER ASSEMBLY	1		
2	RTC3479	• Element air cleaner	1		
3	ERC3896	• Plate-baffle	1		
4	RA607076	• Rivet	3		
5	606247	• Clip	1		
6	STC1120	• Valve assembly air intake	1		
7	ERC3892	Bracket assembly-air cleaner-LH	1		V8
7	ERC3893	Bracket assembly-air cleaner-RH	1		
8	ERC3946	Strap assembly-retaining-front	2		
9	ERC3897	Strap assembly-retaining-rear	2		
10	572994	Pin	2		
11	578023	Nut	2		
12	SH505051	Screw-hexagonal head	4		
13	WL600051L	Washer-spring-5/16"	4		
14	ERC3955	Hose assembly-breather-to filter	1		
15	ERC3954	Hose assembly-breather-to block	1		
16	603183	Filter assembly-in line fuel lines	NLA		Use 606168.
16	606168	Filter assembly-in line fuel lines	1		V8
17	603962	Clip	1		
18	79134	Screw	1		
19	WL700101	Washer-spring	1		

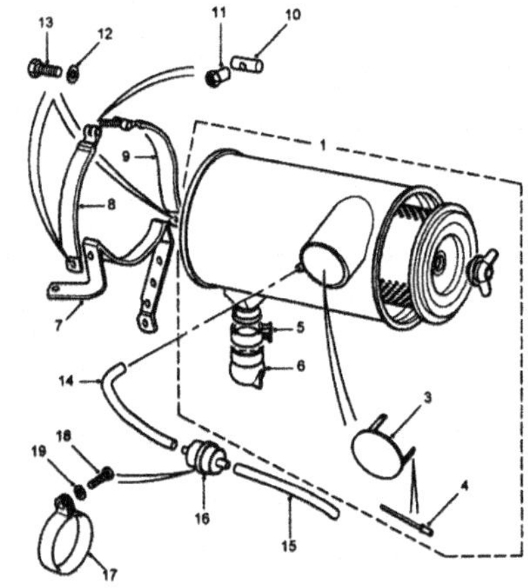

AHJXPA2A

Air Cleaner-V8 EFI-4.0L

Illus	Part Number	Description	Quantity	Change Point	Remarks
1	PHB102560	AIR CLEANER ASSEMBLY	1		
2	RTC4683	• Element air cleaner	1		
3	NTC3751	• Valve assembly air intake	1		
4	ERR2946	• Sensor-air inlet temperature engine-electric control unit	1		
5	PHH100290	Hose-air cleaner	1		
6	PYC101980	Clip	2		
7	ESR1579	Mounting-rubber flexible support	3		
8	ERR5595	Sensor assembly-airflow multi point injection	1		
9	NTC3354	O ring	1		
10	FN106047L	Nut-flange-M6	3		
11	WC106047	Washer-M6	3		
12	PHU102790	Bracket assembly-mounting air cleaner	1		
13	PHU102800	Bracket-support air cleaner/pipe	1		
14	PHU102490	Bracket assembly-mounting air cleaner	1		

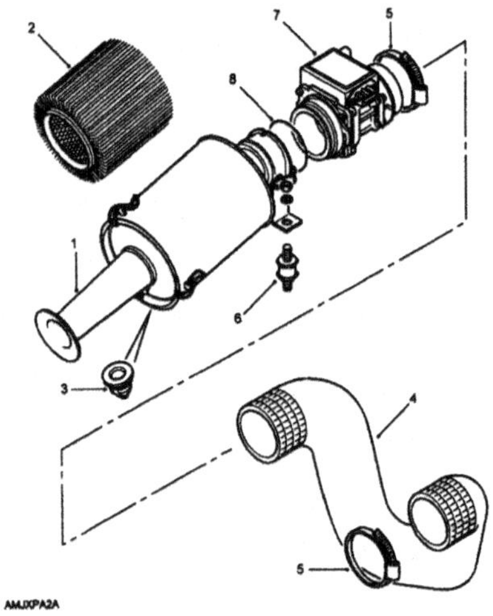

AMJXPA2A

DEFENDER

GROUP J

Fuel & Emission Systems
Fuel-Air Cleaner-Evaporative Loss
Air Cleaner-Nat Asp Diesel

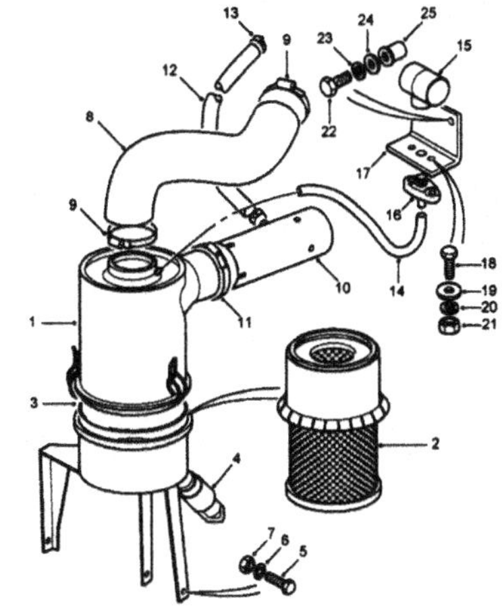

AHJXPC1A

Illus	Part Number	Description	Quantity	Change Point	Remarks
1	RRC4002	AIR CLEANER ASSEMBLY	1	Note (1)	
1	NTC4183	AIR CLEANER ASSEMBLY	1	Note (2)	
2	NRC9238	• Element air cleaner	1		
	NRC9239	• Nut-wing	1		Part of RRC4002.
3	RRC3746	• O ring	1		
4	NRC8955	• Valve assembly air intake	1		Part of RRC4002.
4	NTC3751	• Valve assembly air intake	1		Part of NTC4183.
5	SH106121L	Screw-hexagonal head-M6 x 12	3		
6	WL106001L	Washer-sprung-M6	3		
7	NH106041L	Nut-hexagonal-nyloc-M6	3		
8	NRC8962	Hose-air cleaner	1		
9	CJ600504L	Clip-hose	2		
10	NRC8987	Resonator induction system	1	Note (1)	
10	NTC4612	Resonator induction system	1	Note (2)	
11	CJ600504L	Clip-hose	1		
12	ETC7969	Hose-camshaft cover to inlet manifold breather	1	Note (2)	
13	CJ600164L	Clip-hose	2		
14	NTC4187	Hose-air cleaner-without raised air intake	1		
15	NTC4611	Indicator restriction	1		
16	NTC4224	Connector-inlet manifold adaptor	1		
17	RRC3011	Bracket-air cleaner	1		
18	FS106167L	Screw-flanged head-flanged head-M6 x 16	2		
19	WA106041L	Washer-6mm	2		
20	WL106001L	Washer-sprung-M6	2		
21	NH106041L	Nut-hexagonal-nyloc-M6	2		
22	SH106121L	Screw-hexagonal head-M6 x 12	2		
23	WL106001L	Washer-sprung-M6	2		
24	WA106041L	Washer-6mm	2		
25	NN106011L	Nutsert-blind	2		

CHANGE POINTS:
(1) To (V) FA 375497
(2) From (V) FA 375498

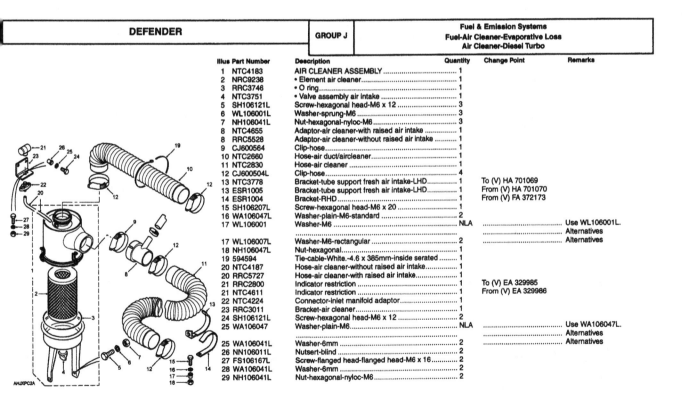

DEFENDER

GROUP J

Fuel & Emission Systems
Fuel-Air Cleaner-Evaporative Loss
Air Cleaner-Diesel Turbo

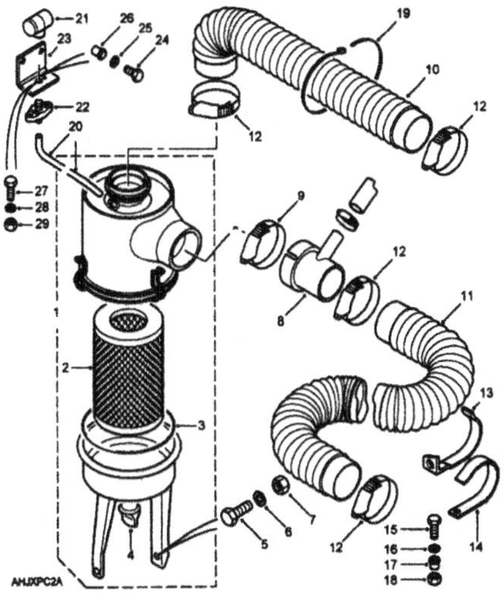

AHJXPC2A

Illus	Part Number	Description	Quantity	Change Point	Remarks
1	NTC4183	AIR CLEANER ASSEMBLY	1		
2	NRC9238	• Element air cleaner	1		
3	RRC3746	• O ring	1		
4	NTC3751	• Valve assembly air intake	1		
5	SH106121L	Screw-hexagonal head-M6 x 12	3		
6	WL106001L	Washer-sprung-M6	3		
7	NH106041L	Nut-hexagonal-nyloc-M6	3		
8	NTC4655	Adaptor-air cleaner-with raised air intake	1		
8	RRC5528	Adaptor-air cleaner-without raised air intake	1		
9	CJ600564	Clip-hose	1		
10	NTC2660	Hose-air duct/aircleaner	1		
11	NTC2830	Hose-air cleaner	1		
12	CJ600504L	Clip-hose	4		
13	NTC3778	Bracket-tube support fresh air intake-LHD	1	To (V) HA 701069	
13	ESR1005	Bracket-tube support fresh air intake-LHD	1	From (V) HA 701070	
14	ESR1004	Bracket-RHD	1	From (V) FA 372173	
15	SH106207L	Screw-hexagonal head-M6 x 20	1		
16	WA106047L	Washer-plain-M6-standard	2		
17	WL106001	Washer-M6	NLA		Use WL106001L.
					Alternatives
17	WL106007L	Washer-M6-rectangular	2		Alternatives
18	NH106047L	Nut-hexagonal	1		
19	594594	Tie-cable-White.-4.6 x 385mm-inside serated	1		
20	NTC4187	Hose-air cleaner-without raised air intake	1		
20	RRC5727	Hose-air cleaner-with raised air intake	1		
21	RRC2800	Indicator restriction	1	To (V) EA 329985	
21	NTC4611	Indicator restriction	1	From (V) EA 329986	
22	NTC4224	Connector-inlet manifold adaptor	1		
23	RRC3011	Bracket-air cleaner	1		
24	SH106121L	Screw-hexagonal head-M6 x 12	2		
25	WA106047	Washer-plain-M6	NLA		Use WA106047L.
					Alternatives
25	WA106041L	Washer-6mm	2		Alternatives
26	NN106011L	Nutsert-blind	2		
27	FS106167L	Screw-flanged head-flanged head-M6 x 16	2		
28	WA106041L	Washer-6mm	2		
29	NH106041L	Nut-hexagonal-nyloc-M6	2		

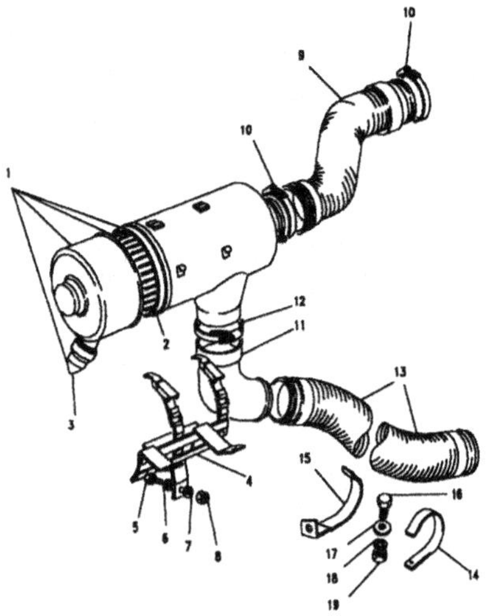

Illus	Part Number	Description	Quantity	Change Point	Remarks
1	ESR370	Air cleaner assembly	1		
2	NTC6660	Element air cleaner	1		
	NRC9239	Nut-wing	1		
3	NRC8955	Valve assembly air intake	1		
4	ESR276	Bracket assembly-air cleaner	1		
5	FS106167L	Screw-flanged head-flanged head-M6 x 16	3		
6	WA106041L	Washer-6mm	3		
7	WL106001L	Washer-sprung-M6	3		
8	NH106041L	Nut-hexagonal-nyloc-M6	3		
9	ESR415	Duct-air cleaner to hose turbocharger	1		
10	STC128	Clip-hose	2		
11	ESR228	Elbow	1		
12	CN100908L	Clip-hose	1		
13	ESR184	Pipe-air cleaner case	1		
14	ESR1004	Bracket-RHD	1		
15	NTC3778	Bracket-tube support fresh air intake-LHD	1	Note (1)	
15	ESR1005	Bracket-tube support fresh air intake-LHD	1	Note (2)	
16	SH106207L	Screw-hexagonal head-M6 x 20	1		
17	WA106047L	Washer-plain-M6-standard	2		
18	WL106007L	Washer-M6-rectangular	2		
19	NH106047L	Nut-hexagonal	1		

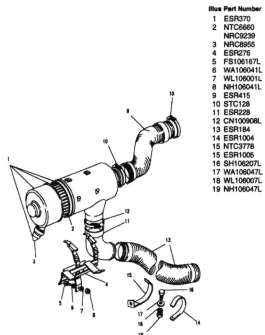

CHANGE POINTS:
(1) To (V) HA 701076
(2) From (V) HA 701077

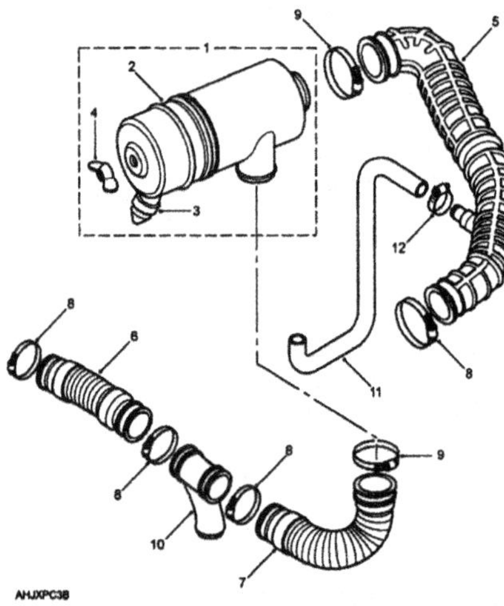

AHJXPC38

Illus	Part Number	Description	Quantity	Change Point	Remarks
1	ESR2102	AIR CLEANER ASSEMBLY	1		
2	ESR2623	• Element air cleaner	1		
3	NRC8955	• Valve assembly air intake	1		
4	NRC9239	• Nut-wing	1		
5	ESR2731	Duct-air cleaner to hose turbocharger	1		Except EGR
5	ESR3111	Duct-air cleaner to hose turbocharger	1		EGR
6	ESR3028	Hose intake-to dump valve	1		
7	ESR3032	Hose-air cleaner	1		
8	CN100708	Clip-hose	4		
9	CN100908L	Clip-hose	2		
10	ESR3162	Dump valve & bracket assy	1		
11	ERR4926	Hose-cyclone-air cleaner	1		
12	CN100258L	Clip-hose-25mm	1		

Air Cleaner Mountings-300TDi

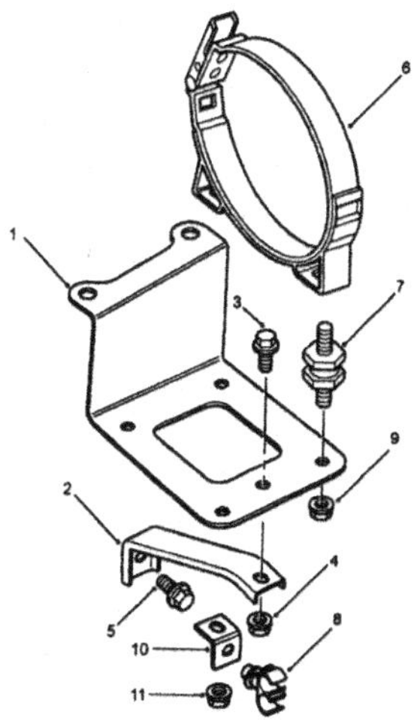

Illus	Part Number	Description	Quantity	Change Point	Remarks
1	ERR2850	Bracket assembly-air cleaner	1		
2	ERR2851	Bracket	1		
3	FS108161L	Screw-to bracket-flanged head-M8 x 16	1		
4	FN108047L	Nut-flange-flanged head-M8	1		
5	FS108207L	Screw-to bracket-flanged head-M8 x 20	1		
6	ERR4688	Strap-air cleaner	2		
7	ERR2337	Mounting-rubber	4		
8	ESR1373	Clip-double-6 - 8mm	1		
9	FN106047L	Nut-flange-M6	2		
10	NRC2089	Bracket-air cleaner	1		
11	FN106047L	Nut-flange-M6	2		

Air Cleaner-Td5

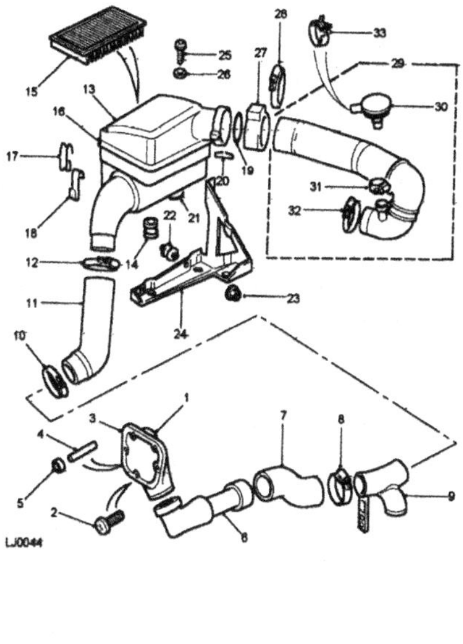

Illus	Part Number	Description	Quantity	Change Point	Remarks
1	ESR3173	Duct air-upper-RH	1		
2	AB608041	Screw-self tapping	5		
3	AFU1926L	Nut-caged	5		
4	AJU1136	Stud	5		
5	359526	Bush	5		
6	ESR3175	Duct air-lower-RH	1		
7	ESR3028	Hose intake	1		
8	CN100708	Clip-hose	1		
9	ESR3162	Dump valve & bracket assy	1		
10	PYC102350	Clip-hose	1		
11	PHD103620	Duct-water separator to air cleaner air intake	1		
12	CN100908L	Clip-hose	1		
13	PHB102360	Air cleaner assembly	1	Note (1)	
13	PHB102880	Air cleaner assembly	1	Note (2)	
14	PYA10008L	Mounting-rubber	3		
15	ESR4238	Element air cleaner	1		
16	PHC100570	Lid-air cleaner	1	Note (1)	
16	PHC100740	Lid-air cleaner	1	Note (2)	
17	WYC100550	Clip-retaining-short	1		
18	WYC100560	Clip-retaining-long	1		

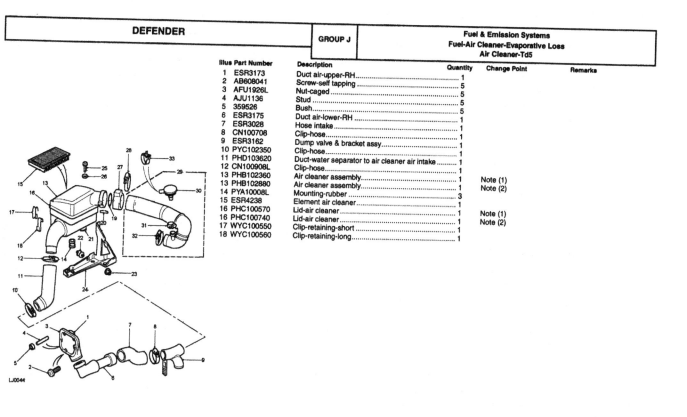

CHANGE POINTS:
(1) To (V) XA 175541
(2) From (V) XA 175542

Illus	Part Number	Description	Quantity	Change Point	Remarks
19	PHN100200	Seal-air cleaner to throttle body induction system	1		
20	WYC100540	Clip-retaining	2		
21	PKS100140	Valve-air cleaner dump	1		
22	ASR2152	Mounting-rubber	1		
23	FN106047L	Nut-flange-M6	3		
24	PHU102860	Bracket assembly-mounting air cleaner	1		
25	DA610054	Screw-self tapping	2		
26	MHK100490	Sensor-multi point injection manifold pressure	1		
27	MHK100620	Sensor-airflow-multi point inject	1		
28	CN100908L	Clip-hose	1	Note (1)	
28	WYC100680	Clip-hose	1	Note (2)	
29	PHD103990	DUCT ASSEMBLY-AIR CLEANER/TURBOCHARGER INDUCTION SYSTEM	1		
30	LLN100140L	• Valve assembly-depression control	1		
31	CN100308L	Clip-hose-30mm	1		
32	CN100808L	Clip-hose	1	Note (1)	
32	WYC100710	Clip-hose	1	Note (2)	
33	PYC101410	Clip-hose	1		

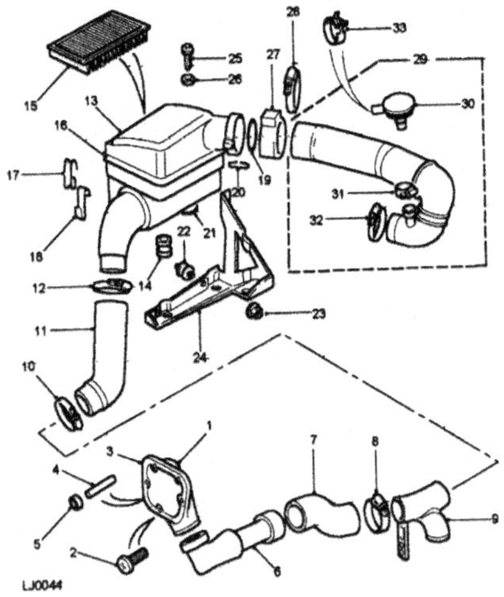

LJ0044

CHANGE POINTS:
(1) To (V) WA 159806
(2) From (V) XA 159807

Illus	Part Number	Description	Quantity	Change Point	Remarks
1	2943328	AIR CLEANER ASSEMBLY	1		
2	2943334	• Element-filter	1		
3	NRC8955	• Valve assembly air intake	1		
4	CN100908	Clip-hose	NLA		Use CN100908L.

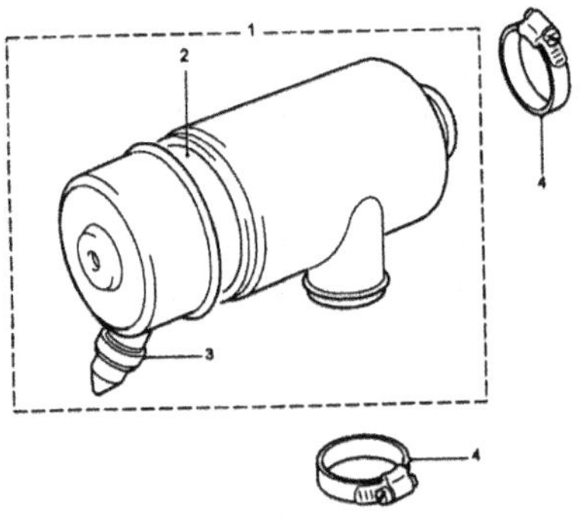

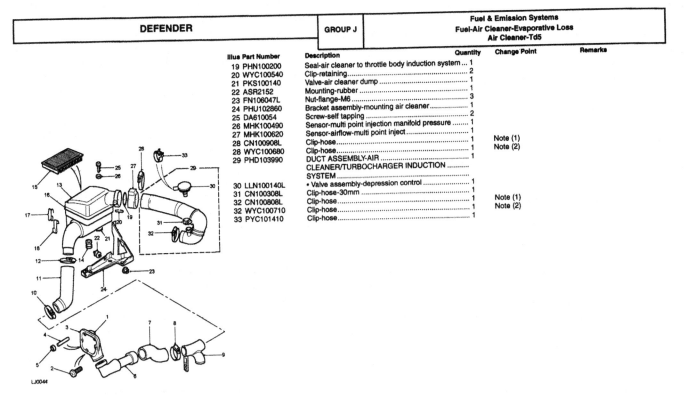

AKJXPC3B

Air Cleaner Mountings-6Cyl Petrol

Illus	Part Number	Description	Quantity	Change Point	Remarks
1	AAU3686	Tie-cable-6.5mm hole-8.0 x 155mm	2		
2	2943358	Bracket-mounting air cleaner	1		
3	FN108041L	Nut-flange-M8	NLA		Use FN108047L.
4	2943129	Plate air cleaner mounting bracket	1`		
5	ERR2337	Mounting-rubber	4		
6	FN106047L	Nut-flange-M6	2		

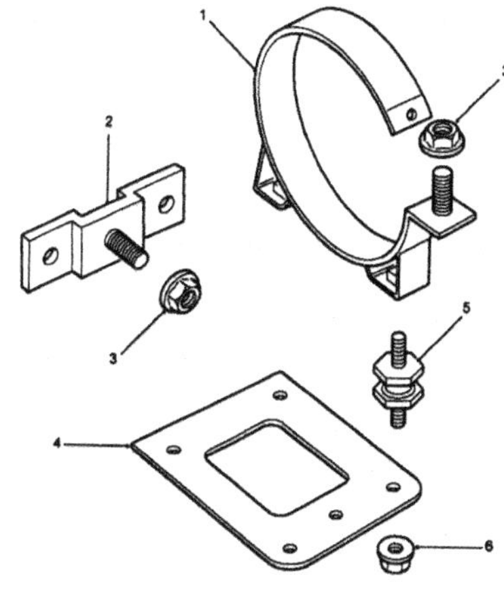

AKJXPC3C

Raised Air Intake-200 TDI

Illus	Part Number	Description	Quantity	Change Point	Remarks
1	NRC6920	Air cleaner assembly-raised	1		
2	NRC6919	Clip	1		
3	SH106207L	Screw-hexagonal head-M6 x 20	1		
4	WA106047L	Washer-plain-M6-standard	1		
5	NH106047L	Nut-hexagonal	1		
6	NRC7457	Hose-air cleaner	1		
7	NTC4257	Clip	2		
8	276426	Seal	2		
9	SH106207L	Screw-hexagonal head-M6 x 20	2		
10	WA106047L	Washer-plain-M6-standard	2		
11	ML106015	Insert-helicoil	2		
12	ESR1128	Hose-air cleaner induction system-vertical	1		
13	ESR1269	Clip-hose	2		
14	ESR1127	Duct assembly-fresh air	1		
15	ESR1225	Clamp	1		
16	ESR1265	Gasket	1		
17	AB608067L	Screw-self tapping	6		
18	WA105001L	Washer-plain-standard-M5	6		
19	AJU1136L	Insert-plain	5		

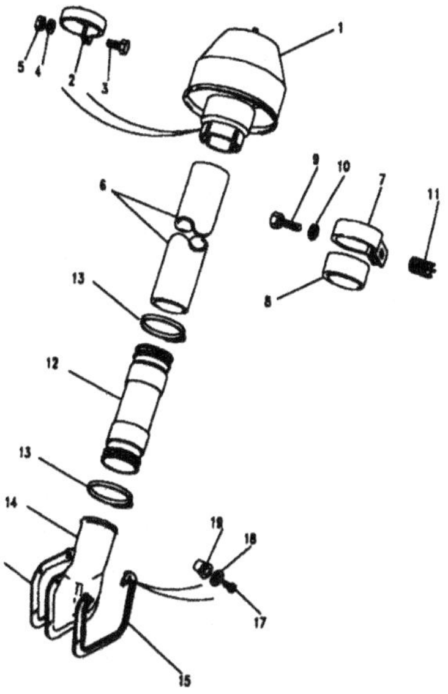

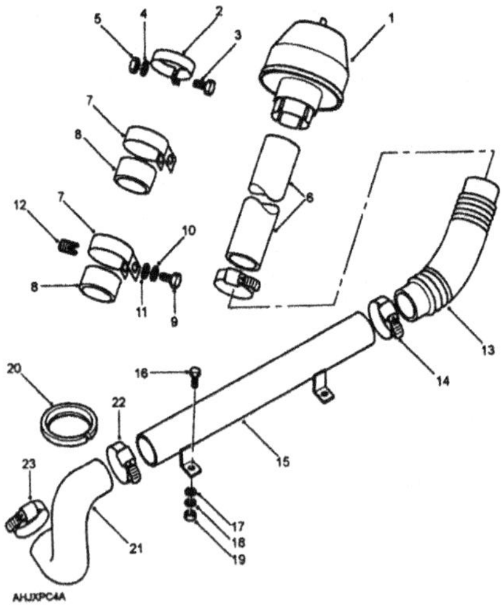

Illus	Part Number	Description	Quantity	Change Point	Remarks
1	NRC6920	Air cleaner assembly-raised	1		
2	NRC6919	Clip	1		
3	FS106201L	Screw-flanged head-M6 x 20	1		
4	WL106001L	Washer-sprung-M6	1		
5	NH106041L	Nut-hexagonal-nyloc-M6	1		
6	NRC7457	Hose-air cleaner	1		
7	NRC7154	Clip	1	Note (1)	
7	NTC4257	Clip	2	Note (2)	
8	276426	Seal	2		
9	FS106201L	Screw-flanged head-M6 x 20	2		
10	WA106041L	Washer-6mm	2		
11	WL106001L	Washer-sprung-M6	2		
12	ML106015	Insert-helicoil	2		
13	NRC6254	Hose-air cleaner	1		
14	CJ600504L	Clip-hose	2		
15	NRC9107	Pipe assembly brake	1		
16	SH106121L	Screw-hexagonal head-M6 x 12	4		
17	WA106041L	Washer-6mm	4		
18	WL106001L	Washer-sprung-M6	4		
19	NH106041L	Nut-hexagonal-nyloc-M6	4		
20	MTC7513	Edging strip	A/R		
21	NRC8984	Hose-air cleaner to pipe	1		
22	CJ600504L	Clip-hose	1		
23	RTC3518	Clip-hose	1		

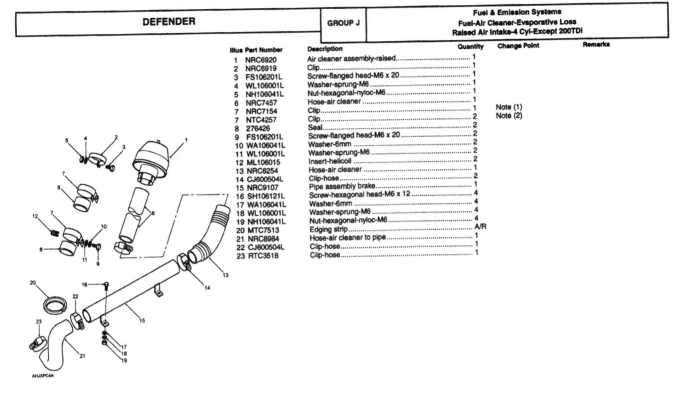

CHANGE POINTS:
(1) To (V) EA 323866
(2) From (V) EA 323867

Illus	Part Number	Description	Quantity	Change Point	Remarks
1	STC61900	Kit-raised air intake	1	Note (1)	Tomb Raider

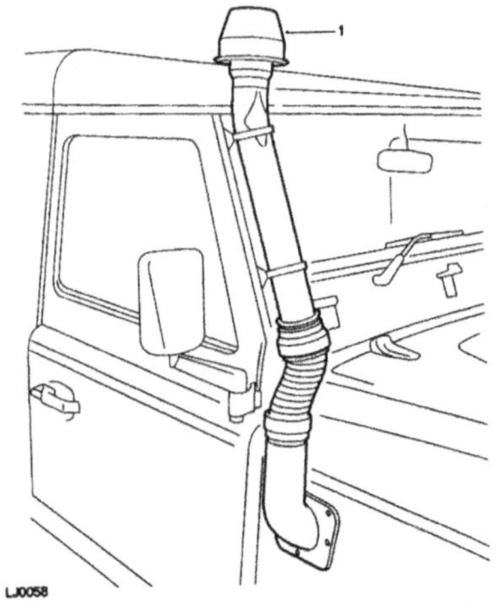

CHANGE POINTS:
(1) From (V) 1A 612404

Illus	Part Number	Description	Quantity	Change Point	Remarks
1	ESR2691	Separator-vapour fuel filler	1		50 LE
1	WLL100100	Separator-vapour fuel filler	1	Note (1)	Petrol except 50 LE
2	AB614061L	Screw-self tapping-No 14 x 3/4	2		
2	AB608047L	Screw-self tapping-No 8 x 1/2	2	Note (1)	Petrol
3	WC106041L	Washer-M6-oversize	4		
	MXC1848	Clip	1	Note (1)	Petrol

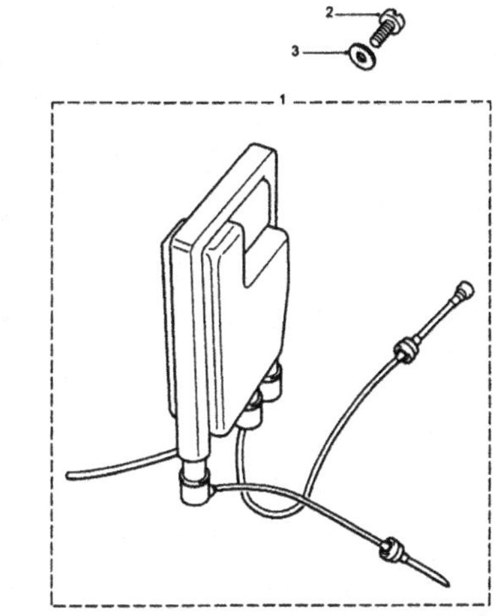

AMJXTA3A

CHANGE POINTS:
(1) From (V) XA 159807

Illus	Part Number	Description	Quantity	Change Point	Remarks
1	NTC2225	Pipe fuel	1		Petrol
2	NTC2227	Connector-straight	1		Petrol
3	NTC2263	Pipe fuel	1		Petrol 110"
3	RRC2487	Pipe fuel	1	Note (1)	V8 Petrol 130"
3	RRC6150	Pipe fuel	1	Note (2)	V8 Petrol 130"
4	NTC2064	Pipe fuel	1		Petrol 110"
4	NTC6750	Pipe fuel	1		Petrol 130"
5	NTC2876	Connector fuel lines	1		Petrol
6	NRC5415	Clip-pipe-double	2		Petrol
7	ETC5340	Elbow fuel tank	1		Petrol
8	CN100168L	Clip-hose	2		Petrol
9	79122	Clip-8mm	4		Petrol

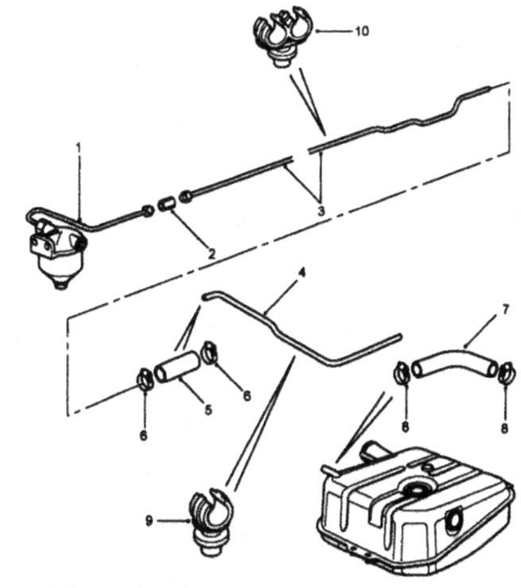

AJJXEA3A

CHANGE POINTS:
(1) To (V) EA 347903
(2) From (V) EA 347904

DEFENDER	GROUP J	Fuel & Emission Systems Fuel-Air Cleaner-Evaporative Loss Twin Tanks Petrol

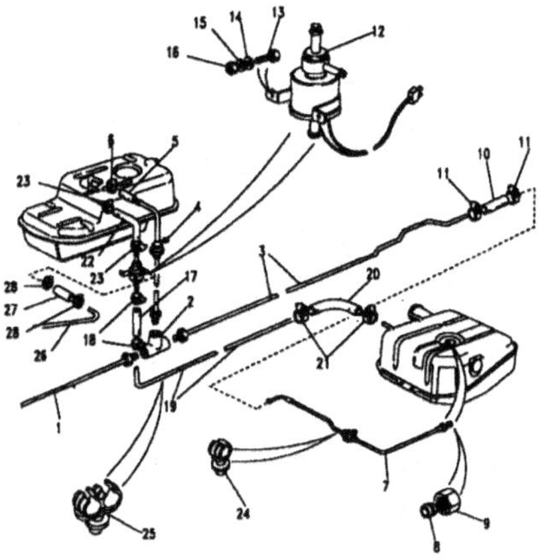

Illus	Part Number	Description	Quantity	Change Point	Remarks
1	NTC2225	Pipe fuel	1		Petrol except 90"
2	NTC2093	T piece	1		Petrol
3	NTC2263	Pipe fuel	1		Petrol
4	NTC6752	Pipe fuel	1		Except Station Wagon
4	NTC6751	Pipe fuel	1		Station Wagon Petrol
5	NTC2876	Connector fuel lines	1		Petrol
6	CN100168L	Clip-hose	2		
7	NTC6750	Pipe fuel	1		
8	NRC9771	Olive-fuel tank pipe	1		
9	NRC9770	Nut-tube-female-M12	1		
10	NTC2876	Connector fuel lines	2		
11	CN100168L	Clip-hose	4		
12	PRC5543	Valve assembly-solenoid	1		
13	FS106201L	Screw-flanged head-M6 x 20	2		
13	SH104201	Screw-hexagonal head-M4 x 20	2		
14	WA104001L	Washer-plain-M4	2		
15	WL104001L	Washer-spring	2		
16	NH104041L	Nut-hexagonal-M4	2		
17	NTC2876	Connector fuel lines	2		
18	CN100168L	Clip-hose	2		
19	NTC2099	Pipe fuel	1		Petrol Defender 110"
19	RRC6716	Pipe fuel	1		Petrol Defender 130"
20	ETC5340	Elbow fuel tank	1		Petrol
21	CN100168L	Clip-hose	2		
22	NTC2097	Hose-fuel	1		
23	CN100168L	Clip-hose	2		
24	79122	Clip-8mm	4		
25	79158	Clip-pipe-double	6		
26	NTC2096	Pipe fuel	1		
27	NTC2876	Connector fuel lines	1		
28	CN100168L	Clip-hose	2		

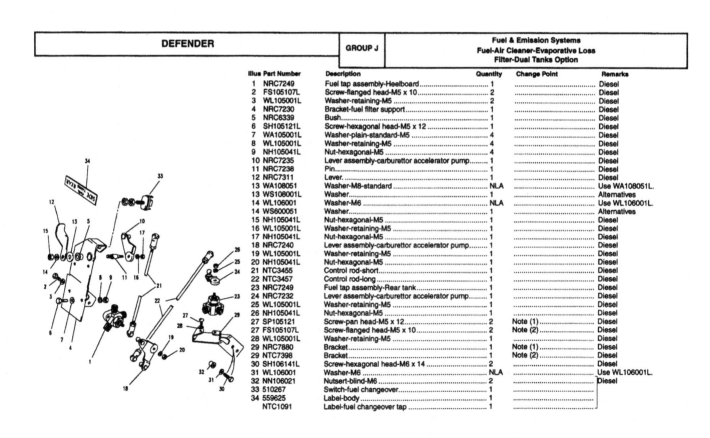

DEFENDER	GROUP J	Fuel & Emission Systems Fuel-Air Cleaner-Evaporative Loss Filter-Dual Tanks Option

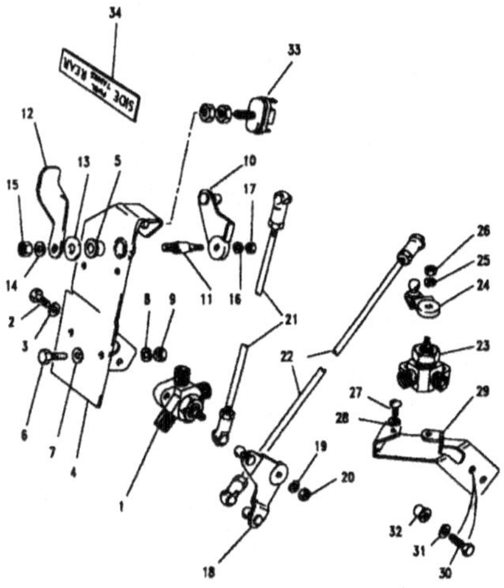

Illus	Part Number	Description	Quantity	Change Point	Remarks
1	NRC7249	Fuel tap assembly-Heelboard	1		Diesel
2	FS105107L	Screw-flanged head-M5 x 10	2		Diesel
3	WL105001L	Washer-retaining-M5	2		Diesel
4	NRC7230	Bracket-fuel filter support	1		Diesel
5	NRC6339	Bush	1		Diesel
6	SH105121L	Screw-hexagonal head-M5 x 12	1		Diesel
7	WA105001L	Washer-plain-standard-M5	4		Diesel
8	WL105001L	Washer-retaining-M5	4		Diesel
9	NH105041L	Nut-hexagonal-M5	4		Diesel
10	NRC7235	Lever assembly-carburettor accelerator pump	1		Diesel
11	NRC7238	Pin	1		Diesel
12	NRC7311	Lever.	1		Diesel
13	WA108051	Washer-M8-standard	NLA		Use WA108051L.
13	WS108001L	Washer	1		Alternatives
14	WL106001	Washer-M6	NLA		Use WL106001L.
14	WS600051	Washer	1		Alternatives
15	NH105041L	Nut-hexagonal-M5	1		Diesel
16	WL105001L	Washer-retaining-M5	1		Diesel
17	NH105041L	Nut-hexagonal-M5	1		Diesel
18	NRC7240	Lever assembly-carburettor accelerator pump	1		Diesel
19	WL105001L	Washer-retaining-M5	1		Diesel
20	NH105041L	Nut-hexagonal-M5	1		Diesel
21	NTC3455	Control rod-short	1		Diesel
22	NTC3457	Control rod-long	1		Diesel
23	NRC7249	Fuel tap assembly-Rear tank	1		Diesel
24	NRC7232	Lever assembly-carburettor accelerator pump	1		Diesel
25	WL105001L	Washer-retaining-M5	1		Diesel
26	NH105041L	Nut-hexagonal-M5	1		Diesel
27	SP105121	Screw-pan head-M5 x 12	2	Note (1)	Diesel
27	FS105107L	Screw-flanged head-M5 x 10	2	Note (2)	Diesel
28	WL105001L	Washer-retaining-M5	1		Diesel
29	NRC7880	Bracket	1	Note (1)	Diesel
29	NTC7398	Bracket	1	Note (2)	Diesel
30	SH106141L	Screw-hexagonal head-M6 x 14	2		Diesel
31	WL106001	Washer-M6	NLA		Use WL106001L.
32	NN106021	Nutsert-blind-M6	2		Diesel
33	510267	Switch-fuel changeover	1		
34	559625	Label-body	1		
	NTC1091	Label-fuel changeover tap	1		

CHANGE POINTS:
(1) To (V) FA 436079
(2) From (V) FA 436080

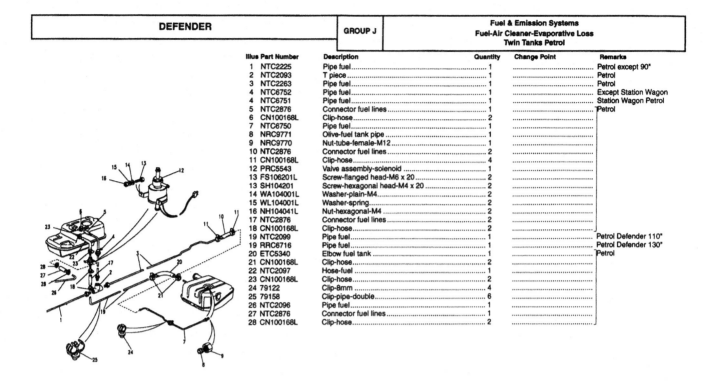

DEFENDER	GROUP J	Fuel & Emission Systems Fuel-Air Cleaner-Evaporative Loss Fuel Filter-Diesel & Diesel Turbo

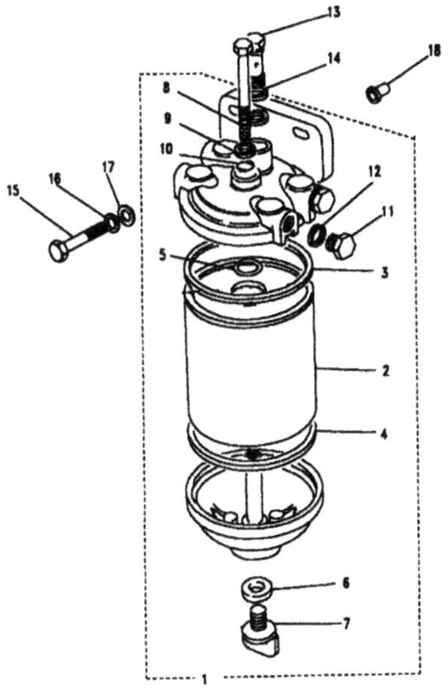

Illus	Part Number	Description	Quantity	Change Point	Remarks
1	563190	ELEMENT-FUEL FILTER DIESEL	1	Note (1)	
2	90517711	• Element-filter	1		
3	AAU9903	• Seal-top	1		
4	AAU9902	• Seal-bottom	1		
5	37H575L	• O ring	1		
6	605011	• Seal-rubber	1		
7	37H7920	• Plug-drain	1		
8	37H8119L	• Bolt	1		
9	522940	• Washer	1		
10	37H770L	Washer-sealing	1	Note (1)	Diesel Turbo
11	517689	Plug-blanking	1	Note (1)	
12	517706	Washer-aluminium	1	Note (1)	
13	13H1515L	Bolt-banjo	1	Note (1)	
14	517976	Washer-copper	1	Note (1)	
15	FS108307L	Screw-flanged head-M8 x 30	2		Diesel Turbo
16	WL108001L	Washer-sprung-M8	2	Note (1)	
17	WA108051L	Washer-8mm	2		
18	NN108021	Nut-blind-M8	2		

CHANGE POINTS:
(1) To (V) MA 962814

DEFENDER	GROUP J	Fuel & Emission Systems Fuel-Air Cleaner-Evaporative Loss Fuel Filter Pipes-Diesel & Diesel Turbo

Illus	Part Number	Description	Quantity	Change Point	Remarks
1	ETC6903	Pipe fuel-lift pump to filter	1	Note (1)	Diesel Naturally Aspirated
1	ERR244	Pipe fuel-lift pump to filter	1	Note (2)	Diesel Naturally Aspirated
1	ETC6903	Pipe fuel-lift pump to filter	1	Note (3)	Diesel Turbo
1	ERR244	Pipe fuel-lift pump to filter	1	Note (4)	Diesel Turbo
2	ETC6901	Pipe fuel-filter to dps pump feed	1		
3	ETC6902	Pipe fuel-dps to pump filter-spill	1		
4	AAU3509	Valve-one way fuel lines	1		
5	517706	Washer-aluminium	1		
6	578293	Clip-hose	6		Sweden

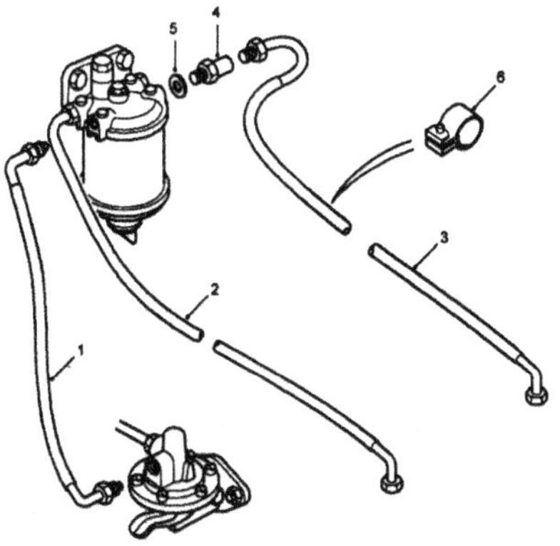

AHJXEC3A

CHANGE POINTS:
(1) To (E)12J 41642C
(2) From (E)12J 41643c
(3) To (E)19J 20835C
(4) From (E)19J 20836C

Fuel Filter-200 TDI

Illus	Part Number	Description	Quantity	Change Point	Remarks
1	NTC1518	FILTER ASSEMBLY-FUEL.-UNHEATED	1		
2	AEU2147L	• Cartridge-diesel fuel filter-unheated	1		
3	AEU2148L	• Screw-bleed-unheated	1		
4	AEU2149L	• Washer-sealing-unheated	1		
5	FS110301L	Screw-flanged head-M10 x 30-top	2		
6	WA110061L	Washer-M10	4		
7	NY110041L	Nut-hexagonal head-nyloc-M10	NLA		Use NY110047L.

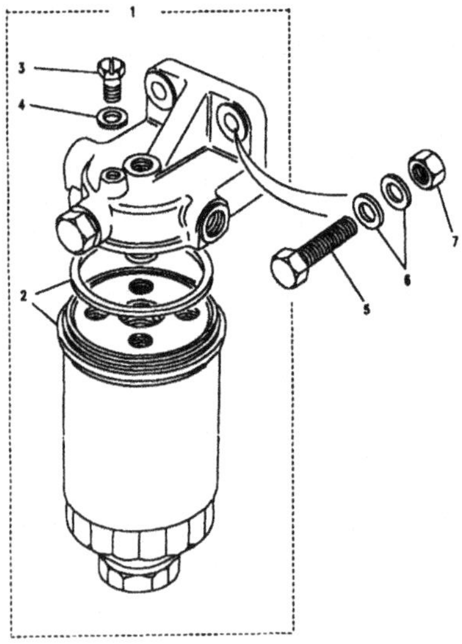

Fuel Filter Pipes-200TDi

Illus	Part Number	Description	Quantity	Change Point	Remarks
1	ESR394	Pipe fuel-lift pump to filter	1	To (V) MA 962814	Diesel TDi
2	NTC3346	Bolt-banjo	2	To (V) MA 962814	
3	ESR354	Washer-copper	4	To (V) MA 962814	
4	ESR395	Pipe fuel-filter to injection pump bolt-banjo	1	To (V) MA 962814	
5	NTC3346	Bolt-banjo	1	To (V) MA 962814	
6	ESR354	Washer-copper	2	To (V) MA 962814	

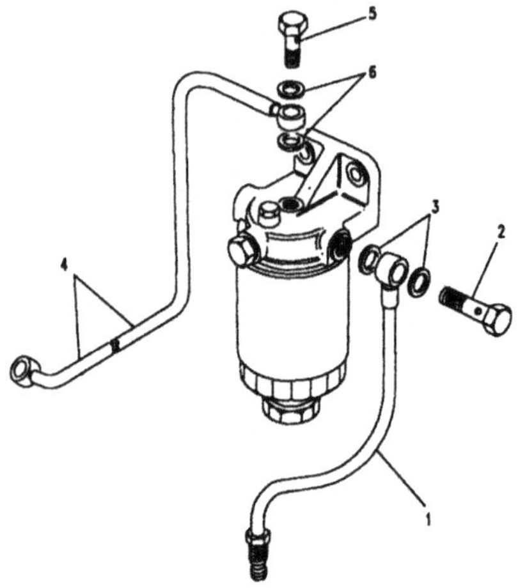

Fuel Filter & Pipes-300TDI

Illus	Part Number	Description	Quantity	Change Point	Remarks
1	NTC1518	FILTER ASSEMBLY-FUEL.-UNHEATED	1		
2	AEU2147L	• Cartridge-diesel fuel filter-unheated	1		
3	AEU2148L	• Screw-bleed-unheated	1		
4	AEU2149L	• Washer-sealing-unheated	1		
5	FS110301L	Screw-flanged head-M10 x 30-top	2		
6	FX110041L	Nut-flange-M10	NLA		Use FX110047L.
7	ESR3118	Pipe fuel	1		
8	ERR1125	Bolt-banjo	1		
9	ESR354	Washer-copper	4		
10	NTC3346	Bolt-banjo	2		
11	ERR894	Washer-sealing	2		
12	ESR3206	Bracket assembly-fuel filter	1		
13	FS108307L	Screw-flanged head-M8 x 30	2		
14	FS108207L	Screw-flanged head-M8 x 20	2		

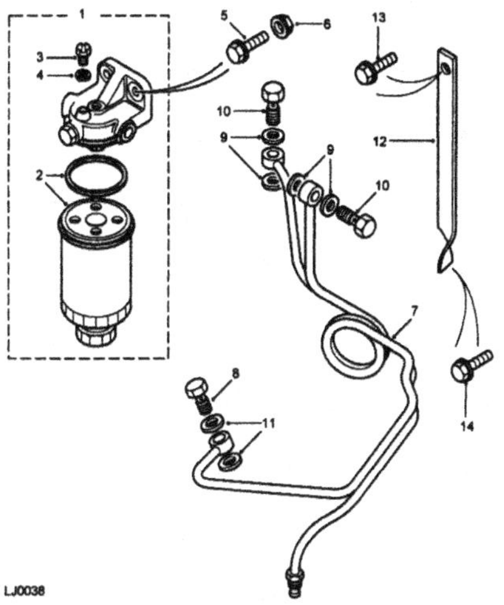
LJ0038

Fuel Filter-V8 & 6 Cylinder Petrol

Illus	Part Number	Description	Quantity	Change Point	Remarks
1	ESR4065	Filter assembly-in line fuel lines	1		V8 EFi
1	ESR4065	Filter assembly-in line fuel lines	1		6 Cylinder 90"
1	NTC6936	Filter assembly-in line fuel lines	1		6 Cylinder 110"
1	WJN101250L	Filter assembly-in line fuel lines	1	Note (1)	V8 Twin Carburettor
2	NTC6937	Bracket-fuel filter	1		V8 EFi
2	NTC6937	Bracket-fuel filter	1		6 Cylinder 90"
2	ESR1935	Bracket-fuel filter	1		6 Cylinder 110"
3	FS108207L	Screw-flanged head-M8 x 20	1	Note (2)	
3	FB108221	Bolt-flanged head-M8 x 110	1	Note (3)	
4	WA108051L	Washer-8mm	2		
5	NN108021	Nut-blind-M8	1		V8 EFi
5	NN108021	Nut-blind-M8	1		6 Cylinder 90"
5	NY108041L	Nut-nyloc-M8	1		6 Cylinder 110"

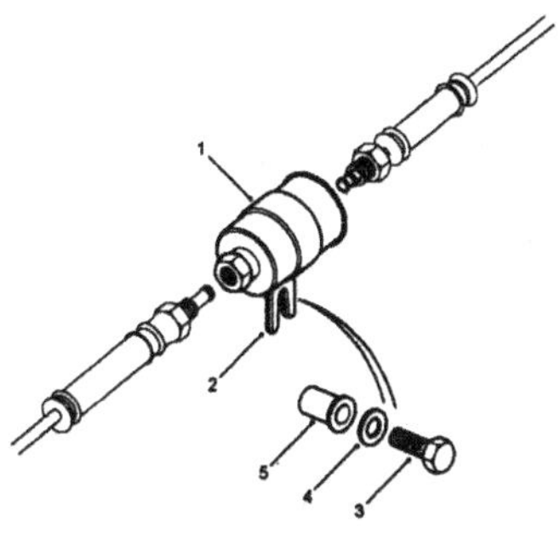
AMJXGA2A

CHANGE POINTS:
(1) From (V) XA 159807
(2) From (V) YA 178325
(3) From (V) YA 178326

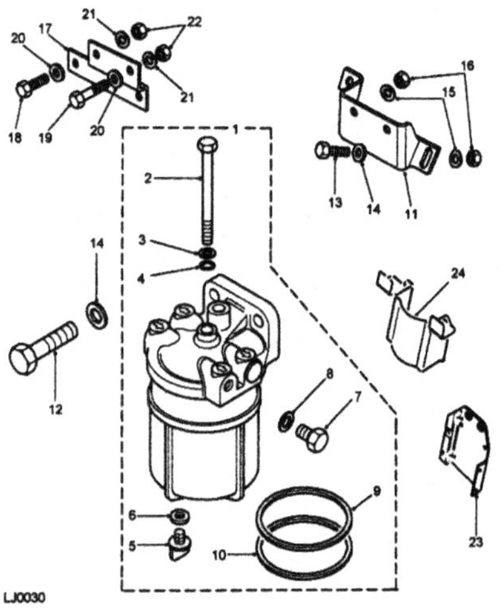

LJ0030

Illus	Part Number	Description	Quantity	Change Point	Remarks
1	562748	Filter/sedimentor assembly-diesel	NLA		Use NRC9708.
1	NRC9708	FILTER/SEDIMENTOR ASSEMBLY-DIESEL	1		
2	37H8119L	• Bolt	1		
3	522940	• Washer	1		
4	37H770	• O ring	1		
5	37H7920	• Plug-drain	1		
6	605011	• Seal-rubber	1		
7	517689	• Plug-blanking	2		
8	517706	• Washer-aluminium	2		
9	AAU9903	• Seal-top	1		
10	AAU9902	• Seal-bottom	1		
11	NRC5623	Bracket-fuel filter support	1		Optional
12	FS108307L	Screw-flanged head-M8 x 30	2		2500 cc
13	FS108207L	Screw-flanged head-M8 x 20	2		
14	WA108051L	Washer-8mm	2		
15	WL108001L	Washer-sprung-M8	2		
16	FN108047L	Nut-flange-flanged head-M8	2		
17	NRC7372	Bracket-fuel filter support	1		Optional
18	FS108257L	Screw-flanged head-M8 x 25	2		
18	FS108307L	Screw-flanged head-M8 x 30	2		Optional
19	FS108207L	Screw-flanged head-M8 x 20	2		Optional
20	WA108051	Washer-M8-standard	NLA		Use WA108051L.
20	WA108051L	Washer-8mm	4		
21	WL108001L	Washer-sprung-M8	4		
22	FN108047L	Nut-flange-flanged head-M8	2		
	NN108021	Nut-blind-M8	1		2500 cc
23	WKT100010	Cover assembly-fuel filter-rear	1	Note (1)	300 TDI
24	WKT100020	Cover assembly-fuel filter-front	1	Note (1)	300 TDI

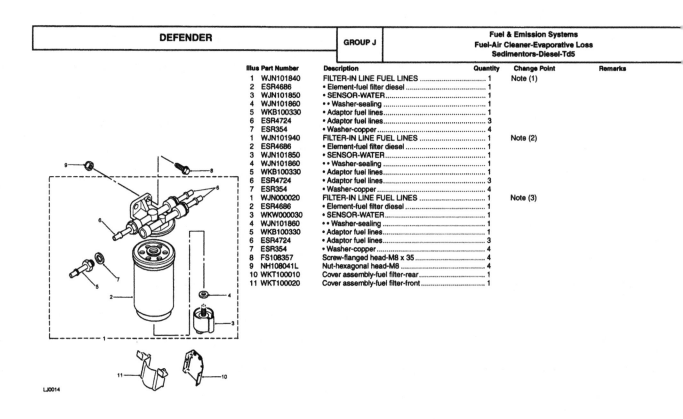

CHANGE POINTS:
(1) From (V) XA 159807

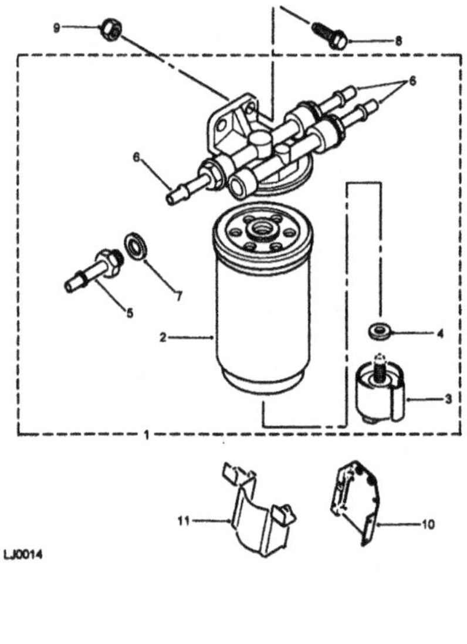

LJ0014

Illus	Part Number	Description	Quantity	Change Point	Remarks
1	WJN101840	FILTER-IN LINE FUEL LINES	1	Note (1)	
2	ESR4686	• Element-fuel filter diesel	1		
3	WJN101850	• SENSOR-WATER	1		
4	WJN101860	• • Washer-sealing	1		
5	WKB100330	• Adaptor fuel lines	1		
6	ESR4724	• Adaptor fuel lines	3		
7	ESR354	• Washer-copper	4		
1	WJN101940	FILTER-IN LINE FUEL LINES	1	Note (2)	
2	ESR4686	• Element-fuel filter diesel	1		
3	WJN101850	• SENSOR-WATER	1		
4	WJN101860	• • Washer-sealing	1		
5	WKB100330	• Adaptor fuel lines	1		
6	ESR4724	• Adaptor fuel lines	3		
7	ESR354	• Washer-copper	4		
1	WJN000020	FILTER-IN LINE FUEL LINES	1	Note (3)	
2	ESR4686	• Element-fuel filter diesel	1		
3	WKW000030	• SENSOR-WATER	1		
4	WJN101860	• • Washer-sealing	1		
5	WKB100330	• Adaptor fuel lines	1		
6	ESR4724	• Adaptor fuel lines	3		
7	ESR354	• Washer-copper	4		
8	FS108357	Screw-flanged head-M8 x 35	4		
9	NH108041L	Nut-hexagonal head-M8	4		
10	WKT100010	Cover assembly-fuel filter-rear	1		
11	WKT100020	Cover assembly-fuel filter-front	1		

CHANGE POINTS:
(1) To (V) YA 600724
(2) From (V) 1A 600725 To (V) ZA 622305
(3) From (V) 1A 622306

Illus	Part Number	Description	Quantity	Change Point	Remarks
1	ETC7193	Duct assembly air cleaner to elbow-S.U.	1		
2	ERC3915	Hose-air duct/aircleaner	2		
3	RTC3519	Clip-hose	4		
4	ERC5247	Elbow-carburettor air inlet	2		
5	ERC3956	Hose-air cleaner	1		
7	ERC3894	Adaptor-air cleaner	1		
8	ERC3899	Seal air intake	1		
9	RTC3519	Clip-hose	1		
10	ETC7199	Hose assembly-breather	1		
11	CN100308L	Clip-hose-30mm	2		
12	594594	Tie-cable-White.-4.6 x 385mm-inside serated	1		
13	ETC7201	Adapter-crankcase breather	1		
14	ERC6878	Valve-air control	1		
15	ETC7189	Hose assembly-breather	1		
16	ETC7188	Flame trap-crankcase breather	1		
17	611092	Hose breather-rocker cover to flame trap-RH	1		
18	611097	Hose breather-carburettor to flame trap-RH	1		

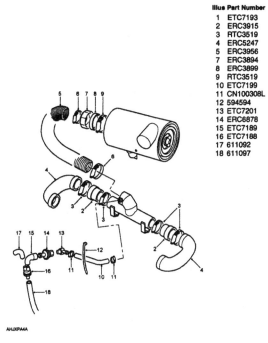

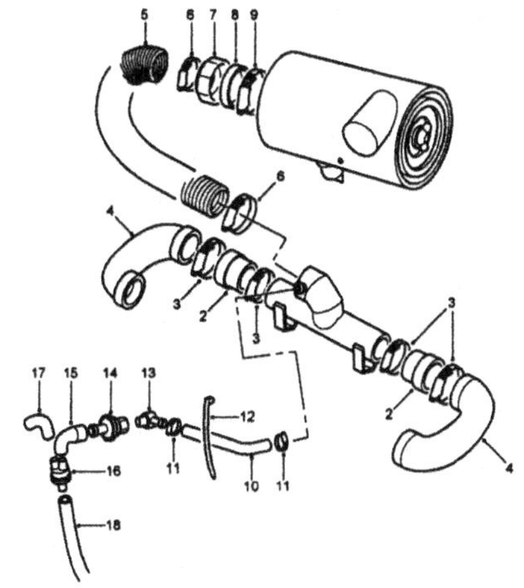

AHJXPA4A

Illus	Part Number	Description	Quantity	Change Point	Remarks
1	ERC5247	Elbow-carburettor air inlet	2		
2	ERC5453	Duct air cleaner to elbow	1		
3	ERC5052	Duct-elbow induction system	2		
4	RTC3518	Clip-hose	1		
5	4594	Washer	2		
6	603851	Grommet	2		
7	ERC5401	Pipe-air cleaner case	1	Note (1)	
7	ERC4074	Pipe-air cleaner case	1	Note (2)	
8	CA600424	Clip	2		
9	ERC3899	Seal air intake	1		
10	ERC5400	Adaptor-air cleaner	1		
11	RTC3502	Clip	1		

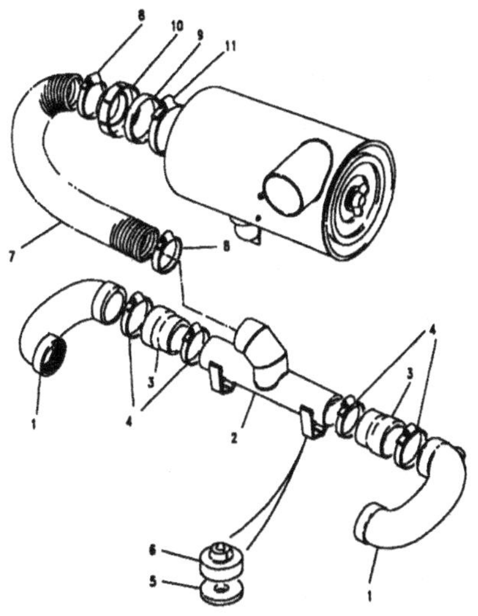

CHANGE POINTS:
(1) To (V) LA 939975
(2) From (V) MA 939976

Illus	Part Number	Description	Quantity	Change Point	Remarks
1	MWC2501	Grille-cold air intake adaptor induction system	1	Note (1)	
2	359526	Bush	5	Note (1)	
3	MWC1826	Duct assembly-fresh air-upper	1	Note (1)	
4	MWC1827	Duct assembly-fresh air-lower	1	Note (1)	
5	MUC2417	Valve assembly air intake	1	Note (1)	
6	AB608047L	Screw-self tapping-No 8 x 1/2	5	Note (1)	
7	AFU1926L	Nut-caged	5		

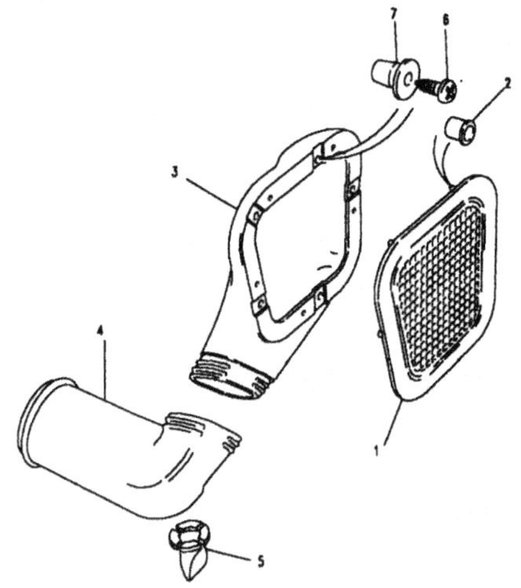

CHANGE POINTS:
(1) To (V) MA 962814

Illus	Part Number	Description	Quantity	Change Point	Remarks
1	BTR6188	Grille-cold air intake adaptor induction system	1		
2	ESR3173	Duct air-upper-RH	1		
3	ESR3175	Duct air-lower-RH	1		
4	ESR2315	Bracket-tube support fresh air intake	1		
5	AB608041	Screw-self tapping	5		
6	AFU1926L	Nut-caged	5		
7	AJU1136	Stud	5	Note (1)	
8	594594	Tie-cable-White.-4.6 x 385mm-inside serated	1		
9	359526	Bush	5		

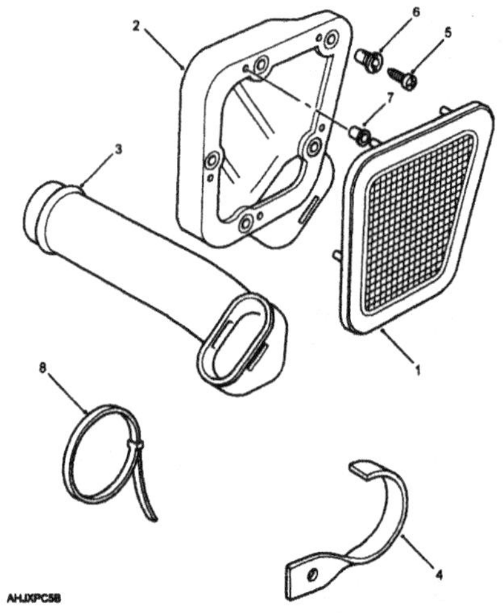

CHANGE POINTS:
(1) From (V) MA 939976

Illus	Part Number	Description	Quantity	Change Point	Remarks
1	BTR6188	Grille-cold air intake adaptor induction system	1		
2	AB608041	Screw-self tapping	5		
3	AFU1926L	Nut-caged	5		
4	AJU1136	Stud	5		
5	2943312	Duct-water separator to air cleaner air intake	1		
6	2943311	Duct-air intake-air cleaner	1		

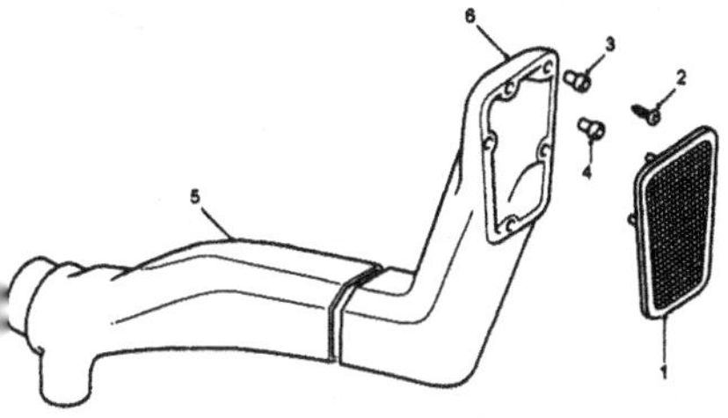

AKJXPC5B

Illus	Part Number	Description	Quantity	Change Point	Remarks
1	AFU1085L	Canister charcoal	1		
2	NRC5844	Bracket-canister support	1		Australia except 90"
2	ESR1277	Bracket-canister support	1		
3	ESR1278	BRACKET ASSEMBLY-CANISTER SUPPORT	1		90"
4	NRC4776	• Clamp	1		
5	SH106141L	• Screw-hexagonal head-M6 x 14	2		
6	SH106351L	• Screw-hexagonal head-M6 x 35	1		
7	WL106001L	• Washer-sprung-M6	2		
8	NY106041L	• Nut-hexagonal head-nyloc-M6	NLA		Use NY106047L.
9	CP108081L	Clip-p-8mm	1		
10	79122	Clip-8mm	3		
11	NRC5818	Pipe-rear elbow	1		Station Wagon
12	NRC9862	Pipe-vent fuel lines-front elbow to rear-LHD	1		Station Wagon
13	NRC9863	Pipe-vent fuel lines-rear elbow to front-LHD	1		Station Wagon
	NTC1304	Pipe-canister to catch tank	1		
14	577458	Elbow-rubber	2		
15	AFU1077L	Clip-swivel	6		
15	NTC3333	Clip-swivel	5		
16	NRC5415	Clip-pipe-double	2		V8
17	79158	Clip-pipe-double	1		
	NTC1310	Clip-fuel pipe edge	3		

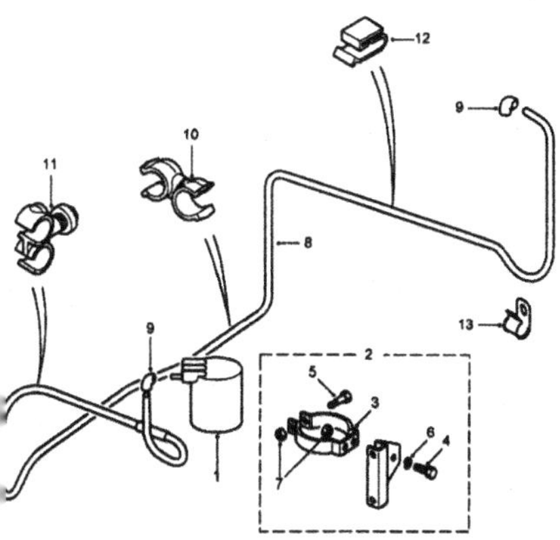

AHJXTA3A

Illus	Part Number	Description	Quantity	Change Point	Remarks
1	ESR4222	CANISTER ASSEMBLY CHARCOAL	1		
2	STC3602	• Bracket assembly-charcoal canister	1		
3	ESR3141	Pipe assembly-canister to separator	1		
4	ESR3663	Hose-charcoal canister to engine purge	1		
5	WJM10006L	Clamp-hose fuel lines	1		
6	AFU1077	Clip-swivel	1		
7	ESR4525	Bracket-purge valve mounting	1		

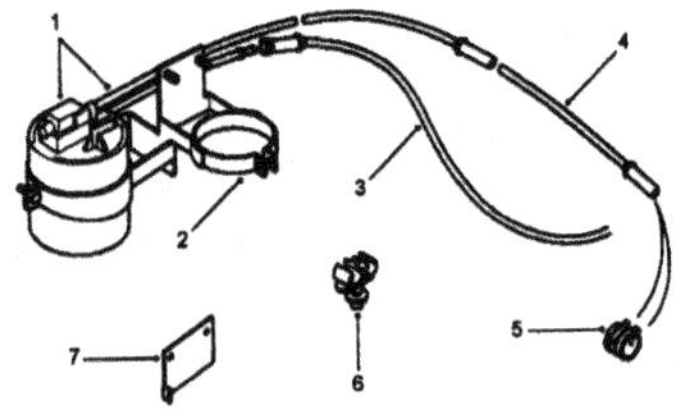

AMJXTA2B

Illus	Part Number	Description	Quantity	Change Point	Remarks
1	WLH100600	Hose-filler fuel filler-petrol	1	Note (1)	V8 Petrol Gulf States
2	NRC2159	Connector fit	1	Note (1)	V8 Petrol Gulf States
3	NRC2652	T piece	1	Note (1)	V8 Petrol Gulf States
4	CP105081	Clip-p	1	Note (1)	V8 Gulf States
5	611110	Hose-crankcase breather flexible	1	Note (1)	V8 Gulf States
6	CP106081	Clip	2	Note (1)	V8 Gulf States
7	577458	Elbow-rubber	2	Note (1)	V8 Gulf States
8	NRC2015	Pipe	1		Petrol Gulf States
9	592326	Catcher-fuel filter fuel tank	1	Note (1)	V8 Gulf States
	NRC2087	Bracket-front	2	Note (1)	V8 Gulf States
	SH105121	Screw-hexagonal head-M5 x 12	3	Note (1)	V8 Gulf States
	WA105001L	Washer-plain-standard-M5	3	Note (1)	V8 Gulf States
	NN105011	Nut	3	Note (1)	V8 Gulf States
	MRC5695	Washer	6	Note (1)	V8 Gulf States
	NRC2195	Pipe catch-Pipe	1	Note (1)	V8 Gulf States
	543589	Clip	2	Note (1)	V8 Gulf States
	NH106041L	Nut-hexagonal-nyloc-M6	6	Note (1)	V8 Gulf States
	NRC2089	Bracket-air cleaner	2	Note (1)	V8 Gulf States
	SE106161	Screw	2	Note (1)	V8 Gulf States
	FS106167L	Screw-flanged head-flanged head-M6 x 16	6	Note (1)	V8 Gulf States
	WL106001L	Washer-sprung-M6	6	Note (1)	V8 Gulf States
	302532	Nut-spiralok	2	Note (1)	V8 Gulf States
	320045	Bolt	2	Note (1)	V8 Gulf States

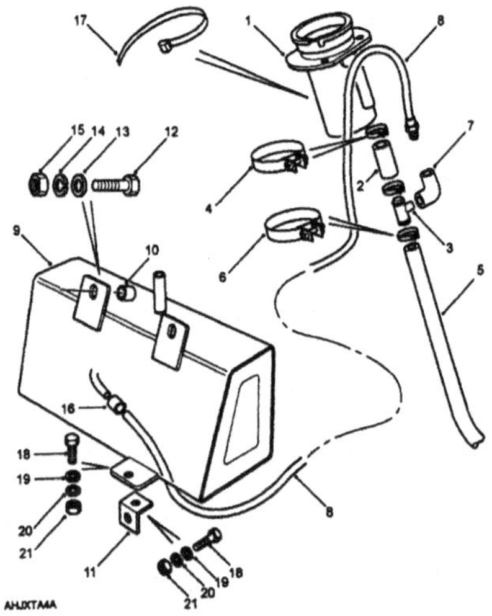

AHJXTA4A

CHANGE POINTS:
(1) From (V) XA 159807

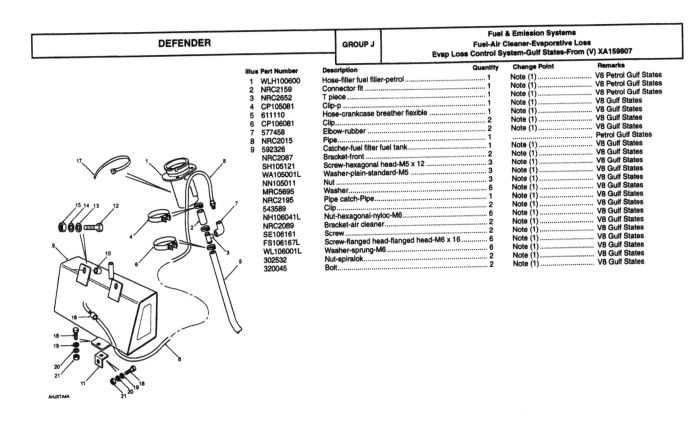

Evap Loss Hoses-4 Cyl Petrol

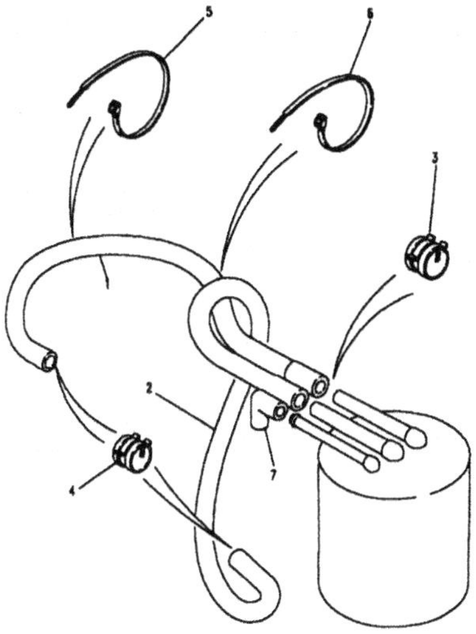

Illus	Part Number	Description	Quantity	Change Point	Remarks
1	ETC6932	Hose-carburettor vent-carburetter to canister	1		
2	ETC5397	Hose-fuel-engine to canister	1		
3	UKC3798L	Clip-hose	2		
4	UKC3803L	Clip-hose	2		
5	C45099	Tie-cable	1		
6	C45099	Tie-cable	1		
7	577458	Elbow-rubber	1		
8	ESR3170	Bracket fusebox	1		
9	ESR3167	CANISTER & BRACKET ASSEMBLY CHARCOAL	1		
	NRC4776	• Clamp	1		
	ESR1277	• Bracket-canister support	1		

Evap Loss Hoses-V8

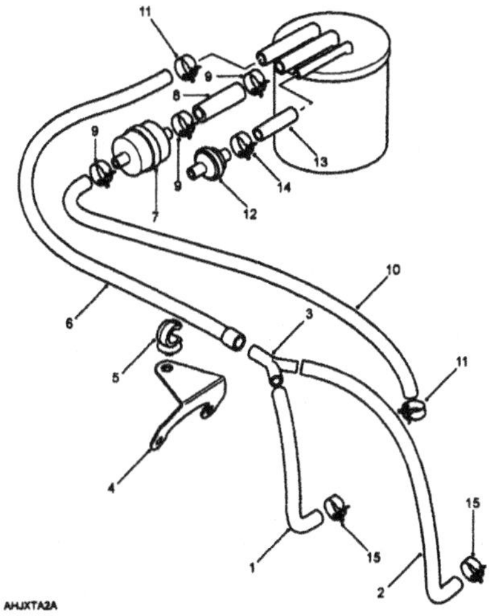

AHJXTA2A

Illus	Part Number	Description	Quantity	Change Point	Remarks
1	NTC3763	Hose-Y piece to carburettor-110mm	1		
2	NTC3764	Hose-Y piece to carburettor-293mm	1		
3	566724L	Y-piece	1		
4	NTC3862	Bracket	1		
5	NTC3863	Clip-hose	1		
6	NTC3766	Hose-moulded-evaporator fuel	1		
7	606168	Filter assembly-in line fuel lines	1		
8	ERC4176	Hose-fuel	1		RHD
8	ETC5397	Hose-fuel	1		LHD
9	UKC3794L	Clip-hose	3		
10	ETC5398	Hose assembly-breather	1		RHD
10	ERC3955	Hose assembly-breather	1		LHD
11	UKC3798L	Clip-hose	2		
12	NTC3891	Valve-pressure vacuum	1		
13	ERC4176	Hose-fuel	1		
14	UKC3795L	Clip-hose-12.7mm	1		
15	UKC3803L	Clip-hose	2		

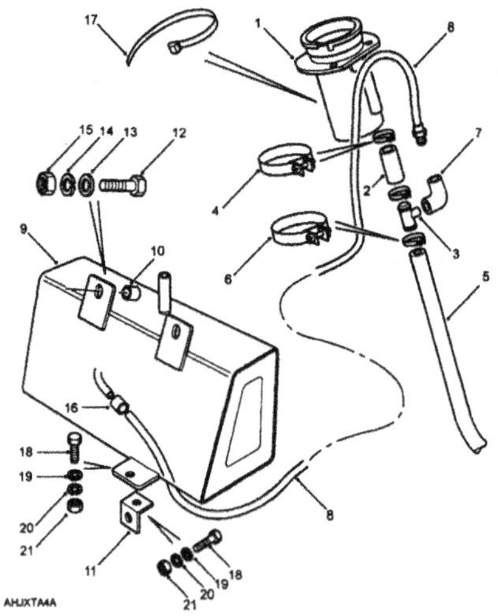

Illus	Part Number	Description	Quantity	Change Point	Remarks
1	NRC9423	Filler assembly-fuel	NLA		Use STC4236. 90°
1	NRC2536	Filler assembly-fuel	1		Except 90°
1	STC4236	FILLER ASSEMBLY-FUEL-NON-VENTED	1		90°
	STC4237	• Cap-filler fuel filler-non-vented-3 lug	1		
2	NRC2159	Connector fit	1		
3	NRC2652	T piece	1		
4	CN100168L	Clip-hose	3		
5	NRC2214	Hose-fuel filler pipe breather	1		Except Australia
5	ESR1287	Hose-fuel filler pipe breather	1		Australia
6	572548	Clip-hose	NLA		Use CN100168L. Station Wagon
6	603887	Clip-hose	1		
7	577458	Elbow-rubber	1		
8	ESR419	Pipe-breather fuel tank-fuel filler to catch tank	1		Chassis Cab 130"
8	ESR421	Pipe-breather fuel tank-fuel filler to catch tank	1		Crew Cab 130"
8	NRC9508	Pipe-breather fuel tank-fuel filler to catch tank	1		110"
8	NTC1305	Pipe-breather fuel tank-fuel filler to catch tank	1		90"
9	NRC9472	Catcher-fuel filter fuel tank	1		Except Station Wagon
9	592326	Catcher-fuel filter fuel tank	1		Station Wagon
10	NTC1306	Spacer	1		
11	NTC1307	Bracket support	1		
12	SH108301L	Screw-hexagonal head-M8 x 30	NLA		Use FS108307L.
12	FS108251L	Screw-flanged head-M8 x 25	NLA		Use FS108257L.
12	FS108307L	Screw-flanged head-M8 x 30	2		90"
13	WA108051L	Washer-8mm	2		Except 90"
13	AFU1079	Washer-M8	2		90"
14	WL108001L	Washer-sprung-M8	2		
15	FN108041L	Nut-flange-M8	NLA		Use FN108047L.
16	577459	Hose-charcoal canister to valve purge	1		

Illus	Part Number	Description	Quantity	Change Point	Remarks
17	C45099	Tie-cable-Pipe to tie bar	1		
17	UKC6683L	Tie-cable-To fuel filler neck	1		HICAP
18	FS108161L	Screw-flanged head-M8 x 16	2		
19	WA108051L	Washer-8mm	2		
20	WL108001L	Washer-sprung-M8	2		
21	FN108041L	Nut-flange-M8	NLA		Use FN108047L.
	NTC3333	Clip-swivel	4		130"
	79122	Clip-8mm	2		

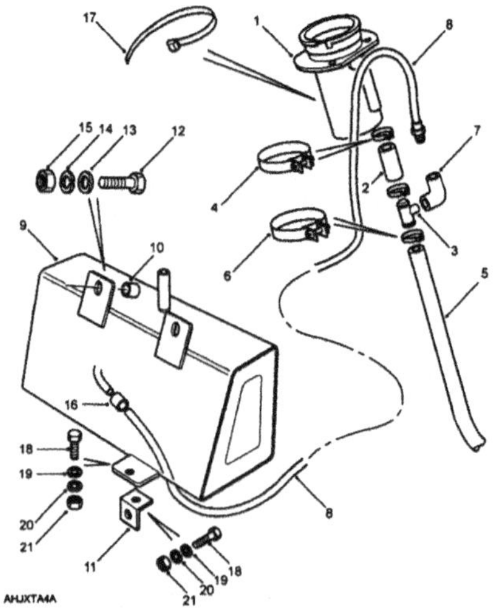

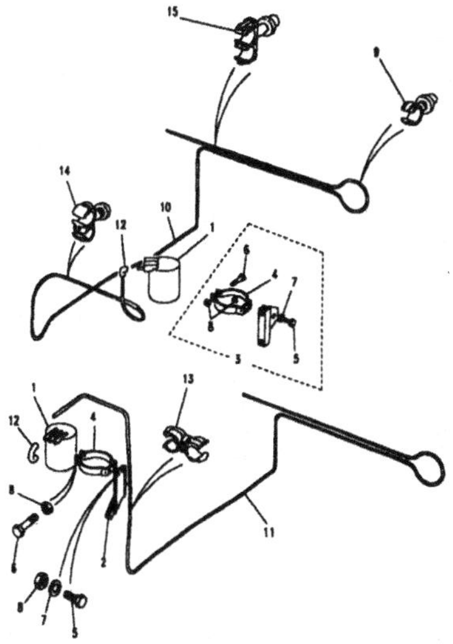

Illus	Part Number	Description	Quantity	Change Point	Remarks
1	AFU1085	Canister charcoal	NLA		Use AFU1085L
1	AFU1085L	Canister charcoal	1		
2	ESR1278	BRACKET ASSEMBLY-CANISTER SUPPORT	1		
4	NRC4776	• Clamp	1		
	ESR1277	• Bracket-canister support	1		
3	ESR3167	CANISTER & BRACKET ASSEMBLY CHARCOAL	1		
4	NRC4776	• Clamp	1		
	ESR1277	• Bracket-canister support	1		
5	SH106141L	Screw-hexagonal head-M6 x 14	2		
6	SH106351L	Screw-hexagonal head-M6 x 35	2		
7	WL106001	Washer-M6	NLA		Use WL106001L.
8	NY106041L	Nut-hexagonal head-nyloc-M6	NLA		Use NY106047L.
9	79122	Clip-8mm	4		
10	NTC1048	Pipe fuel-Canister to catch tank	1		
11	NRC9507	Pipe fuel-Canister to catch tank	1		Australia
12	577458	Elbow-rubber	2		
13	NTC3333	Clip-swivel	7		
14	NRC5415	Clip-pipe-double	2		V8
15	79158	Clip-pipe-double	3		
	CP108081L	Clip-p-8mm	1		

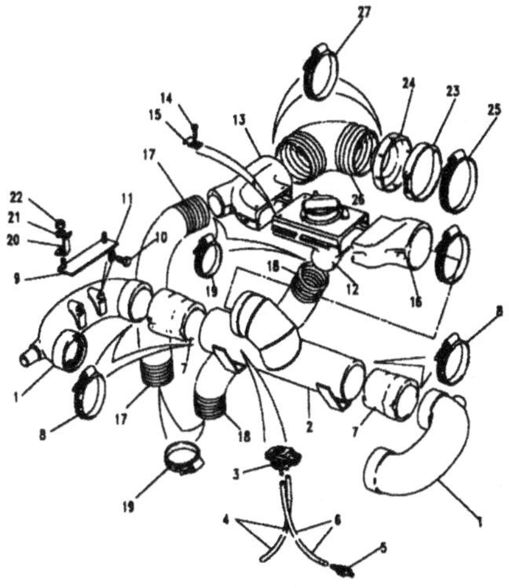

Illus	Part Number	Description	Quantity	Change Point	Remarks
1	ERC7882	Elbow-RH	1		V8 Petrol
1	ERC7881	Elbow-LH	1		V8 Petrol
1	ERC9037	Elbow	2		V8 secondary air injection
2	ERC7144	Duct assembly air cleaner to elbow	1		
3	ERC6399	Sensor-temperature	1		
4	613601	Pipe fuel	1		V8 Petrol
4	614892	Pipe fuel-sensor to non return valve	2	Note (1)	V8 secondary air injection
5	614866	Valve-air control	1		
6	614891	Pipe-carburettor vacuum-sensor to valve-31"	1		
7	ERC5052	Duct-elbow induction system-duct to valve	2		
8	RTC3518	Clip-hose	4		
9	ERC3890	Bracket	1		
10	SH108121L	Screw-hexagonal head-M8 x 12	2		
10	SH505041L	Screw-hexagonal head-5/16UNC x 1/2	2		
11	WL108001L	Washer-sprung-M8	1		
12	ERC4591	Valve assembly air intake	1		
13	ETC4639	Connector-inlet manifold adaptor	1		Except air conditioning
13	ETC5147	Connector-inlet manifold adaptor	1		Air conditioning
14	AB608047L	Screw-self tapping-No 8 x 1/2	4		
14	AB610031L	Screw-10 x 3/8-self tapping	4		
15	216708	Clip	1		
16	ERC3884	Connector-inlet manifold adaptor	1		
17	ERC4293	Pipe fuel	1		
18	ERC4294	Pipe fuel	1		
19	CN100508L	Clip-hose-50mm-less spring assist	4		
20	ERC3891	Clip	2		
21	WL600041L	Washer-plain-M8	2		
22	NH604041L	Nut-hexagonal head-coarse thread-1/4UNF	2		
23	ERC3899	Seal air intake	1		
24	ERC5400	Adaptor-air cleaner	1		
25	RTC3502	Clip	1		
26	ERC4074	Pipe-air cleaner case	1		Except 90"
26	ERC5401	Pipe-air cleaner case	1		90"
	ERC3956	Hose-air cleaner	1		
27	CA600424	Clip	2		

CHANGE POINTS:
(1) To (V) MA 962814

DEFENDER

GROUP J

Fuel & Emission Systems
Fuel-Air Cleaner-Evaporative Loss
Roll Over Anti-Spill System-To (V) MA962814

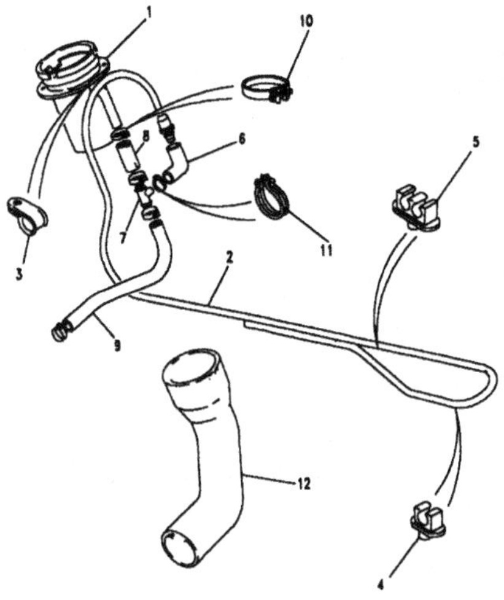

Illus	Part Number	Description	Quantity	Change Point	Remarks
1	NRC9423	Filler assembly-fuel	NLA		Use STC4236.
1	STC4236	FILLER ASSEMBLY-FUEL-NON-VENTED	2		
	STC4237	• Cap-filler fuel filler-non-vented-3 lug	1		
2	NRC2572	Pipe fuel	1		
3	AEU1448	Clip-p	1		
4	79123	Clip-pipe-single	2		
5	AFU1008	Clip-pipe-double	2		
6	577458	Elbow-rubber	1		
7	NRC2652	T piece	1		
8	NRC2159	Connector fit	1		
9	MLH100410	Hose-fuel filler pipe breather	1	Note (1)	
9	ESR1287	Hose-fuel filler pipe breather	1	Note (2)	
10	572839	Clip-hose	4		
11	565656	Clip-hose-double wire	1		
12	NRC9291	Hose-filler fuel filler	1		

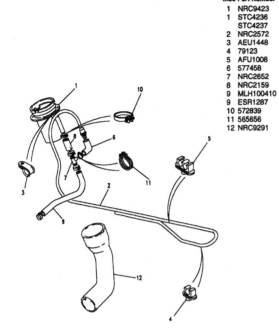

CHANGE POINTS:
(1) To (V) MA 962814
(2) From (V) MA 962815

DEFENDER

GROUP J

Fuel & Emission Systems
Exhaust Gas Recirculation
Valve & Pipes-TDi

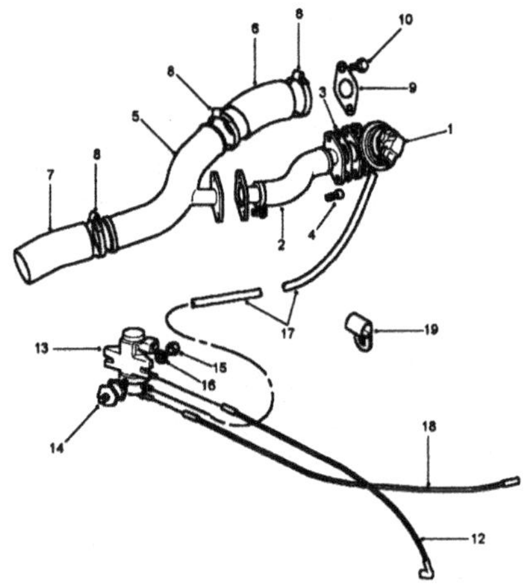

LB0045

Illus	Part Number	Description	Quantity	Change Point	Remarks
1	ERR4047	Valve-exhaust gas recirculation engine exhaust	1	Note (1)	
1	WAV100330	Valve-exhaust gas recirculation engine exhaust	1	Note (2)	
2	ERR3583	Pipe-exhaust gas recirculation	1	Note (3)	
2	ERR5731	Pipe-exhaust gas recirculation	1	Note (4)	90"
2	ERR5732	Pipe-exhaust gas recirculation	1		110"
3	ERR3319	Gasket-exhaust gas recirculation valve to pipe	1		
4	SS108201	Screw-hexagon socket-M8 x 20	2		
5	ERR3579	Pipe-exhaust gas recirculation-15gm	1		
6	ERR3580	Pipe-exhaust gas recirculation	1		
7	ERR3581	Pipe-exhaust gas recirculation	1		
8	PYC101120	Clip-hose	NLA		Use PYC101120L.
8	PYC101120L	Clip-hose-60mm	2		
9	ERR7173	Gasket-exhaust gas recirculation pipe to cylinder head	1		
10	SS108251	Screw-hexagon socket-M8 x 25	2		
12	ESR3105	Hose-modulator valve to air cleaner-Green	1		90"
12	ERR4862	Hose-modulator valve to air cleaner-White.-Green	1	Note (5)	Except 90"
13	ERR3314	Valve-solenoid-exhaust gas recirculation diesel	1		
14	ERR2337	Mounting-rubber	2		
15	NY106047L	Nut-hexagonal head-nyloc-M6	2		
16	WA106001L	Washer-M6	2		
17	ERR5055	Pipe-solenoid valve/exhaust gas recirculation diesel	NLA		Use ESR3533.
17	ESR3533	Pipe-solenoid valve/exhaust gas recirculation diesel-Blue.	1		
17	ESR3308	Pipe-solenoid valve/exhaust gas recirculation diesel-Black	1		
18	ESR3107	Pipe-vacuum exhaust gas recirculation valve solenoid-turbo hose-White.	1		
19	50639	Clip-p-3/8"	1		

CHANGE POINTS:
(1) To (E)25L 08852A
(2) From (E)25L 08853A
(3) To (E)21L 46223A
(4) From (E)21L 46224A
(5) From (V) LA 081991

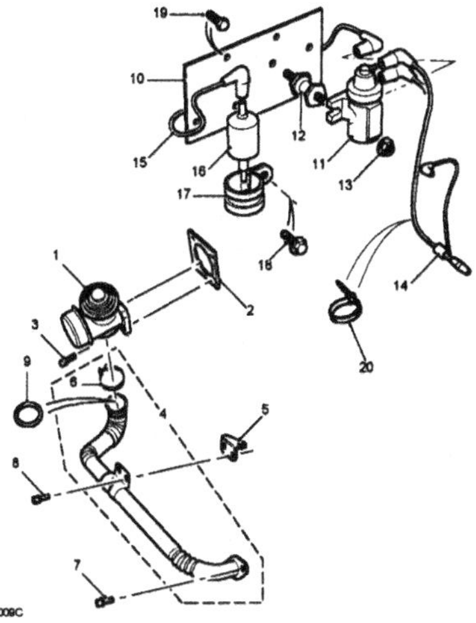

LJ0009C

Illus	Part Number	Description	Quantity	Change Point	Remarks
1	WAV100270	Valve-exhaust gas recirculation engine exhaust	1		
2	ERR6620	Gasket-exhaust gas recirculation valve to inlet manifold	1		
3	FS106207L	Screw-flanged head-M6 x 20	4		
4	WAP101220	Pipe assembly-exhaust gas recirculation	1		
5	WAU100320	Bracket-exhaust gas recirculation pipe support	1		
6	WAC100020	Clip-support-exhaust gas recirculation pipe	1	Note (2)	
6	WAC100030	Clip-support-exhaust gas recirculation pipe	1	Note (3)	
7	WAO100000	Bolt-special EGR pipe to exhaust manifold	2		
7	LYP000050L	Bolt-torx drive-M8-Stainless	2		
8	FS106107L	Screw-flanged head-M6 x 10	2		
9	WAL100240	Gasket-exhaust gas recirculation valve to pipe	1		

CHANGE POINTS:
(2) To (V) XA 163789
(3) From (V) XA 163790

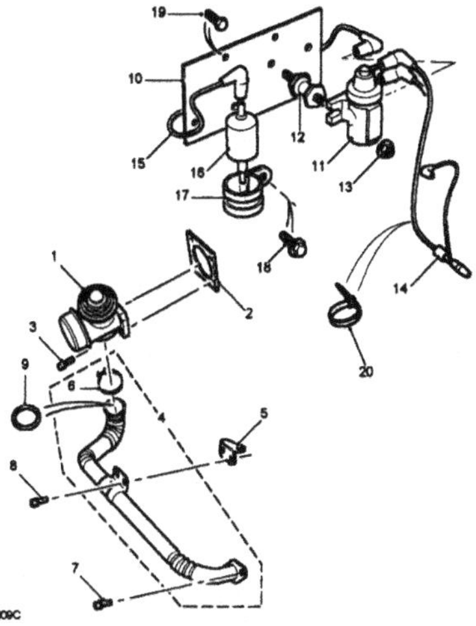

LJ0009C

Illus	Part Number	Description	Quantity	Change Point	Remarks
10	WAU100160	Bracket-exhaust gas recirculation valve engine exhaust	1	Note (1)	
10	WAU100470	Bracket-exhaust gas recirculation valve engine exhaust	1	Note (2)	
11	MSG100110	Valve assembly-exhaust gas recirculation engine exhaust	1		
12	ERR2337	Mounting-rubber	2		
13	FN106047L	Nut-flange-M6	5		
14	WAP100970	Pipe-vacuum exhaust gas recirculation valve solenoid	1	Note (1)	
14	WAP101340	Pipe-vacuum exhaust gas recirculation valve solenoid	1	Note (2)	
15	WAP100980	Pipe-exhaust gas recirculation-Green	1	Note (1)	
15	WAP101390	Pipe-exhaust gas recirculation	1	Note (2)	
16	ESR4323	Filter-exhaust gas recirculation solenoid control valve	1	Note (1)	
17	WYC100470	Clip-p	1	Note (1)	
18	FS106167L	Screw-flanged head-flanged head-M6 x 16	1	Note (1)	
19	FS106167L	Screw-flanged head-flanged head-M6 x 16	2		

CHANGE POINTS:
(1) To (V) XA 175541
(2) From (V) XA 175542

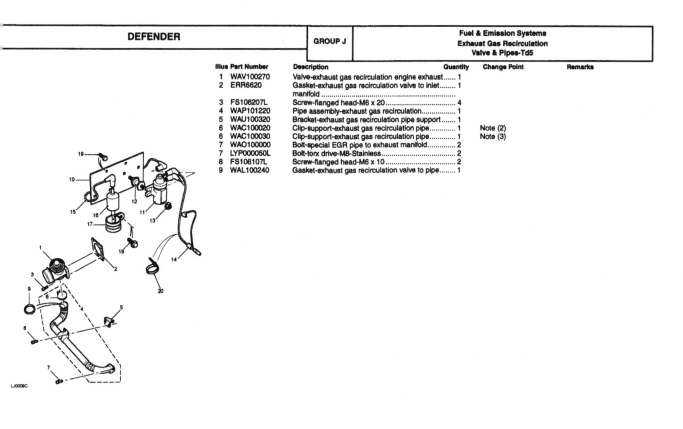

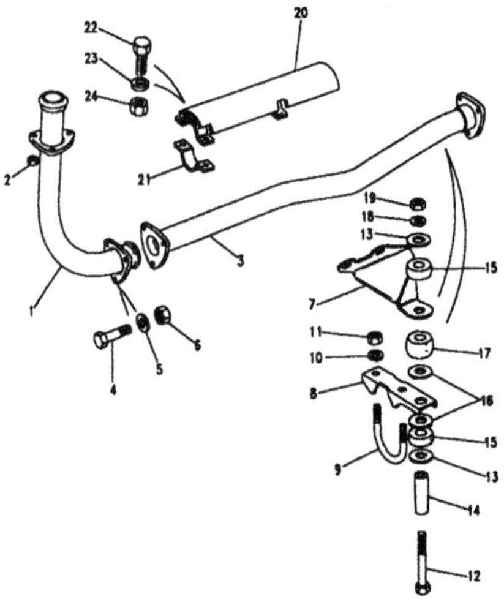

Illus	Part Number	Description	Quantity	Change Point	Remarks
1	NRC8911	Downpipe assembly exhaust system	1	Note (1)	2250 cc
1	NTC2036	Downpipe assembly exhaust system	1		2500 cc
2	AFU2778L	Nut-M10	3		
3	NRC6436	Intermediate assembly exhaust system	1		2250 cc
3	NTC1664	Intermediate assembly exhaust system	1		2500 cc
4	FB108081L	Bolt-flanged head-M8 x 40	3		
5	WL108001L	Washer-sprung-M8	3		
6	FN108041L	Nut-flange-M8	NLA		Use FN108047L.
7	NRC7778	Bracket-exhaust mounting	NLA		Use ESR169.
7	ESR169	Bracket-exhaust mounting	1		
8	NRC6467	Clamp-exhaust intermediate pipe assembly	1	Note (1)	
9	NRC6466	Bolt-u	1		
10	WL108001L	Washer-sprung-M8	2		
11	FN108041L	Nut-flange-M8	NLA		Use FN108047L.
12	SH108701L	Screw-M8 x 70-hexagonal head	1		
13	WP105L	Washer-plain	2		
14	NRC5403	Spacer	1		
15	572166	Bush-exhaust mounting rubber outer	2		
16	572168	Washer	NLA		Use ESR3263.
16	ESR3263	Washer	2		
17	572167	Bush-exhaust mounting rubber middle	1	Note (1)	
18	WL108001L	Washer-sprung-M8	1		
19	FN108041L	Nut-flange-M8	NLA		Use FN108047L.
20	NRC9733	Heatshield engine exhaust	1		2250 cc
21	NRC9722	Clamp	2		
20	NTC5205	Heatshield engine exhaust	1		2500 cc
21	NTC2278	Clamp	1		
22	FS108207L	Screw-flanged head-M8 x 20	4		
23	WL108001L	Washer-sprung-M8	4		
24	FN108041L	Nut-flange-M8	NLA		Use FN108047L.

CHANGE POINTS:
(1) To (V) BA 267063

Exhaust Petrol
Front-4 Cylinder-From (V) AA267064

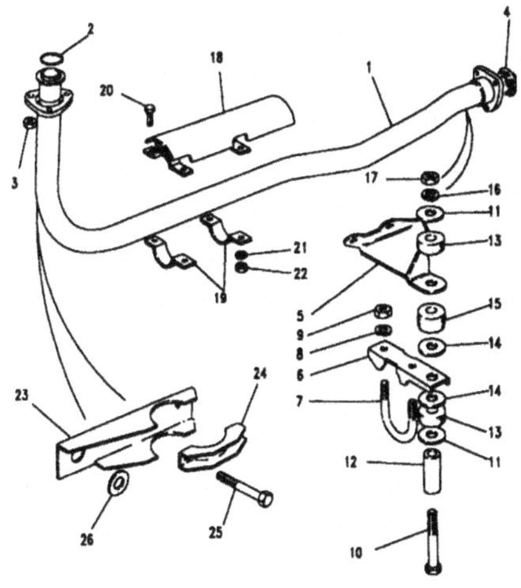

Illus	Part Number	Description	Quantity	Change Point	Remarks
1	NTC1794K	Downpipe assembly exhaust system	NLA		Use NTC1794.
1	NTC1794	Downpipe assembly exhaust system	1	Note (1)	
2	ETC5337	Gasket exhaust system-manifold to downpipe	1		
3	AFU2778L	Nut-M10	3		
4	NTC1030	Olive-intermediate pipe to rear pipe	1		
5	NRC7778	Bracket-exhaust mounting	NLA		Use ESR169.
5	ESR169	Bracket-exhaust mounting	1		
6	NRC6467	Clamp-exhaust intermediate pipe assembly	1	Note (2); Note (3)	
6	90575748	Clamp-exhaust intermediate pipe assembly	1	Note (4); Note (5)	
7	NRC6466	Bolt-u-downpipe support	1	Note (2); Note (3)	
7	NRC6374	Bolt-u-downpipe support	1	Note (4); Note (5)	
8	WL108001L	Washer-sprung-M8	2		
9	FN108041L	Nut-to bracket support-flange-M8	NLA		Use FN108047L.
10	SH108701L	Screw-M8 x 70-hexagonal head	1		
11	WP105L	Washer-plain	2		
12	NRC5403	Spacer	1		
13	572166	Bush-exhaust mounting rubber outer	2		
14	ESR3263	Washer	1	To (V) MA 951419	90"
15	572167	Bush-exhaust mounting rubber middle	1		
16	WL108001L	Washer-sprung-M8	1		
17	FN108041L	Nut-to chassis-flange-M8	NLA		Use FN108047L.
18	NTC5205	Heatshield engine exhaust	1		
19	NTC2278	Clamp	2		
20	FS108207L	Screw-bracket to bracket-flanged head-M8 x 20	4		
21	WL108001L	Washer-sprung-M8	4		
22	FN108041L	Nut-bracket to bracket-flange-M8	NLA		Use FN108047L.
23	NTC4580	Bracket-support downpipe	1	Note (6); Note (7); Note (8); Note (9)	
24	NTC4586	Clamp-exhaust downpipe to manifold	1		
25	BH108131L	Bolt-bracket to body-hexagonal head-M8 x 65	2		
26	WC112081L	Washer-plain-M12 x 28	1		

CHANGE POINTS:
(1) From (V) AA 267064
(2) To (V) 290071 110"
(3) To (V) 290508 90"
(4) From (V) EA 290072 110"
(5) From (V) EA 290509 90"
(6) From (V) EA 290509 To (V) EA 338105 90"
(7) From (V) FA 405285 90"
(8) From (V) EA 290072 To (V) EA 338367 110"
(9) From (V) FA 405333 110"

Exhaust Petrol
Front-Petrol V8-Non Catalyst

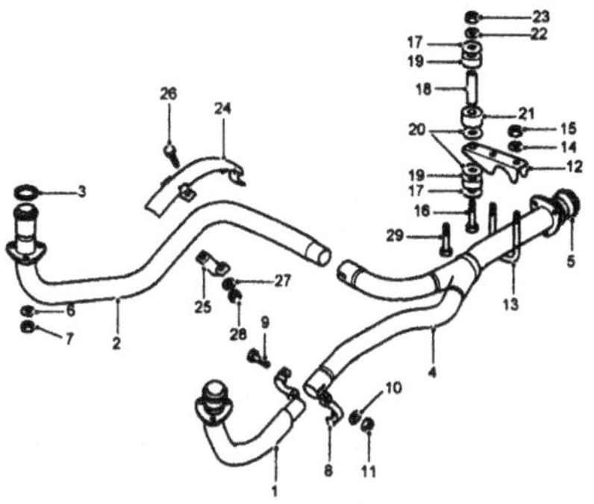

LK0014

Illus	Part Number	Description	Quantity	Change Point	Remarks
1	NRC4219	Downpipe assembly exhaust system-LH	1	Note (1)	
2	NRC6432	Downpipe assembly exhaust system-RH	1		
1	NTC1133K	Downpipe assembly exhaust system-LH	1	Note (2)	
2	NTC1136K	Downpipe assembly exhaust system-RH	1		
1	NRC4219	Downpipe assembly exhaust system-LH	1	Note (3)	
2	NRC6432	Downpipe assembly exhaust system-RH	1		
3	ERC2734	Gasket exhaust system-manifold to downpipe	2	Note (2)	
4	NRC4218	Junction-'y' piece exhaust system	1	Note (1)	
4	NTC2726	Junction-'y' piece exhaust system	1	Note (4)	
5	NTC1030	Olive-exhaust downpipe	1		
6	WM600051L	Washer-spring-5/16"	6	Note (5)	
7	NH605041L	Nut-hexagonal head-5/16UNF	6		
7	NV605041L	Nut-hexagonal head-5/16UNF	6	Note (3)	
7	NTC1966	Nut-self locking-M8	6		
8	90575511	Clamp-'y' piece exhaust	4		
9	BH108091L	Bolt-M8 x 45	4		
10	WL108001L	Washer-sprung-M8	4		
11	NH108041L	Nut-hexagonal head-M8	4		
11	FN108041L	Nut-flange-M8	NLA		Use FN108047L.
12	90575748	Clamp	1		
13	NRC6374	Bolt-u	1		
14	WL108001L	Washer-sprung-M8	2		
15	FN108041L	Nut-flange-M8	NLA		Use FN108047L.
16	SH108701L	Screw-M8 x 70-hexagonal head	1		90"
29	BH108141L	Bolt-bracket to body-hexagonal head-M8 x 70	1		
29	FB108141L	Bolt-bracket to body-flanged head-M8 x 70	1		Except 90"
17	3682	Washer-plain	2		Except 90"
17	WP105L	Washer-plain	2		90"
18	592072	Spacer	1		Except 90"
18	NRC5403	Spacer	1		90"
19	572166	Bush-exhaust mounting rubber outer	2		
20	572168	Washer	NLA	Note (6)	Use ESR3263.
20	ESR3263	Washer	2	Note (7)	
21	572167	Bush-exhaust mounting rubber middle	1		

CHANGE POINTS:
(1) To (V) 267907
(2) From (V) 267908 To (V) FA 404321
(3) From (V) FA 404322
(4) From (V) 267908
(5) To (V) FA 404321
(6) To (V) MA 951418
(7) From (V) MA 951419

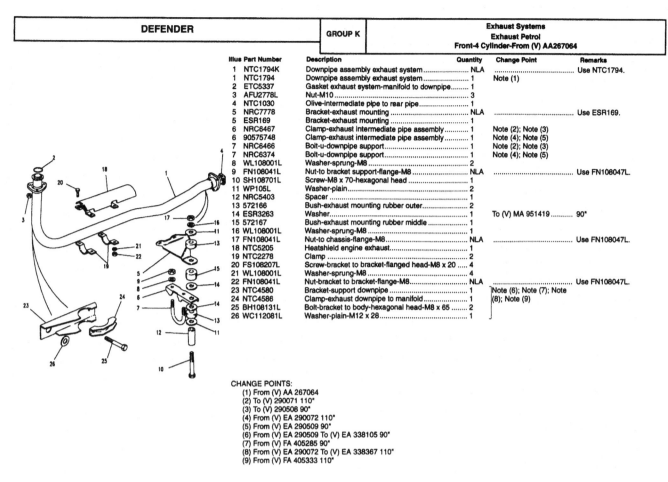

DEFENDER

GROUP K

Exhaust Systems
Exhaust Petrol
Front-Petrol V8-Non Catalyst

Illus	Part Number	Description	Quantity	Change Point	Remarks
22	WL108001L	Washer-sprung-M8	1		
23	NH108041L	Nut-hexagonal head-M8	4		Except 90"
23	FN108041L	Nut-flange-M8	NLA		Use FN108047L.
24	NRC9724	Heatshield engine exhaust	2		
25	NRC9722	Clamp-exhaust intermediate pipe assembly	4		
26	FS108207L	Screw-flanged head-M8 x 20	8	Note (1)	
26	FS108207L	Screw-flanged head-M8 x 20	8		
27	WL108001L	Washer-sprung-M8	8		
28	FN108041L	Nut-flange-M8	NLA		Use FN108047L.

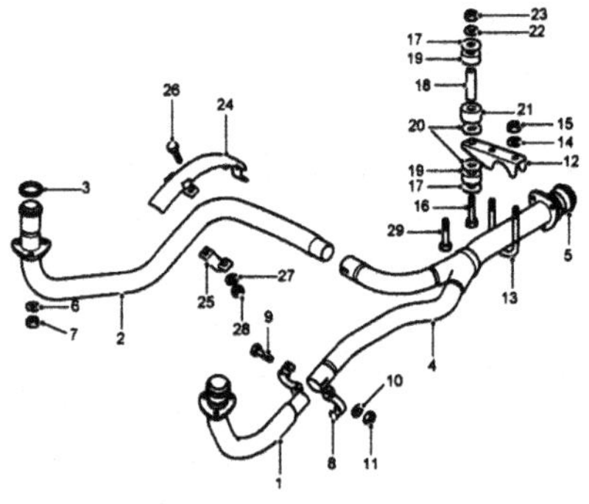

LK0014

CHANGE POINTS:
(1) To (V) 267907

DEFENDER

GROUP K

Exhaust Systems
Exhaust Petrol
Front & Rear-Petrol V8 EFI 4.0L-Catalyst

Illus	Part Number	Description	Quantity	Change Point	Remarks
1	ESR4106	Downpipe assembly exhaust system	1		
2	ETC4524	Gasket exhaust system-manifold to downpipe	2		
3	ERR4245	Nut-M8	6		
4	CRC4579L	Olive-exhaust pipe joint flange	6		
5	ESR2687	Intermediate assembly exhaust system	1		Except 50 LE
5	WCE104630	Intermediate assembly exhaust system	1		50 LE 90"
6	NV110041L	Nut-M10	2		
7	WDV100240	Rear assembly exhaust system	1		Except 50 LE
7	WCG102940	Rear assembly exhaust system	1		50 LE
8	NV110041L	Nut-M10	2		
8	NV110041L	Nut-M10	3		50 LE
9	ESR4227	Heatshield-catalyst exhaust system-LH	1		
10	ESR4226	Heatshield-catalyst exhaust system-RH	1		
11	ANR3138	Heatshield assembly exhaust-downpipe	1		
12	ANR3227	Heatshield-bracket	1		
13	WA110061L	Washer-M10	1		
14	FN110047	Nut-flange-flange-M10	1		
15	AMR6244	Sensor-oxygen multi point injection	4		
16	AMR4238	Bracket assembly-sensor mounting	2		
17	AMR5419	Clip-cable	1		
18	ERR5194	Clip-edge harness	2		
19	FS108161L	Screw-flanged head-M8 x 16	1		
20	PRC2979	Bracket-clipping-steel	2		
21	YYC103160	Clip-cable	2		
22	ESR95	Bracket-mounting-exhaust-rear	1		Except 50 LE
22	ESR3294	Bracket-mounting-exhaust-rear	1		50 LE
23	ESR360	Bracket exhaust system-rear	1		Except 50 LE
23	ESR101	Bracket exhaust system-rear	1		50 LE

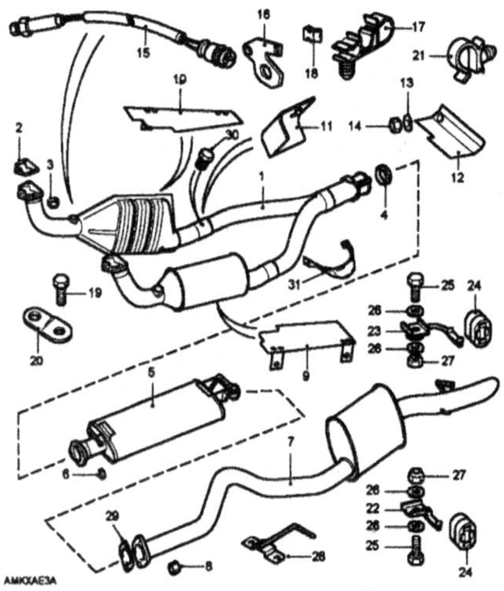

AMKXAE3A

DEFENDER

GROUP K

Exhaust Systems
Exhaust Petrol
Front & Rear-Petrol V8 EFi 4.0L-Catalyst

Illus	Part Number	Description	Quantity	Change Point	Remarks
24	ESR3172	Mounting-rubber exhaust system-front & rear	2		
25	FS108251L	Screw-flanged head-M8 x 25	NLA		Use FS108257L.
26	3663	Washer	4		
27	NV108041L	Nut-M8	2		
28	ESR4438	Bracket assembly-intermediate exhaust mounting	1	Note (1)	
28	WCU101320	Bracket assembly-intermediate exhaust mounting	1	Note (2)	
29	ESR3737	Gasket exhaust system-intermediate to rear pipe	1		
30	WYB10005	Plug-blanking	2		
31	ERR6382	Heatshield-starter motor	1		

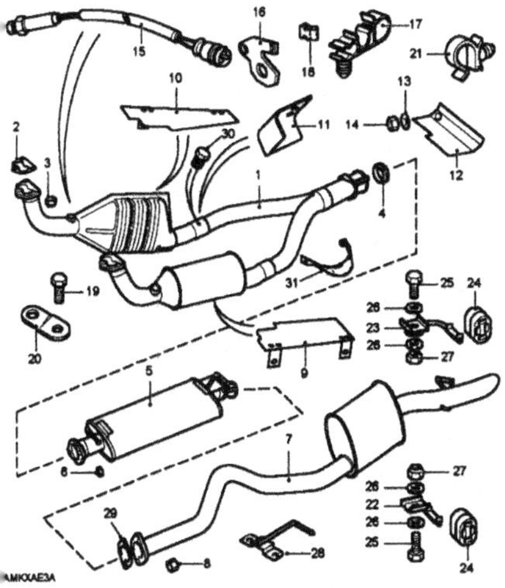
AMKXAE3A

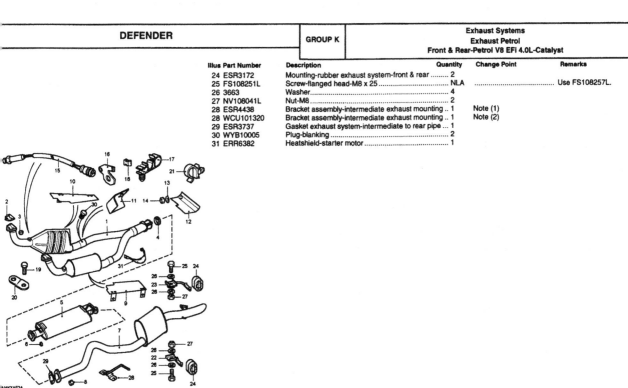

CHANGE POINTS:
(1) To (V) XA 171675
(2) From (V) XA 171676

DEFENDER

GROUP K

Exhaust Systems
Exhaust Petrol
Rear-90-To AA232010 (Soft top) & AA253494 (Hard top)

Illus	Part Number	Description	Quantity	Change Point	Remarks
1	NRC8888	Silencer assembly exhaust system	1	Note (1)	
2	NRC8889	Rear assembly exhaust system	1		
	NRC8238	Finisher-trim exhaust tailpipe	1		
3	FB108081L	Bolt-flanged head-M8 x 40	6		
4	WL108001L	Washer-sprung-M8	6		
5	FN108041L	Nut-flange-M8	NLA		Use FN108047L.
6	SH108701L	Screw-M8 x 70-hexagonal head	2		
7	WP105L	Washer-plain	4		
8	NRC5403	Spacer	2		
9	572166	Bush-exhaust mounting rubber outer	4		
10	572168	Washer	NLA		Use ESR3263.
10	ESR3263	Washer	4		
11	572167	Bush-exhaust mounting rubber middle	2	Note (1)	
12	WL108001L	Washer-sprung-M8	2		
13	FN108041L	Nut-flange-M8	NLA		Use FN108047L.

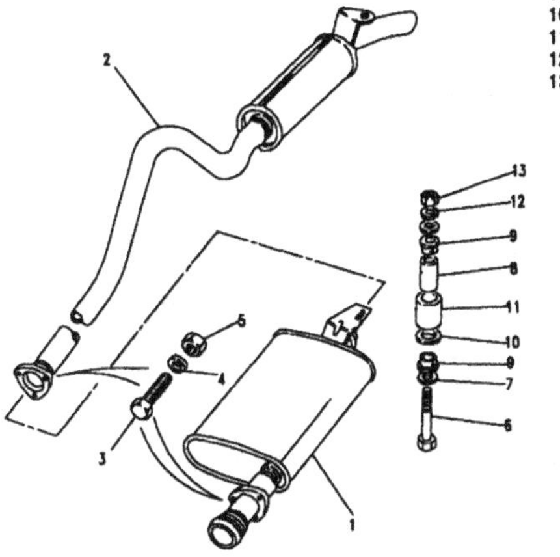

CHANGE POINTS:
(1) To (V) AA 232010 Soft Top; To (V) AA 253494 Hard Top

Exhaust Systems
Exhaust Petrol
Rear-90-From (V) AA232011 (Soft top) & AA253495 (Hard top) To AA267063

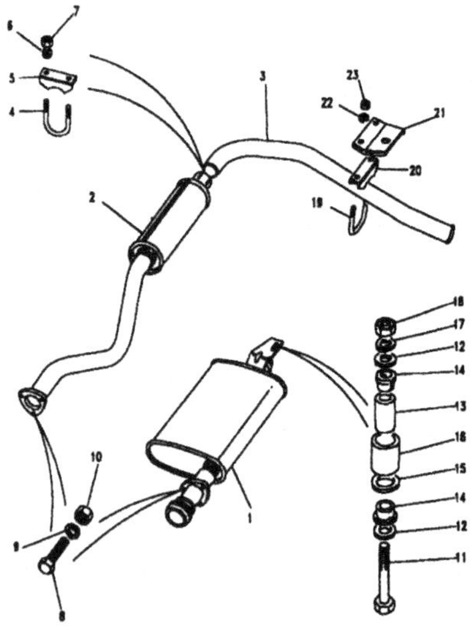

Illus	Part Number	Description	Quantity	Change Point	Remarks
1	NRC8888	Silencer assembly exhaust system	1	Note (1)	
2	NTC1150	Rear assembly exhaust system	1		
3	NTC1149	Tailpipe exhaust system	1		
4	NTC1311	Bolt-u	1		
5	NTC1312	Clamp-tail pipe to rear exhaust	1		
6	WL108001L	Washer-sprung-M8	2	Note (2); Note (3)	
7	FN108041L	Nut-flange-M8	NLA	Note (1)	Use FN108047L.
8	FB108081L	Bolt-flanged head-M8 x 40	6		
9	WL108001L	Washer-sprung-M8	2	Note (2); Note (3)	
10	FN108041L	Nut-flange-M8	NLA	Note (1)	Use FN108047L.
11	SH108701L	Screw-M8 x 70-hexagonal head	2		
12	WP105L	Washer-plain	4		
13	NRC5403	Spacer	2		
14	572166	Bush-exhaust mounting rubber outer	4		
15	572168	Washer	NLA		Use ESR3263.
15	ESR3263	Washer	4		
16	572167	Bush-exhaust mounting rubber middle	2	Note (1)	
17	WL108001	Washer-sprung-M8	NLA		Use WL108001L.
18	FN108041L	Nut-flange-M8	NLA		Use FN108047L.
19	NTC1311	Bolt-u	1		
20	NTC1312	Clamp-tail pipe	1		
21	NTC1313	Bracket-exhaust mounting/lashing hanger	1		
22	WL108001	Washer-sprung-M8	NLA	Note (2); Note (3)	Use WL108001L.
23	FN108041L	Nut-flange-M8	NLA	Note (1)	Use FN108047L.

CHANGE POINTS:
(1) From (V) AA 232011 To (V) BA 267063 Soft Top; From (V) AA 253495 To (V) BA 267063 Hard Top
(2) From (V) AA 232011 To (V) BA 267063 Soft Top
(3) From (V) AA 253495 To (V) BA 267063 Hard Top

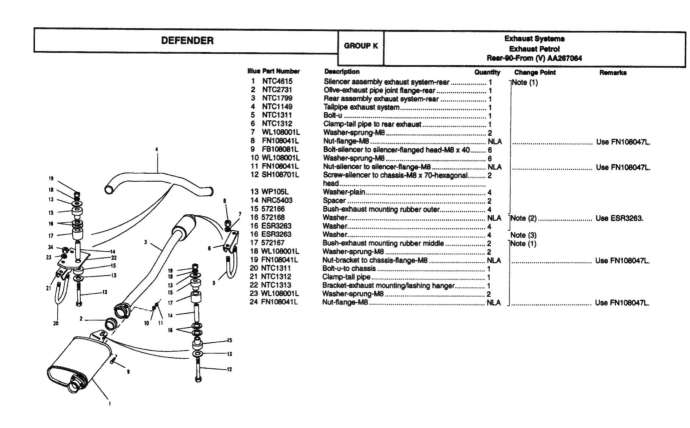

Exhaust Systems
Exhaust Petrol
Rear-90-From (V) AA267064

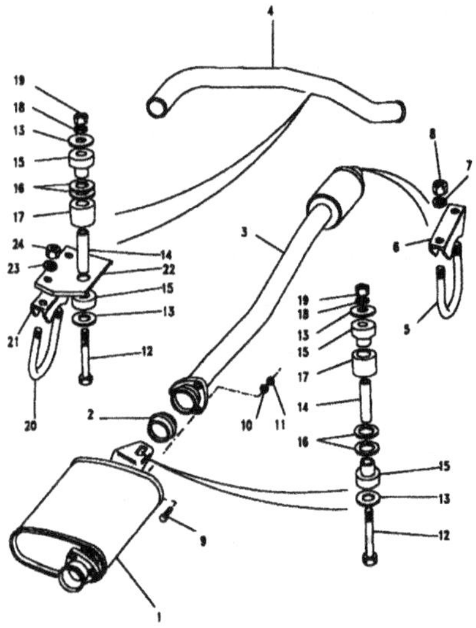

Illus	Part Number	Description	Quantity	Change Point	Remarks
1	NTC4615	Silencer assembly exhaust system-rear	1	Note (1)	
2	NTC2731	Olive-exhaust pipe joint flange-rear	1		
3	NTC1799	Rear assembly exhaust system-rear	1		
4	NTC1149	Tailpipe exhaust system	1		
5	NTC1311	Bolt-u	1		
6	NTC1312	Clamp-tail pipe to rear exhaust	1		
7	WL108001L	Washer-sprung-M8	2		
8	FN108041L	Nut-flange-M8	NLA		Use FN108047L.
9	FB108081L	Bolt-silencer to silencer-flanged head-M8 x 40	6		
10	WL108001L	Washer-sprung-M8	6		
11	FN108041L	Nut-silencer to silencer-flange-M8	NLA		Use FN108047L.
12	SH108701L	Screw-silencer to chassis-M8 x 70-hexagonal head	2		
13	WP105L	Washer-plain	4		
14	NRC5403	Spacer	2		
15	572166	Bush-exhaust mounting rubber outer	4		
16	572168	Washer	NLA	Note (2)	Use ESR3263.
16	ESR3263	Washer	4		
16	ESR3263	Washer	4	Note (3)	
17	572167	Bush-exhaust mounting rubber middle	2	Note (1)	
18	WL108001L	Washer-sprung-M8	2		
19	FN108041L	Nut-bracket to chassis-flange-M8	NLA		Use FN108047L.
20	NTC1311	Bolt-u-to chassis	1		
21	NTC1312	Clamp-tail pipe	1		
22	NTC1313	Bracket-exhaust mounting/lashing hanger	1		
23	WL108001L	Washer-sprung-M8	2		
24	FN108041L	Nut-flange-M8	NLA		Use FN108047L.

CHANGE POINTS:
(1) From (V) AA 267064
(2) From (V) AA 267064 To (V) MA 951418
(3) From (V) MA 951419

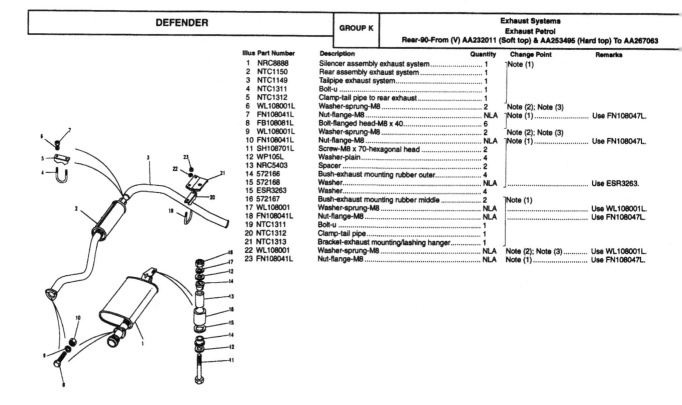

DEFENDER	GROUP K	Exhaust Systems Exhaust Petrol Rear-110-4Cyl & V8

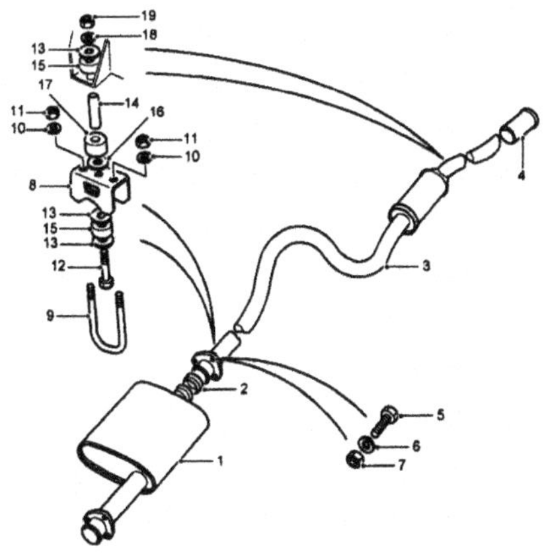

AJKXAA3A

Illus	Part Number	Description	Quantity	Change Point	Remarks
1	NTC4614	Silencer assembly exhaust system	1		
2	NTC2731	Olive-exhaust pipe joint flange-rear	1		Rest of World
2	NTC1030	Olive-exhaust pipe joint flange	1		Switzerland
3	NTC1800	Rear assembly exhaust system	1		Rest of World
3	NTC4617	Rear assembly exhaust system	1		Australia
3	NTC2701	Rear assembly exhaust system	1		Switzerland
4	NRC8238	Finisher-trim exhaust tailpipe	1		Germany
4	NTC2022	Finisher-trim exhaust tailpipe-rear	1		Switzerland
5	BH108091	Bolt-flanged head	6		
6	WL108001L	Washer-sprung-M8	6		
7	NH108041L	Nut-hexagonal head-M8	1		
8	NRC7608	Clamp-rear exhaust	2		
9	NRC7609	Bolt-u	2		
10	WL108001L	Washer-sprung-M8	4		
11	NH108041L	Nut-hexagonal head-M8	1		
12	BH108141L	Bolt-hexagonal head-M8 x 70	2		
12	FB108141L	Bolt-flanged head-M8 x 70	2		
13	3682	Washer-plain	4		
14	592072	Spacer	2		
15	572166	Bush-exhaust mounting rubber outer	4		
16	ESR3263	Washer	4		
17	572167	Bush-exhaust mounting rubber middle	2		
18	WL108001L	Washer-sprung-M8	2		
19	NH108041L	Nut-hexagonal head-M8	1		
	RRC4419	Pipe-exhaust-extension	1		

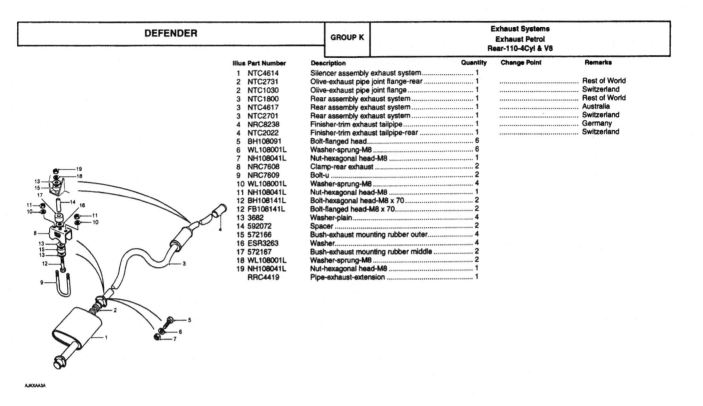

DEFENDER	GROUP K	Exhaust Systems Exhaust Diesel Front-Nat Asp-To (V) AA267063

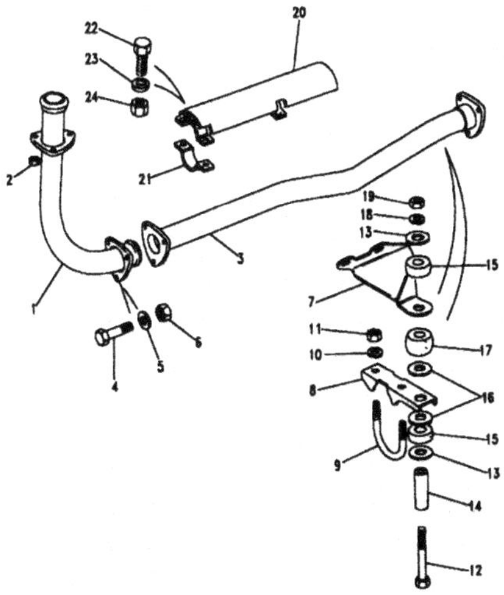

Illus	Part Number	Description	Quantity	Change Point	Remarks
1	NRC9137	Downpipe assembly exhaust system	1		
2	AFU2778L	Nut-M10	3		
3	NRC6436	Intermediate assembly exhaust system	1		
4	FB108081L	Bolt-flanged head-M8 x 40	3		
5	WL108001L	Washer-sprung-M8	3		
6	FN108041L	Nut-flange-M8	NLA		Use FN108047L.
7	NRC7778	Bracket-exhaust mounting	NLA		Use ESR169.
7	ESR169	Bracket-exhaust mounting	1		
8	NRC6467	Clamp-exhaust intermediate pipe assembly	1		
9	NRC6466	Bolt-u	1		
10	WL108001L	Washer-sprung-M8	2		
11	FN108041L	Nut-flange-M8	NLA		Use FN108047L.
12	SH108701L	Screw-M8 x 70-hexagonal head	1		
13	WP105L	Washer-plain	2		
14	NRC5403	Spacer	1		
15	572166	Bush-exhaust mounting rubber outer	2		
16	572168	Washer	NLA		Use ESR3263.
16	ESR3263	Washer	2		
17	572167	Bush-exhaust mounting rubber middle	1		
18	WL108001L	Washer-sprung-M8	1		
19	FN108041L	Nut-flange-M8	NLA		Use FN108047L.
20	NRC9733	Heatshield engine exhaust	1		
21	NRC9722	Clamp	2		
22	FS108207L	Screw-flanged head-M8 x 20	4		
23	WL108001L	Washer-sprung-M8	4		
24	FN108041L	Nut-flange-M8	NLA		Use FN108047L.

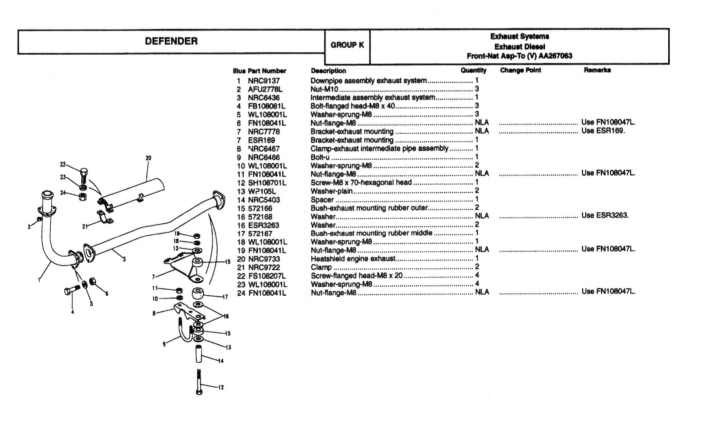

DEFENDER	GROUP K	Exhaust Systems Exhaust Diesel Front-Nat Asp-From (V) AA267064

Illus	Part Number	Description	Quantity	Change Point	Remarks
1	ESR1617	Downpipe assembly exhaust system	1		
2	ETC5337	Gasket exhaust system-manifold to downpipe	1		
3	AFU2778	Nut	NLA		Use AFU2778L.
3	AFU2778L	Nut-M10	3		
4	NTC1030	Olive-exhaust pipe joint flange	1		
5	NRC7778	Bracket-exhaust mounting	NLA		Use ESR169.
5	ESR169	Bracket-exhaust mounting	1		
6	NRC6467	Clamp	1	Note (1); Note (2)	
6	90575748	Clamp-downpipe	1	Note (3); Note (4)	
7	NRC6466	Bolt-u	1	Note (1); Note (2)	
7	NRC6374	Bolt-u-downpipe support	1	Note (3); Note (4)	
8	WL108001L	Washer-sprung-M8	2		
9	FN108041L	Nut-flange-M8	NLA		Use FN108047L.
10	SH108701L	Screw-M8 x 70-hexagonal head	1		
11	WP105L	Washer-plain	2		
12	NRC5403	Spacer	1		
13	572166	Bush-exhaust mounting rubber outer	2		
14	572168	Washer	NLA		Use ESR3263.
					Except 90"
14	572168	Washer	NLA	Note (5)	Use ESR3263.
					90"
14	ESR3263	Washer	1	Note (6)	90"
14	ESR3263	Washer	1		
15	572167	Bush-exhaust mounting rubber middle	1		
16	WL108001L	Washer-sprung-M8	1		
17	FN108041L	Nut-flange-M8	NLA		Use FN108047L.
18	NTC5205	Heatshield engine exhaust	1		
19	NTC2278	Clamp	2		
20	FS108207L	Screw-flanged head-M8 x 20	4		
21	WL108001L	Washer-sprung-M8	4		
22	FN108041L	Nut-flange-M8	NLA		Use FN108047L.

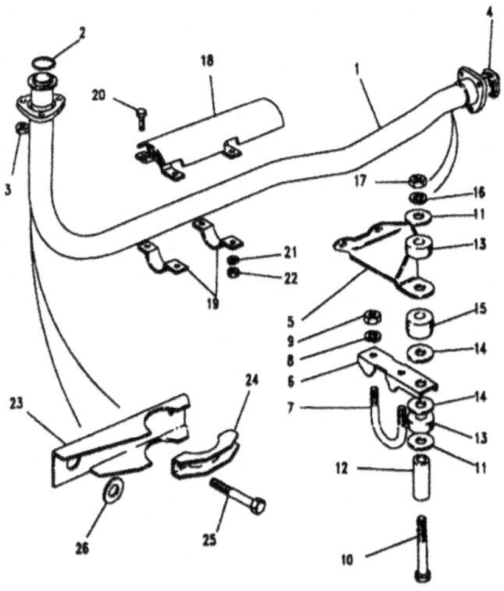

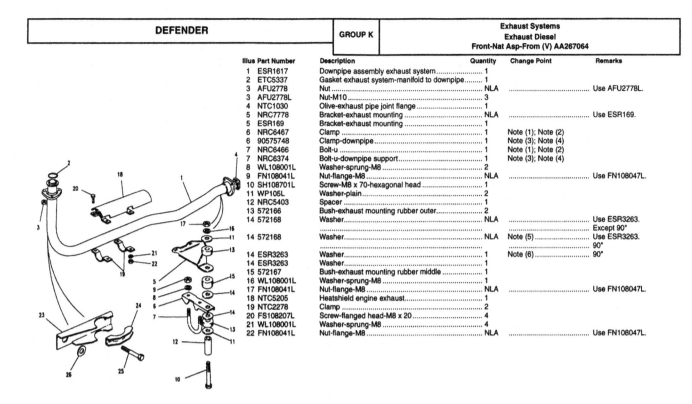

CHANGE POINTS:
(1) To (V) 290508 90"
(2) To (V) 290071 110"
(3) From (V) EA 290509 90"
(4) From (V) EA 290072 110"
(5) From (V) AA 267064 To (V) MA 951418
(6) From (V) MA 951419

DEFENDER	GROUP K	Exhaust Systems Exhaust Diesel Front-Nat Asp-From (V) AA267064

Illus	Part Number	Description	Quantity	Change Point	Remarks
23	NTC4580	Bracket-support downpipe	1	Note (1); Note (2); Note (3); Note (4)	
24	NTC4586	Clamp-exhaust downpipe to manifold	1		
25	BH108131L	Bolt-hexagonal head-M8 x 65	2		
26	WC112081L	Washer-plain-M12 x 28	1		

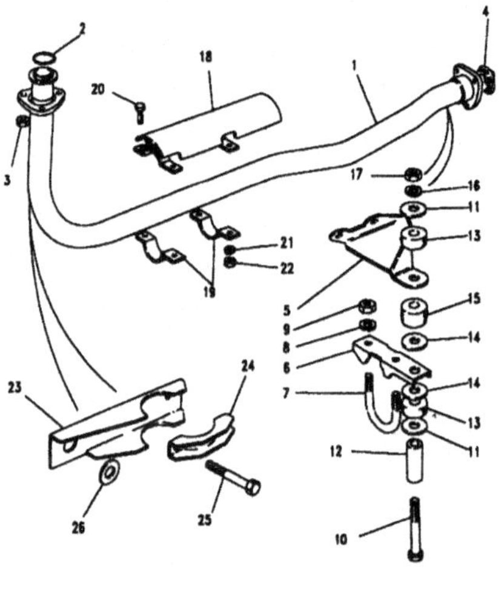

CHANGE POINTS:
(1) From (V) EA 290509 To (V) EA 338105 90"
(2) From (V) FA 405285 90"
(3) From (V) EA 290072 To (V) EA 338367 110"
(4) From (V) FA 405333 110"

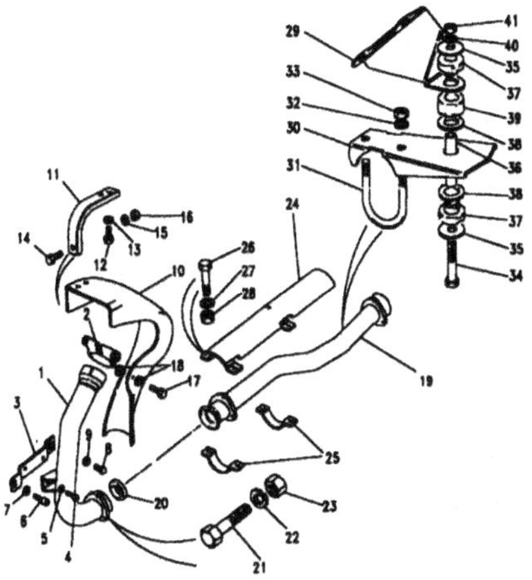

Illus	Part Number	Description	Quantity	Change Point	Remarks
1	NTC4426	Downpipe assembly exhaust system	1	Note (1)	
1	ESR159	Downpipe assembly exhaust system	1	Note (2)	
2	NTC3608	Clamp-exhaust downpipe to manifold	1		
17	SH110161L	Screw-hexagonal head-M10 x 16	1	Note (1)	
18	WA110061L	Washer-M10	1		
3	ESR266	Bracket	1	Note (2)	
4	SS106161L	Screw	2		
5	WJ106001L	Washer-plain-M6	2		
6	SS108161L	Screw-hexagon socket-M8 x 16	1		
7	WA108051L	Washer-8mm	1		
8	SH110141L	Screw-hexagonal head	1		
9	WA110061L	Washer-M10	1		
10	NTC4833	Heatshield assembly exhaust-downpipe	1		
11	NTC4548	Bracket-support	1	Note (3)	
11	ESR219	Bracket-support	1	Note (4)	
12	FS106167L	Screw-flanged head-flanged head-M6 x 16	2		
13	WA106041L	Washer-6mm	2	Note (3)	
13	WA106041L	Washer-6mm	1	Note (4)	
14	FS106167L	Screw-flanged head-flanged head-M6 x 16	1		
15	WL106001L	Washer-sprung-M6	1		
16	NH106041L	Nut-hexagonal-nyloc-M6	1		
17	SH108141L	Screw-hexagonal head-M8 x 14	1		
18	WJ108001	Washer-M8-large	2		
19	NTC4221	Exhaust silencer-intermediate	1		
20	NTC1030	Olive-exhaust pipe joint flange	1		
21	BH108091L	Bolt-M8 x 45	3		
22	WL108001L	Washer-sprung-M8	3		
23	FN108041L	Nut-flange-M8	NLA		Use FN108047L.
24	NTC5205	Heatshield engine exhaust	1		
25	NTC2278	Clamp	2		
26	FS108207L	Screw-flanged head-M8 x 20	4		
27	WL108001L	Washer-sprung-M8	4		
28	FN108041L	Nut-flange-M8	NLA		Use FN108047L.
29	ESR169	Bracket-exhaust mounting	1		
30	90575748	Clamp-exhaust intermediate pipe assembly	1		

CHANGE POINTS:
(1) To (V) FA 450140
(2) From (V) FA 450141
(3) To (V) FA 418962
(4) From (V) FA 418963

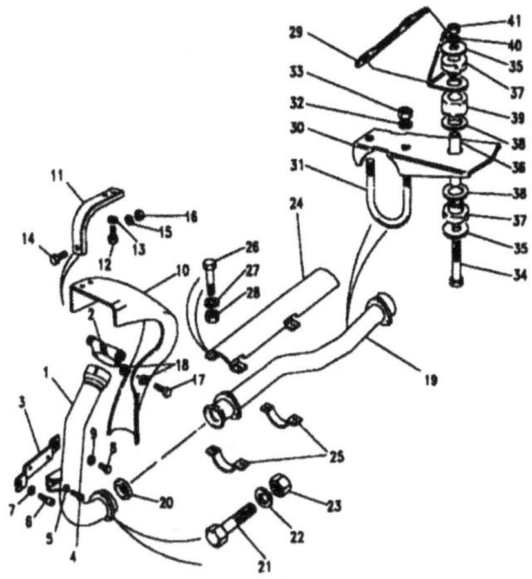

Illus	Part Number	Description	Quantity	Change Point	Remarks
31	NRC6374	Bolt-u	1		
32	WL108001L	Washer-sprung-M8	2		
33	FN108041L	Nut-flange-M8	NLA		Use FN108047L.
34	BH108141L	Bolt-hexagonal head-M8 x 70	1		
34	FB108141L	Bolt-flanged head-M8 x 70	1		
35	WP105L	Washer-plain	2		
36	NRC5403	Spacer	1		
37	572166	Bush-exhaust mounting rubber outer	2		
38	572168	Washer	NLA	Note (1)	Use ESR3263.
38	ESR3263	Washer	2		
38	ESR3263	Washer	2	Note (2)	
39	572167	Bush-exhaust mounting rubber middle	1		
40	WL108001L	Washer-sprung-M8	1		
41	FN108041L	Nut-flange-M8	NLA		Use FN108047L.

CHANGE POINTS:
(1) To (V) MA 951418
(2) From (V) MA 951419

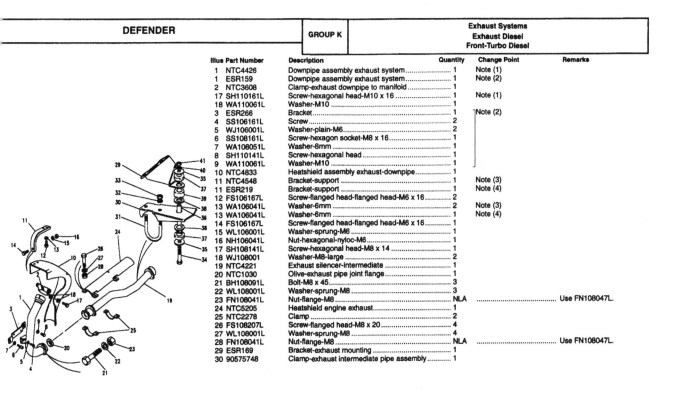

DEFENDER	GROUP K	Exhaust Systems Exhaust Diesel Front-200TDi

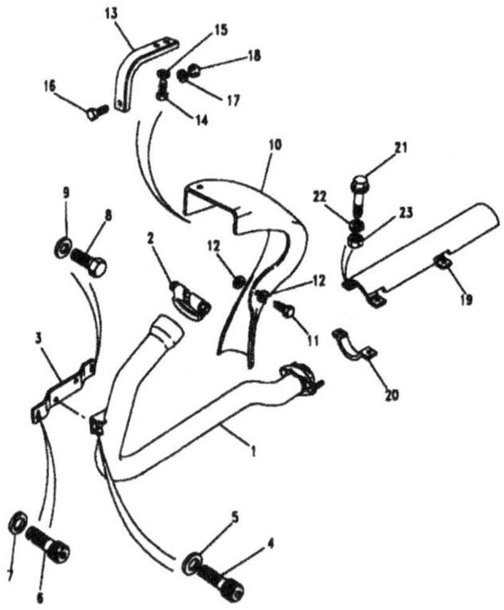

Illus	Part Number	Description	Quantity	Change Point	Remarks
1	ESR158	Downpipe assembly exhaust system	1	Note (1)	
2	NTC3608	Clamp-exhaust downpipe to manifold	1		
3	ESR266	Bracket	1		
4	SS106161L	Screw	2		
5	WJ106001L	Washer-plain-M6	2		
6	SS108161L	Screw-hexagon socket-M8 x 16	1		
7	WA108051L	Washer-8mm	1		
8	SH110141L	Screw-hexagonal head	1		
9	WA110061L	Washer-M10	1		
10	NTC4833	Heatshield assembly exhaust-downpipe	1		
11	SH108141L	Screw-hexagonal head-M8 x 14	2		
12	WJ108001	Washer-M8-large	1		
13	ESR219	Bracket	1		
14	FS106167L	Screw-flanged head-flanged head-M6 x 16	1		
15	WA106041L	Washer-6mm	1		
17	WL106001L	Washer-sprung-M6	1		
17	WL108001L	Washer-sprung-M8	4		
18	NH106041L	Nut-hexagonal-nyloc-M6	1	Note (1)	
19	ESR361	Heatshield engine exhaust	1		
20	ESR208	Clamp	2		
21	FS108207L	Screw-flanged head-M8 x 20	4		
22	WL108001	Washer-sprung-M8	NLA		Use WL108001L.
23	FN108041L	Nut-flange-M8	NLA		Use FN108047L.

CHANGE POINTS:
(1) To (V) LA 939975

DEFENDER	GROUP K	Exhaust Systems Exhaust Diesel Front-300TDi

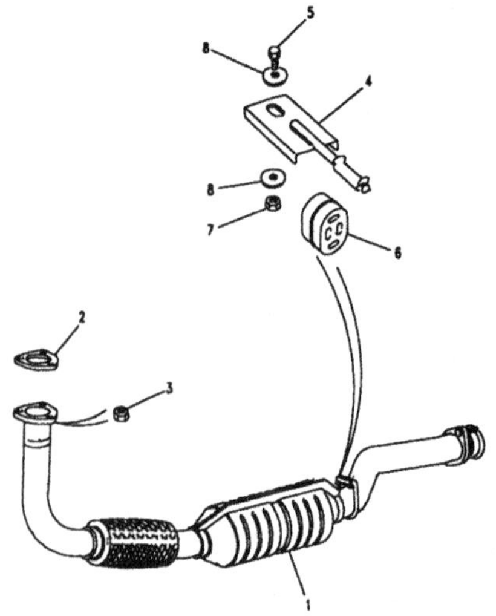

Illus	Part Number	Description	Quantity	Change Point	Remarks
1	ESR2297	Downpipe assembly exhaust system-less catalyst.	1		
1	ESR2739	Downpipe assembly exhaust system-with catalyst.	NLA		Use ESR3495.
1	ESR3495	Downpipe assembly exhaust system-with catalyst.	1		
2	ESR3260	Gasket exhaust system-manifold to downpipe	1		
3	ESR2034	Nut-flange-nyloc-M10	3		
4	ESR2945	Bracket exhaust system-rear	1		Catalyst
5	BH110201	Bolt-bracket to catalyst-hexagonal head-M10 x 100	1		Catalyst
6	ESR3172	Mounting-rubber exhaust system-front & rear	1		
7	FN110047	Nut-flange-flange-M10	1		
8	WA110061L	Washer-M10	2		

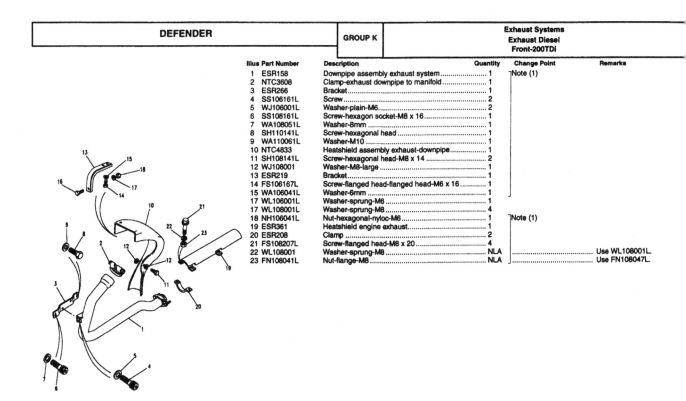

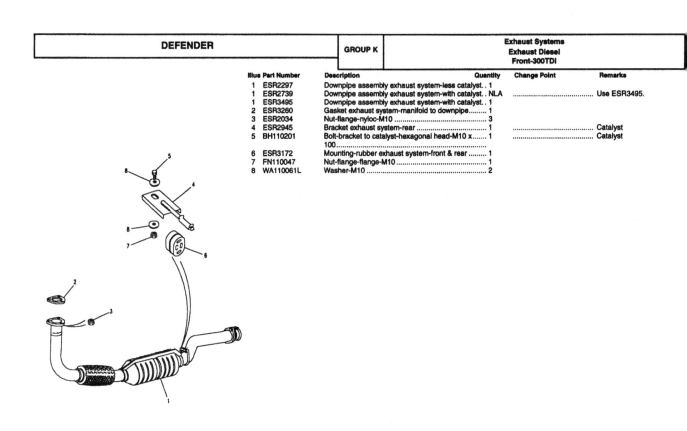

Illus	Part Number	Description	Quantity	Change Point	Remarks
1	WCD105860	Downpipe assembly exhaust system	1		
1	WCD000500	Downpipe assembly-exhaust manifold-with catalyst	1	Note (2)	EGR
2	ESR3737	Gasket exhaust system-turbo outlet to exhaust downpipe	1		
3	ESR2034	Nut-flange-nyloc-M10	3		
4	BH110201	Bolt-hexagonal head-M10 x 100	1		
5	WC110061	Washer-plain	2		
6	ESR2945	Bracket exhaust system-rear	1		
7	FN110047	Nut-flange-flange-M10	1		
8	ESR3172	Mounting-rubber exhaust system-front & rear	1		
9	ESR2034	Nut-flange-nyloc-M10	2		

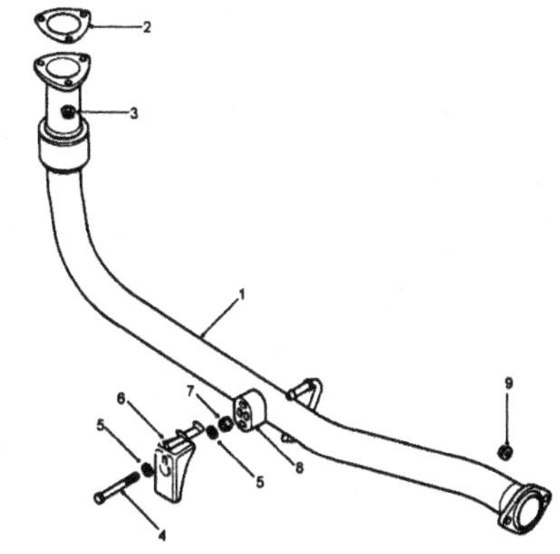

LK0006

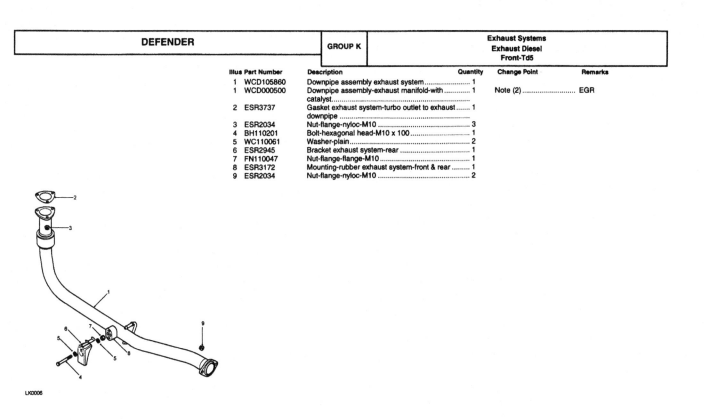

CHANGE POINTS:
(2) From (V) 2A 622424

Illus	Part Number	Description	Quantity	Change Point	Remarks
1	NRC8888	Silencer assembly exhaust system	1		
2	NRC8889	Rear assembly exhaust system	1		
	NRC8238	Finisher-trim exhaust tailpipe	1		Germany
3	FB108081L	Bolt-flanged head-M8 x 40	6		
4	WL108001	Washer-sprung-M8	NLA		Use WL108001L.
4	WL108001L	Washer-sprung-M8	6		
5	FN108041L	Nut-flange-M8	NLA		Use FN108047L.
6	SH108701L	Screw-M8 x 70-hexagonal head	2		
7	WP105L	Washer-plain	4		
8	NRC5403	Spacer	2		
9	572166	Bush-exhaust mounting rubber outer	4		
10	572168	Washer	NLA		Use ESR3263.
11	572167	Bush-exhaust mounting rubber middle	2		
12	WL108001L	Washer-sprung-M8	2		
13	FN108041L	Nut-flange-M8	NLA		Use FN108047L.

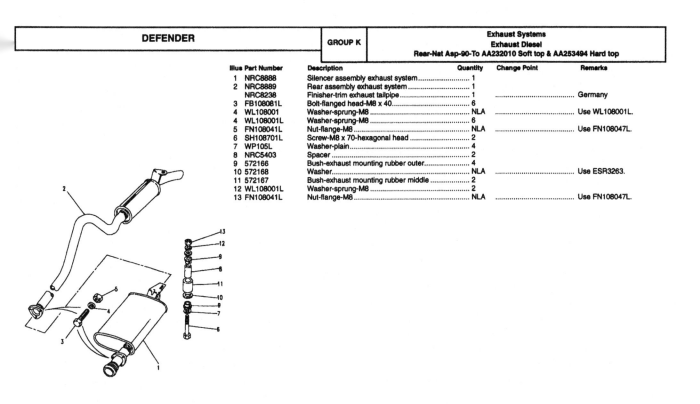

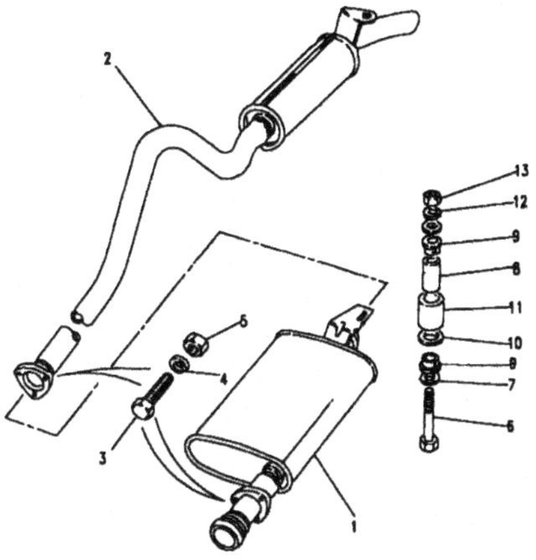

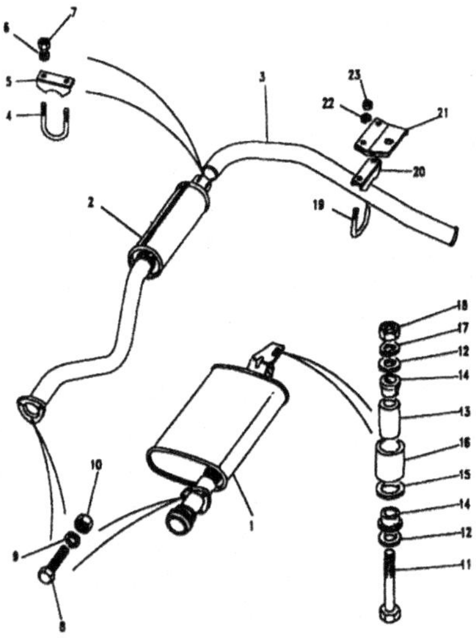

Illus	Part Number	Description	Quantity	Change Point	Remarks
1	NRC8888	Silencer assembly exhaust system	1		
2	NTC1150	Rear assembly exhaust system	1		
3	NTC1149	Tailpipe exhaust system	1		
4	NTC1311	Bolt-u	1		
5	NTC1312	Clamp-tail pipe to rear exhaust	1		
6	WL108001L	Washer-sprung-M8	2		
7	FN108041L	Nut-flange-M8	NLA		Use FN108047L.
8	FB108081L	Bolt-flanged head-M8 x 40	6		
9	WL108001L	Washer-sprung-M8	6		
10	FN108041L	Nut-flange-M8	NLA		Use FN108047L.
11	SH108701L	Screw-M8 x 70-hexagonal head	2		
12	WP105L	Washer-plain	4		
13	NRC5403	Spacer	2		

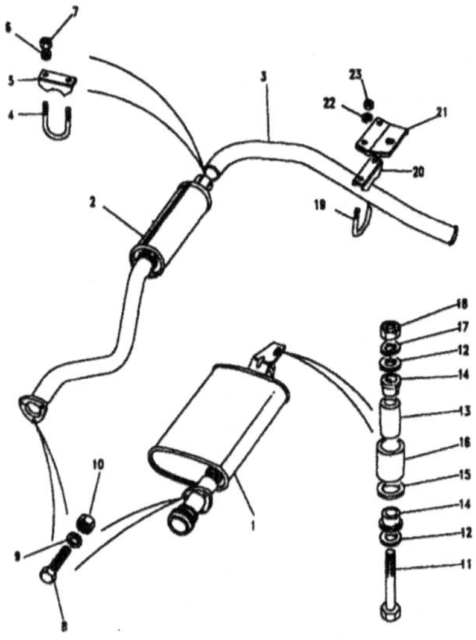

Illus	Part Number	Description	Quantity	Change Point	Remarks
14	572166	Bush-exhaust mounting rubber outer	4		
15	572168	Washer	NLA		Use ESR3263.
16	572167	Bush-exhaust mounting rubber middle	2		
17	WL108001	Washer-sprung-M8	NLA		Use WL108001L.
17	WL108001L	Washer-sprung-M8	2		
18	FN108041L	Nut-flange-M8	NLA		Use FN108047L.
19	NTC1311	Bolt-u	1		
20	NTC1312	Clamp-tail pipe	1		
21	NTC1313	Bracket-exhaust mounting/lashing hanger	1		
22	WL108001	Washer-sprung-M8	NLA		Use WL108001L.
22	WL108001L	Washer-sprung-M8	2		
23	FN108041L	Nut-flange-M8	NLA		Use FN108047L.

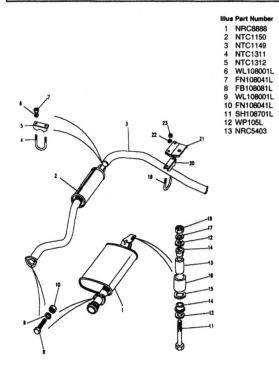

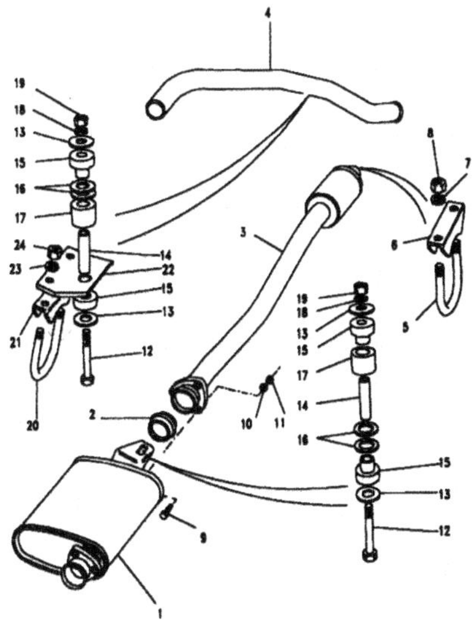

Illus	Part Number	Description	Quantity	Change Point	Remarks
1	NTC4615	Silencer assembly exhaust system-rear	1		
2	NTC2731	Olive-exhaust pipe joint flange-rear	1		
3	NTC1799	Rear assembly exhaust system-rear	1		
4	NTC1149	Tailpipe exhaust system	1		
5	NTC1311	Bolt-u	1		
6	NTC1312	Clamp-tail pipe to rear exhaust	1		
7	WL108001L	Washer-sprung-M8	2		
8	FN108041L	Nut-flange-M8	NLA		Use FN108047L.
9	FB108081L	Bolt-flanged head-M8 x 40	6		
10	WL108001L	Washer-sprung-M8	6		
11	FN108041L	Nut-flange-M8	NLA		Use FN108047L.
12	SH108701L	Screw-M8 x 70-hexagonal head	2		
13	WP105L	Washer-plain	4		
14	NRC5403	Spacer	2		
15	572166	Bush-exhaust mounting rubber outer	4		
16	572168	Washer	NLA	Note (1)	Use ESR3263.
16	ESR3263	Washer	4		
16	ESR3263	Washer	4	Note (2)	
17	572167	Bush-exhaust mounting rubber middle	2		
18	WL108001L	Washer-sprung-M8	2		
19	FN108041L	Nut-flange-M8	NLA		Use FN108047L.
20	NTC1311	Bolt-u	1		
21	NTC1312	Clamp-tail pipe	1		
22	NTC1313	Bracket-exhaust mounting/lashing hanger	1		
23	WL108001L	Washer-sprung-M8	2		
24	FN108041L	Nut-flange-M8	NLA		Use FN108047L.

CHANGE POINTS:
(1) From (V) AA 267064 To (V) MA 951418
(2) From (V) MA 951419

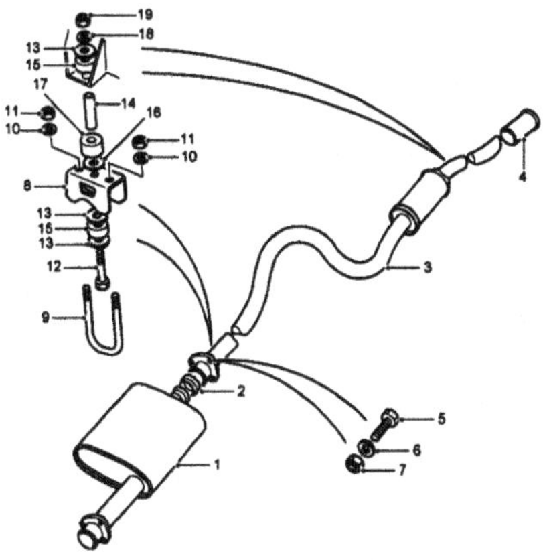

AJKXAA3A

Illus	Part Number	Description	Quantity	Change Point	Remarks
1	NTC4614	Silencer assembly exhaust system	1		
2	NTC2731	Olive-exhaust pipe joint flange-rear	1		Rest of World UK
2	NTC1030	Olive-exhaust pipe joint flange	1		Switzerland
3	NTC1800	Rear assembly exhaust system	1		Rest of World UK
3	NTC4617	Rear assembly exhaust system	1		Australia
3	NTC2701	Rear assembly exhaust system	1		Switzerland
4	NRC8238	Finisher-trim exhaust tailpipe	1		HICAP Germany
4	NTC2022	Finisher-trim exhaust tailpipe-rear	1		Switzerland
5	BH108091	Bolt-flanged head	1		
6	WL108001L	Washer-sprung-M8	6		
7	NH108041	Nut-hexagonal head-M8	NLA		Use NH108041L.
7	NH108041L	Nut-hexagonal head-M8	1		
8	NRC7608	Clamp-rear exhaust	2		
9	NRC7609	Bolt-u	2		
10	WL108001L	Washer-sprung-M8	4		
11	NH108041L	Nut-hexagonal head-M8	1		
12	BH108141	Bolt-hexagonal head	NLA		Use BH108141L.
12	BH108141L	Bolt-hexagonal head-M8 x 70	2		
12	FB108141L	Bolt-flanged head-M8 x 70	2		
13	3682	Washer-plain	4		
14	592072	Spacer	2		
15	572166	Bush-exhaust mounting rubber outer	4		
16	ESR3263	Washer	4		
17	572167	Bush-exhaust mounting rubber middle	2		
18	WL108001L	Washer-sprung-M8	2		
19	NH108041L	Nut-hexagonal head-M8	1		
	RRC4419	Pipe-exhaust-extension	1		130"

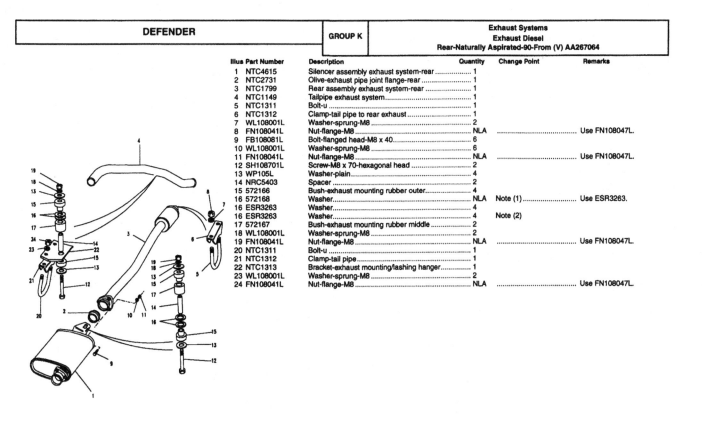

DEFENDER	GROUP K	Exhaust Systems Exhaust Diesel Rear-Turbo Diesel-90

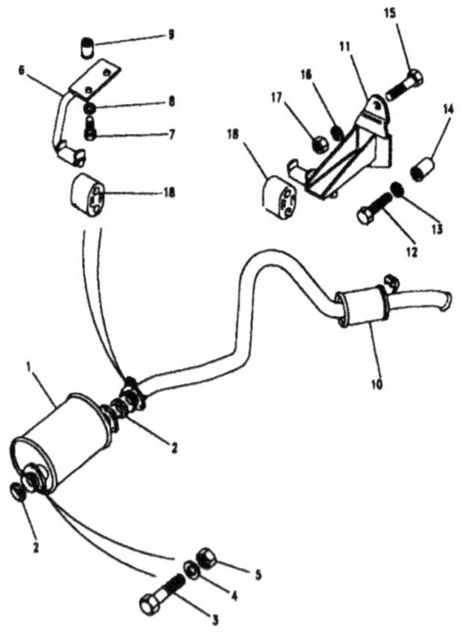

Illus	Part Number	Description	Quantity	Change Point	Remarks
1	NTC1665	Silencer assembly exhaust system	1		
2	NTC1030	Olive-exhaust pipe joint flange	2		
3	BH108091L	Bolt-M8 x 45	6		
4	WL108001L	Washer-sprung-M8	6		
5	FN108041L	Nut-flange-M8	NLA		Use FN108047L.
6	NTC3618	Bracket assembly-intermediate exhaust mounting	1		
7	FS108207L	Screw-flanged head-M8 x 20	2		
8	WL108001L	Washer-sprung-M8	2		
9	NN108021	Nut-blind-M8	2		
10	NTC1802	Rear assembly exhaust system	1		
11	NTC4252	Bracket assembly-exhaust mounting	1		
12	FS108207L	Screw-flanged head-M8 x 20	1		
13	WL108001L	Washer-sprung-M8	1		
14	NN108021	Nut-blind-M8	1		
15	FB108121L	Bolt-flanged head-M8 x 60	1		
16	WL108001L	Washer-sprung-M8	1		
17	FN108041L	Nut-flange-M8	NLA		Use FN108047L.
18	NTC3650	Mounting-rubber exhaust system	2	Note (1)	
18	ESR3172	Mounting-rubber exhaust system-front & rear	2	Note (2)	

CHANGE POINTS:
(1) To (V) MA 988236
(2) From (V) MA 988237

DEFENDER	GROUP K	Exhaust Systems Exhaust Diesel Rear-Turbo Diesel-110/130

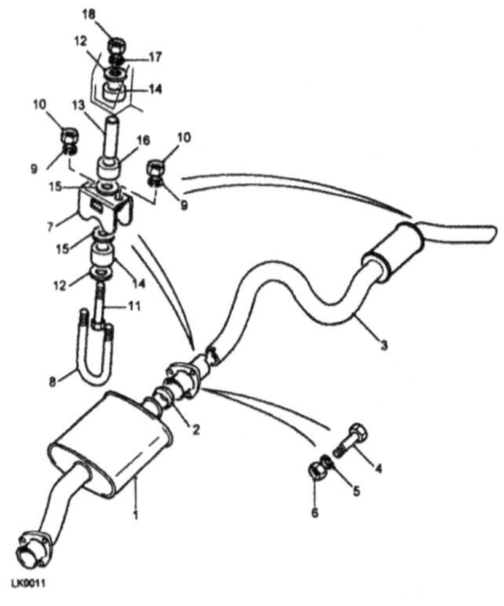

Illus	Part Number	Description	Quantity	Change Point	Remarks
1	NTC1666	Silencer assembly exhaust system	1		
2	NTC1030	Olive	1		
3	NTC2832	Rear assembly exhaust system	1		
4	BH108091L	Bolt-M8 x 45	6		
5	WL108001L	Washer-sprung-M8	6		
6	FN108041L	Nut-flange-M8	NLA		Use FN108047L.
7	NRC7608	Clamp	2		
8	NRC7609	Bolt-u	2		
9	WL108001L	Washer-sprung-M8	4		
10	FN108041L	Nut-flange-M8	NLA		Use FN108047L.
11	SH108701	Screw-hexagonal head-M8 x 70	2		
12	WP105L	Washer-plain	4		
13	NRC5403	Spacer	2		
14	572166	Bush	4		
15	ESR3263	Washer	4		
16	572167	Bush	2		
17	WL108001L	Washer-sprung-M8	2		
18	FN108041L	Nut-flange-M8	NLA		Use FN108047L.
	RRC4419	Pipe-exhaust-extension	1		130"

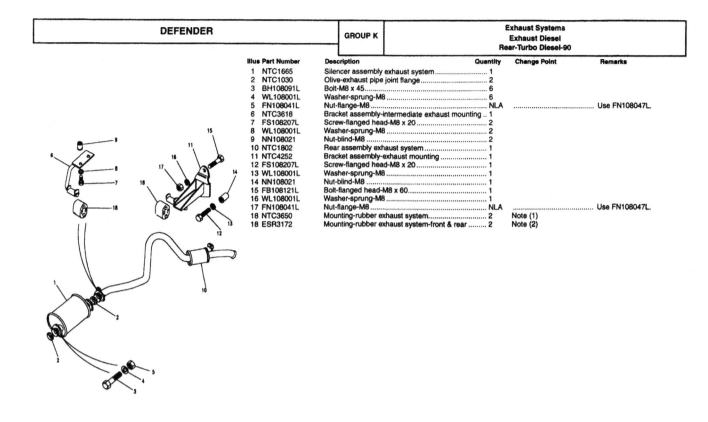

DEFENDER	GROUP K	Exhaust Systems Exhaust Diesel Rear-200TDI-90

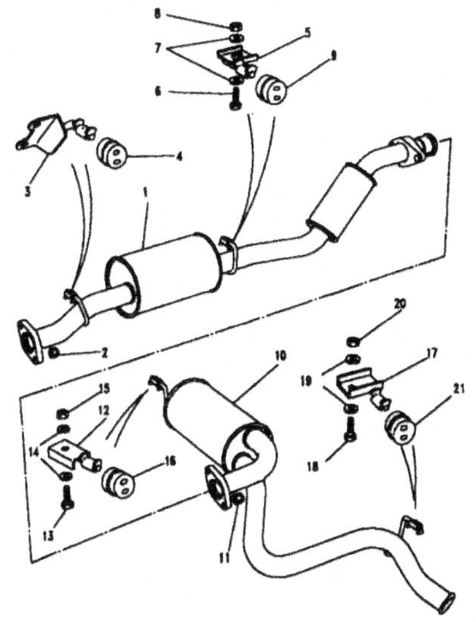

Illus	Part Number	Description	Quantity	Change Point	Remarks
1	ESR358	Silencer assembly exhaust system	1	Note (1)	
2	NV110041L	Nut-M10	2		
3	ESR414	Bracket exhaust system-front	1		
4	NTC5582	Mounting-rubber exhaust system-rear	1		
5	ESR360	Bracket exhaust system-rear	1		
6	FS108251L	Screw-flanged head-M8 x 25	NLA		Use FS108257L.
7	WP185L	Washer-plain-standard	2		
8	NV108041L	Nut-M8	1		
9	NTC5582	Mounting-rubber exhaust system-rear	1		
10	ESR254	Rear assembly exhaust system	1		
11	NV110041L	Nut-M10	2		
12	NTC7348	Bracket-exhaust mounting	NLA		Use ESR2421.
12	ESR2421	Bracket-exhaust mounting	1		
13	FS108251L	Screw-flanged head-M8 x 25	NLA		Use FS108257L.
14	WP185L	Washer-plain-standard	2		
15	NV108041L	Nut-M8	1		
16	NTC5582	Mounting-rubber exhaust system-rear	1		
17	ESR95	Bracket-mounting-exhaust-rear	1		
18	FS108251L	Screw-flanged head-M8 x 25	NLA		Use FS108257L.
19	WP185L	Washer-plain-standard	2		
20	NV108041L	Nut-M8	1		
21	NTC5582	Mounting-rubber exhaust system-rear	1		

CHANGE POINTS:
(1) To (V) LA 939975

DEFENDER	GROUP K	Exhaust Systems Exhaust Diesel Rear-200TDI-110/130

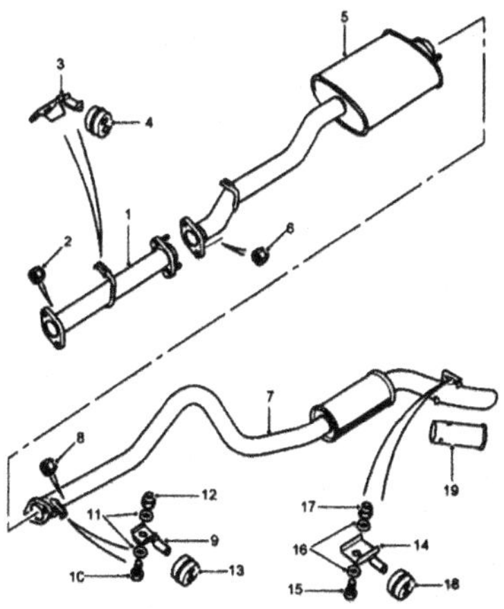

LK0010

Illus	Part Number	Description	Quantity	Change Point	Remarks
1	ESR255	Extension-rear tailpipe aperture	1	Note (1)	130"
2	NV110041L	Nut-M10	2		130"
3	ESR414	Bracket exhaust system-front	1		
4	NTC5582	Mounting-rubber exhaust system-rear	1		
5	ESR54	Silencer assembly exhaust system	1		110"
5	ESR439	Silencer assembly exhaust system	1		130"
6	NV110041L	Nut-M10	2		
7	ESR359	Tailpipe exhaust system	1		Except Australia
7	ESR1696	Tailpipe exhaust system	1		Australia 110"
8	NV110041L	Nut-M10	2		
9	ESR360	Bracket exhaust system-rear	1		
10	FS108251L	Screw-flanged head-M8 x 25	NLA		Use FS108257L.
11	WP185L	Washer-plain-standard	2		
12	NV108041L	Nut-M8	1		
13	NTC5582	Mounting-rubber exhaust system-rear	1		
14	ESR95	Bracket-mounting-exhaust-rear	1		
15	FS108251L	Screw-flanged head-M8 x 25	NLA		Use FS108257L.
16	WP185L	Washer-plain-standard	2		
17	NV108041L	Nut-M8	1		
18	NTC5582	Mounting-rubber exhaust system-rear	1		
19	NTC2022	Finisher-trim exhaust tailpipe-rear	1		HICAP

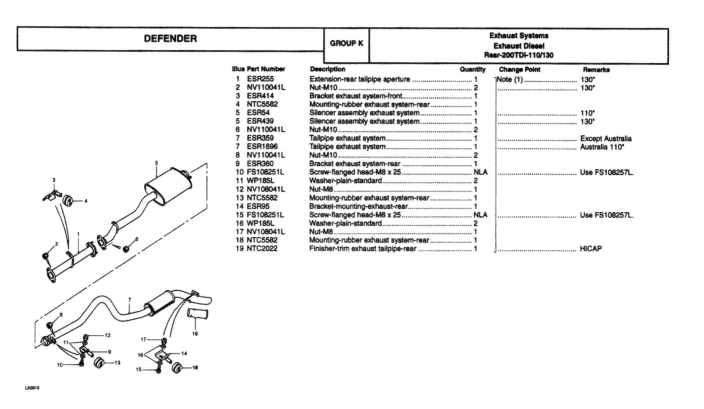

CHANGE POINTS:
(1) To (V) LA 939975

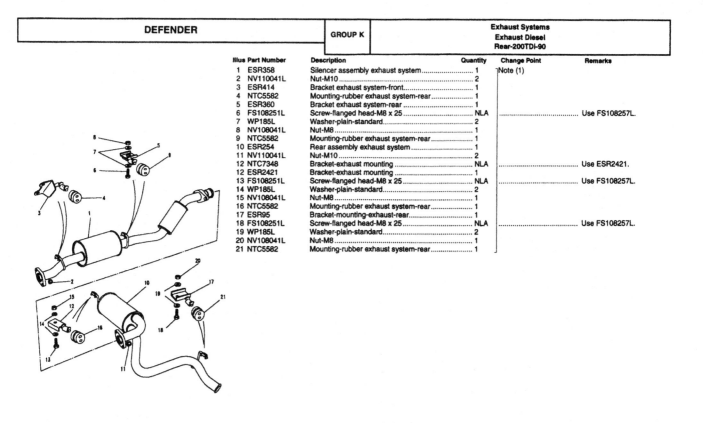

DEFENDER	GROUP K	Exhaust Systems Exhaust Diesel Rear-300TDi-90-To (V) TA999221

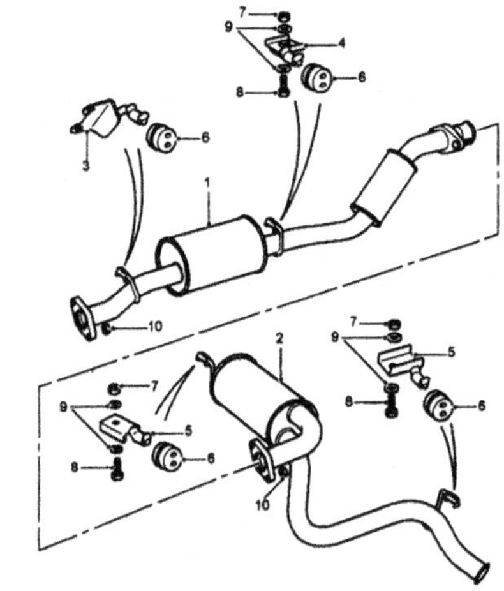

AHKXDE2B

Illus	Part Number	Description	Quantity	Change Point	Remarks
1	ESR2381	Silencer assembly exhaust system-centre	1	Note (1)	
2	ESR2382	Rear assembly exhaust system	1	Note (2)	
2	ESR3463	Rear assembly exhaust system	1	Note (3)	
		BRACKET EXHAUST SYSTEM			
3	ESR2087	front	1	Note (4)	
3	NTC5648	front	1	Note (5)	
3	ESR4578	front	1	Note (6)	
4	ESR2421	Bracket-exhaust mounting	1		
5	ESR3294	Bracket-mounting-exhaust-rear	2		
6	ESR3172	Mounting-rubber exhaust system-front & rear	4		
7	ESR2033	Nut-locking-M8	4		
8	FS108257L	Screw-flanged head-M8 x 25	2		
9	WP185L	Washer-plain-standard	6		
10	NV108041	Nut-M8	4		

CHANGE POINTS:
(1) To (V) TA 999221
(2) To (V) MA 951235
(3) From (V) MA 951236 To (V) TA 999221
(4) To (V) MA 960895
(5) From (V) MA 960896 To (V) TA 999221
(6) From (V) VA 999222

DEFENDER	GROUP K	Exhaust Systems Exhaust Diesel Rear-300TDi-90-From (V) TA999222

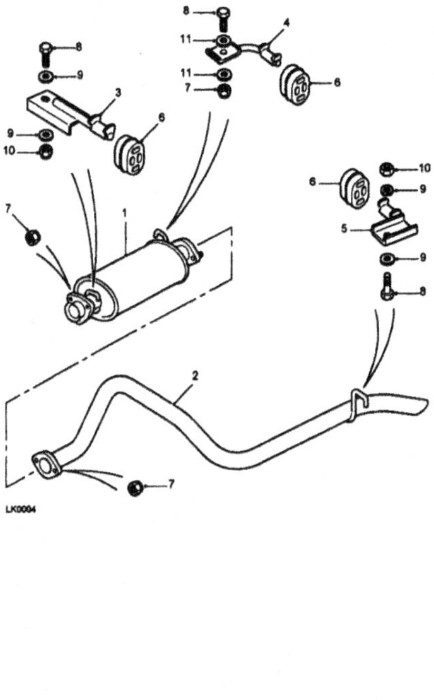

LKX0004

Illus	Part Number	Description	Quantity	Change Point	Remarks
1	ESR4526	Silencer assembly exhaust system-centre	1		
2	ESR4527	Tailpipe assembly-exhaust system	1	To (V) WA 159806	
2	WCG102890	Tailpipe assembly-exhaust system	1	From (V) XA 159807	
3	ESR2087	Bracket exhaust system-front	1		
4	ESR2131	Bracket exhaust system-centre	1		
5	ESR3294	Bracket-mounting-exhaust-rear	1		
6	ESR3172	Mounting-rubber exhaust system-front & rear	3		
7	NV108041L	Nut-M8	5		
8	SH108251	Screw-hexagonal head-M8 x 25	NLA		Use FS108257.
9	3682	Washer-plain	3		
10	ESR2033	Nut-locking-M8	2		
11	3663	Washer	2		

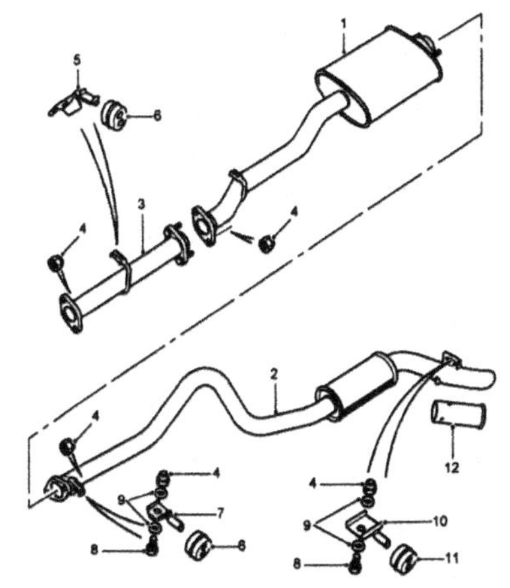

Illus	Part Number	Description	Quantity	Change Point	Remarks
1	ESR2383	Silencer assembly exhaust system	1		110"
1	ESR2385	Silencer assembly exhaust system	1		130"
2	ESR2384	Rear assembly exhaust system	1		Except Australia
2	ESR3152	Rear assembly exhaust system	1		Australia
3	ESR2386	Pipe-exhaust-extension	1		130"
4	NV108041L	Nut-M8	2		
5	ESR2087	Bracket exhaust system-front	1	Note (1)	
5	NTC5648	Bracket exhaust system-front	1	Note (2)	
6	ESR3172	Mounting-rubber exhaust system-front & rear	1		
7	ESR2215	Bracket-mounting-exhaust-rear	1	Note (3)	
7	ESR3294	Bracket-mounting-exhaust-rear	1	Note (4)	
8	FS108251L	Screw-flanged head-M8 x 25	NLA		Use FS108257L.
9	WP185L	Washer-plain-standard	2	Note (5)	
10	ESR95	Bracket-mounting-exhaust-rear	1	Note (3)	
10	ESR3293	Bracket-mounting-exhaust-rear	1	Note (4)	
11	NTC5582	Mounting-rubber exhaust system-rear	1		
12	NTC2022	Finisher-trim exhaust tailpipe-rear	1		HICAP

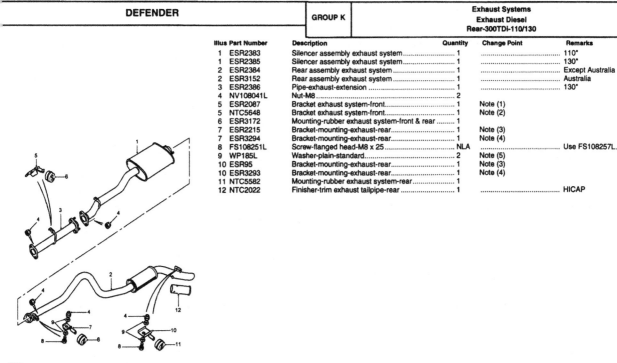

CHANGE POINTS:
(1) To (V) MA 960895
(2) From (V) MA 960896 To (V) TA 999221
(3) To (V) MA 948144
(4) From (V) MA 948145
(5) To (V) LA 939975

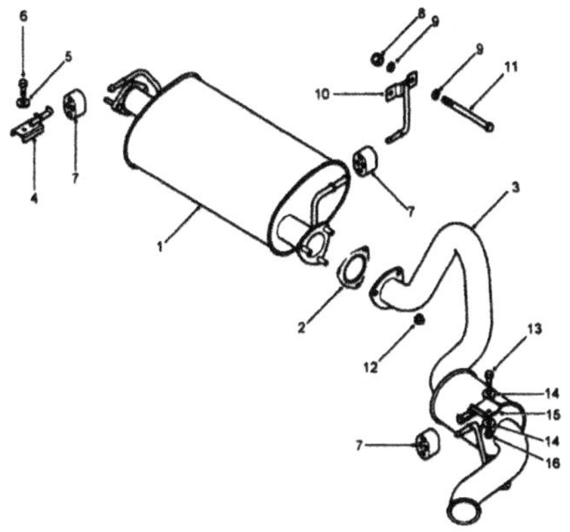

Illus	Part Number	Description	Quantity	Change Point	Remarks
1	WCE104440	Silencer assembly exhaust system	1	Note (1)	
1	WCE105170	Silencer assembly exhaust system	1	Note (2)	
2	ESR3737	Gasket exhaust system-intermediate to rear pipe	1		
3	WCG102940	Rear assembly exhaust system	1		
4	ESR2421	Bracket-exhaust mounting	1		
5	3682	Washer-plain	1		
6	GG108251	Screw	1		
7	ESR3172	Mounting-rubber exhaust system-front & rear	3		
8	NY110041	Nut-hexagonal head-nyloc	2		
9	NRC5758	Washer	4		
10	ESR4438	Bracket assembly-intermediate exhaust mounting	1	Note (3)	
10	WCU101320	Bracket assembly-intermediate exhaust mounting	1	Note (4)	
11	BH110351	Bolt	2		
12	NV110041	Nut	3		
13	FS108257L	Screw-flanged head-M8 x 25	1		
14	3663	Washer	2		
15	ESR3294	Bracket-mounting-exhaust-rear	1		
16	ESR2033	Nut-locking-M8	1		

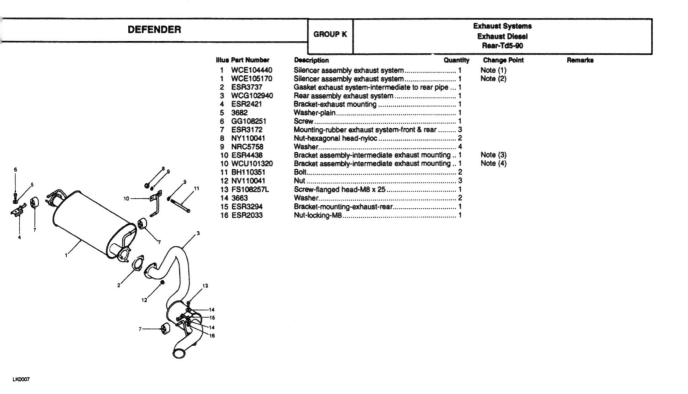

CHANGE POINTS:
(1) To (V) XA 174548
(2) From (V) XA 174548
(3) To (V) XA 171675
(4) From (V) XA 171676

Illus	Part Number	Description	Quantity	Change Point	Remarks
1	WCE104450	Silencer assembly exhaust system	1	Note (1)	110"
1	WCE104460	Silencer assembly exhaust system	1	Note (3)	130"
2	ESR3737	Gasket exhaust system-intermediate to rear pipe	1		110"
2	ESR3737	Gasket exhaust system-intermediate to rear pipe	1		130"
3	WCG103020	Rear assembly exhaust system	1		110"
3	WCG103020	Rear assembly exhaust system	1		130"
4	ESR2421	Bracket-exhaust mounting	1		110"
4	ESR2421	Bracket-exhaust mounting	1		130"
5	3682	Washer-plain	1		110"
5	3682	Washer-plain	1		130"
6	GG108251	Screw	1		110"
6	GG108251	Screw	1		130"
7	ESR3172	Mounting-rubber exhaust system-front & rear	3		110"
7	ESR3172	Mounting-rubber exhaust system-front & rear	3		130"
8	NY110041	Nut-hexagonal head-nyloc	2		110"
8	NY110041	Nut-hexagonal head-nyloc	2		130"
9	NRC5758	Washer	4		110"
9	NRC5758	Washer	4		130"
10	ESR4438	Bracket assembly-intermediate exhaust mounting	1	Note (5)	110"
10	ESR4438	Bracket assembly-intermediate exhaust mounting	1	Note (5)	130"
10	WCU101320	Bracket assembly-intermediate exhaust mounting	1	Note (6)	110"
10	WCU101320	Bracket assembly-intermediate exhaust mounting	1	Note (6)	130"

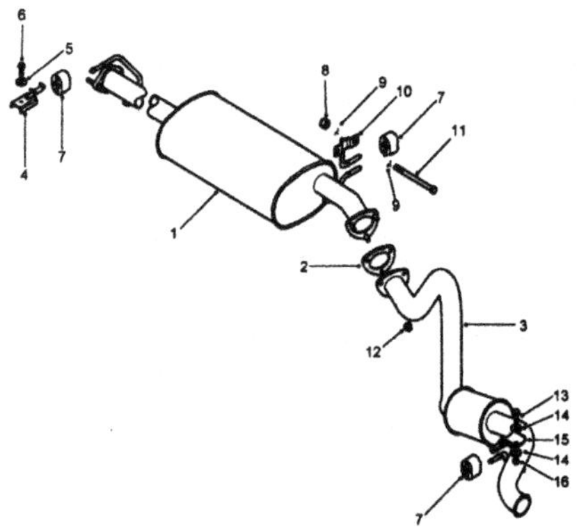

LK0008

CHANGE POINTS:
(1) To (V) XA 174545
(3) To (V) XA 174896
(5) To (V) XA 171675
(6) From (V) XA 171676

Illus	Part Number	Description	Quantity	Change Point	Remarks
11	BH110351	Bolt	2		110"
11	BH110351	Bolt	2		130"
12	NV110041	Nut	3		110"
12	NV110041	Nut	3		130"
13	FS108257L	Screw-flanged head-M8 x 25	1		110"
13	FS108257L	Screw-flanged head-M8 x 25	1		130"
14	3663	Washer	2		110"
14	3663	Washer	2		130"
15	ESR3294	Bracket-mounting-exhaust-rear	1		110"
15	ESR3294	Bracket-mounting-exhaust-rear	1		130"
16	ESR2033	Nut-locking-M8	1		110"
16	ESR2033	Nut-locking-M8	1		130"

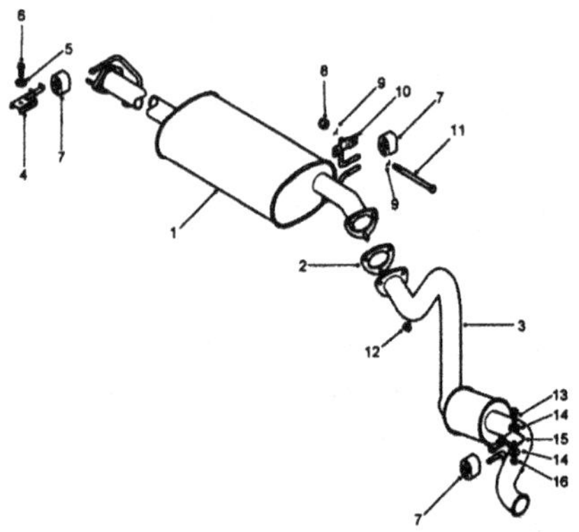

LK0008

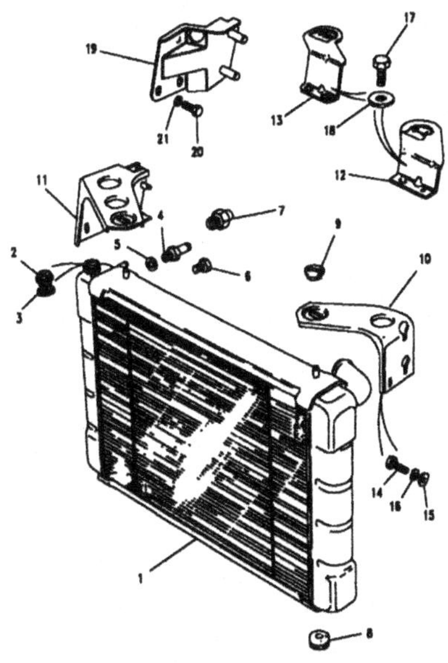

Illus	Part Number	Description	Quantity	Change Point	Remarks
		2.25 PETROL			
1	NRC6888	Radiator assembly	1		Except Heavy duty
1	ESR79	Radiator assembly	1		Heavy duty
		2.5 PETROL			
1	ESR79	Radiator assembly	1	To (V) FA 389980	Except oil cooler (air cooled)
1	ESR77	RADIATOR ASSEMBLY	1	From (V) FA 389981	
1	ESR78	RADIATOR ASSEMBLY	1	To (V) JA 918061	Oil cooler (air cooled)
1	ESR1677	RADIATOR ASSEMBLY	NLA	From (V) JA 918062 To (V) TA 977127	
1	ESR3684	RADIATOR ASSEMBLY	1	From (V) TA 977128	
2	NTC4609	• Plug-drain/filler level	1		
3	NTC5171	• O ring-radiator filler plug	1		
		NAT ASP DIESEL			
1	ESR79	Radiator assembly	1	To (V) FA 389980	Except oil cooler (air cooled)
1	ESR77	RADIATOR ASSEMBLY	1	From (V) FA 389981	
1	ESR78	RADIATOR ASSEMBLY	1	To (V) JA 918061	Oil cooler (air cooled)
1	ESR1677	RADIATOR ASSEMBLY	NLA	From (V) JA 918062 To (V) TA 977127	
1	ESR3684	RADIATOR ASSEMBLY	1	From (V) TA 977128	
2	NTC4609	• Plug-drain/filler level	1		
3	NTC5171	• O ring-radiator filler plug	1		
		DIESEL TURBO			
1	NTC6168	Radiator assembly	1		Except TDi
		200TDI			
1	NTC4893	Radiator assembly	1	To (V) JA 918061	
1	ESR1676	Radiator assembly	1	From (V) JA 918062	

Illus	Part Number	Description	Quantity	Change Point	Remarks
		V8			
1	ESR76	Radiator assembly	1	To (V) FA 428918	Except oil cooler (air cooled)
1	ESR203	RADIATOR ASSEMBLY	1	From (V) FA 428919	
1	ESR204	RADIATOR ASSEMBLY	1	To (V) JA 918061	Oil cooler (air cooled)
1	ESR1678	RADIATOR ASSEMBLY	1	From (V) TA 976036 To (V) TA 977127	
1	ESR3685	RADIATOR ASSEMBLY	1	From (V) TA 977128	Twin Carburettor oil cooler (air cooled)
1	ESR3685	RADIATOR ASSEMBLY	1		4000 cc EFi
2	NTC4609	• Plug-drain/filler level	1		
3	NTC5171	• O ring	1		
4	KTP9024	Penthouse vent-radiator-cooling	1		
5	RRO2125L	Washer	1		
6	RRO2126L	Plug-drain/filler level	1		
7	NTC3858	Adaptor-pipe coolant	2		Diesel Turbo
8	572312	Bush-radiator mounting	2		
9	NRC5544	Mount-radiator rubber	2		
10	NRC4839	Bracket assembly-radiator upper mounting-LH	1	To (V) 4/3/1992 approx	
11	NRC8609	Bracket assembly-radiator upper mounting-RH	1		
12	ESR69	Bracket assembly-radiator mounting-LH	1	From (V) 5/3/1992	
12	ESR68	Bracket assembly-radiator mounting-RH	1		
13	ESR283	Bracket-radiator upper mounting-RH	1		
13	ESR282	Bracket-radiator upper mounting-LH	1		
14	FS106201L	Screw-flanged head-M6 x 20	6	To (V) 4/3/1992 approx	
15	WC106041L	Washer-M6-oversize	6		
16	WL106001L	Washer-sprung-M6	6		
17	SH106207L	Screw-hexagonal head-M6 x 20	4	From (V) 5/3/1992	
18	WC106047	Washer-M6	4		
19	ALR1982	Bracket-bonnet stay	1	From (V) JA 910943	
20	SH106207L	Screw-hexagonal head-M6 x 20	3		
21	WC106047	Washer-M6	4		
	BTR328	Label anti freeze	1		

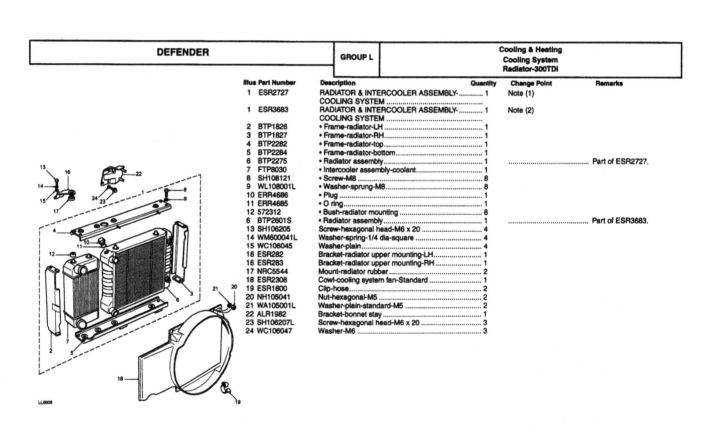

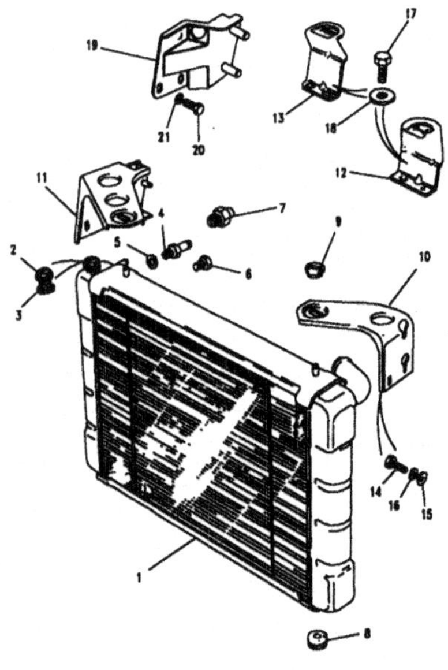

Illus	Part Number	Description	Quantity	Change Point	Remarks
1	ESR2727	RADIATOR & INTERCOOLER ASSEMBLY-COOLING SYSTEM	1	Note (1)	
1	ESR3683	RADIATOR & INTERCOOLER ASSEMBLY-COOLING SYSTEM	1	Note (2)	
2	BTP1826	• Frame-radiator-LH	1		
3	BTP1827	• Frame-radiator-RH	1		
4	BTP2282	• Frame-radiator-top	1		
5	BTP2284	• Frame-radiator-bottom	1		
6	BTP2275	• Radiator assembly	1		Part of ESR2727.
7	FTP8030	• Intercooler assembly-coolant	1		
8	SH108121	• Screw-M8	8		
9	WL108001L	• Washer-sprung-M8	8		
10	ERR4686	• Plug	1		
11	ERR4685	• O ring	1		
12	572312	• Bush-radiator mounting	8		
6	BTP2601S	• Radiator assembly	1		Part of ESR3683.
13	SH106205	Screw-hexagonal head-M6 x 20	4		
14	WM600041L	Washer-spring-1/4 dia-square	4		
15	WC106045	Washer-plain	4		
16	ESR282	Bracket-radiator upper mounting-LH	1		
16	ESR283	Bracket-radiator upper mounting-RH	1		
17	NRC5544	Mount-radiator rubber	2		
18	ESR2308	Cowl-cooling system fan-Standard	1		
19	ESR1800	Clip-hose	2		
20	NH105041	Nut-hexagonal-M5	2		
21	WA105001L	Washer-plain-standard-M5	2		
22	ALR1982	Bracket-bonnet stay	1		
23	SH106207L	Screw-hexagonal head-M6 x 20	3		
24	WC106047	Washer-M6	3		

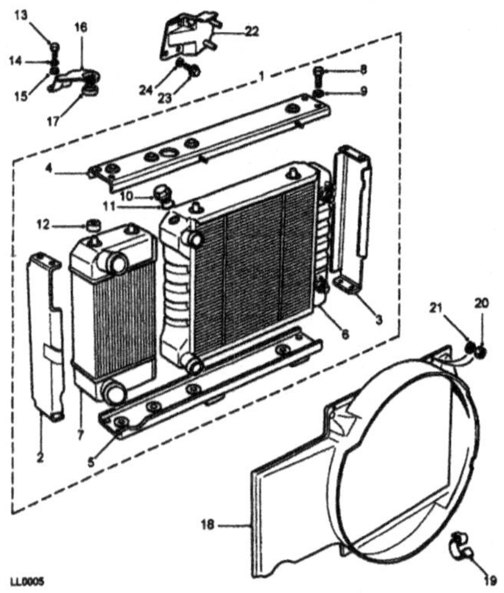

CHANGE POINTS:
(1) To (V) TA 976035
(2) From (V) TA 976036

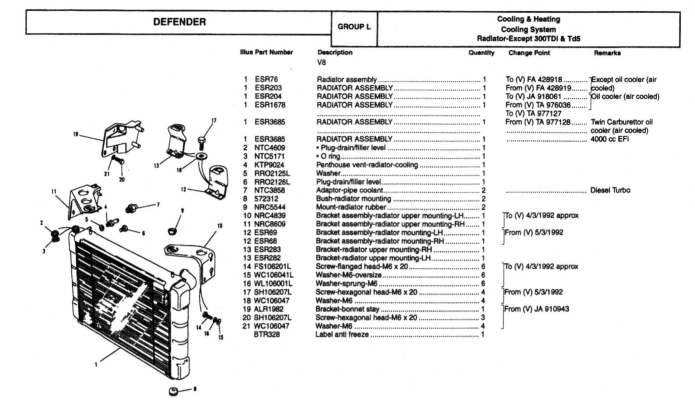

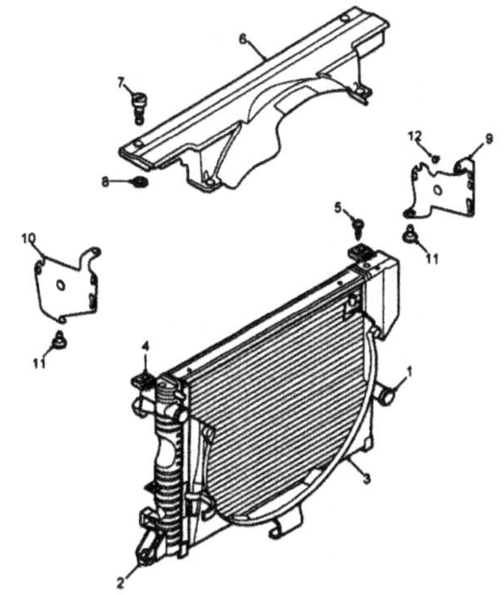

LL0006

Illus	Part Number	Description	Quantity	Change Point	Remarks
1	PCC107480	Radiator-cooling system-diesel-diesel	1	Note (1)	
1	PCC000670	Radiator-cooling system-diesel	1	Note (2)	
1	PCC001020	Radiator-cooling system	1	Note (3)	EGR Td5
2	PCG100300	Mounting-rubber	2		
3	PGK100670	COWL-COOLING SYSTEM FAN-LOWER	1		
4	ANR6462	• Fastener-Dzus-female	4		
5	PYP100550	• Screw-self tapping	2		
6	PGK100680	COWL-COOLING SYSTEM FAN-UPPER HALF	1		
7	ANR6461	• Fastener-Dzus-male	2		
8	PYF100830	• Washer-plastic-retaining	2		
9	PCU103780	Bracket-radiator mounting-RH	1		
10	PCU103790	Bracket-radiator mounting-LH	1		
11	PCG100330	Mount-radiator rubber	2		
12	FS106207L	Screw-flanged head-M6 x 20	4		
13	PCM100210	Intercooler assembly-coolant	1	Note (3)	EGR Td5

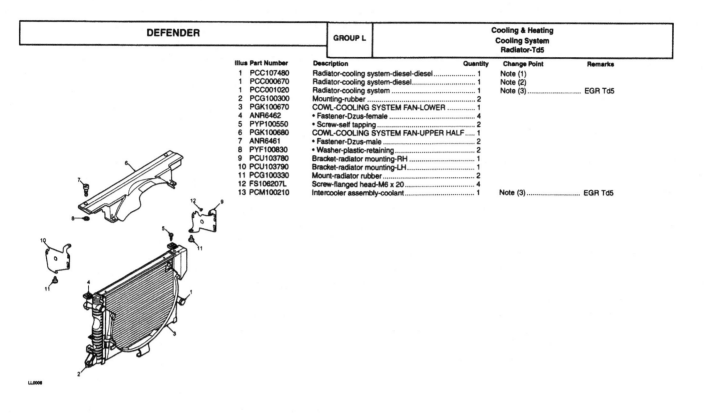

CHANGE POINTS:
(1) To (V) 1A 608153
(2) From (V) 1A 608154 To (V) ZA 999999
(3) From (V) 2A 622424

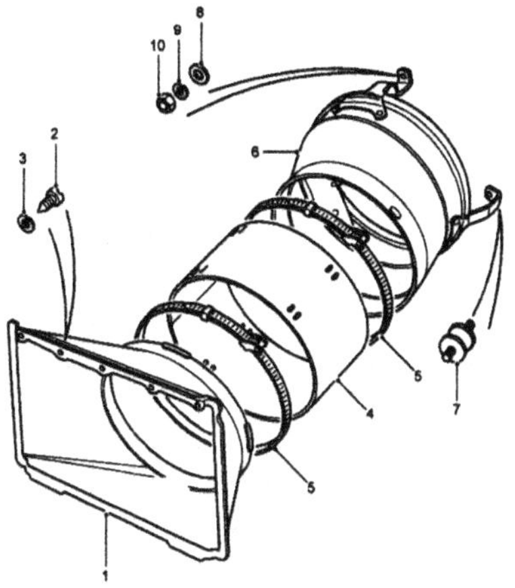

AHLXAA2A

Illus	Part Number	Description	Quantity	Change Point	Remarks
1	NRC3662	Cowl-cooling system fan	1	Note (1)	4 Cylinder Petrol
1	NTC3937	Cowl-cooling system fan-Heavy duty	1	Note (2)	
1	NRC3406	Cowl-cooling system fan	1	Note (3)	V8 Petrol
1	NTC5685	Cowl-cooling system fan	1	Note (4)	
1	NRC3977	Cowl-cooling system fan	1	Note (1)	Diesel Naturally Aspirated
1	NTC3937	Cowl-cooling system fan-Heavy duty	1	Note (2)	
1	NTC3937	Cowl-cooling system fan-Heavy duty	1		Diesel Turbo except TDi
1	ESR335	Cowl-cooling system fan	1	Note (5)	200 TDI
1	ESR2308	Cowl-cooling system fan-Standard	1	Note (6)	300 TDI
2	562979	Screw	5	Note (1)	
2	562979	Screw	4	Note (2)	
3	WS600047L	Washer-spring-fixing radiator cowl-double coil-1/4"-imperial	4	Note (2)	
8	595199	Washer-fixing radiator cowl	2		Diesel
3	WS105001	Washer-spring-fixing radiator cowl-double coil-M5-metric	2		TDi
4	NRC7227	Duct-air inlet heater	1		4 Cylinder
5	NRC6430	Clip	2		
6	ETC4989	Cowl-cooling system fan	1		
7	ETC4993	Mounting-flexible-fan cowl	3		
8	WA108051L	Washer-fixing engine cowl-8mm	2		
9	WL108001L	Washer-fixing engine cowl-sprung-M8	6		
10	FN108041L	Nut-flange-M8	NLA		Use FN108047L.

CHANGE POINTS:
(1) To (V) FA 389798
(2) From (V) FA 389799
(3) To (V) FA 428918
(4) From (V) FA 428919
(5) To (V) LA 939975
(6) From (V) MA 939976

Illus	Part Number	Description	Quantity	Change Point	Remarks
1	2943077	Cowl-cooling system fan	1		
2	562979	Screw	4		

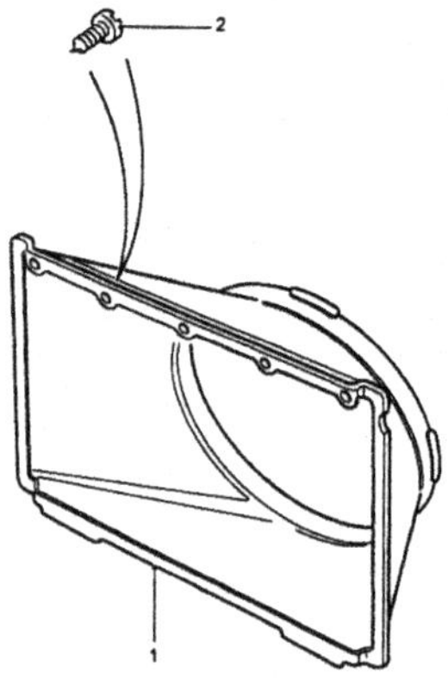

AKLXAA2A

Illus	Part Number	Description	Quantity	Change Point	Remarks
1	ERR7307	Cowl-cooling system fan	1		
2	ESR4588	Bracket	1		
3	ESR3226	Cowl-cooling system fan-upper	1		
4	562979	Screw	5		
5	WS600047L	Washer-spring-double coil-1/4"-imperial	5		
6	ESR2593	Clip	2		

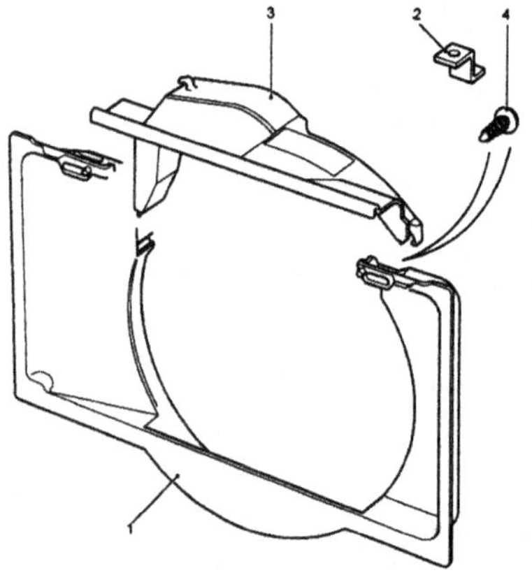

AMLXAA5B

DEFENDER

GROUP L

Cooling & Heating
Cooling System
Expansion Tank-TDi

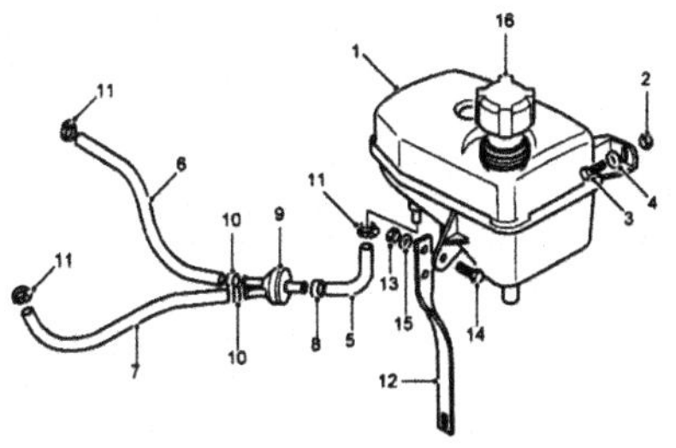

AHLXCC1B

Illus	Part Number	Description	Quantity	Change Point	Remarks
1	ESR63	Tank-radiator expansion	1		
2	NH106041L	Nut-hexagonal-nyloc-M6	2		
3	FS106167L	Screw-flanged head-flanged head-M6 x 16	3		
4	WA106041L	Washer-6mm	5		
5	ESR2343	Hose-expansion tank to pipe	1		
6	ESR3436	HOSE-BLEED PIPE ASSEMBLY TO EXPANSION TANK	1	Note (2)	200 TDI
9	ESR2348	• Pump-expansion tank ejector	1		
6	ESR2344	Hose-bleed pipe assembly to expansion tank	1	Note (1)	300 TDI
7	ESR2345	Hose-engine/ejector-expansion tank	1		
9	ESR2348	Pump-expansion tank ejector	1		
11	CN100208	Clip-hose	3		
12	ESR584	Bracket-expansion tank-for 200TDi	1	Note (2)	
12	ESR2313	Bracket-expansion tank-for 300 TDi	1	Note (1)	
13	NH106041L	Nut-hexagonal-nyloc-M6	1		
14	FS106167L	Screw-flanged head-flanged head-M6 x 16	1		
15	WA106041L	Washer-6mm	1		
16	NTC7161	Cap-expansion tank pressure-15psi	1		

CHANGE POINTS:
(1) From (V) MA 939976
(2) To (V) LA 939975

DEFENDER

GROUP L

Cooling & Heating
Cooling System
Expansion Tank-Except TDi and Td5

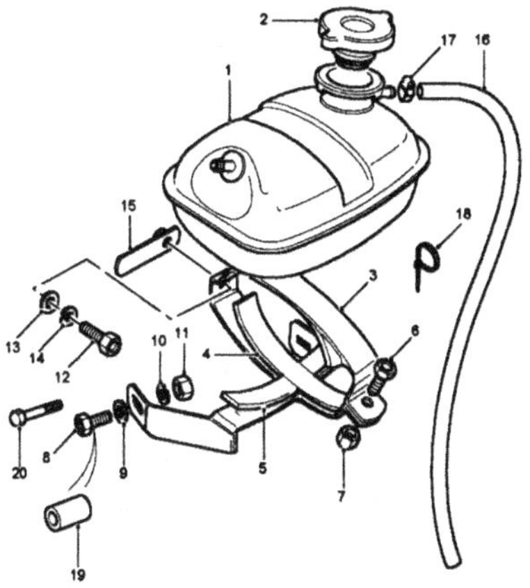

LL0031B

Illus	Part Number	Description	Quantity	Change Point	Remarks
1	ESR2733	Tank-cooling system expansion	1		4 Cylinder
1	ESR2733	Tank-cooling system expansion	1		50 LE
1	ESR2734	Tank-cooling system expansion	1		3500 cc V8
2	RTC3610	Cap-expansion tank pressure	1	Note (1)	4 Cylinder Naturally Aspirated
2	PCD100150	Cap-expansion tank pressure	1	Note (2)	4 Cylinder Naturally Aspirated
2	565540	Cap-expansion tank pressure	NLA		Use PCD100150. 4 Cylinder Diesel Turbo
2	PCD100150	Cap-expansion tank pressure	1	Note (2)	3500 cc V8
3	NRC6692	BRACKET-EXPANSION TANK SUPPORT	1		Except 50 LE
4	NRC5294	• Tape-self adhesive-foam	2		
5	NRC5295	• Tape-self adhesive-foam	2		
3	PCU103630	BRACKET-EXPANSION TANK SUPPORT	1		50 LE
4	NRC5294	• Tape-self adhesive-foam	1		
5	NRC5295	• Tape-self adhesive-foam	1		
6	SH106207L	Screw-hexagonal head-M6 x 20	1	Note (3)	
6	FS106201L	Screw-flanged head-M6 x 20	1	Note (4)	
6	SH106301L	Screw-hexagonal head-M6 x 30	1		50 LE
7	NY106047L	Nut-hexagonal head-nyloc-M6	1		
8	SH106207L	Screw-hexagonal head-M6 x 20	1	Note (3)	
8	FS106201L	Screw-flanged head-M6 x 20	2	Note (4)	
20	FB106081L	Bolt-flanged head-M6 x 40	2		50 LE
9	WC106047	Washer-M6	4	Note (3)	
9	WC106041L	Washer-M6-oversize	4	Note (4)	
10	WL106007L	Washer-M6-rectangular	2	Note (3)	
10	WL106001L	Washer-sprung-M6	2	Note (4)	
11	NH106047	Nut-M6-hexagonal	2	Note (3)	
11	NH106041L	Nut-hexagonal-nyloc-M6	2	Note (4)	
12	SH106207L	Screw-hexagonal head-M6 x 20	2	Note (3)	
12	FS106201L	Screw-flanged head-M6 x 20	1	Note (4)	
13	WC106047	Washer-M6	1	Note (3)	
13	WC106041L	Washer-M6-oversize	1	Note (4)	
14	WL106007L	Washer-M6-rectangular	1	Note (3)	
14	WL106001L	Washer-sprung-M6	1	Note (4)	

CHANGE POINTS:
(1) To (V) LA 932798
(2) From (V) LA 932799
(3) To (V) FA 389798
(4) From (V) FA 389799

Illus	Part Number	Description	Quantity	Change Point	Remarks
15	NRC7133	Nut	1		
16	564724	Hose-expansion tank overflow	1		
17	NRC1360	Clip-hose	1		
18	UKC6684L	Tie-cable-Black-3.5 x 150mm-inside serated	2		50 LE
19	ESR4224	Spacer	2		50 LE

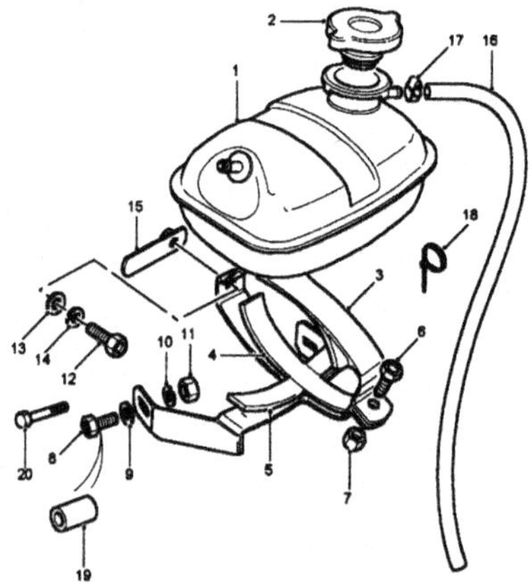

LL0031B

Illus	Part Number	Description	Quantity	Change Point	Remarks
1	PCF101530	Tank-cooling system expansion-diesel	1		
2	PCD100160	Cap-expansion tank pressure	1		
3	FS106167L	Screw-flanged head-flanged head-M6 x 16	1		
4	PCH116750	Hose assembly-expansion tank coolant	1		
5	MXC1848	Clip	2		
6	CP108105L	Clip-pipe-10mm	3		
7	MXC3130PUB	Fastener-drive-Black	3		
8	QYC100230	Clip-hose	2		
	PYC102590	Clip-spring band-14mm	4	Note (1)	

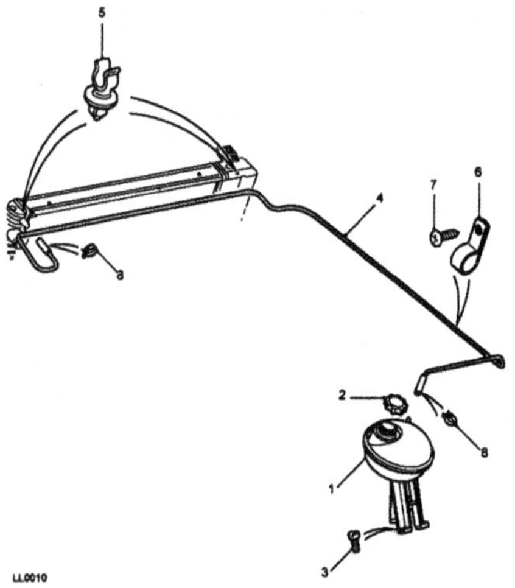

LL0010

CHANGE POINTS:
(1) From (V) XA 159807

Intercooler Hoses-TDi

Illus	Part Number	Description	Quantity	Change Point	Remarks
1	ESR2309	Hose-intercooler to inlet manifold air	1		
2	PYC101120L	Clip-hose-60mm	1		
3	CN100708	Clip-hose	1		
4	ESR2728	PIPE ASSEMBLY-INTERCOOLER TURBOCHARGER	1		300 TDI
5	ESR2055	• Pipe assembly-intercooler turbocharger	1		
6	ESR2119	• Mounting-rubber flexible support	1		
7	ESR2120	• Bracket-coolant bottom hose	1		
8	ESR2729	• Hose assembly-intercooler turbocharger	1		
9	ESR2730	• Hose-turbocharger to pipe	1		
10	PYC101120L	• Clip-hose-60mm	2		
11	NY108041L	• Nut-nyloc-M8	1		
12	SH108161	• Screw-hexagonal head-M8 x 16	1		
13	WA108041	• Washer-plain	1		
10	PYC101120L	• Clip-hose-60mm	2		

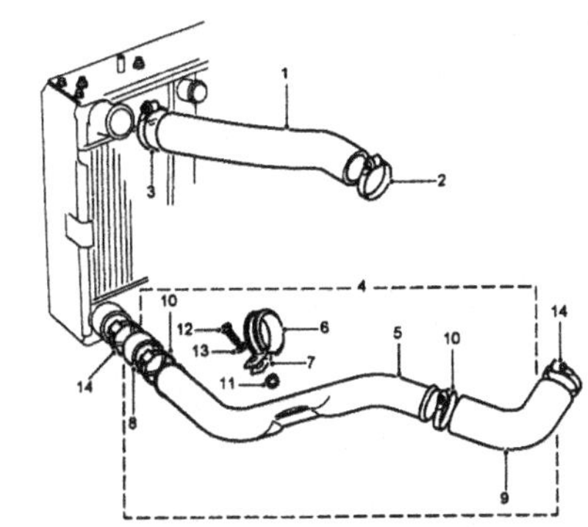

AHLXAA1D

Intercooler Hoses-Td5

Illus	Part Number	Description	Quantity	Change Point	Remarks
1	ESR4504	Intercooler-turbocharger air	1		
2	PNP101250	Pipe assembly-intercooler-metal	1		
3	PNH101590	Hose-intercooler turbocharger-rubber-rubber	1	Note (1)	
3	PNH102080	Hose-intercooler turbocharger-rubber	1	Note (2)	
4	PNH101600	Hose-intercooler turbocharger-rubber	1	Note (1)	
4	PNH102090	Hose-intercooler turbocharger-rubber	1	Note (2)	
5	PYC102340	Clip-hose-spring-band-60mm	4		
6	ESR4640	Hose-intercooler to inlet manifold air-rubber-rubber	1		
7	PYC102360	Clip-hose-spring-band-80mm	1		
8	PYC102350	Clip-hose	1		
9	FS108167PL	Bolt-flanged head-M8 x 16	2		
	WAP000050	Pipe-exhaust gas recirculation	1	Note (2)	Td5
	WIA000030	Cooler assembly-exhaust gas recirculation	1	Note (2)	Td5
	LYR000080	Stud-shoulder	2	Note (2)	Td5
	PYB000030	Plug-blanking.	1	Note (2)	Non EGR Td5

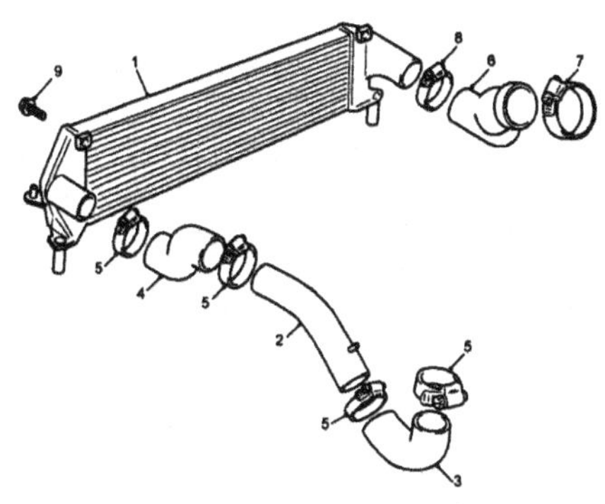

LL0007

CHANGE POINTS:
(1) To (V) ZA 999999
(2) From (V) 2A 622424

Cooling & Heating
Cooling System
Radiator Hoses-2.25 Petrol

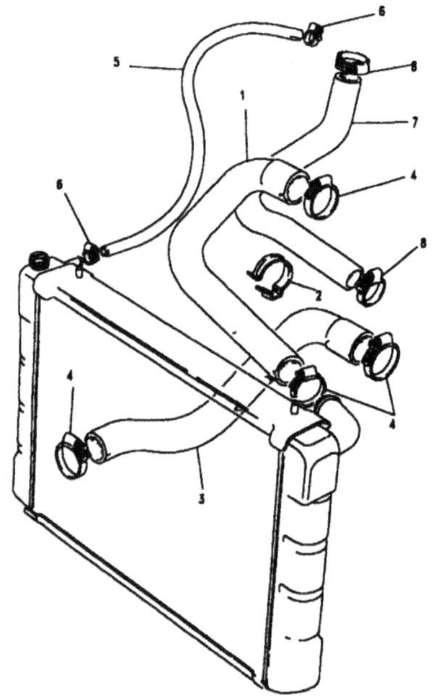

Illus	Part Number	Description	Quantity	Change Point	Remarks
1	NRC6403	Hose-radiator top coolant	1	Note (1)	Except Heavy duty
1	NRC6404	Hose-radiator top coolant	1	Note (1)	Heavy duty
2	NRC7448	Clip	1	Note (1)	
3	NRC3664	Hose-radiator bottom coolant	1	Note (1)	Except Heavy duty
3	NRC3976	Hose-radiator bottom coolant	1	Note (1)	Heavy duty
4	CN100508L	Clip-hose-50mm-less spring assist	4		
5	NRC4852	Hose-bleed pipe assembly to expansion tank	1	Note (1)	
6	AAU1979	Clip-hose	NLA	Note (1)	Use PYC101150.
7	NRC4850	Hose-expansion tank to pipe	1	Note (1)	
8	CN100408	Clip-hose-40mm	2	Note (1)	

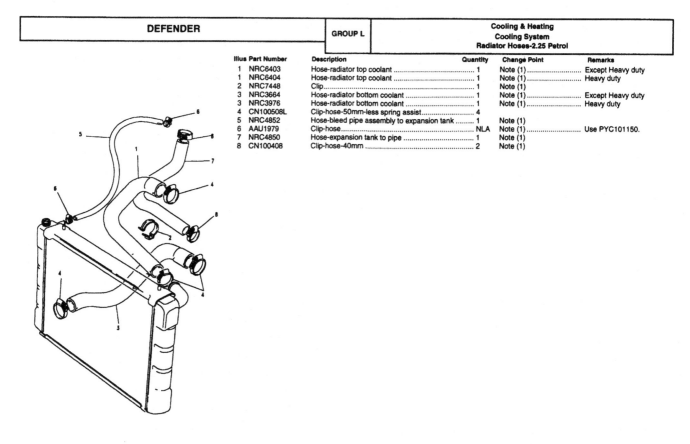

CHANGE POINTS:
(1) To (V) MA 962814

Cooling & Heating
Cooling System
Radiator Hoses-2.5 Petrol & Diesel

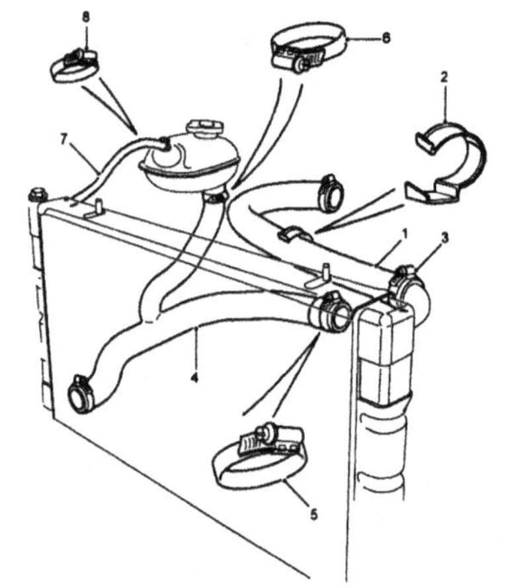

AHLXAAAA

Illus	Part Number	Description	Quantity	Change Point	Remarks
1	NRC6404	Hose-radiator top coolant	1	Note (1)	Petrol
1	NRC6404	Hose-radiator top coolant	1		Diesel Naturally Aspirated
1	NTC2029	Hose-radiator top coolant	1	Note (2)	Petrol
1	NTC2029	Hose-radiator top coolant	1		Diesel Naturally Aspirated
1	ESR2125	Hose-radiator top coolant	1	Note (3)	Petrol
1	ESR2125	Hose-radiator top coolant	1		Diesel Naturally Aspirated
1	ESR2125	Hose-radiator top coolant	1		Diesel Turbo
2	NRC7448	Clip	1		
3	CN100508L	Clip-hose-50mm-less spring assist	6		
	NRC4842	Hose-radiator bottom coolant-to engine	1	Note (1)	
	NRC4843	T piece	1	Note (1)	
	NRC4844	Hose-radiator bottom coolant-to radiator	1	Note (1)	
3	CN100508L	Clip-hose-50mm-less spring assist	4		
4	NRC4837	Hose assembly-expansion tank coolant	1	Note (1)	Diesel
4	NRC5503	Hose assembly-expansion tank coolant	1		Petrol
4	NTC3453	Hose assembly-expansion tank coolant	1	Note (4)	Diesel Turbo
4	NTC3453	Hose assembly-expansion tank coolant	1	Note (4)	4 Cylinder Petrol
4	NTC3453	Hose assembly-expansion tank coolant	1	Note (4)	4 Cylinder Diesel Natural-Aspirated
5	CN100508L	Clip-hose-50mm-less spring assist	2		
5	CN100408	Clip-hose-40mm	2		
6	CN100308L	Clip-hose-30mm	1		
7	NRC9726	Hose-radiator to expansion tank	1		Petrol
7	NRC9726	Hose-radiator to expansion tank	1		Diesel Naturally Aspirated
7	NTC2736	Hose-radiator to expansion tank	1	Note (5)	Diesel Turbo
8	AAU1979	Clip-hose	NLA		Use PYC101150.
8	PYC101150	Clip-hose	2		

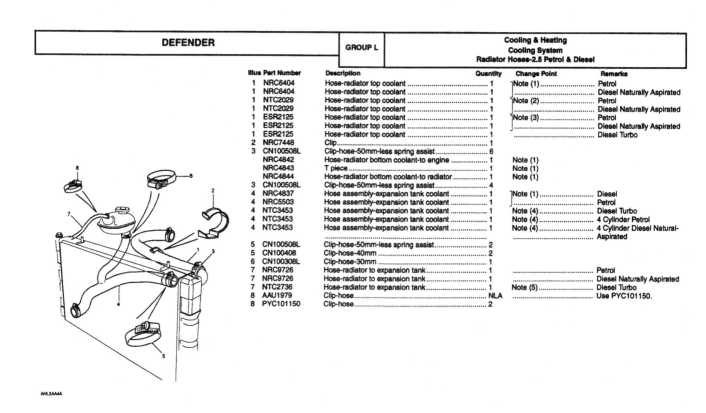

CHANGE POINTS:
(1) To (V) 261252
(2) From (V) 261253 To (V) FA 389798
(3) From (V) FA 389799
(4) From (V) 261253
(5) To (V) MA 962814

DEFENDER

GROUP L

Cooling & Heating
Cooling System
Radiator Hoses-6Cyl 2.8L

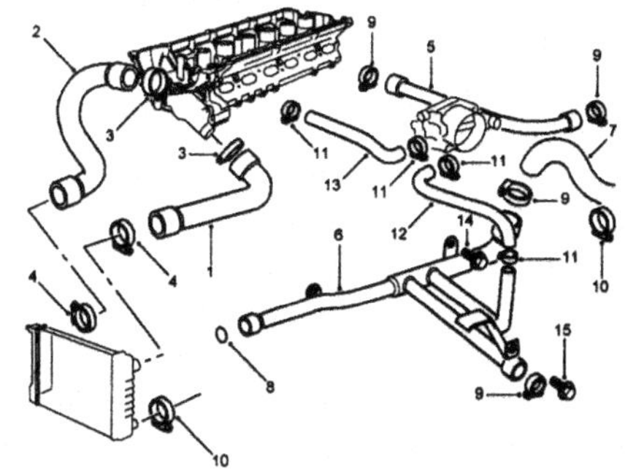

AKBQIG1A

Illus	Part Number	Description	Quantity	Change Point	Remarks
1	2943118	Hose-engine coolant	1		
2	2943119	Hose-engine coolant	1		
3	9952121	Clamp	2		
4	9952119	Clamp	2		
5	2943279	Hose-engine coolant	1		
6	2943342	Pipe assembly-heater	1		
7	2943280	Hose-engine coolant	1		
8	1703848	O ring	2		
9	9952113	Clamp-28mm	3		
10	8367179	Clamp	1		
11	1727509	Clamp	4		
12	1703945	Hose-engine coolant	1		
13	1703865	Hose-engine coolant	1		
14	9915017	Bolt-washer-M6 x 12-M6 x 12	1		
15	9913102	Bolt-washer-M8 x 16	1		

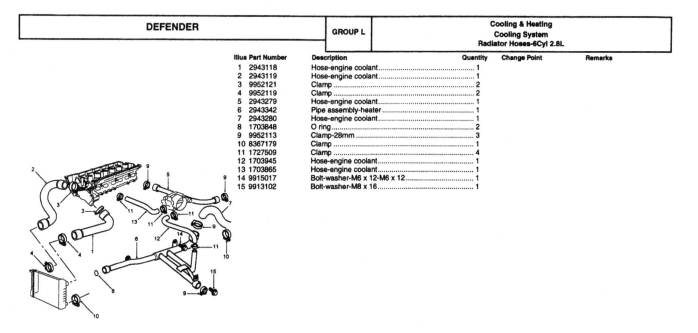

DEFENDER

GROUP L

Cooling & Heating
Cooling System
Radiator Hoses-V8

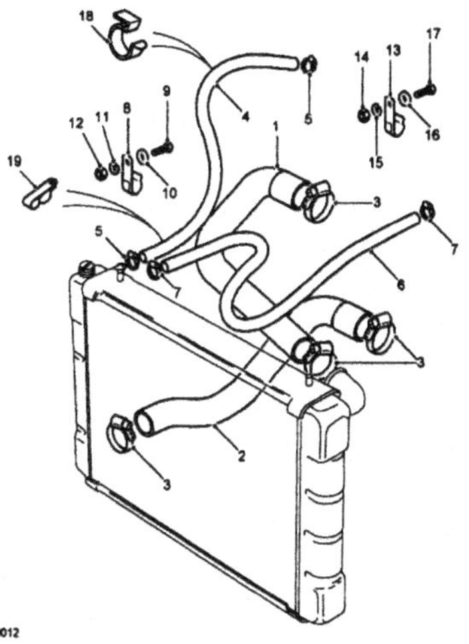

LL0012

Illus	Part Number	Description	Quantity	Change Point	Remarks
1	NRC5985	Hose-radiator top coolant	1	Note (1)	V8 Petrol except air
1	NTC5686	Hose-radiator top coolant	1	Note (2)	conditioning
1	NRC9710	Hose-radiator top coolant	1	Note (3)	V8 Petrol air conditioning
1	NTC5687	Hose-radiator top coolant	1	Note (4)	
2	NRC3405	Hose-radiator bottom coolant	1	Note (5)	Twin Carburettor
2	NTC3543	Hose-radiator bottom coolant	1	Note (6)	
2	ESR4223	Hose-radiator bottom coolant	1		V8 EFi Japan
2	PCH116030	Hose-radiator bottom coolant	1		V8 EFi 50 LE
3	CN100508L	Clip-hose-50mm-less spring assist	4		
4	NRC9726	Hose-radiator to expansion tank-except oil cooler	1		
4	NTC2736	Hose-radiator to expansion tank-with oil cooler	1		
5	PYC101150	Clip-hose	2		
6	90575977	Hose-expansion tank coolant	1		
7	PYC101150	Clip-hose	2		
8	NRC2383	Clip-hose	1		
9	FS106201L	Screw-flanged head-M6 x 20	1		
9	FS106207L	Screw-flanged head-M6 x 20	1		
10	WA106041L	Washer-6mm	1		
11	WM106001L	Washer-spring-M6-square	1		
12	NH106041L	Nut-hexagonal-nyloc-M6	1		
13	239600	Clip-cable-LH	1		Except air conditioning
14	FS108207L	Screw-flanged head-M8 x 20	1		V8 Petrol except air
					conditioning
15	WA108051L	Washer-8mm	1		Except air conditioning
16	WL108001L	Washer-sprung-M8	1		Except air conditioning
17	FN108041L	Nut-flange-M8	NLA		Use FN108047L.
					Except air conditioning
18	PYC102390	Clip-coolant hose	1		V8 EFi
19	PYC102380	Clip-double	1		V8 EFi
	PCH116020	Hose-cooling system bleed	1		50 LE

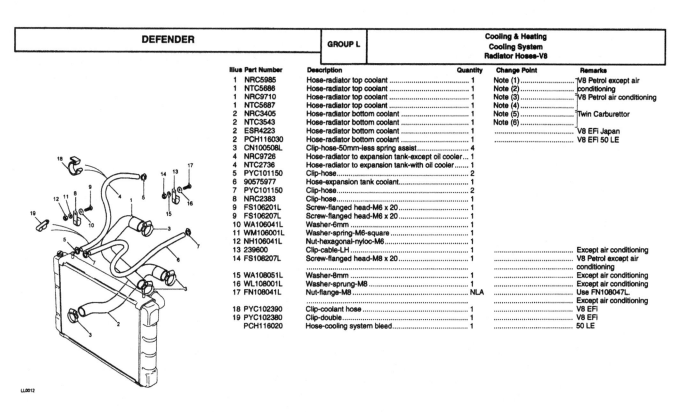

CHANGE POINTS:
(1) To (V) FA 428918
(2) From (V) FA 428919
(3) To (V) FA 429127
(4) From (V) FA 429128
(5) To (V) 257176
(6) From (V) 257177

DEFENDER	GROUP L	Cooling & Heating Cooling System Radiator Hoses-200TDi

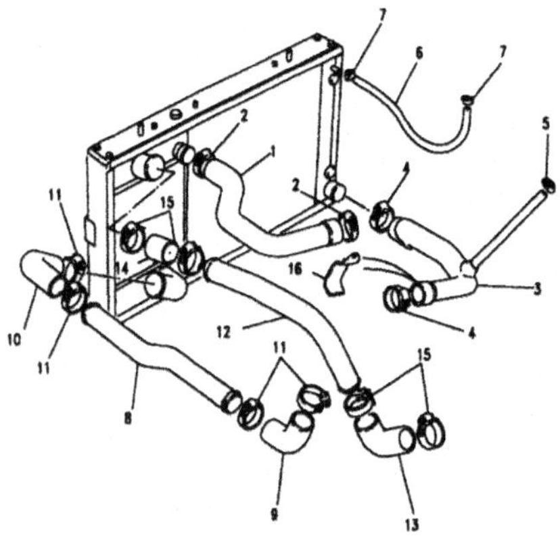

Illus	Part Number	Description	Quantity	Change Point	Remarks
1	NTC4895	Hose-radiator top coolant	1		
2	CN100508	Clip-hose-top hose...	NLA	....	Use CN100508L.
2	CN100508L	Clip-hose-top hose-50mm-less spring assist...........	2		
3	ESR536	Hose-radiator bottom coolant	1	....	Except air conditioning
3	ESR536	Hose-radiator bottom coolant	1	Note (1)...........................	Air conditioning
3	ESR1686	Hose-radiator bottom coolant	1	Note (2)...........................	Air conditioning
4	CN100508L	Clip-hose-bottom hose-50mm-less spring assist.....	2		
5	ESR3607	Clip-hose-26mm	1		
6	NTC4898	Hose-bleed pipe assembly to expansion tank	1	Note (3)	
6	ESR3436	HOSE-BLEED PIPE ASSEMBLY TO EXPANSION TANK..	1	Note (4)	
	ESR2348	• Pump-expansion tank ejector	1		
	PDL100000	• Pump-expansion tank ejector	1		
7	CN100208L	Clip-hose-20mm	2		
8	NTC5628	Hose-intercooler turbocharger	1		
9	ESR299	Hose-intercooler turbocharger	1	Note (5)	
9	ESR1906	Hose-intercooler turbocharger	NLA	Note (6)...........................	Use ESR2934.
9	ESR2934	Hose-intercooler turbocharger	1	Note (6)	
10	ESR298	Hose-intercooler turbocharger	1		
11	CN100608L	Clip-hose..	NLA	....	Use PYC101120.
11	PYC101120	Clip-hose..	NLA	....	Use PYC101120L.
11	PYC101120L	Clip-hose-60mm	4		
12	NTC5627	Pipe-coolant...	1		
13	ESR299	Hose-intercooler turbocharger	1	Note (5)	
13	ESR1906	Hose-intercooler turbocharger	NLA	Note (6)...........................	Use ESR2934.
13	ESR2934	Hose-intercooler turbocharger	1	Note (6)	
14	ESR289	Hose-intercooler to inlet manifold air	1		
15	PYC101120L	Clip-hose-60mm	4		
16	ESR400	Bracket-coolant bottom hose	1	....	Air conditioning

CHANGE POINTS:
(1) To (V) JA 915821
(2) From (V) JA 915822
(3) To (V) MA 948142
(4) From (V) MA 948143
(5) To (V) JA 915341
(6) From (V) JA 915342

DEFENDER	GROUP L	Cooling & Heating Cooling System Radiator Hoses-300TDi

Illus	Part Number	Description	Quantity	Change Point	Remarks
1	ESR2298	Hose-radiator top coolant	1		
2	CN100508L	Clip-hose-50mm-less spring assist..........................	2		
3	ESR3121	Hose-radiator bottom coolant	1		
4	STC7430	Clip-hose-30mm	NLA	....	Use CN100308L.
4	CN100308L	Clip-hose-30mm	2		
5	CN100508L	Clip-hose-50mm-less spring assist..........................	2		
6	ESR2662	Clip-hose..	2		
	594594	Tie-cable-White.-4.6 x 385mm-inside serated	2		

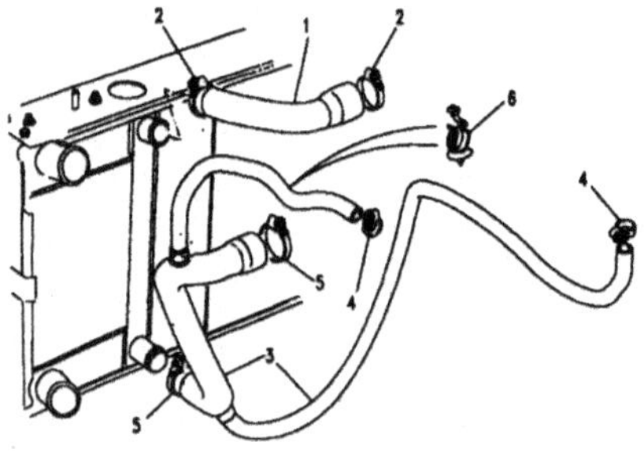

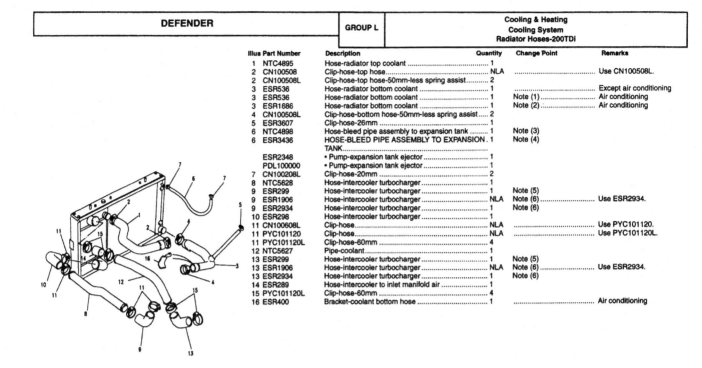

Illus	Part Number	Description	Quantity	Change Point	Remarks
1	PCH114600	Hose-radiator top coolant	1		
2	PYP10008L	Screw-bleed	1		
		HOSE-COOLANT PUMP/EXPANSION TANK/WATER VALVE/THERMOSTAT			
3	PCH116010	Hose-coolant pump/expansion tank/water valve/thermostat	1	Note (2)	
3	PCH117190	Hose-coolant pump/expansion tank/water valve/thermostat	1	Note (3)	
4	PCH115470	Hose-radiator bottom coolant	1		
5	PEM100990	Housing-thermostat	1		
6	PYC102240	Clip-plastic-large	2		
7	PYC102250	Clip-plastic-small	2		
8	PYC102100	Clip-spring band	4		
9	PYC101890	Clip-spring band	1		
10	PYC101910	Clip-spring band	1		
11	PYC102110	Clip-spring band	2		
12	PYC102190	Clip-hose-22mm	5		
13	PCU103610	Bracket-coolant hose support	1		
14	PYC102620	Clip-hose	3		
15	PCH114640	Hose-coolant oil cooler to radiator	1		
16	PCH114650	Hose-fuel cooler to return	1		
17	FS106127L	Screw-flanged head-M6 x 12	1		

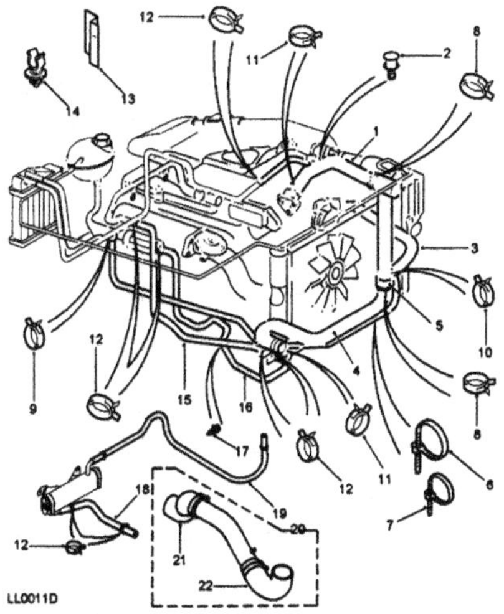

LL0011D

CHANGE POINTS:
(2) To (V) XA 169398
(3) From (V) XA 169399

Illus	Part Number	Description	Quantity	Change Point	Remarks
		VEHICLES WITH COOLED EGR FITTED			
18	PEH000310	Hose-engine to EGR cooler	1	Note (1)	EGR Td5
19	PCH001370	Hose-EGR cooler return	1	Note (1)	EGR Td5

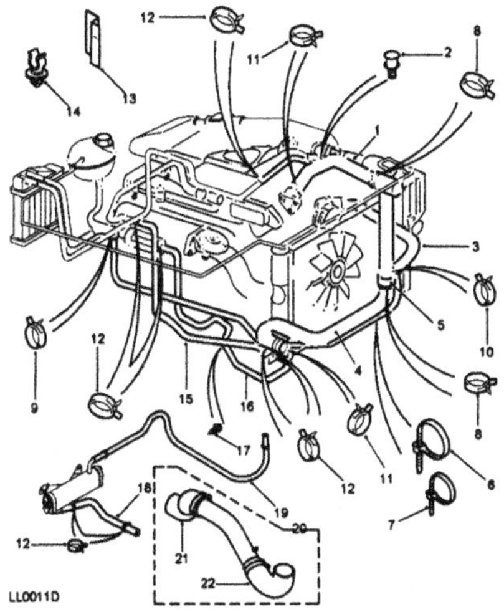

LL0011D

CHANGE POINTS:
(1) From (V) 2A 622424

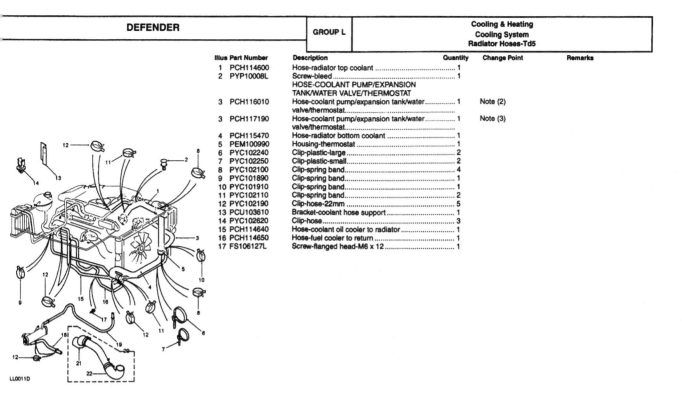

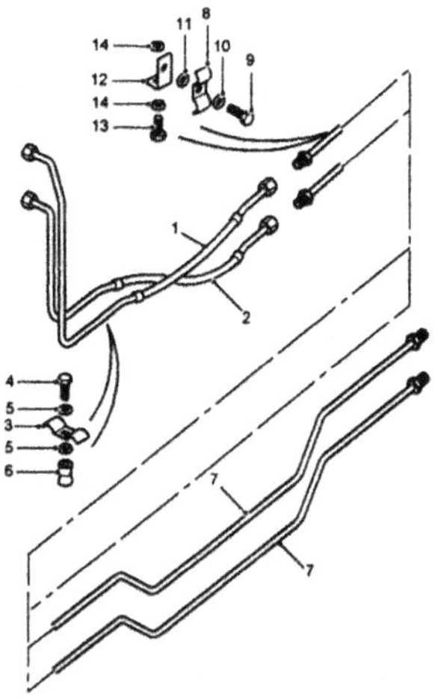

LL0030

Illus	Part Number	Description	Quantity	Change Point	Remarks
		PIPE ASSEMBLY-COOLER TO FILTER OIL			
1	ESR570	RH-front	1	Note (1)	Except air conditioning
1	ESR1919	RH-front	1	Note (2)	
1	ESR530	RH-front	1	Note (1)	Air conditioning
1	ESR1918	RH-front	1	Note (2)	
		PIPE ASSEMBLY-COOLER TO FILTER OIL			
2	ESR571	LH-front	1	Note (1)	Except air conditioning
2	ESR1920	LH-front	1	Note (2)	
2	ESR531	LH-front	1	Note (1)	Air conditioning
2	ESR1917	LH-front	1	Note (2)	
3	594637	Clamp	NLA		Use ESR1584.
3	ESR1584	Clamp	1		
4	FS106167L	Screw-flanged head-flanged head-M6 x 16	1		
5	WA106041L	Washer-6mm	2		
6	NN106011	Nutsert-blind	1		
7	ESR527	Hose-oil cooler to pipe-rear	2	Note (1)	
7	ESR1916	Hose-oil cooler to pipe-rear	2	Note (2)	
8	594637	Clamp	NLA		Use ESR1584.
8	ESR1584	Clamp	1		
9	FS106201L	Screw-flanged head-M6 x 20	1		
10	WA108051L	Washer-8mm	1		
11	WA106041L	Washer-6mm	1		
12	NTC5897	Bracket-mounting oil pipe	1		
13	SH505081L	Screw-hexagonal head-5/8UNC x 1	1		
14	WA106001L	Washer-M6	2		

CHANGE POINTS:
(1) To (V) JA 918061
(2) From (V) JA 918062

Illus	Part Number	Description	Quantity	Change Point	Remarks
1	UBU100450	Bracket-pipe to pipe transmission cooling	1	Note (1)	
2	FS108167PL	Bolt-flanged head-M8 x 16	1		
3	ESR1615	Clamp	4	Note (1)	
4	UBU100440	Bracket-pipe to pipe transmission cooling	1	Note (1)	
5	NTC6847	Clamp	1	Note (1)	
6	FN106047L	Nut-flange-M6	1		
7	UBP101150	PIPE-OIL COOLER TO GEARBOX	1	Note (1)	
	ESR1594	• O ring	NLA		Use ESR1594L.
	ESR1594L	O ring			
8	UBP101160	PIPE-OIL COOLER/TRANSMISSION	1	Note (1)	
	ESR1594	• O ring	NLA		Use ESR1594L.
	ESR1594L	O ring			
9	UBU100430	Bracket-pipe to pipe transmission cooling	1	Note (1)	
10	FS110167	Screw	1	Note (1)	

NOT ILLUSTRATED
PAS ILLUSTREE
NICHT ILLUSTRIERT
SENZA IL DISEGNO
SIN EL DISENO
SEM ILLUSTRACAO
NIET AFGEBEELD

TF 0007

CHANGE POINTS:
(1) From (V) XA 159807

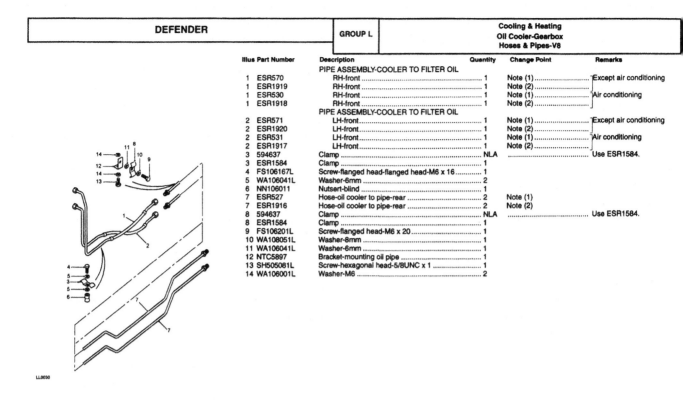

Illus	Part Number	Description	Quantity	Change Point	Remarks
1	ESR488	Oil cooler assembly transmission	1	Note (1)	V8 Petrol
1	ESR1554	Oil cooler assembly transmission	1	Note (2)	
1	ESR3229	Oil cooler assembly transmission	1	Note (3)	
2	ESR489	Bracket-mounting oil cooler	1		
3	FS106167L	Screw-flanged head-flanged head-M6 x 16	2		
4	SH106121L	Screw-hexagonal head-M6 x 12	2		
5	WA106041L	Washer-6mm	4		
6	NH106041L	Nut-hexagonal-nyloc-M6	4		
7	NRC7459	Bolt-u	4		V8 Petrol except air conditioning
8	WA106041L	Washer-6mm	8		
9	NH106041L	Nut-hexagonal-nyloc-M6	8		

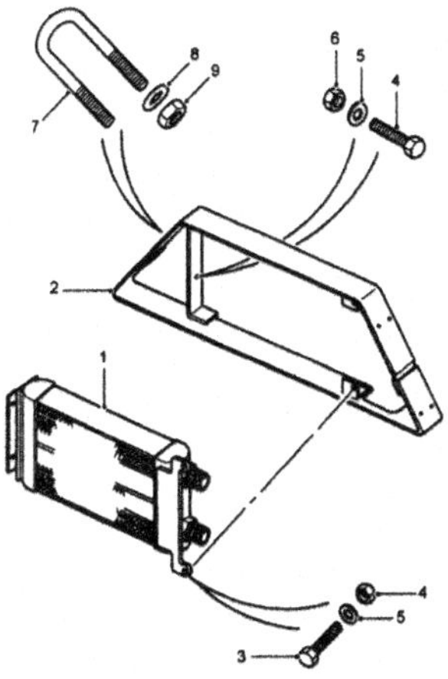

AHLXAG2A

CHANGE POINTS:
(1) To (V) JA 918061
(2) From (V) JA 918062 To (V) MA 951317
(3) From (V) MA 951418

Illus	Part Number	Description	Quantity	Change Point	Remarks
1	FTC5360	Oil cooler assembly transmission	1	Note (1)	V8 Petrol
2	UBP101260	Pipe-transmission/oil cooler	1	Note (1)	V8 Petrol
3	UBP101270	Pipe assembly-oil cooler to transmission	1	Note (1)	V8 Petrol
4	ESR1594	O ring	NLA	Note (1)	Use ESR1594L. V8 Petrol
5	SH106351L	Screw-hexagonal head-M6 x 35	1	Note (1)	V8 Petrol
6	WL106001L	Washer-sprung-M6	1	Note (1)	V8 Petrol

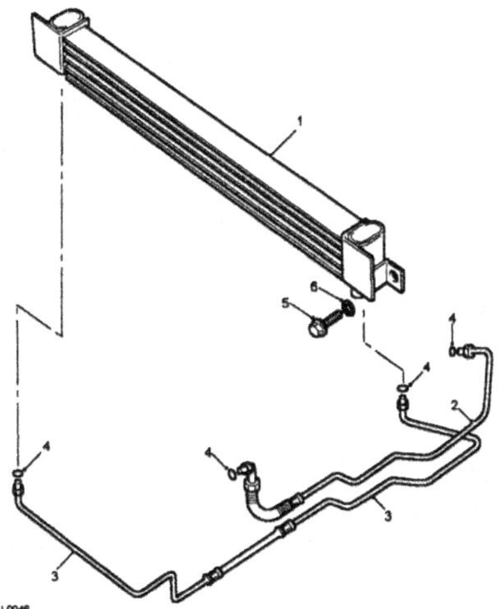

LL0046

CHANGE POINTS:
(1) From (V) XA 159807

Pipes-4 Cylinder-To (V) FA389798

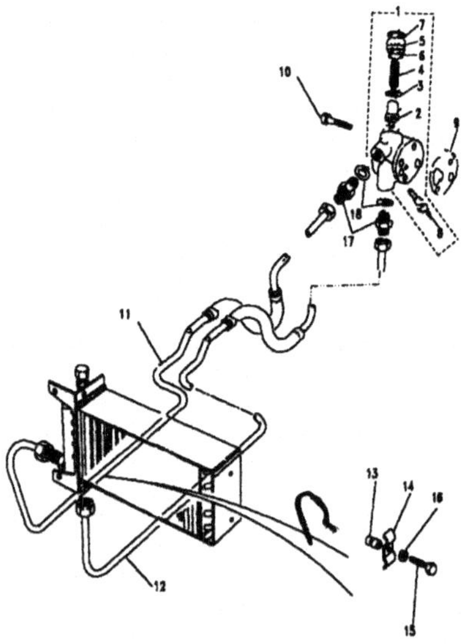

Illus	Part Number	Description	Quantity	Change Point	Remarks
1	ERC7755	VALVE ASSEMBLY-OIL COOLER	1	Note (1)	2250 cc
2	ERC5923	• Thermostat assembly-oil	1		
3	ERC7756	• Washer	1		
4	ERC7757	• Spring	1		
5	ERC5756	• Plug	1		
6	ERC5757	• O ring	1		
7	CR110301	• Circlip	1		
8	PRC2505	• Transducer coolant temperature	1		
9	ERC7773	Washer	1	Note (1)	2250 cc 4 Cylinder
10	ERC9499	Bolt	1		2250 cc 4 Cylinder
11	NRC5820	Pipe assembly-engine oil feed	1		2250 cc 4 Cylinder except air conditioning
11	NRC8196	Pipe assembly-engine oil feed	1		2250 cc 4 Cylinder air conditioning
11	NRC8507	Pipe assembly-engine oil feed	1		2500 cc 4 Cylinder except air conditioning
11	NRC8509	Pipe assembly-engine oil feed	1		2500 cc 4 Cylinder air conditioning
12	NRC5819	Pipe-oil cooler to engine	1		2250 cc 4 Cylinder except air conditioning
12	NRC8197	Pipe-oil cooler to engine	1		2250 cc 4 Cylinder air conditioning
12	NRC8508	Pipe-oil cooler to engine	1		2500 cc 4 Cylinder except air conditioning
12	NRC8510	Pipe-oil cooler to engine	1		2500 cc 4 Cylinder air conditioning
13	NN106011	Nutsert-blind	1		4 Cylinder
14	594637	Clamp	NLA		Use ESR1584. 4 Cylinder
14	ESR1584	Clamp	1		4 Cylinder
15	FS106167L	Screw-flanged head-flanged head-M6 x 16	1		4 Cylinder
16	WL106001L	Washer-sprung-M6	1		4 Cylinder
17	NRC8618	Coupling	2		2500 cc 4 Cylinder
18	ETC7398	Washer-sealing	2		

NOTE:FOR 2.5 VALVE ASSY-REFER TO ENGINE

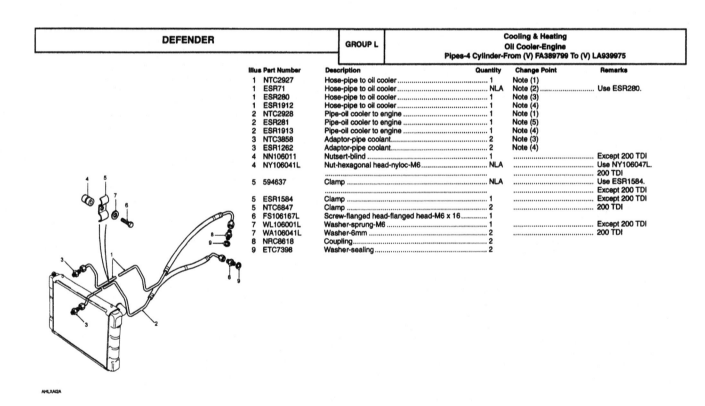

CHANGE POINTS:
(1) To (V) FA 389798

Pipes-4 Cylinder-From (V) FA389799 To (V) LA939975

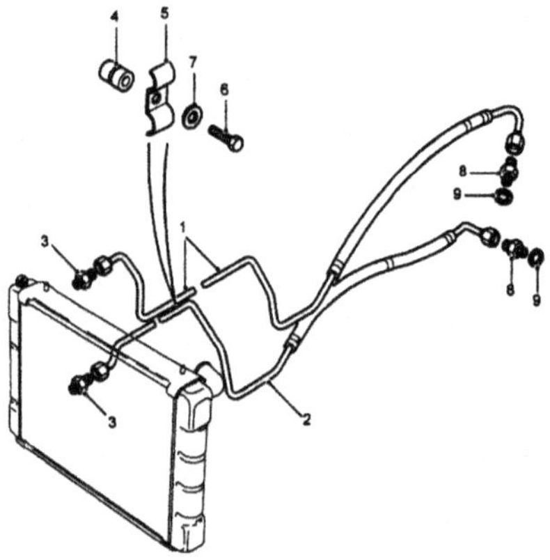

AHLXAI2A

Illus	Part Number	Description	Quantity	Change Point	Remarks
1	NTC2927	Hose-pipe to oil cooler	1	Note (1)	
1	ESR71	Hose-pipe to oil cooler	NLA	Note (2)	Use ESR280.
1	ESR280	Hose-pipe to oil cooler	1	Note (3)	
1	ESR1912	Hose-pipe to oil cooler	1	Note (4)	
2	NTC2928	Pipe-oil cooler to engine	1	Note (1)	
2	ESR281	Pipe-oil cooler to engine	1	Note (5)	
2	ESR1913	Pipe-oil cooler to engine	1	Note (4)	
3	NTC3858	Adaptor-pipe coolant	2	Note (3)	
3	ESR1262	Adaptor-pipe coolant	2	Note (4)	
4	NN106011	Nutsert-blind	1		Except 200 TDI
4	NY106041L	Nut-hexagonal head-nyloc-M6	NLA		Use NY106047L. 200 TDI
5	594637	Clamp	NLA		Use ESR1584. Except 200 TDI
5	ESR1584	Clamp	1		Except 200 TDI
5	NTC6847	Clamp	2		200 TDI
6	FS106167L	Screw-flanged head-flanged head-M6 x 16	1		
7	WL106001L	Washer-sprung-M6	1		Except 200 TDI
7	WA106041L	Washer-6mm	2		200 TDI
8	NRC8618	Coupling	2		
9	ETC7398	Washer-sealing	2		

CHANGE POINTS:
(1) To (V) FA 430160
(2) From (V) FA 430161
(3) To (V) JA 918061
(4) From (V) JA 918062
(5) From (V) FA 430161 To (V) JA 918061

DEFENDER

GROUP L

Cooling & Heating
Oil Cooler-Engine
Pipes-300TDI-From (V) MA939976

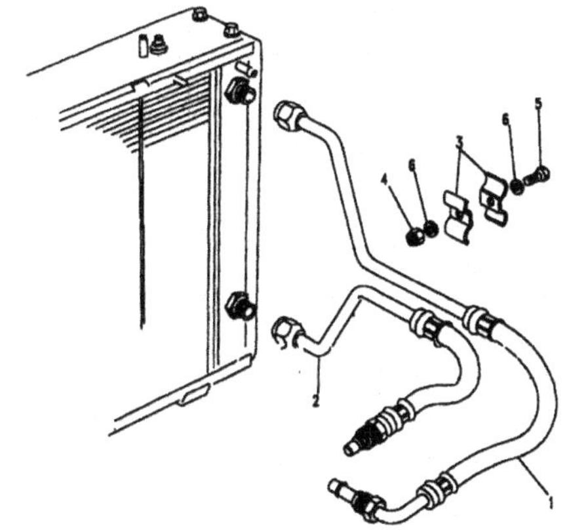

Illus	Part Number	Description	Quantity	Change Point	Remarks
1	ESR1931	PIPE-OIL COOLER TO ENGINE	1	Note (1)	
	ESR1594L	• O ring	4		
1	ESR3690	Pipe-oil cooler to engine	NLA	Note (2)	Use PBP101130 qty 1 When replacing ESR3690 - both oil cooler hoses must be replaced to ensure clamp fits pipes together correctly with PBP101140 qty 1.
1	PBP101130	Pipe-oil cooler to engine	1	Note (2)	
2	ESR2629	PIPE-ENGINE TO OIL COOLER	1	Note (1)	
	ESR1594	• O ring	NLA		Use ESR1594L.
2	ESR3691	PIPE-ENGINE TO OIL COOLER	NLA	Note (2)	Use PBP101130 qty 1 When replacing ESR3691 - both oil cooler hoses must be replaced to ensure clamp fits pipes together correctly with PBP101140 qty 1.
	ESR1594L	• O ring	4		
2	PBP101140	Pipe-engine to oil cooler	1	Note (2)	
3	NTC6847	Clamp	2		
4	NY106041	Nut-flange-nyloc-M6	1		
5	FS106167L	Screw-flanged head-flanged head-M6 x 16	1		
6	WA106041L	Washer-6mm	2		

CHANGE POINTS:
(1) To (V) TA 975349
(2) From (V) TA 975350

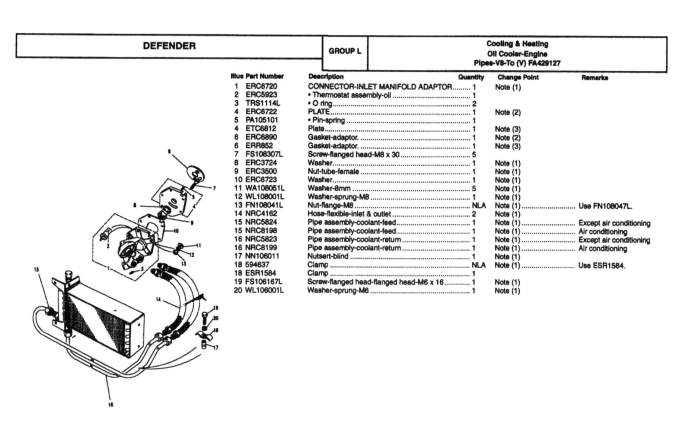

DEFENDER

GROUP L

Cooling & Heating
Oil Cooler-Engine
Pipes-V8-To (V) FA429127

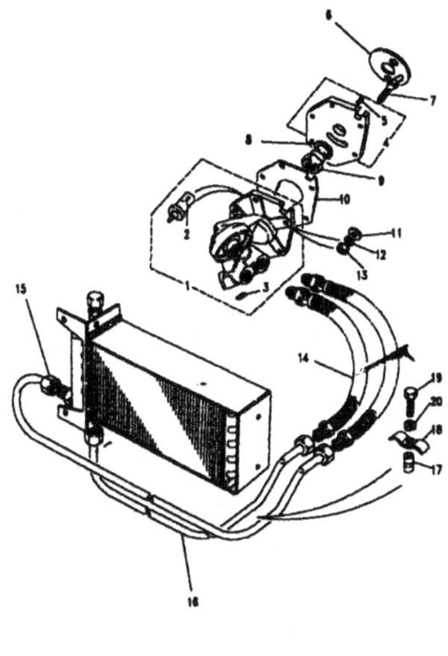

Illus	Part Number	Description	Quantity	Change Point	Remarks
1	ERC6720	CONNECTOR-INLET MANIFOLD ADAPTOR	1	Note (1)	
2	ERC5923	• Thermostat assembly-oil	1		
3	TRS1114L	• O ring	2		
4	ERC6722	PLATE	1	Note (2)	
5	PA105101	• Pin-spring	1		
4	ETC6812	Plate	1	Note (3)	
6	ERC6890	Gasket-adaptor.	1	Note (2)	
6	ERR852	Gasket-adaptor.	1	Note (3)	
7	FS108307L	Screw-flanged head-M8 x 30	5		
8	ERC3724	Washer	1	Note (1)	
9	ERC3500	Nut-tube-female	1	Note (1)	
10	ERC6723	Washer	1	Note (1)	
11	WA108051L	Washer-8mm	5	Note (1)	
12	WL108001L	Washer-sprung-M8	1	Note (1)	
13	FN108041L	Nut-flange-M8	NLA	Note (1)	Use FN108047L.
14	NRC4162	Hose-flexible-inlet & outlet	2	Note (1)	
15	NRC5824	Pipe assembly-coolant-feed	1	Note (1)	Except air conditioning
15	NRC8198	Pipe assembly-coolant-feed	1	Note (1)	Air conditioning
16	NRC5823	Pipe assembly-coolant-return	1	Note (1)	Except air conditioning
16	NRC8199	Pipe assembly-coolant-return	1	Note (1)	Air conditioning
17	NN106011	Nutsert-blind	1	Note (1)	
18	594637	Clamp	NLA	Note (1)	Use ESR1584.
18	ESR1584	Clamp	1		
19	FS106167L	Screw-flanged head-flanged head-M6 x 16	1	Note (1)	
20	WL106001L	Washer-sprung-M6	1	Note (1)	

CHANGE POINTS:
(1) To (V) FA 429127
(2) To (V) 322599
(3) From (V) 322600 To (V) FA 429127

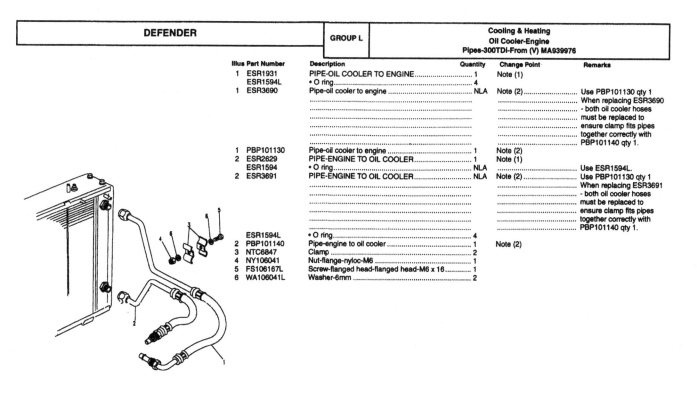

DEFENDER

GROUP L

Cooling & Heating
Oil Cooler-Engine
Pipes-V8-From (V) FA429128

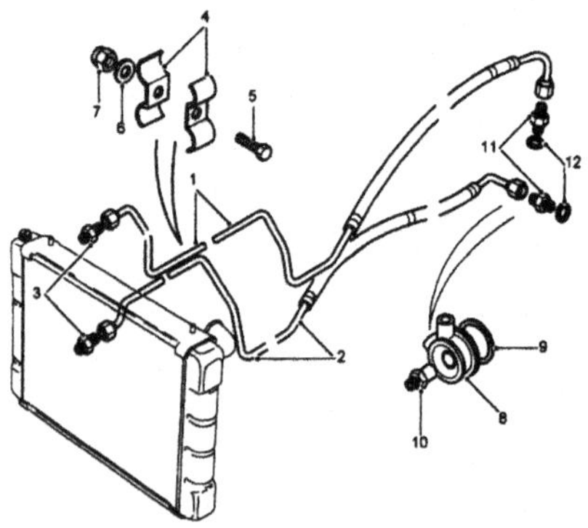

AHLXAI4A

Illus	Part Number	Description	Quantity	Change Point	Remarks
1	ESR399	Hose-pipe to oil cooler	1	Note (2)	V8 Petrol
1	ESR583	Hose-pipe to oil cooler	1	Note (3)	
1	ESR1915	Hose-pipe to oil cooler	1	Note (4)	
2	NTC5624	Pipe-oil cooler to engine-EXCEPT to RHD Gemmer p/s/box fr HA469918	1	Note (5)	
2	ESR398	Pipe-oil cooler to engine- to RHD Gemmer p/s/box. fr HA469818	1		
2	ESR1914	Pipe-oil cooler to engine	1	Note (4)	
3	NTC3858	Adaptor-pipe coolant	2	Note (5)	
3	ESR1262	Adaptor-pipe coolant	2	Note (4)	
4	NTC6847	Clamp	2	Note (1)	
5	FS106167L	Screw-flanged head-flanged head-M6 x 16	1	Note (1)	
6	WA106041L	Washer-6mm	1	Note (1)	
7	NY106047L	Nut-hexagonal head-nyloc-M6	1		V8 Petrol
8	ERC8501	Adaptor-oil filter	1	Note (1)	V8 Petrol
9	ERR852	Gasket-adaptor.	1		
10	ERC2226L	Adaptor-oil filter	1		
11	ETC9064	Adaptor-oil cooler	2		
12	ETC9065	Washer-sealing	2		

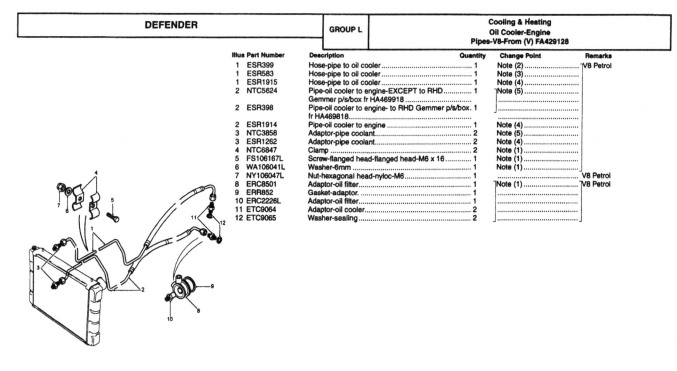

CHANGE POINTS:
(1) From (V) FA 429128
(2) From (V) FA 429128 To (V) HA 906108
(3) From (V) HA 906109 To (V) JA 918061
(4) From (V) JA 918062
(5) From (V) FA 429128 To (V) JA 918061

DEFENDER

GROUP L

Cooling & Heating
Oil Cooler-Engine
Pipes-V8EFI-4.0L

Illus	Part Number	Description	Quantity	Change Point	Remarks
1	PBP101150	Pipe-engine to oil cooler	1		
2	ESR1594L	O ring	2		
3	ESR3098	O ring-small	1		
4	PBP101160	Pipe-oil cooler to engine	1		
5	ESR1594L	O ring	2		
6	NTC6847	Clamp	2		
7	FS106167L	Screw-flanged head-flanged head-M6 x 16	1		
8	WA106001	Washer-plain-M6	1		
9	NY106041	Nut-flange-nyloc-M6	1		

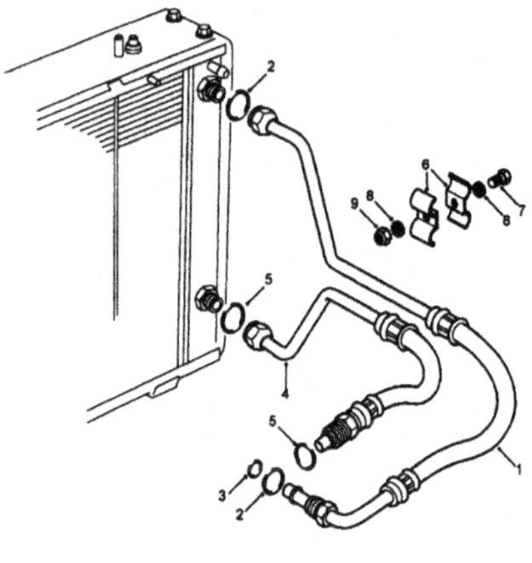

AMLXAI4A

DEFENDER	GROUP L	Cooling & Heating Oil Cooler-Engine Oil Cooler

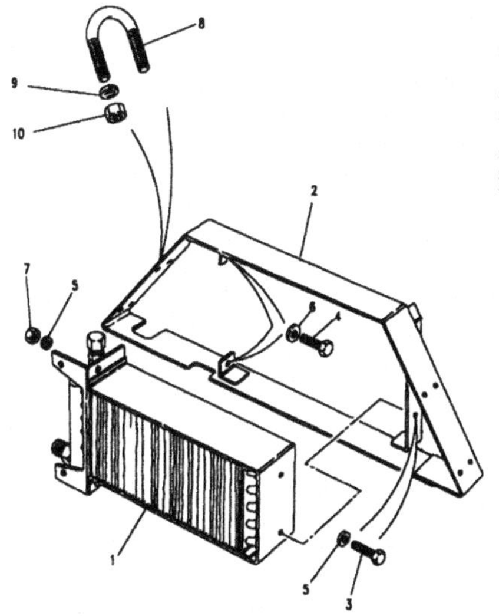

Illus	Part Number	Description	Quantity	Change Point	Remarks
1	NRC7741	Oil cooler-engine	1	Note (1)	4 Cylinder Petrol
1	NRC7741	Oil cooler-engine	1		4 Cylinder Diesel Natural-Aspirated
1	NRC7741	Oil cooler-engine	1	Note (2)	V8 Petrol except air conditioning
1	NRC8201	Oil cooler-engine	1		V8 Petrol air conditioning
2	NRC7458	Bracket-mounting oil cooler	1	Note (2)	Except air conditioning
3	SH106121L	Screw-hexagonal head-M6 x 12	2		
4	SH106167L	Screw-hexagonal head-M6 x 16	2		
5	WL106001L	Washer-sprung-M6	4		
6	WA106041L	Washer-6mm	2		
7	NH106041L	Nut-hexagonal-nyloc-M6	2		
8	NRC7459	Bolt-u	4		
9	WL106001L	Washer-sprung-M6	8		
10	NH106041L	Nut-hexagonal-nyloc-M6	8		
3	SH106121L	Screw-hexagonal head-M6 x 12	2		Air conditioning
5	WL106001L	Washer-sprung-M6	4		
7	NH106041L	Nut-hexagonal-nyloc-M6	2		

CHANGE POINTS:
(1) To (V) FA 389798
(2) To (V) FA 429127

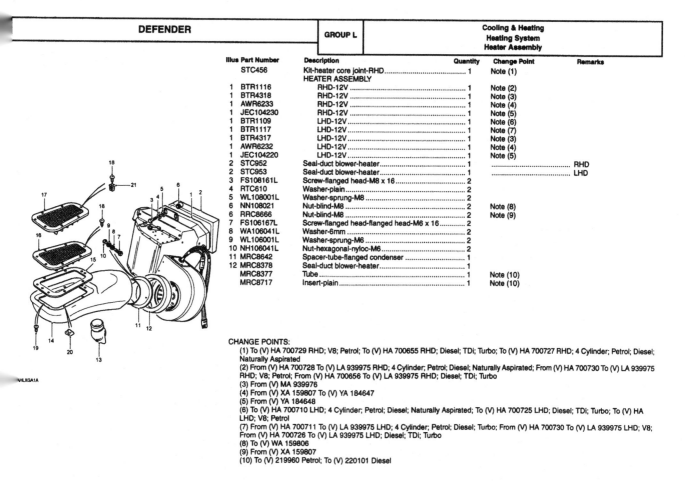

DEFENDER	GROUP L	Cooling & Heating Heating System Heater Assembly

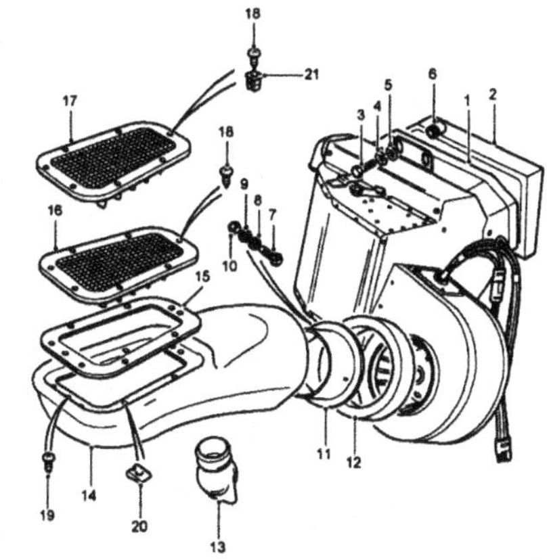

AHLXGA1A

Illus	Part Number	Description	Quantity	Change Point	Remarks
	STC456	Kit-heater core joint-RHD	1	Note (1)	
		HEATER ASSEMBLY			
1	BTR1116	RHD-12V	1	Note (2)	
1	BTR4318	RHD-12V	1	Note (3)	
1	AWR6233	RHD-12V	1	Note (4)	
1	JEC104230	RHD-12V	1	Note (5)	
1	BTR1109	LHD-12V	1	Note (6)	
1	BTR1117	LHD-12V	1	Note (7)	
1	BTR4317	LHD-12V	1	Note (3)	
1	AWR6232	LHD-12V	1	Note (4)	
1	JEC104220	LHD-12V	1	Note (5)	
2	STC952	Seal-duct blower-heater	1		RHD
2	STC953	Seal-duct blower-heater	1		LHD
3	FS108161L	Screw-flanged head-M8 x 16	2		
4	RTC610	Washer-plain	2		
5	WL108001L	Washer-sprung-M8	2		
6	NN108021	Nut-blind-M8	2	Note (8)	
6	RRC8666	Nut-blind-M8	2	Note (9)	
7	FS106167L	Screw-flanged head-flanged head-M6 x 16	2		
8	WA106041L	Washer-6mm	2		
9	WL106001L	Washer-sprung-M6	2		
10	NH106041L	Nut-hexagonal-nyloc-M6	2		
11	MRC8642	Spacer-tube-flanged condenser	1		
12	MRC8378	Seal-duct blower-heater	1		
	MRC8377	Tube	1	Note (10)	
	MRC8717	Insert-plain	1	Note (10)	

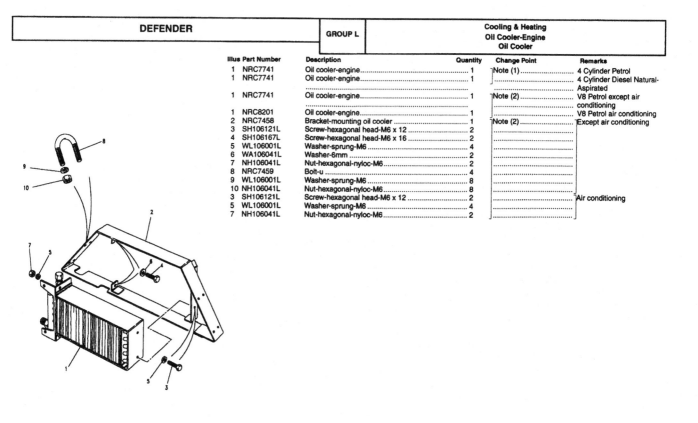

CHANGE POINTS:
(1) To (V) HA 700729 RHD; V8; Petrol; To (V) HA 700655 RHD; Diesel; TDi; Turbo; To (V) HA 700727 RHD; 4 Cylinder; Petrol; Diesel; Naturally Aspirated
(2) From (V) HA 700728 To (V) LA 939975 RHD; 4 Cylinder; Petrol; Diesel; Naturally Aspirated; From (V) HA 700730 To (V) LA 939975 RHD; V8; Petrol; From (V) HA 700656 To (V) LA 939975 RHD; Diesel; TDi; Turbo
(3) From (V) MA 939976
(4) From (V) XA 159807 To (V) YA 184647
(5) From (V) YA 184648
(6) To (V) HA 700710 LHD; 4 Cylinder; Petrol; Diesel; Naturally Aspirated; To (V) HA 700725 LHD; Diesel; TDi; Turbo; To (V) HA LHD; V8; Petrol
(7) From (V) HA 700711 To (V) LA 939975 LHD; 4 Cylinder; Petrol; Diesel; Turbo; From (V) HA 700730 To (V) LA 939975 LHD; V8; From (V) HA 700726 To (V) LA 939975 LHD; Diesel; TDi; Turbo
(8) To (V) WA 159806
(9) From (V) XA 159807
(10) To (V) 219960 Petrol; To (V) 220101 Diesel

Illus	Part Number	Description	Quantity	Change Point	Remarks
13	STC1120	Valve assembly air intake	1	Note (1)	
13	MUC2417	Valve assembly air intake	1	Note (2)	
		DUCT ASSEMBLY-COLD AIR INTAKE INDUCTION SYSTEM			
14	MTC2391	LH-RHD	1	Note (1)	
14	MTC2390	RH-LHD	1		
14	MUC2419	LH-RHD	1	Note (2)	
14	MUC2418	RH-LHD	1		
15	MRC9998	Seal-duct blower-heater	1		
		GRILLE-COLD AIR INTAKE ADAPTOR INDUCTION SYSTEM			
16	MRC9939	LH-RHD	1	Note (3)	
16	MRC9938	RH-LHD	1		
16	AWR2215	LH-RHD	1	Note (4)	
16	AWR2214	RH-LHD	1		
		PLATE-BLANKING AIR INTAKE			
17	MRC9940	RH-RHD	1	Note (3)	
17	MRC9941	LH-LHD	1		
17	AWR2216	RH-RHD	1	Note (4)	
17	AWR2217	LH-LHD	1		
18	AB608065L	Screw-pan	14		
19	AC608041L	Screw-self tapping	4		
20	AJ608041	Clip	9		
21	CZK619	Nut-lokut	9		
22	AWR4782	Gasket-motor blower-heater	1		

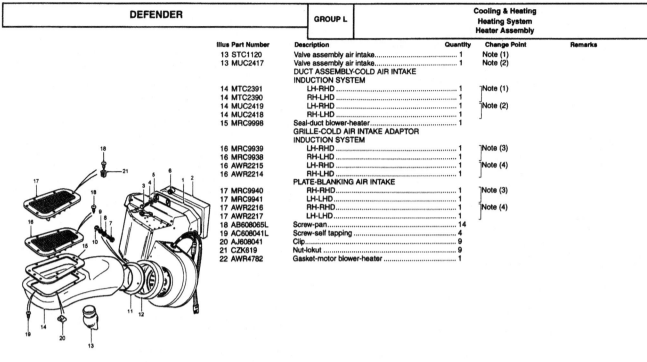

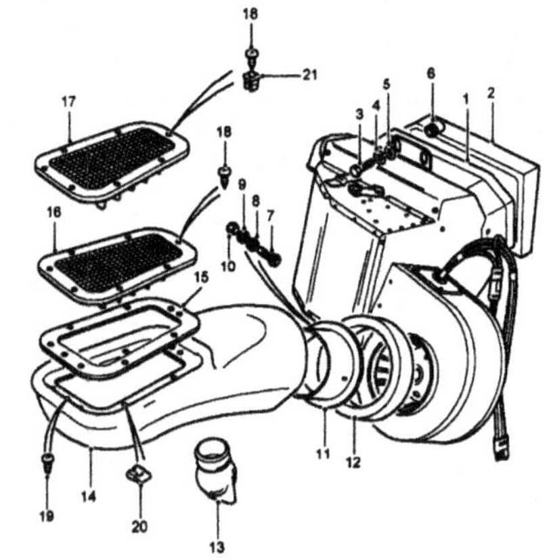

AHLXGA1A

CHANGE POINTS:
(1) To (V) 219960 Petrol; To (V) 220101 Diesel
(2) From (V) 219961 Petrol; From (V) 220102 Diesel
(3) To (V) MA 953171
(4) From (V) MA 953172

Illus	Part Number	Description	Quantity	Change Point	Remarks
		MATRIX-HEATER HEATER			
1	UTP1725	with horizontal inlet/outlet pipes	1	Note (1)	
1	AAP817	with downard facing inlet/outlet pipes	1		
1	UTP1725	with horizontal inlet/outlet pipes	1	Note (2)	RHD
1	JEF100220	with horizontal inlet/outlet pipes	1		LHD
		AIRBOX ASSEMBLY BLOWER-HEATER			
2	AAP810	RHD	1	Note (3)	
2	AAP811	LHD	1		
2	UTP1259	RHD	1	Note (4)	
2	UTP1258	LHD	1		
2	JEN100240	RHD	1	Note (2)	
2	JEN100250	LHD	1		
		BLOWER ASSEMBLY HEATER			
3	RTC4200	RHD	1	Note (3)	
3	RTC4201	LHD	1		
3	UTP1911	RHD	1	Note (4)	
3	UTP1910	LHD	1		
		HARNESS BLOWER-HEATER			
4	UTP1281	RHD	1	Note (3)	
4	UTP1904	RHD	1	Note (6)	
4	UTP1282	LHD	1	Note (1)	
4	JGK100160	RHD	1	Note (2)	
4	JGK100170	LHD	1	Note (2)	

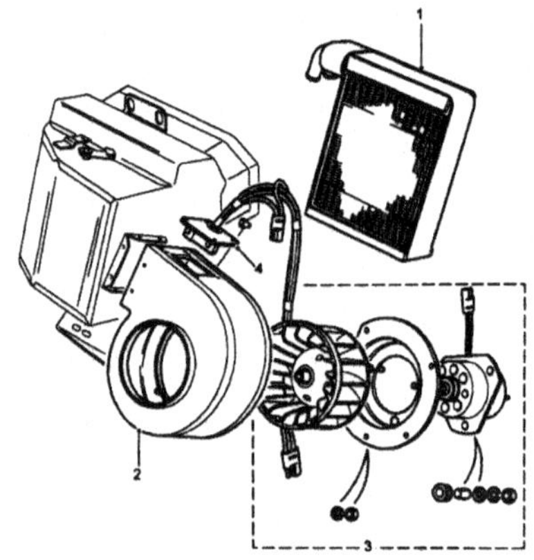

AHLXGA2A

CHANGE POINTS:
(1) To (V) WA 159806
(2) From (V) XA 159807
(3) To (V) LA 939975
(4) From (V) MA 939976
(6) From (V) MA 939976 To (V) WA 159806

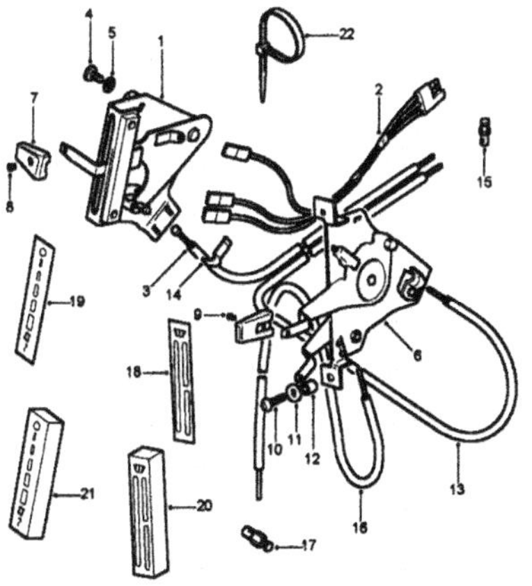

LL0054A

Illus	Part Number	Description	Quantity	Change Point	Remarks
1	UTP1126	Control assembly heater-RHD	1	Note (1)	
1	UTP1125	Control assembly heater-LHD	1		
2	AAP890	Harness-heater	1		
3	AAP876	Cable-control mode control-heater	1		
1	BTR4433	CONTROL ASSEMBLY HEATER-RHD	1	Note (2)	
1	BTR4434	CONTROL ASSEMBLY HEATER-LHD	1	Note (2)	
2	UTP1908	• Harness-heater	1		
3	AAP876	• Cable-control mode control-heater	1		
1	JFT000020	Control assembly heater-RHD	1	Note (3)	
1	JFT000030	Control assembly heater-LHD	1	Note (3)	
3	JFF000070	Cable-control mode control-heater	1	Note (3)	
4	SE105161L	Screw-recessed-pan head-M5 x 16	2	Note (4)	
4	JYP000060	Screw	2	Note (3)	
5	WA105001L	Washer-plain-standard-M5	2		
6	346924	Plate-RHD	1	Note (4)	
6	347586	Plate-LHD	1	Note (4)	
6	JFT000040	Plate-RHD	1	Note (3)	
6	JFT000050	Plate-LHD	1	Note (3)	
7	MTC2805	Knob-control heater	3		
8	SG103084	Screw	1	Note (4)	
8	JYP000070	Screw	1	Note (3)	
9	MTC7737	Screw	2	Note (4)	
9	JYP000070	Screw	2	Note (3)	

CHANGE POINTS:
(1) To (V) LA 939975
(2) From (V) MA 939976 To (V) ZA 999999
(3) From (V) 2A 622424
(4) To (V) ZA 999999

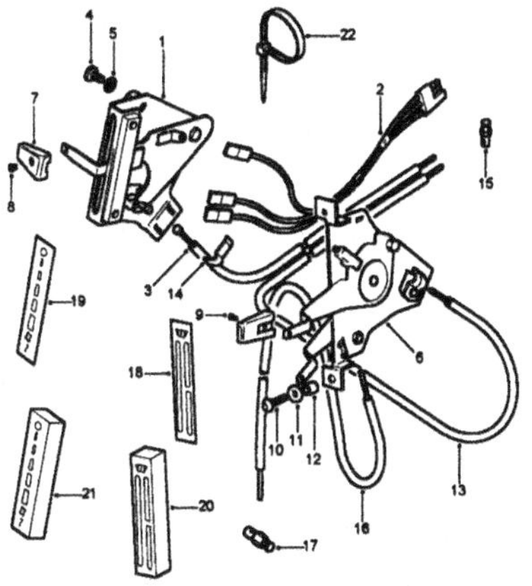

LL0054A

Illus	Part Number	Description	Quantity	Change Point	Remarks
10	SE808244	Screw	2	Note (1)	
10	JYP000060	Screw	2	Note (2)	
11	WA105004L	Washer-plain	2		
12	MRC9922	Spacer	2		
13	MTC6194	Cable-temperature control-heater	1	Note (1)	
13	JFF000060	Cable-temperature control-heater	1	Note (2)	
14	13H7343L	Clip	2		
15	RTC5978	Kit-trunnion	2		
16	347939	Cable-distribution control-heater	1	Note (3)	
16	BTR8736	Cable-distribution control-heater	1	Note (4)	
16	JFF000120	Cable-distribution control-heater	1	Note (5)	
16	JFF000050	Cable-distribution control-heater	1	Note (2)	
17	566902	Pin	1		
18	MTC6006	Label-facia heater control	1	Note (6)	
19	MTC6007	Label-facia heater control	1		
20	YAZ100030	Illumination assembly control-heater-heater	1	Note (7)	
21	YAZ100040	Illumination assembly control-heater-fan	1		
22	UKC6684	Tie-cable	2		

CHANGE POINTS:
(1) To (V) ZA 999999
(2) From (V) 2A 622424
(3) To (V) LA 939975
(4) From (V) MA 939976 To (V) ZA 616951
(5) From (V) 1A 616952 To (V) ZA 999999
(6) To (V) WA 159806
(7) From (V) XA 159807

Cooling & Heating
Heating System
Demisters & Outlet Pipes

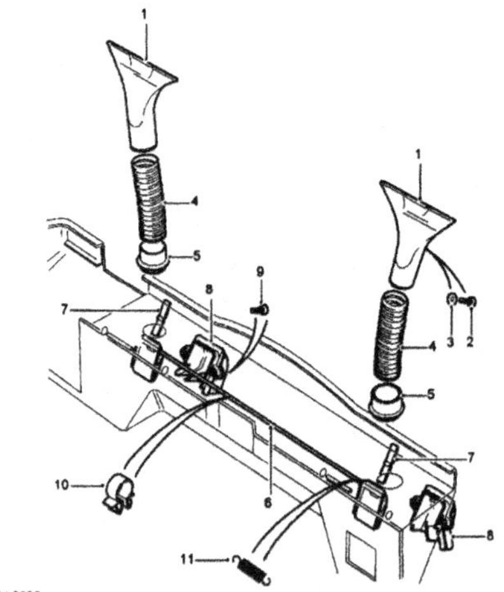

LL0080

Illus	Part Number	Description	Quantity	Change Point	Remarks
		DUCT-DEMIST WINDSCREEN			
1	MRC9668	RH	1		
1	MRC9669	LH	1		
1	MXC3188	RH	1	Note (1)	TDi
1	MXC3189	LH	1		
1	BTR1600	RH	1	Note (2)	
1	BTR1599	LH	1		
1	BTR1600	RH	1		Td5
1	BTR1599	LH	1		
2	AB608047L	Screw-self tapping-No 8 x 1/2	2		
3	WA105001L	Washer-plain-standard-M5	2		
2	AB608054L	Screw-self tapping-No8 x 5/8	4		TDi
	AK608021	Nut-spring-u type	4		
4	MTC6382	Tube	2		
5	MRC7281	Grommet	2		
6	346894	Flap & seals assembly blower-heater	1	Note (3)	
6	BTR1349	Flap & seals assembly blower-heater	1	Note (4)	
6	JDL000030	Flap & seals assembly blower-heater	1	Note (5)	
7	346976	Clip-spring connector	2		
		DUCT ASSEMBLY-AIR FLOOR			
8	395829	RH	1	Note (6)	
8	395830	LH	1		
8	JKB100440	RH	1	Note (7)	
8	JKB100450	LH	1		
8	JKB000080	RH	1	Note (8)	
8	JKB000090	LH	1		
9	MRC1525	Screw	4	Note (6)	
9	AB608055L	Screw-self tapping-No8 x 5/8-Black	4	Note (9)	
10	YYC10037L	Clip	3	Note (5)	
11	FNK000010	Spring	2	Note (5)	

CHANGE POINTS:
(1) To (V) JA 906640
(2) From (V) JA 906641
(3) To (V) HA 905500
(4) From (V) HA 905501 To (V) ZA 999999
(5) From (V) 2A 622424
(6) To (V) VA 135086
(7) From (V) VA 135087 To (V) ZA 616213
(8) From (V) 1A 616214
(9) From (V) VA 135087

Cooling & Heating
Heating System
Heater Pipes-200TDI

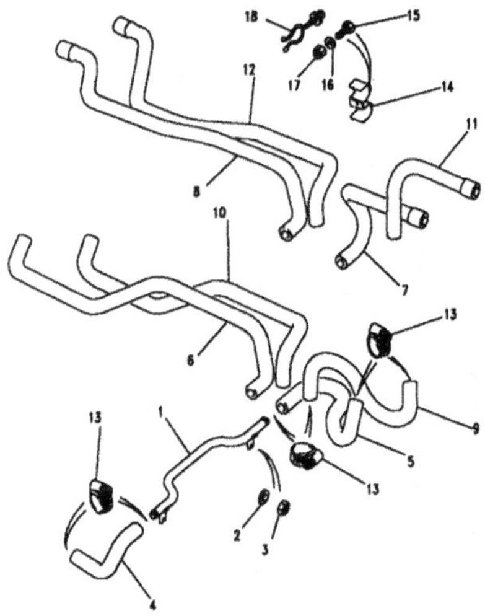

Illus	Part Number	Description	Quantity	Change Point	Remarks
1	ERR371	Pipe-heater to hose coolant	1		Diesel TDi
2	WA110065	Washer-plain	2		
3	NT110041L	Locknut-M10	2		
4	ERR1436	Hose-pipe to heater	1		
5	BTR445	Hose-heater return coolant	1	Note (1)	
6	BTR982	Hose-heater return coolant	1	Note (2)	
7	BTR1130	Hose-heater return coolant	1	Note (3)	
8	BTR1131	Hose-heater return coolant	1	Note (4)	
9	BTR447	Hose-pipe to heater	1	Note (1)	
10	BTR983	Hose-pipe to heater	1	Note (2)	
11	BTR1132	Hose-pipe to heater	1	Note (3)	
12	BTR1133	Hose-pipe to heater	1	Note (4)	
13	CN100258L	Clip-hose-25mm	6		Diesel TDi
14	BTR988	Clip-hose	1		
15	SH105121L	Screw-hexagonal head-M5 x 12	1		
16	WA105001L	Washer-plain-standard-M5	1		
17	NY105041L	Nut-hexagonal-nyloc-M5	1		
18	NRC8332	Clip-cable	1		

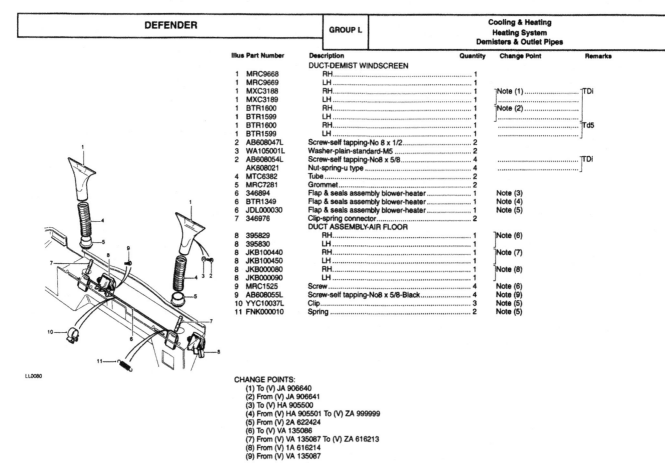

CHANGE POINTS:
(1) To (V) HA 700655 RHD; Diesel; TDi; Turbo
(2) To (V) HA 700725 LHD; Diesel; TDi; Turbo
(3) From (V) HA 700656 RHD; Diesel; TDi; Turbo
(4) From (V) HA 700726 LHD; Diesel; TDi; Turbo

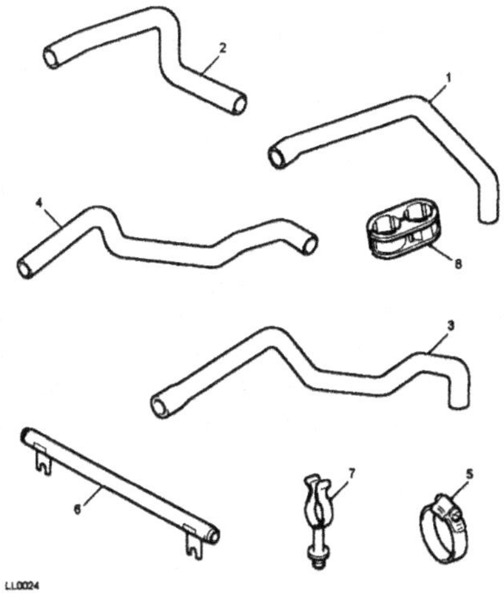

Illus	Part Number	Description	Quantity	Change Point	Remarks
1	BTR6165	Hose-heater-inlet	1		RHD
2	BTR6164	Hose-heater return coolant	1		
3	BTR8396	Hose-heater-inlet	1	Note (1)	LHD
3	JHB100590	HOSE-HEATER-INLET-LHD	1	Note (2)	LHD
5	JYC100870	• Clip-hose-27mm-Green	1		
5	PYC102190	• Clip-hose-22mm	1		
4	BTR8395	Hose-heater-outlet	1	Note (1)	LHD
4	JHC100310	HOSE-HEATER-OUTLET-LHD	1	Note (2)	LHD
5	JYC100870	• Clip-hose-27mm-Green	1		
5	PYC102260	• Clip-hose-26mm	1		
5	CN100258L	Clip-hose-25mm	4	Note (1)	
5	CN100258L	Clip-hose-25mm	2	Note (2)	RHD
6	ERR4531	Pipe-heater to hose coolant	1	Note (3)	
6	ERR6197	Pipe-heater to hose coolant	1	Note (4)	
7	NRC8332	Clip-cable	1		
8	PYC101940	Clip-hose-plastic-double	2	Note (2)	

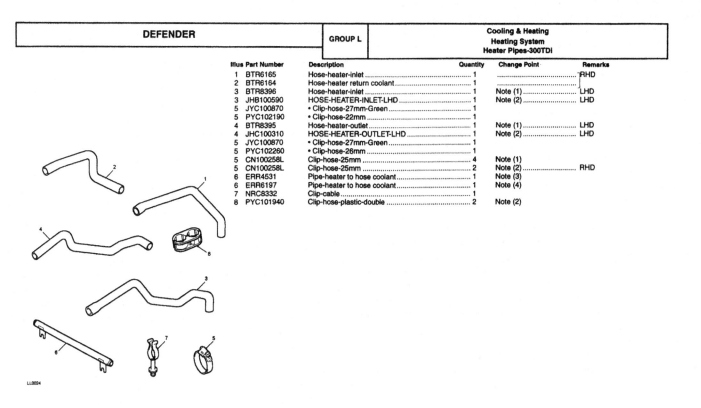

CHANGE POINTS:
(1) To (V) WA 159806
(2) From (V) XA 159807
(3) To (E)18L 12424A Except EGR; To (E)21L 36433A EGR
(4) From (E)18L 12424A Except EGR; From (E)21L 36433A EGR

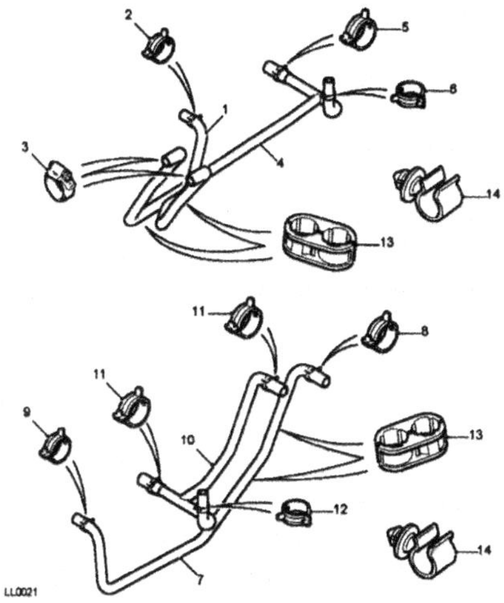

Illus	Part Number	Description	Quantity	Change Point	Remarks
1	AWR6235	HOSE-HEATER-INLET-RHD	1		
2	PYC101880	• Clip-spring band-23mm	1		
3	CN100258L	Clip-hose-heater end-25mm	2		
4	AWR6237	HOSE-HEATER-OUTLET-RHD	1	Note (1)	
5	PYC101890	• Clip-spring band	1		
6	PYC101880	• Clip-spring band-23mm	1		
4	JHC000060	HOSE-HEATER-OUTLET-RHD	1	Note (2)	
5	PYC101890	• Clip-spring band	1		
6	PYC101880	• Clip-spring band-23mm	1		
7	AWR6234	HOSE-HEATER-INLET-LHD	1		
8	JYC100870	• Clip-hose-27mm-Green	1		
9	PYC101880	• Clip-spring band-23mm	1		
10	AWR6236	HOSE-HEATER-OUTLET-LHD	1	Note (1)	
11	JYC100870	• Clip-hose-27mm-Green	1		
12	PYC101880	• Clip-spring band-23mm	1		
10	JHC000050	HOSE-HEATER-OUTLET-LHD	1	Note (2)	
11	JYC100870	• Clip-hose-27mm-Green	1		
12	PYC101880	• Clip-spring band-23mm	1		
13	PYC101940	Clip-hose-plastic-double	2		
14	PYC101370	Clip-plastic-Hose to engine	2		

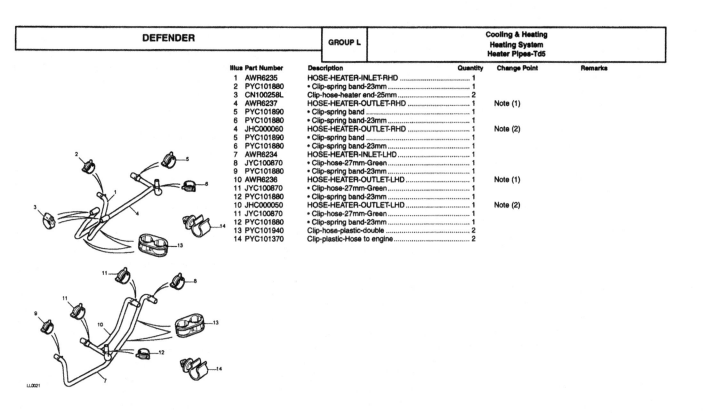

CHANGE POINTS:
(1) To (V) ZA 999999
(2) From (V) 2A 622424

DEFENDER

GROUP L

Cooling & Heating
Heating System
Heater Pipes-4 Cylinder-Except TDi

Illus	Part Number	Description	Quantity	Change Point	Remarks
1	NRC6306	Hose-heater to engine pipe	2	Note (1)	
		PIPE ASSEMBLY-COOLANT TO HEATER			
2	NRC6307	RHD	1		
2	NRC6422	LHD	1	Note (1)	
3	NRC6420	RHD	1		
3	NRC6421	LHD	1	Note (1)	
		HOSE-PIPE TO HEATER			
4	NRC6308	RHD	2	Note (2)	
4	NRC6309	LHD	1	Note (3)	
5	BTR1134	RHD	2	Note (4)	
5	BTR1135	LHD	2	Note (5); Note (6)	
6	CN100258L	Clip-hose-25mm	8	Note (1)	LHD
6	CN100258L	Clip-hose-25mm	8		RHD
7	NRC6417	Bracket-heater feed pipe	1	Note (1)	LHD Petrol
7	NRC6417	Bracket-heater feed pipe	1		RHD Petrol
7	NRC6418	Bracket-heater feed pipe	1	Note (1)	LHD Diesel
7	NRC6418	Bracket-heater feed pipe	1		RHD Diesel
8	NRC6419	Clamp	3	Note (1)	LHD
8	NRC6419	Clamp	3		RHD
9	FS106255L	Screw-flanged head-M6 x 25	2		
10	WL106001L	Washer-sprung-M6	2		
11	NH106041L	Nut-hexagonal-nyloc-M6	2		
12	JHC100330	HOSE-OUTLET HEATER	1	Note (7)	LHD
13	JHB100610	HOSE-INLET HEATER	1	Note (7)	LHD
14	PYC101890	• Clip-spring band-heater end	1		
15	PYC101880	• Clip-spring band-engine end-23mm	1		
16	PYC101940	Clip-hose-plastic-double	2		LHD

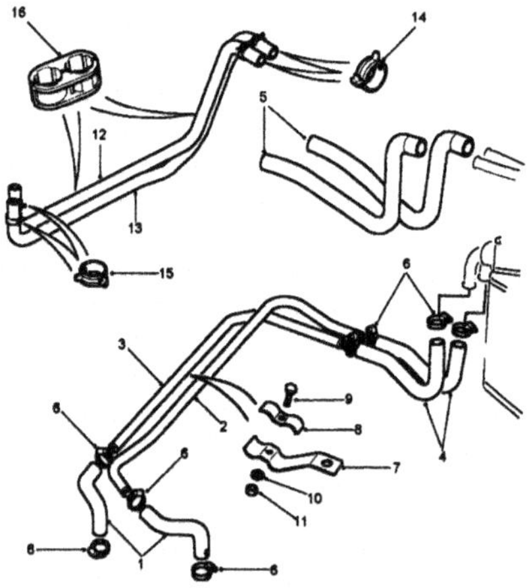

LL0023

CHANGE POINTS:
(1) To (V) WA 159806
(2) To (V) HA 700727 RHD; 4 Cylinder; Petrol; Diesel; Naturally Aspirated; To (V) HA 700727 4 Cylinder; Petrol
(3) To (V) HA 700710 4 Cylinder; Petrol; To (V) HA 700710 4 Cylinder; Diesel; Naturally Aspirated
(4) From (V) HA 700728 RHD; 4 Cylinder; Petrol; Diesel; Naturally Aspirated; From (V) HA 700728 4 Cylinder; Petrol
(5) From (V) HA 700711 To (V) WA 159806 4 Cylinder; Petrol
(6) From (V) HA 700711 To (V) WA 159806 4 Cylinder; Diesel; Naturally Aspirated
(7) From (V) XA 159807

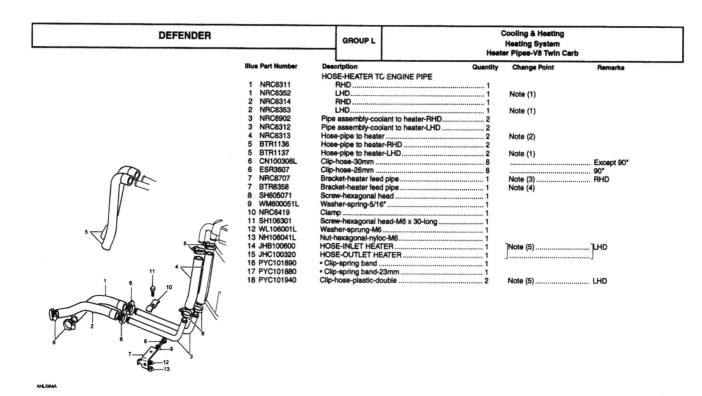

DEFENDER

GROUP L

Cooling & Heating
Heating System
Heater Pipes-V8 Twin Carb

Illus	Part Number	Description	Quantity	Change Point	Remarks
		HOSE-HEATER TO ENGINE PIPE			
1	NRC6311	RHD	1		
1	NRC6352	LHD	1	Note (1)	
2	NRC6314	RHD	1		
2	NRC6353	LHD	1	Note (1)	
3	NRC6902	Pipe assembly-coolant to heater-RHD	2		
3	NRC6312	Pipe assembly-coolant to heater-LHD	2		
4	NRC6313	Hose-pipe to heater	2	Note (2)	
5	BTR1136	Hose-pipe to heater-RHD	2		
5	BTR1137	Hose-pipe to heater-LHD	2	Note (1)	
6	CN100308L	Clip-hose-30mm	8		Except 90"
6	ESR3607	Clip-hose-26mm	8		90"
7	NRC8707	Bracket-heater feed pipe	1	Note (3)	RHD
7	BTR8358	Bracket-heater feed pipe	1	Note (4)	
8	SH605071	Screw-hexagonal head	1		
9	WM600051L	Washer-spring-5/16"	1		
10	NRC6419	Clamp	1		
11	SH106301	Screw-hexagonal head-M6 x 30-long	1		
12	WL106001L	Washer-sprung-M6	1		
13	NH106041L	Nut-hexagonal-nyloc-M6	1		
14	JHB100600	HOSE-INLET HEATER	1	Note (5)	LHD
15	JHC100320	HOSE-OUTLET HEATER	1		
16	PYC101890	• Clip-spring band	1		
17	PYC101880	• Clip-spring band-23mm	1		
18	PYC101940	Clip-hose-plastic-double	2	Note (5)	LHD

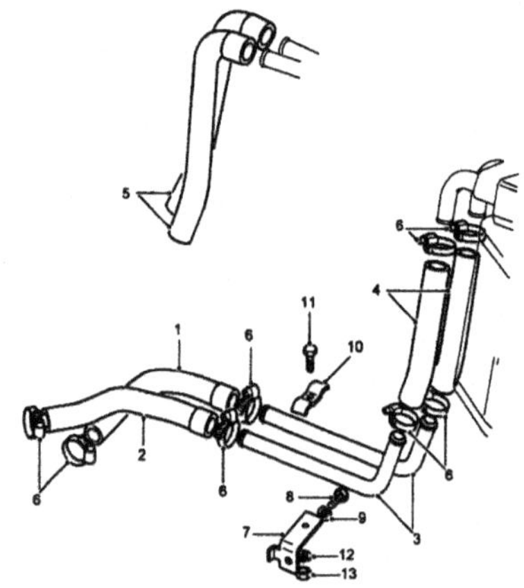

AHLXIA4A

CHANGE POINTS:
(1) To (V) WA 159806
(2) To (V) HA 700729
(3) To (V)24G 12353B
(4) From (V)24G 12354B
(5) From (V) XA 159807

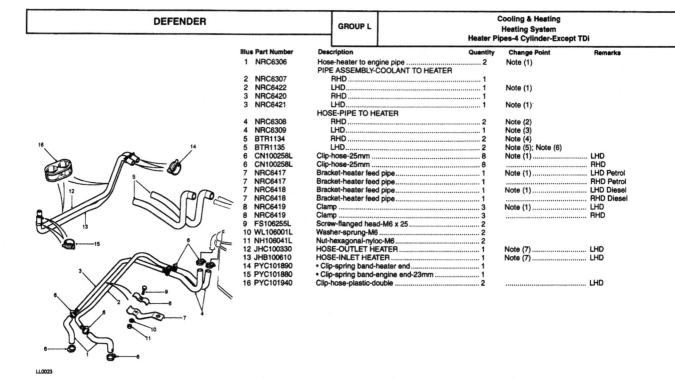

Illus	Part Number	Description	Quantity	Change Point	Remarks
1	AWR6631	Hose-heater-inlet-LHD	1		
1	JHB100650	Hose-heater-inlet-RHD	1		
2	AWR6632	Hose-heater-outlet-LHD	1		
2	JHC100370	Hose-heater-outlet-RHD	1		
3	CN100308L	Clip-hose-30mm	4		

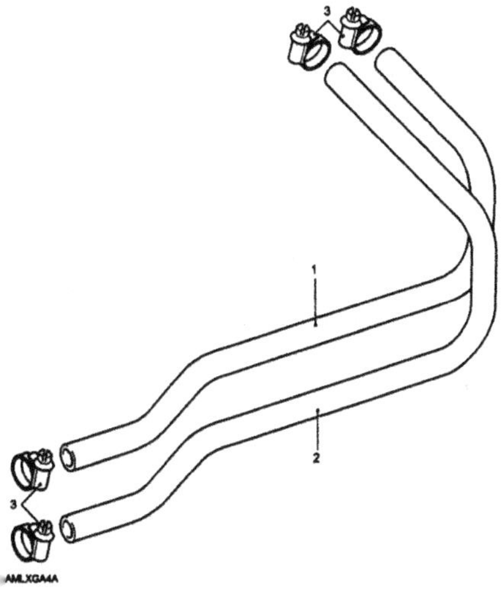

Illus	Part Number	Description	Quantity	Change Point	Remarks
	JMG100380	Kit air conditioning-converting R12 to R134A	1		Cfc-free refrigerant
1	RTC7416	Condenser assembly air conditioning	1		
2	RTC7417	Bracket assembly-support air conditioning	4		
3	RTC7418	Grommet	4		
4	RTC7419	Bracket-lower	1		
5	RTC7420	Bracket	2		
6	RTC7421	Bracket-fan mounting-upper	1		
7	RTC7422	Shroud air conditioning	2		
8	RTC7423	Bracket assembly-support air conditioning	2		
9	RTC7424	Motor-cooling fan condenser	2		
10	RTC7425	Fan-condenser	2		
11	RTC7426	Receiver dryer assembly air conditioning	1		
11	STC2979	Receiver dryer assembly air conditioning	1		Cfc-free refrigerant
12	AEU3068	Switch-pressure air conditioning control-high pressure	NLA		Use BTR3720.
12	BTR3720	Switch-pressure air conditioning control-dual pressure	1		
13	RTC7427	Bracket receiver dryer	1		
14	RTC7428	Bracket	2		
15	RTC7429	Hose-receiver dryer/evaporator air conditioning	1		
16	RTC7430	Hose-compressor/condenser air conditioning	1		Except TDi
16	STC3188	Hose-compressor/condenser air conditioning	1		TDi
16	STC3907	Hose-compressor/condenser air conditioning	NLA		Use STC3188. TDi
16	STC3188	Hose-compressor/condenser air conditioning	1		TDi
17	AEU3067	Valve-charging air conditioning	1		Except cfc-free refrigerant
17	STC3169	Valve-charging air conditioning	1		Cfc-free refrigerant
18	AEU3056	O ring-less cfc free refrigerant	1	Note (1)	
18	STC3191	O ring-11.2mm OD-7.6mm ID-1.8mm thick-with cfc-free refrigerant	1	Note (2)	
19	AEU1626	O ring-5/16"-less cfc free refrigerant	NLA	Note (1)	Use STC3191.
19	STC3191	O ring-11.2mm OD-7.6mm ID-1.8mm thick-with cfc-free refrigerant	2		
19	STC3192	O ring-14.5mm OD-10.8mm ID-1.8mm thick-with cfc-free refrigerant	1	Note (2)	
20	AEU1627	O ring-less cfc free refrigerant-13/32"	NLA	Note (1)	Use STC3192.
20	STC3171	O ring-10mm-with cfc-free refrigerant	1	Note (2)	
21	MTC8500	Coupling-small	1		

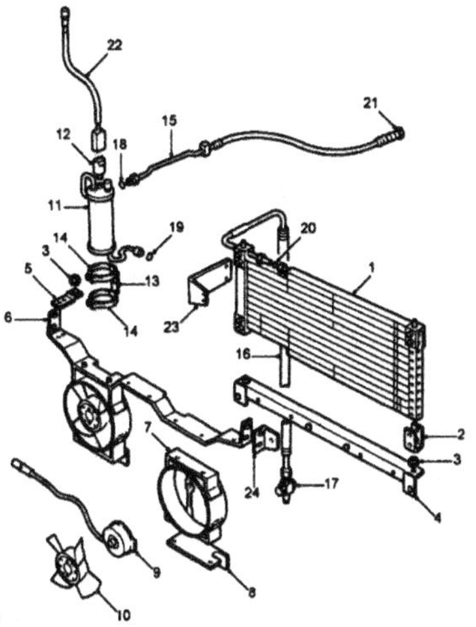

CHANGE POINTS:
(1) To (V) LA 939975
(2) From (V) MA 939976

Illus	Part Number	Description	Quantity	Change Point	Remarks
22	STC2992	Harness pressure switch	1		
23	STC3189	Bracket-support air conditioning	1		
24	STC3190	Bracket	1		

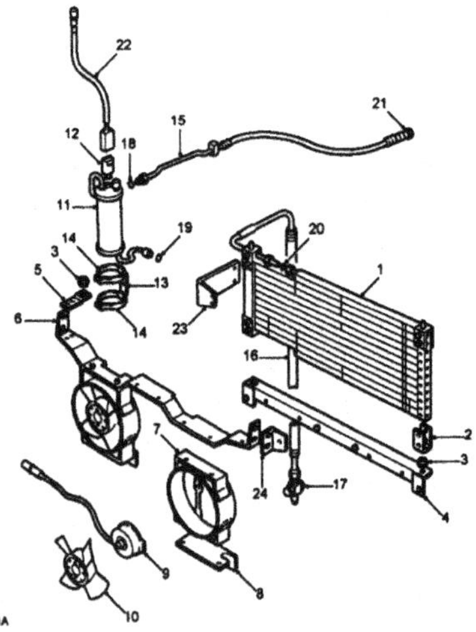

AJLXXA1A

Illus	Part Number	Description	Quantity	Change Point	Remarks
1	JRB100660	CONDENSER/FAN & FRAME ASSEMBLY	1	Note (1)	
2	JRB100850	• Condenser air conditioning	1		
3	JRP100010	• FAN ASSEMBLY-CONDENSER	1		
4	SH106301L	• • Screw-hexagonal head-M6 x 30	4		
5	WJ600041L	• • Washer	4		
6	NY106047L	• • Nut-hexagonal head-nyloc-M6	4		
1	JRB101180	CONDENSER/FAN & FRAME ASSEMBLY	1	Note (2)	
2	JRB100580L	• Condenser air conditioning	1		
3	JRP105080	• FAN ASSEMBLY-CONDENSER	1		
4	SH106301L	• • Screw-hexagonal head-M6 x 30	4		
5	WJ600041L	• • Washer	4		
6	NY106047L	• • Nut-hexagonal head-nyloc-M6	4		
7	FB108087	Bolt-flanged head-M8 x 40	3		
8	FX108047L	Nut-flange-flange-M8	2		
9	JRF100410	Bracket-top mounting condenser	1		

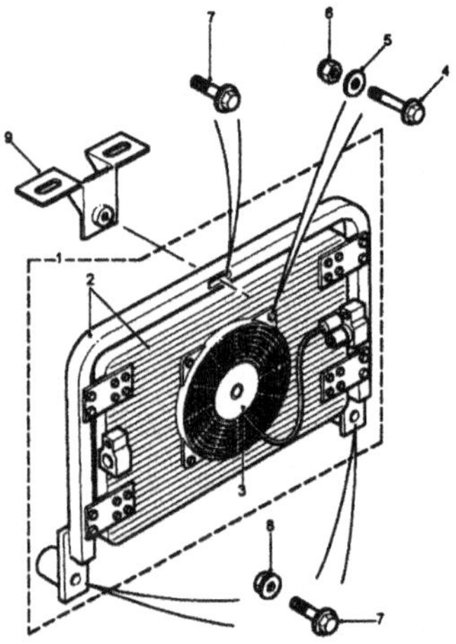

LL0029A

CHANGE POINTS:
(1) To (V) YA 189158
(2) From (V) YA 189159

DEFENDER | GROUP L | Cooling & Heating — Air Conditioning — Condenser Assembly-V8 EFI

Illus	Part Number	Description	Quantity	Change Point	Remarks
1	STC3963	CONDENSER ASSEMBLY AIR CONDITIONING	1		
2	STC3964	• Bracket condenser-LH-top	1		
3	STC3965	• Bracket condenser-RH-top	1		
4	RU612183	• Rivet-pop-aluminium	2		
5	STC3966	• Bracket condenser-LH-bottom	1		
6	STC3967	• Bracket condenser-RH-bottom	1		
7	STC3968	• Screw-self tapping	12		
8	STC3969	Fan-condenser	1		
9	FN106047L	Nut-flange-M6	4		

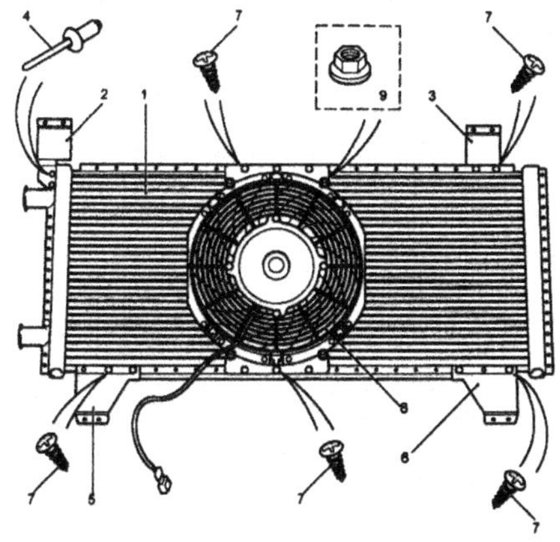

AMLXRA8C

DEFENDER | GROUP L | Cooling & Heating — Air Conditioning — Evaporator Assembly-To (V) WA159806-RHD

Illus	Part Number	Description	Quantity	Change Point	Remarks
		EVAPORATOR ASSEMBLY-AIR CONDITIONING			
1	MUC1663	RHD	1		Except cfc-free refrigerant
1	AWR1168	RHD	1		Petrol cfc-free refrigerant
1	AWR1168	RHD	1		Diesel cfc-free refrigerant
	AWR1242	EVAPORATOR ASSEMBLY-R134A AIR CONDITIONING-RHD	1		TDi cfc-free refrigerant
2	MUC6050	• Matrix-heater	1		
3	MUC6037	• Spacer-evaporator expansion valve	1		
4	MUC6038	• Tube	1		
5	MUC6042	• Thermostat evaporator-air conditioning	1		
6	MUC4375	• Switch assembly-vacuum control-heater	1		
7	MUC1682	• Connector-inlet manifold adaptor	1		
8	MUC6040	• Seal	1		
9	STC3201	• MOTOR AND ROTOR ASSEMBLY	1		
10	MUC6053	• • Wheel blower	1		
11	MUC6054	• • Spacer	1		
12	MUC6055	• • Locknut	1		
13	MUC1675	• • Motor blower-heater	1		
14	MUC6052	• • Seal	1		
15	MUC6056	• Harness blower-heater	1		
16	RTC7470	• Clamp	1		
17	STC760	• Cover-motor blower-heater	1		
18	STC761	• Case-upper evaporator-air conditioning	1		
19	STC762	• Case-lower evaporator-air conditioning	1		
20	STC948	• Adaptor-tube-drain evaporator tube	1		
21	MUC4860	Seal-outlet evaporator-air conditioning	1		
	AWR1173	Kit-matrix & seals heater	1		

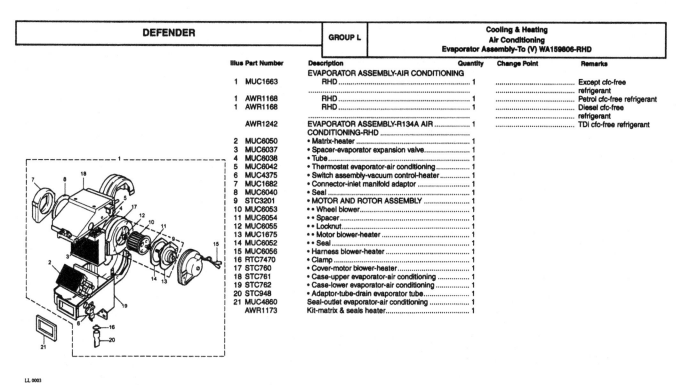

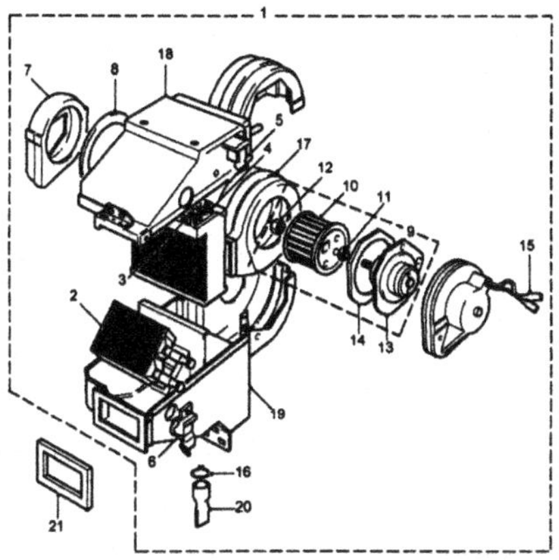

LL 0003

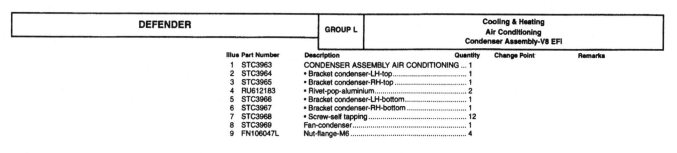

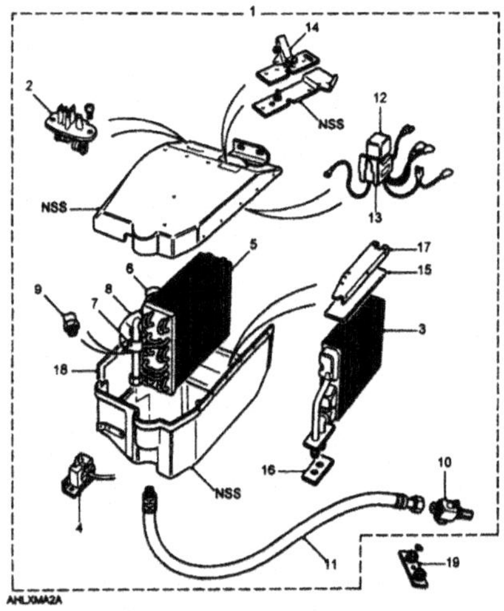

AHLXMA2A

Illus	Part Number	Description	Quantity	Change Point	Remarks
		EVAPORATOR ASSEMBLY-AIR CONDITIONING			
1	RTC7588	LHD	1	Note (1)	Except TDi and cfc-free refrigerant
1	AWR1177	LHD	1	Note (1)	LHD air conditioning cfc-free refrigerant except TDi
1	AWR1249	LHD	1	Note (1)	LHD TDi air conditioning cfc-free refrigerant
2	RTC7456	• Resistor	1		
3	RTC7433	• Matrix-heater	1		
4	RTC7434	• Thermostat evaporator-air conditioning	1		
5	RTC7436	• Evaporator air conditioning	-		Part of RTC7588.
6	AEU1213	• Valve-expansion evaporator-air conditioning	1		
7	AEU1214	• Clamp	1		
8	RTC7458	• Pipe-evaporator air conditioning	1		
9	RTC7457	• Coupling	1		
10	AEU3055	• Valve-suction air conditioning compressor	1		
11	RTC7439	• Hose-evapr/compressor air conditioning	1		
12	RTC7454	• Relay	1		
13	RTC7455	• Harness blower-air conditioning	1		
14	RTC7414	• Switch-vacuum-evaporator-air conditioning	1		
15	RTC7471	• Seal air conditioning	-		Part of RTC7588.
16	RTC7472	• Seal air conditioning	1		
17	RTC7473	• Cover-evaporator servo mechanism	1		
18	RTC7453	• Seal-inlet evaporator-air conditioning	1		
5	RTC7436	• Evaporator air conditioning	1		Part of AWR1177, AWR1249.
15	RTC7471	• Seal air conditioning	1		Part of AWR1177, AWR1249.
19	MUC4358	Adaptor-air conditioning compressor hose	1		
	RTC7452	O ring	2		
	MUC1661	Seal-outlet evaporator-air conditioning	1		
	AWR1173	Kit-matrix & seals heater	1		

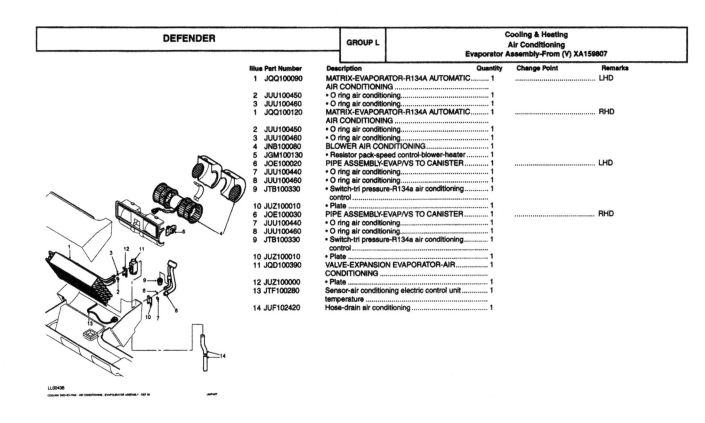

CHANGE POINTS:
(1) To (V) WA 159806

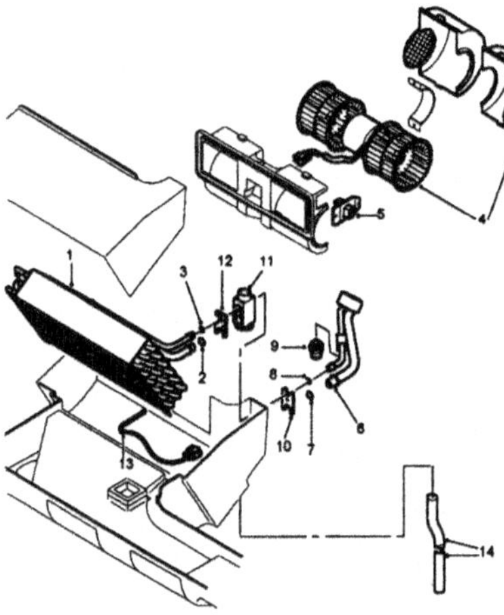

LL0043B

Illus	Part Number	Description	Quantity	Change Point	Remarks
1	JQQ100090	MATRIX-EVAPORATOR-R134A AUTOMATIC AIR CONDITIONING	1		LHD
2	JUU100450	• O ring air conditioning	1		
3	JUU100460	• O ring air conditioning	1		
1	JQQ100120	MATRIX-EVAPORATOR-R134A AUTOMATIC AIR CONDITIONING	1		RHD
2	JUU100450	• O ring air conditioning	1		
3	JUU100460	• O ring air conditioning	1		
4	JNB100080	BLOWER AIR CONDITIONING	1		
5	JGM100130	• Resistor pack-speed control-blower-heater	1		
6	JOE100020	PIPE ASSEMBLY-EVAP/VS TO CANISTER	1		LHD
7	JUU100440	• O ring air conditioning	1		
8	JUU100460	• O ring air conditioning	1		
9	JTB100330	• Switch-tri pressure-R134a air conditioning control	1		
10	JUZ100010	• Plate	1		
6	JOE100030	PIPE ASSEMBLY-EVAP/VS TO CANISTER	1		RHD
7	JUU100440	• O ring air conditioning	1		
8	JUU100460	• O ring air conditioning	1		
9	JTB100330	• Switch-tri pressure-R134a air conditioning control	1		
10	JUZ100010	• Plate	1		
11	JQD100390	VALVE-EXPANSION EVAPORATOR-AIR CONDITIONING	1		
12	JUZ100000	• Plate	1		
13	JTF100280	Sensor-air conditioning electric control unit temperature	1		
14	JUF102420	Hose-drain air conditioning	1		

Illus	Part Number	Description	Quantity	Change Point	Remarks
1	STC4260	EVAPORATOR ASSEMBLY-AIR CONDITIONING	1		RHD
1	STC4261	EVAPORATOR ASSEMBLY-AIR CONDITIONING	1		LHD
2	STC4262	• Valve-expansion evaporator-air conditioning	1		Part of STC4260.
3	STC4263	• O ring-8mm OD-4.5mm ID-1.8mm thick	1		
4	STC3191	• O ring-11.2mm OD-7.6mm ID-1.8mm thick-with cfc-free refrigerant	1		
5	STC3192	• O ring-14.5mm OD-10.8mm ID-1.8mm thick-with cfc-free refrigerant	1		
2	STC3981	• Valve-expansion evaporator-air conditioning	1		Part of STC4261.
6	STC3992	Seal	1		
7	STC3983	Screw	1		
8	STC3982	Blower assembly-air conditioning	1		
9	JUB100140L	Tube-drain evaporator tube	1		

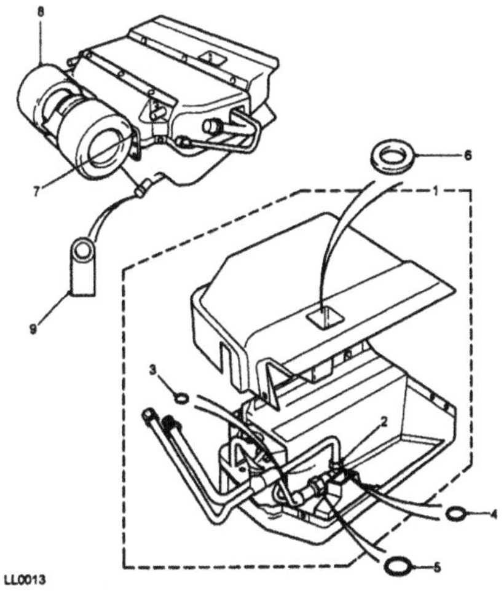

LL0013

Illus	Part Number	Description	Quantity	Change Point	Remarks
1	JRJ100480	Reciever dryer assembly-air con	1		RHD
1	JRJ100490	Reciever dryer assembly-air con	1		LHD
2	FB110201L	Bolt-flanged head-M10 x 100	2		RHD
3	FX106047L	Nut-flange-prevailing torque-M6	2		LHD

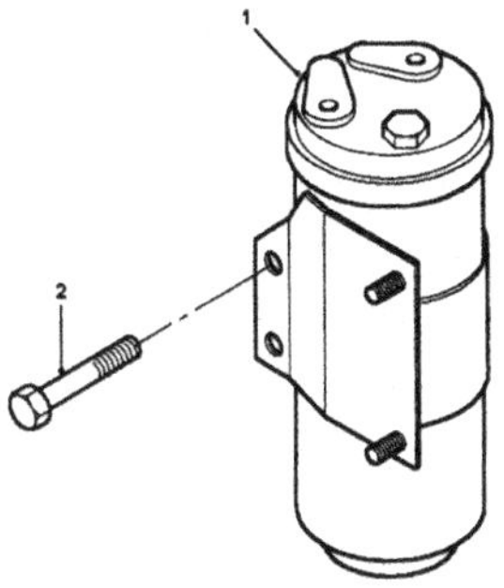

LL0044

Receiver Dryer-V8 EFI-4.0L

Illus	Part Number	Description	Quantity	Change Point	Remarks
1	STC3973	Receiver dryer assembly air conditioning	1		
2	STC3976	SWITCH TRINARY	1		
3	STC3191	• O ring-11.2mm OD-7.6mm ID-1.8mm thick-with cfc-free refrigerant	1		
4	FN108047L	Nut-flange-flanged head-M8	2		
5	FB108181L	Bolt-M8 x 90	2		
6	STC3974	Bracket receiver dryer	1		
7	STC3975	Clip	1		

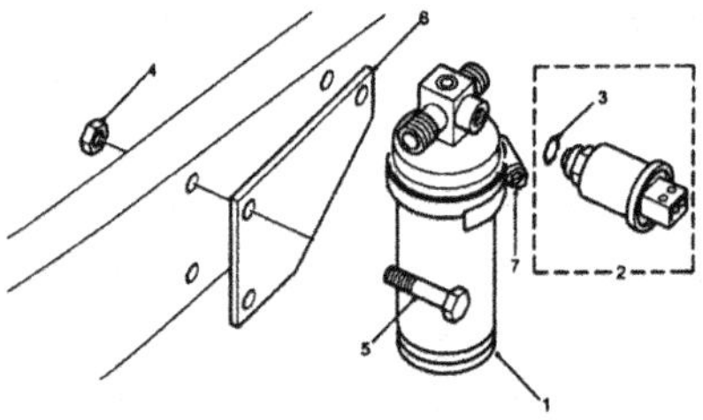

LL0017

Evaporator Bracket-V8 EFI-4.0L

Illus	Part Number	Description	Quantity	Change Point	Remarks
		BRACKET-FAN MOUNTING			
1	STC4266	lower-RHD	1		
1	STC4264	lower-LHD	1		
2	STC4265	upper-RHD	1		
2	STC3991	upper-LHD	1		
3	FN106047L	Nut-flange-M6	5		

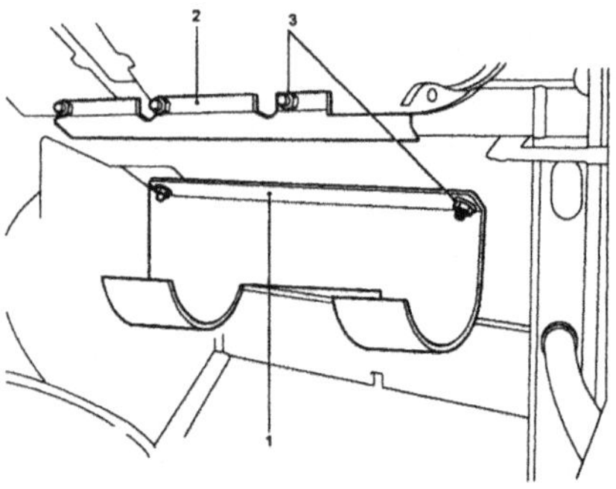

LL0018

Illus	Part Number	Description	Quantity	Change Point	Remarks
1	STC4287	Relay-normally open-Black	3		LHD
2	STC4279	Bracket air conditioning	1		RHD
3	YWB10027L	Relay	1		RHD
4	YWB10004L	Relay-Yellow	3		RHD

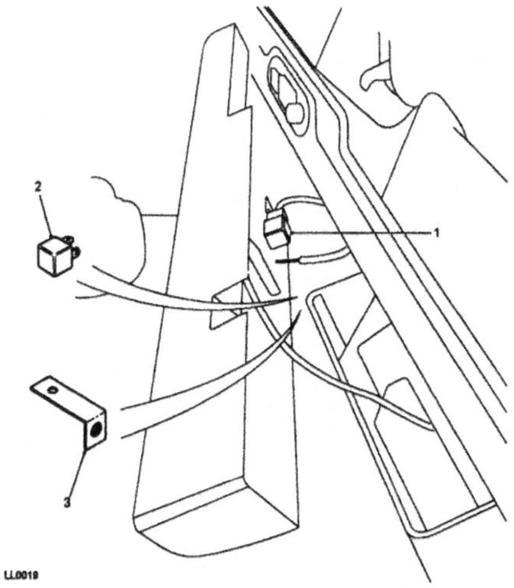

LL0019

Illus	Part Number	Description	Quantity	Change Point	Remarks
1	RTC7440	Motor blower-heater	1		
2	RTC7468	Bracket-blower mounting	1		
3	RTC7441	Fan blower-heater	1		
4	RTC7442	Housing cover	1		
5	RTC7469	Bracket assembly-blower mounting	3		
6	RTC7470	Clamp	1		
7	RTC7446	Seal-facia air duct-heater	1		
	RTC7474	Seal-firewall	1		

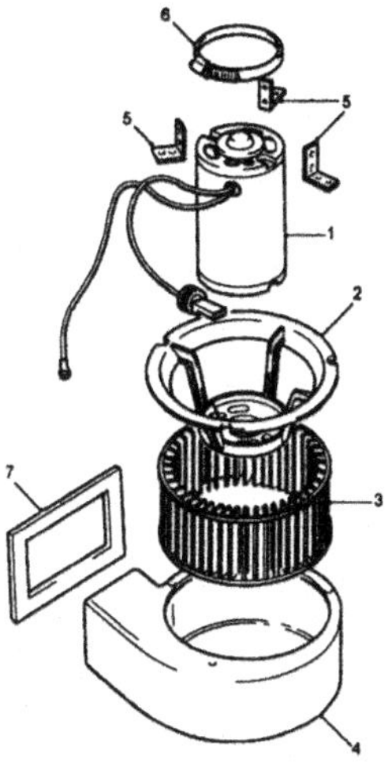

AHLXMA3A

Illus	Part Number	Description	Quantity	Change Point	Remarks
	AWR2473	Hose-vacuum-air temperature control/t induction system	1		RHD Diesel TDi air conditioning
1	RTC7439	Hose-evapr/compressor air conditioning	1		LHD Petrol
1	STC3216	Hose-evapr/compressor air conditioning	1		LHD Diesel
1	MUC4875	Hose-evapr/compressor air conditioning	1		RHD Petrol
1	STC3215	Hose-evapr/compressor air conditioning	1		RHD Diesel
2	AEU3055	Valve-suction air conditioning compressor	1		RHD except cfc-free refrigerant
2	STC3170	Valve-suction air conditioning compressor	1		RHD cfc-free refrigerant
	STC3168	Resistor	1		
3	MUC4874	Seal	1		
4	MUC4872	Hose-condenser/evaporator air conditioning	1		LHD
4	STC3214	Hose-condenser/evaporator air conditioning	1		RHD
5	MUC4358	Adaptor-air conditioning compressor hose	1		
7	RTC7457	Coupling	2		
6	AEU1628	O ring-less cfc free refrigerant-No 10-1/2"diameter	NLA	To (V) MA 962814	Use STC3171. RHD
6	AEU1626	O ring-5/16"-less cfc free refrigerant	NLA	To (V) MA 962814	Use STC3191. RHD
6	AEU1627	O ring-less cfc free refrigerant-13/32"	NLA	To (V) MA 962814	Use STC3192. RHD
6	AEU3056	O ring-less cfc free refrigerant	3	To (V) MA 962814	RHD
6	STC3191	O ring-11.2mm OD-7.6mm ID-1.8mm thick-with cfc-free refrigerant	2	From (V) MA 962815	
6	STC3192	O ring-14.5mm OD-10.8mm ID-1.8mm thick-with cfc-free refrigerant	2	From (V) MA 962815	
6	STC3171	O ring-10mm-with cfc-free refrigerant	2	From (V) MA 962815	

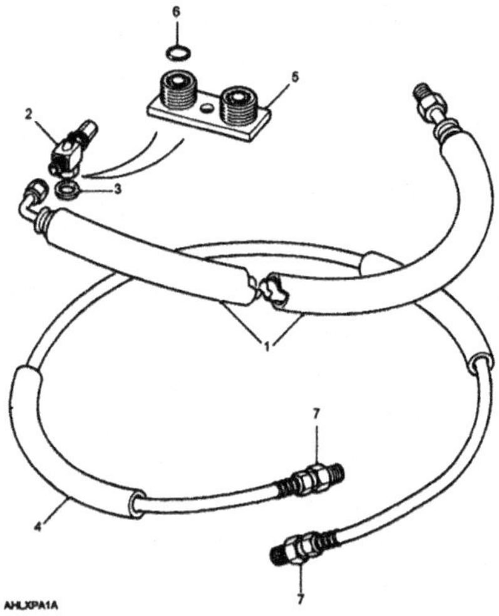

AHLXPA1A

Illus	Part Number	Description	Quantity	Change Point	Remarks
1	MUC1679	Vacuum tank	1		
2	MUC4878	Hose vacuum..-T piece to vacuum tank	1		
3	MUC4878	Hose vacuum..	1		Note (1)
4	MUC4878	Hose vacuum..	1		Note (1)
5	MUC4455	T piece	2		
6	MUC4866	Hose vacuum..	1		
7	MUC4878	Hose vacuum..	1		Note (1)
8	MUC4878	Hose vacuum..	1		Note (1)
9	MUC4865	T piece	1		
10	MUC1671	Harness air conditioning	1		
	STC1569	Pipe-vacuum heater/air conditioning	1		
11	MUC4871	Harness air conditioning	1		
	STC1569	Pipe-vacuum heater/air conditioning	1		
	ATU1041	Ring-retention	8		

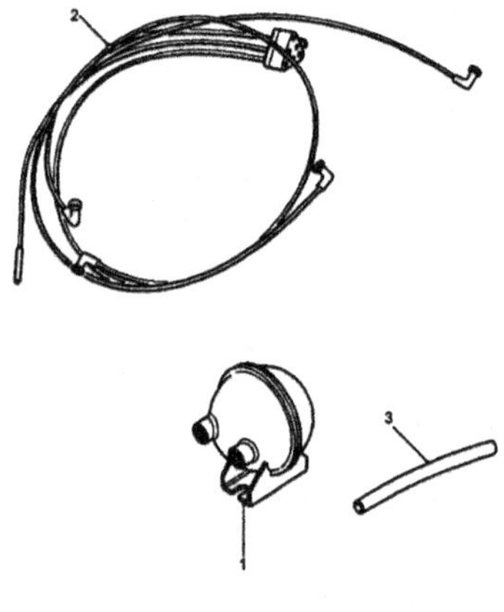

AHLXPA2A

Remarks:
(1) cut to the required length

DEFENDER

GROUP L

Cooling & Heating
Air Conditioning
Heater Pipes-4 Cylinder-RHD

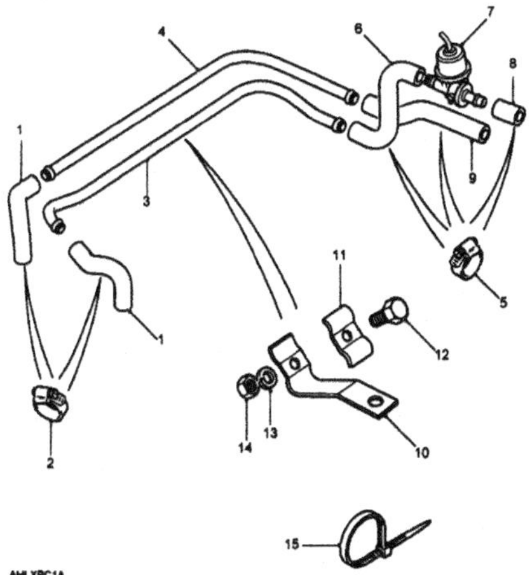

AHLXPC1A

Illus	Part Number	Description	Quantity	Change Point	Remarks
1	NRC6306	Hose-heater to engine pipe	2		
2	CN100308L	Clip-hose-30mm	2		
2	ESR3607	Clip-hose-26mm	2		90°
3	NRC6307	Pipe assembly-coolant to heater-RHD	1		
4	NRC6420	Pipe assembly-coolant to heater-RHD	1		
5	CN100258L	Clip-hose-25mm	8		
6	BTR213	Hose-heater to engine pipe	1	Note (1)	
6	BTR9400	Hose-heater to engine pipe	1	Note (2)	
7	NRC8346	Water control valve	1		
8	ERC3964	Hose-air conditioning	1	Note (1)	
9	BTR214	Hose-heater return coolant	1		
8	BTR9401	Hose-air conditioning	1	Note (2)	
9	BTR9402	Hose-heater return coolant	1		
10	NRC6417	Bracket-heater feed pipe	1		Petrol
10	NRC6418	Bracket-heater feed pipe	1		Diesel
11	NRC6419	Clamp	1		
12	FS106255L	Screw-flanged head-M6 x 25	1		
13	WL106001L	Washer-sprung-M6	1		
14	NH106041L	Nut-hexagonal-nyloc-M6	1		
15	ESR3301	Tie-cable-Black-13.0 x 540mm-inside serated	1		

CHANGE POINTS:
(1) To (V) LA 939975
(2) From (V) MA 939976

DEFENDER

GROUP L

Cooling & Heating
Air Conditioning
Heater Pipes-4 Cylinder-LHD

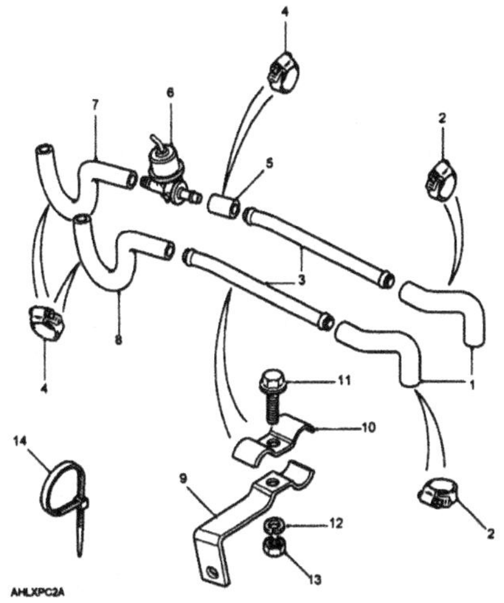

AHLXPC2A

Illus	Part Number	Description	Quantity	Change Point	Remarks
1	NRC6306	Hose-heater to engine pipe	2		
2	CN100258L	Clip-hose-25mm	4		
3	NRC8245	Pipe assembly-coolant to heater	2		
4	CN100258L	Clip-hose-25mm	6		
5	ERC3964	Hose-air conditioning	1		
6	NRC8346	Water control valve	1		
7	NRC8347	Hose-heater to engine pipe	1		
8	NRC8247	Hose-heater to engine pipe	1		
9	NRC8248	Bracket	1		
10	594637	Clamp	NLA		Use ESR1584.
10	ESR1584	Clamp	1		
11	FS106201L	Screw-flanged head-M6 x 20	1		
12	WL106001L	Washer-sprung-M6	1		
13	NH106041L	Nut-hexagonal-nyloc-M6	1		
14	ESR3301	Tie-cable-Black-13.0 x 540mm-inside serated	1		

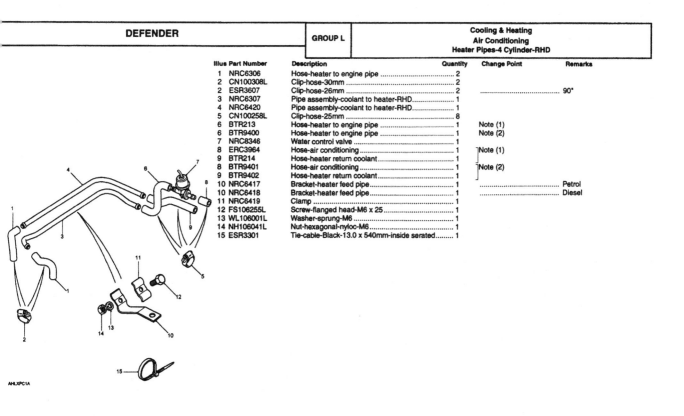

DEFENDER | **GROUP L** | **Cooling & Heating**
Air Conditioning
Heater Pipes-TDi-LHD

Illus	Part Number	Description	Quantity	Change Point	Remarks
1	ERR371	Pipe-heater to hose coolant	1		
2	WA110065	Washer-plain	2		
3	NT110041L	Locknut-M10	2		
4	ERR1436	Hose-pipe to heater	1		
5	BTR984	Hose-heater return coolant	1	Note (1)	
5	AWR2334	Hose-heater return coolant	1	Note (2)	
6	BTR985	Hose-air conditioning	1	Note (1)	
6	AWR2333	Hose-air conditioning	1	Note (2)	
7	BTR986	Hose-heater to engine pipe	1	Note (1)	
7	AWR2332	Hose-heater to engine pipe	1	Note (2)	
8	NRC8346	Water control valve	1		
9	CN100258L	Clip-hose-25mm	8		
10	BTR987	Bracket-hose air conditioning	1		
11	SH105121L	Screw-hexagonal head-M5 x 12	2		
12	MRC9851	Washer-nylon	2		
13	NY105041L	Nut-hexagonal-nyloc-M5	2		
14	BTR988	Clip-hose	2		
15	SH105121L	Screw-hexagonal head-M5 x 12	2		
16	WA105001L	Washer-plain-standard-M5	2		
17	NY105041L	Nut-hexagonal-nyloc-M5	2		
18	ESR3301	Tie-cable-Black-13.0 x 540mm-inside serated	1		

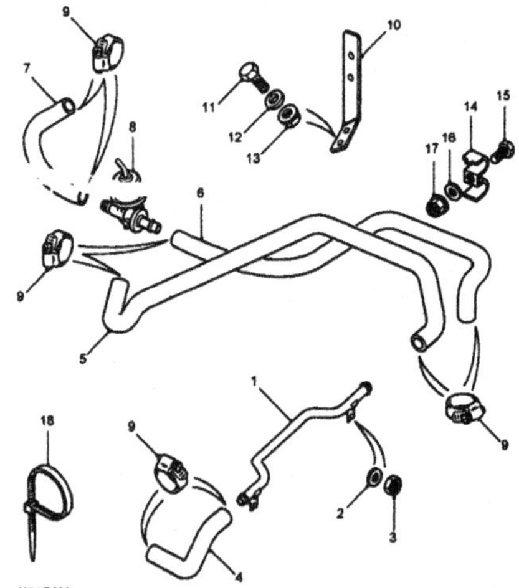

AHLXPC3A

CHANGE POINTS:
(1) To (V) LA 939975
(2) From (V) MA 939976

DEFENDER | **GROUP L** | **Cooling & Heating**
Air Conditioning
Heater Pipes-V8-RHD

Illus	Part Number	Description	Quantity	Change Point	Remarks
1	NRC6314	Hose-heater to engine pipe-RHD	2		
2	CN100308L	Clip-hose-30mm	4		
3	NRC6902	Pipe assembly-coolant to heater-RHD	2		
4	ERC3964	Hose-air conditioning	1		
5	CN100258L	Clip-hose-25mm	10		
6	NRC8346	Water control valve	1		
7	NTC1212	Hose-heater to engine pipe	1		
8	NRC6308	Hose-pipe to heater-RHD	1		
9	NRC6903	Bracket-heater pipe assembly	1		
10	NRC6419	Clamp	1		
11	SH106301L	Screw-hexagonal head-M6 x 30	1		
12	WL106001L	Washer-sprung-M6	1		
13	NH106041L	Nut-hexagonal-nyloc-M6	1		
14	ESR3301	Tie-cable-Black-13.0 x 540mm-inside serated	1		

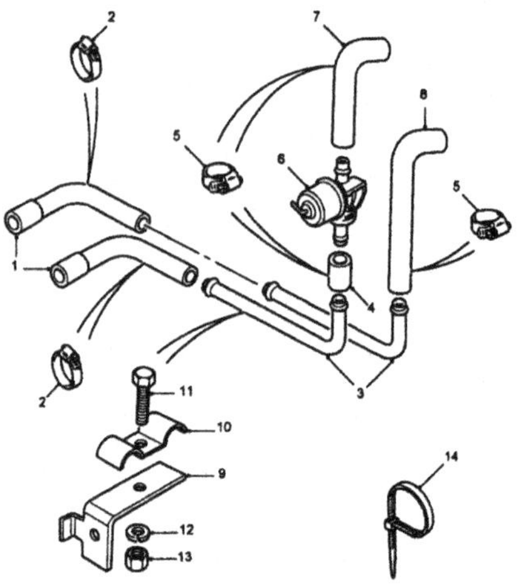

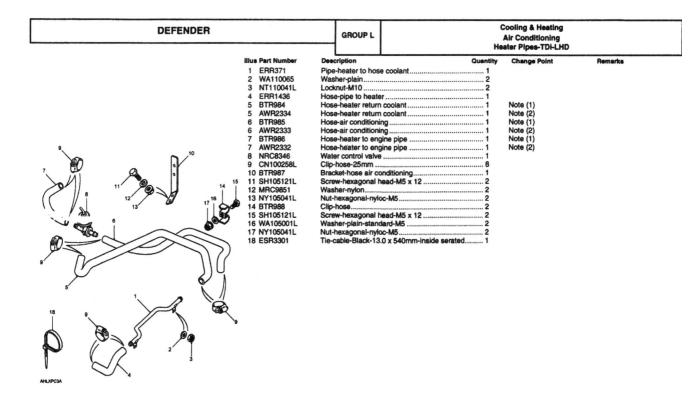

AHLXPC4A

DEFENDER	GROUP L	Cooling & Heating Air Conditioning Heater Pipes-V8-LHD

Illus	Part Number	Description	Quantity	Change Point	Remarks
1	NRC9098	Hose-heater to engine pipe	1		
2	NRC6353	Hose-heater to engine pipe-LHD	1		
3	CN100308L	Clip-hose-30mm	4		
4	NRC9091	Pipe assembly-coolant to heater	1		
5	NTC1090	Pipe assembly-coolant to heater	1		
6	ERC3964	Hose-air conditioning	1		
7	CN100258L	Clip-hose-25mm	7		
8	NRC8346	Water control valve	1		
9	NTC1089	Hose-heater to engine pipe	1		
10	NTC1088	Hose-heater to engine pipe	1		
11	NRC8620	Bracket	1		
12	594637	Clamp	NLA		Use ESR1584.
12	ESR1584	Clamp	1		
13	SH106301L	Screw-hexagonal head-M6 x 30	1		
14	WL106001L	Washer-sprung-M6	1		
15	NH106041L	Nut-hexagonal-nyloc-M6	1		
16	ESR3301	Tie-cable-Black-13.0 x 540mm-inside serated	1		

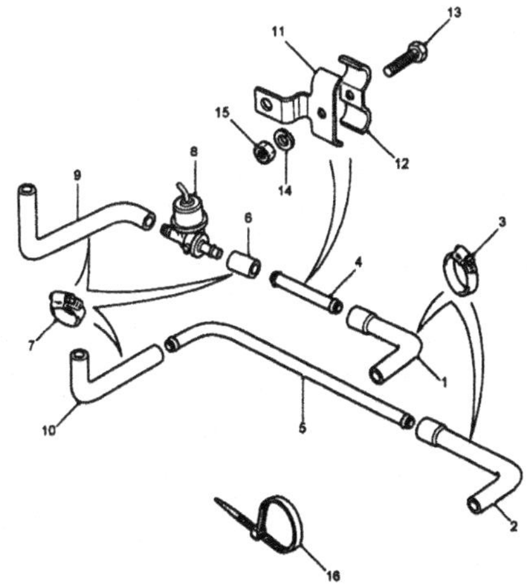

AHLXPC5A

DEFENDER	GROUP L	Cooling & Heating Air Conditioning Fresh Air Duct-RHD

Illus	Part Number	Description	Quantity	Change Point	Remarks
1	MUC1668	Duct assembly-fresh air	1		
2	MUC4884	Motor-vacuum-air con	1		
3	RTC7467	Motor-vacuum-air con	1		
4	MUC4883	Seal	1		
5	MUC4886	Seal-outlet evaporator-air conditioning	1		
6	MUC4888	Seal-facia air duct-air duct to dash-RHD	1	Note (1)	
6	MWC4860	Seal-facia air duct-air duct to dash-RHD	NLA	Note (2)	
7	RTC7470	Clamp	1		

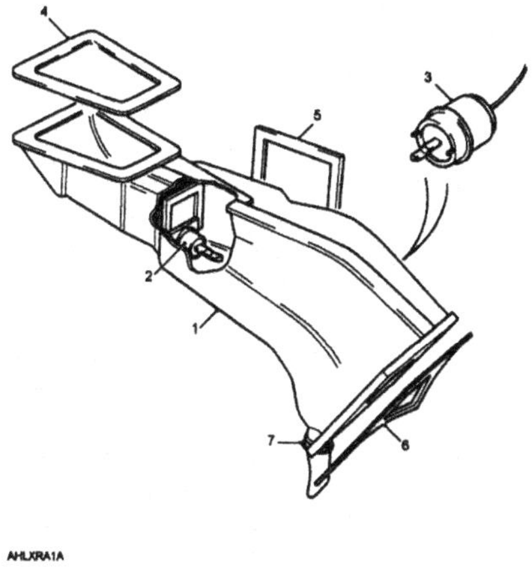

AHLXRA1A

CHANGE POINTS:
(1) To (V) EA 332911
(2) From (V) EA 332912

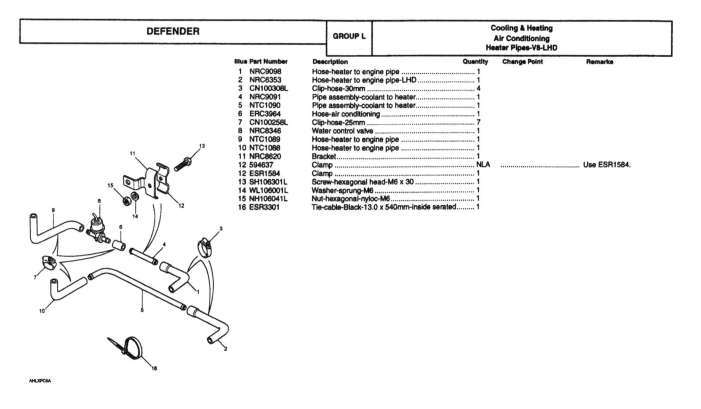

Illus	Part Number	Description	Quantity	Change Point	Remarks
1	MTC5571	Duct-engine intake	1		
2	RTC7461	Gasket	1		
3	RTC7460	Seal-outlet evaporator-air conditioning	1		
4	RTC7459	Seal-air distribution box passenger duct	1		
5	AEU4002	Motor-vacuum-air con	1		
6	MUC4878	Hose vacuum..	1		Note (1)
7	MUC4878	Hose vacuum..	1		Note (1)
8	MUC4878	Hose vacuum..	1		Note (1)
9	MUC4455	T piece	1		
10	RTC7470	Clamp-blower motor	1		
	ATU1041	Ring-retention	8		

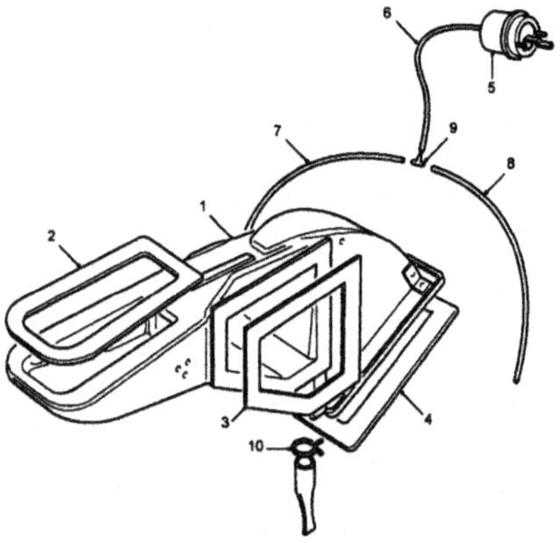

AHLXRA4A

Remarks:
(1) cut to the required length

Illus	Part Number	Description	Quantity	Change Point	Remarks
1	MUC1657	Pad-insulation-air duct-top	1		
2	MUC1658	Pad-insulation-air duct-bottom	1		
3	MUC1659	Pad-insulation-air duct-outer	1		
4	MUC1660	Pad-insulation-air duct-inner	1		

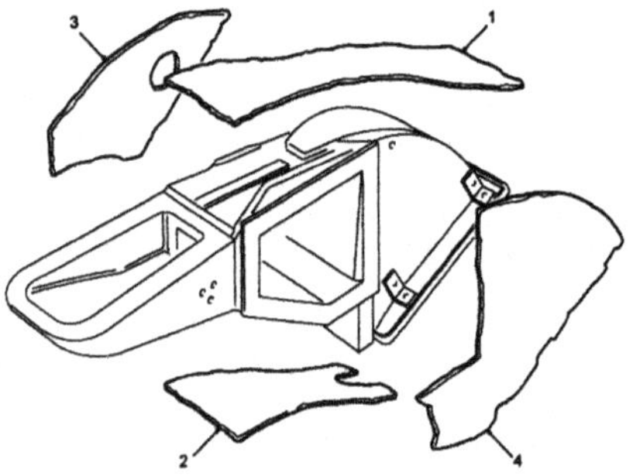

AHLXRA5A

DEFENDER	GROUP L	Cooling & Heating Air Conditioning Heater Controls

Illus	Part Number	Description	Quantity	Change Point	Remarks
1	MTC5573	Control assembly heater-LHD	1	Note (1)	
1	AWR1179	Control assembly heater	1	Note (2)	
2	AEU1205	Switch assembly-pressure condenser fan	1		
3	RTC7443	Switch assembly-vacuum control-heater	1		
4	RTC7451	Switch assembly-vacuum control-heater	1		
5	RTC7445	Cable-control mode control-heater	1		
6	RTC7448	Harness air conditioning	1		
7	RTC7466	Harness air conditioning	1		
8	AEU1198	Knob-control heater	4		

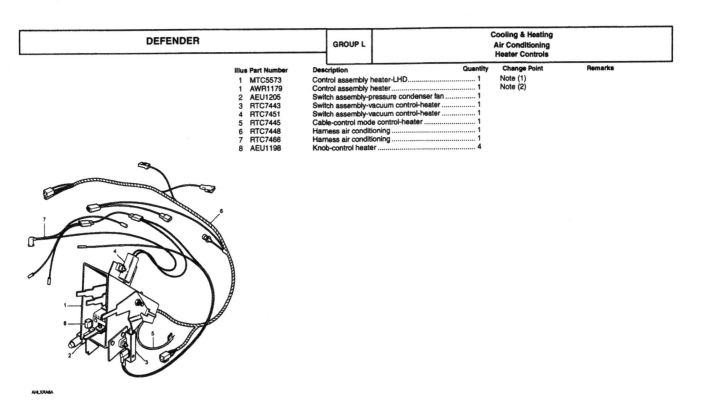

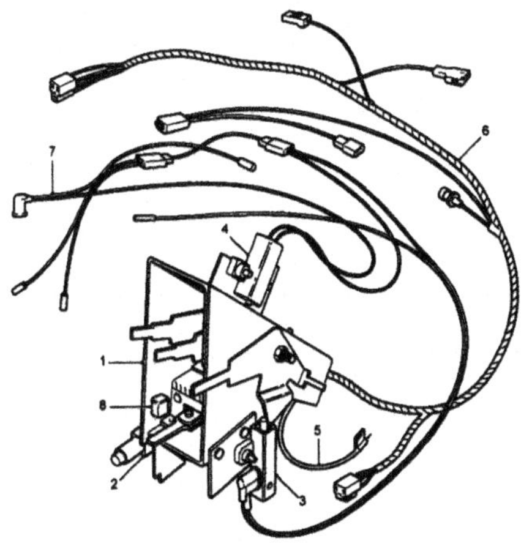

AHLXRA8A

CHANGE POINTS:
(1) To (V) LA 939975
(2) From (V) MA 939976

DEFENDER	GROUP L	Cooling & Heating Air Conditioning Plenum Chamber-LHD

Illus	Part Number	Description	Quantity	Change Point	Remarks
1	RTC7408	Plenum assembly	1	Note (1)	
	AWR1174	Extension assembly-plenum closing	1	Note (2)	
2	RTC7462	Seal air conditioning	1		
3	RTC7463	Seal air conditioning	1		
4	RTC7464	Seal-inlet blower-air conditioning	1		
5	RTC7409	Pipe-plenum chamber breather	1		
6	RTC7415	PANEL-FRONT END TRIM PLENUM CLOSING	1	Note (1)	
6	AWR1448	PANEL-FRONT END TRIM PLENUM CLOSING	1	Note (2)	
7	AEU4002	• Motor-vacuum-air con	1		
8	AB606021	Screw-self tapping AB	22		
	367078	Spacer	A/R		

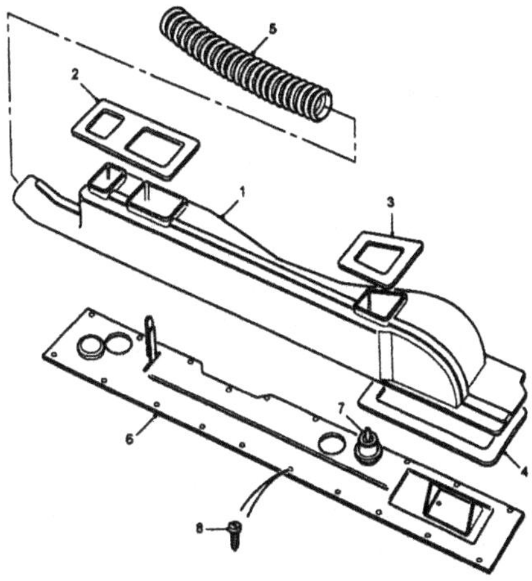

AHLXRA7A

CHANGE POINTS:
(1) To (V) LA 939975
(2) From (V) MA 939976

Plenum Chamber-RHD

Illus	Part Number	Description	Quantity	Change Point	Remarks
1	MUC1665	PLENUM ASSY-DASH TOP	1		
2	AEU4002	• Motor-vacuum-air con	2		
4	MUC4882	Seal air conditioning-RH	1		
5	MUC4881	Seal air conditioning-LH	1		
6	MUC4891	Connector-inlet manifold adaptor	1		
7	MUC1673	Duct-face level vent-LH	1		
8	MUC4892	Hose-manifold to plenum de icer	1		
9	MUC1674	Duct-face level vent-RH	1	Note (1)	
9	AWR1247	Duct-face level vent-RH	1	Note (2)	
10	AB606021L	Screw-self tapping AB-No 6 x 1/4	22		
11	MUC3695	Pad-insulation	1		

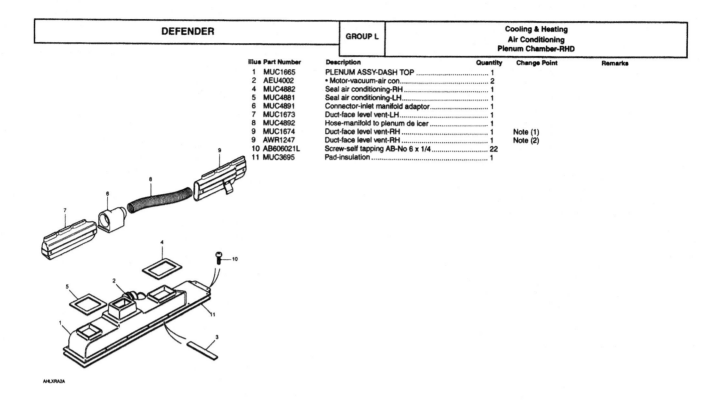

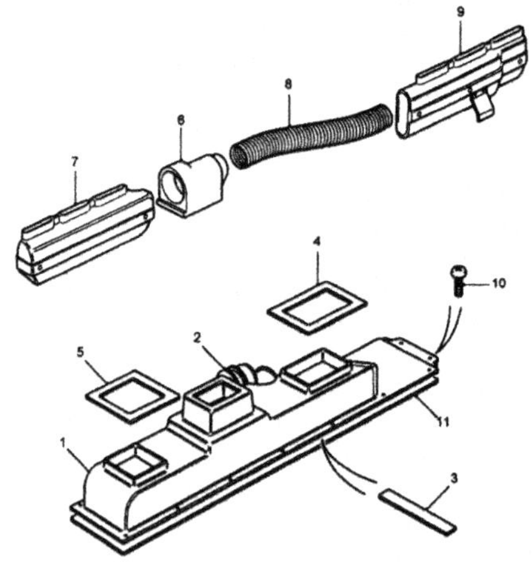

AHLXRA2A

CHANGE POINTS:
(1) To (V) LA 939975
(2) From (V) MA 939976

Facia Panel Assembly-RHD-To (V) WA159806

Illus	Part Number	Description	Quantity	Change Point	Remarks
1	MUC1667	FINISHER ASSEMBLY-FACIA ASSEMBLY	1	Note (1)	
1	AWR1245	FINISHER ASSEMBLY-FACIA ASSEMBLY		Note (2)	
3	AEU4002	• Motor-vacuum-air con	2		
4	MUC1666	• Control assembly heater	1		
5	MUC6011	• Knob-control heater	1		
6	MUC6012	• Switch assembly clutch	1		
7	MUC6013	• Button-switch air conditioning	1		
	573289	• Bulb-504-w10/3-3 Watt	1		
2	MUC6001	• Panel-facia	1		
9	MUC4880	Housing-facia vent louvre	4		
10	MUC1669	VENT ASSEMBLY-FACE LEVEL DRIVER FACIA	1		
11	RTC7411	• Housing-facia vent louvre	1		
12	MUC4895	Hose-air conditioning	1	Note (3)	
12	MXC3418	Hose-air conditioning	1	Note (4)	
13	MXC3357	Adaptor	1		
14	MXC3358	Adaptor	1		
15	MUC1670	Finisher-facia air conditioning control	1		
16	MUC1680	Cable-control mode control-heater	1		
17	RTC7465	Finisher-dash strip	1		

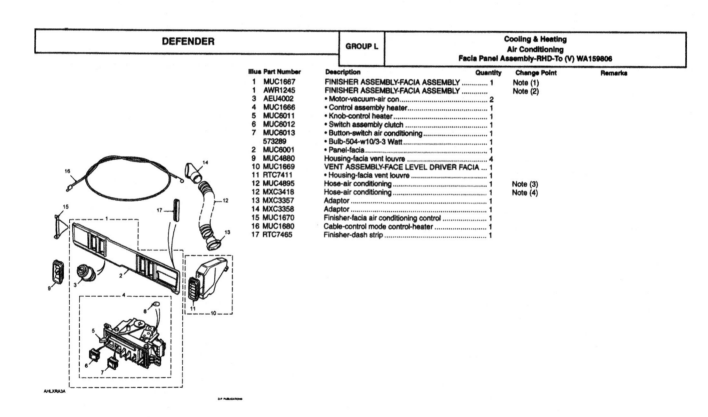

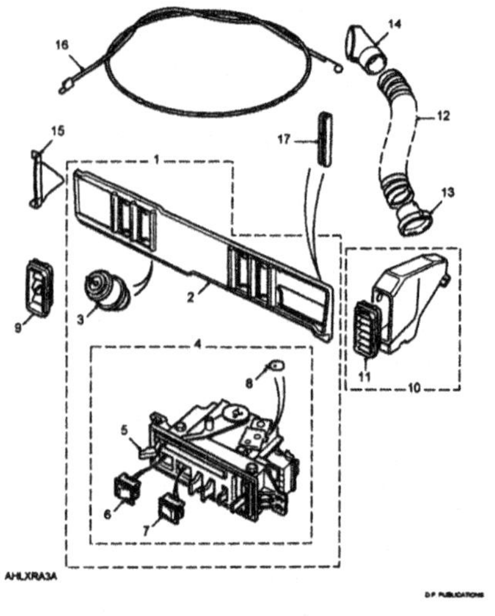

AHLXRA3A

D.P. PUBLICATIONS

CHANGE POINTS:
(1) To (V) LA 939975
(2) From (V) MA 939976
(3) To (V) EA 332911
(4) From (V) EA 332912

Facia Panel Assembly-LHD-To (V) WA159806

Illus	Part Number	Description	Quantity	Change Point	Remarks
1	RTC7450	FACIA ASSEMBLY-FRONT END	1		
2	AEU4000	• Plate	1		
3	AEU4001	• Housing-facia vent louvre-single	5		
3	AWR1169	• Housing-facia vent louvre-set of 5	NLA		Use AEU4001.
4	AC608065	Screw	2		
5	ACU5431	Nut-lokut	2		
6	AB608051	Screw-self tapping	2		
7	WC105001	Washer-plain-M5	2		
8	MTC5581	Finisher-grab handle	1		
9	AW606124	Screw-No 6 x 3/4	1		
10	WA104004	Washer-plain-M4	1		
11	ACU5431	Nut-lokut	1		
12	RTC7410	FINISHER ASSEMBLY COMP-FACIA ASSEMBLY	1	Note (1)	
12	AWR1170	FINISHER ASSEMBLY COMP-FACIA ASSEMBLY	1	Note (2)	
13	RTC7411	• Housing-facia vent louvre	1		
14	79086L	Rivet-plastic-drive	1		
15	MTC7516	Finisher-facia air conditioning control	1		
16	RTC7465	Finisher-dash strip	1		
17	RTC7412	SWITCH-THUMBWHEEL ILLUMINATION CONTROL	1		
	RTC7413	• Bulb illumination assembly	1		

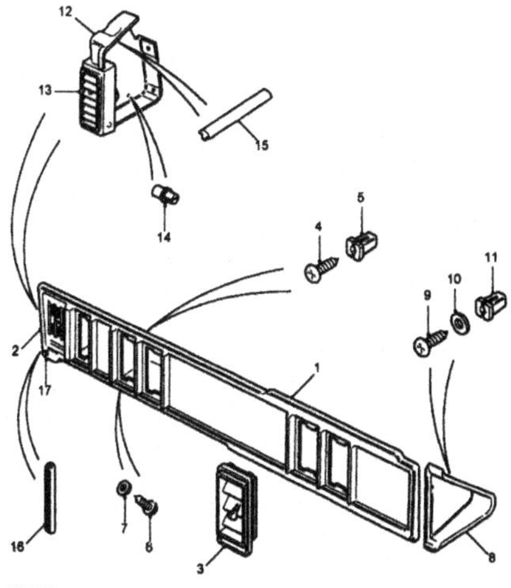

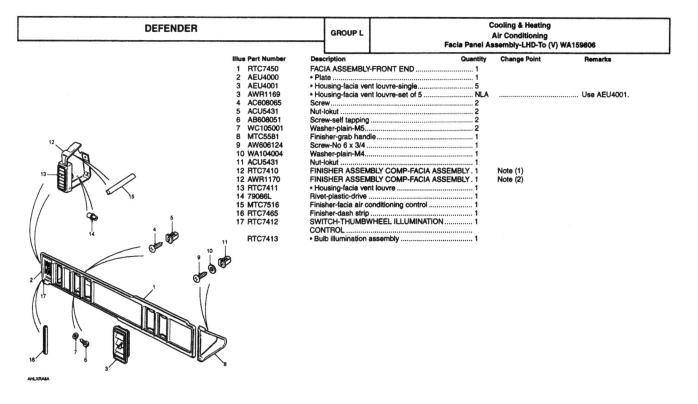

CHANGE POINTS:
(1) To (V) LA 939975
(2) From (V) MA 939976

Facia Panel Assembly-From (V) XA159807

Illus	Part Number	Description	Quantity	Change Point	Remarks
		EVAPORATOR AND FACIA ASSEMBLY			
1	JQB101240	Evaporator assembly-R134a air conditioning	1	Note (1)	RHD
1	JQB101230	Evaporator assembly-R134a air conditioning	1	Note (1)	LHD
1	JQB000020	Evaporator assembly-R134a air conditioning-RHD	1	Note (2)	RHD
1	JQB000030	Evaporator assembly-R134a air conditioning-LHD	1	Note (2)	LHD
		FACIA AND ELECTRICAL COMPONENTS			
2	JTV100000	Housing-air conditioning switches	1		
4	BTR7071	Housing-facia vent louvre	4		
5	YMF101190	Harness air conditioning	1		
6	YWB10027L	Relay	1		
7	JFC101990	Control assembly-air conditioning	1		
8	JTB100340	SWITCH ASSEMBLY-AIR CONDITIONING ROTARY-HEATER CONTROL	1		
3	YUM10001L	• Knob heater/fan control	1		
9	YUK100270	SWITCH ASSEMBLY-AIR CONDITIONING ROTARY-FAN CONTROL	1		
3	YUM10001L	• Knob heater/fan control	1		
10	JQB000010	Duct assembly-air floor	2	Note (2)	

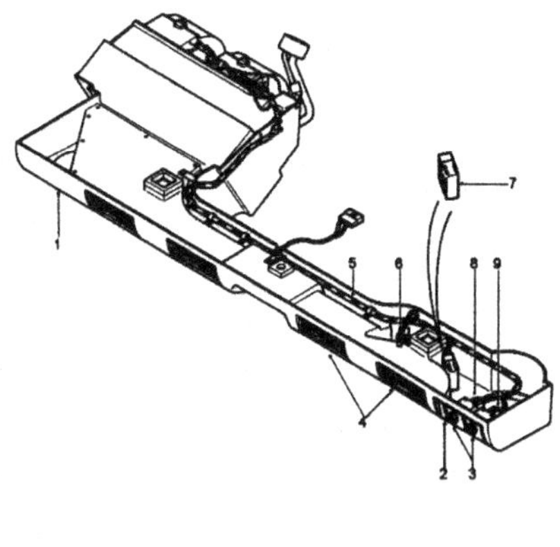

CHANGE POINTS:
(1) From (V) XA 159807 To (V) ZA 608419
(2) From (V) 1A 608420

Illus	Part Number	Description	Quantity	Change Point	Remarks
1	STC4268	Facia assembly	1		LHD
1	STC4267	Facia assembly	1		RHD
2	AB606061	Screw	4		
3	STC4277	Harness air conditioning-under bonnet	1		LHD
3	STC4278	Harness air conditioning-under bonnet	1		RHD
4	NTC1154	Tie-cable-3.5 x 300mm-inside serated	6		
5	STC3986	Switch-rotary heatr/fan control	1		
7	STC3987	Switch-temp control and capillary temp probe	1		
6	YUM10001L	Knob heater/fan control	2		
8	STC3988	Panel-switches mounting	1		
9	DAG100290	Badge-Land Rover-Gold on Green background	1		
9	EMB1542	Badge-Land Rover-Green-Silver	1		
10	BTR7072	Housing-facia vent louvre	4		
11	STC3994	Plug-blanking-9.5mm	4		
12	STC3985	Harness air conditioning-behind facia	1		

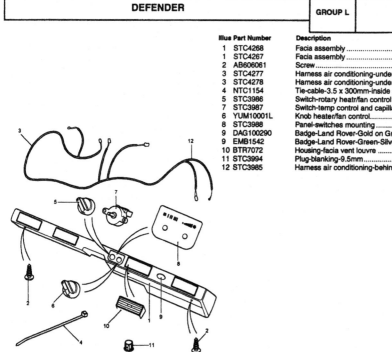

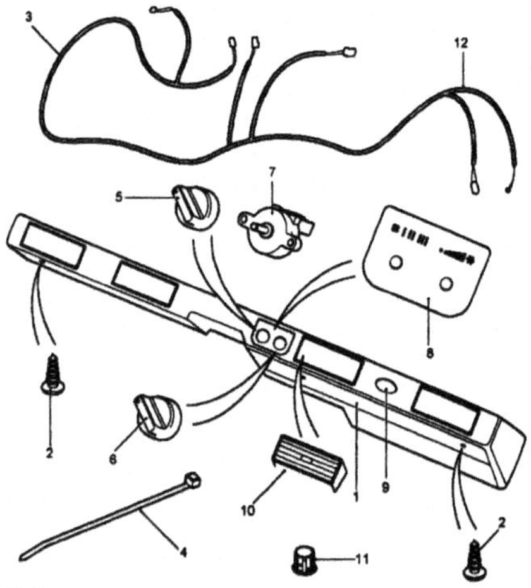

LL0015

Illus	Part Number	Description	Quantity	Change Point	Remarks
		DUCT-DEMIST WINDSCREEN			
1	MRC9668	RH	1		
1	MRC9669	LH	1		
1	MXC3188	RH	1	Note (1)	TDi
1	MXC3189	LH	1		
1	BTR1600	RH	1	Note (2)	
1	BTR1599	LH	1		
1	BTR1600	RH	1		Td5
1	BTR1599	LH	1		
2	AB608047L	Screw-self tapping-No 8 x 1/2	2		
3	WA105001L	Washer-plain-standard-M5	2		
2	AB608054L	Screw-self tapping-No8 x 5/8	4		
	RTC3745	Nut-lokut-RH nozzle	1		
	AK608021	Nut-spring-u type-RH nozzle	1		
4	MRC7279	Tube	2		
5	MRC7281	Grommet	2		

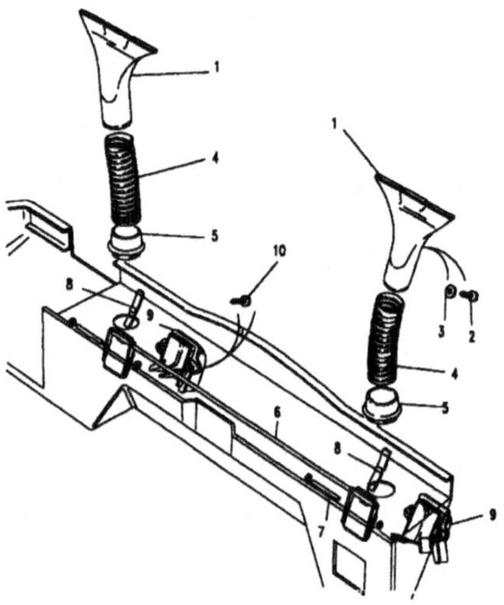

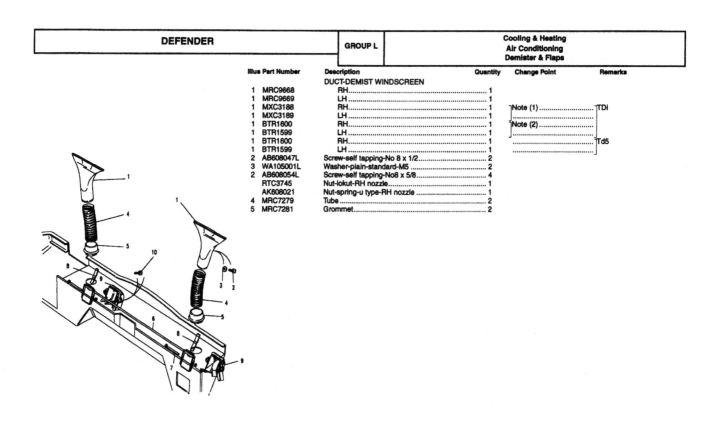

CHANGE POINTS:
(1) To (V) JA 906639
(2) From (V) JA 906640

Illus	Part Number	Description	Quantity	Change Point	Remarks
6	MUC1139	Flap & seals assembly blower-heater	1	Note (1)	LHD TDi
6	BTR1347	Flap & seals assembly blower-heater	1	Note (2)	LHD
6	MUC3278	Flap & seals assembly blower-heater	1	Note (3)	RHD TDi
6	BTR1348	Flap & seals assembly blower-heater	1	Note (4)	RHD
7	MTC5578	Bar-actuating	1		
8	346976	Clip-spring connector	2		
		DUCT ASSEMBLY-AIR FLOOR			
9	395829	RH	1	Note (6)	
9	395830	LH	1	Note (6)	
9	JKB100440	RH	1	Note (7)	
9	JKB100450	LH	1	Note (7)	
10	MRC1525	Screw	4		

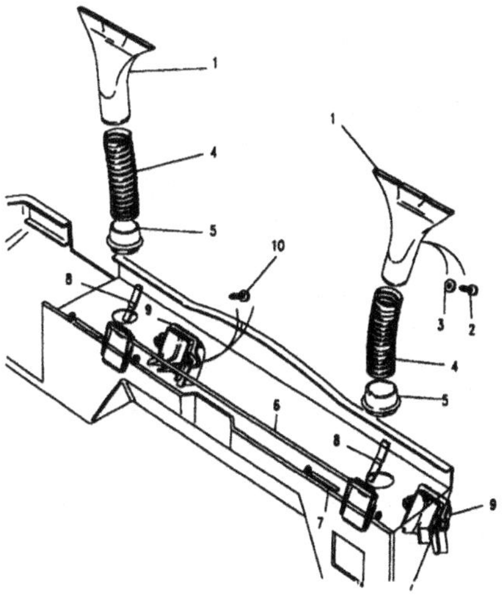

CHANGE POINTS:
(1) To (V) HA 905497
(2) From (V) HA 905498
(3) To (V) JA 908189
(4) From (V) JA 908190
(6) To (V) VA 136611
(7) From (V) VA 136612

Illus	Part Number	Description	Quantity	Change Point	Remarks
1	STC3971	HOSE-COMPRESSOR/CONDENSER AIR CONDITIONING	1		LHD
1	STC4274	HOSE-COMPRESSOR/CONDENSER AIR CONDITIONING	1		RHD
2	STC4271	• O ring-15.7mm OD-10.9mm ID-2.4mm thick	1		
3	STC3192	• O ring-14.5mm OD-10.8mm ID-1.8mm thick-with cfc-free refrigerant	1		
4	STC3972	HOSE-CONDENSER/RECEIVER DRYER AIR CONDITIONING	1		LHD
4	STC4275	HOSE-CONDENSER/RECEIVER DRYER AIR CONDITIONING	1		RHD
5	STC3191	• O ring-11.2mm OD-7.6mm ID-1.8mm thick-with cfc-free refrigerant	2		
6	STC3978	HOSE-RECEIVER DRYER/EVAPORATOR AIR CONDITIONING	1		LHD
6	STC4276	HOSE-RECEIVER DRYER/EVAPORATOR AIR CONDITIONING	1		RHD
5	STC3191	• O ring-11.2mm OD-7.6mm ID-1.8mm thick-with cfc-free refrigerant	2		
7	STC4273	HOSE-EVAPR/COMPRESSOR AIR CONDITIONING	1		RHD
7	STC3977	HOSE-EVAPR/COMPRESSOR AIR CONDITIONING	1		LHD
8	STC4272	• O ring-18.2mm OD-13.5mm ID-2.4mm thick	1		
9	STC4269	• O ring-17.6mm OD-13.5mm ID-1.8mm thick	1		

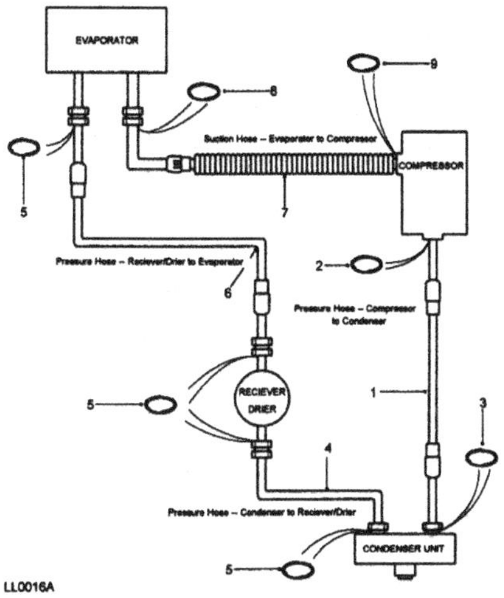

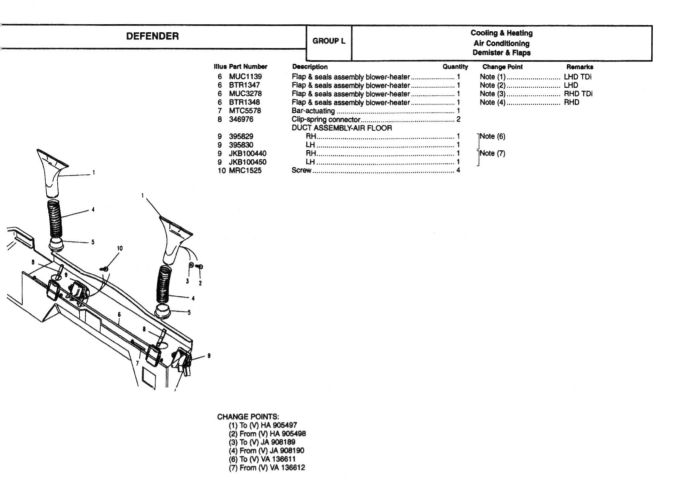

LL0016A

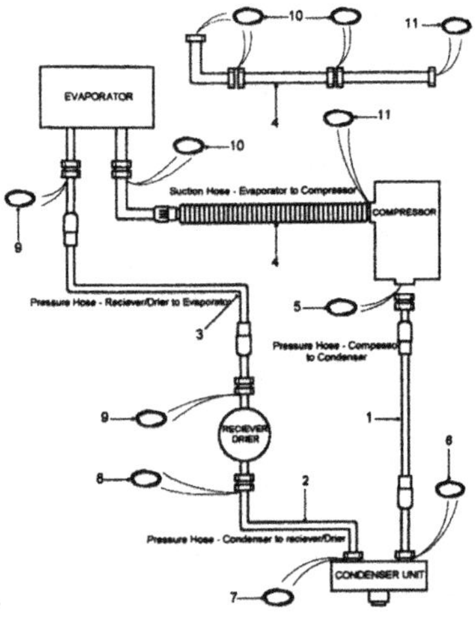

LL0037

Illus	Part Number	Description	Quantity	Change Point	Remarks
1	JUF102190	HOSE-COMPRESSOR/CONDENSER AIR CONDITIONING	1	Note (1)	Td5
5	JUU100480	• O ring air conditioning	2		
1	JUF102210	HOSE-COMPRESSOR/CONDENSER AIR CONDITIONING	1	Note (1)	LHD Petrol
1	JUF102680	HOSE-COMPRESSOR/CONDENSER AIR CONDITIONING	1	Note (1)	TDi
1	JUF102690	HOSE-COMPRESSOR/CONDENSER AIR CONDITIONING	1	Note (2)	RHD V8
1	JUF102930	HOSE-COMPRESSOR/CONDENSER AIR CONDITIONING	1	Note (3)	RHD V8
5	JUU100450	• O ring air conditioning	1		
6	JUU100480	• O ring air conditioning	1		
2	JUE107140	PIPE-CONDENSER/RECEIVER DRYER	1	Note (1)	LHD Td5
2	JUE107150	PIPE-CONDENSER/RECEIVER DRYER	1	Note (4)	RHD Td5
2	JUE110330	PIPE-CONDENSER/RECEIVER DRYER	1	Note (5)	RHD Td5
2	JUE107170	PIPE-CONDENSER/RECEIVER DRYER	1	Note (1)	RHD V8
2	JUE107170	PIPE-CONDENSER/RECEIVER DRYER	1	Note (1)	RHD TDi
2	JUE107290	PIPE-CONDENSER/RECEIVER DRYER	1	Note (2)	LHD V8
2	JUE109920	PIPE-CONDENSER/RECEIVER DRYER	1	Note (3)	LHD V8
2	JUE107290	PIPE-CONDENSER/RECEIVER DRYER	1	Note (1)	LHD Single Carburettor
2	JUE107290	PIPE-CONDENSER/RECEIVER DRYER	1	Note (1)	LHD TDi
7	JUU100470	• O ring air conditioning	1		
8	JUU100480	• O ring air conditioning	1		

CHANGE POINTS:
(1) From (V) XA 159807
(2) From (V) XA 159807 To (V) XA 177875
(3) From (V) XA 177876
(4) From (V) XA 159807 To (V) YA 189158
(5) From (V) YA 189159

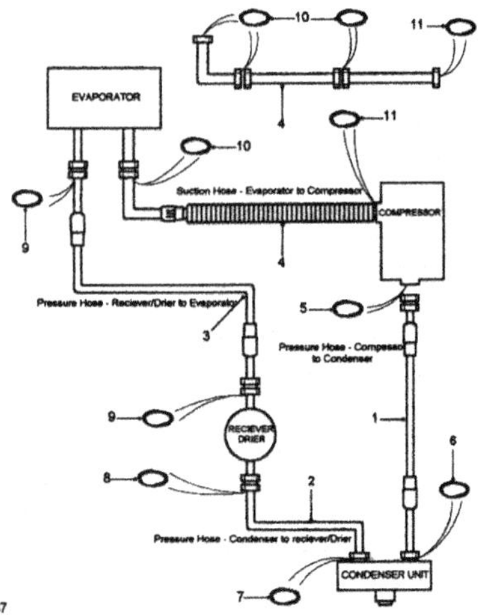

LL0037

Illus	Part Number	Description	Quantity	Change Point	Remarks
3	JUE107180	PIPE-RECEIVER DRY/EVAPORATOR AIR CONDITIONING	1	Note (1)	LHD
3	JUE107190	PIPE-RECEIVER DRY/EVAPORATOR AIR CONDITIONING	1	Note (1)	RHD Diesel
3	JUE107220	PIPE-RECEIVER DRY/EVAPORATOR AIR CONDITIONING	1	Note (1)	RHD V8
9	JUU100470	• O ring air conditioning	2		
4	JUF102250	PIPE-EVAPORATOR/COMPRESSOR AIR CONDITIONING	1	Note (1)	RHD Td5
10	JUU100490	• O ring air conditioning	2		
4	JUF102260	PIPE-EVAPORATOR/COMPRESSOR AIR CONDITIONING	1	Note (1)	LHD TDi
4	JUF102280	PIPE-EVAPORATOR/COMPRESSOR AIR CONDITIONING	1	Note (1)	LHD Petrol
11	JUU100460	• O ring air conditioning	1		
10	JUU100490	• O ring air conditioning	1		
4	JUE107250	PIPE-EVAPORATOR/COMPRESSOR AIR CONDITIONING-PIPE 1	1	Note (1)	RHD TDi
10	JUU100490	• O ring air conditioning	1		
4	JUF102270	PIPE-EVAPORATOR/COMPRESSOR AIR CONDITIONING-PIPE 2	1	Note (1)	RHD TDi
11	JUU100460	• O ring air conditioning	1		
10	JUU100490	• O ring air conditioning	1		
4	JUE109190	PIPE-EVAPORATOR/COMPRESSOR AIR CONDITIONING-PIPE 1	1	Note (1)	LHD Td5
4	JUF102240	PIPE-EVAPORATOR/COMPRESSOR AIR CONDITIONING-PIPE 2	1	Note (2)	LHD Td5
4	JUF103170	PIPE-EVAPORATOR/COMPRESSOR AIR CONDITIONING-PIPE 2	1	Note (3)	LHD Td5
4	JUE107960	PIPE-EVAPORATOR/COMPRESSOR AIR CONDITIONING-PIPE 1	1	Note (1)	RHD V8
4	JUE107280	PIPE-EVAPORATOR/COMPRESSOR AIR CONDITIONING-PIPE 2	1	Note (1)	RHD V8
10	JUU100490	• O ring air conditioning	1		
4	JUE107270	PIPE-EVAPORATOR/COMPRESSOR AIR CONDITIONING-PIPE 3	1	Note (1)	RHD V8
10	JUU100490	• O ring air conditioning	1		
11	JUU100460	• O ring air conditioning	1		

CHANGE POINTS:
(1) From (V) XA 159807
(2) From (V) XA 159807 To (V) YA 189158
(3) From (V) YA 189159

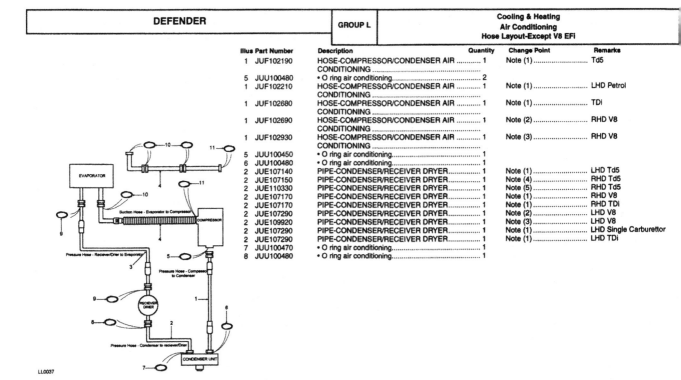

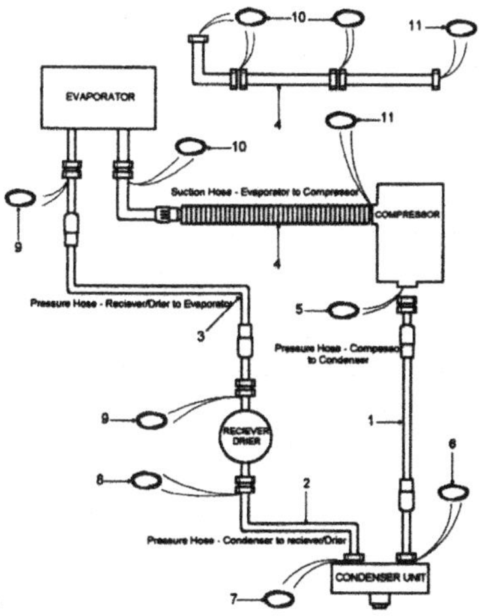

LL0037

Illus	Part Number	Description	Quantity	Change Point	Remarks
12	JPI100000	Adaptor-air conditioning compressor hose	2	Note (1)	Petrol
	FB106067L	Bolt-flanged head-M6	1	Note (1)	LHD air conditioning
	FS106251	Bolt-flanged head-M6 x 25	1	Note (1)	LHD air conditioning
	FB106067L	Bolt-flanged head-M6	1	Note (1)	RHD Diesel
	FS106251	Bolt-flanged head-M6 x 25	1	Note (1)	RHD Diesel
	FB106067L	Bolt-flanged head-M6	1	Note (1)	Td5
	FB106081L	Bolt-flanged head-M6 x 40	1	Note (1)	Td5
	FB106081L	Bolt-flanged head-M6 x 40	1	Note (1)	LHD Petrol air conditioning
	FB106081L	Bolt-flanged head-M6 x 40	1	Note (1)	Tdi
	FB108201L	Bolt-flanged head-M8 x 100	1	Note (1)	Tdi
	FN108047L	Nut-flange-flanged head-M8	1	Note (1)	Tdi
	FB106067L	Bolt-flanged head-M6	1	Note (1)	RHD V8 Petrol
	FB106081L	Bolt-flanged head-M6 x 40	1	Note (1)	LHD Td5
	FS106251	Bolt-flanged head-M6 x 25	1	Note (1)	LHD Td5
	FS106251	Bolt-flanged head-M6 x 25	1	Note (1)	RHD Td5
	FB106081L	Bolt-flanged head-M6 x 40	1	Note (1)	RHD Td5
	78248	Rivet-pop-3/16" x 0.45"lng	1	Note (1)	RHD Td5
	FB106081L	Bolt-flanged head-M6 x 40	1	Note (1)	RHD
	FS106251	Bolt-flanged head-M6 x 25	1	Note (1)	RHD
	FB106081L	Bolt-flanged head-M6 x 40	1	Note (1)	LHD V8
	FS106251	Bolt-flanged head-M6 x 25	1	Note (1)	LHD V8
	78248	Rivet-pop-3/16" x 0.45"lng	2	Note (1)	LHD V8
	FB106067L	Bolt-flanged head-M6	1	Note (1)	RHD V8
	FS106251	Bolt-flanged head-M6 x 25	1	Note (1)	RHD V8

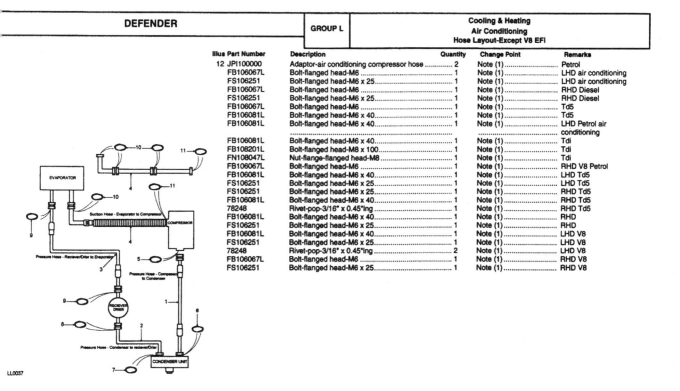

CHANGE POINTS:
(1) From (V) XA 159807

DEFENDER

GROUP M

Body Electrics
Lighting
Headlamps-Without Levelling-To (V) KA922614

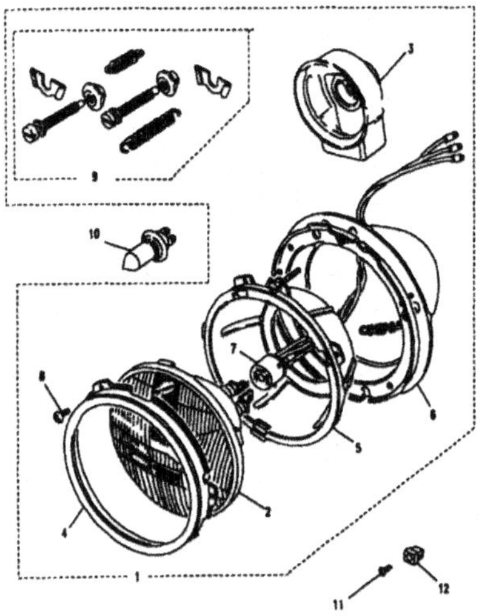

Illus	Part Number	Description	Quantity	Change Point	Remarks
1	AEU1355	HEADLAMP ASSEMBLY-FRONT LIGHTING-SEALED BEAM-RHD	2		
1	27H8207L	HEADLAMP ASSEMBLY-FRONT LIGHTING-SEALED BEAM-LHD	2		
2	RTC3682	• Light unit-headlamp-sealed beam-RHD	2		Part of AEU1355.
4	PRC7992	• Bezel-headlamp-sealed beam-Chrome	2		
5	STC643	• Body-headlamp-sealed beam	2		
6	531586	• Gasket-headlamp lens-sealed beam	2		
7	600226L	• Harness-link-sealed beam	2		
8	AB606022L	• Screw-self tapping-sealed beam-pan head-pointed	6		
9	BHM7058L	• Kit-screw-sealed beam	2		
2	RTC3683	• Light unit-headlamp-sealed beam-LHD	2		Part of 27H8207L.
1	BAU2144	HEADLAMP ASSEMBLY-FRONT LIGHTING-QUARTZ HALOGEN-RHD	2		
1	AEU1742	HEADLAMP ASSEMBLY-FRONT LIGHTING-QUARTZ HALOGEN-LHD	2		
2	RTC4615	• Light unit-headlamp-quartz Halogen-RHD	2		Part of BAU2144.
3	156206	• Cover-headlamp bulb insulation-quartz Halogen	2		
4	PRC7992	• Bezel-headlamp-quartz Halogen-Chrome	2		
5	STC643	• Body-headlamp-quartz Halogen	2		
6	531586	• Gasket-headlamp lens-quartz Halogen	2		
7	600226L	• Harness-link-quartz Halogen	2		
8	AB606022L	• Screw-self tapping-quartz Halogen-pan head-pointed	6		
9	BHM7058L	• Kit-screw-quartz Halogen	2		
2	PRC7994	• Light unit-headlamp-quartz Halogen-LHD	2		Part of AEU1742.
		QUARTZ HALOGEN ONLY			
10	589783	Bulb-headlamp-h4-60/65 Watt-main & dipped front light-Quartz Halogen-Clear.	2		90" except France
10	PRC2167	Bulb-headlamp-h4-60/65 Watt-main & dipped front light-Quartz Halogen-Yellow.	2		France
11	AB608047L	Screw-headlamp to body-self tapping-No 8 x 1/2	8		
12	79051	Nut-lokut-headlamp to body	8		

DEFENDER

GROUP M

Body Electrics
Lighting
Headlamps-Without Levelling-From (V) KA922615

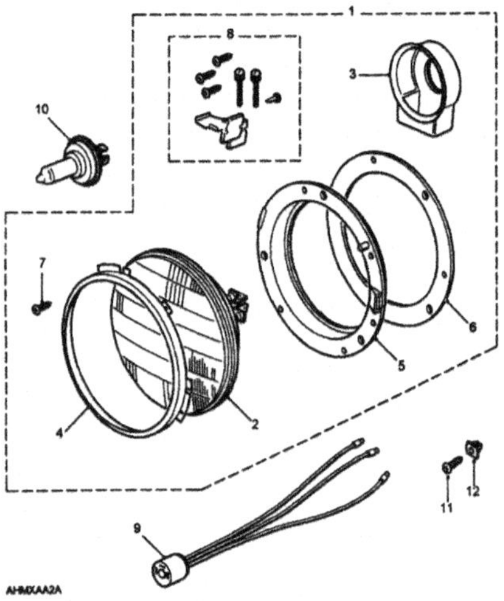

AHMXAA2A

Illus	Part Number	Description	Quantity	Change Point	Remarks
1	AMR2342	HEADLAMP ASSEMBLY-FRONT LIGHTING-WAGNER-SEALED BEAM-RHD	2		
2	STC949	• Light unit-Wagner-RHD-Sealed beam	2		
4	STC1485	• Bezel-headlamp-sealed beam-Black	NLA		Use STC3018.
5	STC1613	• Body-headlamp-sealed beam	2		
6	STC1612	• Gasket-headlamp lens-sealed beam	2		
7	STC1486	• Screw-sealed beam-Black	6		
8	STC1614	• Kit-headlamp fittings-sealed beam	2		
1	AMR2343	HEADLAMP ASSEMBLY-FRONT LIGHTING-WAGNER-SEALED BEAM-LHD	2		
2	STC950	• Light unit-Wagner-LHD-Sealed beam	2		
4	STC1485	• Bezel-headlamp-sealed beam-Black	NLA		Use STC3018.
5	STC1613	• Body-headlamp-sealed beam	2		
6	STC1612	• Gasket-headlamp lens-sealed beam	2		
7	STC1486	• Screw-sealed beam-Black	6		
8	STC1614	• Kit-headlamp fittings-sealed beam	2		
4	STC3018	Bezel-headlamp-sealed beam			RHD except France
4	STC3018	Bezel-headlamp-sealed beam			LHD except France
4	STC3018	Bezel-headlamp-quartz Halogen			RHD except France
4	STC3018	Bezel-headlamp-quartz Halogen			LHD except France

Illus	Part Number	Description	Quantity	Change Point	Remarks
1	AMR2344	HEADLAMP ASSEMBLY-FRONT LIGHTING-BLACK-RHD-WIPAC-QUARTZ HALOGEN	2		
2	STC1209	• Light unit-RHD-Wipac-Quartz Halogen	2		
	STC1851	• Clip-bulb-quartz Halogen	2		
3	STC951	• Cover-headlamp bulb insulation-quartz Halogen	2		
4	STC1485	• Bezel-headlamp-quartz Halogen-Black	NLA		Use STC3018.
5	STC1613	• Body-headlamp-quartz Halogen	2		
6	STC1612	• Gasket-headlamp lens-quartz Halogen	2		
7	STC1486	• Screw-quartz Halogen-Black	6		
8	STC1614	• Kit-headlamp fittings-quartz Halogen	2		
1	AMR2345	HEADLAMP ASSEMBLY-FRONT LIGHTING-BLACK-LHD-WIPAC-QUARTZ HALOGEN	2		
2	STC1210	• Light unit-LHD-Wipac-Quartz Halogen	2		
	STC1851	• Clip-bulb-quartz Halogen	2		
3	STC951	• Cover-headlamp bulb insulation-quartz Halogen	2		
4	STC1485	• Bezel-headlamp-quartz Halogen-Black	NLA		Use STC3018.
5	STC1613	• Body-headlamp-quartz Halogen	2		
6	STC1612	• Gasket-headlamp lens-quartz Halogen	2		
7	STC1486	• Screw-quartz Halogen-Black	6		
8	STC1614	• Kit-headlamp fittings-quartz Halogen	2		

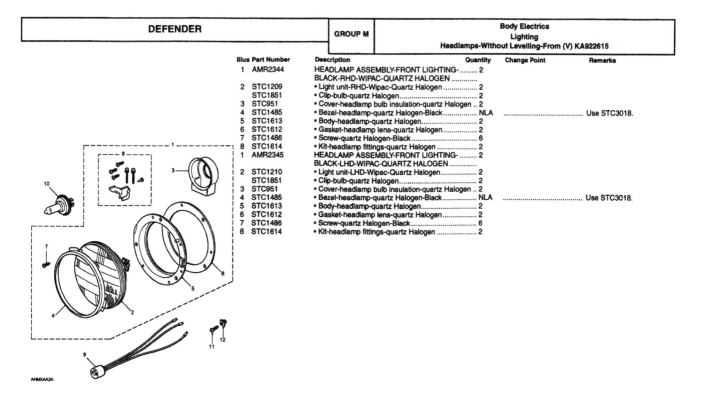

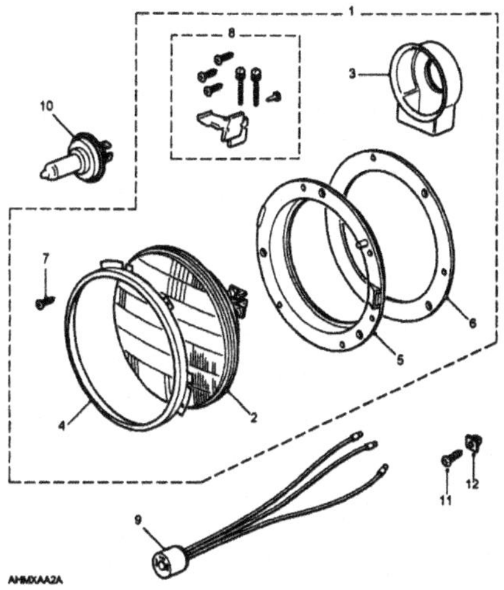

AHMXAA2A

Illus	Part Number	Description	Quantity	Change Point	Remarks
1	AMR2346	Headlamp assembly-front lighting-LHD-Yellow.-Wipac-Quartz Halogen	2		France
9	AMR2357	Harness-link-fitting Wipac in place of Lucas	2		
10	589783	Bulb-headlamp-h4-60/65 Watt-main & dipped front light-Quartz Halogen-Clear.	2		Except France
10	PRC2167	Bulb-headlamp-h4-60/65 Watt-main & dipped front light-Quartz Halogen-Yellow.	2		France
11	AB608047L	Screw-headlamp to body-self tapping-No 8 x 1/2	8		
12	79051	Nut-lokut-headlamp to body	8		

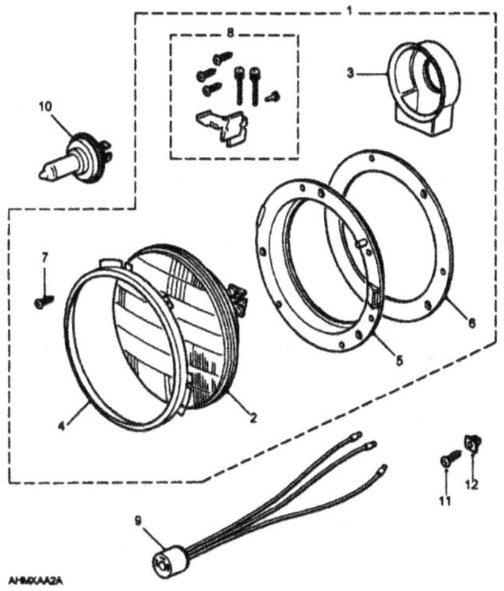

AHMXAA2A

DEFENDER	GROUP M	Body Electrics Lighting Headlamps-With Levelling

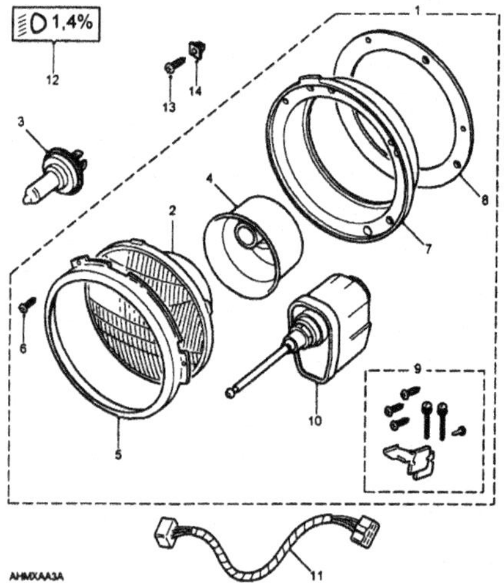

Illus	Part Number	Description	Quantity	Change Point	Remarks
1	AMR3247	HEADLAMP ASSEMBLY-FRONT LIGHTING-LHD-BLACK-WIPAC	2		Germany
2	STC1210	• Light unit-LHD-Wipac-Quartz Halogen	2		
4	STC951	• Cover-headlamp bulb insulation	2		
5	STC1485	• Bezel-headlamp-Black	NLA		Use STC3018.
6	STC1486	• Screw-Black	2		
7	STC4029	• Body-headlamp	2		
8	STC1612	• Gasket-headlamp lens	2		
9	STC1614	• Kit-headlamp fittings	2		
10	AMR2090	• Adjuster unit-headlamp	2		
3	589783	Bulb-headlamp-h4-60/65 Watt-main & dipped front light-Quartz Halogen-Clear.	2		
5	STC3018	Bezel-headlamp			LHD Germany
1	XBC104480	HEADLAMP ASSEMBLY-FRONT LIGHTING	2	From (V) WA 138480	Except Germany
2	STC1209	• Light unit-RHD-Wipac-Quartz Halogen	2		
4	STC951	• Cover-headlamp bulb insulation	2		
5	STC1485	• Bezel-headlamp-Black	NLA		Use STC3018.
6	STC1486	• Screw-Black	2		
7	STC4029	• Body-headlamp	2		
8	STC1612	• Gasket-headlamp lens	2		
9	STC1614	• Kit-headlamp fittings	2		
10	AMR2090	• Adjuster unit-headlamp	2		
5	STC3018	Bezel-headlamp			Except Germany
11	AMR5833	Harness-link	2		
12	PRC8171	Label-headlamp leveling information-fitted to top of radiator	1		
13	AB608047L	Screw-headlamp to body-self tapping-No 8 x 1/2	8		
14	79051	Nut-lokut-headlamp to body	8		

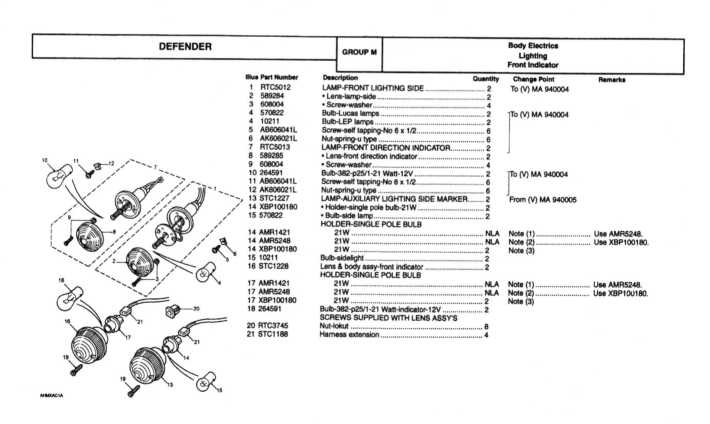

DEFENDER	GROUP M	Body Electrics Lighting Front Indicator

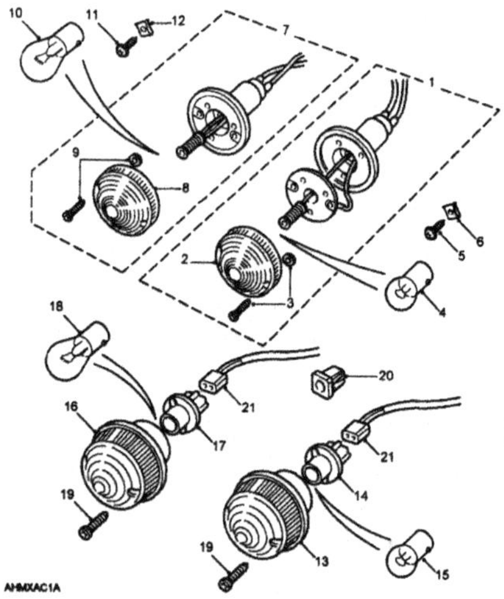

Illus	Part Number	Description	Quantity	Change Point	Remarks
1	RTC5012	LAMP-FRONT LIGHTING SIDE	2	To (V) MA 940004	
2	589284	• Lens-lamp-side	2		
3	608004	• Screw-washer	4		
4	570822	Bulb-Lucas lamps	2	To (V) MA 940004	
4	10211	Bulb-LEP lamps	2		
5	AB606041L	Screw-self tapping-No 6 x 1/2	6		
6	AK606021L	Nut-spring-u type	6		
7	RTC5013	LAMP-FRONT DIRECTION INDICATOR	2		
8	589285	• Lens-front direction indicator	2		
9	608004	• Screw-washer	4		
10	264591	Bulb-382-p25/1-21 Watt-12V	2	To (V) MA 940004	
11	AB606041L	Screw-self tapping-No 6 x 1/2	6		
12	AK606021L	Nut-spring-u type	6		
13	STC1227	LAMP-AUXILIARY LIGHTING SIDE MARKER	2	From (V) MA 940005	
14	XBP100180	• Holder-single pole bulb-21W	2		
15	570822	• Bulb-side lamp	2		
		HOLDER-SINGLE POLE BULB			
14	AMR1421	21W	NLA	Note (1)	Use AMR5248.
14	AMR5248	21W	NLA	Note (2)	Use XBP100180.
14	XBP100180	21W	2	Note (3)	
15	10211	Bulb-sidelight	2		
16	STC1228	Lens & body assy-front indicator	2		
		HOLDER-SINGLE POLE BULB			
17	AMR1421	21W	NLA	Note (1)	Use AMR5248.
17	AMR5248	21W	NLA	Note (2)	Use XBP100180.
17	XBP100180	21W	2	Note (3)	
18	264591	Bulb-382-p25/1-21 Watt-indicator-12V	2		
		SCREWS SUPPLIED WITH LENS ASSY'S			
20	RTC3745	Nut-lokut	8		
21	STC1188	Harness extension	4		

CHANGE POINTS:
(1) From (V) MA 940005 To (V) TA 975885
(2) From (V) TA 975886 To (V) VA 103528
(3) From (V) VA 103529

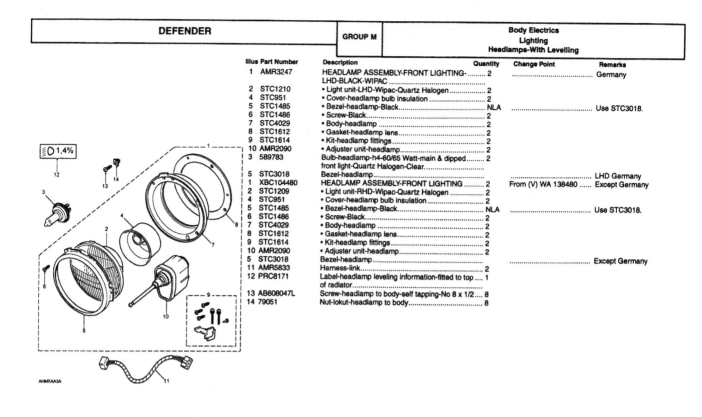

DEFENDER | GROUP M | Body Electrics — Lighting — Side Repeater Lamps-To (V) LA939975

Illus	Part Number	Description	Quantity	Change Point	Remarks
1	589143	LAMP ASSEMBLY-DIRECTION INDICATOR	2	To (V) 331793	
2	27H2403L	• Lens-auxiliary lighting side repeater	2		
3	608311	• Gasket-seating lens	2		
4	608312	• Gasket-seating lamp	2		
5	570822	• Bulb	2		
6	515060	• Boot-cable	2		
7	233243	• Grommet-cable-Black-3 x 25.5mm	2		
8	WM704001L	• Washer-spring	4		
9	257203	• Nut	4		
10	PRC7044	LAMP-AUXILIARY LIGHTING SIDE REPEATER	2	From (V) 331794	
11	570829	• Bulb-501-w10/5-5 Watt-12V	NLA		Use AFU4481.
12	MWC9606	Bush	4	From (V) 331794	
13	AFU1926L	Nut-caged	4	From (V) 331794	

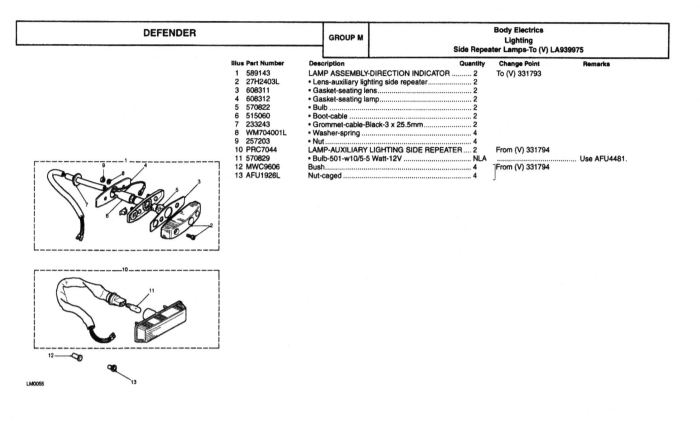

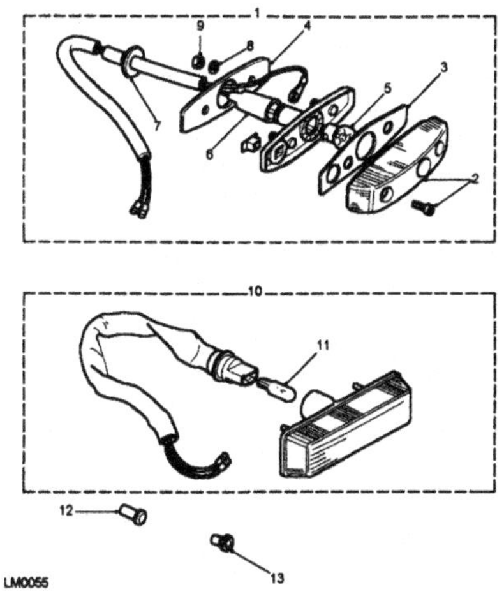

LM0055

DEFENDER | GROUP M | Body Electrics — Lighting — Side Repeater Lamps-From (V) MA939976

Illus	Part Number	Description	Quantity	Change Point	Remarks
1	PRC9916	Lamp-auxiliary lighting side repeater	2	Note (1)	
2	AFU4481	Bulb-501-w10/5-5 Watt-side repeater-12V	2		
3	AFU3112L	O ring	2		
4	STC966	Kit-side repeater harness	2		
1	AMR4103	LAMP-AUXILIARY LIGHTING SIDE REPEATER	2	Note (2)	
1	XGB000030	LAMP-AUXILIARY LIGHTING SIDE REPEATER	2	Note (3)	
2	AFU4481	• Bulb-501-w10/5-5 Watt-12V	2		
5	YPY100220	• Holder-side repeater bulb	2		

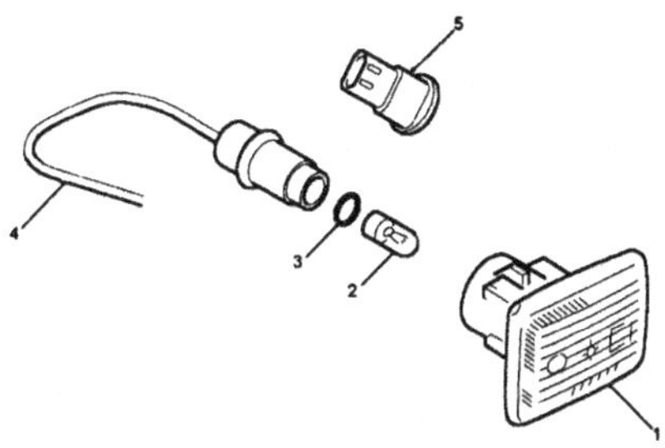

LM0054

CHANGE POINTS:
(1) From (V) MA 939976 To (V) WA 159806
(2) From (V) XA 159807 To (V) ZA 616041
(3) From (V) 1A 616042

Illus	Part Number	Description	Quantity	Change Point	Remarks
1	STC7644	LAMP-FRONT LONG RANGE DRIVING-RALLY 1000	4	Note (1)	Tomb Raider
	RTC9498	• Bulb-headlamp-Quartz Halogen-Cewe-type H2	1		

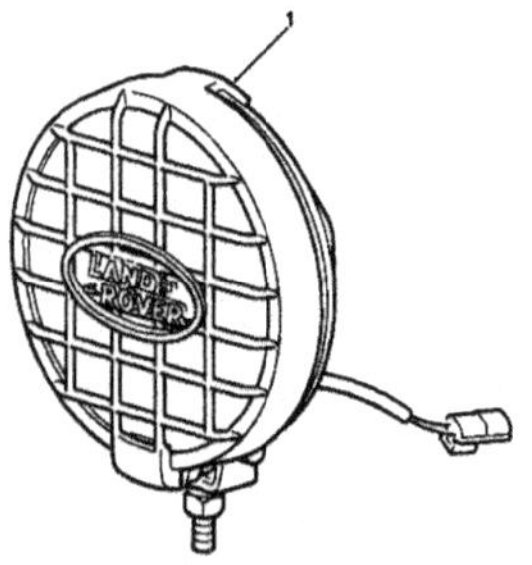

LM0140

CHANGE POINTS:
(1) From (V) 1A 612404

Illus	Part Number	Description	Quantity	Change Point	Remarks
1	RTC5523	LAMP ASSEMBLY-REAR-STOP/TAIL	2		
2	RTC210	• Lens assembly-rear lamp	2		
3	608004	• Screw-washer	4		
4	264590	Bulb-380-p25/2-21/5 Watt-12V	2		
5	77932	Screw	6		
6	RTC5524	LAMP ASSEMBLY-DIRECTION INDICATOR	2		
7	589202	• Lens assembly-rear lamp	2		
8	608004	• Screw-washer	4		
9	264591	Bulb-382-p25/1-21 Watt-indicator-12V	2		
10	77932	Screw	6		
11	AEU1652	LAMP-REAR LICENCE PLATE	1		
12	606211	• Lens-rear licence plate lamp	1		
13	575312	Bulb-233-t8/4-4 Watt-12V	2		
14	589026	Harness-licence plate lamp	1		Except HICAP
15	345597	Plinth-licence plate	1		
14	PRC3617	Harness-licence plate lamp-number plate lamp	1		HICAP
15	PRC3588	Plinth-licence plate	1		
16	257302	Bolt	2		
17	WL105001L	Washer-retaining-M5	2		
18	HN2005L	Nut-UNF	2		
19	235113	Grommet	1		

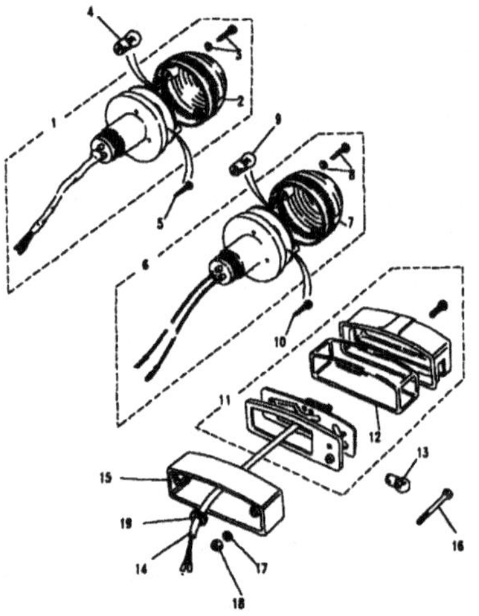

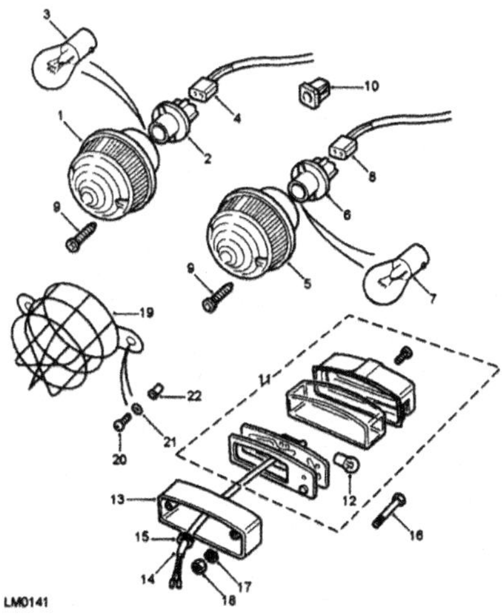

LM0141

Illus	Part Number	Description	Quantity	Change Point	Remarks
1	STC1230	Lens & body-stop/tail	2		
2	AMR1422	Bulbholder-5/21W	2	Note (1)	
2	AMR5249	Bulbholder-5/21W	2	Note (2)	
3	264590	Bulb-380-p25/2-21/5 Watt-12V	2		
4	STC1189	Harness extension-rear stop/tail lamp	NLA		Use STC4637.
4	STC4637	Harness extension-rear stop/tail lamp	2		
5	STC1229	Lens & body-rear indicator	2		
		HOLDER-SINGLE POLE BULB			
6	AMR1421	21W	NLA	Note (1)	Use AMR5248.
6	AMR5248	21W	NLA	Note (3)	Use XBP100180.
6	XBP100180	21W	2	Note (4)	
7	264591	Bulb-382-p25/1-21 Watt-12V	2		
8	STC1188	Harness extension-side indicator lamp	2		
		SCREWS SUPPLIED WITH LENS ASSY			
10	RTC3745	Nut-lokut	8		
11	PRC7255	Lamp-rear licence plate	NLA	Note (5)	Use XFC100550.
11	XFC100550	Lamp-rear licence plate	1	Note (6)	
12	575312	Bulb-233-t8/4-4 Watt-12V	2		

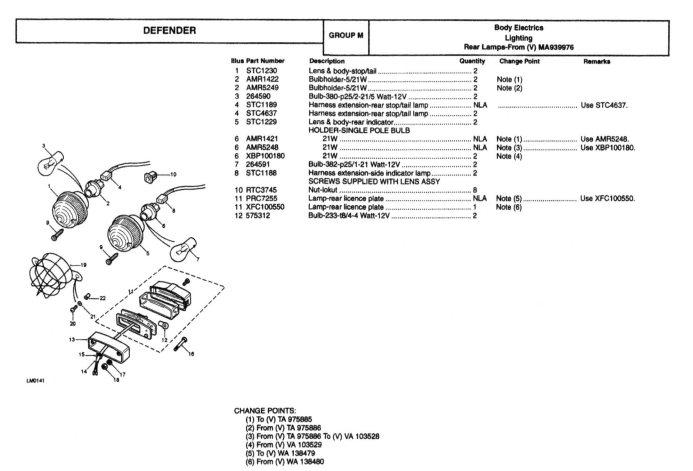

CHANGE POINTS:
(1) To (V) TA 975885
(2) From (V) TA 975886
(3) From (V) TA 975886 To (V) VA 103528
(4) From (V) VA 103529
(5) To (V) WA 138479
(6) From (V) WA 138480

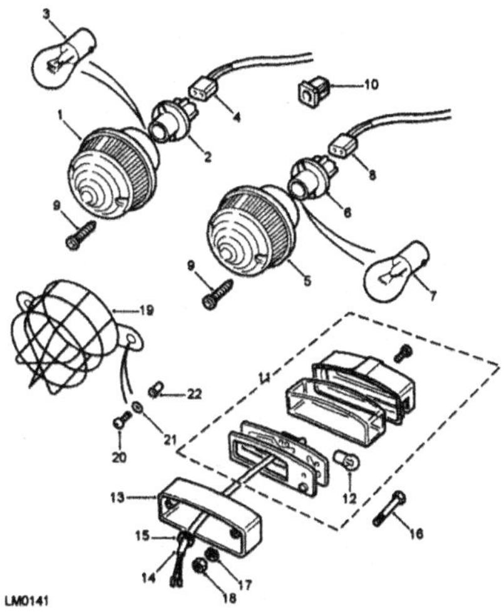

LM0141

Illus	Part Number	Description	Quantity	Change Point	Remarks
13	345597	Plinth-licence plate	1		Except HICAP
13	PRC3588	Plinth-licence plate	1		HICAP
14	589026	Harness-licence plate lamp	1	Note (1)	Except HICAP
14	YND100050	Harness-licence plate lamp	1	Note (2)	Except HICAP
14	PRC3617	Harness-licence plate lamp	1		HICAP
15	233244	Grommet-cable-Black-3 x 19mm	1		
16	SH105551	Screw-hexagonal head-M5	2		
17	WM702001	Washer-spring	2		
18	NH105041	Nut-hexagonal-M5	2		
19	RRC6160	Guard-lamp rear-Black	4	Note (3)	Tomb Raider
20	SE105165L	Screw-M5 x 16-Black	8		
21	WC105007	Washer-plain-large-Black	8		
22	ASR1185	Nutsert-blind-M5-Black	8		

NOTE:HARNESS-EXTENSIONS ARE FOR CONNECTING 95MY LAMPS TO PRE 95MY HARNESSES

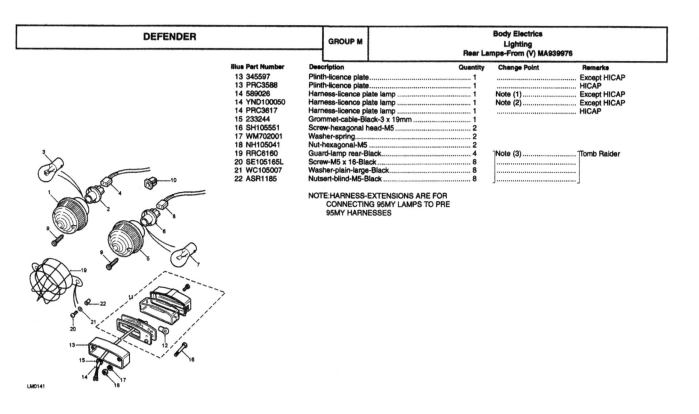

CHANGE POINTS:
(1) To (V) WA 138479
(2) From (V) WA 138480
(3) From (V) 1A 612404

DEFENDER | GROUP M | Body Electrics – Lighting – High Level Stop Lamp

Illus	Part Number	Description	Quantity	Change Point	Remarks
1	XFG100330	LAMP-REAR HIGH MOUNTED STOP	1		
2	264591	• Bulb-382-p25/1-21 Watt-12V	1		
3	BTR2940	Screw-3.5 x 16	2		
4	BTR4414	Cover-high mounted stop lamp integral	1	Note (1)	
4	XFK100290	Cover-high mounted stop lamp integral	1	Note (2)	
5	AWR4639	Adaptor	1		
6	AWR4647	Stud	2		
7	AMR2156	Harness-high mounted stop lamp protected	NLA		Use XFS100050.
7	XFS100050	Harness-high mounted stop lamp protected	1		
8	233244	Grommet-cable-Black-3 x 19mm	1		
9	NY105041L	Nut-hexagonal-nyloc-M5	2		

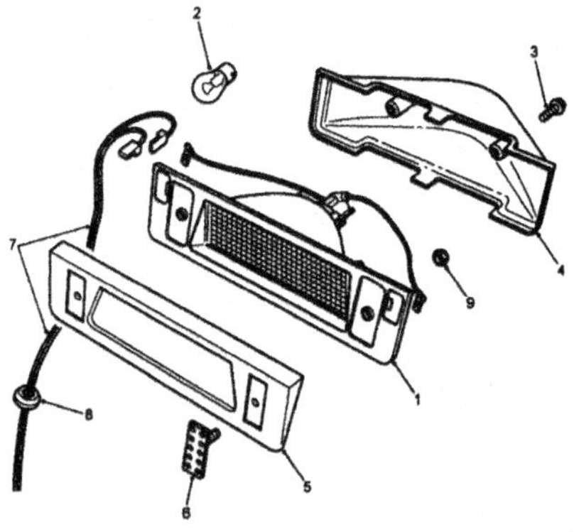

AMMXAC5B

CHANGE POINTS:
(1) To (V) VA 101303
(2) From (V) VA 101304

DEFENDER | GROUP M | Body Electrics – Lighting – Reflectors, Fog Lamp & Reverse Lamp-To (V) LA939975

Illus	Part Number	Description	Quantity	Change Point	Remarks
1	551595	Reflector-rear-round	2		
2	WM702001L	Washer-spring-3/16 dia-square	2		
3	RTC608	Nut	2		
4	MWC1722	Reflector-rear-rectangular	2		
5	AB608047L	Screw-reflector-self tapping-No 8 x 1/2	2		
	PRC2516	LAMP-REAR FOG-RED	NLA		Use PRC7254.
	RTC4183	• Lens-fog-rear-Red	1		
8	RTC4185	• Screw	2		
9	264591	• Bulb-382-p25/1-21 Watt-12V	1		
10	WA105001L	Washer-fog lamp-plain-standard-M5	2		
11	WL105001L	Washer-fog lamp-retaining-M5	2		
12	NH105041L	Nut-hexagonal-fog lamp-M5	2		
6	PRC3299	Lamp-rear reverse	1	To (V) EA 358426	
6	PRC7263	LAMP-REAR REVERSE-CLEAR.	1	From (V) FA 358427	
7	RTC4184	• Lens-reverse-Clear.	1		
8	RTC4185	• Screw	2		
9	264591	• Bulb-382-p25/1-21 Watt-12V	1		
10	WA105001L	Washer-reverse lamp-plain-standard-M5	2		
11	WL105001L	Washer-reverse lamp-retaining-M5	2		
12	NH105041L	Nut-hexagonal-reverse lamp-M5	2		
		VEHICLES WITH LT77 GEARBOX-NOTE 1			
13	PRC2876	Harness rear lamp	1		4 Cylinder
13	PRC4473	Harness rear lamp	1		V8
14	573246	Tie-cable-Black-4.8 x 115mm-inside serated	2		
15	PRC2911	Switch-reverse lamp	1	To (V) FA 410277	4 Cylinder
	PRC3085	Harness-link-reverse lamp switch	1		4 Cylinder
16	PRC8204	Switch-reverse lamp	1	From (V) FA 410278	4 Cylinder
	NT110041L	Locknut-reverse light switch-M10	1		4 Cylinder
17	PRC1039	Switch-reverse lamp	1		V8

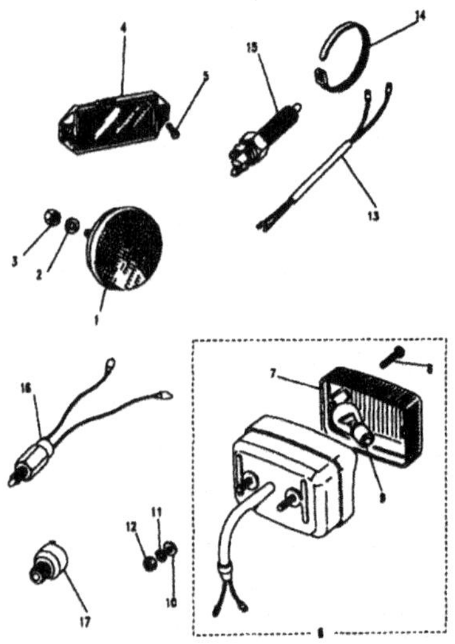

NOTE 1:FOR R380 GEARBOX SWITCHES SEE TRANSMISSION SECTION

Reflector, Fog & Reverse Lamp-From (V) MA939976 To (V)1A612403

Illus	Part Number	Description	Quantity	Change Point	Remarks
1	MWC1722	Reflector-rear-rectangular	2	To (V) WA 138479	
1	XFF100070	Reflector-rear-rectangular	2	From (V) WA 138480	
2	AB608047L	Screw-self tapping-No 8 x 1/2	2		
3	PRC2516	LAMP-REAR FOG-RED	NLA		Use PRC7254.
4	RTC4183	• Lens-fog-rear-Red	1		
5	RTC4185	• Screw	2		
6	264591	• Bulb-382-p25/1-21 Watt-12V	1		
3	PRC7254	Lamp-rear fog	1	Note (1)	
3	XFE100170	Lamp-rear fog	1	Note (2)	
7	WA105001L	Washer-plain-standard-M5	2		
8	WL105001L	Washer-retaining-M5	2		
9	NH105041L	Nut-hexagonal-M5	2		
10	PRC7263	LAMP-REAR REVERSE-CLEAR.	1		
11	RTC4184	• Lens-reverse-Clear.	1		
5	RTC4185	• Screw	2		
6	264591	• Bulb-382-p25/1-21 Watt-12V	1		
10	XFD100050	Lamp-rear reverse	1	Note (2)	
7	WA105001L	Washer-plain-standard-M5	2		
8	WL105001L	Washer-retaining-M5	2		
9	NH105041L	Nut-hexagonal-M5	2		

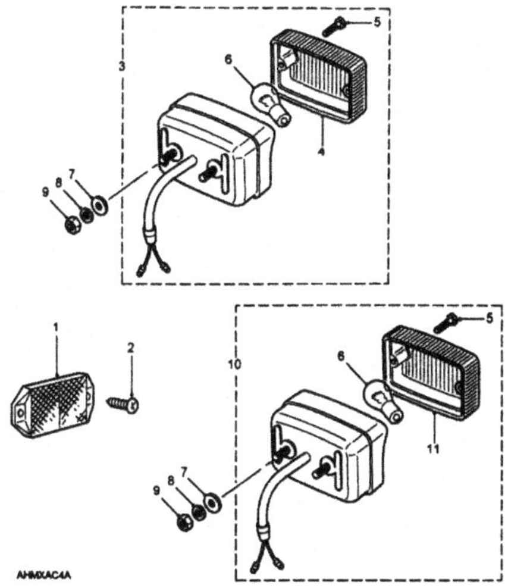

AHMXAC4A

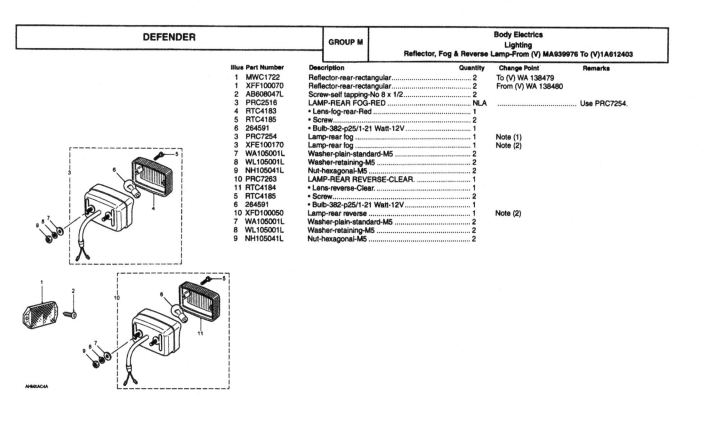

CHANGE POINTS:
(1) To (V) WA 159806
(2) From (V) XA 159807

Reflector, Fog & Reverse Lamp-From (V) 1A612404

Illus	Part Number	Description	Quantity	Change Point	Remarks
1	XFF100070	Reflector-rear-rectangular	2		
2	AB608047L	Screw-self tapping-No 8 x 1/2	4		
3	AMR6522	LAMP-REAR FOG-12V	1		
4	XBP100180	• Holder-single pole bulb-21W	1		
5	264591	• Bulb-382-p25/1-21 Watt-12V	1		
6	AMR3850	• Plinth-lamp	1		
7	DA606059L	• Screw-self tapping	2		
8	SE105161L	• Screw-recessed-pan head-M5 x 16	2		
9	AMR6521	LAMP-REAR REVERSE-12V	1		
10	XBP100180	• Holder-single pole bulb-21W	1		
11	264591	• Bulb-382-p25/1-21 Watt-12V	1		
12	AMR3850	• Plinth-lamp	1		
13	DA606059L	• Screw-self tapping	2		
14	SE105161L	• Screw-recessed-pan head-M5 x 16	2		
15	WA105001L	Washer-plain-standard-M5	4		
16	WL105001L	Washer-retaining-M5	4		
17	NH105041L	Nut-hexagonal-M5	4		

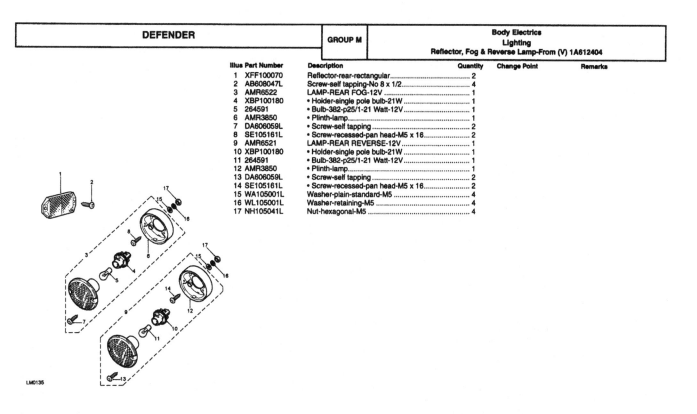

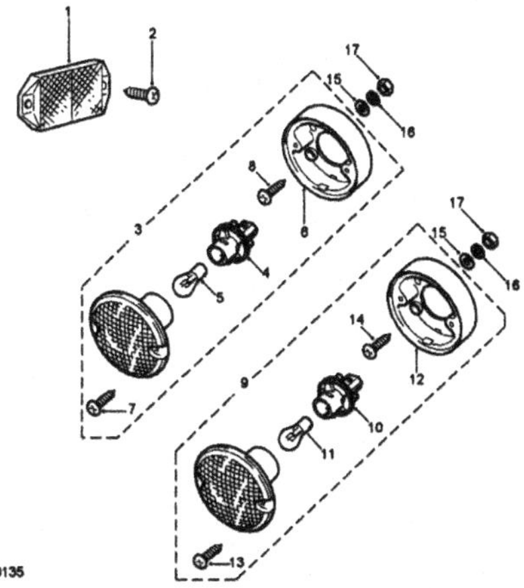

LM0135

DEFENDER	GROUP M	Body Electrics Lighting Interior Lamps-To (V) HA455945

Illus	Part Number	Description	Quantity	Change Point	Remarks
1	265295	LAMP-INTERIOR COURTESY	NLA		Use STC251.
2	320608	• Lens-interior lamp	1		
3	264591	• Bulb-382-p25/1-21 Watt-12V	1		
1	STC251	Lamp-interior courtesy	1		
4	AB606041L	Screw-self tapping-No 6 x 1/2	2		
5	334111	Base-map lamp roof trim cantrail	1		
	MTC4132	Pad-insulation	1		
	MWC9601	Gasket-seating lamp	1	Note (1)	Sunroof
6	312856	Grommet	1		
7	PRC2964	Harness-link-light to roof connection cable	1		
8	PRC3813	Harness-link-roor connection to switch	1		

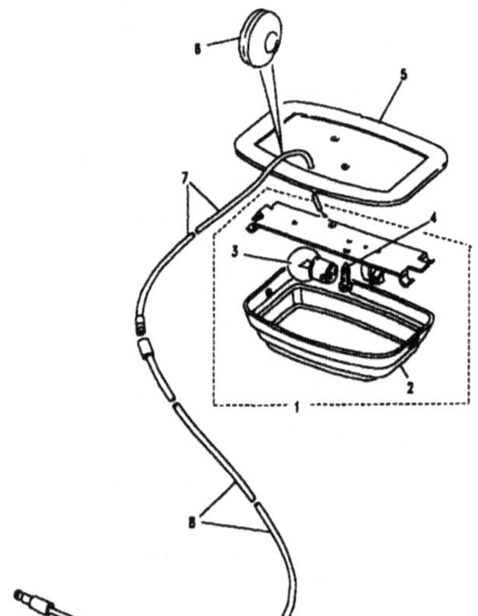

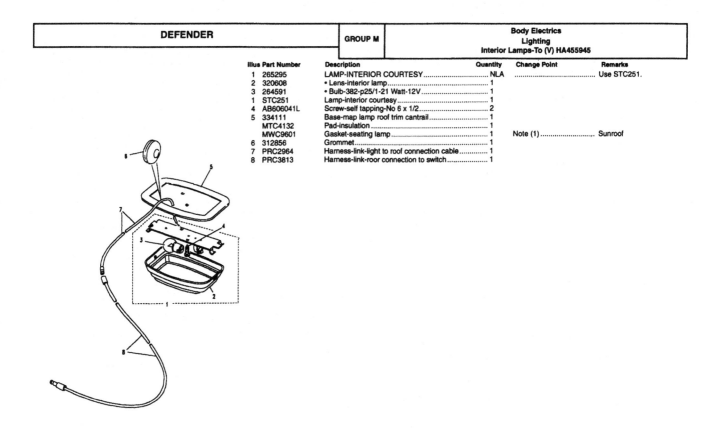

CHANGE POINTS:
(1) From (V) EA 314059 Regular; From (V) EA 314174 Station Wagon

DEFENDER	GROUP M	Body Electrics Lighting Interior Lamps-From (V) HA455946 To (V) LA939975

Illus	Part Number	Description	Quantity	Change Point	Remarks
1	STC251	Lamp-interior courtesy	1		Except Special Vehicles
2	264591	Bulb-382-p25/1-21 Watt-12V	1		
1	AFU4092L	Lamp-interior courtesy-with on/off switch	2		Special Vehicles
9	STC1203	Bulb-245-r19/10-10 Watt	2		
3	AB606041L	Screw-self tapping-No 6 x 1/2	2		
4	MWC9601	Gasket-seating lamp	1		
5	MXC2342	Plate	1		
6	MXC2341	Nut-lokut	2		
7	PRC8231	Switch-contact courtesy light	2	To (V) HA 702829	
8	AFU4241L	Switch-contact courtesy light	2	From (V) HA 702830	

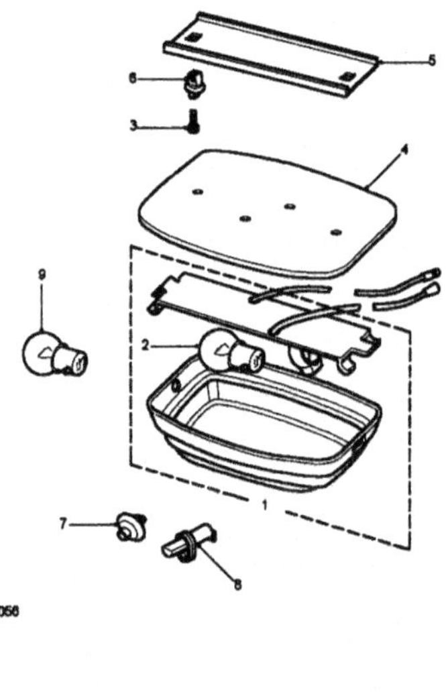

LM0056

Illus	Part Number	Description	Quantity	Change Point	Remarks
		INTERIOR LAMP &MOUNTING BRACKET			
1	AMR3155	LAMP-INTERIOR COURTESY	1/2		
2	586438	• Bulb-272-10 Watt-festoon-36x10.5mm	1/2		
3	AMR3142	Bracket-mounting-lamp-interior	1/2		

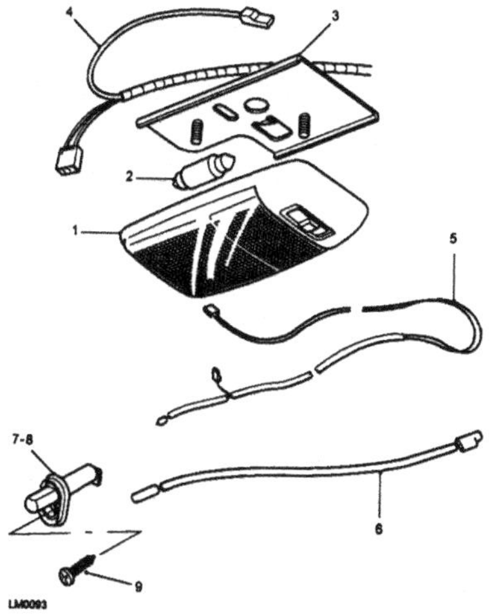

Illus	Part Number	Description	Quantity	Change Point	Remarks
		HARNESS - UP TO 2002MY WITHOUT FACTORY FITTED ALARM			
4	AMR3158	Harness interior light-front	1		Except burglar alarm
5	AMR3322	Harness interior light-rear	1		Except burglar alarm
6	AMR3727	Lead-link-chassis harness to rear light harness	1		
		HARNESS - UP TO 2002MY WITH FACTORY FITTED ALARM			
4	AMR4992	Harness interior light-front	1		Regular burglar alarm Truck Cab except Germany
4	AMR4986	Harness interior light-front	1		Regular burglar alarm Top except Germany
4	AMR5068	Harness interior light-front	1		Station Wagon burglar alarm except Germany
5	AMR4984	Harness interior light-rear	1		Station Wagon burglar alarm 90" except Germa-
5	AMR4990	Harness interior light-rear	1		Station Wagon burglar alarm except Germany 90"
6	AMR4991	Lead-link-rear side door switch	2		Burglar alarm except Germany and 90"
		HARNESS - UP TO 2002MY WITH FACTORY FITTED ALARM-GERMANY			
4	AMR5828	Harness interior light-front	1		Burglar alarm Hard Top Germany
4	AMR5828	Harness interior light-front	1		Burglar alarm Truck Cab Germany
4	AMR5827	Harness interior light-front	1		Burglar alarm Soft Top Germany

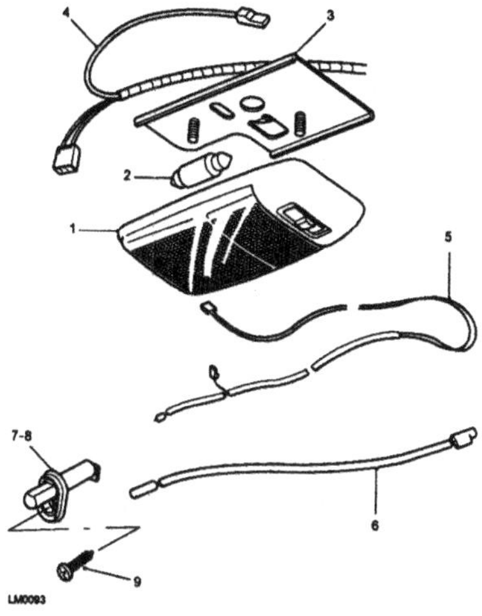

Illus	Part Number	Description	Quantity	Change Point	Remarks
		HARNESS - FROM 2002MY WITHOUT FCATORY FITTED ALARM			
4	YMK000371	Harness interior light	1	Note (1)	Except Station Wagon and alarm and CDL
4	YMK000401	Harness interior light	1	Note (1)	Station Wagon 90" except alarm and CDL
4	YMK000421	Harness interior light	1	Note (1)	Station Wagon 110" except alarm and CDL
4	YMK000511	Harness interior light	1	Note (1)	Regular except burglar alarm and CDL and 130"

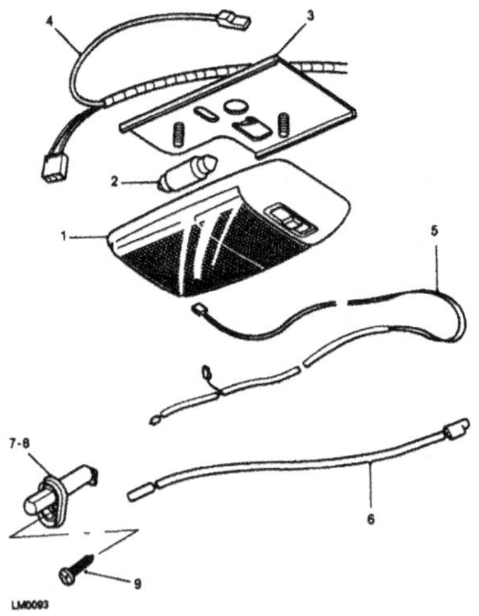

CHANGE POINTS:
(1) From (V) 2A 622424

Illus	Part Number	Description	Quantity	Change Point	Remarks
		HARNESS - FROM 2002MY WITH FACTORY FITTED ALARM			
4	YMK000391	Harness interior light	1	Note (1)	Crew Cab
4	YMK000381	Harness interior light	1	Note (1)	Truck Cab
4	YMK000511	Harness interior light	1	Note (1)	Regular except CDL and 130"
4	YMK000501	Harness interior light	1	Note (1)	Regular CDL 90"
4	YMK000531	Harness interior light	1	Note (1)	Regular CDL 110"
4	YMK000441	Harness interior light	1	Note (1)	Station Wagon 90" except CDL
4	YMK000451	Harness interior light	1	Note (1)	Station Wagon CDL 90"
4	YMK000461	Harness interior light	1	Note (1)	Station Wagon 110" except CDL
4	YMK000471	Harness interior light	1	Note (1)	Station Wagon CDL 110"

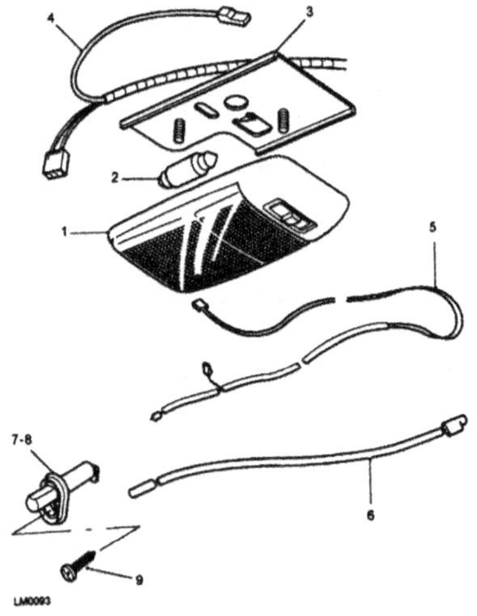

CHANGE POINTS:
(1) From (V) 2A 622424

Illus	Part Number	Description	Quantity	Change Point	Remarks
		DOOR SWITCHES			
7	AFU4241L	Switch-contact courtesy light-front door	2		
8	PRC8548	Switch-contact courtesy light-rear end door	1		
7	AFU4241L	Switch-contact courtesy light-rear side door	2		Burglar alarm
9	YYP100860	Screw-flanged head	A/R		

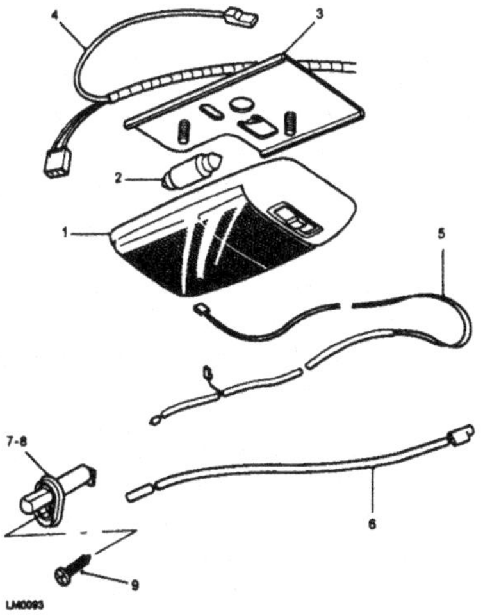

Illus	Part Number	Description	Quantity	Change Point	Remarks
1	STC7039	LAMP ASSEMBLY-REAR-WITH NUMBER PLATE ILLUMINATION	1		
2	STC3287	• Lens assembly-rear lamp-with number plate illumination	1		
3	264591	• Bulb-382-p25/1-21 Watt-12V	1		
4	264591	• Bulb-382-p25/1-21 Watt-12V	1		
5	10211	• Bulb	2		
6	264591	• Bulb-382-p25/1-21 Watt-12V	1		
7	264591	• Bulb-382-p25/1-21 Watt-12V	1		
1	STC7040	LAMP ASSEMBLY-REAR-LESS NUMBER PLATE ILLUMINATION	1		
2	STC3286	• Lens assembly-rear lamp-less number plate illumination	1		
3	264591	• Bulb-382-p25/1-21 Watt-12V	1		
4	264591	• Bulb-382-p25/1-21 Watt-12V	1		
5	10211	• Bulb	2		
6	264591	• Bulb-382-p25/1-21 Watt-12V	1		
7	264591	• Bulb-382-p25/1-21 Watt-12V	1		

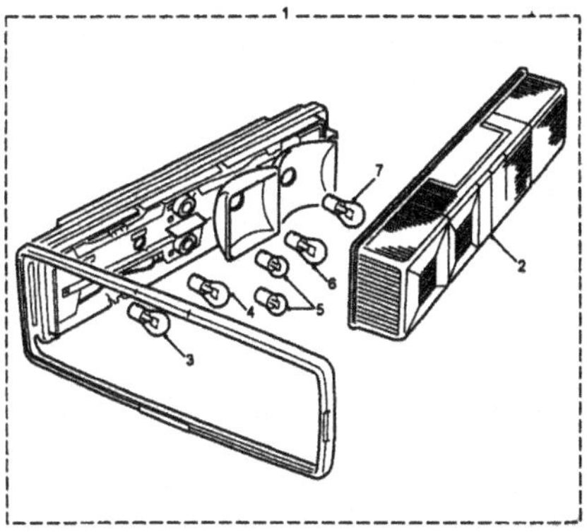

AJMXAC5A

DEFENDER	GROUP M	Body Electrics Lighting Spotlamps-Biaritz LE-Germany Only

Illus	Part Number	Description	Quantity	Change Point	Remarks
1	STC8480	Lamp-front long range driving-Safari 5000	2		
2	STC8813	Kit-auxiliary wiring-safari 500....................................	NLA	....	Use STC8813AA.
2	STC8813AA	Kit-auxiliary wiring-safari 500....................................	1		
3	STC8814	Lamp steady bars-pair..	2		

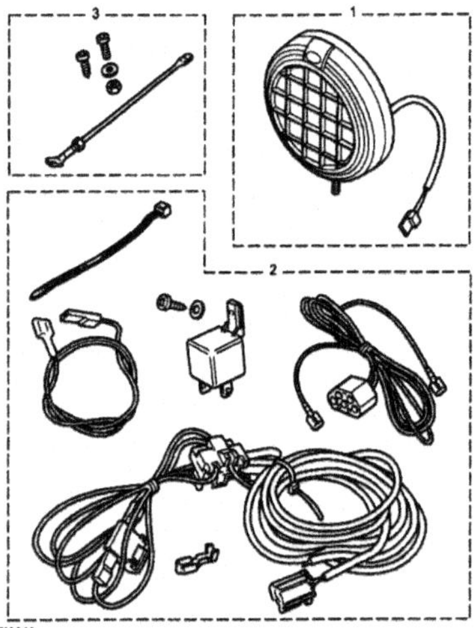

AHMXAA4A

BODY ELECTRICS - LIGHTING - SPOTLAMPS - BIARITZ LE - GERMANY ONLY (DEFENDER 90 1999MY ON)

DEFENDER	GROUP M	Body Electrics Lighting Interior Roof Lamp-Biaritz LE-Germany Only

Illus	Part Number	Description	Quantity	Change Point	Remarks
1	AFU4092L	Lamp-interior courtesy-with on/off switch	1		
2	STC1203	Bulb-245-r19/10-10 Watt..	1		

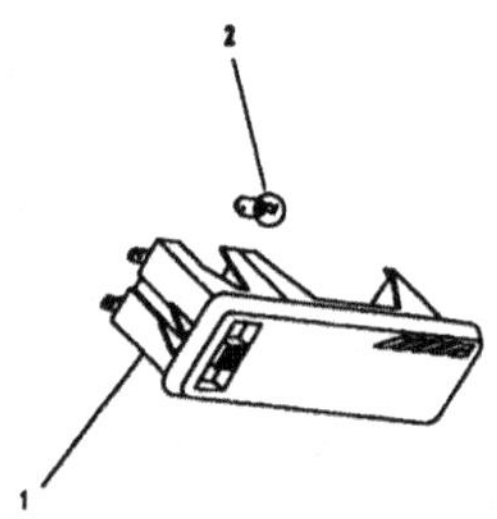

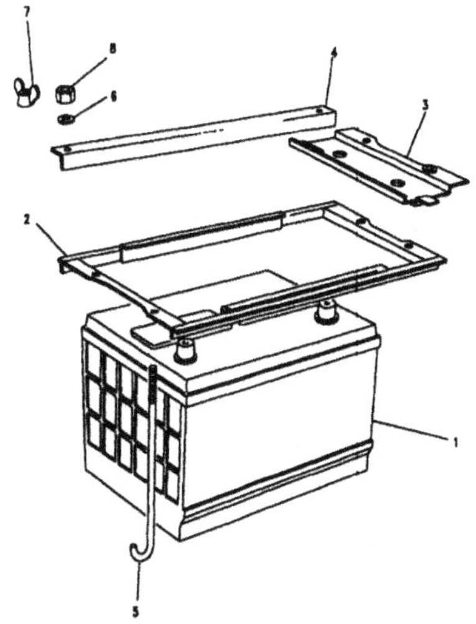

Illus	Part Number	Description	Quantity	Change Point	Remarks
		BATTERY			
1	STC8268	091-bbms-Standard-wet	1		Petrol
1	STC8270	091-bbms-Standard-dry	1		
1	YGD10019	663-bbms-wet	NLA	Note (1)	Use YGD100860.
					Diesel
1	YGD100860	wet-Heavy duty	1		Diesel
1	STC8271	663-bbms-dry	1	Note (1)	Diesel
1	STC8267	072-bbms-wet	1	Note (2)	Diesel
1	STC8269	072-bbms-dry	1		Diesel
2	NRC5338	Cover battery	1	Note (3)	Petrol
2	NRC5387	Cover battery	1		Diesel
3	MTC6302	Spacer	1		Petrol
4	MUC7513	Clamp-fixing battery	1	Note (4)	
5	MUC3201	J bolt-fixing battery	2	Note (3)	
5	MUC7514	J bolt-fixing battery	1	Note (5)	
5	STC307	J bolt-fixing battery	2	Note (6)	
6	WA106041L	Washer-6mm	2	Note (3)	
6	WC106041L	Washer-M6-oversize	2	Note (4)	
7	AFU1272	Nut-wing-M6	2		Alternatives
8	NH106041L	Nut-hexagonal-nyloc-M6	4	Note (3)	
8	NH106041L	Nut-hexagonal-nyloc-M6	4	Note (4)	

CHANGE POINTS:
(1) To (V)APPROX 1/10/84
(2) From (V)APPROX 1/10/84 To (V) MA 962814
(3) To (V) 270511
(4) From (V) 270512
(5) From (V) 270512 To (V) HA 455945
(6) From (V) HA 455946

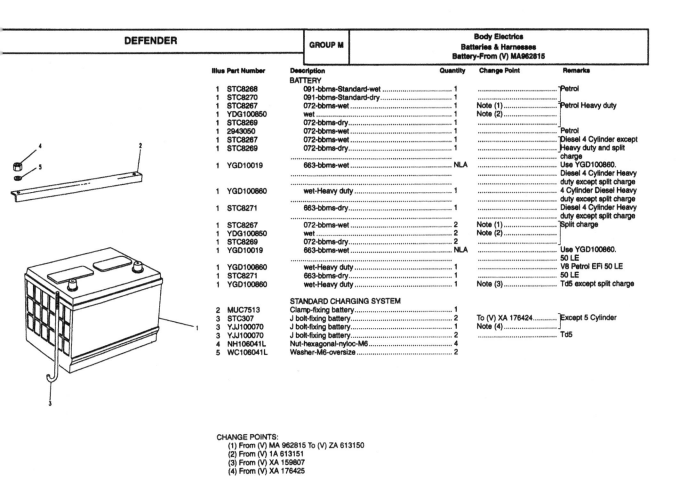

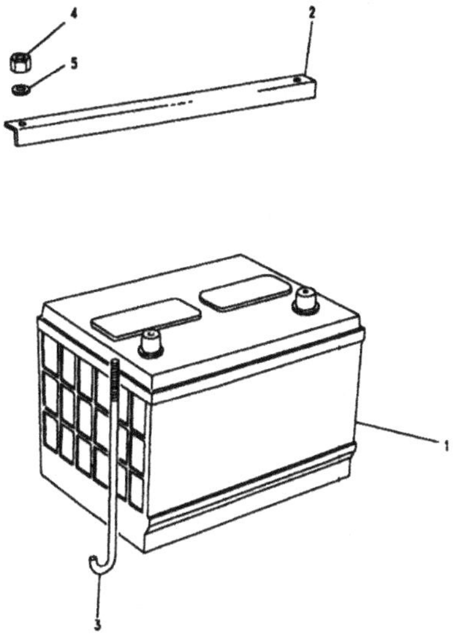

Illus	Part Number	Description	Quantity	Change Point	Remarks
		BATTERY			
1	STC8268	091-bbms-Standard-wet	1		Petrol
1	STC8270	091-bbms-Standard-dry	1		
1	STC8267	072-bbms-wet	1	Note (1)	Petrol Heavy duty
1	YDG100850	wet	1	Note (2)	
1	STC8269	072-bbms-dry	1		
1	2943050	072-bbms-wet	1		Petrol
1	STC8267	072-bbms-wet	1		Diesel 4 Cylinder except
1	STC8269	072-bbms-dry	1		Heavy duty and split
					charge
1	YGD10019	663-bbms-wet	NLA		Use YGD100860.
					Diesel 4 Cylinder Heavy
					duty except split charge
1	YGD100860	wet-Heavy duty	1		4 Cylinder Diesel Heavy
					duty except split charge
1	STC8271	663-bbms-dry	1		Diesel 4 Cylinder Heavy
					duty except split charge
1	STC8267	072-bbms-wet	2	Note (1)	Split charge
1	YDG100850	wet	2	Note (2)	
1	STC8269	072-bbms-dry	2		
1	YGD10019	663-bbms-wet	NLA		Use YGD100860.
					50 LE
1	YGD100860	wet-Heavy duty	1		V8 Petrol EFi 50 LE
1	STC8271	663-bbms-dry	1		50 LE
1	YGD100860	wet-Heavy duty	1	Note (3)	Td5 except split charge
		STANDARD CHARGING SYSTEM			
2	MUC7513	Clamp-fixing battery	1		
3	STC307	J bolt-fixing battery	2	To (V) XA 176424	Except 5 Cylinder
3	YJJ100070	J bolt-fixing battery	1	Note (4)	
3	YJJ100070	J bolt-fixing battery	2		Td5
4	NH106041L	Nut-hexagonal-nyloc-M6	4		
5	WC106041L	Washer-M6-oversize	2		

CHANGE POINTS:
(1) From (V) MA 962815 To (V) ZA 613150
(2) From (V) 1A 613151
(3) From (V) XA 159807
(4) From (V) XA 176425

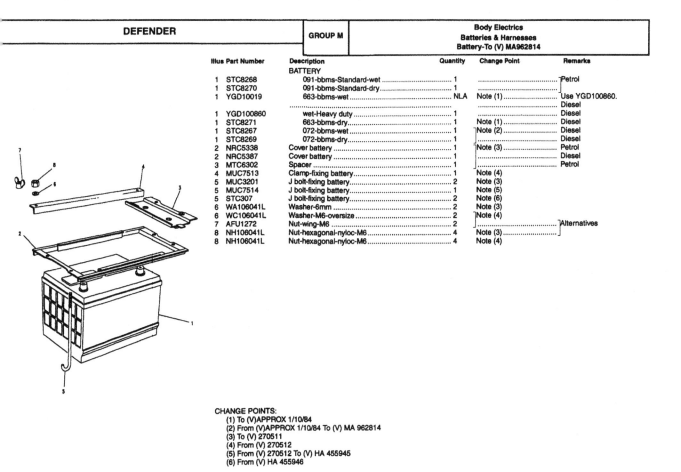

Illus	Part Number	Description	Quantity	Change Point	Remarks
		SPLIT CHARGE BATTERY FIXINGS			
1	RRC7359	Frame assembly-battery box-Split charge	1		
2	RRC7409	Panel battery tray-Split charge	1		
3	FS106167L	Screw-flanged head-panel fixing-flanged head-M6 x 16	4		
4	WL106001L	Washer-panel fixing-sprung-M6	4		
5	WA106041L	Washer-panel fixing-6mm	4		
6	RRC2906	Spacer	1		
7	WA106041L	Washer-spacer fixings-6mm	1		
8	WL106001L	Washer-spacer fixings-sprung-M6	1		
9	NH106041L	Nut-spacer fixings-hexagonal-nyloc-M6	1		
10	STC307	J bolt-fixing battery	2		
11	WA106041L	Washer-6mm	2		
12	NH106041L	Nut-hexagonal-nyloc-M6	4		

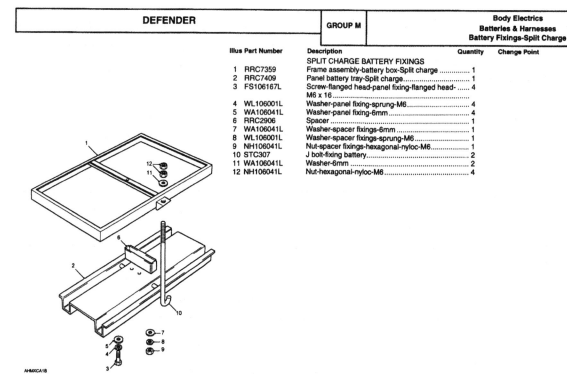

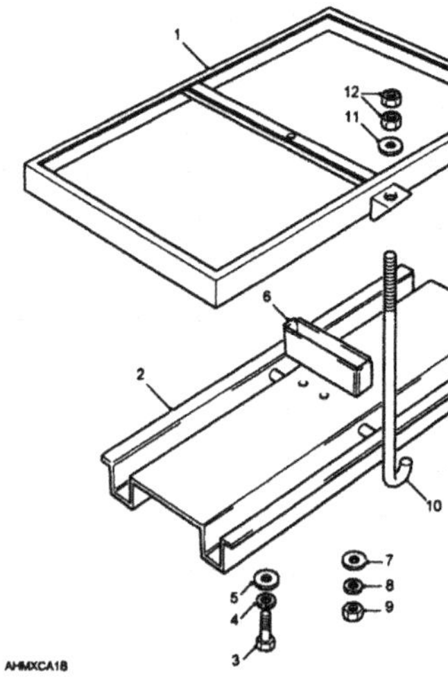

AHMXCA18

Illus	Part Number	Description	Quantity	Change Point	Remarks
		STANDARD CHARGING SYSTEM			
		CABLE-BATTERY POSITIVE			
1	PRC1860	1250MM	1	Note (1)	4 Cylinder Petrol
1	PRC2230	1830MM	1		V8 Twin Carburettor
1	PRC4616	1250MM	1		Diesel Naturally Aspirated
1	PRC4616	1250MM	1	Note (2)	TDi
1	AMR3104	CABLE-BATTERY POSITIVE	1	Note (3)	
1	AMR3843	CABLE-BATTERY POSITIVE-SPLIT CHARGE-ADDITIONAL BATTERY	1	From (V) EA 314059	Split charge
	STC3305	• Bolt-terminal cable-battery	1		
1	YTA101500	Cable-battery positive	1	Note (4)	TDi
1	YTA101510	Cable-battery positive	1		4 Cylinder Petrol
1	YTA101520	Cable-battery positive	1		V8 Petrol
1	YTA101230	Cable-battery positive	1		Td5
1	2943298	Cable-battery positive	1		6 Cylinder Petrol
1	YTA101310	Cable-battery positive	1		50 LE

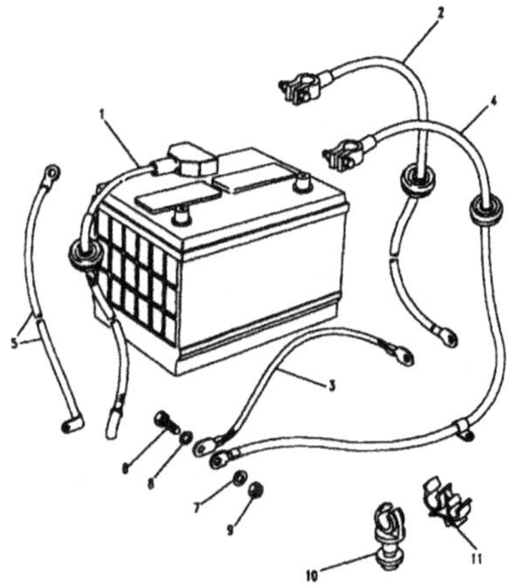

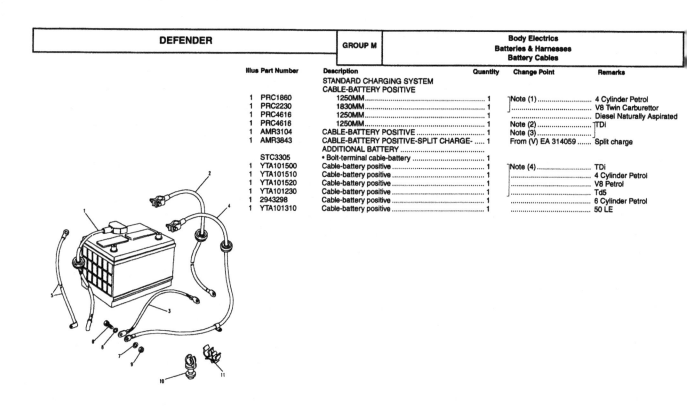

CHANGE POINTS:
(1) To (V) WA 159806
(2) To (V) LA 939975
(3) From (V) MA 939976 To (V) WA 159806
(4) From (V) XA 159807

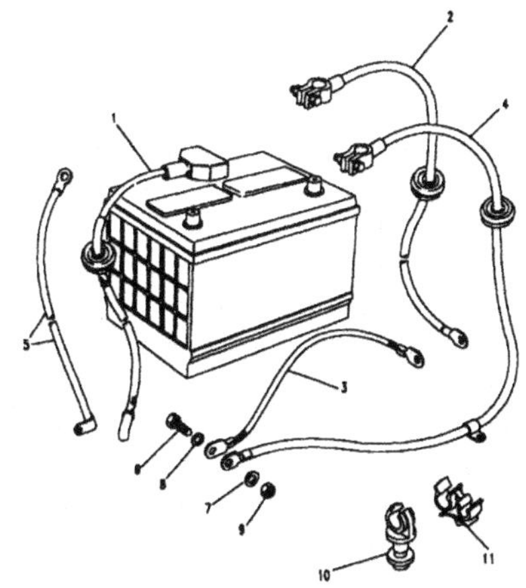

Illus	Part Number	Description	Quantity	Change Point	Remarks
2	PRC1859	Cable-battery negative	1	Note (1)	Petrol
2	PRC7175	Cable-battery negative	1	Note (2)	
2	PRC4333	Cable-battery negative	1	Note (1)	Diesel
2	PRC5524	Cable-battery negative	1	Note (2)	
2	AMR3844	CABLE-BATTERY NEGATIVE-SPLIT CHARGE-ADDITIONAL BATTERY	1	From (V) EA 314059	Split charge
	STC3305	• Bolt-terminal cable-battery	1		
3	PRC3625	Harness earth bond	1	Note (1)	
3	PRC5499	Harness earth bond	1	Note (2)	
		CABLE-BATTERY NEGATIVE			
4	PRC6785	1050MM	1	Note (4)	Note (1)
4	PRC9226	1170MM	1	Note (3)	Petrol
4	PRC9224	1170MM	1		Diesel
	STC3305	• Bolt-terminal cable-battery	1		
4	PRC9224	CABLE-BATTERY NEGATIVE-1170MM	1	Note (5)	
	STC3305	• Bolt-terminal cable-battery	1		
5	PRC2015	Cable assembly starter & earth-300mm	1		Diesel
		FIXINGS-CABLES			
6	FS108201L	Screw-flanged head-M8 x 20	NLA	To (V) 270511	Use FS108207L.
6	FS108251L	Screw-flanged head-M8 x 25	NLA	From (V) 270512	Use FS108257L.
7	WA108051L	Washer-8mm	2		
8	WL108001L	Washer-sprung-M8	2		
9	FN108041L	Nut-flange-M8	NLA		Use FN108047L.
10	PRC3180	Clip-pipe-single	1		
11	PRC3025	Clip-double	2		

CHANGE POINTS:
(1) To (V) 270511
(2) From (V) 270512 To (V) HA 704970
(3) From (V) HA 704971 To (V) WA 159806
(4) From (V) HA 704971
(5) From (V) XA 159807

Remarks:
(1) for vehicles with tool stowage locker under LH front seat

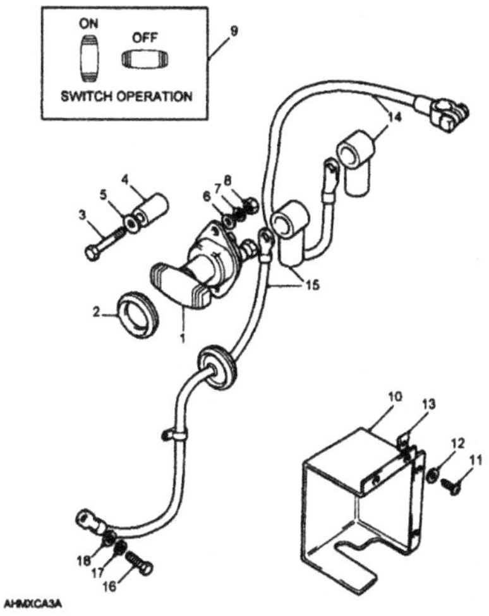

Illus	Part Number	Description	Quantity	Change Point	Remarks
		BATTERY MASTER SWITCH & FIXINGS			
1	PRC4879	Switch-master	1		
3	BH106501L	Bolt-M6 x 50	2		
4	336503	Spacer	2		
5	AFU1080	Washer-plain	2		
6	WA106041L	Washer-6mm	2		
7	WL106001L	Washer-sprung-M6	2		
8	NH106041L	Nut-hexagonal-nyloc-M6	2		
9	RRC3987	Label switch	1		
10	RRC4319	Panel-switch-housing	1		
12	WA104001L	Washer-plain-M4	4		
13	MWC9322	Nut-spring-u type-No 6	4		
		NEGATIVE TO MASTER SWITCH			
14	PRC8166	Cable-battery negative	1		Petrol
14	PRC8248	Cable-battery negative	1		Diesel
		MASTER SWITCH TO CHASSIS & GEARBOX			
15	PRC9229	Cable-Earth	1		Petrol
15	PRC9228	Cable-Earth	1		Diesel
16	FS108201L	Screw-earth cable to gearbox-flanged head-M8 x 20	NLA		Use FS108207L.
17	WL108001L	Washer-earth cable to gearbox-sprung-M8	1		
18	WA108051L	Washer-earth cable to gearbox-8mm	1		

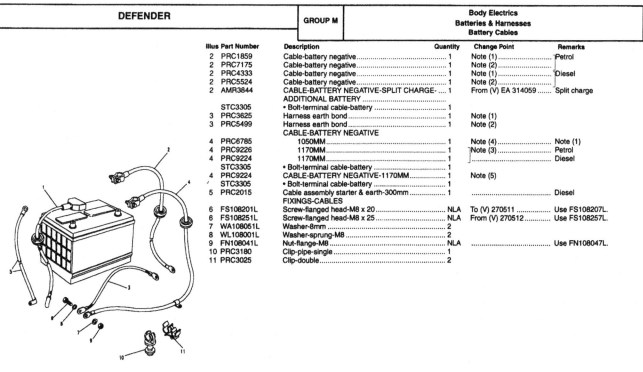

Illus	Part Number	Description	Quantity	Change Point	Remarks
		PETROL 2250CC			
1	PRC3363	HARNESS MAIN	1	Note (1)	2250 cc Petrol
		PETROL 2500CC & V8 - UP TO FA404682			
1	PRC5319	HARNESS MAIN	1	Note (2)	Petrol except 2250 cc
1	PRC6311	HARNESS MAIN	1	Note (3)	
		DIESEL - UP TO FA404682			
1	PRC3969	HARNESS MAIN	1	Note (4)	Diesel UK Rest of World
1	PRC5336	HARNESS MAIN	1		Diesel Norway Finland Germany
1	PRC6311	HARNESS MAIN	1	Note (5)	Diesel
	C46082	• Resistor	NLA		Use PRC9096.

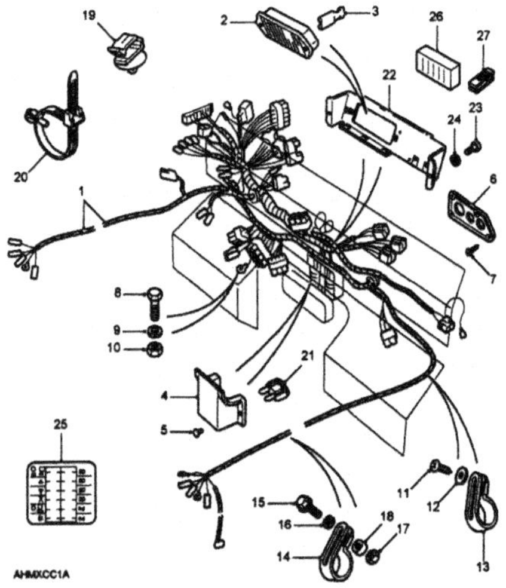

AHMXCC1A

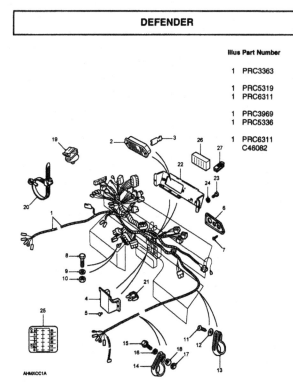

CHANGE POINTS:
(1) To (V) HA 705856
(2) To (V) 270226
(3) From (V) 270227 To (V) FA 404682
(4) To (V) 270483
(5) From (V) 270484 To (V) FA 404682

Illus	Part Number	Description	Quantity	Change Point	Remarks
		ALL VARIANTS - FA404683 TO HA705856			
1	PRC6779	HARNESS MAIN	1	Note (1)	
1	PRC8243	HARNESS MAIN	1	Note (2)	
	C46082	• Resistor	NLA		Use PRC9096.
1	PRC8385	HARNESS MAIN	1	Note (3)	
1	PRC8868	HARNESS MAIN	1	Note (4)	
	PRC9096	• Resistor	1		
	AAU5034	• Diode-Pektron	3		

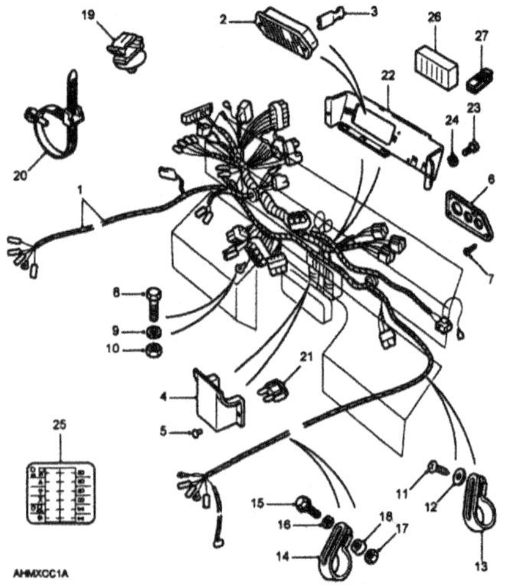

AHMXCC1A

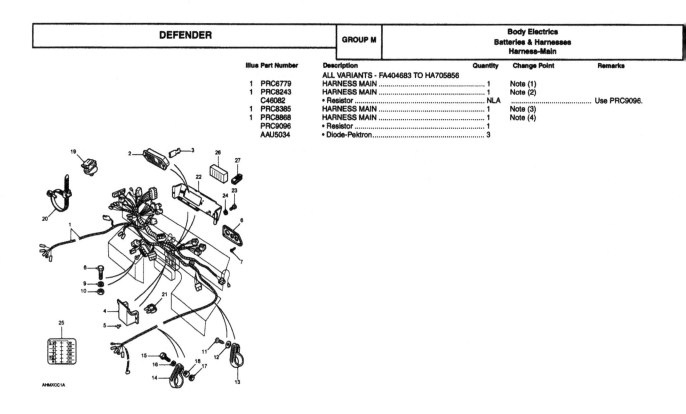

CHANGE POINTS:
(1) From (V) FA 404683 To (V) FA 424037
(2) From (V) FA 424038 To (V) GA 455945
(3) From (V) HA 455946 To (V) HA 702829
(4) From (V) HA 702830 To (V) HA 705856

Illus	Part Number	Description	Quantity	Change Point	Remarks
		PETROL - FROM HA705857 TO WA159806			
1	PRC9810	HARNESS MAIN	1	Note (1)	Petrol
1	AMR1487	HARNESS MAIN	1	Note (2)	
1	AMR2347	HARNESS MAIN	1	Note (3)	
1	AMR3481	HARNESS MAIN	1	Note (4)	Petrol low line
1	AMR4079	HARNESS MAIN	1	Note (5)	
1	AMR3480	HARNESS MAIN	1	Note (4)	Petrol high line
1	AMR4078	HARNESS MAIN	1	Note (6)	
1	AMR5859	HARNESS MAIN	1	Note (7)	
1	YMC129920	HARNESS MAIN	1	Note (8)	Petrol high line except 50 LE
	PRC9096	• Resistor	1		
	AAU5034	• Diode-Pektron	3		
1	YMC133450	Harness main	1	Note (8)	V8 EFi 50 LE Europe UK
1	YMC134410	Harness main	1	Note (8)	V8 EFi 50 LE Japan

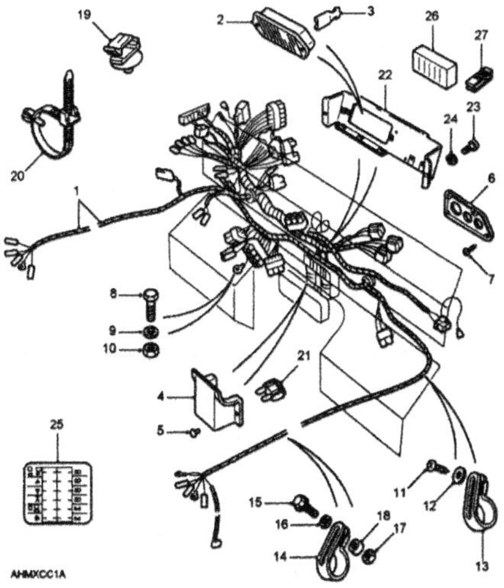

AHMXCC1A

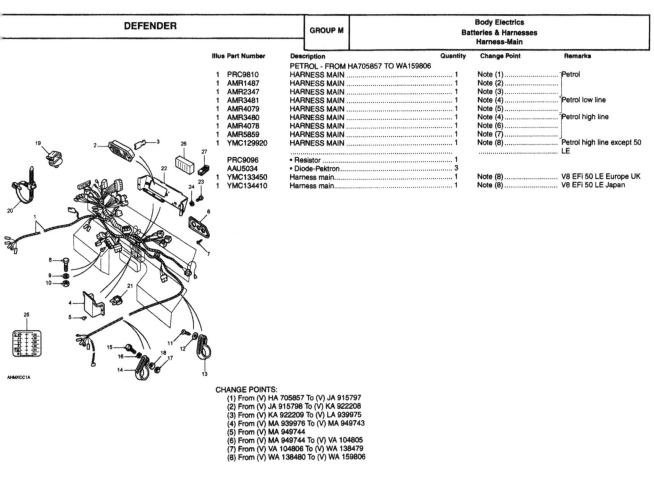

CHANGE POINTS:
(1) From (V) HA 705857 To (V) JA 915797
(2) From (V) JA 915798 To (V) KA 922208
(3) From (V) KA 922209 To (V) LA 939975
(4) From (V) MA 939976 To (V) MA 949743
(5) From (V) MA 949744
(6) From (V) MA 949744 To (V) VA 104805
(7) From (V) VA 104806 To (V) WA 138479
(8) From (V) WA 138480 To (V) WA 159806

Illus	Part Number	Description	Quantity	Change Point	Remarks
		PETROL - FROM XA159807			
1	YMC130400	Harness main	1	Note (1)	RHD V8 Twin Carburettor
1	YMC145980	Harness main	1	Note (2)	
1	YMC000420	Harness main	1	Note (3)	
1	YMC130390	Harness main	1	Note (1)	LHD V8 Twin Carburettor
1	YMC145990	Harness main	1	Note (2)	
1	YMC000450	Harness main	1	Note (3)	
1	YMC130400	Harness main	1	Note (1)	RHD 4 Cylinder
1	YMC145980	Harness main	1	Note (2)	
1	YMC000420	Harness main	1	Note (3)	
1	YMC130390	Harness main	1	Note (1)	LHD 4 Cylinder
1	YMC145990	Harness main	1	Note (2)	
1	YMC000450	Harness main	1	Note (3)	
1	YMC130380	Harness main	1	Note (4)	BMW M52
1	YMC001510	Harness main	1	Note (3)	

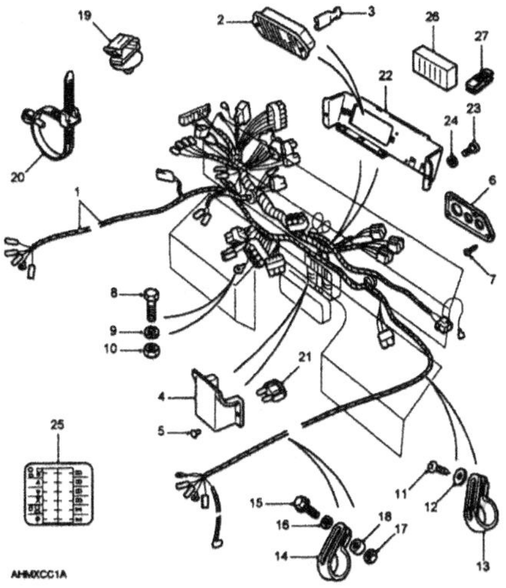

AHMXCC1A

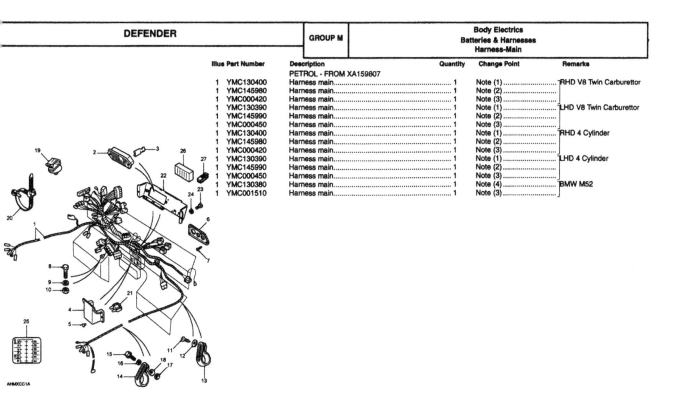

CHANGE POINTS:
(1) From (V) XA 159807 To (V) XA 177484
(2) From (V) XA 177485 To (V) ZA 603383
(3) From (V) 1A 603384 To (V) 1A 622423
(4) From (V) XA 159807 To (V) ZA 603383

Illus	Part Number	Description	Quantity	Change Point	Remarks
		DIESEL NON-TURBO - FROM HA705857			
1	PRC9809	HARNESS MAIN	1	Note (1)	Diesel Naturally Aspirated
1	AMR3482	HARNESS MAIN	1	Note (2)	
1	AMR4080	HARNESS MAIN	1	Note (3)	
1	AMR5858	HARNESS MAIN	1	Note (4)	
	PRC9096	• Resistor	1		
	AAU5034	• Diode-Pektron	3		

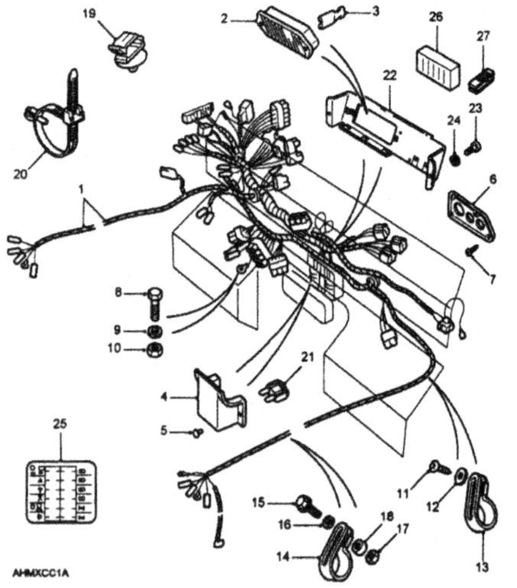

AHMXCC1A

CHANGE POINTS:
(1) From (V) HA 705857 To (V) LA 939975
(2) From (V) MA 939976 To (V) MA 949743
(3) From (V) MA 949744 To (V) VA 104805
(4) From (V) VA 104806 To (V) WA 159806

Illus	Part Number	Description	Quantity	Change Point	Remarks
		200TDI			
1	PRC9810	HARNESS MAIN	1	Note (1)	
1	AMR1488	HARNESS MAIN	1	Note (2)	
1	AMR2348	HARNESS MAIN	1	Note (3)	
	PRC9096	• Resistor	1		
	AAU5034	• Diode-Pektron	3		

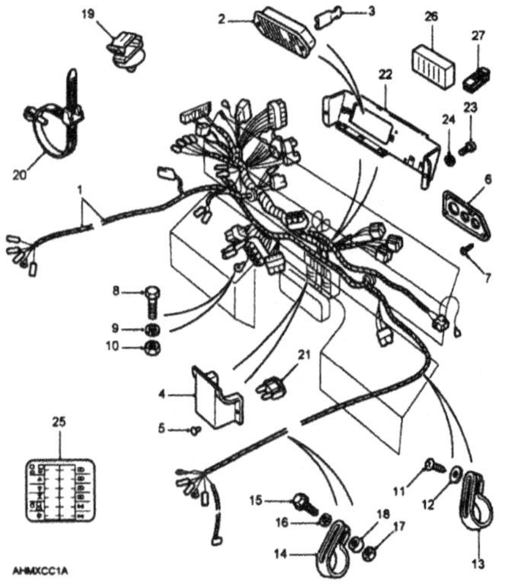

AHMXCC1A

CHANGE POINTS:
(1) From (V) HA 705857 To (V) JA 915323
(2) From (V) JA 915324 To (V) KA 922208
(3) From (V) KA 922209 To (V) LA 939975

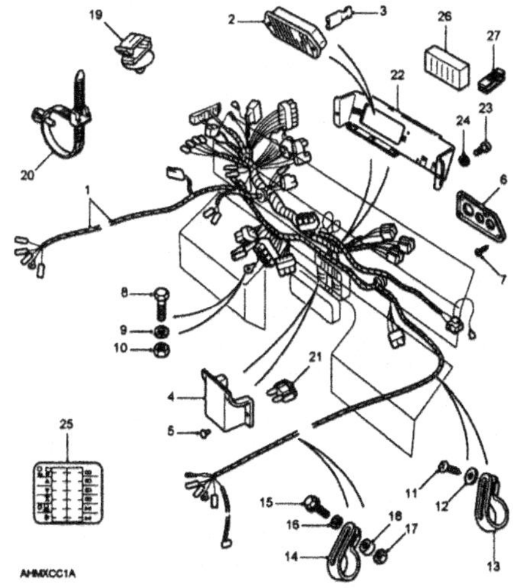
AHMXCC1A

Illus	Part Number	Description	Quantity	Change Point	Remarks
		300TDI-LESS ENGINE IMMOBILISATION			
1	AMR3483	HARNESS MAIN	1	Note (1)	Low line
1	AMR3484	HARNESS MAIN	1	Note (1)	High line
1	AMR4082	HARNESS MAIN	1	Note (2)	Low line
1	AMR4081	HARNESS MAIN	1	Note (2)	High line
1	AMR5856	HARNESS MAIN	1	Note (3)	Low line
1	AMR5857	HARNESS MAIN	1	Note (3)	High line
1	YMC129900	HARNESS MAIN	1	Note (4)	Low line
1	YMC135140	Harness main	1	Note (4)	Headlamp levelling
1	YMC135150	Harness main	1	Note (4)	High line headlamp levelling dim dip
1	YMC130360	Harness main	1	Note (5)	RHD
1	YMC130370	Harness main	1	Note (5)	LHD
1	YMC000400	Harness main	1	Note (6)	RHD
1	YMC000440	Harness main	1	Note (6)	LHD
1	YMC002381	Harness main	1	Note (7)	RHD electric windows Tdi
1	YMC002471	Harness main	1	Note (7)	LHD except electric windows front and CDL
1	YMC002391	Harness main	1	Note (7)	RHD electric windows CDL
1	YMC002481	Harness main	1	Note (7)	LHD TDi electric windows CDL except immobilisation and Td5
		MAIN HARNESS - BRAZIL ONLY			
1	YMC010910	Harness main	1	Note (7)	Tdi Brazil except CDL
1	YMC010920	Harness main	1	Note (7)	CDL Tdi Brazil

CHANGE POINTS:
(1) From (V) MA 939976 To (V) MA 949743
(2) From (V) MA 949744 To (V) VA 104805
(3) From (V) VA 104806 To (V) WA 138479
(4) From (V) WA 138480 To (V) WA 159806
(5) From (V) XA 159807 To (V) ZA 603383
(6) From (V) 1A 603384 To (V) 1A 622423
(7) From (V) 2A 622424

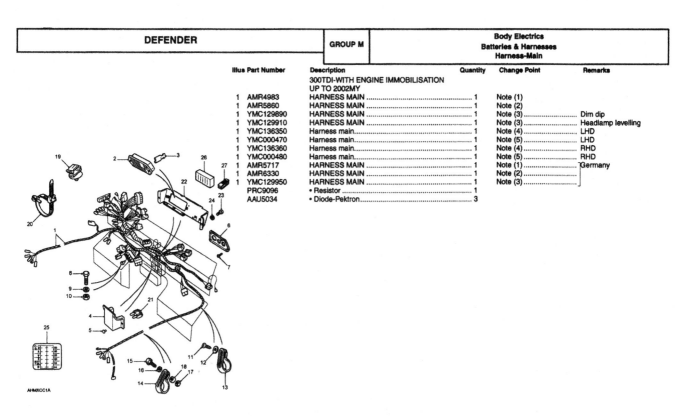

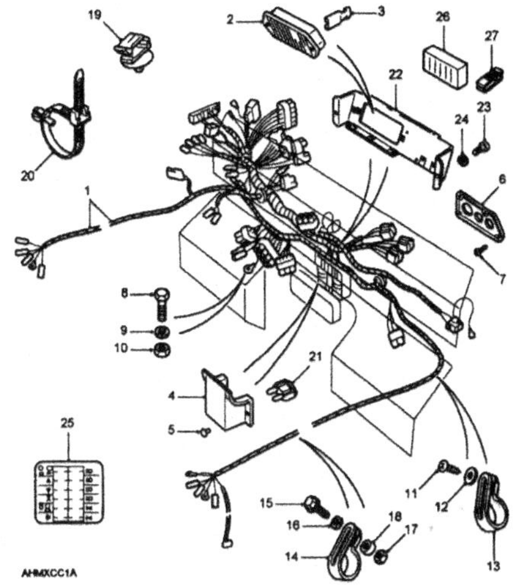
AHMXCC1A

Illus	Part Number	Description	Quantity	Change Point	Remarks
		300TDI-WITH ENGINE IMMOBILISATION UP TO 2002MY			
1	AMR4983	HARNESS MAIN	1	Note (1)	
1	AMR5860	HARNESS MAIN	1	Note (2)	
1	YMC129890	HARNESS MAIN	1	Note (3)	Dim dip
1	YMC129910	HARNESS MAIN	1	Note (3)	Headlamp levelling
1	YMC136350	Harness main	1	Note (4)	LHD
1	YMC000470	Harness main	1	Note (5)	LHD
1	YMC136360	Harness main	1	Note (4)	RHD
1	YMC000480	Harness main	1	Note (5)	RHD
1	AMR5717	HARNESS MAIN	1	Note (1)	Germany
1	AMR6330	HARNESS MAIN	1	Note (2)	
1	YMC129950	HARNESS MAIN	1	Note (3)	
	PRC9096	• Resistor	1		
	AAU5034	• Diode-Pektron	3		

CHANGE POINTS:
(1) From (V) TA 977537 To (V) VA 104805
(2) From (V) VA 104806 To (V) WA 138479
(3) From (V) WA 138480 To (V) WA 159806
(4) From (V) XA 159807 To (V) ZA 603383
(5) From (V) 1A 603384 To (V) 1A 622423

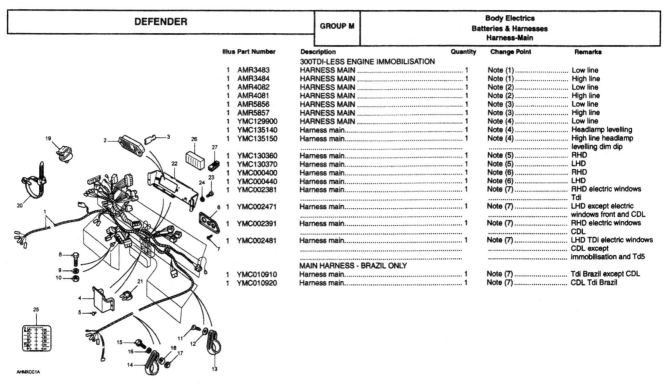

Illus	Part Number	Description	Quantity	Change Point	Remarks
		300TDI-WITH ENGINE IMMOBILISATION FROM 2002MY			
1	YMC002401	Harness main	1	Note (1)	RHD immobilisation Tdi except Antilock Brakes and electric windows and CDL and heated seats South Africa
1	YMC002491	Harness main	1	Note (1)	LHD except electric windows front and CDL
1	YMC002411	Harness main	1	Note (1)	RHD electric windows CDL
1	YMC002501	Harness main	1	Note (1)	LHD electric windows front CDL

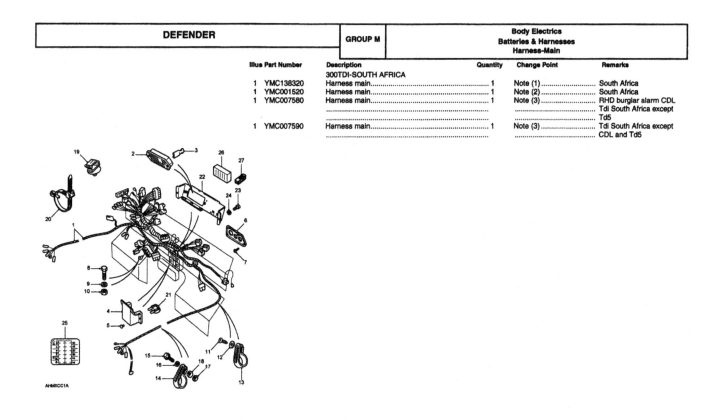

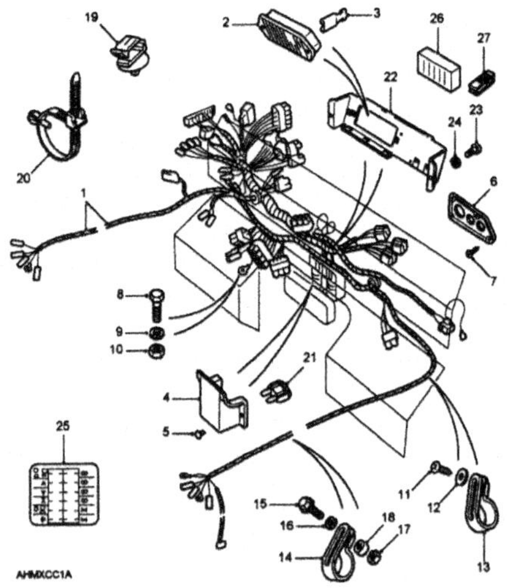

AHMXCC1A

CHANGE POINTS:
(1) From (V) 2A 622424

Illus	Part Number	Description	Quantity	Change Point	Remarks
		300TDI-SOUTH AFRICA			
1	YMC138320	Harness main	1	Note (1)	South Africa
1	YMC001520	Harness main	1	Note (2)	South Africa
1	YMC007580	Harness main	1	Note (3)	RHD burglar alarm CDL Tdi South Africa except Td5
1	YMC007590	Harness main	1	Note (3)	Tdi South Africa except CDL and Td5

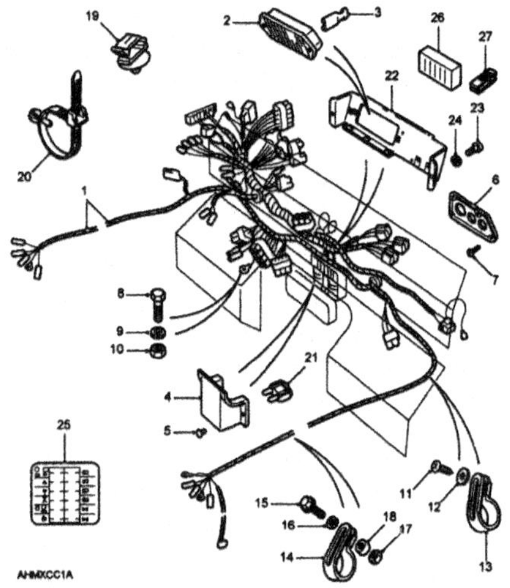

AHMXCC1A

CHANGE POINTS:
(1) From (V) XA 159807 To (V) ZA 603383
(2) From (V) 1A 603384 To (V) 1A 622423
(3) From (V) 2A 622424

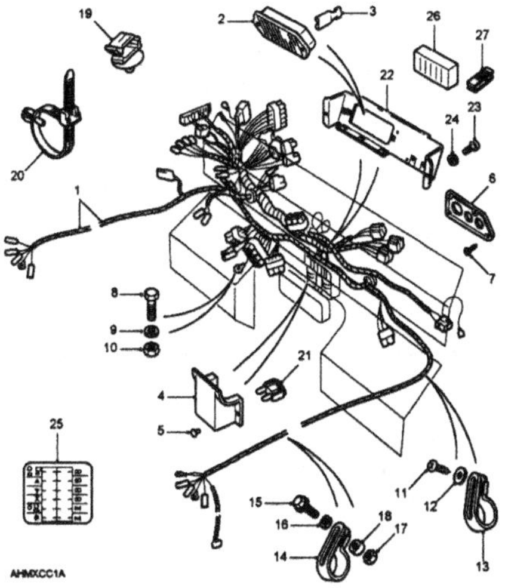

Illus	Part Number	Description	Quantity	Change Point	Remarks
		TD5 - WITH ABS			
1	YMC130350	Harness main	1	Note (1)	RHD high line
1	YMC000530	Harness main	1	Note (2)	RHD high line
1	YMC002341	Harness main	1	Note (3)	RHD except heated seats
1	YMC002351	Harness main	1	Note (3)	RHD heated seats
1	YMC130290	Harness main	1	Note (1)	LHD high line
1	YMC000520	Harness main	1	Note (2)	LHD high line
1	YMC002431	Harness main	1	Note (3)	LHD Antilock Brakes electric windows CDL Td5 except Tdi and heated seats
1	YMC002441	Harness main	1	Note (3)	LHD heated seats
1	STC60703	Harness main	1	Note (4)	Heritage

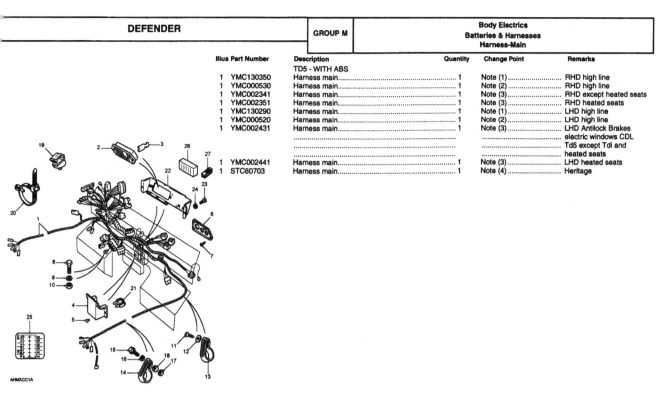

CHANGE POINTS:
(1) From (V) XA 159807 To (V) ZA 603384
(2) From (V) 1A 603385 To (V) 1A 622423
(3) From (V) 2A 622424
(4) From (V) XA 159807 To (V) ZA 999999

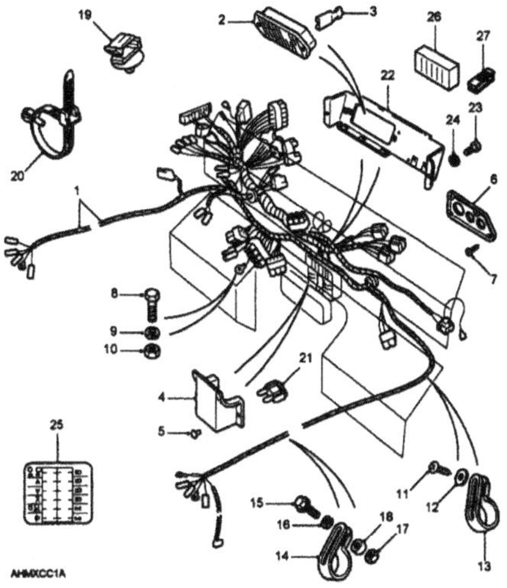

Illus	Part Number	Description	Quantity	Change Point	Remarks
		TD5 - EXCEPT ABS			
1	YMC132360	Harness main	1	Note (1)	RHD low line
1	YMC000550	Harness main	1	Note (2)	RHD low line
1	YMC002361	Harness main	1	Note (3)	RHD except electric windows and CDL
1	YMC004000	Harness main-with tachometer	1	Note (3)	RHD except electric windows and CDL
1	YMC002371	Harness main	1	Note (3)	RHD electric windows front CDL
1	YMC132350	Harness main	1	Note (1)	LHD low line
1	YMC000540	Harness main	1	Note (2)	LHD low line
1	YMC002451	Harness main	1	Note (3)	LHD except electric windows front and CDL
1	YMC002461	Harness main	1	Note (3)	LHD electric windows CDL Td5 except Antilock Brakes and Tdi and heated seats
1	YMC002521	Harness main-LHD	1	Note (3)	Police Italy

CHANGE POINTS:
(1) From (V) XA 159807 To (V) ZA 603384
(2) From (V) 1A 603385 To (V) 1A 622423
(3) From (V) 2A 622424

Illus	Part Number	Description	Quantity	Change Point	Remarks
		TD5 - SOUTH AFRICA			
1	YMC138310	Harness main	1	Note (1)	South Africa
1	YMC000500	Harness main	1	Note (2)	South Africa
1	YMC007560	Harness main	1	Note (3)	RHD CDL Td5 South Africa except burglar and Tdi
1	YMC007570	Harness main	1	Note (3)	Td5 South Africa except alarm and CDL
1	YMC007590	Harness main	1	Note (3)	Tdi South Africa except CDL and Td5

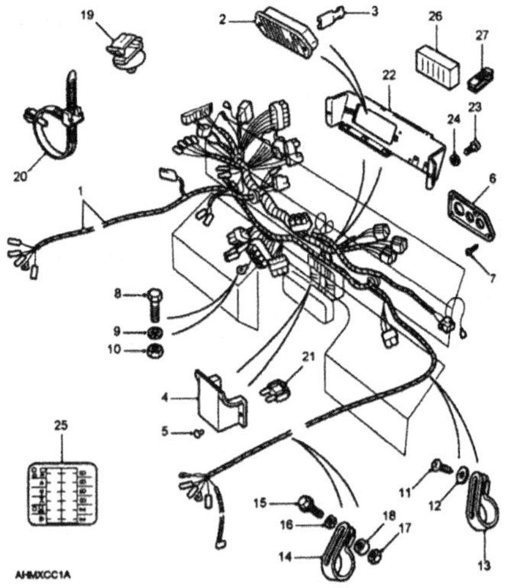

AHMXCC1A

CHANGE POINTS:
(1) From (V) XA 159807 To (V) ZA 603384
(2) From (V) 1A 603385 To (V) 1A 622423
(3) From (V) 2A 622424

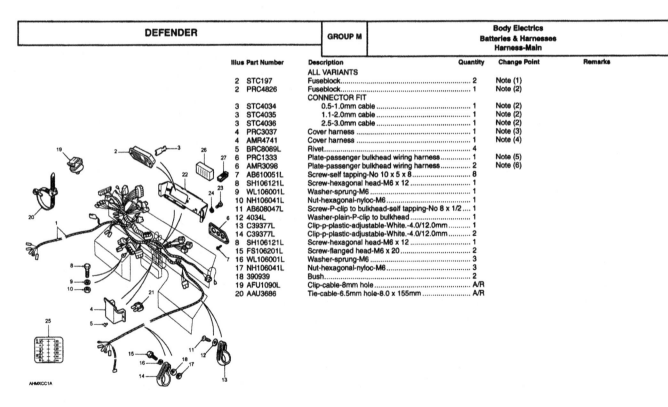

Illus	Part Number	Description	Quantity	Change Point	Remarks
		ALL VARIANTS			
2	STC197	Fuseblock	2	Note (1)	
2	PRC4826	Fuseblock	1	Note (2)	
		CONNECTOR FIT			
3	STC4034	0.5-1.0mm cable	1	Note (2)	
3	STC4035	1.1-2.0mm cable	1	Note (2)	
3	STC4036	2.5-3.0mm cable	1	Note (2)	
4	PRC3037	Cover harness	1	Note (3)	
4	AMR4741	Cover harness	1	Note (4)	
5	BRC8089L	Rivet	4		
6	PRC1333	Plate-passenger bulkhead wiring harness	1	Note (5)	
6	AMR3098	Plate-passenger bulkhead wiring harness	2	Note (6)	
7	AB610051L	Screw-self tapping-No 10 x 5 x 8	8		
8	SH106121L	Screw-hexagonal head-M6 x 12	1		
9	WL106001L	Washer-sprung-M6	1		
10	NH106041L	Nut-hexagonal-nyloc-M6	1		
11	AB608047L	Screw-P-clip to bulkhead-self tapping-No 8 x 1/2	1		
12	4034L	Washer-plain-P-clip to bulkhead	1		
13	C39377L	Clip-p-plastic-adjustable-White.-4.0/12.0mm	1		
14	C39377L	Clip-p-plastic-adjustable-White.-4.0/12.0mm	2		
8	SH106121L	Screw-hexagonal head-M6 x 12	1		
15	FS106201L	Screw-flanged head-M6 x 20	2		
16	WL106001L	Washer-sprung-M6	3		
17	NH106041L	Nut-hexagonal-nyloc-M6	3		
18	390939	Bush	2		
19	AFU1090L	Clip-cable-8mm hole	A/R		
20	AAU3686	Tie-cable-6.5mm hole-8.0 x 155mm	A/R		

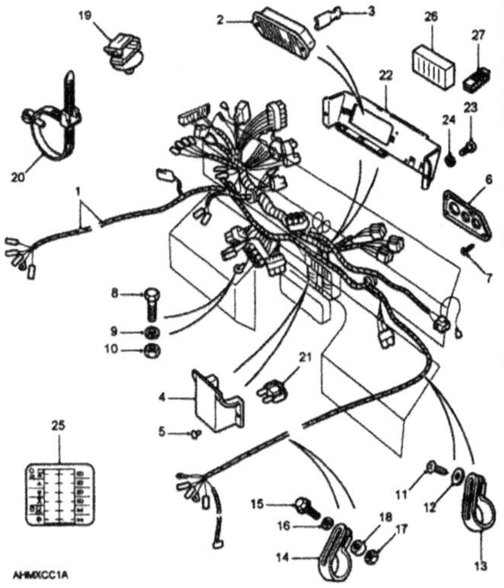

AHMXCC1A

CHANGE POINTS:
(1) To (V) FA 424037
(2) From (V) FA 424038
(3) To (V) MA 963205
(4) From (V) MA 963206
(5) To (V) LA 932798
(6) From (V) LA 932798

Illus	Part Number	Description	Quantity	Change Point	Remarks
		INTERIOR FUSEBOX			
		FUSE			
21	RTC4482	5 amp	A/R	To (V) FA 424037	
21	RTC4500	10 amp	A/R		
21	RTC4502	15 amp	A/R		
21	RTC4785	20 amp	A/R		
21	RTC4505	25 amp	A/R		
21	RTC4510	air conditioning-35 amp	A/R		
21	RTC4497	5 amp-auto-standard	A/R	From (V) FA 424038	
21	RTC4498	7.5 amp-auto-standard.	A/R		
21	RTC4501	10 amp-auto-standard	A/R		
21	RTC4503	15 amp-auto-standard.	A/R		
21	RTC4504	20 amp-auto-standard.	A/R		

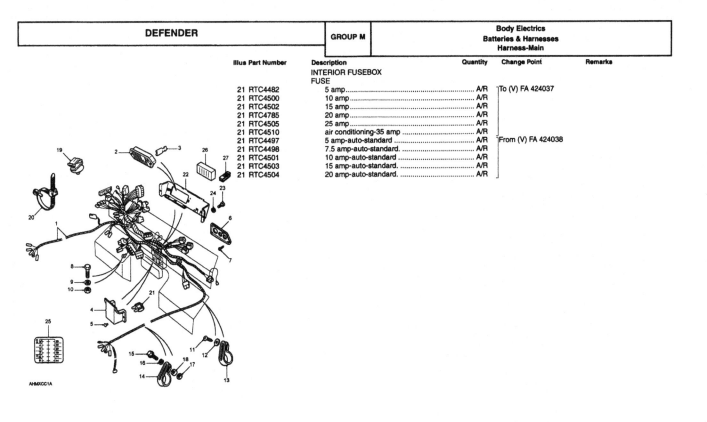

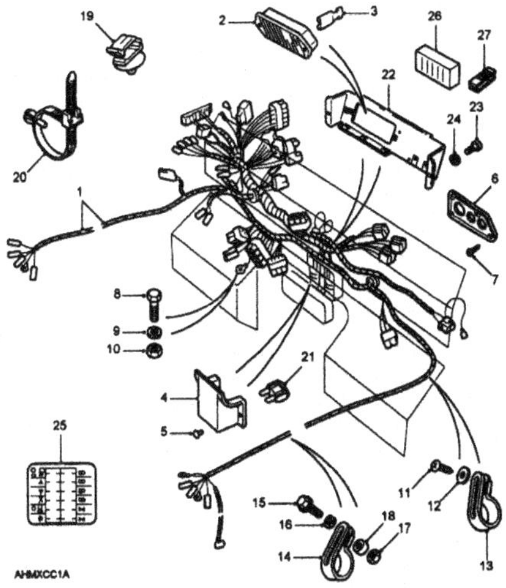
AHMXCC1A

Illus	Part Number	Description	Quantity	Change Point	Remarks
22	PRC2443	Bracket fusebox	1	Note (1)	
22	PRC8072	Bracket fusebox	1	Note (2)	
22	AMR3138	Bracket fusebox	1	Note (3)	
22	YQU104850	Bracket fusebox	1	Note (4)	
23	SE106121L	Screw-pan-pan head-M6 x 12	2		
24	WF600041L	Washer-lock	2		

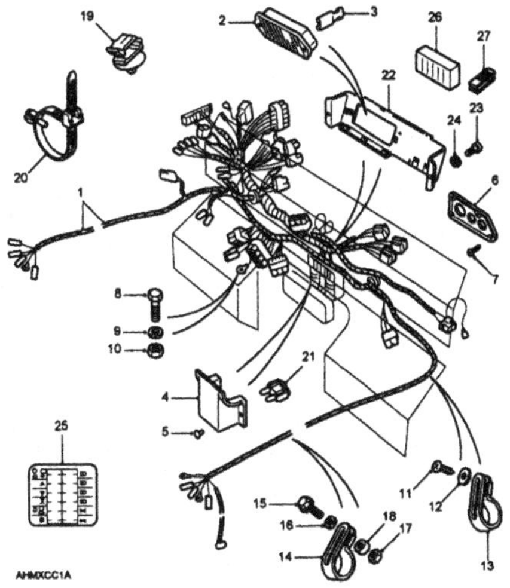
AHMXCC1A

CHANGE POINTS:
(1) To (V) FA 424037
(2) From (V) FA 424038 To (V) LA 933817
(3) From (V) LA 933818 To (V) WA 159806
(4) From (V) XA 159807

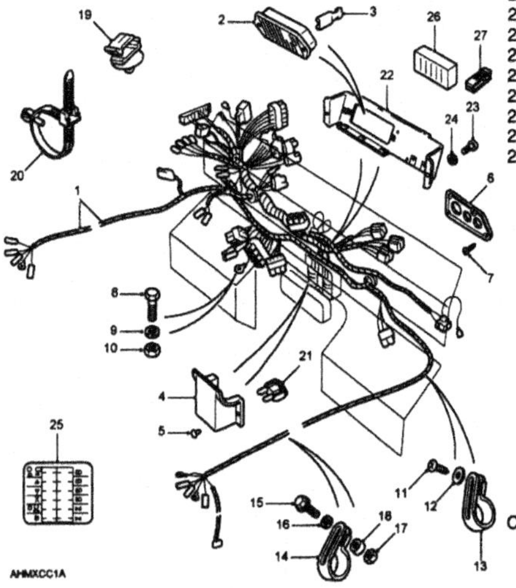

AHMXCC1A

Illus	Part Number	Description	Quantity	Change Point	Remarks
25	PRC3389	Label-fusebox	1	Note (1)	
25	PRC5670	Label-fusebox	1	Note (2)	
25	PRC8245	Label-fusebox	1	Note (3)	
25	PRC9902	Label-fusebox	1	Note (4)	
25	MTC5227	Label-warning	1	Note (11)	Except Germany
25	BTR2308	Label-warning	1	Note (12)	Except Germany
25	AMR3771	Label-fusebox	1	Note (5)	Except burglar alarm
25	AMR5069	Label-fusebox	1		Burglar alarm
25	AMR5861	Label-fusebox	1	Note (6)	
25	YQS101790	Label-fusebox	1	Note (7)	
25	YQS000010	Label-fusebox	1	Note (8)	
25	YQS000060	Label-fusebox	1	Note (9)	Except Germany
25	AMR5718	Label-fusebox	1		Germany
26	HAM4301L	Holder-fuses	1		
27	PRC4412	Extractor blade fuse	1		
28	AHU710040	Bracket-facia	1	Note (10)	RHD
28	AHU710030	Bracket-facia	1		LHD

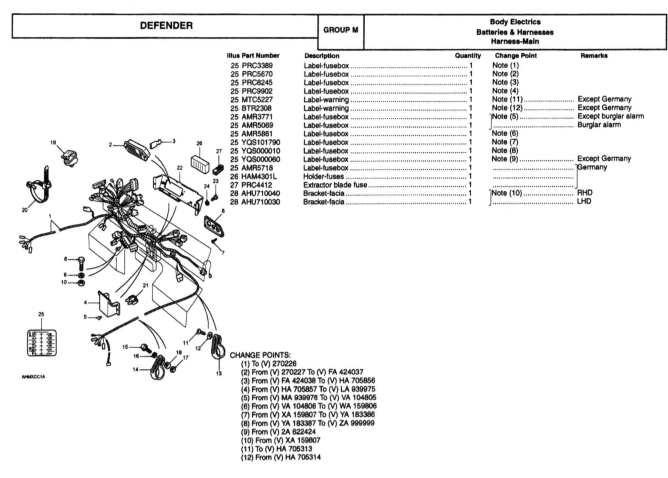

CHANGE POINTS:
(1) To (V) 270226
(2) From (V) 270227 To (V) FA 424037
(3) From (V) FA 424038 To (V) HA 705856
(4) From (V) HA 705857 To (V) LA 939975
(5) From (V) MA 939976 To (V) VA 104805
(6) From (V) VA 104806 To (V) WA 159806
(7) From (V) XA 159807 To (V) YA 183386
(8) From (V) YA 183387 To (V) ZA 999999
(9) From (V) 2A 622424
(10) From (V) XA 159807
(11) To (V) HA 705313
(12) From (V) HA 705314

Illus	Part Number	Description	Quantity	Change Point	Remarks
1	YMB102340	Harness-front wing-RH	1	Note (1)	Except Td5
1	YMD000980	Harness-front wing-RH	1	Note (2)	Except Td5
1	YMB102350	Harness-front wing-LH	1	Note (1)	Except Td5
1	YMD001010	Harness-front wing-LH	1	Note (2)	Except Td5
1	YMB102360	Harness-front wing-RH	1	Note (1)	Td5 headlamp levelling
1	YMD000990	Harness-front wing-RH	1	Note (2)	Td5 headlamp levelling
1	YMB102370	Harness-front wing-LH	1	Note (1)	Burglar alarm Td5
1	YMD001020	Harness-front wing-LH	1	Note (2)	Burglar alarm Td5

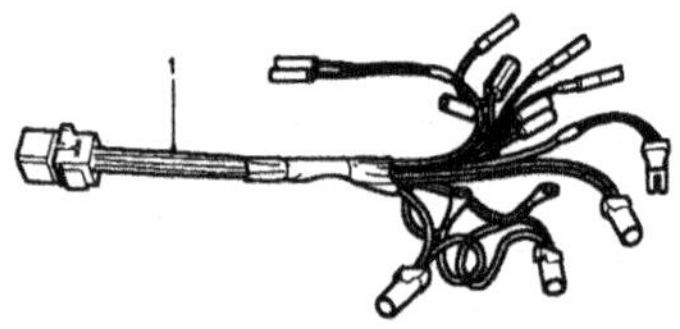

LM0057

CHANGE POINTS:
(1) From (V) XA 159807 To (V) ZA 614032
(2) From (V) 1A 614033

DEFENDER	GROUP M	Body Electrics Batteries & Harnesses Harness-Chassis

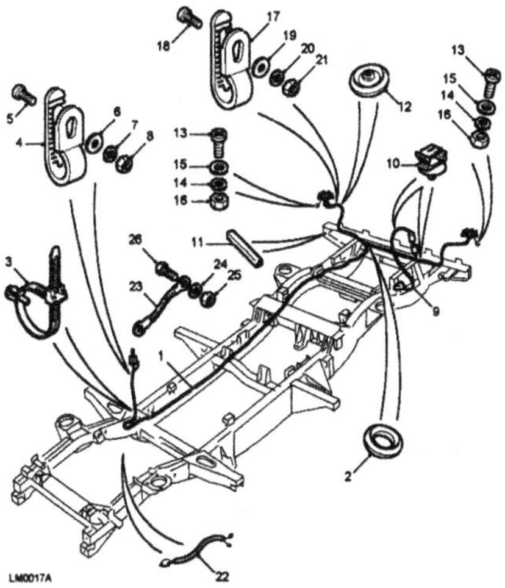

Illus	Part Number	Description	Quantity	Change Point	Remarks
		DEFENDER 90 - UP TO WA159806			
1	PRC3209	Harness-chassis	1	Note (1)	Note (1) Note (3)
1	PRC4590	Harness-chassis	1		Note (1) Note (4)
1	PRC4970	Harness-chassis	1	Note (2)	Note (2) Note (3)
1	PRC7003	Harness-chassis	1	Note (3)	
1	PRC8870	Harness-chassis	1	Note (4)	Petrol Note (2) Note (3)
1	PRC8870	Harness-chassis	1	Note (5)	Diesel Note (2) Note (3)
1	AMR1491	Harness-chassis	1	Note (6)	
1	AMR3448	Harness-chassis	1	Note (7)	Note (2) Note (3)
1	AMR5869	Harness-chassis	1	Note (8)	
1	YMD111090	Harness-chassis	1	Note (9)	Note (2) 90" Note (3)
1	PRC4993	Harness-chassis	1	Note (10)	Note (2) Note (4)
1	PRC7004	Harness-chassis	1	Note (11)	
1	PRC8869	Harness-chassis	1	Note (12)	Diesel Note (2) Note (4)
1	PRC8869	Harness-chassis	1	Note (4)	Petrol Note (2) Note (4)
1	AMR1492	Harness-chassis	1	Note (13)	Diesel Note (2) Note (4)
1	AMR3449	Harness-chassis	1	Note (7)	Note (2) Note (4)
1	AMR5870	Harness-chassis	1	Note (8)	
1	YMD111080	Harness-chassis	1	Note (9)	
1	YMD111800	Harness-chassis	1	Note (9)	4000 cc V8 50 LE

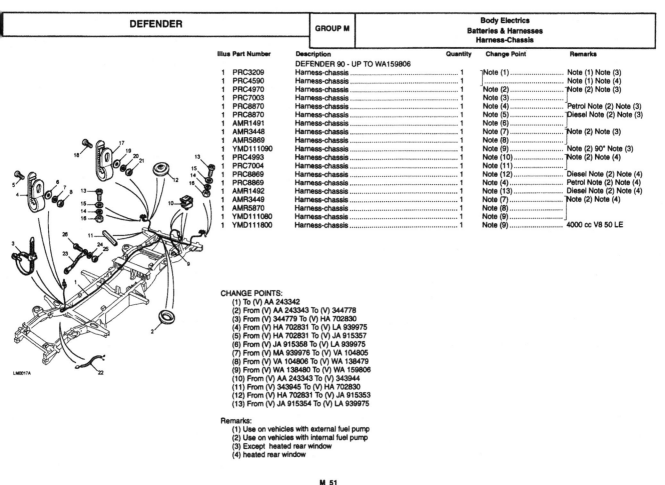

CHANGE POINTS:
(1) To (V) AA 243342
(2) From (V) AA 243343 To (V) 344778
(3) From (V) 344779 To (V) HA 702830
(4) From (V) HA 702831 To (V) LA 939975
(5) From (V) HA 702831 To (V) JA 915357
(6) From (V) JA 915358 To (V) LA 939975
(7) From (V) MA 939976 To (V) VA 104805
(8) From (V) VA 104806 To (V) WA 138479
(9) From (V) WA 138480 To (V) WA 159806
(10) From (V) AA 243343 To (V) 343944
(11) From (V) 343945 To (V) HA 702830
(12) From (V) HA 702831 To (V) JA 915353
(13) From (V) JA 915354 To (V) LA 939975

Remarks:
(1) Use on vehicles with external fuel pump
(2) Use on vehicles with internal fuel pump
(3) Except heated rear window
(4) heated rear window

DEFENDER	GROUP M	Body Electrics Batteries & Harnesses Harness-Chassis

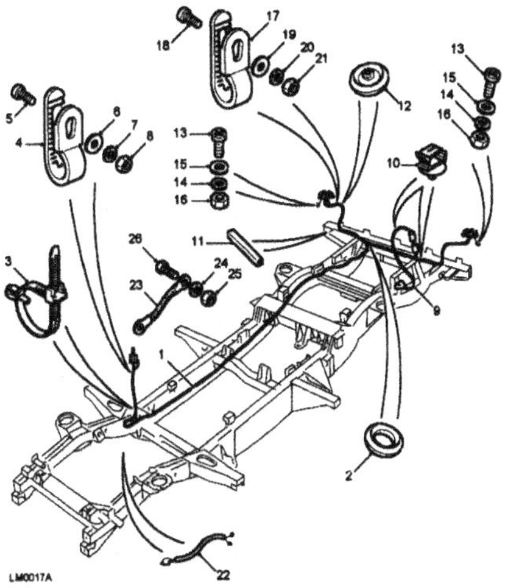

Illus	Part Number	Description	Quantity	Change Point	Remarks
		DEFENDER 90 - FROM XA159807			
1	YMD111210	Harness-chassis	1	Note (1)	Td5
1	YNN000070	Harness-chassis	1	Note (2)	Td5
1	YNN000141	Harness-chassis	1	Note (3)	5 Cylinder Diesel Td5 90" except South Africa
1	YMD111240	Harness-chassis	1	Note (1)	300 TDI
1	YNN000100	Harness-chassis	1	Note (2)	300 TDI
1	YNN000161	Harness-chassis	1	Note (3)	4 Cylinder Diesel Tdi 90" 300 TDI except South Africa
1	YMD111240	Harness-chassis	1	Note (1)	Petrol
1	YNN000100	Harness-chassis	1	Note (2)	Petrol
1	YNN000350	Harness-chassis	1	Note (3)	Td5 South Africa 90"
1	YNN000380	Harness-chassis	1	Note (3)	300 TDI South Africa 90"

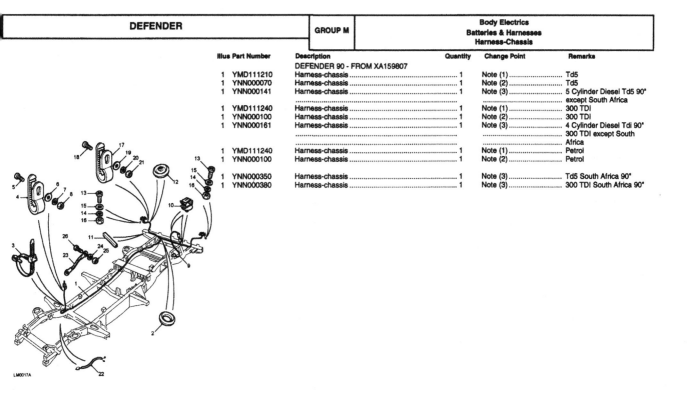

CHANGE POINTS:
(1) From (V) XA 159807 To (V) ZA 612404
(2) From (V) 1A 612404 To (V) 1A 622423
(3) From (V) 2A 622424

Illus	Part Number	Description	Quantity	Change Point	Remarks
		DEFENDER 110 - UP TO LA939975			
		WITHOUT HEATED REAR WINDOW			
1	PRC4970	Harness-chassis	1	Note (1)	
1	PRC7003	Harness-chassis	1	Note (2)	
1	PRC8870	Harness-chassis	1	Note (3)	Petrol
1	PRC8870	Harness-chassis	1	Note (4)	Diesel
1	AMR1491	Harness-chassis	1	Note (5)	Diesel
		REAR WASH WIPE & HEATED REAR WINDOW			
1	PRC4993	Harness-chassis	1	Note (6)	
1	PRC7004	Harness-chassis	1	Note (7)	
1	PRC8869	Harness-chassis	1	Note (3)	Petrol
1	PRC8869	Harness-chassis	1	Note (8)	Diesel
1	AMR1492	Harness-chassis	1	Note (9)	Diesel

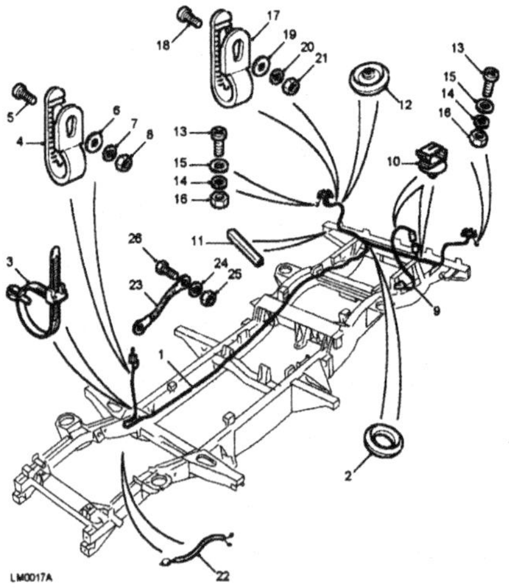

LM0017A

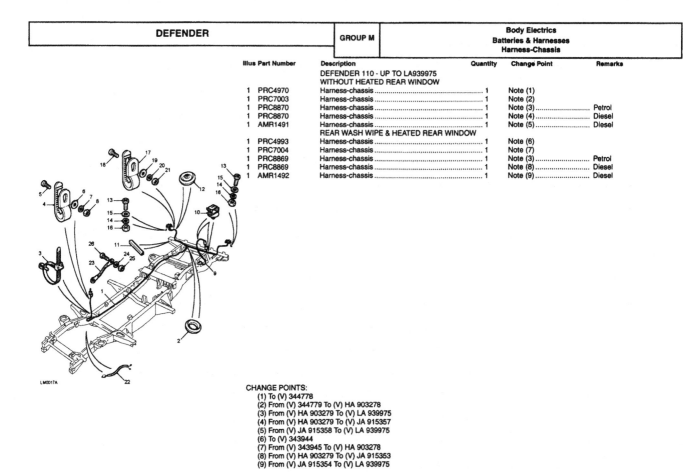

CHANGE POINTS:
(1) To (V) 344778
(2) From (V) 344779 To (V) HA 903278
(3) From (V) HA 903279 To (V) LA 939975
(4) From (V) HA 903279 To (V) JA 915357
(5) From (V) JA 915358 To (V) LA 939975
(6) To (V) 343944
(7) From (V) 343945 To (V) HA 903278
(8) From (V) HA 903279 To (V) JA 915353
(9) From (V) JA 915354 To (V) LA 939975

Illus	Part Number	Description	Quantity	Change Point	Remarks
		DEFENDER 110 - MA939976-WA159806			
		WITHOUT HEATED REAR WINDOW			
1	AMR3448	Harness-chassis	1	Note (1)	Except HICAP
1	AMR5869	Harness-chassis	1	Note (2)	Except HICAP
1	YMD111090	Harness-chassis	1	Note (3)	Except HICAP
		REAR WASH WIPE & HEATED REAR WINDOW			
1	AMR3449	Harness-chassis	1	Note (1)	Except HICAP
1	AMR5870	Harness-chassis	1	Note (2)	Except HICAP
1	YMD111080	Harness-chassis	1	Note (3)	Except HICAP
		HIGH CAPACITY PICK UP			
1	AMR3450	Harness-chassis	1	Note (1)	HICAP
1	AMR5871	Harness-chassis	1	Note (2)	HICAP
1	YMD111100	Harness-chassis	1	Note (3)	HICAP

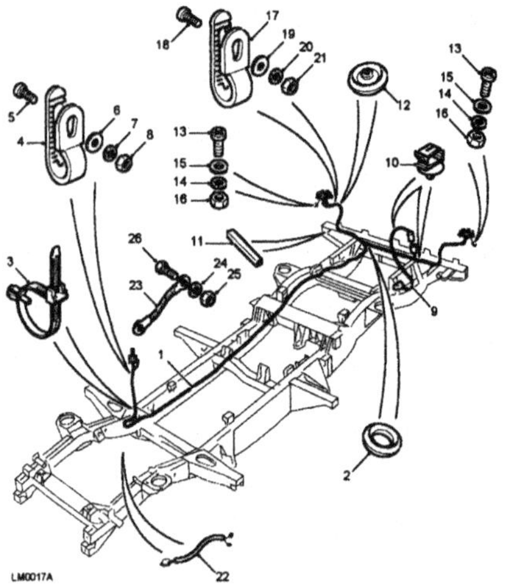

LM0017A

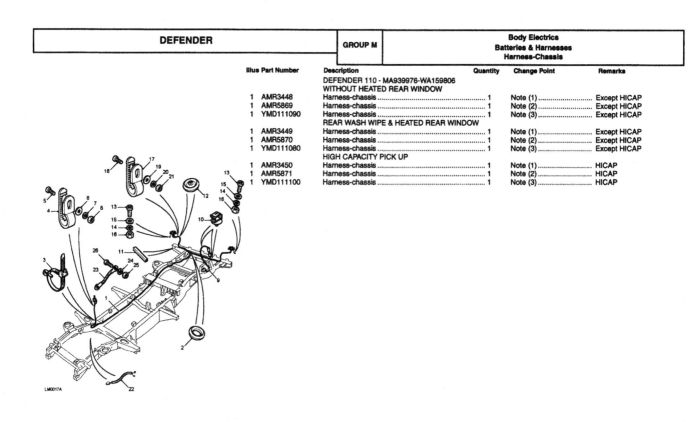

CHANGE POINTS:
(1) From (V) MA 939976 To (V) VA 104805
(2) From (V) VA 104806 To (V) WA 138479
(3) From (V) WA 138480 To (V) WA 159806

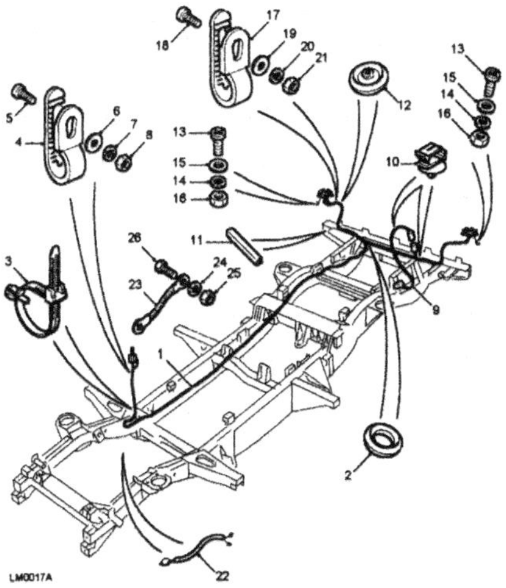

Illus	Part Number	Description	Quantity	Change Point	Remarks
		DEFENDER 110 - FROM XA159807 REGULAR & STATION WAGON			
1	YMD111220	Harness-chassis	1	Note (1)	Td5
1	YNN000080	Harness-chassis	1	Note (2)	Td5
1	YNN000151	Harness-chassis	1	Note (3)	2500 cc 5 Cylinder Diesel Td5 110" except HICAP and South Africa
1	YMD111250	Harness-chassis	1	Note (1)	300 TDI
1	YNN000110	Harness-chassis	1	Note (2)	300 TDI
1	YNN000171	Harness-chassis	1	Note (3)	4 Cylinder Diesel Turbo 110" 300 TDI except HICAP and South Africa
1	YMD111250	Harness-chassis	1	Note (1)	Petrol
1	YNN000110	Harness-chassis	1	Note (2)	Petrol
		HIGH CAPACITY PICK UP			
1	YMD111230	Harness-chassis	1	Note (1)	Td5
1	YNN000090	Harness-chassis	1	Note (2)	Td5
1	YNN000331	Harness-chassis	1	Note (3)	HICAP 2500 cc 5 Cylinder Diesel Td5 110" except South Africa
1	YMD111450	Harness-chassis	1	Note (1)	300 TDI
1	YNN000120	Harness-chassis	1	Note (2)	300 TDI
1	YNN000341	Harness-chassis	1	Note (3)	HICAP 4 Cylinder Diesel 110" 300 TDI except South Africa
1	YMD111450	Harness-chassis	1	Note (1)	Petrol
1	YNN000120	Harness-chassis	1	Note (2)	Petrol
1	YNN000360	Harness-chassis	1	Note (3)	Td5 South Africa
1	YNN000390	Harness-chassis	1	Note (3)	300 TDI South Africa

CHANGE POINTS:
(1) From (V) XA 159807 To (V) ZA 612404
(2) From (V) 1A 612404 To (V) 1A 622423
(3) From (V) 2A 622424

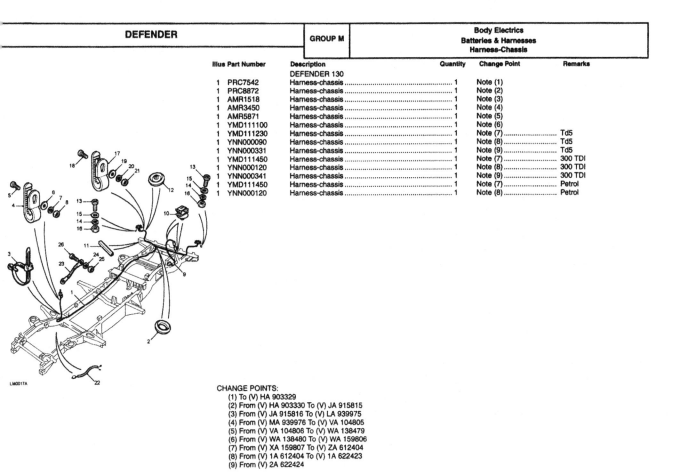

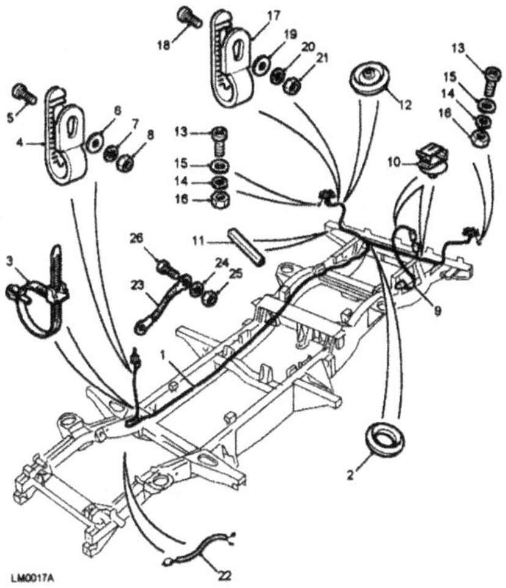

Illus	Part Number	Description	Quantity	Change Point	Remarks
		DEFENDER 130			
1	PRC7542	Harness-chassis	1	Note (1)	
1	PRC8872	Harness-chassis	1	Note (2)	
1	AMR1518	Harness-chassis	1	Note (3)	
1	AMR3450	Harness-chassis	1	Note (4)	
1	AMR5871	Harness-chassis	1	Note (5)	
1	YMD111100	Harness-chassis	1	Note (6)	
1	YMD111230	Harness-chassis	1	Note (7)	Td5
1	YNN000090	Harness-chassis	1	Note (8)	Td5
1	YNN000331	Harness-chassis	1	Note (9)	Td5
1	YMD111450	Harness-chassis	1	Note (7)	300 TDI
1	YNN000120	Harness-chassis	1	Note (8)	300 TDI
1	YNN000341	Harness-chassis	1	Note (9)	300 TDI
1	YMD111450	Harness-chassis	1	Note (7)	Petrol
1	YNN000120	Harness-chassis	1	Note (8)	Petrol

CHANGE POINTS:
(1) To (V) HA 903329
(2) From (V) HA 903330 To (V) JA 915815
(3) From (V) JA 915816 To (V) LA 939975
(4) From (V) MA 939976 To (V) VA 104805
(5) From (V) VA 104806 To (V) WA 138479
(6) From (V) WA 138480 To (V) WA 159806
(7) From (V) XA 159807 To (V) ZA 612404
(8) From (V) 1A 612404 To (V) 1A 622423
(9) From (V) 2A 622424

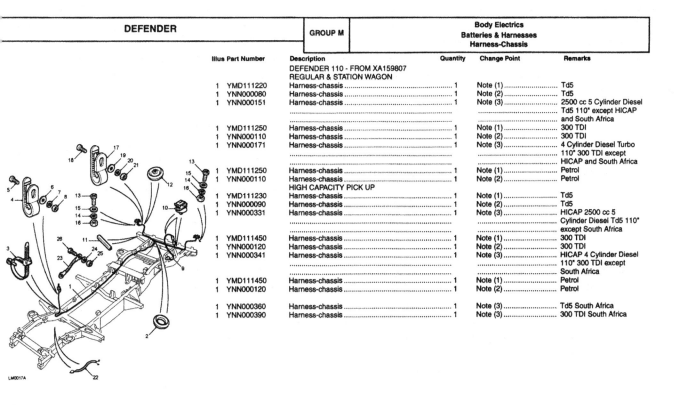

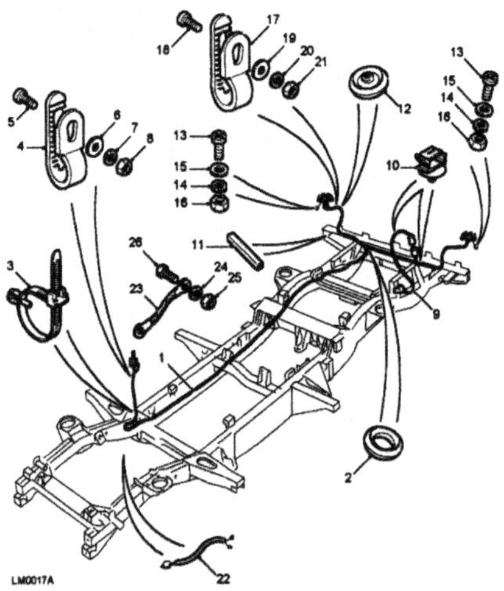

LM0017A

Illus	Part Number	Description	Quantity	Change Point	Remarks
2	589452	Grommet-cable-Black-7 x 53mm	1		
3	AAU3686	Tie-cable-6.5mm hole-8.0 x 155mm	2		
4	C39377L	Clip-p-plastic-adjustable-White.-4.0/12.0mm	1		
5	SE105121L	Screw-pan head-M5 x 12	1		
6	WJ105001L	Washer-plain-M5-oversize	1		
6	WA105001L	Washer-plain-standard-M5	1		50 LE
7	WL105001L	Washer-retaining-M5	1		
8	NH105041L	Nut-hexagonal-M5	1		
9	PRC5602	Harness-fuel tank	1	Note (1)	Petrol 110"
9	PRC7011	Harness-fuel tank	1	Note (2)	
9	PRC9331	Harness-fuel tank	1	Note (3)	
9	AMR1493	Harness-fuel tank-rear	1	From (V) JA 915412	Petrol
9	PRC5544	Harness-fuel tank	1	To (V) 343944	Diesel 110"
9	PRC7012	Harness-fuel tank	1	Note (4)	
9	PRC9332	Harness-fuel tank	1	Note (5)	
9	AMR1494	Harness-fuel tank-rear	1	From (V) JA 915816	Diesel
	RTC6545	Connector harness-to convert PRC5602 where necessary	1		Petrol
10	AFU1090L	Clip-cable-8mm hole	3		
	PRC3537	Clip	1		50 LE

CHANGE POINTS:
(1) To (V) 345778
(2) From (V) 344779 To (V) HA 903305
(3) From (V) HA 903306 To (V) JA 915412
(4) From (V) 343945 To (V) HA 903353
(5) From (V) HA 903354 To (V) JA 915815

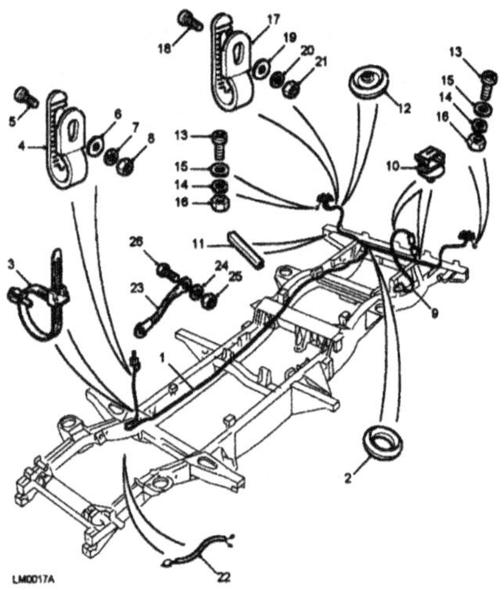

LM0017A

Illus	Part Number	Description	Quantity	Change Point	Remarks
	PRC3537	Clip	1		V8 EFI 50 LE
11	570753	Finisher-edge strip	2		
12	269257	Grommet-cable-Black-6 x 33.5mm	1		
13	SE105121L	Screw-pan head-M5 x 12	2		
14	WM702001L	Washer-spring-3/16 dia-square	2		
15	WA105001L	Washer-plain-standard-M5	2		
16	NH105041L	Nut-hexagonal-M5	2		
17	C393771L	Clip-p-plastic-adjustable-Black-11.0/20.0mm	1		
18	SE105121L	Screw-pan head-M5 x 12	1		
19	WJ105001L	Washer-plain-M5-oversize	1		
19	WA105001L	Washer-plain-standard-M5	2		50 LE
20	WL105001L	Washer-retaining-M5	1		
21	NH105041L	Nut-hexagonal-M5	1		
22	PRC8928	Harness-link-overtemp switch to chassis harness	1	From (V) HA 703223	Except 50 LE
22	PRC8928	Harness-link-overtemp switch to chassis harness	1		50 LE
	AMR2399	Harness extension	1		50 LE
	ERC9404	Bracket harness	2		50 LE
18	FS108161L	Screw-flanged head-M8 x 16	2		50 LE
20	WL108001L	Washer-sprung-M8	1		50 LE
23	RRC8681	Lead-earth bonding	1	From (V) XA 159807	
24	WC108057	Washer-plain-M8	1		
25	NH108041L	Nut-hexagonal head-M8	1		
26	SH108121	Screw-M8	1		

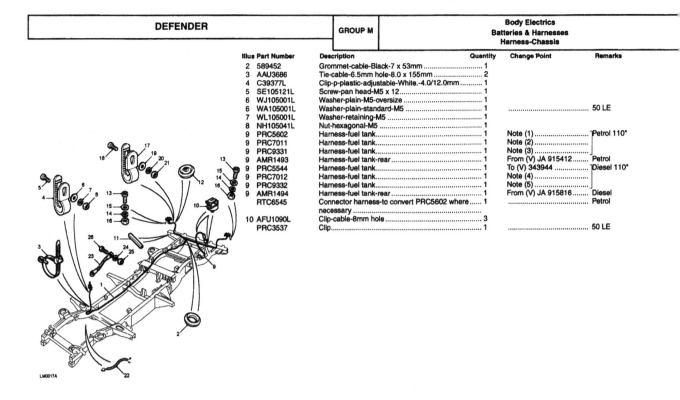

DEFENDER	GROUP M	Body Electrics Batteries & Harnesses Harness-Engine-2.25 Petrol

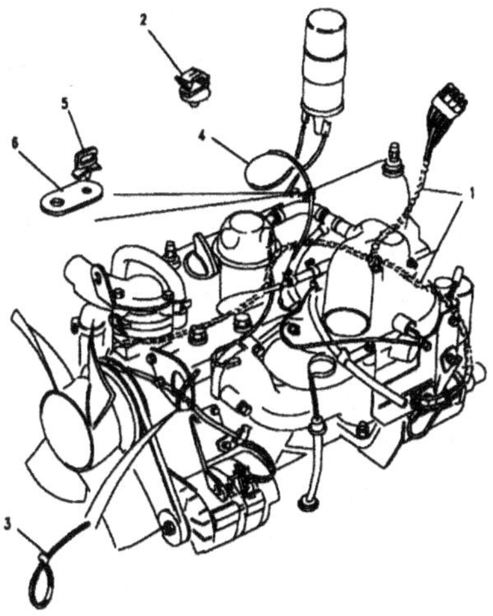

Illus	Part Number	Description	Quantity	Change Point	Remarks
		HARNESS ENGINE			
1	PRC4019	34 amp	1	To (V)11H 05638C	Standard on
1	PRC4020	45 amp	1		Optional
1	PRC4021	65 amp	1		
1	PRC4096	65 amp	1		Air conditioning
1	PRC4785	45 amp	1	From (E)11H 05639c	Standard on
1	PRC4021	65 amp	1		Optional
1	PRC4096	65 amp	1		Air conditioning
2	AFU1090L	Clip-cable-8mm hole	4		
3	RTC3772	Tie-cable-Black-4.8 x 135mm-inside serated	3		
3	568680	Tie-cable-4.8 x 270mm-inside serated	1		
4	PRC4376	Lead-link-solenoid fuel shut off	1		
5	PRC3702	Clip-panel fixing-5mm-4.8mm hole	1		
6	PRC3494	Plate-clips ignition	1		

DEFENDER	GROUP M	Body Electrics Batteries & Harnesses Harness-Engine-2.5 Petrol

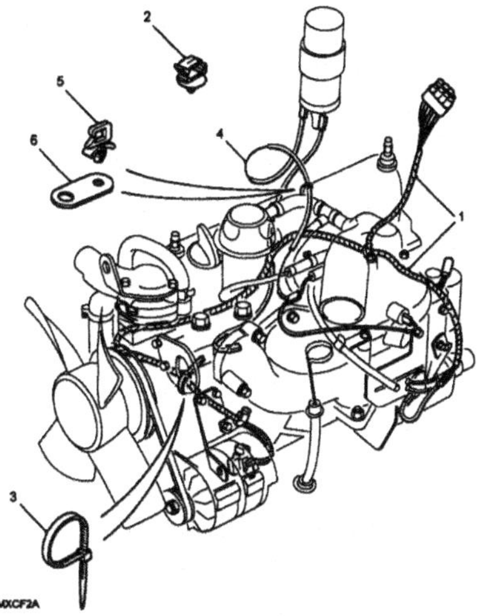

AHMXCF2A

Illus	Part Number	Description	Quantity	Change Point	Remarks
		HARNESS ENGINE			
1	PRC4785	45 amp	1	Note (1)	Standard on
1	PRC4021	65 amp	1		Optional
1	PRC4096	65 amp	1		Air conditioning
1	PRC6080	45 amp	1	Note (2)	Standard on
1	PRC6082	65 amp	1		Optional
1	PRC6081	65 amp	1		Air conditioning
1	PRC6082	65 amp	1	Note (3)	Standard on
1	PRC6081	65 amp	1		Air conditioning
1	AMR2962	65 amp	1	Note (4)	Standard on
1	AMR2982	65 amp	1		Air conditioning
1	AMR4027	65 amp	1	Note (5)	Standard on
1	AMR4029	65 amp	1		Air conditioning
1	AMR4027	65 amp	1	Note (6)	Standard on
1	AMR4849	65 amp	1		Air conditioning
1	YSB105890	Harness engine	1	Note (7)	Except air conditioning
1	YSB105870	Harness engine	1		Air conditioning
2	AFU1090L	Clip-cable-8mm hole	4		
	YQR101600	Clip-harness engine	1	From (V) XA 159807	
3	RTC3772	Tie-cable-Black-4.8 x 135mm-inside serated	2		
3	568680	Tie-cable-4.8 x 270mm-inside serated	1		
4	PRC4376	Lead-link-solenoid fuel shut off	1		
5	PRC3702	Clip-panel fixing-5mm-4.8mm hole	1		
6	PRC3494	Plate-clips ignition	1		

CHANGE POINTS:
(1) To (V) FA 410573
(2) From (V) FA 410574 To (V) KA 922938
(3) From (V) LA 922939 To (V) LA 939975
(4) From (V) MA 939976 To (V) MA 949874
(5) From (V) MA 949875 To (V) MA 965123
(6) From (V) MA 965124 To (V) WA 159806
(7) From (V) XA 159807 To (V) ZA 999999

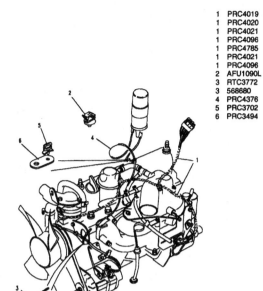

DEFENDER

GROUP M

Body Electrics
Batteries & Harnesses
Harness-Engine-2.8 Petrol

Illus	Part Number	Description	Quantity	Change Point	Remarks
1	2943300	Harness engine	1		
	1744589	Harness-link-low tension ignition coil	1		
	1364507	Clip-cable	1		
	1373669	Clip-cable	1		
	1378529	Clip-cable	1		
	1379136	Clip-cable	1		
	1379351	Clip-cable	1		
	1386642	Clip-cable	1		
	1703531	Cover harness-upper	1		
	1703520	Cover harness-lower	1		
	1703319	Carrier	1		

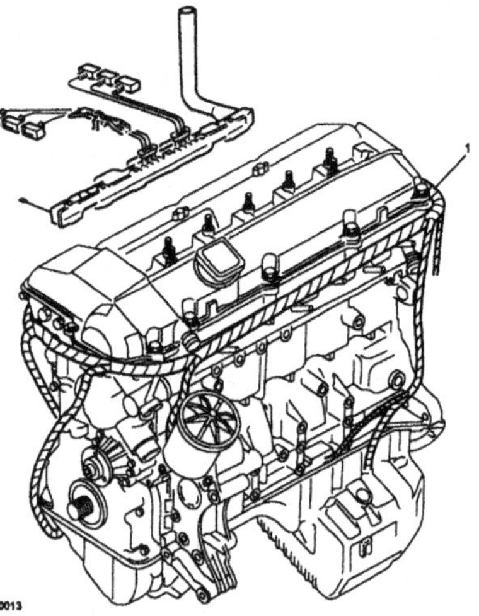

LM0013

DEFENDER

GROUP M

Body Electrics
Batteries & Harnesses
Harness-Engine-V8 Carb

Illus	Part Number	Description	Quantity	Change Point	Remarks
1	PRC4952	Harness engine	1	Note (1)	Note (1) Standard on except air conditioning
1	PRC4954	Harness engine	1	Note (1)	Air conditioning Note (1)
1	PRC4994	Harness engine-45 amp	1	Note (1)	Note (2) Standard on except air conditioning
1	PRC4996	Harness engine-65 amp	1	Note (1)	Note (2) Optional except air conditioning
1	PRC4996	Harness engine-65 amp	1	Note (1)	Air conditioning Note (2)
1	PRC4994	Harness engine-45 amp	1	Note (2)	Standard on except air conditioning
1	PRC5877	Harness engine-65 amp	1		Optional except air conditioning
1	PRC5878	Harness engine-65 amp	1		Air conditioning
1	PRC5877	Harness engine-65 amp	1	Note (3)	Standard on except air conditioning
1	PRC5878	Harness engine-65 amp	1		Air conditioning
1	AMR2959	Harness engine-65 amp	1	Note (4)	Except air conditioning
1	AMR2981	Harness engine-65 amp	1		Air conditioning
1	AMR4023	Harness engine-65 amp	1	Note (5)	Except air conditioning
1	AMR4025	Harness engine-65 amp	1		Air conditioning
1	AMR4023	Harness engine-65 amp	1	Note (6)	Except air conditioning
1	AMR4848	Harness engine-65 amp	1		Air conditioning
1	YSB105900	Harness engine	1	Note (7)	Except air conditioning
1	YSB105880	Harness engine	1		Air conditioning

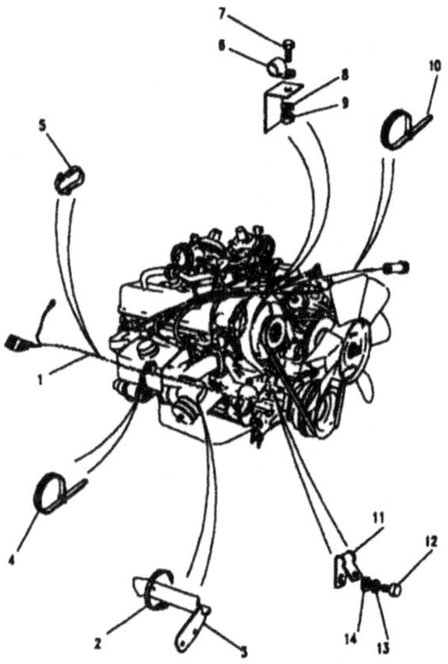

CHANGE POINTS:
(1) To (V) 276551
(2) From (V) 276552 To (V) KA 922938
(3) From (V) LA 922939 To (V) LA 939975
(4) From (V) MA 939976 To (V) MA 949874
(5) From (V) MA 949875 To (V) MA 965123
(6) From (V) MA 965124 To (V) WA 159806
(7) From (V) XA 159807 To (V) ZA 999999

Remarks:
(1) Use on vehicles with external fuel pump
(2) Use on vehicles with internal fuel pump

Illus	Part Number	Description	Quantity	Change Point	Remarks
2	RTC3772	Tie-cable-Black-4.8 x 135mm-inside serated	2		
3	PRC1794	Bracket-support engine cable control	1		
4	568680	Tie-cable-4.8 x 270mm-inside serated	1		
5	AAU3686	Tie-cable-6.5mm hole-8.0 x 155mm	1		
6	CP105061	Clip-p-5mm	1		
7	SH105161L	Screw-hexagonal head-M5 x 16	1		
8	WL105001L	Washer-retaining-M5	1		
9	NH105041L	Nut-hexagonal-M5	1		
10	573246	Tie-cable-Black-4.8 x 115mm-inside serated	2		
11	CP108081L	Clip-p-8mm	1		
12	SH505051L	Screw-hexagonal head-5/16UNC x 5/8	1		
13	WM600051L	Washer-spring-5/16"	1		
14	WA108051L	Washer-8mm	1		
	YQR101600	Clip-harness engine	1	Note (1)	

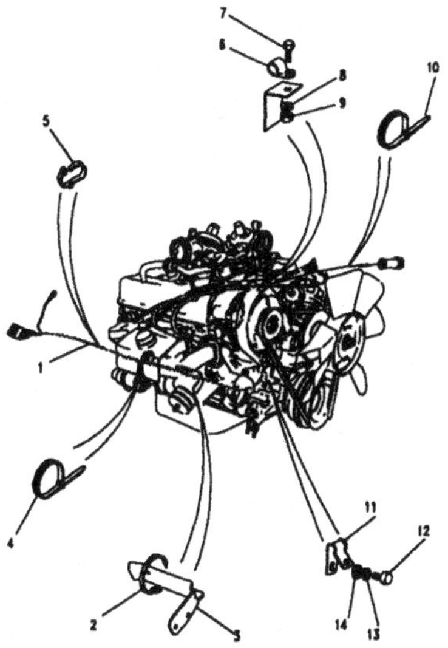

CHANGE POINTS:
(1) From (V) XA 159807

Illus	Part Number	Description	Quantity	Change Point	Remarks
1	YSB106660	Harness engine	1		RHD UK Rest of World
1	YSB106890	Harness engine	1		RHD Japan
1	YSB106660	Harness engine	1		LHD

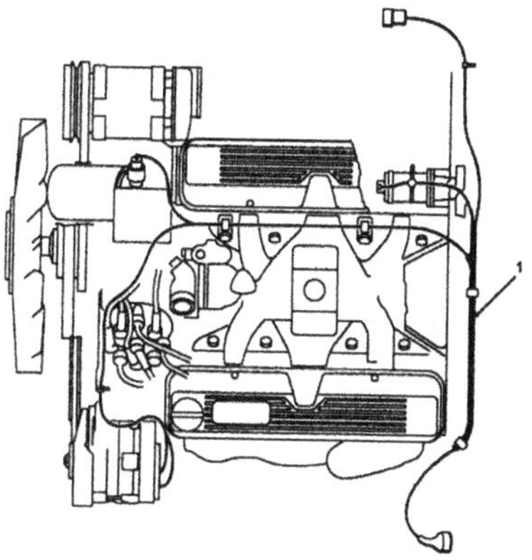

LM0052

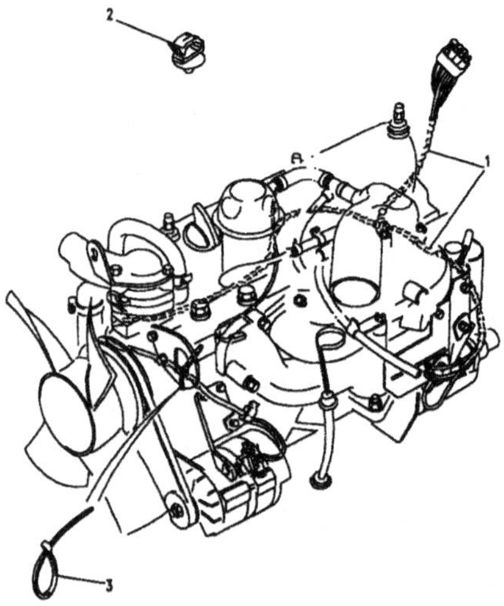

Illus	Part Number	Description	Quantity	Change Point	Remarks
		HARNESS ENGINE			
1	PRC4785	45 amp	1	Note (1)	Standard on
1	PRC4021	65 amp	1		Optional on
1	PRC4096	65 amp	1		Air conditioning
		HARNESS ENGINE			
1	PRC6080	45 amp	1	Note (2)	Standard on
1	PRC6082	65 amp	1		Optional
1	PRC6081	65 amp	1		Air conditioning
		HARNESS ENGINE			
1	PRC6082	65 amp	1	Note (3)	Standard on
1	PRC6081	65 amp	1		Air conditioning
1	AMR2962	65 amp	1	Note (4)	Except air conditioning
1	AMR2982	65 amp	1		Air conditioning
1	AMR4027	65 amp	1	Note (5)	Except air conditioning
1	AMR4029	65 amp	1		Air conditioning
1	AMR4027	65 amp	1	Note (6)	Except air conditioning
1	AMR4849	65 amp	1		Air conditioning
2	AFU1090L	Clip-cable-8mm hole	5		
	YQR101600	Clip-harness engine	1	Note (7)	
3	568680	Tie-cable-4.8 x 270mm-inside serated	1		
3	RTC3772	Tie-cable-Black-4.8 x 135mm-inside serated	2		
	ERC9404	Bracket harness	4		
	ERC9480	Bracket-harness clip to side cover	1		

CHANGE POINTS:
(1) To (V) FA 410573
(2) From (V) FA 410574 To (V) KA 922938
(3) From (V) LA 922939 To (V) LA 939975
(4) From (V) MA 939976 To (V) MA 949874
(5) From (V) MA 949875 To (V) MA 965123
(6) From (V) MA 965124
(7) From (V) XA 159807

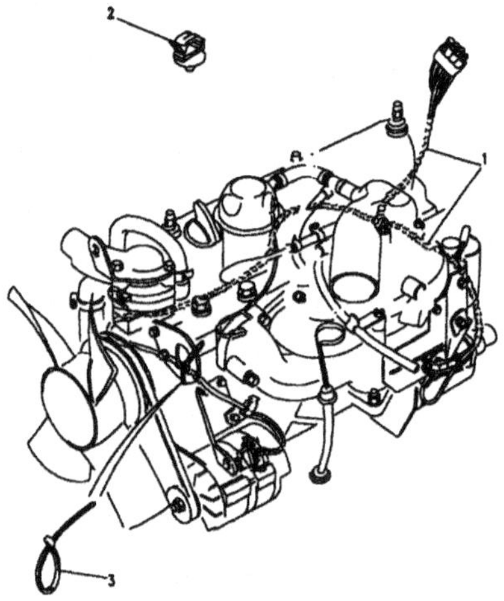

Illus	Part Number	Description	Quantity	Change Point	Remarks
		HARNESS ENGINE			
1	PRC4785	45 amp	1	To (V) FA 410573	Diesel TDi Turbo Standard on except air conditioning
1	PRC4021	65 amp	1		Diesel TDi Turbo Optional except air conditioning
1	PRC4096	65 amp	1		Diesel TDi Turbo air conditioning
1	PRC6080	45 amp	1	From (V) FA 410574 To (V) KA 922938	Diesel TDi Turbo Standard on except air conditioning
1	PRC6082	65 amp	1		Diesel TDi Turbo Optional except air conditioning
1	PRC6081	65 amp	1		Diesel TDi Turbo air conditioning
1	PRC6082	65 amp	1	From (V) LA 922939 To (V) LA 939975	Diesel TDi Turbo Standard on except air conditioning
2	AFU1090L	Clip-cable-8mm hole	5	To (V) MA 962814	Diesel TDi Turbo
3	RTC3772	Tie-cable-Black-4.8 x 135mm-inside serated	2		
3	568680	Tie-cable-4.8 x 270mm-inside serated	1		
	ERC9404	Bracket harness	4	From (V) FA 410574	
	ERC9480	Bracket	1		

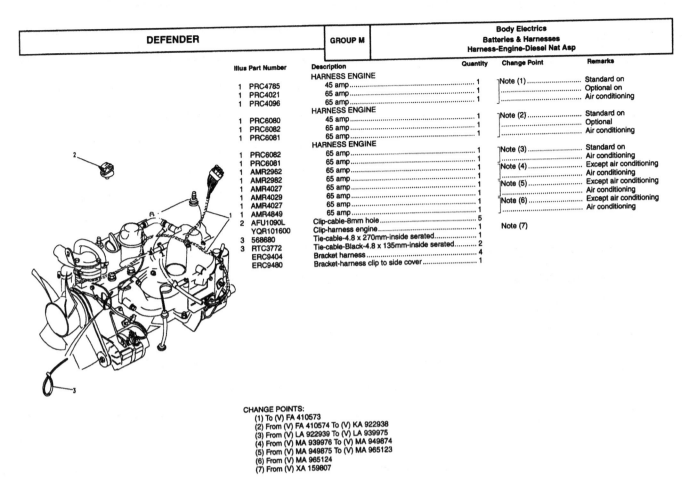

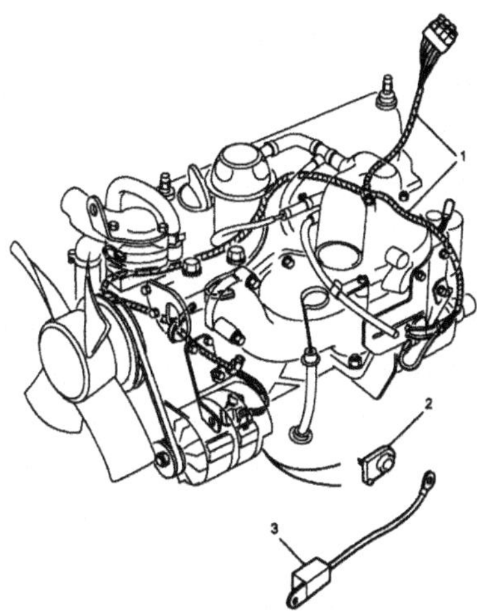

AHMXCF4B

Illus	Part Number	Description	Quantity	Change Point	Remarks
		HARNESS ENGINE			
1	AMR2956	65 amp	1	Note (1)	Standard on
1	AMR2980	65 amp	1		Air conditioning
1	AMR3988	65 amp	1		EGR
1	AMR3987	65 amp	1		EGR air conditioning
1	AMR4019	65 amp	1	Note (2)	Standard on
1	AMR4021	65 amp	1		Air conditioning
1	AMR3988	65 amp	1		EGR
1	AMR3987	65 amp	1		EGR air conditioning
1	AMR4019	65 amp	1	Note (3)	Standard on
1	AMR5415	65 amp	1		Burglar alarm
1	AMR4847	65 amp	1		Air conditioning
1	AMR5416	65 amp	1		Air conditioning burglar alarm
1	AMR3988	65 amp	1		EGR
1	AMR5417	65 amp	1		EGR burglar alarm
1	AMR3987	65 amp	1		EGR air conditioning
1	AMR4019	65 amp	1	Note (4)	Standard on
1	AMR5415	65 amp	1		Burglar alarm
1	AMR4847	65 amp	1		Air conditioning
1	AMR6334	65 amp	1		Air conditioning burglar alarm
1	AMR6661	65 amp	1		EGR
1	AMR5417	65 amp	1		EGR burglar alarm
1	AMR6660	65 amp	1		EGR air conditioning
1	AMR5826	65 amp	1	Note (5)	Burglar alarm Germany
1	AMR6333	65 amp	1		Air conditioning burglar alarm Germany

CHANGE POINTS:
(1) To (V) MA 949874
(2) From (V) MA 949875 To (V) MA 965123
(3) From (V) MA 965124 To (V) VA 107822
(4) From (V) VA 107823 To (V) WA 159806
(5) From (V) TA 977537 To (V) WA 159806

Illus	Part Number	Description	Quantity	Change Point	Remarks
1	YSB106140	Harness engine	1	Note (1)	Non EGR except air conditioning
1	YSB106130	Harness engine	1		Non EGR air conditioning
1	YSB107810	Harness engine	1		TDi EGR air conditioning immobilisation
2	AMR4042	Unit-protection-phase tap-820 ohm	1		EGR
3	AMR4043	Suppressor	1		
	YQR101600	Clip-harness engine	1	Note (1)	

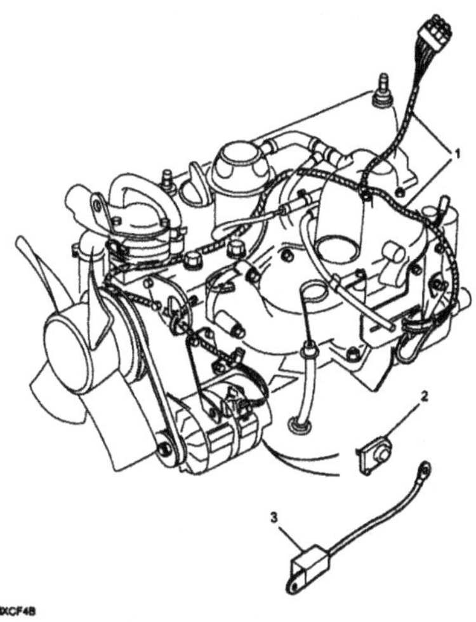

AHMXCF4B

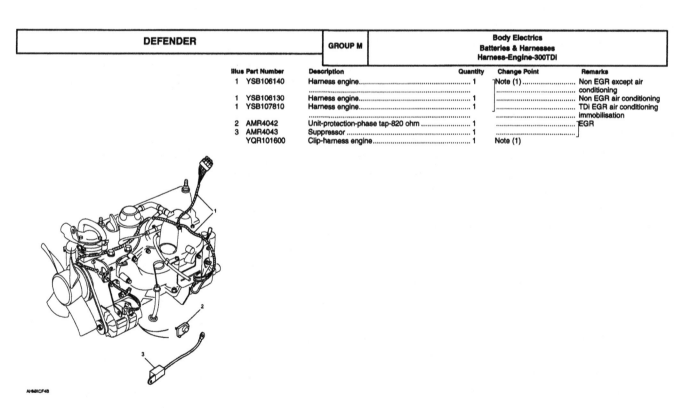

CHANGE POINTS:
(1) From (V) XA 159807

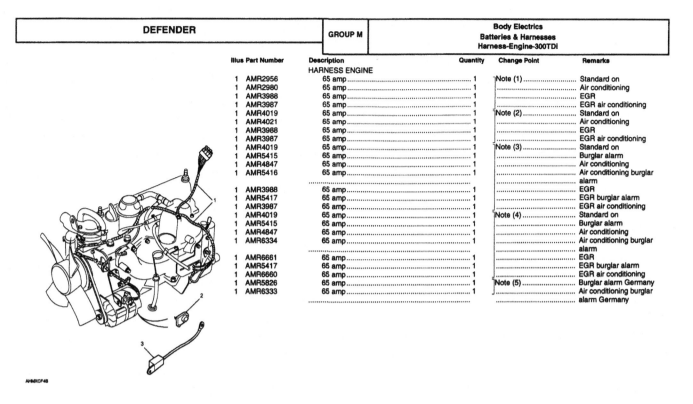

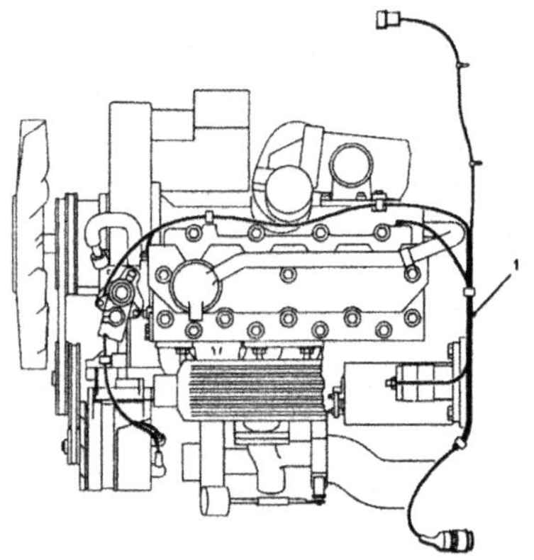

LM0053

Illus	Part Number	Description	Quantity	Change Point	Remarks
1	YSB106902	Harness engine	1	Note (1)	Except air conditioning
1	YSB106901	Harness engine	1		Air conditioning
1	YSB000880	Harness engine	1	Note (2)	Except EGR and air conditioning
1	YSB000860	Harness engine	1		EGR except air conditioning
1	YSB000870	Harness engine	1		Air conditioning except EGR
1	YSB000850	Harness engine	1		EGR air conditioning
2	YSU100520	Bracket-harness engine	2		
3	YQR101600	Clip-harness engine	1		

CHANGE POINTS:
(1) To (V) 1A 622423
(2) From (V) 2A 622424

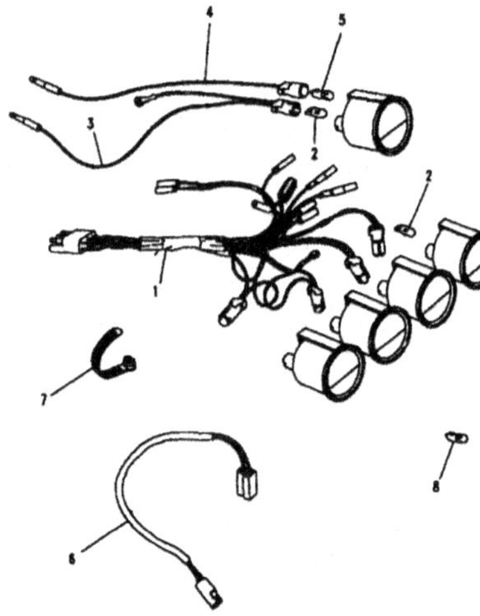

Illus	Part Number	Description	Quantity	Change Point	Remarks
1	PRC7326	HARNESS INSTRUMENT PACK	1	Note (1)	
1	PRC8410	HARNESS INSTRUMENT PACK	1	Note (2)	
1	AMR2625	HARNESS INSTRUMENT PACK	1	Note (3)	
1	AMR3101	HARNESS INSTRUMENT PACK	1	Note (4)	
2	RTC6164	• Bulb-12V-2W	NLA		Use AMR3339.
2	AMR3339	Bulb-12V-2W			
3	PRC7329	HARNESS SUPPLEMENTARY-ADDITIONAL INSTRUMENT	1	To (V) MA 962814	
3	AMR2475	HARNESS SUPPLEMENTARY-VOLT METER	1		
2	RTC6164	• Bulb-12V-2W	NLA		Use AMR3339.
2	AMR3339	Bulb-12V-2W			
4	PRC7060	HARNESS & HOLDER & BULBS INSTRUMENT PACK	1	Note (5)	
4	AMR3444	HARNESS & HOLDER & BULBS INSTRUMENT PACK	1	Note (6)	
4	AMR1647	HARNESS & HOLDER & BULBS INSTRUMENT PACK-CLOCK	1	Note (4)	
5	503352	• Bulb-281-ba7s-2 Watt	1		
6	PRC4318	Lead-brake pad wear warning indicator	1	To (V) MA 962814	
7	C45099	Tie-cable	A/R		
8	573289	Bulb-504-w10/3-3 Watt-air con controls	A/R		
	PRC3095	Harness-link-PDWA switch	1		
		GERMANY ONLY			
	PRC5316	LEAD-LINK-SOLENOID FUEL SHUT OFF	1	To (V) 270226	Germany
	PRC5685	LEAD-LINK-SOLENOID FUEL SHUT OFF	1	From (V) 270227 To (V) MA 962814	
	PRC7894	• Diode	NLA		
	YWB10032L	Relay-changeover-Green	1	To (V) MA 962814	
	AB608031L	Screw-self tapping-No 8 x 3/8	1		
	WA105001L	Washer-plain-standard-M5	1		

CHANGE POINTS:
(1) To (V) FA 450332
(2) From (V) FA 450333 To (V) KA 929567
(3) From (V) KA 929568 To (V) LA 939975
(4) From (V) MA 939976
(5) From (V) 319167 To (V) LA 936689
(6) From (V) LA 936690 To (V) LA 939975

DEFENDER	GROUP M	Body Electrics Batteries & Harnesses Harness-Instrument-From (V) MA939976

Illus	Part Number	Description	Quantity	Change Point	Remarks
1	AMR3101	HARNESS INSTRUMENT PACK	1	Note (1)	
2	RTC6164	• Bulb-12V-2W	NLA		Use AMR3339.
2	AMR3339	Bulb-12V-2W			
		HARNESS INSTRUMENT PACK			
1	AMR5716	Harness instrument pack	1	Note (1)	6 Cylinder
1	YMG109260	with clock	1	Note (2)	4 Cylinder Petrol
1	YMG109260	with clock	1		300 TDI
1	YMG109260	with clock	1		V8 Petrol
1	YMG109280	with clock	1		Td5
1	YMG109270	with tachometer	1		Except Td5
1	YMG111630	with tachometer	1		Td5
2	AMR1647	HARNESS & HOLDER & BULBS INSTRUMENT PACK-CLOCK	1	Note (1)	
2	503352	• Bulb-281-ba7s-2 Watt	1		

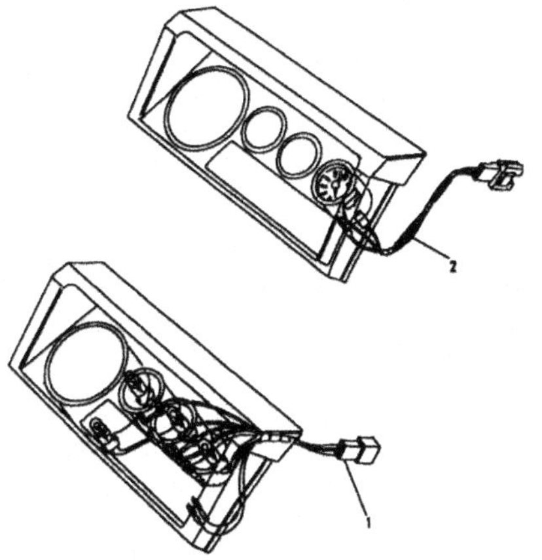

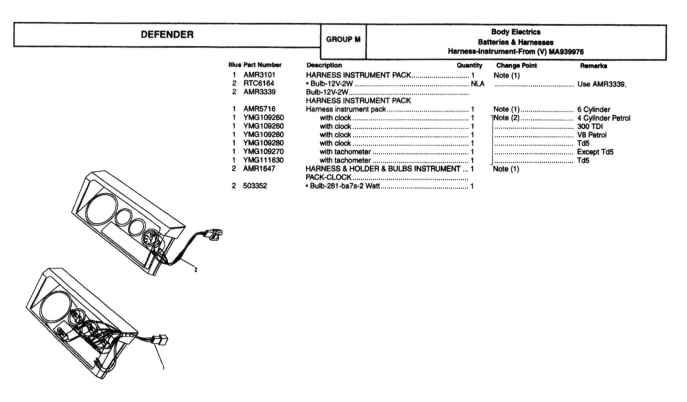

CHANGE POINTS:
(1) From (V) MA 939976 To (V) WA 159806
(2) From (V) XA 159807

DEFENDER	GROUP M	Body Electrics Batteries & Harnesses Harness-Door Front

Illus	Part Number	Description	Quantity	Change Point	Remarks
1	YMM000251	Harness front door	1	Note (1)	Driver CDL except electric windows
1	YMM000271	Harness front door	1	Note (1)	Driver electric windows except CDL
1	YMM000291	Harness front door	1	Note (1)	Driver electric windows CDL
1	YMM000261	Harness front door	1	Note (1)	Passenger CDL except electric windows
1	YMM000281	Harness front door	1	Note (1)	Passenger electric windows except CDL
1	YMM000321	Harness front door	1	Note (1)	Passenger electric windows CDL
2	14A7081L	Plug-blanking	2	Note (1)	Except electric windows and CDL

NOT ILLUSTRATED
PAS ILLUSTREE
NICHT ILLUSTRIERT
SENZA IL DISEGNO
SIN EL DISENO
SEM ILLUSTRACAO
NIET AFGEBEELD

TF 0007

CHANGE POINTS:
(1) From (V) 2A 622424

Harness-Door Rear

Illus	Part Number	Description	Quantity	Change Point	Remarks
1	YMM000351	Harness rear door-rear side	2	Note (1)	CDL
2	YMM000331	Harness-link-rear passenger doors.	1	Note (1)	Station Wagon except CDL
2	YMM000341	Harness-link-rear passenger doors.	1	Note (1)	Station Wagon CDL

NOT ILLUSTRATED
PAS ILLUSTREE
NICHT ILLUSTRIERT
SENZA IL DISEGNO
SIN EL DISENO
SEM ILLUSTRACAO
NIET AFGEBEELD

TF 0007

CHANGE POINTS:
(1) From (V) 2A 622424

Harness-Tailgate

Illus	Part Number	Description	Quantity	Change Point	Remarks
1	PRC4591	Harness-rear end door	1	Note (1)	Heated rear window
1	PRC6290	Harness-rear end door	1	Note (2)	
1	AMR3677	Harness-rear end door	1	Note (3)	
1	YMN000021	Harness-rear end door	1	Note (4)	Heated rear window high mounted stop light rear wash/wipe except CDL
1	YMN000031	Harness-rear end door	1		Heated rear window CDL high mounted stop light rear wash/wipe
1	YMN000081	Harness-rear end door	1		CDL except heated rear window and high mounted stop light and rear wash/wipe

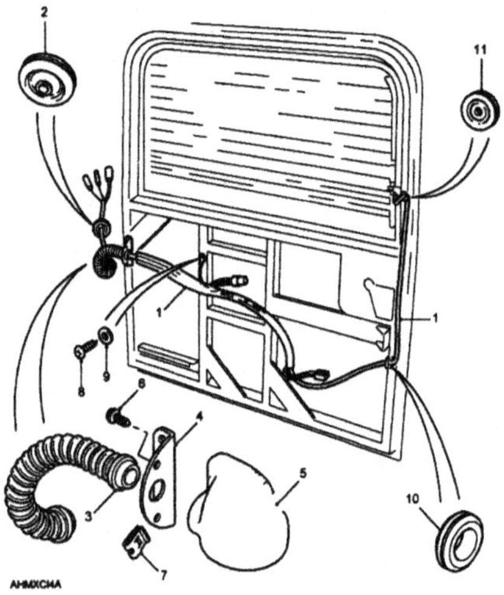

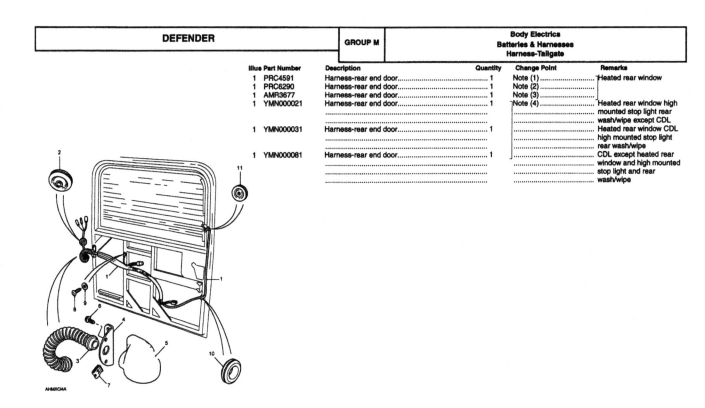

CHANGE POINTS:
(1) To (V) 270226
(2) From (V) 270227 To (V) MA 965105
(3) From (V) MA 965106 To (V) ZA 999999
(4) From (V) 2A 622424

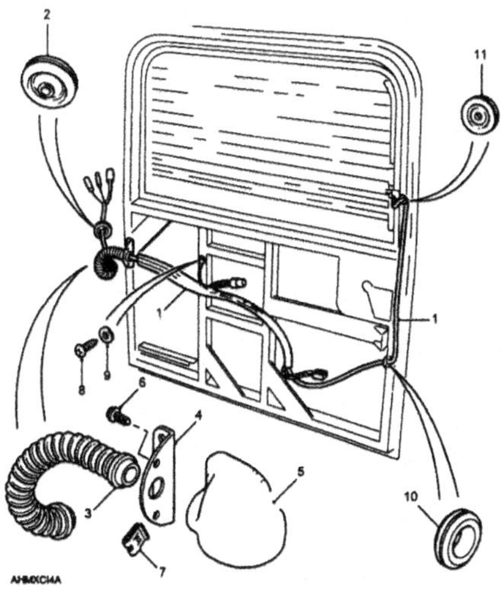

AHMXCI4A

Illus	Part Number	Description	Quantity	Change Point	Remarks
2	BMK1714	Grommet-harness doors	1		Heated rear window
3	PRC4471	Grommet-harness doors-Convolute	1	Note (1)	
3	AMR3963	Grommet-harness doors-Convolute	1	Note (2)	
4	MTC9914	Bracket	1		
5	MTC9915	Cover-grommet-mounting bracket-Black	1	Note (3)	
5	MTC9915LCS	Cover-grommet-mounting bracket-Slate Grey	1	Note (4)	
6	AA606044L	Screw-with rear wash/wipe	2	Note (5)	
7	AK606011L	Nut-spring-flat-with rear wash/wipe	2		
8	AB610041L	Screw-self tapping AB-M8 x 12	1		
9	WA105001L	Washer-plain-standard-M5	1		
		GROMMET			
10	3H822L	lower	1	Note (6)	Heated rear window
10	BHA5131L	lower	1	Note (7)	
11	27H5311	upper	1	Note (6)	
11	235113	Grommet	1	Note (7)	

CHANGE POINTS:
(1) To (V) MA 951244
(2) From (V) MA 951245
(3) To (V) EA 314173
(4) From (V) EA 314174
(5) To (V) MA 962814
(6) To (V) 270226
(7) From (V) 270227

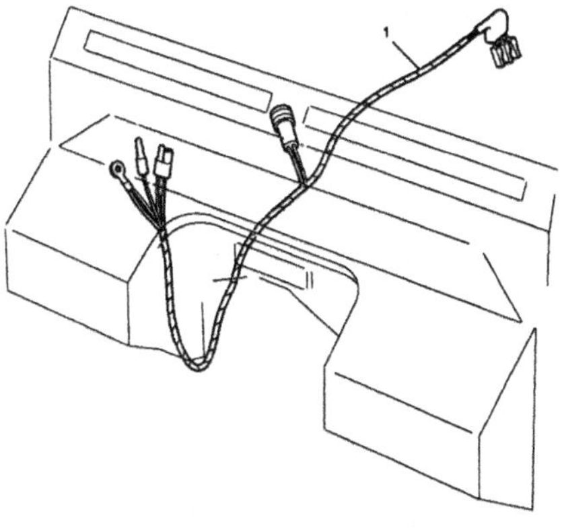

AHMXCE2A

O.P. PUBLICATIONS

Illus	Part Number	Description	Quantity	Change Point	Remarks
		HARNESS-FUEL TANK			
1	PRC5604	with in-tank fuel pump	1	From (V) AA 243343	Petrol
				To (V) 345761	
1	PRC7001	with in-tank fuel pump	1	From (V) 345762	
				To (V) HA 703459	
1	PRC9330	with in-tank fuel pump	1	From (V) HA 703460	
				To (V) LA 939975	
1	AMR3042	with in-tank fuel pump	1	From (V) MA 939976	
1	PRC5601	with in-tank fuel pump	1	From (V) AA 243343	Diesel
				To (V) 343944	
1	PRC7009	with in-tank fuel pump	1	From (V) 343945	
				To (V) HA 702795	
1	PRC9333	with in-tank fuel pump	1	From (V) HA 702796	
				To (V) LA 939975	
1	AMR3041	with in-tank fuel pump	1	From (V) MA 939976	
3	PRC7851	Harness fuel control box	1	From (V) FA 392009	
				To (V) FA 404682	
4	AB608031L	Screw-self tapping-No 8 x 3/8	1		
5	WA105001L	Washer-plain-standard-M5	1		
6	YWB10032L	Relay-changeover-Green	1		
7	PRC5680	Control unit daytime running lamps	1	From (V) 270227	Norway
8	AB608031L	Screw-self tapping-No 8 x 3/8	2		
9	WA105001L	Washer-plain-standard-M5	2		
10	YWB10032L	Relay-changeover-Green	4		
11	PRC6083	Cable-heater plug ignition	1	Note (1)	
12	568680	Tie-cable-4.8 x 270mm-inside serated	5		

CHANGE POINTS:
(1) From (V) HA 455946

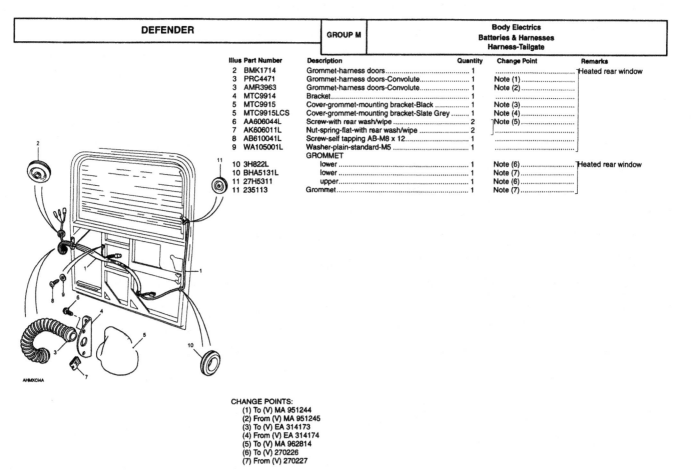

DEFENDER	GROUP M	Body Electrics Batteries & Harnesses Harness-Twin Fuel Tanks

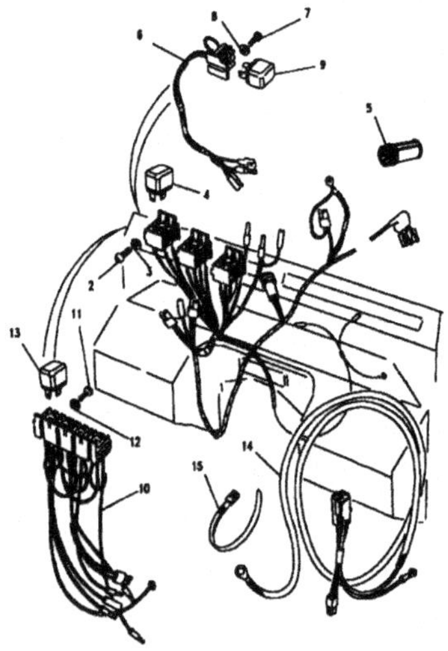

Illus	Part Number	Description	Quantity	Change Point	Remarks
1	PRC5600	Harness-fuel tank-twin tank	1	Note (1)	Petrol 110"
1	PRC7002	Harness-fuel tank-twin tank	1	Note (2)	
1	PRC7867	Harness-fuel tank-twin tank	1	Note (3)	
1	PRC9327	Harness-fuel tank-twin tank	1	Note (4)	
1	AMR2972	Harness-fuel tank-twin tank	1	Note (5)	
1	AMR5530	Harness-fuel tank-twin tank	1	Note (6)	
1	AMR2972	Harness-fuel tank-twin tank	1	Note (5)	Petrol 130"
1	AMR5530	Harness-fuel tank-twin tank	1	Note (6)	
1	PRC5603	Harness-fuel tank-twin tank	1	Note (1)	Diesel 110"
1	PRC7022	Harness-fuel tank-twin tank	1	Note (7)	
1	PRC9329	Harness-fuel tank-twin tank	1	Note (8)	
1	AMR2973	Harness-fuel tank-twin tank	1	Note (9)	
1	AMR2973	Harness-fuel tank-twin tank	1		Diesel 130"
2	AB608047L	Screw-relay base-self tapping-No 8 x 1/2	2		
3	WA105001L	Washer-relay base-plain-standard-M5	2		
4	YWB10032L	Relay-changeover-Green	2		
5	RTC6545	Connector harness-to convert PRC5602 where necessary	1		
6	PRC7851	Harness fuel control box	1	Note (10)	
7	AB608031L	Screw-self tapping-No 8 x 3/8	1		
8	WA105001L	Washer-plain-standard-M5	1		
9	YWB10032L	Relay-changeover-Green	1		
10	PRC5680	Control unit daytime running lamps	1		Norway
11	AB608031L	Screw-self tapping-No 8 x 3/8	2		
12	WA105001L	Washer-plain-standard-M5	2		
13	YWB10032L	Relay-changeover-Green	4		
14	PRC6083	Cable-heater plug ignition	1	From (V) HA 455946	
15	568680	Tie-cable-4.8 x 270mm-inside serated	5		

CHANGE POINTS:
(1) To (V) 343944
(2) From (V) 343945 To (V) 392146
(3) From (V) 392147 To (V) HA 903698
(4) From (V) HA 903699 To (V) LA 939975
(5) From (V) MA 939976 To (V) TA 976209
(6) From (V) TA 976210
(7) From (V) 343945 To (V) HA 903353
(8) From (V) HA 903354 To (V) LA 939975
(9) From (V) MA 939976
(10) From (V) 392009 To (V) FA 404682

DEFENDER	GROUP M	Body Electrics Batteries & Harnesses Harness-Air Conditioning-To (V) MA962814

Illus	Part Number	Description	Quantity	Change Point	Remarks
1	PRC4208	HARNESS-COOLING FAN-AIR CONDITIONING	1	To (V) FA 424037	
2	AAU5034	• Diode-cooling fan harness-Pektron	1		
1	PRC7277	HARNESS-COOLING FAN-AIR CONDITIONING	1	From (V) FA 424038 To (V) HA 903558	
2	AAU5034	• Diode-cooling fan harness-Pektron	1		
1	PRC9324	HARNESS-COOLING FAN-AIR CONDITIONING	1	From (V) HA 903559 To (V) LA 939975	
2	AAU5034	• Diode-cooling fan harness-Pektron	1		
3	AMR2976	HARNESS AIR CONDITIONING-FASCIA	1	From (V) MA 939976	
2	AAU5034	• Diode-cooling fan harness-Pektron	1		
3	PRC3905	Harness air conditioning	1	To (V) GA 455945	
3	PRC9325	Harness air conditioning	1	From (V) HA 455946 To (V) LA 939975	
3	AMR2977	HARNESS AIR CONDITIONING-WING	1	From (V) MA 939976	
2	AAU5034	• Diode-air conditioning harness-Pektron	1		

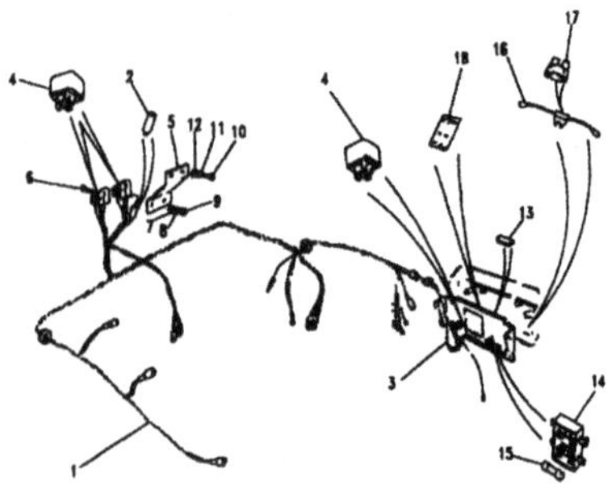

Illus	Part Number	Description	Quantity	Change Point	Remarks
		RELAY			
4	YWB10032L	blower fan-changeover-Green	1	To (V) HA 703459	
4	YWB10032L	condenser fan-changeover-Green	1		
4	YWB10032L	compressor clutch-changeover-Green	1		
4	YWB10027L	a/c blower fan	1	From (V) HA 703460	
4	YWB10027L	a/c condenser fans	1		
4	YWB10027L	a/c compressor clutch	1		
		BRACKET SUPPORT (NO LONGER SERVICED)			
6	SE105121L	Screw-pan head-M5 x 12	2		
7	WA105001L	Washer-plain-standard-M5	2	To (V) MA 962814	
8	WL105001L	Washer-retaining-M5	2		
9	NM105011	Nut-hexagonal	2		
10	SE105121L	Screw-pan head-M5 x 12	2		
11	WA105001L	Washer-plain-standard-M5	2		
12	WL105001L	Washer-retaining-M5	2		
13	DRC1530	Protector-edge	A/R		
14	PRC3737	Fusebox assembly passenger compartment	1	To (V) FA 424037	
15	RTC4510	Fuse-condenser fan-35 amp	1		
15	RTC4500	Fuse-compressor clutch-10 amp	1		
16	PRC4311	LINK-FUSIBLE-IN LINE	1	To (V) MA 962814	
17	RTC4507	• Fuse-30 amp-auto-standard	1		
18	PRC4306	Label-fusebox	1	To (V) FA 424037	

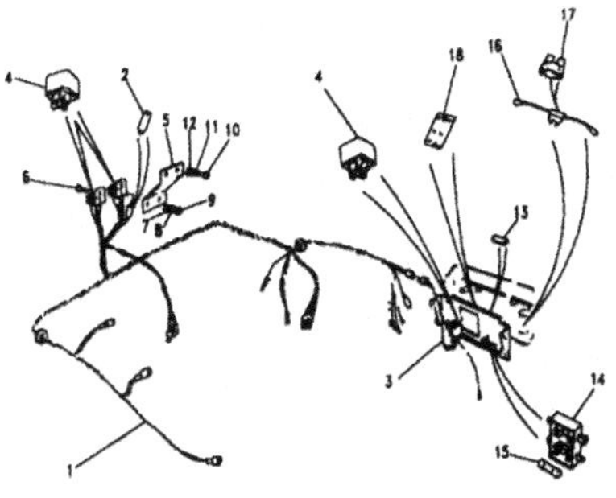

Illus	Part Number	Description	Quantity	Change Point	Remarks
		ALL AIR CONDITIONED VEHICLES			
1	AMR2976	HARNESS AIR CONDITIONING-DASH-FASCIA	1	From (V) MA 939976 To (V) MA 965123	
1	AMR5137	HARNESS AIR CONDITIONING-DASH	1	From (V) MA 965124 To (V) VA 130782	
1	YMF101130	HARNESS AIR CONDITIONING-DASH	1	From (V) VA 130783	
3	AAU5034	• Diode-Pektron	1		
2	AMR2977	HARNESS AIR CONDITIONING-WING-UNDER/BONNET-WING	1	From (V) MA 939976	
3	AAU5034	• Diode-Pektron	1		
		RELAY			
4	YWB10027L	a/c blower fan	1	From (V) MA 962815	
4	YWB10027L	a/c condenser fans	1		
4	YWB10027L	a/c compressor clutch	1		
5	PRC4311	LINK-FUSIBLE-AIR CONDITIONING-IN LINE	1	To (V) MA 965123	
6	RTC4507	• Fuse-30 amp-auto-standard	1		

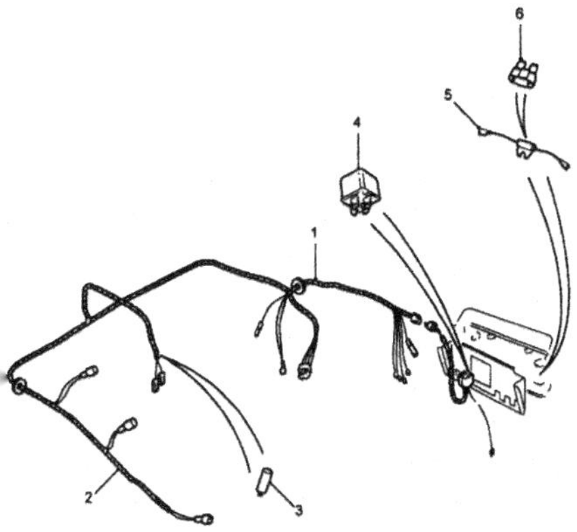

AHMXCE3A

Illus	Part Number	Description	Quantity	Change Point	Remarks
1	AEU1747	Resistor-air conditioning	1		
2	RTC7454	Relay-air conditioning	1		
3	MUC1676	Harness-air conditioning-relay	1		
4	MUC1678	Solenoid-vacuum blower-heater	1		
5	MUC1672	Harness air conditioning	1		
6	MUC1677	Harness-link-lighting	1		

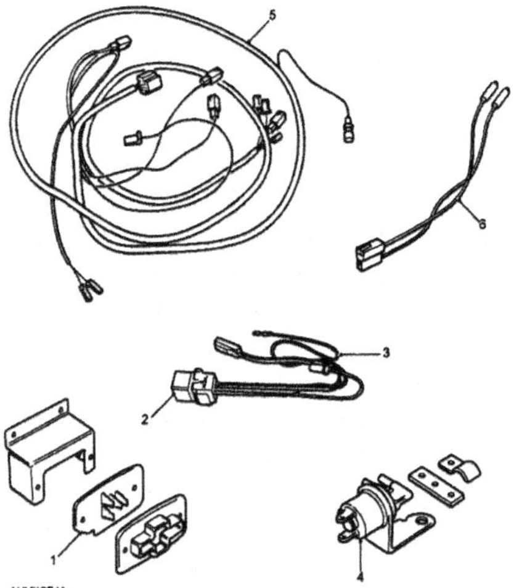

AHMXCE4A

Illus	Part Number	Description	Quantity	Change Point	Remarks
1	PRC4021	Harness engine-65 amp	1		4 Cylinder
1	PRC4953	Harness engine	1	Note (1)	V8
1	PRC4995	Harness engine	1	Note (2)	V8
2	PRC4092	Diode	1	Note (3)	
3	FS108207L	Screw-fixing bracket-flanged head-M8 x 20	2		Split charge
4	WA108001	Washer-plain-fixing bracket-8mm	2	Note (3)	
5	WL108001L	Washer-sprung-M8	2	Note (3)	
6	FN108041L	Nut-flange-M8	NLA	Note (3)	Use FN108047L.
7	PRC4083	Lead link-terminal post to diode	1	Note (3)	Split charge
8	PRC4084	Harness-link-diode to battery	1	Note (3)	
9	PRC4085	Lead-link-diode to terminal box	1	Note (3)	
10	531604	Bracket	1	Note (3)	
11	532736	Terminal connector-plus	1	Note (3)	
12	525569	Terminal connector-minus	1	Note (3)	
13	AR608031L	Screw-self tapping-No 8 x 3/8-long	6	Note (3)	
14	WE703081	Washer	6	Note (3)	
15	SE106201L	Screw-earth-pan head-M6 x 20	1		
16	WL106001L	Washer-sprung-M6	1		
17	NH106041L	Nut-hexagonal-nyloc-M6	1	Note (3)	
18	PRC7100	Post-terminal	1	Note (3)	
20	3830L	Washer-plain	2		
21	575014	Washer-spring	2	Note (3)	
22	90575015	Nut	2	Note (3)	
23	PRC2978	Bracket	1	Note (3)	V8
24	PRC3247	Bracket	1	Note (3)	4 Cylinder
25	FS106167L	Screw-flanged head-flanged head-M6 x 16	2		
26	WA106041L	Washer-6mm	2	Note (3)	
27	WL106001L	Washer-sprung-M6	1		
28	NH106041L	Nut-hexagonal-nyloc-M6	1	Note (3)	
29	PRC3180	Clip-pipe-single	1		
30	13H9157	Clip-pipe-double	5		V8
30	13H9157	Clip-pipe-double	3		4 Cylinder

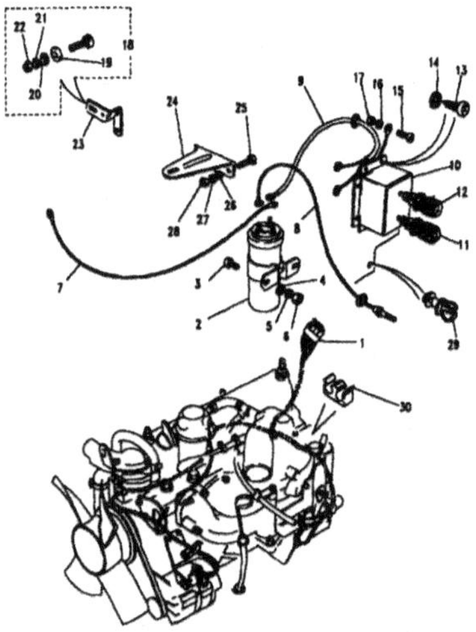

CHANGE POINTS:
(1) To (V) AA 243342
(2) From (V) AA 243343 To (V) DA 310168
(3) To (V) DA 310168

Illus	Part Number	Description	Quantity	Change Point	Remarks
		HARNESS ENGINE			
1	PRC5879	65 amp	1		Note (1)
1	PRC5880	65 amp	1		Note (2)
1	PRC5877	65 amp	1		Note (3)
1	PRC5878	65 amp	1		Note (4)
1	PRC6082	65 amp	1		4 Cylinder
1	PRC5877	65 amp	1		V8 except air conditioning
1	PRC5878	65 amp	1		V8 air conditioning
2	PRC5724	Cable-split charge	1	Note (1)	
2	AMR2350	Cable-split charge	1	Note (2)	
2	AMR3135	Cable-split charge	1	Note (3)	
3	ASU1151	Relay	1	To (V) LA 939975	
3	AMR3324	Relay-33RA w/proof assy	1	From (V) MA 939976 To (V) MA 962814	
4	PRC5723	Bracket	1	To (V) MA 962814	
5	PRC4427	Switch-volt sensitive-45 amp	1	From (V) 270227 To (V) LA 939975	
5	AMR3325	Switch-volt sensitive	1	From (V) MA 939976 To (V) MA 962814	
6	PRC4795	Bracket-relay mounting	1	From (V) 270227 To (V) MA 962814	
7	RA610123	Rivet-pop-aluminium	2		
8	AMR2351	Harness-link-volt sensitive switch	1	From (V) KA 922209 To (V) LA 939975	
9	PRC7100	Post-terminal	1	To (V) DA 310168	
10	PRC7173	Plate-retaining	1	To (V) MA 962814	
11	PRC5003	Cover-terminal post	1		
12	NH104041L	Nut-hexagonal-M4	2		
13	WA704061	Washer	2		
14	SE104161L	Screw-M8 x 16	2		

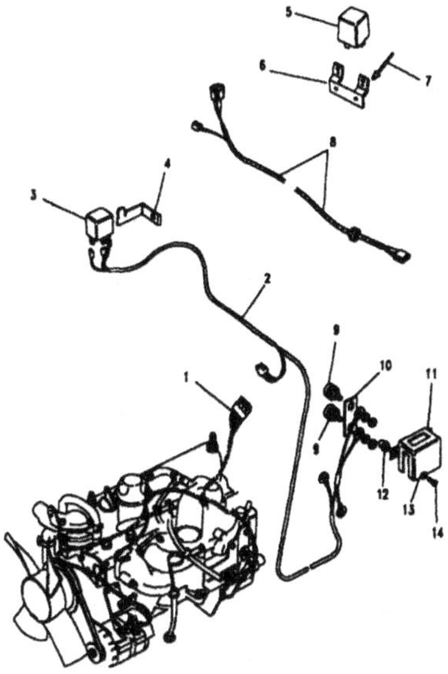

CHANGE POINTS:
(1) To (V) KA 922208
(2) From (V) KA 922209 To (V) LA 939975
(3) From (V) MA 939976 To (V) MA 962814

Remarks:
(1) 4 Cylinder Except air conditioning
(2) 4 Cylinder air conditioning
(3) V8 Except air conditioning
(4) V8 air conditioning

Illus	Part Number	Description	Quantity	Change Point	Remarks
2	AMR3135	Cable-split charge	1	From (V) MA 939976	Split charge
3	AMR3324	Relay-33RA w/proof assy	1		
4	AMR3325	Switch-volt sensitive	1		
5	PRC4795	Bracket-relay mounting	1	From (V) 270227	
6	RA610123	Rivet-pop-aluminium	2		
7	PRC7100	Post-terminal	2	From (V) MA 962815	
8	PRC7173	Plate-retaining	1		
9	PRC5003	Cover-terminal post	1		
10	NH104041L	Nut-hexagonal-M4	2		
11	WA704061	Washer	2		
12	SE104161L	Screw-M8 x 16	2		

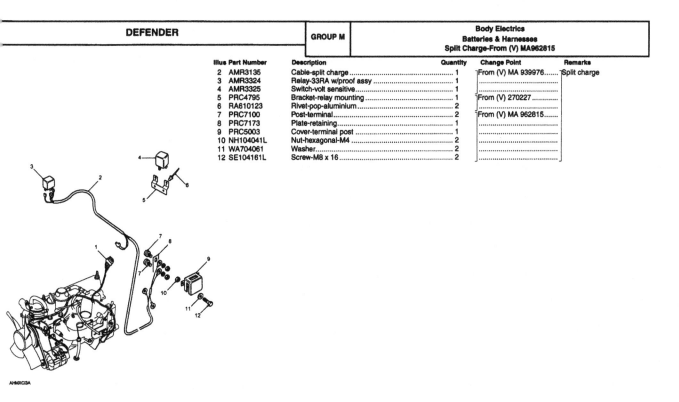

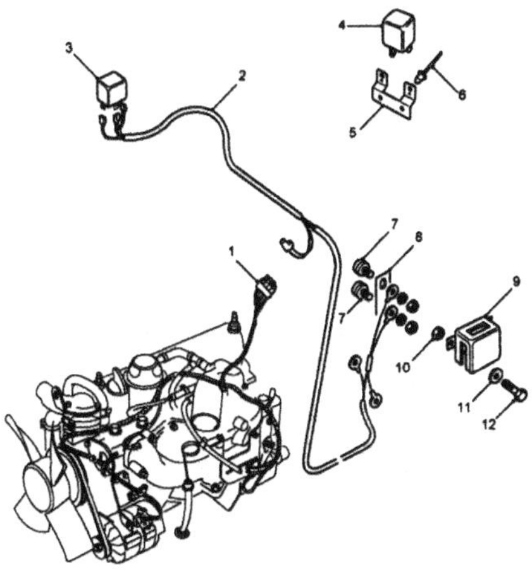

AHMXCI3A

DEFENDER	GROUP M	Body Electrics Batteries & Harnesses Harness Auxiliary

Illus	Part Number	Description	Quantity	Change Point	Remarks
1	STC61820	Harness-supplementary-auxiliary lighting-lower	1	Note (1)	Tomb Raider
2	STC61867	Harness-supplementary-auxiliary lighting-upper	1	Note (1)	Tomb Raider
3	PYD100010	Tie-cable	4	Note (1)	Tomb Raider

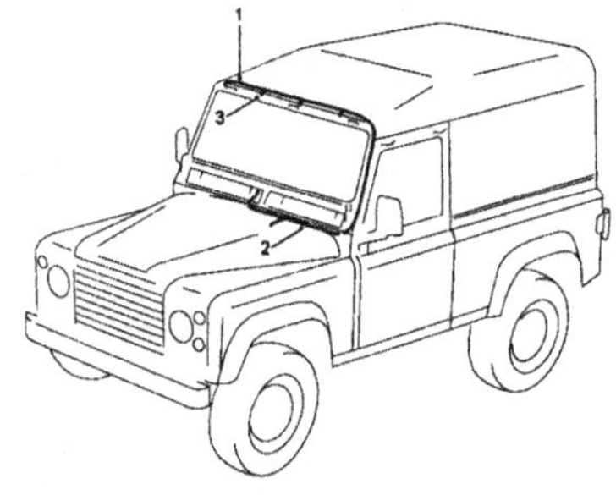

LM0142A

CHANGE POINTS:
(1) From (V) 1A 612404

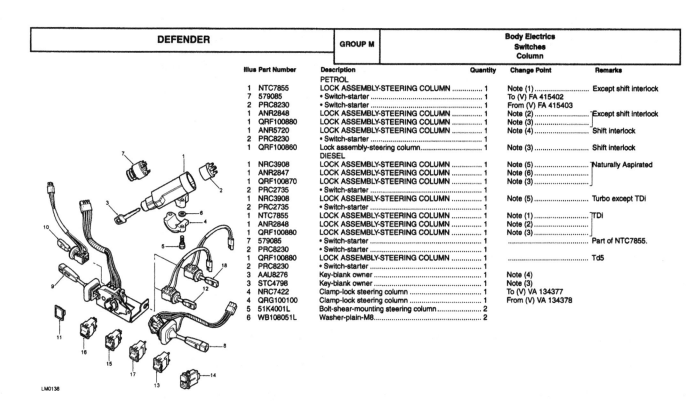

DEFENDER	GROUP M	Body Electrics Switches Column

Illus	Part Number	Description	Quantity	Change Point	Remarks
		PETROL			
1	NTC7855	LOCK ASSEMBLY-STEERING COLUMN	1	Note (1)	Except shift interlock
7	579085	• Switch-starter	1	To (V) FA 415402	
2	PRC8230	• Switch-starter	1	From (V) FA 415403	
1	ANR2848	LOCK ASSEMBLY-STEERING COLUMN	1	Note (2)	Except shift interlock
1	QRF100880	LOCK ASSEMBLY-STEERING COLUMN	1	Note (3)	
1	ANR5720	LOCK ASSEMBLY-STEERING COLUMN	1	Note (4)	Shift interlock
2	PRC8230	• Switch-starter	1		
1	QRF100860	Lock assembly-steering column	1	Note (3)	Shift interlock
		DIESEL			
1	NRC3908	LOCK ASSEMBLY-STEERING COLUMN	1	Note (5)	Naturally Aspirated
1	ANR2847	LOCK ASSEMBLY-STEERING COLUMN	1	Note (6)	
1	QRF100870	LOCK ASSEMBLY-STEERING COLUMN	1	Note (3)	
2	PRC2735	• Switch-starter	1		
1	NRC3908	LOCK ASSEMBLY-STEERING COLUMN	1	Note (5)	Turbo except TDi
2	PRC2735	• Switch-starter	1		
1	NTC7855	LOCK ASSEMBLY-STEERING COLUMN	1	Note (1)	TDi
1	ANR2848	LOCK ASSEMBLY-STEERING COLUMN	1	Note (2)	
1	QRF100880	LOCK ASSEMBLY-STEERING COLUMN	1	Note (3)	
7	579085	• Switch-starter	1		Part of NTC7855.
2	PRC8230	• Switch-starter	1		
1	QRF100880	LOCK ASSEMBLY-STEERING COLUMN	1		Td5
2	PRC8230	• Switch-starter	1		
3	AAU8276	Key-blank owner	1	Note (4)	
3	STC4798	Key-blank owner	1	Note (3)	
4	NRC7422	Clamp-lock steering column	1	To (V) VA 134377	
4	QRG100100	Clamp-lock steering column	1	From (V) VA 134378	
5	51K4001L	Bolt-shear-mounting steering column	2		
6	WB108051L	Washer-plain-M8	2		

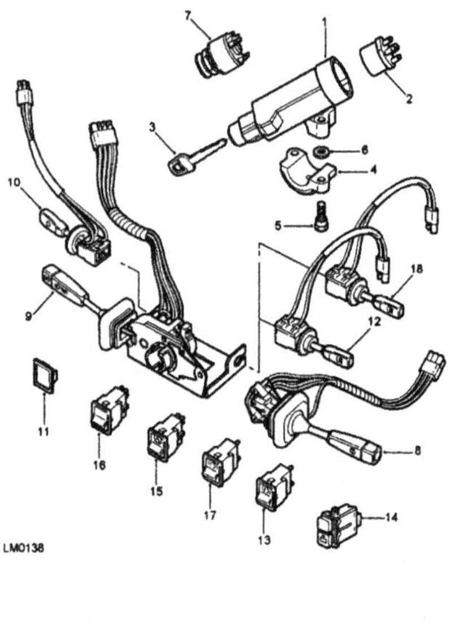

LM0138

CHANGE POINTS:
(1) To (V) LA 932973
(2) From (V) LA 932974 To (V) VA 134377
(3) From (V) VA 134378
(4) To (V) VA 134377
(5) To (V) LA 932971
(6) From (V) LA 932972 To (V) VA 134377

DEFENDER	GROUP M	Body Electrics Switches Column

Illus	Part Number	Description	Quantity	Change Point	Remarks
7	551508	Switch-starter-without steering column lock	1		Petrol
	395141	Lock & keys	1		
7	PRC2734	Switch-starter-without steering column lock	1		Diesel
	RTC3022	Lock & keys-1 barrel/2 keys	1		
8	PRC3900	Switch-wash/wipe windscreen	1	To (V) GA 455945	
8	PRC7370	Switch-wash/wipe windscreen	1	Note (1)	
8	AMR6106	Switch-wash/wipe windscreen	1	From (V) VA 104806	
9	PRC3875	Switch-indicator/horn/ headlamp dip	1	To (V) GA 455945	
9	STC439	Switch-indicator/horn/ headlamp dip	1	Note (1)	
9	AMR6105	Switch-indicator/horn/ headlamp dip	1	Note (2)	
9	XPB101290	Switch-indicator/horn/ headlamp dip	1	From (V) WA 138480	
10	PRC3430	Switch master lighting	1	To (V) VA 104805	
10	AMR6104	Switch master lighting	1	From (V) VA 104806	
11	CZH3827L	Plug-blanking	3	To (V) FA 414356	
11	AAM222L	Plug-blanking	3	Note (3)	

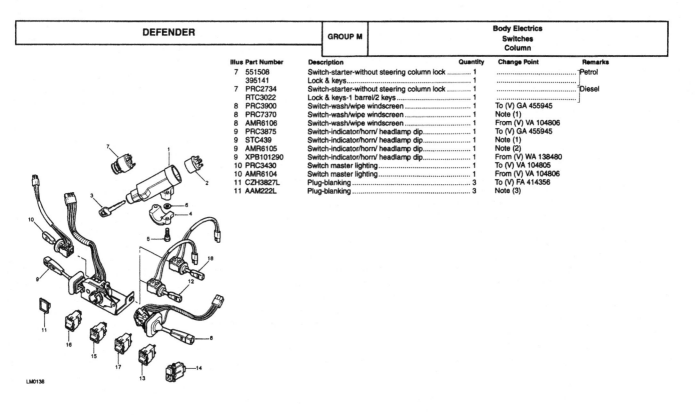

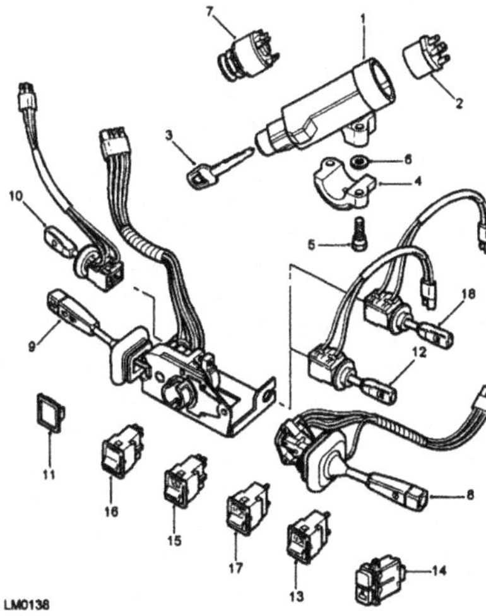
LM0138

CHANGE POINTS:
(1) From (V) HA 455946 To (V) VA 104805
(2) From (V) VA 104806 To (V) WA 138479
(3) From (V) FA 414357

DEFENDER	GROUP M	Body Electrics Switches Column

Illus	Part Number	Description	Quantity	Change Point	Remarks
12	PRC3432	Switch-rear fog lamps	1	To (V) MA 949743	
13	ASU1009	Switch-rocker hazard-24V	1	To (V) WA 138479	
13	YUF101490	Switch-rocker hazard-24V	1	From (V) WA 138480	
14	ADU4791	Switch-rear fog lamp rocker	1	Note (1)	
14	AMR5085	Switch-rear fog lamp rocker	1	Note (2)	
14	YUF101640	Switch-rear fog lamp rocker	1	From (V) WA 138480	
15	AMR6328	Switch-push push fog-rear-one touch	1	Note (3)	
16	YUE100530	Switch-rear fog momentary	1	From (V) WA 138480	
17	C38637L	Switch-fuel changeover	A/R		
18	STC61821	Switch auxiliary-lamp	1	Note (4)	Tomb Raider
	PRC5537	Label-fuel changeover	1		110"
	589511	Switch-accessory push push-non-illuminated	A/R		Police
	PRC2497	Switch-contact courtesy light	1	To (V) GA 455945	
	PRC7371	Switch-contact courtesy light	1	Note (5)	
	PRC5679	Harness interior light	1	Note (6)	
	PRC8470	Harness interior light	1	Note (7)	
	AMR2449	Harness interior light	1	Note (8)	
	STC61851	Bracket-mounting	1	Note (4)	Tomb Raider

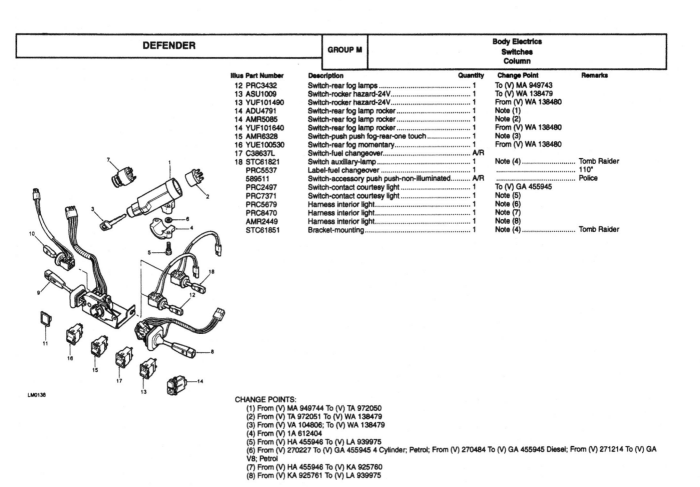

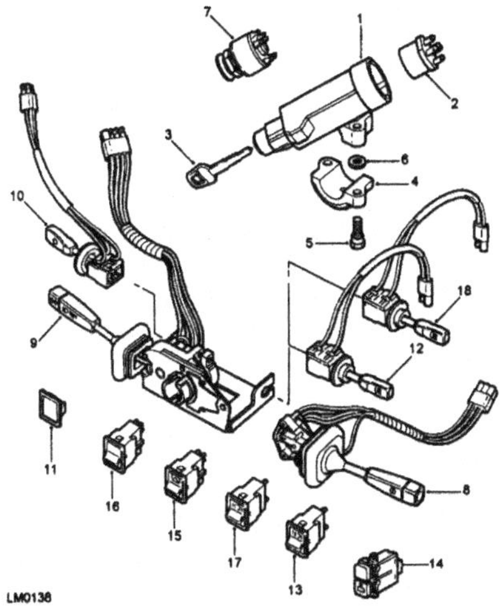
LM0138

CHANGE POINTS:
(1) From (V) MA 949744 To (V) TA 972050
(2) From (V) TA 972051 To (V) WA 138479
(3) From (V) VA 104806; To (V) WA 138479
(4) From (V) 1A 612404
(5) From (V) HA 455946 To (V) LA 939975
(6) From (V) 270227 To (V) GA 455945 4 Cylinder; Petrol; From (V) 270484 To (V) GA 455945 Diesel; From (V) 271214 To (V) GA V8; Petrol
(7) From (V) HA 455946 To (V) KA 925760
(8) From (V) KA 925761 To (V) LA 939975

Body Electrics
Switches
Facia Assembly-From (V) 2A000001

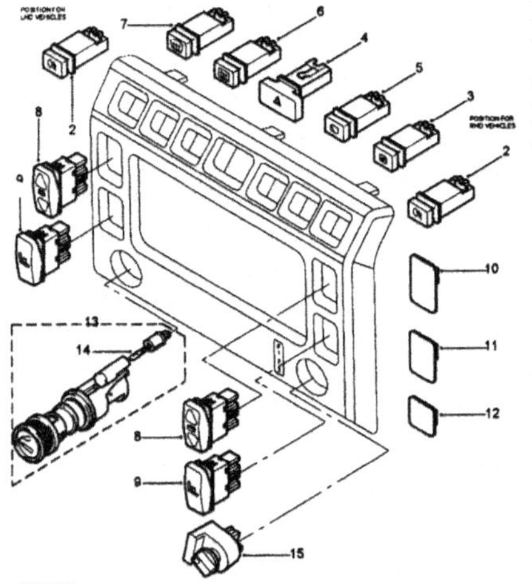

LM0115B

Illus	Part Number	Description	Quantity	Change Point	Remarks
1	YUG000540LNF	Switch-push push fog-front	1	Note (1)	
2	YUG000530LNF	Switch-rear fog lamps	1	Note (1)	
3	YUE000070LNF	Switch-rear wash-momentary	1	Note (1)	
4	YUG000180LNF	Switch-push push hazard-12V	1	Note (1)	
5	YUG000350LNF	Switch-rear wipe push push	1	Note (1)	
6	YUG000470LNF	Switch-push push heated rear window	1	Note (1)	
7	YUG000460LNF	Switch-push push heated windscreen	1	Note (1)	
8	YUF101520LNF	Switch-rocker electric window lift	2	Note (1)	
9	YUG102430LNF	Switch assembly-push push seat-heat	2	Note (1)	
10	YXJ000020LNF	Blank-facia switch	2	Note (1)	
11	YXB100000LNF	Blank assembly-facia switch-electric window lift	2	Note (1)	
12	FBV000070PMA	Blank assembly-facia switch-less headlamp levelling	1	Note (1)	
13	YUJ100650	CIGAR LIGHTER FACIA	1		
14	RTC3635	• Bulb-wedge illumination-12V-1.2 Watt	1		
15	AMR5874	Switch assembly-rotary headlamp leveling	1		90"
15	AMR5875	Switch assembly-rotary headlamp leveling	1		Except 90"

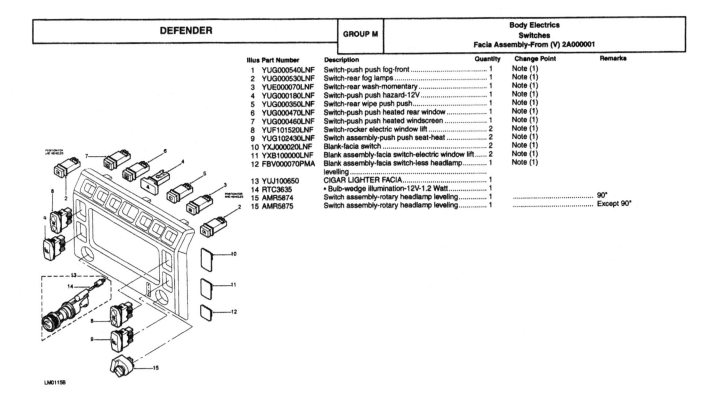

CHANGE POINTS:
(1) From (V) 2A 622424

Body Electrics
Switches
Auxiliary

Illus	Part Number	Description	Quantity	Change Point	Remarks
1	AWR6158LRV	Moulding assembly-facia switch panel	1		
2	EEP118L	Switch assembly-push push heated rear window/cruise	1		
3	EEP119L	Switch-rear wipe push push	1		
4	EEP120L	Switch-rear wash-momentary	1		
5	AFU1897	Fastener-drive-Grey	2		
6	DA610044	Screw-flanged head-No 10 x 1/2	2		
7	STC873	Bulb-illumination	3		

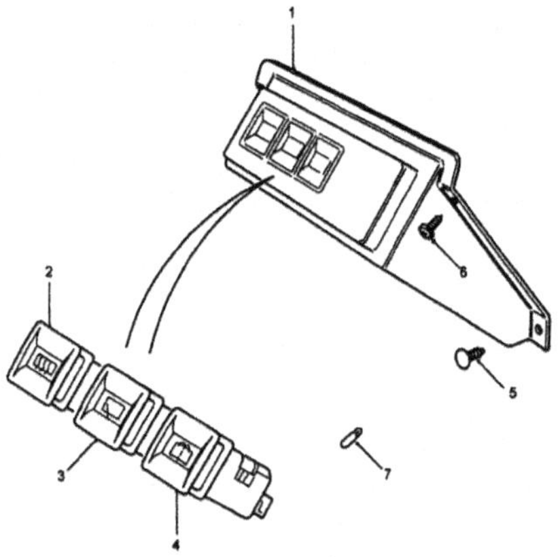

AMMXEC8A

DEFENDER

GROUP M — Body Electrics / Fuse Box / Under Bonnet

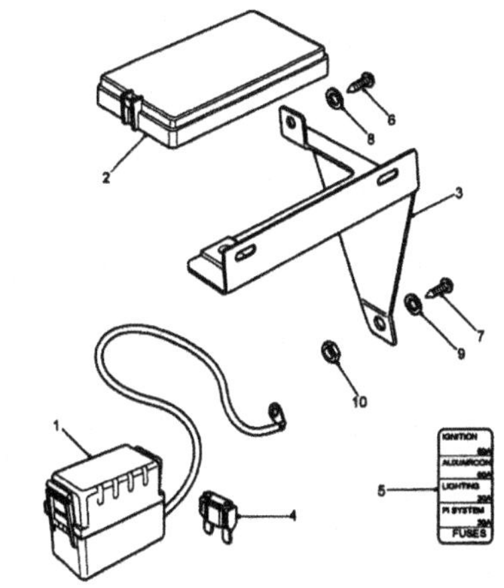

AKMXCC4A

Illus	Part Number	Description	Quantity	Change Point	Remarks
1	AMR1637	Fusebox assembly engine compartment	1	From (V) MA 939976	V8
1	AMR2983	Fusebox assembly engine compartment	1	To (V) MA 953003	4 Cylinder
		FUSEBOX ASSEMBLY ENGINE COMPARTMENT			
1	AMR1637	with long lead to starter motor	1	From (V) MA 953004	V8 except air conditioning
1	AMR1637	with long lead to starter motor	1		LHD V8 air conditioning
1	AMR1637	with long lead to starter motor	1		RHD 4 Cylinder air conditioning
1	AMR2983	with long lead to starter motor	1		4 Cylinder except air conditioning
1	AMR2983	with long lead to starter motor	1		LHD 4 Cylinder air conditioning
1	AMR2983	with long lead to starter motor	1		RHD V8 air conditioning
2	AMR5710	Cover fusebox	1		
2	YQH100940	Cover fusebox	1		50 LE
3	AMR5711	Bracket fusebox	1		Except 6 Cylinder and EFi
3	YQU104670	Bracket fusebox	1		50 LE
3	2943350	Bracket fusebox	1		6 Cylinder
		FUSE			
4	YQG10007	heated rear window-20 amp-maxi-Yellow..	A/R	From (V) MA 939976	
4	YQG10008	Pl/lighting-30 amp-maxi-large-Green	A/R		
4	YQG10011L	ignition/heat & a/c-60 amp-maxi-large-Blue	A/R		
4	YQG10009	military 24v glow plug-40 amp-maxi-Green	A/R		
4	YQG10010	military-50 amp-maxi-Red	A/R		
4	YQG10013	military-80 amp-maxi-Clear	A/R		
5	YQS101830	Label-fusebox	1		50 LE Rest of World UK
5	YQS101890	Label-fusebox	1		50 LE Japan
5	AMR4737	Label-fusebox	1		Japan except EFi
6	SE106161L	Screw-M6 x 16	2		
7	FS106167L	Screw-flanged head-flanged head-M6 x 16	1		
8	WC106041L	Washer-M6-oversize	3		
9	WL106001L	Washer-sprung-M6	1		
10	FN106047L	Nut-flange-M6	2		

DEFENDER

GROUP M — Body Electrics / Fuse Box / Under Seat

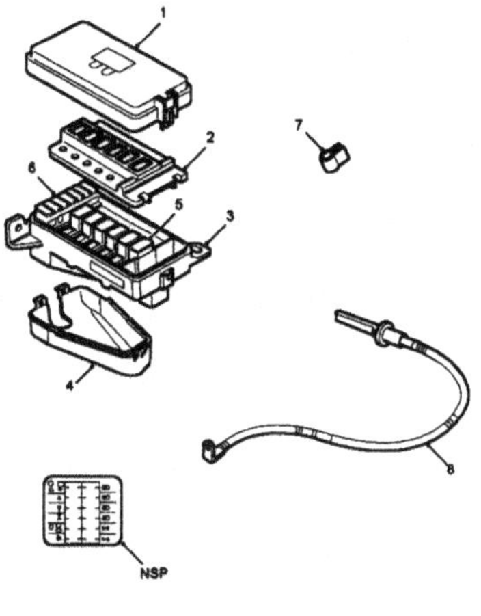

LM0049A

Illus	Part Number	Description	Quantity	Change Point	Remarks
1	YQH100870	Cover fusebox-top	1	Note (1)	
2	YQH000120	Cover fusebox-top	1	Note (2)	
2	YQH10004L	Cover fusebox-inner	1		
3	YPP100310L	Fusebox	1	Note (1)	
3	YQE000180	Fusebox	1	Note (2)	
4	YQH10002L	Cover fusebox-bottom	1		
5	STC1757	Link-fusible-100 amp-Blue.	1		
5	STC1758	Link-fusible-60 amp-Yellow.	1		
5	STC1759	Link-fusible-40 amp-Green	1		
5	STC1760	Link-fusible-30 amp-Pink.	1		
6	RTC4497	Fuse-5 amp-auto-standard	A/R		
6	RTC4498	Fuse-7.5 amp-auto-standard.	A/R		
6	RTC4501	Fuse-10 amp-auto-standard	A/R		
6	RTC4503	Fuse-15 amp-auto-standard.	A/R		
6	RTC4504	Fuse-20 amp-auto-standard.	A/R		
7	AFU3017L	Extractor blade fuse	1		
8	YMZ100990	Harness floor	1		

CHANGE POINTS:
(1) From (V) XA 159807 To (V) ZA 999999
(2) From (V) 2A 622424

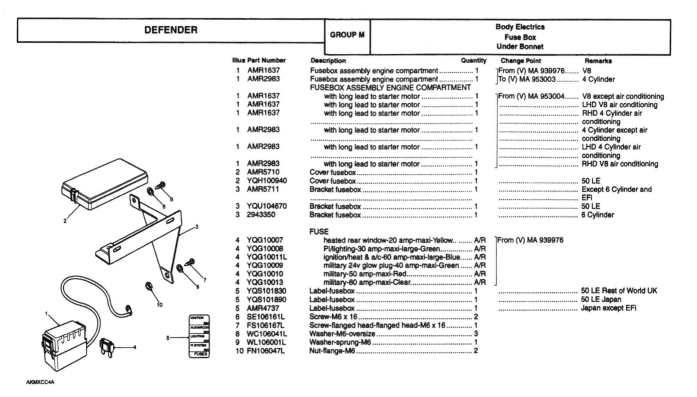

DEFENDER	GROUP M	Body Electrics Relays Relays-To (V) LA939975

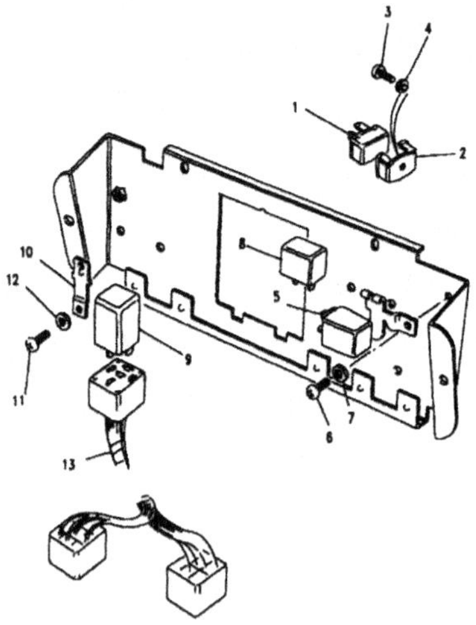

Illus	Part Number	Description	Quantity	Change Point	Remarks
1	RTC3562	Flasher unit electronic-2 pin-without trailer socket	NLA		Use STC4252.
1	STC4252	Flasher unit electronic	1		
2	567959	Clip-retaining-flasher unit	1		
3	SE105101L	Screw-M5	1		
4	WF105001L	Washer-flasher unit-starlock-M5	1		
5	PRC2239	Flasher unit electronic-3 pin-without trailer socket	1		
5	PRC8876	Flasher unit electronic-3 pin-with trailer socket-12V	1		
6	SE106121L	Screw-pan-pan head-M6 x 12	1		
7	WF106001L	Washer-starlock-M6	1		
8	YWB10032L	Relay-brake system check-changeover-Green	1		
8	YWB10032L	Relay-starter-changeover-Green	1		
8	YWB10032L	Relay-fuel changeover option-changeover-Green	1		
8	YWB10032L	Relay-headlamp override-changeover-Green	1		
8	YWB10032L	Relay-changeover-Green	1	From (V) January 1985	Norway
9	PRC6864	Relay-delay unit-12V-Red	1	Note (1)	
9	AMR2341	Relay-delay unit-12V-Red	1	Note (2)	
9	PRC7386	Relay-delay unit-24V	1		
10	DRC1245	Bracket-relay mounting	1	Note (3)	
11	SE105121L	Screw-pan head-M5 x 12	1	Note (3)	
12	WF600041L	Washer-lock	1	Note (3)	
13	PRC8295	Cable-wash/wipe delay	1	Note (3)	

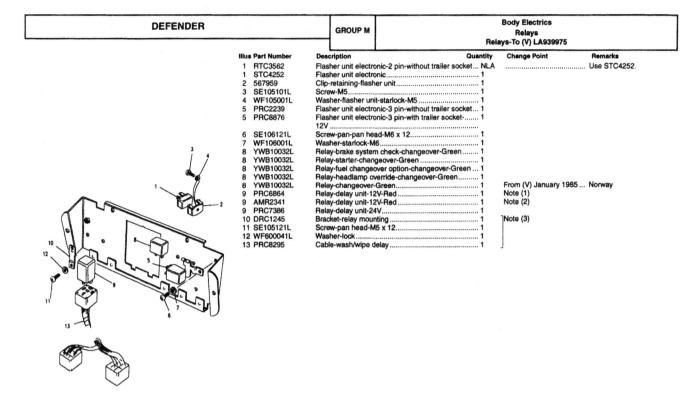

CHANGE POINTS:
(1) To (V) KA 927700
(2) From (V) KA 927701
(3) From (V) HA 455946

DEFENDER	GROUP M	Body Electrics Relays Relays-From (V) MA939976

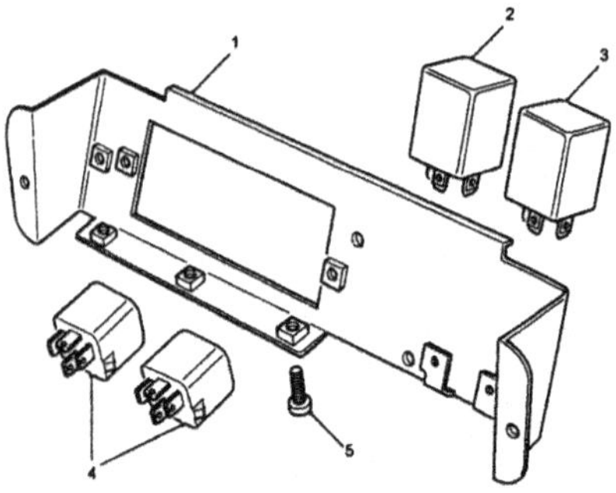

AHMXGA2A

Illus	Part Number	Description	Quantity	Change Point	Remarks
1	AMR3138	Bracket fusebox	1		
2	YWT10003	Flasher unit electronic-3 pin-without trailer socket	1		
2	PRC8876	Flasher unit electronic-3 pin-with trailer socket-12V	1		
3	AMR2341	Relay-wiper-delay unit-12V-Red	1		
3	AMR3773	Relay normally open-Black	1	Note (1)	Antilock Brakes
4	YWB10032L	Relay-changeover-Green	A/R	Note (2)	
4	YWB10027L	Relay	A/R	Note (2)	
4	YWB100820L	Relay assembly multi function	1		V8 EFi 50 LE
5	SE106201L	Screw-pan head-M6 x 20	A/R		
4	PRC6796	Relay-heated front screen-Grey	1	Note (3)	
4	YWB000150	Relay-changeover-Yellow	A/R	Note (3)	
4	YWB000160	Relay-changeover-Green	A/R	Note (3)	
	STC61888	Switch auxiliary-lamp	1	Note (4)	Tomb Raider

CHANGE POINTS:
(1) From (V) XA 159807
(2) From (V) MA 939976 To (V) ZA 999999
(3) From (V) 2A 622424
(4) From (V) 1A 612404

Body Electrics
Relays
Dim Dip Unit & Glow Plug Timer

Illus	Part Number	Description	Quantity	Change Point	Remarks
1	PRC8123	Control unit dim dip-Quartz Halogen	1	Note (1)	Dim dip
1	PRC6336	Control unit dim dip-Sealed beam	1		
2	DA610051L	Screw-flanged head-flanged head-No10	2		
3	YWC10050L	Control unit dim dip	1	Note (2)	UK
3	YWZ10003L	Control unit dim dip	1		Except UK
4	DRC1245	Bracket-relay mounting	1		
5	AB608031L	Screw-self tapping-No 8 x 3/8	1		
6	XBL10003L	Resistor	1		
7	FN106047L	Nut-flange-M6	1		
8	PRC6913	Relay-ignition heater plug-12V	1		
8	ERR4085	Relay-ignition heater plug-24V	1		
9	AB612051L	Screw-self tapping-No 12 x 5/8	1		
10	WE600041L	Washer-starlock	1		

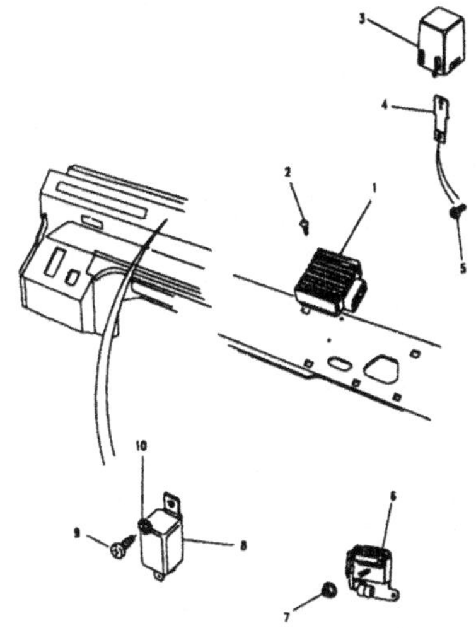

CHANGE POINTS:
(1) From (V) 274311 To (V) HA 705856
(2) From (V) HA 705857

Body Electrics
Electronic Control Units
ECU-Anti-Lock Braking System

Illus	Part Number	Description	Quantity	Change Point	Remarks
1	SRD100490	Electric control unit & traction control-antilock brakes	1	Note (1)	Antilock Brakes
2	FS106167L	Screw-flanged head-flanged head-M6 x 16	3		
3	STC1749	Sensor assembly antilock brakes-front	2		
3	STC1750	Sensor assembly antilock brakes-rear	2		

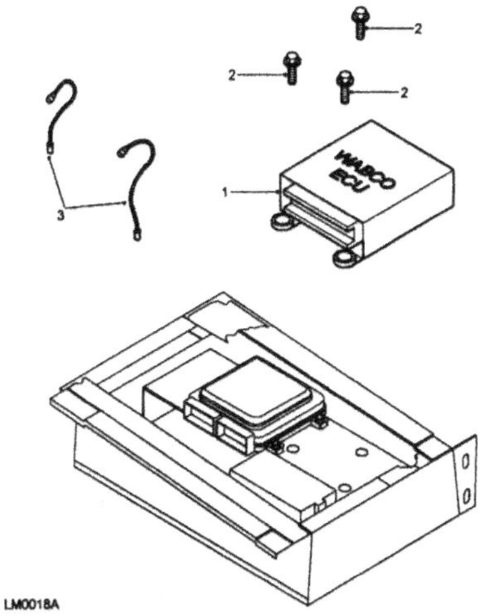

LM0018A

CHANGE POINTS:
(1) From (V) XA 159807

DEFENDER	GROUP M	Body Electrics Electronic Control Units ECU-EGR

Illus	Part Number	Description	Quantity	Change Point	Remarks
1	ERR5033	ECU-EGR-located under front centre seat	1	Note (2)	300 TDI
1	ERR6233	ECU-EGR-located under front centre seat	1	Note (1)	

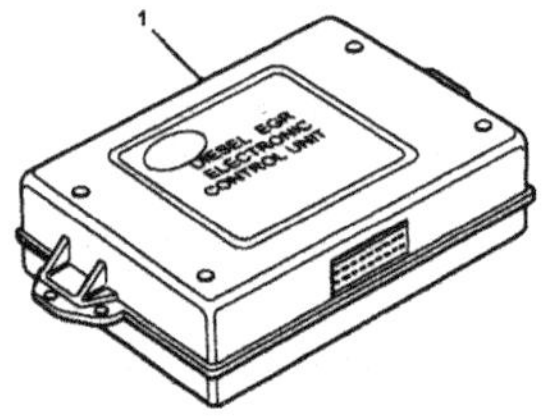

AHMXGC1A

CHANGE POINTS:
(1) From (V) MA 970542 approx
(2) To (V) MA 970541 approx

DEFENDER	GROUP M	Body Electrics Electronic Control Units ECU-One Touch Rear Fog Lamp

Illus	Part Number	Description	Quantity	Change Point	Remarks
1	YWC104430L	ECU-one touch f/lamp	1	From (V) VA 104806	

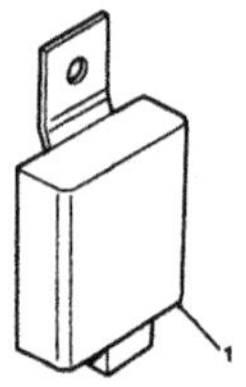

AHMXGC2A

ECU-Fuel Control

Illus	Part Number	Description	Quantity	Change Point	Remarks
		ECU - FUEL CONTROL - V8			
1	MSB100960	Electric control unit-fuel control	1		V8 EFi 50 LE
2	NNU100710	Bracket-mounting engine-electric control unit	1		
3	YQH100960	Cover-electronic box	1		
		ECU - FUEL CONTROL - TD5			
1	MSB101170	Electric control unit-fuel control	1	Note (1)	Td5
1	MSB101171	Electric control unit-fuel control	1	Note (2)	
1	MSB101360	Electric control unit-fuel control	1	Note (3)	
1	MSB000080	Electric control unit-fuel control	1	Note (4)	
1	NNN000120	Electric control unit-fuel control	1	Note (5)	
4	FS106167L	Screw-flanged head-flanged head-M6 x 16	3		

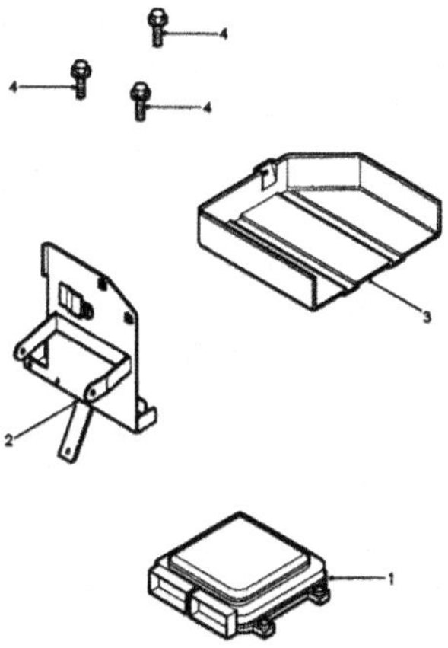

LM0050

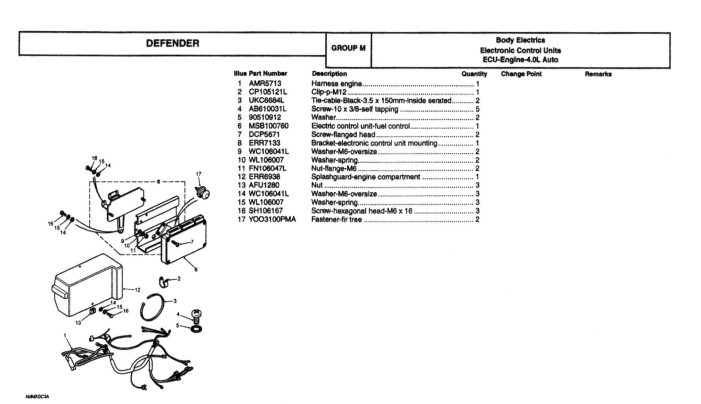

CHANGE POINTS:
(1) To (V) XA 172227
(2) From (V) XA 172228 To (V) YA 199364
(3) From (V) YA 199365 To (V) ZA 605425
(4) From (V) 1A 605426 To (V) ZA 999999
(5) From (V) 2A 622424

ECU-Engine-4.0L Auto

Illus	Part Number	Description	Quantity	Change Point	Remarks
1	AMR5713	Harness engine	1		
2	CP105121L	Clip-p-M12	1		
3	UKC6684L	Tie-cable-Black-3.5 x 150mm-inside serated	2		
4	AB610031L	Screw-10 x 3/8-self tapping	5		
5	90510912	Washer	2		
6	MSB100760	Electric control unit-fuel control	1		
7	DCP5671	Screw-flanged head	2		
8	ERR7133	Bracket-electronic control unit mounting	1		
9	WC106041L	Washer-M6-oversize	2		
10	WL106007	Washer-spring	2		
11	FN106047L	Nut-flange-M6	2		
12	ERR6938	Splashguard-engine compartment	1		
13	AFU1280	Nut	3		
14	WC106041L	Washer-M6-oversize	3		
15	WL106007	Washer-spring	3		
16	SH106167	Screw-hexagonal head-M6 x 16	3		
17	YOO3100PMA	Fastener-fir tree	2		

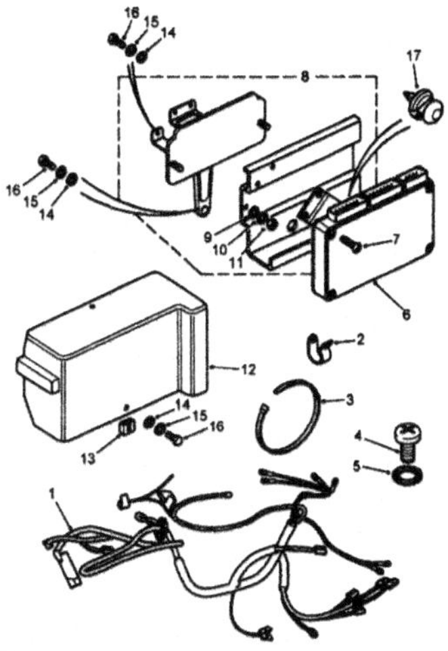

AMMXGC3A

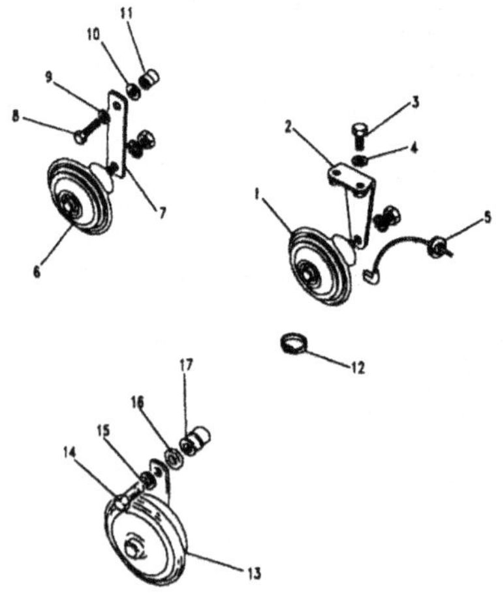

Illus	Part Number	Description	Quantity	Change Point	Remarks
		SINGLE HORN-WITHOUT AIR CONDITIONING			
1	PRC2057	Horn high note-single horn	1		Except 50 LE and Gulf States
2	PRC1984	Bracket-horn mounting	1		
3	SH106141L	Screw-hexagonal head-M6 x 14	2		
4	WL106001L	Washer-sprung-M6	2		
5	235113	Grommet	1		
		ADDITIONAL HORN-WITHOUT AIR CON			
6	PRC2057	Horn high note-additional horn	1		Gulf States except 50 LE
7	PRC4456	Bracket-horn mounting	1		
8	FS108251L	Screw-flanged head-M8 x 25	NLA		Use FS108257L.
9	WL108001L	Washer-sprung-M8	1		
10	4868L	Washer-plain	1		
11	NN108021	Nut-blind-M8	1		
12	C43640	Tie-cable-Black-2.5 x 100mm-outside serated	3		
		SINGLE HORN-WITH AIR CONDITIONING			
13	PRC5912	Horn low note	1		Except 50 LE
14	FS108251L	Screw-flanged head-M8 x 25	NLA		Use FS108257L.
15	WL108001L	Washer-sprung-M8	1		
16	4868L	Washer-plain	1		
17	NN108021	Nut-blind-M8	1		

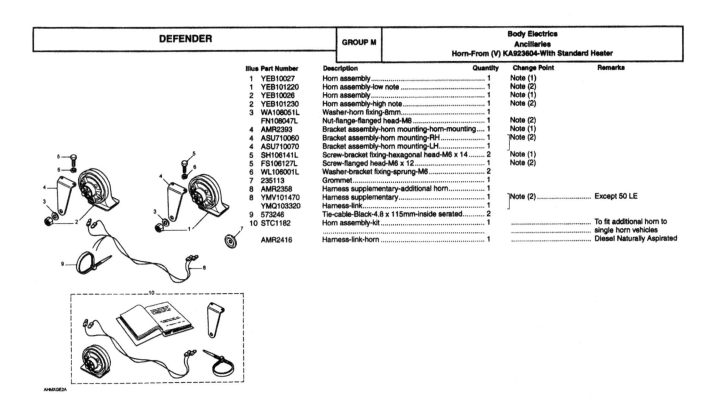

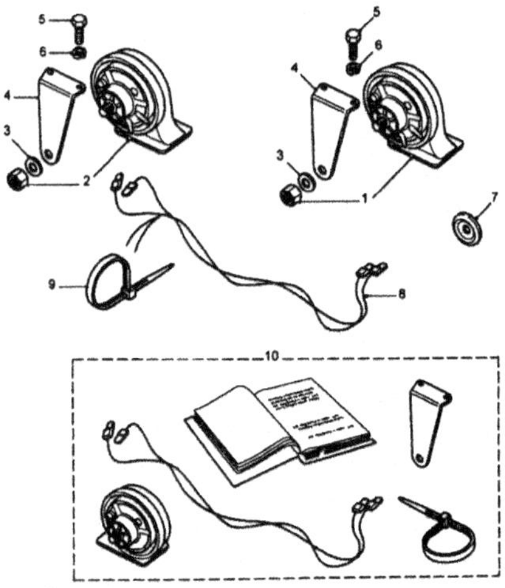

AHMXGE2A

Illus	Part Number	Description	Quantity	Change Point	Remarks
1	YEB10027	Horn assembly	1	Note (1)	
1	YEB101220	Horn assembly-low note	1	Note (2)	
2	YEB10026	Horn assembly	1	Note (1)	
2	YEB101230	Horn assembly-high note	1	Note (2)	
3	WA108051L	Washer-horn fixing-8mm	1		
	FN108047L	Nut-flange-flanged head-M8	1	Note (2)	
4	AMR2393	Bracket assembly-horn mounting-horn-mounting	1	Note (1)	
4	ASU710060	Bracket assembly-horn mounting-RH	1	Note (2)	
4	ASU710070	Bracket assembly-horn mounting-LH	1		
5	SH106141L	Screw-bracket fixing-hexagonal head-M6 x 14	2	Note (1)	
5	FS106127L	Screw-flanged head-M6 x 12	1	Note (2)	
6	WL106001L	Washer-bracket fixing-sprung-M6	2		
7	235113	Grommet	1		
8	AMR2358	Harness supplementary-additional horn	1		
8	YMV101470	Harness supplementary	1	Note (2)	Except 50 LE
	YMQ103320	Harness-link	1		
9	573246	Tie-cable-Black-4.8 x 115mm-inside serated	2		
10	STC1182	Horn assembly-kit	1		To fit additional horn to single horn vehicles
	AMR2416	Harness-link-horn	1		Diesel Naturally Aspirated

CHANGE POINTS:
(1) To (V) WA 159806
(2) From (V) XA 159807

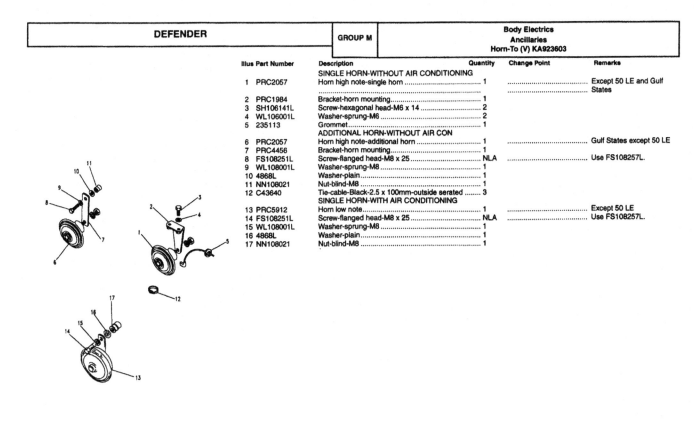

DEFENDER	GROUP M	Body Electrics Ancillaries Horn-From (V) KA923604-With Air Conditioning

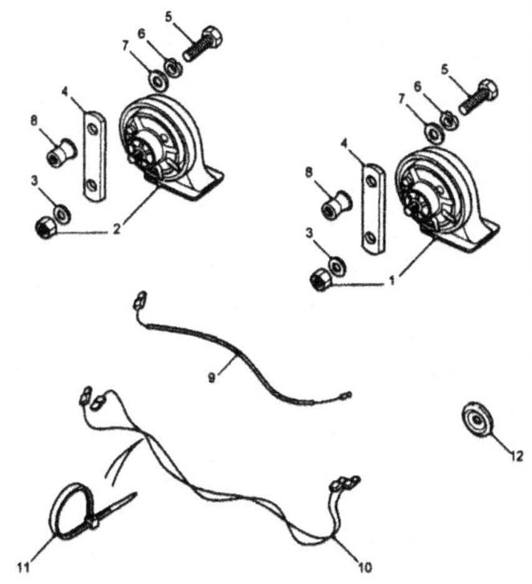

AHMXGE3A

Illus	Part Number	Description	Quantity	Change Point	Remarks
1	YEB10027	Horn assembly	1	Note (1)	
1	YEB101220	Horn assembly-low note	1	Note (2)	
1	YEB101220	Horn assembly-low note	1		50 LE
2	YEB10026	Horn assembly	1	Note (1)	
2	YEB101230	Horn assembly-high note	1	Note (2)	
2	YEB101230	Horn assembly-high note	1		50 LE
3	WA108051L	Washer-horn fixing-8mm	1		
4	AMR2411	Bracket assembly-horn mounting	1	Note (1)	
4	ASU710060	Bracket assembly-horn mounting-RH	1	Note (2)	
4	ASU710070	Bracket assembly-horn mounting-LH	1	Note (2)	
4	ASU710060	Bracket assembly-horn mounting-RH	1		50 LE
4	ASU710070	Bracket assembly-horn mounting-LH	1		50 LE
5	FS108257L	Screw-bracket fixing-flanged head-M8 x 25	1	Note (1)	
5	FS106127L	Screw-flanged head-M6 x 12	1	Note (2)	
6	WL108001L	Washer-bracket fixing-sprung-M8	1		
7	4868L	Washer-plain-bracket fixing	1		
8	NN108021	Nut-blind-M8	1	Note (1)	
8	FN108047L	Nut-flange-flanged head-M8	1	Note (2)	
9	AMR2416	Harness-link-horn	1		Diesel Naturally Aspirated
9	YMQ103320	Harness-link	1		50 LE
9	YMQ103320	Harness-link	1	Note (2)	
10	AMR2358	Harness supplementary-additional horn	1		
10	YMV101470	Harness supplementary	1		Automatic 4000 cc L/R V8 Petrol EFi 50 LE 90"
10	YMV101470	Harness supplementary	1	Note (2)	Except 50 LE
11	573246	Tie-cable-Black-4.8 x 115mm-inside serated	2		
12	235113	Grommet	1		

CHANGE POINTS:
(1) To (V) WA 159806
(2) From (V) XA 159807

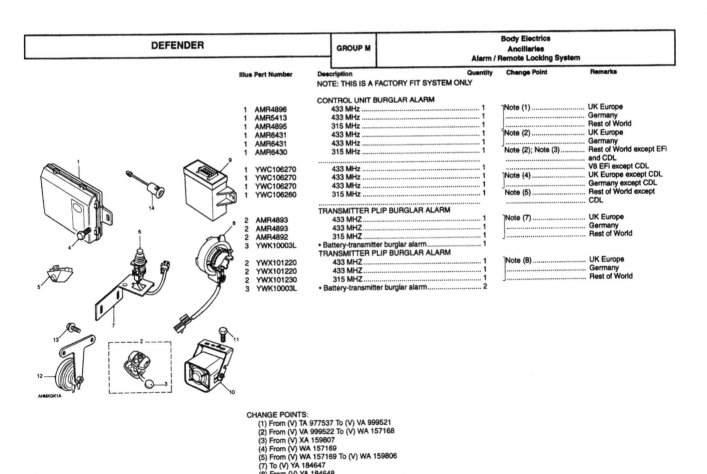

DEFENDER	GROUP M	Body Electrics Ancillaries Alarm / Remote Locking System

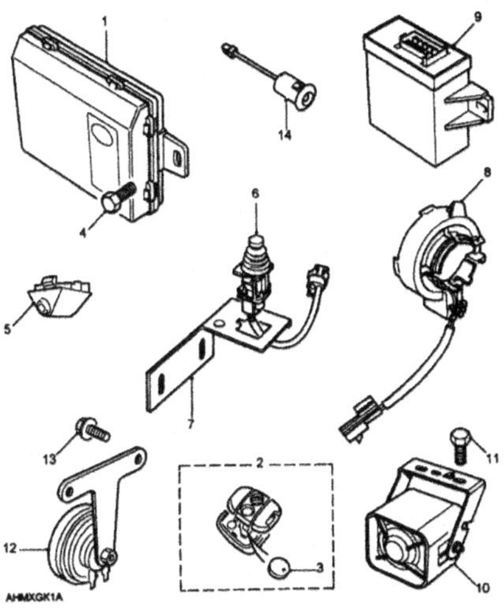

AHMXGK1A

Illus	Part Number	Description	Quantity	Change Point	Remarks
		NOTE: THIS IS A FACTORY FIT SYSTEM ONLY			
		CONTROL UNIT BURGLAR ALARM			
1	AMR4896	433 MHz	1	Note (1)	UK Europe
1	AMR5413	433 MHz	1		Germany
1	AMR4895	315 MHz	1		Rest of World
1	AMR6431	433 MHz	1	Note (2)	UK Europe
1	AMR6431	433 MHz	1		Germany
1	AMR6430	315 MHz	1	Note (2); Note (3)	Rest of World except EFi and CDL
1	YWC106270	433 MHz	1		V8 EFi except CDL
1	YWC106270	433 MHz	1	Note (4)	UK Europe except CDL
1	YWC106270	433 MHz	1		Germany except CDL
1	YWC106260	315 MHz	1	Note (5)	Rest of World except CDL
		TRANSMITTER PLIP BURGLAR ALARM			
2	AMR4893	433 MHZ	1	Note (7)	UK Europe
2	AMR4893	433 MHZ	1		Germany
2	AMR4892	315 MHZ	1		Rest of World
3	YWK10003L	• Battery-transmitter burglar alarm	1		
		TRANSMITTER PLIP BURGLAR ALARM			
2	YWX101220	433 MHZ	1	Note (8)	UK Europe
2	YWX101220	433 MHZ	1		Germany
2	YWX101230	315 MHZ	1		Rest of World
3	YWK10003L	• Battery-transmitter burglar alarm	2		

CHANGE POINTS:
(1) From (V) TA 977537 To (V) VA 999521
(2) From (V) VA 999522 To (V) WA 157168
(3) From (V) XA 159807
(4) From (V) WA 157169
(5) From (V) WA 157169 To (V) WA 159806
(7) To (V) YA 184647
(8) From (V) YA 184648

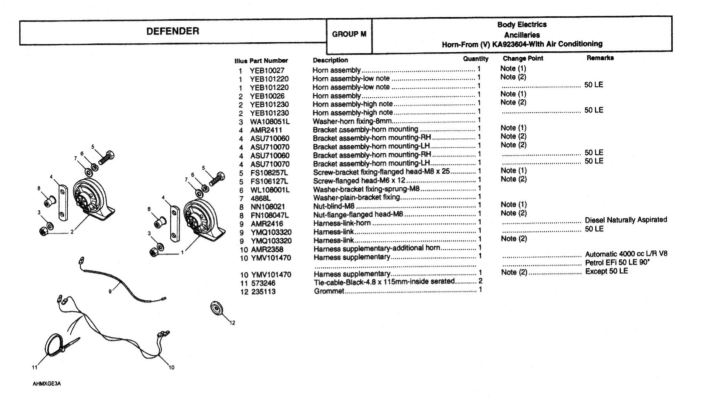

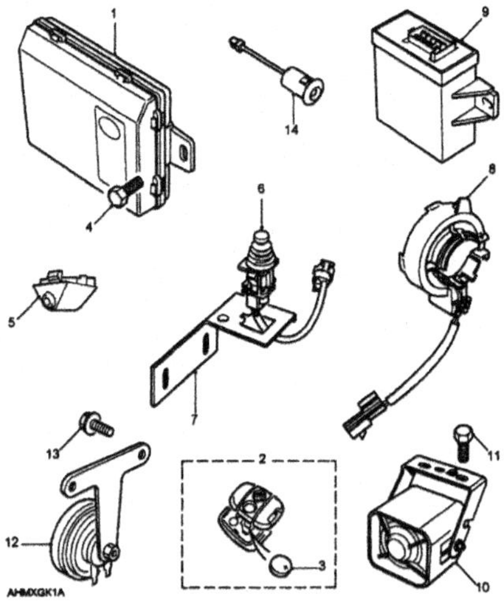

AHMXGK1A

Illus	Part Number	Description	Quantity	Change Point	Remarks
		ALL VARIANTS			
4	SH105201L	Screw-hexagonal head-M5 x 20	1		
5	YWC102900LNF	Sensor ultrasonic	1		
6	AMR2022	Switch-contact-bonnet burglar alarm	1		
7	ALR9158	Switch & bracket assembly-bonnet burglar alarm	1	Note (1)	RHD
7	ABU710160	Switch & bracket assembly-bonnet burglar alarm	1	Note (2)	RHD
7	ALR9159	Switch & bracket assembly-bonnet burglar alarm	1	Note (1)	LHD
7	ABU710170	Switch & bracket assembly-bonnet burglar alarm	1	Note (2)	LHD
8	AMR4897	Coil-engine immobilizer	1		
9	AMR4889	Unit assembly-immobilization-SPIDER	1		
10	AMR4974	Sounder unit burglar alarm-with battery back up	1	Note (3)	
10	YWK100130	Sounder unit burglar alarm-with battery back up	1	Note (4)	
11	FS106167L	Screw-flanged head-flanged head-M6 x 16	1		
12	AMR5611	Sounder unit burglar alarm-without battery back up	1		
13	FS106167L	Screw-flanged head-flanged head-M6 x 16	1		
14	YWN10002L	Indicator-light emitting diode burglar alarm	1		
	AMR1088	Relay-twin make-Brown	1		

NOTE:ECU INCL.DELAY UNIT-INT. LIGHT

CHANGE POINTS:
(1) From (V) TA 977525 To (V) ZA 618333
(2) From (V) 1A 618334
(3) From (V) TA 977525 To (V) WA 159806
(4) From (V) XA 159807

Illus	Part Number	Description	Quantity	Change Point	Remarks
1	AMR5491	Bracket assembly-harness engine	1		
2	RTC4498	Fuse-7.5 amp-auto-standard.	1	Note (1)	
3	YQU10017L	Clip-harness	1	Note (1)	
4	YYC10030L	Clip-harness-adaptor-6.5mm hole	1	Note (1)	
5	RTC4503	Fuse-15 amp-auto-standard.	1	Note (1)	

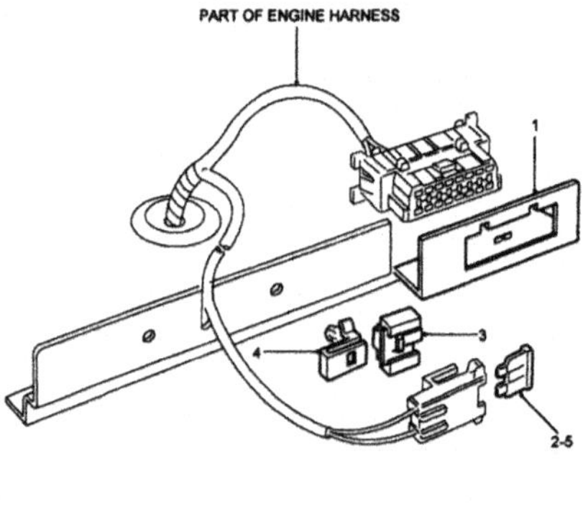

LM0010

CHANGE POINTS:
(1) From (V) TA 977537

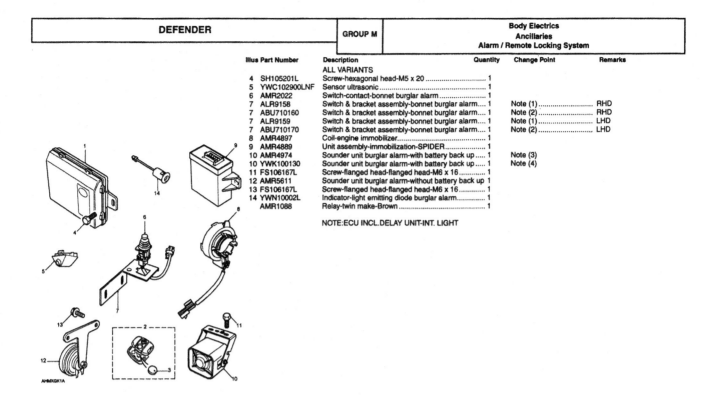

Illus	Part Number	Description	Quantity	Change Point	Remarks
1	SSW100050	KIT-ANTILOCK BRAKE SYSTEM SENSOR-FRONT	1	Note (1)	
2	SSW100060	KIT-ANTILOCK BRAKE SYSTEM SENSOR-REAR	2		
3	FTC1374	• Bush	1		
4	SYL100100	• Grease	1		

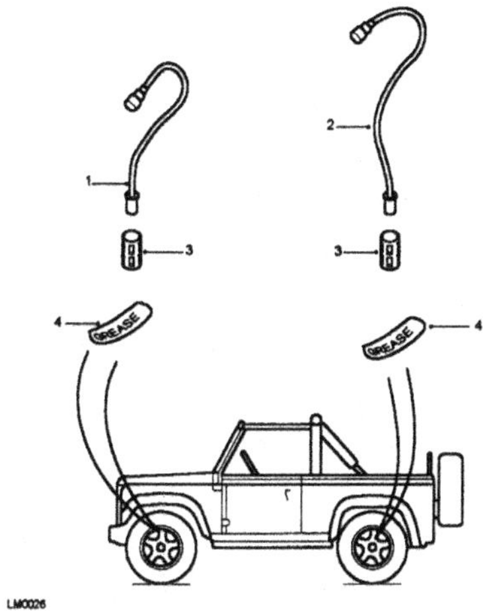

CHANGE POINTS:
(1) From (V) XA 159807

Illus	Part Number	Description	Quantity	Change Point	Remarks
1	YBE100540	Transducer speed	1	Note (1)	V8 Petrol EFi
1	YBE100530	Transducer speed	1	Note (2)	V8 Petrol
1	YBE100530	Transducer speed	1		4 Cylinder Petrol
1	YBE100530	Transducer speed	1		Diesel 300 TDI
1	YBE100530	Transducer speed	1		Diesel Td5
1	YBE100540	Transducer speed	1		BMW M52 Petrol
2	FS106201M	Screw-flanged head-M6 x 20-flanged head-patch lock	1		
3	WA106041L	Washer-6mm	1		
4	571665	O ring	1		
5	AMR5725	Harness-link	1		

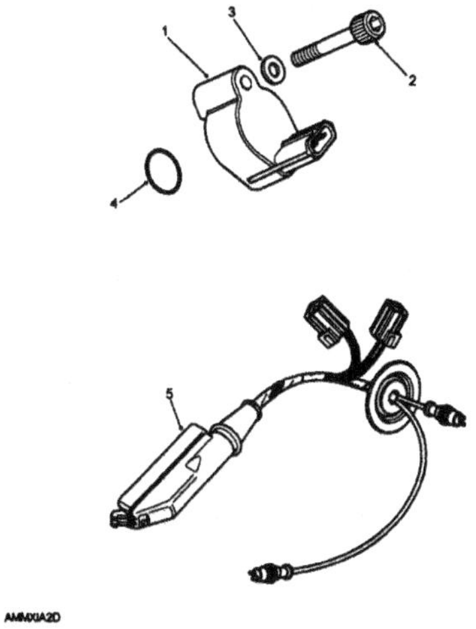

CHANGE POINTS:
(1) To (V) WA 159806
(2) From (V) XA 159807

Illus	Part Number	Description	Quantity	Change Point	Remarks
1	PRC4301	HARNESS FACIA-SEAT BELT & OVERSPEED WARNING	1	Note (1)	
1	AMR3039	HARNESS FACIA-SEAT BELT WARNING	1	Note (2)	
1	YMG109510	HARNESS FACIA-SEAT BELT WARNING	1	Note (3)	
2	AAU5034	• Diode-Pektron	1		
1	YMG109600	Harness facia-with overspeed warning	1	Note (4)	Gulf States
3	PRC4299	Buzzer passive restraint	1		
4	PRC4304	Clip-retaining-buzzer mounting	1		
12	SE105121L	Screw-pan head-M5 x 12	1		
13	WA105041	Washer-plain-M5	1		
14	NH105041	Nut-hexagonal-M5	1		
5	PRC4268	Monitor unit- overspeed-Black	1	Note (5)	
5	YHD100000	Monitor unit- overspeed	1	Note (4)	Gulf States
10	AFU2879	Clip-overspeed monitor-5mm-6.5mm hole	2		
11	DRC1245	Bracket-relay mounting-overspeed monitor	1		
6	PRC4497	Sensor-speed	1		
		CABLE SPEEDOMETER			
7	PRC4298	upper	1	To (V) 299084	Overspeed warning 90°
8	PRC4282	lower	1		
7	PRC6037	upper	1	From (V) 299085	
8	PRC6036	lower	1		
9	C43640	Tie-cable-Black-2.5 x 100mm-outside serated	5		
10	AFU2879	Clip-5mm-6.5mm hole	2		

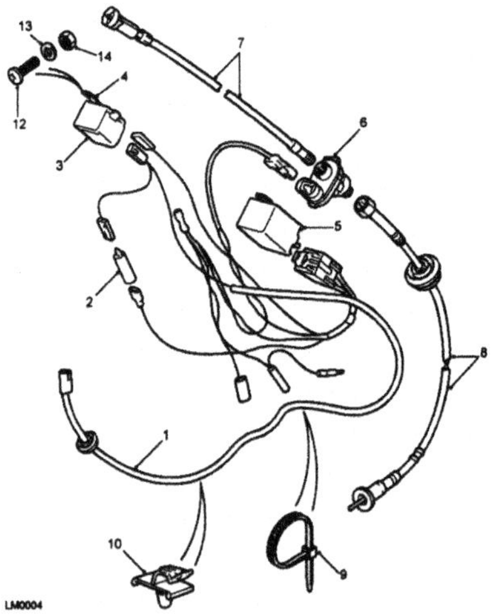

LM0004

CHANGE POINTS:
(1) To (V) LA 939975
(2) From (V) MA 939976 To (V) VA 138479
(3) From (V) WA 138480
(4) From (V) XA 159807
(5) To (V) WA 159806

Illus	Part Number	Description	Quantity	Change Point	Remarks
1	AMR5551	Relay-emissions maintenance	1		
2	RTC6083	Label-underbonnet emissions	1		

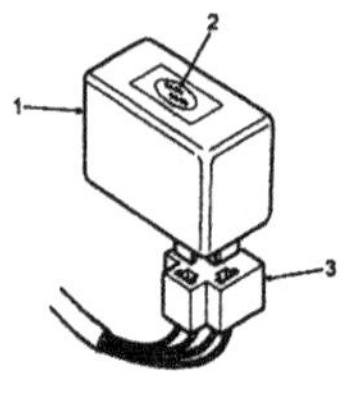

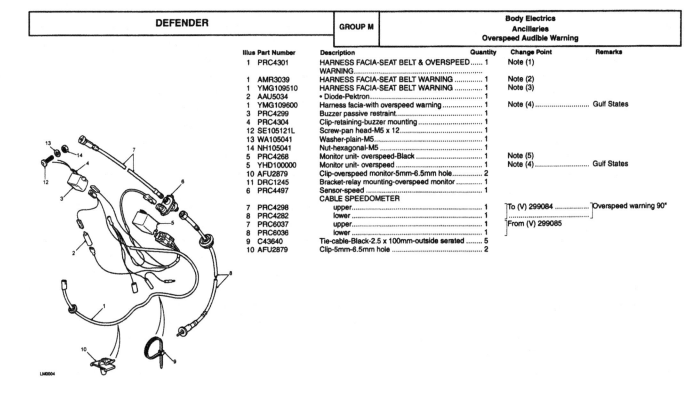

AMMXIA8A

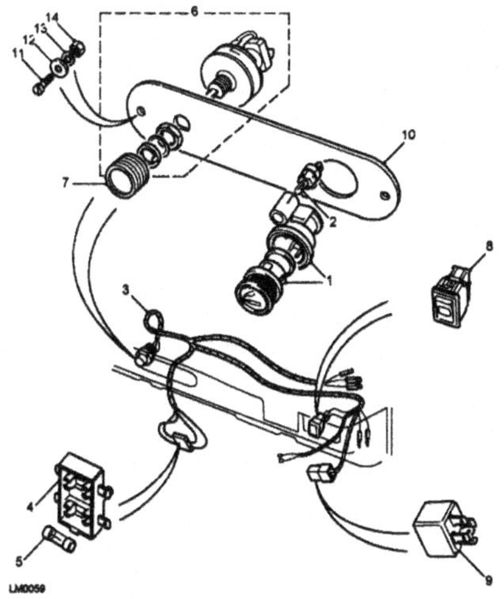

Illus	Part Number	Description	Quantity	Change Point	Remarks
1	PRC4524	CIGAR LIGHTER FACIA	1	Note (1)	
	DRC8398	• Pop out unit cigar lighter	1		
1	PRC9410	CIGAR LIGHTER FACIA	1	Note (2)	
	STC733	• Pop out unit cigar lighter	1		
2	RTC3635	• Bulb-wedge illumination-12V-1.2 Watt	1		
1	YUJ10037L	CIGAR LIGHTER FACIA	1	Note (3)	
1	YUJ100650	CIGAR LIGHTER FACIA	1	Note (4)	
2	RTC3635	• Bulb-wedge illumination-12V-1.2 Watt	1		
3	PRC4438	HARNESS FACIA-RWW/HRW	1	Note (5)	Heated rear window
		HARNESS FACIA			
3	PRC4720	RWW/HRW	1	Note (6)	
3	PRC8246	RWW/HRW	1	Note (7)	
3	PRC8452	RWW/HRW	1	Note (8)	
3	PRC9334	RWW/HRW	1	Note (9)	
3	AMR3124	HRW	1	From (V) MA 939976	Heated rear window
	AAU5034	• Diode-Pektron	1		
3	YMG109510	HARNESS FACIA	1	From (V) WA 138480	
	AAU5034	• Diode-Pektron	1		
	PRC4576	Harness-link-cigar lighter	1	To (V) 270226	
4	PRC3737	Fusebox assembly passenger compartment	1		
5	RTC4502	Fuse-15 amp	1		

CHANGE POINTS:
(1) To (V) JA 913077
(2) From (V) JA 913078 To (V) JA 915407
(3) From (V) JA 915408 To (V) WA 138479
(4) From (V) WA 138480
(5) To (V) 270226
(6) From (V) 270227 To (V) FA 424037
(7) From (V) FA 424038 To (V) GA 455945
(8) From (V) HA 455946 To (V) HA 903278
(9) From (V) HA 903279 To (V) LA 939975

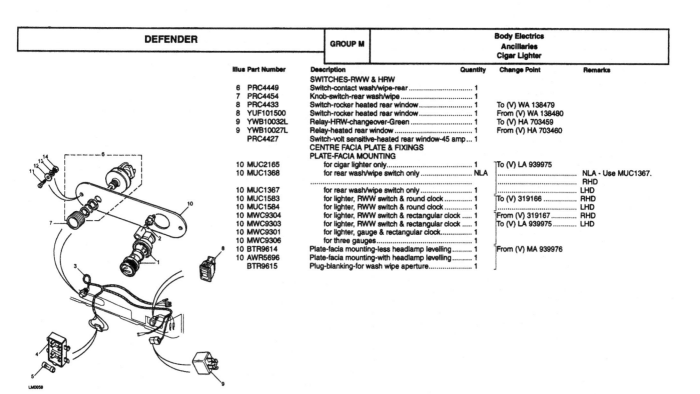

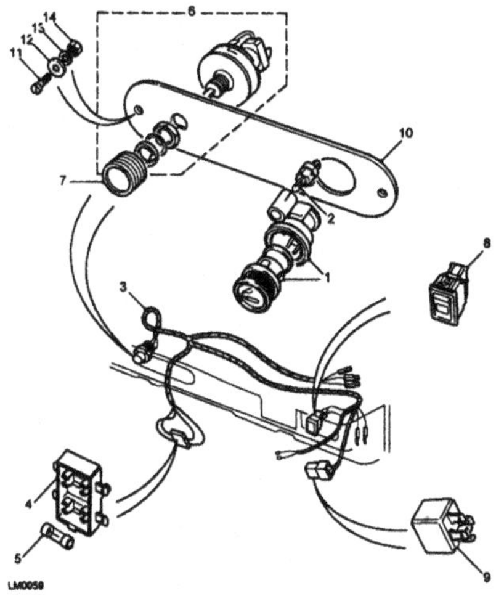

Illus	Part Number	Description	Quantity	Change Point	Remarks
		SWITCHES-RWW & HRW			
6	PRC4449	Switch-contact wash/wipe-rear	1		
7	PRC4454	Knob-switch-rear wash/wipe	1		
8	PRC4433	Switch-rocker heated rear window	1	To (V) WA 138479	
8	YUF101500	Switch-rocker heated rear window	1	From (V) WA 138480	
9	YWB10032L	Relay-HRW-changeover-Green	1	To (V) HA 703459	
9	YWB10027L	Relay-heated rear window	1	From (V) HA 703460	
	PRC4427	Switch-volt sensitive-heated rear window-45 amp	1		
		CENTRE FACIA PLATE & FIXINGS			
		PLATE-FACIA MOUNTING			
10	MUC2165	for cigar lighter only	1	To (V) LA 939975	
10	MUC1368	for rear wash/wipe switch only	NLA		NLA - Use MUC1367.
					RHD
10	MUC1367	for rear wash/wipe switch only	1		LHD
10	MUC1583	for lighter, RWW switch & round clock	1	To (V) 319166	RHD
10	MUC1584	for lighter, RWW switch & round clock	1		LHD
10	MWC9304	for lighter, RWW switch & rectangular clock	1	From (V) 319167	RHD
10	MWC9303	for lighter, RWW switch & rectangular clock	1	To (V) LA 939975	LHD
10	MWC9301	for lighter, gauge & rectangular clock	1		
10	MWC9306	for three gauges	1		
10	BTR9614	Plate-facia mounting-less headlamp levelling	1	From (V) MA 939976	
10	AWR5696	Plate-facia mounting-with headlamp levelling	1		
	BTR9615	Plug-blanking-for wash wipe aperture	1		

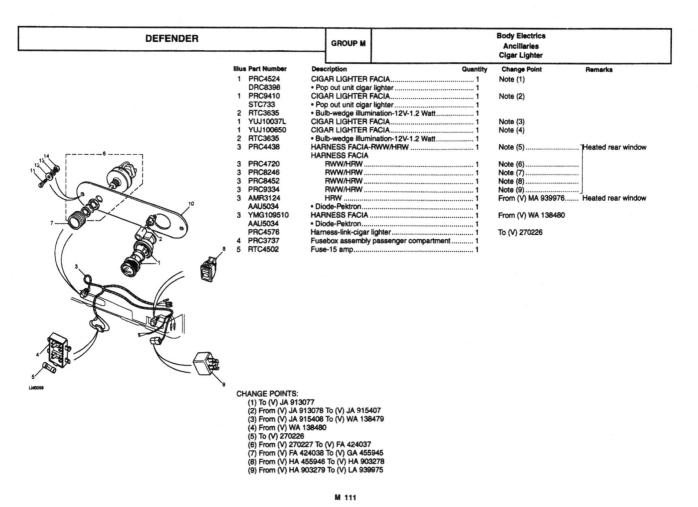

Illus	Part Number	Description	Quantity	Change Point	Remarks
11	SE105121L	Screw-fixing harness cigar lighter-pan head-M5 x 12	1	To (V) LA 939975	
11	SE105204	Screw-fixing facia plate-M5	2		
12	WL105004	Washer-fixing facia plate-sprung-M5	2	To (V) LA 939975	
12	AFU1248	Washer-fixing facia plate-plastic	2	From (V) MA 939976	
13	WC105007	Washer-plain-fixing facia plate-large-Black	2	To (V) LA 939975	
13	WC105001	Washer-plain-fixing facia plate-M5	2	From (V) MA 939976	
14	NH105041L	Nut-hexagonal-fixing facia plate-M5	2		

NOTE:REAR WASH WIPE INCOPORATED
INTO MAIN HARNESS

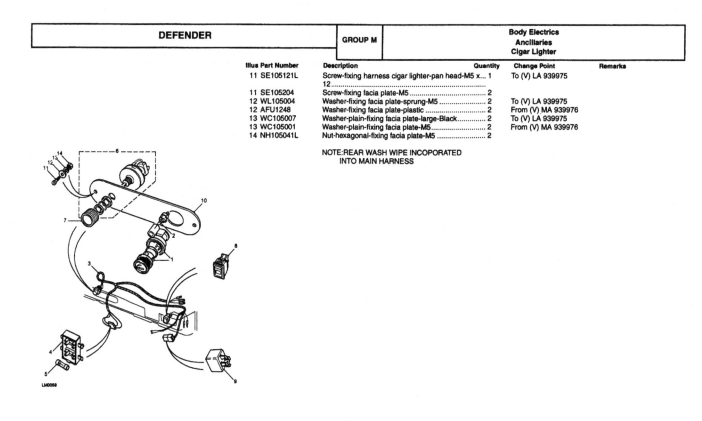

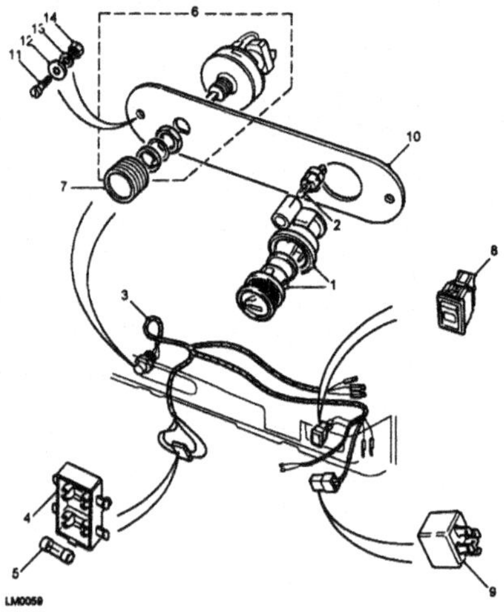

LM0059

Illus	Part Number	Description	Quantity	Change Point	Remarks
		INSTRUMENTS			
1	PRC7373	Speedometer-MPH	1	Note (1)	Except 50 LE
1	PRC7374	Speedometer-KMH-140Km/h	1		Except 50 LE
1	PRC7375	Speedometer-KMH-200km/h	1		Except 6 Cylinder and 50 LE
1	2943301	Speedometer-KMH-200km/h	1		BMW M52 6 Cylinder
3	RTC6164	Bulb-instruments-12V-2W	NLA		Use AMR3339.
3	AMR3339	Bulb-instruments-12V-2W	A/R		
1	YBC101520	Speedometer-MPH	1	Note (2)	Except Heritage
1	STC60688	Speedometer-MPH	1	Note (2)	Heritage
1	YBC101530	Speedometer-KMH	1	Note (2)	Except 6 Cylinder and Heritage
1	YBC101540	Speedometer-KMH	1	Note (2)	6 Cylinder
2	YAJ100370	Bulb & holder assembly	1	Note (2)	
29	STC4779	Ring-retention-speedometer	1	Note (2)	

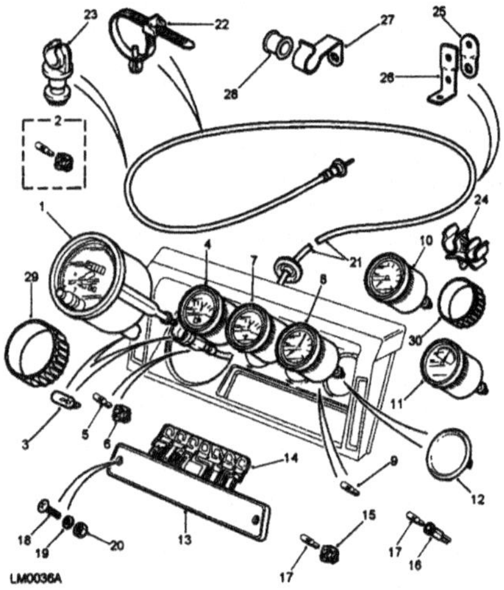
LM0036A

CHANGE POINTS:
(1) To (V) WA 159806
(2) From (V) XA 159807

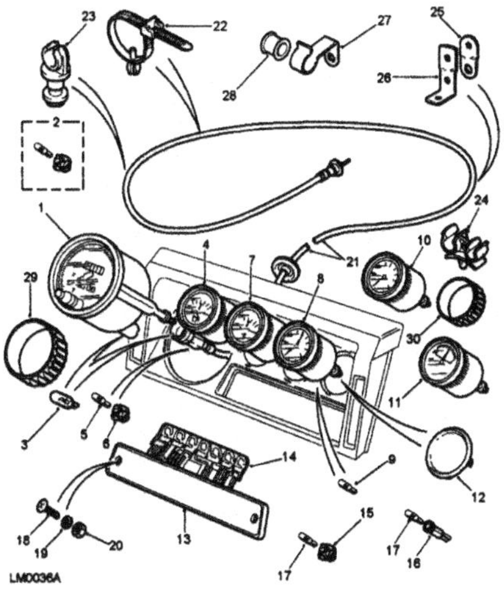

Illus	Part Number	Description	Quantity	Change Point	Remarks
		GAUGE-FUEL			
4	PRC7313	12V	1	Note (1)	
4	2943303	12V	1		6 Cylinder
4	YAD100910	12V	1	Note (2)	Except Heritage
4	STC60691	12V	1		Heritage
5	RTC3635	Bulb-wedge illumination-12V-1.2 Watt	1		
6	YAJ100390	Holder-bulb	1		
		GAUGE-TEMPERATURE			
7	PRC7311	12V	1	Note (3)	Except 6 Cylinder
7	AMR2070	12V	1	Note (4)	
7	AMR2631	12V	1	Note (5)	4 Cylinder
7	AMR2631	12V	1		V8 Petrol
7	2943305	12V	1	Note (1)	6 Cylinder
7	YAD100900	12V	1	Note (2)	Except Heritage
7	STC60690	12V	1		Heritage
5	RTC3635	Bulb-wedge illumination-12V-1.2 Watt	1		
6	YAJ100390	Holder-bulb	1		
8	AMR3443	Clock analogue-round	1	Note (1)	
8	YFB100390	Clock analogue-round	1	Note (2)	
9	503352	Bulb-281-ba7s-2 Watt-clock illumination	1	Note (1)	
10	PRC7315	Ammeter-12V	1		
11	2943302	Tachometer	1	Note (1)	6 Cylinder
11	YAE100760	Tachometer	1	Note (2)	
11	YAE100790	Tachometer	1		Td5 South Africa
11	YAE100800	Tachometer	1		TDi South Africa
11	STC60692	Tachometer	1		Heritage
5	RTC3635	Bulb-wedge illumination-12V-1.2 Watt	1		
6	YAJ100390	Holder-bulb	1		
30	STC4641	Ring-retention-gauge	3	Note (2)	
12	MRC8225	Plug-blanking-clock aperture	1	Note (1)	

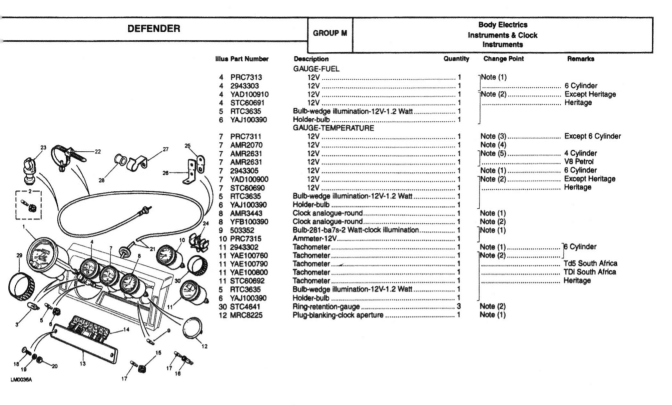

CHANGE POINTS:
(1) To (V) WA 159806
(2) From (V) XA 159807
(3) To (V) JA 916603
(4) From (V) JA 916604 To (V) KA 928139
(5) From (V) KA 928140 To (V) WA 159806

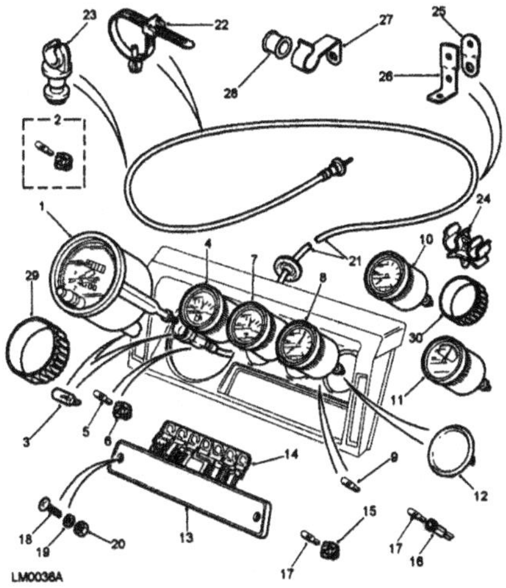

Illus	Part Number	Description	Quantity	Change Point	Remarks
		WARNING LIGHT ASSEMBLY			
13	PRC8879	12V	1	Note (1)	
13	AMR2628	12V	1	Note (2)	
13	AMR2628	12V	1	Note (3)	Petrol
13	AMR4976	12V	1	Note (3)	Diesel
13	AMR5975	12V	1	Note (4)	
14	AEU2721	• Printed circuit board instrument pack	1		
15	RTC3878	• Holder-bulb-direct contact type	13		
16	STC3086	• Holder-bulb-spade connection type	5		
17	RTC3635	• Bulb-wedge illumination-12V-1.2 Watt	18		
13	YAZ100000	Warning light assembly-12V	1	Note (5)	
15	AEU2722	Holder-bulb-Black	NLA	To (V) LA 939975	Use RTC3878.
15	AEU2723	Holder-bulb-Red	NLA	To (V) LA 939975	Use RTC3878.
17	AEU2724	Bulb-wedge illumination-for glow plug warning light to intro of 200TDi engine-6V-1.2 Watt	1		
15	YAJ100400	Holder-bulb-heater switch	1	Note (5)	
17	RTC3635	Bulb-wedge illumination-12V-1.2 Watt	1	Note (5)	
18	SG104165	Screw	1		
19	WE104001L	Washer- shakeproof-M4	2		
20	NH104041L	Nut-hexagonal-M4	2		

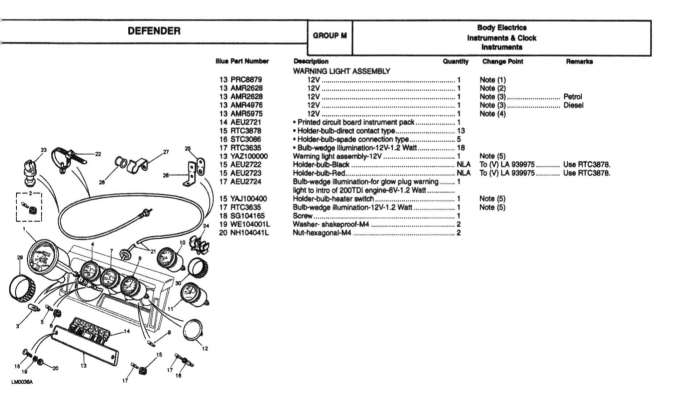

CHANGE POINTS:
(1) To (V) KA 929567
(2) From (V) KA 929568 To (V) MA 969102
(3) From (V) TA 969103 To (V) WA 138479
(4) From (V) WA 138480 To (V) WA 159806
(5) From (V) XA 159807

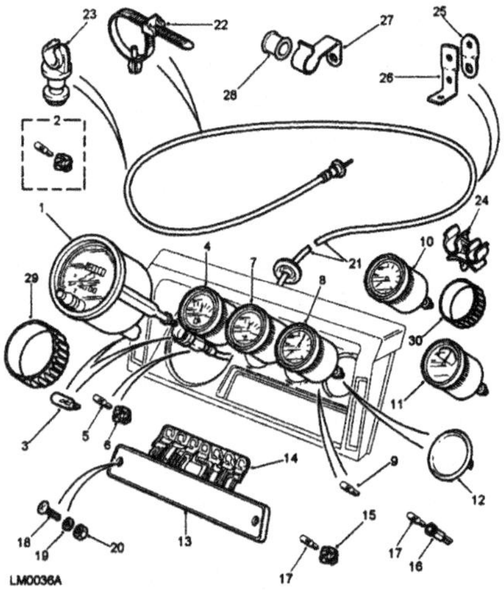

Illus	Part Number	Description	Quantity	Change Point	Remarks
		SPEEDOMETER CABLE-TWO PIECE			
21	PRC3718	Cable speedometer-upper-2 piece	1	To (V) 268134	RHD 4 Cylinder
21	PRC3724	Cable speedometer-lower-2 piece	1		RHD 4 Cylinder
21	PRC3718	Cable speedometer-upper-2 piece	1	To (V) 268016	RHD V8
21	PRC3725	Cable speedometer-lower-2 piece	1		RHD V8
21	PRC3718	Cable speedometer-upper-2 piece	1		LHD
21	PRC3723	Cable speedometer-lower-2 piece	1		LHD
		SPEEDOMETER CABLE-ONE PIECE			
21	PRC6022	Cable speedometer-one piece	1		RHD 4 Cylinder
21	PRC6023	Cable speedometer-one piece	1		RHD V8 Petrol
21	PRC6021	Cable speedometer-one piece	1		LHD
		SPEEDOMETER-POLICE SPEC			
21	ZXC9121	Cable speedometer	NLA		Police
21	ZXC9120	Cable speedometer-gearbox to junction-70"	1		4 Cylinder Police
21	ZXC9119	Cable speedometer-gearbox to junction-80"	1		V8 Police
21	ZXC9117	Cable speedometer-junction to main speedo-26"	1		Police
21	ZXC9118	Cable speedometer-junction to calibrated speedo-18.5"	1		Police
	ZXC9328	Junction unit-speedo cable	1		Police

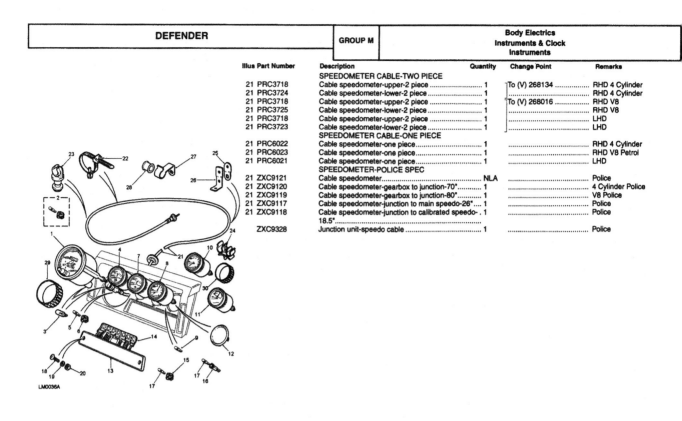

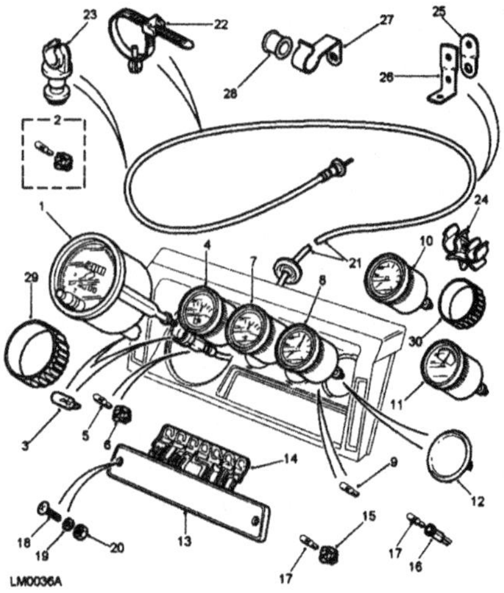

Illus	Part Number	Description	Quantity	Change Point	Remarks
22	AAU3686	Tie-cable-6.5mm hole-8.0 x 155mm	1	Note (1)	
23	PRC3180	Clip-pipe-single	2	Note (2)	
23	79121	Clip-single-9mm	2	Note (3)	
24	PRC3025	Clip-double	2	Note (1)	
25	PRC2979	Bracket-clipping-steel	1		
26	PRC3833	Bracket speedometer cable	1	Note (2)	LHD
26	PRC2980	Bracket speedometer cable	1	Note (3)	4 Cylinder
26	PRC2980	Bracket speedometer cable	1	Note (4)	RHD except 5 Cylinder
26	PRC3678	Bracket speedometer cable	1	Note (1)	V8 Petrol
27	NRC9338	Clip-p	1		
28	589254	Grommet-p-clip-17/32" hole	1		

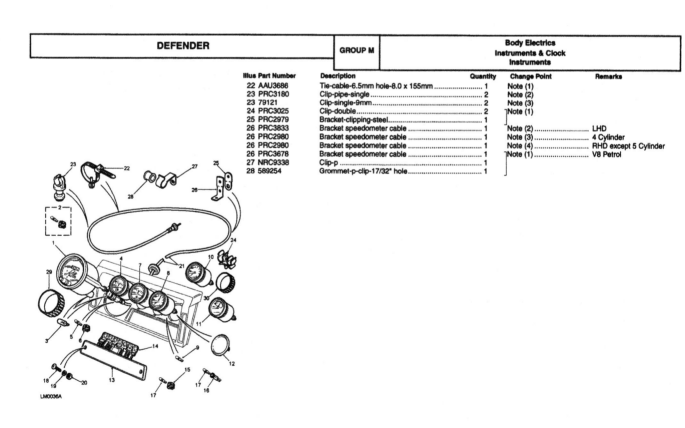

CHANGE POINTS:
(1) To (V) WA 159806
(2) To (V) LA 939975
(3) From (V) MA 939976 To (V) WA 159806
(4) From (V) XA 159807

Illus	Part Number	Description	Quantity	Change Point	Remarks
1	AMR5721	Speedometer-MPH	1		
1	AMR5974	SPEEDOMETER-KMH	1	Note (1)	
2	AMR3339	• Bulb-12V-2W	1		
3	AMR5722	GAUGE-TEMPERATURE	1		
2	AMR3339	• Bulb-12V-2W	1		
4	AMR5723	GAUGE-FUEL	1		
2	AMR3339	• Bulb-12V-2W	1		
5	AMR5724	TACHOMETER	1		
6	STC3313	• Bulb & holder assembly	1		
7	AMR2043	Module-warning light	1		Japan
8	AMR5975	WARNING LIGHT ASSEMBLY-12V	1		Except Japan
	AEU2721	• Printed circuit board instrument pack	1	Note (2)	
	RTC3878	• Holder-bulb-direct contact type	13		
	STC3086	• Holder-bulb-spade connection type	5		
	RTC3635	• Bulb-wedge illumination-12V-1.2 Watt	18		
9	NH104041L	Nut-hexagonal-M4	2		
10	WE104001L	Washer- shakeproof-M4	2		
11	AMR5716	Harness instrument pack	1		
12	YAF100110	Panel-instrument mounting	1		

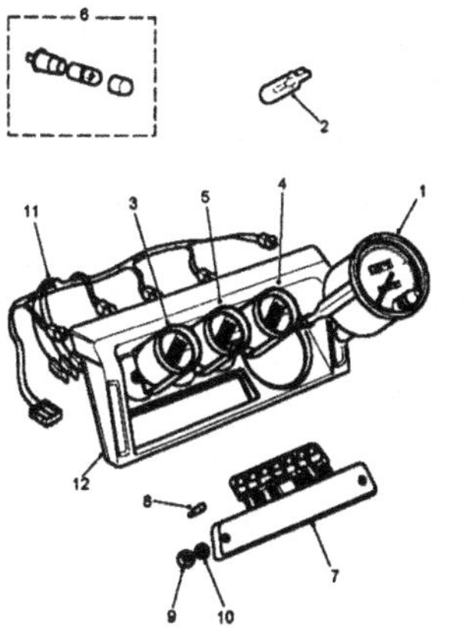

LM0022

CHANGE POINTS:
(1) From (V) WA 138480
(2) To (V) WA 159806

Illus	Part Number	Description	Quantity	Change Point	Remarks
1	RTC6324	Clock analogue-in centre dash panel-round	1	To (V) 319166	
2	PRC4370	CLOCK ANALOGUE-IN CENTRE DASH PANEL-RECTANGULAR	1	Note (1)	
3	PRC4324	• Bezel-clock	1		
	503352	Bulb-281-ba7s-2 Watt-clock illumination	1		
	503352	Bulb-281-ba7s-2 Watt-clock illumination	1		
		GAUGE-OIL			
4	PRC7319	12V	1		4 Cylinder
4	PRC7321	24V	1		
4	PRC7320	12V	1		V8
4	PRC7322	24V	1		
5	PRC7318	Gauge-oil temperature-12V	1		
5	PRC7317	Gauge-oil temperature-24V	1		
	PRC4372	Transducer oil temperature-24V	1		
6	320835	COVER ASSEMBLY-FACIA CONSOLE	1		Except radio
	346786	• Cover-instrument pack	1		
7	AB608031L	• Screw-self tapping-No 8 x 3/8	2		
8	RTC3745	• Nut-lokut	2		
9	SP105204	• Screw-M5 x 20	NLA		Use SE105204.
10	WC105007	• Washer-plain-large-Black	4		
11	WL105004	• Washer-sprung-M5	2		
12	NH105041L	• Nut-hexagonal-M5	2		
9	SE105204	Screw-M5			Except radio

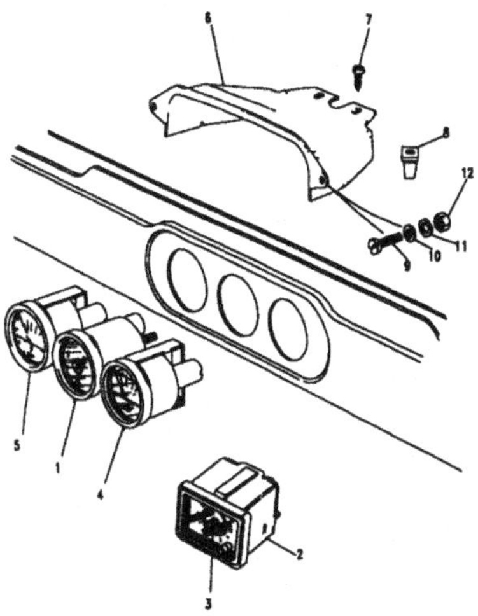

CHANGE POINTS:
(1) From (V) 319167 To (V) LA 936689

DEFENDER	GROUP M	Body Electrics In-Car Entertainment Radio Cassette-To (V) LA939975

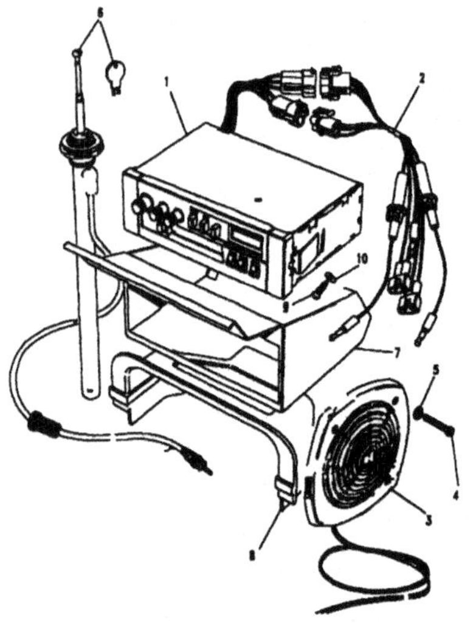

Illus	Part Number	Description	Quantity	Change Point	Remarks
1	PRC9188	Radio cassette assembly- electronic	1	To (V) JA 910822	
1	PRC9937	Radio cassette assembly- electronic	1	From (V) JA 910823	
1	2943370	Radio cassette assembly- electronic	1		6 Cylinder
	PRC9941	Bracket-radio housing-Philips	NLA	From (V) JA 910823	Use XQU000020.
2	PRC6228	Lead-link radio	1	To (V) JA 910822	
2	PRC9938	Lead-link radio	1	From (V) JA 910823	
	2943411	Harness-speaker	1		6 Cylinder Petrol
3	PRC6348	Speaker assembly-front single cone	NLA	To (V) JA 910822	Use PRC9939.
3	PRC9939	Speaker assembly-front single cone-RH	2	From (V) JA 910823	
4	AD606074L	Screw-6 x 7/8	8		
5	WA104001L	Washer-plain-M4	8		
6	PRC4327	Aerial front fender-metal	1		Except 6 Cylinder
6	2943225	Aerial front fender-metal	1		6 Cylinder
7	MWC2526	Bracket assembly-radio housing-(use 95MY radio fixings as replacements.	1		
8	MWC2530	Cover-instrument finisher	1		
9	AV608081	Screw	1		
10	WA105001L	Washer-plain-standard-M5	2		
	STC737	Kit-radio fittings	1		

DEFENDER	GROUP M	Body Electrics In-Car Entertainment Radio Cassette-From (V) MA939976 To MA969102

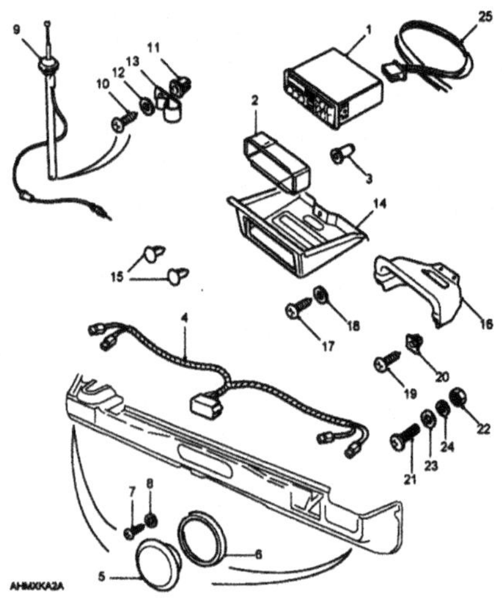

Illus	Part Number	Description	Quantity	Change Point	Remarks
1	AMR3414	Radio cassette assembly- electronic	1		
1	2943370	Radio cassette assembly- electronic	1		6 Cylinder
2	PRC9941	Bracket-radio housing-Philips	NLA	To (V) MA 948147	Use XQU000020.
2	AMR4063	Bracket-radio housing	1	From (V) MA 948148	
3	XQJ10002L	Bung-rubber radio fixing	1		
4	2943411	Harness-speaker	1		6 Cylinder
4	AMR3294	Harness-speaker	1		
5	AMR3417	Speaker assembly-front single cone	2		
6	AMR3840	Bezel-speaker-radio-speaker	2	From (V) MA 943790	
7	AD606074L	Screw-speaker-6 x 7/8	8	To (V) MA 943789	
10	AB606124	Screw-speaker-self tapping-No 6 x 40	8	From (V) MA 943790	
8	WA104001L	Washer-plain-speaker-M4	8	To (V) MA 943789	
8	WA104004	Washer-plain-speaker-M4	8	From (V) MA 943790	
9	AMR3418	Aerial front fender-metal	1		

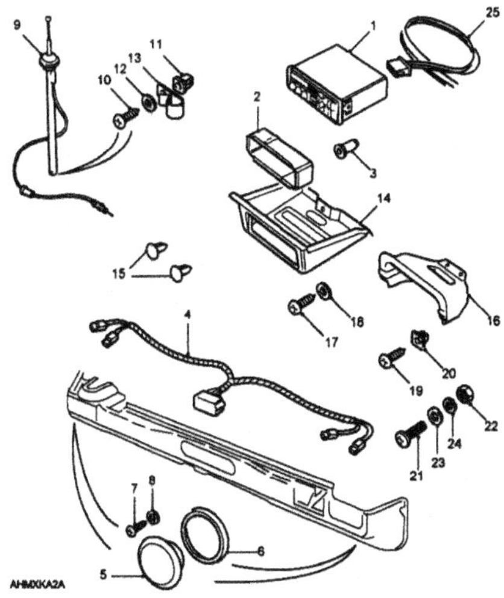

Illus	Part Number	Description	Quantity	Change Point	Remarks
10	AB614061	Screw-antenna-self tapping	1		
11	CZK3164	Nut-lokut-antenna	1		
12	MRC5527	Washer-antenna-plain-M6	1		
13	NRC2383	Clip-hose-antenna	1		
14	BTR8593LDQ	Housing-facia radio/cassette	1	To (V) MA 961247	
14	AWR2277LDQ	Housing-facia radio/cassette	1	From (V) MA 961248 To (V) MA 969102	
15	AFU1897	Fastener-drive-radio housing-Grey	2		
16	BTR9552	Cover-instrument pack	1		
17	AW608081	Screw-8 x 1/2	NLA		Use AV608081.
17	AV608081	Screw	2		
18	WA105001L	Washer-plain-standard-M5	2		
19	AB606034	Screw-pan-instrument cover-8 x 1/2	2		
20	RTC3745	Nut-lokut-instrument cover	2		
21	SE105204	Screw-instrument cover-M5	2		
22	NH105041	Nut-hexagonal-instrument cover-M5	2		
23	WC105004	Washer-instrument cover-M5	4		
24	WL105004	Washer-sprung-M5	2		
25	STC1747	Lead-link radio	NLA	To (V) LA 939975	Use STC7766 Extra lead is for illumination - tape back if not required..
25	STC7766	Lead-link radio	1	From (V) MA 939976	

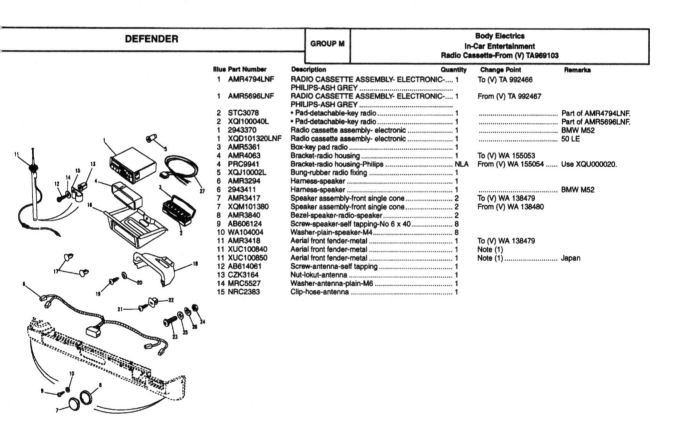

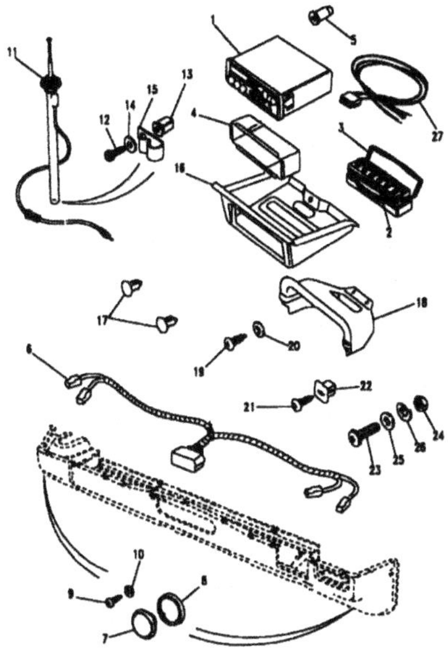

Illus	Part Number	Description	Quantity	Change Point	Remarks
1	AMR4794LNF	RADIO CASSETTE ASSEMBLY- ELECTRONIC-PHILIPS-ASH GREY	1	To (V) TA 992466	
1	AMR5696LNF	RADIO CASSETTE ASSEMBLY- ELECTRONIC-PHILIPS-ASH GREY	1	From (V) TA 992467	
2	STC3078	• Pad-detachable-key radio	1		Part of AMR4794LNF.
2	XQI100040L	• Pad-detachable-key radio	1		Part of AMR5696LNF.
1	2943370	Radio cassette assembly- electronic	1		BMW M52
1	XQD101320LNF	Radio cassette assembly- electronic	1		50 LE
3	AMR5361	Box-key pad radio	1		
4	AMR4063	Bracket-radio housing	1	To (V) WA 155053	
4	PRC9941	Bracket-radio housing-Philips	NLA	From (V) WA 155054	Use XQU000020.
5	XQJ10002L	Bung-rubber radio fixing	1		
6	AMR3294	Harness-speaker	1		
6	2943411	Harness-speaker	1		BMW M52
7	AMR3417	Speaker assembly-front single cone	2	To (V) WA 138479	
7	XQM101380	Speaker assembly-front single cone	2	From (V) WA 138480	
8	AMR3840	Bezel-speaker-radio-speaker	2		
9	AB606124	Screw-speaker-self tapping-No 6 x 40	8		
10	WA104004	Washer-plain-speaker-M4	8		
11	AMR3418	Aerial front fender-metal	1	To (V) WA 138479	
11	XUC100840	Aerial front fender-metal	1	Note (1)	
11	XUC100850	Aerial front fender-metal	1	Note (1)	Japan
12	AB614061	Screw-antenna-self tapping	1		
13	CZK3164	Nut-lokut-antenna	1		
14	MRC5527	Washer-antenna-plain-M6	1		
15	NRC2383	Clip-hose-antenna	1		

CHANGE POINTS:
(1) From (V) WA 138480

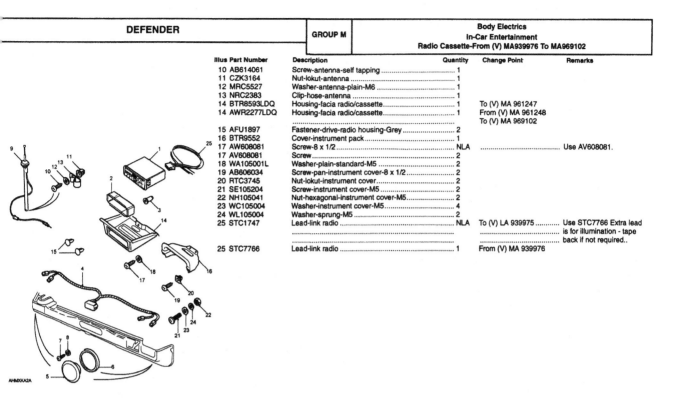

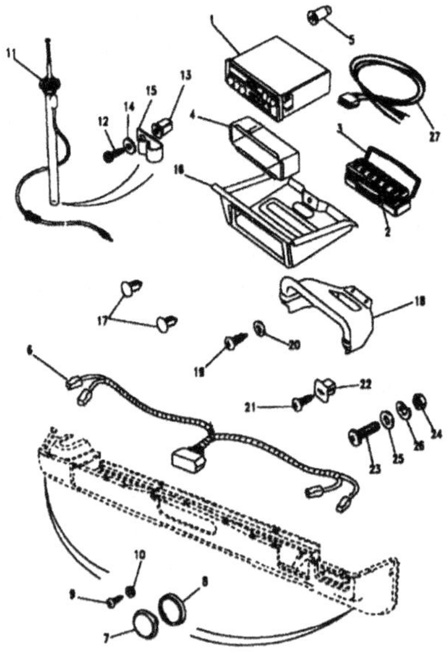

Illus	Part Number	Description	Quantity	Change Point	Remarks
16	AWR2277LDQ	Housing-facia radio/cassette	1	Note (1)	
16	AWR2277LOY	Housing-facia radio/cassette	1	Note (2)	
16	FCA101680LOY	Housing-facia radio/cassette-Dark Granite	1	Note (3)	
16	FCA101680PMA	Housing-facia radio/cassette-Black	1	Note (5)	Tomb Raider
17	AFU1897	Fastener-drive-Grey	2		
17	AFU1897PMP	Fastener-drive-Black	2	Note (5)	Tomb Raider
18	BTR9552	Cover-instrument pack	1	Note (4)	
18	FAR100150	Cover-instrument pack	1	Note (3)	
19	AV608081	Screw-housing	2		
20	WA105001L	Washer-housing-plain-standard-M5	2		
21	AB606034	Screw-pan-instrument cover-8 x 1/2	2		
22	RTC3745	Nut-lokut-instrument cover	2		
23	SE105204	Screw-instrument cover-M5	2		
24	NH105041	Nut-hexagonal-instrument cover-M5	2		
25	WC105004	Washer-instrument cover-M5	4		
26	WL105004	Washer-instrument cover-sprung-M5	2		
27	STC1747	Lead-link radio	NLA		Use STC7766 Extra lead is for illumination - tape back if not required..
27	STC7766	Lead-link radio	1		

CHANGE POINTS:

(1) To (V) VA 104805
(2) From (V) VA 104806 To (V) WA 159806
(3) From (V) XA 159807
(4) To (V) WA 159806
(5) From (V) 1A 612404

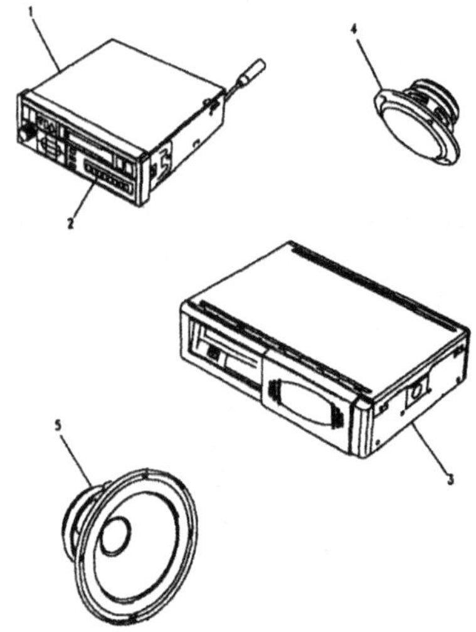

Illus	Part Number	Description	Quantity	Change Point	Remarks
1	STC7005	RADIO CASSETTE ELECTRONIC-AUTO/REVERSAL	1		Except CD compatible
2	STC7008	• Pad-detachable-key radio	1		
1	ZKC6454L	RADIO CASSETTE ELECTRONIC-AUTO/REVERSAL	1		CD compatible
2	STC7009	• Pad-detachable-key radio	1		
3	AMR1783	CD AUTOMATIC CHANGER	NLA		Use AMR3154.
3	AMR3154	CD AUTOMATIC CHANGER-PHILIPS	1		High line
	STC1624	• Magazine-automatic changer compact disc player	1		
4	STC7006	Speaker assembly-front active	2		
5	STC7007	Speaker assembly rear	1		Production fit

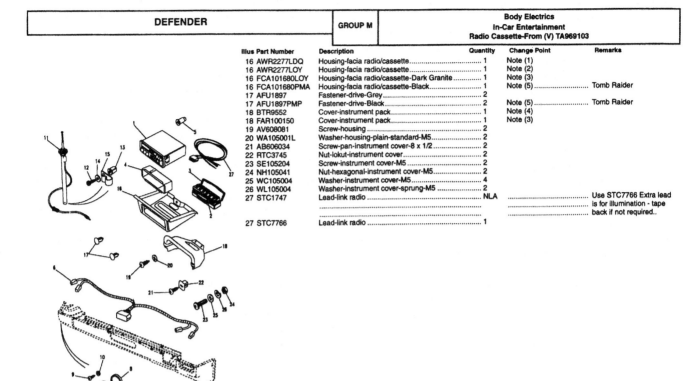

DEFENDER	GROUP M	Body Electrics In-Car Entertainment Aerial & Speakers-V8 EFi

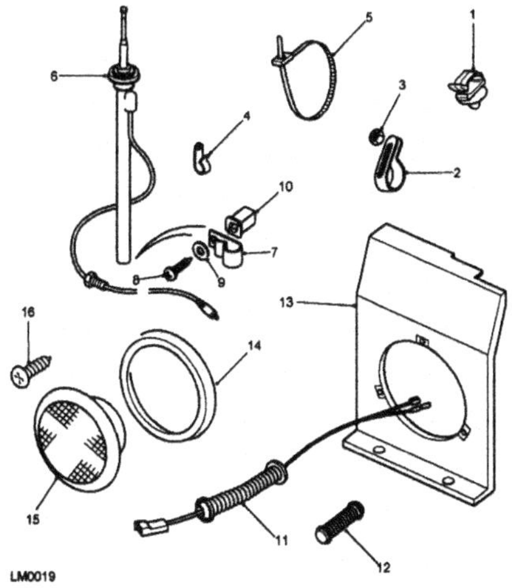

LM0019

Illus	Part Number	Description	Quantity	Change Point	Remarks
1	AFU1090L	Clip-cable-8mm hole	1		
2	C393771L	Clip-p-plastic-adjustable-Black-11.0/20.0mm	1		
3	FN108047L	Nut-flange-flanged head-M8	1		
4	NRC2383	Clip-hose	2		
5	573246	Tie-cable-Black-4.8 x 115mm-inside serated	2		
6	XUC100840	Aerial front fender-metal	1		
6	AMR3976	Aerial front fender-metal	1		
7	NRC2383	Clip-hose	1		
8	AB614061	Screw-self tapping	1		
9	MRC5527	Washer-plain-M6	1		
10	CZK3164	Nut-lokut	1		
11	AMR3262	Harness extension	1		
12	AMR3963	Grommet-harness doors-Convolute	1		
13	AWR4650	Housing-speaker-RH	1		
13	AWR4651	Housing-speaker-LH	1		
14	EKE100000	Plinth-front door speaker	2		
15	XQM101520	SPEAKER-FRONT & REAR SINGLE CONE	4		
	RTC7775	• Speaker-cover	1		
16	AB610061L	Screw-self tapping-No10 x 3/4	6		
16	AB610121L	Screw-No10-self tapping	2		

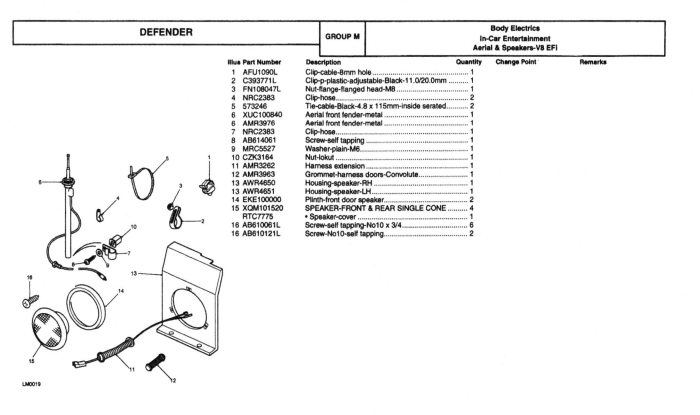

M 127

DEFENDER	GROUP M	Body Electrics Wash Wipe Systems Windscreen Wiper

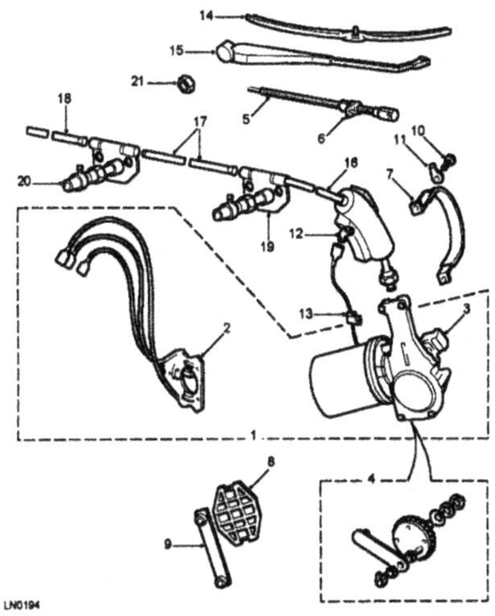

LN0194

Illus	Part Number	Description	Quantity	Change Point	Remarks
1	RTC3867	MOTOR-WINDSCREEN WIPER	1	Note (1)	
2	RTC198	• Brush-wiper motor	1		
3	520160	• Switch parking-screen wipers	1		
1	DLB000200	MOTOR-WINDSCREEN WIPER	1	Note (2)	
2	DLZ000010	• Brush-wiper motor	1		
4	517646	Crank & primary link-windscreen wiper	1	Note (1)	
4	DLW000020	Crank & primary link-windscreen wiper	1	Note (2)	
	DOS000020	Tube	1	Note (2)	
5	37H5208L	Wiper rack	NLA	Note (1)	Use RTC202 Wiper rack and cut to size.
5	DLE000010	Wiper rack	1	Note (2)	
6	37H3694L	Ferrule	1	Note (1)	
6	DLY000010	Ferrule	1	Note (2)	
7	BHA4790L	Bracket-wiper motor	1	Note (1)	
7	DLC000030	Bracket-wiper motor	1	Note (2)	
8	150844	Pad-rubber	1	Note (1)	
8	DKE000010	Pad-rubber	1	Note (2)	
9	MTC2607	Nut-plate	1		
10	SE106161L	Screw-M6 x 16	2		
11	505205	Blade connector-wiper earth	1		
12	STC712	Blade connector-wiper earth	1		
13	570351	Clip-cable	1		

CHANGE POINTS:
(1) To (V) 1A 622423
(2) From (V) 2A 622424

M 128

DEFENDER	GROUP M	Body Electrics Wash Wipe Systems Windscreen Wiper

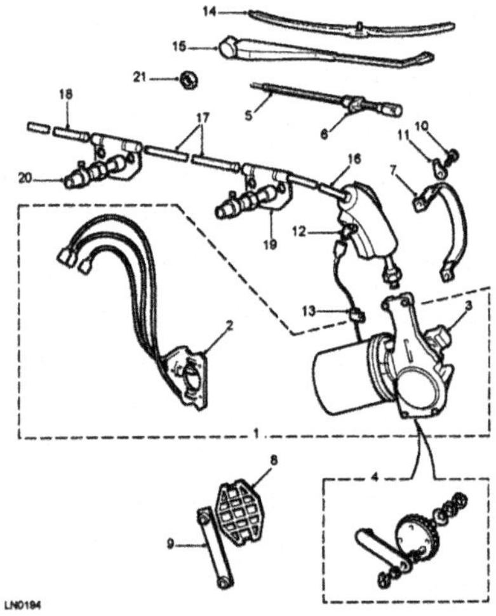

Illus	Part Number	Description	Quantity	Change Point	Remarks
14	PRC8559	Blade-windscreen and backlight wiper-315mm	2	Note (1)	
14	DKC000110PMD	Blade-windscreen and backlight wiper-315mm	2	Note (2)	
15	PRC4276	Arm assembly-windscreen wiper	2	Note (3)	RHD
15	DKB000060PMD	Arm assembly-windscreen wiper	2	Note (4)	RHD
15	PRC4277	Arm assembly-windscreen wiper	2	Note (3)	LHD
15	DKB000050PMD	Arm assembly-windscreen wiper	2	Note (4)	LHD
16	PRC3671	Tube-motor to wheel box-RHD	1		
16	PRC3672	Tube-motor to wheel box-LHD	1		
17	PRC2471	Tube-intermediate section	1		
18	575047	Tube-wheel box to end	1		
19	PRC6283	CASING & WHEELBOX ASSEMBLY-WIPER MOTOR	2	Note (5)	
20	RTC4480	• Drum-splined	1		
19	PRC8495	CASING & WHEELBOX ASSEMBLY-WIPER MOTOR	2	Note (6)	
20	STC987	• Drum-splined	2		
20	DKU000010	Casing & wheelbox assembly-wiper motor	2	Note (4)	
	MUC3933	Cover-wiper pinch bolt	2	Note (7)	Germany
21	DLP000010	Nut-windscreen wiper special	2	Note (4)	
22	YMQ000610	Lead link-windscreen wiper motor-LHD	1	Note (4)	
	DYB000030	Plug-body sealing	1	Note (4)	

CHANGE POINTS:
(1) To (V) XA 170631
(2) From (V) XA 170632
(3) To (V) 1A 622423
(4) From (V) 2A 622424
(5) To (V) FA 434630
(6) From (V) FA 434631 To (V) YA 999999
(7) To (V) MA 962814

DEFENDER	GROUP M	Body Electrics Wash Wipe Systems Windscreen Wash-Non Air Con-To (V) AA270226

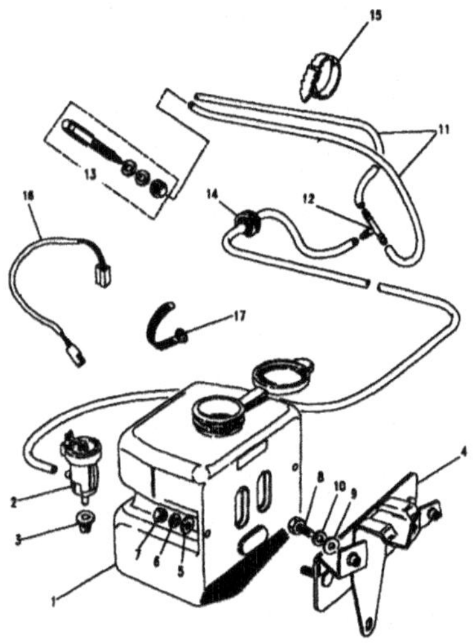

Illus	Part Number	Description	Quantity	Change Point	Remarks
1	PRC3340	Container assembly-windscreen wash	1		
	PRC8664	Cap-container assembly filler neck-55mm	1		
2	ADU3905	Pump assembly-windscreen wash	NLA		Use AMR3849 qty 1 with STC1453 qty 1.
3	RTC3959	Grommet-container assembly pump	1		
4	PRC3978	Bracket-RH	1		
4	PRC3977	Bracket-LH	1		
5	WC106041L	Washer-M6-oversize	2		
6	WL106001L	Washer-sprung-M6	1		
7	NH106041L	Nut-hexagonal-nyloc-M6	3		
8	SE106121L	Screw-pan-pan head-M6 x 12	1		
9	WA106041L	Washer-6mm	1		
10	WL106001L	Washer-sprung-M6	1		
11	RTC3650	Hose-wash system	A/R		
12	C15644L	T piece	1		
13	PRC2437	Jet assembly-nozzle-wash system-single nozzle-front	2		
14	555711	Grommet-cable-Red-6 x 33.5mm	1		
15	RTC222	Fastener-fir tree-2 1/4"	3		
16	PRC3101	Harness-link-washer pump	1		
17	C45099	Tie-cable	4		

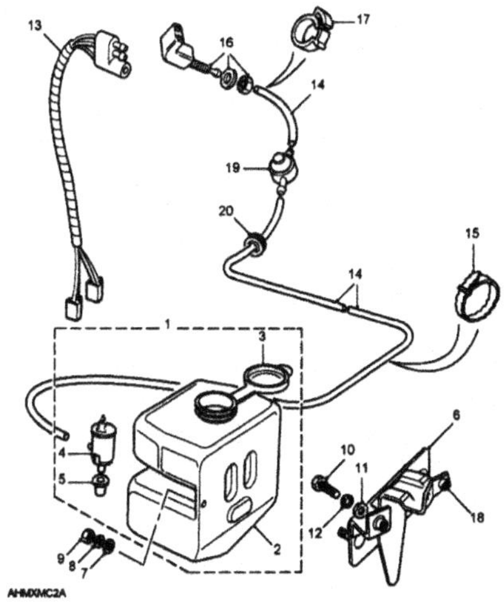

Illus	Part Number	Description	Quantity	Change Point	Remarks
1	AMR3756	CONTAINER-WINDSCREEN WASH	1		
2	PRC5744	• Container-windscreen wash	1		
3	PRC8664	• Cap-container assembly filler neck-55mm	1		
4	ADU3905	• Pump assembly-windscreen wash	NLA		Use AMR3849 qty 1 with STC1453 qty 1.
5	RTC3959	• Grommet-container assembly pump	1		
6	PRC5742	Bracket-washer bottle-RH	NLA	To (V) TA 977374	Use RRC8363.
6	PRC5741	Bracket-washer bottle-LH	1		
6	RRC8363	Bracket-washer bottle-RH	1	From (V) TA 977375	
6	RRC8364	Bracket-washer bottle-LH	1		
7	WC106041L	Washer-M6-oversize	2		
8	WL106001L	Washer-sprung-M6	2		
9	NH106041L	Nut-hexagonal-nyloc-M6	2		
10	SH106121L	Screw-hexagonal head-M6 x 12	1		
11	WA106041L	Washer-6mm	1		
12	WL106001L	Washer-sprung-M6	1		
13	PRC5738	Harness-link-washer pump	1	To (V) LA 939975	
13	AMR1632	Harness-link-washer pump	1	From (V) MA 939976	
14	RTC3650	Hose-wash system	A/R		
15	RTC222	Fastener-fir tree-2 1/4"	3		
16	PRC5736	Jet assembly-nozzle-wash system-single nozzle	NLA	To (V) LA 930671	Use AMR3025.
16	AMR3025	Jet assembly-nozzle-wash system-twin nozzle	1	From (V) LA 930672	
17	AMR3012	Clip-retaining	1		
18	NN106021	Nutsert-blind-M6	2		
19	ACU5037	Valve-wash system non return-4mm	1	From (V) HA 455946	
20	338015	Plug-blanking-plastic-13mm	1		

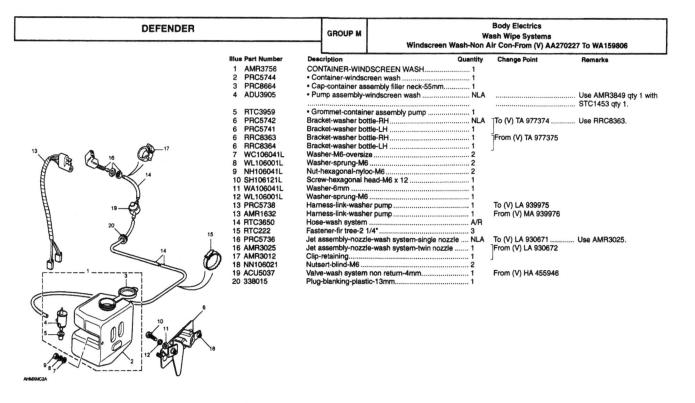

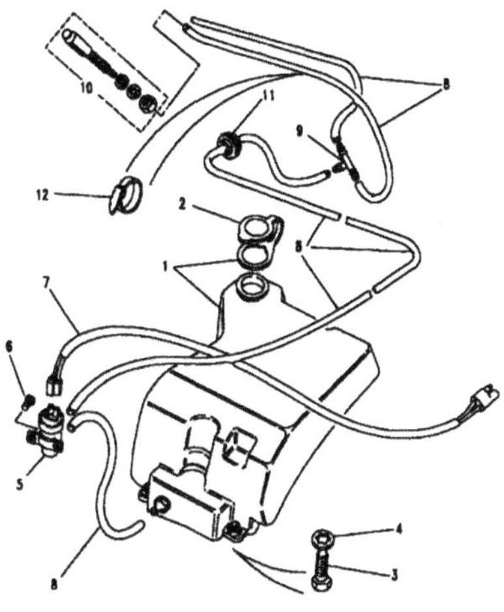

Illus	Part Number	Description	Quantity	Change Point	Remarks
1	PRC3786	Container-windscreen wash	1		
2	PRC2854	Cap-container assembly filler neck-45mm	1		
3	78210	Bolt	3		
4	WF600041L	Washer-lock	3		
5	PRC3369	Pump assembly-windscreen wash	3		
6	AB606051L	Screw-self tapping-No 6 x 5/8	3		
7	PRC3794	Harness-link-pump-windscreen wash	1		
8	RTC3650	Hose-wash system	A/R		
9	C15644	Hose-wash system tee connector/pump-4mm	1		
10	PRC2437	Jet assembly-nozzle-wash system-single nozzle-front	2		
11	555711	Grommet-cable-Red-6 x 33.5mm	1		
12	RTC222	Fastener-fir tree-2 1/4"	3		

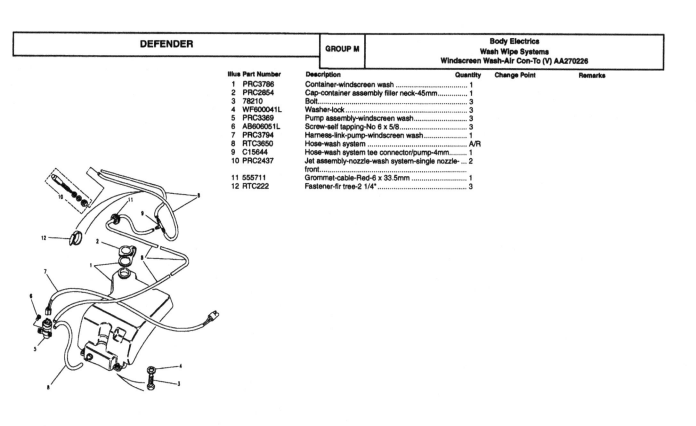

Wash Wipe Systems
Windscreen Wash-Air Con-From (V) AA270227 To WA159806

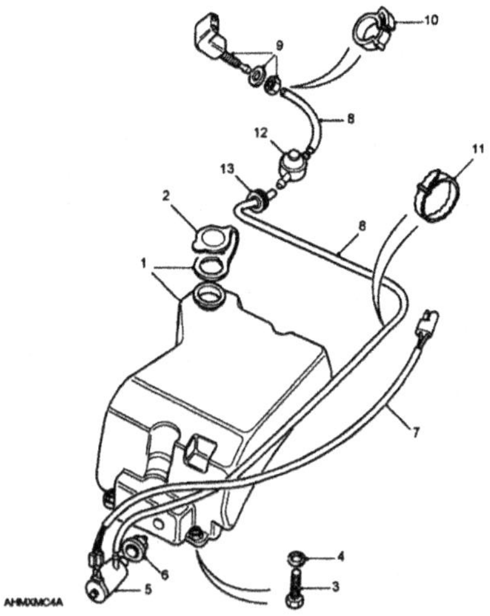

Illus	Part Number	Description	Quantity	Change Point	Remarks
1	PRC5756	Container-windscreen wash	1		
2	PRC2854	Cap-container assembly filler neck-45mm	1		
3	78210	Bolt	3		
4	WF600041L	Washer-lock	3		
5	DRC2713L	Pump assembly-windscreen wash	1		
6	RTC5827	Grommet	1		
7	PRC3794	Harness-link-pump-windscreen wash	1	To (V) LA 939975	
7	AMR2978	Harness-link-pump-windscreen wash	1	From (V) MA 939976	
8	RTC3650	Hose-wash system	A/R		
9	PRC5736	Jet assembly-nozzle-wash system-single nozzle	NLA	To (V) LA 930671	Use AMR3025.
9	AMR3025	Jet assembly-nozzle-wash system-twin nozzle	1	From (V) LA 930672	
10	AMR3012	Clip-retaining	1		
11	RTC222	Fastener-fir tree-2 1/4"	3		
12	ACU5037	Valve-wash system non return-4mm	1	From (V) HA 455946	
13	338015	Plug-blanking-plastic-13mm	1		

Wash Wipe Systems
Windscreen Wash-From (V) XA159807

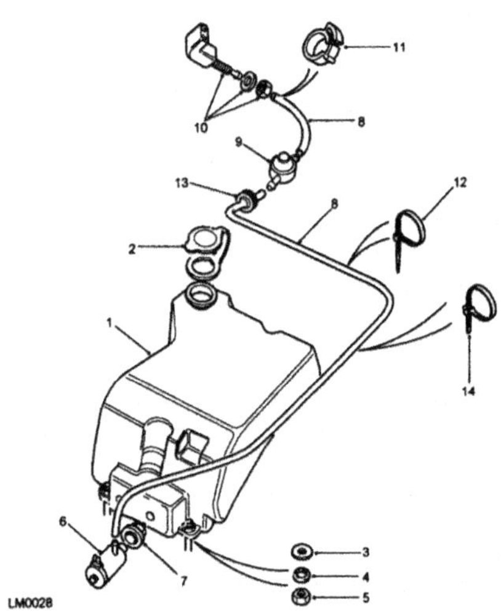

Illus	Part Number	Description	Quantity	Change Point	Remarks
1	DMB103060	Container-windscreen wash	1		
2	DMG10001L	Cap-washer system	1		
3	AFU1069	Washer-plain	3		
4	WF600041L	Washer-lock	3		
5	NH106047L	Nut-hexagonal	3		
6	DMC100550	Pump assembly-windscreen wash	1		
7	AFU4506	Grommet	1		
8	DNC101720	Hose-wash system	A/R		
9	AMR6676	Valve-wash system non return-4mm	1		
10	AMR3025	Jet assembly-nozzle-wash system-twin nozzle	1		
11	AMR3012	Clip-retaining	1		
12	UKC6684L	Tie-cable-Black-3.5 x 150mm-inside serated	3		
13	AMR3550	Grommet	1		
14	YQR10016L	Tie-cable-7mm hole-4.6 x 165mm-4.50mm	1		

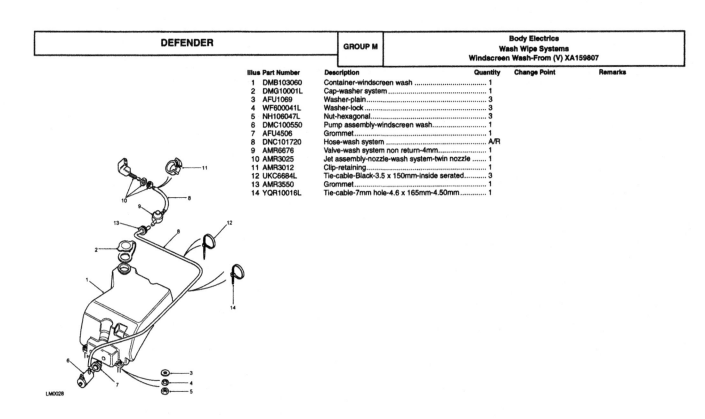

GROUP M	Body Electrics Wash Wipe Systems Windscreen/Backlight Wash-Non Air Con-To (V) WA159806

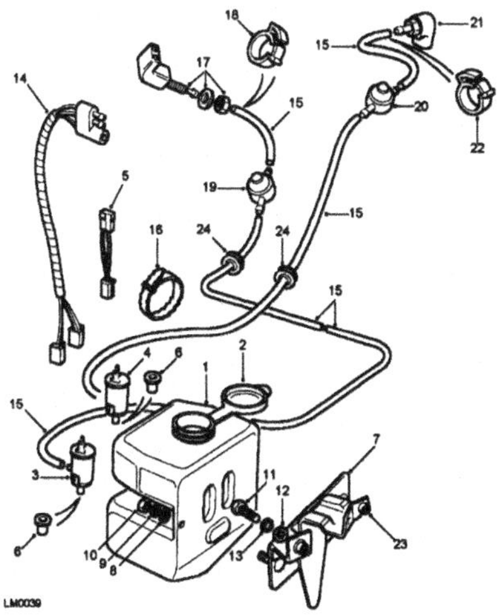

LM0039

Illus	Part Number	Description	Quantity	Change Point	Remarks
1	PRC5747	Container-windscreen wash	1		
2	PRC8664	Cap-container assembly filler neck-55mm	1		
3	ADU3905	Pump assembly-windscreen wash	NLA		Use AMR3849 qty 1 with STC1453 qty 1.
4	STC1453	Pump assembly-backlight wash	1		
5	AMR3849	Lead-link-washer pump-service	1		
6	RTC3959	Grommet-container assembly pump	2		
7	PRC5742	Bracket-washer bottle-RH	NLA	To (V) TA 977374	Use RRC8363.
7	PRC5741	Bracket-washer bottle-LH	1		
7	RRC8363	Bracket-washer bottle-RH	1	From (V) TA 977375	
7	RRC8364	Bracket-washer bottle-LH	1		
8	WC106041L	Washer-M6-oversize	2		
9	WL106001L	Washer-sprung-M6	2		
10	NH106041L	Nut-hexagonal-nyloc-M6	2		
11	SH106121L	Screw-hexagonal head-M6 x 12	1		
12	WA106041L	Washer-6mm	1		
13	WL106001L	Washer-sprung-M6	1		
14	PRC5738	Harness-link	1	To (V) LA 939975	
14	AMR2474	Harness-link	1	From (V) MA 939976	
15	RTC3650	Hose-wash system	A/R		
16	RTC222	Fastener-fir tree-2 1/4"	3		
17	PRC5736	Jet assembly-nozzle-wash system-single nozzle	NLA	To (V) LA 930671	Use AMR3025.
17	AMR3025	Jet assembly-nozzle-wash system-twin nozzle	1	From (V) LA 930672	
18	AMR3012	Clip-retaining	1		
19	ACU5037	Valve-wash system non return-windscreen wash-4mm	1	From (V) HA 455946	
20	ACU5037	Valve-wash system non return-rear screen wash-4mm	1		
21	PRC5802	Jet assembly-nozzle wash system-rear	NLA	To (V) LA 930671	Use AMR3026.
21	AMR3026	Jet assembly-nozzle wash system-rear	1	From (V) LA 930672	
22	AMR3012	Clip-retaining-washer jet	1		
23	NN106021	Nutsert-blind-M6	2		
24	338015	Plug-blanking-plastic-13mm	2		

GROUP M	Body Electrics Wash Wipe Systems Windscreen/Backlight Wash-Air Con-To (V) WA159806

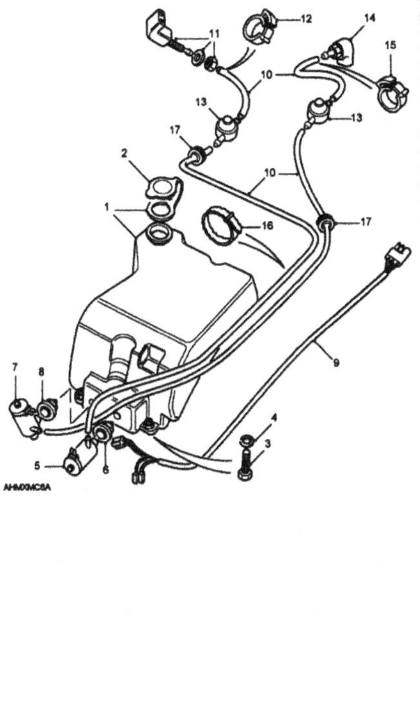

AHM0MC6A

Illus	Part Number	Description	Quantity	Change Point	Remarks
1	PRC5765	Container-windscreen wash	1		
2	PRC2854	Cap-container assembly filler neck-45mm	1		
3	78210	Bolt	3		
4	WF600041L	Washer-lock	3		
5	DRC2713L	Pump assembly-windscreen wash	1		
6	RTC5827	Grommet	1		
7	ADU6693L	Pump assembly-backlight wash	1		
8	RTC5828	Grommet	1		
9	PRC5739	Harness-link-washer pump front & rear	1	To (V) LA 939975	
9	AMR2979	Harness-link-washer pump front & rear	1	From (V) MA 939976	
10	RTC3650	Hose-wash system	A/R		
11	PRC5736	Jet assembly-nozzle-wash system-single nozzle	NLA	To (V) LA 930671	Use AMR3025.
11	AMR3025	Jet assembly-nozzle-wash system-twin nozzle	1	From (V) LA 930672	
12	AMR3012	Clip-retaining	1		
13	ACU5037	Valve-wash system non return-windscreen wash-4mm	1	From (V) HA 455946	
13	ACU5037	Valve-wash system non return-4mm	1		
14	PRC5802	Jet assembly-nozzle wash system-rear	NLA	To (V) LA 930671	Use AMR3026.
14	AMR3026	Jet assembly-nozzle wash system-rear	1	From (V) LA 930672	
15	AMR3012	Clip-retaining	1		
16	RTC222	Fastener-fir tree-2 1/4"	3		
17	338015	Plug-blanking-plastic-13mm	2		

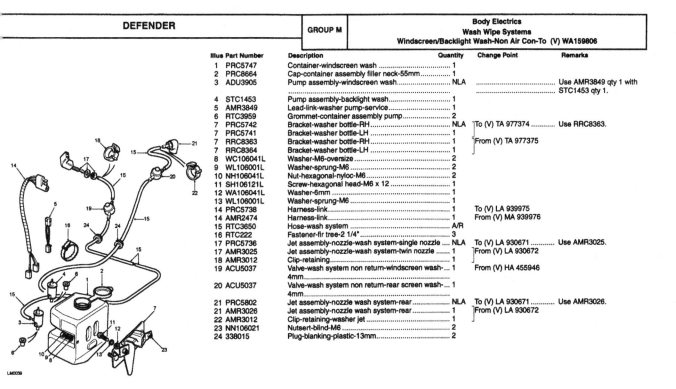

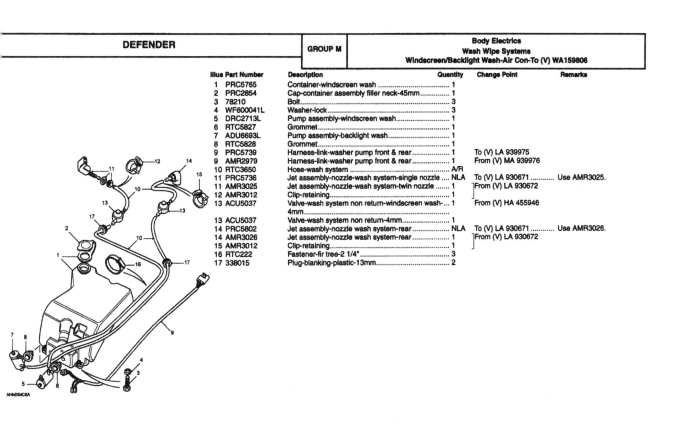

DEFENDER

GROUP M

Body Electrics
Wash Wipe Systems
Windscreen/Backlight Wash-From (V) XA159807

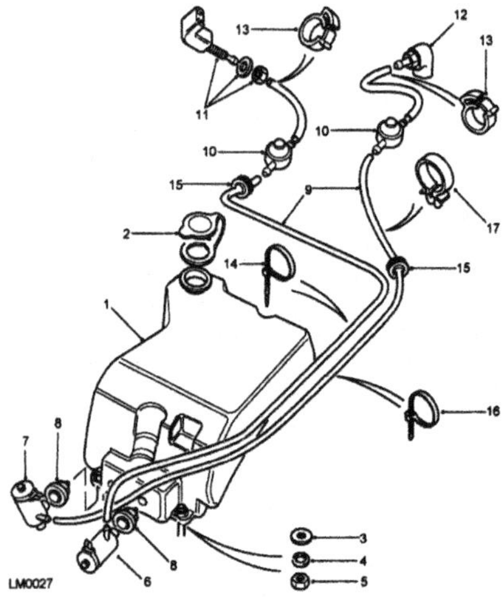

Illus	Part Number	Description	Quantity	Change Point	Remarks
1	DMB103090	Container-windscreen wash	1		
2	DMG10001L	Cap-washer system	1		
3	AFU1069	Washer-plain	3		
4	WF600041L	Washer-lock	3		
5	NH106047L	Nut-hexagonal	3		
6	DMC100550	Pump assembly-windscreen wash	1		
7	DMC100540	Pump assembly-backlight wash-black wire	1		
8	AFU4506	Grommet	2		
9	DNC101720	Hose-wash system	A/R		
10	AMR6676	Valve-wash system non return-4mm	2		
11	AMR3025	Jet assembly-nozzle-wash system-twin nozzle	1		
12	AMR3026	Jet assembly-nozzle wash system-rear	1		
13	AMR3012	Clip-retaining	2		
14	UKC6684L	Tie-cable-Black-3.5 x 150mm-inside serated	3		
15	AMR3550	Grommet	2		
16	YQR10016L	Tie-cable-7mm hole-4.6 x 165mm-4.50mm	2		
17	PRC5273	Clip-omega-Grey-10.5 x 8mm-6.5mm hole	2		

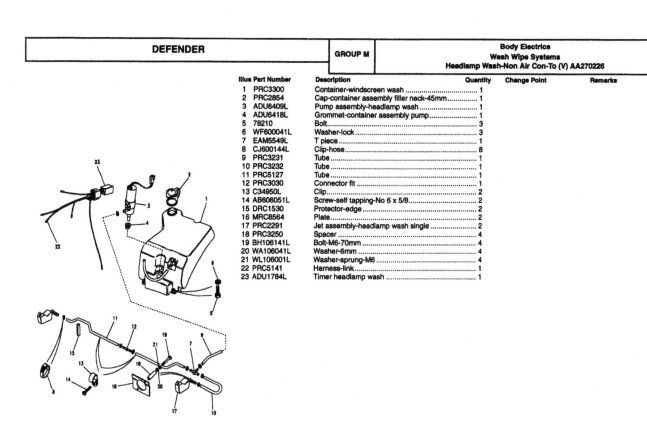

DEFENDER

GROUP M

Body Electrics
Wash Wipe Systems
Headlamp Wash-Non Air Con-To (V) AA270226

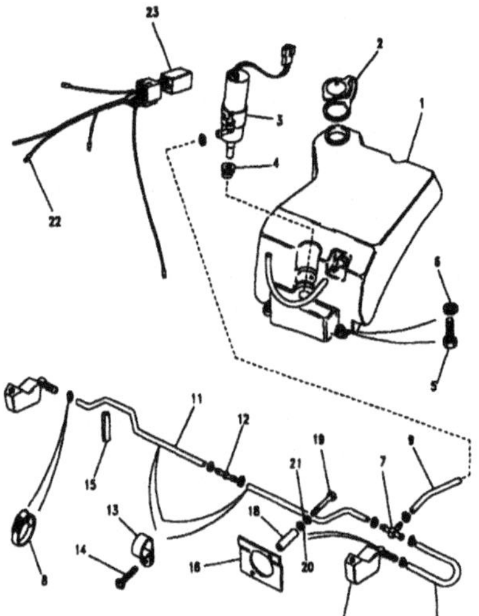

Illus	Part Number	Description	Quantity	Change Point	Remarks
1	PRC3300	Container-windscreen wash	1		
2	PRC2854	Cap-container assembly filler neck-45mm	1		
3	ADU6409L	Pump assembly-headlamp wash	1		
4	ADU6418L	Grommet-container assembly pump	1		
5	78210	Bolt	3		
6	WF600041L	Washer-lock	3		
7	EAM5549L	T piece	1		
8	CJ600144L	Clip-hose	8		
9	PRC3231	Tube	1		
10	PRC3232	Tube	1		
11	PRC5127	Tube	1		
12	PRC3030	Connector fit	1		
13	C34950L	Clip	2		
14	AB606051L	Screw-self tapping-No 6 x 5/8	2		
15	DRC1530	Protector-edge	2		
16	MRC8564	Plate	2		
17	PRC2291	Jet assembly-headlamp wash single	2		
18	PRC3250	Spacer	4		
19	BH106141L	Bolt-M6-70mm	4		
20	WA106041L	Washer-6mm	4		
21	WL106001L	Washer-sprung-M6	4		
22	PRC5141	Harness-link	1		
23	ADU1784L	Timer headlamp wash	1		

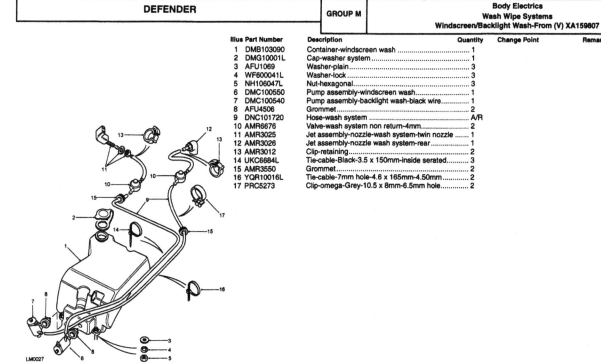

Wash Wipe Systems
Windscreen/Headlamp Wash-Air Con-To (V) AA270226

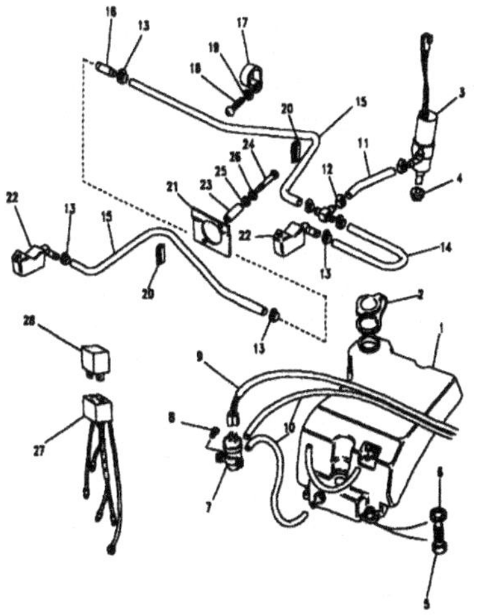

Illus	Part Number	Description	Quantity	Change Point	Remarks
1	PRC3780	Container-windscreen wash	1		
2	PRC2854	Cap-container assembly filler neck-45mm	1		
3	ADU6409L	Pump assembly-headlamp wash	1		
4	ADU6418L	Grommet-container assembly pump	1		
5	78210	Bolt	3		
6	WF600041L	Washer-lock	3		
7	STC575	Pump assembly-windscreen wash	1		
8	AB606051L	Screw-self tapping-No 6 x 5/8	2		
9	PRC3794	Harness-link-pump-windscreen wash	1		
10	RTC3650	Hose-wash system	A/R		
11	PRC3231	Tube	1		
12	EAM5549L	T piece	1		
13	CJ600144L	Clip-hose	8		
14	PRC3232	Tube-to LH jet	1		
15	RTC4848	Hose-headlamp wash-to connector-10mm ID x 5M.	A/R		
15	RTC4848	Hose-headlamp wash-to RH jet-10mm ID x 5M	A/R		
16	PRC3030	Connector fit	1		
17	C34950L	Clip	2		
18	AB606051L	Screw-self tapping-No 6 x 5/8	2		
19	WA104001L	Washer-plain-M4	2		
20	DRC1530	Protector-edge	2		
21	MRC8564	Plate	1		
22	PRC2291	Jet assembly-headlamp wash single	2		
23	PRC3250	Spacer	4		
24	BH106141L	Bolt-M6-70mm	4		
25	WA106041L	Washer-6mm	4		
26	WL106001L	Washer-sprung-M6	1		
27	PRC5141	Harness-link-washer pump-delay unit	1		
28	ADU1784L	Timer headlamp wash	1		

Wash Wipe Systems
Windscreen/Headlamp Wash-Air Con-From (V) AA270227 To WA159806

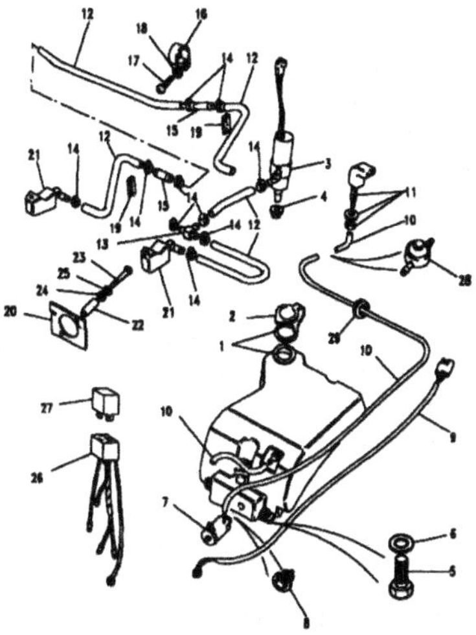

Illus	Part Number	Description	Quantity	Change Point	Remarks
1	PRC5773	Container-windscreen wash	1		
2	PRC2854	Cap-container assembly filler neck-45mm	1		
3	ADU6409L	Pump assembly-headlamp wash	1		
4	ADU6418L	Grommet-container assembly pump	1		
5	78210	Bolt	3		
6	WF600041L	Washer-lock	3		
7	DRC2713L	Pump assembly-windscreen wash	1		
8	RTC5827	Grommet	1		
9	PRC3794	Harness-link-washer pump	1	To (V) LA 939975	
9	AMR2978	Harness-link-washer pump	1	From (V) MA 939976	
10	RTC3650	Hose-wash system	A/R		
11	PRC5736	Jet assembly-nozzle-wash system-single nozzle	NLA	To (V) LA 930671	Use AMR3025.
11	AMR3025	Jet assembly-nozzle-wash system-twin nozzle	1	From (V) LA 930672	
12	RTC4848	Hose-headlamp wash-10mm ID x 5M	A/R		
13	EAM5549L	T piece	1		
14	CJ600144L	Clip-hose	8		
15	PRC3030	Connector fit	2		
16	C34950L	Clip	3		
17	AB606051L	Screw-self tapping-No 6 x 5/8	3		
18	WA104001L	Washer-plain-M4	3		
19	DRC1530	Protector-edge	2		
20	MRC8564	Plate	1		
21	PRC2291	Jet assembly-headlamp wash single	2		
22	PRC3250	Spacer	4		
23	BH106141L	Bolt-M6-70mm	4		
24	WA106041L	Washer-6mm	1		
25	WL106001L	Washer-sprung-M6	1		
26	PRC5141	Harness-link-washer pump-delay unit	1		
27	ADU1784L	Timer headlamp wash	1		
28	ACU5037	Valve-wash system non return-4mm	1	From (V) HA 455946	
29	338015	Plug-blanking-plastic-13mm	2		

DEFENDER	GROUP M	Body Electrics Wash Wipe Systems Windscreen/Backlight/Headlamp Wash-Non Air Con-From (V) AA270227 To WA159806

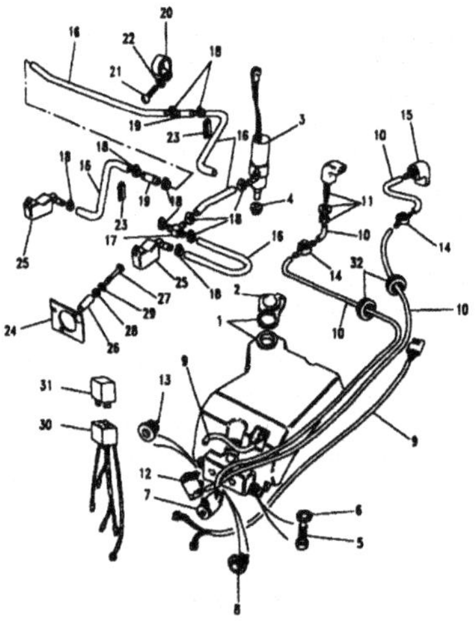

Illus	Part Number	Description	Quantity	Change Point	Remarks
1	PRC5777	Container-windscreen wash	1		
2	PRC2854	Cap-container assembly filler neck-45mm	1		
3	ADU6409L	Pump assembly-headlamp wash	1		
4	ADU6418L	Grommet-container assembly pump	1		
5	78210	Bolt	3		
6	WF600041L	Washer-lock	3		
7	DRC2713L	Pump assembly-windscreen wash	1		
8	RTC5827	Grommet	1		
9	PRC5739	Harness-link-washer pump front & rear	1	To (V) LA 939975	
9	AMR2979	Harness-link-washer pump front & rear	1	From (V) MA 939976	
10	RTC3650	Hose-wash system	A/R		
11	PRC5736	Jet assembly-nozzle-wash system-single nozzle	NLA	To (V) LA 930671	Use AMR3025.
11	AMR3025	Jet assembly-nozzle-wash system-twin nozzle	1	From (V) LA 930672	
12	ADU6693L	Pump assembly-backlight wash	1		
13	RTC5828	Grommet	1		
14	ACU5037	Valve-wash system non return-4mm	2		
15	PRC5802	Jet assembly-nozzle wash system-rear	NLA	To (V) LA 930671	Use AMR3026.
15	AMR3026	Jet assembly-nozzle wash system-rear	1	From (V) LA 930672	
16	RTC4848	Hose-headlamp wash-10mm ID x 5M	A/R		
17	EAM5549L	T piece	1		
18	CJ600144L	Clip-hose	8		
19	PRC3030	Connector fit	2		
20	C34950L	Clip	3		
21	AB606051L	Screw-self tapping-No 6 x 5/8	3		
22	WA104001L	Washer-plain-M4	3		
23	DRC1530	Protector-edge	2		
24	MRC8564	Plate	1		
25	PRC2291	Jet assembly-headlamp wash single	2		
26	PRC3250	Spacer	4		
27	BH106141L	Bolt-M6-70mm	4		
28	WA106041L	Washer-6mm	1		
29	WL106001L	Washer-sprung-M6	1		
30	PRC5141	Harness-link-washer pump-delay unit	1		
31	ADU1784L	Timer headlamp wash	1		
32	338015	Plug-blanking-plastic-13mm	2		

DEFENDER	GROUP M	Body Electrics Wash Wipe Systems Windscreen/Backlight/Headlamp Wash-Finland & Sweden-From (V) AA270227 To (V)

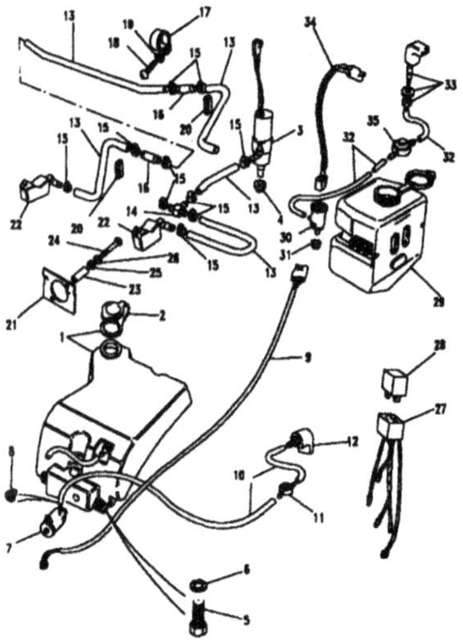

Illus	Part Number	Description	Quantity	Change Point	Remarks
1	PRC5773	Container-windscreen wash	1		
2	PRC2854	Cap-container assembly filler neck-45mm	1		
3	ADU6409L	Pump assembly-headlamp wash	1		
4	ADU6418L	Grommet-container assembly pump	1		
5	78210	Bolt	3		
6	WF600041L	Washer-lock	3		
7	DRC2713L	Pump assembly-windscreen wash	1		
8	RTC5827	Grommet	1		
9	PRC3794	Harness-link-pump-windscreen wash	1		
10	RTC3650	Hose-wash system	A/R		
11	ACU5037	Valve-wash system non return-4mm	1		
12	PRC5802	Jet assembly-nozzle wash system-rear	NLA	To (V) LA 930671	Use AMR3026.
12	AMR3026	Jet assembly-nozzle wash system-rear	1	From (V) LA 930672	
13	RTC4848	Hose-headlamp wash-10mm ID x 5M	A/R		
14	EAM5549L	T piece	1		
15	CJ600144L	Clip-hose	8		
16	PRC3030	Connector fit	2		
17	C34950L	Clip	3		
18	AB605051L	Screw	3		
19	WA104001L	Washer-plain-M4	3		
20	DRC1530	Protector-edge	2		
21	MRC8564	Plate	2		
22	PRC2291	Jet assembly-headlamp wash single	2		
23	PRC3250	Spacer	4		
24	BH106141L	Bolt-M6-70mm	4		
25	WA106041L	Washer-6mm	4		
26	WL106001L	Washer-sprung-M6	4		
27	PRC5141	Harness-link-washer pump-delay unit	1		
28	ADU1784L	Timer headlamp wash	1		
29	PRC5744	Container-windscreen wash	1		
30	ADU3905	Pump assembly-windscreen wash	NLA		Use AMR3849 qty 1 with STC1453 qty 1.
31	RTC3959	Grommet-container assembly pump	1		
32	RTC3650	Hose-wash system	A/R		
33	PRC5736	Jet assembly-nozzle-wash system-single nozzle	NLA	To (V) LA 930671	Use AMR3025.
33	AMR3025	Jet assembly-nozzle-wash system-twin nozzle	1		
34	PRC5739	Harness-link-washer pump	1		
35	ACU5037	Valve-wash system non return-4mm	1	From (V) HA 455946	

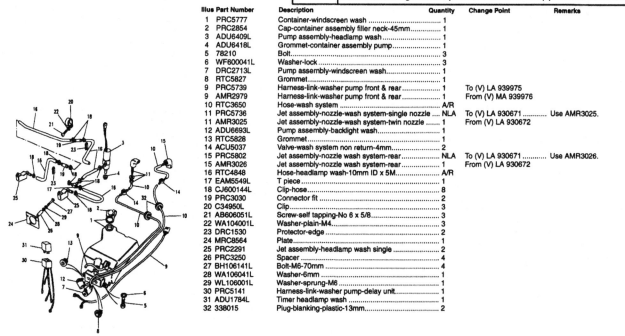

Rear Screen Wiper-To (V) MA965105

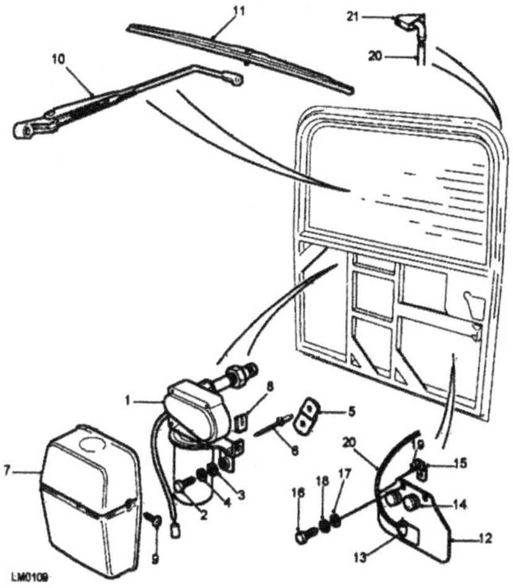

Illus	Part Number	Description	Quantity	Change Point	Remarks
1	PRC4612	Motor & bracket assembly-backlight wiper-Imos	1	Note (1)	
1	AMR1054	Motor & bracket assembly-backlight wiper-Delco	1	From (V) JA 910754	
2	SR106251L	Screw-wiper motor fixing	1		
3	WA106041L	Washer-6mm	1		
4	WL106001L	Washer-sprung-M6	1		
5	MUC1286	Bracket-wiper mounting	1	Note (1)	
5	ALR2622	Bracket-wiper mounting	1	From (V) JA 910754	
6	RA610167	Rivet	1	Note (1)	
6	RA612207L	Rivet	1	From (V) JA 910754	
7	PRC4613	Cover-backlight wiper motor-Black	1	Note (2)	
7	PRC4613LCS	Cover-backlight wiper motor-Grey	1	Note (3)	
7	BTR3792LCS	Cover-backlight wiper motor-Slate Grey	1	From (V) JA 910754	
8	AK608141L	Nut-spring-u type	2		
9	DA608044L	Screw-self tapping-wiper motor fixing-M8 x 13-self tapping	2		
10	STC443	Arm assembly-backlight wiper	1	Note (4)	
10	PRC8558	Arm assembly-backlight wiper	1	From (V) FA 452018	
11	RTC6856	Blade-windscreen and backlight wiper	1	Note (4)	
11	PRC8559	Blade-windscreen and backlight wiper-315mm	1	From (V) FA 452018	
12	PRC4436	Container & pump assembly-windscreen wash	NLA	Note (5)	Original bag no longer available, therefore use washer bag kit STC3803. Note, parts within the new kit will not fit the earlier bag assembly.
13	ADU3905	Pump assembly-windscreen wash	NLA	Note (5)	Use AMR3849 qty 1 with STC1453 qty 1.
14	RTC3175	Cap-washer system	1	Note (5)	
15	MUC1287	Bracket	1	Note (5)	
16	FS106201L	Screw-flanged head-M6 x 20	2	Note (5)	
17	WJ106001L	Washer-plain-M6	2	Note (5)	
18	WL106001L	Washer-sprung-M6	2	Note (5)	
19	RA610167	Rivet	2	Note (5)	
20	RTC3650	Hose-wash system	A/R	Note (5)	
21	EAM9332	Jet assembly-nozzle-wash system-rear	1	Note (5)	

CHANGE POINTS:
- (1) To (V) JA 910753
- (2) To (V) EA 314173
- (3) From (V) EA 314174 To (V) JA 910753
- (4) To (V) FA 452017
- (5) To (V) AA 270226

Rear Screen Wiper-From (V) MA965106

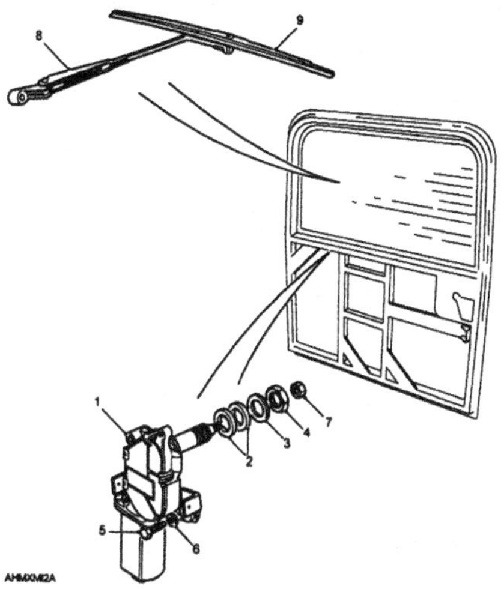

Illus	Part Number	Description	Quantity	Change Point	Remarks
1	AMR3676	Motor & bracket assembly-backlight wiper	1		
1	AMR6108	Motor & bracket assembly-backlight wiper	1		50 LE
2	AMR3932	Grommet	2		
3	AMR3933	Washer-plastic	1		
4	AMR3934	Nut	1		
5	GG106251L	Screw-paint clearing-M6 x 25	1		
6	MRC5527	Washer-plain-M6	1		
7	NH108041L	Nut-hexagonal head-M8	1		
8	PRC8558	Arm assembly-backlight wiper	1		
9	PRC8559	Blade-windscreen and backlight wiper-315mm	1	To (V) XA 170631	
9	DKC100980	Blade-windscreen and backlight wiper-315mm	1	From (V) XA 170632	

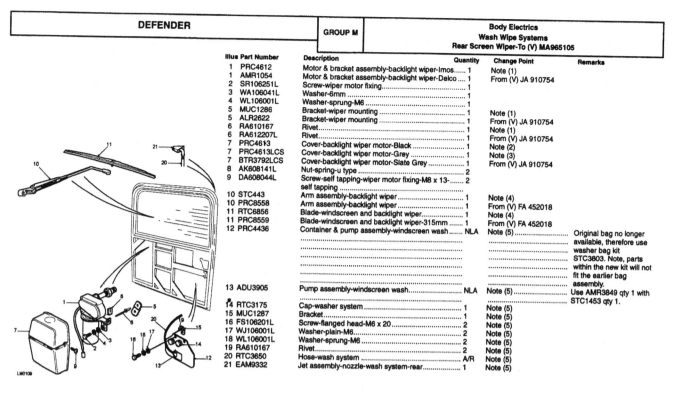

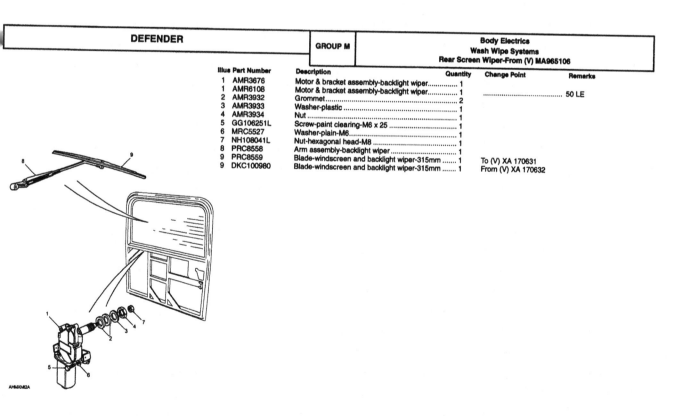

Illus	Part Number	Description	Quantity	Change Point	Remarks
1	AAU3715L	Clip-p-Black-13.6mm-plastic	A/R		
1	PRC4543	Clip-p-Black-17.4/20.0mm-plastic	A/R		
2	C39377L	Clip-p-plastic-adjustable-White.-4.0/12.0mm	A/R		
2	C393771L	Clip-p-plastic-adjustable-Black-11.0/20.0mm	A/R		
3	AFU3081L	Clip-self adhesive-6mm	A/R		
3	DRC5017L	Clip-self adhesive-8mm	A/R		
4	PRC5273	Clip-omega-Grey-10.5 x 8mm-6.5mm hole	A/R		
4	PRC5274	Clip-omega-White.-14 x 10mm-6.5mm hole	A/R		
4	PRC5275	Clip-omega-Blue.-17 x 13mm-6.5mm hole	A/R		

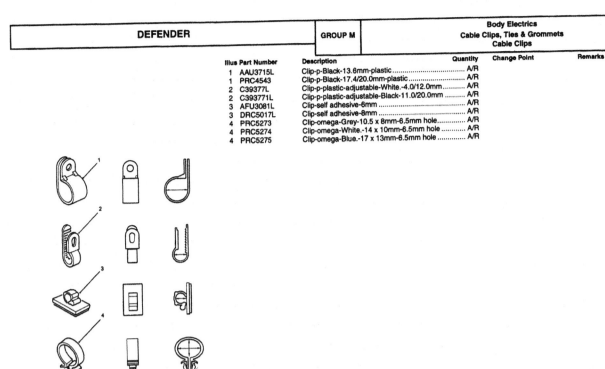

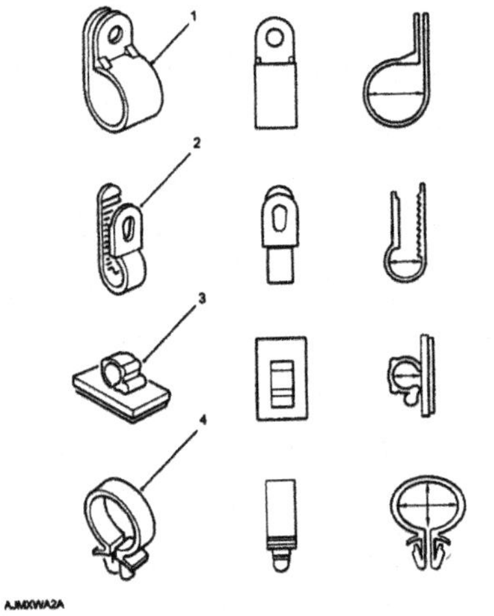

Illus	Part Number	Description	Quantity	Change Point	Remarks
		HARNESS SUPPORT CLIPS-STEEL			
1	240407	Clip-hose-14.5mm-steel-25/64" hole	A/R		
		HARNESS SUPPORT BRACKETS-STEEL			
2	PRC2979	Bracket-clipping-steel	A/R		
3	ERC9404	Bracket harness	A/R		
		CONNECTOR MOUNTING BRACKETS-STEEL			
4	AMR1935	Bracket-mounting-steel	A/R		

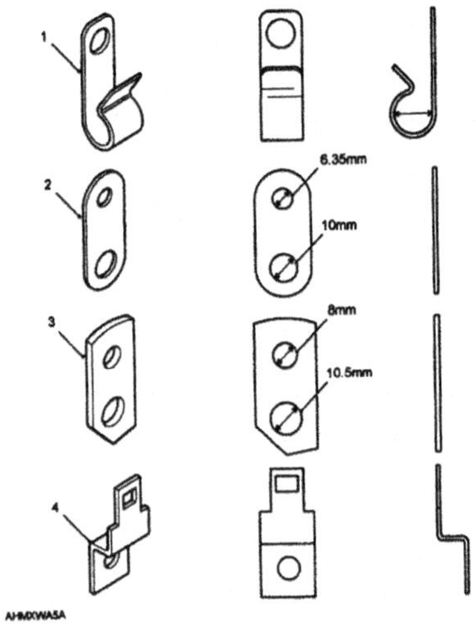

Illus	Part Number	Description	Quantity	Change Point	Remarks
		CABLE TIES-STANDARD-OUTSIDE SERRATED			
1	C43640	Tie-cable-Black-2.5 x 100mm-outside serated	A/R		
		CABLE TIES-STANDARD-INSIDE SERRATED			
		TIE-CABLE			
2	DRC1538	Black-2.5 x 100mm-inside serated	NLA		Use C43640.
2	C43640	Black-2.5 x 100mm-outside serated	A/R		
2	UKC6684L	Black-3.5 x 150mm-inside serated	A/R		
2	NTC1154	3.5 x 300mm-inside serated	A/R		
2	594594	White.-4.6 x 385mm-inside serated	A/R		
2	573246	Black-4.8 x 115mm-inside serated	A/R		
2	RTC3772	Black-4.8 x 135mm-inside serated	A/R		
2	568680	4.8 x 270mm-inside serated	A/R		
2	ESR3301	Black-13.0 x 540mm-inside serated	A/R		
		TIE-CABLE			
3	13H9704L	Black-6.5 x 100mm-releasable	A/R		
3	13H9727L	Black-7.5 x 145mm-releasable	A/R		
3	AFU4173	Black-8.8 x 770mm-releasable	A/R		
		CABLE TIES-PANEL FIXING -TO 4MM THICK			
		TIE-CABLE			
4	YQR10016L	panel fixing-7mm hole-4.6 x 165mm-4.50mm	A/R		
4	YQR10075	panel fixing-Grey-4.6 x 165mm	A/R		
4	YYD10003	panel fixing-8mm hole-4.6 x 215mm	A/R		
		CABLE TIES-PANEL FIXING-TO 2.5MM THICK			
5	AAU3686	Tie-cable-panel fixing-6.5mm hole-8.0 x 155mm	A/R		

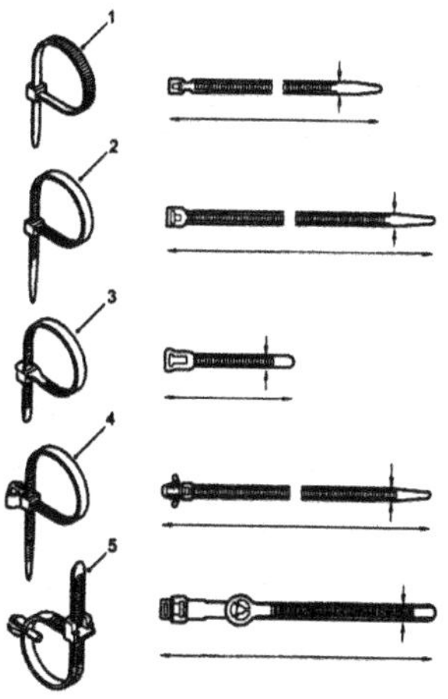

AHMXWA1A

Illus	Part Number	Description	Quantity	Change Point	Remarks
		CABLE STRAPS-PLASTIC ADJUSTABLE PANEL FIXING-FOR 6.4MM HOLE			
1	ADU7981L	Tie-cable-panel fixing-plastic-adjustable-24mm-diameter-97mm-6.4mm hole	A/R		
1	ADU8981	Tie-cable-panel fixing-plastic-adjustable-122mm-32mm diameter-6.4mm hole	A/R		
		CABLE TIE-STUD FIXING			
1	YYC10294L	Tie-cable-stud fixing-fixed contact-Clear	A/R		

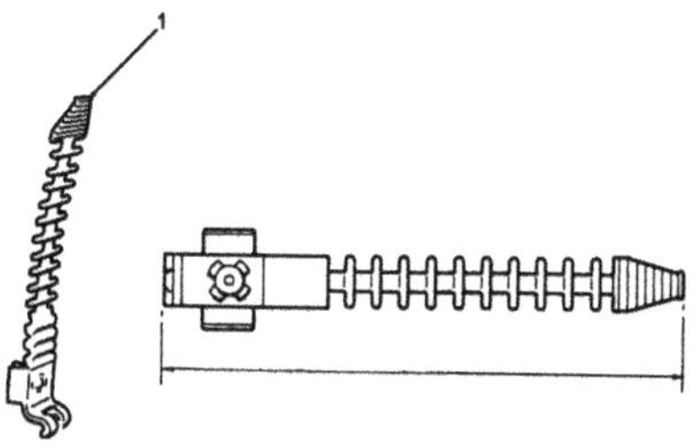

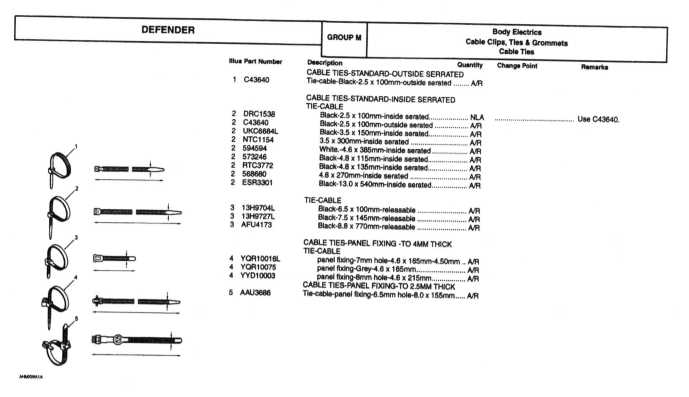

AHMXWA1B

Illus	Part Number	Description	Quantity	Change Point	Remarks
		CRADLE CLIPS-PANEL FIXING			
1	CLP8934	Clip-cradle-panel fixing-13mm-8mm hole	A/R		
		CRADLE CLIPS-STUD FIXING			
2	AMR2323	Clip-cradle-stud fixing-13mm-5mm	A/R		
		SWIVEL CLIPS			
3	ESR301	Clip-swivel-10 x 10mm	A/R		
4	ADU7739L	Clip-swivel-15 x 10mm	A/R		
	AAU3084L	Clip-swivel	6	Note (1)	

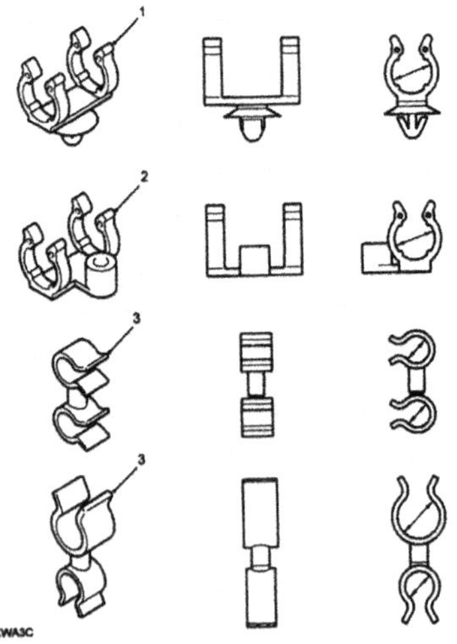

AJMXWA3C

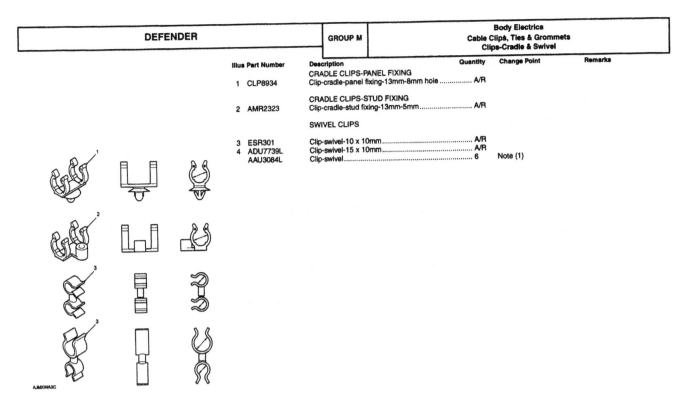

CHANGE POINTS:
(1) From (V) XA 159807

Illus	Part Number	Description	Quantity	Change Point	Remarks
		CLIP-PANEL FIXING			
1	PRC3702	5mm-4.8mm hole	A/R		
2	AFU2879	5mm-6.5mm hole	A/R		
3	AFU1090L	8mm hole	A/R		
		CLIP-EDGE			
4	AFU1296	Clip-edge harness-12mm-Clear.	A/R		
4	AMR5481	Clip-edge harness-15mm	A/R		

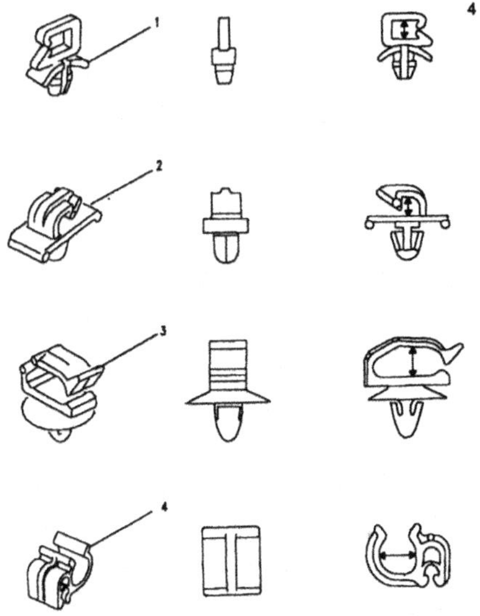

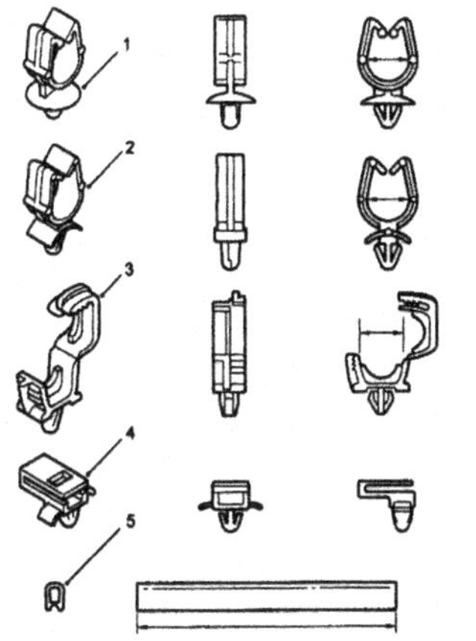

AJMXWA3B

Illus	Part Number	Description	Quantity	Change Point	Remarks
		HARNESS CLIPS-PANEL FIXING			
1	ADU8267	Clip-harness-14mm-6mm hole	A/R		
2	ADU8363L	Clip-harness-14.5mm-6.5mm hole	A/R		
		SNAP CLIPS-PANEL FIXING			
3	DBP8169L	Clip-pivot-snap-13-17mm-7mm hole-Grey	A/R		
		HARNESS ADAPTOR CLIPS-PANEL FIXING			
4	YYC10030L	Clip-harness-adaptor-6.5mm hole	A/R		
		EDGE PROTECTION STRIP			
5	JRC7549	Strip-edge protection-89mm	A/R		

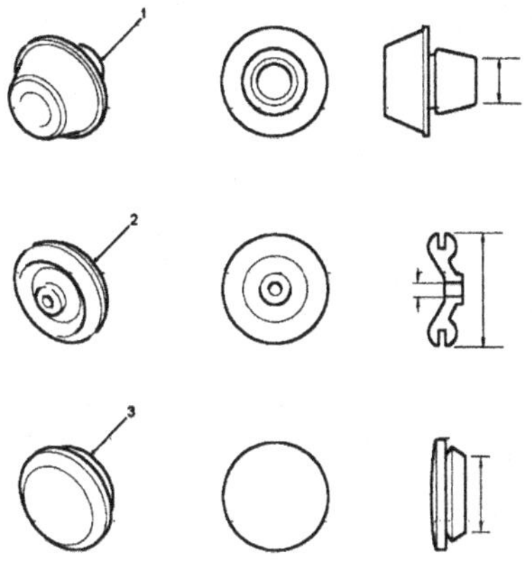

LM0112

Illus	Part Number	Description	Quantity	Change Point	Remarks
		PLASTIC SEALING PLUGS			
1	338029	Plug-blanking-plastic-8mm	A/R		
1	338013	Plug-blanking-plastic-9.5mm	A/R		
1	338014	Plug-blanking-plastic-11mm	A/R		
1	338015	Plug-blanking-plastic-13mm	A/R		
1	ANR1369	Plug-blanking-plastic-13.5mm	A/R		
1	338017	Plug-blanking-plastic-14mm	A/R		
1	338018	Plug-blanking-plastic-16mm	A/R		
1	338019	Plug-blanking-plastic-17.5mm	A/R		
1	338020	Plug-blanking-plastic-19mm	A/R		
1	338021	Plug-blanking-plastic-20.5mm	A/R		
1	338023	Plug-blanking-plastic-25.5mm	A/R		
1	BD155888	Plug-blanking-plastic-32mm	A/R		
1	338025	Plug-blanking-plastic-35mm	A/R		
1	338026	Plug-blanking-plastic-38mm	A/R		
1	AFU2627	Plug-blanking-plastic-41.5mm	A/R		
1	338009	Plug-blanking-plastic-47.5mm	A/R		
1	338028	Plug-blanking-plastic-50mm	A/R		
		RUBBER CABLE GROMMETS			
2	233244	Grommet-cable-Black-3 x 19mm	A/R		
2	233243	Grommet-cable-Black-3 x 25.5mm	A/R		
2	269257	Grommet-cable-Black-6 x 33.5mm	A/R		
2	555711	Grommet-cable-Red-6 x 33.5mm	A/R		
2	276054	Grommet-cable-Black-6 x 41.5mm	A/R		
2	589452	Grommet-cable-Black-7 x 53mm	A/R		
2	233566	Grommet-cable-Red-12.5 x 48mm	A/R		
		RUBBER SEALING GROMMETS			
3	DCP7299L	Plug-blanking-rubber-35mm	A/R		

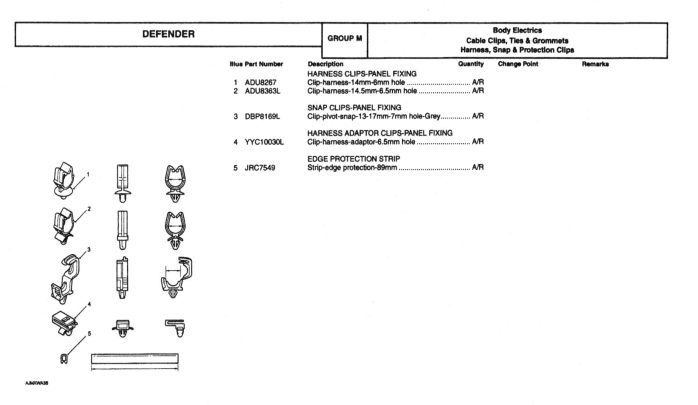

Chassis

Chassis Frame Assembly

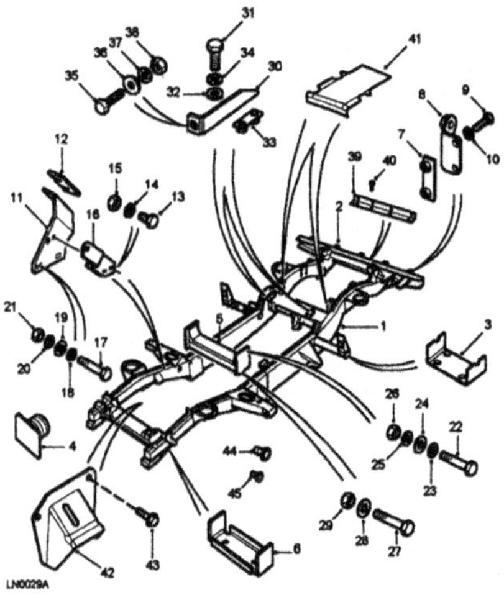

LN0029A

Illus	Part Number	Description	Quantity	Change Point	Remarks
		90" WHEELBASE - UP TO WA159806			
1	NTC7989	FRAME ASSEMBLY-CHASSIS	1	Note (1)	2250 cc Petrol
1	NTC7989	FRAME ASSEMBLY-CHASSIS	1		2500 cc Petrol
1	NTC7989	FRAME ASSEMBLY-CHASSIS	1		Diesel Naturally Aspirated
1	NTC7989	FRAME ASSEMBLY-CHASSIS	1		Diesel Turbo except TDi
1	NTC7989	FRAME ASSEMBLY-CHASSIS	1		200 TDI
1	NTC9473	FRAME ASSEMBLY-CHASSIS	1	Note (2)	4 Cylinder Petrol
1	NTC9473	FRAME ASSEMBLY-CHASSIS	1		Diesel Naturally Aspirated
2	ANR2054	• Crossmember assembly-chassis frame rear	1		
1	NTC1057	FRAME ASSEMBLY-CHASSIS	1	Note (3)	V8 Twin Carburettor
2	ANR2056	• Crossmember assembly-chassis frame rear	1		
1	NTC7807	FRAME ASSEMBLY-CHASSIS	1	Note (4)	V8 Twin Carburettor
1	NTC9476	FRAME ASSEMBLY-CHASSIS	1	Note (2)	V8 Twin Carburettor
1	ANR4742	FRAME ASSEMBLY-CHASSIS	1		300 TDI
1	KVD100120	FRAME ASSEMBLY-CHASSIS	1	Note (5)	4 Cylinder Petrol
1	KVD100120	FRAME ASSEMBLY-CHASSIS	1		Diesel Naturally Aspirated
1	KVD100110	FRAME ASSEMBLY-CHASSIS	1		V8 Twin Carburettor
1	KVD100080	FRAME ASSEMBLY-CHASSIS	1		300 TDI
2	ANR2054	• Crossmember assembly-chassis frame rear	1		

CHANGE POINTS:
(1) To (V) LA 939975
(2) From (V) MA 939976 To (V) VA 138479
(3) To (V) AA 244026
(4) From (V) AA 244027 To (V) LA 939975
(5) From (V) WA 138480 To (V) WA 159806

DEFENDER

GROUP N

Body & Chassis
Chassis
Chassis Frame Assembly

Illus	Part Number	Description	Quantity	Change Point	Remarks
		90" WHEELBASE - FROM XA159807			
1	KVD100340	FRAME ASSEMBLY-CHASSIS	1	Note (1)	4 Cylinder Petrol
1	KVD100320	FRAME ASSEMBLY-CHASSIS	1		300 TDI
1	KVD100330	FRAME ASSEMBLY-CHASSIS	1		Td5
1	KVD100340	FRAME ASSEMBLY-CHASSIS	1		V8 Twin Carburettor
1	KVD100340	FRAME ASSEMBLY-CHASSIS	1		BMW M52
2	STC4456	• Crossmember assembly-chassis frame rear	1		

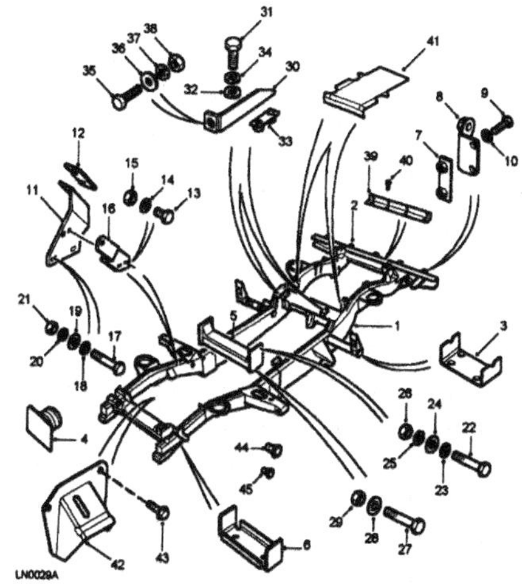

CHANGE POINTS:
(1) From (V) XA 159807

DEFENDER

GROUP N

Body & Chassis
Chassis
Chassis Frame Assembly

Illus	Part Number	Description	Quantity	Change Point	Remarks
		110" WHEELBASE - UP TO WA159806			
1	NTC7843	FRAME ASSEMBLY-CHASSIS	1	Note (1)	4 Cylinder Petrol
1	NTC7843	FRAME ASSEMBLY-CHASSIS	1		Diesel Naturally Aspirated
1	NTC7843	FRAME ASSEMBLY-CHASSIS	1		Diesel Turbo except TDi
1	NTC7843	FRAME ASSEMBLY-CHASSIS	1		200 TDI
1	NTC7844	FRAME ASSEMBLY-CHASSIS	1		V8 Twin Carburettor
1	NTC9481	FRAME ASSEMBLY-CHASSIS	1	Note (2)	4 Cylinder Petrol
1	NTC9481	FRAME ASSEMBLY-CHASSIS	1		Diesel Naturally Aspirated
1	NTC9493	FRAME ASSEMBLY-CHASSIS	1		300 TDI
1	NTC9485	FRAME ASSEMBLY-CHASSIS	1		V8 Twin Carburettor
1	KVD100220	FRAME ASSEMBLY-CHASSIS	1	Note (3)	4 Cylinder Petrol
1	KVD100220	FRAME ASSEMBLY-CHASSIS	1		Diesel Naturally Aspirated
1	KVD100160	FRAME ASSEMBLY-CHASSIS	1		300 TDI
1	KVD100190	FRAME ASSEMBLY-CHASSIS	1		V8 Twin Carburettor
2	ANR2054	• Crossmember assembly-chassis frame rear	1		

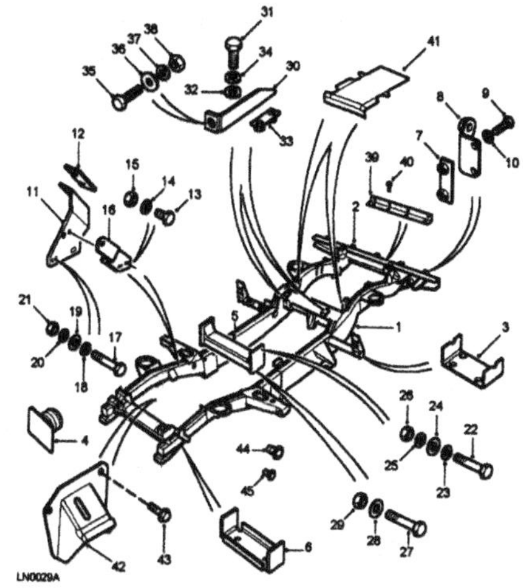

CHANGE POINTS:
(1) To (V) LA 939975
(2) From (V) MA 939976 To (V) VA 138479
(3) From (V) WA 138480 To (V) WA 159806

DEFENDER

GROUP N

Body & Chassis
Chassis
Chassis Frame Assembly

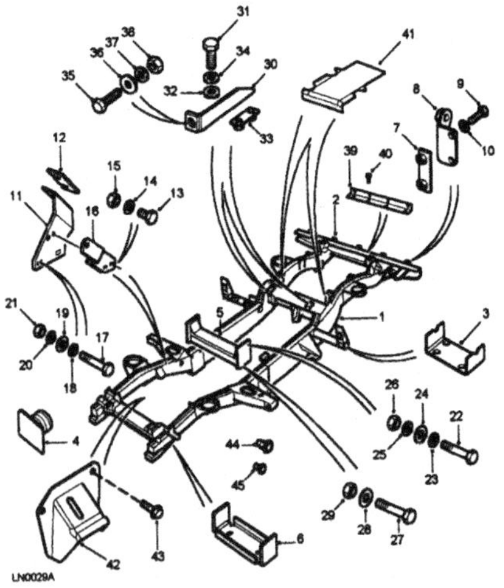

110" WHEELBASE - FROM XA159807

Illus	Part Number	Description	Quantity	Change Point	Remarks
1	KVD100380	FRAME ASSEMBLY-CHASSIS	1	Note (1)	4 Cylinder Petrol normal duty suspension
1	KVD100350	FRAME ASSEMBLY-CHASSIS	1		300 TDI normal duty suspension
1	KVD100360	FRAME ASSEMBLY-CHASSIS	1		300 TDI extra heavy duty
1	KVD100370	FRAME ASSEMBLY-CHASSIS	1		Td5 normal duty suspension
1	KVD100430	FRAME ASSEMBLY-CHASSIS	1		Td5 extra heavy duty
1	KVD100380	FRAME ASSEMBLY-CHASSIS	1		V8 Petrol normal duty suspension
1	KVD100390	FRAME ASSEMBLY-CHASSIS	1		V8 Petrol extra heavy duty
1	KVD100380	FRAME ASSEMBLY-CHASSIS	1		BMW M52
2	STC4456	• Crossmember assembly-chassis frame rear	1		

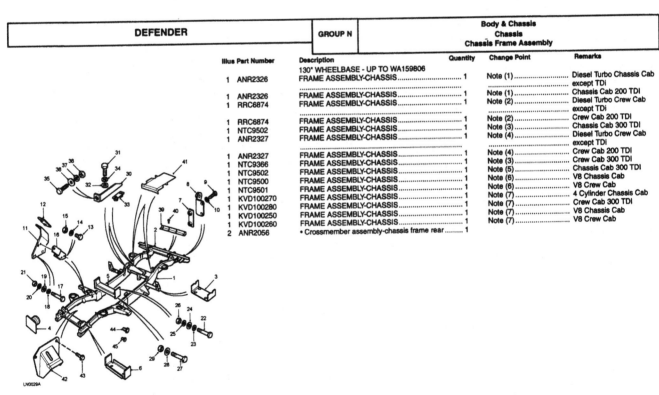

CHANGE POINTS:
(1) From (V) XA 159807

DEFENDER

GROUP N

Body & Chassis
Chassis
Chassis Frame Assembly

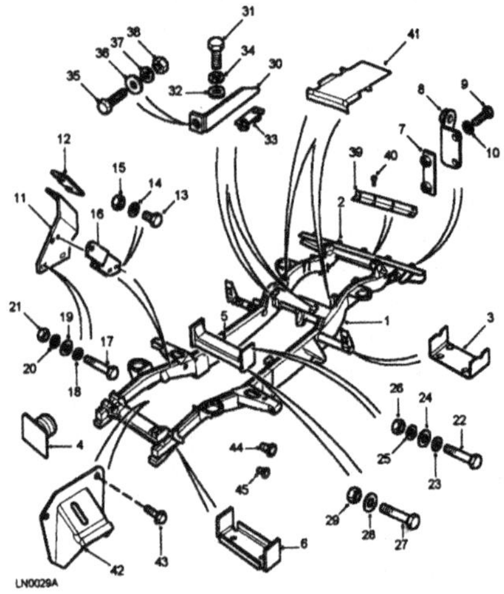

130" WHEELBASE - UP TO WA159806

Illus	Part Number	Description	Quantity	Change Point	Remarks
1	ANR2326	FRAME ASSEMBLY-CHASSIS	1	Note (1)	Diesel Turbo Chassis Cab except TDi
1	ANR2326	FRAME ASSEMBLY-CHASSIS	1	Note (1)	Chassis Cab 200 TDI
1	RRC6874	FRAME ASSEMBLY-CHASSIS	1	Note (2)	Diesel Turbo Crew Cab except TDi
1	RRC6874	FRAME ASSEMBLY-CHASSIS	1	Note (2)	Crew Cab 200 TDI
1	NTC9502	FRAME ASSEMBLY-CHASSIS	1	Note (3)	Chassis Cab 300 TDI
1	ANR2327	FRAME ASSEMBLY-CHASSIS	1	Note (4)	Diesel Turbo Crew Cab except TDi
1	ANR2327	FRAME ASSEMBLY-CHASSIS	1	Note (4)	Crew Cab 200 TDI
1	NTC9366	FRAME ASSEMBLY-CHASSIS	1	Note (3)	Crew Cab 300 TDI
1	NTC9502	FRAME ASSEMBLY-CHASSIS	1	Note (5)	Chassis Cab 300 TDI
1	NTC9500	FRAME ASSEMBLY-CHASSIS	1	Note (6)	V8 Chassis Cab
1	NTC9501	FRAME ASSEMBLY-CHASSIS	1	Note (6)	V8 Crew Cab
1	KVD100270	FRAME ASSEMBLY-CHASSIS	1	Note (7)	4 Cylinder Chassis Cab
1	KVD100280	FRAME ASSEMBLY-CHASSIS	1	Note (7)	Crew Cab 300 TDI
1	KVD100250	FRAME ASSEMBLY-CHASSIS	1	Note (7)	V8 Chassis Cab
1	KVD100260	FRAME ASSEMBLY-CHASSIS	1	Note (7)	V8 Crew Cab
2	ANR2056	• Crossmember assembly-chassis frame rear	1		

CHANGE POINTS:
(1) To (V) LA 939975
(2) To (V) LA 930545
(3) From (V) MA 939976 To (V) WA 159806
(4) From (V) LA 930546 To (V) LA 939975
(5) From (V) MA 939976 To (V) VA 138479
(6) To (V) VA 138479
(7) From (V) WA 138480 To (V) WA 159806

Illus	Part Number	Description	Quantity	Change Point	Remarks
		130" WHEELBASE - FROM XA159807			
1	KVD100400	FRAME ASSEMBLY-CHASSIS	1	Note (1)	300 TDI
1	KVD100420	FRAME ASSEMBLY-CHASSIS	1		V8
1	KVD100410	FRAME ASSEMBLY-CHASSIS	1		Td5
2	STC4456	• Crossmember assembly-chassis frame rear	1		

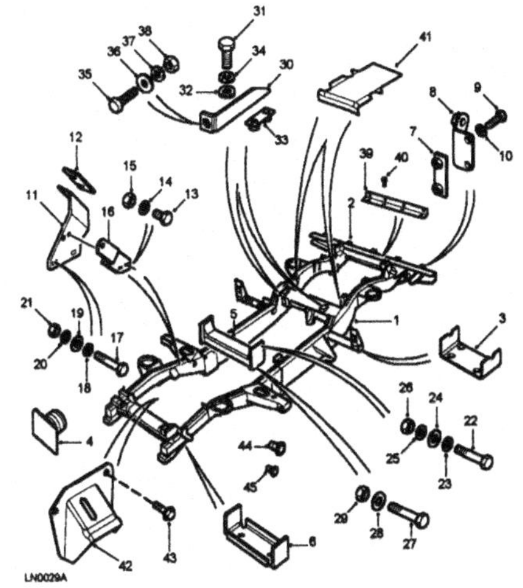

CHANGE POINTS:
(1) From (V) XA 159807

Illus	Part Number	Description	Quantity	Change Point	Remarks
3	ANR4546	Bracket anti roll bar-RH-rear	1		90"
3	ANR4547	Bracket anti roll bar-LH-rear	1		90"
3	NRC5724	Bracket anti roll bar-rear	2		110"
3	NRC5724	Bracket anti roll bar-rear	2		130"
4	NRC6935	Plug	2	Note (1)	
4	KVV100000	Plug	2	Note (2)	
5	NRC7768	Crossmember assembly-chassis frame detachable	1	Note (3)	
5	NTC1963	Crossmember assembly-chassis frame detachable	1	Note (4)	
5	NTC9262	Crossmember assembly-chassis frame detachable	1	Note (5)	
5	ANR3713	Crossmember assembly-chassis frame detachable	1	Note (6)	
5	ANR6386	Crossmember assembly-chassis frame detachable	1	Note (7)	
5	KVB100000	Crossmember assembly-chassis frame detachable	1	Note (2)	
6	NTC7667	Bracket anti roll bar-front	2		
7	MRC5757	Plate & weldnut assembly-to support bracket tailboard	2		
8	NRC9749	Mounting-tailgate hinge	2		
9	FS108207L	Screw-flanged head-M8 x 20	4		
10	WC108051L	Washer-M8	4		
11	NRC7436	Bracket assembly-footrest-RH	1		
11	NRC7435	Bracket assembly-footrest-LH	1		
12	NRC7131	Packing strip	6		
13	AFU1499	Screw-M8 x 25	4	Note (8)	
13	FS108257L	Screw-flanged head-M8 x 25	4	Note (9)	
14	WA108051L	Washer-8mm	16		
15	FN108047L	Nut-flange-flanged head-M8	1		
16	NRC7164	Plate-LH	1		
16	NRC7165	Plate-RH	1		
17	BH108201L	Bolt-hexagonal head-M8 x 100	4		
18	WC108051L	Washer-M8	4		
19	3898	Washer-plain	4	Note (8)	
19	WP185L	Washer-plain-standard	4	Note (9)	
20	WL108001L	Washer-sprung-M8	8		

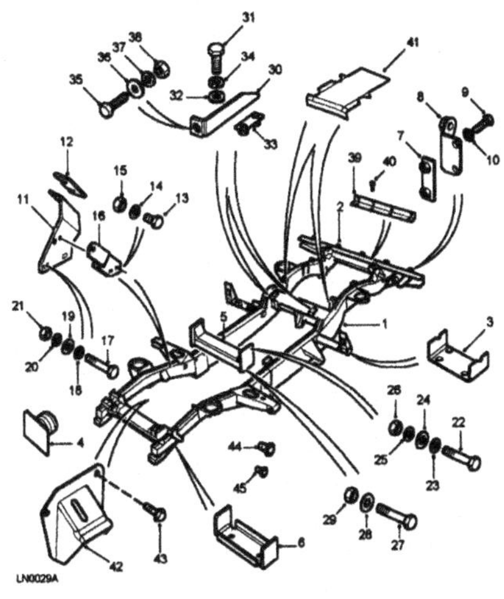

CHANGE POINTS:
(1) To (V) WA 159806
(2) From (V) XA 159807
(3) To (V) AA 270878
(4) From (V) AA 270879 To (V) HA 906307
(5) From (V) HA 906308 To (V) LA 932671
(6) From (V) LA 932672 To (V) LA 939975
(7) From (V) MA 939976 To (V) WA 159806
(8) To (V) LA 939975
(9) From (V) MA 939976

Illus	Part Number	Description	Quantity	Change Point	Remarks
21	FN108047L	Nut-flange-flanged head-M8	1		
22	BH110201L	Bolt-to crossmember-hexagonal head-M10 x 100	4		
13	SH110251L	Screw-to crossmember-hexagonal head-M10 x 25	4		
23	NRC5485	Washer-nylon	4		
24	WC110061L	Washer-plain-M10-oversize	4		
25	217245	Washer-plain-No 10	4		
27	FB108181	Bolt-to crossmember-M8 x 90	6	Note (1)	
27	RYG101360	Bolt-duo taptite-M10 x 25	4	Note (2)	
28	WD108051L	Washer-plain-thin	12		
30	NRC9695	Bracket support-RH	1		
30	NRC9696	Bracket support-LH	1		
31	FS108207L	Screw-bracket support to chassis frame-flanged head-M8 x 20	4		
32	WA108051L	Washer-8mm	4		
33	NRC9698	Plate & weldnut assembly	2		
34	WL108001L	Washer-sprung-M8	1		
35	FS108207L	Screw-flanged head-M8 x 20	2		
36	WL108001L	Washer-sprung-M8	1		
37	WA108051L	Washer-8mm	1		
38	FN108047L	Nut-flange-flanged head-M8	1		
38	FN108047L	Nut-flange-flanged head-M8	1		
20	WL108001L	Washer-sprung-M8	4		
39	KVU101160	Bracket-body/chassis mounting	1		
40	FS108207L	Screw-flanged head-M8 x 20	4		
41	KVW100580	Stiffener-chassis frame-LH	1		130"
41	KVW100580	Stiffener-chassis frame-LH	1		Heavy duty suspension 90"
41	KVW100580	Stiffener-chassis frame-LH	1		Heavy duty suspension 110"
41	KVW100590	Stiffener-chassis frame-RH	1		130"
41	KVW100590	Stiffener-chassis frame-RH	1		Heavy duty suspension 90"
41	KVW100590	Stiffener-chassis frame-RH	1		Heavy duty suspension 110"

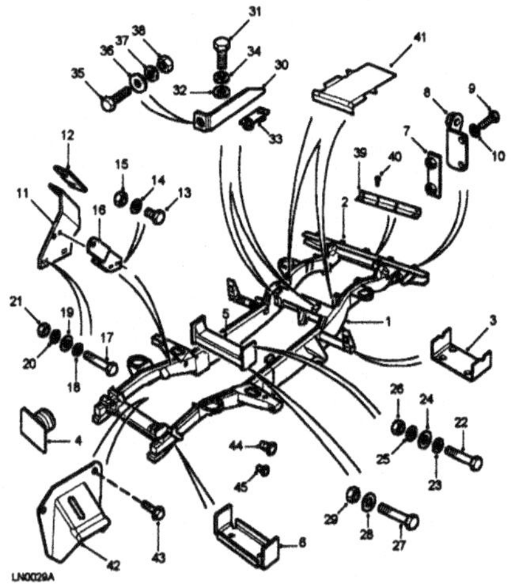

LN0029A

CHANGE POINTS:
(1) To (V) WA 159806
(2) From (V) XA 159807

Illus	Part Number	Description	Quantity	Change Point	Remarks
42	KVU100240	Bracket-engine mounting-RH	1	Note (1)	V8 Twin Carburettor
42	KVU100940	Bracket-engine mounting-LH	1	Note (1)	V8 Twin Carburettor
42	KVU100220	Bracket-engine mounting-RH	1	Note (1)	4 Cylinder Petrol
42	KVU100230	Bracket-engine mounting-LH	1	Note (1)	4 Cylinder Petrol
43	FS108207L	Screw-flanged head-M8 x 20	6	Note (1)	4 Cylinder Petrol
43	FS108207L	Screw-flanged head-M8 x 20	6	Note (1)	V8 Twin Carburettor
44	ANR6563	Nutsert-blind-hexagonal-M8	A/R	Note (1)	
45	BTR8040L	Nutsert-blind-square-M6	A/R	Note (1)	

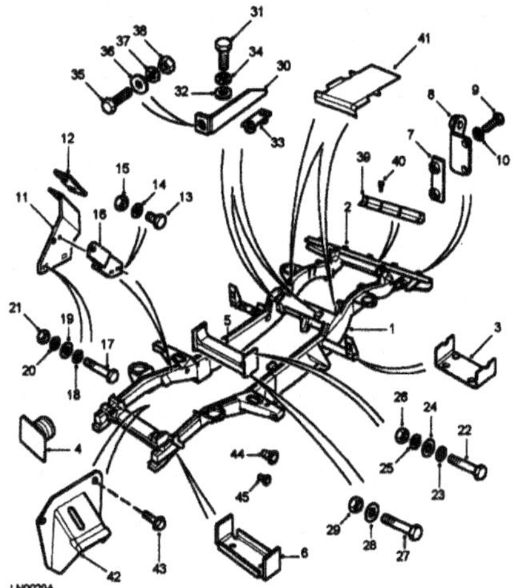

LN0029A

CHANGE POINTS:
(1) From (V) XA 159807

Replacement Outriggers

Illus	Part Number	Description	Quantity	Change Point	Remarks
1	STC8652	Kit-chassis repair-front section-RH	1		
1	STC8653	Kit-chassis repair-front section-LH	1		
2	STC8693	Seat-spring front-RH	1		
2	STC8608	Seat-spring front-LH	1		
3	STC8354	Outrigger assembly-RH-No1-front	1		
3	STC8355	Outrigger assembly-LH-No1-front	1		
4	STC8694	Tie bracket-LH	1		
4	STC8695	Tie bracket-RH	1		
5	STC8604	Bracket assembly-front radius arm mounting-RH	1		
5	STC8605	Bracket assembly-front radius arm mounting-LH	1		
6	STC8606	Bracket assembly-trailing link mounting-RH	1		
6	STC8607	Bracket assembly-trailing link mounting-LH	1		
7	STC8648	Outrigger assembly-RH	1		90"
7	STC8649	Outrigger assembly-LH	1		90"
7	STC8356	Outrigger assembly-Non handed-rear	2		110"
8	STC8610	Seat-spring rear-Non handed	2		90"
8	STC8609	Seat-spring rear-Non handed	2		110"
8	STC8609	Seat-spring rear-Non handed	2		130"
9	STC8650	Crossmember assembly-chassis frame rear	1	Note (1)	90"
9	STC8651	Crossmember assembly-chassis frame rear	1	Note (1)	110"
9	STC8651	Crossmember assembly-chassis frame rear	1	Note (1)	130"
9	STC4456	Crossmember assembly-chassis frame rear	1	Note (2)	

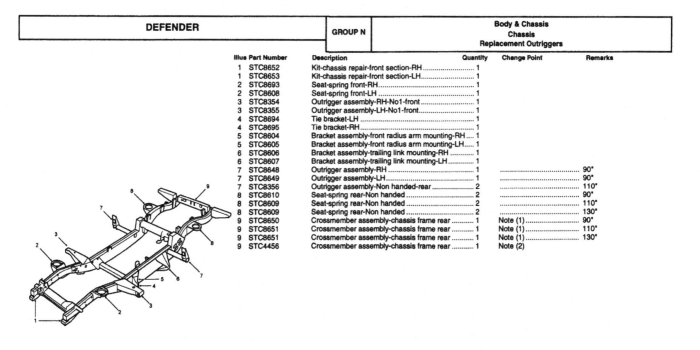

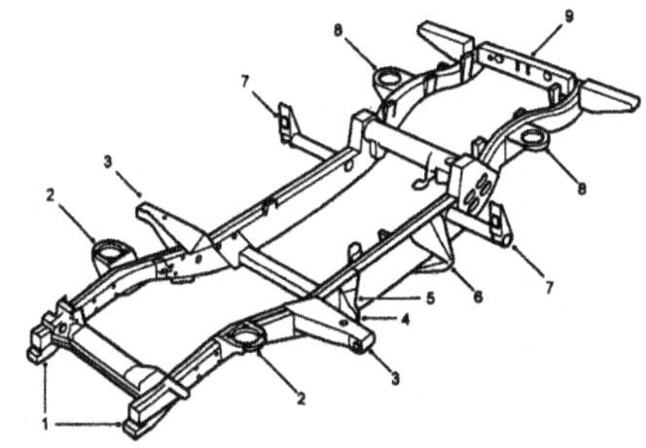

AJNXAA2A

CHANGE POINTS:
(1) To (V) WA 159806
(2) From (V) XA 159807

Chassis Fittings-110/130

Illus	Part Number	Description	Quantity	Change Point	Remarks
1	NRC4661	Bracket support	2		Truck Cab
2	FS106201L	Screw-bracket support to chassis-flanged head-M6 x 20	6		
3	WA106041L	Washer-6mm	6		
4	WL106001L	Washer-sprung-M6	6		
5	NRC5478	Bracket-chassis frame body mounting	2	Note (1)	HICAP 110"
5	NRC5478	Bracket-chassis frame body mounting	2	Note (1)	HICAP 130"
5	KVU101430	Bracket-chassis frame body mounting	1	Note (2)	HICAP 110"
5	KVU101430	Bracket-chassis frame body mounting	1	Note (2)	HICAP 130"
6	FS108257L	Screw-bracket support to chassis-flanged head-M8 x 25	4		
7	WA108051L	Washer-8mm	4		
8	NY108041L	Nut-nyloc-M8	4		
9	NRC4171	Crossmember assembly-rear floor	1		Station Wagon 110"
9	RRC6287	Crossmember assembly-rear floor	1		HICAP 130"
10	SH108701	Screw-crossmember body to chassis-hexagonal head-M8 x 70	4		
11	WA108051L	Washer-8mm	8		
12	NY108041L	Nut-nyloc-M8	4		
13	NRC7053	Bracket mounting body-outer	4		Regular Truck Cab
13	NRC7053	Bracket mounting body-outer	2		Regular Chassis Cab
14	NRC5665	Bracket mounting body	4		Station Wagon
14	NRC6951	Bracket mounting body-inner	2		Regular Chassis Cab
15	NRC4693	Plate	8		
16	FS106201L	Screw-bracket mounting to chassis-flanged head-M6 x 20	16		
17	WC106041L	Washer-M6-oversize	16		
18	WL106041	Washer-spring-6mm	16		
19	NH106041L	Nut-hexagonal-nyloc-M6	16		
20	NRC4966	Plate	1		
21	SL106121	Screw-taptite-plate to chassis-M6 x 12-long	4		

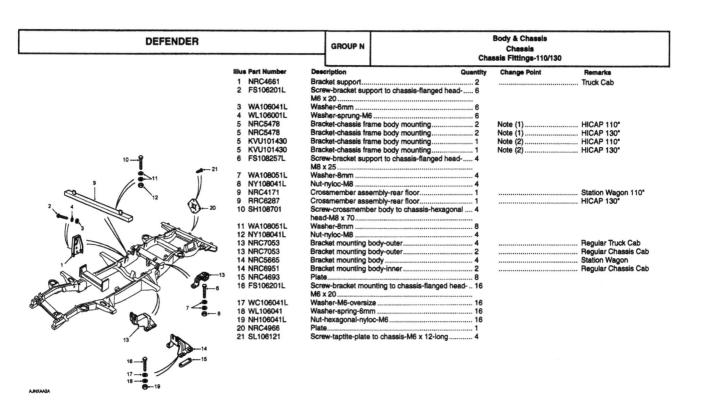

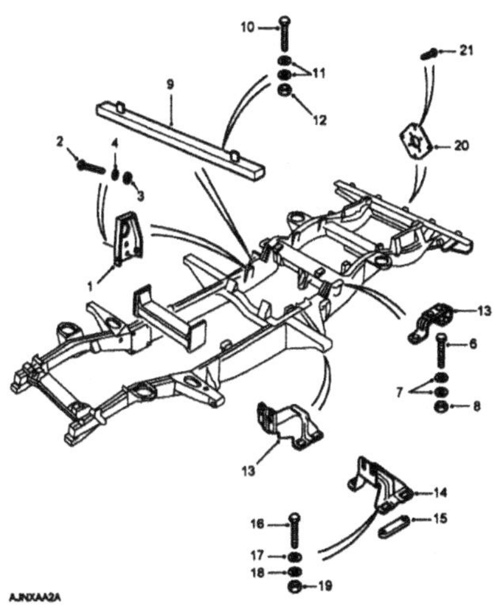

AJNXAA2A

CHANGE POINTS:
(1) To (V) XA 176049
(2) From (V) XA 176050

Engine Mounting-300Tdi

Illus	Part Number	Description	Quantity	Change Point	Remarks
1	ANR2868	Bracket-engine mounting-RH	1		
2	NTC9415	Bracket-engine mounting-LH	1		
3	SH112201	Screw-to bracket mounting-hexagonal head-M12 x 20	8		
4	NTC9416	Bracket-ancillary mounting	2		
5	FX112041L	Nut-flange-M12	2		
6	FX110041L	Nut-flange-M10	NLA		Use FX110047L.
7	FX112041L	Nut-flange-M12	2		

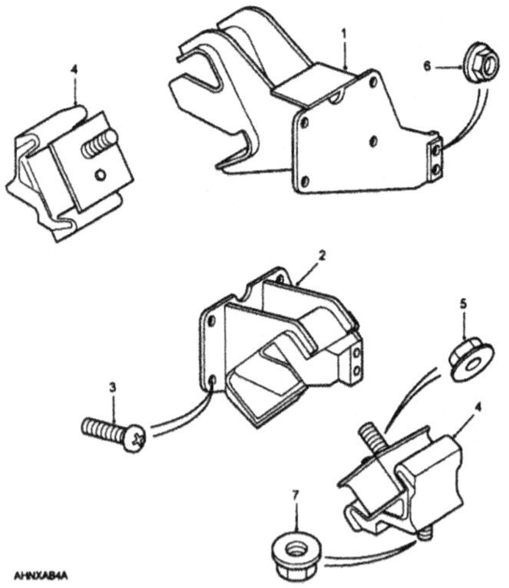

AHNXAB4A

Engine Mountings-Td5

Illus	Part Number	Description	Quantity	Change Point	Remarks
1	KKB102601	Mounting-engine rubber	2	Note (1)	
1	KKB102602	Mounting-engine rubber	2	Note (2)	
2	ANR6623	Bracket-engine mounting-LH	1		
3	ANR6622	Bracket-engine mounting-RH	1		
4	ANR6610	Heatshield	1		
5	FS110301L	Screw-flanged head-M10 x 30-top	8		
6	FS112281L	Screw-flanged head-flanged head-M12 x 28	4		
6	FS112251L	Screw-flanged head-M12 x 25	4		
7	FX112041L	Nut-flange-M12	4		
8	FX112041L	Nut-flange-M12	2		

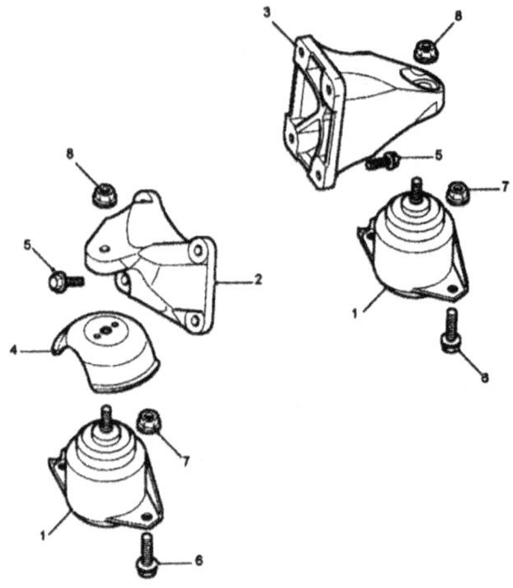

LN0053

CHANGE POINTS:
(1) From (V) XA 159807 To (V) YA 178194
(2) From (V) YA 178195

Illus	Part Number	Description	Quantity	Change Point	Remarks
1	NRC1302	Bracket-engine mounting-RH	NLA		Use ANR4697.
1	ANR4697	Bracket-engine mounting-RH	1		
2	NRC3314	Bracket-engine mounting-LH	1		
3	SH507091L	Screw-mounting to engine-hexagonal head-7/16UNC x 1 1/8	4		
4	WM600071L	Washer-sprung-7/16"	4		
5	SH505071L	Screw-mounting to engine-hexagonal head-5/16UNC x 7/8	2		
6	WM600051L	Washer-spring-5/16"	2		
7	STC434	MOUNTING-ENGINE RUBBER	2		
8	WC110061L	• Washer-plain-M10-oversize	2		
9	WL110001L	• Washer-M10	4		
10	NH110041L	• Nut-hexagonal head-coarse thread-M10	4		

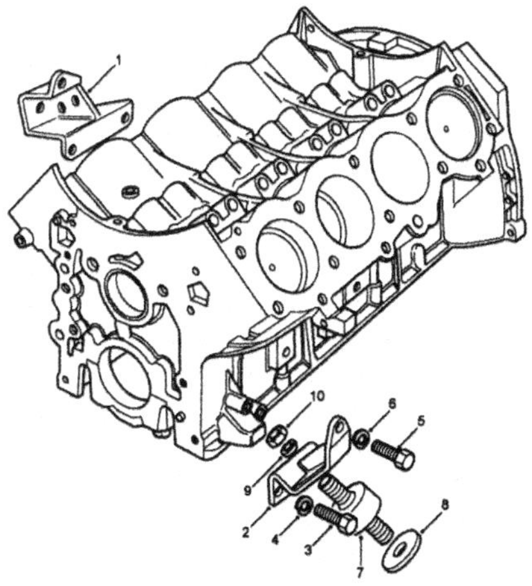

AHNXAB5A

Illus	Part Number	Description	Quantity	Change Point	Remarks
1	NRC5743	Bracket-transmission mounting-LH	1		
2	NRC5742	Bracket-transmission mounting-RH	1		
3	BH108201L	Bolt-to bracket mounting-hexagonal head-M8 x 100	6		
4	WP185L	Washer-plain-standard	6		
5	WA108051L	Washer-8mm	6		
6	WL108001L	Washer-sprung-M8	6		
7	FN108047L	Nut-flange-flanged head-M8	6		
8	NRC9560	Mounting-engine rubber	NLA		Use ANR1808.
8	ANR1808	Mounting-engine rubber	2		
9	WA110061L	Washer-M10	4		
10	WA110061L	Washer-normal o.d.-M10	4		
11	NH110041L	Nut-hexagonal head-coarse thread-M10	4		
11	FN110047	Nut-flange-flange-M10	4		
12	NRC8204	Plate mounting-RH	2		
13	SH112201	Screw-washer to mounting plate-hexagonal head-M12 x 20	8		
14	NRC9561	Washer	8		

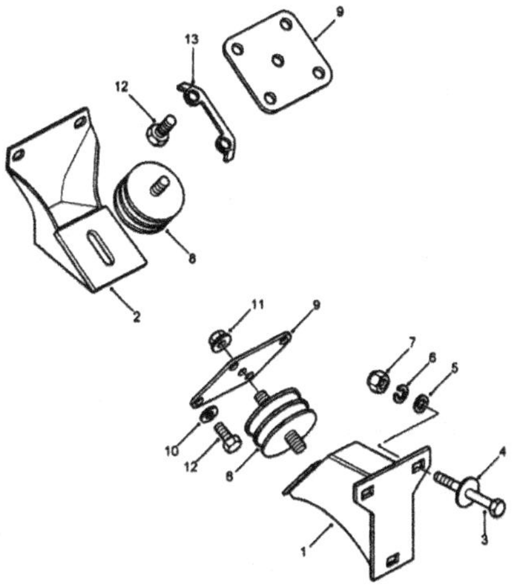

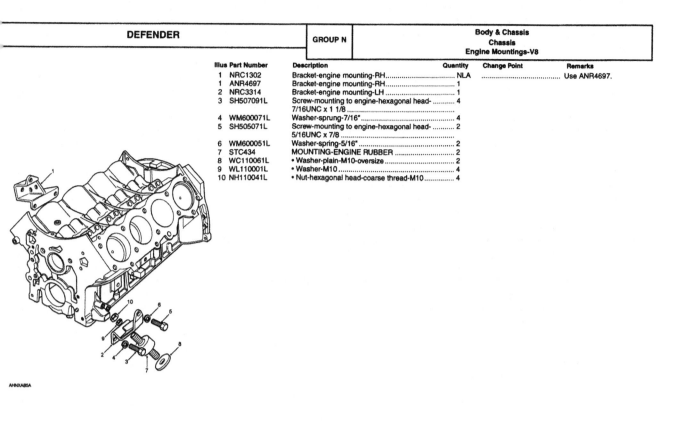

AHNXAB3A

Illus	Part Number	Description	Quantity	Change Point	Remarks
1	90575585	Bracket-transmission mounting-rear-LH	1	Note (1)	
1	ANR2820	Bracket-transmission mounting-rear-LH	1	Note (2)	
2	NTC1201	Bracket-engine mounting-rear-RH	1	Note (1)	
2	ANR4657	Bracket-engine mounting-rear-RH	1	Note (2)	
3	BH108201L	Bolt-to bracket mounting-hexagonal head-M8 x 100	6		
4	WP185L	Washer-plain-standard	6		
5	WA108051L	Washer-8mm	6		
6	NY108041L	Nut-nyloc-M8	6		
7	STC434	Mounting-engine rubber	2	Note (1)	
7	RTC6115	MOUNTING-ENGINE RUBBER	NLA		Use STC434.
4	WC110061L	• Washer-plain-M10-oversize	2		
5	WL110001L	• Washer-M10	4		
6	NH110041L	• Nut-hexagonal head-coarse thread-M10	4		
7	ANR2804	Mounting-engine rubber-M12	2	Note (2)	
8	FX112041L	Nut-flange-M12	4		
9	NTC9224	Bracket assembly-transmission mounting-top-LH	1	Note (1)	
9	ANR4650	Bracket assembly-transmission mounting-top-LH	1	Note (2)	
10	NRC8204	Plate mounting-RH	1	Note (1)	
10	ANR2819	Plate mounting-RH	1	Note (2)	
11	SH112251L	Screw-hexagonal head-M12 x 25	8		
12	WL112001L	Washer	8		

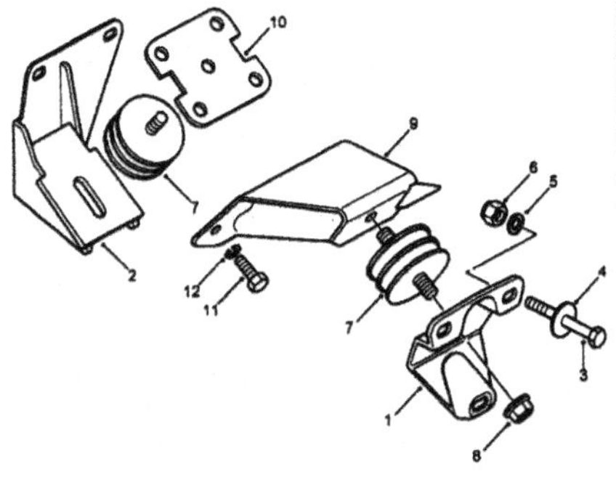

AHNXAB2A

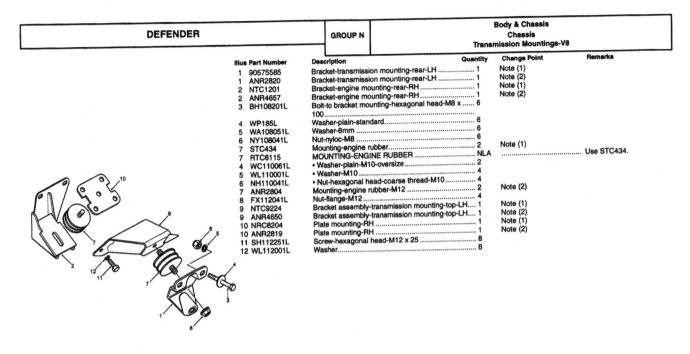

CHANGE POINTS:
(1) To (V) TA 970049
(2) From (V) TA 970050

Illus	Part Number	Description	Quantity	Change Point	Remarks
1	ANR2898	Bracket-transmission mounting-RH	1		
2	ANR3225	Bracket-transmission mounting-LH	1		
3	ANR3200	Mounting-rubber-RH	1		
4	ANR3201	Mounting-rubber-LH	1		
5	ANR3138	Heatshield assembly exhaust-downpipe	1		
6	SH112251L	Screw-to bracket transmission mounting-hexagonal head-M12 x 25	8		
7	WL112001L	Washer	8		
8	FX110041L	Nut-flange-M10	NLA		Use FX110047L.

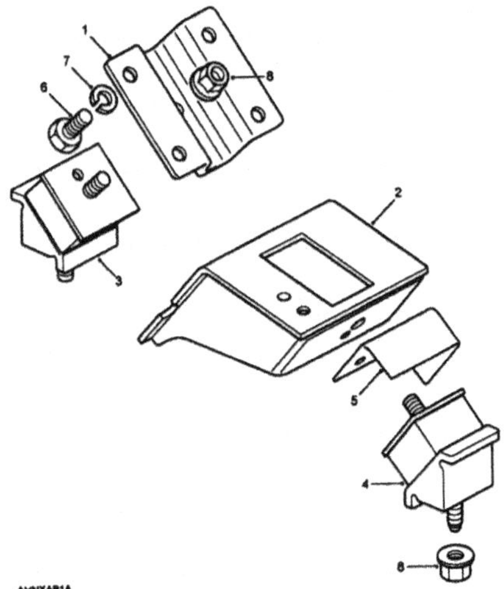

AHNXAB1A

DEFENDER	GROUP N	Body & Chassis Chassis Transmission Mountings-Td5

Illus	Part Number	Description	Quantity	Change Point	Remarks
1	KQB100160	Mounting-gearbox-RH	1		
2	KQB100170	Mounting-gearbox-LH	1		
3	FX110041	Nut-flange-M10	NLA		Use FX110041L.
4	ANR5636	Bracket-mounting-RH	1		
5	ANR5637	Bracket-mounting-LH	1		
6	KRO100030	Heatshield.-LH	1		
7	FS112201L	Screw-flanged head-M12 x 20	4		
8	FS112251L	Screw-flanged head-M12 x 25	4		

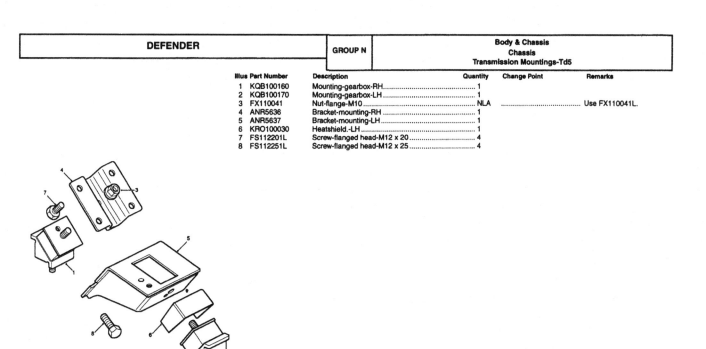

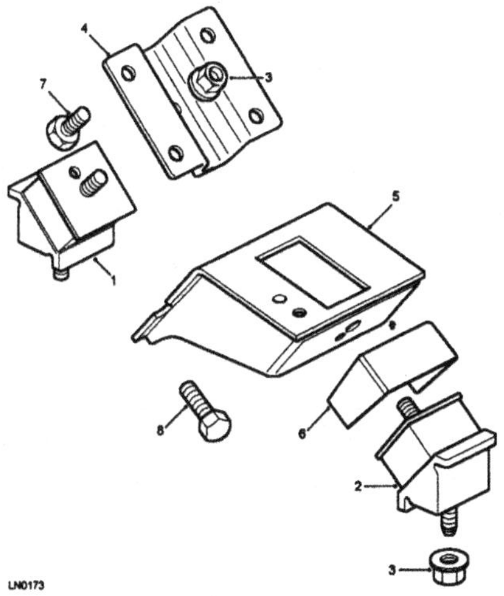

LN0173

DEFENDER	GROUP N	Body & Chassis Chassis Front Bumper & Bumperettes

Illus	Part Number	Description	Quantity	Change Point	Remarks
		BUMPER-FRONT			
1	NRC9211	Galvanised	1	Note (1)	
1	NTC4657	Black	1	Note (2)	
1	DPB103870	Black	1	Note (3)	
1	DPB104270	Black	1	Note (4)	Standard / County
1	STC60705	Silver powder coat	1	Note (4)	Heritage
2	NRC6994	Plate-tapping	2		
3	AFU1386	Bolt-zinc-M10 x 120	4	Note (6)	
3	NTC5401	Bolt-Black-M10 x 120	4	Note (7)	
4	WA110061L	Washer-M10	4	Note (9)	
4	DYF100760	Washer-standard.-Black-10mm	4	Note (10)	
5	DYF100780	Washer-large-Black-M10	4	Note (10)	
6	NRC4733	Bumperette-front-Galvanised	2		Optional
7	SH110251L	Screw-hexagonal head-M10 x 25	16		
8	WA110061L	Washer-M10	16		
9	NY110047L	Nut-flange-nyloc-M10	16		

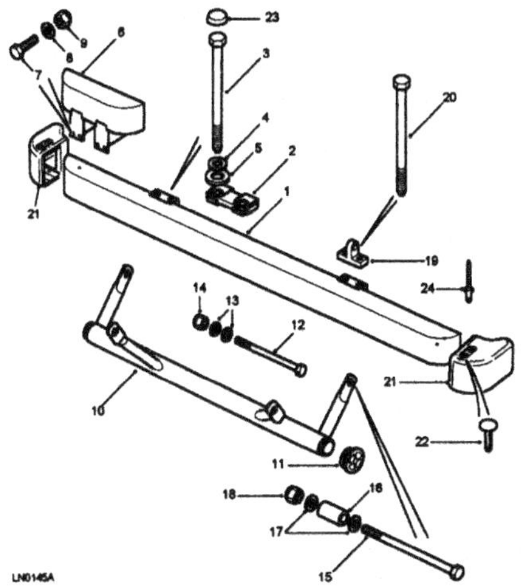

LN0145A

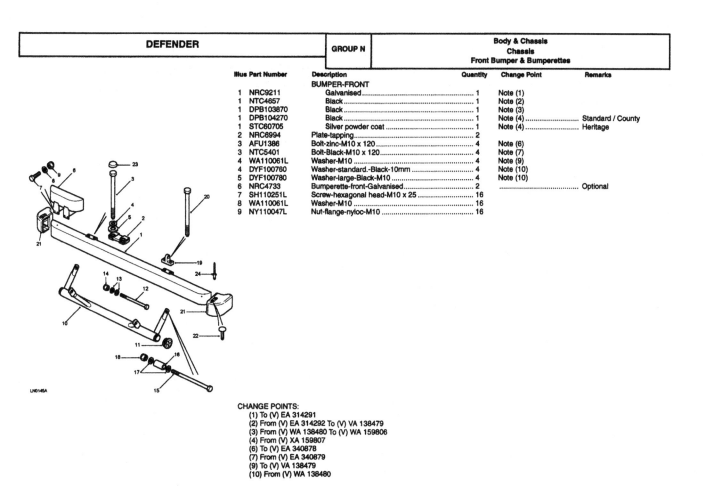

CHANGE POINTS:
(1) To (V) EA 314291
(2) From (V) EA 314292 To (V) VA 138479
(3) From (V) WA 138480 To (V) WA 159806
(4) From (V) XA 159807
(6) To (V) EA 340878
(7) From (V) EA 340879
(9) To (V) VA 138479
(10) From (V) WA 138480

DEFENDER	GROUP N	Body & Chassis Chassis Front Bumper & Bumperettes

Illus	Part Number	Description	Quantity	Change Point	Remarks
10	NRC7009	Bar-underside protection	1		Optional
11	NRC5886	Plug-blanking	2		
12	BH110241L	Bolt-hexagonal head-M10 x 120	2		
13	WA110061L	Washer-M10	4		
14	NY110047L	Nut-flange-nyloc-M10	2		
15	253952	Bolt-1/2UNF x 6 1/2	2	Note (1)	
15	253948	Bolt-1/2UNF x 6 1/4	2	Note (2)	
16	NRC5627	Spacer	2		
17	WC112081	Washer-plain-M12	2		
18	NY608041L	Nut-hexagonal-nyloc-1/2UNF	2		
19	559882	Ring-towing-front	2		Optional
20	BH110261L	Bolt-zinc-M10 x 130	4	Note (3)	
20	NTC5401	Bolt-Black-M10 x 120	4	Note (4)	
21	NRC7439	End cap-front bumper	2	Note (6)	Germany
21	DPT100070	End cap-front bumper	2	Note (7)	
22	DZM100080	Fastener-fir tree	8	Note (7)	
23	NRC7571	Cap-protective	4	Note (6)	Germany
23	BTR1884PMA	Cap-protective-Black	4	Note (7)	
24	78248	Rivet-pop-3/16" x 0.45"lng	8	Note (6)	Germany

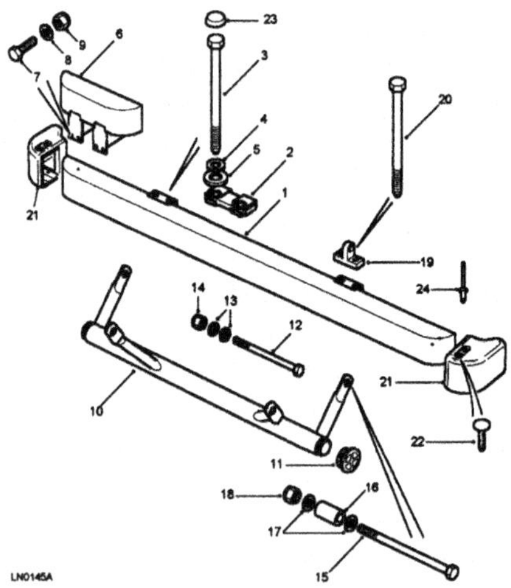

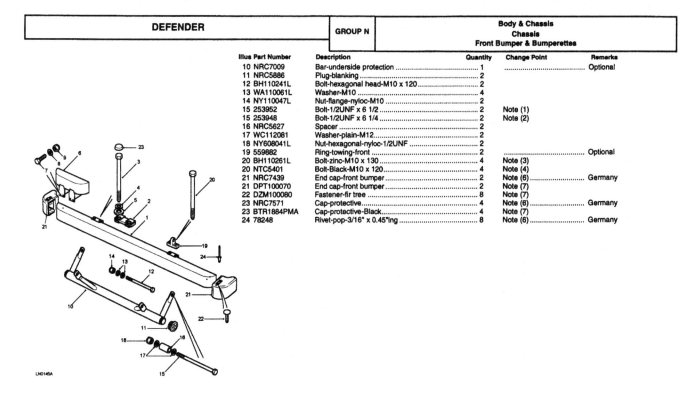

CHANGE POINTS:
(1) To (V) LA 939975
(2) From (V) MA 939976
(3) To (V) EA 340878
(4) From (V) EA 340879
(6) To (V) VA 138479
(7) From (V) WA 138480

DEFENDER	GROUP N	Body & Chassis Chassis Nudge Bar-V8 EFI & France Eastnor LE

Illus	Part Number	Description	Quantity	Change Point	Remarks
1	STC8476	Bar assembly-nudge-front-Black-A frame	1		Eastnor L.E.
1	STC7530	Bar assembly-nudge-front	1		V8 EFI 50 LE

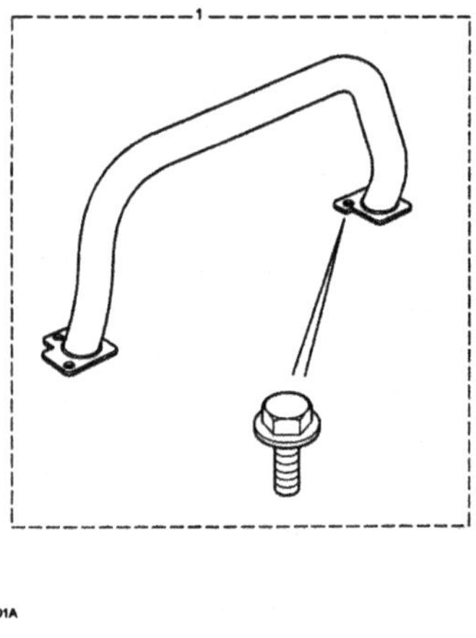

DEFENDER	GROUP N	Body & Chassis Chassis Nudge Bar-90 Sport Only

Illus	Part Number	Description	Quantity	Change Point	Remarks
1	RTC8120	Bar assembly-nudge-front-wrap round with lamp slats	NLA		Use STC50270.
1	STC50270	Bar assembly-nudge-front-wrap round	1		

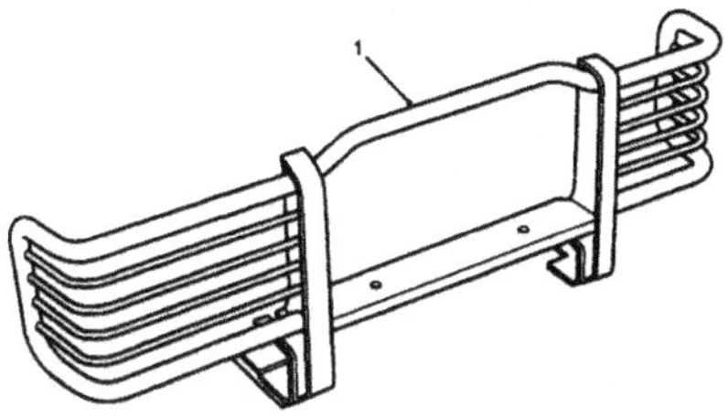

AHNXAD2A

DEFENDER	GROUP N	Body & Chassis Chassis Rear Bumperettes & Lifting Rings

Illus	Part Number	Description	Quantity	Change Point	Remarks
1	RRC2970	Bumperette-rear-RH	1		
1	RRC2971	Bumperette-rear-LH	1		
2	FB110141L	Bolt-to bumperette-flanged head-M10 x 70	8	To (V) WA 138479	
2	AYG100230	Screw-to bumperette-flanged head	8	From (V) WA 138480	
3	WA110061L	Washer-M10	8		
4	WL110001L	Washer-M10	8		
5	NY110047L	Nut-flange-nyloc-M10	8		
6	NRC4853	Lifting ring	2		
7	NRC4854	Plate	2		
8	BH110181L	Bolt-to lifting ring-hexagonal socket	4		
9	WA110061L	Washer-M10	4		
10	WL110001L	Washer-M10	4		
11	NY110047L	Nut-flange-nyloc-M10	4		

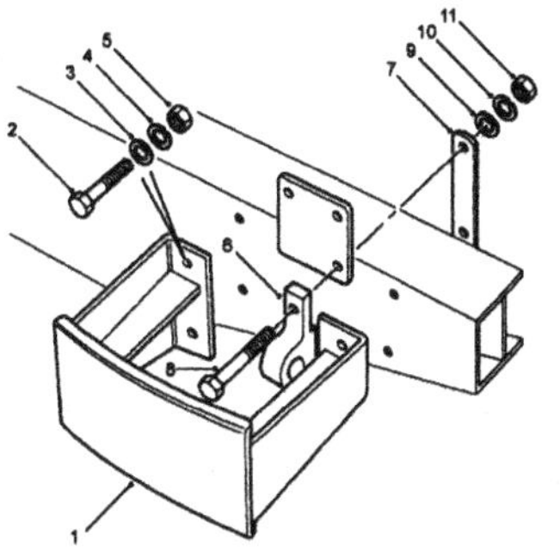

AJNXAE1A

DEFENDER

GROUP N

Body & Chassis
Chassis
Lifting Handle & Lashing Ring

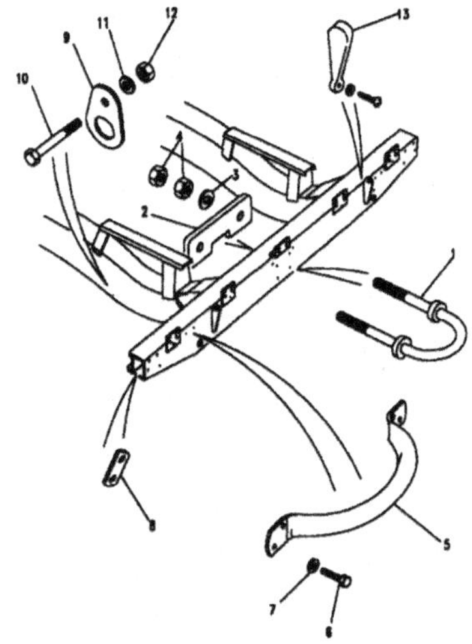

Illus	Part Number	Description	Quantity	Change Point	Remarks
1	NRC5396	Bracket-rear vehicle recovery	1	To (V) LA 939975	
2	562756	Spacer	1		
3	4233	Washer	2		
4	NH116041L	Nut-M16-hexagonal head	4		
5	300816	Handle-grab	1	To (V) EA 314058	
5	NTC5116	Handle-grab-Black	2	From (V) EA 314059	
6	SH108161L	Screw-hexagonal head-M8 x 16	NLA	To (V) LA 939975	Use FS108161L. Except Germany
6	SE108161L	Screw-flanged head	8		Germany
6	FS108161L	Screw-flanged head-M8 x 16	8	From (V) MA 939976 To (V) WA 138479	
6	AYG100230	Screw-flanged head	8	From (V) WA 138480	
7	WA108051L	Washer-8mm	8		
8	NRC5804	Nut	4		
9	90577509	Bracket-towing-front & rear-less spoiler	4		
10	BH110241L	Bolt-hexagonal head-M10 x 120	2	To (V) WA 138479	
10	DYG100720	Bolt-flanged head-M10 x 115	2	From (V) WA 138480	
11	217245	Washer-plain-No 10	4		
12	NY110047L	Nut-flange-nyloc-M10	4		
10	BH110221L	Bolt-to bracket lashing-hexagonal head-M10 x 110	2	Note (1)	
10	DYG100720	Bolt-to bracket lashing-flanged head-M10 x 115	2	Note (2)	
10	KPE100000	Bolt-flanged head-dacromat-Black-M10 x 105	2	Note (3)	90"
10	DYG100720	Bolt-flanged head-M10 x 115	2	Note (3)	110"
10	DYG100720	Bolt-flanged head-M10 x 115	2	Note (3)	130"
11	217245	Washer-plain-No 10	4		
12	NY110047L	Nut-flange-nyloc-M10	4		
13	NRC7425	Cover-tailgate hinge	2	To (V) LA 939975	Germany
	RRC5409	End cap-rear bumper-LH	1		90 SV
	RRC5410	End cap-rear bumper-RH	1		

CHANGE POINTS:
(1) To (V) WA 138479
(2) From (V) WA 138480 To (V) XA 172576
(3) From (V) XA 172577

DEFENDER

GROUP N

Body & Chassis
Chassis
Undertray Assembly

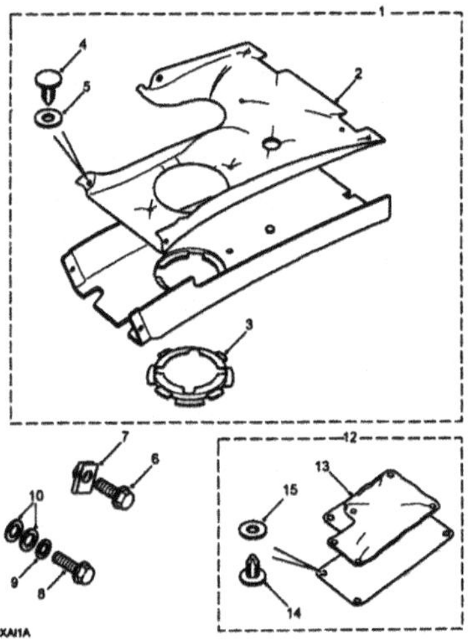

AHNXAI1A

Illus	Part Number	Description	Quantity	Change Point	Remarks
1	AWR5428	UNDERTRAY ASSEMBLY-REAR	1	Note (1)	
2	EUQ100150	• Pad-acoustic	1		
3	STC3712	• Hatch-inspection	1		
4	STC3710	• Fastener-fir tree	8		
5	STC3711	• Washer-plastic	8		
1	KRB100821	Undertray assembly-rear	1	Note (2)	
6	FS108207L	Screw-to hexsert-flanged head-M8 x 20	2		
7	MXC3134	Hexsert	3		
8	FS108307L	Screw-flanged head-M8 x 30	1		
9	WA108051L	Washer-8mm	1		
10	WJ108001	Washer-M8-large	2		
11	AWR6600	Undertray assembly-front	1	Note (1)	
11	KRB100810	Undertray assembly-front	1	Note (2)	
12	AWR6599	HATCH-INSPECTION	1		
13	STC3714	• Pad-engine acoustic	1		
14	STC3710	• Fastener-fir tree	8		
15	STC3711	• Washer-plastic	8		
16	FS108207L	Screw-flanged head-M8 x 20	9		
17	WJ108001	Washer-M8-large	8		
18	MXC3134	Hexsert	2		
19	FN108047L	Nut-flange-flanged head-M8	2		
20	ALR9350	Nut-M8	2		

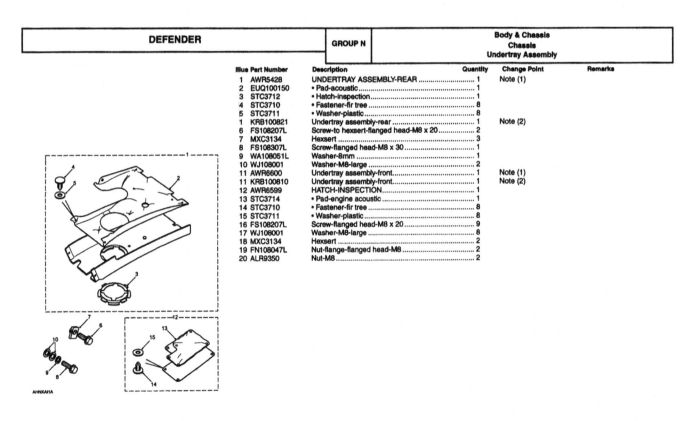

CHANGE POINTS:
(1) To (V) WA 159806
(2) From (V) XA 159807

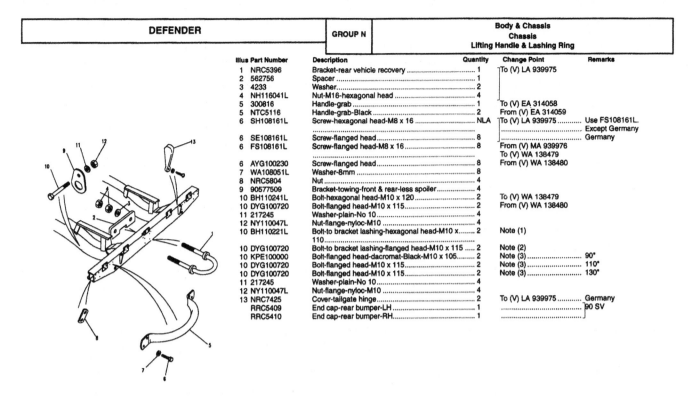

Illus	Part Number	Description	Quantity	Change Point	Remarks
1	STC61862	Guard plate steering	1	Note (1)	Tomb Raider

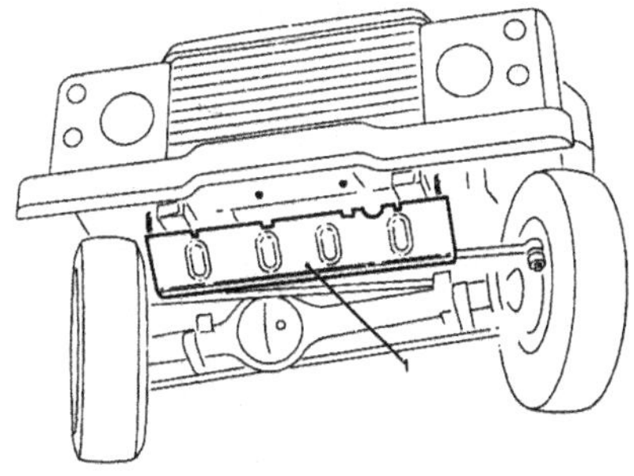

LT0023

CHANGE POINTS:
(1) From (V) 1A 612404

Illus	Part Number	Description	Quantity	Change Point	Remarks
1	ALR6374	Dash assembly-RHD	1	Note (1)	Except air conditioning
1	ALR6375	Dash assembly-LHD	1		
1	ALR2136	Dash assembly-RHD	1	Note (2)	
1	ALR2138	Dash assembly-LHD	1		
1	ALR9946	Dash assembly-RHD	1	Note (3)	
1	ALR9945	Dash assembly-LHD	1		
1	MUC6686	Dash assembly-RHD	1	Note (4)	Air conditioning
1	MXC9012	Dash assembly-RHD	1	Note (5)	
1	MXC9013	Dash assembly-LHD	1		
1	ALR5117	Dash assembly-RHD	1	Note (2)	
1	ALR5118	Dash assembly-LHD	1		
1	ALR9970	Dash assembly-RHD	1	Note (3)	
1	ALR9971	Dash assembly-LHD	1		
1	AHA710010	Dash assembly-RHD	1		V8 EFi 50 LE
1	MXC9015	Dash assembly-LHD	1	Note (6)	Germany
1	AHB710010	Dash assembly-RHD	1	Note (7)	
1	AHB710020	Dash assembly-LHD	1	Note (7)	
1	AHB710050	Dash assembly-RHD	1	Note (8)	RHD
1	AHB710090	Dash assembly-LHD	1	Note (8)	LHD

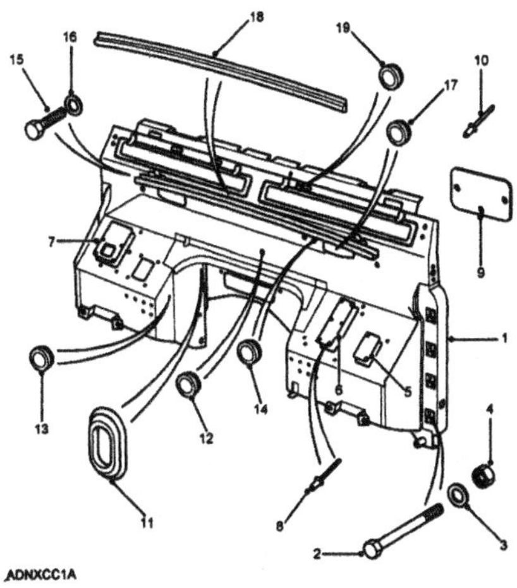

ADNXCC1A

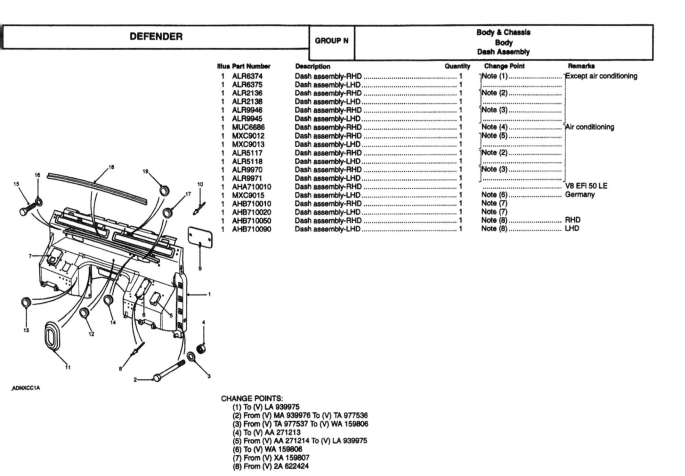

CHANGE POINTS:
(1) To (V) LA 939975
(2) From (V) MA 939976 To (V) TA 977536
(3) From (V) TA 977537 To (V) WA 159806
(4) To (V) AA 271213
(5) From (V) AA 271214 To (V) LA 939975
(6) To (V) WA 159806
(7) From (V) XA 159807
(8) From (V) 2A 622424

Illus	Part Number	Description	Quantity	Change Point	Remarks
2	MRC9420	Bolt-to dash assembly-M12 x 180	2		
3	WA112081L	Washer-plain-standard-M12	5		
4	NH112041L	Nut-hexagonal-M12	2		
5	346981	Plate-cover pedal hole-passenger	1	Note (1)	
6	346599	Plate-cover pedal hole-passenger	1		
7	346598	Plate-cover pedal hole-driver	1		
8	78248	Rivet-pop-3/16" x 0.45"lng	12		
9	395617	Plate-blanking-heater hole	1		
10	RA608123L	Rivet	3		
11	MTC1650	Plug	2	Note (2)	
12	MRC1300	Plug	2	Note (1)	
	DRC1666	Grommet-blind	1		
13	338015	Plug-blanking-plastic-13mm	1	Note (2)	
14	332647	Buffer-bonnet	2		
15	SX108251	Screw-hexagonal socket-high tensile-M8 x 25	4		
16	WA108051L	Washer-8mm	10		
23	ATU1005L	Nutsert-blind-8mm	2	Note (1)	
23	NN108021	Nut-blind-M8	2	Note (3)	
23	RRC8666	Nut-blind-M8	2	Note (4)	
17	BD155888L	Plug	1	Note (2)	
18	MWC2567	Seal-drain channel	1		Except Germany
	MUC6905	Plate-steering column aperture blanking-steering column hole	1	Note (2)	

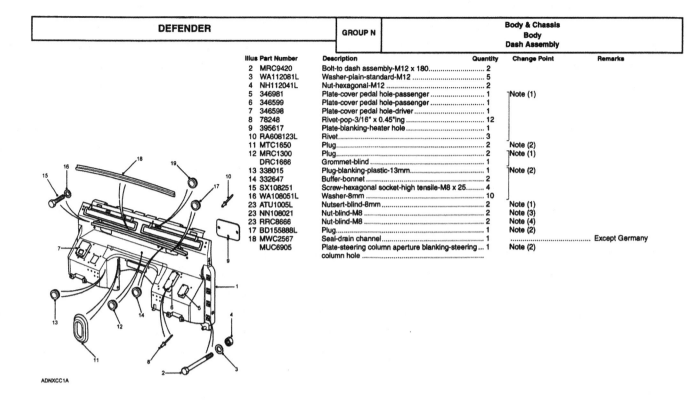

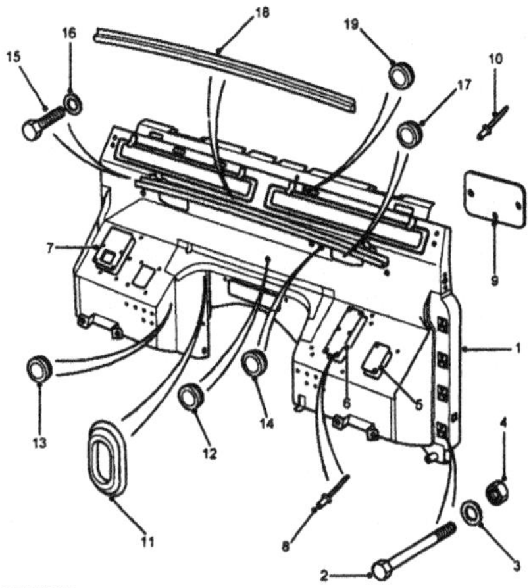

ADNXCC1A

CHANGE POINTS:
(1) To (V) AA 271213
(2) To (V) LA 939975
(3) From (V) AA 271214 To (V) WA 159806
(4) From (V) XA 159807

Illus	Part Number	Description	Quantity	Change Point	Remarks
19	MWC2309	Plug-blanking-wiper spindle	2	Note (1)	
19	AYB100750	Plug-blanking-wiper spindle-12 x 18mm	2	Note (2)	
13	RTC5519	Plug-blanking	2	From (V) AA 271214	
15	AFU1499	Screw-to dash assembly-M8 x 25	4		
20	WC108051L	Washer-M8	4		
21	WL108001L	Washer-sprung-M8	4		
22	FN108047L	Nut-flange-flanged head-M8	4		

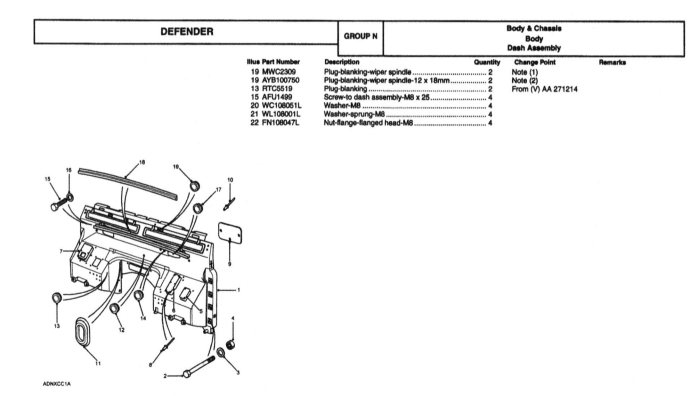

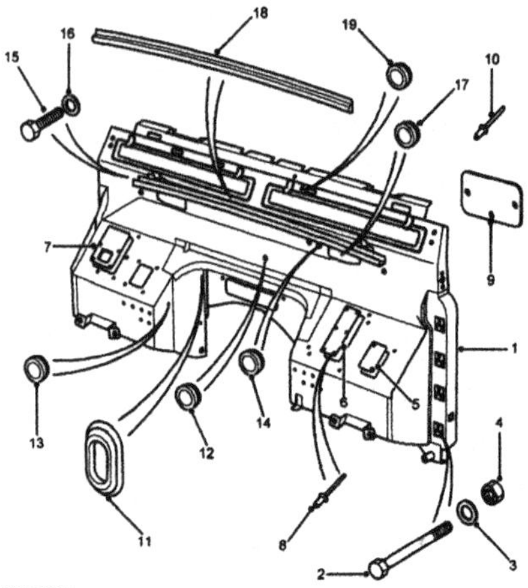

ADNXCC1A

CHANGE POINTS:
(1) To (V) 1A 622423
(2) From (V) 2A 622424

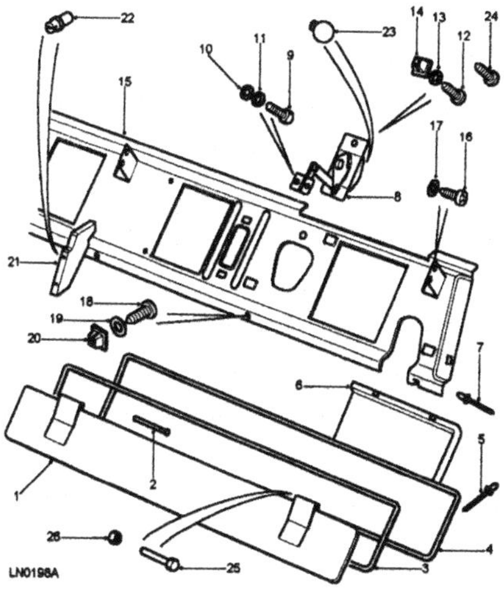

Illus	Part Number	Description	Quantity	Change Point	Remarks
		LID ASSEMBLY-VENTILATOR-DASHBOARD			
1	ALR1618	RH	1	Note (1)	
1	ALR1619	LH	1		
1	ASR1154	RH	1	Note (2)	
1	ASR1153	LH	1		
	ASR1185	Nutsert-blind-M5-Black	2		
2	334121	Pin	4	Note (3)	
25	AIO710010	Stud-bolt	4	Note (4)	
26	AYH100810	Nut-domed	4		
3	MUC4299	Seal-rubber	2	Note (5)	
3	ALR2220	Seal-rubber	2	Note (6)	
3	JAE000030	Seal-rubber	2	Note (7)	Except air conditioning
4	395185	Element-filter-flyscreen	2	To (V) LA 939975	
5	RA610123	Rivet-pop-aluminium	12		
6	MTC2799	Panel-splash-vent-grille-LH ventilator	1		
7	RA610123	Rivet-pop-aluminium	4		
8	346576	Mechanism assembly-air vent operation	2	Note (8)	
9	SH105121L	Screw-to dash ventilator-hexagonal head-M5 x 12	4		
8	AIR710080	Mechanism assembly-air vent operation-RH	1	Note (7)	
8	AIR710090	Mechanism assembly-air vent operation-LH	1		
23	AIT710030	Knob-air vent mechanism operating	2		
24	HYG10013	Bolt-torx-flange	4		
10	WC105001L	Washer-plain-large-M5	4		
11	WL105001L	Washer-retaining-M5	4		
12	DA610051L	Screw-flanged head-flanged head-No10	4		
13	AFU1257	Washer-plain	4		
14	RTC3745	Nut-lokut	4		

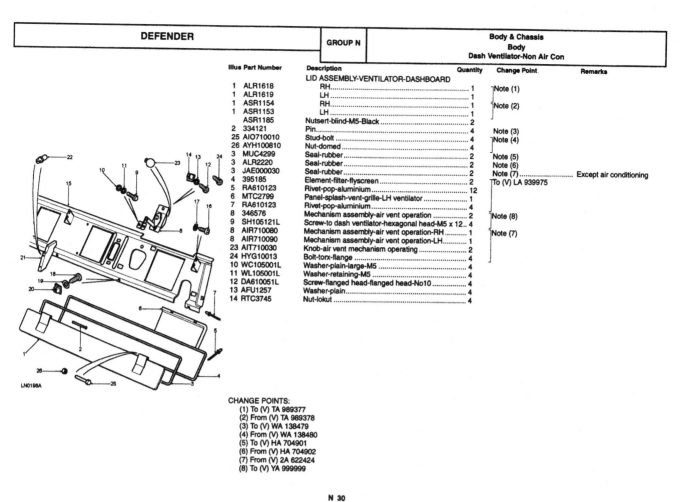

CHANGE POINTS:
(1) To (V) TA 989377
(2) From (V) TA 989378
(3) To (V) WA 138479
(4) From (V) WA 138480
(5) To (V) HA 704901
(6) From (V) HA 704902
(7) From (V) 2A 622424
(8) To (V) YA 999999

Illus	Part Number	Description	Quantity	Change Point	Remarks
15	MXC8574	Plate assembly-front-RHD	1		
15	MXC8573	Plate assembly-front-LHD	1		
16	AB608047L	Screw-to front plate-self tapping-No 8 x 1/2	6		
17	WA105001L	Washer-plain-standard-M5	6		
18	AB608054L	Screw-to plate assembly-self tapping-No8 x 5/8	5	Note (2)	
19	WA104004L	Washer-plain-M4	5		
20	RTC3745	Nut-lokut	5		
21	346941	Panel-air flow divider	1	To (V) LA 939975	
22	79106	Rivet	2		

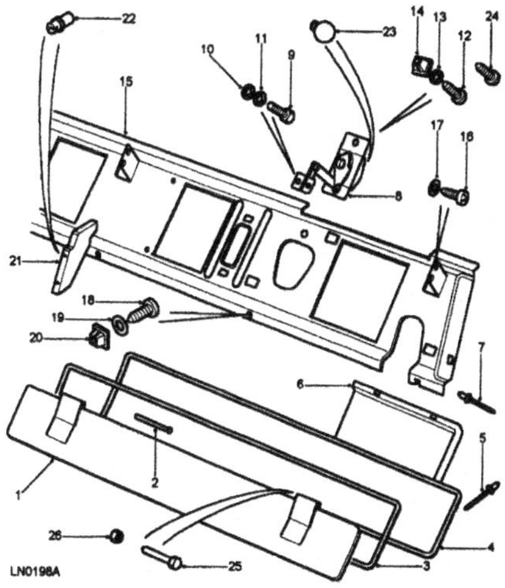

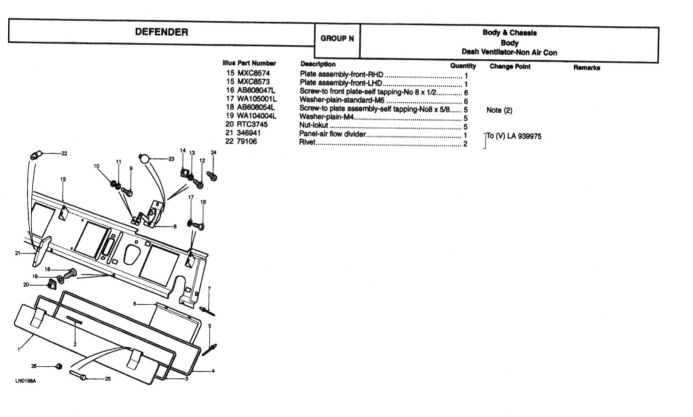

CHANGE POINTS:
(2) To (V) 2A 2002MY

Illus	Part Number	Description	Quantity	Change Point	Remarks
1	MTC6109	Finisher facia vent	2		
2	MTC6015	Washer-sealing	6		
3	WA104001L	Washer-plain-M4	6		
4	WW104001	Washer-waved	6		
5	NH104041L	Nut-hexagonal-M4	6		
6	MUC3498	Plate assembly-front-RHD	1		
6	MXC8575	Plate assembly-front-LHD	1		
7	AB608051L	Screw-front plate to dash-self tapping-No8 x 5/8-Black	5		
8	WA105001L	Washer-front plate to dash-plain-standard-M5	6		
9	RTC3745	Nut-lokut-front plate to dash	5		
10	AFU2636	Screw-front plate to crash rail-No 8	2		

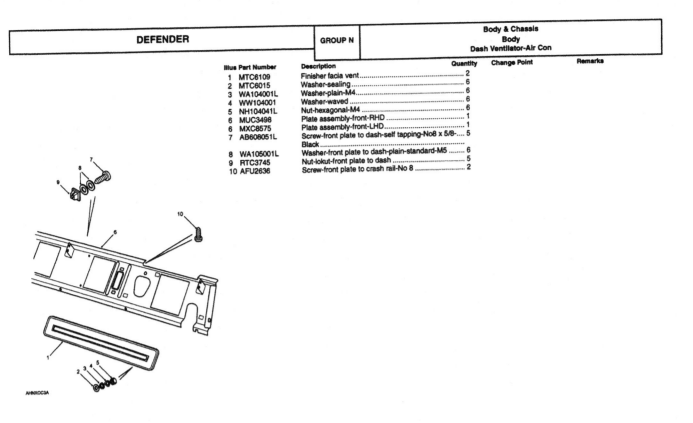

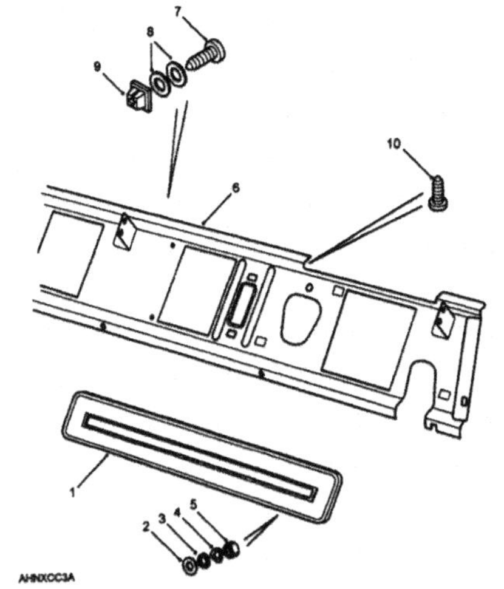

AHNXCC3A

Illus	Part Number	Description	Quantity	Change Point	Remarks
1	MTC2252	Diaphragm assembly-panel	1		4 Cylinder except TDi
1	RTC6826	Diaphragm assembly-panel	1		V8
1	RTC6826	Diaphragm assembly-panel	1		TDi
2	MRC8626	Seal-1.6M-long	1		
3	AB614061L	Screw-panel diaphragm to seal-self tapping-No 14 x 3/4	9		
4	MRC5527	Washer-plain-M6	9		
5	MTC4095	Tunnel assembly-main floor	1	Note (1)	4 Cylinder except TDi
5	MUC4319	Tunnel assembly-main floor	1		LT 85 V8
5	MUC4319	Tunnel assembly-main floor	1		LT 85 TDi
5	ALR1757	Tunnel assembly-main floor	1	Note (2)	LT 77 V8
5	ALR1757	Tunnel assembly-main floor	1		LT 77 TDi
5	ALR7005	Tunnel assembly-main floor	1	Note (3)	R 380 V8 Twin Carburettor
5	ALR7005	Tunnel assembly-main floor	1		4 Cylinder Diesel
5	ADF710030	Tunnel assembly-main floor	1	Note (4)	V8 Twin Carburettor
5	ADF710030	Tunnel assembly-main floor	1		300 TDI
5	ADF710030	Tunnel assembly-main floor	1	Note (6)	Td5
6	MTC6798	Strip-self adhesive packing-front	NLA		Use MUC1237.
7	MTC6798	Strip-self adhesive packing-side	NLA		Note (1)
8	MTC6798	Strip-self adhesive packing-rear	NLA		
6	MUC1237	Strip-self adhesive packing-front	1		Note (2)
7	MUC1237	Strip-self adhesive packing-side	2		
8	MUC1237	Strip-self adhesive packing-rear	1		

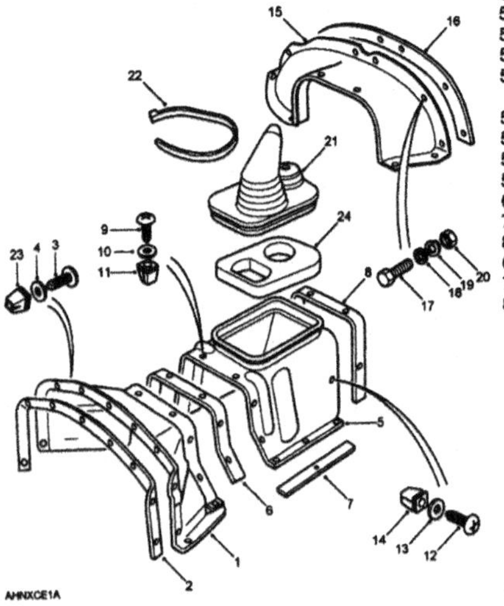

AHNXCE1A

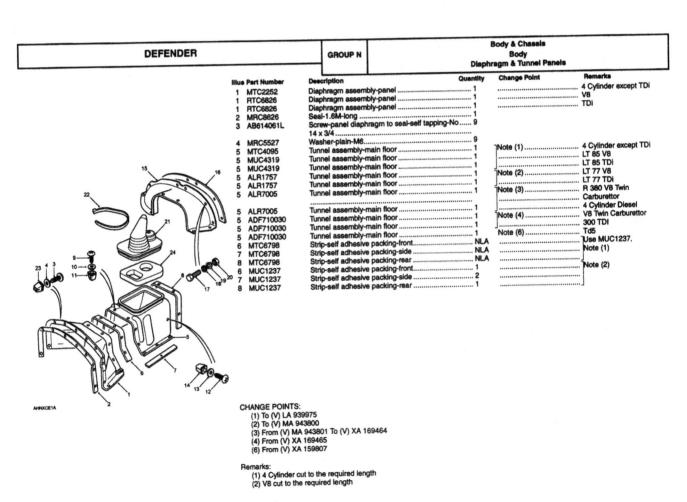

CHANGE POINTS:
(1) To (V) LA 939975
(2) To (V) MA 943800
(3) From (V) MA 943801 To (V) XA 169464
(4) From (V) XA 169465
(6) From (V) XA 159807

Remarks:
(1) 4 Cylinder cut to the required length
(2) V8 cut to the required length

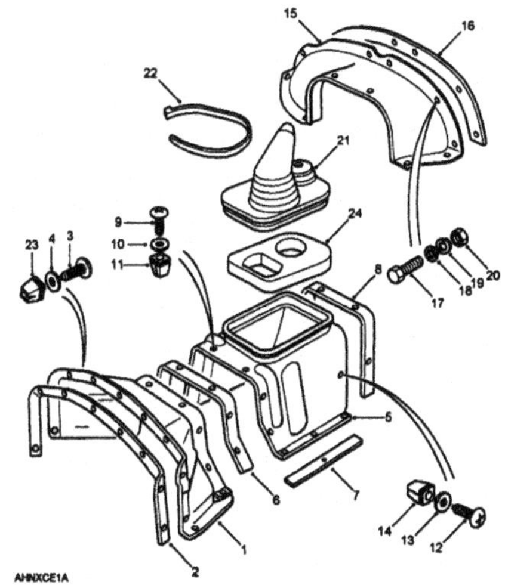

AHNXCE1A

Illus	Part Number	Description	Quantity	Change Point	Remarks
9	AB614061L	Screw-to panel-centre tunnel console-self tapping-No 14 x 3/4	6		4 Cylinder
10	MRC5527	Washer-plain-M6	6		
11	CZA4705L	Nut-lokut	6		
9	AB614061L	Screw-to panel-centre tunnel console-self tapping-No 14 x 3/4	4		V8
10	MRC5527	Washer-plain-M6	4		
11	CZA4705L	Nut-lokut	4		
12	AB614061L	Screw-to panel-centre tunnel console-self tapping-No 14 x 3/4	6		4 Cylinder
13	MRC5527	Washer-plain-M6	6		
14	CZA4705L	Nut-lokut	6		
15	MRC7411	Cover transfer case	1		V8
16	MRC8626	Seal-1.6M-long	1		
17	FS106201L	Screw-cover transfer case to seal-flanged head-M6 x 20	2		
18	WA106041L	Washer-6mm	4		
19	WL106001L	Washer-sprung-M6	2		
20	NH106041L	Nut-hexagonal-nyloc-M6	2		
17	FS108207L	Screw-flanged head-M8 x 20	1	To (V) LA 939975	RHD
19	WL108001L	Washer-sprung-M8	1		
20	FN108041L	Nut-flange-M8	NLA		
17	FS108207L	Screw-flanged head-M8 x 20	2		LHD
19	WL108001L	Washer-sprung-M8	2		
20	FN108041L	Nut-flange-M8	NLA		
21	BTR1698	Gaiter-gear lever assembly-transfer box	1		Except EFi
21	FJL101970	Gaiter-gear lever assembly-transfer box	1		V8 EFi
22	AFU4173	Tie-cable-Black-8.8 x 770mm-releasable	1		
23	CZA4705L	Nut-lokut-panel assembly diaphragm to seal	9		
24	MTC6872	Pad-insulation	1		4 Cylinder
24	MUC4027	Pad-insulation	1		V8

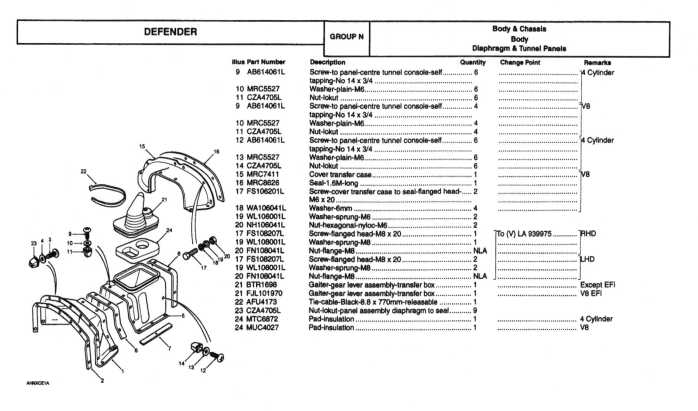

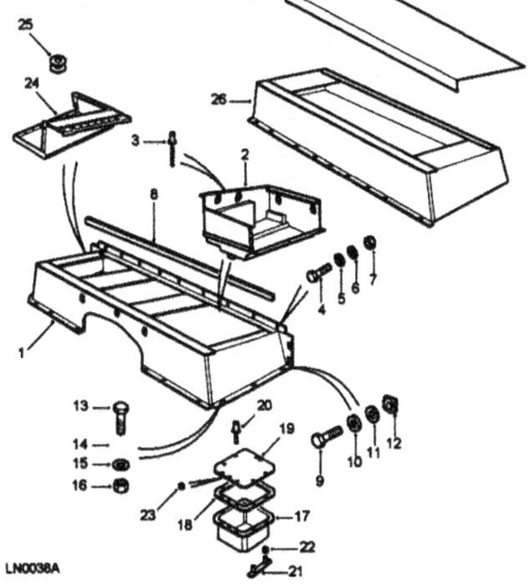

LN0038A

Illus	Part Number	Description	Quantity	Change Point	Remarks
1	MTC6340	BASE ASSEMBLY-FRONT SEAT MOUNTING-WITH TOOL LOCKER	1	Note (1)	4 Cylinder 110"
1	MUC6166	BASE ASSEMBLY-FRONT SEAT MOUNTING-WITH TOOL LOCKER	1		V8 110"
24	MXC5746	• Box-tool stowage	1		
3	78248	• Rivet-pop-3/16" x 0.45"lng	28		
		BASE ASSEMBLY-FRONT SEAT MOUNTING			
1	MXC8551	WITHOUT TOOL LOCKER	1	Note (2)	4 Cylinder 90"
1	MXC8555	WITHOUT TOOL LOCKER	1		LT 85 3500 cc V8 90"
1	ALR1753	WITHOUT TOOL LOCKER	1		LT 77 3500 cc V8 110"
1	ALR6366	WITHOUT TOOL LOCKER	1	Note (3)	LT 77 3500 cc V8 90"
1	ALR6366	WITHOUT TOOL LOCKER	1		R 380 3500 cc V8 90"
1	ALR6366	WITHOUT TOOL LOCKER	1		R 380 4 Cylinder TDi 90"
1	MXC8551	WITHOUT TOOL LOCKER	1	Note (2)	4 Cylinder 110"
1	MXC8555	WITHOUT TOOL LOCKER	1		LT 85 3500 cc V8 110"
1	ALR6366	WITHOUT TOOL LOCKER	1	Note (3)	LT 77 3500 cc V8 110"
1	ALR6366	WITHOUT TOOL LOCKER	1		R 380 3500 cc V8 110"
1	ALR6366	WITHOUT TOOL LOCKER	1		R 380 TDi 110"
2	MXC8556	• Tray battery	1		
3	78248	• Rivet-pop-3/16" x 0.45"lng	28		

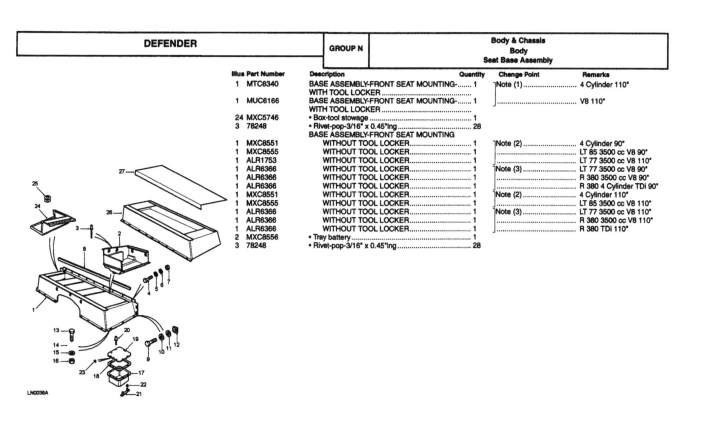

CHANGE POINTS:
(1) To (V) HA 455595
(2) From (V) HA 455596 To (V) WA 159806
(3) To (V) TA 977536

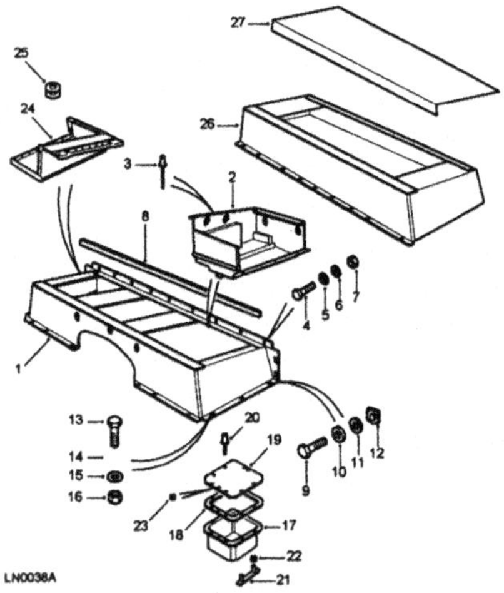

LN0038A

Illus	Part Number	Description	Quantity	Change Point	Remarks
		BASE ASSEMBLY-FRONT SEAT MOUNTING			
1	MXC8552	WITH TOOL LOCKER	1	Note (1)	4 Cylinder 110"
1	MXC8554	WITH TOOL LOCKER	1		LT 85 3500 cc V8 110"
1	ALR1752	WITH TOOL LOCKER	1		LT 77 3500 cc V8 110"
1	ALR6365	WITH TOOL LOCKER	1	Note (2)	LT 77 3500 cc V8 90"
1	ALR6365	WITH TOOL LOCKER	1		R 380 3500 cc V8 90"
1	ALR6365	WITH TOOL LOCKER	1		R 380 TDi 90"
1	ALR6365	WITH TOOL LOCKER	1		LT 77 3500 cc V8 110"
1	ALR6365	WITH TOOL LOCKER	1		R 380 3500 cc V8 110"
1	ALR6365	WITH TOOL LOCKER	1		R 380 TDi 110"
1	ASR1158	WITH TOOL LOCKER	1	Note (3)	TDi 90"
1	ASR1158	WITH TOOL LOCKER	1	Note (3)	TDi 110"
2	MXC8556	• Tray battery	1		
	MXC5746	• Box-tool stowage	1		
3	78248	• Rivet-pop-3/16" x 0.45"lng	53		
1	ASR1157	BASE ASSEMBLY-FRONT SEAT MOUNTING-WITHOUT TOOL LOCKER	1	Note (3)	TDi 90"
1	ASR1157	BASE ASSEMBLY-FRONT SEAT MOUNTING-WITHOUT TOOL LOCKER	1	Note (3)	TDi 110"
2	MXC8556	• Tray battery	1		
3	78248	• Rivet-pop-3/16" x 0.45"lng	53		
1	ASR1870	BASE ASSEMBLY-FRONT SEAT MOUNTING	1		V8 EFi 50 LE
	ALR8075	• Box-tool stowage	1		
2	MXC8556	• Tray battery	1		
3	78248	• Rivet-pop-3/16" x 0.45"lng	53		

CHANGE POINTS:
(1) From (V) HA 455596 To (V) WA 159806
(2) To (V) TA 977536
(3) From (V) TA 977537 To (V) WA 159806

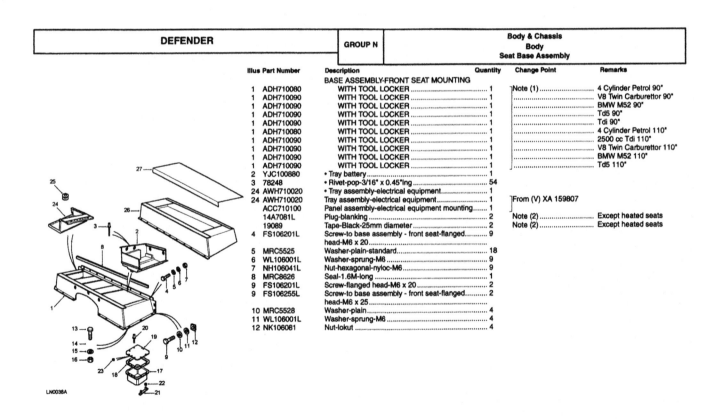

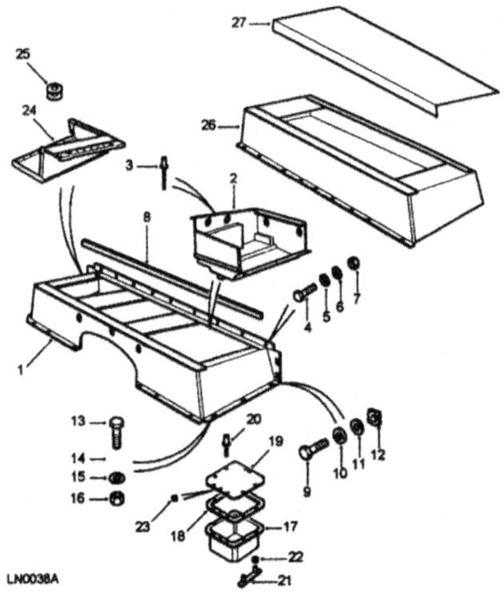

LN0038A

Illus	Part Number	Description	Quantity	Change Point	Remarks
		BASE ASSEMBLY-FRONT SEAT MOUNTING			
1	ADH710080	WITH TOOL LOCKER	1	Note (1)	4 Cylinder Petrol 90"
1	ADH710090	WITH TOOL LOCKER	1		V8 Twin Carburettor 90"
1	ADH710090	WITH TOOL LOCKER	1		BMW M52 90"
1	ADH710090	WITH TOOL LOCKER	1		Td5 90"
1	ADH710090	WITH TOOL LOCKER	1		Tdi 90"
1	ADH710080	WITH TOOL LOCKER	1		4 Cylinder Petrol 110"
1	ADH710090	WITH TOOL LOCKER	1		2500 cc Tdi 110"
1	ADH710090	WITH TOOL LOCKER	1		V8 Twin Carburettor 110"
1	ADH710090	WITH TOOL LOCKER	1		BMW M52 110"
1	ADH710090	WITH TOOL LOCKER	1		Td5 110"
2	YJC100880	• Tray battery	1		
3	78248	• Rivet-pop-3/16" x 0.45"lng	54		
24	AWH710020	• Tray assembly-electrical equipment	1		
24	AWH710020	Tray assembly-electrical equipment	1	From (V) XA 159807	
	ACC710100	Panel assembly-electrical equipment mounting	1		
	14A7081L	Plug-blanking	2	Note (2)	Except heated seats
	19089	Tape-Black-25mm diameter	2	Note (2)	Except heated seats
4	FS106201L	Screw-to base assembly - front seat-flanged head-M6 x 20	9		
5	MRC5525	Washer-plain-standard	18		
6	WL106001L	Washer-sprung-M6	9		
7	NH106041L	Nut-hexagonal-nyloc-M6	9		
8	MRC8626	Seal-1.6M-long	1		
9	FS106201L	Screw-flanged head-M6 x 20	2		
9	FS106255L	Screw-to base assembly - front seat-flanged head-M6 x 25	2		
10	MRC5528	Washer-plain	4		
11	WL106001L	Washer-sprung-M6	4		
12	NK106081	Nut-lokut	4		

CHANGE POINTS:
(1) From (V) XA 159807
(2) From (V) 2A 622424

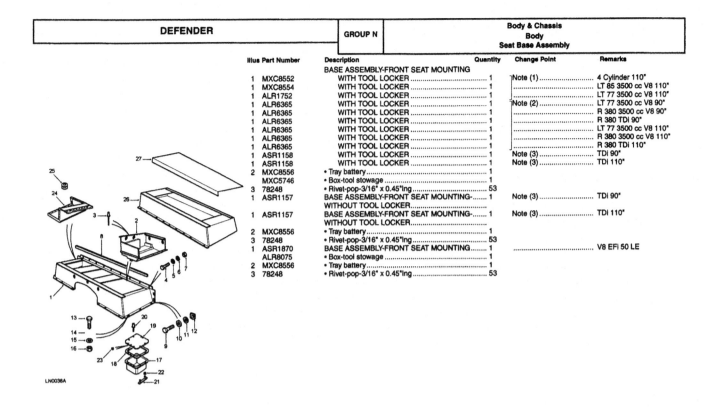

Seat Base Assembly

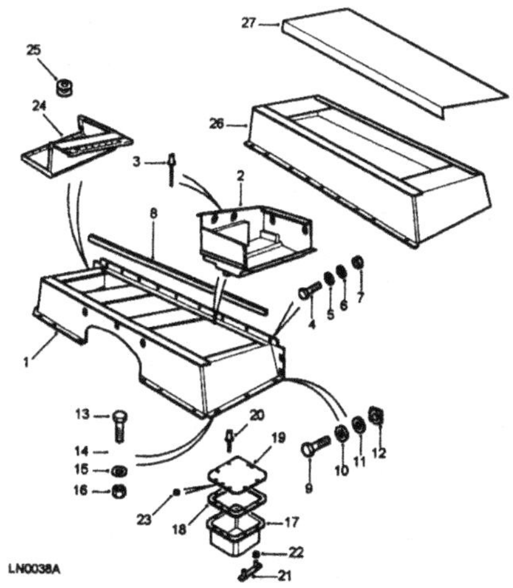

Illus	Part Number	Description	Quantity	Change Point	Remarks
13	FS106201L	Screw-seat base to box immobiliser housing-flanged head-M6 x 20	6		
14	MRC5525	Washer-plain-standard	12		
15	WL106001L	Washer-sprung-M6	6		
16	NH106041L	Nut-hexagonal-nyloc-M6	6		
17	AMR5607	Box-immobiliser housing	1	From (V) TA 977537	
18	AMR5568	Gasket	1	From (V) TA 977537	
19	AMR5566	Lid immobiliser box	1	From (V) TA 977537	
20	AFU1841	Monobolt	6	From (V) TA 977537	
21	MUC1049	Stud	2	From (V) TA 977537	
22	FN106047L	Nut-flange-M6	4	From (V) TA 977537	
23	FN105041L	Nut-flange-M5-D Terminal	2	From (V) TA 977537	
25	YQQ101240	Grommet-harness	1		V8 Twin Carburettor
25	YQQ101240	Grommet-harness	1		4 Cylinder Petrol
26	RRC6239	Base assembly-seat-rear forward facing seat-with tool locker	1		130"
27	RRC6256	Lid-tool locker-rear forward facing seat	1		130"

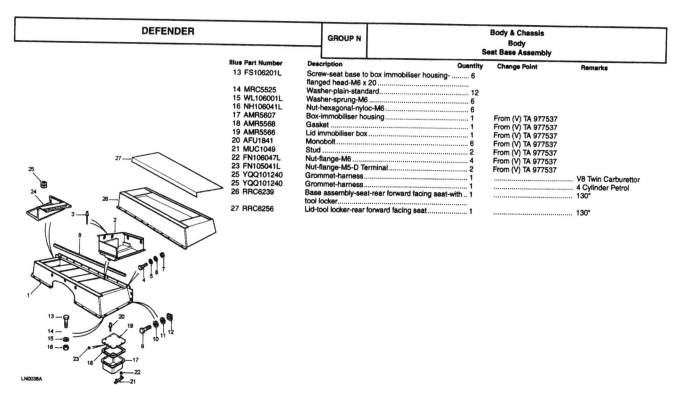

Seatbase Fittings

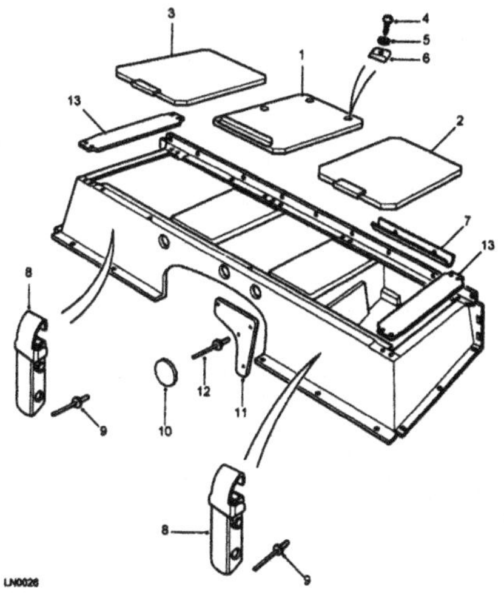

Illus	Part Number	Description	Quantity	Change Point	Remarks
		LID ASSEMBLY-LOCKER			
1	MXC6315	centre	1	Note (1)	4 Cylinder
1	MXC9116	centre	1	Note (2)	
1	ALR5111	centre	1	Note (3)	
		LID ASSEMBLY-LOCKER			
1	MTC4215	centre-less tunnel console	1	Note (4)	V8
1	MTC4197	centre-with tunnel console	1		
1	MXC6312	centre	1	Note (5)	
1	MXC9117	centre	1	Note (2)	
1	ALR5112	centre	1	Note (3)	
2	ALR5110	Lid assembly-locker	1		
3	MUC4499	Lid assembly-locker	1	Note (6)	Note (1)
3	MXC7373	Lid assembly-locker	1	Note (7)	
3	ALR5114	Lid assembly-locker	1	Note (3)	
3	ALR5113	Lid assembly-locker-RH	1	Note (8)	Note (2)
3	AJH710030	Lid assembly-locker-RH	1	Note (9)	
4	AB610051L	Screw-To cover plate centre-self tapping-No 10 x 5 x 8	4		
5	WC106041L	Washer-M6-oversize	4		
6	53K3039L	Nut-spiralok	4		
7	MRC8136	Stop-rear seat locating	2	To (V) HA 455945	
7	MXC6338	Stop-rear seat locating	2	From (V) HA 455946	
	FS106201L	Screw-flanged head-M6 x 20	2	To (V) LA 939975	
	NH106041L	Nut-hexagonal-nyloc-M6	2	To (V) LA 939975	
8	MRC8388	Catch overcentre	2	To (V) LA 939975	
9	RU608123L	Rivet-pop-aluminium-0.125"	2	To (V) LA 939975	

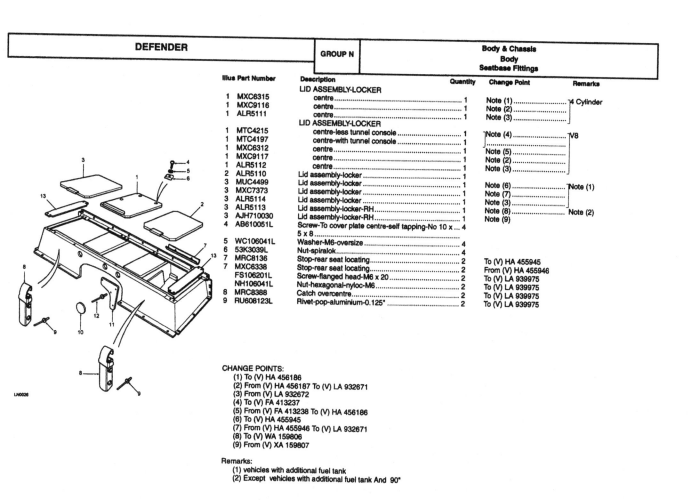

CHANGE POINTS:
(1) To (V) HA 456186
(2) From (V) HA 456187 To (V) LA 932671
(3) From (V) LA 932672
(4) To (V) FA 413237
(5) From (V) FA 413238 To (V) HA 456186
(6) To (V) HA 455945
(7) From (V) HA 455946 To (V) LA 932671
(8) To (V) WA 159806
(9) From (V) XA 159807

Remarks:
(1) vehicles with additional fuel tank
(2) Except vehicles with additional fuel tank And 90"

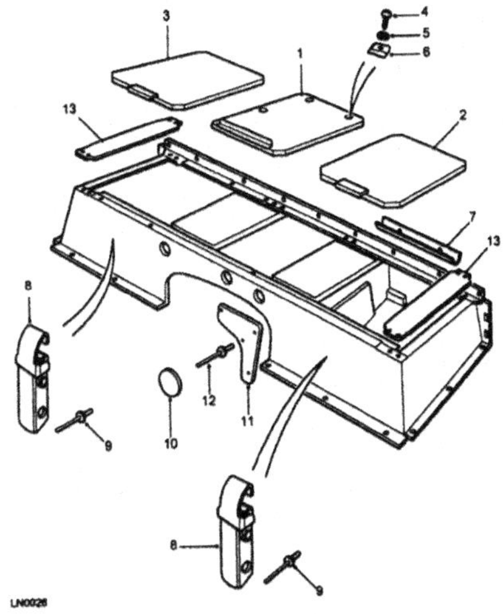

Illus	Part Number	Description	Quantity	Change Point	Remarks
		PLUG-BLANKING			
10	338015	seatbase-plastic-13mm	4		
10	338028	seatbase-plastic-50mm	1		
10	338017	seatbase-plastic-14mm	6		
10	338024	30mm	A/R		
10	338023	plastic-25.5mm	A/R		
11	MTC2203	Plate-RHD	1		4 Cylinder
11	MTC2202	Plate-LHD	1		
11	MUC1234	Plate-RHD	1		V8
11	MUC1233	Plate-LHD	1		
12	78248	Rivet-pop-3/16" x 0.45"lng	4		
		PANEL-EXTENSION			
13	MUC1412	RH	1	Note (1)	
13	334966	RH	1	Note (2)	
13	MUC1412	LH	1	To (V) HA 455945	
		NOTE: FROM HA455946 EXTENSION PANELS ARE PART OF SEAT BASE			
	348859	Cover load space to fuel tank access hole	1	To (V) LA 939975	
	MRC5509	Stud	1		
	RB613102	Rivet-bifurcated	1		
	MUC5376	Pad-insulation-seatbase covers	3		
14	MTC7458	Foam-pad-self adhesive	A/R		

CHANGE POINTS:
(1) To (V) AA 277963
(2) From (V) AA 277964 To (V) HA 455945

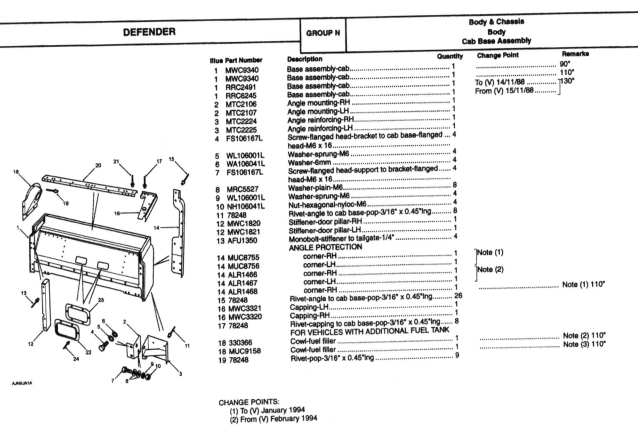

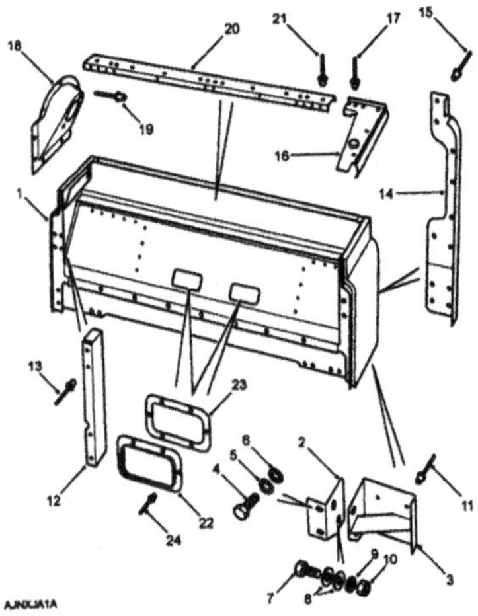

Illus	Part Number	Description	Quantity	Change Point	Remarks
1	MWC9340	Base assembly-cab	1		90"
1	MWC9340	Base assembly-cab	1		110"
1	RRC2491	Base assembly-cab	1	To (V) 14/11/88	130"
1	RRC6245	Base assembly-cab	1	From (V) 15/11/88	
2	MTC2106	Angle mounting-RH	1		
2	MTC2107	Angle mounting-LH	1		
3	MTC2224	Angle reinforcing-RH	1		
3	MTC2225	Angle reinforcing-LH	1		
4	FS106167L	Screw-flanged head-bracket to cab base-flanged head-M6 x 16	4		
5	WL106001L	Washer-sprung-M6	4		
6	WA106041L	Washer-6mm	4		
7	FS106167L	Screw-flanged head-support to bracket-flanged head-M6 x 16	4		
8	MRC5527	Washer-plain-M6	8		
9	WL106001L	Washer-sprung-M6	4		
10	NH106041L	Nut-hexagonal-nyloc-M6	4		
11	78248	Rivet-angle to cab base-pop-3/16" x 0.45"lng	8		
12	MWC1820	Stiffener-door pillar-RH	1		
12	MWC1821	Stiffener-door pillar-LH	1		
13	AFU1350	Monobolt-stiffener to tailgate-1/4"	4		
		ANGLE PROTECTION			
14	MUC8755	corner-RH	1	Note (1)	
14	MUC8756	corner-LH	1		
14	ALR1466	corner-RH	1	Note (2)	
14	ALR1467	corner-LH	1		
14	ALR1468	corner-RH	1		Note (1) 110"
15	78248	Rivet-angle to cab base-pop-3/16" x 0.45"lng	26		
16	MWC3321	Capping-LH	1		
16	MWC3320	Capping-RH	1		
17	78248	Rivet-capping to cab base-pop-3/16" x 0.45"lng	8		
		FOR VEHICLES WITH ADDITIONAL FUEL TANK			
18	330366	Cowl-fuel filler	1		Note (2) 110"
18	MUC9158	Cowl-fuel filler	1		Note (3) 110"
19	78248	Rivet-pop-3/16" x 0.45"lng	9		

CHANGE POINTS:
(1) To (V) January 1994
(2) From (V) February 1994

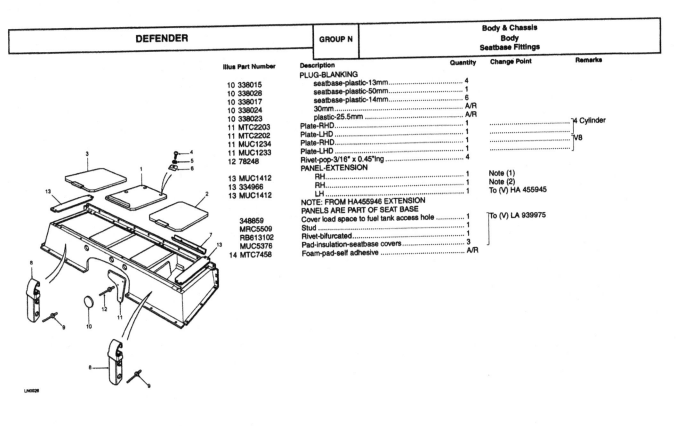

Remarks:
(1) vehicles with additional fuel tank
(2) Galvanised - not suitable for painting
(3) Galvanised and Treated - suitable for painting

Illus	Part Number	Description	Quantity	Change Point	Remarks
		ALL VARIANTS			
20	MWC2938	Capping	1		
21	RU612373L	Rivet-3/16" x 0.575"lng	39		
22	MUC6519	Plate	2		
23	MWC2129	Gasket	2		
24	78248	Rivet-plate to cab base-pop-3/16" x 0.45"lng	12		

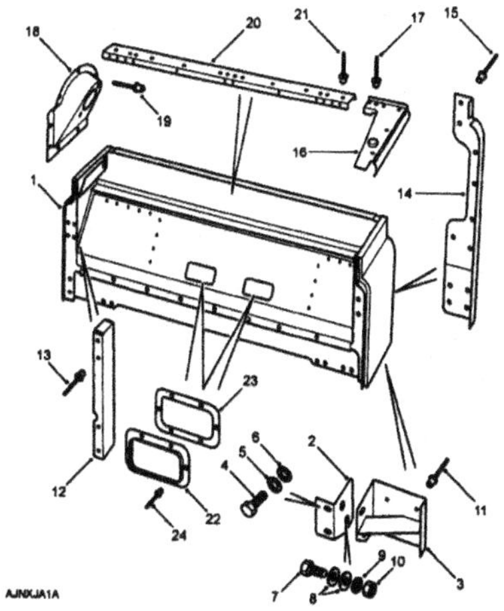

Illus	Part Number	Description	Quantity	Change Point	Remarks
1	MTC4384	Stiffener-cab base assembly-RH	1		
1	MTC4385	Stiffener-cab base assembly-LH	1		
2	MTC5608	Bracket-stiffener mounting-RH	1		
2	MTC5609	Bracket-stiffener mounting-LH	1		
3	FS108257L	Screw-flanged head-M8 x 25	10		
4	WL108001L	Washer-sprung-M8	4		
5	WA108051L	Washer-8mm	4		
6	WC108051L	Washer-M8	10		
7	NY108041L	Nut-nyloc-M8	8		
8	FS106207L	Screw-flanged head-M6 x 20	4		
9	WA106041L	Washer-6mm	8		
10	NY106047L	Nut-hexagonal head-nyloc-M6	4		
11	MTC3052	Bracket-RH	1		
11	MTC3051	Bracket-LH	1		
12	AZF100050	Pad-adhesive-to cab stiffeners	1		HICAP

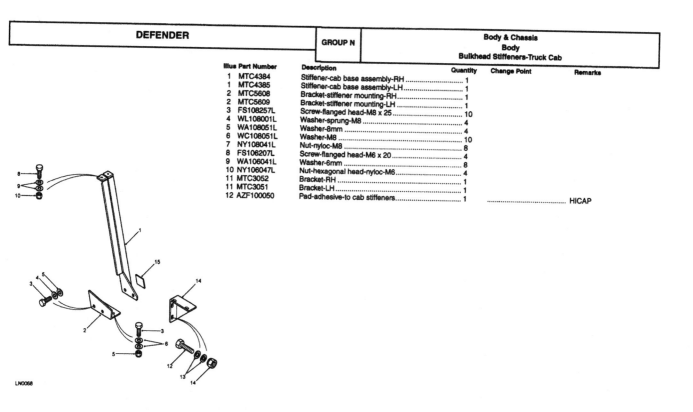

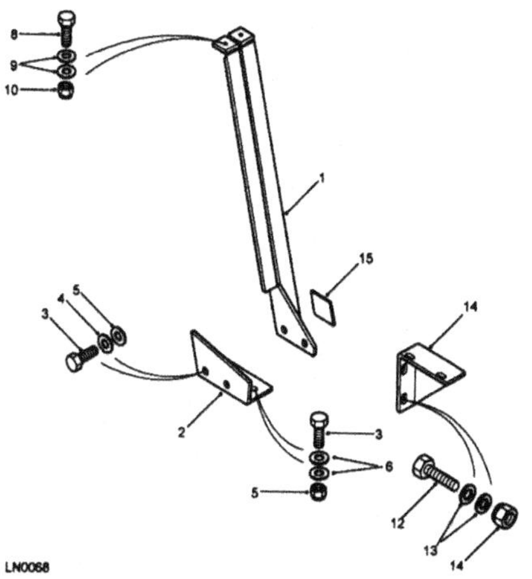

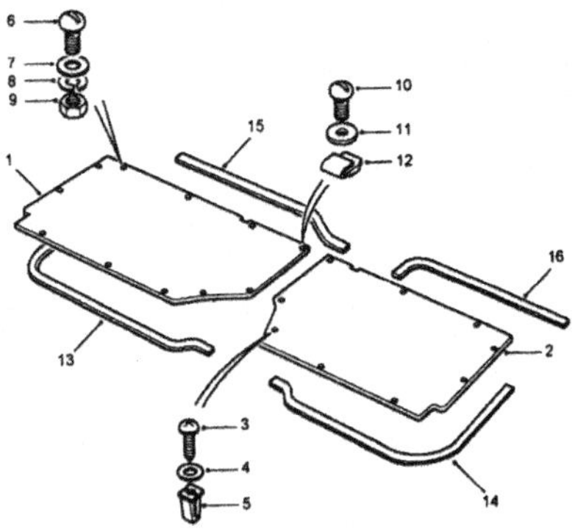

AHNXCG1A

Illus	Part Number	Description	Quantity	Change Point	Remarks
		PANEL-MAIN FLOOR			
1	MRC9720	front-RH	1		4 Cylinder except TDi
1	MUC1228	front-RH	1	Note (1)	LT 85 V8
1	ALR1742	front-RH	1	Note (2)	LT 77 V8
1	ALR1742	front-RH	1		TDi
1	ALR1742	front-RH	1		Td5
		PANEL-MAIN FLOOR			
2	MUC8835	front-LH	1	Note (1)	Diesel Turbo
2	MUC1227	front-LH	1		LT 85 V8
2	MTC2248	front-LH	1	Note (2)	4 Cylinder Petrol
2	MTC2248	front-LH	1		Diesel Naturally Aspirated
2	ALR1743	front-LH	1		LT 77 V8
2	ALR1743	front-LH	1		TDi
2	ALR1743	front-LH	1		Td5
3	AB614061L	Screw-to floor assembly-self tapping-No 14 x 3/4	4		
4	MRC5527	Washer-plain-M6	4		
5	CZA4705L	Nut-lokut	4		
6	SE106201L	Screw-to floor plate-pan head-M6 x 20	4		
7	WC106041L	Washer-M6-oversize	4		
8	WL106001L	Washer-sprung-M6	4		
9	NH106041L	Nut-hexagonal-nyloc-M6	4		
10	320045	Bolt-to floor plate	5		4 Cylinder
11	WC106041L	Washer-M6-oversize	5		
12	AL614011	Nut-spiralok	5		
10	320045	Bolt-to floor plate	6		V8
11	WC106041L	Washer-M6-oversize	6		
12	AL614011	Nut-spiralok	6		
13	MRC8626	Seal-RH-1.6M-long	A/R		
14	MRC8626	Seal-LH-1.6M-long	A/R		
15	MRC8626	Seal-RH-1.6M-long	A/R		
16	MRC8626	Seal-LH-1.6M-long	A/R		
	RRC6198	Rear floor assembly	1		130"
	RRC2497	Support-rear body	1		

CHANGE POINTS:
(1) To (V) LA 939975
(2) From (V) MA 939976

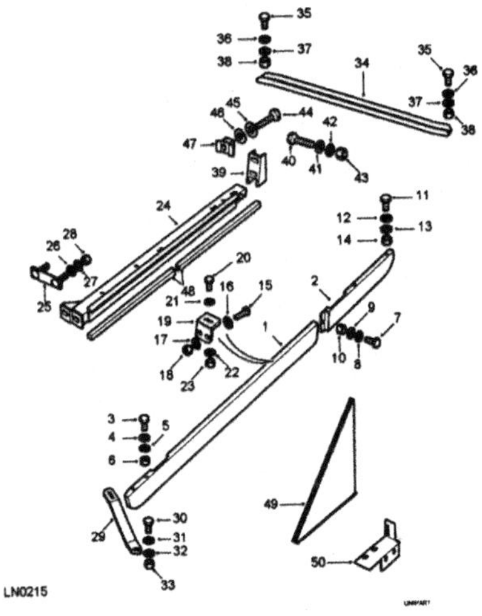

LN0215

Illus	Part Number	Description	Quantity	Change Point	Remarks
		SILL			
1	RTC6205	front-RH	1		Standard / County
1	RTC6206	front-LH	1		
1	ALR3362	front-RH	1		90 SV
1	ALR3363	front-LH	1		
1	ALR3362	front-RH	1		V8 EFi 50 LE
1	ALR3363	front-LH	1		
		SILL			
2	MTC8292	rear-RH	1		90" except Chassis Cab
2	MTC8293	rear-LH	1		
2	337812	rear-RH	1		Chassis Cab
2	337813	rear-LH	1		
2	MRC5049	rear-RH	1		110"
2	MRC5050	rear-LH	1		
2	RRC6234	rear-RH	1		130" except Chassis Cab
2	RRC6233	rear-LH	1		

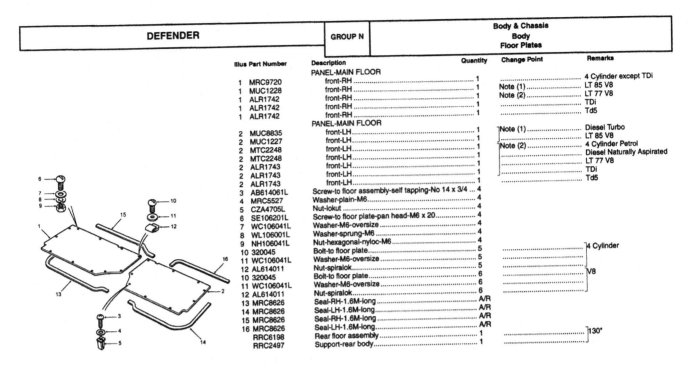

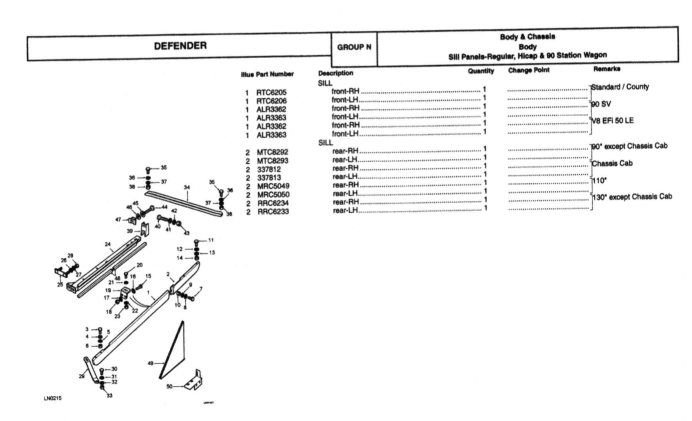

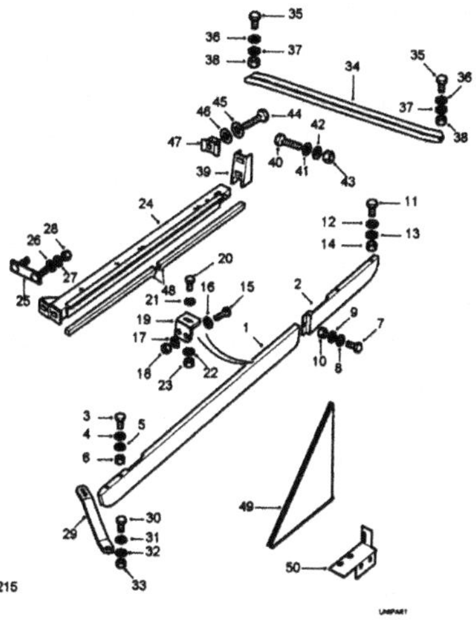

LN0215

Illus	Part Number	Description	Quantity	Change Point	Remarks
3	FS106167L	Screw-flanged head-sill panel to outer wing-flanged head-M6 x 16	4		
4	MRC5525	Washer-plain-sill panel to outer wing-standard	8		
5	WL106001L	Washer-sill panel to outer wing-sprung-M6	4		
6	NH106041L	Nut-sill panel to outer wing-hexagonal-nyloc-M6	4		
7	FS106167L	Screw-flanged head-front to rear sill panel-flanged head-M6 x 16	2		
8	RTC609	Washer-plain-front to rear sill panel-standard	4		
9	WM106001L	Washer-spring-front to rear sill panel-M6-square	2		
10	NH106041L	Nut-front to rear sill panel-hexagonal-nyloc-M6	2		
11	FS106167L	Screw-flanged head-to sill panel rear-flanged head-M6 x 16	14		
12	RTC609	Washer-plain-to sill panel rear-standard	12		
13	WM106001L	Washer-spring-to sill panel rear-M6-square	6		
14	NH106041L	Nut-to sill panel rear-hexagonal-nyloc-M6	14		
15	FS106167L	Screw-flanged head-sill panel to channel bracket-flanged head-M6 x 16	4		
16	RTC609	Washer-plain-sill panel to channel bracket-standard	8		
17	WM106001L	Washer-spring-sill panel to channel bracket-M6-square	4		
18	NH106041L	Nut-sill panel to channel bracket-hexagonal-nyloc-M6	4		
19	MRC9438	Bracket	4		
20	FS106201L	Screw-bracket to sill channel-flanged head-M6 x 20	4		
21	AFU1069	Washer-plain-bracket to sill channel	8		
22	WL106001L	Washer-bracket to sill channel-sprung-M6	4		
23	NH106041L	Nut-bracket to sill channel-hexagonal-nyloc-M6	4		

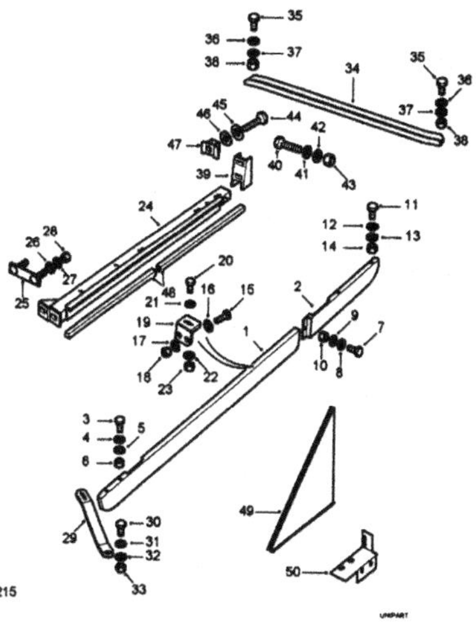

LN0215

Illus	Part Number	Description	Quantity	Change Point	Remarks
24	MWC1086	Channel assembly-sill-RH	1	To (V) LA 924784	
24	MWC1087	Channel assembly-sill-LH	1		
24	ALR5294	Channel assembly-sill-RH	1	Note (1)	
24	ALR5295	Channel assembly-sill-LH	1		
24	AJL710020	Channel assembly-sill-RH	1	Note (2)	
24	AJL710030	Channel assembly-sill-LH	1		
		SILL CHANNEL TO DASH			
25	MRC5765	Stud plate	2		
26	RTC610	Washer-plain	4		
27	WM600051L	Washer-spring-5/16"	4		
28	FN108041L	Nut-flange-M8	NLA		Use FN108047L.
29	MRC5153	Stay-front	2		
30	FS106167L	Screw-flanged head-to front stay-flanged head-M6 x 16	4		
31	WA106041L	Washer-6mm	4		
32	WL106001L	Washer-sprung-M6	4		
33	NH106041L	Nut-hexagonal-nyloc-M6	4		
34	MRC6019	Stay-centre	2		
35	FS106167L	Screw-flanged head-to centre stay-flanged head-M6 x 16	4		
36	WA106041L	Washer-6mm	4		
37	WL106001L	Washer-sprung-M6	4		
38	NH106041L	Nut-hexagonal-nyloc-M6	4		

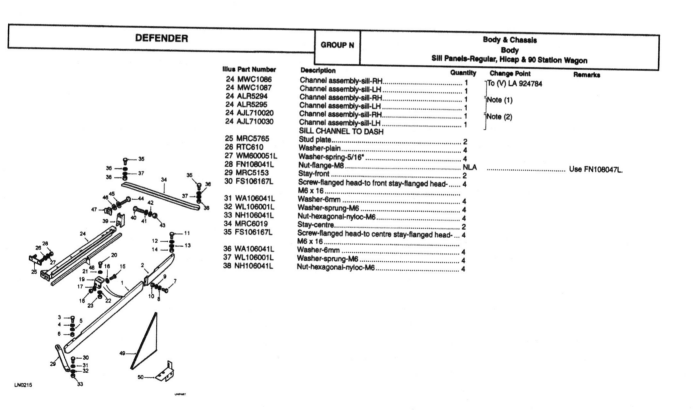

CHANGE POINTS:
(1) From (V) LA 924785 To (V) WA 159806
(2) From (V) XA 159807

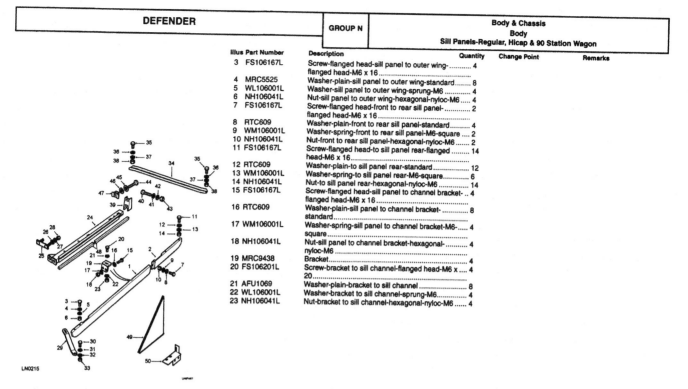

DEFENDER	GROUP N	Body & Chassis Body Sill Panels-Regular, Hicap & 90 Station Wagon

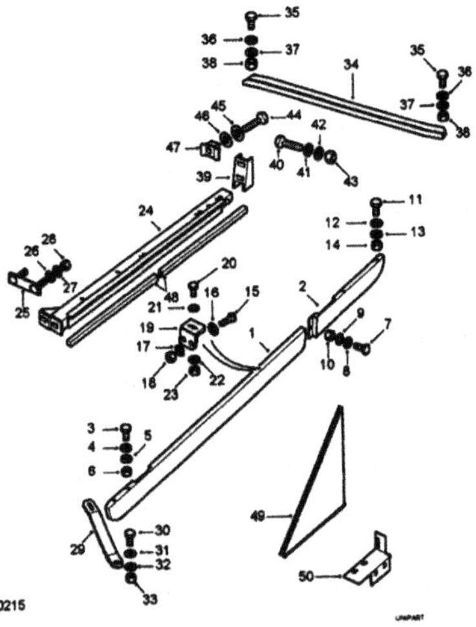

LN0215

Illus	Part Number	Description	Quantity	Change Point	Remarks
39	347436	Bracket	2		
40	FS108207L	Screw-to bracket mounting-flanged head-M8 x 20	4		
41	RTC610	Washer-plain	8		
42	WL108001L	Washer-sprung-M8	4		
43	FN108041L	Nut-flange-M8	NLA		Use FN108047L.
44	FS106201L	Screw-to bracket mounting-flanged head-M6 x 20	4		
45	WL106001L	Washer-sprung-M6	4		
46	MRC5528	Washer-plain	4		
47	NK106081	Nut-lokut	4		
48	ALR6368	Seal-sill/floor	2		
49	ALR9803	Panel rear quarter-LH	1		130"
49	ALR9804	Panel rear quarter-RH	1		130"
50	ALR9801	Bracket-sill extension fixing-LH	1		130"
50	ALR9802	Bracket-sill extension fixing-RH	1		130"

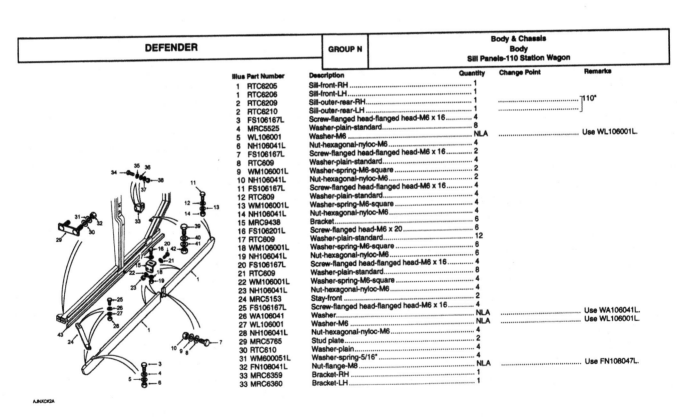

DEFENDER	GROUP N	Body & Chassis Body Sill Panels-110 Station Wagon

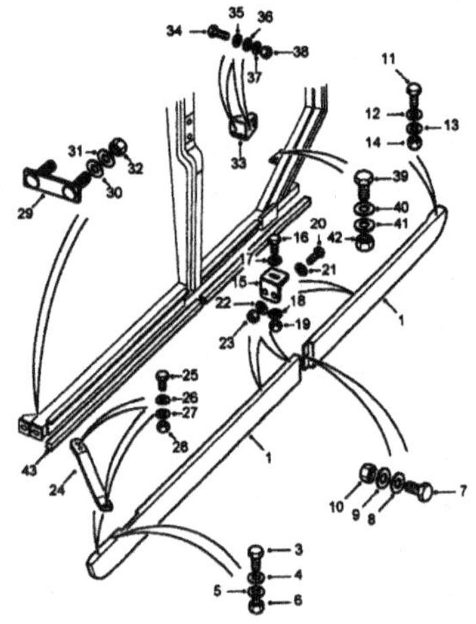

AJNXCK2A

Illus	Part Number	Description	Quantity	Change Point	Remarks
1	RTC6205	Sill-front-RH	1		
1	RTC6206	Sill-front-LH	1		
2	RTC6209	Sill-outer-rear-RH	1		110"
2	RTC6210	Sill-outer-rear-LH	1		
3	FS106167L	Screw-flanged head-flanged head-M6 x 16	4		
4	MRC5525	Washer-plain-standard	8		
5	WL106001	Washer-M6	NLA		Use WL106001L.
6	NH106041L	Nut-hexagonal-nyloc-M6	4		
7	FS106167L	Screw-flanged head-flanged head-M6 x 16	2		
8	RTC609	Washer-plain-standard	4		
9	WM106001L	Washer-spring-M6-square	2		
10	NH106041L	Nut-hexagonal-nyloc-M6	2		
11	FS106167L	Screw-flanged head-flanged head-M6 x 16	4		
12	RTC609	Washer-plain-standard	4		
13	WM106001L	Washer-spring-M6-square	4		
14	NH106041L	Nut-hexagonal-nyloc-M6	4		
15	MRC9438	Bracket	6		
16	FS106201L	Screw-flanged head-M6 x 20	6		
17	RTC609	Washer-plain-standard	12		
18	WM106001L	Washer-spring-M6-square	6		
19	NH106041L	Nut-hexagonal-nyloc-M6	6		
20	FS106167L	Screw-flanged head-flanged head-M6 x 16	4		
21	RTC609	Washer-plain-standard	8		
22	WM106001L	Washer-spring-M6-square	4		
23	NH106041L	Nut-hexagonal-nyloc-M6	4		
24	MRC5153	Stay-front	2		
25	FS106167L	Screw-flanged head-flanged head-M6 x 16	4		
26	WA106041	Washer	NLA		Use WA106041L.
27	WL106001	Washer-M6	NLA		Use WL106001L.
28	NH106041L	Nut-hexagonal-nyloc-M6	4		
29	MRC5765	Stud plate	2		
30	RTC610	Washer-plain	4		
31	WM600051L	Washer-spring-5/16"	4		
32	FN108041L	Nut-flange-M8	NLA		Use FN108047L.
33	MRC6359	Bracket-RH	1		
33	MRC6360	Bracket-LH	1		

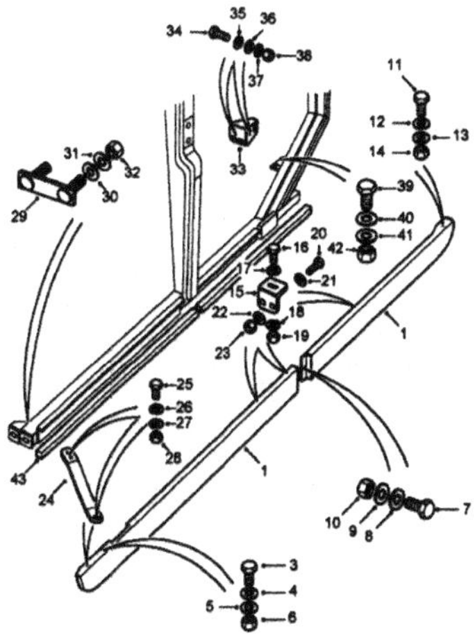

AJNXCK2A

Illus	Part Number	Description	Quantity	Change Point	Remarks
34	SX108251	Screw-to bracket-hexagonal socket-high tensile-M8 x 25	8		
35	WP185	Washer-plain	2		
36	RTC601	Pin-split	16		
37	WM600051L	Washer-spring-5/16"	8		
38	FN108041L	Nut-flange-M8	NLA		Use FN108047L.
39	FS108161L	Screw-to frame-flanged head-M8 x 16	4		
40	WC108051L	Washer-M8	4		
41	WM600051L	Washer-spring-5/16"	4		
42	FN108041L	Nut-flange-M8	NLA		Use FN108047L.
	MUC9110	Nut plate	4		
43	ALR6368	Seal-sill/floor	2		

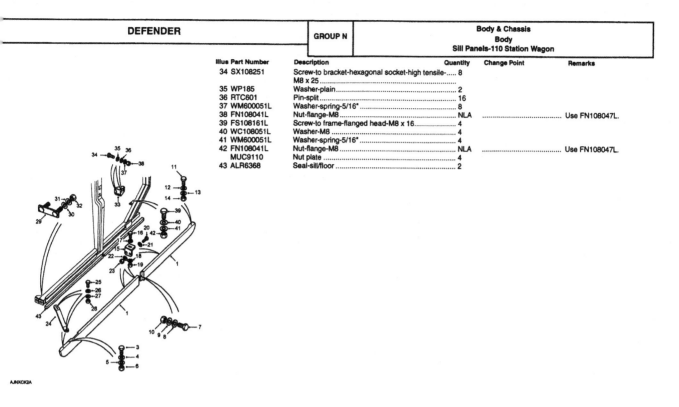

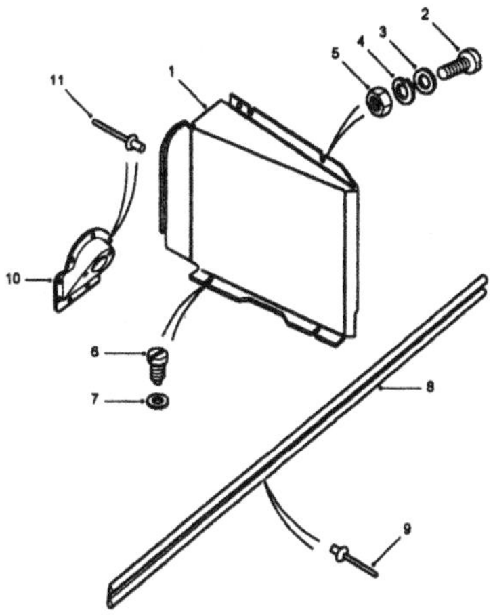

AJNXKC3A

Illus	Part Number	Description	Quantity	Change Point	Remarks
		PANEL COVER			
1	MTC7878	rear lamps-RH	1		90"
1	MTC7879	rear lamps-LH	1		
1	MTC7878	rear lamps-RH	1		Station Wagon 110"
1	MTC7879	rear lamps-LH	1		
1	MRC2244	rear lamps-RH	1		Regular 110"
1	MRC2245	rear lamps-LH	1		
2	SP105121	Screw-panel to body-pan head-M5 x 12	4		
2	SE105121L	Screw-pan head-M5 x 12	4		
3	WC105001L	Washer-plain-large-M5	4		
4	WL105001L	Washer-retaining-M5	4		
5	NM105011	Nut-hexagonal	4		
6	AB608031L	Screw- panel to body-self tapping-No 8 x 3/8	4		
7	WC105001L	Washer-plain-large-M5	4		
8	330615	Tread plate	3		
9	78248	Rivet-pop-3/16" x 0.45"lng	39		
10	MUC9158	Cowl-fuel filler	1	Note (1)	Regular 110"
11	RU612373L	Rivet-3/16" x 0.575"lng	9		

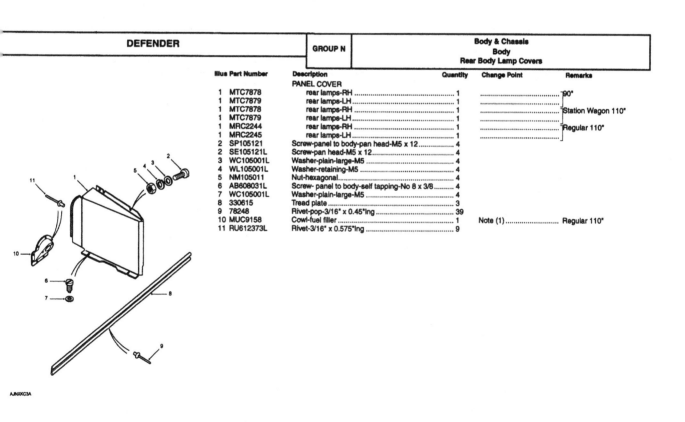

CHANGE POINTS:
(1) To (V) LA 939975

Illus	Part Number	Description	Quantity	Change Point	Remarks
1	DRM10001L	Bracket	2		
2	DYH10048	Nutsert-blind	2		
3	BTR6806	Rivnut	2		

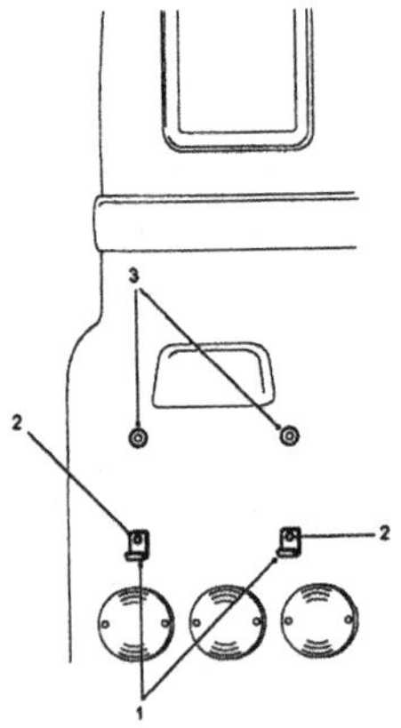

AMNXTA4A

Illus	Part Number	Description	Quantity	Change Point	Remarks
1	395413	Bracket	1		
2	FS106201L	Screw-flanged head-M6 x 20	2		
2	FS106167L	Screw-flanged head-flanged head-M6 x 16	7		
3	RTC609	Washer-plain-standard	9		
4	WM600051L	Washer-spring-5/16"	9		
5	NH106041L	Nut-hexagonal-nyloc-M6	9		
6	FS106167L	Screw-flanged head-flanged head-M6 x 16	4		
7	WC106041L	Washer-M6-oversize	4		
8	WM106001	Washer-spring	4		
9	MRC9388	Nut plate	2		

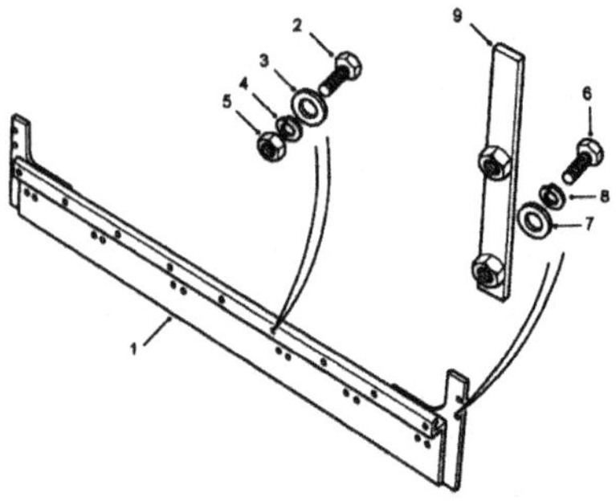

AJNXKE4A

DEFENDER	GROUP N	Body & Chassis Body Front Wing Assembly

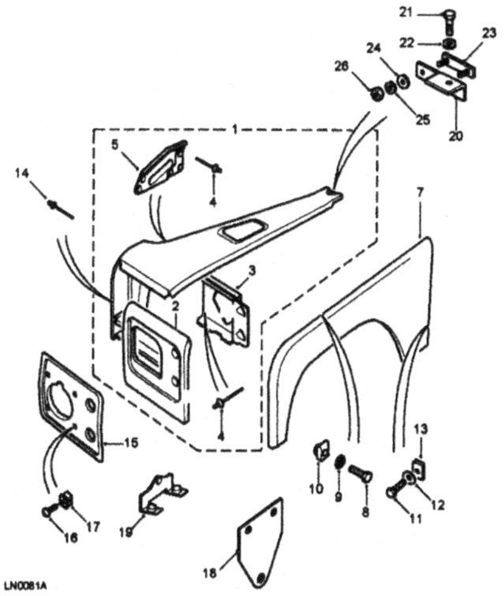

LN0081A

Illus	Part Number	Description	Quantity	Change Point	Remarks
1	MXC9343	FENDER ASSEMBLY-FRONT-RH	1	Note (1)	Except air conditioning
2	RTC6353	• Panel-fender front-RH	1		
3	MTC2062	• Panel-headlamp mounting-RH	1		
4	78248	• Rivet-pop-3/16" x 0.45"lng	16		
5	MRC6051	• Reinforcement assembly-headlamp closing-RH	1		
1	MXC9400	FENDER ASSEMBLY-FRONT-LH	1	Note (1)	Except air conditioning
1	MXC9402	FENDER ASSEMBLY-FRONT-LH	1	Note (1)	Air conditioning
2	RTC6354	• Panel-fender front-LH	1		
3	MTC2063	• Panel-headlamp mounting-LH	1		
4	78248	• Rivet-pop-3/16" x 0.45"lng	16		
5	MRC6052	• Reinforcement assembly-headlamp closing-LH	1		
1	ALR6842	FENDER ASSEMBLY-FRONT-RH	1	Note (2)	
2	ALR5990	• Panel-fender front-RH	1		
3	ALR5324	• Panel-headlamp mounting-RH	1		
4	78248	• Rivet-pop-3/16" x 0.45"lng	16		
5	MRC6051	• Reinforcement assembly-headlamp closing-RH	1		
1	ALR6843	FENDER ASSEMBLY-FRONT-LH	1	Note (2)	Except air conditioning
1	ALR6840	FENDER ASSEMBLY-FRONT-LH	1	Note (2)	Air conditioning
2	ALR5989	• Panel-fender front-LH	1		
3	ALR5323	• Panel-headlamp mounting-LH	1		
4	78248	• Rivet-pop-3/16" x 0.45"lng	16		
5	MRC6052	• Reinforcement assembly-headlamp closing-LH	1		
1	ALR9936	FENDER ASSEMBLY-FRONT-RH	1	Note (3)	Except air conditioning
1	ALR9962	FENDER ASSEMBLY-FRONT-RH	1	Note (3)	Air conditioning
2	ALR5990	• Panel-fender front-RH	1		
3	ALR5324	• Panel-headlamp mounting-RH	1		
4	78248	• Rivet-pop-3/16" x 0.45"lng	16		
5	MRC6051	• Reinforcement assembly-headlamp closing-RH	1		
1	ALR9935	FENDER ASSEMBLY-FRONT-LH	1	Note (3)	
2	ALR5989	• Panel-fender front-LH	1		
3	ALR5323	• Panel-headlamp mounting-LH	1		
4	78248	• Rivet-pop-3/16" x 0.45"lng	16		
5	MRC6052	• Reinforcement assembly-headlamp closing-LH	1		

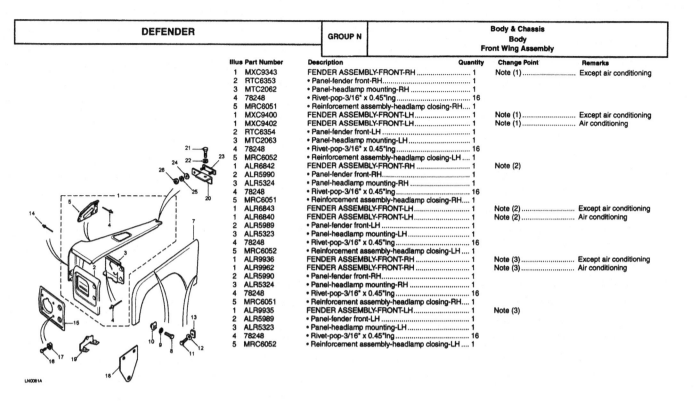

CHANGE POINTS:
(1) To (V) LA 939975
(2) From (V) MA 939976 To (V) TA 977536
(3) From (V) TA 977537 To (V) WA 159806

DEFENDER	GROUP N	Body & Chassis Body Front Wing Assembly

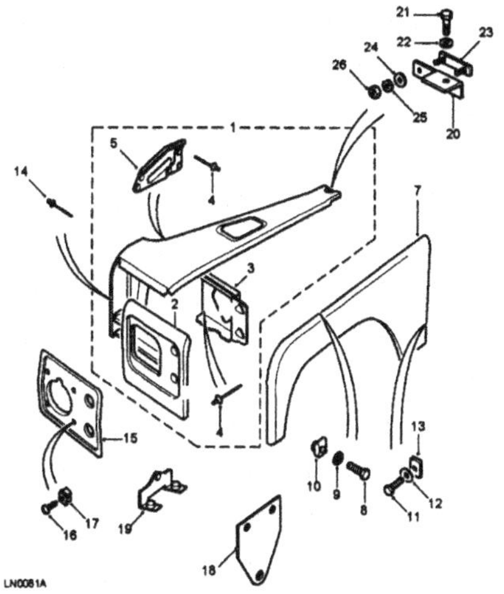

LN0081A

Illus	Part Number	Description	Quantity	Change Point	Remarks
1	STC914	FENDER ASSEMBLY-FRONT-RH	1		90 SV
2	RTC6353	• Panel-fender front-RH	1		
3	MTC2062	• Panel-headlamp mounting-RH	1		
4	78248	• Rivet-pop-3/16" x 0.45"lng	16		
5	MRC6051	• Reinforcement assembly-headlamp closing-RH	1		
1	STC915	FENDER ASSEMBLY-FRONT-LH	1		90 SV
2	RTC6354	• Panel-fender front-LH	1		
3	MTC2063	• Panel-headlamp mounting-LH	1		
4	78248	• Rivet-pop-3/16" x 0.45"lng	16		
5	MRC6052	• Reinforcement assembly-headlamp closing-LH	1		
1	ASR1876	FENDER ASSEMBLY-FRONT-RH	1		V8 EFi Japan
2	ALR7972	• Panel-fender front-RH	1		
3	MTC2062	• Panel-headlamp mounting-RH	1		
4	78248	• Rivet-pop-3/16" x 0.45"lng	16		
5	MRC6051	• Reinforcement assembly-headlamp closing-RH	1		
1	ASR1877	FENDER ASSEMBLY-FRONT-LH	1		V8 EFi Japan
2	ALR7973	• Panel-fender front-LH	1		
3	MTC2063	• Panel-headlamp mounting-LH	1		
4	78248	• Rivet-pop-3/16" x 0.45"lng	16		
5	MRC6052	• Reinforcement assembly-headlamp closing-LH	1		
3	ASW710120	Panel-headlamp mounting-RH	1		V8 EFi 50 LE
3	ASW710130	Panel-headlamp mounting-LH	1		V8 EFi 50 LE
1	ASB710200	FENDER ASSEMBLY-FRONT-RH	1	Note (1)	
2	ASW710140	• Panel-fender front-RH	1		
3	ASW710120	• Panel-headlamp mounting-RH	1		
	ASR2158	• Bracket-radiator closing panel-RH	1		
5	ASR710100	• Reinforcement assembly-headlamp closing-RH	1		
4	RU612253	• Rivet-3/16" x 0.45"lng	8		
1	ASB710210	FENDER ASSEMBLY-FRONT-LH	1	Note (1)	
2	ASW710150	• Panel-fender front-LH	1		
3	ASW710130	• Panel-headlamp mounting-LH	1		
5	ASR710110	• Reinforcement assembly-headlamp closing-LH	1		
4	RU612253	• Rivet-3/16" x 0.45"lng	8		

CHANGE POINTS:
(1) From (V) XA 159807

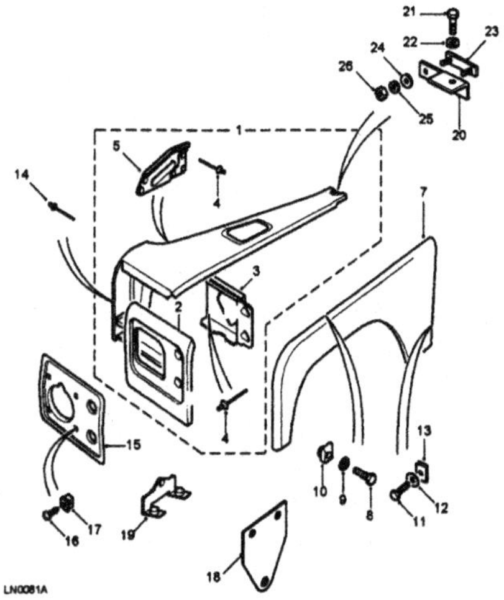

Illus	Part Number	Description	Quantity	Change Point	Remarks
7	RTC6351	Panel assembly-fender side-RH	1	Note (1)	V8 Twin Carburettor
7	RTC6350	Panel assembly-fender side-LH	1		
7	RTC6351	Panel assembly-fender side-RH	1		4 Cylinder Petrol
7	RTC6350	Panel assembly-fender side-LH	1		
7	RTC6351	Panel assembly-fender side-RH	1		Diesel Naturally Aspirated
7	RTC6350	Panel assembly-fender side-LH	1		
7	RTC6351	Panel assembly-fender side-RH	1		Diesel Turbo
7	RTC6352	Panel assembly-fender side-LH	1		
7	ALR5928	Panel assembly-fender side-RH	1		90 SV
7	ALR5927	Panel assembly-fender side-LH	1		
7	ALR6678	Panel assembly-fender side-RH	1	Note (2)	V8 Twin Carburettor
7	ALR6121	Panel assembly-fender side-LH	1	Note (2)	
7	ALR6678	Panel assembly-fender side-RH	1	Note (2)	4 Cylinder Petrol
7	ALR6121	Panel assembly-fender side-LH	1	Note (2)	
7	ALR6678	Panel assembly-fender side-RH	1	Note (2)	Diesel Naturally Aspirated
7	ALR6121	Panel assembly-fender side-LH	1	Note (2)	
7	ALR6121	Panel assembly-fender side-LH	1	Note (3)	TDi except air
7	ALR6122	Panel assembly-fender side-RH	1	Note (3)	conditioning
7	ALR6677	Panel assembly-fender side-LH	1	Note (3)	LHD TDi air conditioning
7	ALR6678	Panel assembly-fender side-RH	1	Note (3)	
7	ASB710040	Panel assembly-fender side-RH	1		V8 EFi 50 LE
7	ASB710050	Panel assembly-fender side-LH	1		
7	ASB710260	Panel assembly-fender side-RH	1	Note (4)	TDi
7	ASB710270	Panel assembly-fender side-LH	1	Note (4)	
7	ASB710260	Panel assembly-fender side-RH	1	Note (4)	Td5
7	ASB710270	Panel assembly-fender side-LH	1	Note (4)	
7	ASB710280	Panel assembly-fender side-RH	1	Note (4)	4 Cylinder Petrol
7	ASB710270	Panel assembly-fender side-LH	1	Note (4)	
7	ASB710280	Panel assembly-fender side-RH	1	Note (4)	V8 Twin Carburettor
7	ASB710270	Panel assembly-fender side-LH	1	Note (4)	
7	ASB710280	Panel assembly-fender side-RH	1	Note (4)	6 Cylinder
7	ASB710290	Panel assembly-fender side-LH	1	Note (4)	

CHANGE POINTS:
(1) To (V) LA 939975
(2) From (V) MA 939976
(3) From (V) MA 939976 To (V) WA 159806
(4) From (V) XA 159807

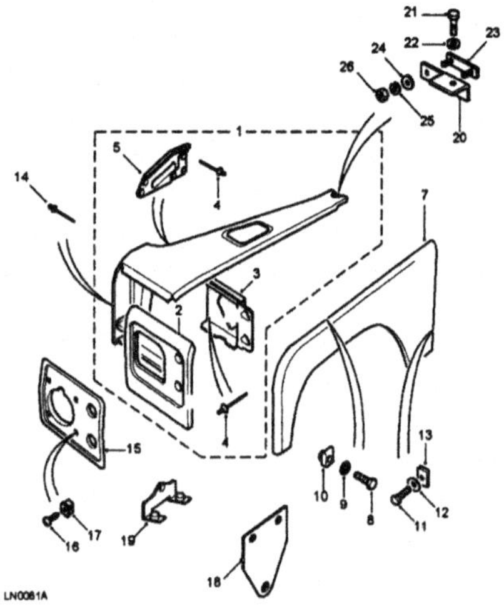

Illus	Part Number	Description	Quantity	Change Point	Remarks
8	MXC2932	Bolt-to panel outer	28		
9	3900L	Washer-standard	28		
10	302532	Nut-spiralok	26		
	AH614011L	Nut-spring-flat	2		
	MUC9339	Washer-fibre	4	To (V) LA 939975	Diesel
11	AM605061	Bolt-nut to panel outer	8		
12	WC108051L	Washer-M8	8		
13	AK616011	Nut-spring-u type	8		
14	RU612373L	Rivet-3/16" x 0.575"lng	8		
		FINISHER-HEADLAMP			
15	MTC7770	Steel Grey-RH-stainless steel.	1	Note (1)	
15	MTC7769	Steel Grey-LH-stainless steel.	1		
15	BTR7850PUC	Black-RH	1	Note (2)	
15	BTR7849PUC	Black-LH	1		
15	DHH100780PUC	Black Spata-RH	1	Note (3)	
15	DHH100790PUC	Black Spata-LH	1		
15	STC60729	Atlantic Green.-RH	1		Heritage
15	STC60730	Atlantic Green.-LH	1		
15	STC60731	Bronze Green-RH	1		
15	STC60732	Bronze Green-LH	1		
16	AB608044L	Screw-finisher to panel nose-self tapping-No 8 x 1/2	2		
17	79051	Nut-lokut	2		

CHANGE POINTS:
(1) To (V) December 1989 approx
(2) To (V) WA 159806
(3) From (V) XA 159807

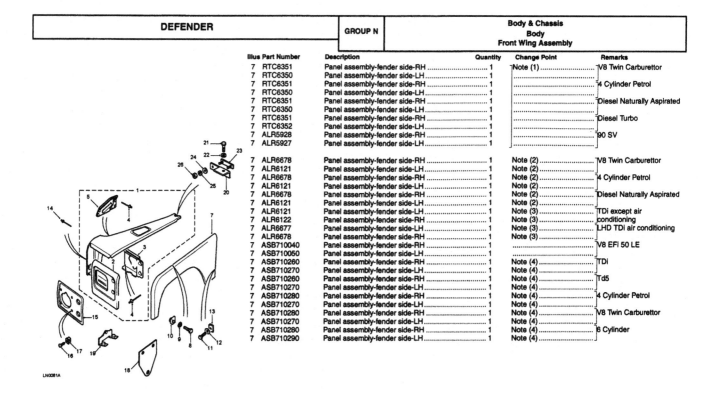

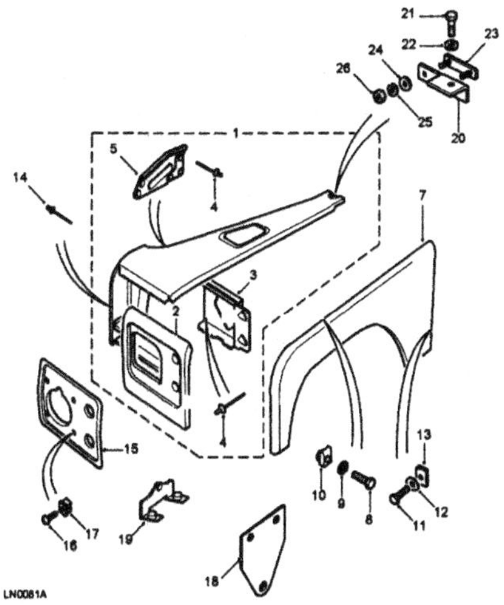

Illus	Part Number	Description	Quantity	Change Point	Remarks
18	MUC3590	Support wing	1		
19	MUC3601	Cleat	1		
20	MTC2136	Bracket-front fender-RH	1	To (V) EA 320821	
20	MRC8926	Bracket-front fender-LH	1		
21	SH106167L	Screw-hexagonal head-M6 x 16	2		
22	AAU9036	Washer-wing to bracket	2		
23	MTC2704	Plate assembly	2		
24	RTC609	Washer-plain-standard	4		
25	WM106001	Washer-spring	4		
26	NH106041L	Nut-hexagonal-nyloc-M6	4		
21	FS106201L	Screw-flanged head-M6 x 20	2	From (V) EA 320822	
25	WM106001L	Washer-spring-M6-square	2	To (V) LA 939975	
	NN106021	Nutsert-blind-M6	2		

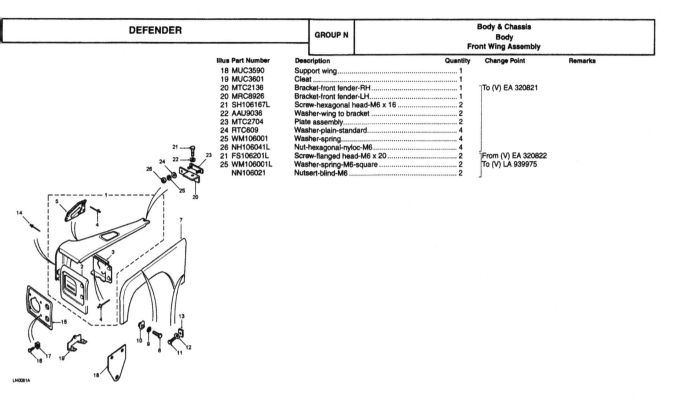

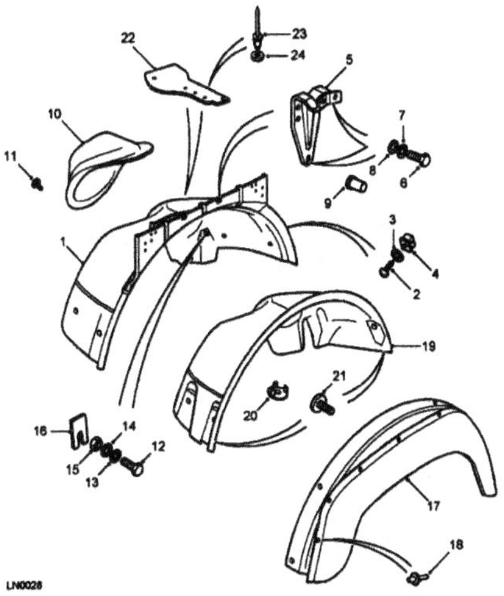

Illus	Part Number	Description	Quantity	Change Point	Remarks
		NON-AIR CON			
		WHEELARCH ASSEMBLY-FRONT			
1	ALR2261	RH	1	Note (1)	Except TDi
1	ASR2250	RH	1	Note (2)	
1	ASR2256	RH	1	Note (2)	TDi
1	ALR2414	RH	1	Note (3)	200 TDI
1	ALR4057	RH	1	Note (1)	300 TDI
1	AWJ710060	RH	1	Note (4)	
		WHEELARCH ASSEMBLY-FRONT			
1	ALR2262	LH	1	Note (3)	Except TDi
1	ALR3970	LH	1	Note (5)	
1	ALR2264	LH	1	Note (6)	
1	ASR2253	LH	1	Note (2)	
1	ALR2265	LH	1	Note (1)	TDi
1	ASR2257	LH	1	Note (2)	
1	AWJ710040	LH	1	Note (4)	

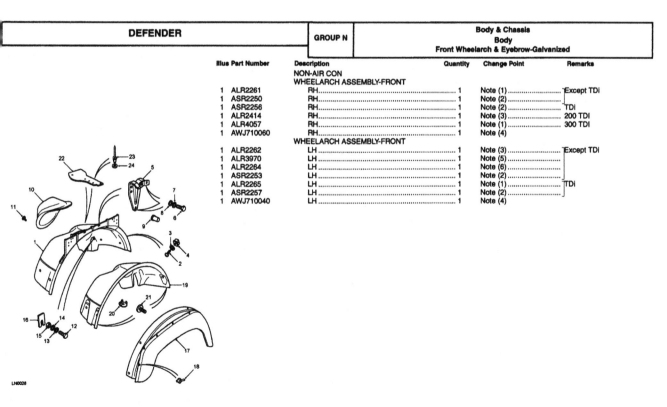

CHANGE POINTS:
(1) To (V) TA 997521
(2) From (V) TA 997522 To (V) WA 159806
(3) To (V) LA 939975
(4) From (V) XA 159807
(5) From (V) MA 939976 To (V) MA 954463
(6) From (V) MA 954464 To (V) TA 997521

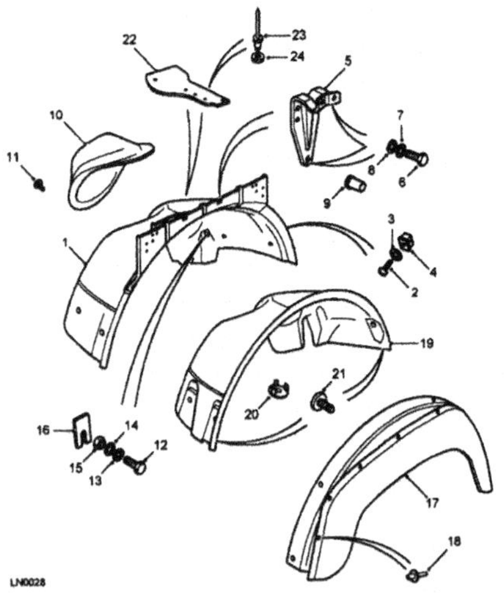
LN0028

Illus	Part Number	Description	Quantity	Change Point	Remarks
		AIR CON			
		WHEELARCH ASSEMBLY-FRONT			
1	MXC4630	RH	1	Note (1)	LHD except TDi
1	ALR2263	RH	1	Note (2)	
1	ASR2252	RH	1	Note (3)	
1	ALR2415	RH	1	Note (1)	LHD TDi
1	ASR2254	RH	1	Note (3)	
1	AWJ710060	RH	1	Note (4)	LHD
		WHEELARCH ASSEMBLY-FRONT			
1	ALR2261	RH	1	Note (1)	RHD except TDi
1	ALR4057	RH	1	Note (2)	RHD TDi
1	ASR2256	RH	1	Note (3)	
1	AWJ710060	RH	1	Note (4)	RHD
		WHEELARCH ASSEMBLY-FRONT			
1	ALR2262	LH	1	Note (1)	LHD except TDi
1	ALR3970	LH	1	Note (2)	
1	ASR2257	LH	1	Note (3)	
1	ALR2265	LH	1	Note (5)	LHD TDi
1	ASR2257	LH	1	Note (3)	
		WHEELARCH ASSEMBLY-FRONT			
1	MXC4631	LH	1	Note (6)	RHD
1	ALR2264	LH	1	Note (7)	
1	ASR2253	LH	1	Note (3)	
1	AWJ710050	LH	1	Note (4)	

CHANGE POINTS:
(1) To (V) LA 939975
(2) From (V) MA 939976 To (V) TA 997521
(3) From (V) TA 997522 To (V) WA 159806
(4) From (V) XA 159807
(5) To (V) TA 997521
(6) To (V) HA 906454
(7) From (V) HA 906455 To (V) TA 997521

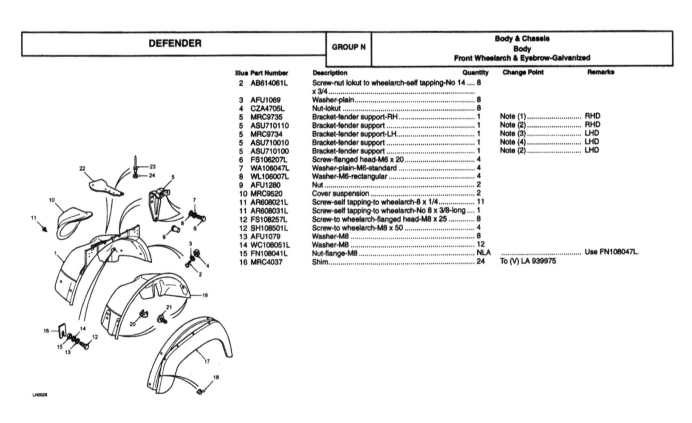

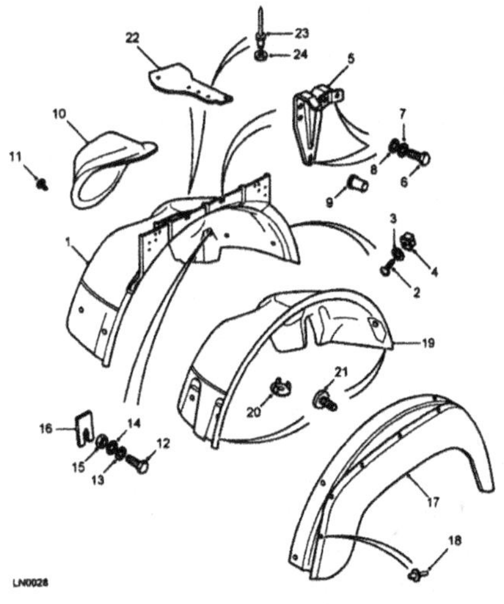
LN0028

Illus	Part Number	Description	Quantity	Change Point	Remarks
2	AB614061L	Screw-nut lokut to wheelarch-self tapping-No 14 x 3/4	8		
3	AFU1069	Washer-plain	8		
4	CZA4705L	Nut-lokut	8		
5	MRC9735	Bracket-fender support-RH	1	Note (1)	RHD
5	ASU710110	Bracket-fender support	1	Note (2)	RHD
5	MRC9734	Bracket-fender support-LH	1	Note (3)	LHD
5	ASU710010	Bracket-fender support	1	Note (4)	LHD
5	ASU710100	Bracket-fender support	1	Note (2)	LHD
6	FS106207L	Screw-flanged head-M6 x 20	4		
7	WA106047L	Washer-plain-M6-standard	4		
8	WL106007L	Washer-M6-rectangular	4		
9	AFU1280	Nut	2		
10	MRC9520	Cover suspension	2		
11	AR608021L	Screw-self tapping-to wheelarch-8 x 1/4	11		
11	AR608031L	Screw-self tapping-to wheelarch-No 8 x 3/8-long	1		
12	FS108257L	Screw-to wheelarch-flanged head-M8 x 25	8		
12	SH108501L	Screw-to wheelarch-M8 x 50	4		
13	AFU1079	Washer-M8	8		
14	WC108051L	Washer-M8	12		
15	FN108041L	Nut-flange-M8	NLA		Use FN108047L.
16	MRC4037	Shim	24	To (V) LA 939975	

CHANGE POINTS:
(1) To (V) XA 175541
(2) From (V) XA 175542
(3) To (V) WA 159806
(4) From (V) XA 159807 To (V) XA 175541

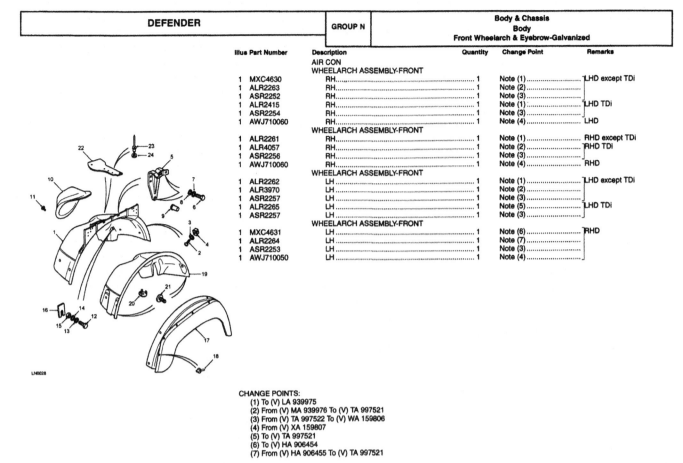

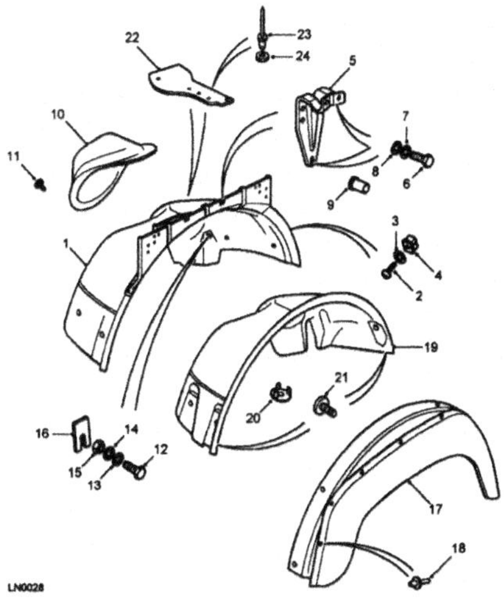

LN0028

Illus	Part Number	Description	Quantity	Change Point	Remarks
		EYEBROW-FRONT WHEELARCH			
17	MRC9378	RH-Black-plastic-Unpainted	1		
17	MRC9377	LH-Black-plastic-Unpainted	1		
17	RRC3043	RH-Matt Black.	1		
17	RRC3044	LH-Matt Black.	1		
17	MTC6874P	RH-Primer	1		
17	MTC6875P	LH-Primer	1		
17	MTC6874NUC	RH-Alpine White	NLA		Use MTC6874P.
17	MTC6875NUC	LH-Alpine White	NLA		Use MTC6875P.
17	MTC6874SUB	RH-Arran Beige	NLA		Use MTC6874P.
17	MTC6875SUB	LH-Arran Beige	NLA		Use MTC6875P.
17	MTC6874AA	RH-Arizona Tan	NLA		Use MTC6874P.
17	MTC6875AA	LH-Arizona Tan	NLA		Use MTC6875P.
17	MTC6874CUF	RH-Arrow Red	NLA		Use MTC6874P.
17	MTC6875CUF	LH-Arrow Red	NLA		Use MTC6875P.
17	STC60708	RH-Atlantic Green.	1		Heritage
17	STC60709	LH-Atlantic Green.	1		Heritage
17	MTC6874HC	RH-Bronze Green	NLA		Use MTC6874P.
17	MTC6875HC	LH-Bronze Green	NLA		Use MTC6875P.
17	STC60733	RH-Bronze Green	1	Note (1)	Heritage Td5
17	STC60711	LH-Bronze Green	1	Note (1)	Heritage
17	MTC6874HUJ	RH-Eastnor Green	NLA		Use MTC6874P.
17	MTC6875HUJ	LH-Eastnor Green	NLA		Use MTC6875P.
17	MTC6874HAF	RH-Epsom Green	NLA		Use MTC6874P.
17	MTC6875HAF	LH-Epsom Green	NLA		Use MTC6875P.
17	MTC6874NM	RH-Ivory	NLA		Use MTC6874P.
17	MTC6875NM	LH-Ivory	NLA		Use MTC6875P.
17	MTC6874HYE	RH-Coniston Green	NLA		Use MTC6874P.
17	MTC6875HYE	LH-Coniston Green	NLA		Use MTC6875P.
17	MTC6874PUE	RH-County Black	NLA		Use MTC6874P.
17	MTC6875PUE	LH-County Black	NLA		Use MTC6875P.
17	MTC6874HUL	RH-County Green	NLA		Use MTC6874P.
17	MTC6875HUL	LH-County Green	NLA		Use MTC6875P.
17	MTC6874CUH	RH-County Red	NLA		Use MTC6874P.
17	MTC6875CUH	LH-County Red	NLA		Use MTC6875P.

CHANGE POINTS:
(1) From (V) XA 159807

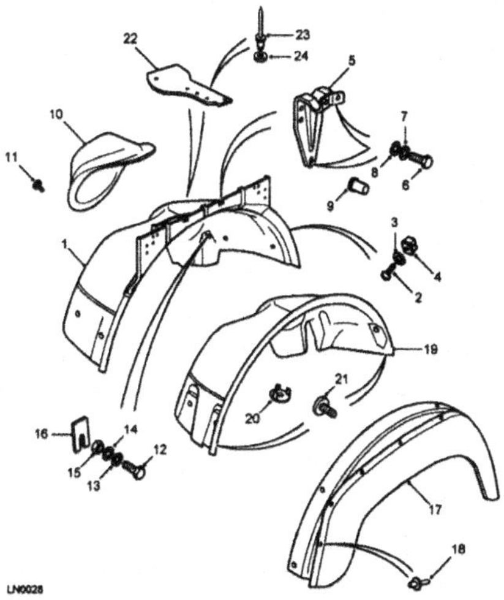

LN0028

Illus	Part Number	Description	Quantity	Change Point	Remarks
		EYEBROW-FRONT WHEELARCH			
17	MTC6875JP	LH-Stratos Blue	NLA		Use MTC6875P.
17	MTC6874HN	RH-Trident Green	NLA		Use MTC6874P.
17	MTC6875HN	LH-Trident Green	NLA		Use MTC6875P.
17	MTC6874CL	RH-Venetian Red	NLA		Use MTC6874P.
17	MTC6875CL	LH-Venetian Red	NLA		Use MTC6875P.
17	MTC6874JC	RH-Marine Blue	NLA		Use MTC6874P.
17	MTC6875JC	LH-Marine Blue	NLA		Use MTC6875P.
17	MTC6874CC	RH-Masai red	NLA		Use MTC6874P.
17	MTC6875CC	LH-Masai red	NLA		Use MTC6875P.
17	MTC6874CUY	RH-Montpellier Red	NLA		Use MTC6874P.
17	MTC6875CUY	LH-Montpellier Red	NLA		Use MTC6875P.
17	MTC6874LVD	RH-Niagara Grey	NLA		Use MTC6874P.
17	MTC6875LVD	LH-Niagara Grey	NLA		Use MTC6875P.
17	MTC6874JUH	RH-Pacific Blue	NLA		Use MTC6874P.
17	MTC6875JUH	LH-Pacific Blue	NLA		Use MTC6875P.
17	MTC6874LUS	RH-Pembroke Grey	NLA		Use MTC6874P.
17	MTC6875LUS	LH-Pembroke Grey	NLA		Use MTC6875P.
17	MTC6874AV	RH-Roan Brown	NLA		Use MTC6874P.
17	MTC6875AV	LH-Roan Brown	NLA		Use MTC6875P.
17	MTC6874JUG	RH-Shire Blue	NLA		Use MTC6874P.
17	MTC6875JUG	LH-Shire Blue	NLA		Use MTC6875P.
17	MTC6874LN	RH-Slate Grey	NLA		Use MTC6874P.
17	MTC6875LN	LH-Slate Grey	NLA		Use MTC6875P.
17	MTC6874JP	RH-Stratos Blue	NLA		Use MTC6874P.
18	AFU1075	Rivet-plastic-drive	16		
19	AWR5476	Liner-front wheelarch-RH	1		
19	AWR5475	Liner-front wheelarch-LH	1		
19	CLF000280	Liner-front wheelarch-RH	1		
19	CLF000290	Liner-front wheelarch-LH	1		
20	BRC5803	Washer	3		
21	MWC9832PMA	Fastener-fir tree-Black	3		
22	MUC9704	Cover-front wheelarch liner	2	To (V) LA 939975	Diesel Turbo
23	78248	Rivet-pop-3/16" x 0.45"lng	6		
24	WA105001L	Washer-plain-standard-M5	6		

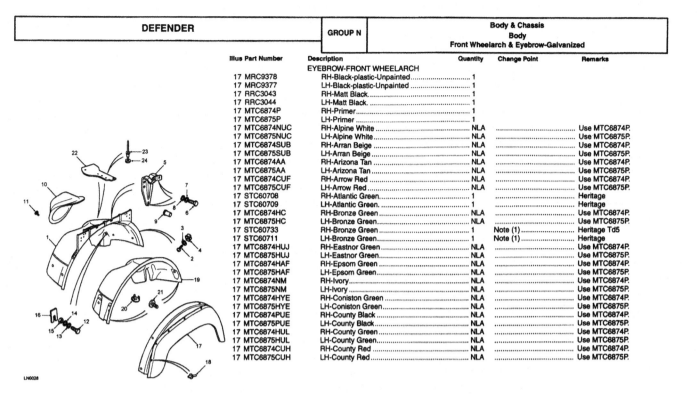

Illus	Part Number	Description	Quantity	Change Point	Remarks
1	KCU100020L	Bracket-warning flare	1		
2	BTR9126	Rivet	1		

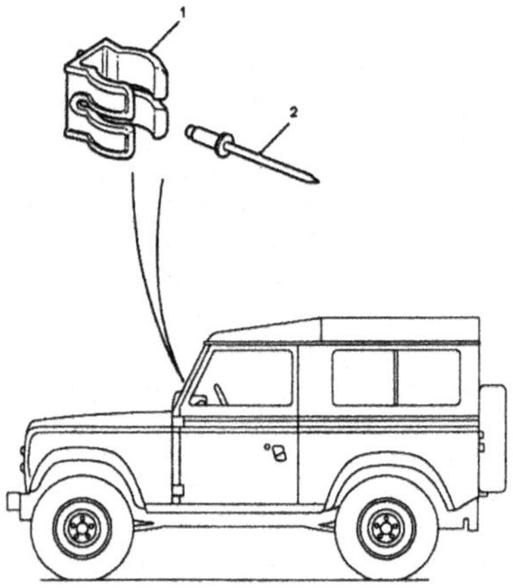

AHNXTA3A

Illus	Part Number	Description	Quantity	Change Point	Remarks
1	RTC6222	Panel outer-rear	1		
		GLASS-REAR QUARTER			
2	MTC3461	5 mm glass-RH	1	Note (1)	
2	MTC3462	5 mm glass-LH	1	Note (1)	
2	MWC4710	4 mm glass-RH	1	Note (2)	
2	MWC4711	4 mm glass-LH	1	Note (2)	
		WEATHERSTRIP-REAR QUARTER			
3	330790	5 mm glass	2	Note (1)	
3	MWC4773	4 mm glass	1	Note (3)	
3	ALR3966	4 mm glass	1	Note (4)	
4	330791	Filler strip	2		
5	MTC5197	GLASS ASSEMBLY-OPENING BACKLIGHT-5MM GLASS	1	Note (5)	
6	MTC6544	• Glass-backlight sliding-5mm glass	1		
7	AEU2805	• Catch assembly-side opening window-5mm glass-LH	1		
7	AEU2806	• Catch assembly-side opening window-5mm glass-RH	1		
5	MWC4762	GLASS ASSEMBLY-OPENING BACKLIGHT-4MM GLASS	1	Note (5)	
6	MWC4726	• Glass-backlight sliding-4mm glass	2		
7	MWC7625	• Catch assembly-side opening window-4mm glass-LH	1		
7	MWC7648	• Catch assembly-side opening window-4mm glass-RH	1		
14	MWC7620	• Felt-nvh	2		
15	MWC7652	• Seal	1		
5	ALR5080	GLASS ASSEMBLY-OPENING BACKLIGHT-4MM GLASS-RH	1	From (V) KA 930144	
6	MWC4726	• Glass-backlight sliding	2		
7	MWC7625	• Catch assembly-side opening window-LH	1		
7	MWC7648	• Catch assembly-side opening window-RH	1		
14	MWC7620	• Felt-nvh	2		
15	MWC7652	• Seal	1		

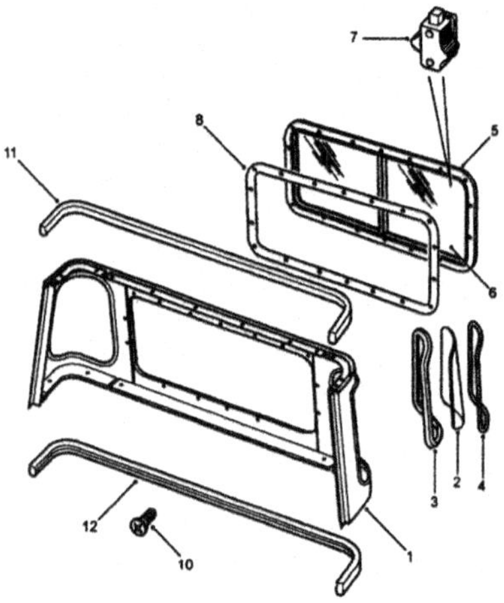

AHNXJC1A

CHANGE POINTS:
(1) To (V) EA 340456
(2) From (V) EA 340457
(3) From (V) EA 340457 To (V) KA 926006
(4) From (V) KA 926007
(5) To (V) KA 930143

Illus	Part Number	Description	Quantity	Change Point	Remarks
8	MTC6233	Seal glazing	1	Note (1)	
8	MWC7641	Seal glazing	1	Note (2)	
9	MTC6232	Finisher-outer	1	Note (3)	
10	AS604044	Rivet	18		
10	RU610253	Rivet	18	Note (4)	
11	334614	Seal-rubber-cantrail-upper	1		
12	333486	Seal-cantrail-waist	1	Note (5)	
12	ALR1161	Seal-cantrail-waist	1	Note (6)	
12	ALR5057	Seal-cantrail-waist	1	Note (7)	
12	AML110060	Seal-waist	1	Note (8)	
13	MTC7513	Edging strip	A/R		

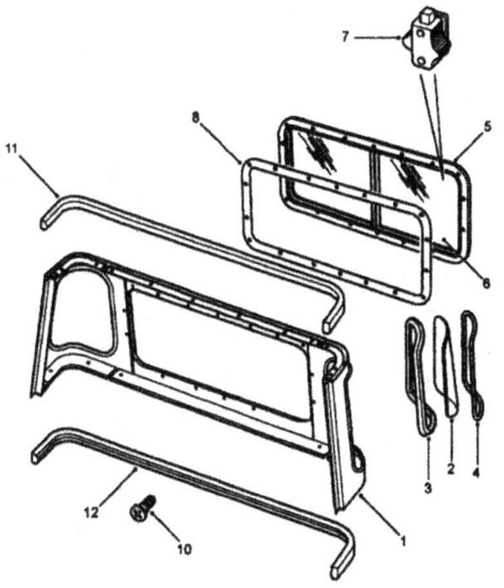

CHANGE POINTS:
(1) To (V) AA 308446
(2) From (V) AA 308447
(3) To (V) KA 930143
(4) From (V) KA 930144
(5) To (V) HA 479307
(6) From (V) HA 479308 To (V) KA 925389
(7) From (V) KA 925390 To (V) ZA 615249
(8) From (V) 1A 615250

Illus	Part Number	Description	Quantity	Change Point	Remarks
1	336577	Bracket mounting	4	To (V) LA 939975	
2	FS106255L	Screw-bracket to body-flanged head-M6 x 25	8		
3	WL106001L	Washer-sprung-M6	8		
4	NH106041L	Nut-hexagonal-nyloc-M6	8		
5	SH607091L	Screw-bracket to cab-hexagonal head	4		
6	WM600071L	Washer-sprung-7/16"	4		
7	4580	Washer-plain-normal o.d.	4		
8	330762	Stud-mounting for cab-5/16UNF	2		
9	WP185L	Washer-normal o.d.-plain-standard	4		
10	3829	Washer-plain-5/16"	6		
11	WM600051L	Washer-spring-5/16"	4		
12	NH605041L	Nut-hexagonal head-5/16UNF	4		
6	WL108001L	Washer-sprung-M8	4		Alternatives
7	WC112081L	Washer-plain-large o.d.-M12 x 28	6		
8	MUC8928	Stud-M8	2		
9	WP185L	Washer-plain-standard	4		
12	FN108041L	Nut-flange-M8	NLA		Use FN108047L.
					Alternatives

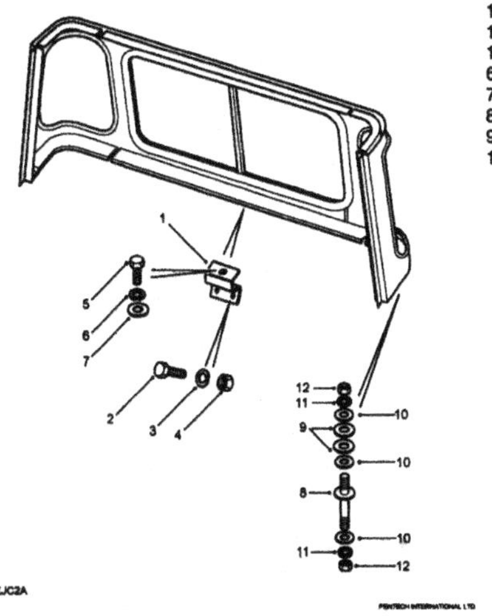

DEFENDER	GROUP N	Body & Chassis Body Rear Body Lower-90-With Bulkhead (Standard/County & X-Tech Hard Top)

Illus	Part Number	Description	Quantity	Change Point	Remarks
1	RTC6280	BODY ASSEMBLY-LOWER REAR-LESS ROPE CLEATS	1	Note (1)	Standard / County
2	MWC6144	• Panel assembly-bodyside trim-front	1		
3	RTC6281	• BODY SIDE ASSEMBLY-REAR-RH	1		
4	RTC6283	• • Panel assembly-bodyside trim-RH	1		
5	MTC7980	• • Panel-rear end-RH	1		
6	RTC6282	• BODY SIDE ASSEMBLY-REAR-LH	1		
7	RTC6284	• • Panel assembly-bodyside trim-LH	1		
8	MTC7981	• • Panel-rear end-LH	1		
9	MTC8184	• Plate assembly-rear-floor	1		
10	330271	• Angle mounting-rear	1		
11	78248	• Rivet-pop-3/16" x 0.45"lng	32		
11	RU612373L	• Rivet-3/16" x 0.575"lng	24		

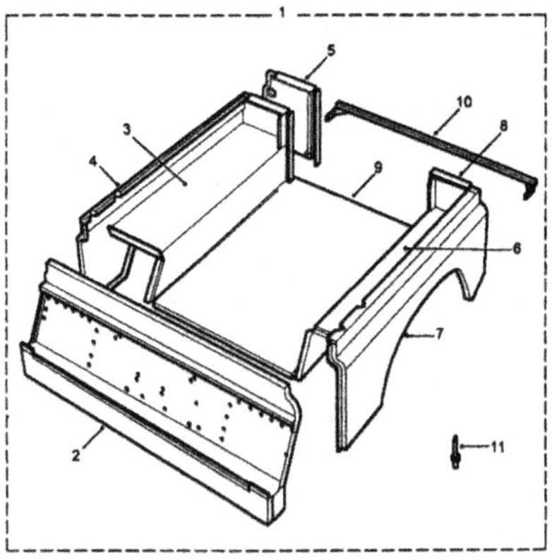

LN0142A

CHANGE POINTS:
(1) To (V) LA 939975

DEFENDER	GROUP N	Body & Chassis Body Rear Body Lower-90-With Bulkhead (Standard/County & X-Tech Hard Top)

Illus	Part Number	Description	Quantity	Change Point	Remarks
1	ALR5985	BODY ASSEMBLY-LOWER REAR-LESS ROPE CLEATS	1	Note (1)	
2	MWC6144	• Panel assembly-bodyside trim-front	1		
3	RTC6281	• BODY SIDE ASSEMBLY-REAR-RH	1		
4	RTC6283	• • Panel assembly-bodyside trim-RH	1		
5	STC1854	• • Panel-rear end-RH	1		
6	RTC6282	• BODY SIDE ASSEMBLY-REAR-LH	1		
7	RTC6284	• • Panel assembly-bodyside trim-LH	1		
8	STC1855	• • Panel-rear end-LH	1		
9	MTC8184	• Plate assembly-rear-floor	1		
10	330271	• Angle mounting-rear	1		
11	78248	• Rivet-pop-3/16" x 0.45"lng	32		
11	RU612373L	• Rivet-3/16" x 0.575"lng	24		

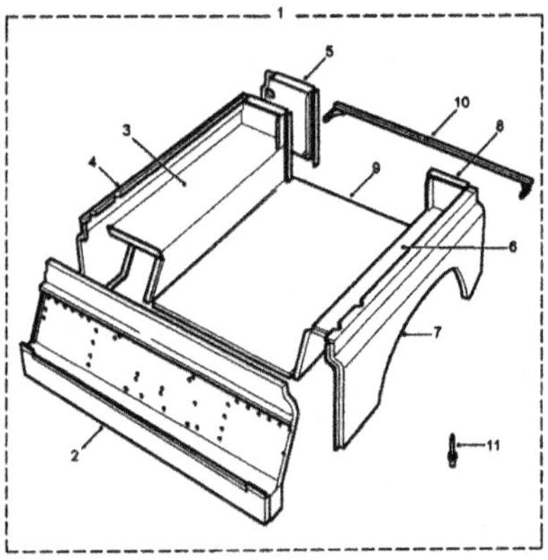

LN0142A

CHANGE POINTS:
(1) From (V) MA 939976 To (V) WA 159806

Illus	Part Number	Description	Quantity	Change Point	Remarks
1	AQA710040	BODY ASSEMBLY-LOWER REAR-LESS ROPE CLEATS	1	Note (1)	
2	MWC6144	• Panel assembly-bodyside trim-front	1		
3	ALA710080	• BODY SIDE ASSEMBLY-REAR-RH	1		
4	ALJ710050	• • Panel assembly-bodyside trim-lower-RH	1		
5	AQH100060	• • Panel-rear end-RH	1		
6	ALA710090	• BODY SIDE ASSEMBLY-REAR-LH	1		
7	RTC6284	• • Panel assembly-bodyside trim-LH	1		
8	AQH100070	• • Panel-rear end-LH	1		
9	MTC8184	• Plate assembly-rear-floor	1		
10	330271	• Angle mounting-rear	1		
11	78248	• Rivet-pop-3/16" x 0.45"lng	32		
11	RU612373L	• Rivet-3/16" x 0.575"lng	24		

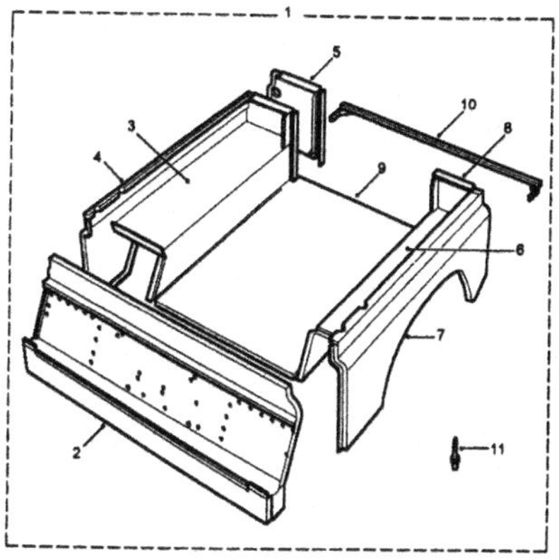

LN0142A

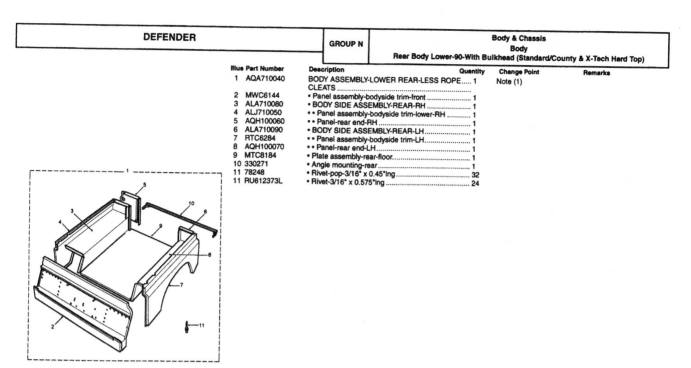

CHANGE POINTS:
(1) From (V) XA 159807 To (V) ZA 612404

Illus	Part Number	Description	Quantity	Change Point	Remarks
1	AQA710380	BODY ASSEMBLY-LOWER REAR-LESS ROPE CLEATS	1	Note (1)	
2	MWC6144	• Panel assembly-bodyside trim-front	1		
3	ALA710540	• BODY SIDE ASSEMBLY-REAR-RH	1		
4	ALA710510	• • Panel assembly-bodyside trim-lower-RH	1		
5	AQH000020	• • Panel-rear end-RH	1		
6	ALA710550	• BODY SIDE ASSEMBLY-REAR-LH	1		
7	RTC6284	• • Panel assembly-bodyside trim-LH	1		
8	AQH000030	• • Panel-rear end-LH	1		
9	MTC8184	• Plate assembly-rear-floor	1		
10	330271	• Angle mounting-rear	1		
11	78248	• Rivet-pop-3/16" x 0.45"lng	32		
11	RU612373L	• Rivet-3/16" x 0.575"lng	24		

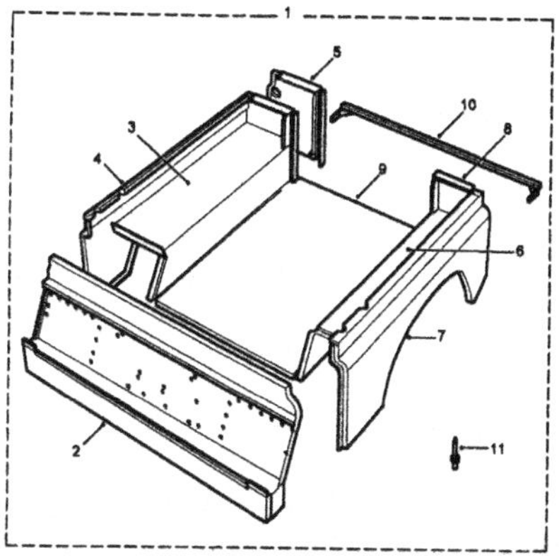

LN0142A

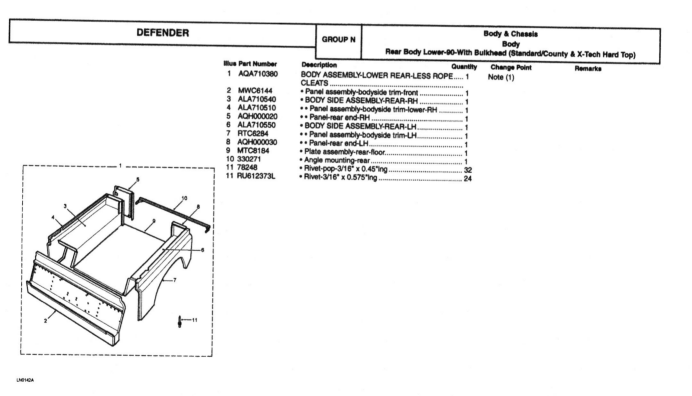

CHANGE POINTS:
(1) From (V) 1A 612404

Illus	Part Number	Description	Quantity	Change Point	Remarks
		90 SV			
1	ALR5921	BODY ASSEMBLY-LOWER REAR	1	Note (1)	90 SV
2	ALR5937	• Panel assembly-bodyside trim-front	1		
3	ALR5922	• BODY SIDE ASSEMBLY-REAR-RH	1		
4	STC1617	• • Panel assembly-bodyside trim-RH	1		
5	STC922	• • Panel-rear end-RH	1		
6	ALR5923	• BODY SIDE ASSEMBLY-REAR-LH	1		
7	STC1616	• • Panel assembly-bodyside trim-LH	1		
8	STC923	• • Panel-rear end-LH	1		
9	MTC8184	• Plate assembly-rear-floor	1		
10	ALR5685	• Bracket-mounting-rear	1		
11	78248	• Rivet-pop-3/16" x 0.45"lng	32		
11	RU612373L	• Rivet-3/16" x 0.575"lng	24		

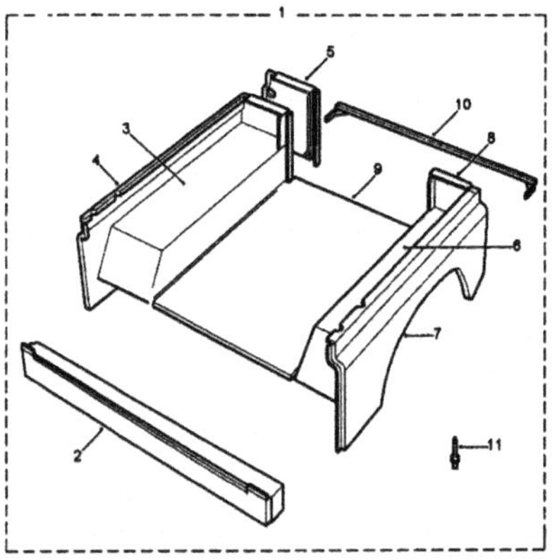

LN0209

CHANGE POINTS:
(1) To (V) LA 939975

Illus	Part Number	Description	Quantity	Change Point	Remarks
		50LE - V8 & M52 - 6 CYLINDER PETROL			
1	ASR2348	BODY ASSEMBLY-LOWER REAR	1	Note (1)	50 LE
2	ALR5937	• Panel assembly-bodyside trim-front	1		
3	ALA710180	• BODY SIDE ASSEMBLY-REAR-RH	1		
4	ALA710510	• • Panel assembly-bodyside trim-lower-RH	1		
5	STC1854	• • Panel-rear end-RH	1		
6	ALA710190	• BODY SIDE ASSEMBLY-REAR-LH	1		
7	RTC6284	• • Panel assembly-bodyside trim-LH	1		
8	STC1855	• • Panel-rear end-LH	1		
9	MTC8184	• Plate assembly-rear-floor	1		
10	330271	• Angle mounting-rear	1		
11	78248	• Rivet-pop-3/16" x 0.45"lng	32		
11	RU612373L	• Rivet-3/16" x 0.575"lng	24		

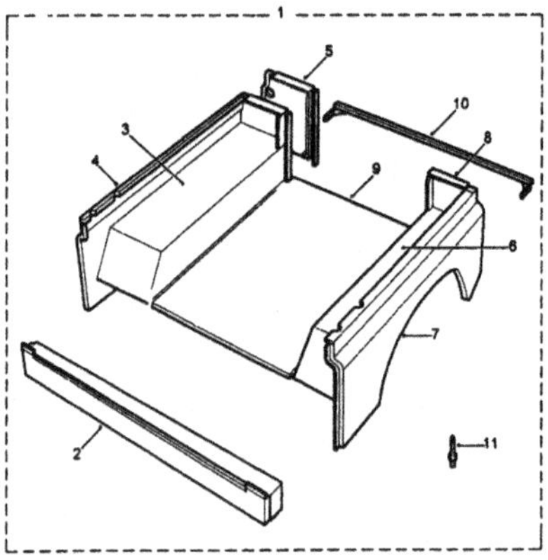

LN0209

CHANGE POINTS:
(1) From (V) MA 939976 To (V) WA 159806

Rear Body Lower-90-Without Bulkhead (90 SV & 50LE V8)

Illus	Part Number	Description	Quantity	Change Point	Remarks
		M52 - 6 CYLINDER PETROL			
1	AQA710110	BODY ASSEMBLY-LOWER REAR-LESS ROPE CLEATS	1	Note (1)	BMW M52
2	ALR5937	• Panel assembly-bodyside trim-front	1		
3	ALA710180	• BODY SIDE ASSEMBLY-REAR-RH	1		
4	ALA710510	• • Panel assembly-bodyside trim-lower-RH	1		
5	STC1854	• • Panel-rear end-RH	1		
6	ALA710190	• BODY SIDE ASSEMBLY-REAR-LH	1		
7	RTC6284	• • Panel assembly-bodyside trim-LH	1		
8	STC1855	• • Panel-rear end-LH	1		
9	MTC8184	• Plate assembly-rear-floor	1		
10	330271	• Angle mounting-rear	1		
11	78248	• Rivet-pop-3/16" x 0.45"lng	32		
11	RU612373L	• Rivet-3/16" x 0.575"lng	24		

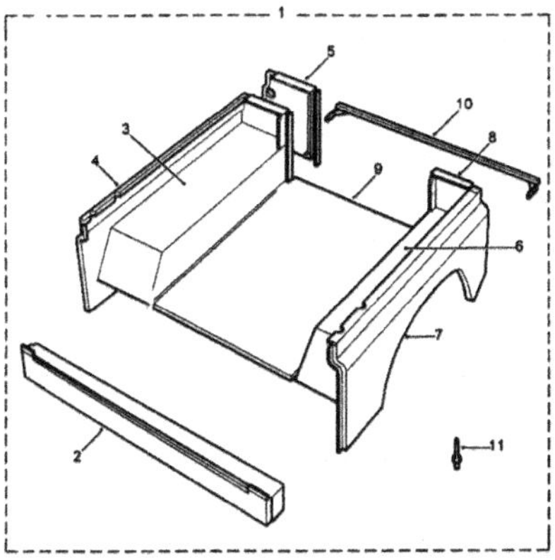

LN0209

CHANGE POINTS:
(1) From (V) XA 159807 To (V) ZA 612404

Rear Body Lower-110 Station Wagon

Illus	Part Number	Description	Quantity	Change Point	Remarks
1	MWC6143	BODY ASSEMBLY-LOWER REAR	1	Note (1)	
2	MTC7886	• BODY SIDE/WHEELARCH ASSEMBLY	1		
3	RTC6291	• • Panel-bodyside-RH	1		
4	MTC7980	• • Panel-rear end-RH	1		
5	MTC7887	• BODY SIDE/WHEELARCH ASSEMBLY	1		
6	MRC5071	• • Panel-bodyside-LH	1		
7	MTC7981	• • Panel-rear end-LH	1		
8	MWC6145	• Floor assembly	1		
9	MTC1039	• Angle mounting-rear	1		
10	78248	• Rivet-pop-3/16" x 0.45"lng	32		
10	RU612373L	• Rivet-3/16" x 0.575"lng	24		

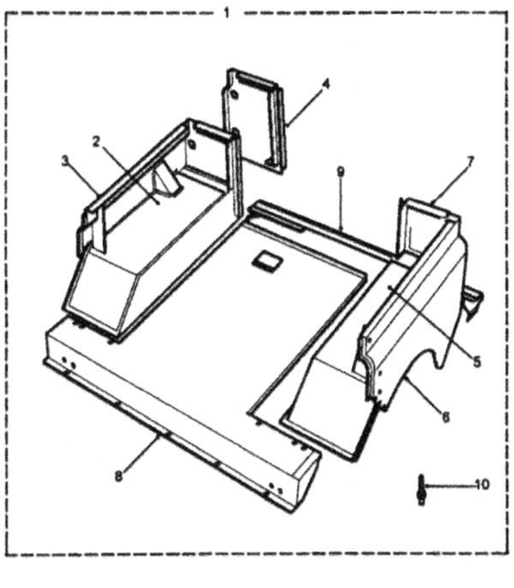

LN0143A

CHANGE POINTS:
(1) To (V) LA 939975

Illus	Part Number	Description	Quantity	Change Point	Remarks
1	ALR5987	BODY ASSEMBLY-LOWER REAR	1	Note (1)	
2	ALR5502	• BODY SIDE/WHEELARCH ASSEMBLY-RH	1		
3	RTC6291	• • Panel-bodyside-RH	1		
4	STC1854	• • Panel-rear end-RH	1		
5	ALR5503	• BODY SIDE/WHEELARCH ASSEMBLY-LH	1		
6	MRC5071	• • Panel-bodyside-LH	1		
7	STC1855	• • Panel-rear end-LH	1		
8	MWC6145	• Floor assembly	1		
9	330271	• Angle mounting-rear	1		
10	78248	• Rivet-pop-3/16" x 0.45"lng	32		
10	RU612373L	• Rivet-3/16" x 0.575"lng	24		

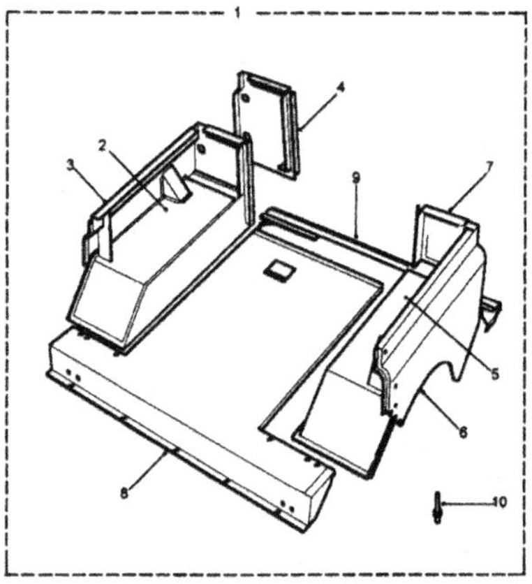

LN0143A

CHANGE POINTS:
(1) From (V) MA 939976 To (V) WA 159806

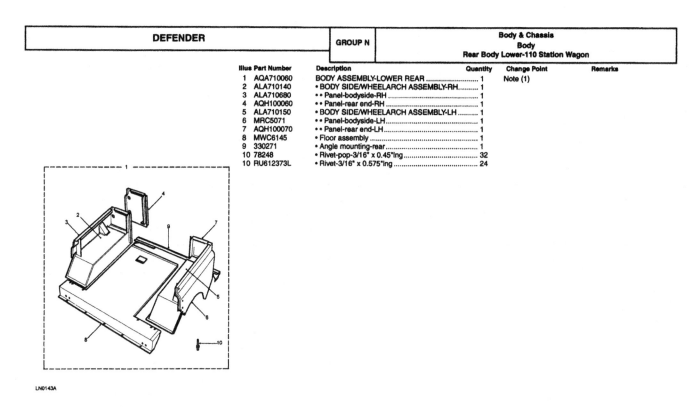

Illus	Part Number	Description	Quantity	Change Point	Remarks
1	AQA710060	BODY ASSEMBLY-LOWER REAR	1	Note (1)	
2	ALA710140	• BODY SIDE/WHEELARCH ASSEMBLY-RH	1		
3	ALA710680	• • Panel-bodyside-RH	1		
4	AQH100060	• • Panel-rear end-RH	1		
5	ALA710150	• BODY SIDE/WHEELARCH ASSEMBLY-LH	1		
6	MRC5071	• • Panel-bodyside-LH	1		
7	AQH100070	• • Panel-rear end-LH	1		
8	MWC6145	• Floor assembly	1		
9	330271	• Angle mounting-rear	1		
10	78248	• Rivet-pop-3/16" x 0.45"lng	32		
10	RU612373L	• Rivet-3/16" x 0.575"lng	24		

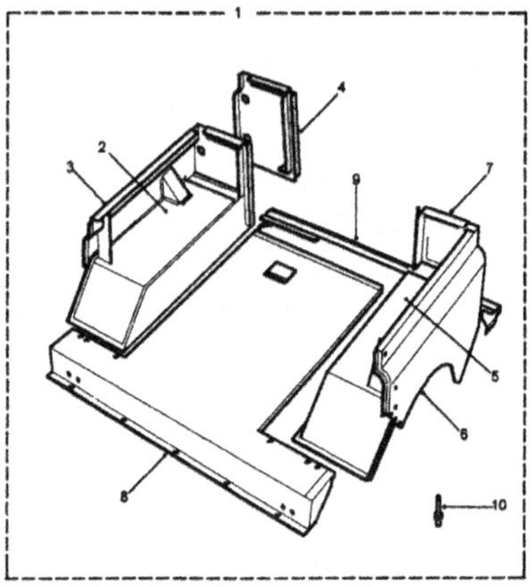

LN0143A

CHANGE POINTS:
(1) From (V) XA 159807 To (V) ZA 612404

Rear Body Lower-110 Station Wagon

Illus	Part Number	Description	Quantity	Change Point	Remarks
1	AQA710390	BODY ASSEMBLY-LOWER REAR	1	Note (1)	
2	ALA710560	• BODY SIDE/WHEELARCH ASSEMBLY-RH	1		
3	ALA710680	• • Panel-bodyside-RH	1		
4	AQH000020	• • Panel-rear end-RH	1		
5	ALA710570	• BODY SIDE/WHEELARCH ASSEMBLY-LH	1		
6	MRC5071	• • Panel-bodyside-LH	1		
7	AQH000030	• • Panel-rear end-LH	1		
8	MWC6145	• Floor assembly	1		
9	330271	• Angle mounting-rear	1		
10	78248	• Rivet-pop-3/16" x 0.45"lng	32		
10	RU612373L	• Rivet-3/16" x 0.575"lng	24		

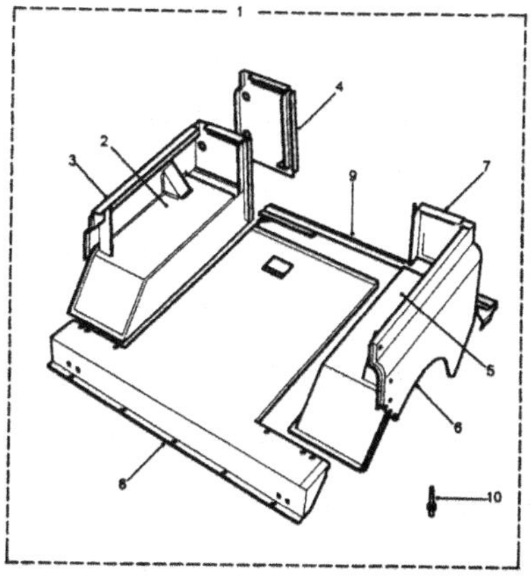

LN0143A

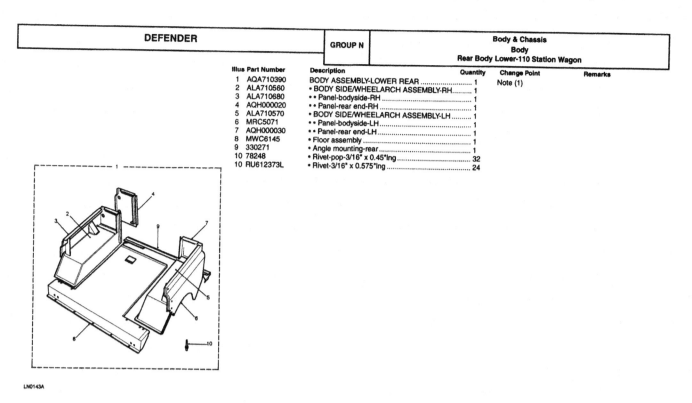

CHANGE POINTS:
(1) From (V) 1A 612404

Rear Body Lower-110 Regular

Illus	Part Number	Description	Quantity	Change Point	Remarks
		REAR FUEL FILLER - WITH ROPE CLEATS			
1	MUC3958	BODY ASSEMBLY-LOWER REAR-REAR FUEL FILLER APERTURE-WITH ROPE CLEATS	1	Note (1)	
2	RTC6246	• Panel assembly-bodyside trim-front-rear fuel filler aperture	1		
3	MUC3964	• BODY SIDE ASSEMBLY-REAR-RH-REAR FUEL FILLER APERTURE-WITH ROPE CLEATS	1		
4	MUC3302	• • Body side-RH-rear fuel filler aperture-with rope cleats	1		
5	MTC7980	• • Panel-rear end-RH	1		
6	MUC3963	• BODY SIDE ASSEMBLY-REAR-LH-WITH ROPE CLEATS	1		
7	MUC3303	• • Body side-LH-with rope cleats	1		
8	MTC7981	• • Panel-rear end-LH	1		
9	MUC3962	• Plate-rear floor	1		
10	330271	• Angle mounting-rear	1		
11	78248	• Rivet-pop-3/16" x 0.45"lng	36		
11	RU612373L	• Rivet-3/16" x 0.575"lng	28		

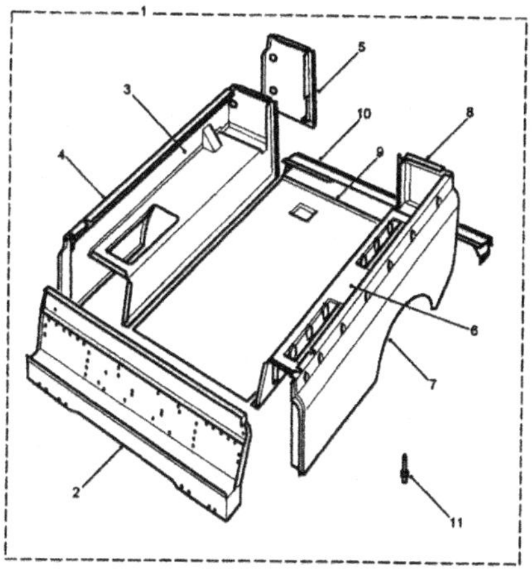

LN0144A

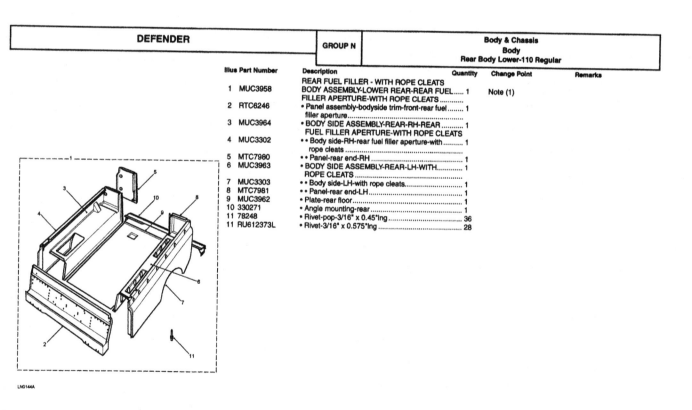

CHANGE POINTS:
(1) To (V) LA 939975

Illus	Part Number	Description	Quantity	Change Point	Remarks
		REAR FUEL FILLER - WITHOUT ROPE CLEATS			
1	RTC5705	BODY ASSEMBLY-LOWER REAR-REAR FUEL FILLER APERTURE-LESS ROPE CLEATS	1	Note (1)	
2	RTC6246	• Panel assembly-bodyside trim-front-rear fuel filler aperture	1		
3	RTC5707	• BODY SIDE ASSEMBLY-REAR-RH-LESS ROPE CLEATS	1		
4	RTC5710	• • Body side-RH-rear fuel filler aperture-less rope cleats	1		
5	MTC7980	• • Panel-rear end-RH	1		
6	RTC5709	• BODY SIDE ASSEMBLY-REAR-LH-LESS ROPE CLEATS	1		
7	RTC5712	• • Body side-LH-less rope cleats	1		
8	MTC7981	• • Panel-rear end-LH	1		
9	MUC3962	• Plate-rear floor	1		
10	330271	• Angle mounting-rear	1		
11	78248	• Rivet-pop-3/16" x 0.45"lng	36		
11	RU612373L	• Rivet-3/16" x 0.575"lng	28		

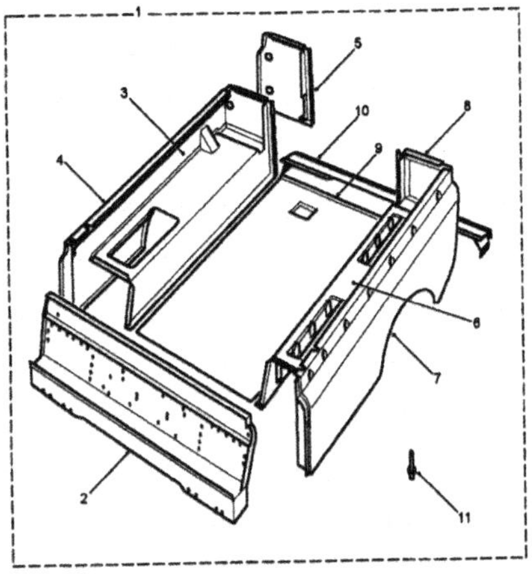

LN0144A

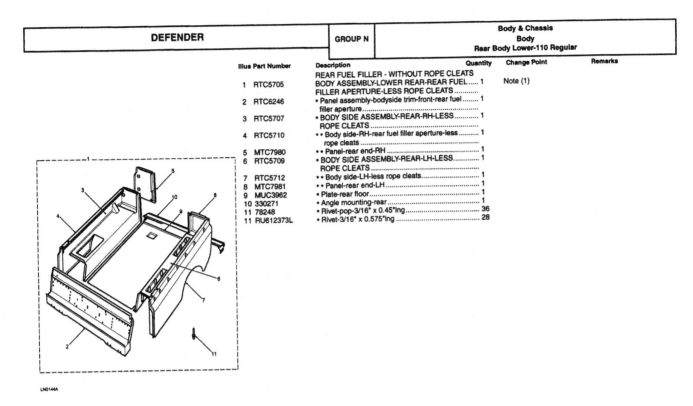

CHANGE POINTS:
(1) To (V) LA 939975

Illus	Part Number	Description	Quantity	Change Point	Remarks
		REAR FUEL FILLER - WITHOUT ROPE CLEATS			
1	ALR7105	BODY ASSEMBLY-LOWER REAR-REAR FUEL FILLER APERTURE-LESS ROPE CLEATS	1	Note (1)	Regular 110"
2	RTC6246	• Panel assembly-bodyside trim-front-rear fuel filler aperture	1		
3	ALR7106	• BODY SIDE ASSEMBLY-REAR-RH-REAR FUEL FILLER APERTURE-LESS ROPE CLEATS	1		
4	RTC5710	• • Body side-RH-rear fuel filler aperture-less rope cleats	1		
5	STC1854	• • Panel-rear end-RH	1		
6	ALR7107	• BODY SIDE ASSEMBLY-REAR-LH-LESS ROPE CLEATS	1		
7	RTC5712	• • Body side-LH-less rope cleats	1		
8	STC1855	• • Panel-rear end-LH	1		
9	MWC7698	• Plate-rear floor	1		
10	330271	• Angle mounting-rear	1		
11	78248	• Rivet-pop-3/16" x 0.45"lng	36		
11	RU612373L	• Rivet-3/16" x 0.575"lng	28		

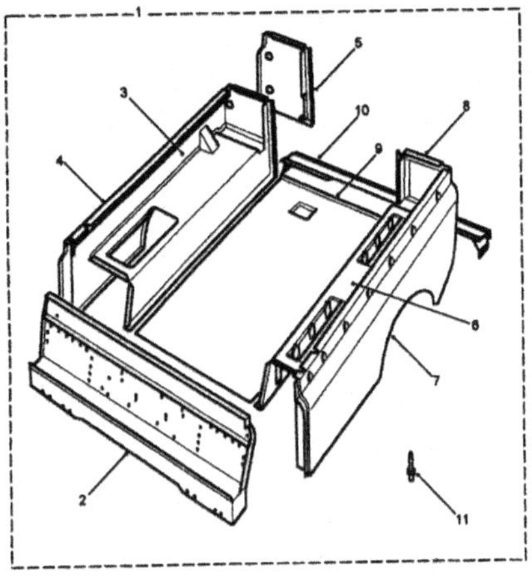

LN0144A

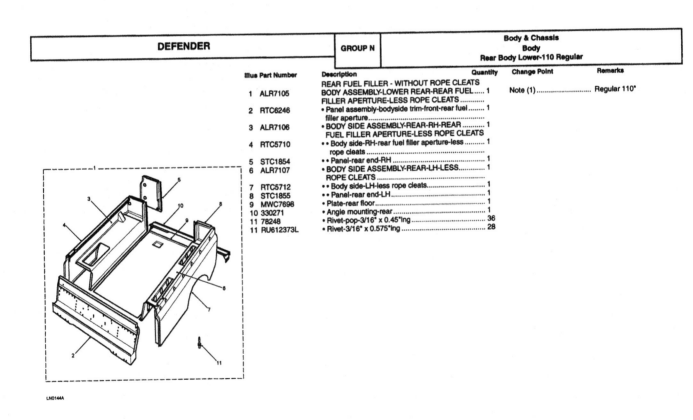

CHANGE POINTS:
(1) From (V) MA 939976 To (V) WA 159806

Illus	Part Number	Description	Quantity	Change Point	Remarks
		REAR FUEL FILLER - WITHOUT ROPE CLEATS			
1	AQA710080	BODY ASSEMBLY-LOWER REAR	1	Note (1)	
2	RTC6246	• Panel assembly-bodyside trim-front-rear fuel filler aperture	1		
3	ALA710160	• BODY SIDE ASSEMBLY-REAR-RH	1		
4	ALA710690	• • Body side-RH-rear fuel filler aperture-less rope cleats	1		
5	AQH100060	• • Panel-rear end-RH	1		
6	ALA710170	• BODY SIDE ASSEMBLY-REAR-LH	1		
7	RTC5712	• • Body side-LH-less rope cleats	1		
8	AQH100070	• • Panel-rear end-LH	1		
9	MWC7698	• Plate-rear floor	1		
10	330271	• Angle mounting-rear	1		
11	78248	• Rivet-pop-3/16" x 0.45"lng	36		
11	RU612373L	• Rivet-3/16" x 0.575"lng	28		

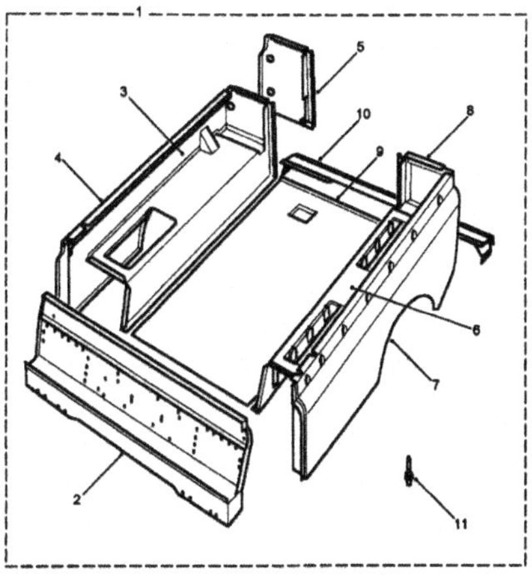

LN0144A

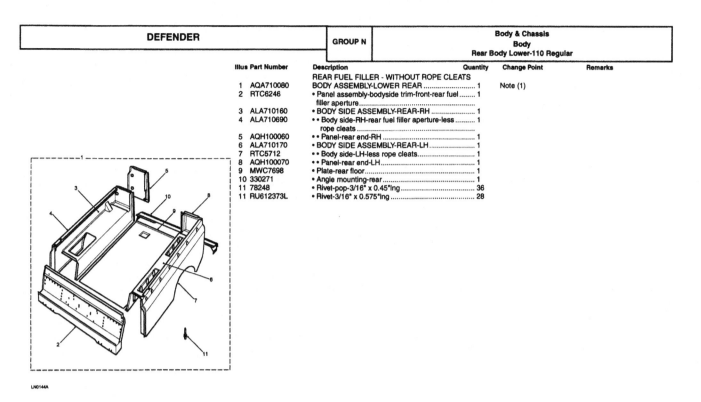

CHANGE POINTS:
(1) From (V) XA 159807 To (V) ZA 612404

Illus	Part Number	Description	Quantity	Change Point	Remarks
		REAR FUEL FILLER - WITHOUT ROPE CLEATS			
1	AQA710400	BODY ASSEMBLY-LOWER REAR	1	Note (1)	
2	RTC6246	• Panel assembly-bodyside trim-front-rear fuel filler aperture	1		
3	ALA710580	• BODY SIDE ASSEMBLY-REAR-RH	1		
4	ALA710690	• • Body side-RH-rear fuel filler aperture-less rope cleats	1		
5	AQH000020	• • Panel-rear end-RH	1		
6	ALA710590	• BODY SIDE ASSEMBLY-REAR-LH	1		
7	RTC5712	• • Body side-LH-less rope cleats	1		
8	AQH000030	• • Panel-rear end-LH	1		
9	MWC7698	• Plate-rear floor	1		
10	330271	• Angle mounting-rear	1		
11	78248	• Rivet-pop-3/16" x 0.45"lng	36		
11	RU612373L	• Rivet-3/16" x 0.575"lng	28		

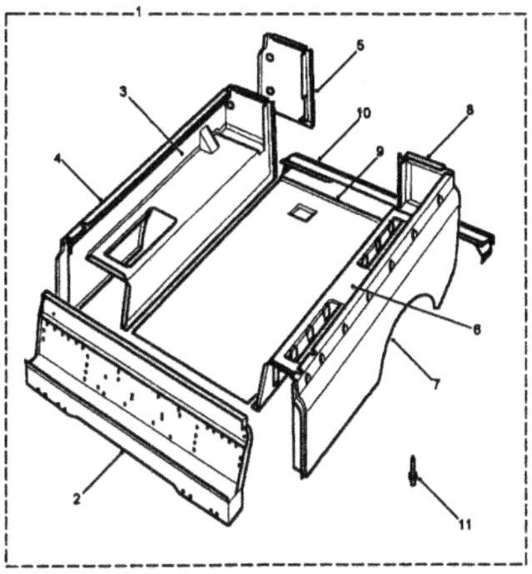

LN0144A

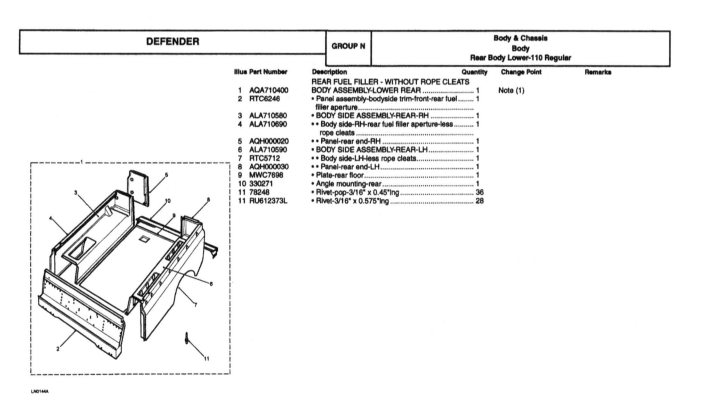

CHANGE POINTS:
(1) From (V) 1A 612404

Illus	Part Number	Description	Quantity	Change Point	Remarks
		FRONT & REAR FILLER - WITH ROPE CLEATS			
1	MUC3971	BODY ASSEMBLY-LOWER REAR-FRONT AND REAR FUEL FILLER APERTURE-WITH ROPE CLEATS	1	Note (1)	
2	MWC7665	• Panel assembly-bodyside trim-front-front fuel filler aperture	1		
3	MUC3974	• BODY SIDE ASSEMBLY-REAR-FRONT AND REAR FUEL FILLER APERTURE-WITH ROPE CLEATS	1		
4	MUC3309	• • Body side-RH-front and rear fuel filler aperture-with rope cleats	1		
5	MTC7980	• • Panel-rear end-RH	1		
6	MUC3963	• BODY SIDE ASSEMBLY-REAR-LH-WITH ROPE CLEATS	1		
7	MUC3303	• • Body side-LH-with rope cleats	1		
8	MTC7981	• • Panel-rear end-LH	1		
9	MUC3962	• Plate-rear floor	1		
10	330271	• Angle mounting-rear	1		
11	78248	• Rivet-pop-3/16" x 0.45"lng	36		
11	RU612373L	• Rivet-3/16" x 0.575"lng	28		

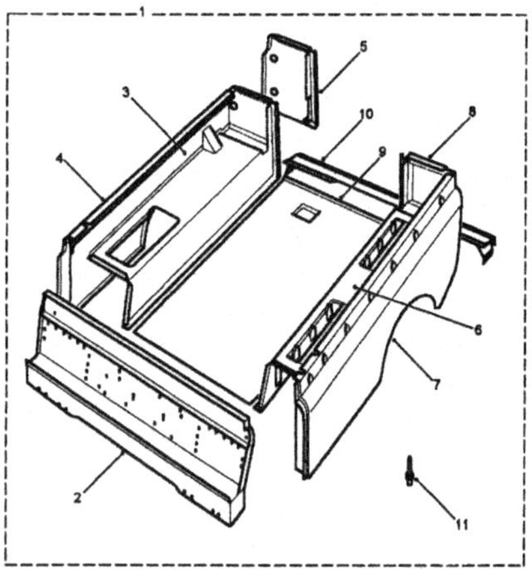

LN0144A

CHANGE POINTS:
(1) To (V) LA 939975

Illus	Part Number	Description	Quantity	Change Point	Remarks
		FRONT FUEL FILLER - WITH ROPE CLEATS			
1	MUC9142	BODY ASSEMBLY-LOWER REAR-FRONT FUEL FILLER APERTURE-WITH ROPE CLEATS	1	Note (1)	
2	MWC7665	• Panel assembly-bodyside trim-front-front fuel filler aperture	1		
3	MUC9136	• BODY SIDE ASSEMBLY-REAR-RH-FRONT FUEL FILLER APERTURE-WITH ROPE CLEATS	1		
4	RTC6257	• • Body side-RH-front fuel filler aperture-with rope cleats	1		
5	MTC7980	• • Panel-rear end-RH	1		
6	MUC3963	• BODY SIDE ASSEMBLY-REAR-LH-WITH ROPE CLEATS	1		
7	MUC3303	• • Body side-LH-with rope cleats	1		
8	MTC7981	• • Panel-rear end-LH	1		
9	MUC3962	• Plate-rear floor	1		
10	330271	• Angle mounting-rear	1		
11	78248	• Rivet-pop-3/16" x 0.45"lng	36		
11	RU612373L	• Rivet-3/16" x 0.575"lng	28		

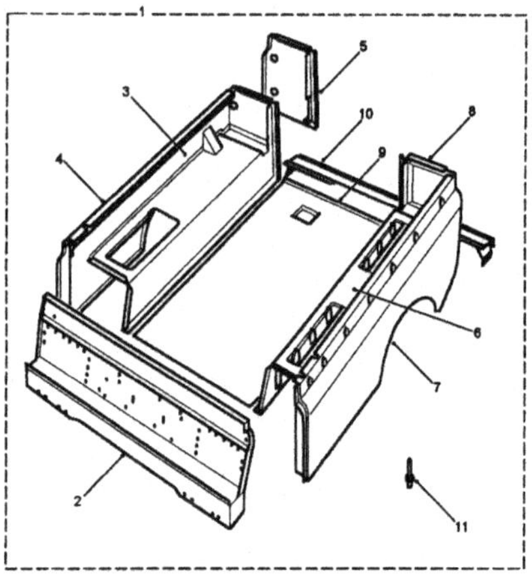

LN0144A

CHANGE POINTS:
(1) To (V) LA 939975

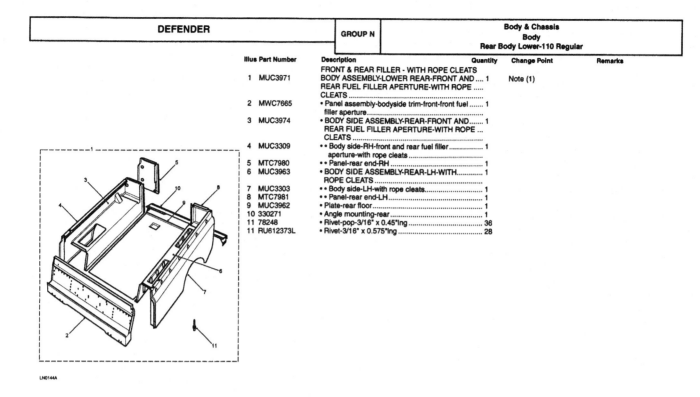

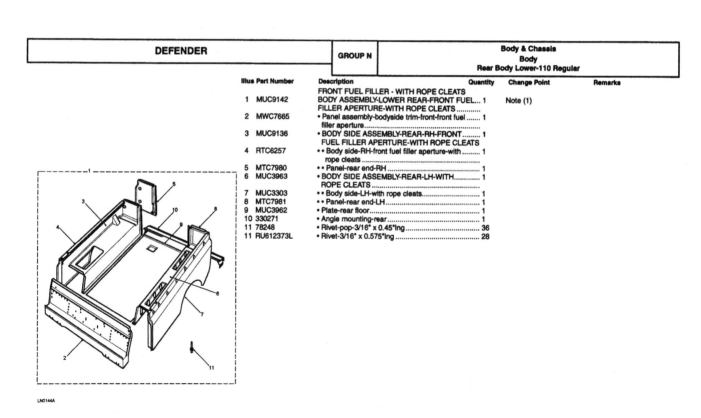

Illus	Part Number	Description	Quantity	Change Point	Remarks
		NO FUEL FILLER - WITHOUT ROPE CLEATS			
1	RTC5706	BODY ASSEMBLY-LOWER REAR-LESS FUEL FILLER APERTURE-LESS ROPE CLEATS	1	Note (1)	
2	RTC6246	• Panel assembly-bodyside trim-front-rear fuel filler aperture	1		
3	RTC5708	• BODY SIDE ASSEMBLY-REAR-RH-LESS FUEL FILLER APERTURE-LESS ROPE CLEATS	1		
4	RTC5711	• • Body side-RH-less fuel filler aperture-less rope cleats	1		
5	MTC7980	• • Panel-rear end-RH	1		
6	RTC5709	• BODY SIDE ASSEMBLY-REAR-LH-LESS ROPE CLEATS	1		
7	RTC5712	• • Body side-LH-less rope cleats	1		
8	MTC7981	• • Panel-rear end-LH	1		
9	MUC3962	• Plate-rear floor	1		
10	330271	• Angle mounting-rear	1		
11	78248	• Rivet-pop-3/16" x 0.45"lng	36		
11	RU612373L	• Rivet-3/16" x 0.575"lng	28		

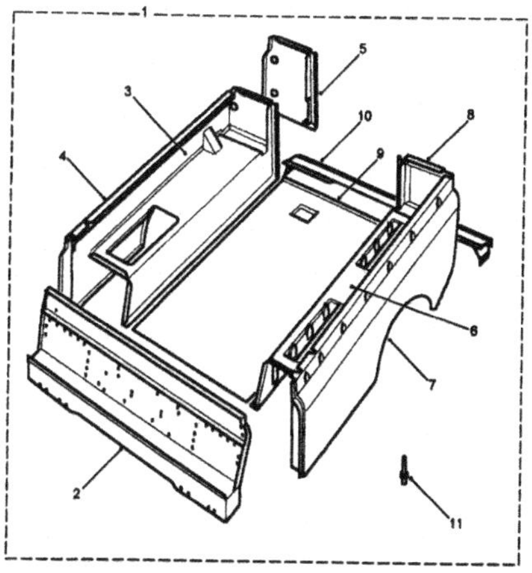

LN0144A

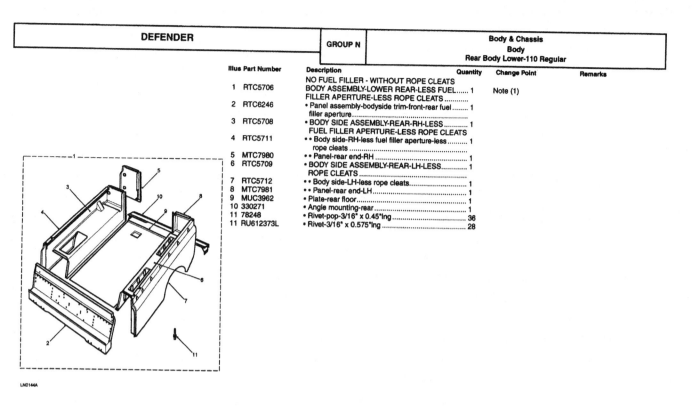

CHANGE POINTS:
(1) To (V) LA 939975

Illus	Part Number	Description	Quantity	Change Point	Remarks
		110 CREW CAB			
1	AQA710290	BODY ASSEMBLY-LOWER REAR	1	Note (1)	
2	ALA710460	• BODY SIDE/WHEELARCH ASSEMBLY-RH	1		
3	ALA710680	• • Panel-bodyside-RH	1		
4	AQH100060	• • Panel-rear end-RH	1		
5	AQU710020	• • Bracket support-upper	1		
6	ALA710470	• BODY SIDE/WHEELARCH ASSEMBLY-LH	1		
7	MRC5071	• • Panel-bodyside-LH	1		
8	AQH100070	• • Panel-rear end-LH	1		
9	AQU710020	• • Bracket support-upper	1		
10	ABB710040	• Bulkhead assembly-body front	1		
11	AFB710070	• FLOOR ASSEMBLY	1		
12	AQU710010	• • Bracket support-lower	2		
13	330271	• Angle mounting-rear	1		
14	78248	• Rivet-pop-3/16" x 0.45"lng	65		
15	RU612373L	• Rivet-3/16" x 0.575"lng	24		

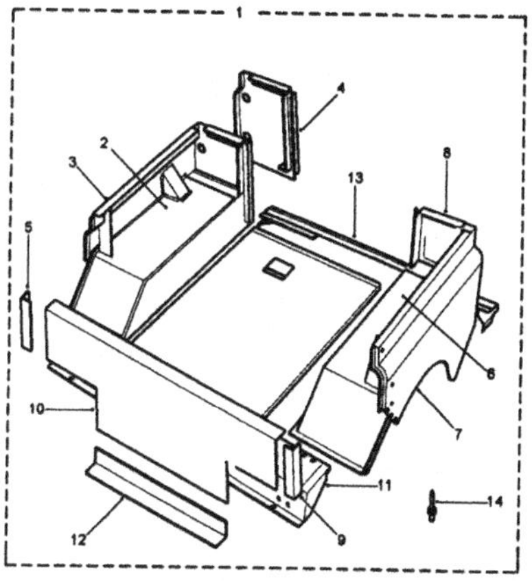

LN0204

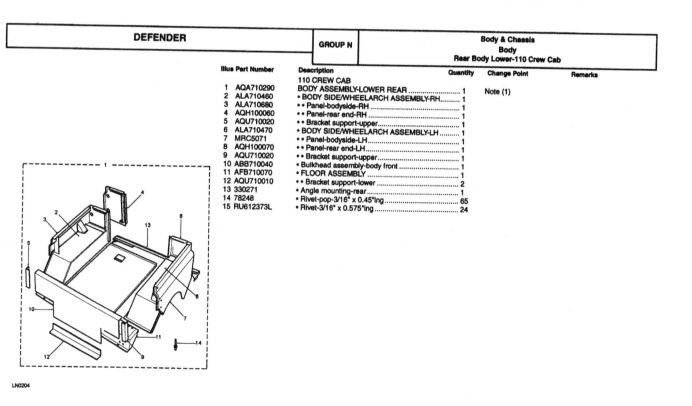

CHANGE POINTS:
(1) From (V) XA 159807 To (V) ZA 612404

DEFENDER	GROUP N	Body & Chassis Body Rear Body Lower-110 Crew Cab

Illus	Part Number	Description	Quantity	Change Point	Remarks
		110 CREW CAB			
1	AQA710420	BODY ASSEMBLY-LOWER REAR	1	Note (1)	
2	ALA710620	• BODY SIDE/WHEELARCH ASSEMBLY-RH	1		
3	ALA710680	• • Panel-bodyside-RH	1		
4	AQH000020	• • Panel-rear end-RH	1		
5	AQU710020	• • Bracket support-upper	1		
6	ALA710630	• BODY SIDE/WHEELARCH ASSEMBLY-LH	1		
7	MRC5071	• • Panel-bodyside-LH	1		
8	AQH000030	• • Panel-rear end-LH	1		
9	AQU710020	• • Bracket support-upper	1		
10	ABB710040	• Bulkhead assembly-body front	1		
11	AFB710070	• FLOOR ASSEMBLY	1		
12	AQU710010	• • Bracket support-lower	2		
13	330271	• Angle mounting-rear	1		
14	78248	• Rivet-pop-3/16" x 0.45"lng	65		
14	RU612373L	• Rivet-3/16" x 0.575"lng	24		

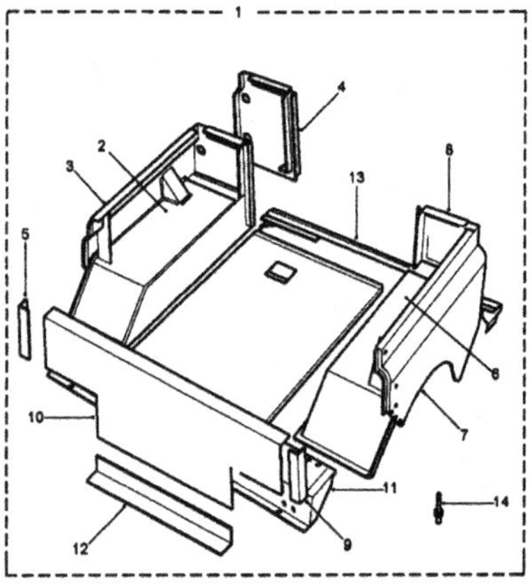

LN0204

CHANGE POINTS:
(1) From (V) 1A 612404

DEFENDER	GROUP N	Body & Chassis Body Rear Body Lower-110/130 HCPU-Assembly

Illus	Part Number	Description	Quantity	Change Point	Remarks
1	MTC3902	Body assembly-lower rear	1	Note (1)	110"
1	RRC6292	Body assembly-lower rear	1		130"
	ALR9186	BODY ASSEMBLY-REAR	1	Note (2)	110"
1	ALR6708	• Body assembly-lower rear	1		
	ALR9187	BODY ASSEMBLY-REAR	1	Note (2)	130"
1	ALR6667	• Body assembly-lower rear	1		
	AQA710200	BODY ASSEMBLY-REAR	1	Note (3)	110"
1	AQA710210	• Body assembly-lower rear	1		
	AQA710180	BODY ASSEMBLY-REAR	1	Note (3)	130"
1	AQA710190	• Body assembly-lower rear	1		

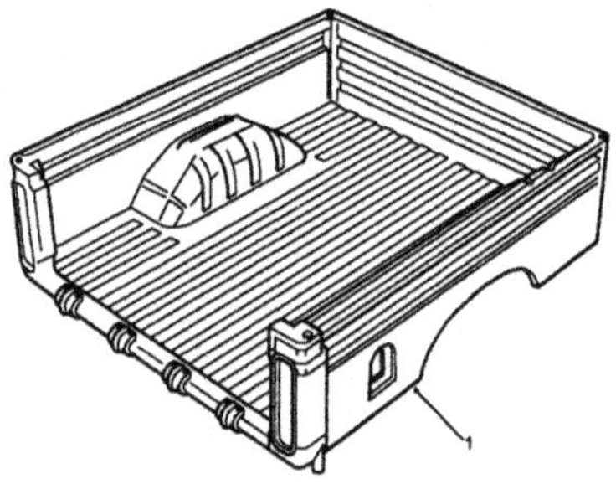

AJNXXG1A

CHANGE POINTS:
(1) To (V) LA 939975
(2) From (V) MA 939976 To (V) WA 159806
(3) From (V) XA 159807

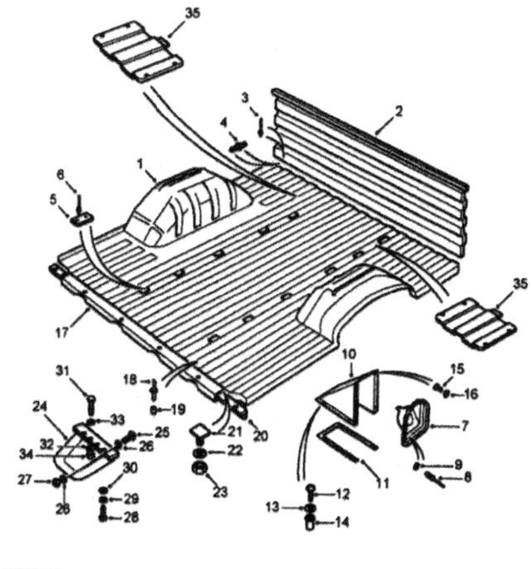

AJNXKG2A

Illus	Part Number	Description	Quantity	Change Point	Remarks
1	MTC3538	Floor assembly	1	Note (1)	110"
1	RRC6296	Floor assembly	1		130"
1	AFB710020	Floor assembly	1	Note (2)	110"
1	AFB710010	Floor assembly	1		130"
2	MTC1409	Bulkhead front assembly	1		
3	RU612183	Rivet-pop-aluminium	15		
4	ACU3777	Monobolt	16		
5	MTC1595	Pad mounting-rear floor	12		110"
5	RRC2443	Pad mounting-rear floor	2		130"
6	RJ612433	Rivet-pop-aluminium	24		
7	MTC3569	Cowl assembly-fuel filler	1	Note (1)	
7	AMP710010	Cowl assembly-fuel filler	1	Note (2)	
8	RA612373L	Rivet-3/16" x 0.575"lng	4		
9	WA105001L	Washer-plain-standard-M5	4		
10	MTC1461	Cover-fuel filler	1		
11	MTC1462	Seal-cap fuel filler	1		
12	SE106161L	Screw-M6 x 16	4		
13	WA106041L	Washer-6mm	4		
14	MR106300	Rivet-M6 x 15	4		
15	AR606031L	Screw-cover-self tapping-No 6 x 3/8	5		
16	WA104001L	Washer-plain-M4	5		
17	MTC3521	Crossmember	1	Note (3)	110"
17	ALR8279	Crossmember	1	Note (4)	
18	AAU6919	Bolt	12		
19	AAU6774	Collar	12		
20	MTC4156	Angle reinforcing	1		
21	MTC3558	Bolt	4		
22	WA108051L	Washer-8mm	4		
23	FN108047L	Nut-flange-flanged head-M8	4		

CHANGE POINTS:
(1) To (V) WA 159806
(2) From (V) XA 159807
(3) To (V) MA 950141
(4) From (V) MA 950142

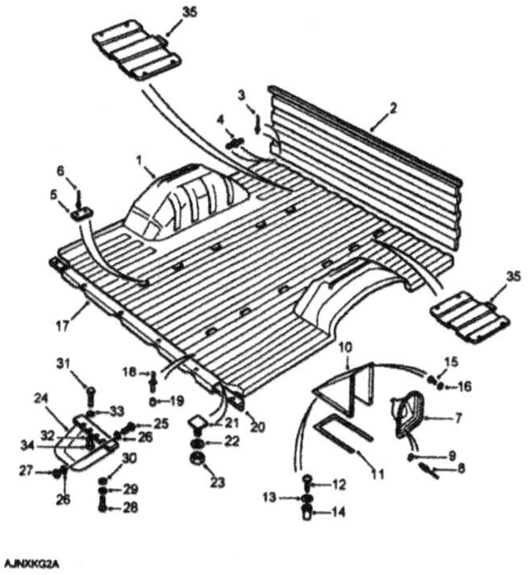

AJNXKG2A

Illus	Part Number	Description	Quantity	Change Point	Remarks
24	MTC3126	Stop-bump-Galvanised-RH	1	To (V) EA 314339	
24	MTC3127	Stop-bump-Galvanised-LH	1		
24	NTC5279	Stop-bump-Black-RH	1	From (V) EA 314340	
24	NTC5278	Stop-bump-Black-LH	1		
25	FS108257L	Screw-flanged head-M8 x 25	4		
26	WA108051L	Washer-8mm	8		
27	FN108047L	Nut-flange-flanged head-M8	4		
28	FS108257L	Screw-bump stop to pillar-flanged head-M8 x 25	2		
29	WL108001L	Washer-sprung-M8	2		
30	WA108051L	Washer-8mm	2		
31	FB108121L	Bolt-bump stop to body-flanged head-M8 x 60	2		
33	WL108001L	Washer-sprung-M8	2		
33	WA108051L	Washer-8mm	2		
34	FN108047L	Nut-flange-flanged head-M8	2		
35	MTC1557	Hatch-inspection	2		

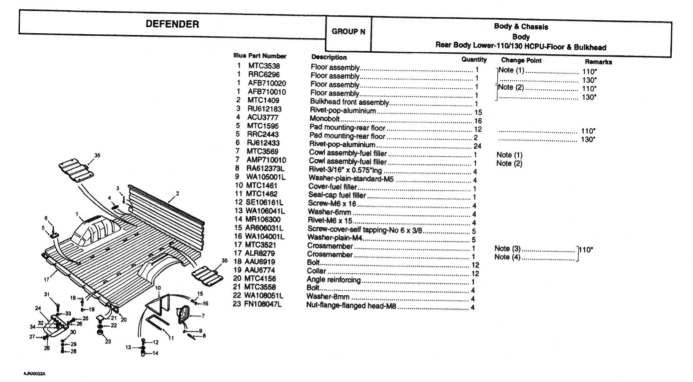

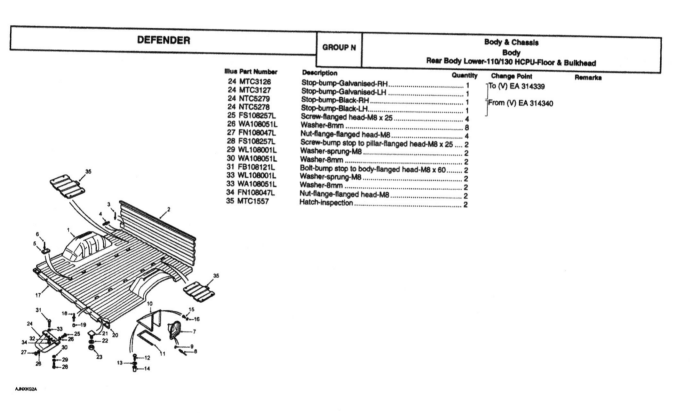

Rear Body Lower-110/130 HCPU-Side Assembly

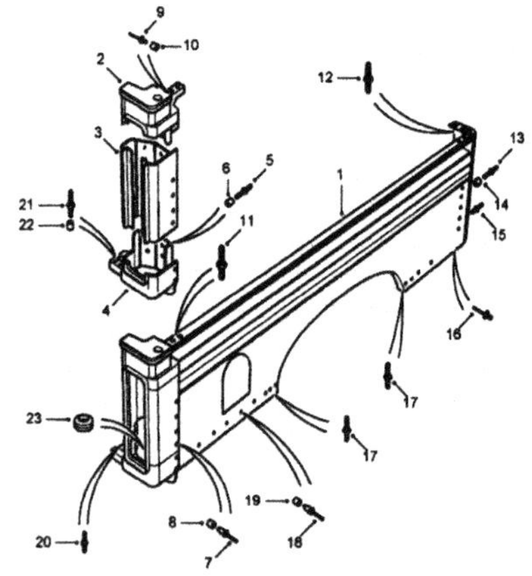

AJNXKG3A

Illus	Part Number	Description	Quantity	Change Point	Remarks
		BODY SIDE ASSEMBLY			
1	MTC3906	RH	1	Note (1)	110"
1	ALR5506	RH	1	Note (2)	
1	ALA710240	RH	1	Note (3)	
1	RRC6304	RH	1		130"
		BODY SIDE ASSEMBLY			
1	MTC3907	LH	1	Note (1)	110"
1	ALR5507	LH	1	Note (2)	
1	ALA710250	LH	1	Note (3)	
1	RRC6305	LH	1		130"
2	MTC5038	Casting-rear pillar-RH	1		
2	MTC5039	Casting-rear pillar-LH	1		
3	MTC1479	Pillar-rear body-lower	2		
4	MTC1481	Quarter-rear lower-RH	1	Note (4)	
4	MTC1482	Quarter-rear lower-LH	1	Note (4)	
4	AGI710020	Quarter-rear lower-RH	1	Note (3)	
4	AGI710030	Quarter-rear lower-LH	1	Note (3)	
5	ACU3530	Rivet	16		
6	AAU6774	Collar	16		
7	ACU1161	Rivet	12		
8	AAU6774	Collar	12		
9	ACU3530	Rivet	4		
10	AAU6774	Collar	4		
11	ACU1762	Monobolt	4		
12	ACU1762	Monobolt	4		
13	AAU8182	Bolt	6		
14	AAU6774	Collar	8		
15	ACU3777	Monobolt	22		
16	RU612183	Rivet-pop-aluminium	8		
18	ACU1161	Rivet	58		
19	AAU6774	Collar	58		
20	ACU1762	Monobolt	4		
21	AAU6919	Bolt	4		
22	AAU6774	Collar	4		
23	3H822L	Grommet-lower	2		

CHANGE POINTS:
(1) To (V) LA 939975
(2) From (V) MA 939976 To (V) WA 159806
(3) From (V) XA 159807
(4) To (V) WA 159806

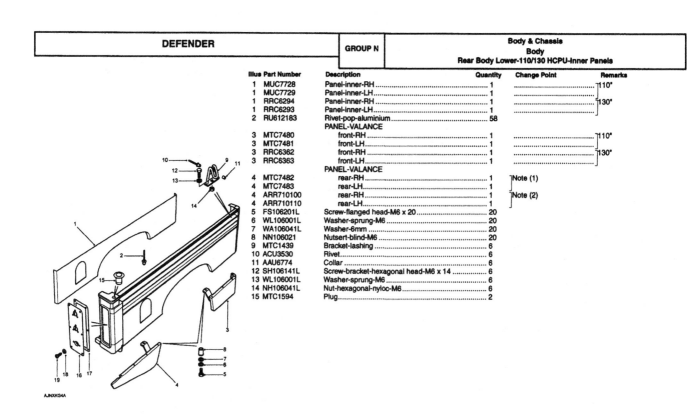

Rear Body Lower-110/130 HCPU-Inner Panels

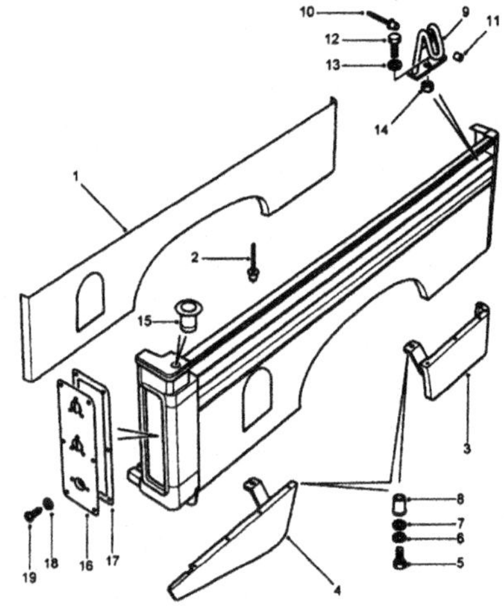

AJNXKG4A

Illus	Part Number	Description	Quantity	Change Point	Remarks
1	MUC7728	Panel-inner-RH	1		110"
1	MUC7729	Panel-inner-LH	1		
1	RRC6294	Panel-inner-RH	1		130"
1	RRC6293	Panel-inner-LH	1		
2	RU612183	Rivet-pop-aluminium	58		
		PANEL-VALANCE			
3	MTC7480	front-RH	1		110"
3	MTC7481	front-LH	1		
3	RRC6362	front-RH	1		130"
3	RRC6363	front-LH	1		
		PANEL-VALANCE			
4	MTC7482	rear-RH	1	Note (1)	
4	MTC7483	rear-LH	1		
4	ARR710100	rear-RH	1	Note (2)	
4	ARR710110	rear-LH	1		
5	FS106201L	Screw-flanged head-M6 x 20	20		
6	WL106001L	Washer-sprung-M6	20		
7	WA106041L	Washer-6mm	20		
8	NN106021	Nutsert-blind-M6	20		
9	MTC1439	Bracket-lashing	6		
10	ACU3530	Rivet	6		
11	AAU6774	Collar	6		
12	SH106141L	Screw-bracket-hexagonal head-M6 x 14	6		
13	WL106001L	Washer-sprung-M6	6		
14	NH106041L	Nut-hexagonal-nyloc-M6	6		
15	MTC1594	Plug	2		

CHANGE POINTS:
(1) To (V) WA 159806
(2) From (V) XA 159807

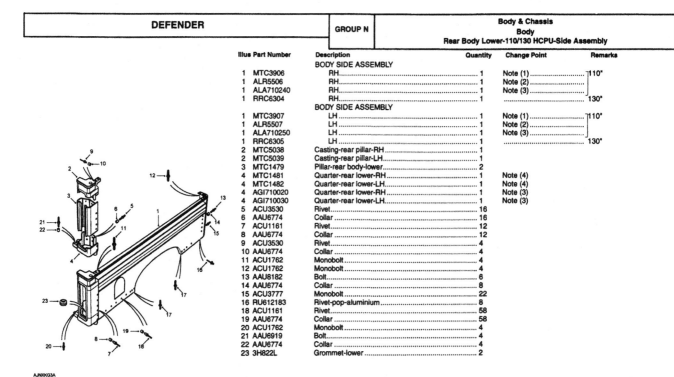

Illus	Part Number	Description	Quantity	Change Point	Remarks
		MOUNTING-REAR LAMP			
16	MTC3350	fog or reverse lamps	1	Note (1)	
16	MTC3515	fog and reverse lamp	1		
16	ALR5330	fog or reverse lamps	1	Note (2)	
16	ALR5329	fog and reverse lamp	1	Note (3)	
16	AQV710010	fog and reverse lamp	1	Note (4)	
17	MTC1448	Seal	2		
18	AR610051L	Screw-self tapping	12		
19	WA105001L	Washer-plain-standard-M5	12		
	MTC7511	Capping-rear valance-corner-LH	1		Germany
	MTC7512	Capping-rear valance-corner-RH	1		

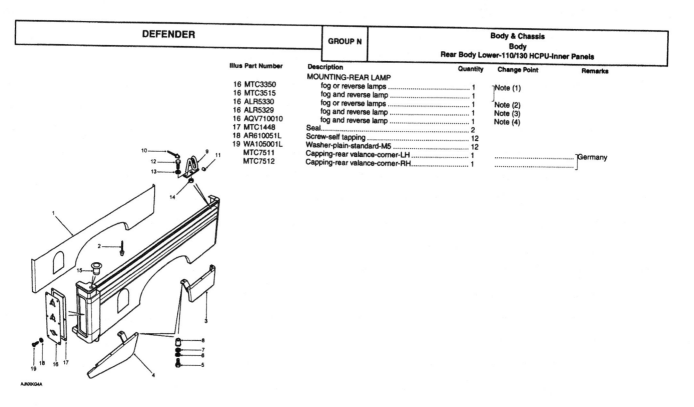

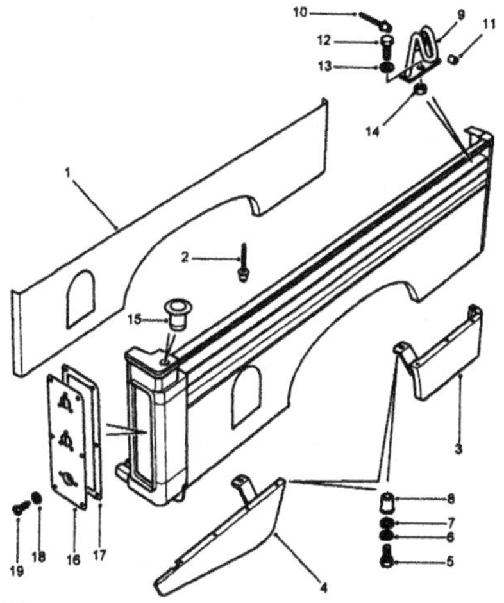

AJNXKG4A

CHANGE POINTS:
(1) To (V) LA 939975
(2) From (V) MA 939976
(3) From (V) MA 939976 To (V) WA 159806
(4) From (V) XA 159807

Illus	Part Number	Description	Quantity	Change Point	Remarks
		CROSSMEMBERS, STAYS AND FIXINGS			
1	MUC8949	Crossmember	3		
2	332582	Pad mounting-rear floor-5.0mm	6		
3	RU612373L	Rivet-3/16" x 0.575"lng	12		
4	78248	Rivet-pop-3/16" x 0.45"lng	12		
5	MUC9220	Stay	2		
6	SE106201L	Screw-pan head-M6 x 20	2		
7	WA106041L	Washer-6mm	4		
8	WL106001L	Washer-sprung-M6	2		
9	NH106041L	Nut-hexagonal-nyloc-M6	2		
10	79281	Pin-42mm	A/R		
10	79283	Pin-38mm	A/R		
10	79293	Pin-35mm	A/R		
11	AAU6774	Collar	A/R		
		BODY TO CHASSIS AT FRONT			
12	FS108257L	Screw-flanged head-M8 x 25	4		
13	AFU1079	Washer-M8	4		
14	WA108051L	Washer-8mm	4		
15	FN108047L	Nut-flange-flanged head-M8	4		
16	305232	Shim	4		
		BODY TO CHASSIS AT REAR			
17	SX108251	Screw-hexagonal socket-high tensile-M8 x 25	10	Note (1)	Except Germany
17	SE108251	Screw-pan head-M8 x 25	10		Germany
17	AYG100240	Screw-torx drive-M8 x 25	10	Note (2)	
18	WA108051L	Washer-8mm	10		
19	WF600051L	Washer-retaining	10		
20	NY108041L	Nut-nyloc-M8	4		
21	305232	Shim	A/R		
22	MRC8736	Nut plate	3		
23	RB610082	Rivet	6		

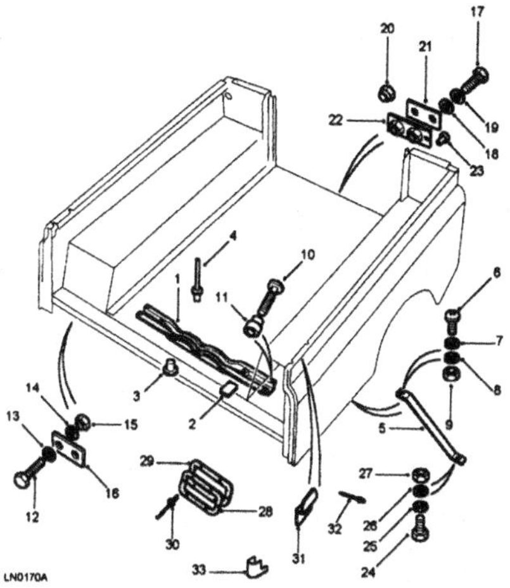

LN0170A

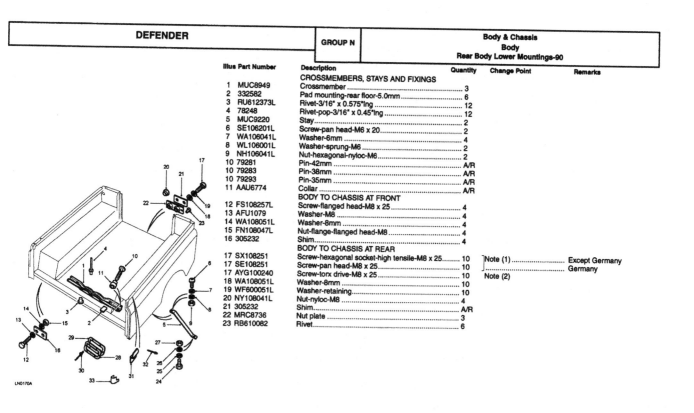

CHANGE POINTS:
(1) To (V) VA 138479
(2) From (V) WA 138480

DEFENDER	GROUP N	Body & Chassis Body Rear Body Lower Mountings-90

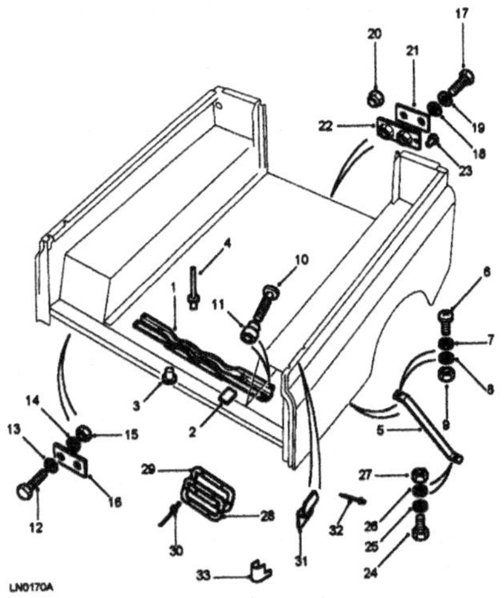

Illus	Part Number	Description	Quantity	Change Point	Remarks
		STAY FIXINGS			
24	FS106201L	Screw-stay to body-flanged head-M6 x 20	2		
25	WA106041L	Washer-6mm	4		
26	WL106001L	Washer-sprung-M6	2		
27	NH106041L	Nut-hexagonal-nyloc-M6	2		
		BULKHEAD ACCESS PLATES			
28	MUC6519	Plate	2		
29	MWC2129	Gasket	2		
30	78248	Rivet-pop-3/16" x 0.45"lng	12		
		ROPE CLEATS			
31	301328	Cleat	6		
32	78248	Rivet-pop-3/16" x 0.45"lng	12		
33	MUC3932	Cover-rope cleat	6		Germany

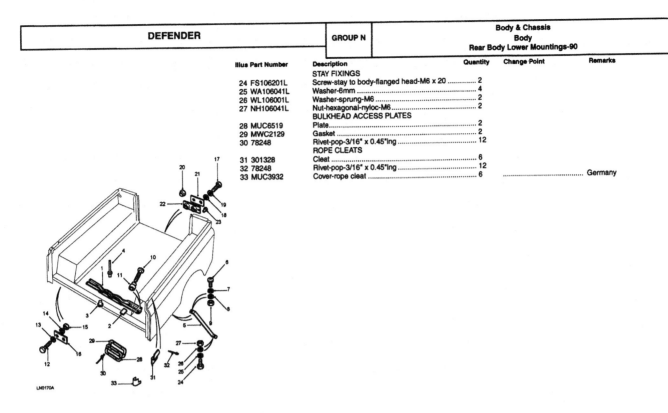

DEFENDER	GROUP N	Body & Chassis Body Rear Body Lower Mountings-110 Regular

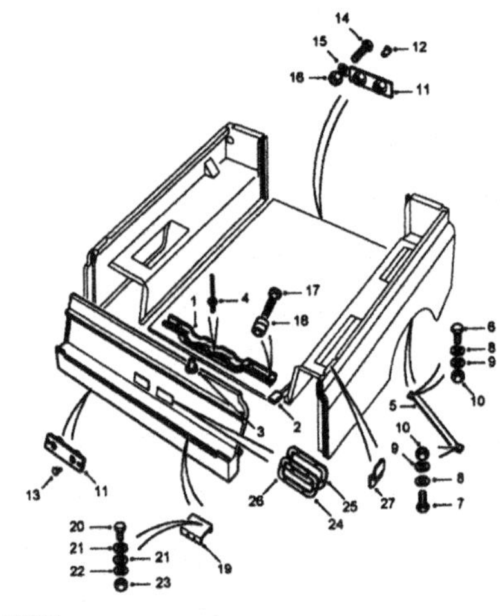

Illus	Part Number	Description	Quantity	Change Point	Remarks
1	MUC8949	Crossmember	6		
2	332582	Pad mounting-rear floor-5.0mm	12		
3	RU612373L	Rivet-3/16" x 0.575"lng	24		
4	78248	Rivet-pop-3/16" x 0.45"lng	36		
5	MRC6027	Stay-RH	1		
5	MRC6028	Stay-LH	1		
6	SE106201L	Screw-stay to body-pan head-M6 x 20	2		
7	FS106201L	Screw-flanged head-M6 x 20	2		
8	WA106041L	Washer-6mm	4		
9	WL106001L	Washer-sprung-M6	4		
10	NH106041L	Nut-hexagonal-nyloc-M6	4		
11	MRC8736	Nut plate	7		
12	RB610082	Rivet	6		
13	78248	Rivet-pop-3/16" x 0.45"lng	8		
14	SX108251	Screw-body to chassis-hexagonal socket-high tensile-M8 x 25	10	Note (1)	
14	AYG100240	Screw-torx drive-M8 x 25	10	Note (2)	
15	WF600051L	Washer-retaining	14		
15	WL108001L	Washer-sprung-M8	14		
16	FN108047L	Nut-flange-flanged head-M8	10		
17	79281	Pin-42mm	A/R		
17	79283	Pin-38mm	A/R		
17	79293	Pin-35mm	A/R		
18	79289	Collar	A/R		
19	MTC3046	Bracket mounting	2		
20	FS108207L	Screw-bracket mounting-flanged head-M8 x 20	4		
21	WA108051L	Washer-8mm	8		
22	WL108001L	Washer-sprung-M8	4		
23	FN108047L	Nut-flange-flanged head-M8	4		
20	FS108207L	Screw-flanged head-M8 x 20	8		
21	WA108051L	Washer-8mm	8		
22	WL108001L	Washer-sprung-M8	8		
23	FN108047L	Nut-flange-flanged head-M8	8		
24	MUC6519	Plate	2		
25	MWC2129	Gasket	2		
26	78248	Rivet-pop-3/16" x 0.45"lng	12		
27	301328	Cleat	10		
	MUC3932	Cover-rope cleat	10		Germany

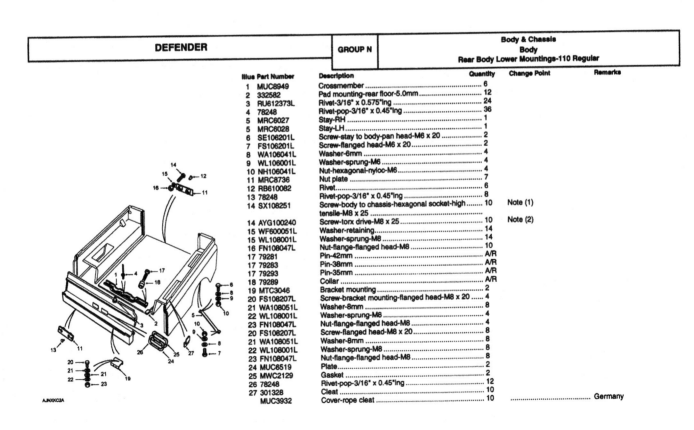

CHANGE POINTS:
(1) To (V) WA 138479
(2) From (V) WA 138480

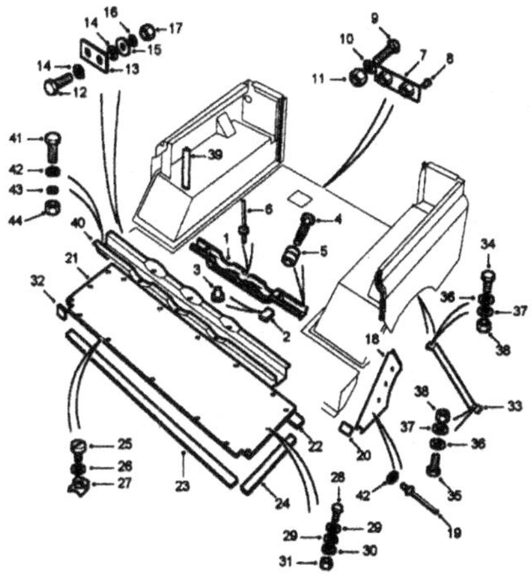

LN0176A

Illus	Part Number	Description	Quantity	Change Point	Remarks
		BODY CROSSMEMBERS AND FIXINGS			
1	MUC8949	Crossmember	4		
2	332582	Pad mounting-rear floor-5.0mm	8		
3	RU612373L	Rivet-3/16" x 0.575"lng	16		
4	79283	Pin-38mm	A/R		
4	79293	Pin-35mm	A/R		
5	79289	Collar	A/R		
6	78248	Rivet-pop-3/16" x 0.45"lng	24		
		BODY TO CHASSIS AT REAR			
7	MRC8736	Nut plate	3		
8	RB610082	Rivet	6		
9	SX108251	Screw-body to chassis-hexagonal socket-high tensile-M8 x 25	10	Note (1)	Except Germany
9	SE108251	Screw-body to chassis-pan head-M8 x 25	10		Germany
9	AYG100240	Screw-torx drive-M8 x 25	10	Note (2)	
10	WF600051L	Washer-retaining	10		
11	FN108047L	Nut-flange-flanged head-M8	4		
		REAR HEELBOARD TO CHASSIS			
12	SH108401L	Screw-heelboard to chassis-hexagonal head-M8 x 40	4		
13	305232	Shim	10		
14	WF600051L	Washer-retaining	8		
15	WA108051L	Washer-8mm	4		
16	WL108001L	Washer-sprung-M8	4		
17	FN108047L	Nut-flange-flanged head-M8	4		
		WHEELARCH EXTENSION PANEL			
18	MRC6436	Panel extension-RH	1		
18	MRC6437	Panel extension-LH	1		
19	78248	Rivet-pop-3/16" x 0.45"lng	22		
20	333263	Seal	2		

CHANGE POINTS:
(1) To (V) VA 138479
(2) From (V) WA 138480

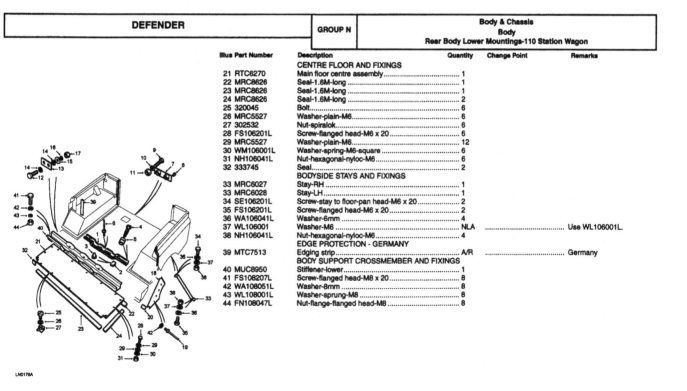

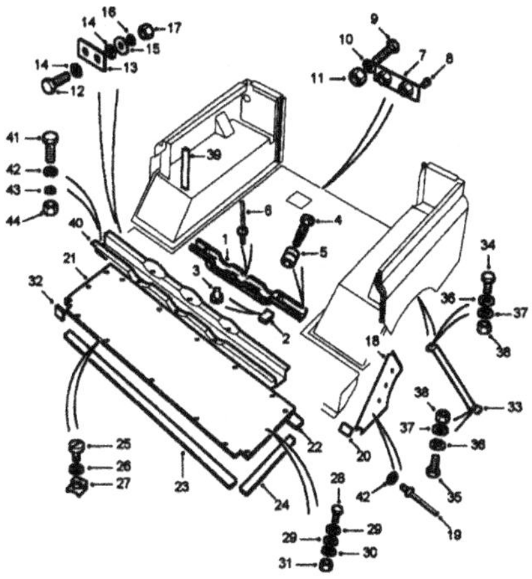

LN0176A

Illus	Part Number	Description	Quantity	Change Point	Remarks
		CENTRE FLOOR AND FIXINGS			
21	RTC6270	Main floor centre assembly	1		
22	MRC8626	Seal-1.6M-long	1		
23	MRC8626	Seal-1.6M-long	1		
24	MRC8626	Seal-1.6M-long	2		
25	320045	Bolt	6		
26	MRC5527	Washer-plain-M6	6		
27	302532	Nut-spiralok	6		
28	FS106201L	Screw-flanged head-M6 x 20	6		
29	MRC5527	Washer-plain-M6	12		
30	WM106001L	Washer-spring-M6-square	6		
31	NH106041L	Nut-hexagonal-nyloc-M6	6		
32	333745	Seal	2		
		BODYSIDE STAYS AND FIXINGS			
33	MRC6027	Stay-RH	1		
33	MRC6028	Stay-LH	1		
34	SE106201L	Screw-stay to floor-pan head-M6 x 20	2		
35	FS106201L	Screw-flanged head-M6 x 20	2		
36	WA106041L	Washer-6mm	4		
37	WL106001	Washer-M6	NLA		Use WL106001L.
38	NH106041L	Nut-hexagonal-nyloc-M6	4		
		EDGE PROTECTION - GERMANY			
39	MTC7513	Edging strip	A/R		Germany
		BODY SUPPORT CROSSMEMBER AND FIXINGS			
40	MUC8950	Stiffener-lower	1		
41	FS108207L	Screw-flanged head-M8 x 20	8		
42	WA108051L	Washer-8mm	8		
43	WL108001L	Washer-sprung-M8	8		
44	FN108047L	Nut-flange-flanged head-M8	8		

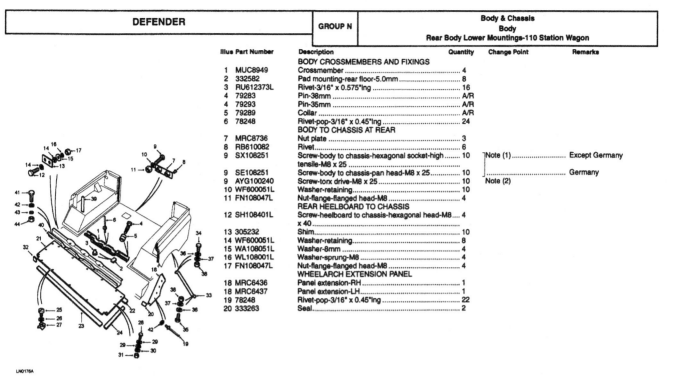

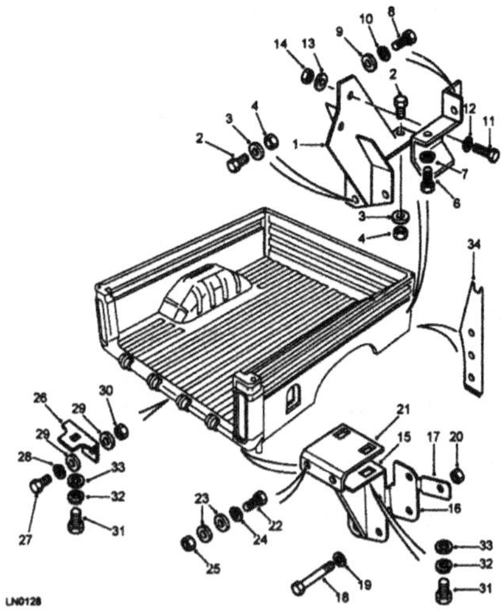

LN0128

Illus	Part Number	Description	Quantity	Change Point	Remarks
1	MTC3481	Bracket-rear body mounting-front-RH	1		
1	MTC3482	Bracket-rear body mounting-front-LH	1		
2	SH110251L	Screw-bracket to chassis-hexagonal head-M10 x 25	6		
3	WA110061L	Washer-M10	6		
4	NY110047L	Nut-flange-nyloc-M10	6		
5	MTC3486	Bracket-chassis frame body mounting-front	2	Note (1)	
5	KVU101420	Bracket-chassis frame body mounting	2	Note (2)	110"
5	KVU101420	Bracket-chassis frame body mounting	2	Note (2)	130"
6	FS110301L	Screw-bracket to body-flanged head-M10 x 30-top	2		
7	WL110001L	Washer-M10	2		
8	SH110251L	Screw-hexagonal head-M10 x 25	2		
9	WA110061L	Washer-M10	2		
10	WL110001L	Washer-M10	2		
11	SH110251L	Screw-bracket to mounting-hexagonal head-M10 x 25	4		
12	WL110001L	Washer-M10	4		
13	WA110061L	Washer-M10	4		
14	NY110047L	Nut-flange-nyloc-M10	4		
15	MTC4992	Bracket assembly-body mounting-rear-RH	1		
15	MTC4993	Bracket assembly-body mounting-rear-LH	1		
16	MTC5086	Packing Piece	2		
17	MTC6154	Plate	4		
18	BH108141L	Bolt-hexagonal head-M8 x 70	8		
19	WA108051L	Washer-8mm	8		
20	FN108047L	Nut-flange-flanged head-M8	8		
21	MTC4002	Bracket-rear sub frame angle-outer	2		
22	FS108207L	Screw-flanged head-M8 x 20	4		
23	WA108051L	Washer-8mm	8		
24	WL108001L	Washer-sprung-M8	4		
25	FN108047L	Nut-flange-flanged head-M8	4		
26	MTC4003	Bracket-rear sub frame angle-inner	3		
27	FS108207L	Screw-flanged head-M8 x 20	6		

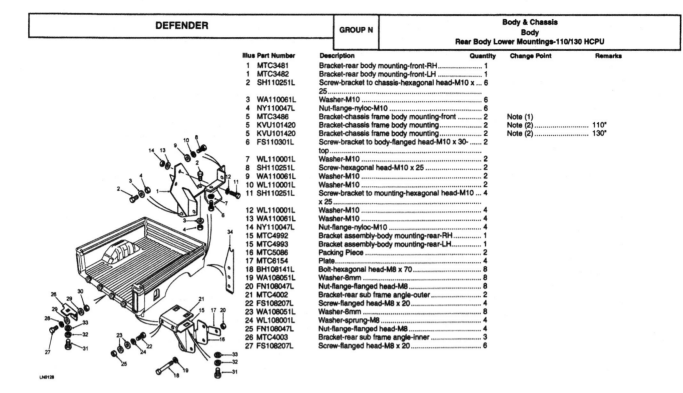

CHANGE POINTS:
(1) To (V) XA 176049
(2) From (V) XA 176050

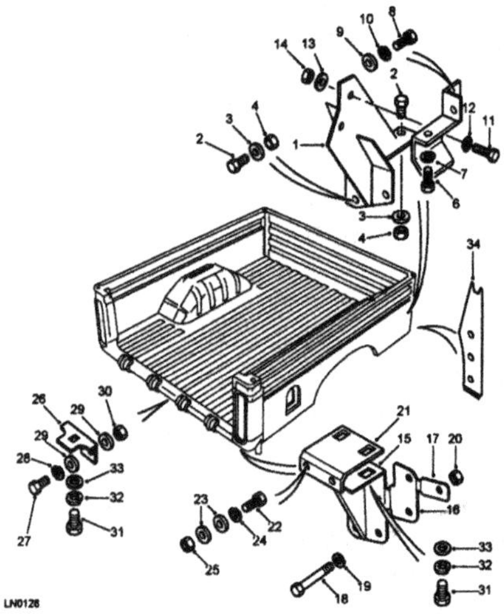

LN0128

Illus	Part Number	Description	Quantity	Change Point	Remarks
29	WA108051L	Washer-8mm	6		
30	FN108047L	Nut-flange-flanged head-M8	6		
31	FS110301L	Screw-flanged head-M10 x 30-top	7		
32	WL110001L	Washer-M10	7		
33	WA110061L	Washer-M10	7		
		DEFENDER 130			
34	RRC6216	Panel extension-RH	1		130"
34	RRC6215	Panel extension-LH	1		130"
		ANGLE MOUNTING			
35	RRC6168	rear	3		
36	RRC6154	RH	1		
36	RRC6155	LH	1		
37	RRC6169	Bracket-chassis frame body mounting-front	2	Note (1)	
38	KVU101440	Bracket-chassis frame body mounting	2	Note (2)	110"
38	KVU101440	Bracket-chassis frame body mounting	2	Note (2)	130"
39	RRC2440	Bracket mounting-body	4		

CHANGE POINTS:
(1) To (V) XA 176049
(2) From (V) XA 176050

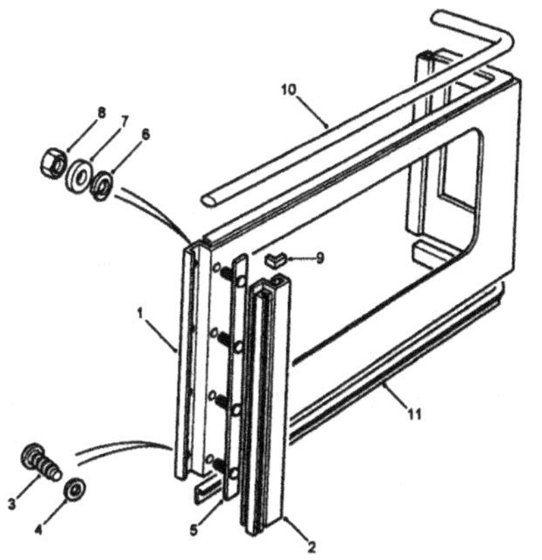

AHNXLE1A

Illus	Part Number	Description	Quantity	Change Point	Remarks
		PANEL-BODYSIDE			
1	MWC9450	end and side window apertures-upper-RH	1		
1	MWC9451	end and side window apertures-upper-LH	1		
1	MWC9452	end window apertures-upper-RH	1		
1	MWC9453	end window apertures-upper-LH	1		
1	STC537	less window aperture-upper-RH	1	Note (2)	
1	STC538	less window aperture-upper-LH	1	Note (2)	
2	MTC5394	Finisher-RH	1		
2	MTC5395	Finisher-LH	1		
3	78832	Screw-taptite	6		
4	AFU1080	Washer-plain	6		
5	332065	Stud plate	2		
6	4034L	Washer-plain	8		
7	WM702001L	Washer-spring-3/16 dia-square	8		
8	RTC608	Nut	8		

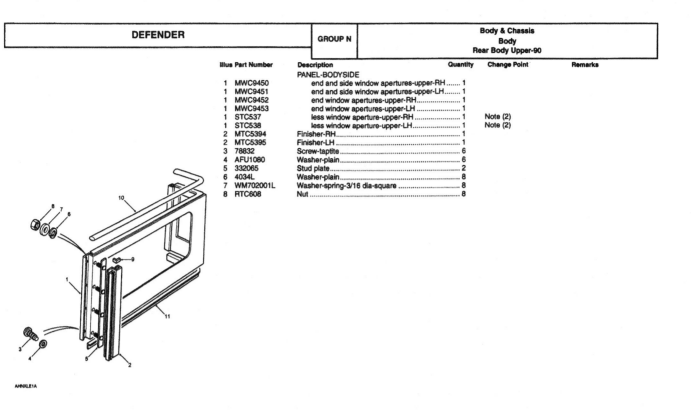

CHANGE POINTS:
(2) To (V) EA 345885

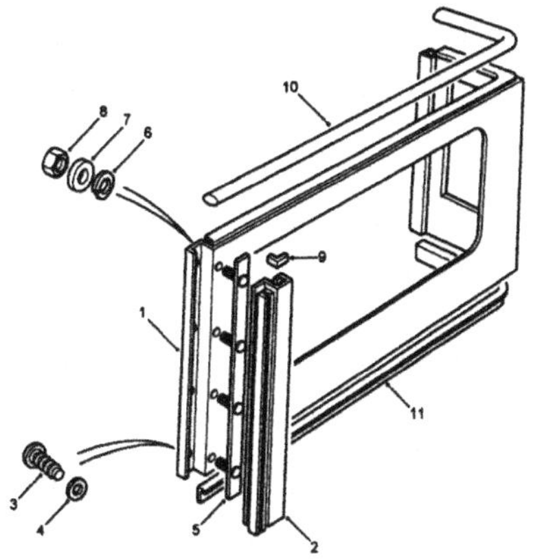

AHNXLE1A

Illus	Part Number	Description	Quantity	Change Point	Remarks
9	332215	Seal-rubber-pillar	4		
10	MUC1006	Seal-upper-RH	1	Note (1)	
10	MUC1007	Seal-upper-LH	1		
10	MXC3676	Seal-upper-RH	1	Note (2)	
10	MXC3677	Seal-upper-LH	1		
10	MXC3684	Seal-upper-front-RH	1		
10	MXC3685	Seal-upper-front-LH	1		
11	MUC1333	Seal-lower	2	Note (1)	Hard Top
11	MXC2031	Seal-lower	2	Note (3)	Hard Top
11	ALR1159	Seal-lower	2	Note (4)	Hard Top
11	ALR5056	Seal-lower	2	Note (5)	Hard Top
11	AML110030	Seal-lower	2	Note (6)	Hard Top
11	MXC2031	Seal-lower	2	Note (7)	Station Wagon
11	ALR1159	Seal-lower	2	Note (8)	Station Wagon
11	ALR5056	Seal-lower	2	Note (5)	Station Wagon
11	AML110030	Seal-lower	2	Note (9)	Station Wagon
11	AML110030	Seal-lower	2	Note (10)	Station Wagon Vehicle with bulkhead
11	AML710020	Seal-lower-RH	1	Note (10)	Station Wagon Vehicle without bulkhead
11	AML710030	Seal-lower-LH	1	Note (10)	Station Wagon Vehicle without bulkhead
	MTC7513	Edging strip	A/R		Germany
	MTC8333	Finisher assembly-d post	2		
	RU608313L	Rivet-aluminium-1/8" x 0.482"lng	2		

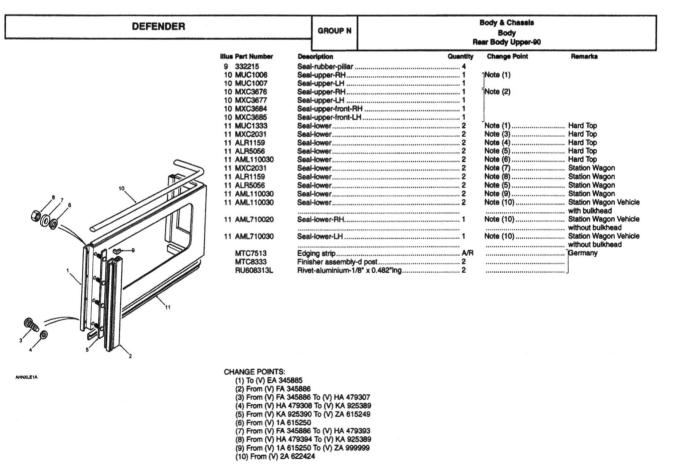

CHANGE POINTS:
(1) To (V) EA 345885
(2) From (V) FA 345886
(3) From (V) FA 345886 To (V) HA 479307
(4) From (V) HA 479308 To (V) KA 925389
(5) From (V) KA 925390 To (V) ZA 615249
(6) From (V) 1A 615250
(7) From (V) FA 345886 To (V) HA 479393
(8) From (V) HA 479394 To (V) KA 925389
(9) From (V) 1A 615250 To (V) ZA 999999
(10) From (V) 2A 622424

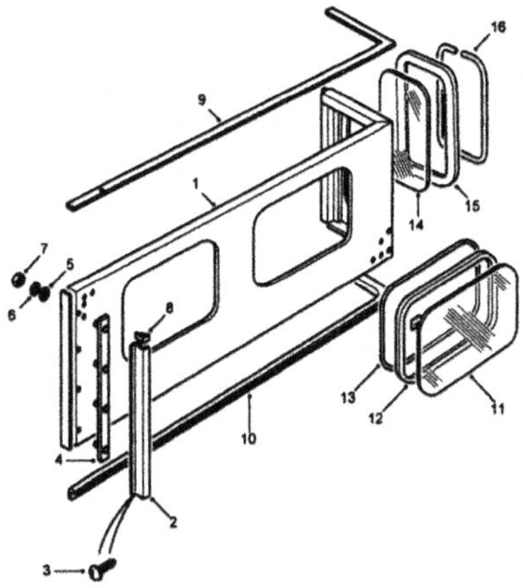

AJNXLC1A

Illus	Part Number	Description	Quantity	Change Point	Remarks
		BODY SIDE			
1	MWC9418	upper-RH-with fixed side window	1		
1	MTC4412	upper-LH-with fixed side window	1	Note (1)	
1	MWC9419	upper-LH-with fixed side window	1	Note (2)	
1	MWC9420	upper-RH-with plain sides	1		
1	MWC9421	upper-LH-with plain sides	1		
1	ALR2302	upper-RH-with sliding side window	1		
1	ALR2303	upper-LH-with sliding side window	1		
2	MTC5394	Finisher-RH	1		
2	MTC5395	Finisher-LH	1		
3	78832	Screw-taptite	6		
4	MUC3566	Stud plate	2		
5	AFU1080	Washer-plain	6	Note (3)	
5	WA105001L	Washer-plain-standard-M5	8	Note (4)	
6	WL105001L	Washer-retaining-M5	8		
7	NM105011	Nut-hexagonal	8		
8	332215	Seal-rubber	4		
9	334610	Seal-upper-RH	1	Note (5)	
9	334611	Seal-upper-LH	1		
9	MXC3680	Seal-upper-RH	1	Note (6)	
9	MXC3681	Seal-upper-LH	1		
9	MXC3684	Seal-upper-front-RH	1		
9	MXC3685	Seal-upper-front-LH	1		
10	333490	Seal-lower	2	Note (5)	
10	MXC2033	Seal-lower	2	Note (7)	
10	ALR1157	Seal-lower	2	Note (8)	
10	ALR5054	Seal-lower	2	Note (9)	
10	AML110010	Seal-lower	2	Note (10)	

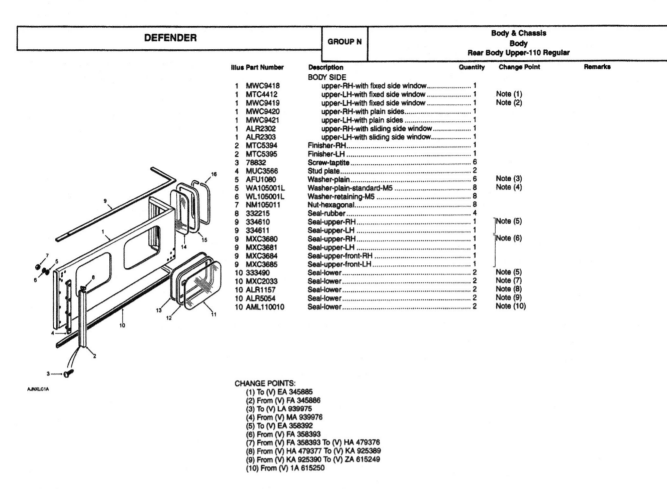

CHANGE POINTS:
(1) To (V) EA 345885
(2) From (V) FA 345886
(3) To (V) LA 939975
(4) From (V) MA 939976
(5) To (V) EA 358392
(6) From (V) FA 358393
(7) From (V) FA 358393 To (V) HA 479376
(8) From (V) HA 479377 To (V) KA 925389
(9) From (V) KA 925390 To (V) ZA 615249
(10) From (V) 1A 615250

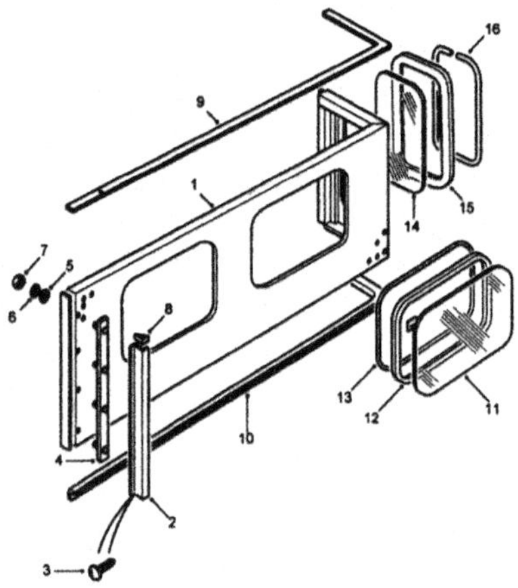

AJNXLC1A

Illus	Part Number	Description	Quantity	Change Point	Remarks
11	MTC5312	Glass side panel-hard top-5mm glass	4	Note (1)	
11	MWC4717	Glass side panel-hard top-4mm glass	4	Note (2)	
12	302177	Weatherstrip-alpine light-5mm glass	4	Note (1)	Hard Top
12	MWC4771	Weatherstrip-alpine light-4mm glass	4	Note (2)	Hard Top
13	302178	Filler strip	4		
14	MTC3476	Glass-rear quarter-5mm glass-back-Clear	2	Note (1)	
14	MWC4715	Glass-rear quarter-4mm glass-back-Clear	2	Note (2)	
15	306287	Strip-glazing-5mm glass	2	Note (1)	
15	MWC4772	Strip-glazing-4mm glass	2	Note (2)	
16	306289	Filler strip	2		
	MTC8333	Finisher assembly-d post	2		Germany
	RU608313L	Rivet-aluminium-1/8" x 0.482"lng	2		
	MUC3810	Stiffener-rear	2		

CHANGE POINTS:
(1) To (V) EA 345885
(2) From (V) FA 345886

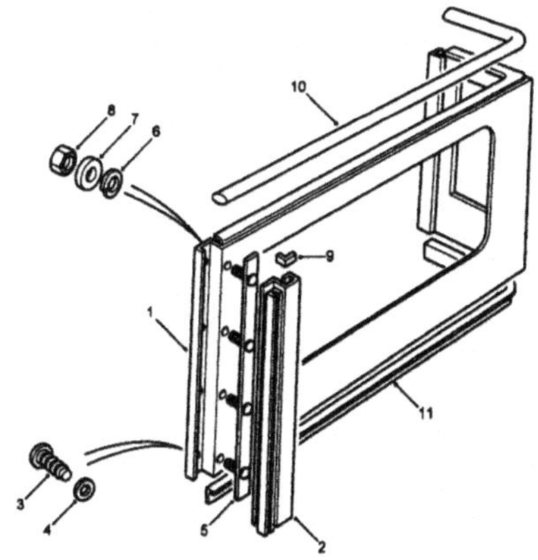

AHNXLE1A

Illus	Part Number	Description	Quantity	Change Point	Remarks
1	MWC8966	Panel-bodyside-end and side window apertures-upper-RH	1		
1	MWC8967	Panel-bodyside-end and side window apertures-upper-LH	1		
2	MTC5394	Finisher-RH	1		
2	MTC5395	Finisher-LH	1		
3	78832	Screw-taptite	6		
4	AFU1080	Washer-plain	6		
5	MUC3566	Stud plate	2		
6	WA105001L	Washer-plain-standard-M5	8		
7	WL105001L	Washer-retaining-M5	8		
8	NM105011	Nut-hexagonal	8		
9	332215	Seal-rubber	4		
10	334610	Seal-upper-RH	1	Note (1)	
10	334611	Seal-upper-LH	1		
10	MXC3676	Seal-upper-RH	1	Note (2)	
10	MXC3677	Seal-upper-LH	1		
10	MXC3684	Seal-upper-front-RH	1		
10	MXC3685	Seal-upper-front-LH	1		
11	333487	Seal-lower	2	Note (1)	
11	MXC2031	Seal-lower	2	Note (3)	
11	ALR1158	Seal-lower	2	Note (4)	
11	ALR5055	Seal-lower	2	Note (5)	

CHANGE POINTS:
(1) To (V) EA 345885
(2) From (V) FA 345886
(3) From (V) FA 345886 To (V) HA 479385
(4) From (V) HA 479386 To (V) KA 925389
(5) From (V) KA 925390

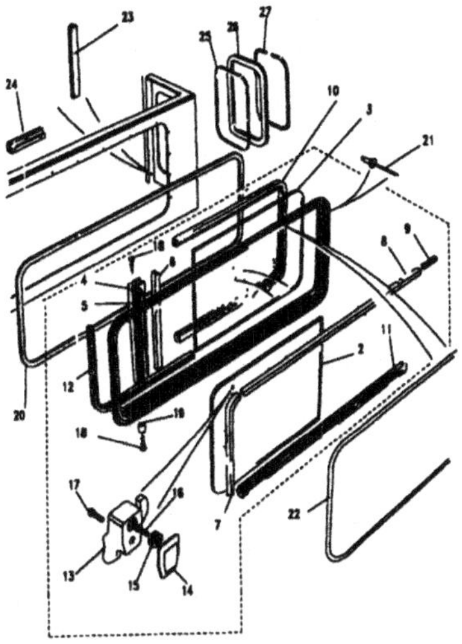

Illus	Part Number	Description	Quantity	Change Point	Remarks
1	MUC3766	GLASS ASSEMBLY-BODYSIDE SLIDING-5 MM GLASS-RH-CLEAR.	1	To (V) EA 344187	
1	MUC3767	GLASS ASSEMBLY-BODYSIDE SLIDING-5 MM GLASS-LH-CLEAR.	1		
2	MUC3791	• Glass-bodyside-sliding-front-Clear.	1		
3	MUC3792	• Glass-bodyside-sliding-rear-Clear.	1		
4	MUC3770	• Rail guide-draught-clear glass	1		
5	MUC3769	• Seal-clear glass	1		
6	MUC1098	• Strip-glazing-clear glass	1		
7	MUC3097	• Felt-nvh-clear glass	1		
8	MUC3096	• Felt-sliding glass-cab-rear panel-top	1		
9	MUC4025	• Buffer-stop-clear glass	1		
10	MUC1484	• Glazing rubber-clear glass	1		
11	MTC8947	• Channel-rear quarter glass run-clear glass	1		
12	MUC3768	• Filler strip-clear glass	1		
13	MTC8270	• Catch-clear glass-RH	1		Part of MUC3766.
13	MTC8271	• Catch-clear glass-LH	1		Part of MUC3767.

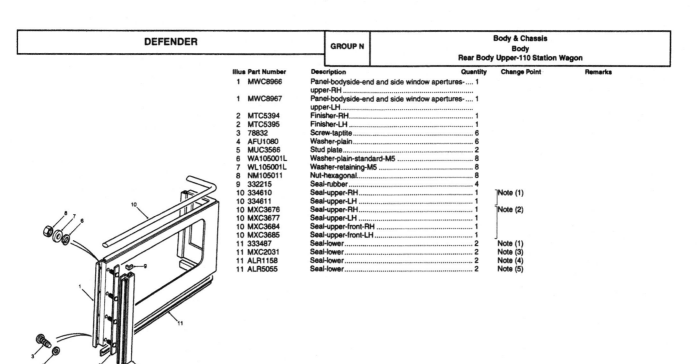

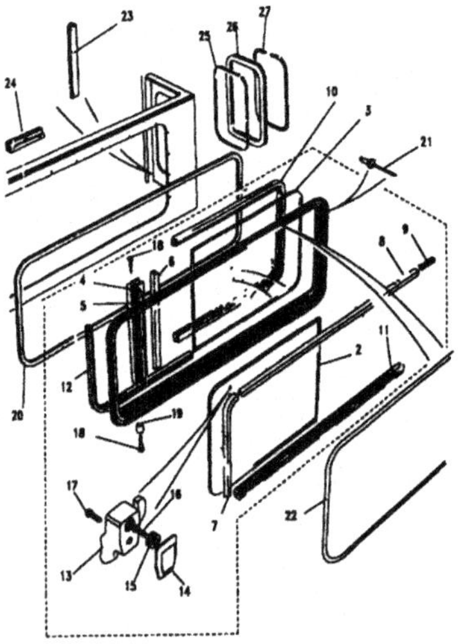

Illus	Part Number	Description	Quantity	Change Point	Remarks
1	MUC3764	GLASS ASSEMBLY-BODYSIDE SLIDING-5 MM GLASS-RH-TINTED	1	To (V) EA 344187	
1	MUC3765	GLASS ASSEMBLY-BODYSIDE SLIDING-5 MM GLASS-LH-TINTED	1		
2	MUC3794	• Glass-bodyside-sliding-front-Tinted	1		
3	MUC3795	• Glass-bodyside-sliding-rear-Tinted	1		
4	MUC3770	• Rail guide-draught-tinted glass	1		
5	MUC3769	• Seal	1		
6	MUC1098	• Strip-glazing	1		
7	MUC3097	• Felt-nvh	1		
8	MUC3096	• Felt-sliding glass-cab-rear panel-top	1		
9	MUC4025	• Buffer-stop-tinted glass	1		
10	MUC1484	• Glazing rubber	1		
11	MTC8947	• Channel-rear quarter glass run	1		
12	MUC3768	• Filler strip-tinted glass	1		
13	MTC8270	• Catch-tinted glass-RH	1		Part of MUC3764.
13	MTC8271	• Catch-tinted glass-LH	1		Part of MUC3765.

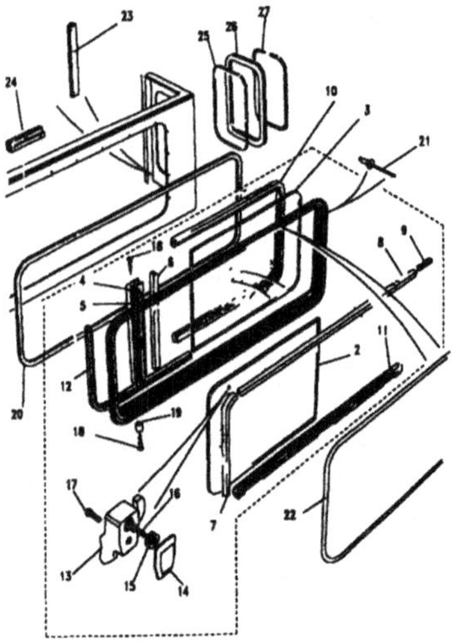

Illus	Part Number	Description	Quantity	Change Point	Remarks
1	MWC4734	GLASS ASSEMBLY-BODYSIDE SLIDING-4 MM GLASS-RH-CLEAR.	1	From (V) EA 344188	
1	MWC4735	GLASS ASSEMBLY-BODYSIDE SLIDING-4 MM GLASS-LH-CLEAR.	1		
2	MWC4728	• Glass-bodyside-sliding-front-Clear.	1		
3	MWC4730	• Glass-bodyside-sliding-rear-Clear.	1		
4	MUC3770	• Rail guide-draught-RH clear	1		
5	MWC7614	• Seal-RH clear	1		
6	MWC7615	• Strip-glazing-RH clear	1		
7	RTC6462	• Felt-nvh-RH clear	1		
9	MUC4025	• Buffer-stop-RH clear	1		
10	MWC7617	• Glazing rubber-RH clear	1		
11	MWC7612	• Channel-rear quarter glass run-RH clear	1		
12	MUC3768	• Filler strip-RH clear	1		
13	MTC8270	• Catch-clear glass-RH	1		Part of MWC4734.
13	MTC8271	• Catch-clear glass-LH	1		Part of MWC4735.

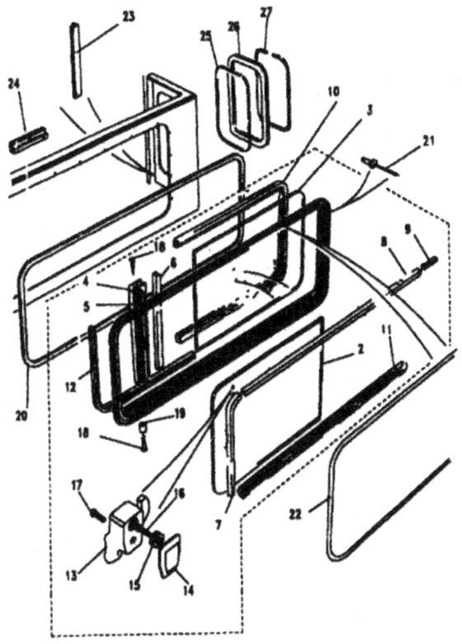

Illus	Part Number	Description	Quantity	Change Point	Remarks
1	MWC4736	GLASS ASSEMBLY-BODYSIDE SLIDING-4 MM GLASS-RH-TINTED..	1	From (V) EA 344188	
1	MWC4737	GLASS ASSEMBLY-BODYSIDE SLIDING-4 MM GLASS-LH-TINTED..	1		
2	MWC4729	• Glass-bodyside-sliding-front-Tinted.	1		
3	MWC4731	• Glass-bodyside-sliding-rear-Tinted	1		
4	MUC3770	• Rail guide-draught-tinted glass	1		
5	MWC7614	• Seal-tinted glass	1		
6	MWC7615	• Strip-glazing-tinted glass	1		
7	RTC6462	• Felt-nvh-tinted glass	1		
9	MUC4025	• Buffer-stop-tinted glass	1		
10	MWC7617	• Glazing rubber-tinted glass	1		
11	MWC7612	• Channel-rear quarter glass run-tinted glass	1		
12	MUC3768	• Filler strip-tinted glass	1		
13	MTC8270	• Catch-tinted glass-RH	1		Part of MWC4736.
13	MTC8271	• Catch-tinted glass-LH	1		Part of MWC4737.

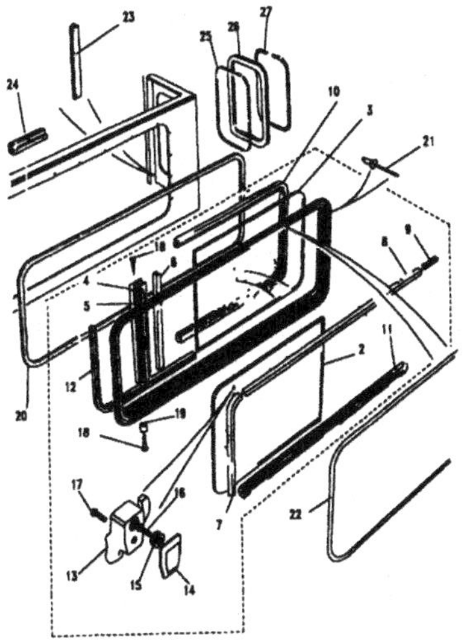

Illus	Part Number	Description	Quantity	Change Point	Remarks
14	MUC1704	Block-fixing-catch slide window	2		
15	MUC1705	Button-quarterlight catch	2		
16	MUC1706	Screw	2		
17	MUC1707	Screw	2		
18	AC606081L	Screw-self tapping-counter sunk	4		
19	MUC3771	Spacer	2		
20	MUC1008	Seal	2		
21	RU610313L	Rivet	48		
22	MUC1005	Filler strip	2		
23	MUC4542	Finisher-front-rear	4		
24	MUC1501	Finisher-upper-lower	12		
		GLASS-REAR QUARTER			
25	MTC3476	5 mm glass-back-Clear.	2	Note (1)	
25	MTC5034	5 mm glass-back-Tinted	2		
25	MWC4715	4 mm glass-back-Clear.	2	Note (2)	
25	MWC4716	4 mm glass-back-Tinted	2		
26	306287	Strip-glazing-5 mm glass	2	Note (1)	
26	MWC4772	Strip-glazing-4 mm glass	2	Note (2)	
27	306289	Filler strip	2		

CHANGE POINTS:
(1) To (V) EA 344187
(2) From (V) EA 344188

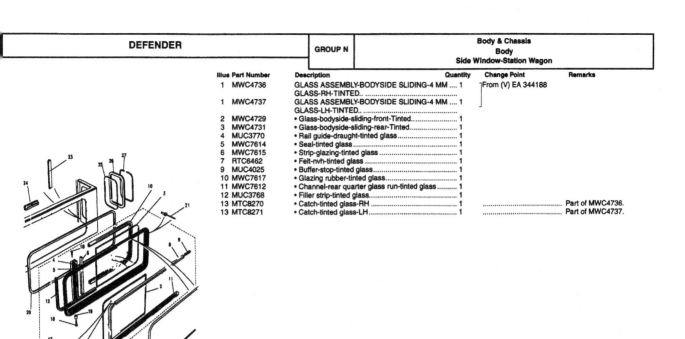

DEFENDER	GROUP N	Body & Chassis Body Side Window-Hard Top-Fixed

Illus	Part Number	Description	Quantity	Change Point	Remarks
1	MTC8251	GLASS ASSEMBLY-BODYSIDE-5 MM GLASS	2	Note (1)	
2	MTC8256	• Glass-bodyside-Clear.	2		
3	MTC8269	• Seal	2		
4	MTC8948	• Filler strip	2		
1	MWC4733	GLASS ASSEMBLY-BODYSIDE-4 MM GLASS	2	Note (2)	
2	MWC4727	• Glass-bodyside-Clear.	2		
3	MWC7686	• Seal	2		
4	MWC7685	• Filler strip	2		
5	MUC1008	Seal	2		
6	RU610313L	Rivet	48		
7	MUC1005	Filler strip	2		

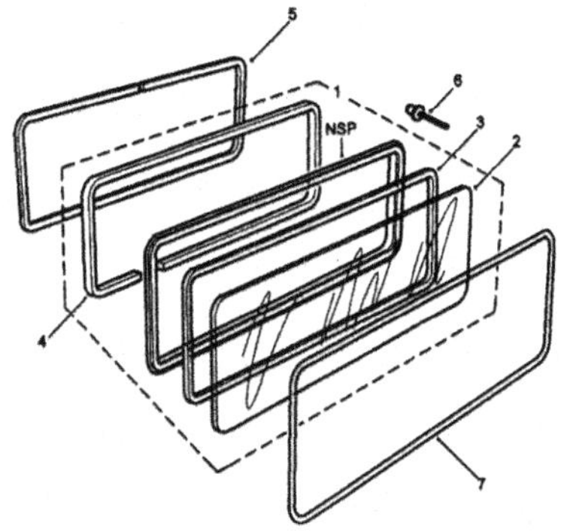

LN0223

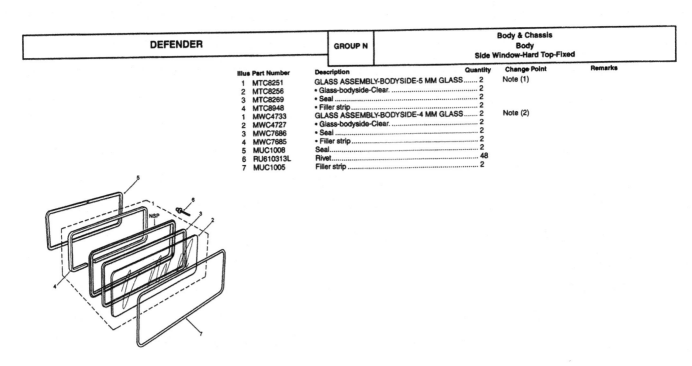

CHANGE POINTS:
(1) To (V) EA 340456
(2) From (V) EA 340457

DEFENDER	GROUP N	Body & Chassis Body Side Window-Hard Top-Sliding

Illus	Part Number	Description	Quantity	Change Point	Remarks
1	ZXC9386	GLASS ASSEMBLY-BODYSIDE SLIDING-RH	1	Note (1)	
1	ZXC9387	GLASS ASSEMBLY-BODYSIDE SLIDING-LH	1		
2	MWC4726	• Glass-backlight sliding	2		
3	MWC7625	• Catch assembly-side opening window-LH	1		
3	MWC7648	• Catch assembly-side opening window-RH	1		
4	MWC7620	• Felt-nvh	2		
5	MWC7652	• Seal	1		
1	ALR5080	GLASS ASSEMBLY-OPENING BACKLIGHT-RH	1	Note (2)	
1	ALR5081	GLASS ASSEMBLY-BODYSIDE SLIDING-LH	1		
2	MWC4726	• Glass-backlight sliding	2		
3	MWC7625	• Catch assembly-side opening window-LH	1		
3	MWC7648	• Catch assembly-side opening window-RH	1		
4	MWC7620	• Felt-nvh-RH	2		
5	MWC7652	• Seal-RH	1		
6	MTC6232	Finisher-outer	4	Note (1)	
7	AS604044	Rivet	72		
7	RU610253	Rivet	72	Note (2)	

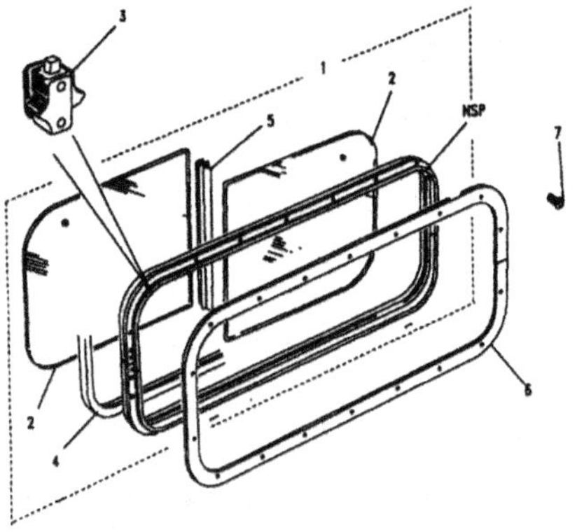

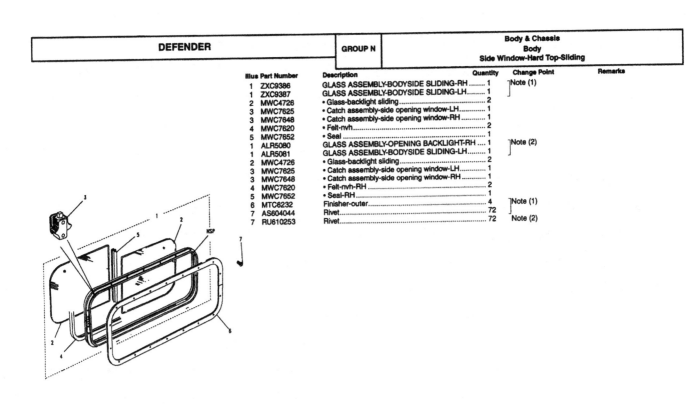

CHANGE POINTS:
(1) To (V) KA 930143
(2) From (V) KA 930144

Rear Body Upper Fixings

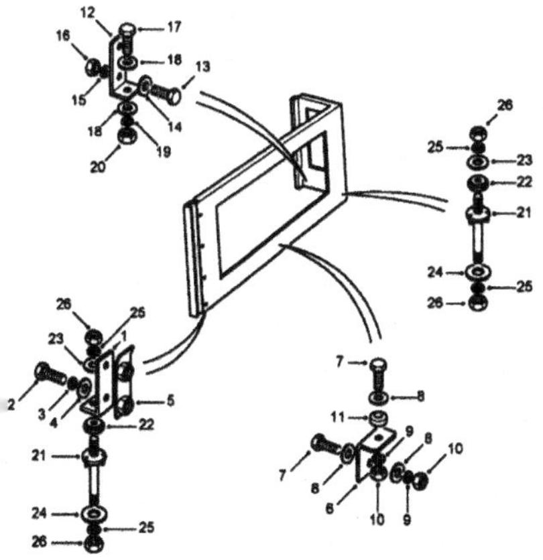

INXLE5A

Illus	Part Number	Description	Quantity	Change Point	Remarks
1	338554	Angle mounting	2		
2	FS108161L	Screw-flanged head-M8 x 16	4		
3	WL108001L	Washer-sprung-M8	2		
4	WC108051L	Washer-M8	4		
5	MUC1324	Nut plate	2		
6	332201	Bracket support	2		
7	FS106201L	Screw-flanged head-M6 x 20	4		Hard Top
8	MRC5527	Washer-plain-M6	8		
9	WL106001L	Washer-sprung-M6	4		
10	NH106041L	Nut-hexagonal-nyloc-M6	4		
7	FS106201L	Screw-flanged head-M6 x 20	8		Station Wagon
8	AFU1080	Washer-plain	12		
9	WL106001L	Washer-sprung-M6	8		
10	NH106041L	Nut-hexagonal-nyloc-M6	8		
11	338550	Buffer-stop	4		
12	338552	Bracket support	2		
13	FS106167L	Screw-flanged head-flanged head-M6 x 16	4		
14	MRC5525	Washer-plain-standard	4		
15	WL106001L	Washer-sprung-M6	4		
16	NH106041L	Nut-hexagonal-nyloc-M6	4		
17	FS108307L	Screw-flanged head-M8 x 30	2		
18	WC108051L	Washer-M8	4		
19	WL108001L	Washer-sprung-M8	8		
20	FN108047L	Nut-flange-flanged head-M8	2		
21	MRC9833	Stud	4		
22	338553	Buffer rubber	4		
23	332293	Washer	4		
24	WC108051	Washer	8		
25	WL108001L	Washer-sprung-M8	8		
26	FN108047L	Nut-flange-flanged head-M8	8		

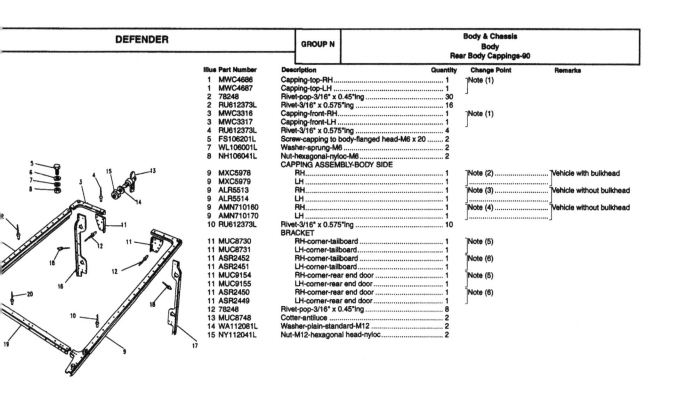

Rear Body Cappings-90

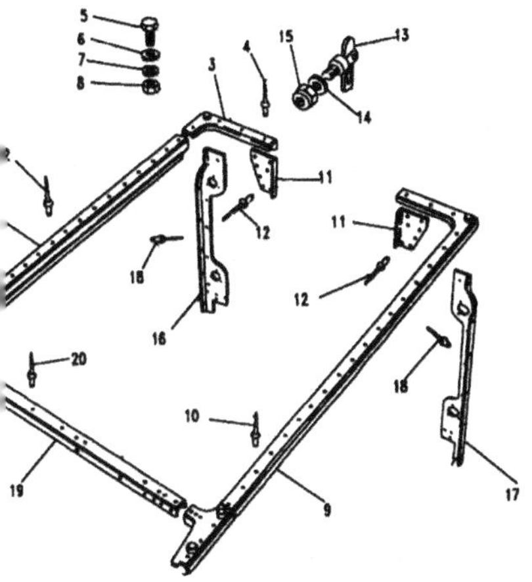

Illus	Part Number	Description	Quantity	Change Point	Remarks
1	MWC4686	Capping-top-RH	1	Note (1)	
1	MWC4687	Capping-top-LH	1		
2	78248	Rivet-pop-3/16" x 0.45"lng	30		
2	RU612373L	Rivet-3/16" x 0.575"lng	16		
3	MWC3316	Capping-front-RH	1	Note (1)	
3	MWC3317	Capping-front-LH	1		
4	RU612373L	Rivet-3/16" x 0.575"lng	4		
5	FS106201L	Screw-capping to body-flanged head-M6 x 20	2		
7	WL106001L	Washer-sprung-M6	2		
8	NH106041L	Nut-hexagonal-nyloc-M6	2		
		CAPPING ASSEMBLY-BODY SIDE			
9	MXC5978	RH	1	Note (2)	Vehicle with bulkhead
9	MXC5979	LH	1		
9	ALR5513	RH	1	Note (3)	Vehicle without bulkhead
9	ALR5514	LH	1		
9	AMN710160	RH	1	Note (4)	Vehicle without bulkhead
9	AMN710170	LH	1		
10	RU612373L	Rivet-3/16" x 0.575"lng	10		
		BRACKET			
11	MUC8730	RH-corner-tailboard	1	Note (5)	
11	MUC8731	LH-corner-tailboard	1		
11	ASR2452	RH-corner-tailboard	1	Note (6)	
11	ASR2451	LH-corner-tailboard	1		
11	MUC9154	RH-corner-rear end door	1	Note (5)	
11	MUC9155	LH-corner-rear end door	1		
11	ASR2450	RH-corner-rear end door	1	Note (6)	
11	ASR2449	LH-corner-rear end door	1		
12	78248	Rivet-pop-3/16" x 0.45"lng	8		
13	MUC8748	Cotter-antiluce	2		
14	WA112081L	Washer-plain-standard-M12	2		
15	NY112041L	Nut-M12-hexagonal head-nyloc	2		

CHANGE POINTS:
(1) To (V) December 1989 approx
(2) From (V) January 1990 approx
(3) To (V) ZA 999999
(4) From (V) 2A 622424
(5) To (V) VA 109548
(6) From (V) VA 109549

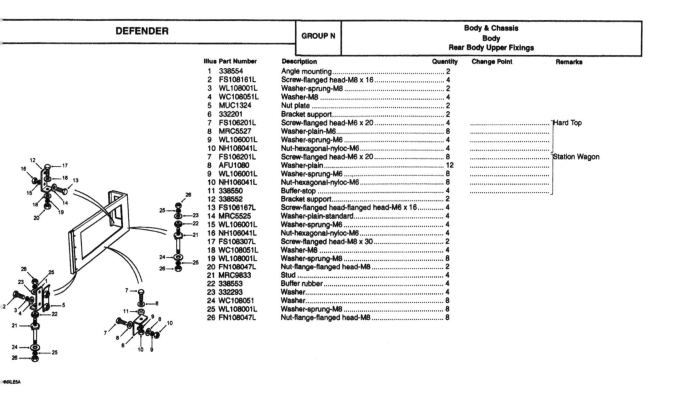

DEFENDER

GROUP N

Body & Chassis
Body
Rear Body Cappings-90

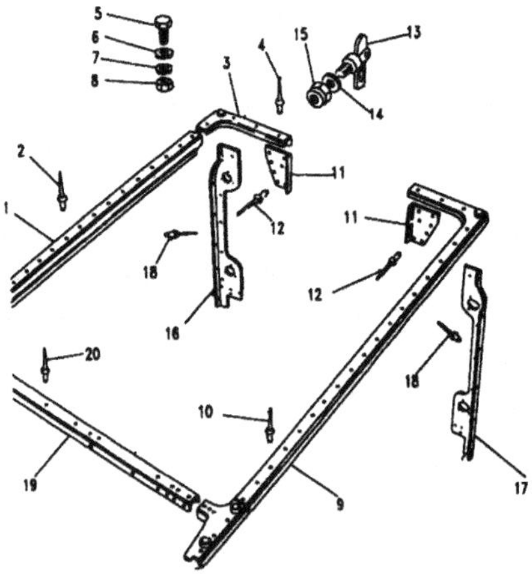

Illus	Part Number	Description	Quantity	Change Point	Remarks
		CAPPING-REAR			
16	MUC8716	RH	1	Note (1)	Note (1)
17	MUC8717	LH	1		
16	MXC8934	RH	1	Note (2)	
17	MXC8935	LH	1		
16	ALR7128	RH	1	Note (3)	
17	ALR7129	LH	1		
16	ALR9104	E prime-RH	1	Note (4)	
17	ALR9103	E prime-LH	1		
16	AQL710020	E prime-RH	1	Note (5)	
17	AQL710030	E prime-LH	1		
16	ALR8082	RH	1	Note (7)	Note (2)
17	ALR8081	LH	1		
16	AQL710060	RH-E prime	1	Note (8)	
17	AQL710070	LH-E prime	1		
18	78248	Rivet-pop-3/16" x 0.45"lng	30		
19	MWC2938	Capping	1		
	MTC7513	Edging strip	A/R	To (V) LA 939975	Germany
	MTC8334	Finisher-corner capping	2		
20	RU608313L	Rivet-aluminium-1/8" x 0.482"lng	2		

CHANGE POINTS:
(1) To (V) March 1990
(2) From (V) April 1990 To (V) LA 939975
(3) From (V) MA 939976 To (V) TA 995738
(4) From (V) TA 995739 To (V) WA 138479
(5) From (V) WA 138480 To (V) 11863BL
(7) To (V) WA 138479
(8) From (V) WA 138480

Remarks:
(1) Rest of World UK
(2) NAS 49 States NAS California

DEFENDER

GROUP N

Body & Chassis
Body
Rear Body Cappings-110 Regular

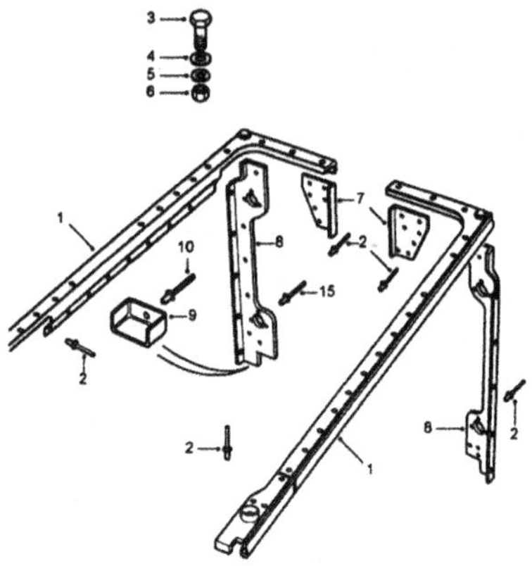

AJNXKESA

Illus	Part Number	Description	Quantity	Change Point	Remarks
		CAPPING ASSEMBLY-BODY SIDE			
1	MWC2120	RH	1	Note (1)	
1	MWC2121	LH	1		
1	MXC5973	RH-Galvanised	1	Note (2)	
1	MXC5974	LH-Galvanised	1		
2	78248	Rivet-pop-3/16" x 0.45"lng	A/R		
2	RU608313L	Rivet-aluminium-1/8" x 0.482"lng	2		
3	FS106207L	Screw-flanged head-M6 x 20	2		
4	WA106001L	Washer-M6	4		
5	WL106001L	Washer-sprung-M6	2		
6	NH106041L	Nut-hexagonal-nyloc-M6	2		
		BRACKET			
7	MUC8730	RH-corner-tailboard	1	Note (3)	
7	MUC8731	LH-corner-tailboard	1		
7	ASR2452	RH-corner-tailboard	1	Note (4)	
7	ASR2451	LH-corner-tailboard	1		
7	MUC9154	RH-corner-rear end door	1	Note (3)	
7	MUC9155	LH-corner-rear end door	1		
7	ASR2450	RH-corner-rear end door	1	Note (4)	
7	ASR2449	LH-corner-rear end door	1		
	MUC8748	Cotter-antiluce	2		
4	WA112081L	Washer-plain-standard-M12	2		
		CAPPING-REAR			
8	ALR9104	E prime-RH	1	Note (5)	
8	ALR9103	E prime-LH	1		
8	AQL710020	E prime-RH	1	Note (6)	
8	AQL710030	E prime-LH	1		
9	MWC2938	Capping	1		
10	RA612373L	Rivet-3/16" x 0.575"lng	39		
	MTC8334	Finisher-corner capping	2		

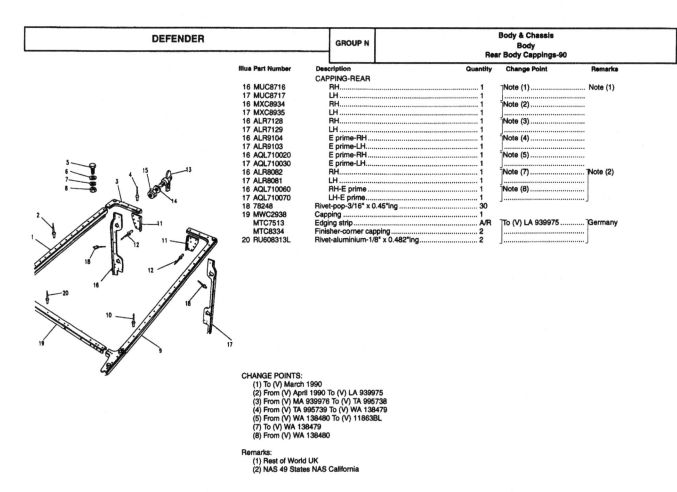

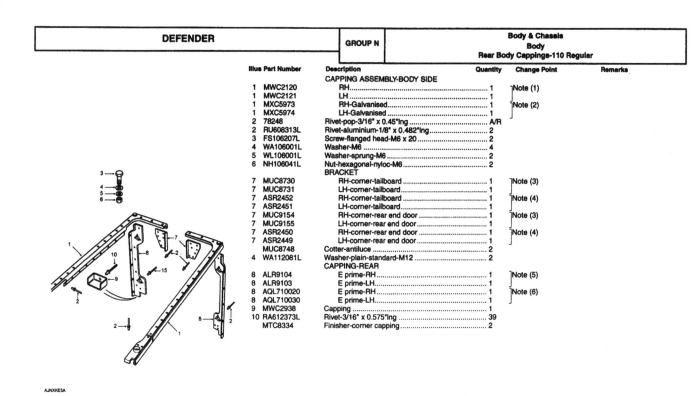

CHANGE POINTS:
(1) To (V) LA 939975
(2) From (V) MA 939976
(3) To (V) VA 109548
(4) From (V) VA 109549
(5) To (V) WA 138479
(6) From (V) WA 138480 To (V) 11863BL

Illus	Part Number	Description	Quantity	Change Point	Remarks
		CAPPING			
1	RTC5066	RH-2 piece	1	Note (1)	
1	RTC5067	LH-2 piece	1		
1	MWC4662	RH-2 piece	1	Note (2)	
1	MWC4663	LH-2 piece	1		
2	78248	Rivet-pop-3/16" x 0.45"lng	32		
3	MWC3316	Capping-front-RH	1		
3	MWC3317	Capping-front-LH	1		
4	RA612373L	Rivet-3/16" x 0.575"lng	12		
4	78248	Rivet-pop-3/16" x 0.45"lng	12		
5	FS106207L	Screw-flanged head-M6 x 20	2		
6	WA106001L	Washer-M6	4		
7	WL106001L	Washer-sprung-M6	2		
8	NH106041L	Nut-hexagonal-nyloc-M6	2		
		CAPPING ASSEMBLY-BODY SIDE			
9	MXC5968	RH-Galvanised-one piece	1	Note (3)	
9	MXC5969	LH-Galvanised-one piece	1		
9	ASR1390	RH-one piece	1	Note (4)	
9	ASR1391	LH-one piece	1		
10	78248	Rivet-pop-3/16" x 0.45"lng	38		
10	RU612373L	Rivet-3/16" x 0.575"lng	6		
		BRACKET			
11	MUC9154	RH-corner-rear end door	1	Note (5)	
11	MUC9155	LH-corner-rear end door	1		
11	ASR2450	RH-corner-rear end door	1	Note (6)	
11	ASR2449	LH-corner-rear end door	1		
12	78248	Rivet-pop-3/16" x 0.45"lng	6		

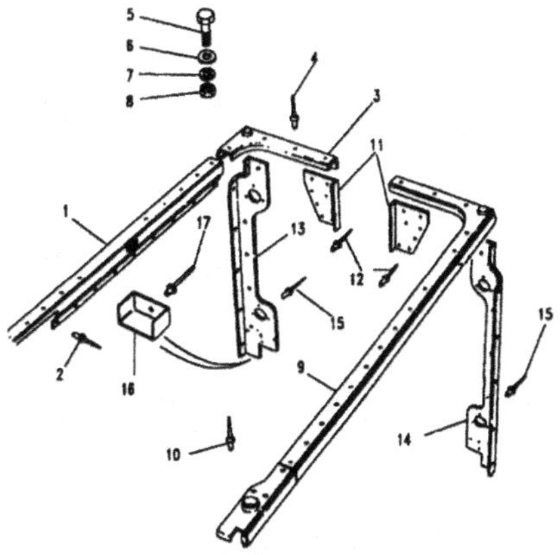

CHANGE POINTS:
(1) To (V) EA 314075
(2) From (V) EA 314076
(3) To (V) WA 138479
(4) From (V) WA 138480
(5) To (V) VA 109548
(6) From (V) VA 109549

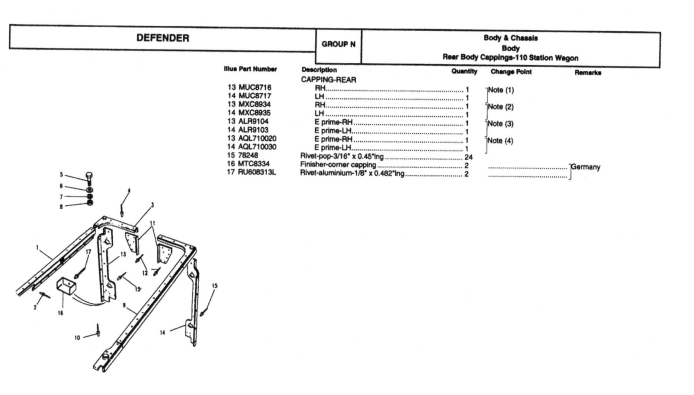

Illus	Part Number	Description	Quantity	Change Point	Remarks
		CAPPING-REAR			
13	MUC8716	RH	1	Note (1)	
14	MUC8717	LH	1		
13	MXC8934	RH	1	Note (2)	
14	MXC8935	LH	1		
13	ALR9104	E prime-RH	1	Note (3)	
14	ALR9103	E prime-LH	1		
13	AQL710020	E prime-RH	1	Note (4)	
14	AQL710030	E prime-LH	1		
15	78248	Rivet-pop-3/16" x 0.45"lng	24		
16	MTC8334	Finisher-corner capping	2		Germany
17	RU608313L	Rivet-aluminium-1/8" x 0.482"lng	2		

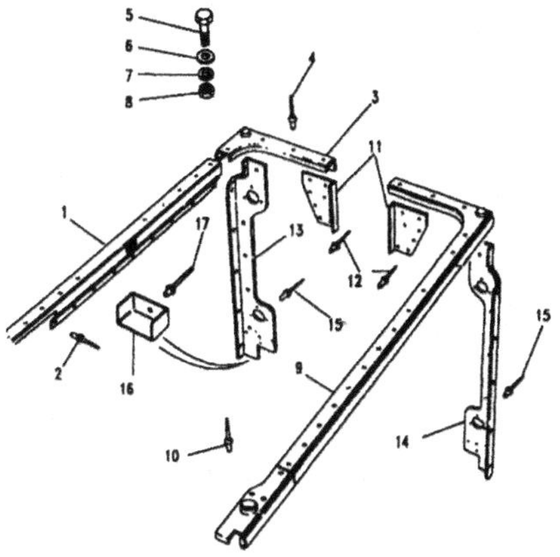

CHANGE POINTS:
(1) To (V) February 1990
(2) From (V) March 1990 To (V) LA 939975
(3) From (V) MA 939976 To (V) WA 138479
(4) From (V) WA 138480

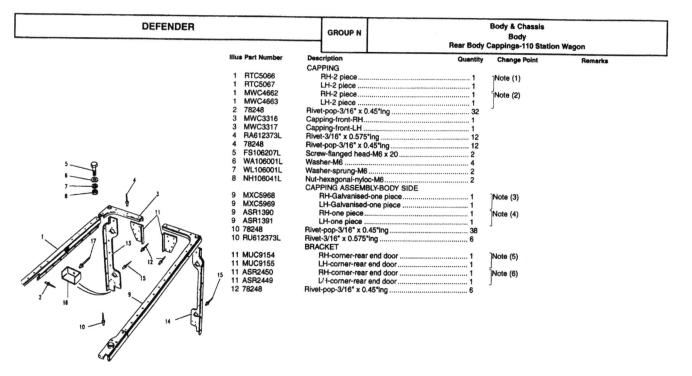

Body
Rear Body Cappings-110 Crew Cab

Illus	Part Number	Description	Quantity	Change Point	Remarks
	AMN710020	Capping assembly-body side-RH	1		Crew Cab 110"
	AMN710030	Capping assembly-body side-LH	1		Crew Cab 110"

NOT ILLUSTRATED
PAS ILLUSTREE
NICHT ILLUSTRIERT
SENZA IL DISEGNO
SIN EL DISENO
SEM ILLUSTRACAO
NIET AFGEBEELD

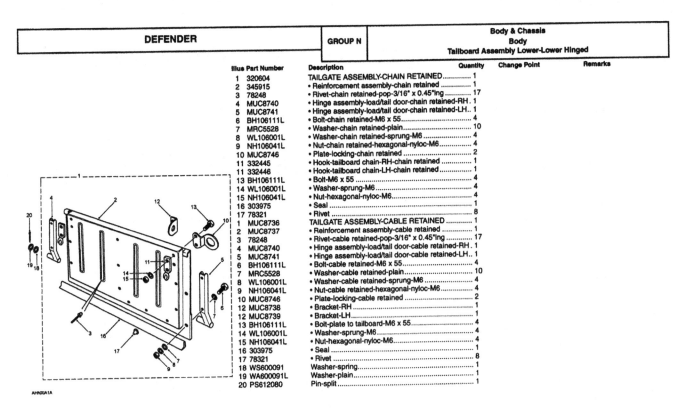

TF 0007

Body
Tailboard Assembly Lower-Lower Hinged

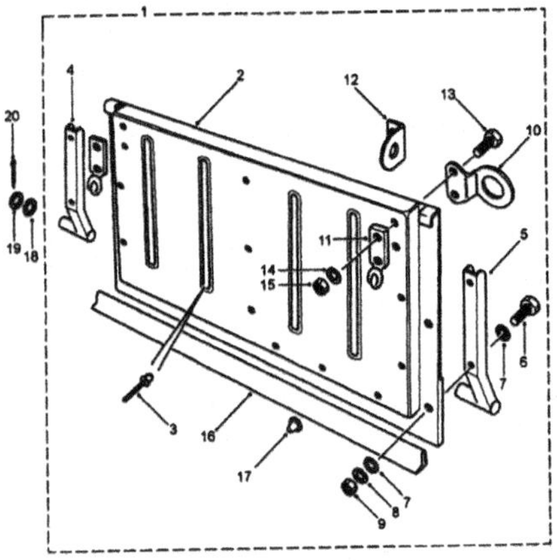

AHNXIA1A

Illus	Part Number	Description	Quantity	Change Point	Remarks
1	320604	TAILGATE ASSEMBLY-CHAIN RETAINED	1		
2	345915	• Reinforcement assembly-chain retained	1		
3	78248	• Rivet-chain retained-pop-3/16" x 0.45"lng	17		
4	MUC8740	• Hinge assembly-load/tail door-chain retained-RH	1		
5	MUC8741	• Hinge assembly-load/tail door-chain retained-LH	1		
6	BH106111L	• Bolt-chain retained-M6 x 55	4		
7	MRC5528	• Washer-chain retained-plain	10		
8	WL106001L	• Washer-chain retained-sprung-M6	4		
9	NH106041L	• Nut-chain retained-hexagonal-nyloc-M6	4		
10	MUC8746	• Plate-locking-chain retained	2		
11	332445	• Hook-tailboard chain-RH-chain retained	1		
11	332446	• Hook-tailboard chain-LH-chain retained	1		
13	BH106111L	• Bolt-M6 x 55	4		
14	WL106001L	• Washer-sprung-M6	4		
15	NH106041L	• Nut-hexagonal-nyloc-M6	4		
16	303975	• Seal	1		
17	78321	• Rivet	8		
1	MUC8736	TAILGATE ASSEMBLY-CABLE RETAINED	1		
2	MUC8737	• Reinforcement assembly-cable retained	1		
3	78248	• Rivet-cable retained-pop-3/16" x 0.45"lng	17		
4	MUC8740	• Hinge assembly-load/tail door-cable retained-RH	1		
5	MUC8741	• Hinge assembly-load/tail door-cable retained-LH	1		
6	BH106111L	• Bolt-cable retained-M6 x 55	4		
7	MRC5528	• Washer-cable retained-plain	10		
8	WL106001L	• Washer-cable retained-sprung-M6	4		
9	NH106041L	• Nut-cable retained-hexagonal-nyloc-M6	4		
10	MUC8746	• Plate-locking-cable retained	2		
12	MUC8738	• Bracket-RH	1		
12	MUC8739	• Bracket-LH	1		
13	BH106111L	• Bolt-plate to tailboard-M6 x 55	4		
14	WL106001L	• Washer-sprung-M6	4		
15	NH106041L	• Nut-hexagonal-nyloc-M6	4		
16	303975	• Seal	1		
17	78321	• Rivet	8		
18	WS600091	Washer-spring	1		
19	WA600091L	Washer-plain	1		
20	PS612080	Pin-split	1		

DEFENDER | **GROUP N** | **Body & Chassis** / **Body** / **Tailboard Assembly Lower-Side Hinged**

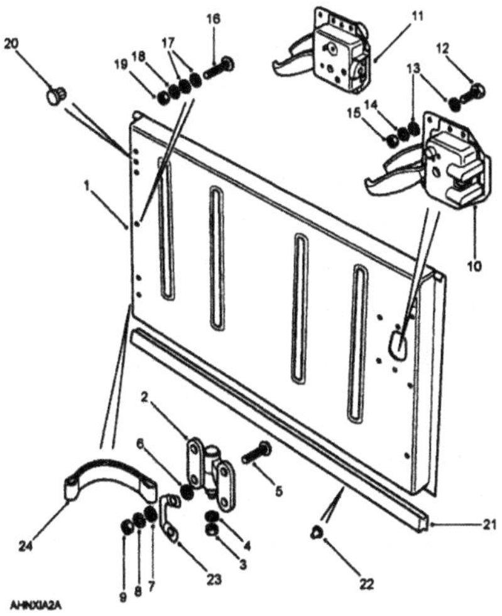

Illus	Part Number	Description	Quantity	Change Point	Remarks
1	ALR7259	Tailgate assembly-spare wheel carrier	1		
1	MUC8707	Tailgate assembly-less spare wheel carrier-slam-type latch	1		
1	RTC6279	TAILGATE ASSEMBLY-LESS SPARE WHEEL CARRIER-ANTI BURST-TYPE LATCH	1		
	MUC8737	• Reinforcement assembly-cable retained	1		
	78248	• Rivet-pop-3/16" x 0.45"lng	17		
	AFU1350	• Monobolt-1/4"	5		
2	346341	Hinge assembly-load/tail door lower-middle	2		
3	257450	Nut-hinge to tailgate	2	Note (1)	
4	WA106041L	Washer-6mm	2		
5	SE108601	Screw-hinge to tailgate-M8 x 60	4		
6	WC108051L	Washer-M8	1		
7	WA108051L	Washer-8mm	2		
8	WL108001L	Washer-sprung-M8	4		
9	NY108041L	Nut-nyloc-M8	4		
10	STC2873	Lock-tailgate-basic-RH	1		
11	395041	Lock-tailgate-anti burst	1		
12	SE106201L	Screw-lock to tailgate-pan head-M6 x 20	4		
13	WA106041L	Washer-6mm	10		
14	WL106001L	Washer-sprung-M6	4		
15	NY106047L	Nut-hexagonal head-nyloc-M6	4		
16	SE106501	Screw-redundant holes	5		
17	WA106041L	Washer-6mm	10		
18	WL106001L	Washer-sprung-M6	5		
19	NY106047L	Nut-hexagonal head-nyloc-M6	5		
20	79086L	Rivet-plastic-drive-redundant holes	1		
21	303975	Seal	1		
22	RT612283	Rivet-seal to tailboard	8	Note (2)	
22	RU612503	Rivet-3/16" x 0.7lng	8	Note (3)	
23	MTC7523	Cleat	1		
24	398776	Check strap	1		

NOTE:CHECK WHAT LOCKS ARE FITTED PRIOR TO ORDERING

CHANGE POINTS:
(1) To (V) TA 989478
(2) To (V) YA 199999
(3) From (V) YA 600001

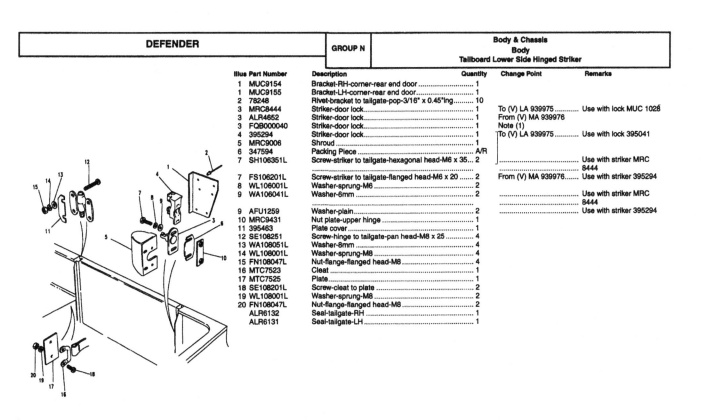

DEFENDER | **GROUP N** | **Body & Chassis** / **Body** / **Tailboard Lower Side Hinged Striker**

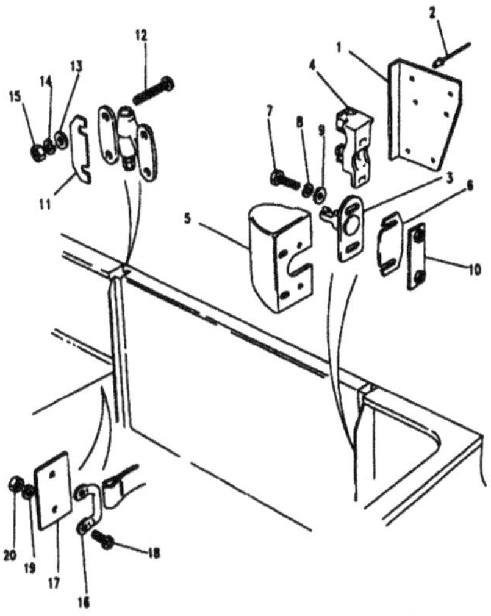

Illus	Part Number	Description	Quantity	Change Point	Remarks
1	MUC9154	Bracket-RH-corner-rear end door	1		
1	MUC9155	Bracket-LH-corner-rear end door	1		
2	78248	Rivet-bracket to tailgate-pop-3/16" x 0.45"lng	10		
3	MRC8444	Striker-door lock	1	To (V) LA 939975	Use with lock MUC 1026
3	ALR4652	Striker-door lock	1	From (V) MA 939976	
3	FQB000040	Striker-door lock	1	Note (1)	
4	395294	Striker-door lock	1	To (V) LA 939975	Use with lock 395041
5	MRC9006	Shroud	1		
6	347594	Packing Piece	A/R		
7	SH106351L	Screw-striker to tailgate-hexagonal head-M6 x 35	2		Use with striker MRC 8444
7	FS106201L	Screw-striker to tailgate-flanged head-M6 x 20	2	From (V) MA 939976	Use with striker 395294
8	WL106001L	Washer-sprung-M6	2		
9	WA106041L	Washer-6mm	2		Use with striker MRC 8444
9	AFU1259	Washer-plain	2		Use with striker 395294
10	MRC9431	Nut plate-upper hinge	1		
11	395463	Plate cover	1		
12	SE108251	Screw-hinge to tailgate-pan head-M8 x 25	4		
13	WA108051L	Washer-8mm	4		
14	WL108001L	Washer-sprung-M8	4		
15	FN108047L	Nut-flange-flanged head-M8	4		
16	MTC7523	Cleat	1		
17	MTC7525	Plate	1		
18	SE108201L	Screw-cleat to plate	2		
19	WL108001L	Washer-sprung-M8	2		
20	FN108047L	Nut-flange-flanged head-M8	2		
	ALR6132	Seal-tailgate-RH	1		
	ALR6131	Seal-tailgate-LH	1		

CHANGE POINTS:
(1) From (V) MA 939976

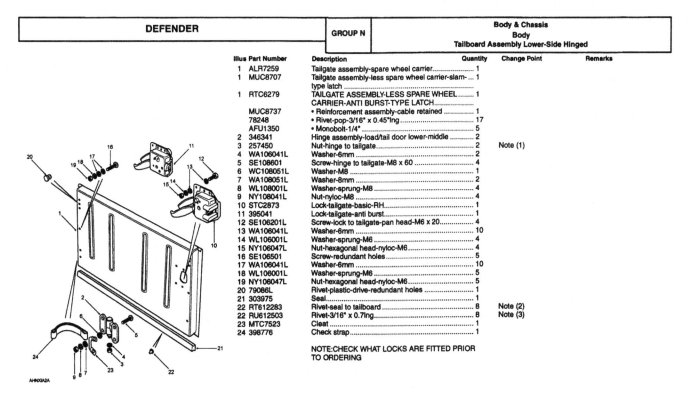

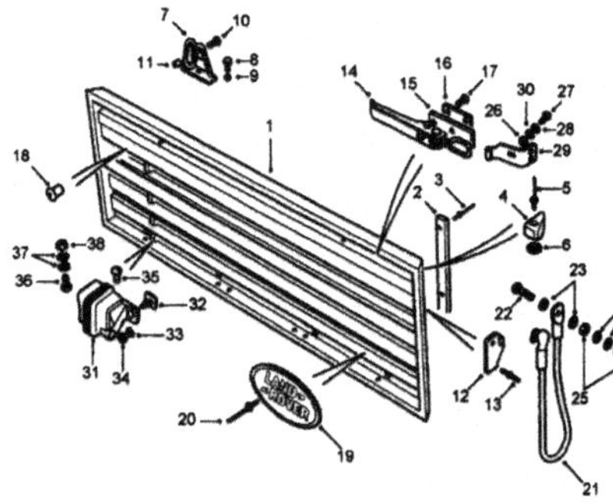

AJNXIA4A

Illus	Part Number	Description	Quantity	Change Point	Remarks
1	MTC3908	Tailgate assembly	1		
2	MTC3139	Rubbing strip-tailgate	3		
3	RU608183L	Rivet	12		
4	MTC1531	Buffer-stop	2		
5	RJ608603	Rivet	2		
6	WA103001L	Washer-plain	2		
7	MTC1439	Bracket-lashing	2		
8	FS106201L	Screw-flanged head-M6 x 20	2		
9	WL106001L	Washer-sprung-M6	2		
10	ACU3530	Rivet	2		
11	AAU6774	Collar	2		
12	MTC4824	Bracket-cable	2		
13	AFU1841	Monobolt	4		
14	MTC3917	Latch assembly-tailgate	2		
15	MTC4846	Plate-rubbing strip fixing	2		
16	MTC4888	Plate	2		
17	SF108251	Screw-fixing plate	4		
18	AFU1876	Rivet	2		
19	MTC4460	Badge	1		
20	AB606031L	Screw-badge-self tapping-No 6 x 3/8	2		
21	RRC5539	Cable-retention	2		
22	FS108307L	Screw-cable-flanged head-M8 x 30	2		
23	WA108051L	Washer-8mm	8		
24	WL108001L	Washer-sprung-M8	2		
	FN108047L	Nut-flange-flanged head-M8	4		
26	MTC4844	Catch-RH	1		
26	MTC4845	Catch-LH	1		
27	FS106255L	Screw-catch-flanged head-M6 x 25	6		
28	WC106041L	Washer-M6-oversize	6		
29	WL106001L	Washer-sprung-M6	6		
30	WC106041L	Washer-M6-oversize	A/R		
31	MTC3556	Hinge assembly-load/tail door	4		
32	MTC3557	Bolt-fixing hinge	8		
33	WA108051L	Washer-8mm	8		
34	FN108047L	Nut-flange-flanged head-M8	8		
35	SH106141L	Screw-hexagonal head-M6 x 14	4		
36	FS108257L	Screw-flanged head-M8 x 25	8		
37	WA108051L	Washer-8mm	16		
38	NY108041L	Nut-nyloc-M8	8		
	MTC3923	Seal-tailgate	1		

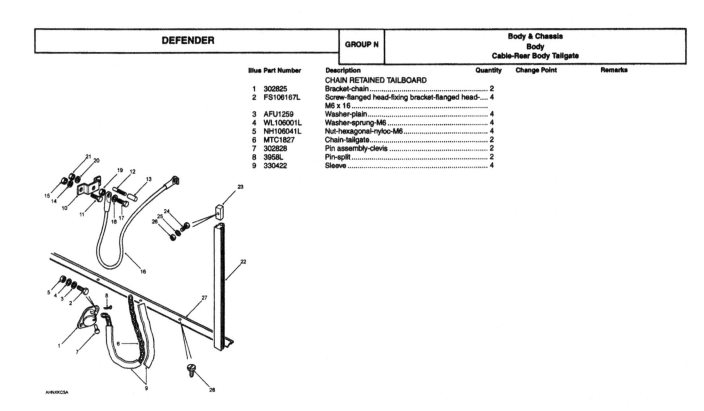

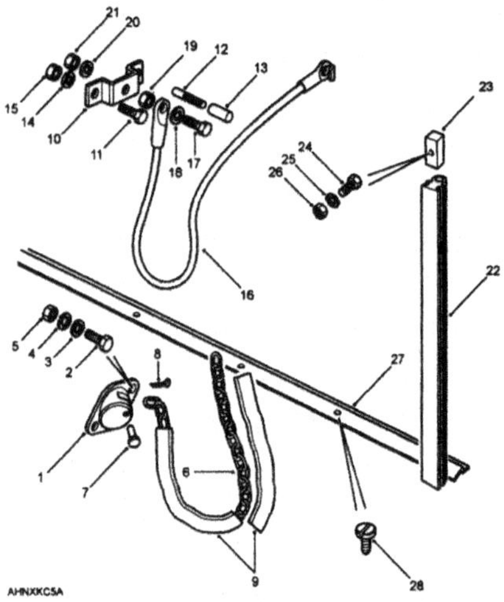

AHNXKC5A

Illus	Part Number	Description	Quantity	Change Point	Remarks
		CHAIN RETAINED TAILBOARD			
1	302825	Bracket-chain	2		
2	FS106167L	Screw-flanged head-fixing bracket-flanged head-M6 x 16	4		
3	AFU1259	Washer-plain	4		
4	WL106001L	Washer-sprung-M6	4		
5	NH106041L	Nut-hexagonal-nyloc-M6	4		
6	MTC1827	Chain-tailgate	2		
7	302828	Pin assembly-clevis	2		
8	3958L	Pin-split	2		
9	330422	Sleeve	4		

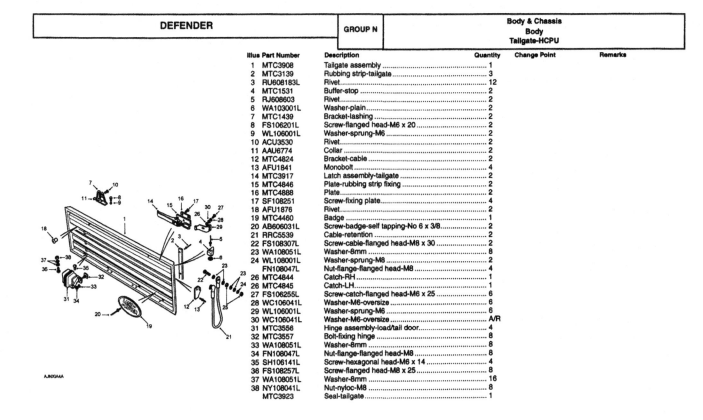

Illus	Part Number	Description	Quantity	Change Point	Remarks
		CABLE RETAINED TAILBOARD			
10	MUC8759	Bracket-cable	2		
11	FS106167L	Screw-flanged head-fixing bracket-flanged head-M6 x 16	4	To (V) EA 351222	
11	FS106167L	Screw-flanged head-fixing bracket-flanged head-M6 x 16	2	From (V) EA 351223	
12	RRC5533	Stud	2		
13	RRC5677	Cover-protector	2		
14	WL106001L	Washer-sprung-M6	4		
15	NH106041L	Nut-hexagonal-nyloc-M6	4		
16	RRC5539	Cable-retention	2		
17	FS108257L	Screw-cable to bracket-flanged head-M8 x 25	2		
18	WC108051L	Washer-M8	2		
19	NT108041L	Nut-hexagonal head	2		
20	WA108051L	Washer-8mm	2	Note (1)	
21	FN108047L	Nut-flange-flanged head-M8	1		
20	WC108051L	Washer-M8	2	Note (2)	
21	NT108041L	Nut-hexagonal head	2		

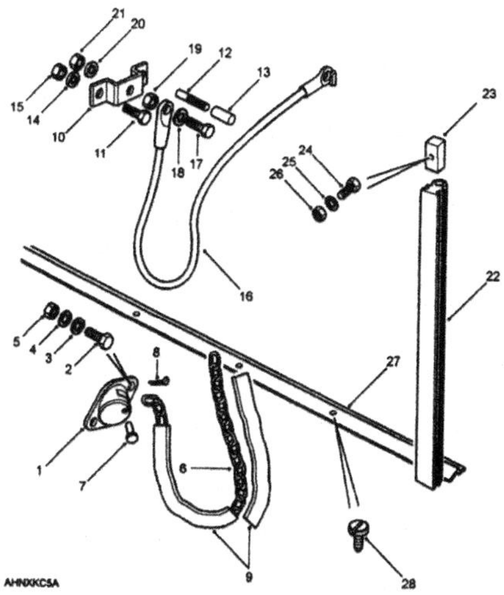

AHNXKC5A

CHANGE POINTS:
(1) To (V) EA 351222
(2) From (V) EA 351223

Illus	Part Number	Description	Quantity	Change Point	Remarks
22	MTC4164	Seal-tailgate-RH	1	Note (1)	
22	MTC4165	Seal-tailgate-LH	1		
22	CKE101100	Seal-tailgate-RH	1	Note (2)	
22	CKE101110	Seal-tailgate-LH	1		
23	332146	Buffer-tailgate	2		
24	SP104121	Screw-fixing buffer	2		
25	WC104001L	Washer-plain	2		
26	NH104041L	Nut-hexagonal-M4	2		
27	330145	Cover-protector	1		
28	AB606041L	Screw-protector fixing-self tapping-No 6 x 1/2	7		

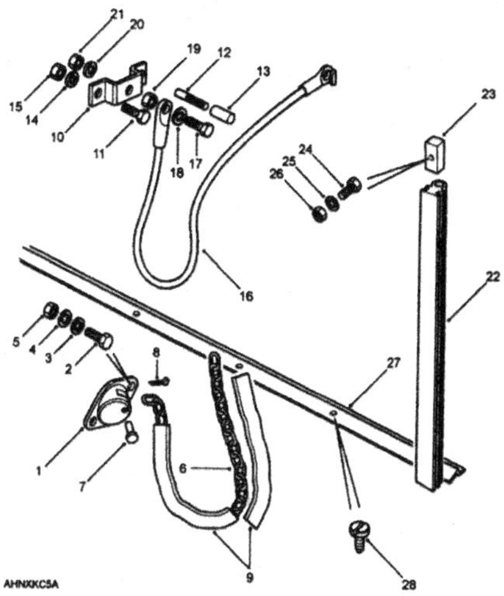

AHNXKC5A

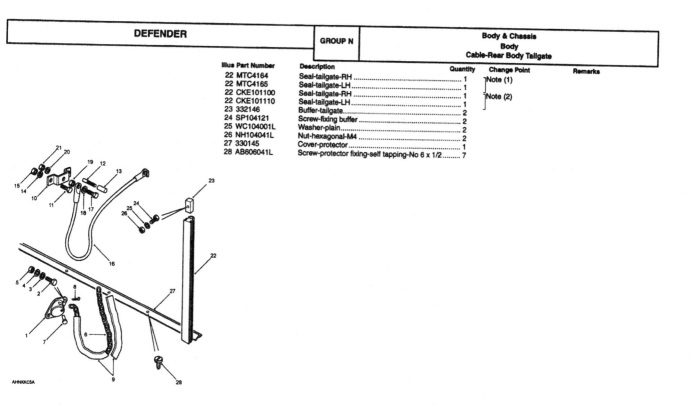

CHANGE POINTS:
(1) To (V) XA 167599
(2) From (V) XA 167600

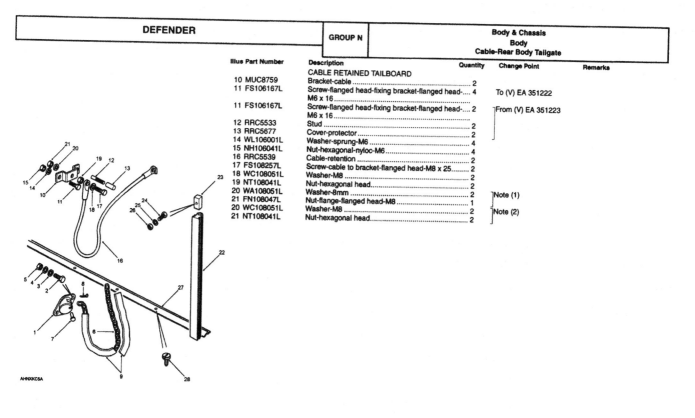

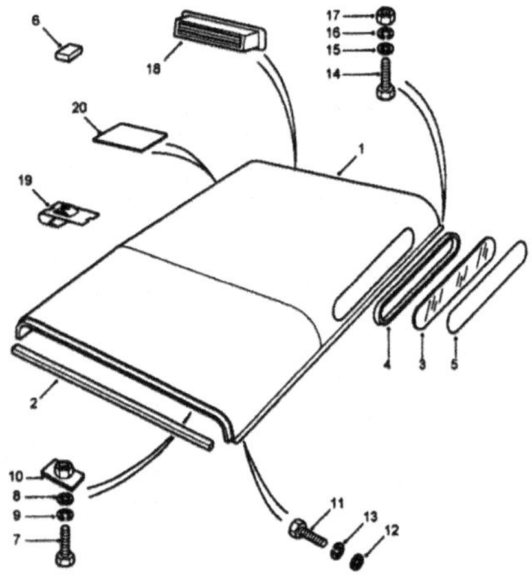

LN0049

Illus	Part Number	Description	Quantity	Change Point	Remarks
		ROOF ASSEMBLY			
1	MWC6697NUC	without Alpine lights-less sunroof-Alpine White	1	Note (1)	
1	AKA710020NUC	without Alpine lights-less sunroof-Alpine White	1	Note (2)	
1	AKA710020NAL	without Alpine lights-less sunroof-Chawton White	1	Note (2)	
1	AKA710170NAL	without Alpine lights-less sunroof-Chawton White	1	Note (3)	
1	MWC6696NUC	Roof assembly-with alpine lights-less sunroof-Alpine White	1	Note (1)	
1	AKA710010NAL	Roof assembly-with alpine lights-less sunroof-Chawton White	1	Note (4)	
		ROOF ASSEMBLY			
1	MWC6273	with alpine lights-with sunroof-Alpine White	1	Note (5)	
1	MWC6907NUC	with alpine lights-with sunroof-Alpine White	1	Note (6)	
1	AKB710010NAL	with alpine lights-with sunroof-Chawton White	1	Note (7)	90" except 50 LE
1	AKB710020NAL	with alpine lights-with sunroof-Chawton White	1	Note (7)	50 LE
1	AKA710620NAL	without Alpine lights-less sunroof-Chawton White	1	Note (8)	90"
1	AKA710610NAL	with alpine lights-less sunroof-Chawton White	1	Note (8)	90"
1	AKB710180NAL	with alpine lights-with sunroof-Chawton White	1	Note (8)	90" except 50 LE

CHANGE POINTS:
(1) To (V) WA 138479
(2) From (V) WA 138480 To (V) WA 159806
(3) From (V) XA 159807
(4) From (V) WA 138480
(5) From (V) EA 314369 To (V) EA 345885
(6) From (V) FA 345886 To (V) WA 138479
(7) From (V) 2002MY
(8) From (V) 2A 622424

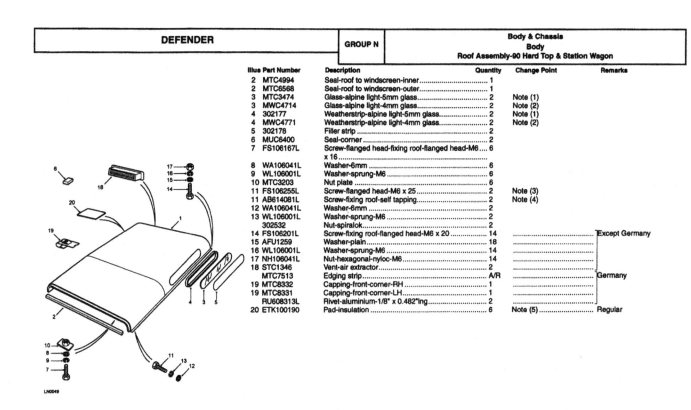

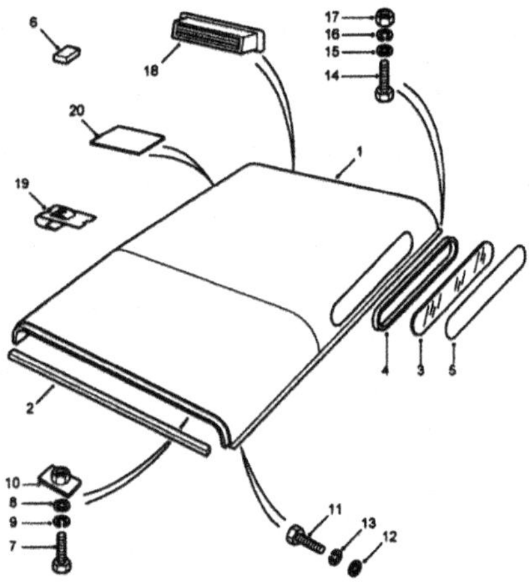

LN0049

Illus	Part Number	Description	Quantity	Change Point	Remarks
2	MTC4994	Seal-roof to windscreen-inner	1		
2	MTC6568	Seal-roof to windscreen-outer	1		
3	MTC3474	Glass-alpine light-5mm glass	2	Note (1)	
3	MWC4714	Glass-alpine light-4mm glass	2	Note (2)	
4	302177	Weatherstrip-alpine light-5mm glass	2	Note (1)	
4	MWC4771	Weatherstrip-alpine light-4mm glass	2	Note (2)	
5	302178	Filler strip	2		
6	MUC6400	Seal-corner	2		
7	FS106167L	Screw-flanged head-fixing roof-flanged head-M6 x 16	6		
8	WA106041L	Washer-6mm	6		
9	WL106001L	Washer-sprung-M6	6		
10	MTC3203	Nut plate	6		
11	FS106255L	Screw-flanged head-M6 x 25	2	Note (3)	
11	AB614081L	Screw-fixing roof-self tapping	2	Note (4)	
12	WA106041L	Washer-6mm	2		
13	WL106001L	Washer-sprung-M6	2		
	302532	Nut-spiralok	2		
14	FS106201L	Screw-fixing roof-flanged head-M6 x 20	14		Except Germany
15	AFU1259	Washer-plain	18		
16	WL106001L	Washer-sprung-M6	14		
17	NH106041L	Nut-hexagonal-nyloc-M6	14		
18	STC1346	Vent-air extractor	2		
	MTC7513	Edging strip	A/R		Germany
19	MTC8332	Capping-front-corner-RH	1		
19	MTC8331	Capping-front-corner-LH	1		
	RU608313L	Rivet-aluminium-1/8" x 0.482"lng	2		
20	ETK100190	Pad-insulation	6	Note (5)	Regular

CHANGE POINTS:
(1) To (V) EA 344187
(2) From (V) EA 344188
(3) To (V) HA 702447
(4) From (V) HA 702448
(5) From (V) XA 159807

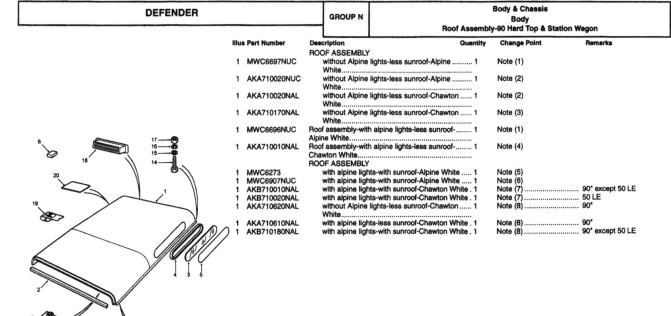

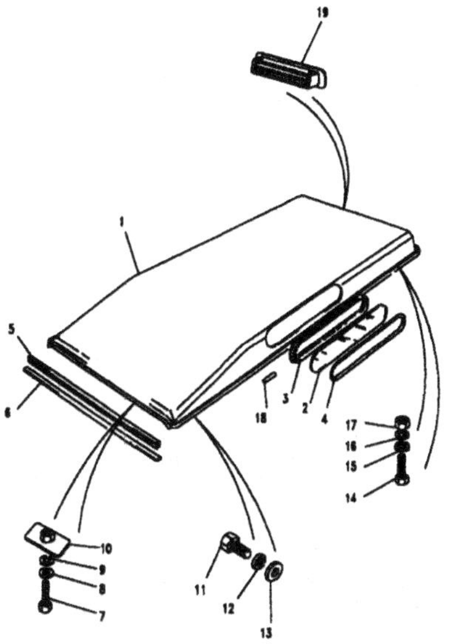

Illus	Part Number	Description	Quantity	Change Point	Remarks
		ROOF ASSEMBLY			
1	MWC6698NUC	Alpine White-less sunroof	1	Note (1)	Station Wagon
1	AKA710060NUC	Alpine White-less sunroof	1	Note (2)	
1	AKA710060NAL	Chawton White-Chawton White-less sunroof-less sunroof	1	Note (3)	
		ROOF ASSEMBLY			
1	MWC5217	with sunroof-external stiffeners	1	Note (4)	Station Wagon
1	MWC6908NUC	Alpine White-with sunroof-internal stiffeners	1	Note (5)	
1	AKB710030NUC	Alpine White-with sunroof	1	Note (2)	
1	AKB710030NAL	Chawton White-with sunroof	1	Note (3)	
		ROOF ASSEMBLY			
1	MWC6699NUC	internal stiffeners-Alpine White	1	Note (1)	Regular Hard Top
1	AKA710070NUC	internal stiffeners-Alpine White	1	Note (2)	Regular Hard Top
1	AKA710070NAL	internal stiffeners-Chawton White	1	Note (6)	Regular Hard Top
1	AKA710180NAL	Chawton White	1	Note (7)	Regular Hard Top
1	AKA710600NAL	Chawton White	1	Note (8)	Regular Hard Top
1	AKA710590NAL	Chawton White-less sunroof	1	Note (8)	Station Wagon
1	AKB710170NAL	Chawton White-with sunroof	1	Note (8)	Station Wagon

CHANGE POINTS:
(1) To (V) WA 138479
(2) From (V) WA 138480 To (V) WA 144978
(3) From (V) WA 144979
(4) From (V) EA 314268 To (V) EA 345885
(5) From (V) FA 345886 To (V) WA 138479
(6) From (V) WA 144979 To (V) WA 159806
(7) From (V) XA 159807 To (V) YA 999999
(8) From (V) 2A 622424

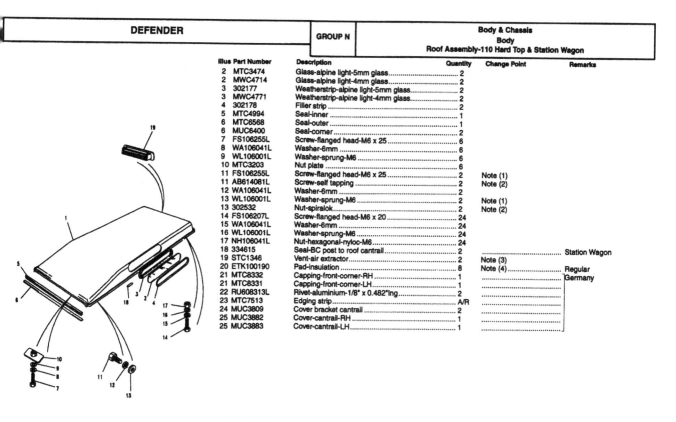

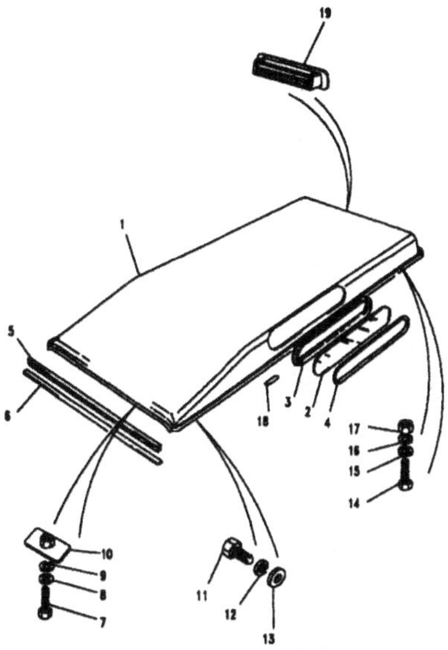

Illus	Part Number	Description	Quantity	Change Point	Remarks
2	MTC3474	Glass-alpine light-5mm glass	2		
2	MWC4714	Glass-alpine light-4mm glass	2		
3	302177	Weatherstrip-alpine light-5mm glass	2		
3	MWC4771	Weatherstrip-alpine light-4mm glass	2		
4	302178	Filler strip	2		
5	MTC4994	Seal-inner	1		
6	MTC6568	Seal-outer	1		
6	MUC6400	Seal-corner	2		
7	FS106255L	Screw-flanged head-M6 x 25	6		
8	WA106041L	Washer-6mm	6		
9	WL106001L	Washer-sprung-M6	6		
10	MTC3203	Nut plate	6		
11	FS106255L	Screw-flanged head-M6 x 25	2	Note (1)	
11	AB614081L	Screw-self tapping	2	Note (2)	
12	WA106041L	Washer-6mm	2		
13	WL106001L	Washer-sprung-M6	2	Note (1)	
13	302532	Nut-spiralok	2	Note (2)	
14	FS106207L	Screw-flanged head-M6 x 20	24		
15	WA106041L	Washer-6mm	24		
16	WL106001L	Washer-sprung-M6	24		
17	NH106041L	Nut-hexagonal-nyloc-M6	24		
18	334615	Seal-BC post to roof cantrail	2		Station Wagon
19	STC1346	Vent-air extractor	2	Note (3)	
20	ETK100190	Pad-insulation	8	Note (4)	Regular
21	MTC8332	Capping-front-corner-RH	1		Germany
21	MTC8331	Capping-front-corner-LH	1		
22	RU608313L	Rivet-aluminium-1/8" x 0.482"lng	2		
23	MTC7513	Edging strip	A/R		
24	MUC3809	Cover bracket cantrail	2		
25	MUC3882	Cover-cantrail-RH	1		
25	MUC3883	Cover-cantrail-LH	1		

CHANGE POINTS:
(1) To (V) HA 903402
(2) From (V) HA 903403
(3) To (V) FA 441847
(4) From (V) XA 159807

DEFENDER	GROUP N	Body & Chassis Body Roof Assembly-Truck Cab

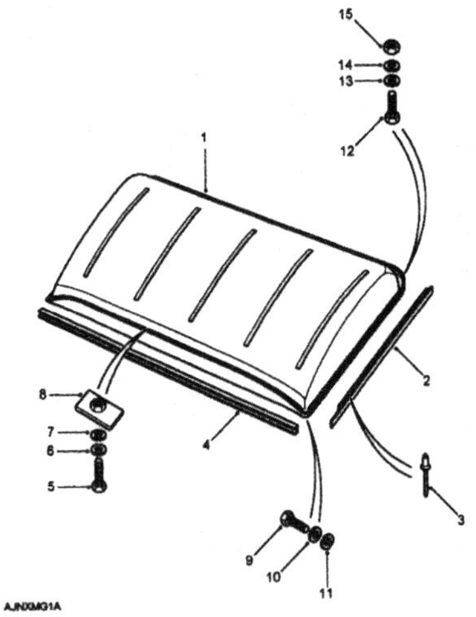

AJNXMG1A

Illus	Part Number	Description	Quantity	Change Point	Remarks
		ROOF ASSEMBLY			
1	MWC6055NUC	Alpine White	1	Note (1)	90"
1	MWC6055NAL	Chawton White	1	Note (2)	
1	MWC6055NUC	Alpine White	1	Note (1)	110"
1	MWC6055NAL	Chawton White	1	Note (3)	110"
1	AKA710640NAL	Chawton White	1	Note (4)	Truck Cab
2	MUC9204	Retainer-RH	1		
2	MUC9205	Retainer-LH	1		
3	78248	Rivet-pop-3/16" x 0.45"lng	10		
4	MTC4994	Seal-roof to windscreen-inner	1		
4	MTC6568	Seal-outer	1		Except 90"
4	MUC6400	Seal-packer-seal to windscreen-corner	2		
5	FS106167L	Screw-flanged head-fixing roof-flanged head-M6 x 16	6		
6	WA106041L	Washer-6mm	6		
7	WL106001L	Washer-sprung-M6	6		
8	MTC3203	Nut plate	6		
9	FS106255L	Screw-flanged head-M6 x 25	2	To (V) HA 702447	
9	AB614081L	Screw-fixing roof-self tapping	2	From (V) HA 702448	
10	WA106041L	Washer-6mm	2		
7	WL106001L	Washer-sprung-M6	2		
11	302532	Nut-spiralok	2		
12	SE105161L	Screw-recessed-pan head-M5 x 16	10		90"
12	FS106207L	Screw-flanged head-M6 x 20	8		Except 90"
13	WA106041L	Washer-6mm	10		90"
13	WA106041L	Washer-6mm	12		Except 90"
14	WL105001L	Washer-retaining-M5	10		90"
14	WL106001L	Washer-sprung-M6	12		Except 90"
15	NH105041L	Nut-hexagonal-M5	10		90"
15	NH105041L	Nut-hexagonal-M5	12		Except 90"
		GERMANY ONLY			
	MTC7513	Edging strip	A/R		Except 90"
	MTC8331	Capping-front-corner-LH	1		
	MTC8332	Capping-front-corner-RH	1		
	RU608313L	Rivet-aluminium-1/8" x 0.482"lng	2		

CHANGE POINTS:
(1) To (V) WA 138479
(2) From (V) WA 138480
(3) From (V) WA 138480 To (V) YA 999999
(4) From (V) 2A 622424

DEFENDER	GROUP N	Body & Chassis Body Roof Assembly-Crew Cab

Illus	Part Number	Description	Quantity	Change Point	Remarks
1	RRC6177NUC	Roof assembly-Alpine White	1	Note (1)	Crew Cab
1	AWR3955NUC	Roof assembly-Alpine White	1	Note (2)	
1	AWR3955NAL	Roof assembly-Chawton White	1	Note (3)	
1	AKA710650NAL	Roof assembly-Chawton White	1	Note (4)	Crew Cab
2	MTC4994	Seal-inner	1		
3	MTC6568	Seal-outer	1		
4	MUC6400	Seal-corner	2		
5	FS106255L	Screw-flanged head-M6 x 25	6		
6	WA106041L	Washer-6mm	6		
7	WL106001L	Washer-sprung-M6	6		
8	MTC3203	Nut plate	6		
9	AB614081L	Screw-self tapping	2		
10	FS106207L	Screw-flanged head-M6 x 20	10		
11	NH106041L	Nut-hexagonal-nyloc-M6	10		

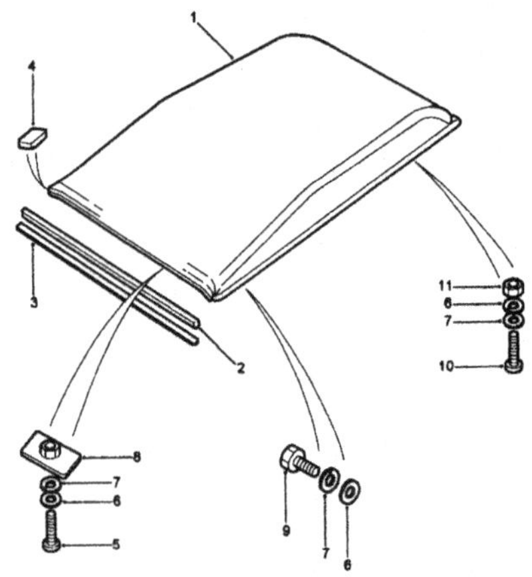

LN0225

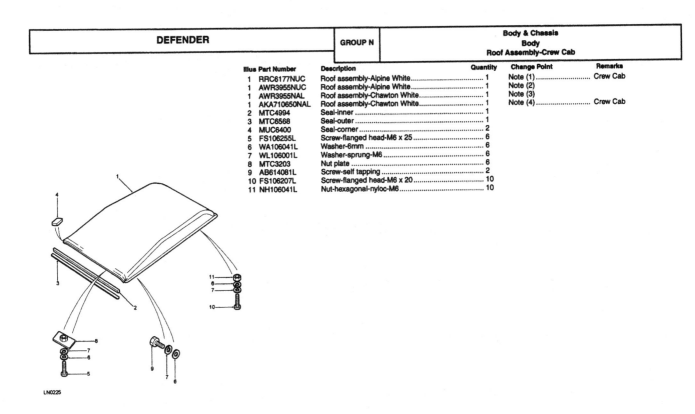

CHANGE POINTS:
(1) To (V) TA 973558
(2) From (V) TA 973559 To (V) WA 138479
(3) From (V) WA 138480 To (V) YA 999999
(4) From (V) 2A 622424

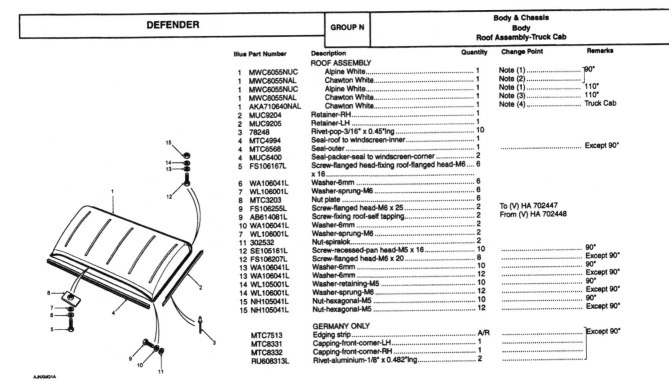

DEFENDER

GROUP N

Body & Chassis
Body
Sunroof Assembly-Manual-From (V) 314174 To (V) HA906679

Illus	Part Number	Description	Quantity	Change Point	Remarks
1	MWC9500	Seal-sunroof to roof	1		
2	RTC5941	Frame-sunroof	1		
3	RTC6790	Lock-tilt & remove sunroof frame	1		
4	AA610031	Screw	14		
5	RTC5942	Seal-glass to frame	1		
6	RTC5943	Panel-sunroof glass lid	NLA		Use STC747 Change to shade pattern only.
6	STC747	Panel-sunroof glass lid	1		
7	MXC5202	Finisher-roof trim sunroof aperture	NLA		Use MXC5011.
7	MXC5011	Finisher-roof trim sunroof aperture	1		
8	MWC5201	Bezel-sunroof handle	NLA		Use MXC5010.
8	MXC5010	Bezel-sunroof handle	1		
9	AB610041L	Screw-self tapping AB-M8 x 12	2		

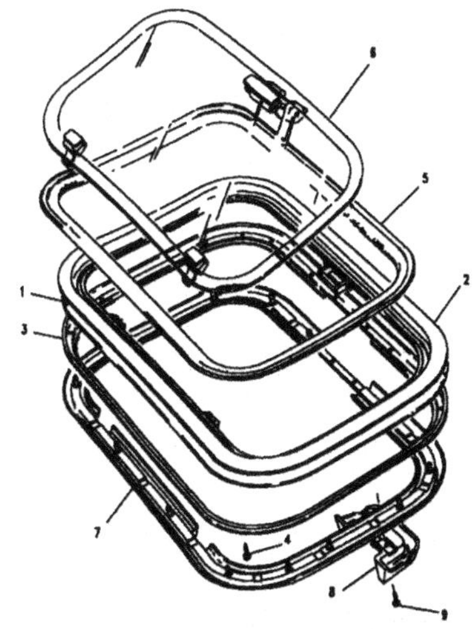

DEFENDER

GROUP N

Body & Chassis
Body
Sunroof Assembly-Manual-From (V) JA906680 To (V) LA939975

Illus	Part Number	Description	Quantity	Change Point	Remarks
1	STC746	Frame-sunroof centre	1		
2	STC747	Panel-sunroof glass lid	1		
3	RTC5942	Seal-glass to frame	1		
4	MWC9500	Seal-sunroof to roof	1		
5	AA610031	Screw-sunroof	14		
6	ALR1460	Escutcheon-sunroof handle	1		
7	STC749	Screw-self tapping	2		
8	STC748	Seal-sunroof to heading	1		
9	ALR2386	Clip	8		

NOTE:THESE PARTS ARE TO SERVICE
FACTORY FIT SUNROOF
ONLY,SUNROOF CANNOT BE
RETROSPECTIVELY FITTED.

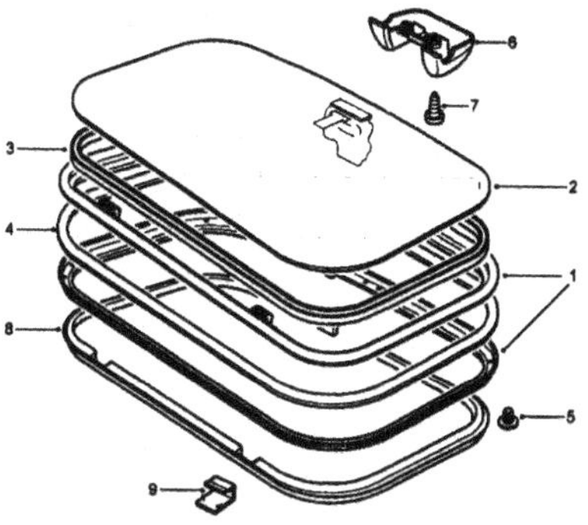

AHNXNA2A

Sunroof Assembly-Twist Handle

Illus	Part Number	Description	Quantity	Change Point	Remarks
1	AWR3321	Frame-sunroof front-upper	1		
2	AWR3323	Panel-sunroof glass lid	1		
3	AWR3324	Frame-sunroof front-lower	1		
4	STC982	Handle assembly-sunroof	1		
5	AWR3320	Finisher-sunroof	1		
6	STC3858	Seal-sunroof	1		
7	STC3859	Screw-sunroof to body	1		
8	STC4321	Label lock operation	1		
	AWR2738	KIT-GLASS SUNROOF ASSEMBLY	1		
1	AWR3321	• Frame-sunroof front-upper	1		
2	AWR3323	• Panel-sunroof glass lid	1		
3	AWR3324	• Frame-sunroof front-lower	1		
5	AWR3320	• Finisher-sunroof	1		

NOTE:SEAL ON UPPER FRAME ONLY
AVAILABLE AS PART
OF UPPER FRAME

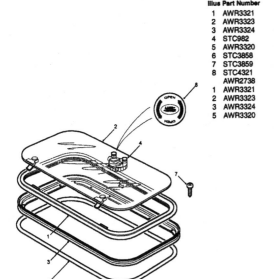

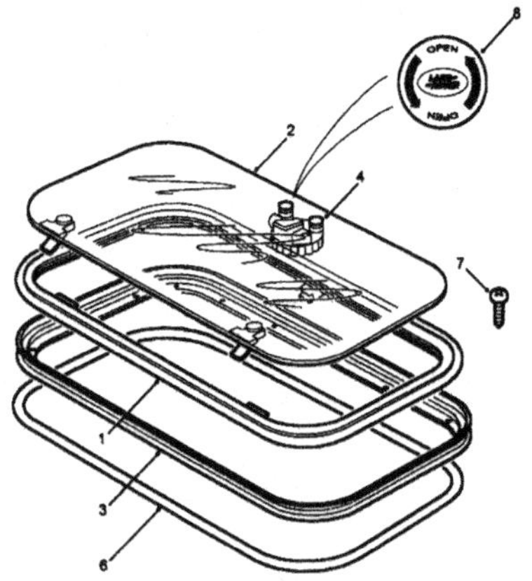

AJNXNA3A

Roof Rack & Mounting Frame Upper

Illus	Part Number	Description	Quantity	Change Point	Remarks
1	STC61855	Front screen hoop assy	1	Note (1)	Tomb Raider
2	STC61854	Rail lower front screen hoop	1		Tomb Raider
3	STC61873	Side rail roof rack support frame-RH	1		Tomb Raider 90"
3	STC61872	Side rail roof rack support frame-LH	1		Tomb Raider 90"
3	STC61879	Side rail roof rack support frame-RH	1		Tomb Raider 110"
3	STC61878	Side rail roof rack support frame-LH	1		Tomb Raider 110"
4	STC61875	Rear rail roof rack support frame	1		Tomb Raider 110"
4	STC61871	Rear rail roof rack support frame	1		Tomb Raider 90"
5	STC61877	Rail diagonal side rear-RH	1		Tomb Raider 110"
5	STC61876	Rail diagonal side rear-LH	1		Tomb Raider 110"
6	ALR5548	Seal	4		Tomb Raider 90"
6	ALR5548	Seal	6		Tomb Raider 110"
7	ALR6871	Screw-torx drive-Black-M10 x 25	20		Tomb Raider 90"
7	ALR6871	Screw-torx drive-Black-M10 x 25	36		Tomb Raider 110"
8	DYF100760	Washer-standard.-Black-10mm	20		Tomb Raider 90"
8	DYF100760	Washer-standard.-Black-10mm	36		Tomb Raider 110"
9	SH108257	Screw-hexagonal head-M8 x 25	A/R		Tomb Raider
10	FS108161L	Screw-flanged head-M8 x 16	A/R		Tomb Raider
11	WA108051L	Washer-8mm	A/R		Tomb Raider
12	STC61874	Clamp-bar	A/R		Tomb Raider
13	STC61890	Pad-rubber	8		Tomb Raider 90"
13	STC61890	Pad-rubber	4		Tomb Raider 110"
14	STC61889	Pad-roof rack rail assembly	8		Tomb Raider 90"
14	STC61889	Pad-roof rack rail assembly	6		Tomb Raider 110"
15	STC61856	Rack assembly-roof	1		Tomb Raider 90"
15	STC61857	Rack assembly-roof	1		Tomb Raider 110"

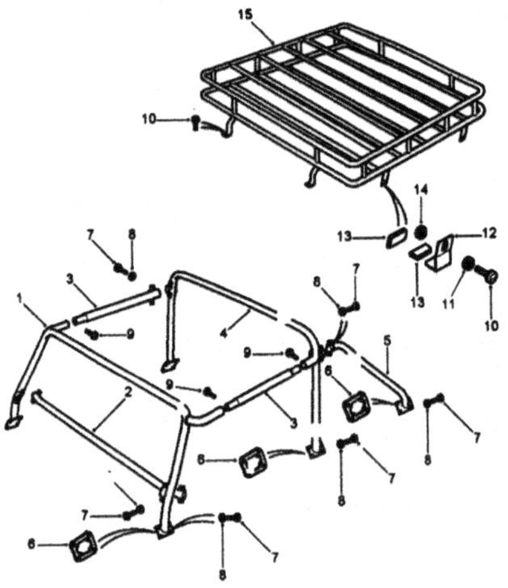

LN0227

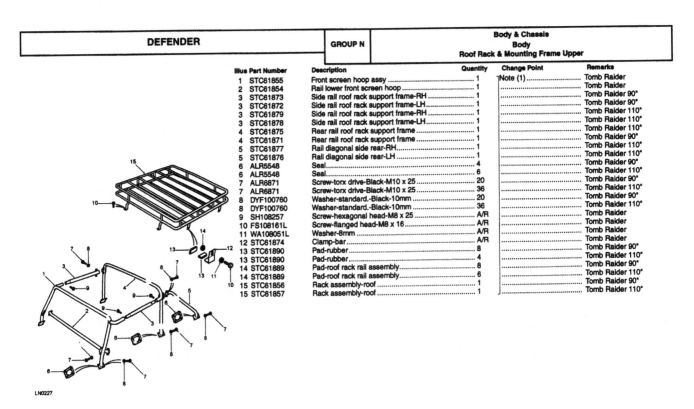

CHANGE POINTS:
(1) From (V) 1A 612404

DEFENDER

GROUP N — **Body & Chassis / Body / Roof Rack-Mounting Frame Lower**

Illus	Part Number	Description	Quantity	Change Point	Remarks
1	ALR7881	Bracket-RH-front	1	Note (1)	Tomb Raider
1	ALR710050	Bracket-LH-front	1	Note (1)	Tomb Raider
2	GG108351	Bolt-M8 x 35	8		Tomb Raider
3	WP8019L	Washer-8mm	8	Note (1)	Tomb Raider
4	ALR9350	Nut-M8	8	Note (1)	Tomb Raider
5	FS108161L	Screw-flanged head-M8 x 16	A/R	Note (1)	Tomb Raider
6	WA108051L	Washer-8mm	A/R	Note (1)	Tomb Raider
7	STC4591	Plate-reinforcement-RH	1	Note (1)	Tomb Raider 90"
7	STC4590	Plate-reinforcement-LH	1	Note (1)	Tomb Raider 90"
8	STC4593	Support-bulkhead-RH	1	Note (1)	Tomb Raider 90"
8	STC4592	Support-bulkhead-LH	1	Note (1)	Tomb Raider 90"
9	ALR5549	Bolt-torx-pan-M10 x 30	4	Note (1)	Tomb Raider 90"
10	WA110061L	Washer-M10	4	Note (1)	Tomb Raider 90"
11	STC4589	Tube-crossmember	1	Note (1)	Tomb Raider 90"
12	AYH100800	Nut-M10-nyloc-Black	4	Note (1)	Tomb Raider 90"
13	DYF100760	Washer-standard.-Black-10mm	4	Note (1)	Tomb Raider 90"
14	STC61884	Bracket mounting-LH-C post	1	Note (1)	Tomb Raider 110"
14	STC61885	Bracket mounting-RH-C post	1	Note (1)	Tomb Raider 110"
15	STC61886	Plate-reinforcement	A/R	Note (1)	Tomb Raider
17	WL108001L	Washer-sprung-M8	A/R	Note (1)	Tomb Raider
18	STC4594	Plate-roll bar stud	2	Note (1)	Tomb Raider 90"
19	STC61880	Bracket-mounting-interior-rear-LH	1	Note (1)	Tomb Raider 90"
19	STC61881	Bracket-mounting-interior-rear-RH	1	Note (1)	Tomb Raider 90"
19	STC61882	Bracket mounting-LH-rear	1	Note (1)	Tomb Raider 110"
19	STC61883	Bracket mounting-RH-rear	1	Note (1)	Tomb Raider 110"
20	NH108041L	Nut-hexagonal head-M8	A/R	Note (1)	Tomb Raider

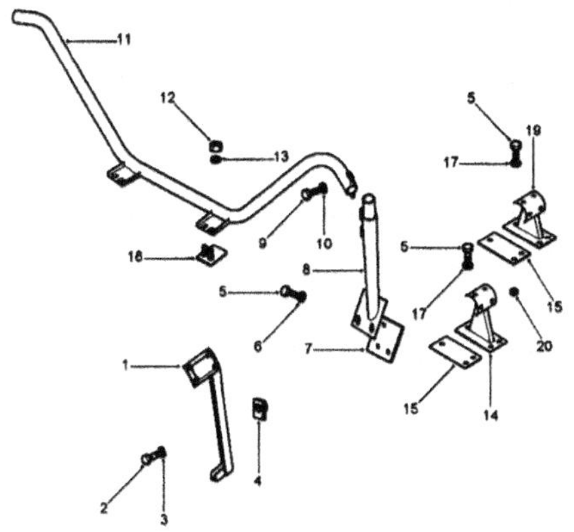

LN0228

CHANGE POINTS:
(1) From (V) 1A 612404

DEFENDER

GROUP N — **Body & Chassis / Body / Bonnet Assembly-Hand Operated**

Illus	Part Number	Description	Quantity	Change Point	Remarks
1	RTC6213	Bonnet assembly	1		
2	MRC9244	Hinge assembly-bonnet	2		
3	SF106161	Screw-M6 x 16	6		
4	WB106041	Washer-plain	6		
5	WL106001L	Washer-sprung-M6	6		
6	NH106041L	Nut-hexagonal-nyloc-M6	6		
7	346849	Bush	2		
8	MRC5016	Buffer-bonnet	4		
9	SE105141	Bolt	8		
10	WA105001L	Washer-plain-standard-M5	16		
11	NY105041L	Nut-hexagonal-nyloc-M5	8		
12	MRC9995	Striker-bonnet	1		
13	MRC4501	Staple-required when bonnet lock fitted	1		
14	78248	Rivet-required when bonnet lock fitted-pop-3/16" x 0.45"lng	2		

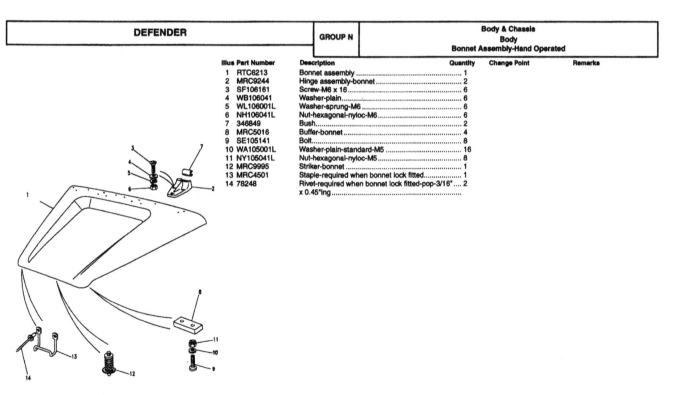

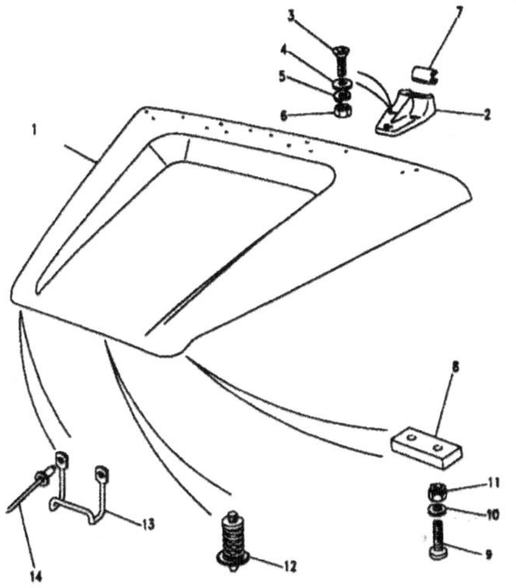

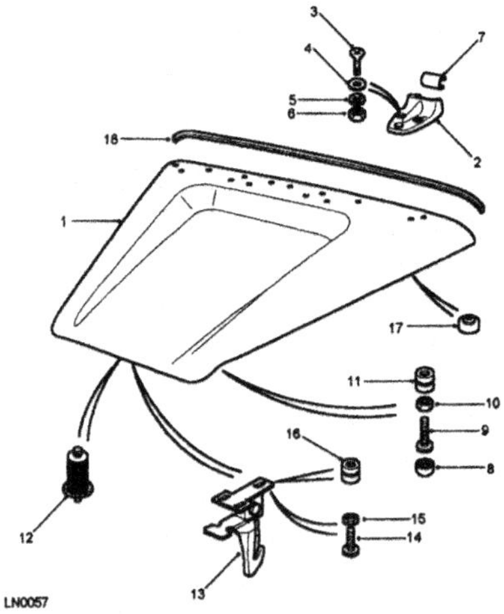

LN0057

Illus	Part Number	Description	Quantity	Change Point	Remarks
1	RTC6213	Bonnet assembly	1	Note (1)	
1	ALR6107	Bonnet assembly-spare wheel carrier	1	Note (2)	Except Td5
1	ALR5835	Bonnet assembly-less spare wheel carrier	1	Note (3)	
1	BKA710030	BONNET ASSEMBLY-LESS SPARE WHEEL CARRIER	1	Note (4)	Td5
	AHU710060	• Bracket-bonnet stay	1		
	BKV710020	• MOUNTING ASSEMBLY-BONNET LOCK	1		
	BKV710010	• • Mounting-bonnet lock	1		
	BYH100110	• • Nut-rivet-steel	1		
	BYH100120	• Nut	8		
	NN108021	• Nut-blind-M8	8		
	RU612253	• Rivet-3/16" x 0.45"lng	45		
1	ALR7544	Bonnet assembly-less spare wheel carrier	1	Note (4)	BMW M52
1	ALR7544	Bonnet assembly-less spare wheel carrier	1	Note (4)	TDi
1	ALR7544	Bonnet assembly-less spare wheel carrier	1	Note (4)	4 Cylinder Petrol
1	ALR7544	Bonnet assembly-less spare wheel carrier	1	Note (4)	V8 Twin Carburettor
2	MRC9244	Hinge assembly-bonnet	2	Note (5)	Standard / County
2	AHU710010	Hinge assembly-bonnet	2	Note (6)	Standard / County
2	STC60719	Hinge assembly-bonnet-Silver powder coat	2		Heritage
3	SF106201L	Screw-hinge to bonnet assembly-M6 x 20-counter sunk-recessed	6		
4	WB106041L	Washer-M6	6		
5	WL106001L	Washer-sprung-M6	6		
6	NH106041L	Nut-hexagonal-nyloc-M6	6		
7	346849	Bush	2		

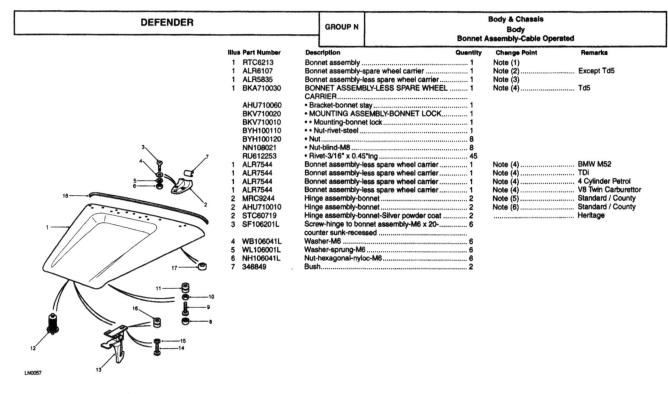

CHANGE POINTS:
(1) To (V) LA 939975
(2) From (V) MA 939976
(3) From (V) MA 939976 To (V) WA 159806
(4) From (V) XA 159807
(5) To (V) WA 138479
(6) From (V) WA 138480

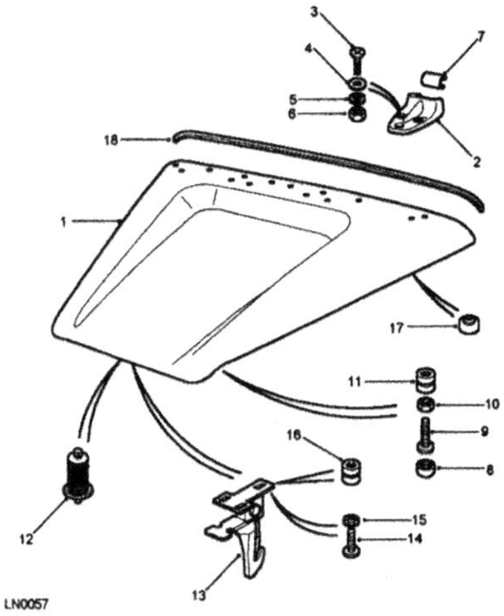

LN0057

Illus	Part Number	Description	Quantity	Change Point	Remarks
8	391287	Buffer-bonnet	4		Spare wheel carrier
9	SE108404L	Screw-pan-to bonnet assembly-M8 x 40	4		
10	NH108044	Nut-hexagonal	4		
8	391287	Buffer-bonnet	2		Except spare wheel carrier
9	SE108404L	Screw-pan-to bonnet assembly-M8 x 40	2		
10	NH108044	Nut-hexagonal	2		
11	NN108021	Nut-blind-M8	4	Note (1)	
11	RRC8666	Nut-blind-M8	4	Note (2)	
12	MWC9361	Striker-bonnet	1	Note (3)	
12	MUC4803	Striker-bonnet	1	Note (4)	Spare wheel carrier
12	ASR1229	Striker-bonnet	1	Note (5)	
12	MUC4803	Striker-bonnet	1	Note (6)	Except spare wheel carrier
12	ASR1227	Striker-bonnet	1	Note (7)	
13	MUC6457	Hook-bonnet safety catch	1		
14	SE106161L	Screw-to bonnet assembly-M6 x 16	3		
15	WF106001L	Washer-starlock-M6	3		
16	NN106021	Nutsert-blind-M6	3	Note (1)	
16	AWR6715	Nutsert-blind-M6	3	Note (2)	
17	MRC6270	Buffer-bonnet	2		
18	CJE100770	Seal-bonnet-rear	1	From (V) XA 159807	
19	FRP100010	Nut-bonnet latch locking	1	Note (2)	
	WA112087	Washer-plain-striker to bonnet-M12-dacromat	1		Td5

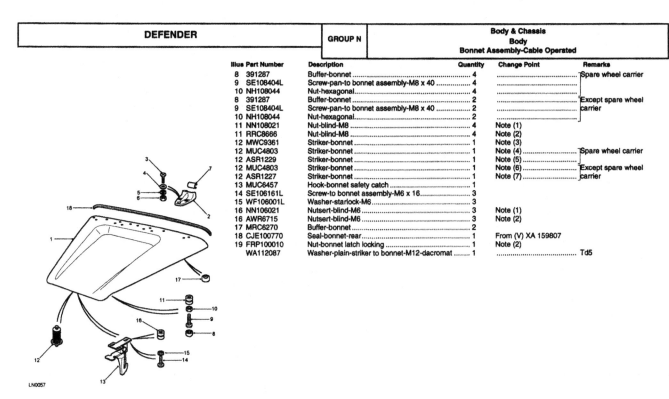

CHANGE POINTS:
(1) To (V) WA 159806
(2) From (V) XA 159807
(3) To (V) MA 949377
(4) From (V) MA 949378 To (V) TA 983377
(5) From (V) TA 983378
(6) From (V) MA 949378 To (V) TA 984993
(7) From (V) TA 984994

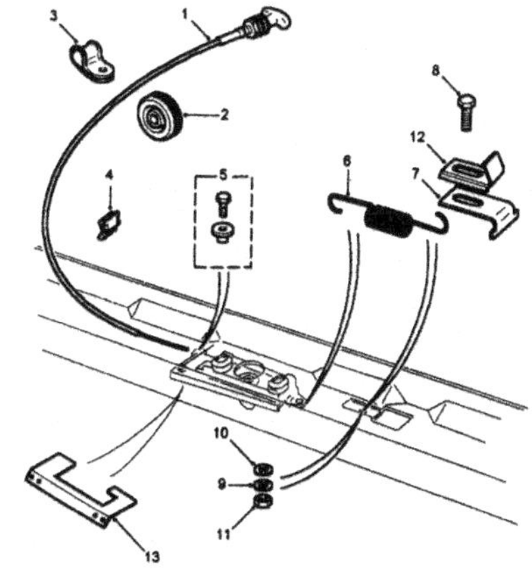

LN0108

Illus	Part Number	Description	Quantity	Change Point	Remarks
1	MXC7354	Cable-bonnet release assembly	1	Note (1)	
1	ALR9556	Cable-bonnet release assembly	1	Note (2)	
1	ASR1457	Cable-bonnet release assembly	1	Note (3)	
1	ALR9555	Cable-bonnet release assembly	1		V8 EFi
2	235113	Grommet	2		
3	3887	Clip-cable	1	To (V) EA 344387	
3	MWC9380	Clip-cable	1	From (V) EA 344388	
4	13H489L	Spring clip.	1		
5	STC926	Kit-bonnet locking-UNF fixing	1	To (V) LA 939975	
5	STC927	Kit-bonnet locking-metric fixing	1	From (V) MA 939976	
6	351991	Spring-return	1		
7	393218	Plate-adjusting-hook	1		
8	FS106207L	Screw-to plate catch-flanged head-M6 x 20	1		
9	WL106001L	Washer-sprung-M6	1		
10	WA106041L	Washer-6mm	1		
11	NH106041L	Nut-hexagonal-nyloc-M6	1		
12	MWC3339	Plate-catch assembly base	1	From (V) EA 321774	
13	ALR9155	Shield-bonnet latch	1	From (V) TA 977537	
14	ALR9157	Nut	1		
15	FN106047L	Nut-flange-M6	2	Note (5)	
16	FSE100460	CABLE-BONNET RELEASE ASSEMBLY	1	Note (5)	
17	ALU710030	• Lever-bonnet release assembly	1		
	SF106201L	Screw-M6 x 20-counter sunk-recessed	6		

CHANGE POINTS:
(1) To (V) MA 965839
(2) From (V) MA 965840 To (V) TA 977536
(3) From (V) TA 977537
(5) From (V) XA 159807

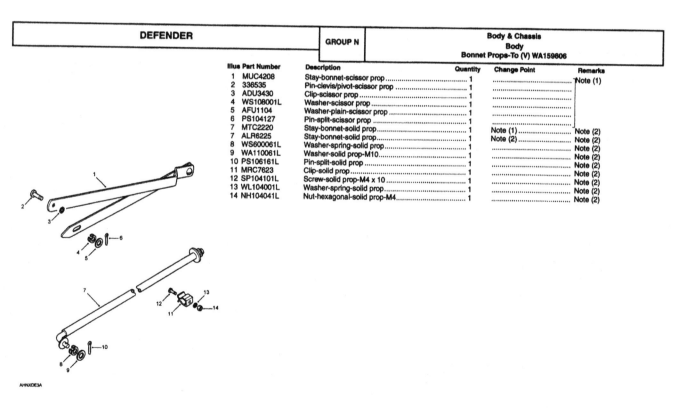

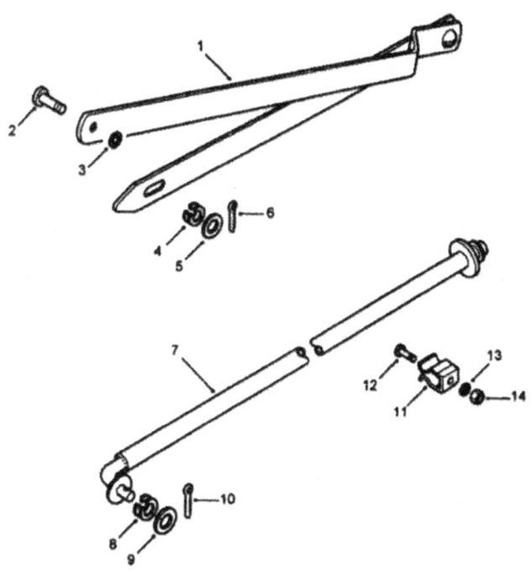

AHNXDE3A

Illus	Part Number	Description	Quantity	Change Point	Remarks
1	MUC4208	Stay-bonnet-scissor prop	1		Note (1)
2	336535	Pin-clevis/pivot-scissor prop	1		
3	ADU3430	Clip-scissor prop	1		
4	WS108001L	Washer-scissor prop	1		
5	AFU1104	Washer-plain-scissor prop	1		
6	PS104127	Pin-split-scissor prop	1		
7	MTC2220	Stay-bonnet-solid prop	1	Note (1)	Note (2)
7	ALR6225	Stay-bonnet-solid prop	1	Note (2)	Note (2)
8	WS600061L	Washer-spring-solid prop	1		Note (2)
9	WA110061L	Washer-solid prop-M10	1		Note (2)
10	PS106161L	Pin-split-solid prop	1		Note (2)
11	MRC7623	Clip-solid prop	1		Note (2)
12	SP104101L	Screw-solid prop-M4 x 10	1		Note (2)
13	WL104001L	Washer-spring-solid prop	1		Note (2)
14	NH104041L	Nut-hexagonal-solid prop-M4	1		Note (2)

CHANGE POINTS:
(1) To (V) LA 939975
(2) From (V) MA 939976

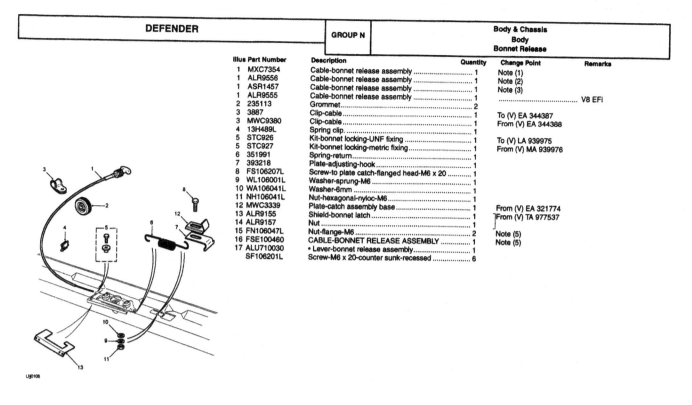

Remarks:
(1) Except spare wheel carrier
(2) spare wheel carrier

Illus	Part Number	Description	Quantity	Change Point	Remarks
1	ALR9022	Stay-bonnet	1		
2	PRC3180	Clip-bonnet prop-single	1		
3	AYA10004L	Grommet	1		

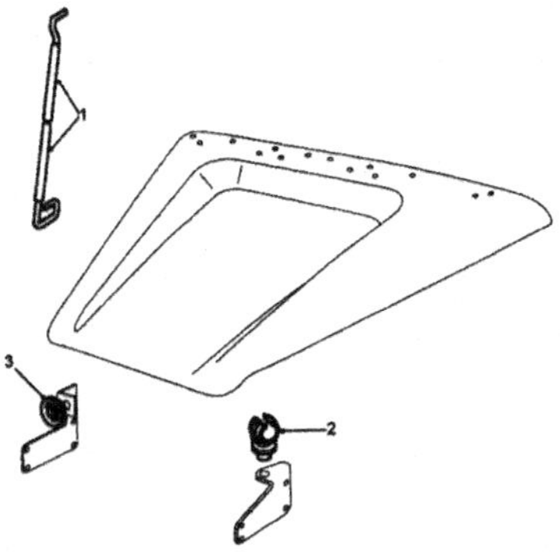

LN0154

Illus	Part Number	Description	Quantity	Change Point	Remarks
		NON AIR CON			
		FRAME-RADIATOR GRILLE			
1	MTC4837	hand operated bonnet release	1	Note (1)	Note (1)
1	MTC1810	hand operated bonnet release	1	Note (1)	Note (2)
1	MWC2926	cable operated bonnet release	1	Note (2)	
1	ALR1339	cable operated bonnet release	1	Note (3)	
1	ASJ710050	Frame-radiator grille	1	Note (4)	Except Td5
1	ASJ710040	Frame-radiator grille-metal	1		Td5
		AIR CON			
1	MUC6112	Frame-radiator grille	1	Note (2)	
1	ALR1522	Frame-radiator grille	1	Note (3)	
1	ASJ710010	Frame-radiator grille-plastic	1	Note (4)	
1	ASR1772	Frame-radiator grille	1		V8 EFI 50 LE
	MRC9544	Seal	1	To (V) LA 939975	
2	AB606057	Screw-to grille assembly-self tapping-No 6 x 5/8-long	4		
3	WC105007	Washer-plain-large-Black	4		
4	RTC3745	Nut-lokut	4		
5	FS108207L	Screw-flanged head-M8 x 20	2		
6	WL108001L	Washer-sprung-M8	2		
7	WA108051L	Washer-8mm	2		
8	NJ108061L	Nut-retaining	2		

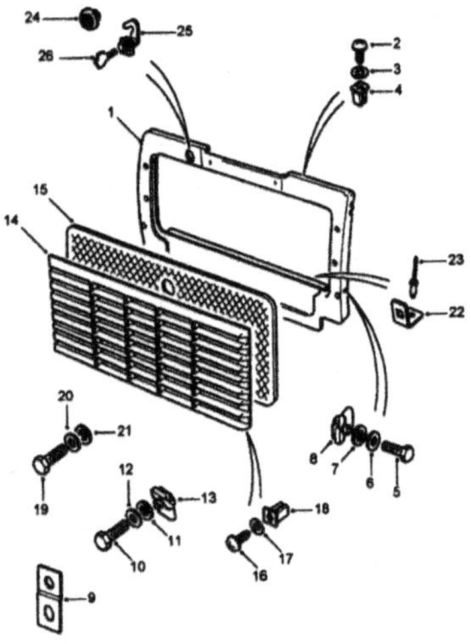

LN0030

CHANGE POINTS:
(1) To (V) LA 939975
(2) To (V) HA 906578
(3) From (V) JA 906579 To (V) WA 159806
(4) From (V) XA 159807

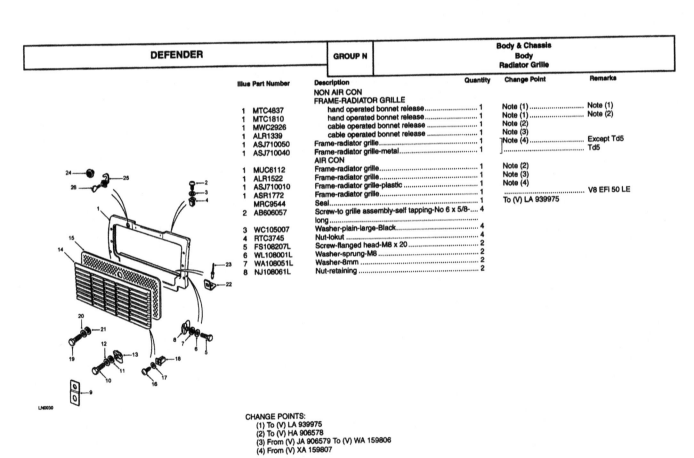

Remarks:
(1) oil cooler is part of radiator
(2) oil cooler is not part of radiator

DEFENDER

GROUP N

Body & Chassis
Body
Radiator Grille

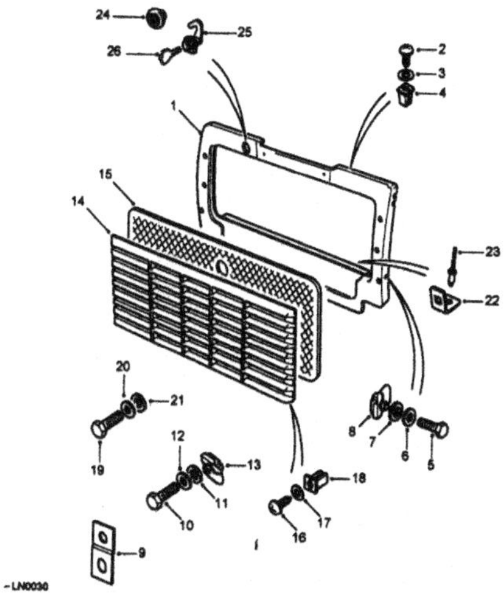

Illus	Part Number	Description	Quantity	Change Point	Remarks
		AIR CON VEHICLES ONLY			
9	MTC6332	Bracket	1		
10	AB614065L	Screw-To nut spring-self tapping	2		
11	WL106005L	Washer-spring-rectangular	2		
12	WA106045L	Washer-plain-standard	2		
13	AK612011L	Nut	2		
		GRILLE-RADIATOR PAINTED			
14	MTC3862	Primer	1		
14	MWC8466PUC	Black	1	To (V) MA 963649	
14	ALR8765PUC	Black	1	From (V) MA 963650	
14	MWC8466NUC	Alpine White	NLA		Use ALR8765PUC.
14	MWC8466SUB	Arran Beige	NLA		
14	MWC8466CUF	Arrow Red	NLA		
14	MWC8466HCC	Bronze Green	NLA		
14	MWC8466HUJ	Eastnor Green	NLA		
14	MWC8466NCM	Ivory	NLA		
14	MWC8466JUH	Pacific Blue	NLA		
14	MWC8466LUS	Pembroke Grey-Pennine Grey	NLA		
14	MWC8466JUG	Shire Blue	NLA		
14	MWC8466LCN	Slate Grey	NLA		
14	MWC8466HCN	Trident Green	NLA		
14	STC60713	Silver powder coat	1		Heritage except air conditioning
14	STC60714	Silver powder coat	1		Heritage air conditioning
15	MTC4220	Guard assembly-hand	1		
		NON AIR CON			
16	AB614088	Screw-To frame grille-No14 x 1.0-long	8		
17	WA106045L	Washer-plain-standard	8		
11	WL106005L	Washer-spring-rectangular	2		
18	RTC3744	Nut-lokut	8		

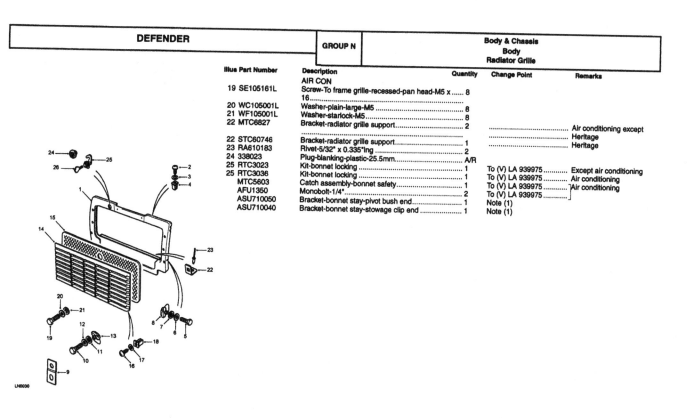

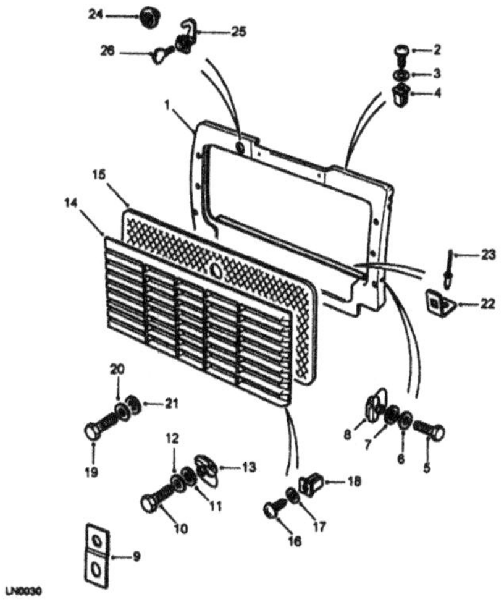

Illus	Part Number	Description	Quantity	Change Point	Remarks
		AIR CON			
19	SE105161L	Screw-To frame grille-recessed-pan head-M5 x 16	8		
20	WC105001L	Washer-plain-large-M5	8		
21	WF105001L	Washer-starlock-M5	8		
22	MTC6827	Bracket-radiator grille support	2		Air conditioning except Heritage
22	STC60746	Bracket-radiator grille support	1		Heritage
23	RA610183	Rivet-5/32" x 0.335"lng	2		
24	338023	Plug-blanking-plastic-25.5mm	A/R		
25	RTC3023	Kit-bonnet locking	1	To (V) LA 939975	Except air conditioning
25	RTC3036	Kit-bonnet locking	1	To (V) LA 939975	Air conditioning
	MTC5603	Catch assembly-bonnet safety	1	To (V) LA 939975	Air conditioning
	AFU1350	Monobolt-1/4"	2	To (V) LA 939975	
	ASU710050	Bracket-bonnet stay-pivot bush end	1	Note (1)	
	ASU710040	Bracket-bonnet stay-stowage clip end	1	Note (1)	

CHANGE POINTS:
(1) From (V) XA 159807

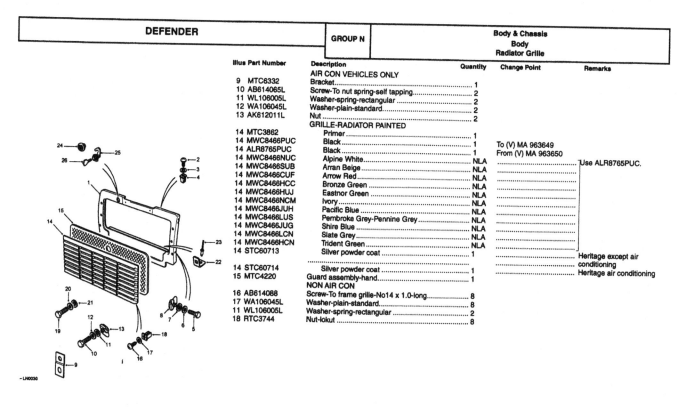

DEFENDER | **GROUP N** | **Body & Chassis — Body — Radiator Grille Chaff Guard**

Illus	Part Number	Description	Quantity	Change Point	Remarks
		GUARD ASSEMBLY-HAND			
1	MTC4220	hand operated bonnet release	1	To (V) LA 939975	Air conditioning
1	MTC4007	hand operated bonnet release	1		Except air conditioning
1	MTC4220	cable operated bonnet release	1		Air conditioning
1	MTC4220	cable operated bonnet release	1		Except air conditioning
2	MTC4829	Seal	1		
3	MTC4826	Clamp	1		
4	78248	Rivet-pop-3/16" x 0.45"lng	7		
5	WA105001L	Washer-plain-standard-M5	2		

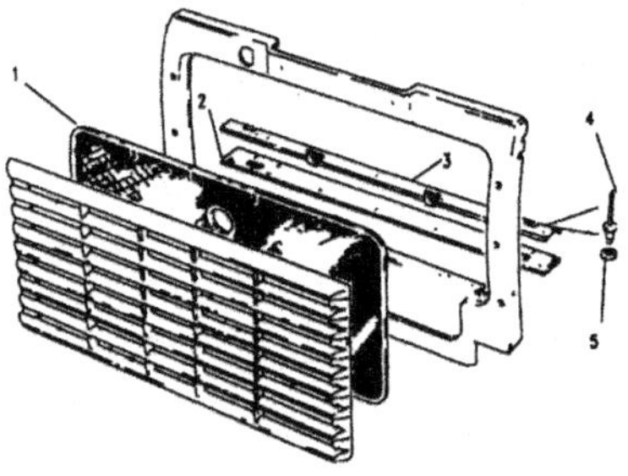

DEFENDER | **GROUP N** | **Body & Chassis — Body — Radiator Baffle Plate**

Illus	Part Number	Description	Quantity	Change Point	Remarks
1	MRC9393	Plate-baffle-RH	1		
1	MRC9394	Plate-baffle-LH	1		
2	MRC8269	Plate	2		
3	MRC8047	Seal	2		
4	RA612183	Rivet-pop-aluminium	8		
5	FS106167L	Screw-flanged head-flanged head-M6 x 16	4		
6	WM106001	Washer-spring	4		
7	WA106041L	Washer-6mm	4		
8	NH106041L	Nut-hexagonal-nyloc-M6	4		
9	235113	Grommet-LH side	1		

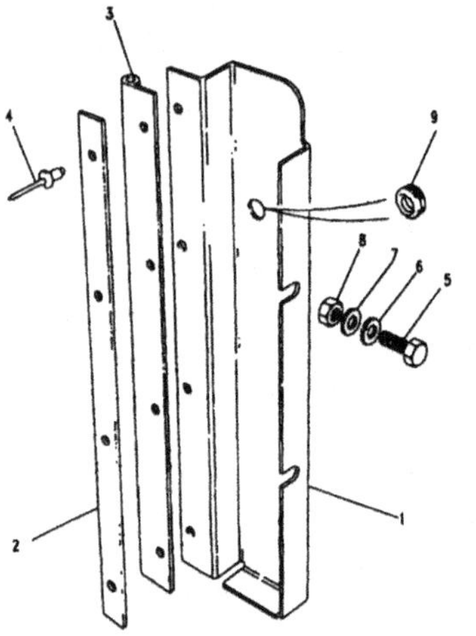

Body

Grille, Top Panel & Braces-Hand Bonnet Release

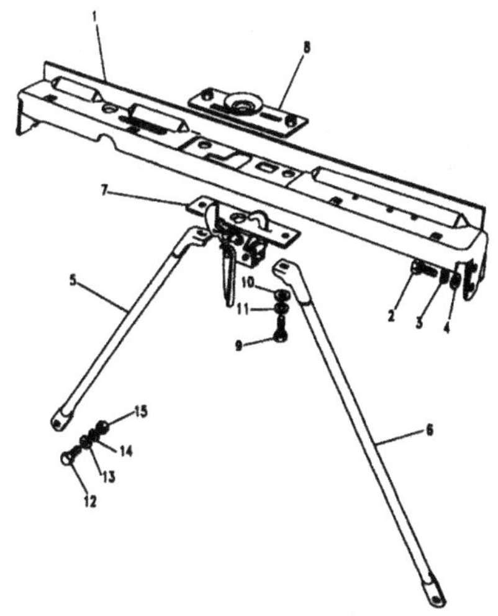

Illus	Part Number	Description	Quantity	Change Point	Remarks
1	MTC7170	Platform assembly-bonnet locking	1		
2	FS108207L	Screw-flanged head-M8 x 20	2		
3	WL108001L	Washer-sprung-M8	4		
4	WA108051L	Washer-8mm	4		
5	MTC3982	Release assembly-bonnet-RH	1		
6	MTC3983	Release assembly-bonnet-LH	1		
7	MRC6977	Catch assembly-bonnet safety	1		Except air conditioning
8	MRC6978	Plate	1		
7	MTC4932	Catch assembly-bonnet safety	1		Air conditioning
8	MTC7140	Plate	1		
15	NH106045	Nut-hexagonal head-nyloc-M6	2		
9	AFU1203	Screw-M6 x 20	2		
10	AFU1080	Washer-plain	2		
11	WL106001L	Washer-sprung-M6	2		
12	FS108207L	Screw-flanged head-M8 x 20	2		
13	WA108051L	Washer-8mm	2		
14	WL108001L	Washer-sprung-M8	2		
15	FN108047L	Nut-flange-flanged head-M8	2		Except air conditioning
15	NY108041L	Nut-nyloc-M8	2		Air conditioning

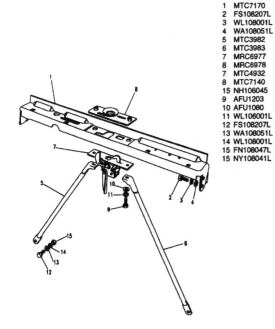

Body

Grille, Top Panel & Braces-Cable Bonnet Release

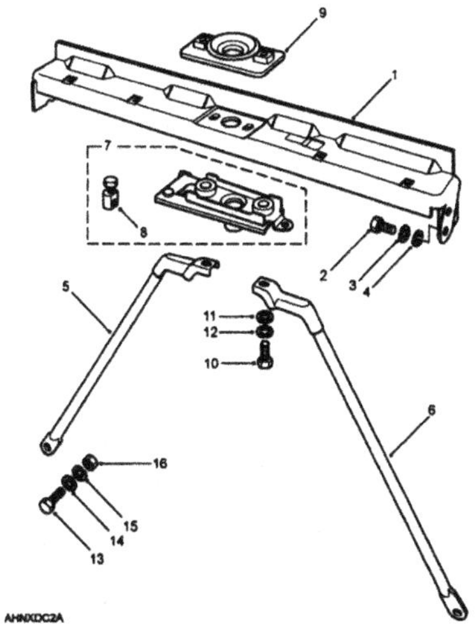

Illus	Part Number	Description	Quantity	Change Point	Remarks
		PLATFORM ASSEMBLY-BONNET LOCKING			
1	MUC4806	top	1	Note (1)	
1	MXC7732	top	1	Note (2)	
1	ALR4564	top	1	Note (3)	
1	ALR9424	top	1	Note (4)	
1	ABG710020	top	1	Note (5)	
1	ABG710040	top	1	Note (6)	
2	FS108257L	Screw-to grille assembly-flanged head-M8 x 25	4		
2	FS108357	Screw-flanged head-M8 x 35	4		Air conditioning
3	WL108001L	Washer-sprung-M8	4		
4	WA108051L	Washer-8mm	4		
5	MUC6658	Crossbrace-RH	1		
6	MUC6659	Crossbrace-LH	1		
7	ALR2385	CATCH ASSEMBLY-BONNET SAFETY	1	To (V) KA 929745	
8	STC927	• Kit-bonnet locking	1		
7	STC925	Catch assembly-bonnet safety	1	From (V) KA 929746	
9	MUC4804	Plate-bonnet latch top	1	Note (7)	
9	RRC8512	Plate-bonnet latch top	1	Note (8)	Td5
9	RRC8512	Plate-bonnet latch top	1	Note (8)	Note (1)
9	MUC4804	Plate-bonnet latch top	1	Note (8)	Note (2)
10	SH106301L	Screw-brace to catch assembly-hexagonal head-M6 x 30	2		
11	WA106041L	Washer-6mm	2		
12	WL106001L	Washer-sprung-M6	2		
13	FS108207L	Screw-to brace-flanged head-M8 x 20	2		
14	WA108051L	Washer-8mm	2		
15	WL108001L	Washer-sprung-M8	2		
16	FN108047L	Nut-flange-flanged head-M8	2		Except air conditioning
16	NY108041L	Nut-nyloc-M8	2		Air conditioning

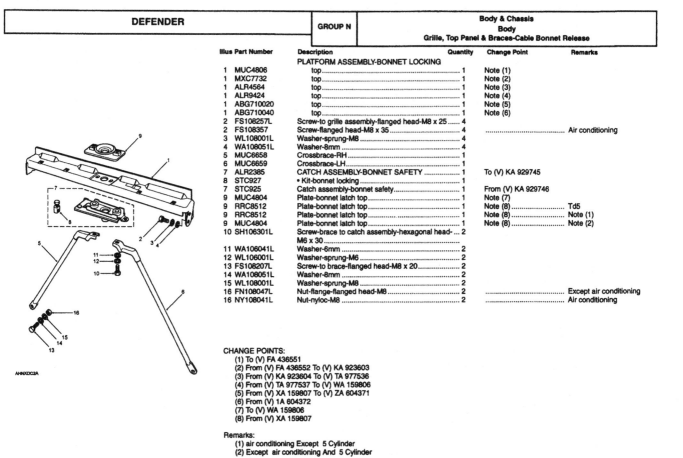

CHANGE POINTS:
(1) To (V) FA 436551
(2) From (V) FA 436552 To (V) KA 923603
(3) From (V) KA 923604 To (V) TA 977536
(4) From (V) TA 977537 To (V) WA 159806
(5) From (V) XA 159807 To (V) ZA 604371
(6) From (V) 1A 604372
(7) To (V) WA 159806
(8) From (V) XA 159807

Remarks:
(1) air conditioning Except 5 Cylinder
(2) Except air conditioning And 5 Cylinder

DEFENDER | GROUP N | Body & Chassis — Body — Body Warning Labels

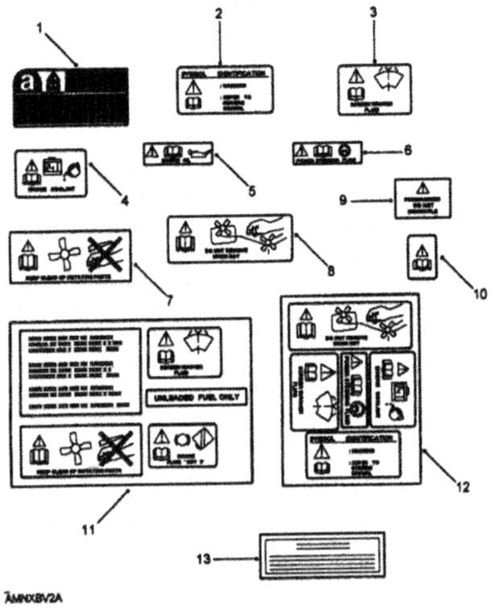

Illus	Part Number	Description	Quantity	Change Point	Remarks
1	BTR389	Label-underbonnet asbestos	1		
2	MUC5307	Label-underbonnet data	1		
3	MUC5308	Label-underbonnet data	1		
4	MUC5309	Label-underbonnet radiator caution	1		
5	MUC5310	Label-oil dip/fill instruction	1		
6	MUC5311	Label power assisted steering reservoir	1		
7	MWC1691	Label-cooling system fan assembly warning	1		
8	MWC1694	Label-underbonnet radiator caution	1		
9	MWC1695	Label-warning	1		
10	MWC1696	Label-warning	1		
11	MWC2698	Label-catalyst	1		
12	MXC2931	Label-air conditioning	1		
12	BAC103320	Label-air conditioning	1	Note (1)	V8 Petrol Twin Carburettor air conditioning
					V8 EFi
13	BAA10082	Label-unleaded fuel only warning	1		
	BAC103370	Label-underbonnet emissions	1	Note (2)	Td5
	BAC001110	Label-underbonnet emissions	1	Note (3)	Td5

CHANGE POINTS:
(1) From (V) XA 159807
(2) To (V) 1A 622423
(3) From (V) 2A 622424

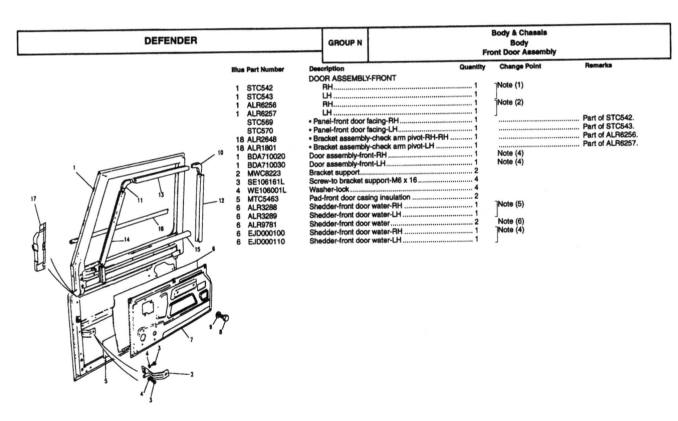

DEFENDER | GROUP N | Body & Chassis — Body — Front Door Assembly

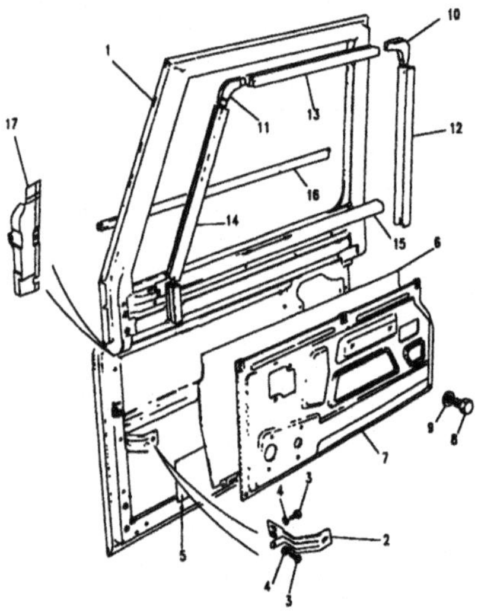

Illus	Part Number	Description	Quantity	Change Point	Remarks
		DOOR ASSEMBLY-FRONT			
1	STC542	RH	1	Note (1)	
1	STC543	LH	1		
1	ALR6256	RH	1	Note (2)	
1	ALR6257	LH	1		
	STC569	• Panel-front door facing-RH	1		Part of STC542.
	STC570	• Panel-front door facing-LH	1		Part of STC543.
18	ALR2648	• Bracket assembly-check arm pivot-RH-RH	1		Part of ALR6256.
18	ALR1801	• Bracket assembly-check arm pivot-LH	1		Part of ALR6257.
1	BDA710020	Door assembly-front-RH	1	Note (4)	
1	BDA710030	Door assembly-front-LH	1	Note (4)	
2	MWC8223	Bracket support	2		
3	SE106161L	Screw-to bracket support-M6 x 16	4		
4	WE106001L	Washer-lock	4		
5	MTC5463	Pad-front door casing insulation	2		
6	ALR3288	Shedder-front door water-RH	1	Note (5)	
6	ALR3289	Shedder-front door water-LH	1		
6	ALR9781	Shedder-front door water	2	Note (6)	
6	EJD000100	Shedder-front door water-RH	1	Note (4)	
6	EJD000110	Shedder-front door water-LH	1		

CHANGE POINTS:
(1) To (V) AA 270226
(2) From (V) AA 270227
(4) From (V) 2A 622424
(5) To (V) MA 970156
(6) From (V) MA 970157 To (V) YA 999999

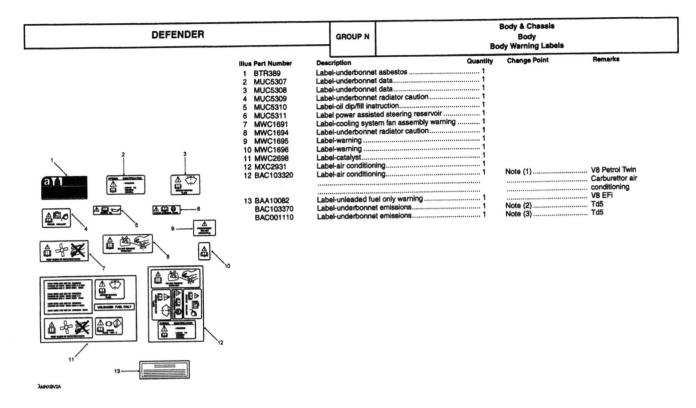

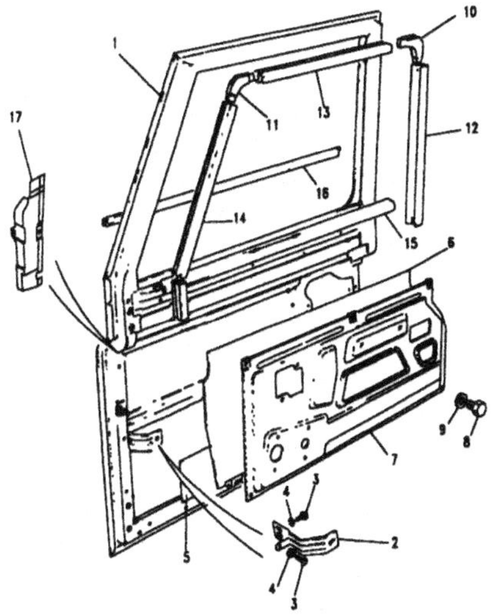

Illus	Part Number	Description	Quantity	Change Point	Remarks
		PANEL-INNER			
7	MUC2074	RH	1	Note (1)	
7	MUC2075	LH	1		
7	MWC8270	RH	1	Note (2)	
7	MWC8271	LH	1		
7	ALR4541	RH	1	Note (3)	
7	ALR4540	LH	1	Note (3)	
7	BDV710080	RH	1	Note (4)	
7	BDV710090	LH	1	Note (4)	
8	FS106101L	Screw-flanged head-to door assembly-M6 x 10	10		
9	WA106041L	Washer-6mm	10		

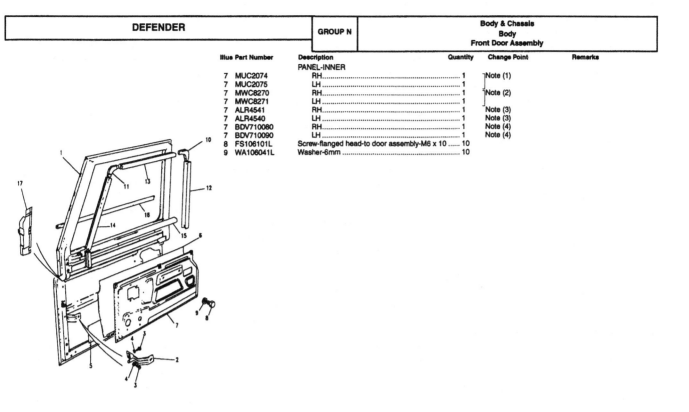

CHANGE POINTS:
(1) To (V) AA 270226
(2) From (V) AA 270227 To (V) LA 932528
(3) From (V) LA 932529 To (V) YA 999999
(4) From (V) 2A 622424

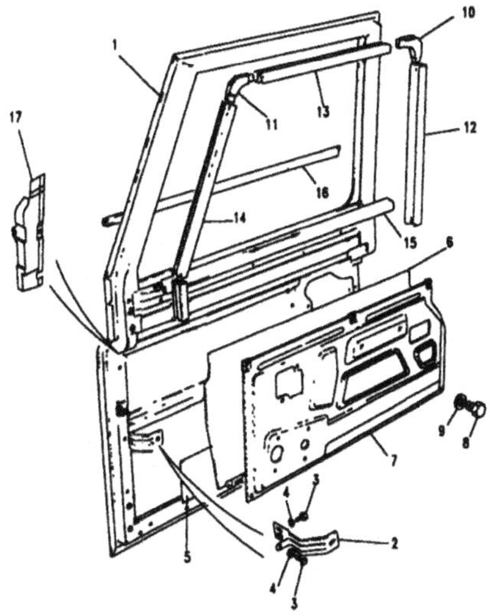

Illus	Part Number	Description	Quantity	Change Point	Remarks
		FILLER			
10	201235	rear-corner	2		
11	201647	front-corner	2		
12	MUC1651	vertical	2		
13	MUC1652	top	2		
14	MUC1730	Filler sloping-RH	1		
14	MUC1731	Filler sloping-LH	1		
		SEAL WAIST			
15	MTC8473	inner	2		
16	MTC8474	outer	2	To (V) LA 937709	
16	ALR5980	outer	2	From (V) LA 937710	
17	MXC7570	Deflector.-RH	1		
17	MXC7571	Deflector.-LH	1		
	MUC3928	Finisher assembly-front door waist-RH	1	To (V) AA 270226	
	MUC3929	Finisher assembly-front door waist-LH	1		
	MUC3186	Clip	10		
	AJU1136L	Insert-plain	10		
	307220	Plug-door bottom-3/8"	4		
	MUC3848	Plug-door lock pocket	2		

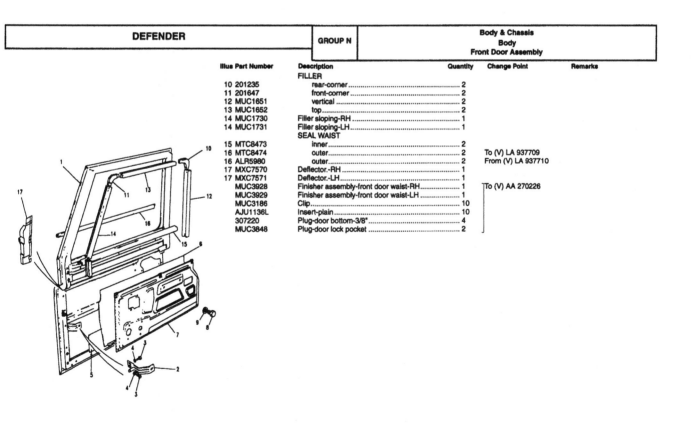

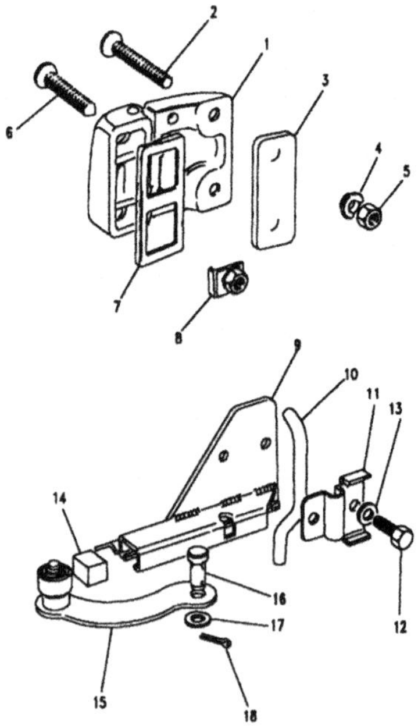

Illus	Part Number	Description	Quantity	Change Point	Remarks
		HINGE ASSEMBLY-DOOR			
1	MXC8284	front door upper-Self Colour-RH	1	Note (1)	
1	MXC8285	front door upper-Self Colour-LH	1		
1	BDB710020	front door upper-Self Colour-RH	1	Note (2)	
1	BDB710030	front door upper-Self Colour-LH	1		
1	BDB710160	front door upper-Self Colour-RH	1	Note (3)	
1	BDB710170	front door upper-Self Colour-LH	1		
1	STC60722	front door upper-Silver powder coat-RH	1		Heritage
1	STC60723	front door upper-Silver powder coat-LH	1		
		HINGE ASSEMBLY-DOOR			
1	MXC8282	front door lower-rear door lower-rear door upper-Self Colour-RH	1	Note (1)	
1	MXC8283	front door lower-rear door lower-rear door upper-Self Colour-LH	1		
1	BDB710040	front door lower-rear door lower-rear door upper-Self Colour-RH	1	Note (2)	
1	BDB710050	front door lower-rear door lower-rear door upper-Self Colour-LH	1		
1	BDB710180	lower-Self Colour-RH	1	Note (3)	
1	BDB710190	lower-Self Colour-LH	1		
1	STC60726	front door lower-rear door lower-rear door upper-Silver powder coat-RH	1		Heritage
1	STC60725	front door lower-rear door lower-rear door upper-Silver powder coat-LH	1		

CHANGE POINTS:
(1) To (V) WA 138479
(2) From (V) WA 138480 To (V) ZA 602283
(3) From (V) 1A 602284

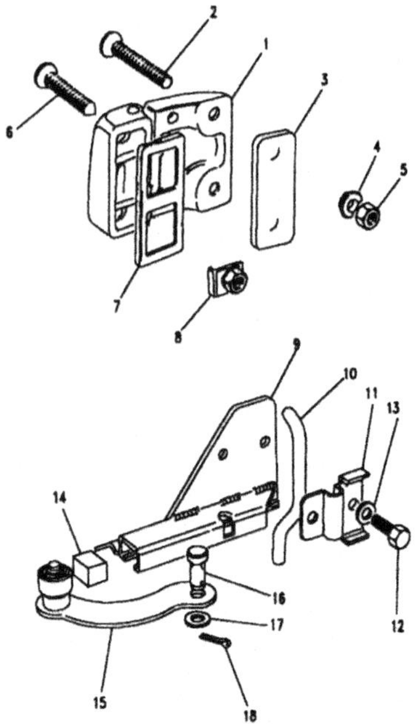

Illus	Part Number	Description	Quantity	Change Point	Remarks
2	MWC1899	Bolt-to hinge assembly-counter sunk	8	Note (1)	
2	ASR1603	Bolt-to hinge assembly-counter sunk	8	Note (2)	
2	BYG100150	Bolt-to hinge assembly-counter sunk-torx drive	8	Note (3)	
2	BYG100220	Bolt-to hinge assembly-counter sunk-torx drive	8	Note (4)	
2	BYG100150L	Bolt-to hinge assembly-counter sunk-torx drive-M8 x 55	8	Note (5)	
3	MWC1898	Shim-door hinge	4		
4	MRC1980	Washer-nylon	8		
5	NH605041L	Nut-hexagonal head-5/16UNF	8	Note (6)	
5	NY108041L	Nut-nyloc-M8	8	Note (7)	
6	79221	Bolt-to hinge assembly-counter sunk	8	Note (6)	
6	BYG100140	Bolt-counter sunk-torx drive	8	Note (3)	
6	BYG100210	Bolt-counter sunk-torx drive	8	Note (4)	
6	BYG100140L	Bolt-counter sunk-torx drive-M8 x 40	8	Note (5)	
7	347369	Shim-door hinge	4	Note (6)	
7	BYF100050	Shim-door hinge	4	Note (8)	
7	BHC710010	Shim-door hinge-plastic	4	Note (9)	
8	MRC2178	Nut	8	Note (6)	
8	ASR1459	Nut	8	Note (7)	

CHANGE POINTS:
(1) To (V) TA 990744
(2) From (V) TA 990745 To (V) VA 138479
(3) From (V) WA 138480 To (V) YA 191331
(4) From (V) YA 191332 To (V) ZA 611581
(5) From (V) 1A 611582
(6) To (V) VA 138479
(7) From (V) WA 138480
(8) From (V) WA 138480 To (V) XA 167557
(9) From (V) XA 167558

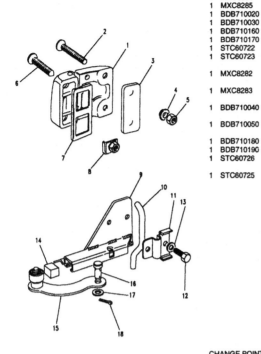

Front Door Hinges & Check Strap

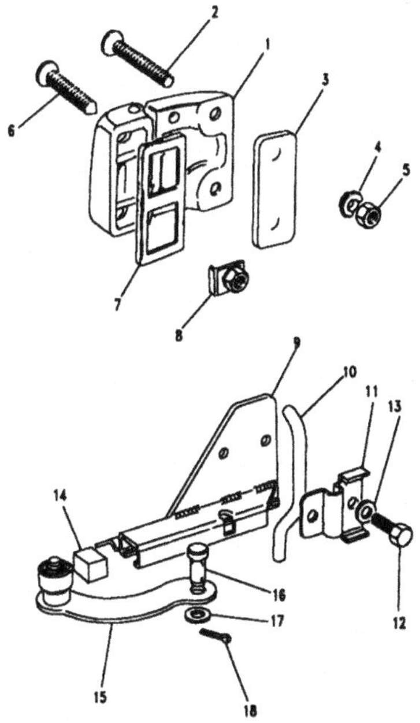

Illus	Part Number	Description	Quantity	Change Point	Remarks
		CHECKER ASSEMBLY-FRONT DOOR			
9	MUC6164	RH	1	To (V) AA 303555	
9	MUC6163	LH	1		
9	MWC5018	RH	1	From (V) AA 303556	
9	MWC5019	LH	1		
		TORSION BAR			
10	ALR2318	RH	1		
10	MUC6159	LH	1	To (V) HA 906552	
10	ALR2319	LH	1	From (V) HA 906553	
11	MUC6157	Bracket-pivot check arm	2	To (V) DA 314368	
11	MWC6450	Bracket-pivot check arm	2	From (V) EA 314369	
12	SH106301	Screw-bracket pivot to strap assembly check squab-hexagonal head-M6 x 30-long	4		
13	WA106041L	Washer-6mm	4		
14	MWC5759	Buffer-front door	2		
		CHECKER-FRONT DOOR			
15	MUC1888	RH	1	To (V) AA 303555	
15	MUC1889	LH	1		
15	ALR2321	RH	1	From (V) AA 303556	
15	ALR2322	LH	1		
16	306564	Pin-clevis/pivot	2	To (V) AA 303555	
16	PC108321L	Pin-clevis/pivot	2	From (V) AA 303556	
17	WA108051L	Washer-8mm	2		
17	302373	Washer-rubber	2		
18	2393	Pin-split	2	To (V) HA 455945	
18	NTC6195	Pin-split	2	From (V) HA 455946	

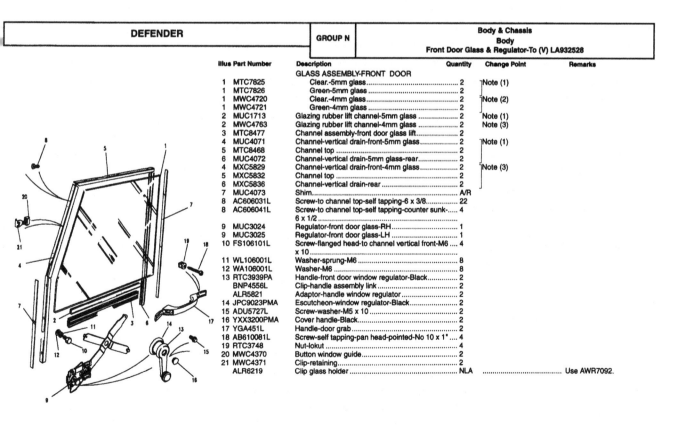

Front Door Glass & Regulator-To (V) LA932528

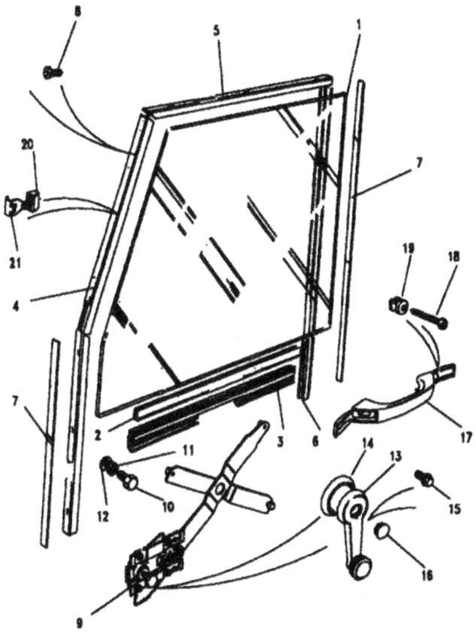

Illus	Part Number	Description	Quantity	Change Point	Remarks
		GLASS ASSEMBLY-FRONT DOOR			
1	MTC7825	Clear.-5mm glass	2	Note (1)	
1	MTC7826	Green-5mm glass	2		
1	MWC4720	Clear.-4mm glass	2	Note (2)	
1	MWC4721	Green-4mm glass	2		
2	MUC1713	Glazing rubber lift channel-5mm glass	2	Note (1)	
2	MWC4763	Glazing rubber lift channel-4mm glass	2	Note (3)	
3	MTC8477	Channel assembly-front door glass lift	2		
4	MUC4071	Channel-vertical drain-front-5mm glass	2	Note (1)	
5	MTC8468	Channel top	2		
6	MUC4072	Channel-vertical drain-5mm glass-rear	2		
4	MXC5829	Channel-vertical drain-front-4mm glass	2	Note (3)	
5	MXC5832	Channel top	2		
6	MXC5836	Channel-vertical drain-rear	2		
7	MUC4073	Shim	A/R		
8	AC606031L	Screw-to channel top-self tapping-6 x 3/8	22		
8	AC606041L	Screw-to channel top-self tapping-counter sunk-6 x 1/2	4		
9	MUC3024	Regulator-front door glass-RH	1		
9	MUC3025	Regulator-front door glass-LH	1		
10	FS106101L	Screw-flanged head-to channel vertical front-M6 x 10	4		
11	WL106001L	Washer-sprung-M6	8		
12	WA106001L	Washer-M6	8		
13	RTC3939PA	Handle-front door window regulator-Black	2		
	BNP4556L	Clip-handle assembly link	2		
	ALR5821	Adaptor-handle window regulator	2		
14	JPC9023PMA	Escutcheon-window regulator-Black	2		
15	ADU5727L	Screw-washer-M5 x 10	2		
16	YXX3200PMA	Cover handle-Black	2		
17	YGA451L	Handle-door grab	2		
18	AB610081L	Screw-self tapping-pan head-pointed-No 10 x 1"	4		
19	RTC3748	Nut-lokut	4		
20	MWC4370	Button window guide	2		
21	MWC4371	Clip-retaining	2		
	ALR6219	Clip glass holder	NLA		Use AWR7092.

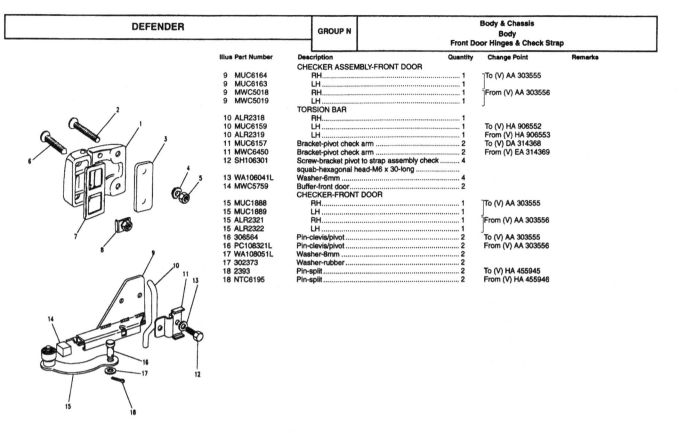

CHANGE POINTS:
(1) To (V) EA 340456 Regular; To (V) EA 344187 Station Wagon
(2) From (V) EA 340457 To (V) LA 932528 Regular; From (V) EA 344188 To (V) LA 932528 Station Wagon
(3) From (V) EA 340457 Regular; From (V) EA 344188 Station Wagon

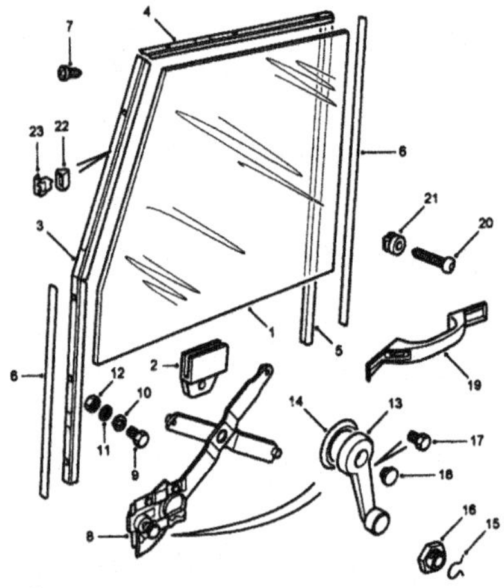

LN0150

Illus	Part Number	Description	Quantity	Change Point	Remarks
		GLASS ASSEMBLY-FRONT DOOR			
1	ALR4773	CLEAR.-RH	1	Note (1)	
1	ALR4771	CLEAR.-LH	1		
1	ALR4774	TINTED..-RH	1		
1	ALR4772	TINTED..-LH	1		
2	AWR7092	• Clip glass holder	2		
		GLASS ASSEMBLY-FRONT DOOR			
1	CUB000060	GREEN-RH	1	Note (2)	
1	CUB000070	GREEN-LH	1		
1	CUB000040	CLEAR.-RH	1		
1	CUB000050	CLEAR.-LH	1		
2	AWR7092	• Clip glass holder	2		
2	ALR6219	Clip glass holder	NLA		Use AWR7092.
3	MXC5829	Channel-vertical drain-front-4mm glass	2	Note (3); Note (4)	
3	CFE000710	Channel-vertical drain-front-4mm glass	2	Note (2)	
4	MXC5832	Channel top	2	Note (3); Note (4)	
5	MXC5836	Channel-vertical drain-rear	2	Note (3); Note (4)	
5	CFE000720	Channel-vertical drain-rear	2	Note (2)	

CHANGE POINTS:
(1) From (V) LA 932529 To (V) YA 999999
(2) From (V) 2A 622424
(3) From (V) EA 340457 To (V) YA 999999 Regular
(4) From (V) EA 344188 To (V) YA 999999 Station Wagon

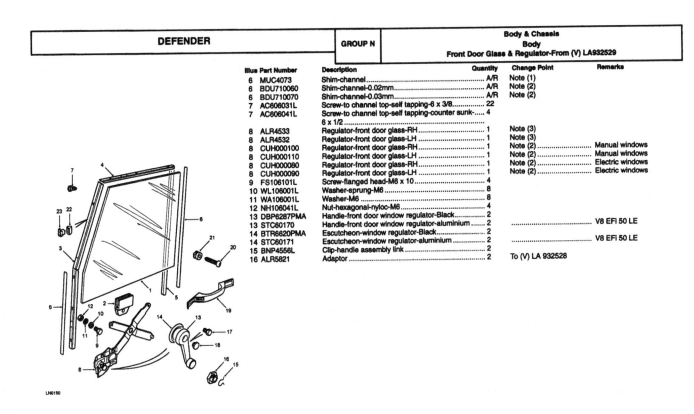

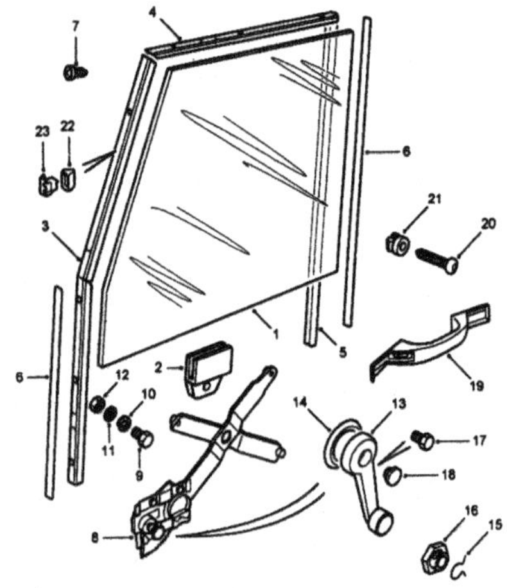

LN0150

Illus	Part Number	Description	Quantity	Change Point	Remarks
6	MUC4073	Shim-channel	A/R	Note (1)	
6	BDU710060	Shim-channel-0.02mm	A/R	Note (2)	
6	BDU710070	Shim-channel-0.03mm	A/R	Note (2)	
7	AC606031L	Screw-to channel top-self tapping-6 x 3/8	22		
7	AC606041L	Screw-to channel top-self tapping-counter sunk-6 x 1/2	4		
8	ALR4533	Regulator-front door glass-RH	1	Note (3)	
8	ALR4532	Regulator-front door glass-LH	1	Note (3)	
8	CUH000100	Regulator-front door glass-RH	1	Note (2)	Manual windows
8	CUH000110	Regulator-front door glass-LH	1	Note (2)	Manual windows
8	CUH000080	Regulator-front door glass-RH	1	Note (2)	Electric windows
8	CUH000090	Regulator-front door glass-LH	1	Note (2)	Electric windows
9	FS106101L	Screw-flanged head-M6 x 10	4		
10	WL106001L	Washer-sprung-M6	8		
11	WA106001L	Washer-M6	8		
12	NH106041L	Nut-hexagonal-nyloc-M6	4		
13	DBP6287PMA	Handle-front door window regulator-Black	2		
13	STC60170	Handle-front door window regulator-aluminium	2		V8 EFi 50 LE
14	BTR6620PMA	Escutcheon-window regulator-Black	2		
14	STC60171	Escutcheon-window regulator-aluminium	2		V8 EFi 50 LE
15	BNP4556L	Clip-handle assembly link	2		
16	ALR5821	Adaptor	2	To (V) LA 932528	

CHANGE POINTS:
(1) To (V) YA 999999
(2) From (V) 2A 622424
(3) From (V) LA 932529 To (V) YA 999999

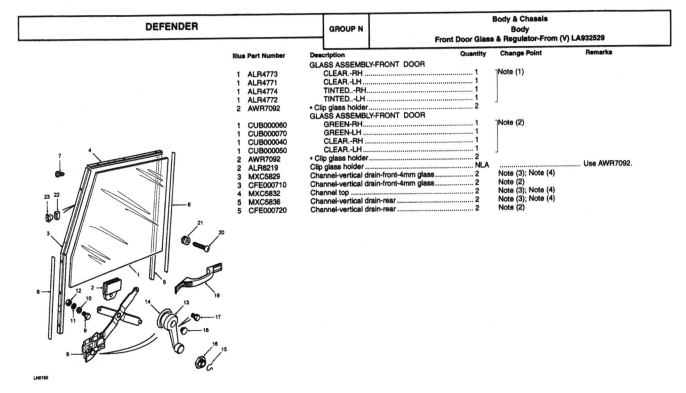

Body
Front Door Glass & Regulator-From (V) LA932529

Illus	Part Number	Description	Quantity	Change Point	Remarks
17	ADU5727L	Screw-washer-handle window regulator to regulator glass-M5 x 10	2		
18	YXX3200PMA	Cover handle-Black	2		
19	YGA451L	Handle-door grab	2		
20	AB610081L	Screw-to pull door-self tapping-pan head-pointed-No 10 x 1"	4		
21	RTC3748	Nut-lokut	4		
22	MWC4370	Button window guide	2	To (V) YA 199364	
22	MXC8603	Button window guide	2	From (V) YA 199365	
23	MWC4371	Clip-retaining	2		

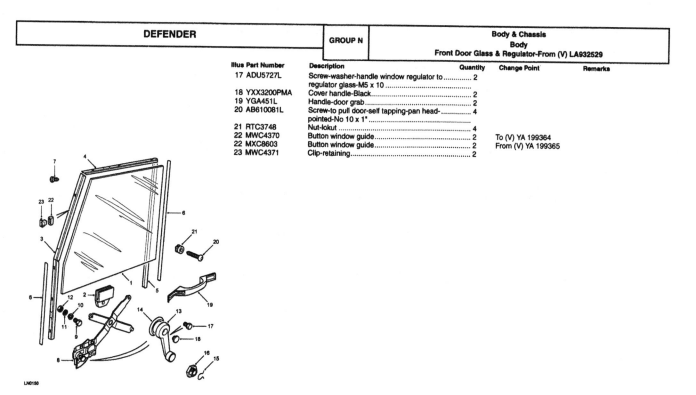

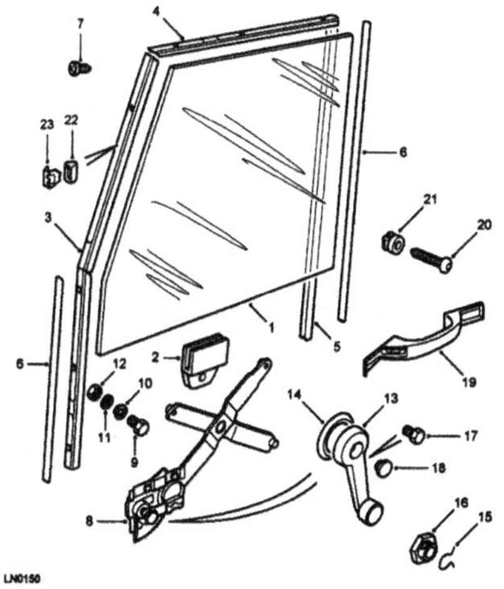

LN0150

Body
Front Door Seals

Illus	Part Number	Description	Quantity	Change Point	Remarks
1	MWC1080	Seal-front door-RH	1	Note (1)	Standard / County
1	MWC1081	Seal-front door-LH	1		
1	ALR4936	Seal-front door-RH	1	Note (2)	
1	ALR4937	Seal-front door-LH	1		
1	CFE102720	Seal-front door-RH	1	Note (3)	
1	CFE102730	Seal-front door-LH	1		
1	CFE102980	Seal-front door-RH	1	Note (4)	
1	CFE102990	Seal-front door-LH	1		
1	ALR6134	Seal-front door-RH-hinge side	1		90 SV
1	ALR6133	Seal-front door-LH-hinge side	1		
1	ALR6136	Seal-front door-RH-lock side	1		
1	ALR6135	Seal-front door-LH-lock side	1		
2	MWC6130	Seal-front door sill	2	Note (6)	
2	ALR6250	Seal-front door sill	2	Note (7)	
3	78248	Rivet-pop-3/16" x 0.45"lng	18	Note (6)	
3	ALR6280	Rivet-pop-steel	20	Note (7)	
4	AWR3140	Foam	4		
	MUC9204	Retainer-RH	1	Note (10)	
	MUC9205	Retainer-LH	1		
	SE105161L	Screw-recessed-pan head-M5 x 16	10		
	AFU1256	Washer-plain	10		
	WL105001L	Washer-retaining-M5	10		
	NH105041L	Nut-hexagonal-M5	10		

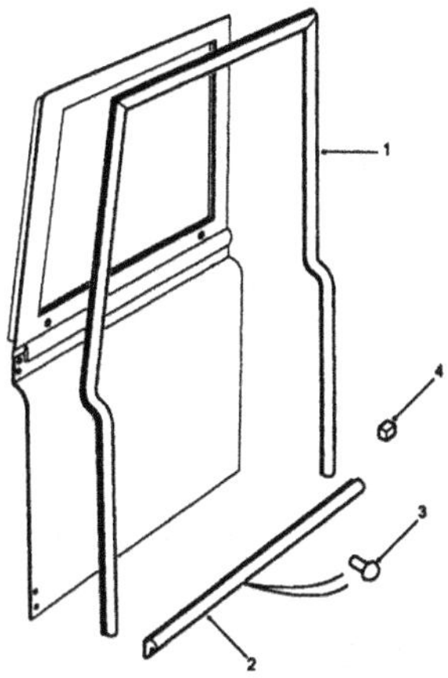

AHNXGA5A

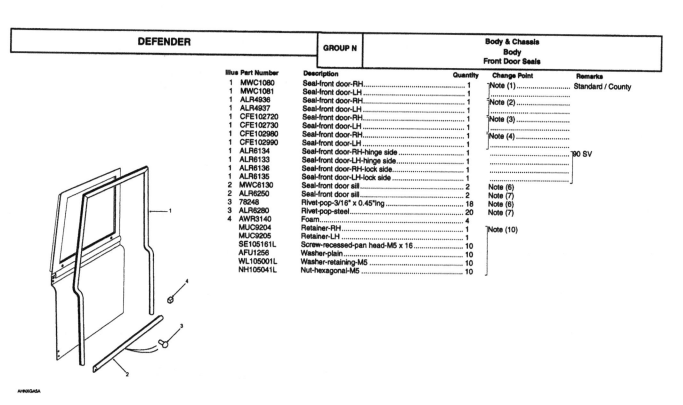

CHANGE POINTS:
(1) To (V) LA 935726
(2) From (V) LA 935727 To (V) VA 134184
(3) From (V) VA 134185 To (V) WA 159806
(4) From (V) XA 159807
(6) To (V) LA 933876
(7) From (V) LA 933877
(10) To (V) AA 270226

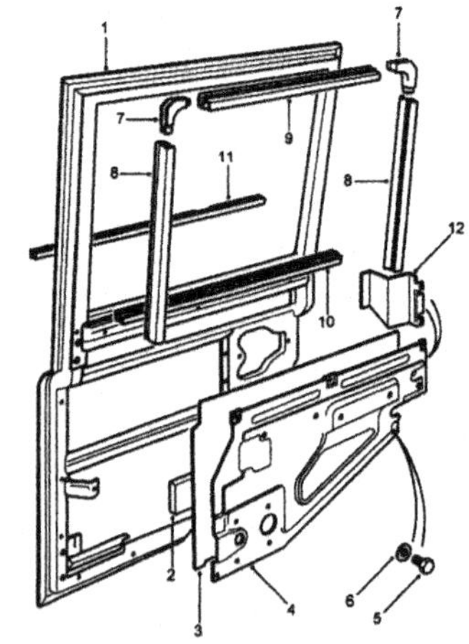

AJNXGI1A

Illus	Part Number	Description	Quantity	Change Point	Remarks
		DOOR ASSEMBLY-REAR			
1	ALR6258	side-RH	1	Note (1)	
1	ALR6259	side-LH	1		
1	ALR9896	side-RH	1	Note (2)	
1	ALR9895	side-LH	1		
1	BFL710020	side-RH	1	Note (3)	
1	BFL710030	side-LH	1	Note (3)	
2	392743	Pad-anti rattle	2		
3	MWC3294	Shedder-rear door water	2	Note (4)	
3	ELD106060	Shedder-rear door water-RH	1	Note (5)	
3	ELD106070	Shedder-rear door water-LH	1		
3	ELD000100	Shedder-rear door water-RH	1	Note (3)	CDL
3	ELD000110	Shedder-rear door water-LH	1		
3	ELD000080	Shedder-rear door water-RH	1		Except CDL
3	ELD000090	Shedder-rear door water-LH	1		
		PANEL-INNER			
4	MWC1602	side-RH	1	Note (6)	
4	MWC1603	side-LH	1		
4	RTC6238	side-RH	1	Note (7)	
4	RTC6239	side-LH	1		
4	ALR4543	side-RH	1	Note (8)	
4	ALR4542	side-LH	1		
4	BFO710020	side-RH	1	Note (3)	CDL
4	BFO710030	side-LH	1		
4	BFO710040	side-RH	1		Except CDL
4	BFO710050	side-LH	1		

CHANGE POINTS:
(1) To (V) TA 977524
(2) From (V) TA 977525 To (V) ZA 999999
(3) From (V) 2A 622424
(4) To (V) YA 191861
(5) From (V) YA 191862 To (V) YA 999999
(6) To (V) EA
(7) From (V) FA To (V) LA 932486
(8) From (V) LA 932487 To (V) YA 999999

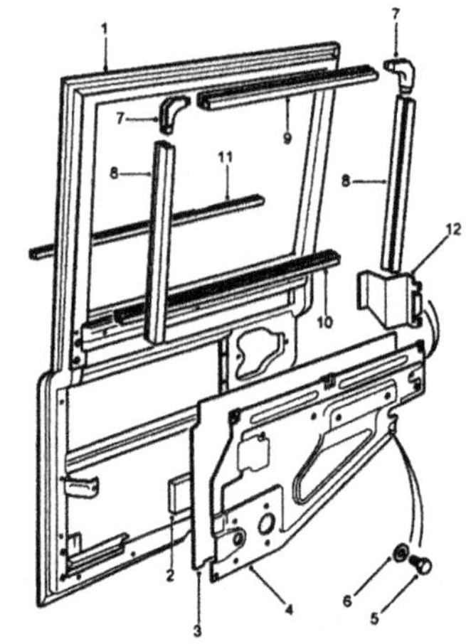

AJNXGI1A

Illus	Part Number	Description	Quantity	Change Point	Remarks
5	FS106167L	Screw-flanged head-to door assembly rear-flanged head-M6 x 16	10		
6	WA106041L	Washer-6mm	10		
7	201235	Filler-rear-corner	4		
8	MUC1651	Filler-vertical	4		
9	MTC8788	Filler-body-RH	1		
9	MTC8789	Filler-body-LH	1		
10	MWC1900	Seal waist inner	2		
		SEAL WAIST OUTER			
11	MUC1604	side-rear door-RH	1	Note (1)	
11	MUC1605	side-rear door-LH	1		
11	ALR5982	side-rear door-RH	1	Note (2)	
11	ALR5981	side-rear door-LH	1		
12	MWC4412	Deflector.-RH	1		
12	MWC4413	Deflector.-LH	1		

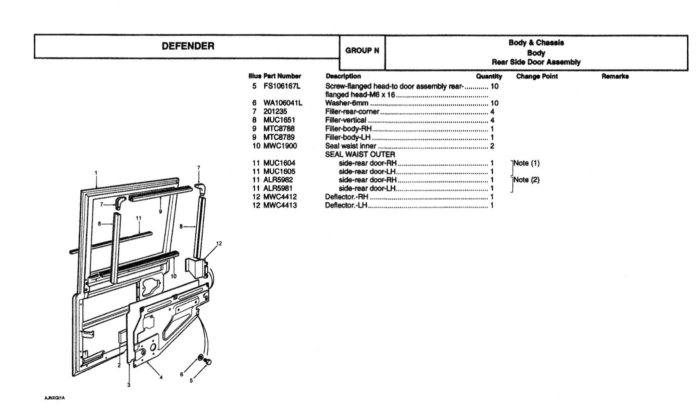

CHANGE POINTS:
(1) To (V) LA 937709
(2) From (V) LA 937710

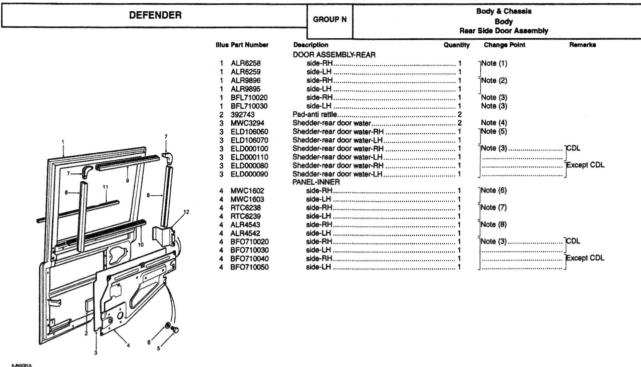

Illus	Part Number	Description	Quantity	Change Point	Remarks
		FRAME ASSEMBLY-BODY SIDE			
1	MWC3336	RH	1	Note (1)	110"
1	MWC3337	LH	1		
1	ALR5308	RH	1	Note (2)	
1	ALR5309	LH	1		
1	AMC710020	RH	1	Note (3)	
1	AMC710030	LH	1		
		FRAME ASSEMBLY-BODY SIDE			
1	RRC6254	RH	1	Note (1)	130"
1	RRC6253	LH	1		
1	ALR5312	RH	1	Note (2)	
1	ALR5313	LH	1		
1	AMC710040	RH	1	Note (3)	
1	AMC710050	LH	1		
		SEAL-REAR DOOR			
2	MWC1082	side-RH	1	Note (4)	
2	MWC1083	side-LH	1		
2	ALR4938	side-RH	1	Note (5)	
2	ALR4939	side-LH	1		
2	CFE103000	side-RH	1	Note (3)	
2	CFE103010	side-LH	1		

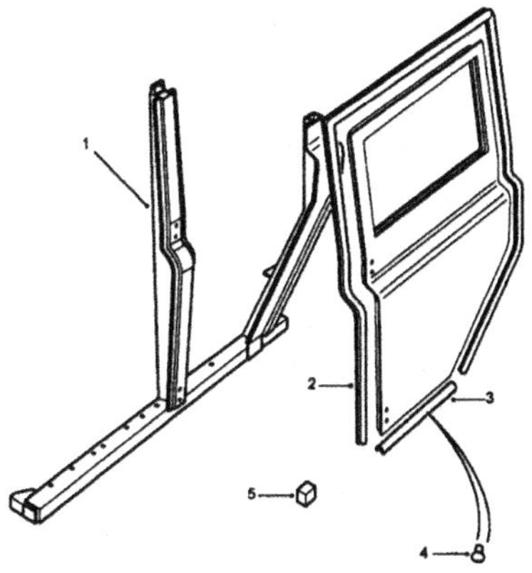

AJNXGK1A

CHANGE POINTS:
(1) To (V) KA 924784
(2) From (V) KA 924785 To (V) WA 159806
(3) From (V) XA 159807
(4) To (V) LA 935726
(5) From (V) LA 935727 To (V) WA 159806

Illus	Part Number	Description	Quantity	Change Point	Remarks
3	MWC6128	Seal-rear door sill-RH	1	Note (1)	
3	MWC6129	Seal-rear door sill-LH	1		
3	ALR6251	Seal-rear door sill	2	Note (2)	
4	RT612283	Rivet	8	Note (5)	
4	RU612503	Rivet-3/16" x 0.7lng	8	Note (6)	
5	AWR3140	Foam	4		
6	EYB10009L	Plug-blanking	2	Note (7)	Station Wagon

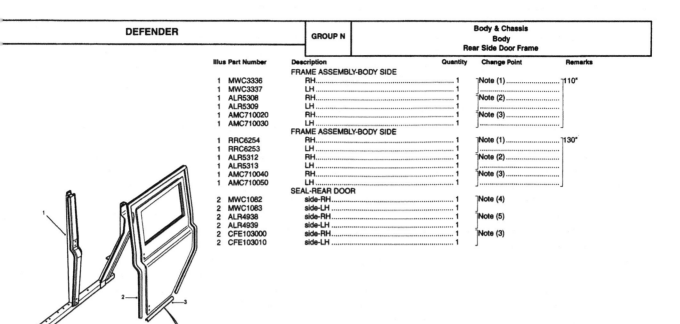

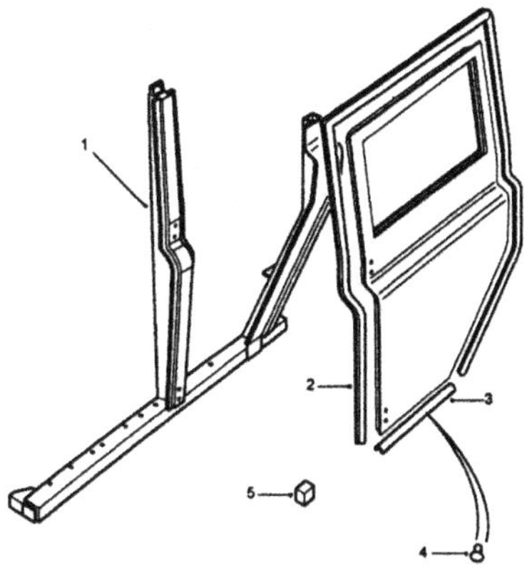

AJNXGK1A

CHANGE POINTS:
(1) To (V) LA 933876
(2) From (V) LA 933877
(5) To (V) YA 199999
(6) From (V) YA 600001
(7) From (V) TA 994833

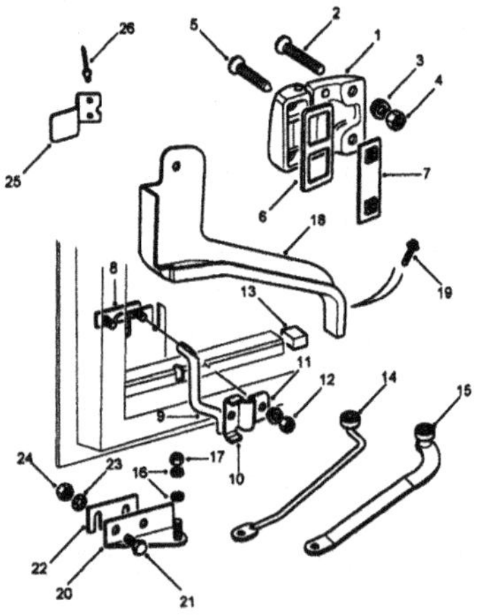

LN0045

Illus	Part Number	Description	Quantity	Change Point	Remarks
		HINGE ASSEMBLY-DOOR			
1	MXC8282	front door lower-rear door lower-rear door upper-Self Colour-RH	2	Note (1)	Standard / County
1	MXC8283	front door lower-rear door lower-rear door upper-Self Colour-LH	2	Note (1)	Standard / County
1	BDB710040	front door lower-rear door lower-rear door upper-Self Colour-RH	2	Note (2)	Standard / County
1	BDB710050	front door lower-rear door lower-rear door upper-Self Colour-LH	2	Note (2)	Standard / County
1	BDB710180	Self Colour-RH	2	Note (3)	Standard / County
1	BDB710190	Self Colour-LH	2	Note (3)	Standard / County
1	STC60725	front door lower-rear door lower-rear door upper-Silver powder coat-LH	1		Heritage
1	STC60726	front door lower-rear door lower-rear door upper-Silver powder coat-RH	1		Heritage
		FIXINGS-HINGE TO DOOR			
2	MRC2762	Bolt-5/16UNF-counter sunk	8	Note (4)	
2	BYG100150	Bolt-counter sunk-torx drive	8	Note (5)	
2	BYG100220	Bolt-counter sunk-torx drive	8	Note (6)	
2	BYG100150L	Bolt-counter sunk-torx drive-M8 x 55	8	Note (7)	
3	MRC1980	Washer-nylon	8		
4	NH605041L	Nut-hexagonal head-5/16UNF	8	Note (4)	
5	NY108041L	Nut-nyloc-M8	8	Note (8)	

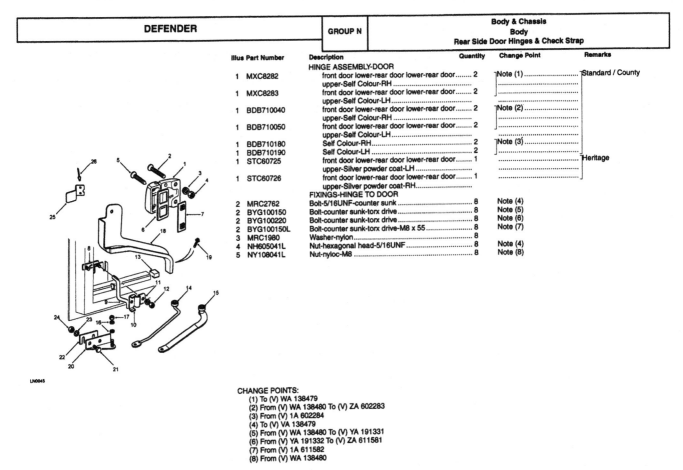

CHANGE POINTS:
(1) To (V) WA 138479
(2) From (V) WA 138480 To (V) ZA 602283
(3) From (V) 1A 602284
(4) To (V) VA 138479
(5) From (V) WA 138480 To (V) YA 191331
(6) From (V) YA 191332 To (V) ZA 611581
(7) From (V) 1A 611582
(8) From (V) WA 138480

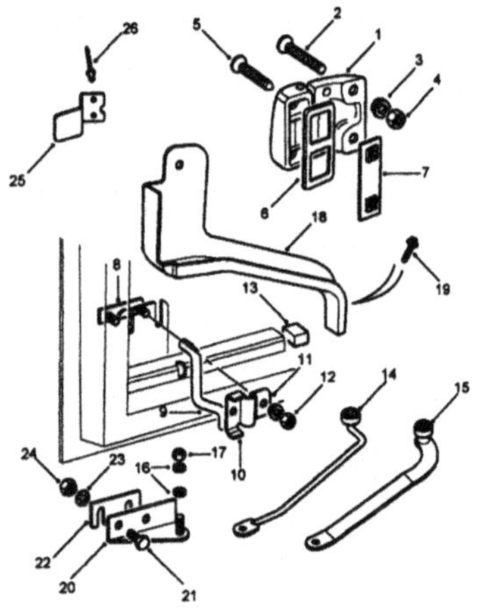

LN0045

Illus	Part Number	Description	Quantity	Change Point	Remarks
		FIXINGS - HINGE TO BODY			
5	MXC1436	Bolt-upper-counter sunk	4	Note (1)	
5	BYG100160	Bolt-upper-counter sunk-torx drive	4	Note (2)	
5	BYG100230	Bolt-upper-counter sunk-torx drive	4	Note (3)	
5	BYG100160L	Bolt-upper-counter sunk-torx drive	4	Note (4)	
5	AFU1036	Bolt-lower-counter sunk	4	Note (1)	
5	BYG100170	Bolt-lower-counter sunk-torx drive	4	Note (2)	
5	BYG100240	Bolt-lower-counter sunk-torx drive	4	Note (3)	
5	BYG100170L	Bolt-lower-counter sunk-torx drive	4	Note (4)	
6	MWC1898	Shim-door hinge	4		
6	347369	Shim-door hinge	4	Note (1)	
6	BHC710010	Shim-door hinge-plastic	4	Note (5)	
7	MUC9110	Nut plate	4		
8	MUC1961	Stud-bolt	2		
		TORSION BAR			
9	ALR2318	RH	1		
9	MUC6159	LH	1	Note (6)	
9	ALR2319	LH	1	Note (7)	
10	MUC6157	Bracket-pivot check arm	2	Note (8)	
10	MWC6450	Bracket-pivot check arm	2	Note (9)	
11	WA106041L	Washer-6mm	4		
12	NH106041L	Nut-hexagonal-nyloc-M6	4		
13	306295	Buffer-stop-rubber-short-1"-3/8	2	Note (8)	
13	MWC6291	Buffer-stop	2	Note (9)	

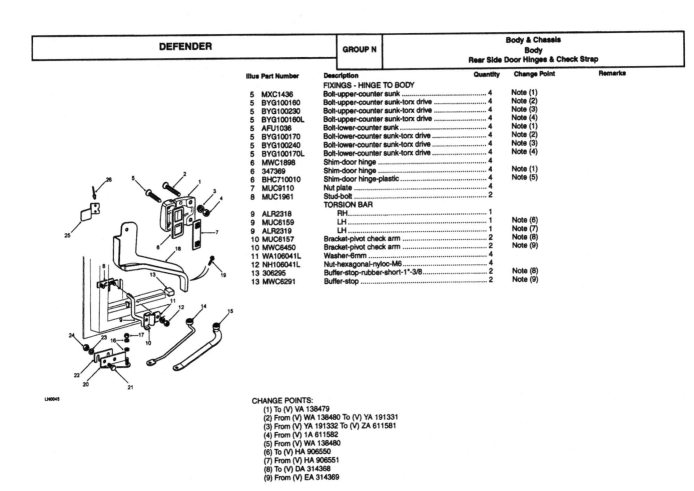

CHANGE POINTS:
(1) To (V) VA 138479
(2) From (V) WA 138480 To (V) YA 191331
(3) From (V) YA 191332 To (V) ZA 611581
(4) From (V) 1A 611582
(5) From (V) WA 138480
(6) To (V) HA 906550
(7) From (V) HA 906551
(8) To (V) DA 314368
(9) From (V) EA 314369

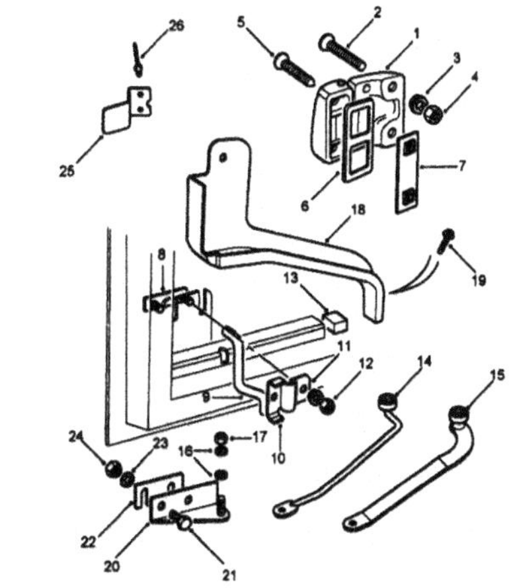

LN0045

Illus	Part Number	Description	Quantity	Change Point	Remarks
		CHECKER ASSEMBLY-REAR DOOR			
14	MWC1838	side-RH	1	Note (1)	
14	MWC1837	side-LH	1		
15	MWC5742	side-RH	1	Note (2)	
15	MWC5741	side-LH	1		
15	BFH710020	side-RH	1	Note (3)	
15	BFH710030	side-LH	1		
16	AFU1262	Washer-plain	4	Note (4)	
16	WA108051L	Washer-8mm	4	Note (3)	
17	NY106047L	Nut-hexagonal head-nyloc-M6	2	Note (4)	
17	NZ108041	Nut-nyloc-M8	2	Note (3)	
18	MXC9586	Panel waterdam-RH	1		
18	MXC9587	Panel waterdam-LH	1		
19	MUC3394	Screw-washer-to panel waterdam-No 8 x 19	2		
20	MRC4753	Bracket assembly-rear door checker-RH	1	Note (4)	
20	MRC4754	Bracket assembly-rear door checker-LH	1		
20	BFU710020	Bracket assembly-rear door checker-RH	1	Note (3)	
20	BFU710030	Bracket assembly-rear door checker-LH	1		
21	FS108257L	Screw-flanged head-M8 x 25	4		
22	305232	Shim	4		
23	WF108001L	Washer-starlock-M8	4		
24	FN108047L	Nut-flange-flanged head-M8	4		
25	ALR9160	Plate	1		
26	RU610183L	Rivet	4		

CHANGE POINTS:
(1) To (V) DA 314368
(2) From (V) EA 314369 To (V) ZA 608986
(3) From (V) 1A 608697
(4) To (V) 1A 608696

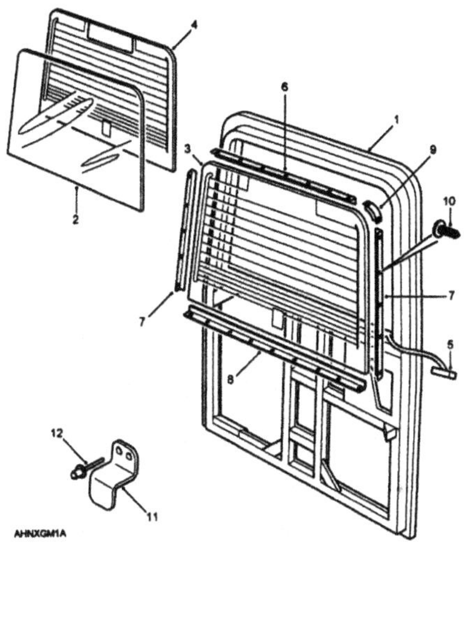

AHNXGM1A

Illus	Part Number	Description	Quantity	Change Point	Remarks
		LOAD/TAIL DOOR ASSEMBLY			
1	RTC6247	spare wheel carrier	1	Note (1)	
1	RTC6266	spare wheel carrier	1	Note (2)	
1	STC1423	spare wheel carrier	1	Note (3)	
1	STC1470	spare wheel carrier	1	Note (4)	
1	ALR6851	spare wheel carrier	1	Note (5)	
1	BIC110030	spare wheel carrier	1	Note (6)	
		LOAD/TAIL DOOR ASSEMBLY			
1	RTC6248	less spare wheel carrier	1	Note (1)	
1	STC1424	less spare wheel carrier	1	Note (7)	
1	STC1471	less spare wheel carrier	1	Note (4)	
1	ALR6852	less spare wheel carrier	1	Note (5)	
1	BIC110040	less spare wheel carrier	1	Note (6)	

CHANGE POINTS:
(1) To (V) AA 241999
(2) From (V) AA 242000 To (V) EA 358392
(3) From (V) FA 358393 To (V) KA 929577
(4) From (V) KA 929578 To (V) LA 939975
(5) From (V) MA 939976
(6) From (V) CO 7825LK
(7) From (V) AA 242000 To (V) KA 929577

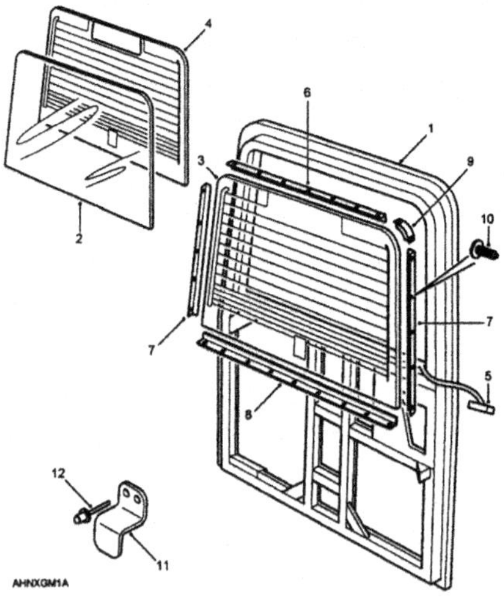

AHNXGM1A

Illus	Part Number	Description	Quantity	Change Point	Remarks
		GLASS - CLEAR			
2	MTC3469	Glass-rear door clear-unheated-5mm glass	1	Note (1); Note (2)	
2	MWC4712	Glass-rear door clear-unheated-4mm glass	1	Note (3); Note (4)	
		GLASS - TINTED			
2	MTC3470	Glass-rear door tinted-Green-unheated-5mm glass	1	Note (1); Note (2)	
2	MTC8951	Glass-rear door tinted-Green-heated-5mm glass	1	Note (1); Note (2)	
2	MWC4713	Glass-rear door tinted-Green-heated-4mm glass	1	Note (3); Note (4)	
4	CQB101560	Glass-high mounted stop light backlight	1	Note (5)	
5	78159	Strip-glazing	A/R		

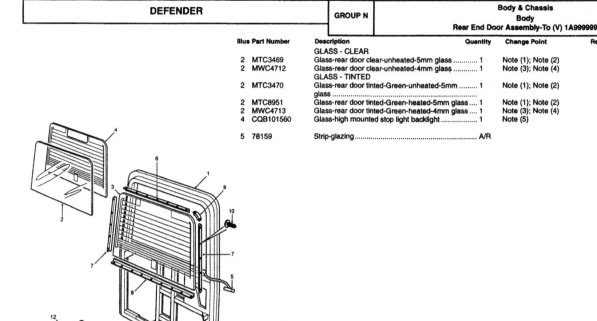

CHANGE POINTS:
(1) To (V) EA 340456 Regular
(2) To (V) EA 344187 Station Wagon
(3) From (V) EA 340457 Regular
(4) From (V) EA 344188 Station Wagon
(5) From (V) WA 138480

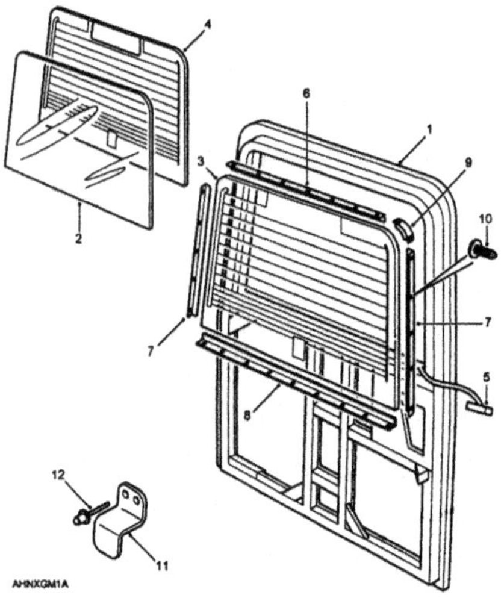

AHNXGM1A

Illus	Part Number	Description	Quantity	Change Point	Remarks
6	333034	Retainer-rear door-top	1		Note (1)
7	333033	Retainer-rear door-side	2		Note (1)
8	333032	Retainer-rear door-bottom	1		Note (1)
9	333035	Retainer-rear door-corner	2		Note (1)
10	AB606031L	Screw-retainer to door rear-self tapping-No 6 x 3/8	30	Note (1)	
10	AR606031L	Screw-retainer to door rear-self tapping-No 6 x 3/8	30	Note (2)	
	MTC9807	Strip-retainer-washer bag-LH	1	Note (3)	
	MTC9981	Retainer-RH	1	Note (3)	
12	RA612157L	Rivet	4	Note (3)	
11	ALR8987	Striker courtesy light	1	Note (4)	
12	RU610183L	Rivet	2	Note (4)	

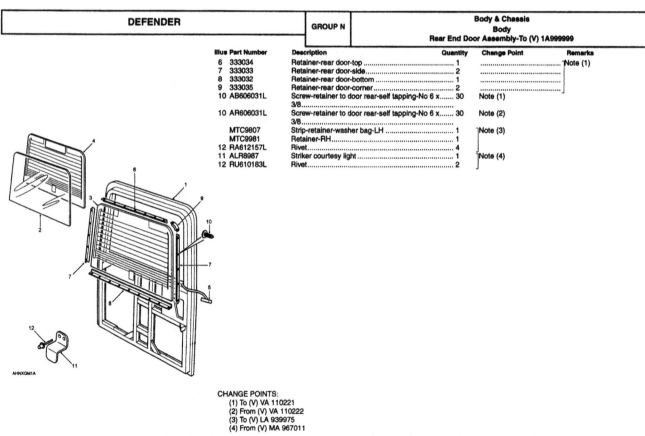

CHANGE POINTS:
(1) To (V) VA 110221
(2) From (V) VA 110222
(3) To (V) LA 939975
(4) From (V) MA 967011

Remarks:
(1) Parts fitted as polished aluminum : may be supplied for service in black primer. Remove if causes concern

Illus	Part Number	Description	Quantity	Change Point	Remarks
1	BIC710200	Load/tail door assembly-spare wheel carrier-with rear wash/wipe	1	Note (1)	
1	BIC710210	Load/tail door assembly-less door mounted spare wheel-with rear wash/wipe	1		
1	BIC710220	Load/tail door assembly-less door mounted spare wheel-less wash wipe	1		
1	BIC710230	Load/tail door assembly-without rear washwipe-less spare wheel carrier-less windows	1		
2	CQB000140	Glass assembly- load/tail door-Clear.	1		Except heated rear window and high mounted stop light
2	CQB000150	Glass assembly- load/tail door-Green-heated	1		Except high mounted stop light
2	CQB000270	Glass assembly- load/tail door-Green-heated-with high mounted stop lamp	1		High mounted stop light
4	CVW000010	Strip-glazing	1		
5	14A7081L	Plug-blanking	1		Except CDL
5	14A7090L	Plug-blanking	1		Except rear wash/wipe
7	BHZ110010	Bolt-M8-domed	6		
8	ESR2033	Nut-locking-M8	6		

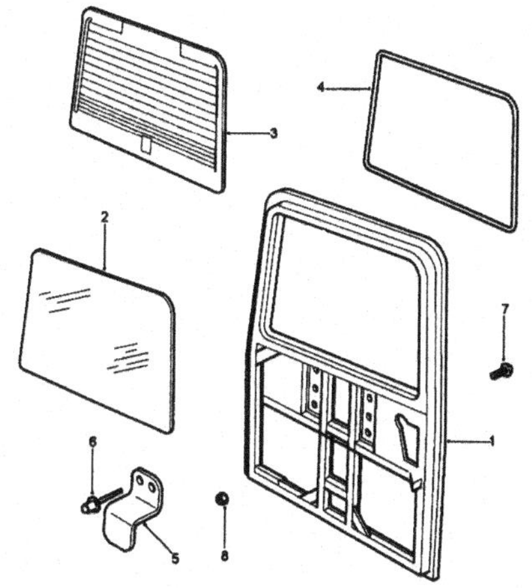
LN0199A

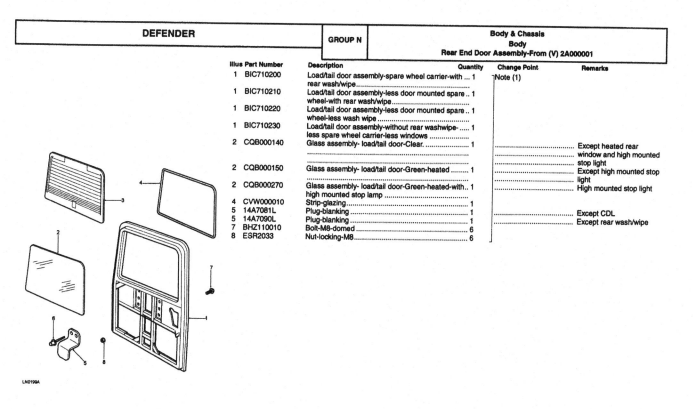

CHANGE POINTS:
(1) From (V) 2A 622424

Illus	Part Number	Description	Quantity	Change Point	Remarks
1	333036	HINGE ASSEMBLY-LOAD/TAIL DOOR UPPER	1	Note (1)	
2	346341	HINGE ASSEMBLY-LOAD/TAIL DOOR LOWER-MIDDLE	1		
3	330954	• Bush	1		
4	330955	• Spring	1		
5	330956	• Washer	1		
6	330953	• Bolt	1		

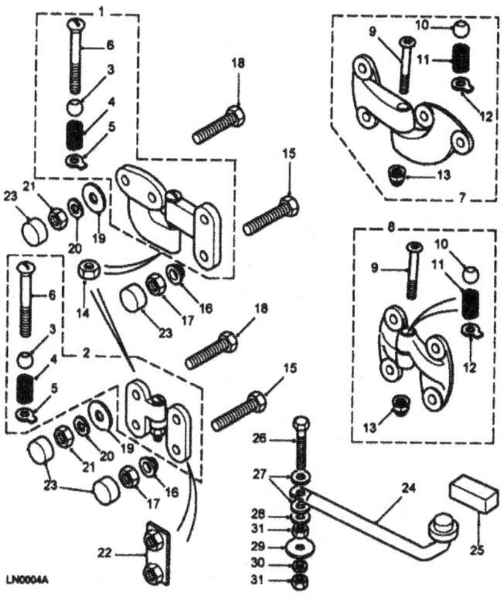
LN0004A

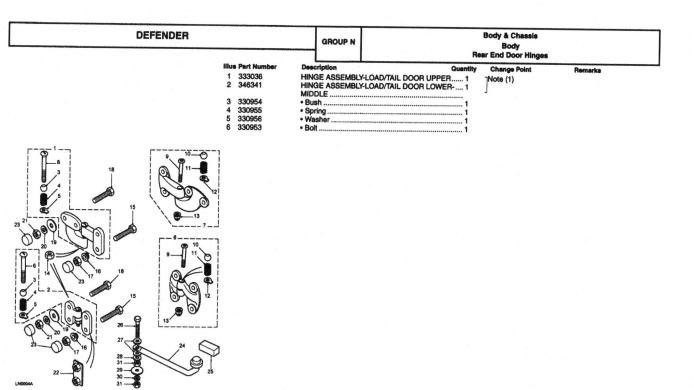

CHANGE POINTS:
(1) To (V) WA 138479

Illus	Part Number	Description	Quantity	Change Point	Remarks
7	BHB710050	HINGE ASSEMBLY-LOAD/TAIL DOOR UPPER-SELF COLOUR	1	Note (1)	
7	BHB710051	HINGE ASSEMBLY-LOAD/TAIL DOOR UPPER-SELF COLOUR	1	Note (2)	
7	STC60720	HINGE ASSEMBLY-LOAD/TAIL DOOR UPPER-SILVER POWDER COAT	1	Note (3)	Heritage
7	BHB710050SVR	HINGE ASSEMBLY-LOAD/TAIL DOOR UPPER-SILVER POWDER COAT	1	Note (4)	Heritage
9	BYG100190	• Bolt-counter sunk-torx drive	1		
10	330954	• Bush	1		
11	330955	• Spring	1		
12	330956	• Washer	1		
13	BYH100130	• Nut-domed	1		

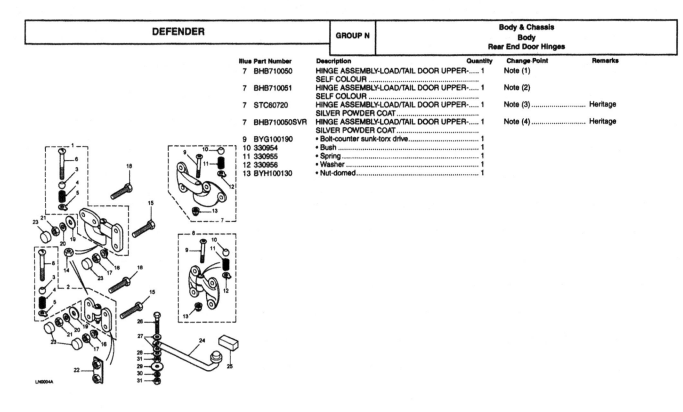

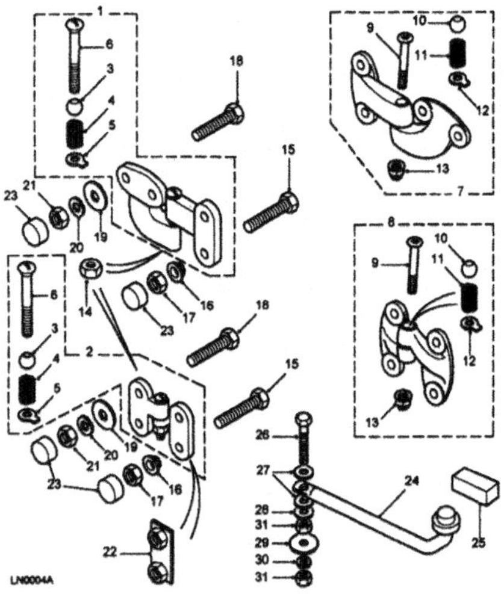

CHANGE POINTS:
(1) From (V) WA 138480 To (V) ZA 613479
(2) From (V) 1A 613480
(3) From (V) WA 138480 To (V) WA 159806
(4) From (V) XA 159807

Illus	Part Number	Description	Quantity	Change Point	Remarks
8	BHB710060	HINGE ASSEMBLY-LOAD/TAIL DOOR LOWER-MIDDLE-SELF COLOUR	1	Note (1)	
8	BHB710061	HINGE ASSEMBLY-LOAD/TAIL DOOR LOWER-SELF COLOUR-LOWER-MIDDLE	1	Note (2)	
8	STC60721	HINGE ASSEMBLY-LOAD/TAIL DOOR LOWER-MIDDLE-SILVER POWDER COAT	1	Note (3)	Heritage
8	BHB710060SVR	HINGE ASSEMBLY-LOAD/TAIL DOOR LOWER-MIDDLE-SILVER POWDER COAT	1	Note (4)	Heritage
9	BYG100190	• Bolt-counter sunk-torx drive	1		
10	330954	• Bush	1		
11	330955	• Spring	1		
12	330956	• Washer	1		
13	BYH100130	• Nut-domed	1		

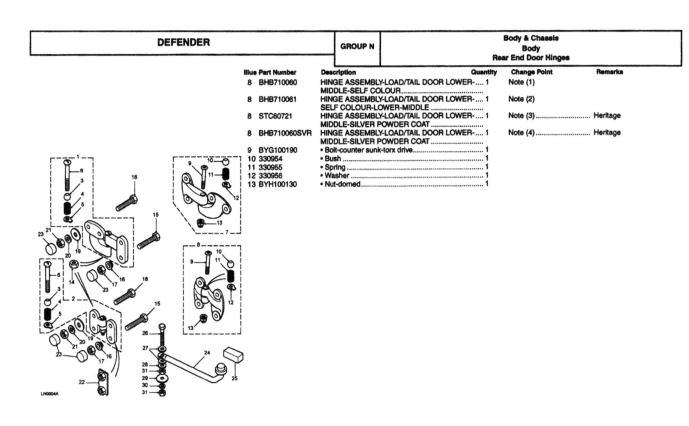

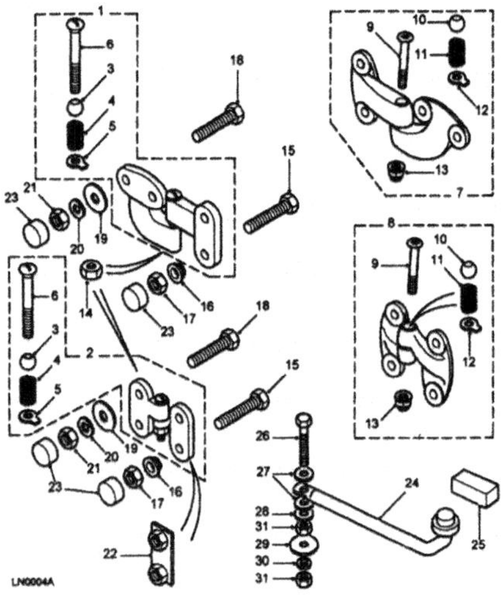

CHANGE POINTS:
(1) From (V) WA 138480 To (V) ZA 613479
(2) From (V) 1A 613480
(3) From (V) WA 138480 To (V) WA 159806
(4) From (V) XA 159807

Illus	Part Number	Description	Quantity	Change Point	Remarks
14	NH604041L	Nut-hexagonal head-coarse thread-1/4UNF	1		
15	SE108501	Screw-pan head-M8 x 50	6	Note (1)	
15	BYG100260	Screw-torx drive-M8 x 50	6	Note (2)	
16	MRC1980	Washer-nylon	6		
17	FN108047L	Nut-flange-flanged head-M8	6		
18	SE108251	Screw-pan head-M8 x 25	6	Note (1)	
18	BYG100250	Screw-torx drive-M8 x 25-Black	6	Note (2)	
19	WC108051L	Washer-M8	6		
20	WL108001L	Washer-sprung-M8	6		
21	FN108047L	Nut-flange-flanged head-M8	4		
22	MTC1042	Nut plate	1		
23	MTC6630	Cover nut-to hinge upper	8		Germany
23	MUC3798	Cover nut-to hinge lower-5/16UNF	2		

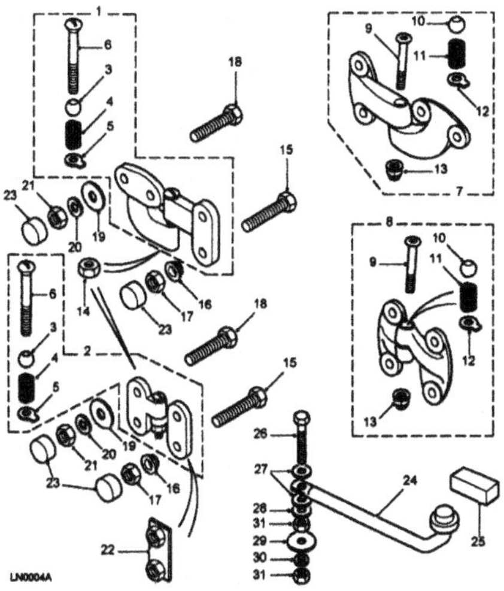

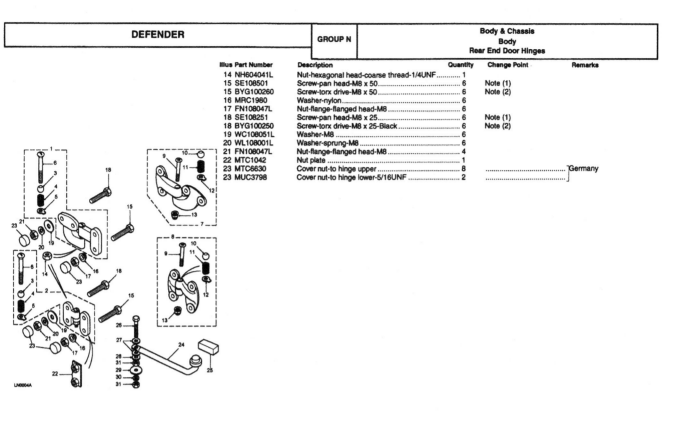

CHANGE POINTS:
(1) To (V) YA 191329
(2) From (V) YA 191330

Illus	Part Number	Description	Quantity	Change Point	Remarks
24	333041	Rod assembly-tie	1	To (V) AA 241999	
25	306295	Buffer-stop-rubber-short-1"-3/8	1		
25	333445	Buffer-stop-rubber-long-1"-1/2"-3/8	1		
26	BH106071	Bolt	1		
27	AFU1262	Washer-plain	2		
28	AFU1078	Washer-plain	1		
29	MRC5525	Washer-plain-standard	1		
30	WL106001L	Washer-sprung-M6	1		
31	NH106041L	Nut-hexagonal-nyloc-M6	2		

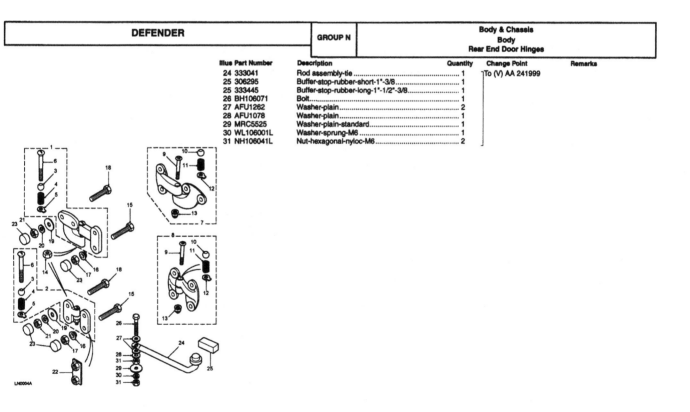

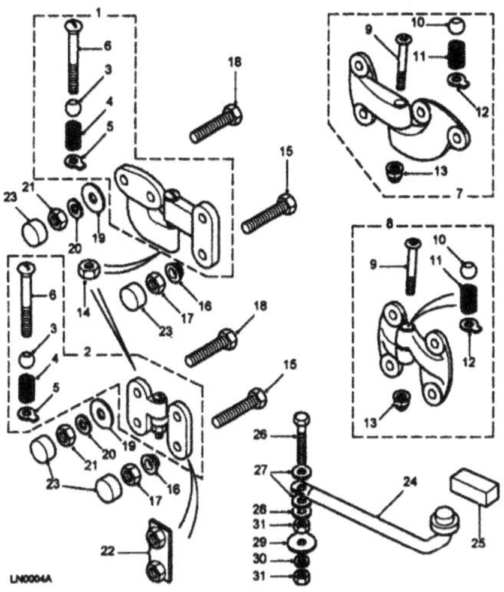

DEFENDER	GROUP N	Body & Chassis Body Rear End Door Check Mechanism-Lever Type

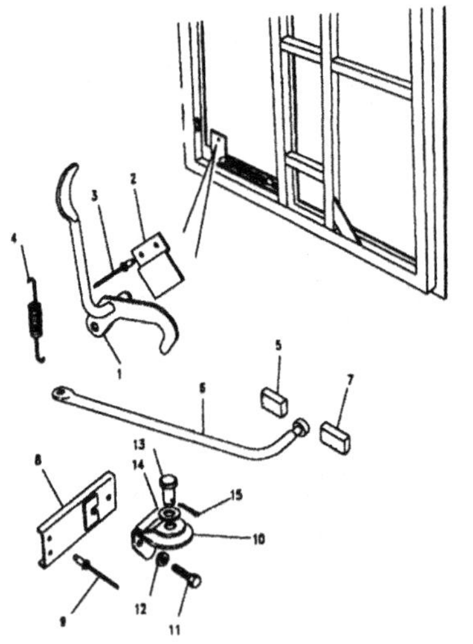

Illus	Part Number	Description	Quantity	Change Point	Remarks
1	MUC4474	Lever assembly-tailgate release	1		
2	MUC4486	Retainer	1		
3	RA608177L	Rivet	2		
4	MUC4481	Spring	1		
5	MUC4545	Buffer-stop-rubber-short	1		
6	MUC4471	Link assembly-drag	1		
7	MUC4544	Buffer-stop-rubber-long	1		
8	MUC4477	Bracket	1		
9	78248	Rivet-pop-3/16" x 0.45"lng	2		
10	346878	Bracket assembly-check arm pivot	1		
11	FS106201L	Screw-flanged head-M6 x 20	2		
12	WL106001L	Washer-sprung-M6	2		
13	306564	Pin-clevis/pivot	1		
14	349931	Washer-plastic	1		
15	2393	Pin-split	1		

DEFENDER	GROUP N	Body & Chassis Body Rear End Door Check Mechanism-With Torsion Bar

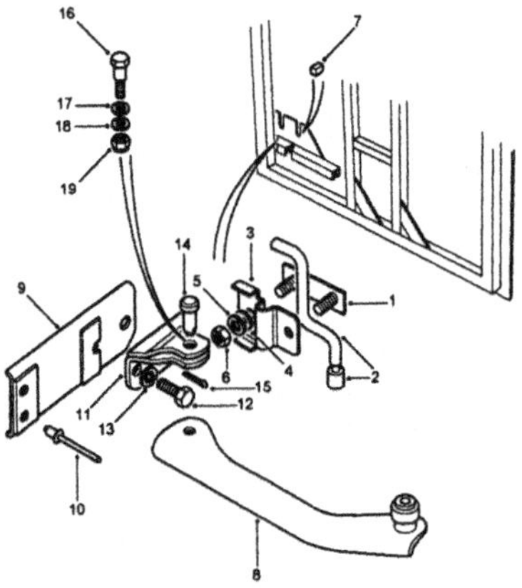

AHNXGM4A

Illus	Part Number	Description	Quantity	Change Point	Remarks
1	MUC1961	Stud-bolt	1		
2	MXC1790	Torsion bar & collar-rear end door	1		
3	MWC6450	Bracket-pivot check arm	1		
4	AFU1080	Washer-plain	2		
5	WL106001L	Washer-sprung-M6	2		
6	NH106041L	Nut-hexagonal-nyloc-M6	2		
7	MWC5759	Buffer-front door	1		
8	MXC5575	Checker assembly-rear door	1	Note (1)	
8	ASR1018	Checker assembly-rear door	1	Note (2)	
8	BHQ710020	Checker assembly-rear door	1	Note (3)	
9	MXC2044	Bracket-rear door checker	1	Note (1)	
9	RRC8517	Bracket-rear door checker	1	Note (2)	
10	78248	Rivet-pop-3/16" x 0.45"lng	2		
11	MXC2047	Bracket assembly-check arm pivot	1		
12	FS108207L	Screw-bracket pivot to bracket checker-flanged head-M8 x 20	2		
13	WL108001L	Washer-sprung-M8	2		
14	306564	Pin-clevis/pivot	1		
15	2393	Pin-split	1		
16	MXC5549	Bolt-shouldered-pin clevis to checker assembly	1		
17	WA108051L	Washer-8mm	1		
18	WA106041L	Washer-6mm	1		
19	NY106047L	Nut-hexagonal head-nyloc-M6	1		

CHANGE POINTS:
- (1) To (V) LA 939975
- (2) From (V) MA 939976
- (3) From (V) 2A 622424

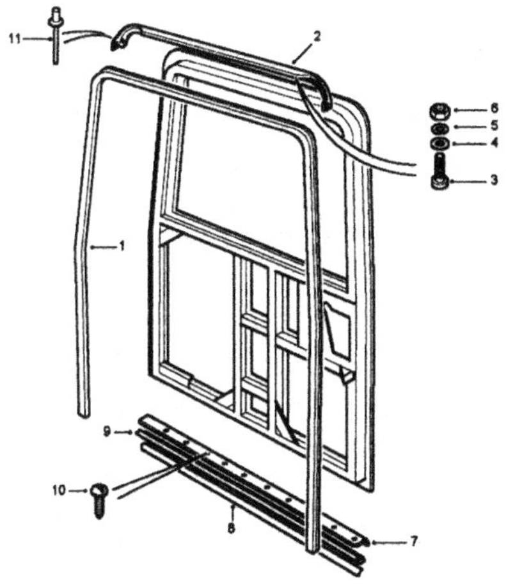

LN0192

Illus	Part Number	Description	Quantity	Change Point	Remarks
1	MTC4111	Seal-load/tail door primary	1	Note (1)	
1	ALR4929	Seal-load/tail door primary	1	Note (2)	
1	CKE101120	Seal-load/tail door primary	1	Note (3)	
2	MTC4290	Retainer-seal	1		
3	SE105161L	Screw-retainer to seal rear door-recessed-pan head-M5 x 16	9		
4	AFU1256	Washer-plain	9		
5	WL105001L	Washer-retaining-M5	9		
6	NH105041L	Nut-hexagonal-M5	9		
7	333203	Protector-tail door	NLA		Use ALR4769 qty 1 with ALR4770 qty 1.
8	ALR4770	Seal-rear door-floor	1		
9	ALR4769	Retainer-mat	1		
10	AB606057	Screw-protector to retainer seal-self tapping-No 6 x 5/8-long	7		
11	RU612373L	Rivet-3/16" x 0.575"lng	9		

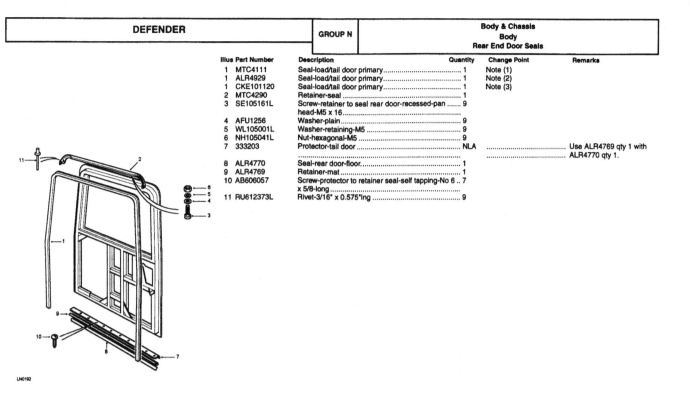

CHANGE POINTS:
(1) To (V) LA 935726
(2) From (V) LA 935727 To (V) XA 167599
(3) From (V) XA 167600

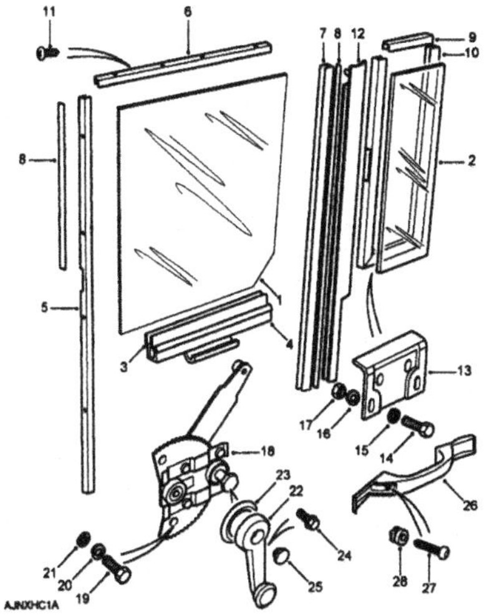

AJNXHC1A

Illus	Part Number	Description	Quantity	Change Point	Remarks
		GLASS-REAR SIDE DOOR			
1	MTC7828	5mm glass-Clear.	2	Note (1)	
1	MTC7829	5mm glass-Tinted..	2		
1	MWC4722	4mm glass-Clear.	2	Note (2)	
1	MWC4723	4mm glass-Tinted..	2		
1	ALR4777	4mm glass-Clear.-RH	1	Note (3)	
1	ALR4775	4mm glass-Clear.-LH	1		
1	ALR4778	4mm glass-Tinted..-RH	1		
1	ALR4776	4mm glass-Tinted..-LH	1		
		GLASS-REAR QUARTER			
2	MTC8460	5mm glass-Clear.	2	Note (1)	
2	MTC8461	5mm glass-Tinted..	2		
2	MWC4724	4mm glass-Clear.	2	Note (4)	
2	MWC4725	4mm glass-Tinted..	2		
3	MUC1714	Glazing rubber lift channel-5mm glass	2	Note (1)	
3	MWC4764	Glazing rubber lift channel-4mm glass	2	Note (4)	
4	MTC8478	Channel-rear door glass lift	2		
5	MUC4072	Channel-vertical drain-5mm glass-rear	2		
5	MXC5837	Channel-vertical drain-4mm glass	2		
6	MTC8471	Channel top-5mm glass	2	Note (1)	
6	MXC5833	Channel top-4mm glass	2	Note (4)	
7	MTC8472	Channel-vertical drain-5mm glass-rear	2	Note (1)	
7	MXC5834	Channel-vertical drain-4mm glass-rear	2	Note (4)	
8	MUC4073	Shim	A/R		
		CHANNEL-REAR QUARTER GLASS RUN			
9	MTC8790	5mm glass-top	2	Note (1)	
9	MXC5835	4mm glass-top	2	Note (4)	
10	MTC8791	5mm glass-lower	2	Note (1)	
10	MXC5830	4mm glass-lower	2	Note (4)	

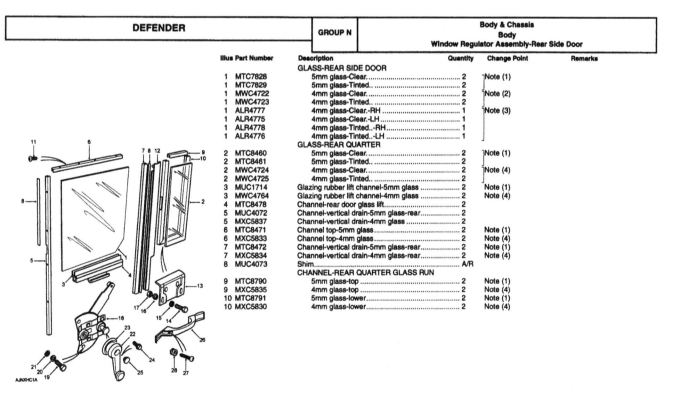

CHANGE POINTS:
(1) To (V) EA 344754
(2) From (V) EA 344755 To (V) LA 932486
(3) From (V) LA 932487
(4) From (V) EA 344755

DEFENDER

GROUP N

Body & Chassis
Body
Window Regulator Assembly-Rear Side Door

Illus	Part Number	Description	Quantity	Change Point	Remarks
11	AC606031L	Screw-to channel top-self tapping-6 x 3/8	16		
11	AC606041L	Screw-to channel top-self tapping-counter sunk-6 x 1/2	2		
12	MUC3492	Channel-rear door glass guide-RH	1		
12	MUC3493	Channel-rear door glass guide-LH	1		
13	MWC1627	Bracket-rear door glass guide	2		
14	SH104101L	Screw-to bracket glass guide-hexagonal head-M4 x 10	4		
15	WA104001L	Washer-plain-M4	4		
16	WE104001L	Washer- shakeproof-M4	4		
17	NH104041L	Nut-hexagonal-M4	4		
		REGULATOR-REAR DOOR GLASS			
18	MUC3026	RH	1	Note (1)	
18	MUC3027	LH	1		
18	ALR4535	RH	1	Note (2)	
18	ALR4534	LH	1		
19	FS106101L	Screw-flanged head-M6 x 10	8		
19	FS106101L	Screw-flanged head-to regulator glass-M6 x 10	8		
20	WA106041L	Washer-6mm	8		
21	WL106001L	Washer-sprung-M6	8		
22	DBP6287PMA	Handle-front door window regulator-Black	2		
	ALR5821	Adaptor	2		
23	BTR6620PMA	Escutcheon-window regulator-Black	2		
	BNP4556	Clip	2		
24	ADU5727L	Screw-washer-to handle window regulator-M5 x 10	2		
25	YXX3200PMA	Cover handle-Black	2		
26	YGA451L	Handle-door grab	2		
27	AB610081L	Screw-to pull door-self tapping-pan head-pointed-No 10 x 1"	4		
28	RTC3748	Nut-lokut	4		

CHANGE POINTS:
(1) To (V) LA 932486
(2) From (V) LA 932487

DEFENDER

GROUP N

Body & Chassis
Body
Windscreen Assembly

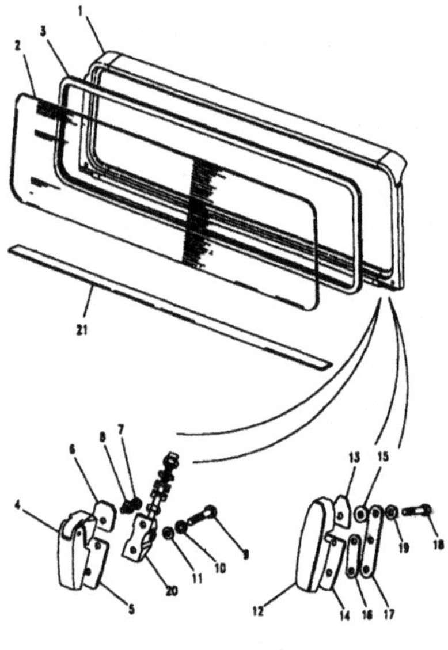

Illus	Part Number	Description	Quantity	Change Point	Remarks
1	MUC2594	Frame assembly-windscreen	1	Note (1)	Standard / County
1	AUH710010	Frame assembly-windscreen	1	Note (2)	Standard / County
1	ALR5705	Frame assembly-windscreen	1		90 SV
		GLASS-WINDSCREEN.			
2	MTC3452	laminated-Green	1	Note (3)	
2	MTC2864	laminated-Clear.	1		
2	MTC2863	toughened-Clear.	1		
2	CMB000420	heated-Clear.	1	Note (4)	
2	CMB000410	heated-Green	1		
3	MUC3733	Glazing rubber-windscreen	1		
4	MXC7847	Hinge windscreen-LH	1	Note (5)	
4	MXC7846	Hinge windscreen-RH	1		
		GASKET-QUARTERLIGHT GLASS HINGE			
5	MXC9982	lower	2		
6	MUC7904	upper	2	Note (6)	
6	MXC9983	upper	2	Note (7)	
7	SE110401	Screw-gasket to hinge-M10 x 40-long	2	Note (5)	
9	SS108404	Screw-clamp to gasket-M8 x 40-long	4		
10	WF108004L	Washer-lock	4		
11	WA108054L	Washer	4		
12	MUC7911	Bracket windscreen-RH	1	Note (8)	
12	MUC7912	Bracket windscreen-LH	1	Note (8)	
13	MXC9982	Gasket-quarterlight glass hinge-lower	2	Note (8)	
14	MXC9983	Gasket-quarterlight glass hinge-upper	2	Note (8)	
15	MUC7907	Washer	2	Note (8)	
16	MUC4289	Spacer	2	Note (8)	
17	MUC4290	Strap-windscreen	2	Note (8)	
18	FB108101L	Bolt-strap to bracket-flanged head-M8 x 50	6	Note (8)	
19	WA108051L	Washer-8mm	6	Note (8)	
20	RTC6159	Clamp	2	Note (8)	
21	ALR1737	Seal-windscreen glazing	1	Note (9)	
21	ALR5058	Seal-windscreen glazing	1	Note (10)	
21	FAJ100020	Seal-windscreen glazing	1	Note (11)	

CHANGE POINTS:
(1) To (V) YA 181358
(2) From (V) YA 181359
(3) To (V) 1A 622423
(4) From (V) 2A 622424
(5) To (V) JA 912345
(6) To (V) HA 466894
(7) From (V) HA 466895 To (V) JA 912345
(8) From (V) JA 912346
(9) From (V) JA 912346 To (V) KA 925389
(10) From (V) KA 925390 To (V) WA 151649
(11) From (V) WA 151650

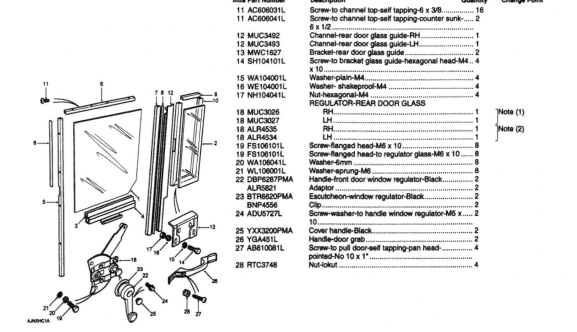

Illus	Part Number	Description	Quantity	Change Point	Remarks
		SPANISH LOCKS-'FAICA/SANTANA'			
		FRONT DOORS			
1	MUC4146	Lock & keys-front door	2	To (V) AA 270226	Spain
2	MUC4145	Key-blank owner	A/R		
		BASIC LOCKS			
		LOCK & KEYS			
1	RTC3022	basic locks-1 barrel/2 keys	1		
1	MTC6503	basic locks-2 barrels/2 keys	1		
1	MTC6504	basic locks-3 barrels/2 keys	1		
1	MTC6505	basic locks-4 barrels/2 keys	1		
1	MTC6506	basic locks-5 barrels/2 keys	1		
1	MTC6507	basic locks-6 barrels/2 keys	1		
2	CZK3438L	Key-blank owner-FT Series	A/R		
2	ALR9811	Key-blank owner-Large head	A/R		
		REAR END DOOR			
1	395141	Lock & keys-rear end door	1	From (V) EA 314174	
2	17H2475L	Key-blank owner-rear end door-square head-FS Series	A/R		
		TAILBOARD SIDE HINGED-LOCK 395041			
1	395141	Lock & keys-tailboard side hinged	1		Rest of World UK
2	17H2475L	Key-blank owner-tailboard side hinged-square head-FS Series	A/R		

NOTE:REAR END DOOR LOCK NOT AVAILABLE SEPERATELY

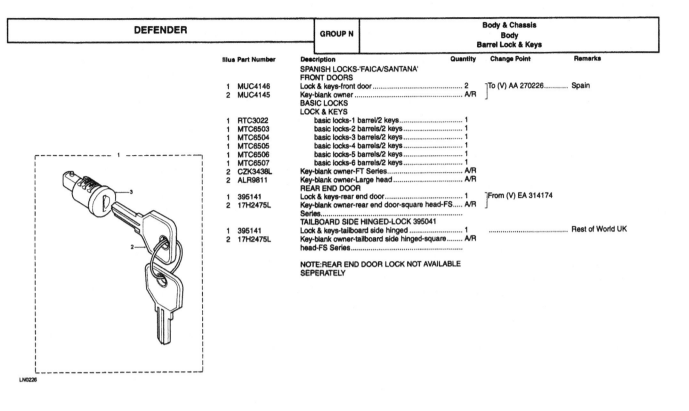

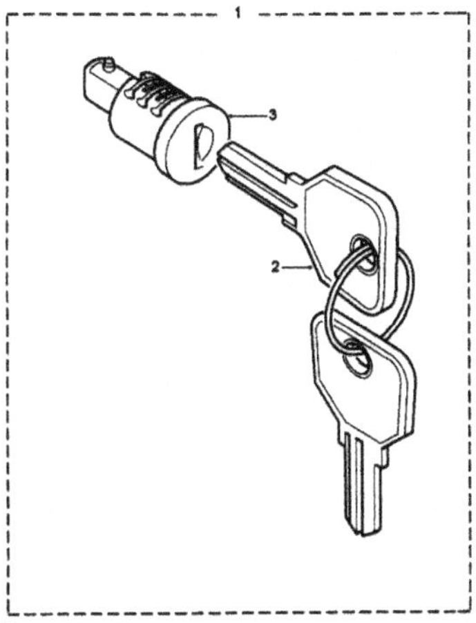

LN0226

Illus	Part Number	Description	Quantity	Change Point	Remarks
		LATCH ASSEMBLY-FRONT DOOR			
1	MUC2290	RH	1	Note (1)	
1	MUC2291	LH	1		
1	MUC6979	RH	1	Note (2)	
1	MUC6980	LH	1		
	MUC4146	• Lock & keys-front door	2		
	MUC4145	Key-blank owner	A/R		
2	MTC5536	Plate-stud-M6	4		
3	WL106001L	Washer-sprung-M6	8		
4	NH106041L	Nut-hexagonal-nyloc-M6	8		
5	MUC3360	Escutcheon-front door release assembly	2		
6	MUC3656	Handle-door grab-RH	1		
6	MUC3657	Handle-door grab-LH	1		
7	AB608061L	Screw-self tapping-No 8 x 3/4	6		
8	WE105001L	Washer-lock	6		
9	CZK3264L	Nut-lokut	6		
7	AB606031L	Screw-self tapping-No 6 x 3/8	2		
10	CZA2259L	Backplate-front & rear door handle	4		
11	WA104001L	Washer-plain-M4	4		
12	WE104001L	Washer- shakeproof-M4	4		
13	NH104041L	Nut-hexagonal-M4	4		
14	MUC4214	Link-front door sill button/latch-RH	1		
14	MUC4215	Link-front door sill button/latch-LH	1		
15	BHA4705L	Clip	2		
16	ADU3307L	Escutcheon-front door release assembly	2		
17	RTC3934AV	Button-front/rear door sill lock-Brushwood	2		

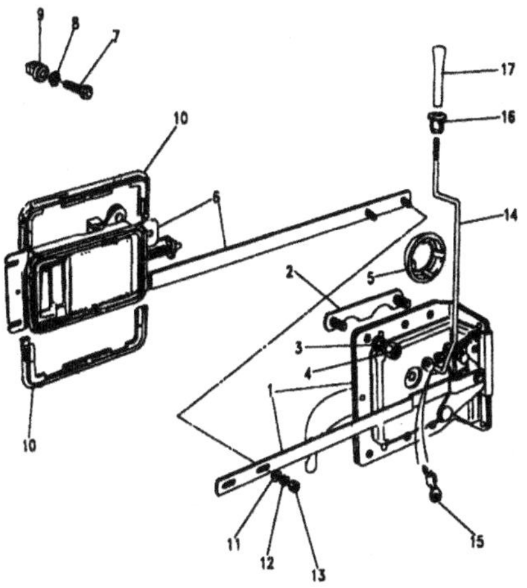

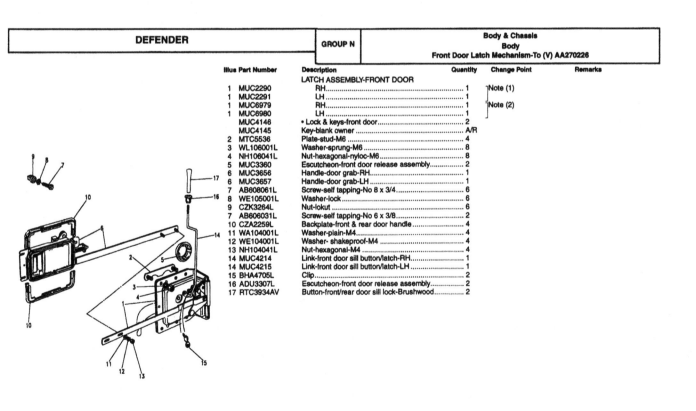

CHANGE POINTS:
(1) To (V) AA 242961
(2) From (V) AA 242962 To (V) AA 270226

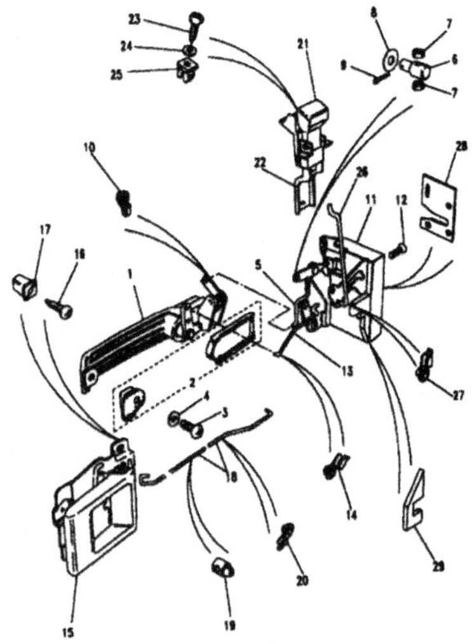

Illus	Part Number	Description	Quantity	Change Point	Remarks
1	MXC7652	Handle assembly-front door-RH	1	Note (1)	
1	CXB000030PMA	Handle assembly-front door-LH	1	Note (2)	
1	MXC7651	Handle assembly-front door-LH	1	Note (1)	
1	CXB000020PMA	Handle assembly-front door-RH	1	Note (2)	
2	STC617	Kit-gasket	2		
3	SE105101L	Screw-gasket kit to handle door outer-M5	4		
4	WA105001L	Washer-plain-standard-M5	4	Note (3)	
4	WC105001L	Washer-plain-large-M5	4	Note (4)	
5	MWC4846	Link threaded-RH	1	Note (1)	
5	FQP000080	Link threaded-RH	1	Note (2)	
5	MWC4847	Link threaded-LH	1		
5	FQP000090	Link threaded-LH	1	Note (2)	
6	MWC4850	Adjuster-door latch	2	Note (5)	
6	ALR4065	Adjuster-door latch	2	Note (6)	
6	FQA000010	Adjuster-door latch	2	Note (2)	
7	NH104041L	Nut-hexagonal-M4	4	Note (5)	
8	MRC5525	Washer-plain-standard	2		
9	PS603041L	Pin-split	2	Note (7)	
9	PS103101L	Pin-split	2	Note (8)	
10	634604	Clip-linkage	4	Note (9)	
10	BRC1393	Clip-linkage	4	Note (10)	
11	MWC1476	Latch-front door-RH	1	Note (11)	
11	FQJ103160	Latch-front door-RH	1	Note (12)	
11	MWC1477	Latch-front door-LH	1	Note (11)	
11	FQJ103170	Latch-front door-LH	1	Note (12)	

CHANGE POINTS:
(1) From (V) AA 270227 To (V) ZA 999999
(2) From (V) 2A 622424
(3) From (V) AA 270227 To (V) HA 455945
(4) From (V) HA 455946
(5) From (V) AA 270227 To (V) KA 930184
(6) From (V) KA 930185
(7) From (V) AA 270227 To (V) FA 446214
(8) From (V) FA 446215
(9) From (V) AA 270227 To (V) HA 703843
(10) From (V) HA 703844
(11) From (V) AA 270227 To (V) YA 194717
(12) From (V) YA 194718

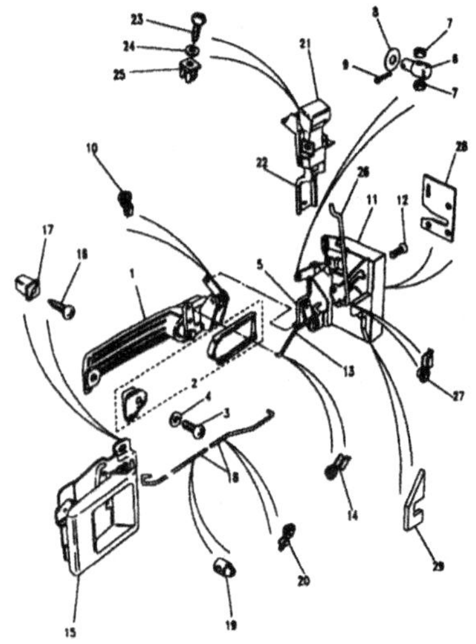

Illus	Part Number	Description	Quantity	Change Point	Remarks
12	SF106161L	Screw-gasket door lockface to latch front door-M6 x 16	6		
12	ALR6350	Screw-gasket door lockface to latch front door-torx drive-M8 x 30	6	Note (1)	
12	FYP101310	Screw-flanged head	6	Note (2)	
13	MWC1480	Link-front door lock/latch-external lock-RH	1		
13	MWC1481	Link-front door lock/latch-external lock-LH	1		
14	634604	Clip-linkage	2	Note (3)	
14	BRC1393	Clip-linkage	2	Note (4)	
15	DBP5840PMA	Handle assembly-door-Black-RH	1		
15	DBP5841PMA	Handle assembly-door-Black-LH	1		
16	MUC3394	Screw-washer-to handle assembly door-No 8 x 19	4		
17	MWC1950	Nut-lokut	4		
18	MWC1486	Link-front door lock/latch-inner handle-RH	1	Note (5)	
18	FQP101200	Link-front door lock/latch-RH	1	Note (2)	
18	MWC1487	Link-front door lock/latch-inner handle-LH	1	Note (5)	
18	FQP101210	Link-front door lock/latch-LH	1	Note (2)	
19	CRC1250L	Clip brake pipe	2		
20	BFP1265L	Clip-linkage	2		
21	JRC1775PMA	Button sill-Black	2		
22	BRC8965PMA	Housing-door lock-Black	2		
23	AB606041L	Screw-to button sill-self tapping-No 6 x 1/2	4		
24	WA104001L	Washer-plain-M4	4		
25	MWC1950	Nut-lokut	4		

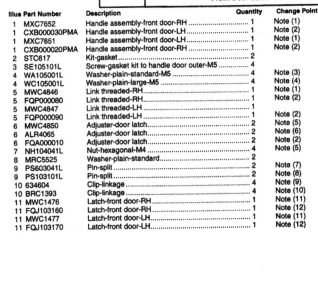

CHANGE POINTS:
(1) To (V) YA 194717
(2) From (V) YA 194718
(3) From (V) AA 270227 To (V) HA 703843
(4) From (V) HA 703844
(5) From (V) AA 270227 To (V) YA 194717

Front Door Latch Mechanism-From (V) AA270227

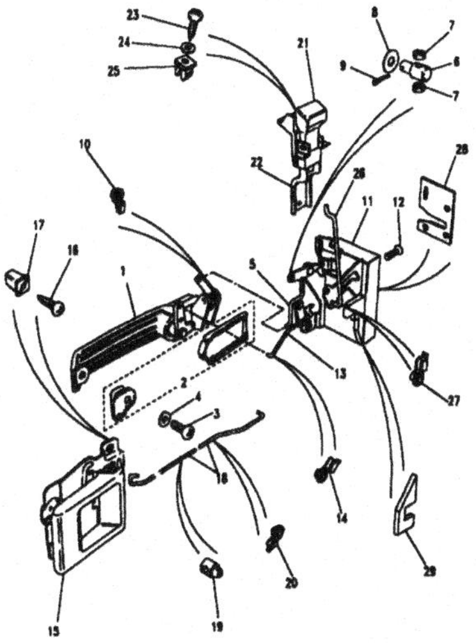

Illus	Part Number	Description	Quantity	Change Point	Remarks
26	MWC1484	Link-front door sill button/latch	2	Note (1)	
26	ALR6224	Link-front door sill button/latch	2	Note (2)	
26	FQK101450	Link-front door sill button/latch	2	Note (3)	
27	BFP1265L	Clip-linkage	2		
28	MXC8222	Gasket door lockface-RH	1	Note (4)	
28	MXC8223	Gasket door lockface-LH	1		
29	MXC8224	Seal-door lock striker-RH	1		
29	MXC8225	Seal-door lock striker-LH	1		

CHANGE POINTS:
(1) From (V) AA 270227 To (V) LA 936068
(2) From (V) LA 936069 To (V) YA 194717
(3) From (V) YA 194718
(4) From (V) FA 419244

Front Door Latch Striker-To (V) AA270226

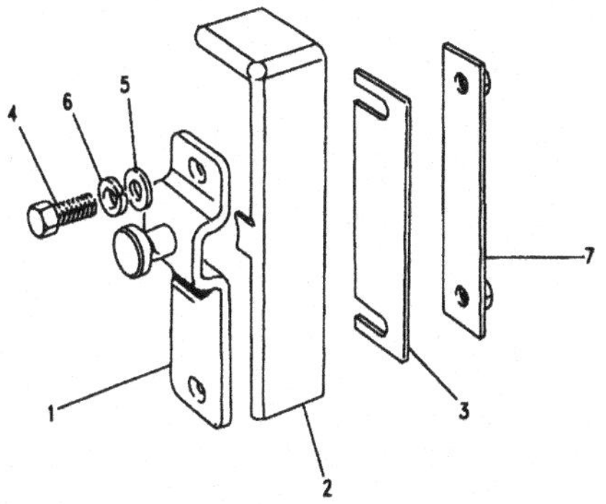

Illus	Part Number	Description	Quantity	Change Point	Remarks
1	MUC2959	Striker-door lock	2		
2	MUC4202	Shroud-central door locking latch-RH	1		
2	MUC4203	Shroud-central door locking latch-LH	1		
3	MUC3038	Shim-0.70mm	A/R		
3	MUC3039	Shim-1.20mm	A/R		
4	FS108207L	Screw-flanged head-M8 x 20	4		
5	WA108051L	Washer-8mm	4		
6	WL108001L	Washer-sprung-M8	4		
7	MUC2961	Plate & weldnut assembly	2		
8	MWC1736	Bracket support-RH	1		Except Station Wagon
8	MWC1737	Bracket support-LH	1		
9	FS106167L	Screw-flanged head-flanged head-M6 x 16	4		
10	WL106001L	Washer-sprung-M6	8		
11	AFU1259	Washer-plain	4		
12	MUC2965	Reinforcement-nut plate	2		
13	MUC1049	Stud	2		
14	AFU1257	Washer-plain	4		
15	NH106041L	Nut-hexagonal-nyloc-M6	4		

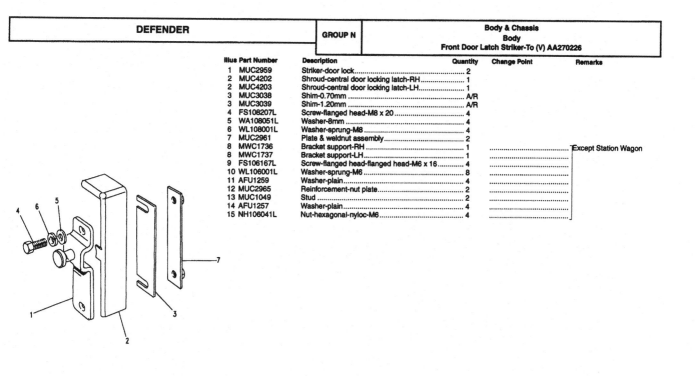

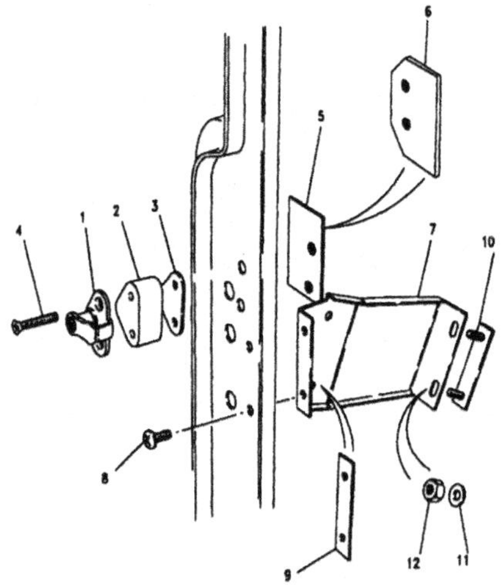

Illus	Part Number	Description	Quantity	Change Point	Remarks
1	MUC8526	Striker-door lock	2		
2	MUC7809	Spacer	2		
3	MWC3148	Spacer	A/R		
4	SF106401	Screw	4	Note (1)	
4	MXC9689	Screw-M6 x 40	4	Note (2)	
5	MWC1812	Reinforcement-RH	1		
5	MWC1813	Reinforcement-LH	1		
6	MWC1622	Nut-plate	2		Station Wagon
7	MWC1736	Bracket support-RH	1		
7	MWC1737	Bracket support-LH	1		
8	SE106161L	Screw-to bracket support-M6 x 16	4		
9	MRC9431	Nut plate	2		
10	MUC1049	Stud	2		
11	WA106041L	Washer-6mm	4		
12	NH106041L	Nut-hexagonal-nyloc-M6	4		

CHANGE POINTS:
(1) From (V) AA 270227 To (V) HA 482027
(2) From (V) HA 482028

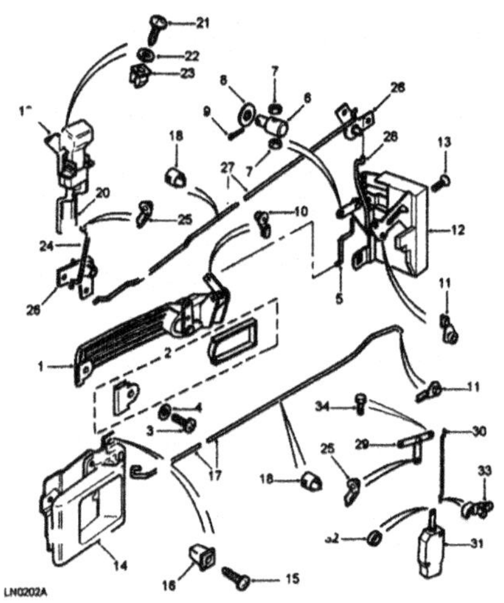

Illus	Part Number	Description	Quantity	Change Point	Remarks
1	MXC2728	Handle assembly-rear door-side-RH	1		
1	MXC2729	Handle assembly-rear door-side-LH	1		
2	STC617	Kit-gasket	2		
3	SE105101L	Screw-to handle assy-M5	4		
4	WA105001L	Washer-plain-standard-M5	4		
5	MWC5002	Link threaded-RH	1		
5	MWC5001	Link threaded-LH	1		
6	MWC4850	Adjuster-door latch	2	To (V) KA 930182	
6	ALR4065	Adjuster-door latch	2	From (V) KA 930183	
7	NH104041L	Nut-hexagonal-M4	4		
8	MRC5525	Washer-plain-standard	2		
9	PS603041L	Pin-split	2	To (V) FA 446199	
9	PS103101L	Pin-split	2	From (V) FA 446200	
10	634604	Clip-linkage	4	To (V) HA 904361	
10	BRC1393	Clip-linkage	4	From (V) HA 904362	
11	BFP1265L	Clip-linkage	4		
12	MWC1488	Latch-rear door-RH	1		
12	FQM100760	Latch-rear door-RH	1	Note (1)	
12	MWC1489	Latch-rear door-LH	1		
12	FQM100770	Latch-rear door-LH	1	Note (1)	
13	SF106161L	Screw-to latch-M6 x 16	6		
13	ALR6350	Screw-to latch-torx drive-M8 x 30	6		
14	DBP5840PMA	Handle assembly-door-Black-RH	1		
14	DBP5841PMA	Handle assembly-door-Black-LH	1		
15	MUC3394	Screw-washer-to handle assy-No 8 x 19	4		
16	MWC1950	Nut-lokut	4		
17	MWC1492	Link - locks-Inner handle-RH	1		
17	MWC1493	Link - locks-Inner handle-LH	1		
18	CRC1250L	Clip brake pipe	4		

CHANGE POINTS:
(1) From (V) YA 194718

DEFENDER | **GROUP N** | **Body & Chassis**

Body
Rear Side Door Latch Mechanism

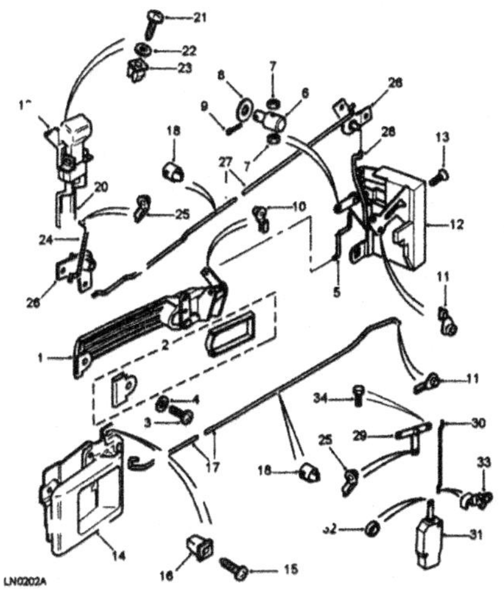

LN0202A

Illus	Part Number	Description	Quantity	Change Point	Remarks
19	JRC1775PMA	Button sill-Black	2		
20	BRC8965PMA	Housing-door lock-Black	2	Note (1)	
21	AB606041L	Screw-to button sill-self tapping-No 6 x 1/2	4		
22	WA104001L	Washer-plain-M4	4		
23	MWC1950	Nut-lokut	4		
24	MUC8364	Link-front door sill button/latch	2	Note (1)	
24	FQK000050	Link-front door sill button/latch	2	Note (2)	
25	634604	Clip-linkage	2	To (V) HA 904361	
25	BRC1393	Clip-linkage	2	From (V) HA 904362	
26	DZA1435L	Bellcrank-door	4		
27	MUC8365	Link intermediate	2	Note (1)	
27	FQK000040	Link intermediate	2	Note (2)	
28	MWC1485	Link door latch	2		
28	FQP000040	Link-rear door crank/latch-with central door locking	2	Note (2)	
29	FQF000040	Crank-door bell-(3 way)-with central door locking	2	Note (2)	
	AB612051	Screw	1	Note (2)	
30	FQP000010	Link rod-Bellcrank to actuator-with central door locking	2	Note (2)	
31	FUD000030	Actuator-central door locking-passenger's door	2	Note (2)	110"
32	CWH000010	Clip-linkage	2	Note (2)	
33	IPN000020	Clip-linkage-Latch to actuator	1	Note (2)	

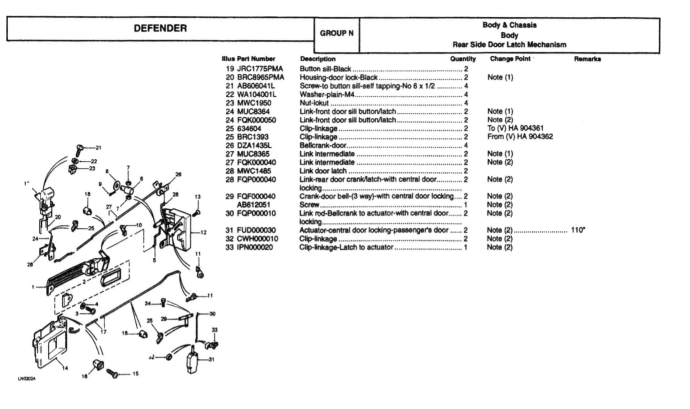

CHANGE POINTS:
(1) To (V) YA 999999
(2) From (V) 2A 622424

DEFENDER | **GROUP N** | **Body & Chassis**

Body
Rear Side Door Latch Striker

Illus	Part Number	Description	Quantity	Change Point	Remarks
1	MUC8526	Striker-door lock	2		
2	MUC7809	Spacer	2		
3	MWC3148	Spacer	A/R		
4	SF106401	Screw-striker to spacer	4	Note (1)	
4	MXC9689	Screw-striker to spacer-M6 x 40	4	Note (2)	
5	MWC1622	Nut-plate	2		

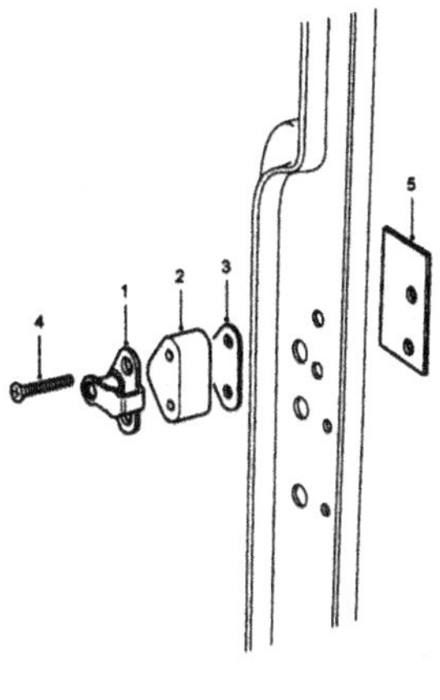

AJNXHG2A

CHANGE POINTS:
(1) To (V) HA 481996
(2) From (V) HA 481997

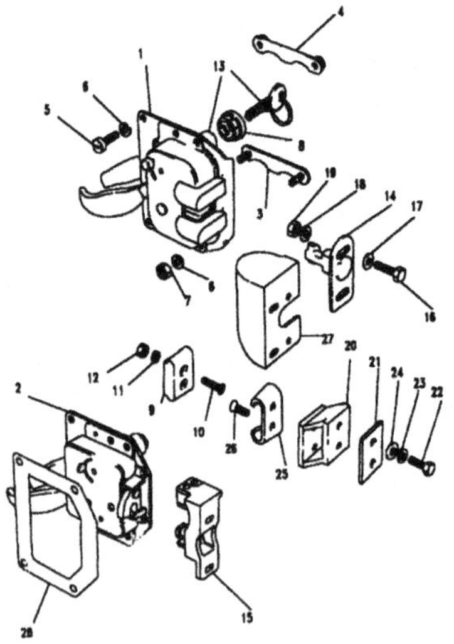

Illus	Part Number	Description	Quantity	Change Point	Remarks
1	STC2871	Kit-door key & lock cylinder-rear-end	1	Note (1)	
2	395037	Lock assembly-door	1	Note (2)	
2	FQM000030	Lock assembly-door	1	Note (3)	CDL
3	MRC9416	Stud plate	1	Note (5)	
3	ASR2667	Stud plate	1	Note (6)	
4	MRC9417	Nut plate	1	Note (5)	
4	ASR2668	Nut plate	1	Note (6)	
5	SE106161L	Screw-to nut plate-M6 x 16	2		
6	WL106001L	Washer-sprung-M6	4		
7	NH106041L	Nut-hexagonal-nyloc-M6	2		
8	347151	Seal	1		
8	CWN100020L	Seal	1	Note (7)	
8	EKC000030PMA	Seal	1	Note (3)	
9	332942	Dovetail male-rear door	1	Note (8)	
10	SA106251	Screw	2	Note (8)	
10	AB612051	Screw	1	Note (3)	
11	FQS000030	Link-load/tail door exterior release handle/latch-with central door locking	2	Note (3)	
12	WL106001L	Washer-sprung-M6	2	Note (8)	
13	NH106041L	Nut-hexagonal-nyloc-M6	2		
14	MRC8444	Striker-door lock	1	Note (9)	
15	395294	Striker-door lock	1	Note (10)	
15	ALR4652	Striker-door lock	1	Note (11)	
15	FQB000040	Striker-door lock	1	Note (12)	
21	395078	Shim	A/R	Note (1)	
	MWC3312	Bracket-roof grab handle rear	1	Note (13)	

CHANGE POINTS:
(1) To (V) LA 939975
(2) From (V) EA 314174
(3) From (V) 2A 622424
(5) To (V) VA 132280
(6) From (V) VA 132281
(7) From (V) CO 7825LK To (V) ZA 999999
(8) To (V) KA 929577
(9) To (V) EA 314173
(10) From (V) EA 314174 To (V) KA 929577
(11) From (V) KA 929578 To (V) YA 199364
(12) From (V) YA 199365
(13) From (V) 289409 To (V) LA 939975

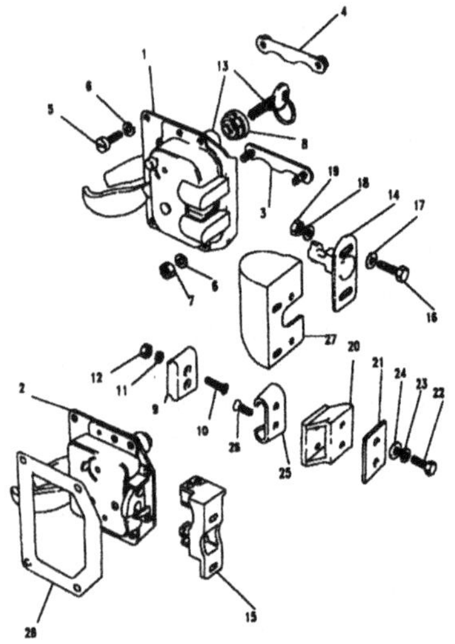

Illus	Part Number	Description	Quantity	Change Point	Remarks
16	SH106351L	Screw-hexagonal head-M6 x 35	2		
17	AFU1259	Washer-plain	2		
18	WL106001L	Washer-sprung-M6	2		
19	NH106041L	Nut-hexagonal-nyloc-M6	2		
20	MRC9619	Spacer	1	Note (1)	
21	305232	Shim	2	Note (1)	
22	FS106201	Screw-flanged head-M6 x 20	2	Note (1)	
23	WL106001L	Washer-sprung-M6	2	Note (1)	
24	AFU1080	Washer-plain	2	Note (1)	
25	332147	Dovetail female-rear door	1	Note (1)	
26	SA106161	Screw	2	Note (1)	
27	MRC9006	Shroud	1		
28	MXC9455	Seal-door lock cover plate	1		
	MTC7155	Cover-lock striker	1		Germany
29	FUD000030	Actuator-central door locking-passenger's door	1	Note (2)	
30	BFU710070	Bracket-mounting-with central door locking	1	Note (2)	
32	CWH000010	Clip-linkage	1	Note (2)	

CHANGE POINTS:
(1) To (V) KA 929577
(2) From (V) 2A 622424

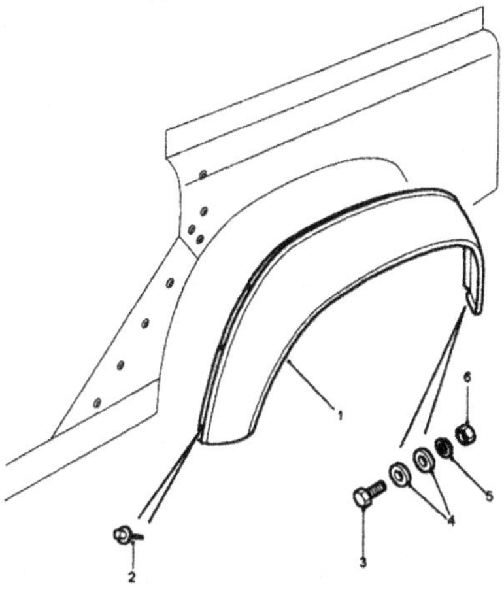

LN0189

Illus	Part Number	Description	Quantity	Change Point	Remarks
		EYEBROW-REAR WHEELARCH			
1	MRC8420	Black-plastic-Unpainted	2	Note (1)	
1	ALO710010	Black-plastic-Unpainted	2	Note (2)	
1	RRC3045	Matt Black.	2		
1	MTC6873P	Primer	2	Note (1)	
1	ALO710020P	Primer	2	Note (2)	
1	MTC6873NUC	Alpine White	NLA		Use MTC6873P.
1	MTC6873AA	Arizona Tan	NLA		Use MTC6873P.
1	MTC6873SUB	Arran Beige	NLA		Use MTC6873P.
1	MTC6873CUF	Arrow Red	NLA		Use MTC6873P.
1	STC60710	Atlantic Green.	2		Heritage
1	MTC6873JRJ	Biaritz Blue	NLA		Use MTC6873P.
1	STC60712	Bronze Green	2		Heritage
1	MTC6873HC	Bronze Green	NLA		Use MTC6873P.
1	MTC6873HYE	Coniston Green	NLA		Use MTC6873P.
1	MTC6873PUE	County Black	NLA		Use MTC6873P.
1	MTC6873HUL	County Green	NLA		Use MTC6873P.
1	MTC6873CUH	County Red	NLA		Use MTC6873P.
1	MTC6873HUJ	Eastnor Green	NLA		Use MTC6873P.
1	MTC6873HAF	Epsom Green	NLA		Use MTC6873P.
1	MTC6873NM	Ivory	NLA		Use MTC6873P.
1	MTC6873JC	Marine Blue	NLA		Use MTC6873P.
1	MTC6873CC	Masai red	NLA		Use MTC6873P.
1	MTC6873CUY	Montpellier Red	NLA		Use MTC6873P.
1	MTC6873LVD	Niagara Grey	NLA		Use MTC6873P.
1	MTC6873JUH	Pacific Blue	NLA		Use MTC6873P.
1	MTC6873LUS	Pembroke Grey	NLA		Use MTC6873P.
1	MTC6873AV	Roan Brown	NLA		Use MTC6873P.
1	MTC6873JUG	Shire Blue	NLA		Use MTC6873P.
1	MTC6873LN	Slate Grey	NLA		Use MTC6873P.
1	MTC6873JP	Stratos Blue	NLA		Use MTC6873P.
1	MTC6873HN	Trident Green	NLA		Use MTC6873P.
1	MTC6873CL	Venetian Red	NLA		Use MTC6873P.
2	AFU1075	Rivet-plastic-drive	24		
3	FS106207L	Screw-flanged head-M6 x 20	2		
4	MRC5525	Washer-plain-standard	4		
5	WL106001L	Washer-sprung-M6	2		
6	NH106041L	Nut-hexagonal-nyloc-M6	2		

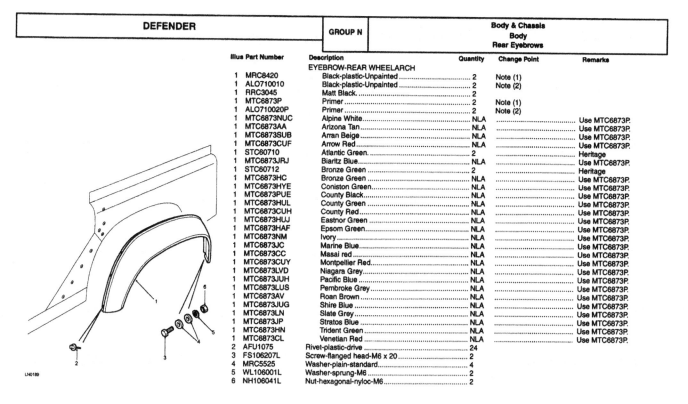

CHANGE POINTS:
(1) To (V) WA 138479
(2) From (V) WA 138480

Illus	Part Number	Description	Quantity	Change Point	Remarks
1	MTC7861	Mudshield-rear lamp	2	Note (1)	
1	BTR1790	Mudshield-rear lamp	2	Note (2)	
2	AFU1218L	Washer-plain	4		
3	AR610051L	Screw-self tapping	4		
4	AK610021L	Nut	4		
5	MRC8094	Plate	1		Except 90"
6	AR610051L	Screw-self tapping	4		Except 90"
7	AK610021L	Nut	4		Except 90"

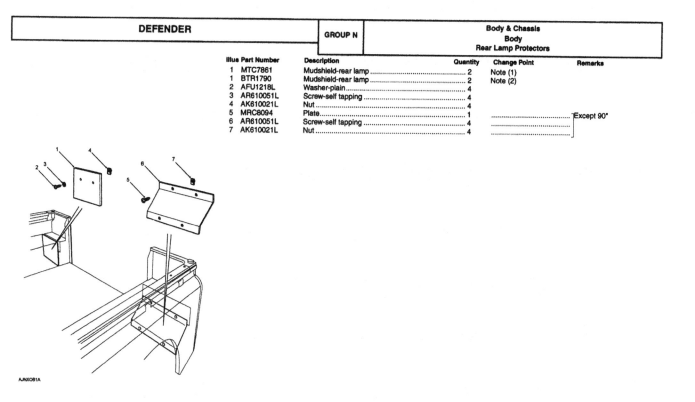

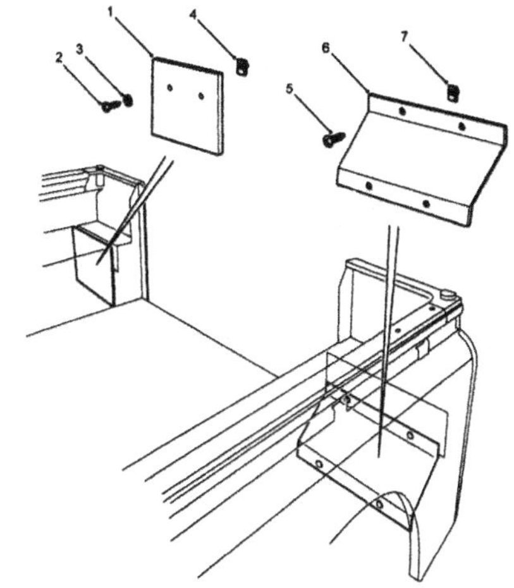

AJNXO81A

CHANGE POINTS:
(1) To (V) HA 704532
(2) From (V) HA 704533

Stirrup Step-Side Doors

Illus	Part Number	Description	Quantity	Change Point	Remarks
1	MTC2138	Step assembly-side-stirrup type	NLA		Use MTC2138AA.
1	MTC2138AA	Step assembly-side-stirrup type	1		Production fit except Germany
2	SE108251	Screw-pan head-M8 x 25	2		
3	WC108051L	Washer-M8	2		
4	WL108001L	Washer-sprung-M8	2		
5	FN108047L	Nut-flange-flanged head-M8	2		
6	MTC2548	Finisher	1		Germany

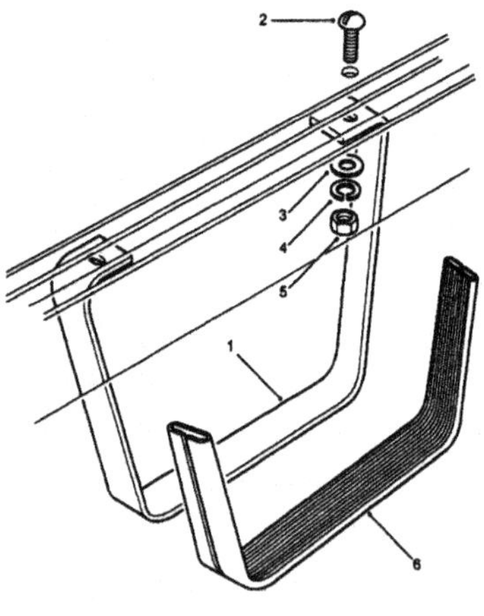

AHNXPA1A

Step Assembly Folding-Side Doors

Illus	Part Number	Description	Quantity	Change Point	Remarks
1	MTC7466	STEP ASSEMBLY-SIDE-FOLDING	1		Production fit except Germany
2	MTC3021	• Kit-side step	1		
3	MTC3076	• Tread plate	1		
4	RT612253	• Rivet	4		
5	WA105001L	• Washer-plain-standard-M5	4		
6	MTC7465	• Bracket	1		
7	MTC1233	• Spring	1		
8	MTC7464	• Bolt	2		
9	WB114001L	• Washer-plain	2		
10	NY108041L	• Nut-nyloc-M8	2		
11	MXC1624	Support assembly-side step	1		
12	FS108257L	Screw-step to sill-flanged head-M8 x 25	2		Except Germany
13	WA108051L	Washer-step to sill-8mm	2		
14	NY108041L	Nut-step to sill-nyloc-M8	2		
15	FS108257L	Screw-brace to chassis-flanged head-M8 x 25	1		Except Germany
16	WL108001L	Washer-brace to chassis-sprung-M8	1		
17	WC108051L	Washer-brace to chassis-M8	A/R		
18	NN108021	Nut-brace to chassis-blind-M8	1	Note (2)	
18	AYH101200	Nut-brace to chassis-hexagonal-M8	1	Note (3)	
19	SE108201	Screw-brace to step	1		
20	NY108041L	Nut-brace to step-nyloc-M8	1		

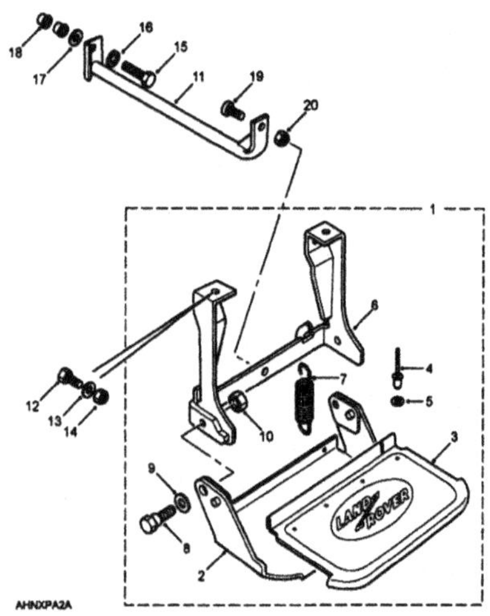

AHNXPA2A

CHANGE POINTS:
(2) To (V) WA 159806
(3) From (V) XA 159807

Illus	Part Number	Description	Quantity	Change Point	Remarks
1	STC8438AA	Step-side runner-Black-pair	1		Biaritz L.E. Germany
1	STC61858	Step-side runner-RH	1	Note (1)	Tomb Raider 90"
1	STC61859	Step-side runner-LH	1		
1	STC61860	Step-side runner-LH	1		Tomb Raider 110"
1	STC61861	Step-side runner-RH	1		

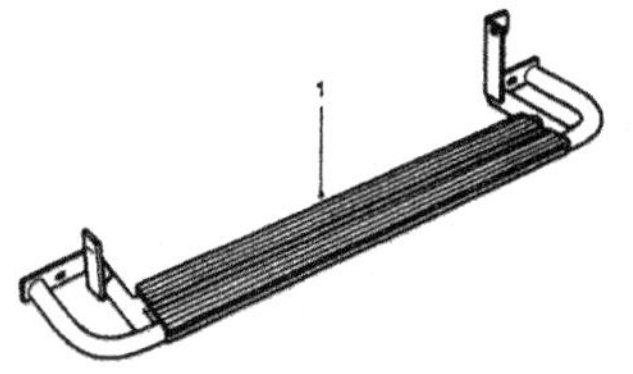

AHNXPASA

CHANGE POINTS:
(1) From (V) 1A 612404

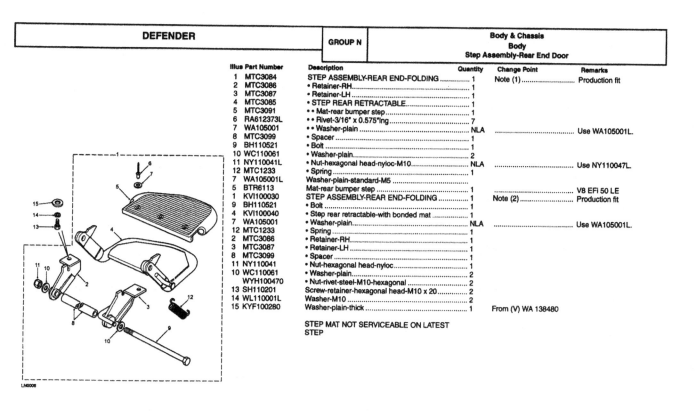

Illus	Part Number	Description	Quantity	Change Point	Remarks
1	MTC3084	STEP ASSEMBLY-REAR END-FOLDING	1	Note (1)	Production fit
2	MTC3086	• Retainer-RH	1		
3	MTC3087	• Retainer-LH	1		
4	MTC3085	• STEP REAR RETRACTABLE	1		
5	MTC3091	• • Mat-rear bumper step	1		
6	RA612373L	• • Rivet-3/16" x 0.575"lng	7		
7	WA105001	• • Washer-plain	NLA		Use WA105001L.
8	MTC3099	• Spacer	1		
9	BH110521	• Bolt	1		
10	WC110061	• Washer-plain	2		
11	NY110041L	• Nut-hexagonal head-nyloc-M10	NLA		Use NY110047L.
12	MTC1233	• Spring	1		
7	WA105001L	Washer-plain-standard-M5			
5	BTR6113	Mat-rear bumper step	1		V8 EFi 50 LE
1	KVI100030	STEP ASSEMBLY-REAR END-FOLDING	1	Note (2)	Production fit
9	BH110521	• Bolt	1		
4	KVI100040	• Step rear retractable-with bonded mat	1		
7	WA105001	• Washer-plain	NLA		Use WA105001L.
12	MTC1233	• Spring	1		
2	MTC3086	• Retainer-RH	1		
3	MTC3087	• Retainer-LH	1		
8	MTC3099	• Spacer	1		
11	NY110041	• Nut-hexagonal head-nyloc	1		
10	WC110061	• Washer-plain	2		
	WYH100470	• Nut-rivet-steel-M10-hexagonal	2		
13	SH110201	Screw-retainer-hexagonal head-M10 x 20	2		
14	WL110001L	Washer-M10	2		
15	KYF100280	Washer-plain-thick	1	From (V) WA 138480	

STEP MAT NOT SERVICEABLE ON LATEST STEP

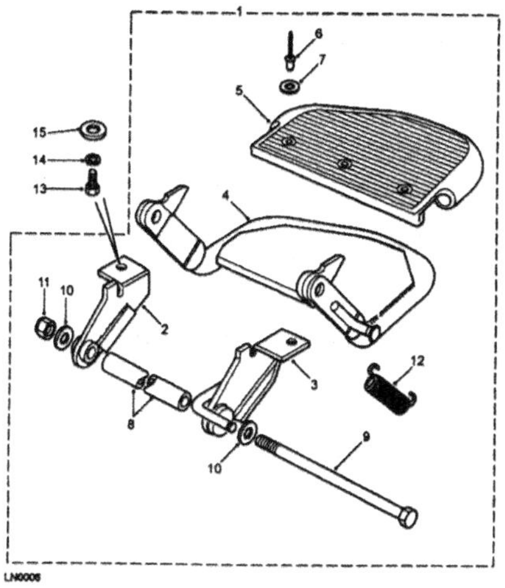

LN0006

CHANGE POINTS:
(1) To (V) WA 138479
(2) From (V) WA 138480

DEFENDER

GROUP N — **Body & Chassis** / **Body** / **Rear Step Assembly-Fixed**

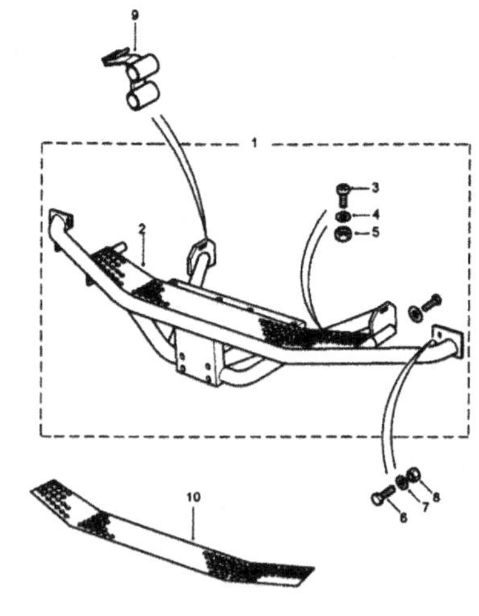

LN0229

Illus	Part Number	Description	Quantity	Change Point	Remarks
1	STC7016	STEP ASSEMBLY-REAR END-FIXED CONTACT	1		Eastnor L.E. France
2	BTR6113	• Mat-rear bumper step	1		
3	BTR8311	• Screw-plastic	8		
4	BTR8313	• Washer-plastic	8		
5	BTR8312	• Nut-plastic	8		
2	STC60168	Plate-chequer-rear step	1		V8 EFi 50 LE
6	BH110221L	Bolt-hexagonal head-M10 x 110	4		
7	WC110061L	Washer-plain-M10-oversize	12		
8	NY110047L	Nut-flange-nyloc-M10	4		
9	ANR3821	Spacer-twintube	2		
1	DQB102390	Step assembly-rear end-less tread plate	1		V8 EFi 50 LE
1	STC50269	Step assembly-rear end-less tread plate	1	Note (1)	Tomb Raider 90"
1	STC50301	Step assembly-rear end-less tread plate	1		Tomb Raider 110"
10	STC61868	Plate-chequer-rear step	1		Tomb Raider
	STC61894	Grommet-in bumper-rear	2	Note (1)	Tomb Raider
	STC61895	Rivet-long	A/R	Note (1)	Tomb Raider

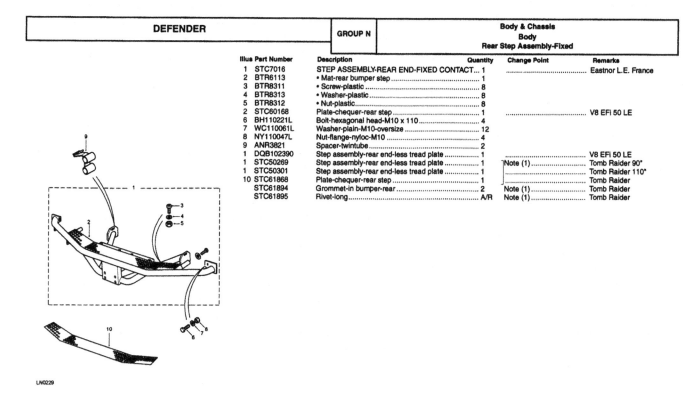

CHANGE POINTS:
(1) From (V) 1A 612404

DEFENDER

GROUP N — **Body & Chassis** / **Body** / **Decals & Badges-90-To (V) GA455945**

Illus	Part Number	Description	Quantity	Change Point	Remarks
1	MTC8305	Badge-front-Silver on Black background	1	Note (1)	
2	MXC6396	Badge-front-Silver on Black background	1	Note (2)	
3	MUC2002	Badge-Land Rover-rear-Silver on Black background	NLA	Note (1)	Use MXC6401.
4	MXC6401	Badge-Land Rover-rear-Silver on Black background	1	Note (2)	
5	MXC6402	Badge-grille-Land Rover-Silver.	1	Note (3)	

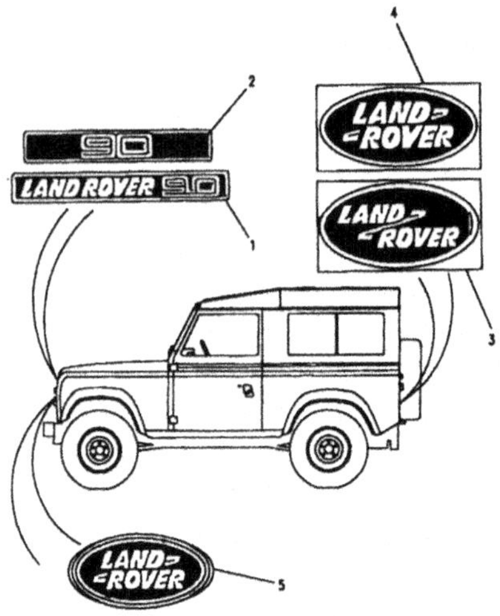

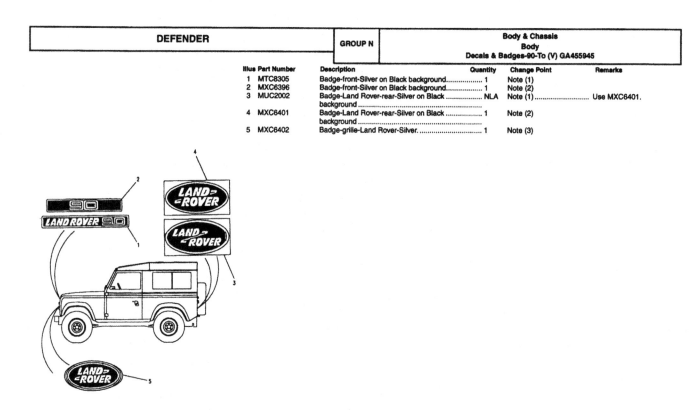

CHANGE POINTS:
(1) To (V) FA 414686
(2) From (V) FA 414687 To (V) GA 455945
(3) To (V) GA 455945

Decals & Badges- 90-From (V) HA455946

Illus	Part Number	Description	Quantity	Change Point	Remarks
1	MXC6402	Badge-grille-Land Rover-Silver.	1	Note (1)	
1	DAS100150	Badge-grille-Land Rover-Gold	1	Note (2)	
2	BTR1045	Tape-grille-Defender-Silver on Black background	1		
3	BTR1047	Badge-Land Rover-rear-Gold on Green background	1	Note (1)	
3	DAH100680	Badge-Land Rover-rear-Gold	1	Note (2)	
4	BTR1048	Tape-rear-Defender 90-Silver on clear background	1	Note (3)	
4	BTR2981LVA	Tape-rear-Defender 90-Light Grey on clear background	1	Note (4)	
4	BTR2981LYV	Tape-rear-Defender 90-Black	1	Note (5)	
5	DAF105360MMG	Badge-Td5 -no pattern-Silver	2	Note (6)	5 Cylinder Td5
5	DAF105360LYV	Badge-Td5 -no pattern-Black	2	Note (5)	5 Cylinder Td5
5	DAM100750LQQ	Badge-Td5 -moulded-plastic-Dark Grey	2	Note (5)	5 Cylinder Td5

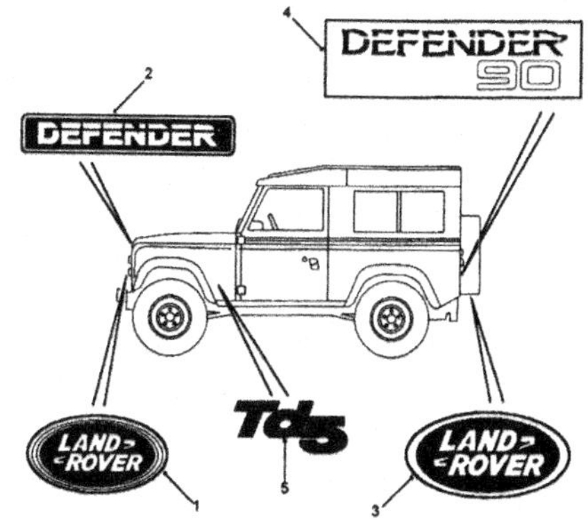

LN0178

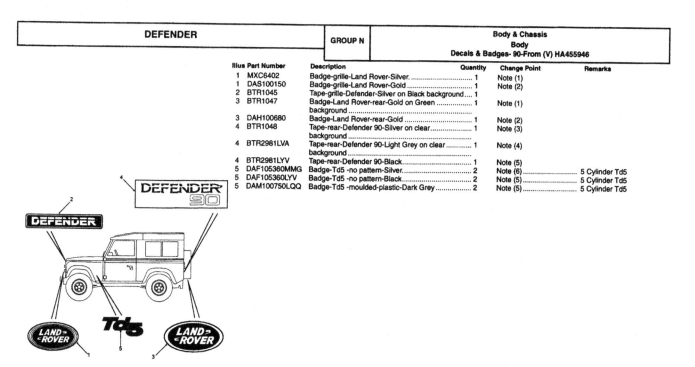

CHANGE POINTS:
(1) From (V) HA 455946 To (V) WA 138479
(2) From (V) WA 138480
(3) From (V) HA 455946 To (V) HA 906578
(4) From (V) JA 906579
(5) From (V) 1A 600725
(6) From (V) XA 159807

Decals & Badges-110/130-To (V) GA455945

Illus	Part Number	Description	Quantity	Change Point	Remarks
1	MUC2003	Badge-front-Silver on Black background	1	Note (1)	110"
					130"
2	MXC6397	Badge-front-Silver on Black background	1	Note (2)	110"
3	MUC2002	Badge-Land Rover-rear-Silver on Black background	NLA	Note (1)	Use MXC6401.
4	MXC6401	Badge-Land Rover-rear-Silver on Black background	1	Note (2)	
5	MXC6402	Badge-grille-Land Rover-Silver.	1		
6	MXC6398	Badge-front-Silver on Black background	1	From (V) FA 414616	130"

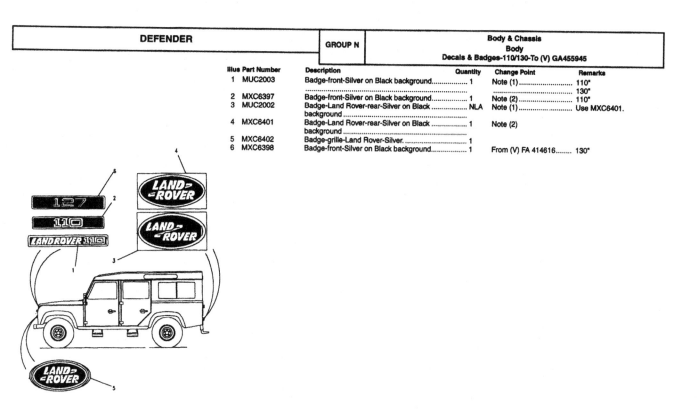

CHANGE POINTS:
(1) To (V) FA 414615
(2) From (V) FA 414616

DEFENDER	GROUP N	Body & Chassis Body Decals & Badges-110/130-From (V) HA455946

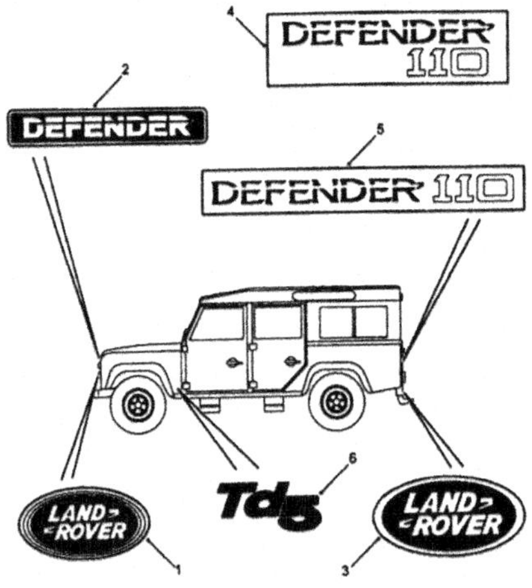

LN0043

Illus	Part Number	Description	Quantity	Change Point	Remarks
1	MXC6402	Badge-grille-Land Rover-Silver.	1	Note (1)	
1	DAS100130	Badge-grille-Land Rover-Gold	1	Note (2)	
2	BTR1045	Tape-grille-Defender-Silver on Black background	1		
3	BTR1047	Badge-Land Rover-rear-Gold on Green background	1		
4	BTR1049	Tape-Defender 110-Silver on clear background	1		110"
4	BTR2982LVA	Tape-Defender 110-Light Grey-On clear background	1		110"
4	BTR2982LYV	Tape-Defender 110-Black	1	Note (3)	110"
5	BTR1050	Tape-Defender 110-Silver on clear background	1		HICAP 110"
5	BTR2983LVA	Tape-Defender 110-Light Grey-On clear background	1		HICAP 110"
5	BTR2983LYV	Tape-Defender 110-Black	1	Note (3)	HICAP 110"
5	BTR1051	Tape-Defender 130-Silver on clear background	1		130"
5	BTR2984LVA	Tape-Defender 130-Light Grey-On clear background	1		130"
5	BTR2984LYV	Tape-Defender 130-Black	1	Note (3)	130"
6	DAF105360MMG	Badge-Td5 -no pattern-Silver.	2	Note (4)	Td5
6	DAF105360LYV	Badge-Td5 -no pattern-Black	2	Note (3)	Td5
6	DAM100750LQQ	Badge-Td5 -moulded-plastic-Dark Grey	2	Note (3)	Td5

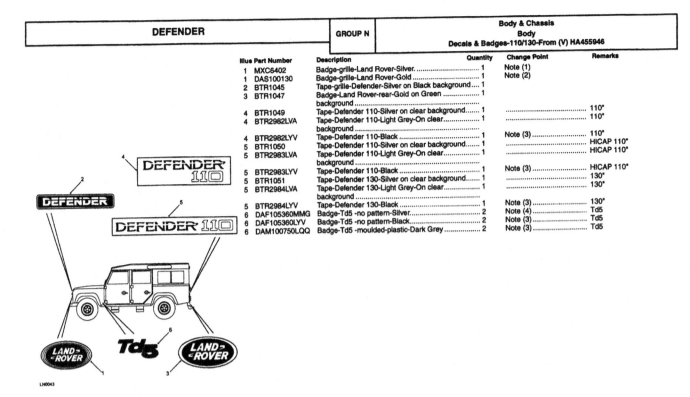

CHANGE POINTS:
(1) To (V) WA 138479
(2) From (V) WA 138480
(3) From (V) 1A 600725
(4) From (V) XA 159807

DEFENDER	GROUP N	Body & Chassis Body Decals & Badges-Special Editions

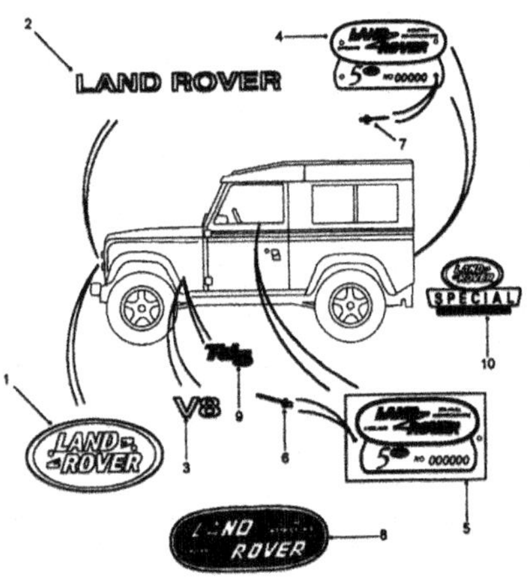

LN0060B

Illus	Part Number	Description	Quantity	Change Point	Remarks
1	MXC6402	Badge-grille-Land Rover-Silver.	1		
2	BTR8704MUL	Decal-Land Rover	1		
3	BTR8705MUL	Decal-body side-V8	2		
4	DAG100390H	Badge-rear panel	1		50 LE
5	DAG100400H	Badge-cubby box	1		50 LE
6	RRC4583	Rivet	2		
7	RRC4583	Rivet	2		
8	DAG000040	Badge-Land Rover	1		X-Tech LE
8	STC60511	Badge-Land Rover	1		Tdi Hardtop 50th
8	STC60752	Badge-Land Rover	1		Heritage
9	DAM100750LQQ	Badge-Td5 -moulded-plastic-Dark Grey	1		X-Tech LE
10	STC7052	Decal-Special-small	2		Special Vehicles
10	STC7053	Decal-Special-large	1		Special Vehicles

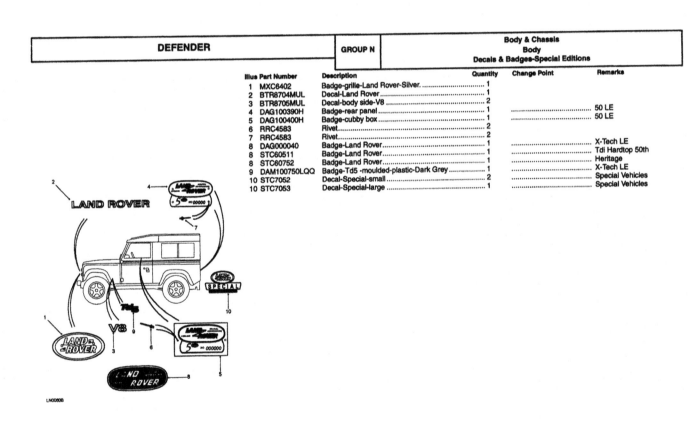

Bodytapes-90-County-V8 To (V) AA271214

Illus	Part Number	Description	Quantity	Change Point	Remarks
		TAPE			
1	RTC6474	door/wing-Beige-RH	1	To (V) AA 271214	
1	RTC6476	door/wing-Beige-LH	1		
1	RTC6475	door/wing-Blue.-RH	1		
1	RTC6477	door/wing-Blue.-LH	1		
2	MUC3172AF	Tape-door-Beige-RH	1		
		TAPE			
3	MUC3174AF	bodyside-front-Beige-RH	1		
3	MUC3175AF	bodyside-front-Beige-LH	1		
3	MUC3174JU	bodyside-front-Blue.-RH	1		
3	MUC3175JU	bodyside-front-Blue.-LH	1		
		TAPE			
4	MUC3532AF	bodyside-rear-Beige-RH	1		
4	MUC3533AF	bodyside-rear-Beige-LH	1		
4	MUC3532JU	bodyside-rear-Blue.-RH	1		
4	MUC3533JU	bodyside-rear-Blue.-LH	1		
5	MUC3373AF	Tape-V8-Beige	2		
5	MUC3373JU	Tape-V8-Blue.	2		

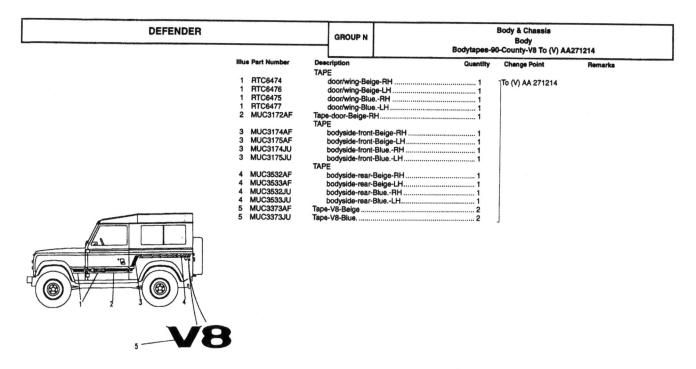

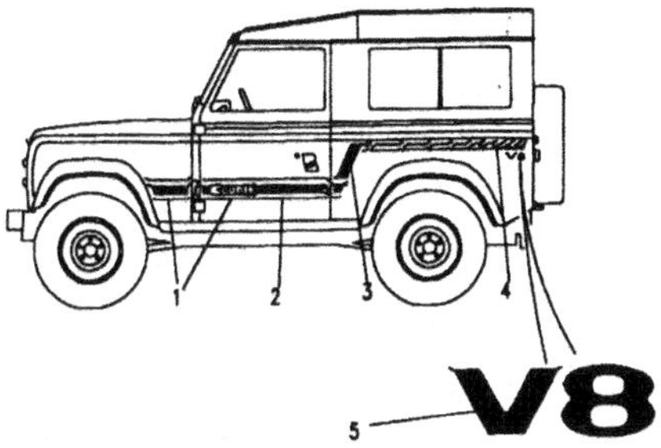

Bodytapes-90/110-County-Turbo From (V) AA270227 To (V) DA314368

Illus	Part Number	Description	Quantity	Change Point	Remarks
		TAPE			
1	MUC6932	'Turbo'-rear	1	From (V) AA 270227 To (V) DA 314368	
2	MWC2238HA	front door-Green-RH	1		
2	MWC2237HA	front door-Green-LH	1		
2	MWC2238LB	front door-Grey-RH	1		
2	MWC2237LB	front door-Grey-LH	1		
3	MWC2239HA	rear door-side-Green-LH	1		110"
3	MWC2239LB	rear door-side-Grey-LH	1		
3	MWC2240HA	rear door-side-Green-RH	1		
3	MWC2240LB	rear door-side-Grey-RH	1		
4	MWC2241HA	body front-upper-Green-LH	1		
4	MWC2241LB	body front-upper-Grey-LH	1		
4	MWC2242HA	body front-upper-Green-RH	1		
4	MWC2242LB	body front-upper-Grey-RH	1		
4	MWC2248HA	body front-upper-Green-RH	1		90"
4	MWC2247HA	body front-upper-Green-LH	1		
4	MWC2248LB	body front-upper-Grey-RH	1		
4	MWC2247LB	body front-upper-Grey-LH	1		
5	MWC2244HA	body strobe-Green-RH	1		
5	MWC2243HA	body strobe-Green-LH	1		
5	MWC2244LB	body strobe-Grey-RH	1		
5	MWC2243LB	body strobe-Grey-LH	1		
6	MWC2246HA	Green-RH	1		
6	MWC2245HA	Green-LH	1		
6	MWC2246LB	Grey-RH	1		
6	MWC2245LB	Grey-LH	1		
7	MWC2250HA	body front-lower-Green-RH	1		90"
7	MWC2249HA	body front-lower-Green-LH	1		
7	MWC2250LB	body front-lower-Grey-RH	1		
7	MWC2249LB	body front-lower-Grey-LH	1		

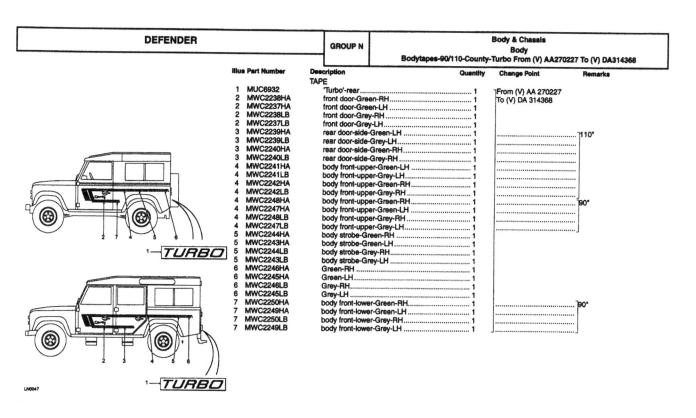

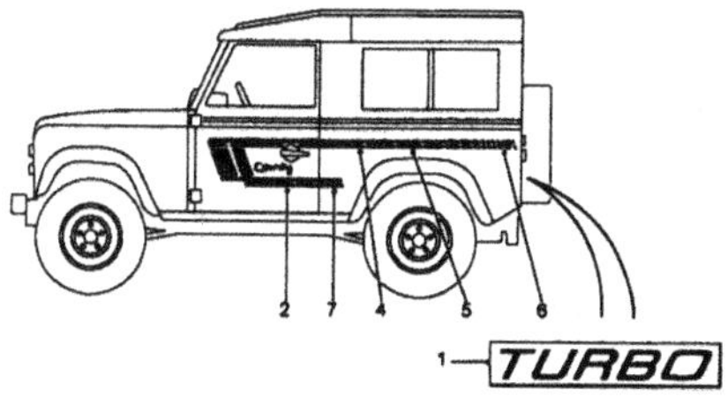

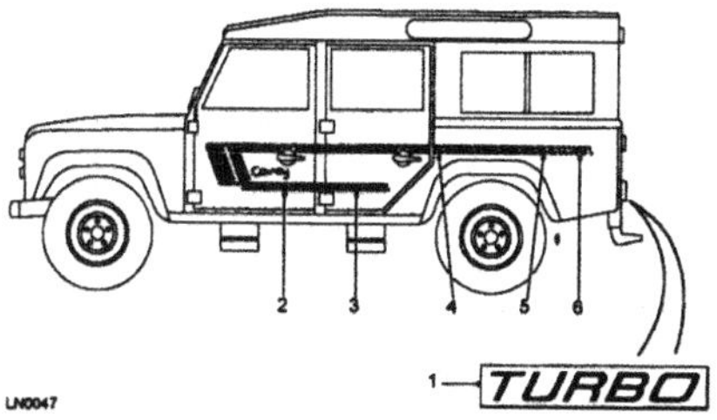

LN0047

Bodytapes-90/110-Station Wagon-From (V) DA314369 To (V) FA456152

Illus	Part Number	Description	Quantity	Change Point	Remarks
		TAPE			
1	MWC8256LUJ	'Turbo'-rear-Grey	1	From (V) DA 314369 To (V) FA 414686	
1	MWC8256MUB	'Turbo'-rear-Silver on Black background	1	From (V) FA 414687	
2	MWC8257LUJ	rear-Grey-V8	1	From (V) DA 314369 To (V) FA 414686	
2	MWC8257MUB	Silver on Black background-rear-V8	1	From (V) FA 414687	
3	MWC7188RUM	front door-Dark Silver-RH	1	From (V) DA 314369 To (V) FA 456152	
3	MWC7189RUM	front door-Dark Silver-LH	1	From (V) DA 314369 To (V) FA 456152	
4	MWC7190RUM	rear side door-Dark Silver-RH	1		110"
4	MWC7191RUM	rear side door-Dark Silver-LH	1		110"
5	MWC7194RUM	rear quarter-Dark Silver-RH	1	From (V) DA 314369 To (V) FA 456152	90"
5	MWC7195RUM	rear quarter-Dark Silver-LH	1	From (V) DA 314369 To (V) FA 456152	90"
5	MWC8590RUM	rear quarter-Dark Silver-RH	1		110"
5	MWC8591RUM	rear quarter-Dark Silver-LH	1		110"

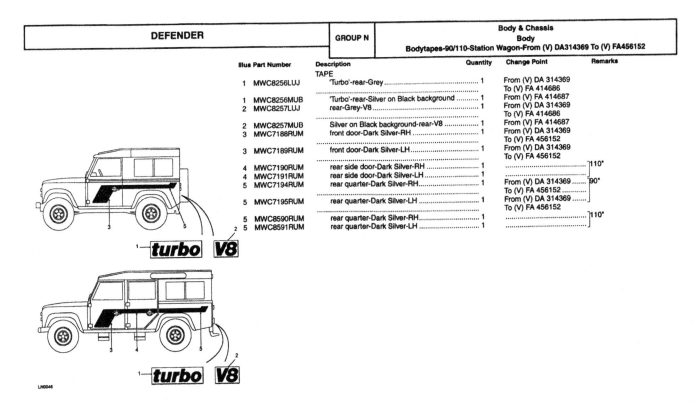

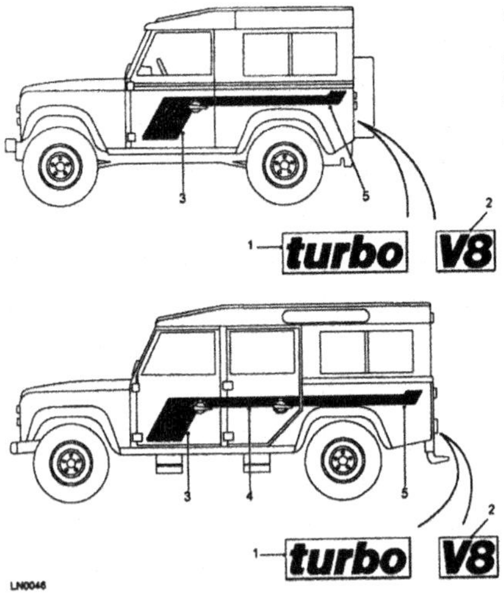

Bodytapes-Except Station Wagon-90/110-From (V) FA345886 To (V) FA456152

Illus	Part Number	Description	Quantity	Change Point	Remarks
		TAPE			
1	MWC8256LUJ	'Turbo'-rear-Grey	1	From (V) FA 345886 To (V) FA 414686	
1	MWC8256MUB	'Turbo'-rear-Silver on Black background	1	From (V) FA 414687 To (V) FA 456152	
2	MWC8257LUJ	'V8'-rear-Grey-V8	1	From (V) FA 345886 To (V) FA 414686	
2	MWC8257MUB	'V8'-Silver on Black background-rear-V8	1	From (V) FA 414687 To (V) FA 456152	
3	MXC1872RUP	front door-RH-Silver.-Mid Grey-Dark Grey	1	From (V) FA 345886	90"
3	MXC1873RUP	front door-LH-Silver.-Mid Grey-Dark Grey	1	To (V) FA 456152	90"
3	MXC1874RUP	front door-RH-Silver-Mid Grey-Dark Grey	1		110"
3	MXC1875RUP	front door-LH-Silver-Mid Grey-Dark Grey	1		110"
4	MXC5015RUP	chassis cab-500mm-Silver-Mid Grey-Dark Grey	A/R		90"
4	MXC5015RUP	except chassis cab-1200mm-Silver-Mid Grey-Dark Grey	A/R		90"
4	MXC5015RUP	chassis cab-500mm-Silver-Mid Grey-Dark Grey	A/R		110"
4	MXC5015RUP	hard/soft top-2600mm-Silver-Mid Grey-Dark Grey	A/R		110"
4	MXC5015RUP	HCPU-3100mm-Silver-Mid Grey-Dark Grey	A/R		110"

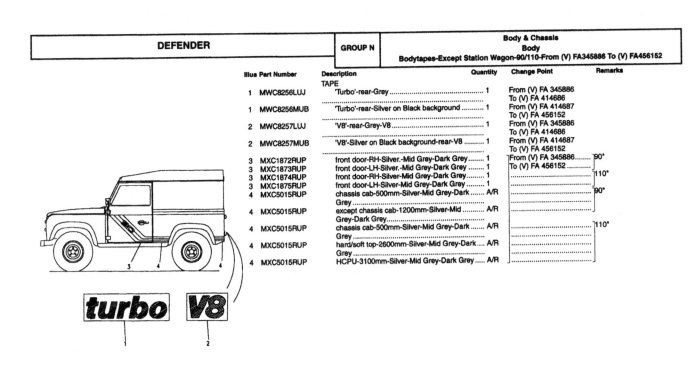

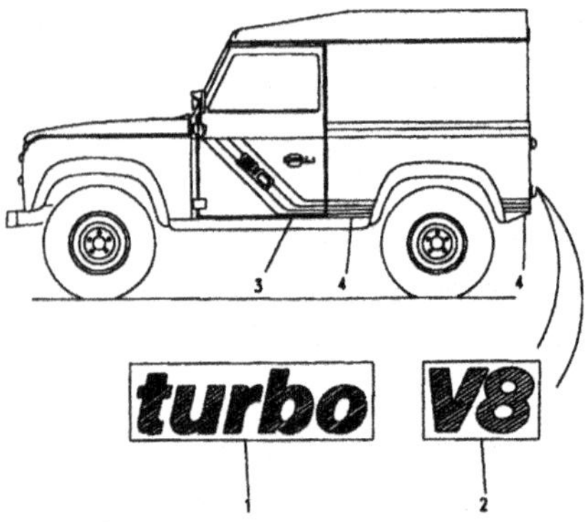

Illus	Part Number	Description	Quantity	Change Point	Remarks
1	BTR516MUB	Badge-TDI-front-wing-Silver on Black background	2	From (V) HA 456061 To (V) HA 906595	
2	BTR514MUB	Badge-V8-front-wing-Silver on Black background	2		
		TAPE			
3	BTR1052RUK	front door-Multi Green-RH	1		90"
3	BTR1053RUK	front door-Multi Green-LH	1		
4	BTR98RUK	chassis cab-500mm-Multi Green	A/R		Except Station Wagon
4	BTR98RUK	except chassis cab-1200mm-Multi Green	A/R		
5	BTR166RUV	bodyside-Strobe Blue-RH	1		Station Wagon
5	BTR167RUV	bodyside-Strobe Blue-LH	1		

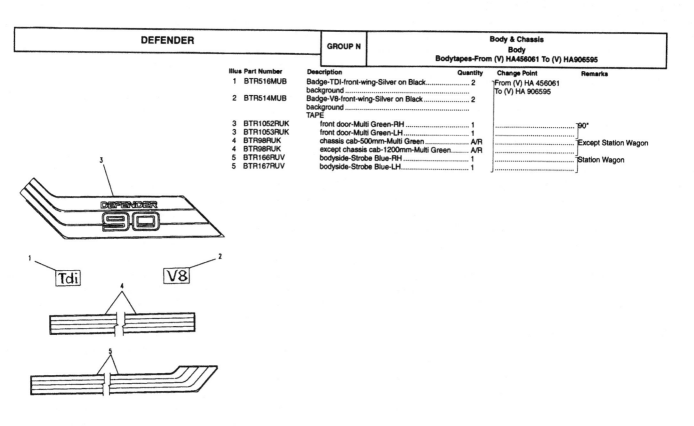

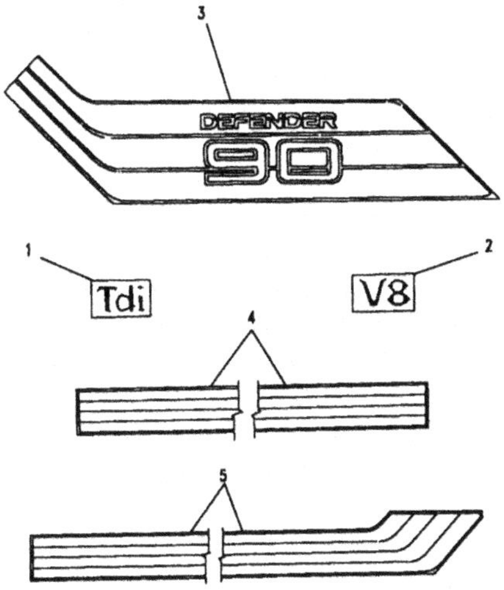

Illus	Part Number	Description	Quantity	Change Point	Remarks
1	BTR516LVA	Badge-Tdi-front-wing-Light Grey	2		TDI
1	BTR516LYV	Badge-TDI-front-wing-Black	2	Note (1)	TDI
2	BTR514LVA	Badge-V8-front-wing-Light Grey	2		V8
2	BTR514LYV	Badge-V8-front-wing-Black	2	Note (1)	V8
		TAPE			
3	BTR2406RWF	front door-Light Grey-Dark Grey-RH	1		
3	BTR2407RWF	front door-Light Grey-Dark Grey-LH	1		
4	BTR2413SUJ	bodyside 'county'-Beige	2		
5	BTR2416RWF	bodyside-Light Grey-Dark Grey-RH	1		
5	BTR2417RWF	bodyside-Light Grey-Dark Grey-LH	1		
6	MWC8256LVA	Badge-Turbo-rear-Light Grey	1		
7	BTR2414RWF	Tape-Light Grey-Dark Grey-RH	1		Chassis Cab
7	BTR2415RWF	Tape-Light Grey-Dark Grey-LH	1		

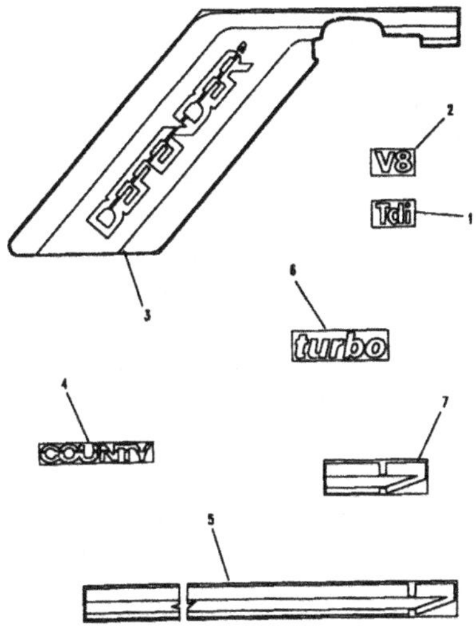

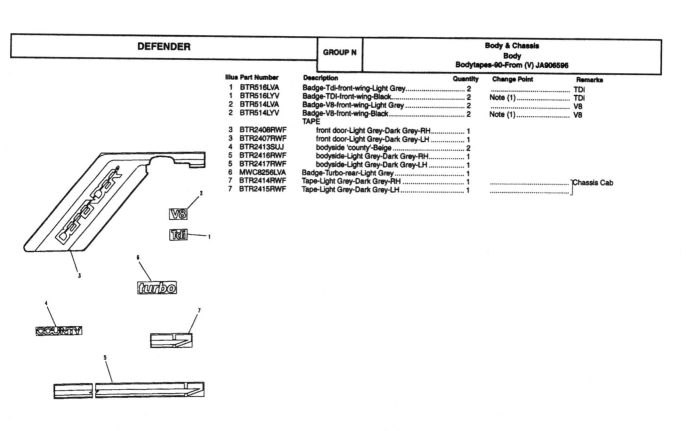

CHANGE POINTS:
(1) From (V) 1A 600725

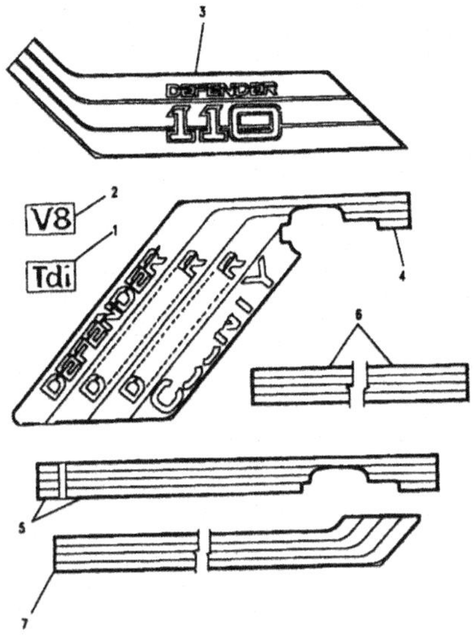

Illus	Part Number	Description	Quantity	Change Point	Remarks
1	BTR516MUB	Badge-TDI-front-wing-Silver on Black background	2	From (V) HA 455946	
2	BTR514MUB	Badge-V8-front-wing-Silver on Black background	2		
		EXCEPT COUNTY STATION WAGON			
3	BTR1054RUK	Tape-front door-Multi Green-RH	1	From (V) HA 455962	
3	BTR1055RUK	Tape-front door-Multi Green-LH	1		
		COUNTY STATION WAGON			
		TAPE			
4	BTR1056RUV	front door-Strobe Blue-RH	1	From (V) HA 455646	
4	BTR1057RUV	front door-Strobe Blue-LH	1		
4	BTR1056RUW	front door-Strobe Green-RH	1	From (V) HA 455962	
4	BTR1057RUW	front door-Strobe Green-LH	1		
5	BTR164RUV	rear door-side-Strobe Blue-RH	1	From (V) HA 455946	
5	BTR165RUV	rear door-side-Strobe Blue-LH	1		
5	BTR164RUW	rear door-side-Strobe Green-RH	1	From (V) HA 455962	
5	BTR165RUW	rear door-side-Strobe Green-LH	1		
		COUNTY STATION WAGON			
		TAPE SIDESTRIPE			
7	BTR162RUV	Strobe Blue-RH	1	From (V) HA 455946	
7	BTR163RUV	Strobe Blue-LH	1		
7	BTR162RUW	Strobe Green-RH	1	From (V) HA 455962	
7	BTR163RUW	Strobe Green-LH	1		

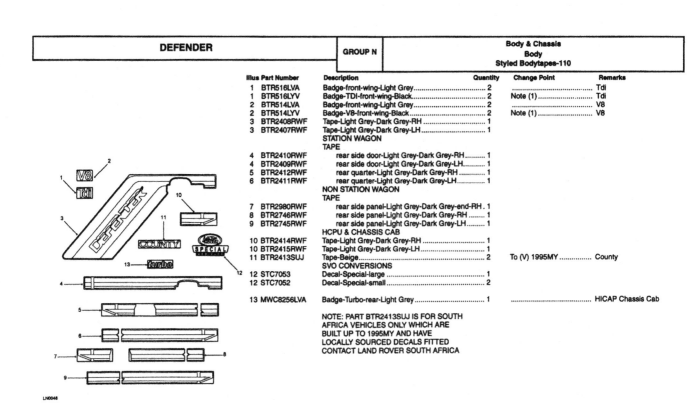

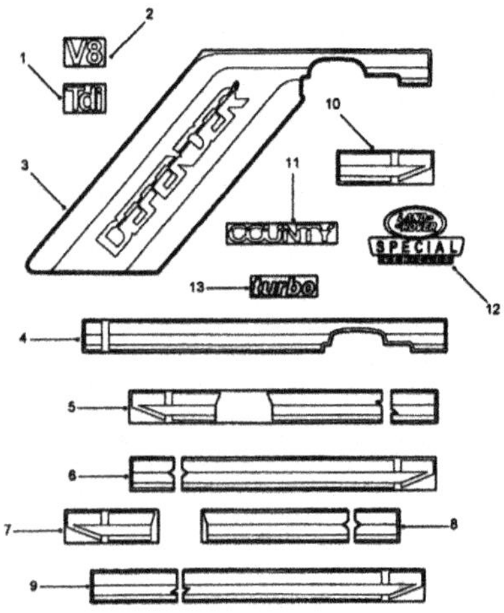

LN0048

Illus	Part Number	Description	Quantity	Change Point	Remarks
1	BTR516LVA	Badge-front-wing-Light Grey	2		Tdi
1	BTR516LYV	Badge-TDI-front-wing-Black	2	Note (1)	Tdi
2	BTR514LVA	Badge-front-wing-Light Grey	2		V8
2	BTR514LYV	Badge-V8-front-wing-Black	2	Note (1)	V8
3	BTR2408RWF	Tape-Light Grey-Dark Grey-RH	1		
3	BTR2407RWF	Tape-Light Grey-Dark Grey-LH	1		
		STATION WAGON			
		TAPE			
4	BTR2410RWF	rear side door-Light Grey-Dark Grey-RH	1		
4	BTR2409RWF	rear side door-Light Grey-Dark Grey-LH	1		
5	BTR2412RWF	rear quarter-Light Grey-Dark Grey-RH	1		
6	BTR2411RWF	rear quarter-Light Grey-Dark Grey-LH	1		
		NON STATION WAGON			
		TAPE			
7	BTR2980RWF	rear side panel-Light Grey-Dark Grey-end-RH	1		
8	BTR2746RWF	rear side panel-Light Grey-Dark Grey-RH	1		
9	BTR2745RWF	rear side panel-Light Grey-Dark Grey-LH	1		
		HCPU & CHASSIS CAB			
10	BTR2414RWF	Tape-Light Grey-Dark Grey-RH	1		
10	BTR2415RWF	Tape-Light Grey-Dark Grey-LH	1		
11	BTR2413SUJ	Tape-Beige	2	To (V) 1995MY	County
		SVO CONVERSIONS			
12	STC7053	Decal-Special-large	1		
12	STC7052	Decal-Special-small	2		
13	MWC8256LVA	Badge-Turbo-rear-Light Grey	1		HICAP Chassis Cab

NOTE: PART BTR2413SUJ IS FOR SOUTH AFRICA VEHICLES ONLY WHICH ARE BUILT UP TO 1995MY AND HAVE LOCALLY SOURCED DECALS FITTED CONTACT LAND ROVER SOUTH AFRICA

CHANGE POINTS:
(1) From (V) 1A 600725

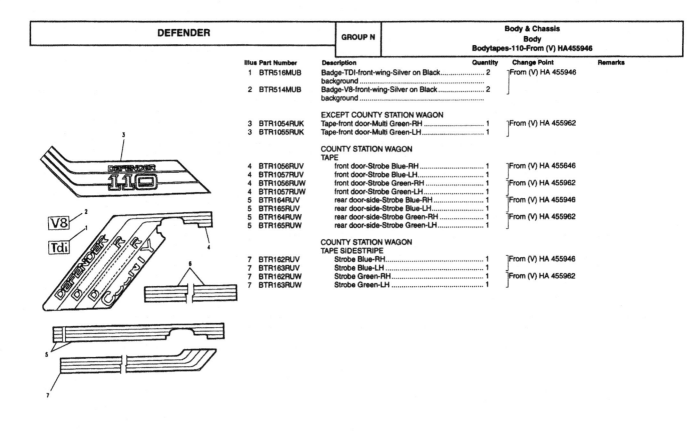

Ladder Rack

Illus	Part Number	Description	Quantity	Change Point	Remarks
1	MUC1086	RACK-LADDER	1		HICAP
2	MTC4942	• Stop ladder-bracket	2		
3	PC106641	• Pin assembly-clevis	2		
4	WA106041L	• Washer-6mm	2		
5	PS103121L	• Pin-split	2		
6	FS108307L	Screw-flanged head-M8 x 30	2		
7	WL108001L	Washer-sprung-M8	2		
8	WA108051L	Washer-8mm	2		

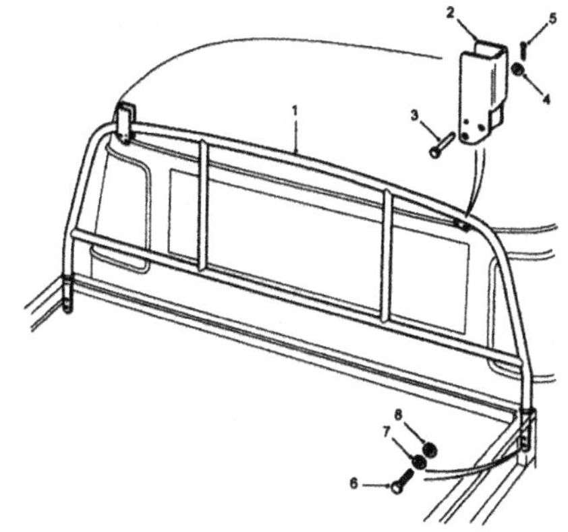

AJNXUC8A

Roll Protection Bar

Illus	Part Number	Description	Quantity	Change Point	Remarks
1	RRC3264	Bar-roll over	1		
2	BH110301L	Bolt-bar to body	8		
3	WL110001L	Washer-M10	8		
4	WA110061L	Washer-M10	8		
5	MTC5519	Nut plate	4		
6	BH110251	Bolt-bar to body	4		
7	WL110001L	Washer-M10	4		
8	WA110061L	Washer-M10	4		
9	MTC5519	Nut plate	2		
10	RRC3584	Plate-sliding	2		
11	SA106161	Screw-plate to bar	4		
12	WA106041L	Washer-6mm	8		
13	NY106047L	Nut-hexagonal head-nyloc-M6	4		
14	SD106401L	Screw-plate to bar	4		
15	NS106011	Nut-square	4		
16	WA106041L	Washer-6mm	4		
17	NY106047L	Nut-hexagonal head-nyloc-M6	4		

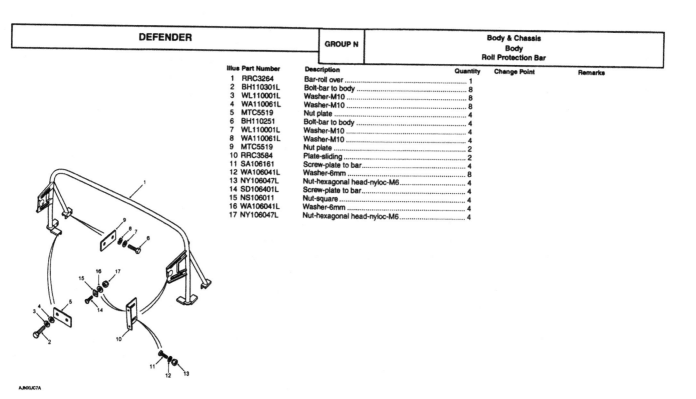

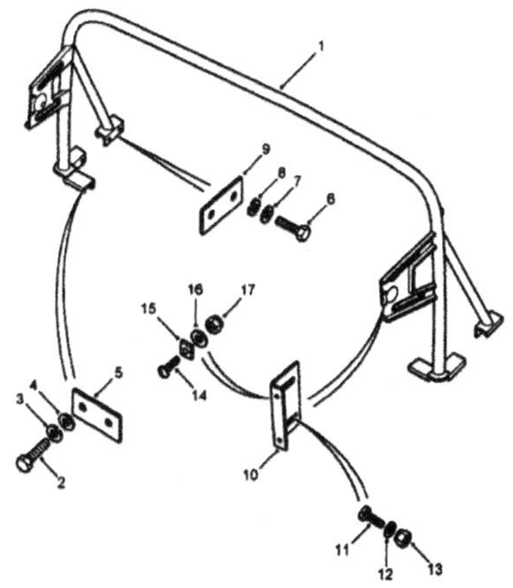

AJNXUC7A

Protection Bar-Eastnor LE & 90 Sport Only

Illus	Part Number	Description	Quantity	Change Point	Remarks
1	STC7014	Reinforcement-BC post	1		
2	ALR7822	Stay-back-RH	1		
2	ALR7823	Stay-back-LH	1		
3	MTC5519	Nut plate	2		
4	ALR6871	Screw-torx drive-Black-M10 x 25	12		

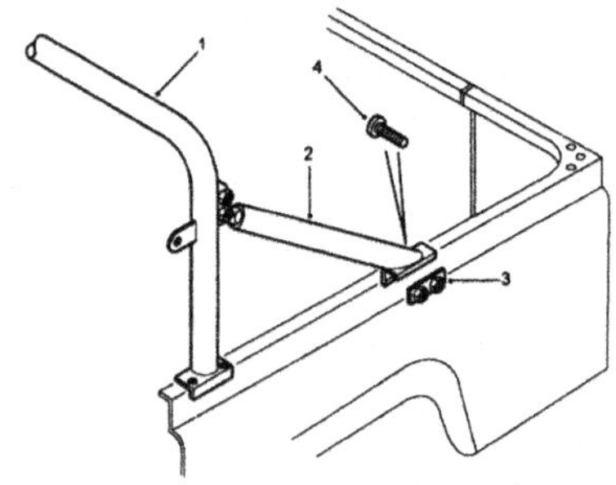

AHHXUE1A

Mirrors-Interior & Exterior

Illus	Part Number	Description	Quantity	Change Point	Remarks
1	MRC9564	Mirror assembly-interior-non dipping	1		
1	MTC6376	Mirror assembly-interior-Black-dipping	1		Standard / County
1	MXC3340	Mirror assembly-interior-Black-dipping	1		90 SV 90 Sport Biaritz L.E. Eastnor L.E. 50 LE
1	STC60728	Mirror assembly-interior-Bronze Green-dipping	1		Heritage
1	STC60727	Mirror assembly-interior-Atlantic Green.-dipping	1		Heritage
2	372336	Plate	1		
3	SF104204L	Screw-with trim	3		
3	SF104164	Screw-less trim	3		
	MXC3341	Slug-windscreen mirror fixing	1		
	STC2404	Adhesive	1		
4	MTC5084	MIRROR ASSEMBLY-EXTERNAL HEAD-CONVEX	2		
	RTC4341	• Glass-exterior mirror assembly-convex	2		
4	AWR6525	MIRROR ASSEMBLY-EXTERNAL HEAD-FLAT	2		Gulf States
	AWR6874	• Glass-exterior mirror assembly-flat	2		
4	MRC9747	MIRROR ASSEMBLY-EXTERNAL HEAD-FLAT	2		Except Australia and Gulf States
	RTC4340	• Glass-exterior mirror assembly flat	2		
4	MUC3707	MIRROR ASSEMBLY-EXTERNAL HEAD-FLAT-RH	1		Australia
	RTC4342	• Glass-exterior mirror assembly flat	1		
4	MUC3708	MIRROR ASSEMBLY-EXTERNAL HEAD-FLAT-LH	1		Australia
	RTC4342	• Glass-exterior mirror assembly flat	1		
5	MTC5083	Arm-mirror	2		Use with MTC 5084 Use with MUC 3707/8
6	MRC4583	Arm-mirror	2		Use with MRC 9747
7	SE604071L	Screw-fixing mirror-1/4UNF x 7/8	4		
8	MRC1979	Washer-nylon	4		

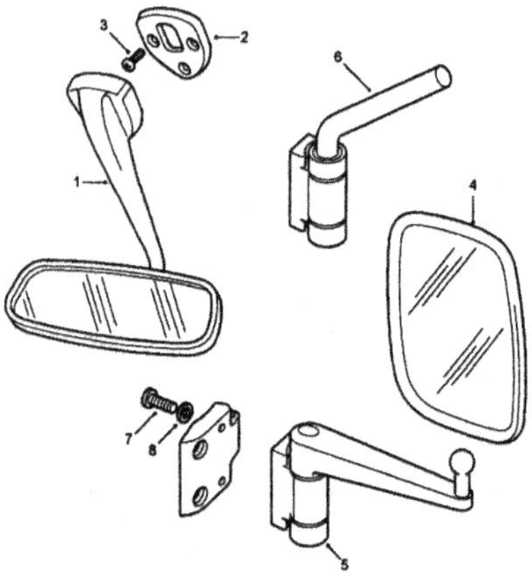

AJNXRA1A

DEFENDER

GROUP N

Body & Chassis
Body
Hard Top-Eastnor LE & Biaritz LE Only

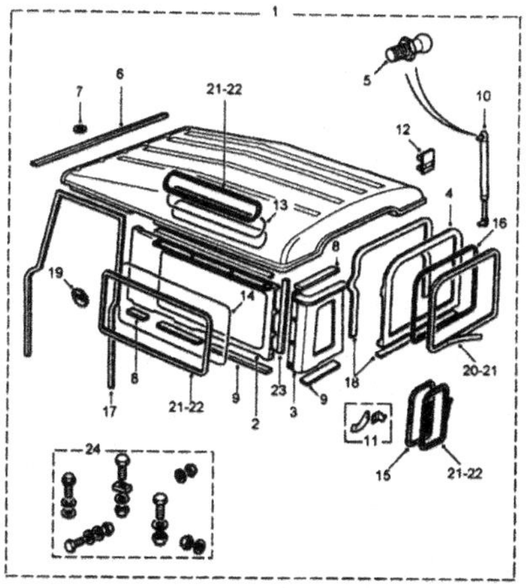

AHNXUA4A

Illus	Part Number	Description	Quantity	Change Point	Remarks
1	STC3271	HARDTOP ASSEMBLY	1		
	STC8692	• Hood assembly-full length-glazed	1		
2	STC3207	• Panel side -hard top-glazed-RH	1		
2	STC3208	• Panel side -hard top-glazed-LH	1		
3	STC3209	• Panel rear quarter-glazed-RH	1		
3	STC3210	• Panel rear quarter-glazed-LH	1		
4	ALR8327	• Tailgate assembly-glazed	1		
5	STC3320	• Joint-ball	2		
6	STC3289	• Seal-15m rolls	A/R		
7	ALR8333	• Spacer	6		
8	STC3291	• Seal-25m rolls	A/R		
9	STC3290	• Seal-20m rolls	A/R		
10	ALR8360	• Strut-tailgate gas	2		
11	STC3221	• Bracket-RH	1		
11	STC3220	• Bracket-LH	1		
12	ALR8329	• Hinge assembly-bonnet	2		
13	MWC4714	• Glass-alpine light-4mm glass	2		
14	MWC4727	• Glass-bodyside-Clear.	2		
15	MWC4715	• Glass-rear quarter-back-Clear.	2		
16	MWC4712	• Glass-rear door clear-unheated-4mm glass	1		
17	ALR4936	• Seal-front door-RH	1		
17	ALR4937	• Seal-front door-LH	1		
18	ALR8357	• Seal-tailgate	1		
19	BTR1047	• Badge-Land Rover-rear-Gold on Green background	2		
20	ALR8348	• Seal-tailgate	1		
21	ALR8364	• Seal-body side glass run	2		
22	ALR8337	• Seal	2		
23	306290	• Lock strip	2		
24	ALR8352	• Kit-hardtop installation fitting	1		

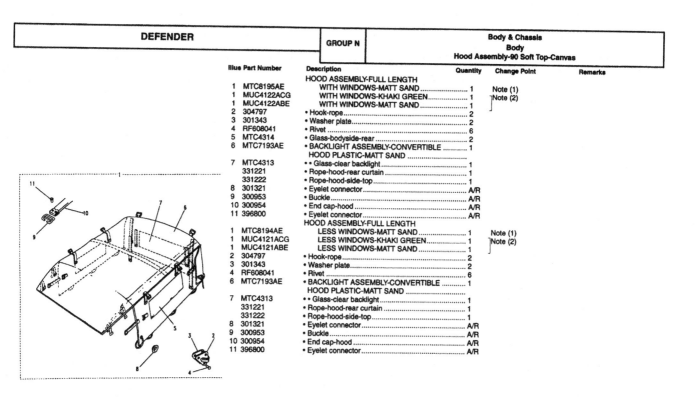

DEFENDER

GROUP N

Body & Chassis
Body
Hood Assembly-90 Soft Top-Canvas

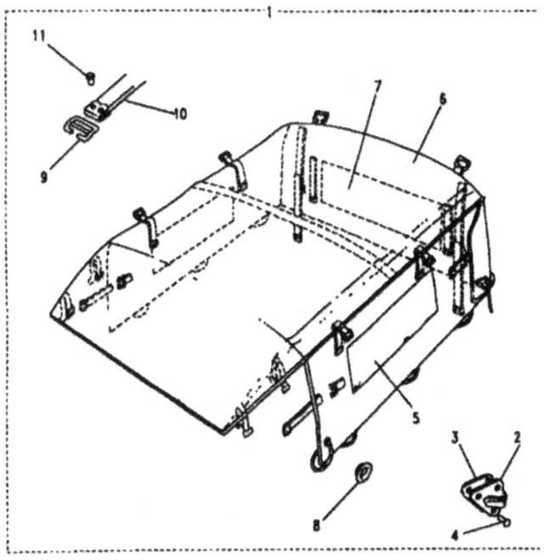

Illus	Part Number	Description	Quantity	Change Point	Remarks
		HOOD ASSEMBLY-FULL LENGTH			
1	MTC8195AE	WITH WINDOWS-MATT SAND	1	Note (1)	
1	MUC4122ACG	WITH WINDOWS-KHAKI GREEN	1	Note (2)	
1	MUC4122ABE	WITH WINDOWS-MATT SAND	1		
2	304797	• Hook-rope	2		
3	301343	• Washer plate	2		
4	RF608041	• Rivet	6		
5	MTC4314	• Glass-bodyside-rear	2		
6	MTC7193AE	• BACKLIGHT ASSEMBLY-CONVERTIBLE HOOD PLASTIC-MATT SAND	1		
7	MTC4313	• • Glass-clear backlight	1		
	331221	• Rope-hood-rear curtain	1		
	331222	• Rope-hood-side-top	1		
8	301321	• Eyelet connector	A/R		
9	300953	• Buckle	A/R		
10	300954	• End cap-hood	A/R		
11	396800	• Eyelet connector	A/R		
		HOOD ASSEMBLY-FULL LENGTH			
1	MTC8194AE	LESS WINDOWS-MATT SAND	1	Note (1)	
1	MUC4121ACG	LESS WINDOWS-KHAKI GREEN	1	Note (2)	
1	MUC4121ABE	LESS WINDOWS-MATT SAND	1		
2	304797	• Hook-rope	2		
3	301343	• Washer plate	2		
4	RF608041	• Rivet	6		
6	MTC7193AE	• BACKLIGHT ASSEMBLY-CONVERTIBLE HOOD PLASTIC-MATT SAND	1		
7	MTC4313	• • Glass-clear backlight	1		
	331221	• Rope-hood-rear curtain	1		
	331222	• Rope-hood-side-top	1		
8	301321	• Eyelet connector	A/R		
9	300953	• Buckle	A/R		
10	300954	• End cap-hood	A/R		
11	396800	• Eyelet connector	A/R		

CHANGE POINTS:
(1) To (V) AA 224093
(2) From (V) AA 224094

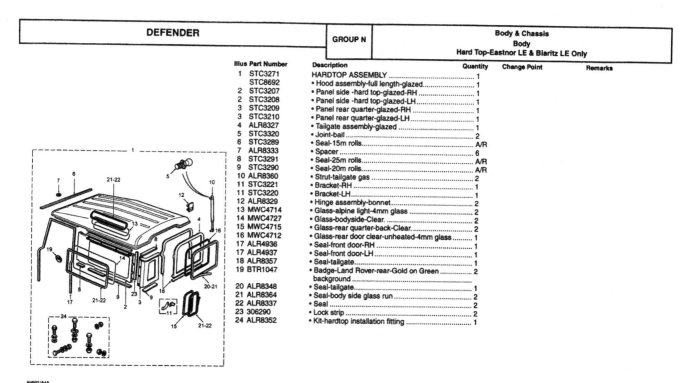

DEFENDER	GROUP N	Body & Chassis Body Hood Assembly-110 Soft Top-Canvas

Illus	Part Number	Description	Quantity	Change Point	Remarks
		HOOD ASSEMBLY-FULL LENGTH			
1	MTC7710AG	KHAKI GREEN-WITH SIDE WINDOWS	1		
1	MTC7710AE	MATT SAND-WITH SIDE WINDOWS	1		
1	MTC7711AG	KHAKI GREEN-WITH PLAIN SIDES	1		
1	MTC7711ABE	MATT SAND-WITH PLAIN SIDES	1		
4	304797	• Hook-rope	2		
5	301343	• Washer plate	2		
6	3547	• Rivet	6		
7	MTC4314	• Glass-bodyside-rear	3		Part of MTC7710AG, MTC7710AE.
	331221	• Rope-hood-rear curtain	1		
	331222	• Rope-hood-side-top	1		
12	301321	• Eyelet connector	A/R		
13	300953	• Buckle	A/R		
14	300954	• End cap-hood	A/R		
15	396800	• Eyelet connector	A/R		
7	MTC4314	• Glass-bodyside-rear	1		Part of MTC7711AG, MTC7711ABE.
2	331249	Strap-retaining	1		
3	90301332	Strap-retaining	2		

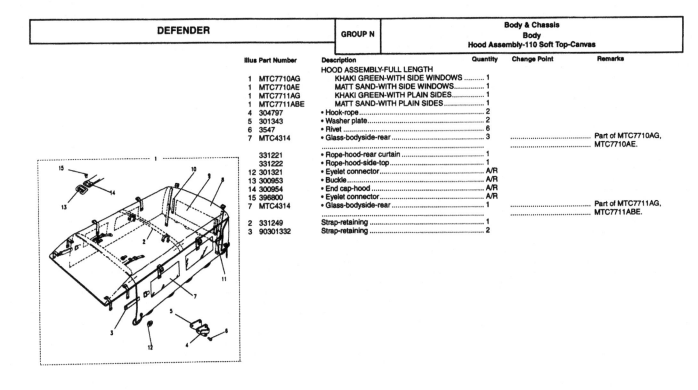

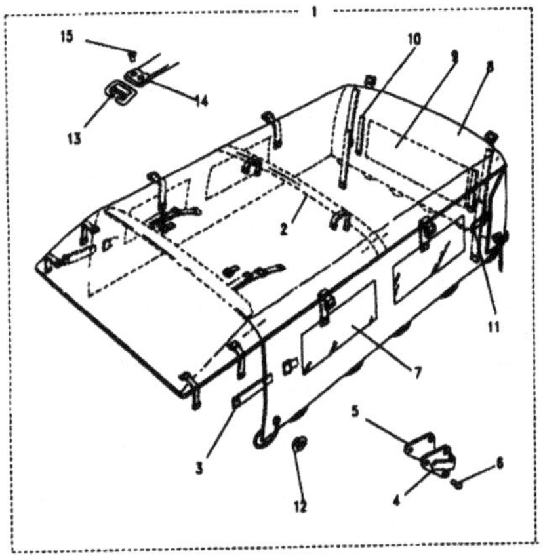

DEFENDER	GROUP N	Body & Chassis Body Hood Assembly-90 Soft Top-PVC

Illus	Part Number	Description	Quantity	Change Point	Remarks
1	DSB000080ABE	HOOD ASSEMBLY-FULL LENGTH-PVC-MATT SAND-WITH PLAIN SIDES	1		
2	STC4627ABE	• Rope-hood side curtain	2		
3	STC4005	• Rope-hood-elastic	5		
1	DSB000090ABE	HOOD ASSEMBLY-FULL LENGTH-PVC-MATT SAND-WITH SIDE WINDOWS	1		
2	STC4627ABE	• Rope-hood side curtain	2		
3	STC4005	• Rope-hood-elastic	5		

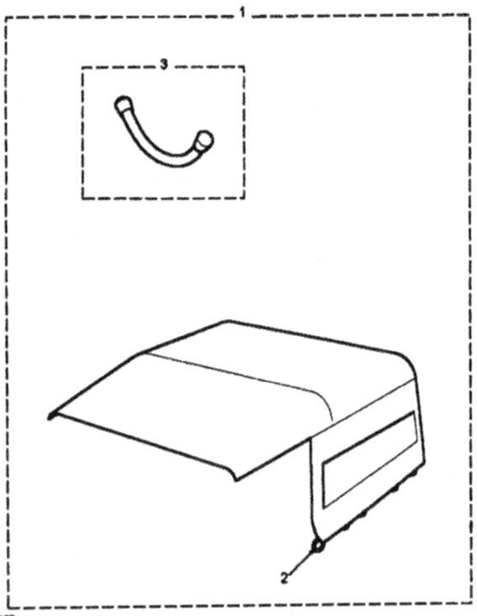

LN0187

Body & Chassis
Body
Hood Assembly-110 Soft Top-PVC

Illus	Part Number	Description	Quantity	Change Point	Remarks
1	DSB000100ABE	HOOD ASSEMBLY-FULL LENGTH-PVC-MATT SAND-WITH PLAIN SIDES	1		
2	STC4627ABE	• Rope-hood side curtain	2		
3	STC4005	• Rope-hood-elastic	5		
1	DSB000110ABE	HOOD ASSEMBLY-FULL LENGTH-PVC-MATT SAND-WITH SIDE WINDOWS	1		
2	STC4627ABE	• Rope-hood side curtain	2		
3	STC4005	• Rope-hood-elastic	5		

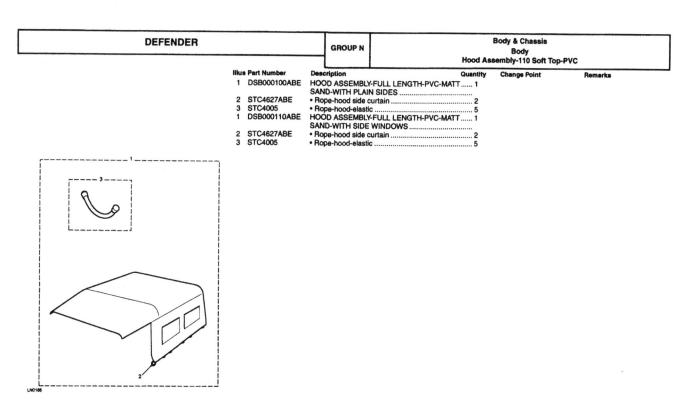

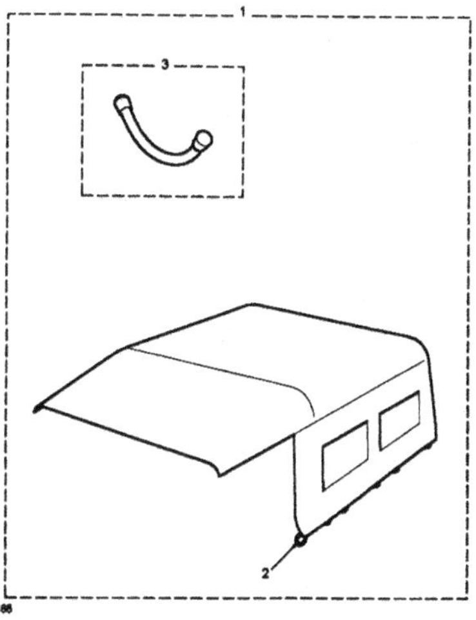

LN0166

Body & Chassis
Body
Hood Assembly-90 Truck Cab-Canvas-Cab Fixing

Illus	Part Number	Description	Quantity	Change Point	Remarks
		HOOD ASSEMBLY-3/4 LENGTH			
1	MTC8197AG	WITH SIDE WINDOWS-KHAKI GREEN	1		90"
1	MTC8197AE	WITH SIDE WINDOWS-MATT SAND	1		
1	MTC8196AG	LESS WINDOWS-KHAKI GREEN	1		
1	MTC8196AE	LESS WINDOWS-MATT SAND	1		
2	304797	• Hook-rope	2		
3	301343	• Washer plate	2		
4	RF608041	• Rivet	6		
5	MTC4314	• Glass-bodyside-rear	2		Part of MTC8197AG, MTC8197AE.
6	MWC1092AG	• BACKLIGHT ASSEMBLY-CONVERTIBLE HOOD PLASTIC-KHAKI GREEN	1		Part of MTC8197AG, MTC8196AG.
7	MTC4313	• • Glass-clear backlight	1		
	331221	• Rope-hood-rear curtain	1		
	331222	• Rope-hood-side-top	1		
8	301321	• Eyelet connector	A/R		
9	300953	• Buckle	A/R		
10	300954	• End cap-hood	A/R		
11	396800	• Eyelet connector	A/R		
6	MTC7193AE	• BACKLIGHT ASSEMBLY-CONVERTIBLE HOOD PLASTIC-MATT SAND	1		Part of MTC8197AE, MTC8196AE.
7	MTC4313	• • Glass-clear backlight	1		

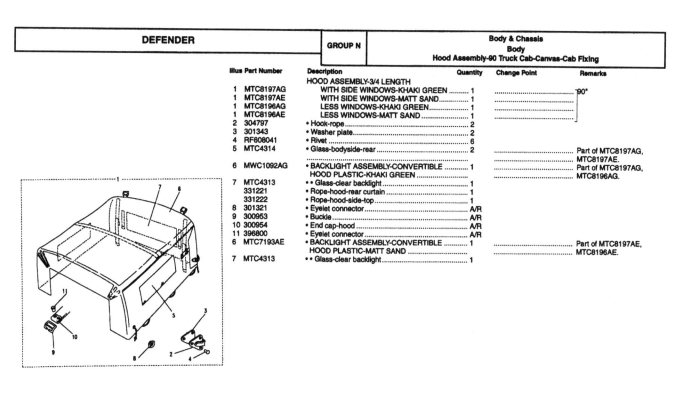

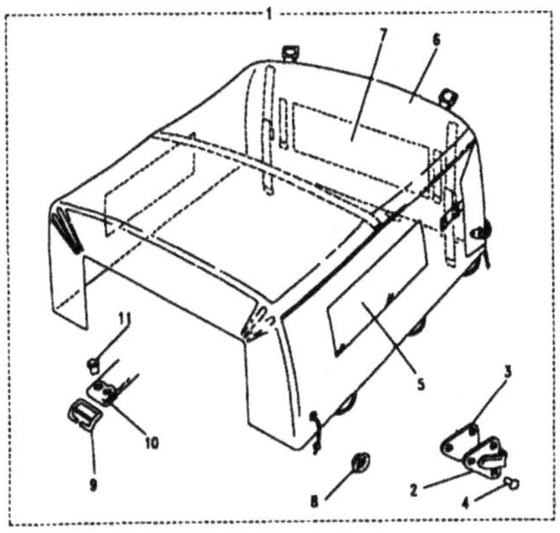

Illus	Part Number	Description	Quantity	Change Point	Remarks
		HOOD ASSEMBLY-3/4 LENGTH			
1	MUC7914ACG	WITH SIDE WINDOWS-KHAKI GREEN	1		90"
1	MUC7914ABE	WITH SIDE WINDOWS-MATT SAND	1		
1	MUC7913ACG	LESS WINDOWS-KHAKI GREEN	1		
1	MUC7913ABE	LESS WINDOWS-MATT SAND	1		
2	304797	• Hook-rope	2		
3	301343	• Washer plate	2		
4	RF608041	• Rivet	6		
5	MTC4314	• Glass-bodyside-rear	2		Part of MUC7914ACG, MUC7914ABE.
6	MTC7193AE	• BACKLIGHT ASSEMBLY-CONVERTIBLE HOOD PLASTIC-MATT SAND	1		
7	MTC4313	• • Glass-clear backlight	1		
	331221	• Rope-hood-rear curtain	1		
	331222	• Rope-hood-side-top	1		
8	301321	• Eyelet connector	A/R		
9	300953	• Buckle	A/R		
10	300954	• End cap-hood	A/R		
11	396800	• Eyelet connector	A/R		

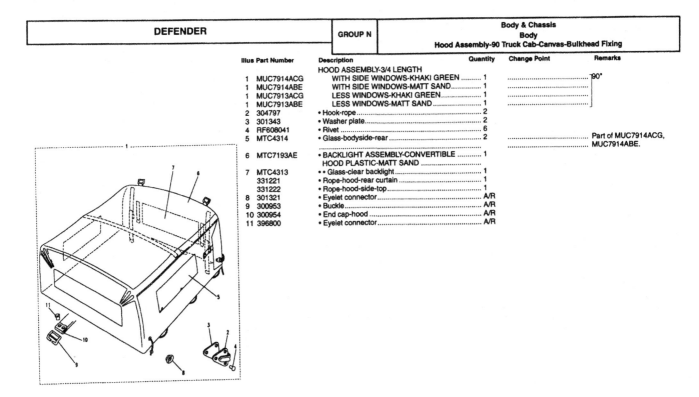

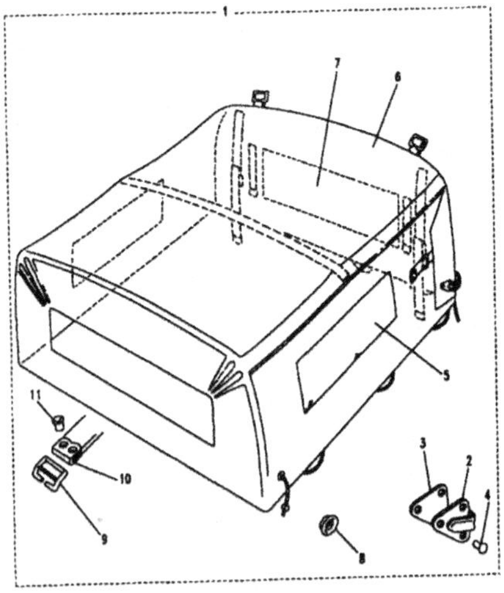

Illus	Part Number	Description	Quantity	Change Point	Remarks
1	DSB000060ABE	HOOD ASSEMBLY-3/4 LENGTH-PVC-MATT SAND-WITH PLAIN SIDES	1		
2	STC4627ABE	• Rope-hood side curtain	2		
3	STC4005	• Rope-hood-elastic	5		
1	DSB000070ABE	HOOD ASSEMBLY-3/4 LENGTH-PVC-MATT SAND-WITH SIDE WINDOWS	1		
2	STC4627ABE	• Rope-hood side curtain	2		
3	STC4005	• Rope-hood-elastic	5		

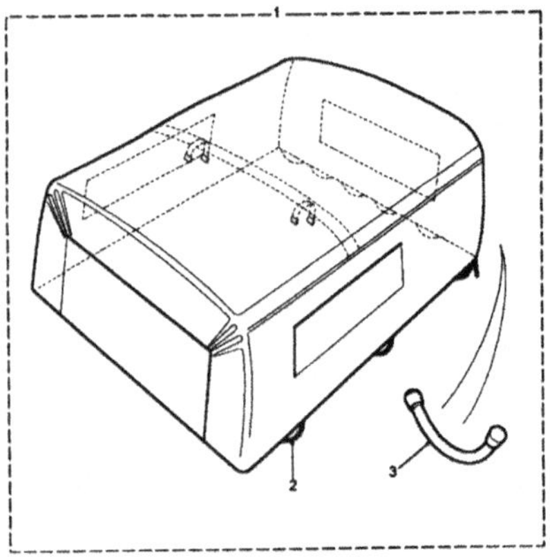

LN0186

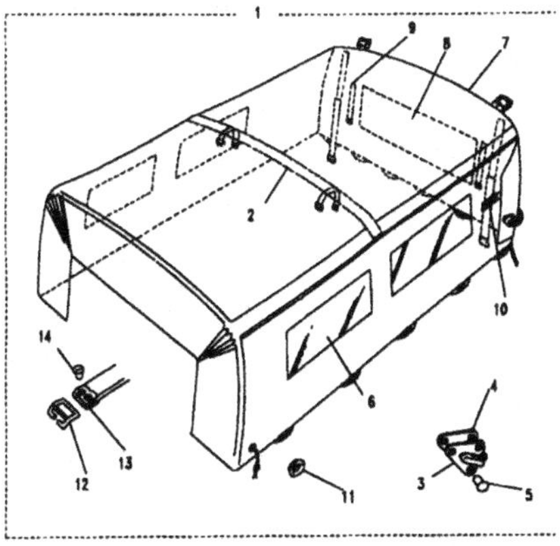

Illus	Part Number	Description	Quantity	Change Point	Remarks
		HOOD ASSEMBLY-3/4 LENGTH			
1	MTC7200AG	WITH SIDE WINDOWS-KHAKI GREEN	1	Note (1)	
1	MTC7200AE	WITH SIDE WINDOWS-MATT SAND	1	Note (1)	
1	MTC7471AG	LESS WINDOWS-KHAKI GREEN	1	Note (2)	
1	MTC7471AE	LESS WINDOWS-MATT SAND	1	Note (2)	
3	304797	• Hook-rope	2		
4	301343	• Washer plate	2		
5	RF608041	• Rivet	6		
6	MTC4314	• Glass-bodyside-rear	2		Part of MTC7200AG, MTC7200AE.
7	MWC1092AG	• BACKLIGHT ASSEMBLY-CONVERTIBLE HOOD PLASTIC-KHAKI GREEN	1		Part of MTC7200AG, MTC7471AG.
8	MTC4313	• • Glass-clear backlight	1		
	331221	• Rope-hood-rear curtain	1		
	331222	• Rope-hood-side-top	1		
11	301321	• Eyelet connector	A/R		
12	300953	• Buckle	A/R		
13	300954	• End cap-hood	A/R		
14	396800	• Eyelet connector	A/R		
7	MTC7193AE	• BACKLIGHT ASSEMBLY-CONVERTIBLE HOOD PLASTIC-MATT SAND	1		Part of MTC7200AE, MTC7471AE.
8	MTC4313	• • Glass-clear backlight	1		
9	339935	Strap-retaining	2		
10	90301332	Strap-retaining	2		

CHANGE POINTS:
(1) To (V) AA 283701
(2) To (V) AA 285842

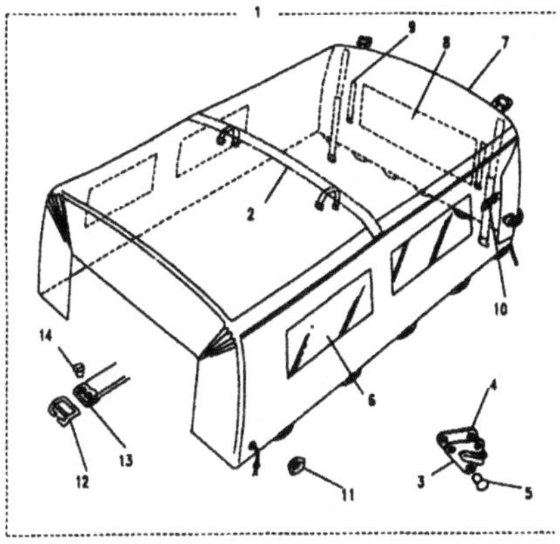

Illus	Part Number	Description	Quantity	Change Point	Remarks
		HOOD ASSEMBLY-3/4 LENGTH			
1	MUC7916AG	KHAKI GREEN-WITH SIDE WINDOWS	1	Note (1)	
1	MUC7916AE	MATT SAND-WITH SIDE WINDOWS	1	Note (1)	
1	MUC7915AG	KHAKI GREEN-WITH PLAIN SIDES	1	Note (2)	
1	MUC7915AE	MATT SAND-WITH PLAIN SIDES	1	Note (2)	
2	304797	• Hook-rope	2		
3	301343	• Washer plate	2		
4	RF608041	• Rivet	6		
5	MTC4314	• Glass-bodyside-rear	3		Part of MUC7916AG, MUC7916AE.
8	331221	• Rope-hood-rear curtain	1		
8	331222	• Rope-hood-side-top	1		
9	301321	• Eyelet connector	A/R		
10	300953	• Buckle	A/R		
11	300954	• End cap-hood	A/R		
12	396800	• Eyelet connector	A/R		
5	MTC4314	• Glass-bodyside-rear	1		Part of MUC7915AG, MUC7915AE.
6	MWC1092AG	BACKLIGHT ASSEMBLY-CONVERTIBLE HOOD PLASTIC-KHAKI GREEN	1		
7	MTC4313	• Glass-clear backlight	1		

CHANGE POINTS:
(1) From (V) AA 283702
(2) From (V) AA 285843

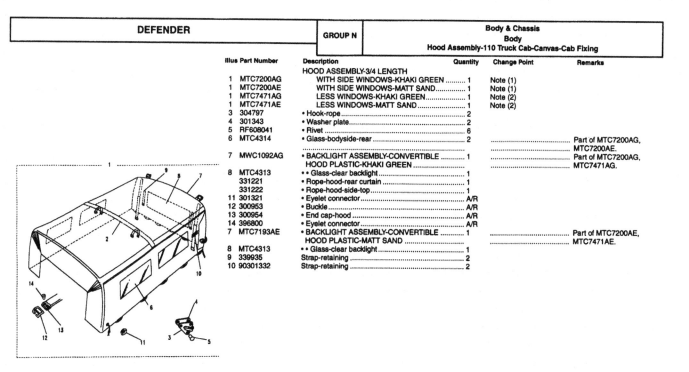

Hood Assembly-110 Truck Cab-PVC

Illus	Part Number	Description	Quantity	Change Point	Remarks
1	DSB100410ABE	HOOD ASSEMBLY-3/4 LENGTH-PVC-MATT SAND-WITH PLAIN SIDES	1		
2	STC4627ABE	• Rope-hood side curtain	2		
3	STC4005	• Rope-hood-elastic	5		
1	DSB100430ABE	HOOD ASSEMBLY-3/4 LENGTH-PVC-MATT SAND-WITH SIDE WINDOWS	1		
2	STC4627ABE	• Rope-hood side curtain	2		
3	STC4005	• Rope-hood-elastic	5		

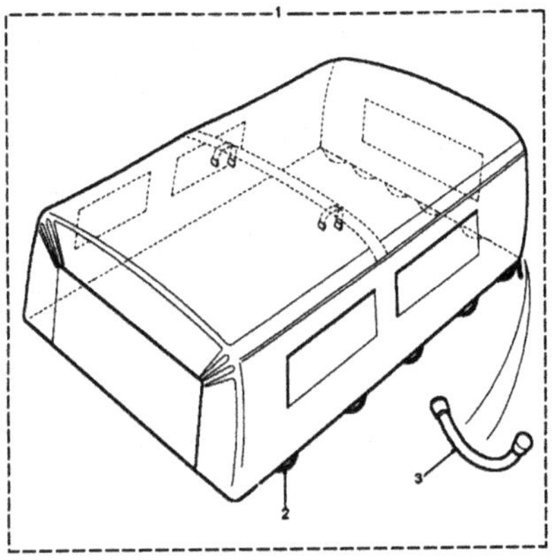

LN0174

Hood Assembly-110 HCPU & 130-Canvas

Illus	Part Number	Description	Quantity	Change Point	Remarks
		HOOD ASSEMBLY-3/4 LENGTH			
1	MTC2575AG	KHAKI GREEN-WITH SIDE WINDOWS	1		110"
1	MTC2575AE	MATT SAND-WITH SIDE WINDOWS	1		
1	RRC2963ABE	MATT SAND-WITH SIDE WINDOWS	1		130"
2	304797	• Hook-rope	4		
3	301343	• Washer plate	4		
4	RF608041	• Rivet	12		
5	MTC4314	• Glass-bodyside-rear	5		
6	MTC4313	• Glass-clear backlight	1		
7	MTC4061AG	• Curtain assembly-rear-Khaki Green	1		Part of MTC2575AG.
8	301321	• Eyelet connector	A/R		
9	300953	• Buckle	A/R		
10	300954	• End cap-hood	A/R		
11	396800	• Eyelet connector	A/R		
12	MTC4315	• Rope-hood-side	2		
12	331221	• Rope-hood-rear curtain	1		
	MTC4319	• Rope-top and sides-hood	1		
7	MTC4061AE	• Curtain assembly-rear-Matt sand	1		Part of MTC2575AE, RRC2963ABE.

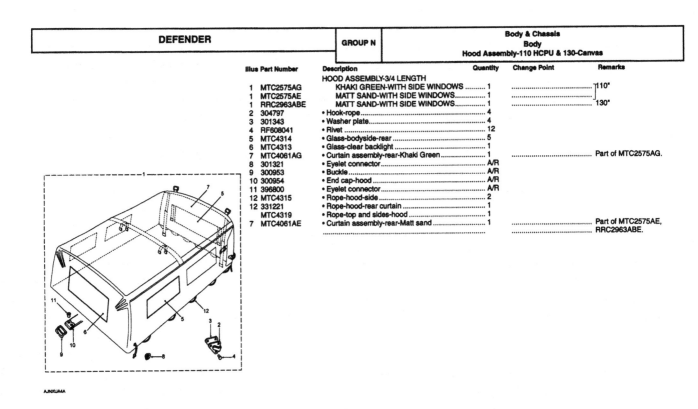

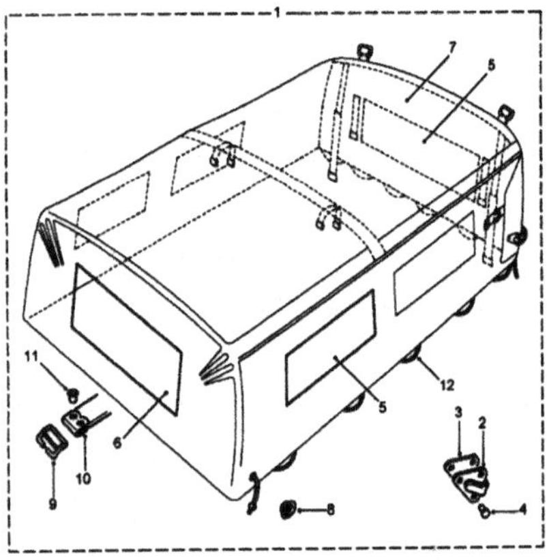

AJNXJA4A

Illus	Part Number	Description	Quantity	Change Point	Remarks
		HOOD ASSEMBLY-3/4 LENGTH			
1	MTC2574AG	KHAKI GREEN-WITH PLAIN SIDES	1		110"
1	MTC2574AE	MATT SAND-WITH PLAIN SIDES	1		110"
1	RRC2481ABE	MATT SAND-WITH PLAIN SIDES	1		130"
2	304797	• Hook-rope	4		
3	301343	• Washer plate	4		
4	RF608041	• Rivet	12		
5	MTC4314	• Glass-bodyside-rear	1		
6	MTC4313	• Glass-clear backlight	1		
7	MTC4061AG	• Curtain assembly-rear-Khaki Green	1		Part of MTC2574AG.
8	301321	• Eyelet connector	A/R		
9	300953	• Buckle	A/R		
10	300954	• End cap-hood	A/R		
11	396800	• Eyelet connector	A/R		
12	MTC4315	• Rope-hood-side	2		
12	331221	• Rope-hood-rear curtain	1		
	MTC4319	• Rope-top and sides-hood	1		
7	MTC4061AE	• Curtain assembly-rear-Matt sand	1		Part of MTC2574AE, RRC2481ABE.

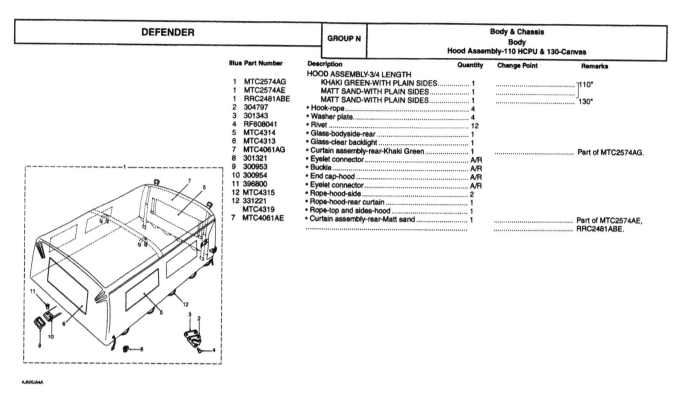

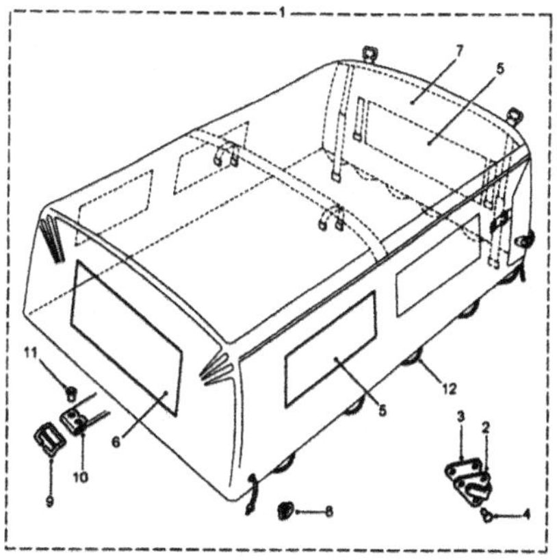

AJNXUA4A

Illus	Part Number	Description	Quantity	Change Point	Remarks
		HOOD ASSEMBLY-3/4 LENGTH			
1	DSB100400ABE	PVC-MATT SAND-WITH PLAIN SIDES	1		110"
1	DSB100440ABE	PVC-MATT SAND-WITH SIDE WINDOWS	1		110"
1	DSB100390ABE	PVC-MATT SAND-WITH PLAIN SIDES	1		130"
1	DSB100420ABE	PVC-MATT SAND-WITH SIDE WINDOWS	1		130"
2	STC4627ABE	• Rope-hood side curtain	2		
3	STC4005	• Rope-hood-elastic	5		

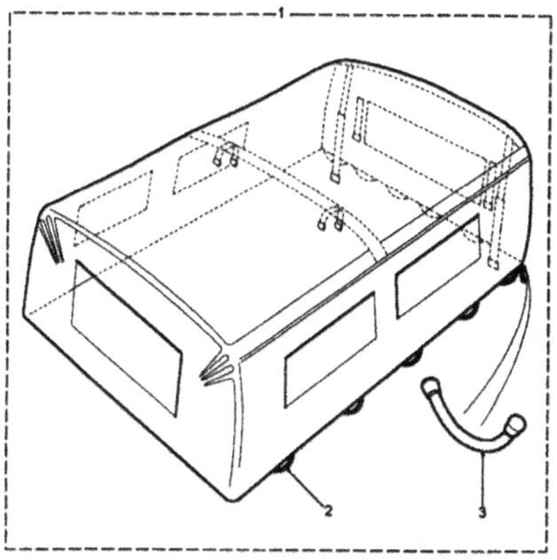

LN0175

DEFENDER	GROUP N	Body & Chassis Body Hood Assembly-110 Crew Cab

Illus	Part Number	Description	Quantity	Change Point	Remarks
1	DSB000020ABE	HOOD ASSEMBLY-3/4 LENGTH	1	Note (1)	Crew Cab 110"
2	STC4627ABE	• Rope-hood side curtain	2		
3	STC4005	• Rope-hood-elastic	5		

NOT ILLUSTRATED
PAS ILLUSTREE
NICHT ILLUSTRIERT
SENZA IL DISEGNO
SIN EL DISENO
SEM ILLUSTRACAO
NIET AFGEBEELD

TF 0007

CHANGE POINTS:
(1) From (V) 001033

DEFENDER	GROUP N	Body & Chassis Body Header Rail-90 Sport Only

Illus	Part Number	Description	Quantity	Change Point	Remarks
1	ALR6777	Panel header roof	1		

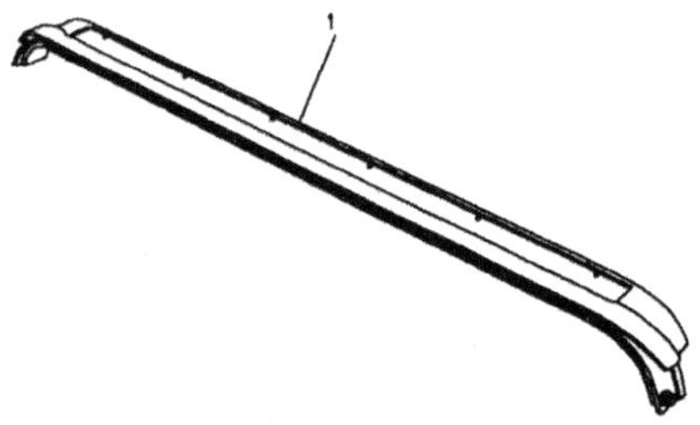

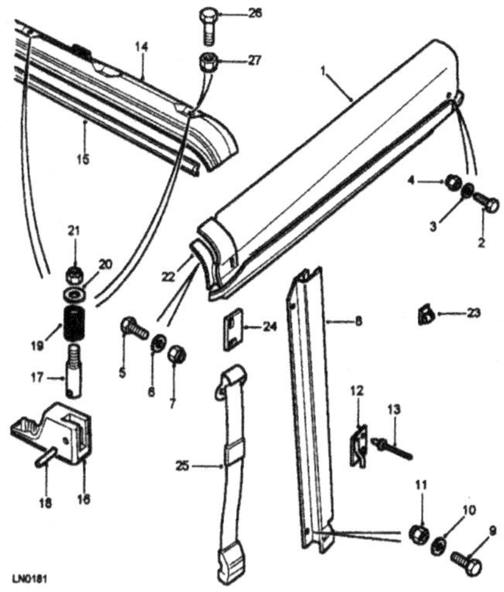

LN0181

Illus	Part Number	Description	Quantity	Change Point	Remarks
		DRAIN CHANNEL			
1	MTC6992	top-RH	1	Note (1)	
1	MTC6993	top-LH	1		
1	RRC3972	top-RH	1	Note (2)	
1	RRC3973	top-LH	1		
2	FS106207L	Screw-fixing channel-flanged head-M6 x 20	2		
3	AFU1080	Washer-plain	2		
4	NY106047L	Nut-hexagonal head-nyloc-M6	2		
5	FS106167L	Screw-flanged head-fixing channel-flanged head-M6 x 16	2		
6	AFU1080	Washer-plain	2		
7	NY106047L	Nut-hexagonal head-nyloc-M6	2		
8	MTC5428	Drain channel-side-RH	1		
8	MTC5429	Drain channel-side-LH	1		
9	FS106167L	Screw-flanged head-fixing channel-flanged head-M6 x 16	4		
10	AFU1080	Washer-plain	8		
11	NY106047L	Nut-hexagonal head-nyloc-M6	4		
12	330578	Hook-rope-front-RH	1		
12	330579	Hook-rope-front-LH	1		
13	78248	Rivet-pop-3/16" x 0.45"lng	4		
14	MTC6626	Header rail-canvas	1	Note (1)	
14	MTC9773	Header rail-canvas	1	Note (2)	
14	RRC8597	Header rail-vinyl.	1		
15	MTC7252	Seal	1		
16	MTC4581	Handle-grab	4		
17	MTC4583	Spindle-hood ret	4		
18	PA106201	Pin-spring	4		
19	MTC4584	Spring	4		
20	WC106041L	Washer-M6-oversize	4		
21	NY106047L	Nut-hexagonal head-nyloc-M6	4		
22	MTC7431	Seal	2		
23	AFU4162	Hook-drain channel	6	Note (2)	
24	MUC4538	Seal-top drain channel to hoodstick	1		
25	MUC4061ACG	Strap-hood-Khaki Green	2		
25	MUC4061ABE	Strap-hood-Matt sand	2		
26	SE106251	Screw-pan-M6 x 25	6		
27	NY106047L	Nut-hexagonal head-nyloc-M6	6		

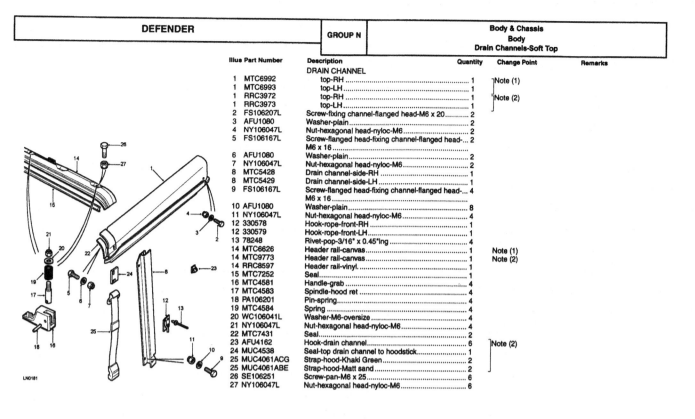

CHANGE POINTS:
(1) To (V) AA 224093
(2) From (V) AA 224094

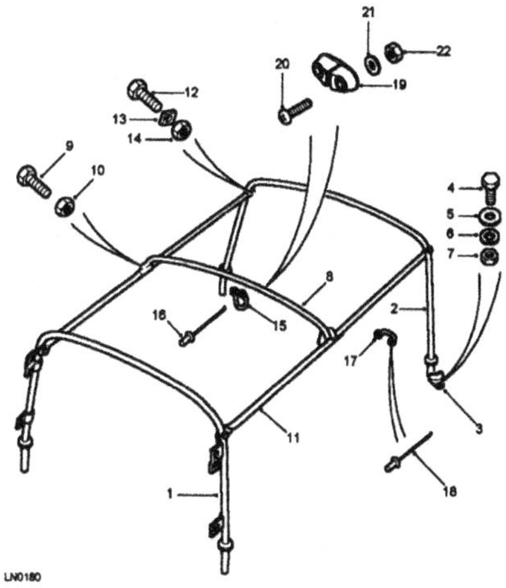

LN0180

Illus	Part Number	Description	Quantity	Change Point	Remarks
		SUPPORT ASSEMBLY-HOOD			
1	330551	front	1	Note (1)	
1	MUC4524	front	1	Note (2)	
2	330553	rear	1		
3	304301	Clamp	4		
4	FS108257L	Screw-clamp to body-flanged head-M8 x 25	4		
5	WA108051L	Washer-8mm	4		
6	WL108001L	Washer-sprung-M8	4		
7	FN108047L	Nut-flange-flanged head-M8	4		
8	330557	Support assembly-hood-intermediate	1		
9	FS106167L	Screw-flanged head-flanged head-M6 x 16	4		
10	NH106041L	Nut-hexagonal-nyloc-M6	4		
11	MUC1081	Tie bar	2		
12	SA106351	Screw-M6 x 35	4		
13	NS106011	Nut-square	4		
14	NY106047L	Nut-hexagonal head-nyloc-M6	4		
15	345699	Hook-rope-rear	2		
16	RR612103	Rivet	4		
17	395143	Staple	NLA		Use RRC3966.
17	RRC3966	Staple	2		
18	RA612373L	Rivet-3/16" x 0.575"lng	4		
19	RRC8002	Cleat	2		
20	SE105301L	Screw-recessed-pan head-M5 x 30	4		
21	WA105001L	Washer-plain-standard-M5	4		
22	NY105041L	Nut-hexagonal-nyloc-M5	4		

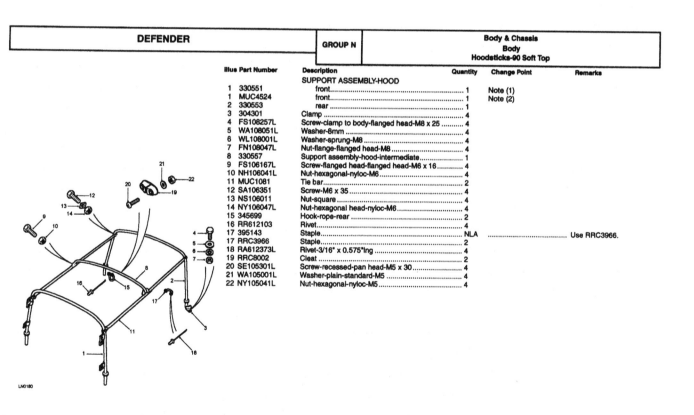

CHANGE POINTS:
(1) To (V) AA 224093
(2) From (V) AA 224094

Hoodsticks-110 Soft Top

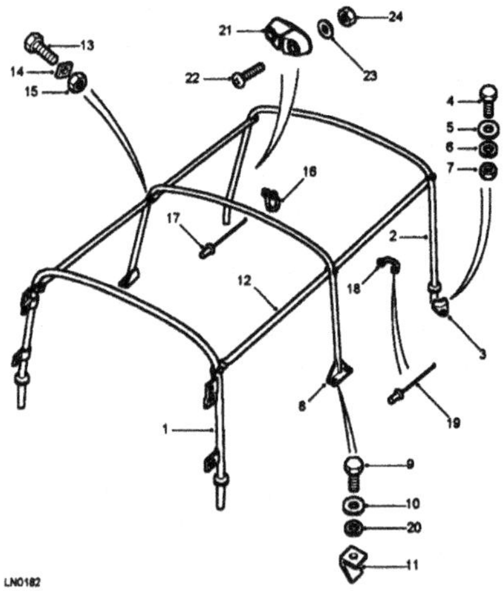

LN0182

Illus	Part Number	Description	Quantity	Change Point	Remarks
1	MUC4524	Support assembly-hood-front	1		
2	330553	Support assembly-hood	1		
3	304301	Clamp	4		
4	FS108257L	Screw-flanged head-M8 x 25	4		
5	WA108051L	Washer-8mm	4		
6	WL108001L	Washer-sprung-M8	4		
7	FN108047L	Nut-flange-flanged head-M8	4		
8	330699	Support assembly-hood-intermediate	1		
9	SR106201	Bolt-M6 x 20	4		
10	WL106001L	Washer-sprung-M6	4		
11	MRC9603	Nut plate	4		
12	330896	Tie bar-rear	4		
13	SA106451	Screw-hoodsticks-M6 x 45	4		
14	NS106011	Nut-square	6		
15	NY106047L	Nut-hexagonal head-nyloc-M6	6		
16	345699	Hook-rope-rear	2		
17	RR612103	Rivet	4		
18	RRC3966	Staple	4		
19	RA612373L	Rivet-3/16" x 0.575"lng	4		
20	MRC5527	Washer-plain-M6	4		
21	RRC8002	Cleat	2		
22	SE105301L	Screw-recessed-pan head-M5 x 30	4		
23	WA105001L	Washer-plain-standard-M5	4		
24	NY105041L	Nut-hexagonal-nyloc-M5	4		

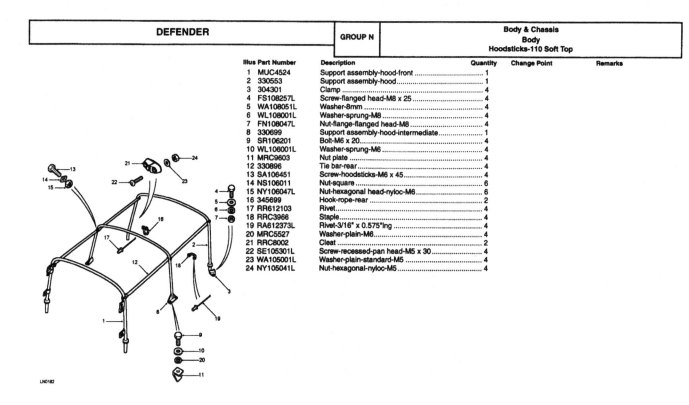

Hoodsticks-90 Truck Cab-Cab Fixing

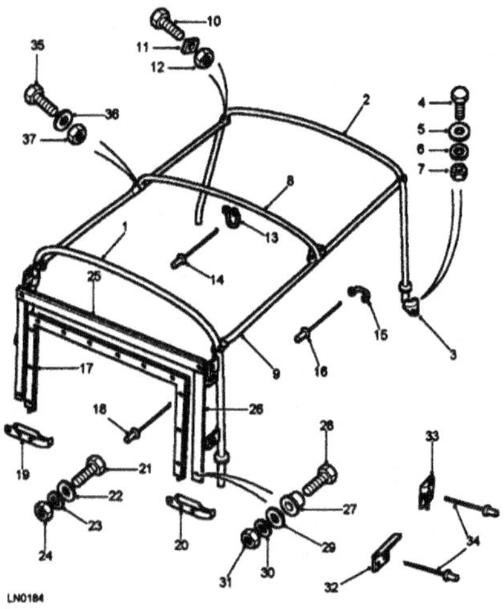

LN0184

Illus	Part Number	Description	Quantity	Change Point	Remarks
1	330553	Support assembly-hood-front	1		
2	330553	Support assembly-hood-rear	1		
3	304301	Clamp	4		
4	FS108257L	Screw-hoodsticks-flanged head-M8 x 25	4		
5	WA108051L	Washer-8mm	4		
6	WL108001L	Washer-sprung-M8	4		
7	FN108041L	Nut-flange-M8	NLA		Use FN108047L.
8	330557	Support assembly-hood-intermediate	1		
9	MUC1082	Tie bar-front and rear	2		
10	SA106351	Screw-M6 x 35	4		
11	NS106011	Nut-square	4		
12	NY106041L	Nut-hexagonal head-nyloc-M6	NLA		Use NY106047L.
13	345699	Hook-rope-rear	2		
14	RR612103	Rivet	4		
15	395143	Staple	NLA		Use RRC3966.
16	RA612373L	Rivet-3/16" x 0.575"lng	4		
17	MTC7384	Frame assembly-manual convertible hood	1		
18	RU612183	Rivet-pop-aluminium	12		
19	331673	Drain channel	1		
20	331674	Drain channel	1		
21	SE106201L	Screw-pan head-M6 x 20	4		
22	AFU1080	Washer-plain	4		
23	WL106001L	Washer-sprung-M6	4		
24	NH106041L	Nut-hexagonal-nyloc-M6	4		
25	331675	Strap-convertible hood tonneau retaining	1		
26	331676	Strap-convertible hood tonneau retaining	2		
27	348430	Stud	2		
28	SE105351L	Screw-pan	2		
29	WA105001L	Washer-plain-standard-M5	2		
30	WL105001L	Washer-retaining-M5	2		
31	NM105011	Nut-hexagonal	2		
32	334245	Hook retaining-RH	1		
32	334246	Hook retaining-LH	1		
33	330578	Hook-rope-front-RH	1		
33	330579	Hook-rope-front-LH	1		
34	78248	Rivet-pop-3/16" x 0.45"lng	4		
35	FS106167L	Screw-flanged head-flanged head-M6 x 16	4		
36	WA106041L	Washer-6mm	4		
37	NH106041L	Nut-hexagonal-nyloc-M6	4		

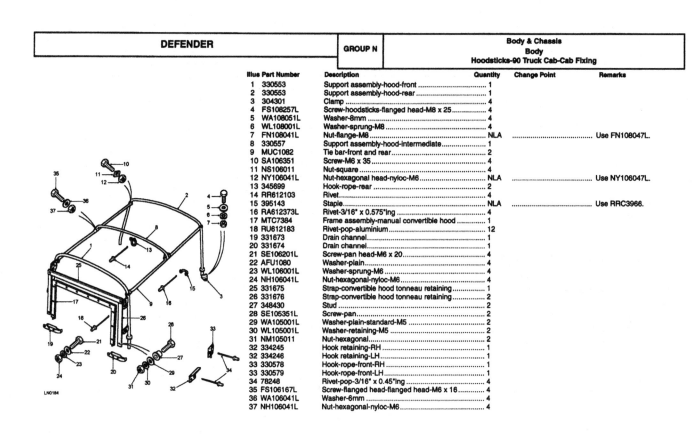

Body & Chassis
Body
Hoodsticks-90 Truck Cab-Bulkhead Fixing

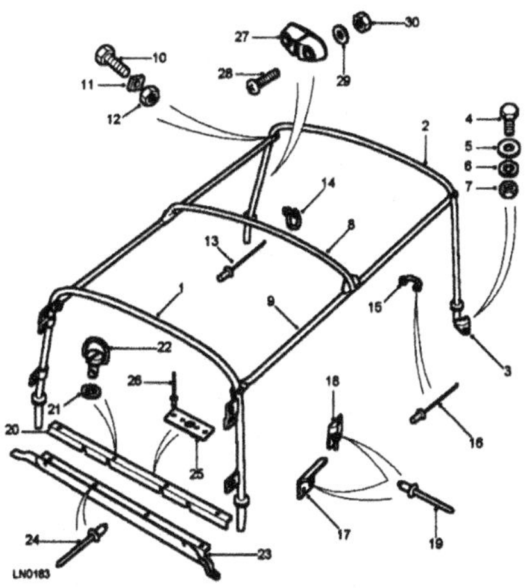

Illus	Part Number	Description	Quantity	Change Point	Remarks
1	330553	Support assembly-hood	1		
2	330553	Support assembly-hood	1		
3	304301	Clamp	4		
4	FS108257L	Screw-flanged head-M8 x 25	4		
5	WA108051L	Washer-8mm	4		
6	WL108001L	Washer-sprung-M8	4		
7	FN108047L	Nut-flange-flanged head-M8	4		
8	330557	Support assembly-hood-intermediate	1		
9	MUC1082	Tie bar	2		
10	SA106351	Screw-M6 x 35	4		
11	NS106011	Nut-square	4		
12	NY106047L	Nut-hexagonal head-nyloc-M6	4		
13	345699	Hook-rope-rear	2		
14	RR612103	Rivet	4		
15	395143	Staple	NLA		Use RRC3966.
15	RRC3966	Staple	2		
16	RA612373L	Rivet-3/16" x 0.575"lng	4		
17	334245	Hook retaining-RH	1		
17	334246	Hook retaining-LH	1		
18	330578	Hook-rope-front-RH	1		
18	330579	Hook-rope-front-LH	1		
19	78248	Rivet-pop-3/16" x 0.45"lng	4		
20	MTC4054	Retaining-strip	1		
21	AAU2367	Retainer	4		
22	AFU2503	Stud	4		
23	MUC7923	Drain channel	1		
24	RU612373L	Rivet-3/16" x 0.575"lng	7		
25	AFU2504	Plate-retaining	4		
26	RA610183	Rivet-5/32" x 0.335"lng	8		
27	RRC8002	Cleat	2		
28	SE105301L	Screw-recessed-pan head-M5 x 30	4		
29	WA105001L	Washer-plain-standard-M5	4		
30	NY105041L	Nut-hexagonal-nyloc-M5	4		

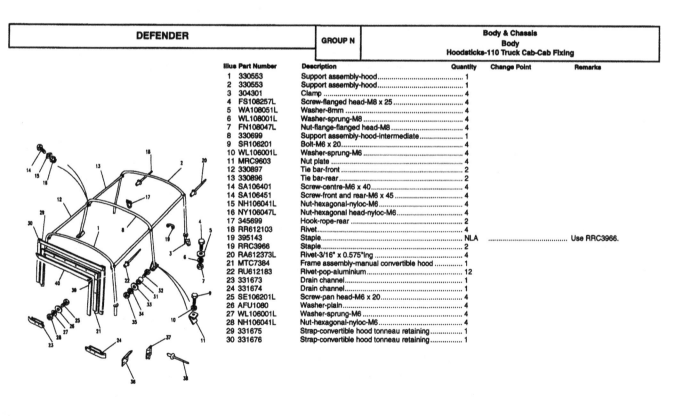

Body & Chassis
Body
Hoodsticks-110 Truck Cab-Cab Fixing

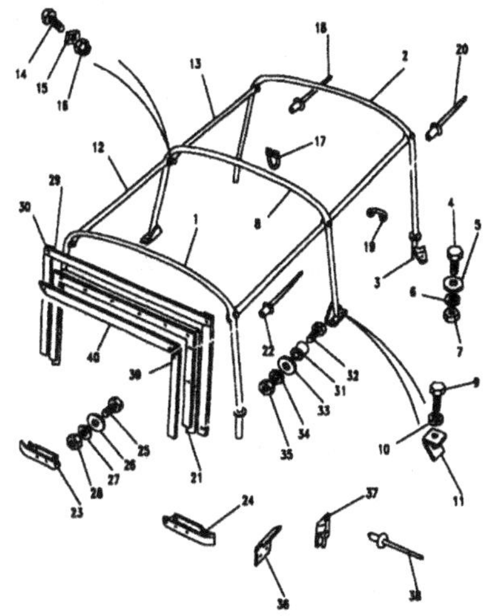

Illus	Part Number	Description	Quantity	Change Point	Remarks
1	330553	Support assembly-hood	1		
2	330553	Support assembly-hood	1		
3	304301	Clamp	4		
4	FS108257L	Screw-flanged head-M8 x 25	4		
5	WA108051L	Washer-8mm	4		
6	WL108001L	Washer-sprung-M8	4		
7	FN108047L	Nut-flange-flanged head-M8	4		
8	330699	Support assembly-hood-intermediate	1		
9	SR106201	Bolt-M6 x 20	4		
10	WL106001L	Washer-sprung-M6	4		
11	MRC9603	Nut plate	4		
12	330897	Tie bar-front	2		
13	330896	Tie bar-rear	2		
14	SA106401	Screw-centre-M6 x 40	4		
14	SA106451	Screw-front and rear-M6 x 45	4		
15	NH106041L	Nut-hexagonal-nyloc-M6	4		
16	NY106047L	Nut-hexagonal head-nyloc-M6	4		
17	345699	Hook-rope-rear	2		
18	RR612103	Rivet	4		
19	395143	Staple	NLA		Use RRC3966.
19	RRC3966	Staple	2		
20	RA612373L	Rivet-3/16" x 0.575"lng	4		
21	MTC7384	Frame assembly-manual convertible hood	1		
22	RU612183	Rivet-pop-aluminium	12		
23	331673	Drain channel	1		
24	331674	Drain channel	1		
25	SE106201L	Screw-pan head-M6 x 20	4		
26	AFU1080	Washer-plain	4		
27	WL106001L	Washer-sprung-M6	4		
28	NH106041L	Nut-hexagonal-nyloc-M6	4		
29	331675	Strap-convertible hood tonneau retaining	1		
30	331676	Strap-convertible hood tonneau retaining	1		

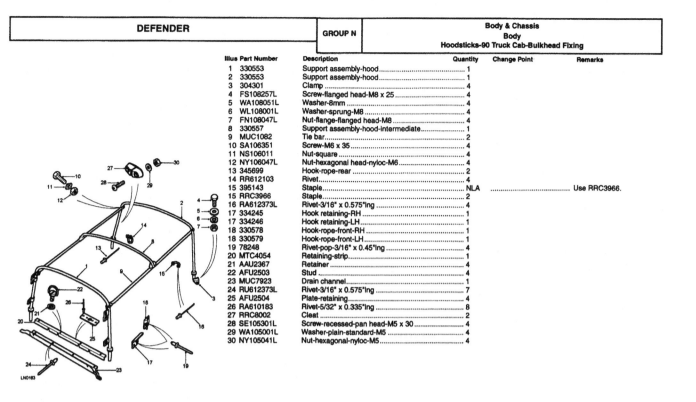

DEFENDER	GROUP N	Body & Chassis Body Hoodsticks-110 Truck Cab-Cab Fixing

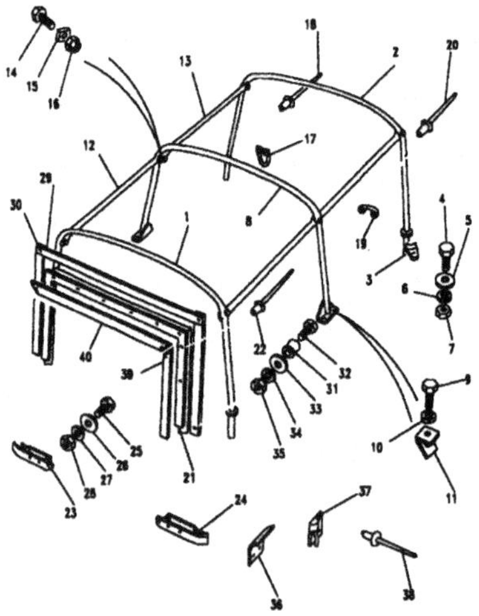

Illus	Part Number	Description	Quantity	Change Point	Remarks
31	MXC4657	Stud	2		
32	SE105351L	Screw-pan	2		
33	WA105001L	Washer-plain-standard-M5	2		
34	WL105001L	Washer-retaining-M5	2		
35	NM105011	Nut-hexagonal	2		
36	334245	Hook retaining-RH	1		
36	334246	Hook retaining-LH	1		
37	330578	Hook-rope-front-RH	1		
37	330579	Hook-rope-front-LH	1		
38	78248	Rivet-pop-3/16" x 0.45"lng	4		
39	MTC8145	Seal	2		
40	MTC8146	Seal	1		

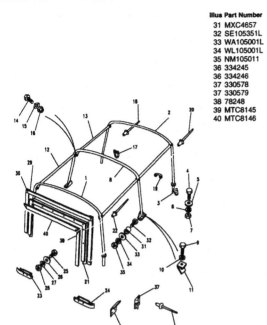

DEFENDER	GROUP N	Body & Chassis Body Hoodsticks-110 Truck Cab-Bulkhead Fixing

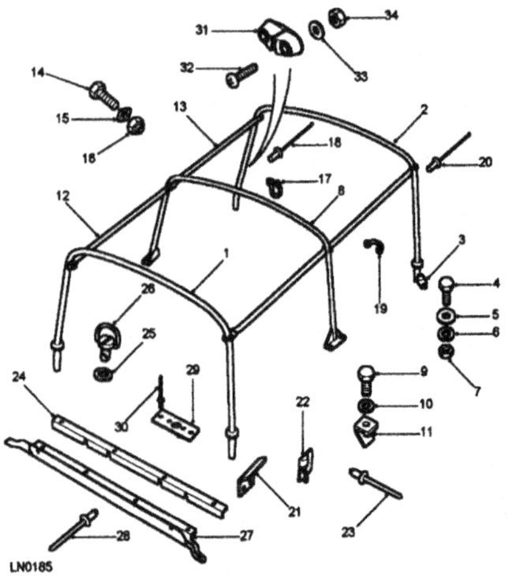

Illus	Part Number	Description	Quantity	Change Point	Remarks
1	330553	Support assembly-hood	1		
2	330553	Support assembly-hood	1		
3	304301	Clamp	4		
4	FS108251L	Screw-flanged head-M8 x 25	NLA		Use FS108257L.
5	WA108051L	Washer-8mm	4		
6	WL108001L	Washer-sprung-M8	4		
7	FN108047L	Nut-flange-flanged head-M8	4		
8	330699	Support assembly-hood-intermediate	1		
9	SR106201	Bolt-M6 x 20	4		
10	WL106001L	Washer-sprung-M6	4		
11	MRC9603	Nut plate	4		
12	330897	Tie bar-front	2		
13	330896	Tie bar-rear	2		
14	SA106401	Screw-M6 x 40	2		
14	SA106351	Screw-M6 x 35	4		
15	NS106011	Nut-square	6		
16	NY106041L	Nut-hexagonal head-nyloc-M6	NLA		Use NY106047L.
17	345699	Hook-rope-rear	2		
18	RR612103	Rivet	4		
19	395143	Staple	NLA		Use RRC3966.
20	RA612373L	Rivet-3/16" x 0.575"lng	4		
21	334245	Hook retaining-RH	1		
21	334246	Hook retaining-LH	1		
22	330578	Hook-rope-front-RH	1		
22	330579	Hook-rope-front-LH	1		
23	78248	Rivet-pop-3/16" x 0.45"lng	4		
24	MTC4054	Retaining-strip	1		
25	AAU2367	Retainer	4		
26	AFU2503	Stud	4		
27	MUC7923	Drain channel	1		
28	RU612373L	Rivet-3/16" x 0.575"lng	7		
29	AFU2504	Plate-retaining	4		
30	RA610183	Rivet-5/32" x 0.335"lng	8		
31	RRC8002	Cleat	2		
32	SE105301L	Screw-recessed-pan head-M5 x 30	4		
33	WA105001L	Washer-plain-standard-M5	4		
34	NY105041L	Nut-hexagonal-nyloc-M5	4		

DEFENDER | GROUP N | Body & Chassis — Body — Hoodsticks-110 HCPU & 130

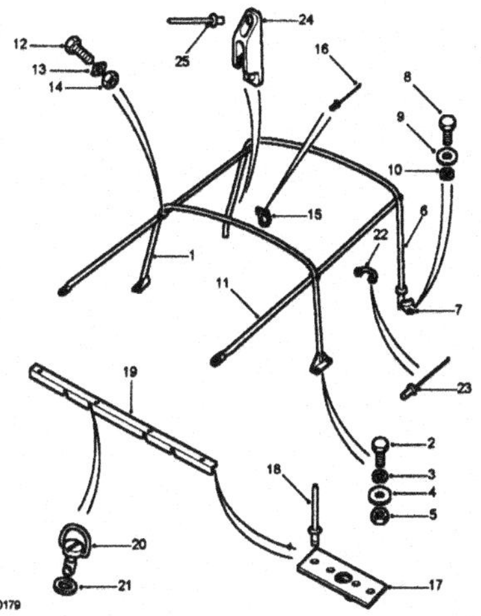

LN0179

Illus	Part Number	Description	Quantity	Change Point	Remarks
1	MTC4943	Support assembly-hood-intermediate	1		
2	FS106201L	Screw-flanged head-M6 x 20	4		
3	WL106001L	Washer-sprung-M6	4		
4	WA106041L	Washer-6mm	4		
5	NH106041L	Nut-hexagonal-nyloc-M6	4		
6	MTC4944	Support assembly-hood-rear	1		
7	304301	Clamp	2		
8	FS108207L	Screw-flanged head-M8 x 20	2		
9	WA108051L	Washer-8mm	2		
10	WL108001	Washer-sprung-M8	NLA		Use WL108001L.
11	MTC4945	Tie bar	4		110"
11	330897	Tie bar-front	2	To (V) 20/8/89	130"
11	RRC4422	Tie bar-rear	2		
11	RRC6365	Tie bar	4	From (V) 21/8/89	
12	SA106451	Screw-M6 x 45	6		
13	NS106011	Nut-square	6		
14	NY106041L	Nut-hexagonal head-nyloc-M6	NLA		Use NY106047L.
15	345699	Hook-rope-rear	2		
16	RU612373L	Rivet-3/16" x 0.575"lng	4		
17	AFU2504	Plate-retaining	4		
18	RJ610243	Rivet-pop-aluminium	8		
19	MTC4054	Retaining-strip	1		
20	AFU2503	Stud	4		
21	AAU2367	Retainer	4		
22	RRC3966	Staple	2		
23	RU612373L	Rivet-3/16" x 0.575"lng	4		
24	DJL000010	Cleat	2		
25	RRC4583	Rivet	4		

DEFENDER | GROUP N | Body & Chassis — Body — Hoodsticks-110 Crew Cab

Illus	Part Number	Description	Quantity	Change Point	Remarks
	DJH000010	Tube assembly-hood stick tie	2	Note (1)	Crew Cab 110"

ILLUSTRATION TO FOLLOW
L'ILLUSTRATION A SUIVRE
DAS BILD IST ZU FOLGEN
IL DISEGNO SEGUIRA
EL DISENO SIGUE
A ILLUSTRACAO SEGUIRA MAIS TARDE

TF 0007

CHANGE POINTS:
(1) From (V) 001033

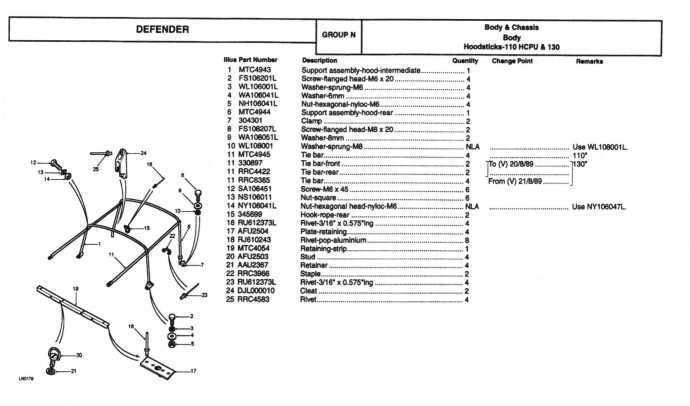

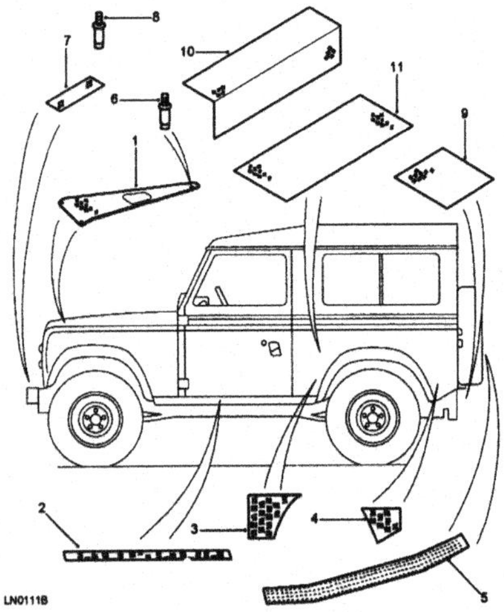

LN0111B

Illus	Part Number	Description	Quantity	Change Point	Remarks
		TREAD PLATE			
1	STC60162	front fender-counter sunk-Bright-RH	1		V8 EFi 50 LE
1	STC60163	front fender-counter sunk-Bright-LH	1		
1	STC60846	front fender-counterbored-Matt-RH	1		Extreme Belgium
1	STC60847	front fender-counterbored-Matt-LH	1		
1	STC7048	front fender-counterbored-Bright-RH	1		Special Vehicles
1	STC7049	front fender-counterbored-Bright-LH	1		
1	STC61822	front fender-RH-RHD	1	Note (1)	Tomb Raider
1	STC61825	front fender-LH-RHD	1		
1	STC61824	front fender-RH-LHD	1		
1	STC61823	front fender-LH-LHD	1		
		PLATE-CHEQUER			
2	STC60164	sill.-RH	1		V8 EFi 50 LE
2	STC60165	sill.-LH	1		
2	STC60848	sill.-RH	1		Extreme Belgium
2	STC60849	sill.-LH	1		
2	STC61827	sill.-RH	1	Note (1)	Tomb Raider 90"
2	STC61826	sill.-LH	1		
2	STC61831	sill.-RH	1		Tomb Raider 110"
2	STC61830	sill.-LH	1		
		PLATE-CHEQUER			
3	STC61834	side-LH	1	Note (1)	Tomb Raider 90"
3	STC61835	side-RH	1		
3	STC61836	side-LH	1		Tomb Raider 110"
3	STC61837	side-RH	1		

CHANGE POINTS:
(1) From (V) 1A 612404

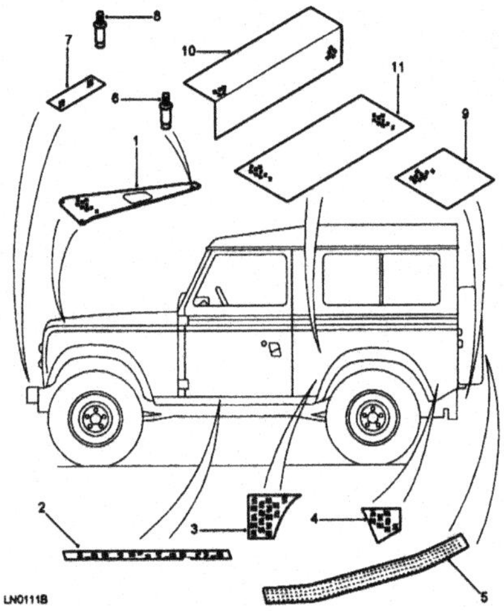

LN0111B

Illus	Part Number	Description	Quantity	Change Point	Remarks
		PLATE-CHEQUER			
4	STC60166	corner-rear-RH	1		V8 EFi 50 LE
4	STC60167	corner-rear-LH	1		
4	STC60850	corner-rear-RH	1		Extreme Belgium
4	STC60851	corner-rear-LH	1		
4	STC61829	corner-rear-RH	1	Note (1)	Tomb Raider 90"
4	STC61828	corner-rear-LH	1		
4	STC61832	corner-rear-LH	1		Tomb Raider 110"
4	STC61833	corner-rear-RH	1		
5	STC60168	Plate-chequer-rear step	1		V8 EFi 50 LE
5	STC60852	Plate-chequer-rear step	1		Extreme Belgium
6	STC61896	Rivet-short	A/R	Note (1)	Tomb Raider
7	STC61842	Plate-chequer-in bumper-front	2		Tomb Raider 90"
7	STC61843	Plate-chequer-in bumper-front-LH	1		Tomb Raider 110"
7	STC61844	Plate-chequer-in bumper-front-RH	1		
8	STC61895	Rivet-long	A/R		Tomb Raider
9	STC61841	Tread plate-tailboard	1		Tomb Raider 110"
10	STC61838	Plate-chequer-loadspace area-LH	1		
10	STC61839	Plate-chequer-loadspace area-RH	1		
11	STC61840	Plate-chequer-loadspace area-floor	1		
12	SF106161L	Screw-M6 x 16	A/R		
13	WJ106001L	Washer-plain-M6	A/R		
14	NY106047L	Nut-hexagonal head-nyloc-M6	A/R		

CHANGE POINTS:
(1) From (V) 1A 612404

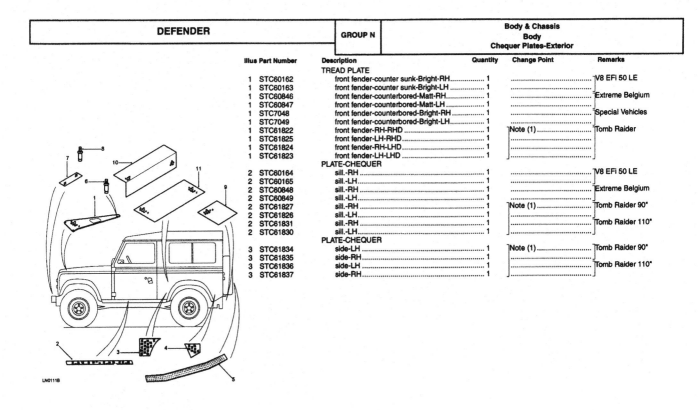

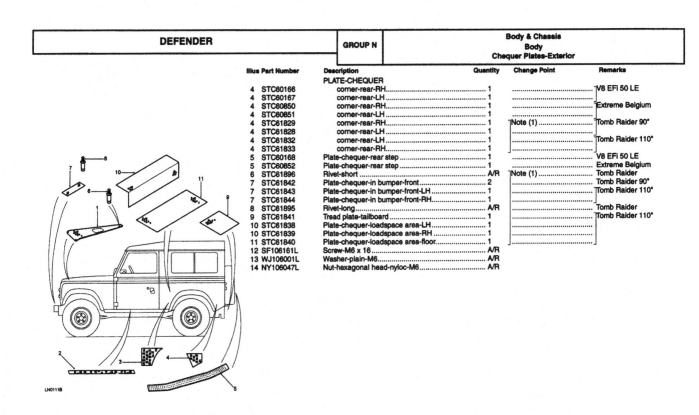

DEFENDER

GROUP N

Body & Chassis
Roll Cage
Lower-Station Wagon

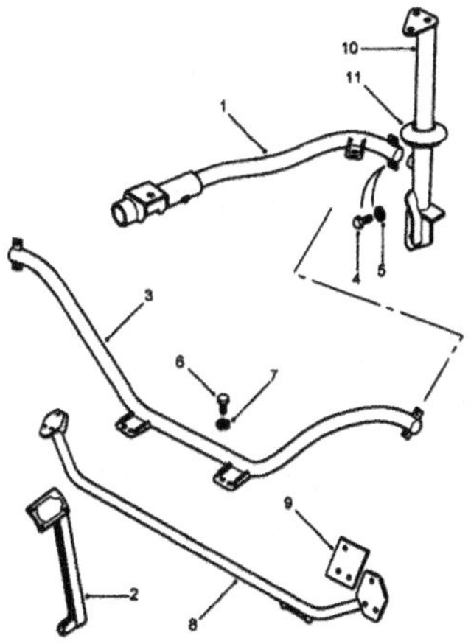

AMNXO88C

Illus	Part Number	Description	Quantity	Change Point	Remarks
1	ASR1097	Bar-transverse-roll cage-LH	1		
1	ASR1096	Bar-transverse-roll cage-RH	1		
2	ALR7881	Bracket-RH-front	1		
2	ALR7843	Bracket-LH-front	1		
3	ASR1109	Stay-roll cage hoop-inner	1		
4	ALR5549	Bolt-torx-pan-M10 x 30	4		
5	WA110061L	Washer-M10	4		
6	SH607091L	Screw-hexagonal head	2		
7	WA600071L	Washer	2		
8	ALR5557	Stay-roll cage hoop-lower	1		
9	ALR5558	Seal	2		
		SUPPORT-ROLL CAGE			
10	ASR1105	LH	1		V8 EFi
10	ASR1104	RH	1		V8 EFi
10	2943364	LH	1		6 Cylinder
10	2943363	RH	1		6 Cylinder
11	ALR7812	Grommet	2		
	AQF710010	Plate-roll bar stud	1		V8 EFi 50 LE

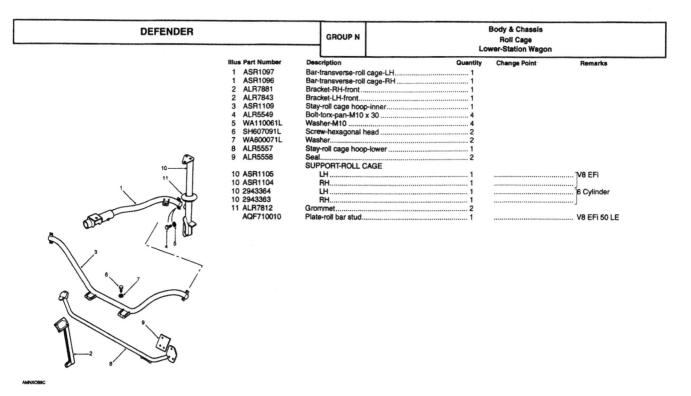

DEFENDER

GROUP N

Body & Chassis
Roll Cage
Lower-Regular

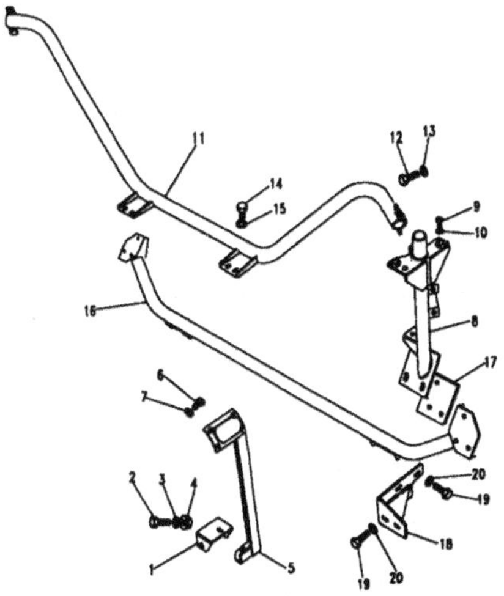

Illus	Part Number	Description	Quantity	Change Point	Remarks
1	ALR3220	Bracket-mounting-RH	1		
1	ALR3219	Bracket-mounting-LH	1		
2	SH110251L	Screw-hexagonal head-M10 x 25	2		
3	WA110061L	Washer-M10	4		
4	FN110047	Nut-flange-flange-M10	2		
5	ALR7843	Bracket-LH-front	1		
5	ALR7881	Bracket-RH-front	1		
6	MXC6676	Screw-M8	8		
7	4594L	Washer-plain	8		
8	2943361	Bracket-LH	1		
8	2943360	Bracket-RH	1		
9	ALR5549	Bolt-torx-pan-M10 x 30	10		
10	WA110065	Washer-plain	10		
11	ALR5556	Cage assembly-roll	1		
12	SH110251L	Screw-hexagonal head-M10 x 25	4		
13	WA110061L	Washer-M10	4		
14	SH607091L	Screw-hexagonal head	2		
15	WA600071L	Washer	2		
16	ALR5557	Stay-roll cage hoop-lower	1		
17	ALR5558	Seal	2		
18	ALR5560	Bracket-mounting cage-LH	1		
18	ALR5561	Bracket-mounting cage-RH	1		
19	SH110251L	Screw-hexagonal head-M10 x 25	10		
20	WA110061L	Washer-M10	10		

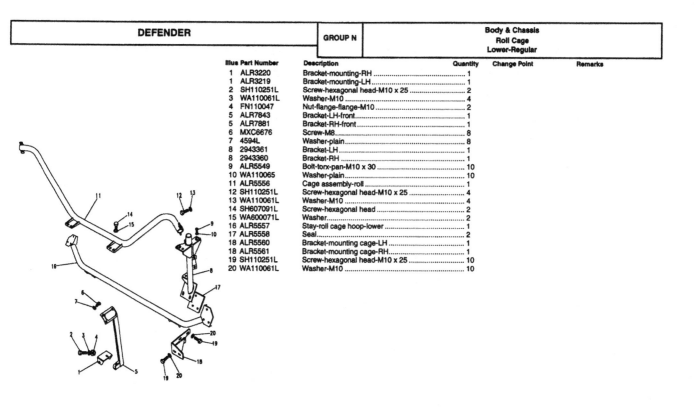

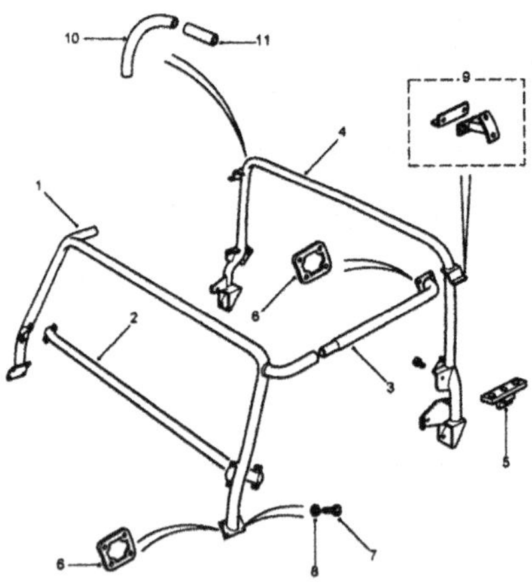

AMNXOB7C

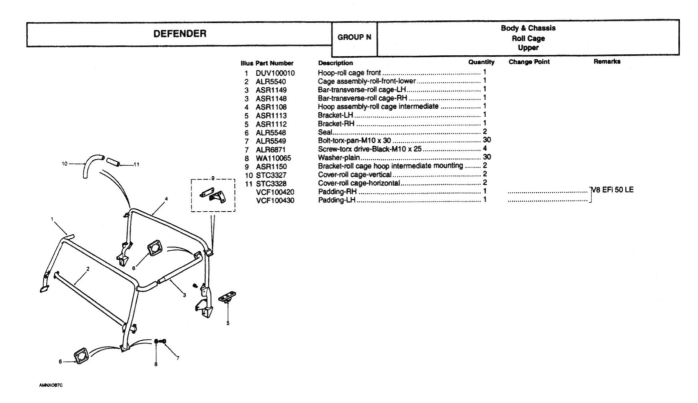

Illus	Part Number	Description	Quantity	Change Point	Remarks
1	DUV100010	Hoop-roll cage front	1		
2	ALR5540	Cage assembly-roll-front-lower	1		
3	ASR1149	Bar-transverse-roll cage-LH	1		
3	ASR1148	Bar-transverse-roll cage-RH	1		
4	ASR1108	Hoop assembly-roll cage intermediate	1		
5	ASR1113	Bracket-LH	1		
5	ASR1112	Bracket-RH	1		
6	ALR5548	Seal	2		
7	ALR5549	Bolt-torx-pan-M10 x 30	30		
7	ALR6871	Screw-torx drive-Black-M10 x 25	4		
8	WA110065	Washer-plain	30		
9	ASR1150	Bracket-roll cage hoop intermediate mounting	2		
10	STC3327	Cover-roll cage-vertical	2		
11	STC3328	Cover-roll cage-horizontal	2		
	VCF100420	Padding-RH	1		V8 EFi 50 LE
	VCF100430	Padding-LH	1		V8 EFi 50 LE

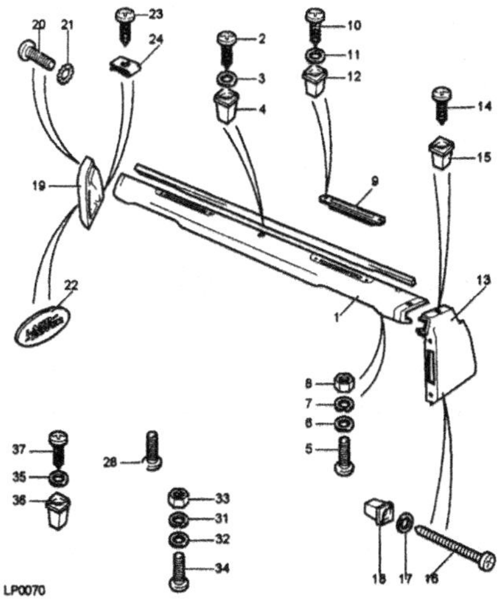

LP0070

Illus	Part Number	Description	Quantity	Change Point	Remarks
1	MWC9327PMA	Pad-facia crash assembly-Black	1	Note (1)	
1	MXC6084PMA	Pad-facia crash assembly-Black	1	Note (2)	
2	AB614064	Screw-self tapping-No 14 x 3/4	8		
3	WC106044L	Washer-plain-M6	3		
4	CZA4705L	Nut-lokut	3		
5	SE104124L	Screw-M4 x 12	2		
6	WA104004L	Washer-plain-M4	2		
7	WL104004	Washer-spring-M4	2		
8	NH104044	Nut-hexagonal-M4	2		
9	MTC6040	Finisher-demist vent windscreen	2	Note (3)	
9	BTR912	Finisher-demist vent windscreen	2	Note (4)	
10	AB606064L	Screw-self tapping AB-No 6 x 3/4	4		
11	WA105001L	Washer-plain-standard-M5	4		
12	RTC3745	Nut-lokut	4		
		NON AIR CONDITIONING			
		PANEL-FACIA			
13	MWC9338PMA	RHD-less air conditioning-Black	1		
13	MTC4571	LHD-less air conditioning-Black	1	Note (5)	
13	MWC9339PUA	LHD-less air conditioning-Black	1	Note (6)	
13	MWC9339PMA	LHD-less air conditioning-Black	1	Note (7)	
		WITH A/CON NO13 IS A VENT (SEE COOLING/HEATING)			
14	AD606044L	Screw-No 6 x 1/2	1		
15	RTC3745	Nut-lokut	1		
16	AB610124L	Screw-self tapping-No 10 x 1 1/2	1		
17	AFU1248	Washer-plastic	1		
18	RTC3748	Nut-lokut	1		90"
18	CZA4705L	Nut-lokut	1		110"

CHANGE POINTS:
(1) To (V) HA 455945
(2) From (V) HA 455946
(3) To (V) FA 453191
(4) From (V) FA 453192
(5) To (V) AA 343015
(6) From (V) AA 343016 To (V) LA 939975
(7) From (V) MA 939976

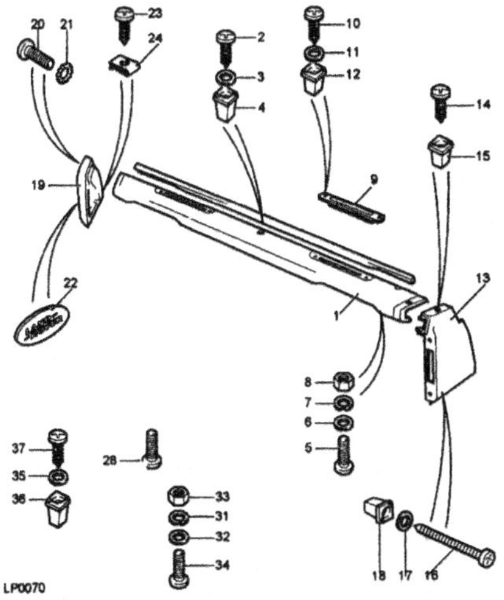

LP0070

Illus	Part Number	Description	Quantity	Change Point	Remarks
		HANDLE ASSEMBLY-GRAB			
19	MTC6142	RH-LHD	1		Except air conditioning
19	MTC6143	LH-RHD	1		Except air conditioning
19	AWR1175	RH-LHD	1		Air conditioning
20	SE105121L	Screw-pan head-M5 x 12	1		
21	WF105001L	Washer-starlock-M5	1		
22	MTC5851	Badge	1		
23	AC606104	Screw-self tapping-counter sunk-No 6 x 1 1/4	1		
24	AK606031	Nut-spring-u type-No 6	1		
		NON AIR CONDITIONING			
28	AB608047L	Screw-self tapping-No 8 x 1/2	6		
11	WA105001L	Washer-plain-standard-M5	6		
31	WM702001L	Washer-spring-3/16 dia-square	2		
32	WC105001L	Washer-plain-large-M5	4		
33	NH105041L	Nut-hexagonal-M5	2		
34	AB608051L	Screw-self tapping-No8 x 5/8-Black	2		
35	AK606031	Nut-spring-u type-No 6	1		
36	RTC3745	Nut-lokut	2		
37	SE105121L	Screw-pan head-M5 x 12	2		

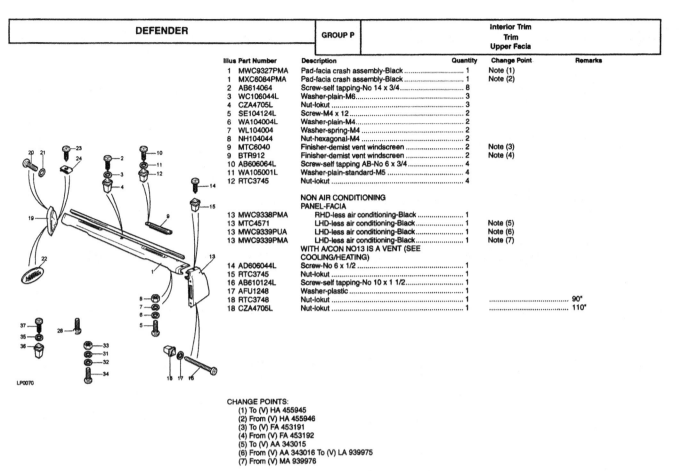

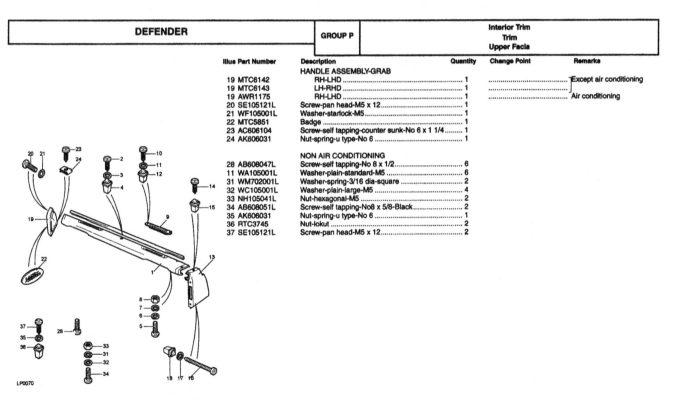

DEFENDER	GROUP P	Interior Trim Trim Facia Moulding-To (V) 1A999999

NOT ILLUSTRATED
PAS ILLUSTREE
NICHT ILLUSTRIERT
SENZA IL DISEGNO
SIN EL DISENO
SEM ILLUSTRACAO
NIET AFGEBEELD

TF 0007

Illus	Part Number	Description	Quantity	Change Point	Remarks
		PANEL-FACIA			
1	MTC4617LDQ	Panel-facia-RHD-less air conditioning-Vince Grey.	1	Note (1)	RHD except air conditioning
1	MTC4618LDQ	Panel-facia-LHD-less air conditioning-Vince Grey.	1	Note (1)	LHD except air conditioning
1	MTC4617LOY	Panel-facia-RHD-less air conditioning-Dark Granite	1	Note (2)	RHD except air conditioning
1	MTC4618LOY	Panel-facia-LHD-less air conditioning-Dark Granite	1	Note (2)	LHD except air conditioning
1	FBS100920LOY	Panel-facia-RHD-less air conditioning-Dark Granite	1	Note (3)	
1	FBS100930LOY	Panel-facia-LHD-less air conditioning-Dark Granite	1	Note (3)	
1	FBS100920PMA	Panel-facia-RHD-less air conditioning-Black	1	Note (3)	Tomb Raider
1	FBS100930PMA	Panel-facia-LHD-less air conditioning-Black	1	Note (3)	Tomb Raider
2	AFU1897	Fastener-drive-Grey	2		
2	AFU1897PMP	Fastener-drive-Black	2		
3	AFU2813	Fastener-drive	6		
4	AB606044L	Screw-self tapping-No 6 x 1/2	2		
5	WA104004L	Washer-plain-M4	2		
6	AJ606011L	Nut-M6	2		

CHANGE POINTS:
(1) To (V) TA 999221
(2) From (V) VA 999222 To (V) WA 159806
(3) From (V) XA 159807

DEFENDER	GROUP P	Interior Trim Trim Facia Moulding-From (V) 2A000001

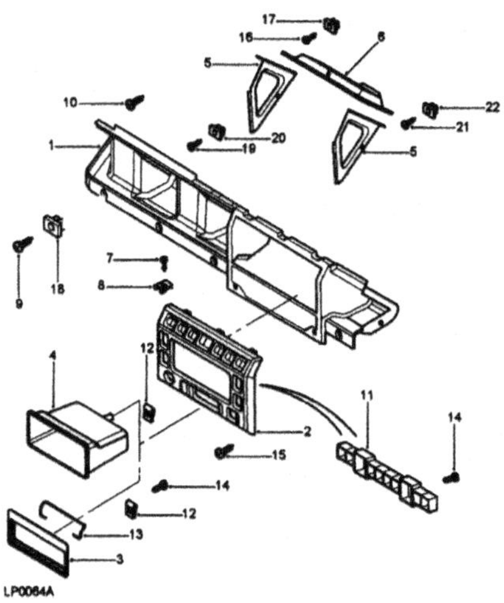

LP0064A

Illus	Part Number	Description	Quantity	Change Point	Remarks
1	FAB012860PMA	Moulding-facia stowage shelf-RHD	1	Note (1)	
1	FAB012870PMA	Moulding-facia stowage shelf-LHD	1	Note (1)	
2	FWJ000110PMA	Moulding-centre console switch pack	1	Note (1)	
3	FHF000070PMA	Bezel-radio	1	Note (1)	
4	FHM000040PMA	Bin-facia console stowage	1	Note (1)	Except radio
5	FHC000180	Bracket-facia console mounting-RH	1	Note (1)	
5	FHC000190	Bracket-facia console mounting-LH	1	Note (1)	
6	FHF000020	Support assembly-centre facia-radio	1	Note (1)	
7	DA608054	Screw	3		
8	FBT000010	Nut-spire	3	Note (1)	
9	DA608054	Screw	4		
10	DA608055L	Screw-self tapping	3		
11	YUD000310PMA	Insert-facia	1	Note (1)	
12	EYC106690	Clip	2		Radio
12	EYC106690	Clip	6		Except radio
13	FBT000020	Wire-trim retention	2	Note (1)	Radio
14	DA608031	Screw	10		Radio
14	DA608031	Screw	6		Except radio
15	DA608084	Screw-flanged head	2		
16	DA608054	Screw	4		
17	AFU2692	Nut-lokut	4		
18	DRC5582	Nut-lokut	4		
19	DA608054	Screw	2		
20	CZH677L	Nut-lokut	2		
21	AB614065L	Screw-self tapping	4		
22	CZA4705L	Nut-lokut	4		

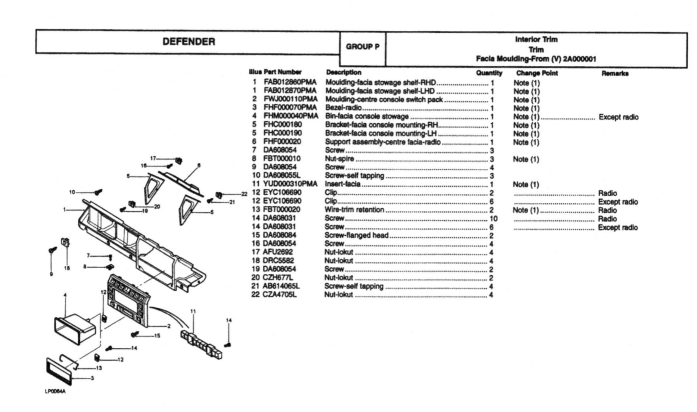

CHANGE POINTS:
(1) From (V) 2A 622424

Illus	Part Number	Description	Quantity	Change Point	Remarks
1	RTC8071	Kit-ashtray	1		

KIT INCLUDES ASHTRAY, SHROUD, & FIXINGS

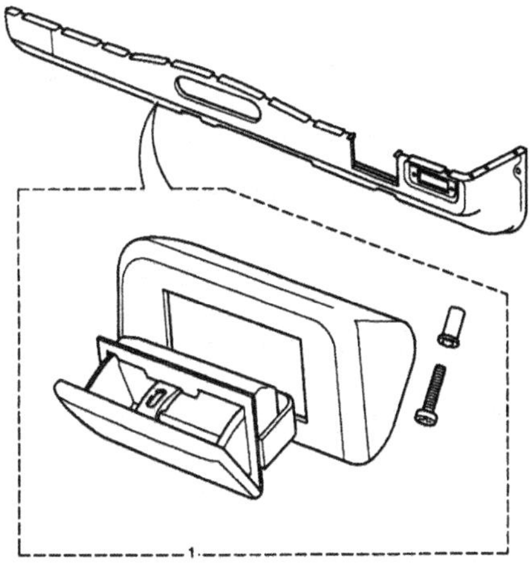

AHPXAA2A

Illus	Part Number	Description	Quantity	Change Point	Remarks
1	DZA5097L	Ashtray assembly-facia	1		
2	MUC1582	Retainer	1		

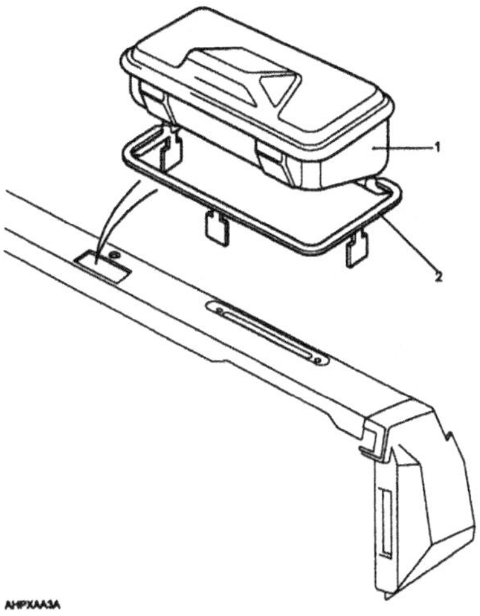

AHPXAA3A

Cowl Instrument Binnacle

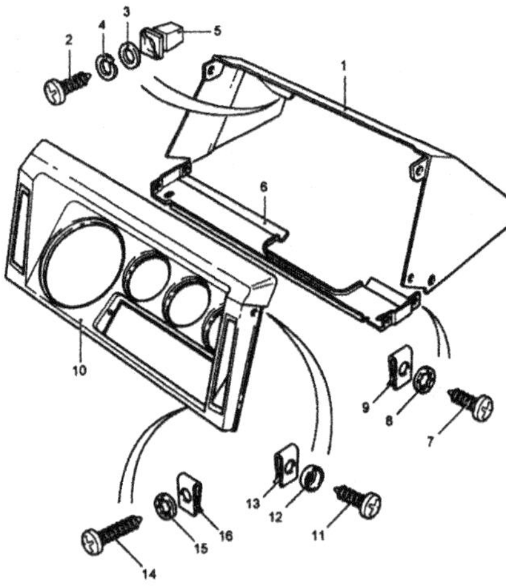

AHPXAA4A

Illus	Part Number	Description	Quantity	Change Point	Remarks
1	MTC2808	Cowl assembly instrument pack	1		RHD
1	MUC3023	Cowl assembly instrument pack	1		LHD
	FAR100130	Cover-instrument pack	1	Note (1)	
	FCA101680	Housing-facia radio/cassette	1	Note (1)	
	JQY100170	Blank-evaporator speaker	1	Note (1)	Air conditioning
2	AZ610081	Screw-No 10 x 1"	5		
3	AFU1218L	Washer-plain	5		
4	WL105001L	Washer-retaining-M5	5		
5	CZA4705L	Nut-lokut	5		
6	MUC7598	Stiffener-inst cowl-RH-RHD	1		
6	MUC7599	Stiffener-inst cowl-LH-LHD	1		
	AAM222L	Plug-blanking	1		110"
7	AB608044L	Screw-self tapping-No 8 x 1/2	4		RHD air conditioning
7	AFU2636	Screw-No 8	4		LHD air conditioning
8	WF703084	Washer-starlock-No 8-3mm	4		Air conditioning
9	AJ608031	Nut-spring-u type-No 8	4		Air conditioning
10	MTC5458	Panel-instrument mounting-RHD	1	Note (2)	
10	MTC5459	Panel-instrument mounting-LHD	1	Note (2)	
10	AWR3812	Panel-instrument mounting-alarm LED aperture-RHD	1	Note (2)	
10	AWR3813	Panel-instrument mounting-alarm LED aperture-LHD	1	Note (2)	
10	YAF100080	Panel-instrument mounting	1	Note (1)	RHD Td5
10	YAF100080	Panel-instrument mounting	1	Note (1)	RHD TDi
10	YAF100080	Panel-instrument mounting	1	Note (1)	RHD V8 Twin Carburettor
10	YAF100080	Panel-instrument mounting	1	Note (1)	RHD 4 Cylinder Petrol
10	YAF100080	Panel-instrument mounting	1	Note (1)	2800 cc BMW M52
10	YAF100090	Panel-instrument mounting	1	Note (1)	LHD Td5
10	YAF100090	Panel-instrument mounting	1	Note (1)	LHD TDi
10	YAF100090	Panel-instrument mounting	1	Note (1)	LHD V8 Twin Carburettor
10	YAF100090	Panel-instrument mounting	1	Note (1)	LHD 4 Cylinder Petrol
11	AD606044L	Screw-No 6 x 1/2	2		
12	WK606214L	Washer-cup-No 6	2		
13	MWC9322	Nut-spring-u type-No 6	2		
14	AB606044L	Screw-self tapping-No 6 x 1/2	2		
15	WF704064	Washer-starlock-No 6-4mm	2		
16	MWC9322	Nut-spring-u type-No 6	2		

CHANGE POINTS:
(1) From (V) XA 159807
(2) To (V) WA 159806

Cover Auxiliary Instruments

Illus	Part Number	Description	Quantity	Change Point	Remarks
1	320835	COVER ASSEMBLY-FACIA CONSOLE	1		
2	346786	• Cover-instrument pack	1		
3	AB608031L	• Screw-self tapping-No 8 x 3/8	2		
4	RTC3745	• Nut-lokut	2		
5	SP105204	• Screw-M5 x 20	NLA		Use SE105204.
6	WC105007	• Washer-plain-large-Black	4		
7	WL105004	• Washer-sprung-M5	2		
8	NH105041L	• Nut-hexagonal-M5	2		
5	SE105204	Screw-M5			

FOR VEHICLES WITHOUT FACTORY FITTED RADIO ONLY.
FOR VEHICLES WITH RADIO SEE ELECTRICAL - RADIO

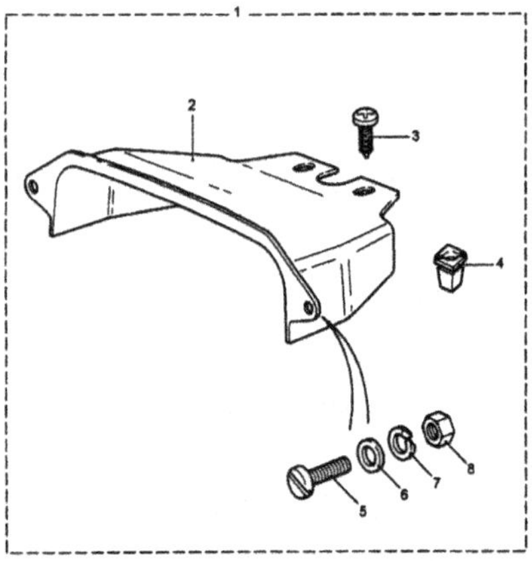

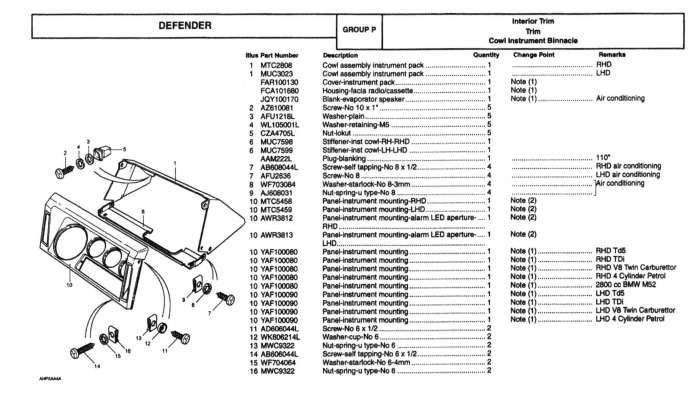

AHPXAA5A

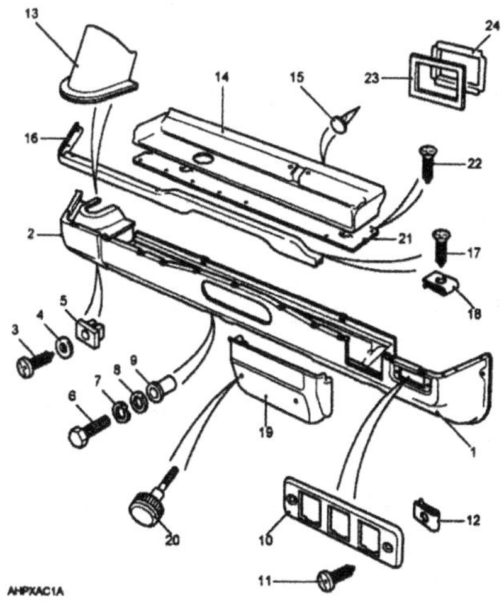

AHPXAC1A

Illus	Part Number	Description	Quantity	Change Point	Remarks
		DUCT-HEATER			
1	MTC2826	RHD-without speaker-less immobilisation	1		Except air conditioning
1	MTC2827	LHD-without speaker-less immobilisation	1		
1	AWR5007	RHD-without speaker-with immobilisation	1		
1	MUC1384	RHD-with speaker-less immobilisation	1		
1	MUC1383	LHD-with speaker-less immobilisation	1		
1	AWR5035	RHD-with speaker-with immobilisation	1		
1	MUC3249	RHD-without speaker-less immobilisation	1		Air conditioning
1	AWR5036	RHD-without speaker-with immobilisation	1		
1	MUC3244	RHD-with speaker-less immobilisation	1		
1	AWR5037	RHD-with speaker-with immobilisation	1		
1	MUC1703	LHD-without speaker-less immobilisation	1		Air conditioning 90"
1	MUC1716	LHD-with speaker-less immobilisation	1		
1	MUC1703	LHD-without speaker-less immobilisation	1	Note (1)	110" except headlamp levelling
1	MUC1716	LHD-with speaker-less immobilisation	1		
1	FAE101360LOY	LHD-with speaker-less immobilisation	1	Note (2)	110" headlamp levelling
		DUCT-HEATER			
1	FAY000220PMA	RHD-with speaker	1	Note (3)	
1	FAY000230PMA	LHD-with speaker	1	Note (3)	
1	FAY000240PMA	RHD-without speaker	1	Note (3)	
1	FAY000250PMA	LHD-without speaker	1	Note (3)	

CHANGE POINTS:
(1) To (V) WA 138479
(2) From (V) WA 138480 To (V) ZA 999999
(3) From (V) 2A 622424

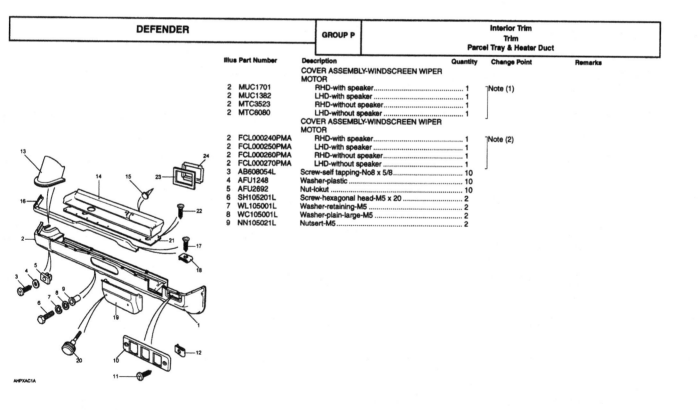

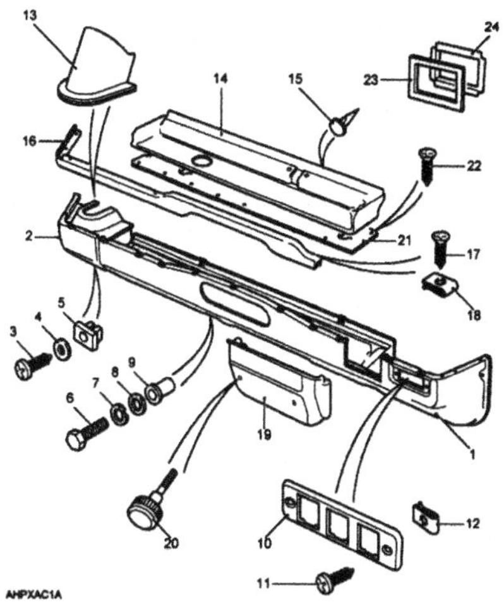

AHPXAC1A

Illus	Part Number	Description	Quantity	Change Point	Remarks
		COVER ASSEMBLY-WINDSCREEN WIPER MOTOR			
2	MUC1701	RHD-with speaker	1	Note (1)	
2	MUC1382	LHD-with speaker	1		
2	MTC3523	RHD-without speaker	1		
2	MTC6080	LHD-without speaker	1		
		COVER ASSEMBLY-WINDSCREEN WIPER MOTOR			
2	FCL000240PMA	RHD-with speaker	1	Note (2)	
2	FCL000250PMA	LHD-with speaker	1		
2	FCL000260PMA	RHD-without speaker	1		
2	FCL000270PMA	LHD-without speaker	1		
3	AB608054L	Screw-self tapping-No8 x 5/8	10		
4	AFU1248	Washer-plastic	10		
5	AFU2692	Nut-lokut	10		
6	SH105201L	Screw-hexagonal head-M5 x 20	2		
7	WL105001L	Washer-retaining-M5	2		
8	WC105001L	Washer-plain-large-M5	2		
9	NN105021L	Nutsert-M5	2		

CHANGE POINTS:
(1) To (V) ZA 999999
(2) From (V) 2A 622424

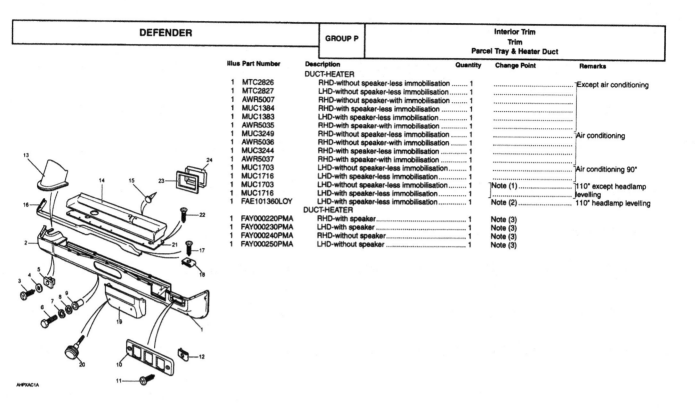

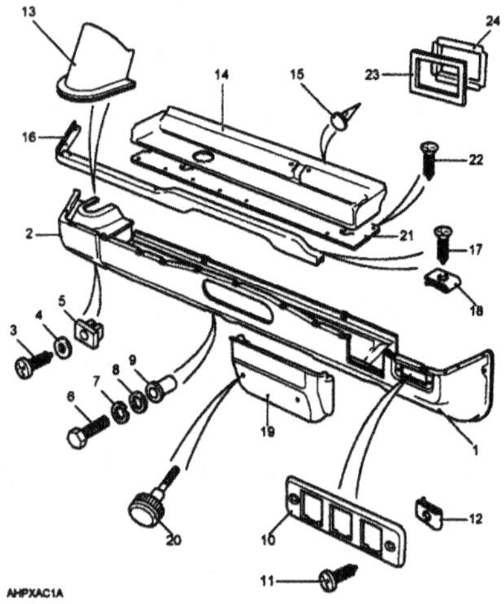

AHPXAC1A

Illus	Part Number	Description	Quantity	Change Point	Remarks
10	MTC2640	Panel assembly-switch mounting-RHD	1		
11	AD606041L	Screw-self tapping	2		
12	AK606011L	Nut-spring-flat-with rear wash/wipe	2		
13	MTC3705LDQ	Cover-wiper-cable drive-Vince Grey	1	Note (1)	
13	MTC3705LOY	Cover-wiper-cable drive-Dark Granite	1	Note (2)	
13	MTC3705PMA	Cover-wiper-cable drive-Black	1	Note (3)	Tomb Raider
14	MRC7282	PARCEL SHELF-FRONT-RHD	1	Note (4)	
15	RTC3750	• Fastener-drive	5		
11	AB606044L	• Screw-self tapping-No 6 x 1/2	5		
4	WA104004L	• Washer-plain-M4	5		
14	MRC7283	PARCEL SHELF-FRONT-LHD	1	Note (4)	
15	AFU2813	• Fastener-drive	5		
11	AB606044L	• Screw-self tapping-No 6 x 1/2	5		
4	WA104004L	• Washer-plain-M4	5		
14	AHL710020	Parcel shelf-front-RHD	1	Note (5)	
14	AHL710030	Parcel shelf-front-LHD	1		
15	YOO5098LOY	Fastener-drive-Dark Granite	5	Note (5)	
15	YOO5098PMP	Fastener-drive-Black	5		Tomb Raider

CHANGE POINTS:
(1) To (V) TA 999221
(2) From (V) VA 999222
(3) From (V) 1A 612404
(4) To (V) WA 159806
(5) From (V) XA 159807

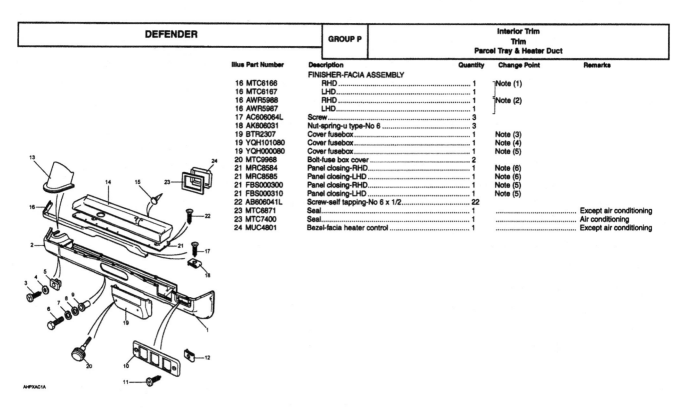

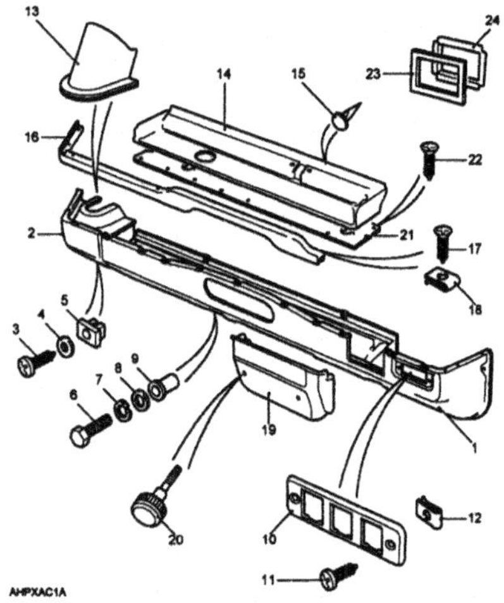

AHPXAC1A

Illus	Part Number	Description	Quantity	Change Point	Remarks
		FINISHER-FACIA ASSEMBLY			
16	MTC6166	RHD	1	Note (1)	
16	MTC6167	LHD	1		
16	AWR5988	RHD	1	Note (2)	
16	AWR5987	LHD	1		
17	AC606064L	Screw	3		
18	AK606031	Nut-spring-u type-No 6	3		
19	BTR2307	Cover fusebox	1	Note (3)	
19	YQH101080	Cover fusebox	1	Note (4)	
19	YQH000080	Cover fusebox	1	Note (5)	
20	MTC9968	Bolt-fuse box cover	2		
21	MRC8584	Panel closing-RHD	1	Note (6)	
21	MRC8585	Panel closing-LHD	1	Note (6)	
21	FBS000300	Panel closing-RHD	1	Note (5)	
21	FBS000310	Panel closing-LHD	1	Note (5)	
22	AB606041L	Screw-self tapping-No 6 x 1/2	22		
23	MTC6871	Seal	1		Except air conditioning
23	MTC7400	Seal	1		Air conditioning
24	MUC4801	Bezel-facia heater control	1		Except air conditioning

CHANGE POINTS:
(1) To (V) TA 999221
(2) From (V) VA 999222
(3) To (V) WA 159806
(4) From (V) XA 159807 To (V) ZA 999999
(5) From (V) 2A 622424
(6) To (V) ZA 999999

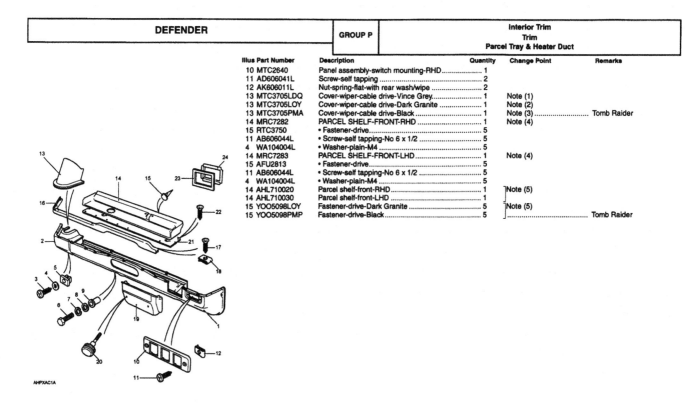

Illus	Part Number	Description	Quantity	Change Point	Remarks
1	BTR9926LNF	ILLUMINATION ASSEMBLY SELECTOR MECHANISM-ASH GREY	1		
2	AMR1192	• HARNESS-LINK-SELECTOR ILLUMIATION SELECTION MECHANISM	1		
3	STC881	• • Bulb-wedge illumination	2		
4	SE104161L	Screw-M8 x 16	4		
5	WA104001L	Washer-plain-M4	4		
6	FTC5193	Bracket-mounting	1		
7	SE106121	Screw-M6 x 12	4		
8	SE106251	Screw-pan-M6 x 25	2		
9	AFU1080	Washer-plain	2		
10	WL106001L	Washer-sprung-M6	6		
11	FTC5236	Retainer	1		
12	FTC5237	Seal-selector cable automatic transmission	1		

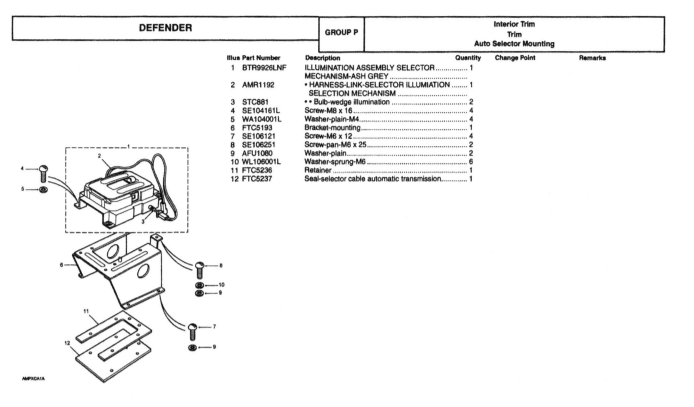

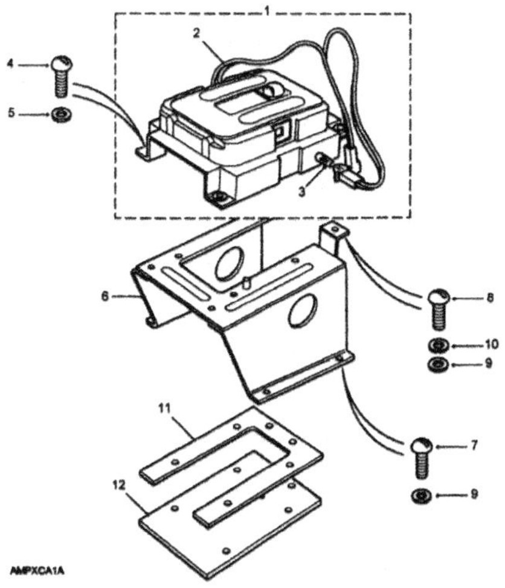

AMPXCA1A

Illus	Part Number	Description	Quantity	Change Point	Remarks
1	MXC2611	Cubby box	1	To (V) MA 962814	
2	MTC4520	Tray-console picnic	1		
3	RTC3024	Lock set	1		
4	AB606061L	Screw-self tapping-No 6 x 3/4	2		
5	CZK3882	Key	A/R		
6	SE106351L	Screw-pan-M6 x 35	4		
7	WA106041L	Washer-6mm	4		
8	NN106021	Nutsert-blind-M6	4		
9	AFU2501	Plug	4		

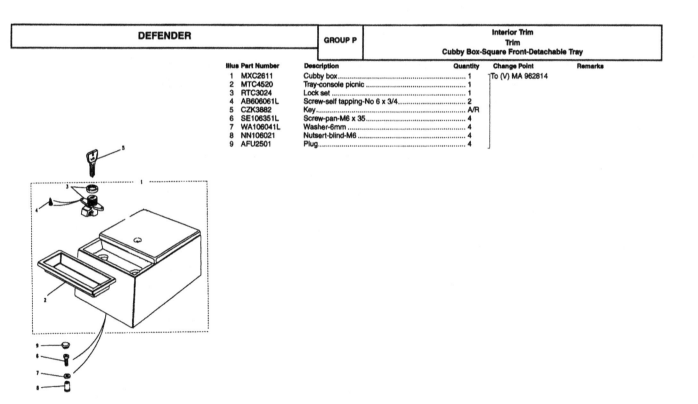

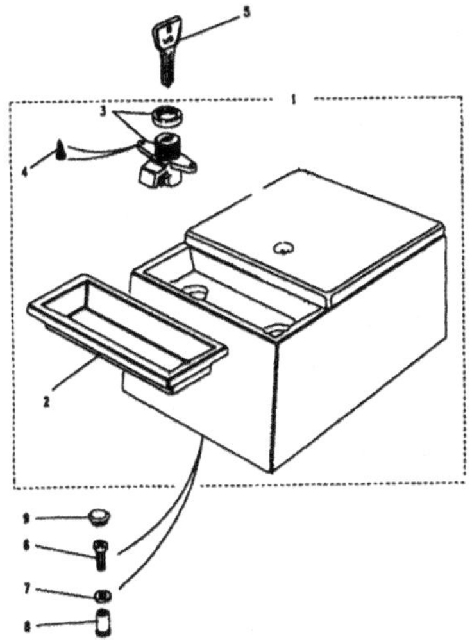

DEFENDER	GROUP P	Interior Trim Trim Cubby Box-Square Front-Fixed Tray

Illus	Part Number	Description	Quantity	Change Point	Remarks
1	MUC6681	CUBBY BOX	1	To (V) HA 455631	
2	MUC6682	• Striker-centre console stowage box lid	1		
3	MUC6452	• Latch assembly-tunnel console lid	1		
4	MUC6453	• Lock set	1		
	MUC2153	Key-blank owner	A/R		
5	SE106351L	Screw-pan-M6 x 35	4		
6	WA106041L	Washer-6mm	1		
7	NN106021	Nutsert-blind-M6	4		
8	AFU2501	Plug	4		

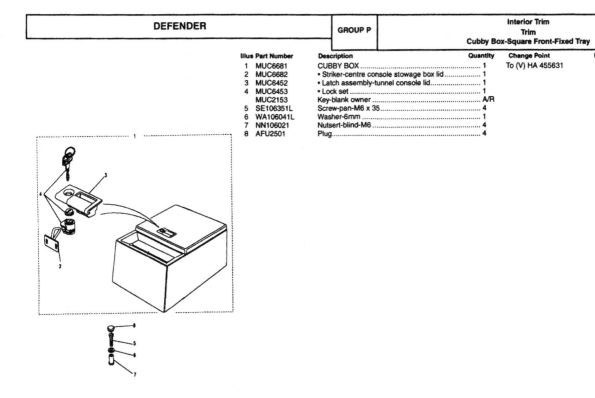

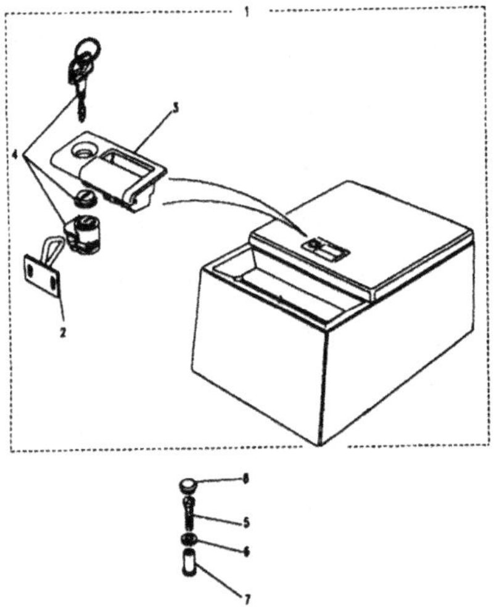

DEFENDER	GROUP P	Interior Trim Trim Cubby Box-Sloping Front

Illus	Part Number	Description	Quantity	Change Point	Remarks
1	AWR1607	CUBBY BOX	1	Note (1)	
1	AWR5986LOY	CUBBY BOX-DARK GRANITE	1	Note (2); Note (3)	
2	BTR695	• Striker assembly-door lock	1		
3	MUC6452	• Latch assembly-tunnel console lid	1		
4	MUC6453	• Lock set	1		
	MUC2153	Key-blank owner	A/R		
1	FJG000010LOY	CUBBY BOX-DARK GRANITE	1	Note (4)	
5	FJH000010PMA	• Striker-centre console stowage box lid	1		
6	FJF000030	• Latch assembly-tunnel console lid	1		
1	FJG000010PMA	CUBBY BOX-BLACK	1	Note (5)	Tomb Raider
5	FJH000010PMA	• Striker-centre console stowage box lid	1		
6	FJF000030	• Latch assembly-tunnel console lid	1		
7	SE106551	Screw-flanged head	4	Note (6)	
7	SE106651	Screw-pan head-M6 x 65	4	Note (7)	
8	WA106041L	Washer-6mm	4		
9	NN106021	Nutsert-blind-M6	4		
10	AFU2501	Plug	4		
11	STC61865	Holder-cup	1	Note (5)	Tomb Raider
12	STC61866	Trim panel-aluminium	2	Note (5)	Tomb Raider

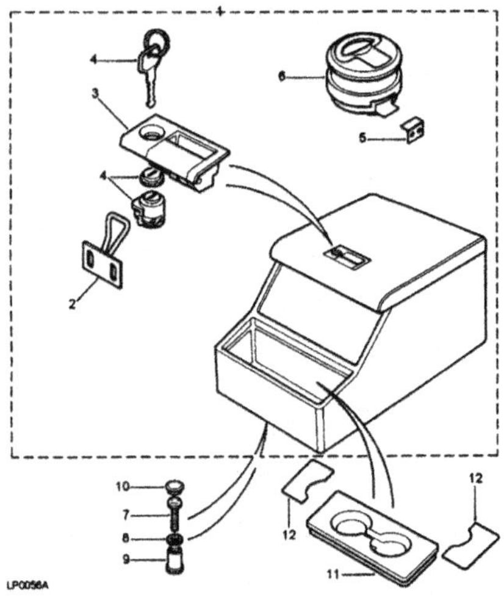

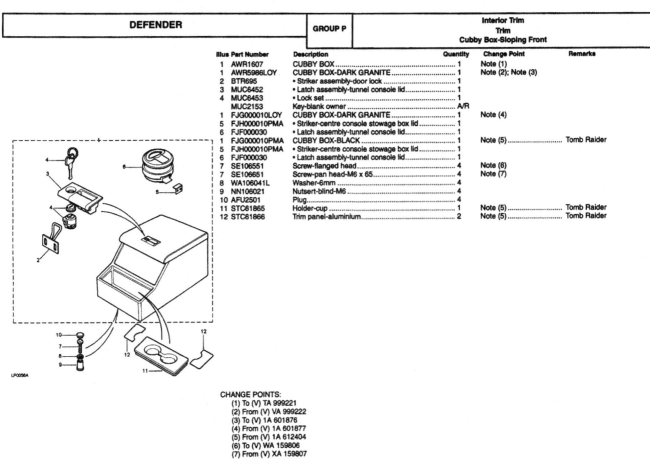

CHANGE POINTS:
(1) To (V) TA 999221
(2) From (V) VA 999222
(3) To (V) 1A 601876
(4) From (V) 1A 601877
(5) From (V) 1A 612404
(6) To (V) WA 159806
(7) From (V) XA 159807

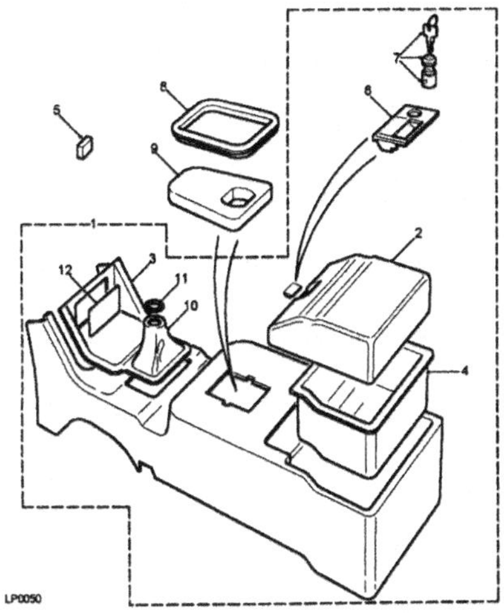

LP0050

Illus	Part Number	Description	Quantity	Change Point	Remarks
1	FHS101520	CONSOLE ASSEMBLY-TUNNEL	1		
2	AWR5520	• Lid-tunnel console	1		
3	AWR5522	• Lid assembly-facia fuse box	1		
4	AWR5695	• Cubby box	1		
5	BTR6506	• Foam	2		
6	FNC100050L	• Latch assembly-tunnel console lid	1		
7	FN310013L	• Lock & keys	1		
8	BTR3100LNF	Finisher-front console automatic selector-Ash Grey	1		
9	AWR6175	Pad-insulation	1		
10	FJL101970	Gaiter-gear lever assembly-transfer box	1		
11	BTR7958	Retainer-gear lever assembly gaiter-upper	1		
12	BTR9547	Label-warning-automatic	1		
13	FIF100110	Mat-centre console	1		
14	AFU1897LDE	Fastener-drive-Slate Grey	2		
15	AWR6683	Bracket-console trim	1		
16	AWR6715	Nutsert-blind-M6	3		
17	DA608044L	Screw-self tapping-M8 x 13-self tapping	6		
18	FS106167L	Screw-flanged head-flanged head-M6 x 16	3		
19	MTC4771	Bracket fixing	1		
20	MWC3136	Clip-snap-sack	2		
21	RA607076	Rivet	2		
22	RU612373L	Rivet-3/16" x 0.575"lng	4		

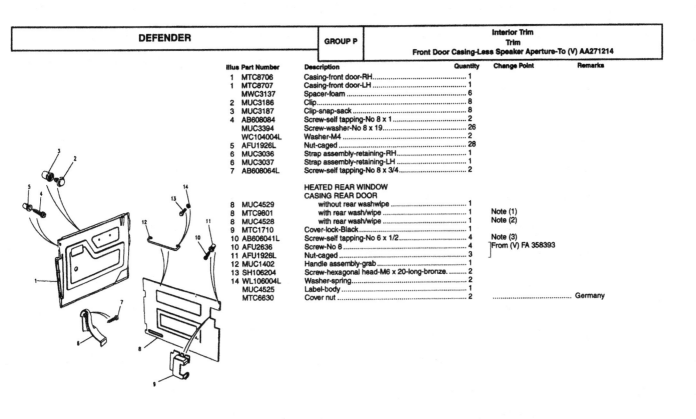

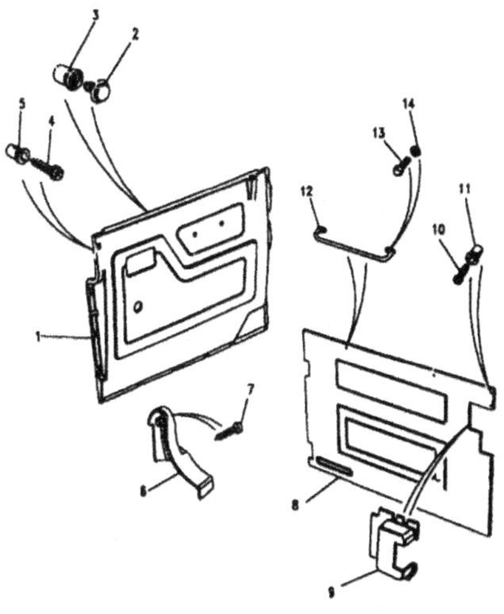

Illus	Part Number	Description	Quantity	Change Point	Remarks
1	MTC8706	Casing-front door-RH	1		
1	MTC8707	Casing-front door-LH	1		
	MWC3137	Spacer-foam	6		
2	MUC3186	Clip	8		
3	MUC3187	Clip-snap-sack	8		
4	AB608084	Screw-self tapping-No 8 x 1	2		
	MUC3394	Screw-washer-No 8 x 19	26		
	WC104004L	Washer-M4	2		
5	AFU1926L	Nut-caged	28		
6	MUC3036	Strap assembly-retaining-RH	1		
6	MUC3037	Strap assembly-retaining-LH	1		
7	AB608064L	Screw-self tapping-No 8 x 3/4	2		
		HEATED REAR WINDOW			
		CASING REAR DOOR			
8	MUC4529	without rear washwipe	1		
8	MTC9801	with rear wash/wipe	1	Note (1)	
8	MUC4528	with rear wash/wipe	1	Note (2)	
9	MTC1710	Cover-lock-Black	1		
10	AB606041L	Screw-self tapping-No 6 x 1/2	4	Note (3)	
10	AFU2636	Screw-No 8	4	From (V) FA 358393	
11	AFU1926L	Nut-caged	3		
12	MUC1402	Handle assembly-grab	1		
13	SH106204	Screw-hexagonal head-M6 x 20-long-bronze.	2		
14	WL106004L	Washer-spring	2		
	MUC4525	Label-body	1		
	MTC6630	Cover nut	2		Germany

CHANGE POINTS:
(1) To (V) AA 241999
(2) From (V) AA 242000
(3) To (V) EA 358392

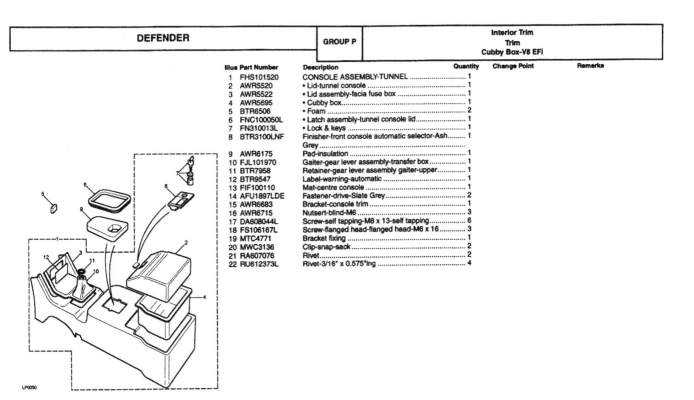

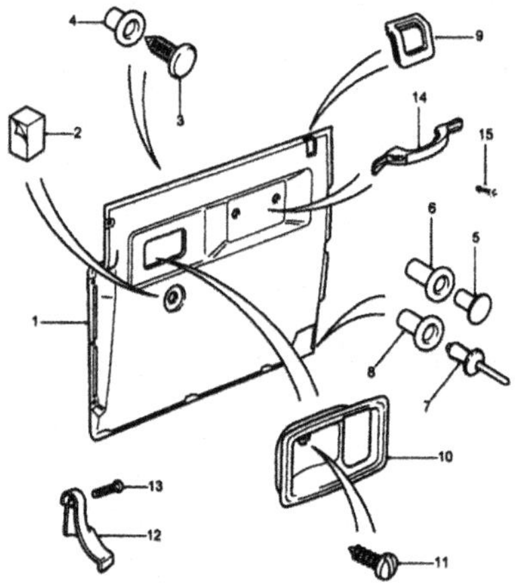

LP0045

Illus	Part Number	Description	Quantity	Change Point	Remarks
		CASING-FRONT DOOR			
1	MWC2780	RH-Black	1	Note (1)	
1	MWC2781	LH-Black	1		
1	MXC1858LCS	RH-Slate Grey	1	Note (2)	
1	MXC1859LCS	LH-Slate Grey	1		
1	BTR6700LCS	RH-Slate Grey	1	Note (3)	
1	BTR6701LCS	LH-Slate Grey	1		
1	BTR6700LOY	RH-Dark Granite	1	Note (4); Note (5)	
1	BTR6701LOY	LH-Dark Granite	1		
1	EJB120040LOY	RH-Dark Granite	1	Note (6)	Except electric windows and CDL
1	EJB120050LOY	LH-Dark Granite	1		
1	EJB000720LOY	RH-Dark Granite	1	Note (7)	Electric windows CDL
1	EJB000730LOY	LH-Dark Granite	1		
1	EJB001020LOY	RH-Dark Granite	1		CDL except electric windows
1	EJB001030LOY	LH-Dark Granite	1		

CHANGE POINTS:
(1) To (V) EA 314058
(2) From (V) EA 314059 To (V) LA 932528
(3) From (V) LA 932529 To (V) TA 999221
(4) From (V) VA 999222
(5) To (V) VA 128269
(6) From (V) VA 128270
(7) From (V) 2A 622424

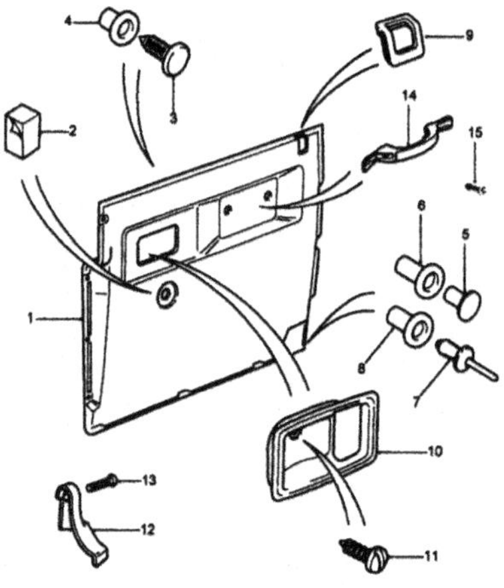

LP0045

Illus	Part Number	Description	Quantity	Change Point	Remarks
2	MWC3137	Spacer-foam	4		
3	MWC1474	Fastener-fir tree	24	Note (1)	
3	MXC1800	Fastener-fir tree	24	Note (2)	
4	MWC3136	Clip-snap-sack	24		
5	79118PH	Stud-Black	4	Note (3)	
6	13H2475L	Clip-snap-sack	4		
7	MWC9918LCS	Nut-lokut-Grey	4	Note (4)	
7	MWC9918LOY	Nut-lokut-Dark Granite	4	Note (5)	
8	MWC9917	Clip-snap-sack	4	Note (6)	
9	MXC4738PMA	Escutcheon-door-lock-Black	2		
10	DBP6532PMA	Bezel-door handle-Black-RH	1		
10	DBP6533PMA	Bezel-door handle-Black-LH	1		
11	DA608044L	Screw-self tapping-M8 x 13-self tapping	2		
12	MUC3036	Strap assembly-retaining-RH	1		
12	MUC3037	Strap assembly-retaining-LH	1		
13	AB608064L	Screw-self tapping-No 8 x 3/4	2		
14	YOO451PMA	Handle-door grab	2		
15	AB610081	Screw-self tapping	4		

CHANGE POINTS:
(1) To (V) AA 339423
(2) From (V) AA 339424
(3) To (V) EA 314058
(4) From (V) EA 314059 To (V) TA 999221
(5) From (V) VA 999222
(6) From (V) EA 314059

DEFENDER

GROUP P

Interior Trim
Trim
Front Door Casing-With Speaker Aperture

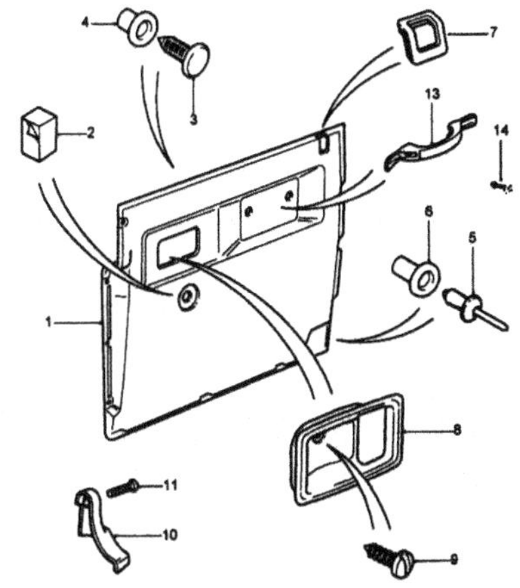

LP0044

Illus	Part Number	Description	Quantity	Change Point	Remarks
1	AWR4648LOY	Casing-front door-RH	1		
1	EJB120040PMA	Casing-front door-RH-Black	1	Note (1)	Tomb Raider
1	AWR4649LOY	Casing-front door-LH	1		
1	EJB120050PMA	Casing-front door-LH-Black	1	Note (1)	Tomb Raider
2	MWC3137	Spacer-foam	4		
3	MXC1800	Fastener-fir tree	24		
4	MWC3136	Clip-snap-sack	24		
5	MWC9918PMA	Rivet-plastic-drive-Black	4	Note (1)	Tomb Raider
6	MWC9917	Clip-snap-sack	4		
7	MXC4738PMA	Escutcheon-door-lock-Black	2		
8	DBP6532PMA	Bezel-door handle-Black-RH	1		
8	DBP6533PMA	Bezel-door handle-Black-LH	1		
9	DA608044L	Screw-self tapping-M8 x 13-self tapping	2		
10	MUC3036	Strap assembly-retaining-RH	1		
10	MUC3037	Strap assembly-retaining-LH	1		
11	AB608064L	Screw-self tapping-No 8 x 3/4	2		
12	STC3312	Spacer	1		
13	YOO451PMA	Handle-door grab	2		
14	AB610081	Screw-self tapping	4		
	MWC9918LCS	Nut-lokut-Grey	4		

CHANGE POINTS:
(1) From (V) 1A 612404

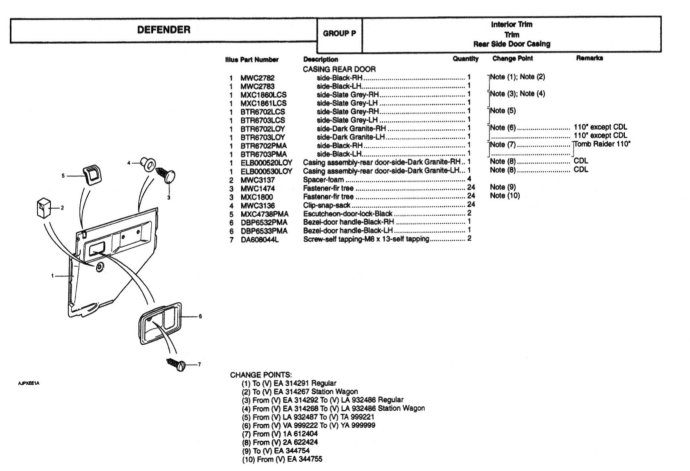

DEFENDER

GROUP P

Interior Trim
Trim
Rear Side Door Casing

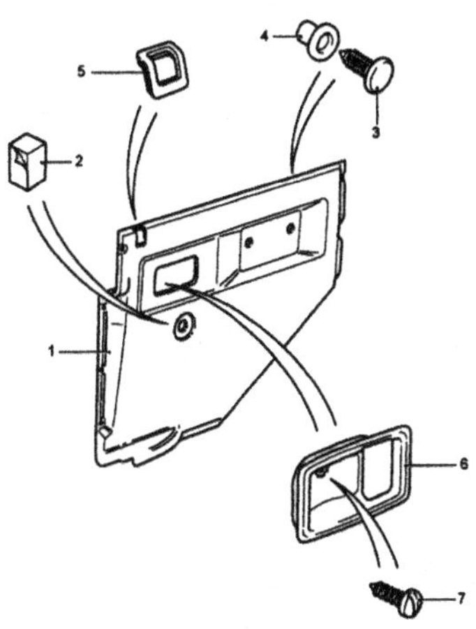

AJPXEE1A

Illus	Part Number	Description	Quantity	Change Point	Remarks
		CASING REAR DOOR			
1	MWC2782	side-Black-RH	1	Note (1); Note (2)	
1	MWC2783	side-Black-LH	1		
1	MXC1860LCS	side-Slate Grey-RH	1	Note (3); Note (4)	
1	MXC1861LCS	side-Slate Grey-LH	1		
1	BTR6702LCS	side-Slate Grey-RH	1	Note (5)	
1	BTR6703LCS	side-Slate Grey-LH	1		
1	BTR6702LOY	side-Dark Granite-RH	1	Note (6)	110" except CDL
1	BTR6703LOY	side-Dark Granite-LH	1		110" except CDL
1	BTR6702PMA	side-Black-RH	1	Note (7)	Tomb Raider 110"
1	BTR6703PMA	side-Black-LH	1		
1	ELB000520LOY	Casing assembly-rear door-side-Dark Granite-RH	1	Note (8)	CDL
1	ELB000530LOY	Casing assembly-rear door-side-Dark Granite-LH	1	Note (8)	CDL
2	MWC3137	Spacer-foam	4		
3	MWC1474	Fastener-fir tree	24	Note (9)	
3	MXC1800	Fastener-fir tree	24	Note (10)	
4	MWC3136	Clip-snap-sack	24		
5	MXC4738PMA	Escutcheon-door-lock-Black	2		
6	DBP6532PMA	Bezel-door handle-Black-RH	1		
6	DBP6533PMA	Bezel-door handle-Black-LH	1		
7	DA608044L	Screw-self tapping-M8 x 13-self tapping	2		

CHANGE POINTS:
(1) To (V) EA 314291 Regular
(2) To (V) EA 314267 Station Wagon
(3) From (V) EA 314292 To (V) LA 932486 Regular
(4) From (V) EA 314268 To (V) LA 932486 Station Wagon
(5) From (V) LA 932487 To (V) TA 999221
(6) From (V) VA 999222 To (V) YA 999999
(7) From (V) 1A 612404
(8) From (V) 2A 622424
(9) To (V) EA 344754
(10) From (V) EA 344755

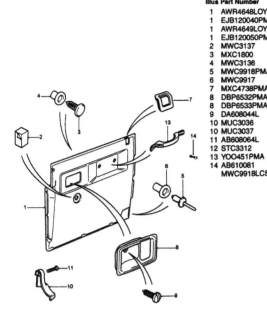

DEFENDER

GROUP P — Interior Trim / Trim / Rear End Door Casing-To (V) MA965105

Illus	Part Number	Description	Quantity	Change Point	Remarks
		CASING ASSEMBLY-TAIL DOOR			
1	MWC1743	BLACK-WITHOUT REAR WASHWIPE	1	Note (1)	
1	MWC1743LCS	SLATE GREY-WITHOUT REAR WASHWIPE	1	Note (2)	
1	MXC1989LCS	SLATE GREY-WITHOUT REAR WASHWIPE	1	Note (3)	
1	BTR7964LCS	SLATE GREY-WITHOUT REAR WASHWIPE	1	Note (4)	
		CASING ASSEMBLY-TAIL DOOR			
1	MWC1744	BLACK-WITH REAR WASH/WIPE	1	Note (1)	
1	MWC1744LCS	SLATE GREY-WITH REAR WASH/WIPE	1	Note (2)	
1	MXC1992LCS	SLATE GREY-WITH REAR WASH/WIPE	1	Note (5)	
1	BTR3793LCS	SLATE GREY-WITH REAR WASH/WIPE	1	Note (6)	
1	BTR7959LCS	SLATE GREY-WITH REAR WASH/WIPE	1	Note (4)	
	73037	• Clip	8		
2	MTC1710	Cover-lock-Black	1	Note (7)	
2	395191LCS	Cover-lock-Slate Grey	1	Note (8)	
3	AB606041	Screw-self tapping-No 6 x 1/2	7		
3	AFU2636	Screw-No 8	1		
4	AA606044L	Screw-with rear wash/wipe	2		
5	AK606011L	Nut-spring-flat-with rear wash/wipe	2		
6	MUC1402	Handle assembly-grab	1		
7	SH106204	Screw-hexagonal head-M6 x 20-long-bronze.	2		
8	WL106004	Washer-spring-M6	2		
9	MUC4525	Label-body	1		
10	MTC9915LCS	Cover-grommet-mounting bracket-Slate Grey	1		
11	BTR3792LCS	Cover-backlight wiper motor-Slate Grey	1		
12	AA606044L	Screw-cover grommet fixing-with rear wash/wipe	2		
13	AK606011L	Nut-spring-flat-cover grommet fixing-with rear wash/wipe	2		
14	DA608044L	Screw-self tapping-wiper motor fixing-M8 x 13-self tapping	2		
15	AK608141L	Nut-spring-u type-wiper motor fixing	2		

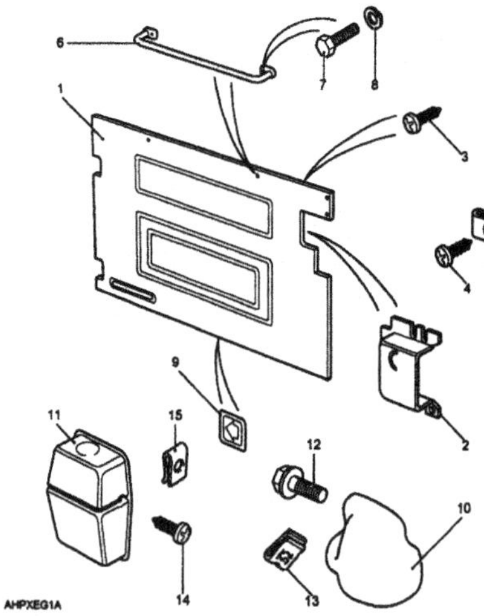

AHPXEG1A

CHANGE POINTS:
(1) To (V) EA 314058
(2) From (V) EA 314059 To (V) FA 358392
(3) From (V) FA 358393 To (V) KA 929577
(4) From (V) KA 929578 To (V) MA 965105
(5) From (V) FA 358393 To (V) JA 910753
(6) From (V) JA 910754 To (V) KA 929577
(7) To (V) EA 314058 Regular; To (V) EA 314173 Station Wagon
(8) From (V) EA 314059 Regular; From (V) EA 314174 Station Wagon

DEFENDER

GROUP P — Interior Trim / Trim / Rear End Door Casing-From (V) MA965106 To (V) 1A999999

Illus	Part Number	Description	Quantity	Change Point	Remarks
		CASING ASSEMBLY-TAIL DOOR			
1	AWR1609LCS	except rear wash/wipe-Slate Grey	1	Note (1)	
2	BTR9712LCS	with rear wash/wipe-Slate Grey	1		
1	AWR1609LOY	except rear wash/wipe-Dark Granite	1	Note (2)	
2	BTR9712LOY	with rear wash/wipe-Dark Granite	1		
2	BTR9712PMA	with rear wash/wipe-Black	1	Note (3)	Tomb Raider 90"
3	BTR9714LCS	Cover-lock-Slate Grey	1	Note (1)	
3	BTR9714LOY	Cover-lock-Dark Granite	1	Note (2)	
3	BTR9714PMA	Cover-lock-Black	1	Note (3)	Tomb Raider 90"
4	BTR9715LCS	Cover-grommet-mounting bracket-Slate Grey	1	Note (1)	
4	BTR9715LOY	Cover-grommet-mounting bracket-Dark Granite	1	Note (2)	
4	BTR9715PMA	Cover-grommet-mounting bracket-Black	1	Note (3)	Tomb Raider 90"
5	BTR9723LCS	Cover-backlight wiper motor-Slate Grey	1	Note (1)	
5	BTR9723LOY	Cover-backlight wiper motor-Dark Granite	1	Note (2)	
5	BTR9723PMA	Cover-backlight wiper motor-Black	1	Note (3)	Tomb Raider 90"
6	AFU1926L	Nut-caged	3		
7	AFU2636	Screw-No 8	7		
8	MUC1402	Handle assembly-grab	1		
9	FS106201L	Screw-flanged head-M6 x 20	2		
9	SH106204	Screw-hexagonal head-M6 x 20-long-bronze.	2		
10	WL106004	Washer-spring-M6	2		
11	WL106001L	Washer-sprung-M6	1		
12	73037	Clip	8		
13	AA606044L	Screw-cover grommet fixing-with rear wash/wipe	2		
14	AK606011L	Nut-spring-flat-cover grommet fixing-with rear wash/wipe	2		
15	DA608044L	Screw-self tapping-wiper motor fixing-M8 x 13-self tapping	2		
16	AK608141L	Nut-spring-u type-wiper motor fixing	2		

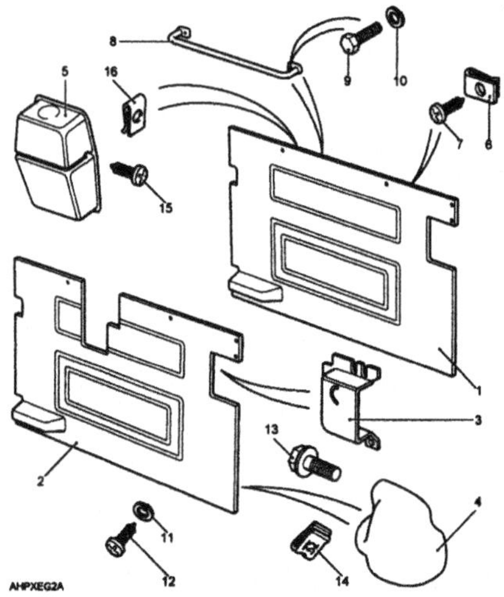

AHPXEG2A

CHANGE POINTS:
(1) From (V) MA 965106 To (V) TA 999221
(2) From (V) VA 999222
(3) From (V) 1A 612404

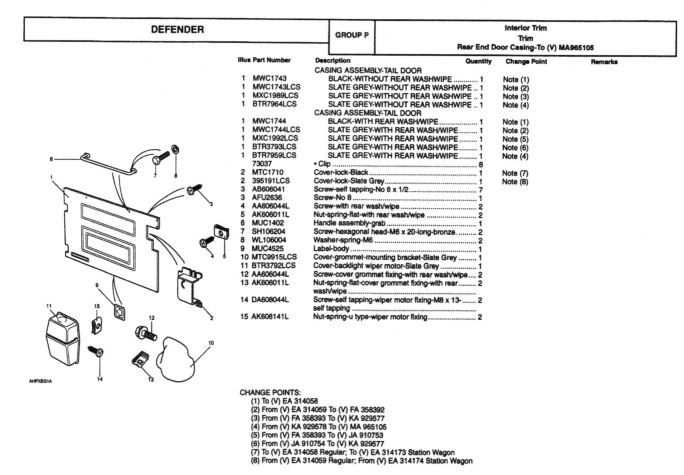

Rear End Door Casing-From (V) 2A000001

Illus	Part Number	Description	Quantity	Change Point	Remarks
1	ESN000200LOY	Casing assembly-tail door-Dark Granite	1	Note (1)	
2	EKM100100L	Clip-cup retainer	9	Note (1)	
3	EYC000300	Clip-retaining	9	Note (1)	
4	FVJ000010LOY	Escutcheon-rear door release assembly	1	Note (1)	
5	EST000010PMA	Handle-grab	1	Note (1)	
6	DYP101480	Screw-torx-pan	4	Note (1)	
7	BTR8039	Nut-lokut	4	Note (1)	

NOT ILLUSTRATED
PAS ILLUSTREE
NICHT ILLUSTRIERT
SENZA IL DISEGNO
SIN EL DISENO
SEM ILLUSTRACAO
NIET AFGEBEELD

TF 0007

CHANGE POINTS:
(1) From (V) 2A 622424

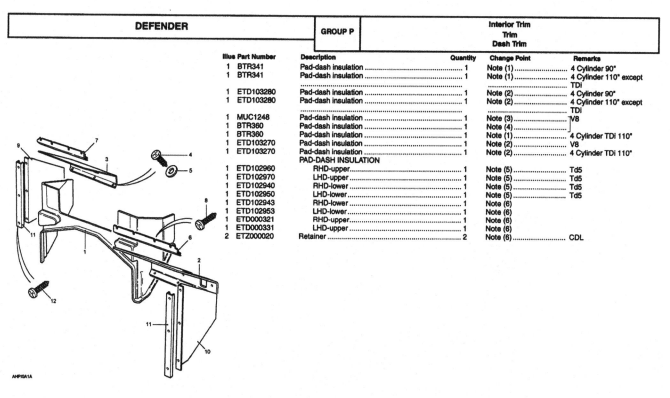

Dash Trim

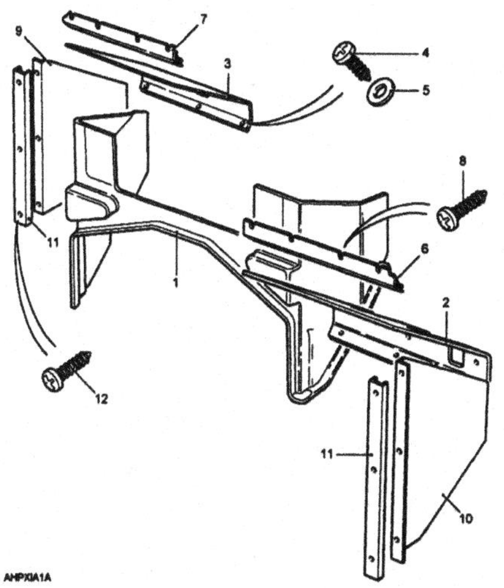

AHPXIA1A

Illus	Part Number	Description	Quantity	Change Point	Remarks
1	BTR341	Pad-dash insulation	1	Note (1)	4 Cylinder 90"
1	BTR341	Pad-dash insulation	1	Note (1)	4 Cylinder 110" except TDi
1	ETD103280	Pad-dash insulation	1	Note (2)	4 Cylinder 90"
1	ETD103280	Pad-dash insulation	1	Note (2)	4 Cylinder 110" except TDi
1	MUC1248	Pad-dash insulation	1	Note (3)	V8
1	BTR360	Pad-dash insulation	1	Note (4)	
1	BTR360	Pad-dash insulation	1	Note (1)	4 Cylinder TDi 110"
1	ETD103270	Pad-dash insulation	1	Note (2)	V8
1	ETD103270	Pad-dash insulation	1	Note (2)	4 Cylinder TDi 110"
		PAD-DASH INSULATION			
1	ETD102960	RHD-upper	1	Note (5)	Td5
1	ETD102970	LHD-upper	1	Note (5)	Td5
1	ETD102940	RHD-lower	1	Note (5)	Td5
1	ETD102950	LHD-lower	1	Note (5)	Td5
1	ETD102943	RHD-lower	1	Note (6)	
1	ETD102953	LHD-lower	1	Note (6)	
1	ETD000321	RHD-upper	1	Note (6)	
1	ETD000331	LHD-upper	1	Note (6)	
2	ETZ000020	Retainer	2	Note (6)	CDL

CHANGE POINTS:
(1) To (V) XA 171960
(2) From (V) XA 171961
(3) To (V) FA 424037
(4) From (V) FA 424038 To (V) XA 171960
(5) To (V) ZA 999999
(6) From (V) 2A 622424

Illus	Part Number	Description	Quantity	Change Point	Remarks
		DASH CENTRE - CARPET			
	MUC1356RD	Carpet-front floor-Brushwood	1	Note (1)	4 Cylinder
	MXC2949LDE	Carpet-front floor-Slate Grey	1	Note (2)	4 Cylinder 90"
	MXC2949LOY	Carpet-front floor-Dark Granite	1	Note (3)	
	EAD102240LOY	Carpet-front floor-Dark Granite	1	Note (4)	
	MXC2949LDE	Carpet-front floor-Slate Grey	1	Note (5)	4 Cylinder 110" except
	MXC2949LOY	Carpet-front floor-Dark Granite	1	Note (6)	TDi
	MXC2948LDE	Carpet-front floor-Slate Grey	1		4 Cylinder TDi 110"
	MXC2948LOY	Carpet-front floor-Dark Granite	1		
	MUC1256RD	Carpet-front floor-Brushwood	1	Note (1)	V8
	MXC2948LDE	Carpet-front floor-Slate Grey	1	Note (2)	
	MXC2948LOY	Carpet-front floor-Dark Granite	1	Note (3)	

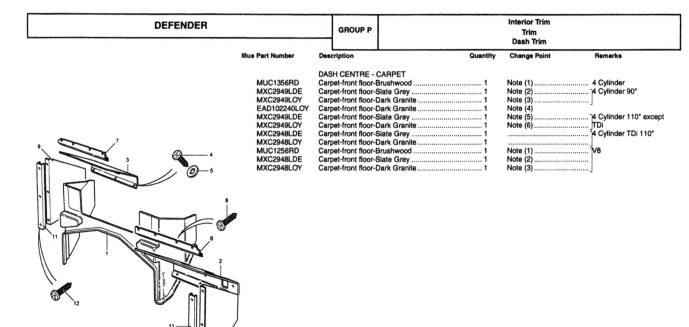

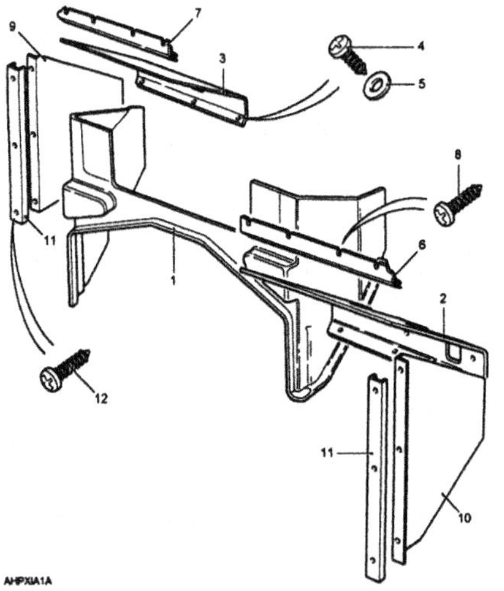

AHPXIA1A

CHANGE POINTS:
(1) To (V) EA 314173
(2) From (V) EA 314174 To (V) TA 999221
(3) From (V) VA 999222
(4) From (V) XA 172150
(5) To (V) TA 999221
(6) From (V) TA 999222

Illus	Part Number	Description	Quantity	Change Point	Remarks
		RHD-NON AIR CON			
2	MUC9167	Finisher-footwell upper-RH	1	Note (1)	
3	MTC4866	Finisher-footwell upper-LH	1	Note (1)	
2	MXC6538	Finisher-footwell upper-RH	1	Note (2)	
3	MXC6539	Finisher-footwell upper-LH	1	Note (2)	
2	BTR5232	Finisher-footwell upper-RH-RHD-rubber	1	Note (3)	
3	BTR5233	Finisher-footwell upper-LH-RHD-rubber	1	Note (3)	
2	AWR1612	Finisher-footwell upper-RH-cardboard	1	Note (4)	
		RHD-AIR CON			
2	MUC9167	Finisher-footwell upper-RH	1	Note (1)	
3	MUC2210	Finisher-footwell upper-LH	1	Note (1)	
2	MXC6538	Finisher-footwell upper-RH	1	Note (2)	
2	BTR5232	Finisher-footwell upper-RH-RHD-rubber	1	Note (3)	
3	MXC6543	Finisher-footwell upper-LH	1	Note (5)	
2	AWR1612	Finisher-footwell upper-RH-cardboard	1	Note (4)	
3	AWR1604	Finisher-footwell upper-LH	1	Note (4)	

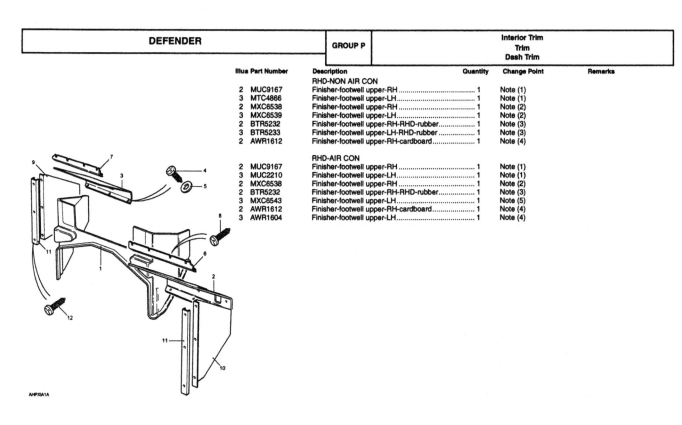

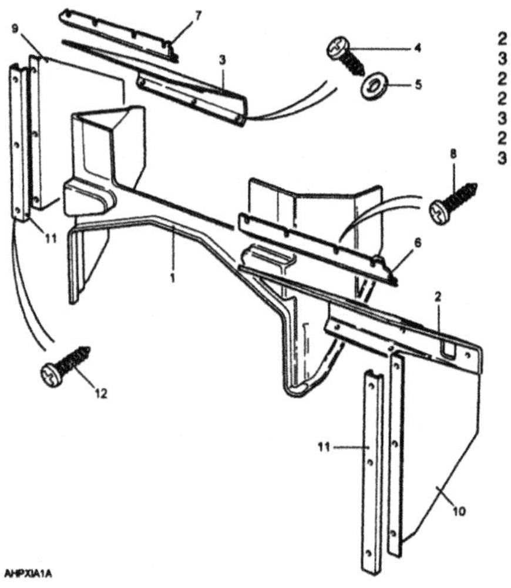

AHPXIA1A

CHANGE POINTS:
(1) To (V) FA 440581
(2) From (V) FA 440582 To (V) KA 922165
(3) From (V) KA 922166
(4) From (V) MA 948148
(5) From (V) FA 440582 To (V) MA 948147

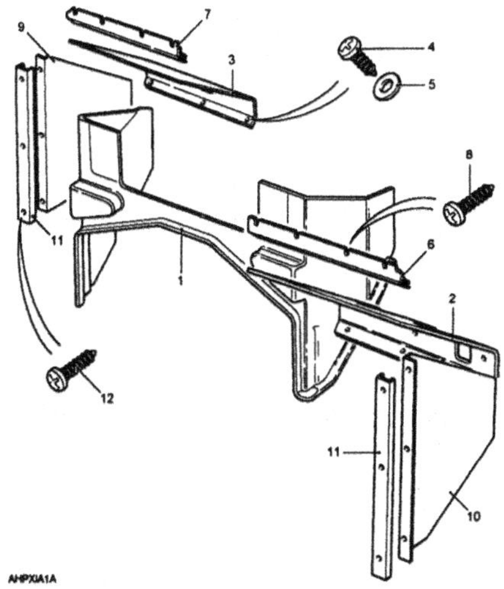

AHPXIA1A

Illus	Part Number	Description	Quantity	Change Point	Remarks
		LHD-NON AIR CON			
2	MUC9168	Finisher-footwell upper-RH	1	Note (1)	
3	MTC4865	Finisher-footwell upper-LH	1	Note (1)	
2	MXC6540	Finisher-footwell upper-RH	1	Note (2)	
2	BTR5234	Finisher-footwell upper-RH-rubber	1	Note (3)	
3	MXC6541	Finisher-footwell upper-LH	1	Note (4)	
3	BTR5235	Finisher-footwell upper-LH-rubber	1	Note (5)	
3	AWR1611	Finisher-footwell upper-LH-cardboard	1	Note (6)	
		LHD-AIR CON			
2	MTC8360	Finisher-footwell upper-RH	1	Note (7)	
2	MUC9169	Finisher-footwell upper-RH	1	Note (8)	
2	MXC6542	Finisher-footwell upper-RH	1	Note (9)	
2	BTR5236	Finisher-footwell upper-RH	1	Note (10)	
2	BTR5234	Finisher-footwell upper-RH-rubber	1	Note (11)	300 TDI
2	FAG100290	Finisher-footwell upper-RH	1	Note (11)	2500 cc Petrol
2	FAG100290	Finisher-footwell upper-RH	1	Note (11)	V8 Twin Carburettor
2	FAG100240	Finisher-footwell upper-RH	1		V8 EFi 50 LE
3	MTC4865	Finisher-footwell upper-LH	1	Note (1)	
3	BTR5235	Finisher-footwell upper-LH-rubber	1	Note (3)	
3	AWR1611	Finisher-footwell upper-LH-cardboard	1	Note (6)	

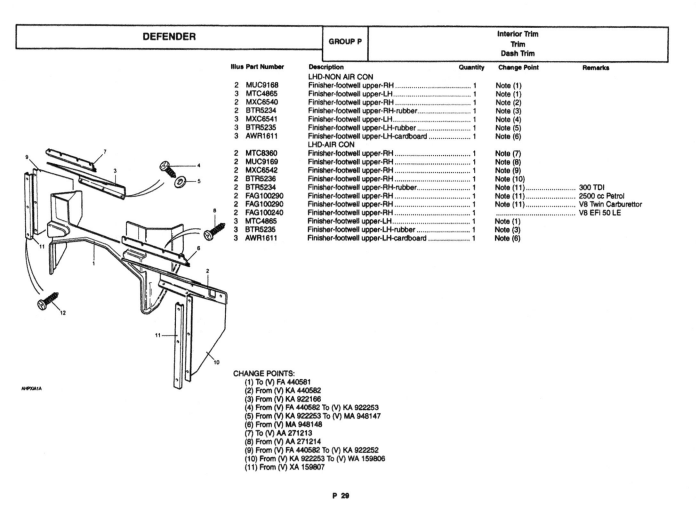

CHANGE POINTS:
(1) To (V) FA 440581
(2) From (V) KA 440582
(3) From (V) KA 922166
(4) From (V) FA 440582 To (V) KA 922253
(5) From (V) KA 922253 To (V) MA 948147
(6) From (V) MA 948148
(7) To (V) AA 271213
(8) From (V) AA 271214
(9) From (V) FA 440582 To (V) KA 922252
(10) From (V) KA 922253 To (V) WA 159806
(11) From (V) XA 159807

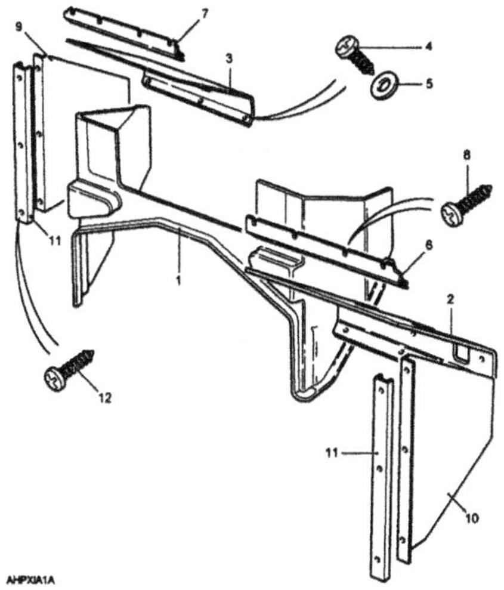

AHPXIA1A

Illus	Part Number	Description	Quantity	Change Point	Remarks
	AID710010	Panel-toe box	1		V8 EFi 50 LE
	MTC8349	Panel-rubber	1		Air conditioning
4	AB606041L	Screw-self tapping-No 6 x 1/2	6		
5	WC104001L	Washer-plain	6		
		RETAINER			
6	MWC6254	RH	1	Note (1)	
6	MXC6550	RH	1	Note (2); Note (3)	
6	BTR6194	RH	1	Note (4); Note (5)	
7	396416	LH	1	Note (6)	
7	MWC6253	LH	1	Note (7)	
7	MXC6551	LH	1	Note (2); Note (3)	
7	BTR6193	LH	1	Note (4); Note (5)	
8	AB608054L	Screw-self tapping-No8 x 5/8	10		
	AFU1248	Washer-plastic	10		
	AFU2692	Nut-lokut	10		

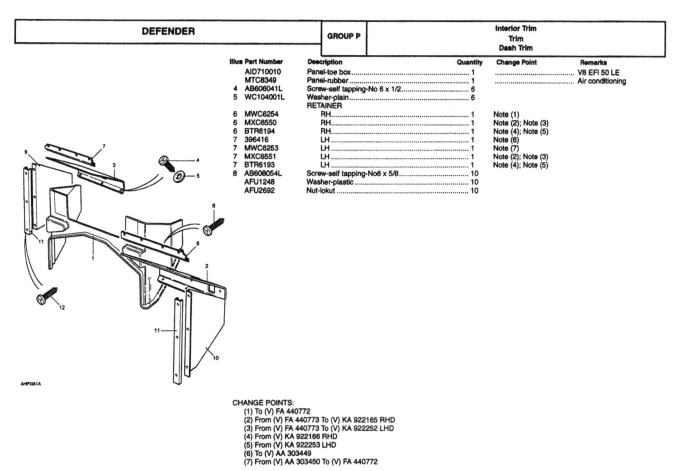

CHANGE POINTS:
(1) To (V) FA 440772
(2) From (V) FA 440773 To (V) KA 922165 RHD
(3) From (V) FA 440773 To (V) KA 922252 LHD
(4) From (V) KA 922166 RHD
(5) From (V) KA 922253 LHD
(6) To (V) AA 303449
(7) From (V) AA 303450 To (V) FA 440772

Illus	Part Number	Description	Quantity	Change Point	Remarks
		FINISHER-FACIA ASSEMBLY			
9	MRC5394	LH	1	Note (1)	
10	MTC6820	RH	1		
9	BTR981	LH	1	Note (2)	
10	BTR980	RH	1		
11	MUC9347	Retainer	2	Note (1)	
		RETAINER			
11	BTR978	RH	1	Note (3)	
11	BTR979	LH	1		
11	BTR2372	RH	1	Note (4)	
11	BTR2371	LH	1		
12	AB606041L	Screw-self tapping-No 6 x 1/2	6	Note (5)	
12	YYP100860	Screw-flanged head	4	Note (6)	

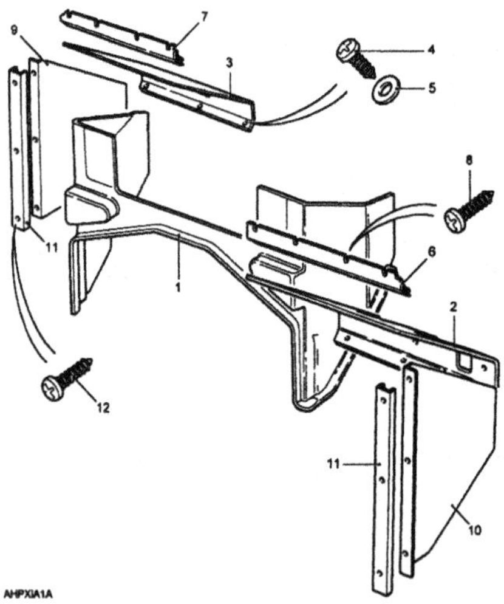

AHPXIA1A

CHANGE POINTS:
(1) To (V) HA 455595
(2) From (V) HA 455596
(3) From (V) HA 455596 To (V) HA 903278
(4) From (V) HA 903279
(5) To (V) VA 138479
(6) From (V) WA 138480

Illus	Part Number	Description	Quantity	Change Point	Remarks
1	EAY10010L	Footrest assembly-front floor	1		
2	BTR1875	Bracket assembly-footrest	1		
3	GT106205L	Screw-M6 x 20	2		
4	GL108351	Screw-M8	3		

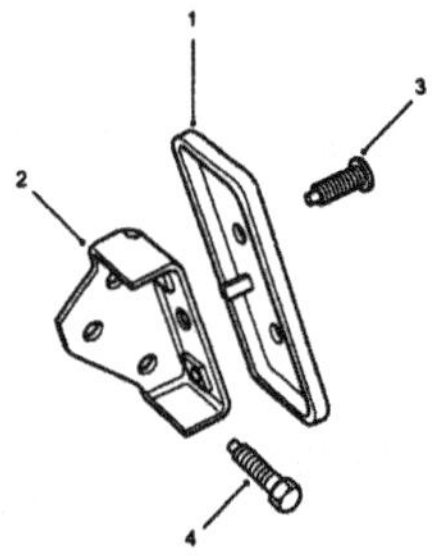

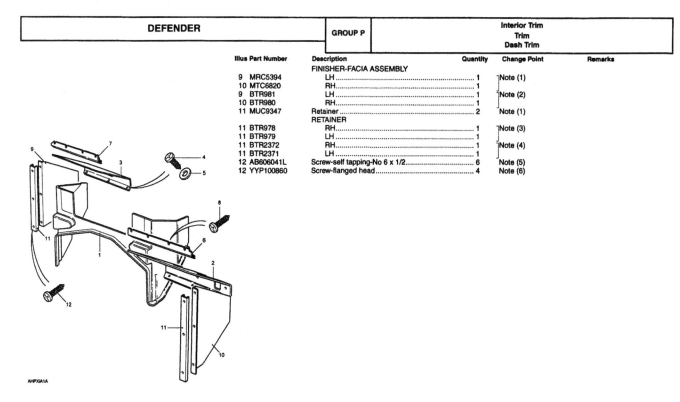

AMPXIA4A

Illus	Part Number	Description	Quantity	Change Point	Remarks
		SUNVISOR ASSEMBLY-FRONT HEADER			
1	MTC5698	RH	1	Note (1)	
1	MXC1394LUH	RH-Ripple Grey	1	Note (2)	Standard / County
1	BTR6334PUC	RH-Black Spata	1		90 SV
1	AWR1548LNF	RH-Ash Grey	1		Soft Top Germany
		SUNVISOR ASSEMBLY-FRONT HEADER			
2	MTC5699	LH	1	Note (1)	
2	MXC1395LUH	LH-Ripple Grey	1	Note (2)	
2	BTR6333PUC	LH-Black Spata	1		90 SV
2	STC7015	LH	1		Eastnor L.E. France
2	AWR6421LNF	LH-Ash Grey	1		Soft Top Germany
		SCREW			
3	SE106201L	for untrimmed vehicles-pan head-M6 x 20	4	Note (3)	
3	SE106251L	for trimmed vehicles-pan head-M6 x 25	4		
3	AB614061L	for untrimmed vehicles-self tapping-No 14 x 3/4	4	Note (4)	
3	AB614081L	for trimmed vehicles-self tapping	4		
4	WL106001L	Washer-sprung-M6	4		
5	WA106041L	Washer-6mm	4		
6	79246	Nut-spiralok	4	Note (4)	
	NN106021	Nutsert-blind-M6	4	Note (5)	

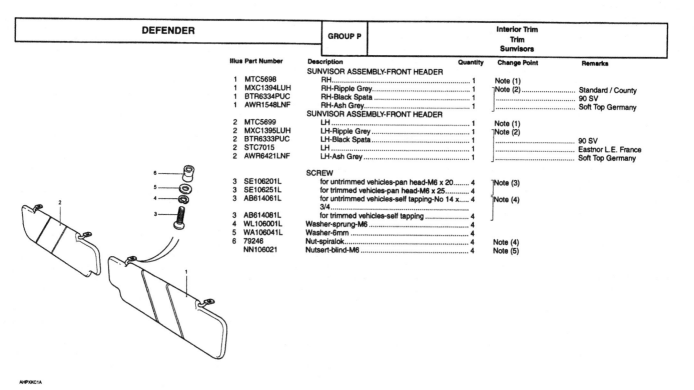

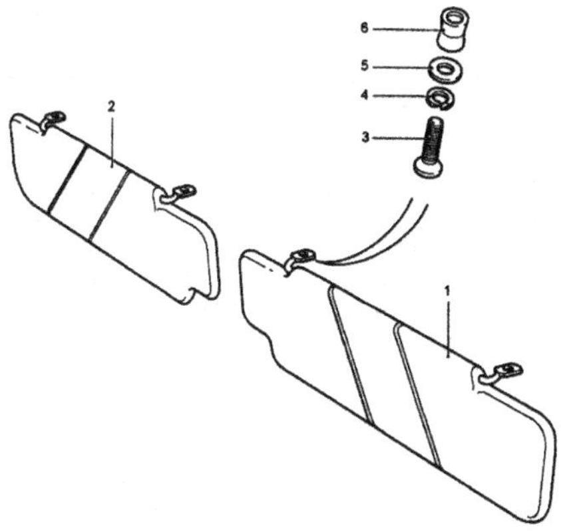

AHPXXC1A

CHANGE POINTS:
(1) To (V) EA 314058
(2) From (V) EA 314059
(3) To (V) KA 926045
(4) From (V) KA 926046
(5) From (V) FA 413835 To (V) KA 926045

Illus	Part Number	Description	Quantity	Change Point	Remarks
1	BTR3415	Pad-insulation bonnet	1	Note (1)	
1	BTR6189	Pad-insulation bonnet	1	Note (2)	
1	AWR2896	Pad-insulation bonnet	1	Note (3)	
1	AWR4147	Pad-insulation bonnet	1	Note (4)	
2	MTC4657	Bracket	2	Note (5)	
3	AR608061	Screw-pan	13		
3	AR608061	Screw-pan	9	Note (6)	90"
4	AFU1071	Washer	9		
5	AFU1497	Spacer	9	Note (5)	
	RU612373L	Rivet-3/16" x 0.575"lng	9		

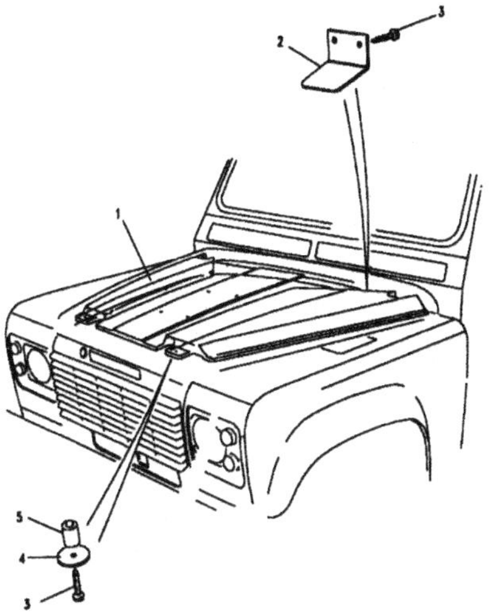

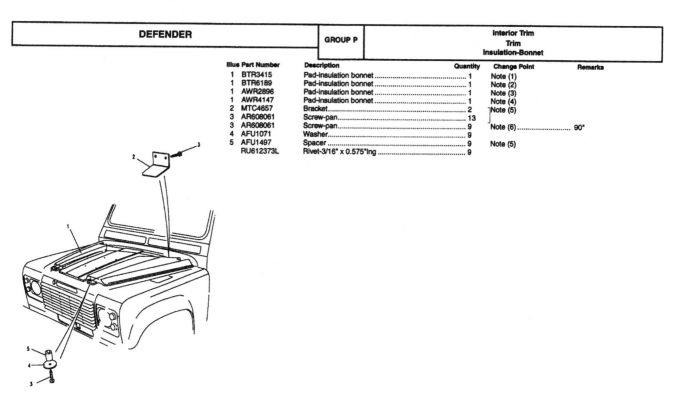

CHANGE POINTS:
(1) To (V) LA 939975
(2) From (V) MA 939976 To (V) MA 959646
(3) From (V) MA 959647 To (V) TA 974652
(4) From (V) TA 974653
(5) To (V) JA 915268
(6) From (V) JA 915269

DEFENDER	GROUP P	Interior Trim Trim Carpets-Front Floor-To (V) WA159806

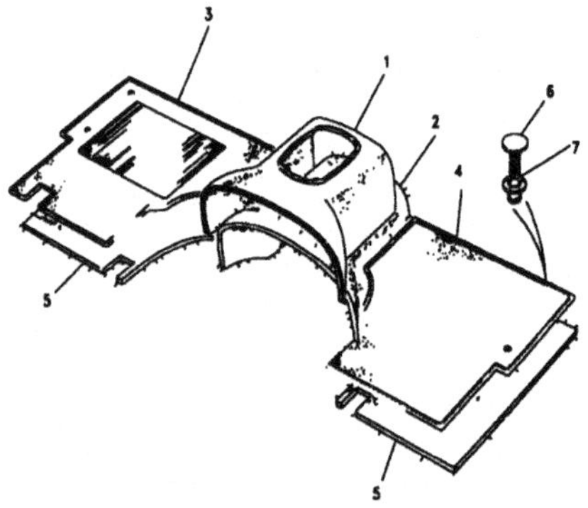

Illus	Part Number	Description	Quantity	Change Point	Remarks
		CARPET-TUNNEL			
1	MUC1361RD	Brushwood-carpet	1	Note (1)	4 Cylinder
1	MUC1257RD	Brushwood-carpet	1		V8 Twin Carburettor
1	MUC1361LDE	Slate Grey-carpet	1	Note (2)	4 Cylinder
1	MUC1257LDE	Slate Grey-carpet	1		LT 85 V8
1	BTR1200LDE	Slate Grey-carpet	1		LT 77 V8
1	BTR9321LDE	Slate Grey-carpet	1	Note (3)	
1	AWR6713LOY	Dark Granite-carpet	1	Note (4)	Petrol except 50 LE
1	AWR6713LOY	Dark Granite-carpet	1		Diesel TDi 90"
2	MUC1499	Felt-tunnel	1		4 Cylinder
2	MUC1494	Felt-tunnel	1		V8
		CARPET-FRONT FLOOR			
3	MUC1358RD	RH-RHD-Brushwood	1	Note (1)	4 Cylinder
3	MUC1362RD	RH-LHD-Brushwood	1		
3	MUC1258RD	RH-RHD	1		V8 Twin Carburettor
3	MUC1264RD	RH-LHD	1		
		CARPET-FRONT FLOOR			
3	MUC1358LDE	RH-RHD-Slate Grey-with eyelets	1	Note (2)	4 Cylinder
3	MUC1362LDE	RH-LHD-Slate Grey-with eyelets	1		
3	MUC1258LDE	RH-RHD-Slate Grey-with eyelets	1		V8 Twin Carburettor
3	MUC1264LDE	RH-LHD-Slate Grey-with eyelets	1		
		CARPET-FRONT FLOOR			
3	AWR5395LDE	RH-RHD-Slate Grey-without eyelets	1	Note (3)	4 Cylinder except TDi
3	AWR5396LDE	RH-LHD-Slate Grey-without eyelets	1		
3	AWR5393LDE	RH-RHD-Slate Grey-without eyelets	1		V8 Twin Carburettor
3	AWR5394LDE	RH-LHD-Slate Grey-without eyelets	1		
3	AWR5393LDE	RH-RHD-Slate Grey-without eyelets	1		TDi
3	AWR5394LDE	RH-LHD-Slate Grey-without eyelets	1		

CHANGE POINTS:
(1) To (V) DA 314368
(2) From (V) EA 314369 To (V) LA 939975
(3) From (V) MA 939976 To (V) TA 999221
(4) From (V) VA 999222 To (V) WA 159806

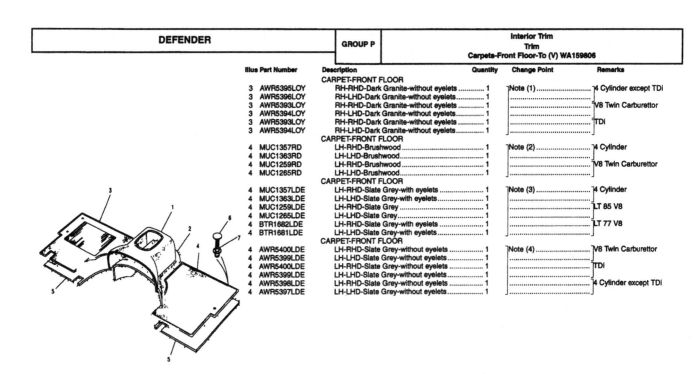

DEFENDER	GROUP P	Interior Trim Trim Carpets-Front Floor-To (V) WA159806

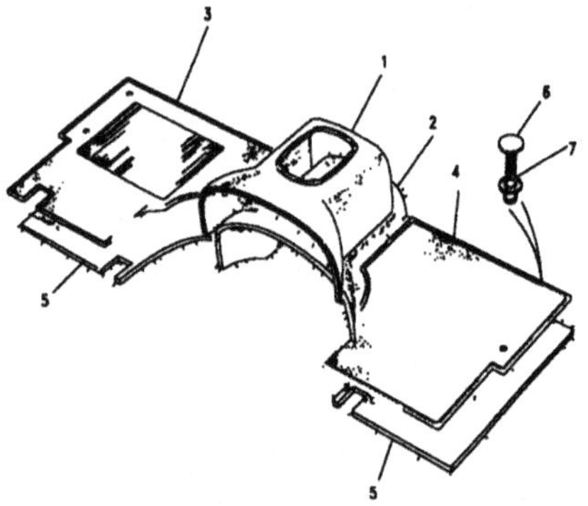

Illus	Part Number	Description	Quantity	Change Point	Remarks
		CARPET-FRONT FLOOR			
3	AWR5395LOY	RH-RHD-Dark Granite-without eyelets	1	Note (1)	4 Cylinder except TDi
3	AWR5396LOY	RH-LHD-Dark Granite-without eyelets	1		
3	AWR5393LOY	RH-RHD-Dark Granite-without eyelets	1		V8 Twin Carburettor
3	AWR5394LOY	RH-LHD-Dark Granite-without eyelets	1		
3	AWR5393LOY	RH-RHD-Dark Granite-without eyelets	1		TDi
3	AWR5394LOY	RH-LHD-Dark Granite-without eyelets	1		
		CARPET-FRONT FLOOR			
4	MUC1357RD	LH-RHD-Brushwood	1	Note (2)	4 Cylinder
4	MUC1363RD	LH-LHD-Brushwood	1		
4	MUC1259RD	LH-RHD-Brushwood	1		V8 Twin Carburettor
4	MUC1265RD	LH-LHD-Brushwood	1		
		CARPET-FRONT FLOOR			
4	MUC1357LDE	LH-RHD-Slate Grey-with eyelets	1	Note (3)	4 Cylinder
4	MUC1363LDE	LH-LHD-Slate Grey-with eyelets	1		
4	MUC1259LDE	LH-RHD-Slate Grey	1		LT 85 V8
4	MUC1265LDE	LH-LHD-Slate Grey	1		
4	BTR1682LDE	LH-RHD-Slate Grey-with eyelets	1		LT 77 V8
4	BTR1681LDE	LH-LHD-Slate Grey-with eyelets	1		
		CARPET-FRONT FLOOR			
4	AWR5400LDE	LH-RHD-Slate Grey-without eyelets	1	Note (4)	V8 Twin Carburettor
4	AWR5399LDE	LH-LHD-Slate Grey-without eyelets	1		
4	AWR5400LDE	LH-RHD-Slate Grey-without eyelets	1		TDi
4	AWR5399LDE	LH-LHD-Slate Grey-without eyelets	1		
4	AWR5398LDE	LH-RHD-Slate Grey-without eyelets	1		4 Cylinder except TDi
4	AWR5397LDE	LH-LHD-Slate Grey-without eyelets	1		

CHANGE POINTS:
(1) From (V) VA 999222 To (V) WA 159806
(2) To (V) DA 314368
(3) From (V) EA 314369 To (V) LA 939975
(4) From (V) MA 939976 To (V) TA 999221

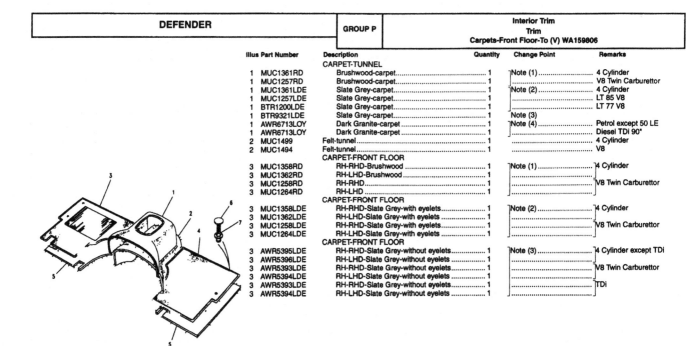

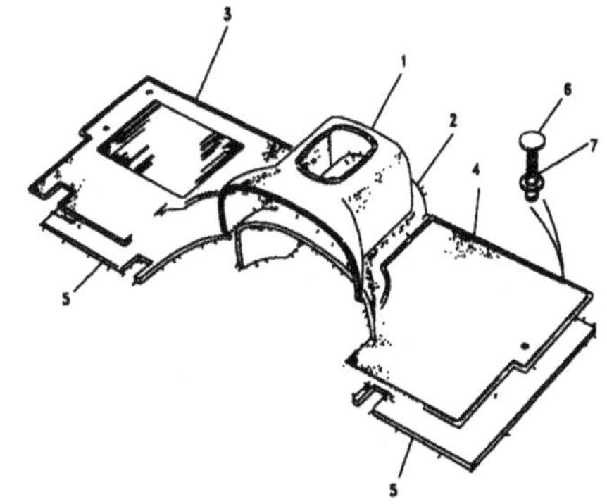

Illus	Part Number	Description	Quantity	Change Point	Remarks
		CARPET-FRONT FLOOR			
4	AWR5400LOY	LH-RHD-Dark Granite-without eyelets	1	Note (1)	V8 Twin Carburettor
4	AWR5399LOY	LH-LHD-Dark Granite-without eyelets	1		
4	AWR5400LOY	LH-RHD-Dark Granite-without eyelets	1		TDi
4	AWR5399LOY	LH-LHD-Dark Granite-without eyelets	1		
4	AWR5398LOY	LH-RHD-Dark Granite-without eyelets	1		4 Cylinder except TDi
4	AWR5397LOY	LH-LHD-Dark Granite-without eyelets	1		
		UNDERLAY-FRONT FLOOR INSULATION			
5	MUC1498	RH	1	Note (2)	4 Cylinder except TDi
5	MUC1497	LH	1		4 Cylinder except TDi
5	BTR8114	RH	1	Note (3)	4 Cylinder except TDi
5	BTR8115	LH	1		4 Cylinder except TDi
5	MUC1268	RH	1	Note (2)	V8
5	MUC1269	LH	1		LT 85 V8
5	BTR1683	LH	1		LT 77 V8
5	BTR8116	RH	1	Note (3)	V8
5	BTR8117	LH	1		
5	BTR8116	RH	1		TDi 90"
5	BTR8117	LH	1		TDi 90"
6	RTC3938LDE	Fastener-drive-Slate Grey	4	Note (4)	
6	MXC5451LOY	Fastener-drive-Dark Granite	4	Note (5)	
7	13H2475L	Clip-snap-sack	4		

CHANGE POINTS:
(1) From (V) VA 999222 To (V) WA 159806
(2) To (V) KA 929547
(3) From (V) KA 929548
(4) To (V) TA 999221
(5) From (V) VA 999222

NOT ILLUSTRATED
PAS ILLUSTREE
NICHT ILLUSTRIERT
SENZA IL DISEGNO
SIN EL DISENO
SEM ILLUSTRACAO
NIET AFGEBEELD

Illus	Part Number	Description	Quantity	Change Point	Remarks
	EAD102070LOY	Carpet-front floor tunnel surround-Dark Granite-carpet	1	Note (1)	
	EAD102060LOY	Carpet-tunnel-Dark Granite-carpet	1	Note (1)	
	EAD102200LOY	Carpet-front floor-RH-RHD-Dark Granite	1	Note (1)	V8 air conditioning
	EAD102200LOY	Carpet-front floor-RH-RHD-Dark Granite	1	Note (1)	TDi air conditioning
	EAD102180LOY	Carpet-front floor-RH-RHD-Dark Granite	1	Note (1)	4 Cylinder Petrol air conditioning
	EAD102040LOY	Carpet-front floor-RH-RHD-Dark Granite	1	Note (1)	Td5
	EAD102030LOY	Carpet-front floor-LH-LHD-Dark Granite	1	Note (1)	Td5 except air conditioning
	EAD102160LOY	Carpet-front floor-RHD-passenger side-Dark Granite	1	Note (1)	Air conditioning Td5
	EAD102170LOY	Carpet-front floor-LHD-passenger side-Dark Granite	1	Note (1)	Air conditioning Td5
	EAD102190LOY	Carpet-front floor-LH-LHD-Dark Granite	1	Note (1)	4 Cylinder Petrol air conditioning
	EAD102210LOY	Carpet-front floor-LH-Dark Granite	1	Note (1)	V8 air conditioning
	EAD102020LOY	Carpet-front floor-LH-RHD-Dark Granite	1	Note (1)	Td5 except air conditioning
	EAD102050LOY	Carpet-front floor-LH-LHD-Dark Granite	1	Note (1)	LHD V8 except air conditioning
	EAD102050LOY	Carpet-front floor-LH-LHD-Dark Granite	1	Note (1)	LHD TDi except air conditioning
	EAD102050LOY	Carpet-front floor-LH-LHD-Dark Granite	1	Note (1)	LHD Td5 except air conditioning
	EAE101180LOY	Carpet-front floor wheelarch-RH-Dark Granite	1	Note (2)	Station Wagon Td5
	EAE101190LOY	Carpet-front floor wheelarch-LH-Dark Granite	1	Note (2)	Station Wagon Td5
	EAE101200LOY	Carpet-front floor wheelarch-RH-Dark Granite	1	Note (2)	Except Station Wagon
	EAE101210LOY	Carpet-front floor wheelarch-LH-Dark Granite	1	Note (2)	Except Station Wagon
	EAE000060LOY	Carpet-centre floor wheelarch-Dark Granite-RH	1	Note (3)	
	EAE000070LOY	Carpet-centre floor wheelarch-Dark Granite-LH	1	Note (3)	
	ADU8026LOYL	Fastener-drive	4	Note (1)	
	AJU1136	Stud	4	Note (1)	

TF 0007

CHANGE POINTS:
(1) From (V) XA 159807
(2) From (V) XA 159807 To (V) YA 999999
(3) From (V) 2A 622424

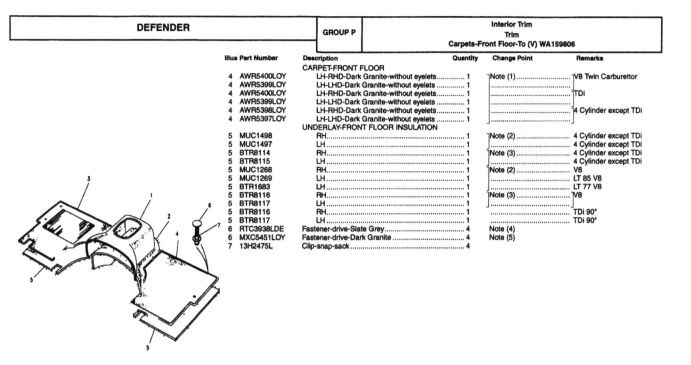

Illus	Part Number	Description	Quantity	Change Point	Remarks
1	MUC1621	Cover-tunnel-rubber	1	Note (1)	4 Cylinder
1	MUC1253	Cover-tunnel-rubber	1		LT 85 V8
1	BTR1198	Cover-tunnel-rubber	1		LT 77 V8
1	BTR9320	Cover-tunnel-rubber	1	Note (2)	
		MAT-FRONT FLOOR DROP IN			
2	MUC2268	RH-RHD	1	Note (3)	LT 77 4 Cylinder
3	MUC2269	LH-RHD	1	Note (3)	
2	MUC2270	RH-LHD	1	Note (3)	
3	MUC2271	LH-LHD	1	Note (3)	
2	BTR7896	RH	1	Note (4)	
3	BTR7895	LH	1	Note (4)	
3	BTR1680	LH-RHD	1	Note (3)	LT 77 V8
3	BTR1679	LH-LHD	1	Note (3)	
2	MUC1250	RH-RHD	1	Note (3)	LT 85 V8
3	MUC1249	LH-RHD	1	Note (3)	
2	MUC1254	RH-LHD	1	Note (3)	
3	MUC1255	LH-LHD	1	Note (3)	
2	BTR7898	RH	1	Note (5)	
3	BTR7897	LH	1		
4	ETL100440	Pad-front footwell insulation-LHD	1	Note (6)	LHD 2500 cc L/R 5 Cylinder Diesel Turbo Td5
4	ETL100430	Pad-front footwell insulation-RHD	1	Note (6)	RHD 2500 cc L/R 5 Cylinder Diesel Turbo Td5

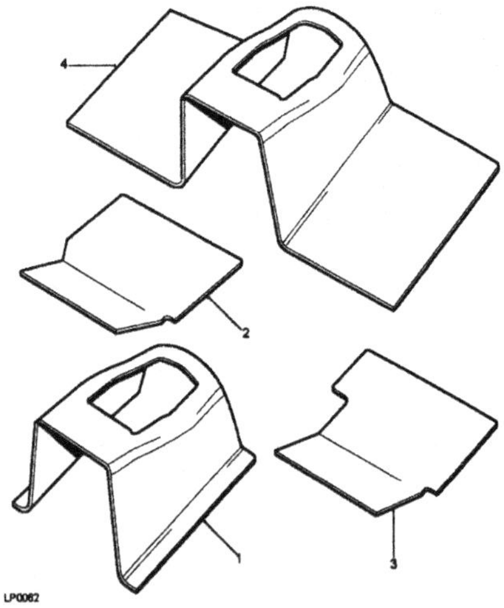

LP0062

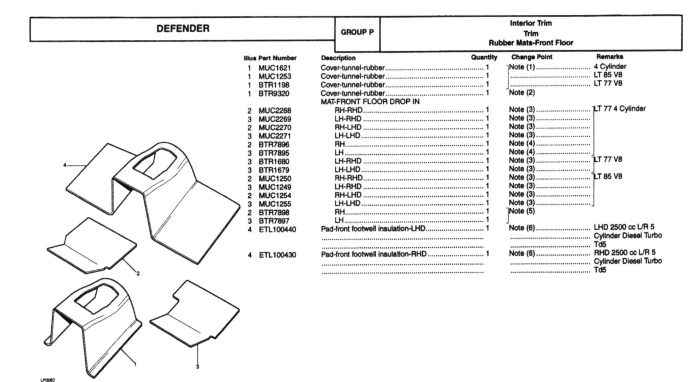

CHANGE POINTS:
(1) To (V) LA 939975
(2) From (V) MA 939976
(3) To (V) KA 929549
(4) From (V) KA 929550 To (V) LA 939975
(5) From (V) KA 929550
(6) From (V) XA 159807

Illus	Part Number	Description	Quantity	Change Point	Remarks
		CARPET-CENTRE FLOOR HEELBOARD			
1	MUC1360RD	RH-RHD-Brushwood	1	Note (1); Note (2)	RHD 4 Cylinder Note (1)
1	MUC1364RD	RH-LHD-Brushwood	1	Note (1); Note (2)	LHD 4 Cylinder Note (1)
1	MUC2160RD	RH-RHD-Brushwood	1	Note (1); Note (2)	RHD 4 Cylinder Note (2)
1	MUC2161RD	RH-LHD-Brushwood	1	Note (1); Note (2)	LHD 4 Cylinder Note (2)
1	MUC1260RD	RH-RHD-Brushwood	1	Note (1); Note (2)	RHD V8
1	MUC1261RD	LH-RHD-Brushwood	1	Note (1); Note (2)	RHD V8
1	MUC1266RD	LHD-Brushwood	1	Note (1); Note (2)	LHD V8
1	MUC3567RD	RH-RHD-Brushwood	1	Note (3); Note (4)	RHD 4 Cylinder
1	MUC3568RD	RH-LHD-Brushwood	1	Note (3); Note (4)	LHD 4 Cylinder
1	MUC1359RD	LH-RHD-Brushwood	1		RHD 4 Cylinder
1	MUC1365RD	LH-LHD-Brushwood	1		LHD 4 Cylinder
1	MWC7658LDE	RH-RHD-Slate Grey	1	Note (5); Note (6)	RHD 4 Cylinder
1	MWC7657LDE	LH-RHD-Slate Grey	1	Note (5); Note (6)	RHD 4 Cylinder
1	MWC7662LDE	RH-LHD-Slate Grey	1	Note (5); Note (6)	LHD 4 Cylinder
1	MWC7661LDE	LH-LHD-Slate Grey	1	Note (5); Note (6)	LHD 4 Cylinder
1	MWC7660LDE	RH-RHD-Slate Grey	1	Note (5); Note (6)	RHD V8
1	MWC7659LDE	LH-RHD-Slate Grey	1	Note (5); Note (6)	RHD V8
1	MWC7663LDE	LHD-Slate Grey	1	Note (5); Note (6)	LHD V8
1	MWC9370LDE	RH-Slate Grey	1	Note (7)	4 Cylinder
1	MWC9371LDE	LH-Slate Grey	1	Note (7)	4 Cylinder
1	MWC9369LDE	Slate Grey	1	Note (7)	V8
1	MXC2338LDE	RH-Slate Grey	1	Note (8)	4 Cylinder
1	MXC2339LDE	LH-Slate Grey	1	Note (8)	4 Cylinder
1	MXC2340LDE	Slate Grey	1	Note (8)	LT 85 V8
1	BTR1194LDE	Slate Grey	1	Note (8)	LT 77 V8
1	BTR1194LOY	Dark Granite	1	Note (9)	V8
1	MXC2338LOY	RH-Dark Granite	1	Note (9)	4 Cylinder
1	MXC2339LOY	LH-Dark Granite	1	Note (9)	4 Cylinder
1	BTR1194LOY	Dark Granite	1	Note (10)	Td5

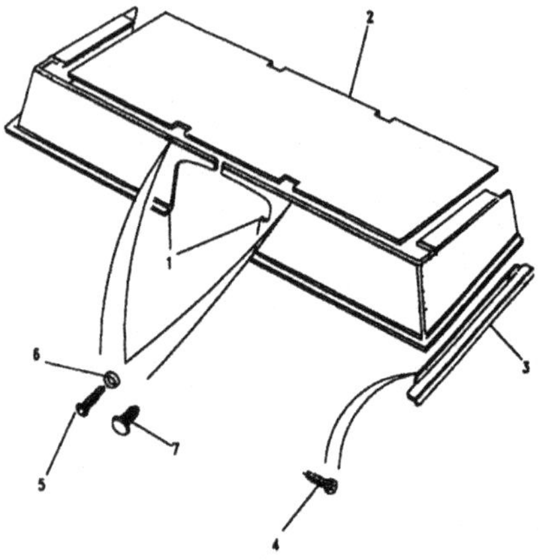

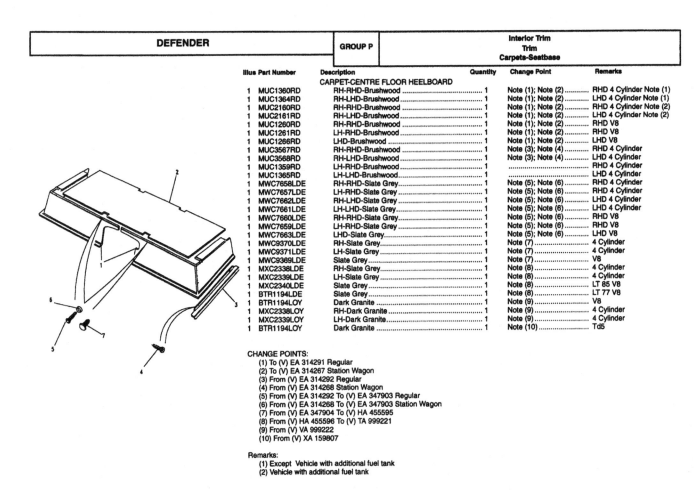

CHANGE POINTS:
(1) To (V) EA 314291 Regular
(2) To (V) EA 314267 Station Wagon
(3) From (V) EA 314292 Regular
(4) From (V) EA 314268 Station Wagon
(5) From (V) EA 314292 To (V) EA 347903 Regular
(6) From (V) EA 314268 To (V) EA 347903 Station Wagon
(7) From (V) EA 347904 To (V) HA 455595
(8) From (V) HA 455596 To (V) TA 999221
(9) From (V) VA 999222
(10) From (V) XA 159807

Remarks:
(1) Except Vehicle with additional fuel tank
(2) Vehicle with additional fuel tank

Trim
Carpets-Seatbase

Illus	Part Number	Description	Quantity	Change Point	Remarks
2	MUC1757	Carpet-intermediate-top	1	Note (1); Note (2)	
2	MUC1757LDE	Carpet-intermediate-top-Slate Grey	1	Note (3); Note (4)	
2	MXC2337LDE	Carpet-intermediate-top-Slate Grey	1	Note (5)	
3	MUC1500	Retainer	2	Note (8)	Station Wagon
3	MWC9376	Retainer	2	Note (8)	Except Station Wagon
4	AB606054L	Screw-pan	6	Note (8)	
5	MTC9428	Screw	16	Note (1); Note (2)	
6	MTC9429	Washer-cup	16	Note (1); Note (2)	
7	AFU1897LDE	Fastener-drive-Slate Grey	9	Note (6)	
7	AFU1897LOY	Fastener-drive-Dark Granite	9	Note (7)	

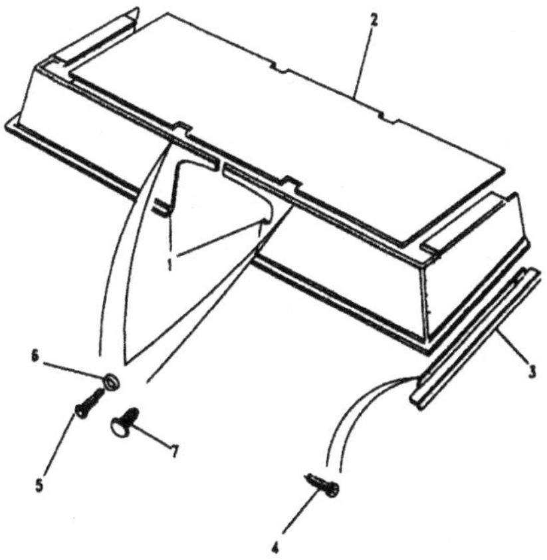

CHANGE POINTS:
(1) To (V) EA 314291 Regular
(2) To (V) EA 314267 Station Wagon
(3) From (V) EA 314292 To (V) HA 455595 Regular
(4) From (V) EA 314268 To (V) HA 455595 Station Wagon
(5) From (V) HA 455596
(6) To (V) TA 999221
(7) From (V) VA 999222 To (V) WA 159806
(8) To (V) KA 924784

Trim
Insulation-Seatbase-To (V) WA159806

Illus	Part Number	Description	Quantity	Change Point	Remarks
1	MXC1804PMA	Pad-insulation-RH-Black	1	Note (1)	4 Cylinder
2	MXC1805PMA	Pad-insulation-LH-Black	1	Note (1)	4 Cylinder
1	MXC1806PMA	Pad-insulation-Black	1	Note (1)	V8
1	BTR1197PMA	Pad-insulation-Black	1	Note (2)	LT 77 V8
1	MXC5088PMA	Pad-insulation-RH-Black	1	Note (2)	4 Cylinder
2	MXC5089PMA	Pad-insulation-LH-Black	1	Note (2)	4 Cylinder
1	MXC5090PMA	Pad-insulation-Black	1	Note (2)	LT 85 V8
1	BTR1197PMA	Pad-insulation-Black	1	Note (3)	
3	396950	Pad-front seat pan insulation-RH	1		
3	396951	Pad-front seat pan insulation-LH	1		

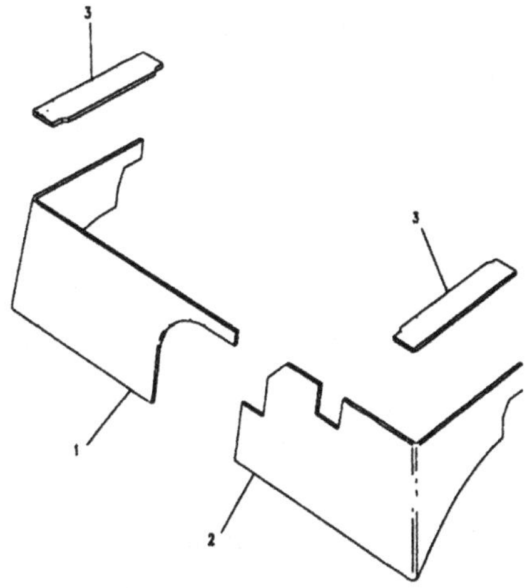

CHANGE POINTS:
(1) To (V) GA 455945
(2) From (V) HA 455946 To (V) LA 939975
(3) From (V) MA 939976

DEFENDER	GROUP P	Interior Trim Trim Insulation-Seatbase-From (V) XA159807

Illus	Part Number	Description	Quantity	Change Point	Remarks
1	ETT100230	Pad-front seat pan insulation-RHD	1	Note (1)	RHD 2500 cc L/R 5 Cylinder Diesel Turbo Td5
1	ETT100240	Pad-front seat pan insulation-LHD	1	Note (1)	LHD 2500 cc L/R 5 Cylinder Diesel Turbo Td5
2	YOO5098PMP	Fastener-drive-Black	4	Note (1)	2500 cc L/R 5 Cylinder Diesel Turbo Td5

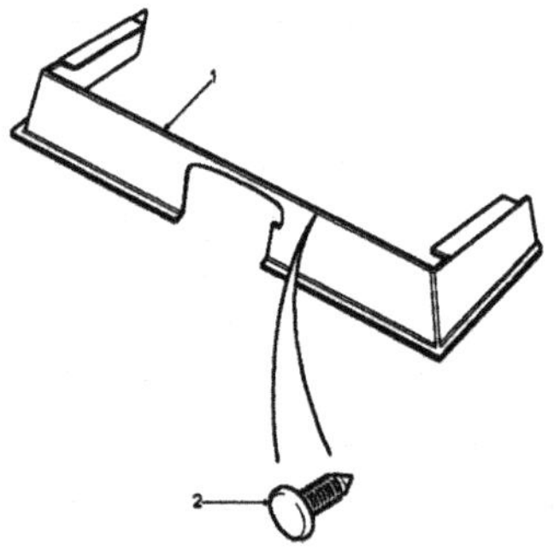

LP0063

CHANGE POINTS:
(1) From (V) XA 159807

DEFENDER	GROUP P	Interior Trim Trim Carpets-Intermediate Floor

Illus	Part Number	Description	Quantity	Change Point	Remarks
		CARPET-TOE PANEL			
1	MUC6667RD	Brushwood/Berber	1	Note (1); Note (2)	Except Regular and 90"
1	MUC6667LDE	Slate Grey	1	Note (3); Note (4)	
1	MUC6667LOY	Dark Granite	1	Note (5); Note (6)	
1	EAD101960LOY	rear-Dark Granite	1	Note (7)	
2	396541	Retainer-outer	2		
3	396542	Retainer-centre	1		
4	AB606041L	Screw-self tapping-No 6 x 1/2	6		
		CARPET ASSEMBLY- INTERMEDIATE			
5	MUC1353AV	with eyelets-Brushwood	1	Note (1); Note (2)	
5	MUC1353LDE	with eyelets-Slate Grey	1	Note (9); Note (10)	
5	AWR5401LDE	without eyelets-Slate Grey	1	Note (11)	
5	AWR5401LOY	without eyelets-Dark Granite	1	Note (5)	
6	MUC1495	Felt-nvh-intermediate	1		
		FASTENER-DRIVE			
7	RTC3938AV	Brushwood-plastic	4	Note (1); Note (2)	
7	RTC3938LDE	Slate Grey	4	Note (3); Note (4)	
7	MXC5451LOY	Dark Granite	4	Note (5)	
8	13H2475L	Clip-snap-sack	4		

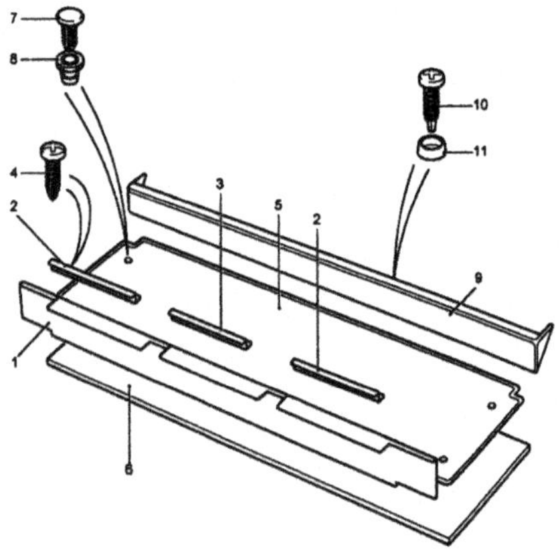

AJPXPA3A

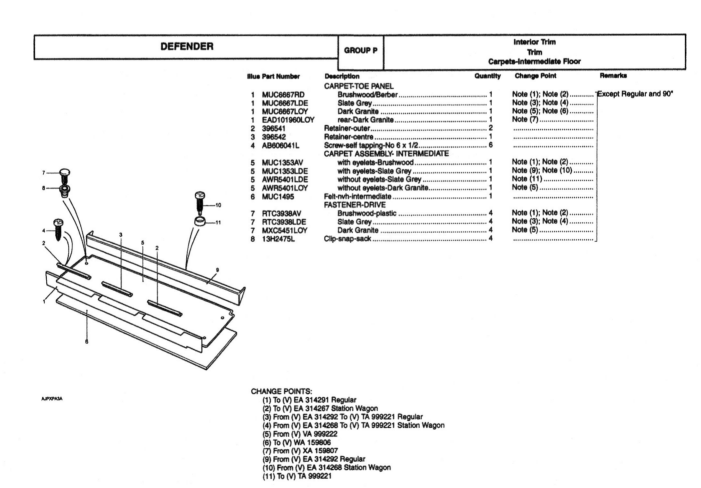

CHANGE POINTS:
(1) To (V) EA 314291 Regular
(2) To (V) EA 314267 Station Wagon
(3) From (V) EA 314292 To (V) TA 999221 Regular
(4) From (V) EA 314268 To (V) TA 999221 Station Wagon
(5) From (V) VA 999222
(6) To (V) WA 159806
(7) From (V) XA 159807
(9) From (V) EA 314292 Regular
(10) From (V) EA 314268 Station Wagon
(11) To (V) TA 999221

Carpets-Intermediate Floor

Illus	Part Number	Description	Quantity	Change Point	Remarks
		CARPET-CENTRE FLOOR HEELBOARD			
9	MWC2315AV	10 seats-Brushwood	1	Note (1)	Except Regular and 90"
9	MUC1759	12 seats	1		
9	MWC2315LDE	10 seats-Slate Grey	1	Note (2)	
9	MUC1759LDE	12 seats-Slate Grey	1		
9	MWC2315LOY	10 seats-Dark Granite	1	Note (3)	
9	MUC1759LOY	12 seats-Dark Granite	1		
10	MTC9428	Screw	12		
11	MTC9429	Washer-cup	12		
	ADU8026LOYL	Fastener-drive	4	Note (4)	
	AJU1136	Stud	2		
	MWC9917	Clip-snap-sack	2		
	RU612253	Rivet-3/16" x 0.45"lng	7		

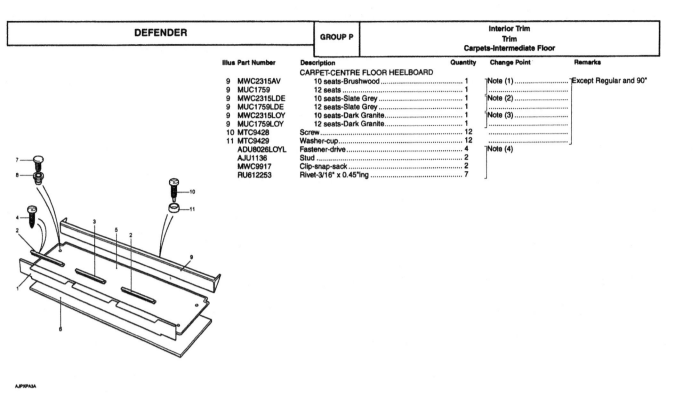

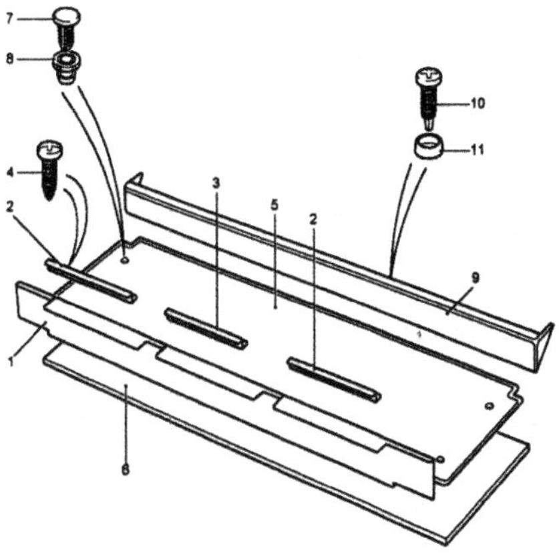

AJPXPA3A

CHANGE POINTS:
(1) To (V) EA 314291
(2) From (V) EA 314292 To (V) TA 999221
(3) From (V) VA 999222
(4) From (V) XA 159807

Rubber Mats-Intermediate Floor

Illus	Part Number	Description	Quantity	Change Point	Remarks
1	396540	Cover-toe box	1	Note (1)	Except Regular and 90"
1	MXC6142PMA	Cover-toe box-Black	1	Note (2)	
2	396541	Retainer-outer	2		
3	396542	Retainer-centre	1		
4	AB606041L	Screw-self tapping-No 6 x 1/2	6		
5	331481	Mat-intermediate floor-rubber	1		
6	MUC1495	Felt-nvh-intermediate	1		
7	331480	Retainer	2		
8	336780	Retainer-RH	1		
8	336781	Retainer-LH	1		
9	78248	Rivet-pop-3/16" x 0.45"lng	4		

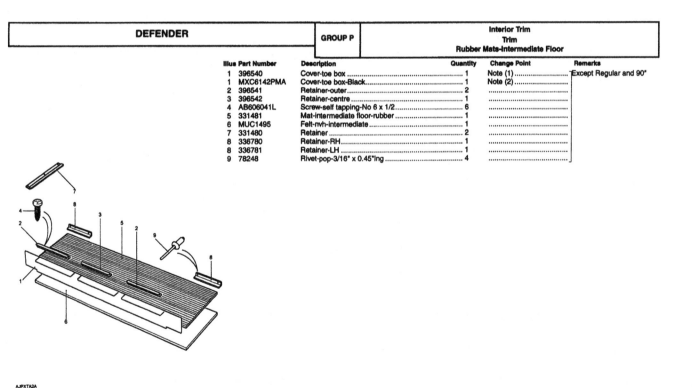

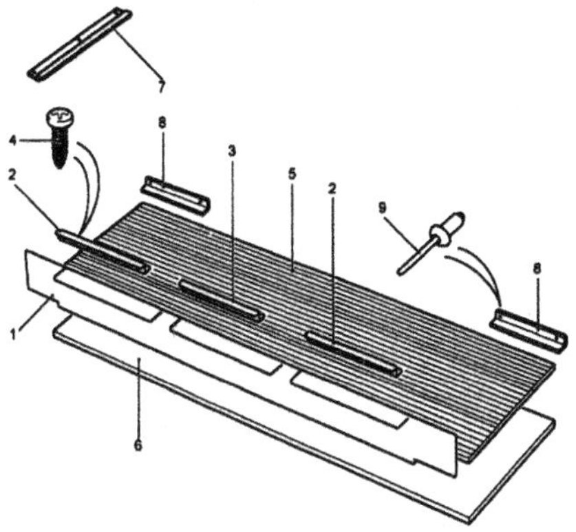

AJPXTA3A

CHANGE POINTS:
(1) To (V) HA 455595
(2) From (V) HA 455596 To (V) WA 159806

Illus	Part Number	Description	Quantity	Change Point	Remarks
		CARPET-REAR FLOOR			
1	MUC2400LDE	Slate Grey	1	Note (1)	90"
1	AWR2703LDE	Slate Grey	1	Note (2)	
1	AWR2703LOY	Dark Granite	1	Note (3)	
		CARPET-REAR FLOOR			
1	MUC1758RD	Brushwood/Berber	1	Note (4); Note (5)	110"
1	MUC1758LDE	Slate Grey	1	Note (6); Note (7)	
1	AWR2704LDE	Slate Grey	1	Note (2)	
1	AWR2704LOY	Dark Granite	1	Note (3)	
		CARPET-REAR FLOOR WHEELARCH			
2	AWR2700LDE	RH-Slate Grey	1	Note (2)	County 90"
2	AWR2700LDE	RH-Slate Grey	1	Note (8)	County Hard Top 90"
2	AWR2700LOY	RH-Dark Granite	1	Note (3)	90" except EFi
2	AWR4652LOY	RH-Dark Granite	1		V8 EFi 50 LE
2	AWR2702LDE	RH-Slate Grey	1	Note (2)	110"
2	AWR2702LOY	RH-Dark Granite	1	Note (3)	110"
		CARPET-REAR FLOOR WHEELARCH			
3	AWR2699LDE	LH-Slate Grey	1	Note (2)	County 90"
3	AWR2699LDE	LH-Slate Grey	1	Note (8)	County Hard Top 90"
3	AWR2699LOY	LH-Dark Granite	1	Note (3)	90" except EFi
3	AWR4653LOY	LH-Dark Granite	1		V8 EFi 50 LE
3	AWR2701LDE	LH-Slate Grey	1	Note (2)	110"
3	AWR2701LOY	LH-Dark Granite	1	Note (3)	110"

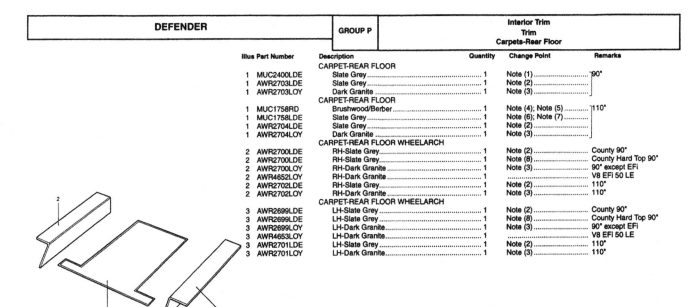

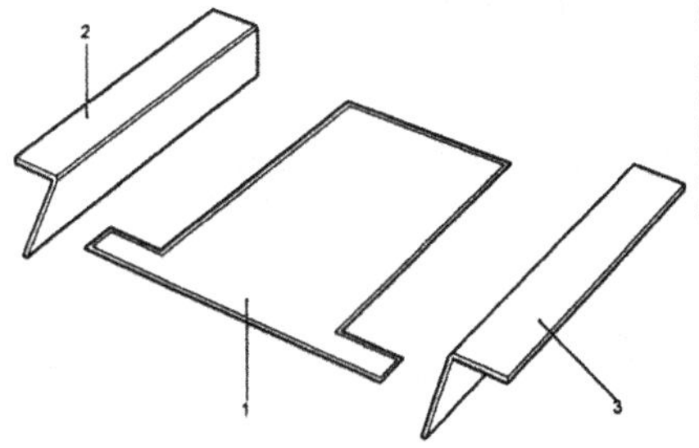

AHPXPC1A

CHANGE POINTS:
(1) To (V) MA 955468
(2) From (V) MA 955469 To (V) TA 999221
(3) From (V) VA 999222
(4) To (V) EA 314291 Regular
(5) To (V) EA 314267 Station Wagon
(6) From (V) EA 314292 To (V) MA 955468 Regular
(7) From (V) EA 314268 To (V) MA 955468 Station Wagon
(8) From (V) MA 955617 To (V) TA 999221

Illus	Part Number	Description	Quantity	Change Point	Remarks
1	MTC8294	Mat-loadspace	1	Note (1)	
1	AWR2705	Mat-loadspace	1	Note (2)	
1	EAH105070	Mat-loadspace	1	Note (3)	

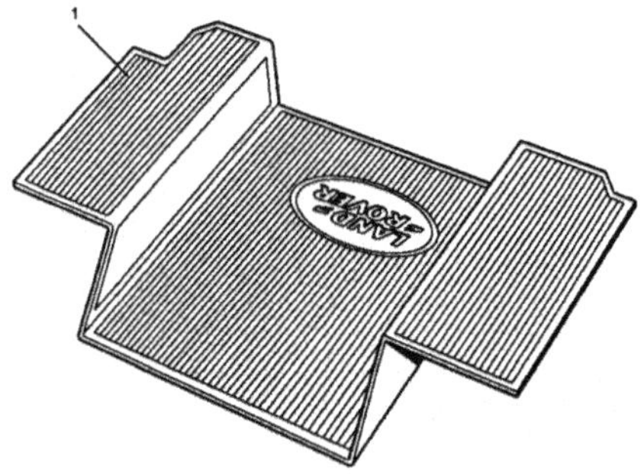

AHPXTA2B

CHANGE POINTS:
(1) To (V) MA 955616
(2) From (V) MA 955617 To (V) WA 159806
(3) From (V) XA 159807

Rubber Mats-Rear Floor-110/130

Illus	Part Number	Description	Quantity	Change Point	Remarks
1	331670	Mat-rear floor drop in-cab floor	1		110"
1	RRC6186	Mat-rear floor drop in-cab floor	1		130"
2	336780	Retainer-RH	1		
3	336781	Retainer-LH	1		
4	78248	Rivet-pop-3/16" x 0.45"lng	4		

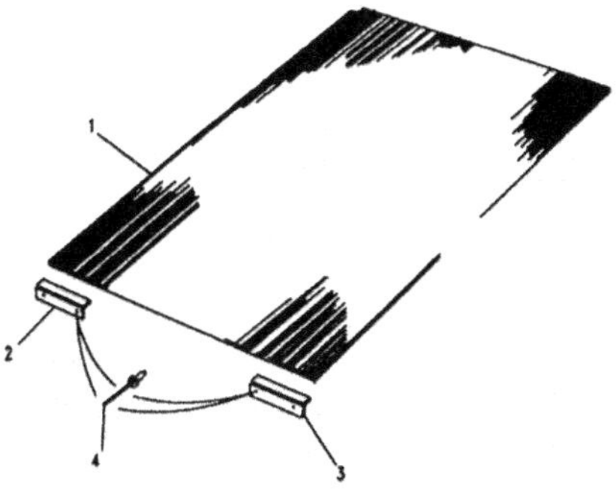

Insulation-Turbo Diesel

Illus	Part Number	Description	Quantity	Change Point	Remarks
		PAD-INSULATION			
1	MWC8203	toebox-LH-RHD	1		TDi
1	MWC8201	toebox-LH-LHD	1		TDi
2	MWC8202	toebox-inner-RH	1		TDi
		PAD-DASH INSULATION			
3	MWC8205	dash vent	1		TDi
4	MWC8206	centre	1		TDi
5	MWC8207	centre lower	1		TDi
6	MWC8208	Pad-tunnel insulation-RH	1		TDi
7	MWC8209	Pad-tunnel insulation-LH	1		TDi
8	MWC8210	Pad-insulation-diaphragm	1		TDi
9	MWC8211	Pad-front floor insulation-LH	1		TDi
		PAD-HEELBOARD INSULATION			
10	MWC8212	centre-RHD	1	Note (1)	TDi
10	MWC8213	centre-LHD	1		TDi
10	BTR362	centre-RHD	1	Note (2)	TDi
10	BTR361	centre-LHD	1		TDi
11	MWC8214	LH	1	Note (1)	TDi
11	BTR363	LH	1	Note (2)	TDi
12	MWC8215	Pad-mid floor insulation-LH	1		TDi
		PAD-INSULATION			
13	MWC8216	battery box-front	1	Note (1)	TDi
14	MWC8217	battery box-side	1		TDi
13	BTR364	battery box-front	1	Note (2)	TDi
14	BTR365	battery box-side	1		TDi
15	MWC8218	battery box lid	1		TDi
16	MWC8219	Pad-insulation-diaphragm flange-LH	1		TDi

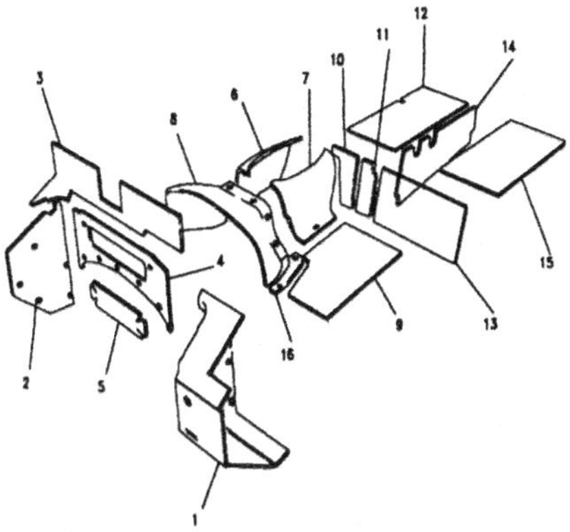

CHANGE POINTS:
(1) To (V) HA 455945
(2) From (V) HA 455946

DEFENDER | **GROUP P** | **Interior Trim**

Trim

Insulation-Turbo Diesel

Illus	Part Number	Description	Quantity	Change Point	Remarks
		ONE PIECE DASH INSULATION			

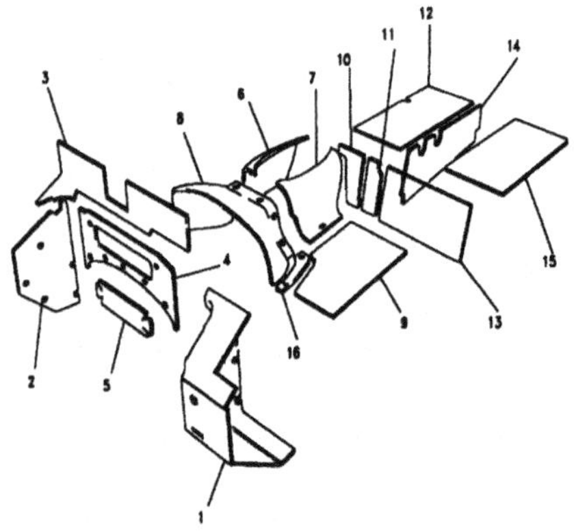

DEFENDER | **GROUP P** | **Interior Trim**

Trim

Chequer Plates-Interior

Illus	Part Number	Description	Quantity	Change Point	Remarks
		PLATE-CHEQUER			
1	STC61848	front footwell.-drivers side-RHD	1	Note (1)	Tomb Raider
1	STC61846	front footwell.-drivers side-LHD	1		
2	STC61847	front footwell.-passenger side-RHD	1		
2	STC61845	front footwell.-passenger side-LHD	1		
3	STC61870	rear-floor.	1		Tomb Raider 110"
4	STC61850	floor.-rear	1		Tomb Raider 90"
5	STC61849	Retainer-mat-floor.	2		Tomb Raider

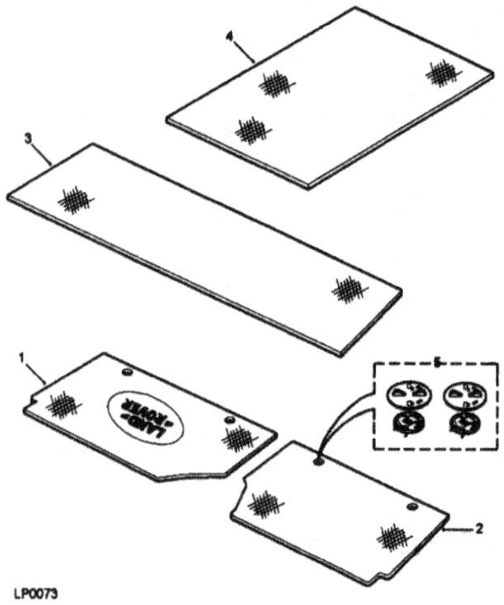

LP0073

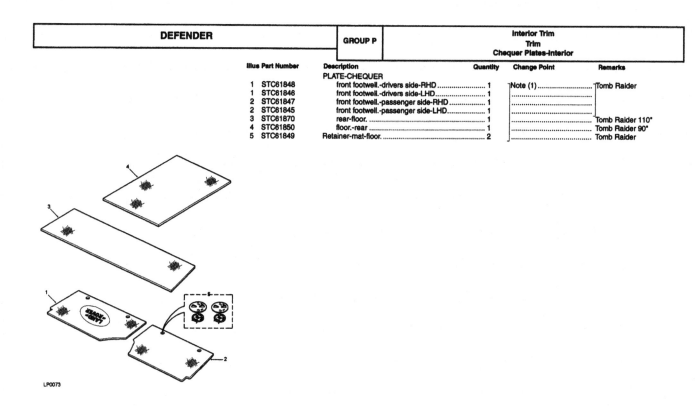

CHANGE POINTS:
(1) From (V) 1A 612404

Trim
Body Trim-Station Wagon-To (V) EA314173

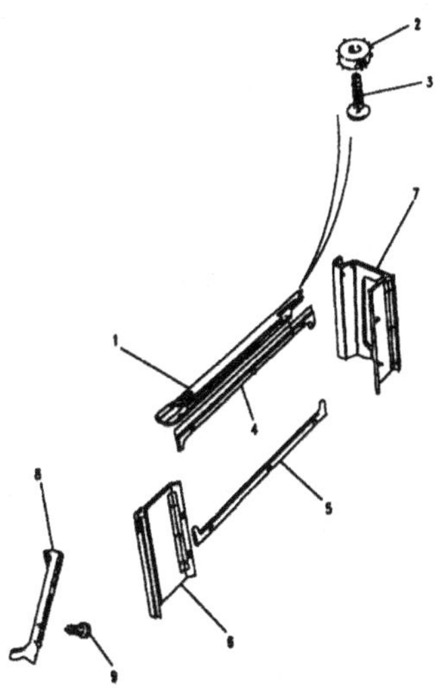

Illus	Part Number	Description	Quantity	Change Point	Remarks
1	MUC6494	Finisher-assembly-cantrail-RH	1		
1	MUC6495	Finisher-assembly-cantrail-LH	1		
2	MUC1508	Spacer	8		
3	AFU1900	Fastener-fir tree-White.	8		
4	MUC1474	Finisher-sixthlight upper	2		
5	MUC3242	Finisher-sixthlight lower	2		
6	MTC8296	Sixthlight assembly-front-RH	1		
6	MTC8297	Sixthlight assembly-front-LH	1		
7	MTC8298	Finisher assembly-quarterlight-RH	1		
7	MTC8299	Finisher assembly-quarterlight-LH	1		
8	MTC5212	Finisher-windscreen A post-RH	1		
8	MWC2314	Finisher-windscreen A post-LH	1		
9	AB606084	Screw-self tapping-No 6 x 1"	4		
		GERMANY			
	MUC3630	Cover-quarter trim casing-RH	1		
	MUC3631	Cover-quarter trim casing-LH	1		
9	AB608047L	Screw-self tapping-No 8 x 1/2	4		

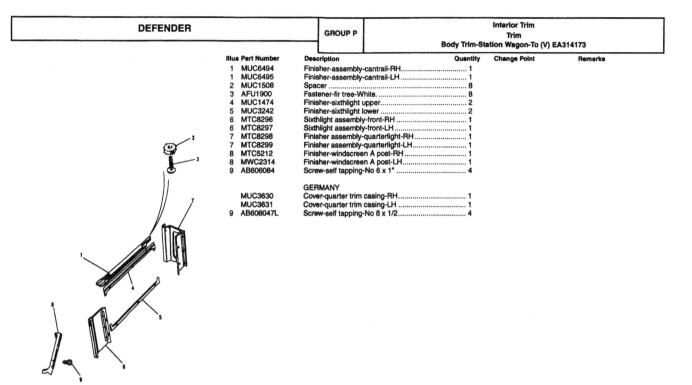

Trim
Body Trim-Station Wagon-From (V) EA314174

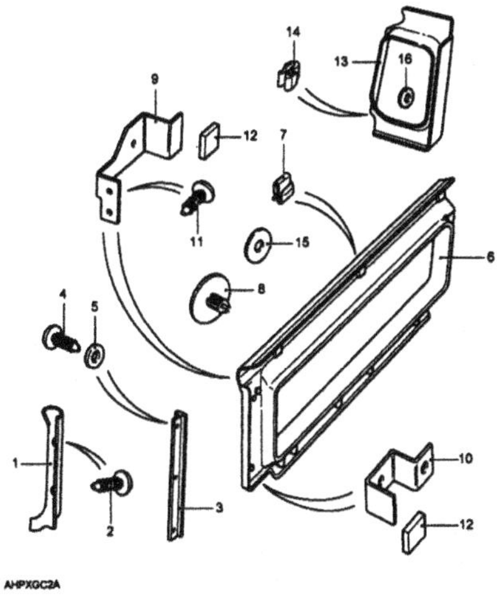

AHPXGC2A

Illus	Part Number	Description	Quantity	Change Point	Remarks
1	MTC5212	Finisher-windscreen A post-RH	1		
1	MWC2314	Finisher-windscreen A post-LH	1		
2	AB606084	Screw-self tapping-No 6 x 1"	4		
		TRIM PANEL			
3	MXC3319LNP	front-Mid Grey	2	Note (1)	
3	MXC3319LOY	front-Dark Granite	2	Note (2)	
3	MWC9823LNP	front-Mid Grey	2	Note (3)	90"
	MWC8901LNP	Finisher-BC post-Mid Grey	2	Note (1)	110"
	MWC8901LOY	Finisher-BC post-Dark Granite	2	Note (2)	
4	77869	Screw	6		
5	3852L	Washer	6		
		PANEL-BODYSIDE TRIM			
6	MWC5832LNP	RH-Mid Grey	1	Note (1)	90" except burglar alarm
6	MWC5832LOY	RH-Dark Granite	1	Note (2)	
6	AWR3151LNP	RH-Mid Grey	1	Note (4)	Burglar alarm 90"
6	AWR3151LOY	RH-Dark Granite	1	Note (2)	
6	BTR306LNP	RH-Mid Grey	1	Note (1)	12 seats 110"
6	BTR306LOY	RH-Dark Granite	1	Note (2)	
6	BTR5438LNP	RH-Mid Grey	1	Note (1)	10 seats 110"
6	BTR5438LOY	RH-Dark Granite	1	Note (2)	
		PANEL-BODYSIDE TRIM			
6	MWC5833LNP	LH-Mid Grey	1	Note (1)	90"
6	MWC5833LOY	LH-Dark Granite	1	Note (2)	
6	BTR305LNP	LH-Mid Grey	1	Note (1)	12 seats 110"
6	BTR305LOY	LH-Dark Granite	1	Note (2)	
6	BTR5437LNP	LH-Mid Grey	1	Note (1)	10 seats 110"
6	BTR5437LOY	LH-Dark Granite	1	Note (2)	

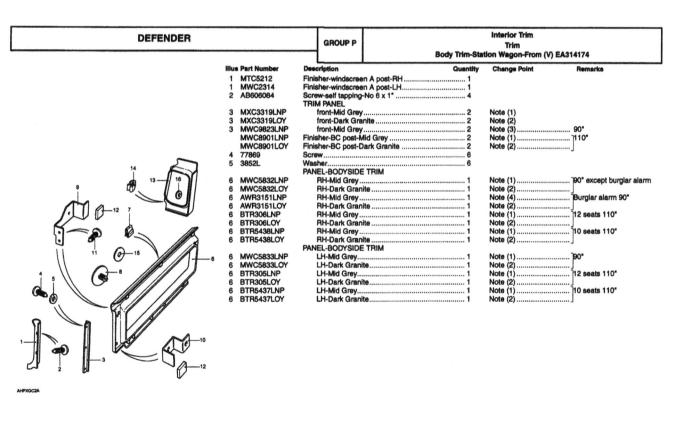

CHANGE POINTS:
(1) To (V) TA 999221
(2) From (V) VA 999222
(3) To (V) FA 365455
(4) From (V) TA 969103 To (V) TA 999221

Body Trim-Station Wagon-From (V) EA314174

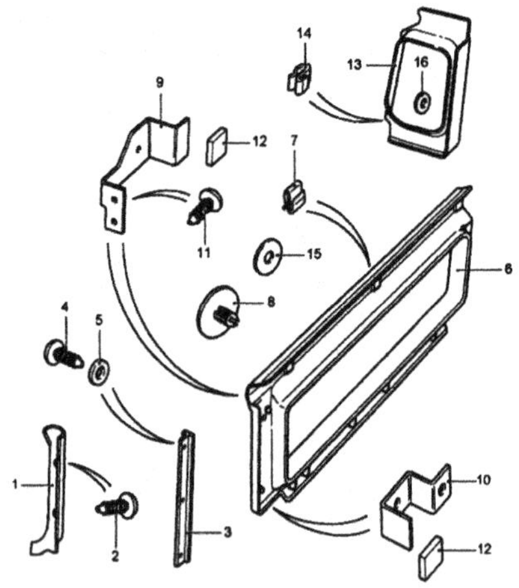

AHPXGC2A

Illus	Part Number	Description	Quantity	Change Point	Remarks
7	MWC6203	Clip-edge harness	6		
	SE106401	Screw-pan-10 Seats-M6 x 40	1		110"
18	WC600045L	Washer-10 Seats-plain-1/4 dia	2		
	MTC3203	Nut plate-10 Seats	1		
	SE106401	Screw-pan-12 Seats-M6 x 40	3		
18	WC600045L	Washer-12 Seats-plain-1/4 dia	6		
	MTC3203	Nut plate-12 Seats	3		
8	MWC5763LNP	Fastener-fir tree-Mid Grey	2	Note (1)	
8	MWC5763LOY	Fastener-fir tree-Dark Granite	2	Note (2)	
	MWC5764	Guide-front seat belt webbing	2		110"
9	MXC3278	Bracket-upper-RH	1		
9	MXC3279	Bracket-upper-LH	1		
10	MXC3276	Bracket-lower	2		90"
10	MXC3277	Bracket-lower	2		110"
11	AB608044L	Screw-upper bracket-self tapping-No 8 x 1/2	4		
12	MUC6400	Seal-corner	4		
		FINISHER-TRIM RETENTION			
13	MWC8910LNP	RH-Mid Grey	1	Note (1)	
13	MWC8910LOY	RH-Dark Granite	1	Note (2)	
13	MWC8911LNP	LH-Mid Grey	1	Note (1)	
13	MWC8911LOY	LH-Dark Granite	1	Note (2)	
14	BTR6682	Clip-edge harness	4		
	MXC1130PMA	Plug-Black	2		110"
		SEAT BELT ANCHORAGE/TRIM PROTECTION			
15	MWC9482	Washer	2		90"
15	MWC9482	Washer	4		110"
16	STC3165	Cover-rivet-head	16		

CHANGE POINTS:
(1) To (V) TA 999221
(2) From (V) VA 999222

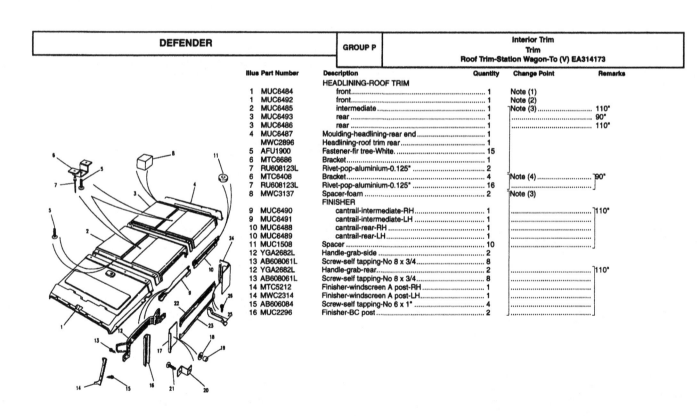

Roof Trim-Station Wagon-To (V) EA314173

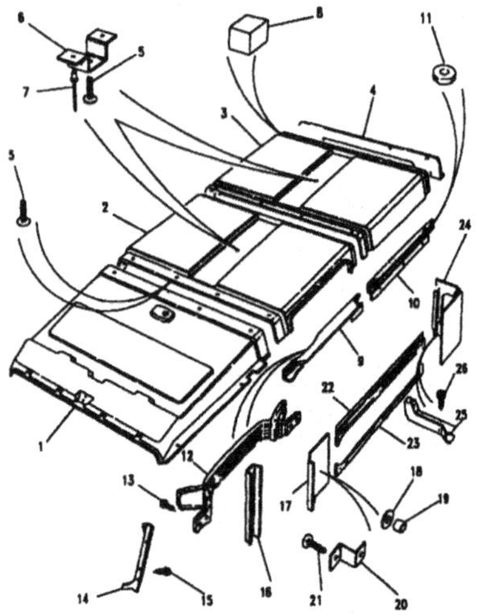

Illus	Part Number	Description	Quantity	Change Point	Remarks
		HEADLINING-ROOF TRIM			
1	MUC6484	front	1	Note (1)	
1	MUC6492	front	1	Note (2)	
2	MUC6485	intermediate	1	Note (3)	110"
3	MUC6493	rear	1		90"
3	MUC6486	rear	1		110"
4	MUC6487	Moulding-headlining-rear end	1		
	MWC2896	Headlining-roof trim rear	1		
5	AFU1900	Fastener-fir tree-White.	15		
6	MTC6686	Bracket	1		
7	RU608123L	Rivet-pop-aluminium-0.125"	2		
6	MTC6408	Bracket	4	Note (4)	90"
7	RU608123L	Rivet-pop-aluminium-0.125"	16		
8	MWC3137	Spacer-foam	2	Note (3)	
		FINISHER			
9	MUC6490	cantrail-intermediate-RH	1		110"
9	MUC6491	cantrail-intermediate-LH	1		
10	MUC6488	cantrail-rear-RH	1		
10	MUC6489	cantrail-rear-LH	1		
11	MUC1508	Spacer	10		
12	YGA2682L	Handle-grab-side	2		
13	AB608061L	Screw-self tapping-No 8 x 3/4	8		
12	YGA2682L	Handle-grab-rear	2		110"
13	AB608061L	Screw-self tapping-No 8 x 3/4	8		
14	MTC5212	Finisher-windscreen A post-RH	1		
14	MWC2314	Finisher-windscreen A post-LH	1		
15	AB606084	Screw-self tapping-No 6 x 1"	4		
16	MUC2296	Finisher-BC post	2		

CHANGE POINTS:
(1) To (V) AA 232401
(2) From (V) AA 232402 To (V) EA 314267
(3) To (V) EA 314267
(4) To (V) AA 238316

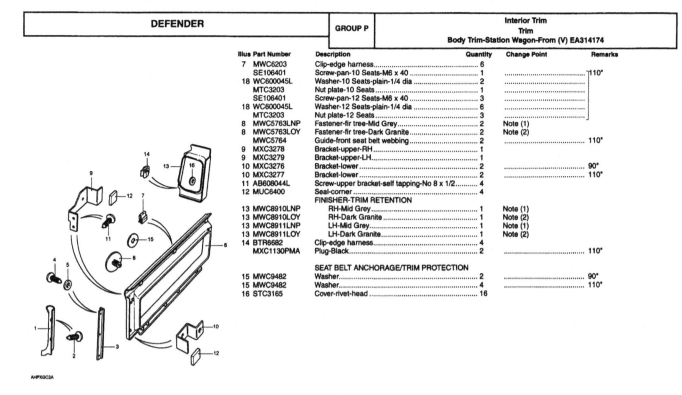

Illus	Part Number	Description	Quantity	Change Point	Remarks
		FINISHER-D POST			
17	MWC1628	static-RH	1	Note (1)	110"
17	MWC1629	static-LH	1		
17	MWC1624	inertia reel-RH	1		
17	MWC1625	inertia reel-LH	1		
18	MUC6075	Spacer-inertia reel seat belts	2		
19	WA112081L	Washer-inertia reel seat belts-plain-standard-M12	2		
20	MUC6074	Bracket-inertia reel seat belts	2		
21	AFU1900	Fastener-fir tree-inertia reel seat belts-White	2		
22	MUC1474	Finisher-sixthlight upper	2		
23	MUC3242	Finisher-sixthlight lower	2		
24	MUC1554	Finisher-quarter trim strip-RH	1		
24	MUC1555	Finisher-quarter trim strip-LH	1		
		GERMANY			
25	MUC3630	Cover-quarter trim casing-RH	1		
25	MUC3631	Cover-quarter trim casing-LH	1		
26	AB60804	Screw	4		

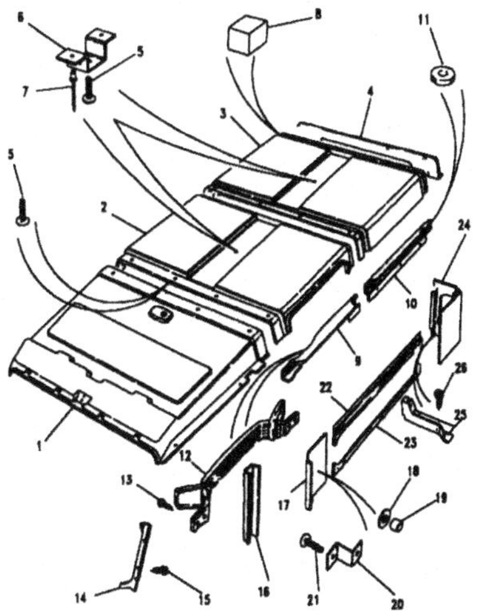

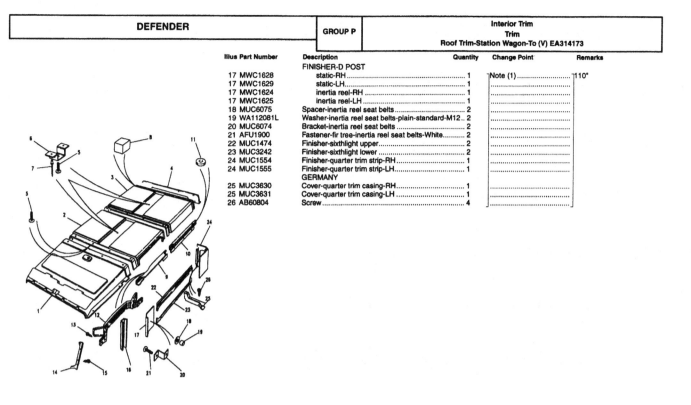

CHANGE POINTS:
(1) To (V) EA 314267

Illus	Part Number	Description	Quantity	Change Point	Remarks
		HEADLINING-ROOF TRIM			
1	MXC2343LUH	front-Ripple Grey-less sunroof	1	Note (1)	
1	BTR9176LUH	front-Ripple Grey-less sunroof	1	Note (2)	
1	AWR2735LUH	front-Ripple Grey	1	Note (3)	
1	MWC9491LUH	front-Ripple Grey-with sunroof	1	To (V) EA	90"
1	MWC9490LUH	front-Ripple Grey-with sunroof	1		110"
1	MXC5856LUH	front-Ripple Grey-with sunroof	NLA	Note (4)	Use MXC2344LUH.
1	MXC2344LUH	front-Ripple Grey-with sunroof	1	Note (5)	
1	BTR1886LUH	front-Ripple Grey-with sunroof	NLA	Note (6)	Use BTR4525LUH.
1	BTR4525LUH	front-Ripple Grey-with sunroof	1	Note (7)	
1	BTR9181LUH	front-Ripple Grey-with sunroof	1	Note (2)	
1	AWR2736LUH	front-Ripple Grey-with sunroof	1	Note (8)	
1	AWR3044LUH	front-Ripple Grey-with sunroof	1	Note (9)	

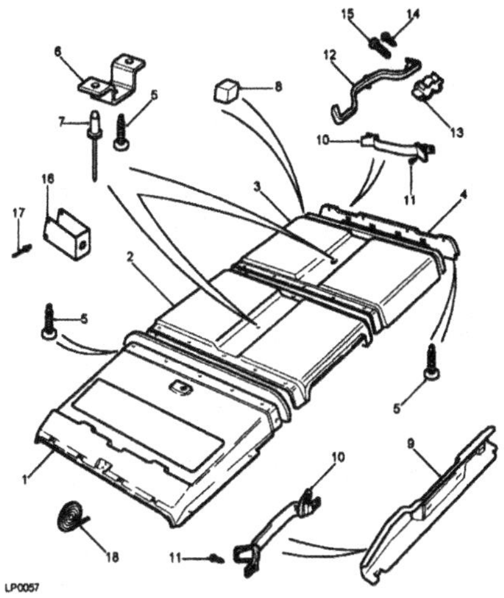

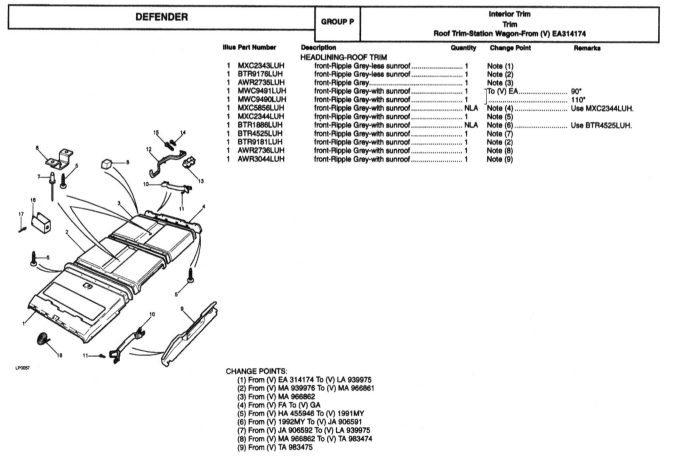

CHANGE POINTS:
(1) From (V) EA 314174 To (V) LA 939975
(2) From (V) MA 939976 To (V) MA 966861
(3) From (V) MA 966862
(4) From (V) FA To (V) GA
(5) From (V) HA 455946 To (V) 1991MY
(6) From (V) 1992MY To (V) JA 906591
(7) From (V) JA 906592 To (V) LA 939975
(8) From (V) MA 966862 To (V) TA 983474
(9) From (V) TA 983475

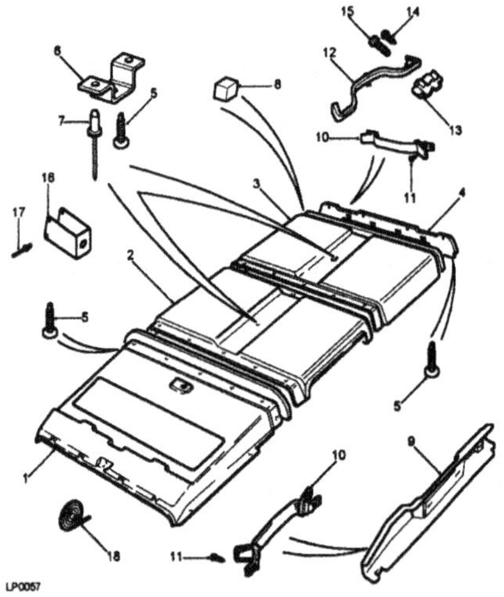

LP0057

Illus	Part Number	Description	Quantity	Change Point	Remarks
		HEADLINING-ROOF TRIM			
2	MWC9484LUH	intermediate-Ripple Grey	1	Note (1)	110"
2	MXC2347LUH	intermediate-Ripple Grey	1	Note (2)	
2	BTR9385LUH	intermediate-Ripple Grey	1	Note (3)	
2	AWR3029LUH	intermediate-Ripple Grey	1	Note (4)	
2	EDB103130LUH	intermediate-Ripple Grey	1	Note (5)	
		HEADLINING-ROOF TRIM			
3	BTR9177LUH	rear-Ripple Grey	1	Note (6)	90"
3	AWR4710LUH	rear-Ripple Grey	1	Note (7)	
3	MXC2346LUH	rear-Ripple Grey	1	Note (8)	
3	MWC9485LUH	rear-Ripple Grey	1	Note (8)	110"
3	BTR9180LUH	rear-Ripple Grey	1	Note (9)	
3	AWR3273LUH	rear-Ripple Grey	1	Note (10)	
		FINISHER-HEADLINING			
4	MWC9486LUH	rear-Ripple Grey	1	Note (11)	
4	MXC1645LUH	rear-Ripple Grey	1	Note (12)	
4	BTR586LUH	rear-Ripple Grey	1	Note (13)	
4	AWR4709LUH	rear-Ripple Grey	1	Note (14)	

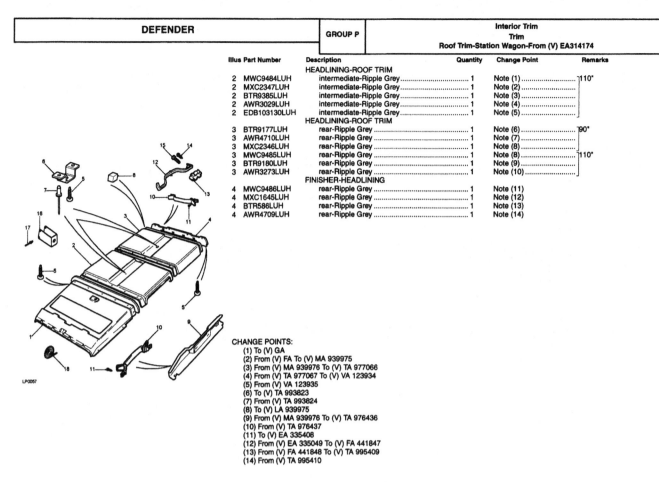

CHANGE POINTS:
(1) To (V) GA
(2) From (V) FA To (V) MA 939975
(3) From (V) MA 939976 To (V) TA 977066
(4) From (V) TA 977067 To (V) VA 123934
(5) From (V) VA 123935
(6) To (V) TA 993823
(7) From (V) TA 993824
(8) To (V) LA 939975
(9) From (V) MA 939976 To (V) TA 976436
(10) From (V) TA 976437
(11) To (V) EA 335408
(12) From (V) EA 335049 To (V) FA 441847
(13) From (V) FA 441848 To (V) TA 995409
(14) From (V) TA 995410

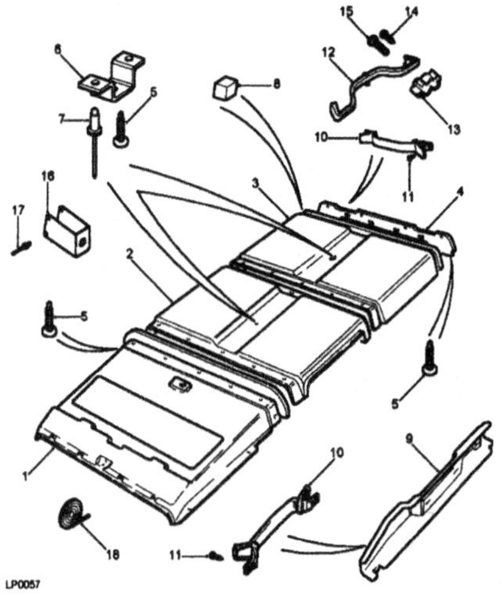

LP0057

Illus	Part Number	Description	Quantity	Change Point	Remarks
5	MWC9832LUH	Fastener-fir tree-Light Grey	15		90"
5	MWC9832LUH	Fastener-fir tree-Light Grey	30		110"
5	AFU1900	Fastener-fir tree-White.	20		50 LE
6	MTC6686	Bracket	1		90"
6	MTC6686	Bracket	2		110"
7	RU608123L	Rivet-pop-aluminium-0.125"	2		90"
7	RU608123L	Rivet-pop-aluminium-0.125"	4		110"
8	MUC4199	Spacer	2	Note (1)	
8	MWC3137	Spacer-foam	2	Note (2)	
		FINISHER-ROOF CANTRAIL			
9	MWC8914LNP	RH-Mid Grey	1	Note (3)	110" except burglar alarm
9	MWC8916LOY	RH-Dark Granite	1	Note (4)	
9	AWR3032LNP	RH-Mid Grey	1	Note (5)	Burglar alarm 110"
9	AWR3032LOY	RH-Dark Granite	1	Note (4)	
9	MWC8915LNP	LH-Mid Grey	1	Note (3)	110"
9	MWC8917LOY	LH-Dark Granite	1	Note (4)	

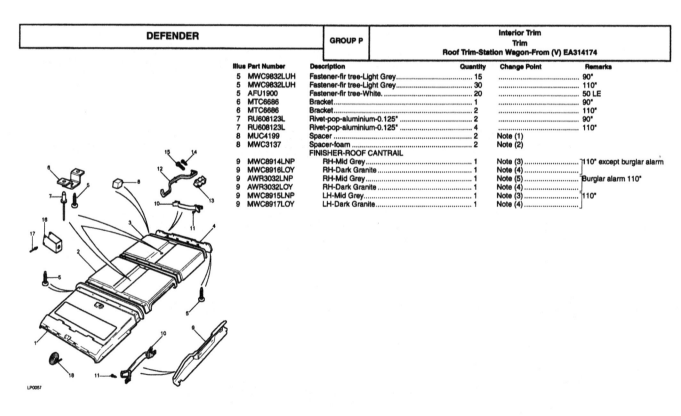

CHANGE POINTS:
(1) From (V) EA 314174 To (V) EA 335120
(2) From (V) EA 335121
(3) To (V) TA 999221
(4) From (V) VA 999222
(5) From (V) TA 977525 To (V) TA 999221

Illus	Part Number	Description	Quantity	Change Point	Remarks
10	YGA2682L	Handle-grab	2	Note (1)	90"
11	AB608061L	Screw-self tapping-No 8 x 3/4	8		
		HANDLE ASSEMBLY-ROOF TRIM GRAB			
12	JPC5641LUN	Ash	2	Note (2)	90"
12	JPC5641LUN	Ash	4	Note (3)	110"
12	JPC5641LNF	Ash Grey	2	Note (4)	90"
12	JPC5641LNF	Ash Grey	4	Note (4)	110"
13	PAM4356L	Spacer	4	Note (5)	90"
13	PAM4356L	Spacer	8		110"
14	AB608107	Screw-self tapping-No 8 x 1 1/4	4	Note (5)	90"
14	AB608107	Screw-self tapping-No 8 x 1 1/4	8		110"
15	SE105351L	Screw-pan	4	Note (5)	90"
15	SE105351L	Screw-pan	8		110"
16	MXC5859	Bracket	2		90"
17	RU612373L	Rivet-3/16" x 0.575"lng	8		90"
18	MUC1237	Strip-self adhesive packing	A/R	Note (6)	Cut to the required length

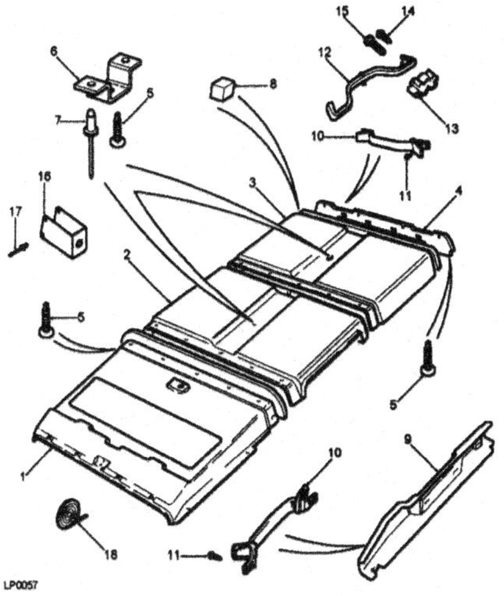

LP0057

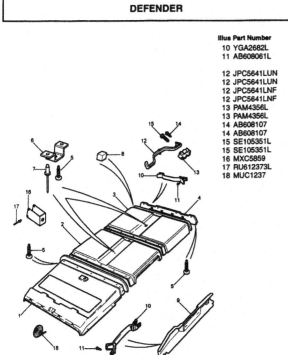

CHANGE POINTS:
(1) From (V) EA 314174 To (V) JA 917889
(2) From (V) JA 917890 To (V) TA 999221
(3) To (V) TA 999221
(4) From (V) VA 999222
(5) From (V) JA 917890
(6) From (V) YA 198811

Illus	Part Number	Description	Quantity	Change Point	Remarks
		HEADLINING-ROOF TRIM			
1	MUC6651	front-less sunroof	1	Note (1)	
1	MXC5857LUH	front-Ripple Grey-less sunroof	1	Note (2)	
1	MXC2345LUH	front-Ripple Grey-less sunroof	1	Note (3)	
1	BTR9178LUH	front-Ripple Grey-less sunroof	1	Note (4)	
1	AWR2735LUH	front-Ripple Grey	1	Note (5)	
1	AWR3030LUH	with hole for alarm-front-Ripple Grey-less sunroof	1	Note (6)	Burglar alarm
		HEADLINING-ROOF TRIM			
1	BTR1886LUH	front-Ripple Grey-with sunroof	NLA	Note (7)	Use BTR4525LUH.
1	BTR4525LUH	front-Ripple Grey-with sunroof	1	Note (8)	
1	BTR9181LUH	front-Ripple Grey-with sunroof	1	Note (4)	
1	AWR2736LUH	front-Ripple Grey-with sunroof	1	Note (5)	
1	AWR3044LUH	with hole for alarm-front-Ripple Grey-with sunroof	1	Note (6)	Burglar alarm

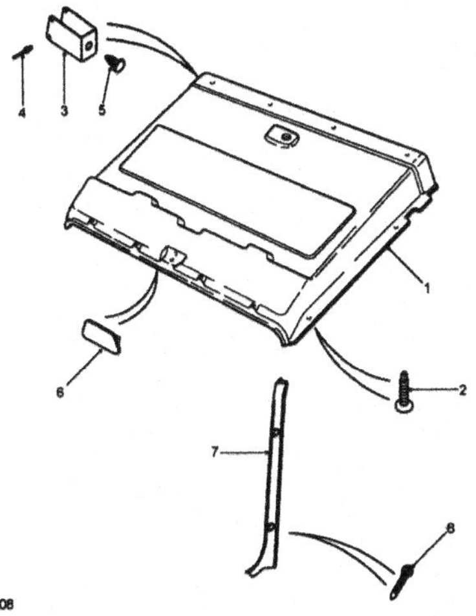

LP0008

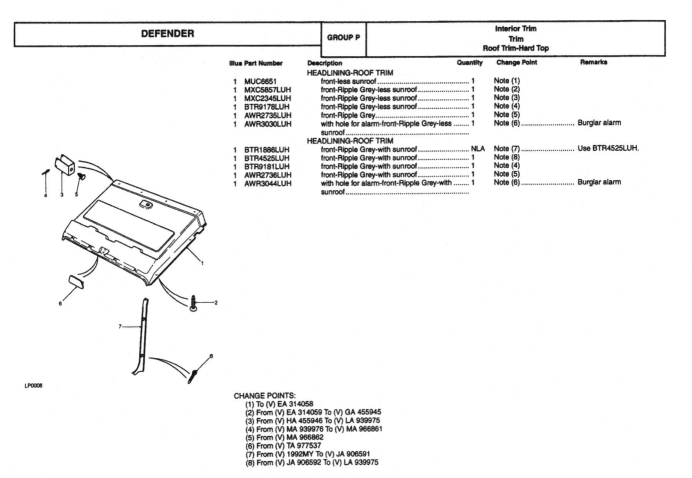

CHANGE POINTS:
(1) To (V) EA 314058
(2) From (V) EA 314059 To (V) GA 455945
(3) From (V) HA 455946 To (V) LA 939975
(4) From (V) MA 939976 To (V) MA 966861
(5) From (V) MA 966862
(6) From (V) TA 977537
(7) From (V) 1992MY To (V) JA 906591
(8) From (V) JA 906592 To (V) LA 939975

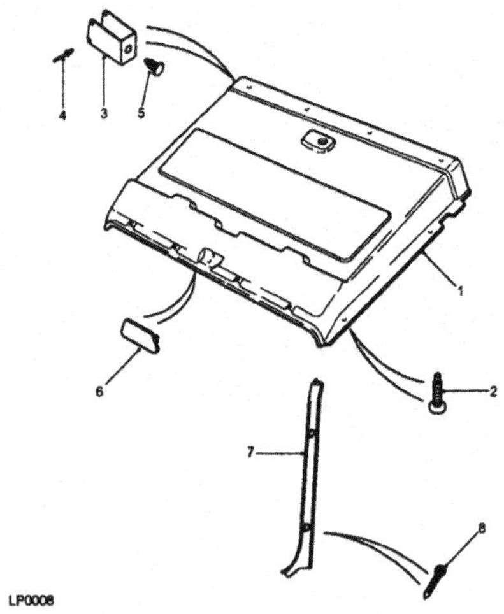

LP0008

Illus	Part Number	Description	Quantity	Change Point	Remarks
2	AFU1900	Fastener-fir tree-White.	8	Note (1)	
2	MWC9832LUH	Fastener-fir tree-Light Grey	8	Note (2)	
3	MXC5859	Bracket	2		90"
4	RU612373L	Rivet-3/16" x 0.575"lng	8		
5	MWC9832LUH	Fastener-fir tree-Light Grey	2		
6	BTR7006LUH	Panel-blanking-headlining-Ripple Grey	1	Note (3)	
7	MTC5212	Finisher-windscreen A post-RH	1		110"
7	MWC2314	Finisher-windscreen A post-LH	1		
8	AB606084	Screw-self tapping-No 6 x 1"	4		
	MUC3844	Finisher-B post-RH	1	Note (4)	Germany 110"
	MUC3845	Finisher-B post-LH	1		
	MUC3630	Cover-quarter trim casing-RH	1		
	MUC3631	Cover-quarter trim casing-LH	1		
8	AB608047L	Screw-self tapping-No 8 x 1/2	4		
9	AWR4710LUH	Headlining-roof trim-rear-Ripple Grey	1		
	MUC1237	Strip-self adhesive packing	A/R	Note (5)	Cut to the required length

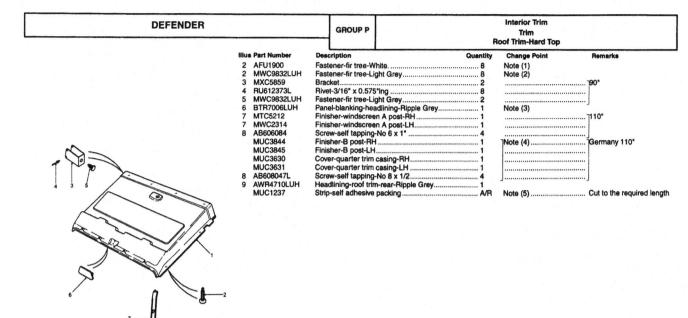

CHANGE POINTS:
(1) To (V) EA 314058
(2) From (V) EA 314059
(3) From (V) TA 976436 To (V) TA 978042
(4) To (V) EA 314291
(5) From (V) YA 198811

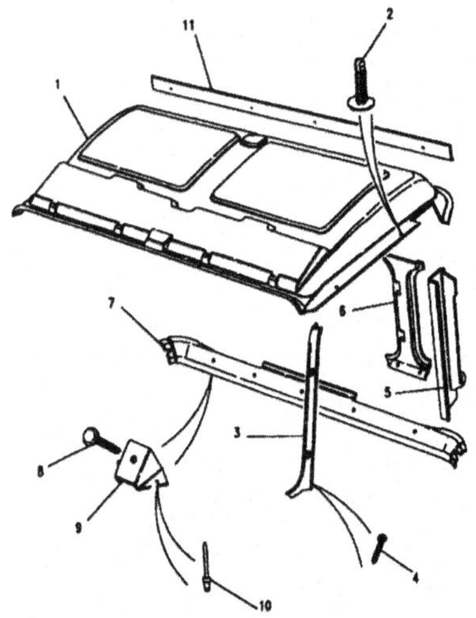

Illus	Part Number	Description	Quantity	Change Point	Remarks
1	MTC5206	Headlining-roof trim	1	Note (1)	Except burglar alarm
1	MUC6496	Headlining-roof trim-front	1	Note (2)	Except burglar alarm
1	MXC2348LUH	Headlining-roof trim-front-Ripple Grey	1	Note (3)	Except burglar alarm
1	BTR9179LUH	Headlining-roof trim-Ripple Grey	1	Note (4)	Except burglar alarm
1	AWR3844LUH	Headlining-roof trim-Ripple Grey	NLA	Note (5)	Use AWR3031LUH. Except burglar alarm
1	AWR3031LUH	Headlining-roof trim-with hole for alarm-Ripple Grey	1	Note (6)	Burglar alarm
2	AFU1900	Fastener-fir tree-White.	4	Note (7)	
2	MWC9832LUH	Fastener-fir tree-Light Grey	4	Note (3)	
3	MTC5212	Finisher-windscreen A post-RH	1		
3	MWC2314	Finisher-windscreen A post-LH	1		
4	AB606084	Screw-self tapping-No 6 x 1"	4		
		FINISHER-B POST			
5	MUC6498	RH	1	Note (7)	
5	MUC6499	LH	1		
5	MWC5712LUH	RH-Ripple Grey	1	Note (8)	
5	MWC5713LUH	LH-Ripple Grey	1		
5	AWR4706LUH	RH-Ripple Grey	1	Note (9)	
5	AWR4707LUH	LH-Ripple Grey	1		

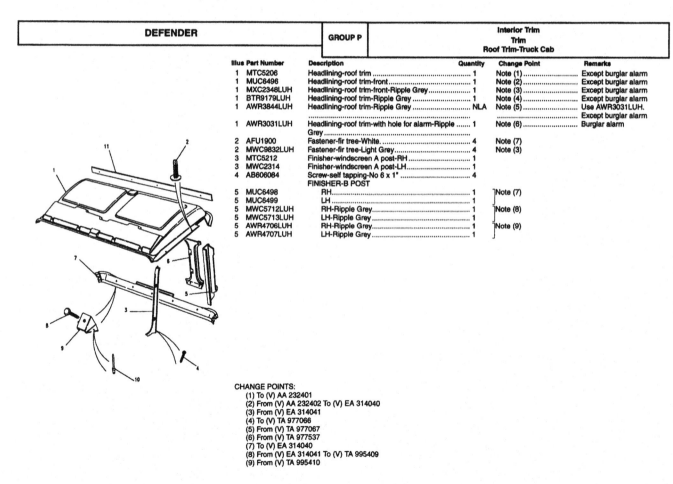

CHANGE POINTS:
(1) To (V) AA 232401
(2) From (V) AA 232402 To (V) EA 314040
(3) From (V) EA 314041
(4) To (V) TA 977066
(5) From (V) TA 977067
(6) From (V) TA 977537
(7) To (V) EA 314040
(8) From (V) EA 314041 To (V) TA 995409
(9) From (V) TA 995410

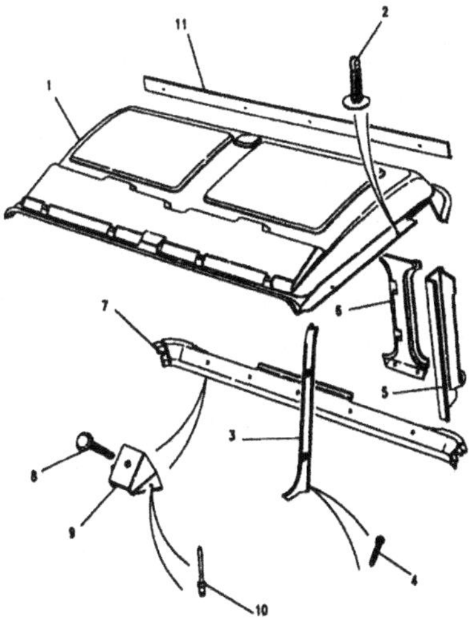

Illus	Part Number	Description	Quantity	Change Point	Remarks
		FINISHER-PILLAR-CAB			
6	MUC6652	rear-RH	1	Note (1)	
6	MUC6653	rear-LH	1		
6	MWC5710LUH	rear-RH-Ripple Grey	1	Note (2)	
6	MWC5711LUH	rear-LH-Ripple Grey	1		
6	AWR4704LUH	rear-RH-Ripple Grey	1	Note (3)	
6	AWR4705LUH	rear-LH-Ripple Grey	1		
7	MUC6497	Panel-lower rear trim	1	Note (1)	
7	MWC5708LUH	Panel-lower rear trim-Ripple Grey	1	Note (2)	
7	AWR4708LUH	Panel-lower rear trim-Ripple Grey	1	Note (3)	
8	AFU1900	Fastener-fir tree-White.	7	Note (1)	
8	MWC9832LUH	Fastener-fir tree-Light Grey	7	Note (4)	
9	MTC5486	Bracket	7		
10	RA608236L	Rivet	14		
11	MWC9604	Retainer-headlining	1	Note (5)	
4	AB608054L	Screw-self tapping-No8 x 5/8	4		
1	MUC6496	Headlining-roof trim-front	1	Note (6)	130"
1	MXC2348LUH	Headlining-roof trim-front-Ripple Grey	1	Note (7)	
1	RRC2409	Headlining-roof trim-centre	1	Note (8)	
1	RRC2476	Headlining-roof trim-rear	1		
	RRC2595	Finisher-cab back-RH	1		
	RRC2596	Finisher-cab back-LH	1		
	RRC2626	Finisher-cantrail rear-RH	1		
	RRC2629	Finisher-cantrail rear-LH	1		

CHANGE POINTS:
(1) To (V) EA 314040
(2) From (V) EA 314041 To (V) TA 995409
(3) From (V) TA 995410
(4) From (V) EA 314041
(5) From (V) EA 314041 To (V) KA 930143
(6) To (V) DA 314368
(7) From (V) EA 314369 To (V) GA
(8) To (V) GA

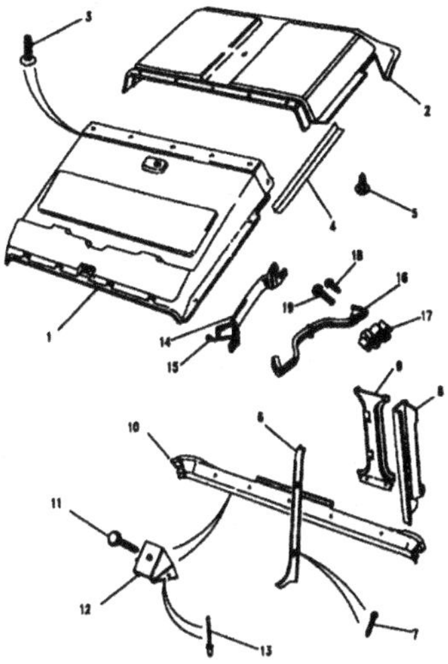

Illus	Part Number	Description	Quantity	Change Point	Remarks
		HEADLINING-ROOF TRIM			
1	RRC7587LUH	front-Ripple Grey	1	Note (1)	
1	BTR9183LUH	front-Ripple Grey	1	Note (2)	
1	AWR2735LUH	front-Ripple Grey	1	Note (3)	
		HEADLINING-ROOF TRIM			
2	RRC7190LUH	rear-Ripple Grey	1	Note (1)	
2	AWR1049LUH	rear-Ripple Grey	1	Note (4)	
2	AWR3953LUH	rear-Ripple Grey	1	Note (5)	
3	MWC9832LUH	Fastener-fir tree-Light Grey	17		
4	RRC7198LUH	Side angle roof trim-Ripple Grey	2	Note (6)	
4	AWR3942LUH	Side angle roof trim-Ripple Grey	2	Note (7)	
5	AB606051L	Screw-self tapping-No 6 x 5/8	2		
6	MTC5212	Finisher-windscreen A post-RH	1		
6	MWC2314	Finisher-windscreen A post-LH	1		
7	AB606084	Screw-self tapping-No 6 x 1"	4		
		FINISHER-B POST			
8	MWC5712LUH	RH-Ripple Grey	1	Note (8)	
8	MWC5713LUH	LH-Ripple Grey	1		
8	AWR4706LUH	RH-Ripple Grey	1	Note (9)	
8	AWR4707LUH	LH-Ripple Grey	1		
		FINISHER-PILLAR-CAB			
9	MWC5710LUH	rear-RH-Ripple Grey	1	Note (8)	
9	MWC5711LUH	rear-LH-Ripple Grey	1		
9	AWR4704LUH	rear-RH-Ripple Grey	1	Note (9)	
9	AWR4705LUH	rear-LH-Ripple Grey	1		
10	MWC5708LUH	Panel-lower rear trim-Ripple Grey	1	Note (8)	
10	AWR4708LUH	Panel-lower rear trim-Ripple Grey	1	Note (9)	
11	AFU1900	Fastener-fir tree-White.	7		

CHANGE POINTS:
(1) To (V) MA 943975
(2) From (V) MA 943976 To (V) MA 966978
(3) From (V) MA 966979
(4) From (V) MA 943976 To (V) TA 973531
(5) From (V) TA 973532
(6) To (V) TA 970132
(7) From (V) TA 970133
(8) To (V) TA 995409
(9) From (V) TA 995410

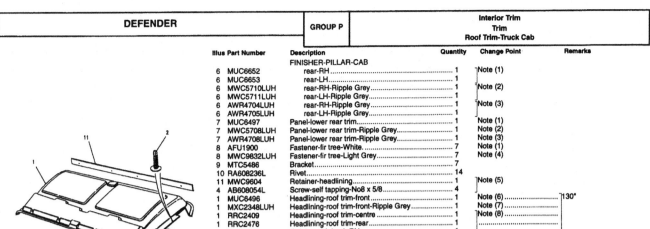

Illus	Part Number	Description	Quantity	Change Point	Remarks
12	MTC5486	Bracket	7		
13	RA608236L	Rivet	14		
14	YGA2682L	Handle-grab	4	Note (1)	
15	AB608061L	Screw-self tapping-No 8 x 3/4	16		
14	YGA2682L	Handle-grab	2	Note (2)	
15	AB608061L	Screw-self tapping-No 8 x 3/4	8		
16	JPC5641LUN	Handle assembly-roof trim grab-Ash	2	Note (3)	
17	PAM4356L	Spacer	4		
18	AB608107	Screw-self tapping-No 8 x 1 1/4	4		
19	SE105351L	Screw-pan	4		
	MUC1237	Strip-self adhesive packing	A/R	Note (4)	Cut to the required length

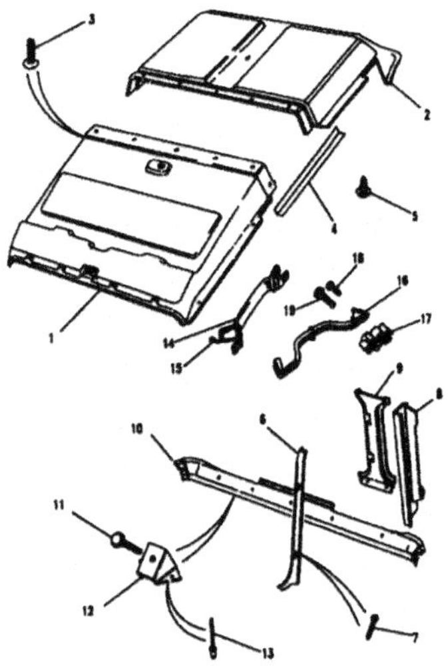

CHANGE POINTS:
(1) To (V) HA 904417
(2) From (V) HA 904418 To (V) JA 917889
(3) From (V) JA 917890
(4) From (V) YA 198811

Illus	Part Number	Description	Quantity	Change Point	Remarks
		PANEL TRIM-WINDSCREEN			
1	AWR1547LNF	RH-Ash Grey	1		
2	AWR1545LNF	LH-Ash Grey	1		
3	AWR1546LNF	centre-Ash Grey	1		

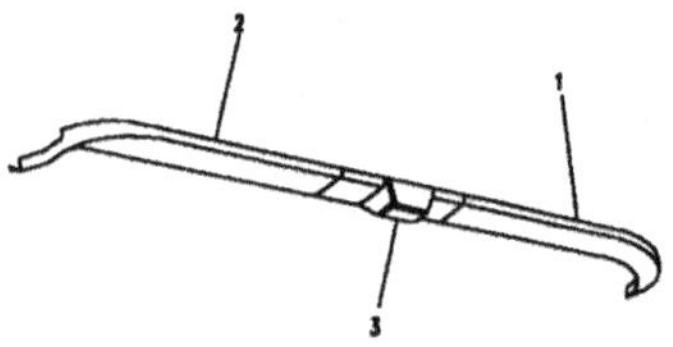

Illus	Part Number	Description	Quantity	Change Point	Remarks
		MAT-FRONT FLOOR DROP IN			
1	MUC2380	RH-RHD	1	Note (1)	4 Cylinder
1	MUC2379	LH-RHD	1		
1	MUC2382	RH-LHD	1		
1	MUC2381	LH-LHD	1		
1	MUC4150	RH-RHD	1		V8
1	MUC4149	LH-RHD	1		
1	MUC4152	RH-LHD	1		
1	MUC4153	LH-LHD	1		

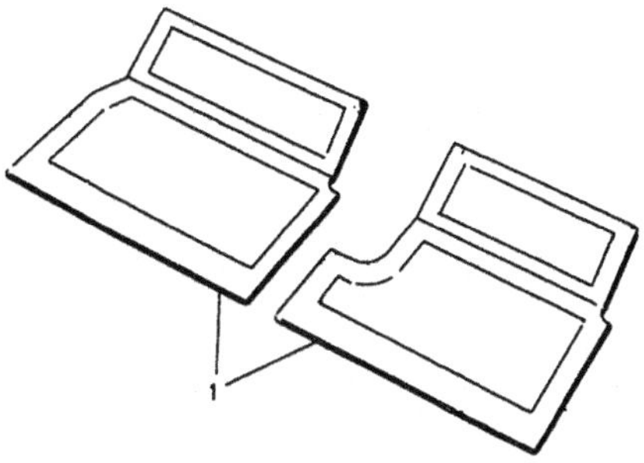

CHANGE POINTS:
(1) To (V) HA 467836

DEFENDER

GROUP R

Seats
Seating
Support & Slides-Basic Vinyl

Illus	Part Number	Description	Quantity	Change Point	Remarks
1	349996	Frame assembly-manual front seat	2	Note (1)	
2	MRC9492	Slide-front seat right hand side-RH-control	1	Note (2)	
3	MRC9481	Slide-front seat left hand side-RH-basic	2		
3	MRC9493	Slide-front seat left hand side-LH-basic	1		
2	MXC3258	Slide-front seat right hand side-RH-control	2	Note (3)	
3	MXC3259	Slide-front seat left hand side-LH-basic	2		
4	NT108041L	Nut-frame to slide-hexagonal head	8		
5	WF108001L	Washer-interior tooth-starlock-M8	8		
5	4075L	Washer-fixing seat frame assy-plain-M8	8		
6	SF106201L	Screw-seat slide to floor-M6 x 20-counter sunk-recessed	16		
7	MTC7631	Nut plate	8		
8	RU608253L	Rivet-pop-aluminium	16		
6	SA106201	Screw-slotted head-M6 x 20-counter sunk	8	Note (4)	
12	MRC5525	Washer-plain-standard	8	Note (4)	
13	WL106001L	Washer-sprung-M6	8	Note (4)	
9	MTC1714	Support-seat-RH-centre	1	Note (1)	
10	MTC1715	Support-seat-LH-centre	1	Note (1)	
11	FS106201L	Screw-centre support to floor-flanged head-M6 x 20	4		
12	MRC5525	Washer-plain-fixing seat support -standard	4		
13	WL106001L	Washer-sprung-M6	4		
14	NH106041L	Nut-centre support to floor-hexagonal-nyloc-M6	4		

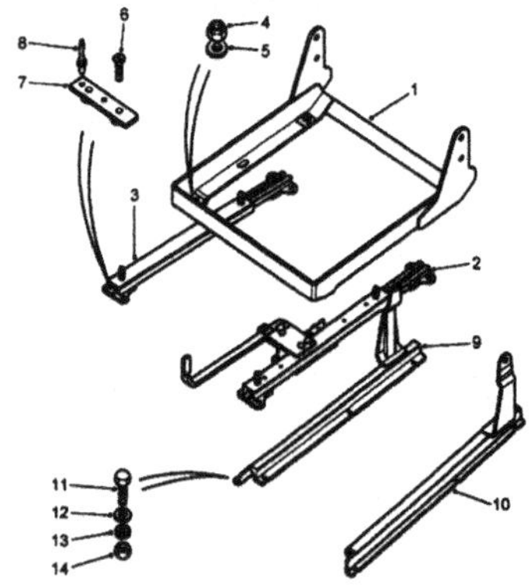

AHRXCA1A

CHANGE POINTS:
(1) To (V) TA 999221
(2) To (V) FA 410573
(3) From (V) FA 410574 To (V) TA 999221
(4) From (V) FA 410574 To (V) MA 962814

DEFENDER

GROUP R

Seats
Seating
Front-Basic Vinyl

Illus	Part Number	Description	Quantity	Change Point	Remarks
		SQUAB-ASSEMBLY			
1	MUC1520	FRONT SEAT-VINYL-BLACK	2	Note (1)	
1	MWC5599LCS	FRONT SEAT-VINYL-SLATE GREY	2	Note (2)	90°
1	MWC5599LCS	FRONT SEAT-VINYL-SLATE GREY	2	Note (3)	110°
2	337873	• Foam-squab-driver & passenger side seats	2		
3	RTC3764	• Clip	16		
		SQUAB-ASSEMBLY			
1	MUC1488	CENTRE-VINYL-BLACK	1	Note (1)	
1	MWC5607LCS	CENTRE-VINYL-SLATE GREY	1	Note (4)	90°
1	MWC5607LCS	CENTRE-VINYL-SLATE GREY	1	Note (3)	110°
2	337880	• Foam-squab-centre	1		
3	RTC3764	• Clip	16		
4	331709	Bolt-shouldered	8		
5	WC108051L	Washer-drivers & passenger squab-M8	8		
6	345213	Washer-rubber-drivers & passenger squab	4		
7	349931	Washer-plastic	4		90°
7	349931	Washer-plastic	2		110°
8	RTC614	Pin-centre squab	2	Note (4)	
9	320699	CUSHION-ASSEMBLY-FRONT SEAT-VINYL-BLACK	2	Note (1)	
9	MWC5573LCS	CUSHION-ASSEMBLY-FRONT SEAT-VINYL-SLATE GREY	2	Note (2)	
10	337899	• Foam cushion-driver & passenger side seats	2		
11	349943	• Capping corner-protective-front seats	12		Part of 320699.
11	349943	• Capping corner-protective-front seats	8		Part of MWC5573LCS.
9	320726	CUSHION-ASSEMBLY-CENTRE-VINYL-BLACK	1	Note (1)	
9	MWC5613LCS	CUSHION-ASSEMBLY-CENTRE-VINYL-SLATE GREY	1	Note (2)	
10	337859	• Foam cushion-centre seat	1		
11	349943	• Capping corner-protective-front seats	12		Part of 320726.
11	349943	• Capping corner-protective-front seats	8		Part of MWC5613LCS.
12	331974	Strap-centre cushion-front seats	1		
13	RTC3755	Rivet	1		
14	348430	Stud	1		
15	SE105251L	Screw-pan	1		
16	WL105001L	Washer-retaining-M5	1		
17	NH105041L	Nut-hexagonal-M5	1		

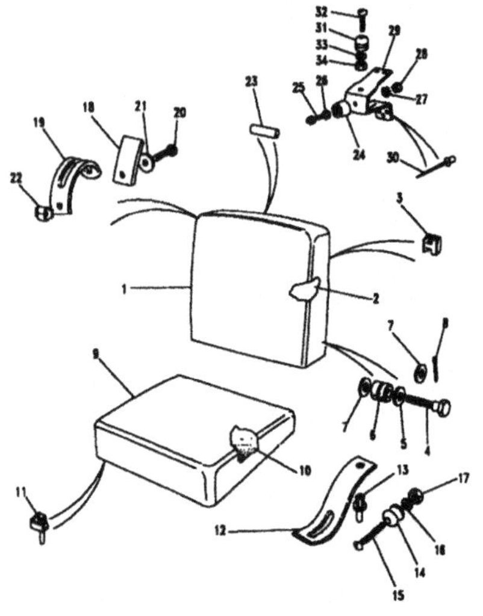

CHANGE POINTS:
(1) To (V) EA 314058
(2) From (V) EA 314059
(3) To (V) TA 999221
(4) To (V) HA 900379

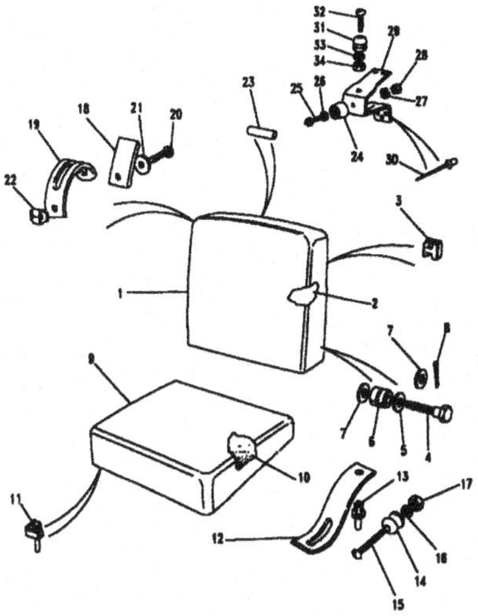

Illus	Part Number	Description	Quantity	Change Point	Remarks
18	339986	Packing rubber-drivers & passenger squab	4	Note (1)	Station Wagon 90"
20	AB610081	Screw-drivers & passenger squab-self tapping	4	Note (1)	Station Wagon 90"
18	339986	Packing rubber-drivers & passenger squab	4		Station Wagon 110"
21	WJ105001L	Washer-drivers & passenger squab-plain-M5-oversize	4		Station Wagon 90"
22	78237	Nut-spiralok-drivers & passenger squab	4	Note (1)	Station Wagon 90"
20	AB610081	Screw-drivers & passenger squab-self tapping	4		Station Wagon 110"
22	78237	Nut-spiralok-drivers & passenger squab	4		Station Wagon 110"
21	WJ105001L	Washer-drivers & passenger squab-plain-M5-oversize	4		Station Wagon 110"
19	331273	Strap-retaining-centre squab	2	Note (1)	Except Station Wagon
20	AB610061L	Screw-centre squab-self tapping-No10 x 3/4	2	Note (1)	Except Station Wagon
21	WJ105001L	Washer-centre squab-plain-M5-oversize	2	Note (1)	Except Station Wagon
22	78237	Nut-spiralok-centre squab	2	Note (1)	Except Station Wagon
23	346410	Tube-centre squab	3	Note (1)	Except Station Wagon
24	304125	Buffer rubber-seat front-centre squab	2	Note (1)	Except Station Wagon
25	SE105251L	Screw-pan-centre squab	2	Note (1)	Except Station Wagon
26	WC702101L	Washer-plain-centre squab	2	Note (1)	Except Station Wagon
27	WE702101L	Washer-starlock-centre squab	2	Note (1)	Except Station Wagon
28	NH105041L	Nut-hexagonal-centre squab-M5	2	Note (1)	Except Station Wagon
29	347553	Bracket-front seat support	6	Note (1)	
30	RU612373L	Rivet-3/16" x 0.575"lng	24	Note (1)	
31	348430	Stud	2		
32	SE105251L	Screw-pan	2		
33	WL105001L	Washer-retaining-M5	2		
34	NH105041L	Nut-hexagonal-M5	2		
18	347869	Packing rubber-centre seat	1		Station Wagon 110"
19	332355	Strap-retaining	1		Station Wagon 110"
20	AB610061L	Screw-centre seat-self tapping-No10 x 3/4	1		Station Wagon 110"
21	WJ105001L	Washer-centre squab-plain-M5-oversize	2		Station Wagon 110"
22	78237	Nut-spiralok-centre squab	2		Station Wagon 110"
20	AB606041L	Screw-strap to grab rail-self tapping-No 6 x 1/2	1		Station Wagon 110"
21	AFU1247	Washer-strap to grab rail	1		Station Wagon 110"

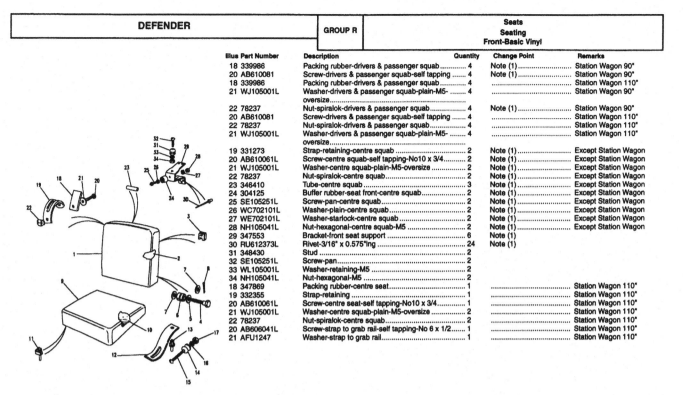

CHANGE POINTS:
(1) To (V) EA 314058

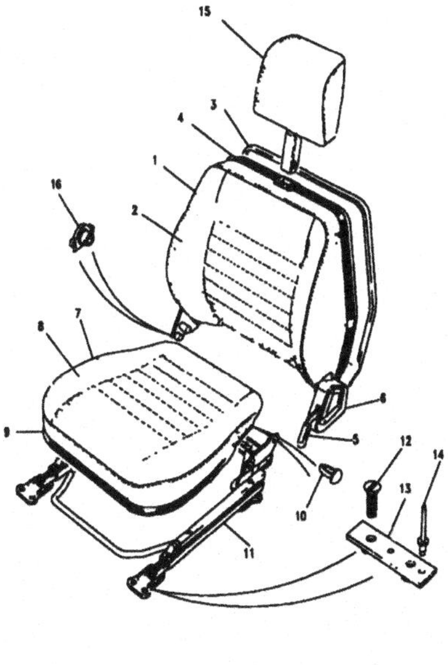

Illus	Part Number	Description	Quantity	Change Point	Remarks
		SEAT ASSEMBLY FRONT			
	MUC8428RD	RH-cloth-Brushwood-driver's seat	1	Note (1)	
	MUC8429RD	LH-cloth-Brushwood-driver's seat	1		
	MWC3306	RH-Vinyl-Black-driver's seat	1	Note (2)	
	MWC3307	LH-Vinyl-Black-driver's seat	1		
		SQUAB-ASSEMBLY			
1	MUC8448RD	cloth-Brushwood	1		
1	MUC8449RD	cloth-Brushwood	1		
1	MWC3302	Vinyl-Black	1		
1	MWC3303	Vinyl-Black	1		
2	MTC1933RD	Overlay-front seat squab-cloth	2		
2	MTC1923	Overlay-front seat squab-Vinyl			
3	STC354AV	Panel-front seat squab face-Brushwood	2		
3	STC354PB	Panel-front seat squab face-Black	2		
4	MTC9956	Trim panel	2		
5	MUC8754	Knob-front seat tip lever	2		
6	MWC7636	Plate-front seat recline mechanism cover-RH	1		
6	MWC7635	Plate-front seat recline mechanism cover-LH	1		
7	MUC8780RD	Cushion-manual front seat-cloth	2		
7	MWC4535	Cushion-manual front seat-Vinyl	2		
8	MTC1932RD	Cover assembly-front seat cushion-cloth	2		
8	MWC4534	Cover assembly-front seat cushion-Vinyl	2		
9	MTC9967	Finisher-trim retention	2		
10	MTC9962	Finisher-trim retention	12		
11	MXC5778	Subframe & slide assembly-front seat-RH	1		
11	MXC5779	Subframe & slide assembly-front seat-LH	1		
12	SF106201L	Screw-M6 x 20-counter sunk-recessed	16		
13	MTC7631	Nut plate	8		
14	RU608253L	Rivet-pop-aluminium	16		
15	MWC1018RD	Headrestraint-fixed bolster front-cloth	2		
15	MWC1010	Headrestraint-fixed bolster front-Vinyl	2		
16	MXC5212	Location rear-seat cushion-front seat	2		

CHANGE POINTS:
(1) To (V) AA 277963 approx
(2) To (V) AA 276736

DEFENDER

GROUP R

Seats
Seating
Front-With Headrestraint-From (V) AA277964 To DA314040

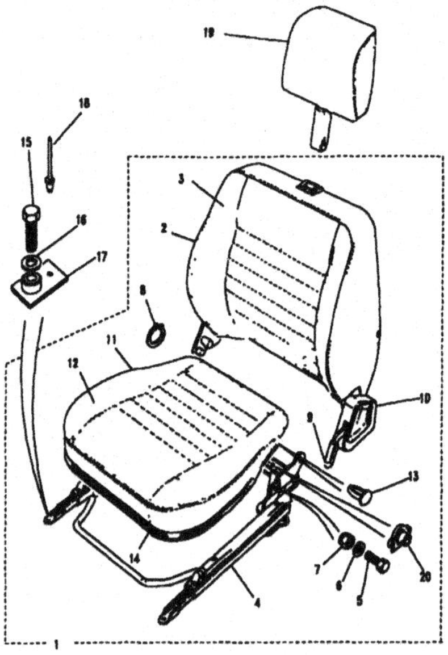

Illus	Part Number	Description	Quantity	Change Point	Remarks
		SEAT ASSEMBLY FRONT			
1	MUC8428RD	RH-cloth-Brushwood-driver's seat	1	Note (1)	RHD
1	MUC8430RD	LH-cloth-Brushwood-passenger's seat	1	Note (1)	RHD
1	MUC8429RD	LH-cloth-Brushwood-driver's seat	1	Note (1)	LHD
1	MUC8431RD	RH-cloth-Brushwood-passenger's seat	1	Note (1)	LHD
1	MWC3306	RH-Vinyl-Black-driver's seat	1	Note (2)	RHD
1	MWC3307	LH-Vinyl-Black-driver's seat	1	Note (2)	LHD
1	MWC3301	Vinyl-Black-passenger's seat	1		
		SQUAB-ASSEMBLY			
2	MUC8448RD	cloth-Brushwood	1		RHD
2	MUC8449RD	cloth-Brushwood	1		LHD
2	MWC3302	Vinyl-Black	1		RHD
2	MWC3303	Vinyl-Black	1		LHD
3	MUC8409RD	Cover assembly-front seat squab-cloth-Brushwood	1		
3	MUC8414	Cover assembly-front seat squab-Vinyl-Black	1		
		SUBFRAME & SLIDE ASSEMBLY			
4	MXC5778	front seat-RH	1		RHD
4	MXC5779	front seat-LH	1		LHD
4	MUC8439	LH-cloth	1		RHD
4	MUC8438	RH-cloth	1		LHD
5	SH108151	Screw-hexagonal head-M8 x 15	1		
6	WA108041	Washer-plain	2		
7	NY108041L	Nut-nyloc-M8	2		
8	CR120205	Circlip	1		
9	MUC8754	Knob-front seat tip lever	1		
10	MWC7636	Plate-front seat recline mechanism cover-RH	1		
10	MWC7635	Plate-front seat recline mechanism cover-LH	1		
11	MUC8780RD	Cushion-manual front seat-cloth	1		
11	MWC4535	Cushion-manual front seat-Vinyl	1		
12	MTC1932RD	Cover assembly-front seat cushion-cloth	1		
12	MWC4534	Cover assembly-front seat cushion-Vinyl	1		
13	MTC9962	Finisher-trim retention	4		
14	MTC9967	Finisher-trim retention	1		
15	FS108257L	Screw-flanged head-M8 x 25	4		
16	WA108051L	Washer-8mm	4		

CHANGE POINTS:
(1) From (V) AA 277964
(2) From (V) AA 276737

DEFENDER

GROUP R

Seats
Seating
Front-With Headrestraint-From (V) AA277964 To DA314040

Illus	Part Number	Description	Quantity	Change Point	Remarks
	4075L	Washer-plain-M8	4		
17	MUC7947	Nut-plate	4		
18	RU608313L	Rivet-aluminium-1/8" x 0.482"lng	1		
19	MWC1018RD	Headrestraint-fixed bolster front-cloth	1		
19	MWC1010	Headrestraint-fixed bolster front-Vinyl	1		
20	MXC5212	Location rear-seat cushion-front seat	2		

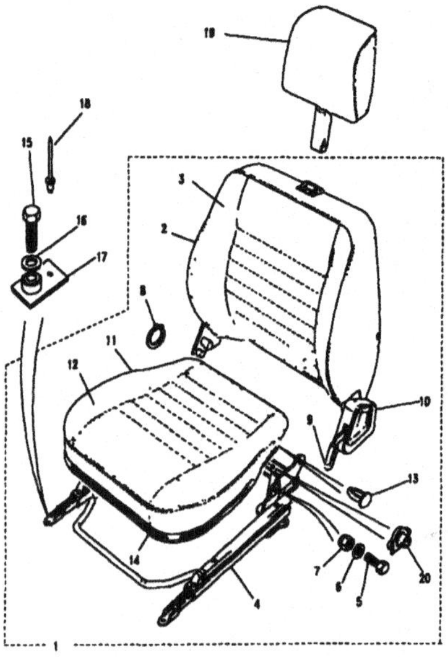

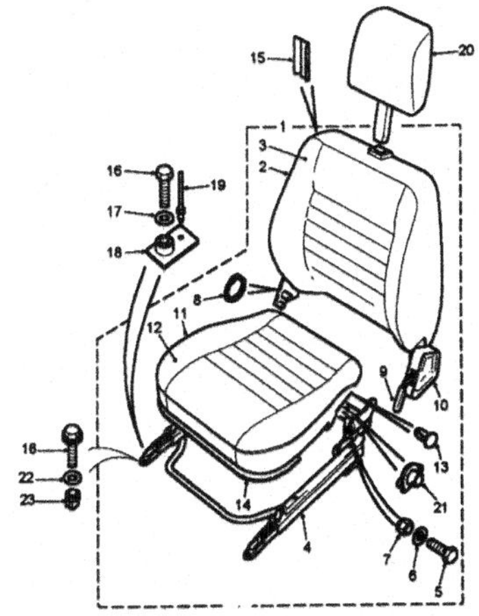

LR0025

Illus	Part Number	Description	Quantity	Change Point	Remarks
		SEAT ASSEMBLY FRONT			
1	MWC5630RCF	RH-cloth-Blue Grey-without pocket	1	Note (1)	
1	MWC5676RCF	LH-cloth-Blue Grey-without pocket	1		
1	MWC5667LCS	RH-Vinyl-Slate Grey-without pocket	1		
1	MWC5674LCS	LH-Vinyl-Slate Grey-without pocket	1		
1	MWC8944RCF	RH-cloth-Blue Grey-without pocket	1	Note (2)	
1	MWC8945RCF	LH-cloth-Blue Grey-without pocket	1		
1	MWC8946LCS	RH-Vinyl-Slate Grey-without pocket	1	Note (3)	
1	MWC8947LCS	LH-Vinyl-Slate Grey-without pocket	1		
1	MXC3254RUY	RH-cloth-Morland Grey-without pocket	1	Note (4)	
1	MXC3255RUY	LH-cloth-Morland Grey-without pocket	1		
1	MXC3256LCS	RH-Vinyl-Slate Grey-without pocket	1	Note (5)	
1	MXC3257LCS	LH-Vinyl-Slate Grey-without pocket	1		
1	AWR5688RFI	RH-cloth-Rayleigh-without pocket	1	Note (6); Note (7)	
1	AWR5687RFI	LH-cloth-Rayleigh-without pocket	1		
1	AWR5686RPI	RH-Vinyl-Twill-without pocket	1		
1	AWR5685RPI	LH-Vinyl-Twill-without pocket	1		
1	BTR1764RUY	RH-cloth-Morland Grey-with pocket	1	Note (8)	110"
1	BTR1765RUY	LH-cloth-Morland Grey-with pocket	1		
1	BTR1766LCS	RH-Vinyl-Slate Grey-with pocket	1		
1	BTR1767LCS	LH-Vinyl-Slate Grey-with pocket	1		
1	AWR5684RFI	RH-cloth-Rayleigh-with pocket	1	Note (9)	110"
1	AWR5683RFI	LH-cloth-Rayleigh-with pocket	1		
1	AWR5682RPI	RH-Vinyl-Twill-with pocket	1		
1	AWR5681RPI	LH-Vinyl-Twill-with pocket	1		

CHANGE POINTS:
(1) To (V) FA 358426
(2) From (V) FA 358427 To (V) HA 456060
(3) From (V) FA 358427 To (V) HA 455631
(4) From (V) HA 456061 To (V) TA 999221
(5) From (V) HA 455632 To (V) TA 999221
(6) From (V) VA 999222 To (V) VA 999999
(7) From (V) VA 000001 To (V) WA 138479
(8) To (V) TA 999221
(9) From (V) VA 999222 To (V) WA 138479

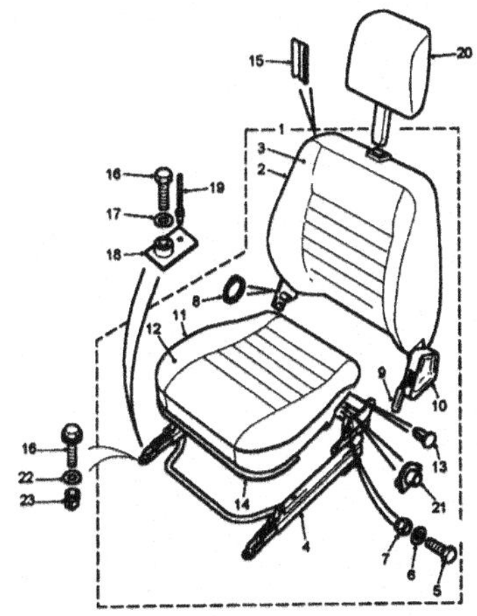

LR0025

Illus	Part Number	Description	Quantity	Change Point	Remarks
		SEAT ASSEMBLY FRONT			
1	HAD132800RFI	RH-cloth-Rayleigh-without pocket	1	Note (1)	Except 50 LE
1	HAD132810RFI	LH-cloth-Rayleigh-without pocket	1	Note (1)	
1	HAD132760RFI	RH-cloth-Rayleigh-without pocket	1	Note (1)	4000 cc L/R V8 Petrol EFi 50 LE
1	HAD132770RFI	LH-cloth-Rayleigh-without pocket	1	Note (1)	4000 cc L/R V8 Petrol EFi 50 LE
1	HAD132780RPI	RH-Vinyl-Twill-without pocket	1	Note (2)	
1	HAD132790RPI	LH-Vinyl-Twill-without pocket	1	Note (2)	
1	HAD132740RPI	RH-Vinyl-Twill-with pocket	1	Note (2)	
1	HAD132750RPI	LH-Vinyl-Twill-with pocket	1	Note (2)	
1	HAD132540LOY	RH-cloth-Dark Granite-without pocket	1	Note (3)	
1	HAD132550LOY	LH-cloth-Dark Granite-without pocket	1	Note (3)	
1	HAD132560LOY	RH-cloth-Dark Granite-with pocket	1	Note (3)	
1	HAD132570LOY	LH-cloth-Dark Granite-with pocket	1	Note (3)	
		SEAT ASSEMBLY FRONT			
1	HAD001340LOY	RH-cloth-Dark Granite-with pocket-heated	1	Note (4)	
1	HAD001350LOY	LH-cloth-Dark Granite-with pocket-heated	1	Note (4)	
1	HAD001300RPI	RH-Vinyl-Twill-with pocket-heated	1	Note (4)	
1	HAD001310RPI	LH-Vinyl-Twill-with pocket-heated	1	Note (4)	

CHANGE POINTS:
(1) From (V) WA 138480 To (V) WA 159806
(2) From (V) WA 138480
(3) From (V) XA 159807
(4) From (V) 2A 622424

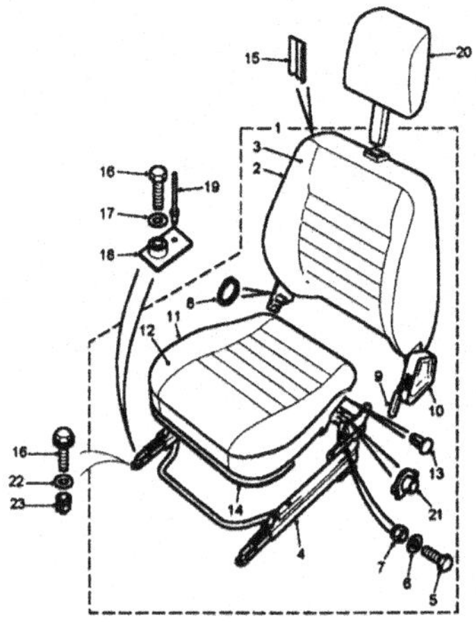

LR0025

Illus	Part Number	Description	Quantity	Change Point	Remarks
		SQUAB ASSEMBLY-SIDE			
2	MWC5677RCF	RH-cloth-Blue Grey-without pocket	1	Note (1)	
2	MWC5668LCS	RH-Vinyl-Slate Grey-without pocket	1	Note (1)	
2	MWC5679RCF	LH-cloth-Blue Grey-without pocket	1	Note (1)	
2	MWC5675LCS	LH-Vinyl-Slate Grey-without pocket	1	Note (1)	
2	MWC9842RCF	RH-cloth-Blue Grey-without pocket	1	Note (2)	
2	MWC9841RCF	LH-cloth-Blue Grey-without pocket	1	Note (2)	
2	MWC9842RUY	RH-cloth-Morland Grey-without pocket	1	Note (3)	
2	MWC9841RUY	LH-cloth-Morland Grey-without pocket	1	Note (3)	
2	AWR5900RFI	RH-cloth-Rayleigh-without pocket	1	Note (4)	
2	AWR5901RFI	LH-cloth-Rayleigh-without pocket	1	Note (4)	
2	AWR5902RPI	RH-Vinyl-Twill-without pocket	1	Note (4)	
2	AWR5903RPI	LH-Vinyl-Twill-without pocket	1	Note (4)	
2	MWC9844LCS	RH-Vinyl-Slate Grey-without pocket	1	Note (5)	
2	MWC9843LCS	LH-Vinyl-Slate Grey-without pocket	1	Note (5)	
2	AWR5704RFI	RH-cloth-Rayleigh-with pocket	1		
2	AWR5703RFI	LH-cloth-Rayleigh-with pocket	1		
2	AWR5704RFI	RH-cloth-Rayleigh-with pocket	1	Note (6)	Station Wagon 110"
2	AWR5703RFI	LH-cloth-Rayleigh-with pocket	1	Note (6)	Station Wagon 110"
2	MWC9842RUY	RH-cloth-Morland Grey-without pocket	1	Note (7)	110" except Station Wagon
2	MWC9841RUY	LH-cloth-Morland Grey-without pocket	1	Note (7)	
2	MWC9844LCS	RH-Vinyl-Slate Grey-without pocket	1	Note (7)	
2	MWC9843LCS	LH-Vinyl-Slate Grey-without pocket	1	Note (7)	
2	AWR5900RFI	RH-cloth-Rayleigh-without pocket	1	Note (6)	
2	AWR5901RFI	LH-cloth-Rayleigh-without pocket	1	Note (6)	
2	AWR5902RPI	RH-Vinyl-Twill-without pocket	1	Note (6)	
2	AWR5903RPI	LH-Vinyl-Twill-without pocket	1	Note (6)	

CHANGE POINTS:
(1) To (V) FA 358426
(2) From (V) FA 358427 To (V) HA 456060
(3) From (V) HA 456061 To (V) TA 999221
(4) From (V) VA 999222 To (V) WA 159806
(5) From (V) FA 358427 To (V) TA 999221
(6) From (V) VA 999222
(7) To (V) TA 999221

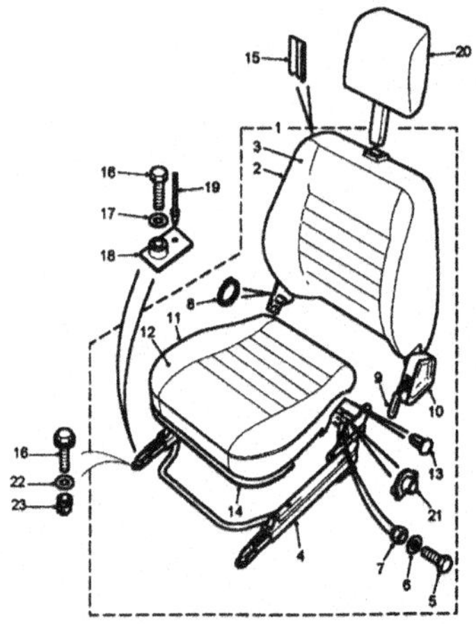

LR0025

Illus	Part Number	Description	Quantity	Change Point	Remarks
		SQUAB ASSEMBLY-SIDE			
2	BTR1760RUY	RH-cloth-Morland Grey-with pocket	1	Note (1)	Station Wagon 110"
2	BTR1761RUY	LH-cloth-Morland Grey-with pocket	1	Note (1)	Station Wagon 110"
2	BTR1762LCS	RH-Vinyl-Slate Grey-with pocket	1	Note (1)	Station Wagon 110"
2	BTR1763LCS	LH-Vinyl-Slate Grey-with pocket	1	Note (1)	Station Wagon 110"
2	AWR5698RPI	RH-Vinyl-Twill-with pocket	1	Note (2)	Station Wagon 110"
2	AWR5699RPI	LH-Vinyl-Twill-with pocket	1	Note (2)	Station Wagon 110"
2	HAJ101380LOY	RH-cloth-Dark Granite-with pocket	1	Note (3)	
2	HAJ101390LOY	LH-cloth-Dark Granite-with pocket	1	Note (3)	110" except South Africa
2	HAJ101400LOY	RH-cloth-Dark Granite-without pocket	1	Note (3)	
2	HAJ101410LOY	LH-cloth-Dark Granite-without pocket	1	Note (3)	BMW M52 110"
2	STC60736	RH-leather-Green	1	Note (3)	Heritage
2	STC60748	LH-leather-Green	1	Note (3)	Heritage
		SQUAB ASSEMBLY-SIDE			
2	HAJ000160LOY	RH-CLOTH-DARK GRANITE-WITH POCKET-HEATED	1	Note (4)	
2	HAJ000170LOY	LH-CLOTH-DARK GRANITE-WITH POCKET-HEATED	1	Note (4)	
2	HAJ000180RPI	RH-VINYL-TWILL-WITH POCKET-HEATED	1	Note (4)	
2	HAJ000190RPI	LH-VINYL-TWILL-WITH POCKET-HEATED	1	Note (4)	

CHANGE POINTS:
(1) To (V) TA 999221
(2) From (V) VA 999222
(3) From (V) XA 159807
(4) From (V) 2A 622424

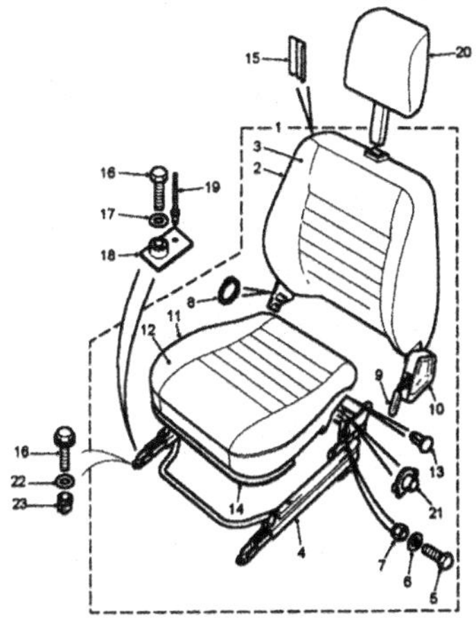

LR0025

Illus	Part Number	Description	Quantity	Change Point	Remarks
		COVER ASSEMBLY-FRONT SEAT SQUAB			
3	MWC5632RCF	cloth-Blue Grey-without pocket	2	Note (1)	
3	MWC8942RCF	cloth-Blue Grey-without pocket	2	Note (2)	
3	MWC8942RUY	cloth-Morland Grey-without pocket	2	Note (3)	
3	BTR1758RUY	cloth-Morland Grey-with pocket	2	Note (4)	110"
3	AWR5905RFI	cloth-Rayleigh-without pocket	2	Note (5)	
3	AWR5706RFI	cloth-Rayleigh-with pocket	2		V8 EFi
3	HBA106180LOY	cloth-Dark Granite-with pocket	2	Note (6)	Station Wagon 110"
3	HBA106190LOY	cloth-Dark Granite-without pocket	2	Note (6)	Station Wagon 110"
3	AWR5706RFI	cloth-Rayleigh-with pocket	2	Note (7)	110"
		COVER ASSEMBLY-FRONT SEAT SQUAB			
3	MWC5669LCS	Vinyl-Slate Grey-without pocket	2	Note (1)	
3	MWC8943LCS	Vinyl-Slate Grey-without pocket	2	Note (8)	
3	BTR1759LCS	Vinyl-Slate Grey-with pocket	2	Note (4)	110"
3	AWR5904RPI	Vinyl-Twill-without pocket	2	Note (5)	
3	BTR1762RPI	Vinyl-Twill-with pocket-RH	1		90"
3	BTR1763RPI	Vinyl-Twill-with pocket-LH	1		90"
3	AWR5702RPI	Vinyl-Twill-with pocket	2	Note (7)	110"
3	HBA000660PMA	Cover assembly-front seat squab	2	Note (9)	Tomb Raider

CHANGE POINTS:
(1) To (V) FA 358426
(2) From (V) FA 358427 To (V) HA 456060
(3) From (V) HA 456061 To (V) TA 999221
(4) To (V) TA 999221
(5) From (V) VA 999222 To (V) WA 159806
(6) From (V) XA 159807
(7) From (V) VA 999222
(8) From (V) FA 358427 To (V) TA 999221
(9) From (V) 1A 612404

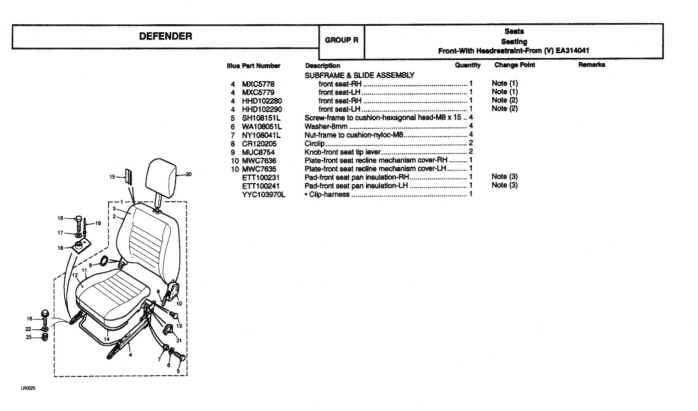

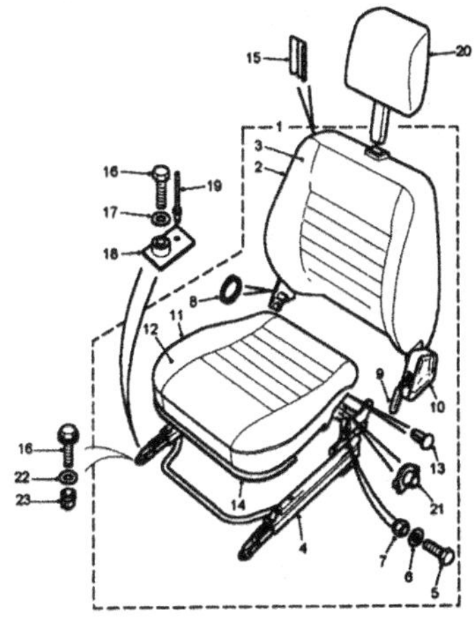

LR0025

Illus	Part Number	Description	Quantity	Change Point	Remarks
		SUBFRAME & SLIDE ASSEMBLY			
4	MXC5778	front seat-RH	1	Note (1)	
4	MXC5779	front seat-LH	1	Note (1)	
4	HHD102280	front seat-RH	1	Note (2)	
4	HHD102290	front seat-LH	1	Note (2)	
5	SH108151L	Screw-frame to cushion-hexagonal head-M8 x 15	4		
6	WA108051L	Washer-8mm	4		
7	NY108041L	Nut-frame to cushion-nyloc-M8	4		
8	CR120205	Circlip	2		
9	MUC8754	Knob-front seat tip lever	2		
10	MWC7636	Plate-front seat recline mechanism cover-RH	1		
10	MWC7635	Plate-front seat recline mechanism cover-LH	1		
	ETT100231	Pad-front seat pan insulation-RH	1	Note (3)	
	ETT100241	Pad-front seat pan insulation-LH	1	Note (3)	
	YYC103970L	• Clip-harness	1		

CHANGE POINTS:
(1) To (V) WA 158374
(2) From (V) WA 158375
(3) From (V) 2A 622424

Illus	Part Number	Description	Quantity	Change Point	Remarks
		CUSHION ASSEMBLY-FRONT SEAT			
11	MWC5670LCS	Vinyl-Slate Grey	2	Note (2)	
11	AWR5700RPI	Vinyl-Twill	2	Note (4)	
11	MWC5648RCF	cloth-Blue Grey	2	Note (5)	
11	MWC5648RUY	cloth-Morland Grey	2	Note (3)	
11	AWR5705RFI	cloth-Rayleigh	2	Note (6)	
11	HAG100970LOY	cloth-Dark Granite	2	Note (1)	
11	STC60734	leather-Green	2	Note (1)	Heritage
11	HAG000130LOY	cloth-Dark Granite-heated	1	Note (7)	
11	HAG000140RPI	Vinyl-Twill-heated	1	Note (7)	
		COVER ASSEMBLY-FRONT SEAT CUSHION			
12	MWC5649RCF	cloth-Blue Grey	2	Note (5)	
12	MWC5649RUY	cloth-Morland Grey	2	Note (3)	
12	AWR5707RFI	cloth-Rayleigh	2	Note (6)	
12	HCA106010LOY	cloth-Dark Granite	2	Note (1)	
12	MWC5671LCS	Vinyl-Slate Grey	2	Note (2)	
12	AWR5701RPI	Vinyl-Twill	2	Note (4)	
12	HCA000660PMA	Cover assembly-front seat cushion	2	Note (8)	Tomb Raider

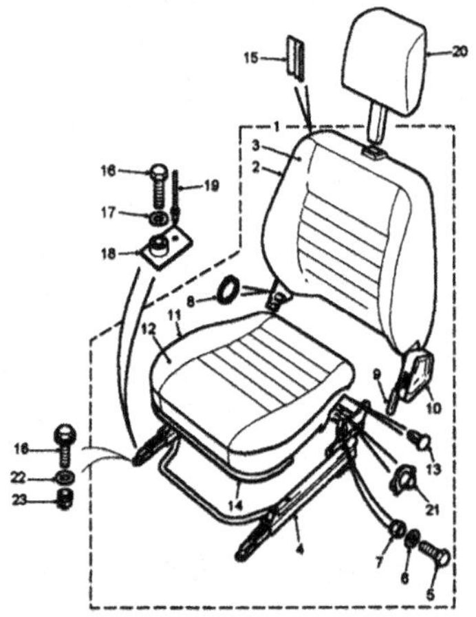

LR0025

CHANGE POINTS:
(1) From (V) XA 159807
(2) To (V) TA 999221
(3) From (V) HA 456061 To (V) TA 999221
(4) From (V) VA 999222
(5) To (V) HA 456060
(6) From (V) VA 999222 To (V) WA 159806
(7) From (V) 2A 622424
(8) From (V) 1A 612404

Illus	Part Number	Description	Quantity	Change Point	Remarks
13	MTC9962	Finisher-trim retention	8		
14	MTC9967	Finisher-trim retention	2		
15	MWC6106PCB	Strip-rubbing-Black	4		
15	AWR5899PCB	Strip-rubbing-Black	2		V8 EFi 50 LE
		WHEN CENTRE SEATS NOT FITTED			
16	FS108257L	Screw-flanged head-M8 x 25	8	Note (1)	2 front seats
16	FS108405	Screw-seat slide to floor-flanged head-M8 x 40	8	Note (2)	2 front seats
17	WA108051L	Washer-8mm	8		2 front seats
24	4075L	Washer-plain-M8	8		2 front seats
18	MUC7947	Nut-plate	8	Note (1)	2 front seats
19	RU608313L	Rivet-aluminium-1/8" x 0.482"lng	8		2 front seats
		WHEN CENTRE SEAT IS FITTED			
16	FS108257L	Screw-flanged head-M8 x 25	8	Note (1)	3 front seats
16	FS108405	Screw-seat slide to floor-flanged head-M8 x 40	8	Note (2)	3 front seats
17	WA108051L	Washer-8mm	10		3 front seats
24	4075L	Washer-plain-M8	48		3 front seats
18	MUC7947	Nut-plate	6	Note (1)	3 front seats
19	RU608313L	Rivet-aluminium-1/8" x 0.482"lng	6		3 front seats
25	FN108047L	Nut-flange-flanged head-M8	2		
26	MWC4536	Bracket-front seat slide frame	2		RHD
		HEADRESTRAINT ASSEMBLY			
20	MWC5626RUY	cloth-Morland Grey	2	Note (3)	
20	MWC5628LCS	Vinyl-Slate Grey	2		
20	AWR5712RFI	cloth-Rayleigh	2	Note (4)	
20	AWR5708RPI	Vinyl-Twill	2		
20	HAH103510LOY	cloth-Dark Granite	2	Note (2)	
20	STC60738	leather-Green	2		Heritage
20	HAH000330PMA	Black	2	Note (6)	Tomb Raider
21	MXC5212	Location rear-seat cushion-front seat	2		
22	AYF10001L	Washer-plain-M8	2		
23	AWR4731	Nutsert-blind-for seat runner to seat base bolt-M8	8	Note (5)	

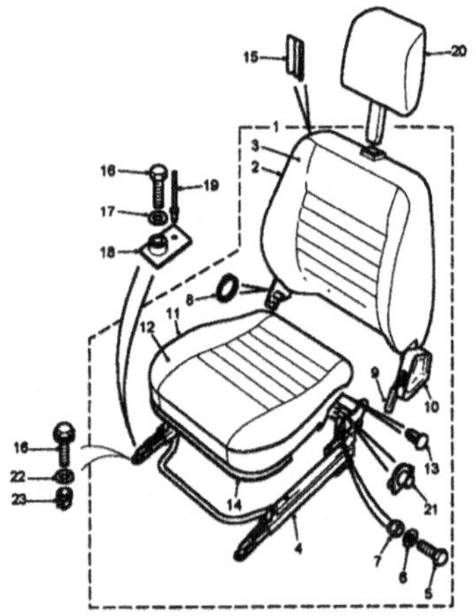

LR0025

CHANGE POINTS:
(1) To (V) WA 159806
(2) From (V) XA 159807
(3) To (V) TA 999221
(4) From (V) VA 999222 To (V) WA 159806
(5) From (V) TA 976927
(6) From (V) 1A 612404

DEFENDER	GROUP R	Seats Seating Centre Front-To (V) AA277963

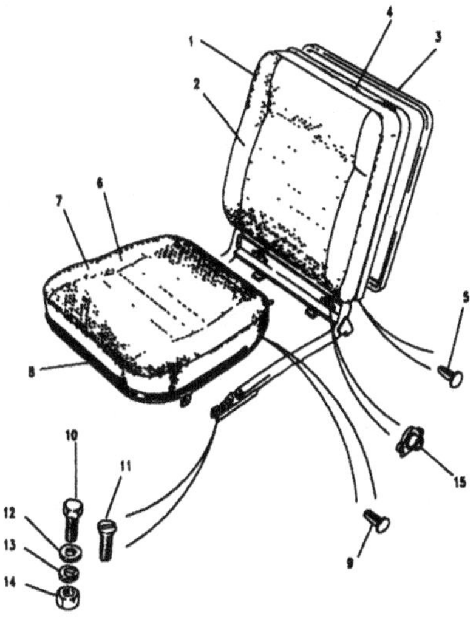

Illus	Part Number	Description	Quantity	Change Point	Remarks
	MUC8432RD	Seat assembly-centre-cloth-Brushwood	1		
	MWC4548	Seat assembly-centre-Vinyl-Black	1		
1	MUC8450RD	Squab assembly-front-centre-seat-cloth	1		
1	MUC8447	Squab assembly-front-centre-seat-Vinyl	1		
2	MTC1950RD	Overlay-front seat squab centre-cloth	1		
2	MTC1944	Overlay-front seat squab centre-Vinyl	1		
3	STC355AV	Panel-back-seat-front-squab-Brushwood	1		
3	STC355PB	Panel-back-seat-front-squab-Black	1		
4	MTC9958	Finisher-seat plinth	1		
5	MTC9962	Finisher-trim retention	1		
6	MUC8779RD	Cushion assembly-front seat-cloth	1		
6	MWC4549	Cushion assembly-front seat-Vinyl	1		
7	MTC1949RD	Overlay-seat-front-cushion-centre-cloth	1		
7	MTC1943	Overlay-seat-front-cushion-centre-Vinyl	1		
8	MTC9959	Finisher-trim retention	1		
9	MTC9962	Finisher-trim retention	4		
10	BH106071	Bolt	2		
11	SF106201L	Screw-M6 x 20-counter sunk-recessed	2		
12	MRC5525	Washer-plain-standard	4		
13	WL106001L	Washer-sprung-M6	4		
14	NH106041L	Nut-hexagonal-nyloc-M6	4		
15	MXC5212	Location rear-seat cushion-front seat	2		

DEFENDER	GROUP R	Seats Seating Centre Front-From (V) AA277964 To (V) DA314040

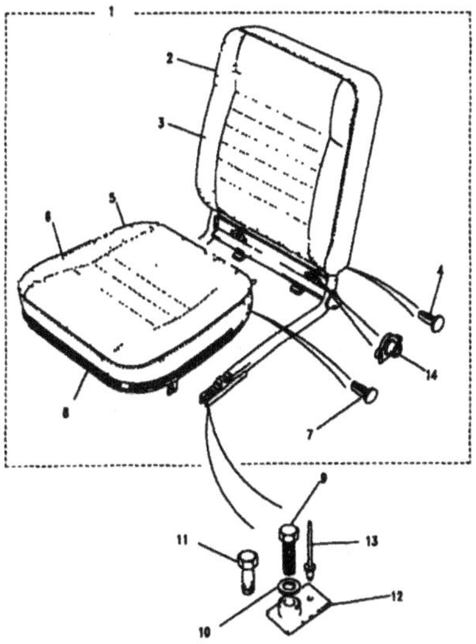

Illus	Part Number	Description	Quantity	Change Point	Remarks
1	MUC8432RD	Seat assembly-centre-cloth-Brushwood	1		
1	MWC4548	Seat assembly-centre-Vinyl-Black	1		
2	MUC8450RD	Squab assembly-front-centre-seat-cloth	1		
2	MUC8447	Squab assembly-front-centre-seat-Vinyl	1		
3	MUC8411RD	Cover assembly-front seat squab-cloth	1		
3	MUC8412	Cover assembly-front seat squab-Vinyl	1		
4	MTC9962	Finisher-trim retention	4		
5	MUC8779RD	Cushion assembly-front seat-cloth	1		
5	MWC4549	Cushion assembly-front seat-Vinyl	1		
6	MTC1949RD	Overlay-seat-front-cushion-centre-cloth	1		
6	MWC4950	Overlay-seat-front-cushion-centre-Vinyl	1		
7	MTC9962	Finisher-trim retention	4		
8	MTC9959	Finisher-trim retention	1		
9	FS108257L	Screw-flanged head-M8 x 25	4		
10	WC108051L	Washer-M8	4		
11	FS108307L	Screw-flanged head-M8 x 30	2		
12	MUC7947	Nut-plate	2		
13	FN108047L	Nut-flange-flanged head-M8	2		
14	MXC5212	Location rear-seat cushion-front seat	2		

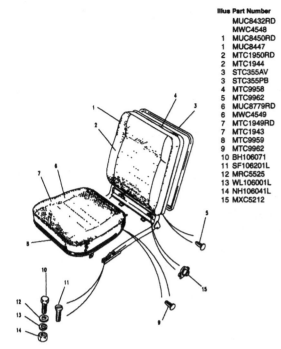

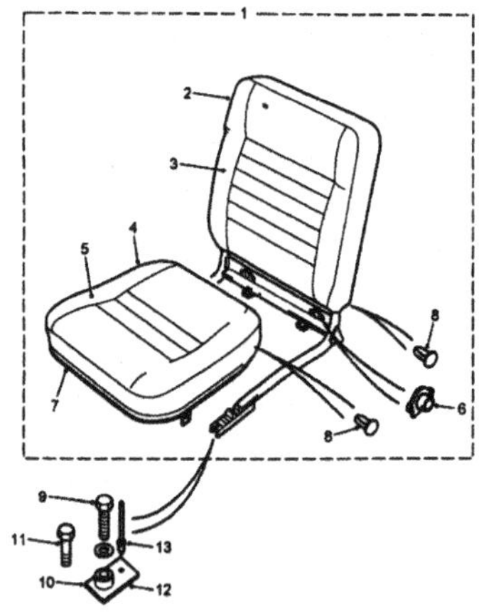

AHRXEA8A

Illus	Part Number	Description	Quantity	Change Point	Remarks
1	MWC5685LCS	SEAT ASSEMBLY-CENTRE-GREY-VINYL	1	Note (1)	
2	MWC5686LCS	• SQUAB ASSEMBLY-FRONT-CENTRE-SEAT-VINYL-SLATE GREY	1		
3	MWC5687LCS	• • Cover assembly-front seat squab-centre-Grey-Vinyl	1		
4	MWC5688LCS	• CUSHION ASSEMBLY-FRONT SEAT-VINYL-SLATE GREY	1		
5	MWC5689LCS	• • Cover assembly-front seat cushion-centre-Slate Grey-Vinyl	1		
1	MWC5680RCF	SEAT ASSEMBLY-CENTRE-CLOTH-BLUE GREY	1	Note (2)	
2	MWC5681RCF	• SQUAB ASSEMBLY-FRONT-CENTRE-SEAT-CLOTH-BLUE GREY	1		
3	MWC5682RCF	• • Cover assembly-front seat squab-centre-Grey-cloth	1		
4	MWC5683RCF	• CUSHION ASSEMBLY-FRONT SEAT-CLOTH-BLUE GREY	1		
5	MWC5684RCF	• • Cover assembly-front seat cushion-centre-cloth-Blue Grey	1		
1	MXC2646RUY	SEAT ASSEMBLY-CENTRE-CLOTH-MORLAND GREY	1	Note (3)	
2	MXC2650RUY	• SQUAB ASSEMBLY-FRONT-CENTRE-SEAT-CLOTH-MORLAND GREY	1		
3	MXC2641RUY	• • Cover assembly-front seat squab-centre-cloth-Morland Grey	1		
4	MXC2649RUY	• CUSHION ASSEMBLY-FRONT SEAT-CLOTH-MORLAND GREY	1		
5	MXC2640RUY	• • Cover assembly-front seat cushion-centre-cloth-Morland Grey	1		
6	MXC5212	• Location rear-seat cushion-front seat	2		
7	MTC9959	• Finisher-trim retention	1		
8	MTC9962	• Finisher-trim retention	2		

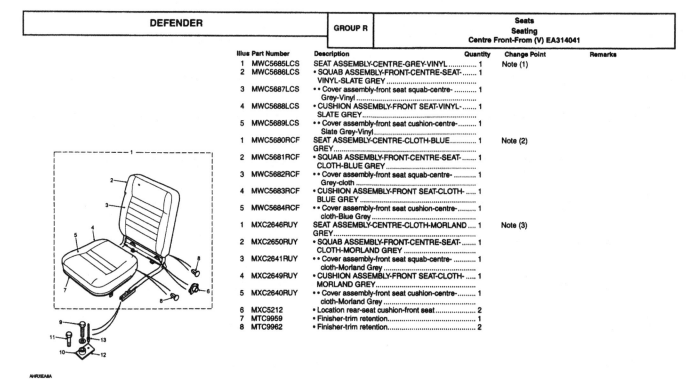

CHANGE POINTS:
(1) To (V) HA 455631
(2) To (V) HA 456060
(3) From (V) HA 456061 To (V) TA 999221

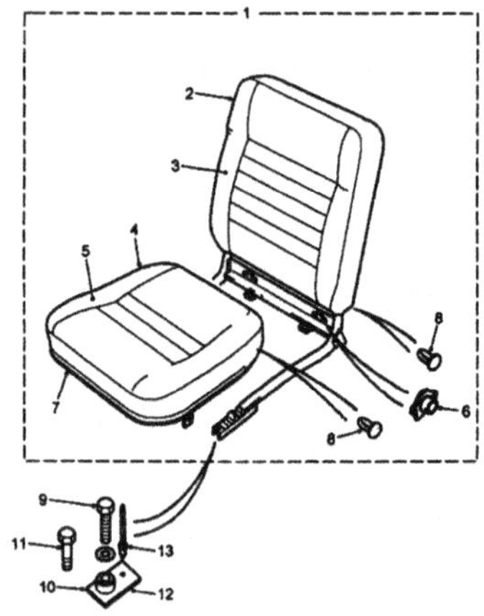

AHRXEA8A

Illus	Part Number	Description	Quantity	Change Point	Remarks
1	AWR5722RFI	SEAT ASSEMBLY-CENTRE-CLOTH-RAYLEIGH	1	Note (1)	
2	AWR5724RFI	• SQUAB ASSEMBLY-FRONT-CENTRE-SEAT-CLOTH-RAYLEIGH	1		
3	AWR5726RFI	• • Cover assembly-front seat squab-centre-cloth-Rayleigh	1		
4	AWR5723RFI	• CUSHION ASSEMBLY-FRONT SEAT-CLOTH-RAYLEIGH	1		
5	AWR5725RFI	• • Cover assembly-front seat cushion-centre-cloth-Rayleigh	1		
6	MXC5212	• Location rear-seat cushion-front seat	2		
7	MTC9959	• Finisher-trim retention	1		
8	MTC9962	• Finisher-trim retention	2		
1	HAD129870RFI	SEAT ASSEMBLY-CENTRE-CLOTH-RAYLEIGH	1	Note (2)	
2	HAJ101300RFI	• SQUAB ASSEMBLY-FRONT-CENTRE-SEAT-CLOTH-RAYLEIGH	1		
3	HBA105650RFI	• • Cover assembly-front seat squab-centre-cloth-Rayleigh	1		
4	HAG100720RFI	• CUSHION ASSEMBLY-FRONT SEAT-CLOTH-RAYLEIGH	1		
5	HCA105550RFI	• • Cover assembly-front seat cushion-centre-cloth-Rayleigh	1		
6	MXC5212	• Location rear-seat cushion-front seat	2		
7	MTC9959	• Finisher-trim retention	1		
8	MTC9962	• Finisher-trim retention	2		
1	MXC2645LCS	SEAT ASSEMBLY-CENTRE-VINYL-SLATE GREY	1	Note (3)	
2	MXC2648LCS	• SQUAB ASSEMBLY-FRONT-CENTRE-SEAT-VINYL-SLATE GREY	1		
3	MXC2652LCS	• • Cover assembly-front seat squab-centre-Vinyl-Slate Grey	1		
4	MXC2647LCS	• CUSHION ASSEMBLY-FRONT SEAT-VINYL-RAYLEIGH	1		
5	MXC2651LCS	• • Cover assembly-front seat cushion-centre-Vinyl-Slate Grey	1		
6	MXC5212	• Location rear-seat cushion-front seat	2		
7	MTC9959	• Finisher-trim retention	1		

CHANGE POINTS:
(1) From (V) VA 999222 To (V) WA 138479
(2) From (V) WA 138480
(3) From (V) HA 456061 To (V) TA 999221

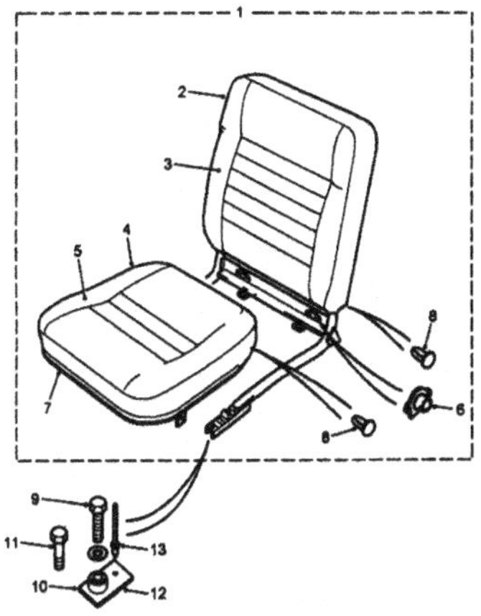

AHRXEA8A

Illus	Part Number	Description	Quantity	Change Point	Remarks
8	MTC9962	• Finisher-trim retention	2		
1	AWR5716RPI	SEAT ASSEMBLY-CENTRE-VINYL-TWILL	1	Note (1)	
2	AWR5718RPI	• SQUAB ASSEMBLY-FRONT-CENTRE-SEAT-VINYL-TWILL	1		
3	AWR5719RPI	• • Cover assembly-front seat squab-centre-Vinyl-Twill	1		
4	AWR5717RPI	• CUSHION ASSEMBLY-FRONT SEAT-VINYL-TWILL	1		
5	AWR5721RPI	• • Cover assembly-front seat cushion-centre-Vinyl-Twill	1		
6	MXC5212	• Location rear-seat cushion-front seat	2		
7	MTC9959	• Finisher-trim retention	1		
8	MTC9962	• Finisher-trim retention	2		
1	HAD129860RPI	SEAT ASSEMBLY-CENTRE-VINYL-TWILL	1	Note (2)	
2	HAJ101070RPI	• SQUAB ASSEMBLY-FRONT-CENTRE-SEAT-VINYL-TWILL	1		
3	HBA105640RPI	• • Cover assembly-front seat squab-centre-Vinyl-Twill	1		
4	HAG100650RPI	• CUSHION ASSEMBLY-FRONT SEAT-VINYL-TWILL	1		
5	HCA105540RPI	• • Cover assembly-front seat cushion-Vinyl-Twill-centre	1		
6	MXC5212	• Location rear-seat cushion-front seat	2		
7	MTC9959	• Finisher-trim retention	1		
8	MTC9962	• Finisher-trim retention	2		

CHANGE POINTS:
(1) From (V) VA 999222 To (V) WA 138479
(2) From (V) WA 138480

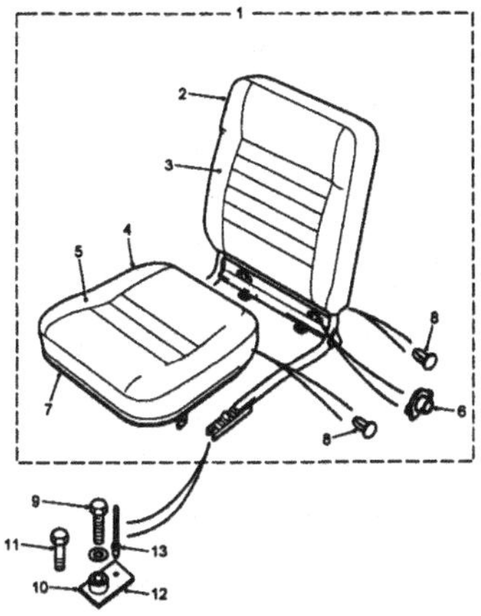

AHRXEA8A

Illus	Part Number	Description	Quantity	Change Point	Remarks
1	HAD132530LOY	SEAT ASSEMBLY-CENTRE-CLOTH-DARK GRANITE	1	Note (1)	
2	HAJ101310LOY	• SQUAB ASSEMBLY-FRONT-CENTRE-SEAT-CLOTH-DARK GRANITE	1		
3	HBA106200LOY	• • Cover assembly-front seat squab-centre-cloth-Dark Granite	1		
4	HAG101020LOY	• CUSHION ASSEMBLY-FRONT SEAT-CLOTH-DARK GRANITE	1		
5	HCA106020LOY	• • Cover assembly-front seat cushion-cloth-Dark Granite-without pocket	1		
2	STC60737	Squab assembly-front-centre-seat-Green-leather	1	Note (1)	Heritage
4	STC60735	Cushion assembly-front seat-Green-centre-leather	1	Note (1)	Heritage

CHANGE POINTS:
(1) From (V) XA 159807

Illus	Part Number	Description	Quantity	Change Point	Remarks
9	FS108257L	Screw-to floor-flanged head-M8 x 25	2	Note (1)	
9	FB108101L	Bolt-flanged head-M8 x 50	2	Note (2)	
10	WC108051L	Washer-M8	4		
11	FS108307L	Screw-to floor-flanged head-M8 x 30	2		
12	MUC7947	Nut-plate	2		
13	RU608313L	Rivet-aluminium-1/8" x 0.482"lng	2		
	FN108047L	Nut-flange-flanged head-M8	2		

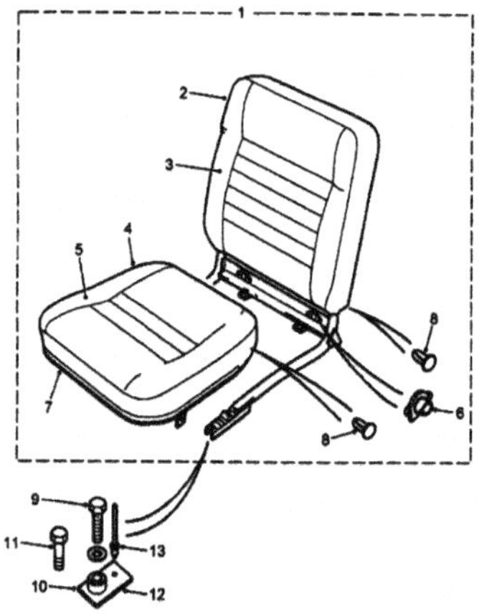

AHRXEA8A

CHANGE POINTS:
(1) To (V) WA 138479
(2) From (V) WA 138480

Illus	Part Number	Description	Quantity	Change Point	Remarks
		SEAT-SMALL SPLIT REAR			
1	MWC3111RD	cloth-Brushwood/Berber	1	Note (1)	
1	MWC5533RCF	cloth-Blue Grey	1	Note (2)	
1	MXC5822RUY	cloth-Morland Grey	1	Note (3)	
1	AWR5735RFI	cloth-Rayleigh	1	Note (4)	
1	HLD103660LOY	cloth-Dark Granite	1	Note (5)	
1	MWC3112PB	Vinyl-Black	1	Note (1)	
1	MWC5534LCS	Vinyl-Grey	1	Note (2)	
1	MXC5823LCS	Vinyl-Slate Grey	1	Note (3)	
1	AWR5745RPI	Vinyl-Twill	1	Note (4)	
1	HLD001600PMA	Black	1	Note (10)	Tomb Raider 110"
		SQUAB-SMALL SPLIT REAR SEAT			
2	MUC9974RD	cloth-Brushwood/Berber	1	Note (1)	
2	MWC5536RCF	cloth-Blue Grey	1	Note (2)	
2	RRC6271RCF	cloth-Blue Grey	1	Note (7)	130"
2	MXC3169RUY	cloth-Morland Grey	1	Note (3)	
2	RRC6271RUY	cloth-Morland Grey	1	Note (8)	130"
2	AWR5738RFI	cloth-Rayleigh	1	Note (6)	
2	HLE110110LOY	cloth-Dark Granite	1	Note (5)	2 front seats
2	HLE110060LOY	cloth-Dark Granite	1	Note (5)	3 front seats
2	AWR5764RFI	cloth-Rayleigh	1	Note (4)	130"
2	MUC9975PB	Vinyl-Black	1	Note (1)	
2	MWC5537LCS	Vinyl-Grey	1	Note (2)	
2	MXC3170LCS	Vinyl-Slate Grey	1	Note (3)	
2	RRC6270LCS	Vinyl-Slate Grey	1	Note (9)	130"
2	AWR5748RPI	Vinyl-Twill	1	Note (6)	
2	AWR5758RPI	Vinyl-Twill	1	Note (4)	130"

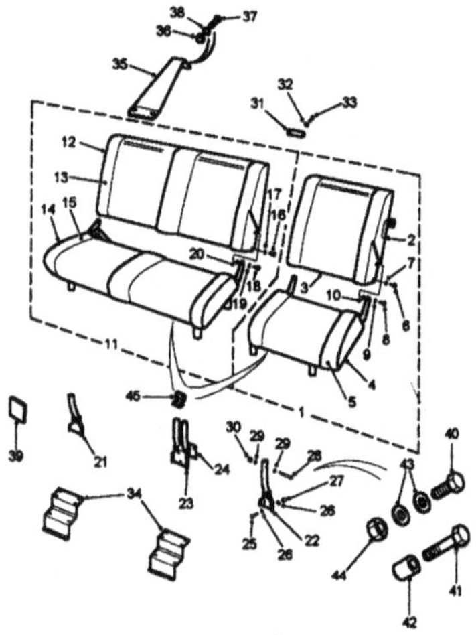

LR0048

CHANGE POINTS:
(1) To (V) EA 314267
(2) From (V) EA 314268 To (V) FA 418702
(3) From (V) FA 418703 To (V) TA 999221
(4) From (V) VA 999222
(5) From (V) XA 159807
(6) From (V) VA 999222 To (V) WA 159806
(7) To (V) GA 456658
(8) From (V) GA 456659 To (V) TA 999221
(9) To (V) TA 999221
(10) From (V) 1A 612404

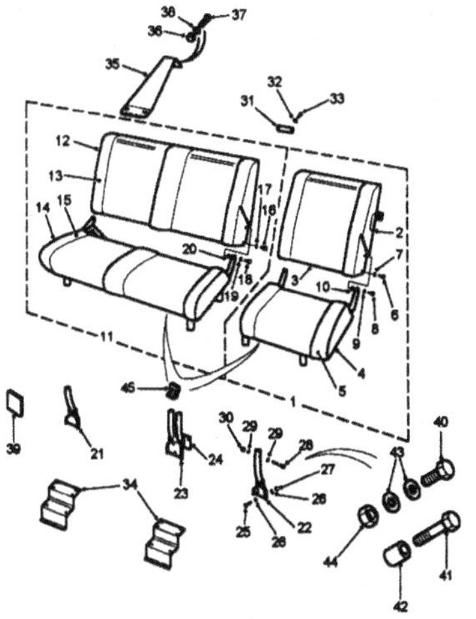

LR0046

Illus	Part Number	Description	Quantity	Change Point	Remarks
		COVER ASSEMBLY-REAR SEAT SMALL SPLIT SQUAB			
3	MWC1707RD	cloth-Brushwood/Berber	1	Note (1)	
3	MWC5539RCF	cloth-Blue Grey	1	Note (2)	
3	MXC1827RUY	cloth-Morland Grey	1	Note (3)	
3	AWR5742RFI	cloth-Rayleigh	1	Note (4)	
3	HMA111310LOY	cloth-Dark Granite	1	Note (5)	
3	MWC1708PB	Vinyl-Black	1	Note (1)	
3	MWC5540LCS	Vinyl-Grey	1	Note (2)	
3	MXC1831LCS	Vinyl-Slate Grey	1	Note (3)	
3	AWR5752RPI	Vinyl-Twill	1	Note (4)	
		CUSHION-SMALL SPLIT REAR SEAT			
4	MWC3107RD	cloth-Brushwood/Berber	1	Note (1)	
4	MWC5546RCF	cloth-Blue Grey	1	Note (2)	
4	RRC6393RCF	cloth-Blue Grey	1	Note (6)	130"
4	MXC5814RUY	cloth-Morland Grey	1	Note (3)	
4	RRC6393RUY	cloth-Morland Grey	1	Note (7)	130"
4	AWR5739RFI	cloth-Rayleigh	1	Note (4)	
4	AWR5765RFI	cloth-Rayleigh	1	Note (4)	130"
4	HLF105580LOY	cloth-Dark Granite	1	Note (5)	
4	HLF105530LOY	cloth-Dark Granite	1	Note (5)	130"
4	MWC3108PB	Vinyl-Black	1	Note (1)	
4	MWC5547LCS	Vinyl-Grey	1	Note (2)	
4	MXC5815LCS	Vinyl-Slate Grey	1	Note (3)	
4	RRC6392LCS	Vinyl-Slate Grey	1	Note (8)	130"
4	AWR5749RPI	Vinyl-Twill	1	Note (4)	
4	AWR5759RPI	Vinyl-Twill	1	Note (4)	130"

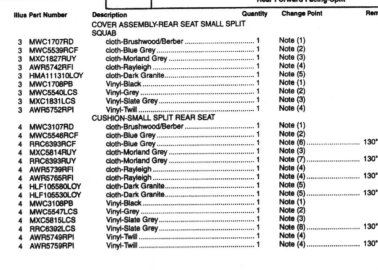

CHANGE POINTS:
(1) To (V) EA 314267
(2) From (V) EA 314268 To (V) FA 418702
(3) From (V) FA 418703 To (V) TA 999221
(4) From (V) VA 999222 To (V) WA 159806
(5) From (V) XA 159807
(6) To (V) GA 456658
(7) From (V) GA 456659 To (V) TA 999221
(8) To (V) TA 999221

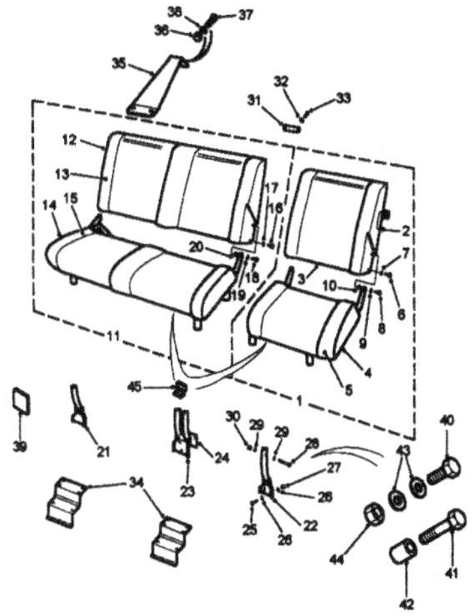

LR0046

Illus	Part Number	Description	Quantity	Change Point	Remarks
		COVER ASSEMBLY-REAR SEAT SMALL SPLIT CUSHION			
5	MWC3103RD	cloth-Brushwood/Berber	1	Note (1)	
5	MWC5549RCF	cloth-Blue Grey	1	Note (2)	
5	MXC1826RUY	cloth-Morland Grey	1	Note (3)	
5	AWR5743RFI	cloth-Rayleigh	1	Note (4)	
5	HPA106710LOY	cloth-Dark Granite	1	Note (5)	
5	MWC3105PB	Vinyl-Black	1	Note (1)	
5	MWC5550LCS	Vinyl-Slate Grey	1	Note (2)	
5	MXC1830LCS	Vinyl-Slate Grey	1	Note (3)	
5	AWR5753RPI	Vinyl-Twill	1	Note (4)	
6	MWC2522	Bolt-shouldered	1		
7	WC108051L	Washer-M8	1		
8	MWC2522	Bolt-shouldered	2		
9	WC110061L	Washer-plain-M10-oversize	2		
10	WL108001L	Washer-sprung-M8	2		
		SEAT-LARGE SPLIT REAR			
11	MWC3113RD	cloth-Brushwood/Berber	1	Note (1)	110"
11	MWC5555RCF	cloth-Blue Grey	1	Note (2)	
11	MXC5820RUY	cloth-Morland Grey	1	Note (3)	
11	AWR5734RFI	cloth-Rayleigh	1	Note (4)	
11	HLD103670LOY	cloth-Dark Granite	1	Note (5)	
11	MWC3114PB	Vinyl-Black	1	Note (1)	
11	MWC5556LCS	Vinyl-Slate Grey	1	Note (2)	
11	MXC5821LCS	Vinyl-Slate Grey	1	Note (3)	
11	AWR5744RPI	Vinyl-Twill	1	Note (4)	
11	HLD001610PMA	Black	1	Note (6)	Tomb Raider 110"

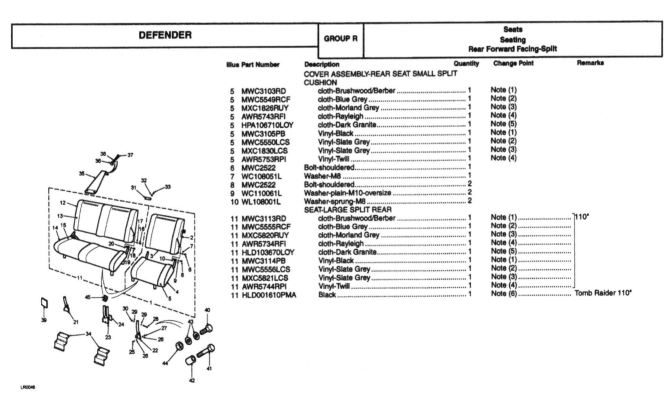

CHANGE POINTS:
(1) To (V) EA 314267
(2) From (V) EA 314268 To (V) FA 418702
(3) From (V) FA 418703 To (V) TA 999221
(4) From (V) VA 999222 To (V) WA 159806
(5) From (V) XA 159807
(6) From (V) 1A 612404

DEFENDER	GROUP R	Seats Seating Rear Forward Facing-Split

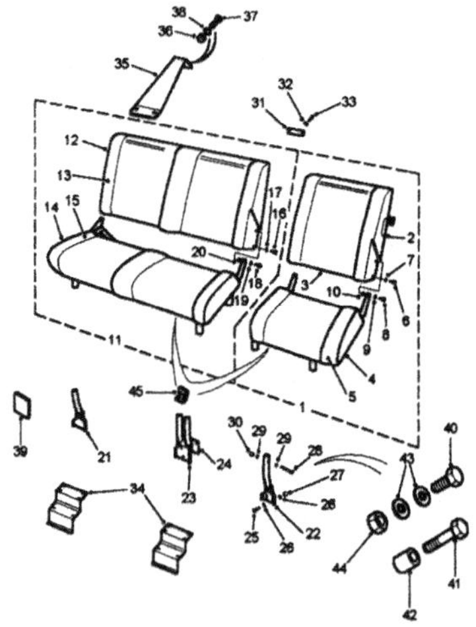

LR0048

Illus	Part Number	Description	Quantity	Change Point	Remarks
		SQUAB-LARGE SPLIT REAR SEAT			
12	MUC9971RD	cloth-Brushwood/Berber	1	Note (1)	110"
12	MWC5558RCF	cloth-Blue Grey	1	Note (2)	110"
12	RRC6269RCF	cloth-Blue Grey	1	Note (6)	130"
12	MXC3167RUY	cloth-Morland Grey	1	Note (3)	110"
12	RRC6269RUY	cloth-Morland Grey	1	Note (7)	130"
12	AWR5736RFI	cloth-Rayleigh	1	Note (4)	110"
12	AWR5762RFI	cloth-Rayleigh	1	Note (8)	130"
12	HLE110050LOY	cloth-Dark Granite	1	Note (5)	3 front seats
12	HLE110100LOY	cloth-Dark Granite	1	Note (5)	2 front seats
12	MUC9972PB	Vinyl-Black	1	Note (1)	110"
12	MWC5559LCS	Vinyl-Grey	1	Note (2)	110"
12	MXC3168LCS	Vinyl-Slate Grey	1	Note (3)	110"
12	RRC6268LCS	Vinyl-Slate Grey	1	Note (9)	130"
12	AWR5746RPI	Vinyl-Twill	1	Note (4)	110"
12	AWR5756RPI	Vinyl-Twill	1	Note (8)	130"
		COVER ASSEMBLY-REAR SEAT LARGE SPLIT SQUAB			
13	MWC1705RD	cloth-Brushwood/Berber	1	Note (1)	110"
13	MWC5561RCF	cloth-Blue Grey	1	Note (2)	
13	MXC1829RUY	cloth-Morland Grey	1	Note (3)	
13	AWR5740RFI	cloth-Rayleigh	1	Note (8)	
13	HMA111350LOY	cloth-Dark Granite	1	Note (5)	
13	MWC1706PB	Vinyl-Black	1	Note (1)	110"
13	MWC5562LCS	Vinyl-Grey	1	Note (2)	
13	MXC1833LCS	Vinyl-Slate Grey	1	Note (3)	
13	AWR5750RPI	Vinyl-Twill	1	Note (8)	

CHANGE POINTS:

(1) To (V) EA 314267
(2) From (V) EA 314268 To (V) FA 418702
(3) From (V) FA 418703 To (V) TA 999221
(4) From (V) VA 999222 To (V) WA 159806
(5) From (V) XA 159807
(6) To (V) FA 419177
(7) From (V) FA 419178 To (V) TA 999221
(8) From (V) VA 999222
(9) To (V) TA 999221

DEFENDER	GROUP R	Seats Seating Rear Forward Facing-Split

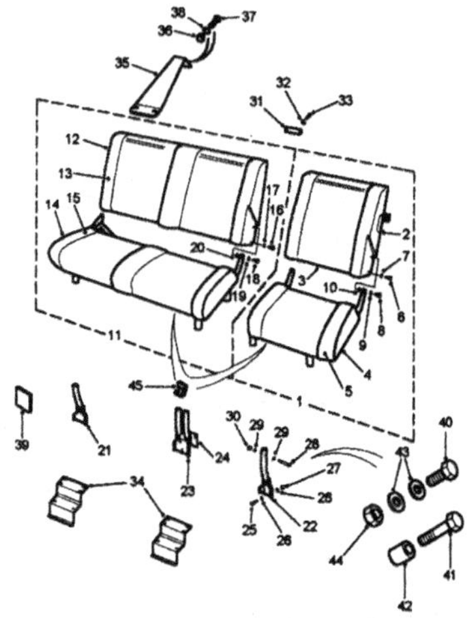

LR0048

Illus	Part Number	Description	Quantity	Change Point	Remarks
		CUSHION-LARGE SPLIT REAR SEAT			
14	MWC3109RD	cloth-Brushwood/Berber	1	Note (1)	110"
14	MWC5568RCF	cloth-Blue Grey	1	Note (2)	110"
14	RRC6391RCF	cloth-Blue Grey	1	Note (6)	130"
14	MXC5812RUY	cloth-Morland Grey	1	Note (3)	110"
14	RRC6391RUY	cloth-Morland Grey	1	Note (7)	130"
14	AWR5737RFI	cloth-Rayleigh	1	Note (4)	110"
14	AWR5763RFI	cloth-Rayleigh	1	Note (8)	130"
14	HLF105520LOY	cloth-Dark Granite	1	Note (5)	3 front seats 110"
14	HLF105610LOY	cloth-Dark Granite	1	Note (5)	2 front seats 110"
14	MWC3110PB	Vinyl-Black	1	Note (1)	110"
14	MWC5569LCS	Vinyl-Slate Grey	1	Note (2)	110"
14	MXC5813LCS	Vinyl-Slate Grey	1	Note (3)	110"
14	RRC6390LCS	Vinyl-Slate Grey	1	Note (9)	130"
14	AWR5747RPI	Vinyl-Twill	1	Note (4)	110"
14	AWR5757RPI	Vinyl-Twill	1	Note (8)	130"
		COVER ASSEMBLY-REAR SEAT LARGE SPLIT CUSHION			
15	MWC3104RD	cloth-Brushwood/Berber	1	Note (1)	110"
15	MWC5592RCF	cloth-Blue Grey	1	Note (2)	
15	MXC1828RUY	cloth-Morland Grey	1	Note (3)	
15	AWR5741RFI	cloth-Rayleigh	1	Note (4)	
15	HPA106700LOY	cloth-Dark Granite	1	Note (5)	
15	MWC3106PB	Vinyl-Black	1	Note (1)	
15	MWC5593LCS	Vinyl-Slate Grey	1	Note (2)	
15	MXC1832LCS	Vinyl-Slate Grey	1	Note (3)	
15	AWR5751RPI	Vinyl-Twill	1	Note (4)	

CHANGE POINTS:

(1) To (V) EA 314267
(2) From (V) EA 314268 To (V) FA 418702
(3) From (V) FA 418703 To (V) TA 999221
(4) From (V) VA 999222 To (V) WA 159806
(5) From (V) XA 159807
(6) To (V) FA 419177
(7) From (V) FA 419178 To (V) TA 999221
(8) From (V) VA 999222
(9) To (V) TA 999221

Illus	Part Number	Description	Quantity	Change Point	Remarks
16	MWC2522	Bolt-shouldered	1		
17	WC108051L	Washer-M8	1		
18	MWC2522	Bolt-shouldered	2		
19	WC110061L	Washer-plain-M10-oversize	2		
20	WJ108001	Washer-M8-large	2		
		BRACKET-MOUNTING			
21	MUC9874	outer-RH	1	Note (1)	110"
22	MUC9875	outer-LH	1		
23	MUC9864	inner	1		
		BRACKET-MOUNTING			
21	RRC6104	outer-RH	1		130"
22	RRC6105	outer-LH	1		130"
23	RRC6106	inner	1		130"
		BRACKET-MOUNTING			
21	MUC9872	outer-RH	1	Note (2)	
22	MUC9873	outer-LH	1		
23	MUC9871	inner	1		
24	MWC1623	Plate-reinforcement	1		
25	FS108257L	Screw-bracket to floor-flanged head-M8 x 25	9		
26	WC108051L	Washer-bracket to floor-M8	18		
27	FN108047L	Nut-flange-bracket to floor-flanged head-M8	9		

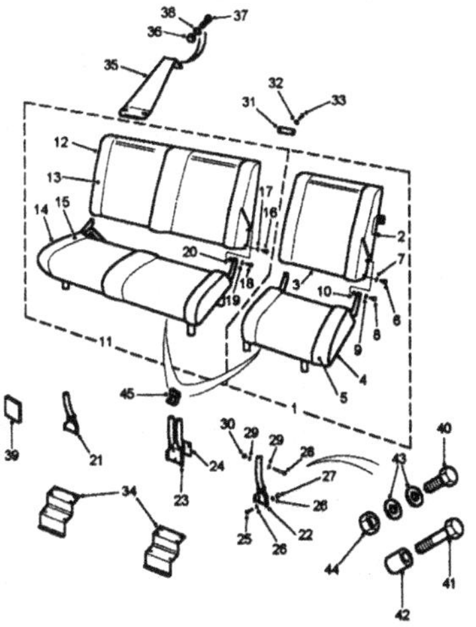

LR0048

CHANGE POINTS:
(1) To (V) TA 999221
(2) From (V) VA 999222

Illus	Part Number	Description	Quantity	Change Point	Remarks
		SEAT FIXINGS			
28	SH108401L	Screw-seat to bracket-hexagonal head-M8 x 40	4	Note (1)	
29	WC108051L	Washer-seat to bracket-M8	8	Note (1)	
30	FN108047L	Nut-flange-seat to bracket-flanged head-M8	4		
31	MWC1141	Plate-rear seat squab retention	1		Australia
32	SE108201	Screw	2		
33	WA108051L	Washer-8mm	2		
34	MTC6757	Bracket-front seat support	2		
		LONG SEAT TO BULKHEAD & FIXINGS			
35	AWR2816	Bracket-rear seat mounting	2	Note (2)	
36	NN106021	Nutsert-blind-M6	4	Note (2)	
37	FS106167L	Screw-flanged head-flanged head-M6 x 16	4		110"
38	MRC5525	Washer-plain-standard	4	Note (2)	
39	RRC6111	Pad-rubber	4		130"
		SEAT PIVOT - LATER TYPE			
40	FB108101L	Bolt-flanged head-M8 x 50	2	Note (3)	110"
41	FB108181L	Bolt-M8 x 90	2		
42	AWR5871	Spacer	2		
43	WC108051L	Washer-M8	8		
44	NY108041L	Nut-nyloc-M8	4		
		SEAT CUSHION TRIM CLIPS			
45	315264	Clip-trim retention	4		
		FIXED SEAT BRACKETS - 110 CREW CAB			
46	ALU710080	Bracket-rear seat mounting	2		110"
47	ALU710090	Bracket-rear seat mounting	2		
48	FS106167L	Screw-flanged head-flanged head-M6 x 16	4		
49	MRC5525	Washer-plain-standard	4		

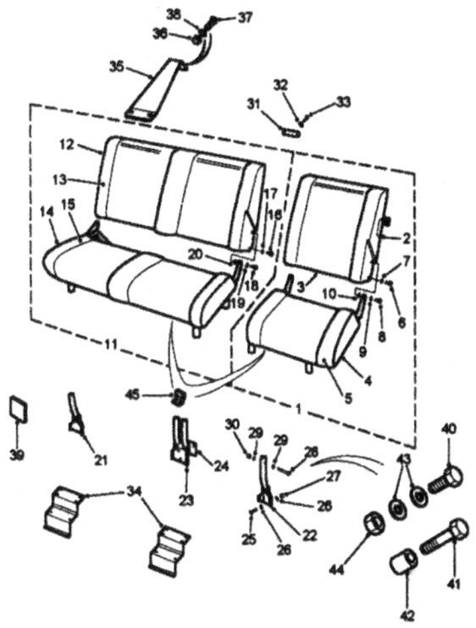

LR0048

CHANGE POINTS:
(1) To (V) TA 999221
(2) From (V) MA 959195
(3) From (V) VA 999222

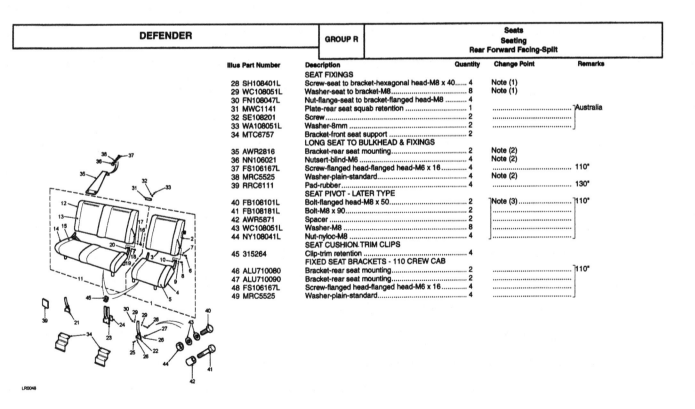

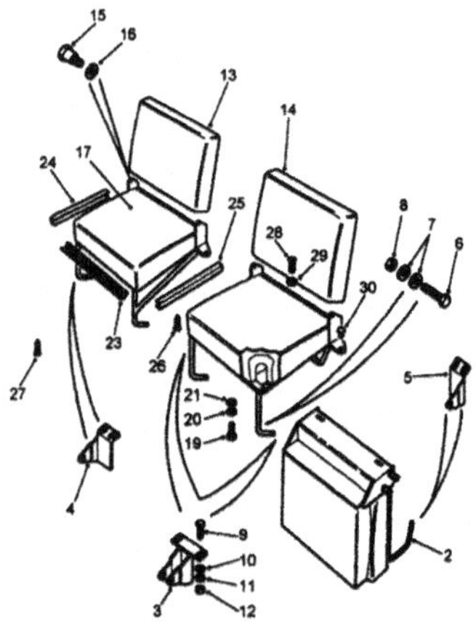

AJRXGE1A

Illus	Part Number	Description	Quantity	Change Point	Remarks
1	347343	Frame-seat assembly-centre	1		110"
2	347344	Frame-seat assembly outer	2		
		BRACKET-REAR SEAT MOUNTING			
3	MTC6793	inner	2		
4	MTC6794	outer-RH	1		
5	MTC6795	outer-LH	1		
6	331709	Bolt-shouldered	6		
7	AFU1263	Washer	12		
8	NH106041L	Nut-hexagonal-nyloc-M6	6		
9	SE106204	Screw-bracket to floor	14		
10	WA106041L	Washer-bracket to floor-6mm	14		
11	WL106001L	Washer-bracket to floor-sprung-M6	14		
12	NH106041L	Nut-bracket to floor-hexagonal-nyloc-M6	14		110"
		SQUAB-REAR SEAT INDIVIDUAL			
13	MTC4489RD	Brushwood/Berber-cloth	3	Note (1)	
13	MXC2780RCF	Blue Grey-Grey-cloth	3	Note (2)	
13	349514	Black-Vinyl	3	Note (1)	
13	MXC2780RUY	MORLAND GREY-CLOTH	3	Note (3)	
13	AWR5787RFI	RAYLEIGH-CLOTH	3	Note (4)	
13	MWC5525LCS	SLATE GREY-VINYL	3	Note (5)	
13	AWR5789RPI	TWILL-VINYL	3	Note (6)	
14	349529	• Foam-squab	3		
15	331709	• Bolt-shouldered	6		
16	WC108051L	• Washer-M8	6		
	349955	• Washer-rubber	6		
	349931	• Washer-plastic	6		
13	HLE110070LOY	Squab-rear seat individual-Dark Granite-cloth-without pocket	1	Note (7)	
13	STC60742	Squab-rear seat individual-Green-leather	1	Note (7)	Heritage

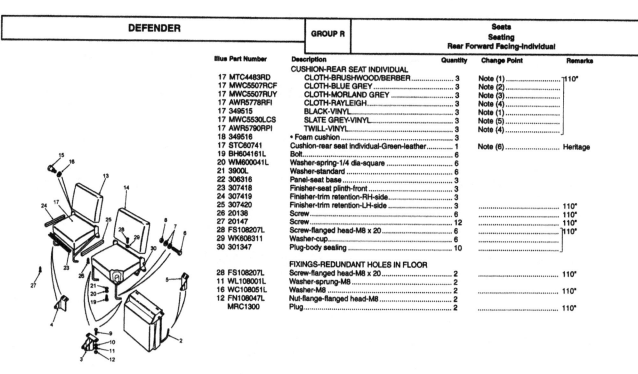

CHANGE POINTS:
(1) To (V) EA 314267
(2) From (V) EA 314268 To (V) HA 455595
(3) From (V) HA 455596 To (V) TA 999221
(4) From (V) VA 999222 To (V) WA 159806
(5) From (V) EA 314268 To (V) TA 999221
(6) From (V) VA 999222
(7) From (V) XA 159807

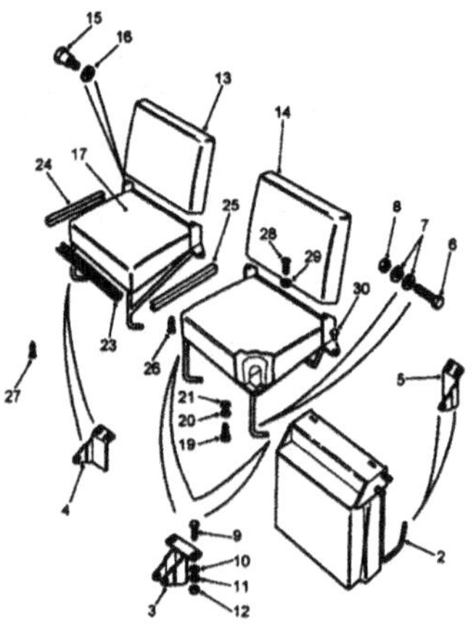

AJRXGE1A

Illus	Part Number	Description	Quantity	Change Point	Remarks
		CUSHION-REAR SEAT INDIVIDUAL			
17	MTC4483RD	CLOTH-BRUSHWOOD/BERBER	3	Note (1)	110"
17	MWC5507RCF	CLOTH-BLUE GREY	3	Note (2)	
17	MWC5507RUY	CLOTH-MORLAND GREY	3	Note (3)	
17	AWR5778RFI	CLOTH-RAYLEIGH	3	Note (4)	
17	349515	BLACK-VINYL	3	Note (1)	
17	MWC5530LCS	SLATE GREY-VINYL	3	Note (5)	
17	AWR5790RPI	TWILL-VINYL	3	Note (4)	
18	349516	• Foam cushion	3		
17	STC60741	Cushion-rear seat individual-Green-leather	1	Note (6)	Heritage
19	BH604161L	Bolt	6		
20	WM600041L	Washer-spring-1/4 dia-square	6		
21	3900L	Washer-standard	6		
22	306316	Panel-seat base	3		
23	307418	Finisher-seat plinth-front	3		
24	307419	Finisher-trim retention-RH-side	3		
25	307420	Finisher-trim retention-LH-side	3		110"
26	20138	Screw	6		110"
27	20147	Screw	12		110"
28	FS108207L	Screw-flanged head-M8 x 20	6		110"
29	WK608311	Washer-cup	6		
30	301347	Plug-body sealing	10		
		FIXINGS-REDUNDANT HOLES IN FLOOR			
28	FS108207L	Screw-flanged head-M8 x 20	2		110"
11	WL108001L	Washer-sprung-M8	2		
16	WC108051L	Washer-M8	2		110"
12	FN108047L	Nut-flange-flanged head-M8	2		
	MRC1300	Plug	2		110"

CHANGE POINTS:
(1) To (V) EA 314267
(2) From (V) EA 314268 To (V) HA 455595
(3) From (V) HA 455596 To (V) TA 999221
(4) From (V) VA 999222
(5) From (V) EA 314268 To (V) TA 999221
(6) From (V) XA 159807

Illus	Part Number	Description	Quantity	Change Point	Remarks
1	347863	Nut-plate	3		
2	RA612156L	Rivet	6		
3	MRC4798	Bolt-shouldered	3		
		STRIKER-REAR SEAT SQUAB			
4	347861	RH	1		
4	347861	centre	1		
4	347862	LH	1		
5	SE106161L	Screw-M6 x 16	3		
6	AFU1080	Washer-plain	6		
7	NY106047L	Nut-hexagonal head-nyloc-M6	3		
8	79134	Screw	3		
9	MTC6801	Spring	3		
10	MTC6802	Plate	3		
11	SH106204	Screw-hexagonal head-M6 x 20-long-bronze.	1		
12	NH106044	Nut-hexagonal	1		

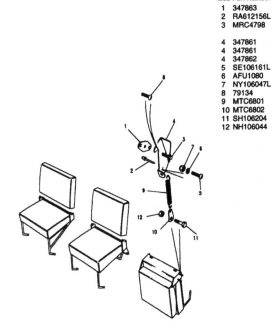

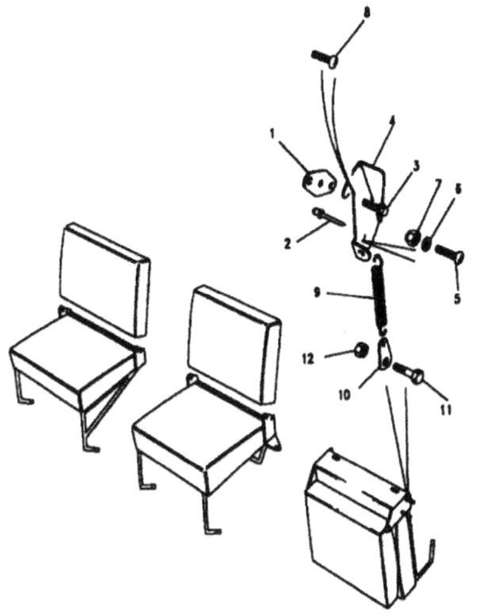

Illus	Part Number	Description	Quantity	Change Point	Remarks
		SQUAB-REAR SEAT INDIVIDUAL			
1	MWC5508RUY	cloth-Morland Grey	4	Note (1)	
1	MTC4484RD	cloth-Brushwood/Berber	4	Note (2)	
1	MWC5508RCF	cloth-Blue Grey	4	Note (3)	
1	AWR5779RFI	cloth-Rayleigh	4	Note (4)	
1	HLE110140LOY	cloth-Dark Granite	4	Note (5)	
1	AWR5964RPI	Vinyl-Twill	4	Note (6)	
1	STC60739	leather-Green	4		Heritage
1	HLE001720PMA	Black	4	Note (10)	Tomb Raider 90"
		SUPPORT-SEAT			
2	MTC8302	RH	4	Note (7)	
2	MTC8303	LH	4		
2	MWC8666	RH	4	Note (8)	
2	MWC8667	LH	4		
2	AWR2444	RH	4	Note (9)	
2	AWR2443	LH	4		

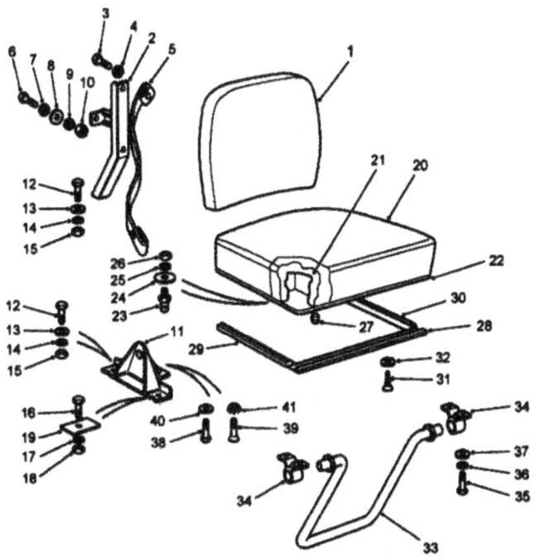

AHRXXA3A

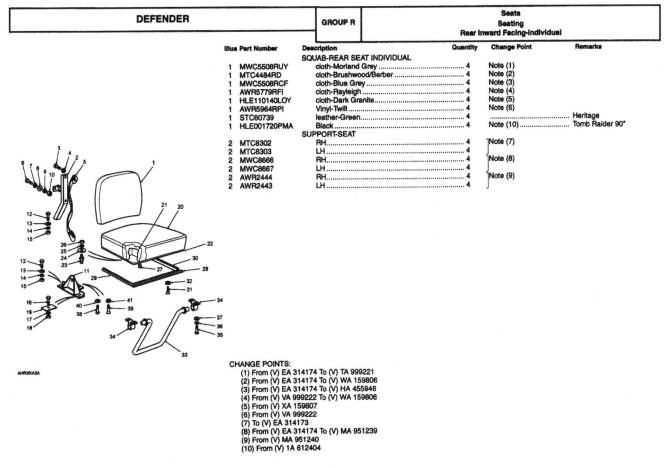

CHANGE POINTS:
(1) From (V) EA 314174 To (V) TA 999221
(2) From (V) EA 314174 To (V) WA 159806
(3) From (V) EA 314174 To (V) HA 455946
(4) From (V) VA 999222 To (V) WA 159806
(5) From (V) XA 159807
(6) From (V) VA 999222
(7) To (V) EA 314173
(8) From (V) EA 314174 To (V) MA 951239
(9) From (V) MA 951240
(10) From (V) 1A 612404

Illus	Part Number	Description	Quantity	Change Point	Remarks
3	FS106167L	Screw-flanged head-backrest to support-flanged head-M6 x 16	16		
4	WL106001L	Washer-sprung-M6	16		
5	RTC6453	Strap assembly-retaining-Black	4	Note (1)	
5	339878	Strap assembly-retaining-Green	4	Note (1)	
5	IPM000010	Strap assembly-retaining	4	Note (2)	
6	FS106167L	Screw-flanged head-support to capping-flanged head-M6 x 16	6		
7	WB106041L	Washer-M6	6		
8	WC106041L	Washer-M6-oversize	6		
9	WL106001L	Washer-sprung-M6	6		
10	NH106041L	Nut-support to capping-hexagonal-nyloc-M6	6		
11	MUC4108	Pivot bracket-RH	4		
11	MUC4109	Pivot bracket-LH	4		
12	SH604051L	Screw-to wheelarch-hexagonal head-1/4UNF x 5/8	16		
13	WC600045L	Washer-plain-1/4 dia	16		
14	WM600041L	Washer-spring-1/4 dia-square	16		
15	NH604041L	Nut-to wheelarch-hexagonal head-coarse thread-1/4UNF	16		
16	SH604071L	Screw-to wheelarch-hexagonal head-1/4UNF x 7/8	4		
17	WM600041L	Washer-spring-1/4 dia-square	4		
18	NH604041L	Nut-to wheelarch-hexagonal head-coarse thread-1/4UNF	4		
19	346804	Clamp-bar	4		

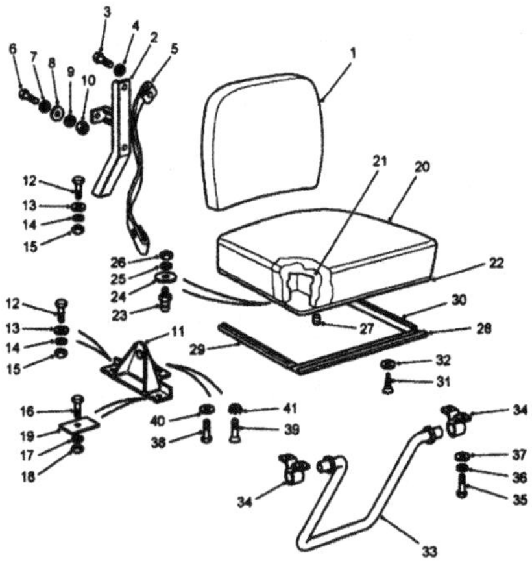

AHRXKA3A

CHANGE POINTS:
(1) To (V) YA 195270
(2) From (V) YA 195271

Illus	Part Number	Description	Quantity	Change Point	Remarks
20	MWC5507RUY	CUSHION-REAR SEAT INDIVIDUAL-CLOTH-MORLAND GREY	4	Note (1)	
21	349516	• Foam cushion	3		
20	AWR5778RFI	CUSHION-REAR SEAT INDIVIDUAL-CLOTH-RAYLEIGH	4	Note (2)	
21	349516	• Foam cushion	3		
20	MTC4483RD	CUSHION-REAR SEAT INDIVIDUAL-CLOTH-BRUSHWOOD/BERBER	4	Note (3)	
21	349516	• Foam cushion	3		
20	MWC5507RCF	CUSHION-REAR SEAT INDIVIDUAL-CLOTH-BLUE GREY	4	Note (4)	
21	349516	• Foam cushion	3		
20	HLF105540LOY	CUSHION-REAR SEAT INDIVIDUAL-CLOTH-DARK GRANITE	4	Note (5)	
21	349516	• Foam cushion	1		
20	AWR5963RPI	CUSHION-REAR SEAT INDIVIDUAL-VINYL-TWILL	4	Note (6)	
21	349516	• Foam cushion	1		
20	STC60740	CUSHION-REAR SEAT INDIVIDUAL-LEATHER-GREEN	4	Note (5)	Heritage
21	349516	• Foam cushion	1		
20	HLF000930PMA	Cushion-rear seat individual-Black	4	Note (7)	Tomb Raider 90"

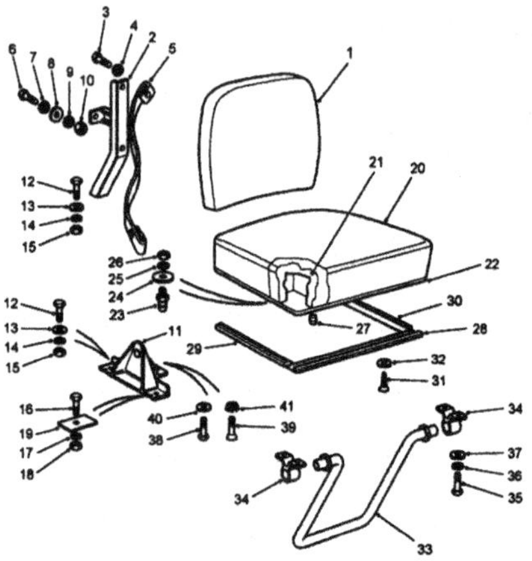

AHRXKA3A

CHANGE POINTS:
(1) To (V) TA 999221
(2) From (V) VA 999222 To (V) WA 159806
(3) To (V) EA 314173
(4) From (V) EA 314174 To (V) HA 455945
(5) From (V) XA 159807
(6) From (V) VA 999222
(7) From (V) 1A 612404

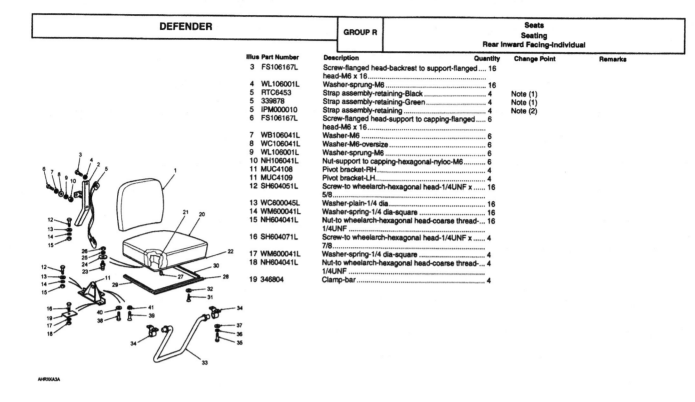

Rear Inward Facing-Individual

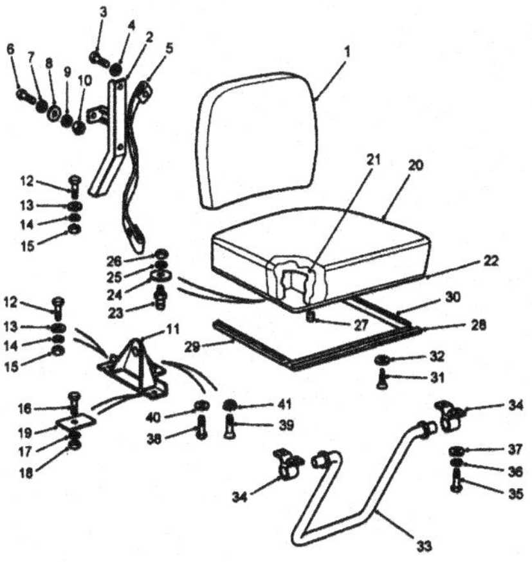

AHRXXA3A

Illus	Part Number	Description	Quantity	Change Point	Remarks
22	306316	Panel-seat base	4		
23	243618	Stud	4		
24	3852L	Washer	4		
25	WM702001L	Washer-spring-3/16 dia-square	4		
26	RTC608	Nut	4		
27	312028	Buffer rubber-seat rear	4		
28	307418	Finisher-seat plinth-front	4		
29	307419	Finisher-trim retention-RH-side	4		
30	307420	Finisher-trim retention-LH-side	4		
31	20147	Screw-to finisher	16		
31	AF608081	Screw-to seat base	8		
32	WK608213	Washer-cup	8		
33	MUC4083	Tube-inward facing rear seats support	4		
34	90306199	Tube bearing	8		
35	SH604071L	Screw-bearing to cushion frame-hexagonal head-1/4UNF x 7/8	16		
36	WM600041L	Washer-spring-1/4 dia-square	16		
37	WB106045	Washer-plain-thin	16		
38	SH604071	Screw-pivot bracket to cushion frame-hexagonal head	8		
39	SF604101	Screw-pivot bracket to cushion frame	8		
40	WB106045	Washer-plain-thin	16		
41	WH600041L	Washer-starlock	8		
		SEAT FIXINGS - SOUTH AFRICA			
42	AWR6715	Nutsert-blind-M6	8		BMW M52 South Africa

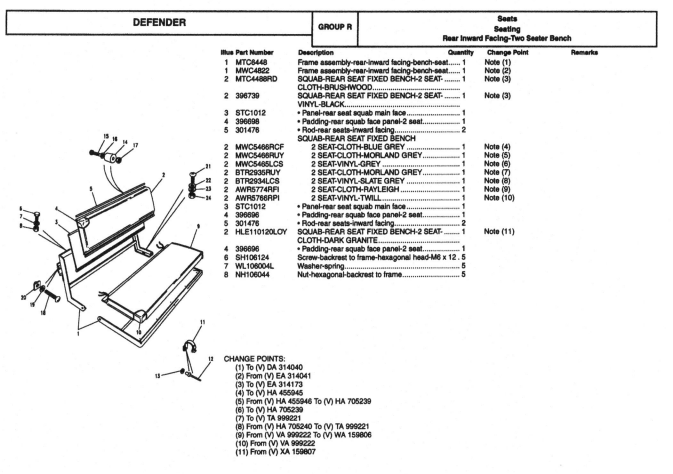

Rear Inward Facing-Two Seater Bench

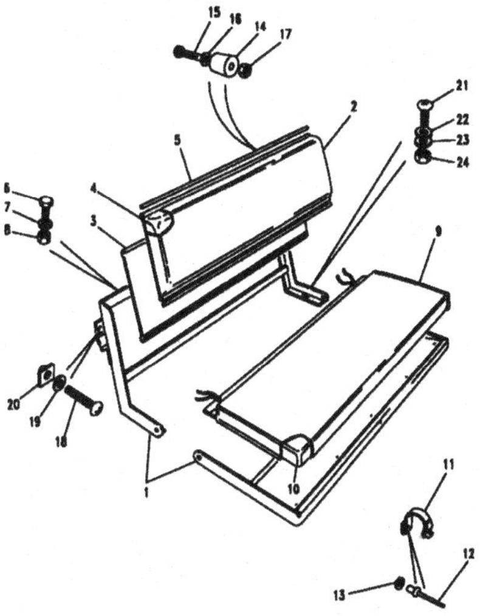

Illus	Part Number	Description	Quantity	Change Point	Remarks
1	MTC6448	Frame assembly-rear-inward facing-bench-seat	1	Note (1)	
1	MWC4822	Frame assembly-rear-inward facing-bench-seat	1	Note (2)	
2	MTC4488RD	SQUAB-REAR SEAT FIXED BENCH-2 SEAT-CLOTH-BRUSHWOOD	1	Note (3)	
2	396739	SQUAB-REAR SEAT FIXED BENCH-2 SEAT-VINYL-BLACK	1	Note (3)	
3	STC1012	• Panel-rear seat squab main face	1		
4	396698	• Padding-rear squab face panel-2 seat	1		
5	301476	• Rod-rear seats-inward facing	2		
		SQUAB-REAR SEAT FIXED BENCH			
2	MWC5466RCF	2 SEAT-CLOTH-BLUE GREY	1	Note (4)	
2	MWC5466RUY	2 SEAT-CLOTH-MORLAND GREY	1	Note (5)	
2	MWC5465LCS	2 SEAT-VINYL-GREY	1	Note (6)	
2	BTR2935RUY	2 SEAT-CLOTH-MORLAND GREY	1	Note (7)	
2	BTR2934LCS	2 SEAT-VINYL-SLATE GREY	1	Note (8)	
2	AWR5774RFI	2 SEAT-CLOTH-RAYLEIGH	1	Note (9)	
2	AWR5766RPI	2 SEAT-VINYL-TWILL	1	Note (10)	
3	STC1012	• Panel-rear seat squab main face	1		
4	396696	• Padding-rear squab face panel-2 seat	1		
5	301476	• Rod-rear seats-inward facing	2		
2	HLE110120LOY	SQUAB-REAR SEAT FIXED BENCH-2 SEAT-CLOTH-DARK GRANITE	1	Note (11)	
4	396696	• Padding-rear squab face panel-2 seat	1		
6	SH106124	Screw-backrest to frame-hexagonal head-M6 x 12	5		
7	WL106004L	Washer-spring	5		
8	NH106044	Nut-hexagonal-backrest to frame	5		

CHANGE POINTS:

(1) To (V) DA 314040
(2) From (V) EA 314041
(3) To (V) EA 314173
(4) To (V) HA 455945
(5) From (V) HA 455946 To (V) HA 705239
(6) To (V) HA 705239
(7) To (V) TA 999221
(8) From (V) HA 705240 To (V) TA 999221
(9) From (V) VA 999222 To (V) WA 159806
(10) From (V) VA 999222
(11) From (V) XA 159807

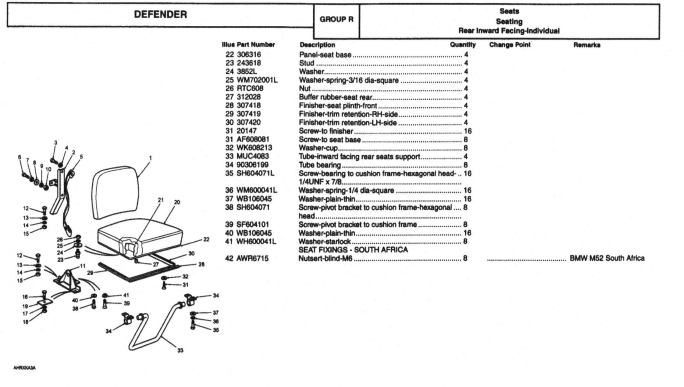

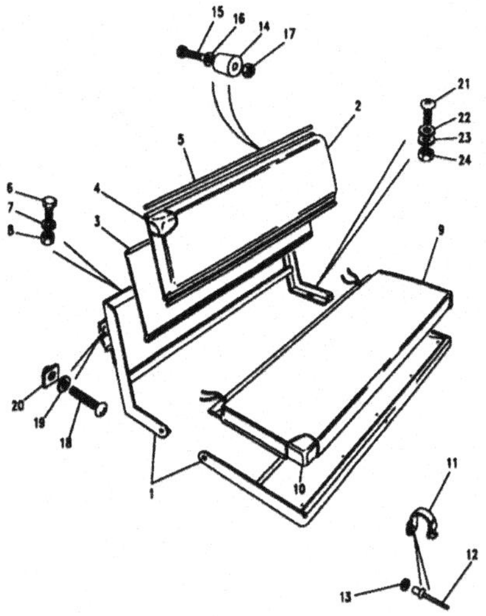

Illus	Part Number	Description	Quantity	Change Point	Remarks
		CUSHION-REAR SEAT FIXED BENCH			
9	MTC4487RD	CLOTH-BRUSHWOOD	1	Note (1)	
9	320674	VINYL-BLACK	1		
9	MWC5464RCF	CLOTH-BLUE GREY	1	Note (2)	
9	AWR5775RFI	CLOTH-RAYLEIGH	1	Note (3)	
9	AWR5767RPI	VINYL-TWILL	1	Note (4)	
9	MWC5464RUY	CLOTH-MORLAND GREY	1	Note (5)	
9	MWC5463LCS	VINYL-SLATE GREY	1		
10	331835	• Foam cushion	1		
9	HLF105570LOY	CUSHION-REAR SEAT FIXED BENCH-CLOTH-DARK GRANITE	1	Note (6)	9 seats
10	331835	• Foam cushion	1		
11	302648	Straps-load	1		
12	RU612373L	Rivet-3/16" x 0.575"lng	2		
13	WC702101L	Washer-plain	2		
14	304125	Buffer rubber-seat front	2		
15	SE105251L	Screw-pan-squab to frame	2		
16	WA105001L	Washer-plain-standard-M5	2		
17	NH105041L	Nut-hexagonal-M5	2		
18	SE106401	Screw-pan-seat frame to body-M6 x 40	2		90"
18	SE106401	Screw-pan-M6 x 40	1		110"
19	WC600045L	Washer-plain-1/4 dia	2		90"
19	WC600045L	Washer-plain-1/4 dia	1		110"
20	MTC3203	Nut plate-seat frame to body	2		
	MWC5661	Plate-2 seats	1		110"
18	SE604051L	Screw-pan-1/4UNF x 5/8	2		
19	WA106044L	Washer-plain-6mm	2		
20	334177	Nut plate-rear seat squab-1/4UNF	1		
18	SE106401	Screw-pan-M6 x 40	1		110"
19	WC600045L	Washer-plain-1/4 dia	2		
24	NH106041L	Nut-hexagonal-nyloc-M6	1		

CHANGE POINTS:
(1) To (V) EA 314173
(2) To (V) HA 455945
(3) From (V) VA 999222 To (V) WA 159806
(4) From (V) VA 999222
(5) To (V) TA 997521
(6) From (V) XA 159807

Illus	Part Number	Description	Quantity	Change Point	Remarks
21	SE106201L	Screw-seat frame to wheelarch-pan head-M6 x 20	2		
22	MRC5528	Washer-plain	2		
23	AFU1070	Washer	2		
24	NH106041L	Nut-seat frame to wheelarch-hexagonal-nyloc-M6	2		
	MTC8335	Cover edge upper	2		Germany 110"
	MTC7513	Edging strip	A/R		
12	RU608313L	Rivet-aluminium-1/8" x 0.482"lng	2		

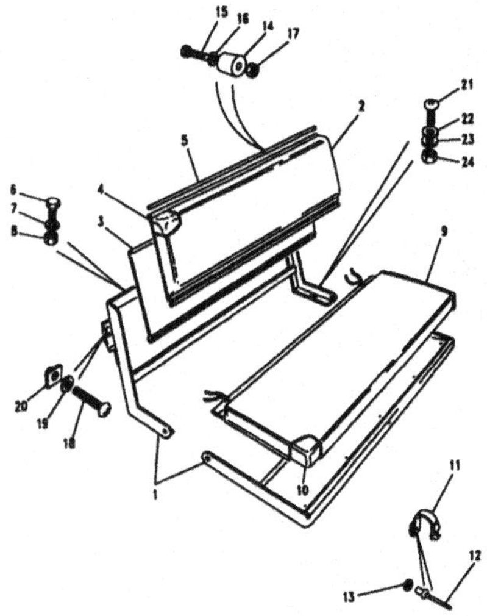

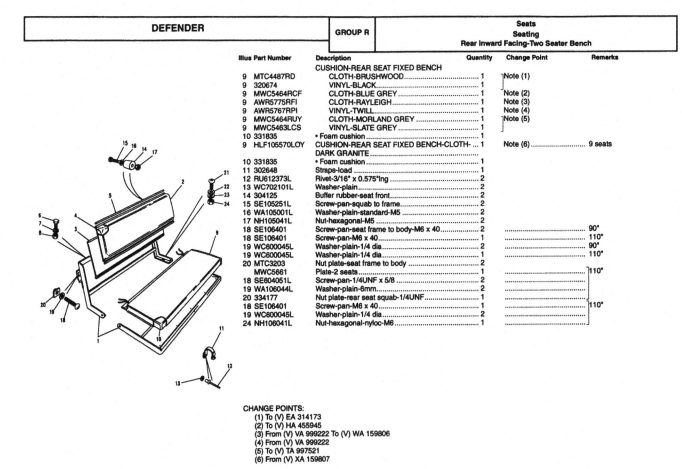

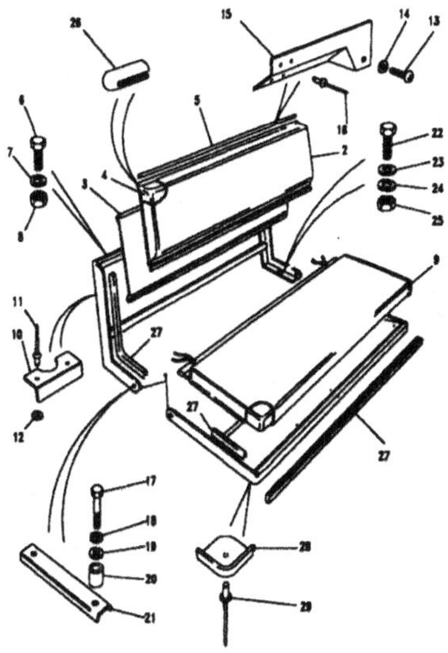

Illus	Part Number	Description	Quantity	Change Point	Remarks
		FRAME ASSEMBLY-BENCH SEAT			
1	MWC8548	RH	1		110" except Hard Top and Spain
1	MWC8547	LH	1		
1	BTR5818	LH-9 seats	1		Hard Top Spain 110"
		SQUAB-REAR SEAT FIXED BENCH			
2	MWC5494RCF	Blue Grey-Grey-cloth	1	Note (1)	110"
2	MWC5494RUY	Morland Grey-cloth	1	Note (2)	110"
2	BTR2937RUY	Morland Grey-cloth	1	Note (3)	110"
2	AWR7044RFI	Rayleigh-cloth	1	Note (4)	110"
2	HLE110090LOY	3 SEAT-CLOTH-DARK GRANITE	1	Note (5)	
4	AWR6863	• Foam-squab-3 seat	1		
2	MWC5493LCS	SQUAB-REAR SEAT FIXED BENCH-GREY-VINYL	1	Note (6)	110"
3	STC1013	• Panel-rear seat squab main face	1	Note (7)	
4	396697	• Foam-squab	1		
2	BTR2936LCS	SQUAB-REAR SEAT FIXED BENCH-SLATE GREY-VINYL	1	From (V) HA 906384 To (V) TA 999221	110"
4	396697	• Foam-squab	1		
2	AWR7046RPI	SQUAB-REAR SEAT FIXED BENCH-TWILL-VINYL	1	From (V) VA 999222	110"
4	AWR6863	• Foam-squab-3 seat	1		
2	STC60744	Squab-rear seat fixed bench-Green-leather	2	Note (5)	Heritage
5	334540	Rod-rear seats-inward facing	2		110"
6	SH106124	Screw-hexagonal head-M6 x 12	6		
7	WL106004L	Washer-spring	6		
8	NH106044	Nut-hexagonal	6		

CHANGE POINTS:
(1) To (V) GA
(2) From (V) HA To (V) HA 906383
(3) From (V) HA 906384 To (V) TA 999221
(4) From (V) VA 999222 To (V) WA 159806
(5) From (V) XA 159807
(6) To (V) HA 906383
(7) To (V) HA 905791

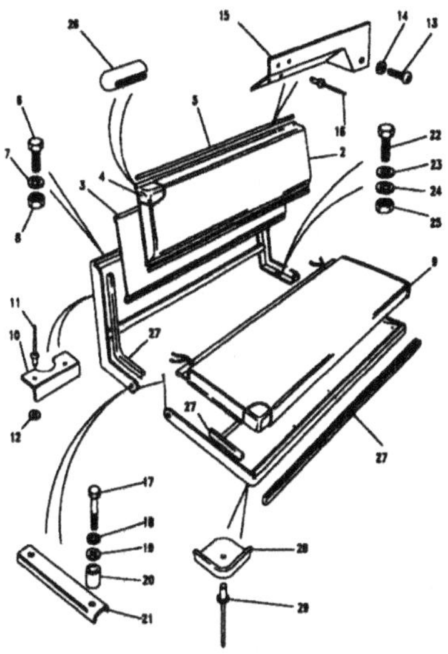

Illus	Part Number	Description	Quantity	Change Point	Remarks
		CUSHION-REAR SEAT FIXED BENCH			
9	MWC5492RCF	Blue Grey-Grey-cloth	1	Note (1)	110"
9	MWC5492RUY	Morland Grey-cloth	1	Note (2)	110"
9	AWR5771RFI	Rayleigh-cloth	1	Note (3)	110"
9	MWC5491LCS	Slate Grey-Vinyl	1	Note (4)	110"
9	AWR5783RPI	Twill-Vinyl	1	Note (3)	110"
9	STC60743	Green-leather	2	Note (5)	Heritage
9	HLF105560LOY	cloth-Dark Granite	1	Note (5)	110"
10	334601	Bracket-rear seat retention	1		110"
11	RA612237	Rivet	2		110"
12	WA110061L	Washer-M10	2		110"
13	SE106164	Screw	1		110"
14	WC600045L	Washer-plain-1/4 dia	1		
15	MWC6924	Bracket-RH	1		
15	MWC6925	Bracket-LH	1		
16	RA612157	Rivet	4		
17	FB108101L	Bolt-flanged head-M8 x 50	2		110"
18	WL108001L	Washer-sprung-M8	2		
19	WC108051L	Washer-M8	2		110"
20	MRC6845	Spacer	2		
21	MRC6843	Stiffener-seat frame	1		
22	FS108207L	Screw-flanged head-M8 x 20	2		110" except Spain
23	WC108051L	Washer-M8	2		
24	WL108001L	Washer-sprung-M8	2		
25	FN108047L	Nut-flange-flanged head-M8	2		
22	SE106201L	Screw-pan head-M6 x 20	2		110"
23	MRC5528	Washer-plain	2		
25	NH106041L	Nut-hexagonal-nyloc-M6	1		
	AFU1070	Washer	2		
		GERMANY ONLY			
26	MTC8335	Cover edge upper	2		110"
27	MTC7513	Edging strip	A/R		
29	RU608313L	Rivet-aluminium-1/8" x 0.482"lng	2		

CHANGE POINTS:
(1) To (V) EA 314267
(2) From (V) EA 314268 To (V) TA 999221
(3) From (V) VA 999222
(4) To (V) TA 999221
(5) From (V) XA 159807

DEFENDER	GROUP R	Seats Seating Rear Inward Facing-130

Illus	Part Number	Description	Quantity	Change Point	Remarks
1	RRC2485	Seat-rear fixed bench	2		

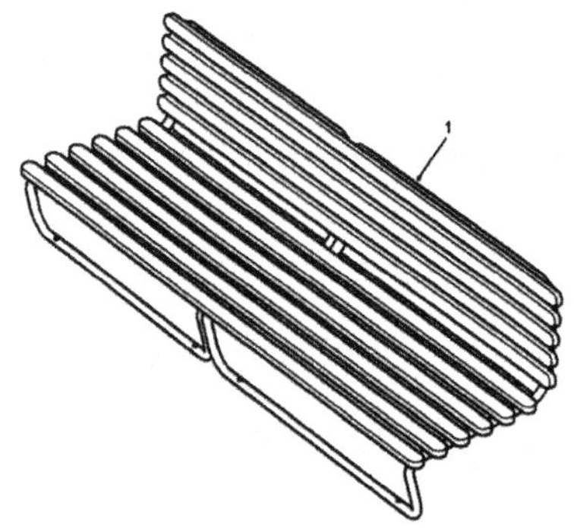

AJRXXA8A

DEFENDER	GROUP R	Seats Seating Rear-Grab Rail

Illus	Part Number	Description	Quantity	Change Point	Remarks
1	MWC4380	Handle assembly-roof trim grab	1		Station Wagon 110"
2	FS108207L	Screw-grab rail to BC post-flanged head-M8 x 20	4		110"
3	WC108051L	Washer-M8	4		
4	WL108001L	Washer-grab rail to BC post-sprung-M8	4		

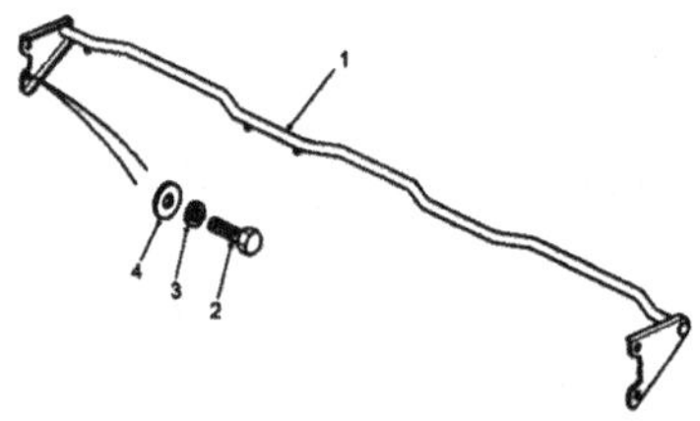

AJRXEA8A

Seating
Lock-Rear Forward Facing Split

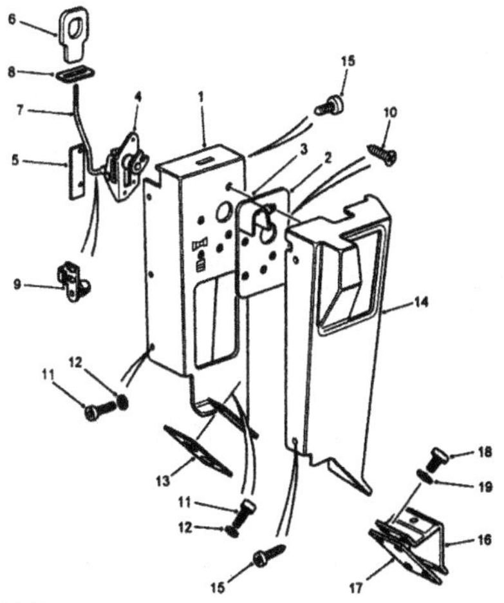

AJRXIA1A

Illus	Part Number	Description	Quantity	Change Point	Remarks
1	MWC1496	Bracket-front seat support-RH	1		
1	MWC1497	Bracket-front seat support-LH	1		
2	MWC3138	PLATE ASSEMBLY-RH	1	Note (1)	
2	MWC3139	PLATE ASSEMBLY-LH	1	Note (1)	
3	MUC5456	• Buffer rubber	2		
2	HWE100740	Plate assembly-RH	1	Note (2)	
2	HWE100750	Plate assembly-LH	1	Note (2)	
4	MWC2532	Latch assembly-rear seat cushion-RH	1		
4	MWC2533	Latch assembly-rear seat cushion-LH	1		
5	MUC9999	Plate	2		
6	MUC5743	Ring pull-seat lock-rear seats	NLA		Use MWC2722.
6	MWC2722	Ring pull-seat lock-rear seats	2		
7	MWC1614	Link-squab hinge-RH	1		
7	MWC1615	Link-squab hinge-LH	1		
8	MWC2891	Washer	2		
9	ADU3469L	Clip-linkage	2		
10	SF910141L	Screw	10		
11	SE105101L	Screw-M5	16		
12	WA105001L	Washer-plain-standard-M5	16		
13	MWC1608	Plate-safety harness reinforcement mounting-RH	1		
13	MWC1609	Plate-safety harness reinforcement mounting-LH	1		
14	MWC1632	Cover-lock striker-RH	1		
14	MWC1633	Cover-lock striker-LH	1		
15	AV608081L	Screw	12		
16	MWC5417	Support-seat-10 seats	2		
17	MWC5455	Plate-10 seats	2		
18	SE105165L	Screw-M5 x 16-Black	8		
19	WA105001L	Washer-plain-standard-M5	8		

CHANGE POINTS:
(1) To (V) VA 133066
(2) From (V) VA 133067

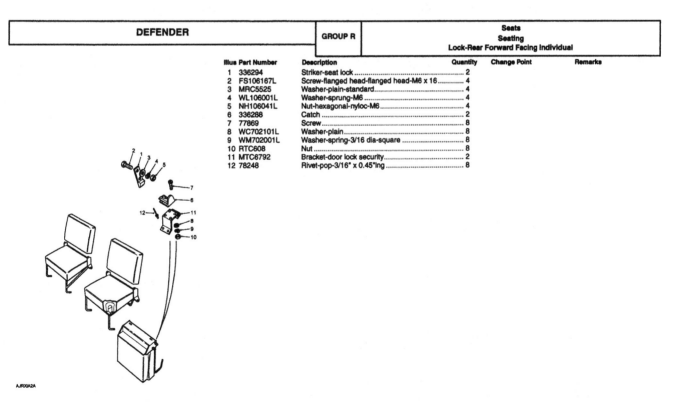

Seating
Lock-Rear Forward Facing Individual

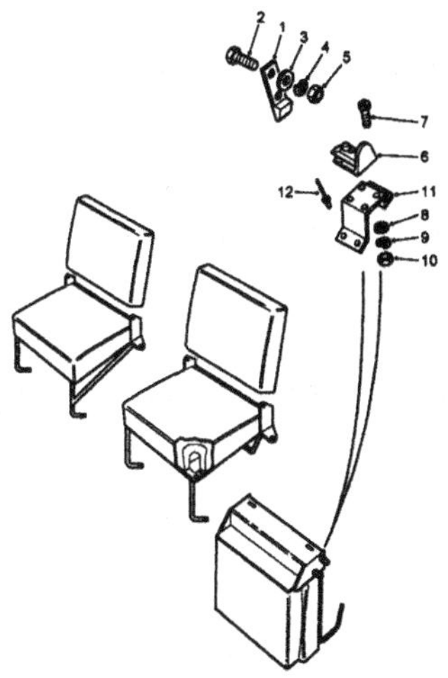

AJRXIA2A

Illus	Part Number	Description	Quantity	Change Point	Remarks
1	336294	Striker-seat lock	2		
2	FS106167L	Screw-flanged head-flanged head-M6 x 16	4		
3	MRC5525	Washer-plain-standard	4		
4	WL106001L	Washer-sprung-M6	4		
5	NH106041L	Nut-hexagonal-nyloc-M6	4		
6	336288	Catch	2		
7	77869	Screw	8		
8	WC702101L	Washer-plain	8		
9	WM702001L	Washer-spring-3/16 dia-square	8		
10	RTC608	Nut	8		
11	MTC6792	Bracket-door lock security	2		
12	78248	Rivet-pop-3/16" x 0.45"lng	8		

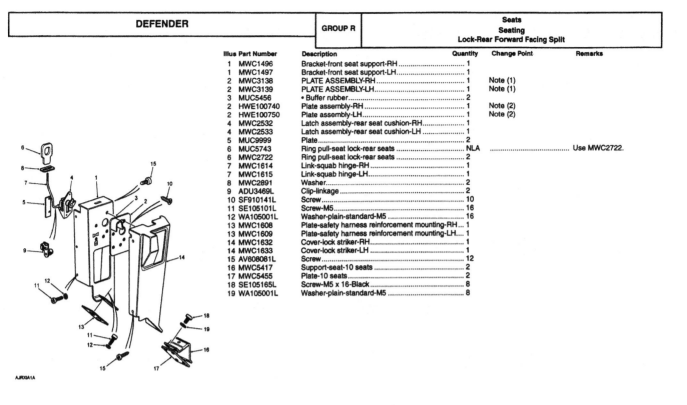

DEFENDER	GROUP R	Seats Seating Squab Lock-Rear Forward Facing Individual

Illus	Part Number	Description	Quantity	Change Point	Remarks
1	MXC2744	Catch-RH-centre	1		
1	MXC2745	Catch-LH	1		
2	SE106164	Screw	3		
3	WC600045L	Washer-plain-1/4 dia	3		
4	NY106041L	Nut-hexagonal head-nyloc-M6	NLA		Use NY106047L.
5	SH604071L	Screw-hexagonal head-1/4UNF x 7/8	3		
6	MXC2751	Spacer	3		
7	WC600045L	Washer-plain-1/4 dia	3		
8	79134	Screw	3		
9	MTC6801	Spring	3		
10	MTC6802	Plate	3		
11	SE106164	Screw	3		
12	WL106004L	Washer-spring	3		
13	NH106044	Nut-hexagonal	3		
		EXCEPT CENTRE SQUAB			
14	336294	Striker-seat lock-except centre squab	2		
15	SE106164	Screw-except centre squab	2		
16	WC600045L	Washer-except centre squab-plain-1/4 dia	2		
17	WL106004L	Washer-spring-except centre squab	2		
18	NH106044	Nut-hexagonal-except centre squab	2		
19	MXC1813LCS	Squab cover-RH-centre	1		
19	MXC1814LCS	Squab cover-LH	1		
20	MTC9424	Screw	6	Note (1)	
20	SF104164	Screw	6	Note (2)	

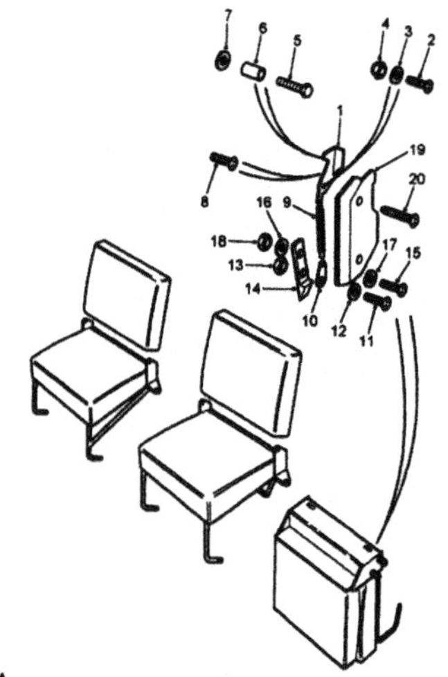

AJRX0A4A

CHANGE POINTS:
(1) To (V) FA 419520
(2) From (V) FA 419521

DEFENDER	GROUP R	Seats Seat Belts Front Seatbelt Assembly-Full Length Hood-To (V) 87MY

Illus	Part Number	Description	Quantity	Change Point	Remarks
1	MTC1608	Seat belt-RH	1	Note (1)	
1	MTC1609	Seat belt-LH	1	Note (1)	
	AFU2875	Clip	2		
	AB610051L	Screw-self tapping-No 10 x 5 x 8	4		

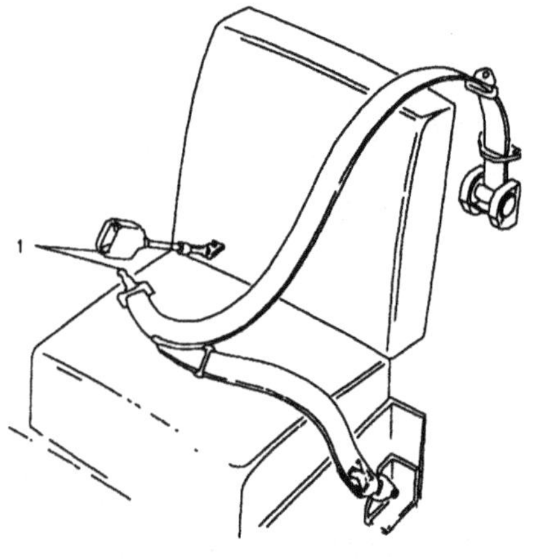

CHANGE POINTS:
(1) To (V) AA 271214

DEFENDER	GROUP R	Seats Seat Belts Front Seatbelt Assembly-Except Length Hood-To (V) 87MY

Illus	Part Number	Description	Quantity	Change Point	Remarks
1	MWC3284	Seat belt-RH-non audible	1	Note (1)	
1	MWC3285	Seat belt-LH-non audible	1	Note (1)	
1	MTC7798	Seat belt-LH-audible	1	Note (1)	
	AFU2875	Clip	2		
	AB610051L	Screw-self tapping-No 10 x 5 x 8	4		

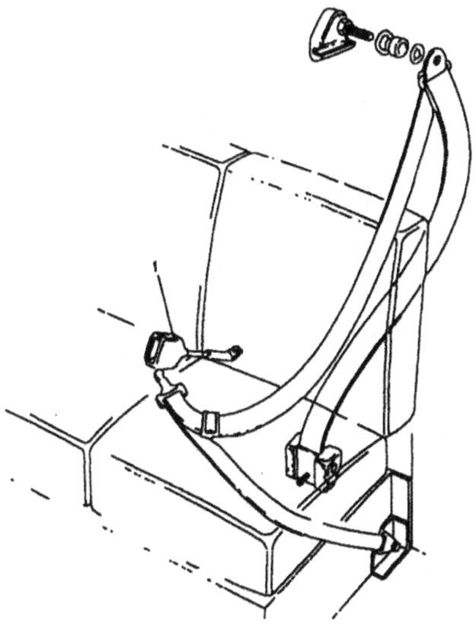

CHANGE POINTS:
(1) To (V) AA 271214

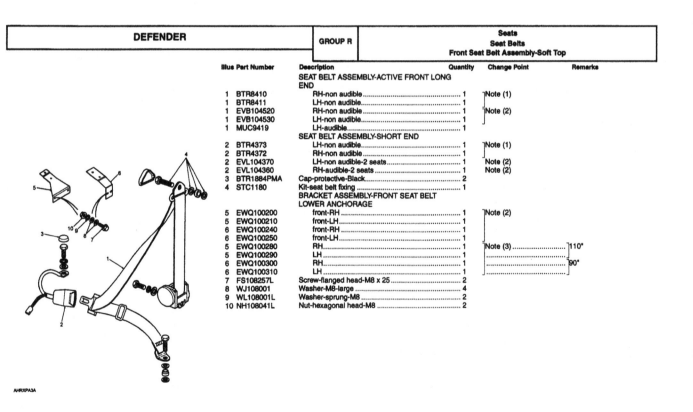

DEFENDER	GROUP R	Seats Seat Belts Front Seat Belt Assembly-Soft Top

Illus	Part Number	Description	Quantity	Change Point	Remarks
		SEAT BELT ASSEMBLY-ACTIVE FRONT LONG END			
1	BTR8410	RH-non audible	1	Note (1)	
1	BTR8411	LH-non audible	1		
1	EVB104520	RH-non audible	1	Note (2)	
1	EVB104530	LH-non audible	1		
1	MUC9419	LH-audible	1		
		SEAT BELT ASSEMBLY-SHORT END			
2	BTR4373	LH-non audible	1	Note (1)	
2	BTR4372	RH-non audible	1		
2	EVL104370	LH-non audible-2 seats	1	Note (2)	
2	EVL104360	RH-audible-2 seats	1	Note (2)	
3	BTR1884PMA	Cap-protective-Black	2		
4	STC1180	Kit-seat belt fixing	1		
		BRACKET ASSEMBLY-FRONT SEAT BELT LOWER ANCHORAGE			
5	EWQ100200	front-RH	1	Note (2)	
5	EWQ100210	front-LH	1		
6	EWQ100240	front-RH	1		
6	EWQ100250	front-LH	1		
5	EWQ100280	RH	1	Note (3)	110"
5	EWQ100290	LH	1		
6	EWQ100300	RH	1		90"
6	EWQ100310	LH	1		
7	FS108257L	Screw-flanged head-M8 x 25	2		
8	WJ108001	Washer-M8-large	4		
9	WL108001L	Washer-sprung-M8	2		
10	NH108041L	Nut-hexagonal head-M8	2		

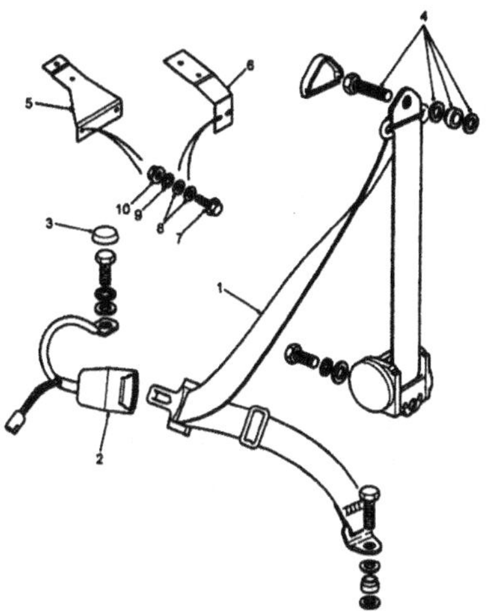

AHRXPA3A

CHANGE POINTS:
(1) To (V) WA 138479
(2) From (V) WA 138480
(3) From (V) XA 159807

Illus	Part Number	Description	Quantity	Change Point	Remarks
		SEAT BELT ASSEMBLY-ACTIVE FRONT LONG END			
1	MXC5492	RH-non audible	1	Note (1)	
1	MXC5493	LH-non audible	1		
1	MXC5491	LH-audible	1		
1	MXC5488	RH-non audible	1	Note (2)	
1	MXC5489	LH-non audible	1	Note (2)	
1	MWC8615	LH-audible	1	Note (2)	
1	BTR6562	RH-non audible	1	Note (3)	Regular Hard Top
1	BTR6561	LH-non audible	1		Regular Hard Top
1	AWR2001	LH-non audible	1		Station Wagon 110"
1	AWR2002	RH-non audible	1		Station Wagon 110"
1	BTR4376	RH	1	Note (4)	TDi Australia Chassis Cab
		SEAT BELT ASSEMBLY-SHORT END			
2	BTR4372	RH-non audible	1	Note (5)	
2	BTR4373	LH-non audible	1	Note (5)	
2	MXC5509	LH-audible	1	Note (5)	
2	EVL104370	LH-non audible-2 seats	1	Note (6)	
2	EVL104360	RH-audible-2 seats	1	Note (6)	
2	EVB104200	LH-audible-3 seats	1	Note (6)	
2	EVB104150	LH-audible-2 seats	1	Note (6)	
3	STC1180	Kit-seat belt fixing	1		
4	BTR1884PMA	Cap-protective-Black	2		

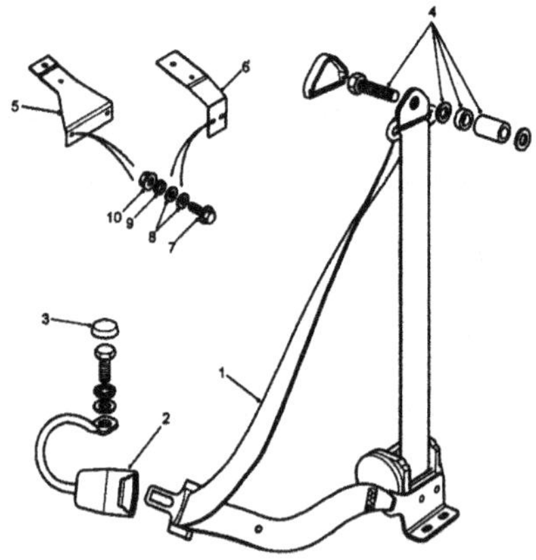

AHRXPA4A

CHANGE POINTS:
(1) To (V) EA 354677
(2) From (V) EA 354678 To (V) KA 924692
(3) From (V) KA 924693
(4) From (V) JA 907021 To (V) KA 924692
(5) To (V) VA 138479
(6) From (V) WA 138480

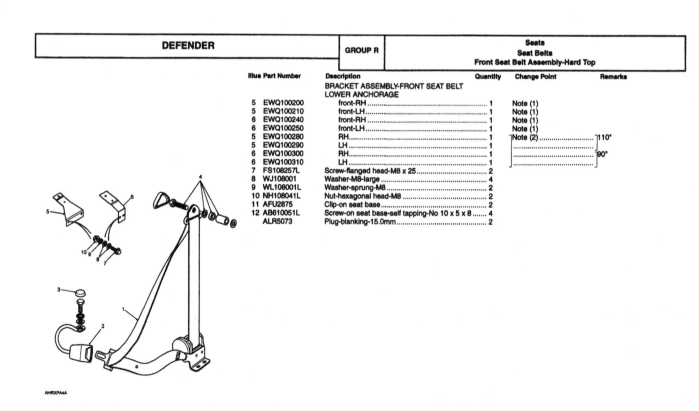

Illus	Part Number	Description	Quantity	Change Point	Remarks
		BRACKET ASSEMBLY-FRONT SEAT BELT LOWER ANCHORAGE			
5	EWQ100200	front-RH	1	Note (1)	
5	EWQ100210	front-LH	1	Note (1)	
6	EWQ100240	front-RH	1	Note (1)	
6	EWQ100250	front-LH	1	Note (1)	
5	EWQ100280	RH	1	Note (2)	110"
5	EWQ100290	LH	1		
6	EWQ100300	RH	1		90"
6	EWQ100310	LH	1		
7	FS108257L	Screw-flanged head-M8 x 25	2		
8	WJ108001	Washer-M8-large	4		
9	WL108001L	Washer-sprung-M8	2		
10	NH108041L	Nut-hexagonal head-M8	2		
11	AFU2875	Clip-on seat base	2		
12	AB610051L	Screw-on seat base-self tapping-No 10 x 5 x 8	4		
	ALR5073	Plug-blanking-15.0mm	2		

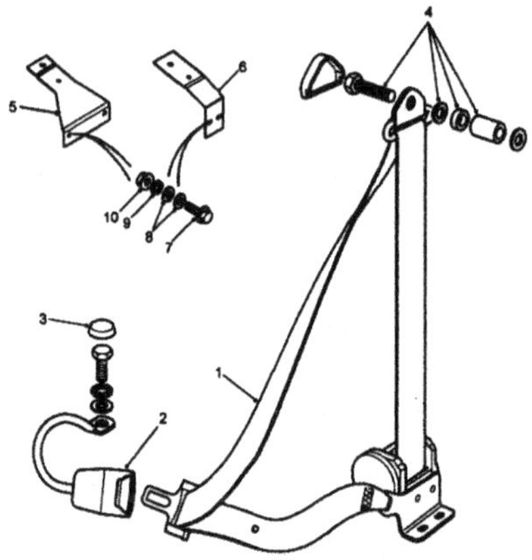

AHRXPA4A

CHANGE POINTS:
(1) From (V) WA 138480 To (V) WA 159806
(2) From (V) XA 159807

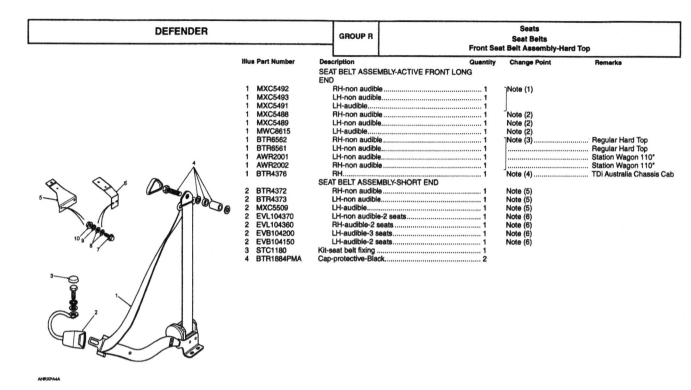

DEFENDER	GROUP R	Seats Seat Belts Front Seat Belt Assembly-V8 EFI-4.0L

Illus	Part Number	Description	Quantity	Change Point	Remarks
1	AWR4656	SEAT BELT ASSEMBLY-PASSIVE FRONT-LH	1		Except Japan
	MXC5509	• Seat belt assembly-short end-LH-audible	1		
1	AWR4316	SEAT BELT ASSEMBLY-PASSIVE FRONT-RH	1		Except Japan
	MXC5510	• Seat belt assembly-short end	1		
	BTR6561	Seat belt assembly-active front long end-LH-non audible	1		Japan
	BTR6562	Seat belt assembly-active front long end-RH-non audible	1		
	EVB104450	Seat belt assembly-short end-RH-non audible-2 seats	1		
	EVL104370	Seat belt assembly-short end-LH-non audible-2 seats	1		
2	MTC8338	Clip	2		
3	AB610051L	Screw-on seat base-self tapping-No 10 x 5 x 8	4		
	STC1180	Kit-seat belt fixing	1		
	BTR1884PMA	Cap-protective-Black	2		
	WL106001L	Washer-sprung-M6	1		
3	FS106255L	Screw-flanged head-M6 x 25	1		
	NH106041L	Nut-hexagonal-nyloc-M6	1		
	MRC5527	Washer-plain-M6	2		

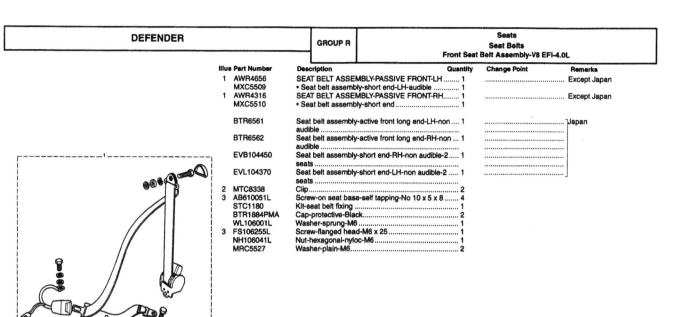

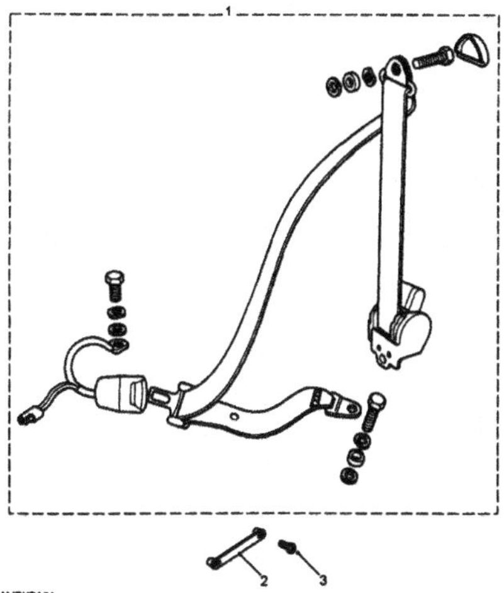

AMRXPA2A

DEFENDER	GROUP R	Seats Seat Belts Centre Front Seat Belt Assembly-To (V) WA138479

Illus	Part Number	Description	Quantity	Change Point	Remarks
	MXC2537	Seat belt assembly-active front lap	NLA	Note (1)	Use BTR4348.
	BTR4348	SEAT BELT ASSEMBLY-ACTIVE FRONT LAP	1	Note (2)	3 front seats
2	BTR4346	• Seat belt assembly-short end	1		
1	BTR4347	• Seat belt assembly-front long end	1		
3	STC1180	Kit-seat belt fixing	1	Note (3)	

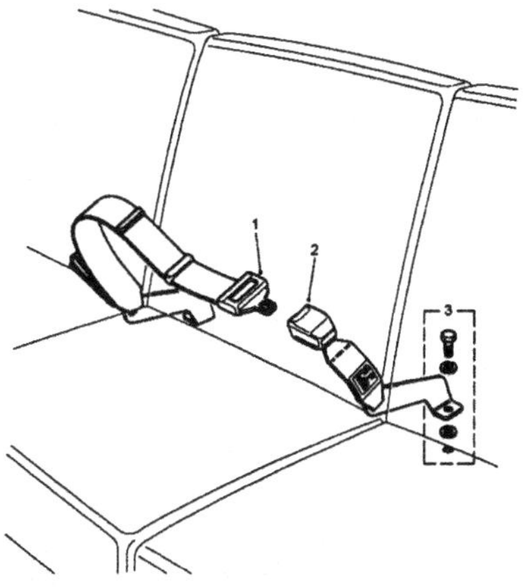

AHRXPA5A

CHANGE POINTS:
(1) To (V) KA 924692
(2) From (V) KA 924693 To (V) WA 138479
(3) From (V) KA 924693

Centre Front Seat Belt Assembly-From (V) WA138480

Illus	Part Number	Description	Quantity	Change Point	Remarks
1	EVB104100	Seat belt assembly-short end-RH	1		
2	EVB104110	Seat belt assembly-short end-LH	1		

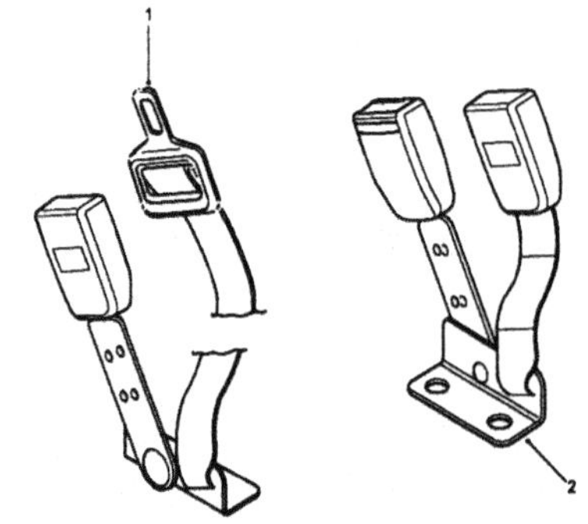

LR0037

Rear Seat Belt-Forward Facing-Outer-Inertia Reel Type

Illus	Part Number	Description	Quantity	Change Point	Remarks
1	BTR304	SEAT BELT ASSEMBLY-ACTIVE FRONT LONG END	2	Note (1)	110" except Crew Cab
3	MXC5521	• Seat belt assembly-short end	1		
2	BTR5779	SEAT BELT ASSEMBLY-ACTIVE FRONT LONG END	2	Note (2)	110" except Crew Cab
3	MXC5521	• Seat belt assembly-short end	1		
4	BTR1884PMA	Cap-protective-Black	4	Note (2)	110"
5	MWC1055PMA	Clip-rear seat belt stowage-Black	2		110"
6	AC606044L	Screw-long	2		110"
2	MXC5488	SEAT BELT ASSEMBLY-ACTIVE FRONT LONG END-RH-NON AUDIBLE	2	Note (1)	130"
3	MXC5510	• Seat belt assembly-short end	1		
2	MXC5489	Seat belt assembly-active front long end-LH-non audible	2	Note (1)	130"
3	BTR4372	Seat belt assembly-short end-RH-non audible	1	Note (2)	130"
3	BTR4373	Seat belt assembly-short end-LH-non audible	1	Note (2)	130"
4	BTR1884PMA	Cap-protective-Black	2	Note (2)	130"
	STC1180	Kit-seat belt fixing	1		130"
7	MRC4655	Plate-rear seat belt male anchor-single	A/R		130"
7	MXC7264	Plate-rear seat belt male anchor-twin	2		110"
	AFU2875	Clip	2		130"
	AB610051L	Screw-self tapping-No 10 x 5 x 8	4		130"

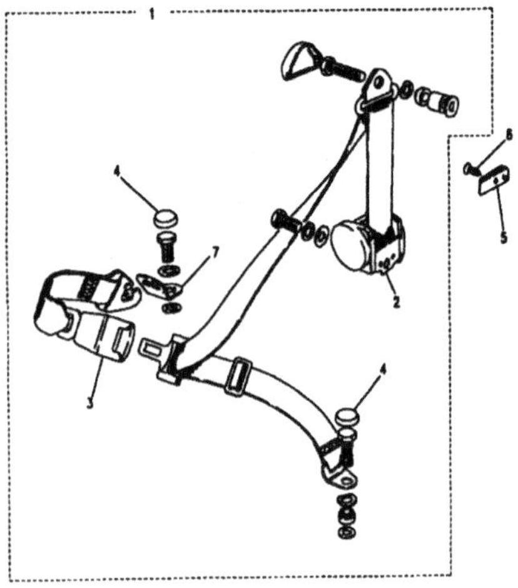

CHANGE POINTS:
(1) To (V) KA 924692
(2) From (V) KA 924693

Illus	Part Number	Description	Quantity	Change Point	Remarks
1	STC79	Seat belt assembly.-rear-outer-static	2		

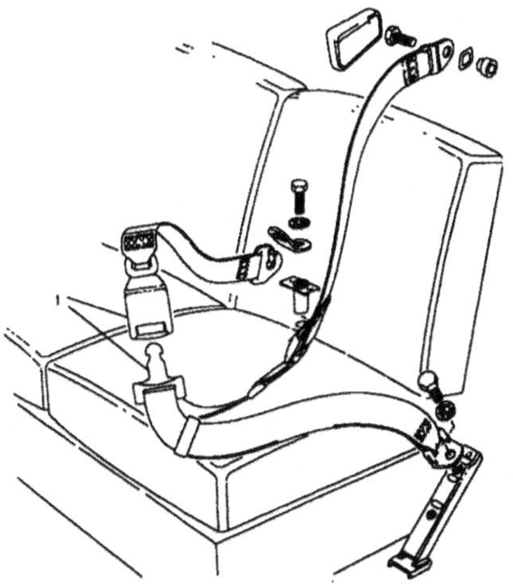

Illus	Part Number	Description	Quantity	Change Point	Remarks
1	MXC5497	Seat belt assembly-rear-centre lap	1	Note (1)	110"
	BTR5782	Seat belt assembly-long end-rear-centre lap	1	Note (2)	
	BTR5781	Seat belt assembly-short end	1		
	MRC4655	Plate-rear seat belt male anchor-single	2		
1	BTR1155	Seat belt assembly-rear-centre lap	1	Note (3)	130"
2	AWR1587	Seat belt assembly-rear-centre lap	1	Note (4)	

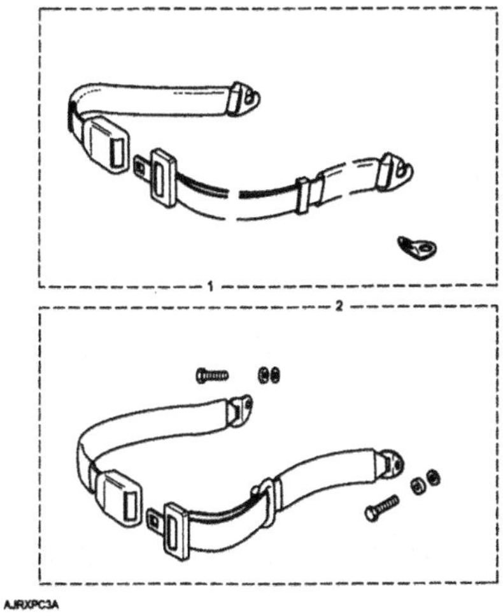

CHANGE POINTS:
(1) To (V) KA 924692
(2) From (V) KA 924693
(3) To (V) MA 945907
(4) From (V) MA 945908

Illus	Part Number	Description	Quantity	Change Point	Remarks
1	MXC5495	Seat belt assembly-individual rear	4	Note (1)	90"
1	BTR9627	Seat belt assembly-individual rear	4	Note (2)	90"
1	AWR4406	SEAT BELT ASSEMBLY-INDIVIDUAL REAR	1		V8 EFi 90"
3	AWR4685	• Seat belt assembly-short end-rear	2		
2	AWR4686	• Tongue assembly-seat belt-double-rear-centre-front	1		
		FOUR INWARD FACING SEATS			
1	MXC5495	Seat belt assembly-individual rear	4		4 seats 110"
		SIX INWARD FACING SEAT OPTION			
2	BTR9626	Tongue assembly-seat belt	6	Note (2)	6 seats 110"
3	BTR9884	Seat belt assembly-short end-rear-centre	2	Note (2)	6 seats 110"
4	BTR9625	Seat belt assembly-short end-side	4	Note (2)	6 seats 110"

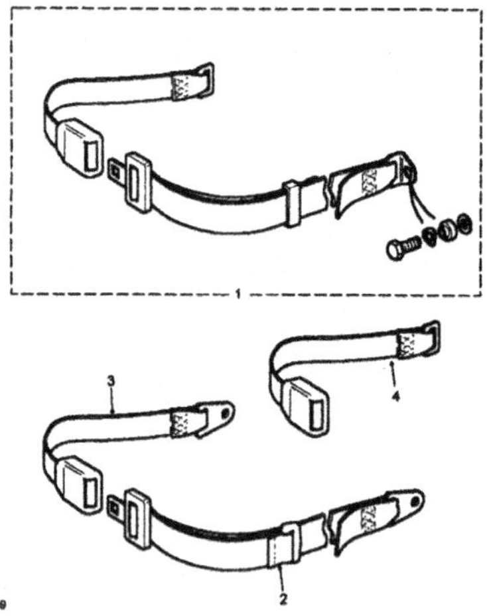

LR0039

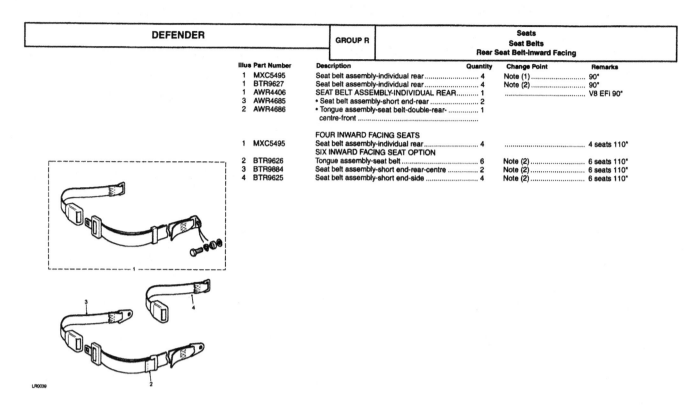

CHANGE POINTS:
(1) To (V) MA 951239
(2) From (V) MA 951240

Illus	Part Number	Description	Quantity	Change Point	Remarks
1	MWC4393	Tube assy-child s/belt mtg	1		110"
2	SH110251L	Screw-hexagonal head-M10 x 25	2		110"
3	WA110061L	Washer-M10	2		110"
4	WA110061L	Washer-M10	A/R		110"
5	MWC8276	Bracket assembly-safety harness mounting-RH	1		110"
5	MWC8277	Bracket assembly-safety harness mounting-LH	1		110"
6	FS108207L	Screw-flanged head-M8 x 20	4		110"
7	WA108051L	Washer-8mm	4		110"
8	FN108041L	Nut-flange-M8	NLA		Use FN108047L.
9	MWC4398	Footrest assembly-front floor-RH	1		110"
9	MWC4399	Footrest assembly-front floor-LH	1		110"
10	FS108207L	Screw-flanged head-M8 x 20	4		110"
11	WA108051L	Washer-8mm	4		110"
12	FN108041L	Nut-flange-M8	NLA		Use FN108047L.
					110"

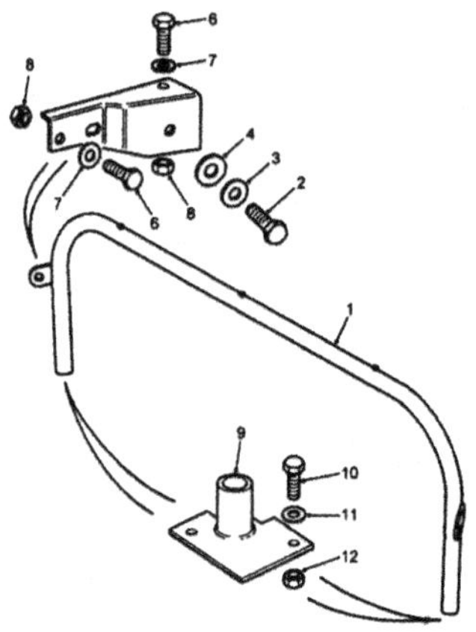

AJRXRC2A

DEFENDER

GROUP R

Seats
Seat Belts
Seat Belt-Front SeatBase Anchorage-Hard & Soft Top

Illus	Part Number	Description	Quantity	Change Point	Remarks
1	395252	Bracket assembly-harness	2		
2	MRC4885	Bar-tie-bent machining-RH	1		
2	MRC4886	Bar-tie-bent machining-LH	1		
3	BH108071L	Bolt-M8 x 35	4		
4	AFU1079	Washer-M8	6		
5	WL108001L	Washer-sprung-M8	4		
6	FN108041L	Nut-flange-M8	NLA		Use FN108047L.
8	AFU1079	Washer-M8	4		
9	WL108001L	Washer-sprung-M8	2		
10	FN108041L	Nut-flange-M8	NLA		Use FN108047L.
11	345100	Gusset-seat belt reinforcement-RH	1		
11	345101	Gusset-seat belt reinforcement-LH	1		

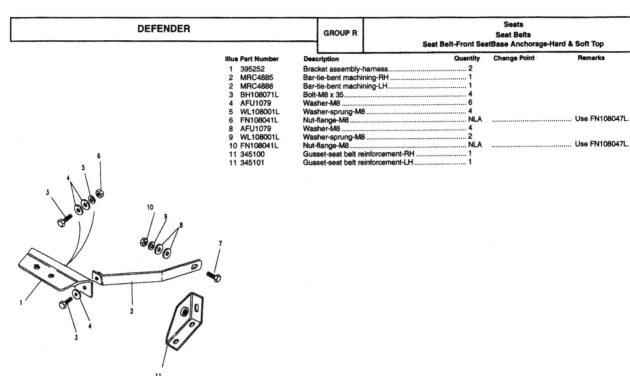

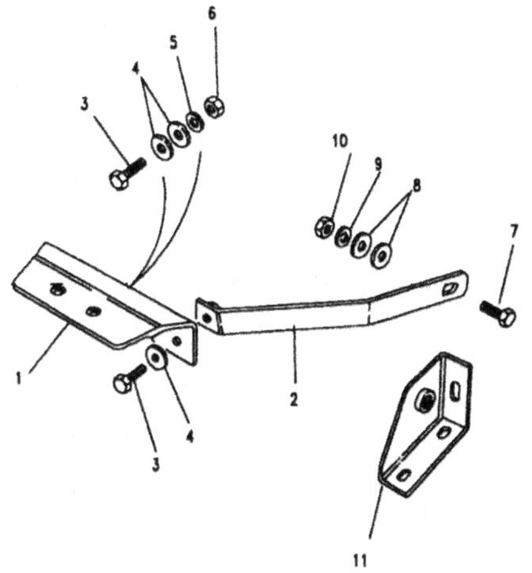

DEFENDER

GROUP R

Seats
Seat Belts
Front Seatbelt Anchorage-50 LE

Illus	Part Number	Description	Quantity	Change Point	Remarks
1	395252	Bracket assembly-harness	2		
2	FS108257L	Screw-flanged head-M8 x 25	2		
3	WC108051	Washer	4		
4	WL108001L	Washer-sprung-M8	2		
5	WL108001L	Washer-sprung-M8	1		
6	FN108047L	Nut-flange-flanged head-M8	2		
7	MRC8524	Bracket	2		
8	RU612373L	Rivet-3/16" x 0.575"lng	4		
9	WC108051L	Washer-M8	4		
10	FN108047L	Nut-flange-flanged head-M8	4		

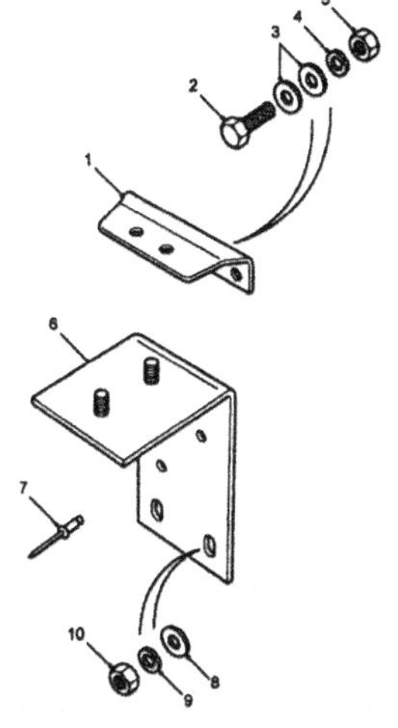

AMRXRA2A

DEFENDER | GROUP R | Seats — Seat Belts — Soft Top Front Seat Anchorage Rail

Illus	Part Number	Description	Quantity	Change Point	Remarks
1	MRC7354	Rail-anchorage-s/harness	1		
2	FS108257L	Screw-flanged head-M8 x 25	4		
3	WA108051L	Washer-8mm	4		
4	WL108001L	Washer-sprung-M8	4		
5	FN108041L	Nut-flange-M8	NLA		Use FN108047L.
6	MRC199	Bar-tie-bent forging-RH	1		
6	MRC200	Bar-tie-bent forging-LH	1		
7	SH112251	Screw-hexagonal head-M12 x 25	2		
8	WL112001L	Washer	2		
9	WA112081L	Washer-plain-standard-M12	2		
10	SH110201L	Screw-hexagonal head-M10 x 20	2		
11	WL110001L	Washer-M10	2		
12	WA110061L	Washer-M10	2		
13	MRC7610	Nut plate	2		
14	MRC8329	Cap-finishing-RH	1		
14	MRC8330	Cap-finishing-LH	1		
15	MRC8389	Plug	4		
16	MRC8390	Lug-fixing-front seat	14		
17	MRC8392	Cover-tie bar-RH	1		
17	MRC8393	Cover-tie bar-LH	1		

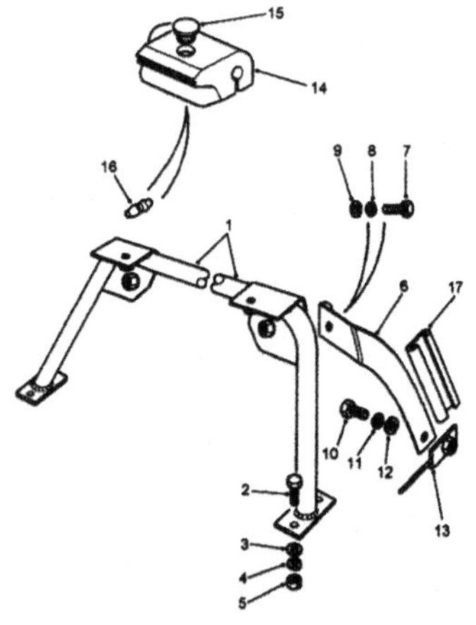

AHRXRA1A

DEFENDER | GROUP R | Seats — Seat Belts — Front Seats-Safety Harness Anchorage-To (V) MA962814

Illus	Part Number	Description	Quantity	Change Point	Remarks
1	MRC7755	Loop-hood	1		
2	345937	Plate	2		
3	BH605101L	Bolt-hexagonal head-5/16UNF x 1 1/4	4		
4	WA108051L	Washer-8mm	4		
5	WL600051	Washer-spring	4		
6	NH605041L	Nut-hexagonal head-5/16UNF	4		
7	MTC1631	Plate	2		
8	RU612373L	Rivet-3/16" x 0.575"lng	8		
9	FS106201L	Screw-flanged head-M6 x 20	8		
10	MRC5524	Washer-plain	8		
11	WL106001L	Washer-sprung-M6	8		
12	NH106041L	Nut-hexagonal-nyloc-M6	8		

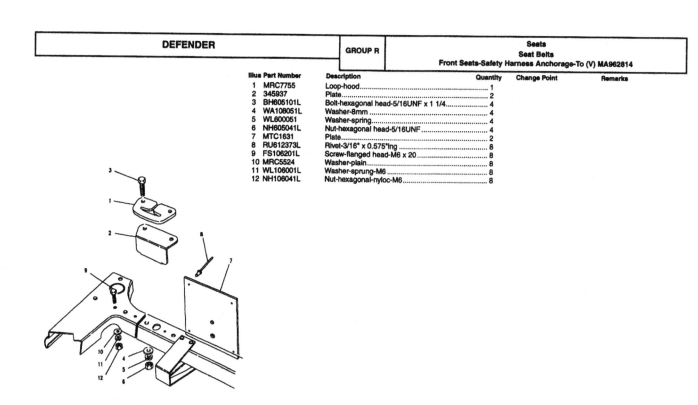

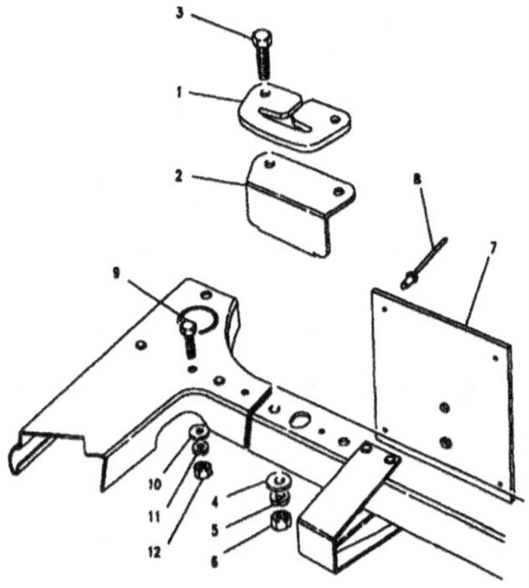

Illus	Part Number	Description	Quantity	Change Point	Remarks
		HARD TOP			
1	395586	Bracket-RH	1		
1	395587	Bracket-LH	1		
2	MRC7626	Bolt	2		
3	WB106041L	Washer-M6	2		
4	WL106001L	Washer-sprung-M6	2		
5	NH106041L	Nut-hexagonal-nyloc-M6	2		

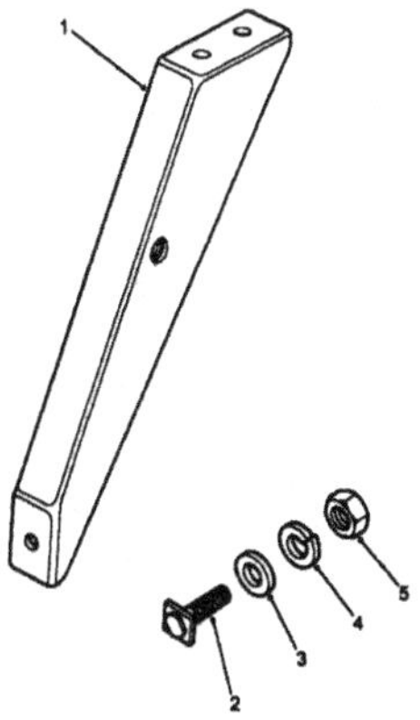

AHRXRA3A

Illus	Part Number	Description	Quantity	Change Point	Remarks
		CHASSIS CAB & HARD TOP			
1	MTC4090	Bracket-for reel	2		
2	WC108051L	Washer-M8	4		
3	WL108001L	Washer-sprung-M8	4		
4	FN108041L	Nut-bracket to bracket-flange-M8	NLA		Use FN108047L.
5	MRC8524	Bracket-to bulkhead	2		
6	RA612347L	Rivet	4		
7	FS108257L	Screw-bracket to bulkhead-flanged head-M8 x 25	4		
8	WA108051L	Washer-8mm	4		
9	WL108001L	Washer-sprung-M8	4		
10	FN108041L	Nut-bracket to bulkhead-flange-M8	NLA		Use FN108047L.

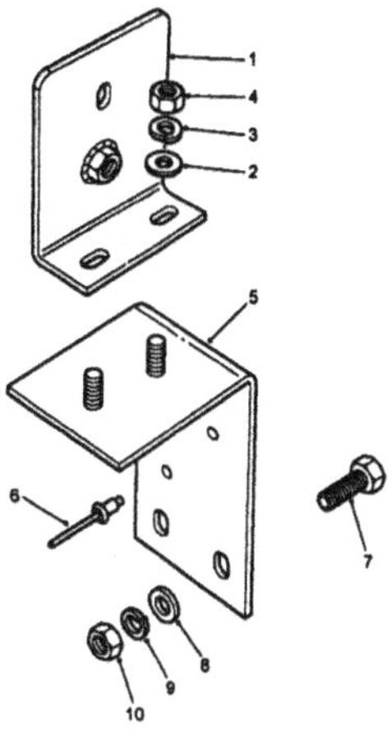

AHRXRA4A

Illus	Part Number	Description	Quantity	Change Point	Remarks
1	345100	Gusset-seat belt reinforcement-RH	1		110"
1	345101	Gusset-seat belt reinforcement-LH	1		
2	395249	Bracket assembly-harness	2		
3	MRC4731	Nut plate	2		
4	RU612373L	Rivet-3/16" x 0.575"lng	2		

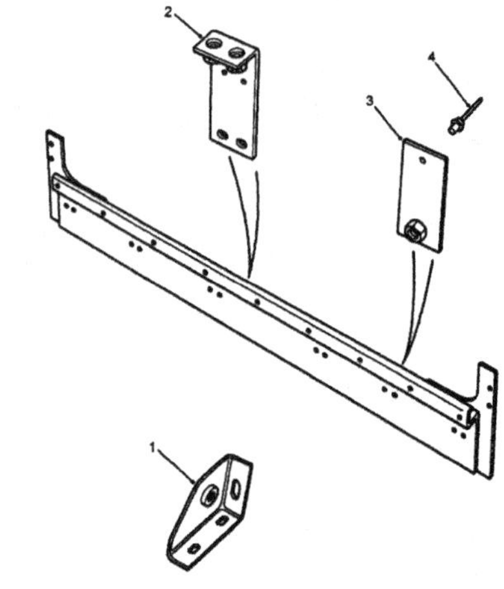

Illus	Part Number	Description	Quantity	Change Point	Remarks
		BRACKET-REAR SEAT BELT ANCHORAGE			
1	MRC9362	upper-RH	1		
1	MRC9361	upper-LH	1		
2	MRC9368	lower-RH	1		
2	MRC9367	lower-LH	1		
3	AFU1298	Monobolt	12		
4	AFU1350	Monobolt-1/4"	6		
5	AFU1298	Monobolt	12		
6	345100	Gusset-seat belt reinforcement-RH	1		
6	345101	Gusset-seat belt reinforcement-LH	1		
7	FS106255L	Screw-flanged head-M6 x 25	2		
8	AFU1069	Washer-plain	2		
9	WL106001L	Washer-sprung-M6	2		
10	NH106041L	Nut-hexagonal-nyloc-M6	2		

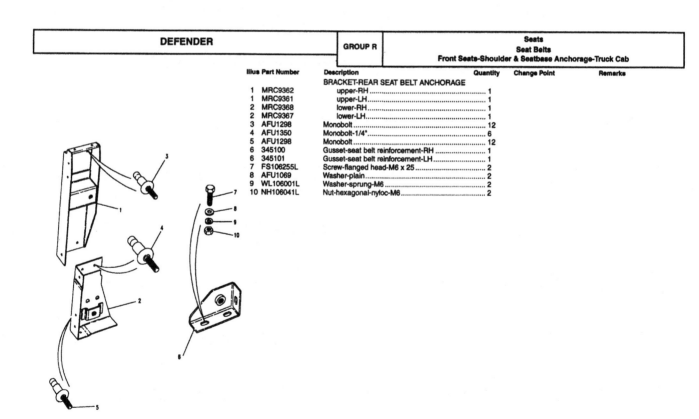

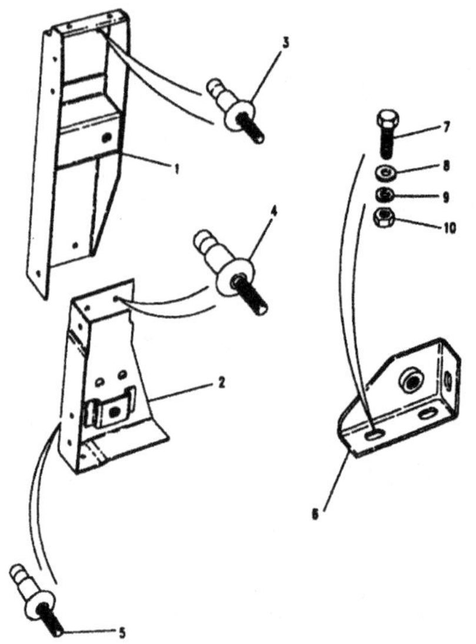

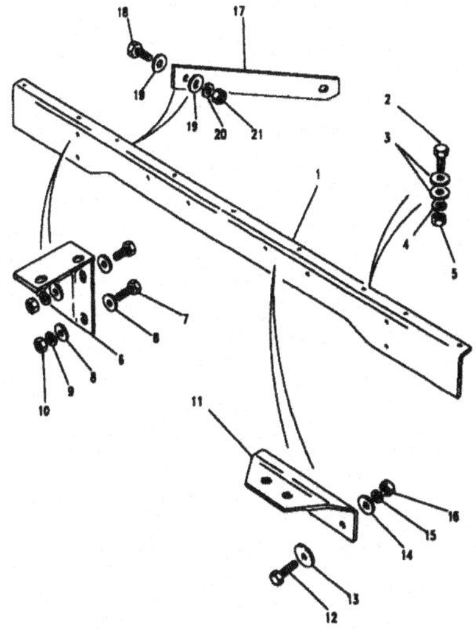

Illus	Part Number	Description	Quantity	Change Point	Remarks
1	MTC3042	Reinforcement	1		Truck Cab
2	FS108257L	Screw-flanged head-M8 x 25	9		
3	WC108051L	Washer-M8	18		
4	WL108001L	Washer-sprung-M8	9		
5	FN108041L	Nut-flange-M8	NLA		Use FN108047L.
6	MTC3051	Bracket-LH	1		
6	MTC3052	Bracket-RH	1		
7	FS108257L	Screw-flanged head-M8 x 25	2		
7	FS108307L	Screw-flanged head-M8 x 30	2		
8	WC108051L	Washer-M8	8		
9	WL108001L	Washer-sprung-M8	4		
10	FN108041L	Nut-flange-M8	NLA		Use FN108047L.
11	395252	Bracket assembly-harness	2		
12	FS108257L	Screw-flanged head-M8 x 25	4		
13	AFU1079	Washer-M8	4		
14	WC108051L	Washer-M8	4		
15	WL108001L	Washer-sprung-M8	4		
16	FN108041L	Nut-flange-M8	NLA		Use FN108047L.
17	MTC3032	Bar-tie-bent forging	2		
18	FS108257L	Screw-flanged head-M8 x 25	4		
19	WC108051L	Washer-M8	8		
20	WL108001L	Washer-sprung-M8	4		
21	FN108041L	Nut-flange-M8	NLA		Use FN108047L.

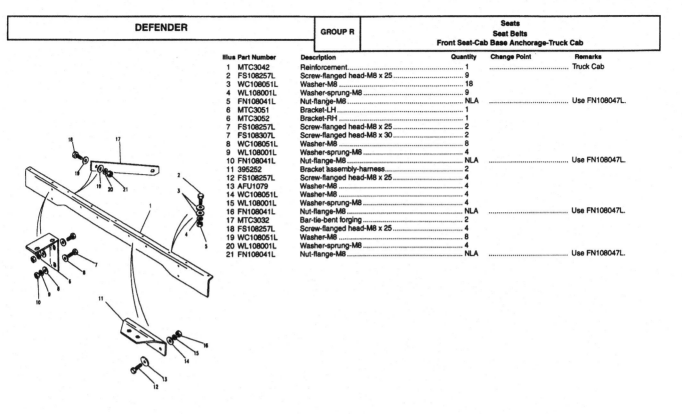

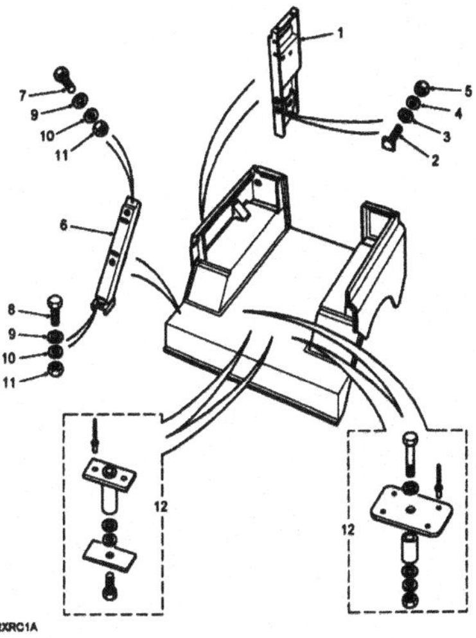

AJRXRC1A

Illus	Part Number	Description	Quantity	Change Point	Remarks
		BRACKET-REAR SEAT BELT ANCHORAGE			
1	MWC5054	upper-RH	1	Note (1)	
1	MWC5055	upper-LH	1		
1	MXC3282	upper-RH	1	Note (2)	
1	MXC3283	upper-LH	1		
2	MRC7626	Bolt	2		
3	WB106041L	Washer-M6	2		
4	WL106001L	Washer-sprung-M6	2		
5	NH106041L	Nut-hexagonal-nyloc-M6	2		
6	347844	Bracket-rear seat belt anchorage-to wheelarch	2		
7	255227	Screw-upper	2		
8	SH605081L	Screw-hexagonal head-5/16UNF x 1	2		
9	3830L	Washer-plain	4		
10	WM600051L	Washer-spring-5/16"	4		
11	NH605041L	Nut-hexagonal head-5/16UNF	4		
12	RTC6065	Kit-seat belt fixing	1		

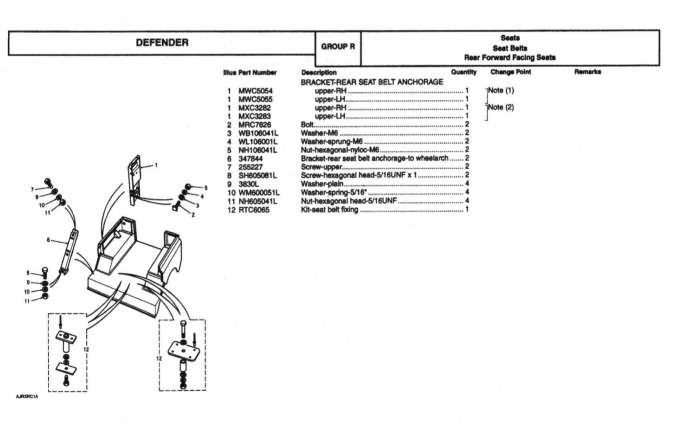

CHANGE POINTS:
(1) To (V) EA
(2) From (V) FA

DEFENDER

GROUP R

Seats
Seat Belts
Anchorage-Rear Inward Facing Seats-To (V) MA951239

Illus	Part Number	Description	Quantity	Change Point	Remarks
1	MTC6836	Stiffener-wheel arch rear floor-front	2	Note (1)	
2	MUC1331	Stiffener-wheel arch rear floor-LH-centre-rear	2		90"
3	MUC1330	Stiffener-wheel arch rear floor-RH-centre-rear	2		90"
2	MTC6835	Stiffener-wheel arch rear floor-centre	2		110"
3	MRC1638	Stiffener-wheel arch rear floor-rear	2		110"
4	MTC6840	Bracket-front subframe-front	2		
4	MTC6839	Bracket-front subframe-centre	2		110"
5	MUC1327	Bracket-rear subframe-centre	2		90"
6	AFU1350	Monobolt-1/4"	12		
7	RA612156L	Rivet	8		
8	RA612236	Rivet	4		

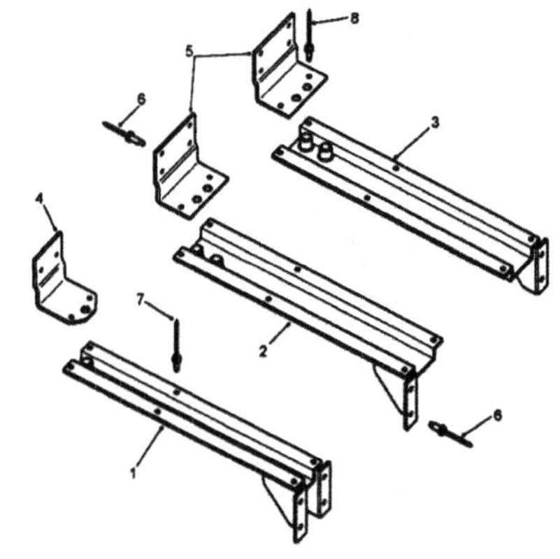

AHRXRE1A

CHANGE POINTS:
(1) To (V) MA 951239

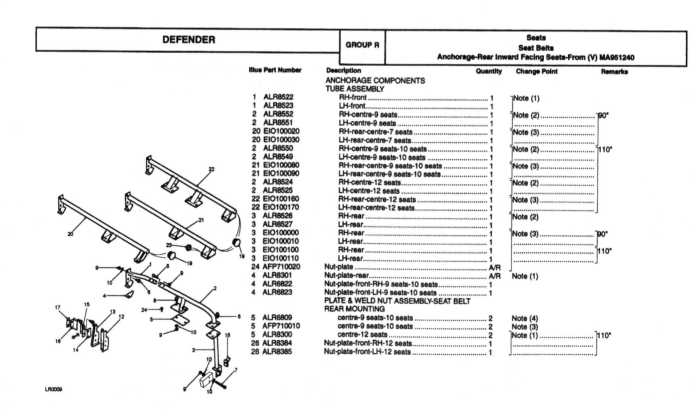

DEFENDER

GROUP R

Seats
Seat Belts
Anchorage-Rear Inward Facing Seats-From (V) MA951240

Illus	Part Number	Description	Quantity	Change Point	Remarks
		ANCHORAGE COMPONENTS			
		TUBE ASSEMBLY			
1	ALR8522	RH-front	1	Note (1)	
1	ALR8523	LH-front	1		
2	ALR8552	RH-centre-9 seats	1	Note (2)	90"
2	ALR8551	LH-centre-9 seats	1		
20	EIO100020	RH-rear-centre-7 seats	1	Note (3)	
20	EIO100030	LH-rear-centre-7 seats	1		
2	ALR8550	RH-centre-9 seats-10 seats	1	Note (2)	110"
2	ALR8549	LH-centre-9 seats-10 seats	1		
21	EIO100080	RH-rear-centre-9 seats-10 seats	1	Note (3)	
21	EIO100090	LH-rear-centre-9 seats-10 seats	1		
2	ALR8524	RH-centre-12 seats	1	Note (2)	
2	ALR8525	LH-centre-12 seats	1		
22	EIO100160	RH-rear-centre-12 seats	1	Note (3)	
22	EIO100170	LH-rear-centre-12 seats	1		
3	ALR8526	RH-rear	1	Note (2)	
3	ALR8527	LH-rear	1		
3	EIO100000	RH-rear	1	Note (3)	90"
3	EIO100010	LH-rear	1		
3	EIO100100	RH-rear	1		110"
3	EIO100110	LH-rear	1		
24	AFP710020	Nut-plate	A/R		
4	ALR8301	Nut-plate-rear	A/R	Note (1)	
4	ALR6822	Nut-plate-front-RH-9 seats-10 seats	1		
4	ALR6823	Nut-plate-front-LH-9 seats-10 seats	1		
		PLATE & WELD NUT ASSEMBLY-SEAT BELT			
		REAR MOUNTING			
5	ALR6809	centre-9 seats-10 seats	2	Note (4)	
5	AFP710010	centre-9 seats-10 seats	2	Note (3)	
5	ALR8300	centre-12 seats	2	Note (1)	110"
26	ALR8384	Nut-plate-front-RH-12 seats	1		
26	ALR8385	Nut-plate-front-LH-12 seats	1		

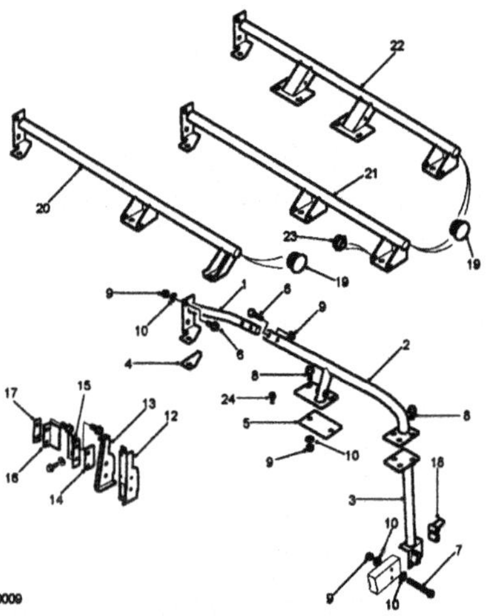

LR0009

CHANGE POINTS:
(1) From (V) MA 951240
(2) From (V) MA 951240 To (V) WA 159806
(3) From (V) XA 159807
(4) To (V) WA 159806

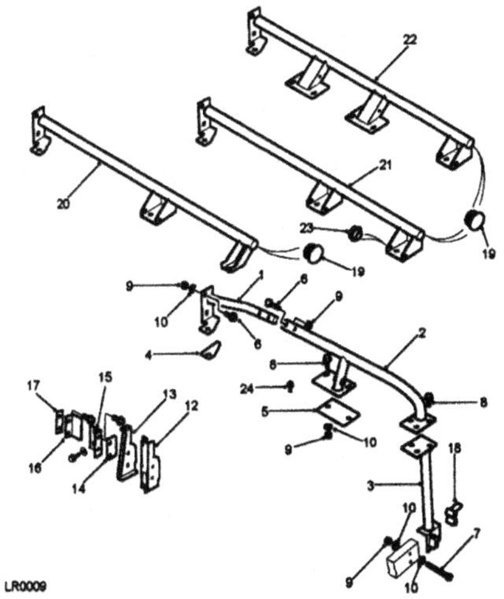

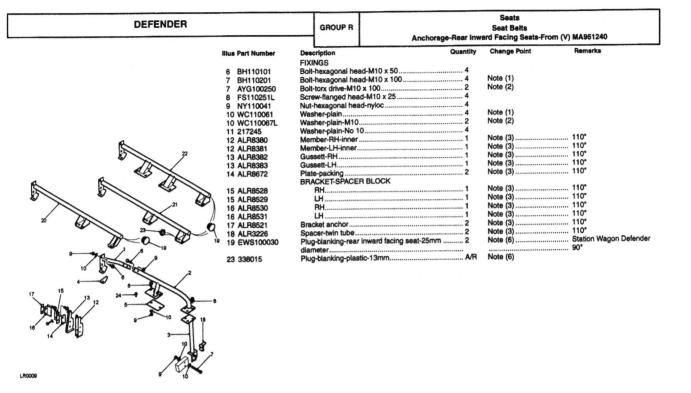

Illus	Part Number	Description	Quantity	Change Point	Remarks
		FIXINGS			
6	BH110101	Bolt-hexagonal head-M10 x 50	4		
7	BH110201	Bolt-hexagonal head-M10 x 100	4	Note (1)	
7	AYG100250	Bolt-torx drive-M10 x 100	2	Note (2)	
8	FS110251L	Screw-flanged head-M10 x 25	4		
9	NY110041	Nut-hexagonal head-nyloc	4		
10	WC110061	Washer-plain	4	Note (1)	
10	WC110067L	Washer-plain-M10	2	Note (2)	
11	217245	Washer-plain-No 10	4		
12	ALR8380	Member-RH-inner	1	Note (3)	110"
12	ALR8381	Member-LH-inner	1	Note (3)	110"
13	ALR8382	Gussett-RH	1	Note (3)	110"
13	ALR8383	Gussett-LH	1	Note (3)	110"
14	ALR8672	Plate-packing	2	Note (3)	110"
		BRACKET-SPACER BLOCK			
15	ALR8528	RH	1	Note (3)	110"
15	ALR8529	LH	1	Note (3)	110"
16	ALR8530	RH	1	Note (3)	110"
16	ALR8531	LH	1	Note (3)	110"
17	ALR8521	Bracket anchor	2	Note (3)	110"
18	ALR3226	Spacer-twin tube	2	Note (3)	110"
19	EWS100030	Plug-blanking-rear inward facing seat-25mm diameter	2	Note (6)	Station Wagon Defender 90"
23	338015	Plug-blanking-plastic-13mm	A/R	Note (6)	

CHANGE POINTS:
(1) To (V) WA 138479
(2) From (V) WA 138480
(3) From (V) MA 951240
(6) From (V) XA 159807

Tool Stowage

Illus	Part Number	Description	Quantity	Change Point	Remarks
1	MWC9313	Bracket-jack stowage mounting	1	Note (1)	
2	78248	Rivet-pop-3/16" x 0.45"lng	2		
3	371144	Ring-retention-rubber	1		
4	MTC1359	Strap-spare wheel jack retention	1		
5	AFU1256	Washer-plain	1		
6	78248	Rivet-pop-3/16" x 0.45"lng	1		
7	MWC2145	Bracket-jack stowage-LH	1		
7	MWC2146	Bracket-jack stowage-RH	1		
8	78248	Rivet-pop-3/16" x 0.45"lng	2		
9	90508035	Clip	4		
10	78248	Rivet-pop-3/16" x 0.45"lng	4		

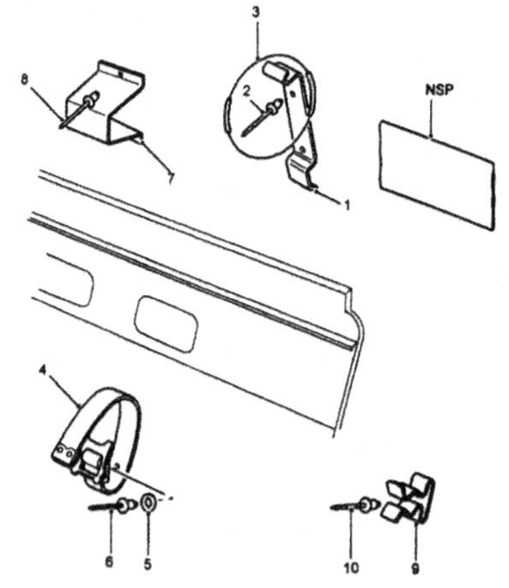

AHSXAA2A

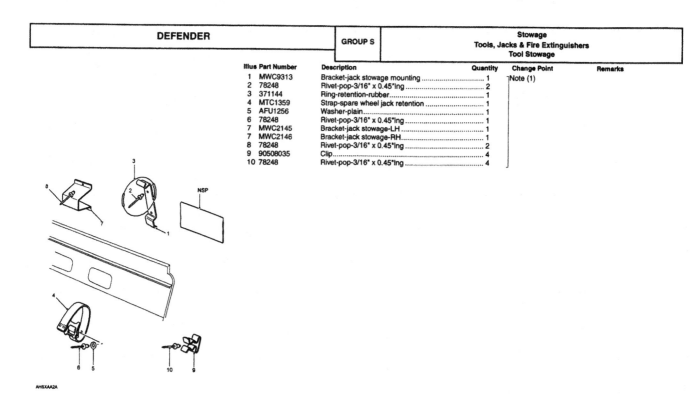

CHANGE POINTS:
(1) From (V) AA 270227

Tool Stowage(Cont)

Illus	Part Number	Description	Quantity	Change Point	Remarks
1	MWC9313	Bracket-jack stowage mounting	1		
2	RU612123L	Rivet	1		
3	371144	Ring-retention-rubber	1		
4	MTC7449	Clip	4		
5	RU612123L	Rivet	1		
6	MWC9313	Bracket-jack stowage mounting	1		
7	RU612123L	Rivet	2		
8	371144	Ring-retention-rubber	1		
9	MTC1359	Strap-spare wheel jack retention	2		
10	AFU1256	Washer-plain	2		
11	RU612373L	Rivet-3/16" x 0.575"lng	2		
12	90508035	Clip	3		
13	RU612123L	Rivet	3		
14	MTC7457	Pad-anti rattle	NLA		

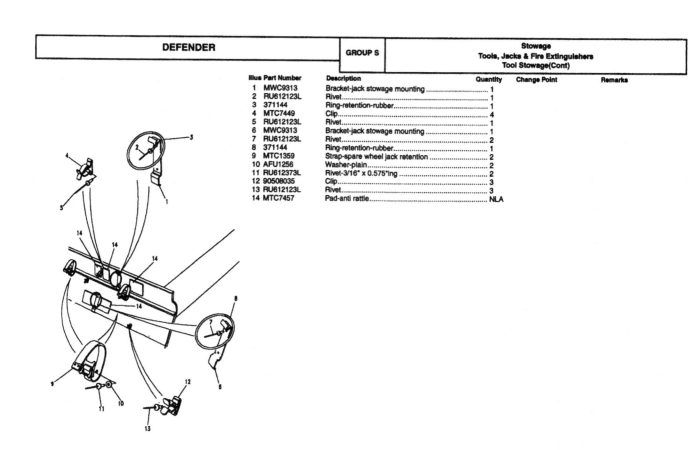

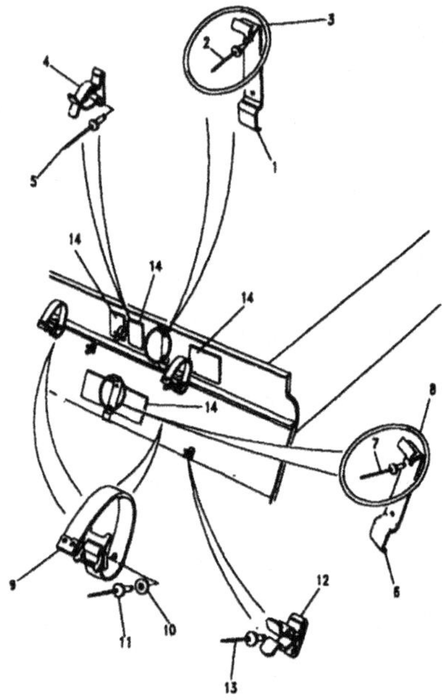

Tool Curtain

Illus	Part Number	Description	Quantity	Change Point	Remarks
1	MXC6321PMA	Tool curtain-Black	1	Note (1)	
2	78248	Rivet-pop-3/16" x 0.45"lng	3		

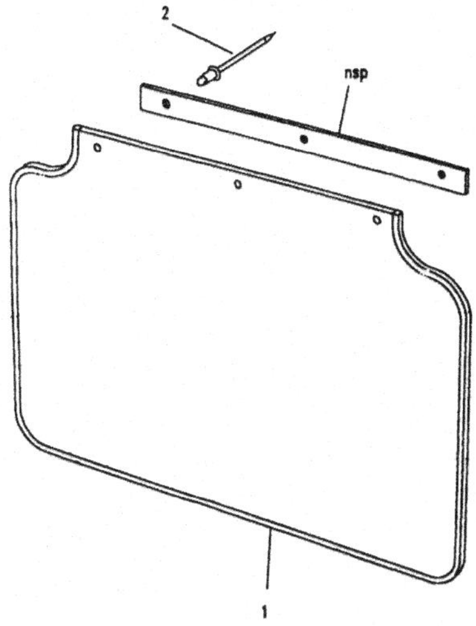

CHANGE POINTS:
(1) From (V) AA 270227

DEFENDER | GROUP S | Stowage
Tools, Jacks & Fire Extinguishers

Tool Curtain(Cont)

Illus	Part Number	Description	Quantity	Change Point	Remarks
1	MTC3165	Tool curtain	1	Note (1)	Germany
2	MTC3166	Plate	1		
3	FS106255L	Screw-flanged head-M6 x 25	8		
4	MTC4601	Washer plate	4		
5	WL106001L	Washer-sprung-M6	8		
6	NH106041L	Nut-hexagonal-nyloc-M6	8		

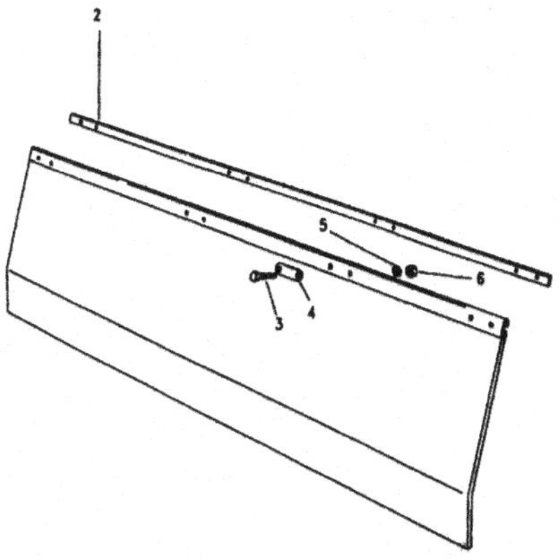

CHANGE POINTS:
(1) To (V) GA 456152

Tool Stowage-Station Wagon

Illus	Part Number	Description	Quantity	Change Point	Remarks
1	MTC1359	Strap-spare wheel jack retention	2		
2	AFU1256	Washer-plain	1		
3	78248	Rivet-pop-3/16" x 0.45"lng	2		
4	MTC1357	Bracket	1		
5	MTC1356	Retainer	1		
6	MWC9313	Bracket-jack stowage mounting	2		
7	78248	Rivet-pop-3/16" x 0.45"lng	2		
8	371144	Ring-retention-rubber	2		

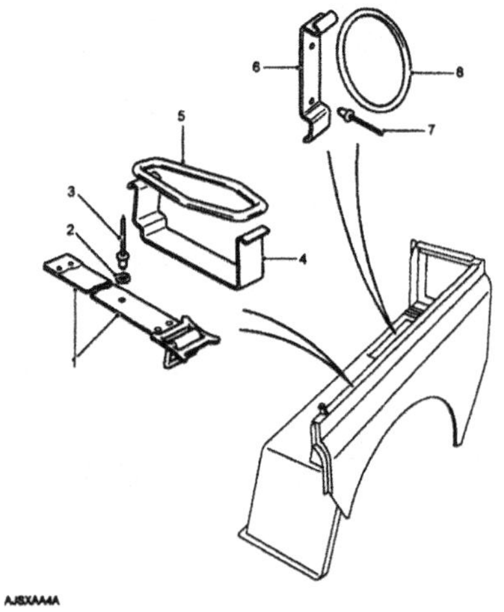

AJSXAA4A

Toolroll

Illus	Part Number	Description	Quantity	Change Point	Remarks
1	NTC7955	Jack-side lift	1		
2	NRC6481	Spanner-tool kit	1		
3	MUC4291	Pliers-tool kit	1		
4	NRC7455	Bag-jack assembly stowage	1		
5	219704	Roll-tool stowage	1		
6	AFU1024L	Pliers-tool kit	1		
7	276396	Spanner-tool kit-13mm x 11mm-1/2" x 7/16"	1		
7	AFU1004	Spanner-tool kit-10mm x 13mm	1		
8	MUC4275	Spanner-tool kit plug	1		
9	NRC6993	Screwdriver-tool kit	1		
10	NTC7829	Wheelbrace	1		
11	NTC7937	Chock-spare wheel stowage	1	Note (2)	
11	ANR3052	Chock-spare wheel stowage	1	Note (3)	
12	NTC7956	Jack assembly-screw	NLA	Note (4)	Use ANR4489 Screw jack is NLA - use hydraulic type.
13	543301	Handle-jack-wooden	1	Note (4)	
14	592514	Handle-jack	1		
15	592513	Handle-jack	1		

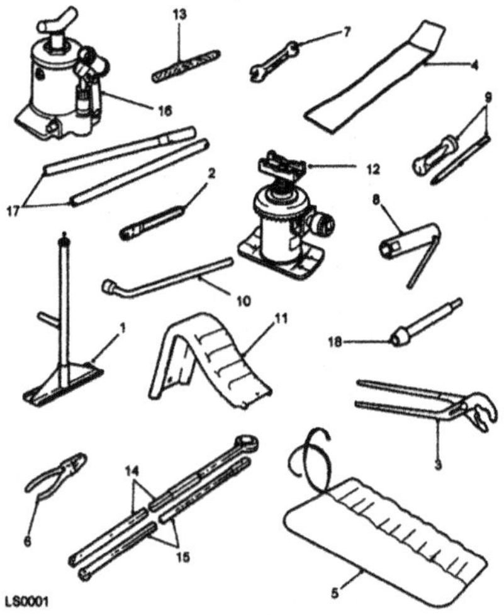

LS0001

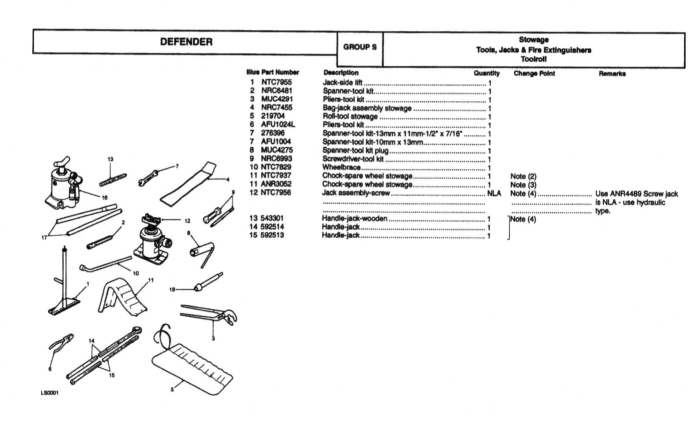

CHANGE POINTS:
(2) To (V) MA 941926
(3) From (V) MA 941927
(4) From (V) FA 454476 To (V) MA 951317

DEFENDER	GROUP S	Stowage Tools, Jacks & Fire Extinguishers Toolroll

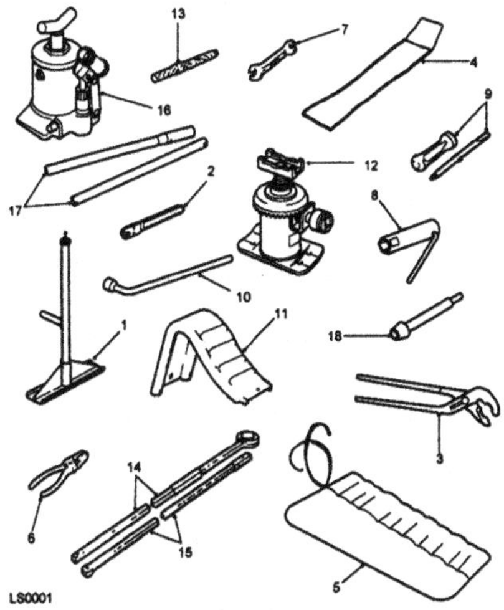

LS0001

Illus	Part Number	Description	Quantity	Change Point	Remarks
16	ANR4489	JACK-HYDRAULIC	1	Note (1)	
17	ANR4510	• Handle-jack	NLA		Use KAH000050.
16	KAJ100610	JACK-HYDRAULIC	1	Note (2)	
17	ANR4510	• Handle-jack	NLA		Use KAH000050.
18	562019	Gauge-tyre pressure	NLA		Use STC724.
18	STC724	Gauge-tyre pressure	1		
	NRC8605	KIT-TOOL & STOWAGE ASSEMBLY	1		
	3290	• Plug-coolant drain	1		
7	AFU1004	• Spanner-tool kit-10mm x 13mm	1		
8	MUC4275	• Spanner-tool kit plug	1		
9	NRC6993	• Screwdriver-tool kit	1		
5	219704	• Roll-tool stowage	1		
7	276396	• Spanner-tool kit-13mm x 11mm-1/2" x 7/16"	1		

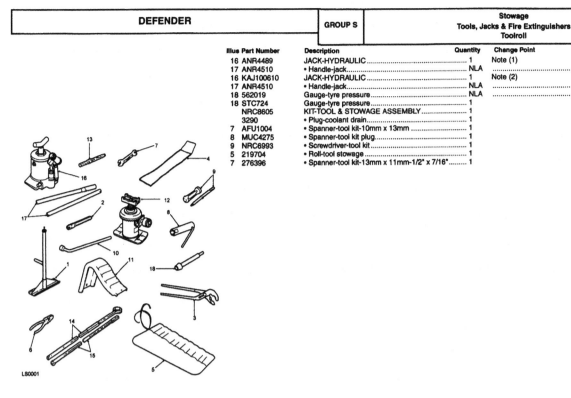

CHANGE POINTS:
(1) From (V) MA 951318 To (V) WA 159806
(2) From (V) XA 159807

DEFENDER	GROUP S	Stowage Tools, Jacks & Fire Extinguishers Spare Wheel-Bonnet-Bar Type

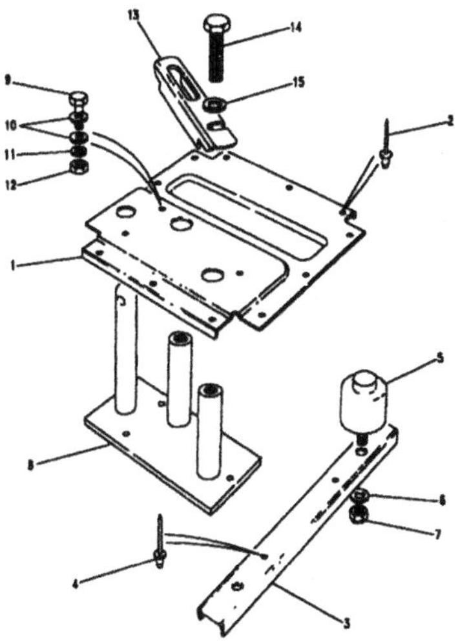

Illus	Part Number	Description	Quantity	Change Point	Remarks
1	MTC3594	Plate	1	Note (1)	
2	RA612183	Rivet-pop-aluminium	11		
3	MTC4570	Reinforcement assembly-load door spare wheel mounting	2		
4	RA612183	Rivet-pop-aluminium	4		
5	MRC4619	Buffer-spare wheel	4		
6	WB108051L	Washer-plain-M8	4		
7	NY108041L	Nut-nyloc-M8	4		
8	MTC3598	Plate	1		
9	SH105161L	Screw-hexagonal head-M5 x 16	3		
10	WA105001L	Washer-plain-standard-M5	6		
11	WL105001L	Washer-retaining-M5	3		
12	NH105041L	Nut-hexagonal-M5	3		
13	MRC5063	Retainer	1		
14	MRC4473	Bolt	2		
15	WD112081L	Washer-plain	2		

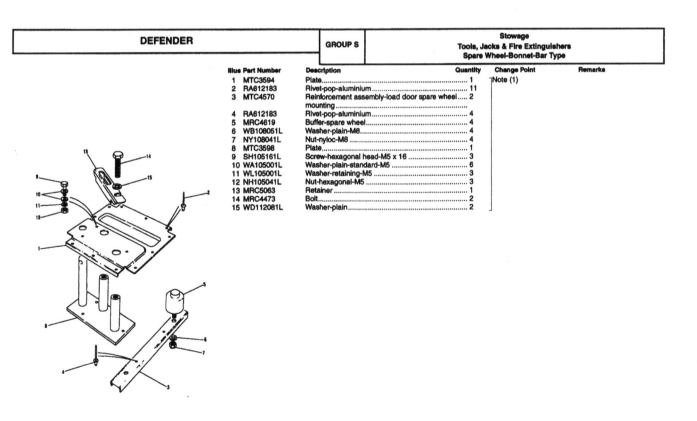

CHANGE POINTS:
(1) To (V) LA 939975

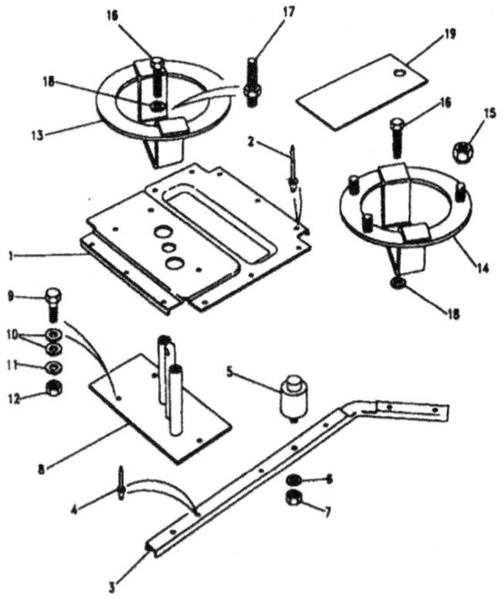

Illus	Part Number	Description	Quantity	Change Point	Remarks
1	MUC2443	Plate-spare wheel support	1		
2	RA612183	Rivet-pop-aluminium	11		
3	MUC6418	Reinforcement-RH	1		
3	MUC6419	Reinforcement-LH	1		
4	RA612183	Rivet-pop-aluminium	10		
5	MRC4619	Buffer-spare wheel	4		
6	WB108051L	Washer-plain-M8	4		
7	NY108041L	Nut-nyloc-M8	4		
8	MUC2442	Plate-spare wheel retention	1	Note (1)	
8	AQU110010	Plate-spare wheel retention	1	Note (2)	
9	SH105161L	Screw-plate to bonnet-hexagonal head-M5 x 16	3		
10	WA105001L	Washer-plain-standard-M5	6		
11	WL105001L	Washer-retaining-M5	3		
12	NH105041L	Nut-hexagonal-M5	3		
13	MUC2440	Retainer-except 3 stud fixing-spare wheel	1	Note (1)	
13	AQU110020	Retainer-except 3 stud fixing-spare wheel	1	Note (2)	
14	MWC4309	Retainer-3 stud fixing	1	Note (3)	
14	ALR2380	Retainer-3 stud fixing	1	Note (4)	
15	90577473	Nut wheel retention-16mm-steel wheel	3		
16	MRC4473	Bolt	2		
17	BTR549	Screw	1		
18	WD112081L	Washer-plain	2		
19	BTR550	Plate cover	1		

CHANGE POINTS:
(1) To (V) 1A 622423
(2) From (V) 2A 622424
(3) To (V) HA 906597
(4) From (V) JA 906598

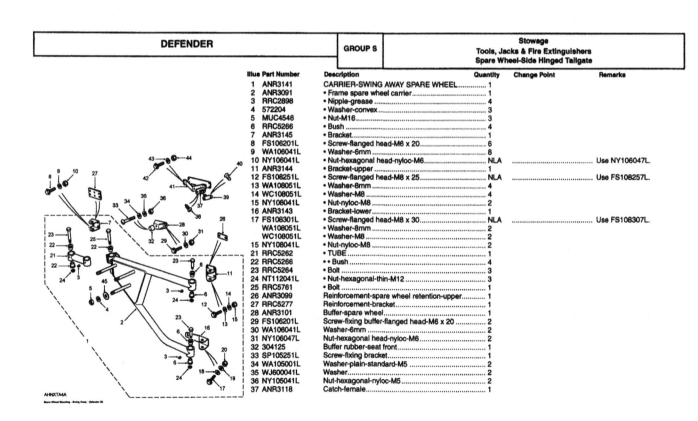

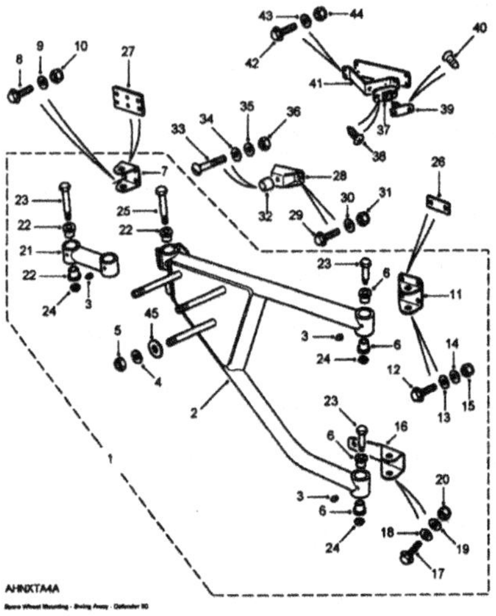

Illus	Part Number	Description	Quantity	Change Point	Remarks
1	ANR3141	CARRIER-SWING AWAY SPARE WHEEL	1		
2	ANR3091	• Frame spare wheel carrier	1		
3	RRC2898	• Nipple-grease	4		
4	572204	• Washer-convex	3		
5	MUC4546	• Nut-M16	3		
6	RRC5266	• Bush	4		
7	ANR3145	• Bracket	1		
8	FS106201L	• Screw-flanged head-M6 x 20	6		
9	WA106041L	• Washer-6mm	8		
10	NY106041L	• Nut-hexagonal head-nyloc-M6	NLA		Use NY106047L.
11	ANR3144	• Bracket-upper	1		
12	FS108251L	• Screw-flanged head-M8 x 25	NLA		Use FS108257L.
13	WA108051L	• Washer-8mm	4		
14	WC108051L	• Washer-M8	4		
15	NY108041L	• Nut-nyloc-M8	2		
16	ANR3143	• Bracket-lower	1		
17	FS108301L	• Screw-flanged head-M8 x 30	NLA		Use FS108307L.
	WA108051L	• Washer-8mm	2		
	WC108051L	• Washer-M8	2		
15	NY108041L	• Nut-nyloc-M8	2		
21	RRC5262	• TUBE	1		
22	RRC5266	• • Bush	4		
23	RRC5264	• Bolt	3		
24	NT112041L	• Nut-hexagonal-thin-M12	3		
25	RRC5761	• Bolt	1		
26	ANR3099	Reinforcement-spare wheel retention-upper	1		
27	RRC5277	Reinforcement-bracket	1		
28	ANR3101	Buffer-spare wheel	1		
29	FS106201L	Screw-fixing buffer-flanged head-M6 x 20	2		
30	WA106041L	Washer-6mm	2		
31	NY106047L	Nut-hexagonal head-nyloc-M6	2		
32	304125	Buffer rubber-seat front	1		
33	SP105251L	Screw-fixing bracket	1		
34	WA105001L	Washer-plain-standard-M5	2		
35	WJ600041L	Washer	2		
36	NY105041L	Nut-hexagonal-nyloc-M5	2		
37	ANR3118	Catch-female	1		

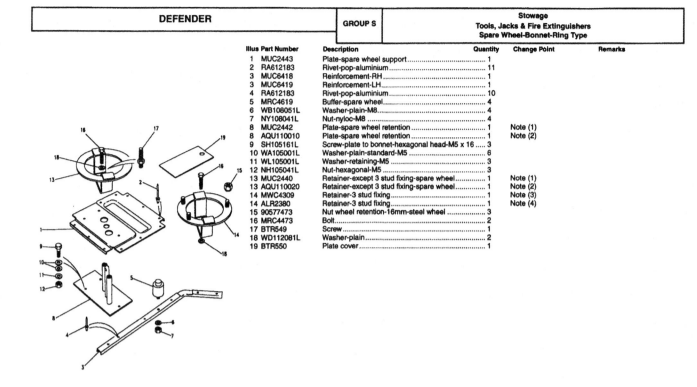

DEFENDER

GROUP S

Stowage
Tools, Jacks & Fire Extinguishers
Spare Wheel-Side Hinged Tailgate

Illus	Part Number	Description	Quantity	Change Point	Remarks
38	SF105121L	Screw-fixing catch	2		
39	ANR3117	Catch-male	1		
40	SF105121L	Screw-fixing catch	2		
41	ANR3100	Bracket-female catch	1		
42	FS106201L	Screw-fixing bracket-flanged head-M6 x 20	4		
42	FS106207L	Screw-fixing bracket-flanged head-M6 x 20	6		
43	WA106041L	Washer-6mm	8		
44	NY106047L	Nut-hexagonal head-nyloc-M6	2		
45	NRC5602	Retainer-inner	3		

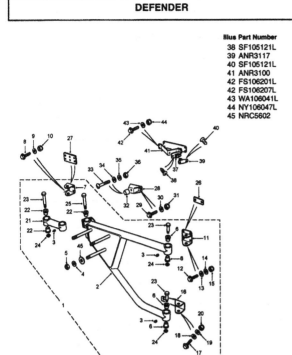

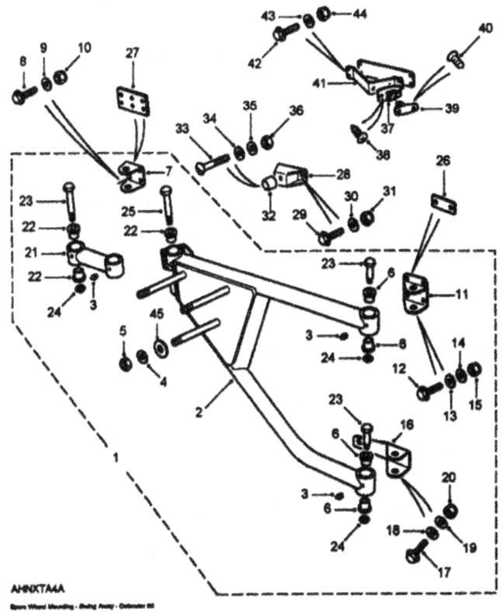

DEFENDER

GROUP S

Stowage
Tools, Jacks & Fire Extinguishers
Spare Wheel-Rear End Door-To (V) 1A999999

Illus	Part Number	Description	Quantity	Change Point	Remarks
1	MUC2366	Carrier-spare wheel	1	Note (1)	
1	ALR2377	Carrier-spare wheel	1	Note (2)	
2	MUC2934	Plate-spare wheel retention	1	Note (3)	
2	MXC7228	Plate-spare wheel retention	1	Note (4)	
2	ALR2378	Plate-spare wheel retention	1	Note (5)	
3	SE106251L	Screw-fixing clamp-pan head-M6 x 25	7	Note (3)	
4	WL106001L	Washer-sprung-M6	7	Note (3)	
5	NH106041L	Nut-hexagonal-nyloc-M6	7	Note (3)	
3	SE106251L	Screw-fixing clamp-pan head-M6 x 25	11	Note (6)	
3	FS106257L	Screw-flanged head-M6 x 25	8		
4	WL106001L	Washer-sprung-M6	11	Note (6)	
5	NH106041L	Nut-hexagonal-nyloc-M6	11	Note (6)	
5	NY106041	Nut-flange-nyloc-M6	11		
6	MUC2364	Bolt-u	1	Note (7)	
7	NH112041L	Nut-hexagonal-M12	4	Note (7)	
7	RRD100650	Nut-spare wheel retention	20		V8 EFi 50 LE
8	MUC2368	Spacer spare wheel retention	3		
9	90577473	Nut wheel retention-16mm-steel wheel	3		
10	MXC7226	Stiffener-RH	1	Note (6)	
11	MXC7227	Stiffener-LH	1	Note (6)	
12	78248	Rivet-pop-3/16" x 0.45"lng	22	Note (6)	

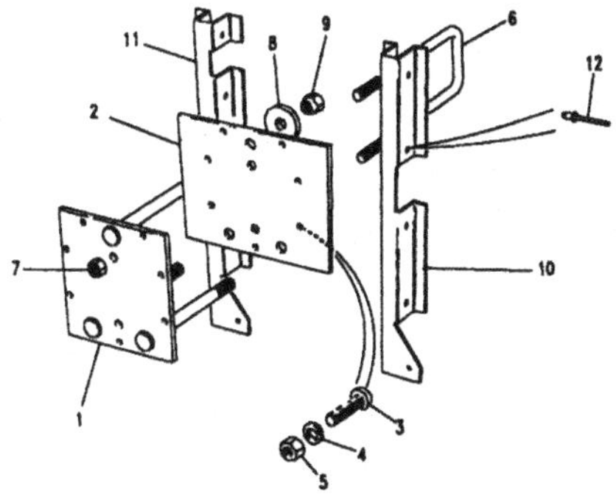

CHANGE POINTS:
(1) To (V) JA 906582
(2) From (V) JA 906583
(3) To (V) FA 423115
(4) From (V) FA 423116 To (V) HA 906580
(5) From (V) JA 906581
(6) From (V) FA 423116
(7) To (V) HA 906580

Illus	Part Number	Description	Quantity	Change Point	Remarks
1	BHI710030	Carrier-load/tail door spare wheel mounting	1		
2	VYG000020	Bolt-washer-M8 x 50	6		
3	566580	Washer-plain-10mm ID	6		
4	NY108047	Nut-nyloc-M8	6		
5	NTC7396	Nut wheel retention-M16-steel wheel	3		
6	ANR4914	Nut wheel retention-M16-alloy wheel	3		

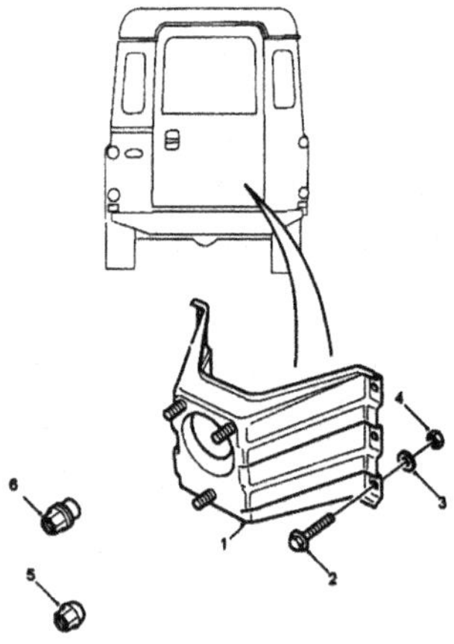

LS0021

Illus	Part Number	Description	Quantity	Change Point	Remarks
1	MUC6332	Plate-spare wheel retention	1		
2	RA612237	Rivet	3		
3	MXC5479	Bar-tie straight-spare wheel clamp	1		
3	ANR6578	Bar-tie straight-extended-alloy wheel	1		
4	FB106081L	Bolt-flanged head-M6 x 40	1		
5	WC106041L	Washer-M6-oversize	2		
6	NY106047L	Nut-hexagonal head-nyloc-M6	1		
7	MXC5477	Clamp	1		
8	MXC5478	Disc-clamping-spare wheel	1		
9	WA116101L	Washer-plain	1		
10	MXC5480	Spacer	1		
11	250053	Nut-wing	1		
12	90577473	Nut wheel retention-16mm-steel wheel	1		
13	MUC1649	STRIP-PROTECTION MOUNTING BRACKET	1		
14	330212	• Rubbing strip-spare wheel retention	1	To (V) VA 133527	
14	KTH100000	• Rubbing strip-spare wheel retention	1	From (V) VA 133528	
15	RA612346	• Rivet	2		
16	RA612237	Rivet	4		
17	STC61869	Adaptor-spare wheel	1	Note (1)	Tomb Raider 110"
18	ANR2763MMM	Nut-alloy road wheels	3		

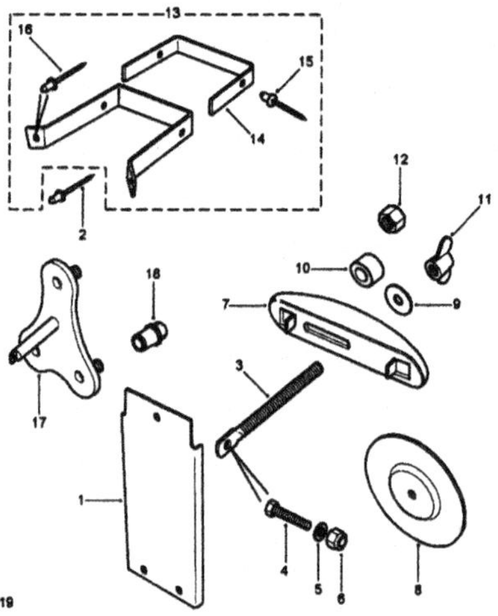

LS0019

CHANGE POINTS:
(1) From (V) 1A 612404

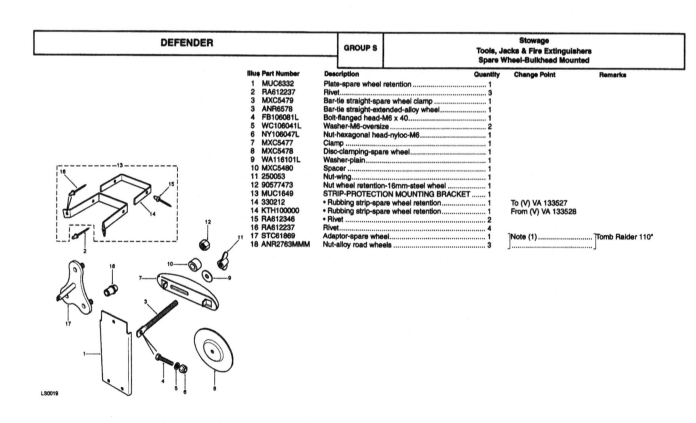

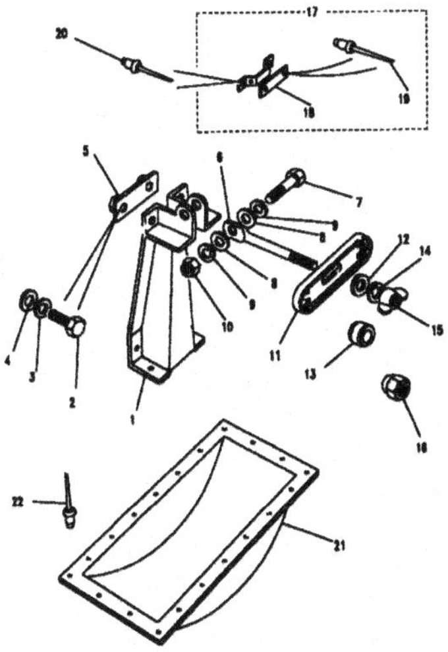

Illus	Part Number	Description	Quantity	Change Point	Remarks
1	MRC4846	Bracket-load/tail door spare wheel mounting	1		
2	FS108201L	Screw-flanged head-M8 x 20	NLA		Use FS108207L.
3	WC108051L	Washer-M8	2		
4	WL108001	Washer-sprung-M8	NLA		Use WL108001L.
5	MRC5757	Plate & weldnut assembly	1		
6	347866	Bar-tie straight	1	Note (1)	
6	MXC5479	Bar-tie straight	1	Note (2)	
7	FB106081L	Bolt-flanged head-M6 x 40	1		
8	WC106041L	Washer-M6-oversize	2		
9	WS106001	Washer-spring	2		
10	NY106041L	Nut-hexagonal head-nyloc-M6	NLA		Use NY106047L.
11	303847	Clamp	1	Note (1)	
11	MXC5477	Clamp	1	Note (2)	
12	AFU1265	Washer	1	Note (1)	
13	MXC5480	Spacer	1	Note (2)	
14	WL110001L	Washer-M10	1	Note (1)	
15	250053	Nut-wing	1	Note (1)	
16	90577473	Nut wheel retention-16mm-steel wheel	1	Note (2)	
17	332672	BRACKET-SPARE WHEEL RETENTION MOUNTING	2		
18	332674	• Rubbing strip-spare wheel retention	1	To (V) VA 133481	
18	KTH100010	• Rubbing strip-spare wheel retention	1	From (V) VA 133482	
19	78248	• Rivet-pop-3/16" x 0.45"lng	2		
20	78248	Rivet-pop-3/16" x 0.45"lng	2		
21	330602	Well-spare wheel	1		
22	78248	Rivet-pop-3/16" x 0.45"lng	2		

CHANGE POINTS:
(1) To (V) FA 450453
(2) From (V) FA 450454

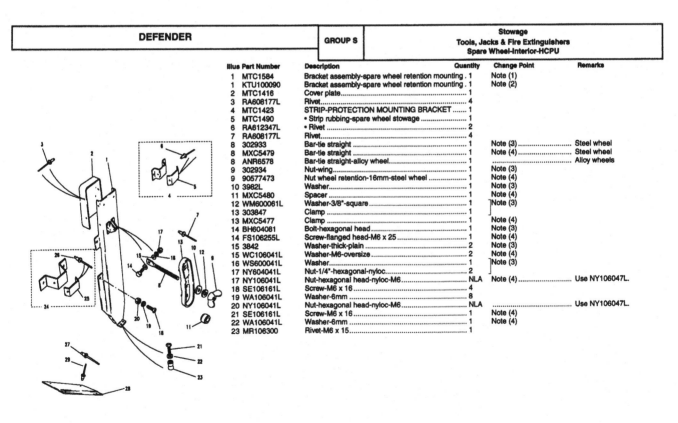

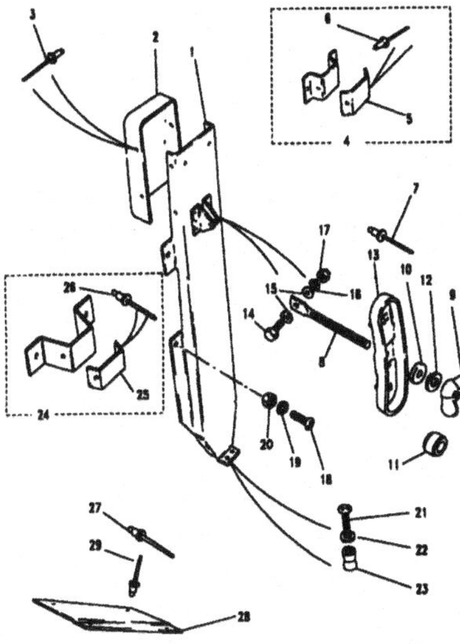

Illus	Part Number	Description	Quantity	Change Point	Remarks
1	MTC1584	Bracket assembly-spare wheel retention mounting	1	Note (1)	
1	KTU100090	Bracket assembly-spare wheel retention mounting	1	Note (2)	
2	MTC1416	Cover plate	1		
3	RA608177L	Rivet	4		
4	MTC1423	STRIP-PROTECTION MOUNTING BRACKET	1		
5	MTC1490	• Strip rubbing-spare wheel stowage	1		
6	RA612347L	• Rivet	2		
7	RA608177L	Rivet	4		
8	302933	Bar-tie straight	1	Note (3)	Steel wheel
8	MXC5479	Bar-tie straight	1	Note (4)	Steel wheel
8	ANR6578	Bar-tie straight-alloy wheel	1		Alloy wheels
9	302934	Nut-wing	1	Note (3)	
9	90577473	Nut wheel retention-16mm-steel wheel	1	Note (4)	
10	3982L	Washer	1	Note (3)	
11	MXC5480	Spacer	1	Note (4)	
12	WM600061L	Washer-3/8"-square	1	Note (3)	
13	303847	Clamp	1		
13	MXC5477	Clamp	1	Note (4)	
14	BH604081	Bolt-hexagonal head	1	Note (3)	
14	FS106255L	Screw-flanged head-M6 x 25	1	Note (4)	
15	3842	Washer-thick-plain	2	Note (3)	
15	WC106041L	Washer-M6-oversize	2	Note (4)	
16	WS600041L	Washer	1	Note (3)	
17	NY604041L	Nut-1/4"-hexagonal-nyloc	2		
17	NY106041L	Nut-hexagonal head-nyloc-M6	NLA	Note (4)	Use NY106047L.
18	SE106161L	Screw-M6 x 16	4		
19	WA106041L	Washer-6mm	8		
20	NY106041L	Nut-hexagonal head-nyloc-M6	NLA		Use NY106047L.
21	SE106161L	Screw-M6 x 16	1	Note (4)	
22	WA106041L	Washer-6mm	1	Note (4)	
23	MR106300	Rivet-M6 x 15	1		

CHANGE POINTS:
(1) To (V) WA 159806
(2) From (V) XA 159807
(3) To (V) FA 450453
(4) From (V) FA 450454

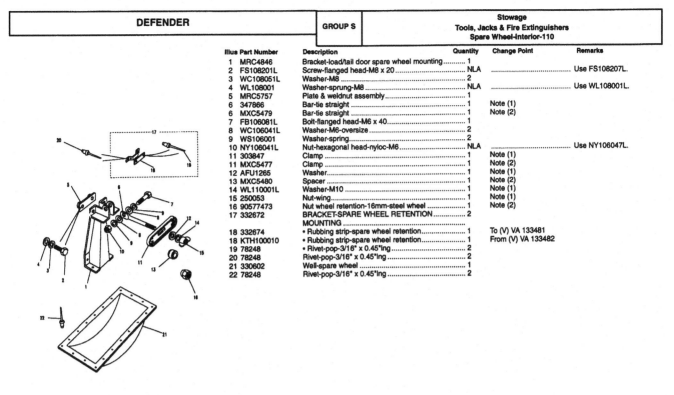

Illus	Part Number	Description	Quantity	Change Point	Remarks
24	332672	BRACKET-SPARE WHEEL RETENTION MOUNTING	2		
25	332674	• Rubbing strip-spare wheel retention	1	To (V) VA 133481	
25	KTH100010	• Rubbing strip-spare wheel retention	1	From (V) VA 133482	
26	78248	• Rivet-pop-3/16" x 0.45"lng	2		
27	RU612503	Rivet-3/16" x 0.7lng	4		
28	MTC1592	Plate	1		
29	RU612183	Rivet-pop-aluminium	4		

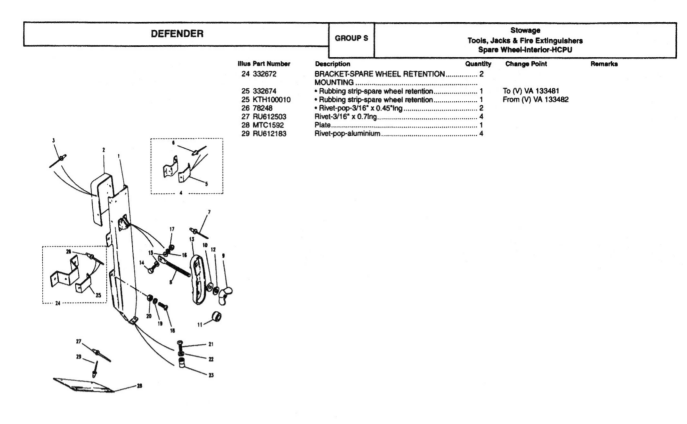

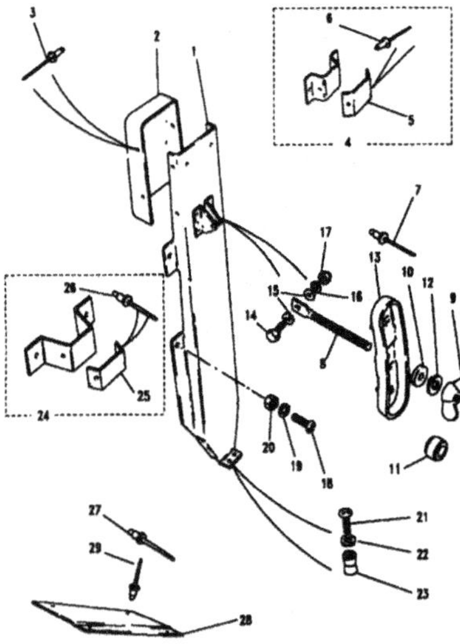

Illus	Part Number	Description	Quantity	Change Point	Remarks
1	2705	Spanner-tool kit-3/16" x 1/4"	1		
1	230736	Spanner-tool kit-5/16" x 7/16"	1		
1	276396	Spanner-tool kit-13mm x 11mm-1/2" x 7/16"	1		
1	277217	Spanner-tool kit-11/16" x 3/4"	1		
1	AFU1005	Spanner-tool kit-10mm x 13mm-6/16 x 1/2	1		
2	MUC4291	Pliers-tool kit	1		
3	MUC4275	Spanner-tool kit plug	1		
4	276322	Spanner-tool kit plug	NLA		Use MUC4275.
4	MUC4275	Spanner-tool kit plug	1		
5	276323	Spanner-tool kit plug	NLA		Extension for plug spanner no longer available, use latest plug spanner MUC4275.
6	549840	Spanner-tool kit-5/16" x 3/8"	1		
7	562019	Gauge-tyre pressure	NLA		Use STC724.
7	STC724	Gauge-tyre pressure	1		
8	NRC6993	Screwdriver-tool kit	1		
9	NTC7829	Wheelbrace	1		
10	523638	Pump-foot	1		
11	NTC7937	Chock-spare wheel stowage	1	Note (1)	
11	ANR3052	Chock-spare wheel stowage	1	Note (2)	
	MXC7648	Strap-tool kit retention	1		

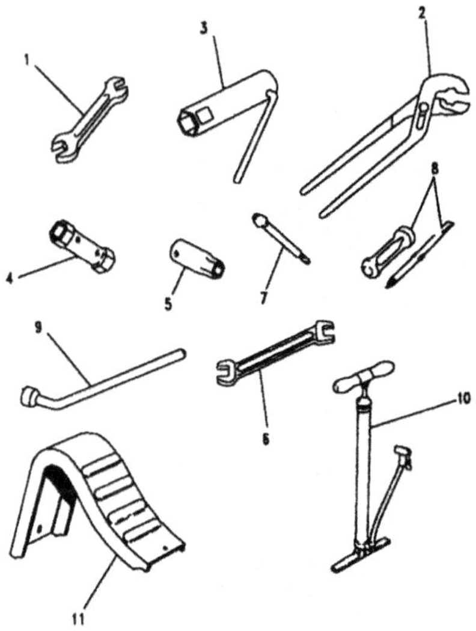

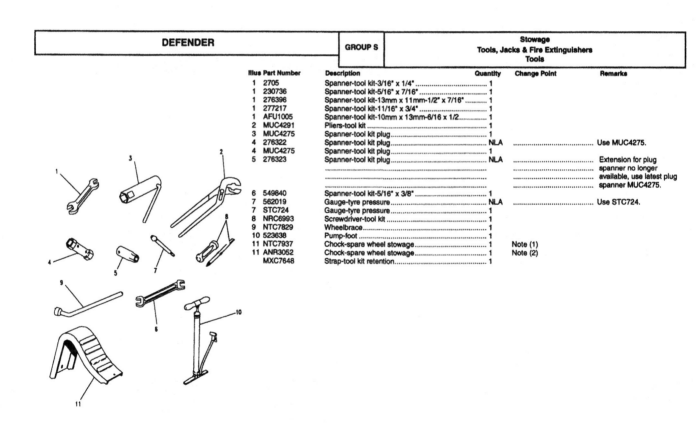

CHANGE POINTS:
(1) To (V) MA 941926
(2) From (V) MA 941927

Illus	Part Number	Description	Quantity	Change Point	Remarks
1	EOZ100000	Loop-luggage tie down	6		
2	FS108257L	Screw-flanged head-M8 x 25	6		
3	FY108047	Nut-flange-nyloc-M8	6		
4	WJ108001	Washer-M8-large	6		

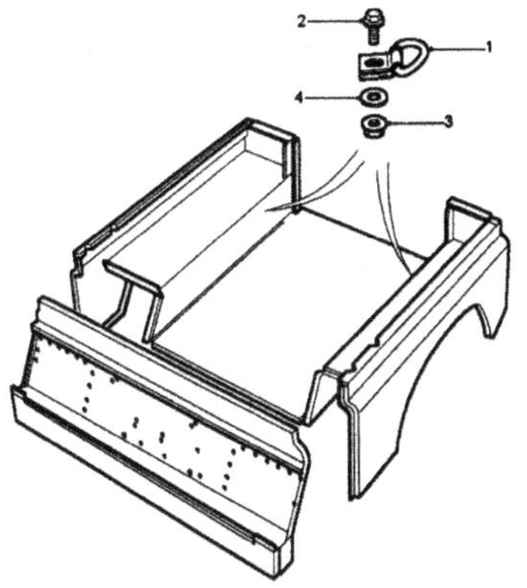

LS0016

Illus	Part Number	Description	Quantity	Change Point	Remarks
		TYRON SAFETY BAND			
	STC7803	6.5"-steel wheel-tubed-Dunlop-single	1		
	STC7804	6.5"-steel wheel-tubed-Dunlop-set of 5	1		
	STC7778	6.5"-steel wheel-tubeless-Dunlop-set of 5	1		
	STC7777	6.5"-steel wheel-tubeless-Dunlop-single	1		
	STC7800	6.5"-steel wheel-tubeless-Lemmerz-set of 5	1		
	STC7779	6.5"-steel wheel-tubeless-Lemmerz-single	1		
	STC7806	6.5"-steel wheel-tubed-Lemmerz-set of 5	1		
	STC7805	6.5"-steel wheel-tubed-Lemmerz-single	1		
	STC7802	5.5"-6"-steel wheel-tubed-set of 5	1		
	STC7801	5.5"-6"-steel wheel-tubed-single	1		
	STC7776	5.5"-6"-steel wheel-tubeless-set of 5	1		
	STC7775	5.5"-6"-steel wheel-tubeless-single	1		
	STC7647	7"-set of 5	1		

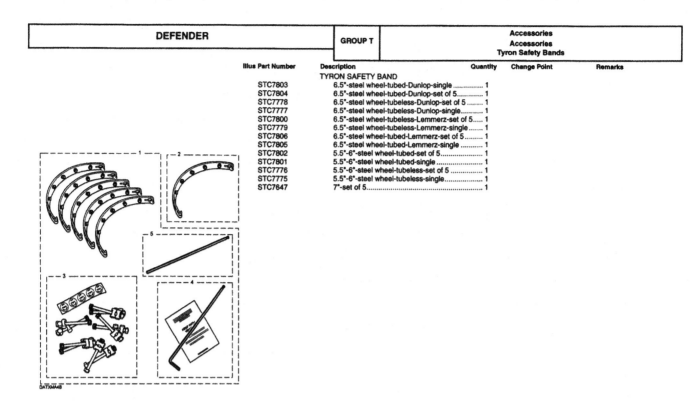

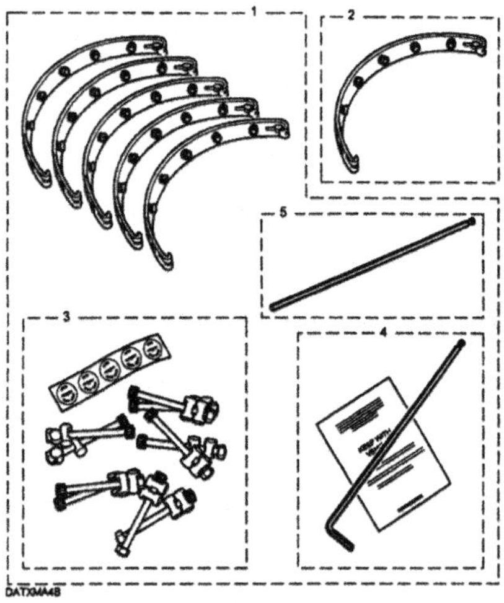

Illus	Part Number	Description	Quantity	Change Point	Remarks
1	STC7664	Set-snow chains-pair-750 x 16-265 x 16-235 x 16	1		
1	RTC9589	Set-snow chains-205 x 16-600 x 16	1		

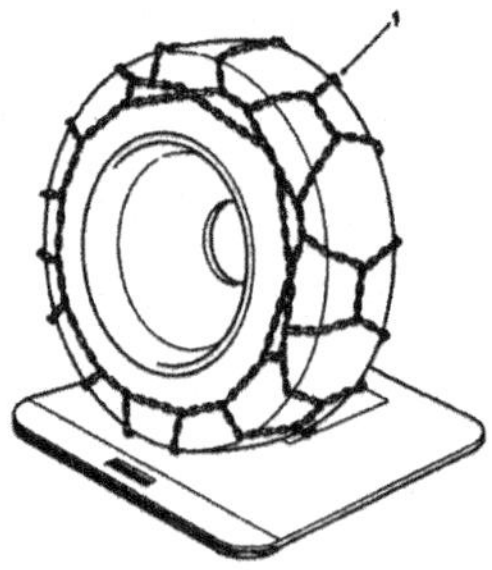

DEFENDER	GROUP T	Accessories Accessories Covers-Spare Wheel

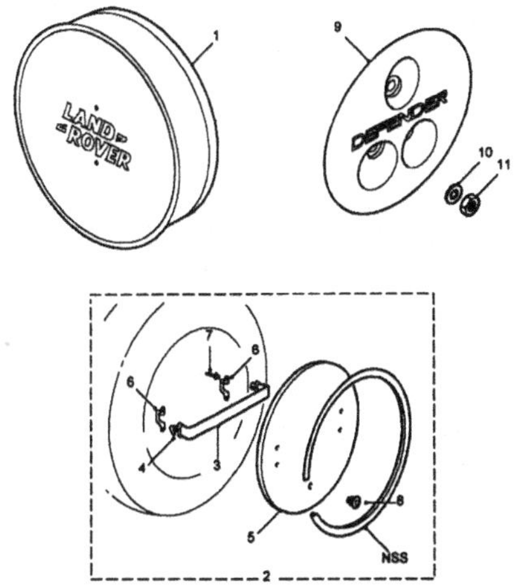

LT0005

Illus	Part Number	Description	Quantity	Change Point	Remarks
		COVER-SPARE WHEEL			
1	MRC7365	750 x 16	NLA	Note (1)	
1	MUC4161	750 x 16	1		Germany
1	MUC3628	205 x 16	1		
1	MXC6405	750 x 16	1	Note (2)	
1	MXC6406	205 x 16	1		
1	STC8487	265 x 16	1		Freestyle 90"
1	STC7665	235 x 16	1		Freestyle 110"
2	395576	KIT SPARE WHEEL RETENTION	1	Note (3)	Germany
3	395579	• STRAP ASSEMBLY-RETAINING	1		
4	301005	• • Hook-seat lockdown catch	2		
5	395577	• Plate-spare wheel cover location/retention	1		
6	395143	• Staple	NLA		Use RRC3966.
7	79194	• Rivet	4		
8	395580	• Knob-push selector handle	1		
6	RRC3966	Staple			Germany
9	BTR2129NAL	Plate-spare wheel retention-Chawton White	1		
9	BTR2129NUC	Plate-spare wheel retention-Alpine White	1		
10	MXC7335	Washer-plastic	3		
11	MXC7887	Nut-M16	3		
1	STC50266	Cover-spare wheel-265 x 16	1		Except Freestyle

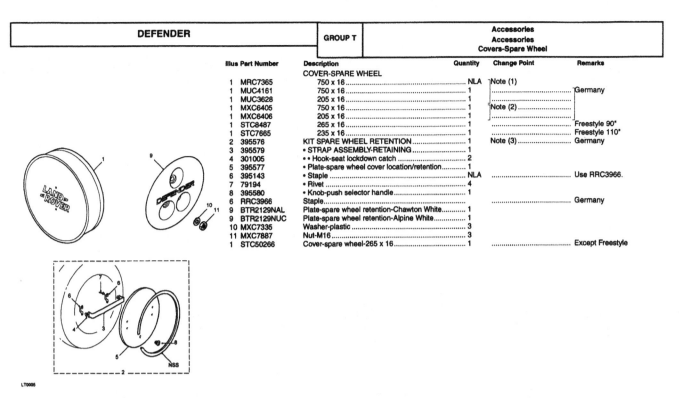

CHANGE POINTS:
(1) To (V) FA 414686
(2) From (V) FA 414687 To (V) HA 906580
(3) To (V) MA 962814

DEFENDER	GROUP T	Accessories Accessories Gaiter Kit-Swivel Pin Housing

Illus	Part Number	Description	Quantity	Change Point	Remarks
1	RTC3826	KIT-GAITER-OUTER JOINT DRIVESHAFT	1		
2	RTC3519	• Clip-hose	2		

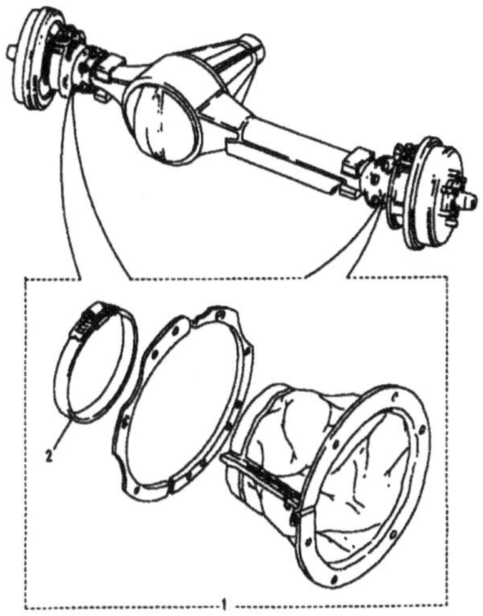

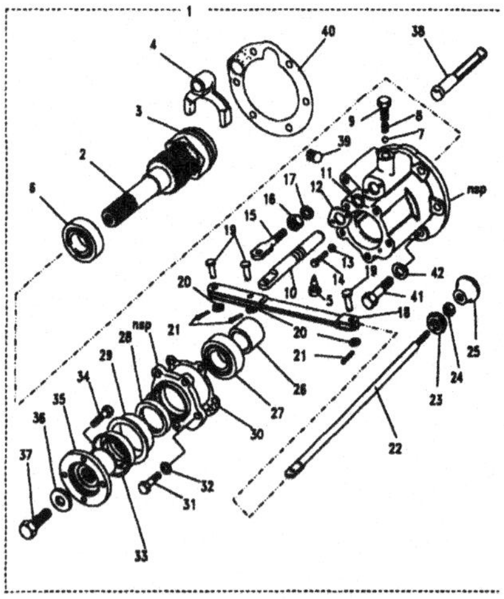

Illus	Part Number	Description	Quantity	Change Point	Remarks
1	FTC988	SOCKET-POWER TAKE OFF ACCESSORY	1		4 Cylinder
1	FRC8541	SOCKET-POWER TAKE OFF ACCESSORY	1		V8
2	FRC5376	• Shaft-front output	1		
3	FRC5381	• Dog starting	1		
4	FRC5379	• Fork-selector	1		
5	FTC4536	• Screw-grub	1		
6	217325	• Bearing-ball	1		
7	BLS112L	• Ball-detent manual transmission	1		
8	NRC255	• Spring	1		
9	SH112201	• Screw-hexagonal head-M12 x 20	1		
10	FRC5380	• Shaft-selector manual transmission	1		
11	FRC3477	• O ring	1		
12	FRC5388	• Plate	1		
13	WL106001L	• Washer-sprung-M6	2		
14	SH106141L	• Screw-hexagonal head-M6 x 14	2		
15	576303	• Pin	1		
16	FN110041L	• Nut-flange-M10	NLA		Use FN110047.
17	WM600071L	• Washer-sprung-7/16"	1		
18	FRC5383	• Lever assembly-operating/selector automatic transmission	1		
19	PC106291	• Pin-clevis/pivot	3		
20	WA106041L	• Washer-6mm	3		
21	PS103121L	• Pin-split	3		
22	FRC5391	• Rod assembly-connecting	3		Part of FTC988.
23	508571	• Grommet	1		
24	NT110041L	• Locknut-M10	1		
25	FRC3470	• Knob-push selector handle	1		
26	FRC5385	• Spacer	1		
27	STC1130	• Bearing-ball	1		
28	FRC5387	• Seal	1		
29	236548	• Mudguard-power take off	1		
30	FRC5386	• Gasket	1		

DEFENDER | GROUP T | Accessories
Accessories
Centre Power Take Off-To (V) MA962814

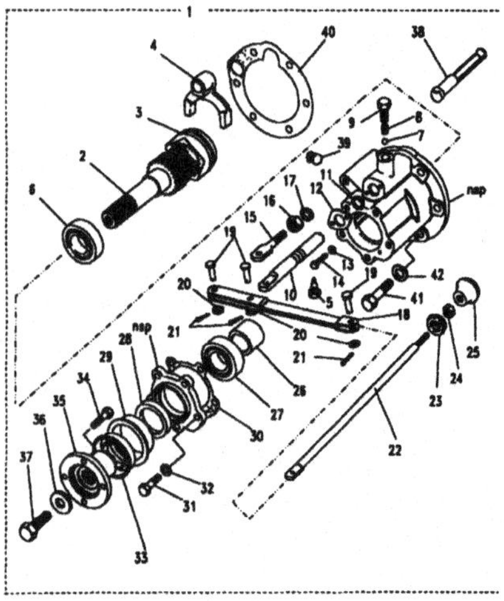

Illus	Part Number	Description	Quantity	Change Point	Remarks
31	FS108251L	• Screw-flanged head-M8 x 25	NLA		Use FS108257L.
32	WL108001L	• Washer-sprung-M8	5		
33	236074	• Mudguard-power take off	1		
34	509045P	• Bolt-3/8-UNF	4		
35	FRC5378	• Flange-coupling	1		
36	571174	• Washer	1		
37	SH116301	• Screw-flanged head	1		
38	FRC6933	• Catcher-manual transmission oil	1		
40	FRC5389	• Washer	1		
41	BH110091L	• Bolt-M10 x 45	6		
42	WL110001L	• Washer-M10	6		
22	FRC8538	• Rod assembly-connecting	1		Part of FRC8541.
16	FN110047	Nut-flange-flange-M10			

Illus	Part Number	Description	Quantity	Change Point	Remarks
		KIT-ELECTRIC WINCH			
1	RTC8137	Husky	1		Except air conditioning
1	RTC9588	X6 2,270Kg	1		Except air conditioning
1	RTC8965	low profile 3,360Kg	1		Air conditioning
	STC50104	WINCH-ELECTRIC-M6000-C/W FITTINGS	1		
	STC50105	• Bumper mounting-front	1		
1	STC8818	KIT-ELECTRIC WINCH-XD9000I 4,080KG	1		Except air conditioning
	STC7812	• Wire rope-winch	1		
2	RTC9520	Kit-winch accessories	1		
	STC50299	Winch-electric-Warn-cut-out	1		

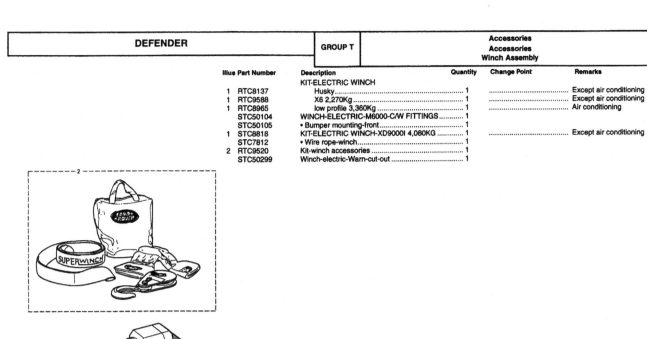

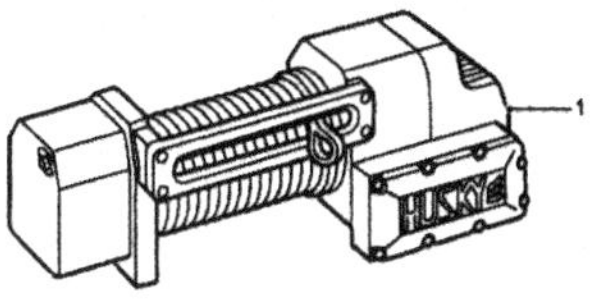

AHTXKA1A

Illus	Part Number	Description	Quantity	Change Point	Remarks
1	STC7050	Kit-raised air intake	NLA		Use STC7050AA. 2500 cc L/R 4 Cylinder Diesel TDi Turbo
1	STC7050AA	Kit-raised air intake	NLA		Use STC7050AB. 2500 cc L/R Diesel TDi Turbo
2	STC7050AB	Kit-raised air intake	1		
1	STC50265	Kit-raised air intake	1		2500 cc L/R 5 Cylinder Diesel Turbo Td5
1	STC50265	Kit-raised air intake	1		2500 cc L/R 4 Cylinder Diesel TDi Turbo

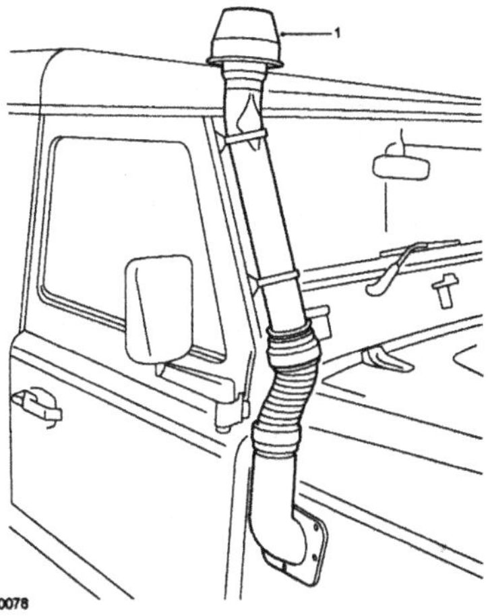

LT0078

Illus	Part Number	Description	Quantity	Change Point	Remarks
1	STC8480	LAMP-FRONT LONG RANGE DRIVING-SAFARI 5000	1		
	606178	• Bulb-headlamp-h3-55 Watt-type H3	1		
2	STC8481	LAMP ASSEMBLY-FRONT LIGHTING FOG-SAFARI 5000	1		
	606178	• Bulb-headlamp-h3-55 Watt-type H3	1		
3	STC8813	Kit-auxiliary wiring-safari 500	NLA		Use STC8813AA.
3	STC8813AA	Kit-auxiliary wiring-safari 500	1		
4	STC8814	Lamp steady bars-pair	1		
5	STC8842	Protector-driving lamp-pair	1		
6	STC8811	Lens-replacement	1		
7	STC8812	Lens-fog	1		

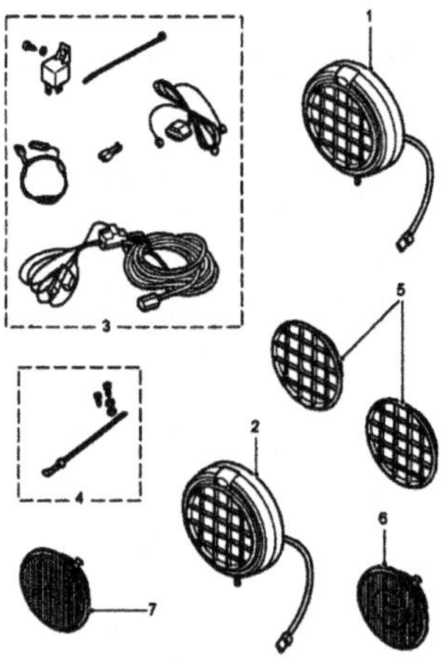

AHTXCC1A

Illus	Part Number	Description	Quantity	Change Point	Remarks
1	STC8870	Switch-rocker	1		
2	606178	Bulb-headlamp-h3-55 Watt-type H3	1		
3	RTC9521	Lamp-front lighting fog-Rally 1000	NLA		Use STC7643.
3	STC7643	Lamp-front lighting fog-Rally 1000	1		
3	RTC9523	Lamp-front lighting fog-Cewe-rectangular	NLA		
4	RTC9522	LAMP-FRONT LONG RANGE DRIVING-RALLY 1000	NLA		Use STC7644.
7	RTC9498	• Bulb-headlamp-Quartz Halogen-Cewe-type H2	1		
4	STC7644	Lamp-front long range driving-Rally 1000	1		
5	RTC9586AA	Kit-driving lamp wiring-Cewe	1		
6	STC8107	Lens-replacement-Rally 1000	1		
7	RTC9498	Bulb-headlamp-Quartz Halogen-Cewe-type H2	1		
8	RTC8917	Lamp-auxiliary front lighting	NLA		Use RTC8917AA.
8	RTC8917AA	Lamp-auxiliary front lighting	1		
9	RTC8921	Lamp-auxiliary front lighting	NLA		Use RTC8921AA.
9	RTC8921AA	Lamp-auxiliary front lighting-	1		

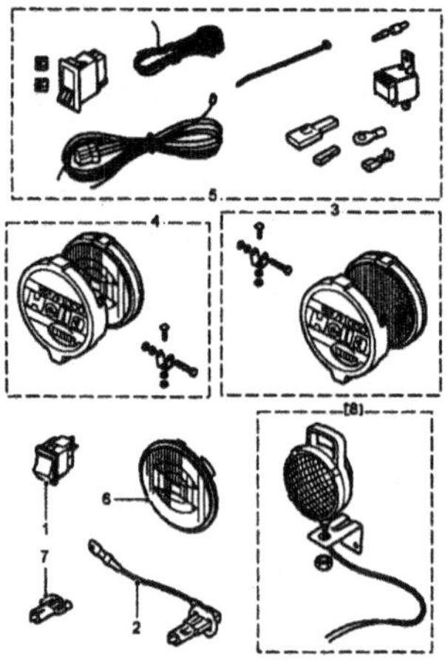

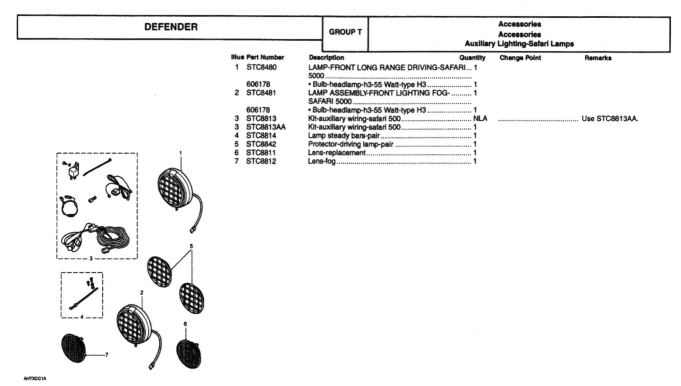

AHTXCC2A

Auxiliary Lighting-Fog Lamps

Illus	Part Number	Description	Quantity	Change Point	Remarks
1	RTC8922	Kit-front lighting fog lamp-rectangular	1		

LT0120

Radio Upgrade Kit

Illus	Part Number	Description	Quantity	Change Point	Remarks
1	STC7763	Radio cassette assembly- electronic	1		
2	STC7764	Kit-radio fittings	1	Note (1)	
2	STC7764AA	Kit-radio fittings	1	Note (2)	
3	STC7765	Speaker assembly-front active	1		
4	STC7766	Lead-link radio	1		
5	STC8059	Kit-radio fittings	1		
6	PRC4244	Speaker assembly rear-Bokhara-Philips	1		Accessory fit
7	STC8058	Aerial front fender-rubberised	1		Production fit

NOT ILLUSTRATED
PAS ILLUSTREE
NICHT ILLUSTRIERT
SENZA IL DISEGNO
SIN EL DISENO
SEM ILLUSTRACAO
NIET AFGEBEELD

TF 0007

CHANGE POINTS:
(1) To (V) WA 159806
(2) From (V) XA 159807

Illus	Part Number	Description	Quantity	Change Point	Remarks
1	STC1371	Kit-sumpguard-engine compartment	1		

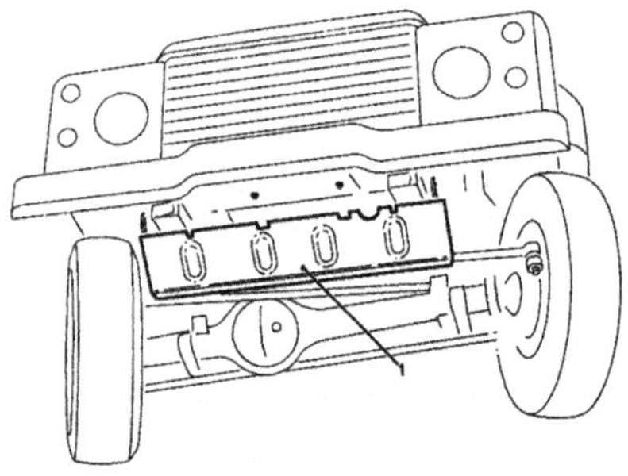

LT0023

Illus	Part Number	Description	Quantity	Change Point	Remarks
		TREAD PLATE			
1	STC7667	front fender-counter sunk-Matt-with aerial aperture	1		RHD Matched pair
1	STC7693	front fender-counter sunk-Matt-with aerial aperture	1		LHD Matched pair
1	STC7668	front fender-counter sunk-Matt-less aerial aperture	1		Matched pair
2	STC50245	Kit-checker plate	1		90"
2	STC50381	Kit-checker plate	1		110"
3	AFU1843	Monobolt-3/16 dia	A/R		
4	SF106161L	Screw-M6 x 16	A/R		
5	WJ106001L	Washer-plain-M6	A/R		
6	NY106047L	Nut-hexagonal head-nyloc-M6	A/R		

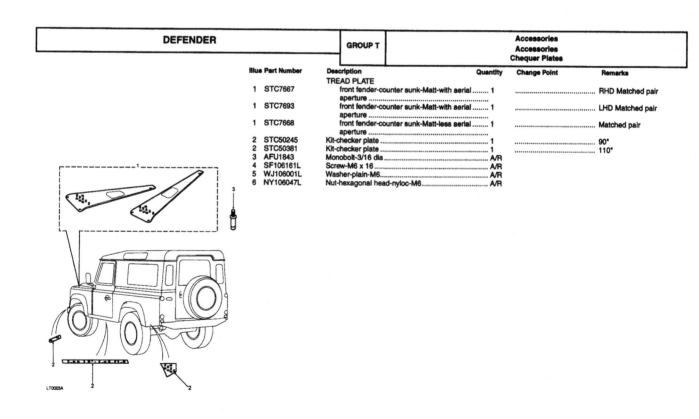

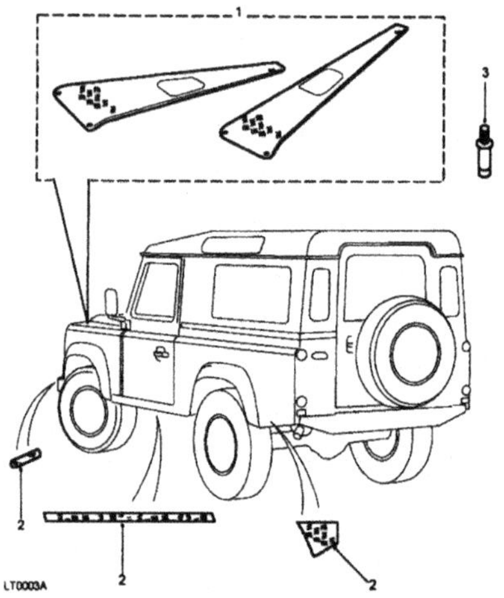

LT0003A

Illus	Part Number	Description	Quantity	Change Point	Remarks
1	RTC8120	Bar assembly-nudge-front-compatable with winch RTC8965-wrap round with lamp slats	NLA		Use STC50270.
1	STC50270	Bar assembly-nudge-front-wrap round	1		Except air conditioning
2	RTC9547	Bar assembly-nudge-front-compatable with winch RTC8965-straight	1		
3	STC8476	Bar assembly-nudge-front-compatable with winch RTC8965-Black-A frame	1		
3	STC50264	Bar assembly-nudge-front-Black-A frame	1		Except air conditioning
3	STC50478	Bar assembly-nudge-front-Black-A frame	1		Air conditioning
3	STC8477	Bar assembly-nudge-front-stainless steel.-A frame	1		Except air conditioning
3	STC53037	Bar assembly-nudge-front-stainless steel.-A frame	1		Air conditioning
4	STC8143	Bar assembly-nudge-front-compatable with winch RTC8965 + air con vehicles-wrap round	1		

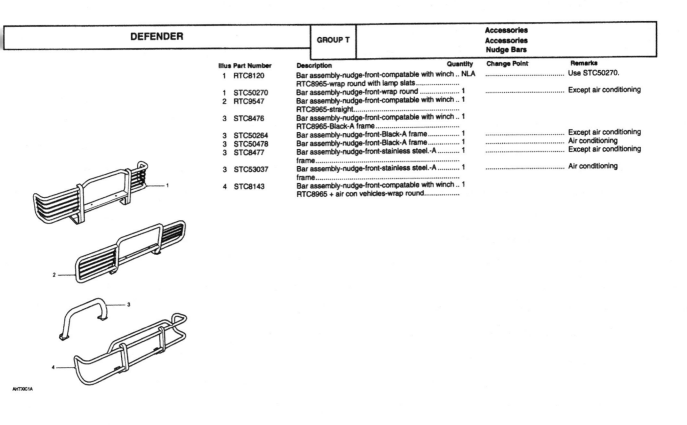

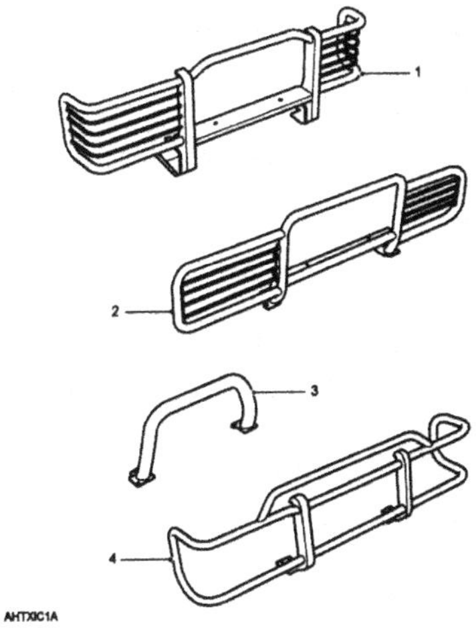

AHTXC1A

Illus	Part Number	Description	Quantity	Change Point	Remarks
1	RTC8969	Lamp guards-hinged-front	1		Except headlamp wash
		LAMP GUARDS-HINGED			
2	RTC8860	rear-with door mounted spare wheel	NLA		Use RTC8860AA.
					Except HICAP
2	RTC8860AA	with door mounted spare wheel	1		Except HICAP
2	RTC8859	rear-less door mounted spare wheel	NLA		Use RTC8859AA.
					Except HICAP
2	RTC8859AA	less door mounted spare wheel	1		Except HICAP
3	STC8056	Lamp guards-hinged-rear	1		HICAP 110"
4	345985	LAMP GUARDS-FIXED-FRONT	1		
	78384	• Screw-10UNF x 3/4	2		
	WL700101L	• Washer-spring-No 10-single coil-rectangular	2		
	AFU1876	• Rivet	2		
	AB608047L	• Screw-self tapping-No 8 x 1/2	2		
	WC702101L	• Washer-plain	2		
5	RTC8064	KIT-LAMP GUARD FIXING-REAR	1		
	78384	• Screw-10UNF x 3/4	4		
	WC702101L	• Washer-plain	4		
	WL700101L	• Washer-spring-No 10-single coil-rectangular	4		
	AFU1876	• Rivet	4		
5	RTC8065	KIT-LAMP GUARD FIXING	1		HICAP
	AB608101L	• Screw-self tapping B-No 8 x 1 1/4	8		
	244009	• Spacer	8		
	MRC316	Guard-lamp-protection-rear-single	1		
	STC7561	Protector-headlamp-perspex-pair	1		

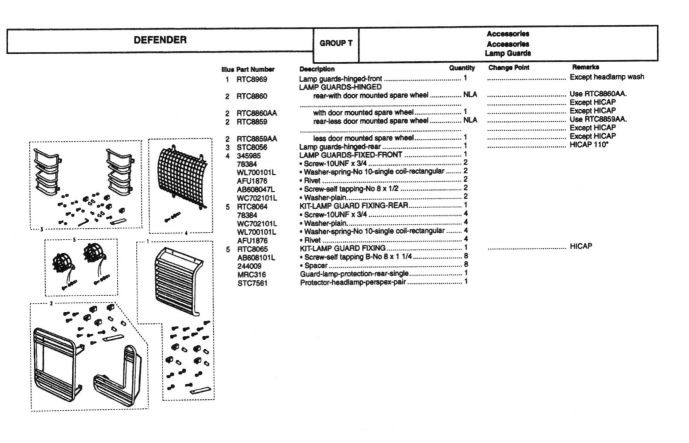

Illus	Part Number	Description	Quantity	Change Point	Remarks
1	RTC8161A	Rack assembly-roof-1600mm	1		
2	RTC8141A	Rack assembly-roof-2400mm	1		
3	RTC8131A	Rack-ladder	1		Hard Top except HICAP
4	RTC8849	Ladder-roof rack access	NLA		Use RTC8849AA.
4	RTC8849AA	Ladder-roof rack access	1		

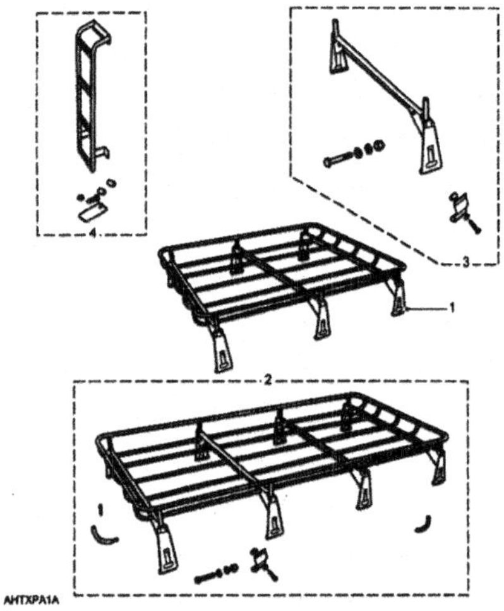

AHTXPA1A

Illus	Part Number	Description	Quantity	Change Point	Remarks
1	STC7582	Bar-roof sports	1		
2	STC7627	Luggage top box	NLA		Use STC50149.
2	STC50149	Luggage top box-RH & LH side opening	NLA		Use STC50149AA.
2	STC50149AA	Luggage top box-RH & LH side opening	1		
3	STC7628	Box-skis	1		
4	STC8435	Carrier-sailboard-use with sports bars	1		
5	STC7568	Carrier-ski roof rack-use with sports bars	1		
6	RTC9477	Load stop adjustable-set of 4	1		
7	STC7566	Strap-roof rack lashing-pair-2 metres	1		
8	STC50358	Kit-hardtop stowage fitting	1		
9	CAR10003L	Strap-roof rack lashing-5.0m	1		
10	STC53014	Carrier-roof rack luggage	1		

NOT ILLUSTRATED
PAS ILLUSTREE
NICHT ILLUSTRIERT
SENZA IL DISEGNO
SIN EL DISENO
SEM ILLUSTRACAO
NIET AFGEBEELD

ND 0007

Illus	Part Number	Description	Quantity	Change Point	Remarks
1	RTC8098	Mat-front floor-front footwell.-pair	NLA	Note (1)	Use RTC8098AA.
1	RTC8098AA	Mat-front floor-front footwell.-pair	NLA	Note (1)	Use RTC8098AB.
1	RTC8098AB	Mat-front floor-front footwell.-pair	1	Note (1)	Accessory fit
1	STC50172	Mat-front floor-front footwell.-pair	1	Note (2)	Accessory fit
2	RTC8099	Mat-rear floor drop in-rear-pair	1		Accessory fit
3	RTC8938	Mat-floor cover heel	1		4 Cylinder
	STC50173	Mat-footwell set-intermediate-footwell	1		Station Wagon 110"

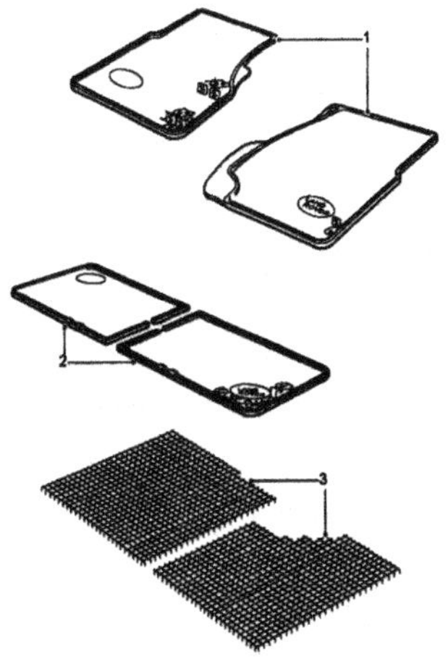

AHTXMC5A

CHANGE POINTS:
(1) To (V) WA 159806
(2) From (V) XA 159807

Illus	Part Number	Description	Quantity	Change Point	Remarks
		COVER-SEAT-WATERPROOF			
1	STC8178	Grey-front pair-outer	NLA		Use STC8178AA.
					2 front seats
1	STC8178AA	Grey-front pair-outer	1		2 front seats
1	RTC8931	front single seat-Beige	1		
		COVER-SEAT-WATERPROOF			
2	STC8179	Grey-front set	NLA		Use STC8179AA.
					3 front seats
2	STC8179AA	Grey-front set	1		3 front seats
2	RTC8932	front single seat-Beige	1		
		COVER-SEAT-WATERPROOF			
3	STC8180	12 seats-Grey	NLA		Use STC8180AA.
3	STC8180AA	12 seats-Grey	1		
3	STC8181	Grey-inward facing set	NLA		Use STC8181AA.
3	STC8181AA	Grey-inward facing set	1		
3	RTC8933	Beige-inward facing set-12 seats	1		Station Wagon 110"
		COVER-SEAT-WATERPROOF			
4	STC8182	Grey-side bench pair-10 seats	NLA		Use STC8182AA.
4	STC8182AA	Grey-side bench pair-10 seats	1		
4	STC7637AA	12 seats-bench type seats	1		110"
5	STC8183	Grey-bench type seats-60/40 split	NLA		Use STC8183AA.
5	STC8183AA	Grey-bench type seats-60/40 split	1		
		COVER-HEAD RESTRAINT-WATERPROOF			
6	STC50480	Cover-headrestraint-pair	1		

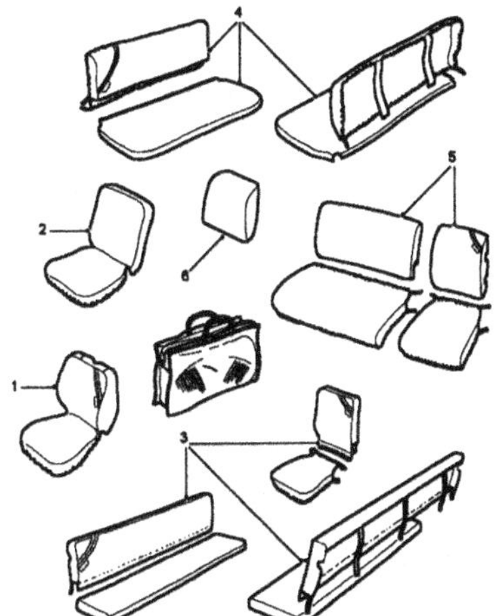

LT0129

Illus	Part Number	Description	Quantity	Change Point	Remarks
1	RTC9534AB	Seat-child restraint	NLA		Use STC50013.
1	STC50013	Seat-child restraint	1		
2	STC8154	Cushion-child restraint booster	1		

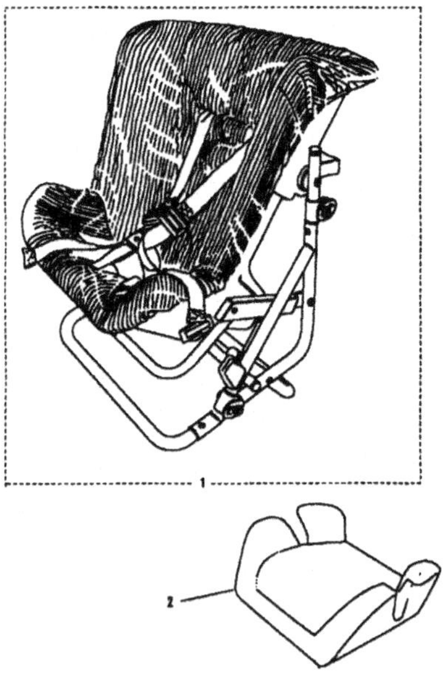

Illus	Part Number	Description	Quantity	Change Point	Remarks
1	RTC8936	Liner-carpet protection-loadspace	NLA		Use RTC8936AA.
1	RTC8936AA	Liner-carpet protection-loadspace	1		
2	STC8109	Mat-loadspace-full-Nylon	1		

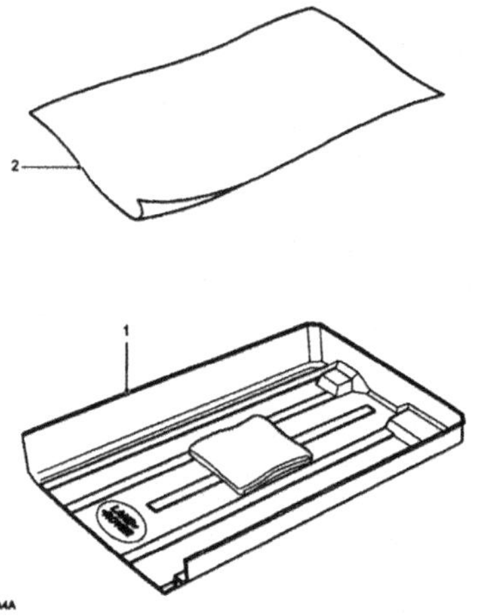

AHTXMA4A

Loadspace Protection-Stowable

Illus	Part Number	Description	Quantity	Change Point	Remarks
1	STC7619	Mat-loadspace	1		90" except Station Wagon
1	STC7898	Mat-loadspace	1		Station Wagon 90"
1	STC7620	Mat-loadspace	1		110" except Station Wagon
1	STC7899	Mat-loadspace	1		Station Wagon 110"

NOT ILLUSTRATED
PAS ILLUSTREE
NICHT ILLUSTRIERT
SENZA IL DISEGNO
SIN EL DISENO
SEM ILLUSTRACAO
NIET AFGEBEELD

TF 0007

Tonneau Cover-90SV

Illus	Part Number	Description	Quantity	Change Point	Remarks
1	BTR8691	Cover assembly-convertible hood tonneau	1		

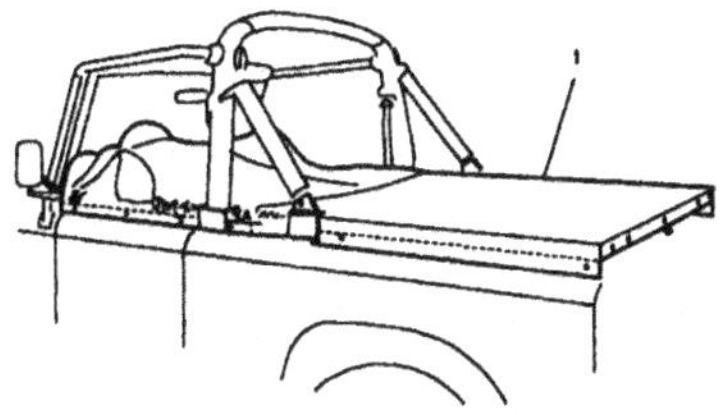

Illus	Part Number	Description	Quantity	Change Point	Remarks
		GUARD-DOG-LOADSPACE			
1	RTC8095	mesh type	1		90"
1	RTC8095	mesh type	1		Regular 110"
2	STC8070	mesh type	NLA		Use STC7555.
					Station Wagon 110"
2	STC7555	mesh type-Grey	1		Station Wagon 110"
	RTC8951	Clip-Black-mesh type	1		

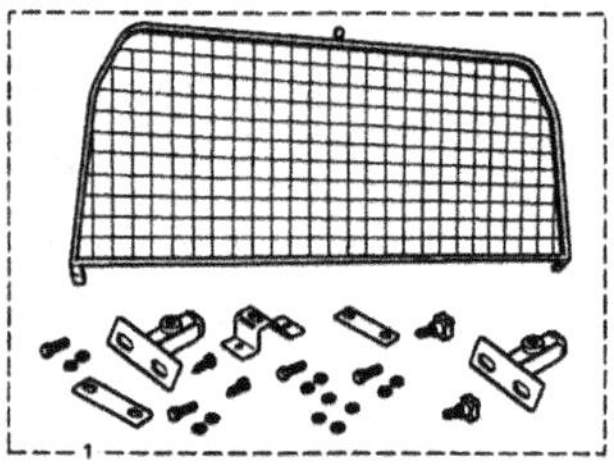

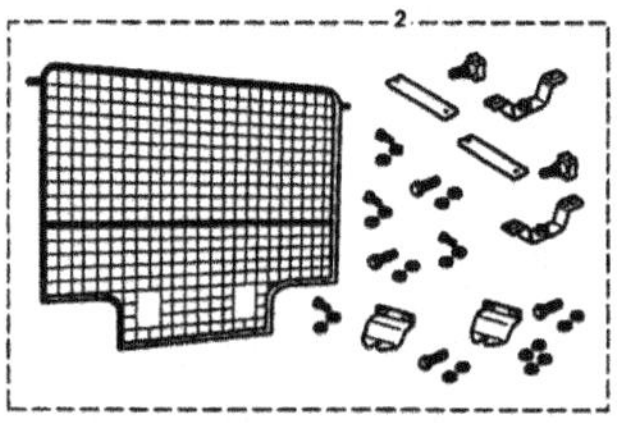

AJTXMC2A

Illus	Part Number	Description	Quantity	Change Point	Remarks
1	RTC9472AA	Guard-radiator cowl-animal ingress prevention	1		Diesel Turbo
1	RTC9473AA	Guard-radiator cowl-animal ingress prevention	1		Petrol Single Carburettor
1	RTC9473AA	Guard-radiator cowl-animal ingress prevention	1		Diesel Naturally Aspirated
1	STC8866	Guard-radiator cowl-animal ingress prevention	1		TDi

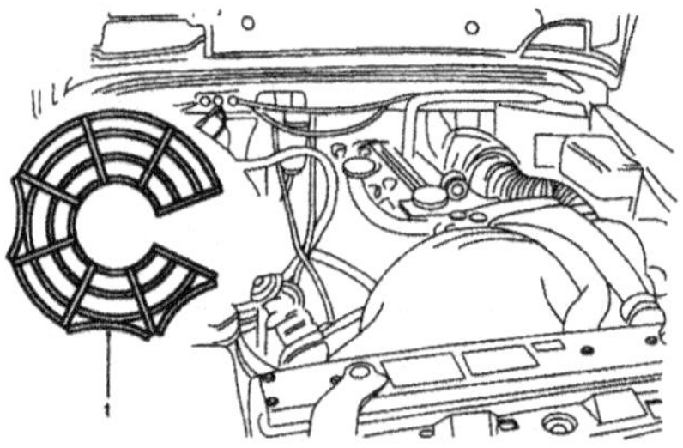

LT0079

Safety & Security-Fire Extinguisher

Illus	Part Number	Description	Quantity	Change Point	Remarks
1	MRC7350	Extinguisher-fire	NLA	Note (1)	Use ANR2948.
1	ANR2948	Extinguisher-fire-1 kg	NLA	Note (2)	Use STC8529.
1	STC8529	Extinguisher-fire-1 kg	NLA		Use STC8529AA.
1	STC8529AA	Extinguisher-fire-1 kg	1		
1	STC8138AA	Extinguisher-fire-2 kg	NLA		Use STC8138AB.
1	STC8138AB	Extinguisher-fire-2 kg	1		
2	SF106161	Screw-M6 x 16	2		Accessory fit
2	SF105251L	Screw-M5 x 25	2		Production fit
3	MM106301L	Nutsert-M6	2		Accessory fit
3	NN105021L	Nutsert-M5	2		Production fit

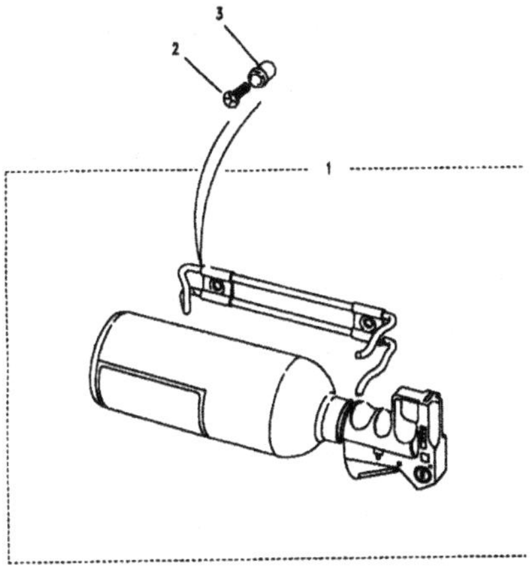

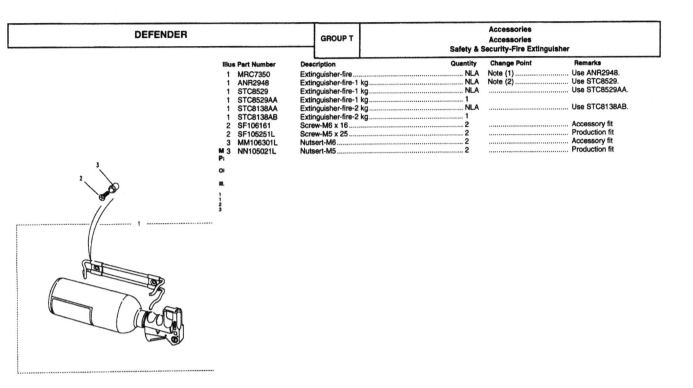

CHANGE POINTS:
(1) To (V) KA 922469
(2) From (V) KA 922470

Safety & Security-Security Box

Illus	Part Number	Description	Quantity	Change Point	Remarks
1	STC8018L	Box-gun	NLA		Use STC8018AB.
1	STC8018AB	Box-gun	1		
2	STC8124	Kit-gun box fixing	1		

BOX = 870MM X 190MM
INTERNAL TRAY = 850MM X 165MM

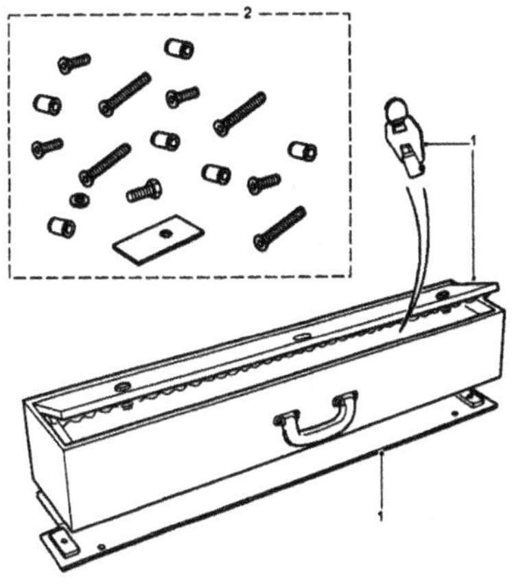

AHTXMA3A

Towing Equipment-Adjustable Height Assembly

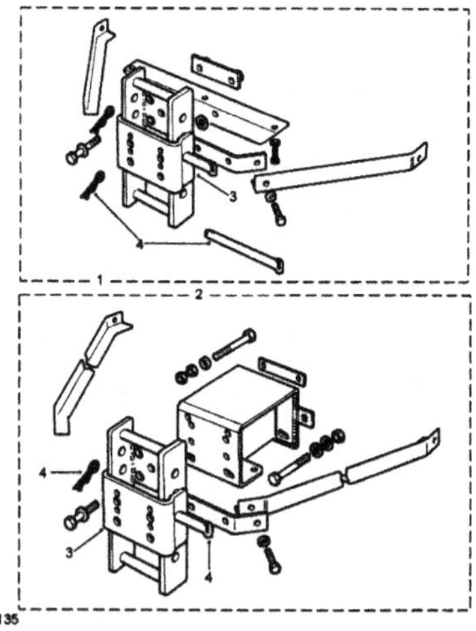

LT0135

Illus	Part Number	Description	Quantity	Change Point	Remarks
1	RTC8828AA	Towing attachment assembly-adjustable	1	Note (1)	Except HICAP
2	RTC9580A	TOWING ATTACHMENT ASSEMBLY-ADJUSTABLE	1		HICAP
3	RTC8831	• Plate-tow bar bracket slider	1		
4	RTC9581	• Pin-towing pintle	1		
1	STC50255	TOWING ATTACHMENT ASSEMBLY-ADJUSTABLE	1	Note (2)	90" except HICAP
1	STC50256	TOWING ATTACHMENT ASSEMBLY-ADJUSTABLE	1		110" except HICAP
2	STC50257	TOWING ATTACHMENT ASSEMBLY-ADJUSTABLE	1		HICAP
3	STC50259	• Plate-tow bar bracket slider-sliding	1		
4	STC50258	• Pin-towing pintle	1		
1	STC50255AA	TOWING ATTACHMENT ASSEMBLY-ADJUSTABLE	1	Note (3)	90" except HICAP
1	STC50256AA	TOWING ATTACHMENT ASSEMBLY-ADJUSTABLE	1		110" except HICAP
2	STC50257AA	TOWING ATTACHMENT ASSEMBLY-ADJUSTABLE	1		HICAP
3	STC50259AA	• Plate-tow bar bracket slider	1		
4	STC50258	• Pin-towing pintle	1		

CHANGE POINTS:
(1) To (V) WA 159806
(2) From (V) XA 159807 To (V) YA 194717
(3) From (V) YA 194718

Towing Equipment-Towing Drop Plate With Tow Ball-To (V) VA138479-Except HCPU

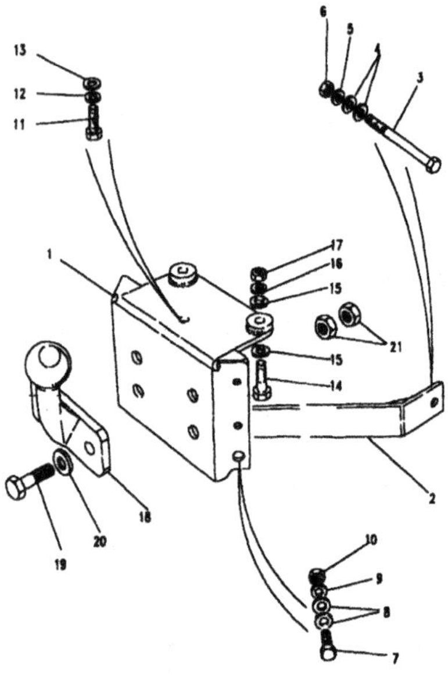

Illus	Part Number	Description	Quantity	Change Point	Remarks
1	NRC8208	Bracket-towing	1		Except BMW M52
2	NRC8210	Bar-tie straight-RH	1		
2	NRC8211	Bar-tie straight-LH	1		
3	BH110201L	Bolt-tie bar to chassis-hexagonal head-M10 x 100	2		
4	WA110061L	Washer-tie bar to chassis-M10	4		
5	WL110001L	Washer-tie bar to chassis-M10	2		
6	NY110047L	Nut-flange-nyloc-M10	2		
7	SH110301	Screw-tie bar to bracket-flanged head-M10 x 30	2		
8	WA110061L	Washer-tie bar to bracket-M10	4		
9	WL110001L	Washer-tie bar to bracket-M10	2		
10	NY110047L	Nut-flange-nyloc-M10	2		
11	SH110251L	Screw-bracket to rear crossmember-hexagonal head-M10 x 25	1		
12	WL110001L	Washer-bracket to rear crossmember-M10	1		
13	WA110061L	Washer-bracket to rear crossmember-M10	1		
14	BH110081L	Bolt-bracket to rear crossmember-hexagonal head-M10 x 40	2		
15	WA110061L	Washer-bracket to rear crossmember-M10	4		
16	WL110001L	Washer-bracket to rear crossmember-M10	2		
17	NY110047L	Nut-flange-nyloc-M10	2		
18	RTC8891AA	Ball-towing attachment-bracket to rear crossmember-50mm	1		
19	BH116121L	Bolt-towing ball to bracket	2		
20	RTC625	Washer-towing ball to bracket	2		
21	NY116041L	Nut-towing ball to bracket-hexagonal head-nyloc-M16	4		

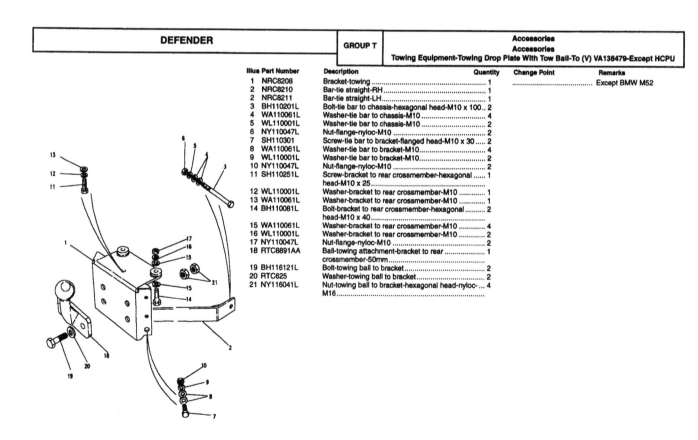

DEFENDER	GROUP T	Accessories Accessories Towing Equipment-Towing Drop Plate With Tow Ball-To (V) VA138479-HCPU

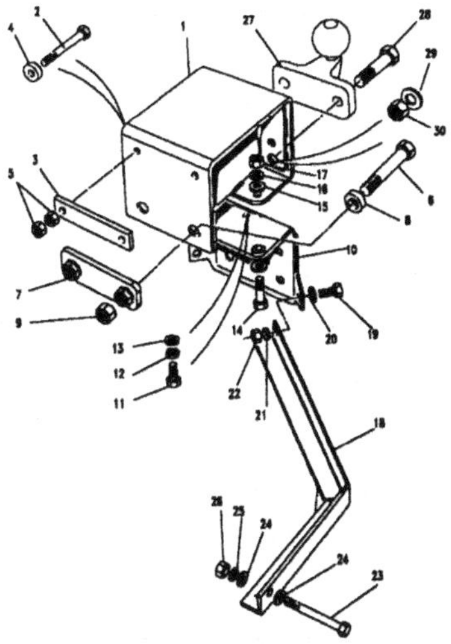

Illus	Part Number	Description	Quantity	Change Point	Remarks
1	NRC7758	Towing attachment assembly	1		
2	BH110181L	Bolt-extention to rear crossmembers-hexagonal socket	2		
4	NRC6324	Spacer-extention to rear crossmembers	2		
5	NY110047L	Nut-flange-nyloc-M10	2		
6	BH116201	Bolt-extention to rear crossmembers	2		
7	NRC6636	Plate-towing equipment nut-extention to rear crossmembers	1		
8	4233	Washer-extention to rear crossmembers	2		
9	NY116041L	Nut-Tie-bar to chassis-hexagonal head-nyloc-M16	2		
10	NRC8208	Bracket-towing	1	Note (1)	
11	SH110301	Screw-tie bar to bracket-flanged head-M10 x 30	1		
12	WL110001L	Washer-Tie-bar to chassis-M10	1		
13	WA110001L	Washer-plain-M10	1		
14	BX110071M	Bolt-Bracket to extension assy-hexagonal head-M10 x 35	2		
15	WA110001L	Washer-plain-M10	4		
16	WL110001L	Washer-Bracket to extension assy-M10	2		
17	NY110047L	Nut-flange-nyloc-M10	2		
18	NRC8229	Bar-tie straight-Bracket to extension assy-LH	1		
18	NRC8230	Bar-tie straight-Bracket to extension assy-RH	1		
19	SH110301	Screw-Bracket to extension assy-flanged head-M10 x 30	2	Note (1)	
20	WA110001L	Washer-plain-M10	4		
21	WL110001L	Washer-Bracket to extension assy-M10	2		
22	NY110047L	Nut-flange-nyloc-M10	2		
23	BH110201L	Bolt-tie bar to chassis-hexagonal head-M10 x 100	2	Note (1)	
24	WA110001L	Washer-plain-M10	4		
25	WL110001L	Washer-Bracket to extension assy-M10	2		
26	NY110047L	Nut-flange-nyloc-M10	2		
27	RTC8891	Ball-towing attachment-Tie-bar to chassis-50mm	NLA		Use RTC8891AA.
27	RTC8891AA	Ball-towing attachment-Tie-bar to chassis-50mm	1		
28	BH116101	Bolt	2		
29	RTC625	Washer-towing ball to bracket	2	Note (1)	
30	NY116041L	Nut-extention to rear crossmembers-hexagonal head-nyloc-M16	2		

CHANGE POINTS:
(1) To (V) MA 962814

DEFENDER	GROUP T	Accessories Accessories Towing Equipment-Towing Jaw-To (V) WA159806

Illus	Part Number	Description	Quantity	Change Point	Remarks
1	90518674	Tow jaw-3500Kg	1		
2	559636	Jaw assembly-towing	1		
3	562756	Spacer-towing jaw to rear crossmember	1		
4	BH116261	Bolt-towing jaw to rear crossmember	2		
5	NY116041L	Nut-towing jaw to rear crossmember-hexagonal head-nyloc-M16	2		
6	BH116161L	Bolt-towing jaw to bracket	2		
7	NY116041L	Nut-towing jaw to bracket-hexagonal head-nyloc-M16	4		

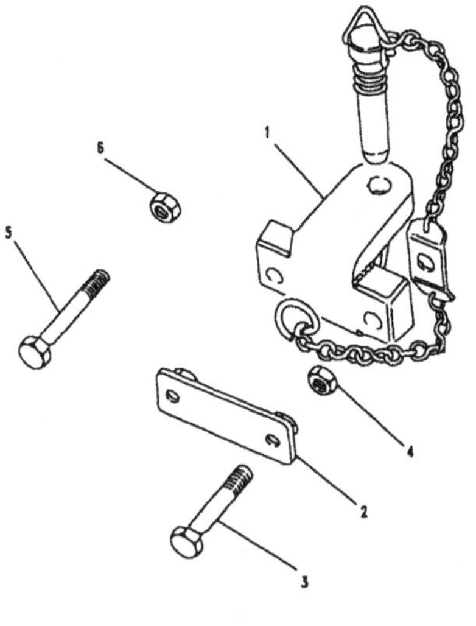

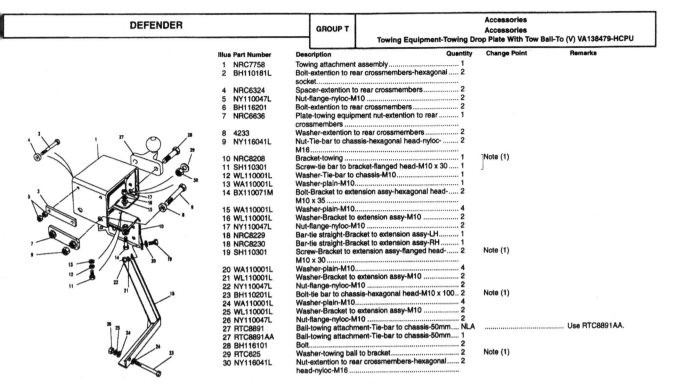

Illus	Part Number	Description	Quantity	Change Point	Remarks
1	246109	Hook-front sub frame towing	NLA		
2	NRC8323	Plate assembly-tow bar mounting	1		
3	BX112201	Bolt-towing hook to crossmember-M12 x 100-hexagonal head	4		
4	WA112081L	Washer-towing hook to crossmember-plain-standard-M12	4		
5	NH112041L	Nut-towing hook to crossmember-hexagonal-M12	8		
3	BH112101L	Bolt-towing hook to drop plate-M12 x 50	4		
5	NH112041L	Nut-towing hook to drop plate-hexagonal-M12	8		

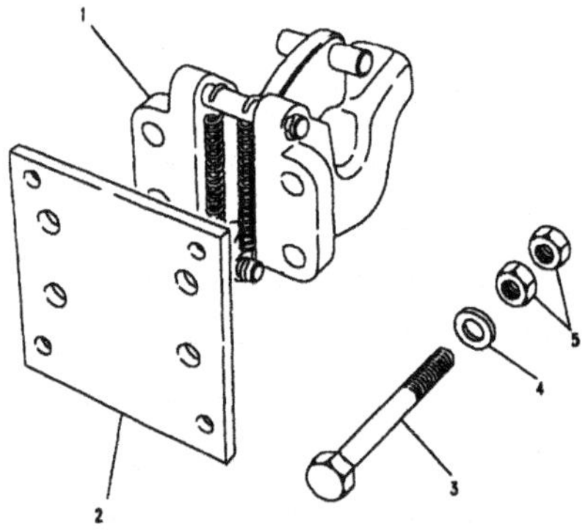

Illus	Part Number	Description	Quantity	Change Point	Remarks
1	535068	Tow jaw-5000Kg	1		
2	NRC8323	Plate assembly-tow bar mounting	1		
3	BH110181L	Bolt-pintle to crossmember-hexagonal socket	4		
4	NH110041L	Nut-pintle to crossmember-hexagonal head-coarse thread-M10	8		
3	BH110081L	Bolt-pintle to drop plate-hexagonal head-M10 x 40	4		
4	NH110041L	Nut-pintle to drop plate-hexagonal head-coarse thread-M10	8		

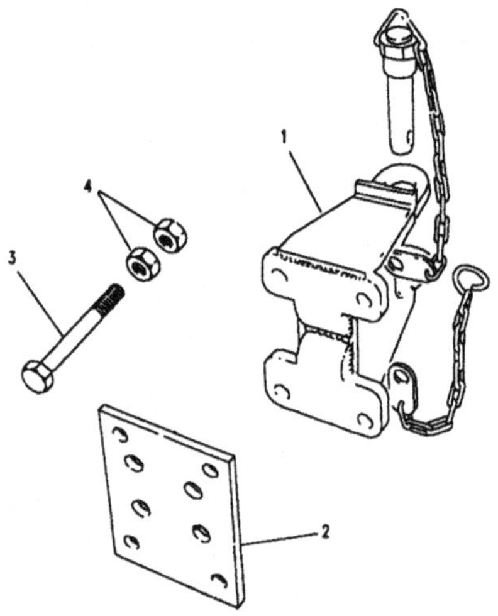

Illus	Part Number	Description	Quantity	Change Point	Remarks
1	NRC2051	Towing attachment assembly	1		
2	RTC5597	Pin-towing pintle	1		
3	STC3430	Pin-locking	1		
4	STC3431	Clip-retainer pin	1		
5	531447	Plate-packing	1		
6	BH112241L	Bolt-pintle to crossmember	4		
7	NH112041L	Nut-pintle to crossmember-hexagonal-M12	8		
8	NRC8323	Plate assembly-tow bar mounting	1		
9	BH112141L	Bolt-hexagonal socket-pintle to crossmember-M12 x 70.	4		

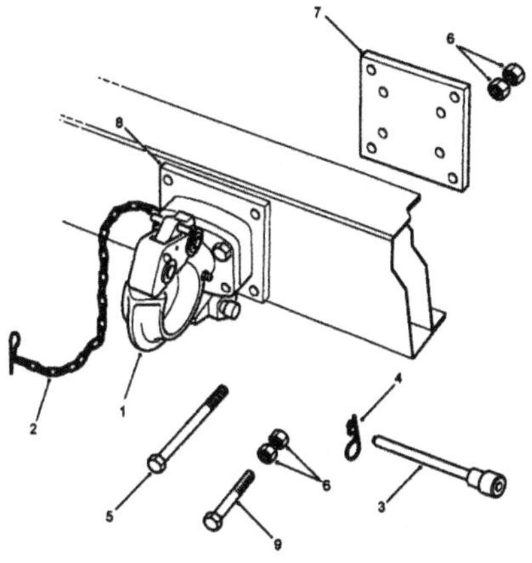

LT0094

Illus	Part Number	Description	Quantity	Change Point	Remarks
1	STC8051	Kit-towing-removable towball	1	Note (1)	

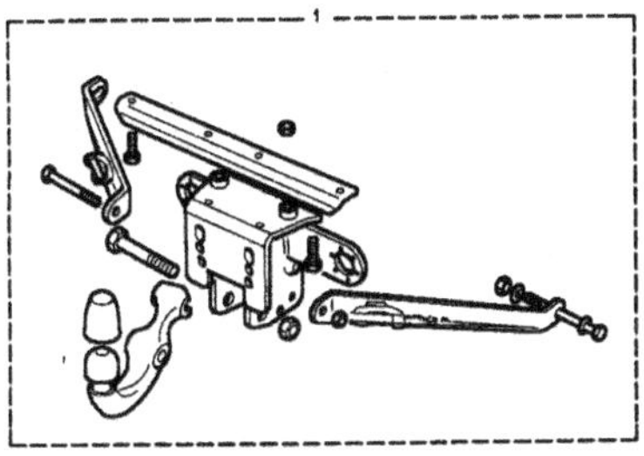

LT0092

CHANGE POINTS:
(1) To (V) WA 159806

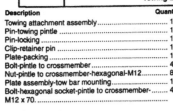

Towing Equipment-Drop Plate With Tow Ball-From (V) WA138480-Except HCPU

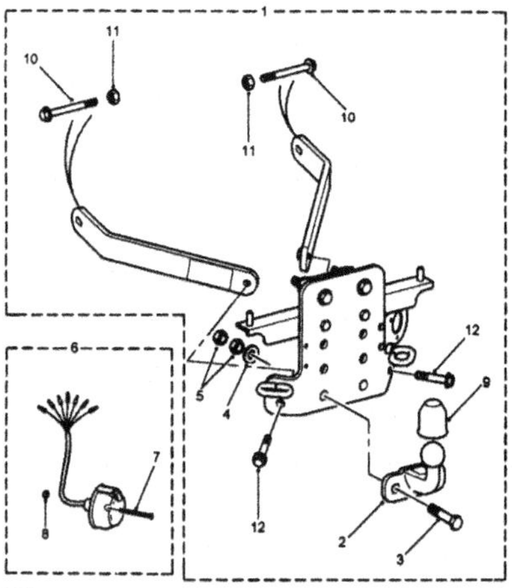

LT0095

Illus	Part Number	Description	Quantity	Change Point	Remarks
1	VUB105440	TOWING ATTACHMENT ASSEMBLY	1	Note (1)	90"
1	VUB105440	TOWING ATTACHMENT ASSEMBLY	1	Note (1)	110"
2	RTC8891AA	• Ball-towing attachment-50mm	1		
3	BH116127	• Bolt-M16 x 60-dacromat	2		
4	WC116101	• Washer	2		
5	NH116041L	• Nut-M16-hexagonal head	4		
9	ANR3635	• Cover-towing attachment ball-50mm	1		
6	YWJ101490	KIT-TOWING ELECTRICS	1	Note (1)	
7	SE105401	• Screw-pan head-M5 x 40	3		
8	NY105041L	• Nut-hexagonal-nyloc-M5	3		
2	RTC8891AA	Ball-towing attachment-50mm			
3	BH116127	Bolt-M16 x 60-dacromat			
1	VUB105460	TOWING ATTACHMENT ASSEMBLY	1	Note (2)	90"
1	VUB105470	TOWING ATTACHMENT ASSEMBLY	1	Note (2)	110"
2	RTC8891AA	• Ball-towing attachment-50mm	1		
3	BH116127	• Bolt-M16 x 60-dacromat	2		
4	WC116101	• Washer	2		
5	NH116041L	• Nut-M16-hexagonal head	4		
9	ANR3635	• Cover-towing attachment ball-50mm	1		
6	YWJ101500	KIT-TOWING ELECTRICS-N TYPE	1	Note (2)	
7	SE105401	• Screw-pan head-M5 x 40	3		
8	NY105041L	• Nut-hexagonal-nyloc-M5	3		
2	RTC8891AA	Ball-towing attachment-50mm			
3	BH116127	Bolt-M16 x 60-dacromat			
10	DYG100720	Bolt-flanged head-M10 x 115	2		
11	FX110047L	Nut-flange-M10	2		
12	FS110301L	Screw-flanged head-M10 x 30-top	2		

CHANGE POINTS:
(1) From (V) WA 138480 To (V) WA 159806
(2) From (V) XA 159807

Towing Equipment-Drop Plate With Tow Ball-From (V) WA138480-HCPU

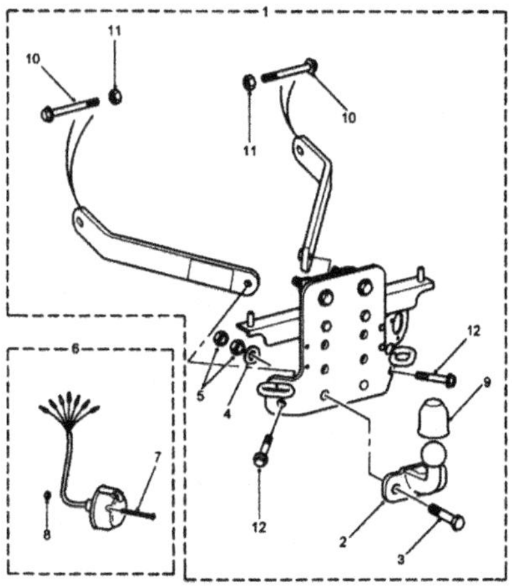

LT0095

Illus	Part Number	Description	Quantity	Change Point	Remarks
1	VUB105450	TOWING ATTACHMENT ASSEMBLY	1	Note (1)	110"
1	VUB105450	TOWING ATTACHMENT ASSEMBLY	1	Note (1)	130"
2	RTC8891AA	• Ball-towing attachment-50mm	1		
3	BH116127	• Bolt-M16 x 60-dacromat	2		
4	WC116101	• Washer	2		
5	NH116041L	• Nut-M16-hexagonal head	4		
9	ANR3635	• Cover-towing attachment ball-50mm	1		
6	YWJ101490	KIT-TOWING ELECTRICS		Note (1)	
7	SE105401	• Screw-pan head-M5 x 40	3		
8	NY105041L	• Nut-hexagonal-nyloc-M5	3		
2	RTC8891AA	Ball-towing attachment-50mm			
3	BH116127	Bolt-M16 x 60-dacromat			
1	VUB105480	TOWING ATTACHMENT ASSEMBLY	1	Note (2)	110"
1	VUB105480	TOWING ATTACHMENT ASSEMBLY	1	Note (2)	130"
2	RTC8891AA	• Ball-towing attachment-50mm	1		
3	BH116127	• Bolt-M16 x 60-dacromat	2		
4	WC116101	• Washer	2		
5	NH116041L	• Nut-M16-hexagonal head	4		
9	ANR3635	• Cover-towing attachment ball-50mm	1		
6	YWJ101500	KIT-TOWING ELECTRICS-N TYPE	1	Note (2)	
7	SE105401	• Screw-pan head-M5 x 40	3		
8	NY105041L	• Nut-hexagonal-nyloc-M5	3		
2	RTC8891AA	Ball-towing attachment-50mm			
3	BH116127	Bolt-M16 x 60-dacromat			
10	DYG100720	Bolt-flanged head-M10 x 115	2		
11	FX110047L	Nut-flange-M10	2		
12	FS110301L	Screw-flanged head-M10 x 30-top	2		

CHANGE POINTS:
(1) From (V) WA 138480 To (V) WA 159806
(2) From (V) XA 159807

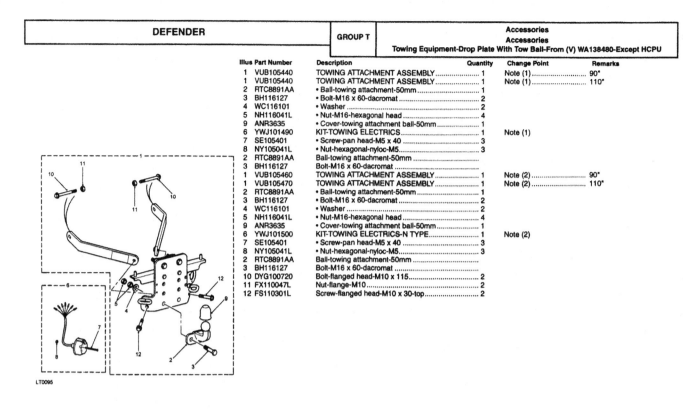

DEFENDER	GROUP T	Accessories Accessories Towing Equipment-Towing Jaw-From (V) XA159807

Illus	Part Number	Description	Quantity	Change Point	Remarks
1	KNB100640	JAW ASSEMBLY-TOWING	1		
2	KNS100000	• Pin	1		
3	KYP000020	• Rivet	2		
4	562756	Spacer	1		
5	BH116261	Bolt	2		
6	NY116041L	Nut-hexagonal head-nyloc-M16	2		

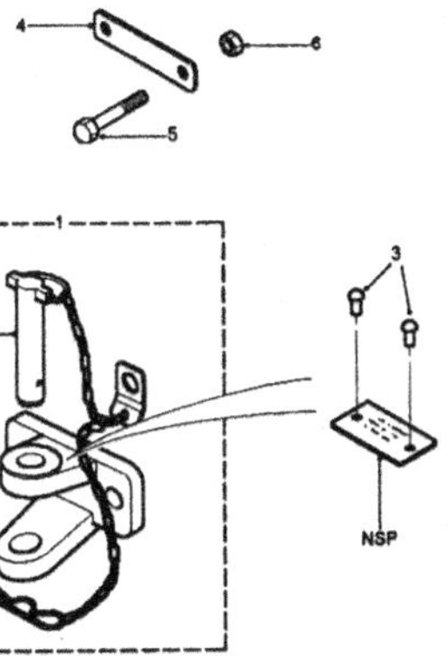

LT0096A

DEFENDER	GROUP T	Accessories Accessories Towing Equipment-Towing Jaw/Ball Fixings-Direct to Crossmember-From (V) XA159807

Illus	Part Number	Description	Quantity	Change Point	Remarks
1	KNK100090	Plate assembly-tow bar mounting	1		
2	KNK100080	Plate-tow bar mounting	1		
3	KNL100010	Stiffener-tow equipment angle iron	1		
4	FS110251	Screw-flanged head-M10 x 25	3		
5	FS110301L	Screw-flanged head-M10 x 30-top	2		
6	NY110041	Nut-hexagonal head-nyloc	2		
7	FB112081	Bolt-flanged head-M12 x 40	2		
8	BH116107	Bolt-dacromat-M16 x 50	2		
9	562756	Spacer	1		
10	BH116127	Bolt-M16 x 60-dacromat	2		

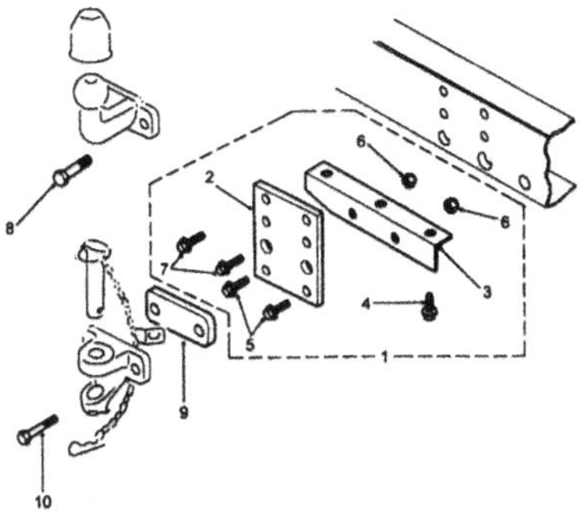

LT0097

Illus	Part Number	Description	Quantity	Change Point	Remarks
1	STC8919	Rope-towing	1		

LT0093

Illus	Part Number	Description	Quantity	Change Point	Remarks
1	RTC8891AA	Ball-towing attachment-50mm	1		
2	RTC8159	Jaw assembly-towing	1		

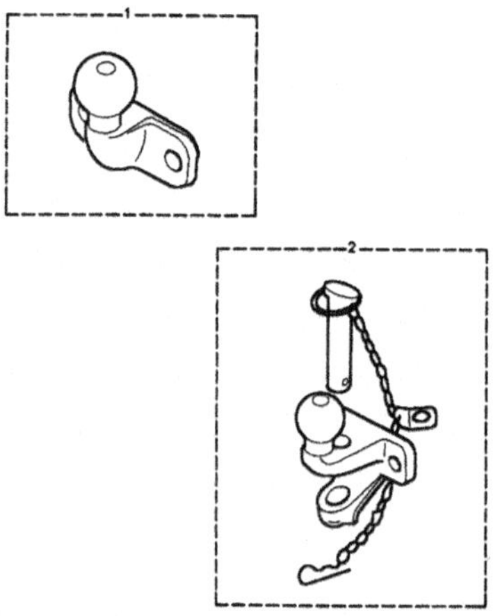

LT0091

Illus	Part Number	Description	Quantity	Change Point	Remarks
1	RTC8977	Split charge-towing electrics	1		
2	STC8874	Towing socket-S type	1		
3	RTC8872	KIT-ELECTRICAL ASSEMBLY TOWING KIT-N TYPE	1	Note (1)	
3	YWJ101500	KIT-TOWING ELECTRICS-N TYPE	1	Note (2)	
4	SE105401	• Screw-pan head-M5 x 40	3		
5	NY105041L	• Nut-hexagonal-nyloc-M5	3		

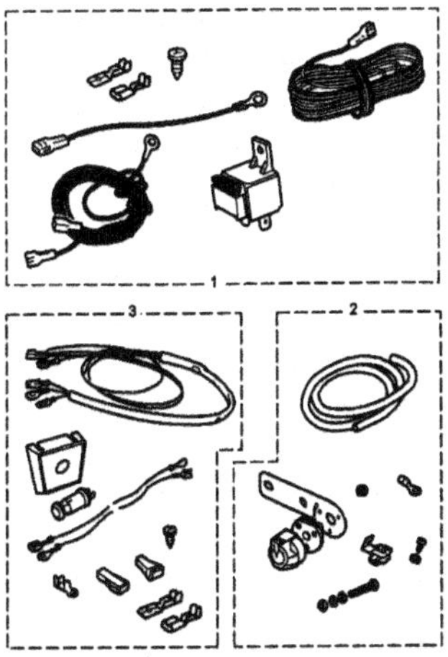

AHTXCA3A

CHANGE POINTS:
(1) To (V) WA 159806
(2) From (V) XA 159807

Illus	Part Number	Description	Quantity	Change Point	Remarks
1	STC50303	Kit-towing electrics-Type S	1		Split charge 90"
1	STC50324	Kit-towing electrics-Type S	1		Split charge 110"
1	STC50325	Kit-towing electrics-Type S	1		Split charge 130"

NOT ILLUSTRATED
PAS ILLUSTREE
NICHT ILLUSTRIERT
SENZA IL DISEGNO
SIN EL DISENO
SEM ILLUSTRACAO
NIET AFGEBEELD

ND 0007

Towing Electrics-Trailer Socket-To (V) MA962814

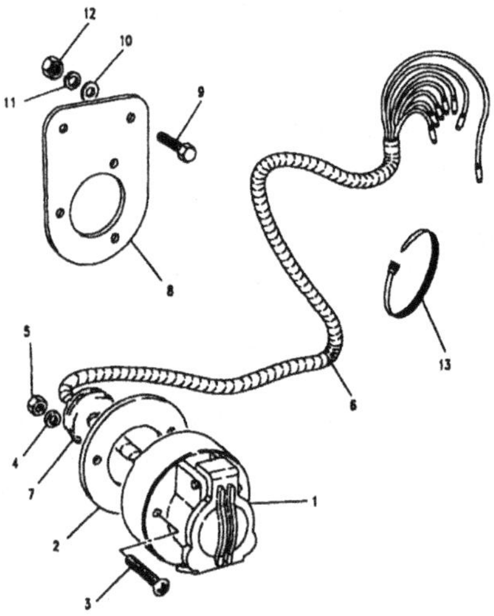

Illus	Part Number	Description	Quantity	Change Point	Remarks
1	579409	Socket-electrical towing-7 pin	NLA		Use STC4286.
1	STC4286	Socket-electrical towing-7 pin-12N	1		Except Switzerland
1	RTC3729	Socket-electrical towing-7 pin	1		
2	560553	Seal	1	Note (1)	
2	PRC4540	Seal	2	Note (2)	
3	SE105351L	Screw-pan	6		
4	WL105001L	Washer-retaining-M5	6		
5	NH105041L	Nut-hexagonal-M5	6		
		UK & EUROPE			
6	PRC2403	Harness towing	1	Note (1)	UK Europe
6	PRC5357	Harness towing	1	Note (2)	UK Europe
6	PRC3543	Harness towing	1	Note (3)	UK Europe
6	PRC5874	Harness towing	1	Note (4)	UK Europe
		REST OF WORLD - EXCEPT SWITZERLAND			
6	PRC4209	Harness towing	1	Note (1)	
6	PRC3542	Harness towing	1	Note (3)	
6	PRC5356	Harness towing	1	Note (2)	
6	PRC6167	Harness towing	1	Note (4)	
		WHEN UNIVERSAL TOW HITCH FITTED			
6	PRC8131	Harness towing	1		
7	PRC2439	Grommet	1		
8	NRC8048	Plate-trailer socket mounting	2		
9	SH106251	Screw-hexagonal head-M6 x 25	4		
10	WA106041L	Washer-6mm	4		
11	WL106001L	Washer-sprung-M6	4		
12	NH106041L	Nut-hexagonal-nyloc-M6	4		
13	UKC6684L	Tie-cable-Black-3.5 x 150mm-inside serated	2		

CHANGE POINTS:
(1) To (V) AA 283269
(2) From (V) AA 283270
(3) To (V) 283346
(4) From (V) 283347

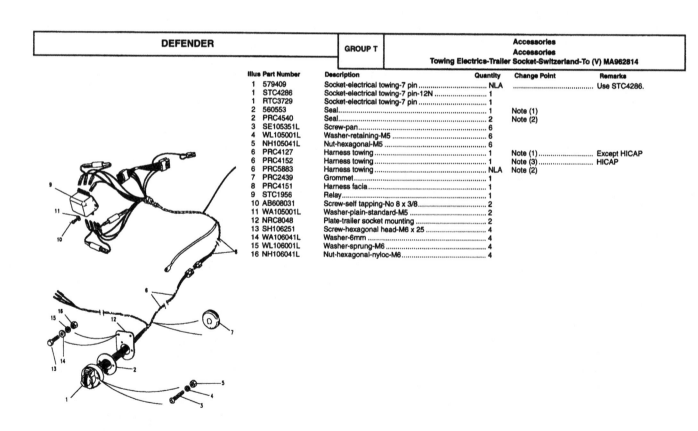

Towing Electrics-Trailer Socket-Switzerland-To (V) MA962814

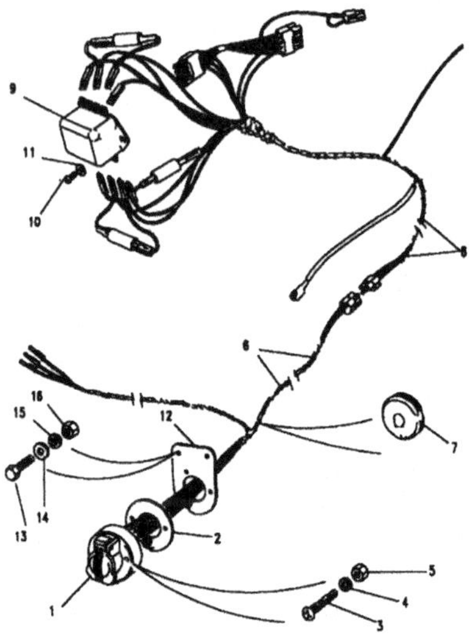

Illus	Part Number	Description	Quantity	Change Point	Remarks
1	579409	Socket-electrical towing-7 pin	NLA		Use STC4286.
1	STC4286	Socket-electrical towing-7 pin-12N	1		
1	RTC3729	Socket-electrical towing-7 pin	1		
2	560553	Seal	1	Note (1)	
2	PRC4540	Seal	2	Note (2)	
3	SE105351L	Screw-pan	6		
4	WL105001L	Washer-retaining-M5	6		
5	NH105041L	Nut-hexagonal-M5	6		
6	PRC4127	Harness towing	1	Note (1)	Except HICAP
6	PRC4152	Harness towing	1	Note (3)	HICAP
6	PRC5883	Harness towing	NLA	Note (2)	
7	PRC2439	Grommet	1		
8	PRC4151	Harness facia	1		
9	STC1956	Relay	1		
10	AB608031	Screw-self tapping-No 8 x 3/8	2		
11	WA105001L	Washer-plain-standard-M5	2		
12	NRC8048	Plate-trailer socket mounting	2		
13	SH106251	Screw-hexagonal head-M6 x 25	4		
14	WA106041L	Washer-6mm	4		
15	WL106001L	Washer-sprung-M6	4		
16	NH106041L	Nut-hexagonal-nyloc-M6	4		

CHANGE POINTS:
(1) To (V) AA 283269
(2) From (V) AA 283270
(3) To (V) 283346

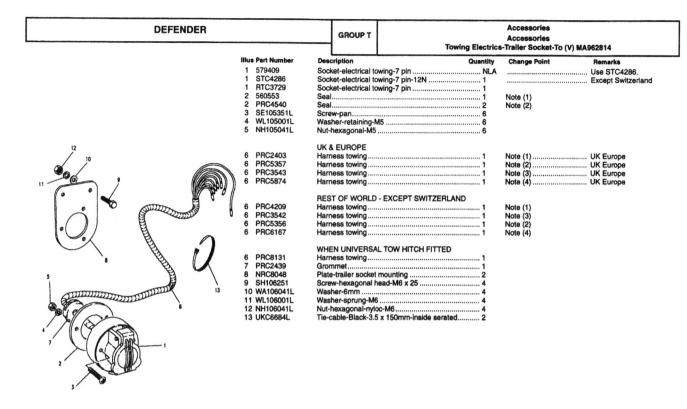

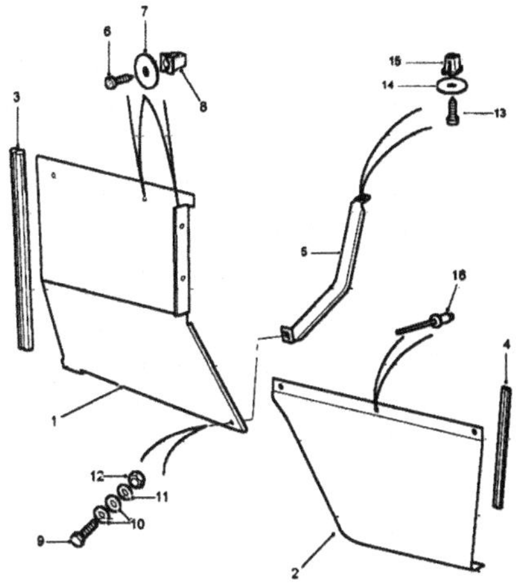

LT0012

Illus	Part Number	Description	Quantity	Change Point	Remarks
1	MRC7359	Wheelguard-RH	1		
2	MRC7360	Wheelguard-LH	1		
3	MRC7361	Seal-RH	1		
4	MRC7362	Seal-LH	1		
5	MRC8732	Stay	2		
6	AB608047L	Screw-self tapping-No 8 x 1/2	4		
7	AFU1218L	Washer-plain	4		
8	RTC3745	Nut-lokut	4		
9	FS106167L	Screw-flanged head-flanged head-M6 x 16	1	Note (1)	
10	WA106041	Washer	NLA		Use WA106041L.
11	WL106001	Washer-M6	NLA		Use WL106001L.
12	NH106041	Nut-hexagonal head-M6	NLA		Use NH106041L.
13	AB608047L	Screw-self tapping-No 8 x 1/2	1		
14	AFU1218L	Washer-plain	1		
15	RTC3745	Nut-lokut	1		
16	78248	Rivet-pop-3/16" x 0.45"lng	3		

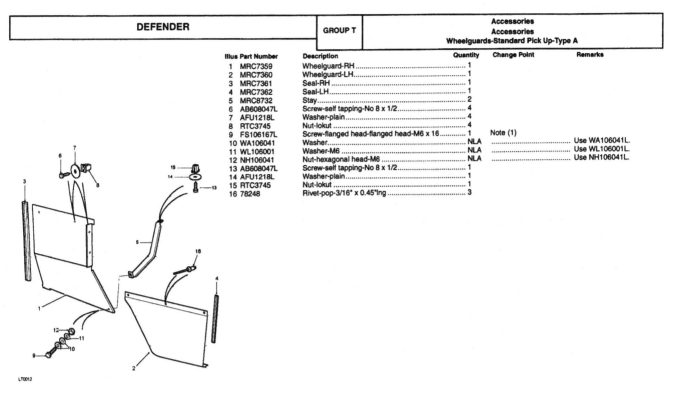

CHANGE POINTS:
(1) To (V) LA 939975

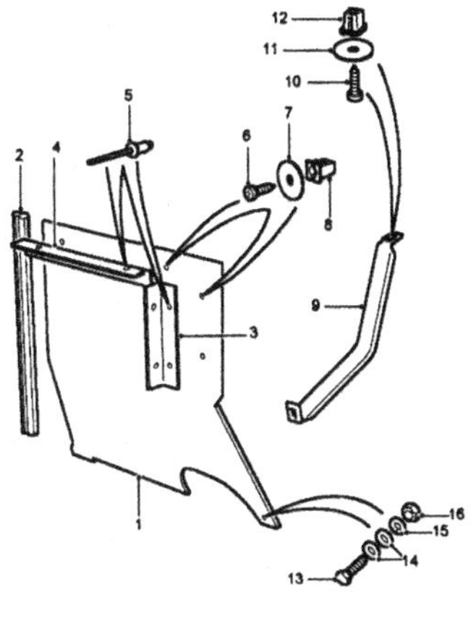

LT0011

Illus	Part Number	Description	Quantity	Change Point	Remarks
1	MWC1058	Wheelguard-RH	1		110"
1	MWC1059	Wheelguard-LH	1		
2	MRC7361	Seal-RH	2		
3	MWC1062	Bracket-side	2		
4	MWC1063	Bracket-top	2		
5	78248	Rivet-pop-3/16" x 0.45"lng	8		
6	AB608047L	Screw-self tapping-No 8 x 1/2	8		
7	AFU1218L	Washer-plain	8		
8	RTC3745	Nut-lokut	8		
9	MRC8732	Stay	2		
10	AB608047L	Screw-self tapping-No 8 x 1/2	2		
11	AFU1218L	Washer-plain	2		
12	RTC3745	Nut-lokut	2		
13	FS106167L	Screw-flanged head-flanged head-M6 x 16	2		
14	WA106001L	Washer-M6	4		
15	WL106001L	Washer-sprung-M6	4		
16	NH106041L	Nut-hexagonal-nyloc-M6	2		110"

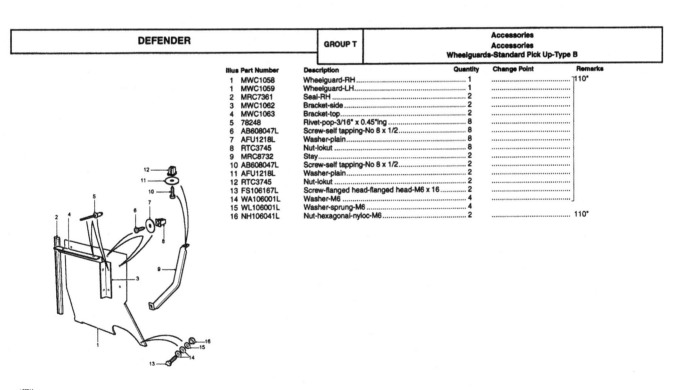

Illus	Part Number	Description	Quantity	Change Point	Remarks
1	STC7635	Step & bumper-rear	1	Note (1)	
1	STC50269AA	Step & bumper-rear	1	Note (2)	90"
1	STC50301	Step assembly-rear end	1	Note (2)	110"
2	STC7631	Step assembly-side-Black	1		
3	STC7632	Step assembly-rear end	1		

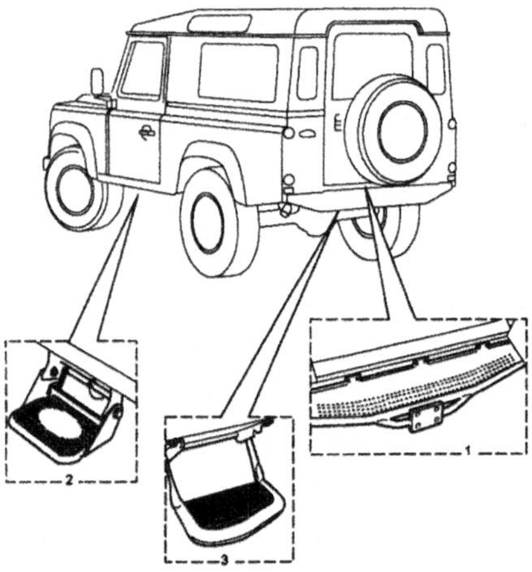

CHANGE POINTS:
(1) To (V) WA 159806
(2) From (V) XA 159807

Illus	Part Number	Description	Quantity	Change Point	Remarks
		90" WHEELBASE			
1	STC8438	Step-side runner-Black-pair	NLA		Use STC8438AA.
					90"
1	STC8438AA	Step-side runner-Black-pair	1		90"
1	STC60853	Step-side runner-Black-RH	1		90" Extreme Belgium
1	STC60854	Step-side runner-Black-LH	1		90" Extreme Belgium
1	STC60706	Step-side runner-Silver powder coat-pair	1		90" Heritage
1	STC50141	Step-side runner-Bright-stainless steel.-pair	1		90"
1	STC60160	Step-side runner-Bright-stainless steel.-RH	1		90" 50 LE
1	STC60161	Step-side runner-Bright-stainless steel.-LH	1		90" 50 LE
		110" WHEELBASE			
1	STC8015	Step-side runner-Black-pair	NLA		Use STC8015AA.
					110"
1	STC8015AA	Step-side runner-Black-pair	1		110"
1	STC60707	Step-side runner-Silver powder coat-pair	1		110" Heritage

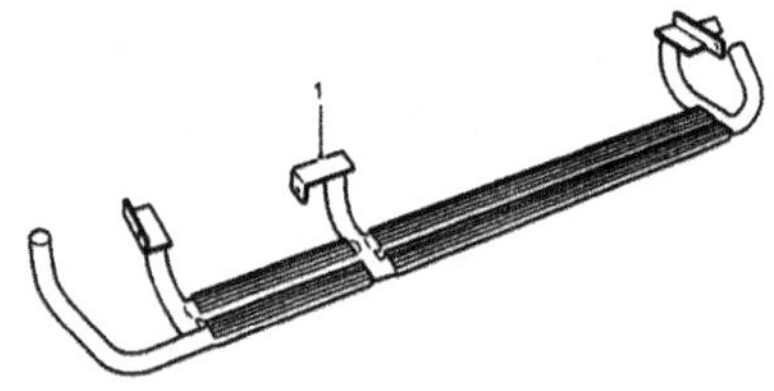

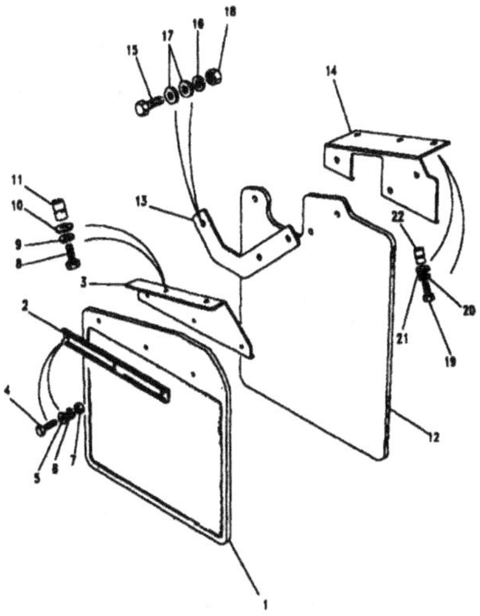

Illus	Part Number	Description	Quantity	Change Point	Remarks
1	RTC4685	Mudflaps-front-pair	1		
2	MTC3874	Stiffener-front mudflap	2		
3	MTC3000	Bracket-front mudflap retention-RH	1		
3	MTC3001	Bracket-front mudflap retention-LH	1		
4	FS106255L	Screw-mudflap attachment-flanged head-M6 x 25	6		
5	WA106041L	Washer-6mm	6		
6	WL106001L	Washer-sprung-M6	6		
7	NH106041L	Nut-mudflap attachment-hexagonal-nyloc-M6	6		
8	FS106201L	Screw-mudflap mounting bracket to body-flanged head-M6 x 20	4		
9	WL106001L	Washer-sprung-M6	4		
10	WA106041L	Washer-6mm	4		
11	NN106021	Nutsert-blind-M6	4		
		MUDFLAP-REAR			
12	MUC2344	RH	1	Note (1)	
12	MXC6412	RH	1	Note (2)	
12	CAT100960	RH-with bracket	1	Note (3)	Td5
12	MUC2345	LH	1	Note (4)	Soft Top
12	MUC3990	LH	1	Note (5)	
12	MXC6413	LH	1	Note (2)	
12	MUC2345	LH	1	Note (6)	Hard Top
12	MUC3990	LH	1	Note (7)	
12	MXC6413	LH	1	Note (2)	
12	CAT101110	LH-with bracket	1		V8 EFi 50 LE
12	CAT101110	LH-with bracket	1	Note (3)	Td5
13	MUC1512	Plate-mudflap support	2		

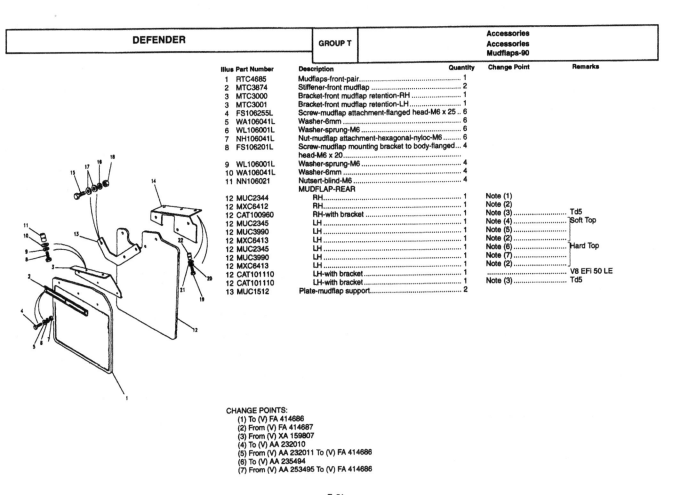

CHANGE POINTS:
(1) To (V) FA 414686
(2) From (V) FA 414687
(3) From (V) XA 159807
(4) To (V) AA 232010
(5) From (V) AA 232011 To (V) FA 414686
(6) To (V) AA 235494
(7) From (V) AA 253495 To (V) FA 414686

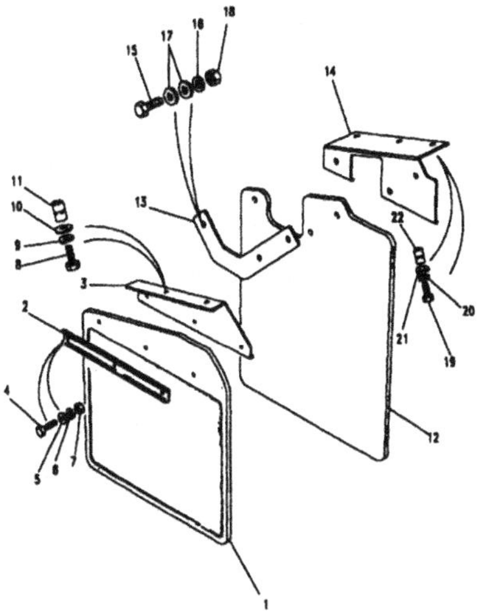

Illus	Part Number	Description	Quantity	Change Point	Remarks
		BRACKET-REAR MUDFLAP RETENTION			
14	MUC3984	RH	1	Note (1)	Soft Top
14	MUC3985	LH	1		
14	MUC3986	RH	1	Note (2)	
14	MUC3987	LH	1		
14	MUC3984	RH	1	Note (3)	Hard Top
14	MUC3985	LH	1		
14	MUC3986	RH	1	Note (4)	
14	MUC3987	LH	1		
14	CAX100140	RH	1	Note (5)	
14	CAX100150	LH	1		
15	FS106255L	Screw-mudflap attachment-flanged head-M6 x 25	6		
16	WL106001L	Washer-sprung-M6	6		
17	WA106041L	Washer-6mm	6		
18	NH106041L	Nut-mudflap attachment-hexagonal-nyloc-M6	6		
19	FS106167L	Screw-flanged head-flanged head-M6 x 16	4		
20	WL106001L	Washer-sprung-M6	6		
21	NN106021	Nutsert-blind-M6	2		
22	WA106041L	Washer-6mm	6		
	CYF000020	Spacer	2		
23	MTC7513	Edging strip	A/R		Germany

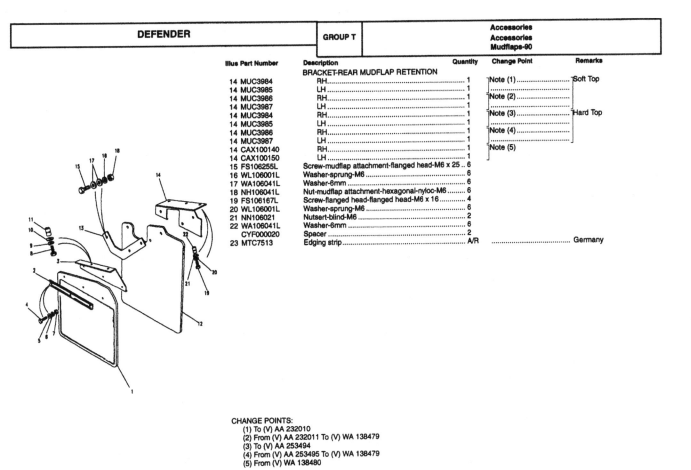

CHANGE POINTS:
(1) To (V) AA 232010
(2) From (V) AA 232011 To (V) WA 138479
(3) To (V) AA 253494
(4) From (V) AA 253495 To (V) WA 138479
(5) From (V) WA 138480

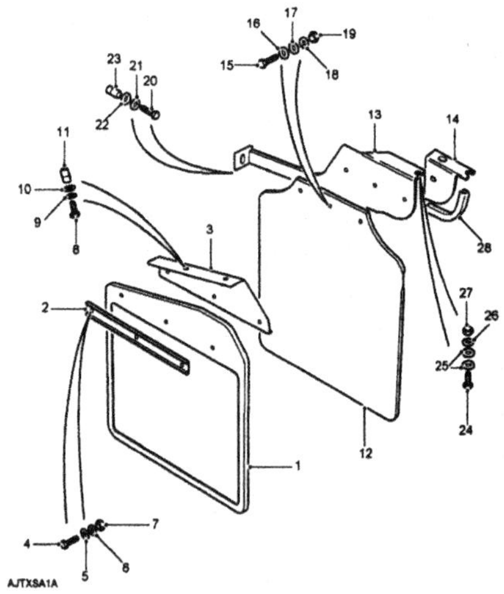

Illus	Part Number	Description	Quantity	Change Point	Remarks
1	RTC4685	Mudflaps-front-pair	1		
2	MTC3874	Stiffener-front mudflap	2		
3	MTC3000	Bracket-front mudflap retention-RH	1		
3	MTC3001	Bracket-front mudflap retention-LH	1		
4	FS106255L	Screw-flanged head-M6 x 25	6		
5	WA106041L	Washer-6mm	6		
6	WL106001L	Washer-sprung-M6	6		
7	NH106041L	Nut-hexagonal-nyloc-M6	6		
8	FS106201L	Screw-flanged head-M6 x 20	4		
9	WL106001L	Washer-sprung-M6	4		
10	WA106041L	Washer-6mm	4		
	CYF000020	Spacer	2		
11	NN106021	Nutsert-blind-M6	4		
12	RTC4686	Mudflap-rear	2	Note (1)	
12	MXC6411	Mudflap-rear-rubber	NLA	Note (2)	Use BTR277.
12	BTR277	Mudflap-rear-ribbed rubber	2		
13	MTC8358	Bracket-mounting-rear-RH	1		
13	MTC8357	Bracket-mounting-rear-LH	1		
14	MTC8440	Bracket-rear mudflap retention-rear-RH	1		HICAP
14	MTC8441	Bracket-rear mudflap retention-rear-LH	1		HICAP
15	FS106167L	Screw-flanged head-flanged head-M6 x 16	6		
16	WJ600041L	Washer	6		
17	WC106041L	Washer-M6-oversize	6		
18	WL106001L	Washer-sprung-M6	6		
19	NH106041L	Nut-hexagonal-nyloc-M6	6		
20	FS106167L	Screw-flanged head-flanged head-M6 x 16	6		
20	FS106201L	Screw-flanged head-M6 x 20	2		
21	WL106001L	Washer-sprung-M6	2		
22	WA106041L	Washer-6mm	2		
23	NN106011	Nutsert-blind	2		
24	FS106167L	Screw-flanged head-flanged head-M6 x 16	4		
25	WA108041L	Washer-plain-8mm	8		
26	WL106001L	Washer-sprung-M6	4		
27	NH106041L	Nut-hexagonal-nyloc-M6	6		
28	MTC7513	Edging strip	A/R		Germany

CHANGE POINTS:
(1) To (V) FA 414615
(2) From (V) FA 414616

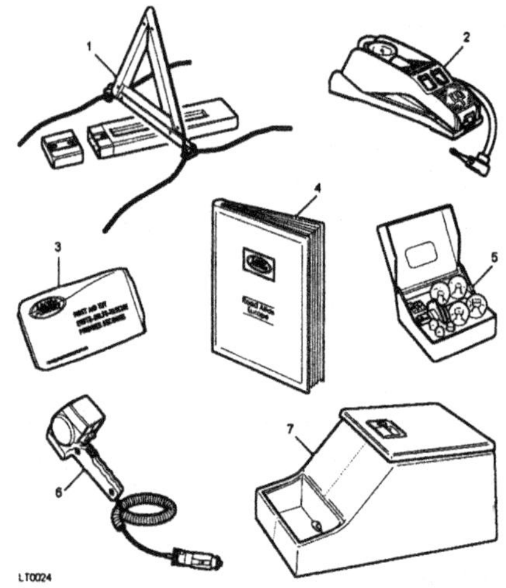

Illus	Part Number	Description	Quantity	Change Point	Remarks
1	STC7641	Triangle-warning	1		
2	STC8243	Pump-foot	1		
3	STC7642	Kit-first aid	1		
4	STC8784	Road atlas	1		
5	STC8247AA	Kit-bulb-white,	1		
6	RTC9527	Lamp-hand-Cewe	1		
7	STC7634	Cubby box-with lock	1		
8	STC8888	Kit-seat belt reel & fixings-inward facing set	1		110" Station Wagon 11 seats 12 seats
9	STC8212	Scraper-ice	1		
10	STC720	Kit-window care	1		
11	VUB112530L	Bag-accessory-umbrella	1		

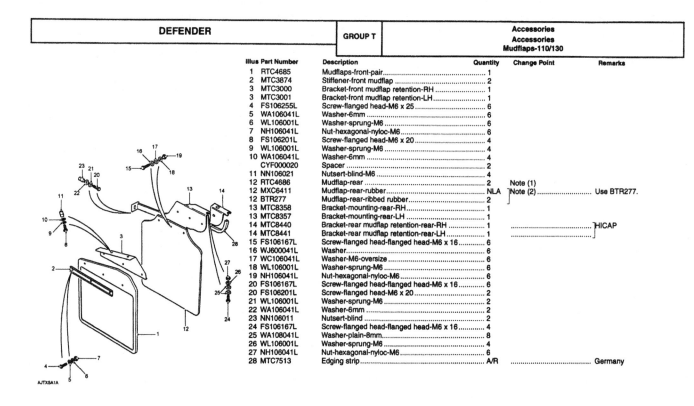

Illus	Part Number	Description	Quantity	Change Point	Remarks
		SEALANTS			
1	STC50541	Stripper-gasket-200ml	1		
2	STC50542	Lubricant-silicone-aerosol-200ml	1		
3	STC50543	Cleaner-liquid-200ml	1		
4	STC50544	Cleaner-liquid-400ml	1		
5	STC50545	Lubricant-Penetrating-150ml	1		
6	STC50550	Gasket-sealing-50ml	1		
7	STC50551	Adhesive-sealing-300ml	1		
8	STC50546	Adhesive-5ml	1		
9	STC50552	Thread-locking-sealing-10ml	1		
10	STC50553	Sealant-stud & bearing-10ml	1		
11	STC50554	Retainer-10ml	1		
12	STC4404	Sealant-Hylomar 607 (300ml)	A/R		Manual

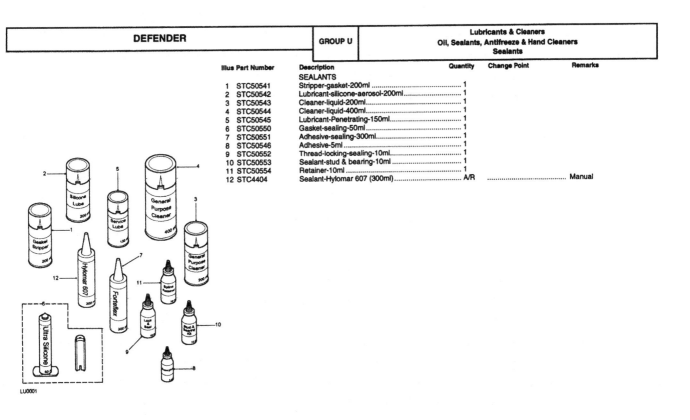

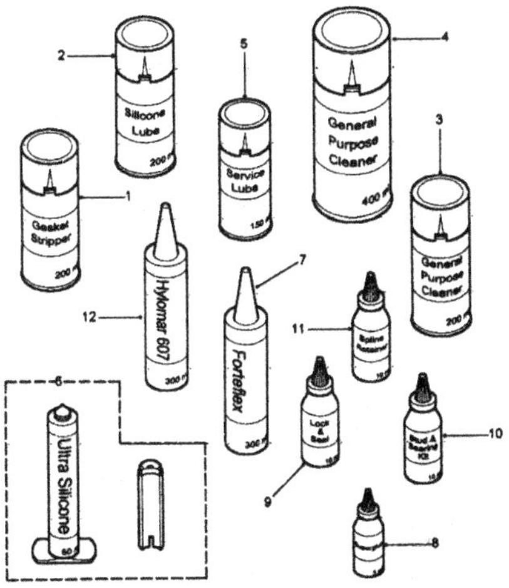

LU0001

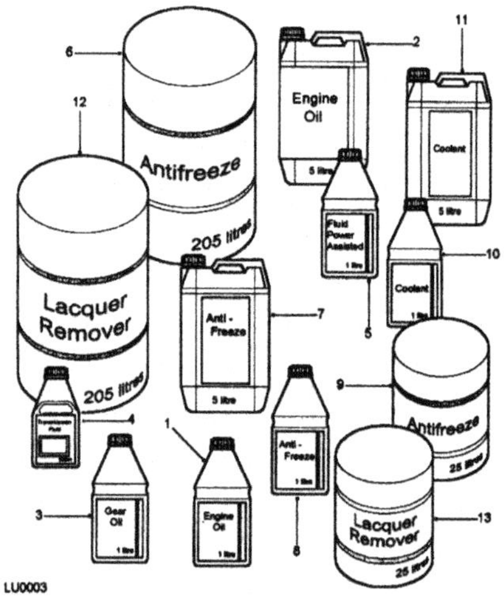

LU0003

Illus	Part Number	Description	Quantity	Change Point	Remarks
		OIL			
1	STC8257	SHPD-1ltr	A/R		UK
2	STC8256	SHPD-5ltr	A/R		
1	STC8255	15W-40-1ltr	A/R		
2	STC8254	15W-40-5ltr	A/R		
3	STC8259	EP90	A/R		
4	STC8261	Fluid-automatic transmission-DEXTRON 2	A/R		
4	STC8263	Fluid-automatic transmission-Type G	A/R		
5	STC8292	Brake fluid	A/R		
		ANTIFREEZE			
8	RTC5779A	1ltr	A/R		Except 5 Cylinder
	RTC5781A	5ltr	A/R		Except 5 Cylinder
9	STC50524	25 Litres.	1		Td5
6	RTC5782A	205ltr	A/R		Except 5 Cylinder
10	STC50529	Coolant-1ltr	1		Td5
11	STC50530	Coolant-5ltr	1		Td5
		LACQUER REMOVER			
12	STC2774LGE	Fluid-de-lacquering-205ltr	A/R		
13	STC2774SML	Fluid-de-lacquering-25 Litres.	A/R		
		LUBRICANT ANTI-SQUEAK			
	CYK100070L	Lubricant-aerosol	1		
	CYK100050L	Lubricant	1		

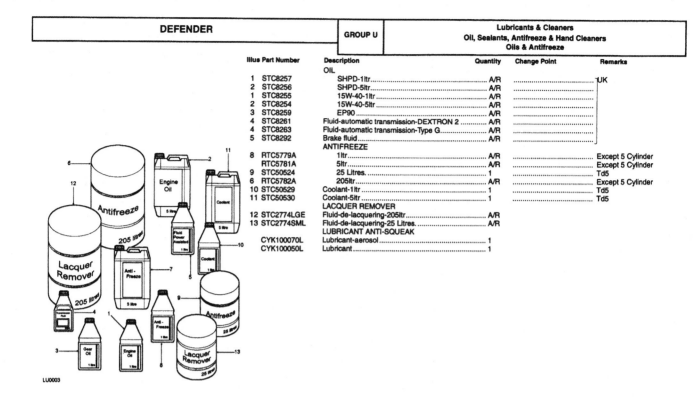

Illus	Part Number	Description	Quantity	Change Point	Remarks
		HAND CLEANERS			
1	STC50547	Cleaner-liquid-hand-Orange-400ml	1`		
2	STC50548	Cleaner-liquid-hand-Orange-3L	1		
3	STC50549	Cleaner-liquid-hand-400ml	1		

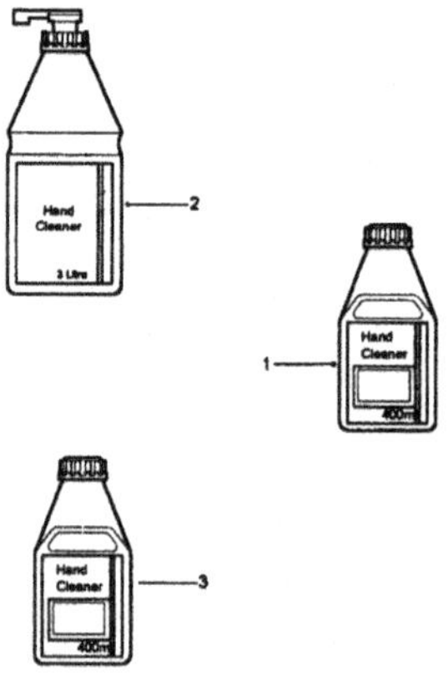

LU0002

Illus	Part Number	Description	Quantity	Change Point	Remarks
1	STC7032	Intermediate assembly exhaust system-6x6-3 hole. flange	1		
1	STC60137	Intermediate assembly exhaust system-6x6-2 hole. flange	1		

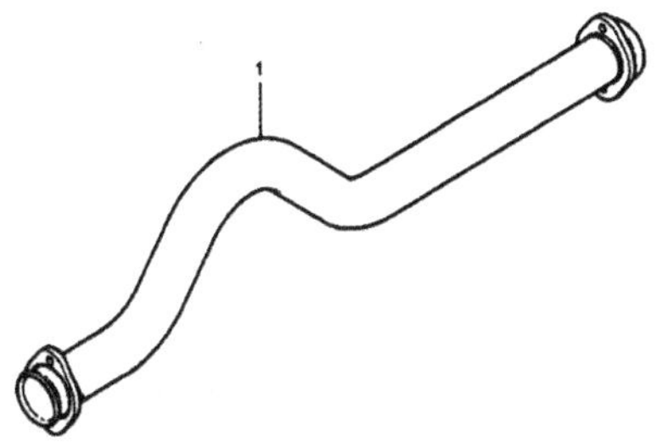

LK0003

Special Vehicle Options
SVO Options
Mudflaps-Police

Illus	Part Number	Description	Quantity	Change Point	Remarks
1	STC7343	Kit-mudflaps	1		90"
1	STC7336	Kit-mudflaps	1		110"

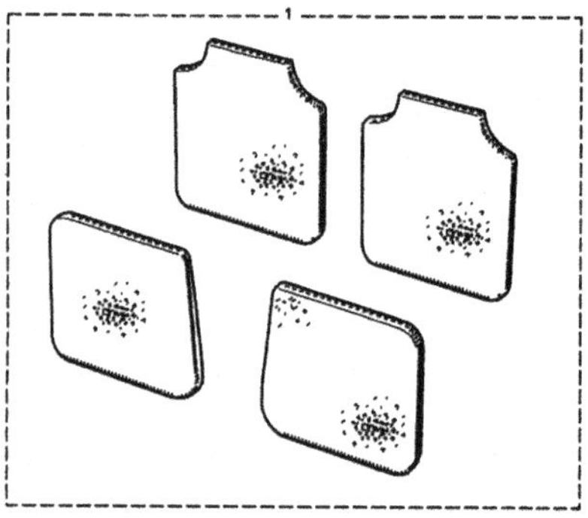

AHVXSA1A

Special Vehicle Options
SVO Options
Roll Cage Upper-90SV

Illus	Part Number	Description	Quantity	Change Point	Remarks
	ALR6777	Panel header roof	1		
		CAGE ASSEMBLY-ROLL			
1	ALR5539	front	1		
2	ALR5540	front-lower	1		
3	ALR5541	front-side	1		
4	ALR5543	centre	1		
5	ALR5544	Tie bar-roll cage	1		
6	ALR5545	Bracket-roll cage hoop intermediate mounting-LH	1		
6	ALR5546	Bracket-roll cage hoop intermediate mounting-RH	1		
	ALR5548	Seal-front wing	2		
7	STC1379	Cage assembly-roll-rear-longitudinal	1		
8	STC1378	Cage assembly-roll-rear	1		

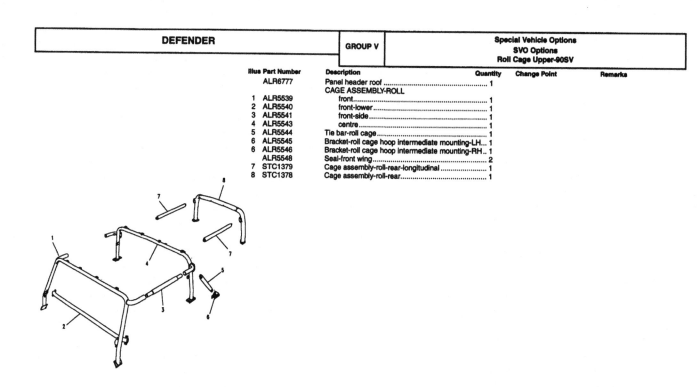

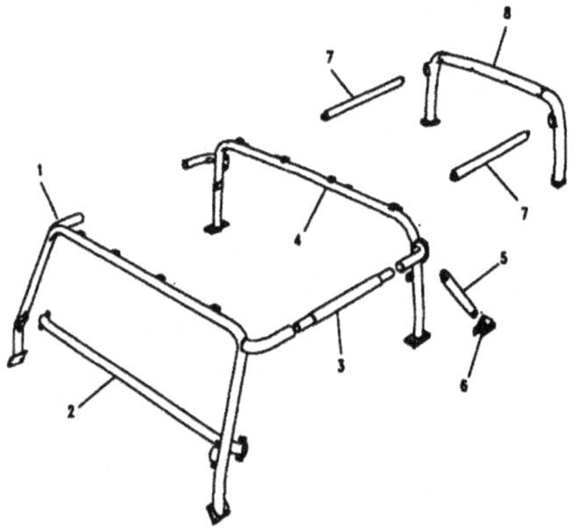

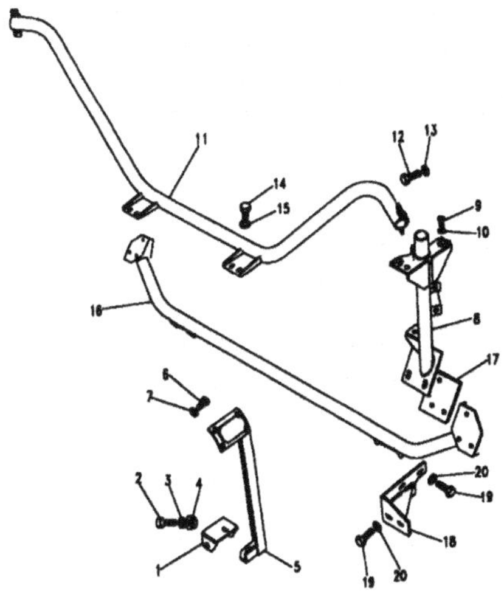

Illus	Part Number	Description	Quantity	Change Point	Remarks
1	ALR3219	Bracket-mounting-LH	1		
1	ALR3220	Bracket-mounting-RH	1		
2	SH110251L	Screw-hexagonal head-M10 x 25	2		
3	WA110061L	Washer-M10	4		
4	FN110047	Nut-flange-flange-M10	2		
5	ALR3221	Bracket-front fender-LH	1		
5	ALR3222	Bracket-front fender-RH	1		
6	MXC6676	Screw-M8	8		
7	4594L	Washer-plain	8		
8	ALR6109	Bracket-support-LH	1		
8	ALR6110	Bracket-support-RH	1		
9	ALR5549	Bolt-torx-pan-M10 x 30	10		
10	ALR5550	Washer-fibre	10		
11	ALR5556	Cage assembly-roll	1		
12	SH110251L	Screw-crosstube to hoop-hexagonal head-M10 x 25	4		
13	WA110061L	Washer-M10	4		
14	SH607091L	Screw-hexagonal head	2		
15	WA600071L	Washer	2		
16	ALR5557	Stay-roll cage hoop-lower	1		
17	ALR5558	Seal	2		
18	ALR5561	Bracket-mounting cage-RH	1		
18	ALR5560	Bracket-mounting cage-LH	1		
19	SH110251L	Screw-hexagonal head-M10 x 25	10		
20	WA110061L	Washer-M10	10		

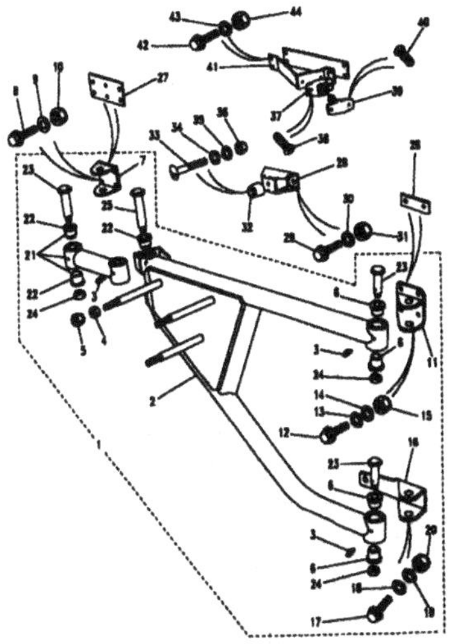

Illus	Part Number	Description	Quantity	Change Point	Remarks
1	BTR8714	CARRIER-LOAD/TAIL DOOR SPARE WHEEL MOUNTING	1	Note (1)	
2	BTR8720	• Frame spare wheel carrier	1		
3	RRC2898	• Nipple-grease	4		
4	MUC4546	• Nut-M16	3		
5	90577473	• Nut wheel retention-16mm-steel wheel	4		
6	RRC5266	• Bush	4		
7	ANR3145	• Bracket	1		
8	FS106201	• Screw-flanged head-M6 x 20	6		
9	WA106041L	• Washer-6mm	8		
10	NY106041L	• Nut-hexagonal head-nyloc-M6	NLA		Use NY106047L.
11	RRC5739	• Pivot-spare wheel harness	1		
12	FS108251L	• Screw-flanged head-M8 x 25	NLA		Use FS108257L.
13	WA108051L	• Washer-8mm	4		
14	WC108051L	• Washer-M8	1		
15	NY108041L	• Nut-nyloc-M8	2		
16	RRC5115	• Pivot-spare wheel harness	1		
17	FS108301L	• Screw-flanged head-M8 x 30	NLA		Use FS108307L.
18	WA108051L	• Washer-8mm	2		
19	WC108051L	• Washer-M8	2		
20	NY108041L	• Nut-nyloc-M8	2		
21	RRC5262	• TUBE	1		
22	RRC5266	• • Bush	4		
23	RRC5264	• Bolt	3		
24	NT112041L	• Nut-hexagonal-thin-M12	3		
25	RRC5761	• Bolt	1		
17	FS108307L	Screw-flanged head-M8 x 30			
26	ANR3099	Reinforcement-spare wheel retention-upper	1		
27	RRC5277	Reinforcement	1		
28	RRC2241	Bracket-spare wheel retention mounting	1		
29	FS106201	Screw-flanged head-M6 x 20	2		
30	WA106041L	Washer-6mm	2		
31	NY106041L	Nut-hexagonal head-nyloc-M6	NLA		Use NY106047L.
32	304125	Buffer rubber-seat front	1		
33	SP105251	Screw	1		
34	WA105001L	Washer-plain-standard-M5	2		
35	WJ600041L	Washer	2		
36	NY105041L	Nut-hexagonal-nyloc-M5	1		
37	ANR3118	Catch-female	1		
39	ANR3117	Catch-male	1		

CHANGE POINTS:
(1) To (V) LA 939975

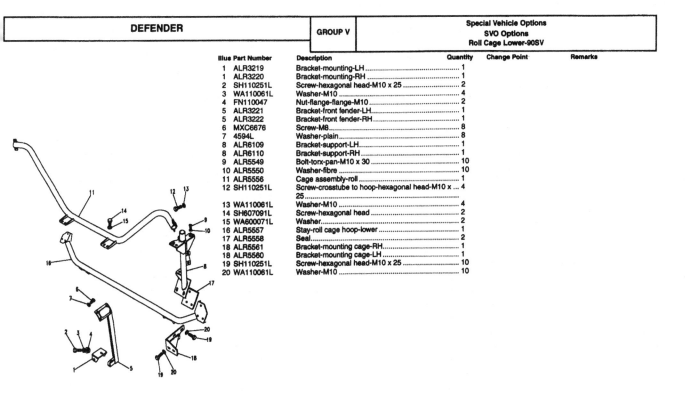

Carrier Spare Wheel-90SV

Illus	Part Number	Description	Quantity	Change Point	Remarks
40	SF105121	Screw	2		
41	RRC5278	Bracket	1		
42	FS106201	Screw-flanged head-M6 x 20	4		
43	WA106041L	Washer-6mm	8		
44	NY106041L	Nut-hexagonal head-nyloc-M6	NLA		Use NY106047L.

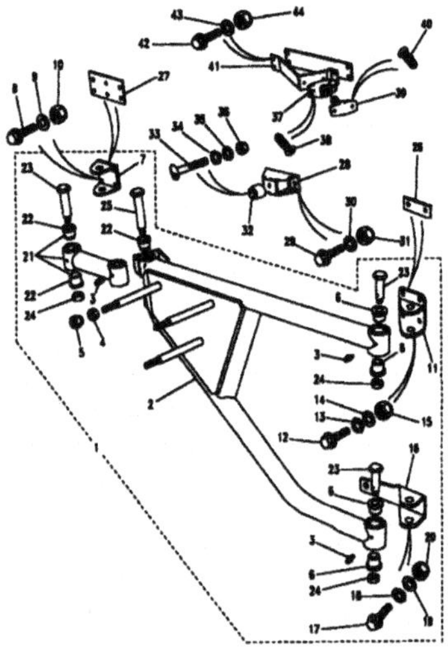

Bodytapes-90SV

Illus	Part Number	Description	Quantity	Change Point	Remarks
1	STC7011	Decal-tailgate-90SV	1		
2	STC7012	Decal front fender-90SV-rear	2		

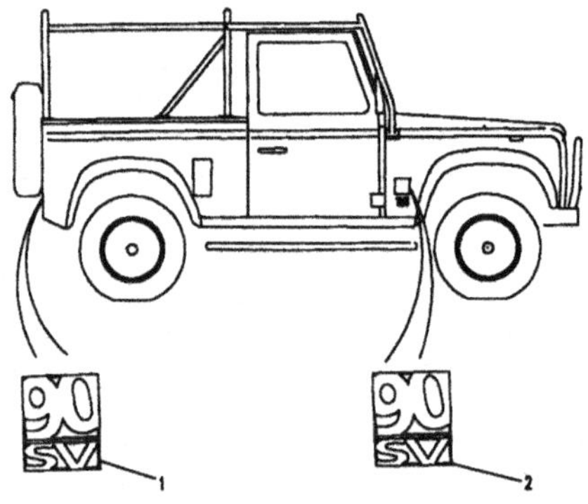

Illus	Part Number	Description	Quantity	Change Point	Remarks
1	STC60123	Badge-Camel Trophy-large	NLA		Contact Special Vehicle Operations @ Land Rover for supply.
2	STC60124	Badge-Camel Trophy-small	NLA		Contact Special Vehicle Operations @ Land Rover for supply.
3	STC60125	Badge-Camel Trophy-front door	NLA		Contact Special Vehicle Operations @ Land Rover for supply.

LV0001

Illus	Part Number	Description	Quantity	Change Point	Remarks
1	STC7000	Hood assembly-full length-with windows	1		
1	STC3117	Hood assembly-full length-less windows	1		
2	STC7001	Kit-fixing-screw	1		
3	STC7002	Pad-anti rattle	1		
4	STC7003	Strap-convertible hood tonneau retaining	1		
5	RRC5802	Clip	6		

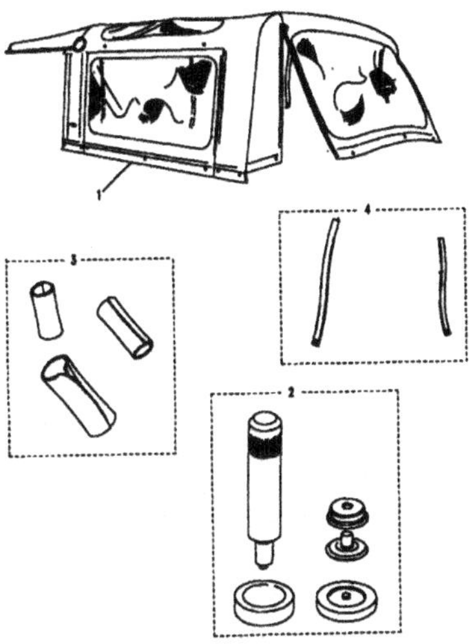

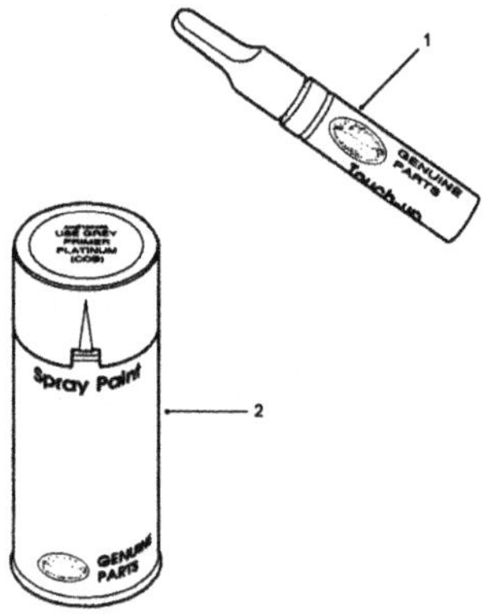

AHTXAA1A

Illus	Part Number	Description	Quantity	Change Point	Remarks
		PAINT-PENCIL			
1	RTC6870T	Alpine White-Solid-(LRC456)	1		
1	STC4325T	Alveston Red-Micatallic-(LRC696)	1		
1	RTC6634T	Ardennes Green-County Green-Micatallic-(LRC413)	1		
1	RTC6401T	Arles Blue-Pacific Blue-Windjammer Blue-Solid-(LRC424)	1		
1	RTC5728T	Arrow Red-Portofino Red-Solid-(LRC390)	1		
1	RTC4051T	Arizona Tan	1		
1	RTC5980T	Arran Beige-Solid-(LRC433)	1		
1	STC60747T	Atlantic Green.	1	Note (1)	Heritage
1	STC3915T	Atlantis Blue-Micatallic-(LRC632)	1	Note (2)	50 LE
1	RTC5979T	Beluga Black-Solid-(LRC416)	1		
1	STC1773T	Biaritz Blue-Micatallic-(LRC965)	1		
1	STC4597T	Bonatti Grey-Metallic-(LRC659)	1		
1	RTC4042T	Bronze Green	1		
1	STC3822T	Caledonian Blue-Micatallic-(LRC507)	1		
1	STC3828T	Chawton White-Micatallic-(LRC603)	1		
1	STC3825T	Cobar Blue-Metallic-(LRC624)	1		
1	STC1348T	Coniston Green-Solid-(LRC570)	1		
1	STC3824T	Coniston Green-Micatallic-(LRC637)	1		

CHANGE POINTS:
(1) From (V) XA 159807
(2) From (V) WA 138480 To (V) WA 159806

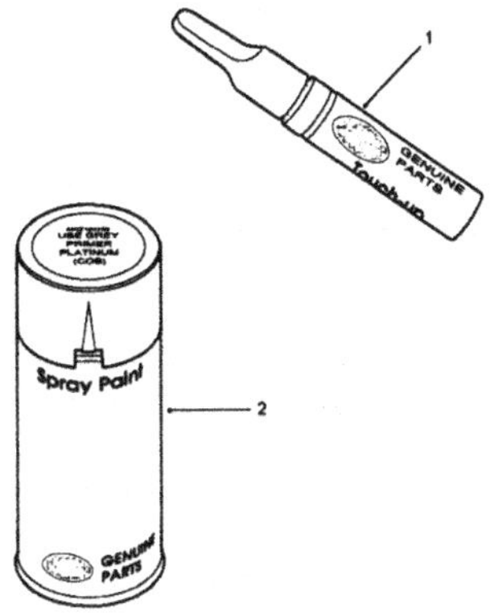

AHTXAA1A

Illus	Part Number	Description	Quantity	Change Point	Remarks
		PAINT-PENCIL			
1	RTC5983T	County Red-Trocadero Red-Micatallic-(LRC467)	1		
1	RTC4058T	Davas White-Ivory-Solid-(LRC354)	1		
1	RTC5981T	Eastnor Green-Solid-(LRC419)	1		
1	STC1774T	Epsom Green-Micatallic-(LRC961)	1		
1	STC4323T	Icelandic Blue-Micatallic-(LRC621)	1		
1	STC4324T	Kent Green-Micatallic-(LRC647)	1		
1	STC4238T	Kinversand-Micatallic-(LRC609)	1		
1	STC4595T	Monte Carlo Blue-Micatallic-(LRC608)	1		
1	STC1349T	Montpellier Red-Micatallic-(LRC536)	1		
1	STC1449T	Niagara Grey-Metallic-(LRC574)	1		
1	STC4596T	Oslo Blue-Micatallic-(LRC644)	1		
1	RTC6869T	Pennine Grey-Solid-(LRC476)	1		
1	STC7552T	Quicksilver-(LRC468)	1		
1	STC2828T	Rioja Red-Micatallic-(LRC601)	1		
1	STC2863T	Riviera Blue-Metallic-(LRC588)	1		
1	STC3823T	Rutland Red-Solid-(LRC607)	1		
1	RTC5727T	Shire Blue	1		
1	RTC4054T	Slate Grey-Cambrian Grey	1		
1	RTC4049T	Stratos Blue-Tasman Blue	1		
1	STC8927T	Silver Sparkle	1		
1	RTC4035T	Venetian Red	1		
1	STC3827T	Woodcote Green-Micatallic-(LRC623)	1		

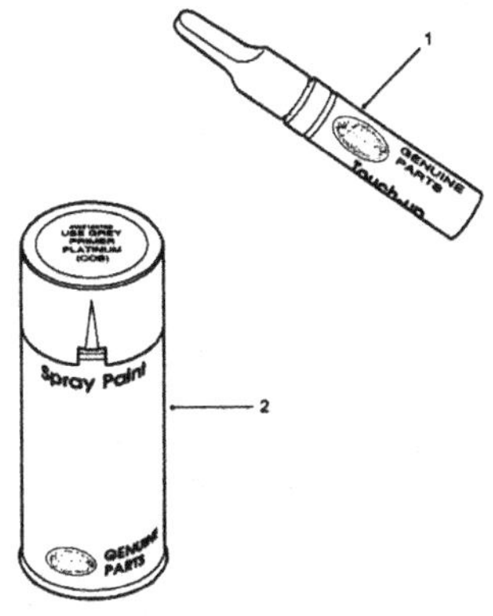

AHTXAA1A

Illus	Part Number	Description	Quantity	Change Point	Remarks
		PAINT-AEROSOL SPRAY			
2	RTC6870A	Alpine White-Solid-(LRC456)	1		
2	STC4325A	Alveston Red-Micatallic-(LRC696)	1		
2	RTC6634A	Ardennes Green-County Green-Micatallic-(LRC413)	1		
2	RTC4051A	Arizona Tan	1		
2	RTC5980A	Arran Beige-Solid-(LRC433)	1		
2	RTC5728A	Arrow Red-Portofino Red-Solid-(LRC390)	1		
2	RTC4042A	Ascot Green-Bronze Green	1		
2	STC60747A	Atlantic Green.	1	Note (1)	Heritage
2	STC3915A	Atlantis Blue-Micatallic-(LRC632)	1	Note (2)	50 LE
2	RTC5979A	Beluga Black-County Black-Solid-(LRC416)	1		
2	STC1773A	Biaritz Blue-Micatallic-(LRC965)	1		
2	STC4597A	Bonatti Grey-Metallic-(LRC659)	1		
2	RTC4054A	Cambrian Grey-Slate Grey	1		
2	STC1348A	Coniston Green-Solid-(LRC570)	1		
2	STC3822A	Caledonian Blue-Solid-(LRC507)	1		
2	STC3828A	Chawton White-Metallic-(LRC603)	1		
2	STC3825A	Cobar Blue-Metallic-(LRC624)	1		
2	STC3824A	Coniston Green-Micatallic-(LRC637)	1		
2	RTC5983A	Foxfire Red-Micatallic-(LRC467)	1		

CHANGE POINTS:
(1) From (V) XA 159807
(2) From (V) WA 138480 To (V) WA 159806

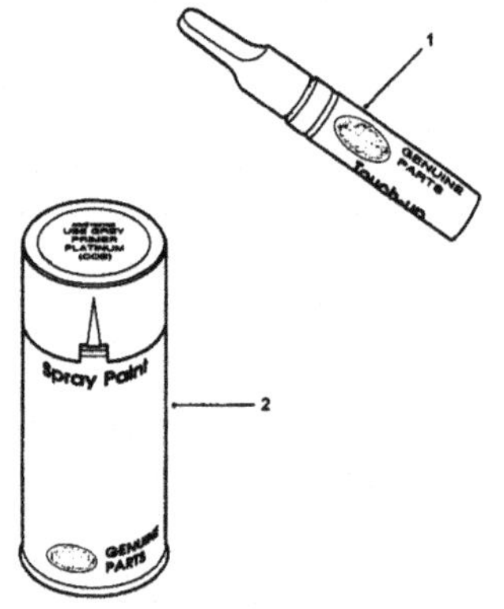

AHTXAA1A

Illus	Part Number	Description	Quantity	Change Point	Remarks
		PAINT-AEROSOL SPRAY			
2	RTC4058A	Davas White-Ivory-Solid-(LRC354)	1		
2	RTC5981A	Eastnor Green-Solid-(LRC419)	1		
2	STC1774A	Epsom Green-Micatallic-(LRC961)	1		
2	STC4323A	Icelandic Blue-Micatallic-(LRC621)	1		
2	STC4324A	Kent Green-Micatallic-(LRC647)	1		
2	STC4238A	Kinversand-Micatallic-(LRC609)	1		
2	RTC4043A	Marine Blue	1		
2	RTC4032A	Masai red	1		
2	STC4595A	Monte Carlo Blue-Micatallic-(LRC608)	1		
2	STC1349A	Montpellier Red-Micatallic-(LRC536)	1		
2	STC1449A	Niagara Grey-Metallic-(LRC574)	1		
2	STC4596A	Oslo Blue-Micatallic-(LRC644)	1		
2	RTC6401A	Pacific Blue-Windjammer Blue-Solid-(LRC424)	1		
2	RTC6869A	Pennine Grey-Solid-(LRC476)	1		
2	STC2828A	Rioja Red-Micatallic-(LRC601)	1		
2	STC2863A	Riviera Blue-Metallic-(LRC588)	1		
2	STC3823A	Rutland Red-Solid-(LRC607)	1		
2	RTC5727A	Shire Blue	1		
2	RTC4049A	Stratos Blue-Tasman Blue	1		
2	RTC4047A	Trident Green	1		
2	RTC4035A	Venetian Red	1		
2	STC3827A	Woodcote Green-Micatallic-(LRC623)	1		

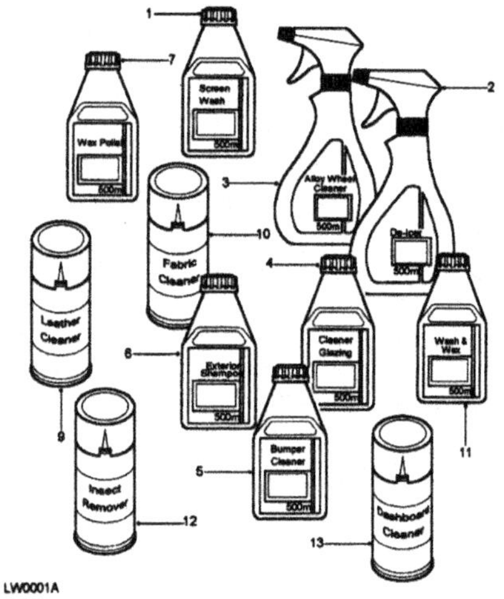

LW0001A

Illus	Part Number	Description	Quantity	Change Point	Remarks
		CAR CARE			
1	STC4672	Screen Wash-250ml	A/R		Europe
1	STC4687	Screen Wash-500ml	1		
1	STC8249	Screen Wash-1ltr	A/R		Europe
1	STC4674	Screen Wash-5ltr	1		
2	STC717	Deicer-500ml	NLA		Use STC4676. Europe
2	STC4676	Deicer-500ml	A/R		Europe
2	STC4677	Deicer-300ml	1		
2	STC4678	Deicer-100ml	1		
3	STC718	Cleaner-alloy wheel-500ml	A/R		Europe
3	STC4675	Cleaner-alloy wheel-500ml	A/R		Europe
4	STC719	Cleaner-glazing-500ml	A/R		Europe
4	STC4681	Cleaner-glazing-300ml	A/R		Europe
5	STC721	Bumper cleaner-black-500ml	A/R		Europe
6	STC722	Shampoo-500ml	A/R		Europe
7	STC723	Wax Polish-500ml	NLA		Use STC4682. Europe
7	STC4682	Wax Polish-300ml	A/R		Europe
8	STC4680	Wash 'n' Wax-300ml	A/R		Europe
9	STC4684	Cleaner Leather-300ml	1		
10	STC4685	Cleaner fabric-300ml	1		
11	STC4686	Insect remover-300ml	1		
12	STC4683	Cleaner dashboard	1		

This page is intentionally left blank

10211	M 06	17H8764L	H 26	2217L	B341	232046	B163	240407	H 05	247127	B 03	247965	B152	267837	J 09
10211	M 24	18G8619L	B 44	2217L	B342	233220	G 04	240555	B 15	247127	B 51	250053	S 15	267837	J 11
10802070	B119	18G8619L	B 91	2217L	B343	233220	G 05	240708	G 07	247127	B 52	250053	S 14	268887	B 22
10802070	B167	18G8619L	B138	2217L	B363	233243	M152	240708	G 08	247127	B102	250830	B166	269257	M152
11009L	F 15	18G8619L	B358	2265L	J 01	233243	M 07	242522	E 01	247127	B104	250830	B118	269257	M 58
11011L	F 13	18G8619L	B359	2265L	J 08	233244	M 13	242522	E 02	247127	B152	252513	B303	269783	G 07
11011L	F 14	18G8951L	H 01	2265L	J 10	233244	M152	242522	E 03	247127	B153	252514	B323	269783	G 08
11015L	F 13	18G8953L	H 01	2266L	B 95	233244	M 12	243618	R 35	247153	B120	252516	B308	2705	S 18
1180237	J 23	19089	N 37	2266L	B142	233326	B 11	243958	B 73	247153	B168	252516	B309	272632	G 07
11820L	H 20	1943711	J 07	2266L	B188	233328	B 11	243958	J 01	247179	B129	252623	B326	272712	G 07
11987L	F 13	201235	N165	2266L	H 19	233566	M152	243958	J 08	247179	B176	252623	B327	272712	G 08
11988L	F 13	201235	N155	2266L	B 45	234124	B 11	243958	J 10	247212	B 42	253205	B 42	272713	G 07
11H1781L	G 01	20138	R 30	2266L	B363	234532	E 01	243958	B 25	247212	B 90	253942	B337	272713	G 08
1247357	C 40	20147	R 30	2266L	B227	234532	E 02	243958	J 03	247554	B 53	253948	E 57	272714	G 07
12H220L	B129	20147	R 35	22G1988L	C 69	234532	E 03	243959	B207	247555	B197	253948	N 20	272714	G 08
12H220L	B176	201647	N155	22G1988L	C 24	234957	H 28	243959	B 03	247555	B 04	253952	E 57	272819	G 07
12H4636L	B267	213700	B 03	22G1989L	C 69	235113	M 75	243959	B 07	247555	B 53	253952	E 62	272819	G 08
12H4636L	B271	213700	B 19	22G1989L	C 24	235113	N142	243959	B 24	247555	B105	253952	N 20	273069	B209
1364507	M 61	213700	B 67	230313	B212	235113	M102	243959	B 72	247555	B123	253963	F 07	273069	B246
1373669	M 61	213961	B200	230313	B 23	235113	M103	243959	B125	247555	B211	255227	R 68	273069	B251
1378529	M 61	213961	B306	230313	B 71	235113	M 10	243959	B172	247583	B107	257011	B336	273069	B 21
1379136	M 61	213961	B376	230313	B124	235113	M101	243959	B 51	247583	B156	257017	B303	273069	B 22
1379351	M 61	213961	B 65	230313	B171	235113	N149	243959	B102	247614	B 20	257020	B336	273069	B 70
1386642	M 61	213961	B116	230511	E 21	235770	B198	243959	B152	247614	B 68	257064	B323	273069	B122
139082	G 04	213961	B 52	230736	S 18	235770	B 05	243960	B119	247624	B 22	257071	B337	273069	B129
13H1515L	J 52	213961	B104	232037	B 22	235770	B 54	243960	B167	247634	B 22	257123	B336	273069	B170
13H2023L	C 17	213961	B 17	232039	B165	235770	B106	243967	B314	247665	B205	257203	M 07	273069	B176
13H2023L	C 20	214228	B 32	232039	D 05	235770	B155	243967	B378	247665	B 15	257302	M 10	273069	B169
13H2475L	P 37	214228	B 78	232039	C 56	236022	B323	243967	B385	247665	B 63	257450	N122	273069	B121
13H2475L	P 44	214229	B 32	232039	C 83	236067	B 11	243968	B314	247665	B 64	264024	E 60	273069	B 69
13H2475L	P 20	214229	B 78	232039	C 86	236070	E 21	244009	T 16	247665	B115	264024	E 68	273166	B314
13H489L	N142	214995	B 15	232039	C 37	236072	E 35	244487	B205	247665	B164	264590	M 10	273370	B334
13H7343L	L 37	216708	J 73	232039	B 66	236074	T 06	244487	B 15	247683	B119	264590	M 11	273521	B129
13H9157	M 82	216962	D 18	232039	B117	236257	B205	244487	B 63	247683	B167	264591	M 13	273521	B176
13H9704L	M147	216962	D 19	232039	E 50	236257	B 15	244487	B 64	247723	B119	264591	M 06	273711	B 15
13H9727L	M147	217245	N 24	232039	E 51	236257	B 63	244487	B115	247723	B167	264591	M 24	275234	B 60
14A7081L	N 37	217245	R 71	232039	B 18	236257	B 64	244487	B164	247726	B129	264591	M 17	275234	B 11
14A7081L	M 72	217245	F 07	232042	D 07	236257	B115	244488	B205	247726	B176	264591	M 18	275234	B 12
14A7081L	N174	217245	F 08	232042	C 56	236257	B164	244488	B 15	247737	B120	264591	M 10	275679	B 19
14A7090L	N174	217245	F 10	232042	C 08	236406	B200	244488	B 63	247737	B168	264591	M 11	275679	B 67
150844	M128	217245	F 11	232043	B323	236548	T 05	244488	B 64	247738	B120	264591	M 14	275679	B119
154545	B307	217245	F 09	232043	B390	236632	E 35	244488	B115	247738	B168	264591	M 15	275679	B167
154545	B319	217245	N 08	232043	B324	236993	H 29	244488	B164	247742	B 16	264591	M 16	276054	M152
154545	B382	217325	T 05	232044	B205	236995	H 29	245003	B 90	247755	B102	264767	G 04	276322	S 18
156206	M 01	217352	E 23	232044	B 15	238542	H 29	246109	T 33	247766	B307	265169	B 06	276323	S 18
1703319	M 61	217352	E 47	232044	B 63	2393	N158	247040	B 20	247766	B 09	265175	B 06	276396	S 06
1703520	M 61	217353	E 23	232044	B 64	2393	N181	247040	B 68	247766	B 58	265175	B 55	276396	S 07
1703531	M 61	217353	E 47	232044	B115	2393	N180	247040	B120	247874	B 24	265295	M 17	276396	S 18
1703848	L 16	218983	H 29	232044	B164	239600	B334	247040	B168	247874	B 72	266945	B199	276426	J 46
1703865	L 16	219704	S 06	232046	B 13	239600	L 17	247051	B 19	247874	B125	266945	B236	276426	J 45
1703945	L 16	219704	S 07	232046	B 61	239673	G 12	247051	B 67	247874	B172	266945	B107	276483	E 01
1727509	L 16	2204L	B325	232046	B 62	239673	G 13	247051	B119	247912	B 11	266945	B156	276484	E 01
1742636	C 70	2215L	E 69	232046	B113	240407	M146	247051	B167	247965	B 03	267451	B 11	277217	S 18
1744589	M 61	2215L	H 32	232046	B114	240407	G 03	247127	B195	247965	B 51	267604	B323	277388	B 11
17H2475L	N186	2215L	H 30	232046	B162	240407	H 02	247127	B233	247965	B102	267837	J 01	277956	B 20

277956	B 68	2943370	M121	302373	N158	306564	N181	330271	N 85	330956	N177	333034	N173	338015	M135
277956	B120	2943411	M122	302532	N 57	306564	N180	330271	N 86	331083	F 04	333035	N173	338015	M136
277956	B168	2943411	M124	302532	N132	307220	N155	330271	N 68	331221	N223	333036	N175	338015	M131
278109	B 15	2943411	M121	302532	N 99	307418	R 30	330271	N 69	331221	N233	333041	N179	338015	M133
278166	G 07	2943433	E 53	302532	J 67	307418	R 35	330271	N 70	331221	N234	333203	N182	338015	M140
279648	B 19	2943486	J 07	302532	N129	307419	R 30	330271	N 71	331221	N227	333263	N 98	338015	M141
279648	B 67	2995	B 23	302532	N131	307419	R 35	330271	N 87	331221	N228	333445	N179	338017	M152
27H2403L	M 07	2995	B 71	302648	R 37	307420	R 30	330271	N 88	331221	N224	333486	N 66	338017	N 40
27H5311	M 75	2995	B124	302825	N125	307420	R 35	330271	N 73	331221	N230	333487	N106	338018	M152
27H5932L	B143	2995	B171	302828	N125	3101	J 01	330271	N 74	331221	N231	333490	N104	338019	M152
27H8207L	M 01	2K8686L	G 05	302933	S 16	3101	J 09	330366	N 41	331222	N223	333745	N 99	338020	M152
2943050	M 28	300816	N 24	302934	S 16	3101	J 11	330422	N125	331222	N227	334111	M 17	338021	M152
2943077	L 06	300953	N223	3036L	B386	312028	R 35	330551	N239	331222	N228	334121	N 30	338023	M152
2943111	C 40	300953	N233	3036L	B363	312856	M 17	330553	N239	331222	N224	334177	R 37	338023	N 40
2943111	C 53	300953	N234	3036L	B364	315264	R 28	330553	N240	331222	N230	334245	N241	338023	N147
2943116	F 24	300953	N227	3036L	B326	320045	N 99	330553	N241	331222	N231	334245	N242	338024	N 40
2943117	F 24	300953	N228	3036L	B327	320045	N 44	330553	N242	331249	N224	334245	N244	338025	M152
2943118	L 16	300953	N224	303847	S 16	320045	J 67	330553	N243	331273	R 03	334245	N245	338026	M152
2943119	L 16	300953	N230	303847	S 15	320604	N121	330553	N245	331480	P 46	334246	N241	338028	M152
2943124	G 04	300953	N231	303975	N121	320608	M 17	330557	N239	331481	P 46	334246	N242	338028	N 40
2943129	J 44	300954	N223	303975	N122	320674	R 37	330557	N241	331670	P 49	334246	N244	338029	M152
2943144	G 05	300954	N233	304125	R 03	320699	R 02	330557	N242	331673	N241	334246	N245	338550	N114
2943144	C 44	300954	N234	304125	V 05	320726	R 02	330578	N238	331673	N243	334540	R 39	338552	N114
2943147	J 23	300954	N227	304125	R 37	320835	P 08	330578	N241	331674	N241	334601	R 40	338553	N114
2943224	G 03	300954	N228	304125	S 10	320835	M120	330578	N242	331674	N243	334610	N104	338554	N114
2943225	M121	300954	N224	304301	N239	3259	E 35	330578	N244	331675	N241	334610	N106	339878	R 33
2943279	L 16	300954	N230	304301	N246	3259	E 08	330578	N245	331675	N243	334611	N104	339935	N230
2943280	L 16	300954	N231	304301	N240	3261	F 07	330579	N238	331676	N241	334611	N106	339986	R 03
2943286	J 23	301005	T 03	304301	N241	3261	F 08	330579	N241	331676	N243	334614	N 66	345100	R 65
2943288	G 05	301321	N223	304301	N242	3261	F 09	330579	N242	331709	R 29	334615	N131	345100	R 59
2943289	E 54	301321	N233	304301	N243	3261L	F 10	330579	N244	331709	R 02	334966	N 40	345100	R 66
2943298	M 30	301321	N234	304301	N245	3261L	F 11	330579	N245	331835	R 37	336288	R 44	345101	R 65
2943300	M 61	301321	N227	304797	N223	3290	B303	330602	S 15	331974	R 02	336294	R 44	345101	R 59
2943301	M114	301321	N228	304797	N233	3290	B 47	330615	N 51	332065	N102	336294	R 45	345101	R 66
2943302	M115	301321	N224	304797	N234	3290	C 29	330699	N240	332146	N127	336503	M 32	345213	R 02
2943303	M115	301321	N230	304797	N227	3290	S 07	330699	N243	332147	N197	336535	N143	345597	M 10
2943305	M115	301321	N231	304797	N228	3290	E 20	330699	N245	332201	N114	336577	N 67	345597	M 12
2943311	J 64	301328	N 97	304797	N224	3290	C 51	330762	N 67	332215	N103	336780	P 46	345662	H 02
2943312	J 64	301328	N 96	304797	N230	3291	E 20	330790	N 65	332215	N104	336780	P 49	345699	N239
2943328	J 43	301343	N223	304797	N231	3292	C 30	330791	N 65	332215	N106	336781	P 46	345699	N246
2943334	J 43	301343	N233	3052	G 07	3292	C 37	330896	N240	332293	N114	336781	P 49	345699	N240
2943337	J 18	301343	N234	305232	N170	3292	C 04	330896	N243	332355	R 03	337812	N 45	345699	N241
2943342	L 16	301343	N227	305232	N197	3292	C 05	330896	N245	332445	N121	337813	N 45	345699	N242
2943344	C 44	301343	N228	305232	N 98	3292	E 21	330897	N246	332446	N121	337859	R 02	345699	N243
2943346	C 70	301343	N224	305232	N 95	330145	N127	330897	N243	332582	N 97	337873	R 02	345699	N245
2943348	C 70	301343	N230	306287	N111	330212	S 14	330897	N245	332582	N 98	337880	R 02	345915	N121
2943349	C 70	301343	N231	306287	N105	330271	N 76	330953	N175	332582	N 95	337899	R 02	345937	R 62
2943350	M 91	301347	R 30	306289	N111	330271	N 77	330954	N175	332647	N 28	338009	M152	345985	T 16
2943358	J 44	301476	R 36	306289	N105	330271	N 78	330954	N176	332672	S 17	338013	M152	346341	N175
2943360	N251	302177	N105	306290	N222	330271	N 79	330954	N177	332672	S 15	338013	G 09	346341	N122
2943361	N251	302177	N129	306295	N169	330271	N 80	330955	N175	332674	S 17	338014	M152	346410	R 03
2943363	N250	302177	N131	306295	N179	330271	N 81	330955	N176	332674	S 15	338015	N 28	346576	N 30
2943364	N250	302178	N105	306316	R 30	330271	N 82	330955	N177	332942	N196	338015	M152	346598	N 28
2943370	M122	302178	N129	306316	R 35	330271	N 83	330956	N175	333032	N173	338015	N 40	346599	N 28
2943370	M124	302178	N131	306564	N158	330271	N 84	330956	N176	333033	N173	338015	R 71	346722	F 05

346786	P 08	3682	K 10	395185	N 30	4095	B 88	501593	B153	516028	B 09	527269	B 03	538132	B 54
346786	M120	3682	K 31	395191LCS	P 23	4095	B136	502116	B230	516028	B 58	527269	B 51	538132	B106
346804	R 33	3682	K 29	395249	R 65	4095	B 41	502116	B263	516951	B332	528004	B 06	538132	B155
346849	N139	3682	K 23	395252	R 59	4095	B185	502116	B 47	517646	M128	528004	B 55	538133	B198
346849	N140	3682	K 32	395252	R 67	4233	N 24	502116	B 98	517689	J 58	529364	B399	538133	B 05
346878	N180	371144	S 01	395252	R 60	4233	T 31	502116	B191	517689	J 52	530178	B 16	538134	B198
346894	L 38	371144	S 05	395294	N196	4421	B308	502116	B146	517706	J 58	530179	B 16	538134	B 05
346924	L 36	371144	S 02	395294	N123	4421	B309	502116	B148	517706	J 53	531447	T 35	538134	B 54
346941	N 31	372336	N221	395413	N 53	4478	B342	50216	B147	517706	J 52	531586	M 01	538134	B106
346976	L 38	3739	B 11	395463	N123	4478	B343	502473	B209	517976	B175	531604	M 82	538134	B155
346976	L 76	3748	B 15	395576	T 03	4580	N 67	502473	B246	517976	B176	531689	G 10	538890L	G 06
346981	N 28	37D2260L	B267	395577	T 03	4581	B342	502473	B 21	517976	J 52	531893	H 29	539706	E 14
347151	N196	37D2260L	B279	395579	T 03	4581	B343	502473	B169	517976	B296	532323	D 40	539706	E 40
347343	R 29	37D2260L	B285	395580	T 03	4589L	B204	502473	B121	518653	B332	532323	D 17	539706	E 42
347344	R 29	37H3694L	M128	395586	R 63	4589L	B 14	502473	B 69	519965	J 04	532387	B200	539706	E 43
347369	N157	37H4558L	D 41	395587	R 63	4589L	B 62	502951	J 14	51K4001L	M 86	532387	B 07	539707	E 35
347369	N169	37H5208L	M128	395617	N 28	4589L	B114	502951	J 15	520160	M128	532387	B 56	539707	E 39
347436	N 48	37H575L	J 52	395829	L 38	4589L	B311	503352	M115	520455	B 46	532387	B108	539707	E 08
347553	R 03	37H6171L	B143	395829	L 76	4589L	B162	503352	M 70	520455	B 96	532387	B157	539707	E 11
347586	L 36	37H7618L	B143	395830	L 38	4589L	B163	503352	M 71	521452	G 12	532736	M 82	539718	E 35
347594	N123	37H770	J 58	395830	L 76	4594	J 61	503352	M120	521452	B336	532943	C 23	539718	E 08
347844	R 68	37H770L	J 52	3958L	N125	4594L	B323	503805	C 32	521452	B335	533765	D 19	539720	E 35
347861	R 31	37H7920	J 58	396416	P 30	4594L	B357	503805	C 33	521453	B336	534790	J 19	539720	E 08
347862	R 31	37H7920	J 52	396540	P 46	4594L	B112	503805	C 34	521453	B335	534790	B333	539722	E 35
347863	R 31	37H8119L	J 58	396541	P 44	4594L	B161	503981	H 29	522745	B 16	534790	B330	539722	E 08
347866	S 15	37H8119L	J 52	396541	P 46	4594L	B341	504006	B 03	522745	B 63	534790	B331	539724	E 35
347869	R 03	3829	N 67	396542	P 44	4594L	G 07	504006	B 51	522745	B115	534797	J 19	539724	E 08
347939	L 37	3830L	M 82	396542	P 46	4594L	B365	504006	B102	522745	B164	534897	B323	539745	E 35
348430	R 02	3830L	R 68	396696	R 36	4594L	B366	504006	B152	52278	B 42	535068	T 34	539745	E 39
348430	R 03	3842	S 16	396697	R 39	4594L	V 04	504233	J 16	52278	B 90	535781	B399	539745	E 08
348430	N241	3852L	R 35	396698	R 36	4594L	N251	50446	G 09	522932	B323	535782	B399	539745	E 11
348747	F 05	3852L	P 54	396739	R 36	4866L	B348	50446	G 07	522932	G 11	536373	B340	53K3039L	N 39
348859	N 40	3887	N142	396800	N223	4866L	B365	50446	G 08	522940	J 58	536382	B340	541010	B105
349514	R 29	3890	J 09	396800	N233	4868L	M103	504673	J 16	522940	J 52	536577	B 03	541010	B154
349515	R 30	3890	J 11	396800	N234	4868L	M101	505205	M128	523203	B334	536577	B 07	541010	B211
349516	R 30	3898	N 07	396800	N227	4868L	B364	506069	B 22	523638	S 18	536577	B102	541215	B330
349516	R 34	3900L	N 57	396800	N228	4905	F 07	50639	J 75	524765	B207	536577	B152	542636	B 10
349529	R 29	3900L	R 30	396800	N224	4905	F 08	50641	B334	524765	B244	538038	B202	542636	B 59
349931	R 29	3900L	G 10	396800	N230	4905	F 10	507829	B 21	524765	B251	538038	B 09	542846	J 19
349931	R 02	390939	B244	396800	N231	4905	F 11	507829	B169	524765	B 19	538038	B110	542846	J 30
349931	N180	390939	M 46	396950	P 42	4905	F 09	507829	B121	524765	B 67	538038	B159	542846	J 27
349943	R 02	391287	N141	396951	P 42	500447	J 03	507829	B 69	524765	B166	538039	B202	542846	J 21
349955	R 29	392743	N164	3972	J 01	500710	J 14	508571	T 05	524765	B118	538039	B 09	542846	J 25
349996	R 01	393218	N142	3972	J 11	500746	E 58	509045P	E 01	525389	B 20	538039	B 58	542846	J 28
351991	N142	395037	N196	3982L	S 16	500746	E 63	509045P	E 03	525389	B 68	538039	B110	543301	S 06
3547	N224	395041	N122	398776	N122	500746	E 65	509045P	T 06	525428	B214	538039	B159	543589	B 19
359526	J 63	395078	N196	3H822L	M 75	500746	E 66	510267	J 51	525428	B173	538131	B198	543589	B 67
359526	J 62	395141	M 87	3H822L	N 92	501593	B195	512646	B 32	525428	B126	538131	B235	543589	J 67
359526	J 41	395141	N186	4034L	M 46	501593	B233	512646	B 78	525497	B207	538131	B 05	543765	J 16
3663	K 31	395143	N239	4034L	N102	501593	B 03	515060	M 07	525497	B244	538131	B 54	543767	J 16
3663	K 06	395143	T 03	4067	B348	501593	B 51	515291	B 22	525497	B 19	538131	B106	543819	F 18
3663	K 29	395143	N241	4075L	B307	501593	B 52	515466	D 41	525497	B 67	538131	B155	546026	B 11
3663	K 33	395143	N242	4075L	R 06	501593	B102	515467	D 41	525497	B166	538132	B198	546194	B399
367078	L 69	395143	N243	4075L	R 01	501593	B104	515468	D 41	525497	B118	538132	B235	546198	B399
3682	K 03	395143	N245	4075L	R 14	501593	B152	515470	D 41	525569	M 82	538132	B 05	546198	C 72

546798	B 21	549611	B 42	563132	B113	568680	J 23	571161	C 02	572167	K 21	576137	C 43	586440	B320
546798	B 69	549611	B 90	563190	J 52	568680	H 02	571161	C 43	572167	K 22	576159	E 33	586440	C 84
546799	B209	549702	B 19	563195	B129	568680	H 05	571163	C 28	572167	K 23	576159	E 34	586440	C 51
546799	B246	549702	B 67	564258	B320	568680	H 09	571163	C 45	572167	K 25	576159	E 36	586440	C 52
546799	B169	549840	S 18	564258	B383	568680	M 65	571163	C 02	572168	K 03	576159	E 37	587405	B 73
546799	B121	549909	B 15	564258	B 22	568680	J 17	571163	C 43	572168	K 12	576159	E 07	587405	B 74
546841	B 07	549911	B304	564307	B 73	568680	M 63	571174	T 06	572168	K 01	576159	E 09	587405	B 25
546841	B 56	549911	B374	564307	B 25	568686	B 19	571439	C 24	572168	K 11	576203	C 28	587405	B 26
546841	B108	550732	G 04	564308	B173	568686	B 67	571468	D 18	572168	K 15	576203	C 45	587405	B364
548169	H 29	551508	M 87	564308	B126	568687	B 19	571468	D 19	572168	K 07	576203	C 02	587405	B162
549229	E 01	551595	M 14	564308	B 74	568687	B 67	571536	D 07	572168	K 08	576203	C 43	587405	B163
549229	E 02	552818	E 58	564308	B 26	568688	B166	571536	D 08	572168	K 09	576220	C 30	587477	B395
549229	E 03	552818	E 63	564332	B176	568688	B118	571665	D 19	572168	K 19	576236	E 14	587517	B 25
549230	E 14	552818	E 65	564332E	B129	568689	B166	571665	D 40	572168	K 21	576236	E 41	587684	B 33
549230	E 41	552818	E 66	564332E	B176	568689	B118	571665	M108	572168	K 22	576236	E 44	589026	M 10
549230	E 44	552819	E 60	564455	B205	568788	B 43	571682	D 18	572204	S 10	576237	E 14	589026	M 12
549232	E 14	552819	E 68	564455	B 15	568788	B 91	571682	D 19	572312	L 02	576237	E 41	589143	M 07
549232	E 41	554621	B 19	564455	B 63	568788	B138	571718	E 18	572312	L 03	576237	E 44	589202	M 10
549232	E 44	554621	B 67	564455	B 64	568858	F 18	571752	E 49	572337	E 62	576238	E 14	589254	C 84
549234	E 14	554880	B341	564455	B115	568883	G 07	571752	E 26	572338	E 62	576238	E 41	589254	M118
549234	E 41	554880	B342	564455	B164	568883	G 08	571755	E 19	572535	J 12	576238	E 44	589254	B334
549234	E 44	554971	B 88	564456	B205	568895	G 07	571944	C 30	572548	H 02	576239	E 14	589284	M 06
549236	E 14	554971	B136	564456	B 15	569006	J 10	571970	D 19	572548	H 05	576239	E 41	589285	M 06
549236	E 41	554971	B 41	564456	B 63	569291	G 09	572077	F 07	572548	J 14	576239	E 44	589452	M152
549236	E 44	554971	B185	564456	B 64	569522	F 02	572077	F 08	572548	J 16	576303	T 05	589452	M 57
549238	E 14	555711	M152	564456	B115	569522	F 03	572077	F 10	572548	J 70	576476	B370	589511	M 88
549238	E 41	555711	M130	564456	B164	569701	G 07	572077	F 11	572839	B 33	576557	B 47	589783	M 05
549238	E 44	555711	M132	564724	L 10	569701	G 08	572077	F 09	572839	J 74	576557	B 98	589783	M 01
549240	E 14	557523	B 60	564813	G 09	569714	H 01	572087	E 59	572839	J 16	576723	C 28	589783	M 04
549240	E 41	557523	B 11	564816	G 09	569714	H 05	572166	K 03	572994	J 34	576723	C 45	591039	H 29
549240	E 44	557523	B 12	565540	L 09	570351	M128	572166	K 10	573246	M147	576723	C 02	591227	C 30
549242	E 14	559625	J 51	565656	J 74	570753	M 58	572166	K 02	573246	M102	576723	C 43	591231	C 03
549242	E 41	559636	T 32	566580	S 13	570822	M 06	572166	K 12	573246	M103	576973	H 29	591394	C 31
549242	E 44	559882	N 20	56667	H 08	570822	M 07	572166	K 01	573246	M 14	577458	J 65	591519	C 35
549244	E 14	560553	T 45	566724L	J 69	570829	M 07	572166	K 11	573246	M127	577458	B334	591988	C 03
549244	E 41	560553	T 46	566737	B331	571043	C 36	572166	K 15	573246	M 63	577458	J 68	592072	K 03
549244	E 44	561195	E 06	566902	L 37	571134	B399	572166	K 07	573256	B334	577458	J 72	592072	K 10
549246	E 14	561195	E 31	567959	M 93	571134	D 09	572166	K 08	573289	M 70	577458	J 74	592072	K 23
549246	E 41	561196	E 06	568244	J 13	571134	C 31	572166	K 09	573289	L 71	577458	J 70	592324	H 01
549246	E 44	561196	E 31	568333	B 05	571134	D 10	572166	K 19	574469	B 10	577458	J 67	592326	J 70
549248	E 14	56140	B147	568333	B 54	571134	C 51	572166	K 21	574469	B 59	577459	J 70	592326	J 67
549248	E 41	562019	S 07	568431	B230	571134	D 06	572166	K 22	574654	B173	577643	G 05	592358	G 04
549248	E 44	562019	S 18	568431	B263	571142	C 32	572166	K 23	574654	B126	577703	E 69	592443	H 08
549250	E 14	562481	G 03	568431	B191	571146	D 22	572166	K 25	574658	B 22	577846	B303	592445	E 62
549250	E 41	562481	G 10	568431	B146	571146	D 28	572167	K 03	575014	M 82	577873	H 24	592513	S 06
549250	E 44	562748	J 58	568431	B148	571146	C 36	572167	K 10	575047	M129	577873	H 20	592514	S 06
549252	E 14	562756	N 24	568680	M147	571146	C 24	572167	K 02	575312	M 10	577873	H 22	592773	E 68
549252	E 41	562756	T 32	568680	M 77	571146	D 24	572167	K 12	575312	M 11	577898	F 17	593692	E 13
549252	E 35	562756	T 40	568680	M 76	571146	D 29	572167	K 01	575615	E 62	578023	J 34	593692	E 40
549252	E 44	562756	T 39	568680	B334	571158	C 36	572167	K 11	575616	E 62	578293	J 53	593692	E 43
549473	E 49	562979	L 05	568680	M 59	571160	C 28	572167	K 15	575707	E 56	578620	B323	593693	E 14
549473	E 24	562979	L 07	568680	M 60	571160	C 45	572167	K 07	575882	E 69	579085	M 86	593693	E 40
549473	E 26	562979	L 06	568680	M 66	571160	C 02	572167	K 08	576137	C 28	579409	T 45	593693	E 42
549473	E 47	563132	B 14	568680	E 50	571161	C 28	572167	K 09	576137	C 45	579409	T 46	593693	E 43
549610	B 42	563132	B 61	568680	E 51	571161	C 45	572167	K 19	576137	C 02	586438	M 19	593802	C 36

594087	C 72	597586	B 51	602148	B382	603183	J 34	605833	B332	608004	M 06	611097	B339	614106	B312
594087	C 54	597586	B 52	602152	B303	603184	B320	605848	B332	608004	M 10	611110	J 67	614154	B349
594091	H 26	597586	B102	602152	B323	603224	B323	606168	J 69	608065	F 13	611114	B321	614154	B225
594091	H 33	597586	B104	602152	B373	603224	B324	606168	J 34	608065	F 14	611212	B342	614188	B322
594091	C 42	597586	B152	602153	B319	603237	G 12	606178	T 09	608066	F 14	611212	B343	614202	B314
594091	H 31	597586	B153	602153	B382	603237	B336	606178	T 10	608068	F 13	611213	B342	614443	B386
594091	C 41	598006	B323	602154	B319	603277	B323	606207	J 12	608068	F 14	611213	B343	614443	B326
594091	C 43	599552	B 07	602154	B382	603301	B304	606211	M 10	608069	F 13	611215	B342	614443	B327
594134	C 72	599552	B 56	602172	B319	603330	B321	606247	J 34	608073	F 15	611215	B343	614538L	B335
594134	C 54	599552	B108	602186	B319	603340	B399	606474	D 28	608197	B350	611323	B370	614555	B330
594290	D 17	599552	B157	602186	B382	603376	B321	606474	D 29	608246	E 06	611351	B321	614555	B331
594493	E 13	599552	D 09	602191	B317	603378	B319	606538	F 15	608246	E 31	611379	B342	614585	B303
594594	M147	599552	D 10	602191	B381	603378	B382	606542	F 15	608246	D 07	611440	B342	614617	H 02
594594	G 06	599944	E 43	602192	B317	603428	B310	606543	F 15	608246	C 30	611440	B343	614617	H 05
594594	B334	599945	E 12	602193	B317	603431	J 19	606544	F 13	608246	C 24	611514	B314	614670	B313
594594	J 60	599945	E 40	602199	B306	603431	J 30	606544	F 14	608246	D 10	611659L	B319	614718	B349
594594	J 63	599945	E 42	602200	B317	603431	J 27	606545	F 13	608246	E 35	611659L	B382	614718	B225
594594	L 19	600226L	M 01	602200	B381	603431	J 21	606545	F 14	608246	E 32	611660	B382	614743	B343
594594	J 37	600265	F 08	602200	B365	603431	J 25	606551	F 13	608246	E 08	611786	B324	614866	J 73
594594	B338	600265	F 10	602201	B307	603431	J 28	606551	F 14	608266	B350	612064	B333	614891	B337
594594	B339	600265	F 11	602201	B385	603441	B323	606553	F 15	608266	B351	612320	B336	614891	B330
594594	E 50	601845	B332	602212	B303	603446	B350	606564	F 13	608311	M 07	612326	B308	614891	B331
594594	E 51	602040	B316	602227	B322	603446	B352	606567	F 15	608312	M 07	612326	B309	614891	J 73
594637	L 61	602040	B385	602236	B385	603535	B304	606666	E 20	608352	B 46	612435	B334	614892	J 73
594637	L 64	602040	B381	602236	B325	603554	B315	606666	E 22	608395	B 46	612505	B330	614939	B363
594637	L 29	602061	B305	602289	B315	603561	B323	606683	H 26	608395	B 97	612505	B331	614939	B364
594637	L 26	602067	B314	602289	B316	603622	B336	606688	H 27	608400	H 28	612689	B327	61K738	G 09
594637	L 27	602070	B306	602289	B166	603622	B335	606733	C 42	610020	B340	612710	B306	61K738	G 07
594637	L 22	602070	B376	602289	B381	603659	B200	606733	C 41	610178	B304	612898	B303	61K738	G 08
594753	J 14	602071	B314	602289	B118	603659	B306	606733	C 43	610246	B323	612898	B373	622324	C 37
594753	J 16	602076	B385	602388	B307	603659	B376	607163	E 32	610289	B322	612989	B304	622324	E 51
594946	F 07	602076	B325	602411	B304	603672	B395	607165	E 45	610327	B334	613087	B310	622324	D 36
594946	F 08	602082	B305	602505	B358	603672	B324	607166	E 45	610333	B336	613244	B363	622324	C 51
594946	F 10	602087	B306	602505	B359	603672	B350	607167	E 45	610489	B303	613402	B321	622388	C 36
594946	F 11	602087	B376	602512	B320	603672	B353	607168	E 45	610489	B377	613514	B330	624091	B207
594946	F 09	602097	B319	602512	B383	603673	B350	607169	E 45	610578	B310	613514	B331	624091	B244
594947	F 07	602097	B382	602545	B303	603673	B353	607173	E 32	610736	B399	613540	B349	624091	B 24
594947	F 08	602098	B317	602545	B377	603675	B320	607177	E 45	610789	B342	613601	J 73	624091	B 72
594947	F 10	602098	B381	602582	B310	603713	B347	607178	E 45	610789	B343	613620	B363	624091	B125
594947	F 11	602099	B325	602587	B304	603713	B313	607179	E 45	610792	B343	613620	B364	624091	B172
594947	F 09	602123	B315	602609	B305	603734	B319	607180	E 45	610833	B331	613671	B304	625038	B320
595199	F 18	602123	B316	602634	B334	603734	B382	607181	E 32	610849	B330	613718L	B321	625038	B 22
595199	L 05	602123	B381	602687	B 24	603796	B316	607182	E 32	611015	B330	613857	B350	634604	N193
595478	D 05	602130	B303	602687	B 72	603851	J 61	607183	E 32	611015	B331	613857	B351	634604	N194
595478	C 56	602130	B373	602687	B125	603887	J 70	607185	E 32	611019	B304	613857	B352	634604	N188
595478	C 83	602141	B303	602687	B172	603962	J 34	607187	E 45	611022	B363	613910	G 12	634604	N189
595478	C 37	602141	B373	602687	B324	603972	B342	607188	E 45	611022	B364	613910	G 13	6395L	B202
595478	E 50	602142	B319	602910	B314	603972	B343	607189	E 45	611026	B330	613915	G 11	6395L	B238
595478	E 51	602142	B382	602912	B314	605011	J 58	607190	E 45	611089	B303	613915	G 12	6395L	B370
596490	B 73	602146	B303	602913	B314	605011	J 52	607191	E 45	611089	B373	613915	G 13	6395L	B 09
596490	B 25	602146	B373	602953	B350	605061	F 15	607197	E 45	611092	J 60	613916	G 12	6395L	B 58
597586	B195	602146	D 10	602953	B351	605174	B340	607357	E 32	611092	B338	613916	G 13	6395L	B110
597586	B 03	602147	B303	602953	B352	605180	B340	607567	F 16	611092	B339	614037	B314	6395L	B159
597586	C 69	602147	B373	603031	B317	605181	B340	608000	F 15	611097	J 60	614106	B313	6395L	B268
597586	C 24	602148	B319	603127	B320	605800	B332	608000	F 16	611097	B338	614106	B341	6397	C 32

6860L	G 03	78248	N238	79051	M 04	79293	N 97	90575511	K 03	9952121	L 16	AAU6919	N 92	AB606061	L 74
73037	P 24	78248	R 44	79086L	N122	79293	N 98	90575585	C 38	AA606044L	M 75	AAU7219L	B344	AB606061L	B 09
73037	P 23	78248	P 46	79086L	L 72	79293	N 95	90575585	N 16	AA606044L	P 24	AAU7604	B332	AB606061L	B 58
7316	E 15	78248	P 49	79106	N 31	8367179	L 16	90575597	F 18	AA606044L	P 23	AAU7803	H 16	AB606061L	P 14
7316	E 41	78248	N 79	79118PH	P 20	850641	J 03	90575748	K 03	AA610031	N135	AAU7803	H 17	AB606064L	P 01
77869	R 44	78248	N 80	79121	M118	8566L	B198	90575748	K 02	AA610031	N134	AAU7803	H 10	AB606084	P 54
77869	P 54	78248	N 81	79121	G 03	8566L	B235	90575748	K 12	AAM222L	P 07	AAU7803	H 13	AB606084	P 63
77932	M 10	78248	N 82	79121	G 10	8566L	B 05	90575748	K 14	AAM222L	M 87	AAU7803	H 15	AB606084	P 64
77941	J 14	78248	N 83	79121	J 19	8566L	B 54	90575789	E 61	AAP810	L 35	AAU8182	N 92	AB606084	P 66
77941	J 15	78248	N 84	79121	J 30	8566L	B106	90575878	E 69	AAP811	L 35	AAU8276	M 86	AB606084	P 53
78159	N172	78248	N 85	79121	J 27	8566L	B155	90575977	L 17	AAP817	L 35	AAU8452	B350	AB606084	P 56
78210	M136	78248	N 86	79121	J 21	8566L	B268	90577064	J 12	AAP876	L 36	AAU8452	B351	AB606124	M122
78210	M132	78248	N117	79121	J 22	8G7019L	D 41	90577473	E 54	AAP890	L 36	AAU9036	N 58	AB606124	M124
78210	M133	78248	N 68	79121	J 25	8G8587L	H 32	90577473	S 16	AAU1700	H 11	AAU9902	J 58	AB608031	T 46
78210	M139	78248	N 69	79121	J 28	8G8587L	H 30	90577473	S 15	AAU1979	B 80	AAU9902	J 52	AB608031L	F 04
78210	M140	78248	N 70	79122	J 65	8G8837L	G 04	90577473	S 14	AAU1979	L 14	AAU9903	J 58	AB608031L	M 77
78210	M141	78248	N 71	79122	J 49	90301332	N224	90577473	V 05	AAU1979	L 15	AAU9903	J 52	AB608031L	N 51
78210	M142	78248	N148	79122	J 50	90301332	N230	90577473	S 09	AAU2249L	B226	AB605051L	M142	AB608031L	M 76
78210	M138	78248	N139	79122	J 19	90306199	R 35	90577473	S 12	AAU2249L	B356	AB606021	L 69	AB608031L	G 10
78227	G 07	78248	N180	79122	J 30	90508035	S 01	90577509	N 24	AAU2249L	B 94	AB606021L	B 22	AB608031L	P 08
78227	G 08	78248	N 95	79122	J 72	90508035	S 02	90577642	G 05	AAU2249L	B141	AB606021L	L 70	AB608031L	M 70
78237	R 03	78248	N 96	79122	J 27	90508545	J 01	90577704	E 69	AAU2249L	B362	AB606022L	M 01	AB608031L	M120
78248	N 28	78248	T 47	79122	J 71	90508545	J 08	90602025	B304	AAU2249L	B187	AB606031L	N124	AB608031L	M 95
78248	N 35	78248	T 48	79122	J 21	90508545	J 10	90602064	B314	AAU2304	D 19	AB606031L	N187	AB60804	P 57
78248	N 36	78248	L 80	79122	J 22	90510912	M100	90602068	B306	AAU2304	D 40	AB606031L	N173	AB608041	J 63
78248	N 37	78248	S 12	79123	G 05	90513171	B 73	90602072	B314	AAU2367	N246	AB606034	M123	AB608041	J 41
78248	N 54	78248	N163	79123	E 50	90513171	B 25	90602202	B307	AAU2367	N242	AB606034	M125	AB608041	J 64
78248	N 55	78248	N 87	79123	E 51	90513220	B321	90602202	B373	AAU2367	N245	AB606041	P 23	AB608044L	N 57
78248	N181	78248	N 88	79123	J 74	90513454	E 35	90602372	B304	AAU2825	E 32	AB606041L	N194	AB608044L	P 07
78248	N121	78248	N241	79124	H 22	90513454	E 08	90606261	J 12	AAU2967	B344	AB606041L	P 12	AB608044L	P 55
78248	N 75	78248	N242	79125	H 10	90513454	E 11	90606262	J 12	AAU3084L	M149	AB606041L	P 30	AB608047L	P 02
78248	N 76	78248	N244	79127	H 24	90517711	J 52	90606566	F 13	AAU3509	J 53	AB606041L	P 31	AB608047L	M 46
78248	N 77	78248	N245	79127	H 13	90518466	B119	90607170	E 45	AAU3686	M 46	AB606041L	C 84	AB608047L	M 05
78248	N 78	78248	N 72	79127	H 15	90518466	B167	90608178	B 46	AAU3686	M118	AB606041L	M 06	AB608047L	M 77
78248	N132	78248	N 73	79127	H 20	90518674	T 32	90608178	B 97	AAU3686	M147	AB606041L	N127	AB608047L	T 16
78248	H 36	78248	N 74	79127	H 22	90519054	B 03	90608178	B367	AAU3686	M 57	AB606041L	R 03	AB608047L	N 31
78248	S 01	78321	N121	79134	R 45	90519054	B 51	90608545	E 32	AAU3686	G 03	AB606041L	P 44	AB608047L	L 38
78248	N 20	78384	T 16	79134	J 34	90519054	B102	90610796	B342	AAU3686	J 44	AB606041L	P 46	AB608047L	P 63
78248	N 40	78593	B320	79134	R 31	90519054	B152	90610796	B343	AAU3686	M 63	AB606041L	M 17	AB608047L	L 75
78248	N122	78782	B307	79158	J 65	90519055	B195	90611014	B330	AAU3715L	M145	AB606041L	M 18	AB608047L	M 01
78248	N123	78832	N102	79158	J 50	90519055	B233	90611014	B331	AAU5034	M 34	AB606041L	P 18	AB608047L	M 14
78248	N 97	78832	N104	79158	J 20	90519055	B 03	90611112	B321	AAU5034	M 35	AB606041L	H 09	AB608047L	M 15
78248	N 51	78832	N106	79158	J 72	90519055	B 51	90611439	B342	AAU5034	M 37	AB606041L	N189	AB608047L	M 04
78248	N115	78861	B320	79158	J 23	90519055	B 52	90611504	B325	AAU5034	M 38	AB606044L	P 07	AB608047L	J 62
78248	N116	78862	B303	79158	J 22	90519055	B102	90611812	B317	AAU5034	M 40	AB606044L	P 11	AB608047L	J 73
78248	N 98	78862	B320	79194	T 03	90519055	B104	90613049	B 87	AAU5034	M111	AB606044L	P 03	AB608047L	P 53
78248	N118	79004	E 50	79221	N157	90519055	B152	90613049	B 40	AAU5034	M109	AB606051L	P 66	AB608047L	J 48
78248	N119	79004	E 51	79246	P 33	90519055	B153	90613442	B365	AAU5034	M 78	AB606051L	M132	AB608047L	T 47
78248	S 03	79004	H 20	79281	N 97	90568054	B213	90613913	G 12	AAU5034	M 80	AB606051L	M139	AB608047L	T 48
78248	S 05	79026	B123	79281	N 95	90568054	B324	90613913	G 13	AAU6774	N124	AB606051L	M140	AB608047L	M 16
78248	S 17	79026	B211	79283	N 97	90571086	C 30	90614584	B316	AAU6774	N 90	AB606051L	M141	AB608051	L 72
78248	S 15	79027	B248	79283	N 98	90571104	C 30	9913102	L 16	AAU6774	N 92	AB606051L	M138	AB608051L	P 02
78248	N 63	79051	N 57	79283	N 95	90571104	C 08	9915017	L 16	AAU6774	N 93	AB606054L	P 41	AB608051L	N 32
78248	N 41	79051	M 05	79289	N 97	90571104	C 07	9952113	L 16	AAU6774	N 95	AB606057	N182	AB608054L	P 10
78248	N 42	79051	M 01	79289	N 98	90575015	M 82	9952119	L 16	AAU6919	N 90	AB606057	N145	AB608054L	P 30

AB608054L	N 31	AB614061L	B 89	AD606074L	M121	ADU8846L	H 15	AEU1616	B140	AEU1694	B 85	AEU1775	B223	AEU1780	B134
AB608054L	L 38	AB614061L	N 44	ADF710030	N 33	ADU8981	M148	AEU1616	B358	AEU1694	B182	AEU1775	B183	AEU1780	B346
AB608054L	P 65	AB614061L	N 61	ADH710080	N 37	ADU9081L	F 23	AEU1616	B359	AEU1694	B 86	AEU1776	B222	AEU1780	B347
AB608054L	L 75	AB614061L	J 19	ADH710090	N 37	AEU1029	F 13	AEU1616	B361	AEU1694	B134	AEU1776	B 38	AEU1780	B 39
AB608055L	L 38	AB614061L	J 20	ADP710040	H 34	AEU1034	B 42	AEU1626	L 45	AEU1694	B346	AEU1776	B 85	AEU1780	B135
AB608061L	P 67	AB614061L	J 48	ADU1784L	M139	AEU1034	B 90	AEU1626	L 58	AEU1694	B347	AEU1776	B182	AEU1780	B223
AB608061L	P 56	AB614064	P 01	ADU1784L	M140	AEU1044	H 01	AEU1627	L 45	AEU1694	B 39	AEU1776	B 86	AEU1780	B183
AB608061L	P 61	AB614065L	N146	ADU1784L	M141	AEU1045	H 01	AEU1627	L 58	AEU1694	B135	AEU1776	B134	AEU1782	B222
AB608061L	N187	AB614065L	P 04	ADU1784L	M142	AEU1147	J 12	AEU1628	L 58	AEU1694	B223	AEU1776	B346	AEU1782	B 38
AB608064L	P 18	AB614081L	N132	ADU1784L	M138	AEU1192	B222	AEU1652	M 10	AEU1694	B183	AEU1776	B347	AEU1782	B 85
AB608064L	P 21	AB614081L	P 33	ADU2003L	H 10	AEU1192	B 38	AEU1684	B 42	AEU1706	B 44	AEU1776	B 39	AEU1782	B182
AB608064L	P 20	AB614081L	N129	ADU3307L	N187	AEU1192	B 85	AEU1688	B222	AEU1706	B 91	AEU1776	B135	AEU1782	B 86
AB608065L	L 34	AB614081L	N133	ADU3430	N143	AEU1192	B182	AEU1688	B 38	AEU1706	B 93	AEU1776	B223	AEU1782	B134
AB608067L	J 45	AB614081L	N131	ADU3469L	R 43	AEU1192	B 86	AEU1688	B 85	AEU1706	B138	AEU1776	B183	AEU1782	B346
AB608084	P 18	AB614088	N146	ADU3905	M135	AEU1192	B134	AEU1688	B182	AEU1706	B140	AEU1777	B222	AEU1782	B347
AB608101L	T 16	ABB710040	N 87	ADU3905	M143	AEU1192	B346	AEU1688	B 86	AEU1706	B358	AEU1777	B 38	AEU1782	B 39
AB608107	P 67	ABB710040	N 88	ADU3905	M130	AEU1192	B347	AEU1688	B134	AEU1706	B359	AEU1777	B 85	AEU1782	B135
AB608107	P 61	ABG710020	N151	ADU3905	M131	AEU1192	B 39	AEU1688	B346	AEU1706	B361	AEU1777	B182	AEU1782	B223
AB610031L	B321	ABG710040	N151	ADU3905	M142	AEU1192	B135	AEU1688	B347	AEU1708	B 44	AEU1777	B 86	AEU1782	B183
AB610031L	B324	ABU710160	M105	ADU4791	M 88	AEU1192	B223	AEU1688	B 39	AEU1708	B 93	AEU1777	B134	AEU1784	B222
AB610031L	J 73	ABU710170	M105	ADU4928L	B 44	AEU1192	B183	AEU1688	B135	AEU1708	B140	AEU1777	B346	AEU1784	B 38
AB610031L	M100	ABU7142	B340	ADU4928L	B 93	AEU1198	L 68	AEU1688	B223	AEU1708	B361	AEU1777	B347	AEU1784	B 85
AB610041L	B395	ABU7145	B340	ADU4928L	B140	AEU1205	L 68	AEU1688	B183	AEU1709	B 44	AEU1777	B 39	AEU1784	B182
AB610041L	M 75	AC606031L	N184	ADU4928L	B361	AEU1213	L 50	AEU1689	B222	AEU1709	B 93	AEU1777	B135	AEU1784	B 86
AB610041L	B377	AC606031L	N159	ADU5727L	N184	AEU1214	L 50	AEU1689	B 38	AEU1709	B140	AEU1777	B223	AEU1784	B134
AB610041L	G 10	AC606031L	N161	ADU5727L	N159	AEU1248	F 15	AEU1689	B 85	AEU1709	B361	AEU1777	B183	AEU1784	B346
AB610041L	N134	AC606041L	N184	ADU5727L	N162	AEU1248	F 16	AEU1689	B182	AEU1710	B 44	AEU1778	B222	AEU1784	B347
AB610041L	B298	AC606041L	N159	ADU6409L	M139	AEU1355	M 01	AEU1689	B 86	AEU1710	B 91	AEU1778	B 38	AEU1784	B 39
AB610051L	M 46	AC606041L	N161	ADU6409L	M140	AEU1356	F 15	AEU1689	B134	AEU1710	B 93	AEU1778	B 85	AEU1784	B135
AB610051L	N 39	AC606044L	R 54	ADU6409L	M141	AEU1357	F 15	AEU1689	B346	AEU1710	B138	AEU1778	B182	AEU1784	B223
AB610051L	R 54	AC606064L	P 12	ADU6409L	M142	AEU1358	F 13	AEU1689	B347	AEU1710	B140	AEU1778	B 86	AEU1784	B183
AB610051L	R 50	AC606081L	N111	ADU6409L	M138	AEU1359	F 13	AEU1689	B 39	AEU1710	B358	AEU1778	B134	AEU1785	B222
AB610051L	R 46	AC606104	P 02	ADU6418L	M139	AEU1422	B350	AEU1689	B135	AEU1710	B359	AEU1778	B346	AEU1785	B 38
AB610051L	R 47	AC608041L	L 34	ADU6418L	M140	AEU1446	H 36	AEU1689	B223	AEU1710	B361	AEU1778	B347	AEU1785	B 85
AB610051L	R 51	AC608065	L 72	ADU6418L	M141	AEU1448	J 74	AEU1689	B183	AEU1725	B 43	AEU1778	B 39	AEU1785	B182
AB610061L	R 03	ACC710100	N 37	ADU6418L	M142	AEU1449	B330	AEU1690	B222	AEU1725	B 93	AEU1778	B135	AEU1785	B 86
AB610061L	M127	ACU1161	N 92	ADU6418L	M138	AEU1488	E 45	AEU1690	B 38	AEU1725	B140	AEU1778	B223	AEU1785	B134
AB610081	R 03	ACU1762	N 92	ADU6693L	M136	AEU1489	E 45	AEU1690	B 85	AEU1725	B361	AEU1778	B183	AEU1785	B346
AB610081	P 21	ACU3530	N124	ADU6693L	M141	AEU1527	B 43	AEU1690	B182	AEU1726	B 43	AEU1779	B222	AEU1785	B347
AB610081	P 20	ACU3530	N 92	ADU6847L	B243	AEU1527	B 93	AEU1690	B 86	AEU1726	B 44	AEU1779	B 38	AEU1785	B 39
AB610081L	N184	ACU3530	N 93	ADU6847L	B293	AEU1527	B140	AEU1690	B134	AEU1726	B 93	AEU1779	B 85	AEU1785	B135
AB610081L	N159	ACU3777	N 90	ADU7346	B398	AEU1527	B361	AEU1690	B346	AEU1726	B140	AEU1779	B182	AEU1785	B223
AB610081L	N162	ACU3777	N 92	ADU7739L	M149	AEU1532	B 43	AEU1690	B347	AEU1726	B361	AEU1779	B 86	AEU1785	B183
AB610121L	M127	ACU5037	M135	ADU7828L	B395	AEU1532	B 44	AEU1690	B 39	AEU1742	M 01	AEU1779	B134	AEU1786	B222
AB610124L	P 01	ACU5037	M136	ADU7981L	M148	AEU1532	B 91	AEU1690	B135	AEU1747	M 81	AEU1779	B346	AEU1786	B 38
AB612051	N194	ACU5037	M131	ADU8026LOYL	P 45	AEU1532	B 93	AEU1690	B223	AEU1775	B222	AEU1779	B347	AEU1786	B 85
AB612051	N196	ACU5037	M133	ADU8026LOYL	P 38	AEU1532	B138	AEU1690	B183	AEU1775	B 38	AEU1779	B 39	AEU1786	B182
AB612051L	M 95	ACU5037	M140	ADU8267	M151	AEU1532	B140	AEU1691	B 86	AEU1775	B 85	AEU1779	B135	AEU1786	B 86
AB614061	M123	ACU5037	M141	ADU8363L	M151	AEU1532	B358	AEU1691	B347	AEU1775	B182	AEU1779	B223	AEU1786	B134
AB614061	M124	ACU5037	M142	ADU8363L	F 23	AEU1532	B359	AEU1691	B 39	AEU1775	B 86	AEU1779	B183	AEU1786	B346
AB614061	M127	ACU5431	L 72	ADU8363L	F 25	AEU1532	B361	AEU1691	B135	AEU1775	B134	AEU1780	B222	AEU1786	B347
AB614061L	B 42	AD606041L	P 11	ADU8363L	F 27	AEU1547	H 27	AEU1691	B223	AEU1775	B346	AEU1780	B 38	AEU1786	B 39
AB614061L	P 33	AD606044L	P 01	ADU8460	G 03	AEU1613	B143	AEU1691	B183	AEU1775	B347	AEU1780	B 85	AEU1786	B135
AB614061L	N 33	AD606044L	P 07	ADU8846L	H 17	AEU1616	B 44	AEU1694	B222	AEU1775	B 39	AEU1780	B182	AEU1786	B223
AB614061L	N 34	AD606074L	M122	ADU8846L	H 12	AEU1616	B 93	AEU1694	B 38	AEU1775	B135	AEU1780	B 86	AEU1786	B183

AEU1787	B222	AEU1792	B347	AEU2566	B 76	AEU2721	M119	AEU4119	B 36	AFU1085L	J 72	AFU1350	N 41	AFU1926L	P 24
AEU1787	B 38	AEU1792	B 39	AEU2566	B 31	AEU2722	M116	AEU4147	B143	AFU1090L	B 04	AFU1350	R 69	AFU1926L	M 07
AEU1787	B 85	AEU1792	B135	AEU2566	B 28	AEU2723	M116	AEU4148	B143	AFU1090L	B 53	AFU1350	R 66	AFU1926L	P 18
AEU1787	B182	AEU1792	B223	AEU2567	B 28	AEU2724	M116	AEU4149	B143	AFU1090L	B 59	AFU1386	N 19	AFU1926L	J 62
AEU1787	B 86	AEU1792	B183	AEU2568	B 28	AEU2733	D 41	AEU4150	B143	AFU1090L	B 98	AFU1400	D 42	AFU1926L	J 41
AEU1787	B134	AEU1814	B 43	AEU2569	B 77	AEU2734	D 41	AEU4151	B143	AFU1090L	M 46	AFU1400	D 41	AFU1926L	J 64
AEU1787	B346	AEU1814	B358	AEU2569	B 31	AEU2735	D 41	AF608081	R 35	AFU1090L	M150	AFU1497	P 34	AFU2501	P 16
AEU1787	B347	AEU1891	H 01	AEU2569	B 28	AEU2736	D 41	AFB710010	N 90	AFU1090L	M 57	AFU1499	N 29	AFU2501	P 14
AEU1787	B 39	AEU1942	B 44	AEU2572	B 31	AEU2737	D 41	AFB710020	N 90	AFU1090L	M 59	AFU1499	N 07	AFU2501	P 15
AEU1787	B135	AEU1942	B 91	AEU2572	B 28	AEU2738	D 41	AFB710070	N 87	AFU1090L	M 60	AFU1499	N 38	AFU2503	N246
AEU1787	B223	AEU1942	B138	AEU2573	B 77	AEU2741	H 01	AFB710070	N 88	AFU1090L	M 66	AFU1841	N124	AFU2503	N242
AEU1787	B183	AEU1942	B358	AEU2573	B 31	AEU2761	F 07	AFP710010	R 70	AFU1090L	E 50	AFU1843	T 14	AFU2503	N245
AEU1788	B222	AEU1942	B359	AEU2574	B 77	AEU2792	B143	AFP710020	R 70	AFU1090L	M127	AFU1848L	B126	AFU2504	N246
AEU1788	B 38	AEU2129L	B217	AEU2574	B 31	AEU2805	N 65	AFU1004	S 06	AFU1090L	M 65	AFU1848L	B 73	AFU2504	N242
AEU1788	B 85	AEU2147L	J 54	AEU2575	B 76	AEU2806	N 65	AFU1004	S 07	AFU1104	N143	AFU1848L	B 25	AFU2504	N245
AEU1788	B182	AEU2147L	J 56	AEU2575	B 31	AEU3015	H 01	AFU1005	S 18	AFU1107	J 21	AFU1876	N124	AFU2627	M152
AEU1788	B 86	AEU2148L	J 54	AEU2575	B 28	AEU3055	L 50	AFU1008	J 74	AFU1107	J 28	AFU1876	T 16	AFU2627	G 09
AEU1788	B134	AEU2148L	J 56	AEU2577	B 76	AEU3055	L 58	AFU1024L	S 06	AFU1180	H 25	AFU1879L	B196	AFU2636	P 07
AEU1788	B346	AEU2149L	J 54	AEU2577	B 31	AEU3056	L 45	AFU1031	H 27	AFU1203	N150	AFU1879L	B103	AFU2636	N 32
AEU1788	B347	AEU2149L	J 56	AEU2577	B 28	AEU3056	L 58	AFU1036	N169	AFU1217	H 20	AFU1879L	B104	AFU2636	P 24
AEU1788	B 39	AEU2462	B332	AEU2578	B 76	AEU3067	L 45	AFU1069	N 46	AFU1218L	N199	AFU1879L	B153	AFU2636	P 18
AEU1788	B135	AEU2464L	B 43	AEU2578	B 31	AEU3068	L 45	AFU1069	N 61	AFU1218L	P 07	AFU1882L	B196	AFU2636	P 23
AEU1788	B223	AEU2464L	B358	AEU2578	B 28	AEU3076	B 43	AFU1069	R 66	AFU1218L	T 47	AFU1882L	B234	AFU2692	P 10
AEU1788	B183	AEU2496	H 28	AEU2579	B 77	AEU3076	B 91	AFU1069	M134	AFU1218L	T 48	AFU1882L	B 08	AFU2692	P 30
AEU1790	B222	AEU2497	H 28	AEU2579	B 31	AEU3076	B 93	AFU1069	M137	AFU1234	E 19	AFU1882L	B 57	AFU2692	P 04
AEU1790	B 38	AEU2498	H 29	AEU2579	B 28	AEU3076	B138	AFU1070	R 40	AFU1234	E 20	AFU1882L	B103	AFU2778	K 12
AEU1790	B 85	AEU2502	B 46	AEU2580	B 76	AEU3076	B140	AFU1070	R 38	AFU1247	R 03	AFU1882L	B153	AFU2778L	K 02
AEU1790	B182	AEU2502	B 96	AEU2580	B 31	AEU3076	B359	AFU1071	P 34	AFU1248	P 01	AFU1887L	B196	AFU2778L	K 12
AEU1790	B 86	AEU2507	B 43	AEU2580	B 28	AEU3076	B361	AFU1075	N198	AFU1248	P 10	AFU1887L	B243	AFU2778L	K 01
AEU1790	B134	AEU2507	B 91	AEU2581	B 31	AEU3077	B332	AFU1075	N 63	AFU1248	P 30	AFU1887L	B103	AFU2778L	K 11
AEU1790	B346	AEU2507	B138	AEU2581	B 28	AEU4000	L 72	AFU1077	J 66	AFU1248	M113	AFU1887L	B104	AFU2813	P 11
AEU1790	B347	AEU2507	B359	AEU2582	B 76	AEU4001	L 72	AFU1077L	J 65	AFU1256	N182	AFU1887L	B153	AFU2813	P 03
AEU1790	B 39	AEU2508	E 32	AEU2582	B 31	AEU4002	L 70	AFU1077L	G 03	AFU1256	S 01	AFU1890L	B 19	AFU2875	R 54
AEU1790	B135	AEU2515	E 32	AEU2582	B 28	AEU4002	L 66	AFU1077L	J 19	AFU1256	S 05	AFU1890L	B 67	AFU2875	R 50
AEU1790	B223	AEU2520	E 16	AEU2583	B 76	AEU4002	L 69	AFU1078	N179	AFU1256	S 02	AFU1890L	B119	AFU2875	R 46
AEU1790	B183	AEU2521	E 16	AEU2583	B 31	AEU4002	L 71	AFU1079	N 61	AFU1256	N163	AFU1890L	B167	AFU2875	R 47
AEU1791	B222	AEU2522	E 16	AEU2583	B 28	AEU4013	F 12	AFU1079	R 59	AFU1257	N191	AFU1897	M 90	AFU2879	M109
AEU1791	B 38	AEU2539	H 27	AEU2584	B 76	AEU4014	F 12	AFU1079	R 67	AFU1257	N 30	AFU1897	M123	AFU2879	M150
AEU1791	B 85	AEU2557	B 30	AEU2584	B 31	AEU4015	F 12	AFU1079	J 70	AFU1259	N197	AFU1897	M125	AFU3017L	M 92
AEU1791	B182	AEU2560	B 77	AEU2584	B 28	AEU4016	F 12	AFU1079	N 95	AFU1259	N191	AFU1897	P 03	AFU3061L	M145
AEU1791	B 86	AEU2560	B 31	AEU2585	B 76	AEU4017	F 12	AFU1080	N181	AFU1259	N123	AFU1897LDE	H 35	AFU3112L	M 08
AEU1791	B134	AEU2560	B 28	AEU2585	B 31	AEU4018	F 12	AFU1080	N197	AFU1259	N125	AFU1897LDE	P 41	AFU4092L	M 26
AEU1791	B346	AEU2561	B 28	AEU2585	B 28	AEU4019	F 12	AFU1080	M 32	AFU1259	N129	AFU1897LDE	P 17	AFU4092L	M 18
AEU1791	B347	AEU2562	B 77	AEU2586	B 28	AEU4020	F 12	AFU1080	P 13	AFU1262	N170	AFU1897LOY	P 41	AFU4162	N238
AEU1791	B 39	AEU2562	B 31	AEU2587	B 28	AEU4021	F 12	AFU1080	N238	AFU1262	N179	AFU1897PMP	M125	AFU4173	C 69
AEU1791	B135	AEU2562	B 28	AEU2718	B220	AEU4023	F 12	AFU1080	N114	AFU1263	R 29	AFU1897PMP	P 03	AFU4173	M147
AEU1791	B223	AEU2563	B 77	AEU2718	B131	AEU4024	F 12	AFU1080	N150	AFU1265	S 15	AFU1900	P 63	AFU4173	N 34
AEU1791	B183	AEU2563	B 31	AEU2718	B180	AEU4025	F 07	AFU1080	R 31	AFU1272	M 27	AFU1900	P 64	AFU4173	C 24
AEU1792	B222	AEU2563	B 28	AEU2719	B220	AEU4025	F 12	AFU1080	N102	AFU1280	N 61	AFU1900	P 65	AFU4214	F 18
AEU1792	B 38	AEU2564	B 77	AEU2719	B131	AEU4025	F 09	AFU1080	N104	AFU1280	M100	AFU1900	P 66	AFU4241L	M 18
AEU1792	B 85	AEU2564	B 31	AEU2719	B180	AEU4026	F 07	AFU1080	N106	AFU1296	M150	AFU1900	P 53	AFU4241L	M 23
AEU1792	B182	AEU2564	B 28	AEU2720	B220	AEU4026	F 12	AFU1080	N241	AFU1298	R 66	AFU1900	P 56	AFU4481	M 08
AEU1792	B 86	AEU2565	B 76	AEU2720	B131	AEU4026	F 09	AFU1080	N243	AFU1342L	B334	AFU1900	P 57	AFU4506	M134
AEU1792	B134	AEU2565	B 31	AEU2720	B180	AEU4119	B 83	AFU1085	J 72	AFU1350	N147	AFU1900	P 60	AFU4506	M137
AEU1792	B346	AEU2565	B 28	AEU2721	M116	AEU4119	B132	AFU1085L	J 65	AFU1350	N122	AFU1926L	J 63	AGI710020	N 92

AGI710030	N 92	AKA710180NAL	N130	ALR1467	N 41	ALR3970	N 59	ALR5313	N166	ALR5981	N165	ALR7105	N 81	ALR8987	N173
AH614011L	N 57	AKA710590NAL	N130	ALR1468	N 41	ALR3970	N 60	ALR5323	N 54	ALR5982	N165	ALR7106	N 81	ALR9022	N144
AHA710010	N 27	AKA710600NAL	N130	ALR1522	N145	ALR4057	N 59	ALR5324	N 54	ALR5985	N 69	ALR7107	N 81	ALR9103	N116
AHB710010	N 27	AKA710610NAL	N128	ALR1618	N 30	ALR4057	N 60	ALR5329	N 94	ALR5987	N 76	ALR7128	N116	ALR9103	N119
AHB710020	N 27	AKA710620NAL	N128	ALR1619	N 30	ALR4065	N193	ALR5330	N 94	ALR5989	N 54	ALR7129	N116	ALR9103	N117
AHB710050	N 27	AKA710640NAL	N132	ALR1737	N185	ALR4065	N188	ALR5502	N 76	ALR5990	N 54	ALR7259	N122	ALR9104	N116
AHB710090	N 27	AKA710650NAL	N133	ALR1742	N 44	ALR4532	N161	ALR5503	N 76	ALR6107	N140	ALR7544	N140	ALR9104	N119
AHL710020	P 11	AKB710010NAL	N128	ALR1743	N 44	ALR4533	N161	ALR5506	N 92	ALR6109	V 04	ALR7812	N250	ALR9104	N117
AHL710030	P 11	AKB710020NAL	N128	ALR1752	N 36	ALR4534	N184	ALR5507	N 92	ALR6110	V 04	ALR7822	N220	ALR9155	N142
AHU710010	N140	AKB710030NAL	N128	ALR1753	N 35	ALR4535	N184	ALR5513	N115	ALR6121	N 56	ALR7823	N220	ALR9157	N142
AHU710030	M 49	AKB710030NUC	N130	ALR1757	N 33	ALR4540	N154	ALR5514	N115	ALR6122	N 56	ALR7843	N250	ALR9158	M105
AHU710040	M 49	AKB710170NAL	N130	ALR1801	N153	ALR4541	N154	ALR5539	V 03	ALR6131	N123	ALR7843	N251	ALR9159	M105
AHU710060	N140	AKB710180NAL	N128	ALR1982	L 02	ALR4542	N164	ALR5540	N252	ALR6132	N123	ALR7881	N250	ALR9160	N170
AID710010	P 30	AL614011	N 44	ALR1982	L 03	ALR4543	N164	ALR5540	V 03	ALR6133	N163	ALR7881	N251	ALR9186	N 89
AIO710010	N 30	ALA710080	N 70	ALR2136	N 27	ALR4564	N151	ALR5541	V 03	ALR6134	N163	ALR7881	N138	ALR9187	N 89
AIR710080	N 30	ALA710090	N 70	ALR2138	N 27	ALR4652	N196	ALR5543	V 03	ALR6135	N163	ALR7972	N 55	ALR9350	N 25
AIR710090	N 30	ALA710140	N 77	ALR2220	N 30	ALR4652	N123	ALR5544	V 03	ALR6136	N163	ALR7973	N 55	ALR9350	N138
AIT710030	N 30	ALA710150	N 77	ALR2261	N 59	ALR4769	N182	ALR5545	V 03	ALR6219	N159	ALR8075	N 36	ALR9424	N151
AJ606011L	P 03	ALA710160	N 82	ALR2261	N 60	ALR4770	N182	ALR5546	V 03	ALR6219	N160	ALR8081	N116	ALR9555	N142
AJ608031	P 07	ALA710170	N 82	ALR2262	N 59	ALR4771	N160	ALR5548	N252	ALR6224	N190	ALR8082	N116	ALR9556	N142
AJ608041	L 34	ALA710180	N 73	ALR2262	N 60	ALR4772	N160	ALR5548	V 03	ALR6225	N143	ALR8279	N 90	ALR9781	N153
AJH710030	N 39	ALA710180	N 74	ALR2263	N 60	ALR4773	N160	ALR5548	N137	ALR6250	N163	ALR8300	R 70	ALR9801	N 48
AJL710020	N 47	ALA710190	N 73	ALR2264	N 59	ALR4774	N160	ALR5549	N252	ALR6251	N167	ALR8301	R 70	ALR9802	N 48
AJL710030	N 47	ALA710190	N 74	ALR2264	N 60	ALR4775	N183	ALR5549	N250	ALR6256	N153	ALR8327	N222	ALR9803	N 48
AJU1136	J 63	ALA710240	N 92	ALR2265	N 59	ALR4776	N183	ALR5549	V 04	ALR6257	N153	ALR8329	N222	ALR9804	N 48
AJU1136	P 45	ALA710250	N 92	ALR2265	N 60	ALR4777	N183	ALR5549	N251	ALR6258	N164	ALR8333	N222	ALR9811	N186
AJU1136	J 41	ALA710460	N 87	ALR2302	N104	ALR4778	N183	ALR5549	N138	ALR6259	N164	ALR8337	N222	ALR9895	N164
AJU1136	J 64	ALA710470	N 87	ALR2303	N104	ALR4929	N182	ALR5550	V 04	ALR6280	N163	ALR8348	N222	ALR9896	N164
AJU1136	P 38	ALA710510	N 71	ALR2318	N158	ALR4936	N222	ALR5556	V 04	ALR6350	N193	ALR8352	N222	ALR9935	N 54
AJU1136L	N155	ALA710510	N 73	ALR2318	N169	ALR4936	N163	ALR5556	N251	ALR6350	N189	ALR8357	N222	ALR9936	N 54
AJU1136L	J 45	ALA710510	N 74	ALR2319	N158	ALR4937	N222	ALR5557	N250	ALR6365	N 36	ALR8360	N222	ALR9945	N 27
AK606011L	P 11	ALA710540	N 71	ALR2319	N169	ALR4937	N163	ALR5557	V 04	ALR6366	N 35	ALR8364	N222	ALR9946	N 27
AK606011L	M 75	ALA710550	N 71	ALR2321	N158	ALR4938	N166	ALR5557	N251	ALR6368	N 50	ALR8380	R 71	ALR9962	N 54
AK606011L	P 24	ALA710560	N 78	ALR2322	N158	ALR4939	N166	ALR5558	N250	ALR6368	N 48	ALR8381	R 71	ALR9970	N 27
AK606011L	P 23	ALA710570	N 78	ALR2377	S 12	ALR5054	N104	ALR5558	V 04	ALR6374	N 27	ALR8382	R 71	ALR9971	N 27
AK606021L	M 06	ALA710580	N 83	ALR2378	S 12	ALR5055	N106	ALR5558	N251	ALR6375	N 27	ALR8383	R 71	ALU1403L	B237
AK606031	P 02	ALA710590	N 83	ALR2380	S 09	ALR5056	N103	ALR5560	V 04	ALR6667	N 89	ALR8384	R 70	ALU1403L	D 04
AK606031	P 12	ALA710620	N 88	ALR2385	N151	ALR5057	N 66	ALR5560	N251	ALR6677	N 56	ALR8385	R 70	ALU1403L	C 55
AK608021	L 38	ALA710630	N 88	ALR2386	N135	ALR5058	N185	ALR5561	V 04	ALR6678	N 56	ALR8521	R 71	ALU710030	N142
AK608021	L 75	ALA710680	N 77	ALR2414	N 59	ALR5073	R 50	ALR5561	N251	ALR6708	N 89	ALR8522	R 70	ALU710080	R 28
AK608141L	M143	ALA710680	N 78	ALR2415	N 60	ALR5080	N 65	ALR5685	N 72	ALR6777	N237	ALR8523	R 70	ALU710090	R 28
AK608141L	P 24	ALA710680	N 87	ALR2622	M143	ALR5080	N113	ALR5705	N185	ALR6777	V 03	ALR8524	R 70	AM605061	N 57
AK608141L	P 23	ALA710680	N 88	ALR2648	N153	ALR5081	N113	ALR5821	N184	ALR6809	R 70	ALR8525	R 70	AMC710020	N166
AK610021L	N199	ALA710690	N 82	ALR3219	V 04	ALR5110	N 39	ALR5821	N159	ALR6822	R 70	ALR8526	R 70	AMC710030	N166
AK612011L	N146	ALA710690	N 83	ALR3219	N251	ALR5111	N 39	ALR5821	N161	ALR6823	R 70	ALR8527	R 70	AMC710040	N166
AK612011L	H 09	ALJ710050	N 70	ALR3220	V 04	ALR5112	N 39	ALR5835	N140	ALR6840	N 54	ALR8528	R 71	AMC710050	N166
AK616011	N 57	ALO710010	N198	ALR3220	N251	ALR5113	N 39	ALR5921	N 72	ALR6842	N 54	ALR8529	R 71	AML110010	N104
AKA710010NAL	N128	ALO710020P	N198	ALR3221	V 04	ALR5114	N 39	ALR5922	N 72	ALR6843	N 54	ALR8530	R 71	AML110030	N103
AKA710020NAL	N128	ALR1157	N104	ALR3222	V 04	ALR5117	N 27	ALR5923	N 72	ALR6851	N171	ALR8531	R 71	AML110060	N 66
AKA710020NUC	N128	ALR1158	N106	ALR3226	R 71	ALR5118	N 27	ALR5927	N 56	ALR6852	N171	ALR8549	R 70	AML710020	N103
AKA710060NAL	N130	ALR1159	N103	ALR3288	N153	ALR5294	N 47	ALR5928	N 56	ALR6871	N220	ALR8550	R 70	AML710030	N103
AKA710060NUC	N130	ALR1161	N 66	ALR3289	N153	ALR5295	N 47	ALR5937	N 72	ALR6871	N252	ALR8551	R 70	AMN710020	N120
AKA710070NAL	N130	ALR1339	N145	ALR3362	N 45	ALR5308	N166	ALR5937	N 73	ALR6871	N137	ALR8552	R 70	AMN710030	N120
AKA710070NUC	N130	ALR1460	N135	ALR3363	N 45	ALR5309	N166	ALR5937	N 74	ALR7005	N 33	ALR8672	R 71	AMN710160	N115
AKA710170NAL	N128	ALR1466	N 41	ALR3966	N 65	ALR5312	N166	ALR5980	N155	ALR710050	N138	ALR8765PUC	N146	AMN710170	N115

DEFENDER

GROUP X

Numeric Index "AMP710010 " TO "ANR5265"

AMP710010 N 90	AMR2449 M 88	AMR3135 M 83	AMR3850 M 16	AMR4991 M 20	AMR5975 M116	ANR2485 F 24	ANR3118 V 05
AMR1054 M143	AMR2474 M135	AMR3135 M 84	AMR3859 C 55	AMR4992 M 20	AMR5975 M119	ANR2485 F 26	ANR3118 S 10
AMR1088 M105	AMR2475 M 70	AMR3138 M 48	AMR3918 C 55	AMR5068 M 20	AMR6103 B288	ANR2487 F 26	ANR3138 K 05
AMR1192 P 13	AMR2625 M 70	AMR3138 M 94	AMR3932 M144	AMR5069 M 49	AMR6104 M 87	ANR2503 H 14	ANR3138 N 17
AMR1421 M 06	AMR2628 M116	AMR3142 M 19	AMR3933 M144	AMR5085 M 88	AMR6105 M 87	ANR2512 G 10	ANR3141 S 10
AMR1421 M 11	AMR2631 M115	AMR3154 M126	AMR3934 M144	AMR5137 M 80	AMR6106 M 87	ANR2763MMM E 54	ANR3143 S 10
AMR1422 M 11	AMR2896 B354	AMR3155 M 19	AMR3963 M 75	AMR5248 M 06	AMR6108 M144	ANR2763MMM S 14	ANR3144 S 10
AMR1425 B385	AMR2956 M 67	AMR3158 M 20	AMR3963 M127	AMR5248 M 11	AMR6244 K 05	ANR2775 H 21	ANR3145 V 05
AMR1487 M 35	AMR2959 M 62	AMR3247 M 05	AMR3976 M127	AMR5249 M 11	AMR6328 M 88	ANR2776 H 21	ANR3145 S 10
AMR1488 M 38	AMR2962 M 60	AMR3262 M127	AMR3987 M 67	AMR5361 M124	AMR6330 M 40	ANR2777 H 21	ANR3200 N 17
AMR1491 M 51	AMR2962 M 65	AMR3294 M122	AMR3988 M 67	AMR5413 M104	AMR6333 M 67	ANR2778 H 21	ANR3201 N 17
AMR1491 M 53	AMR2972 M 77	AMR3294 M124	AMR4019 M 67	AMR5415 M 67	AMR6334 M 67	ANR2779 H 22	ANR3225 N 17
AMR1492 M 51	AMR2973 M 77	AMR3321 B250	AMR4021 M 67	AMR5416 M 67	AMR6430 M104	ANR2780 H 16	ANR3227 D 08
AMR1492 M 53	AMR2976 M 78	AMR3322 M 20	AMR4023 M 62	AMR5417 M 67	AMR6431 M104	ANR2783 H 04	ANR3227 D 09
AMR1493 M 57	AMR2976 M 80	AMR3324 M 83	AMR4025 M 62	AMR5419 K 05	AMR6521 M 16	ANR2784 H 04	ANR3227 K 05
AMR1494 M 57	AMR2977 M 78	AMR3324 M 84	AMR4027 M 60	AMR5481 M150	AMR6522 M 16	ANR2804 N 16	ANR3231 F 01
AMR1495 J 04	AMR2977 M 80	AMR3325 M 83	AMR4027 M 65	AMR5491 M106	AMR6660 M 67	ANR2819 N 16	ANR3231 F 03
AMR1496 J 04	AMR2978 M133	AMR3325 M 84	AMR4029 M 60	AMR5530 M 77	AMR6661 M 67	ANR2820 C 38	ANR3327 F 20
AMR1518 M 56	AMR2978 M140	AMR3339 M114	AMR4029 M 65	AMR5551 M110	AMR6676 M134	ANR2820 N 16	ANR3400 G 08
AMR1632 M131	AMR2979 M136	AMR3339 M 70	AMR4042 M 68	AMR5566 N 38	AMR6676 M137	ANR2847 M 86	ANR3410 E 57
AMR1637 M 91	AMR2979 M141	AMR3339 M 71	AMR4043 M 68	AMR5568 N 38	ANR1338 G 10	ANR2848 M 86	ANR3563 H 04
AMR1647 M 70	AMR2980 M 67	AMR3339 M119	AMR4063 M122	AMR5607 N 38	ANR1339 G 10	ANR2858 F 17	ANR3564 H 04
AMR1647 M 71	AMR2981 M 62	AMR3412 B261	AMR4063 M124	AMR5611 M105	ANR1369 M152	ANR2859 F 17	ANR3578 E 64
AMR1783 M126	AMR2982 M 60	AMR3412E B261	AMR4078 M 35	AMR5696LNF M124	ANR1415 H 14	ANR2860 F 17	ANR3598 F 24
AMR1935 M146	AMR2982 M 65	AMR3414 M122	AMR4079 M 35	AMR5710 M 91	ANR1419 G 03	ANR2868 N 12	ANR3615 H 16
AMR2022 M105	AMR2983 M 91	AMR3417 M122	AMR4080 M 37	AMR5711 M 91	ANR1534PM E 53	ANR2898 N 17	ANR3615 H 12
AMR2043 M119	AMR3012 M135	AMR3417 M124	AMR4081 M 39	AMR5713 M100	ANR1689MNH E 53	ANR2914 F 26	ANR3631MNH E 53
AMR2070 M115	AMR3012 M136	AMR3418 M122	AMR4082 M 39	AMR5716 M 71	ANR1799 E 62	ANR2945 G 04	ANR3635 T 37
AMR2090 M 05	AMR3012 M131	AMR3418 M124	AMR4103 M 08	AMR5716 M119	ANR1808 B 08	ANR2946 H 17	ANR3635 T 38
AMR2092 B314	AMR3012 M133	AMR3443 M115	AMR4238 K 05	AMR5717 M 40	ANR1808 B 57	ANR2946 H 18	ANR3692 H 34
AMR2156 M 13	AMR3012 M134	AMR3444 M 70	AMR4247 B396	AMR5718 M 49	ANR1808 B109	ANR2946 H 14	ANR3693 H 34
AMR2217 B261	AMR3012 M137	AMR3448 M 51	AMR4247E B261	AMR5721 M119	ANR1808 B158	ANR2947 H 17	ANR3713 N 07
AMR2218 B396	AMR3025 M135	AMR3448 M 54	AMR4249 B261	AMR5722 M119	ANR1808 B201	ANR2947 H 18	ANR3770 H 14
AMR2323 M149	AMR3025 M136	AMR3449 M 51	AMR4249E B261	AMR5723 M119	ANR1808 N 15	ANR2947 H 14	ANR3821 N204
AMR2341 M 93	AMR3025 M131	AMR3449 M 54	AMR4737 M 91	AMR5724 M119	ANR1895 E 63	ANR2948 T 27	ANR3861 E 54
AMR2341 M 94	AMR3025 M133	AMR3450 M 54	AMR4741 M 46	AMR5725 M108	ANR1895 E 65	ANR2967 C 44	ANR4188 E 56
AMR2342 M 02	AMR3025 M140	AMR3450 M 56	AMR4794LNF M124	AMR5826 M 67	ANR1895 E 66	ANR2985 F 27	ANR4189 E 61
AMR2343 M 02	AMR3025 M141	AMR3480 M 35	AMR4847 M 67	AMR5827 M 20	ANR1969 F 24	ANR2994 F 07	ANR4344 E 68
AMR2344 M 03	AMR3025 M142	AMR3481 M 35	AMR4848 M 62	AMR5828 M 20	ANR1972 F 03	ANR2994 F 08	ANR4489 S 07
AMR2345 M 03	AMR3025 M134	AMR3482 M 37	AMR4849 M 60	AMR5833 M 05	ANR1998 F 20	ANR2994 F 11	ANR4510 S 07
AMR2346 M 04	AMR3025 M137	AMR3483 M 39	AMR4849 M 65	AMR5856 M 39	ANR2003 B341	ANR3036 E 69	ANR4546 N 07
AMR2347 M 35	AMR3026 M135	AMR3484 M 39	AMR4889 M105	AMR5857 M 39	ANR2054 N 01	ANR3037 E 62	ANR4547 N 07
AMR2348 M 38	AMR3026 M136	AMR3550 M134	AMR4892 M104	AMR5858 M 37	ANR2054 N 03	ANR3052 S 06	ANR4548 E 68
AMR2350 M 83	AMR3026 M141	AMR3550 M137	AMR4893 M104	AMR5859 M 35	ANR2056 N 01	ANR3052 S 18	ANR4583PM E 53
AMR2351 M 83	AMR3026 M142	AMR3676 M144	AMR4895 M104	AMR5860 M 40	ANR2056 N 05	ANR3060 E 64	ANR4635PM E 53
AMR2357 M 04	AMR3026 M137	AMR3677 M 74	AMR4896 M104	AMR5861 M 49	ANR2135 F 24	ANR3060 E 67	ANR4636PM E 53
AMR2358 M102	AMR3039 M109	AMR3727 M 20	AMR4897 M105	AMR5869 M 51	ANR2136 F 26	ANR3069 H 14	ANR4650 N 16
AMR2358 M103	AMR3041 M 76	AMR3756 M131	AMR4939 B396	AMR5869 M 54	ANR2157 B258	ANR3091 S 10	ANR4657 C 38
AMR2393 M102	AMR3042 M 76	AMR3771 M 49	AMR4948 C 86	AMR5870 M 51	ANR2162 G 04	ANR3099 V 05	ANR4657 N 16
AMR2399 M 58	AMR3095 H 34	AMR3773 M 94	AMR4974 M105	AMR5870 M 54	ANR2183 G 05	ANR3099 S 10	ANR4696 B377
AMR2411 M103	AMR3098 M 46	AMR3840 M122	AMR4976 M116	AMR5871 M 54	ANR2326 N 05	ANR3100 S 11	ANR4697 N 14
AMR2416 M102	AMR3101 M 70	AMR3840 M124	AMR4983 M 40	AMR5871 M 56	ANR2327 N 05	ANR3101 S 10	ANR4697 B377
AMR2416 M103	AMR3101 M 71	AMR3843 M 30	AMR4984 M 20	AMR5874 M 89	ANR2391LAL E 54	ANR3107 H 07	ANR4742 N 01
AMR2425 B207	AMR3104 M 30	AMR3844 M 31	AMR4986 M 20	AMR5875 M 89	ANR2391MNH E 54	ANR3117 V 05	ANR4914 S 13
AMR2425 B244	AMR3124 M111	AMR3849 M135	AMR4990 M 20	AMR5974 M119	ANR2391MUE E 54	ANR3117 S 11	ANR5265 H 07

DEFENDER

GROUP X

Numeric Index "ANR5307MNH " TO "AWR6599 "

ANR5307MNH E 53	AQH000030 N 71	ASR1096 N250	ASU1151 M 83	AWR1548LNF P 33	AWR3273LUH P 59	AWR5398LDE P 36	AWR5744RPI R 24
ANR5307RJQ E 53	AQH000030 N 88	ASR1097 N250	ASU710010 N 61	AWR1587 R 56	AWR3320 N136	AWR5398LOY P 37	AWR5745RPI R 22
ANR5308 G 04	AQH100060 N 77	ASR1104 N250	ASU710040 N147	AWR1604 P 28	AWR3321 N136	AWR5399LDE P 36	AWR5746RPI R 25
ANR5311 G 08	AQH100060 N 82	ASR1105 N250	ASU710050 N147	AWR1607 P 16	AWR3323 N136	AWR5399LOY P 37	AWR5747RPI R 26
ANR5435 E 55	AQH100060 N 70	ASR1108 N252	ASU710060 M102	AWR1609LCS P 24	AWR3324 N136	AWR5400LDE P 36	AWR5748RPI R 22
ANR5436 E 55	AQH100060 N 87	ASR1109 N250	ASU710060 M103	AWR1609LOY P 24	AWR3812 P 07	AWR5400LOY P 37	AWR5749RPI R 23
ANR5593PM E 53	AQH100070 N 77	ASR1112 N252	ASU710070 M102	AWR1611 P 29	AWR3813 P 07	AWR5401LDE P 44	AWR5750RPI R 25
ANR5636 N 18	AQH100070 N 82	ASR1113 N252	ASU710070 M103	AWR1612 P 28	AWR3844LUH P 64	AWR5401LOY P 44	AWR5751RPI R 26
ANR5637 N 18	AQH100070 N 70	ASR1148 N252	ASU710100 N 61	AWR2001 R 49	AWR3942LUH P 66	AWR5428 N 25	AWR5752RPI R 23
ANR5720 M 86	AQH100070 N 87	ASR1149 N252	ASU710110 N 61	AWR2002 R 49	AWR3953LUH P 66	AWR5475 N 63	AWR5753RPI R 24
ANR5782 F 24	AQL710020 N116	ASR1150 N252	ASW710120 N 55	AWR2214 L 34	AWR3955NAL N133	AWR5476 N 63	AWR5756RPI R 25
ANR5782 F 26	AQL710020 N119	ASR1153 N 30	ASW710130 N 55	AWR2215 L 34	AWR3955NUC N133	AWR5520 P 17	AWR5757RPI R 26
ANR5783 H 25	AQL710020 N117	ASR1154 N 30	ASW710140 N 55	AWR2216 L 34	AWR4147 P 34	AWR5522 P 17	AWR5758RPI R 22
ANR5783 E 21	AQL710030 N116	ASR1157 N 36	ASW710150 N 55	AWR2217 L 34	AWR4316 R 51	AWR5681RPI R 07	AWR5759RPI R 23
ANR5784 H 25	AQL710030 N119	ASR1158 N 36	ATU1005L N 28	AWR2277LDQ M123	AWR4406 R 57	AWR5682RPI R 07	AWR5762RFI R 25
ANR5784 E 21	AQL710030 N117	ASR1185 N 30	ATU1017L E 50	AWR2277LDQ M125	AWR4639 M 13	AWR5683RFI R 07	AWR5763RFI R 26
ANR6222 F 20	AQL710060 N116	ASR1185 M 12	ATU1017L E 51	AWR2277LOY M125	AWR4647 M 13	AWR5684RFI R 07	AWR5764RFI R 22
ANR6332 G 08	AQL710070 N116	ASR1227 N141	ATU1041 L 59	AWR2332 L 62	AWR4648LOY P 21	AWR5685RPI R 07	AWR5765RFI R 23
ANR6333 G 09	AQU110010 S 09	ASR1229 N141	ATU1041 L 66	AWR2333 L 62	AWR4649LOY P 21	AWR5686RPI R 07	AWR5766RPI R 36
ANR6373 G 10	AQU110020 S 09	ASR1390 N118	AUD2437L B336	AWR2334 L 62	AWR4650 M127	AWR5687RFI R 07	AWR5767RPI R 37
ANR6386 N 07	AQU710010 N 87	ASR1391 N118	AUD2437L B335	AWR2443 R 32	AWR4651 M127	AWR5688RFI R 07	AWR5771RFI R 40
ANR6461 L 04	AQU710010 N 88	ASR1457 N142	AUD3306L B333	AWR2444 R 32	AWR4652LOY P 47	AWR5695 P 17	AWR5774RFI R 36
ANR6462 L 04	AQU710020 N 87	ASR1459 N157	AUD3577L B388	AWR2473 L 58	AWR4653LOY P 47	AWR5696 M112	AWR5775RFI R 37
ANR6472 G 09	AQU710020 N 88	ASR1603 N157	AUD4398L B333	AWR2699LDE P 47	AWR4656 R 51	AWR5698RPI R 10	AWR5778RFI R 30
ANR6476 G 09	AQV710010 N 94	ASR1772 N145	AUD4771L B333	AWR2699LOY P 47	AWR4685 R 57	AWR5699RPI R 10	AWR5778RFI R 34
ANR6563 N 09	AR606031L N 90	ASR1870 N 36	AUH710010 N185	AWR2700LDE P 47	AWR4686 R 57	AWR5700RPI R 13	AWR5779RFI R 32
ANR6578 S 16	AR606031L N173	ASR1876 N 55	AV608081 M123	AWR2700LOY P 47	AWR4704LUH P 65	AWR5701RPI R 13	AWR5783RPI R 40
ANR6578 S 14	AR608021L N 61	ASR1877 N 55	AV608081 M125	AWR2701LDE P 47	AWR4704LUH P 66	AWR5702RPI R 11	AWR5787RFI R 29
ANR6610 N 13	AR608031L M 82	ASR2152 J 42	AV608081 M121	AWR2701LOY P 47	AWR4705LUH P 65	AWR5703RFI R 09	AWR5789RPI R 29
ANR6622 N 13	AR608031L N 61	ASR2158 N 55	AV608081L R 43	AWR2702LDE P 47	AWR4705LUH P 66	AWR5704RFI R 09	AWR5790RPI R 30
ANR6623 N 13	AR608041 H 35	ASR2250 N 59	AW606124 L 72	AWR2702LOY P 47	AWR4706LUH P 64	AWR5705RFI R 13	AWR5871 R 28
ANR6655 F 26	AR608061 P 34	ASR2252 N 60	AW608081 M123	AWR2703LDE P 47	AWR4706LUH P 66	AWR5706RFI R 11	AWR5899PCB R 14
ANR6656 F 26	AR610051L N199	ASR2253 N 59	AWH710020 N 37	AWR2703LOY P 47	AWR4707LUH P 64	AWR5707RFI R 13	AWR5900RFI R 09
ANR6885 G 10	AR610051L N 94	ASR2253 N 60	AWJ710040 N 59	AWR2704LDE P 47	AWR4707LUH P 66	AWR5708RPI R 14	AWR5901RFI R 09
ANR6971 E 56	ARA1501L J 01	ASR2254 N 60	AWJ710050 N 60	AWR2704LOY P 47	AWR4708LUH P 65	AWR5712RFI R 14	AWR5902RPI R 09
AQA710040 N 70	ARA1501L J 09	ASR2256 N 59	AWJ710060 N 59	AWR2705 P 48	AWR4708LUH P 66	AWR5716RPI R 19	AWR5903RPI R 09
AQA710060 N 77	ARA1501L J 04	ASR2256 N 60	AWJ710060 N 60	AWR2735LUH P 62	AWR4709LUH P 59	AWR5717RPI R 19	AWR5904RPI R 11
AQA710080 N 82	ARA1502L J 01	ASR2257 N 59	AWR1049LUH P 66	AWR2735LUH P 66	AWR4710LUH P 63	AWR5718RPI R 19	AWR5905RFI R 11
AQA710110 N 74	ARA1502L J 09	ASR2257 N 60	AWR1168 L 49	AWR2735LUH P 58	AWR4710LUH P 59	AWR5719RPI R 19	AWR5963RPI R 34
AQA710180 N 89	ARR710100 N 93	ASR2348 N 73	AWR1169 L 72	AWR2736LUH P 62	AWR4731 R 14	AWR5721RPI R 19	AWR5964RPI R 32
AQA710190 N 89	ARR710110 N 93	ASR2449 N115	AWR1170 L 72	AWR2736LUH P 58	AWR4782 L 34	AWR5722RFI R 18	AWR5986LOY P 16
AQA710200 N 89	AS604044 N 66	ASR2449 N118	AWR1173 L 49	AWR2738 N136	AWR5007 P 09	AWR5723RFI R 18	AWR5987 P 12
AQA710210 N 89	AS604044 N113	ASR2449 N117	AWR1173 L 50	AWR2816 R 28	AWR5035 P 09	AWR5724RFI R 18	AWR5988 P 12
AQA710290 N 87	ASB710040 N 56	ASR2450 N115	AWR1174 L 69	AWR2896 P 34	AWR5036 P 09	AWR5725RFI R 18	AWR6158LRV M 90
AQA710380 N 71	ASB710050 N 56	ASR2450 N118	AWR1175 P 02	AWR3029LUH P 59	AWR5037 P 09	AWR5726RFI R 18	AWR6175 P 17
AQA710390 N 78	ASB710200 N 55	ASR2450 N117	AWR1177 L 50	AWR3030LUH P 62	AWR5393LDE P 35	AWR5734RFI R 24	AWR6232 L 33
AQA710400 N 83	ASB710210 N 55	ASR2451 N115	AWR1179 L 68	AWR3031LUH P 64	AWR5393LOY P 36	AWR5735RFI R 22	AWR6233 L 33
AQA710420 N 88	ASB710260 N 56	ASR2451 N117	AWR1242 L 49	AWR3032LNP P 60	AWR5394LDE P 35	AWR5736RFI R 25	AWR6234 L 41
AQF710010 N250	ASB710270 N 56	ASR2452 N115	AWR1245 L 71	AWR3032LOY P 60	AWR5394LOY P 36	AWR5737RFI R 26	AWR6235 L 41
AQH000020 N 78	ASB710280 N 56	ASR2452 N117	AWR1247 L 70	AWR3044LUH P 62	AWR5395LDE P 35	AWR5738RFI R 22	AWR6236 L 41
AQH000020 N 83	ASB710290 N 56	ASR2667 N196	AWR1249 L 50	AWR3044LUH P 58	AWR5395LOY P 36	AWR5739RFI R 23	AWR6237 L 41
AQH000020 N 71	ASJ710010 N145	ASR2668 N196	AWR1448 L 69	AWR3140 N167	AWR5396LDE P 35	AWR5740RFI R 25	AWR6421LNF P 33
AQH000020 N 88	ASJ710040 N145	ASR710100 N 55	AWR1545LNF P 68	AWR3140 N163	AWR5396LOY P 36	AWR5741RFI R 26	AWR6506 H 04
AQH000030 N 78	ASJ710050 N145	ASR710110 N 55	AWR1546LNF P 68	AWR3151LNP P 54	AWR5397LDE P 36	AWR5742RFI R 23	AWR6525 N221
AQH000030 N 83	ASR1018 N181	ASU1009 M 88	AWR1547LNF P 68	AWR3151LOY P 54	AWR5397LOY P 37	AWR5743RFI R 24	AWR6599 N 25

AWR6600	N 25
AWR6631	L 44
AWR6632	L 44
AWR6683	P 17
AWR6713LOY	P 35
AWR6715	R 35
AWR6715	E 69
AWR6715	P 17
AWR6715	N141
AWR6863	R 39
AWR6874	N221
AWR7044RFI	R 39
AWR7046RPI	R 39
AWR7092	N160
AYA10004L	N144
AYB100750	N 29
AYF10001L	R 14
AYG100230	N 23
AYG100230	N 24
AYG100240	N 97
AYG100240	N 98
AYG100240	N 95
AYG100250	R 71
AYH100800	N138
AYH100810	N 30
AYH101200	N201
AZ610081	P 07
AZF100050	N 43
BAA10082	N152
BAC001110	N152
BAC103320	N152
BAC103370	N152
BAU1689	D 05
BAU1689	C 37
BAU1689	E 50
BAU1825	B 43
BAU1825	B 91
BAU1825	B138
BAU1825	B358
BAU1825	B359
BAU2144	M 01
BAU2193	B 43
BAU2193	B 91
BAU2193	B138
BAU2195	B 43
BAU2195	B 91
BAU2195	B138
BAU2195L	B358
BAU2195L	B359
BAU4611L	B128
BAU4611L	B175
BAU4865	F 12
BAU4870	F 12
BAU4871	F 12
BAU5325L	B387

BD155888	M152
BD155888L	N 28
BDA710020	N153
BDA710030	N153
BDB710020	N156
BDB710030	N156
BDB710040	N156
BDB710040	N168
BDB710050	N156
BDB710050	N168
BDB710160	N156
BDB710170	N156
BDB710180	N156
BDB710180	N168
BDB710190	N156
BDB710190	N168
BDU1496L	B249
BDU1649L	B267
BDU710060	N161
BDU710070	N161
BDV710080	N154
BDV710090	N154
BFH710020	N170
BFH710030	N170
BFL710020	N164
BFL710030	N164
BFO710020	N164
BFO710030	N164
BFO710040	N164
BFO710050	N164
BFP1265L	N193
BFP1265L	N189
BFP1265L	N190
BFU710020	N170
BFU710030	N170
BFU710070	N197
BH106051L	B303
BH106051L	B 13
BH106051L	B 62
BH106051L	D 31
BH106051L	D 33
BH106061L	H 10
BH106061L	H 19
BH106061L	H 22
BH106061L	C 08
BH106061L	C 07
BH106061L	H 11
BH106071	N179
BH106071	R 15
BH106091L	H 14
BH106091L	H 11
BH106111L	N121
BH106111L	H 11
BH106141L	B125
BH106141L	M139

BH106141L	M140
BH106141L	M141
BH106141L	M142
BH106141L	M138
BH106151L	B 24
BH106151L	B 72
BH106151L	B125
BH106151L	B172
BH106501L	M 32
BH108061M	E 20
BH108061M	E 22
BH108071L	R 59
BH108077	F 06
BH108081L	B142
BH108081L	C 24
BH108091	K 10
BH108091	K 23
BH108091L	H 36
BH108091L	F 06
BH108091L	B 95
BH108091L	B142
BH108091L	B188
BH108091L	K 03
BH108091L	F 02
BH108091L	H 19
BH108091L	B 45
BH108091L	B227
BH108091L	K 14
BH108091L	K 24
BH108091L	K 25
BH108111L	D 31
BH108111L	D 33
BH108131L	B 10
BH108131L	B 58
BH108131L	B110
BH108131L	B159
BH108131L	K 02
BH108131L	K 13
BH108141	K 23
BH108141L	N100
BH108141L	B 73
BH108141L	B 74
BH108141L	K 03
BH108141L	K 10
BH108141L	B 25
BH108141L	B 26
BH108141L	K 15
BH108141L	K 23
BH108151L	B 09
BH108151L	B 10
BH108151L	B 13
BH108151L	B 20
BH108151L	B 58
BH108151L	B 68
BH108151L	B 61

BH108151L	B 62
BH108151L	B113
BH108151L	B114
BH108151L	B162
BH108151L	B163
BH108161L	B 13
BH108161L	B 61
BH108161L	B 62
BH108161L	B 95
BH108161L	B113
BH108161L	B114
BH108161L	B142
BH108161L	B188
BH108161L	B 45
BH108161L	B227
BH108161L	B162
BH108161L	B163
BH108171L	B 13
BH108171L	B 61
BH108171L	B 62
BH108171L	B113
BH108171L	B114
BH108171L	B162
BH108171L	B163
BH108181L	B221
BH108181L	B181
BH108181L	D 04
BH108181L	B 87
BH108181L	B137
BH108181L	B 83
BH108181L	B 84
BH108181L	B132
BH108181L	B133
BH108181L	B 36
BH108181L	B 37
BH108181L	B 40
BH108181L	B224
BH108181L	B184
BH108201L	B 10
BH108201L	B 58
BH108201L	B110
BH108201L	B159
BH108201L	B 95
BH108201L	B 45
BH108201L	B 26
BH108201L	N 15
BH108201L	N 16
BH108201L	N 07
BH110081L	D 09
BH110081L	T 30
BH110081L	T 34
BH110081L	D 10
BH110081L	D 06
BH110091L	B230
BH110091L	B191

BH110091L	D 08
BH110091L	D 09
BH110091L	C 30
BH110091L	T 06
BH110091L	B143
BH110091L	B144
BH110091L	B146
BH110091L	B148
BH110091L	B229
BH110091L	B189
BH110091L	D 10
BH110091L	J 03
BH110091L	D 06
BH110101	R 71
BH110101L	C 30
BH110101L	B 87
BH110101L	B137
BH110101L	B 40
BH110101L	B224
BH110101L	B184
BH110121L	C 30
BH110121L	F 18
BH110121L	D 11
BH110181L	N 23
BH110181L	T 34
BH110181L	T 31
BH110201	K 17
BH110201	R 71
BH110201	K 18
BH110201L	B 87
BH110201L	B137
BH110201L	T 30
BH110201L	B 40
BH110201L	B224
BH110201L	B184
BH110201L	T 31
BH110201L	N 08
BH110221L	B348
BH110221L	N 24
BH110221L	N204
BH110221L	C 51
BH110221L	E 63
BH110221L	E 66
BH110241L	N 20
BH110241L	B348
BH110241L	N 24
BH110251	N219
BH110261	C 83
BH110261L	N 20
BH110301L	N219
BH110351	E 69
BH110351	K 31
BH110351	K 33
BH110521	N203
BH112091L	C 06

BH112101L	T 33
BH112101L	E 33
BH112101L	E 34
BH112101L	E 35
BH112101L	E 36
BH112101L	E 37
BH112101L	E 07
BH112101L	E 09
BH112121L	F 07
BH112121L	F 08
BH112121L	F 11
BH112141L	C 29
BH112141L	T 35
BH112241L	T 35
BH114167	E 57
BH116101	T 31
BH116107	T 40
BH116121L	T 30
BH116127	T 37
BH116127	T 38
BH116127	T 40
BH116161L	T 32
BH116187	E 56
BH116201	T 31
BH116207	E 56
BH116261	T 32
BH116261	T 39
BH504101L	B308
BH504101L	B309
BH504121L	B341
BH504121L	B342
BH504121L	B343
BH504151L	B308
BH504151L	B309
BH504151L	B349
BH504161L	B308
BH504161L	B309
BH505111L	B334
BH505111L	B363
BH505111L	B364
BH505121L	B308
BH505121L	B309
BH505161L	B309
BH505201L	B348
BH505241L	B307
BH505401L	B308
BH505401L	B309
BH505401L	B341
BH505441L	B349
BH506111L	B348
BH506111L	B363
BH506111L	B364
BH506121L	B325
BH506161L	C 73
BH506161L	B325

BH506161L	G 05
BH506161L	C 51
BH506201L	B363
BH506201L	B364
BH506441L	B327
BH604081	S 16
BH604151L	F 17
BH604161L	R 30
BH605101L	B349
BH605101L	R 62
BH605101L	B225
BH605111L	B365
BH605121L	B304
BH605121L	B363
BH605131L	B304
BH605201L	B363
BH605261L	B 45
BH607161L	F 08
BH607161L	F 10
BH607161L	F 11
BH607161L	F 09
BH607381	F 07
BH608381	E 57
BH608461	E 57
BH610281L	E 56
BH610321L	E 61
BH612321	E 62
BHA4705L	N187
BHA4790L	M128
BHA5131L	M 75
BHB710050	N176
BHB710050SVR	N176
BHB710051	N176
BHB710060	N177
BHB710060SVR	N177
BHB710061	N177
BHC710010	N157
BHC710010	N169
BHI710030	S 13
BHM1079L	B344
BHM7058L	M 01
BHM7063L	C 28
BHM7063L	C 45
BHM7063L	C 02
BHQ710020	N181
BHZ110010	N174
BIC110030	N171
BIC110040	N171
BIC710200	N174
BIC710210	N174
BIC710220	N174
BIC710230	N174
BKA710030	N140
BKV710010	N140
BKV710020	N140

BLS108L	C 32
BLS108L	C 33
BLS108L	C 34
BLS108L	F 13
BLS112L	C 46
BLS112L	C 21
BLS112L	T 05
BMK1714	M 75
BMK1903	G 09
BMK2466	H 23
BMK2466	H 19
BMK2466	H 21
BNP2227L	H 24
BNP2227L	H 22
BNP4556	N184
BNP4556L	N159
BNP4556L	N161
BRC1393	N193
BRC1393	N194
BRC1393	N188
BRC1393	N189
BRC5803	N 63
BRC8089L	M 46
BRC8965PMA	N194
BRC8965PMA	N189
BT606101L	D 18
BTP1826	L 03
BTP1827	L 03
BTP2275	L 03
BTP2282	L 03
BTP2284	L 03
BTP2601S	L 03
BTR1045	N206
BTR1045	N208
BTR1047	N222
BTR1047	N206
BTR1047	N208
BTR1048	N206
BTR1049	N208
BTR1050	N208
BTR1051	N208
BTR1052RUK	N214
BTR1053RUK	N214
BTR1054RUK	N216
BTR1055RUK	N216
BTR1056RUV	N216
BTR1056RUW	N216
BTR1057RUV	N216
BTR1057RUW	N216
BTR1109	L 33
BTR1116	L 33
BTR1117	L 33
BTR1130	L 39
BTR1131	L 39
BTR1132	L 39

BTR1133	L 39
BTR1134	L 42
BTR1135	L 42
BTR1136	L 43
BTR1137	L 43
BTR1155	R 56
BTR1194LDE	P 40
BTR1194LOY	P 40
BTR1197PMA	P 42
BTR1198	P 39
BTR1200LDE	P 35
BTR1347	L 76
BTR1348	L 76
BTR1349	L 38
BTR1599	L 38
BTR1599	L 75
BTR1600	L 38
BTR1600	L 75
BTR162RUV	N216
BTR162RUW	N216
BTR163RUV	N216
BTR163RUW	N216
BTR164RUV	N216
BTR164RUW	N216
BTR165RUV	N216
BTR165RUW	N216
BTR166RUV	N214
BTR1679	P 39
BTR167RUV	N214
BTR1680	P 39
BTR1681LDE	P 36
BTR1682LDE	P 36
BTR1683	P 37
BTR1698	C 69
BTR1698	N 34
BTR1758RUY	R 11
BTR1759LCS	R 11
BTR1760RUY	R 10
BTR1761RUY	R 10
BTR1762LCS	R 10
BTR1762RPI	R 11
BTR1763LCS	R 10
BTR1763RPI	R 11
BTR1764RUY	R 07
BTR1765RUY	R 07
BTR1766LCS	R 07
BTR1767LCS	R 07
BTR1790	N199
BTR1875	P 32
BTR1884PMA	N 20
BTR1884PMA	R 54
BTR1884PMA	R 48
BTR1884PMA	R 49
BTR1884PMA	R 51
BTR1886LUH	P 62

BTR1886LUH	P 58
BTR2129NAL	T 03
BTR2129NUC	T 03
BTR213	L 60
BTR214	L 60
BTR2307	P 12
BTR2308	M 49
BTR2371	P 31
BTR2372	P 31
BTR2407RWF	N215
BTR2407RWF	N217
BTR2408RWF	N215
BTR2408RWF	N217
BTR2409RWF	N217
BTR2410RWF	N217
BTR2411RWF	N217
BTR2412RWF	N217
BTR2413SUJ	N215
BTR2413SUJ	N217
BTR2414RWF	N215
BTR2414RWF	N217
BTR2415RWF	N215
BTR2415RWF	N217
BTR2416RWF	N215
BTR2417RWF	N215
BTR2745RWF	N217
BTR2746RWF	N217
BTR277	T 53
BTR2934LCS	R 36
BTR2935RUY	R 36
BTR2936LCS	R 39
BTR2937RUY	R 39
BTR2940	M 13
BTR2980RWF	N217
BTR2981LVA	N206
BTR2981LYV	N206
BTR2982LVA	N208
BTR2982LYV	N208
BTR2983LVA	N208
BTR2983LYV	N208
BTR2984LVA	N208
BTR2984LYV	N208
BTR304	R 54
BTR305LNP	P 54
BTR305LOY	P 54
BTR306LNP	P 54
BTR306LOY	P 54
BTR3100LNF	P 17
BTR328	L 02
BTR341	P 26
BTR3415	P 34
BTR360	P 26
BTR361	P 50
BTR362	P 50
BTR363	P 50

BTR364	P 50
BTR365	P 50
BTR3720	L 45
BTR3792LCS	M143
BTR3792LCS	P 23
BTR3793LCS	P 23
BTR389	N152
BTR4317	L 33
BTR4318	L 33
BTR4346	R 52
BTR4347	R 52
BTR4348	R 52
BTR4372	R 54
BTR4372	R 48
BTR4372	R 49
BTR4373	R 54
BTR4373	R 48
BTR4373	R 49
BTR4376	R 49
BTR4414	M 13
BTR4433	L 36
BTR4434	L 36
BTR445	L 39
BTR447	L 39
BTR4525LUH	P 62
BTR4525LUH	P 58
BTR514LVA	N215
BTR514LVA	N217
BTR514LYV	N215
BTR514LYV	N217
BTR514MUB	N214
BTR514MUB	N216
BTR516LVA	N215
BTR516LVA	N217
BTR516LYV	N215
BTR516LYV	N217
BTR516MUB	N214
BTR516MUB	N216
BTR5232	P 28
BTR5233	P 28
BTR5234	P 29
BTR5235	P 29
BTR5236	P 29
BTR5437LNP	P 54
BTR5437LOY	P 54
BTR5438LNP	P 54
BTR5438LOY	P 54
BTR549	S 09
BTR550	S 09
BTR5750	B394
BTR5779	R 54
BTR5781	R 56
BTR5782	R 56
BTR5818	R 39
BTR586LUH	P 59

BTR6113	N203
BTR6113	N204
BTR6141	B213
BTR6141	B 24
BTR6164	L 40
BTR6165	L 40
BTR6188	J 63
BTR6188	J 64
BTR6189	P 34
BTR6193	P 30
BTR6194	P 30
BTR6333PUC	P 33
BTR6334PUC	P 33
BTR6506	P 17
BTR6561	R 49
BTR6561	R 51
BTR6562	R 49
BTR6562	R 51
BTR6620PMA	N184
BTR6620PMA	N161
BTR6682	P 55
BTR6700LCS	P 19
BTR6700LOY	P 19
BTR6701LCS	P 19
BTR6701LOY	P 19
BTR6702LCS	P 22
BTR6702LOY	P 22
BTR6702PMA	P 22
BTR6703LCS	P 22
BTR6703LOY	P 22
BTR6703PMA	P 22
BTR6806	N 52
BTR695	P 16
BTR7006LUH	P 63
BTR7071	L 73
BTR7072	L 74
BTR7849PUC	N 57
BTR7850PUC	N 57
BTR7895	P 39
BTR7896	P 39
BTR7897	P 39
BTR7898	P 39
BTR7958	P 17
BTR7959LCS	P 23
BTR7964LCS	P 23
BTR8039	P 25
BTR8040L	N 09
BTR8114	P 37
BTR8115	P 37
BTR8116	P 37
BTR8117	P 37
BTR8311	N204
BTR8312	N204
BTR8313	N204
BTR8332PMA	C 84

BTR8334PMA	C 84
BTR8335PMA	C 84
BTR8336	C 84
BTR8358	L 43
BTR8395	L 40
BTR8396	L 40
BTR8410	R 48
BTR8411	R 48
BTR8505	B259
BTR8593LDQ	M123
BTR8691	T 24
BTR8704MUL	N209
BTR8705MUL	N209
BTR8714	V 05
BTR8720	V 05
BTR8736	L 37
BTR912	P 01
BTR9126	N 64
BTR9176LUH	P 58
BTR9177LUH	P 59
BTR9178LUH	P 62
BTR9179LUH	P 64
BTR9180LUH	P 59
BTR9181LUH	P 62
BTR9181LUH	P 58
BTR9183LUH	P 66
BTR9270	C 69
BTR9320	P 39
BTR9321LDE	P 35
BTR9385LUH	P 59
BTR9400	L 60
BTR9401	L 60
BTR9402	L 60
BTR9419	B222
BTR9419	B 85
BTR9419	B 86
BTR9419	B134
BTR9419	B346
BTR9419	B347
BTR9419	B135
BTR9419	B223
BTR9547	P 17
BTR9552	M123
BTR9552	M125
BTR9614	M112
BTR9615	M112
BTR9623	C 84
BTR9625	R 57
BTR9626	R 57
BTR9627	R 57
BTR9712LCS	P 24
BTR9712LOY	P 24
BTR9712PMA	P 24
BTR9714LCS	P 24
BTR9714LOY	P 24

BTR9714PMA	P 24
BTR9715LCS	P 24
BTR9715LOY	P 24
BTR9715PMA	P 24
BTR9723LCS	P 24
BTR9723LOY	P 24
BTR9723PMA	P 24
BTR978	P 31
BTR979	P 31
BTR980	P 31
BTR981	P 31
BTR982	L 39
BTR983	L 39
BTR984	L 62
BTR985	L 62
BTR986	L 62
BTR987	L 62
BTR988	L 62
BTR988	L 39
BTR9884	R 57
BTR98RUK	N214
BTR9926LNF	P 13
BX108130	E 43
BX110071M	B212
BX110071M	B 23
BX110071M	B 47
BX110071M	B 71
BX110071M	B 98
BX110071M	B124
BX110071M	B171
BX110071M	D 08
BX110071M	E 20
BX110071M	E 21
BX110071M	E 48
BX110071M	D 10
BX110071M	T 31
BX110091L	E 62
BX110095M	E 49
BX110095M	E 26
BX110111L	E 62
BX110111L	E 48
BX112091	B249
BX112201	T 33
BX112201	F 07
BX112201	F 08
BX112201	F 11
BX112201	F 09
BX116201L	E 57
BYF100050	N157
BYG100140	N157
BYG100140L	N157
BYG100150	N157
BYG100150	N168
BYG100150L	N157
BYG100150L	N168

BYG100160	N169
BYG100160L	N169
BYG100170	N169
BYG100170L	N169
BYG100190	N176
BYG100190	N177
BYG100210	N157
BYG100220	N157
BYG100220	N168
BYG100230	N169
BYG100240	N169
BYG100250	N178
BYG100260	N178
BYH100110	N140
BYH100120	N140
BYH100130	N176
BYH100130	N177
BZV1051	C 55
C15644	M132
C15644L	M130
C34950L	M139
C34950L	M140
C34950L	M141
C34950L	M142
C34950L	M138
C37222L	B 44
C37222L	B 91
C37222L	B138
C37222L	B358
C37222L	B359
C38637L	M 88
C393771L	M145
C393771L	M 58
C393771L	M127
C39377L	M 46
C39377L	M145
C39377L	M 57
C43231L	B391
C435996L	B 30
C43640	B318
C43640	M109
C43640	M147
C43640	B334
C43640	M101
C45099	J 68
C45099	M 70
C45099	M130
C45099	J 71
C457593	B385
C457593	B 24
C457593	B 72
C457593	B172
C457593L	B125
C457593L	B324
C46082	M 33

C46082	M 34
CA600424	J 73
CA600424	J 61
CAR10003L	T 18
CAT100960	T 51
CAT101110	T 51
CAX100140	T 52
CAX100150	T 52
CCN110L	E 12
CCN110L	E 40
CCN110L	E 42
CDU1001L	B270
CDU51	C 55
CFE000710	N160
CFE000720	N160
CFE102720	N163
CFE102730	N163
CFE102980	N163
CFE102990	N163
CFE103000	N166
CFE103010	N166
CJ600144L	B324
CJ600144L	M139
CJ600144L	M140
CJ600144L	M141
CJ600144L	M142
CJ600144L	M138
CJ600164L	J 36
CJ600224	B170
CJ600304L	B213
CJ600504L	J 33
CJ600504L	J 46
CJ600504L	J 37
CJ600504L	J 36
CJ600564	J 37
CJE100770	N141
CKE101100	N127
CKE101110	N127
CKE101120	N182
CLF000280	N 63
CLF000290	N 63
CLP3180	G 08
CLP8934	M149
CMB000410	N185
CMB000420	N185
CN100148L	B 22
CN100148L	B 70
CN100168L	J 49
CN100168L	J 50
CN100168L	J 20
CN100168L	J 23
CN100168L	H 05
CN100168L	J 70
CN100168L	J 22
CN100208	L 08

CN100208L B248
CN100208L B 22
CN100208L B 70
CN100208L B123
CN100208L F 23
CN100208L F 25
CN100208L F 27
CN100208L L 18
CN100208L B211
CN100258L B248
CN100258L B 24
CN100258L B 72
CN100258L B125
CN100258L B172
CN100258L B123
CN100258L J 39
CN100258L L 60
CN100258L L 61
CN100258L L 62
CN100258L L 63
CN100258L L 64
CN100258L L 42
CN100258L F 23
CN100258L F 24
CN100258L F 26
CN100258L L 39
CN100258L L 40
CN100258L B211
CN100258L B178
CN100258L L 41
CN100308L B241
CN100308L J 60
CN100308L L 60
CN100308L L 63
CN100308L L 64
CN100308L L 43
CN100308L L 19
CN100308L B339
CN100308L J 18
CN100308L L 44
CN100308L L 15
CN100308L B329
CN100308L J 42
CN100408 L 14
CN100408 L 15
CN100408L B204
CN100408L B 14
CN100408L B 61
CN100408L B 62
CN100408L B113
CN100408L B114
CN100408L B162
CN100408L B163
CN100508 L 18
CN100508L E 01

CN100508L L 17
CN100508L L 19
CN100508L J 73
CN100508L L 18
CN100508L L 14
CN100508L L 15
CN100608L L 18
CN100708 J 39
CN100708 L 12
CN100708 J 41
CN100808L J 42
CN100908 J 43
CN100908L J 38
CN100908L J 39
CN100908L J 16
CN100908L J 41
CN100908L J 42
CP105061 M 63
CP105081 J 18
CP105081 J 67
CP105121L M100
CP105121L H 08
CP106081 J 67
CP108081L J 65
CP108081L J 72
CP108081L M 63
CP108105L L 11
CP108251L B244
CP110161 B178
CQB000140 N174
CQB000150 N174
CQB000270 N174
CQB101560 N172
CR110301 L 26
CR110625 B273
CR120081L G 11
CR120105L C 68
CR120105L C 22
CR120115L B 34
CR120115L B 81
CR120125L D 29
CR120171L B 87
CR120171L B 40
CR120195 B 83
CR120195 B132
CR120195 B 36
CR120205 R 05
CR120205 R 12
CR120215 D 30
CR120215L D 32
CR120215L D 35
CR120215L D 33
CR120305 B205
CR120335L C 68
CR120335L C 23

CRC1226 B323
CRC1250 H 10
CRC1250 H 11
CRC1250L N193
CRC1250L H 12
CRC1250L H 13
CRC1250L H 15
CRC1250L H 20
CRC1250L H 22
CRC1250L N189
CRC1487 H 16
CRC1487 H 17
CRC1487 H 18
CRC1487 H 10
CRC1487 H 12
CRC1487 H 13
CRC1487 H 14
CRC1487 H 19
CRC1487 H 22
CRC1487 H 11
CRC2015 F 01
CRC209 F 01
CRC209 F 03
CRC2128 H 04
CRC2130 H 04
CRC2131 H 01
CRC2131 H 04
CRC2131 H 08
CRC2131 H 09
CRC2133 H 08
CRC2134 H 08
CRC2135 H 01
CRC2135 H 04
CRC2135 H 08
CRC2143 H 04
CRC2144 H 08
CRC4579L K 05
CS600244L H 02
CS600244L H 05
CS600244L H 08
CS600244L H 09
CUB000040 N160
CUB000050 N160
CUB000060 N160
CUB000070 N160
CUD2399L B333
CUD2785L B333
CUD2788L B333
CUH000080 N161
CUH000090 N161
CUH000100 N161
CUH000110 N161
CVW000010 N174
CWH000010 N194
CWH000010 N197

CWN100020L N196
CXB000020PMA N188
CXB000030PMA N188
CYF000020 T 52
CYF000020 T 53
CYK100050L U 02
CYK100070L U 02
CZA2259L N187
CZA4705L P 01
CZA4705L P 07
CZA4705L N 34
CZA4705L N 44
CZA4705L N 61
CZA4705L P 04
CZG1946 B298
CZH3827L M 87
CZH677L P 04
CZK3164 M123
CZK3164 M124
CZK3164 M127
CZK3264L N187
CZK3438L N186
CZK3882 P 14
CZK619 L 34
DA606059L M 16
DA608031 P 04
DA608044L P 22
DA608044L M143
DA608044L P 24
DA608044L P 23
DA608044L P 17
DA608044L P 21
DA608044L P 20
DA608054 P 04
DA608055L P 04
DA608084 P 04
DA610044 M 90
DA610051L N 30
DA610051L M 95
DA610054 J 42
DAF105360LYV N206
DAF105360LYV N208
DAF105360MMG N206
DAF105360MMG N208
DAG000040 N209
DAG100290 L 74
DAG100390H N209
DAG100400H N209
DAH100680 N206
DAM100750LQQ N209
DAM100750LQQ N206
DAM100750LQQ N208
DAS100130 N208
DAS100150 N206
DBP5840PMA N193

DBP5840PMA N189
DBP5841PMA N193
DBP5841PMA N189
DBP6287PMA N184
DBP6287PMA N161
DBP6532PMA P 22
DBP6532PMA P 21
DBP6532PMA P 20
DBP6533PMA P 22
DBP6533PMA P 21
DBP6533PMA P 20
DBP8169L M151
DCP3212L G 08
DCP3969L H 16
DCP5671 M100
DCP7299L M152
DCP7384L B254
DHH100780PUC N 57
DHH100790PUC N 57
DJH000010 N247
DJL000010 N246
DKB000050PMD M129
DKB000060PMD M129
DKC000110PMD M129
DKC100980 M144
DKE000010 M128
DKU000010 M129
DLB000200 M128
DLC000030 M128
DLE000010 M128
DLP000010 M129
DLW000020 M128
DLY000010 M128
DLZ000010 M128
DMB103060 M134
DMB103090 M137
DMC100540 M137
DMC100550 M134
DMC100550 M137
DMG10001L M134
DMG10001L M137
DNC101720 M134
DNC101720 M137
DOS000020 M128
DPB103870 N 19
DPB104270 N 19
DPT100070 N 20
DQB102390 N204
DRC1245 M109
DRC1245 M 93
DRC1245 M 95
DRC1530 M 79
DRC1530 M139
DRC1530 M140
DRC1530 M141

DRC1530 M142
DRC1530 M138
DRC1538 B318
DRC1538 M147
DRC1666 N 28
DRC2479 B314
DRC2713L M136
DRC2713L M133
DRC2713L M140
DRC2713L M141
DRC2713L M142
DRC5017L M145
DRC5582 P 04
DRC8398 M111
DRM10001L N 52
DSB000020ABE N236
DSB000060ABE N229
DSB000070ABE N229
DSB000080ABE N225
DSB000090ABE N225
DSB000100ABE N226
DSB000110ABE N226
DSB100390ABE N235
DSB100400ABE N235
DSB100410ABE N232
DSB100420ABE N235
DSB100430ABE N232
DSB100440ABE N235
DUV100010 N252
DYB000030 M129
DYC101410L H 06
DYF100760 N 19
DYF100760 N137
DYF100760 N138
DYF100780 N 19
DYG100720 N 24
DYG100720 T 37
DYG100720 T 38
DYH10048 N 52
DYP101480 P 25
DZA1435L N194
DZA5097L P 06
DZM100080 N 20
EAC2414L B387
EAC32151 B389
EAC32151 B 79
EAD101960LOY P 44
EAD102020LOY P 38
EAD102030LOY P 38
EAD102040LOY P 38
EAD102050LOY P 38
EAD102060LOY P 38
EAD102070LOY P 38
EAD102160LOY P 38
EAD102170LOY P 38

EAD102180LOY P 38
EAD102190LOY P 38
EAD102200LOY P 38
EAD102210LOY P 38
EAD102240LOY P 27
EAE000060LOY P 38
EAE000070LOY P 38
EAE101180LOY P 38
EAE101190LOY P 38
EAE101200LOY P 38
EAE101210LOY P 38
EAH105070 P 48
EAM5549L M139
EAM5549L M140
EAM5549L M141
EAM5549L M142
EAM5549L M138
EAM9332 M143
EAY10010L P 32
EDB103130LUH P 59
EDP7510L G 08
EEP118L M 90
EEP119L M 90
EEP120L M 90
EEP191L H 34
EGP1661L E 68
EGP1889 E 68
EIO100000 R 70
EIO100010 R 70
EIO100020 R 70
EIO100030 R 70
EIO100080 R 70
EIO100090 R 70
EIO100100 R 70
EIO100110 R 70
EIO100160 R 70
EIO100170 R 70
EIQ100020 B373
EJB000720LOY P 19
EJB000730LOY P 19
EJB001020LOY P 19
EJB001030LOY P 19
EJB120040LOY P 19
EJB120040PMA P 21
EJB120050LOY P 19
EJB120050PMA P 21
EJD000100 N153
EJD000110 N153
EJP7738L C 66
EKC000030PMA N196
EKE100000 M127
EKM100100L P 25
ELB000520LOY P 22
ELB000530LOY P 22
ELD000080 N164

ELD000090 N164
ELD000100 N164
ELD000110 N164
ELD106060 N164
ELD106070 N164
EMB1542 L 74
EOZ100000 S 19
ERC1351 B314
ERC1353 B350
ERC1353 B351
ERC1353 B352
ERC1561 B212
ERC1561 B 23
ERC1561 B 71
ERC1561 B124
ERC1561 B171
ERC1637 B319
ERC1637 B381
ERC2042L B337
ERC210 B315
ERC210 B316
ERC211 B315
ERC211 B316
ERC2135 B323
ERC2139 B324
ERC2143 B324
ERC2144 B320
ERC215 B315
ERC2154 B330
ERC2154 B331
ERC2226L L 30
ERC224 B315
ERC224 B316
ERC224 B381
ERC225 B315
ERC225 B316
ERC2254 B 19
ERC2254 B 67
ERC2254 B119
ERC2254 B167
ERC2297 B323
ERC2319 B324
ERC2320 B324
ERC2446 B336
ERC255 B388
ERC256 B323
ERC2734 K 03
ERC2838 B322
ERC2839 B322
ERC2866 B 22
ERC2869 B 04
ERC2869 B 53
ERC2920 B318
ERC2973 B303
ERC298 B 80

ERC298 B 30
ERC2989 B320
ERC3102 B326
ERC3163 B336
ERC3256 B 42
ERC3256 B 90
ERC3345 B361
ERC3346 B315
ERC3346L B315
ERC3458 B328
ERC3489 B324
ERC3493 B323
ERC3500 L 29
ERC3561 B323
ERC3562 B324
ERC3563 B324
ERC3579 B388
ERC3579 B391
ERC3588 B329
ERC3690 B328
ERC3690 B327
ERC3699 B327
ERC3724 L 29
ERC3729 B323
ERC3792L B391
ERC3884 J 73
ERC3890 J 73
ERC3891 J 73
ERC3892 J 34
ERC3893 J 34
ERC3894 J 60
ERC3896 J 34
ERC3897 J 34
ERC3899 J 60
ERC3899 J 73
ERC3899 J 61
ERC3915 J 60
ERC3915 B338
ERC3915 B339
ERC3930 B321
ERC3931 B321
ERC3946 J 34
ERC3954 J 34
ERC3955 J 69
ERC3955 J 34
ERC3956 J 60
ERC3956 B338
ERC3956 B339
ERC3956 J 73
ERC3964 L 60
ERC3964 L 61
ERC3964 L 63
ERC3964 L 64
ERC4074 J 73
ERC4074 J 61

ERC416 B304
ERC416 B374
ERC417 B304
ERC417 B374
ERC4176 J 69
ERC4193 B337
ERC4203 B329
ERC4204 B329
ERC4215 B391
ERC4293 J 73
ERC4294 J 73
ERC4480 B129
ERC4536 B350
ERC4591 J 73
ERC4644 B195
ERC4644 B 03
ERC4644 B 51
ERC4644 B102
ERC4644 B152
ERC4658 B230
ERC4658 B 47
ERC4658 B 98
ERC4658 B191
ERC4658 B147
ERC4670 B321
ERC4820 B323
ERC4877 B304
ERC4878 B304
ERC4879 B304
ERC4880 B304
ERC4949 B319
ERC4949 B382
ERC4989 B327
ERC4995 B 03
ERC4995 B 51
ERC4995 B 52
ERC4995 B102
ERC4995 B104
ERC4995 B152
ERC4995 B153
ERC4996 B195
ERC4996 B233
ERC4996 B 03
ERC4996 B 51
ERC4996 B 52
ERC4996 B102
ERC4996 B104
ERC4996 B152
ERC4996 B153
ERC5014 B 05
ERC5052 J 73
ERC5052 J 61
ERC5068 B326
ERC5068 B327
ERC5086 B 08

ERC5086 B 57
ERC5086 B103
ERC5086 B153
ERC5127 B 05
ERC5127 B 54
ERC5128 B 05
ERC5128 B 54
ERC5139 B 95
ERC5139 B142
ERC5139 B188
ERC5139 B 45
ERC5145 B 83
ERC5145 B132
ERC5145 B 36
ERC5146 B 83
ERC5146 B132
ERC5146 B 36
ERC5152 B 87
ERC5152 B137
ERC5152 B 40
ERC5152 B224
ERC5152 B184
ERC5155 B 87
ERC5155 B137
ERC5155 B 40
ERC5155 B224
ERC5155 B184
ERC5247 J 60
ERC5247 B338
ERC5247 B339
ERC5247 J 61
ERC5293 B 47
ERC5293 B 98
ERC5349 B 05
ERC5349 B 54
ERC5361 B 09
ERC5361 B 58
ERC5386 B 87
ERC5386 B 40
ERC5387 B 87
ERC5387 B 40
ERC5400 J 73
ERC5400 J 61
ERC5401 J 73
ERC5401 J 61
ERC5453 J 61
ERC5512 B320
ERC5545 B 13
ERC5545 B 61
ERC5545 B113
ERC5578 B 13
ERC5578 B 61
ERC5578 B113
ERC5600 B204
ERC5600 B 13

ERC5600 B 61
ERC5600 B 62
ERC5600 B113
ERC5600 B114
ERC5600 B162
ERC5600 B163
ERC5654 B 14
ERC5654 B 61
ERC5654 B 62
ERC5654 B113
ERC5654 B114
ERC5654 B162
ERC5654 B163
ERC5655 B204
ERC5655 B 13
ERC5655 B 61
ERC5655 B 62
ERC5655 B113
ERC5655 B114
ERC5655 B162
ERC5655 B163
ERC5705 B309
ERC5707 B311
ERC5708 B 14
ERC5708 B 62
ERC5708 B114
ERC5708 B311
ERC5709 B204
ERC5709 B 14
ERC5709 B 62
ERC5709 B114
ERC5709 B311
ERC5709 B162
ERC5709 B163
ERC573 B381
ERC5745 B350
ERC5749 B322
ERC5756 L 26
ERC5757 L 26
ERC5761 B303
ERC5786 B328
ERC5830 B357
ERC5830 B364
ERC5830 B365
ERC5830 B366
ERC5875 B386
ERC5875 B328
ERC5913 B206
ERC5913 B243
ERC5913 B 65
ERC5913 B116
ERC5913 B165
ERC5913 B 66
ERC5913 B117
ERC5913 B 17

ERC5913 B 18
ERC5923 B206
ERC5923 B243
ERC5923 B165
ERC5923 B 66
ERC5923 B117
ERC5923 L 29
ERC5923 L 26
ERC5923 B 18
ERC5925 B327
ERC6047 B126
ERC6071 B 87
ERC6071 B 40
ERC6072 B 86
ERC6072 B 39
ERC614 B320
ERC614 B381
ERC6200 B 22
ERC6200 B 70
ERC6266 B 95
ERC6266 B142
ERC6266 B188
ERC6266 B227
ERC6337 B 20
ERC6337 B 68
ERC6337 B120
ERC6337 B168
ERC6341 B 20
ERC6341 B 68
ERC6341 B120
ERC6341 B168
ERC6362 B331
ERC6363 B331
ERC6364 B330
ERC6365 B330
ERC6380 B 19
ERC6380 B 67
ERC6399 J 73
ERC6408 B 47
ERC6408 B 98
ERC6432 B 47
ERC6432 B146
ERC6478 B125
ERC6479 B 10
ERC6479 B 59
ERC6479 B110
ERC6479 B159
ERC6480 B222
ERC6480 B 38
ERC6480 B 85
ERC6480 B182
ERC6480 B 86
ERC6480 B134
ERC6480 B346
ERC6480 B347

ERC6480 B 39
ERC6480 B135
ERC6480 B223
ERC6480 B183
ERC6504 B163
ERC6538 B365
ERC6540 B311
ERC6545 B348
ERC6547 B365
ERC6551 B230
ERC6551 B 47
ERC6551 B 98
ERC6551 B191
ERC6551 B147
ERC6552 B322
ERC6683 B 45
ERC6691 B 25
ERC6720 L 29
ERC6722 L 29
ERC6723 L 29
ERC675 B313
ERC675 B341
ERC675 B312
ERC676 B315
ERC6761 B128
ERC6761E B128
ERC6821 B 19
ERC6821 B 67
ERC6821 B119
ERC6821 B167
ERC6859 B198
ERC6859 B106
ERC6859 B155
ERC6860 B106
ERC6860 B155
ERC6861 B198
ERC6861 B106
ERC6861 B155
ERC6869 B 09
ERC6869 B 58
ERC6878 J 60
ERC6878 B338
ERC6878 B339
ERC6878 B329
ERC6886 B138
ERC6890 L 29
ERC6934 B303
ERC6939 B126
ERC6974 B181
ERC6974 B 83
ERC6974 B 84
ERC6974 B132
ERC6974 B133
ERC6974 B 36
ERC6974 B 37

ERC6975 B 83
ERC6975 B132
ERC6975 B 36
ERC6976 B 83
ERC6976 B132
ERC6976 B 36
ERC6977 B 83
ERC6977 B132
ERC6977 B 36
ERC6996 B 32
ERC6996 B 78
ERC6997 B331
ERC7082 B 87
ERC7082 B137
ERC7082 B 40
ERC7082 B224
ERC7082 B184
ERC7089 B 05
ERC7089 B 54
ERC7131 B350
ERC7144 J 73
ERC7295 B230
ERC7295 B263
ERC7295 B 47
ERC7295 B 98
ERC7295 B110
ERC7295 B159
ERC7295 B191
ERC7295 B146
ERC7295 B148
ERC7312 B 13
ERC7312 B 61
ERC7312 B 62
ERC7312 B113
ERC7312 B114
ERC7312 B162
ERC7312 B163
ERC7313 B 13
ERC7321 B386
ERC7321 B326
ERC7321 B327
ERC7343 B 29
ERC7489 B 13
ERC7489 B 61
ERC7489 B113
ERC7489 B162
ERC7494 B348
ERC7510 B 24
ERC7510 B 72
ERC7510 B125
ERC7510 B172
ERC7530 B 15
ERC7530 B 63
ERC7530 B 64
ERC7530 B115

ERC7530 B164
ERC7548 B365
ERC7611 B327
ERC7629 B329
ERC7630 B329
ERC7631 B329
ERC7744 B336
ERC7755 L 26
ERC7756 L 26
ERC7757 L 26
ERC7773 L 26
ERC7834 B163
ERC7865 B316
ERC7871 B 13
ERC7881 J 73
ERC7882 J 73
ERC7896 B327
ERC7897 B327
ERC7922 B 80
ERC7922 B 29
ERC7929 B322
ERC7929 B384
ERC7940 B 15
ERC7940 B 63
ERC7940 B 64
ERC7940 B115
ERC7940 B164
ERC7974 B142
ERC7974 B188
ERC7974 B227
ERC7987 B 09
ERC7987 B 58
ERC8049 B170
ERC8119 B 32
ERC8119 B 78
ERC8124 B 73
ERC8124 B 25
ERC8164 B311
ERC8406 B 15
ERC8408 B115
ERC8408 B164
ERC8447 B 83
ERC8447 B132
ERC8447 B 36
ERC8450 B119
ERC8450 B167
ERC8460 B 73
ERC8460 B 25
ERC8501 L 30
ERC8505 J 34
ERC8520 B 42
ERC8626 B335
ERC8631 B 29
ERC8639 B324
ERC8645 B 73

ERC8645	B 25
ERC8663	B166
ERC8663	B118
ERC8712	B 74
ERC8712	B 26
ERC8722	B 46
ERC8722	B 97
ERC8722	B 75
ERC8751	B 06
ERC8751	B 55
ERC8751	B107
ERC8751	B156
ERC8757	B125
ERC8758	B 24
ERC8758	B 72
ERC8758	B125
ERC8758	B172
ERC8847	B212
ERC8847	B124
ERC8847	B171
ERC8849	B212
ERC8849	B124
ERC8849	B171
ERC8851	B361
ERC8861	B112
ERC8861	B161
ERC8864	B196
ERC8864	B103
ERC8864	B153
ERC8890	B 13
ERC8890	B 62
ERC8906	B334
ERC8907	B334
ERC8938	B 14
ERC8938	B 62
ERC8964	B 09
ERC8964	B 10
ERC8964	B 58
ERC8964	B142
ERC8964	B188
ERC8964	B227
ERC8973	B 19
ERC8973	B 67
ERC8975	B 11
ERC8976	B 16
ERC8980	B200
ERC8980	B 07
ERC8980	B 56
ERC8980	B108
ERC8980	B157
ERC8986	B 43
ERC8986	B 93
ERC8986	B140
ERC8987	B 44
ERC8987	B 93
ERC8987	B140
ERC9031	B 22
ERC9031	B 70
ERC9032	B 22
ERC9032	B 70
ERC9033	B 22
ERC9033	B 70
ERC9035	B329
ERC9037	J 73
ERC9039	B329
ERC9054	B 20
ERC9054	B 68
ERC9054	B120
ERC9054	B168
ERC9055	B120
ERC9055	B168
ERC9056	B120
ERC9056	B168
ERC9059	B120
ERC9059	B168
ERC9060	B120
ERC9060	B168
ERC9069	B 73
ERC9069	B 25
ERC9071	B 73
ERC9071	B 25
ERC9073	B105
ERC9073	B154
ERC9102	B 20
ERC9102	B 68
ERC9103	B 20
ERC9103	B 68
ERC9106	B 20
ERC9106	B 68
ERC9107	B 20
ERC9107	B 68
ERC9110	B390
ERC9137	B120
ERC9137	B168
ERC9138	B 20
ERC9138	B 68
ERC9188	B107
ERC9188	B 52
ERC9188	B104
ERC9199	B110
ERC9199	B159
ERC9201	B110
ERC9201	B160
ERC9213	B334
ERC9220	B 22
ERC9220	B 70
ERC9220	B122
ERC9220	B170
ERC9240	B230
ERC9240	B191
ERC9240	B146
ERC9240	B148
ERC9278	B 20
ERC9278	B 68
ERC9294	B 32
ERC9294	B 78
ERC9348	B 03
ERC9398	B339
ERC9404	B230
ERC9404	B244
ERC9404	B253
ERC9404	B257
ERC9404	B263
ERC9404	B 47
ERC9404	B 59
ERC9404	B 98
ERC9404	B159
ERC9404	B191
ERC9404	M146
ERC9404	M 58
ERC9404	B146
ERC9404	B148
ERC9404	M 66
ERC9404	B153
ERC9404	M 65
ERC9410	B196
ERC9410	B234
ERC9410	B 08
ERC9410	B 57
ERC9410	B103
ERC9410	B153
ERC9432	B119
ERC9432	B167
ERC9448	B 19
ERC9448	B 67
ERC9448	B119
ERC9448	B167
ERC9468	B 10
ERC9468	B 58
ERC9480	B197
ERC9480	B 04
ERC9480	B 53
ERC9480	B105
ERC9480	B154
ERC9480	M 66
ERC9480	M 65
ERC9499	L 26
ERC9501	B166
ERC9501	B118
ERC9519	B 09
ERC9519	B 58
ERC9528	B 09
ERC9528	B 58
ERC9631	B166
ERC9631	B118
ERC9688	B126
ERC9693	B 34
ERC9693	B 81
ERC9704	B 34
ERC9704	B 81
ERC9706	B205
ERC9706	B 15
ERC9706	B 63
ERC9706	B 64
ERC9706	B115
ERC9706	B164
ERC9708	B 34
ERC9708	B 81
ERC9728	B122
ERC9765	B106
ERC9765	B155
ERC9884	B 65
ERC9884	B116
ERC9884	B 17
ERC9896	B 29
ERR1019	B207
ERR1019	B244
ERR1040	B238
ERR1041	B238
ERR1063	B205
ERR1063	B 15
ERR1063	B 63
ERR1063	B 64
ERR1063	B115
ERR1063	B164
ERR1084	B238
ERR1085	B238
ERR1086	B238
ERR1088	B205
ERR1088	B 15
ERR1088	B 63
ERR1088	B 64
ERR1088	B115
ERR1088	B164
ERR1092	B240
ERR1094	B234
ERR1101	B374
ERR1107	B208
ERR1117	B 15
ERR1117	B 63
ERR1117	B115
ERR1117	B164
ERR1125	B216
ERR1125	B218
ERR1125	B253
ERR1125	B255
ERR1125	B177
ERR1125	J 56
ERR1125	B178
ERR1156	B209
ERR1156	B246
ERR1157	B209
ERR117	B386
ERR1178	B205
ERR118	B203
ERR1181	B198
ERR1181	B 54
ERR1181	B106
ERR1181	B155
ERR1197	B208
ERR1200	B217
ERR1200	B254
ERR1201	B208
ERR1202	B208
ERR1203	B208
ERR1203	B245
ERR1208	B214
ERR1209	B208
ERR1209	B245
ERR1210	B208
ERR1223	B166
ERR1223	B118
ERR1230	B121
ERR1253	B202
ERR1256	B202
ERR1259	B176
ERR1260	B177
ERR1261	B388
ERR1262	B388
ERR1264	B221
ERR1266	B129
ERR1266	B176
ERR1273	B202
ERR1274	B202
ERR1291	B200
ERR1299	B206
ERR1304	B217
ERR1304	B254
ERR1330	B230
ERR1333	B216
ERR1333E	B216
ERR1347	B165
ERR1347	B 66
ERR1347	B117
ERR1347	B 18
ERR1351	B248
ERR1390	B199
ERR1391	B199
ERR1424	B204
ERR1435	B214
ERR1436	L 62
ERR1436	L 39
ERR1440	B230
ERR1454	B 22
ERR1454	B 70
ERR1454	B122
ERR1458	B218
ERR1471	B248
ERR1471	B123
ERR1471	B211
ERR1475	B197
ERR1475	B 04
ERR1475	B 53
ERR1475	B105
ERR1475	B154
ERR1499	B213
ERR1509	B217
ERR1510	B 67
ERR1510	B166
ERR1510	B118
ERR1521	B205
ERR1530	B210
ERR1535	B230
ERR1535	B 05
ERR1535	B 47
ERR1535	B 54
ERR1535	B 98
ERR1535	B106
ERR1535	B155
ERR1535	B191
ERR1536	B207
ERR1553	B202
ERR1560	B239
ERR1561	B239
ERR1564	B235
ERR1570	B108
ERR1574	B357
ERR1574	B366
ERR1605	B123
ERR1605	B211
ERR1607	B202
ERR1607	B 09
ERR1607	B 58
ERR1607	B110
ERR1607	B159
ERR1621	B210
ERR1630	B198
ERR1630	B235
ERR1630	B 05
ERR1630	B 54
ERR1630	B106
ERR1630	B155
ERR1632	B307
ERR1632	B110
ERR1632	B159
ERR1642	B198
ERR1653	B234
ERR1653	B237
ERR1662	B216
ERR1729	B123
ERR1729	B211
ERR1756	B388
ERR1772	B375
ERR1773	B375
ERR1780	B316
ERR1780	B381
ERR1782	B316
ERR1782	B381
ERR1790	B200
ERR1885	B357
ERR1885	B366
ERR1919	B233
ERR1921	B319
ERR1922L	B303
ERR1939	B244
ERR1972	B240
ERR1973	B240
ERR1976	B221
ERR1976	B181
ERR1976	B 84
ERR1976	B133
ERR1990	B314
ERR2023	B253
ERR2026	B197
ERR2026	B248
ERR2026	B 04
ERR2026	B 53
ERR2026	B105
ERR2026	B154
ERR2026	B123
ERR2026	B211
ERR2027	B257
ERR2028	B215
ERR2028	B252
ERR2028	B127
ERR2028	B174
ERR2073	B356
ERR2073	B313
ERR2073	B362
ERR2081	B244
ERR2081	B279
ERR2081	B289
ERR2081	B287
ERR2100	B235
ERR2109	B255
ERR2112	B235
ERR2215	B259
ERR2216	B249
ERR2216	B253
ERR2220	B235
ERR2228	B258
ERR2241	B206
ERR2241	B243
ERR2264	B370
ERR2266	B242
ERR2317	B243
ERR2337	J 40
ERR2337	J 44
ERR2337	J 75
ERR2337	J 77
ERR2344	B239
ERR2375	B202
ERR2393	B210
ERR2396	B244
ERR2405	B245
ERR2409	B247
ERR2410	B236
ERR2418	B236
ERR2419	B236
ERR2428	B308
ERR2428	B309
ERR2429	B385
ERR2429	B324
ERR244	J 53
ERR25	B202
ERR2529	B210
ERR2530	B203
ERR2532	B230
ERR2532	B 05
ERR2532	B 47
ERR2532	B 54
ERR2532	B 98
ERR2532	B106
ERR2532	B155
ERR2532	B191
ERR2532	B147
ERR2532	B148
ERR2533	B326
ERR2535	B326
ERR2551	B316
ERR2605	B221
ERR2605	B181
ERR2605	B 84
ERR2605	B133
ERR2609	B384
ERR2623	B206
ERR2639	B104
ERR2640	B303
ERR2640	B373
ERR2711	B206
ERR2732	B245
ERR2767	B233
ERR2789	B242
ERR2798	B260
ERR2803	B213
ERR2846	B304
ERR2846	B374
ERR2850	J 40
ERR2851	J 40
ERR2860	B166

ERR2860	B118
ERR2861	B166
ERR2861	B118
ERR2943	B317
ERR2943	B381
ERR2944	B317
ERR2944	B381
ERR2946	J 35
ERR2958	B304
ERR2958	B374
ERR2966	B387
ERR2970	B395
ERR3	B195
ERR3062	B394
ERR3062	B393
ERR3081	B166
ERR3081	B118
ERR3082	B166
ERR3082	B118
ERR3084	B248
ERR309	B205
ERR3091	B 87
ERR3091	B137
ERR3091	B224
ERR3091	B184
ERR314	B209
ERR3283	B243
ERR3284	B241
ERR3286	B239
ERR3287	B242
ERR3291	B250
ERR3299	B237
ERR3314	J 75
ERR3319	J 75
ERR333	B218
ERR3330	B373
ERR3331	B373
ERR3339	B254
ERR3339E	B254
ERR334	B218
ERR3340	B206
ERR3340	B243
ERR3340	B314
ERR3340	B378
ERR3340	B 65
ERR3340	B116
ERR3340	B165
ERR3340	B 66
ERR3340	B117
ERR3340	B 17
ERR3340	B 18
ERR3342	B245
ERR3343	B245
ERR335	B218
ERR335	B255
ERR335	B178
ERR3356	B238
ERR3359	B388
ERR3359	B398
ERR3368	B210
ERR3380	B204
ERR3380	B 13
ERR3380	B 62
ERR3380	B114
ERR3380	B162
ERR3380	B163
ERR3417	B237
ERR3419	B233
ERR3424	B247
ERR3439	B380
ERR3440	B379
ERR3440	B394
ERR3443	B380
ERR3457	B245
ERR3468	B254
ERR3479	B250
ERR3481	B251
ERR3490	B250
ERR3494	B218
ERR3494	B178
ERR3495	B218
ERR3495	B178
ERR3539	B257
ERR3545	B249
ERR3545	B253
ERR3547	B249
ERR3579	J 75
ERR3580	J 75
ERR3581	J 75
ERR3583	J 75
ERR359	B216
ERR3592	B374
ERR3604	B202
ERR3604	B111
ERR3604	B160
ERR3605	B197
ERR3605	B 04
ERR3605	B 53
ERR3605	B105
ERR3605	B154
ERR3605	B123
ERR3605	B211
ERR3606	B205
ERR3606	B 15
ERR3606	B 63
ERR3606	B115
ERR3606	B164
ERR3607	B206
ERR3607	B165
ERR3614	B110
ERR3614	B160
ERR3615	B110
ERR3615	B159
ERR3616	B110
ERR3616	B160
ERR3617	B128
ERR3617	B175
ERR3618	B119
ERR3618	B167
ERR362	B126
ERR3622	B250
ERR3633	B237
ERR3648	B315
ERR3648	B316
ERR3648	B381
ERR3650	B316
ERR3652	B217
ERR3671	B394
ERR3677	B306
ERR3677	B376
ERR3682	B213
ERR3682	B 24
ERR3682	B 72
ERR3682	B125
ERR3682	B172
ERR3683	B237
ERR3683	B272
ERR3693	B373
ERR371	L 62
ERR371	L 39
ERR3712	B391
ERR3720	B384
ERR3733	B258
ERR3734	B241
ERR3735	B242
ERR3736	B241
ERR3737	B250
ERR3738	B250
ERR3753	B244
ERR3754	B249
ERR3756	B249
ERR3758	B374
ERR3759	B374
ERR3760	B374
ERR3777	B246
ERR3779	B245
ERR3780	B254
ERR3785	B251
ERR3788	B306
ERR3788	B376
ERR3799	B 90
ERR3799	B395
ERR3799	B350
ERR3799	B351
ERR3807	B260
ERR3809	B237
ERR3907	B279
ERR3907	B283
ERR3920	B146
ERR3920	B148
ERR3924	B230
ERR394	B202
ERR3987	B235
ERR4000	B251
ERR4001	B251
ERR4021	B390
ERR4046	B253
ERR4047	J 75
ERR4052	B394
ERR4053	B393
ERR4054	B393
ERR4060	B304
ERR4066	B393
ERR4077	B379
ERR4085	M 95
ERR4120	B239
ERR4157	B373
ERR4175	B209
ERR4175	B246
ERR4175	B169
ERR4175	B121
ERR4175	B 69
ERR4179	B233
ERR4194	B380
ERR4199	B373
ERR4225	B388
ERR4235	B390
ERR4237	B383
ERR4245	K 05
ERR4248	B316
ERR4258	B383
ERR4258	B389
ERR4278	B388
ERR4278	B398
ERR4285	B352
ERR4309	B385
ERR4314	B373
ERR4315	B373
ERR4318	B388
ERR4352	B388
ERR4352	B398
ERR4381	B330
ERR4381	B331
ERR4383	B331
ERR4384	B 80
ERR4384	B 29
ERR4385	B 73
ERR4385	B 25
ERR4386	B 73
ERR4386	B 25
ERR4387	B 73
ERR4387	B 25
ERR4388	B389
ERR4389	B385
ERR4410	B395
ERR4415	B395
ERR4419	B253
ERR4419E	B253
ERR4427	B393
ERR4450	B377
ERR4513	B394
ERR4519L	B363
ERR4519L	B364
ERR4524	B348
ERR4531	L 40
ERR4541	B387
ERR4543	B260
ERR455	B210
ERR4556	B303
ERR4563	B383
ERR4566	B390
ERR4574	B230
ERR4574	B263
ERR4574	B 47
ERR4574	B 98
ERR4574	B191
ERR4574	B147
ERR4574	B148
ERR4575	B238
ERR4576	B238
ERR4578	B238
ERR4598	B280
ERR4621	B217
ERR4621	B254
ERR4628	B319
ERR4628	B381
ERR4632	B247
ERR4633	B306
ERR4633	B376
ERR4638	B259
ERR4639	B259
ERR4640	B209
ERR4640	B246
ERR4640	B 21
ERR4640	B169
ERR4640	B121
ERR4640	B 69
ERR4664	B238
ERR4679	B393
ERR4682	B208
ERR4685	B250
ERR4685	L 03
ERR4686	B250
ERR4686	L 03
ERR4687	B245
ERR4688	J 40
ERR4691	B247
ERR4696	B237
ERR4697	B237
ERR4698	B256
ERR4699	B251
ERR4706	B248
ERR4707	B235
ERR4708	B241
ERR4709	B249
ERR4710	B235
ERR4716	B 07
ERR4716	B 56
ERR4716	B108
ERR4716	B157
ERR4723	B263
ERR4725	B253
ERR4735	B316
ERR477	B 52
ERR478	B104
ERR479	B153
ERR4802	B255
ERR4802E	B255
ERR4815	B398
ERR4818	B383
ERR4819	B383
ERR4820	B385
ERR4821	B250
ERR4824	B239
ERR4834	B247
ERR4837	B375
ERR4848	B245
ERR4852	B255
ERR4859	B261
ERR4860	B238
ERR4861	B233
ERR4862	J 75
ERR4868	B393
ERR4883	B245
ERR4886	B385
ERR4894	B255
ERR4895	B255
ERR4905	B377
ERR4908	B230
ERR4908	B263
ERR4922	B374
ERR4923	B325
ERR4926	B248
ERR4926	J 39
ERR4933	B 22
ERR4933	B 70
ERR4934	B 65
ERR4934	B116
ERR4934	B 66
ERR4934	B117
ERR4934	B 17
ERR4934	B 18
ERR4935	B323
ERR4936	B307
ERR4937	B387
ERR4944	B388
ERR500	B205
ERR5000	B383
ERR5007	B388
ERR5008	B386
ERR5009	B262
ERR5009	B228
ERR5009	B144
ERR5009	B145
ERR5009	B229
ERR5009	B189
ERR5009	B190
ERR5009E	B262
ERR5009E	B228
ERR5009E	B145
ERR5009E	B190
ERR5010	B386
ERR5023	B386
ERR5024	B386
ERR5027	B244
ERR5032	B398
ERR5033	M 97
ERR5034	B195
ERR5034	B233
ERR5034	B 51
ERR5034	B 52
ERR5034	B102
ERR5034	B104
ERR5034	B152
ERR5034	B153
ERR5039	B389
ERR5041	B210
ERR5041	B247
ERR5045	B385
ERR5055	J 75
ERR5057	B252
ERR506	B197
ERR506	B123
ERR506	B211
ERR5086	B384
ERR5087	B235
ERR5090	B374
ERR5098	B250
ERR5099	B241
ERR5103	B388
ERR5194	K 05
ERR5194	C 53
ERR5215	B235
ERR5215	B268
ERR5217	B383
ERR5218	B383
ERR5219	B383
ERR5238	B385
ERR5259	B241
ERR5261	B207
ERR5261	B244
ERR5262	B207
ERR5262	B244
ERR5263	B207
ERR5263	B244
ERR5278	B267
ERR528	B205
ERR5285	B273
ERR5291	B268
ERR530	B205
ERR531	B205
ERR531	B 52
ERR531	B104
ERR531	B153
ERR532	B205
ERR5345	B268
ERR535	B220
ERR535	B131
ERR535	B180
ERR5369	B280
ERR5384	B280
ERR539	B 80
ERR539	B 29
ERR5391	B374
ERR541	B205
ERR5439	B383
ERR5448	B316
ERR5473	B385
ERR5474	B385
ERR551L	B214
ERR551L	B218
ERR551L	B386
ERR551L	B293
ERR5529	B280
ERR5529	B282
ERR5553	B375
ERR5575	B370
ERR5579	B380
ERR5579	B394
ERR559	B208
ERR5594	B398
ERR5595	J 35
ERR560	B208
ERR560	B245
ERR561	B209
ERR561	B246
ERR561	B 21
ERR561	B169
ERR561	B121
ERR561	B 69

ERR5617	B279	ERR6417	B287	ERR696	B213	ERR7249	B239	ERR896	B178	ESR1594L	L 28	ESR2215	K 30	ESR2756	J 07
ERR5658	B399	ERR6490	B307	ERR6977	B267	ERR7266	B284	ERR900	B203	ESR1615	L 23	ESR228	J 38	ESR276	J 38
ERR5691	B241	ERR6490	B378	ERR6978	B269	ERR7280	B378	ERR900	B240	ESR1617	K 12	ESR2297	K 17	ESR280	L 27
ERR5731	J 75	ERR6490	B110	ERR6996	B296	ERR7283	B385	ERR913	B195	ESR1650	J 15	ESR2298	L 19	ESR2806	C 86
ERR5732	J 75	ERR6490	B159	ERR6997	B296	ERR7283	B325	ERR913	B233	ESR1676	L 01	ESR2308	L 05	ESR281	L 27
ERR5795	B386	ERR6493	B278	ERR6999	B296	ERR7288	B320	ERR928	B205	ESR1677	L 01	ESR2308	L 03	ESR282	L 02
ERR586	B 52	ERR6505	B275	ERR6999E	B296	ERR7288	B383	ERR977	B 24	ESR1678	L 02	ESR2309	L 12	ESR282	L 03
ERR586	B104	ERR6581	B268	ERR7000	B296	ERR7293	B239	ERR977	B172	ESR1686	L 18	ESR2313	L 08	ESR2821	J 07
ERR586	B153	ERR6611	B279	ERR7002	B237	ERR7296	B260	ERR978	B207	ESR169	K 02	ESR2315	J 63	ESR283	L 02
ERR5911	B242	ERR6611	B283	ERR7004	B279	ERR7297	B260	ESN000200LOY	P 25	ESR169	K 12	ESR2343	L 08	ESR283	L 03
ERR593	B107	ERR6612	B279	ERR7004	B287	ERR7306	B385	ESR1004	J 38	ESR169	K 01	ESR2344	L 08	ESR289	L 18
ERR593	B156	ERR6612	B283	ERR703	B199	ERR7306	B325	ESR1004	J 37	ESR169	K 11	ESR2345	L 08	ESR2934	L 18
ERR595	B 55	ERR6616	B279	ERR703	B236	ERR7307	L 07	ESR1005	J 38	ESR169	K 14	ESR2348	L 08	ESR2945	K 17
ERR5958	B278	ERR6616	B287	ERR7032	B289	ERR7338	B381	ESR1005	J 37	ESR1696	K 27	ESR2348	L 18	ESR2945	K 18
ERR597	B214	ERR6620	J 76	ERR7033	B294	ERR7340	B248	ESR101	K 05	ESR1800	L 03	ESR2381	K 28	ESR298	L 18
ERR5992	B273	ERR663	B210	ERR7042	B273	ERR736	B 22	ESR1127	J 45	ESR184	J 38	ESR2382	K 28	ESR299	L 18
ERR6013	B279	ERR6658	B295	ERR7043	B273	ERR736	B 70	ESR1128	J 45	ESR1906	L 18	ESR2383	K 30	ESR301	M149
ERR6013	B283	ERR6658	B277	ERR7047	B275	ERR736	B122	ESR1225	J 45	ESR1912	L 27	ESR2384	K 30	ESR301	G 03
ERR605	B198	ERR6658	B278	ERR7049	B279	ERR736	B170	ESR1253	C 86	ESR1913	L 27	ESR2385	K 30	ESR301	J 30
ERR605	B 54	ERR6659	B295	ERR705	B198	ERR737	B122	ESR1262	L 30	ESR1914	L 30	ESR2386	K 30	ESR301	J 27
ERR605	B106	ERR6659	B277	ERR705	B 54	ERR737	B170	ESR1262	L 27	ESR1915	L 30	ESR2421	K 28	ESR301	J 25
ERR605	B155	ERR6659	B278	ERR705	B106	ERR7386	B260	ESR1265	J 45	ESR1916	L 22	ESR2421	K 31	ESR301	J 28
ERR6064	B279	ERR666	B212	ERR705	B155	ERR7387	B260	ESR1269	J 45	ESR1917	L 22	ESR2421	K 26	ESR3028	J 39
ERR6064	B287	ERR667	B216	ERR7050	B279	ERR743	B 90	ESR1277	J 65	ESR1918	L 22	ESR2421	K 32	ESR3028	J 41
ERR6066	B279	ERR6674	B279	ERR7060	B279	ERR751	B198	ESR1277	J 68	ESR1919	L 22	ESR2422	B251	ESR3032	J 39
ERR607	B209	ERR6676	B279	ERR7065	B280	ERR765	B207	ESR1277	J 72	ESR1920	L 22	ESR245	J 29	ESR3098	L 31
ERR607	B246	ERR6689	B290	ERR7065	B282	ERR806	B229	ESR1278	J 65	ESR1931	L 28	ESR246	J 26	ESR3105	J 75
ERR607	B 21	ERR6700	B253	ERR7070	B274	ERR807	B229	ESR1278	J 72	ESR1935	J 57	ESR247	J 27	ESR3107	J 75
ERR607	B169	ERR6704	B388	ERR7072	B285	ERR808	B229	ESR1287	J 74	ESR203	L 02	ESR254	K 26	ESR3111	J 39
ERR607	B121	ERR6704	B391	ERR7094	B284	ERR848	B205	ESR1287	J 14	ESR2033	K 28	ESR255	K 27	ESR3118	J 56
ERR607	B 69	ERR6709	B284	ERR7097	B289	ERR850	B205	ESR1287	J 16	ESR2033	K 31	ESR2593	L 07	ESR3121	L 19
ERR6087	B369	ERR6711	B275	ERR7098	B291	ERR850	B 15	ESR1287	J 70	ESR2033	B286	ESR2623	J 39	ESR3124	J 29
ERR6087E	B369	ERR6711	B294	ERR7133	M100	ERR850	B 63	ESR1373	J 30	ESR2033	B293	ESR2629	L 28	ESR3124	J 26
ERR6107	B378	ERR6761	B279	ERR7134	B284	ERR850	B115	ESR1373	J 23	ESR2033	K 29	ESR2657	J 07	ESR3125	J 25
ERR6117	B374	ERR6761	B287	ERR7135	B284	ERR850	B164	ESR1373	J 27	ESR2033	K 33	ESR266	K 16	ESR3125	J 28
ERR6119	B398	ERR6768	B286	ERR7143	B238	ERR852	L 29	ESR1373	J 40	ESR2033	N174	ESR266	K 14	ESR3127	J 29
ERR6126	B378	ERR678	B214	ERR7154	B244	ERR852	L 30	ESR1373	J 25	ESR2034	K 17	ESR2662	L 19	ESR3127	J 26
ERR6170	B398	ERR6794	B388	ERR7155	B284	ERR874	B248	ESR1373	J 28	ESR2034	K 18	ESR2681	J 18	ESR3128	J 29
ERR6189	B388	ERR6811	B233	ERR7173	J 75	ERR874	B123	ESR1404	J 23	ESR2034	B293	ESR2687	K 05	ESR3129	J 28
ERR6192	B279	ERR6818	B233	ERR7177	B269	ERR874	B211	ESR1554	L 24	ESR204	L 02	ESR2691	J 48	ESR3130	J 29
ERR6192	B289	ERR6824	B280	ERR719	B230	ERR877	B123	ESR1579	J 35	ESR2055	L 12	ESR2692	J 07	ESR3132	J 25
ERR6192	B287	ERR6825	B280	ERR719	B263	ERR877	B211	ESR158	K 16	ESR208	K 16	ESR2693	J 07	ESR3133	J 26
ERR6197	L 40	ERR6835	B253	ERR7217	B381	ERR878	B123	ESR1584	L 61	ESR2087	K 28	ESR2694	J 18	ESR3134	J 26
ERR6220	B278	ERR6859	B284	ERR7218	B316	ERR878	B211	ESR1584	L 64	ESR2087	K 30	ESR2727	L 03	ESR3135	J 30
ERR6233	M 97	ERR6862	B279	ERR722	B387	ERR879	B123	ESR1584	L 29	ESR2087	K 29	ESR2728	L 12	ESR3135	J 27
ERR6269	B395	ERR6885	B274	ERR7220	B291	ERR879	B211	ESR1584	L 26	ESR2102	J 39	ESR2729	L 12	ESR3135	J 24
ERR6299	B291	ERR6938	M100	ERR7225	B279	ERR886	B216	ESR1584	L 27	ESR2119	L 12	ESR2730	L 12	ESR3135	J 25
ERR631	B216	ERR6948	B276	ERR7231	B280	ERR886	B251	ESR1584	L 22	ESR2120	L 12	ESR2731	J 39	ESR3135	J 28
ERR635	B202	ERR6949	B295	ERR7231	B282	ERR886	B253	ESR159	K 14	ESR2125	L 15	ESR2732	J 18	ESR3141	J 66
ERR6354	B279	ERR6949	B277	ERR7233	B283	ERR894	B216	ESR1594	L 23	ESR2131	K 29	ESR2733	L 09	ESR3152	K 30
ERR6354	B283	ERR6949	B278	ERR7234	B280	ERR894	B244	ESR1594	L 25	ESR219	K 16	ESR2734	L 09	ESR3162	J 39
ERR6378	B274	ERR6951	B277	ERR7234	B283	ERR894	B251	ESR1594	L 28	ESR219	K 14	ESR2739	K 17	ESR3162	J 41
ERR6382	K 06	ERR6951	B278	ERR7236	B283	ERR894	B253	ESR1594L	C 86	ESR2191	B369	ESR2750	J 23	ESR3167	J 68
ERR6401	B271	ERR6953	B269	ERR7237	B283	ERR894	J 56	ESR1594L	L 31	ESR2204	J 04	ESR2751	J 23	ESR3167	J 72
ERR6417	B279	ERR6954L	B269	ERR7247	B291	ERR896	B218	ESR1594L	L 23	ESR2212	J 23	ESR2752	J 23	ESR3170	J 68

ESR3172	K 17	ESR3301	L 64	ESR4065	J 57	ESR95	K 05	ETC4122	B159	ETC4371	B183	ETC4751	B 19	ETC5065	B159
ESR3172	K 28	ESR3308	J 75	ESR4106	K 05	ESR95	K 30	ETC4124	B202	ETC4390	B198	ETC4751	B 67	ETC5090	B351
ESR3172	K 18	ESR335	L 05	ESR414	K 26	ESR95	K 27	ETC4124	B111	ETC4390	B106	ETC4751	B166	ETC5147	J 73
ESR3172	K 31	ESR3353	E 01	ESR414	K 27	EST000010PMA	P 25	ETC4124	B160	ETC4390	B155	ETC4751	B118	ETC5155	B 06
ESR3172	K 24	ESR3436	L 08	ESR415	B218	ETC4006	G 13	ETC4133	B 46	ETC4417	B128	ETC4752	B128	ETC5155	B 55
ESR3172	K 06	ESR3436	L 18	ESR415	J 38	ETC4014	B124	ETC4133	B 97	ETC4417	B175	ETC4752	B175	ETC5155	B107
ESR3172	K 30	ESR3463	K 28	ESR419	J 70	ETC4014	B171	ETC4140	B 23	ETC4420	B110	ETC4761	B 24	ETC5155	B156
ESR3172	K 29	ESR3482	J 18	ESR421	J 70	ETC4021	B206	ETC4140	B 71	ETC4420	B160	ETC4761	B 72	ETC5155	B147
ESR3172	K 32	ESR3495	K 17	ESR4218	C 86	ETC4021	B 65	ETC4153	B 83	ETC4421	B110	ETC4761	B125	ETC5157	B 06
ESR3173	J 63	ESR352	J 29	ESR4219	C 86	ETC4021	B116	ETC4153	B132	ETC4421	B159	ETC4761	B172	ETC5172	B 23
ESR3173	J 41	ESR352	J 26	ESR4222	J 66	ETC4021	B165	ETC4153	B 36	ETC4422	B110	ETC4763	B 24	ETC5172	B 71
ESR3175	J 63	ESR3533	J 75	ESR4223	L 17	ETC4021	B 66	ETC4154	B202	ETC4422	B159	ETC4763	B 72	ETC5182	G 11
ESR3175	J 41	ESR3535	J 23	ESR4224	L 10	ETC4021	B117	ETC4154	B110	ETC4440	B128	ETC4765	B385	ETC5183	G 11
ESR3206	J 56	ESR3536	J 23	ESR4226	K 05	ETC4021	B 17	ETC4154	B159	ETC4460	B 20	ETC4785	B204	ETC5187	B 09
ESR3226	L 07	ESR354	J 56	ESR4227	K 05	ETC4021	B 18	ETC4156	B129	ETC4460	B 68	ETC4785	B162	ETC5187	B 58
ESR3229	L 24	ESR354	J 55	ESR4238	J 41	ETC4022	B206	ETC4156	B176	ETC4460	B120	ETC4785	B163	ETC5190	B 60
ESR3260	K 17	ESR354	J 59	ESR4290	J 17	ETC4022	B165	ETC4197	B137	ETC4460	B168	ETC4799	B 04	ETC5190	B 12
ESR3263	K 03	ESR358	K 26	ESR4323	J 77	ETC4022	B 66	ETC4197	B224	ETC4466	B 90	ETC4799	B 53	ETC5191	B 60
ESR3263	K 10	ESR359	K 27	ESR439	K 27	ETC4022	B117	ETC4197	B184	ETC4498	B 19	ETC4873	B111	ETC5191	B 12
ESR3263	K 02	ESR360	K 26	ESR4414	J 17	ETC4022	B 18	ETC4212	B 88	ETC4498	B 67	ETC4873	B160	ETC5276	B206
ESR3263	K 12	ESR360	K 05	ESR4438	K 31	ETC4033	B116	ETC4212	B136	ETC4498	B119	ETC4880	B205	ETC5276	B165
ESR3263	K 01	ESR360	K 27	ESR4438	K 06	ETC4033	B165	ETC4212	B 41	ETC4498	B167	ETC4880	B 15	ETC5301	B119
ESR3263	K 11	ESR3607	B385	ESR4438	K 32	ETC4033	B117	ETC4212	B185	ETC4499	B 11	ETC4880	B 63	ETC5305	B 31
ESR3263	K 15	ESR3607	L 60	ESR4504	L 13	ETC4034	B116	ETC4217	B125	ETC4524	K 05	ETC4880	B 64	ETC5305	B 28
ESR3263	K 07	ESR3607	L 43	ESR4525	J 66	ETC4034	B165	ETC4246	B209	ETC4529	B195	ETC4880	B115	ETC5306	B 31
ESR3263	K 08	ESR3607	B339	ESR4526	K 29	ETC4034	B117	ETC4246	B246	ETC4529	B 52	ETC4880	B164	ETC5306	B 28
ESR3263	K 09	ESR3607	L 18	ESR4527	K 29	ETC4058	B110	ETC4246	B 21	ETC4529	B102	ETC4882	B 87	ETC5312	B126
ESR3263	K 22	ESR3607	B329	ESR4578	K 28	ETC4058	B159	ETC4246	B169	ETC4529	B104	ETC4882	B137	ETC5329	B326
ESR3263	K 23	ESR361	K 16	ESR4588	L 07	ETC4063	B110	ETC4246	B121	ETC4529	B152	ETC4882	B 40	ETC5330	B 73
ESR3263	K 25	ESR3663	J 66	ESR4640	L 13	ETC4063	B159	ETC4246	B 69	ETC4529	B153	ETC4882	B224	ETC5331	B126
ESR3277	J 01	ESR3683	L 03	ESR4686	J 59	ETC4067	B 21	ETC4272	B 83	ETC4596	B385	ETC4882	B184	ETC5337	K 02
ESR3277	J 09	ESR3684	L 01	ESR4687	J 24	ETC4067	B 69	ETC4272	B132	ETC4616	B220	ETC4922	B195	ETC5337	K 12
ESR3277	J 11	ESR3685	L 02	ESR4687	J 31	ETC4068	B209	ETC4272	B 36	ETC4616	B131	ETC4922	B233	ETC5340	J 49
ESR3278	J 02	ESR3690	L 28	ESR4687	J 32	ETC4068	B246	ETC4276	B314	ETC4616	B180	ETC4922	B 51	ETC5340	J 50
ESR3278	J 09	ESR3691	L 28	ESR4724	J 59	ETC4068	B 21	ETC4291	B129	ETC4630	B202	ETC4925	B 33	ETC5347	B 65
ESR3278	J 04	ESR3695	C 86	ESR488	L 24	ETC4068	B169	ETC4291	B176	ETC4630	B111	ETC4959	B 80	ETC5347	B116
ESR3281	J 18	ESR370	J 38	ESR489	L 24	ETC4068	B121	ETC4292	B129	ETC4630	B160	ETC4959	B 30	ETC5347	B 17
ESR3281	J 17	ESR3710	J 05	ESR527	L 22	ETC4068	B 69	ETC4292	B176	ETC4639	J 73	ETC4989	L 05	ETC5354	B351
ESR3293	K 30	ESR3737	K 18	ESR530	L 22	ETC4069	B209	ETC4293	B129	ETC4643	B166	ETC4993	L 05	ETC5397	J 68
ESR3294	K 28	ESR3737	K 31	ESR531	L 22	ETC4069	B246	ETC4293	B176	ETC4643	B118	ETC4994	B 09	ETC5397	J 69
ESR3294	K 31	ESR3737	K 06	ESR536	L 18	ETC4069	B 21	ETC4294	B129	ETC4649	B166	ETC4994	B 10	ETC5398	J 69
ESR3294	K 05	ESR3737	K 32	ESR54	K 27	ETC4069	B169	ETC4294	B176	ETC4649	B118	ETC4994	B 58	ETC5412	B 19
ESR3294	K 30	ESR3806	J 05	ESR570	L 22	ETC4069	B121	ETC4308	B129	ETC4650	B113	ETC4995	B 10	ETC5412	B 67
ESR3294	K 29	ESR3806	J 06	ESR571	L 22	ETC4069	B 69	ETC4308	B176	ETC4670	B212	ETC4995	B 58	ETC5524	B391
ESR3294	K 33	ESR3807	J 05	ESR583	L 30	ETC4070	B128	ETC4330	B304	ETC4670	B124	ETC4996	B110	ETC5576	B357
ESR3298	J 23	ESR3807	J 06	ESR584	L 08	ETC4070	B175	ETC4354	B304	ETC4670	B171	ETC4996	B159	ETC5576	B366
ESR3299	J 30	ESR3808	J 05	ESR63	L 08	ETC4076	B212	ETC4357	B 95	ETC4678	G 11	ETC5027	B 79	ETC5577	B244
ESR3299	J 27	ESR3808	J 06	ESR68	L 02	ETC4076	B124	ETC4357	B142	ETC4686	G 11	ETC5040	B 74	ETC5577	B251
ESR3300	J 30	ESR387	J 18	ESR69	L 02	ETC4076	B171	ETC4357	B188	ETC4697	B103	ETC5040	B 26	ETC5577	B 07
ESR3300	J 27	ESR3928	J 07	ESR71	L 27	ETC4077	B198	ETC4357	B 45	ETC4706	B115	ETC5064	B202	ETC5577	B 52
ESR3301	M147	ESR394	J 55	ESR76	L 02	ETC4077	B106	ETC4357	B227	ETC4706	B164	ETC5064	B110	ETC5577	B104
ESR3301	L 60	ESR395	J 55	ESR77	L 01	ETC4077	B155	ETC4369	B304	ETC4709	B 19	ETC5064	B159	ETC5588	B122
ESR3301	L 61	ESR398	L 30	ESR78	L 01	ETC4105	B106	ETC4371	B 86	ETC4715	B351	ETC5065	B202	ETC5588	B170
ESR3301	L 62	ESR399	L 30	ESR79	L 01	ETC4105	B155	ETC4371	B135	ETC4717	B351	ETC5065	B307	ETC5592	B196
ESR3301	L 63	ESR400	L 18	ESR95	K 26	ETC4122	B110	ETC4371	B223	ETC4728L	B335	ETC5065	B110	ETC5592	B234

ETC5592	B103	ETC5958	B125	ETC6492	B173	ETC6932	J 68	ETC7336	B146	ETC7867	B 07	ETC8074	B153	ETC8617	B353
ETC5592	B104	ETC5958	B172	ETC6496	B340	ETC6970	B173	ETC7339	B304	ETC7867	B 56	ETC8086	B199	ETC8618	B353
ETC5592	B153	ETC5964	B381	ETC6510	B 19	ETC6976	B352	ETC7345	B307	ETC7867	B108	ETC8095	B208	ETC8620	B166
ETC5594	B320	ETC5965	B 24	ETC6510	B 67	ETC7012	B339	ETC7351	B218	ETC7867	B157	ETC8103	B208	ETC8620	B118
ETC5603	B 30	ETC5965	B 72	ETC6510	B119	ETC7058	B218	ETC7351	B178	ETC7869	B215	ETC8191	B199	ETC8636	B170
ETC5605	B 30	ETC5965	B125	ETC6510	B167	ETC7058	B177	ETC7353	B388	ETC7869	B127	ETC8191	B236	ETC8663	B209
ETC5609	B 64	ETC5965	B172	ETC6531	B196	ETC7059	B170	ETC7357	B199	ETC7869	B174	ETC8191	B 55	ETC8663	B246
ETC5617	B350	ETC5967	B213	ETC6531	B234	ETC7061	B335	ETC7357	B236	ETC7884	B391	ETC8191	B107	ETC8666	B178
ETC5617	B351	ETC5967	B 24	ETC6531	B103	ETC7091	B175	ETC7357	B 55	ETC7884	D 30	ETC8191	B156	ETC8670S	B156
ETC5665	B341	ETC5967	B 72	ETC6531	B104	ETC7122	B333	ETC7357	B107	ETC7884	D 35	ETC8193	B209	ETC8676	B156
ETC5672	B110	ETC5967	B125	ETC6531	B153	ETC7123	B333	ETC7357	B156	ETC7887	B391	ETC8193	B246	ETC8720	B353
ETC5672	B159	ETC5967	B172	ETC6532	B196	ETC7126	B334	ETC7385	B307	ETC7909	B170	ETC8194	B207	ETC8751	B218
ETC5675	B110	ETC5989	B339	ETC6532	B234	ETC7127	B333	ETC7388	B385	ETC7915	B323	ETC8194	B279	ETC8751E	B218
ETC5675	B159	ETC5990	B339	ETC6532	B103	ETC7128	B212	ETC7390	B364	ETC7917	B173	ETC8352	B195	ETC8765	B357
ETC5689	B340	ETC5994	B 55	ETC6532	B104	ETC7128	B 23	ETC7393	G 12	ETC7929	B197	ETC8352	B233	ETC8765	B366
ETC5700	B149	ETC6081	B 09	ETC6532	B153	ETC7128	B 71	ETC7394	B355	ETC7929	B105	ETC8362	B 52	ETC8767	B152
ETC5710	B218	ETC6081	B 58	ETC6535	B326	ETC7128	B124	ETC7394	B312	ETC7929	B154	ETC8362	B104	ETC8808	B207
ETC5710	B177	ETC6082	B 09	ETC6547	B385	ETC7128	B171	ETC7394	B359	ETC7934	B 05	ETC8412	B217	ETC8808	B244
ETC5717	B128	ETC6137	B 16	ETC6549	B339	ETC7135	B 19	ETC7394	B360	ETC7934	B 54	ETC8412E	B217	ETC8809	B207
ETC5717	B175	ETC6137	B 63	ETC6550	B339	ETC7135	B 67	ETC7395	B214	ETC7934	B106	ETC8440	B365	ETC8810	B207
ETC5739	B169	ETC6137	B115	ETC6579	B339	ETC7135	B119	ETC7395	B173	ETC7934	B155	ETC8441	B357	ETC8810	B244
ETC5739	B121	ETC6137	B164	ETC6581	B339	ETC7136	B175	ETC7398	B200	ETC7939	B204	ETC8441	B364	ETC8820	B218
ETC5740	B169	ETC6138	B 16	ETC6586	B352	ETC7136E	B175	ETC7398	B206	ETC7939	B226	ETC8441	B366	ETC8820	B255
ETC5752	B178	ETC6138	B 63	ETC6607	B341	ETC7144	B 76	ETC7398	L 26	ETC7939	B114	ETC8442	B195	ETC8820	B178
ETC5755	B178	ETC6138	B115	ETC6630	G 11	ETC7184	B218	ETC7398	L 27	ETC7939	B 91	ETC8442	B233	ETC8829	B 54
ETC5755	B153	ETC6138	B164	ETC6640	B178	ETC7184	B177	ETC7503	B173	ETC7939	B 92	ETC8442	B 52	ETC8829	B106
ETC5780	B191	ETC6139	B 16	ETC6647	B341	ETC7186	B177	ETC7530	B208	ETC7939	B 93	ETC8442	B104	ETC8829	B155
ETC5780	B146	ETC6139	B 63	ETC6661	B387	ETC7187	B170	ETC7553L	B311	ETC7939	B 94	ETC8442	B153	ETC8833	B314
ETC5780	B148	ETC6139	B115	ETC6663	B178	ETC7188	J 60	ETC7554	B204	ETC7939	B138	ETC8445	B300	ETC8843	B218
ETC5783	B221	ETC6139	B164	ETC6669	B178	ETC7188	B338	ETC7554	B163	ETC7939	B139	ETC8470	B217	ETC8843	B178
ETC5783	B181	ETC6142	B 16	ETC6675	B128	ETC7188	B339	ETC7558	B178	ETC7939	B140	ETC8494	B387	ETC8847	B207
ETC5783	B 84	ETC6142	B 63	ETC6675	B175	ETC7189	J 60	ETC7582	B 65	ETC7939	B141	ETC8496	B398	ETC8847	B244
ETC5783	B133	ETC6142	B115	ETC6812	L 29	ETC7189	B338	ETC7582	B116	ETC7939	B186	ETC8511	B336	ETC8853	B202
ETC5783	B 37	ETC6142	B164	ETC6841	B162	ETC7189	B339	ETC7582	B 66	ETC7939	B187	ETC8511	B335	ETC8854	B221
ETC5815	B221	ETC6155	B 79	ETC6841	B163	ETC7190	B166	ETC7582	B117	ETC7939	B162	ETC8513	B336	ETC8854	B181
ETC5815	B181	ETC6156	B 79	ETC6849	B322	ETC7193	J 60	ETC7582	B 17	ETC7939	B163	ETC8513	B335	ETC8854	B 84
ETC5815	B 84	ETC6222	B388	ETC6850L	B322	ETC7193	B338	ETC7582	B 18	ETC7947	B 58	ETC8530	B153	ETC8854	B133
ETC5815	B133	ETC6243	B 79	ETC6852	B162	ETC7195	B339	ETC7596	B 03	ETC7969	B122	ETC8550	B203	ETC9064	L 30
ETC5815	B 37	ETC6249	B339	ETC6852	B163	ETC7199	J 60	ETC7596	B 51	ETC7969	J 36	ETC8559	B357	ETC9065	L 30
ETC5816	B167	ETC6278	B 19	ETC6874	B388	ETC7199	B338	ETC7596	B102	ETC7970	B215	ETC8559	B364	ETC9077	B181
ETC5835	B 90	ETC6278	B 67	ETC6881	B149	ETC7199	B339	ETC7596	B152	ETC7970	B127	ETC8559	B365	ETC9077	B 83
ETC5866	B 21	ETC6331	B339	ETC6882	B149	ETC7201	J 60	ETC7633	B173	ETC7970	B174	ETC8559	B366	ETC9077	B 84
ETC5866	B 69	ETC6350	B 76	ETC6883	B149	ETC7201	B338	ETC7654	B178	ETC8001	B207	ETC8560	B240	ETC9077	B133
ETC5898	B218	ETC6375	B387	ETC6884	B149	ETC7201	B339	ETC7667	B177	ETC8002	B207	ETC8579	B357	ETC9077	B 37
ETC5898	B177	ETC6394	B 47	ETC6885	B149	ETC7203	B 21	ETC7668M	B391	ETC8003	B207	ETC8579	B366	ETD000321	P 26
ETC5900N	B 48	ETC6394	B 98	ETC6886	B149	ETC7207	B178	ETC7714	B302	ETC8007	B213	ETC8596	B381	ETD000331	P 26
ETC5918	B339	ETC6408	B341	ETC6887	B149	ETC7238	B204	ETC7750	B173	ETC8031	B207	ETC8600	B170	ETD102940	P 26
ETC5944	B 84	ETC6438	B122	ETC6901	J 53	ETC7238	B162	ETC7750	B126	ETC8031	B244	ETC8604	B320	ETD102943	P 26
ETC5944	B133	ETC6438	B170	ETC6902	J 53	ETC7238	B163	ETC7756	B 88	ETC8036	B207	ETC8610	B353	ETD102950	P 26
ETC5944	B 37	ETC6439	B 22	ETC6903	J 53	ETC7286	B199	ETC7756	B136	ETC8036	B244	ETC8611	B353	ETD102953	P 26
ETC5955	B 22	ETC6439	B 70	ETC6910	B173	ETC7305	B387	ETC7756	B 41	ETC8042	B217	ETC8612	B353	ETD102960	P 26
ETC5955	B 70	ETC6471	B315	ETC6912	B339	ETC7331	B177	ETC7756	B185	ETC8074	B195	ETC8613	B353	ETD102970	P 26
ETC5958	B213	ETC6474	B318	ETC6924	B122	ETC7333	B112	ETC7769	B391	ETC8074	B233	ETC8614	B353	ETD103270	P 26
ETC5958	B 24	ETC6484	B353	ETC6924	B170	ETC7333	B161	ETC7774	B170	ETC8074	B 52	ETC8615	B353	ETD103280	P 26
ETC5958	B 72	ETC6486	B341	ETC6929	B 73	ETC7336	B191	ETC7867	B200	ETC8074	B104	ETC8616	B353	ETK100190	N129

ETK100190	N131	FAY000220PMA	P 09	FB108101L	E 57	FB108181	N 08	FB506267	B393	FN106047L	J 42	FN108041L	J 71	FN108047L	N242
ETL100430	P 39	FAY000230PMA	P 09	FB108101L	N185	FB108181L	R 28	FBS000300	P 12	FN106047L	J 44	FN108041L	J 44	FN108047L	N243
ETL100440	P 39	FAY000240PMA	P 09	FB108101L	R 28	FB108181L	L 54	FBS000310	P 12	FN106047L	L 23	FN108041L	K 25	FN108047L	N245
ETT100230	P 43	FAY000250PMA	P 09	FB108101L	B 73	FB108181M	D 04	FBS100920LOY	P 03	FN106047L	J 77	FN108041L	N241	FN110041	B240
ETT100231	R 12	FB105051L	D 36	FB108101L	C 45	FB108181ML	D 04	FBS100920PMA	P 03	FN106047L	M 95	FN108047L	B245	FN110041	J 03
ETT100240	P 43	FB106067L	L 80	FB108101L	R 40	FB108197	B394	FBS100930LOY	P 03	FN108041	J 08	FN108047L	B254	FN110041L	T 05
ETT100241	R 12	FB106081L	B213	FB108101L	C 41	FB108201L	B202	FBS100930PMA	P 03	FN108041L	B204	FN108047L	B259	FN110041L	D 10
ETZ000020	P 26	FB106081L	S 15	FB108101L	C 08	FB108201L	B238	FBT000010	P 04	FN108041L	B214	FN108047L	B262	FN110047	B240
EUQ100150	N 25	FB106081L	S 14	FB108101L	C 07	FB108201L	L 80	FBT000020	P 04	FN108041L	B216	FN108047L	B396	FN110047	B241
EVB104100	R 53	FB106081L	L 09	FB108101L	B 25	FB108221	B238	FBV000070PMA	M 89	FN108041L	B217	FN108047L	E 56	FN110047	B262
EVB104110	R 53	FB106081L	L 80	FB108101L	R 21	FB108221	J 57	FC106087M	B271	FN108041L	B251	FN108047L	E 57	FN110047	D 09
EVB104150	R 49	FB106111L	B248	FB108111	C 55	FB108227	B396	FC108137	B202	FN108041L	B253	FN108047L	N 25	FN110047	C 69
EVB104200	R 49	FB106121L	B123	FB108111L	B 13	FB108251	B200	FC108137	B241	FN108041L	B354	FN108047L	N 29	FN110047	K 17
EVB104450	R 51	FB106121L	B211	FB108111L	B110	FB108251	B261	FC108175	B282	FN108041L	B 60	FN108047L	N170	FN110047	C 06
EVB104520	R 48	FB108051	B253	FB108111L	B120	FB108251	B110	FC108247	B241	FN108041L	R 58	FN108047L	N239	FN110047	C 24
EVB104530	R 48	FB108061	G 08	FB108111L	B159	FB108251	B159	FC110107L	E 47	FN108041L	M 31	FN108047L	R 27	FN110047	T 06
EVL104360	R 48	FB108071L	B204	FB108111L	B168	FB108251	F 02	FC506267S	B394	FN108041L	M 82	FN108047L	R 28	FN110047	B229
EVL104360	R 49	FB108071L	B238	FB108111L	D 05	FB108261	B241	FC506267S	B393	FN108041L	N 34	FN108047L	R 30	FN110047	V 04
EVL104370	R 48	FB108081	C 55	FB108111L	C 69	FB108267	B280	FCA101680	P 07	FN108041L	N 49	FN108047L	H 35	FN110047	K 18
EVL104370	R 49	FB108081L	B238	FB108111L	B 61	FB108267	B270	FCA101680LOY	M125	FN108041L	N 50	FN108047L	N178	FN110047	K 05
EVL104370	R 51	FB108081L	B123	FB108111L	B113	FB110071L	B263	FCA101680PMA	M125	FN108041L	B 73	FN108047L	N123	FN110047	B294
EWQ100200	R 48	FB108081L	C 69	FB108111L	D 32	FB110071ML	D 09	FCL000240PMA	P 10	FN108041L	B 87	FN108047L	N124	FN110047	B296
EWQ100200	R 50	FB108081L	B 87	FB108111L	D 35	FB110081ML	D 08	FCL000250PMA	P 10	FN108041L	J 01	FN108047L	N 97	FN110047	B297
EWQ100210	R 48	FB108081L	B 95	FB108111L	C 24	FB110081S	B294	FCL000260PMA	P 10	FN108041L	L 05	FN108047L	N126	FN110047	C 51
EWQ100210	R 50	FB108081L	B137	FB108111L	H 14	FB110087	B297	FCL000270PMA	P 10	FN108041L	N 47	FN108047L	N 98	FN110047	N251
EWQ100240	R 48	FB108081L	B188	FB108111L	D 33	FB110087	B273	FHC000180	P 04	FN108041L	N 48	FN108047L	N 99	FN110047	N 15
EWQ100240	R 50	FB108081L	B 40	FB108111L	D 34	FB110091L	C 53	FHC000190	P 04	FN108041L	N 61	FN108047L	N 90	FN310013L	P 17
EWQ100250	R 48	FB108081L	B 45	FB108111L	D 06	FB110091ML	D 08	FHF000020	P 04	FN108041L	R 61	FN108047L	N 91	FNC100050L	P 17
EWQ100250	R 50	FB108081L	B211	FB108117	B291	FB110091ML	D 09	FHF000070PMA	P 04	FN108041L	R 64	FN108047L	N100	FNK000010	L 38
EWQ100280	R 48	FB108081L	B364	FB108117	B293	FB110101	C 53	FHM000040PMA	P 04	FN108041L	L 17	FN108047L	N101	FQA000010	N188
EWQ100280	R 50	FB108081L	B365	FB108121L	B200	FB110101L	C 52	FHS101520	P 17	FN108041L	K 03	FN108047L	H 07	FQB000040	N196
EWQ100290	R 48	FB108081L	B227	FB108121L	B110	FB110127	B296	FIF100110	P 17	FN108041L	K 04	FN108047L	J 58	FQB000040	N123
EWQ100290	R 50	FB108081L	B224	FB108121L	B159	FB110131	B240	FJF000030	P 16	FN108041L	J 10	FN108047L	N151	FQF000040	N194
EWQ100300	R 48	FB108081L	B184	FB108121L	N 91	FB110137	B373	FJG000010LOY	P 16	FN108041L	N 67	FN108047L	N200	FQJ103160	N188
EWQ100300	R 50	FB108081L	K 01	FB108121L	B364	FB110141L	B203	FJG000010PMA	P 16	FN108041L	R 59	FN108047L	R 40	FQJ103170	N188
EWQ100310	R 48	FB108081L	K 11	FB108121L	K 24	FB110141L	C 73	FJH000010PMA	P 16	FN108041L	R 67	FN108047L	N114	FQK000040	N194
EWQ100310	R 50	FB108081L	K 07	FB108141L	B202	FB110141L	N 23	FJL101970	N 34	FN108041L	H 01	FN108047L	M102	FQK000050	N194
EWS100030	R 71	FB108081L	K 08	FB108141L	K 03	FB110151L	B379	FJL101970	P 17	FN108041L	L 29	FN108047L	M103	FQK101450	N190
EYB10009L	N167	FB108081L	K 09	FB108141L	K 10	FB110151L	B394	FN105041L	B261	FN108041L	D 36	FN108047L	R 16	FQM000030	N196
EYC000300	P 25	FB108081L	K 19	FB108141L	K 15	FB110201L	C 52	FN105041L	N 38	FN108041L	K 02	FN108047L	M127	FQM100760	N193
EYC106690	P 04	FB108081L	K 20	FB108141L	K 23	FB110201L	L 53	FN105047L	B261	FN108041L	K 12	FN108047L	R 60	FQM100770	N193
FA105201	J 05	FB108081L	K 22	FB108141S	C 55	FB110221L	C 53	FN106047L	B387	FN108041L	K 01	FN108047L	L 54	FQP000010	N194
FA105201	J 06	FB108087	B293	FB108151L	B202	FB110227	B296	FN106047L	N 38	FN108041L	K 11	FN108047L	N150	FQP000040	N194
FA108207	J 05	FB108087	B270	FB108151L	B204	FB110301L	C 73	FN106047L	M 91	FN108041L	K 16	FN108047L	R 14	FQP000080	N188
FA108207	J 06	FB108087	L 47	FB108161L	B214	FB112081	T 40	FN106047L	C 54	FN108041L	K 14	FN108047L	R 21	FQP000090	N188
FAB012860PMA	P 04	FB108091L	C 43	FB108161L	B238	FB112101L	C 53	FN106047L	H 07	FN108041L	K 15	FN108047L	J 40	FQP101200	N189
FAB012870PMA	P 04	FB108101L	B202	FB108161L	D 09	FB112201L	C 53	FN106047L	N142	FN108041L	K 24	FN108047L	B280	FQP101210	N189
FAE101360LOY	P 09	FB108101L	B208	FB108161L	C 41	FB504117S	B388	FN106047L	F 20	FN108041L	K 07	FN108047L	B285	FQS000030	N196
FAG100240	P 29	FB108101L	B238	FB108161L	C 53	FB505171S	B378	FN106047L	F 25	FN108041L	K 08	FN108047L	N 95	FRC1032	C 35
FAG100290	P 29	FB108101L	B245	FB108167	B291	FB505181	B390	FN106047L	F 27	FN108041L	K 09	FN108047L	B273	FRC1034	C 35
FAJ100020	N185	FB108101L	B253	FB108167	B270	FB505241S	B378	FN106047L	M100	FN108041L	K 19	FN108047L	L 80	FRC1035	C 35
FAM9270	C 66	FB108101L	B 09	FB108171	B251	FB506115	B385	FN106047L	J 35	FN108041L	K 20	FN108047L	N 15	FRC1193	E 35
FAM9270	C 67	FB108101L	B 10	FB108171	C 55	FB506155	B385	FN106047L	L 48	FN108041L	K 21	FN108047L	N 07	FRC1193	E 08
FAR100130	P 07	FB108101L	B 58	FB108171L	B204	FB506211	B393	FN106047L	L 55	FN108041L	K 22	FN108047L	N 08	FRC1195	E 35
FAR100150	M125	FB108101L	E 56	FB108177	B295	FB506267	B394	FN106047L	J 40	FN108041L	J 70	FN108047L	N240	FRC1195	E 08

FRC1197	E 35
FRC1197	E 08
FRC1199	E 35
FRC1199	E 08
FRC1201	E 35
FRC1201	E 08
FRC1203	E 35
FRC1203	E 08
FRC167	D 05
FRC168	D 05
FRC2301	C 32
FRC2301	C 33
FRC2309	C 30
FRC2310	E 49
FRC2310	E 23
FRC2310	E 26
FRC2317	D 17
FRC2334	C 32
FRC2334	C 33
FRC2361	C 31
FRC2365	D 14
FRC2365	D 40
FRC2365	C 30
FRC2365	C 08
FRC2365	C 07
FRC2365	C 26
FRC2368	C 36
FRC2370	C 30
FRC2370	C 36
FRC2381	C 36
FRC2390	C 36
FRC2402	C 28
FRC2402	C 45
FRC2402	C 42
FRC2402	C 41
FRC2402	C 02
FRC2445	C 32
FRC2446	C 32
FRC2447	C 32
FRC2448	C 32
FRC2449	C 32
FRC2454	E 46
FRC2455	E 46
FRC2457	C 34
FRC2464	D 18
FRC2464	D 19
FRC2464	D 40
FRC2465	C 30
FRC2468	C 30
FRC2470	C 35
FRC2479	C 33
FRC2481	C 28
FRC2481	C 36
FRC2481	C 45
FRC2481	C 41
FRC2481	C 02
FRC2481	B295
FRC2481	C 53
FRC2481	C 43
FRC2481	B277
FRC2481	B278
FRC2482	B233
FRC2482	D 09
FRC2482	C 30
FRC2482	D 10
FRC2482	B267
FRC2482	D 06
FRC2487	C 37
FRC2488	C 32
FRC2488	C 33
FRC2528	C 28
FRC2528	C 45
FRC2528	C 02
FRC2542	C 30
FRC2554	C 32
FRC2555	C 32
FRC2556	C 32
FRC2577	C 36
FRC2578	C 35
FRC2583	C 37
FRC2587	C 37
FRC2612	C 37
FRC2622	C 37
FRC2623	C 37
FRC2626	C 55
FRC2626	C 69
FRC2626	C 37
FRC2626	C 25
FRC2644	E 18
FRC2648	C 37
FRC2671	B 47
FRC2671	B 98
FRC2859	C 72
FRC2859	C 54
FRC2883	E 20
FRC2883	E 21
FRC2884	E 20
FRC2884	E 21
FRC2885	E 20
FRC2885	E 21
FRC2886	E 20
FRC2886	E 21
FRC2889	E 18
FRC2894	E 20
FRC2894	E 21
FRC2906	E 20
FRC2916	E 20
FRC2933	E 12
FRC2933	E 40
FRC2975	C 28
FRC2975	C 45
FRC2975	C 02
FRC2975	C 43
FRC3002	E 35
FRC3002	E 39
FRC3002	E 08
FRC3002	E 11
FRC3072	C 31
FRC3073	C 30
FRC3099	E 23
FRC3112	C 35
FRC3117	C 36
FRC3118	C 36
FRC3132	E 46
FRC3146	C 37
FRC3147	E 46
FRC3162	D 19
FRC3166	C 30
FRC3196	D 17
FRC3282	C 36
FRC3286	D 19
FRC3310	D 19
FRC3311	D 19
FRC3312	D 19
FRC3313	D 19
FRC3319	C 35
FRC3327	C 42
FRC3327	C 41
FRC3327	C 03
FRC3416	C 42
FRC3416	C 41
FRC3416	C 03
FRC3417	C 03
FRC3470	T 05
FRC3477	T 05
FRC3481	C 36
FRC3502	D 42
FRC3502	D 41
FRC3511	E 20
FRC3602	D 19
FRC3725	E 20
FRC3725	E 22
FRC3731	C 30
FRC3732	C 35
FRC3806	C 35
FRC3890	E 16
FRC3891	E 16
FRC3896	C 33
FRC3897	C 33
FRC3898	C 32
FRC3898	C 33
FRC3987	C 35
FRC3988	E 23
FRC3988	E 47
FRC4062	C 37
FRC4078	B230
FRC4078	B370
FRC4078	B 47
FRC4078	B 98
FRC4078	B191
FRC4078	C 28
FRC4078	B147
FRC4078	C 02
FRC4078	C 03
FRC4112	E 33
FRC4112	E 34
FRC4112	E 35
FRC4112	E 36
FRC4112	E 37
FRC4112	E 07
FRC4112	E 09
FRC4142	E 19
FRC4206	E 19
FRC4282	C 08
FRC4282	C 07
FRC4307	E 06
FRC4319	E 23
FRC4320	E 23
FRC4321	C 14
FRC4327	C 09
FRC4329	C 09
FRC4331	C 09
FRC4333	C 09
FRC4335	C 09
FRC4337	C 09
FRC4339	C 09
FRC4341	C 09
FRC4343	C 09
FRC4345	C 09
FRC4347	C 09
FRC4349	C 10
FRC4351	C 10
FRC4353	C 10
FRC4355	C 10
FRC4357	C 10
FRC4359	C 10
FRC4361	C 10
FRC4363	C 10
FRC4365	C 10
FRC4367	C 10
FRC4369	C 10
FRC4377	E 24
FRC4377	E 47
FRC4434	C 68
FRC4434	C 22
FRC4435	C 68
FRC4435	C 22
FRC4449	C 08
FRC4449	C 07
FRC4489	C 24
FRC4489	C 26
FRC4490	C 24
FRC4490	C 26
FRC4493	C 08
FRC4493	C 07
FRC4494	C 34
FRC4494	C 08
FRC4494	C 07
FRC4499	D 30
FRC4499	D 32
FRC4499	D 35
FRC4499	D 36
FRC4499	D 37
FRC4499	D 39
FRC4499	D 38
FRC4499	D 33
FRC4501	C 08
FRC4501	C 07
FRC4501	C 26
FRC4505	D 37
FRC4505	D 39
FRC4505	D 38
FRC4509	D 40
FRC4509	D 32
FRC4509	C 22
FRC4509	D 33
FRC4565	D 32
FRC4565	D 33
FRC4586	E 35
FRC4714	C 32
FRC4718	E 50
FRC4719	E 50
FRC4803	C 28
FRC4803	C 45
FRC4803	C 02
FRC4808	B218
FRC4808	B244
FRC4808	B255
FRC4808	B 07
FRC4808	B 56
FRC4808	B108
FRC4808	B157
FRC4808	B177
FRC4808	D 09
FRC4808	D 40
FRC4808	D 10
FRC4810	C 30
FRC4810	C 08
FRC4810	C 07
FRC4810	C 26
FRC4838	E 20
FRC4839	E 20
FRC4840	E 20
FRC4841	E 20
FRC4845	C 10
FRC4856	C 09
FRC4873	C 09
FRC4873	C 26
FRC4875	C 31
FRC4905	C 23
FRC4946	C 17
FRC4947	C 17
FRC4947	C 20
FRC4951	D 40
FRC4951	C 68
FRC4951	D 30
FRC4951	D 35
FRC4951	C 22
FRC4951	D 34
FRC5053	D 06
FRC5076	D 30
FRC5076	D 32
FRC5076	D 35
FRC5076	D 33
FRC5095	C 17
FRC5095	C 20
FRC5162	C 16
FRC5180	C 03
FRC5186	C 17
FRC5186	C 20
FRC5204	E 33
FRC5204	E 34
FRC5204	E 36
FRC5204	E 37
FRC5204	E 07
FRC5204	E 09
FRC5235	C 14
FRC5243	C 13
FRC5244	C 13
FRC5245	C 13
FRC5246	C 13
FRC5247	C 13
FRC5253	C 13
FRC5255	C 42
FRC5255	C 41
FRC5255	C 03
FRC5279	C 12
FRC5280	C 64
FRC5280	C 14
FRC5284	C 15
FRC5286	C 15
FRC5288	C 15
FRC5290	C 15
FRC5292	C 15
FRC5294	C 15
FRC5296	C 15
FRC5298	C 15
FRC5300	C 15
FRC5302	C 15
FRC5305	C 10
FRC5306	C 30
FRC5317	C 34
FRC5376	T 05
FRC5378	T 06
FRC5379	T 05
FRC5380	T 05
FRC5381	T 05
FRC5383	T 05
FRC5385	T 05
FRC5386	T 05
FRC5387	T 05
FRC5388	T 05
FRC5389	T 06
FRC5391	T 05
FRC5409	D 07
FRC5409	D 40
FRC5409	D 10
FRC5413	D 08
FRC5413	D 40
FRC5413	D 10
FRC5415	D 09
FRC5415	D 10
FRC5416	D 09
FRC5416	D 40
FRC5416	D 10
FRC5419	D 40
FRC5419	D 10
FRC5424	D 17
FRC5425	D 29
FRC5428	D 12
FRC5435	D 29
FRC5436	D 29
FRC5438	D 19
FRC5439	D 18
FRC5440	D 20
FRC5440	D 23
FRC5442	D 18
FRC5446	D 19
FRC5449	D 20
FRC5449	D 23
FRC5450	D 19
FRC5454	D 17
FRC5458	D 28
FRC5459	D 29
FRC5460	D 29
FRC5461	D 29
FRC5465	D 29
FRC5468	D 21
FRC5468	D 24
FRC5469	D 21
FRC5469	D 24
FRC5473	D 21
FRC5473	D 40
FRC5473	D 24
FRC5478	D 30
FRC5478	D 31
FRC5478	D 35
FRC5478	D 33
FRC5479	D 40
FRC5479	D 30
FRC5479	D 32
FRC5479	D 35
FRC5479	D 33
FRC5480	D 30
FRC5480	D 32
FRC5480	D 35
FRC5480	D 33
FRC5486	D 40
FRC5494	D 17
FRC5498	D 24
FRC5562	D 22
FRC5562	D 28
FRC5562	D 24
FRC5562	D 29
FRC5564	D 14
FRC5566	E 01
FRC5574	D 30
FRC5574	D 32
FRC5574	D 35
FRC5574	D 33
FRC5575	D 05
FRC5575	D 20
FRC5575	D 28
FRC5575	D 40
FRC5575	C 83
FRC5575	D 35
FRC5575	D 29
FRC5576	D 21
FRC5576	D 40
FRC5576	D 24
FRC5594	D 07
FRC5594	D 10
FRC5595	D 07
FRC5595	D 10
FRC5596	C 24
FRC5602	C 34
FRC5603	C 34
FRC5604	C 34
FRC5605	C 34
FRC5606	C 34
FRC5607	C 34
FRC5608	C 34
FRC5609	C 34
FRC5610	C 34
FRC5611	C 34
FRC5612	C 34
FRC5613	C 34
FRC5614	C 34
FRC5615	C 34
FRC5616	C 34

FRC5622	D 06
FRC5661	E 33
FRC5661	E 34
FRC5661	E 36
FRC5661	E 37
FRC5661	E 07
FRC5661	E 09
FRC5674	C 30
FRC5678	C 12
FRC5679	C 13
FRC5681	D 29
FRC5690	E 33
FRC5690	E 34
FRC5690	E 35
FRC5690	E 36
FRC5690	E 37
FRC5690	E 07
FRC5690	E 09
FRC5698	C 37
FRC5806	E 23
FRC5806	E 47
FRC5859	C 68
FRC5859	C 23
FRC5864	C 68
FRC5864	C 22
FRC5926	E 49
FRC5926	E 25
FRC5928E	C 01
FRC5978	C 33
FRC5981	C 73
FRC5998	D 39
FRC6000	D 36
FRC6000	D 37
FRC6000	D 39
FRC6030	D 21
FRC6030	D 24
FRC6066	D 37
FRC6066	D 39
FRC6069	D 24
FRC6098	D 29
FRC6103	D 04
FRC6103	D 40
FRC6104	D 04
FRC6105	D 04
FRC6105	D 40
FRC6106	D 05
FRC6109	D 21
FRC6109	D 24
FRC6110	D 22
FRC6110	D 24
FRC6110	C 51
FRC6117	D 32
FRC6117	D 33
FRC6121	D 18
FRC6125	D 31
FRC6125	D 33
FRC6137	E 23
FRC6137	E 46
FRC6139	E 23
FRC6141	E 46
FRC6145	C 46
FRC6145	C 04
FRC6145	C 05
FRC6154	C 06
FRC6243	E 01
FRC6244	C 08
FRC6244	C 07
FRC6246	C 07
FRC6306	D 40
FRC6306	C 37
FRC6306	D 32
FRC6306	D 33
FRC6316	C 24
FRC6317	C 24
FRC6318	C 24
FRC6375	C 06
FRC6402	H 25
FRC6403	H 25
FRC6578	D 10
FRC6595	D 32
FRC6595	D 34
FRC6670	C 12
FRC6782	E 24
FRC6782	E 26
FRC6783	E 24
FRC6783	E 26
FRC6784	E 24
FRC6784	E 26
FRC6785	E 24
FRC6785	E 26
FRC6786	E 24
FRC6786	E 26
FRC6787	E 24
FRC6787	E 26
FRC6788	E 24
FRC6788	E 26
FRC6789	E 24
FRC6789	E 26
FRC6790	E 24
FRC6790	E 26
FRC6861	D 17
FRC6872	D 30
FRC6872	D 31
FRC6872	D 35
FRC6872	D 33
FRC6873	D 30
FRC6873	D 31
FRC6873	D 35
FRC6873	D 33
FRC6915	C 84
FRC6933	T 06
FRC6943	D 08
FRC6943	D 10
FRC6956	D 11
FRC6958	D 11
FRC6960	D 11
FRC6968	D 11
FRC7018	D 28
FRC7018	D 29
FRC7021	D 29
FRC7026	D 10
FRC7043	D 18
FRC7043	D 19
FRC7043	D 40
FRC7065	E 18
FRC7098	D 22
FRC7098	D 24
FRC7155	C 69
FRC7155	C 24
FRC7160	C 69
FRC7160	C 24
FRC7192	C 23
FRC7195	C 21
FRC7201	H 25
FRC7201	E 21
FRC7202	H 25
FRC7202	E 21
FRC7214	C 16
FRC7214	C 20
FRC7231	E 31
FRC7257	E 46
FRC7313	C 24
FRC7315	D 37
FRC7315	D 39
FRC7325	D 37
FRC7325	D 39
FRC7325	D 38
FRC7326	D 29
FRC7329	H 25
FRC7330	C 22
FRC7332	C 22
FRC7333	C 68
FRC7333	C 22
FRC7334	C 68
FRC7334	C 22
FRC7335	C 68
FRC7335	C 22
FRC7362	C 24
FRC7414	C 69
FRC7414	C 24
FRC7427	D 27
FRC7428	D 15
FRC7429	D 27
FRC7434	D 25
FRC7437	D 16
FRC7439	D 15
FRC7439	D 16
FRC7439	D 40
FRC7441	D 28
FRC7447	D 07
FRC7452	D 16
FRC7453	D 16
FRC7454	D 16
FRC7487	D 30
FRC7487	D 34
FRC7493	C 69
FRC7493	C 25
FRC7499	D 11
FRC7500	C 83
FRC7569	D 11
FRC7575	C 16
FRC7602	C 17
FRC7630	C 84
FRC7652	D 24
FRC7680	E 46
FRC7681	E 46
FRC7686	D 21
FRC7686	D 24
FRC7706	C 73
FRC7707	C 73
FRC7732	E 02
FRC7752	C 32
FRC7752	C 33
FRC7752	C 34
FRC7753	C 34
FRC7754	C 36
FRC7757	C 34
FRC7761	C 33
FRC7763	C 33
FRC7764	C 32
FRC7766	C 36
FRC7767	C 36
FRC7769	C 36
FRC7810	D 15
FRC7852	C 32
FRC7855	C 55
FRC7860	C 69
FRC7860	C 25
FRC7871	D 21
FRC7871	D 24
FRC7884	D 15
FRC7885	D 27
FRC7886	C 69
FRC7886	C 24
FRC7904E	C 27
FRC7926	D 11
FRC7929	D 28
FRC7941	D 31
FRC7941	D 33
FRC7944	D 31
FRC7944	D 33
FRC7946	D 38
FRC7948	D 21
FRC7970	D 28
FRC7998	D 05
FRC7998	D 40
FRC8002	E 47
FRC8033	D 38
FRC8041	D 21
FRC8075	D 36
FRC8075	D 37
FRC8075	D 38
FRC8093	D 41
FRC8094	E 46
FRC8095	E 46
FRC8104	C 08
FRC8104	C 07
FRC8119	C 24
FRC8120	C 24
FRC8127	C 68
FRC8127	C 21
FRC8129	C 33
FRC8139	C 32
FRC8141	C 16
FRC8154	E 35
FRC8154	E 39
FRC8154	E 08
FRC8154	E 11
FRC8170	C 68
FRC8170	C 23
FRC8176	C 34
FRC8187	E 43
FRC8188	E 43
FRC8189	E 43
FRC8190	E 43
FRC8202	D 36
FRC8203	D 30
FRC8203	D 35
FRC8204	D 36
FRC8208	C 33
FRC8209	C 33
FRC8210	C 32
FRC8211	C 34
FRC8211	C 35
FRC8213	C 35
FRC8214	C 32
FRC8215	C 31
FRC8220	E 35
FRC8220	E 39
FRC8220	E 08
FRC8220	E 11
FRC8221	E 23
FRC8221	E 46
FRC8222	E 47
FRC8227	E 47
FRC8232	C 11
FRC8232	C 12
FRC8232	C 14
FRC8239	C 68
FRC8239	C 23
FRC8240	C 23
FRC8246	C 17
FRC8246	C 20
FRC8250	C 37
FRC8270	C 36
FRC8271	C 37
FRC8285	C 17
FRC8285	C 20
FRC8291	D 15
FRC8292	D 07
FRC8292	D 15
FRC8292	D 40
FRC8292	D 30
FRC8292	D 35
FRC8299	D 04
FRC8380	C 35
FRC8382	C 17
FRC8382	C 20
FRC8383	C 04
FRC8383	C 05
FRC8384	C 17
FRC8385	E 02
FRC8386	E 01
FRC8389	E 03
FRC8390	E 01
FRC8391	E 03
FRC8392	E 02
FRC8393	E 02
FRC8397	C 30
FRC8400	C 33
FRC8401	C 33
FRC8402	C 33
FRC8403	C 33
FRC8404	C 33
FRC8405	C 33
FRC8406	C 33
FRC8409	C 34
FRC8421	C 35
FRC8422	C 33
FRC8452	C 36
FRC8454	C 36
FRC8455	C 36
FRC8468	C 84
FRC8529	C 29
FRC8530	E 19
FRC8531	C 42
FRC8538	T 06
FRC8540	E 46
FRC8541	T 05
FRC8544	D 21
FRC8547	D 36
FRC8548	D 36
FRC8549	D 41
FRC8555	E 46
FRC8558	D 06
FRC8561	D 30
FRC8561	D 35
FRC8611	E 34
FRC8667	E 43
FRC8700	E 49
FRC8700	E 23
FRC8700	E 25
FRC8700	E 47
FRC8707	C 84
FRC8709	C 84
FRC8711	C 84
FRC8712	C 84
FRC8722	C 37
FRC8722	C 25
FRC8724	C 69
FRC8724	C 24
FRC8743	C 84
FRC8744	C 84
FRC8751	D 30
FRC8751	D 35
FRC8751	D 06
FRC8758	C 06
FRC8766	D 30
FRC8766	D 35
FRC8767	D 36
FRC8768	D 36
FRC8769	D 36
FRC8773	C 24
FRC8775	H 19
FRC8777	C 32
FRC8777	C 33
FRC8777	C 34
FRC8782	E 04
FRC8782	E 05
FRC8783	E 04
FRC8783	E 05
FRC8786	E 27
FRC8787	E 27
FRC8859	D 38
FRC8863	C 37
FRC8899	D 28
FRC8900	D 28
FRC8917	D 12
FRC8917	D 13
FRC9310	D 36
FRC9359	C 84
FRC9386	C 12
FRC9389	C 14
FRC9427	D 05
FRC9427	C 83
FRC9428	C 56
FRC9428	C 06
FRC9429	C 37
FRC9430	D 05
FRC9430	C 56
FRC9430	C 37
FRC9454	E 04
FRC9455	E 04
FRC9460	D 15
FRC9462	D 15
FRC9468N	D 01
FRC9469N	D 01
FRC9470N	D 01
FRC9471N	D 01
FRC9513	D 28
FRC9524	C 30
FRC9526	C 15
FRC9546	D 28
FRC9549	D 28
FRC9551	D 27
FRC9552	D 15
FRC9555	D 30
FRC9556	C 33
FRC9568	B230
FRC9568	B370
FRC9568	B 47
FRC9568	B 98
FRC9568	B191
FRC9568	C 28
FRC9568	C 45
FRC9568	B147
FRC9568	C 41
FRC9568	C 02
FRC9568	C 03
FRC9620	C 31
FRC9621	C 32
FRC9758	C 20
FRC9761	C 18
FRC9792L	C 11
FRC9803	C 46
FRC9803	C 04
FRC9812	C 15
FRC9845	D 11
FRC9847	D 11
FRC9849	D 11
FRC9851	D 11
FRC9853	D 11
FRC9865	C 06
FRC9926	D 08
FRC9926	D 14
FRC9928	D 14
FRC9930	D 14
FRC9932	D 14
FRC9934	D 14
FRC9936	D 14

FRC9938	D 14
FRC9940	D 14
FRC9942	D 14
FRC9944	D 14
FRC9946	D 14
FRC9948	D 14
FRC9950	D 14
FRC9952	D 14
FRC9954	D 14
FRC9956	D 14
FRC9958	D 14
FRC9960	D 14
FRC9963	D 08
FRC9979	E 43
FRP100010	N141
FS104147M	B388
FS104207M	B388
FS105101	B251
FS105107L	J 51
FS105107L	B229
FS106101	C 43
FS106101L	B202
FS106101L	N184
FS106101L	C 84
FS106101L	C 28
FS106101L	N154
FS106101L	C 45
FS106101L	C 02
FS106101L	C 53
FS106101L	N159
FS106101L	N161
FS106107L	B272
FS106107L	J 76
FS106125L	E 19
FS106125L	B274
FS106127L	B387
FS106127L	M102
FS106127L	M103
FS106127L	L 20
FS106127L	B293
FS106127L	B298
FS106161M	C 56
FS106167	B249
FS106167L	B212
FS106167L	B237
FS106167L	B243
FS106167L	B249
FS106167L	B354
FS106167L	B 23
FS106167L	B 71
FS106167L	B 90
FS106167L	B124
FS106167L	N165
FS106167L	N132
FS106167L	N239
FS106167L	R 28
FS106167L	R 33
FS106167L	M 91
FS106167L	L 24
FS106167L	L 33
FS106167L	C 69
FS106167L	C 73
FS106167L	C 86
FS106167L	M 96
FS106167L	M105
FS106167L	M 29
FS106167L	M 82
FS106167L	N 49
FS106167L	N191
FS106167L	N125
FS106167L	N126
FS106167L	N 53
FS106167L	J 38
FS106167L	G 10
FS106167L	N 46
FS106167L	N 47
FS106167L	N 41
FS106167L	N238
FS106167L	R 44
FS106167L	N114
FS106167L	L 08
FS106167L	J 37
FS106167L	C 23
FS106167L	C 24
FS106167L	B341
FS106167L	M 99
FS106167L	B103
FS106167L	F 23
FS106167L	F 25
FS106167L	F 27
FS106167L	L 31
FS106167L	P 17
FS106167L	L 29
FS106167L	L 30
FS106167L	L 26
FS106167L	L 27
FS106167L	N149
FS106167L	K 16
FS106167L	K 14
FS106167L	L 11
FS106167L	J 36
FS106167L	B267
FS106167L	B291
FS106167L	B284
FS106167L	B285
FS106167L	T 52
FS106167L	T 53
FS106167L	T 47
FS106167L	T 48
FS106167L	J 77
FS106167L	L 22
FS106167L	J 67
FS106167L	L 28
FS106167L	N129
FS106167L	G 01
FS106167L	N241
FS106167P	B171
FS106201	N197
FS106201	V 05
FS106201	V 06
FS106201L	B221
FS106201L	B 10
FS106201L	B 59
FS106201L	B159
FS106201L	B181
FS106201L	N 37
FS106201L	N 38
FS106201L	N 58
FS106201L	M 46
FS106201L	C 69
FS106201L	N 11
FS106201L	N 34
FS106201L	N 39
FS106201L	N 49
FS106201L	N123
FS106201L	N124
FS106201L	N 97
FS106201L	N115
FS106201L	N 99
FS106201L	N 53
FS106201L	N 93
FS106201L	N246
FS106201L	E 69
FS106201L	J 50
FS106201L	J 46
FS106201L	N 46
FS106201L	N 48
FS106201L	L 61
FS106201L	D 30
FS106201L	D 31
FS106201L	N114
FS106201L	J 20
FS106201L	L 02
FS106201L	L 09
FS106201L	L 17
FS106201L	M143
FS106201L	P 24
FS106201L	C 24
FS106201L	B 83
FS106201L	B 84
FS106201L	B132
FS106201L	B133
FS106201L	J 13
FS106201L	R 62
FS106201L	F 23
FS106201L	R 01
FS106201L	B 36
FS106201L	B 37
FS106201L	C 07
FS106201L	D 33
FS106201L	N180
FS106201L	N 96
FS106201L	J 22
FS106201L	T 51
FS106201L	T 53
FS106201L	L 22
FS106201L	N129
FS106201L	S 10
FS106201L	S 11
FS106201M	D 08
FS106201M	M108
FS106207L	B110
FS106207L	B159
FS106207L	N132
FS106207L	N198
FS106207L	N118
FS106207L	N142
FS106207L	N 61
FS106207L	N238
FS106207L	D 35
FS106207L	L 17
FS106207L	N117
FS106207L	H 30
FS106207L	B 84
FS106207L	L 04
FS106207L	B291
FS106207L	J 76
FS106207L	N 43
FS106207L	S 11
FS106207L	N133
FS106207L	N131
FS106251	L 80
FS106251M	D 30
FS106251ML	D 30
FS106255L	B210
FS106255L	B379
FS106255L	N 37
FS106255L	N132
FS106255L	C 72
FS106255L	C 54
FS106255L	N124
FS106255L	S 16
FS106255L	L 60
FS106255L	L 42
FS106255L	N 67
FS106255L	S 04
FS106255L	R 66
FS106255L	F 20
FS106255L	R 51
FS106255L	H 20
FS106255L	T 51
FS106255L	T 52
FS106255L	T 53
FS106255L	N129
FS106255L	N133
FS106255L	N131
FS106257L	C 37
FS106257L	B275
FS106257L	S 12
FS106307L	B274
FS106307L	B284
FS108127L	B239
FS108127L	B241
FS108127L	B242
FS108127L	B258
FS108127L	B380
FS108127L	B276
FS108127L	B286
FS108127L	B294
FS108127ML	B393
FS108127ML	B292
FS108161L	B195
FS108161L	B204
FS108161L	B221
FS108161L	B237
FS108161L	B244
FS108161L	B249
FS108161L	B253
FS108161L	B258
FS108161L	B 07
FS108161L	B 13
FS108161L	B 56
FS108161L	B 59
FS108161L	B157
FS108161L	L 33
FS108161L	M 58
FS108161L	N 50
FS108161L	N 24
FS108161L	N114
FS108161L	B162
FS108161L	B153
FS108161L	J 40
FS108161L	J 71
FS108161L	K 05
FS108161L	N137
FS108161L	N138
FS108167PL	B354
FS108167PL	H 07
FS108167PL	L 13
FS108167PL	L 23
FS108201L	B205
FS108201L	B 90
FS108201L	M 31
FS108201L	M 32
FS108201L	S 15
FS108201L	B393
FS108207	B167
FS108207L	B198
FS108207L	B202
FS108207L	B216
FS108207L	B234
FS108207L	B237
FS108207L	B244
FS108207L	B253
FS108207L	B255
FS108207L	B257
FS108207L	B258
FS108207L	B357
FS108207L	B 04
FS108207L	B 10
FS108207L	B 15
FS108207L	B 19
FS108207L	B 53
FS108207L	B 59
FS108207L	B 60
FS108207L	B 67
FS108207L	B 90
FS108207L	B105
FS108207L	B110
FS108207L	B 63
FS108207L	B 64
FS108207L	B115
FS108207L	B154
FS108207L	B159
FS108207L	B164
FS108207L	E 56
FS108207L	E 61
FS108207L	E 62
FS108207L	E 68
FS108207L	D 16
FS108207L	N 25
FS108207L	N181
FS108207L	R 30
FS108207L	R 58
FS108207L	C 83
FS108207L	M 82
FS108207L	N 34
FS108207L	N145
FS108207L	N191
FS108207L	N 97
FS108207L	N 99
FS108207L	N100
FS108207L	N246
FS108207L	B 74
FS108207L	B142
FS108207L	B188
FS108207L	J 08
FS108207L	J 58
FS108207L	R 42
FS108207L	N 48
FS108207L	N151
FS108207L	R 40
FS108207L	L 17
FS108207L	K 04
FS108207L	B341
FS108207L	B119
FS108207L	J 56
FS108207L	F 03
FS108207L	J 57
FS108207L	B 12
FS108207L	B393
FS108207L	B366
FS108207L	B227
FS108207L	N150
FS108207L	B167
FS108207L	D 17
FS108207L	K 02
FS108207L	K 12
FS108207L	K 01
FS108207L	K 11
FS108207L	K 16
FS108207L	K 14
FS108207L	K 24
FS108207L	J 40
FS108207L	B291
FS108207L	B280
FS108207L	B289
FS108207L	B292
FS108207L	B294
FS108207L	B296
FS108207L	N 07
FS108207L	N 08
FS108207L	N 09
FS108251	J 10
FS108251L	B197
FS108251L	B200
FS108251L	B202
FS108251L	B205
FS108251L	B207
FS108251L	B213
FS108251L	B221
FS108251L	B 04
FS108251L	B 07
FS108251L	B 15
FS108251L	B105
FS108251L	B106
FS108251L	B108
FS108251L	B110
FS108251L	B128
FS108251L	B115
FS108251L	B154
FS108251L	B155
FS108251L	B159
FS108251L	B164
FS108251L	B175
FS108251L	B181
FS108251L	D 04
FS108251L	C 28
FS108251L	M 31
FS108251L	B 87
FS108251L	B 95
FS108251L	B137
FS108251L	C 45
FS108251L	G 10
FS108251L	J 08
FS108251L	J 10
FS108251L	C 09
FS108251L	C 23
FS108251L	C 24
FS108251L	B341
FS108251L	B 83
FS108251L	B 84
FS108251L	T 06
FS108251L	B132
FS108251L	B133
FS108251L	M101
FS108251L	C 02
FS108251L	C 03
FS108251L	B 36
FS108251L	B 37
FS108251L	B 40
FS108251L	B 45
FS108251L	B211
FS108251L	B365
FS108251L	B224
FS108251L	V 05
FS108251L	B184
FS108251L	D 37
FS108251L	D 39
FS108251L	D 38
FS108251L	D 24
FS108251L	D 34
FS108251L	K 26
FS108251L	J 70
FS108251L	K 06
FS108251L	K 30
FS108251L	K 27
FS108251L	S 10
FS108251L	N245
FS108251ML	D 07
FS108251ML	D 09
FS108251ML	D 04
FS108251ML	D 05
FS108251ML	D 16
FS108251ML	D 21
FS108251ML	D 35
FS108251ML	D 24
FS108251ML	C 43
FS108251S	C 57
FS108257L	B198

FS108257L	B233
FS108257L	B238
FS108257L	B244
FS108257L	B248
FS108257L	B250
FS108257L	B260
FS108257L	B354
FS108257L	B 07
FS108257L	B 42
FS108257L	B 56
FS108257L	B105
FS108257L	B 63
FS108257L	B 64
FS108257L	B123
FS108257L	E 68
FS108257L	D 05
FS108257L	D 21
FS108257L	N170
FS108257L	N239
FS108257L	R 27
FS108257L	C 55
FS108257L	C 69
FS108257L	F 05
FS108257L	H 34
FS108257L	H 35
FS108257L	N 11
FS108257L	N124
FS108257L	N126
FS108257L	N 91
FS108257L	N201
FS108257L	C 42
FS108257L	G 10
FS108257L	J 58
FS108257L	N151
FS108257L	N 61
FS108257L	K 28
FS108257L	R 61
FS108257L	R 64
FS108257L	D 35
FS108257L	M103
FS108257L	R 48
FS108257L	R 50
FS108257L	C 24
FS108257L	R 05
FS108257L	R 16
FS108257L	R 67
FS108257L	F 03
FS108257L	R 60
FS108257L	R 14
FS108257L	R 21
FS108257L	K 31
FS108257L	B291
FS108257L	N 95
FS108257L	B270
FS108257L	K 33
FS108257L	N 43
FS108257L	N 07
FS108257L	N240
FS108257L	N241
FS108257L	N242
FS108257L	N243
FS108257L	S 19
FS108301L	B252
FS108301L	D 04
FS108301L	B 87
FS108301L	V 05
FS108301L	B162
FS108301L	B163
FS108301L	D 10
FS108301L	S 10
FS108301S	C 57
FS108307	B291
FS108307L	B200
FS108307L	B221
FS108307L	B241
FS108307L	B261
FS108307L	B181
FS108307L	D 09
FS108307L	D 04
FS108307L	N 25
FS108307L	N218
FS108307L	C 55
FS108307L	C 84
FS108307L	C 35
FS108307L	C 36
FS108307L	N124
FS108307L	B 73
FS108307L	B 95
FS108307L	B113
FS108307L	B114
FS108307L	G 04
FS108307L	J 58
FS108307L	N114
FS108307L	C 24
FS108307L	B 83
FS108307L	B 84
FS108307L	B132
FS108307L	B133
FS108307L	R 16
FS108307L	J 52
FS108307L	J 56
FS108307L	R 67
FS108307L	B 11
FS108307L	C 03
FS108307L	B 36
FS108307L	B 37
FS108307L	B 40
FS108307L	B 45
FS108307L	L 29
FS108307L	C 08
FS108307L	B 25
FS108307L	V 05
FS108307L	B162
FS108307L	B163
FS108307L	R 21
FS108307L	J 70
FS108307L	B285
FS108307L	G 02
FS108351L	C 70
FS108357	C 86
FS108357	J 08
FS108357	N151
FS108357	B 45
FS108357	B363
FS108357	B364
FS108357	B365
FS108357	B274
FS108357	B279
FS108357	B280
FS108357	B287
FS108357	B295
FS108357	B273
FS108357	J 59
FS108405	R 14
FS108807	B294
FS110141M	B399
FS110167	B299
FS110167	L 23
FS110207L	B273
FS110251	T 40
FS110251L	R 71
FS110251M	B399
FS110301L	B206
FS110301L	B230
FS110301L	B243
FS110301L	B259
FS110301L	B260
FS110301L	B262
FS110301L	B263
FS110301L	B384
FS110301L	B 47
FS110301L	B 65
FS110301L	B 98
FS110301L	B116
FS110301L	B165
FS110301L	B191
FS110301L	D 07
FS110301L	D 08
FS110301L	N100
FS110301L	N101
FS110301L	B 66
FS110301L	B117
FS110301L	B142
FS110301L	B348
FS110301L	B188
FS110301L	B143
FS110301L	B144
FS110301L	B146
FS110301L	B148
FS110301L	J 54
FS110301L	J 56
FS110301L	F 01
FS110301L	F 03
FS110301L	J 07
FS110301L	B 17
FS110301L	B 18
FS110301L	B229
FS110301L	B227
FS110301L	D 10
FS110301L	C 44
FS110301L	N 13
FS110301L	T 37
FS110301L	T 38
FS110301L	T 40
FS110301L	E 67
FS110307	B274
FS110307	J 05
FS110307	J 06
FS112201L	N 18
FS112251L	N 13
FS112251L	N 18
FS112281L	N 13
FS112301P	E 39
FS112301P	E 11
FS112401	C 51
FS112401L	B249
FS112401L	C 53
FS112401L	C 52
FS504047	B391
FS504047	B337
FS504047	B324
FS504047	B335
FS504087S	B388
FS505077	B385
FSE100460	N142
FT106257M	B271
FT108207	B280
FTC1010	C 44
FTC1074	C 18
FTC1084	D 25
FTC1085	D 27
FTC1112	C 10
FTC1117	B399
FTC1249	E 03
FTC1250	E 03
FTC1271	C 41
FTC1282	C 10
FTC1293	C 10
FTC1301	C 13
FTC1310	C 11
FTC1311	C 59
FTC1311	C 63
FTC1311	C 65
FTC1311	C 13
FTC1312	C 12
FTC1313	C 11
FTC1327	C 12
FTC1332	E 16
FTC1333	E 16
FTC1356	C 74
FTC1361	C 12
FTC1368	H 25
FTC1368	H 32
FTC1368	H 30
FTC1374	H 33
FTC1374	M107
FTC1379	H 33
FTC1381	H 32
FTC1381	H 30
FTC1384	E 31
FTC1384	E 29
FTC1403	C 08
FTC1403	C 07
FTC1404	C 08
FTC1406	C 10
FTC1416	C 18
FTC1428	C 10
FTC1435	C 20
FTC1438	C 09
FTC1441	C 55
FTC1441	C 08
FTC1446	C 10
FTC1455	C 14
FTC1488	C 68
FTC1489	C 23
FTC1490	C 21
FTC1518	C 08
FTC1518	C 07
FTC1525	C 86
FTC1533	C 08
FTC1533	C 07
FTC159	B 47
FTC159	B 98
FTC160	B370
FTC1616	E 22
FTC1617	E 22
FTC1633	E 27
FTC1636	E 27
FTC1667	C 44
FTC1680	B399
FTC1681	B399
FTC1682	B399
FTC1683	B399
FTC1684	B399
FTC1685	B399
FTC1686	B399
FTC1687	B399
FTC1688	B399
FTC1689	B399
FTC1692	C 44
FTC1724	E 48
FTC1725	E 48
FTC1740	E 48
FTC1741	D 27
FTC1748	D 07
FTC1752	C 13
FTC1760	C 13
FTC1764	C 21
FTC1765	C 21
FTC1791	C 14
FTC1814	C 21
FTC1823	D 27
FTC1919	D 08
FTC1977	B399
FTC1989	C 13
FTC1994	B230
FTC1994	B263
FTC2005	C 62
FTC2005	C 65
FTC2005	C 13
FTC2006	C 13
FTC2007	C 13
FTC2008	C 13
FTC2009	C 13
FTC2061	D 08
FTC2061	D 10
FTC2084	C 13
FTC2089	C 13
FTC2090	C 13
FTC2102	C 08
FTC2104	C 55
FTC2104	C 08
FTC2149	B230
FTC2149	B263
FTC2149	B191
FTC2149	B147
FTC2149	B148
FTC2162	C 53
FTC2167	C 53
FTC2168	C 53
FTC2169	C 44
FTC2170	C 44
FTC2174	C 44
FTC2175	E 50
FTC2176	E 50
FTC2177	E 50
FTC2177	E 51
FTC2178	E 50
FTC2178	E 51
FTC2179	E 51
FTC2189	C 44
FTC2190	C 08
FTC2192	C 05
FTC2193	C 22
FTC2210	C 08
FTC2210	C 07
FTC2212	E 28
FTC2223	E 06
FTC2282	C 12
FTC2283	C 13
FTC2284	C 14
FTC2285	C 12
FTC2352	E 28
FTC2353	E 28
FTC2383	C 55
FTC2385	C 66
FTC2392	C 55
FTC2396	C 59
FTC2396	C 62
FTC2396	C 63
FTC2397	C 59
FTC2397	C 63
FTC2450	C 21
FTC2462	C 12
FTC248	C 66
FTC248	C 18
FTC2504	C 11
FTC2505	C 11
FTC2528	E 20
FTC2529	E 20
FTC2530	E 20
FTC2531	E 20
FTC254	E 16
FTC2582	C 67
FTC263	C 19
FTC265	C 19
FTC267	C 19
FTC2687	C 55
FTC269	C 19
FTC2694	C 53
FTC271	C 19
FTC2712	C 63
FTC2714	C 59
FTC2716	C 61
FTC2725	C 67
FTC2727	C 64
FTC273	C 19
FTC2731	C 63
FTC2731	C 64
FTC2733	C 59
FTC2737	C 58
FTC275	C 19
FTC2750	E 33
FTC2750	E 07
FTC2750E	E 33
FTC2750E	E 07
FTC277	C 19
FTC2783	E 23
FTC2783	E 25
FTC2783	E 46
FTC279	C 19
FTC281	C 19
FTC2822	C 09
FTC2827	D 28
FTC2827	D 29
FTC283	C 19
FTC285	C 19
FTC2859	D 28
FTC2859	D 29
FTC287	C 19
FTC2882	E 21
FTC2885	C 68
FTC2887	C 63
FTC289	C 19
FTC291	C 19
FTC293	C 19
FTC2941	C 66
FTC2945	C 66
FTC2948	C 60
FTC295	C 19
FTC2957	C 42
FTC2957	C 41
FTC2957	C 03
FTC2974	C 66
FTC311	C 09
FTC3145	E 22
FTC3146	E 17
FTC3147	E 17
FTC3148	E 17
FTC3149	E 17
FTC3154	E 22
FTC3154	E 25
FTC316	C 09
FTC316	C 26
FTC317	C 66
FTC317	C 18
FTC3178	D 08
FTC3179	E 49
FTC3179	E 26
FTC3185	E 49
FTC3185	E 25
FTC3188	E 48
FTC3196	B 98
FTC322E	C 27
FTC322N	C 27
FTC3232	E 29
FTC3245	E 03
FTC3269	E 12
FTC3269	E 42
FTC3270	E 48

DEFENDER | GROUP X | Numeric Index "FTC3271 " TO "FTC5360"

FTC3271	E 48	FTC3586	E 40	FTC3769	C 48	FTC3883	E 38	FTC4085	C 44	FTC4322	C 49	FTC4846	D 15	FTC5099	D 26
FTC3272	E 36	FTC3586	E 42	FTC3771	C 48	FTC3883	E 10	FTC4095	D 36	FTC4324	C 49	FTC4847	D 27	FTC5100	C 59
FTC3272	E 09	FTC3587	C 56	FTC3773	C 48	FTC3885	E 38	FTC4108	C 46	FTC4326	C 49	FTC4848	D 07	FTC5100	C 62
FTC3272E	E 36	FTC3620	E 13	FTC3775	C 48	FTC3885	E 10	FTC4108	C 68	FTC4388	B399	FTC4849	D 07	FTC5101	C 63
FTC3272E	E 09	FTC3620	E 40	FTC3777	C 48	FTC3887	E 38	FTC4111	E 22	FTC4392	C 53	FTC4850	D 14	FTC5102	C 64
FTC3276	E 18	FTC3620	E 42	FTC3779	C 48	FTC3887	E 10	FTC4112	C 46	FTC4413	E 06	FTC4866	D 08	FTC5105	E 18
FTC3278	H 25	FTC3620	E 43	FTC3781	C 48	FTC3889	E 38	FTC4112	C 04	FTC4449	C 55	FTC4889	H 19	FTC5120	C 68
FTC3279	H 25	FTC3623	C 08	FTC3783	C 48	FTC3889	E 10	FTC4112	C 05	FTC4458	C 68	FTC4889	H 21	FTC5142	E 36
FTC3280	E 04	FTC3623	C 07	FTC3785	C 48	FTC3891	E 38	FTC4112	C 26	FTC4461	C 40	FTC4939	D 18	FTC5142	E 09
FTC3280	E 05	FTC3627	D 28	FTC3787	C 48	FTC3891	E 10	FTC4131	C 46	FTC4461	C 53	FTC4939	D 19	FTC5150	E 13
FTC3281	E 04	FTC3646	E 18	FTC382	D 26	FTC3893	E 38	FTC4171	C 59	FTC4465	H 33	FTC4940	D 18	FTC5150	E 42
FTC3281	E 05	FTC3647	E 20	FTC3846	H 30	FTC3893	E 10	FTC4171	C 62	FTC4465	H 31	FTC4941	D 19	FTC5193	P 13
FTC3283	C 84	FTC3647	E 22	FTC3847	C 67	FTC3895	E 38	FTC4171	C 63	FTC4474	C 74	FTC4942	D 19	FTC5199	C 41
FTC3299	H 33	FTC3648	E 22	FTC3848	C 46	FTC3895	E 10	FTC4171	C 64	FTC4483	C 56	FTC4962	D 13	FTC5199	C 43
FTC3299	H 31	FTC3648	E 48	FTC3850	C 67	FTC3904	E 51	FTC4172	C 59	FTC4502	C 01	FTC4962	D 14	FTC5200	B230
FTC3300	E 04	FTC3648	E 23	FTC3852	D 32	FTC3905	E 03	FTC4172	C 63	FTC4504	C 10	FTC4969	C 71	FTC5200	B370
FTC3300	E 05	FTC3649	E 48	FTC3852	D 34	FTC3911	C 41	FTC4173	C 42	FTC4506	C 01	FTC4978	C 66	FTC5200	B 47
FTC3301	E 04	FTC3649	E 46	FTC3853	E 15	FTC3912	C 41	FTC4174	C 42	FTC4510	C 69	FTC4978	C 67	FTC5200	B 98
FTC3301	E 05	FTC3650	E 48	FTC3853	E 42	FTC3915	C 69	FTC4177	C 42	FTC4510	C 24	FTC4982	C 66	FTC5200	C 28
FTC3302	E 04	FTC3670	E 21	FTC3853	E 44	FTC3921	C 51	FTC4178	D 04	FTC4510	C 26	FTC4984	C 66	FTC5200	C 45
FTC3303	E 04	FTC3674	D 22	FTC3855	E 15	FTC3922	C 51	FTC4185	D 07	FTC4522	C 55	FTC4989	C 64	FTC5200	B147
FTC3304	E 29	FTC3675	D 36	FTC3855	E 42	FTC3927	C 58	FTC4187	D 07	FTC4524	C 64	FTC4990	C 64	FTC5200	C 41
FTC3306	H 31	FTC3675	D 37	FTC3855	E 44	FTC3928	C 58	FTC4188	D 13	FTC4536	D 28	FTC4991	C 55	FTC5200	C 02
FTC3308	E 21	FTC3675	D 39	FTC3857	E 15	FTC3951	C 65	FTC4189	D 27	FTC4536	C 68	FTC4991	C 64	FTC5200	C 03
FTC3309	E 21	FTC3688	E 27	FTC3857	E 42	FTC3953	C 65	FTC419	C 20	FTC4536	C 23	FTC4992	C 59	FTC5200	C 43
FTC3310	E 21	FTC3696	C 57	FTC3857	E 44	FTC3955	C 65	FTC4190	D 15	FTC4536	T 05	FTC4992	C 62	FTC5202	C 41
FTC3311	E 21	FTC3697	C 64	FTC3859	E 15	FTC3957	C 65	FTC4204	B263	FTC4536	D 29	FTC4992	C 63	FTC5202	C 43
FTC3366	C 58	FTC3698	D 21	FTC3859	E 42	FTC3959	C 65	FTC4204	B148	FTC4539	C 64	FTC4992	C 64	FTC5207	D 11
FTC3370	C 68	FTC3699	C 64	FTC3859	E 44	FTC3961	C 65	FTC4206	C 55	FTC4540	E 43	FTC4994	D 09	FTC5210	E 04
FTC3371	C 64	FTC3700	C 64	FTC3861	E 15	FTC3963	C 65	FTC4209	C 42	FTC4585	C 68	FTC5013	D 11	FTC5213	C 52
FTC3373	C 12	FTC3701	C 55	FTC3861	E 42	FTC3965	C 65	FTC4210	E 33	FTC4588	C 68	FTC5018	C 63	FTC5218	C 41
FTC3375	H 27	FTC3703	C 58	FTC3861	E 44	FTC3967	C 65	FTC4210	E 34	FTC4596	C 46	FTC5018	C 64	FTC5236	P 13
FTC3375	H 33	FTC3711	C 56	FTC3863	E 15	FTC3969	C 65	FTC4210	E 36	FTC4596	C 68	FTC5019	C 59	FTC5237	P 13
FTC3375	H 31	FTC3713	C 56	FTC3863	E 42	FTC3974	E 27	FTC4210	E 37	FTC4597	C 68	FTC5019	C 62	FTC5241	E 49
FTC3382	C 46	FTC3721	E 28	FTC3863	E 44	FTC3975	C 56	FTC4210	E 07	FTC4606	B399	FTC5019	C 63	FTC5241	E 25
FTC3382	C 68	FTC3721	E 29	FTC3865	E 15	FTC4007	C 12	FTC4210	E 09	FTC4607	B399	FTC503	C 24	FTC5258	E 39
FTC3382	C 21	FTC3727	C 84	FTC3865	E 42	FTC4008	C 14	FTC4229	C 42	FTC4608	B399	FTC5036	C 61	FTC5258	E 11
FTC3387	C 55	FTC3730	C 55	FTC3865	E 44	FTC4009	C 13	FTC4234	E 43	FTC4616	C 51	FTC5037	C 60	FTC5268	E 22
FTC3391	C 67	FTC3731	E 46	FTC3867	E 15	FTC4010	C 14	FTC4238	C 57	FTC4617	C 68	FTC5038	C 59	FTC5268	E 48
FTC3401	E 18	FTC3732	E 46	FTC3867	E 42	FTC4011	C 12	FTC4241	C 55	FTC4630	B299	FTC5041	C 63	FTC5269	C 84
FTC3429	E 43	FTC3739	C 47	FTC3867	E 44	FTC4018	C 51	FTC4242	C 65	FTC4631	B299	FTC5043	C 64	FTC5287	C 58
FTC3434	E 31	FTC3741	C 47	FTC3869	E 38	FTC4021	C 55	FTC4245	C 64	FTC4661	B 98	FTC5044	C 58	FTC5288	C 64
FTC3437	E 31	FTC3743	C 47	FTC3869	E 10	FTC4036	D 40	FTC4296	C 49	FTC4662	B370	FTC5046	C 58	FTC5296	E 21
FTC3454	E 18	FTC3745	C 47	FTC3871	E 38	FTC4036	C 37	FTC4298	C 49	FTC4663	E 37	FTC5056	C 58	FTC5297	E 21
FTC3456	E 18	FTC3747	C 47	FTC3871	E 10	FTC4036	D 32	FTC4300	C 49	FTC4663E	E 37	FTC5070	C 64	FTC5298	E 21
FTC347	C 10	FTC3749	C 47	FTC3873	E 38	FTC4036	D 35	FTC4302	C 49	FTC4720	C 43	FTC5070	C 65	FTC5299	E 21
FTC357	C 12	FTC3751	C 47	FTC3873	E 10	FTC4036	D 33	FTC4304	C 49	FTC4735	D 35	FTC5071	C 28	FTC5300	E 27
FTC358	C 11	FTC3753	C 47	FTC3875	E 38	FTC4037	D 40	FTC4306	C 49	FTC4738	B268	FTC5071	C 45	FTC5303	C 57
FTC3581	C 68	FTC3755	C 47	FTC3875	E 10	FTC4037	D 30	FTC4308	C 49	FTC4785	E 48	FTC5071	C 02	FTC5303	C 09
FTC3582	C 68	FTC3757	C 47	FTC3877	E 38	FTC4037	D 31	FTC4310	C 49	FTC4785	E 25	FTC5072	C 41	FTC5317	E 39
FTC3584	C 59	FTC3759	C 48	FTC3877	E 10	FTC4037	D 35	FTC4312	C 49	FTC4832	C 53	FTC5085	E 06	FTC5317	E 11
FTC3584	C 62	FTC3761	C 48	FTC3879	E 38	FTC4037	D 33	FTC4314	C 49	FTC4833	C 53	FTC5085	E 51	FTC5322	E 39
FTC3584	C 63	FTC3763	C 48	FTC3879	E 10	FTC4053	C 55	FTC4316	C 49	FTC4838	H 25	FTC5085	E 27	FTC5322	E 11
FTC3584	C 64	FTC3765	C 48	FTC3881	E 38	FTC4056	C 46	FTC4318	C 49	FTC4839	H 25	FTC5085	E 29	FTC5360	C 86
FTC3586	E 13	FTC3767	C 48	FTC3881	E 10	FTC4056	C 52	FTC4320	C 49	FTC4845	D 14	FTC5090	C 83	FTC5360	C 70

DEFENDER | GROUP X | Numeric Index "FTC5360" TO "KVD100330 "

FTC5360	L 25	FTC748	D 23	FTP8030	L 03	HAD132750RPI	R 08	HLF105530LOY	R 23	IGM100000	D 04	JQB101230	L 73	JUU100450	L 78
FTC5361	C 86	FTC750	D 20	FUD000030	N194	HAD132760RFI	R 08	HLF105540LOY	R 34	IPM000010	R 33	JQB101240	L 73	JUU100450	L 51
FTC5361	C 70	FTC750	D 23	FUD000030	N197	HAD132770RFI	R 08	HLF105560LOY	R 40	IPN000020	N194	JQD100390	L 51	JUU100460	L 79
FTC5371	C 57	FTC752	D 20	FVJ000010LOY	P 25	HAD132780RPI	R 08	HLF105570LOY	R 37	IPV000010	E 61	JQQ100090	L 51	JUU100460	L 51
FTC5372	C 57	FTC752	D 23	FWJ000110PMA	P 04	HAD132790RPI	R 08	HLF105580LOY	R 23	IYR100000	D 09	JQQ100120	L 51	JUU100470	L 78
FTC5399	E 12	FTC754	D 20	FX106047L	L 53	HAD132800RFI	R 08	HLF105610LOY	R 26	IYR100010	D 09	JQY100170	P 07	JUU100470	L 79
FTC5399	E 42	FTC754	D 23	FX108041	B241	HAD132810RFI	R 08	HMA111310LOY	R 23	JAE000030	N 30	JRB100580L	L 47	JUU100480	L 78
FTC5401	E 12	FTC756	D 20	FX108047L	B261	HAG000130LOY	R 13	HMA111350LOY	R 25	JDL000030	L 38	JRB100660	L 47	JUU100490	L 79
FTC5401	E 42	FTC756	D 23	FX108047L	L 47	HAG000140RPI	R 13	HN2005L	B303	JEC104220	L 33	JRB100850	L 47	JUZ100000	L 51
FTC5402	E 12	FTC758	D 20	FX110041	N 18	HAG100650RPI	R 19	HN2005L	B320	JEC104230	L 33	JRB101180	L 47	JUZ100010	L 51
FTC5402	E 42	FTC758	D 23	FX110041L	B214	HAG100720RFI	R 18	HN2005L	M 10	JEF100220	L 35	JRC1775PMA	N194	JYC100870	L 40
FTC5409	C 56	FTC760	D 20	FX110041L	B240	HAG100970LOY	R 13	HN2005L	B336	JEN100240	L 35	JRC1775PMA	N189	JYC100870	L 41
FTC5409	C 83	FTC760	D 23	FX110041L	B251	HAG101020LOY	R 20	HPA106700LOY	R 26	JEN100250	L 35	JRC7549	M151	JYP000060	L 36
FTC5409	C 37	FTC762	D 20	FX110041L	N 12	HAH000330PMA	R 14	HPA106710LOY	R 24	JFC101990	L 73	JRF100410	L 47	JYP000060	L 37
FTC5409	C 06	FTC762	D 23	FX110041L	J 56	HAH103510LOY	R 14	HWE100740	R 43	JFF000050	L 37	JRJ100480	L 53	JYP000070	L 36
FTC5409	E 50	FTC764	D 20	FX110041L	N 17	HAJ000160LOY	R 10	HWE100750	R 43	JFF000060	L 37	JRJ100490	L 53	JZX1039L	B333
FTC5409	E 51	FTC764	D 23	FX110047L	D 09	HAJ000170LOY	R 10	HYG10013	N 30	JFF000070	L 36	JRP100010	L 47	JZX1181L	B333
FTC5413	E 39	FTC766	D 20	FX110047L	T 37	HAJ000180RPI	R 10	IAB100020	D 03	JFF000120	L 37	JRP105080	L 47	JZX1303L	B333
FTC5413	E 11	FTC766	D 23	FX110047L	T 38	HAJ000190RPI	R 10	IAB100030	D 03	JFT000020	L 36	JS499L	B332	JZX1394L	B333
FTC5414	E 49	FTC768	D 20	FX112041	B377	HAJ101070RPI	R 19	IAB100040	D 03	JFT000030	L 36	JS657L	J 12	KAJ100610	S 07
FTC5414	E 26	FTC768	D 23	FX112041L	N 12	HAJ101300RFI	R 18	IAB100050	D 03	JFT000040	L 36	JS660L	J 20	KCU100020L	N 64
FTC5421	D 05	FTC770	D 20	FX112041L	N 13	HAJ101310LOY	R 20	IAI100030	D 09	JFT000050	L 36	JS660L	J 12	KKB102601	N 13
FTC5422	D 05	FTC770	D 23	FX112041L	N 16	HAJ101380LOY	R 10	ICB100070	D 04	JGK100160	L 35	JS660L	J 22	KKB102602	N 13
FTC5427	D 05	FTC772	D 20	FY108047	H 06	HAJ101390LOY	R 10	ICL100010	D 42	JGK100170	L 35	JTB100330	L 51	KKB103120	B377
FTC56	E 22	FTC772	D 23	FY108047	S 19	HAJ101400LOY	R 10	ICN100000	D 18	JGM100130	L 51	JTB100340	L 73	KKJ100110	B386
FTC566	C 84	FTC774	D 20	FY110057	J 05	HAJ101410LOY	R 10	ICV100000	D 14	JHB100590	L 40	JTF100280	L 51	KNB100640	T 39
FTC575	B230	FTC774	D 23	FY110057	J 06	HAM4301L	M 49	ICW100000	D 42	JHB100600	L 43	JTV100000	L 73	KNK100080	T 40
FTC575	B263	FTC776	D 20	FYP101310	N189	HBA000660PMA	R 11	ICW100010	D 42	JHB100610	L 42	JUB100140L	L 52	KNK100090	T 40
FTC575	B191	FTC776	D 23	GG106201	H 32	HBA105640RPI	R 19	ICW100030	D 42	JHB100650	L 44	JUE107140	L 78	KNL100010	T 40
FTC575	B147	FTC781	E 13	GG106251L	F 05	HBA105650RFI	R 18	ICW100050	D 42	JHC000050	L 41	JUE107150	L 78	KNS100000	T 39
FTC575	B148	FTC782E	E 33	GG106251L	M144	HBA106180LOY	R 11	IEC100020	D 18	JHC000060	L 41	JUE107170	L 78	KPE100000	N 24
FTC576	B230	FTC782E	E 07	GG108251	K 31	HBA106190LOY	R 11	IEE100050	D 28	JHC100310	L 40	JUE107180	L 79	KQB100160	N 18
FTC726	D 20	FTC782N	E 33	GG108251	K 32	HBA106200LOY	R 20	IEJ100010	D 16	JHC100320	L 43	JUE107190	L 79	KQB100170	N 18
FTC726	D 23	FTC782N	E 07	GG108251L	F 05	HCA000660PMA	R 13	IEJ100030	D 16	JHC100330	L 42	JUE107220	L 79	KRB100810	N 25
FTC728	D 20	FTC785	E 34	GG108251L	G 09	HCA105540RPI	R 19	IEJ100050	D 16	JHC100370	L 44	JUE107250	L 79	KRB100821	N 25
FTC728	D 23	FTC785	E 37	GG108351	N138	HCA105550RFI	R 18	IEJ100070	D 16	JKB000080	L 38	JUE107270	L 79	KRO100030	N 18
FTC730	D 20	FTC785R	E 34	GG605081	G 07	HCA106010LOY	R 13	IEJ100090	D 16	JKB000090	L 38	JUE107280	L 79	KSP101410	B299
FTC730	D 23	FTC785R	E 37	GL108351	P 32	HCA106020LOY	R 20	IEJ100110	D 16	JKB100440	L 38	JUE107290	L 78	KTH100000	S 14
FTC732	D 20	FTC840	E 22	GS108081L	C 31	HHD102280	R 12	IEJ100130	D 16	JKB100440	L 76	JUE107960	L 79	KTH100010	S 17
FTC732	D 23	FTC859	E 49	GS110501	C 69	HHD102290	R 12	IEJ100150	D 16	JKB100450	L 38	JUE109190	L 79	KTH100010	S 15
FTC734	D 20	FTC859	E 26	GS110501	C 24	HLD001600PMA	R 22	IEJ100170	D 16	JKB100450	L 76	JUE109920	L 78	KTP9024	L 02
FTC734	D 23	FTC861	E 22	GS112141L	C 37	HLD001610PMA	R 24	IEJ100190	D 16	JMG100380	L 45	JUE110330	L 78	KTU100090	S 16
FTC736	D 20	FTC890	D 09	GT106205L	P 32	HLD103660LOY	R 22	IEJ100210	D 16	JNB100080	L 51	JUF102190	L 78	KVB100000	N 07
FTC736	D 23	FTC890	C 83	HAD001300RPI	R 08	HLD103670LOY	R 24	IEJ100230	D 16	JOE100020	L 51	JUF102210	L 78	KVD100080	N 01
FTC738	D 20	FTC890	C 08	HAD001310RPI	R 08	HLE001720PMA	R 32	IEJ100250	D 16	JOE100030	L 51	JUF102240	L 79	KVD100110	N 01
FTC738	D 23	FTC890	C 07	HAD001340LOY	R 08	HLE110050LOY	R 25	IEJ100270	D 16	JPB101200	B259	JUF102250	L 79	KVD100120	N 01
FTC740	D 20	FTC902	H 25	HAD001350LOY	R 08	HLE110060LOY	R 22	IEJ100290	D 16	JPB101330	B295	JUF102260	L 79	KVD100160	N 03
FTC740	D 23	FTC916	C 14	HAD129860RPI	R 19	HLE110070LOY	R 29	IEJ100310	D 16	JPC5641LNF	P 61	JUF102270	L 79	KVD100190	N 03
FTC742	D 20	FTC918	C 05	HAD129870RFI	R 18	HLE110090LOY	R 39	IEJ100330	D 16	JPC5641LUN	P 67	JUF102280	L 79	KVD100220	N 03
FTC742	D 23	FTC942	E 49	HAD132530LOY	R 20	HLE110100LOY	R 25	IEJ100350	D 16	JPC5641LUN	P 61	JUF102420	L 51	KVD100250	N 05
FTC744	D 20	FTC942	E 25	HAD132540LOY	R 08	HLE110110LOY	R 22	IEJ100370	D 16	JPC9023PMA	N159	JUF102680	L 78	KVD100260	N 05
FTC744	D 23	FTC943	E 49	HAD132550LOY	R 08	HLE110120LOY	R 36	IEJ100390	D 16	JPI100000	L 80	JUF102690	L 78	KVD100270	N 05
FTC746	D 20	FTC943	E 26	HAD132560LOY	R 08	HLE110140LOY	R 32	IEQ100000	D 26	JQB000010	L 73	JUF102930	L 78	KVD100280	N 05
FTC746	D 23	FTC943	E 47	HAD132570LOY	R 08	HLF000930PMA	R 34	IGC100010	D 35	JQB000020	L 73	JUF103170	L 79	KVD100320	N 02
FTC748	D 20	FTC988	T 05	HAD132740RPI	R 08	HLF105520LOY	R 26	IGC100020	D 35	JQB000030	L 73	JUU100440	L 51	KVD100330	N 02

KVD100340	N 02	LFT100300	B269	LVB000210	B280	MRC1980	N157	MRC5527	N 34	MRC7626	R 63	MRC9416	N196	MSX100080	B287
KVD100350	N 04	LGC107280	B281	LVB101770	B280	MRC1980	N168	MRC5527	N 99	MRC7626	R 68	MRC9417	N196	MTC1039	N 75
KVD100360	N 04	LGJ100690	B274	LVC100260	B320	MRC1980	N178	MRC5527	N 44	MRC7755	R 62	MRC9420	N 28	MTC1042	N178
KVD100370	N 04	LGJ100880	B244	LVF100380	B270	MRC199	R 61	MRC5527	N 41	MRC8047	N149	MRC9431	N123	MTC1078	F 05
KVD100380	N 04	LGJ100900	B316	LVG100340	B271	MRC200	R 61	MRC5527	N114	MRC8094	N199	MRC9431	N192	MTC1233	N203
KVD100390	N 04	LGJ100900	B381	LVH100230	B291	MRC2178	N157	MRC5527	M123	MRC8136	N 39	MRC9438	N 49	MTC1233	N201
KVD100400	N 06	LGQ000020	B274	LVJ000010	B289	MRC2244	N 51	MRC5527	M124	MRC8225	M115	MRC9438	N 46	MTC1356	S 05
KVD100410	N 06	LGQ100500	B274	LVP000020	B284	MRC2245	N 51	MRC5527	M144	MRC8269	N149	MRC9481	R 01	MTC1357	S 05
KVD100420	N 06	LGV000020	B282	LWQ100270	B286	MRC2762	N168	MRC5527	M127	MRC8329	R 61	MRC9492	R 01	MTC1359	S 01
KVD100430	N 04	LHA000030	B274	LXB100090	B274	MRC316	T 16	MRC5527	R 51	MRC8330	R 61	MRC9493	R 01	MTC1359	S 05
KVI100030	N203	LHG100580	B268	LXI100000	B274	MRC4037	N 61	MRC5527	N240	MRC8377	L 33	MRC9520	N 61	MTC1359	S 02
KVI100040	N203	LHH100660	B235	LXU100050	B274	MRC4473	S 08	MRC5528	N 37	MRC8378	L 33	MRC9544	N145	MTC1382	F 05
KVU100220	N 09	LHP000020	B274	LYG000230	B284	MRC4473	S 09	MRC5528	N121	MRC8388	N 39	MRC9564	N221	MTC1409	N 90
KVU100230	N 09	LHP100700	B274	LYG101190	B268	MRC4501	N139	MRC5528	N 48	MRC8389	R 61	MRC9570	H 34	MTC1416	S 16
KVU100240	N 09	LHP100860	B240	LYG101200	B284	MRC4583	N221	MRC5528	R 40	MRC8390	R 61	MRC9571	H 34	MTC1423	S 16
KVU100940	N 09	LHV100150	B240	LYG101210	B274	MRC4619	S 08	MRC5528	R 38	MRC8392	R 61	MRC9603	N240	MTC1439	N124
KVU101160	N 08	LJC100270	B246	LYG101510	B280	MRC4619	S 09	MRC5695	J 67	MRC8393	R 61	MRC9603	N243	MTC1439	N 93
KVU101420	N100	LJC100270	B121	LYG101510	B282	MRC4655	R 54	MRC5757	S 15	MRC8420	N198	MRC9603	N245	MTC1448	N 94
KVU101430	N 11	LJC100270	B 69	LYH100500	B240	MRC4655	R 56	MRC5757	N 07	MRC8444	N196	MRC9619	N197	MTC1461	N 90
KVU101440	N101	LJQ100940	B280	LYP000050L	J 76	MRC4731	R 65	MRC5765	N 49	MRC8444	N123	MRC9668	L 38	MTC1462	N 90
KVV100000	N 07	LJQ100940	B283	LYP101160	B271	MRC4753	N170	MRC5765	N 47	MRC8524	R 64	MRC9668	L 75	MTC1479	N 92
KVW100580	N 08	LJR103670	B273	LYQ100040	B279	MRC4754	N170	MRC6019	N 47	MRC8524	R 60	MRC9669	L 38	MTC1481	N 92
KVW100590	N 08	LJR104820	B274	LYQ100050	C 55	MRC4796	R 31	MRC6027	N 97	MRC8564	M139	MRC9669	L 75	MTC1482	N 92
KVX000010	E 61	LKB108110	B285	LYQ100080	B267	MRC4846	S 15	MRC6027	N 99	MRC8564	M140	MRC9720	N 44	MTC1490	S 16
KYF100280	N203	LKC102020	B286	LYQ100080L	B267	MRC4885	R 59	MRC6028	N 97	MRC8564	M141	MRC9734	N 61	MTC1531	N124
KYP000020	T 39	LKG100470	B286	LYQ100090	C 46	MRC4886	R 59	MRC6028	N 99	MRC8564	M142	MRC9735	N 61	MTC1557	N 91
LBB001190	B264	LLH000070	B284	LYQ100120L	B267	MRC5016	N139	MRC6051	N 54	MRC8564	M138	MRC9747	N221	MTC1584	S 16
LBB001200	B266	LLH102680	B284	LYQ100170	B279	MRC5049	N 45	MRC6051	N 55	MRC8584	P 12	MRC9833	N114	MTC1592	S 17
LBB111670	B264	LLN100140L	B284	LYR000080	L 13	MRC5050	N 45	MRC6052	N 54	MRC8585	P 12	MRC9851	L 62	MTC1594	N 93
LBB111680	B265	LLN100140L	J 42	LZX1505	B333	MRC5063	S 08	MRC6052	N 55	MRC8626	N 37	MRC9922	L 37	MTC1595	N 90
LBB111690	B266	LLO100000	B248	LZX1600L	B333	MRC5071	N 75	MRC6270	N141	MRC8626	N 33	MRC9938	L 34	MTC1608	R 46
LBH000090	B284	LLO100000	B123	LZX1988L	B333	MRC5071	N 76	MRC6359	N 49	MRC8626	N 34	MRC9939	L 34	MTC1609	R 46
LBH100360	B284	LLO100000	B211	LZX1989L	B333	MRC5071	N 77	MRC6360	N 49	MRC8626	N 99	MRC9940	L 34	MTC1631	R 62
LBH100370	B284	LNL100000	B274	LZX2107L	B333	MRC5071	N 78	MRC6436	N 98	MRC8626	N 44	MRC9941	L 34	MTC1650	N 28
LBL100000	B284	LPD100010	B291	MAE100010	B279	MRC5071	N 87	MRC6437	N 98	MRC8642	L 33	MRC9995	N139	MTC1650	G 10
LCF104560	B373	LPF101250	B271	MAE100010	B287	MRC5071	N 88	MRC6843	R 40	MRC8717	L 33	MRC9998	L 34	MTC1710	P 18
LCF104860	B373	LPX100590	B291	MBD100050	B279	MRC5153	N 49	MRC6845	R 40	MRC8732	T 47	MSB000080	M 99	MTC1710	P 23
LCL100020L	B267	LPY100160	B291	MBD100050	B287	MRC5153	N 47	MRC6977	N150	MRC8732	T 48	MSB100760	M100	MTC1714	R 01
LCM100150	B267	LQC100270L	B284	MDY100080L	B243	MRC5394	P 31	MRC6978	N150	MRC8736	N 97	MSB100960	M 99	MTC1715	R 01
LCM100160	B267	LQM100880	B272	MHK100490	J 42	MRC5509	N 40	MRC7279	L 75	MRC8736	N 98	MSB101170	M 99	MTC1810	N145
LCM100170	B279	LQN101070	B272	MHK100620	J 42	MRC5524	R 62	MRC7281	L 38	MRC8736	N 95	MSB101171	M 99	MTC1827	N125
LDF000890	B281	LQP100680	B291	MHK100640	B285	MRC5525	N 37	MRC7281	L 75	MRC8926	N 58	MSB101360	M 99	MTC1923	R 04
LDF107860	B279	LQS105070	B243	MJN100910	B254	MRC5525	N 38	MRC7282	P 11	MRC9006	N197	MSC000030	B287	MTC1932RD	R 04
LDF108080	B316	LQX100130	B274	ML106015	J 46	MRC5525	N193	MRC7283	P 11	MRC9006	N123	MSC000040	B287	MTC1932RD	R 05
LDF108090	B381	LRJ100000	B291	ML106015	J 45	MRC5525	N198	MRC7350	T 27	MRC9244	N139	MSC100670	B279	MTC1933RD	R 04
LDI100030	B280	LSB102550	B270	MLH100410	J 74	MRC5525	R 28	MRC7354	R 61	MRC9244	N140	MSC100670	B287	MTC1943	R 15
LDR000020	B284	LSB102610	B237	MM106301L	T 27	MRC5525	N 49	MRC7359	T 47	MRC9361	R 66	MSC100670E	B287	MTC1944	R 15
LDU100350	B280	LSF100040L	B237	MR106300	N 90	MRC5525	N179	MRC7360	T 47	MRC9362	R 66	MSG100110	J 77	MTC1949RD	R 15
LDU100380	B280	LSO100000	B306	MR106300	S 16	MRC5525	N 46	MRC7361	T 47	MRC9367	R 66	MSK100050	G 05	MTC1949RD	R 16
LDU100470	B280	LSO100000	B376	MRC1300	N 28	MRC5525	R 44	MRC7361	T 48	MRC9368	R 66	MSO000060	B287	MTC1950RD	R 15
LFB101630	B268	LSP100640	B271	MRC1300	R 30	MRC5525	N114	MRC7362	T 47	MRC9377	N 62	MSO000080	B287	MTC2062	N 54
LFL000460	B269	LUD100040L	B284	MRC1525	L 38	MRC5525	R 15	MRC7365	T 03	MRC9378	N 62	MSO100010	B279	MTC2062	N 55
LFL105300	B269	LUF100420	B267	MRC1525	L 76	MRC5525	R 01	MRC7411	N 34	MRC9388	N 53	MSO100010	B287	MTC2063	N 54
LFN10006L	B269	LUF100430	B233	MRC1638	R 69	MRC5525	N188	MRC7610	R 61	MRC9393	N149	MSX000010	B287	MTC2063	N 55
LFQ100310	B267	LVB000200	B280	MRC1979	N221	MRC5527	N 33	MRC7623	N143	MRC9394	N149	MSX100080	B279	MTC2106	N 41

MTC2107	N 41	MTC3203	N129	MTC4111	N182	MTC4826	N148	MTC5581	L 72	MTC6827	N147	MTC6874P	N 62	MTC7483	N 93
MTC2136	N 58	MTC3203	N133	MTC4132	M 17	MTC4829	N148	MTC5603	N147	MTC6835	R 69	MTC6874PUE	N 62	MTC7511	N 94
MTC2138	N200	MTC3203	N131	MTC4156	N 90	MTC4837	N145	MTC5608	N 43	MTC6836	R 69	MTC6874SUB	N 62	MTC7512	N 94
MTC2138AA	N200	MTC3350	N 94	MTC4164	N127	MTC4844	N124	MTC5609	N 43	MTC6839	R 69	MTC6875AA	N 62	MTC7513	N132
MTC2202	N 40	MTC3452	N185	MTC4165	N127	MTC4845	N124	MTC5698	P 33	MTC6840	R 69	MTC6875AV	N 63	MTC7513	N 66
MTC2203	N 40	MTC3461	N 65	MTC4197	N 39	MTC4846	N124	MTC5699	P 33	MTC6871	P 12	MTC6875CC	N 63	MTC7513	N116
MTC2220	N143	MTC3462	N 65	MTC4215	N 39	MTC4865	P 29	MTC5851	P 02	MTC6872	N 34	MTC6875CL	N 63	MTC7513	N 99
MTC2224	N 41	MTC3469	N172	MTC4220	N146	MTC4866	P 28	MTC6006	L 37	MTC6873AA	N198	MTC6875CUF	N 62	MTC7513	J 46
MTC2225	N 41	MTC3470	N172	MTC4220	N148	MTC4888	N124	MTC6007	L 37	MTC6873AV	N198	MTC6875CUH	N 62	MTC7513	R 40
MTC2248	N 44	MTC3474	N129	MTC4290	N182	MTC4932	N150	MTC6015	N 32	MTC6873CC	N198	MTC6875CUY	N 63	MTC7513	R 38
MTC2252	N 33	MTC3474	N131	MTC4313	N223	MTC4942	N218	MTC6040	P 01	MTC6873CL	N198	MTC6875HAF	N 62	MTC7513	T 52
MTC2390	L 34	MTC3476	N111	MTC4313	N233	MTC4943	N246	MTC6080	P 10	MTC6873CUF	N198	MTC6875HC	N 62	MTC7513	T 53
MTC2391	L 34	MTC3476	N105	MTC4313	N234	MTC4944	N246	MTC6109	N 32	MTC6873CUH	N198	MTC6875HN	N 63	MTC7513	N103
MTC2548	N200	MTC3481	N100	MTC4313	N227	MTC4945	N246	MTC6142	P 02	MTC6873CUY	N198	MTC6875HUJ	N 62	MTC7513	N129
MTC2574AE	N234	MTC3482	N100	MTC4313	N228	MTC4992	N100	MTC6143	P 02	MTC6873HAF	N198	MTC6875HUL	N 62	MTC7513	N131
MTC2574AG	N234	MTC3486	N100	MTC4313	N230	MTC4993	N100	MTC6154	N100	MTC6873HC	N198	MTC6875HYE	N 62	MTC7516	L 72
MTC2575AE	N233	MTC3499	F 04	MTC4313	N231	MTC4994	N132	MTC6166	P 12	MTC6873HN	N198	MTC6875JC	N 63	MTC7523	N122
MTC2575AG	N233	MTC3515	N 94	MTC4314	N223	MTC4994	N129	MTC6167	P 12	MTC6873HUJ	N198	MTC6875JP	N 63	MTC7523	N123
MTC2607	M128	MTC3521	N 90	MTC4314	N233	MTC4994	N133	MTC6194	L 37	MTC6873HUL	N198	MTC6875JUG	N 63	MTC7525	N123
MTC2640	P 11	MTC3523	P 10	MTC4314	N234	MTC4994	N131	MTC6232	N 66	MTC6873HYE	N198	MTC6875JUH	N 63	MTC7631	R 04
MTC2704	N 58	MTC3538	N 90	MTC4314	N227	MTC5034	N111	MTC6232	N113	MTC6873JC	N198	MTC6875LN	N 63	MTC7631	R 01
MTC2799	N 30	MTC3556	N124	MTC4314	N228	MTC5038	N 92	MTC6233	N 66	MTC6873JP	N198	MTC6875LUS	N 63	MTC7710AE	N224
MTC2805	L 36	MTC3557	N124	MTC4314	N224	MTC5039	N 92	MTC6302	M 27	MTC6873JRJ	N198	MTC6875LVD	N 63	MTC7710AG	N224
MTC2808	P 07	MTC3558	N 90	MTC4314	N230	MTC5083	N221	MTC6332	N146	MTC6873JUG	N198	MTC6875NM	N 62	MTC7711ABE	N224
MTC2826	P 09	MTC3569	N 90	MTC4314	N231	MTC5084	N221	MTC6340	N 35	MTC6873JUH	N198	MTC6875NUC	N 62	MTC7711AG	N224
MTC2827	P 09	MTC3594	S 08	MTC4315	N233	MTC5086	N100	MTC6376	N221	MTC6873LN	N198	MTC6875P	N 62	MTC7737	L 36
MTC2863	N185	MTC3598	S 08	MTC4315	N234	MTC5197	N 65	MTC6382	L 38	MTC6873LUS	N198	MTC6875PUE	N 62	MTC7769	N 57
MTC2864	N185	MTC3611	G 10	MTC4319	N233	MTC5206	P 64	MTC6408	P 56	MTC6873LVD	N198	MTC6875SUB	N 62	MTC7770	N 57
MTC3000	T 51	MTC3705LDQ	P 11	MTC4319	N234	MTC5212	P 54	MTC6448	R 36	MTC6873NM	N198	MTC6992	N238	MTC7798	R 47
MTC3000	T 53	MTC3705LOY	P 11	MTC4320	J 15	MTC5212	P 63	MTC6503	N186	MTC6873NUC	N198	MTC6993	N238	MTC7825	N159
MTC3001	T 51	MTC3705PMA	P 11	MTC4384	N 43	MTC5212	P 64	MTC6504	N186	MTC6873P	N198	MTC7140	N150	MTC7826	N159
MTC3001	T 53	MTC3801	F 04	MTC4385	N 43	MTC5212	P 66	MTC6505	N186	MTC6873PUE	N198	MTC7155	N197	MTC7828	N183
MTC3021	N201	MTC3862	N146	MTC4412	N104	MTC5212	P 53	MTC6506	N186	MTC6873SUB	N198	MTC7170	N150	MTC7829	N183
MTC3032	R 67	MTC3874	T 51	MTC4460	N124	MTC5212	P 56	MTC6507	N186	MTC6874AA	N 62	MTC7193AE	N223	MTC7861	N199
MTC3042	R 67	MTC3874	T 53	MTC4483RD	R 30	MTC5227	M 49	MTC6544	N 65	MTC6874AV	N 63	MTC7193AE	N227	MTC7878	N 51
MTC3046	N 97	MTC3902	N 89	MTC4483RD	R 34	MTC5312	N105	MTC6568	N132	MTC6874CC	N 63	MTC7193AE	N228	MTC7879	N 51
MTC3051	R 67	MTC3906	N 92	MTC4484RD	R 32	MTC5394	N102	MTC6568	N129	MTC6874CL	N 63	MTC7193AE	N230	MTC7886	N 75
MTC3051	N 43	MTC3907	N 92	MTC4487RD	R 37	MTC5394	N104	MTC6568	N133	MTC6874CUF	N 62	MTC7200AE	N230	MTC7887	N 75
MTC3052	R 67	MTC3908	N124	MTC4488RD	R 36	MTC5394	N106	MTC6568	N131	MTC6874CUH	N 62	MTC7200AG	N230	MTC7980	N 75
MTC3052	N 43	MTC3917	N124	MTC4489RD	R 29	MTC5395	N102	MTC6626	N238	MTC6874CUY	N 63	MTC7252	N238	MTC7980	N 79
MTC3076	N201	MTC3923	N124	MTC4520	P 14	MTC5395	N104	MTC6630	N178	MTC6874HAF	N 62	MTC7384	N241	MTC7980	N 80
MTC3084	N203	MTC3982	N150	MTC4570	S 08	MTC5395	N106	MTC6630	P 18	MTC6874HC	N 62	MTC7384	N243	MTC7980	N 84
MTC3085	N203	MTC3983	N150	MTC4571	P 01	MTC5428	N238	MTC6686	P 56	MTC6874HN	N 63	MTC7400	P 12	MTC7980	N 85
MTC3086	N203	MTC4002	N100	MTC4581	N238	MTC5429	N238	MTC6686	P 60	MTC6874HUJ	N 62	MTC7431	N238	MTC7980	N 86
MTC3087	N203	MTC4003	N100	MTC4583	N238	MTC5458	P 07	MTC6757	R 28	MTC6874HUL	N 62	MTC7449	S 02	MTC7980	N 68
MTC3091	N203	MTC4007	N148	MTC4584	N238	MTC5459	P 07	MTC6792	R 44	MTC6874HYE	N 62	MTC7457	S 02	MTC7981	N 75
MTC3099	N203	MTC4054	N246	MTC4601	S 04	MTC5463	N153	MTC6793	R 29	MTC6874JC	N 63	MTC7458	N 40	MTC7981	N 79
MTC3126	N 91	MTC4054	N242	MTC4617LDQ	P 03	MTC5486	P 65	MTC6794	R 29	MTC6874JP	N 63	MTC7464	N201	MTC7981	N 80
MTC3127	N 91	MTC4054	N245	MTC4617LOY	P 03	MTC5486	P 67	MTC6795	R 29	MTC6874JUG	N 63	MTC7465	N201	MTC7981	N 84
MTC3139	N124	MTC4061AE	N233	MTC4618LDQ	P 03	MTC5519	N219	MTC6798	N 33	MTC6874JUH	N 63	MTC7466	N201	MTC7981	N 85
MTC3165	S 04	MTC4061AE	N234	MTC4618LOY	P 03	MTC5519	N220	MTC6801	R 45	MTC6874LN	N 63	MTC7471AE	N230	MTC7981	N 86
MTC3166	S 04	MTC4061AG	N233	MTC4657	P 34	MTC5536	N187	MTC6801	R 31	MTC6874LUS	N 63	MTC7471AG	N230	MTC7981	N 68
MTC3203	N132	MTC4061AG	N234	MTC4771	F 05	MTC5571	L 66	MTC6802	R 45	MTC6874LVD	N 63	MTC7480	N 93	MTC8145	N244
MTC3203	P 55	MTC4090	R 64	MTC4771	P 17	MTC5573	L 68	MTC6802	R 31	MTC6874NM	N 62	MTC7481	N 93	MTC8146	N244
MTC3203	R 37	MTC4095	N 33	MTC4824	N124	MTC5578	L 76	MTC6820	P 31	MTC6874NUC	N 62	MTC7482	N 93	MTC8184	N 68

MTC8184	N 69	MTC8468	N159	MUC1008	N112	MUC1359RD	P 40	MUC1666	L 71	MUC2291	N187	MUC3302	N 79	MUC3794	N108
MTC8184	N 70	MTC8471	N183	MUC1049	N 38	MUC1360RD	P 40	MUC1667	L 71	MUC2296	P 56	MUC3303	N 79	MUC3795	N108
MTC8184	N 71	MTC8472	N183	MUC1049	N191	MUC1361LDE	P 35	MUC1668	L 65	MUC2344	T 51	MUC3303	N 84	MUC3798	N178
MTC8184	N 72	MTC8473	N155	MUC1049	N192	MUC1361RD	P 35	MUC1669	L 71	MUC2345	T 51	MUC3303	N 85	MUC3809	N131
MTC8184	N 73	MTC8474	N155	MUC1081	N239	MUC1362LDE	P 35	MUC1670	L 71	MUC2364	S 12	MUC3309	N 84	MUC3810	N105
MTC8184	N 74	MTC8477	N159	MUC1082	N241	MUC1362RD	P 35	MUC1671	L 59	MUC2366	S 12	MUC3360	N187	MUC3844	P 63
MTC8194AE	N223	MTC8478	N183	MUC1082	N242	MUC1363LDE	P 36	MUC1672	M 81	MUC2368	S 12	MUC3373AF	N210	MUC3845	P 63
MTC8195AE	N223	MTC8500	L 45	MUC1086	N218	MUC1363RD	P 36	MUC1673	L 70	MUC2379	P 69	MUC3373JU	N210	MUC3848	N155
MTC8196AE	N227	MTC8706	P 18	MUC1098	N107	MUC1364RD	P 40	MUC1674	L 70	MUC2380	P 69	MUC3394	N170	MUC3882	N131
MTC8196AG	N227	MTC8707	P 18	MUC1098	N108	MUC1365RD	P 40	MUC1675	L 49	MUC2381	P 69	MUC3394	N193	MUC3883	N131
MTC8197AE	N227	MTC8788	N165	MUC1139	L 76	MUC1367	M112	MUC1676	M 81	MUC2382	P 69	MUC3394	P 18	MUC3928	N155
MTC8197AG	N227	MTC8789	N165	MUC1227	N 44	MUC1368	M112	MUC1677	M 81	MUC2400LDE	P 47	MUC3394	N189	MUC3929	N155
MTC8251	N112	MTC8790	N183	MUC1228	N 44	MUC1382	P 10	MUC1678	M 81	MUC2417	L 34	MUC3492	N184	MUC3932	N 97
MTC8256	N112	MTC8791	N183	MUC1233	N 40	MUC1383	P 09	MUC1679	L 59	MUC2417	J 62	MUC3493	N184	MUC3932	N 96
MTC8269	N112	MTC8947	N107	MUC1234	N 40	MUC1384	P 09	MUC1679	H 09	MUC2418	L 34	MUC3498	N 32	MUC3933	M129
MTC8270	N107	MTC8947	N108	MUC1237	N 33	MUC1402	P 24	MUC1680	L 71	MUC2419	L 34	MUC3532AF	N210	MUC3958	N 79
MTC8270	N108	MTC8948	N112	MUC1237	P 63	MUC1402	P 18	MUC1682	L 49	MUC2440	S 09	MUC3532JU	N210	MUC3962	N 79
MTC8270	N109	MTC8951	N172	MUC1237	P 67	MUC1402	P 23	MUC1701	P 10	MUC2442	S 09	MUC3533AF	N210	MUC3962	N 80
MTC8270	N110	MTC9424	R 45	MUC1237	P 61	MUC1412	N 40	MUC1703	P 09	MUC2443	S 09	MUC3533JU	N210	MUC3962	N 84
MTC8271	N107	MTC9428	P 41	MUC1248	P 26	MUC1474	P 53	MUC1704	N111	MUC2594	N185	MUC3566	N104	MUC3962	N 85
MTC8271	N108	MTC9428	P 45	MUC1249	P 39	MUC1474	P 57	MUC1705	N111	MUC2934	S 12	MUC3566	N106	MUC3962	N 86
MTC8271	N109	MTC9429	P 41	MUC1250	P 39	MUC1484	N107	MUC1706	N111	MUC2959	N191	MUC3567RD	P 40	MUC3963	N 79
MTC8271	N110	MTC9429	P 45	MUC1253	P 39	MUC1484	N108	MUC1707	N111	MUC2961	N191	MUC3568RD	P 40	MUC3963	N 84
MTC8292	N 45	MTC9773	N238	MUC1254	P 39	MUC1488	R 02	MUC1713	N159	MUC2965	N191	MUC3590	N 58	MUC3963	N 85
MTC8293	N 45	MTC9801	P 18	MUC1255	P 39	MUC1494	P 35	MUC1714	N183	MUC3023	P 07	MUC3601	N 58	MUC3964	N 79
MTC8294	P 48	MTC9807	N173	MUC1256RD	P 27	MUC1495	P 44	MUC1716	P 09	MUC3024	N159	MUC3628	T 03	MUC3971	N 84
MTC8296	P 53	MTC9914	M 75	MUC1257LDE	P 35	MUC1495	P 46	MUC1730	N155	MUC3025	N159	MUC3630	P 63	MUC3974	N 84
MTC8297	P 53	MTC9915	M 75	MUC1257RD	P 35	MUC1497	P 37	MUC1731	N155	MUC3026	N184	MUC3630	P 53	MUC3984	T 52
MTC8298	P 53	MTC9915LCS	M 75	MUC1258LDE	P 35	MUC1498	P 37	MUC1757	P 41	MUC3027	N184	MUC3630	P 57	MUC3985	T 52
MTC8299	P 53	MTC9915LCS	P 23	MUC1258RD	P 35	MUC1499	P 35	MUC1757LDE	P 41	MUC3036	P 18	MUC3631	P 63	MUC3986	T 52
MTC8302	R 32	MTC9956	R 04	MUC1259LDE	P 36	MUC1500	P 41	MUC1758LDE	P 47	MUC3036	P 21	MUC3631	P 53	MUC3987	T 52
MTC8303	R 32	MTC9958	R 15	MUC1259RD	P 36	MUC1501	N111	MUC1758RD	P 47	MUC3036	P 20	MUC3631	P 57	MUC3990	T 51
MTC8305	N205	MTC9959	R 15	MUC1260RD	P 40	MUC1508	P 53	MUC1759	P 45	MUC3037	P 18	MUC3656	N187	MUC4025	N107
MTC8331	N132	MTC9959	R 16	MUC1261RD	P 40	MUC1508	P 56	MUC1759LDE	P 45	MUC3037	P 21	MUC3657	N187	MUC4025	N108
MTC8331	N129	MTC9959	R 17	MUC1264LDE	P 35	MUC1512	T 51	MUC1759LOY	P 45	MUC3037	P 20	MUC3695	L 70	MUC4025	N109
MTC8331	N131	MTC9959	R 18	MUC1264RD	P 35	MUC1520	R 02	MUC1888	N158	MUC3038	N191	MUC3707	N221	MUC4025	N110
MTC8332	N132	MTC9959	R 19	MUC1265LDE	P 36	MUC1554	P 57	MUC1889	N158	MUC3039	N191	MUC3708	N221	MUC4027	N 34
MTC8332	N129	MTC9962	R 04	MUC1265RD	P 36	MUC1555	P 57	MUC1961	N169	MUC3096	N107	MUC3733	N185	MUC4061ABE	N238
MTC8332	N131	MTC9962	R 05	MUC1266RD	P 40	MUC1582	P 06	MUC1961	N181	MUC3096	N108	MUC3764	N108	MUC4061ACG	N238
MTC8333	N103	MTC9962	R 15	MUC1268	P 37	MUC1583	M112	MUC2002	N207	MUC3097	N107	MUC3765	N108	MUC4071	N159
MTC8333	N105	MTC9962	R 16	MUC1269	P 37	MUC1584	M112	MUC2002	N205	MUC3097	N108	MUC3766	N107	MUC4072	N183
MTC8334	N116	MTC9962	R 14	MUC1286	M143	MUC1604	N165	MUC2003	N207	MUC3172AF	N210	MUC3767	N107	MUC4072	N159
MTC8334	N119	MTC9962	R 17	MUC1287	M143	MUC1605	N165	MUC2074	N154	MUC3174AF	N210	MUC3768	N107	MUC4073	N183
MTC8334	N117	MTC9962	R 18	MUC1324	N114	MUC1621	P 39	MUC2075	N154	MUC3174JU	N210	MUC3768	N108	MUC4073	N159
MTC8335	R 40	MTC9962	R 19	MUC1327	R 69	MUC1649	S 14	MUC2153	P 16	MUC3175AF	N210	MUC3768	N109	MUC4073	N161
MTC8335	R 38	MTC9967	R 04	MUC1330	R 69	MUC1651	N165	MUC2153	P 15	MUC3175JU	N210	MUC3768	N110	MUC4083	R 35
MTC8338	R 51	MTC9967	R 05	MUC1331	R 69	MUC1651	N155	MUC2160RD	P 40	MUC3186	N155	MUC3769	N107	MUC4108	R 33
MTC8349	P 30	MTC9967	R 14	MUC1333	N103	MUC1652	N155	MUC2161RD	P 40	MUC3186	P 18	MUC3769	N108	MUC4109	R 33
MTC8357	T 53	MTC9968	P 12	MUC1353AV	P 44	MUC1657	L 67	MUC2165	M112	MUC3187	P 18	MUC3770	N107	MUC4121ABE	N223
MTC8358	T 53	MTC9981	N173	MUC1353LDE	P 44	MUC1658	L 67	MUC2210	P 28	MUC3201	M 27	MUC3770	N108	MUC4121ACG	N223
MTC8360	P 29	MUC1005	N111	MUC1356RD	P 27	MUC1659	L 67	MUC2268	P 39	MUC3242	P 53	MUC3770	N109	MUC4122ABE	N223
MTC8440	T 53	MUC1005	N112	MUC1357LDE	P 36	MUC1660	L 67	MUC2269	P 39	MUC3242	P 57	MUC3770	N110	MUC4122ACG	N223
MTC8441	T 53	MUC1006	N103	MUC1357RD	P 36	MUC1661	L 50	MUC2270	P 39	MUC3244	P 09	MUC3771	N111	MUC4145	N186
MTC8460	N183	MUC1007	N103	MUC1358LDE	P 35	MUC1663	L 49	MUC2271	P 39	MUC3249	P 09	MUC3791	N107	MUC4145	N187
MTC8461	N183	MUC1008	N111	MUC1358RD	P 35	MUC1665	L 70	MUC2290	N187	MUC3278	L 76	MUC3792	N107	MUC4146	N186

MUC4146	N187	MUC4872	L 58	MUC6452	P 16	MUC7912	N185	MUC8740	N121	MUC9974RD	R 22	MWC1691	N152	MWC2244LB	N211
MUC4149	P 69	MUC4874	L 58	MUC6452	P 15	MUC7913ABE	N228	MUC8741	N121	MUC9975PB	R 22	MWC1694	N152	MWC2245HA	N211
MUC4150	P 69	MUC4875	L 58	MUC6453	P 16	MUC7913ACG	N228	MUC8746	N121	MUC9999	R 43	MWC1695	N152	MWC2245LB	N211
MUC4152	P 69	MUC4878	L 59	MUC6453	P 15	MUC7914ABE	N228	MUC8748	N115	MUI000040	B282	MWC1696	N152	MWC2246HA	N211
MUC4153	P 69	MUC4878	L 66	MUC6457	N141	MUC7914ACG	N228	MUC8748	N117	MWC1010	R 04	MWC1705RD	R 25	MWC2246LB	N211
MUC4161	T 03	MUC4880	L 71	MUC6484	P 56	MUC7915AE	N231	MUC8754	R 04	MWC1010	R 06	MWC1706PB	R 25	MWC2247HA	N211
MUC4199	P 60	MUC4881	L 70	MUC6485	P 56	MUC7915AG	N231	MUC8754	R 05	MWC1018RD	R 04	MWC1707RD	R 23	MWC2247LB	N211
MUC4202	N191	MUC4882	L 70	MUC6486	P 56	MUC7916AE	N231	MUC8754	R 12	MWC1018RD	R 06	MWC1708PB	R 23	MWC2248HA	N211
MUC4203	N191	MUC4883	L 65	MUC6487	P 56	MUC7916AG	N231	MUC8755	N 41	MWC1055PMA	R 54	MWC1722	M 14	MWC2248LB	N211
MUC4206	N143	MUC4884	L 65	MUC6488	P 56	MUC7923	N242	MUC8756	N 41	MWC1058	T 48	MWC1722	M 15	MWC2249HA	N211
MUC4212	B354	MUC4886	L 65	MUC6489	P 56	MUC7923	N245	MUC8759	N126	MWC1059	T 48	MWC1736	N191	MWC2249LB	N211
MUC4214	N187	MUC4888	L 65	MUC6490	P 56	MUC7947	R 06	MUC8779RD	R 15	MWC1062	T 48	MWC1736	N192	MWC2250HA	N211
MUC4215	N187	MUC4891	L 70	MUC6491	P 56	MUC7947	R 16	MUC8779RD	R 16	MWC1063	T 48	MWC1737	N191	MWC2250LB	N211
MUC4275	S 06	MUC4892	L 70	MUC6492	P 56	MUC7947	R 14	MUC8780RD	R 04	MWC1080	N163	MWC1737	N192	MWC2309	N 29
MUC4275	S 07	MUC4895	L 71	MUC6493	P 56	MUC7947	R 21	MUC8780RD	R 05	MWC1081	N163	MWC1743	P 23	MWC2314	P 54
MUC4275	S 18	MUC5307	N152	MUC6494	P 53	MUC8364	N194	MUC8835	N 44	MWC1082	N166	MWC1743LCS	P 23	MWC2314	P 63
MUC4289	N185	MUC5308	N152	MUC6495	P 53	MUC8365	N194	MUC8928	N 67	MWC1083	N166	MWC1744	P 23	MWC2314	P 64
MUC4290	N185	MUC5309	N152	MUC6496	P 64	MUC8409RD	R 05	MUC8949	N 97	MWC1086	N 47	MWC1744LCS	P 23	MWC2314	P 66
MUC4291	S 06	MUC5310	N152	MUC6496	P 65	MUC8411RD	R 16	MUC8949	N 98	MWC1087	N 47	MWC1812	N192	MWC2314	P 53
MUC4291	S 18	MUC5311	N152	MUC6497	P 65	MUC8412	R 16	MUC8949	N 95	MWC1092AG	N227	MWC1813	N192	MWC2314	P 56
MUC4299	N 30	MUC5376	N 40	MUC6498	P 64	MUC8414	R 05	MUC8950	N 99	MWC1092AG	N230	MWC1820	N 41	MWC2315AV	P 45
MUC4319	N 33	MUC5456	R 43	MUC6499	P 64	MUC8428RD	R 04	MUC9110	N169	MWC1092AG	N231	MWC1821	N 41	MWC2315LDE	P 45
MUC4358	L 50	MUC5743	R 43	MUC6519	N 97	MUC8428RD	R 05	MUC9110	N 50	MWC1141	R 28	MWC1826	J 62	MWC2315LOY	P 45
MUC4358	L 58	MUC6001	L 71	MUC6519	N 42	MUC8429RD	R 04	MUC9136	N 85	MWC1474	P 22	MWC1827	J 62	MWC2501	J 62
MUC4375	L 49	MUC6011	L 71	MUC6519	N 96	MUC8429RD	R 05	MUC9142	N 85	MWC1474	P 20	MWC1837	N170	MWC2522	R 24
MUC4455	L 59	MUC6012	L 71	MUC6651	P 62	MUC8430RD	R 05	MUC9154	N123	MWC1476	N188	MWC1838	N170	MWC2522	R 27
MUC4455	L 66	MUC6013	L 71	MUC6652	P 65	MUC8431RD	R 05	MUC9154	N115	MWC1477	N188	MWC1898	N157	MWC2526	M121
MUC4471	N180	MUC6037	L 49	MUC6653	P 65	MUC8432RD	R 15	MUC9154	N118	MWC1480	N189	MWC1898	N169	MWC2530	M121
MUC4474	N180	MUC6038	L 49	MUC6658	N151	MUC8432RD	R 16	MUC9154	N117	MWC1481	N189	MWC1899	N157	MWC2532	R 43
MUC4477	N180	MUC6040	L 49	MUC6659	N151	MUC8438	R 05	MUC9155	N123	MWC1484	N190	MWC1900	N165	MWC2533	R 43
MUC4481	N180	MUC6042	L 49	MUC6667LDE	P 44	MUC8439	R 05	MUC9155	N115	MWC1485	N194	MWC1950	N193	MWC2567	N 28
MUC4486	N180	MUC6050	L 49	MUC6667LOY	P 44	MUC8447	R 15	MUC9155	N118	MWC1486	N189	MWC1950	N194	MWC2698	N152
MUC4499	N 39	MUC6052	L 49	MUC6667RD	P 44	MUC8447	R 16	MUC9155	N117	MWC1487	N189	MWC1950	N189	MWC2722	R 43
MUC4524	N239	MUC6053	L 49	MUC6681	P 15	MUC8448RD	R 04	MUC9158	N 51	MWC1488	N193	MWC2120	N117	MWC2780	P 19
MUC4524	N240	MUC6054	L 49	MUC6682	P 15	MUC8448RD	R 05	MUC9158	N 41	MWC1489	N193	MWC2121	N117	MWC2781	P 19
MUC4525	P 18	MUC6055	L 49	MUC6686	N 27	MUC8449RD	R 04	MUC9167	P 28	MWC1492	N193	MWC2129	N 97	MWC2782	P 22
MUC4525	P 23	MUC6056	L 49	MUC6905	N 28	MUC8449RD	R 05	MUC9168	P 29	MWC1493	N193	MWC2129	N 42	MWC2783	P 22
MUC4528	P 18	MUC6074	P 57	MUC6932	N211	MUC8450RD	R 15	MUC9169	P 29	MWC1496	R 43	MWC2129	N 96	MWC2891	R 43
MUC4529	P 18	MUC6075	P 57	MUC6979	N187	MUC8450RD	R 16	MUC9204	N132	MWC1497	R 43	MWC2145	S 01	MWC2896	P 56
MUC4538	N238	MUC6112	N145	MUC6980	N187	MUC8526	N195	MUC9204	N163	MWC1602	N164	MWC2146	S 01	MWC2926	N145
MUC4542	N111	MUC6157	N158	MUC7000	F 05	MUC8526	N192	MUC9205	N132	MWC1603	N164	MWC2237HA	N211	MWC2938	N116
MUC4544	N180	MUC6157	N169	MUC7505	G 07	MUC8707	N122	MUC9205	N163	MWC1608	R 43	MWC2237LB	N211	MWC2938	N 42
MUC4545	N180	MUC6159	N158	MUC7506	G 09	MUC8716	N116	MUC9220	N 95	MWC1609	R 43	MWC2238HA	N211	MWC2938	N117
MUC4546	V 05	MUC6159	N169	MUC7513	M 27	MUC8716	N119	MUC9339	N 57	MWC1614	R 43	MWC2238LB	N211	MWC3103RD	R 24
MUC4546	S 10	MUC6163	N158	MUC7513	M 28	MUC8717	N116	MUC9347	P 31	MWC1615	R 43	MWC2239HA	N211	MWC3104RD	R 26
MUC4801	P 12	MUC6164	N158	MUC7514	M 27	MUC8717	N119	MUC9419	R 48	MWC1622	N195	MWC2239LB	N211	MWC3105PB	R 24
MUC4803	N141	MUC6166	N 35	MUC7598	P 07	MUC8730	N115	MUC9704	N 63	MWC1622	N192	MWC2240HA	N211	MWC3106PB	R 26
MUC4804	N151	MUC6332	S 14	MUC7599	P 07	MUC8730	N117	MUC9864	R 27	MWC1623	R 27	MWC2240LB	N211	MWC3107RD	R 23
MUC4806	N151	MUC6400	N132	MUC7728	N 93	MUC8731	N115	MUC9871	R 27	MWC1624	P 57	MWC2241HA	N211	MWC3108PB	R 23
MUC4860	L 49	MUC6400	P 55	MUC7729	N 93	MUC8731	N117	MUC9872	R 27	MWC1625	P 57	MWC2241LB	N211	MWC3109RD	R 26
MUC4865	L 59	MUC6400	N129	MUC7809	N195	MUC8736	N121	MUC9873	R 27	MWC1627	N184	MWC2242HA	N211	MWC3110PB	R 26
MUC4865	H 09	MUC6400	N133	MUC7809	N192	MUC8737	N121	MUC9874	R 27	MWC1628	P 57	MWC2242LB	N211	MWC3111RD	R 22
MUC4866	L 59	MUC6400	N131	MUC7904	N185	MUC8737	N122	MUC9875	R 27	MWC1629	P 57	MWC2243HA	N211	MWC3112PB	R 22
MUC4866	H 09	MUC6418	S 09	MUC7907	N185	MUC8738	N121	MUC9971RD	R 25	MWC1632	R 43	MWC2243LB	N211	MWC3113RD	R 24
MUC4871	L 59	MUC6419	S 09	MUC7911	N185	MUC8739	N121	MUC9972PB	R 25	MWC1633	R 43	MWC2244HA	N211	MWC3114PB	R 24

MWC3136	P 22
MWC3136	H 35
MWC3136	P 17
MWC3136	P 21
MWC3136	P 20
MWC3137	P 22
MWC3137	P 18
MWC3137	P 56
MWC3137	P 60
MWC3137	P 21
MWC3137	P 20
MWC3138	R 43
MWC3139	R 43
MWC3148	N195
MWC3148	N192
MWC3284	R 47
MWC3285	R 47
MWC3294	N164
MWC3301	R 05
MWC3302	R 04
MWC3302	R 05
MWC3303	R 04
MWC3303	R 05
MWC3306	R 04
MWC3306	R 05
MWC3307	R 04
MWC3307	R 05
MWC3312	N196
MWC3316	N115
MWC3316	N118
MWC3317	N115
MWC3317	N118
MWC3320	N 41
MWC3321	N 41
MWC3336	N166
MWC3337	N166
MWC3339	N142
MWC4309	S 09
MWC4370	N159
MWC4370	N162
MWC4371	N159
MWC4371	N162
MWC4380	R 42
MWC4393	R 58
MWC4398	R 58
MWC4399	R 58
MWC4412	N165
MWC4413	N165
MWC4534	R 04
MWC4534	R 05
MWC4535	R 04
MWC4535	R 05
MWC4536	R 14
MWC4548	R 15
MWC4548	R 16
MWC4549	R 15
MWC4549	R 16
MWC4662	N118
MWC4663	N118
MWC4686	N115
MWC4687	N115
MWC4710	N 65
MWC4711	N 65
MWC4712	N222
MWC4712	N172
MWC4713	N172
MWC4714	N222
MWC4714	N129
MWC4714	N131
MWC4715	N222
MWC4715	N111
MWC4715	N105
MWC4716	N111
MWC4717	N105
MWC4720	N159
MWC4721	N159
MWC4722	N183
MWC4723	N183
MWC4724	N183
MWC4725	N183
MWC4726	N 65
MWC4726	N113
MWC4727	N222
MWC4727	N112
MWC4728	N109
MWC4729	N110
MWC4730	N109
MWC4731	N110
MWC4733	N112
MWC4734	N109
MWC4735	N109
MWC4736	N110
MWC4737	N110
MWC4762	N 65
MWC4763	N159
MWC4764	N183
MWC4771	N105
MWC4771	N129
MWC4771	N131
MWC4772	N111
MWC4772	N105
MWC4773	N 65
MWC4822	R 36
MWC4846	N188
MWC4847	N188
MWC4850	N193
MWC4850	N188
MWC4854	H 09
MWC4860	L 65
MWC4950	R 16
MWC5001	N193
MWC5002	N193
MWC5018	N158
MWC5019	N158
MWC5054	R 68
MWC5055	R 68
MWC5201	N134
MWC5217	N130
MWC5417	R 43
MWC5455	R 43
MWC5463LCS	R 37
MWC5464RCF	R 37
MWC5464RUY	R 37
MWC5465LCS	R 36
MWC5466RCF	R 36
MWC5466RUY	R 36
MWC5491LCS	R 40
MWC5492RCF	R 40
MWC5492RUY	R 40
MWC5493LCS	R 39
MWC5494RCF	R 39
MWC5494RUY	R 39
MWC5507RCF	R 30
MWC5507RCF	R 34
MWC5507RUY	R 30
MWC5507RUY	R 34
MWC5508RCF	R 32
MWC5508RUY	R 32
MWC5525LCS	R 29
MWC5530LCS	R 30
MWC5533RCF	R 22
MWC5534LCS	R 22
MWC5536RCF	R 22
MWC5537LCS	R 22
MWC5539RCF	R 23
MWC5540LCS	R 23
MWC5546RCF	R 23
MWC5547LCS	R 23
MWC5549RCF	R 24
MWC5550LCS	R 24
MWC5555RCF	R 24
MWC5556LCS	R 24
MWC5558RCF	R 25
MWC5559LCS	R 25
MWC5561RCF	R 25
MWC5562LCS	R 25
MWC5568RCF	R 26
MWC5569LCS	R 26
MWC5573LCS	R 02
MWC5592RCF	R 26
MWC5593LCS	R 26
MWC5599LCS	R 02
MWC5607LCS	R 02
MWC5613LCS	R 02
MWC5626RUY	R 14
MWC5628LCS	R 14
MWC5630RCF	R 07
MWC5632RCF	R 11
MWC5648RCF	R 13
MWC5648RUY	R 13
MWC5649RCF	R 13
MWC5649RUY	R 13
MWC5661	R 37
MWC5667LCS	R 07
MWC5668LCS	R 09
MWC5669LCS	R 11
MWC5670LCS	R 13
MWC5671LCS	R 13
MWC5674LCS	R 07
MWC5675LCS	R 09
MWC5676RCF	R 07
MWC5677RCF	R 09
MWC5679RCF	R 09
MWC5680RCF	R 17
MWC5681RCF	R 17
MWC5682RCF	R 17
MWC5683RCF	R 17
MWC5684RCF	R 17
MWC5685LCS	R 17
MWC5686LCS	R 17
MWC5687LCS	R 17
MWC5688LCS	R 17
MWC5689LCS	R 17
MWC5708LUH	P 65
MWC5708LUH	P 66
MWC5710LUH	P 65
MWC5710LUH	P 66
MWC5711LUH	P 65
MWC5711LUH	P 66
MWC5712LUH	P 64
MWC5712LUH	P 66
MWC5713LUH	P 64
MWC5713LUH	P 66
MWC5741	N170
MWC5742	N170
MWC5759	N158
MWC5759	N181
MWC5763LNP	P 55
MWC5763LOY	P 55
MWC5764	P 55
MWC5832LNP	P 54
MWC5832LOY	P 54
MWC5833LNP	P 54
MWC5833LOY	P 54
MWC6055NAL	N132
MWC6055NUC	N132
MWC6106PCB	R 14
MWC6128	N167
MWC6129	N167
MWC6130	N163
MWC6143	N 75
MWC6144	N 68
MWC6144	N 69
MWC6144	N 70
MWC6144	N 71
MWC6145	N 75
MWC6145	N 76
MWC6145	N 77
MWC6145	N 78
MWC6203	P 55
MWC6253	P 30
MWC6254	P 30
MWC6273	N128
MWC6291	N169
MWC6450	N158
MWC6450	N169
MWC6450	N181
MWC6696NUC	N128
MWC6697NUC	N128
MWC6698NUC	N130
MWC6699NUC	N130
MWC6907NUC	N128
MWC6908NUC	N130
MWC6924	R 40
MWC6925	R 40
MWC7188RUM	N212
MWC7189RUM	N212
MWC7190RUM	N212
MWC7191RUM	N212
MWC7194RUM	N212
MWC7195RUM	N212
MWC7612	N109
MWC7612	N110
MWC7614	N109
MWC7614	N110
MWC7615	N109
MWC7615	N110
MWC7617	N109
MWC7617	N110
MWC7620	N 65
MWC7620	N113
MWC7625	N 65
MWC7625	N113
MWC7635	R 04
MWC7635	R 05
MWC7635	R 12
MWC7636	R 04
MWC7636	R 05
MWC7636	R 12
MWC7641	N 66
MWC7648	N 65
MWC7648	N113
MWC7652	N 65
MWC7652	N113
MWC7657LDE	P 40
MWC7658LDE	P 40
MWC7659LDE	P 40
MWC7660LDE	P 40
MWC7661LDE	P 40
MWC7662LDE	P 40
MWC7663LDE	P 40
MWC7665	N 84
MWC7665	N 85
MWC7685	N112
MWC7686	N112
MWC7698	N 81
MWC7698	N 82
MWC7698	N 83
MWC8201	P 50
MWC8202	P 50
MWC8203	P 50
MWC8205	P 50
MWC8206	P 50
MWC8207	P 50
MWC8208	P 50
MWC8209	P 50
MWC8210	P 50
MWC8211	P 50
MWC8212	P 50
MWC8213	P 50
MWC8214	P 50
MWC8215	P 50
MWC8216	P 50
MWC8217	P 50
MWC8218	P 50
MWC8219	P 50
MWC8223	N153
MWC8256LUJ	N212
MWC8256LUJ	N213
MWC8256LVA	N215
MWC8256LVA	N217
MWC8256MUB	N212
MWC8256MUB	N213
MWC8257LUJ	N212
MWC8257LUJ	N213
MWC8257MUB	N212
MWC8257MUB	N213
MWC8270	N154
MWC8271	N154
MWC8276	R 58
MWC8277	R 58
MWC8466CUF	N146
MWC8466HCC	N146
MWC8466HCN	N146
MWC8466HUJ	N146
MWC8466JUG	N146
MWC8466JUH	N146
MWC8466LCN	N146
MWC8466LUS	N146
MWC8466NCM	N146
MWC8466NUC	N146
MWC8466PUC	N146
MWC8466SUB	N146
MWC8547	R 39
MWC8548	R 39
MWC8590RUM	N212
MWC8591RUM	N212
MWC8615	R 49
MWC8666	R 32
MWC8667	R 32
MWC8901LNP	P 54
MWC8901LOY	P 54
MWC8910LNP	P 55
MWC8910LOY	P 55
MWC8911LNP	P 55
MWC8911LOY	P 55
MWC8914LNP	P 60
MWC8915LNP	P 60
MWC8916LOY	P 60
MWC8917LOY	P 60
MWC8942RCF	R 11
MWC8942RUY	R 11
MWC8943LCS	R 11
MWC8944RCF	R 07
MWC8945RCF	R 07
MWC8946LCS	R 07
MWC8947LCS	R 07
MWC8966	N106
MWC8967	N106
MWC9301	M112
MWC9303	M112
MWC9304	M112
MWC9306	M112
MWC9313	S 01
MWC9313	S 05
MWC9313	S 02
MWC9322	P 07
MWC9322	M 32
MWC9327PMA	P 01
MWC9338PMA	P 01
MWC9339PMA	P 01
MWC9339PUA	P 01
MWC9340	N 41
MWC9361	N141
MWC9369LDE	P 40
MWC9370LDE	P 40
MWC9371LDE	P 40
MWC9376	P 41
MWC9380	N142
MWC9418	N104
MWC9419	N104
MWC9420	N104
MWC9421	N104
MWC9450	N102
MWC9451	N102
MWC9452	N102
MWC9453	N102
MWC9482	P 55
MWC9484LUH	P 59
MWC9485LUH	P 59
MWC9486LUH	P 59
MWC9490LUH	P 58
MWC9491LUH	P 58
MWC9500	N135
MWC9500	N134
MWC9601	M 17
MWC9601	M 18
MWC9604	P 65
MWC9606	M 07
MWC9823LNP	P 54
MWC9832LUH	P 63
MWC9832LUH	P 64
MWC9832LUH	P 65
MWC9832LUH	P 66
MWC9832LUH	P 60
MWC9832PMA	N 63
MWC9841RCF	R 09
MWC9841RUY	R 09
MWC9842RCF	R 09
MWC9842RUY	R 09
MWC9843LCS	R 09
MWC9844LCS	R 09
MWC9917	P 45
MWC9917	P 21
MWC9917	P 20
MWC9918LCS	P 21
MWC9918LCS	P 20
MWC9918LOY	P 20
MWC9918PMA	P 21
MXC1130PMA	P 55
MXC1394LUH	P 33
MXC1395LUH	P 33
MXC1436	N169
MXC1624	N201
MXC1645LUH	P 59
MXC1790	N181
MXC1800	P 22
MXC1800	P 21
MXC1800	P 20
MXC1804PMA	P 42
MXC1805PMA	P 42
MXC1806PMA	P 42
MXC1813LCS	R 45
MXC1814LCS	R 45
MXC1826RUY	R 24
MXC1827RUY	R 23
MXC1828RUY	R 26
MXC1829RUY	R 25
MXC1830LCS	R 24
MXC1831LCS	R 23

MXC1832LCS	R 26
MXC1833LCS	R 25
MXC1848	B387
MXC1848	J 48
MXC1848	L 11
MXC1858LCS	P 19
MXC1859LCS	P 19
MXC1860LCS	P 22
MXC1861LCS	P 22
MXC1872RUP	N213
MXC1873RUP	N213
MXC1874RUP	N213
MXC1875RUP	N213
MXC1989LCS	P 23
MXC1992LCS	P 23
MXC2031	N103
MXC2031	N106
MXC2033	N104
MXC2044	N181
MXC2047	N181
MXC2337LDE	P 41
MXC2338LDE	P 40
MXC2338LOY	P 40
MXC2339LDE	P 40
MXC2339LOY	P 40
MXC2340LDE	P 40
MXC2341	M 18
MXC2342	M 18
MXC2343LUH	P 58
MXC2344LUH	P 58
MXC2345LUH	P 62
MXC2346LUH	P 59
MXC2347LUH	P 59
MXC2348LUH	P 64
MXC2348LUH	P 65
MXC2537	R 52
MXC2611	P 14
MXC2640RUY	R 17
MXC2641RUY	R 17
MXC2645LCS	R 18
MXC2646RUY	R 17
MXC2647LCS	R 18
MXC2648LCS	R 18
MXC2649RUY	R 17
MXC2650RUY	R 17
MXC2651LCS	R 18
MXC2652LCS	R 18
MXC2728	N193
MXC2729	N193
MXC2744	R 45
MXC2745	R 45
MXC2751	R 45
MXC2780RCF	R 29
MXC2780RUY	R 29
MXC2931	N152
MXC2932	N 57
MXC2948LDE	P 27
MXC2948LOY	P 27
MXC2949LDE	P 27
MXC2949LOY	P 27
MXC3130PUB	L 11
MXC3134	N 25
MXC3167RUY	R 25
MXC3168LCS	R 25
MXC3169RUY	R 22
MXC3170LCS	R 22
MXC3188	L 38
MXC3188	L 75
MXC3189	L 38
MXC3189	L 75
MXC3254RUY	R 07
MXC3255RUY	R 07
MXC3256LCS	R 07
MXC3257LCS	R 07
MXC3258	R 01
MXC3259	R 01
MXC3276	P 55
MXC3277	P 55
MXC3278	P 55
MXC3279	P 55
MXC3282	R 68
MXC3283	R 68
MXC3319LNP	P 54
MXC3319LOY	P 54
MXC3340	N221
MXC3341	N221
MXC3357	L 71
MXC3358	L 71
MXC3418	L 71
MXC3676	N103
MXC3676	N106
MXC3677	N103
MXC3677	N106
MXC3680	N104
MXC3681	N104
MXC3684	N103
MXC3684	N104
MXC3684	N106
MXC3685	N103
MXC3685	N104
MXC3685	N106
MXC4630	N 60
MXC4631	N 60
MXC4657	N244
MXC4738PMA	P 22
MXC4738PMA	P 21
MXC4738PMA	P 20
MXC5010	N134
MXC5011	N134
MXC5015RUP	N213
MXC5088PMA	P 42
MXC5089PMA	P 42
MXC5090PMA	P 42
MXC5202	N134
MXC5212	R 04
MXC5212	R 06
MXC5212	R 15
MXC5212	R 16
MXC5212	R 14
MXC5212	R 17
MXC5212	R 18
MXC5212	R 19
MXC5451LOY	P 37
MXC5451LOY	P 44
MXC5477	S 16
MXC5477	S 15
MXC5477	S 14
MXC5478	S 14
MXC5479	S 16
MXC5479	S 15
MXC5479	S 14
MXC5480	S 16
MXC5480	S 15
MXC5480	S 14
MXC5488	R 54
MXC5488	R 49
MXC5489	R 54
MXC5489	R 49
MXC5491	R 49
MXC5492	R 49
MXC5493	R 49
MXC5495	R 57
MXC5497	R 56
MXC5509	R 49
MXC5509	R 51
MXC5510	R 54
MXC5510	R 51
MXC5521	R 54
MXC5549	N181
MXC5575	N181
MXC5714	J 05
MXC5714	J 06
MXC5746	N 35
MXC5746	N 36
MXC5778	R 04
MXC5778	R 05
MXC5778	R 12
MXC5779	R 04
MXC5779	R 05
MXC5779	R 12
MXC5812RUY	R 26
MXC5813LCS	R 26
MXC5814RUY	R 23
MXC5815LCS	R 23
MXC5820RUY	R 24
MXC5821LCS	R 24
MXC5822RUY	R 22
MXC5823LCS	R 22
MXC5829	N159
MXC5829	N160
MXC5830	N183
MXC5832	N159
MXC5832	N160
MXC5833	N183
MXC5834	N183
MXC5835	N183
MXC5836	N159
MXC5836	N160
MXC5837	N183
MXC5856LUH	P 58
MXC5857LUH	P 62
MXC5859	P 63
MXC5859	P 61
MXC5968	N118
MXC5969	N118
MXC5973	N117
MXC5974	N117
MXC5978	N115
MXC5979	N115
MXC6084PMA	P 01
MXC6142PMA	P 46
MXC6312	N 39
MXC6315	N 39
MXC6321PMA	S 03
MXC6338	N 39
MXC6396	N205
MXC6397	N207
MXC6398	N207
MXC6401	N207
MXC6401	N205
MXC6402	N209
MXC6402	N207
MXC6402	N206
MXC6402	N208
MXC6402	N205
MXC6405	T 03
MXC6406	T 03
MXC6411	T 53
MXC6412	T 51
MXC6413	T 51
MXC6538	P 28
MXC6539	P 28
MXC6540	P 29
MXC6541	P 29
MXC6542	P 29
MXC6543	P 28
MXC6550	P 30
MXC6551	P 30
MXC6676	V 04
MXC6676	N251
MXC7226	S 12
MXC7227	S 12
MXC7228	S 12
MXC7264	R 54
MXC7335	T 03
MXC7354	N142
MXC7373	N 39
MXC7570	N155
MXC7571	N155
MXC7648	S 18
MXC7651	N188
MXC7652	N188
MXC7732	N151
MXC7846	N185
MXC7847	N185
MXC7887	T 03
MXC8222	N190
MXC8223	N190
MXC8224	N190
MXC8225	N190
MXC8282	N156
MXC8282	N168
MXC8283	N156
MXC8283	N168
MXC8284	N156
MXC8285	N156
MXC8551	N 35
MXC8552	N 36
MXC8554	N 36
MXC8555	N 35
MXC8556	N 35
MXC8556	N 36
MXC8573	N 31
MXC8574	N 31
MXC8575	N 32
MXC8603	N162
MXC8934	N116
MXC8934	N119
MXC8935	N116
MXC8935	N119
MXC9012	N 27
MXC9013	N 27
MXC9015	N 27
MXC9116	N 39
MXC9117	N 39
MXC9343	N 54
MXC9400	N 54
MXC9402	N 54
MXC9455	N197
MXC9586	N170
MXC9587	N170
MXC9689	N195
MXC9689	N192
MXC9982	N185
MXC9983	N185
MYC100230L	B293
NAD10038	B369
NAD10038E	B369
NAD10039	B144
NAD10039	B229
NAD10039	B189
NAD10040	B 96
NAD10040E	B 96
NAD101190	B369
NAD101190E	B397
NAD101190E	B369
NAD101240	B297
NAD101240E	B297
NAD101490	B397
NAD101490	B369
NAD101490E	B397
NAD101490E	B369
NAF100170	B 96
NAJ100100	B 96
NAK100050	B 96
NC112041	E 60
NC112041	E 68
NC112041	F 17
NC112041	F 18
NH104041L	B244
NH104041L	B 19
NH104041L	B 67
NH104041L	N184
NH104041L	N193
NH104041L	M116
NH104041L	N 32
NH104041L	N127
NH104041L	J 50
NH104041L	M 83
NH104041L	M 84
NH104041L	F 23
NH104041L	M119
NH104041L	N187
NH104041L	N188
NH104041L	N143
NH104044	P 01
NH105041	F 04
NH105041	H 36
NH105041	M109
NH105041	L 03
NH105041	M123
NH105041	M125
NH105041	M 12
NH105041L	B218
NH105041L	B 80
NH105041L	B128
NH105041L	B175
NH105041L	N182
NH105041L	N132
NH105041L	P 02
NH105041L	M113
NH105041L	M 57
NH105041L	M 58
NH105041L	J 51
NH105041L	R 02
NH105041L	R 03
NH105041L	G 13
NH105041L	P 08
NH105041L	T 45
NH105041L	T 46
NH105041L	M 14
NH105041L	M 15
NH105041L	M120
NH105041L	B 29
NH105041L	B178
NH105041L	R 37
NH105041L	C 51
NH105041L	M 63
NH105041L	S 08
NH105041L	S 09
NH105041L	N163
NH105041L	M 16
NH106041	T 47
NH106041	H 11
NH106041L	B303
NH106041L	B354
NH106041L	N 37
NH106041L	N 38
NH106041L	N 58
NH106041L	N169
NH106041L	N181
NH106041L	N196
NH106041L	N197
NH106041L	N121
NH106041L	N198
NH106041L	N239
NH106041L	M 46
NH106041L	R 29
NH106041L	R 33
NH106041L	L 24
NH106041L	L 33
NH106041L	C 69
NH106041L	C 29
NH106041L	H 25
NH106041L	N 11
NH106041L	M 29
NH106041L	M 32
NH106041L	M 82
NH106041L	N 34
NH106041L	N 39
NH106041L	N 49
NH106041L	N179
NH106041L	N191
NH106041L	N 97
NH106041L	N115
NH106041L	N125
NH106041L	N126
NH106041L	N 99
NH106041L	N 53
NH106041L	N118
NH106041L	N 93
NH106041L	N246
NH106041L	E 69
NH106041L	J 38
NH106041L	J 33
NH106041L	J 46
NH106041L	N 44
NH106041L	N 46
NH106041L	N 47
NH106041L	N142
NH106041L	N 41
NH106041L	R 44
NH106041L	R 40
NH106041L	L 60
NH106041L	L 61
NH106041L	L 63
NH106041L	L 64
NH106041L	R 63
NH106041L	R 68
NH106041L	N114
NH106041L	J 20
NH106041L	L 09
NH106041L	L 08
NH106041L	L 17
NH106041L	L 42
NH106041L	L 43
NH106041L	M135
NH106041L	J 37
NH106041L	N117
NH106041L	L 32
NH106041L	N 67
NH106041L	C 24
NH106041L	T 45
NH106041L	T 46
NH106041L	S 04
NH106041L	B147
NH106041L	M 27
NH106041L	M 28
NH106041L	R 15
NH106041L	J 13
NH106041L	R 62
NH106041L	R 66
NH106041L	F 23
NH106041L	M130
NH106041L	M131
NH106041L	R 01
NH106041L	R 51
NH106041L	H 10
NH106041L	H 14
NH106041L	H 19

Part No.	Ref.	Part No.	Ref.	Part No.	Ref.	Part No.	Ref.	Part No.	Ref.	Part No.	Ref.	Part No.	Ref.	Part No.	Ref.
NH106041L	H 22	NH108041L	B126	NH110041L	B148	NJ108061L	N145	NRC1302	N 14	NRC4733	N 19	NRC5415	J 25	NRC6221	E 68
NH106041L	B224	NH108041L	H 34	NH110041L	F 02	NK106081	N 37	NRC1360	L 10	NRC4757	J 03	NRC5415	J 28	NRC6235	E 63
NH106041L	N149	NH108041L	M 58	NH110041L	F 03	NK106081	N 48	NRC2015	J 67	NRC4765	J 01	NRC5434	B 08	NRC6235	E 65
NH106041L	N139	NH108041L	B 73	NH110041L	H 01	NK106081	F 01	NRC2051	T 35	NRC4765	J 08	NRC5434	B 57	NRC6235	E 66
NH106041L	N140	NH108041L	B 75	NH110041L	B189	NM105011	N 51	NRC2087	J 67	NRC4765	J 10	NRC5434	B109	NRC6254	J 46
NH106041L	N187	NH108041L	B 87	NH110041L	D 06	NM105011	M 79	NRC2089	J 40	NRC4772	H 01	NRC5434	B158	NRC6302	F 23
NH106041L	R 37	NH108041L	B137	NH110041L	N 15	NM105011	N104	NRC2089	J 67	NRC4775	H 01	NRC5434	B201	NRC6302	F 25
NH106041L	R 38	NH108041L	J 08	NH110041L	N 16	NM105011	N106	NRC2159	J 74	NRC4776	J 65	NRC5478	N 11	NRC6302	F 27
NH106041L	N192	NH108041L	M144	NH110041L	E 63	NM105011	N241	NRC2159	J 70	NRC4776	J 68	NRC5485	N 08	NRC6306	L 60
NH106041L	K 16	NH108041L	K 03	NH110041L	E 66	NM105011	N244	NRC2159	J 67	NRC4776	J 72	NRC5494	G 03	NRC6306	L 61
NH106041L	K 14	NH108041L	K 04	NH112041L	B128	NN105011	J 67	NRC2195	J 67	NRC4837	L 15	NRC5502	G 03	NRC6306	L 42
NH106041L	J 36	NH108041L	R 48	NH112041L	B175	NN105021L	P 10	NRC2211	G 05	NRC4839	L 02	NRC5503	L 15	NRC6307	L 60
NH106041L	N 95	NH108041L	R 50	NH112041L	N 28	NN105021L	T 27	NRC2214	J 70	NRC4842	L 15	NRC5544	L 02	NRC6307	L 42
NH106041L	N 96	NH108041L	J 10	NH112041L	T 33	NN106011	E 69	NRC223	B334	NRC4843	L 15	NRC5544	L 03	NRC6308	L 63
NH106041L	J 22	NH108041L	K 10	NH112041L	T 35	NN106011	F 23	NRC2383	L 17	NRC4844	L 15	NRC5582	F 17	NRC6308	L 42
NH106041L	T 51	NH108041L	B341	NH112041L	S 12	NN106011	L 29	NRC2383	M123	NRC4850	L 14	NRC5593	E 63	NRC6309	L 42
NH106041L	T 52	NH108041L	B103	NH116041L	N 24	NN106011	L 26	NRC2383	M124	NRC4852	L 14	NRC5593	E 65	NRC6311	L 43
NH106041L	T 53	NH108041L	B 11	NH116041L	T 37	NN106011	L 27	NRC2383	F 20	NRC4853	N 23	NRC5593	E 66	NRC6312	L 43
NH106041L	N161	NH108041L	B 12	NH116041L	T 38	NN106011	T 53	NRC2383	M127	NRC4854	N 23	NRC5602	S 11	NRC6313	L 43
NH106041L	T 48	NH108041L	B 40	NH604041L	B 32	NN106011	L 22	NRC2536	J 70	NRC4966	N 11	NRC5602	E 63	NRC6314	L 63
NH106041L	J 67	NH108041L	B 25	NH604041L	B 78	NN106011L	J 37	NRC255	T 05	NRC5088	H 36	NRC5602	E 65	NRC6314	L 43
NH106041L	N129	NH108041L	B 26	NH604041L	R 33	NN106011L	J 36	NRC2572	J 74	NRC5089	H 36	NRC5602	E 66	NRC6320	E 69
NH106041L	S 12	NH108041L	B 27	NH604041L	N178	NN106021	N 58	NRC2652	J 74	NRC5104	H 36	NRC5603	E 63	NRC6324	T 31
NH106041L	N133	NH108041L	B363	NH604041L	B377	NN106021	P 33	NRC2652	J 70	NRC5110	H 36	NRC5603	E 65	NRC6339	J 51
NH106041L	G 01	NH108041L	B364	NH604041L	J 13	NN106021	R 28	NRC2652	J 67	NRC5220	G 01	NRC5603	E 66	NRC6352	L 43
NH106041L	N241	NH108041L	B365	NH604041L	J 73	NN106021	C 86	NRC2744	H 34	NRC5281	F 01	NRC5623	J 58	NRC6353	L 64
NH106041L	N243	NH108041L	B366	NH604041L	G 07	NN106021	N 93	NRC2864	B323	NRC5294	L 09	NRC5627	N 20	NRC6353	L 43
NH106041L	N131	NH108041L	B224	NH604041L	G 08	NN106021	J 51	NRC3301	B303	NRC5295	L 09	NRC5665	N 11	NRC6372	E 59
NH106044	R 45	NH108041L	B184	NH604041L	B365	NN106021	M135	NRC3314	N 14	NRC5338	M 27	NRC5674	E 68	NRC6374	K 03
NH106044	R 39	NH108041L	D 36	NH605041L	B304	NN106021	P 16	NRC3405	L 17	NRC5346	E 32	NRC5707	E 69	NRC6374	K 02
NH106044	R 36	NH108041L	B299	NH605041L	B307	NN106021	P 14	NRC3406	L 05	NRC5387	M 27	NRC5724	N 07	NRC6374	K 12
NH106044	R 31	NH108041L	K 23	NH605041L	E 59	NN106021	P 15	NRC3662	L 05	NRC5396	N 24	NRC5742	N 15	NRC6374	K 15
NH106045	H 25	NH108041L	J 59	NH605041L	N157	NN106021	F 25	NRC3664	L 14	NRC5403	K 03	NRC5743	N 15	NRC6388	E 67
NH106045	N150	NH108041L	N138	NH605041L	N168	NN106021	F 27	NRC3908	M 86	NRC5403	K 02	NRC5758	E 69	NRC6389	E 67
NH106047	B354	NH108044	N141	NH605041L	H 29	NN106021	M131	NRC3923	E 62	NRC5403	K 12	NRC5758	K 31	NRC6403	L 14
NH106047	L 09	NH108065L	B218	NH605041L	B334	NN106021	N141	NRC3976	L 14	NRC5403	K 01	NRC5758	K 32	NRC6404	L 14
NH106047	F 19	NH108065L	B173	NH605041L	R 68	NN106021	T 51	NRC3977	L 05	NRC5403	K 11	NRC5804	N 24	NRC6404	L 15
NH106047L	J 38	NH110041L	B 08	NH605041L	K 03	NN106021	T 52	NRC4162	L 29	NRC5403	K 15	NRC5818	J 65	NRC6417	L 60
NH106047L	J 37	NH110041L	B 46	NH605041L	N 67	NN106021	T 53	NRC4171	N 11	NRC5403	K 07	NRC5819	L 26	NRC6417	L 42
NH106047L	J 45	NH110041L	B 47	NH605041L	B330	NN108021	N 28	NRC4218	K 03	NRC5403	K 08	NRC5820	L 26	NRC6418	L 60
NH106047L	M134	NH110041L	B 57	NH605041L	B331	NN108021	L 33	NRC4219	K 03	NRC5403	K 09	NRC5823	L 29	NRC6418	L 42
NH106047L	M137	NH110041L	B 97	NH605041L	R 62	NN108021	F 05	NRC4251	H 10	NRC5403	K 19	NRC5824	L 29	NRC6419	L 60
NH108041	K 23	NH110041L	B 98	NH605041L	B 45	NN108021	N201	NRC4251	H 19	NRC5403	K 20	NRC5844	J 65	NRC6419	L 63
NH108041L	B357	NH110041L	B109	NH605041L	B363	NN108021	J 58	NRC4251	H 22	NRC5403	K 22	NRC5886	N 20	NRC6419	L 42
NH108041L	B 07	NH110041L	B158	NH605041L	G 01	NN108021	M103	NRC4251	H 11	NRC5403	K 25	NRC5975	F 21	NRC6419	L 43
NH108041L	B 09	NH110041L	B201	NH606041L	C 38	NN108021	J 52	NRC4317	E 67	NRC5414	J 11	NRC5976	F 22	NRC6420	L 60
NH108041L	B 10	NH110041L	N 14	NH606041L	B341	NN108021	M101	NRC4318	E 67	NRC5415	J 65	NRC5977	F 22	NRC6420	L 42
NH108041L	B 56	NH110041L	C 30	NH606041L	B342	NN108021	J 57	NRC4365	E 58	NRC5415	J 49	NRC5982	F 19	NRC6421	L 42
NH108041L	B 59	NH110041L	C 38	NH606041L	B343	NN108021	N140	NRC4475	G 01	NRC5415	J 19	NRC5985	L 17	NRC6422	L 42
NH108041L	B 60	NH110041L	C 04	NH608061L	B119	NN108021	N141	NRC4514	E 56	NRC5415	J 20	NRC6058	G 09	NRC6430	L 05
NH108041L	B108	NH110041L	C 05	NH608061L	B167	NN108021	K 24	NRC4515	E 56	NRC5415	J 30	NRC6097	J 03	NRC6432	K 03
NH108041L	B129	NH110041L	T 34	NH614041	F 08	NNN000120	M 99	NRC4516	E 56	NRC5415	J 72	NRC62	J 01	NRC6436	K 01
NH108041L	B175	NH110041L	B143	NH614041	F 10	NNU100710	M 99	NRC4661	N 11	NRC5415	J 23	NRC62	J 08	NRC6436	K 11
NH108041L	B176	NH110041L	B144	NH910011L	B335	NR604090L	B328	NRC4665	G 09	NRC5415	J 27	NRC62	J 10	NRC6466	K 02
NH108041L	B177	NH110041L	B146	NH910241L	B335	NR604090L	B327	NRC4693	N 11	NRC5415	J 21	NRC62	J 03	NRC6466	K 12

Part No.	Ref.	Part No.	Ref.	Part No.	Ref.	Part No.	Ref.	Part No.	Ref.	Part No.	Ref.	Part No.	Ref.	Part No.	Ref.
NRC6466	K 01	NRC7240	J 51	NRC7791	G 06	NRC8199	L 29	NRC8507	L 26	NRC9107	J 46	NRC9462	E 64	NRC9726	L 17
NRC6466	K 11	NRC7249	J 51	NRC7792	G 06	NRC8201	L 32	NRC8508	L 26	NRC9115	H 34	NRC9463	E 64	NRC9726	L 15
NRC6467	K 02	NRC7284	J 13	NRC7799	H 16	NRC8204	N 15	NRC8509	L 26	NRC9121	G 01	NRC9472	J 70	NRC9729	E 57
NRC6467	K 12	NRC7303	J 27	NRC7799	H 12	NRC8204	N 16	NRC8510	L 26	NRC9123	H 34	NRC9474	J 01	NRC9731	H 11
NRC6467	K 01	NRC7310	J 30	NRC7799	H 13	NRC8208	T 30	NRC8518	E 69	NRC9137	K 11	NRC9474	J 08	NRC9733	K 01
NRC6467	K 11	NRC7310	J 27	NRC7799	H 11	NRC8208	T 31	NRC8560	G 10	NRC9138	J 10	NRC9492	F 23	NRC9733	K 11
NRC6481	S 06	NRC7311	J 51	NRC7801	H 11	NRC8210	T 30	NRC8588	F 07	NRC9169	G 09	NRC9501	C 38	NRC9741	F 17
NRC6515	H 11	NRC7318	J 30	NRC7827	G 01	NRC8211	T 30	NRC8589	F 07	NRC9183	G 09	NRC9507	J 72	NRC9742	F 17
NRC6526	J 08	NRC7319	J 30	NRC7835	F 04	NRC8213	H 20	NRC8593	H 08	NRC9211	N 19	NRC9508	J 70	NRC9743	F 17
NRC6558	J 10	NRC7351	J 30	NRC7836	F 04	NRC8214	H 20	NRC8605	S 07	NRC9217	G 07	NRC9529	H 01	NRC9749	N 07
NRC6561	E 69	NRC7351	J 27	NRC7869	G 09	NRC8215	H 14	NRC8609	L 02	NRC9224	G 09	NRC9536	J 19	NRC9757	H 19
NRC6636	T 31	NRC7372	J 58	NRC7869	G 07	NRC8215	H 19	NRC8618	B206	NRC9225	J 01	NRC9543	J 01	NRC9770	J 50
NRC6653	H 35	NRC7387	F 06	NRC7871	H 11	NRC8229	T 31	NRC8618	B165	NRC9233	G 09	NRC9543	J 09	NRC9770	J 20
NRC6658	E 68	NRC7387	F 02	NRC7874	H 16	NRC8230	T 31	NRC8618	B 66	NRC9233	H 01	NRC9543	J 11	NRC9770	J 30
NRC6692	L 09	NRC7415	E 54	NRC7874	H 17	NRC8231	F 17	NRC8618	B117	NRC9238	J 33	NRC9551	F 19	NRC9770	J 27
NRC6747	F 01	NRC7422	M 86	NRC7874	H 18	NRC8232	F 17	NRC8618	L 26	NRC9238	J 37	NRC9552	F 19	NRC9770	J 04
NRC6795	H 35	NRC7425	N 24	NRC7874	H 10	NRC8238	K 10	NRC8618	L 27	NRC9238	J 36	NRC9557	B 08	NRC9770	J 25
NRC6799	G 10	NRC7435	N 07	NRC7874	H 12	NRC8238	K 07	NRC8620	L 64	NRC9239	J 38	NRC9557	B 57	NRC9770	J 28
NRC6836	J 10	NRC7436	N 07	NRC7874	H 13	NRC8238	K 19	NRC8626	G 06	NRC9239	J 39	NRC9557	B109	NRC9771	J 50
NRC6888	L 01	NRC7439	N 20	NRC7874	H 14	NRC8238	K 23	NRC8627	G 06	NRC9239	J 33	NRC9557	B158	NRC9771	J 20
NRC6902	L 63	NRC7441	C 42	NRC7874	H 11	NRC8245	L 61	NRC8629	H 08	NRC9239	J 36	NRC9557	B201	NRC9771	J 30
NRC6902	L 43	NRC7441	G 05	NRC7880	J 51	NRC8247	L 61	NRC8690	H 01	NRC9246	E 50	NRC9560	B 08	NRC9771	J 27
NRC6903	L 63	NRC7448	L 14	NRC7893	J 27	NRC8248	L 61	NRC8707	L 43	NRC9246	E 51	NRC9560	B109	NRC9771	J 04
NRC6904	E 67	NRC7448	L 15	NRC7901	H 11	NRC8286	F 21	NRC8721	H 11	NRC9284	G 10	NRC9560	B158	NRC9771	J 25
NRC6919	J 46	NRC7454	J 13	NRC7902	H 11	NRC8287	F 22	NRC8734	G 10	NRC9285	G 10	NRC9560	B201	NRC9771	J 28
NRC6919	J 45	NRC7455	S 06	NRC7903	H 11	NRC8290	F 21	NRC8888	K 07	NRC9291	J 74	NRC9560	N 15	NRC9772	J 19
NRC6920	J 46	NRC7457	J 46	NRC7904	H 11	NRC8291	F 22	NRC8888	K 08	NRC9291	J 14	NRC9561	N 15	NRC9772	J 20
NRC6920	J 45	NRC7457	J 45	NRC7905	H 19	NRC8323	T 33	NRC8888	K 19	NRC9304	H 10	NRC9562	J 09	NRC9786	J 20
NRC6935	N 07	NRC7458	L 32	NRC7906	H 19	NRC8323	T 34	NRC8888	K 20	NRC9305	H 10	NRC9572	J 14	NRC9786	J 22
NRC6951	N 11	NRC7459	L 24	NRC7930	J 19	NRC8323	T 35	NRC8889	K 07	NRC9338	M118	NRC9575	H 16	NRC9862	J 65
NRC6993	S 06	NRC7459	L 32	NRC7930	J 13	NRC8329	G 04	NRC8889	K 19	NRC9338	H 02	NRC9575	H 12	NRC9863	J 65
NRC6993	S 07	NRC7571	N 20	NRC7930	J 21	NRC8330	G 04	NRC8897	H 19	NRC9338	H 05	NRC9575	H 13	NS106011	N239
NRC6993	S 18	NRC7578PM	E 53	NRC7979	J 26	NRC8332	B210	NRC8902	H 19	NRC9423	J 74	NRC9575	H 11	NS106011	N219
NRC6994	N 19	NRC7605	G 03	NRC7981	E 63	NRC8332	G 06	NRC8911	K 01	NRC9423	J 14	NRC9595	G 05	NS106011	N246
NRC7000	E 67	NRC7606	G 03	NRC7981	E 66	NRC8332	L 39	NRC8916	J 25	NRC9423	J 70	NRC9607	E 32	NS106011	N240
NRC7009	N 20	NRC7608	K 10	NRC7984	H 35	NRC8332	L 40	NRC8916	J 28	NRC9424	J 14	NRC9678	J 01	NS106011	N241
NRC7044	H 36	NRC7608	K 23	NRC7987	F 22	NRC8333	G 06	NRC8917	J 21	NRC9429	J 14	NRC9678	J 11	NS106011	N242
NRC7050	E 69	NRC7608	K 25	NRC7988	F 21	NRC8346	L 60	NRC8918	J 19	NRC9431	H 10	NRC9682	J 01	NS106011	N245
NRC7053	N 11	NRC7609	K 10	NRC8007	E 69	NRC8346	L 61	NRC8919	J 19	NRC9432	H 10	NRC9683	H 10	NSC100790	B298
NRC7066	E 69	NRC7609	K 23	NRC8024	E 32	NRC8346	L 62	NRC8919	J 21	NRC9434	H 10	NRC9690	H 10	NT108041L	B 20
NRC7124	H 36	NRC7609	K 25	NRC8044	E 59	NRC8346	L 63	NRC8920	J 25	NRC9435	H 10	NRC9695	N 08	NT108041L	B 68
NRC7127	F 02	NRC7616	F 10	NRC8045	E 59	NRC8346	L 64	NRC8921	J 21	NRC9436	H 10	NRC9696	N 08	NT108041L	B120
NRC7127	F 03	NRC7635	F 01	NRC8048	T 45	NRC8347	L 61	NRC8922	J 28	NRC9437	H 10	NRC9698	N 08	NT108041L	B168
NRC7131	N 07	NRC7636	F 01	NRC8048	T 46	NRC8349	H 08	NRC8923	J 28	NRC9438	H 10	NRC9700	E 59	NT108041L	N126
NRC7133	L 10	NRC7636	F 03	NRC8059	H 36	NRC8349	H 09	NRC8955	J 38	NRC9446	E 59	NRC9700	E 64	NT108041L	R 01
NRC7135	J 13	NRC7648	H 36	NRC8087	J 27	NRC8352	H 08	NRC8955	J 39	NRC9447	E 59	NRC9708	J 58	NT108041L	D 36
NRC7139	G 05	NRC7704	F 06	NRC8103	J 29	NRC8352	H 09	NRC8955	J 33	NRC9448	E 59	NRC9710	L 17	NT108041L	D 37
NRC7154	J 46	NRC7704	F 02	NRC8104	J 30	NRC8375	E 69	NRC8955	J 36	NRC9448	E 64	NRC9711	F 01	NT108041L	D 38
NRC7164	N 07	NRC7741	L 32	NRC8104	J 27	NRC8404	F 23	NRC8955	J 43	NRC9449	E 59	NRC9711	F 03	NT110041L	B214
NRC7165	N 07	NRC7758	T 31	NRC8108	J 30	NRC8405	F 23	NRC8962	J 36	NRC9449	E 64	NRC9713	E 08	NT110041L	D 22
NRC7227	L 05	NRC7768	N 07	NRC8116	G 03	NRC8405	F 27	NRC8984	J 46	NRC9455	H 19	NRC9713	E 11	NT110041L	L 62
NRC7230	J 51	NRC7778	K 02	NRC8117	G 03	NRC8408	F 23	NRC8987	J 36	NRC9455	H 21	NRC9722	K 04	NT110041L	T 05
NRC7232	J 51	NRC7778	K 12	NRC8196	L 26	NRC8462	J 29	NRC9035	H 19	NRC9456	H 19	NRC9722	K 01	NT110041L	M 14
NRC7235	J 51	NRC7778	K 01	NRC8197	L 26	NRC8502	G 10	NRC9091	L 64	NRC9456	H 21	NRC9722	K 11	NT110041L	L 39
NRC7238	J 51	NRC7778	K 11	NRC8198	L 29	NRC8503	G 10	NRC9098	L 64	NRC9461	H 36	NRC9724	K 04	NT112041	E 20

NT112041L	E 19
NT112041L	H 25
NT112041L	G 03
NT112041L	E 22
NT112041L	V 05
NT112041L	S 10
NT604041L	G 05
NT605041L	B308
NT605041L	B309
NT605041L	G 04
NT605041L	B363
NT605041L	B364
NT607041L	G 05
NT614041L	F 11
NTC1030	K 03
NTC1030	K 10
NTC1030	K 02
NTC1030	K 12
NTC1030	K 14
NTC1030	K 24
NTC1030	K 23
NTC1030	K 25
NTC1048	J 72
NTC1049	J 14
NTC1049	J 16
NTC1057	N 01
NTC1088	L 64
NTC1089	L 64
NTC1090	L 64
NTC1091	J 51
NTC1112	G 07
NTC1133K	K 03
NTC1136K	K 03
NTC1149	K 08
NTC1149	K 09
NTC1149	K 20
NTC1149	K 22
NTC1150	K 08
NTC1150	K 20
NTC1154	M147
NTC1154	L 74
NTC1175	G 05
NTC1175	H 10
NTC1175	H 12
NTC1176	H 10
NTC1176	H 12
NTC1176	H 15
NTC1177	H 12
NTC1177	H 13
NTC1177	H 15
NTC1201	C 38
NTC1201	N 16
NTC1210	G 09
NTC1212	L 63
NTC1224	H 35
NTC1304	J 65
NTC1305	J 70
NTC1306	J 70
NTC1307	J 70
NTC1310	J 65
NTC1311	K 08
NTC1311	K 09
NTC1311	K 20
NTC1311	K 21
NTC1311	K 22
NTC1312	K 08
NTC1312	K 09
NTC1312	K 20
NTC1312	K 21
NTC1312	K 22
NTC1313	K 08
NTC1313	K 09
NTC1313	K 21
NTC1313	K 22
NTC1384	G 06
NTC1385	G 06
NTC1518	J 54
NTC1518	J 56
NTC1557	H 34
NTC1582	F 09
NTC1582E	F 09
NTC1583	F 09
NTC1583E	F 09
NTC1612	J 04
NTC1636	H 19
NTC1643	H 36
NTC1650	J 33
NTC1664	K 01
NTC1665	K 24
NTC1666	K 25
NTC1683	F 22
NTC1685	F 21
NTC1686	F 22
NTC1687	F 21
NTC1691	F 21
NTC1772	E 61
NTC1773	E 62
NTC1775	F 18
NTC1792	H 19
NTC1794	K 02
NTC1794K	K 02
NTC1799	K 09
NTC1799	K 22
NTC1800	K 10
NTC1800	K 23
NTC1802	K 24
NTC1888	E 60
NTC1888	E 68
NTC1963	N 07
NTC1966	K 03
NTC2017	J 03
NTC2022	K 10
NTC2022	K 30
NTC2022	K 23
NTC2022	K 27
NTC2029	L 15
NTC2036	K 01
NTC2064	J 49
NTC2069	J 20
NTC2069	J 22
NTC2072	J 20
NTC2072	J 22
NTC2073	J 20
NTC2077	J 20
NTC2077	J 22
NTC2078	J 20
NTC2078	J 22
NTC2086	G 03
NTC2087	G 03
NTC2088	J 01
NTC2089	J 08
NTC2093	J 50
NTC2096	J 50
NTC2097	J 50
NTC2099	J 50
NTC2110	J 10
NTC2120	J 22
NTC2122	J 22
NTC2156	J 04
NTC2157	J 29
NTC2157	J 26
NTC2159	J 01
NTC2179	J 30
NTC2179	J 27
NTC2180	J 09
NTC2223	J 20
NTC2224	J 20
NTC2225	J 49
NTC2225	J 50
NTC2225	J 22
NTC2227	J 49
NTC2229	J 15
NTC2263	J 49
NTC2263	J 50
NTC2278	K 02
NTC2278	K 12
NTC2278	K 01
NTC2278	K 14
NTC2292	B334
NTC2333	J 11
NTC2334	J 11
NTC2337	J 18
NTC2337	J 16
NTC2338	J 16
NTC2590	F 07
NTC2590E	F 07
NTC2591	F 07
NTC2591E	F 07
NTC2595	F 21
NTC2595	F 24
NTC2595	F 26
NTC2597	F 21
NTC2597	F 24
NTC2655	J 15
NTC2660	J 37
NTC2676	J 15
NTC2681	J 03
NTC2690	J 15
NTC2699	J 16
NTC2701	K 10
NTC2701	K 23
NTC2705	E 56
NTC2706	E 62
NTC2707	E 62
NTC2723	F 20
NTC2726	K 03
NTC2731	K 10
NTC2731	K 09
NTC2731	K 22
NTC2731	K 23
NTC2736	L 17
NTC2736	L 15
NTC2743	G 03
NTC2757	J 15
NTC2830	J 37
NTC2832	K 25
NTC2837	J 03
NTC2876	J 49
NTC2876	J 50
NTC2876	J 20
NTC2876	J 22
NTC2914	J 15
NTC2927	L 27
NTC2928	L 27
NTC3066	F 21
NTC3333	J 65
NTC3333	J 72
NTC3333	J 71
NTC3346	J 56
NTC3346	J 55
NTC3354	J 35
NTC3372	H 01
NTC3372	H 04
NTC3372	H 09
NTC3391	J 10
NTC3396	G 03
NTC3453	L 15
NTC3455	J 51
NTC3457	J 51
NTC3459	G 03
NTC3460	G 03
NTC3480	H 36
NTC3483	G 10
NTC3484	G 10
NTC3489	J 30
NTC3489	J 27
NTC3490	J 25
NTC3490	J 28
NTC3491	J 29
NTC3491	J 26
NTC3492	J 25
NTC3492	J 28
NTC3543	L 17
NTC3608	K 16
NTC3608	K 14
NTC3618	K 24
NTC3650	K 24
NTC3686	G 06
NTC3687	G 06
NTC3692	J 22
NTC3751	J 33
NTC3751	J 37
NTC3751	J 35
NTC3751	J 36
NTC3763	J 69
NTC3764	J 69
NTC3766	J 69
NTC3778	J 38
NTC3778	J 37
NTC3791	F 23
NTC3791	F 25
NTC3791	F 27
NTC3793	B334
NTC3794	B334
NTC3858	L 02
NTC3858	L 30
NTC3858	L 27
NTC3862	J 69
NTC3863	J 69
NTC3866	J 20
NTC3867	J 20
NTC3891	J 69
NTC3932	G 06
NTC3933	G 06
NTC3937	L 05
NTC4135PM	E 53
NTC4183	J 33
NTC4183	J 37
NTC4183	J 36
NTC4187	J 37
NTC4187	J 36
NTC4205	B377
NTC4221	K 14
NTC4224	J 37
NTC4224	J 36
NTC4252	K 24
NTC4257	J 46
NTC4257	J 45
NTC4260	E 62
NTC4414	H 01
NTC4414	H 03
NTC4414	H 06
NTC4426	K 14
NTC4517	J 07
NTC4548	K 14
NTC4571	E 58
NTC4571	E 63
NTC4571	E 65
NTC4571	E 66
NTC4578	H 19
NTC4580	K 02
NTC4580	K 13
NTC4586	K 02
NTC4586	K 13
NTC4595	J 27
NTC4596	J 30
NTC4596	J 27
NTC4597	J 30
NTC4598	J 25
NTC4598	J 28
NTC4599	J 27
NTC4600	J 25
NTC4601	J 28
NTC4604	J 29
NTC4604	J 26
NTC4604	J 25
NTC4604	J 28
NTC4609	B385
NTC4609	L 01
NTC4609	L 02
NTC4611	J 37
NTC4611	J 36
NTC4612	J 36
NTC4614	K 10
NTC4614	K 23
NTC4615	K 09
NTC4615	K 22
NTC4617	K 10
NTC4617	K 23
NTC4618	E 62
NTC4655	J 37
NTC4657	N 19
NTC4720	E 61
NTC4833	K 16
NTC4833	K 14
NTC4844	F 01
NTC4893	L 01
NTC4895	L 18
NTC4898	L 18
NTC4944	G 03
NTC4945	G 03
NTC5000	F 22
NTC5001	F 21
NTC5017	G 09
NTC5116	N 24
NTC5171	B385
NTC5171	L 01
NTC5171	L 02
NTC5193MUE	E 53
NTC5205	K 02
NTC5205	K 12
NTC5205	K 01
NTC5205	K 14
NTC5278	N 91
NTC5279	N 91
NTC5351	J 10
NTC5401	N 19
NTC5401	N 20
NTC5418	J 18
NTC5582	K 26
NTC5582	K 30
NTC5582	K 27
NTC5624	L 30
NTC5627	L 18
NTC5628	L 18
NTC5648	K 28
NTC5648	K 30
NTC5685	L 05
NTC5686	L 17
NTC5687	L 17
NTC5708	H 16
NTC5708	H 13
NTC5708	H 14
NTC5709	H 12
NTC5711	H 16
NTC5711	H 12
NTC5728	J 25
NTC5728	J 28
NTC5729	J 29
NTC5729	J 26
NTC5750	J 30
NTC5750	J 27
NTC5858	J 07
NTC5859	J 07
NTC5879	J 07
NTC5897	L 22
NTC5900	C 38
NTC5916	J 18
NTC5916	J 17
NTC6106	E 64
NTC6168	L 01
NTC6195	N158
NTC6660	J 38
NTC6730	F 22
NTC6731	F 21
NTC6750	J 49
NTC6750	J 50
NTC6751	J 50
NTC6752	J 50
NTC6776	E 60
NTC6781	E 56
NTC6790	F 22
NTC6828	E 60
NTC6837	E 60
NTC6847	C 86
NTC6847	L 31
NTC6847	L 30
NTC6847	L 27
NTC6847	L 23
NTC6847	L 28
NTC6863	F 21
NTC6936	J 57
NTC6937	J 57
NTC6994	E 22
NTC7097	G 10
NTC7161	L 08
NTC7224	F 23
NTC7240	G 10
NTC7307	E 56
NTC7331	E 56
NTC7348	K 26
NTC7349	J 17
NTC7394	E 68
NTC7396	E 54
NTC7396	S 13
NTC7398	J 51
NTC7503	J 11
NTC7503	J 15
NTC7503	J 17
NTC7667	N 07
NTC7676	H 22
NTC7689	H 22
NTC7731	F 01
NTC7807	N 01
NTC7829	S 06
NTC7829	S 18
NTC7843	N 03
NTC7844	N 03
NTC7855	M 86
NTC7933	G 09
NTC7937	S 06
NTC7937	S 18
NTC7955	S 06
NTC7956	S 06
NTC7961	H 14
NTC7962	H 14
NTC7964	H 22
NTC7968	H 14
NTC7970	H 14
NTC7989	N 01

NTC7989	N 01
NTC8011	G 10
NTC8191	F 22
NTC8192	F 21
NTC8193	F 21
NTC8202	E 60
NTC8202	E 68
NTC8223	F 08
NTC8224	F 08
NTC8242	H 24
NTC8242	H 22
NTC8263	F 23
NTC8263	F 25
NTC8263	F 27
NTC8287	B221
NTC8287	B181
NTC8287	B 84
NTC8287	B133
NTC8328	E 61
NTC8450	H 13
NTC8451	H 13
NTC8452	H 12
NTC8453	H 16
NTC8453	H 13
NTC8454	H 16
NTC8454	H 12
NTC8455	H 19
NTC8456	H 19
NTC8543	H 19
NTC8544	G 10
NTC8553	G 10
NTC8554	G 10
NTC8592	H 09
NTC8836	H 14
NTC8847	F 01
NTC8848	F 01
NTC8848	F 03
NTC8860	F 27
NTC8861	F 22
NTC8861	F 24
NTC9027	E 61
NTC9055	G 05
NTC9068	F 01
NTC9068	F 03
NTC9070	B221
NTC9070	B181
NTC9070	B 84
NTC9070	B133
NTC9071	F 24
NTC9071	F 26
NTC9072	F 24
NTC9073	F 24
NTC9073	F 26
NTC9074	F 26
NTC9099	F 26
NTC9198	B341
NTC9208	F 27
NTC9224	N 16
NTC9262	N 07
NTC9359	G 03
NTC9360	G 03
NTC9366	N 05
NTC9415	N 12
NTC9416	N 12
NTC9461	E 57
NTC9462	E 57
NTC9473	N 01
NTC9476	N 01
NTC9481	N 03
NTC9485	N 03
NTC9493	N 03
NTC9500	N 05
NTC9501	N 05
NTC9502	N 05
NTC9531	H 17
NTC9543	H 17
NTC9543	H 18
NTC9543L	H 16
NTC9543L	H 15
NTC9704	F 26
NTC9726	H 16
NTC9726	H 14
NTC9859	D 42
NTC9932	E 62
NTC9976MNH	E 53
NTC9976MUE	E 53
NUC10003	B291
NUC100280L	B243
NV108041	K 28
NV108041L	K 26
NV108041L	K 06
NV108041L	K 30
NV108041L	K 29
NV108041L	K 27
NV110041	K 31
NV110041	K 33
NV110041L	K 26
NV110041L	K 05
NV110041L	K 27
NV114047	E 57
NV116041L	E 60
NV116041L	E 68
NV116047	E 56
NV605041L	K 03
NV608041L	E 63
NY105041L	N239
NY105041L	M 13
NY105041L	T 43
NY105041L	L 62
NY105041L	D 31
NY105041L	L 39
NY105041L	N139
NY105041L	V 05
NY105041L	D 36
NY105041L	D 33
NY105041L	T 37
NY105041L	T 38
NY105041L	S 10
NY105041L	N240
NY105041L	N242
NY105041L	N245
NY106041	D 08
NY106041	C 86
NY106041	H 33
NY106041	L 31
NY106041	L 28
NY106041	S 12
NY106041L	J 65
NY106041L	N246
NY106041L	S 16
NY106041L	S 15
NY106041L	R 45
NY106041L	J 72
NY106041L	F 23
NY106041L	H 20
NY106041L	L 27
NY106041L	V 05
NY106041L	V 06
NY106041L	S 10
NY106041L	N241
NY106041L	N245
NY106047L	N170
NY106047L	N181
NY106047L	N239
NY106047L	N219
NY106047L	N122
NY106047L	S 14
NY106047L	N238
NY106047L	L 09
NY106047L	L 30
NY106047L	T 14
NY106047L	R 31
NY106047L	J 75
NY106047L	N 43
NY106047L	L 47
NY106047L	N249
NY106047L	S 10
NY106047L	S 11
NY106047L	N240
NY106047L	N242
NY106047L	N243
NY108041L	B128
NY108041L	B112
NY108041L	B161
NY108041L	B175
NY108041L	E 56
NY108041L	E 61
NY108041L	E 68
NY108041L	D 21
NY108041L	D 28
NY108041L	N157
NY108041L	N168
NY108041L	R 28
NY108041L	N 11
NY108041L	N122
NY108041L	N124
NY108041L	N201
NY108041L	F 06
NY108041L	B309
NY108041L	B 95
NY108041L	B142
NY108041L	B188
NY108041L	G 04
NY108041L	J 01
NY108041L	J 08
NY108041L	N151
NY108041L	L 12
NY108041L	R 05
NY108041L	F 02
NY108041L	F 03
NY108041L	J 57
NY108041L	H 03
NY108041L	H 14
NY108041L	H 19
NY108041L	B 45
NY108041L	B227
NY108041L	N150
NY108041L	V 05
NY108041L	D 36
NY108041L	D 37
NY108041L	D 39
NY108041L	D 38
NY108041L	R 12
NY108041L	N 95
NY108041L	J 03
NY108041L	N 43
NY108041L	N 16
NY108041L	S 08
NY108041L	S 09
NY108041L	S 10
NY108041L	G 02
NY108047	J 17
NY108047	S 13
NY110041	E 61
NY110041	N203
NY110041	R 71
NY110041	K 31
NY110041	K 32
NY110041	T 40
NY110041L	N203
NY110041L	C 37
NY110041L	E 69
NY110041L	J 54
NY110041L	E 46
NY110047L	E 60
NY110047L	E 68
NY110047L	C 69
NY110047L	C 83
NY110047L	F 18
NY110047L	N 19
NY110047L	N 20
NY110047L	N 23
NY110047L	N100
NY110047L	N 24
NY110047L	N204
NY110047L	C 25
NY110047L	T 30
NY110047L	E 48
NY110047L	T 31
NY110051L	E 61
NY110051L	E 62
NY112041	E 63
NY112041	E 65
NY112041	E 66
NY112041L	N115
NY112041L	F 07
NY112041L	F 08
NY112041L	F 11
NY112041L	E 63
NY112041L	E 66
NY114041	E 57
NY116041L	E 68
NY116041L	T 30
NY116041L	T 32
NY116041L	E 39
NY116041L	T 31
NY116041L	E 08
NY116041L	E 11
NY116041L	T 39
NY116051L	E 57
NY120041L	E 56
NY120041L	E 61
NY120041L	D 18
NY120041L	D 19
NY604041L	F 17
NY604041L	S 16
NY605041L	G 04
NY606041L	E 33
NY606041L	E 34
NY606041L	E 36
NY606041L	E 37
NY606041L	E 07
NY606041L	E 09
NY607041L	F 07
NY607041L	F 08
NY607041L	F 10
NY607041L	F 11
NY607041L	F 09
NY608041L	E 57
NY608041L	E 58
NY608041L	E 62
NY608041L	N 20
NY608041L	F 07
NY608041L	F 08
NY608041L	F 10
NY608041L	F 11
NY608041L	F 09
NY608041L	E 63
NY610041	E 56
NY610041L	E 61
NY612041	E 62
NYH100090	B297
NYX100080	B288
NZ108041	N170
NZ606041L	E 01
NZ606041L	E 03
NZX8076L	B333
PA103061	C 84
PA105101	L 29
PA105101L	B166
PA105101L	B118
PA105161L	G 01
PA106201	N238
PA108101L	C 64
PA120801L	C 69
PA120801L	C 24
PAM4356L	P 67
PAM4356L	P 61
PBC101270	B291
PBP101130	L 28
PBP101140	L 28
PBP101150	L 31
PBP101160	L 31
PC105401L	D 37
PC105401L	D 39
PC105401L	D 38
PC106291	T 05
PC106561L	C 36
PC106641	N218
PC108291L	H 34
PC108291L	H 36
PC108321L	N158
PC108321L	D 32
PC108321L	D 37
PC108321L	D 39
PC108321L	D 38
PC108321L	D 33
PC112291	G 09
PCC000670	L 04
PCC001020	L 04
PCC107480	L 04
PCD100150	L 09
PCD100160	L 11
PCF101530	L 11
PCG100300	L 04
PCG100330	L 04
PCH001370	L 21
PCH114600	L 20
PCH114640	L 20
PCH114650	L 20
PCH115470	L 20
PCH116010	L 20
PCH116020	L 17
PCH116030	L 17
PCH116750	L 11
PCH117190	L 20
PCM100210	L 04
PCU103610	L 20
PCU103630	L 09
PCU103780	L 04
PCU103790	L 04
PDL100000	L 18
PEH000310	L 21
PEH101170	B385
PEM100990	L 20
PEP102670	B290
PEP102840	B241
PEP102840	B250
PET100790	B241
PEU102770	B294
PFQ10001L	B275
PGG101050	B276
PGK100670	L 04
PGK100680	L 04
PHB102360	J 41
PHB102560	J 35
PHB102880	J 41
PHC100570	J 41
PHC100740	J 41
PHD103620	J 41
PHD103990	J 42
PHH100290	J 35
PHN100200	J 42
PHU102490	J 35
PHU102790	J 35
PHU102800	J 35
PHU102860	J 42
PIB000060	B292
PIB000070	B292
PIB100050	B292
PIP100030	B290
PKS100140	J 42
PKX100030	B334
PMF000040	B293
PMF100460	B293
PMF100460E	B293
PMK100130	B293
PNH101570	B293
PNH101590	L 13
PNH101600	L 13
PNH101670	B293
PNH101680	B293
PNH101840	B293
PNH102080	L 13
PNH102090	L 13
PNP101250	L 13
PNP101280	B293
PNT100030	B293
PQR101050	B380
PQR101070	B295
PQR101150	B295
PQS101490	B278
PQS101500	B277
PRC1039	C 30
PRC1039	M 14
PRC1333	M 46
PRC1794	M 63
PRC1859	M 31
PRC1860	M 30
PRC1984	M101
PRC2015	M 31
PRC2057	M101
PRC2167	M 01
PRC2167	M 04
PRC2230	M 30
PRC2239	M 93
PRC2291	M139
PRC2291	M140
PRC2291	M141
PRC2291	M142
PRC2291	M138
PRC2403	T 45
PRC2437	M130
PRC2437	M132
PRC2439	T 45
PRC2439	T 46
PRC2443	M 48
PRC2471	M129
PRC2476	J 01
PRC2497	M 88
PRC2505	B 19
PRC2505	B 65
PRC2505	B 67
PRC2505	B 66
PRC2505	B119
PRC2505	L 26
PRC2505	B 17
PRC2505	B 18
PRC2505	B167
PRC2506	B324

PRC2507	B314	PRC3299	M 14	PRC3900	M 87	PRC4412	M 49	PRC5141	M140	PRC5773	M142	PRC6387	B 17	PRC7370	M 87
PRC2516	M 14	PRC3300	M138	PRC3901	J 12	PRC4427	M112	PRC5141	M141	PRC5777	M141	PRC6387	B 18	PRC7371	M 88
PRC2516	M 15	PRC3340	M130	PRC3905	M 78	PRC4427	M 83	PRC5141	M142	PRC5802	M135	PRC6574	B354	PRC7373	M114
PRC2734	M 87	PRC3359	B213	PRC3969	M 33	PRC4430	B324	PRC5141	M138	PRC5802	M136	PRC6613E	B 46	PRC7374	M114
PRC2735	M 86	PRC3359	B172	PRC3977	M130	PRC4433	M112	PRC5273	M145	PRC5802	M141	PRC6613E	B 96	PRC7375	M114
PRC2854	M136	PRC3359	B324	PRC3978	M130	PRC4436	M143	PRC5273	M137	PRC5802	M142	PRC6613N	B 46	PRC7386	M 93
PRC2854	M132	PRC3363	M 33	PRC4019	M 59	PRC4438	M111	PRC5274	M145	PRC5852	J 01	PRC6613N	B 96	PRC7542	M 56
PRC2854	M133	PRC3366	B 24	PRC4020	M 59	PRC4449	M112	PRC5275	M145	PRC5852	J 09	PRC6663	B 67	PRC7851	M 77
PRC2854	M139	PRC3366	B 72	PRC4021	M 82	PRC4454	M112	PRC5316	M 70	PRC5852	J 11	PRC6663	B119	PRC7851	M 76
PRC2854	M140	PRC3366	B125	PRC4021	M 59	PRC4456	M101	PRC5319	M 33	PRC5852	J 04	PRC6663	B167	PRC7867	M 77
PRC2854	M141	PRC3369	M132	PRC4021	M 60	PRC4471	M 75	PRC5336	M 33	PRC5874	T 45	PRC6779	M 34	PRC7894	M 70
PRC2854	M142	PRC3389	M 49	PRC4021	M 66	PRC4473	M 14	PRC5356	T 45	PRC5877	M 83	PRC6785	M 31	PRC7992	M 01
PRC2854	M138	PRC3430	M 87	PRC4021	M 65	PRC4497	M109	PRC5357	T 45	PRC5877	M 62	PRC6796	M 94	PRC7994	M 01
PRC2876	M 14	PRC3432	M 88	PRC4043	B116	PRC4503	B354	PRC5499	M 31	PRC5878	M 83	PRC6864	M 93	PRC8072	M 48
PRC2911	D 22	PRC3494	M 59	PRC4043	B165	PRC4524	M111	PRC5524	M 31	PRC5878	M 62	PRC6913	M 95	PRC8123	M 95
PRC2911	M 14	PRC3494	M 60	PRC4043	B117	PRC4540	T 45	PRC5537	M 88	PRC5879	M 83	PRC6947	B207	PRC8131	T 45
PRC2911	D 24	PRC3494	B 30	PRC4083	M 82	PRC4540	T 46	PRC5538	B144	PRC5880	M 83	PRC7001	M 76	PRC8166	M 32
PRC2964	M 17	PRC3505	B385	PRC4084	M 82	PRC4543	M145	PRC5538	B229	PRC5883	T 46	PRC7002	M 77	PRC8171	M 05
PRC2978	M 82	PRC3505	B172	PRC4085	M 82	PRC4576	M111	PRC5538	B189	PRC5912	M101	PRC7003	M 51	PRC8204	M 14
PRC2978	C 51	PRC3505	B324	PRC4092	M 82	PRC4590	M 51	PRC5543	J 50	PRC6021	M117	PRC7003	M 53	PRC8230	M 86
PRC2979	B244	PRC3537	M 57	PRC4096	M 59	PRC4591	M 74	PRC5544	M 57	PRC6022	M117	PRC7004	M 51	PRC8231	M 18
PRC2979	D 08	PRC3537	M 58	PRC4096	M 60	PRC4612	M143	PRC5600	M 77	PRC6023	M117	PRC7004	M 53	PRC8243	M 34
PRC2979	M118	PRC3541	B 24	PRC4096	M 66	PRC4613	M143	PRC5601	M 76	PRC6036	M109	PRC7009	M 76	PRC8245	M 49
PRC2979	M146	PRC3541	B 72	PRC4096	M 65	PRC4613LCS	M143	PRC5602	M 57	PRC6037	M109	PRC7011	M 57	PRC8246	M111
PRC2979	K 05	PRC3541	B125	PRC4127	T 46	PRC4616	M 30	PRC5603	M 77	PRC6080	M 60	PRC7012	M 57	PRC8248	M 32
PRC2980	M118	PRC3542	T 45	PRC4151	T 46	PRC4720	M111	PRC5604	M 76	PRC6080	M 66	PRC7018	J 09	PRC8295	M 93
PRC3025	M118	PRC3543	T 45	PRC4152	T 46	PRC4785	M 59	PRC5670	M 49	PRC6080	M 65	PRC7019	J 01	PRC8385	M 34
PRC3025	M 31	PRC3588	M 10	PRC4208	M 78	PRC4785	M 60	PRC5679	M 88	PRC6081	M 60	PRC7019	J 11	PRC8410	M 70
PRC3030	M139	PRC3588	M 12	PRC4209	T 45	PRC4785	M 66	PRC5680	M 77	PRC6081	M 66	PRC7020	J 04	PRC8452	M111
PRC3030	M140	PRC3617	M 10	PRC4244	T 12	PRC4785	M 65	PRC5680	M 76	PRC6081	M 65	PRC7022	M 77	PRC8463	J 04
PRC3030	M141	PRC3617	M 12	PRC4262	J 01	PRC4795	M 83	PRC5685	M 70	PRC6082	M 60	PRC7044	M 07	PRC8470	M 88
PRC3030	M142	PRC3625	M 31	PRC4268	M109	PRC4795	M 84	PRC5723	M 83	PRC6082	M 66	PRC7060	M 70	PRC8495	M129
PRC3030	M138	PRC3671	M129	PRC4276	M129	PRC4826	M 46	PRC5724	M 83	PRC6082	M 83	PRC7100	M 82	PRC8548	M 23
PRC3037	M 46	PRC3672	M129	PRC4277	M129	PRC4879	M 32	PRC5736	M135	PRC6082	M 65	PRC7100	M 83	PRC8558	M143
PRC3085	M 14	PRC3678	M118	PRC4282	M109	PRC4951	B354	PRC5736	M136	PRC6083	M 77	PRC7100	M 84	PRC8558	M144
PRC3095	M 70	PRC3702	M150	PRC4297	G 09	PRC4952	M 62	PRC5736	M131	PRC6083	M 76	PRC7173	M 83	PRC8559	M129
PRC3098	J 11	PRC3702	M 59	PRC4298	M109	PRC4953	M 82	PRC5736	M133	PRC6133	B354	PRC7173	M 84	PRC8559	M143
PRC3101	M130	PRC3702	M 60	PRC4299	M109	PRC4954	M 62	PRC5736	M140	PRC6141	B354	PRC7175	M 31	PRC8559	M144
PRC3131	B354	PRC3702	B 30	PRC4301	M109	PRC4970	M 51	PRC5736	M141	PRC6144	B354	PRC7204	B314	PRC8593	B213
PRC3180	D 08	PRC3718	M117	PRC4304	M109	PRC4970	M 53	PRC5736	M142	PRC6167	T 45	PRC7254	M 15	PRC8664	M135
PRC3180	M118	PRC3723	M117	PRC4306	M 79	PRC4993	M 51	PRC5738	M135	PRC6228	M121	PRC7255	M 11	PRC8664	M130
PRC3180	M 31	PRC3724	M117	PRC4311	M 79	PRC4993	M 53	PRC5738	M131	PRC6283	M129	PRC7263	M 14	PRC8664	M131
PRC3180	M 82	PRC3725	M117	PRC4311	M 80	PRC4994	M 62	PRC5739	M136	PRC6290	M 74	PRC7263	M 15	PRC8707	J 04
PRC3180	N144	PRC3737	M111	PRC4318	M 70	PRC4995	M 82	PRC5739	M141	PRC6295	B119	PRC7277	M 78	PRC8708	J 08
PRC3209	M 51	PRC3737	M 79	PRC4324	M120	PRC4996	M 62	PRC5739	M142	PRC6295	B167	PRC7311	M115	PRC8868	M 34
PRC3231	M139	PRC3780	M139	PRC4327	M121	PRC5003	M 83	PRC5741	M135	PRC6311	M 33	PRC7313	M115	PRC8869	M 51
PRC3231	M138	PRC3786	M132	PRC4333	M 31	PRC5003	M 84	PRC5741	M131	PRC6336	M 95	PRC7315	M115	PRC8869	M 53
PRC3232	M139	PRC3794	M132	PRC4370	M120	PRC5109E	B144	PRC5742	M135	PRC6348	M121	PRC7317	M120	PRC8870	M 51
PRC3232	M138	PRC3794	M133	PRC4372	B116	PRC5109E	B229	PRC5742	M131	PRC6387	B206	PRC7318	M120	PRC8870	M 53
PRC3247	M 82	PRC3794	M139	PRC4372	B165	PRC5109E	B189	PRC5744	M131	PRC6387	B243	PRC7319	M120	PRC8872	M 56
PRC3250	M139	PRC3794	M140	PRC4372	B117	PRC5109N	B144	PRC5744	M142	PRC6387	B 65	PRC7320	M120	PRC8873	C 56
PRC3250	M140	PRC3794	M142	PRC4372	M120	PRC5109N	B229	PRC5747	M135	PRC6387	B116	PRC7321	M120	PRC8873	C 08
PRC3250	M141	PRC3813	M 17	PRC4376	M 59	PRC5109N	B189	PRC5756	M133	PRC6387	B165	PRC7322	M120	PRC8876	M 93
PRC3250	M142	PRC3833	M118	PRC4376	M 60	PRC5127	M138	PRC5765	M136	PRC6387	B 66	PRC7326	M 70	PRC8876	M 94
PRC3250	M138	PRC3875	M 87	PRC4376	B 30	PRC5141	M139	PRC5773	M140	PRC6387	B117	PRC7329	M 70	PRC8879	M116

PRC8928	M 58	PS104127L	D 34	PYC102060	J 06	QVB101350	B294	RF608041	N233	RRC2898	S 10	RRC5728	B170	RRC6874	N 05
PRC9096	M 34	PS104161	H 34	PYC102070	J 17	QVU10037	B294	RF608041	N234	RRC2906	M 29	RRC5739	V 05	RRC7190LUH	P 66
PRC9096	M 35	PS104161	H 36	PYC102100	L 20	QYC100230	L 11	RF608041	N227	RRC2963ABE	N233	RRC5761	V 05	RRC7198LUH	P 66
PRC9096	M 37	PS106161L	N143	PYC102110	L 20	QYC100290	F 25	RF608041	N228	RRC2970	N 23	RRC5761	S 10	RRC7359	M 29
PRC9096	M 38	PS106201	G 09	PYC102190	L 40	QYC100290	F 27	RF608041	N230	RRC2971	N 23	RRC5802	V 09	RRC7409	M 29
PRC9096	M 40	PS106251L	E 60	PYC102190	L 20	QYX100280	F 24	RF608041	N231	RRC3011	J 37	RRC6104	R 27	RRC7587LUH	P 66
PRC9188	M121	PS106321L	E 60	PYC102240	L 20	QYX100280	F 26	RFD100000	E 49	RRC3011	J 36	RRC6105	R 27	RRC8002	N239
PRC9224	M 31	PS106321L	E 62	PYC102250	L 20	RA607076	P 17	RFD100000	E 25	RRC3043	N 62	RRC6106	R 27	RRC8002	N240
PRC9226	M 31	PS106321L	E 68	PYC102260	L 40	RA607076	J 34	RJ608603	B 09	RRC3044	N 62	RRC6111	R 28	RRC8002	N242
PRC9228	M 32	PS106321L	F 17	PYC102340	L 13	RA608123L	N 28	RJ608603	B 58	RRC3045	N198	RRC6149	J 22	RRC8002	N245
PRC9229	M 32	PS603041L	N193	PYC102350	J 18	RA608177L	S 16	RJ608603	N124	RRC3264	N219	RRC6150	J 49	RRC8363	M135
PRC9324	M 78	PS603041L	G 03	PYC102350	J 16	RA608177L	J 08	RJ610243	N246	RRC3266	E 67	RRC6154	N101	RRC8363	M131
PRC9325	M 78	PS603041L	G 10	PYC102350	L 13	RA608177L	N180	RJ612433	N 90	RRC3352	E 67	RRC6155	N101	RRC8364	M135
PRC9327	M 77	PS603041L	N188	PYC102350	J 41	RA608236L	P 65	RKB101111	E 67	RRC3355	E 67	RRC6160	M 12	RRC8364	M131
PRC9329	M 77	PS606101L	B319	PYC102350	J 17	RA608236L	P 67	RKB101230	E 64	RRC3584	N219	RRC6168	N101	RRC8512	N151
PRC9330	M 76	PS606101L	B382	PYC102360	L 13	RA610123	N 30	RKB101240	E 64	RRC3746	J 33	RRC6169	N101	RRC8517	N181
PRC9331	M 57	PS608101L	E 62	PYC102380	L 17	RA610123	M 83	RKC5098L	C 14	RRC3746	J 37	RRC6177NUC	N133	RRC8597	N238
PRC9332	M 57	PS608101L	E 35	PYC102390	L 17	RA610123	M 84	RNF100090	E 63	RRC3746	J 36	RRC6186	P 49	RRC8666	N 28
PRC9333	M 76	PS608101L	E 39	PYC102590	L 11	RA610167	M143	RNF100090	E 65	RRC3966	N239	RRC6198	N 44	RRC8666	L 33
PRC9334	M111	PS608101L	E 08	PYC102620	L 20	RA610183	N147	RNF100090	E 66	RRC3966	N246	RRC6215	N101	RRC8666	N141
PRC9410	M111	PS608101L	E 11	PYD100010	M 85	RA610183	N242	RPM100070	E 63	RRC3966	T 03	RRC6216	N101	RRC8681	M 58
PRC9677	C 84	PS612080	N121	PYF100830	L 04	RA610183	N245	RPM100080	E 65	RRC3966	N240	RRC6233	N 45	RRD100650	S 12
PRC9809	M 37	PSD103040	B299	PYG10006L	B277	RA612156L	R 69	RPM100080	E 66	RRC3966	N242	RRC6234	N 45	RRJ100120	E 55
PRC9810	M 35	PSD103470	B299	PYG10006L	B278	RA612156L	R 31	RR612103	N239	RRC3966	N243	RRC6239	N 38	RRO2125L	L 02
PRC9810	M 38	PSF100140	B299	PYH100400	B292	RA612157	R 40	RR612103	N240	RRC3972	N238	RRC6245	N 41	RRO2126L	L 02
PRC9858	B 42	PYA10008L	J 41	PYP10008L	L 20	RA612157L	N173	RR612103	N241	RRC3973	N238	RRC6253	N166	RRW100010	E 55
PRC9858	B 89	PYA10011L	B284	PYP100550	L 04	RA612183	B391	RR612103	N242	RRC3987	M 32	RRC6254	N166	RSC100040	E 58
PRC9859	C 84	PYB000030	L 13	QAF000140	F 11	RA612183	N149	RR612103	N243	RRC4002	J 33	RRC6256	N 38	RSC100050	E 58
PRC9902	M 49	PYC101120	L 18	QAF000150	F 11	RA612183	S 08	RR612103	N245	RRC4002	J 36	RRC6268LCS	R 25	RT612253	N201
PRC9916	M 08	PYC101120	J 75	QEH102380	F 27	RA612183	S 09	RRC110870MNH	E 53	RRC4319	M 32	RRC6269RCF	R 25	RT612283	N167
PRC9937	M121	PYC101120L	L 12	QEH102390	F 26	RA612207L	M143	RRC110870RHO	E 53	RRC4418	J 16	RRC6269RUY	R 25	RT612283	N122
PRC9938	M121	PYC101120L	L 18	QEH102400	F 26	RA612207L	H 19	RRC2241	V 05	RRC4419	K 10	RRC6270LCS	R 22	RTC1115	H 28
PRC9939	M121	PYC101120L	J 75	QEH102460	F 24	RA612236	R 69	RRC2281	E 57	RRC4419	K 23	RRC6271RCF	R 22	RTC1139	E 32
PRC9941	M122	PYC101150	B 80	QEH102570	F 24	RA612237	S 14	RRC2303	E 03	RRC4419	K 25	RRC6271RUY	R 22	RTC1148	J 11
PRC9941	M124	PYC101150	L 17	QEH102570	F 26	RA612237	R 40	RRC2409	P 65	RRC4422	N246	RRC6287	N 11	RTC1481	B344
PRC9941	M121	PYC101150	L 15	QEP104961	F 24	RA612346	S 14	RRC2440	N101	RRC4583	N246	RRC6292	N 89	RTC1526	H 26
PS102081L	G 03	PYC101370	L 41	QEP104971	F 27	RA612347L	S 16	RRC2443	N 90	RRC4583	N209	RRC6293	N 93	RTC1526	H 33
PS102081L	G 10	PYC101410	J 42	QEP105122	F 24	RA612347L	R 64	RRC2475	J 29	RRC5115	V 05	RRC6294	N 93	RTC1526	H 31
PS103081L	G 03	PYC101410L	B284	QEP105130	F 26	RA612373L	N203	RRC2476	P 65	RRC5262	V 05	RRC6296	N 90	RTC1718	B304
PS103101L	N193	PYC101800L	B255	QEP105410	F 24	RA612373L	N239	RRC2479	H 19	RRC5262	S 10	RRC6304	N 92	RTC171810	B304
PS103101L	N188	PYC101880	L 42	QEP105450	F 27	RA612373L	N118	RRC2481ABE	N234	RRC5264	V 05	RRC6305	N 92	RTC171820	B304
PS103101L	D 37	PYC101880	L 43	QEP105760	F 24	RA612373L	N 90	RRC2485	R 41	RRC5264	S 10	RRC6362	N 93	RTC1730	B 06
PS103101L	D 39	PYC101880	L 41	QEP105770	F 26	RA612373L	N117	RRC2486	J 20	RRC5266	V 05	RRC6363	N 93	RTC173010	B 06
PS103101L	D 38	PYC101890	L 42	QEU101060	E 11	RA612373L	N240	RRC2487	J 49	RRC5266	S 10	RRC6365	N246	RTC173020	B 06
PS103121L	D 22	PYC101890	L 43	QFX000030	F 20	RA612373L	N241	RRC2491	N 41	RRC5277	V 05	RRC6390LCS	R 26	RTC1956	D 33
PS103121L	N218	PYC101890	L 20	QLC100080	F 06	RA612373L	N242	RRC2497	N 44	RRC5277	S 10	RRC6391RCF	R 26	RTC198	M128
PS103121L	C 36	PYC101890	L 41	QLG100000	F 06	RA612373L	N243	RRC2593	J 16	RRC5278	V 06	RRC6391RUY	R 26	RTC2057	C 07
PS103121L	T 05	PYC101910	L 20	QMB101620	F 03	RA612373L	N245	RRC2595	P 65	RRC5409	N 24	RRC6392LCS	R 23	RTC207	H 29
PS104121L	D 38	PYC101940	L 42	QRF100860	M 86	RB610082	N 97	RRC2596	P 65	RRC5410	N 24	RRC6393RCF	R 23	RTC210	M 10
PS104127	N143	PYC101940	L 43	QRF100870	M 86	RB610082	N 98	RRC2626	P 65	RRC5528	J 37	RRC6393RUY	R 23	RTC2104	B345
PS104127L	C 84	PYC101940	L 40	QRF100880	M 86	RB610082	N 95	RRC2629	P 65	RRC5533	N126	RRC6716	J 50	RTC2117	B305
PS104127L	H 34	PYC101940	L 41	QRG100100	M 86	RB613102	N 40	RRC2644	J 26	RRC5539	N124	RRC6744	J 29	RTC211710	B305
PS104127L	H 36	PYC101980	J 35	QTB102760	F 03	RBI100000	E 57	RRC2645	J 26	RRC5539	N126	RRC6745	J 27	RTC211720	B305
PS104127L	D 37	PYC102060	J 05	QTB102760PMA	F 03	RDB100070	E 56	RRC2800	J 37	RRC5677	N126	RRC6746	J 27	RTC218620	B305
PS104127L	D 39	PYC102060	J 17	QTF100220	F 03	RF608041	N223	RRC2898	V 05	RRC5727	J 37	RRC6747	J 30	RTC2186S	B305

RTC222	M135	RTC3022	M 87	RTC3388	H 01	RTC3650	M139	RTC3938AV	P 44	RTC4282	C 74	RTC4482	M 47	RTC4685	T 53
RTC222	M136	RTC3022	N186	RTC3397	D 11	RTC3650	M140	RTC3938LDE	P 37	RTC4285	C 73	RTC4485	B 83	RTC4686	T 53
RTC222	M130	RTC3022	J 15	RTC3403	D 41	RTC3650	M141	RTC3938LDE	P 44	RTC4286	C 73	RTC4485	B132	RTC473420	B 55
RTC222	M131	RTC3023	N147	RTC3418	H 28	RTC3650	M142	RTC3939PA	N159	RTC4288	C 73	RTC4485	B 36	RTC4734S	B 55
RTC222	M132	RTC3024	P 14	RTC3429	E 23	RTC3663	B 77	RTC3948	B 28	RTC4289	C 73	RTC4487	E 43	RTC4738	F 06
RTC222	M133	RTC3036	N147	RTC3429	E 25	RTC3663	B 31	RTC3948	B 30	RTC4290	C 73	RTC4488	E 45	RTC4738	F 02
RTC2348	B320	RTC3056	F 19	RTC3429	E 46	RTC3663	B 29	RTC3949	B 30	RTC4291	C 73	RTC4490	D 11	RTC4740	J 15
RTC2349	B320	RTC3058	F 19	RTC3458	E 01	RTC3664	B 31	RTC3959	M135	RTC4295	C 83	RTC4497	M 47	RTC4741	J 15
RTC2408	B305	RTC306	F 15	RTC3458	E 02	RTC3664	B 29	RTC3959	M130	RTC4300	C 83	RTC4497	M 92	RTC477820	B107
RTC240820	B305	RTC307	F 13	RTC3458	E 03	RTC3665	B 77	RTC3959	M131	RTC4301	C 83	RTC4498	M 47	RTC4778S	B107
RTC2626	B 05	RTC308	F 15	RTC3472	B350	RTC3665	B 31	RTC3959	M142	RTC4307	C 83	RTC4498	M106	RTC4783	B198
RTC262610	B 05	RTC3095	E 42	RTC3474	B 42	RTC3665	B 29	RTC3962	F 19	RTC4308	C 83	RTC4498	M 92	RTC4783	B235
RTC262620	B 05	RTC3095	E 43	RTC3474	B 90	RTC3682	M 01	RTC3985	B 51	RTC4313	C 83	RTC4500	M 47	RTC4783	B 54
RTC2726	E 14	RTC315	B 42	RTC3479	J 34	RTC3683	M 01	RTC4032A	W 04	RTC4314	C 83	RTC4500	M 79	RTC4783	B106
RTC2726	E 40	RTC3163	H 27	RTC3497	B324	RTC3729	T 45	RTC4035A	W 04	RTC4315	C 83	RTC4501	M 47	RTC4783	B155
RTC2762	F 15	RTC3166	H 28	RTC3499	B122	RTC3729	T 46	RTC4035T	W 02	RTC4320	C 74	RTC4501	M 92	RTC478310	B198
RTC2825	B198	RTC3167	H 28	RTC3499	B329	RTC3744	N146	RTC4042A	W 03	RTC4335	C 75	RTC4502	M 47	RTC478310	B235
RTC2825	B235	RTC3168	H 28	RTC3502	J 73	RTC3745	P 01	RTC4042T	W 01	RTC4336	C 75	RTC4502	M111	RTC478310	B 54
RTC2825	B 05	RTC3169	H 28	RTC3502	J 61	RTC3745	P 02	RTC4043A	W 04	RTC4338	C 75	RTC4503	M 47	RTC478310	B106
RTC2825	B 54	RTC3170	H 29	RTC3511	E 23	RTC3745	M 06	RTC4047A	W 04	RTC4339	C 75	RTC4503	M106	RTC478310	B155
RTC2825	B106	RTC3171	H 28	RTC3511	E 46	RTC3745	N 32	RTC4049A	W 04	RTC4340	N221	RTC4503	M 92	RTC4785	M 47
RTC2825	B155	RTC3175	M143	RTC3518	J 46	RTC3745	N145	RTC4049T	W 02	RTC4341	N221	RTC4504	M 47	RTC4820	E 16
RTC2889	B 35	RTC3176	H 29	RTC3518	B338	RTC3745	N 30	RTC4051A	W 03	RTC4342	N221	RTC4504	M 92	RTC4825	F 22
RTC2889	B 82	RTC3188	B354	RTC3518	B339	RTC3745	N 31	RTC4051T	W 01	RTC4373	D 26	RTC4505	M 47	RTC4825	F 25
RTC2890	B 35	RTC3197	B350	RTC3518	J 73	RTC3745	P 08	RTC4054A	W 03	RTC437420	B 55	RTC4507	M 79	RTC4825	F 27
RTC2890	B 82	RTC3197	B351	RTC3518	J 61	RTC3745	L 75	RTC4054T	W 02	RTC4374S	B 55	RTC4507	M 80	RTC4826	F 22
RTC2913	B345	RTC3197	B352	RTC3519	E 52	RTC3745	M123	RTC4058A	W 04	RTC4391	F 14	RTC4510	M 47	RTC4841	B 07
RTC2914	C 15	RTC3198	B351	RTC3519	J 60	RTC3745	M125	RTC4058T	W 02	RTC4392	F 14	RTC4510	M 79	RTC4841	B 56
RTC2918N	B 01	RTC3198	B352	RTC3519	T 04	RTC3745	M 11	RTC4059E	B100	RTC4393	F 14	RTC4595R	B 49	RTC4841	B108
RTC294	F 13	RTC3201	B351	RTC3562	M 93	RTC3745	M120	RTC4183	M 14	RTC4394	F 14	RTC4615	M 01	RTC4848	M139
RTC295	F 13	RTC3201	B352	RTC3566	B333	RTC3745	T 47	RTC4183	M 15	RTC4395	F 14	RTC4635	E 58	RTC4848	M140
RTC297	F 13	RTC3215	B 43	RTC3570	B 42	RTC3745	T 48	RTC4184	M 14	RTC4398	F 14	RTC4636	E 63	RTC4848	M141
RTC2972E	B301	RTC3215	B 91	RTC3570	B350	RTC3748	N184	RTC4184	M 15	RTC4399	F 14	RTC4637	E 58	RTC4848	M142
RTC2972N	B301	RTC3215	B138	RTC3570	B351	RTC3748	P 01	RTC4185	M 14	RTC4400	F 14	RTC4638	E 65	RTC4849	B 76
RTC2973N	B301	RTC3215	B358	RTC3570	B353	RTC3748	N159	RTC4185	M 15	RTC4401	F 14	RTC4639	E 65	RTC4850	B 76
RTC2978	B 02	RTC3215	B359	RTC3571	B 42	RTC3748	N162	RTC418820	B 06	RTC4402	F 16	RTC4643	C 73	RTC4850	B 31
RTC298	F 13	RTC3254	D 08	RTC3610	L 09	RTC3750	P 11	RTC418840	B 06	RTC4403	F 16	RTC4644	C 73	RTC4850	B 28
RTC299	F 13	RTC3254	D 09	RTC3614	B 42	RTC3755	R 02	RTC4188S	B 06	RTC4404	F 16	RTC4645	C 73	RTC4851	B 77
RTC2991	B102	RTC3254	D 04	RTC3614	B 90	RTC3764	R 02	RTC419020	B 06	RTC4405	F 16	RTC4647	C 74	RTC4851	B 31
RTC2992	B 54	RTC3254	D 05	RTC3618	B350	RTC3772	B 59	RTC419040	B 06	RTC4406	F 16	RTC4648	C 73	RTC4852	B 76
RTC2992	B106	RTC3254	E 15	RTC3626	H 28	RTC3772	B110	RTC4190S	B 06	RTC4407	F 16	RTC4649	C 74	RTC4853	B 77
RTC299210	B 54	RTC327	B340	RTC3627	H 28	RTC3772	M147	RTC4198	F 07	RTC4408	F 16	RTC4650	C 83	RTC4853	B 31
RTC299210	B106	RTC3278	B 42	RTC3635	M111	RTC3772	M 59	RTC4198	F 08	RTC4409	F 16	RTC4652	C 74	RTC4854	C 73
RTC2993	B199	RTC3278	B 90	RTC3635	M115	RTC3772	M 60	RTC4198	F 10	RTC4410	F 16	RTC4653	C 74	RTC4857	B 76
RTC2993	B236	RTC3282	B 42	RTC3635	M116	RTC3772	M 66	RTC4198	F 11	RTC4419	B 76	RTC4655	C 74	RTC4858	B 76
RTC2993	B 55	RTC3286	B350	RTC3635	M119	RTC3772	M 65	RTC4198	F 09	RTC4419	B 31	RTC4656	C 74	RTC4859	B 76
RTC2993	B107	RTC3292	B 43	RTC3635	M 89	RTC3772	M 63	RTC4200	L 35	RTC4420	B 76	RTC4657	C 74	RTC4860	B 77
RTC2993	B156	RTC3292	B 93	RTC3644	B 13	RTC3812	B 90	RTC4201	L 35	RTC4420	B 31	RTC4658	C 73	RTC4860	B 31
RTC299310	B199	RTC3292	B140	RTC3650	M135	RTC3826	E 52	RTC4268	C 74	RTC4421	B 76	RTC4659	C 83	RTC4861	B 77
RTC299310	B236	RTC3292	B361	RTC3650	M136	RTC3826	T 04	RTC4276	C 74	RTC4421	B 31	RTC4660	C 79	RTC4896	B 76
RTC299310	B 55	RTC3346	E 01	RTC3650	M143	RTC3867	M128	RTC4277	C 74	RTC4425	G 05	RTC4661	C 83	RTC4896	B 31
RTC299310	B107	RTC3346	E 02	RTC3650	M130	RTC3878	M116	RTC4278	C 74	RTC4428	H 01	RTC4662	C 83	RTC4897	B 76
RTC299310	B156	RTC3380	H 26	RTC3650	M131	RTC3878	M119	RTC4279	C 74	RTC4472	F 18	RTC4663	C 83	RTC4898	B 76
RTC300	F 13	RTC3381	H 26	RTC3650	M132	RTC3890	D 40	RTC4280	C 74	RTC4477	B314	RTC4683	J 35	RTC4898	B 31
RTC301	F 13	RTC3387	H 01	RTC3650	M133	RTC3934AV	N187	RTC4281	C 74	RTC4480	M129	RTC4685	T 51	RTC4899	B 76

RTC4900	B 76	RTC5048	B368	RTC5121	C 77	RTC5181	C 82	RTC5674	B 83	RTC5686	B362	RTC5816	G 06	RTC5967	B 46
RTC4900	B 31	RTC5049	B 46	RTC5122	C 77	RTC5182	C 82	RTC5674	B 84	RTC5686	B186	RTC5818	C 74	RTC5967	B 96
RTC4901	B 76	RTC5049	B 96	RTC5122	C 80	RTC5183	C 82	RTC5674	B133	RTC5686	B187	RTC5827	M136	RTC5970	B 77
RTC4901	B 31	RTC5049	B367	RTC5123	C 77	RTC5184	C 82	RTC5674	B 37	RTC5687	B226	RTC5827	M133	RTC5971	B351
RTC4903	B 77	RTC5049	B368	RTC5123	C 80	RTC5185	C 82	RTC5675	B181	RTC5687	B356	RTC5827	M140	RTC5971	B352
RTC4903	B 31	RTC5050	B367	RTC5124	C 77	RTC5186	C 82	RTC5675	B 83	RTC5687	B 92	RTC5827	M141	RTC5978	L 37
RTC4904	B 77	RTC5050	B368	RTC5125	C 81	RTC5187	C 82	RTC5675	B 84	RTC5687	B 94	RTC5827	M142	RTC5979A	W 03
RTC4906	B 77	RTC5064	D 26	RTC5126	C 80	RTC5188	C 82	RTC5675	B133	RTC5687	B139	RTC5828	M136	RTC5979T	W 01
RTC4908	B 77	RTC5066	N118	RTC5126	C 81	RTC5190	C 82	RTC5675	B 37	RTC5687	B141	RTC5828	M141	RTC5980A	W 03
RTC4908	B 31	RTC5067	N118	RTC5127	C 81	RTC5191	C 82	RTC5679	B387	RTC5687	B362	RTC5841	E 16	RTC5980T	W 01
RTC4932	B 42	RTC5068	F 09	RTC5128	C 81	RTC5192	C 82	RTC5680E	B226	RTC5687	B186	RTC5841	E 17	RTC5981A	W 04
RTC4933	B 42	RTC5069	F 09	RTC5129	C 82	RTC5193	C 82	RTC5680E	B356	RTC5687	B187	RTC5856E	B301	RTC5981T	W 02
RTC4934	B 42	RTC5070	F 09	RTC5134	C 79	RTC5203	C 73	RTC5680E	B 94	RTC5688	B355	RTC5856N	B301	RTC5983A	W 03
RTC4935	B 42	RTC5071	F 09	RTC5135	C 79	RTC5209	C 74	RTC5680E	B141	RTC5688	B356	RTC5863	B 77	RTC5983T	W 02
RTC4936	B 42	RTC5072	F 09	RTC5135	C 78	RTC5211	C 83	RTC5680E	B362	RTC5688	B360	RTC5863	B 31	RTC599320	B156
RTC4937	C 73	RTC5073	F 09	RTC5136	C 79	RTC5212	C 83	RTC5680E	B187	RTC5688	B362	RTC5863	B 30	RTC601	N 50
RTC4978	B144	RTC5074	F 09	RTC5137	C 79	RTC5218E	B 43	RTC5680N	B226	RTC5689	B226	RTC5869	F 17	RTC6061N	B368
RTC4978	B229	RTC5077	B128	RTC5137	C 78	RTC5218E	B 93	RTC5680N	B356	RTC5689	B355	RTC5870	F 17	RTC6065	R 68
RTC4978	B189	RTC5077	B175	RTC5138	C 78	RTC5218E	B140	RTC5680N	B 94	RTC5689	B356	RTC5891	B128	RTC6072	B333
RTC4979	B144	RTC5083E	B 43	RTC5139	C 78	RTC5218E	B361	RTC5680N	B141	RTC5689	B 92	RTC5891	B175	RTC6074	B340
RTC4979	B229	RTC5083E	B 91	RTC5141	C 76	RTC5228E	B367	RTC5680N	B362	RTC5689	B 94	RTC5906	F 12	RTC6075	B340
RTC4979	B189	RTC5083E	B138	RTC5142	C 76	RTC5249E	B143	RTC5680N	B187	RTC5689	B139	RTC5909	F 12	RTC6077	B 88
RTC4980	B144	RTC5085E	B359	RTC5143	C 76	RTC5249N	B143	RTC5681E	B356	RTC5689	B141	RTC5918	B322	RTC6077	B136
RTC4980	B229	RTC5086E	B358	RTC5144	C 76	RTC5265E	B150	RTC5681E	B362	RTC5689	B360	RTC5925	B226	RTC6077	B 41
RTC4980	B189	RTC5087E	B361	RTC5145	C 77	RTC5519	N 29	RTC5681N	B356	RTC5689	B362	RTC5925	B355	RTC6077	B185
RTC4981	B144	RTC5088E	B 43	RTC5146	C 77	RTC5523	M 10	RTC5681N	B362	RTC5689	B186	RTC5925	B356	RTC608	R 35
RTC4981	B229	RTC5090	B352	RTC5147	C 77	RTC5524	M 10	RTC5682E	B226	RTC5689	B187	RTC5925	B 92	RTC608	R 44
RTC4981	B189	RTC5092	B352	RTC5148	C 77	RTC5563	B 46	RTC5682E	B 92	RTC5705	N 80	RTC5925	B139	RTC608	M 14
RTC4982	B144	RTC5099	B218	RTC5149	C 77	RTC5563	B 96	RTC5682E	B139	RTC5706	N 86	RTC5925	B360	RTC608	J 14
RTC4982	B229	RTC5099	B177	RTC5150	C 83	RTC5572	H 26	RTC5682E	B186	RTC5707	N 80	RTC5925	B362	RTC608	J 15
RTC4982	B189	RTC5100	C 85	RTC5151	C 81	RTC5573	H 26	RTC5682N	B226	RTC5708	N 86	RTC5925	B186	RTC608	N102
RTC4983	B144	RTC5100	C 77	RTC5152	C 81	RTC5574	H 27	RTC5682N	B 92	RTC5709	N 80	RTC5926	B226	RTC6083	M110
RTC4983	B229	RTC5100	C 78	RTC5153	C 81	RTC5577	B 46	RTC5682N	B139	RTC5709	N 86	RTC5926	B355	RTC6084	B130
RTC4983	B189	RTC5100	C 80	RTC5154	C 81	RTC5577	B 97	RTC5682N	B186	RTC5710	N 80	RTC5926	B356	RTC609	B307
RTC4998	H 26	RTC5100	C 81	RTC5155	C 79	RTC5577	B368	RTC5683E	B355	RTC5710	N 81	RTC5926	B 92	RTC609	B 32
RTC4999	H 26	RTC5101	C 76	RTC5156	C 79	RTC5597	T 35	RTC5683E	B360	RTC5711	N 86	RTC5926	B 94	RTC609	B 78
RTC5001	H 27	RTC5101	C 79	RTC5157	C 79	RTC5608	B 77	RTC5683N	B355	RTC5712	N 80	RTC5926	B139	RTC609	N 58
RTC5012	M 06	RTC5101	C 82	RTC5158	C 79	RTC5628	B354	RTC5683N	B360	RTC5712	N 81	RTC5926	B141	RTC609	N 49
RTC5013	M 06	RTC5101	C 85	RTC5159	C 79	RTC5629	B 89	RTC5684	B226	RTC5712	N 82	RTC5926	B360	RTC609	N 53
RTC5014	B350	RTC5101	C 77	RTC5160	C 79	RTC5670	B226	RTC5684	B 92	RTC5712	N 83	RTC5926	B362	RTC609	B328
RTC5044	B355	RTC5101	C 78	RTC5161	C 78	RTC5670	B356	RTC5684	B139	RTC5712	N 86	RTC5926	B186	RTC609	N 46
RTC5044	B360	RTC5102	C 75	RTC5162	C 78	RTC5670	B 92	RTC5684	B186	RTC5727A	W 04	RTC5926	B187	RTC609	B327
RTC5045	B355	RTC5103	C 75	RTC5163	C 78	RTC5670	B 94	RTC5685	B355	RTC5727T	W 02	RTC5935	B221	RTC6093	B218
RTC5045	B360	RTC5105	C 75	RTC5164	C 78	RTC5670	B139	RTC5685	B 92	RTC5728A	W 03	RTC5935	B181	RTC6093	B177
RTC5046	B226	RTC5106	C 75	RTC5171	C 82	RTC5670	B141	RTC5685	B139	RTC5728T	W 01	RTC5935	B341	RTC6094	B218
RTC5046	B356	RTC5107	C 75	RTC5171	C 78	RTC5670	B362	RTC5685	B360	RTC5733	C 74	RTC5935	B 84	RTC6094	B177
RTC5046	B 94	RTC5108	C 75	RTC5172	C 82	RTC5670	B186	RTC5685	B186	RTC5734	C 74	RTC5935	B133	RTC610	L 33
RTC5046	B141	RTC5109	C 75	RTC5173	C 80	RTC5670	B187	RTC5686	B226	RTC5735	C 74	RTC5935	B 37	RTC610	N 49
RTC5046	B362	RTC5111	C 75	RTC5174	C 80	RTC5671	B226	RTC5686	B355	RTC5756	H 27	RTC5935	B340	RTC610	N 47
RTC5046	B187	RTC5112	C 75	RTC5175	C 80	RTC5671	B356	RTC5686	B356	RTC5774	B179	RTC5941	N134	RTC610	N 48
RTC5047	B355	RTC5113	C 75	RTC5176	C 80	RTC5671	B 94	RTC5686	B 92	RTC5775	B179	RTC5942	N135	RTC610	G 07
RTC5047	B360	RTC5114	C 75	RTC5177	C 80	RTC5671	B141	RTC5686	B 94	RTC5779A	U 02	RTC5942	N134	RTC6110	F 13
RTC5048	B 46	RTC5115	C 75	RTC5178	C 80	RTC5671	B362	RTC5686	B139	RTC5781A	U 02	RTC5943	N134	RTC6110	F 14
RTC5048	B 96	RTC5116	C 75	RTC5179	C 80	RTC5671	B187	RTC5686	B141	RTC5782A	U 02	RTC5947	B 90	RTC6114	B226
RTC5048	B367	RTC5117	C 75	RTC5180	C 82	RTC5674	B181	RTC5686	B360	RTC5792	C 83	RTC5965	B388	RTC6114	B355

RTC6114	B356	RTC6283	N 68	RTC6702	B253	RTC7428	L 45	RTC8098AB	T 19	RTC9547	T 15	RU612373L	R 03	SA506081L	B318
RTC6114	B 94	RTC6283	N 69	RTC6751	C 57	RTC7429	L 45	RTC8099	T 19	RTC9563	E 54	RU612373L	N 42	SA506081L	B365
RTC6114	B141	RTC6284	N 68	RTC6751	C 10	RTC7430	L 45	RTC8120	T 15	RTC9580A	T 29	RU612373L	P 63	SAD000010PMA	G 02
RTC6114	B360	RTC6284	N 69	RTC6754	E 16	RTC7433	L 50	RTC8120	N 22	RTC9581	T 29	RU612373L	P 34	SB106121	B267
RTC6114	B362	RTC6284	N 70	RTC6755	E 16	RTC7434	L 50	RTC8131A	T 17	RTC9586AA	T 10	RU612373L	R 65	SB108201L	C 35
RTC6114	B187	RTC6284	N 71	RTC6760	B341	RTC7436	L 50	RTC8137	T 07	RTC9588	T 07	RU612373L	N 79	SBB104100	G 03
RTC6115	C 38	RTC6284	N 73	RTC6782	F 13	RTC7439	L 50	RTC8141A	T 17	RTC9589	T 02	RU612373L	N 80	SD106401L	N219
RTC6115	N 16	RTC6284	N 74	RTC6783	F 13	RTC7439	L 58	RTC8159	T 42	RU608123L	N 39	RU612373L	N 81	SDB000330	H 32
RTC6129	F 12	RTC6291	N 75	RTC6790	N134	RTC7440	L 57	RTC8161A	T 17	RU608123L	P 56	RU612373L	N 82	SDB000330	H 30
RTC613	B386	RTC6291	N 76	RTC6793	B 50	RTC7441	L 57	RTC844	E 32	RU608123L	P 60	RU612373L	N 83	SDB100980	H 32
RTC613	B328	RTC6324	M120	RTC6795	B151	RTC7442	L 57	RTC845	E 32	RU608183L	N124	RU612373L	N 84	SDB100980	H 30
RTC6130	F 12	RTC6333	B 13	RTC6797	C 26	RTC7443	L 68	RTC8828AA	T 29	RU608253L	R 04	RU612373L	N 85	SE104124L	P 01
RTC614	R 02	RTC6337	B309	RTC6799	H 27	RTC7445	L 68	RTC8831	T 29	RU608253L	R 01	RU612373L	N 86	SE104124L	H 34
RTC6159	N185	RTC6338	B309	RTC6800N	B 49	RTC7446	L 57	RTC8849	T 17	RU608313L	N132	RU612373L	N 68	SE104161L	P 13
RTC6164	M114	RTC6350	N 56	RTC6800R	B 49	RTC7448	L 68	RTC8849AA	T 17	RU608313L	N116	RU612373L	N 69	SE104161L	M 83
RTC6164	M 70	RTC6351	N 56	RTC6801E	B100	RTC7450	L 72	RTC8859	T 16	RU608313L	N119	RU612373L	N 70	SE104161L	M 84
RTC6164	M 71	RTC6352	N 56	RTC6801N	B100	RTC7451	L 68	RTC8859AA	T 16	RU608313L	R 40	RU612373L	N 71	SE104201L	C 84
RTC6167	B115	RTC6353	N 54	RTC6802E	B150	RTC7452	L 50	RTC8860	T 16	RU608313L	N117	RU612373L	S 02	SE105101L	N193
RTC6167	B164	RTC6353	N 55	RTC6802N	B150	RTC7453	L 50	RTC8860AA	T 16	RU608313L	R 06	RU612373L	R 62	SE105101L	R 43
RTC6168	B115	RTC6354	N 54	RTC6826	N 33	RTC7454	L 50	RTC8872	T 43	RU608313L	R 14	RU612373L	P 61	SE105101L	N188
RTC6168	B164	RTC6354	N 55	RTC6851	B 65	RTC7454	M 81	RTC8891	T 31	RU608313L	R 21	RU612373L	P 17	SE105101L	M 93
RTC617420	B156	RTC6398	F 07	RTC6851	B116	RTC7455	L 50	RTC8891AA	T 30	RU608313L	R 38	RU612373L	R 60	SE105121L	P 02
RTC6174S	B156	RTC6398	F 09	RTC6851	B119	RTC7456	L 50	RTC8891AA	T 31	RU608313L	N103	RU612373L	R 37	SE105121L	M113
RTC6179	D 41	RTC6399	F 07	RTC6851	B 17	RTC7457	L 50	RTC8891AA	T 37	RU608313L	N105	RU612373L	N 95	SE105121L	M109
RTC6180	B127	RTC6399	F 09	RTC6851	B167	RTC7457	L 58	RTC8891AA	T 38	RU608313L	N129	RU612373L	N 87	SE105121L	M 57
RTC6205	N 49	RTC6401A	W 04	RTC6856	M143	RTC7458	L 50	RTC8891AA	T 42	RU608313L	N131	RU612373L	N 88	SE105121L	M 58
RTC6205	N 45	RTC6401T	W 01	RTC6862	E 16	RTC7459	L 66	RTC8917	T 10	RU610183L	N170	RU612373L	N242	SE105121L	N 51
RTC6206	N 49	RTC644220	B107	RTC6868E	C 01	RTC7460	L 66	RTC8917AA	T 10	RU610183L	N173	RU612373L	N245	SE105121L	J 02
RTC6206	N 45	RTC6442S	B107	RTC6869A	W 04	RTC7461	L 66	RTC8921	T 10	RU610253	N 66	RU612373L	N 72	SE105121L	J 09
RTC6209	N 49	RTC6453	R 33	RTC6869T	W 02	RTC7462	L 69	RTC8921AA	T 10	RU610253	N113	RU612373L	N 73	SE105121L	J 11
RTC6210	N 49	RTC6457	B199	RTC6870A	W 03	RTC7463	L 69	RTC8922	T 11	RU610313L	N111	RU612373L	N 74	SE105121L	M 79
RTC6213	N139	RTC645720	B199	RTC6870T	W 01	RTC7464	L 69	RTC8931	T 20	RU610313L	N112	RU612503	N167	SE105121L	J 04
RTC6213	N140	RTC645740	B199	RTC6896	B207	RTC7465	L 71	RTC8932	T 20	RU612123L	S 02	RU612503	N122	SE105121L	M 93
RTC6222	N 65	RTC6462	N109	RTC6999E	C 01	RTC7465	L 72	RTC8933	T 20	RU612183	N 90	RU612503	S 17	SE105141	N139
RTC6238	N164	RTC6462	N110	RTC7408	L 69	RTC7466	L 68	RTC8936	T 22	RU612183	N 92	RU612503	J 15	SE105161	F 04
RTC6239	N164	RTC6474	N210	RTC7409	L 69	RTC7467	L 65	RTC8936AA	T 22	RU612183	N 93	RUB101740	E 49	SE105161	H 36
RTC6246	N 79	RTC6475	N210	RTC7410	L 72	RTC7468	L 57	RTC8938	T 19	RU612183	S 17	RUB101740	E 25	SE105161L	N182
RTC6246	N 80	RTC6476	N210	RTC7411	L 71	RTC7469	L 57	RTC8951	T 25	RU612183	L 48	RYG101010L	E 23	SE105161L	N132
RTC6246	N 81	RTC6477	N210	RTC7411	L 72	RTC7470	L 49	RTC8965	T 07	RU612183	N241	RYG101360	N 06	SE105161L	N147
RTC6246	N 82	RTC6540	B177	RTC7412	L 72	RTC7470	L 57	RTC8969	T 16	RU612183	N243	SA106161	N197	SE105161L	L 36
RTC6246	N 83	RTC6541	B177	RTC7413	L 72	RTC7470	L 65	RTC8977	T 43	RU612253	N 55	SA106161	N219	SE105161L	N163
RTC6246	N 86	RTC6542	B177	RTC7414	L 50	RTC7470	L 66	RTC9472AA	T 26	RU612253	P 45	SA106201	R 01	SE105161L	M 16
RTC6247	N171	RTC6543	B177	RTC7415	L 69	RTC7471	L 50	RTC9473AA	T 26	RU612253	N140	SA106251	N196	SE105165L	R 43
RTC6248	N171	RTC6545	M 57	RTC7416	L 45	RTC7472	L 50	RTC9477	T 18	RU612373L	N 57	SA106351	N239	SE105165L	M 12
RTC625	T 30	RTC6545	M 77	RTC7417	L 45	RTC7473	L 50	RTC9498	M 09	RU612373L	N182	SA106351	N241	SE105201L	H 34
RTC625	T 31	RTC6545	J 01	RTC7418	L 45	RTC7474	L 57	RTC9498	T 10	RU612373L	N 75	SA106351	N242	SE105204	M113
RTC6257	N 85	RTC6545	J 09	RTC7419	L 45	RTC7588	L 50	RTC9520	T 07	RU612373L	N 76	SA106351	N245	SE105204	P 08
RTC6266	N171	RTC6564	B209	RTC7420	L 45	RTC773	E 45	RTC9521	T 10	RU612373L	N 77	SA106401	N243	SE105204	M123
RTC6270	N 99	RTC6564	B246	RTC7421	L 45	RTC7775	M127	RTC9522	T 10	RU612373L	N 78	SA106401	N245	SE105204	M125
RTC6279	N122	RTC6594	C 73	RTC7422	L 45	RTC8064	T 16	RTC9523	T 10	RU612373L	N 97	SA106451	N246	SE105204	M120
RTC6280	N 68	RTC6627	B 90	RTC7423	L 45	RTC8065	T 16	RTC9526	E 53	RU612373L	N 51	SA106451	N240	SE105251L	R 02
RTC6281	N 68	RTC6634A	W 03	RTC7424	L 45	RTC8071	P 05	RTC9526POL	E 53	RU612373L	N115	SA106451	N243	SE105251L	R 03
RTC6281	N 69	RTC6634T	W 01	RTC7425	L 45	RTC8095	T 25	RTC9527	T 54	RU612373L	N 98	SA108161	H 29	SE105251L	R 37
RTC6282	N 68	RTC6635	B194	RTC7426	L 45	RTC8098	T 19	RTC9534AB	T 21	RU612373L	N118	SA108201L	D 42	SE105301L	N239
RTC6282	N 69	RTC6702	B216	RTC7427	L 45	RTC8098AA	T 19	RTC9535	E 54	RU612373L	N246	SA108201L	D 41	SE105301L	N240

SE105301L	N242	SE106551	P 16	SFR47	B166	SGB114450	H 16	SH106121L	J 13	SH106351L	C 86	SH108701	N 11	SH116301	T 06
SE105301L	N245	SE106651	P 16	SFR47	B118	SGB114490	H 21	SH106121L	F 23	SH106351L	C 54	SH108701	K 25	SH214141	D 07
SE105351L	P 67	SE108161L	N 24	SG103084	L 36	SGB114500	H 21	SH106121L	M131	SH106351L	N123	SH108701L	K 03	SH214141	D 04
SE105351L	T 45	SE108201	R 28	SG104165	M116	SGI100010	H 17	SH106121L	B 11	SH106351L	J 72	SH108701L	K 02	SH406061L	E 08
SE105351L	T 46	SE108201	N201	SGB000640	H 23	SGI100020	H 16	SH106121L	B 12	SH106351L	L 25	SH108701L	K 12	SH406061L	E 11
SE105351L	P 61	SE108201L	N123	SGB000650	H 23	SGI100020	H 17	SH106121L	J 36	SH106451	G 01	SH108701L	K 01	SH504041L	B337
SE105351L	N241	SE108251	N178	SGB000660	H 23	SGI100020	H 18	SH106124	R 39	SH108121	M 58	SH108701L	K 11	SH504041L	B324
SE105351L	N244	SE108251	N123	SGB000670	H 23	SGI100020	H 15	SH106124	R 36	SH108121	L 03	SH108701L	K 07	SH504051L	B307
SE105401	F 04	SE108251	N 98	SGB111890	H 17	SGI100040	H 24	SH106141L	B206	SH108121L	B202	SH108701L	K 08	SH504051L	G 12
SE105401	T 43	SE108251	N200	SGB111900	H 17	SGI100040	H 21	SH106141L	B 65	SH108121L	B159	SH108701L	K 09	SH504051L	G 13
SE105401	T 37	SE108251	N 95	SGB111910	H 17	SGK100860	H 16	SH106141L	B116	SH108121L	J 73	SH108701L	K 19	SH504051L	B310
SE105401	T 38	SE108404L	N141	SGB111920	H 17	SGK100860	H 17	SH106141L	B165	SH108141L	B221	SH108701L	K 20	SH504051L	B330
SE106121	P 13	SE108501	N178	SGB111930	H 17	SGK100860	H 15	SH106141L	J 65	SH108141L	B181	SH108701L	K 22	SH504051L	B336
SE106121L	B110	SE108601	N122	SGB111931	H 17	SGK100870	H 16	SH106141L	N124	SH108141L	B 75	SH110141L	K 16	SH504061L	B323
SE106121L	B160	SE110401	N185	SGB111940	H 17	SGK100870	H 17	SH106141L	N 93	SH108141L	B 83	SH110141L	K 14	SH504061L	B376
SE106121L	M 48	SE604051L	R 37	SGB111941	H 17	SGK100870	H 18	SH106141L	B 66	SH108141L	B 84	SH110161L	F 01	SH504061L	B385
SE106121L	F 01	SE604071L	N221	SGB111950	H 18	SGK100870	H 15	SH106141L	B117	SH108141L	B132	SH110161L	F 03	SH505041L	J 73
SE106121L	M130	SE808244	L 37	SGB111960	H 18	SGK100890	H 16	SH106141L	J 51	SH108141L	B133	SH110161L	K 14	SH505051	J 34
SE106121L	M 93	SEE000010	H 32	SGB111970	H 18	SGL100000	H 22	SH106141L	M102	SH108141L	B 36	SH110201	N203	SH505051L	B162
SE106161	J 67	SEE000010	H 30	SGB111980	H 18	SGL100010	H 24	SH106141L	J 72	SH108141L	B 37	SH110201L	B123	SH505051L	B163
SE106161L	B354	SF104164	N221	SGB111990	H 18	SGL100020	H 21	SH106141L	T 05	SH108141L	B 27	SH110201L	R 61	SH505051L	M 63
SE106161L	N196	SF104164	R 45	SGB111991	H 18	SH104081L	F 23	SH106141L	M101	SH108141L	K 16	SH110201L	B211	SH505061L	B384
SE106161L	M 91	SF104204L	N221	SGB112000	H 18	SH104101L	N184	SH106141L	B 17	SH108141L	K 14	SH110251L	E 59	SH505061L	B310
SE106161L	N153	SF105121	V 06	SGB112001	H 18	SH104121L	B 19	SH106141L	B 18	SH108141L	C 51	SH110251L	R 58	SH505071L	N 14
SE106161L	M128	SF105121L	S 11	SGB112020	H 23	SH104121L	B 67	SH106161M	C 68	SH108151	R 05	SH110251L	N 19	SH505071L	B377
SE106161L	N 90	SF105251L	T 27	SGB112020	H 21	SH104201	J 50	SH106161S	C 46	SH108151L	R 12	SH110251L	N100	SH505071L	B341
SE106161L	S 16	SF106161	T 27	SGB112021	H 23	SH105121	F 04	SH106167	B354	SH108161	L 12	SH110251L	T 30	SH505071L	B342
SE106161L	N141	SF106161	N139	SGB112350	H 23	SH105121	J 67	SH106167	F 19	SH108161L	N 24	SH110251L	V 04	SH505071L	B343
SE106161L	N192	SF106161L	N193	SGB112350	H 21	SH105121L	N 30	SH106167	M100	SH108201L	J 10	SH110251L	N251	SH505081L	L 22
SE106161L	R 31	SF106161L	N189	SGB112351	H 23	SH105121L	J 51	SH106167L	N 58	SH108251	K 29	SH110251L	E 64	SH505091L	B307
SE106164	R 45	SF106161L	T 14	SGB112370	H 16	SH105121L	L 62	SH106167L	L 32	SH108251L	B108	SH110251L	E 67	SH505091L	B386
SE106164	R 40	SF106161L	N249	SGB112380	H 24	SH105121L	L 39	SH106204	P 24	SH108251L	B155	SH110251L	N 08	SH505091L	B381
SE106167	B354	SF106201L	N142	SGB112380	H 22	SH105161	C 84	SH106204	P 18	SH108251L	D 31	SH110301	E 61	SH505091L	B324
SE106201L	P 33	SF106201L	D 30	SGB112390	H 24	SH105161L	C 51	SH106204	P 23	SH108251L	D 33	SH110301	T 30	SH506031	C 24
SE106201L	M 82	SF106201L	D 32	SGB112390	H 22	SH105161L	C 52	SH106204	R 31	SH108251L	D 06	SH110301	T 31	SH506071L	B318
SE106201L	N122	SF106201L	D 35	SGB112400	H 24	SH105161L	M 63	SH106205	L 03	SH108257	N137	SH110301L	B144	SH506071L	B320
SE106201L	N 97	SF106201L	R 04	SGB112400	H 22	SH105161L	S 08	SH106207L	J 38	SH108301L	B 73	SH110301L	B189	SH506071L	B357
SE106201L	N 99	SF106201L	R 15	SGB112410	H 24	SH105161L	S 09	SH106207L	L 02	SH108301L	J 70	SH110351L	E 60	SH506071L	B381
SE106201L	N 44	SF106201L	R 01	SGB112410	H 22	SH105201L	P 10	SH106207L	L 09	SH108401L	B357	SH110351L	E 68	SH506071L	B342
SE106201L	R 40	SF106201L	N140	SGB112420	H 16	SH105201L	M105	SH106207L	L 03	SH108401L	R 28	SH110401L	D 06	SH506071L	B343
SE106201L	R 38	SF106201L	D 33	SGB112421	H 16	SH105201L	G 13	SH106207L	J 37	SH108401L	C 28	SH112201	N 12	SH506071L	B365
SE106201L	N 95	SF106401	N195	SGB112430	H 16	SH105251L	B218	SH106207L	J 45	SH108401L	C 31	SH112201	T 05	SH506071L	B366
SE106201L	M 94	SF106401	N192	SGB112430	H 14	SH105251L	B178	SH106251	T 45	SH108401L	C 37	SH112201	N 15	SH506081L	B306
SE106201L	N241	SF108251	N124	SGB112440	H 14	SH105551	M 12	SH106251	T 46	SH108401L	N 98	SH112251	R 61	SH506091L	B327
SE106201L	N243	SF108251L	D 08	SGB112450	H 14	SH106121L	B 60	SH106301	N158	SH108401L	J 01	SH112251L	B 08	SH506095L	B386
SE106204	R 29	SF108251L	D 10	SGB112451	H 16	SH106121L	E 19	SH106301	E 69	SH108401L	B 83	SH112251L	B 57	SH506101L	B357
SE106251	P 13	SF604101	R 35	SGB112460	H 16	SH106121L	M 46	SH106301	L 43	SH108401L	B132	SH112251L	B109	SH506101L	B366
SE106251	N238	SF910141L	R 43	SGB112461	H 16	SH106121L	L 24	SH106301L	C 29	SH108401L	C 02	SH112251L	B158	SH506101L	B326
SE106251L	P 33	SFP000130	H 33	SGB113700	H 21	SH106121L	C 83	SH106301L	N151	SH108401L	B 36	SH112251L	B201	SH506121L	B350
SE106251L	S 12	SFP000130	H 31	SGB113701	H 21	SH106121L	H 25	SH106301L	L 63	SH108401L	B 45	SH112251L	C 38	SH506121L	B352
SE106351L	P 14	SFP000140	H 27	SGB113780	H 16	SH106121L	J 33	SH106301L	L 64	SH108401L	C 06	SH112251L	N 16	SH507091L	N 14
SE106351L	P 15	SFP000150	H 33	SGB114380	H 23	SH106121L	J 46	SH106301L	L 09	SH108401L	B366	SH112251L	N 17	SH507091L	B377
SE106401	P 55	SFP000150	H 31	SGB114381	H 23	SH106121L	M135	SH106301L	L 47	SH108451L	B357	SH112301L	C 06	SH604031L	B303
SE106401	R 37	SFP000160	H 33	SGB114390	H 23	SH106121L	J 37	SH106351L	N197	SH108451L	B366	SH112505	H 25	SH604031L	G 07
SE106501	N122	SFP000160	H 31	SGB114391	H 23	SH106121L	L 32	SH106351L	J 65	SH108501L	N 61	SH112505	E 22	SH604041L	B320

SH604051L	B 32	SMC000190	H 32	SS108301L	B127	STC1180	R 54	STC1250	B228	STC128	J 16	STC1549N	C 01	STC1773A	W 03
SH604051L	B 78	SMC000190	H 30	SS108301L	B131	STC1180	R 48	STC1250	B397	STC1280	H 27	STC1557	B219	STC1773T	W 01
SH604051L	R 33	SMD100260	H 32	SS108301L	B174	STC1180	R 49	STC1250	B144	STC1281	H 32	STC1558	B179	STC1774A	W 04
SH604061L	B342	SMD100260	H 30	SS108301L	B180	STC1180	R 51	STC1250	B145	STC1281	H 30	STC1559	B130	STC1774T	W 02
SH604061L	B343	SMD100270	H 32	SS108404	N185	STC1182	M102	STC1250	B229	STC130	B 43	STC1562	B130	STC1796	B261
SH604071	R 35	SMD100270	H 30	SS108555	B388	STC1184	B352	STC1250	B369	STC130	B 93	STC1566	B345	STC1836	C 75
SH604071L	R 33	SMG000010	H 26	SS108701S	C 55	STC1188	M 06	STC1250	B189	STC130	B140	STC1569	L 59	STC1845	E 43
SH604071L	R 35	SMG000010	H 33	SS108801	B388	STC1188	M 11	STC1250	B190	STC130	B358	STC1601	H 33	STC1846	E 12
SH604071L	B377	SMG000010	H 31	SS110555	B373	STC1189	M 11	STC1251	B262	STC130	B361	STC1601	H 31	STC1846	E 42
SH604071L	R 45	SMN000060	H 32	SS110801	B230	STC1190	B215	STC1251	B228	STC1346	N129	STC1602	E 14	STC1851	M 03
SH604081L	G 07	SMN000060	H 30	SS506060	B341	STC1190	B127	STC1251	B144	STC1346	N131	STC1611	B308	STC1854	N 76
SH604081L	G 08	SN106127L	H 24	SS506121L	B367	STC1190	B174	STC1251	B145	STC1348A	W 03	STC1612	M 05	STC1854	N 81
SH605051L	B386	SN106307	H 24	SS506121L	B368	STC1203	M 26	STC1251	B229	STC1348T	W 01	STC1612	M 02	STC1854	N 69
SH605051L	B328	SP104101L	N143	SS607160	B399	STC1203	M 18	STC1251	B189	STC1349A	W 04	STC1612	M 03	STC1854	N 73
SH605061L	B342	SP104121	N127	SSW100050	M107	STC1209	M 05	STC1251	B190	STC1349T	W 02	STC1613	M 02	STC1854	N 74
SH605061L	B343	SP105121	N 51	SSW100060	M107	STC1209	M 03	STC1252	B369	STC1371	T 13	STC1613	M 03	STC1855	N 76
SH605071	L 43	SP105121	J 51	ST606080	B388	STC1210	M 05	STC1253	B397	STC1378	V 03	STC1614	M 05	STC1855	N 81
SH605081L	E 62	SP105204	P 08	STC100410	G 04	STC1210	M 03	STC1253	B369	STC1379	V 03	STC1614	M 02	STC1855	N 69
SH605081L	R 68	SP105204	M120	STC100440	G 04	STC1212	B352	STC1254	B262	STC1423	N171	STC1614	M 03	STC1855	N 73
SH605081L	B342	SP105251	V 05	STC1004E	C 01	STC1227	M 06	STC1254	B228	STC1424	N171	STC1616	N 72	STC1855	N 74
SH605081L	B343	SP105251L	S 10	STC1005E	C 01	STC1228	M 06	STC1254	B144	STC1427	B375	STC1617	N 72	STC1857	B351
SH605121L	B351	SQB000300	H 04	STC1006E	C 01	STC1229	M 11	STC1254	B145	STC1449A	W 04	STC1624	M126	STC1857	B352
SH606061L	B370	SQB000300	H 06	STC1007E	C 01	STC1230	M 11	STC1254	B229	STC1449T	W 02	STC1628	C 46	STC1889	C 10
SH606061L	H 36	SQB000310	H 04	STC1012	R 36	STC1241	B369	STC1254	B189	STC1453	M135	STC1633	B221	STC1891	B372
SH607081L	B370	SQB000310	H 06	STC1013	R 39	STC1242	B369	STC1254	B190	STC1467	B 35	STC1633	B181	STC1896	B218
SH607091L	N 67	SQB102910	H 04	STC1017	D 01	STC1243	B369	STC1255	B262	STC1467	B 82	STC1633	B341	STC1956	T 46
SH607091L	N250	SQB102910	H 06	STC1036	C 05	STC1244	B262	STC1255	B228	STC1470	N171	STC1633	B 84	STC1961	B373
SH607091L	V 04	SQB102911	H 04	STC1040	F 14	STC1244	B228	STC1255	B397	STC1471	N171	STC1633	B133	STC197	M 46
SH607091L	N251	SQB102911	H 06	STC1041	F 15	STC1244	B144	STC1255	B144	STC1481	B101	STC1633	B 37	STC199	B 55
SH910101	B335	SQB102920	H 04	STC1041	F 16	STC1244	B145	STC1255	B145	STC1482	J 04	STC1633	B340	STC19920	B 55
SH910241L	B335	SQB102920	H 06	STC1042	F 13	STC1244	B229	STC1255	B229	STC1485	M 05	STC1639	B392	STC201	H 26
SHB101370	H 24	SQB102921	H 04	STC1042	F 14	STC1244	B189	STC1255	B369	STC1485	M 02	STC1639	B345	STC205	B333
SHB101370	H 21	SQB102921	H 06	STC1044	F 08	STC1244	B190	STC1255	B189	STC1485	M 03	STC1640	B 35	STC234	B226
SHB101430	H 24	SQB103220	H 04	STC1044	F 10	STC1245	B262	STC1255	B190	STC1486	M 05	STC1640	B 82	STC234	B356
SHU100340	H 24	SQQ100000	H 03	STC1044	F 11	STC1245	B228	STC1257	B 99	STC1486	M 02	STC1641	B392	STC234	B 94
SHU100340	H 22	SQQ100000	H 06	STC1045	F 08	STC1245	B144	STC1262	H 26	STC1486	M 03	STC1675	B232	STC234	B141
SIH100010	H 06	SR106201	N240	STC1045	F 10	STC1245	B145	STC1263	H 26	STC1518	B143	STC1693	B379	STC234	B362
SJC100420	H 06	SR106201	N243	STC1045	F 11	STC1245	B229	STC1264	H 32	STC1519	B 46	STC1694	B254	STC234	B187
SJC100421	H 06	SR106201	N245	STC1052020	B199	STC1245	B189	STC1264	H 30	STC1519	B 96	STC1695	B254	STC2404	N221
SJC100460	H 03	SR106251L	M143	STC1052040	B199	STC1245	B190	STC1265	H 32	STC1525	D 42	STC1696	B254	STC244	D 41
SJG100240	H 06	SRB101550	H 07	STC1055	F 12	STC1246	B262	STC1265	H 30	STC1526	D 42	STC1697	B254	STC245	D 41
SJJ100350	H 06	SRD100490	M 96	STC1060	C 74	STC1246	B228	STC1266	H 26	STC1527	D 42	STC1736E	B231	STC246	D 41
SJJ100351	H 03	SRU101920	H 07	STC1086	B241	STC1246	B144	STC1267	H 26	STC1530	H 36	STC1736N	B231	STC251	M 17
SJJ100351	H 06	SRU101970	H 07	STC1120	L 34	STC1246	B145	STC1268	H 32	STC1532	D 42	STC1738	B254	STC251	M 18
SJL100200	H 03	SRU102200	H 07	STC1120	J 34	STC1246	B229	STC1268	H 30	STC1533	D 42	STC1739	B254	STC262	B216
SJL100200	H 06	SS106161L	K 16	STC1121	B316	STC1246	B189	STC1269	H 32	STC1536	D 42	STC1747	M123	STC2770	C 01
SJO100080	H 06	SS106161L	K 14	STC1122	B316	STC1246	B190	STC1269	H 30	STC1538	D 42	STC1747	M125	STC2774LGE	U 02
SL106121	N 11	SS108161L	B242	STC1130	D 18	STC1247	B262	STC1270	H 32	STC1546E	C 39	STC1749	M 96	STC2774SML	U 02
SL510031	H 24	SS108161L	K 16	STC1130	D 19	STC1247	B228	STC1270	H 30	STC1546N	C 39	STC1750	M 96	STC2796	H 28
SL510031	H 20	SS108161L	K 14	STC1130	T 05	STC1247	B144	STC1275	H 27	STC1547E	C 39	STC1757	M 92	STC2797	H 28
SL510031	H 22	SS108201	B255	STC1137	F 10	STC1247	B145	STC1276	H 33	STC1547N	C 39	STC1758	M 92	STC2798	H 28
SLC000010PMA	G 02	SS108201	J 75	STC1138	F 10	STC1247	B229	STC1276	H 31	STC1548E	C 39	STC1759	M 92	STC2801	B256
SLC100210	G 02	SS108251	J 75	STC1139	J 01	STC1247	B189	STC1279	H 32	STC1548N	C 39	STC1760	M 92	STC2802	B256
SMC000180	H 32	SS108251L	B220	STC1172	B219	STC1247	B190	STC1279	H 30	STC1549E	C 39	STC1768	E 12	STC2818	C 41
SMC000180	H 30	SS108301L	B215	STC1180	R 52	STC1250	B262	STC128	J 38	STC1549N	C 39	STC1768	E 40	STC2818	C 44

STC2828A	W 04	STC3169	L 45	STC3328	N252	STC361	H 28	STC3971	L 77	STC4274	L 77	STC4593	N138	STC50172	T 19
STC2828T	W 02	STC3170	L 58	STC334	C 82	STC3610	D 02	STC3972	L 77	STC4275	L 77	STC4594	N138	STC50173	T 19
STC2845	F 11	STC3171	L 45	STC3372	B378	STC3610E	D 02	STC3973	L 54	STC4276	L 77	STC4595A	W 04	STC50245	T 14
STC2846	F 11	STC3171	L 58	STC3374	B 28	STC3611	D 02	STC3974	L 54	STC4277	L 74	STC4595T	W 02	STC50255	T 29
STC2847	F 14	STC3176	B295	STC3375	C 62	STC3615K	D 09	STC3975	L 54	STC4278	L 74	STC4596A	W 04	STC50255AA	T 29
STC2847	F 16	STC3177	B295	STC3376	C 63	STC3624	B253	STC3976	L 54	STC4279	L 56	STC4596T	W 02	STC50256	T 29
STC2848	F 13	STC3185	D 15	STC3377	C 64	STC363	B219	STC3977	L 77	STC4286	T 45	STC4597A	W 03	STC50256AA	T 29
STC2848	F 14	STC3188	L 45	STC3378	C 67	STC3710	N 25	STC3978	L 77	STC4286	T 46	STC4597T	W 01	STC50257	T 29
STC2851	E 58	STC3189	L 46	STC3395	B198	STC3711	N 25	STC398	F 11	STC4287	L 56	STC4614	B255	STC50257AA	T 29
STC2852	E 63	STC3190	L 46	STC3395	B235	STC3712	N 25	STC3981	L 52	STC4299	B374	STC4615	B255	STC50258	T 29
STC2853	E 58	STC3191	L 45	STC3395	B 54	STC3714	N 25	STC3982	L 52	STC4321	N136	STC4617	B255	STC50259	T 29
STC2854	E 65	STC3191	L 58	STC3395	B106	STC3715	B262	STC3983	L 52	STC4322	H 03	STC4627ABE	N225	STC50259AA	T 29
STC2855	E 65	STC3191	L 52	STC3395	B155	STC3715	B228	STC3985	L 74	STC4323A	W 04	STC4627ABE	N235	STC50264	T 15
STC2856	E 65	STC3191	L 77	STC3407	B238	STC3715	B144	STC3986	L 74	STC4323T	W 02	STC4627ABE	N229	STC50265	T 08
STC2856	E 66	STC3191	L 54	STC3410	E 55	STC3715	B145	STC3987	L 74	STC4324A	W 04	STC4627ABE	N236	STC50266	T 03
STC2863A	W 04	STC3192	L 45	STC3411	E 55	STC3715	B229	STC3988	L 74	STC4324T	W 02	STC4627ABE	N226	STC50269	N204
STC2863T	W 02	STC3192	L 58	STC3412	E 55	STC3715	B189	STC3991	L 55	STC4325A	W 03	STC4627ABE	N232	STC50269AA	T 49
STC2871	N196	STC3192	L 52	STC3413	E 55	STC3715	B190	STC3992	L 52	STC4325T	W 01	STC4637	M 11	STC50270	T 15
STC2873	N122	STC3192	L 77	STC3414	E 55	STC3722	E 39	STC3994	L 74	STC434	N 14	STC4641	M115	STC50270	N 22
STC2878	H 01	STC3201	L 49	STC3415	E 55	STC3722	E 11	STC4005	N225	STC434	C 38	STC4668	B269	STC50299	T 07
STC2879	H 01	STC3202	B261	STC3416	E 55	STC3766	E 58	STC4005	N235	STC434	N 16	STC467	H 28	STC50301	N204
STC288	E 58	STC3207	N222	STC3417	E 55	STC3767	E 63	STC4005	N229	STC4348	C 63	STC4672	W 05	STC50301	T 49
STC289	E 63	STC3208	N222	STC3418	E 55	STC3769	E 58	STC4005	N236	STC4370	D 18	STC4674	W 05	STC50303	T 44
STC290	E 58	STC3209	N222	STC3419	E 55	STC3770	E 65	STC4005	N226	STC4373	J 17	STC4675	W 05	STC50324	T 44
STC291	E 65	STC3210	N222	STC3420	E 55	STC3771	E 65	STC4005	N232	STC4378	B379	STC4676	W 05	STC50325	T 44
STC292	E 65	STC3214	L 58	STC3421	E 55	STC3772	E 65	STC4029	M 05	STC4382	E 48	STC4677	W 05	STC50358	T 18
STC293	E 65	STC3215	L 58	STC3422	E 55	STC3772	E 66	STC4034	M 46	STC4382	E 23	STC4678	W 05	STC50381	T 14
STC293	E 66	STC3216	L 58	STC3423	E 55	STC3822A	W 03	STC4035	M 46	STC4382	E 25	STC468	H 28	STC50478	T 15
STC2940	D 11	STC3220	N222	STC3424	E 55	STC3822T	W 01	STC4036	M 46	STC4385	F 14	STC4680	W 05	STC50480	T 20
STC2955	E 01	STC3221	N222	STC3425	E 55	STC3823A	W 04	STC4104	B314	STC4389	B253	STC4681	W 05	STC50501	B263
STC2955	E 02	STC3252	B253	STC3426	E 55	STC3823T	W 02	STC4104	B378	STC439	M 87	STC4682	W 05	STC50503	B370
STC2979	L 45	STC3253	B253	STC3427	E 55	STC3824A	W 03	STC416	F 14	STC4391	H 34	STC4683	W 05	STC50524	U 02
STC298210	B236	STC3254	B253	STC3428	E 55	STC3824T	W 01	STC418	F 14	STC4401	E 32	STC4684	W 05	STC50529	U 02
STC298220	B236	STC3271	N222	STC3429	E 55	STC3825A	W 03	STC4236	J 74	STC4403	E 32	STC4685	W 05	STC50530	U 02
STC2992	L 46	STC3272	B399	STC3430	T 35	STC3825T	W 01	STC4236	J 14	STC4404	U 01	STC4686	W 05	STC50541	U 01
STC3018	M 05	STC3286	M 24	STC3431	T 35	STC3827A	W 04	STC4236	J 70	STC441	H 03	STC4687	W 05	STC50542	U 01
STC3018	M 02	STC3287	M 24	STC3432	D 18	STC3827T	W 02	STC4237	J 74	STC442	H 03	STC469	H 29	STC50543	U 01
STC3049	E 17	STC3289	N222	STC3433	D 19	STC3828A	W 03	STC4237	J 14	STC443	M143	STC471	C 04	STC50544	U 01
STC3050	E 17	STC3290	N222	STC3435	E 20	STC3828T	W 01	STC4237	J 70	STC4456	N 10	STC4745	B269	STC50545	U 01
STC3051	E 17	STC3291	N222	STC3435	E 22	STC3858	N136	STC4238A	W 04	STC4456	N 02	STC4779	M114	STC50546	U 01
STC307	M 29	STC3295	F 11	STC354AV	R 04	STC3859	N136	STC4238T	W 02	STC4456	N 04	STC4786	B287	STC50547	U 03
STC307	M 27	STC3297	B217	STC354PB	R 04	STC3860	C 30	STC4252	M 93	STC4456	N 06	STC4798	M 86	STC50548	U 03
STC307	M 28	STC3297	B254	STC355AV	R 15	STC3867	B101	STC4260	L 52	STC4462	B397	STC4807	E 01	STC50549	U 03
STC3078	M124	STC3299	B268	STC355PB	R 15	STC3907	L 45	STC4261	L 52	STC4462	B369	STC4808	E 01	STC50550	B237
STC308	B192	STC330	C 82	STC359	H 28	STC3915A	W 03	STC4262	L 52	STC4464	B397	STC487	B309	STC50550	U 01
STC3084	B255	STC3300	B268	STC3592	B255	STC3915T	W 01	STC4263	L 52	STC4464	B369	STC488	B309	STC50551	U 01
STC3086	M116	STC3305	M 30	STC3597	B253	STC3943	J 14	STC4264	L 55	STC4465	B397	STC491	H 03	STC50552	U 01
STC3086	M119	STC3305	M 31	STC360	H 28	STC3947	F 11	STC4265	L 55	STC4465	B369	STC492	H 03	STC50553	U 01
STC309E	B193	STC3312	P 21	STC3600	C 73	STC3963	L 48	STC4266	L 55	STC4509	B279	STC493	H 03	STC50554	U 01
STC309N	B193	STC3313	M119	STC3601	E 55	STC3964	L 48	STC4267	L 74	STC4509	B287	STC50013	T 21	STC509	B333
STC3117	V 09	STC3314	C 34	STC3602	J 66	STC3965	L 48	STC4268	L 74	STC456	L 33	STC50104	T 07	STC510	B333
STC3159	B255	STC3314	C 35	STC3608	D 02	STC3966	L 48	STC4269	L 77	STC4589	N138	STC50105	T 07	STC53014	T 18
STC3164	B 99	STC3319	B371	STC3608E	D 03	STC3967	L 48	STC4271	L 77	STC4590	N138	STC50141	T 50	STC53037	T 15
STC3165	P 55	STC3320	N222	STC3609	D 02	STC3968	L 48	STC4272	L 77	STC4591	N138	STC50149	T 18	STC536	C 07
STC3168	L 58	STC3327	N252	STC3609E	D 03	STC3969	L 48	STC4273	L 77	STC4592	N138	STC50149AA	T 18	STC537	N102

UKC8677L	C 02	WA104004L	P 01	WA105001L	D 38	WA106041L	N218	WA106041L	M131	WA108051	J 51	WA108051L	N239	WA108051L	J 57
UKC8L	C 58	WA104004L	P 11	WA105001L	B178	WA106041L	N219	WA106041L	M139	WA108051	J 58	WA108051L	N218	WA108051L	G 08
UKC8L	C 10	WA104004L	N 31	WA105001L	D 33	WA106041L	P 33	WA106041L	M140	WA108051	J 10	WA108051L	R 28	WA108051L	B 12
UKJ000010	C 69	WA104004L	P 03	WA105001L	R 37	WA106041L	R 29	WA106041L	M141	WA108051	B366	WA108051L	R 58	WA108051L	B 37
ULC1796L	C 16	WA105001	N203	WA105001L	C 51	WA106041L	L 24	WA106041L	M142	WA108051	B184	WA108051L	C 83	WA108051L	B 40
URB100760	B263	WA105001L	B218	WA105001L	J 04	WA106041L	L 33	WA106041L	H 22	WA108051	D 10	WA108051L	C 84	WA108051L	H 03
URB100760	B191	WA105001L	B128	WA105001L	C 52	WA106041L	C 83	WA106041L	L 30	WA108051	D 24	WA108051L	F 05	WA108051L	H 14
URB100760	B147	WA105001L	B175	WA105001L	J 67	WA106041L	C 36	WA106041L	L 27	WA108051	J 03	WA108051L	H 34	WA108051L	H 19
URB100760	B148	WA105001L	N193	WA105001L	N104	WA106041L	F 05	WA106041L	B 17	WA108051L	B197	WA108051L	H 36	WA108051L	L 29
UTJ100210	C 42	WA105001L	N203	WA105001L	N106	WA106041L	F 17	WA106041L	B 18	WA108051L	B202	WA108051L	N 11	WA108051L	C 08
UTP1125	L 36	WA105001L	N239	WA105001L	S 08	WA106041L	N154	WA106041L	B336	WA108051L	B205	WA108051L	M 31	WA108051L	B 25
UTP1126	L 36	WA105001L	P 01	WA105001L	S 09	WA106041L	M108	WA106041L	B335	WA108051L	B215	WA108051L	M 32	WA108051L	B 27
UTP1258	L 35	WA105001L	P 02	WA105001L	S 10	WA106041L	N 11	WA106041L	N149	WA108051L	B216	WA108051L	N145	WA108051L	B336
UTP1259	L 35	WA105001L	M 75	WA105001L	N240	WA106041L	M 29	WA106041L	V 05	WA108051L	B218	WA108051L	N191	WA108051L	B335
UTP1281	L 35	WA105001L	C 84	WA105001L	N241	WA106041L	M 32	WA106041L	V 06	WA108051L	B221	WA108051L	N122	WA108051L	B363
UTP1282	L 35	WA105001L	F 04	WA105001L	N242	WA106041L	M 82	WA106041L	D 36	WA108051L	B307	WA108051L	N123	WA108051L	B364
UTP1725	L 35	WA105001L	H 34	WA105001L	N244	WA106041L	N 34	WA106041L	N192	WA108051L	B354	WA108051L	N124	WA108051L	B365
UTP1904	L 35	WA105001L	M 57	WA105001L	N245	WA106041L	N122	WA106041L	K 16	WA108051L	B357	WA108051L	N 97	WA108051L	B224
UTP1908	L 36	WA105001L	M 58	WA105001L	M 16	WA106041L	N123	WA106041L	K 14	WA108051L	B386	WA108051L	N126	WA108051L	N150
UTP1910	L 35	WA105001L	M 77	WA105004L	L 37	WA106041L	N 97	WA106041L	J 36	WA108051L	B388	WA108051L	N 98	WA108051L	V 05
UTP1911	L 35	WA105001L	N 32	WA105041	M109	WA106041L	N 99	WA106041L	N 95	WA108051L	B 10	WA108051L	N 99	WA108051L	D 37
UYF100160	D 22	WA105001L	N 90	WA106001	L 31	WA106041L	N 90	WA106041L	N 96	WA108051L	B 15	WA108051L	N 90	WA108051L	D 39
UYF100160	D 24	WA105001L	N 94	WA106001L	E 19	WA106041L	N 93	WA106041L	T 51	WA108051L	B 42	WA108051L	N 91	WA108051L	D 38
VCF100420	N252	WA105001L	N201	WA106001L	N118	WA106041L	N246	WA106041L	T 52	WA108051L	B 58	WA108051L	N100	WA108051L	D 17
VCF100430	N252	WA105001L	M 76	WA106001L	D 30	WA106041L	S 16	WA106041L	T 53	WA108051L	B 60	WA108051L	N101	WA108051L	D 33
VUB105440	T 37	WA105001L	N 31	WA106001L	J 20	WA106041L	B 66	WA106041L	M138	WA108051L	B 90	WA108051L	N201	WA108051L	D 34
VUB105450	T 38	WA105001L	J 02	WA106001L	N117	WA106041L	B377	WA106041L	L 22	WA108051L	B105	WA108051L	N246	WA108051L	B153
VUB105460	T 37	WA105001L	J 09	WA106001L	C 23	WA106041L	B117	WA106041L	N 43	WA108051L	B110	WA108051L	B308	WA108051L	R 12
VUB105470	T 37	WA105001L	J 51	WA106001L	C 08	WA106041L	J 38	WA106041L	L 28	WA108051L	B127	WA108051L	B309	WA108051L	R 14
VUB105480	T 38	WA105001L	L 36	WA106001L	C 07	WA106041L	J 46	WA106041L	N129	WA108051L	B128	WA108051L	B 73	WA108051L	K 16
VUB112530L	T 54	WA105001L	L 38	WA106001L	J 22	WA106041L	N 47	WA106041L	S 10	WA108051L	B 63	WA108051L	B 75	WA108051L	K 14
VYG000020	S 13	WA105001L	N 63	WA106001L	N159	WA106041L	N151	WA106041L	S 11	WA108051L	B 64	WA108051L	B 87	WA108051L	J 70
WA103001L	N124	WA105001L	R 43	WA106001L	N161	WA106041L	N142	WA106041L	N133	WA108051L	B115	WA108051L	B137	WA108051L	J 71
WA104001L	B244	WA105001L	L 62	WA106001L	T 48	WA106041L	N 41	WA106041L	G 01	WA108051L	B154	WA108051L	N 24	WA108051L	N 95
WA104001L	B 19	WA105001L	L 75	WA106001L	J 75	WA106041L	G 12	WA106041L	N241	WA108051L	B159	WA108051L	G 09	WA108051L	L 22
WA104001L	B 67	WA105001L	D 31	WA106001L	L 22	WA106041L	G 13	WA106041L	N131	WA108051L	B164	WA108051L	G 04	WA108051L	N 43
WA104001L	N184	WA105001L	L 03	WA106041	N 49	WA106041L	L 08	WA106044L	R 37	WA108051L	B173	WA108051L	J 01	WA108051L	M 63
WA104001L	N194	WA105001L	M123	WA106041	H 20	WA106041L	L 17	WA106045L	N146	WA108051L	B175	WA108051L	J 58	WA108051L	N 15
WA104001L	M 32	WA105001L	M125	WA106041	T 47	WA106041L	M135	WA106047	J 37	WA108051L	B177	WA108051L	L 05	WA108051L	N 16
WA104001L	N 32	WA105001L	J 11	WA106041L	B206	WA106041L	M143	WA106047L	B354	WA108051L	B126	WA108051L	N151	WA108051L	S 10
WA104001L	N 90	WA105001L	T 46	WA106041L	B303	WA106041L	J 37	WA106047L	J 38	WA108051L	E 56	WA108051L	G 11	WA108051L	N 07
WA104001L	P 13	WA105001L	M 14	WA106041L	B354	WA106041L	L 32	WA106047L	N 61	WA108051L	E 57	WA108051L	R 61	WA108051L	N 08
WA104001L	J 50	WA105001L	M 15	WA106041L	B 65	WA106041L	T 45	WA106047L	J 37	WA108051L	E 68	WA108051L	R 64	WA108051L	G 02
WA104001L	M122	WA105001L	M 70	WA106041L	B110	WA106041L	T 46	WA106047L	F 19	WA108051L	D 09	WA108051L	D 32	WA108051L	N240
WA104001L	F 23	WA105001L	M 79	WA106041L	B116	WA106041L	T 05	WA106047L	J 45	WA108051L	D 04	WA108051L	L 17	WA108051L	N241
WA104001L	M121	WA105001L	J 45	WA106041L	B159	WA106041L	B103	WA108001	M 82	WA108051L	D 05	WA108051L	M102	WA108051L	N242
WA104001L	M139	WA105001L	M121	WA106041L	B165	WA106041L	B147	WA108001	D 36	WA108051L	D 16	WA108051L	M103	WA108051L	N243
WA104001L	M140	WA105001L	B 29	WA106041L	D 08	WA106041L	M 27	WA108041	L 12	WA108051L	D 21	WA108051L	C 09	WA108051L	N245
WA104001L	M141	WA105001L	L 39	WA106041L	D 22	WA106041L	J 13	WA108041	R 05	WA108051L	D 28	WA108051L	C 23	WA108051L	N137
WA104001L	M142	WA105001L	N148	WA106041L	N158	WA106041L	P 16	WA108041L	T 53	WA108051L	N 25	WA108051L	B341	WA108051L	N138
WA104001L	N187	WA105001L	N139	WA106041L	N165	WA106041L	P 14	WA108051	B174	WA108051L	N 28	WA108051L	B 84	WA108054L	N185
WA104001L	N189	WA105001L	V 05	WA106041L	N169	WA106041L	P 15	WA108051	B175	WA108051L	N185	WA108051L	B133	WA108251L	H 34
WA104004	M122	WA105001L	N188	WA106041L	N184	WA106041L	F 20	WA108051	B181	WA108051L	N158	WA108051L	R 05	WA110001L	D 09
WA104004	M124	WA105001L	D 37	WA106041L	N181	WA106041L	F 23	WA108051	C 36	WA108051L	N170	WA108051L	J 52	WA110001L	T 31
WA104004	L 72	WA105001L	D 39	WA106041L	N132	WA106041L	M130	WA108051	J 08	WA108051L	N181	WA108051L	R 62	WA110001L	E 67

WA110061L	B214	WA110065	L 62	WB106041L	R 63	WC106041L	J 48	WC108051L	S 10	WCE104630	K 05	WF600041L	M133	WJ108001	N 25
WA110061L	B230	WA110065	N252	WB106041L	R 68	WC106041L	M130	WC108051L	N 07	WCE105170	K 31	WF600041L	M139	WJ108001	R 27
WA110061L	B263	WA110065	L 39	WB106041L	N140	WC106041L	M131	WC108057	M 58	WCG102890	K 29	WF600041L	M140	WJ108001	R 48
WA110061L	B357	WA110065	N251	WB106045	R 35	WC106041L	H 10	WC110061	N203	WCG102940	K 31	WF600041L	M141	WJ108001	R 50
WA110061L	B 47	WA110068L	B284	WB108051L	M 86	WC106041L	H 19	WC110061	R 71	WCG102940	K 05	WF600041L	M142	WJ108001	K 16
WA110061L	B 98	WA112081L	N 28	WB108051L	B 88	WC106041L	T 53	WC110061	K 18	WCG103020	K 32	WF600041L	M138	WJ108001	K 14
WA110061L	B191	WA112081L	N115	WB108051L	B136	WC106041L	H 11	WC110061L	B 08	WCU101320	K 31	WF600041L	M134	WJ108001	S 19
WA110061L	E 60	WA112081L	G 03	WB108051L	B 41	WC106044L	P 01	WC110061L	B 57	WCU101320	K 06	WF600041L	M137	WJ110001	B260
WA110061L	E 68	WA112081L	G 09	WB108051L	B185	WC106045	L 03	WC110061L	B109	WCU101320	K 32	WF600041L	M 93	WJ110001L	F 18
WA110061L	D 08	WA112081L	R 61	WB108051L	S 08	WC106047	L 02	WC110061L	B158	WD108051L	N 08	WF600051L	N 97	WJ110001L	J 03
WA110061L	N219	WA112081L	N117	WB108051L	S 09	WC106047	L 09	WC110061L	B201	WD112081L	S 08	WF600051L	N 98	WJ600041L	V 05
WA110061L	R 58	WA112081L	C 06	WB112081L	E 22	WC106047	L 03	WC110061L	E 62	WD112081L	S 09	WF600051L	N 95	WJ600041L	T 53
WA110061L	C 83	WA112081L	T 33	WB114001L	N201	WC106047	J 35	WC110061L	N 14	WDV100240	K 05	WF600071L	G 05	WJ600041L	L 47
WA110061L	C 37	WA112081L	F 07	WB120001	E 62	WC108051	J 08	WC110061L	R 24	WE104001L	B244	WF703084	P 07	WJ600041L	S 10
WA110061L	F 18	WA112081L	F 08	WB600071L	B 34	WC108051	N114	WC110061L	R 27	WE104001L	N184	WF704064	P 07	WJC100680	J 24
WA110061L	N 19	WA112081L	F 11	WB600071L	B 81	WC108051	R 60	WC110061L	C 69	WE104001L	M116	WFH101710	J 17	WJC100680	J 31
WA110061L	N 20	WA112081L	F 09	WC104001L	P 30	WC108051L	E 68	WC110061L	C 38	WE104001L	M119	WFH101730	J 06	WJC100680	J 32
WA110061L	N 23	WA112081L	P 57	WC104001L	N127	WC108051L	N 29	WC110061L	B377	WE104001L	N187	WFH101750	J 05	WJM10006	B387
WA110061L	N100	WA112087	N141	WC104004L	P 18	WC108051L	N 57	WC110061L	N204	WE105001L	N187	WFH101790	J 06	WJM10006L	J 66
WA110061L	N101	WA116101L	S 14	WC105001	M113	WC108051L	R 24	WC110061L	N 16	WE106001L	N153	WFH101820	J 17	WJN000020	J 59
WA110061L	B 87	WA120001	E 61	WC105001	L 72	WC108051L	R 27	WC110061L	E 63	WE114001	F 03	WFI100070	J 05	WJN101250L	J 57
WA110061L	B137	WA600071L	F 07	WC105001L	P 02	WC108051L	R 28	WC110061L	E 66	WE114001L	F 01	WFI100070	J 06	WJN101840	J 59
WA110061L	B348	WA600071L	F 10	WC105001L	P 10	WC108051L	R 29	WC110061L	N 08	WE600041L	M 95	WFI100080	J 05	WJN101850	J 59
WA110061L	R 40	WA600071L	N250	WC105001L	N147	WC108051L	R 30	WC110067L	R 71	WE600071L	G 05	WFI100080	J 06	WJN101860	J 59
WA110061L	K 17	WA600071L	V 04	WC105001L	N 51	WC108051L	N 50	WC112081	N 20	WE600081L	F 01	WFI100100	J 05	WJN101940	J 59
WA110061L	R 61	WA600071L	N251	WC105001L	N 30	WC108051L	N178	WC112081L	E 57	WE600101L	G 05	WFI100100	J 06	WJP107880	J 32
WA110061L	C 04	WA600091L	N121	WC105001L	G 10	WC108051L	N122	WC112081L	E 60	WE702101L	R 03	WFS100520	J 05	WJP107890	J 32
WA110061L	C 05	WA702101L	B303	WC105001L	N188	WC108051L	N126	WC112081L	E 68	WE703081	M 82	WFS100520	J 06	WJP107900	J 32
WA110061L	C 06	WA702101L	B320	WC105004	M123	WC108051L	N201	WC112081L	F 17	WF104001L	H 34	WFS100530	J 05	WJP107910	J 32
WA110061L	C 25	WA702101L	C 84	WC105004	M125	WC108051L	S 15	WC112081L	F 18	WF105001L	P 02	WFS100530	J 06	WJP107920	J 32
WA110061L	T 30	WA702101L	B337	WC105007	M113	WC108051L	B 87	WC112081L	N 67	WF105001L	N147	WFU100820	J 05	WJP107930	J 32
WA110061L	B146	WA702101L	B336	WC105007	N145	WC108051L	B 95	WC112081L	K 02	WF105001L	M 93	WFU100820	J 06	WJP107940	J 32
WA110061L	B148	WA702101L	B335	WC105007	P 08	WC108051L	B142	WC112081L	K 13	WF106001L	B354	WGE100110	J 05	WJP107950	J 31
WA110061L	J 54	WA704061	M 83	WC105007	M 12	WC108051L	B188	WC116101	E 68	WF106001L	N141	WGE100110	J 06	WJP107960	J 31
WA110061L	F 01	WA704061	M 84	WC105007	M120	WC108051L	J 01	WC116101	T 37	WF106001L	M 93	WGE100120	J 05	WJP107970	J 31
WA110061L	F 03	WAC100020	J 76	WC106041L	R 33	WC108051L	R 02	WC116101	T 38	WF108001L	B354	WGE100120	J 06	WJP107980	J 31
WA110061L	N250	WAC100030	J 76	WC106041L	M 91	WC108051L	R 42	WC600045L	R 33	WF108001L	N170	WH600041L	R 35	WJP107990	J 31
WA110061L	B 40	WAL100240	J 76	WC106041L	N 11	WC108051L	N 61	WC600045L	R 45	WF108001L	R 01	WHK100040	J 06	WJP108000	J 24
WA110061L	B366	WAO100000	J 76	WC106041L	N 39	WC108051L	N200	WC600045L	R 40	WF108004L	N185	WHK100050	J 06	WJP108010	J 24
WA110061L	B224	WAP000050	L 13	WC106041L	N124	WC108051L	R 40	WC600045L	P 55	WF110001L	H 16	WHK100060	J 05	WJP108020	J 24
WA110061L	B367	WAP100970	J 77	WC106041L	N 53	WC108051L	R 64	WC600045L	R 37	WF110001L	H 17	WHK100070	J 05	WJP108030	J 24
WA110061L	B368	WAP100980	J 77	WC106041L	S 16	WC108051L	N114	WC702101	H 22	WF110001L	H 18	WIA000030	L 13	WJP108040	J 24
WA110061L	V 04	WAP101220	J 76	WC106041L	S 15	WC108051L	J 10	WC702101L	T 16	WF110001L	F 03	WJ105001L	M 57	WJP108050	J 24
WA110061L	B184	WAP101340	J 77	WC106041L	B308	WC108051L	B103	WC702101L	R 03	WF110001L	H 10	WJ105001L	M 58	WJP108060	J 24
WA110061L	D 10	WAP101390	J 77	WC106041L	B309	WC108051L	R 16	WC702101L	R 44	WF110001L	H 12	WJ105001L	R 03	WJP108070	J 24
WA110061L	K 16	WAU100160	J 77	WC106041L	G 10	WC108051L	R 67	WC702101L	H 24	WF110001L	H 13	WJ106001L	B 42	WK606214L	P 07
WA110061L	K 14	WAU100320	J 76	WC106041L	S 14	WC108051L	F 02	WC702101L	H 20	WF110001L	H 14	WJ106001L	B 89	WK608213	R 35
WA110061L	K 05	WAU100470	J 77	WC106041L	N 44	WC108051L	F 03	WC702101L	R 37	WF110001L	H 19	WJ106001L	J 19	WK608311	R 30
WA110061L	C 51	WAV100270	J 76	WC106041L	N238	WC108051L	R 60	WC702101L	J 14	WF110001L	H 22	WJ106001L	J 20	WKB100330	J 59
WA110061L	N251	WAV100330	J 75	WC106041L	L 02	WC108051L	B 40	WC702101L	J 15	WF110001L	H 11	WJ106001L	M143	WKT100010	J 58
WA110061L	N 15	WB106041	N139	WC106041L	L 09	WC108051L	B 45	WCD000500	K 18	WF112001L	G 03	WJ106001L	K 16	WKT100010	J 59
WA110061L	E 64	WB106041L	B320	WC106041L	M135	WC108051L	B227	WCD105860	K 18	WF116001L	H 36	WJ106001L	K 14	WKT100020	J 58
WA110061L	E 67	WB106041L	B 42	WC106041L	M 27	WC108051L	V 05	WCE104440	K 31	WF600041L	M 48	WJ106001L	T 14	WKT100020	J 59
WA110061L	N143	WB106041L	B 90	WC106041L	M 28	WC108051L	R 21	WCE104450	K 32	WF600041L	M136	WJ106001L	N249	WKW000030	J 59
WA110061L	N138	WB106041L	R 33	WC106041L	M100	WC108051L	N 43	WCE104460	K 32	WF600041L	M132	WJ108001	B173	WL104001L	J 50

WL104001L	N143	WL106001L	B 13	WL106001L	P 13	WL106001L	B 36	WL106007L	F 19	WL108001L	B181	WL108001L	J 08	WL108001L	B224
WL104004	P 01	WL106001L	B 24	WL106001L	J 38	WL106001L	B 37	WL106041	N 11	WL108001L	B191	WL108001L	J 58	WL108001L	N150
WL105001L	B 80	WL106001L	B 59	WL106001L	J 33	WL106001L	H 10	WL108001	B155	WL108001L	B126	WL108001L	L 05	WL108001L	B184
WL105001L	N182	WL106001L	B 72	WL106001L	J 46	WL106001L	H 14	WL108001	N246	WL108001L	E 56	WL108001L	R 42	WL108001L	B162
WL105001L	N132	WL106001L	B 90	WL106001L	N 44	WL106001L	H 19	WL108001	S 15	WL108001L	E 57	WL108001L	N 48	WL108001L	B163
WL105001L	P 07	WL106001L	B124	WL106001L	N 46	WL106001L	L 29	WL108001	J 08	WL108001L	E 61	WL108001L	N151	WL108001L	B167
WL105001L	P 10	WL106001L	B125	WL106001L	N 47	WL106001L	C 07	WL108001	J 10	WL108001L	E 68	WL108001L	N200	WL108001L	K 02
WL105001L	H 36	WL106001L	B131	WL106001L	N 48	WL106001L	L 26	WL108001	B162	WL108001L	N 29	WL108001L	R 40	WL108001L	K 12
WL105001L	M 57	WL106001L	B171	WL106001L	N151	WL106001L	L 27	WL108001	B163	WL108001L	N181	WL108001L	R 61	WL108001L	D 33
WL105001L	M 58	WL106001L	B172	WL106001L	N142	WL106001L	N150	WL108001	K 16	WL108001L	N239	WL108001L	R 64	WL108001L	K 01
WL105001L	N 51	WL106001L	B180	WL106001L	N 41	WL106001L	N139	WL108001	K 08	WL108001L	N216	WL108001L	D 31	WL108001L	K 11
WL105001L	N 30	WL106001L	B181	WL106001L	R 44	WL106001L	N140	WL108001	K 19	WL108001L	R 24	WL108001L	N114	WL108001L	K 16
WL105001L	J 02	WL106001L	E 19	WL106001L	L 60	WL106001L	B162	WL108001	K 21	WL108001L	R 30	WL108001L	L 17	WL108001L	K 14
WL105001L	J 09	WL106001L	N 37	WL106001L	L 61	WL106001L	B163	WL108001L	B197	WL108001L	L 33	WL108001L	L 03	WL108001L	K 15
WL105001L	J 51	WL106001L	N 38	WL106001L	L 63	WL106001L	N187	WL108001L	B198	WL108001L	C 28	WL108001L	M103	WL108001L	K 24
WL105001L	R 02	WL106001L	N184	WL106001L	L 64	WL106001L	D 34	WL108001L	B204	WL108001L	C 31	WL108001L	K 03	WL108001L	K 07
WL105001L	R 03	WL106001L	N181	WL106001L	R 63	WL106001L	N180	WL108001L	B205	WL108001L	C 35	WL108001L	K 04	WL108001L	K 08
WL105001L	G 13	WL106001L	N196	WL106001L	R 68	WL106001L	K 16	WL108001L	B221	WL108001L	C 37	WL108001L	R 48	WL108001L	K 09
WL105001L	J 11	WL106001L	N197	WL106001L	N114	WL106001L	K 14	WL108001L	B230	WL108001L	F 05	WL108001L	R 50	WL108001L	K 19
WL105001L	T 45	WL106001L	N121	WL106001L	J 20	WL106001L	J 36	WL108001L	B263	WL108001L	H 34	WL108001L	K 10	WL108001L	K 20
WL105001L	T 46	WL106001L	N132	WL106001L	L 02	WL106001L	N 95	WL108001L	B357	WL108001L	H 35	WL108001L	N 67	WL108001L	K 21
WL105001L	M 10	WL106001L	N198	WL106001L	L 09	WL106001L	N 96	WL108001L	B 07	WL108001L	H 36	WL108001L	C 23	WL108001L	K 22
WL105001L	M 14	WL106001L	P 33	WL106001L	L 42	WL106001L	J 22	WL108001L	B 09	WL108001L	C 54	WL108001L	C 24	WL108001L	J 70
WL105001L	M 15	WL106001L	M 46	WL106001L	L 43	WL106001L	T 51	WL108001L	B 10	WL108001L	M 31	WL108001L	B 83	WL108001L	J 71
WL105001L	M 79	WL106001L	R 29	WL106001L	M102	WL106001L	T 52	WL108001L	B 13	WL108001L	M 32	WL108001L	B 84	WL108001L	D 06
WL105001L	C 51	WL106001L	R 33	WL106001L	M135	WL106001L	T 53	WL108001L	B 14	WL108001L	M 58	WL108001L	T 06	WL108001L	K 23
WL105001L	J 04	WL106001L	M 91	WL106001L	M143	WL106001L	N159	WL108001L	B 15	WL108001L	M 82	WL108001L	B119	WL108001L	N 43
WL105001L	C 52	WL106001L	J 65	WL106001L	P 24	WL106001L	N161	WL108001L	B 19	WL108001L	N 34	WL108001L	B132	WL108001L	K 25
WL105001L	N104	WL106001L	L 33	WL106001L	J 37	WL106001L	T 48	WL108001L	B 20	WL108001L	N145	WL108001L	B133	WL108001L	N 15
WL105001L	N106	WL106001L	C 86	WL106001L	N117	WL106001L	M138	WL108001L	B 42	WL108001L	N178	WL108001L	B147	WL108001L	N 07
WL105001L	M 63	WL106001L	C 37	WL106001L	L 32	WL106001L	J 67	WL108001L	B 47	WL108001L	N191	WL108001L	B148	WL108001L	N 08
WL105001L	S 08	WL106001L	F 05	WL106001L	N 67	WL106001L	L 25	WL108001L	B 53	WL108001L	N122	WL108001L	E 20	WL108001L	N240
WL105001L	S 09	WL106001L	H 25	WL106001L	C 23	WL106001L	N129	WL108001L	B 56	WL108001L	N123	WL108001L	J 52	WL108001L	N241
WL105001L	N163	WL106001L	N 11	WL106001L	T 45	WL106001L	S 12	WL108001L	B 58	WL108001L	N124	WL108001L	R 59	WL108001L	N242
WL105001L	N241	WL106001L	M 29	WL106001L	T 46	WL106001L	N133	WL108001L	B 59	WL108001L	N 97	WL108001L	R 67	WL108001L	N243
WL105001L	N244	WL106001L	M 32	WL106001L	B 83	WL106001L	G 01	WL108001L	B 67	WL108001L	N 98	WL108001L	M101	WL108001L	N245
WL105001L	M 16	WL106001L	M 82	WL106001L	B 84	WL106001L	N240	WL108001L	B 68	WL108001L	N 99	WL108001L	J 73	WL108001L	N138
WL105004	M113	WL106001L	N 34	WL106001L	T 05	WL106001L	N241	WL108001L	B 90	WL108001L	N 91	WL108001L	R 60	WL110001L	B206
WL105004	P 08	WL106001L	N179	WL106001L	S 04	WL106001L	N243	WL108001L	B 98	WL108001L	N100	WL108001L	B 11	WL110001L	B 08
WL105004	M123	WL106001L	N191	WL106001L	B133	WL106001L	N245	WL108001L	B105	WL108001L	N201	WL108001L	C 02	WL110001L	B 46
WL105004	M125	WL106001L	N122	WL106001L	B147	WL106001L	N131	WL108001L	B106	WL108001L	B 61	WL108001L	C 03	WL110001L	B 47
WL105004	M120	WL106001L	N123	WL106001L	R 15	WL106004	P 24	WL108001L	B108	WL108001L	B 62	WL108001L	B 36	WL110001L	B 57
WL106001	N 49	WL106001L	N124	WL106001L	J 13	WL106004	P 23	WL108001L	B110	WL108001L	B 73	WL108001L	B 37	WL110001L	B 65
WL106001	N 99	WL106001L	N 97	WL106001L	R 62	WL106004L	R 45	WL108001L	B120	WL108001L	B 74	WL108001L	B 40	WL110001L	B 96
WL106001	J 51	WL106001L	N115	WL106001L	R 66	WL106004L	R 39	WL108001L	B129	WL108001L	B 75	WL108001L	H 01	WL110001L	B 98
WL106001	J 37	WL106001L	N125	WL106001L	M101	WL106004L	P 18	WL108001L	B 63	WL108001L	B 87	WL108001L	B 45	WL110001L	B109
WL106001	J 72	WL106001L	N126	WL106001L	F 23	WL106004L	R 36	WL108001L	B 64	WL108001L	B 95	WL108001L	L 29	WL110001L	B116
WL106001	T 47	WL106001L	N118	WL106001L	M130	WL106005L	N146	WL108001L	B115	WL108001L	B113	WL108001L	C 08	WL110001L	B158
WL106001	H 11	WL106001L	N 93	WL106001L	M131	WL106007	B354	WL108001L	B154	WL108001L	B114	WL108001L	C 07	WL110001L	B165
WL106001L	B204	WL106001L	N246	WL106001L	M139	WL106007	M100	WL108001L	B155	WL108001L	B137	WL108001L	B 25	WL110001L	B201
WL106001L	B212	WL106001L	E 69	WL106001L	M140	WL106007L	B354	WL108001L	B157	WL108001L	B142	WL108001L	B 26	WL110001L	D 09
WL106001L	B220	WL106001L	B 61	WL106001L	M141	WL106007L	J 38	WL108001L	B159	WL108001L	C 42	WL108001L	B 27	WL110001L	N 14
WL106001L	B221	WL106001L	B 62	WL106001L	M142	WL106007L	N 61	WL108001L	B164	WL108001L	B188	WL108001L	B365	WL110001L	N203
WL106001L	B303	WL106001L	B113	WL106001L	R 01	WL106007L	L 09	WL108001L	B168	WL108001L	G 09	WL108001L	B366	WL110001L	N219
WL106001L	B 10	WL106001L	B114	WL106001L	R 51	WL106007L	J 37	WL108001L	B176	WL108001L	J 01	WL108001L	B227	WL110001L	C 30

WL110001L	C 38	WL700101	J 34	WM600051L	E 59	WM702001L	B303	WW104001	N 32	YBC101540	M114	YMC002411	M 41	YMD111230	M 56
WL110001L	H 25	WL700101L	T 16	WM600051L	E 62	WM702001L	B323	WYB10005	K 06	YBE100530	D 08	YMC002431	M 43	YMD111240	M 52
WL110001L	N 23	WL700101L	J 14	WM600051L	N 14	WM702001L	P 02	WYC100470	J 77	YBE100530	M108	YMC002441	M 43	YMD111250	M 55
WL110001L	N100	WL700101L	J 15	WM600051L	H 29	WM702001L	R 35	WYC100540	J 42	YBE100540	M108	YMC002451	M 44	YMD111450	M 55
WL110001L	N101	WLD100730	J 17	WM600051L	N 49	WM702001L	M 58	WYC100550	J 41	YCB100390	B 67	YMC002461	M 44	YMD111450	M 56
WL110001L	S 15	WLD100820	J 18	WM600051L	N 50	WM702001L	R 44	WYC100560	J 41	YCB100390	B119	YMC002471	M 39	YMD111800	M 51
WL110001L	B 87	WLH100570	J 17	WM600051L	N 53	WM702001L	M 14	WYC100570	J 06	YCB100400	B324	YMC002481	M 39	YMF101130	M 80
WL110001L	B377	WLH100600	J 18	WM600051L	B308	WM702001L	B336	WYC100680	J 42	YDG100850	M 28	YMC002491	M 41	YMF101190	L 73
WL110001L	B117	WLH100600	J 17	WM600051L	B309	WM702001L	B335	WYC100710	J 42	YEB10026	M102	YMC002501	M 41	YMG109260	M 71
WL110001L	B137	WLH100600	J 67	WM600051L	B377	WM702001L	N102	WYH100470	N203	YEB10026	M103	YMC002521	M 44	YMG109270	M 71
WL110001L	R 61	WLK100110	J 17	WM600051L	B334	WM704001L	M 07	WYH100470	J 05	YEB10027	M102	YMC004000	M 44	YMG109280	M 71
WL110001L	C 04	WLL100100	J 48	WM600051L	B349	WP105L	K 03	WYH100470	J 06	YEB10027	M103	YMC007560	M 45	YMG109510	M111
WL110001L	C 05	WM106001	N 58	WM600051L	N 47	WP105L	K 02	WYQ100040	J 05	YEB101220	M102	YMC007570	M 45	YMG109510	M109
WL110001L	T 30	WM106001	N 53	WM600051L	R 68	WP105L	K 12	WYQ100040	J 06	YEB101220	M103	YMC007580	M 42	YMG109600	M109
WL110001L	T 06	WM106001	N149	WM600051L	L 43	WP105L	K 01	WZX1505	B333	YEB101230	M102	YMC007590	M 42	YMG111630	M 71
WL110001L	B143	WM106001L	N 58	WM600051L	K 03	WP105L	K 11	XBC104480	M 05	YEB101230	M103	YMC007590	M 45	YMK000371	M 21
WL110001L	B144	WM106001L	C 28	WM600051L	B324	WP105L	K 15	XBL10003L	M 95	YFB100390	M115	YMC010910	M 39	YMK000381	M 22
WL110001L	E 20	WM106001L	N 49	WM600051L	N 67	WP105L	K 07	XBP100180	M 06	YGA2682L	P 67	YMC010920	M 39	YMK000391	M 22
WL110001L	F 01	WM106001L	N 99	WM600051L	B341	WP105L	K 08	XBP100180	M 11	YGA2682L	P 56	YMC129890	M 40	YMK000401	M 21
WL110001L	F 02	WM106001L	N 46	WM600051L	B310	WP105L	K 09	XBP100180	M 16	YGA2682L	P 61	YMC129900	M 39	YMK000421	M 21
WL110001L	F 03	WM106001L	L 17	WM600051L	B330	WP105L	K 19	XFC100550	M 11	YGA451L	N184	YMC129910	M 40	YMK000441	M 22
WL110001L	J 07	WM106001L	C 02	WM600051L	B331	WP105L	K 20	XFD100050	M 15	YGA451L	N159	YMC129920	M 35	YMK000451	M 22
WL110001L	B 40	WM110001L	E 59	WM600051L	G 07	WP105L	K 22	XFE100170	M 15	YGA451L	N162	YMC129950	M 40	YMK000461	M 22
WL110001L	H 01	WM110001L	E 63	WM600051L	B 45	WP105L	K 25	XFF100070	M 15	YGD10019	M 27	YMC130290	M 43	YMK000471	M 22
WL110001L	B 17	WM110001L	E 64	WM600051L	B342	WP185	N 50	XFF100070	M 16	YGD10019	M 28	YMC130350	M 43	YMK000501	M 22
WL110001L	B229	WM110001L	E 66	WM600051L	B343	WP185L	J 01	XFG100330	M 13	YGD100860	M 27	YMC130360	M 39	YMK000511	M 21
WL110001L	B224	WM110001L	E 67	WM600051L	B363	WP185L	J 08	XFK100290	M 13	YGD100860	M 28	YMC130370	M 39	YMK000511	M 22
WL110001L	B189	WM600041L	B306	WM600051L	B364	WP185L	K 28	XFS100050	M 13	YHD100000	M109	YMC130380	M 36	YMK000531	M 22
WL110001L	B184	WM600041L	B307	WM600051L	B365	WP185L	N 67	XGB000030	M 08	YJC100880	N 37	YMC130390	M 36	YMM000251	M 72
WL110001L	D 10	WM600041L	B320	WM600051L	B225	WP185L	K 26	XPB101290	M 87	YJJ100070	M 28	YMC130400	M 36	YMM000261	M 72
WL110001L	E 23	WM600041L	B323	WM600051L	M 63	WP185L	K 30	XQD101320LNF	M124	YKL100120	B296	YMC132350	M 44	YMM000271	M 72
WL110001L	J 03	WM600041L	B370	WM600061	B365	WP185L	K 27	XQI100040L	M124	YMB102340	M 50	YMC132360	M 44	YMM000281	M 72
WL110001L	T 31	WM600041L	B376	WM600061	B367	WP185L	N 15	XQJ10002L	M122	YMB102350	M 50	YMC133450	M 35	YMM000291	M 72
WL110001L	D 06	WM600041L	B385	WM600061L	B318	WP185L	N 16	XQJ10002L	M124	YMB102360	M 50	YMC134410	M 35	YMM000321	M 72
WL110001L	N 16	WM600041L	B 32	WM600061L	B320	WP185L	N 07	XQM101380	M124	YMB102370	M 50	YMC135140	M 39	YMM000331	M 73
WL110001L	E 47	WM600041L	B 42	WM600061L	B357	WP8019L	N138	XQM101520	M127	YMC000400	M 39	YMC135150	M 39	YMM000341	M 73
WL110301L	B 66	WM600041L	B 78	WM600061L	B381	WQB100410	J 06	XUC100840	M124	YMC000420	M 36	YMC136350	M 40	YMM000351	M 73
WL112001L	B 08	WM600041L	R 30	WM600061L	H 36	WQB100420	J 06	XUC100840	M127	YMC000440	M 39	YMC136360	M 40	YMN000021	M 74
WL112001L	B 57	WM600041L	R 33	WM600061L	S 16	WQB100430	J 06	XUC100850	M124	YMC000450	M 36	YMC138310	M 45	YMN000031	M 74
WL112001L	B109	WM600041L	R 35	WM600061L	G 05	WQB100440	J 06	YAD100900	M115	YMC000470	M 40	YMC138320	M 42	YMN000081	M 74
WL112001L	B158	WM600041L	C 73	WM600061L	B341	WQB100450	J 05	YAD100910	M115	YMC000480	M 40	YMC145980	M 36	YMQ000610	M129
WL112001L	B201	WM600041L	B377	WM600061L	B342	WQB100460	J 05	YAE100760	M115	YMC000500	M 45	YMC145990	M 36	YMQ103320	M102
WL112001L	C 29	WM600041L	B337	WM600061L	B343	WQB100470	J 05	YAE100790	M115	YMC000520	M 43	YMD000980	M 50	YMQ103320	M103
WL112001L	C 38	WM600041L	L 03	WM600061L	B363	WQT100030L	B398	YAE100800	M115	YMC000530	M 43	YMD000990	M 50	YMV101470	M102
WL112001L	H 27	WM600041L	B324	WM600061L	B364	WQT100030L	B298	YAF100080	P 07	YMC000540	M 44	YMD001010	M 50	YMV101470	M103
WL112001L	R 61	WM600041L	B310	WM600061L	B365	WS105001	L 05	YAF100090	P 07	YMC000550	M 44	YMD001020	M 50	YMZ100990	M 92
WL112001L	C 06	WM600041L	B330	WM600061L	B366	WS106001	S 15	YAF100110	M119	YMC001510	M 36	YMD111080	M 51	YND100050	M 12
WL112001L	N 16	WM600041L	J 13	WM600061L	B368	WS108001L	J 51	YAJ100370	M114	YMC001520	M 42	YMD111080	M 54	YNN000070	M 52
WL112001L	N 17	WM600041L	B342	WM600061L	E 08	WS108001L	N143	YAJ100390	M115	YMC002341	M 43	YMD111090	M 51	YNN000080	M 55
WL1O8001L	B 04	WM600041L	B343	WM600061L	E 11	WS600041L	S 16	YAJ100400	M116	YMC002351	M 43	YMD111090	M 54	YNN000090	M 55
WL600041L	J 73	WM600041L	B335	WM600071L	N 14	WS600047L	L 05	YAZ100000	M116	YMC002361	M 44	YMD111100	M 54	YNN000090	M 56
WL600051	R 62	WM600051L	B220	WM600071L	B377	WS600047L	L 07	YAZ100030	L 37	YMC002371	M 44	YMD111100	M 56	YNN000100	M 52
WL600051L	J 34	WM600051L	B131	WM600071L	N 67	WS600051	J 51	YAZ100040	L 37	YMC002381	M 39	YMD111210	M 52	YNN000110	M 55
WL600061L	C 73	WM600051L	B180	WM600071L	T 05	WS600061L	N143	YBC101520	M114	YMC002391	M 39	YMD111220	M 55	YNN000120	M 55
WL600061L	C 38	WM600051L	B381	WM702001	M 12	WS600091	N121	YBC101530	M114	YMC002401	M 41	YMD111230	M 55	YNN000120	M 56

N000120	M 56	YSB000860	M 69	YWB10032L	M 94
N000141	M 52	YSB000870	M 69	YWB100820L	M 94
N000151	M 55	YSB000880	M 69	YWC10050L	M 95
N000161	M 52	YSB105870	M 60	YWC102900LNF	M105
N000171	M 55	YSB105880	M 62	YWC104430L	M 98
N000331	M 55	YSB105890	M 60	YWC106260	M104
N000331	M 56	YSB105900	M 62	YWC106270	M104
N000341	M 55	YSB106130	M 68	YWJ101490	T 37
N000341	M 56	YSB106140	M 68	YWJ101490	T 38
N000350	M 52	YSB106660	M 64	YWJ101500	T 43
N000360	M 55	YSB106890	M 64	YWJ101500	T 37
N000380	M 52	YSB106901	M 69	YWJ101500	T 38
N000390	M 55	YSB106902	M 69	YWK10003L	M104
O3100PMA	M100	YSB107810	M 68	YWK100130	M105
O451PMA	P 21	YSU100520	M 69	YWN10002L	M105
O451PMA	P 20	YTA101230	M 30	YWT10003	M 94
O5098LOY	P 11	YTA101310	M 30	YWX101220	M104
O5098PMP	P 11	YTA101500	M 30	YWX101230	M104
O5098PMP	P 43	YTA101510	M 30	YWZ10003L	M 95
P100310L	M 92	YTA101520	M 30	YXB100000LNF	M 89
Y100220	M 08	YUD000310PMA	P 04	YXJ000020LNF	M 89
E000180	M 92	YUE000070LNF	M 89	YXX3200PMA	N184
G10007	M 91	YUE100530	M 88	YXX3200PMA	N159
G10008	M 91	YUF101490	M 88	YXX3200PMA	N162
G10009	M 91	YUF101500	M112	YYC10017	B395
G10010	M 91	YUF101520LNF	M 89	YYC10030L	M151
G10011L	M 91	YUF101640	M 88	YYC10030L	M106
G10013	M 91	YUG000180LNF	M 89	YYC10037L	L 38
H000080	P 12	YUG000350LNF	M 89	YYC10294L	M148
H000120	M 92	YUG000460LNF	M 89	YYC103160	K 05
H10002L	M 92	YUG000470LNF	M 89	YYC103970L	R 12
H10004L	M 92	YUG000530LNF	M 89	YYD10003	M147
H100870	M 92	YUG000540LNF	M 89	YYG10015	J 17
H100940	M 91	YUG102430LNF	M 89	YYP100860	P 31
H100960	M 99	YUJ10037L	M111	YYP100860	M 23
H101080	P 12	YUJ100650	M111	ZKC6454L	M126
Q101240	N 38	YUJ100650	M 89	ZXC9117	M117
R10016L	M147	YUK100270	L 73	ZXC9118	M117
R10016L	M134	YUM10001L	L 74	ZXC9119	M117
R10016L	M137	YUM10001L	L 73	ZXC9120	M117
R10075	M147	YWB000150	M 94	ZXC9121	M117
R101600	M 60	YWB000160	M 94	ZXC9328	M117
R101600	M 68	YWB10004L	L 56	ZXC9386	N113
R101600	M 65	YWB10027L	M112	ZXC9387	N113
R101600	M 69	YWB10027L	M 79		
R101600	M 63	YWB10027L	M 80		
S000010	M 49	YWB10027L	L 56		
S000060	M 49	YWB10027L	L 73		
S101790	M 49	YWB10027L	M 94		
S101830	M 91	YWB10032L	M112		
S101890	M 91	YWB10032L	M 77		
U10017L	M106	YWB10032L	M 76		
U104670	M 91	YWB10032L	M 70		
U104850	M 48	YWB10032L	M 79		
B000850	M 69	YWB10032L	M 93		

Brooklands Books Ltd., PO Box 146, Cobham,
Surrey KT11 1LG, England

ISBN: 9781855207127 Part No. STC9021CC Ref: LR87PH 1T4/2212

LAND ROVER OFFICIAL FACTORY PUBLICATIONS

Land Rover Series 1 Workshop Manual	4291
Land Rover Series 1 1948-53 Parts Catalogue	4051
Land Rover Series 1 1954-58 Parts Catalogue	4107
Land Rover Series 1 Instruction Manual	4277
Land Rover Series 1 and II Diesel Instruction Manual	4343
Land Rover Series II and IIA Workshop Manual	AKM8159
Land Rover Series II and Early IIA Bonneted Control Parts Catalogue	605957
Land Rover Series IIA Bonneted Control Parts Catalogue	RTC9840CC
Land Rover Series IIA, III and 109 V8 Optional Equipment Parts Catalogue	RTC9842CE
Land Rover Series IIA/IIB Instruction Manual	LSM64IM
Land Rover Series 2A and 3 88 Parts Catalogue Supplement (USA Spec)	606494
Land Rover Series III Workshop Manual	AKM3648
Land Rover Series III Workshop Manual V8 Supplement (edn. 2)	AKM8022
Land Rover Series III 88, 109 and 109 V8 Parts Catalogue	RTC9841CE
Land Rover Series III Owners Manual 1971-1978	607324B
Land Rover Series III Owners Manual 1979-1985	AKM8155
Military Land Rover (Lightweight) Series III Parts Catalogue	61278
Military Land Rover Series III (L.W.B.) User Handbook	608179
Military Land Rover (Lightweight) Series III User Manual	608180
Land Rover 90/110 and Defender Workshop Manual 1983-1992	SLR621ENWM
Land Rover Defender Workshop Manual 1993-1995	LDAWMEN93
Land Rover Defender 300 Tdi and Supplements Workshop Manual 1996-1998	LRL0097ENGBB
Land Rover Defender Td5 Workshop Manual and Supplements 1999-2006	LRL0410BB
Land Rover Defender Electrical Manual Td5 1999-06 and 300Tdi 2002-2006	LRD5EHBB
Land Rover 110 Parts Catalogue 1983-1986	RTC9863CE
Land Rover Defender Parts Catalogue 1987-2006	STC9021CC
Land Rover 90 • 110 Handbook 1983-1990 MY	LSM0054
Land Rover Defender 90 • 110 • 130 Handbook 1991 MY - Feb. 1994	LHAHBEN93
Land Rover Defender 90 • 110 • 130 Handbook Mar. 1994 - 1998 MY	LRL0087ENG/2
Military Land Rover 90/110 All Variants (Excluding APV and SAS) User Manual	2320-D-122-201
Military Land Rover 90 and 110 2.5 Diesel Engine Versions User Handbook	SLR989WDHB
Military Land Rover Defender XD - Wolf Workshop Manual - 2320D128 -	302 522 523 524
Military Land Rover Defender XD - Wolf Parts Catalogue	2320D128711
Discovery Workshop Manual 1990-1994 (petrol 3.5, 3.9, Mpi and diesel 200 Tdi)	SJR900ENWM
Discovery Workshop Manual 1995-1998 (petrol 2.0 Mpi, 3.9, 4.0 V8 and diesel 300 Tdi)	LRL0079BB
Discovery Series II Workshop Manual 1999-2003 (petrol 4.0 V8 and diesel Td5 2.5)	VDR100090/6
Discovery Parts Catalogue 1989-1998 (2.0 Mpi, 3.5, 3.9 V8 and 200 Tdi and 300 Tdi)	RTC9947CF
Discovery Parts Catalogue 1999-2003 (petrol 4.0 V8 and diesel Td5 2.5)	STC9049CA
Discovery Owners Handbook 1990-1991 (petrol 3.5 V8 and diesel 200 Tdi)	SJR820ENHB90
Discovery Series II Handbook 1999-2004 MY (petrol 4.0 V8 and Td5 diesel)	LRL0459BB
Freelander Workshop Manual 1998-2000 (petrol 1.8 and diesel 2.0)	LRL0144
Freelander Workshop Manual 2001-2003 ON (petrol 1.8L, 2.5L and diesel Td4 2.0)	LRL0350ENG/4
Land Rover 101 1 Tonne Forward Control Workshop Manual	RTC9120
Land Rover 101 1 Tonne Forward Control Parts Catalogue	608294B
Land Rover 101 1 Tonne Forward Control User Manual	608239
Range Rover Workshop Manual 1970-1985 (petrol 3.5)	AKM3630
Range Rover Workshop Manual 1986-1989	SRR660ENWM &
(petrol 3.5 and diesel 2.4 Turbo VM)	LSM180WS4/2
Range Rover Workshop Manual 1990-1994	
(petrol 3.9, 4.2 and diesel 2.5 Turbo VM, 200 Tdi)	LHAWMENA02
Range Rover Workshop Manual 1995-2001 (petrol 4.0, 4.6 and BMW 2.5 diesel)	LRL0326ENGBB
Range Rover Workshop Manual 2002-2005 (BMW petrol 4.4 and BMW 3.0 diesel)	LRL0477
Range Rover Electrical Manual 2002-2005 UK version (petrol 4.4 and 3.0 diesel)	RR02KEMBB
Range Rover Electrical Manual 2002-2005 USA version (BMW petrol 4.4)	RR02AEMBB
Range Rover Parts Catalogue 1970-1985 (petrol 3.5)	RTC9846CH
Range Rover Parts Catalogue 1986-1991 (petrol 3.5, 3.9 and diesel 2.4 and 2.5 Turbo VM)	RTC9908CB
Range Rover Parts Catalogue 1992-1994 MY and 95 MY Classic	
(petrol 3.9, 4.2 and diesel 2.5 Turbo VM, 200 Tdi and 300 Tdi)	RTC9961CB
Range Rover Parts Catalogue 1995-2001 MY (petrol 4.0, 4.6 and BMW 2.5 diesel)	RTC9970CE
Range Rover Owners Handbook 1970-1980 (petrol 3.5)	606917
Range Rover Owners Handbook 1981-1982 (petrol 3.5)	AKM8139
Range Rover Owners Handbook 1983-1985 (petrol 3.5)	LSM0001HB
Range Rover Owners Handbook 1986-1987 (petrol 3.5 and diesel 2.4 Turbo VM)	LSM129HB

Engine Overhaul Manuals for Land Rover and Range Rover

300 Tdi Engine, R380 Manual Gearbox and LT230T Transfer Gearbox Overhaul Manuals	LRL003, 070 & 081
Petrol Engine V8 3.5, 3.9, 4.0, 4.2 and 4.6 Overhaul Manuals	LRL004 & 164
Land Rover/Range Rover Driving Techniques	LR369
Working in the Wild - Manual for Africa	SMR684MI
Winching in Safety - Complete guide to winching Land Rovers and Range Rovers	SMR699MI

Workshop Manual Owners Edition

Land Rover 2 / 2A / 3 Owners Workshop Manual 1959-1983
Land Rover 90, 110 and Defender Workshop Manual Owners Edition 1983-1995
Land Rover Discovery Workshop Manual Owners Edition 1990-1998

Printed and bound in Great Britain by
Marston Book Services Ltd, Oxfordshire

Printed by Printforce, United Kingdom